POCKET
ROMANIZED
JAPANESE-ENGLISH
DICTIONARY

By Hiroshi Takahashi
Kyoko Takahashi

TAISEIDO

GENERAL INTRODUCTION

This Japanese-English dictionary was completed after four years work to meet the essential needs of the foreigners who want to know the meaning of a Japanese word and some important facts of usage.

To bring the dictionary up to date, the primary consideration in the selection of entries was to collect the standard words and to omit time-worn words and the trite ways of expression, and newfangled words which are likely to become obsolete soon.

Entries total about 24,000 words, which should prove to be practical enough for everyday life. It is my pleasure that you should have frequent recourse to the dictionary.

November 1984   *Authors*

HOW TO USE THIS DICTIONARY

The entries (gothic typed) are presented in the Romanized Japanese, followed by the letters in the Japanese and Chinese characters. Then the English words applicable to them come.

METHODS OF PRESENTATION

(1) The American English is given priority.

(2) The words are arranged alphabetically.

    (a) When a word has some long-vowel, the order of presentation is as following:

        ex. ① dasu ② dasû ③ dâsu.

    (b) When the words have the same Romanized spelling, the word using the hyphen or dot between syllables is put ahead.

        ① *ex.* **mei-an** 〈めいあん：明暗〉 light and darkness.

        ② *ex.* **meian** 〈めいあん：名案〉 a good idea, a splendid idea.

        ① *ex.* **an·i** 〈あんい：安易〉

        ② *ex.* **ani** 〈あに：兄〉 an elder brother, an older brother.

    (c) Homonyms are given priority to the word the accent of which is ahead.

        ① *ex.* **dōshi** 〈どうし：同志〉 a kindred mind, a comrade.

        ② *ex.* **dōshi** 〈どうし：動詞〉 a verb.

    (d) When the words have the same accent, priority is given to the word which functions only as noun, and then come the words having some verb or adjective meaning or both.

(3) Unless it is particularly inconvenient to search for words, the verb or adjective form derived from a noun is presented in the basic form.

(4) When an entry has another popular or current way of expression (especially in some colloquial way), it should follow the direction by *see*.

        ex. **yuki-ataru** 〈ゆきあたる：行き当たる〉 *see*. iki-ataru.

(5) As for prefix, suffix, auxiliary verb and particle, dash is attached before or after the entry.

        ex. **-nagara** 〈-ながら〉 while, as, ...ing, with, over; though, but, yet, in spite of.

(6) In the case of having a little different way of expression though completely or nearly same in the meaning, the words are presented together using 'or.' (This is also applicable to a usage and an idiom.)

　　ex. **obekka** or **obenchara** 〈おべっか, おべんちゃら〉 flattery.

REFERENCES TO THE ROMANIZED LETTERS

(1) The romanized letters are used according to the system of the attached table.

(2) Considering the practical pronunciation, *m* is used in spelling before the bilabial sounds (b, m and p), though in this case of the Japanese system *n* is usually preferred.

　　ex. empitsu ← enpitsu

(3) Considering the system of the Japanese *kana* (仮名), a Romanized spelling is sometimes changed.

('Tôri' and 'ôkii' are common in the Japanese spelling, but they are hard to distinguish from 'touri' (とうり) and 'oukii' (おうきい) in *kana*.)

　　ex. toori (とおり), ookii (おおきい).

　But when a current spelling is fixed, this system is not followed. For example Ôsaka is not 'Oosaka.'

REFERENCES TO THE MEANING OF A WORD

Each meaning of a word is distinguished by semicolon(;).

The order of meanings is arranged from the general to the particular.

(　) used in the explanation means that the part is omissible.

((　)) is used to point out some relation of meaning between the entry and the other words.

〔　〕 is used to compliment the meaning.

EXAMPLES AND IDIOMS

Most of the entries are chosen from the noun form and the other forms such as verb, adjective, adverb and idioms are presented in italic.

Examples (also in the form of a sentence) and compound words are presented in the Romanized letters for the most part.

REFERENCES TO THE ROMANIZED LETTERS

	a (あ)(ア)	i (い)(イ)	u (う)(ウ)	e (え)(エ)	o (お)(オ)
①	ka (か)(カ)	ki (き)(キ)	ku (く)(ク)	ke (け)(ケ)	ko (こ)(コ)
②	sa (さ)(サ)	shi (し)(シ)	su (す)(ス)	se (せ)(セ)	so (そ)(ソ)
③	ta (た)(タ)	chi (ち)(チ)	tsu (つ)(ツ)	te (て)(テ)	to (と)(ト)
	na (な)(ナ)	ni (に)(ニ)	nu (ぬ)(ヌ)	ne (ね)(ネ)	no (の)(ノ)
④	ha (は)(ハ)	hi (ひ)(ヒ)	fu (ふ)(フ)	he (へ)(ヘ)	ho (ほ)(ホ)
	ma (ま)(マ)	mi (み)(ミ)	mu (む)(ム)	me (め)(メ)	mo (も)(モ)
	ya (や)(ヤ)		yu (ゆ)(ユ)		yo (よ)(ヨ)
	ra (ら)(ラ)	ri (り)(リ)	ru (る)(ル)	re (れ)(レ)	ro (ろ)(ロ)
	wa (わ)(ワ)				
	n (ん)(ン)				

①'	ga (が)(ガ)	gi (ぎ)(ギ)	gu (ぐ)(グ)	ge (げ)(ゲ)	go (ご)(ゴ)
②'	za (ざ)(ザ)	ji (じ,ぢ)(ジ,ヂ)	zu (ず,づ)(ズ,ヅ)	ze (ぜ)(ゼ)	zo (ぞ)(ゾ)
③'	da (だ)(ダ)			de (で)(デ)	do (ど)(ド)
④'	ba (ば)(バ)	bi (び)(ビ)	bu (ぶ)(ブ)	be (べ)(ベ)	bo (ぼ)(ボ)
④"	pa (ぱ)(パ)	pi (ぴ)(ピ)	pu (ぷ)(プ)	pe (ぺ)(ペ)	po (ぽ)(ポ)

kya (きゃ)(キャ)	kyu (きゅ)(キュ)	kyo (きょ)(キョ)
sha (しゃ)(シャ)	shu (しゅ)(シュ) she (しぇ)(シェ)	sho (しょ)(ショ)
cha (ちゃ)(チャ)	chu (ちゅ)(チュ) che (ちぇ)(チェ)	cho (ちょ)(チョ)
nya (にゃ)(ニャ)	nyu (にゅ)(ニュ)	nyo (にょ)(ニョ)
hya (ひゃ)(ヒャ)	hyu (ひゅ)(ヒュ)	hyo (ひょ)(ヒョ)
mya (みゃ)(ミャ)	myu (みゅ)(ミュ)	myo (みょ)(ミョ)
rya (りゃ)(リャ)	ryu (りゅ)(リュ)	ryo (りょ)(リョ)
gya (ぎゃ)(ギャ)	gyu (ぎゅ)(ギュ)	gyo (ぎょ)(ギョ)
ja (じゃ)(ジャ)	ju (じゅ)(ジュ) je (じぇ)(ジェ)	jo (じょ)(ジョ)
bya (びゃ)(ビャ)	byu (びゅ)(ビュ)	byo (びょ)(ビョ)
pya (ぴゃ)(ピャ)	pyu (ぴゅ)(ピュ)	pyo (ぴょ)(ピョ)

	di (ディ)	
fa (ファ)	fi (フィ)	fo (フォ)
	ti (ティ)	
	wi (ウィ) we (ウェ)	wo (ウォ)

o is used instead of wo (ウォ).

chĕ (ちえっ) → an assimilated sound in the last syllable of a word.

A dot mark(·) put between the syllables is used to separate *n* sound from the next one.

　　ex.　nya (にゃ)

　　ex.　n·ya (んや)

A hyphen-liked line(·) put between the Japanese *kata-kana* letters is equivalent to '¨' put above a vowel.

PRESENTATION OF JAPANESE

(1)　Japanese *kana* is presented in 〈　　〉 (a loan word in *kata-kana*) and after colon (：) *Kanji* (Chinese character) comes.

(2)　The official standard *kanjis* (containing 1945 letters), the use of which cover a wide range in laws, official documents, school textbooks and newspapers, are adopted in this dictionary.

　　(The official standard letters — *Jyôyo-kanji* in Japanese — were selected by Japanese Language Council and notified Oct. 1, 1981 by the Cabinet. The standard presents a guide-line for the use of *kanji* easy to understand and communicate in a social life.)

(3)　*Okuri-gana* (declentional *kana*) also follows the system by the Council.

(4)　In a usage and an idiom the current style mixing kana is omitted.

(5)　When more than two *kanjis* are applicable to a word, all but a common one are put in (　　).

　　ex.　膨張(脹)

And some subtle differences of usage in *kanjis* are shown in the examples, if necessary.

　　ex.　**katai** 〈硬(固, 堅)い〉

　　　　katai ishi (硬い石) a hard stone

　　　　katai kesshin (固い決心) a firm resolution

　　　　katai hito (堅い人) a man of strict morals

(6)　When *kanji* is not used for some consideration of the subtle meaning or *kana* is used in a colloquial way, though *kanji* is presented in the entry, *kana* is used in the usage.

　　ex.　**tokoro** 〈ところ：所〉a place.

　　　　Koko-wa　watashi-ga　umareta-tokoro-desu.（ここは私が生まれた所です.）This is the place where I was born.

Kare-wa　ii　tokoro-ga-aru.（彼はいいところがある。）He　has　a　good
point.

(7) As the voiceless sound sometimes turns into the voiced one
(particularly in compound words) such as t → d, s → j or z, under
some phonological condition, the example of usage follows the
Japanese usual practice.

　　　ex.　**kassen**〈かっせん：合戦〉a battle, a fight.

　　　　　uta-gassen（歌合戦）a singing contest

(8) ? and ! are not used and a full stop puts an end in Japanese.

A

a 〈あ〉 Oh! / Ah! / Dear me! / Look!
    A-ita! (あ, 痛.) Ouch!
â 〈ああ〉 Oh! / Ah!; Yes.
abaku 〈あばく：暴く〉 disclose, expose; dig open.
    himitsu o abaku (秘密を暴く) disclose a secret
    imbô o abaku (陰謀を暴く) expose a plot
    shôtai-o-abaku (正体を暴く) show ((a person)) in his true colors
    haka o abaku (墓を暴く) dig a grave open
abara-bone 〈あばらぼね：あばら骨〉 a rib.
abareru 〈あばれる：暴れる〉 act violently.
    abare-dasu (暴れ出す) get rowdy, get riotous
    abare-mawaru (暴れ回る) run about wildly
abekku 〈アベック〉 a (young) couple.
abekobe 〈あべこべ〉 *see.* gyaku.
abiru 〈あびる：浴びる〉 bathe, take a bath.
    shawâ o abiru (シャワーを浴びる) take a shower
abu 〈あぶ〉 a horsefly, a gadfly.
abuna-ge 〈あぶなげ：危な気〉
  abuna-ge-na 〈危な気な〉 dangerous, unreliable, doubtful, unsteady.
    abuna-ge-nai (危な気ない) safe, secure, reliable, steady
abunai 〈あぶない：危ない〉 dangerous, risky, narrow.
    Abunai! (危ない.) Look out! / Take care!
    abunai-koto o suru (危ないことをする) run a risk
    abunai-tokoro-o-tasukaru (危ないところを助かる) have a narrow escape
    abunai-tokoro-o-tasukerareru (危ないところを助けられる) be rescued from danger
  abunaku 〈危なく〉 nearly, almost, on the point of ((doing)).

abura〈あぶら：油〉oil.

   abura-ga-kireru（油が切れる）run short of oil

   abura-de ageru（油で揚げる）fry in oil

   abura-o-sasu〈油を差す〉oil.

   abura-darake-no or *abura-ke-no-aru*〈油だらけの，油気のある〉oily.

abura〈あぶら：脂〉fat, lard.

   abura-mi（脂身）the fat

abura-e〈あぶらえ：油絵〉(an) oil painting.

   abura-e-o-kaku（油絵をかく）paint in oils

abura-enogu〈あぶらえのぐ：油絵の具〉oil colors.

abura-kasu〈あぶらかす：油かす〉oil cake, rape cake.

aburakkoi〈あぶらっこい：脂っこい〉greasy, fatty, oily.

   aburakkoi tabe-mono（脂っこい食べ物）rich food

abura-mushi〈あぶらむし：油虫〉a cockroach, a plant louse.

achi-kochi〈あちこち〉here and there.

   achi-kochi o miru（あちこちを見る）look here and there

   achi-kochi-kara atsumaru（あちこちから集まる）flock from far and
   near

achira〈あちら〉there, the other.

   achira-gawa（あちら側）the other side

   achira-e or *achira-ni*〈あちらへ，あちらに〉there, over there.

adana〈あだな：あだ名〉a nickname.

   hito o adana-de yobu（人をあだ名で呼ぶ）call a person by his nickname

adokenai〈あどけない〉innocent, childish, naïve.

   adokenai kao（あどけない顔）an innocent face

   adokenai-koto-o-iu〈あどけないことを言う〉talk like a child.

   adokenaku〈あどけなく〉innocently, childishly, naïvely.

aegu〈あえぐ〉pant, gasp.

   aegi-nagara〈あえぎながら〉gaspingly, out of breath.

aen〈あえん：亜鉛〉zinc.

aenai〈あえない〉

   aenai-saigo-o-togeru〈あえない最後を遂げる〉come to a sad end.

aete〈あえて〉daringly, boldly.

   aete~(-suru)〈あえて～（する）〉dare ((to do)), venture ((to do)), make
   bold ((to do)).

Afuganisutan〈アフガニスタン〉Afghanistan.

afureru〈あふれる〉overflow.

　　　kankyaku-de afureru（観客であふれる）be overflowed with spectators

　　　namida-ga-afureru（涙があふれる）be filled with tears

Afurika〈アフリカ〉Africa.

　　　Afurika-jin（アフリカ人）an African

　　　Afurika(-jin)-no（アフリカ(人)の）African

afutâ-sâbisu〈アフターサービス〉after-sale service.

agaki〈あがき〉struggling.

　　　agaki-ga-tore-nai（あがきがとれない）be in a fix

　agaku〈あがく〉struggle.

agari〈あがり：上がり〉a rise, an advance.

　　　kaidan o agari-ori-suru（階段を上がり降りする）go up and down the stairs

-agari〈-あがり：-上がり〉

　　　yakunin-agari（役人上がり）an ex-official

　　　ame-agari-no michi（雨上がりの道）a road after the rain

agaru〈あがる：上がる〉rise, go up; come out; be raised; make progress, improve; enter; be over; get excited, get nervous.

　　　yane-ni agaru（屋根に上がる）go up on the roof

　　　furo-kara agaru（風ろから上がる）come out of a bath

　　　kyûryô-ga-agaru（給料が上がる）get a raise in salary

　　　gakkô-no-seiseki-ga-agaru（学校の成績が上がる）show a better school record

　　　ude-ga-agaru（腕が上がる）improve in one's skill

　　　gakkô ni agaru（学校に上がる）enter a school

　　　Ame-ga-agatta.（雨が上がった.）It has stopped raining.

　　　butai-de agaru（舞台で上がる）get nervous on a stage

age-ashi〈あげあし：挙(揚)げ足〉

　age-ashi-o-toru〈挙(揚)げ足を取る〉catch ((a person)) tripping, trip ((a person)) up.

ageru〈あげる：上げる〉lift (up); raise; increase; give.

　　　koe o ageru（声を上げる）lift up one's voice

　　　kyûryô o agete-morau（給料を上げてもらう）get one's salary raised

　　　supîdo o ageru（スピードを上げる）increase speed

　　　Kono hon o kimi-ni age-yô.（この本を君に上げよう.）I'll give you this book.

ageru〈あげる：挙げる〉give; hold.

　　　jitsurei o ageru（実例を挙げる）give an example

kekkon-shiki o ageru〈結婚式を挙げる〉 hold a wedding

ageru〈あげる：揚げる〉fly, set off, shoot; fry.

tako o ageru（たこを揚げる）fly a kite

niku o batâ-de ageru（肉をバターで揚げる） fry meat in butter

-ageru〈-あげる〉do ((something)) for ((a person)), be kind enough ((to do)).

ageshio〈あげしお：上げ潮〉the flowing tide.

age-zoko〈あげぞこ：上げ底〉a raised bottom, a false bottom.

Kono hako wa age-zoko-da.（この箱は上げ底だ。）This box has a false bottom.

ago〈あご〉the jaw, the chin.

uwa-ago（上あご） the upper jaw

shita-ago（下あご） the lower jaw

ago-hige（あごひげ） a beard

hito o ago-de-tsukau（人をあごで使う）have a person at one's beck (and call)

agumu〈あぐむ〉grow weary ((of)), get tired ((of)).

machi-agumu（待ちあぐむ） become weary of waiting

agura〈あぐら〉

agura-o-kaku〈あぐらをかく〉 sit cross-legged.

ahen〈あへん：阿片〉opium.

ahen o suu（阿片を吸う） smoke opium

ahen-chûdoku（阿片中毒） opium poisoning

ahiru〈あひる〉a duck.

ahiru-no-ko（あひるの子）a duckling

ahô-dori〈あほうどり：あほう鳥〉an albatross.

ai〈あい〉indigo.

ai-iro(-no)（あい色(の)） indigo, deep blue

ai〈あい：愛〉love.

ai-suru〈愛する〉love; dear, beloved.

aibu〈あいぶ：愛ぶ〉caress.

aibu-suru〈愛ぶする〉caress, fondle.

aichaku〈あいちゃく：愛着〉attachment, love.

〜-ni-aichaku-o-kanjiru〈〜に愛着を感じる〉become attached to... .

aida〈あいだ：間〉interval, space, an opening, a gap, distance.

aida-o-tsumete-kaku（間を詰めて書く） write close

aida-o-oite〈間をおいて〉at intervals.

aida-no, aida-de, aida-ni or **aida-wa**〈あいだの，あいだで，あいだに，

あいだは：間の，間で，間に，間は〉during, for, while; as long as; between, among.

   watashi-ga-Itaria-ni-iru-aida-ni（私がイタリアにいる間に）during my stay in Italy

   tō-ka-no-aida（10日の間）for ten days

   watashi-ga ikite-iru-aida-wa（私が生きている間は）as long as I live

   shokuji-to-shokuji-no-aida-ni（食事と食事の間に）between meals

   wareware-yo-nin-no-aida-de（我々四人の間で）among us four

aidagara〈あいだがら：間柄〉relation.

   oya-ko-no aidagara（親子の間柄）the relation between(or of) father and son

aidoku〈あいどく：愛読〉

   aidoku-sha（愛読者）an ardent reader

   aidoku-sho（愛読書）one's favorite book

   aidoku-suru〈愛読する〉read with pleasure(or interest).

ai-fuku〈あいふく：合い服〉a spring suit.

aigo〈あいご：愛護〉kind treatment; protection.

   aigo-suru〈愛護する〉treat kindly, protect.

aijin〈あいじん：愛人〉a lover, a love, a sweetheart.

aijō〈あいじょう：愛情〉love, affection.

   aijō o idaku（愛情を抱く）feel affection ((toward))

   aijō-no-aru〈愛情のある〉affectionate, warmhearted.

   aijō-no-nai（愛情のない）cold

   aijō-o-komete〈愛情を込めて〉affectionately.

ai-kagi〈あいかぎ：合いかぎ〉a duplicate key, a masterkey.

ai-kawarazu〈あいかわらず：相変わらず〉as usual, as...as ever.

   ai-kawarazu isogashii（相変わらず忙しい）be busy as usual

   ai-kawarazu utsukushii（相変わらず美しい）be as beautiful as ever

aiken〈あいけん：愛犬〉one's pet dog.

aikō〈あいこう：愛好〉love, fondness.

   ongaku no aikō-sha（音楽の愛好者）a lover of music

   aikō-suru〈愛好する〉love, be fond ((of)).

aikoku〈あいこく：愛国〉

   aikoku-sha（愛国者）a patriot

   aikoku-shin（愛国心）patriotism

   aikoku-teki-na〈愛国的な〉patriotic.

ai-kotoba〈あいことば：合い言葉〉a password, a watchword.

aikuchi〈あいくち〉a dagger, a dirk.

aikyô 〈あいきょう：愛きょう〉 charms.

　aikyô-no-aru 〈愛きょうのある〉 charming.

aima 〈あいま：合間〉 an interval.

　aima-ni 〈合間に〉 in the intervals, when one has time to spare.

　　shigoto no aima-ni 〈仕事の合間に〉 in the intervals of business

aimai 〈あいまい〉 vagueness, obscurity, ambiguity.

　aimai-na 〈あいまいな〉 vague, obscure, ambiguous; doubtful, suspicious.

　　aimai-na henji 〈あいまいな返事〉 a vague answer

　aimai-na-koto-o-iu 〈あいまいなことを言う〉 equivocate, talk ambiguously.

　aimai-ni 〈あいまいに〉 vaguely, doubtfully.

ainiku 〈あいにく〉 unfortunately, unluckily, I am sorry, but... .

　ainiku-no 〈あいにくの〉 unfortunate, unlucky, unseasonable.

ainoko 〈あいのこ：合いの子〉 a half blood.

ainori 〈あいのり：相乗り〉

　ainori-suru 〈相乗りする〉 ride together.

Ainu 〈アイヌ〉 an Ainu, an Aino.

　　Ainu-go 〈アイヌ語〉 Ainu, Aino

airashii 〈あいらしい：愛らしい〉 lovely, charming, sweet.

　airashiku 〈愛らしく〉 charmingly.

airo 〈あいろ：あい路〉 a narrow path, a bottleneck.

　　airo-to-naru 〈あい路となる〉 cause a bottleneck

airon 〈アイロン〉 an iron.

　airon-o-kakeru 〈アイロンをかける〉 iron, press.

Airurando 〈アイルランド〉 Ireland.

　　Airurando-jin 〈アイルランド人〉 an Irishman *or* an Irishwoman

　　Airurando-go 〈アイルランド語〉 Irish

　　Airurando(-jin)-no 〈アイルランド（人）の〉 Irish

aisatsu 〈あいさつ〉 a greeting.

　　aisatsu-jô 〈あいさつ状〉 a letter of greeting

　aisatsu-suru 〈あいさつする〉 greet.

aiseki 〈あいせき：相席〉

　aiseki-suru 〈相席する〉 share a table 〔with another at a lunchroom〕.

aishô 〈あいしょう：相性〉 affinity, congeniality.

　aishô-no-ii 〈相性のいい〉 of congenial disposition.

　　aishô-no-warui 〈相性の悪い〉 uncongenial

aishô 〈あいしょう：愛称〉 a pet name.

aishô-ka 〈あいしょうか：愛唱歌〉 one's favorite song(s).

aiso *or* **aisô** 〈あいそ，あいそう：愛想〉

aiso-(or *aisô*-)o-tsukasu〈愛想を尽かす〉be disgusted ((at, by *or* with)).

aiso-(or *aisô*-)no-ii〈愛想のいい〉amiable, sociable.

    aiso-(or aisô-)no-warui *or* aiso-(*or* aisô-)no-nai（愛想の悪い，愛想のない）cold

aiso-(or *aisô*)*yoku*〈愛想よく〉amiably, sociably.

aita〈あいた：開(空)いた〉open, empty, vacant.

    aita heya（空いた部屋）a vacant room

aite〈あいて：相手〉a companion, a partner; an opponent, a rival.

    asobi-aite（遊び相手）a playmate, a playfellow

    hanashi-aite（話し相手）someone to talk to

    sôdan-aite（相談相手）an adviser

    aite-kata（相手方）the other party

    ∼-*o-aite-ni-suru*（〜を相手にする）deal with... , make a companion of... .

    ∼-*o-aite-ni-shi-nai*（〜を相手にしない）do not care for...

aite-iru〈あいている：開(空)いている〉be open; be empty, be unoccupied, be free.

    aite-iru toire（空いているトイレ）an unoccupied toilet

    Kyô-yûgata-wa　jikan-ga-aite-iru.（今日夕方は時間が空いている.）I am free this evening.

aitô〈あいとう：哀悼〉condolence, sympathy, regret, grief.

    aitô-no-i o hyô-suru（哀悼の意を表する）express one's regret〔over the death of a person〕

aitsu〈あいつ〉that fellow, that guy.

ai-tsuide〈あいついで：相次いで〉one after another, in succession.

â-iu〈ああいう〉*see.* anna.

aiyô〈あいよう：愛用〉

aiyô-suru〈愛用する〉use regularly(*or* habitually), patronize.

aiyoku〈あいよく：愛欲〉love and lust, sexual passion.

    aiyoku no toriko-ni-naru（愛欲のとりこになる）become a slave of passion

aizu〈あいず：合図〉a sign, a signal.

aizu-suru〈合図する〉sign, make a sign, signal.

aizuchi〈あいづち：相づち〉

aizuchi-o-utsu〈相づちを打つ〉chime in.

aji〈あじ〉a horse mackerel.

aji〈あじ：味〉taste, savor, flavor.

aji-ga-suru〈味がする〉taste.

    myô-na aji-ga-suru（妙な味がする）have a strange taste

～-no-aji-ga-suru〈～の味がする〉taste of... .

aji-ga-ii〈味がいい〉taste sweet.

　aji-ga-warui（味が悪い）taste bad

aji-o-tsukeru〈味を付ける〉season.

aji-no-ii〈味のいい〉nice, delicious, savory, palatable.

　aji-no-warui（味の悪い）unsavory, unpalatable

aji-no-aru〈味のある〉tasteful.

　aji-no-nai（味のない）tasteless, insipid

Ajia〈アジア〉Asia.

　Ajia-jin（アジア人）an Asian

　Ajia(-jin)-no（アジア(人)の）Asian

aji-kagen〈あじかげん：味加減〉

aji-kagen-ga-ii〈味加減がいい〉be well seasoned.

　aji-kagen-ga-warui（味加減が悪い）be badly seasoned

aji-kagen-o-miru〈味加減を見る〉taste ((something)) to see how it is seasoned.

ajike-nai〈あじけない：味気ない〉*see.* ajiki-nai.

ajiki-nai〈あじきない：味気ない〉weary, dreary, insipid, jejune, arid.

　ajiki-nai yo-no-naka（味気ない世の中）a dreary world

ajisai〈あじさい〉a hydrangea.

ajito〈アジト〉an agitating point, a hideout.

ajiwau〈あじわう：味わう〉taste; appreciate; enjoy.

　shi o ajiwau（詩を味わう）appreciate poetry

　tabi o ajiwau（旅を味わう）enjoy one's journey

aka〈あか：赤〉red.

　aka-shingō（赤信号）a red light

　aka-no tanin（赤の他人）a perfect stranger

akai〈赤い〉red.

akaku-naru〈赤くなる〉turn red.

kao-o-akaku-suru〈顔を赤くする〉blush.

kao-o-akaku-shite〈顔を赤くして〉with a blush, blushingly.

aka〈あか〉dirt, filth.

　aka o otosu（あかを落とす）wash off the dirt

aka-darake-no〈あかだらけの〉dirty, filthy.

akaaka〈あかあか：明々〉

akaaka-to〈明々と〉brightly.

aka-chan〈あかちゃん：赤ちゃん〉*see.* akambô.

aka-gai〈あかがい：赤貝〉an ark shell.

akagire〈あかぎれ〉chaps, cracks.
 akagire-ga-kireru〈あかぎれが切れる〉get chapped, get cracked.
aka-haji〈あかはじ：赤恥〉
 hito-mae-de aka-haji-o-kaku〈人前で赤恥をかく〉be put to shame in
   public.
akaji〈あかじ：赤字〉red figures, a deficit.
   akaji-keiei（赤字経営）deficit operation
akambō〈あかんぼう：赤ん坊〉a baby.
akami〈あかみ：赤身〉the lean.
akami〈あかみ：赤み〉
 akami-gakatta or *akami-o-obita*〈赤みがかった，赤みを帯びた〉reddish.
aka-nuke〈あかぬけ：あか抜け〉
 aka-nuke-no-shita〈あか抜けのした〉polished, refined.
akarasama〈あからさま〉
 akarasama-na〈あからさまな〉plain; candid, openhearted, honest, direct,
   straightforward.
 akarasama-ni〈あからさまに〉plainly; candidly, openheartedly, honestly,
   directly, straightforwardly.
   akarasama-ni-ieba（あからさまに言えば）to be frank with you,
    frankly speaking
akari〈あかり：明かり〉a light.
   akari o tsukeru（明かりを付ける）turn on the light
   akari o kesu（明かりを消す）turn off the light
akarui〈あかるい：明るい〉light, bright, cheerful; be familiar ((with)), be
   learned ((in)).
   akarui heya（明るい部屋）a light room
   akarui-tokoro-de（明るい所で）in the light
   akarui-uchi-ni（明るいうちに）while it is light, before dark
   akarui mirai（明るい未来）a bright future
   akarui kao（明るい顔）a cheerful look
   bungaku-ni-akarui（文学に明るい）be well read in literature
 akaruku〈明るく〉bright, brightly.
   akaruku-naru（明るくなる）lighten, grow light
   akaruku-suru（明るくする）lighten, make brighter
akarumi〈あかるみ：明るみ〉
 akarumi-ni〈明るみに〉in the light.
   akarumi-ni-deru（明るみに出る）come to light, be brought to light
akashi〈あかし〉

mi-no-akashi-o-tateru〈身のあかしを立てる〉prove one's innocence.

akashia〈アカシア〉an acacia.

akashio〈あかしお：赤潮〉a red tide.

akasu〈あかす：明かす〉pass, spend; tell, disclose, reveal.
　　ichi-ya o akasu（一夜を明かす）pass a night
　　nezu-ni-yo-o-akasu（寝ずに夜を明かす）sit up all night
　　na o akasu（名を明かす）disclose one's name
　　tejina-no-tane o akasu（手品の種を明かす）reveal the trick, show
　　　one's hand

akasu〈あかす：飽かす〉cloy, satiate.
　　kane-ni-akashite ie o tateru（金に飽かして家を建てる）build a house
　　　regardless of expenses

aka-tombo〈あかとんぼ：赤とんぼ〉a red dragonfly.

aka-tsuchi〈あかつち：赤土〉red clay.

akatsuki〈あかつき：暁〉dawn, daybreak.
　　akatsuki-ni（暁に）at dawn

~-no-akatsuki-niwa〈〜の暁には〉in case of... .
　　seikô-no-akatsuki-niwa（成功の暁には）when one has succeeded

-ake-〈-あけ-：-明け-〉
　　akegata-ni（明け方に）at dawn
　　ake-kure（明け暮れ）morning and evening, day and night
　　ake-no-myôjô（明けの明星）the morning star, Venus
　　tsuyu-ake（梅雨明け）the end of the rainy season

akeppanashi〈あけっぱなし：開けっ放し〉
akeppanashi-ni-shite-oku〈開けっ放しにしておく〉leave ((a door)) open.

akeru〈あける：開(空)ける〉open, untie; bore, make; draw aside; absent
　　oneself ((from)); make way ((for)).
　　to o akeru（戸を開ける）open a door
　　kuchi o ookiku-akete（口を大きく開けて）with mouth wide open
　　ana o akeru（穴をあける）make a hole
　　kâten o akeru（カーテンを開ける）draw aside a curtain
　　ie-o-akeru（家を空ける）stay away from home
　　rôjin-ni michi o akeru（老人に道を空ける）make way for an old man

akeru〈あける：明ける〉dawn; open, begin; end, be over.
　　Yo-ga-akeru.（夜が明ける.）It dawns.
　　Akemashite-omedetô!（明けましておめでとう.）A Happy New Year!
　　Tsuyu ga aketa.（梅雨が明けた.）The rainy season is over.

aki〈あき：秋〉autumn, fall.

    aki-bare〈秋晴れ〉 a fine autumn day
    aki-guchi〈秋口〉 the beginning of autumn
    aki-kaze〈秋風〉an autumn breeze

aki〈あき：飽き〉wearisomeness, tiresomeness.
    aki-shō〈飽き性〉 fickle nature

akiru〈飽きる〉 get tired ((of)).

akiaki-suru〈飽き飽きする〉 be sick ((of)), be bored ((with)).
    akiaki-suru shigoto〈飽き飽きする仕事〉 wearisome work

aki-yasui〈飽きやすい〉 get tired easily.

aki〈あき：空き〉a gap, an opening; (a) space; room; vacancy.

aki-〈あき-：空き-〉
    aki-bin〈空き瓶〉 an empty bottle
    aki-ya〈空き家〉 a vacant house
    akichi〈空き地〉 a vacant lot

akinai〈あきない：商い〉trade.

akinau〈商う〉 trade ((in)), deal ((in)).

akiraka〈あきらか：明らか〉

akiraka-ni-suru〈明らかにする〉 make ((a matter)) clear, clear (up).
    gen·in o akiraka-ni-suru〈原因を明らかにする〉 clear up the cause
    taido o akiraka-ni-suru〈態度を明らかにする〉 define one's attitude

akiraka-ni-naru〈明らかになる〉 become clear, be ascertained, be known.

akiraka-na〈明らかな〉 clear, plain, evident, obvious.
    akiraka-na jijitsu〈明らかな事実〉 an obvious fact

akirame〈あきらめ〉resignation, abandonment.
    akirame-no-ii-hito（あきらめのいい人） a person who knows how to resign oneself to one's lot

akirameru〈あきらめる〉 give up, abandon, resign oneself to.

akireru〈あきれる〉be amazed ((at)); be disgusted ((at, by *or* with)).

akire-kaeru〈あきれかえる〉 be thoroughly disgusted ((at, by *or* with)).

akirete-mono-ga-ie-nai〈あきれてものが言えない〉 be speechless with amazement.

akireta〈あきれた〉amazed, disgusting, absurd.
    akireta kao（あきれた顔） an amazed look
    akireta yatsu（あきれたやつ） a disgusting fellow
    akireta nedan（あきれた値段） an absurd price

Akiresu-ken〈アキレスけん〉the Achilles' tendon.

akisu〈あきす：空き巣〉sneak-thieving; a sneak thief, snooper.

akka〈あっか：悪化〉

akka-suru〈悪化する〉make worse.

akke〈あっけ〉

akke-ni-torareru〈あっけに取られる〉be astonished, be astounded, be taken aback, be dumbfounded.

akke-ni-torarete〈あっけに取られて〉in astonishment.

akkenai〈あっけない〉too little, too soon.

akkenaku〈あっけなく〉all too soon, suddenly.

akkenaku shinu（あっけなく死ぬ）die so suddenly

akogare〈あこがれ〉longing, yearning.

akogareru〈あこがれる〉long ((for)), yearn ((after or for)).

akoya-gai〈あこやがい：あこや貝〉a pearl oyster.

aku〈あく：悪〉badness, evil, wickedness, vice.

aku-ni somaru（悪に染まる）be steeped in vice

aku〈あく〉lye, harshness.

aku〈あく：開(空)く〉open, begin; be empty, become vacant; be free.

akubi〈あくび〉a yawn.

akubi-o-suru〈あくびをする〉yawn, give a yawn.

akudoi〈あくどい〉loud, fulsome, vicious.

aku-eikyô〈あくえいきょう：悪影響〉a bad influence.

aku-eikyô o oyobosu（悪影響を及ぼす）exert a bad influence ((upon))

akueki〈あくえき：悪疫〉a plague.

akuheki〈あくへき：悪癖〉a bad habit, a vice.

inshu no akuheki（飲酒の悪癖）the vice of intemperance

akuhyô〈あくひょう：悪評〉a bad reputation, ill fame, an unfavorable criticism.

akuhyô-no-aru hito（悪評のある人）a person of ill fame

akuhyô o tateru〈悪評を立てる〉circulate scandal ((about)).

akuhyô-o-ukeru〈悪評を受ける〉be criticized unfavorably.

akui〈あくい：悪意〉ill will, an evil intention.

akui-no-aru〈悪意のある〉ill-willed.

akui-no-nai（悪意のない）innocent

akuji〈あくじ：悪事〉an evil deed, (a) wrong; a crime.

akuji o hataraku（悪事を働く）do evil(or wrong), commit a crime

aku-jôken〈あくじょうけん：悪条件〉unfavorable conditions.

aku-junkan〈あくじゅんかん：悪循環〉a vicious cycle.

aku-kanjô〈あくかんじょう：悪感情〉bad feeling, an unfavorable impression.

　　aku-kanjô o ataeru（悪感情を与える）　make an unfavorable impression ((on))

akuma〈あくま：悪魔〉a devil, a demon, a fiend.

　akuma-no-yô-na〈悪魔のような〉devilish, fiendish.

akumade(-mo)〈あくまで(も)：飽くまで(も)〉to the last, to the end; to the utmost.

　　akumade-mo tatakau（飽くまでも戦う）　fight to the death

akumei〈あくめい：悪名〉

　akumei-takai〈悪名高い〉notorious.

akumu〈あくむ：悪夢〉a nightmare, a bad dream.

　　akumu-ni-osowareru（悪夢に襲われる）　suffer from a nightmare

akunin〈あくにん：悪人〉a bad man.

akuratsu〈あくらつ：悪らつ〉

　akuratsu-na〈悪らつな〉villainous, foul, crafty, wily.

　　akuratsu-na　shudan（悪らつな手段）　a villainous measure, a foul means

akurei〈あくれい：悪例〉a bad example.

　　akurei o nokosu（悪例を残す）　set a bad example

akuriru〈アクリル〉acryl(yl).

　akuriru-kei(-no) or *akuriru-no*〈アクリル系(の)，アクリルの〉acrylic.

akuru-〈あくる-：明くる-〉*see.*　yoku-.

akuryoku〈あくりょく：握力〉grip.

　　akuryoku-kei（握力計）　a dynamometer

akusei〈あくせい：悪性〉

　akusei-no〈悪性の〉malignant, vicious.

　　akusei-no shuyô（悪性のしゅよう）　a vicious tumor

akusen〈あくせん：悪銭〉

　　Akusen-mi-ni-tsukazu.（悪銭身に付かず.）　Ill gotten, ill spent.

akusento〈アクセント〉an accent, a stress.

　akusento-o-tsukeru〈アクセントを付ける〉accent, stress.

akuseru〈アクセル〉an accelerator.

　　akuseru-o fumu（アクセルを踏む）　step on the accelerator

akushitsu〈あくしつ：悪質〉

　akushitsu-na〈悪質な〉vicious, malignant, wicked.

　　akushitsu-na sagi（悪質な詐欺）　a vicious fraud

　　akushitsu-na gyôsha（悪質な業者）　a wicked trader

akushu〈あくしゅ：握手〉a handshake.

　akushu-suru〈握手する〉shake hands.

akushû 〈あくしゅう：悪臭〉a bad smell, an offensive odor.
　akushû o hanatsu（悪臭を放つ）give out a bad smell
akushû 〈あくしゅう：悪習〉a bad habit.
aku-shumi 〈あくしゅみ：悪趣味〉vulgar taste.
aku-tenkô 〈あくてんこう：悪天候〉bad weather.
akutô 〈あくとう：悪党〉a rascal, a villain, a scoundrel.
akutô 〈あくとう：悪投〉a wild throw.
akutoku 〈あくとく：悪徳〉vice, immorality.
akuun 〈あくうん：悪運〉the devil's own luck.
　akuun-ga-tsuyoi（悪運が強い）have the devil's own luck
akuyaku 〈あくやく：悪役〉a villain's part.
　akuyaku o enjiru（悪役を演じる）play the part of a villain
akuyô 〈あくよう：悪用〉abuse, misuse.
　akuyô-suru 〈悪用する〉make a bad use ((of)), abuse.
akuyû 〈あくゆう：悪友〉a bad friend, bad company.
　akuyû to majiwaru（悪友と交わる）keep bad company
aku-zairyô 〈あくざいりょう：悪材料〉unfavorable factors.
ama 〈あま：亜麻〉flax.
ama 〈あま：海女〉a woman diver.
ama 〈あま：尼〉a nun.
　ama-dera（尼寺）a nunnery, a convent
amachua 〈アマチュア〉an amateur.
ama-dare 〈あまだれ：雨垂れ〉raindrops, eavesdrops.
ama-do 〈あまど：雨戸〉a sliding door, a shutter.
　amado o akeru（雨戸を開ける）pull open the shutters
　amado o shimeru（雨戸を閉める）put up the shutters
amaeru 〈あまえる：甘える〉behave like a spoilt child, play the baby
((to)); fawn ((on)).
ama-gaeru 〈あまがえる：雨がえる〉a tree frog.
ama-gasa 〈あまがさ：雨傘〉an umbrella.
ama-gu 〈あまぐ：雨具〉rain gear, rainwear.
ama-gumo 〈あまぐも：雨雲〉a rain cloud.
amai 〈あまい：甘い〉sweet; indulgent, fond; liberal; optimistic.
　amai-mono（甘いもの）sweets, candy
　amai chichi（甘い父）an indulgent father
　amai haha（甘い母）a fond mother
　amai-ten-o-tsukeru（甘い点を付ける）mark ((papers)) liberally
　amai kangae（甘い考え）an optimistic view

hito-o-amaku-miru〈人を甘く見る〉hold a person cheap.

ama-kuchi〈あまくち：甘口〉
    ama-kuchi-no sake〈甘口の酒〉light *sake*

amaku-suru〈あまくする：甘くする〉sweeten.

ama-mi〈あまみ：甘み〉
    ama-mi-ga-aru〈甘みがある〉taste sweet, be sweetened.

ama-mizu〈あまみず：雨水〉rainwater.

ama-mori〈あまもり：雨漏り〉a leak in the roof.
    ama-mori o tomeru〈雨漏りを止める〉stop the leaks

amanjiru〈あまんじる：甘んじる〉content oneself ((with)), put up ((with)),
    be resigned ((to)).
    kyôgû-ni-amanjiru〈境遇に甘んじる〉be content with one's lot
    ummei-ni-amanjiru〈運命に甘んじる〉be resigned to one's fate
    amanjite〈甘んじて〉contentedly, resignedly.

Ama-no-gawa〈あまのがわ：天の川〉the Milky Way.

amari〈あまり：余り〉the remainder, the rest, leavings.
    amari-mono（余り物）remnants
    amari-no〈余りの〉remaining, surplus.

amari〈あまり：余り〉too.
    amari ookii（余り大きい）too large
    amari~nai〈余り~ない〉too...to, not many, not much, not quite, not
    very.

-amari〈-あまり：-余り〉over, more than; excess.
    ni-nen-amari（二年余り）over(*or* more than) two years
    ureshisa-no-amari（うれしさの余り）in the excess of one's joy
    kanashisa-no-amari（悲しさの余り）in one's grief

amaru〈あまる：余る〉remain, be left (over); be beyond, exceed.
    Jû-kara-ni-o-hiku-to　hachi-amaru.（十から二を引くと八余る。）Two
        from ten leaves eight.
    amatta kane（余った金）the money left over
    chikara-ni-amaru（力に余る）be beyond one's ability
    te-ni-amaru（手に余る）be beyond control
    me-ni-amaru（目に余る）cannot be overlooked

amasu〈あます：余す〉leave (over), save.
    amasu-tokoro-naku〈余すところなく〉exhaustively, thoroughly.

ama-to〈あまとう：甘党〉a person who has a sweet tooth.

amattarui〈あまったるい：甘ったるい〉too sweet, sugary, honeyed.
    amattarui kuchô-de（甘ったるい口調で）in a honeyed tone

ama-yadori 〈あまやどり：雨宿り〉
  ama-yadori-suru 〈雨宿りする〉 take shelter from the rain.
amayakasu 〈あまやかす：甘やかす〉 indulge, pet, spoil.
  amayakashite ko o sodateru 〈甘やかして子を育てる〉 bring up a child
    indulgently
ama-zuppai 〈あまずっぱい：甘酸っぱい〉 sour-sweet.
amba 〈あんば：あん馬〉 a side horse, a pommeled horse.
ame 〈あめ：雨〉 (a) rain, a rainfall, a shower.
  ame-ga-ooi 〈雨が多い〉 have a lot of rain
  ame-ni-au 〈雨に遭う〉 be caught in a rain
  ame-ni-nureru 〈雨にぬれる〉 be wet with rain
  ame-no-sukunai-kuni 〈雨の少ない国〉 a country of little rain
  ame-moyô 〈雨模様〉 a threatening weather
  ame-tsuzuki 〈雨続き〉 a long rain
  kiri-no-yô-na ame 〈霧のような雨〉 a fine rain, a misty rain
  oo-ame 〈大雨〉 a heavy rain
  ame-ga-furu 〈雨が降る〉 rain.
  Ame-ga-furi-sô-da. 〈雨が降りそうだ.〉 It looks like rain.
  ame-ga-furi-dasu 〈雨が降り出す〉 begin to rain
  ame-ga-furi-tsuzuku 〈雨が降り続く〉 keep raining
  ame-ga futtari-yandari-suru 〈雨が降ったりやんだりする〉 rain on and
    off
  Ame ga hageshiku futteiru. 〈雨が激しく降っている.〉 It's raining
    heavily.
  ame-ga-yamu 〈雨がやむ〉 stop raining
  ame-no or *ame-no-ooi* 〈雨の, 雨の多い〉 rainy.
  ame-no-furu-hi-ni 〈雨の降る日に〉 on a rainy day
  ame-no-furu-naka-o 〈雨の降る中を〉 in the rain
ame 〈あめ〉 a candy, a lollipop.
  ame o shaburu 〈あめをしゃぶる〉 eat candy
ame-agari 〈あめあがり：雨上がり〉
  ame-agari-no utsukushii niji 〈雨上がりの美しいにじ〉 a beautiful
    rainbow just after the rain
ame-furi 〈あめふり：雨降り〉 a rainfall; a rainy day.
  ame-furi-ni dete-iku 〈雨降りに出て行く〉 go out in the rain
Amerika 〈アメリカ〉 America.
  Amerika-gasshû-koku 〈アメリカ合衆国〉 the United States of
    America

Amerika-jin〈アメリカ人〉an American
Amerika(-jin)-no〈アメリカ(人)の〉 American

ami〈あみ：網〉a net.
　　ami o haru（網を張る）stretch a net
　　ami o hiku（網を引く）draw a net
　　ami o utsu（網を打つ）cast a net
　　ami-ni-kakaru（網に掛かる）be caught in a net
amība〈アミーバ〉an amoeba.
ami-bari〈あみばり：編み針〉a knitting needle.
amidana〈あみだな：網棚〉a rack.
amido〈あみど：網戸〉a window screen, a screen door.
ami-me〈あみめ：編み目〉a stitch.
ami-mono〈あみもの：編み物〉knitting, (a) knitwork.
　ami-mono-o-suru〈編み物をする〉knit, do knitting.
ami-no-me〈あみのめ：網の目〉meshes〔of a net〕, a network.
amino-san〈アミノさん：アミノ酸〉an amino acid.
amma〈あんま〉massage; a masseur, a masseuse.
　amma-o-suru〈あんまをする〉massage.
ammari〈あんまり〉
　　Sorya ammari-da.（そりゃあんまりだ。）That's too much. / That's
　　the limit. / It's too heartless of you.
ammin〈あんみん：安眠〉a good(quiet *or* sound) sleep.
　　ammin-ga-deki-nai（安眠ができない）have a bad night, be wakeful
　　ammin o bôgai-suru（安眠を妨害する）disturb((a person's)) sleep
　ammin-suru〈安眠する〉sleep well, have a good night's rest.
ammoku〈あんもく：暗黙〉
　ammoku-no〈暗黙の〉tacit.
　　ammoku-no ryôkai（暗黙の了解）a tacit understanding
　ammoku-no-uchi-ni〈暗黙のうちに〉tacitly.
ampi〈あんぴ：安否〉safety.
　　ampi-o-ki-zukau（安否を気遣う）be concerned about ((a person's))
　　safety
　　ampi-o-tazuneru（安否を尋ねる）ask after ((a person's)) safety
ampu〈アンプ〉an amplifier.
amu〈あむ：編む〉knit; braid, plait; crochet.
　　kami o o-sage-ni-amu（髪をお下げに編む）braid one's hair
　ami-awaseru〈編み合わせる〉knit together, intertwine.
an〈あん〉bean jam.

an 〈あん：案〉 a proposal; an idea; a plan, a scheme; expectation; a bill, a draft.

    an o tateru 〈案を立てる〉 make a plan

    mei-an 〈名案〉 a very good idea

  an-ni-sôi-shite 〈案に相違して〉 contrary to one's expectations.

ana 〈あな：穴〉 a hole, a deficit.

    ana o horu 〈穴を掘る〉 dig a hole

    ana o fusagu 〈穴をふさぐ〉 close up a hole

    ana o umeru *or* ana-ume-suru 〈穴を埋める，穴埋めする〉 make up a deficit

anadori 〈あなどり：侮り〉 contempt, scorn.

  anadoru 〈侮る〉 despise, make light ((of)).

anago 〈あなご〉 a sea eel.

anata 〈あなた〉 I say, dear, sir, madam.

anata 〈あなた〉 you.

    anata-wa *or* anata-ga 〈あなたは，あなたが〉 you

    anata-no 〈あなたの〉 your

    anata-ni *or* anata-o 〈あなたに，あなたを〉 you

    anata-no-mono 〈あなたのもの〉 yours

    anata-jishin 〈あなた自身〉 yourself

anata-gata 〈あなたがた：あなた方〉 you.

    anata-gata-wa *or* anata-gata-ga 〈あなた方は，あなた方が〉 you

    anata-gata-no 〈あなた方の〉 your

    anata-gata-ni *or* anata-gata-o 〈あなた方に，あなた方を〉 you

    anata-gata-no-mono 〈あなた方のもの〉 yours

    anata-gata-jishin 〈あなた方自身〉 yourselves

anchaku 〈あんちゃく：安着〉 safe arrival.

  anchaku-suru 〈安着する〉 arrive safely.

anchi 〈あんち：安置〉

  anchi-suru 〈安置する〉 enshrine, lay in state.

anchû-mosaku 〈あんちゅうもさく：暗中模索〉

  anchû-mosaku-suru 〈暗中模索する〉 grope in the dark.

anda 〈あんだ：安打〉 a hit.

andâ-rain 〈アンダーライン〉 an underline.

  andâ-rain-o-hiku 〈アンダーラインを引く〉 underline.

andâ-surô 〈アンダースロー〉 an underhand throw.

ando 〈あんど：安ど〉 *see.* anshin.

ane 〈あね：姉〉 an elder sister, an older sister.

giri-no-ane〈義理の姉〉a sister-in-law

a-nettai〈あねったい：亜熱帯〉the subtropical zones, the subtropics.

a-nettai-no〈亜熱帯の〉subtropical.

angai〈あんがい：案外〉contrary to one's expectations, unexpectedly, surprisingly.

angai-na〈案外な〉unexpected, surprising.

angô〈あんごう：暗号〉a code, a cipher, a secret language.

angô-de dempô o utsu〈暗号で電報を打つ〉 send a telegram in code

angô-dempô〈暗号電報〉 a cipher telegram

angô-de-kaku〈暗号で書く〉cipher.

angô-o-kaidoku-suru〈暗号を解読する〉decipher.

Anguro-Sakuson-minzoku〈アングロサクソンみんぞく：アングロサクソン民族〉the Anglo-Saxon race.

ani〈あに：兄〉an elder brother, an older brother.

giri-no-ani〈義理の兄〉 a brother-in-law

an·i〈あんい：安易〉

an·i-na〈安易な〉easy, easygoing.

an·i-na seikatsu〈安易な生活〉 an easy life

aniyome〈あによめ：兄嫁〉an elder brother's wife, a sister-in-law.

anji〈あんじ：暗示〉a hint, a suggestion.

anji o ataeru〈暗示を与える〉 give a hint

anji-suru〈暗示する〉hint, suggest.

anji-teki-na〈暗示的な〉suggestive.

anjiru〈あんじる：案じる〉be anxious ((about *or* for)), be concerned ((about, for *or* over)), worry ((about *or* over)).

anjū〈あんじゅう：安住〉

anjū-no chi o motomeru〈安住の地を求める〉seek a place for peaceful living.

ankā〈アンカー〉an anchor.

ankâ-o-tsutomeru〈アンカーを務める〉anchor.

ankan〈あんかん：安閑〉

ankan-to(-shite)〈安閑と(して)〉idly, in idleness.

ankan-to-shite kurasu〈安閑として暮らす〉 pass one's time in idleness

ankêto〈アンケート〉a questionnaire.

anki〈あんき：暗記〉

anki-mono〈暗記物〉 memory work

anki-ryoku〈暗記力〉 retentive power

anki-suru〈暗記する〉learn by heart, memorize.
anki-shite-iru〈暗記している〉know by heart.

ankô〈あんこう〉an angler.

ankoku〈あんこく：暗黒〉darkness.
    ankoku-gai（暗黒街）a gangland
ankoku-no〈暗黒の〉dark.

ankôru〈アンコール〉an encore.

ankyo〈あんきょ：暗きょ〉an underdrain, a culvert, a blind ditch.

anna〈あんな〉such, so, like that.
    anna hito（あんな人）such a person
anna-fû-ni〈あんなふうに〉like that, in such a way, (in) that way.

annai〈あんない：案内〉guidance; (an) invitation; a notice, advices.
    annai-jô（案内状）a letter of invitation, an invitation
    annai-sha（案内者）a guide
    annai-sho（案内書）a guidebook
    annai-jo（案内所）an information bureau
    annai-gakari（案内係）a desk clerk, an usher
annai-suru〈案内する〉guide, show, lead.
    michi o annai-suru（道を案内する）show ((a person)) the way
    saki-ni-tatte annai-suru（先に立って案内する）lead the way

ano〈あの〉that, the, those.
    ano hito（あの人）that person
    ano hito-tachi（あの人たち）those people
    ano-yô-ni（あのように）like that, (in) that way
    ano-koro-wa（あのころは）in those days
    ano-toki-irai（あの時以来）since then

ano or **anô**〈あの，あのう〉Well, I say, Why, If you please.

ano-nê〈あのねえ〉Well, Look here, Listen, I say.

ano-yô-na〈あのような〉*see*. anna.

anraku〈あんらく：安楽〉ease, comfort.
    anraku-isu（安楽いす）an easy chair
    anraku-shi（安楽死）mercy killing
anraku-na〈安楽な〉easy, comfortable.
    anraku-na kurashi（安楽な暮らし）a comfortable living
anraku-ni〈安楽に〉easily, comfortably, in comfort.
    anraku-ni kurasu（安楽に暮らす）live in comfort

ansatsu〈あんさつ：暗殺〉assassination.
    ansatsu-o-kuwadateru（暗殺を企てる）make an attempt on another's

life
ansatsu-sha〈暗殺者〉an assassin
ansatsu-suru〈暗殺する〉assassinate.

ansei〈あんせい：安静〉rest, repose.
zettai-ansei（絶対安静）an absolute rest
ansei-ni-shite-iru〈安静にしている〉keep quiet.

anshin〈あんしん：安心〉
anshin-suru〈安心する〉feel easy ((about)), feel relieved, rest assured.
anshin-saseru〈安心させる〉set ((a person)) at ease.
anshin-shite〈安心して〉feeling at rest.
anshin-shite shinu（安心して死ぬ）die without regret

anshitu〈あんしつ：暗室〉a darkroom.

anshô〈あんしょう：暗礁〉a sunken rock, a deadlock.
anshô-ni-nori-ageru〈暗礁に乗り上げる〉run on a rock, be deadlocked.

anshô〈あんしょう：暗唱〉recitation, recital.
anshô-suru〈暗唱する〉recite, repeat from memory.

antai〈あんたい：安泰〉
antai-de-aru〈安泰である〉be safe, be secure.
Kare-no chii wa antai-da.（彼の地位は安泰だ。）His position is secure.

antan〈あんたん：暗たん〉
antan-taru〈暗たんたる〉dark, gloomy, dismal.
antan-taru zento（暗たんたる前途）gloomy prospects

antei〈あんてい：安定〉stability, steadiness, balance.
antei o tamotsu（安定を保つ）keep balance
antei o ushinau（安定を失う）lose balance
antei o kaku（安定を欠く）lack stability
seikatsu no antei o uru（生活の安定を得る）secure a sure means of living
antei-kan（安定感）a sense of stability
antei-saseru〈安定させる〉stabilize.
antei-shita or *antei-shite-iru*〈安定した，安定している〉stable.
antei-shita shokugyô（安定した職業）stable occupation

antena〈アンテナ〉an antenna.
antena o haru（アンテナを張る）stretch an antenna

an・yaku〈あんやく：暗躍〉
an・yaku-suru〈暗躍する〉engage in secret maneuvers.

anzan〈あんざん：安産〉

anzan-o-suru〈安産をする〉have an easy delivery〔to a boy〕.

anzan〈あんざん：暗算〉mental calculation.

   anzan-o-suru〈暗算をする〉calculate mentally.

anzen〈あんぜん：安全〉safety, security.

   anzen-beruto（安全ベルト）　a safety belt, a seat belt

   anzen-chitai（安全地帯）　a safety zone

   anzen-dai-ichi（安全第一）　Safety First

   anzen-shūkan（安全週間）　Safety Week

   anzen-sōchi（安全装置）　a safety device

   anzen-hoshō-jōyaku（安全保障条約）　a security pact

   anzen-unten（安全運転）　careful driving

   anzen-na〈安全な〉safe, secure.

   anzen-ni〈安全に〉safely, in safety.

anzu〈あんず〉an apricot.

ao〈あお：青〉blue, green.

   ao-shingō（青信号）　a green light

   aoi〈青い〉blue, green, pale.

   aoi-me（青い目）　blue eyes

   kao-iro-ga-aoi（顔色が青い）　look pale

   aoku-naru〈青くなる〉turn pale.

aoba〈あおば：青葉〉green leaves.

   aoba-ga-de-hajimeru（青葉が始める）　begin to show green

aogu〈あおぐ〉fan.

aogu〈あおぐ：仰ぐ〉look up ((at)); respect, look up ((to)).

   sora-o aogu（空を仰ぐ）　look up at the sky

   shi-to aogu（師と仰ぐ）　look up to ((a person)) as his teacher

aojashin〈あおじゃしん：青写真〉a blueprint.

aojiroi〈あおじろい：青白い〉pale, pallid.

aomi〈あおみ：青み〉

   aomi-gakatta〈青みがかった〉bluish, greenish.

aomono〈あおもの：青物〉greens, vegetables.

aomuke〈あおむけ：仰向け〉

   aomuke-ni〈仰向けに〉on one's back.

   aomuke-ni neru（仰向けに寝る）　lie on one's back

aori〈あおり〉

   fu-keiki-no-aori-o-kutte tōsan-suru〈不景気のあおりを食って倒産する〉fail as a result of business depression.

   aoru〈あおる〉stir up, inflame.

han-nichi-kanjô o aoru〈反日感情をあおる〉stir up anti-Japanese feeling

ao-suji〈あおすじ：青筋〉

ao-suji-o-tatete-okoru〈青筋を立てて怒る〉turn purple with rage.

aozameru〈あおざめる：青ざめる〉turn pale.

aozameta〈青ざめた〉pale, pallid.

aozora〈あおぞら：青空〉the blue sky.

apâto〈アパート〉an apartment house, flats; an apartment, a flat.

apîru〈アピール〉an appeal.

apîru-suru〈アピールする〉appeal ((to)).

taishû-ni apîru-suru（大衆にアピールする） appeal to the masses

appaku〈あっぱく：圧迫〉pressure, oppression.

appaku o kuwaeru（圧迫を加える） put pressure ((upon))

appaku-o-ukeru〈圧迫を受ける〉be pressed.

appaku-o-ukete〈圧迫を受けて〉under pressure.

appare〈あっぱれ〉

Appare!（あっぱれ.）Bravo! / Well done!

appare-na〈あっぱれな〉admirable, splendid, excellent.

ara〈あら〉Oh! / Why! / Good gracious! / Dear me!

Ara, hontô?（あら，本当.）Really?

araara-shii〈あらあらしい：荒々しい〉rude, rough, harsh.

araara-shiku〈荒々しく〉rudely, roughly, harshly.

Arabia〈アラビア〉Arabia.

Arabia-jin（アラビア人） an Arab

Arabia-go（アラビア語） Arabic

Arabia-sûji（アラビア数字） Arabic numerals

Arabia(-jin)-no（アラビア(人)の） Arabian

Arabu-rengô-kyôwa-koku〈アラブれんごうきょうわこく：アラブ連合共和国〉the United Arab Republic.

ara-dateru〈あらだてる：荒ら立てる〉aggravate, make serious, make ((a matter)) worse.

arai〈あらい：粗い〉coarse, rough.

me-no-arai kiji（目の粗い生地） coarse fabric

kime-no-arai hada（きめの粗い肌） a rough skin

arai shima（粗いしま） large stripes

arai〈あらい：荒い〉rude, wild, rough, harsh, violent, heavy, strong.

kishô-no-arai hito（気性の荒い人） a man of violent temper

kotoba-zukai-ga-arai（言葉遣いが荒い） be rough in speech

Umi ga arai. 〔海が荒い。〕 The sea is rough.

arai 〈あらい：洗い〉 wash, washing.

　arai-no-kiku 〈洗いのきく〉 washable.

arai-mono 〈あらいもの：洗い物〉 washing, laundry; the dishes.

　arai-mono o suru 〔洗い物をする〕 do one's washing, do the dishes

arakajime 〈あらかじめ〉 beforehand, in advance, previously.

ara-kasegi 〈あらかせぎ：荒稼ぎ〉

　ara-kasegi-o-suru 〈荒稼ぎをする〉 make a big hit in speculation, make quick money, commit burglary.

aranami 〈あらなみ：荒波〉 angry waves, a troubled sea.

　jinsei no aranami-ni-momareru 〔人生の荒波にもまれる〕 be tossed about in the storms of life

arappoi 〈あらっぽい：荒っぽい〉 wild, rough.

arare 〈あられ〉 hail, a hailstone.

　Arare-ga-furu. 〔あられが降る。〕 It hails.

ara-ryôji 〈あらりょうじ：荒療治〉 a drastic treatment, a drastic measure.

　ara-ryôji o yaru 〔荒療治をやる〕 take a drastic measure

ara-sagashi 〈あらさがし：粗探し〉 faultfinding.

　ara-sagashi-o-suru 〈粗探しをする〉 find fault ((with)).

arashi 〈あらし〉 a storm, a tempest.

　arashi-no-mae-no shizukesa 〔あらしの前の静けさ〕 the calm before a storm

　arashi-ni au 〔あらしに遭う〕 be overtaken by a storm

　arashi-no 〈あらしの〉 stormy.

　arashi-no yoru-ni 〔あらしの夜に〕 on a stormy night

ara-shigoto 〈あらしごと：荒仕事〉 hard manual labor.

arasoi 〈あらそい：争い〉 a dispute, an argument, a quarrel; a competition, (a) rivalry; a discord, a strife.

　arasoi no tane o maku 〔争いの種をまく〕 sow the seeds of strife

arasou 〈あらそう：争う〉 dispute, argue, quarrel; compete with ((a person)) for, contest with ((a person)) for; be at discord ((with)), fight ((against)).

　hôtei-de arasou 〔法廷で争う〕 contest ((the point)) at law

　seki-o-arasou 〔席を争う〕 scramble for good places

　arasowarenu 〈争われぬ〉 incontestable, undeniable.

　arasowarenu shôko 〔争われぬ証拠〕 a positive proof

arasu 〈あらす：荒らす〉 ruin, devastate, harm, damage; raid, break ((into)).

　sakumotsu-o-arasu 〔作物を荒らす〕 do damage to the crops

ginkô-o-arasu〈銀行を荒らす〉 break into a bank

ara-suji〈あらすじ：粗筋〉an outline, a plot.

aratamaru〈あらたまる：改まる〉be renewed; change, be changed, be revised, be improved, be reformed; become formal.

aratamatta-mono-no-ii-kata-o-suru〈改まったものの言い方をする〉 use formal language

aratameru〈あらためる：改める〉change, alter; renew, innovate; correct, reform, revise.

okonai o aratameru〈行いを改める〉 mend one's ways

aratamete〈あらためて：改めて〉again, over again, another time.

arate〈あらて：新手〉a new type.

arate-no-sagi〈新手の詐欺〉 a new type of swindling

arau〈あらう：洗う〉wash, cleanse, rinse.

mizu-de arau〈水で洗う〉 wash in water

atama o arau〈頭を洗う〉 shampoo one's hair

kampan o arau〈甲板を洗う〉 sweep the deck

ara-umi〈あらうみ：荒海〉a rough sea.

arawareru〈あらわれる：現(表)れる〉come out, appear, come in sight; show itself, be revealed; be found (out), be discovered.

yo-ni-arawareru〈世に現れる〉 become famous(*or* known)

arawasu〈あらわす：現(表)す〉show, manifest, display, prove, speak ((for)); reveal, betray, expose; express; stand ((for)), symbolize; distinguish.

shuwan o arawasu〈手腕を現す〉 display one's ability

kanjô o arawasu〈感情を表す〉 betray one's feeling

jibun-no-kangae o kotoba-de arawasu〈自分の考えを言葉で表す〉 express oneself in words

na-o-arawasu〈名を現す〉 distinguish oneself, become famous

arawasu〈あらわす：著す〉write.

hon o arawasu〈本を著す〉 write a book

arayuru〈あらゆる：有らゆる〉every, all.

arayuru shudan o tsukusu〈あらゆる手段を尽くす〉 try every possible means

arayuru-ten-de〈あらゆる点で〉 in all respects

are〈あれ〉There! / Look!.

Are, tasukete!〈あれ，助けて．〉 Help, help!

are〈あれ：荒れ〉chapping, roughness.

hifu-no-are-ni-yoku-kiku〈皮膚の荒れによく効く〉 be very good for

chapped skin

are 〈あれ〉 that.

    are-kore *or* are-ya-kore-ya（あれこれ，あれやこれや） this and that

        are-kore-kangaeta-sue（あれこれ考えた末） after fully considering the matter

    are-hodo（あれほど） so much, to that extent

    are-hodo-no（あれほどの） such

    are-irai *or* are-kara（あれ以来，あれから） since then, after that

  are-ra〈あれら〉 those, they.

are-chi〈あれち：荒れ地〉 wasteland.

are-hateru〈荒れ果てる〉 be ruined, lie waste, be desolated.

  are-hateta〈荒れ果てた〉 ruined, waste, desolate.

are-hôdai〈あれほうだい：荒れ放題〉

  are-hôdai-de-aru〈荒れ放題である〉 be left to run waste, be left to dilapidation.

are-kuruu〈あれくるう：荒れ狂う〉 rage.

    are-kuruu umi（荒れ狂う海） raging waves

areru〈あれる：荒れる〉 get rough, be stormy; be devastrated, go to ruin, be dilapidated; become rough, get chappy.

    Umi ga arete-iru.（海が荒れている。） The sea is rough.

  areta〈荒れた〉 dilapidated, ill-kept, desolate, rough.

    areta ie（荒れた家） a dilapidated house

    areta tochi（荒れた土地） desolate land

    areta te（荒れた手） rough hands

arerugî〈アレルギー〉 allergy.

    arerugî-hannô（アレルギー反応） allergic reaction

    arerugî-taishitsu（アレルギー体質） an allergic constitution

  arerugî-sei(-no)〈アレルギー性(の)〉 allergic.

    arerugî-sei shikkan（アレルギー性疾患） an allergic disease

are-shô〈あれしょう：荒れ性〉

    are-shô-no-hito（荒れ性の人） a person who is liable to have a chappy skin

ari〈あり〉 an ant.

    ari-jigoku（あり地獄） an ant lion

ari-amaru〈ありあまる：有り余る〉

  ari-amaru-hodo(-no)〈有り余るほど(の)〉 enough and to spare.

    ari-amaru-hodo kane-ga-aru（有り余るほど金がある） have enough money and to spare

ariari-to 〈ありありと〉 vividly, distinctly, clearly.
    ariari-to-me-ni-ukabu（ありありと目に浮かぶ） have a vivid recollection ((of))

ari-awase 〈ありあわせ：有り合わせ〉
  ari-awase-no 〈有り合わせの〉 ready, in(*or* on) hand.
    ari-awase-no ryôri（有り合わせの料理） ready dishes
    ari-awase-no-mono-de-shokuji-o-suru（有り合わせの物で食事をする） take potluck

aribai 〈アリバイ〉 an alibi.
    Aribai ga kuzureta.（アリバイが崩れた.） The alibi was broken down.

ari-fure-ta 〈ありふれた：有り触れた〉 common, commonplace, familiar.
    ari-fure-ta koto（ありふれた事） a commonplace event
    ari-fure-ta hanashi（ありふれた話） an old story

ari-gachi 〈ありがち：有りがち〉
  ari-gachi-de-aru 〈有りがちである〉 be apt ((to do)).
  ari-gachi-na 〈有りがちな〉 frequent, common.

arigane 〈ありがね：有り金〉 all the money one has in hand.

arigatai 〈ありがたい：有り難い〉 kind, welcome, gracious, thankful, grateful.
    arigatai kotoba（有り難い言葉） one's kind words
    arigatai okuri-mono（有り難い贈り物） a welcome gift
    arigataku-nai（有り難くない） unwelcome
  arigataku-omou 〈有り難く思う〉 be thankful ((for)), be obliged ((to)), appreciate.
  arigatai-koto-ni-wa 〈有り難いことには〉 fortunately.

arigata-meiwaku 〈ありがためいわく：有り難迷惑〉 misplaced kindness.

arigata-mi 〈ありがたみ：有り難み〉 value, blessing.
    arigata-mi o shiru（有り難みを知る） know the true value
    kane no arigata-mi（金の有り難み） the value of money
    kenkô no arigata-mi（健康の有り難み） the blessing of health

Arigatô. 〈ありがとう。：有り難う。〉 Thank you. / Many thanks. / It's very kind of you ((to)).

ari-no-mama 〈ありのまま：有りのまま〉 as it is.
    ari-no-mama o iu（有りのままを言う） tell the truth
  ari-no-mama-no 〈有りのままの〉 plain, actual, frank, candid, undisguised, unexaggerated.
  ari-no-mama-ni 〈有りのままに〉 plainly, frankly, candidly, without

concealment, without exaggeration.

　　ari-no-mama-ni-ieba（有りのままに言えば）　to tell the truth

arisama〈ありさま：有様〉a state, (a) condition, circumstances; a sight, a scene, a spectacle.

　　ima-no　arisama-dewa（今の有様では）　under the present circumstances

　　santan-taru　arisama　o　teisuru（惨たんたる有様を呈する）　present a wretched spectacle

arishi-hi〈ありしひ：在りし日〉

　　arishi-hi-no　Mihara-san（在りし日の三原さん）　the late Mr. Mihara while in life

ari-sô-na〈ありそうな：有りそうな〉probable, likely.

　　ari-sô-na-koto（ありそうな事）　a probability

ari-sô-ni-nai〈ありそうにない〉improbable, unlikely.

　　ari-sô-ni-nai hanashi（ありそうにない話）　a tall story

aritsuku〈ありつく〉

　　go-chisô-ni-aritsuku（ごちそうにありつく）　get treated〔to a dinner〕

　　shoku-ni-aritsuku（職にありつく）　get employment

arittake〈ありったけ：有りったけ〉

arittake-no〈有りったけの〉all.

　　arittake-no kane（有りったけの金）　all the money one has

　　arittake-no　chikara　o　dasu（有りったけの力を出す）　put forth all one's strength

ari-uru〈ありうる：有り得る〉*see.* ari-sô-na.

ari-e-nai〈あり得ない〉*see.* ari-sô-ni-nai.

aru〈ある：在(有)る〉be, there is, there are, exist, be found; be situated, stand, lie, run; have, possess, own, keep; happen, occur, take place; be held, come off; consist ((in)).

aru〈ある〉a, one, some, a certain.

　　aru hi（ある日）　one day

　　aru hito（ある人）　some one

　　aru teido-made（ある程度まで）　to a certain extent

　　aru-toki（ある時）　once, on a certain occasion

　　aru tokoro-de（ある所で）　at a certain place

arubaito〈アルバイト〉a part-time job.

　　arubaito-no gakusei（アルバイトの学生）　a working student

　　arubaito-o-suru（アルバイトをする）　work at a part-time job

aru-chû〈アルちゅう：アル中〉an abbreviation of 'arukôru-chûdoku'.

arudake〈あるだけ：有るだけ〉*see.* arittake.

arufa〈アルファ〉alpha.

kyûryô ni-ka-getsu-bun purasu-arufa-no-bônasu（給料二か月分プラス
アルファのボーナス）a bonus equivalent to two months' pay plus
something

arufabetto〈アルファベット〉the alphabet.

arufabetto-jun-ni〈アルファベット順に〉alphabetically, in alphabetical
order.

aruiwa〈あるいは〉or, either...or; perhaps, maybe.

kore-ka aruiwa sore（これかあるいはそれ）this or that

Aruiwa sô-kamo-shirenai.（あるいはそうかも知れない。）It may be so.

aruji〈あるじ〉*see.* shujin.

arukari〈アルカリ〉alkali.

arukari-sei(-no)〈アルカリ性(の)〉alkaline.

arukôru〈アルコール〉alcohol.

arukôru-inryô（アルコール飲料）alcoholic drinks

arukôru-chûdoku（アルコール中毒）alcoholism; an alcoholic.

arukôru(-sei)-no〈アルコール(性)の〉alcoholic.

aruku〈あるく：歩く〉walk, go on foot.

toori-o aruku（通りを歩く）walk along the street

aruite gakkô-e iku（歩いて学校へ行く）go to school on foot

aruite kaeru（歩いて帰る）walk home

kyôkai-made aruite-go-fun（教会まで歩いて5分）five minutes' walk
to the church

aruki-mawaru（歩き回る）walk about

aruminiumu〈アルミニウム〉aluminum, aluminium.

Arupusu〈アルプス〉the Alps.

Nihon Arupusu（日本アルプス）the Japan Alps

aruto〈アルト〉alto.

aruto-kashu（アルト歌手）an alto

Aruzenchin〈アルゼンチン〉Argentina.

Aruzenchin-jin（アルゼンチン人）an Argentine

Aruzenchin(-jin)-no（アルゼンチン(人)の）Argentine

aryûsan〈ありゅうさん：亜硫酸〉sulfurous acid.

asa〈あさ：朝〉morning.

asa(-ni)（朝(に)）in the morning

getsuyô-no-asa-ni（月曜の朝に）on Monday morning

asa-hayaku（朝早く）early in the morning

asa-kara ban-made〔朝から晩まで〕 from morning till night

asa-ban〔朝晩〕 morning and evening, day and night

mai-asa〔毎朝〕 every morning

asa〈あさ：麻〉hemp(-cloth), hemp(-plant).

asa-nawa〔麻縄〕 a hemp rope

asagao〈あさがお：朝顔〉a morning glory.

asa-gohan〈あさごはん：朝御飯〉breakfast.

asa-guroi〈あさぐろい：浅黒い〉swarthy.

asahaka〈あさはか：浅はか〉

asahaka-na〈浅はかな〉 shallow, thoughtless; silly.

asahaka-na kangae〔浅はかな考え〕 a shallow idea

asahi〈あさひ：朝日〉the morning sun, the rising sun.

asai〈あさい：浅い〉shallow, superficial; light; slight; short.

asai ike〔浅い池〕 a shallow pond

asai chishiki〔浅い知識〕 a superficial knowledge

asai nemuri〔浅い眠り〕 a light sleep

asai kizu〔浅い傷〕 a slight wound

shôbai-no-keiken-ga-asai〔商売の経験が浅い〕 have little experience in business

asamashii〈あさましい：浅ましい〉shameful, base, mean; wretched.

asamashii okonai〔浅ましい行い〕 a shameful conduct, a mean action

asamashii kangae〔浅ましい考え〕 a base idea

asamashii yo-no-naka〔浅ましい世の中〕 a wretched world

asamashiku-omou〈浅ましく思う〉 be ashamed ((of oneself)).

asa-meshi〈あさめし：朝飯〉*see.* asa-gohan.

asa-meshi-mae-no〈朝飯前の〉 easy.

asa-meshi-mae-no shigoto〔朝飯前の仕事〕 an easy task

asane〈あさね：朝寝〉late rising.

asane-suru〈朝寝する〉 get up late.

asa-nebô〈あさねぼう：朝寝坊〉a late riser.

asaru〈あさる〉search ((for)), hunt ((for)).

hon-o-asaru〔本をあさる〕 hunt for books

asase〈あさせ：浅瀬〉a shoal, shallows, a ford.

asase-ni-nori-ageru〈浅瀬に乗り上げる〉 run aground.

asatte〈あさって〉the day after tomorrow.

asatte-no-asa〔あさっての朝〕 the morning after next

asa-yake〈あさやけ：朝焼け〉the morning glow.

ase〈あせ：汗〉sweat, perspiration.

　　　ase o fuku（汗をふく）　wipe the sweat
　　　ase-bamu（汗ばむ）　be slightly moist with perspiration
　　　ase-bisshori-da（汗びっしょりだ）　be wet with perspiration
　　　Watashi-wa ase-kaki-da.（私は汗かきだ.）　I sweat easily.
　　ase-o-kaku〈汗をかく〉sweat.
asedaku〈あせだく：汗だく〉
　　asedaku-ni-natte〈汗だくになって〉dripping with sweat.
asemo〈あせも：汗も〉prickly heat, (a) heat rash.
　　　asemo-ga-dekiru（汗もができる）　have prickly heat
aseru〈あせる：焦る〉be in a hurry; be impatient, be too eager.
　　　Aseru-na.（焦るな.）　Don't be in a hurry. / Go easy.
　　　seikō-o-aseru（成功を焦る）　be too eager for success
aseru〈あせる〉fade, discolor.
　　iro-aseta〈色あせた〉faded, discolored.
ashi〈あし：足(脚)〉a foot, a leg; a paw; a pace, a step.
　　　ashi-ga-hayai（脚が速い）　be swift of foot
　　　ashi-ga-osoi（脚が遅い）　be slow of foot
　　　ashi-ga-itai（足が痛い）　have a sore foot
　　　ashi-ga-bô-no-yô-ni-naru（足が棒のようになる）　walk one's legs off
　　　ashi-no-kô（足の甲）　the instep of a foot
　　　ashi-no-ura（足の裏）　the sole of a foot
　　　ashi-no-yubi（足の指）　a toe
　　　sambon-ashi-no têburu（三本脚のテーブル）　a three-legged table
　　　ashi-o fumu（足を踏む）　step on ((another's)) foot
　　　ashi o nobasu（足を伸ばす）　stretch out one's legs
　　　tsukareta ashi o hikizutte-aruku（疲れた足を引きずって歩く）　drag
　　　　one's weary feet
　　　ashi o hayameru（脚を速める）　quicken one's pace
　　　watashi-no ie-kara honno hito-ashi（私の家からほんのひと足）　only a
　　　　step from my house
　　ashi-ga-tsuku〈足が付く〉be traced, be tracked.
　　ashi-o-arau〈足を洗う〉wash one's hands ((of)).
　　ashi o hipparu〈足を引っ張る〉drag ((a person)) down.
ashi〈あし〉a reed, a rush.
ashi-ato〈あしあと：足跡〉a footprint, a footmark, a footstep.
　　　ashi-ato o nokosu（足跡を残す）　leave one's footprints
　　　ashi-ato o tadotte-iku（足跡をたどって行く）　follow up ((a person's))
　　　　footsteps, follow in ((a person's)) tracks

ashiba 〈あしば：足場〉 scaffolding, a scaffold.

ashi-bumi 〈あしぶみ・足踏み〉
  ashi-bumi-suru〈足踏みする〉 mark time; be at a standstill.

ashidori 〈あしどり：足取り〉 a step, a pace.
  karui ashidori-de（軽い足取りで） with a light step
  omoi ashidori-de（重い足取りで） with a heavy step

ashi-gakari 〈あしがかり：足掛かり〉 a foothold, a footing; a clue, a key.
  ashi-gakari-ga-dekiru（足掛かりができる） secure a footing

ashika 〈あしか〉 a sea lion.

ashi-kake 〈あしかけ：足掛け〉
  ashi-kake-go-nen（足掛け五年） five calendar years

ashikarazu 〈あしからず〉
  Ashikarazu go-ryōshō-kudasai.（あしからずご了承ください。） I beg you
    to understand my position.

ashi-koshi 〈あしこし：足腰〉 legs and loins.
  ashi-koshi-no-tatsu-uchi-wa〈足腰の立つうちは〉 while one is strong
    enough for work.

ashi-kubi 〈あしくび：足首〉 an ankle.

ashi-moto 〈あしもと：足下〉
  ashi-moto-ni〈足下に〉 at one's feet.
    Ashi-moto-ni-ki-o-tsukete!（足下に気を付けて。） Watch your step!

ashi-nami 〈あしなみ：足並み〉 pace, step.
  ashi-nami o soroeru（足並みをそろえる） keep pace ((with))
  ashi-nami-ga-midareru（足並みが乱れる） walk out of step

ashi-oto 〈あしおと：足音〉 a footstep, a step.
  ashi-oto o tateru（足音を立てる） make the sound of footsteps
  ashi-oto-o-tatezu-ni（足音を立てずに） with silent steps

ashirai 〈あしらい〉
  kyaku-ashirai-ga-ii〈客あしらいがいい〉 be hospitable, give good service.

ashirau 〈あしらう〉
  hito o tsumetaku ashirau〈人を冷たくあしらう〉 treat a person in a cold
    way.

ashita 〈あした〉 *see.* asu.

asobaseru 〈あそばせる：遊ばせる〉 amuse; leave ((a person *or* a thing))
    idle.
  kane o asobaseru（金を遊ばせる） have one's money idle

asobi 〈あそび：遊び〉 play, recreation, amusement, pleasure.
  asobi-ni inaka-e iku（遊びに田舎へ行く） go into the country for

    pleasure

    Asobi-ni-kite-kudasai.〔遊びに来てください.〕 Come and see me.

    soto-e asobi-ni-iku〔外へ遊びに行く〕 go out to play

    asobi-tomodachi〔遊び友達〕 a playmate

    asobi-ba〔遊び場〕 a playground

    asobi-jikan〔遊び時間〕 playtime, a recess

    asobi-hambun-ni〔遊び半分に〕 partly for pleasure

asobu〈あそぶ：遊ぶ〉play, amuse oneself, enjoy oneself; go on an excursion, visit; be idle.

    karuta-o-shite-asobu〔かるたをして遊ぶ〕 play cards

    uta-o-utatte asobu〔歌を歌って遊ぶ〕 amuse oneself with singing

    asonde-kurasu〔遊んで暮らす〕 loaf one's time away; live in idleness

asoko〈あそこ〉that place.

    asoko-made〔あそこまで〕 as far as there

    asoko-no, asoko-e or asoko-ni〔あそこの, あそこへ, あそこに〕 there, over there

assaku〈あっさく：圧搾〉compression.

    assaku-ki〔圧搾機〕 a compressor

    assaku-kûki〔圧搾空気〕 compressed air

assaku-suru〈圧搾する〉compress.

assari(-to)〈あっさり（と）〉easily, simply, briefly, lightly, frankly.

    shiai ni assari katsu〔試合にあっさり勝つ〕 win a game easily

assari-shita〈あっさりした〉plain, simple, light, openhearted.

    assari-shita tabe-mono〔あっさりした食べ物〕 a plain meal, light food

    assari-shita hito〔あっさりした人〕 an openhearted person

assen〈あっせん：あっ旋〉good offices, mediation.

    Takata-shi no assen-de〔高田氏のあっ旋で〕 through the good offices of Mr. Takata

assen-suru〈あっ旋する〉use one's good offices, mediate ((between)).

    shûshoku-o-assen-suru〔就職をあっ旋する〕 help ((a person)) (to) find employment

asshi〈あっし：圧死〉

asshi-suru〈圧死する〉be crushed to death.

asshuku〈あっしゅく：圧縮〉compression, condensation.

    asshuku-ki or asshuku-pompu〔圧縮器, 圧縮ポンプ〕 a compressor

asshuku-suru〈圧縮する〉compress, condense.

asu〈あす：明日〉tomorrow.

asu-no-asa（明日の朝）tomorrow morning

âsu〈アース〉a ground, an earth.

ataeru〈あたえる：与える〉give, bestow; award; provide, furnish; set; cause.

    kane o ataeru（金を与える）give money

    shô o ataeru（賞を与える）award ((a person)) a prize

    shigoto o ataeru（仕事を与える）provide ((a person)) with work

    mondai o ataeru（問題を与える）set ((a pupil)) a problem

    songai-o-ataeru（損害を与える）do damage ((to)), inflict an injury ((on))

atai〈あたい：値〉

    atai-suru〈値する〉be worth, be worthy ((of)), deserve.

    yomu-ni-atai-suru（読むに値する）be worth reading

atakamo〈あたかも〉just, like, just as, as...as, as if.

atama〈あたま：頭〉a head; brains; hair.

    atama-no-teppen-kara　ashi-no-saki-made（頭のてっぺんから足の先まで）from head to foot

    atama-ga-itai（頭が痛い）have a headache

    atama-ga-aru（頭がある）have brains

    atama-ga-nai（頭がない）have no brains

    atama-ga-ii（頭がいい）have a clear head

    atama-ga-warui（頭が悪い）have a dull head

    atama-ga-furui（頭が古い）have old-fashioned ideas

    atama o tsukau（頭を使う）use one's head, exercise one's brains

    atama-o-nayamasu（頭を悩ます）rack one's brains ((over)), be worried ((about))

    atama o katte-morau（頭を刈ってもらう）have one's hair cut

atama-kazu〈あたまかず：頭数〉the number of persons.

    atama-kazu-o-soroeru〈頭数をそろえる〉make up the number.

atama-kin〈あたまきん：頭金〉down payment, a deposit.

    atama-kin-o-harau（頭金を払う）make a down payment

atama-uchi〈あたまうち：頭打ち〉

    kyûryô-ga-atama-uchi-ni-naru〈給料が頭打ちになる〉reach the top of the pay list for one's rank.

atarashii〈あたらしい：新しい〉new, fresh, recent, hot, modern.

    atarashii ie（新しい家）a new house

    atarashii sakana（新しい魚）fresh fish

    atarashii nyûsu（新しいニュース）hot news

    kioku-ni-atarashii（記憶に新しい）be fresh in one's memory

atarashiku〈新しく〉newly.

    atarashiku-tateta ie（新しく建てた家）a newly-built house

    atarashiku-kita sensei（新しく来た先生）the new teacher

atari〈あたり：辺り〉

    atari-ichimen-ni（辺り一面に）all over the place

    tsugi-no nichiyō-atari（次の日曜あたり）about next Sunday

atari-ni or *atari-o*〈辺りに，辺りを〉about, around, near.

    kono-atari-ni（この辺りに）about here

    atari-o-mi-mawasu（辺りを見回す）look around

atari〈あたり：当たり〉a hit, a success.

    ii atari（いい当たり）a nice hit

    oo-atari（大当たり）a great hit

    atari-hazure（当たり外れ）hit or miss, success or failure

    atari-doshi（当たり年）a luck year, a fruitful year

    atari-kuji（当たりくじ）a winning number

    atari-chirasu（当たり散らす）find faults with everybody

-atari〈－あたり：－当たり〉per, a.

atarimae〈あたりまえ：当たり前〉

~*-no-wa atarimae-da* .〈～のは当たり前だ。〉It is natural that... .

    Kare-ga　okoru-no-wa-atarimae-da.（彼が怒るのは当たり前だ。）lt is natural that he should be angry.

atarimae-no〈当たり前の〉usual, common, ordinary, proper, right, just, reasonable, natural.

    atarimae-no koto（当たり前のこと）a matter of course

        atarimae-no-koto　to　omou（当たり前のことと思う）take ((it)) for granted

atari-sawari〈あたりさわり：当たり障り〉

atari-sawari-no-nai〈当たり障りのない〉noncommittal.

    atari-sawari-no-nai　henji（当たり障りのない返事）a noncommittal answer

    atari-sawari-no-nai-koto-o-iu（当たり障りのないことを言う）talk harmlessly, talk harmless remarks

ataru〈あたる：当たる〉hit, strike; shine ((upon)), be exposed; warm oneself; come true, be right, guess right; fall on; be equal ((to)); lie; disagree ((with)), be poisoned; undertake; make a hit; treat.

    tama-ni-ataru（弾に当たる）be hit by a bullet

    hi-no-atara-nai basho（日の当たらない場所）a place out of the sun

　　yo-tsuyu-ni-ataru（夜露に当たる）　be exposed to the night dew

　　hi-ni-ataru（火に当たる）　warm oneself at the fire

　　mato ni ataru（的に当たる）　hit the target

　　nichiyô-ni ataru（日曜に当たる）　fall on Sunday

　　go-mêtoru-ni-ataru（五メートルに当たる）　be equal to 5 meters

　　higashi-ni-atatte（東に当たって）　to the east

　　mizu-ni-ataru（水に当たる）　be poisoned by bad water

　　atsusa-ni-ataru（暑さに当たる）　be affected by the summer heat

　　atatta shibai（当たった芝居）　a hit play

　　tsuraku ataru（つらく当たる）　treat harshly

atatakai〈あたたかい：暖(温)かい〉warm.

　　atatakai fuyu（暖かい冬）　a mild winter

　　atatakai kokoro（温かい心）　a warm heart

　atatakaku〈暖(温)かく〉warmly, kindly.

　　atatakaku-shite-iru（暖かくしている）　keep oneself warm

　　hi-mashi-ni atatakaku-naru（日増しに暖かくなる）　be getting warmer and warmer

atatakami〈あたたかみ：温かみ〉warmth.

　　ningen-teki-na atatakami（人間的な温かみ）　human warmth

　atatakami-no-aru〈温かみのある〉warm-hearted.

　　atatakami-no-nai（温かみのない）　cold-hearted

atatamaru〈あたたまる：暖(温)まる〉warm oneself, get warm.

　atatameru〈暖(温)める〉warm, heat; renew.

　　kyûkô o atatameru（旧交を温める）renew one's old friendship ((with))

atchi〈あっち〉*see.* achira.

　　Atchi-e ike!（あっちへ行け。）　Go away!

ate〈あて：当て〉an object, an aim, an end; hope(s), expectation(s); reliance, dependence.

　ate-ni-suru〈当てにする〉expect, rely ((on)).

　ate-ga-hazureru〈当てが外れる〉be disappointed, miss one's aim.

　ate-ni-nara-nai〈当てにならない〉unreliable, uncertain.

　ate-no-nai〈当てのない〉aimless.

　ate-mo-naku〈当てもなく〉aimlessly.

atehamaru〈あてはまる：当てはまる〉apply ((to)), hold true ((of)), come ((under)), fit, be fit ((for)).

　atehameru〈当てはめる〉apply ((to)), fit, adapt.

ate-ji〈あてじ：当て字〉a false substitute character.

atekosuri〈あてこすり：当てこすり〉a sly hint, an indirect cut.

atekosuri-o-iu or *atekosuru* 〈当てこすりを言う，当てこする〉make a sly hint, give an indirect cut.

atena 〈あてな：あて名〉an address.

atena-ga-chigau 〈あて名が違う〉be wrongly addressed.

-ate-no 〈-あての〉addressed to... .

ateru 〈あてる：当(充)てる〉apply, put, lay; guess; devote; expose.

　　　juwa-ki o mimi-ni ateru (受話器を耳に当てる) put a receiver to one's ear

　　　umaku ateru (うまく当てる) hit the mark, guess right

　　　ate-sokonau (当て損なう) miss the mark, guess wrong

　　　asa-no jikan o benkyô-ni ateru (朝の時間を勉強に充てる) devote morning hours to study

　　　hi-ni ateru (日に当てる) expose ((a thing)) to the sun

atetsuke 〈あてつけ：当て付け〉

atetsuke-gamashii 〈当て付けがましい〉insinuative.

　　　atetsuke-gamashii koe (当て付けがましい声) an insinuative voice

atetsuke-gamashiku 〈当て付けがましく〉insinuatively.

ate-zuiryô 〈あてずいりょう：当て推量〉a guess, guesswork.

　　　ton-demo-nai ate-zuiryô (とんでもない当て推量) a wild guess

ate-zuiryô-o-suru 〈当て推量をする〉make a random guess.

atezuppô 〈あてずっぽう：当てずっぽう〉a random guess, guesswork, a conjecture.

　　　atezuppô-o-iu (当てずっぽうを言う) hazard a conjecture

ato 〈あと：後〉the back, the rear, the next, the following, the rest.

　　　ato-o-furi-muku (後を振り向く) look back

ato-ni-tsuzuku 〈後に続く〉follow.

ato-ni-mawasu 〈後に回す〉postpone, put off.

ato-de or *ato-ni* 〈後で，後に〉after, later (on).

　　　mikka-ato-ni (三日後に) after three days

　　　Mata ato-de. (又後で。) See you later.

ato-ni 〈後に〉behind.

　　　ato-ni nokosu (後に残す) remain behind

ato-kara-ato-kara 〈後から後から〉one after another.

ato 〈あと：跡〉a mark, a trace, a track; ruins.

　　　ato-ga-tsuku (跡が付く) leave a mark ((on))

　　　ato o nokosu (跡を残す) leave one's traces behind ((one))

　　　ato o nokosa-nai (跡を残さない) leave no trace behind ((one))

　　　〜-no ato-ga-nai (〜の跡がない) there is no trace of...

chi no ato（血の跡） marks of blood

kuruma no ato（車の跡） the track of a car

shiro no ato（城の跡） the ruins of a castle

shujutsu-no ato（手術の跡） a surgical scar

ato-o-tsukeru〈跡をつける〉trace.

ato-o-kuramasu〈跡をくらます〉abscond.

ato-aji〈あとあじ：後味〉(an) aftertaste.

ato-aji-ga-warui（後味が悪い） leave a bad taste in one's mouth (behind)

ato-ashi〈あとあし：後足〉a hind leg.

atogama〈あとがま：後がま〉a successor.

atogama-ni-suwaru（後がまに座る） sit in ((a person's)) place

atogama-ni-sueru（後がまに据える） put ((a person)) in one's place

ato-kata〈あとかた：跡形〉traces, marks, proof, evidence.

ato-kata-mo-naku（跡形もなく） without leaving any trace

ato-katazuke〈あとかたづけ：後片付け〉

ato-katazuke-o-suru〈後片付けをする〉put ((things)) in order, clear away.

shokuji-no-ato-katazuke-o-suru（食事の後片付けをする） clear the table

ato-kusare〈あとくされ：後腐れ〉

ato-kusare-no-nai-yô-ni〈後腐れのないように〉so that there may be no trouble left behind.

ato-mawashi〈あとまわし：後回し〉

ato-mawashi-ni-suru〈後回しにする〉let ((a matter)) wait.

Sono-koto-wa-ato-mawashi-ni-shite-ii.（その事は後回しにしていい.） The matter can wait. / You can let the matter wait.

ato-modori〈あともどり：後戻り〉

ato-modori-suru〈後戻りする〉turn back.

ato-no-matsuri〈あとのまつり：後の祭り〉

Ima-sara ato-no-matsuri-da.（今更後の祭りだ.） It's too late now. / It's a day after the fair.

ato-oshi〈あとおし：後押し〉

ato-oshi-suru〈後押しする〉push ((a cart)) from behind; support, back up.

atorie〈アトリエ〉an *atelier*, a studio.

ato-saki〈あとさき：後先〉

ato-saki-o-kangaezu-ni〈後先を考えずに〉regardless of the consequences, without thinking of what it may cause.

ato-shimatsu〈あとしまつ：後始末〉settlement.

ato-shimatsu-suru 〈後始末する〉 settle, wind up.

ato-tori 〈あととり：跡取り〉 a successor; an heir, an heiress.

ato-tsugi 〈あとつぎ：跡継ぎ〉 see. ato-tori.

ato-zusari 〈あとざり：後ざり〉

ato-zusari-suru 〈後ずさりする〉 step back.

atsugari 〈あつがり：暑がり〉

　　atsugari-ya 〈暑がり屋〉 a person who is sensitive to the heat

atsugaru 〈暑がる〉 feel hot, feel the heat, complain of the heat.

atsu-geshô 〈あつげしょう：厚化粧〉 a thick makeup.

atsu-geshô-o-suru 〈厚化粧をする〉 be thickly painted, be heavily powdered.

atsugi 〈あつぎ：厚着〉 thick dressing.

atsugi-suru 〈厚着する〉 be thickly dressed.

atsui 〈あつい：厚い〉 thick, heavy; warm, kind, cordial.

　　atsui ita 〈厚い板〉 a thick board

atsuku 〈厚く〉 thickly; warmly, kindly, cordially.

　　atsuku kiru 〈厚く切る〉 slice off ((a piece)) thick

　　atsuku rei-o-noberu 〈厚く礼を述べる〉 thank ((a person)) warmly

　　atsuku motenasu 〈厚くもてなす〉 receive ((a person)) cordially

atsui 〈あつい：暑(熱)い〉 hot, warm, heated.

atsuku-suru 〈熱くする〉 heat.

atsuku-naru 〈暑(熱)くなる〉 get warm, be heated.

atsukai 〈あつかい：扱い〉 treatment, dealing.

　　kodomo-atsukai-ni-suru 〈子供扱いにする〉 treat ((a person)) as a child

　　kyaku-atsukai-ga-ii 〈客扱いがいい〉 be hospitable, give good service

　　kyaku-atsukai-ga-warui 〈客扱いが悪い〉 be inhospitable, give bad service

atsukai-yasui 〈扱いやすい〉 be easy to deal with.

　　atsukai-nikui 〈扱いにくい〉 be hard to deal with

atsukamashii 〈あつかましい：厚かましい〉 impudent, bold.

atsukamashiku 〈厚かましく〉 impudently, boldly.

atsukau 〈あつかう：扱う〉 treat, deal ((in or with)), handle.

　　kôhei-ni atsukau 〈公平に扱う〉 deal justly ((with))

　　chûi-shite atsukau 〈注意して扱う〉 handle ((a thing)) with care

　　teara-ni atsukau 〈手荒に扱う〉 handle ((a thing)) roughly

atsukurushii 〈あつくるしい：暑苦しい〉 close, sultry, stuffy.

atsumari 〈あつまり：集まり〉 a gathering, a meeting, a party.

atsumaru〈集まる〉gather, come(*or* get) together, crowd, swarm, meet, be collected.

atsumeru〈あつめる：集める〉get together, gather, collect, raise, attract.

    zairyô o atsumeru（材料を集める）gather materials

    kitte o atsumeru（切手を集める）collect stamps

    kifu-kin-o-atsumeru（寄附金を集める）call for contributions

    seken-no chûmoku o atsumeru（世間の注目を集める）attract public attention

atsurae〈あつらえ〉an order; an article ordered.

atsurae-no〈あつらえの〉ordered, custom-made.

atsuraeru〈あつらえる〉order, give an order.

atsureki〈あつれき〉friction, discord.

    atsureki o shôjiru（あつれきを生じる）cause discord

atsuryoku〈あつりょく：圧力〉pressure.

    atsuryoku-kei（圧力計）a pressure gauge

atsuryoku-o-kuwaeru〈圧力を加える〉give pressure ((to)), press ((on)).

atsusa〈あつさ：厚さ〉thickness.

atsusa〈あつさ：熱[暑]さ〉heat, warmth, hot weather.

    atsusa-ni yowai（暑さに弱い）be sensitive to the heat

    atsusa-ni-makeru（暑さに負ける）be affected by the heat

    yaketsuku-yô-na atsusa（焼き付くような暑さ）scorching heat

atto〈あっと〉

    atto iwaseru（あっと言わせる）take ((a person)) aback

    atto odoroku（あっと驚く）be taken aback

    atto sakebu（あっと叫ぶ）utter a cry

    atto-iu-ma-ni（あっという間に）in a moment

attô〈あっとう：圧倒〉

attô-suru〈圧倒する〉overwhelm, overpower.

attô-teki(-na)〈圧倒的(な)〉overwhelming.

    attô-teki tasû（圧倒的多数）an overwhelming majority

    attô-teki shôri（圧倒的勝利）a sweeping victory, a landslide

attô-teki-ni〈圧倒的に〉overwhelmingly.

au〈あう：会[遭]う〉see, meet, come across; be caught ((in)).

    jiko-ni-au（事故に遭う）meet with an accident

    yûjin ni battari-au（友人にばったり会う）come across a friend

    niwaka-ame-ni-au（にわか雨に遭う）be caught in a shower

    abunai-me-ni-au（危い目に遭う）be exposed to danger

    ai-ni-iku（会いに行く）go to see

au〈あう：合う〉fit, suit, be suited ((to)), become; agree ((with)); be right, be correct; pay.

    pittari au（ぴったり合う）fit perfectly

    shumi ni au（趣味に合う）suit one's taste

    hito-to iken-ga-awa-nai（人と意見が合わない）do not agree with a person

    jikan-ga-yoku-au（時間がよく合う）keep good time

    Kanjô wa atte-iru.（勘定は合っている．）The accounts are correct.

auto〈アウト〉out.

auto-ni-naru〈アウトになる〉be put out.

awa〈あわ：泡〉a bubble, foam, lather.

awa-ga-tatsu〈泡が立つ〉bubble, foam, lather.

awa-dachi-ga-ii〈泡立ちがいい〉lather well.

awabi〈あわび〉an ear shell, an abalone.

awai〈あわい：淡い〉light, faint, pale.

    awai iro（淡い色）a light color

    awai nozomi（淡い望み）a faint hope

aware〈あわれ：哀れ〉misery, sorrow, pity.

aware-ni-omou〈哀れに思う〉have pity ((on)), feel pity ((for)).

aware-na〈哀れな〉miserable, wretched, sad, piteous, poor.

awaremi〈あわれみ〉pity, compassion.

awaremi-bukai〈あわれみ深い〉compassionate, charitable.

awaremu〈あわれむ〉pity, feel pity ((for)), have compassion ((on)).

awase〈あわせ〉a lined *kimono*.

awaseru〈あわせる：合わせる〉put together, combine; add up, sum up; set.

    te o awaseru（手を合わせる）clasp one's hands

    tokei o awaseru（時計を合わせる）set a watch right

    kao-o-awaseru（顔を合わせる）meet, see

awasete〈合わせて〉in all, all told, altogether.

    chikara-o-awasete（力を合わせて）with combined efforts

awatadashii〈あわただしい：慌ただしい〉busy, hurried, restless.

    awatadashii ichinichi o sugosu（慌ただしい一日を過ごす）pass a restless day

    awatadashii ryokô（慌ただしい旅行）a flying tour

awatadashiku〈慌ただしく〉hurriedly, hastily, in a hurry.

awate-mono〈あわてもの：慌て者〉a careless person, a hasty person.

awateru 〈あわてる：慌てる〉be confused, lose one's head, be in a hurry.
sukoshi-mo awate-nai 〈少しも慌てない〉keep quite cool.
awatete 〈慌てて〉confusedly, in a flurry, in a hurry.
 awatezu-ni 〈慌てずに〉calmly
awayokuba 〈あわよくば〉if chance favors one.
ayafuya 〈あやふや〉
ayafuya-na 〈あやふやな〉uncertain, dubious, doubtful, vague, ambiguous.
 ayafuya-na taido 〈あやふやな態度〉a dubious attitude
 ayafuya-na henji 〈あやふやな返事〉a vague answer
ayakaru 〈あやかる〉
 Kimi-ni-ayakari-tai-ne. 〈君にあやかりたいね.〉 I wish I were as lucky as you.
ayamachi 〈あやまち：過ち〉a fault, a mistake, an error.
 ayamachi o okasu 〈過ちを犯す〉commit a fault
 ayamachi o mitomeru 〈過ちを認める〉admit one's fault
ayamari 〈あやまり：謝り〉an excuse, an apology.
ayamaru 〈謝る〉apologize, beg pardon ((of)), beg ((a person's)) pardon.
 hira-ayamari-ni-ayamaru 〈平謝りに謝る〉 make a humble apology
ayamari 〈あやまり：誤り〉an error, a mistake, a slip.
 ayamari o tadasu 〈誤りを正す〉correct errors
ayamaru 〈誤る〉mistake, make a mistake, err.
 handan-o-ayamaru 〈判断を誤る〉misjudge
 hôshin-o-ayamaru 〈方針を誤る〉take a wrong course
 mi o ayamaru 〈身を誤る〉ruin oneself
 sentaku-o-ayamaru 〈選択を誤る〉make a wrong choice
ayamatta 〈誤った〉mistaken, wrong, false, incorrect.
 ayamatta-handan 〈誤った判断〉misjudgment
 ayamatta kangae 〈誤った考え〉a mistaken idea
ayamatte 〈誤(過)って〉by mistake, through one's fault.
ayame 〈あやめ〉an iris, a sweet flag.
aya-ori 〈あやおり：あや織り〉twill, figured cloth.
aya-ori-no 〈あや織りの〉twilled, figured.
ayashii 〈あやしい：怪しい〉doubtful, questionable, uncertain; suspicious; strange.
 ayashii jimbutsu 〈怪しい人物〉a suspicious-looking man, a suspicious character
 ayashii tenki 〈怪しい天気〉threatening weather

ayashii-mono-oto-ga-suru〈怪しい物音がする〉 sound strange
ayashinde〈怪しんで〉doubtfully, suspiciously.
ayashimu〈あやしむ：怪しむ〉doubt, suspect, wonder.
　～(-wa)-ayashimu-ni-tari-nai((～は)怪しむに足りない） It is no
　　wonder that... .
　ayashimu-beki〈怪しむべき〉doubtful, suspicious.
　ayashimareru〈怪しまれる〉incur(*or* excite) suspicion.
ayasu〈あやす〉fondle, dandle, humor.
ayatori〈あやとり：あや取り〉
　ayatori-o-suru〈あや取りをする〉play at cat's cradle.
ayatsuri-ningyô〈あやつりにんぎょう：操り人形〉a puppet, a mario-
　nette.
ayatsuru〈あやつる：操る〉handle, manage, operate, work.
　ningyô o ayatsuru（人形を操る） work puppets
　hito-o-jiyû-ni-ayatsuru（人を自由に操る） make a puppet of a person
　Doitsu-go o jiyû-ni-ayatsuru（ドイツ語を自由に操る） have a good
　　command of German
ayauku〈あやうく：危うく〉nearly, almost.
　ayauku～(-suru)-tokoro-de-aru（危うく～(する)ところである） come
　　close to ((doing))...
ayu〈あゆ〉an *ayu*.
ayumi-yori〈あゆみより：歩み寄り〉mutual concessions.
　ayumi-yoru〈歩み寄る〉make mutual concessions, compromise.
　ayumi-yotte〈歩み寄って〉by mutual concessions.
aza〈あざ〉a birthmark, a bruise.
azakeru〈あざける〉ridicule, sneer ((at)), scorn, scoff ((at)).
azami〈あざみ〉a thistle.
azamuku〈あざむく：欺く〉deceive, cheat.
azarashi〈あざらし〉a seal.
azawarau〈あざわらう：あざ笑う〉*see*. chôshô-suru.
azayaka〈あざやか：鮮やか〉
　azayaka-na〈鮮やかな〉bright, vivid, clear, splendid; fine.
　　azayaka-na aka（鮮やかな赤） bright red
　　azayaka-na inshô（鮮やかな印象） a vivid impression
　　azayaka-na purei（鮮やかなプレイ） a fine play
　azayaka-ni〈鮮やかに〉brightly, vividly, splendidly.
azen〈あぜん：啞然〉
　azen-to-suru〈啞然とする〉be quite stunned ((by)), be struck speechless

　with astonishment.

　azen-to-shite〈あぜんとして〉in utter amazement, in open-mouthed sur-
　prise.

azukari〈あずかり：預かり〉

　　azukari-kin（預かり金）　money on deposit

　　azukari-mono（預かり物）　a thing received in charge

　　azukari-nushi（預かり主）　a depositary

　　azukari-shō（預かり証）　a deposit receipt

azukaru〈あずかる：預かる〉keep; take charge ((of)); take care ((of)).

　azukeru〈預ける〉deposit, leave ((a thing)) with ((a person)).

　　kane o ginkô-ni azukeru（金を銀行に預ける）　deposit money in a
　　bank

　　sûtsukêsu o eki-ni azukeru（スーツケースを駅に預ける）　leave one's
　　suitcase on check at a station

azuki〈あずき：小豆〉a red bean.

　azuki-iro-no〈小豆色の〉reddish-brown.

B

ba〈ば：場〉a place, a spot, a scene.

　　sono-ba-de（その場で）　on the spot

　　sono-ba-ni（その場に）　on the scene

baai〈ばあい：場合〉an occasion, circumstances, a situation, a case.

　　baai-ni-yotte(wa)（場合によって（は））　according to circumstances

　　ikanaru-baai-ni-mo（いかなる場合にも）　in all cases

　　　ikanaru-baai-ni-mo～nai（いかなる場合にも～ない）　in no case

　　sono-baai-ni-wa（その場合には）　in that case

　　taitei-no baai（大抵の場合）　in most cases

　～-no-baai-ni-wa〈～の場合には〉in case of, if, when.

　　uten-no-baai-ni-wa（雨天の場合には）　in case of rain

bachabacha〈ばちゃばちゃ〉
　bachabacha-saseru〈ばちゃばちゃさせる〉splash〔one's feet in the water〕.
bachi〈ばち〉a drum stick, a plectrum.
bachi〈ばち：罰〉punishment, a curse.
　bachi-ga-ataru〈罰が当たる〉be punished, have punishment inflicted ((on)).
bai〈ばい：倍〉double, twice.
　fudan-no ne-no-bai-harau〈普段の値の倍払う〉pay double the usual price
　hito-no-bai-hataraku〈人の倍働く〉work twice as hard as others
-bai〈-ばい：-倍〉times.
　ni-bai〈二倍〉twice, double
　sambai〈三倍〉three times
　go-bai〈五倍〉five times
　San-no-roku-bai wa jû-hachi.〈三の六倍は十八。〉Six times three is eighteen.
bai-bai〈ばいばい：売買〉
　baibai-keiyaku〈売買契約〉a sales contract
　bai-bai-suru〈売買する〉buy and sell, deal ((in)), trade ((in)), handle.
baidoku〈ばいどく：梅毒〉syphilis.
baien〈ばいえん：ばい煙〉smoke, soot.
　baien-no-ooi〈ばい煙の多い〉smoky.
　baien-no-nai〈ばい煙のない〉smokeless
baika〈ばいか：売価〉the (selling) price.
baika〈ばいか：買価〉the purchase price.
baikai〈ばいかい：媒介〉mediation.
　baikai-suru〈媒介する〉mediate, carry.
　Densen-byô wa shibashiba ka-ni-yotte baikai-sareru.〈伝染病はしばしば蚊によって媒介される。〉Infectious disease is often carried by mosquitoes.
　〜-no-baikai-ni-yori〈〜の媒介により〉through the medium of... .
baikin〈ばいきん：ばい菌〉a bacterium, a germ.
　baikin o korosu〈ばい菌を殺す〉destroy germs
baikingu-ryôri〈バイキングりょうり：バイキング料理〉smorgasbord.
baiku〈バイク〉a motorbike.
baimei〈ばいめい：売名〉self-advertisement.
　baimei-kôi〈売名行為〉a publicity stunt

baiorin 〈バイオリン〉a violin.

baiorin o hiku（バイオリンを弾く） play the violin

bairitsu 〈ばいりつ：倍率〉magnification, magnifying power.

bairitsu-no-takai〈倍率の高い〉of high magnifying power; highly competitive.

baishaku 〈ばいしゃく：媒酌〉

baishaku-nin（媒酌人） a go-between

〜-*no-baishaku-de*〈〜の媒酌で〉 through the good offices of... .

baishin-in 〈ばいしんいん：陪審員〉a juryman, a juror; a jury.

baishō 〈ばいしょう：賠償〉reparation, compensation.

baishō o yōkyū-suru（賠償を要求する） demand reparation

baishō-kin（賠償金） indemnities, reparations, damages

baishō-suru〈賠償する〉indemnify, compensate, make up ((for)), pay.

baishū 〈ばいしゅう：買収〉

baishū-suru〈買収する〉purchase, buy up; bribe, buy off.

baishun 〈ばいしゅん：売春〉prostitution.

baishun-kôi-o-suru（売春行為をする） practice prostitution

baishun-fu（売春婦） a prostitute

baisū 〈ばいすう：倍数〉a multiple.

baiten 〈ばいてん：売店〉a stand, a stall, a kiosk.

eki-no baiten（駅の売店） a station stall

baiu 〈ばいう：梅雨〉*see*. tsuyu（梅雨）.

baiyaku 〈ばいやく：売薬〉a patent medicine.

baiyaku-zumi 〈ばいやくずみ：売約済み〉Sold.

baiyō 〈ばいよう：培養〉cultivation, culture.

baiyō-suru〈培養する〉cultivate, culture, grow.

bajji 〈バッジ〉a badge.

bajji o tsukeru（バッジを着ける） wear a badge

bajutsu 〈ばじゅつ：馬術〉horsemanship, horseback riding.

baka 〈ばか〉a fool.

Sonna koto o suru-nante omae-mo-baka-danâ!（そんなことをするなんてお前もばかだなあ.） What a fool you are to do such a thing!

baka-ni-suru〈ばかにする〉treat with contempt, look down ((on)), make light ((of)), make a fool ((of)).

baka-na〈ばかな〉foolish, silly, stupid, absurd.

baka-na-koto（ばかなこと） a foolish thing, nonsense

Baka-na-koto o iu-na.（ばかなことを言うな.） Don't talk nonsense.

bakabakashii〈ばかばかしい〉absurd, silly.

Bakabakashii!（ばかばかしい.）Fiddlesticks!

baka-ni〈ばかに〉awfully, exceedingly, ridiculously, abnormally.

baka-ni samui（ばかに寒い）be awfully cold

baka-ni yasui（ばかに安い）be ridiculously cheap

-bakari〈-ばかり〉about, some, or so; only, nothing but; just; almost.

sen-en-bakari（千円ばかり）about 1,000 yen

go-nen bakari-mae（五年ばかり前）some five years ago

Kare-wa Eigo-bakari benkyô-suru.（彼は英語ばかり勉強する.）He studies only English.

Kare-wa Furansu-go-bakari-de-naku Doitsu-go-mo hanasu.（彼はフランス語ばかりでなくドイツ語も話す.）He speaks German as well as French.

Kare-no haha-oya wa naku-bakari-datta.（彼の母親は泣くばかりだった.）His mother did nothing but cry.

Kanojo-wa ima-kaetta-bakari-desu.（彼女は今帰ったばかりです.）She has just come back.

Ane-no mune wa kanashimi-de hari-saken-bakari-datta.（姉の胸は悲しみで張り裂けんばかりだった.）My sister's heart almost burst with grief.

baka-sawagi〈ばかさわぎ：ばか騒ぎ〉

baka-sawagi-o-yaru〈ばか騒ぎをやる〉go on the spree, have high jinks.

baka-shôjiki〈ばかしょうじき：ばか正直〉

baka-shôjiki-na〈ばか正直な〉too honest, honest to a fault.

baka-teinei〈ばかていねい：ばか丁寧〉

baka-teinei-na〈ばか丁寧な〉excessively polite.

baka-teinei-ni〈ばか丁寧に〉with overdone politeness.

bakazu〈ばかず：場数〉

bakazu-o-funde-iru〈場数を踏んでいる〉have a great deal of experience.

bake-mono〈ばけもの：化け物〉a monster, a ghost.

bake-mono-yashiki（化け物屋敷）a haunted house

baken〈ばけん：馬券〉a pari-mutuel ticket.

baken-uri-ba（馬券売り場）a betting-ticket window

jôgai-baken-uri-ba（場外馬券売り場）an off-track betting place

bakeru〈ばける：化ける〉disguise oneself〔as a woman〕.

baketsu〈バケツ〉a bucket.

baketsu-ippai-no mizu〈バケツ一杯の水〉a bucketful of water.

bakkin〈ばっきん：罰金〉a fine, a penalty.

bakkin-o-kasuru〈罰金を課する〉fine.

bakkin-o-kaserareru 〈罰金を課せられる〉 be fined.

 go-sen-en bakkin-o-kaserareru （五千円罰金を課せられる） be fined 5,000 yen

bakku 〈バック〉 back, the background.

 Fuji-san-o-bakku-ni-shite （富士山をバックにして） with Mt. Fuji for the background

bakku-suru 〈バックする〉 back, go back.

 kuruma o bakku-saseru （車をバックさせる） back (up) a car

bakku-de-oyogu 〈バックで泳ぐ〉 swim backstroke.

bakku-mirâ 〈バックミラー〉 a rearview mirror.

bakkuru 〈バックル〉 a buckle.

bakkuru-no-tsuita 〈バックルの付いた〉 buckled.

bakuchi 〈ばくち〉 gambling.

 bakuchi-uchi （ばくち打ち） a gambler

bakuchi-o-utsu 〈ばくちを打つ〉 gamble.

bakudai 〈ばくだい：ばく大〉

bakudai-na 〈ばく大な〉 vast, immense, enormous.

 bakudai-na sonshitsu （ばく大な損失） an enormous loss

bakudan 〈ばくだん：爆弾〉 a bomb.

 kô-seinô-bakudan （高性能爆弾） a TNT bomb

bakudan-o-tôka-suru 〈爆弾を投下する〉 drop bombs, bomb.

bakufu 〈ばくふ：幕府〉 the shogunate, the feudal government.

bakufû 〈ばくふう：爆風〉 a blast.

bakugeki 〈ばくげき：爆撃〉 bombing.

 bakugeki-ki （爆撃機） a bomber

bakugeki-suru 〈爆撃する〉 bomb.

bakuha 〈ばくは：爆破〉

bakuha-suru 〈爆破する〉 blow up, blast.

bakuhatsu 〈ばくはつ：爆発〉 explosion, burst, eruption.

 gasu-bakuhatsu （ガス爆発） explosion of gas

 bakuhatsu-butsu （爆発物） an explosive

bakuhatsu-suru 〈爆発する〉 explode, burst, blow up, erupt.

 ikari-ga-bakuhatsu-suru （怒りが爆発する） burst into a rage

bakuhatsu-teki(-na) 〈爆発的(な)〉 explosive, tremendous.

 bakuhatsu-teki ninki （爆発的人気） tremendous popularity

bakuro 〈ばくろ：暴露〉

 bakuro-kiji （暴露記事） an exposé

bakuro-suru 〈暴露する〉 disclose, expose.

bakuryô 〈ばくりょう：幕僚〉a staff officer; the staff.

bakushi 〈ばくし：爆死〉

　bakushi-suru 〈爆死する〉be bombed to death.

bakushin-chi 〈ばくしんち：爆心地〉a blast center, the center of explosion.

bakushô 〈ばくしょう：爆笑〉a burst of laughter.

　bakushô-suru 〈爆笑する〉burst into laughter, burst out laughing.

bakuteria 〈バクテリア〉a bacterium.

bakuyaku 〈ばくやく：爆薬〉see. bakuhatsu-butsu.

bakuzen 〈ばくぜん：漠然〉

　bakuzen-to-shita 〈漠然とした〉vague, obscure.

　　bakuzen-to-shita kotae〈漠然とした答え〉 a vague answer

　bakuzen-to〈漠然と〉vaguely, obscurely.

bamen 〈ばめん：場面〉a scene, a spectacle.

bampaku 〈ばんぱく：万博〉an abbreviation of 'bankoku-haku(ran-kai)'.

ban 〈ばん：番〉one's turn, order, number; watch, guard.

　　Kondo-wa watashi-no ban-da.（今度は私の番だ。） This is my turn.

　　ban o kuruwasu（番を狂わす） disturb the order

　　Nan-ban-desu-ka?（何番ですか。） What number, please?

　　Nihon-de ni-ban-me-ni-ookii toshi（日本で二番目に大きい都市） the second largest city in Japan

　ban-o-suru〈番をする〉watch, tend, look ((after)), keep watch.

　　mise-no-ban-o-suru（店の番をする） tend a shop

ban 〈ばん：晩〉an evening, a night.

　　ban-ni（晩に） in the evening, at night

　　　getsuyô-bi-no-ban-ni（月曜日の晩に） on Monday evening

　　　itsuka no ban-ni（五日の晩に） on the evening of the 5th

　　komban（今晩） this evening, tonight

　　mai-ban（毎晩） every evening, every night

banana 〈バナナ〉a banana.

　　banana-hito-fusa（バナナ一房） a bunch of bananas

ba-nare 〈ばなれ：場慣れ〉

　　ba-nare-shita hito（場慣れした人） an experienced person, a practiced person

　ba-nare-suru〈場慣れする〉get over one's stage fright.

bancha 〈ばんちゃ：番茶〉coarse tea.

banchi 〈ばんち：番地〉a lot number, a house number.

　　O-taku-wa-nambanchi-desu-ka?（お宅は何番地ですか。） What is the

street number of your house?

bando 〈バンド〉 a belt, a band; a band.

bane 〈ばね〉 a spring.

bangô 〈ばんごう：番号〉 a number.

 bangô-o-tsukeru or *bangô-o-utsu* 〈番号を付ける，番号を打つ〉 give a number ((to)), number.

 bangô-jun-ni 〈番号順に〉 in numerical order.

ban-gohan 〈ばんごはん：晩御飯〉 supper, dinner.

bangumi 〈ばんぐみ：番組〉 a program.

bangumi o tsukuru 〈番組を作る〉 arrange a program

bangumi-ni noseru 〈番組に載せる〉 put on the program

bangumi-ni notte-iru 〈番組に載っている〉 be on the program

terebi-bangumi 〈テレビ番組〉 a TV program

banji 〈ばんじ：万事〉 everything, all things.

Banji-kô-tsugô. 〈万事好都合.〉 All goes well.

Banji-kyûsu. 〈万事休す.〉 All is up (with me).

bankai 〈ばんかい：ばん回〉 retrieval, restoration, revival.

 bankai-suru 〈ばん回する〉 retrieve, restore, revive.

banken 〈ばんけん：番犬〉 a watchdog.

bankoku 〈ばんこく：万国〉 all nations.

bankok(u)-ki 〈万国旗〉 the flags of all nations

bankoku-haku(ran-kai) 〈万国博(覧会)〉 a world fair

 bankoku(-kyôtsû)-no 〈万国(共通)の〉 international, universal.

bankon 〈ばんこん：晩婚〉

 bankon-datta 〈晩婚だった〉 married late in life.

ban-kuruwase 〈ばんくるわせ：番狂わせ〉 a surprise, an upset, an unexpected result.

ban-kuruwase-de-katsu 〈番狂わせで勝つ〉 score an upset victory ((over))

ban-meshi 〈ばんめし：晩飯〉 *see.* ban-gohan.

bannan 〈ばんなん：万難〉

 bannan-o-haishite 〈万難を排して〉 at all risks, in spite of all difficulties.

bannen 〈ばんねん：晩年〉 one's later years.

 bannen-ni 〈晩年に〉 late in life.

bannin 〈ばんにん：番人〉 a watchman, a keeper; a watch, a guard.

bannin 〈ばんにん：万人〉

 bannin-muki-de-aru 〈万人向きである〉 suit everybody.

bannô 〈ばんのう：万能〉

bannô-senshu〈万能選手〉an all-round player

bannô-no〈万能の〉almighty, all-round.

bansaku〈ばんさく：万策〉

bansaku-ga-tsukiru〈万策が尽きる〉be at the end of one's resources.

bansan〈ばんさん：晩さん〉dinner, supper.

bansan-kai〈晩さん会〉a dinner party

-ban-sen〈-ばんせん：-番線〉a track.

go-ban-sen〈五番線〉the fifth track, Track No. Five

banshaku〈ばんしゃく：晩酌〉a daily drink at supper.

banshû〈ばんしゅう：晩秋〉late fall, late autumn.

banshû-ni〈晩秋に〉late in fall, late in autumn.

banshun〈ばんしゅん：晩春〉late spring.

banshun-ni〈晩春に〉late in spring.

bansô〈ばんそう：伴奏〉accompaniment.

piano no bansô-de *or* piano no bansô-ni-awasete〈ピアノの伴奏で，ピアノの伴奏に合わせて〉to the accompaniment of the piano

bansô-sha〈伴奏者〉an accompanist

bansô-suru〈伴奏する〉accompany, play ((a person's)) accompaniment.

bansô-kô〈ばんそうこう〉an adhesive plaster.

bansô-kô o haru〈ばんそうこうをはる〉apply an adhesive plaster ((to))

bantamu-kyû〈バンタムきゅう：バンタム級〉the bantamweight class.

bantamu-kyû-no〈バンタム級の〉bantamweight.

bantan〈ばんたん：万端〉everything, all.

Yôi-bantan-totonotta.〈用意万端整った.〉Everything is ready.

banto〈バント〉a bunt.

banto-suru〈バントする〉bunt.

banzai〈ばんざい：万歳〉hurrah, cheers.

banzai-o-san-shô-suru〈万歳を三唱する〉give three cheers ((for))

banzen〈ばんぜん：万全〉perfectness.

banzen-o-kisuru〈万全を期する〉make assurance doubly sure.

banzuke〈ばんづけ：番付〉a graded list, a ranking list.

bara〈ばら〉

bara-de〈ばらで〉in bulk.

bara-de uru〈ばらで売る〉sell in bulk

bara〈ばら〉a rose.

bara-iro-no〈ばら色の〉rosy, rose-colored.

barabara〈ばらばら〉

barabara-ni〈ばらばらに〉scatteringly, separately; in pieces.

barabara-ni ie-ni-kaeru〈ばらばらに家に帰る〉 come home separately
barabara-ni-naru〈ばらばらになる〉 scatter, break up; fall in pieces.
barabara-ni-suru〈ばらばらにする〉 take to pieces.

barakku〈バラック〉a shack, a barrack.

bara-maku〈ばらまく〉scatter, broadcast.

bara-ni〈ばらに：ばら荷〉a bulk cargo, a cargo in bulk.

baransu〈バランス〉balance.

baransu o tamotsu（バランスを保つ） keep balance
baransu o ushinau（バランスを失う） lose balance
baransu-no-toreta〈バランスのとれた〉well-balanced.

barasu〈ばらす〉take to pieces; make away ((with)), dispose ((of)), bump
off; expose, disclose, reveal.

barê-bôru〈バレーボール〉volleyball.

bareru〈ばれる〉come out, come to light, be discovered, be revealed.

baribari〈ばりばり〉
baribari-kajiru（ばりばりかじる） crunch
baribari-hataraku（ばりばり働く） work like a tiger

barikan〈バリカン〉hair clippers.

barikêdo〈バリケード〉a barricade.
barikêdo o kizuku（バリケードを築く） set up a barricade

bariki〈ばりき：馬力〉horsepower.
go-jû-bariki-no môtâ（五十馬力のモーター） a 50 horsepower motor

bariton〈バリトン〉baritone.
bariton-kashu（バリトン歌手） a baritone

bariumu〈バリウム〉barium meal.

basabasa〈ばさばさ〉
Kami-no-ke ga basabasa-da.（髪の毛がばさばさだ。） My hair is dry
and loose.

Basedô-shi-byô〈バセドーしびょう：バセドー氏病〉Basedow's disease.

basha〈ばしゃ：馬車〉a coach, a cart.

bashin〈ばしん：馬身〉a horse's length.
hambashin-no-sa-de katsu（半馬身の差で勝つ） win by a half length

basho〈ばしょ：場所〉a place, a spot, room, space.
kaigô no basho（会合の場所） a place of meeting
basho o akeru（場所を空ける） make room ((for))
basho o toru（場所を取る） occupy space
sangatsu-basho（三月場所） the March *sumo* tournament

basho-gara〈ばしょがら：場所柄〉the situation, the location, the occasion.

basho-gara-mo-kangaezu-ni〈場所柄も考えずに〉 regardless of where one is, regardless of the occasion

bassai〈ばっさい：伐採〉felling, deforestation.
bassai-suru〈伐採する〉fell, cut off.

basshi〈ばっし：抜糸〉extraction of the stitches.
basshi-suru〈抜糸する〉take out the stitches.

basshi〈ばっし：抜歯〉extraction of a tooth.
basshi-suru〈抜歯する〉pull out a tooth.

bassoku〈ばっそく：罰則〉penal regulations.
bassoku-ni-fureru〈罰則に触れる〉 infringe the penal regulations

bassui〈ばっすい：抜粋〉extraction, selection; an extract, a selection.
bassui-suru〈抜粋する〉extract, select ((from)).

bassuru〈ばっする：罰する〉punish.
basserareru〈罰せられる〉be punished.

basu〈バス〉a bus.
basu ni noru〈バスに乗る〉 take a bus
basu o oriru〈バスを降りる〉 get off a bus
basu-tei〈バス停〉 a bus stop
kankô-basu〈観光バス〉 a sightseeing bus

basu〈バス〉bass.
basu-kashu〈バス歌手〉 a bass

basu〈バス〉a bath.
basu-toire-tsuki-no heya〈バストイレ付きの部屋〉 a room with bath and toilet

batâ〈バター〉butter.
pan ni batâ-o tsukeru〈パンにバターを付ける〉 spread bread with butter

batabata〈ばたばた〉
rôka o batabata-aruku〈廊下をばたばた歩く〉 walk along the passage noisily
batabata-tôsan-suru〈ばたばた倒産する〉 fail one after another
shigoto o batabata-katazukeru〈仕事をばたばた片付ける〉 finish one's business with dispatch

batafurai〈バタフライ〉the butterfly stroke.

batan〈ばたん〉
batan-to〈ばたんと〉with a bang.
to o batan-to shimeru〈戸をばたんと閉める〉 shut a door with a

bang

bâten〈バーテン〉a bartender, a barman.

bateru〈ばてる〉crack up, be played out, be done in, be done up.

baton〈バトン〉a baton.
　baton o watasu（バトンを渡す）hand over the baton ((to))
　baton-gâru（バトンガール）a baton twirler

batsu〈ばつ：罰〉punishment, penalty.
　batsu o kuwaeru（罰を加える）inflict punishment ((on))
　batsu-o-ukeru〈罰を受ける〉be punished, suffer punishment.

batsu〈ばつ：閥〉a clique.
　batsu o tsukuru（閥を作る）form a clique
　gaku-batsu（学閥）an academic clique

batsugun〈ばつぐん：抜群〉
　batsugun-no〈抜群の〉conspicuous, distinguished.
　batsugun-no-seiseki-de　sotsugyô-suru（抜群の成績で卒業する）graduate with honors

batta〈ばった〉a grasshopper.

battâ〈バッター〉a batter, a batsman.
　migi-battâ（右バッター）a right-handed batter
　hidari-battâ（左バッター）a left-handed batter

battari〈ばったり〉with a thud; suddenly, abruptly, unexpectedly.
　battari taoreru（ばったり倒れる）fall with a thud
　battari-de-au（ばったり出会う）fall in with ((a person)), come across

batteki〈ばってき：抜てき〉
　batteki-suru〈抜てきする〉pick out for promotion.

batto〈バット〉a bat.
　batto o furu（バットを振る）swing one's bat
　batto-de-utsu〈バットで打つ〉bat.

baundo〈バウンド〉bound, bounce.
　bôru　o　wan-baundo-de　toru（ボールをワンバウンドで捕る）catch a ball on the first bounce
　baundo-suru〈バウンドする〉bound, bounce.

bazâ〈バザー〉a bazaar.
　bazâ o hiraku（バザーを開く）hold a bazaar

bebî-〈ベビー-〉
　bebî-kâ（ベビーカー）a baby carriage, a baby buggy
　bebî-sâkuru（ベビーサークル）a playpen

bechabecha〈べちゃべちゃ〉*see.* pechakucha.

beddo-taun 〈ベッドタウン〉 a bedroom town, a dormitory town.

Bei-Chū 〈べいちゅう：米中〉

　Bei-Chū-no 〈米中の〉 Sino-American.

Beigo 〈べいご：米語〉 American English.

beika 〈べいか：米価〉 the price of rice.

Beika 〈べいか：米貨〉 American money, the U.S.dollar.

Beikoku 〈べいこく：米国〉 *see.* Amerika.

beisaku 〈べいさく：米作〉 cultivation of rice; rice crop.

Bei-So 〈ベイソ：米ソ〉

　Bei-So-no 〈米ソの〉 American-Soviet, Russo-American.

bēju(-iro-no) 〈ベージュ（いろの）：ベージュ（色の）〉 beige.

-(su-)bekarazu 〈-（す）べからず〉 must not ((do)), should not ((do)), ought not to ((do)).

-(su-)beki 〈-（す）べき〉 should ((do)), ought to ((do)).

bekkan 〈べっかん：別館〉 an annex ［to a hotel］.

bekko 〈べっこ：別個〉

　bekko-no 〈別個の〉 different, another.

　　bekko-no mondai（別個の問題）　another question

bekkō 〈べっこう：べっ甲〉 tortoiseshell.

　　bekkō-zaiku（べっ甲細工）　tortoiseshell work

bekkyo 〈べっきょ：別居〉

　bekkyo-suru 〈別居する〉 live separately, live apart ((from)).

bemmaku 〈べんまく：弁膜〉 a valve.

　　bemmaku-shō〈弁膜症〉 valvular disease

bemmei 〈べんめい：弁明〉

　　bemmei-sho（弁明書）　a written explanation

bempi 〈べんぴ：便秘〉 constipation.

　bempi-suru 〈便秘する〉 be constipated.

ben 〈べん：便〉 convenience, facilities, service.

　　basu-no ben（バスの便）　a bus service

　　　basu-no-ben-ga-ii（バスの便がいい）　be convenient to the bus

ben 〈べん：便〉 feces, stool.

　　ben o kensa-suru（便を検査する）　examine the feces

　　katai ben（硬い便）　hard feces

　　yawarakai ben（軟らかい便）　loose feces

ben 〈べん：弁〉 a petal; a valve.

-ben 〈-べん：-弁〉 a dialect, an accent.

　　Nagoya-ben-de　hanasu（名古屋弁で話す）　speak　with　a　Nagoya

accent

bengi 〈べんぎ：便宜〉 convenience, accommodation, facility.

    bengi-jô〈便宜上〉 for convenience(') sake

    〜-no-bengi-o-hakatte（〜の便宜を図って） for the convenience of...

bengo 〈べんご：弁護〉 defense, justification, pleading.

    jiko-bengo（自己弁護） self-justification

bengo-suru〈弁護する〉 defend, plead ((for)).

bengo-nin 〈べんごにん：弁護人〉 a counsel, a pleader.

bengo-shi 〈べんごし：弁護士〉 a lawyer.

    bengo-shi o tanomu（弁護士を頼む） engage a lawyer

beni 〈べに：紅〉 rouge.

    beni o tsukeru（紅をつける） apply rouge ((to))

beniya-ita 〈ベニヤいた：ベニヤ板〉 a veneer board, a plywood board.

benjin 〈ベンジン〉 benzine.

benjo 〈べんじょ：便所〉 a lavatory, a water closet, a toilet (room), a washroom, a rest room.

        Benjo wa doko-desu-ka?（便所はどこですか。） Where can I wash my hands? / Where is the bathroom?

benkai 〈べんかい：弁解〉 explanation, an excuse, a plea, an apology.

benkai-suru〈弁解する〉 explain, excuse oneself, make an excuse ((for)).

benki 〈べんき：便器〉 a toilet stool, a chamber pot.

benkyô 〈べんきょう：勉強〉 study.

    benkyô o namakeru（勉強を怠ける） neglect one's studies

    Kimi-tachi-futari wa benkyô-ga-tari-nai.（君たち二人は勉強が足りない。） Both of you do not work hard enough.

    benkyô-beya（勉強部屋） a study

    benkyô-jikan（勉強時間） study hours

    benkyô-ka（勉強家） a diligent person, a hard worker

benkyô-suru〈勉強する〉 study.

    kotsukotsu-benkyô-suru（こつこつ勉強する） dig ((at))

benkyô-shi-sugiru〈勉強しすぎる〉 overstudy.

benri 〈べんり：便利〉 convenience, handiness.

benri-de-aru〈便利である〉 be convenient.

    chika-tetsu-ni benri-de-aru（地下鉄に便利である） be convenient for the subway

benri-na〈便利な〉 convenient, handy.

    benri-na basho（便利な場所） a convenient location

    benri-na jisho（便利な辞書） a handy dictionary

benron〈べんろん：弁論〉discussion, controversy, debate, argument, pleading.

benron-taikai〈弁論大会〉a speech contest

benron-suru〈弁論する〉have a discussion, conduct a controversy ((with)), argue, plead.

bensai〈べんさい：弁済〉repayment, payment, settlement.

shakkin no bensai〈借金の弁済〉payment of debts

bensai-suru〈弁済する〉repay, pay (off), settle.

benshō〈べんしょう：弁償〉compensation, indemnification.

benshō-suru〈弁償する〉compensate, indemnify, make up ((for)).

songai-o-benshô-suru〈損害を弁償する〉compensate ((a person)) for his loss, indemnify ((a person)) for a loss

benshō-hō〈べんしょうほう：弁証法〉dialectic.

benshô-hô-teki〈弁証法的〉dialectic.

benshô-hô-teki-ni〈弁証法的に〉dialectically.

bentō〈べんとう：弁当〉lunch, a box lunch.

bentô o motte-iku〈弁当を持って行く〉take a lunch with one

bentô o taberu〈弁当を食べる〉eat lunch

bentô-bako〈弁当箱〉a lunch box

bentsū〈べんつう：便通〉a motion, a passage, a movement, an evacuation.

bentsû-ga-aru〈便通がある〉have a motion

bentsû-ga-nai〈便通がない〉be constipated.

benzetsu〈べんぜつ：弁舌〉speech, eloquence.

benzetsu-ka〈弁舌家〉an eloquent speaker

benzetsu-sawayaka-na〈弁舌さわやかな〉eloquent, fluent.

benzetsu-sawayaka-ni〈弁舌さわやかに〉eloquently, fluently.

beppyō〈べっぴょう：別表〉an attached table.

berabera〈べらべら〉

berabera-shaberu〈べらべらしゃべる〉chatter, prattle, talk volubly, shoot off one's mouth.

beranda〈ベランダ〉a veranda(h), a porch.

berê-bô〈ベレーぼう：ベレー帽〉a beret.

beru〈ベル〉a bell, a doorbell.

beru o osu〈ベルを押す〉press the bell

beru o narasu〈ベルを鳴らす〉ring the bell

bêru〈ベール〉a veil.

bêru-o-kaburu〈ベールをかぶる〉veil one's face.

Berugî 〈ベルギー〉 Belgium.

    Berugî-jin 〈ベルギー人〉 a Belgian

    Berugî(-jin)-no 〈ベルギー(人)の〉 Belgian

beruto 〈ベルト〉 a belt.

    beruto o shimeru 〈ベルトを締める〉 fasten a belt

beso 〈べそ〉

    beso-o-kaku 〈べそをかく〉 laugh on the other side of one's mouth.

bessatsu 〈べっさつ：別冊〉 a separate volume, an extra number.

bessekai 〈べっせかい：別世界〉 another world.

besshi 〈べっし：別紙〉 an accompanying paper, an attached sheet.

    besshi-no-toori 〈別紙のとおり〉 as stated in the attached sheet

bessô 〈べっそう：別荘〉 a villa, a country place, a cottage.

bêsu 〈ベース〉 a base, a basis; a base bag.

    chingin-bêsu 〈賃金ベース〉 the wage base

    bêsu-o-fumu 〈ベースを踏む〉 step on a base

    bêsu-appu-suru 〈ベースアップする〉 raise the wage base.

besuto 〈ベスト〉 best.

    besuto o tsukusu 〈ベストを尽くす〉 do one's best

    besuto-ten-ni-hairu 〈ベストテンに入る〉 come out among the best ten

betabeta 〈べたべた〉

    kabe-ni-betabeta-posutâ-o-haru 〈壁にべたべたポスターをはる〉 paste
        posters all over a wall

    oshiroi-o-betabeta-nuru 〈おしろいをべたべた塗る〉 paint oneself
        thickly

    enogu o betabeta-nuru 〈絵の具をべたべた塗る〉 daub paint

    Shita-gi ga karada-ni-betabeta-kuttsuku. 〈下着が体にべたべたくっ付
        く.〉 My undershirt clings to my body.

beta-tsuku or **beto-tsuku** 〈べたつく，べとつく〉 be sticky.

betobeto 〈べとべと〉

    betobeto-shite-iru 〈べとべとしている〉 be wet and smeary.

Betonamu 〈ベトナム〉 Vietnam.

    Betonamu-jin 〈ベトナム人〉 a Vietnamese

    Betonamu(-jin)-no 〈ベトナム(人)の〉 Vietnamese

betsu 〈べつ：別〉 distinction, discrimination, difference; an exception.

betsu-no 〈別の〉 another, different.

    Iu-no-to okonau-no-to-wa betsu-no koto da. 〈言うのと行うのとは別の
        ことだ.〉 To say is one thing, and to do is another (thing).

  ～*-no-betsu-naku* 〈～の別なく〉 regardless of... .

dan-jo-no-betsu-naku〈男女の別なく〉regardless of sex

betsu-ni〈別に〉particularly.

Kesa wa betsu-ni-suru-koto-ga-nai.（今朝は別にする事がない．）I have nothing particular to do this morning.

～-wa-betsu-ni(-shite)〈～は別に（して）〉apart from, except, excepting, extra, in addition, particularly.

jôdan-wa-betsu-ni-shite（冗談は別にして）jesting apart

kisha-chin-wa-betsu-ni-shite（汽車賃は別にして）exclusive of the railway fare

futsû-ryôkin-to-wa-betsu-ni（普通料金とは別に）in addition to the ordinary fare

betsu-atsurae〈べつあつらえ：別あつらえ〉a special order.

betsubetsu〈べつべつ：別々〉

betsubetsu-no〈別々の〉separate.

betsubetsu-no ie-ni sumu（別々の家に住む）live in separate houses

betsubetsu-ni〈別々に〉separately.

betsubetsu-ni tsutsumu（別々に包む）wrap up separately

betsubin〈べつびん：別便〉

betsubin-de〈別便で〉by separate mail.

betsujin〈べつじん：別人〉a different person, another person.

betsu-kanjô〈べつかんじょう：別勘定〉a separate account, an extra bill.

betsu-mei〈べつめい：別名〉another name, an alias.

Yamada-betsu-mei-Hongô（山田別名本郷）Yamada alias Hongo

betsu-mondai〈べつもんだい：別問題〉another question, a different story.

Sore-wa betsu-mondai-da.（それは別問題だ．）That is another story.

～-wa-betsu-mondai-to-shite〈～は別問題として〉apart from... .

betsuri〈べつり：別離〉parting.

betsuri no kanashimi（別離の悲しみ）the sorrow of parting

bettari〈べったり〉

bettari-kuttsuku〈べったりくっ付く〉stick fast ((to)).

bi〈び：美〉beauty.

nikutai-bi（肉体美）physical beauty

bibi〈びび：微々〉

bibi-taru〈微々たる〉insignificant, trifling.

bibi-taru mondai（微々たる問題）a matter of little significance

bibô〈びぼう：美ぼう〉good looks.

bibô-no〈美ぼうの〉good-looking.

bibun〈びぶん：微分〉differential calculus.
bichiku〈びちく：備蓄〉
　bichiku-suru〈備蓄する〉save for emergency.
bīchi-parasoru〈ビーチパラソル〉a beach umbrella.
bidan〈びだん：美談〉a praiseworthy episode.
bi-danshi〈びだんし：美男子〉a handsome man.
bidō〈びどう：微動〉
　bidō-da-ni-shi-nai〈微動だにしない〉stand as firm as rock.
bifū〈びふう：微風〉a breeze, a gentle wind.
bifū〈びふう：美風〉a laudable custom.
bifuteki〈ビフテキ〉(a) beefsteak, (a) steak.
bigaku〈びがく：美学〉esthetics.
bigan-〈びがん：美顔-〉
　　bigan-jutsu〈美顔術〉beauty culture, a facial
　　bigan-sui〈美顔水〉a beauty wash
bihin〈びひん：備品〉fixtures, furnishings, equipments.
bijin〈びじん：美人〉a beauty, a beautiful woman.
bijutsu〈びじゅつ：美術〉art, the fine arts.
　　bijutsu-hin〈美術品〉a work of art
　　bijutsu-kan〈美術館〉an art museum
　bijutsu-teki(-na)〈美術的(な)〉artistic.
　bijutsu-teki-ni〈美術的に〉artistically.
bika〈びか：美化〉beautification.
　bika-suru〈美化する〉beautify, make beautiful, idealize.
bikan〈びかん：美観〉a fine view, beauty.
　　bikan o sokonau〈美観を損なう〉spoil the beauty ((of))
bi-kataru〈びカタル：鼻カタル〉nasal catarrh.
-biki〈-びき：-引き〉
　　gomu-biki-no〈ゴム引きの〉coated with india rubber
　　sambu-biki-de〈三分引きで〉at 3% discount
bikkuri〈びっくり〉
　bikkuri-suru〈びっくりする〉be surprised, be astonished, be amazed, be startled.
　bikkuri-saseru〈びっくりさせる〉surprise, astonish, startle.
　bikkuri-suru-yō-na〈びっくりするような〉surprising, astonishing, startling.
　bikkri-shita〈びっくりした〉surprised, startled, frightened.
　bikkuri-shite〈びっくりして〉in surprise, in astonishment.

bikô〈びこう：備考〉a note, remarks.

bikô-ran〈備考欄〉 a remarks column

bikô(-sha)〈びこう（しゃ）：尾行（者）〉a shadow(er), a tail.

bikô o tsukeru〈尾行を付ける〉 put a tail ((on))

itsu-mo bikô-ga-tsuite-iru〈いつも尾行が付いている〉be always wearing a tail

bikô o maku〈尾行をまく〉 shake off a shadow

bikô-suru〈尾行する〉shadow, follow, trail, tail.

bikô-sareru〈尾行される〉be shadowed, be followed, be trailed, be tailed.

bikubiku〈びくびく〉

bikubiku-suru〈びくびくする〉be nervous, be timid, be in fear, be afraid.

bikubiku-shi-nagara〈びくびくしながら〉nervously, timidly, in great fear.

biku-to-mo〈びくとも〉

biku-to-mo-shi-nai〈びくともしない〉be unshaken, be unperturbed, be not at all daunted, do not budge an inch.

biku-to-mo-sezu-ni〈びくともせずに〉nothing daunted.

bimbô〈びんぼう：貧乏〉poverty.

bimbô-shite-iru〈貧乏している〉be in poverty, be poor.

bimbô-na〈貧乏な〉poor.

bimei〈びめい：美名〉

〜-no-bimei-no-moto-ni〈〜の美名の下に〉under the cloak of... .

bimyô〈びみょう：微妙〉

bimyô-na〈微妙な〉delicate, subtle.

bin〈びん：瓶〉a bottle, a phial, a decanter.

bin-ni-ireru, bin-ni-tsumeru or *bin-zume-ni-suru*〈瓶に入れる，瓶に詰める，瓶詰めにする〉bottle.

bin-zume-no〈瓶詰めの〉bottled.

bin〈びん：便〉mail, post, service, a flight.

kôkû-bin-de〈航空便で〉 by air mail

Sapporo-yuki hyaku-go-bin-de（札幌行き105便で）on the 105 flight to Sapporo

binetsu〈びねつ：微熱〉a slight fever.

binetsu-ga-aru〈微熱がある〉have a slight fever, be slightly feverish.

binjô〈びんじょう：便乗〉

binjô-suru〈便乗する〉avail (oneself) ((of)), take advantage ((of)).

binkan〈びんかん：敏感〉

binkan-na〈敏感な〉sensitive.

    binkan-na mimi（敏感な耳）　a sensitive ear

binsen〈びんせん：便せん〉a writing pad, letter paper.

binshō〈びんしょう：敏しょう〉

    dôsa-ga-binshô-de-aru（動作が敏しょうである）　be quick in action

  binshô-na〈敏しょうな〉quick, smart.

  binshô-ni〈敏しょうに〉quickly.

binsoku〈びんそく：敏速〉*see.* binshô.

binwan-ka〈びんわんか：敏腕家〉an able person, a man of capacity, a hustler.

bira〈ビラ〉a bill, a handbill, a placard, a poster.

    bira o maku（ビラをまく）　distribute bills

    bira o haru（ビラをはる）　put up a poster

biri〈びり〉the last, the bottom.

    biri-kara-ni-bamme（びりから二番目）　the last but one

biribiri〈びりびり〉

  biribiri-saku〈びりびり裂く〉tear up into pieces.

birôdo〈ビロード〉velvet.

biru〈ビル〉a (an office) building.

bîru〈ビール〉beer.

    bîru-ippon（ビール一本）　a bottle of beer

Biruma〈ビルマ〉Burma.

    Biruma-jin（ビルマ人）　a Burmese

    Biruma(-jin)-no（ビルマ(人)の）　Burmese

bîrusu〈ビールス〉a virus.

biryō〈びりょう：微量〉a very small amount.

biryoku〈びりょく：微力〉

  biryoku-o-tsukusu〈微力を尽くす〉do one's bit, do what one can.

bi-ryûshi〈びりゅうし：微粒子〉a minute particle, a corpuscle.

bi-seibutsu〈びせいぶつ：微生物〉a microbe, a microorganism.

bishibishi〈びしびし〉severely.

    bishibishi shobun-suru（びしびし処分する）　deal severely ((with))

bishin〈びしん：微震〉a slight shock of an earthquake.

bishi-teki(-na)〈びしてき(な)：微視的(な)〉microscopic.

bishō〈びしょう：微笑〉a smile.

  bishô-suru〈微笑する〉smile.

  bishô-o-ukabete〈微笑を浮かべて〉with a smile, smilingly.

bishoku〈びしょく：美食〉

    bishoku-ka（美食家）　an epicure, a gourmet

bishoku-suru〈美食する〉live on dainty food.
bisho-nure〈びしょぬれ〉
　bisho-nure-ni-naru〈びしょぬれになる〉be wet through, be drenched to the skin.
bisshori〈びっしょり〉
　　bisshori-ase-o-kaku（びっしょり汗をかく）be all of a sweat
　　ase-de-bisshori-ni-naru（汗でびっしょりになる）be sweated through
bitamin〈ビタミン〉vitamin.
　　bitamin-zai（ビタミン剤）a vitamin pill
biteikotsu〈びていこつ：尾てい骨〉the coccyx.
biteki-kankaku〈びてきかんかく：美的感覚〉an esthetic sense.
biten〈びてん：美点〉a merit, a good point.
bitoku〈びとく：美徳〉a virtue.
biwa〈びわ〉a loquat.
biyô〈びよう：美容〉beauty culture.
　　biyô-in（美容院）a beauty salon, a beauty parlor
　　biyô-shi（美容師）a beauty artist
　　biyô-seikei（美容整形）cosmetic surgery
　　biyô-taisô（美容体操）calisthenics
biza〈ビザ〉a visa.
　ryoken ni biza-o-shite-morau〈旅券にビザをしてもらう〉have one's passport visaed.
bizai〈びざい：微罪〉a minor offense.
bô〈ぼう：棒〉a stick, a pole, a bar.
　bô-ni-furu〈棒に振る〉lose all, ruin.
　　isshô-o-bô-ni-furu（一生を棒に振る）ruin one's life
bô-〈ぼう-：某-〉a certain, so-and-so; certain.
　　bô-jitsu（某日）a certain day, one day
　　Bô-shi（某氏）Mr. So-and-so
　　bô-sho（某所）a certain place
bôbi〈ぼうび：防備〉defense.
　bôbi-suru〈防備する〉defend.
　mu-bôbi-no〈無防備の〉defenseless.
bô-biki〈ぼうびき：棒引き〉cancellation.
　bô-biki-ni-suru〈棒引きにする〉cancel (out).
　　shakkin o bô-biki-ni-suru（借金を棒引きにする）cancel a debt
bôbô〈ぼうぼう〉
　　hige-o-bôbô-to-nobashite-iru　otoko（ひげをぼうぼうと伸ばしている男）

　　a man with a shaggy growth of beard

　　kusa-ga-bôbô-to-haete-iru〈草がぼうぼうと生えている〉be　overgrown
　　　with grass

　　bôbô-moe-agaru〈ぼうぼう燃え上がる〉burst into flames

bochi〈ぼち：墓地〉a graveyard, a churchyard, a cemetery.

bôchô〈ぼうちょう：膨脹〉swelling, expansion.

　　tsûka no bôchô〈通貨の膨脹〉expansion of currency

　bôchô-suru〈膨脹する〉swell, expand.

bôchô〈ぼうちょう：傍聴〉

　　bôchô-nin〈傍聴人〉a hearer, an audience ; the public admitted

　　bôchô-seki〈傍聴席〉seats for the public admitted

　bôchô-suru〈傍聴する〉hear, listen ((to)), attend.

bôchû-zai〈ぼうちゅうざい：防虫剤〉an insect repellent.

bôdai〈ぼうだい：ぼう大〉

　bôdai-na〈ぼう大な〉huge, bulky, massive, extensive, enormous.

　　bôdai-na yosan〈ぼう大な予算〉a huge budget

　　bôdai-na kingaku〈ぼう大な金額〉an enormous amount of money

bodai-ju〈ぼだいじゅ：ぼだい樹〉a linden tree.

bôdan〈ぼうだん：防弾〉

　　bôdan-garasu〈防弾ガラス〉bulletproof glass

　bôdan-no〈防弾の〉bulletproof.

bodi-biru〈ボディービル〉body-building.

bôdô〈ぼうどう：暴動〉a riot.

　　Bôdô ga okiru.〈暴動が起きる。〉A riot breaks out.

　　bôdô o okosu〈暴動を起こす〉start a riot

　　bôdô o chin・atsu-suru〈暴動を鎮圧する〉suppress a riot

bôdoku〈ぼうどく：防毒〉

　　bôdoku-masuku〈防毒マスク〉a gas mask

bôei〈ぼうえい：防衛〉defense.

　　jiko-bôei〈自己防衛〉self-defense

　bôei-suru〈防衛する〉defend ((against)).

bôeki〈ぼうえき：貿易〉trade, commerce.

　　bôeki-aite-koku〈貿易相手国〉a trade partner

　　bôeki-gaisha〈貿易会社〉a trading company

　　kaigai-bôeki〈海外貿易〉foreign trade

　bôeki-suru〈貿易する〉trade ((with)), commerce.

bôeki〈ぼうえき：防疫〉prevention of epidemics.

bôen-〈ぼうえん-：望遠-〉

bôen-kyô〈望遠鏡〉 a telescope

tentai-bôen-kyô〈天体望遠鏡〉 an astronomical telescope

bôen-renzu〈望遠レンズ〉 a telephoto lens

bôfura〈ぼうふら〉a mosquito larva.

bôfû-rin〈ぼうふうりん：防風林〉a windbreak (forest).

bôfû-u〈ぼうふうう：暴風雨〉a rainstorm, a storm.

bôfû-u-keihô〈暴風雨警報〉 a storm warning

bôfu-zai〈ぼうふざい：防腐剤〉an antiseptic.

bôgai〈ぼうがい：妨害〉disturbance, obstruction, interruption, interference.

eigyô-bôgai〈営業妨害〉 obstruction of business

bôgai-suru〈妨害する〉disturb, obstruct, interrupt, interfere ((with)).

ammin o bôgai-suru〈安眠を妨害する〉 disturb one's sleep

bôgen〈ぼうげん：暴言〉violent language, one's abusive use of language.

bôgen-o-haku〈暴言を吐く〉use violent language, abuse.

bôgi〈ぼうぎ：謀議〉

bôgi-o-korasu〈謀議を凝らす〉conspire together.

bôgyo〈ぼうぎょ：防御〉defense.

bôgyo-suru〈防御する〉defend.

bôhan〈ぼうはん：防犯〉prevention of crimes.

bôhan-beru〈防犯ベル〉 a burglar alarm

bôha-tei〈ぼうはてい：防波堤〉a breakwater.

bôhatsu〈ぼうはつ：暴発〉an accidental discharge.

raifuru no bôhatsu〈ライフルの暴発〉 an accidental firing of a rifle

bôhatsu-suru〈暴発する〉go off accidentally.

bohi〈ぼひ：墓碑〉a tombstone, a gravestone.

bohi o tateru〈墓碑を建てる〉 set up a tombstone

boikotto〈ボイコット〉a boycott.

boikotto-suru〈ボイコットする〉boycott.

boin〈ぼいん：母音〉a vowel.

boin〈ぼいん：母印〉a thumbmark, a thumbprint.

boin-o-osu〈ぼ印を押す〉seal ((a document)) with the thumb.

bôin-bôshoku〈ぼういんぼうしょく：暴飲暴食〉

bôin-bôshoku-suru〈暴飲暴食する〉drink and eat too much.

bôju〈ぼうじゅ：傍受〉

bôju-suru〈傍受する〉intercept, monitor, pick up, tap.

muden o bôju-suru〈無電を傍受する〉 intercept a radio message

bôka〈ぼうか：防火〉fire prevention.

bôka-kôzô（防火構造） fireproof construction
bôka-setsubi（防火設備） fire prevention equipment
bôkan〈ぼうかん：防寒〉 protection against the cold.
bôkan-gu（防寒具） an outfit for protection against the cold
bôkan〈ぼうかん：傍観〉
bôkan-sha（傍観者） a looker-on, a bystander
bôkan-suru〈傍観する〉 look on, stand by idly.
bôkan〈ぼうかん：暴漢〉a ruffian.
bôkan-ni osowareru（暴漢に襲われる） be assaulted by a ruffian
bokashi〈ぼかし〉 gradation, shading off.
bokasu〈ぼかす〉 gradate, shade off.
bokei〈ぼけい：母系〉 the maternal line.
bokei-kazoku（母系家族） a maternal family
bokei-no〈母系の〉 maternal.
bôkei〈ぼうけい：傍系〉
bôkei-gaisha（傍系会社） a subsidiary company
bôkei-no〈傍系の〉 subsidiary, collateral.
bôken〈ぼうけん：冒険〉an adventure, a venture, a hazard, a risk.
bôken-suru〈冒険する〉 venture, make a venture, run a risk.
bôken-teki(-na)〈冒険的(な)〉 adventurous, hazardous.
bokeru〈ぼける〉 dote, become mentally weak.
atama-ga sukoshi-bokete-iru（頭が少しぼけている） be a little weak-
headed
boketsu〈ぼけつ：墓穴〉
mizukara-boketsu-o-horu〈自ら墓穴を掘る〉 bring about one's own ruin.
boki〈ぼき：簿記〉 bookkeeping.
boki-o-tsukeru〈簿記を付ける〉 keep books, keep accounts.
bokin〈ぼきん：募金〉 fund-raising, collection of contributions (*or* subscriptions).
bokin-undô（募金運動） a fund-raising campaign
gaitô-bokin（街頭募金） a street collection of subscriptions
bokin-suru〈募金する〉 raise money, collect contributions, invite
subscriptions.
bokka〈ぼっか：牧歌〉a pastoral.
bokka-teki(-na)〈牧歌的(な)〉 pastoral.
bokkô〈ぼっこう：ぼっ興〉a sudden rise.
bokkô-suru〈ぼっ興する〉 rise suddenly.
bokkôshô〈ぼっこうしょう：没交渉〉

bokkôshô-de-aru 〈没交渉である〉 have nothing to do ((with)), have no relation ((with)), be independent ((of)).

bokô 〈ぼこう：母校〉 one's Alma Mater.

bokô 〈ぼこう：母港〉 a home port.

bôkô 〈ぼうこう：暴行〉 violence, an outrage, an assault.

   bôkô-o-kuwaeru 〈暴行を加える〉 do violence ((to)), commit an outrage ((on)), assault.

bôkô 〈ぼうこう〉 the bladder.

   bôkô-en (ぼうこう炎) inflammation of the bladder

bokoku 〈ぼこく：母国〉 one's mother country, the homeland.

   bokoku-go (母国語) one's mother tongue

boku 〈ぼく：僕〉 *see.* wata(ku)shi.

bôkû 〈ぼうくう：防空〉 air defense.

bokuchiku 〈ぼくちく：牧畜〉 stock farming, stock raising, cattle breeding.

   bokuchiku-gyô-sha (牧畜業者) a stock farmer, a cattle breeder

bokujô 〈ぼくじょう：牧場〉 a stock farm, a pasture, a meadow, a ranch.

bokujû 〈ぼくじゅう：墨汁〉 India ink.

bokumetsu 〈ぼくめつ：撲滅〉 eradication, extirpation, extermination.

   gan-bokumetsu-undô (がん撲滅運動) an anti-cancer campaign

   bokumetsu-suru 〈撲滅する〉 exterminate, stamp out.

bôkun 〈ぼうくん：暴君〉 a tyrant, a despot.

bokusatsu 〈ぼくさつ：撲殺〉 slaughter.

   bokusatsu-suru 〈撲殺する〉 beat ((a person)) to death.

bokushi 〈ぼくし：牧師〉 a pastor, a minister, a clergyman.

bokusô 〈ぼくそう：牧草〉 grass.

   bokusô-chi (牧草地) a pasture, a meadow

bokutotsu 〈ぼくとつ〉

   bokutotsu-na 〈ぼくとつな〉 unsophisticated.

bôkyo 〈ぼうきょ：暴挙〉 a reckless act, outrage, violence.

   bôkyo-ni-deru 〈暴挙に出る〉 act recklessly, resort to violence.

bôkyo(-no-nen) 〈ぼうきょう（のねん）：望郷（の念）〉 homesickness, nostalgia.

bombe 〈ボンベ〉 a cylinder.

   gasu-bombe (ガスボンベ) a gas cylinder

bombon 〈ぼんぼん〉

   Hanabi ga bombon-agari-dashita. (花火がぼんぼん揚がり出した.) The fireworks began to crack up in the air.

bômei 〈ぼうめい：亡命〉
  bômei-sha (亡命者) an exile, a (political) refugee, a fugitive
  bômei-seifu (亡命政府) a government in exile
 bômei-suru 〈亡命する〉 flee from one's own country, seek refuge.
bon 〈ぼん：盆〉 a tray, a server; the *Bon* Festival.
  bon-odori (盆踊り) a *Bon* Festival dance
bonchi 〈ぼんち：盆地〉 a basin.
  Kôfu-bonchi (甲府盆地) the Kofu Basin
bonda 〈ぼんだ：凡打〉
 bonda-suru 〈凡打する〉 hit an easy grounder(*or* a pop fly).
bônen-kai 〈ぼうねんかい：忘年会〉 a year-end (dinner) party.
bon-furai 〈ぼんフライ：凡フライ〉
 bon-furai o uchi-ageru 〈凡フライを打ち上げる〉 fly an easy fly.
bongo 〈ぼんご：ぼん語〉 Sanscrit.
bôn-heddo 〈ボーンヘッド〉 a bonehead play.
  bôn-heddo-o-yaru (ボーンヘッドをやる) pull a bonehead play
bonjin 〈ぼんじん：凡人〉 an ordinary person, a mediocrity.
bonkura 〈ぼんくら〉 a stupid, a blockhead, a dunderhead.
 bonkura-na 〈ぼんくらな〉 stupid, half-witted.
bonsai 〈ぼんさい：盆栽〉 a potted plant.
  matsu-no-bonsai (松の盆栽) a dwarf pine tree
bontai 〈ぼんたい：凡退〉
 bontai-suru 〈凡退する〉 be easily put out.
 bontai-saseru 〈凡退させる〉 retire.
bon·yari 〈ぼんやり〉
 bon·yari-shita 〈ぼんやりした〉 stupid, vacant, absentminded; vague, dim.
  bon·yari-shita kao (ぼんやりした顔) a vacant look
  bon·yari-shita sugata (ぼんやりした姿) a vague figure
 bon·yari(-to) 〈ぼんやり（と）〉 stupidly, vacantly, absentmindedly; vaguely, dimly.
  bon·yari(-to) mi-tsumeru (ぼんやり（と）見詰める) stare vacantly ((at))
  bon·yari oboete-iru (ぼんやり覚えている) remember vaguely
  kiri-no-naka-ni bon·yari(-to) mizuumi-ga-mieru (霧の中にぼんやり（と）湖が見える) be able to see the lake dimly through the haze
bonyû 〈ぼにゅう：母乳〉 mother's milk.
  bonyû-de sodateru (母乳で育てる) feed ((a baby)) on mother's milk
bôon 〈ぼうおん：防音〉 soundproofing.

bôon-no〈防音の〉soundproof.

boppatsu〈ぼっぱつ：ぼっ発〉an outbreak.

boppatsu-suru〈ぼっ発する〉break out.

bôraku〈ぼうらく：暴落〉a slump, a heavy decline.

　　kabu-no bôraku（株の暴落）　a slump in stocks

bôraku-suru〈暴落する〉slump, plunge.

bôri〈ぼうり：暴利〉excessive profits.

　　bôri o tori-shimaru（暴利を取り締まる）　control profiteering

bôri-o-musaboru〈暴利をむさぼる〉profiteer.

boribori〈ぼりぼり〉

　　boribori-kajiru（ぼりぼりかじる）　munch, crunch

　　boribori-kaku（ぼりぼりかく）　scratch violently

bôringu〈ボーリング〉boring, drilling; bowling.

　　bôringu-jô（ボーリング場）　a bowling alley

bôringu-o-suru〈ボーリングをする〉bowl.

boro〈ぼろ〉rags, tatters.

　　boro-o-kite-iru（ぼろを着ている）　be in rags

　　boro-gire（ぼろ切れ）　a rag, old cloth

　　boro-jidôsha（ぼろ自動車）　a shabby car, a jalopy

boroboro〈ぼろぼろ〉

　　namida-o-boroboro-kobosu（涙をぼろぼろこぼす）　shed big drops of tears

boroboro〈ぼろぼろ〉

boroboro-no〈ぼろぼろの〉ragged, tattered.

boroboro-ni〈ぼろぼろに〉in pieces, in rags, in tatters, in shreds.

　　boroboro-ni-naru（ぼろぼろになる）　be worn to tatters

boroi〈ぼろい〉

　　boroi shôbai（ぼろい商売）　a lucrative job

boro(i)-môke〈ぼろ(い)もうけ〉

boro-môke-o-yaru〈ぼろもうけをやる〉make easy money, make undue profits.

boro-kuso〈ぼろくそ〉

boro-kuso-ni-iu〈ぼろくそに言う〉speak very ill ((of)), speak very disparagingly ((of)).

bôron〈ぼうろん：暴論〉a wild argument.

　　bôron-o-haku（暴論を吐く）　make a wild argument, make absurd remarks

bôru-〈ボール-〉

bôru-gami〈ボール紙〉 cardboard
bôru-bako〈ボール箱〉 a cardboard case, a carton

boruto〈ボルト〉a volt, voltage; a bolt.
    hyaku-boruto-no denryû（百ボルトの電流） a 100-volt current
    boruto o shimeru（ボルトを締める） tighten a bolt

bôryaku〈ぼうりゃく：謀略〉a stratagem, a plot.
    bôryaku-o-megurasu（謀略をめぐらす） devise a stratagem, work out a plot

bôryoku〈ぼうりょく：暴力〉violence, force.
    bôryoku-ni-uttaeru（暴力に訴える） resort to violence
    bôryoku-kôi（暴力行為） an act of violence
    bôryoku-dan（暴力団） a band of ruffians; a gangster
    bôryoku-de（暴力で） by force.

boryûmu〈ボリューム〉volume.
    boryûmu o ageru（ボリュームを上げる） turn up the volume

bôsai〈ぼうさい：防災〉prevention against disasters.

bosan〈ぼさん：墓参〉a visit to a grave.
    bosan-ni kaeru（墓参に帰る） return home to visit the family grave

bôsa-rin〈ぼうさりん：防砂林〉trees for preventing sand shifting.

bosei〈ぼせい：母性〉motherhood, maternity.
    bosei-ai（母性愛） maternal love
    bosei-honnô（母性本能） maternal instinct

bôseki〈ぼうせき：紡績〉spinning, cotton-spinning.
    bôseki-kôjô（紡績工場） a cotton mill, a spinning mill

bosen〈ぼせん：母船〉a mother ship.

bôsen〈ぼうせん：防戦〉a defensive fight.
    bôsen-suru〈防戦する〉fight in defense.

bôsetsu-rin〈ぼうせつりん：防雪林〉a snow forest.

bôshi〈ぼうし：帽子〉a hat, a cap.
    bôshi o kaburu（帽子をかぶる） put on a hat
    bôshi o nugu（帽子を脱ぐ） take off one's hat
    bôshi-o-kabutta-mama(-de)（帽子をかぶったまま（で）） with one's hat on.

bôshi〈ぼうし：防止〉prevention, check.
    bôshi-suru〈防止する〉prevent, check.

bôshin〈ぼうしん：防振〉
    bôshin-no〈防振の〉vibrationproof.

bôshitsu〈ぼうしつ：防湿〉
    bôshitsu-no〈防湿の〉dampproof, moistureproof.

bôshô 〈ぼうしょう：傍証〉
　　bôshô o katameru 〈傍証を固める〉collect supporting evidence.
bôshoku 〈ぼうしょく：防しょく〉
　　bôshoku-no 〈防しょくの〉corrosionproof.
boshû 〈ぼしゅう：募集〉
　　　boshû-gaku 〈募集額〉the amount to be raised
　　　boshû-jin-in 〈募集人員〉the number of persons to be admitted
　　boshû-suru 〈募集する〉invite, collect, raise, appeal ((for)), float.
　　　shigan-sha o boshû-suru 〈志願者を募集する〉invite applications
　　　kaiin o boshû-suru 〈会員を募集する〉collect members
　　　kikin o boshû-suru 〈基金を募集する〉raise a fund
　　　kifu(-kin)-o-boshû-suru 〈寄附(金)を募集する〉appeal for contributions
　　　kôsai o boshû-suru 〈公債を募集する〉float a loan
　　　kôkoku-de-boshû-suru 〈広告で募集する〉advertise ((for))
　　boshû-ni-ôjiru 〈募集に応じる〉apply ((for)), subscribe ((for)).
bôshû 〈ぼうしゅう：防臭〉
　　　bôshû-zai 〈防臭剤〉a deodorant
bôshuku 〈ぼうしゅく：防縮〉
　　bôshuku-kakô-no-shite-aru 〈防縮加工のしてある〉shrinkproof.
bôsô 〈ぼうそう：暴走〉reckless driving; a reckless run.
bosoboso 〈ぼそぼそ〉
　　bosoboso-hanasu 〈ぼそぼそ話す〉talk in a subdued tone.
bosshû 〈ぼっしゅう：没収〉confiscation, forfeiture, seizure.
　　bosshû-suru 〈没収する〉confiscate, forfeit, seize.
　　bosshû-sareru 〈没収される〉be confiscated, be forfeited.
bôsui 〈ぼうすい：防水〉
　　bôsui-no or *bôsui-shita* 〈防水の，防水した〉waterproof, watertight.
botabota 〈ぼたぼた〉in drops.
　　botabota-tareru 〈ぼたぼたたれる〉drip, trickle down.
botai 〈ぼたい：母体〉the mother's body.
　　　senkyo-botai 〈選挙母体〉an electorate
bô-taka-tobi 〈ぼうたかとび：棒高跳び〉pole jump, pole vault.
botan 〈ぼたん〉a peony.
　　　botan-yuki 〈ぼたん雪〉large snowflakes
botan 〈ボタン〉a button.
　　　Botan ga toreta. 〈ボタンが取れた.〉A Button has come off.
　　　botan-ana 〈ボタン穴〉a buttonhole

botan-o-kakeru 〈ボタンを掛ける〉 button, fasten a button.

    botan-o-hazusu（ボタンを外す） unbutton, undo a button

botchan 〈ぼっちゃん：坊ちゃん〉 your son, a boy, a son, a green boy; sonny.

    Kare-wa marude-botchan-da.（彼はまるで坊ちゃんだ.） He knows nothing of the world.

bôto 〈ぼうと：暴徒〉 a mob, rioters.

bôto 〈ボート〉 a boat.

    bôto-o-kogi-ni-iku（ボートをこぎに行く） go boating, go for a row

    bôto-rêsu（ボートレース） a boat race, a regatta

bôtô 〈ぼうとう：暴騰〉 a sudden rise, a jump.

    bukka no bôtô（物価の暴騰） a sharp rise of prices

bôtô-suru 〈暴騰する〉 rise suddenly, jump, soar, skyrocket.

bôtô 〈ぼうとう：暴投〉 a wild pitch, a wild throw.

bôtô-chinjutsu 〈ぼうとうちんじゅつ：冒頭陳述〉 an opening statement.

bôtoku 〈ぼうとく：冒とく〉

kami-o-bôtoku-suru 〈神を冒とくする〉 blaspheme, profane, defile.

botsubotsu 〈ぼつぼつ〉 little by little, slowly, gradually.

    Botsubotsu atatakaku-natte-kita.（ぼつぼつ暖かくなってきた.） It has been getting warmer and warmer.

    Botsubotsu dekake-yô.（ぼつぼつ出掛けよう.） Now, let's be getting along.

botsuraku 〈ぼつらく：没落〉 downfall, ruin.

botsuraku-suru 〈没落する〉 fall, be ruined.

botto or **bôtto** 〈ぼっと，ぼうっと〉

    botto-moe-agaru（ぼっと燃え上がる） blaze up, flame up

    atama ga nan-to-naku bôtto-shite-iru（頭が何となくぼうっとしている） feel somehow dazed

    uttori-shite-bôtto-naru（うっとりしてぼうっとなる） be fascinated

    bôtto-kasunde mieru（ぼうっとかすんで見える） be seen dimly, be seen faintly

    bôtto-shita shashin（ぼうっとした写真） a blurred photograph

bottô 〈ぼっとう：没頭〉

bottô-suru 〈没頭する〉 be absorbed ((in)), immerse oneself ((in)), devote oneself ((to)).

boya 〈ぼや〉 a small fire.

bô-ya 〈ぼうや：坊や〉 a boy; my boy, sonny.

boyaboya 〈ぼやぼや〉

boyaboya-suru 〈ぼやぼやする〉 be careless, be absentminded, be woolgathering, fool around.

   Boyaboya-suru-na! 〈ぼやぼやするな.〉 Look alive! / Look sharp!

boyakeru 〈ぼやける〉 become dim, get blurred.

boyaku 〈ぼやく〉 grumble, complain.

bô-yomi 〈ぼうよみ：棒読み〉

bô-yomi-suru 〈棒読みする〉 read straight on, read in a singsong manner.

bôzen 〈ぼうぜん：ぼう然〉

bôzen-to 〈ぼう然と〉 vacantly, absentmindedly.

bôzen-to-suru or *bôzen-jishitsu-suru* 〈ぼう然とする，ぼう然自失する〉 be stupefied.

   kanashimi-de bôzen-to-suru 〈悲しみでぼう然とする〉 be stupefied with grief

bôzu 〈ぼうず：坊主〉 a Buddhist priest, a monk.

   bôzu-atama 〈坊主頭〉 a shaven head

   bôzu-gari 〈坊主刈り〉 a close crop

bu 〈ぶ：部〉 a part; a department, a club; a copy.

   dai-sambu 〈第三部〉 Part III

   shoseki-bu 〈書籍部〉 the book department

   tenisu-bu 〈テニス部〉 the tennis club

   ichi-bu sen-en 〈一部千円〉 one thousand yen per copy

bu 〈ぶ：分，歩〉 rate, percentage, percent.

   hachi-bu no tesû-ryô 〈八分の手数料〉 a commission of 8 percent

   Kôji wa hachi-bu-doori kansei-shita. 〈工事は八分どおり完成した.〉 The work is 80 percent finished.

   Kimi-no-hô-ni bu-ga-aru. 〈君の方に歩がある.〉 The odds are in your favor.

buai 〈ぶあい：歩合〉 rate, percentage; a commission.

buai-sei-de 〈歩合制で〉 on a percentage basis.

bu-aisô 〈ぶあいそう：無愛想〉

bu-aisô-na 〈無愛想な〉 cold, unsociable, unaffable, gruff, sullen.

   bu-aisô-na taido 〈無愛想な態度〉 cold manner

bu-atsui 〈ぶあつい：分厚い〉 thick, massive, heavy.

   bu-atsui hon 〈分厚い本〉 a thick book

bûbû 〈ぶうぶう〉

   bûbû-iu 〈ぶうぶう言う〉 grumble ((about, at *or* over)), complain ((of)), bellyache ((about))

   keiteki-o-bûbû-narashite-hashiru 〈警笛をぶうぶう鳴らして走る〉 run

honking

bubun〈ぶぶん：部分〉a part, a portion.

ichi-bubun（一部分）(a) part ((of))

bubun-teki(-na)〈部分的（な）〉partial.

bubun-teki-ni〈部分的に〉partially.

bubun-hin〈ぶぶんひん：部分品〉*see.* buhin.

buchi〈ぶち〉spots, specks.

shiro-kuro-no-buchi-inu（白黒のぶち犬）a black and white dog

buchi-no〈ぶちの〉spotted, speckled.

buchi-komu〈ぶちこむ：ぶち込む〉throw ((a thing *or* a person)) into.

buchi-kowashi〈ぶちこわし：ぶち壊し〉destruction, demolition; spoiling.

Sekkaku-no keikaku mo buchi-kowashi-da.（せっかくの計画もぶち壊しだ。）The plan has been destroyed.

buchi-kowasu〈ぶち壊す〉break, destroy, pull down; spoil, knock ((something)) into a cocked hat.

buchi-makeru〈ぶちまける〉

ikari-o-buchi-makeru（怒りをぶちまける）give vent to one's anger

kimochi o buchi-makeru（気持ちをぶちまける）pour out one's feelings

buchi-nuku〈ぶちぬく：ぶち抜く〉

shikiri o buchi-nuite ookina heya o tsukuru（仕切りをぶち抜いて大きな部屋を作る）remove the partition walls to make a larger room

budô〈ぶどう〉a grape, a vine.

budô-hito-fusa（ぶどう一房）a bunch of grapes

budô-en（ぶどう園）a vineyard

budô-shu（ぶどう酒）wine

budô-jô-kyûkin〈ぶどうじょうきゅうきん：ぶどう状球菌〉a staphylococcus.

bu-enryo〈ぶえんりょ：無遠慮〉

bu-enryo-na〈無遠慮な〉unceremonious, forward, bold, unreserved, frank.

bu-enryo-ni〈無遠慮に〉unceremoniously, forwardly, boldly, unreservedly, frankly.

bugai-sha〈ぶがいしゃ：部外者〉an outsider.

buhin〈ぶひん：部品〉(spare) parts.

bui〈ブイ〉a buoy.

kyûmei-bui（救命ブイ）a life buoy

buji〈ぶじ：無事〉safety; peace.

buji-na〈無事な〉safe; peaceful.

buji-ni〈無事に〉safe(ly), in safety, without any trouble; in peace, peacefully.

    buji-ni kaeru（無事に帰る）come back safe

    buji-ni tsuku（無事に着く）arrive in good condition

    buji-ni kurasu（無事に暮らす）live in peace

bujoku〈ぶじょく：侮辱〉insult.

    bujoku o shinobu（侮辱を忍ぶ）swallow an insult

bujoku-suru〈侮辱する〉insult.

bujoku-o-ukeru〈侮辱を受ける〉suffer an insult, be insulted.

buka〈ぶか：部下〉a subordinate, a follower, one's men.

bukabuka〈ぶかぶか〉

bukabuka-no〈ぶかぶかの〉baggy.

bu-kakkô〈ぶかっこう：不(無)かっ好〉

bu-kakkô-na〈不(無)かっ好な〉ill-shaped, awkward, clumsy.

bukan〈ぶかん：武官〉a military(*or* naval) officer.

    taishi-kan-zuki riku-gun-bukan（大使館付き陸軍武官）a military attaché to an embassy

buki〈ぶき：武器〉arms, a weapon.

    buki o toru（武器を取る）take up arms

bu-kimi〈ぶきみ：無(不)気味〉

bu-kimi-na〈無(不)気味な〉uncanny, weird, eerie, gruesome.

bu-kiryô〈ぶきりょう：不(無)器量〉

bu-kiryô-na〈不(無)器量な〉plain, plain-looking, homely.

bu-kiyô〈ぶきよう：不(無)器用〉

bu-kiyô-na〈不(無)器用な〉awkward, clumsy, unskillful.

bu-kiyô-ni〈不(無)器用に〉awkwardly, clumsily.

bukka〈ぶっか：物価〉prices〔of commodities〕.

    Bukka ga agatta.（物価が上がった。）Prices have gone up.

    Bukka ga sagatta.（物価が下がった。）Prices have come down.

    bukka-shisû（物価指数）a price index

    bukka-tôki（物価騰貴）a rise in prices

    bukka-no antei（物価の安定）price stability

bukken〈ぶっけん：物件〉a thing, an article.

    shôko-bukken（しょうこぶっけん：証拠物件）material evidence

bukken〈ぶっけん：物権〉a real right.

bukkirabô〈ぶっきらぼう〉

bukkirabô-na〈ぶっきらぼうな〉abrupt, curt, blunt.
  bukkirabô-na taido（ぶっきらぼうな態度）abrupt manner
bukkirabô-ni〈ぶっきらぼうに〉abruptly, curtly, bluntly.
bukkyô〈ぶっきょう：仏教〉Buddhism.
  bukkyô-to（仏教徒）a Buddhist
bukubuku〈ぶくぶく〉
  bukubuku-futotta hito（ぶくぶく太った人）a plump person
  bukubuku-awa-ga-tatsu（ぶくぶく泡が立つ）bubble up
  bukubuku-shizumu（ぶくぶく沈む）sink bubbling
bukyoku〈ぶきょく：舞曲〉dance music.
bukyoku〈ぶきょく：部局〉a department, a bureau.
  bukyoku-sei（部局制）a departmental system
bumben〈ぶんべん：分べん〉childbirth, delivery.
bumben-suru〈分べんする〉give birth ((to)), be delivered ((of)).
bumbo〈ぶんぼ：分母〉a denominator.
bumbun〈ぶんぶん〉humming, buzzing, a hum, a buzz, a whir(r).
bumbun-iu〈ぶんぶんいう〉hum, buzz, whir.
bummei〈ぶんめい：文明〉civilization.
  bummei-shakai（文明社会）civilized society
bummei-no〈文明の〉civilized.
bummyaku〈ぶんみゃく：文脈〉the context〔of a passage〕.
bumon〈ぶもん：部門〉a class, a division, a department, a section, a branch.
bumon-betsu-ni-suru〈部門別にする〉classify, departmentalize.
bumpa〈ぶんぱ：分派〉a sect, a faction.
  bumpa-katsudô（分派活動）factional activities
bumpai〈ぶんぱい：分配〉division, sharing, distribution, allotment.
  rieki-no bumpai（利益の分配）profit sharing
bumpai-suru〈分配する〉divide, share, distribute, allot.
  byôdô-ni bumpai-suru（平等に分配する）distribute equally
bumpitsu〈ぶんぴつ：分泌〉secretion.
  bumpitsu-butsu（分泌物）a secretion
bumpitsu-suru〈分泌する〉secrete.
bumpitsu〈ぶんぴつ：文筆〉literary art, writing.
  bumpitsu-de seikei-o-tateru（文筆で生計を立てる）live by one's pen
  bumpitsu-ka（文筆家）a literary man, a writer
bumpô〈ぶんぽう：文法〉grammar.
bumpô-jô-no or *bumpô-teki(-na)*〈文法上の，文法的(な)〉grammatical.

bumpô-jô(-wa) or *bumpô-teki-ni* 〈文法上(は)，文法的に〉grammatically.
bumpu 〈ぶんぷ：分布〉distribution.
  chiri-teki bumpu（地理的分布）geographical distribution
  bumpu-suru〈分布する〉be distributed.
bûmu 〈ブーム〉a boom.
  kankô-bûmu（観光ブーム）a sightseeing boom
bun 〈ぶん：文〉writings, a composition, a sentence, style.
  bun o tsukuru（文を作る）make a composition
  senren-sareta bun（洗練された文）a refined sentence
  Kanojo-wa bun-ga-umai.（彼女は文がうまい。）She is a good writer.
  Kare-wa bun-ga-heta-da.（彼は文が下手だ。）He is a poor writer.
-bun 〈-ぶん：-分〉a share, a part, a ration, a portion; a fraction.
  Kore-wa kimi-no bun-desu.（これは君の分です。）This is for you.
  ichi-nichi-bun-no shokuryô（一日分の食糧）a day's ration
  arukôru-bun（アルコール分）alcoholic content
  sambun-no-ichi（三分の一）a third, one third
  sambun-no-ni（三分の二）two thirds
  yombun-no-ichi（四分の一）a quarter
  yombun-no-ni（四分の二）two quarters
  jû-bun-no-roku（十分の六）six tenths
bunai 〈ぶない：部内〉circles, the department.
  seifu-bunai（政府部内）government circles
bunan 〈ぶなん：無難〉
  bunan-na〈無難な〉safe, secure; faultless, flawless.
bunchin 〈ぶんちん：文鎮〉a paperweight.
bunchô 〈ぶんちょう：文鳥〉a paddy bird.
bundan 〈ぶんだん：文壇〉
  bundan-ni-deru〈文壇に出る〉enter upon a literary career.
bundo-ki 〈ぶんどき：分度器〉a protractor.
bungaku 〈ぶんがく：文学〉literature.
  bungaku-bu（文学部）the department of literature
  bungaku-hakase（文学博士）a doctor of literature, Doctor of Literature (Litt. D.)
  bungaku-sakuhin（文学作品）a literary work
  bungaku-sha（文学者）a literary man, a man of letters
  bungaku-shi（文学史）a history of literature
  jun-bungaku（純文学）polite literature
  Nihon-bungaku（日本文学）Japanese literature

taishû-bungaku（大衆文学） popular literature

bungaku-no or *bungaku-teki(-na)*〈文学の，文学的(な)〉literary.

bungei〈ぶんげい：文芸〉literature, literary art.

bungei-sakuhin（文芸作品） *see.* bungaku-sakuhin

bungo〈ぶんご：文語〉written language, literary language.

bungo-tai（文語体） literary style

bungô〈ぶんごう：文豪〉a master writer, a great man of letters.

bungu〈ぶんぐ：文具〉stationery.

bungu-ya（文具屋） a stationer; a stationer's, a stationery store

bungyô〈ぶんぎょう：分業〉division of labor, specialization.

bun·i〈ぶんい：文意〉the meaning〔of a sentence〕, the effect〔of a letter〕.

bunjô〈ぶんじょう：分譲〉

bunjô-chi（分譲地） lots for sale

bunjô-suru〈分譲する〉sell ((land)) in lots.

bunka〈ぶんか：文化〉culture.

bunka-jin（文化人） a man of culture

bunka-shisan *or* bunka-zai（文化資産，文化財） cultural assets

bunka-no〈文化の〉cultural.

bunka-no kôryû（文化の交流） cultural exchange

bunka-teki(-na)〈文化的(な)〉cultural, cultured, civilized.

bunka〈ぶんか：文科〉a literature course, the department of literature.

bunka〈ぶんか：分科〉a department, a branch.

bunka-kai（分科会） a subcommittee

bunka〈ぶんか：分化〉specialization, differentiation.

bunka-suru〈分化する〉specialize, differentiate.

bunkai〈ぶんかい：分解〉analysis, resolution, dissolution.

bunkai-suru〈分解する〉analyze, resolve ((into)), dissolve ((into)).

bunkan〈ぶんかん：文官〉a civil officer; the civil service.

bunkatsu〈ぶんかつ：分割〉division, partition.

bunkatsu-barai（分割払い） payment in installments, an installment plan

bunkatsu-suru〈分割する〉divide (up), partition.

bunke〈ぶんけ：分家〉a branch family.

bunken〈ぶんけん：文献〉literature, documents.

sankô-bunken（参考文献） literature cited, a bibliography

bunken〈ぶんけん：分権〉decentralization of authorities.

chihô-bunken（地方分権） decentralization of power

bunki-ten 〈ぶんきてん：分岐点〉a turning point, a junction.

bunko 〈ぶんこ：文庫〉a library; *bunko*.
Iwanami-bunko（岩波文庫） the Iwanami Library
bunko-ban（文庫版） *bunko* size
bunko-bon（文庫本） a pocket edition, a paperback

bunkô 〈ぶんこう：分光〉spectrum.
bunkô-ki（分光器） a spectroscope

bunkyô 〈ぶんきょう：文教〉education, culture.
bunkyô-(chi)ku（文教(地)区） a school zone
bunkyô-seisaku（文教政策） an educational policy

bunkyoku 〈ぶんきょく：分極〉polarization.
bunkyoku-ka-suru〈分極化する〉polarize.

bunnô 〈ぶんのう：分納〉
bunnô-suru〈分納する〉pay by installments; deliver in parts.

bunrei 〈ぶんれい：文例〉an example〔for writing〕.

bunretsu 〈ぶんれつ：分裂〉dissolution, disintegration, breakup, division, split.
kaku-bunretsu（核分裂） nuclear division(*or* fission)
bunretsu-suru〈分裂する〉break up, be divided, split.

bunri 〈ぶんり：分離〉separation, secession, severance, segregation.
chûô-bunri-tai（中央分離帯） a median strip
bunri-suru〈分離する〉separate, secede, sever, segregate.

bunritsu 〈ぶんりつ：分立〉separation, independence.
san-ken-bunritsu（三権分立） the separation of the three powers
bunritsu-suru〈分立する〉separate ((from)).

bunrui 〈ぶんるい：分類〉classification, grouping.
bunrui-suru〈分類する〉classify, divide into classes, group.

bunryô 〈ぶんりょう：分量〉a quantity, an amount; a dose.

bunsai 〈ぶんさい：文才〉
bunsai-ga-aru〈文才がある〉have a talent for writing.

bunsan 〈ぶんさん：分散〉breakup, dispersion, decentralization.
bunsan-suru〈分散する〉break up, disperse, decentralize.

bunsatsu 〈ぶんさつ：分冊〉a separate volume.
bunsatsu-de shuppan-suru（分冊で出版する） publish in parts
bunsatsu-uri-o-suru（分冊売りをする） sell ((the volumes)) singly

bunseki 〈ぶんせき：分析〉analysis.
bunseki-suru〈分析する〉analyze.

bunshi 〈ぶんし：分子〉a numerator; a molecule; an element.

    tô-nai-no fuhei-bunshi (党内の不平分子) discontented elements in the party

bunshi 〈ぶんし：分詞〉a participle.

bunsho 〈ぶんしょ：文書〉a document, a record.

bunshô 〈ぶんしょう：文章〉*see.* bun.

bunshô 〈ぶんしょう：文相〉*see.* mombu-daijin.

bunshû 〈ぶんしゅう：文集〉a collection of works.

bunshuku 〈ぶんしゅく：分宿〉

  bunshuku-suru 〈分宿する〉put up separately 〔at several hotels〕.

bunsû 〈ぶんすう：分数〉a fraction.

    bunsû-shiki (分数式) a fractional expression

  bunsû-no 〈分数の〉fractional.

bunsui-rei 〈ぶんすいれい：分水れい〉a watershed, a divide.

buntai 〈ぶんたい：文体〉a (literary) style.

    heii-na buntai-de (平易な文体で) in a plain style

buntai 〈ぶんたい：分隊〉a squad, a division, a detachment.

buntan 〈ぶんたん：分担〉partial charge, allotment, one's share.

    buntan-kin (分担金) a share of expenses

  buntan-suru 〈分担する〉take partial charge ((of)), share.

    hiyô o buntan-suru (費用を分担する) share the expenses with one another

    shigoto o buntan-suru (仕事を分担する) divide the work ((among))

buntsû 〈ぶんつう：文通〉correspondence.

  buntsû-suru 〈文通する〉correspond ((with)), exchange letters ((with)).

bun·ya 〈ぶんや：分野〉a field, a sphere.

    katsudô-bun·ya (活動分野) one's field of activity

bunzai 〈ぶんざい：分際〉

  bunzai o shiru 〈分際を知る〉know one's station in life.

buppin 〈ぶっぴん：物品〉an article, a commodity, goods.

    buppin-zei (物品税) a commodity tax

burabura(-to) 〈ぶらぶら(と)〉aimlessly, idly, lazily.

    burabura(-to)-aruku (ぶらぶら(と)歩く) walk aimlessly, stroll about

    burabura-shite-hi-o-sugosu (ぶらぶらして日を過ごす) lead an idle life

Burajiru 〈ブラジル〉Brazil.

    Burajiru-jin (ブラジル人) a Brazilian

    Burajiru(-jin)-no (ブラジル(人)の) Brazilian

burakku 〈ブラック〉black.

    kôhî o burakku-de-nomu (コーヒーをブラックで飲む) have coffee

black

burakku-risuto〈ブラックリスト〉a blacklist.
　burakku-risuto-ni-noru〈ブラックリストに載る〉be blacklisted, be on a blacklist.

buranko〈ぶらんこ〉a swing.
　buranko-ni noru（ぶらんこに乗る）get on a swing

burari〈ぶらり〉
　burari-to〈ぶらりと〉aimlessly.
　　burari-to-tachi-yoru（ぶらりと立ち寄る）drop in

bura-sagaru〈ぶらさがる：ぶら下がる〉hang down ((from)), dangle.
　　tsuri-kawa-ni bura-sagaru（つり革にぶら下がる）hang on to a strap

bura-sageru〈ぶら下げる〉hang, dangle; carry.
　　te-ni kamera o bura-sagete（手にカメラをぶら下げて）carrying a camera in one's hand

burashi〈ブラシ〉a brush.
　burashi-o-kakeru〈ブラシをかける〉brush.

buratsuku〈ぶらつく〉stroll about, take a stroll, loiter about.
　　kôen o buratsuku（公園をぶらつく）loiter about a park

buraun-kan〈ブラウンかん：ブラウン管〉a cathode-ray tube.

burei〈ぶれい：無礼〉
　burei-na〈無礼な〉rude, impolite, insolent, impertinent.
　　burei-na koto o iu（無礼なことを言う）say a rude thing

burei-kô〈ぶれいこう：無礼講〉
　burei-kô-de〈無礼講で〉without ceremony.

burêki〈ブレーキ〉a brake.
　　burêki o kakeru（ブレーキをかける）put on the brakes
　　　burêki o kyû-ni-kakeru（ブレーキを急にかける）jam on the brakes
　　Burêki ga kika-nai.（ブレーキが効かない.）The brakes do not work.

bureru〈ぶれる〉
　　Kamera ga bureta.（カメラがぶれた.）The camera moved.

buri〈ぶり〉a yellowtail.

-buri〈-ぶり〉a way, a manner, a style; an interval, lapse.
　　hanashi-buri（話しぶり）one's way of talking
　　roku-nen-buri-ni（六年ぶりに）after an interval of six years
　　shitta-ka-buri-o-suru（知ったかぶりをする）pretnd to know

buriiji〈ブリッジ〉a bridge.
　　buriiji-o-kakeru（ブリッジをかける）fix a bridge, bridge〔a tooth〕
　　buriiji o yaru（ブリッジをやる）play bridge

buri-kaesu 〈ぶりかえす：ぶり返す〉
  byôki-ga-buri-kaesu〈病気がぶり返す〉 have a relapse
  Atsusa ga buri-kaeshita.（暑さがぶり返した.） The hot weather has returned.

buriki 〈ブリキ〉 tinplate.
  buriki-kan（ブリキ缶） a can, a tin.
  buriki-ya（ブリキ屋） a tinman; a tinsmith

-buru 〈-ぶる〉 assume airs, pose ((as)), pretend ((to)).
  geijutsu-ka-buru（芸術家ぶる） assume an air of an artist

buruburu 〈ぶるぶる〉
  osoroshikute buruburu-furueru（恐ろしくてぶるぶる震える） tremble with fear
  samusa-de buruburu-furueru（寒さでぶるぶる震える） shiver with cold
  Te ga buruburu-furueru.（手がぶるぶる震える.） My hands shake.

burudôzâ 〈ブルドーザー〉 a bulldozer.
  burudôzâ-de-ji-narashi-suru or *burudôzâ-de-tori-harau*〈ブルドーザーで地ならしする，ブルドーザーで取り払う〉bulldoze (out).

Burugaria 〈ブルガリア〉 Bulgaria.
  Burugaria-jin（ブルガリア人） a Bulgarian
  Burugaria-go（ブルガリア語） Bulgarian
  Burugaria(-jin)-no（ブルガリア(人)の） Bulgarian

burui 〈ぶるい：部類〉 a class, a head, a category, an order.
  〜-no-burui-ni-hairu（〜の部類に入る） come under the head of...

burujoa 〈ブルジョア〉 a bourgeois.
  burujoa-kaikyū（ブルジョア階級） the bourgeoisie

buryoku 〈ぶりょく：武力〉 military power, force of arms.
  buryoku-ni uttaeru（武力に訴える） appeal to arms

bu-sahô 〈ぶさほう：不(無)作法〉 bad manners, impoliteness.
  bu-sahô-de-aru〈不(無)作法である〉 have no manners.
  bu-sahô-na〈不(無)作法な〉 ill-mannered, impolite.

bu-saiku 〈ぶさいく：不(無)細工〉
  bu-saiku-na〈不(無)細工な〉 awkward, clumsy.
  bu-saiku-na-koto-o-yaru〈不(無)細工なことをやる〉 bungle, make a mess of it.

bu-sata 〈ぶさた〉 *see.* go-bu-sata.

busho 〈ぶしょ：部署〉 one's post.
  busho ni tsuku（部署に就く） take up one's post

bushô 〈ぶしょう：不(無)精〉indolence, laziness.
　　bushô-mono （不(無)精者） a lazybones
　bushô-na 〈不(無)精な〉indolent, lazy.
busô 〈ぶそう：武装〉armament.
　　busô-kaijo （武装解除） disarmament
　busô-suru 〈武装する〉arm, arm oneself ((with)).
bussan 〈ぶっさん：物産〉a product, produce.
　　shuyô-bussan （主要物産） the staple products
busshi 〈ぶっし：物資〉goods, materials, commodities.
busshiki 〈ぶっしき：仏式〉
　busshiki-ni-yori 〈仏式により〉 according to Buddhist rites.
busshitsu 〈ぶっしつ：物質〉matter, substance, material.
　　busshitsu-bummei （物質文明） material civilization
　busshitsu-teki(-na) 〈物質的(な)〉material, physical.
　busshitsu-teki-ni 〈物質的に〉materially, physically.
busshoku 〈ぶっしょく：物色〉
　busshoku-suru 〈物色する〉look ((for)), search ((for)).
　　kônin-o-busshoku-suru （後任を物色する） look for a successor
bussô 〈ぶっそう：物騒〉
　bussô-na 〈物騒な〉troubled, unsafe, dangerous.
　　bussô-na yo-no-naka （物騒な世の中） troubled times
busû 〈ぶすう：部数〉the number of copies, circulation.
　　busû-ga-deru （部数が出る） have a large circulation
buta 〈ぶた：豚〉a pig.
　　buta o kau （豚を飼う） breed pigs
　　buta-niku （豚肉） pork
buta-bako 〈ぶたばこ：豚箱〉a police cell.
butai 〈ぶたい：舞台〉the stage, the scene, one's sphere.
　　butai-ni tatsu （舞台に立つ） appear on the stage, go on the stage
　　butai-chûkei （舞台中継） a stage relay
　　butai-dokyô （舞台度胸） stage nerve
　　butai-haiyû （舞台俳優） a stage actor, a stage actress
　　butai-keiken （舞台経験） stage experience
　　butai-kôka （舞台効果） stage effect
　　butai-shômei （舞台照明） stage lighting
　　butai-sôchi （舞台装置） stage setting
　　mawari-butai （回り舞台） a revolving stage
　　shôsetsu no butai （小説の舞台） the scene of a story

   katsudô-butai〈活動舞台〉one's sphere of action

   butai-ura-no tori-hiki〈舞台裏の取り引き〉a backdoor dealing

butai〈ぶたい：部隊〉a (military) unit, a corps, a force, troops.

butô-kai〈ぶとうかい：舞踏会〉a ball, a dance.

   kasô-butô-kai〈仮装舞踏会〉a masked ball

butsubutsu〈ぶつぶつ〉

  butsubutsu-iu〈ぶつぶつ言う〉grumble, complain.

butsubutsu-kôkan〈ぶつぶつこうかん：物々交換〉barter.

  butsubutsu-kôkan-suru〈物々交換する〉barter ((A for B)).

  butsubutsu-kôkan-de〈物々交換で〉by barter, on the barter system.

butsudan〈ぶつだん：仏壇〉a family Buddhist altar.

butsujô〈ぶつじょう：物情〉

   Butsujô-sôzen-to-shite-iru.〈物情騒然としている.〉 Public feelings are excited.

butsukaru〈ぶつかる〉strike, hit, run ((against)), collide ((with)); come ((upon)), meet ((with)).

   omoi-mo-kake-nai konnan-ni-butsukaru〈思いもかけない困難にぶつかる〉 meet with an unexpected difficulty

butsukeru〈ぶつける〉throw ((at)), strike ((against)), knock ((against)).

   inu-ni ishi o butsukeru〈犬に石をぶつける〉 throw a stone at a dog

   doa-ni atama o butsukeru〈ドアに頭をぶつける〉 knock one's head against a door

butsuri(-gaku)〈ぶつり(がく)：物理(学)〉physics.

   butsuri-gaku-sha〈物理学者〉 a physicist

   butsuri-ryôhô〈物理療法〉 physiotherapy

  butsuri(-gaku)-no, butsuri(-gaku)-jô-no or *butsuri-teki(-na)*〈物理(学)の, 物理(学)上の, 物理的(な)〉physical.

   butsuri-teki genshô〈物理的現象〉 a physical phenomenon

  butsuri(-gaku)-jô or *butsuri(-gaku)-teki-ni*〈物理(学)上, 物理(学)的に〉physically.

butsuryô〈ぶつりょう：物量〉the amount of materials.

   butsuryô-ni-mono-o-iwasete〈物量にものをいわせて〉 on the strength of material superiority

butsuyoku〈ぶつよく：物欲〉worldly desires.

  butsuyoku-ni-torawareta〈物欲に捕らわれた〉worldly-minded.

butsuzen〈ぶつぜん：仏前〉

  butsuzen-ni-sonaeru〈仏前に供える〉offer ((something)) before the tablet of the deceased.

butsuzô〈ぶつぞう：仏像〉an image of Buddha, a Buddhist image.

buttai〈ぶったい：物体〉a body, an object, a substance.

butteki〈ぶってき：物的〉material, physical.
　　butteki-shigen（物的資源）　material resources
　　butteki-shôko（物的証拠）　physical evidence

buttooshi〈ぶっとおし：ぶっ通し〉
　buttooshi-ni〈ぶっ通しに〉all through, consecutively, without stopping, on end, running.
　　go-jikan buttooshi-ni（五時間ぶっ通しに）　for five hours running

buttsuke-homban〈ぶっつけほんばん：ぶっつけ本番〉
　buttsuke-homban-no〈ぶっつけ本番の〉unrehearsed.
　buttsuke-homban-de〈ぶっつけ本番で〉without rehearsal.

buyo〈ぶよ〉a gnat, a midge.

buyô〈ぶよう：舞踊〉dancing, a dance.
　　Nihon-buyô（日本舞踊）　Japanese dancing

bu-yôjin〈ぶようじん：不(無)用心〉
　bu-yôjin-na〈不(無)用心な〉unsafe; careless.

buzâ〈ブザー〉a buzzer.
　buzâ-o-narashite-yobu〈ブザーを鳴らして呼ぶ〉buzz ((for)).

buzoku〈ぶぞく：部族〉a tribe.

byô〈びょう〉a drawing pin, a thumb tack; a tack; a rivet.
　byô-de-tomeru〈びょうで留める〉pin up, tack down.

byô〈びょう：秒〉a second.
　　byô-shin（秒針）　the second hand

byôbu〈びょうぶ〉a (folding) screen.
　　byôbu o tateru（びょうぶを立てる）　set up a screen

byôdô〈びょうどう：平等〉equality, impartiality.
　byôdô-na〈平等な〉equal, even, impartial.
　byôdô-ni〈平等に〉equally, evenly, without discrimination.
　　byôdô-ni wakeru（平等に分ける）　divide equally

byôgen-tai〈びょうげんたい：病原体〉a pathogen.

byôgo〈びょうご：病後〉
　byôgo-no〈病後の〉convalescent.
　byôgo-de or *byôgo-ni*〈病後で，病後に〉after one's illness.

byôin〈びょういん：病院〉a hospital.
　　byôin-e katsugi-komareru（病院へ担ぎ込まれる）　be carried to hospital
　　byôin-ni-haitte-iru（病院に入っている）　be in (the) hospital

　　　sôgô-byôin（総合病院）　a general hospital

byôjaku〈びょうじゃく：病弱〉see. byôshin.

byôjô〈びょうじょう：病状〉the condition of a disease, the condition of a patient.

　　　O-kâ-san-no-go-byôjô-wa-ikaga-desu-ka?（お母さんのご病状はいかがですか。）　How is your sick mother?

byôki〈びょうき：病気〉sickness, illness, a disease.

　　　byôki-ni-kakaru（病気にかかる）　be taken ill, get sick, fall ill

　　　byôki-de-aru（病気である）　be sick

　　　byôki-de-nete-iru（病気で寝ている）　be sick in bed

　　　byôki-ga-naoru（病気が治る）　get well, recover from one's sickness

　byôki-no（病気の）　sick, indisposed.

byôki-agari-no〈びょうきあがりの：病気上がりの〉see.　byôgo-no.

byômei〈びょうめい：病名〉the name of a disease.

byônin〈びょうにん：病人〉a sick person, a patient; the sick.

byôri-gaku〈びょうりがく：病理学〉pathology.

byôsei〈びょうせい：病勢〉see.　byôjô.

byôsha〈びょうしゃ：描写〉description.

　byôsha-suru（描写する）describe.

byôshi〈びょうし：病死〉death from sickness.

　byôshi-suru（病死する）die of illness, die from a disease.

byôshin〈びょうしん：病身〉infirmity.

　byôshin-no（病身の）sickly, invalid, infirm.

byôshitsu〈びょうしつ：病室〉a sickroom, a ward.

byôshô〈びょうしょう：病床〉a sickbed.

byôsoku〈びょうそく：秒速〉the speed a second.

　　　byôsoku-yon-jû-mêtoru-no　kyôfû（秒速四十メートルの強風）　the gale at a speed of 40 meters a second

byôteki(-na)〈びょうてき（な）：病的（な）〉morbid, unsound, abnormal.

　　　byôteki-na seikaku（病的な性格）　abnormal character

　byôteki-ni（病的に）morbidly, abnormally.

byôtô〈びょうとう：病棟〉a ward.

　　　kakuri-byôtô（隔離病棟）　an isolation ward

byô-yomi〈びょうよみ：秒読み〉countdown.

　byô-yomi-o-suru〈秒読みをする〉count down.

byûbyû〈びゅうびゅう〉

　　　Kaze　ga　byûbyû-fuiteiru.（風がびゅうびゅう吹いている。）　The wind is whistling.

byuffe 〈ビュッフェ〉 a buffet.
byun 〈びゅん〉
 byun-to-tobu〈びゅんと飛ぶ〉zing, zip.

C

cha 〈ちゃ：茶〉tea.
 cha o dasu（茶を出す）serve tea ((to))
 cha o ireru（茶を入れる）make tea
 cha o nomu（茶を飲む）take tea
  cha-o-ippai nomu（茶を一杯飲む）have a cup of tea
 koi cha（濃い茶）strong tea
 usui cha（薄い茶）weak tea
 cha-dansu（茶だんす）a tea cabinet
 cha-dōgu（茶道具）tea-things
 cha-gashi（茶菓子）tea cake
chachi 〈ちゃち〉
 chachi-na〈ちゃちな〉cheap, mean, toylike, jerry-built.
 chachi-na ie（ちゃちな家）a jerry-built house
cha-iro(-no) 〈ちゃいろ(の)：茶色(の)〉light brown.
cha-kasshoku(-no) 〈ちゃかっしょく(の)：茶褐色(の)〉brown.
chakichaki 〈ちゃきちゃき〉
 chakichaki-no Edokko（ちゃきちゃきの江戸っ子）a truebred *Edokko*
chakkari 〈ちゃっかり〉
 chakkari-shita〈ちゃっかりした〉shrewd, smart, cunning.
chakkō 〈ちゃっこう：着工〉
 chakkō-suru〈着工する〉start work.
chakku 〈チャック〉a zipper, a zip fastener.
 chakku-o-kakeru〈チャックを掛ける〉zip (up), run up a zipper.
 chakku-o-hazusu（チャックを外す）unzip, zip open

chaku 〈ちゃく：着〉
  chaku-shidai〈着次第〉 as soon as one arrives
-chaku 〈-ちゃく：-着〉
  itchaku-ni-naru〈一着になる〉 come in first〔in a race〕
  go-ji Tôkyô-chaku-no-ressha〈五時東京着の列車〉 the train due at Tokyo at 5
chakuchaku(-to) 〈ちゃくちゃく(と)：着々(と)〉 step by step, steadily.
chakufuku 〈ちゃくふく：着服〉
  chakufuku-suru〈着服する〉 pocket, embezzle.
chakugan-ten 〈ちゃくがんてん：着眼点〉 the point aimed at, a point of view.
chakuhyô 〈ちゃくひょう：着氷〉 icing.
chakujitsu 〈ちゃくじつ：着実〉 steadiness.
  chakujitsu-na〈着実な〉 steady.
    chakujitsu-na shimpo〈着実な進歩〉 steady progress
  chakujitsu-ni〈着実に〉 steadily.
chakunin 〈ちゃくにん：着任〉
  chakunin-suru〈着任する〉 arrive at one's post.
chakuriku 〈ちゃくりく：着陸〉 landing.
  mu-chakuriku hikô〈無着陸飛行〉 a nonstop flight
  chakuriku-suru〈着陸する〉 land, make a landing.
  buji-chakuriku-suru〈無事着陸する〉 make a safe landing
chakuseki 〈ちゃくせき：着席〉
  chakuseki-suru〈着席する〉 take one's seat, sit (down).
chakushi 〈ちゃくし：嫡子〉 the heir, a legitimate child.
chakushoku 〈ちゃくしょく：着色〉 coloring.
  chakushoku-suru〈着色する〉 color.
chakushu 〈ちゃくしゅ：着手〉
  chakushu-suru〈着手する〉 start, begin, set about, undertake.
    atarashii jigyô ni chakushu-suru〈新しい事業に着手する〉 start a new enterprise
chakusô 〈ちゃくそう：着想〉 an idea, a conception.
  chakusô-ga-ii〈着想がいい〉 be well conceived, be a clever idea.
chakusui 〈ちゃくすい：着水〉 landing on the water, (a) splashdown.
  chakusui-suru〈着水する〉 land on the water, splash down.
chame 〈ちゃめ：茶目〉
  chame-na〈茶目な〉 playful.
    chame-na hito〈茶目な人〉 a playful fellow.

champon〈ちゃんぽん〉
champon-ni〈ちゃんぽんに〉alternately, by turns.
  bîru to uisukî o champon-ni nomu（ビールとウイスキーをちゃんぽんに飲む）take beer and whisky alternately

channeru〈チャンネル〉a channel.
  channeru o kiri-kaeru（チャンネルを切り替える）change the channel
  dai-yon-channeru-de（第四チャンネルで）on Channel 4

cha-no-ma〈茶の間〉a living room, a sitting room.

chansu〈チャンス〉a chance.

chan-to〈ちゃんと〉neatly, tidily, properly.
  chan-to kimono-o-kiru（ちゃんと着物を着る）dress neatly
  chan-to suwaru（ちゃんと座る）sit properly

charamporan〈ちゃらんぽらん〉
  charamporan-na hito（ちゃらんぽらんな人）an irresponsible person
  iu-koto-ga-charamporan-da〈言うことがちゃらんぽらんだ〉talk irresponsibly.

charin〈ちゃりん〉
  charin-to〈ちゃりんと〉with a clink.
  charin-to-iu（ちゃりんという）clink

cha-saji〈茶さじ：茶さじ〉a teaspoon.
  cha-saji-ippai-no satô（茶さじ一杯の砂糖）a teaspoonful of sugar.

châtâ〈チャーター〉
  châtâ-ki（チャーター機）a chartered plane
  châtâ-suru〈チャーターする〉charter.

chawan〈ちゃわん：茶わん〉a (rice) bowl, a teacup.

chě〈ちぇっ〉tut!, phew!, pshaw!, shucks!

chekku〈チェック〉check.
  chekku-suru〈チェックする〉check (off).

Cheko-Surobakia〈チェコスロバキア〉Czechoslovakia.
  Cheko-Surobakia-jin（チェコスロバキア人）a Czechoslovak
  Cheko-Surobakia-no（チェコスロバキアの）Czechoslovakian

chero〈チェロ〉a cello.
  chero-sôsha（チェロ奏者）a cellist

chesu〈チェス〉chess.
  chesu o suru（チェスをする）play chess
  chesu-no-ban（チェスの盤）a chessboard
  chesu-no-koma（チェスのこま）a chessman

chi〈ち：血〉blood.

chi o haku〈血を吐く〉 spit blood, vomit blood

chi-no-tsunagatta kyôdai〈血のつながった兄弟〉 brothers of the same blood

chi-ga-deru or *chi-ga-nagareru*〈血が出る，血が流れる〉 bleed.

chi-ga-tomaru〈血が止まる〉 stop bleeding

chi-darake-no〈血だらけの〉 bloody.

chi〈ち：地〉 the earth, the ground, land.

chi-no-ri〈地の利〉 advantages of position

chi〈ち：智〉 wisdom, intellect, intelligence.

chian〈ちあん：治安〉(the) public peace.

chian o iji-suru〈治安を維持する〉 maintain public peace

chian o midasu〈治安を乱す〉 break public peace

chibashiru〈ちばしる：血走る〉be bloodshot.

chibashitta me-de〈血走った目で〉 with bloodshot eyes.

Chibetto〈チベット〉Tibet.

Chibetto-jin（チベット人） a Tibetan

Chibtto-go（チベット語） Tibetan

Chibetto(-jin)-no（チベット(人)の） Tibetan

chibusa〈ちぶさ：乳房〉the breast(s).

chichi〈ちち：乳〉milk.

chichi-o-nomaseru〈乳を飲ませる〉suckle〔a baby〕.

chichi-o-shiboru〈乳を搾る〉 milk〔a cow〕.

chichi〈ちち：父〉a father.

chichi-no or *chichi-rashii*〈父の，父らしい〉fatherly, fatherlike.

chichi〈ちち：遅々〉

chichi-to-shite〈遅々として〉slowly, languidly.

chichi-to-shite-susuma-nai〈遅々として進まない〉 progress at a snail's pace

chichû〈ちちゅう：地中〉

chichû-no〈地中の〉underground.

chichû-ni〈地中に〉in the ground.

Chichûkai〈ちちゅうかい：地中海〉the Mediterranean (Sea).

chie〈ちえ：知恵〉wisdom, wit.

seikatsu-no chie（生活の知恵） wisdom for living

chie-no-aru〈知恵のある〉wise.

chie-no-nai〈知恵のない〉 unwise, stupid, silly

chie-no-tari-nai〈知恵の足りない〉 shallow-brained

chien〈ちえん：遅延〉delay.

chien-suru〈遅延する〉delay, be delayed.

chifusu〈チフス〉typhoid (fever), typhus (fever).

chigaeru〈ちがえる：違える〉

    basu-o-nori-chigaeru（バスを乗り違える）take the wrong bus

chigai〈ちがい：違い〉(a) difference, (a) distinction.

    taihen-na chigai ni naru（大変な違いになる）make a great difference

    taishita-chigai-wa-nai（大した違いはない）make little difference

chigai-hôken〈ちがいほうけん：治外法権〉extraterritoriality, extraterritorial rights.

(-ni)-chigai-nai〈(-に)ちがいない：(-に)違いない〉must ((be)), I am sure, certainly, surely.

chigaku〈ちがく：地学〉earth science, physical geography.

chigau〈ちがう：違う〉differ ((from)), be different ((from)); be wrong, be mistaken; no, not.

    amari-chigawa-nai（余り違わない）do not make much difference, make little difference

    maru-de chigau（まるで違う）be quite different ((from))

    ookisa-ga chigau（大きさが違う）be different in size

    Kono kotae wa chigau.（この答えは違う。）This answer is wrong.

    "Kore-wa kimi-no empitsu-desu-ka?" "Chigai-masu."（"これは君の鉛筆ですか。" "違います。"）"Is this your pencil?" "No."

chigatta〈違った〉different, distinct, another; wrong, mistaken.

chigireru〈ちぎれる〉be torn to pieces, be torn off.

chigiru〈ちぎる〉tear (off), pick.

chiguhagu〈ちぐはぐ〉

    chiguhagu-na hanashi（ちぐはぐな話）an incoherent story

chigyo〈ちぎょ：稚魚〉a young fish.

chihai〈ちはい：遅配〉a delay in rationing.

    kyûryô-no-chihai（給料の遅配）a delay in the payment of wages

    yûbin-no-chihai（郵便の遅配）a delay in mail delivery

chihei-sen〈ちへいせん：地平線〉the horizon.

    chihei-sen-jô-ni（地平線上に）above the horizon

    chihei-sen-ka-ni（地平線下に）below the horizon

chihô〈ちほう：地方〉a locality, a district, a region, an area, the provinces, the country.

    Kansai-chihô（関西地方）the Kansai district

    chihô-jichi-tai（地方自治体）a local self-governing body

    chihô-shoku（地方色）local color

chihô-teki(-na) or *chihô-no* 〈地方的(な), 地方の〉local, regional, provincial.

chihyô 〈ちひょう：地表〉the surface of the earth.

chii 〈ちい：地位〉a position, standing, a post.

     chii o uru（地位を得る） get a position

     chii o ushinau（地位を失う） lose one's position

     shakai-teki chii（社会的地位） one's social standing

        shakai-teki chii-ga-takai（社会的地位が高い） be of high social standing

        shakai-teki chii-ga-hikui（社会的地位が低い） be of low social standing

chiiki 〈ちいき：地域〉a region, an area, a zone.

     chiiki-shakai（地域社会） a community

chiiki-teki(-na) 〈地域的(な)〉local, regional.

chiiki-teki-ni 〈地域的に〉locally, regionally.

chiisai 〈ちいさい：小さい〉small, little, tiny; trifling, trivial; low.

     chiisai ie（小さい家） a small house

     chiisai kodomo（小さい子供） a small child, a little child

     chiisai koto-gara（小さい事柄） a trivial matter

     chiisai koe-de（小さい声で） in a low voice

     chiisai-toki-ni（小さい時に） in one's childhood

chiisaku-naru 〈小さくなる〉become smaller.

     chiisaku-kiru（小さく切る） cut ((a thing)) small

chiji 〈ちじ：知事〉a (prefectural) governor.

chijiku 〈ちじく：地軸〉the earth's axis.

chijimeru 〈ちぢめる：縮める〉shorten, reduce, abridge.

     jumyô o chijimeru（寿命を縮める） shorten one's life

     kikan o chijimeru（期間を縮める） reduce the term

     bunshô o chijimeru（文章を縮める） abridge a composition

chijimi-agaru 〈ちぢみあがる：縮み上がる〉cower.

     osoroshikute chijimi-agaru（恐ろしくて縮み上がる） shrink with fear

chijimu 〈ちぢむ：縮む〉shrink, wrinkle.

chijin 〈ちじん：知人〉an acquaintance.

chijirasu 〈ちぢらす：縮らす〉frizzle, curl, wave.

chijireru 〈縮れる〉be frizzled, become curly, be wavy.

chijireta 〈縮れた〉frizzled, curled, curly, wavy.

     chijire-ge（縮れ毛） curly hair, curls

chijô 〈ちじょう：地上〉

chijô-kimmu〈地上勤務〉 ground service

chijô-no, chijô-de or *chijô-ni*〈地上の，地上で，地上に〉on the ground, on (the) earth.

chijô〈ちじょう：痴情〉blind passion.

chijô-ni-yoru hanzai〈痴情による犯罪〉 a crime of blind passion

chijô-ken〈ちじょうけん：地上権〉superficies.

chijoku〈ちじょく：恥辱〉disgrace, dishonor, shame.

chijoku-o-ataeru〈恥辱を与える〉disgrace, dishonor, make ((a person)) ashamed.

chika〈ちか：地下〉

chika-dô〈地下道〉 an underpass, a subway

chika-gai〈地下街〉 an underground market

chika-shitsu〈地下室〉 a basement, a cellar

chika-sui〈地下水〉 underground water, ground water

chika-undô〈地下運動〉 underground activities

chika-no, chika-de or *chika-ni*〈地下の，地下で，地下に〉underground.

chika〈ちか：地価〉the price of land.

chikagoro〈ちかごろ：近ごろ〉recently, lately, nowadays, today.

chikagoro-no〈近ごろの〉recent, late, present-day.

chikagoro-no deki-goto〈近ごろの出来事〉 a recent event

chikagoro-no wakai mono〈近ごろの若い者〉 young people of today

chikagoro-made〈近ごろまで〉until recently.

chikai〈ちかい：近い〉near, near(*or* close) by, close, nearly.

chikai shinseki〈近い親せき〉 a near relative

Gakkô wa eki-ni-chikai-tokoro-ni-aru.〈学校は駅に近い所にある．〉 The school is near the station.

Kurisumasu ga chikai.〈クリスマスが近い．〉 Christmas is near at hand.

roku-jussai-ni-chikai〈六十歳に近い〉 be nearly sixty years old

kansei-ni-chikai〈完成に近い〉 be nearly completed(*or* finished)

chikai shôrai-ni〈近い将来に〉in the near future.

chikai-uchi-ni〈近いうちに〉shortly, before long.

chikai〈ちかい：誓い〉an oath, a vow.

chikai-o-tateru〈誓いを立てる〉 make (an) oath ((that)), take (an) oath ((to do))

chikai o mamoru〈誓いを守る〉 keep one's vow

chikai o yaburu〈誓いを破る〉 break one's vow

chikau〈誓う〉swear, vow, make a vow, take an oath.

chikatte 〈誓って〉 upon my word.

chikai 〈ちかい：地階〉 a basement.

chikajika 〈ちかぢか：近々〉 shortly, before long, in a short time.

chikaku 〈ちかく：近く〉 shortly, before long, in a short time; nearly, about.

     Kare-wa chikaku Amerika-kara kaette-kimasu. 〈彼は近くアメリカから帰って来ます。〉 He will be back from America before long.

     hachi-ji-chikaku-made 〈八時近くまで〉 till nearly eight o'clock

     go-jû-nin-chikaku 〈五十人近く〉 nearly fifty persons

〜-no-chikaku-ni 〈〜の近くに〉 near.

     kono-chikaku-ni 〈この近くに〉 near here

chikaku 〈ちかく：知覚〉 perception.

chikaku-suru 〈知覚する〉 perceive.

chikaku 〈ちかく：地殻〉 the earth's crust.

     chikaku-hendô 〈地殻変動〉 movements of the earth's crust

chika-michi 〈ちかみち：近道〉 a shorter way, a shortcut.

     chika-michi o suru 〈近道をする〉 take a shortcut

chikan 〈ちかん：痴漢〉 a molester.

chikara 〈ちから：力〉 strength, force, power, energy; effort; aid; ability.

     chikara-ippai 〈力いっぱい〉 with all one's strength

       chikara-ippai-yaru 〈力いっぱいやる〉 do one's best

     jôki no chikara 〈蒸気の力〉 the power of steam

chikara-ga-tsuku 〈力が付く〉 gain strength, make progress.

chikara-ni-naru 〈力になる〉 help, assist.

chikara-zukeru 〈力付ける〉 cheer up, encourage.

chikara-o-otosu 〈力を落とす〉 be discouraged, be disheartened.

chikara-no-aru 〈力のある〉 strong, powerful, forceful, able.

     chikara-no-nai 〈力のない〉 weak, incapable

chikara-zuku-de 〈力尽くで〉 by force.

chikara-o-awasete 〈力を合わせて〉 by united effort.

chikara-no-oyobu-kagiri 〈力の及ぶ限り〉 to the best of one's ability.

chikara-kobu 〈ちからこぶ〉

chikara-kobu-o-tsukuru 〈力こぶを作る〉 flex one's arm to make the muscle of the upper one swell up.

chika-tetsu 〈ちかてつ：地下鉄〉 a subway, an underground.

     chika-tetsu-de iku 〈地下鉄で行く〉 go by subway

chikayoru 〈ちかよる：近寄る〉 come near, approach.

chikayoseru 〈ちかよせる：近寄せる〉 *see.* chikazukeru.

chikazukeru〈ちかづける：近付ける〉put ((a thing)) close ((to)); allow ((a person)) to come near, keep company ((with)).

chikazuki〈ちかづき：近付き〉acquaintance.
　chikazuki-ni-naru〈近付きになる〉make ((a person's)) acquaintance, become acquainted ((with)).

chikazuku〈ちかづく：近付く〉approach, near, come near, draw near; become acquainted ((with)).
　　kansei ni chikazuku（完成に近付く）be nearing completion
　　Natsu-yasumi ga chikazuku.（夏休みが近付く.）The summer vacation is drawing near.
　　Anna　grûpu-ni-wa　chikazuku-na.（あんなグループには近付くな.）Keep away from such a group.

chikei〈ちけい：地形〉topography, geographical features.

chikin〈チキン〉chicken.
　　chikin-katsu(retsu)（チキンカツ(レツ)）a chicken cutlet
　　chikin-raisu（チキンライス）chicken and rice

chikki〈チッキ〉a check.
　nimotsu　o　chikki-ni-suru〈荷物をチッキにする〉have　one's　baggage checked.

chikoku〈ちこく：遅刻〉
　chikoku-suru〈遅刻する〉be late, be behind time.

chiku〈ちく：地区〉a district, an area, a region, a zone.
　　Kansai-chiku（関西地区）the Kansai area

chikubi〈ちくび：乳首〉a nipple, a teat.

chikuchiku〈ちくちく〉
　chikuchiku-itamu〈ちくちく痛む〉prick, prickle.

chikudenchi〈ちくでんち：蓄電池〉a storage battery, a storage cell.

chikunô-shô〈ちくのうしょう：蓄のう症〉empyema.

chikuri-to〈ちくりと〉
　　chikuri-to sasu（ちくりと刺す）prick
　　chikuri-to-itai-koto-o-iu（ちくりと痛いことを言う）prick ((a person)) on the raw

chikusan(-gyô)〈ちくさん(ぎょう)：畜産(業)〉livestock breeding.
　　chikusan-gyô-sha（畜産業者）a livestock raiser

chikuseki〈ちくせき：蓄積〉accumulation.
　　hirô no chikuseki（疲労の蓄積）the accumulation of fatigue
　chikuseki-suru〈蓄積する〉accumulate.

chikushô〈ちくしょう：畜生〉a beast, a brute.

　　　Chikushô!〈畜生.〉 Confound it! / You brute!

chikushô-no-yô-na〈畜生のような〉beastly, brutal.

chikyô〈ちきょう：地峡〉an isthmus.

chikyû〈ちきゅう：地球〉the earth.

　　　chikyû-gi〈地球儀〉a globe

chimame〈ちまめ：血豆〉a blood blister.

　　　chimame ga dekiru〈血豆ができる〉get a blood blister

chimamire〈ちまみれ：血まみれ〉

chimamire-ni-naru〈血まみれになる〉be smeared with blood, be bloodied.

chimamire-no〈血まみれの〉bloodstained, bloody, gory.

chimanako〈ちまなこ：血眼〉bloodshot eyes.

chimanako-ni-natte sagasu〈血眼になって捜す〉look for ((a thing))
　　　desperately.

chimayou〈ちまよう：血迷う〉run wild, lose one's mind, be in a frenzy.

chimbotsu〈ちんぼつ：沈没〉

chimbotsu-suru〈沈没する〉sink, go down, go to the bottom.

chimei〈ちめい：地名〉the name of a place.

chimei〈ちめい：知名〉

chimei-no〈知名の〉noted, well-known.

chimei-shô〈ちめいしょう：致命傷〉a fatal wound.

chimei-shô-o-ukeru〈致命傷を受ける〉be fatally wounded.

chimei-teki(-na)〈ちめいてき(な)：致命的(な)〉fatal.

　　　chimei-teki dageki o ataeru〈致命的打撃を与える〉deal ((a person)) a
　　　fatal blow

chimitsu〈ちみつ：ち密〉

chimitsu-na〈ち密な〉minute, fine, close, exact, accurate.

　　　chimitsu-na zunô〈ち密な頭脳〉a fine brain

　　　chimitsu-na kansatsu〈ち密な観察〉a close observation

chimitsu-ni〈ち密に〉minutely, closely, exactly, accurately.

chimmi〈ちんみ：珍味〉a dainty, a delicacy.

　　　sankai-no-chimmi〈山海の珍味〉all sorts of delicacies

chimmoku〈ちんもく：沈黙〉silence.

　　　chimmoku o mamoru〈沈黙を守る〉keep silence(*or* silent)

　　　chimmoku o yaburu〈沈黙を破る〉break one's silence

chimmoku-suru〈沈黙する〉hold one's tongue.

chimmoku-saseru〈沈黙させる〉silence, put ((a person)) to silence.

chimpira〈ちんぴら〉an urchin; a punk.

chimpu〈ちんぷ：陳腐〉

chimpu-na〈陳腐な〉out-of-date, commonplace, trite, worn-out.

　chimpu-na kotoba（陳腐な言葉）a hackneyed remark

chimpunkampun〈ちんぷんかんぷん〉

　chimpunkampun-na　henji（ちんぷんかんぷんな返事）an　incoherent
　　reply

　chimpunkampun-na-koto o iu（ちんぷんかんぷんなことを言う）talk
　　nonsense

　Chimpunkampun-de-sukoshi-mo-wakara-nai.（ちんぷんかんぷんで少し
　　も分からない。）It is all Greek to me.

chîmu-wâku〈チームワーク〉teamwork.

　chîmu-wâku-ga torete-i-nai（チームワークがとれていない）be poor in
　　teamwork

chin·age〈ちんあげ：賃上げ〉a raise in (one's) wages.

　chin·age-tôsô（賃上げ闘争）a struggle for higher wages

chi-namagusai〈ちなまぐさい：血なまぐさい〉sanguinary.

(-ni)-chinande〈(-に)ちなんで〉after... .

chin·atsu〈ちんあつ：鎮圧〉suppression.

　chin·atsu-suru〈鎮圧する〉suppress.

chinchaku〈ちんちゃく：沈着〉composure.

　chinchaku-na〈沈着な〉composed, calm, cool.

　chinchaku-ni〈沈着に〉composedly, calmly, coolly.

chinchô〈ちんちょう：珍重〉

　chinchô-suru〈珍重する〉value highly, make much ((of)).

chinden〈ちんでん：沈でん〉deposition, settlement.

　chinden-butsu（沈でん物）a deposit, a sediment

　chinden-suru〈沈でんする〉be deposited, settle.

chinetsu〈ちねつ：地熱〉terrestrial heat.

chingin〈ちんぎん：賃金〉wages, pay.

　jisshitsu-chingin（実質賃金）real wages

chinjô(-sho)〈ちんじょう(しょ)：陳情(書)〉a petition.

　chinjô o uke-tsukeru（陳情を受け付ける）accept a petition

　chinjô o hane-tsukeru（陳情をはねつける）reject a petition

　chinjô-dan（陳情団）a group of lobbyists

　chinjô-suru〈陳情する〉petition, make an appeal ((to)).

chinjutsu〈ちんじゅつ：陳述〉a statement.

　itsuwarazaru chinjutsu（偽らざる陳述）a true statement

　chinjutsu-sho（陳述書）a written statement

　chinjutsu-suru〈陳述する〉state.

chinka 〈ちんか：沈下〉 subsidence, sinking.

    jiban-chinka〈地盤沈下〉 ground subsidence

  chinka-suru〈沈下する〉 subside, sink.

chinka 〈ちんか：鎮火〉 extinguishment of a fire.

  chinka-suru〈鎮火する〉 be put out, be extinguished.

chinkyaku 〈ちんきゃく：珍客〉 a welcome guest, an unexpected visitor.

chinō 〈ちのう：知能〉 mental faculties, intelligence, intellect.

    chinō-han〈知能犯〉 a mental offense

    chinō-shisū〈知能指数〉 an intelligence quotient

chi-no-ke 〈ちのけ：血の気〉

    chi-no-ke-no-nai〈血の気のない〉 as white as a sheet

    chi-no-ke-no-ooi〈血の気の多い〉 sanguine, hot-blooded

chinomigo 〈ちのみご：乳飲み子〉 a suckling (child).

chinretsu 〈ちんれつ：陳列〉 exhibition, show, display.

    chinretsu-hin〈陳列品〉 articles on show

  chinretsu-suru〈陳列する〉 exhibit, put on show, display.

chinsei-zai 〈ちんせいざい：鎮静剤〉 a sedative, a tranquilizer.

chin-shigoto 〈ちんしごと：賃仕事〉 job work, piecework.

chintai 〈ちんたい：沈滞〉

  chintai-shita〈沈滞した〉 dull, slack, stagnant.

    chintai-shita kûki〈沈滞した空気〉 a stagnant atmosphere

chintai-keiyaku 〈ちんたいけいやく：賃貸契約〉 a lease.

chin-taishaku 〈ちんたいしゃく：賃貸借〉 letting and hiring.

chintsû 〈ちんつう：沈痛〉

  chintsû-na〈沈痛な〉 grave, serious, sad.

    chintsû-na kao-tsuki-de〈沈痛な顔つきで〉 with a sad look

chintsû-zai 〈ちんつうざい：鎮痛剤〉 an anodyne, a lenitive.

chippu 〈チップ〉 a tip.

  chippu-o-yaru〈チップをやる〉 tip.

chirabaru 〈ちらばる：散らばる〉 see. chirakaru.

chirachira 〈ちらちら〉

    Me ga chirachira-suru.（目がちらちらする.） My eyes are dazzled.

    Yuki-ga-chirachira-futteiru.（雪がちらちら降っている.） It is snowing lightly.

chirahora 〈ちらほら〉 here and there, in twos and threes, sparsely.

    Sakura ga chirahora saki-hajimeta.（桜がちらほら咲き始めた.） Cherry blossoms are coming out here and there.

chirakaru 〈ちらかる：散らかる〉 be scattered about, be in disorder.

    Omocha ga chirakatte-iru. (おもちゃが散らかっている。) Toys lie scattered about.

chirakasu 〈散らかす〉 scatter about, put in disorder.

    heya o chirakashite-oku (部屋を散らかしておく) leave a room in disorder

chirari-to 〈ちらりと〉

    chirari-to-miru (ちらりと見る) glance ((at))

    chirari-to-mimi-ni-suru (ちらりと耳にする) happen to hear, hear by chance

chirashi 〈ちらし：散らし〉 a leaflet, a handbill.

    chirashi o maku (散らしをまく) distribute handbills

chiratsuku 〈ちらつく〉 *see.* chirachira.

chiri 〈ちり：地理〉 geography.

chiri-teki(-na) or *chiri-jô-no* 〈地理的(な)，地理上の〉 geographical.

chiri-teki-ni or *chiri-jô* 〈地理的に，地理上〉 geographically.

Chiri 〈チリ〉 Chile.

    Chiri-jin (チリ人) a Chilean

    Chiri(-jin)-no (チリ(人)の) Chilean

chiri 〈ちり〉 dust, rubbish, dirt.

    Chiri-mo-tsumoreba yama-to-naru. (ちりも積もれば山となる。) Many a little makes a mickle.

    chiri-tori (ちり取り) a dustpan

chiri-o-harau 〈ちりを払う〉 dust.

chiribameru 〈ちりばめる〉 set, inlay, stud.

    takusan-no hôseki-o-chiribameta yubi-wa (たくさんの宝石をちりばめた指輪) a ring studded with many jewels

chirigami 〈ちりがみ：ちり紙〉 toilet paper, tissue paper.

chirijiri(-barabara) 〈ちりぢり(ばらばら)：散り散り(ばらばら)〉

chirijiri(-barabara)-ni 〈散り散り(ばらばら)に〉 scatteredly, separately.

    chirijiri-barabara-ni ie-ni-kaeru (散り散りばらばらに家に帰る) return home separately

chirijiri(-barabara)-ni-naru 〈散り散り(ばらばら)になる〉 scatter, be scattered, disperse, break up.

    Kare-no ikka wa chirijiri-ni-natta. (彼の一家は散り散りになった。) His family broke up.

chirimen 〈ちりめん〉 crepe, silk crape.

chirinchirin 〈ちりんちりん〉 tinkle-tinkle, ting-a-ling.

chirinchirin-naru 〈ちりんちりん鳴る〉 tinkle, clink, jingle.

chiru〈ちる：散る〉scatter, fall.

chiryō〈ちりょう：治療〉medical treatment.
　　chiryô-chû-de-aru（治療中である）be under medical treatment
　　chiryô-hi（治療費）a doctor's fee
　　chiryô-hô（治療法）a remedy, a cure
　chiryô-o-ukeru〈治療を受ける〉take medical treatment, be treated.
　chiryô-suru〈治療する〉treat.

chisei〈ちせい：知性〉intellect, intelligence.
　chisei-teki(-na)〈知性的(な)〉intellectual, intelligent.

chisei〈ちせい：治世〉a reign, a regime.

chisei〈ちせい：地勢〉*see.* chikei.

chishiki〈ちしき：知識〉knowledge, learning, information.
　　kiso-chishiki（基礎知識）a basic knowledge
　　tashō　hôritsu-no-chishiki-ga-aru（多少法律の知識がある）have some legal knowledge
　　chishiki-jin（知識人）an intellectual
　　chishiki-kaikyû（知識階級）the educated class

chishi-ryō〈ちしりょう：致死量〉a fatal dose.

chishitsu(-gaku)〈ちしつ(がく)：地質(学)〉geology.

chisō〈ちそう：地層〉a stratum.

chisô〈ちそう：ち走〉*see.* go-chisô.

chisso〈ちっそ：窒素〉nitrogen.

chissoku〈ちっそく：窒息〉suffocation.
　chissoku-suru〈窒息する〉be suffocated, be choked.
　　chissoku-shite-shinu（窒息して死ぬ）be suffocated to death

chisui〈ちすい：治水〉river improvement, flood control.
　　chisui-kôji（治水工事）embankment works

chisuji〈ちすじ：血筋〉blood, lineage.
　chisuji-o-hiku〈血筋を引く〉be descended ((from)), run in one's blood.

chitai〈ちたい：地帯〉a zone, an area, a belt.
　　sangaku-chitai（山岳地帯）a mountainous area
　　ryoku-chitai（緑地帯）a green belt

chitai〈ちたい：遅滞〉
　chitai-naku〈遅滞なく〉without delay.

chitan〈チタン〉titanium.

chiteki(-na)〈ちてき(な)：知的(な)〉intellectual, mental.
　　chiteki-na seikatsu（知的な生活）intellectual life
　　chiteki-na shigoto（知的な仕事）brain work

chiten 〈ちてん：地点〉a spot, a point.

chitsujo 〈ちつじょ：秩序〉order.

    chitsujo o tamotsu（秩序を保つ）keep order

    chitsujo o midasu（秩序を乱す）disturb order

  chitsujo-tadashii or *chitsujo-no-aru*〈秩序正しい，秩序のある〉orderly.

    chitsujo-no-nai（秩序のない）disorderly, disordered

  chitsujo-tadashiku〈秩序正しく〉in good order.

chittomo 〈ちっとも〉*see.* sukoshi-mo〜nai.

chiyahoya 〈ちやほや〉

  chiyahoya-suru〈ちやほやする〉make a lion ((of)), dance attendance ((on)).

  chiyahoya-sareru〈ちやほやされる〉be lionized, be much waited upon.

chiyu 〈ちゆ：治癒〉healing, cure.

    chiyu-ritsu（治癒率）a cure rate

  chiyu-suru〈治癒する〉heal, cure.

chizu 〈ちず：地図〉a map, an atlas.

-cho 〈-ちょ：-著〉

    Takahashi-cho（高橋著）written by Takahashi

chô 〈ちょう：町〉a street, a block.

    Suda-chô（須田町）Suda Street

chô 〈ちょう：腸〉the intestines, the bowels.

    dai-chô（大腸）the large intestine

    shô-chô（小腸）the small intestine

chô 〈ちょう〉a butterfly.

chô 〈ちょう：兆〉a trillion, a billion.

chô 〈ちょう：長〉the head, the chief, the leader, the boss.

    ikka no chô（一家の長）the head of a family

chô 〈ちょう：朝〉a dynasty, a reign, a regime, a period, an age.

    Bikutoria-chô（ビクトリア朝）the reign of Victoria

    Heian-chô（平安朝）the Heian period

chô- 〈ちょう-：超-〉super-, ultra-.

    chô-kokka-shugi（超国家主義）ultranationalism

    chô-man・in-de-aru（超満員である）be packed to overflowing

chôai 〈ちょうあい：寵愛〉

  chôai-suru〈ちょう愛する〉make a favorite ((of)), love ((a person)) tenderly.

chôba 〈ちょうば：跳馬〉long horse; vaulting horse.

chôbatsu 〈ちょうばつ：懲罰〉discipline, punishment, chastisement.

　　chôbatsu-iin-kai〈懲罰委員会〉a disciplinary committee

chôbatsu-ni-kakeru〈懲罰にかける〉discipline, punish, chastise.

chobi-hige〈ちょびひげ〉

chobi-hige-o-hayashite-iru〈ちょびひげを生やしている〉wear a toothbrush mustache.

chôbo〈ちょうぼ：帳簿〉a book, an account book.

　　chôbo o tsukeru（帳簿を付ける）　keep accounts

　　chôbo o gomakasu（帳簿をごまかす）　falsify accounts

chôbô〈ちょうぼう：眺望〉a view, a prospect.

　　chôbô-ga-ii（眺望がいい）　have a fine view

chôbun〈ちょうぶん：弔文〉a funeral address.

chochiku〈ちょちく：貯蓄〉saving, savings.

　chochiku-suru〈貯蓄する〉save (up).

chôchin〈ちょうちん〉a (paper) lantern.

chô-chô〈ちょうちょう：長調〉a major key.

chôchô〈ちょうちょう：町長〉a town headman, a town manager.

chôdai〈ちょうだい〉

　　Kono hon o chôdai.（この本をちょうだい。）　Please give me this book.

　　Kekkô-na shina-o-chôdai-shimashite-arigatô.（結構な品をちょうだいしましてありがとう。）　Many thanks for your nice present.

　　Jûbun chôdai-shimashita.（十分ちょうだいしました。）　I've had enough.

chôden〈ちょうでん：弔電〉a telegram of condolence.

　　chôden o utsu（弔電を打つ）　send a telegram of condolence

chôdo〈ちょうど：丁度〉just, right, exactly.

　　chôdo-go-ji-ni（ちょうど五時に）　just at five

　　chôdo-ii-toki-ni（ちょうどいい時に）　just in time

　　chôdo-sono-toki-ni（ちょうどその時に）　just then

　　Chôdo kono shôsetsu o yomi-oeta-tokoro-desu.（ちょうどこの小説を読み終えたところです。）　I have just finished reading this novel.

　　chôdo mannaka-ni（ちょうど真ん中に）　right in the middle

　　Kono bôshi wa anata-ni chôdo-ii.（この帽子はあなたにちょうどいい。）　This hat fits you exactly.

chôdo〈ちょうど：調度〉supplies, furniture.

chôeki〈ちょうえき：懲役〉penal servitude.

chôen〈ちょうえん：腸炎〉inflammation of the intestines.

chôfuku〈ちょうふく：重複〉(an) overlap, overlapping.

chôfuku-suru〈重複する〉overlap.

chôgô〈ちょうごう：調合〉

chôgô-suru〈調合する〉compound, mix.

　　shohô-doori-ni-chôgô-suru〈処方どおりに調合する〉 make up a pre-scription

chô-hachô〈ちょうはちょう：長波長〉a long-wave length.

chôhatsu〈ちょうはつ：長髪〉

chôhatsu-no〈長髪の〉long-haired.

chôhatsu〈ちょうはつ：挑発〉provocation, excitement, suggestion.

chôhatsu-suru〈挑発する〉provoke, excite, arouse.

chôhatsu-teki(-na)〈挑発的(な)〉provocative, suggestive.

　　chôhatsu-teki-na taido（挑発的な態度） a provocative attitude

chôhei〈ちょうへい：徴兵〉conscription.

chô-heisoku〈ちょうへいそく：腸閉そく〉ileus, intestinal obstruction.

chôhen〈ちょうへん：長編〉a long piece.

　　chôhen-shôsetsu（長編小説） a long novel

chôhô〈ちょうほう：重宝〉

chôhô-na〈重宝な〉convenient, handy, useful.

　　chôhô-na jisho（重宝な辞書） a handy dictionary

　　chôhô-na hito（重宝な人） a useful person

chôhô〈ちょうほう：ちょう報〉intelligence.

　　chôhô-kikan（ちょう報機関） a secret service

　　chôhô-mô（ちょう報網） an intelligence network

chô-hôkei〈ちょうほうけい：長方形〉a rectangle.

chô-hôkei-no〈長方形の〉rectangular.

chôhon-nin〈ちょうほんにん：張本人〉the ringleader.

choichoi〈ちょいちょい〉now and then, occasionally, frequently.

chôin〈ちょういん：調印〉signature, signing.

chôin-suru〈調印する〉sign.

chôji〈ちょうじ：弔辞〉a message of condolence, a memorial address.

　　chôji o noberu（弔辞を述べる） express one's condolence

chô-jikan(-ni-watatte)〈ちょうじかん(にわたって)：長時間(にわたって)〉for many hours.

chôjin〈ちょうじん：超人〉a superman.

chôjin-teki(-na)〈超人的(な)〉superhuman.

　　chôjin-teki doryoku（超人的努力） superhuman efforts

chôjiri〈ちょうじり：帳じり〉the balance of accounts.

chôjiri-o-awasu〈帳じりを合わす〉make the accounts balance.

Chôjiri ga awa-nai.〔帳じりが合わない.〕 The accounts do not balance.

chôjo〈ちょうじょ：長女〉one's eldest daughter.

chôjô〈ちょうじょう：頂上〉the top, the summit.
yama no chôjô-ni（山の頂上に）on the top of the mountain
chôjô-kaidan（頂上会談）a summit conference

chôju〈ちょうじゅ：長寿〉(a) long life, longevity.
chôju-o-tamotsu（長寿を保つ）live long, enjoy longevity.

chojutsu〈ちょじゅつ：著述〉writing.
chojutsu-ni-jûji-suru（著述に従事する）be engaged in writing
chojutsu-gyô（著述業）the profession of letters

chôka〈ちょうか：超過〉excess.
yunyû-chôka（輸入超過）an excess of imports over exports
yushutsu-chôka（輸出超過）an excess of exports over imports
chôka-suru〈超過する〉exceed, be more than.

chôkai〈ちょうかい：町会〉a town assembly.
chôkai-giin（町会議員）a member of a town assembly

chôkai-menshoku〈ちょうかいめんしょく：懲戒免職〉a disciplinary dismissal.
chôkai-menshoku-ni-naru〈懲戒免職になる〉be dismissed by way of disciplinary punishment.

chôka-kimmu〈ちょうかきんむ：超過勤務〉overtime work.
chôka-kimmu-o-suru〈超過勤務をする〉work overtime.

chôkaku〈ちょうかく：聴覚〉hearing, auditory sense.
chôkaku-ga-surudoi（聴覚が鋭い）have a keen sense of hearing

chôkan〈ちょうかん：朝刊〉a morning paper, a morning edition.

chôkan〈ちょうかん：長官〉a director, a head, a chief, a governor.

chôkan-zu〈ちょうかんず：鳥かん図〉a bird's-eye view.

chô-kataru〈ちょうカタル：腸カタル〉intestinal catarrh, enteritis.

chôkeshi〈ちょうけし：帳消し〉
Kore-de chôkeshi-da.（これで帳消しだ.）Now we are quits.
chôkeshi-ni-suru〈帳消しにする〉write off, call quits, offset.
Kore-de-chôkeshi-ni-shiyô.（これで帳消しにしよう.）Let's call quits.

chôki〈ちょうき：弔旗〉
chôki-o-kakageru〈弔旗を掲げる〉hang a flag at half-mast.

chôki〈ちょうき：長期〉a long term, a long period of time.
chôki-keikaku（長期計画）a long-range plan
chôki-taizai（長期滞在）a long stay

chôki-ni-wataru 〈長期にわたる〉 extend over a long period of time.
chôki-ni-watatte 〈長期にわたって〉 over an extended period of time.

chokin 〈ちょきん：貯金〉 savings, saving.
    chokin o orosu (貯金を下ろす) draw one's savings
    chokin-bako (貯金箱) a savings box
    chokin-tsûchô (貯金通帳) a savings passbook
chokin-suru 〈貯金する〉 save money.

chokin(-to) 〈ちょきん（と）〉
chokin-to-kiru 〈ちょきんと切る〉 snip (off).

chokka 〈ちょっか：直下〉
chokka-no, chokka-ni or *chokka-o* 〈直下の，直下に，直下を〉 directly under.

chokkai 〈ちょっかい〉
chokkai-o-dasu 〈ちょっかいを出す〉 meddle ((in)), poke one's nose ((into)); make a pass ((at)).

chokkaku 〈ちょっかく：直角〉 a right angle.
    chokkaku-ni majiwaru (直角に交わる) cross at right angles
    chokkaku-sankaku-kei (直角三角形) a right-angled triangle
chokkaku-no 〈直角の〉 right-angled.
~-to-chokkaku-ni 〈～と直角に〉 at the right angle to... .

chokkan 〈ちょっかん：直感〉 intuition.
chokkan-teki-ni 〈直感的に〉 intuitively.

chokkatsu 〈ちょっかつ：直轄〉
~-no-chokkatsu-de-aru 〈～の直轄である〉 be under direct control of... .

chokkei 〈ちょっけい：直系〉 a direct descent, a direct line.
    chokkei-no shison (直系の子孫) a direct descendant

chokkei 〈ちょっけい：直径〉 a diameter.
    chokkei-hachi-mêtoru (直径八メートル) eight meters in diameter, eight meters across

chokketsu 〈ちょっけつ：直結〉
chokketsu-suru 〈直結する〉 be connected directly ((with)), have direct bearings ((on)).

chokki 〈チョッキ〉 a vest, a waistcoat.

chokkô 〈ちょっこう：直行（航）〉
chokkô-suru 〈直行（航）する〉 go straight ((to)), run through ((to)), sail direct ((for *or* to)), fly nonstop ((for *or* to)).

chokkyû 〈ちょっきゅう：直球〉 a straight ball.

chôkô 〈ちょうこう：徴（兆）候〉 a sign, an indication, a symptom.

haien no chôkô （肺炎の徴(兆)候） symptoms of pneumonia

chôkô 〈ちょうこう：聴講〉

chôkô-sei （聴講生） an irregular student, an auditor

chôkô-suru 〈聴講する〉 attend ［a lecture］, audit ［a course］.

chokochoko 〈ちょこちょこ〉

chokochoko-aruku （ちょこちょこ歩く） toddle about

chokochoko-suru （ちょこちょこする） bustle about

chôkoku 〈ちょうこく：彫刻〉 (a) sculpture, (a) carving.

chôkoku-ka （彫刻家） a sculptor

chôkoku-suru 〈彫刻する〉 carve, sculpture.

chokomaka 〈ちょこまか〉 *see.* chokochoko.

choku 〈ちょく〉 a small cup for drinking *sake*.

chokubai 〈ちょくばい：直売〉 direct sales.

chokubai-ten （直売店） a direct store

chokubai-suru 〈直売する〉 sell direct ((to)).

chokuchô 〈ちょくちょう：直腸〉 the rectum.

chokuei 〈ちょくえい：直営〉 direct management.

chokugeki(-dan) 〈ちょくげき(だん)：直撃(弾)〉 a direct hit.

chokugeki-o-ukeru 〈直撃を受ける〉 be hit directly by a bomb.

chokugo 〈ちょくご：直後〉

chokugo-no or *chokugo-ni* 〈直後の，直後に〉 immediately after, directly after.

chokujô 〈ちょくじょう：直情〉

chokujô-keikô-no hito （直情径行の人） a man of impulsive disposition

chokumen 〈ちょくめん：直面〉

chokumen-suru 〈直面する〉 face, confront, be faced ((with)), be confronted ((by *or* with)).

shi-ni-chokumen-suru （死に直面する） be confronted by death

chokuretsu 〈ちょくれつ：直列〉

denchi o chokuretsu-ni-tsunagu （電池を直列につなぐ） connect cells in series

chokuritsu 〈ちょくりつ：直立〉

chokuritsu-suru 〈直立する〉 stand upright, rise perpendicularly.

chokuritsu-no or *chokuritsu-shita* 〈直立の，直立した〉 upright.

chokuritsu-shite 〈直立して〉 upright.

chokuryû 〈ちょくりゅう：直流〉 direct current (D.C.).

chokusen 〈ちょくせん：直線〉 a straight line.

　　chokusen-kôsu〈直線コース〉a straight course

　itchokusen-ni〈一直線に〉in a straight line.

chokusetsu〈ちょくせつ：直接〉

　chokusetsu-no〈直接の〉direct, immediate, personal.

　chokusetsu-ni〈直接に〉direct(ly), immediately, in person, personally.

　　chokusetsu-kansetsu-ni〈直接間接に〉directly or indirectly

chokusha〈ちょくしゃ：直射〉

　　chokusha-nikkô〈直射日光〉direct sunlight

　chokusha-suru〈直射する〉shine directly ((upon)), fall directly ((upon)).

chokushi〈ちょくし：直視〉

　chokushi-suru〈直視する〉look ((a person *or* a thing)) in the face.

　　genjitsu o chokushi-suru〈現実を直視する〉face up to the reality

chokusô〈ちょくそう：直送〉direct delivery.

　chokusô-suru〈直送する〉send direct(ly) ((to)).

chokutsû〈ちょくつう：直通〉direct service, through service.

　　chokutsû-denwa〈直通電話〉a direct telephone line, a hot line

　　chokutsû-ressha〈直通列車〉a through train

chokuyaku〈ちょくやく：直訳〉literal translation.

　chokuyaku-suru〈直訳する〉translate literally.

chokuzen〈ちょくぜん：直前〉

　chokuzen-no or　*chokuzen-ni*〈直前の，直前に〉immediately before, directly before.

chokuzoku〈ちょくぞく：直属〉

　chokuzoku-no〈直属の〉under one's direct orders.

chôkyô〈ちょうきょう：調教〉

　　chôkyô-shi〈調教師〉a (horse) trainer

　chôkyô-suru〈調教する〉train, break (in).

chô-kyori〈ちょうきょり：長距離〉a long distance, a long range.

　　chô-kyori-denwa〈長距離電話〉a long-distance call

　　　chô-kyori-denwa o kakeru〈長距離電話を掛ける〉talk long distance ((to))

　　chô-kyori-kyôsô〈長距離競走〉a long-distance race, a marathon (race)

chomei〈ちょめい：著名〉

　chomei-na〈著名な〉eminent, famous, well-known.

chômei〈ちょうめい：長命〉a long life.

　chômei-no〈長命の〉long-lived.

chômen〈ちょうめん：帳面〉a notebook.

chômi 〈ちょうみ：調味〉
　　chômi-ryô〈調味料〉 a seasoning, a flavoring
　chômi-suru〈調味する〉season, flavor.
chômin 〈ちょうみん：町民〉a townsman, townspeople.
chômon 〈ちょうもん：弔問〉
　　chômon-kyaku〈弔問客〉 a caller for condolence
　chômon-suru〈弔問する〉make a call of condolence.
chônai 〈ちょうない：町内〉
　　chônai-no hitobito（町内の人々） people living in the same street
chônan 〈ちょうなん：長男〉one's eldest son.
chô-nekutai or **chô-tai** 〈ちょうネクタイ，ちょうタイ：蝶ネクタイ，蝶タイ〉a bow (tie).
chô-nenten 〈ちょうねんてん：腸ねん転〉volvulus, a twist in the intestines.
chongiru 〈ちょんぎる：ちょん切る〉chop off, snip off.
chô-ompa 〈ちょうおんぱ：超音波〉supersonic waves.
chô-onsoku 〈ちょうおんそく：超音速〉supersonic speed.
　chô-onsoku-no〈超音速の〉supersonic.
chôrei 〈ちょうれい：朝礼〉a morning meeting.
chôri 〈ちょうり：調理〉cooking.
　　chôri-dai〈調理台〉 a dresser, a kitchen table
　　chôri-hô〈調理法〉 recipe
　　chôri-nin〈調理人〉 a cook
chôritsu 〈ちょうりつ：調律〉tuning.
　　chôritsu-shi〈調律師〉 a tuner
　chôritsu-suru〈調律する〉tune.
chôrô 〈ちょうろう：長老〉an elder, a senior, a doyen, a dean.
　　seikai-no-chôrô（政界の長老） an elder statesman
chorochoro 〈ちょろちょろ〉
　　chorochoro-nagareru（ちょろちょろ流れる） trickle
　　chorochoro-suru（ちょろちょろする） flit about, sneak about
choromakasu 〈ちょろまかす〉pilfer, swindle, peculate, embezzle.
chôrui 〈ちょうるい：鳥類〉birds, fowls.
　　chôrui-gaku〈鳥類学〉 ornithology
chôryoku 〈ちょうりょく：張力〉tension.
　　hyômen-chôryoku（表面張力） surface tension
chôryoku 〈ちょうりょく：聴力〉the power of hearing.
chôryû 〈ちょうりゅう：潮流〉a tide, a (tidal) current.

chôsa〈ちょうさ：調査〉(an) investigation, (an) examination, (an) inquiry, (a) survey.

   chôsa-suru〈調査する〉investigate, examine, inquire ((into)), survey.

chosaku〈ちょさく：著作〉writing.

     chosaku-ken（著作権）copyright

chôsei〈ちょうせい：調整〉regulation, adjustment.

   chôsei-suru〈調整する〉regulate, adjust.

chôsen〈ちょうせん：挑戦〉a challenge.

     chôsen ni ôjiru（挑戦に応じる）accept a challenge

     chôsen-sha（挑戦者）a challenger

   chôsen-suru〈挑戦する〉challenge.

Chôsen〈ちょうせん：朝鮮〉Korea.

     Chôsen-jin（朝鮮人）a Korean

     Chôsen-go（朝鮮語）Korean

     Chôsen(-jin)-no（朝鮮(人)の）Korean

chôsetsu〈ちょうせつ：調節〉regulation, adjustment, control.

   chôsetsu-suru〈調節する〉regulate, adjust, control.

     heya no ondo o chôsetsu-suru（部屋の温度を調節する）regulate the temperature of a room

chosha〈ちょしゃ：著者〉a writer, an author.

chôshi〈ちょうし：調子〉a tune, a tone; a way, a manner; a condition.

     chôshi-ga-atte-iru（調子が合っている）be in tune ((with))

     chôshi-ga-hazurete-iru（調子が外れている）be out of tune ((with))

     chôshi o ageru（調子を上げる）raise the tone

     chôshi o sageru（調子を下げる）lower the tone

     karada-no-chôshi-ga-ii（体の調子がいい）be in good condition

     Kono terebi wa chôshi-ga-warui.（このテレビは調子が悪い.）This TV doesn't work well.

   chôshi-o-awaseru〈調子を合わせる〉tune, play along ((with)).

   chôshi-no-ii〈調子のいい〉melodious, harmonious, rhythmical.

   kô-iu-chôshi-ni〈こういう調子に〉in this way.

   kono-chôshi-dewa〈この調子では〉at this rate.

chôshin〈ちょうしん：長針〉the minute hand.

chôshin〈ちょうしん：長身〉high stature.

   chôshin-no〈長身の〉tall.

chôshin-ki〈ちょうしんき：聴診器〉a stethoscope.

chosho〈ちょしょ：著書〉a book, a work.

     Kanojo-ni-wa chosho-ga-ooi.（彼女には著書が多い.）She has written

many books.

chôsho 〈ちょうしょ：長所〉 a strong point, a good point, a merit.

chôsho 〈ちょうしょ：調書〉 a written evidence.
　chôsho-ni-toru 〈調書に取る〉 put on record.

chôshô 〈ちょうしょう：ちょう笑〉 derision, ridicule, sneer.
　chôshô-suru 〈ちょう笑する〉 deride, ridicule, sneer ((at)).

chôshoku 〈ちょうしょく：朝食〉 breakfast.
　chôshoku o toru 〈朝食を取る〉 have breakfast

chôshu 〈ちょうしゅ：聴取〉
　chôshu-suru 〈聴取する〉 listen ((to)), hear.

chôshû 〈ちょうしゅう：聴衆〉 an audience, hearers.
　takusan-no chôshû 〈たくさんの聴衆〉 a large audience
　wazuka-na chôshû 〈わずかな聴衆〉 a small audience

chôshû 〈ちょうしゅう：徴収〉 collection, levy.
　chôshû-suru 〈徴収する〉 collect, levy.
　zei o chôshû-suru 〈税を徴収する〉 collect taxes

chôsoku 〈ちょうそく：長足〉
　chôsoku-no-shimpo-o-togeru 〈長足の進歩を遂げる〉 make rapid progress.

chosui-chi 〈ちょすいち：貯水池〉 a reservoir.

chô-tampa 〈ちょうたんぱ：超短波〉 ultrashort waves.
　chô-tampa-jushin-ki 〈超短波受信器〉 an ultrashort wave receiver

chôtatsu 〈ちょうたつ：調達〉
　chôtatsu-suru 〈調達する〉 supply, provide, furnish, raise.

chôtei 〈ちょうてい：調停〉 mediation, arbitration, intervention.
　chôtei-an 〈調停案〉 a mediation plan
　chôtei-nin 〈調停人〉 a mediator, an arbitrator
　chôtei-suru 〈調停する〉 mediate, arbitrate, intervene ((in)).
　arasoi o chôtei-suru 〈争いを調停する〉 mediate a dispute

chôten 〈ちょうてん：頂点〉 the peak, the climax, the top.
　chôten ni tassuru 〈頂点に達する〉 reach the peak

chô-tôha 〈ちょうとうは：超党派〉
　chô-tôha-gaikô 〈超党派外交〉 a nonpartisan diplomacy, a bipartisan diplomacy
　chô-tôha-no 〈超党派の〉 nonpartisan, bipartisan.

chô-tokkyû 〈ちょうとっきゅう：超特急〉 a superexpress.

chototsu 〈ちょとつ：ちょ突〉
　chototsu-môshin-suru 〈ちょ突猛進する〉 make a reckless rush.

chôtsugai 〈ちょうつがい〉 a hinge.

chotto 〈ちょっと〉 just a moment; a little, a bit; rather, pretty.

    Chotto matte-kudasai. （ちょっと待ってください。） Just a moment.

    Chotto kore-o kite-goran. （ちょっとこれを着てごらん。） Just try this on.

    chotto-shita shinsetsu （ちょっとした親切） a little act of kindness

    chotto-shita kaze （ちょっとした風邪） a slight cold

    chotto-shita kissa-ten （ちょっとした喫茶店） a decent-looking tea-room

chotto 〈ちょっと〉 Say, I say.

chôwa 〈ちょうわ：調和〉 harmony.

    chôwa o kaku （調和を欠く） lack harmony

   chôwa-suru 〈調和する〉 harmonize ((with)), be in harmony ((with)).

    chôwa-shi-nai （調和しない） be out of harmony ((with))

   chôwa-no-toreta 〈調和のとれた〉 harmonious.

chôyaku 〈ちょうやく：跳躍〉 a jump, jumping.

    chôyaku-dai （跳躍台） a springboard

   chôyaku-suru 〈跳躍する〉 jump, leap.

chôzai 〈ちょうざい：調剤〉 *see.* chôgô.

chôzei 〈ちょうぜい：徴税〉 tax collection.

   chôzei-suru 〈徴税する〉 collect taxes.

chôzen 〈ちょうぜん：超然〉

   〜-kara-chôzen-to-shite-iru 〈〜から超然としている〉 rise above... .

chozô 〈ちょぞう：貯蔵〉 storage, stock.

    chozô-ga-jûbun-aru （貯蔵が十分ある） have a large stock ((of))

   chozô-suru 〈貯蔵する〉 store, lay up.

chôzô 〈ちょうぞう：彫像〉 a statue, statuary.

chû 〈ちゅう：中〉 average; the middle.

    chû-ijô （中以上） above the average

    chû-ika （中以下） below the average

chû 〈ちゅう：宙〉 the air.

    chû-ni-uku （宙に浮く） float in the air

chû 〈ちゅう：注〉 notes.

-chû 〈-ちゅう：-中〉 during, in the course of, in, on, under.

    rusu-chû （留守中） during one's absence

    gozen-chû （午前中） in the morning

    jugyô-chû （授業中） in class

    kimmu-chû （勤務中） on duty

    kenchiku-chû （建築中） under construction

jutchû-hakku〈十中八九〉 nine cases out of ten, ten to one

chûbu〈チューブ〉a tube.

    chûbu-iri-no-neri-hamigaki (チューブ入りの練り歯磨き) a tube of toothpaste

chûbu〈ちゅうぶ : 中部〉the central part.

    Chûbu-Nihon (中部日本) Central Japan

chûbû〈ちゅうぶう : 中風〉*see.* chûki.

chûburu〈ちゅうぶる : 中古〉*see.* chûko.

chûcho〈ちゅうちょ〉hesitation.

 chûcho-suru〈ちゅうちょする〉hesitate.

 chûcho-shite or *chûcho-shi-nagara*〈ちゅうちょして，ちゅうちょしながら〉hesitatingly.

    chûcho-sezu-ni (ちゅうちょせずに) without hesitation

chûchû〈ちゅうちゅう〉

 chûchû-naku〈ちゅうちゅう鳴く〉twitter, chirp, squeak.

chûdan〈ちゅうだん : 中断〉discontinuance, interruption.

 chûdan-suru〈中断する〉discontinue, interrupt.

 chûdan-sareru〈中断される〉be discontinued, be interrupted.

chûdô〈ちゅうどう : 中道〉

    chûdô-ha (中道派) a middle of the roader, a Centrist

    chûdô-seiji (中道政治) the middle-of-the-road politics

chûdoku〈ちゅうどく : 中毒〉poisoning.

 chûdoku-o-okosu〈中毒を起こす〉be poisoned ((by)).

    shoku-chûdoku-o-okosu (食中毒を起こす) be poisoned by food

chûfuku〈ちゅうふく : 中腹〉

    yama-no-chûfuku-ni (山の中腹に) halfway up(*or* down) the mountain

chûgaeri〈ちゅうがえり : 宙返り〉a somersault, looping.

 chûgaeri-suru〈宙返りする〉turn a somersault, turn loops.

chûgaku〈ちゅうがく : 中学〉

    chûgakkô (中学校) a junior high school, a lower secondary school

    chûgaku-sei (中学生) a junior high school boy(*or* girl).

chûgata〈ちゅうがた : 中型〉a medium size.

 chûgata-no〈中型の〉medium-sized.

chûgen〈ちゅうげん : 中元〉a midyear present.

chûgi〈ちゅうぎ : 忠義〉loyalty, devotion.

 chûgi-na〈忠義な〉loyal, faithful, devoted.

Chûgoku〈ちゅうごく : 中国〉China.

　　　Chûgoku-jin（中国人）　a Chinese

　　　Chûgoku-go（中国語）　Chinese

　　　Chûgoku(-jin)-no（中国(人)の）　Chinese

chû-gurai〈ちゅうぐらい：中位〉

　chû-gurai-no〈中位の〉medium, middling, middle, average, mediocre.

　　　chû-gurai-no-se-no-takasa-da（中位の背の高さだ）be of middle height

　　　Kare-no seiseki wa chû-gurai-da.（彼の成績は中位だ.）His school
　　　record is mediocre.

chûi〈ちゅうい：中位〉*see.* chû-gurai.

chûi〈ちゅうい：注意〉attention, care, caution, advice, (a) warning.

　　　chûi o harau（注意を払う）pay attention ((to))

　　　chûi o hiku（注意を引く）draw ((a person's)) attention

　　　chûi o unagasu（注意を促す）call one's attention ((to))

　　　chûi o ataeru（注意を与える）give ((a person)) advice

　　　Ashi-moto-ni-chûi.（足下に注意.）Watch your step.

　　　kyôfû-chûi-hô（強風注意報）a storm warning

　　　chûi-jikô（注意事項）matters to be attended to

　　　chûi-jimbutsu（注意人物）a dangerous character

　chûi-suru〈注意する〉pay attention ((to)), take care ((of)), be careful
　　((of)), be cautious ((of)), mind, watch, advise, warn.

　　　karada-ni-chûi-suru（体に注意する）take care of oneself

　　　tabe-mono-ni chûi-suru（食べ物に注意する）be careful about what
　　　one eats

　chûi-bukai〈注意深い〉careful, attentive, cautious.

　　　chûi-no-tari-nai（注意の足りない）careless, inattentive

　chûi-bukaku　or　*chûi-shite*〈注意深く，注意して〉carefully, attentively,
　　cautiously.

chûi〈ちゅうい：中尉〉a first lieutenant, a lieutenant; a lieutenant junior
　grade, a sublieutenant.

chûji-en〈ちゅうじえん：中耳炎〉otitis media, tympanitis.

chûjitsu〈ちゅうじつ：忠実〉faithfulness.

　chûjitsu-na〈忠実な〉faithful.

　chûjitsu-ni〈忠実に〉faithfully.

chûjo〈ちゅうじょう：中将〉a lieutenant general; a vice admiral.

chûjun〈ちゅうじゅん：中旬〉the middle ten days of a month.

　　　ichigatsu-chûjun-ni（一月中旬に）about the middle of January

Chûka〈ちゅうか：中華〉

　　　Chûka-jimmin-kyôwa-koku（中華人民共和国）the People's Republic

of China.

Chûka-ryôri（中華料理） Chinese cooking; Chinese dishes

chûkai〈ちゅうかい：仲介〉mediation, intermediation.

chûkai-sha（仲介者） a mediator, a go-between, an agent

chûkai-suru〈仲介する〉mediate.

chûkai-no-rô-o-toru〈仲介の労を取る〉act as go-between.

chûkaku〈ちゅうかく：中核〉the kernel, the core.

chûkan〈ちゅうかん：中間〉the middle.

chûkan-hôkoku（中間報告） an interim report

chûkan-no〈中間の〉middle.

～*-no-chûkan-ni*〈～の中間に〉halfway between... .

Nagoya wa Tôkyô-to-Himeji-no-chûkan-ni-aru.（名古屋は東京と姫路の中間にある.） Nagoya is halfway between Tokyo and Himeji.

chûkan-shoku〈ちゅうかんしょく：中間色〉neutral tints.

chûkei〈ちゅうけい：中継〉relay.

chûkei-hôsô（中継放送） relay broadcasting

chûkei-kyoku（中継局） a relay station

butai-chûkei（舞台中継） a stage relay broadcast

chûkei-suru〈中継する〉relay.

chûken〈ちゅうけん：中堅〉the backbone.

waga-sha no chûken（我が社の中堅） the backbone of our firm

chûki〈ちゅうき：中気〉palsy, paralysis.

Chû-kintô〈ちゅうきんとう：中近東〉the Middle and Near East.

chûko〈ちゅうこ：中古〉

chûko-hin（中古品） secondhand goods

chûko-sha（中古車） a used car

chûko-no〈中古の〉secondhand, used.

chûkoku〈ちゅうこく：忠告〉advice, warning.

chûkoku ni shitagau（忠告に従う） follow ((a person's)) advice

chûkoku-suru〈忠告する〉advise, give ((a person)) warning.

chûkô-shoku〈ちゅうこうしょく：昼光色〉

chûkô-shoku-denkyû（昼光色電球） a daylight lamp

chû-kyori-kyôsô〈ちゅうきょりきょうそう：中距離競走〉a middle-distance race.

chûkyû〈ちゅうきゅう：中級〉the medium grade.

chûkyû-Eigo-kôza（中級英語講座） the intermediate English course

chûmoku〈ちゅうもく：注目〉attention, notice.

seken-no chûmoku o hiku（世間の注目を引く） attract public attention

　　chûmoku-ni-atai-suru〈注目に値する〉be worth notice

　chûmoku-suru〈注目する〉pay attention ((to)), keep one's eye ((upon)), take notice ((of)).

　chûmoku-su-beki〈注目すべき〉noticeable, noteworthy, remarkable.

chûmon〈ちゅうもん：注文〉an order.

　　chûmon-hin〈注文品〉goods ordered

　chûmon-suru〈注文する〉order, give an order.

Chū-Nambei〈ちゅうなんべい：中南米〉Central and South America.

chûnen〈ちゅうねん：中年〉middle age.

　chûnen-no〈中年の〉middle-aged.

chû-nikai〈ちゅうにかい：中二階〉a mezzanine.

chûniku〈ちゅうにく：中肉〉

　　chûniku-chûzei-no hito〈中肉中背の人〉a person of medium height and build, a middle-sized person

chûnin〈ちゅうにん：仲人〉see. nakôdo.

chûnyû〈ちゅうにゅう：注入〉

　chûnyû-suru〈注入する〉pour ((into)), infuse, implant.

chûô〈ちゅうおう：中央〉the center, the middle.

　　chûô-shûken〈中央集権〉centralization of government

　chûô-no〈中央の〉central.

　chûô-ni〈中央に〉in the center ((of)).

chûritsu〈ちゅうりつ：中立〉neutrality.

　　chûritsu o mamoru〈中立を守る〉maintain neutrality

　　chûritsu-chitai〈中立地帯〉a neutral zone

　　chûritsu-koku〈中立国〉a neutral power

　　chûritsu-shugi〈中立主義〉neutralism

　chûritsu-no〈中立の〉neutral.

chûryû〈ちゅうりゅう：中流〉the middle courses; the middle class(es).

chûryû〈ちゅうりゅう：駐留〉

　　chûryû-gun〈駐留軍〉stationary troops, occupation forces

chûsa〈ちゅうさ：中佐〉a lieutenant colonel; a commander.

chûsai〈ちゅうさい：仲裁〉arbitration, mediation.

　　chûsai-sha〈仲裁者〉an arbitrator, a mediator

　chûsai-suru〈仲裁する〉arbitrate, mediate.

chûsan-kaikyū〈ちゅうさんかいきゅう：中産階級〉the middle class(es).

chûsei〈ちゅうせい：中世〉the Middle Ages, medieval times.

　chûsei-no〈中世の〉medieval.

chûsei 〈ちゅうせい：中性〉 neutrality.
    chûsei-senzai（中性洗剤） a neutral detergent
  chûsei-no〈中性の〉 neutral.
chûsen 〈ちゅうせん：抽せん〉 (lot) drawing, a lottery.
    chûsen-ken（抽せん券） a lottery ticket
  chûsen-suru〈抽せんする〉 draw lots.
  chûsen-de〈抽せんで〉 by lot, by lottery.
chûsha 〈ちゅうしゃ：注射〉 (an) injection.
    kinniku-chûsha（筋肉注射） intramuscular injection
    chûsha-ki（注射器） an injector, a syringe
  chûsha-suru〈注射する〉 inject.
chûsha 〈ちゅうしゃ：駐車〉 parking.
    chûsha-ihan（駐車違反） a parking violation
    Chûsha-kinshi.（駐車禁止.） No Parking.
    chûsha-jô（駐車場） a parking lot, a parking zone
  chûsha-suru〈駐車する〉 park.
chûshaku 〈ちゅうしゃく：注釈〉 *see*. chû（注）.
chûshi 〈ちゅうし：中止〉 discontinuance, suspension, stoppage.
  chûshi-suru〈中止する〉 discontinue, suspend, stop, call off.
  chûshi-ni-naru〈中止になる〉 be suspended, be stopped, be called off.
chûshi 〈ちゅうし：注視〉 *see*. chûmoku.
chûshin 〈ちゅうしん：中心〉 the center, the core.
    shi no chûshin-ni（市の中心に） in the center of a city
    chûshin-chi（中心地） a center
    chûshin-jimbutsu（中心人物） the leader, a spark plug
  chûshin-no〈中心の〉 central.
chûshin 〈ちゅうしん：衷心〉
  chûshin-kara-no〈衷心からの〉 hearty, heartfelt, sincere.
  chûshin-kara or *chûshin-yori*〈衷心から，衷心より〉 heartily, sincerely.
    chûshin-kara kansha-suru（衷心から感謝する） thank （(a person)) from one's heart
    Chûshin-yori-o-kuyami-môshi-agemasu.（衷心よりお悔やみ申し上げます.） Please accept my sincere condolence.
chûshô(-suru) 〈ちゅうしょう（する）：中傷（する）〉 slander.
    chûshô-suru-hito（中傷する人） a slanderer
chûshô 〈ちゅうしょう：抽象〉 abstraction.
    chûshô-meishi（抽象名詞） an abstract noun
    chûshô-ron（抽象論） an abstract argument

chûshô-teki(-na)〈抽象的(な)〉abstract.

chûshô-teki-ni〈抽象的に〉abstractly, in the abstract.

    chûshô-teki-ni iu〈抽象的に言う〉 speak in the abstract

chûshoku〈ちゅうしょく：昼食〉lunch.

    chûshoku o toru（昼食を取る） have lunch

    chûshoku-go（昼食後） after lunch

chûshû-no-meigetsu〈ちゅうしゅうのめいげつ：仲秋の名月〉the harvest moon.

chûshutsu〈ちゅうしゅつ：抽出〉abstraction, extraction; sampling.

    nin·i·chûshutsu-hô（任意抽出法） a random sampling method

chûshutsu-suru〈抽出する〉abstract, extract.

Chû-So〈ちゅうソ：中ソ〉

Chû-So-no〈中ソの〉Sino-Soviet.

chûsû〈ちゅうすう：中枢〉the center, the backbone; a mainstay, a key man.

    shinkei-chûsû（神経中枢） a nerve center

chûsui-en〈ちゅうすいえん：中垂炎〉appendicitis.

chûtai〈ちゅうたい：中隊〉a company.

    chûtai-chô（中隊長） a company commander

chûtai〈ちゅうたい：中退〉an abbreviation of 'chûto-taigaku'.

    chûtai-sha（中退者） a dropout

chûtai-suru〈中退する〉leave school in mid-course.

chûten〈ちゅうてん：中点〉the middle point〔of a line〕.

chûtetsu〈ちゅうてつ：鋳鉄〉cast iron.

Chûtô〈ちゅうとう：中東〉the Middle East.

chûto-hampa〈ちゅうとはんぱ：中途半端〉

    chûto-hampa-na-koto-o-yaru（中途半端なことをやる）do ((things)) by halves

    chûto-hampa-ni-shite-oku（中途半端にしておく） leave ((things)) unfinished

chûton〈ちゅうとん：駐屯〉

    chûton-gun（駐屯軍） a garrison, occupation forces

chûton-suru〈駐屯する〉be stationed.

chûto-taigaku〈ちゅうとたいがく：中途退学〉*see.* chûtai（中退）.

chûwa〈ちゅうわ：中和〉neutralization, counteraction.

chûwa-suru〈中和する〉neutralize, counteract.

chûya〈ちゅうや：昼夜〉day and night, night and day.

    itchûya（一昼夜） (for) twenty-four hours

chûya-kenkô-de-hataraku〈昼夜兼行で働く〉 work night and day

chûyô〈ちゅうよう：中庸〉the mean, moderation.

chûyô-o-eta〈中庸を得た〉mean, moderate, reasonable.

chûyu〈ちゅうゆ：注油〉oiling, lubrication.

chûyu-suru〈注油する〉oil, lubricate.

chûzai〈ちゅうざい：駐在〉

chûzai-in〈駐在員〉 a resident reporter, a resident officer

chûzai-sho〈駐在所〉 a police substation

chûzetsu〈ちゅうぜつ：中絶〉interruption, suspension, intermission.

ninshin-chûzetsu〈妊娠中絶〉(an) artificial abortion, interrupted pregnancy

chûzetsu-suru〈中絶する〉be interrupted, be suspended.

chûzô〈ちゅうぞう：鋳造〉casting, founding, coinage, minting.

chûzô-sho〈鋳造所〉 a foundry, a mint

chûzô-suru〈鋳造する〉cast, found, coin, mint.

D

dabô〈だぼう：打棒〉batting.

dabô o fûjiru〈打棒を封じる〉 throttle the bats

daboku-shô〈だぼくしょう：打撲傷〉a bruise, a contusion.

daboku-shô-o-ukeru〈打撲傷を受ける〉get a bruise ((on)), be bruised.

dabora〈だぼら：駄ぼら〉a big talk, a brag.

dabora-o-fuku〈駄ぼらを吹く〉talk big, brag.

dabudabu〈だぶだぶ〉

dabudabu-no〈だぶだぶの〉baggy, loose.

dabudabu-no zubon（だぶだぶのズボン） baggy trousers

daburu〈ダブル〉double.

daburu-haba-no（ダブル幅の） of double width

daburu-no uwagi（ダブルの上着） a double-breasted coat

dabu-tsuku 〈だぶつく〉 be oversupplied, be glutted.

dachō 〈だちょう〉 an ostrich.

dada 〈だだ：駄々〉
  dada-o-koneru 〈駄々をこねる〉 fret, be fretful.

dadakko 〈だだっこ：駄々っ子〉 a spoilt child, a fretful child.

daeki 〈だえき：だ液〉 saliva.

daen 〈だえん：だ円〉 an ellipse, an oval.

daen-kei 〈だえんけい：だ円形〉 an oval.
  daen-kei-no 〈だ円形の〉 oval.

daga 〈だが〉 but, however, yet, nevertheless, though.

da-gakki 〈だがっき：打楽器〉 a percussion instrument.

dageki 〈だげき：打撃〉 a blow, a shock; batting.
    dageki o ataeru （打撃を与える） give a blow ((to))
    dageki-o-ukeru （打撃を受ける） suffer a blow, be shocked
    dageki-ō （打撃王） the batting champion

daha 〈だは：打破〉
  daha-suru 〈打破する〉 break down, overthrow, destroy, do away ((with)).
    inshū-o-daha-suru （因習を打破する） do away with conventionalities

daho 〈だほ：だ捕〉 capture, seizure.
    daho-sen （だ捕船） a prize
  daho-suru 〈だ捕する〉 capture, seize, make prize ((of)).

dai 〈だい：代〉 a generation, a time.
    chichi-no dai-ni （父の代に） in my father's time
    ichi-dai-de （一代で） in one's lifetime
    jū-dai-de-aru （十代である） be in one's teens
    sen-kyū-hyaku-nana-jū-nen-dai-ni （1970年代に） in the 1970s

dai 〈だい：題〉 a subject, a theme, a title.
  dai-suru or *dai-o-tsukeru* 〈題する，題を付ける〉 entitle.
    jiyū-to-dai-suru rombun （「自由」と題する論文） an essay entitled 'Liberty'

dai 〈だい：台〉 a stand, a rest.
    gakufu-dai （楽譜台） a music stand

dai 〈だい：大〉 largeness, greatness; size.
    dai-shō-no-ni-shurui （大小の二種類） two sizes, large and small
    hagaki-dai-no （はがき大の） of postcard size

dai- 〈だい-：第-〉 No.
    dai-ichi （第一） No. 1, the first
    dai-ni （第二） No. 2, the second

dai-san〈第三〉 No. 3, the third

dai-jû〈第十〉 No. 10, the tenth

daiben〈だいべん：大便〉feces, stool.

daiben-o-suru〈大便をする〉go to stool, relieve nature.

daibu〈だいぶ〉very, much, pretty.

daibu kibun-ga-ii（だいぶ気分がいい）feel much better

Kyô-wa daibu samui.（今日はだいぶ寒い．）It is pretty cold today.

dai-bubun〈だいぶぶん：大部分〉the greater part ((of)), the majority ((of)); for the most part, mostly.

gakusei no dai-bubun（学生の大部分）the majority of the students

Kare-ra-wa dai-bubun Doitsu-jin-desu.（彼らは大部分ドイツ人です．）They are mostly German.

dai-bubun-no〈大部分の〉most.

daichi〈だいち：大地〉the earth, the ground.

daichi〈だいち：台地〉a tableland, a plateau, a height.

daichô-kin〈だいちょうきん：大腸菌〉a colon bacillus.

daida〈だいだ：代打〉

daida-suru〈代打する〉pinch-hit ((for)).

dai-dai〈だいだい：代々〉for generations, from generation to generation.

daidai〈だいだい〉a bitter orange.

daidai-iro-no〈だいだい色の〉orange-colored.

daidai-teki〈だいだいてき：大々的〉

daidai-teki-ni〈大々的に〉on a large scale.

daidai-teki-ni senden-suru（大々的に宣伝する）advertise extensively

daidokoro〈だいどころ：台所〉a kitchen.

daidokoro-dôgu（台所道具）kitchen utensils

daidokoro-shigoto（台所仕事）kitchen work

daidô-shôi〈だいどうしょうい：大同小異〉

Dochira-mo daidô-shôi-da.（どちらも大同小異だ．）Both of them are much the same. / There is little to choose between the two.

daigaku〈だいがく：大学〉a university, a college.

daigaku-sei（大学生）a university student, a college student, an undergraduate

daigaku-in〈だいがくいん：大学院〉a graduate school, the postgraduate course.

daigi-in〈だいぎいん：代議員〉a representative, a delegate.

daigishi〈だいぎし：代議士〉a member of the Diet.

daigishi-ni-rikkôho-suru（代議士に立候補する）run for the Diet

daihon 〈だいほん：台本〉 a script, a scenario.

daihyō 〈だいひょう：代表〉 representation; a representative.

   daihyō-suru 〈代表する〉 represent.

   daihyō-teki(-na) 〈代表的(な)〉 representative, typical.

   ～-o-daihyō-shite 〈～を代表して〉 on(*or* in) behalf of... .

dai-ichi 〈だいいち：第一〉 the first, No. 1.

     dai-ichi-inshô 〈第一印象〉 the first impression

   dai-ichi-no 〈第一の〉 first, initial, primary.

   dai-ichi-ni 〈第一に〉 first, firstly, in the first place, first of all.

dai-ichiji 〈だいいちじ：第一次〉

     dai-ichiji-sekai-taisen 〈第一次世界大戦〉 the First World War, World War I

dai-ippo 〈だいいっぽ：第一歩〉 the first step, a start.

     dai-ippo o fumi-dasu 〈第一歩を踏み出す〉 take the first step, make a start

dai-issen 〈だいいっせん：第一線〉 the first line, the front.

     dai-issen-de katsuyaku-suru 〈第一線で活躍する〉 be active in the first line

daiji 〈だいじ：大事〉 *see.* taisetsu.

   daiji-o-totte 〈大事を取って〉 as a precaution.

dai-jimbutsu 〈だいじんぶつ：大人物〉 a great character.

daijin 〈だいじん：大臣〉 a minister.

daijōbu 〈だいじょうぶ：大丈夫〉 safe, secure, all right; assuredly, certainly.

     Daijôbu, kare-wa kuru-yo. 〈大丈夫，彼は来るよ．〉 He is sure to come. (He will surely(certainly) come.)

daikan 〈だいかん：大寒〉 the coldest season, midwinter.

dai-kibo 〈だいきぼ：大規模〉

   dai-kibo-na 〈大規模な〉 large-scale.

   dai-kibo-ni 〈大規模に〉 on a large scale.

daikin 〈だいきん：代金〉 a price.

   daikin-o-harau 〈代金を払う〉 pay the price ((for)), pay ((for)).

dai-kirai 〈だいきらい：大嫌い〉

   dai-kirai-de-aru 〈大嫌いである〉 detest, abhor, loathe.

daikō 〈だいこう：代行〉

     daikô-kikan 〈代行機関〉 an agency

   daikô-suru 〈代行する〉 act ((for)).

daikoku-bashira 〈だいこくばしら：大黒柱〉 the central pillar; the prop.

　　ikka no daikoku-bashira（一家の大黒柱）the breadwinner of a family

daikon〈だいこん：大根〉a radish.

daiku〈だいく：大工〉a carpenter.
　　daiku-shigoto（大工仕事）carpenter's work

daimei〈だいめい：題名〉a title.

dai-meishi〈だいめいし：代名詞〉a pronoun.

daimyô〈だいみょう：大名〉a *daimyo*, a feudal lord.
　　daimyô-ryokô-o-suru（大名旅行をする）travel like a lord

dai-nashi〈だいなし：台無し〉
　dai-nashi-ni-suru（台無しにする）ruin, mar, spoil, mess.
　　isshô o dai-nashi-ni-suru（一生を台無しにする）ruin one's life
　dai-nashi-ni-naru（台無しになる）be ruined, be spoiled, come to nothing.

dai-niji〈だいにじ：第二次〉
　　dai-niji-sekai-taisen（第二次世界大戦）the Second World War, World War II

dai-ôjô〈だいおうじょう：大往生〉
　dai-ôjô-o-togeru〈大往生を遂げる〉die a peaceful death.

dairi〈だいり：代理〉proxy, agency; a proxy, an agent, a representative.
　　dairi-ten（代理店）an agency
　dairi-o-suru（代理をする）act ((for)).
　~-no-dairi-to-shite（〜の代理として）in(*or* on) behalf of... .

dai-rîgu〈だいリーグ：大リーグ〉a major league.
　　dai-rigâ（大リーガー）a major leaguer

dairiseki〈だいりせき：大理石〉marble.

dai-rokkan〈だいろっかん：第六感〉a sixth sense, intuition.

dai-san-sha〈だいさんしゃ：第三者〉a third person, a third party, an outsider.
　　kôhei-na dai-san-sha（公平な第三者）an impartial observer

dai-sharin〈だいしゃりん：大車輪〉a giant swing.

daishin〈だいしん：代診〉an assistant doctor.
　daishin-suru〈代診する〉examine ((a patient)) in behalf of ((another doctor)).

dai-shizen〈だいしぜん：大自然〉Mother Nature.

dai-shô〈だいしょう：大小〉
　　dai-shô-no（大小の）large and small
　　dai-shô-samazama-no（大小さまざまの）of various sizes
　　dai-shô-ni-kakawarazu（大小にかかわらず）regardless of size

daishô〈だいしょう：代償〉compensation.

～-no-daishô-to-shite〈～の代償として〉in compensation for... .

daisô〈だいそう：代走〉

daisô-sha（代走者）a pinch runner

daisô-suru〈代走する〉run for another.

dai-sôjô〈だいそうじょう：大僧正〉an archbishop.

daisoreta〈だいそれた：大それた〉audacious, inordinate, outrageous, atrocious.

daisoreta nozomi（大それた望み）an inordinate desire

daisû〈だいすう：代数〉algebra.

daisuki〈だいすき：大好き〉

daisuki-de-aru〈大好きである〉like very much, be very fond ((of)).

daisuki-na〈大好きな〉favorite.

watashi-no daisuki-na supôtsu（私の大好きなスポーツ）my favorite sport

daitai〈だいたい：大たい〉the thigh.

daitai-kotsu（大たい骨）a thighbone

daitai〈だいたい：大隊〉a battalion.

daitai-chô（大隊長）a battalion commander

daitai〈だいたい：大体〉an outline, a summary; generally, on the whole.

daitai o noberu（大体を述べる）give an outline ((of))

daitai-kara-ieba（大体から言えば）generally speaking

daitai-no〈大体の〉general, rough.

daitai-no mitsumori（大体の見積もり）a rough estimate

daitan〈だいたん：大胆〉boldness, daring.

daitan-na〈大胆な〉bold, daring.

daitan-ni〈大胆に〉boldly, daringly.

dai-tasû〈だいたすう：大多数〉a large majority, the greater part ((of)).

attô-teki dai-tasû（圧倒的大多数）an overwhelming majority

daitôryô〈だいとうりょう：大統領〉the President.

daiya〈ダイヤ〉a railroad schedule; a diamond.

Daiya ga midarete-iru.（ダイヤが乱れている。）The railroad schedule is in confusion.

daiyaku〈だいやく：代役〉a substitute, a stand-in, a double.

daiyaku-o-tsutomeru〈代役を務める〉play as a substitute ((for)), play the part of another actor, fill in ((for)).

daiyaru〈ダイヤル〉a dial (plate).

daiyaru-o-mawasu〈ダイヤルを回す〉turn a dial, dial.

daiyô 〈だいよう：代用〉 substitution.
    daiyô-hin（代用品）a substitute ((for))
  daiyô-suru〈代用する〉substitute ((A for B)).
daizai 〈だいざい：題材〉a subject matter, a theme.
daizu 〈だいず：大豆〉a soybean.
dajun 〈だじゅん：打順〉a batting order.
dakai 〈だかい：打開〉
  dakai-suru〈打開する〉break.
    nankyoku-o-dakai-suru（難局を打開する）find one's way out of the
      difficulties
dakara 〈だから〉so, so that, therefore; as, because, since.
-dake 〈-だけ〉only, alone; as...as; enough, worth; by.
    ichi-do-dake（一度だけ）only once
    kondo-dake（今度だけ）for this once
    tada-kore-dake（ただこれだけ）only this
    Watashi-dake ie-ni-imasu.（私だけ家にいます。）I'll be home alone.
    dekiru-dake-hayaku（できるだけ早く）as soon as possible
    Kore-dake-de-jûbun-de-shô.（これだけで十分でしょう。）This will be
      enough.
    yomu-dake-no-kachi-ga-aru（読むだけの価値がある）be worth read-
      ing
    jussenchi-dake nagai（十センチだけ長い）be too long by ten cen-
      timeters
  〜*-dake-de-naku*〜*-mo(-mata)*〈〜だけでなく〜も（又）〉not only...but (also)
    ... .
daketsu 〈だけつ：妥結〉an agreement.
    daketsu-suru（妥結する）reach an agreement ((with))
daki-ageru 〈だきあげる：抱き上げる〉lift ((a child)) in one's arms.
daki-au 〈だきあう：抱き合う〉embrace each other.
daki-kakaeru 〈だきかかえる：抱きかかえる〉hold ((a person)) in one's
  arms.
  daki-kakaerarete〈抱きかかえられて〉carried in the arms ((of)).
daki-komu 〈だきこむ：抱き込む〉win ((a person)) over to one's side.
daki-okosu 〈だきおこす：抱き起こす〉raise ((a person)) in one's arms.
daki-shimeru 〈だきしめる：抱き締める〉embrace ((a person)) closely,
  hug ((a person)) tightly.
daki-tsuku 〈だきつく：抱き付く〉
    kubi-ni-daki-tsuku（首に抱き付く）throw one's arms around

another's neck

koshi-ni-daki-tsuku〈腰に抱き付く〉seize ((a person)) round the waist

daki-yoseru〈だきよせる：抱き寄せる〉draw ((a person)) close(r) to one's breast.

dakkai(-suru)〈だっかい（する）：奪回（する）〉recapture.

dakkô〈だっこう：脱こう〉prolapse of the anus.

dakkyû〈だっきゅう：脱きゅう〉dislocation.

dakkyû-suru〈脱きゅうする〉dislocate, be dislocated, be put out of joint.

daku〈だく：抱く〉hold in one's arms, embrace; sit.

tamago-o-daku〈卵を抱く〉sit on eggs

akambô-o-daite〈赤ん坊を抱いて〉with a baby in one's arms.

dakuon〈だくおん：濁音〉a voiced sound.

dakuryû〈だくりゅう：濁流〉a muddy stream.

dakyô〈だきょう：妥協〉compromise.

Dakyô-no-yochi-ga-nai.〈妥協の余地がない.〉There is no room for compromise.

dakyô-ten〈妥協点〉a meeting point, a point of compromise

dakyô-suru〈妥協する〉compromise, come to terms ((with)).

dakyô-teki(-na)〈妥協的（な）〉compromising, concessive.

damari-komu〈だまりこむ：黙り込む〉sink into silence, fall dumb.

damari-konde〈黙り込んで〉in stony silence.

damaru〈だまる：黙る〉become silent, stop speaking.

Damare!〈黙れ.〉Shut up! / Silence!

damatte〈黙って〉in silence, silently, without a word.

damatte-iru〈黙っている〉keep silent

damashi-ai〈だましあい：だまし合い〉

kitsune-to-tanuki-no-damashi-ai-o-suru〈きつねとたぬきのだまし合いをする〉try to outfox each other.

damasu〈だます〉deceive, cheat, take in.

dambô〈だんぼう：暖房〉heating.

dambô-kigu〈暖房器具〉a heater

dambô-sôchi〈暖房装置〉heating

dambôru〈ダンボール〉corrugated cardboard.

dame〈だめ：駄目〉useless, vain, of no use, no good, hopeless; must not.

Naitatte-dame-da.〈泣いたって駄目だ.〉It's no use crying.

Ano kanja wa mô-dame-da.〈あの患者はもう駄目だ.〉The case is hopeless.

Kare-wa mô-dame-da.〈彼はもう駄目だ.〉It's all up with him.

Kare-ni atte-wa-dame-da.〈彼に会っては駄目だ。〉 You must not see him.

dame-ni-suru〈駄目にする〉spoil, ruin.

dame-ni-naru〈駄目になる〉be spoiled, be ruined, be futile, fail, come to naught.

dame-oshi〈だめおし：駄目押し〉

dame-oshi-no-itten-o-kuwaeru〈駄目押しの一点を加える〉score an insurance run.

dammen〈だんめん：断面〉a cross section.

shihon-shugi-keizai no ichi-dammen（資本主義経済の一断面）a cross section of the capitalistic economy

dampen〈だんぺん：断片〉a fragment, a piece.

dampen-teki(-na)〈断片的(な)〉fragmentary.

dampingu〈ダンピング〉dumping.

dampingu-suru〈ダンピングする〉dump.

dampukâ〈ダンプカー〉a dump truck.

dan〈だん：段〉a step, a stair; a column.

dan〈だん：壇〉a platform, a stage.

-dan〈-だん：-団〉a body, a group, a party.

chôsa-dan（調査団）a survey group

kankô-dan（観光団）a tourist party

shisetsu-dan（使節団）a mission, a delegation

dan·atsu〈だんあつ：弾圧〉suppression, crackdown.

dan·atsu-suru〈弾圧する〉suppress.

danchi〈だんち：団地〉a housing development.

danchigai〈だんちがい：段違い〉

danchigai-ni-tsuyoi（段違いに強い）be incomparably strong

danchigai-heikô-bô（段違い平行棒）uneven parallel bars

danchô〈だんちょう：団長〉the leader, the head.

ikkô no danchô（一行の団長） the leader of a party

dandan〈だんだん：段々〉gradually, little by little, step by step, more and more, less and less.

Dandan kuraku-natte-kuru.（だんだん暗くなってくる。） It's getting darker and darker.

dandan-batake〈だんだんばたけ：段々畑〉a terraced farm.

dandô-dan〈だんどうだん：弾道弾〉a ballistic missile.

dandori〈だんどり：段取り〉a program, a plan, arrangements.　「ments

dandori-o-kimeru（段取りを決める） map out a plan, make arrange-

    asu-no dandori（明日の段取り） the program for tomorrow

dangai〈だんがい：断崖〉a precipice, a cliff, a bluff.
    dangai-zeppeki（断がい絶壁） an overhanging cliff

dangai〈だんがい：弾劾〉impeachment.
    dangai-saiban-sho（弾劾裁判所） a Court of Impeachment
    dangai-suru〈弾劾する〉impeach.

dangan〈だんがん：弾丸〉a bullet, a cannon ball.

dangen〈だんげん：断言〉assertion, affirmation, declaration.
    dangen-suru〈断言する〉assert, affirm, declare.

dango〈だんご：団子〉a dumpling.

dangô〈だんごう：談合〉consultation, conference.
    dangô-suru〈談合する〉consult ((with)), confer ((with)).

dani〈だに〉a tick.

danjiki〈だんじき：断食〉a fast, fasting.
    danjiki-suru〈断食する〉fast.

dan-jo〈だんじょ：男女〉man and woman.
    dan-jo-o-towazu（男女を問わず） regardless of sex
    dan-jo-kyôgaku（男女共学） coeducation
      dan-jo-kyôgaku-no（男女共学の） coeducational

danka〈だんか：だん家〉a parishioner.

dankai〈だんかい：段階〉a step, a stage, a phase.
    shin-dankai（新段階） a new phase
    dankai-teki(-na)〈段階的(な)〉staged, phased.
    dankai-teki haishi（段階的廃止） staged reduction

danketsu〈だんけつ：団結〉unity, union, combination.
    danketsu-suru〈団結する〉unite, band together, combine.
    danketsu-shite〈団結して〉in union, in combination, in a body.

danko〈だんこ：断固〉
danko-taru〈断固たる〉firm, decisive, determined, resolute, positive, drastic.
    danko-taru taido（断固たる態度） a determined attitude
    danko-taru shochi（断固たる処置） a drastic measure
    danko-to-shite〈断固として〉firmly, decisively, resolutely, positively.
    danko-to-shite hantai-suru（断固として反対する） oppose positively

dankô〈だんこう：団交〉an abbreviation of 'dantai-kôshô'.

dankô〈だんこう：断行〉
dankô-suru〈断行する〉carry ((a thing)) into effect resolutely.

dankô〈だんこう：断交〉(a) rupture.

keizai-dankô〈経済断交〉a rupture of economic relations

dankô-suru〈断交する〉break off relations ((with)).

dankon〈だんこん：弾こん〉a bullet mark.

dannen〈だんねん：断念〉

dannen-suru〈断念する〉give up, abandon.

dannetsu〈だんねつ：断熱〉

dannetsu-zai〈断熱材〉heat insulating material

danraku〈だんらく：段落〉a pause; the end of a paragraph.

Kore-de wareware-no shigoto mo ichi-danraku-tsuita.（これで我々の
仕事も一段落付いた.）This brings our work to a pause for the
present.

danran〈だんらん：団らん〉

ikka-danran no tanoshimi（一家団らんの楽しみ）the pleasure of a
happy home

danro〈だんろ：暖炉〉a fireplace, a hearth, a stove.

danryoku〈だんりょく：弾力〉elasticity.

danryoku-no-aru〈弾力のある〉elastic.

danryoku-sei-no-aru〈弾力性のある〉flexible.

danryû〈だんりゅう：暖流〉a warm current.

dansei〈だんせい：男性〉the male (sex).

dansei-teki(-na)〈男性的(な)〉manly, masculine.

dansei〈だんせい：男声〉a male voice.

dansei-gasshô〈男声合唱〉a male chorus

dansen〈だんせん：断線〉disconnection.

dansen-suru〈断線する〉snap, be down.

danshi〈だんし：男子〉a man, a male, a boy.

danshô〈だんしょう：談笑〉

danshô-suru〈談笑する〉have a pleasant chat ((with)).

dansô〈だんそう：断層〉a dislocation; a gap.

sedai-no-dansô〈世代の断層〉a generation gap

dansu〈ダンス〉dancing, a dance.

dansu-pâtî（ダンスパーティー）a dance, a ball

dansu-o-suru〈ダンスをする〉dance, have a dance ((with)).

dansui〈だんすい：断水〉suspension of water supply.

dansui-suru〈断水する〉cut off water supply.

dantai〈だんたい：団体〉a party, a group, a body, a team.

dantai-kôdô〈団体行動〉a collective action

dantai-kôshô〈団体交渉〉collective bargaining

　　　dantai-kyaku〈団体客〉 party travelers
　　　dantai-kyôgi〈団体競技〉 a team sport
　　　dantai-ryokô〈団体旅行〉 a group tour
　　　　dantai-ryokô-o-suru〈団体旅行をする〉 travel in a party
　　　dantai-seikatsu〈団体生活〉 a group life
dantei〈だんてい：断定〉a conclusion, a decision.
　dantei-suru〈断定する〉conclude, come to a conclusion.
dantô〈だんとう：暖冬〉a mild winter.
　　　dantô-ihen〈暖冬異変〉 an abnormally warm winter
dantô〈だんとう：弾頭〉a warhead.
　　　kaku-dantô〈核弾頭〉 a nuclear warhead
danwa〈だんわ：談話〉(a) talk, (a) conversation.
　danwa-suru〈談話する〉talk ((with)), have a conversation ((with)).
dan･yaku〈だんやく：弾薬〉ammunition.
dan･yû〈だんゆう：男優〉an actor.
danzen〈だんぜん：断然〉decidedly, positively, absolutely.
danzetsu〈だんぜつ：断絶〉severance, (a) rupture; extinction.
　　　kokkô no danzetsu〈国交の断絶〉 a rupture of diplomatic relations
　danzetsu-suru〈断絶する〉sever, break off; become extinct.
danzoku〈だんぞく：断続〉intermittence.
　danzoku-teki(-na)〈断続的(な)〉intermittent.
　　　Danzoku-teki-na-ame-ga-isshû-kan-tsuzuiteiru.〈断続的な雨が一週間続
　　　いている。〉 It has been raining off and on for one week.
　danzoku-teki-ni〈断続的に〉off and on.
dappi〈だっぴ：脱皮〉
　dappi-suru〈脱皮する〉cast off the skin; outgrow.
　　　kyûtai-kara-dappi-suru〈旧態から脱皮する〉 outgrow the covention
daradara〈だらだら〉
　　　daradara-shigoto-o-suru〈だらだら仕事をする〉 work in a slovenly
　　　　way
　　　Ase ga daradara-nagareru.〈汗がだらだら流れる。〉 Sweat drips.
-darake〈-だらけ〉full of... , filled with... , covered with... .
　　　goshoku-darake-no kôsei-zuri〈誤植だらけの校正刷り〉 a proof full of
　　　　misprints
　　　hokori-darake-no têburu〈ほこりだらけのテーブル〉 a table covered
　　　　with dust
darakeru〈だらける〉feel languid, feel dull, be loose, be lazy.
　daraketa〈だらけた〉dull, loose, lazy.

    daraketa shiai（だらけた試合）a dull game

    daraketa seikatsu（だらけた生活）a lazy life

daraku〈だらく：堕落〉depravity, (moral) corruption.

 daraku-suru〈堕落する〉become depraved, go to the bad.

 daraku-shita〈堕落した〉depraved, corrupt.

darashi(-no)-nai〈だらし(の)ない〉slovenly, untidy, slack, loose.

    darashi-nai aruki-kata-o-suru（だらしない歩き方をする）walk with slovenly gait

dare〈だれ〉who, whose, whom.

    Kare-wa dare-desu-ka?（彼は誰ですか.）Who is he?

    Kore-wa dare-no hon-desu-ka?（これはだれの本ですか.）Whose book is this?

    Dare-ni atta-no-ka?（だれに会ったのか.）Whom(*or* Who) did you see?

    Dare-o matteiru-no-desu-ka?（だれを待っているのですか.）Whom(*or* Who) are you waiting for?

 dare-ka〈だれか〉someone, somebody; anyone, anybody.

    Dare-ka ima-ni-iru.（だれか居間にいる.）Someone is in the living room.

    Watashi-no-gaishutsu-chū-ni dare-ka kimashita-ka?（私の外出中にだれか来ましたか.）Did anyone come while I was out?

 dare-demo〈だれでも〉everyone, everybody; anyone, anybody.

    Dare-demo sore-o shitte-iru.（だれでもそれを知っている.）Everyone knows it.

    Dare-demo kono hon-wa-yomeru.（だれでもこの本は読める.）Anybody can read this book.

 dare-mo～-nai〈だれも～ない〉no one, nobody.

    Dare-mo sore-o shira-nai.（だれもそれを知らない.）No one knows it.

 dare-mo-kare-mo-mina〈だれも彼も皆〉every man jack.

dareru〈だれる〉be bored ((with)), flag.

daritsu〈だりつ：打率〉a batting average.

-darō〈-だろう〉I think, I suppose, I hope, I am afraid, maybe, perhaps, probably.

darui〈だるい〉languid, weary, dull, heavy.

 daru-sō-ni〈だるそうに〉languidly, wearily.

daryoku〈だりょく：打力〉hitting power.

dasaku〈ださく：駄作〉a poor work, trash, rubbish.

dasan〈ださん：打算〉

dasan-teki(-na) 〈打算的（な）〉 selfish, calculating.

dasei 〈だせい：惰性〉 inertia, momentum.

dasei-de 〈惰性で〉 by sheer force of habit.

daseki 〈だせき：打席〉 *see.* **dasû.**

dasen 〈だせん：打線〉 the batting lineup.

dasha 〈だしゃ：打者〉 a batter.

　　kyô-dasha 〈強打者〉 a hard hitter, a slugger.

dashi 〈だし：出し〉 (soup) stock.

　　dashi o toru 〈出しを取る〉 prepare stock

dashi-au 〈だしあう：出し合う〉 club together.

dashi-ire 〈だしいれ：出し入れ〉

　　ginkô-de-no　kane-no-dashi-ire〈銀行での金の出し入れ〉 depositing
　　and drawing money in a bank

dashi-mono 〈だしもの：出し物〉 a program.

　　omo-na dashi-mono〈主な出し物〉 the principal feature〔of the day〕,
　　the highlight〔on the program〕

dashin 〈だしん：打診〉 percussion.

dashin-suru 〈打診する〉 examine by percussion, sound.

　　ikô-o-dashin-suru〈意向を打診する〉 sound ((a person's)) opinion, feel
　　((a person)) out

dashinuke 〈だしぬけ：出し抜け〉

dashinuke-ni〈出し抜けに〉 suddenly, unexpectedly, without notice.

dashi-nuku〈だしぬく：出し抜く〉 forestall, scoop, outwit.

dassen 〈だっせん：脱線〉 derailment; (a) digression.

dassen-suru 〈脱線する〉 be derailed, run off the rails; get sidetracked.

dasshi- 〈だっし：脱脂〉

　　dasshi-men（脱脂綿） absorbent cotton

　　dasshi-nyû（脱脂乳） skim milk

dasshoku 〈だっしょく：脱色〉

　　dasshoku-zai（脱色剤） a decolorant

dasshoku-suru〈脱色する〉 decolorize.

dasshu 〈だっしゅ：奪取〉

dasshu-suru〈奪取する〉 capture, carry, seize.

dasshû 〈だっしゅう：脱臭〉

　　dasshû-zai（脱臭剤） a deodorant

dasshû-suru〈脱臭する〉 deodorize.

dasshutsu 〈だっしゅつ：脱出〉

dasshutsu-suru〈脱出する〉 escape ((from)), get out.

dassô〈だっそう：脱走〉(an) escape, (a) desertion.
dassô o kuwadateru（脱走を企てる）attempt an escape
dassô-hei（脱走兵）a deserter
dassô-suru〈脱走する〉escape, run away ((from)).

dassui〈だっすい：脱水〉dehydration.
dassui-ki（脱水機）a spin-drier
dassui-suru〈脱水する〉dehydrate.

dassuru〈だっする：脱する〉escape ((from)), get rid ((of)), get out of.
kiki-o-dassuru（危機を脱する）get out of the woods

dasu〈だす：出す〉hold out, put out, take out; hand in, present; send, post, mail; put forth; serve.
te o dasu（手を出す）hold out one's hand
mado-kara kubi o dasu（窓から首を出す）put one's head out of the window
poketto-kara hankachi o dasu（ポケットからハンカチを出す）take out a handkerchief from one's pocket
sakubun o dasu（作文を出す）hand in a composition
ko-zutsumi o dasu（小包を出す）send a package
tegami o dasu（手紙を出す）post a letter
chikara o dasu（力を出す）put forth one's strength
chôshoku o dasu（朝食を出す）serve breakfast

-dasu〈-だす：-出す〉begin.
Ame ga furi-dashita.（雨が降り出した．）It has begun to rain.
watto-naki-dasu（わっと泣き出す）burst into tears
watto-warai-dasu（わっと笑い出す）burst out laughing

dasû〈だすう：打数〉
go-dasû（五打数）five at bats

dâsu〈ダース〉a dozen.
ichi-dâsu（一ダース）a dozen
han-dâsu（半ダース）half a dozen, a half dozen
ichi-dâsu-han（一ダース半）a dozen and a half

datai〈だたい：堕胎〉abortion.
datai-suru〈堕胎する〉have an abortion.
datai-saseru〈堕胎させる〉cause abortion.

datchô〈だっちょう：脱腸〉hernia, rupture.

-date〈-だて：-建て〉
hachi-kai-date-no biru（八階建てのビル）an eight-storied building

daten〈だてん：打点〉runs batted in (RBI).

　　　daten-ô（打点王）　the RBI winner

datô(-suru)〈だとう(する)：打倒(する)〉overthrow.

datô〈だとう：妥当〉

　　　datô-na〈妥当な〉proper, appropriate, reasonable, fit.

datsugoku〈だつごく：脱獄〉prison breaking.

　　　datsugoku-shû（脱獄囚）a prison-breaker

　　　datsugoku-suru〈脱獄する〉break prison, escape from prison.

datsui〈だつい：脱衣〉

　　　datsui-jo（脱衣所）a dressing room, a bathing booth.

datsumô〈だつもう：脱毛〉loss of hair.

datsuraku〈だつらく：脱落〉an omission; defection, desertion.

　　　bunchû-no datsuraku（文中の脱落）omissions in the sentences

　　　datsuraku-suru〈脱落する〉be omitted; fall away, drop away.

datsuzei〈だつぜい：脱税〉tax evasion.

　　　datsuzei-suru〈脱税する〉evade a tax.

dattai〈だったい：脱退〉withdrawal, secession.

　　　dattai-suru〈脱退する〉withdraw ((from)), secede ((from)).

datte〈だって〉but, because.

　　　"Dôshite motto-hayaku oki-nakatta-no?" "Datte nemu-katta-n-da-
　　　mono."（"どうしてもっと早く起きなかったの.""だって眠かったんだ
　　　もの."）"Why didn't you get up earlier?" "Because I was
　　　sleepy."

-datte〈-だって〉even; also, too.

　　　kodomo-datte（子供だって）even a child

　　　Kare-datte tsukarete-iru.（彼だって疲れている.）He is tired, too.

Dau-heikin〈ダウへいきん：ダウ平均〉the Dow-Jones average.

de〈で：出〉appearance; flow, outflow; origin, birth.

　　　tsuki no de（月の出）the rise of the moon

　　　inku-no-de-ga-warui（インクの出が悪い）do not have a good flow of
　　　ink

　　　daigaku-de（大学出）a university graduate

　　　meimon-no-de-de-aru（名門の出である）come of a noble family

-de〈-で〉in, at, on; in, within; of, from, with, through, because of; on,
　　for; in, with; at, for; at, in; at, by; of, from; by, on, in, with.

　　　Tôkyô-de（東京で）in Tôkyô

　　　Tôkyô-no-Shinjuku-de（東京の新宿で）at Shinjuku in Tôkyô

　　　Ginza-de（銀座で）on the Ginza

　　　ichi-jikan-de（一時間で）in an hour

    ichi-nen-de （一年で）　within a year

    gan-de shinu （がんで死ぬ）　die of cancer

    karô-de shinu （過労で死ぬ）　die from hard work

    samusa-de furueteiru （寒さで震えている）　be shivering with cold

    fu-chûi-de （不注意で）　through one's carelessness

    byôki-de （病気で）　because of illness

    shigoto-de （仕事で）　on business

    chiisai koe-de （小さい声で）　in a low voice

    yorokonde （喜んで）　with pleasure

    ichi-yâdo hyaku-en-de （一ヤード百円で）　at one hundred yen a yard

    go-sen-en-de uru （五千円で売る）　sell ((a thing)) for 5,000 yen

    ni-jû-ni-sai-de （二十二歳で）　at (the age of) twenty-two

    san-jû-dai-de （三十代で）　in one's thirties

    zen-sokuryoku-de （全速力で）　at full speed

    dâsu-de uru （ダースで売る）　sell by the dozen

    watashi-no tokei-de （私の時計で）　by my watch

    renga-de sôko o tateru （レンガで倉庫を建てる）　build a warehouse of brick

    jitensha-de （自転車で）　by bicycle, on a bicycle

    terebi-de （テレビで）　on television

    Eigo-de kaku （英語で書く）　write in English

    empitsu-de kaku （鉛筆で書く）　write with a pencil

de-aruku 〈であるく：出歩く〉gad about, go out.

de-ashi 〈であし：出足〉start.

    de-ashi-ga-ii （出足がいい）　make a good start, there is a good turnout

    de-ashi-ga-warui （出足が悪い）　make a bad start, there is a slow turnout

de-au 〈であう：出会う〉meet (with), come across.

    tochû-de de-au （途中で出会う）　meet ((a person)) on the way

deba(-bôchô) 〈でば（ぼうちょう）：出刃（包丁）〉a kitchen knife.

deban 〈でばん：出番〉one's turn, one's time.

debana 〈でばな：出ばな〉

  debana-o-kujikareru 〈出ばなをくじかれる〉be baffled at the outset.

de-bushô 〈でぶしょう：出不(無)精〉a stay-at-home.

  de-bushô-no 〈出不(無)精の〉stay-at-home.

debyû 〈デビュー〉a debut.

  debyû-suru 〈デビューする〉make one's debut.

dedashi 〈でだし：出だし〉
 dedashi-ga-ii 〈出だしがいい〉 make a good start.
deddo-bôru 〈デッドボール〉 a dead ball.
 deddo-bôru-o-kuu 〈デッドボールを食う〉 be hit by a pitch.
defure 〈デフレ〉 deflation.
degake 〈でがけ：出掛け〉
 degake-ni 〈出掛けに〉 just when one is going out.
degarashi 〈でがらし：出がらし〉
 degarashi-no cha（出がらしの茶）thin tea
deguchi 〈でぐち：出口〉 a way out, an exit.
de-hajime 〈ではじめ：出始め〉 the first appearance.
 takenoko-no-de-hajime（たけのこの出始め）early bamboo shoots
 de-hajimeru 〈出始める〉 begin to appear, begin to come in.
de-iri 〈でいり：出入り〉 going in and out.
 hito-no-de-iri-ga-ooi（人の出入りが多い）have a large number of visitors
 de-iri-guchi（出入り口）an entrance, a doorway, a gateway
 de-iri-suru 〈出入りする〉 go in and out.
deisui 〈でいすい：泥酔〉 dead drunkenness.
 deisui-suru 〈泥酔する〉 get dead drunk.
dekadeka(-to) 〈でかでか（と）〉
 dekadeka-to kaki-tateru 〈でかでかと書き立てる〉 play up ((a thing)) with a banner.
dekakeru 〈でかける：出掛ける〉 go out, start, set out.
 sampo-ni dekakeru（散歩に出掛ける）go out for a walk
 ryokô-ni dekakeru（旅行に出掛ける）start on a journey
 Haha wa ima dekakete-imasu.（母は今出掛けています。）Mother is out now.
dekata 〈でかた：出方〉
 Banji sempô-no-dekata-shidai-da.（万事先方の出方次第だ。）Everything depends upon how they will act.
deki 〈でき：出来〉 make, workmanship; the result; a crop.
 gakkô-no-deki-ga-ii（学校の出来がいい）do well at school
 kome no deki-ga-ii（米の出来がいい）have a good harvest of rice
 ko-mugi no deki-ga-warui（小麦の出来が悪い）have a poor crop of wheat
 deki-no-ii 〈出来のいい〉 of good make, of fine workmanship.
 deki-no-warui（出来の悪い）of poor make, of poor workmanship

dekiagari〈できあがり：出来上がり〉completion, finish.

　　Dekiagari-wa-itsu-goro-desu-ka?（出来上がりはいつごろですか。）When will it be completed?

　deki-agaru〈出来上がる〉be completed, be finished, be ready.

dekiai〈できあい：出来合い〉

　dekiai-no〈出来合いの〉ready-made.

　　dekiai-no fuku（出来合いの服）ready-made clothes

deki-bae〈できばえ：出来栄え〉

　　Kono mozaiku wa subarashii-deki-bae-da.（このモザイクはすばらしい出来栄えだ。）This mosaic is of excellent workmanship.

deki-daka〈できだか：出来高〉a yield, a crop, production; volume.

　　shigoto no deki-daka（仕事の出来高）the amount of work done

　　deki-daka-barai（出来高払い）piecework payment

deki-gokoro〈できごころ：出来心〉(an) impulse.

　　honno-ichiji-no-deki-gokoro-kara（ほんの一時の出来心から）on the impulse of the moment

deki-goto〈できごと：出来事〉an occurrence, a happening, an event, an accident.

　　fusoku-no deki-goto（不測の出来事）an unforeseen occurrence

　　kotoshi no omo-na deki-goto（今年の主な出来事）main events of this year

deki-mono〈できもの：出来物〉a tumor, a boil, a swelling.

dekiru〈できる：出来る〉can, be able to; be good ((at)), be skillful ((in)); be ready, be finished; be made; grow.

　　Kare-wa oyogu-koto-ga-dekiru.（彼は泳ぐことができる。）He can swim.

　　Kare-wa oyogu-koto-ga-deki-nai.（彼は泳ぐことができない。）He cannot swim.

　　Kare-wa sûgaku-ga-yoku-dekiru.（彼は数学がよくできる。）He is good at mathematics.

　　Kare-wa Eigo-ga-deki-nai.（彼は英語ができない。）He is poor at English.

　　Shokuji-no-yôi-ga-dekimashita.（食事の用意ができました。）Dinner is ready.

　　Kono ie wa renga-de-dekite-iru.（この家はレンガで出来ている。）This house is made of brick.

　　Koko-dewa ringo wa deki-nai.（ここではりんごは出来ない。）Apples do not grow here.

dekiru-dake〈できるだけ〉as...as one can, as...as possible.
   dekiru-dake-hayaku〈できるだけ早く〉as soon as one can
   dekiru-dake-ooku〈できるだけ多く〉as much as possible
dekireba〈できれば〉if possible, if one can.
dekishi〈できし：でき死〉death from drowning.
   dekishi-tai〈でき死体〉a drowned body
dekishi-suru〈でき死する〉be drowned, drown.
deki-tate〈できたて：出来たて〉
deki-tate-no〈出来たての〉newly-made, bran(d)-new, fresh.
   deki-tate-no kêki〈出来たてのケーキ〉cake hot from the oven
dekki〈デッキ〉the deck, the platform.
dekoboko〈でこぼこ：凸凹〉
   dekoboko-michi〈凸凹道〉a rough road
dekoboko-no〈凸凹の〉uneven, rough, rugged, bumpy.
dekorêshon-kêki〈デコレーションケーキ〉a fancy cake.
de-kuwasu〈でくわす：出くわす〉*see.* de-au.
dema〈デマ〉a false rumor.
   dema-o-tobasu〈デマを飛ばす〉start a false rumor
de-mado〈でまど：出窓〉a bay window.
demae〈でまえ：出前〉outside catering, dishes to order.
   demae o suru〈出前をする〉do outside catering
   chûshoku-no-demae-o-tanomu〈昼食の出前を頼む〉order lunch delivered to one's house
de-makase〈でまかせ：出任せ〉
de-makase-o-iu〈出任せを言う〉talk at random.
demawaru〈でまわる：出回る〉appear on the market.
   Nashi ga demawatte-iru.（なしが出回っている。）The pear is in season.
dembun〈でんぶん：電文〉a telegraphic message, a telegram.
Demmâku〈デンマーク〉Denmark.
   Demmâku-jin〈デンマーク人〉a Dane
   Demmâku-go〈デンマーク語〉Danish
   Demmâku(-jin)-no〈デンマーク(人)の〉Danish
demo〈デモ〉a demonstration.
   demo-kôshin〈デモ行進〉a demonstration parade
   demo-tai〈デモ隊〉demonstrators
demo-o-yaru〈デモをやる〉demonstrate ((against)), hold a demonstration.
(-)demo〈(-)でも〉even; any; even if, even though, though; whether...

or, either... or; and, also, as well; but.

   ima-demo（今でも）even now

   kodomo-demo（子供でも）even a child

   Itsu-demo kinasai.（いつでも来なさい。）Come any time you like.

   ame-demo（雨でも）even if it rains

   iya-demo-ô-demo（いやでも応でも）whether you like it or not

   donna muzukashii shigoto-demo（どんな難しい仕事でも）however hard the work may be

   Dochira-demo ii.（どちらでもいい。）Either will do.

   Kare-wa isha-de-ari ongaku-ka-demo-aru.（彼は医者であり音楽家でもある。）He is a doctor and musician.

   Demo watashi-wa sô-omowa-nai.（でも私はそう思わない。）But I don't think so.

dempa〈でんぱ：電波〉an electric wave.

dempa〈でんぱ：伝ぱ〉propagation, spread.

 dempa-suru〈伝ぱする〉propagate, be propagated, spread.

dempô〈でんぽう：電報〉a telegram, a wire.

   dempô-ryô（電報料）a telegram fee

   angô-dempô（暗号電報）a code telegram

 dempô-o-utsu〈電報を打つ〉send a telegram, telegraph, wire, cable.

dempun〈でんぷん：でん粉〉starch.

 dempun-shitsu-no〈でん粉質の〉starchy.

dempyô〈でんぴょう：伝票〉a chit, a slip.

   dempyô o kiru（伝票を切る）give a chit, issue a slip

demukae〈でむかえ：出迎え〉meeting, reception.

 demukae-o-ukeru〈出迎えを受ける〉be met.

 de-mukaeru〈出迎える〉meet, greet.

de-nakereba〈でなければ：出直す〉otherwise, or, else.

de-naosu〈でなおす：出直す〉call again, make a fresh start.

den·atsu〈でんあつ：電圧〉voltage.

   Den·atsu ga takai.（電圧が高い。）The voltage is high.

   den·atsu-kei（電圧計）a voltmeter

denchi〈でんち：電池〉an electric cell, a battery.

   denchi o jûden-suru（電池を充電する）charge a battery

denchû〈でんちゅう：電柱〉a pole, a telephone pole.

dendô〈でんどう：伝道〉missionary work.

   dendô-shi（伝道師）a missionary

 dendô-suru〈伝道する〉preach.

dendô〈でんどう：伝導〉conduction, transmission.

    dendô-tai（伝導体）a conductor

  dendô-suru〈伝導する〉conduct, transmit.

dendô〈でんどう：殿堂〉a palace, a shrine, a temple.

    gakumon no dendô（学問の殿堂）a sanctuary of learning

dendô-ki〈でんどうき：電動機〉an electromotor.

den·en〈でんえん：田園〉the country, rural districts.

    den·en-seikatsu（田園生活）a country(or rural) life

    den·en-toshi（田園都市）a rural(or garden) city

  den·en-no〈田園の〉rural.

dengen〈でんげん：電源〉a power supply; a power source.

    dengen o kiru（電源を切る）cut the power supply

    dengen-kaihatsu（電源開発）development of power resources

dengon〈でんごん：伝言〉a message.

    dengon-ban（伝言板）a message board

denguri-gaeru〈でんぐりがえる：でんぐり返る〉turn a somersault, turn head over heels.

denjishaku〈でんじしゃく：電磁石〉an electromagnet.

denju〈でんじゅ：伝授〉initiation, instruction.

  denju-suru〈伝授する〉initiate, instruct.

    hiketsu-o-denju-suru（秘けつを伝授する）initiate ((a person)) into the secrets ((of))

denka〈でんか：殿下〉Your Highness, His Highness, Her Highness.

denka〈でんか：電化〉electrification.

    tetsudô no denka（鉄道の電化）electrification of railways

  denka-suru〈電化する〉electrify.

denki〈でんき：電気〉electricity, an electric light.

    denki o tsukeru（電気を付ける）turn(switch or put) on the electric light

    denki o kesu（電気を消す）turn(switch or put) off the electric light

    denki-kigu or denki-seihin（電気器具, 電気製品）an electric appliance

    denki-ryôkin（電気料金）electric charges

  denki-no〈電気の〉electric(al).

denki〈でんき：伝記〉a life (story), a biography.

denkô〈でんこう：電光〉electric light, lightning.

    denkô-nyûsu（電光ニュース）an electric news tape

denkyoku〈でんきょく：電極〉an electrode.

denkyû〈でんきゅう：電球〉an electric bulb.

dennetsu-ki〈でんねつき：電熱器〉an electric heater, an electric hot plate.

denrai〈でんらい：伝来〉transmission, introduction.

denrai-suru〈伝来する〉be transmitted, be introduced.

denrai-no〈伝来の〉ancestral, traditional, imported.

　senzo-denrai-no takara（先祖伝来の宝）one's family treasure

denrei〈でんれい：伝令〉an official message; an orderly.

denri-sô〈でんりそう：電離層〉the ionosphere.

denryoku〈でんりょく：電力〉electric power.

　denryoku-jijô（電力事情）the electric power condition

denryû〈でんりゅう：電流〉an electric current.

　denryû o kiru（電流を切る）turn off the current

densanki〈でんさんき：電算機〉an abbreviation of 'denshi-keisan-ki'.

densen〈でんせん：電線〉an electric wire, a telephone line.

　kaitei-densen（海底電線）a submarine cable

densen〈でんせん：伝染〉contagion, infection.

　kûki-densen（空気伝染）airborne infection

densen-suru〈伝染する〉be contagious, be infectious, be catching, infect, be infected ((with)).

densen-sei(-no)〈伝染性(の)〉contagious, infectious, catching, epidemic.

densen〈でんせん：伝線〉

　densen-shita kutsu-shita（伝線した靴下）laddered stockings

densen-byô〈でんせんびょう：伝染病〉a contagious(*or* an infectious) disease, an epidemic.

　densen-byô-kanja（伝染病患者）an infectious case

densetsu〈でんせつ：伝説〉a legend, a tradition.

densetsu-no or *densetsu-teki(-na)*〈伝説の，伝説的(な)〉legendary, traditional.

densha〈でんしゃ：電車〉an electric train, a train, a streetcar, a trolley (car), a tram(-car).

　densha-de iku（電車で行く）go by train

　densha ni noru（電車に乗る）get on a train, take a train

　densha o oriru（電車を降りる）get off a train

　densha-chin（電車賃）carfare

denshi〈でんし：電子〉an electron.

　denshi-keisan-ki（電子計算機）an electronic computer

　denshi-kembikyô（電子顕微鏡）an electron microscope

denshi-kôgaku〔電子工学〕 electronics

denshi-zunô〔電子頭脳〕 an electronic brain

denshin〈でんしん：電信〉telegraph, a wire, a cable.

denshin-gawase〔電信為替〕a telegraphic transfer

densho-bato〈でんしょばと：伝書ばと〉a carrier pigeon.

densô〈でんそう：電送〉

densô-shashin〔電送写真〕telephoto service; a telephotograph, a radiophotograph

densô-suru〈電送する〉send ((a photograph)) over the wires, radio〔a photograph〕.

dentatsu〈でんたつ：伝達〉

dentatsu-suru〈伝達する〉transmit, communicate.

dentô〈でんとう：電灯〉an electric light.

dentô o tsukeru〔電灯を付ける〕 switch on the (electric) light

dentô o kesu〔電灯を消す〕 switch off the (electric) light

dentô〈でんとう：伝統〉tradition, convention.

dentô-teki(-na)〈伝統的(な)〉traditional, conventional.

denwa〈でんわ：電話〉a telephone.

denwa o kakeru〔電話を掛ける〕 telephone, phone, ring up, call ((a person)) up

denwa de yobi-dasu〔電話で呼び出す〕 call ((a person)) on the telephone

denwa ni deru〔電話に出る〕 answer the telephone

denwa-de hanasu〔電話で話す〕 talk with ((a person)) over the telephone

denwa-o-kiru〔電話を切る〕 ring off

Nakata-san-kara denwa-desu.〔中田さんから電話です。〕 A call for you from Mr. Nakata.

Anata-ni denwa-desu.〔あなたに電話です。〕 A phone for you.

denwa-ni-dete-iru〔電話に出ている〕 be on the phone

Ato-de denwa-shimasu.〔後で電話します。〕 I'll call you back.

Chotto denwa-o-o-kari-shitai-no-desu-ga.〔ちょっと電話をお借りしたいのですが。〕 May I use your phone a minute?

Denwa-o-kira-nai-de o-machi-kudasai.〔電話を切らないでお待ちください。〕 Hold the line, please.

denwa-bangô〔電話番号〕a telephone number

denwa-bokkusu〔電話ボックス〕a telephone booth, a kiosk, a telephone box

denwa-chô〈電話帳〉 a telephone directory
denwa-kôkan-shu〈電話交換手〉 a telephone operator
denwa-kyoku〈電話局〉 a telephone office
denwa-ryôkin〈電話料金〉 telephone charges
kokusai-denwa〈国際電話〉 international telephone service
shinai-denwa〈市内電話〉 a local call

depâto〈デパート〉a department store.

derikêto〈デリケート〉
derikêto-na〈デリケートな〉delicate, subtle, sensitive.

deru〈でる：出る〉go out, come out, get out; appear, come out; attend; start, leave, set out; leave, graduate; join, take part ((in)).
sampo-ni-deru〈散歩に出る〉 go out for a walk
heya-kara-deru〈部屋から出る〉 go out of a room
butai-e deru〈舞台へ出る〉 appear on the stage
Tsuki ga kumo-ma-kara deta.〈月が雲間から出た。〉 The moon came out from behind the clouds.
pâtî ni deru〈パーティーに出る〉 attend a party
tabi-ni deru〈旅に出る〉 set out on a journey
daigaku-o-deru〈大学を出る〉 graduate from a university
shiai-ni-deru〈試合に出る〉 take part in a game

desaki〈でさき：出先〉the place where one has gone.
desaki-kikan〈出先機関〉 local agencies of the central government

deshabari〈でしゃばり：出しゃばり〉intrusion; an intruder, a forward person.
deshabaru〈出しゃばる〉intrude, be forward, poke one's nose ((into)).

deshi〈でし：弟子〉a pupil, a follower, an apprentice.
mana-deshi〈まな弟子〉 one's favorite pupil

-deshô〈-でしょう〉*see.* -darô.

de-sorou〈でそろう：出そろう〉come out fully, be all present.

dessan〈デッサン〉a (rough) sketch.

de-sugiru〈ですぎる：出過ぎる〉be impudent; be too strong.
O-cha ga de-sugita.〈お茶が出過ぎた。〉 The tea is too strong.
de-sugita〈出過ぎた〉uncalled-for, obtrusive.

detarame〈でたらめ：出たら目〉a wild talk, nonsense.
Kare-no-iu-koto wa subete detarame-da.〈彼の言うことはすべてでたらめだ。〉 What he says is all nonsense.
detarame-na〈でたらめな〉random, unreliable.
detarame-na henji〈でたらめな返事〉 a random answer

　　　detarame-na hanashi〈でたらめな話〉a tall story

　　detarame-ni〈でたらめに〉at random.

detchi-age〈でっちあげ：でっち上げ〉a fabrication, a concoction, a frame-up.

　　detchi-age-no〈でっち上げの〉made-up, put-up.

　　detchi-ageru〈でっち上げる〉fabricate, concoct, make up.

dêto〈デート〉a date.

　　dêto-suru〈デートする〉date (with), have a date ((with)).

dewa〈では〉then, well, now.

　　　Dewa, mata ashita.（ではまたあした.）Well, see you again tomorrow.

-dewa〈-では〉

　　　Kyûshû-dewa（九州では）in Kyushu

　　　Nihon-go-dewa（日本語では）in Japanese

　　　watashi-no-hô-dewa（私の方では）as for me

　　　watashi-no tokei-dewa（私の時計では）by my watch

　　　watashi-no-shitte-iru-kagiri-dewa（私の知っている限りでは）so far as I know

　　　kono sora-moyô-dewa（この空模様では）(judging) from the look of the sky

　　　kono-bun-dewa（この分では）if things go on at this rate

do〈ど：度〉a time; a degree; an extent, a limit.

　　　ichi-do（一度）once

　　　ni-do（二度）twice

　　　san-do（三度）three times

　　　sesshi jû-go-do（摂氏十五度）fifteen degrees centigrade

　　　hokui-go-jû-ichi-do-ni（北緯五十一度に）in latitude 51°N

　　　san-jû-do no kaku（三十度の角）an angle of 30 degrees

　　　ni-jû-do no megane（二十度の眼鏡）spectacles of 20 degrees

　　do-o-sugosu〈度を過ごす〉go to excess, go too far.

dô〈どう：銅〉copper.

　　　dô-ka（銅貨）a copper (coin)

dô〈どう：胴〉the trunk, the body; the frame.

dô〈どう〉how, what.

　　　Kyô-wa dô-desu-ka?（今日はどうですか.）How are you today?

　　　Soko-e　itte-mite-wa-dô-desu-ka?（そこへ行ってみてはどうですか.）How about going there?

　　　Ano　shibai wa　dô-deshita-ka?（あの芝居はどうでしたか.）How did

you like the play?

Kono jisho o dô-omoimasu-ka? (この辞書をどう思いますか.) What do you think of this dictionary?

Dô-shitara-ii-ka wakara-nai. (どうしたらいいか分からない.) I don't know what to do.

Dô-shitara-ii-darô? (どうしたらいいだろう.) What shall I do?

Kare wa dô-shimashita? (彼はどうしました.) What has become of him?

Ano tokei wa dô-shimashita? (あの時計はどうしました.) What have you done with that watch?

Dô-shimashita. (どうしました.) What's the matter with you?

Dô-itashimashite. (どういたしまして.) You are welcome. / Not at all.

dô-mitemo (どう見ても) to all appearances, in every respect

dô-〈どう-：同-〉the same.

dôjitsu (同日) (on) the same day

dô-age〈どうあげ：胴上げ〉

dô-age-suru〈胴上げする〉carry ((a person)) shoulder-high, toss ((a person)).

dôban〈どうばん：銅板〉a copperplate.

dobei〈どべい：土塀〉a mud wall.

dobin〈どびん：土瓶〉an earthen teapot.

doboku〈どぼく：土木〉civil engineering.

doboku-gishi (土木技師) a civil engineer

doboku-kôji (土木工事) engineering works

dobu〈どぶ〉a ditch.

dobu-mizu (どぶ水) ditch water

dôbun〈どうぶん：同文〉an identical text.

Ika-dôbun. (以下同文.) The following sentences are the same as above.

dôbutsu〈どうぶつ：動物〉an animal.

dôbutsu-kai (動物界) the animal kingdom

dôbutsu-en (動物園) a zoo

dôbutsu-gaku (動物学) zoology

dôbutsu-gaku-sha (動物学者) a zoologist

dochaku〈どちゃく：土着〉

dochaku-no〈土着の〉native.

dochaku-no-hito (土着の人) a native

dochira 〈どちら〉 which, whichever, where, who.

Dochira-ga anata-no kasa desu-ka?（どちらがあなたの傘ですか。） Which is your umbrella?

Bîru to wain to dochira-ga suki-desu-ka?（ビールとワインとどちらが好きですか。） Which do you like better, beer or wine?

Dochira-demo hoshii-hô o tori-nasai.（どちらでも欲しい方を取りなさい。） Take whichever you like.

Dochira-demo yoroshii.（どちらでもよろしい。） Either will do.

Dochira-ni o-sumai-desu-ka?（どちらにお住まいですか。） Where do you live?

Dochira-sama-desu-ka?（どちら様ですか。） Who shall I say?

dochira-ka 〈どちらか〉 either...or.

anata-ka watashi-ka-dochira-ka（あなたか私かどちらか） either you or I

dochira-ka-to-iu-to 〈どちらかというと〉 rather.

Kare-wa dochira-ka-to-iu-to e-ga-umai-hô-da.（彼はどちらかというと絵がうまい方だ。） He is rather good at painting.

dochira-mo 〈どちらも〉 both (and), neither (nor).

Dochira-mo-suki-desu.（どちらも好きです。） I like both of them.

Dochira-mo-suki-dewa-ari-masen.（どちらも好きではありません。） I like neither of them.

Chichi-mo-watashi-mo dochira-mo genki-desu.（父も私もどちらも元気です。） Both father and I are well.

Watashi-wa pen-mo-empitsu-mo dochira-mo mochi-awasete-i-nai.（私はペンも鉛筆もどちらも持ち合わせていない。） I have neither a pen nor a pencil with me.

Watashi-wa tabako-mo-sake-mo dochira-mo yara-nai.（私はたばこも酒もどちらもやらない。） I neither smoke nor drink.

dochira-ni-shite-mo 〈どちらにしても〉 in either case, anyhow.

dodai 〈どだい：土台〉 a foundation, groundwork, a base.

dodai o sueru（土台を据える） lay the foundation ((of))

dô-demo 〈どうでも〉

dô-demo-ii 〈どうでもいい〉 do not matter, don't care (at all) ((for)), never mind, make no difference ((to)).

dô-demo-ii-koto（どうでもいい事） a matter of no importance, an immaterial thing

dô-demo-suki-na-yô-ni 〈どうでも好きなように〉 as you please.

dôdô 〈どうどう：堂々〉

dôdô-taru 〈堂々たる〉 stately, grand, dignified.

  dôdô-taru teitaku 〈堂々たる邸宅〉 a stately mansion

  dôdô-taru fûsai 〈堂々たる風さい〉 a dignified appearance

dôdô-to 〈堂々と〉 in grand style, in a dignified manner.

dôfû 〈どうふう：同封〉

dôfû-suru 〈同封する〉 enclose.

dôfû-no 〈同封の〉 enclosed.

dôga 〈どうが：動画〉 an animation.

dogaishi 〈どがいし：度外視〉

dogaishi-suru 〈度外視する〉 leave ((a matter)) out of consideration.

dôgi 〈どうぎ：動議〉 a motion.

dôgi-o-teishutsu-suru 〈動議を提出する〉 make a motion, move ((that)).

dôgi 〈どうぎ：道義〉 morality.

  dôgi-shin 〈道義心〉 moral sense

dôgi-go 〈どうぎご：同義語〉 *see.* dôi-go.

dogimagi 〈どぎまぎ〉

dogimagi-suru 〈どぎまぎする〉 be flurried, be bewildered, be disconcerted, fall into a flutter.

dogimagi-shite 〈どぎまぎして〉 in confusion, in a flurry, in a flutter.

dogimo 〈どぎも：度ぎも〉

dogimo-o-nuku 〈度ぎもを抜く〉 strike ((a person)) out of his wits, strike ((a person)) dumb, take ((a person)) aback.

dogimo-o-nukareru 〈度ぎもを抜かれる〉 be frightened out of one's senses, be taken aback.

dôgu 〈どうぐ：道具〉 an instrument, a utensil, a tool.

  daiku-dôgu 〈大工道具〉 a carpenter's tools

dôgyô 〈どうぎょう：同業〉

  dôgyô-kumiai 〈同業組合〉 a trade association

  dôgyô-sha 〈同業者〉 the profession, the trade; a fellow trader, a person of the same business

dôhai 〈どうはい：同輩〉 one's equal, a colleague.

dôhan 〈どうはん：同伴〉 company.

  dôhan-sha 〈同伴者〉 a companion

dôhan-suru 〈同伴する〉 accompany, go in company ((with)).

dôhan-de 〈同伴で〉 in company ((with)).

dohyô 〈どひょう：土俵〉 the (*sumo* wrestling) ring.

dôi 〈どうい：同意〉 agreement, consent.

  dôi o uru 〈同意を得る〉 obtain ((a person's)) consent

dôi-suru〈同意する〉agree ((to *or* with)), consent ((to)).

   teian-ni dôi-suru〈提案に同意する〉consent to ((a person's)) proposal

dôi-go〈どうご：同意語〉a synonym.

dôin〈どういん：動員〉mobilization.

dôin-suru〈動員する〉mobilize, call out.

   Ooku-no keikan ga dôin-sareta.（多くの警官が動員された.）Many policemen were called out.

   ichi-man-nin-no kankyaku o dôin-suru（一万人の観客を動員する）draw 10,000 audience

Doitsu〈ドイツ〉Germany.

   Higashi-Doitsu（東ドイツ）East Germany

   Nishi-Doitsu（西ドイツ）West Germany

   Doitsu-jin（ドイツ人）a German

   Doitsu-go（ドイツ語）German

   Doitsu(-jin)-no（ドイツ(人)の）German

dôitsu〈どういつ：同一〉

   dôitsu-jimbutsu（同一人物）one and the same person

dôitsu-no〈同一の〉the same, identical.

dô-iu〈どういう〉what kind of, what.

   Dô-iu-kudamono ga ichiban-suki-desu-ka?（どういう果物が一番好きですか.）What kind of fruit do you like best?

   Kare-wa dô-iu-hito-desu-ka?（彼はどういう人ですか.）What is he like?

   Sore wa dô-iu-imi-desu-ka?（それはどういう意味ですか.）What do you mean by that?

doji〈どじ〉

doji-o-fumu〈どじを踏む〉bungle, make a mess of it.

dôji〈どうじ：同時〉the same time.

   dôji-tsûyaku（同時通訳）simultaneous interpretation

dôji-ni〈同時に〉at the same time; at a time; on the other hand.

dôjin〈どうじん：同人〉a literary coterie, a member.

   dôjin-zasshi（同人雑誌）a literary coterie magazine

dôjiru〈どうじる：動じる〉be perturbed, be upset.

   dôji-nai（動じない）remain unperturbed

dôji-yasui〈動じやすい〉(easily) excitable.

dojô〈どじょう〉a loach.

dôjô〈どうじょう：道場〉an exercise hall, a training hall.

   kendôjô（剣道場）a fencing hall

dôjô〈どうじょう：同情〉sympathy.
　dôjô-suru〈同情する〉sympathize ((with)).
　dôjô-shin-no-aru〈同情心のある〉sympathetic, warmhearted.
　　dôjô-shin-no-nai（同情心のない）unsympathetic, coldhearted

dôjô〈どうじょう：同乗〉
　　dôjô-sha（同乗者）a fellow passenger
　dôjô-suru〈同乗する〉ride together.

dôjô〈どうじょう：同上〉the same as (the) above, ditto.

dôka〈どうか〉*see.* dôzo.

(-ka)-dô-ka〈(-か)どうか〉whether, if.
　　Kare-ga komban kuru-ka-dô-ka ayashii-mono-da.（彼が今晩来るかどうか怪しいものだ。）It is doubtful whether he will come tonight.

dokadoka〈どかどか〉
　dokadoka-to heya-ni-hairu〈どかどかと部屋に入る〉troop boisterously into the room.

dôka-kôka〈どうかこうか〉somehow (or other), by some means (or other), with difficulty.

dokan〈どかん〉
　dokan-to〈どかんと〉with a thump, with a bang.

dokan〈どかん：土管〉an earthen pipe.

dôkan〈どうかん：同感〉
　dôkan-de-aru〈同感である〉agree ((to *or* with)), be of the same opinion.

dôka-sen〈どうかせん：導火線〉a fuse; a cause.
　dôka-sen-to-naru〈導火線となる〉give rise ((to)), cause.

dôka-shite〈どうかして〉in some way, by some means.

dôka-suru〈どうかする〉something is the matter ((with)).
　　Kare-wa dôka-shite-iru.（彼はどうかしている。）Something is the matter with him.

dôke-〈どうけ-：道化-〉
　　dôke-shi（道化師）a clown, a buffoon
　　dôke-shibai（道化芝居）a farce

dôkei〈どうけい：同型〉
　dôkei-no〈同型の〉of the same type.

dôkei〈どうけい：同系〉
　　dôkei-gaisha（同系会社）an affiliated company
　dôkei-no〈同系の〉akin, of the same stock.

doken〈どけん：土建〉
　　doken-gyô-sha（土建業者）a civil engineering and building construc-

tor

dôken〈どうけん：同権〉equal rights.

dan-jo-dôken（男女同権）equal rights for both sexes

doki〈どき：土器〉an earthen vessel; earthenware.

dôki〈どうき：銅器〉a copper utensil; copperware.

dôki〈どうき：同期〉the same period; the same class.

dôki-sei（同期生）a classmate, a graduate in the same class

dôki〈どうき：動機〉a motive.

dôki〈どうき：動悸〉beating of the heart, (a) palpitation, throbbing.

dôki-ga-suru〈動悸がする〉beat, palpitate, throb.

dokidoki〈どきどき〉

dokidoki-suru〈どきどきする〉throb.

dokitto〈どきっと〉

dokitto-suru（どきっとする）feel a shock, be startled ((at *or* by))

dokitto-saseru（どきっとさせる）give ((a person)) a shock, startle

dokkai-ryoku〈どっかいりょく：読解力〉reading comprehension.

dokkari *or* **dokka-to**〈どっかり，どっかと〉plump, heavily.

dokka-to isu-ni-koshi-o-orosu（どっかといすに腰を下ろす）plump down into a chair

dokke〈どっけ：毒気〉

dokke-o-nukareru〈毒気を抜かれる〉see. dogimo-o-nukareru.

dokkingu〈ドッキング〉docking.

dokkingu-suru〈ドッキングする〉dock ((with)).

dokkingu-o-toku〈ドッキングを解く〉undock ((from)).

dokkin-hô〈どっきんほう：独禁法〉*see.* dokusen-kinshi-hô.

dokkoi〈どっこい〉

Dokkoi sô-wa-ika-nai!（どっこいそうは行かない．）No, no, that won't do!

dokkoi-sho〈どっこいしょ〉

dokkoi-sho-to ishi o mochi-ageru（どっこいしょと石を持ち上げる）lift a stone with an effort.

dokku〈ドック〉a dock.

dokku-iri-suru（ドック入りする）go into dock

doko〈どこ〉where.

Doko-e iku-tokoro-desu-ka?（どこへ行くところですか．）Where are you going?

Doko-kara kimashita-ka?（どこから来ましたか．）Where did you come from?

doko-ka〈どこか〉 somewhere, anywhere.

　doko-ka sono-atari-ni（どこかその辺りに）　somewhere about there

　Kinô-no　ban　doko-ka-e　ikimashita-ka?（昨日の晩どこかへ行きましたか。）　Did you go anywhere last night?

doko(-de)-demo〈どこ(で)でも〉 anywhere, everywhere, wherever.

　Doko-de-demo　sore-ra　wa　kaemasu.（どこででもそれらは買えます。）　You can get them anywhere.

　anata-gata-ga　iku-tokoro-nara　doko-demo（あなた方が行く所ならどこでも）　wherever you go

doko-e-mo or *doko-ni-mo* ～*(-nai)*〈どこへも，どこにも～(ない)〉 nowhere.

　Doko-ni-mo sore-o mitsukeru-koto-ga-deki-nakatta.（どこにもそれをみつけることができなかった。）　It was to be found nowhere.

doko-made〈どこまで〉 how far.

　Kare-no hanashi wa doko-made hontô-nan-darô?（彼の話はどこまで本当なんだろう。）　How far is his story true?

doko-made-mo〈どこまでも〉 to the end, persistently.

　doko-made-mo hantai-suru（どこまでも反対する）　oppose stubbornly

doko-kara-mitemo〈どこから見ても〉 in every respect.

dôkô〈どうこう：どう孔〉 the pupil.

dôkô〈どうこう：動向〉 a tendency, a trend.

　seron no dôkô（世論の動向）　the trend of public opinion

dôkô〈どうこう：同好〉 the same taste.

　dôkô no shi（同好の士）　persons of the similar tastes

dôkô〈どうこう：同行〉

　dôkô-hachi-nin（同行八人）　a party of eight

　dôkô-sha（同行者）　a companion, a fellow traveler

dôkô-suru〈同行する〉 go (along) with, accompany, travel together.

-dokoro-ka〈－どころか〉 far from; not to speak of, to say nothing of.

　Kanojo-wa kenkô-dokoro-ka.（彼女は健康どころか。）　She is far from healthy.

　Kare-wa Supein-go-dokoro-ka Eigo-mo-shira-nai.（彼はスペイン語どころか英語も知らない。）　He knows no English, to say nothing of Spanish.

sore-dokoro-ka〈それどころか〉 on the contrary.

doko-soko〈どこそこ〉 such and such a place.

doku〈どく：毒〉 poison.

doku-no-aru〈毒のある〉 poisonous.

doku〈どく〉 get out of the way, step aside.

Doite-kudasai!〈どいてください.〉 Get out of my way!

dokubō〈どくぼう：独房〉a solitary cell.

dokudan〈どくだん：独断〉

dokudan-de〈独断で〉on one's own authority(judgment *or* responsibility).

dokudoku〈どくどく〉

dokudoku-nagareru〈どくどく流れる〉flow profusely, gush out ((of)).

dokudoku-shii〈どくどくしい：毒々しい〉heavy, gross, gaudy.

dokudoku-shii iro（毒々しい色） a gaudy color

dokuen-kai〈どくえんかい：独演会〉a solo recital, a one-man show.

dokuga〈どくが：毒が〉

dokuga-ni-kakaru〈毒がに掛かる〉fall a victim ((to)).

dokugaku〈どくがく：独学〉self-education.

dokugaku-suru〈独学する〉study by oneself, teach oneself.

dokugaku-no〈独学の〉self-educated.

dokugaku-no hito（独学の人） a self-educated person

doku-gasu〈どくガス：毒ガス〉poison gas.

doku-gasu-de-yarareru〈毒ガスでやられる〉be gassed.

doku-hebi〈どくへび：毒蛇〉a venomous serpent, a poisonous snake.

dokuja〈どくじゃ：毒蛇〉*see.* doku-hebi.

dokuji〈どくじ：独自〉

dokuji-no〈独自の〉original, of one's own, personal, individual.

dokuji-no kenkai（独自の見解） one's personal views

dokuji-no-kôdô-o-toru（独自の行動をとる） go one's own way

doku-mushi〈どくむし：毒虫〉a poisonous insect.

dokuritsu〈どくりつ：独立〉independence.

dokuritsu o sengen-suru（独立を宣言する） declare independence

dokuritsu-koku（独立国） an independent nation

dokuritsu-shin（独立心） a spirit of independence

dokuritsu-suru〈独立する〉become independent.

dokuritsu-no〈独立の〉independent.

dokuryoku〈どくりょく：独力〉

dokuryoku-de〈独力で〉single-handed, by one's own efforts.

nani-mo-kamo dokuryoku-de yaru（何もかも独力でやる） do everything single-handed

dokusai〈どくさい：独裁〉dictatorship.

dokusai-sha（独裁者） a dictator

dokusai-teki(-na)〈独裁的(な)〉dictatorial.

dokusai-teki-ni〈独裁的に〉dictatorially.

dokusatsu〈どくさつ：毒殺〉

dokusatsu-suru〈毒殺する〉kill by poison.

dokusen〈どくせん：独占〉exclusive possession, (a) monopoly.

dokusen-ken（独占権）a monopoly

dokusen-kinshi-hô（独占禁止法）the Anti-monopoly Law

dokusen-suru〈独占する〉monopolize.

dokusen-teki(-na)〈独占的(な)〉monopolistic.

dokusha〈どくしゃ：読者〉a reader, a subscriber.

dokusha-ran（読者欄）the readers' column

dokushin〈どくしん：独身〉bachelorhood, spinsterhood.

dokushin-sha（独身者）an unmarried person; a single man, a bachelor; a single woman, a spinster

dokushin-no〈独身の〉unmarried, single.

dokushin-de kurasu（独身で暮らす）live single

dokusho〈どくしょ：読書〉reading.

dokusho-ka（読書家）a great reader

dokusho-suru〈読書する〉read.

dokushô〈どくしょう：独唱〉a (vocal) solo.

dokushô-kai（独唱会）a (vocal) recital

dokushô-suru〈独唱する〉sing (a) solo.

dokushû〈どくしゅう：独習〉self-study, self-teaching.

dokushû-sho（独習書）a teach-yourself book; a pony, a crib

dokushû-suru〈独習する〉teach oneself, study by oneself.

dokuso〈どくそ：毒素〉a toxin.

dokusô〈どくそう：独奏〉a solo.

dokusô-sha（独奏者）a soloist

dokusô-kai（独奏会）a recital

dokusô-suru〈独奏する〉play a solo.

dokusô(-ryoku)〈どくそう(りょく)：独創(力)〉originality.

dokusô-teki(-na)〈独創的(な)〉original, creative.

dokutoku〈どくとく：独特〉

dokutoku-no〈独特の〉peculiar, special, of one's own.

Nihon-dokutoku-no shûkan（日本独特の習慣）a custom peculiar to Japan

kanojo-dokutoku-no-yari-kata-de（彼女独特のやり方で）in her own way

dôkutsu〈どうくつ：洞くつ〉a cave, a cavern.

dokuyaku 〈どくやく：毒薬〉 a poisonous medicine, poison.

dokuzen(-shugi) 〈どくぜん（しゅぎ）：独善(主義)〉 self-righteousness.

   dokuzen-teki(-na) 〈独善的(な)〉 self-righteous, self-justified.

dokuzetsu 〈どくぜつ：毒舌〉 blistering remarks.

   dokuzetsu-o-abiseru 〈毒舌を浴びせる〉 blister.

doku-zuku 〈どくづく：毒づく〉 curse, call ((a person)) names.

dokyô 〈どきょう：度胸〉 courage, pluck, mettle.

   dokyô-no-aru 〈度胸のある〉 bold, courageous, plucky, mettlesome.

      dokyô-no-nai（度胸のない）timid, cowardly

dôkyo 〈どうきょ：同居〉

      dôkyo-nin（同居人）a lodger; a roomer, a paying guest

   dôkyo-suru 〈同居する〉 live together, live with.

dôkyô 〈どうきょう：同郷〉 the same province.

      dôkyô-jin（同郷人）a person from the same province

dôkyû 〈どうきゅう：同級〉 the same class.

      dôkyû-sei（同級生）a classmate

doma 〈どま：土間〉 an unfloored part 〔of a house〕.

dô-mawari 〈どうまわり：胴回り〉 one's girth.

domburi 〈どんぶり〉 a porcelain bowl.

      domburi-kanjô（どんぶり勘定）collecting and spending money without keeping accounts

dômei 〈どうめい：同盟〉 an alliance, a league, a union, a confederation.

      dômei o musubu（同盟を結ぶ）form an alliance ((with))

      dômei-jôyaku（同盟条約）a treaty of alliance

dô-meishi 〈どうめいし：動名詞〉 a gerund.

dô-mo 〈どうも〉 (very) much, very, quite, really; somehow.

      Dô-mo arigatô.（どうもありがとう。）Thank you very much.

      Dô-mo sumi-masen.（どうもすみません。）I'm very sorry.

      Dô-mo kare wa suka-nai.（どうも彼は好かない。）Somehow I don't like him.

dômô 〈どうもう：どう猛〉

   dômô-na 〈どう猛な〉 fierce, savage.

domoru 〈どもる〉 stammer, stutter.

   domori-nagara 〈どもりながら〉 stammeringly, stutteringly.

dômyaku 〈どうみゃく：動脈〉 an artery.

      dai-dômyaku（大動脈）the main artery

      dômyaku-kôka(-shô)（動脈硬化(症)）hardening of arteries

don 〈どん〉

　　　Yôi, don!〈用意，どん .〉 Ready! *Go!*

　　don-to-butsukaru（どんとぶつかる） bump ((against *or* into))

donabe〈どなべ：土なべ〉an earthen pot.

dô-naga〈どうなが：胴長〉

　dô-naga-no〈胴長の〉long-torsoed.

donari-chirasu〈どなりちらす：怒鳴り散らす〉rant to right and left.

donari-tsukeru〈どなりつける：怒鳴りつける〉storm ((at)).

donaru〈どなる：怒鳴る〉cry, shout, roar, yell.

donata〈どなた〉

　　　Donata-desu-ka?（どなたですか .） What's your name, please? / What
　　　　name shall I say? / May I ask who is speaking, please?

dônatsu〈ドーナツ〉a doughnut.

donchan-sawagi〈どんちゃんさわぎ：どんちゃん騒ぎ〉

　donchan-sawagi-o-yaru〈どんちゃん騒ぎをやる〉drink and make a racket.

dondon（どんどん）rapidly, freely, on and on; loudly.

　　dondon susumu（どんどん進む） advance rapidly

　　dondon kane o tsukau（どんどん金を使う） spend money freely

　　dondon ureru（どんどん売れる） sell like hot cakes

　　dondon taiko o tataku（どんどん太鼓をたたく） beat a drum loudly

　　dondon-to-o-tataku（どんどん戸をたたく） pound on a door

dô-nempai〈どうねんぱい：同年輩〉

　dô-nempai-de-aru〈同年輩である〉be of the same age.

donguri〈どんぐり〉an acorn.

dô-nika〈どうにか〉in some way, somehow, by some means or other.

　dô-nika～(-suru)〈どうにか～(する)〉manage ((to do)).

　　dô-nika-kurashite-iru（どうにか暮らしている） manage to live

dônimo〈どうにも〉((not)) in any way.

　　　Dônimo-shiyô-ga-nai.（どうにも仕様がない .） There is no help for it.

donkaku〈どんかく：鈍角〉an obtuse angle.

donkan〈どんかん：鈍感〉

　donkan-na〈鈍感な〉insensible, dull.

donki〈どんき：鈍器〉a blunt weapon.

donkô(-ressha)〈どんこう（れっしゃ）：鈍行（列車）〉a slow train.

donna〈どんな〉what, what kind of, what...like.

　　　Donna eiga ga suki-desu-ka?（どんな映画が好きですか .） What movie
　　　　do you like?

　　　Kare-wa donna-hito-desu-ka?（彼はどんな人ですか .） What is he like?

　donna～demo〈どんな～でも〉any.

Donna-hito-demo sore wa dekiru.（どんな人でもそれはできる．） Anybody can do it.

Anata-no-tame-nara donna-koto-demo shimasu.（あなたのためならどんなことでもします．） I will do anyting I can for you.

Donna-hito-demo sore wa deki-nai.（どんな人でもそれはできない．） Nobody can do it.

donna-koto-ga-attemo 〈どんなことがあっても〉whatever may happen, in any circumstances.

donna-koto-ga-attemo~nai 〈どんなことがあっても～ない〉on no account.

donna-ni 〈どんなに〉how, how much.

Sore-o kiitara kare-no o-kâ-san wa donna-ni yorokobu-deshô!（それを聞いたら彼のお母さんはどんなに喜ぶでしょう．） How glad his mother will be to hear it!

donna-ni~demo 〈どんなに～でも〉however... , no matter how... .

donna-ni isshô-kemmei-yattemo（どんなに一生懸命やっても） however hard you may work

dono 〈どの〉which, what; any, every, where.

Dono kisetsu ga ichiban-suki-desu-ka?（どの季節が一番好きですか．） Which season do you like best?

Dono michi o itte-mo eki-ni-demasu.（どの道を行っても駅に出ます．） Whichever road you take, you will come to the station.

Dono empitsu-demo hoshii-mono-o tori-nasai.（どの鉛筆でも欲しい物を取りなさい．） Take any pencil you want.

Dono yûkan mo sono jiken o hôdô-shite-iru.（どの夕刊もその事件を報道している．） Every evening paper reports the event.

Hongô-no-dono-hen-ni-o-sumi-desu-ka?（本郷のどの辺にお住みですか．） Where do you live in Hongô? / In what part of Hongo do you live?

dono~-mo-nai 〈どの～もない〉none.

Dono mondai mo toke-nakatta.（どの問題も解けなかった．） I could solve none of the problems.

-dono 〈-どの：-殿〉 *see.* -sama.

donô 〈どのう：土のう〉a sandbag.

dono-kurai 〈どのくらい：どの位〉how far, how long, how soon, how many, how much, how high, how large, how wide, how thick, how many times, how often.

Koko-kara eki-made dono-kurai-arimasu-ka?（ここから駅までどのくらいありますか．） How far is it from here to the station?

Kono tsuri-bashi-no-nagasa wa dono-kurai-arimasu-ka?〈この釣り橋の長さはどのくらいありますか。〉 How long is this suspension bridge?

Dono-kurai Eigo o naratte-oraremasu-ka?〈どのくらい英語を習っておられますか。〉 How long have you been studying English?

Kono hako-no-naka-ni dono-kurai ringo ga arimasu-ka?〈この箱の中にどのくらいりんごがありますか。〉 How many apples are there in this box?

Dono-kurai o-kane-ga-irimasu-ka?〈どのくらいお金が要りますか。〉 How much money do you want?

Ano sentô wa dono-kurai-takasa-ga-arimasu-ka?〈あのせん塔はどのくらい高さがありますか。〉 How high is that steeple?

Shinchô wa dono-kurai-arimasu-ka?〈身長はどのくらいありますか。〉 How tall are you?

Hito-tsuki-ni dono-kurai o-kâ-san-ni tegami-o-kakimasu-ka?〈一月にどのくらいお母さんに手紙を書きますか。〉 How many times do you write to your mother in a month?

dono-michi〈どのみち：どの道〉anyhow, anyway, in any case, at any rate, sooner or later.

dono-yô-ni〈どのように〉how, in what manner.

donten〈どんてん：曇天〉cloudy weather.

dontsû〈どんつう：鈍痛〉a dull pain.

don·yoku〈どんよく：どん欲〉avarice, greed.
 don·yoku-na〈どん欲な〉avaricious, greedy.

don·yori〈どんより〉
 don·yori-to-shita〈どんよりとした〉leaden, dull.
  don·yori-to-shita sora〈どんよりとした空〉a leaden sky

dônyû〈どうにゅう：導入〉introduction.
  gaishi-dônyû〈外資導入〉introduction of foreign capital
 dônyû-suru〈導入する〉introduce.

donzoko〈どんぞこ：どん底〉the bottom, the depths.
  bimbô no donzoko-ni-iru〈貧乏のどん底にいる〉be in the depths of poverty

dôon〈どうおん：同音〉homophony.
  dôon-igi-go〈同音異義語〉a homonym

-doori(-ni)〈-どおり(に)〉as, according to, in accordance with.
  yakusoku-doori-ni〈約束どおりに〉according to one's promise
  jikan-doori-ni〈時間どおりに〉on time, punctually

-dooshi〈-どおし：-通し〉all through, throughout.

yo-dooshi〈夜通し〉all the night through, all night (long), throughout the night

yo-dooshi okite-iru〈夜通し起きている〉sit up all night

tachi-dooshi-de-iru〈立ち通している〉keep standing all the time

Nagoya-made tachi-dooshi-datta.（名古屋まで立ち通しだった。）I was kept standing all the way to Nagoya

dora〈どら〉a gong.

doraibu〈ドライブ〉a drive.

doraibu-ni-iku〈ドライブに行く〉go for a drive

dôraku〈どうらく：道楽〉a hobby, a pastime, a pleasure; dissipation.

dôraku-ni e o kaku（道楽に絵をかく）draw pictures for pleasure

dôraku-mono（道楽者）a libertine

dôraku-suru〈道楽する〉lead a dissipated life.

dorama〈ドラマ〉a drama, a play.

doramu-kan〈ドラムかん：ドラム缶〉a drum.

dôran〈どうらん：動乱〉an upheaval, disturbance, a riot.

dôran o okosu（動乱を起こす）cause a riot

dôran〈ドーラン〉grease paint.

dore〈どれ〉which.

Dore-ga ichiban suki-desu-ka?（どれが一番好きですか。）Which do you like best?

dore-demo〈どれでも〉any, whichever.

Dore-demo suki-na mono o tori-nasai.（どれでも好きな物を取りなさい。）Take any one you like. / Take whichever you like.

dore-hodo〈どれほど〉how many, how much.

dore-ka〈どれか〉any, either, some.

dore-mo〈どれも〉all, every, any.

Dore-mo hoshiku-nai.（どれも欲しくない。）I don't want any of them.

dorei〈どれい：奴隷〉a slave.

doremifa〈ドレミファ〉the musical scale: do, re, mi, fa, sol, la, and si.

dôri〈どうり：道理〉reason.

mono-no-dôri ga wakaru（物の道理が分かる）see reason

dôri-ni-kanatta or *dôri-no-aru*〈道理にかなった，道理のある〉reasonable.

doro〈どろ：泥〉mud.

doro-darake-ni-naru（泥だらけになる）be covered with mud

doro-mizu（泥水）muddy water

dronko-michi（泥んこ道）a muddy road

doro-darake-no,   *doro-mamire-no*   or   *doronko-no*〈泥だらけの，泥まみれの，泥んこの〉muddy.

dôro〈どうろ：道路〉a road, a way, a street.
     dôro-hyôshiki（道路標識）a road sign
     dôro-kôji（道路工事）road repairing

dorobô〈どろぼう：泥棒〉theft; a thief, a robber, a burglar.
     dorobô-ni-hairu（泥棒に入る）break into a house

dorodoro〈どろどろ〉
     dorodoro-no sûpu（どろどろのスープ）thick soup
     dorodoro-ni-naru（どろどろになる）become muddy; be reduced to jelly

doro-jiai〈どろじあい：泥試合〉
     doro-jiai-o-enjiru〈泥試合を演じる〉sling mud at each other.

doro-kusai〈どろくさい：泥臭い〉with a muddy odor; unrefined, uncouth.

doronko〈どろんこ：泥んこ〉
     doronko-asobi-o-suru〈泥んこ遊びをする〉play with mud, make mud pies.

doro-numa〈どろぬま：泥沼〉
     doro-numa-ni-ochi-komu   or   *doro-numa-ni-hamari-komu*〈泥沼に落ち込む，泥沼にはまり込む〉bog, be bogged (down), mire oneself.

doru〈ドル〉a dollar.
     doru-bako（ドル箱）a gold mine, a money-maker

dôrui-kô〈どうるいこう：同類項〉a similar term.

doryô〈どりょう：度量〉generocity.
     doryô-no-hiroi〈度量の広い〉generous, broad-minded.
     doryô-no-semai（度量の狭い）narrow-minded

dôryô〈どうりょう：同僚〉a colleague, an associate, a co-worker, a *confrère*.

doryôkô〈どりょうこう：度量衡〉weights and measures.

doryoku〈どりょく：努力〉(an) effort, an endeavor.
     doryoku no kesshô（努力の結晶）the fruit of one's efforts
     doryoku-ka（努力家）a hard worker, a man of industry
     doryoku-suru〈努力する〉make efforts, endeavor, strive.

dôryoku〈どうりょく：動力〉(motive) power.

dôsa〈どうさ：動作〉action, motion, movement.
     dôsa-ga-kamman-de-aru（動作が緩慢である）be slow in movement

dosakusa〈どさくさ〉
     dosakusa-ni-magirete〈どさくさに紛れて〉in the confusion, taking advan-

tage of the confusion.

dosa-mawari〈どさまわり：どさ回り〉
　　dosa-mawari-o-yaru〈どさ回りをやる〉barnstorm.

dôsan〈どうさん：動産〉movables.

dôsatsu-ryoku〈どうさつりょく：洞察力〉an insight.
　　dôsatsu-ryoku-no-aru hito〈洞察力のある人〉a man of insight

dôse〈どうせ〉anyway, anyhow, at any rate, after all, at best, at all.

dosei〈どせい：土星〉Saturn.

dôsei〈どうせい：同姓〉the same surname.
　　Kare-wa watashi-to dôsei-dômei-da.（彼は私と同姓同名だ.）He has
　　the same name as myself.

dôsei〈どうせい：同性〉the same sex.

dôsei〈どうせい：同せい〉
　　dôsei-suru〈同せいする〉cohabit ((with)).

dôsei〈どうせい：動静〉movements.
　　teki-jin·ei no dôsei-o-saguru（敵陣営の動静を探る）spy on the move-
　　ments of the enemy camp

dôsei-ai〈どうせいあい：同性愛〉homosexual love, lesbianism.

dôseki〈どうせき：同席〉
　　dôseki-no hitobito（同席の人々）those present
　　dôseki-suru〈同席する〉sit with ((a person)).

dosha-buri〈どしゃぶり：どしゃ降り〉a heavy rain.
　　Dosha-buri-da.（どしゃ降りだ.）It is raining cats and dogs.

dosha-kuzure〈どしゃくずれ：土砂崩れ〉a landslide, a washout.

dôshi〈どうし：同士〉a fellow.
　　gakusei-dôshi（学生同士）fellow students

dôshi〈どうし：同志〉a kindred mind, a comrade.

dôshi〈どうし：動詞〉a verb.

doshidoshi〈どしどし〉
　　Doshidoshi shitsumon-na-sai.（どしどし質問なさい.）Ask questions
　　without any hesitation.

doshin〈どしん〉
　　doshin-to〈どしんと〉plump, with a thud.
　　doshin-to ochiru（どしんと落ちる）fall plump

dôshin〈どうしん：童心〉the child's mind.
　　dôshin o kizutsukeru（童心を傷つける）disillusion the child

dôshin-en〈どうしんえん：同心円〉a concentric circle.

dô-shite〈どうして〉how, why.

Kimi-wa dô-shite kono hako o tsukutta-no?（君はどうしてこの箱を作ったの．） How did you make this box?

Dô-shite kare-wa Kimiko o koroshita-no-ka?（どうして彼は君子を殺したのか．） Why did he kill Kimiko?

dô-shite-mo〈どうしても〉at any cost, by all means; will not.

Dô-shite-mo to ga aka-nai.（どうしても戸が開かない．） The door won't open.

dôshitsu〈どうしつ：同室〉the same room.

dôshitsu-sha（同室者）a roommate

dôshitsu-suru〈同室する〉room ((with)).

dôshokubutsu〈どうしょくぶつ：動植物〉animals and plants.

dôsô〈どうそう：同窓〉

dôsô-kai（同窓会）an alumni association, an alumni meeting

dôsô-sei（同窓生）a schoolfellow, a schoolmate, an alumnus

dosoku〈どそく：土足〉

dosoku-no-mama-de〈土足のままで〉without removing one's shoes.

dossari〈どっさり〉*see.* takusan.

dosshiri〈どっしり〉

dosshiri-shita〈どっしりした〉massive, substantial, heavy-built, dignified.

dosu〈どす〉

dosu-no-kiita koe（どすのきいた声）a voice with a threatening tone

dosû〈どすう：度数〉the number of times, frequency; the degree.

dôsû〈どうすう：同数〉the same number.

dôsû-no〈同数の〉as many ((as...)).

dosuguroi〈どすぐろい：どす黒い〉dark(ish), dusky.

dota-bata〈どたばた〉

dota-bata-kigeki（どたばた喜劇）a slapstick comedy

dôtai〈どうたい：胴体〉a body, a trunk.

dôtai-chakuriku（胴体着陸）a belly landing

dôtai〈どうたい：動態〉movement.

jinkô no dôtai（人口の動態）the movement of population

dôtai〈どうたい：導体〉a conductor.

ryô-dôtai（良導体）a good conductor

dotamba〈どたんば：土壇場〉

dotamba-ni-oi-komareru（土壇場に追い込まれる）be driven to bay

dotamba-de〈土壇場で〉at the last moment.

dotchi〈どっち〉*see.* dochira.

dotchi-michi〈どっちみち〉*see.* dochira-ni-shite-mo.

dotchi-tsukazu 〈どっちつかず：どっち付かず〉
  dotchi-tsukazu-no 〈どっち付かずの〉noncommittal, evasive.
    dotchi-tsukazu-no henji（どっち付かずの返事）an evasive answer
dote 〈どて：土手〉a bank, an embankment.
dôtei 〈どうてい：童貞〉virginity, chastity.
    dôtei o mamoru（童貞を守る）keep one's chastity
dô-teki(-na) 〈どうてき（な）：動的（な）〉dynamic.
dôten 〈どうてん：同点〉a tie, a draw.
  dôten-ni-naru〈同点になる〉tie ((with)), draw ((with)).
dotô 〈どとう：怒とう〉raging billows.
  dotô-no-yô-ni-oshi-yoseru〈怒とうのように押し寄せる〉surge ((to *or* upon)).
dôtô 〈どうとう：同等〉equality.
  dôtô-no〈同等の〉equal.
  dôtô-ni〈同等に〉equally.
    hitobito o dôtô-ni tori-atsukau（人々を同等に取り扱う）treat persons equally
dôtoku 〈どうとく：道徳〉morality, morals.
  dôtoku-teki(-na) or *dôtoku-jô-no*〈道徳的（な），道徳上の〉moral.
  dôtoku-teki-ni or *dôtoku-jô*〈道徳的に，道徳上〉morally.
dotto 〈どっと〉
    dotto-ittoki-ni dete-kuru（どっといっときに出て来る）come out with a rush
    dotto-warai-dasu（どっと笑い出す）burst into laughter
    Kanojo-no me-ni dotto-namida-ga-afureta.（彼女の目にどっと涙があふれた.）Tears welled up into her eyes.
dôwa 〈どうわ：童話〉a fairy tale, a juvenile story.
    dôwa-geki（童話劇）a juvenile play
    dôwa-sakka（童話作家）a writer of juvenile stories
do-wasure 〈どわすれ：度忘れ〉
  do-wasure-suru〈度忘れする〉slip out of one's memory.
doyadoya 〈どやどや〉
  doyadoya-to〈どやどやと〉in a crowd, noisily.
    doyadoya-to heya-ni-haitte-kuru（どやどやと部屋に入って来る）throng noisily into a room
dôyara 〈どうやら〉likely.
    Dôyara ame-ni-nari-sô-da.（どうやら雨になりそうだ.）It's likely to rain.
doyô 〈どよう：土用〉dog days, the hottest period of summer.

doyô-nami〈土用波〉high waves in the dog days

dôyô〈どうよう：童謡〉a nursery rhyme.

dôyô〈どうよう：動揺〉

dôyô-suru〈動揺する〉tremble, shake, jolt; be restless, be disturbed.

dôyô〈どうよう：同様〉

Kore-wa shimpin-dôyô-da.（これは新品同様だ。） This is just as good as new.

dôyô-na or *dôyô-no*〈同様な，同様の〉the same ((as)), like, similar ((to)).

dôyô-ni〈同様に〉in the same way, likewise.

doyô-bi〈どようび：土曜日〉Saturday.

doyomeki〈どよめき〉a stir.

doyomeku〈どよめく〉stir, make a stir.

dôzai〈どうざい：同罪〉the same crime.

Kimi-tachi-wa-dochira-mo dôzai-da.（君たちはどちらも同罪だ。） Both of you are equally to blame.

dôzen〈どうぜん：同然〉*see.* dôyô.

dozô〈どぞう：土蔵〉a godown, a storehouse.

dôzo〈どうぞ〉please.

Dôzo kochira-e.（どうぞこちらへ。） This way, please.

dôzô〈どうぞう：銅像〉a bronze statue.

dôzoku〈どうぞく：同族〉

dôzoku-gaisha（同族会社） a family partnership

E

e〈え〉*see.* esa.

e〈え：柄〉a handle, a grip, a haft.

e〈え：絵〉a picture, a drawing, a painting, a sketch.

e-o-kaku〈絵をかく〉draw a picture, paint〔a picture〕.

e-no-yô-na〈絵のような〉picturesque.

e *or* **ê** 〈え，ええ〉 yes; er-.

e, e? *or* **ê, ê?** 〈え，え？；ええ，ええ？〉 oh; yes; eh?, what?

-e 〈-へ〉 for, to, toward; in, into; on.
　　Tôkyô-e tatsu（東京へ立つ） leave for Tokyo
　　ike-e ochiru（池へ落ちる） fall into a pond
　　hon o tana-e ageru（本を棚へ上げる） put the books on the shelf

ebi 〈えび〉 a lobster, a prawn, a shrimp.

ebi-cha-iro(-no) 〈えびちゃいろ(の)：えび茶色(の)〉 maroon.

ê-bî-shî 〈エービーシー〉 ABC, the alphabet.
　ê-bî-shî-jun-ni 〈エービーシー順に〉 in alphabetical order.

echiketto 〈エチケット〉 etiquette.
　　echiketto-ni-hansuru（エチケットに反する） be against etiquette

Echiopia 〈エチオピア〉 Ethiopia.
　　Echiopia-jin（エチオピア人） an Ethiopian
　　Echiopia(-jin)-no（エチオピア(人)の） Ethiopian

eda 〈えだ：枝〉 a branch, a bough, a twig.

eda-mame 〈えだまめ：枝豆〉 green soybeans.

e-fude 〈えふで：絵筆〉 a paintbrush.

efu-emu 〈エフエム〉 FM.
　　efu-emu-hôsô（ＦＭ放送） an FM broadcast

egaku 〈えがく：描く〉 paint, draw, sketch, describe.
　　kokoro-ni egaku（心に描く） picture ((a thing)) to oneself

egao 〈えがお：笑顔〉 a smiling face.
　　egao-de mukaeru（笑顔で迎える） greet ((a person)) with a smile

e-gatai 〈えがたい：得難い〉 hard to get.
　e-gatai-shina（得難い品） a rare article.

eguru 〈えぐる〉 gouge.

e-hagaki 〈えはがき：絵はがき〉 a picture postcard.

ehen 〈えへん〉 ahem! hem!
　ehen-to-seki-barai-suru〈えへんとせき払いする〉 hem.

e-hon 〈えほん：絵本〉 a picture book.

eibin 〈えいびん：鋭敏〉
　eibin-na〈鋭敏な〉 sharp, keen, sensitive.
　　eibin-na kankaku（鋭敏な感覚） keen sense

eibun 〈えいぶん：英文〉
　　eibun-wayaku（英和訳） translation from English into Japanese, English-Japanese translation

Ei-bungaku 〈えいぶんがく：英文学〉 English literature.

eichi 〈えいち：英知〉 sagacity, wisdom, acumen.

eidan 〈えいだん：英断〉 decision, decisive judgment, a drastic measure.
 eidan o kaku（英断を欠く）lack decision
 eidan o kudasu（英断を下す）take a drastic measure

eidan 〈えいだん：営団〉 a corporation.

eien 〈えいえん：永遠〉 eternity, permanence.
 eien-no〈永遠の〉 eternal, permanent.
 eien-ni〈永遠に〉 eternally, permanently.

eiga 〈えいが：映画〉 a movie, a moving picture, a motion picture, a film, the movies.
 eiga-o-mini-iku（映画を見に行く）go to a movie
 eiga-fan（映画ファン）a movie fan
 eiga-haiyû（映画俳優）a movie actor, a movie actress
 eiga-kan（映画館）a movie theater, a cinema
 eiga-kantoku（映画監督）a director, a producer
 eiga-satsuei-jo（映画撮影所）a film studio

Eigo 〈えいご：英語〉 English, the English language.
 Eigo-ga-umai（英語がうまい）be good at English
 Eigo o hanasu（英語を話す）speak English
 Eigo o kaku（英語を書く）write English
 Eigo o yomu（英語を読む）read English
 Eigo-kaiwa（英語会話）English conversation
 Eigo-no〈英語の〉 English.
 Eigo-no-shiken（英語の試験）an examination in English

eigyô 〈えいぎょう：営業〉 business.
 eigyô-sho（営業所）a business place, an office
 eigyô-bu（営業部）the business department
 eigyô-jikan（営業時間）business(*or* office) hours
 eigyô-suru〈営業する〉 do business.

ei-ji 〈えいじ：英字〉 an English letter.
 ei-ji-shimbun（英字新聞）an English paper

Ei-jin 〈えいじん：英人〉 *see.* Eikoku-jin.

eijû 〈えいじゅう：永住〉 permanent residence.
 eijû-suru〈永住する〉 settle down, reside permanently.

Eika 〈えいか：英貨〉 British money, sterling.

eikaku 〈えいかく：鋭角〉 an acute angle.

eikan 〈えいかん：栄冠〉 the crown.
 shôri-no-eikan-o-itadaku〈勝利の栄冠をいただく〉be crowned with

victory.

eiki 〈えいき：英気〉 vigor, energy.

  eiki o yashinau〈英気を養う〉 store up one's energy

eikō 〈えいこう：栄光〉a glory, a halo.

Eikoku 〈えいこく：英国〉England, Great Britain, the United Kingdom.

  Eikoku-jin〈英国人〉 an Englishman, an Englishwoman

  Eikoku(-jin)-no〈英国(人)の〉 English, British

eiko-seisui 〈えいこせいすい：栄枯盛衰〉prosperity and decline.

  Eiko-seisui wa yo-no-narai.〈栄枯盛衰は世の習い.〉 A man's life has its ups and downs.

eikyō 〈えいきょう：影響〉influnece, effect.

  eikyô-o-ataeru〈影響を与える〉influence, affect, have an influence(*or* effect) ((on)).

  eikyô-o-ukeru〈影響を受ける〉be influenced ((by)), be affected ((by)).

eikyū 〈えいきゅう：永久〉see. eien.

  eikyū-shi〈永久歯〉 a permanent tooth

eimin 〈えいみん：永眠〉eternal rest.

  eimin-suru〈永眠する〉pass away, die.

Ei-rempō 〈えいれんぽう：英連邦〉the British Commonwealth of Nations.

eiri 〈えいり：鋭利〉sharpness.

  eiri-na〈鋭利な〉sharp, sharp-edged.

  eiri-na hamono〈鋭利な刃物〉 a sharp-edged tool

eiri 〈えいり：営利〉money-making, gain.

  eiri-shugi〈営利主義〉 commercialism

eisai-kyôiku 〈えいさいきょういく：英才教育〉special education for the gifted.

eisei 〈えいせい：衛星〉a satellite.

  eisei-toshi〈衛星都市〉 a satellite city

  jinkô-eisei〈人工衛星〉 an artificial satellite

eisei 〈えいせい：衛生〉hygiene, sanitation, health.

  eisei-jô-ii〈衛生上いい〉be good for health, be wholesome, be healthy.

  eisei-jô-warui〈衛生上悪い〉 be injurious to health, be un-wholesome, be unhealthy

  eisei-jô-no or eisei-teki(-na)〈衛生上の，衛生的(な)〉hygienic, sanitary.

eisha 〈えいしゃ：映写〉projection.

  eisha-ki〈映写機〉 a projector

  eisha-maku〈映写幕〉 a screen

  eisha-suru〈映写する〉project ((a picture)) on a screen.

eitai-shakuchi-ken〈えいたいしゃくちけん：永代借地権〉a perpetual lease.

eiten〈えいてん：栄転〉promotion.

eiten-suru〈栄転する〉be promoted and transfered ((to)).

ei-wa〈えいわ：英和〉English-Japanese.

 ei-wa-jiten（英和辞典）an English-Japanese dictionary

ei-yaku〈えいやく：英訳〉an English translation.

ei-yaku-suru〈英訳する〉translate into English.

eiyo〈えいよ：栄誉〉honor, glory.

eiyo-aru〈栄誉ある〉honorable, glorious.

eiyō〈えいよう：栄養〉nutrition, nourishment.

 eiyō-ka（栄養価）nutritive value

 eiyō-furyō（栄養不良）undernourishment

 eiyō-shitchō（栄養失調）malnutrition

eiyō-ni-naru or *eiyō-bun-ni-tomu*〈栄養になる，栄養分に富む〉nutritious, nourishing.

eiyō-no-ii〈栄養のいい〉well-fed.

 eiyō-furyō-no（栄養不良の）ill-fed

eiyū〈えいゆう：英雄〉a hero.

eiyū-teki(-na)〈英雄的(な)〉heroic.

eizen〈えいぜん：営繕〉building and repairs.

 eizen-hi（営繕費）building and repairing expenses

eizō〈えいぞう：映像〉an image, a picture.

eizoku〈えいぞく：永続〉

eizoku-suru〈永続する〉last long, endure.

 eizoku-shi-nai（永続しない）be short-lived

eizoku-teki(-na)〈永続的(な)〉lasting, everlasting, enduring, permanent.

ejiki〈えじき：え食〉a prey, a victim.

ejiki-ni-naru〈え食になる〉fall a prey ((to)).

Ejiputo〈エジプト〉Egypt.

 Ejiputo-jin（エジプト人）an Egyptian

 Ejiputo-go（エジプト語）Egyptian

 Ejiputo(-jin)-no（エジプト(人)の）Egyptian

eki〈えき：駅〉a station, a depot, a stop.

 eki-chō（駅長）a stationmaster

 eki-in（駅員）a station employee

 eki-ben（駅弁）a lunch sold on a railroad platform

 shūchaku-eki（終着駅）a terminal station

eki〈えき：液〉juice, sap, liquid, a solution.

eki〈えき：易〉fortune-telling, divination.
　　ekisha（易者）a fortune-teller
　eki o mite-morau〈易を見てもらう〉have one's fortune told.

ekibyō〈えきびょう：疫病〉an epidemic.

ekichō〈えきちょう：益鳥〉a useful bird.

ekichū〈えきちゅう：益虫〉a beneficial insect.

ekiden-kyōsō〈えきでんきょうそう：駅伝競走〉a long-distance relay race.

ekika〈えきか：液化〉liquefaction.
　　ekika-gasu（液化ガス）liquefied gas

ekiri〈えきり：疫痢〉children's dysentery.

ekisu〈エキス〉an extract, an essence.
　ekisu o toru〈エキスを採る〉extract essence ((from)).

ekisupandā〈エキスパンダー〉a chest expander.

ekisutora〈エキストラ〉an extra (hand).
　　ekisutora o yaru（エキストラをやる）play an extra part

ekitai〈えきたい：液体〉a liquid, fluid.
　　ekitai-nenryō（液体燃料）liquid fuel

ekken〈えっけん：越権〉arrogation.
　　ekken-kôi（越権行為）an arrogation

ekkusu-sen〈エックスせん：エックス線〉X-rays.
　ekkusu-sen-ni-kakeru〈エックス線に掛ける〉X-ray.

ekkyō〈えっきょう：越境〉
　ekkyō-suru〈越境する〉cross the border ((into)).

eko-hiiki〈えこひいき：依こひいき〉partiality.
　eko-hiiki-suru〈えこひいきする〉be partial ((to)).
　eko-hiiki-no〈えこひいきの〉partial, unfair.
　　eko-hiiki-no-nai〈えこひいきのない〉impartial, fair

ekoji〈えこじ：依こ地〉
　ekoji-na〈依こ地な〉perverse, cross-grained.
　ekoji-ni-natte〈依こ地になって〉out of perversity.

ekubo〈えくぼ〉a dimple.
　ekubo-ga-dekiru〈えくぼが出来る〉dimple.

emaki-mono〈えまきもの：絵巻き物〉a picture scroll.

emban〈えんばん：円盤〉a disk, a disc; a discus.
　　emban-nage（円盤投げ）the discus throw

embi-fuku〈えんびふく：えん尾服〉a swallow-tailed coat, a full-dress coat.

embun〈えんぶん：塩分〉salinity.

  embun-no-aru or *embun-o-fukunda*〈塩分のある，塩分を含んだ〉saline, saltish.

emi〈えみ：笑み〉a smile.

  emi-o-ukabete〈笑みを浮かべて〉with a smile.

emmaku〈えんまく：煙幕〉a smoke screen.

    emmaku o haru（煙幕を張る）lay down a smoke screen

emman〈えんまん：円満〉

  emman-na〈円満な〉harmonious, peaceful, happy.

    emman-na kaiketsu（円満な解決）a peaceful settlement

    emman-na katei（円満な家庭）a happy home

  emman-ni〈円満に〉harmoniously, peacefully.

emono〈えもの：獲物〉game, spoils, a catch, a prize.

empitsu〈えんぴつ：鉛筆〉a pencil.

    empitsu-de kaku（鉛筆で書く）write in pencil

    empitsu no sin（鉛筆のしん）the lead of a pencil

    empitsu-kezuri（鉛筆削り）a pencil sharpener

    iro-empitsu（色鉛筆）a colored pencil

empô〈えんぽう：遠方〉a great(*or* long) distance, a distant place.

    empô-kara kuru（遠方から来る）come from a long way off

  empô-no〈遠方の〉distant, faraway.

  empô-ni〈遠方に〉in the distance.

en〈えん：円〉a circle; a yen (Japanese currency).

    en o egaku（円を描く）draw a circle

    sen-en（千円）one thousand yen

en〈えん：縁〉a relation, a connection.

    en-ga-nai（縁がない）have no connection ((with))

    en-mo-yukari-mo-nai（縁もゆかりもない）have nothing to do ((with)), be a perfect stranger ((to))

    en-o-kiru（縁を切る）cut one's connections ((with)), break off ((with))

    fushigi-na en-de（不思議な縁で）by happy chance

en-bi〈えんビ：塩ビ〉an abbreviation of 'enka-binîru.'

enchaku〈えんちゃく：延着〉delayed arrival.

  enchaku-suru〈延着する〉be delayed, arrive late.

enchô〈えんちょう：園長〉the head, the chief.

    dôbutsu-en no enchô（動物園の園長）the head of a zoo

　　　yôchi-en no enchô〈幼稚園の園長〉 the head of a kindergarten

enchô〈えんちょう：延長〉extension, prolongation.

　　　enchô-sen〈延長戦〉 an extra-inning game

　enchô-suru〈延長する〉extend, prolong.

enchû〈えんちゅう：円柱〉a column.

　enchû-jô-no, enchû-kei-no or *enchû-no*〈円柱状の，円柱形の，円柱の〉columnar.

endai〈えんだい：遠大〉

　endai-na〈遠大な〉farseeing, long-ranged, great.

　　　endai-na keikaku o tateru〈遠大な計画を立てる〉 make a farseeing plan

endan〈えんだん：演壇〉a platform.

endan〈えんだん：縁談〉an offer of marriage.

　　　Kanojo-ni-wa endan-ga-takusan-aru.（彼女には縁談がたくさんある.）She has had many offers of marriage.

endate〈えんだて：円建て〉a yen base.

endô〈えんどう〉a pea.

　　　ao-endô〈青えんどう〉 green peas

endoku〈えんどく：鉛毒〉lead poisoning.

en‧ei〈えんえい：遠泳〉a long-distance swim.

　en‧ei-suru〈遠泳する〉have a long-distance swim.

en‧en〈えんえん：炎々〉

　en‧en-to-moe-agaru〈炎々と燃え上がる〉be in flames, blaze up.

en‧en〈えんえん：延々〉

　　　en‧en　chôda-no-retsu-o-nashite〈延々長蛇の列を成して〉 in a long queue

　　　en‧en go-jikan-mo-tsuzuku〈延々五時間も続く〉 last as long as five hours

　　　en‧en-to-tsuranaru-sammyaku〈延々と連なる山脈〉 a long chain of mountains

enerugî〈エネルギー〉energy.

engan〈えんがん：沿岸〉the coast, the shore.

engawa〈えんがわ：縁側〉a veranda(h), a porch; a balcony.

engei〈えんげい：演芸〉a performance, entertainments.

　　　engei-kai〈演芸会〉 an entertainment

engei〈えんげい：園芸〉gardening.

engeki〈えんげき：演劇〉a play, a theatrical performance.

　　　engeki o yaru〈演劇をやる〉 give a play, perform a play on the

stage

Engeru-keisû〈エンゲルけいすう：エンゲル係数〉Engel's coefficient.

engi〈えんぎ：演技〉performance.

　　engi-sha〈演技者〉a performer

engi〈えんぎ：縁起〉an omen.

　　engi-o-katsugu〈縁起を担ぐ〉believe in omens

　engi-no-ii〈縁起のいい〉of a good omen.

　　engi-no-warui〈縁起の悪い〉ill-omened

engo〈えんご：援護〉protection, cover(ing).

　　engo-shageki〈援護射撃〉covering fire

　engo-suru〈援護する〉protect, cover.

engumi〈えんぐみ：縁組み〉a marriage, (an) adoption.

　engumi-suru〈縁組みする〉marry, adopt.

engun〈えんぐん：援軍〉reinforcement(s).

　engun-o-okuru〈援軍を送る〉send reinforcement(s) ((to)), reinforce.

en·in〈えんいん：遠因〉a remote cause.

enji〈えんじ：園児〉a kindergarten child.

enji-iro(-no)〈えんじいろ(の)：えんじ色(の)〉deep red.

enjin〈エンジン〉an engine.

　　enjin o kakeru〈エンジンをかける〉start an engine

　　enjin o tomeru〈エンジンを止める〉stop an engine

enjin〈えんじん：円陣〉a circle.

　　enjin-o-tsukutte-tatsu〈円陣を作って立つ〉stand in a circle

enjiru〈えんじる：演じる〉perform, play.

　　〜-no yaku o enjiru〈〜の役を演じる〉play the part of...

enjo〈えんじょ：援助〉help, aid, assistance, support.

　　enjo o ataeru〈援助を与える〉give assistance ((to))

　　enjo-o-motomeru〈援助を求める〉ask for ((a person's)) assistance

　enjo-suru〈援助する〉help, aid, assist, support.

enjō〈えんじょう：炎上〉

　enjō-suru〈炎上する〉burst into flames.

enjuku〈えんじゅく：円熟〉maturity, mellowness.

　　enjuku-no-iki ni tassuru〈円熟の域に達する〉attain maturity

　enjuku-suru〈円熟する〉mature, mellow.

　enjuku-shita〈円熟した〉mature, ripe, perfect.

enka-binîru〈えんかビニール：塩化ビニール〉vinyl chloride.

enkai〈えんかい：沿海〉the inshore, the coast.

　　enkai-gyogyō〈沿海漁業〉inshore fishery

enkai-no 〈沿海の〉 coastal, inshore.

enkai 〈えんかい：宴会〉 a dinner party, a banquet, a feast.

enkai o hiraku 〈宴会を開く〉 give a dinner party, hold a banquet

enkan 〈えんかん：鉛管〉 a leaden pipe.

enkan-kôji 〈鉛管工事〉 plumbing

enkatsu 〈えんかつ：円滑〉 smoothness, harmony.

enkatsu-na 〈円滑な〉 smooth, harmonious.

enkatsu-ni 〈円滑に〉 smoothly, harmoniously, without a hitch.

enkei 〈えんけい：円形〉 a circle.

enkei-gekijô 〈円形劇場〉 an amphitheater

enkei-no 〈円形の〉 circular, round.

enki 〈えんき：延期〉 postponement.

enki-suru 〈延期する〉 postpone, put off.

enki-ni-naru 〈延期になる〉 be postponed, be put off.

enkin-hô 〈えんきんほう：遠近法〉 perspective.

enko 〈えんこ：縁故〉 relation, connection; a relative.

enko-o-tayotte 〈縁故を頼って〉 through one's relative(s).

enko 〈えんこ〉

enko-suru 〈えんこする〉 break down, get stuck.

enkyoku 〈えんきょく：遠曲〉

enkyoku-na 〈遠曲な〉 euphemistic, roundabout, indirect.

enkyoku-ni 〈遠曲に〉 in a roundabout way, in an indirect expression.

en-kyori 〈えんきょり：遠距離〉 a long distance.

en-kyori-no 〈遠距離の〉 long-distance.

en-musubi-no-kami 〈えんむすびのかみ：縁結びの神〉 Cupid, Hymen.

ennô 〈えんのう：延納〉 delayed payment.

en-no-shita 〈えんのした：縁の下〉

en-no-shita-no-chikara-mochi 〈縁の下の力持ち〉 a thankless job

enogu 〈えのぐ：絵の具〉 paints, colors, oils, watercolors.

enogu-o-nuru 〈絵の具を塗る〉 paint, color.

enrai 〈えんらい：遠来〉

enrai-no kyaku 〈遠来の客〉 a visitor from afar

enro 〈えんろ：遠路〉 a long way.

enryo 〈えんりょ：遠慮〉 reserve, reservation.

enryo-suru 〈遠慮する〉 be reserved.

Koko-dewa tabako go-enryo-kudasai. (ここではたばこ御遠慮ください。)
Please refrain from smoking here.

enryo-bukai 〈遠慮深い〉 modest, shy.

enryo-no-nai〈遠慮のない〉unreserved, free.

enryo-naku〈遠慮なく〉without reserve, freely.

ensan〈えんさん：塩酸〉hydrochloric acid.

ensei(-tai)〈えんせい（たい）：遠征（隊）〉an expedition.

ensei-suru〈遠征する〉go on an expedition.

ensei〈えんせい：えん世〉

ensei-ka（えん世家）a pessimist

ensei-shugi（えん世主義）pessimism

ensei-teki(-na)〈えん世的(な)〉pessimistic.

ensen〈えんせん：沿線〉

ensen-no or *ensen-ni*〈沿線の，沿線に〉along a railway line.

enshi〈えんし：遠視〉farsightedness, longsightedness.

enshi-no〈遠視の〉farsighted, longsighted.

enshin〈えんしん：遠心〉

enshin-bunri-ki（遠心分離機）a centrifugal machine

enshin-ryoku（遠心力）centrifugal force

enshō〈えんしょう：炎症〉inflammation.

enshō-o-okosu〈炎症を起こす〉be inflamed, inflame.

enshō〈えんしょう：延焼〉

enshō-o-manugareru（延焼を免れる）escape spreading flames

enshō-suru〈延焼する〉spread, catch fire.

enshū〈えんしゅう：円周〉circumference.

enshū-ritsu（円周率）pi

enshū〈えんしゅう：演習〉practice, an exercise, maneuvers, a seminar.

dai-enshū（大演習）great maneuvers

enshū-shitsu（演習室）a seminar room

enshutsu〈えんしゅつ：演出〉production.

enshutsu-ka（演出家）a producer, a director

enshutsu-suru〈演出する〉produce.

enso〈えんそ：塩素〉chlorine.

ensō〈えんそう：演奏〉a musical performance, a recital.

ensō-kai（演奏会）a concert, a recital

ensō-sha（演奏者）a performer

ensō-suru〈演奏する〉perform, play.

ensoku〈えんそく：遠足〉an excursion, a walking tour, an outing, a hike.

ensoku-ni-iku（遠足に行く）go on an excursion, go on a hike

ensui〈えんすい：円すい〉a (circular) cone.

ensui(-kei)-no 〈円すい(形)の〉 conical, coniform.

en-suto 〈エンスト〉 stalling of an engine.
En-suto-o-okoshita. 〈エンストを起こした.〉 The engine stalled.

entai 〈えんたい：延滞〉
    entai-kin（延滞金） arrears
    entai-rishi（延滞利子） overdue interest
entai-suru 〈延滞する〉 be in arrear(s), be delayed.

entaku 〈えんたく：円卓〉 a round table.
    entaku-kaigi（円卓会議） a round table conference

enten 〈えんてん：炎天〉 hot weather.
enten-ka-de 〈炎天下で〉 under the scorching sun.

entô 〈えんとう：円筒〉 a cylinder.
entô-kei-no 〈円筒形の〉 cylindrical.

entotsu 〈えんとつ：煙突〉 a chimney, a funnel, a stovepipe.
    entotsu o sôji-suru（煙突を掃除する） sweep a chimney

en-tsuzuki 〈えんつづき：縁続き〉 relationship.
    tooi en-tsuzuki（遠い縁続き） a distant relation
en-tsuzuki-de-aru 〈縁続きである〉 be related ((to)).

en·yô 〈えんよう：遠洋〉 an ocean, a deep sea.
    en·yô-kôkai（遠洋航海） ocean navigation
      en·yô-kôkai-ni deru（遠洋航海に出る） set out on ocean navigation
    en·yô-gyogyô（遠洋漁業） deep-sea fishing

en·yô 〈えんよう：援用〉 claim, quotation.
en·yô-suru 〈援用する〉 claim, quote, invoke.

en·yû-kai 〈えんゆうかい：園遊会〉 a garden party.
    en·yû-kai o moyoosu（園遊会を催す） give a garden party

enzai 〈えんざい：えん罪〉 a false charge.
    enzai-o-sosogu（えん罪をそそぐ） clear oneself of a false charge

enzetsu 〈えんぜつ：演説〉 a speech, an address, an oration.
    enzetsu-ka（演説家） a speaker, an orator
    enzetsu-kaijô（演説会場） a meeting hall
enzetsu-suru 〈演説する〉 make a speech, deliver an address.

enzuku 〈えんづく：縁付く〉 marry, get married ((to)).

eppei 〈えっぺい：閲兵〉
eppei-suru 〈閲兵する〉 inspect troops.

epuron 〈エプロン〉 an apron, a pinafore.
    epuron o shite-iru（エプロンをしている） wear an apron

era 〈えら〉 a gill.

erâ 〈エラー〉 an error.

    erâ o suru 〈エラーをする〉 make an error

erabu 〈えらぶ：選ぶ〉 choose, select, sort; elect.

    shinchô-ni erabu 〈慎重に選ぶ〉 choose carefully

    shi-chô ni erabareru 〈市長に選ばれる〉 be elected mayor

erai 〈えらい：偉い〉 great, extraordinary, superior.

    erai hito 〈偉い人〉 a great man

    jibun-o-erai-ningen-da-to-omou 〈自分を偉い人間だと思う〉 have a high opinion of oneself

erai 〈えらい〉 great, serious, heavy, violent, severe.

    erai son 〈えらい損〉 a serious loss

    erai-me-ni-au 〈えらい目に遭う〉 have a hard time

erasô 〈えらそう：偉そう〉

    erasô-na 〈偉そうな〉 important-looking.

    erasô-na-kao-o-suru 〈偉そうな顔をする〉 look big

    erasô-na-koto-o-iu 〈偉そうなことを言う〉 talk big

erebêtâ 〈エレベーター〉 an elevator, a lift.

    erebêtâ ni noru 〈エレベーターに乗る〉 take an elevator

eri 〈えり：襟〉 the neck, a neckband, a collar, a neck.

    eri-o-tsukamu 〈襟をつかむ〉 seize ((a person)) by the collar

    ôbâ no eri o tateru 〈オーバーの襟を立てる〉 turn up the collar of one's overcoat

eri-gonomi 〈えりごのみ：えり好み〉

    eri-gonomi-suru 〈えり好みする〉 be particular ((about)).

erinuki 〈えりぬき：えり抜き〉 pick; the pick, the choice, the cream.

    erinuki-no 〈えり抜きの〉 picked, choice, select.

    erinuki-no shina 〈えり抜きの品〉 choice articles

erîto 〈エリート〉 the elite.

ero 〈エロ〉 eroticism.

    ero-shashin 〈エロ写真〉 a pornographic picture

    ero-na 〈エロな〉 erotic, obscene.

eru 〈える：得る〉 get, have, obtain, acquire, secure, find, earn, win, gain; can.

    shoku o eru 〈職を得る〉 get a job

    chishiki o eru 〈知識を得る〉 acquire knowledge

    chii o eru 〈地位を得る〉 secure a position

    hôshû o eru 〈報酬を得る〉 earn a reward

    shin·yô o eru 〈信用を得る〉 win the confidence ((of))

～(-se)-zaru-o-e-nai 〈～(せ)ざるを得ない〉 cannot help ((doing)).

eru-pî-rekôdo 〈エルピーレコード〉 an LP (record).

esa 〈えさ〉 a bait, food, feed.

esa-o-yaru 〈えさをやる〉 feed.

ese- 〈えせ-〉 false, pretended, would-be.

 ese-gakusha 〈えせ学者〉 a pretended scholar

 ese-shinshi 〈えせ紳士〉 a would-be gentleman

eshaku 〈えしゃく：会釈〉 a bow, a salutation.

eshaku-suru 〈会釈する〉 bow, make a bow, salute.

 karuku eshaku-suru 〈軽く会釈する〉 bow slightly

eso 〈えそ〉 gangrene.

esu-efu 〈エスエフ〉 science fiction.

esukarêtâ 〈エスカレーター〉 an escalator.

 esukarêtâ-de agaru 〈エスカレーターで上がる〉 go up on an escalator

 esukarêtâ-de oriru 〈エスカレーターで降りる〉 go down on an escalator

esukarêto 〈エスカレート〉

esukarêto-suru 〈エスカレートする〉 escalate.

Esukimô 〈エスキモー〉 an Eskimo.

esu-ô-esu 〈エスオーエス〉 an SOS.

 esu-ô-esu o hassuru 〈SOSを発する〉 send an SOS by radio, flash an SOS

Esuperanto 〈エスペラント〉 Esperanto.

etai 〈えたい：得体〉

etai-no-shire-nai 〈得体の知れない〉 strange, mysterious, nondescript.

 etai-no-shire-nai otoko 〈得体の知れない男〉 a mysterious man

 etai-no-shire-nai byôki 〈得体の知れない病気〉 a nondescript disease

ete 〈えて：得手〉 one's forte.

 ete to fu-ete 〈得手と不得手〉 one's strong and weak points

ete-katte 〈えてかって：得手勝手〉

ete-katte-na 〈得手勝手な〉 selfish, egoistic.

 ete-katte-na otoko 〈得手勝手な男〉 an egoistic man

êteru 〈エーテル〉 ether.

ê-to 〈ええと〉 let me see, well, er—.

etoku 〈えとく：会得〉

etoku-suru 〈会得する〉 understand, comprehend, grasp, catch, see.

etoku-shi-yasui 〈会得しやすい〉 easy to understand, easy to learn.

 etoku-shi-nikui 〈会得しにくい〉 hard to understand, hard to learn

etsu 〈えつ：悦〉joy, rapture.
　hitori-etsu-ni-iru 〈一人悦に入る〉be pleased with oneself.
etsunen 〈えつねん：越年〉
　Beppu-de etsunen-suru 〈別府で越年する〉greet the New Year at Beppu.
etsuran 〈えつらん：閲覧〉perusal, reading.
　　etsuran-shitsu（閲覧室）a reading room
　etsuran-suru 〈閲覧する〉peruse, read.
ettô 〈えっとう：越冬〉
　　ettô-tai（越冬隊）a wintering party
　ettô-suru 〈越冬する〉pass the winter.

F

faindâ 〈ファインダー〉a viewfinder.
fairu 〈ファイル〉a file.
　fairu-suru 〈ファイルする〉file.
fakushimiri 〈ファクシミリ〉(a) facsimile.
fasunâ 〈ファスナー〉a fastener, a zipper.
　fasunâ-o-shimeru 〈ファスナーを締める〉zip.
　　fasunâ-o-hazusu（ファスナーを外す）unzip
fauru 〈ファウル〉(a) foul.
　fauru-suru 〈ファウルする〉foul.
fên-genshô 〈フェーンげんしょう：フェーン現象〉a föhn phenomenon.
fenshingu 〈フェンシング〉fencing, foils.
　　fenshingu-no-senshu（フェンシングの選手）a fencer, a foilsman
fezâ-kyû 〈フェザー級〉the featherweight.
　fezâ-kyû-no 〈フェザー級の〉featherweight.
fianse 〈フィアンセ〉one's fiance, one's fiancee.
figyua-sukêto 〈フィギュアスケート〉figure skating.
　　figyua-sukêto-no-senshu（フィギュアスケートの選手）a figurer

figyua-sukêto-o-suru〈フィギュアスケートをする〉skate figures.

Finrando〈フィンランド〉Finland.

Finrando-jin（フィンランド人）a Finn

Finrando-go（フィンランド語）Finnish

Finrando(-jin)-no（フィンランド(人)の）Finnish

Firipin〈フィリピン〉the Philippines.

Firipin-guntô（フィリピン群島）the Philippine Islands

Firipin-jin（フィリピン人）a Filipino, a Filipina

Firipin(-jin)-no（フィリピン(人)の）Philippine

firudo-shumoku〈フィールド種目〉a field event.

firumu〈フィルム〉(a) film.

esu-esu-firumu-ippon（ＳＳフィルム一本）a reel of SS film

kamera-ni-firumu-o-ireru〈カメラにフィルムを入れる〉load a camera.

firutâ〈フィルター〉a (color) filter; a filter tip.

firutâ-tsuki-no〈フィルター付きの〉filter-tipped.

fito〈フィート〉foot.

ichi-fito go-inchi（一フィート五インチ）one foot five inches

ni-fito roku-inchi（二フィート六インチ）two feet six inches

foa-bôru〈フォアボール〉a base on balls.

foa-bôru-o-dasu（フォアボールを出す）give ((a batter)) a base on balls

foa-bôru-de-ichirui-ni-deru（フォアボールで一塁に出る）get a base on balls

fôku〈フォーク〉a fork; a folk song.

fu〈ふ：府〉a prefecture.

Kyôto-fu（京都府）Kyoto Prefecture

fu〈ふ：歩〉a pawn.

fu o tsuku（歩を突く）advance a pawn

fu〈ふ：譜〉a (sheet) music, a (musical) note.

fu-o-mizu-ni-ensô-suru（譜を見ずに演奏する）play from memory

fu〈ふ：負〉

fu-no〈負の〉negative, minus.

fu-no kazu（負の数）a negative number, a minus quantity

fu〈ふ〉

fu-ni-ochi-nai〈ふに落ちない〉cannot understand, be hard to understand.

fû〈ふう：封〉seal.

fû o kiru（封を切る）break the seal

fû-o-suru〈封をする〉seal.

fû〈ふう：風〉a look, an air; a way, a manner; a style, a type.

Sono otoko wa donna-fû-no-hito-deshita-ka? (その男はどんなふうの人でしたか。) What did that man look like?

Furansu-fû-no ryôri (フランス風の料理) cooking in a French style

donna-fû-ni 〈どんなふうに〉 in what way, how.

konna-fû-ni 〈こんなふうに〉 in this way, like this.

fuan 〈ふあん：不安〉 uneasiness, anxiety.

fuan-kan (不安感) a feeling of uneasiness

fuan-ni-omou 〈不安に思う〉 feel uneasy ((about)), be anxious ((about)), be uncertain ((over)).

fuan-na 〈不安な〉 uneasy, anxious.

fuan-na ichi-ya (不安な一夜) an uneasy night

fu-annai 〈ふあんない：不案内〉 ignorance.

Watashi-wa koko-wa mattaku fu-annai-de. (私はここは全く不案内で。) I am quite a stranger here.

fu-antei 〈ふあんてい：不安定〉 instability.

fu-antei-na 〈不安定な〉 unstable.

fûatsu 〈ふうあつ：風圧〉 wind pressure.

fubai-dômei 〈ふばいどうめい：不買同盟〉 a boycott.

shôhi-sha-fubai-dômei (消費者不買同盟) a consumers' boycott

fu-barai 〈ふばらい：不払い〉 nonpayment.

fuben 〈ふべん：不便〉 inconvenience.

fuben o kanjiru (不便を感じる) feel inconvenience

fuben-na 〈不便な〉 inconvenient.

fuben-na-tokoro-ni-aru (不便な所にある) be inconveniently situated

fuben-na-omoi-o-suru (不便な思いをする) experience inconveniences

fu-benkyô 〈ふべんきょう：不勉強〉

fu-benkyô-na 〈不勉強な〉 idle.

fubi 〈ふび：不備〉 imperfection, lack, a defect.

eisei-setsubi no fubi (衛生設備の不備) lack of proper sanitation

fubi-na 〈不備な〉 deficient, imperfect, defective.

fubin 〈ふびん：不びん〉

fubin-ni-omou 〈不びんに思う〉 pity, take pity ((on)), feel pity ((for)).

fubin-na 〈不びんな〉 poor, pitiful, pitiable, miserable.

fubin-na ko (不びんな子) a poor child

fubo 〈父母〉 one's father and mother, one's parents.

fûbô 〈ふうぼう：風ぼう〉 features, appearance.

fûbô 〈ふうぼう：風防〉

fûbô-garasu (風防ガラス) a windshield, a windscreen

fubuki〈ふぶき：吹雪〉a snowstorm, a snowdrift.

fubun-ritsu〈ふぶんりつ：不文律〉an unwritten law.

fûbutsu〈ふうぶつ：風物〉

    Nihon-no fûbutsu（日本の風物） things Japanese

fu-byôdô〈ふびょうどう：不平等〉inequality.

  fu-byôdô-na〈不平等な〉unequal.

fuchaku〈ふちゃく：付着〉

  fuchaku-suru〈付着する〉adhere ((to)), stick ((to)), cling ((to)).

    Shita-gi-ni kekkon ga fuchaku-shite-ita.〔下着に血こんが付着してい
    た.〕There were some stains of blood on the underwear.

fuchi〈ふち：縁〉an edge, a brim, a rim.

    gake no fuchi（がけの縁） the edge of a precipice

    fuchi-nashi-no megane（縁なしの眼鏡） rimless spectacles

fûchi-chiku〈ふうちちく：風致地区〉a scenic zone.

fuchin〈ふちん：浮沈〉

  shôgai-no-fuchin-ni-kakawaru〈生涯の浮沈にかかわる〉affect one's whole
  career.

fuchô〈ふちょう：不調〉failure; a bad condition.

    fuchô-ni-owaru（不調に終わる） end in failure, fail

    fuchô-de-aru（不調である） be in a bad condition

fûchô〈ふうちょう：風潮〉a tendency, a trend, the current, the tide, the
  stream.

    yo no fûchô（世の風潮） the stream of the times

fu-chôwa〈ふちょうわ：不調和〉disharmony, discord.

  fu-chôwa-de-aru〈不調和である〉do not harmonize ((with)), do not go
  ((with)).

fu-chûi〈ふちゅうい：不注意〉carelessness.

  fu-chûi-na〈不注意な〉careless.

    fu-chûi-na ayamari o suru（不注意な誤りをする） make a careless
    mistake

  fu-chûi-ni(-mo)〈不注意に（も）〉carelessly.

  fu-chûi-kara〈不注意から〉through one's carelessness.

fuda〈ふだ：札〉a card, a label, a tag, check.

fuda-dome〈ふだどめ：札止め〉House Full. / a sellout.

    renjitsu fuda-dome-no-seikyô-de-aru（連日札止めの盛況である） draw
    a full house every day

fudan〈ふだん：普段〉usually, always.

    Watashi-wa fudan jû-ji-ni neru.（私は普段十時に寝る.）I usually go

to bed at ten.

fudan-yori-hayaku（普段より早く） earlier than usual

fudan-no〈普段の〉usual.

fudan-no-toori（普段のとおり） as usual

fudan-gi〈ふだんぎ：普段着〉everyday wear, everyday clothes, home wear.

fudan-gi-no-mama-de（普段着のままで） in everyday clothes

fuda-tsuki〈ふだつき：札付き〉

fuda-tsuki-no〈札付きの〉notorious.

fuda-tsuki-no akkan（札付きの悪漢） a notorious scoundrel

fude〈ふで：筆〉a writing brush, a paintbrush.

fude-tate（筆立て） a pen stand, a pencil vase

fu-deki〈ふでき：不出来〉

Kotoshi-wa kome ga fu-deki-da.（今年は米が不出来だ.） The rice crop has turned out badly this year.

fudô〈ふどう：不同〉

Junjo-fudô.（順序不同.） No special order is observed.

fudô〈ふどう：不動〉

fudô-no〈不動の〉immovable, unshakable.

fudô-no chii（不動の地位） an unshakable position

fudô〈ふどう：浮動〉

fudô-hyô（浮動票） a floating vote

fûdo〈ふうど：風土〉climate.

fûdo-byô（風土病） an endemic.

fûdô〈ふうどう：風洞〉a wind tunnel.

fu-dôi〈ふどうい：不同意〉disagreement, disapproval.

fu-dôi-de-aru〈不同意である〉disagree ((to)), disapprove ((of)).

fu-dôsan〈ふどうさん：不動産〉real estate.

fu-dôsan-gyô-sha（不動産業者） a real estate broker

fu-dôtoku〈ふどうとく：不道徳〉immorality.

fu-dôtoku-na〈不道徳な〉immoral, depraved.

fue〈ふえ：笛〉a flute, a pipe, a whistle.

fue o fuku（笛を吹く） play a flute, blow a whistle

fu-eisei〈ふえいせい：不衛生〉

fu-eisei-na〈不衛生な〉insanitary, unhealthy, unwholesome.

fueru（ふえる：増(殖)える）increase, multiply, gain, swell; breed, multiply.

go-jû-fueru（五十増える） increase by 50

taijû-ga-fueru〈体重が増える〉 gain in weight

Hae ga fueru.（はえが殖える.） Flies multiply (themselves).

fu·ete〈ふえて：不得手〉

fu·ete-de-aru〈不得手である〉be a poor hand ((at)), be poor ((in)).

Watashi-wa gogaku-ga-fu·ete-de-aru.（私は語学が不得手である.） I am a poor linguist.

fu·ete-na〈不得手な〉poor, weak.

fûfu〈ふうふ：夫婦〉husband and wife, a (married) couple.

fûfû〈ふうふう〉

fûfû-fuki-nagara sûpu o nomu（ふうふう吹きながらスープを飲む）eat soup blowing on it

fûfû-iu（ふうふういう） puff and pant

fufuku〈ふふく：不服〉dissatisfaction, disagreement, an objection, a complaint.

fufuku no môshi-tate（不服の申し立て） an appeal of dissatisfaction

fufun〈ふふん〉pooh!, humph!

fûfu-naka〈ふうふなか：夫婦仲〉conjugal relations, conjugal affection.

Ryôshin wa fûfu-naka-ga-ii.（両親は夫婦仲がいい.）My parents live happily together.

fugai-nai〈ふがいない〉

Ware-nagara-fugai-nai.（我ながらふがいない.）I am ashamed of myself.

fû-gawari〈ふうがわり：風変わり〉

fû-gawari-na〈風変わりな〉eccentric, queer, quaint, odd, singular.

fû-gawari-na otoko（風変わりな男） a queer character, an eccentric

fugi〈ふぎ：不義〉

fugi-mittsû-o-suru〈不義密通をする〉commit infidelities.

fu-giri〈ふぎり：不義理〉dishonesty, injustice, ingratitude.

fu-giri-o-suru〈不義理をする〉do ((a person)) wrong, be ungrateful.

fu-giri-na〈不義理な〉dishonest, unjust, ungrateful.

fu-giri-na otoko（不義理な男） an ungrateful man

fû-giri〈ふうぎり：封切り〉a release.

fû-giri-kan（封切り館） a first-run theater, a first runner

fû-giri-suru〈封切りする〉release.

fû-girareru〈封切られる〉be released.

fû-giri-no〈封切りの〉newly-released.

fugô〈ふごう：富豪〉a man of great wealth, a mammoth millionaire.

fugô〈ふごう：符号〉a mark, a sign, a symbol.

  fugô-o-tsukeru〈符号を付ける〉mark.

fugô〈ふごう：符合〉

  fugô-suru〈符合する〉coincide ((with)), agree ((with)), accord ((with)), correspond ((with)), tally ((with)).

fu-gôkaku〈ふごうかく：不合格〉disqualification, failure, rejection.

    fu-gôkaku-hin〈不合格品〉 a rejected article

  fu-gôkaku-ni-naru〈不合格になる〉be disqualfied, fail to pass, be rejected.

  fu-gôkaku-no〈不合格の〉disqualified.

fu-gôri〈ふごうり：不合理〉irrationality, unreasonableness.

  fu-gôri-na〈不合理な〉irrational, unreasonable, illogical.

fugu〈ふぐ〉a swellfish, a globefish.

fugû〈ふぐう：不遇〉ill fortune, ill fate, obscurity.

    fugû-o-kakotsu〈不遇をかこつ〉 complain of one's ill fate

    isshô fugû-de-owaru〈一生不遇で終わる〉 live in obscurity all one's life

fuhai〈ふはい：腐敗〉decomposition, putrefaction; corruption.

  fuhai-suru〈腐敗する〉rot, become rotten, go bad; corrupt.

  fuhai-shi-yasui〈腐敗しやすい〉putrefactive.

  fuhai-shita〈腐敗した〉putrid, rotten, bad; corrupt(ed).

fuhai〈ふはい：不敗〉

  fuhai-no〈不敗の〉undefeated, invincible.

fuhatsu〈ふはつ：不発〉

    fuhatsu-dan〈不発弾〉 a blind shell

  fuhatsu-ni-owaru〈不発に終わる〉misfire.

fuhei〈ふへい：不平〉discontent, dissatisfaction; a complaint.

  fuhei-o-idaku〈不平を抱く〉feel discontented.

  fuhei-o-iu〈不平を言う〉grumble ((about, at *or* over)), complain ((of)), make a complaint ((about *or* of)).

fuhen〈ふへん：普遍〉

    fuhen-sei〈普遍性〉 universality

  fuhen-teki(-na)〈普遍的(な)〉universal.

fuhen〈ふへん：不変〉

  fuhen-no〈不変の〉unchangeable, invariable, constant, permanent.

fu-hitsuyô〈ふひつよう：不必要〉

  fu-hitsuyô-na〈不必要な〉unnecessary, needless.

fuhô〈ふほう：不法〉unlawfulness, lawlessness.

    fuhô-kôi〈不法行為〉 an unlawful act

    fuhô-nyûgoku〈不法入国〉illegal entry

fuhô-na〈不法な〉unlawful, illegal.

fuhô〈ふほう：ふ報〉a report of ((a person's)) death.

    fuhô-ni-sessuru〈ふ報に接する〉hear of ((a person's)) death

fu-hon·i〈ふほんい：不本意〉reluctance, unwillingness.

fu-hon·i-na〈不本意な〉reluctant, unwilling.

fu-hon·i-nagara or *fu-hon·i-ni*〈不本意ながら，不本意に〉reluctantly, unwillingly, against one's will.

fuhyô〈ふひょう：不評〉a bad reputation, unpopularity.

fuhyô-o-maneku〈不評を招く〉lose popularity, become unpopular.

fuhyô-na〈不評な〉disreputable, unpopular.

fui〈ふい〉

    fui-ni-naru〈ふいになる〉be lost, come to naught

    fui-ni-suru〈ふいにする〉lose, waste, bring to naught

fui〈ふい：不意〉

fui-no〈不意の〉sudden, incidental, unexpected.

    fui-no deki-goto〈不意の出来事〉an unexpected event

    fui-no raikyaku〈不意の来客〉an unexpected guest

fui-ni〈不意に〉suddenly, by chance, unexpectedly.

fûin〈ふういん：封印〉a (stamped) seal.

fûin-suru〈封印する〉seal.

fu-iri〈ふいり：不入り〉a small audience, an empty house, a failure.

fu-itchi〈ふいっち：不一致〉discord, disagreement, inconsistency.

fui-uchi〈ふいうち：不意打ち〉a surprise attack.

fui-uchi-o-kuu〈不意打ちを食う〉be taken by surprise.

fuji〈ふじ：不治〉

fuji-no〈不治の〉incurable, fatal.

    fuji-no yamai〈不治の病〉an incurable disease

fuji〈ふじ〉a wisteria.

    fuji-iro(-no)〈ふじ色(の)〉light purple

fuji-chaku(riku)〈ふじちゃく(りく)：不時着(陸)〉an emergency landing.

fuji-chaku(riku)-suru〈不時着(陸)する〉make an emergency landing.

fûji-komu〈ふうじこむ：封じ込む〉enclose ((something in)).

fuji-mi〈ふじみ：不死身〉

fuji-mi-de-aru〈不死身である〉be insensible to pain, have nine lives.

fujin〈ふじん：婦人〉a woman, a lady.

    fujin-keikan〈婦人警官〉a policewoman

fujin-rashii〈婦人らしい〉womanly, womanlike, ladylike.

fujin-yô(-no) 〈婦人用(の)〉 women's, ladies'.
    fujin-yô akusesarî（婦人用アクセサリー） women's accessories
fujin 〈ふじん：夫人〉 a wife, Mrs.
    Yamada-fujin（山田夫人） Mrs. Yamada
fu-jiyû 〈ふじゆう：不自由〉 inconvenience, want, poverty.
    fu-jiyû-o-shinobu（不自由を忍ぶ） put up with inconveniences
fu-jiyû-suru 〈不自由する〉 want, be in need of ((of)).
    kane-ni-fu-jiyû-suru（金に不自由する） be in need of money
fu-jiyû-na 〈不自由な〉 inconvenient, needy.
fu-jiyû-naku 〈不自由なく〉 in comfort.
    fu-jiyû-naku kurasu（不自由なく暮らす） live in comfort
fujo 〈ふじょ：扶助〉
    fujo-ryô（扶助料） a maintenance, an allowance to a bereaved family, a pension
    sôgo-fujo（相互扶助） mutual aid
fujo-suru 〈扶助する〉 aid, help, support, render ((a person)) assistance.
fujo-o-ukeru 〈扶助を受ける〉 depend on ((a person)) for support, receive allowance ((from)).
fujô 〈ふじょう：浮上〉
fujô-suru 〈浮上する〉 come up to the surface, surface.
fujô 〈ふじょう：不浄〉
fujô-no 〈不浄の〉 unclean.
    fujô-no kane（不浄の金） ill-gotten money
fujo(-shi) 〈ふじょ(し)；婦女(了)〉 womenfolk(s), the fair sex.
fu-jûbun 〈ふじゅうぶん：不十分〉 insufficiency, want, imperfection.
    shôko-fu-jûbun-de（証拠不十分で） for want of evidence
fu-jûbun-na 〈不十分な〉 insufficient, not enough, imperfect.
fu-jûjun 〈ふじゅうじゅん：不従順〉 disobedience, indocility.
fu-jûjun-na 〈不従順な〉 disobedient, indocile.
fujun 〈ふじゅん：不純〉
    fujun-butsu（不純物） impurities
fujun-na 〈不純な〉 impure.
fujun 〈ふじゅん：不順〉
fujun-na 〈不順な〉 unseasonable, changeable, irregular.
    fujun-na tenkô（不順な天候） the unseasonable weather
fuka 〈ふか：付加〉 addition, supplement.
    fuka-kachi（付加価値） value added
    fuka-zei（付加税） an additional tax, a surtax

fuka-suru 〈付加する〉 add ((to)), supplement.

fuka 〈ふか：ふ化〉 hatching, incubation.

jinkô-fuka（人工ふ化）　artificial incubation

fuka-suru 〈ふ化する〉 hatch.

fuka 〈ふか〉 a shark.

fûka(-sayô) 〈ふうか(さよう)：風化(作用)〉 weathering.

fûka-suru 〈風化する〉 weather.

fukabuka-to 〈ふかぶかと：深々と〉

fukabuka-to-isu-ni-suwaru〈深々といすに座る〉sit deep in a chair.

fu-kabun 〈ふかぶん：不可分〉

fu-kabun-na〈不可分な〉indivisible, inseparable.

fu-kabun-na kankei（不可分な関係）　an inseparable relation

fukahi 〈ふかひ：不可避〉

fukahi-na〈不可避な〉inevitable, unavoidable.

fukai 〈ふかい：深い〉 deep; dense, thick; profound, deep.

fukai ido（深い井戸）　a deep well

fukai kiri（深い霧）　a dense fog

fukai kangae（深い考え）　a deep thought

fukaku〈深く〉deep(ly).

fukaku horu（深く掘る）　dig deep

fukaku iki-o-suu（深く息を吸う）　breathe deep

fukaku kangaeru（深く考える）　think deeply

fukaku-naru〈深くなる〉deepen, become deeper.

fukaku-suru〈深くする〉deepen, make deeper.

fukai 〈ふかい：不快〉 displeasure, discomfort.

fukai-shisû（不快指数）　a discomfort index

fukai-na〈不快な〉unpleasant, disagreeable, uncomfortable, displeased.

fu-kainyû 〈ふかいにゅう：不介入〉 noninvolvement, nonintervention.

fuka-iri 〈ふかいり：深入り〉

fuka-iri-suru〈深入りする〉go too far ((in or into)), be taken up ((with)).

fukakai 〈ふかかい：不可解〉

fukakai-na〈不可解な〉beyond comprehension, baffling, inscrutable.

fukaketsu 〈ふかけつ：不可欠〉

fukaketsu-na〈不可欠な〉indispensable ((to)).

fukakô-ryoku 〈ふかこうりょく：不可抗力〉 an act of God, inevitability.

fukakô-ryoku-no〈不可抗力の〉inevitable, beyond control.

fukakô-ryoku-no jiko（不可抗力の事故）　an accident beyond ((a person's)) control

fukaku 〈ふかく：ふ角〉 an angle of depression.

fukaku 〈ふかく：不覚〉 lack of care, a defeat, a mistake.

 fukaku-o-toru (不覚を取る) be beaten, suffer a defeat

 zengo-fukaku-ni-naru (前後不覚になる) become unconscious

fûkaku 〈ふうかく：風格〉 appearance, personality, character, style.

 fûkaku-no-aru hito (風格のある人) a man of noble appearance

 dokutoku-no fûkaku-ga-aru (独特の風格がある) have a distinctive style

fu-kakudai 〈ふかくだい：不拡大〉

 fu-kakudai-hôshin (不拡大方針) a nonexpansion policy

fu-kakujitsu 〈ふかくじつ：不確実〉

 fu-kakujitsu-na 〈不確実な〉 uncertain, unreliable.

fukameru 〈ふかめる：深める〉 deepen, intensify, strengthen.

 rikai-o-fukameru (理解を深める) promote a better understanding

 kankei-o-fukameru (関係を深める) make the connection closer

fukami 〈ふかみ：深み〉 a depth, a deep place.

 fukami-ni-hamaru (深みにはまる) fall into a depth

fu-kanô 〈ふかのう：不可能〉 impossibility.

 fu-kanô-na 〈不可能な〉 impossible.

fu-kanshô 〈ふかんしょう：不干渉〉 nonintervention.

fukan-shô 〈ふかんしょう：不感症〉 frigidity.

fu-kanzen 〈ふかんぜん：不完全〉 imperfection, incompleteness.

 fu-kanzen-na 〈不完全な〉 imperfect.

 fu-kanzen-ni 〈不完全に〉 imperfectly.

fu-kappatsu 〈ふかっぱつ：不活発〉

 fu-kappatsu-na 〈不活発な〉 dull, inactive, sluggish, languid, stagnant, flat.

fukasa 〈ふかさ：深さ〉 depth.

 fukasa o hakaru (深さを測る) plumb the depth

fukashin 〈ふかしん：不可侵〉

 fukashin-jôyaku (不可侵条約) a nonaggression treaty

fukasu 〈ふかす〉 steam.

 satsuma-imo o fukasu (さつま芋をふかす) steam sweet potatoes

fukasu 〈ふかす：吹かす〉

 enjin o fukasu (エンジンを吹かす) rev (up) a motor

 tabako o fukasu (たばこを吹かす) smoke a cigarette

fukasu 〈ふかす：更かす〉

 yo-o-fukasu 〈夜を更かす〉 sit up till late.

fuka-zake 〈ふかざけ：深酒〉
  fuka-zake-suru 〈深酒する〉 drink excessively.

fuka-zume 〈ふかづめ：深づめ〉
  fuka-zume-o-kiru 〈深づめを切る〉 cut a nail to the quick.

fuke 〈ふけ〉 dandruff, scurf.
  fuke-darake-no 〈ふけだらけの〉 scurfy, dandruffy.

fukei 〈ふけい：父兄〉 one's parents.
  fukei-kai 〈父兄会〉 a parents' association

fûkei 〈ふうけい：風景〉 a landscape, a scene, a view.
  fûkei-ga 〈風景画〉 a landscape (painting)

fu-keiki 〈ふけいき：不景気〉 bad times; economic depression.
  fu-keiki-na 〈不景気な〉 inactive, dull, slack, depressed.

fu-keizai 〈ふけいざい：不経済〉
  fu-keizai-na 〈不経済な〉 uneconomical, expensive.

fu-ken 〈ふけん：府県〉 prefectures.
  fu-ken-no 〈府県の〉 prefectural.

fu-kenkô 〈ふけんこう：不健康〉 bad health.
  fu-kenkô-na 〈不健康な〉 unhealthy.

fu-kenshiki 〈ふけんしき：不見識〉
  fu-kenshiki-na 〈不見識な〉 undignified, disgraceful.

fu-kenzen 〈ふけんぜん：不健全〉
  fu-kenzen-na 〈不健全な〉 unwholesome, unsound.

fukeru 〈ふける：老ける〉 grow old.
  toshi-yori-fukete-mieru 〈年より老けて見える〉 look old for one's age

fukeru 〈ふける：更ける〉 grow late, advance, wear on.
  yoru ga fukeru-ni-tsurete 〈夜が更けるにつれて〉 as the night wears on

fukeru 〈ふける〉 be absorbed ((in)); indulge oneself ((in)).
  dokusho-ni-fukeru 〈読書にふける〉 be absorbed in reading

fuketsu 〈ふけつ：不潔〉
  fuketsu-na 〈不潔な〉 unclean, dirty, filthy.

fuke-yaku 〈ふけやく：老け役〉
  fuke-yaku o enjiru 〈老け役を演じる〉 do the part of an aged person.

fuki 〈ふき〉 a butterbur(r).

fûki 〈ふうき：風紀〉 public morals, discipline.
  fûki o midasu 〈風紀を乱す〉 corrupt public morals

fuki-ageru 〈ふきあげる：吹き上げる〉 blow up, throw up ((water)) into the air.

fuki-buri 〈ふきぶり：吹き降り〉wind and rain, a driving rain.
    Kinô-wa ichi-nichi-jû fuki-buri-datta.（昨日は一日中吹き降りだった.）We had a driving rain all day yesterday.

fuki-damari 〈ふきだまり：吹きだまり〉a snowdrift.

fuki-dasu 〈ふきだす：吹き出す〉begin to blow; burst into laughter, burst out laughing.

fuki-dasu 〈ふきだす：噴き出す〉spout (out), blow off.
    Chi ga fuki-dashiteiru.（血が噴き出している.）Blood is spouting.

fukide-mono 〈ふきでもの：吹き出物〉a skin eruption, a rash, a pimple.
    kao-ni fukide-mono-ga-dekiru（顔に吹き出物が出来る）have eruptions in the face

fu-kigen 〈ふきげん：不機嫌〉displeasure, bad humor.
  fu-ki-gen-de-aru 〈不機嫌である〉be in an ill humor.
  fu-kigen-na 〈不機嫌な〉ill-humored, displeased, sullen, cross.
    fu-kigen-na-kao-o-suru（不機嫌な顔をする）look displeased

fuki-harau 〈ふきはらう：吹き払う〉blow away, sweep off, puff away.

fuki-kae 〈ふきかえ：吹き替え〉dubbing.
  fuki-kaeru 〈吹き替える〉dub.
    Nihon-go-ni fuki-kaeru（日本語に吹き替える）dub in Japanese

fuki-kaesu 〈ふきかえす：吹き返す〉
  iki-o-fuki-kaesu 〈息を吹き返す〉come to life again.

fuki-kakeru 〈ふきかける：吹き掛ける〉blow upon, breathe upon, spray upon.
    gurasu-ni iki-o-fuki-kakeru（ガラスに息を吹き掛ける）breathe on a glass

fuki-kesu 〈ふきけす：吹き消す〉blow out.

fuki-kesu 〈ふきけす：拭き消す〉wipe out.

fuki-komu 〈ふきこむ：吹き込む〉blow in; record.
    rekôdo-ni-fuki-komu（レコードに吹き込む）put ((a song)) on a record

fuki-makuru 〈ふきまくる：吹きまくる〉sweep along, blow about, rage.
    Kaze ga sakuya-hito-ban-jû fuki-makutta.（風が昨夜一晩中吹きまくった.）The wind raged all last night.

fukin 〈ふきん：布きん〉a dishcloth.

fukin 〈ふきん：付近〉the neighborhood, the vicinity.
    kono-fukin-ni（この付近に）in this neighborhood, near here, around here
  fukin-no 〈付近の〉neighboring, nearby.

fuki-nagashi 〈ふきながし：吹き流し〉a streamer, a wind vane.

fu-kinkô 〈ふきんこう：不均衡〉imbalance, disproportion, disparity, inequality.

fu-kinkô-na 〈不均衡な〉ill-balanced, disproportionate, unequal.

fu-kinshin 〈ふきんしん：不謹慎〉imprudence, indiscretion.

fu-kinshin-na 〈不謹慎な〉imprudent, indiscreet.

fuki-orosu 〈ふきおろす：吹き下ろす〉blow down.

> yama-kara fuki-orosu-kaze（山から吹き下ろす風）the wind blowing down the mountains

fuki-sarashi 〈ふきさらし：吹きさらし〉

fuki-sarashi-no 〈吹きさらしの〉wind-swept, exposed to the wind.

> fuki-sarashi-no hômu-de（吹きさらしのホームで）at a wind-swept platform

fu-kiso 〈ふきそ：不起訴〉

> Kanojo-wa fu-kiso-ni-natta.（彼女は不起訴になった.）She was acquitted.

> Jiken wa fu-kiso-ni-natta.（事件は不起訴になった.）The case was dropped.

fuki-sôji 〈ふきそうじ：ふき掃除〉

fuki-sôji-suru 〈ふき掃除する〉sweep and dust〔a room〕.

fu-kisoku 〈ふきそく：不規則〉irregularity.

fu-kisoku-na 〈不規則な〉irregular.

> fu-kisoku-na seikatsu（不規則な生活）an irregular life

fu-kisoku-ni 〈不規則に〉irregularly.

fuki-susabu 〈ふきすさぶ：吹きすさぶ〉blow violently.

> fuki-susabu kaze（吹きすさぶ風）a blustering wind

fuki-taosu 〈ふきたおす：吹き倒す〉blow down, blow to the ground.

fuki-tobasu 〈ふきとばす：吹き飛ばす〉blow away, blow off.

> bôshi o fuki-tobasareru（帽子を吹き飛ばされる）have one's hat blown off

fuki-toru 〈ふきとる：ふき取る〉wipe off, mop up.

fukitsu 〈ふきつ：不吉〉an ill omen.

fukitsu-na 〈不吉な〉ill-omened, unlucky, ominous, sinister.

> fukitsu-na yokan（不吉な予感）an ominous presentiment

fuki-tsuke 〈ふきつけ：吹き付け〉spraying.

> fuki-tsuke-tosô（吹き付け塗装）spray painting

fuki-tsukeru 〈ふきつける：吹き付ける〉blow against ((something)).

fuki-yamu 〈ふきやむ：吹き止む〉cease to blow, blow itself out.

fukkakeru 〈ふっかける：吹っ掛ける〉

　　　kenka o fukkakeru〈けんかを吹っ掛ける〉 pick a quarrel ((with))

　　　ne-o-fukkakeru〈値を吹っ掛ける〉 make an exorbitant demand, rush ((a person))

fukkan〈ふっかん：副官〉an adjutant.

fukkatsu〈ふっかつ：復活〉rebirth, resurgence.

　　　gunkoku-shugi no fukkatsu〈軍国主義の復活〉 the resurgence of militarism

　fukkatsu-suru〈復活する〉come to life again, revive.

Fukkatsu-sai〈ふっかつさい：復活祭〉Easter.

fukki〈ふっき：復帰〉a return, a comeback.

　fukki-suru〈復帰する〉return ((to)), make a comeback, revert ((to)).

　　　shokuba-ni-fukki-suru〈職場に復帰する〉 return to work

fukkin〈ふっきん：腹筋〉an abdominal muscle.

fukko〈ふっこ：復古〉restoration, revival.

　　　fukko-chō〈復古調〉 a reactionary tendency, a revival mood

fukkō〈ふっこう：復興〉revival, restoration, reconstruction.

　fukkô-suru〈復興する〉be revived, be reconstructed.

fukkura〈ふっくら〉

　fukkura-shita〈ふっくらした〉plump, full.

　　　fukkura-shita hoo〈ふっくらしたほお〉 full cheeks

fukkyū〈ふっきゅう：復旧〉restoration.

　　　fukkyû-kōji〈復旧工事〉 restoration work

　fukkyû-suru〈復旧する〉be restored, resume normal services.

fukō〈ふこう：不幸〉unhappiness, misery; misfortune, ill luck.

　fukô-na〈不幸な〉unhappy, unfortunate, unlucky.

　　　fukô-na hito〈不幸な人〉 an unhappy person

　fukô-nimo〈不幸にも〉unfortunately, unluckily.

fukō〈ふこう：不孝〉undutifulness (to one's parents).

　fukô-na〈不孝な〉undutiful.

fu-kōhei〈ふこうへい：不公平〉unfairness, injustice, inequity.

　fu-kôhei-na〈不公平な〉unfair, unjust, inequitable.

fukoku〈ふこく：布告〉proclamation, declaration.

　fukoku-suru〈布告する〉proclaim, declare.

　　　sensen o fukoku-suru〈宣戦を布告する〉 declare war ((on))

fûkô-meibi〈ふうこうめいび：風光明び〉

　　　Tôchi-wa　fûkô-meibi-de-aru.〈当地は風光明びである。〉 This place is famous for its scenic beauty. / The scenery here is quite beautiful.

fuku 〈ふく：服〉 clothes, a dress, a suit.

    fuku o kiru（服を着る） put on clothes

    fuku o nugu（服を脱ぐ） take off one's clothes

    fuku o ki-gaeru（服を着替える） change one's clothes

fuku 〈ふく：福〉 (good) fortune, blessing, (good) luck.

fuku 〈ふく：吹く〉 blow.

    Kaze ga tsuyoku fuiteiru.（風が強く吹いている.） It is blowing hard.

    torampetto o fuku（トランペットを吹く） blow a trumpet

fuku 〈ふく：噴く〉 emit, spout.

    hi o fuku（火を噴く） emit fire

fuku 〈ふく〉 tile〔a roof〕, shingle, slate.

fuku 〈ふく〉 wipe, mop.

    tsukue o fuku（机をふく） wipe a desk

fuku- 〈ふく-：副-〉 vice-, assistant.

    fuku-daitôryô（副大統領） a vice-president

    fuku-chiji（副知事） a vice-governor

    fuku-gichô（副議長） a vice-chairman

    fuku-shihai-nin（副支配人） an assistant manager

fukuan 〈ふくあん：腹案〉 a plan (in one's mind).

    fukuan o tateru（腹案を立てる） draw up a plan

fuku-biki 〈ふくびき：福引き〉 a lottery.

    fuku-biki-o-suru〈福引きをする〉 draw lots.

fuku-bu 〈ふくぶ：腹部〉 the abdomen, the belly.

fukubun 〈ふくぶん：複文〉 a complex sentence.

fukuchô 〈ふくちょう：副長〉 an executive (officer).

fukudoku 〈ふくどく：服毒〉

    fukudoku-jisatsu-o-suru（服毒自殺をする） kill oneself by taking poison

fuku-dokuhon 〈ふくどくほん：副読本〉 a supplementary reader.

fukueki 〈ふくえき：服役〉

    fukueki-kikan（服役期間） a term of sentence

    fukueki-suru〈服役する〉 serve a prison term.

fukuen 〈ふくえん：復縁〉 reconciliation.

    fukuen-suru〈復縁する〉 be reinstated〔as a wife〕.

fukugan 〈ふくがん：複眼〉 compound eyes.

fukugen 〈ふくげん：復元〉

    fukugen-suru〈復元する〉 restore to the original state.

fukugô 〈ふくごう：複合〉

    fukugô-go（複合語） a compound (word)

fukugô-tai〈複合体〉 a complex

fukugô-no〈複合の〉compound, complex.

fukugyô〈ふくぎょう：副業〉a side job, a sideline.

fuku-hi(rei)〈ふくひ(れい)：複比(例)〉a compound ratio.

fukuin〈ふくいん：復員〉demobilization.

fukuin-suru〈復員する〉be demobilized, be discharged, be demobbed.

fukuin〈ふくいん：福音〉the gospel.

fukuin o toku（福音を説く） preach the gospel

fukuji〈ふくじ：服地〉cloth, dress material, fabric material, suiting.

fukujin〈ふくじん：副じん〉adrenal glands.

fukujû〈ふくじゅう：服従〉obedience.

fukujû-suru〈服従する〉obey, be obedient ((to)).

fukujû-teki(-na)〈服従的(な)〉obedient.

fukuju-sô〈ふくじゅそう：福寿草〉an adonis.

fukuma-den〈ふくまでん：伏魔殿〉a pandemonium, a hotbed of iniquity.

fukumaku〈ふくまく：腹膜〉the peritoneum.

fukumaku-en（腹膜炎） peritonitis

fukumen〈ふくめん：覆面〉a mask.

fukumen-gôtô（覆面強盗） a masked burglar

fukumi〈ふくみ：含み〉an implication, a hidden meaning.

fukumi-no-aru kotoba（含みのある言葉） words with a hidden meaning

fukumi-warai〈ふくみわらい：含み笑い〉a chuckle.

fukumi-warai-o-suru〈含み笑いをする〉chuckle.

fukumu〈ふくむ：含む〉contain, include.

Kaisui-ni-wa donna busshitsu ga fukumarete-imasu-ka?（海水にはどんな物質が含まれていますか。） What substances does sea water contain?

Ryôkin-ni-wa zeikin-wa-fukumarete-i-nai.（料金には税金は含まれていない。） The charge does not include the tax.

Watashi-o-fukumete jû-nin-ga-shusseki-shita.（私を含めて十人が出席した。） Ten were present, including me.

fukurahagi〈ふくらはぎ〉the calf.

fukuramasu〈ふくらます：膨らます〉swell (out), inflate, plump up, puff.

kûki-makura o fukuramasu（空気まくらを膨らます） plump up a pillow

hoo o fukuramasu（ほおを膨らます） puff out one's cheeks

fukuramu〈膨らむ〉swell (out), become inflated.

　　Tsubomi ga fukurami-hajimeta.（つぼみが膨らみ始めた.）　The buds began to swell.

fukurami〈膨らみ〉a swelling, a bulge.

　　kanojo-no mune no yutaka-na fukurami（彼女の胸の豊かな膨らみ）the rich bulge of her breast

fukurashi-ko〈ふくらしこ：膨らし粉〉baking powder.

fukureru〈ふくれる：膨れる〉swell out, be inflated, rise; get sulky.

fukurettsura〈ふくれっつら：膨れっ面〉a sulky look, a sullen look.

fukurettsura-o-suru〈膨れっ面をする〉pout.

fukuri〈ふくり：複利〉compound interest.

　　fukuri-de keisan-suru（複利で計算する）calculate at compound interest

fukuro〈ふくろ：袋〉a bag, a sack.

　　fukuro-ni-ireru（袋に入れる）　put into a bag

fukurô〈ふくろう〉an owl.

fukuro-dataki〈ふくろだたき：袋だたき〉

fukuro-dataki-ni-suru〈袋だたきにする〉gang up on ((a person)) and beat him up.

fukuro-kôji〈ふくろこうじ：袋小路〉a blind alley, an impasse.

fukuro-no-nezumi〈ふくろのねずみ：袋のねずみ〉a mouse in a trap.

fukusa〈ふくさ〉a (small) crape wrapper.

fuku-sambutsu〈ふくさんぶつ：副産物〉a by-product.

fuku-sayô〈ふくさよう：副作用〉a side effect ((on)).

fukusei〈ふくせい：複製〉reproduction.

　　Fukyo-fukusei.（不許複製.）　All rights reserved.

fukusei-suru〈複製する〉reproduce.

fukusen〈ふくせん：複線〉a double track.

fukusen-ka-suru〈複線化する〉double-track.

fukusha〈ふくしゃ：ふく射〉radiation.

　　fukusha-netsu（ふく射熱）　radiant heat

fukusha-suru〈ふく射する〉radiate.

fukusha〈ふくしゃ：複写〉reproduction, a copy.

fukusha-suru〈複写する〉reproduce, copy, take a copy ((of)).

fukushi〈ふくし：福祉〉welfare.

　　shakai-fukushi（社会福祉）　social welfare

fukushi〈ふくし：副詞〉an adverb.

fukushiki-boki〈ふくしきぼき：複式簿記〉double-entry bookkeeping.

fukushiki-kokyû〈ふくしきこきゅう：腹式呼吸〉abdominal breathing.

fukushin 〈ふくしん：腹心〉
    fukushin-no-buka（腹心の部下） one of one's trusted men

fukushoku 〈ふくしょく：復職〉 reinstatement.
  fukushoku-suru（復職する） be reinstated〔in one's former office〕.

fukushoku 〈ふくしょく：副食〉 a side dish.

fukushoku-dezainâ 〈ふくしょくデザイナー：服飾デザイナー〉 a dress designer.

fukushû 〈ふくしゅう：復習〉 review.
  fukushû-suru〈復習する〉 review〔one's lesson〕.

fukushû 〈ふくしゅう：復しゅう〉 revenge.
  fukushû-suru〈復しゅうする〉 revenge oneself ((on)), be revenged ((upon)).

fuku-shûnyû 〈ふくしゅうにゅう：副収入〉 an additional income.

fukusô 〈ふくそう：服装〉 dress, costume, clothes.
    seishiki-no fukusô（正式の服装） formal dress
  rippa-na-fukusô-o-shite-iru〈立派な服装をしている〉 be well dressed.

fukusû 〈ふくすう：複数〉 the plural (number).
  fukusû-no〈複数の〉 plural.

fukusuru 〈ふくする：服する〉 submit ((to)), obey.
    tsumi-ni-fukusuru（罪に服する） submit to the sentence
    meirei ni fukusuru（命令に服する） obey the orders

fukusuru 〈ふくする：復する〉
  heijô-no jôtai-ni fukusuru〈平常の状態に復する〉 return to the normal conditions.

fukutsu 〈ふくつ：不屈〉
  fukutsu-no〈不屈の〉 indomitable.
    fukutsu-no seishin（不屈の精神） an indomitable spirit

fukutsû 〈ふくつう：腹痛〉 a stomachache.
  fukutsû-ga-suru（腹痛がする） have a stomachache

fukuwa-jutsu 〈ふくわじゅつ：腹話術〉 ventriloquy.
    fukuwa-jutsu-sha（腹話術者） a ventriloquist

fukuyô 〈ふくよう：服用〉
  fukuyô-suru〈服用する〉 take.
    kusuri o shokugo-ni fukuyô-suru（薬を食後に服用する） take medicine after meals

fukuzatsu 〈ふくざつ：複雑〉
  fukuzatsu-na〈複雑な〉 complicated, complex, intricate.
    fukuzatsu-na jijô（複雑な事情） complicated circumstances

　　　fukuzatsu-na kikô〈複雑な機構〉 intricate mechanism
fukuzô〈ふくぞう：腹蔵〉
　fukuzô-no-nai〈腹蔵のない〉 unreserved, frank, outspoken.
　fukuzô-naku〈腹蔵なく〉 without reserve, frankly, freely.
　　　fukuzô-naku-ieba〈腹蔵なく言えば〉 frankly speaking
fukyô〈ふきょう：不況〉 depression, slump, bad business.
　　　fukyô-jidai〈不況時代〉 depression days
　　　sekai-teki-na fukyô〈世界的な不況〉 worldwide depression
fukyô〈ふきょう：布教〉 propagandism.
　fukyô-suru〈布教する〉 propagandize.
fukyô〈ふきょう：不興〉 displeasure.
　　　fukyô o kau〈不興を買う〉 incur ((a person's)) displeasure
fu-kyôwa-on〈ふきょうわおん：不協和音〉 a discord, a dissonance.
fukyû〈ふきゅう：普及〉 spread, diffusion; popularization.
　　　kyôiku no fukyû〈教育の普及〉 the spread of education
　　　fukyû-ritsu〈普及率〉 the rate of diffusion
　　　fukyû-ban〈普及版〉 a popular edition
　fukyû-suru〈普及する〉 spread, diffuse; popularize.
fukyû〈ふきゅう：不朽〉
　fukyû-no〈不朽の〉 immortal.
　　　fukyû-no meisaku〈不朽の名作〉 an immortal work
fu-majime〈ふまじめ：不まじめ〉
　fu-majime-na〈不まじめな〉 not serious.
fuman〈ふまん：不満〉 dissatisfaction, discontent.
　fuman-de-aru, fuman-ni-omou or *fuman-o-idaku*〈不満である、不満に思う、不満を抱く〉 be dissatisfied ((at *or* with)), feel discontented ((with)).
　fuman-na or *fuman-sô-na*〈不満な、不満そうな〉 dissatisfied, discontented.
　　　fuman-sô-na kao-tsuki o suru〈不満そうな顔つきをする〉 wear a dissatisfied look
fumbaru〈ふんばる〉 brace one's legs and stand firm; hold out, make an effort.
fumbetsu〈ふんべつ：分別〉 discretion, prudence, good sense, judg(e)ment.
　fumbetsu-no-aru〈分別のある〉 discreet, prudent, thoughtful, judicious.
　　　fumbetsu-no-nai〈分別のない〉 indiscreet, imprudent, thoughtless, injudicious
fumei〈ふめい：不明〉 obscurity, indistinctness.

fumei-no 〈不明の〉 obscure, indistinct, unknown, dubious.

  gen·in-fumei-no kaji（原因不明の火事） a fire of unknown origin

  kokuseki-fumei-no sempaku（国籍不明の船舶） a vessel∖of dubious nationality

  mimoto-fumei-no-shitai（身元不明の死体） an unidentified body

fu-meirô 〈ふめいろう：不明朗〉

fu-meirô-na 〈不明朗な〉 gloomy, dubious, underhand, unfair.

fu-meiryô 〈ふめいりょう：不明りょう〉

fu-meiryô-na 〈不明りょうな〉 indistinct, obscure, unclear.

fu-meiryô-ni 〈不明りょうに〉 indistinctly, obscurely.

fu-meiyo 〈ふめいよ：不名誉〉 dishonor, disgrace, shame.

fu-meiyo-na 〈不名誉な〉 dishonorable, disgraceful, shameful.

fumetsu 〈ふめつ：不滅〉 immortality.

fumetsu-no 〈不滅の〉 immortal, monumental.

fûmi 〈ふうみ：風味〉 flavor, savor, taste.

fûmi-no-ii 〈風味のいい〉 delicious, savory, tasty.

  fûmi-no-nai（風味のない） insipid, tasteless

fumi-dai 〈ふみだい：踏み台〉 a footstool, a springboard.

  hito-o-fumi-dai-ni-suru（人を踏み台にする） make a stepping-stone of a person

fumi-dasu 〈ふみだす：踏み出す〉 step forward, advance.

  ippo fumi-dasu（一歩踏み出す） take a step ((toward))

fumi-hazusu 〈ふみはずす：踏み外す〉 miss one's foot, make a false step.

fumi-ireru 〈ふみいれる：踏み入れる〉 tread on, step in, set one's foot in.

fumi-katameru 〈ふみかためる：踏み固める〉 stamp down.

fumikiri 〈ふみきり：踏切〉 a railroad crossing, a level crossing.

  mujin-fumikiri（無人踏切） an unattended (railroad) crossing

fumi-kiru 〈ふみきる：踏み切る〉 take the plunge ((on)).

fumi-komu 〈ふみこむ：踏み込む〉 step into; make a raid ((on)).

fumin 〈ふみん：不眠〉

  fumin-shô（不眠症） insomnia

fumin-fukyû-de 〈不眠不休で〉 without sleeping or resting.

fumi-nijiru 〈ふみにじる：踏みにじる〉 trample underfoot.

fumi-taosu 〈ふみたおす：踏み倒す〉 bilk.

  kanjô o fumi-taosu（勘定を踏み倒す） bilk a bill

fumi-todomaru 〈ふみとどまる：踏みとどまる〉 hold one's own, make a stand ((against)), hold on.

fumi-tsubusu 〈ふみつぶす：踏みつぶす〉 crush ((a thing)) under one's foot.

fumi-tsukeru 〈ふみつける：踏み付ける〉trample down, tread on; despise.

fummatsu 〈ふんまつ：粉末〉powder.
  fummatsu-ni-suru〈粉末にする〉powder, reduce to powder.
  fummatsu(-jô)-no〈粉末(状)の〉powdered.

fummu-ki 〈ふんむき：噴霧器〉a spray(er).
  fummu-ki-de-kakeru〈噴霧器でかける〉spray.

fumô 〈ふもう：不毛〉
  fumô-no〈不毛の〉barren; sterile.
    fumô-no chi (不毛の地) barren land

fumoto 〈ふもと〉the foot.
    yama no fumoto-ni (山のふもとに) at the foot of a mountain

fumu 〈ふむ：踏む〉step ((on)), tread ((on)).
    hito-no ashi o fumu (人の足を踏む) step on a person's foot

fumuki 〈ふむき：不向き〉
  fumuki-de-aru〈不向きである〉be not cut out ((for)).

fun 〈ふん：分〉a minute.
    jû-go-fun (十五分) fifteen minutes, a quarter
    san-juppun (三十分) thirty minutes, half an hour
    jû-ji sampun (十時三分) three minutes past ten, ten three
    ku-ji go-jû-nana-fun or jû-ji sampun-mae (九時五十七分, 十時三分前)
      nine fifty-seven, three minutes to ten
    Aruite go-fun-desu. (歩いて五分です。) It's (a) five minutes' walk.

fun 〈ふん〉excrement(s), dung, droppings.

fun 〈ふん〉hum(ph)!, hmm!, pshaw!

funa 〈ふな〉a crucian (carp).

funa-ashi 〈ふなあし：船脚〉speed.
  funa-ashi-no-hayai fune〈船脚の速い船〉a fast boat.
    funa-ashi-no-osoi fune (船脚の遅い船) a slow boat

funa-bin 〈ふなびん：船便〉shipping service; sea mail.

funa-chin 〈ふなちん：船賃〉passage, a boat fare, freight.

funa-gaisha 〈ふながいしゃ：船会社〉a steamship company.

funa-kaji 〈ふなかじ：船火事〉a fire on a ship.

funa-ni 〈ふなに：船荷〉a (ship's) cargo, a freight.
    funa-ni-shôken (船荷証券) a bill of lading

funa-nori 〈ふなのり：船乗り〉*see.* sen·in.

funa-nushi 〈ふなぬし：船主〉*see.* senshu.

funare 〈ふなれ：不慣れ〉

funare-na 〈不慣れな〉 inexperienced, unaccustomed, unfamiliar.
　　funare-na hito 〈不慣れな人〉 an inexperienced person
　　funare-na shigoto 〈不慣れな仕事〉 an unaccustomed job
　　funare-na tochi 〈不慣れな土地〉 an unfamiliar place

funa-tabi 〈ふなたび：船旅〉 a voyage, a sea trip.

funa-yoi 〈ふなよい：船酔い〉 seasickness.
funa-yoi-suru 〈船酔いする〉 get seasick.

funa-zumi 〈ふなづみ：船積み〉
funa-zumi-suru 〈船積みする〉 ship, load.

fundan 〈ふんだん〉
fundan-ni 〈ふんだんに〉 in plenty, abundantly, fully, lavishly.
　　fundan-ni kane o tsukau 〈ふんだんに金を使う〉 spend money lavishly

fundari-kettari 〈ふんだりけったり：踏んだりけったり〉
　　Sore-jâ fundari-kettari-da. （それじゃあ踏んだりけったりだ。） It is adding insult to injury.

fundō 〈ふんどう：分銅〉 a weight.

fune 〈ふね：舟，船〉 a boat, a vessel, a ship, a motorship.
　　fune ni noru 〈船に乗る〉 go on board a ship
　　fune o oriru 〈船を降りる〉 leave a ship
　　fune-ni-tsuyoi 〈船に強い〉 be a good sailor
　　fune-ni-yowai 〈船に弱い〉 be a poor sailor

funen(-sei) 〈ふねん（せい）：不燃(性)〉
funen-sei-no 〈不燃性の〉 noninflammable, incombustible.

fu-nesshin 〈ふねっしん：不熱心〉 lack of enthusiasm, indifference.
fu-nesshin-de-aru 〈不熱心である〉 take little interest ((in)), be indifferent ((to)).
fu-nesshin-na 〈不熱心な〉 unenthusiastic, halfhearted, indifferent.
fu-nesshin-ni 〈不熱心に〉 unenthusiastically, halfheartedly, indifferently.

fungai 〈ふんがい：憤慨〉 indignation, resentment.
fungai-suru 〈憤慨する〉 be indignant ((at *or* over)), resent.

fungiri 〈ふんぎり〉
fungiri-ga-tsuka-nai 〈ふんぎりが付かない〉 be unable to make up one's mind, hesitate.

fu-niai 〈ふにあい：不似合い〉
fu-niai-de-aru 〈不似合いである〉 do not become ((a person)).
fu-niai-na 〈不似合いな〉 unbecoming ((to)), unfit ((for)), unsuitable ((for)).

fun·iki 〈ふんいき：雰囲気〉 an atmosphere.

funin 〈ふにん：赴任〉
funin-suru 〈赴任する〉 leave for one's new post, proceed to one's post.

fu-ninjō 〈ふにんじょう：不人情〉
fu-ninjô-na 〈不人情な〉 unkind, inhuman, hardhearted, heartless.

fu-ninki 〈ふにんき：不人気〉 unpopularity.
fu-ninki-na 〈不人気な〉 unpopular.

funin-shô 〈ふにんしょう：不妊症〉 sterility.
funin-shô-no 〈不妊症の〉 sterile.

funka 〈ふんか：噴火〉 an eruption.
　　funka-shite-iru 〈噴火している〉 be in eruption
　　funka-kô 〈噴火口〉 a crater
funka-suru 〈噴火する〉 erupt, burst into eruption.

funki 〈ふんき：奮起〉
funki-suru 〈奮起する〉 rouse oneself (up), be stirred up.
funki-saseru 〈奮起させる〉 rouse, stir up.

funkyû 〈ふんきゅう：紛糾〉 complication, tangle.
funkyû-suru 〈紛糾する〉 become complicated, tangle.

funô 〈ふのう：不能〉
　　sei-teki-funô-sha 〈性的不能者〉 an impotent

funsai 〈ふんさい：粉砕〉
funsai-suru 〈粉砕する〉 smash to pieces, crush, annihilate.

funsen 〈ふんせん：奮戦〉 hard fighting, a desperate fight.
funsen-suru 〈奮戦する〉 fight hard, fight desperately.

funsha 〈ふんしゃ：噴射〉 jet.
funsha-suru 〈噴射する〉 jet, fire.

funshitsu 〈ふんしつ：紛失〉 loss.
　　funshitsu-butsu 〈紛失物〉 a lost article, a missing article
funshitsu-suru 〈紛失する〉 lose, miss, be lost, be missing.
funshitsu-shita 〈紛失した〉 lost, missing.

funshoku-kessan 〈ふんしょくけっさん：粉飾決算〉 a rigged account.

funsô 〈ふんそう：紛争〉 (a) dispute, (a) trouble.
　　funsô o kaiketsu-suru 〈紛争を解決する〉 settle a dispute

funsô 〈ふんそう：ふん装〉 makeup, disguise.
funsô-suru 〈ふん装する〉 make up, disguise oneself ((as)).
　　onna-ni-funsô-suru 〈女にふん装する〉 disguise oneself as a woman

funsui 〈ふんすい：噴水〉 a jet, a fountain.

funsuru 〈ふんする〉 act the part ((of)), impersonate, disguise oneself ((as)).

funtô〈ふんとう：奮闘〉a struggle, strenuous efforts.
funtô-suru〈奮闘する〉struggle, make strenuous efforts.

fu-nyoi〈ふによい：不如意〉
te-moto-fu-nyoi-de-aru〈手もと不如意である〉be pressed for money.

fûnyû〈ふうにゅう：封入〉
　　fûnyû-butsu（封入物）　an enclosure
fûnyû-suru〈封入する〉enclose.
fûnyû-no〈封入の〉enclosed, under cover.

funzen〈ふんぜん：憤然〉
funzen-to(-shite)〈憤然と（して）〉indignantly, in a rage.

funzori-kaeru〈ふんぞりかえる：ふんぞり返る〉assume a high and
mighty attitude.

fuon〈ふおん：不穏〉
fuon-na〈不穏な〉disquieting, alarming, disorderly, threatening.
　　fuon-na-kôdô-ni-deru（不穏な行動に出る）　disturb the peace and
　　order of society

fu-ontô〈ふおんとう：不穏当〉
fu-ontô-na〈不穏当な〉improper, unjust, unfair, violent.
　　fu-ontô-na shochi（不穏当な処置）　an unfair dealing

furafura〈ふらふら〉
　　atama-ga-furafura-suru（頭がふらふらする）　feel dizzy
　　ashi-moto-ga-furafura-suru（足下がふらふらする）　be unsteady on
　　one's feet
　　furafura-tachi-agaru（ふらふら立ち上がる）　stagger to one's feet
　　tsukarete furafura-ni-natte-iru（疲れてふらふらになっている）　be faint
　　with fatigue

furai〈フライ〉a fly.
　　furai o toru（フライを捕る）　catch a fly
furai-o-ageru〈フライを上げる〉fly, pop.

furai〈フライ〉fry.
　　ebi-furai（えびフライ）　fried lobster
　　furai-pan（フライパン）　a frying pan, a skillet
furai-ni-suru〈フライにする〉fry.
furai-ni-shita〈フライにした〉fried.

furai-kyû〈フライきゅう：フライ級〉the flyweight.
furai-kyû-no〈フライ級の〉flyweight.

furan〈ふらん：腐乱〉decomposition.
　　furan-shitai（腐乱死体）　a decomposed body

Furansu〈フランス〉France.

    Furansu-jin（フランス人）a Frenchman, a Frenchwoman

    Furansu-go（フランス語）French

    Furansu(-jin)-no（フランス(人)の）French

furareru〈ふられる：振られる〉be rejected, be refused, be jilted.

furari〈ふらり〉

furari-to〈ふらりと〉by chance, unexpectedly, without any definite purpose.

    furari-to dekakeru（ふらりと出掛ける）go out without any definite purpose

    furari-to-tachi-yoru（ふらりと立ち寄る）drop in

furasshu〈フラッシュ〉a flash, (a) flashlight.

    furasshu-o-abiru（フラッシュを浴びる）be in a flood of flashlights

    furasshu o taku（フラッシュをたく）light a flashbulb

furasuko〈フラスコ〉a flask.

fura-tsuku〈ふらつく〉

ashi-moto-ga-fura-tsuku〈足下がふらつく〉see. furafura(ashi-moto-ga-furafura-suru).

furatto〈フラット〉a flat.

    san-jû-byô-furatto-de（三十秒フラットで）in 30 seconds flat

fure-ai〈ふれあい：触れ合い〉contact, touch.

fure-au〈触れ合う〉come in touch ((with)).

    kokoro-to-kokoro-ga-fure-au（心と心が触れ合う）sympathize ((with)), hold communion ((with)).

fure-komi〈ふれこみ：触れ込み〉announcement, a herald.

    Kare-wa isha-da-to-iu-fure-komi-datta.（彼は医者だという触れ込みだった。）It was given out that he was a doctor.

fure-mawaru〈ふれまわる：触れ回る〉trumpet, spread, circulate.

    kinjo-jû fure-mawaru（近所中触れ回る）trumpet ((a story)) among the whole neighborhood

fu-renzoku-sen〈ふれんぞくせん：不連続線〉a line of discontinuity.

fureru〈ふれる：振れる〉shake, oscillate.

fureru〈ふれる：触れる〉touch; touch ((on)), mention, refer ((to)).

    migi-te-de fureru（右手で触れる）touch ((a thing)) with the right hand

    mondai-ni-fure-nai（問題に触れない）do noy touch the question

furi〈ふり：不利〉disadvantage.

furi-na〈不利な〉disadvantageous, unfavorable.

furi-na tachiba-ni-aru〈不利な立場にある〉 be in a disadvantageous position

furi〈ふり：降り〉rainfall.

Hidoi-furi-da!（ひどい降りだ.）How it rains!

furi〈ふり：振り〉

　furi-o-suru〈振りをする〉pretend, affect, feign.

byōki-no-furi-o-suru（病気の振りをする）feign sickness, feign to be sick

kikoe-nai-furi-o-suru（聞こえない振りをする）pretend not to hear

mite-mi-nai-furi-o-suru（見て見ない振りをする）pretend not to see

shira-nai-furi-o-suru（知らない振りをする）affect ignorance

furi-ageru〈ふりあげる：振り上げる〉fling up, swing up.

furi-ai〈ふりあい：振り合い〉consideration, comparison.

hoka-to-no-furi-ai-mo-aru-kara（ほかとの振り合いもあるから）as we must take other people into consideration

furi-ateru〈ふりあてる：振り当てる〉assign, allot.

furi-dashi〈ふりだし：振り出し〉a beginning, the starting point; drawing.

furi-dashi-ni-modoru（振り出しに戻る）make a fresh start

　furi-dasu〈振り出す〉draw, issue.

tegata o furi-dasu（手形を振り出す）draw a bill

furi-gana〈ふりがな：振り仮名〉

seimei-ni-furi-gana-o-tsukeru（姓名に振り仮名を付ける）give the reading of ((a person's)) name in *kana*

furi-hanasu〈ふりはなす：振り離す〉shake off, shake oneself free ((from)).

furi-harau or **furi-hodoku**〈ふりはらう, ふりほどく：振り払う, 振りほどく〉*see.* furi-hanasu.

furi-kaburu〈ふりかぶる：振りかぶる〉hold ((a ball)) aloft.

furikae〈ふりかえ：振替〉change, transfer.

furikae-de sōkin-suru（振替で送金する）send money by postal transfer

furikae-chokin（振替貯金）transfer savings

furikae-dempyō（振替伝票）a transfer slip

furi-kaeru〈ふりかえる：振り返る〉look back, turn about.

jibun-no kako o furi-kaeru（自分の過去を振り返る）look back upon one's past

furi-kakaru〈ふりかかる：降りかかる〉befall, happen ((to)), overhang.

　　mi-ni　furi-kakatta　sainan〈身に降りかかった災難〉 the misfortune which befell a person

furi-kakeru〈ふりかける：振り掛ける〉sprinkle.

　　niku-ni　koshô o furi-kakeru（肉にこしょうを振り掛ける） sprinkle pepper over meat

furi-kata〈ふりかた：振り方〉

　　mi-no-furi-kata o kimeru（身の振り方を決める） make up a plan for ((a person's)) future

furi-kiru〈ふりきる：振り切る〉shake off, sever by force.

　　furi-kitte-nigeru（振り切って逃げる） tear oneself away ((from))

furi-ko〈ふりこ：振り子〉a pendulum.

fu-rikô〈ふりこう：不履行〉nonfulfillment, nonperformance, nonobservance, breach.

　　keiyaku-fu-rikô（契約不履行） nonfulfillment of a contract

furi-komu〈ふりこむ：降り込む〉rain into.

furi-maku〈ふりまく：振りまく〉sprinkle, scatter.

furi-mawasu〈ふりまわす：振り回す〉brandish; display, show off; abuse.

　furi-mawasareru〈振り回される〉be turned round ((a person's)) (little) finger, be led by the nose.

furi-mukeru〈ふりむける：振り向ける〉appropriate(*or* apply) ((something to)).

furi-muku〈ふりむく：振り向く〉*see.* furi-kaeru.

furin〈ふりん：不倫〉

　furin-na〈不倫な〉immoral, illicit.

　　furin-na koi（不倫な恋） illicit love

fûrin〈ふうりん：風鈴〉a wind-bell.

furî-pasu〈フリーパス〉a free ticket.

furi-shikiru〈ふりしきる：降りしきる〉

　furi-shikiru-ame-no-naka-o（降りしきる雨の中を）in a downpour.

furi-sode〈ふりそで：振りそで〉a long-sleeved *kimono.*

furi-tsuke〈ふりつけ：振り付け〉dance composition, choreography.

　　furi-tsuke-shi（振り付け師） a dance composer, choreographer

　furi-tsuke-o-suru〈振り付けをする〉compose〔a dance〕, choreograph.

furi-tsuzuku〈ふりつづく：降り続く〉continue to rain, rain continuously, snow incessantly.

　　furi-tsuzuku-naga-ame（降り続く長雨） a long spell of rain

furi-wakeru〈ふりわける：振り分ける〉put in two, distribute ((among *or* to)).

furo 〈ふろ：風ろ〉a bath.

    Furo ga waita. (風ろが沸いた.)　The bath is ready.

    furo ni hairu (風ろに入る)　take a bath

    furo-kara-agaru (風ろから上がる)　get out of a bath

    furo-ni-ireru (風ろに入れる)　give a bath ((to))

    furo-ba (風ろ場)　a bathroom

    furo-oke (風ろおけ)　a bathtub

    furo-ya (風ろ屋)　a bathhouse, a public bath

furokku 〈フロック〉a fluke.

furoku 〈ふろく：付録〉a supplement, extra.

furonto 〈フロント〉the front desk.

furonto-garasu 〈フロントガラス〉a windshield.

furô-sha 〈ふろうしゃ：浮浪者〉a vagabond, a vagrant.

furoshiki 〈ふろしき：風ろ敷〉a (cloth) wrapper, a kerchief.

    furoshiki-de tsutsumu (風ろ敷で包む)　wrap in a kerchief

    furoshiki-zutsumi (風ろ敷包み)　a parcel in a wrapper, a bundle

furô-shotoku 〈ふろうしょとく：不労所得〉an unearned income, an investment income.

furu 〈フル〉

    ichi-nichi-jû furu-ni hataraku (一日中フルに働く)　work all the day without rest

    kikai o furu-ni-ugokasu (機械をフルに動かす)　keep all the machines in motion

    setsubi-o-furu-ni-katsuyô-suru (設備をフルに活用する)　make full use of the facilities

furu 〈ふる：降る〉fall, come down.

    Ame ga furu. (雨が降る.)　It rains.

    Yuki ga furu. (雪が降る.)　It snows.

    Ame ga futtari-yandari-shita. (雨が降ったりやんだりした.)　It rained off and on.

    futte-mo furanakute-mo (降っても降らなくても)　rain or shine

furu 〈ふる：振る〉wave, shake, swing; wag.

    te o furu (手を振る)　wave one's hand

    kubi-o-yoko-ni-furu (首を横に振る)　shake one's head

    batto o furu (バットを振る)　swing a bat

furubita or **furu-boketa** 〈ふるびた，ふるぼけた：古びた，古ぼけた〉old, worn-out, ((a thing)) that has been long used, ((a thing)) that has seen long service.

furubite-kiiroku-natta shorui（古びて黄色くなった書類）the documents yellowed with age

furu-danuki〈ふるだぬき：古だぬき〉an old stager, an old fox.

furu-dôgu〈ふるどうぐ：古道具〉a secondhand article.

furu-dôgu-ya（古道具屋）a dealer in secondhand articles, a junk dealer; a secondhand store, a junk shop

furue〈ふるえ：震え〉shivering, shudder, tremble, a quiver.

furue-goe（震え声）a trembling voice

furue-agaru〈ふるえあがる：震え上がる〉tremble violently.

furueru〈ふるえる：震える〉tremble, shiver.

kowagatte-furueru（怖がって震える）tremble for fear

samukute-furueru（寒くて震える）shiver with cold

furu-gi〈ふるぎ：古着〉old clothes, secondhand clothing.

furu-gi-ya（古着屋）an old-clothes dealer; a secondhand clothing store

furu-hon〈ふるほん：古本〉a secondhand book.

furu-hon-ya（古本屋）a secondhand bookseller; a secondhand bookstore.

furui〈ふるい：古い〉old, antiquated, old-fashioned.

furui hanashi（古い話）an old story

furuku〈古く〉

furuku-naru（古くなる）become old, become out of date

furuku-kara（古くから）from old (times)

furui〈ふるい〉a sieve, a sifter.

furui-ni-kakeru〈ふるいに掛ける〉put ((something)) through a sieve, screen, winnow, sift out.

furui-okosu〈ふるいおこす：奮い起こす〉muster up, summon up.

furui-otosu〈ふるいおとす：ふるい落とす〉*see.* furui-ni-kakeru.

furui-tatsu〈ふるいたつ：奮い立つ〉*see.* funki-suru.

furu-kabu〈ふるかぶ：古株〉an old stump; an old-timer.

furu-kizu〈ふるきず：古傷〉an old wound.

furu-kizu o abaku（古傷を暴く）open up old wounds, expose ((a person's)) past scandals

furu-kusai〈ふるくさい：古臭い〉antiquated, old-fashioned, hackneyed.

furumai〈ふるまい：振る舞い〉behavior, conduct.

furumau〈振る舞う〉behave oneself, conduct oneself.

enryo-naku furumau（遠慮なく振る舞う）conduct oneself without reserve(*or* without ceremony)

furu-sato 〈ふるさと：古里〉 *see.* kokyô.

furu-su 〈ふるす：古巣〉 one's former haunt.

furûto 〈フルート〉 a flute.
　　furûto o fuku（フルートを吹く） play the flute

furuu 〈ふるう：振るう〉 show, display, wield; be prosperous.
　　shuwan o furuu（手腕を振るう） show one's ability
　　kenryoku o furuu（権力を振るう） wield one's power
　furuwa-nai 〈振るわない〉 be dull, be in a bad way, be at a low ebb.
　　Kanojo-no shôbai wa chikagoro furuwa-nai.（彼女の商売は近ごろ振る
　　わない。） Her business has been dull these days.

furuwaseru 〈ふるわせる：震わせる〉 shake, tremble.
　　okotte karada-o-furuwaseru（怒って体を震わせる） tremble with rage

furyo 〈ふりょ：不慮〉
　furyo-no 〈不慮の〉 unforeseen, unexpected, accidental.
　　furyo-no deki-goto（不慮の出来事） an unforeseen event
　　furyo-no shi（不慮の死） a sudden death
　　furyo-no-sainan（不慮の災難） an accident

furyô 〈ふりょう：不良〉 badness; delinquency.
　　furyô-hin（不良品） inferior goods
　　furyô-shônen（不良少年） a delinquent boy
　furyô-no 〈不良の〉 bad, inferior; delinquent.

furyô 〈ふりょう：不漁（猟）〉 a poor catch, little game.

furyoku 〈ふりょく：浮力〉 buoyancy, lift.

fûryoku 〈ふうりょく：風力〉 wind force.

fûryû 〈ふうりゅう：風流〉
　fûryû-na 〈風流な〉 elegant, tasteful, refined, graceful.
　　fûryû-na hito（風流な人） a man of refined taste

fusa 〈ふさ：房〉 a tuft, a fringe, a tassel; a bunch, a cluster.
　　budô-hito-fusa（ぶどう一房） a bunch of grapes

fûsa 〈ふうさ：封鎖〉 a blockade.
　　gakuen-fûsa（学園封鎖） a campus blockade
　fûsa-suru 〈封鎖する〉 blockade, block (up), freeze.
　　fûsa-o-toku（封鎖を解く） lift a blockade, unfreeze

fusafusa 〈ふさふさ〉
　fusafusa-shita 〈ふさふさした〉 tufty, fringy.
　　fusafusa-shita kami（ふさふさした髪） tufty hair

fusagaru 〈ふさがる〉 be closed, be shut; be occupied, be engaged, be busy.

Kizu-guchi ga fusagatta. (傷口がふさがった.) The wound has closed up.

Kono heya wa fusagatte-iru. (この部屋はふさがっている.) This room is occupied.

Watashi-wa ima te-ga-fusagatte-iru. (私は今手がふさがっている.) I am busy now.

fusagu 〈ふさぐ〉 close (up), shut (up), stop up, fill (up).

ana o fusagu (穴をふさぐ) stop up a hole

fusagi-komu 〈ふさぎこむ：ふさぎ込む〉 be cast down, be in low spirits, be depressed, mope.

fusai 〈ふさい：負債〉 a debt.

fusai o kaesu (負債を返す) pay off a debt

fusai-ga-aru 〈負債がある〉 be indebted ((to a person)).

fusai 〈ふさい：夫妻〉 husband and wife.

Takata-fusai (高田夫妻) Mr. and Mrs. Takata

fûsai 〈ふうさい：風さい〉 appearance, presence.

fûsai-no-agara-nai hito (風さいのあがらない人) a man of no presence

fusaku 〈ふさく：不作〉 a poor crop, a bad harvest.

kome no fusaku (米の不作) a poor crop of rice

fu-sanka 〈ふさんか：不参加〉 nonparticipation.

fu-sansei 〈ふさんせい：不賛成〉 disapproval, disagreement.

fu-sansei-de-aru 〈不賛成である〉 object ((to)), disapprove ((of)), disagree ((with)).

Watashi-wa sore-ni-wa-fu-sansei-desu. (私はそれには不賛成です.) I am against it.

fûsatsu 〈ふうさつ：封殺〉 a force-out.

fûsatsu-suru 〈封殺する〉 force ((a runner)) out.

fusawashii 〈ふさわしい〉 suitable ((for *or* to)), becoming ((to)), worthy ((of)), appropriate ((for *or* to)).

sono ba-ni-fusawashii kotoba (その場にふさわしい言葉) words suitable for the occasion

fuse 〈ふせ：布施〉 alms, an offering.

fusegu 〈ふせぐ：防ぐ〉 defend, protect ((against *or* from)), keep off, prevent.

jikoku o teki-no-shinryaku-kara fusegu (自国を敵の侵略から防ぐ) defend one's country against the invaders

samusa-kara mi o fusegu (寒さから身を防ぐ) protect oneself from the cold hae o fusegu〈はえを防ぐ〉 keep off the flies

densen o fusegu〈伝染を防ぐ〉 prevent infection

fusei〈ふせい：不正〉injustice, wrong, unlawfulness, dishonesty, impropriety.

fusei-o-hataraku〈不正を働く〉 do a dishonest thing, do wrong

fusei-kôi〈不正行為〉 a dishonest act

fusei-shudan〈不正手段〉 a dishonest means

fusei-na〈不正な〉unjust, wrong, unlawful, dishonest, improper.

fu-seijitsu〈ふせいじつ：不誠実〉insincerity, unfaithfulness.

fu-seijitsu-na〈不誠実な〉insincere, unfaithful.

fusei-jôsha〈ふせいじょうしゃ：不正乗車〉an illegal ride.

fusei-jôsha-o-suru〈不正乗車をする〉steal a ride ((on)).

fu-seikaku〈ふせいかく：不正確〉inaccuracy, incorrectness.

fu-seikaku-na〈不正確な〉inaccurate, incorrect.

fu-seikaku-ni〈不正確に〉inaccurately, incorrectly.

fu-seikô〈ふせいこう：不成功〉ill success, failure.

fu-seikô-ni-owaru〈不成功に終わる〉 end in failure

fu-seimyaku〈ふせいみゃく：不整脈〉an irregular pulse.

fu-seiritsu〈ふせいりつ：不成立〉

fu-seiritsu-ni-owaru or *fu-seiritsu-to-naru*〈不成立に終わる，不成立となる〉 end in failure, fall through.

fu-seiseki〈ふせいせき：不成績〉a poor result.

fu-semmei〈ふせんめい：不鮮明〉

fu-semmei-na〈不鮮明な〉indistinct, unclear.

fusen〈ふせん：付せん〉a tag, a slip, a label.

fusen-o-tsukeru〈付せんを付ける〉tag, label.

fusen-o-tsukete-dasu〈付せんを付けて出す〉 readdress ((a letter)) and forward it

fûsen〈ふうせん：風船〉a balloon.

fûsen o fukuramasu〈風船を膨らます〉 inflate a balloon

fûsen-dama〈風船玉〉 a toy balloon

fusen-shô〈ふせんしょう：不戦勝〉an unearned win.

fusen-shô-to-naru〈不戦勝となる〉get a win without playing.

fuseru〈ふせる：伏せる〉

me o fuseru〈目を伏せる〉 cast down one's eyes

mi-o-fuseru〈身を伏せる〉 lie down, prostrate oneself

fu-sessei〈ふせっせい：不摂生〉neglect of health.

fu-sessei-o-suru〈不摂生をする〉neglect one's health.

fu-sessei 〈ふせっせい：不節制〉 intemperance, excesses.
  fu-sessei-o-suru 〈不節制をする〉 be intemperate, commit excesses.
  fu-sessei-na 〈不節制な〉 intemperate.

fusetsu 〈ふせつ：敷設〉
  fusetsu-suru 〈敷設する〉 lay (down), build.
      kaitei-densen o fusetsu-suru (海底電線を敷設する) lay a (submarine) cable

fûsha 〈ふうしゃ：風車〉 a windmill.

fushi 〈ふし：節〉 a joint, a knob; a tune.
      take-no fushi (竹の節) a bamboo joint
      fushibushi-ga-itamu (節々が痛む) feel pain in every joint
      yukai-na fushi (愉快な節) a merry tune

fûshi 〈ふうし：風刺〉 a satire.
      tsûretsu-na fûshi (痛烈な風刺) a keen satire
      fûshi-teki(-na) 〈風刺的（な）〉 satirical, sarcastic, ironical.

fu-shiawase 〈ふしあわせ：不幸せ〉 *see.* fukô (不幸).

fushidara 〈ふしだら〉
  fushidara-na 〈ふしだらな〉 loose, dissolute.
      fushidara-na seikatsu o suru (ふしだらな生活をする) lead a loose life

fushigi 〈ふしぎ：不思議〉 a wonder, a mystery.
      sekai no nana-fushigi (世界の七不思議) the seven wonders of the world
  〜-to-wa-fushigi-da. 〈〜とは不思議だ。〉 It is strange that... ., It is a wonder that... .
  〜-ni-fushigi-wa-nai 〈〜に不思議はない〉 It is natural that... , It is little wonder that... .
  fushigi-na 〈不思議な〉 wonderful, strange, mysterious.
  fushigi-ni 〈不思議に〉 wonderfully, strangely, mysteriously.
  fushigi-ni-mo 〈不思議にも〉 strange to say.

fu-shimatsu 〈ふしまつ：不始末〉 mismanagement, carelessness, misconduct.

fushimban 〈ふしんばん：不寝番〉 night watch; a night watch.
  fushimban-o-suru 〈不寝番をする〉 keep a night watch, keep vigil.

fushin 〈ふしん：不審〉 doubt, suspicion.
      fushin o idaku (不審を抱く) harbor suspicion
  fushin-ni-omou 〈不審に思う〉 doubt, think ((something)) suspicious, suspect.
  fushin-na 〈不審な〉 doubtful, suspicious, strange.

　　　fushin-na kasho〈不審な箇所〉 a doubtful point

　　　kyodô-fushin-na otoko〈挙動不審な男〉 a suspicious-looking man

　　fushin-sô-ni〈不審そうに〉doubtfully, inquiringly, suspiciously.

fuˑshin〈ふしん：不振〉dullness, depression, inactivity, a slump.

　　　yushutsu no kyokudo-no fushin（輸出の極度の不振） extreme inactivity of the export trade

　　fushin-no〈不振の〉dull, depressed, inactive, flat, slack.

fushin〈ふしん：普請〉building, construction.

　　　yasu-bushin-no ie（安普請の家） a jerry-built house

fushin-jimmon〈ふしんじんもん：不審尋問〉

　　fushin-jimmon-suru〈不審尋問する〉question ((a person)).

　　fushin-jimmon-o-ukeru〈不審尋問を受ける〉be questioned〔by a policeman〕.

fu-shinjin〈ふしんじん：不信心〉impiety, infidelity.

　　fu-shinjin-na〈不信心な〉impious, infidel.

fushin-kan〈ふしんかん：不信感〉(a) distrust.

　　　fushin-kan o idaku（不信感を抱く） have a distrust ((of))

fushin-kôi〈ふしんこうい：不信行為〉

　　fushin-kôi o suru〈不信行為をする〉commit a breach of faith.

fu-shinnin〈ふしんにん：不信任〉nonconfidence.

　　　naikaku-fu-shinnin-an（内閣不信任案） a nonconfidence bill in the Cabinet

fu-shinsetsu〈ふしんせつ：不親切〉unkindness, unfriendness.

　　fu-shinsetsu-na〈不親切な〉unkind, unfriendly.

　　fu-shinsetsu-ni〈不親切に〉unkindly.

fu-shizen〈ふしぜん：不自然〉

　　fu-shizen-na〈不自然な〉unnatural, artificial, affected.

　　fu-shizen-ni〈不自然に〉unnaturally, artificially, affectedly.

fushô〈ふしょう：負傷〉an injury, a wound.

　　　fushô-sha（負傷者） an injured person, a wounded person

　　fushô-suru〈負傷する〉be injured, be wounded.

fushô〈ふしょう：不詳〉*see.* fumei.

fûsho〈ふうしょ：封書〉a sealed letter.

fushôbushô〈ふしょうぶしょう：不承不承〉reluctantly, unwillingly, against one's will.

fu-shôchi〈ふしょうち：不承知〉disapproval, disagreement, objection, denial, refusal.

　　fu-shôchi-de-aru〈不承知である〉disapprove ((of)), object ((to)), refuse to consent ((to)).

fushô-ji 〈ふしょうじ：不祥事〉 a scandal; a deplorable event.

fu-shôjiki 〈ふしょうじき：不正直〉 dishonesty.

　fu-shôjiki-na 〈不正直な〉 dishonest.

fu-shôka 〈ふしょうか：不消化〉 indigestion.

　fu-shôka-butsu（不消化物）　indigestibles

fushoku 〈ふしょく：腐食〉 corrosion, erosion, rot.

　fushoku-suru 〈腐食する〉 corrode, erode, rot.

fûshû 〈ふうしゅう：風習〉 (manners and) customs.

fu-shubi 〈ふしゅび：不首尾〉 *see.* shippai.

　fu-shubi-ni owaru（不首尾に終わる）　*see.* shippai-ni owaru

fusoku 〈ふそく：不足〉 want, lack, shortage.

　suimin-busoku（睡眠不足）　lack of sleep

　undô-busoku（運動不足）　lack of exercise

　fusoku-shite-iru or　*fusoku-suru* 〈不足している，不足する〉 be short ((of)), be lacking ((in)), be in need ((of)), want, lack.

　　shokuryô-ga-fusoku-shite-iru（食糧が不足している）　be short of food

fusoku 〈ふそく：不測〉 *see.* furyo.

fûsoku 〈ふそく：風速〉 the velocity of the wind.

　sai-dai-fûsoku-go-jû-mêtoru（最大風速五十メートル）　a maximum wind velocity of 50 meters per second

fuson 〈ふそん：不そん〉

　fuson-na 〈不そんな〉 haughty, arrogant, insolent.

　　fuson-na taido（不そんな態度）　an insolent manner

fu-sôô 〈ふそうおう：不相応〉

　fu-sôô-na 〈不相応な〉 unsuitable, unsuited, unfit, unbecoming, out of proportion ((to)).

　　bun-fu-sôô-na-seikatsu-o-suru（分不相応な生活をする）　live beyond one's means

fusso 〈ふっそ：ふっ素〉 fluorine.

fusû 〈ふすう：負数〉 a negative number.

fûsui-gai 〈ふうすいがい：風水害〉 damage from a storm and flood.

futa 〈ふた〉 a cover, a cap, a lid.

　futa-o-suru 〈ふたをする〉 cover, cap, put on the lid.

　futa-o-toru 〈ふたを取る〉 open, uncover, lift the lid.

futa-e-mabuta 〈ふたえまぶた：二重まぶた〉 a double eyelid.

futa-go 〈ふたご：双子〉 twins, a twin.

　futa-go-no kyôdai（双子の兄弟）　twin brothers

futa-gokoro〈ふたごころ：二心〉duplicity.
 futa-gokoro-no-aru〈二心のある〉double-faced.
  futa-gokoro-no-nai（二心のない） sincere, loyal

futai〈ふたい：付帯〉
  futai-jikō（付帯事項） a supplementary item.
  futai-jōken（付帯条件） an incidental condition

fûtai〈ふうたい：風袋〉tare, packing.
 fûtai-komi-de〈風袋込みで〉in gross weight.

futa-mata〈ふたまた：二また〉
  futa-mata-soketto（二またソケット） a two-way socket
 futa-mata-o-kakeru〈二またを掛ける〉have it both ways, sit on the fence.

futan〈ふたん：負担〉a burden, a charge.
  futan o kakeru（負担を掛ける） be a burden ((on))
  futan o karuku-suru（負担を軽くする） lighten a burden
 futan-suru〈負担する〉bear, stand, shoulder, share.
  seikatsu-hi-no-ichibu-o-futan-suru（生活費の一部を負担する） share the living expenses

futa-oya〈ふたおや：二親〉both parents.

futari〈ふたり：二人〉two persons, a couple.
  futari(-kiri)-de（二人(切り)で） between the two, between you and me
  futari-tomo（二人とも） both (of them)
  futari-zutsu（二人ずつ） two and two

fu-tashika〈ふたしか：不確か〉uncertainty.
 fu-tashika-na〈不確かな〉uncertain.
  fu-tashika-na henji（不確かな返事） an uncertain answer

futatabi〈ふたたび：再び〉again, for the second time, once more.

futa-te〈ふたて：二手〉
 futa-te-ni-wakareru〈二手に分かれる〉divide into two groups.

futa-toori〈ふたとおり：二通り〉two kinds ((of)), two ways.
  futa-toori-no-kangae-kata（二通りの考え方） two ways of thinking

futatsu〈ふたつ：二つ〉two.
  futatsu-ni（二つに） in two
  futatsu-zutsu（二つずつ） by twos
 futatsu-tomo〈二つとも〉both... ((and)); neither... ((nor)).

futatsu-henji〈ふたつへんじ：二つ返事〉
 futatsu-henji-de-hiki-ukeru〈二つ返事で引き受ける〉give a ready consent ((to)), accept ((something)) most willingly.

futebute-shii〈ふてぶてしい〉impudent, insolent, shameless.

fu-tegiwa〈ふてぎわ：不手際〉clumsiness, awkwardness.

fu-tegiwa-na〈不手際な〉clumsy, awkward, unskillful.

futei〈ふてい：不定〉

fotei-no〈不定の〉unsettled, indefinite, unfixed, undecided.

    jûsho-futei-no〈住所不定の〉wandering, having no fixed abode

futei〈ふてい：不貞〉unchastity.

futei-no〈不貞の〉unchaste, unfaithful.

    futei-no tsuma〈不貞の妻〉an unfaithful wife

fu-teiki〈ふていき：不定期〉

    fu-teiki-kôro〈不定期航路〉a tramp route

fu-teiki-no〈不定期の〉irregular.

futei-shi〈ふていし：不定詞〉an infinitive.

futeki〈ふてき：不敵〉

futeki-na〈不敵な〉daring, fearless, dauntless; audacious.

    futeki-na furumai〈不敵な振る舞い〉a fearless conduct

fu-tekinin-sha〈ふてきにんしゃ：不適任者〉an unqualified person.

fu-tekitô〈ふてきとう：不適当〉

fu-tekitô-na〈不適当な〉unsuitable, unfit ((for)), out of place, improper.

fute-kusareru〈ふてくされる：ふて腐れる〉go into the sulks; become desperate.

fu-tettei〈ふてってい：不徹底〉

fu-tettei-na〈不徹底な〉not thorough(going), unconvincing, lukewarm, halfway.

    fu-tettei-na shiji〈不徹底な指示〉not thoroughgoing directions

futo〈ふと〉suddenly, by chance, accidentally, unexpectedly.

    futo-me-o-samasu〈ふと目を覚ます〉chance to awake

    futo-shita-koto-de shiri-ai-ni-naru〈ふとしたことで知り合いになる〉get acquainted by chance

futo-mune-ni-ukabu〈ふと胸に浮かぶ〉occur ((to)), flash across one's mind.

futô〈ふとう：ふ頭〉a wharf, a quay, a pier.

futô〈ふとう：不当〉injustice, unfairness, unreasonableness.

futô-na〈不当な〉unjust, unfair, unreasonable, unlawful; undeserved, exorbitant.

    futô-na tori-atsukai〈不当な取り扱い〉unjust treatment

    futô-na rieki〈不当な利益〉unfair profits

    futô-na nedan〈不当な値段〉an exorbitant price

futô-〈ふとう‐：不凍‐〉
　　futô-eki（不凍液）　an antifreezing solution
　　futô-kô（不凍港）　an ice-free port
fûtô〈ふうとう：封筒〉an envelope.
　　fûtô ni ate-na-o-kaku（封筒にあて名を書く）　address an envelope
futodoki〈ふとどき：不届き〉
　futodoki-na〈不届きな〉outrageous, insolent, rude, unpardonable.
futo-gaki〈ふとがき：太書き〉
　futo-gaki-no〈太書きの〉broad-pointed.
futoi〈ふとい：太い〉big, thick; deep.
　　futoi ude（太い腕）　a big arm
　　futoi ito（太い糸）　a thick thread
　　futoi koe（太い声）　a deep voice
　futoku〈太く〉thickly, deeply.
　　futoku-naru（太くなる）　become big, become thick
　　futoku-suru（太くする）　make thick
fu-tôitsu〈ふとういつ：不統一〉lack of unity, disunity.
　fu-tôitsu-na〈不統一な〉lacking in unity, disunited.
futokoro〈ふところ：懐〉
　　haha-oya no futokoro-ni-idakarete-iru akambô（母親の懐に抱かれてい
　　る赤ん坊）　a baby carried in the bosom of its mother
　　futokoro-ga-atatakai（懐が暖かい）　have a heavy purse
　　futokoro-ga-sabishii（懐が寂しい）　have a light purse
　　jibun-no futokoro-o-itameru（自分の懐を痛める）　pay out of one's
　　own pocket
futoku〈ふとく：不徳〉lack of virtue.
　　Mina-watashi-no-futoku-no-itasu-tokoro-desu.（皆私の不徳の致すとこ
　　ろです。）　I am solely to blame for it.
fu-tokutei〈ふとくてい：不特定〉
　　fu-tokutei-tasû-no hitobito（不特定多数の人々）　many and unspecified
　　persons
　fu-tokutei-no〈不特定の〉unspecified.
futoku-yôryô〈ふとくようりょう：不得要領〉
　futoku-yôryô-na〈不得要領な〉vague, ambiguous, indefinite, evasive.
　　futoku-yôryô-na henji（不得要領な返事）　an evasive answer
fu-tômei〈ふとうめい：不透明〉opacity.
　fu-tômei-na〈不透明な〉opaque, milky.
futo-momo〈ふともも：太もも〉a thigh.

futon 〈ふとん：布団〉 bedding; a mattress, a quilt, a counterpane.

    futon o shiku〈布団を敷く〉 make a bed

    futon o kakeru〈布団を掛ける〉 put on a quilt

    futon o tatamu〈布団を畳む〉 fold up the bedding

futoppara 〈ふとっぱら：太っ腹〉

  futoppara-na〈太っ腹な〉 generous, broad-minded.

futoru 〈ふとる：太る〉 grow fat, gain flesh, put on weight.

  futorasu〈太らす〉 fatten, feed up; enrich.

  futotta〈太った〉 fat, fleshy, plump.

futosa 〈ふとさ：太さ〉 thickness.

fu-tôshiki 〈ふとうしき：不等式〉 an inequality.

futsū 〈ふつう：不通〉

  futsū-ni-naru〈不通になる〉 be suspended, be blocked, be interrupted, be paralyzed, be tied up.

futsū 〈ふつう：普通〉 normally, commonly, usually, generally.

    Chôshoku wa futsū roku-ji-ni taberu. (朝食は普通六時に食べる.) I usually take breakfast at six.

  futsū-no〈普通の〉 normal, common, usual, general.

    futsū-no yari-kata(-de) (普通のやり方(で)) the normal way

futsū- 〈ふつう-：普通-〉

    futsū-ka (普通科) a regular course

    futsū-ressha (普通列車) a local train, an accommodation train

    futsū-yokin (普通預金) an ordinary deposit

    futsū-yûbin (普通郵便) ordinary mail, ordinary post

fu-tsugô 〈ふつごう：不都合〉 inconvenience, wrong.

  fu-tsugô-na〈不都合な〉 inconvenient, wrong.

    fu-tsugô-na-koto-o-suru (不都合なことをする) do wrong, misconduct

futsuka 〈ふつか：二日〉 two days; the second (day).

    futsuka-me-ni (二日目に) on the second day〔after one's arrival〕

    futsuka-oki-ni (二日おきに) every three days

futsuka-yoi 〈ふつかよい：二日酔い〉 a hangover, the morning after.

fu-tsuriai 〈ふつりあい：不釣り合い〉 imbalance, disproportion.

  fu-tsuriai-na〈不釣り合いな〉 ill-matched, ill-balanced, out of proportion ((to)), incommensurate ((with)).

    fu-tsuriai-na fûfu (不釣り合いな夫婦) an ill-matched couple

futsutsuka 〈ふつつか〉

  futsutsuka-na〈ふつつかな〉 incompetent; unmannerly.

futtei 〈ふってい：払底〉 shortage, scarcity, dearth.

jinzai no futtei（人材の払底）a dearth of talent

futto〈ふっと〉

rôsoku o futto-fuki-kesu〈ろうそくをふっと吹き消す〉whiff out a candle.

futtô〈ふっとう：沸騰〉boiling.

futtô-ten（沸騰点）the boiling point

futtô-suru〈沸騰する〉boil.

futto-bôru〈フットボール〉football.

futto-bôru o yaru（フットボールをやる）play football

futto-bôru-kyôgi-jô（フットボール競技場）a football field, a gridiron

futtobu〈ふっとぶ：吹っ飛ぶ〉be blown off.

futtoraito〈フットライト〉footlights.

fûu〈ふうう：風雨〉wind and rain, a (rain)storm.

fûu-o-tsuite（風雨をついて）in spite of the storm

fûu-chûi-hô（風雨注意報）a storm warning

fuun〈ふうん：不運〉(a) misfortune, ill luck.

fuun-na〈不運な〉unfortunate, unlucky.

fuun-ni-mo〈不運にも〉unfortunately, unluckily.

fuwa〈ふわ：不和〉discord, trouble, disharmony.

katei-no fuwa（家庭の不和）family trouble

fuwafuwa〈ふわふわ〉

fuwafuwa-shita〈ふわふわした〉soft, spongy; unsteady.

fuwafuwa-shite kimochi-ga-ii（ふわふわして気持ちがいい）be soft and feel comfortable

fuwari(-to)〈ふわり（と）〉gently, softly, lightly.

fu-watari〈ふわたり：不渡り〉dishonor, nonpayment.

fu-watari-tegata（不渡手形）a dishonored bill

fu-watari-ni-naru〈不渡りになる〉be dishonored.

fuyakeru〈ふやける〉swell up, become sodden.

fuyaketa〈ふやけた〉swollen, sodden.

fuyasu〈ふやす：増（殖）やす〉increase, add ((to)).

shokunin-no-kazu o fuyasu（職人の数を増やす）increase the hands

fuyo〈ふよ：付与〉

fuyo-suru〈付与する〉give, bestow, grant, vest.

kengen o fuyo-suru（権限を付与する）give ((a person)) an authority

fuyô〈ふよう：扶養〉support, maintenance.

fuyô-kazoku（扶養家族）a (family) dependent

fuyô-suru〈扶養する〉support, maintain.

fuyô〈ふよう：不用〉

　　fuyô-hin〈不用品〉 a disused(*or* useless) thing
　fuyô-to-naru〈不用となる〉become useless.
　fuyô-na〈不用な〉disused, useless.
fu-yôi〈ふようい：不用意〉
　fu-yôi-na〈不用意な〉unprepared; heedless, careless.
　　fu-yôi-na kotoba（不用意な言葉） careless remarks
fu-yôjô〈ふようじょう：不養生〉neglect of one's health.
　　Isha-no-fu-yôjô.（医者の不養生.） It is a good doctor who follows his
　　own directions.
fuyu〈ふゆ：冬〉winter.
　　fuyu-jû（冬中） during the winter
　　fuyu-fuku（冬服） winter clothes
　　fuyu-jitaku-o-suru（冬支度をする） prepare for the winter
　　fuyu-yasumi（冬休み） a winter vacation
fu-yukai〈ふゆかい：不愉快〉
　fu-yukai-na〈不愉快な〉unpleasant, disagreeable.
fu-yukitodoki〈ふゆきとどき：不行き届き〉negligence, inattentiveness,
　mismanagement, poor service.
　fu-yukitodoki-na〈不行き届きな〉negligent, inattentive, poor.
fuzai〈ふざい：不在〉absence.
　　watashi-no fuzai-chû-ni（私の不在中に） during my absence
　　fuzai-tôhyô（不在投票） absentee voting
　fuzai-de-aru〈不在である〉be absent, be out, be not at home.
fuzakeru〈ふざける〉romp (about); joke.
　fuzakete〈ふざけて〉in fun, for a joke.
fuzei〈ふぜい：風情〉taste, elegance.
　fuzei-no-aru〈風情のある〉tasteful, elegant, refined.
　　fuzei-no-nai（風情のない） tasteless, dry, dull
fuzen〈ふぜん：不全〉
　　jin-fuzen（じん不全） a kidney malfunction
fûzen-no-tomoshibi〈ふうぜんのともしび：風前のともしび〉
　　Kare-no ummei wa fûzen-no-tomoshibi-da.（彼の運命は風前のともしび
　　だ.） His life hangs by a thread.
-fuzoku-〈-ふぞく-：-付属-〉
　　〜-fuzoku-shô-gakklô（〜付属小学校） an elementary school attached
　　((to))
　　〜-fuzoku-byôin（〜付属病院） a hospital attached ((to))
　　fuzoku-hin（付属品） an accessory, fittings

fuzoku-suru 〈付属する〉 be attached ((to)), belong ((to)).

fûzoku 〈ふうぞく：風俗〉 manners.
　　fûzoku-shûkan（風俗習慣）　manners and customs

fu-zoroi 〈ふぞろい：不ぞろい〉
　fu-zoroi-no 〈不ぞろいの〉 uneven, irregular, out of sort, odd.

fuzui 〈ふずい：不随〉 paralysis.
　　hanshin-fuzui（半身不随）　partial paralysis
　fuzui-ni-naru 〈不随になる〉 be paralyzed.

G

ga 〈が〉 a moth.

ga 〈が：我〉 self, ego.
　ga-o-toosu 〈我を通す〉 have one's own way.
　ga-no-tsuyoi 〈我の強い〉 self-willed, self-assertive.

-ga 〈-が〉
　　Natsu-yasumi ga owatta.（夏休みが終わった.）The summer vacation
　　　is over.
　　I ga itai.（胃が痛い.）I have a stomachache.
　　Watashi-wa mikan ga suki-da.（私はみかんが好きだ.）I like oranges.
　　Kare-wa yakyû-ga-umai.（彼は野球がうまい.）He is good at
　　　baseball.
　　Watashi-wa wakai-ga, anata-wa toshi-o-totte-iru.（私は若いが, あなた
　　　は年を取っている.）I am young, but you are old.
　　Watashi-wa kinô kanojo-ni atta-ga, totemo kao-iro-ga-warukatta.（私
　　　は昨日彼女に会ったが, とても顔色が悪かった.）Yesterday I saw
　　　her, and she looked quite pale.

gabugabu 〈がぶがぶ〉
　gabugabu-nomu 〈がぶがぶ飲む〉 quaff, swill, drink heavily.

gabyô 〈がびょう：画びょう〉 a thumbtack, a drawing pin.

gabyô-de-tomeru〈画びょうで留める〉tack.

gachagacha〈がちゃがちゃ〉

　　gachagacha-iu-oto（がちゃがちゃいう音）a clattering noise

　　gachagacha-saseru〈がちゃがちゃさせる〉clatter, rattle.

gachan〈がちゃん〉

　gachan-to-denwa-o-kiru〈がちゃんと電話を切る〉ring off sharply.

-gachi〈-がち〉be apt ((to do)), be liable ((to do)), be prone ((to do)).

　　Wareware-wa mina machigai-o-shi-gachi-da.（我々は皆間違いをしがちだ。）We are all apt to make mistakes.

　　Haha wa rusu-gachi-da.（母は留守がちだ。）My mother is away from home most of the time.

gachigachi〈がちがち〉

　　Samukute ha ga gachigachi-naru.（寒くて歯ががちがち鳴る。）My teeth chatter with cold.

gachô〈がちょう〉a goose.

gadai〈がだい：画題〉the subject of a painting.

gadan〈がだん：画壇〉painting circles.

gaden-insui〈がでんいんすい：我田引水〉arguing ((a matter)) only from a self-centered angle.

　gaden-insui-no〈我田引水の〉self-centered.

gâdo〈ガード〉a railroad overpass, an elevated railroad bridge; a guard.

　　gâdo-man（ガードマン）a guard

gafû〈がふう：画風〉a style of painting.

gagô〈がごう：雅号〉a pen name.

gahaku〈がはく：画伯〉a (great) painter, a (great) artist.

gahô〈がほう：画法〉the art of drawing.

gahô〈がほう：画報〉a pictorial, a graphic.

gai〈がい：害〉harm, injury, damage, evil effects.

　　gai o kuwaeru（害を加える）inflict harm ((on))

　gaisuru〈害する〉harm, injure, hurt, damage.

　　kenkô o gaisuru（健康を害する）injure ((a person's)) health

　　kanjô o gaisuru（感情を害する）hurt ((a person's)) feeling

　gai-no-aru〈害のある〉harmful, injurious.

　　gai-no-nai（害のない）harmless

-gai〈-がい：-外〉

　　shi-gai-ni（市外に）outside the city

　　semmon-gai-de-aru（専門外である）be out of one's line

-gai〈-がい：-街〉

shôten-gai（商店街）a shopping street

jûtaku-gai（住宅街）a residential district

gaibu〈がいぶ：外部〉the outside, the exterior.

gaibu-ni-moreru〈外部に漏れる〉leak out.

gaibu-no〈外部の〉outside, outer, exterior, external.

gaibu-kara〈外部から〉from the outside.

gaibun〈がいぶん：外聞〉

haji-mo-gaibun-mo-nai〈恥も外聞もない〉do not care about decency.

gaichi〈がいち：外地〉an oversea(s) land.

gaichi-kimmu（外地勤務）overseas service

gaichô〈がいちょう：害鳥〉an injurious bird.

gaichû〈がいちゅう：害虫〉a harmful insect.

gaichû〈がいちゅう：外注〉an outside order.

gaichû-ni-dasu〈外注に出す〉place an order outside.

gaiden〈がいでん：外電〉a foreign telegram, foreign news.

gaido〈ガイド〉a guide.

gaidoku〈がいどく：害毒〉evil, harm, poison.

shakai-ni-gaidoku-o-nagasu〈社会に害毒を流す〉poison society.

gaien〈がいえん：外えん〉the outer gardens.

gaihaku〈がいはく：外泊〉

gaihaku-suru〈外泊する〉sleep out, stay out for the night.

gaihi〈がいひ：外皮〉cuticle, a crust, a shell, a husk, a hull.

gaijin〈がいじん：外人〉a foreigner.

gaika〈がいか：外貨〉foreign currency(*or* money).

gaikaku〈がいかく：外角〉an external angle; the outside.

gaikakkyû（外角球）an outside ball

gaikaku〈がいかく：外郭〉

gaikaku-dantai（外郭団体）an auxiliary organization, an extra-governmental organization

gaikan〈がいかん：外観〉(external) appearance, an exterior view.

Gaikan wa ate-ni-nara-nai.（外観は当てにならない。）Appearances are deceptive.

hito o gaikan-de handan-suru（人を外観で判断する）judge a person by his appearance

tatemono no gaikan（建物の外観）the exterior of a building

gaikan-wa〈外観は〉in appearance.

gaikei〈がいけい：外形〉an outward form.

gaiken〈がいけん：外見〉*see.* gaikan.

gaiken-wa 〈外見は〉in appearance, apparently.

gaiki 〈がいき：外気〉the (outside) air.
  gaiki-ni-ataru 〈外気に当たる〉expose oneself to the air

gaikin 〈がいきん：外勤〉outside duty.
  gaikin-no 〈外勤の〉on outside duty.

gaikō 〈がいこう：外交〉diplomacy, a foreign policy, diplomatic intercourse.
  gaikō-jirei 〈外交辞令〉diplomatic language
  gaikō-kan 〈外交官〉a diplomat, a diplomatist
  gaikō-kankei 〈外交関係〉diplomatic relations
  gaikō-shisetsu-dan 〈外交使節団〉a diplomatic mission
  gaikō-jō-no or *gaikō-teki(-na)* 〈外交上の，外交的(な)〉diplomatic.
  gaikō-jō 〈外交上〉diplomatically.

gaikoku 〈がいこく：外国〉a foreign country.
  gaikoku-kara kaeru 〈外国から帰る〉return from abroad
  gaikoku-go 〈外国語〉a foreign language
  gaikoku-jin 〈外国人〉a foreigner
  gaikoku-sei-no 〈外国製の〉foreign-made
  gaikoku-no 〈外国の〉foreign.
  gaikoku-de, gaikoku-e or *gaikoku-ni* 〈外国で，外国へ，外国に〉abroad, oversea.
  gaikoku-e iku 〈外国へ行く〉go abroad

gaikō-sei 〈がいこうせい：外向性〉extroversion.
  gaikō-sei-no 〈外向性の〉extrovert(ed).

gaikotsu 〈がいこつ：がい骨〉a skeleton.
  gaikotsu-no-yō-ni-yasete-iru 〈がい骨のようにやせている〉be reduced to a skeleton

gaikyō 〈がいきょう：概況〉a general condition.

gaimen 〈がいめん：外面〉the outside, the exterior.
  gaimen-wa 〈外面は〉outwardly.

gaimu 〈がいむ：外務〉
  gaimu-shō 〈外務省〉the Ministry of Foreign Affairs
  gaimu-daijin 〈外務大臣〉the Minister of Foreign Affairs

gainen 〈がいねん：概念〉a general idea, a concept.
  gainen-teki(-na) 〈概念的(な)〉conceptual.
  gainen-teki-ni 〈概念的に〉conceptually.

gairai 〈がいらい：外来〉
  gairai-go 〈外来語〉a loan word

gairai-kanja〈外来患者〉an outpatient
gairai-no〈外来の〉from abroad, foreign, imported.
gairo〈がいろ：街路〉a street, a road.
gairo-ju〈街路樹〉street trees
gairon〈がいろん：概論〉an outline, general remarks, an introduction.
gairyaku〈がいりゃく：概略〉an outline.
gairyaku o noberu〈概略を述べる〉give an outline ((of))
gaisan〈がいさん：概算〉a rough estimate.
gaisan-suru〈概算する〉estimate roughly.
gaisan-de〈概算で〉at a rough estimate.
gaisen〈がいせん：がい旋〉a triumphal return.
gaisen-suru〈がい旋する〉return in triumph.
gaisetsu〈がいせつ：概説〉a general statement.
gaisetsu-suru〈概説する〉give an outline ((of)).
gaisha〈がいしゃ：外車〉a foreign car, an imported car.
gaishi〈がいし：外資〉foreign capital.
gaishi-dônyû〈外資導入〉the introduction of foreign capital
gaishi〈がいし：がい子〉an insulator.
gaishite〈がいして：概して〉generally, as a rule.
gaishite-ieba〈概して言えば〉generally speaking
gaishō〈がいしょう：外傷〉an external injury, a trauma.
gaishô〈がいしょう：外相〉*see.* gaimu-daijin.
gaishoku〈がいしょく：外食〉
gaishoku-suru〈外食する〉dine out.
gaishutsu〈がいしゅつ：外出〉
gaishutsu-suru〈外出する〉go out.
gaishutsu-shi-nai〈外出しない〉stay at home
gaishutsu-chû-ni〈外出中に〉while one is out.
gaisû〈がいすう：概数〉round numbers.
gaisû-de〈概数で〉in round numbers
gaitan〈がいたん：慨嘆〉
gaitan-suru〈慨嘆する〉deplore, lament, regret.
gaitan-su-beki〈慨嘆すべき〉deplorable, lamentable, regrettable.
gaiteki〈がいてき：外敵〉a foreign enemy(*or* invader).
gaitô〈がいとう：外とう〉an overcoat.
gaitô〈がいとう：街灯〉a street light.
gaitô〈がいとう：街頭〉a street.
gaitô-ni-tatte senden-suru〈街頭に立って宣伝する〉propagandize in

    the street

    gaitô-rokuon〈街頭録音〉 a street-corner transcription

gaitô〈がいとう：該当〉

 gaitô-suru〈該当する〉 come ((under)), be applicable ((to)), correspond ((to)).

gaiya〈がいや：外野〉 the outfield.

    gaiya-shu〈外野手〉 an outfielder

gaiyô〈がいよう：概要〉 *see.* gairyaku.

gaiyô〈がいよう：外用〉

    gaiyô-yaku〈外用薬〉 a medicine for external application

gaiyû〈がいゆう：外遊〉traveling abroad.

 gaiyû-suru〈外遊する〉travel abroad.

 gaiyû-chû-ni〈外遊中に〉while abroad.

gaka〈がか：画家〉a painter, an artist.

gaka〈がか：画架〉an easel.

gakai〈がかい：瓦解〉*see.* hôkai.

-gakari〈-がかり〉

    futari-gakari-de〈二人がかりで〉by two, between the two

    san-nin-gakari-de〈三人がかりで〉among the three

      san-nin-gakari-de tsukue o hakobu〈三人がかりで机を運ぶ〉 carry a table with the combined labor of three

    go-nin-gakari-no shigoto〈五人がかりの仕事〉 a job requiring five persons to do

-gakaru〈-がかる〉

    akami-gakatta〈赤みがかった〉 reddish

    ki-iro-gakatta〈黄色がかった〉 yellowish

gake〈がけ〉a cliff, a precipice, a bluff.

    gake-kara-ochiru〈がけから落ちる〉 fall over a precipice

 gake-no-ooi〈がけの多い〉cliffy.

-gake〈-がけ：-掛け〉

    go-nin-gake-no isu〈五人掛けのいす〉 a bench for five

    yukata-gake-de〈浴衣掛けで〉 informally dressed

    teika no roku-gake-de〈定価の六掛けで〉 at 60 per cent of the price

    kaeri-gake-ni〈帰り掛けに〉 on one's way home

gaki〈がき：餓鬼〉

    gaki-daishô〈餓鬼大将〉 the king of the kids, a bully

gakka〈がっか：学科〉a subject, a course of study.

gakka〈がっか：学課〉a lesson, school work.

gakkai〈がっかい：学会〉an academic society, an academic meeting.

gakkai〈がっかい：学界〉learned circles.

gakkari〈がっかり〉

　gakkari-suru〈がっかりする〉be discouraged, be disappointed.

　　hidoku gakkari-suru（ひどくがっかりする）be greatly disappointed

gakki〈がっき：学期〉a term, a semester.

　　shin-gakki（新学期）a fresh term

　　ichi-gakki（一学期）the first term

　　gakki-matsu（学期末）the end of a term

gakki〈がっき：楽器〉a musical instrument.

gakkō〈がっこう：学校〉a school, a college, an academy; an educational institution.

　　gakkō e hairu（学校へ入る）enter a school

　　kodomo o gakkō-ni ireru（子供を学校に入れる）send a child to school

　　gakkō-e-iku（学校へ行く）go to school, attend school

　　gakkō-kara kaeru（学校から帰る）come home from school

　　gakkō-o-yasumu（学校を休む）be absent from school

　　gakkō-o-saboru（学校をさぼる）play truant (from school)

　　gakkō o yameru（学校をやめる）leave school

　　gakkō-o-deru　*or*　gakkō-o-sotsugyō-suru（学校を出る，学校を卒業する）graduate from a school

　　gakkō-kyūshoku（学校給食）school meal

　　gakkō-seikatsu（学校生活）school life

　　gakkō-tomodachi（学校友達）a schoolfellow, schoolmate

　gakkō-de〈学校で〉at school.

　gakkō-ga-hikete-kara〈学校が引けてから〉after school.

gakku〈がっく：学区〉a school district.

　　gakku-sei（学区制）the school district system

gakkuri〈がっくり〉

　gakkuri-kuru〈がっくりくる〉be given a sad shock.

gakkyū〈がっきゅう：学級〉a class; a grade, a form.

gakkyū〈がっきゅう：学究〉a scholar.

　gakkyū-teki(-na)〈学究的(な)〉scholastic, academic.

gaku〈がく：額〉a sum, an amount.

gaku〈がく：額〉a tablet, a framed picture.

　　gaku o kakeru（額を掛ける）hang a framed picture ((on))

　gaku-ni-ireru〈額に入れる〉frame, set ((a picture)) in a frame.

gaku〈がく〉a calyx, a cup.

gakubatsu〈がくばつ：学閥〉an academic clique, academical affiliations.

gakubu〈がくぶ：学部〉a college, a faculty, a department.
    gakubu-chô（学部長）a dean

gaku-buchi〈がくぶち：額縁〉a frame.

gakuchô〈がくちょう：学長〉a president.

gakudan〈がくだん：楽団〉an orchestra, a band.

gakudan〈がくだん：楽壇〉musical circles.

gakudô〈がくどう：学童〉school children; a schoolboy, a schoolgirl.

gakuen〈がくえん：学園〉an educational institution, a campus.
    gakuen-funsô（学園紛争）a campus dispute
    gakuen-sai（学園祭）a campus festival

gakufu〈がくふ：学府〉
    saikô-gakufu（最高学府）the highest institution of learning

gakufu〈がくふ：楽譜〉a sheet of music, a score; music.
    gakufu-nashi-de ensô-suru（楽譜なしで演奏する）play without music
    gakufu-shû（楽譜集）a music book

gakufû〈がくふう：学風〉academic traditions; a method of study.

gakugaku〈がくがく〉
    Hiza ga gakugaku-suru.（ひざががくがくする。）My knees wobble.

gakugei〈がくげい：学芸〉art and science.
    gakugei-kai（学芸会）a literary exhibition, literary exercises

gakugyô〈がくぎょう：学業〉studies, schoolwork; scholarship.
    gakugyô-ni-hagemu（学業に励む）work hard in one's studies

gakuha〈がくは：学派〉a school, a sect.

gakuhi〈がくひ：学費〉*see.* gakushi（学資）.

gakui〈がくい：学位〉a degree, a title, a doctorate.
    gakui o toru（学位を取る）take a degree
    gakui-rombun（学位論文）a (master's *or* doctor's) thesis

gakujutsu〈がくじゅつ：学術〉science, learning, scholarship.
    gakujutsu-kaigi（学術会議）the Science Council
    gakujutsu-rombun（学術論文）a scientific essay

gakumei〈がくめい：学名〉a scientific name.

gakumen〈がくめん：額面〉face value, par; denomination.
    uwasa o gakumen-doori-ni uke-toru（うわさを額面どおりに受け取る）
        take a report at face value
   gakumen-de〈額面で〉at par.

gakumon〈がくもん：学問〉learning, studies.

　　gakumon-no-aru hito〈学問のある人〉a learned person, a person of learning

gakunen〈がくねん：学年〉a school year.

　　gakunen-shiken〈学年試験〉an annual examination

gakureki〈がくれき：学歴〉one's school career.

gakuri〈がくり：学理〉a theory.

　gakuri-teki(-na) or *gakuri-jō-no*〈学理的(な), 学理上の〉theoretical.

　gakuri-teki-ni or *gakuri-jō*〈学理的に, 学理上〉theoretically, in theory.

gakuryoku〈がくりょく：学力〉scholarship.

　　gakuryoku-no-aru-hito〈学力のある人〉a good scholar

　　gakuryoku-no-nai-hito〈学力のない人〉a poor scholar

　　gakuryoku-tesuto〈学力テスト〉an achievement test

gakusei〈がくせい：学生〉a student.

　　gakusei-jidai〈学生時代〉one's student days

　　gakusei-seikatsu〈学生生活〉student life

　　gakusei-undō〈学生運動〉a student movement

gakusei〈がくせい：学制〉an educational system.

gakusei〈がくせい：楽聖〉a master of music.

gakuseki(-bo)〈がくせき(ぼ)：学籍(簿)〉a school register.

　　gakuseki-bo-kara na o sakujo-suru〈学籍簿から名を削除する〉strike ((a person's)) name off the school register

gakusetsu〈がくせつ：学説〉a theory, a doctrine.

　　gakusetsu o tateru〈学説を立てる〉set up a theory

gakusha〈がくしゃ：学者〉a scholar, a learned person.

　gakusha-rashii〈学者らしい〉scholarlike, scholarly.

　gakusha-butta〈学者ぶった〉pedantic.

gakushi〈がくし：学士〉a university graduate; a bachelor.

　　bun-gakushi〈文学士〉(a) Bachelor of Arts

　　gakushi-gō〈学士号〉a bachelor's degree

gakushi〈がくし：学資〉school expenses.

　　gakushi o okuru〈学資を送る〉supply ((a student)) with his school expenses

Gakushi-in〈がくしいん：学士院〉the Academy.

gakushiki〈がくしき：学識〉learning.

　　gakushiki-keiken-sha〈学識経験者〉a man of learning and experience

　gakushiki-no-aru〈学識のある〉learned.

gakushō〈がくしょう：楽章〉a movement.

　　　dai-san-gakushô〈第三楽章〉 the third movement

gakushû〈がくしゅう：学習〉learning, study.
　gakushû-suru〈学習する〉learn, study.

gakusoku〈がくそく：学則〉school regulations.

gakuwari〈がくわり：学割〉a special fare reduction for students.

gakuya〈がくや：楽屋〉a dressing room, a greenroom.
　　　gakuya o tazuneru〈楽屋を訪ねる〉 visit ((an actor)) backstage
　gakuya-ura-de(-no)〈楽屋裏で(の)〉behind the scenes.
　　　gakuya-ura-de-no kôsaku〈楽屋裏での工作〉 backstage maneuver

gakuyô-hin〈がくようひん：学用品〉school things, school supplies.

gakuyû〈がくゆう：学友〉a schoolmate, a schoolfellow, a fellow student.

gakuzen〈がくぜん：がく然〉
　gakuzen-to-suru〈がく然とする〉be amazed, be startled, be shocked.
　gakuzen-to-shite〈がく然として〉in amazement, aghast.

gama〈がま〉a toad.

gaman〈がまん：我慢〉patience, perseverance, endurance, self-control.
　gaman-suru〈我慢する〉be patient, persevere, endure, put up ((with)),
　　control oneself.
　　　gaman-deki-nai〈我慢できない〉 cannot bear, cannot stand, lose
　　　patience ((with))
　gaman-zuyoi〈我慢強い〉patient, persevering.
　gaman-zuyoku〈我慢強く〉patiently, perseveringly.

gambari〈がんばり：頑張り〉
　　　gambari-ya〈頑張りや〉 a bitter-ender
　gambaru〈頑張る〉hold out, stand out.
　　　Gambare!〈頑張れ.〉 Hold out!

gamen〈がめん：画面〉a picture, a screen.

gamigami〈がみがみ〉
　gamigami-iu〈がみがみ言う〉snap ((at)), scold vehemently.

gammei〈がんめい：頑迷〉bigotry.
　gammei-na〈頑迷な〉bigoted.

gammen〈がんめん：顔面〉the face.
　　　gammen-shinkei-tsû〈顔面神経痛〉 facial neuralgia
　gammen-no〈顔面の〉facial.

gampeki〈がんぺき：岸壁〉a quay, a wharf.

gamu〈ガム〉chewing gum.
　　　gamu-o-kamu〈ガムをかむ〉 have a chew of gum

gamushara〈がむしゃら〉

gamushara-na〈がむしゃらな〉daredevil, reckless.

gamushara-ni〈がむしゃらに〉in a daredevil manner, recklessly.

gan〈がん〉a wild goose.

gan〈がん〉cancer.

　　hifu-gan（皮膚がん）　skin cancer

gan〈がん：願〉

gan-o-kakeru〈願をかける〉offer a prayer with a vow ((at *or* to)).

ganchiku〈がんちく：含蓄〉an implication.

ganchiku-no-aru〈含蓄のある〉significant, pregnant, suggestive.

　　ganchiku-no-aru kotoba（含蓄のある言葉）　pregnant words

ganchû〈がんちゅう：眼中〉

ganchû-ni-nai〈眼中にない〉take no notice ((of)), think nothing ((of)), disregard, ignore, be beyond one's notice.

gangan〈がんがん〉

　　Atama ga gangan-suru.（頭ががんがんする。）　My head hums.

　　Mimi ga gangan-naru.（耳ががんがん鳴る。）　My ears ring.

gangu〈がんぐ：がん具〉a toy, a plaything.

gani-mata〈がにまた〉bandy legs.

gani-mata-no or *gani-mata-de*〈がにまたの，がにまたで〉bandy-legged.

ganji-garame〈がんじがらめ〉

ganji-garame-ni-shibaru〈がんじがらめに縛る〉bind ((a person)) firmly hand and foot.

ganjitsu〈がんじつ：元日〉New Year's Day.

ganjô〈がんじょう：頑丈〉

ganjô-na〈頑丈な〉stout, strong, sturdy, robust.

ganjô-ni〈頑丈に〉stoutly, strongly, sturdily.

ganka〈がんか：眼下〉

ganka-no or *ganka-ni*〈眼下の，眼下に〉under one's eyes, right below one's eyes.

ganka〈がんか：眼科〉ophthalmology.

　　ganka-i（眼科医）　an eye doctor, an oculist

ganken〈がんけん：頑健〉

ganken-na〈頑健な〉very strong, robust.

gankin〈がんきん：元金〉the principal.

ganko〈がんこ：頑固〉stubbornness, obstinacy.

ganko-na〈頑固な〉stubborn, obstinate.

ganko-ni〈頑固に〉stubbornly, obstinately.

gankyô〈がんきょう：頑強〉

gankyô-na〈頑強な〉dogged, stubborn.

gankyô-ni〈頑強に〉doggedly, stubbornly.

　　　gankyô-ni teikô-suru（頑強に抵抗する）resist stubbornly

gankyû〈がんきゅう：眼球〉an eyeball.

gannen〈がんねん：元年〉the first year.

ganrai〈がんらい：元来〉originally, fundamentally, primarily, by nature, essentially, in itself, in the first place; really, properly speaking.

　　　ganrai shôjiki-de-aru（元来正直である）be honest by nature

gan-ri〈がんり：元利〉principal and interest.

　　　gan-ri-gôkei(-gaku)（元利合計(額)）an amount with interest added

ganryô〈がんりょう：顔料〉cosmetics; a paint, a color, a pigment.

ganseki〈がんせき：岩石〉(a) rock, a crag.

　ganseki-no-ooi〈岩石の多い〉rocky, craggy.

gansho〈がんしょ：願書〉an application.

　　　gansho o dasu（願書を出す）present an application

ganshoku〈がんしょく：顔色〉

　ganshoku-nakara-shimeru〈顔色なからしめる〉put ((a person)) into the shade, put ((a person)) to shame.

ganso〈がんそ：元祖〉the originator, the founder, the father, the inventor.

gantai〈がんたい：眼帯〉an eye bandage.

gantan〈がんたん：元たん(旦)〉New Year's Day.

gantei〈がんてい：眼底〉

　　　gantei-shukketsu（眼底出血）cerebral hemorrhage in one's eyes

gan-to-shite〈がんとして：頑として〉

　gan-to-shite-kiki-ire-nai or *gan-to-shite-ôji-nai*〈頑として聞き入れない，頑として応じない〉refuse flatly, turn a deaf ear ((to)).

gan‧yaku〈がんやく：丸薬〉a pill.

gan‧yû〈がんゆう：含有〉

　　　gan‧yû-ryô（含有量）content

　gan‧yû-suru〈含有する〉contain, hold, have ((in)).

ganzô〈がんぞう：がん造〉counterfeiting, forgery.

　　　ganzô-shihei（がん造紙幣）a forged note

　ganzô-suru〈がん造する〉counterfeit, forge.

　ganzô-no〈がん造の〉counterfeit, forged.

gappei〈がっぺい：合併〉combination, amalgamation, merger.

　gappei-suru〈合併する〉combine, amalgamate, merge.

gappon〈がっぽん：合本〉a bound volume.

gappon-ni-suru 〈合本にする〉 combine in one volume.

gara 〈がら：柄〉 a pattern, a design; build; character; pertinence.

    gara-mono-no waishatsu（柄物のワイシャツ）a patterned shirt

    gara-no-ookii（柄の大きい）of a large build

    gara-no-chiisai（柄の小さい）of a small build

    Watashi-wa hito o rîdo-suru-gara-dewa-nai.（私は人をリードする柄ではない。）It is not for me to lead others.

    Ano otoko wa gakusha-nado-to-ieta-gara-dewa-nai.（あの男は学者などと言えた柄ではない。）He has no claim to the name of scholar.

gara-no-warui 〈柄の悪い〉 vulgar, raffish.

gara-aki 〈がらあき：がら空き〉

gara-aki-de-aru 〈がら空きである〉 be quite empty.

garagara 〈がらがら〉 a rattle, rattling.

    garagara-hebi（がらがら蛇）a rattlesnake

    garagara-ochiru（がらがら落ちる）rattle down

    garagara no gekijô（がらがらの劇場）an empty theater

garakuta 〈がらくた〉 rubbish, trash, junk.

-garami 〈-がらみ〉

    go-jû-garami-no otoko（五十がらみの男）a man about fifty

garan 〈がらん〉 a Buddhist temple, a cathedral.

garan 〈がらん〉

garan-to-shita 〈がらんとした〉 empty, bare, deserted.

garangaran 〈がらんがらん〉

garangaran-to-naru 〈がらんがらんと鳴る〉 clang.

garari 〈がらり〉

garari-to 〈がらりと〉 with a clatter; suddenly, completely.

    garari-to to o akeru（がらりと戸を開ける）open the door with a clatter

    garari-to taido o kaeru（がらりと態度を変える）suddenly change one's attitude

garasu 〈ガラス〉 glass, a pane.

    garasu-kigu（ガラス器具）glassware

    mado-garasu（窓ガラス）a window pane

garasu-bari 〈ガラスばり：ガラス張り〉

    garasu-bari-no-naka-de okonawareru-beki seiji（ガラス張りの中で行われるべき政治）the state affairs to be administered before a public

garasu-bari-no 〈ガラス張りの〉 glazed, glassed-in.

garêji 〈ガレージ〉 a garage.

gareki〈がれき〉rubbles and pebbles.

gari-ban〈がりばん：がり版〉*see.* tôsha-ban.

gari-ben〈がりべん：がり勉〉grinding; a grind.
gari-ben-suru〈がり勉する〉grind.

garigari〈がりがり〉
garigari-kaku〈がりがりかく〉 scratch
garigari-kamu〈がりがりかむ〉 crunch

garô〈がろう：画廊〉a picture gallery.

-garu〈－がる〉
samu-garu〈寒がる〉feel cold.

garyô〈がりょう：雅量〉tolerance, generosity.
garyô-no-aru〈雅量のある〉tolerant, broad-minded.
garyô-no-nai〈雅量のない〉 intolerant, narrow-minded

garyû〈がりゅう：我流〉
garyû-de-yaru〈我流でやる〉do ((a thing)) in one's own way.
garyû-no〈我流の〉self-taught.

gasagasa〈がさがさ〉
shigemi-no-naka-kara gasagasa-dete-kuru（茂みの中からがさがさ出て
来る） come rustling out of the bush
gasagasa-suru〈がさがさする〉rustle; feel rough.

gasatsu〈がさつ〉
gasatsu-na〈がさつな〉rude, rough, unrefined.
gasatsu-na yatsu〈がさつなやつ〉 a rude fellow

gashi〈がし：餓死〉death from hunger.
gashi-suru〈餓死する〉die of hunger, be starved to death.

gashitsu〈がしつ：画室〉a studio, an *atelier*.

gashô〈がしょう：画商〉a picture dealer.

gashû〈がしゅう：画集〉a book of drawings.

gasorin〈ガソリン〉gasoline, gas, petrol.
gasorin-sutando（ガソリンスタンド） a gas(*or* filling) stand

gassaku〈がっさく：合作〉collaboration, a joint work.
gassaku-suru〈合作する〉collaborate with ((a person)) on.

gassan〈がっさん：合算〉adding up.
gassan-suru〈合算する〉add up, add together.

gasshiri〈がっしり〉
gasshiri-shita〈がっしりした〉sturdy, stalwart, stout, massive.

gasshô〈がっしょう：合唱〉chorus.
konsei-gasshô（混声合唱） a mixed chorus

     gasshô-dan〈合唱団〉 a chorus, a choir

    gasshô-suru〈合唱する〉 sing in chorus.

gasshô〈がっしょう：合掌〉

    gasshô-suru〈合掌する〉 put one's hands flat together in prayer.

Gasshûkoku〈がっしゅうこく：合衆国〉 the United States (of America).

gasshuku〈がっしゅく：合宿〉

     gasshuku-jo〈合宿所〉 a training camp, a dormitory

    gasshuku-suru〈合宿する〉 lodge together.

gassô〈がっそう：合奏〉 (a) concert, (an) ensemble.

    gassô-suru〈合奏する〉 play in concert.

gasu〈ガス〉 gas.

     gasu o tsukeru（ガスを付ける） turn on the gas

     gasu o kesu（ガスを消す） turn off the gas

     Gasu ga morete-iru.（ガスが漏れている。） The gas leaks.

     gasu-chûdoku（ガス中毒） gas poisoning

     gasu-jisatsu-suru（ガス自殺する） kill oneself by inhaling gas

gata〈がた〉

    gata-ga-kuru〈がたがくる〉 break down, become rickety.

-gata〈-がた：-型〉

     sen-kyū-hyaku-hachi-jû-go-nen-gata（1985年型） the 1985 model

-gata〈-がた：-方〉

     san-wari-gata（三割方） by some thirty percent

     Genji-gata（源氏方） the Genji's side

gatagata〈がたがた〉

     Mado ga gatagata-iu.（窓ががたがたいう。） The windows rattle.

     samukute gatagata-furueru（寒くてがたがた震える） shiver with cold

     gatagata-no hashigo-dan（がたがたのはしご段） a rickety staircase

gatagoto〈がたごと〉

    gatagoto-hashiru〈がたごと走る〉 rattle along.

-gatai〈-がたい：難い〉 *see.* -nikui.

gatan〈がたん〉

    gatan-to〈がたんと〉 with a bang.

     gatan-to tomaru（がたんと止まる） stop with a jolt

gata-ochi〈がたおち：がた落ち〉

    ninki-ga-gata-ochi-ni-naru〈人気ががた落ちになる〉 have a sudden fall in one's popularity.

gatchi〈がっち：合致〉 *see.* itchi.

gatchiri〈がっちり〉

gatchiri-shita〈がっちりした〉strongly-built; tightfisted, shrewd.

gaten〈がてん：合点〉

　　gaten-ga-iku-made（合点がいくまで）till one thoroughly understands

　　gaten-no-ika-nai（合点のいかない）incomprehensible

gatsugatsu〈がつがつ〉

　　gatsugatsu-taberu（がつがつ食べる）eat greedily

　　gatsugatsu-shite-iru（がつがつしている）be greedy

gawa〈がわ：側〉a side.

　　hidari-gawa（左側）the left side

　　migi-gawa（右側）the right side

　　kochira-gawa（こちら側）this side

　　achira-gawa（あちら側）the other side

　　seifu-gawa（政府側）the Government side

　　rôdô-gawa-no iken（労働側の意見）the opinion on the part of the workers

　　uchi-gawa（内側）the inside

　　soto-gawa（外側）the outside

〜-no-gawa-ni-tsuku〈〜の側につく〉take sides with... , take part with... .

gayagaya〈がやがや〉noisily.

gayagaya-sawagu〈がやがや騒ぐ〉make a noise, fuss.

gayôshi〈がようし：画用紙〉drawing paper.

gâze〈ガーゼ〉gauze.

gazen〈がぜん：俄然〉all of a sudden, suddenly.

gazô〈がぞう：画像〉a portrait, one's likeness, an image, a picture.

ge〈げ：下〉the low grade; the last volume.

　　ge-no-ge（下の下）the worst of all

geba-hyô〈げばひょう：下馬評〉an outsider's advanced rumor.

gedan〈げだん：下段〉the lower berth.

gedoku-zai〈げどくざい：解毒剤〉an antidote.

gehin〈げひん：下品〉

gehin-na〈下品な〉vulgar, low, indecent, coarse.

　　gehin-na kotoba（下品な言葉）a vulgar expression

gei〈げい：芸〉an art, an accomplishment, acting; a trick.

　　gei-de-mi-o-tateru（芸で身を立てる）earn one's living as an artist

　　Gei wa mi-o-tasukeru.（芸は身を助ける.）Accomplishments are a benefit in need.

　　gei o suru（芸をする）do a trick

　　gei-ga-komakai（芸が細かい）be mindful of particulars

geigeki〈げいげき：迎撃〉

geigeki-yō-misairu（迎撃用ミサイル） an interceptor missile

geigeki-suru〈迎撃する〉 intercept.

geigō〈げいごう：迎合〉

geigō-suru〈迎合する〉 ingratiate oneself ((with)), flatter, echo.

geigō-teki(-na)〈迎合的（な）〉 ingratiating.

geihin-kan〈げいひんかん：迎賓館〉 a (Government) guest house.

geijutsu〈げいじゅつ：芸術〉 art, fine arts.

geijutsu-sakuhin（芸術作品） a work of art

geijutsu-ka（芸術家） an artist

geijutsu-teki(-na)〈芸術的（な）〉 artistic.

geijutsu-teki-ni〈芸術的に〉 artistically.

geimei〈げいめい：芸名〉 a stage name, a screen name.

geinō〈げいのう：芸能〉 public entertainment, accomplishments.

geinō-jin（芸能人） an artiste, a performer, a public entertainer

geinō-kai（芸能界） the world of show business

geitō〈げいとう：芸当〉 an art, a performance, a feat, a stunt, a trick.

abunai-geitō-o-suru（危ない芸当をする） do a stunt, try a risky attempt

geiyu〈げいゆ：鯨油〉 whale oil.

gejigeji〈げじげじ〉 a millepede; a worm.

gejun〈げじゅん：下旬〉 the last ten days of a month.

shichi-gatsu-gejun-ni（七月下旬に） towards the end of July, late in July

geka〈げか：外科〉 surgery.

geka-i（外科医） a surgeon

geka-iin（外科医院） a surgery

geka-shujutsu（外科手術） a surgical operation

gekai〈げかい：下界〉 the earth.

gekai-o-mi-orosu（下界を見下ろす） look down upon the earth

geki〈げき：劇〉 a drama, a play.

geki o jōen-suru（劇を上演する） stage a drama

geki-teki(-na)〈劇的（な）〉 dramatic.

gekichin〈げきちん：撃沈〉

gekichin-suru〈撃沈する〉 sink.

gekidan〈げきだん：劇団〉 a dramatic company, a troupe.

gekidan〈げきだん：劇壇〉 the stage.

gekidan-ni-tatsu（劇壇に立つ） come on the stage

gekido 〈げきど：激怒〉 violent anger, fury.
　gekido-suru 〈激怒する〉 rage, be enraged.
　gekido-saseru 〈激怒させる〉 enrage.
gekidô 〈げきどう：激動〉 excitement; violent shaking.
　gekidô-suru 〈激動する〉 be excited; shake violently.
gekigen 〈げきげん：激減〉
　gekigen-suru 〈激減する〉 decrease sharply.
gekihen 〈げきへん：激(劇)変〉 a sudden change.
　gekihen-suru 〈激変する〉 change suddenly, undergo a sudden change.
gekihyô 〈げきひょう：劇評〉 dramatic criticism.
　gekihyô-ka（劇評家） a dramatic critic
gekijô 〈げきじょう：劇場〉 a theater, a playhouse.
gekijô 〈げきじょう：激情〉 a violent emotion, passion.
　gekijô-ni-kararete〈激情に駆られて〉 carried away by a fit of passion.
gekimu 〈げきむ：劇務〉 hard work, press of business.
　gekimu-ni taoreru（劇務に倒れる） break down under the strain
gekirei 〈げきれい：激励〉 encouragement.
　gekirei no kotoba（激励の言葉） words of encouragement
　gekirei-suru〈激励する〉 encourage.
gekiretsu 〈げきれつ：激烈〉
　gekiretsu-na〈激烈な〉 vehement, violent, fierce, acute, keen.
　gekiretsu-na kotoba（激烈な言葉） vehement language
　gekiretsu-na kyôsô（激烈な競争） fierce competition
gekirô 〈げきろう：激浪〉 raging waves, a high sea.
gekiron 〈げきろん：激論〉 a hot argument, a heated discussion.
　gekiron-suru〈激論する〉 have a heated discussion, argue hotly.
gekiryû 〈げきりゅう：激流〉 a violent stream, a raging torrent.
gekisaku 〈げきさく：劇作〉 playwriting.
　gekisakka（劇作家） a playwriter, a dramatist
　gekisaku-suru〈劇作する〉 write a play.
gekisen 〈げきせん：激戦〉 a severe fight, heavy fighting, a hot contest.
　gekisen-chi（激戦地） a hard-fought field, a closely contested constituency
gekishin 〈げきしん：激震〉 a severe shock.
gekishô 〈げきしょう：激賞〉 high praise.
　gekishô-suru〈激賞する〉 praise highly.
gekisuru 〈げきする：激する〉 get excited, be enraged.
　gekishi-yasui〈激しやすい〉 excitable.

gekitai 〈げきたい：撃退〉

  gekitai-suru 〈撃退する〉 drive back, repulse; reject, refuse.

gekitotsu 〈げきとつ：激突〉 a crash.

  gekitotsu-suru 〈激突する〉 crash ((into)).

gekitsū 〈げきつう：劇(激)痛〉 an acute pain.

gekitsui 〈げきつい：撃墜〉

  gekitsui-suru 〈撃墜する〉 shoot down, (bring) down.

gekiyaku 〈げきやく：劇薬〉 a powerful medicine, a deadly poison.

gekizō 〈げきぞう：激増〉

  gekizô-suru 〈激増する〉 increase suddenly.

gekka 〈げっか：激化〉

  gekka-suru 〈激化する〉 become intensified.

gekkan 〈げっかん：月刊〉 monthly publication.

    gekkan-shi（月刊誌） a monthly

  gekkan-no 〈月刊の〉 monthly.

gekkei 〈げっけい：月経〉 menstruation, menses, periods.

    gekkei-ga-aru（月経がある） have the menses

    gekkei-fujun（月経不順） menstrual irregularity

gekkei-ju 〈げっけいじゅ：月けい樹〉 a laurel tree.

gekkei-kan 〈げっけいかん：月けい冠〉 a laurel wreath.

gekkō 〈げっこう：月光〉 moonlight.

gekkō 〈げっこう：激こう〉 excitement, rage, fury.

  gekkô-suru 〈激こうする〉 become excited, be enraged.

  gekkô-shite 〈激こうして〉 in excitement, in a fit of passion.

gekkyū 〈げっきゅう：月給〉 a monthly pay, a monthly salary.

    gekkyû-tori（月給取り） a salaried man

    gekkyû-bi（月給日） the payday

geko 〈げこ：下戸〉 a poor drinker, a nondrinker.

gekokujō 〈げこくじょう：下こく上〉 the tail wags the dog.

gemba 〈げんば：現場〉 the spot, the scene.

    jiko-gemba（事故現場） the scene of the accident

    gemba-kenshō（現場検証） an inspection of the scene of crime

    gemba-kantoku（現場監督） a field overseer

gembaku 〈げんばく：原爆〉 see. genshi-bakudan.

gembatsu 〈げんばつ：厳罰〉 a severe punishment.

  gembatsu-ni-shosuru 〈厳罰に処する〉 punish ((a person)) severely.

gembo 〈げんぼ：原簿〉 a ledger, the original register.

gembu-gan 〈げんぶがん：玄武岩〉 basalt.

gembun 〈げんぶん：原文〉 the original, the text.
    gembun-de yomu〈原文で読む〉 read ((a book)) in the original
gembutsu 〈げんぶつ：原物〉 the original.
    gembutsu-dai-no〈原物大の〉 life-sized, full-sized.
gembutsu 〈げんぶつ：現物〉 the actual article, spot goods.
    gembutsu-tori-hiki（現物取引） spot transaction
    gembutsu-shusshi（現物出資） investment in kind
gemmai 〈げんまい：玄米〉 unpolished rice.
gemmei 〈げんめい：言明〉 declaration, statement.
    gemmei-suru〈言明する〉 declare.
gemmei 〈げんめい：厳命〉
    gemmei-suru〈厳命する〉 give a strict order.
gemmen 〈げんめん：原綿〉 raw cotton.
gemmetsu 〈げんめつ：幻滅〉 disillusion.
    gemmetsu-no-hiai-o-kanjiru〈幻滅の悲哀を感じる〉 be disillusioned.
gemmitsu 〈げんみつ：厳密〉 strictness.
    gemmitsu-na〈厳密な〉 strict, rigid, close.
    gemmitsu-ni〈厳密に〉 strictly, rigidly, closely, exactly.
    gemmitsu-ni-ieba（厳密に言えば） strictly speaking
gempai 〈げんぱい：減配〉 a dividend cut.
    gempai-suru〈減配する〉 reduce a dividend.
gempin 〈げんぴん：現品〉 the actual thing, stocks.
    gempin-hiki-kae-barai（現品引換払い） cash on delivery(C.O.D.)
    gempin-zaiko（現品在庫） the goods in stock
gempô 〈げんぼう：減俸〉 see. genkyû（減給）.
gempon 〈げんぽん：原本〉 the original book, the text.
gêmu 〈ゲーム〉 a game.
    gêmu o suru（ゲームをする） play a game
    san-gêmu-han-no-sa-de（三ゲーム半の差で） by three and a half
    games
gen 〈げん：弦〉 a string, gut.
    gen-gakki（弦楽器） a stringed instrument
gen 〈げん：減〉 (a) decrease, (a) reduction.
    ni-juppâsento-gen（二十パーセント減） a decrease of 20 percent
gen- 〈げん-：現-〉 present, existing.
    gen-naikaku（現内閣） the present Cabinet
gen·an 〈げんあん：原案〉 the original bill, the original plan.
    gen·an-doori kaketsu-suru（原案どおり可決する） pass ((a bill)) in its

original form

genchi 〈げんち：現地〉the spot, the actual place.

genchi-chôsa（現地調査）an on-the-spot survey

genchi-hôkoku（現地報告）a report from the spot

genchi-jikan（現地時間）local time

genchi 〈げんち：言質〉a pledge, a promise, a commitment.

genchi o toru（言質を取る）obtain ((a person's)) pledge

gencho 〈げんちょ：原著〉the original work.

gencho-sha（原著者）an author

gendai 〈げんだい：現代〉the present age, modern times, today.

gendai-Eigo（現代英語）present-day English

gendai-no 〈現代の〉present-day, modern, current.

gendai-teki(-na) 〈現代的(な)〉modern, up-to-date.

gendai-teki-na tate-mono（現代的な建物）a building in modern style

gendo 〈げんど：限度〉a limit, limits.

gendo ni tassuru（限度に達する）reach the limit

〜-o-gendo-to-shite（〜を限度として）within the limits of...

gen-dô 〈げんどう：言動〉one's speech and conduct.

gendô-ryoku 〈げんどうりょく：原動力〉motive power, driving force.

gen·ei 〈げんえい：幻影〉a vision, a phantom, an illusion.

gen·eki 〈げんえき：現役〉active service, active duty.

gen·eki-o-shirizoku（現役を退く）retire from active service

gen·eki-de-nyûgaku-suru（現役で入学する）enter ((a college))
directly upon graduation〔from high school〕

genetsu-zai 〈げねつざい：解熱剤〉an antifebrile.

genga 〈げんが：原画〉the original picture.

gengaku 〈げんがく：弦楽〉string music.

gengaku-shijû-sô（弦楽四重奏）a string quartet

gengaku 〈げんがく：減額〉a reduction, a cut.

gengaku-suru 〈減額する〉reduce, cut down.

gengo 〈げんご：言語〉language, speech, words.

gengo-shôgai（言語障害）a speech defect

gengo-gaku（言語学）linguistics, philology

gengo-ni-zessuru 〈言語に絶する〉be beyond words.

gengo 〈げんご：原語〉the original word.

gen·in 〈げんいん：原因〉a cause, a factor, the source.

gen·in o akiraka-ni-suru（原因を明らかにする）clear up the cause

〜-ni-gen·in-suru 〈〜に原因する〉be caused by... , arise from... .

gen·in-fumei-no〈原因不明の〉of an unknown origin.

gen·in〈げんいん：減員〉

gen·in-suru〈減員する〉reduce the staff.

genjitsu〈げんじつ：現実〉actuality, reality.

genjitsu-shugi〈現実主義〉realism

genjitsu-ka-suru〈現実化する〉actualize, realize.

genjitsu-no〈現実の〉actual, real.

genjitsu-teki(-na)〈現実的(な)〉realistic, down-to-earth.

genjitsu-ni〈現実に〉actually, really.

genjitsu-ni-naru〈現実になる〉become reality, come true

genjō〈げんじょう：現状〉the present condition.

genjô o iji-suru〈現状を維持する〉maintain the existing state of things

genjô-de-wa〈現状では〉under the existing circumstances

genjū〈げんじゅう：厳重〉strictness, severity.

genjû-na〈厳重な〉strict, severe, rigorous, close.

genjû-na keikai〈厳重な警戒〉(a) strict watch

genjû-na kôgi o suru〈厳重な抗議をする〉make a strong protest ((against))

genjû-ni〈厳重に〉strictly, severely, rigorously, closely.

gen-jūmin〈げんじゅうみん：原住民〉a native.

gen-jūsho〈げんじゅうしょ：現住所〉one's present address.

genka〈げんか：原価〉the cost price.

genka-keisan〈原価計算〉cost accounting

shi-ire-genka〈仕入れ原価〉purchasing cost

genka-ika-de〈原価以下で〉below cost.

genkai〈げんかい：限界〉a boundary, a limit, limitation.

genkai o sadameru〈限界を定める〉fix the limit

genkai o koeru〈限界を越える〉pass the limit

jibun-no nôryoku-no-genkai o shiru〈自分の能力の限界を知る〉know one's limitations

genkaku〈げんかく：幻覚〉a hallucination.

genkaku-o-okosu〈幻覚を起こす〉hallucinate, have hallucinations.

genkaku〈げんかく：厳格〉

genkaku-na〈厳格な〉strict, stern, rigorous, severe.

genkaku-ni〈厳格に〉strictly, sternly, rigorously, severely.

genkan〈げんかん：玄関〉the front door, the entrance, the porch.

genkan-kara hairu〈玄関から入る〉enter at the front door

genkan-barai-o-kuwaseru（玄関払いを食わせる） turn ((a person)) away at the door

genkan〈げんかん：厳寒〉intense cold.

genka-shōkyaku〈げんかしょうきゃく：減価償却〉depreciation.

genkei〈げんけい：原形〉the original form.

genkei o tamotsu（原形を保つ） keep ((its)) original form

genkei〈げんけい：減刑〉reduction of penalty.

genkei-suru〈減刑する〉reduce〔penalty〕.

genki〈げんき：元気〉vigor, energy, spirits, pep.

genki o ushinau（元気を失う） lose heart

genki o tori-modosu（元気を取り戻す） recover one's spirits

genki-ni kurasu（元気に暮らす） live in good health

genki-hatsuratsu-to-shite-iru or *genki-ôsei-de-aru*〈元気はつらつとしている、元気おう盛である〉be full of pep.

genki-zuku or *genki-o-dasu*〈元気付く、元気を出す〉cheer up, get encouraged.

genki-zukeru〈元気付ける〉cheer up, encourage, pep up.

genki-na or *genki-no-ii*〈元気な、元気のいい〉cheerful, high-spirited, healthy.

genki-no-nai（元気のない） cheerless, low-spirited, depressed

genki-yoku〈元気よく〉cheerfully, in high spirits.

genki-naku（元気なく） cheerlessly, dispiritedly

genkin〈げんきん：現金〉cash, ready money.

genkin-de harau（現金で払う） pay in cash

genkin-de kau（現金で買う） buy for cash

genkin-kakitome（現金書留） a cash registered mail

genkin-ni-kaeru〈現金に換える〉cash.

ko-gitte o genkin-ni-kaeru（小切手を現金に換える） have a check cashed

genkin-na〈現金な〉mercenary, calculating.

genkin-na otoko（現金な男） a calculating man

genkin〈げんきん：厳禁〉strict prohibition.

genkin-suru〈厳禁する〉prohibit strictly.

gen-kō〈げんこう：言行〉one's sayings and doings.

gen-kô-ga-itchi-suru（言行が一致する） act up to what one says

gen-kô-ga-itchi-shi-nai（言行が一致しない） say one thing and do another

genkō〈げんこう：原稿〉a manuscript, a copy.

genkô-ryô〈原稿料〉 manuscript fee

genkô-yôshi〈原稿用紙〉 manuscript paper, a writing pad

genkô〈げんこう：現行〉

genkô-seido〈現行制度〉 the present system

genkô-no〈現行の〉 existing, present.

genkô-no kyôka-sho〈現行の教科書〉 the textbooks now in use

genkô-han〈げんこうはん：現行犯〉

genkô-han-de toraerareru〈現行犯で捕らえられる〉 be caught in the act 〔of stealing〕.

genkoku〈げんこく：原告〉 a plaintiff.

genkotsu〈げんこつ：げん骨〉 a fist.

genkotsu-de naguru〈げん骨で殴る〉 strike ((a person)) with one's fist

genkyô〈げんきょう：現況〉 see. genjô.

genkyû〈げんきゅう：言及〉 reference.

genkyû-suru〈言及する〉 refer ((to)), mention.

genkyû〈げんきゅう：減給〉 reduction of one's salary.

genkyû-sareru〈減給される〉 have one's salary reduced.

gennari〈げんなり〉

gennari-suru〈げんなりする〉 be sick and tired ((of)), be fed up ((with)).

gen-ni〈げんに：現に〉 actually, really, with one's own eyes, with one's own ears; for instance.

Gen-ni watashi-wa sore-o mimashita.（現に私はそれを見ました.） I saw it with my own eyes.

genri〈げんり：原理〉 a principle, a theory.

genrô〈げんろう：元老〉 an elder, a senior, an old-timer.

seikai-no-genrô〈政界の元老〉 an elder statesman

jitsugyô-kai-no genrô-tachi〈実業界の元老たち〉 old-timers in business circles

genron〈げんろん：言論〉 speech, discussion.

genron no jiyû〈言論の自由〉 freedom of speech

genron-kikan〈言論機関〉 an organ of public opinion

genron〈げんろん：原論〉 the principles〔of economics〕.

genryô〈げんりょう：原料〉 raw material(s).

genryô〈げんりょう：減量〉

genryô-suru〈減量する〉 reduce one's weight.

gensaku〈げんさく：原作〉 the original work.

gensan〈げんさん：減産〉 a decrease in production, curtailment of production.

gensan-suru〈減産する〉curtail production.

gensan-chi〈げんさんち：原産地〉the country of origin, the original home.

gense〈げんせ：現世〉this world, this life.

gensei〈げんせい：厳正〉strictness, impartiality.

gensei-chûritsu（厳正中立）strict neutrality

gensei-na〈厳正な〉strict, impartial.

gensei-na hihan（厳正な批判）an impartial criticism

gensei-ni〈厳正に〉strictly, impartially.

gensen〈げんせん：源泉〉a wellspring, a source.

chishiki no gensen（知識の源泉）a source of knowledge

gensen-chôshû（源泉徴収）taxation at the source of income

gensen〈げんせん：厳選〉

gensen-suru〈厳選する〉select carefully.

genshi〈げんし：原始〉the beginning, genesis, origin.

genshi-jidai（原始時代）the primitive ages

genshi-jin（原始人）primitive man

genshi-rin（原始林）a virgin forest

genshi-teki(-na)〈原始的(な)〉primitive, pristine.

genshi〈げんし：原子〉an atom.

genshi-bakudan（原子爆弾）an atomic bomb, an A-bomb

genshi-gumo（原子雲）an atomic cloud

genshi-kaku（原子核）an atomic nucleus

genshi-ro（原子炉）a nuclear reactor

genshi-no〈原子の〉atomic.

genshi〈げんし：減資〉reduction of capital.

genshi-suru〈減資する〉reduce the capital.

genshi-ryoku〈げんしりょく：原子力〉atomic energy, nuclear power.

genshi-ryoku-hatsuden-sho（原子力発電所）an atomic power station

genshi-ryoku-sensui-kan（原子力潜水艦）an atomic(-powered) submarine

gensho〈げんしょ：原書〉the original (work).

Chikamatsu o gensho-de yomu（近松を原書で読む）read *Chikamatsu* in the original

genshô〈げんしょう：現象〉a phenomenon.

shizen-genshô（自然現象）a natural phenomenon

genshô〈げんしょう：減少〉(a) decrease, (a) diminution, (a) reduction.

genshô-suru〈減少する〉decrease, diminish, lessen, be reduced.

genshoku〈げんしょく：現職〉the present post.

genshoku-no〈現職の〉in active service, on the active list.

　genshoku-no keikan（現職の警官）a policeman in active service

genshoku〈げんしょく：原色〉a primary color.

　genshoku-ban（原色版）a heliotype

genshoku〈げんしょく：減食〉reduction of diet.

genshoku-suru〈減食する〉reduce one's diet.

genshu〈げんしゅ：元首〉the chief of a nation, the sovereign.

genshu〈げんしゅ：厳守〉

genshu-suru〈厳守する〉observe strictly.

　jikan-o-genshu-suru（時間を厳守する）be very punctual

　kisoku-o-genshu-suru（規則を厳守する）observe the rules to the letter

　yakusoku-o-genshu-suru（約束を厳守する）keep one's promise strictly

genshû〈げんしゅう：減収〉a decrease in income.

genshuku〈げんしゅく：厳粛〉gravity, solemnity.

genshuku-na〈厳粛な〉grave, solemn.

　genshuku-na-kimochi-ni-naru（厳粛な気持ちになる）be inspired with awe

genshuku-ni〈厳粛に〉gravely, solemnly.

genso〈げんそ：元素〉an element.

gensô〈げんそう：幻想〉a fantasy, an illusion, a vision, a dream.

　gensô-kyoku（幻想曲）a fantasia, a fantasy

gensô-teki(-na)〈幻想的(な)〉visionary, dreamy.

gensô〈げんそう：げん窓〉a porthole.

gensoku〈げんそく：原則〉a principle, a general rule.

gensoku-to-shite or *gensoku-teki-ni*〈原則として，原則的に〉as a rule, in principle.

gensoku〈げんそく：げん側〉the (ship's) side, the broadside.

gensoku〈げんそく：減速〉deceleration.

gensoku-suru〈減速する〉decelerate, reduce the speed, slow down.

genson〈げんそん：現存〉

genson-suru〈現存する〉exist, be in existence.

genson-no〈現存の〉existing, living, alive.

gensui〈げんすい：元帥〉a marshal, a general of the army, an admiral of the fleet, a fleet admiral.

gensui 〈げんすい：減水〉low water.

  gensui-suru 〈減水する〉fall, go down.

gen-sui-baku 〈げんすいばく：原水爆〉atomic and hydrogen bombs, A and H bombs.

gentai 〈げんたい：減退〉decline, loss.

    shokuyoku no gentai （食欲の減退）loss of appetite

  gentai-suru 〈減退する〉decline, fall off.

gentei 〈げんてい：限定〉limitation.

    gentei-ban （限定版）a limited edition

  gentei-suru 〈限定する〉limit.

genten 〈げんてん：原典〉the original text.

genten 〈げんてん：原点〉the starting point.

    genten-ni tachi-kaeru （原点に立ち返る）go back to the starting point

genten 〈げんてん：減点〉

  genten-suru 〈減点する〉give ((a person)) a demerit mark.

genwaku 〈げんわく：げん惑〉dazzlement.

  genwaku-suru 〈げん惑する〉dazzle.

gen·ya 〈げんや：原野〉a field, a plain, a wilderness.

gen·yu 〈げんゆ：原油〉crude petroleum.

gen·yû 〈げんゆう：現有〉

    gen·yû-seiryoku （現有勢力）effective(*or* existing) strength

genzai 〈げんざい：現在〉the present time; now, at present.

  genzai-no 〈現在の〉present.

  genzai-made 〈現在まで〉up to now.

  genzai-no-tokoro-dewa 〈現在のところでは〉at present, for the time being.

genzai 〈げんざい：原罪〉the original sin.

genzei 〈げんぜい：減税〉a tax reduction.

  genzei-suru 〈減税する〉reduce taxes.

genzen 〈げんぜん：厳然〉

  genzen-taru 〈厳然たる〉solemn, grave, stern, solid.

    genzen-taru jijitsu （厳然たる事実）a stern reality

  genzen-to 〈厳然と〉solemnly, gravely, sternly.

genzô 〈げんぞう：現像〉development.

    genzô-eki （現像液）a developer

  genzô-suru 〈現像する〉develop.

geppô 〈げっぽう：月報〉a monthly bulletin.

geppu 〈げっぷ：月賦〉a monthly instal(l)ment.

geppu-de ichi-man-en-zutsu-harau （月賦で一万円ずつ払う） pay ((for a thing)) by monthly installments of 10,000 yen

geppu 〈げっぷ〉

geppu-ga-deru 〈げっぷが出る〉 belch.

gera 〈ゲラ〉 a galley.

gera-zuri （ゲラ刷り） a galley proof

geragera 〈げらげら〉

geragera-warau 〈げらげら笑う〉 guffaw.

geraku 〈げらく：下落〉 a fall.

beika-no geraku （米価の下落） a fall in the price of rice

geraku-suru 〈下落する〉 fall, decline, come down, go down, become lower.

gerende 〈ゲレンデ〉 a slope.

geretsu 〈げれつ：下劣〉 baseness, meanness.

geretsu-na 〈下劣な〉 base, mean, low, vulgar.

geri 〈げり：下痢〉 diarrhea.

geri-dome （下痢止め） a binding medicine

geri-suru 〈下痢する〉 have diarrhea, have loose bowels.

gerira 〈ゲリラ〉 guer(r)illa.

gerira-katsudō （ゲリラ活動） guerilla activities

Geruman-minzoku 〈ゲルマンみんぞく：ゲルマン民族〉 the Germanic race.

gesha 〈げしゃ：下車〉

gesha-suru 〈下車する〉 get off.

geshi 〈げし：夏至〉 the summer solstice.

geshuku 〈げしゅく：下宿〉 lodgings, boarding.

geshuku-seikatsu-o-suru （下宿生活をする） live in lodgings

geshuku-dai （下宿代） the charge for board and lodging

geshuku-nin （下宿人） a lodger, a boarder

geshuku-ya （下宿屋） a lodging house, a boarding house

geshuku-suru 〈下宿する〉 lodge ((at)), board ((at)).

geshu-nin 〈げしゅにん：下手人〉 a perpetrator, a murderer.

gessan 〈げっさん：月産〉 a monthly production.

gessha 〈げっしゃ：月謝〉 a monthly tuition fee.

gesshoku 〈げっしょく：月食〉 a lunar eclipse.

gesshū 〈げっしゅう：月収〉 a monthly income.

gessori 〈げっそり〉

gessori-yaseru 〈げっそりやせる〉 lose much flesh, grow very thin.

gesui 〈げすい：下水〉 sewerage, drainage, a sewer system; a sewer, a drain; sewage.

　　gesui-kan（下水管）a drainpipe

　　gesui-kōji（下水工事）drainage works

geta 〈げた〉a *geta*, clogs.

　geta-baki-de 〈げた履きで〉in clogs.

getsugaku 〈げつがく：月額〉a monthly sum.

getsumatsu 〈げつまつ：月末〉the end of the month.

getsumen 〈げつめん：月面〉the surface of the moon.

　　getsumen-chakuriku（月面着陸）a lunar landing

getsuyō-bi 〈げつようび：月曜日〉Monday.

gettsū 〈ゲッツー〉a double play.

　　gettsū-ni-naru（ゲッツーになる）become victims of a double play

gezai 〈げざい：下剤〉a purgative, a laxative.

gia 〈ギア〉a gear.

　　gia o kaeru（ギアを変える）shift gears

gian 〈ぎあん：議案〉a bill.

　　gian o teishutsu-suru（議案を提出する）introduce a bill

　　gian o tsūka-saseru（議案を通過させる）pass a bill

　　gian o hiketsu-suru（議案を否決する）reject a bill

gibo 〈ぎぼ：義母〉a mother-in-law, a stepmother, a foster mother.

gichō 〈ぎちょう：議長〉the president, the chairman, the chairwoman, the Speaker.

gida 〈ぎだ：犠打〉sacrifice batting.

gidai 〈ぎだい：議題〉a subject for discussion.

　　gidai-ni-noboru（議題に上る）be taken up for discussion

gien-kin 〈ぎえんきん：義えん金〉a contribution, a subscription.

　　gien-kin o tsunoru（義えん金を募る）collect contributions for the relief ((of))

gifu 〈ぎふ：義父〉a father-in-law, a stepfather, a foster father.

gifun 〈ぎふん：義憤〉righteous indignation.

　　gifun-o-kanjiru（義憤を感じる）have righteous indignation ((against or with))

gigan 〈ぎがん：義眼〉an artificial eye.

gigi 〈ぎぎ：疑義〉*see.* gimon-no ten.

gīgī 〈ぎいぎい〉

　gīgī-to-kishimu 〈ぎいぎいときしむ〉creak.

　gīgī-to-oto-no-suru 〈ぎいぎいと音のする〉creaky.

gigoku 〈ぎごく：疑獄〉a scandal.

　gigoku-ni renza-suru〈疑獄に連座する〉be involved in a scandal

gihitsu 〈ぎひつ：偽筆〉forged handwriting.

　gihitsu-no〈偽筆の〉forged.

　gihitsu-de〈偽筆で〉in a forged hand.

giin 〈ぎいん：議員〉a member〔of an assembly〕.

　giin-ni-erabareru〈議員に選ばれる〉be elected a member ((of)).

giji 〈ぎじ：議事〉proceedings.

　giji no shinkô〈議事の進行〉progress of proceedings

　giji-nittei〈議事日程〉the order of the day, the agenda

　giji-roku〈議事録〉minutes

giji 〈ぎじ：疑似〉

　giji-korera〈疑似コレラ〉false cholera, a suspected case of cholera

giji-dô 〈ぎじどう：議事堂〉an assembly hall, the Diet, the Capitol.

gijin 〈ぎじん：擬人〉

　gijin-ka-suru〈擬人化する〉personify, impersonate.

gijô 〈ぎじょう：議場〉an assembly hall, a chamber, the House.

gijô-hei 〈ぎじょうへい：儀じょう兵〉a guard of honor.

gijutsu 〈ぎじゅつ：技術〉an art, technique

　gijutsu-ka〈技術家〉a technical expert.

　gijutsu-no, gijutsu-teki(-na) or *gijutsu-jô-no* 〈技術の，技術的(な)，技術上
の〉technical.

　gijutsu-teki-ni〈技術的に〉technically.

gikai 〈ぎかい：議会〉an assembly, the Diet, Congress, Parliament.

　gikai-o-shôshû-suru〈議会を召集する〉call the Diet in session

　gikai o kaisan-suru〈議会を解散する〉dissolve the Diet

　gikai-seiji〈議会政治〉parliamentary government

gikei 〈ぎけい：義兄〉an elder brother-in-law.

giketsu 〈ぎけつ：議決〉a decision, a resolution.

　giketsu-ken〈議決権〉the right to vote

　giketsu-suru〈議決する〉decide, resolve, pass a vote ((of)).

gikô 〈ぎこう：技巧〉art, technical skill, technique.

　gikô o korasu〈技巧を凝らす〉exert one's technical skill

gikochi-nai 〈ぎこちない〉awkward, stiff, clumsy.

　gikochi-nai taido〈ぎこちない態度〉an awkward manner

　gikochi-nai-kanji-ga-suru〈ぎこちない感じがする〉feel awkward

　gikochi-nai dôsa〈ぎこちない動作〉stiff manners

gikuri-to or **gikutto** 〈ぎくりと，ぎくっと〉

gikuri-to-suru *or* gikutto-suru（ぎくりとする，ぎくっとする）be
startled ((at))
gikuri-to-mune-ni-kotaeru *or* gikutto-mune-ni-kotaeru（ぎくりと胸に
こたえる，ぎくっと胸にこたえる）come home ((to))
gikuri-to-saseru *or* gikutto-saseru（ぎくりとさせる，ぎくっとさせる）
give ((a person)) a start ((at))

gikushaku〈ぎくしゃく〉
gikushaku-suru〈ぎくしゃくする〉be jerky.
gikushaku-shita〈ぎくしゃくした〉jerky.

gikyō(-shin)〈ぎきょう（しん）：義きょう（心）〉chivalry.
gikyō-teki(-na)〈義きょう的（な）〉chivalrous.

gi-kyōdai〈ぎきょうだい：義兄弟〉a brother-in-law.
gi-kyōdai-no-sakazuki-o-tori-kawasu（義兄弟の杯を取り交わす）swear
to be brothers

gikyoku〈ぎきょく：戯曲〉a drama, a play.

gimai〈ぎまい：義妹〉a younger sister-in-law.

giman〈ぎまん：欺まん〉deception, deceit, fraud.
giman-teki(-na)〈欺まん的（な）〉deceptive, deceitful, fraudulent.
giman-teki kōi（欺まん的行為）a fraudulent act

-gime〈-ぎめ：-決め〉
tsuki-gime-de（月決めで）by the month

gimei〈ぎめい：偽名〉a false name.
gimei o tsukau（偽名を使う）use a false name
〜-to-iu-gimei-de（〜という偽名で）under the false name of...

-gimi〈-ぎみ：-気味〉a touch, a dash, a shade.
kaze-gimi-de-aru（風邪気味である）have a touch of cold

gimmi〈ぎんみ：吟味〉
gimmi-suru〈吟味する〉examine closely, inquire ((into)), select carefully.
gimmi-shita〈吟味した〉carefully selected.
gimmi-shite〈吟味して〉carefully, with care.

gimon〈ぎもん：疑問〉a question, a doubt.
gimon-o-idaku or gimon-o-sashi-hasamu〈疑問を抱く，疑問を差し挟む〉
have doubts ((about)), doubt.
〜-ka-dō-ka-gimon-de-aru.〈〜かどうか疑問である。〉It is doubtful
whether... .
gimon-no〈疑問の〉questionable, doubtful.
gimon-no ten（疑問の点）a doubtful point
Gimon-no-yochi-ga-nai.（疑問の余地がない。）There is no room for

doubt.

gimu 〈ぎむ：義務〉(a) duty, an obligation.

    gimu o hatasu（義務を果たす）do one's duty

    gimu o okotaru（義務を怠る）neglect one's duty

    gimu-kyôiku（義務教育）compulsory education

~(-suru)-gimu-ga-aru〈～(する)義務がある〉ought to ((do)), be under an obligation ((to do)).

gimu-o-owaseru or *gimu-zukeru*〈義務を負わせる，義務づける〉put ((a person)) under an obligation.

gimu-teki(-na)〈義務的(な)〉obligatory, compulsory.

tada-gimu-teki-ni〈ただ義務的に〉from a mere sense of obligation.

gin(-no)〈ぎん：銀(の)〉silver.

gin-iro-no〈銀色の〉silver, silvery.

ginen〈ぎねん：疑念〉*see.* utagai.

ginga〈ぎんが：銀河〉the Milky Way.

    ginga-kei（銀河系）the galactic system

ginga(-kei)-no〈銀河(系)の〉galactic.

ginka〈ぎんか：銀貨〉a silver coin.

ginkô〈ぎんこう：銀行〉a bank.

    ginkô-tsûchô（銀行通帳）a bankbook

    ginkô-yokin（銀行預金）bank deposits

    ginkô-tori-hiki-ga-aru（銀行取引がある）have an account with a bank

    ginkô-in（銀行員）a bank clerk

    toshi-ginkô（都市銀行）a city bank

    chihô-ginkô（地方銀行）a local bank

ginkon-shiki〈ぎんこんしき：銀婚式〉a silver wedding.

ginnan〈ぎんなん〉a ginkgo nut.

ginô〈ぎのう：技能〉skill, ability.

    ginô-shô（技能賞）a prize for skill, the technical award

gin-sekai〈ぎんせかい：銀世界〉a silver world.

    Ichimen-no-gin-sekai-da.（一面の銀世界だ。）All is covered with snow.

gipusu〈ギプス〉gyps, a plaster cast.

    gipusu o hameru（ギプスをはめる）apply a plaster cast ((to))

giragira〈ぎらぎら〉

giragira-suru〈ぎらぎらする〉glitter, glare.

    giragira-suru taiyô（ぎらぎらする太陽）the glaring sun

girei〈ぎれい：儀礼〉courtesy, etiquette.

girei-teki(-na) 〈儀礼的(な)〉 formal.

  girei-teki-na hômon o suru（儀礼的な訪問をする） pay a formal visit

girei-jô〈儀礼上〉out of courtesy.

giri〈ぎり：義理〉justice, duty, obligation, honor, courtesy.

  giri-ga-aru（義理がある）have an obligation ((to))

  giri-o-tateru（義理を立てる） do one's duty ((by))

  giri-gatai（義理堅い）have a strong sense of duty

  giri-o-shira-nai *or* giri-shirazu-de-aru（義理を知らない，義理知らずである） have no sense of duty

  giri-o-kaku（義理を欠く）fail in one's (social) duties ((to))

  giri-no-oji（義理の叔(伯)父）one's uncle by marriage

  giri-ninjô（義理人情） duty and humanity

o-giri-nimo~-deki-nai〈お義理にも〜できない〉cannot bring oneself ((to do)).

girigiri〈ぎりぎり〉

  jôho-dekiru girigiri-no-sen（譲歩できるぎりぎりの線） the very limit to which one can concede

  girigiri-no nedan（ぎりぎりの値段） the lowest price

  shukkin-jikan-girigiri-ni-suberi-komu（出勤時間ぎりぎりに滑り込む） slide into the office at the last moment

Girisha〈ギリシャ〉Greece.

  Girisha-jin（ギリシャ人） a Greek

  Girisha-go（ギリシャ語） Greek

  Girisha(-jin)-no（ギリシャ(人)の） Greek

giron〈ぎろん：議論〉an argument, a discussion, a dispute.

  giron-de hito o yari-komeru（議論で人をやり込める） corner a person in an argument, argue a person down

  giron-no-yochi-ga-nai（議論の余地がない） be beyond dispute

giron-suru〈議論する〉argue, discuss, dispute.

  nagai-aida-giron-suru（長い間議論する） have a long argument

giryô〈ぎりょう：техн量〉ability, capacity, skill, competence.

  giryô o hakki-suru（技量を発揮する） show one's ability ((in))

giryô-no-aru〈技量のある〉able, capable, skilled, competent.

gisaku〈ぎさく：偽作〉a spurious work.

gisaku-no〈偽作の〉forged, faked.

gisei〈ぎせい：犠牲〉a sacrifice.

  gisei-banto（犠牲バント） a sacrifice bunt

  gisei-sha（犠牲者） a victim

gisei-ni-suru〈犠牲にする〉sacrifice, make a sacrifice ((of)).

　　mi o gisei-ni-suru〈身を犠牲にする〉 sacrifice oneself

gisei-ni-naru〈犠牲になる〉fall a victim ((to)).

gisei-o-harau〈犠牲を払う〉make sacrifices.

　　tadai-no-gisei-o-harau〈多大の犠牲を払う〉 pay dearly ((for))

〜-o-gisei-ni-shite〈〜を犠牲にして〉at the sacrifice of... , at the cost of ... .

ikanaru-gisei-o-haratte-mo〈いかなる犠牲を払っても〉at any cost.

giseki〈ぎせき：議席〉a seat.

　　giseki ni tsuku（議席に着く） take one's seat

　　giseki o ushinau（議席を失う） lose one's seat

gishi〈ぎし：技師〉an engineer.

　　denki-gishi（電気技師） an electrical engineer

gishi〈ぎし：義姉〉an elder sister-in-law.

gishi〈ぎし：義歯〉*see.* ire-ba.

gishigishi〈ぎしぎし〉

gishigishi-to-oto-ga-suru〈ぎしぎしと音がする〉creak.

gishiki〈ぎしき：儀式〉a ceremony, a rite, a service.

　　gishiki o okonau（儀式を行う） perform a ceremony

gishiki-baru〈儀式張る〉stand on ceremony, be too formal.

gishiki-batte〈儀式張って〉ceremoniously, formally.

gishin〈ぎしん：疑心〉suspicion, doubt.

　　Gishin-anki-o-shôzu.（疑心暗鬼を生ず.） Suspicion will raise bogies.

gishô〈ぎしょう：偽証〉false evidence, perjury.

gishô-suru or *gishô-zai-o-okasu*〈偽証する，偽証罪を犯す〉give false evidence, commit perjury.

gishu〈ぎしゅ：義手〉an artificial arm.

gisô〈ぎそう：艤装〉equipment〔of a ship〕.

gisô-suru〈艤装する〉equip, fit out.

gisô(-suru)〈ぎそう（する）：偽（擬）装（する）〉camouflage, disguise.

gisoku〈ぎそく：義足〉an artificial leg.

gisshiri〈ぎっしり〉

gisshiri-tsumeru or *gisshiri-tsume-komu*〈ぎっしり詰める，ぎっしり詰め込む〉pack closely, fill to the utmost, cram, jam.

gisshiri-tsumaru or *gisshiri-tsumatte-iru*〈ぎっしり詰まる，ぎっしり詰まっている〉be packed to the full, be filled closely, be crammed ((with)), be jammed ((with)), be chock-full ((of)), be full ((of)).

gitâ〈ギター〉a guitar.

gitâ o hiku〈ギターを弾く〉 play the guitar

gitei〈ぎてい：義弟〉a younger brother-in-law.

giwaku〈ぎわく：疑惑〉suspicion, doubt.

giwaku o maneku〈疑惑を招く〉 arouse ((a person's)) suspicion

giwaku o toku〈疑惑を解く〉 clear one's suspicions

giyū-gun〈ぎゆうぐん：義勇軍〉a volunteer army.

gizagiza〈ぎざぎざ〉notches.

gizagiza-no-tsuita〈ぎざぎざの付いた〉notched, corrugated.

gizen〈ぎぜん：偽善〉hypocrisy.

gizen-sha〈偽善者〉 a hypocrite

gizen-teki(-na)〈偽善的(な)〉hypocritical.

gizō〈ぎぞう：偽造〉forgery, fabrication.

bunsho-gizō〈文書偽造〉 forgery of a document

gizō-suru〈偽造する〉forge, fabricate.

ko-gitte o gizō-suru〈小切手を偽造する〉 forge a check

go〈ご：五〉five.

dai-go〈第五〉 the fifth

go〈ご：語〉a word, language.

go〈ご：碁〉(the game of) *go*.

go o utsu〈碁を打つ〉 play *go*

go-ishi〈碁石〉 a *go* stone

-go〈-ご：-後〉after, later, since.

san-juppun-go〈三十分後〉 after thirty minutes, thirty minutes later

sono-go〈その後〉 after that, afterward

sono-go-zutto〈その後ずっと〉 ever since

gō〈ごう：号〉a number, an issue; a pen name.

'Kaji' no sangatsu-gō〈「家事」の三月号〉 the March number of the *'Kaji'*

Tatsuo-to-iu-gô-de〈竜雄という号で〉 under the pen name of *Tatsuo*

gō〈ごう：郷〉

Gô-ni-ittewa gô-ni-shitagae.〈郷に入っては郷に従え.〉 When in Rome, do as the Romans do.

gō〈ごう：業〉

gô-o-niyasu〈業を煮やす〉be vexed ((at)), be impatient ((with)).

goba〈ごば：後場〉the afternoon session.

goban〈ごばん：碁盤〉a *go* board, a checkerboard.

goban-no-me〈碁盤の目〉 squares, a grid

gôban〈ごうばん：合板〉plywood.

gôben 〈ごうべん：合弁〉joint undertaking.

    gôben-gaisha〈合弁会社〉a joint corporation

gobi 〈ごび：語尾〉the ending of a word.

    gobi-henka〈語尾変化〉inflection

gobô 〈ごぼう〉a burdock.

    gobô-nuki-ni-suru〈ごぼう抜きにする〉pull ((persons)) out one after another.

gobu-gobu 〈ごぶごぶ：五分五分〉evenness, a tie.

    Chansu wa gobu-gobu-da.（チャンスは五分五分だ。）The chances are even.

    gobu-gobu-no〈五分五分の〉even, drawn.

go-bu-sata 〈ごぶさた：御無さた〉silence, neglect to call.

    Go-bu-sata-shite môshi-wake-ari-masen.（ごぶさたして申し訳ありません。）Excuse me for my long absence.

gochagocha 〈ごちゃごちゃ〉

    gochagocha-ni〈ごちゃごちゃに〉in disorder, in confusion.

        gochagocha-ni-naru（ごちゃごちゃになる）get confused

        gochagocha-ni-natte-iru（ごちゃごちゃになっている）be in confusion, be in a mess

        gochagocha-ni-suru（ごちゃごちゃにする）mix up, throw into disorder

go-chisô 〈ごちそう：御ち走〉an entertainment, a treat, a feast, hospitality, dainty dishes.

    sukiyaki-o-go-chisô-ni-naru（すき焼きをごちそうになる）be treated to *sukiyaki*

    Go-chisô-sama-deshita.（ごちそうさまでした。）Thank you for your hospitality.

    go-chisô-suru〈ごちそうする〉entertain, treat, feast.

gochô 〈ごちょう：ご長〉a corporal.

gochô 〈ごちょう：語調〉an accent, a tone.

    gochô o tsuyomeru（語調を強める）raise one's voice

gôdatsu 〈ごうだつ：強奪〉seizure, robbery.

    gôdatsu-suru〈強奪する〉seize, rob with violence.

gôdô 〈ごうどう：合同〉combination, union; congruence.

    gôdô-suru〈合同する〉combine, unite.

    gôdô-shite〈合同して〉unitedly, jointly.

goei 〈ごえい：護衛〉a guard, an escort, convoy.

    goei-suru〈護衛する〉guard, escort, convoy.

gofuku〈ごふく：呉服〉dry goods, drapery.

 gofuku-ya（呉服屋）a dry-goods dealer, a draper; a dry-goods store, a draper's shop

gogaku〈ごがく：語学〉language study, linguistics.

 gogaku-ga-tassha-de-aru（語学が達者である）be a good linguist

 gogaku-ryoku（語学力）linguistic ability

gogan-kôji〈ごがんこうじ：護岸工事〉bank(*or* shore) protection works.

gogatsu〈ごがつ：五月〉May.

gogen〈ごげん：語源〉the origin of a word.

gôgi〈ごうぎ：合議〉consultation, counsel.

 gôgi-sei（合議制）a council system

gogo〈ごご：午後〉afternoon.

 gogo(-ni)（午後(に)）in the afternoon

 kyô-gogo（今日午後）this afternoon

 gogo-yo-ji-ni（午後四時に）at four in the afternoon

 kayô-no-gogo-ni（火曜の午後に）on Tuesday afternoon

gôgô〈ごうごう〉

 gôgô-to-iu〈ごうごうという〉roaring, rumbling.

 gôgô-to-iu-oto-o-tatete-hashiri-saru（ごうごうという音を立てて走り去る）roar by

gohai〈ごはい：誤配〉misdelivery.

gohan〈ごはん：御飯〉boiled rice, a meal.

 gohan o taku（御飯を炊く）cook rice

 gohan o taberu（御飯を食べる）take a meal

gohei〈ごへい：語弊〉

 gohei-ga-aru〈語弊がある〉be misleading.

gôhô〈ごほう：語法〉usage, (a mode of) expression.

gohô〈ごほう：誤報〉a false report.

 Sore-wa-gohô-datta.（それは誤報だった.）The report proved to be incorrect.

gôhô〈ごうほう：合法〉lawfulness, legality.

 gôhô-ka（合法化）legalization

  gôhô-ka-suru（合法化する）legalize

 gôhô-teki(-na)〈ごうほうてき(な)：合法的(な)〉lawful, legal, legitimate.

  gôhô-teki-na shudan（合法的な手段）lawful means

 gôhô-teki-ni〈合法的に〉lawfully, legally, legitimately.

gôhô〈ごうほう：豪放〉

 gôhô-na〈豪放な〉openhearted and manly.

gohon 〈ごほん〉
　gohon-to-seki-o-suru 〈ごほんとせきをする〉 cough, 'hack, hack, hack'.

goi 〈ごい：語彙〉 a vocabulary.
　goi-ga-hôfu-de-aru 〈語いが豊富である〉 be rich in vocabulary
　goi-ga-hinjaku-de-aru 〈語いが貧弱である〉 be poor in vocabulary

gôi 〈ごうい：合意〉 mutual agreement.
　gôi ni tassuru 〈合意に達する〉 reach (an) agreement
　gôi-no-ue-de 〈合意の上で〉 by mutual agreement

gôin 〈ごういん：強引〉 (main) force.
　gôin-na 〈強引な〉 forcing.
　gôin-ni 〈強引に〉 by force.
　gôin-ni-dôi-saseru 〈強引に同意させる〉 force ((a person)) to consent

goji 〈ごじ：誤字〉 a wrong word, a misprint.

gojippo-hyappo 〈ごじっぽひゃっぽ：五十歩百歩〉
　Gojippo-hyappo-da. 〈五十歩百歩だ。〉 There is not much difference between the two.

gojitsu 〈ごじつ：後日〉 in the future, some day.
　gojitsu-no-tame-ni 〈後日のために〉 for future reference.

gôjô 〈ごうじょう：強情〉 obstinacy, stubbornness.
　gôjô-o-haru 〈強情を張る〉 be obstinate, be stubborn.
　gôjô-na 〈強情な〉 obstinate, stubborn.

go-jū 〈ごじゅう：五十〉 fifty.
　dai-go-jū 〈第五十〉 the fiftieth

gojun 〈ごじゅん：語順〉 word order.

go-jû-no-tô 〈ごじゅうのとう：五重の塔〉 a five-storied pagoda.

gojû-on 〈ごじゅうおん：五十音〉 the Japanese syllabary.

gôka 〈ごうか：豪華〉
　gôka-ban 〈豪華版〉 a deluxe edition
　gôka-sen 〈豪華船〉 a luxury vessel
　gôka-na 〈豪華な〉 gorgeous, luxurious.

gokai 〈ごかい：誤解〉 misunderstanding.
　gokai o maneku 〈誤解を招く〉 cause misunderstanding
　gokai-suru 〈誤解する〉 misunderstand, have a false idea ((of)).

gokai 〈ごかい〉 a lugworm.

gôkai 〈ごうかい：豪快〉
　gôkai-na 〈豪快な〉 heroic and large-minded.

gokakkei 〈ごかっけい：五角形〉 a pentagon.

gokaku 〈ごかく：互角〉 equality, evenness, a good match.

gokaku-de-aru〈互角である〉be equal ((with)).

gokaku-no〈互角の〉equal, even, well-matched.

    gokaku-no shôbu（互角の勝負）a well-matched game

gôkaku〈ごうかく：合格〉

    gôkaku-sha（合格者）a successful candidate

gôkaku-suru〈合格する〉pass.

    nyûshi ni gôkaku-suru（入試に合格する）pass an entrance examination

gokan〈ごかん：五官〉the five organs of sense.

gokan〈ごかん：五感〉the (five) senses.

gokan〈ごかん：語感〉a linguistic sense.

    gokan-ga-surudoi（語感が鋭い）have a keen sense of language

gôkan(-suru)〈ごうかん（する）：強かん（する）〉rape.

goke〈ごけ：後家〉a widow.

gokei〈ごけい：互恵〉reciprocity, mutual benefits.

    gokei-jôyaku（互恵条約）a reciprocal treaty

gôkei〈ごうけい：合計〉the total amount, the sum total.

    Gôkei-ikura-desu-ka?（合計幾らですか。）What is the total?

gôkei-suru〈合計する〉sum up, total.

gôkei～-ni-naru〈合計～になる〉amount to...in all.

gôkei-de〈合計で〉in all, all told.

gôken〈ごうけん：合憲〉

    gôken-sei（合憲性）constitutionality

gôken-teki(-na)〈合憲的（な）〉constitutional.

goki〈ごき：語気〉a tone.

goki-surudoku〈語気鋭く〉in a sharp tone.

goki〈ごき：誤記〉an error in writing.

gôki〈ごうき：剛き〉fortitude.

gôki-na〈剛きな〉plucky, stouthearted.

gokiburi〈ごきぶり〉a cockroach.

go-kigen〈ごきげん：御機嫌〉

    Go-kigen-ikaga-desu-ka?（御機嫌いかがですか。）How are you getting along?

    Go-kigen-yô!（ごきげんよう。）Good-by(e)! / Good luck to you!

gôkin〈ごうきん：合金〉an alloy.

goku〈ごく：語句〉words and phrases.

goku〈ごく〉

goku-sukoshi〈ごく少し〉only a little.

gokuaku-hidô〈ごくあくひどう：極悪非道〉
　gokuaku-hidô-na〈極悪非道な〉most wicked, atrocious, devilish.

gokugoku〈ごくごく〉
　gokugoku-nomu〈ごくごく飲む〉drink ((water)) in big swallows.

gokuhi〈ごくひ：極秘〉a strict secret, a top secret.
　gokuhi-ni-suru〈極秘にする〉keep ((a matter)) strictly confidential.
　gokuhi-no〈極秘の〉strictly confidential.
　gokuhi-no-uchi-ni〈極秘のうちに〉in profound secrecy.

gokui〈ごくい：極意〉the secret (point).
　　gokui-o-kiwameru（極意を極める）master the secret ((of))

gokujô〈ごくじょう：極上〉
　　gokujô-hin（極上品）an Al article
　gokujô-no〈極上の〉the best, of the highest quality.

gokuraku〈ごくらく：極楽〉paradise.

gokuri〈ごくり〉
　gokuri-to〈ごくりと〉at a gulp.
　　gokuri-to-nomu（ごくりと飲む）gulp down

goku-saishiki〈ごくさいしき：極彩色〉
　goku-saishiki-no〈極彩色の〉richly colored.

goku-tsubushi〈ごくつぶし：穀つぶし〉a good-for-nothing.
　goku-tsubushi-de-aru〈穀つぶしである〉be not worth one's salt.

goma〈ごま〉a sesami (seed).
　　goma-abura（ごま油）sesami oil

gomakashi〈ごまかし〉deception.
　gomakashi-no〈ごまかしの〉false, fraudulent.
　gomakasu〈ごまかす〉deceive, cheat, evade, gloss over, falsify, pocket, misrepresent.

gôman〈ごうまん：ごう慢〉arrogance, haughtiness.
　gôman-na〈ごう慢な〉arrogant, haughty.

goma-shio〈ごましお：ごま塩〉
　　goma-shio-atama-no（ごま塩頭の）with gray-white hair

gômei-gaisha〈ごうめいがいしゃ：合名会社〉an unlimited partnership.
　　gômei-gaisha-Matsuki-shôkai（合名会社松木商会）Matsuki & Co.

gomen〈ごめん：御免〉pardon; decline.
　　Gomen-nasai.（御免なさい。）Excuse me. / Pardon me. / I beg your
　　　pardon. / May I come in?
　　Sore-wa-gomen-kômuri-tai.（それは御免こうむりたい。）I wish to be
　　　excused from doing such a thing.

gomi 〈ごみ〉 dust, litter, trash, rubbish, garbage.
　　Koko-ni　gomi-o-sute-nai-de-kudasai.（ここにごみを捨てないでください。） No litter here.
　　gomi-bako（ごみ箱） a dust bin, a garbage can
　　gomi-shôkyaku-ro（ごみ焼却炉） a garbage furnace

gomigomi 〈ごみごみ〉
　gomigomi-shita〈ごみごみした〉 squalid.

gomoku-narabe 〈ごもくならべ：五目並べ〉 gobang.

gômon 〈ごうもん：拷問〉 torture.
　　gômon-ni-kakeru（拷問に掛ける） put ((a person)) to torture

gomu 〈ゴム〉 gum, rubber.
　　gomu-nori（ゴムのり） gum arabic
　　gomu-gutsu（ゴム靴） rubber shoes, rubber boots
　　gomu-in（ゴム印） a rubber stamp
　　gomu-himo（ゴムひも） an elastic cord
　　wa-gomu（輪ゴム） a rubber band

gongo-dôdan 〈ごんごどうだん：言語道断〉
　gongo-dôdan-na〈言語道断な〉 outrageous, absurd.

gonin 〈ごにん：誤認〉 a mistake, misconception.

gôon 〈ごうおん：ごう音〉 a roaring sound, a thundering noise.
　　gôon-o-hasshite（ごう音を発して） with a roaring sound

goraku 〈ごらく：娯楽〉 amusement(s), entertainment, recreation.
　　goraku-gai（娯楽街） an amusement center
　　goraku-bangumi（娯楽番組） an entertainment program
　　goraku-setsubi（娯楽設備） recreation facilities
　　goraku-shitsu（娯楽室） a recreation room

goran 〈ごらん：御覧〉 see, look; try.
　　Sore-goran!（それごらん。） There, didn't I tell you?
　　Mô-ichido-yatte-goran.（もう一度やってごらん。） Try and do it again.
　goran-no-toori〈御覧のとおり〉 as you see.

gôrei 〈ごうれい：号令〉 a command, an order.
　gôrei-o-kakeru〈号令を掛ける〉 give a command, give an order.

gôri(-sei) 〈ごうり（せい）：合理（性）〉 rationality.
　　gôri-ka（合理化） rationalization
　　　gôri-ka-suru（合理化する） rationalize
　　gôri-shugi（合理主義） rationalism
　gôri-teki(-na)〈合理的（な）〉 rational, reasonable.

gôri-teki-ni 〈合理的に〉 rationally, reasonablly.

gori-muchû 〈ごりむちゅう：五里霧中〉

gori-muchû-de-aru 〈五里霧中である〉 be in a fog, be all at sea.

gorira 〈ゴリラ〉 a gorilla.

go-riyaku 〈ごりやく：御利益〉 divine favor.

Go-riyaku-ga-atta. (御利益があった.) My prayers were answered.

goro 〈ごろ：語ろ〉

goro-ga-ii 〈語ろがいい〉 sound well, be euphonic.

goro-ga-warui (語ろが悪い) lack euphony

goro 〈ゴロ〉 a grounder.

goro o utsu (ゴロを打つ) hit a grounder

-goro 〈-ごろ〉 about, around.

o-hiru-goro (お昼ごろ) about noon

yo-ji-goro (四時ごろ) about four o'clock

rai-shû no hajime-goro (来週の初めごろ) around the beginning of next week

gorogoro 〈ごろごろ〉

gorogoro-naru (ごろごろ鳴る) roll, rumble

Kaminari ga gorogoro-naru. (雷がごろごろ鳴る.) The thunder rolls.

neko-ga-nodo-o-gorogoro-narasu (猫がのどをごろごろ鳴らす) purr

ie-de gorogoro-suru (家でごろごろする) idle away one's time at home

goro-ne 〈ごろね：ごろ寝〉

goro-ne-suru 〈ごろ寝する〉 sleep with one's clothes on.

gorori 〈ごろり〉

gorori-to-yoko-ni-naru 〈ごろりと横になる〉 throw oneself down.

gorotsuki 〈ごろつき〉 a ruffian, a rowdy, a rough, a bully.

gôru 〈ゴール〉 a goal, a basket.

gôru-suru (ゴールする) make a goal, score a basket

gôru-in-suru (ゴールインする) reach the goal

gôruden-awâ 〈ゴールデンアワー〉 (the) prime time.

gorufu 〈ゴルフ〉 golf.

gorufu o suru (ゴルフをする) play golf

gorufu-jô (ゴルフ場) a golf course, golf links

goryô 〈ごりょう：御陵〉 an Imperial mausoleum.

gôryû 〈ごうりゅう：合流〉

gôryû-ten (合流点) the junction 〔of two rivers〕

gôryû-suru〈合流する〉join.

    Yodo-gawa ni gôryû-suru（淀川に合流する）join the *Yodo* River

    undô-ni gôryû-suru（運動に合流する）join in some movement

gosa〈ごさ：誤差〉an accidental error, an aberration.

gosai〈ごさい：後妻〉a second wife.

  gosai-o-mukaeru〈後妻を迎える〉marry a second wife, remarry.

gosan〈ごさん：午さん〉a luncheon, a lunch.

gosan〈ごさん：誤算〉miscalculation.

  gosan-o-suru〈誤算をする〉miscalculate, make a miscalculation.

gôsei〈ごうせい：豪勢〉

  gôsei-na〈豪勢な〉grand, luxurious, gorgeous, plush.

gôsei〈ごうせい：合成〉composition, synthesis.

    gôsei-go（合成語）a compound word

    gôsei-hikaku（合成皮革）synthetic leather

    gôsei-jushi（合成樹脂）synthetic resins, plastics

  gôsei-suru〈合成する〉compose, synthesize.

  gôsei-no〈合成の〉compound, synthetic.

gosen〈ごせん：互選〉mutual election.

    gosen-tôhyô（互選投票）mutual vote

gôsetsu〈ごうせつ：豪雪〉a very heavy snowfall.

gôsha〈ごうしゃ：豪しゃ〉

  gôsha-na〈豪しゃな〉luxurious, sumptuous, extravagant.

-goshi〈-ごし：-越し〉

    kakine-goshi-ni（垣根越しに）over the fence

    go-nen-goshi-no kôsai（五年越しの交際）an intercourse of five years'
    standing

gôshi-gaisha〈ごうしがいしゃ：合資会社〉a limited partnership.

    gôshi-gaisha-Yamaguchi-shôkai（合資会社山口商会）Yamaguchi &
    Co., Ltd.

goshigoshi〈ごしごし〉

  goshigoshi-kosuru〈ごしごしこする〉rub briskly.

Goshikku〈ゴシック〉Gothic.

    Goshikku-kenchiku（ゴシック建築）Gothic architecture

    Goshikku-tai（ゴシック体）Gothic type

goshin〈ごしん：護身〉self-defense.

    goshin-jutsu（護身術）the art of self-defense

  goshin-yô-no or *goshin-yô-ni*〈護身用の，護身用に〉for self-protection.

goshin〈ごしん：誤診〉a wrong diagnosis.

goshin-suru〈誤診する〉diagnose wrongly, make an error in diagnosis.

goshin〈ごしん：誤審〉wrong refereeing; misjudgment, mistrial.

goshin-suru〈誤審する〉referee wrongly, misjudge.

goshô〈ごしょう：後生〉

goshô-dakara〈後生だから〉for Heaven's sake, for the love of God.

goshô-daiji-ni-motte-iru〈後生大事に持っている〉treasure.

goshoku〈ごしょく：誤植〉a misprint, a printer's error.

goshu-kyôgi〈ごしゅきょうぎ：五種競技〉pentathlon.

gosô〈ごそう：護送〉escort.

　　gosô-sha〈護送車〉a patrol wagon, a prison van

gosô-suru〈護送する〉escort, send ((a criminal)) under police escort [to some place].

gôsô〈ごうそう：豪壮〉

gôsô-na〈豪壮な〉splendid, magnificent.

gosogoso〈ごそごそ〉

　　gosogoso-oto-ga-suru〈ごそごそ音がする〉rustle

　　gosogoso-hai-dasu〈ごそごそはい出す〉crawl out

gossori〈ごっそり〉all, entirely.

　　Yôfuku-dansu-no sûtsu-ga-gossori nusumareta.〈洋服だんすのスーツがごっそり盗まれた。〉All my suits in the bureau were stolen.

gosuru〈ごする〉rank ((among *or* with)).

　　〜-to-goshite-hataraku〈〜とごして働く〉work side by side with...

go-tabun〈ごたぶん：御多分〉

go-tabun-ni-morezu〈御多分にもれず〉like the rest, as is usual ((with)).

gotagota〈ごたごた〉trouble; confusion, disorder.

　　katei-no gotagota〈家庭のごたごた〉domestic trouble

gotagota-o-okosu〈ごたごたを起こす〉make trouble, get into trouble ((with)).

gotagota-shite-iru〈ごたごたしている〉be confused, be in disorder.

gôtan〈ごうたん：豪胆〉

gôtan-na〈豪胆な〉bold, dauntless, fearless.

gotcha〈ごっちゃ〉

gotcha-ni-suru〈ごっちゃにする〉mix up, confuse, confound.

gote〈ごて：後手〉

gote-ni-naru〈後手になる〉be forestalled.

goten〈ごてん：御殿〉a palace.

-goto〈-ごと〉

sakana o kawa-goto-taberu〈魚を皮ごと食べる〉eat a fish, skin and all.

gôtô〈ごうとう：強盗〉burglary, robbery; a burglar, a robber.

　　ginkô-gôtô（銀行強盗）　bank robbery, a bank robber

　　kenjū-gôtô（けん銃強盗）　a holdup, a gunman

　gôtô-ni-hairareru〈強盗に入られる〉be robbed by a burglar, be burglarized.

-goto-ni〈－ごとに〉every.

　　juppun-goto-ni（十分ごとに）　every ten minutes

　　au-hito-goto-ni（会う人ごとに）　everyone one meets

　　koko-e kuru-tabi-goto-ni（ここへ来るたびごとに）　every time one comes here

　　hito-ame-goto-ni（一雨ごとに）　with every rainfall

go-tsugô〈ごつごう：御都合〉

　　go-tsugô-shugi（御都合主義）　opportunism

gotsugotsu〈ごつごつ〉

　gotsugotsu-shita〈ごつごつした〉rugged, angular, horny.

　　gotsugotsu-shita te（ごつごつした手）　a horny hand

gotsun〈ごつん〉

　gotsun-to〈ごつんと〉with a thump.

　　hashira-ni atama o gotsun-to-butsukeru（柱に頭をごつんとぶつける）　bump one's head against a pillar

gotta-gaesu〈ごったがえす：ごった返す〉be in confusion; be overcrowded ((with)).

gôu〈ごうう：豪雨〉a heavy rain, a downpour.

gowagowa〈ごわごわ〉

　gowagowa-shita〈ごわごわした〉stiff, starchy.

　　gowagowa-shita shîtsu（ごわごわしたシーツ）　a starchy sheet

goyaku〈ごやく：誤訳〉mistranslation.

　goyaku-suru〈誤訳する〉mistranslate.

go-yô〈ごよう：御用〉business; an order; government service.

　　Nani-ka go-yô-wa-ari-masen-ka?（何か御用はありませんか．）　What can I do for you? / Can I help you?

　　Kyô-wa go-yô-wa-ari-masen-ka?（今日は御用はありませんか．）　Do you have any order today, madam?

　　go-yô-kiki（御用聞き）　an order taker

　　go-yô-kumiai（御用組合）　a company union

　　go-yô-shimbun（御用新聞）　a kept press

goyô(-suru)〈ごよう（する）：誤用（する）〉misuse.

gôyoku〈ごうよく：強欲〉

gôyoku-na〈強欲な〉greedy, avaricious, covetous.

gôyû〈ごうゆう：豪遊〉

    gôyû-suru〈豪遊する〉spend extravagant money in merrymaking.

goza〈ござ〉a mat.

    goza o shiku（ござを敷く）spread a mat

gozen〈ごぜん：午前〉morning.

    gozen(-ni)（午前(に)）in the morning

    gozen-ku-ji-ni（午前九時に）at nine in the morning

    suiyô-no-gozen-ni（水曜の午前に）on Wednesday morning

go-zonji〈ごぞんじ：御存知〉

    Tôkyô-ni go-zonji-no-kata-wa-irasshai-masen-ka?（東京に御存知の方は
いらっしゃいませんか．）Do you have any acquaintances in Tokyo?

gu〈ぐ：愚〉

    gu no kotchô（愚の骨頂）the height of folly

guai〈ぐあい：具合〉a condition; health; convenience; a manner, a way.

    tenki-guai（天気具合）the condition of the weather

    Byônin-no-guai wa dô-desu-ka?（病人の具合はどうですか．）How is
the patient?

guai-ga-ii〈具合がいい〉be in good order, feel well, be convenient.

    Kyô-wa karada-no-guai-ga-totemo-ii.（今日は体の具合がとてもいい．）
I feel much better today.

guai-ga-warui〈具合が悪い〉be out of order, feel ill, be inconvenient.

    Koko-ni-san-nichi karada-no-guai-ga-warui.（ここ二、三日体の具合が悪
い．）I have been ill for these few days.

    Kono-kikai-wa-guai-ga-warui.（この機械は具合が悪い．）Something is
wrong with this machine.

guai-yoku〈具合よく〉luckily, conveniently.

donna-guai-ni〈どんな具合に〉in what way, how.

konna-guai-ni〈こんな具合に〉in this way, like this.

guchi〈ぐち：愚痴〉an idle complaint.

    guchi-o-iu〈愚痴を言う〉grumble ((at)), complain ((about *or* of)).

    guchippoi〈愚痴っぽい〉grumbling, querulous.

gudenguden〈ぐでんぐでん〉

    gudenguden-ni-you〈ぐでんぐでんに酔う〉be dead drunk.

gûgû〈ぐうぐう〉

    gûgû-ibiki-o-kaku（ぐうぐういびきをかく）snore loudly

    O-naka ga gûgû-natteiru.（おなかがぐうぐう鳴っている．）My berry
is growling.

gūhatsu〈ぐうはつ：偶発〉occur by chance.
　gūhatsu-suru〈偶発する〉occur by chance.
　gūhatsu-teki(-na)〈偶発的(な)〉accidental.
　　gūhatsu-teki-jiken（偶発的事件）an accident
　gūhatsu-teki-ni〈偶発的に〉accidentally.
guigui〈ぐいぐい〉
　　guigui-hiku（ぐいぐい引く）pull with jerks
　　guigui-osu（ぐいぐい押す）press hard
　　guigui-nomu（ぐいぐい飲む）gulp down
gui-nomi〈ぐいのみ：ぐい飲み〉
　gui-nomi-suru〈ぐい飲みする〉take a swig ((at)).
gumbai〈ぐんばい：軍配〉an umpire's fan.
　gumbai-o-ageru〈軍配を挙げる〉declare ((a person)) the winner.
gumbi〈ぐんび：軍備〉armaments.
　　gumbi-kakuchō（軍備拡張）the expansion of armaments
　　gumbi-shukushō（軍備縮小）*see.* gunshuku
gumbu〈ぐんぶ：軍部〉the military authorities, the military.
gumi〈ぐみ〉an cleaster.
gummu〈ぐんむ：軍務〉military service.
　gummu-ni-fukusuru〈軍務に服する〉serve in the army(*or* navy).
gumpō-kaigi〈ぐんぽうかいぎ：軍法会議〉a court-martial.
　gumpō-kaigi-ni-kakerareru〈軍法会議にかけられる〉be court-martialed.
gumpuku〈ぐんぷく：軍服〉a military(*or* naval) uniform.
gun〈ぐん：軍〉a force, an army, troops.
　　gun o okosu（軍を起こす）raise an army
gun〈ぐん：郡〉a district, a county.
gun〈ぐん：群〉a group, a crowd.
　　gun-o-nashite（群を成して）in a group, in schools
　gun-o-nuku〈群を抜く〉be well above the average, tower above the rest.
gungaku-tai〈ぐんがくたい：軍楽隊〉a military band.
gungun〈ぐんぐん〉
　　gungun-shimpo-suru（ぐんぐん進歩する）make steady progress
　　byōki-ga-gungun-yoku-naru（病気がぐんぐんよくなる）get steadily
　　　better
　　se-ga-gungun-nobiru（背がぐんぐん伸びる）grow taller and taller
gunji〈ぐんじ：軍事〉military and naval affairs.
　　gunji-hyōron-ka（軍事評論家）a military writer
　　gunji-kichi（軍事基地）a military(*or* naval) base

gunji-kôdô（軍事行動） military activities

gunjin〈ぐんじん：軍人〉a soldier, a sailor, an airman.

gunju〈ぐんじゅ：軍需〉

gunju-hin（軍需品） munitions, war supplies

gunju-keiki（軍需景気） munitions boom

gunju-sangyô（軍需産業） the munitions industry

gunka〈ぐんか：軍歌〉a martial song.

gunkan〈ぐんかん：軍艦〉a warship.

gunki〈ぐんき：軍紀〉military discipline.

gunki〈ぐんき：軍旗〉the colors.

gunki〈ぐんき：軍機〉a military secret.

gunkô〈ぐんこう：軍港〉a naval port.

gunkoku-shugi〈ぐんこくしゅぎ：軍国主義〉militarism.

gunkoku-shugi-sha（軍国主義者） a militarist

gunkoku-shugi-no or *gunkoku-shugi-teki(-na)*〈軍国主義の，軍国主義的（な）〉militaristic.

gû-no-ne〈ぐうのね：ぐうの音〉

gû-no-ne-mo-de-nai〈ぐうの音も出ない〉be completely defeated.

gunsei〈ぐんせい：軍政〉military administration.

gunsei o shiku（軍政をしく） establish a military government

gunsei〈ぐんせい：群生〉

gunsei-suru〈群生する〉grow in crowds.

gunsei〈ぐんせい：群棲〉

gunsei-suru〈群せいする〉live in flocks.

gunshû〈ぐんしゅう：群集〉a crowd.

gunshû-shinri（群集心理） mob psychology

gunshuku〈ぐんしゅく：軍縮〉(an abbreviation of 'gumbi-shukushô'): the reduction of armaments.

gunsô〈ぐんそう：軍曹〉a sergeant.

guntai〈ぐんたい：軍隊〉the forces, an army, the troops, the military.

guntô〈ぐんとう：群島〉a group of islands, an archipelago.

Firipin-guntô（フィリピン群島） the Philippine Islands

gunyagunya〈ぐにゃぐにゃ〉

gunyagunya-ni-naru〈ぐにゃぐにゃになる〉become flabby, become limp.

gunyagunya-no or *gunyagunya-shita*〈ぐにゃぐにゃの，ぐにゃぐにゃした〉flabby, limp.

gun·yô〈ぐんよう：軍用〉

gun·yô-ressha（軍用列車） a troop train

gun·yô-no 〈軍用の〉 for military use.

gun·yû 〈ぐんゆう：群雄〉

gun·yû-kakkyo no jidai 〈群雄割拠の時代〉 the age of rival leaders

gunzô 〈ぐんぞう：群像〉 a group.

gunzoku 〈ぐんぞく：軍属〉 a civilian employee in the army(*or* navy).

gurabia 〈グラビア〉 photogravure, gravure.

gurabu 〈グラブ〉 a glove, a pair of gloves.

gurafu 〈グラフ〉 a graph.

gurafu ni suru 〈グラフにする〉 make a graph ((of))

gurafu-yôshi 〈グラフ用紙〉 graph paper, section paper

guragura 〈ぐらぐら〉

guragura-suru 〈ぐらぐらする〉 totter, shake, be shaky, be unstable, wobble, waver.

guragura-suru isu 〈ぐらぐらするいす〉 an unstable chair

guragura-suru tsukue 〈ぐらぐらする机〉 a wobbly desk

guragura-suru ha 〈ぐらぐらする歯〉 a loose tooth

kokoro-ga mada guragura-shiteiru 〈心がまだぐらぐらしている〉 be still wavering in one's mind

Yu ga guragura-ni-tatteiru. 〈湯がぐらぐら煮立っている.〉 Water is boiling up.

-gurai 〈-ぐらい〉 *see.* -kurai.

gurando 〈グランド〉 *see.* guraundo.

gurasu 〈グラス〉 a glass.

gurasu-ippai-no-wain 〈グラス一杯のワイン〉 a glass of wine

guratan 〈グラタン〉 *gratin.*

guratsuku 〈ぐらつく〉 totter, shake, be unsteady, waver.

guraundo 〈グラウンド〉 a ground, a stadium, a playground.

gureru 〈ぐれる〉 go astray, stray from the right path.

guriguri 〈ぐりぐり〉 a hard lump 〔under one's armpit〕.

gurô 〈ぐろう：愚弄ろう〉 mockery, derision.

gurô-suru 〈愚弄ろうする〉 make a fool ((of)), mock ((at)), deride, ridicule.

gurokkî 〈グロッキー〉

gurokkî-ni-naru 〈グロッキーになる〉 become groggy.

gurotesuku 〈グロテスク〉 grotesquerie.

gurotesuku-na 〈グロテスクな〉 grotesque.

guru 〈ぐる〉

guru-ni-naru 〈ぐるになる〉 conspire ((with)), plot together.

guru-ni-natte 〈ぐるになって〉 in league ((with)), hand in glove ((with)).

guruguru 〈ぐるぐる〉
    guruguru hashiru（ぐるぐる走る） run round and round
    ki-no-mawari-ni rôpu o guruguru-maku〔木の周りにロープをぐるぐる巻く〕 wind a rope several and several times round a tree
-gurumi 〈-ぐるみ〉 (together) with.
    machi-gurumi（町ぐるみ） an entire city, throughout the city
gurûpu 〈グループ〉 a group.
    gurûpu o tsukuru（グループを作る） form a group
    gurûpu-katsudô（グループ活動） group activities
    gurûpu-ni-natte（グループになって） in groups
gururi 〈ぐるり〉 environs.
  gururi-ni or *gururi-o* 〈ぐるりに，ぐるりを〉 (a)round.
gurutamin-san 〈グルタミンさん：グルタミン酸〉 glutamic acid.
gushin 〈ぐしん：具申〉 reporting, representation.
    gushin-sho（具申書） a (full) report, a representation
  gushin-suru 〈具申する〉 report in detail, make a representation ((to)).
gussuri(-to) 〈ぐっすり(と)〉 fast, sound, soundly.
    gussuri nemuru（ぐっすり眠る） sleep soundly
gûsû 〈ぐうすう：偶数〉 an even number.
gutai 〈ぐたい：具体〉
    gutai-an（具体案） a definite plan
    gutai-saku（具体策） a concrete measure
    gutai-ka（具体化） concretization, embodiment, materialization
      gutai-ka-suru（具体化する） concretize, embody, materialize
  gutai-teki(-na) 〈具体的(な)〉 definite, concrete.
  gutai-teki-ni 〈具体的に〉 definitely, concretely.
    gutai-teki-ni-ieba（具体的に言えば） to put it concretely
gûtara 〈ぐうたら〉 a lazybones.
  gûtara-na 〈ぐうたらな〉 lazy, idle.
gutsugutsu 〈ぐつぐつ〉
  gutsugutsu-niru 〈ぐつぐつ煮る〉 boil down, simmer.
guttari(-to) 〈ぐったり(と)〉
  tsukare-hatete-guttari-to-naru 〈疲れ果ててぐったりとなる〉 feel as limp as a doll.
gutto 〈ぐっと〉
    gutto-nomi-hosu（ぐっと飲み干す） take a deep swallow ((of))
    gutto-osaeru（ぐっと抑える） bite one's lip(s)
    mune-ni-gutto-kuru（胸にぐっとくる） feel a lump in one's throat

gûwa〈ぐうわ：ぐう話〉an allegory, a fable.

gûzen〈ぐうぜん：偶然〉by chance, accidentally, unexpectedly.
gûzen au（偶然会う）meet ((a person)) by chance, come across.
gûzen-no〈偶然の〉accidental.
gûzen-no-deki-goto（偶然の出来事）an accident
gûzen-no-itchi（偶然の一致）a coincidence

gûzô〈ぐうぞう：偶像〉an idol, an icon.
gûzô o sûhai-suru（偶像を崇拝する）worship idols
gûzô-sûhai（偶像崇拝）idol worship
gûzô-hakai（偶像破壊）iconoclasm
gûzô-ka-suru〈偶像化する〉idolize, make an idol ((of)).

guzuguzu〈ぐずぐず〉
guzuguzu-suru〈ぐずぐずする〉be slow, linger, dawdle ((over)), hesitate.
Guzuguzu-suru-na!（ぐずぐずするな。）Don't be slow!
guzuguzu-iu〈ぐずぐず言う〉complain, grumble.
guzuguzu-iwazu-ni〈ぐずぐず言わずに〉without grumbling.
guzuguzu-sezu-ni〈ぐずぐずせずに〉without delay.

guzu-tsuku〈ぐずつく〉
Asu-wa tenki ga guzu-tsuku-deshô.（明日は天気がぐずつくでしょう。）
The weather will remain unsettled tomorrow.

gyă〈ぎゃっ〉
gyatto-sakebu〈ぎゃっと叫ぶ〉yell.

gyabajin〈ギャバジン〉gabardine.

gyafun〈ぎゃふん〉
gyafun-to-iwaseru〈ぎゃふんと言わせる〉squelch.
gyafun-to-iu〈ぎゃふんと言う〉be squelched.

gyagu〈ギャグ〉a gag.
gyagu o tobasu（ギャグを飛ばす）pull a gag

gyâgyâ〈ぎゃあぎゃあ〉
gyâgyâ-naku〈ぎゃあぎゃあ泣(鳴)く〉squall, caterwaul, squawk.

gyakkô〈ぎゃっこう：逆行〉
gyakkô-suru〈逆行する〉go back.
jisei-ni-gyakkô-suru（時勢に逆行する）go against the times

gyakkô〈ぎゃっこう：逆光〉
gyakkô-de shashin o toru（逆光で写真を撮る）take a picture against the light

gyakkyô〈ぎゃっきょう：逆境〉adversity.
gyakkyô-ni-aru（逆境にある）be in adversity

gyakkyô-to-tatakau〈逆境と闘う〉 struggle with adversity

gyaku〈ぎゃく：逆〉the inverse, reverse.

　gyaku-no〈逆の〉contrary, reverse, inverse, opposite.

　　gyaku-no-hôkô-ni〈逆の方向に〉in the opposite direction

　gyaku-ni〈逆に〉conversely, the wrong way about.

　　gyaku-ni ieba〈逆に言えば〉conversely speaking

　gyaku-ni-suru〈逆にする〉turn the other way, turn upside down, turn inside out, reverse.

　　junjo o gyaku-ni-suru〈順序を逆にする〉reverse the order.

gyaku-fû〈ぎゃくふう：逆風〉a contrary(*or* an unfavorable) wind.

gyakujô〈ぎゃくじょう：逆上〉

　gyakujô-suru〈逆上する〉go to ((a person's)) head, be beside oneself.

gyaku-kôka〈ぎゃくこうか：逆効果〉a contrary effect.

　　gyaku-kôka o shôjiru〈逆効果を生じる〉produce a contrary result

gyaku-modori〈ぎゃくもどり：逆戻り〉

　gyaku-modori-suru〈逆戻りする〉go backward, turn back.

gyakuryû〈ぎゃくりゅう：逆流〉a back current.

　gyakuryû-suru〈逆流する〉flow backward.

gyakusan〈ぎゃくさん：逆算〉

　gyakusan-suru〈逆算する〉count backward.

gyakusatsu(-suru)〈ぎゃくさつ(する)：虐殺(する)〉slaughter, massacre.

gyaku-senden〈ぎゃくせんでん：逆宣伝〉counterpropaganda.

　gyaku-senden-o-yaru〈逆宣伝をやる〉conduct counterpropaganda.

gyakusetsu〈ぎゃくせつ：逆説〉a paradox.

　gyakusetsu-teki(-na)〈逆説的(な)〉paradoxical.

　gyakusetsu-teki-ni-ieba〈逆説的に言えば〉paradoxically speaking.

gyakushû〈ぎゃくしゅう：逆襲〉a counterattack.

　gyakushû-suru〈逆襲する〉make a counterattack ((against *or* on)).

gyaku(-suishin)-roketto〈ぎゃく(すいしん)ロケット：逆(推進)ロケット〉a retro-rocket.

gyakutai〈ぎゃくたい：虐待〉ill-treatment, cruelty.

　gyakutai-suru〈虐待する〉ill-treat, treat ((a person *or* an animal)) cruelly.

gyaku-tanchi〈ぎゃくたんち：逆探知〉

　gyaku-tanchi-suru〈逆探知する〉trace.

　　denwa o gyaku-tanchi-suru〈電話を逆探知する〉trace the telephone call

gyakuten〈ぎゃくてん：逆転〉a reversal.

　　gyakuten-gachi-suru〈逆転勝ちする〉win a come-from-behind victory ((over))

gyakuten-suru 〈逆転する〉 go into reverse, be reversed.

Keisei ga gyakuten-shita.（形勢が逆転した．） The tables were turned.

gyakuyô 〈ぎゃくよう：逆用〉

gyakuyô-suru 〈逆用する〉 make a reverse use ((of)), take advantage ((of)).

gyaku-yunyû 〈ぎゃくゆにゅう：逆輸入〉

gyaku-yunyû-suru 〈逆輸入する〉 reimport.

gyaku-yushutsu 〈ぎゃくゆしゅつ：逆輸出〉

gyaku-yushutsu-suru 〈逆輸出する〉 reexport.

gyangu 〈ギャング〉 a gangster, a gang.

gyappu 〈ギャップ〉 a gap.

gyappu o umeru（ギャップを埋める） fill a gap

gyara 〈ギャラ〉 a guarantee.

gyô 〈ぎょう：行〉 a line.

gyô o aratameru（行を改める） begin a new line

ichi-gyô-oki-ni（一行おきに） on every other line

ue-kara ni-gyô-me（上から二行目） the second line from the top

gyofu 〈ぎょふ：漁夫〉 a fisherman.

gyofu-no-ri-o-shimeru 〈漁夫の利を占める〉 fish in troubled waters, gain the third party's profit.

gyôgi 〈ぎょうぎ：行儀〉 manners, behavior.

gyôgi-sahô（行儀作法） good manners, etiquette

gyôgi-no-ii 〈行儀のいい〉 well-mannered.

gyôgi-no-warui（行儀の悪い） ill-mannered

gyogun 〈ぎょぐん：魚群〉 a school of fish.

gyogyô 〈ぎょぎょう：漁業〉 fishery.

gyogyô-ken（漁業権） a fishery right

gyôgyô-shii 〈ぎょうぎょうしい：仰々しい〉 exaggerated, ostentatious, high-sounding.

gyôgyô-shii kata-gaki（仰々しい肩書き） a high-sounding title

gyôgyô-shiku 〈仰々しく〉 exaggeratedly, ostentatiously.

gyôgyô-shiku-iu（仰々しく言う） exaggerate

gyôji 〈ぎょうじ：行事〉 an event, a function.

nenjû-gyôji（年中行事） the chief events of the year.

gyôji 〈ぎょうじ：行司〉 a *sumo* (wrestling) referee.

gyojô 〈ぎょじょう：漁場〉 a fishing ground, a fishery.

gyokai〈ぎょかい：魚介〉fishes and shellfishes, sea food.

gyôkai〈ぎょうかい：業界〉business world, the trade.

   gyôkai-shi（業界紙）a trade paper

gyôkaku〈ぎょうかく：仰角〉an angle of elevation.

gyokaku-daka〈ぎょかくだか：漁獲高〉a haul (of fish).

gyôkan〈ぎょうかん：行間〉space between lines.

   gyôkan o akeru（行間を空ける）leave space between lines

gyokô〈ぎょこう：漁港〉a fishing port.

gyôko〈ぎょうこ：凝固〉solidification, congelation, coagulation, fixation.

  gyôko-suru〈凝固する〉solidify, congeal, coagulate, fix.

gyôkô〈ぎょうこう〉good luck.

gyokuro〈ぎょくろ：玉露〉refined green tea.

gyomin〈ぎょみん：漁民〉fishermen.

gyômu〈ぎょうむ：業務〉business, service, duty.

   gyômu-ni-hagemu（業務に励む）attend to one's business with diligence

   gyômu-shikkô-bôgai（業務執行妨害）interference in the execution of one's duty

gyorai〈ぎょらい：魚雷〉a torpedo.

gyôretsu〈ぎょうれつ：行列〉a queue, a procession, a parade.

  gyôretsu-suru〈行列する〉queue up, stand in a line.

gyorogyoro〈ぎょろぎょろ〉

  me o gyorogyoro-saseru〈目をぎょろぎょろさせる〉goggle one's eyes.

gyorui〈ぎょるい：魚類〉fishes.

gyôsei〈ぎょうせい：行政〉administration.

   gyôsei-ken（行政権）administrative power

   gyôsei-kikan（行政機関）an administrative organ

   gyôsei-kaikaku（行政改革）an administrative reform

  gyôsei-jô-no or *gyôsei-teki(-na)*〈行政上の，行政的(な)〉executive, administrative.

   gyôsei-teki shuwan（行政的手腕）administrative ability

gyôseki〈ぎょうせき：業績〉achievements, results.

   gyôseki o ageru（業績を上げる）produce achievements

gyosen〈ぎょせん：漁船〉a fishing boat.

gyosha〈ぎょしゃ：御者〉a driver, a cabman.

gyôsha〈ぎょうしゃ：業者〉traders (concerned), the trade.

gyôshu〈ぎょうしゅ：業種〉a type of industry.

   gyôshu-betsu-ni-suru（業種別にする）classify by industry

gyôshuku 〈ぎょうしゅく：凝縮〉 condensation.
 gyôshuku-suru 〈凝縮する〉 condense.
gyoson 〈ぎょそん：漁村〉 a fishing village.
gyosuru 〈ぎょする：御する〉 manage, control.
 gyoshi-yasui 〈御しやすい〉 manageable, easy to manage.
  gyoshi-nikui 〈御しにくい〉 unmanageable, hard to control
gyotaku 〈ぎょたく：魚拓〉 a fish print.
gyotto 〈ぎょっと〉
 gyotto-suru 〈ぎょっとする〉 be startled ((at)), be frightened ((at)).
gyôza 〈ギョーザ〉 a Chinese-style dumpling stuffed with minced pork.
gyûgyû 〈ぎゅうぎゅう〉
  gyûgyû-naru （ぎゅうぎゅう鳴る） creak
  gyûgyû-tsume-komu （ぎゅうぎゅう詰め込む） squeeze ((into))
  gyûgyû-iu-me-ni-awaseru （ぎゅうぎゅう言う目に遭わせる） bring ((a person)) to cry mercy
gyûjiru 〈ぎゅうじる：牛耳る〉 take the lead ((in)), control, dominate.
gyûniku 〈ぎゅうにく：牛肉〉 beef.
gyûnyû 〈ぎゅうにゅう：牛乳〉 milk.
  gyûnyû-de akambô o sodateru （牛乳で赤ん坊を育てる） feed a baby on cow's milk
 gyûnyû-o-shiboru 〈牛乳を搾る〉 milk 〔a cow〕.
gyutto 〈ぎゅっと〉
  gyutto shibaru （ぎゅっと縛る） bind fast
  gyutto-te-o-nigiru （ぎゅっと手を握る） squeeze ((a person's)) hand
  gyutto tsukamu （ぎゅっとつかむ） grasp firmly

H

ha 〈は：葉〉 a leaf, foliage, a needle, a blade.
 ha-no-ooi 〈葉の多い〉 leafy.

ha-no-nai〈葉のない〉leafless.

ha〈は：刃〉an edge, a blade.

surudoi ha（鋭い刃）a keen edge

ha o tsukeru（刃を付ける）give an edge ((to))

ha〈は：歯〉a tooth.

ha ga haeru（歯が生える）cut a tooth

ha-ga-ii（歯がいい）have good teeth

ha-ga-warui（歯が悪い）have bad teeth

ha-ga-itamu（歯が痛む）have a toothache

ha-ga-uku（歯が浮く）set one's teeth on edge

ha o migaku（歯を磨く）clean one's teeth

ha o chiryô-shite-morau（歯を治療してもらう）have one's tooth treated

ha o nuku（歯を抜く）pull out a tooth

ha-burashi（歯ブラシ）a toothbrush

ha-migaki（歯磨き）dentifrice

ha-o-kuishibatte-gaman-suru（歯を食いしばって我慢する）take it (on the chin)

ha〈は：派〉a party, a faction, a school, a sect, a group.

ha or **hâ**〈は，はあ〉yes, indeed, well, I see.

haaku〈はあく：把握〉

haaku-suru〈把握する〉grasp, get hold ((of)), seize.

imi o haaku-suru（意味を把握する）grasp the meaning

ha-ari〈はあり：羽あり〉see. hane-ari.

haba〈はば：幅〉width, breadth.

haba-go-mêtoru（幅五メートル）five meters in width, five meters wide

haba-tobi（幅跳び）a broad jump

haba-o-hirogeru〈幅を広げる〉widen, broaden.

haba-no-hiroi〈幅の広い〉wide, broad.

haba-no-semai（幅の狭い）narrow

haba-ga-kiku〈幅が利く〉have influence ((over)), be influential ((in)).

habakaru〈はばかる〉be afraid ((of)), hesitate ((to do)), shrink ((from)), be diffident ((to)).

hito-mae-o-habakaru（人前をはばかる）be in diffidence to others

habakaru-tokoro-naku（はばかるところなく）without reserve

habamu〈はばむ：阻む〉hinder, check, prevent, keep ((from)).

habataki〈はばたき：羽ばたき〉a flutter, flapping of the wings.

habataku〈羽ばたく〉flutter, flap the wings.

habatsu〈はばつ：派閥〉a faction, a clique.

habikoru〈はびこる〉spread, overgrow, grow thick.

　　Hatake　niwa　zassô-ga-habikotte-iru.（畑には雑草がはびこっている.）
　　　　The field is overgrown with weeds.

habuku〈はぶく：省く〉leave out, omit, save, spare.

　　jikan to rôryoku o habuku（時間と労力を省く）　save time and labor

haburi〈はぶり：羽振り〉

haburi-ga-ii〈羽振りがいい〉be influential, have great influence ((on, over
or with)); be popular.

hachi〈はち：鉢〉a pot, a basin.

hachi〈はち：八〉eight.

dai-hachi〈第八〉the eighth.

hachi〈はち〉a bee, a wasp.

　　hachi-ni sasareru（はちに刺される）　be stung by a wasp
　　hachi-no-su（はちの巣）　a beehive, a hive, a honeycomb
　　hachi-mitsu（はちみつ）　honey

hachigatsu〈はちがつ：八月〉August.

hachi-jû〈はちじゅう：八十〉eighty.

dai-hachi-jû〈第八十〉the eightieth.

hachi-kireru〈はちきれる：はち切れる〉burst, break open.

〜-de-hachi-kire-sô-da〈〜ではち切れそうだ〉be bursting with... .
　　Kare-wa　genki-de-hachi-kire-sô-da.（彼は元気ではち切れそうだ.）　He
　　is bursting with vigor.

hachi-maki〈はちまき：はち巻き〉

hachi-maki-suru〈はち巻きする〉wear a towel around one's head.

hachi-miri〈はちミリ：八ミリ〉an 8 mm cinecamera, an 8 mm projector.

hachi-ue〈はちうえ：鉢植え〉

hachi-ue-no〈鉢植えの〉potted.

　　hachi-ue-no kiku（鉢植えの菊）　a potted chrysanthemum

hachô〈はちょう：波長〉(a) wavelength.

hachô-o-awaseru〈波長を合わせる〉tune in.

hachû-rui〈はちゅうるい：は虫類〉the reptiles.

hada〈はだ：肌〉the skin; (a) temperament, (a) type.

　　hada-ga-shiroi（肌が白い）　have a fair skin
　　hada-o-sasu-yô-na samusa（肌を刺すような寒さ）　biting cold
　　hada-ga-awa-nai（肌が合わない）　cannot get along ((with)), cannot go
　　together ((with))

gakusha-hada-de-aru〈学者肌である〉 have something of the scholar in one

hada-gi〈肌着〉 underwear, undershirts

hadaka〈はだか：裸〉
hadaka-ni-naru〈裸になる〉become naked, strip oneself of one's clothes.
hadaka-ni-suru〈裸にする〉strip ((a person)) of his clothes.
hadaka-no〈裸の〉naked, bare, nude.

hadakeru〈はだける〉open, bare, expose, stretch.
mune o hadakeru〈胸をはだける〉 expose one's breast

hada-mi〈はだみ：肌身〉the body.
hada-mi-hanasazu-motte-iru〈肌身離さず持っている〉 carry ((a thing)) on ((a person's)) body

hadan〈はだん：破談〉rupture, rejection.
hadan-ni-naru〈破談になる〉be ruptured, be broken off, be rejected.

hadashi〈はだし〉bare feet.
hadashi-de〈はだしで〉with bare feet.
hadashi-de aruku〈はだしで歩く〉 walk barefoot

hada-zamui〈はだざむい：肌寒い〉chill(y).

hada-zawari〈はだざわり：肌触り〉the touch, the feel.
hada-zawari-ga-ii〈肌触りがいい〉 be agreeable to the touch

hade〈はで：派手〉
hade-na〈派手な〉gay, showy.
hade-na-fukusō-o-suru〈派手な服装をする〉 be gaily dressed
hade-na-kurashi-o-suru〈派手な暮らしをする〉 live in a showy way
hade-na-senden-o-suru〈派手な宣伝をする〉 advertise in a big way

ha-dome〈はどめ：歯止め〉a brake.
ha-dome-o-kakeru〈歯止めをかける〉brake, apply the brakes, put the brakes ((on)).

hâdoru〈ハードル〉a hurdle.
hâdoru-o-tobi-koeru〈ハードルを跳び越える〉hurdle.

hae〈はえ〉a fly.
hae o tataku〈はえをたたく〉 flap a fly
hae-tataki〈はえたたき〉 a flyflap

hae-giwa〈はえぎわ：生え際〉a hairline.

hae-nuki〈はえぬき：生え抜き〉
hae-nuki-no〈はえ抜きの〉trueborn, born and bred.
hae-nuki-no Edokko〈はえ抜きの江戸っ子〉 a trueborn *Edokko*

haeru〈はえる：生える〉grow, come out, sprout; cut.

    Zassô ga haeru.（雑草が生える.） Weeds grow.

haeru 〈はえる：映える〉 shine.

    asahi-ni haeru（朝日に映える） shine in the rising sun

hagaki 〈はがき〉 a postal card, a postcard.

    hagaki o dasu（はがきを出す） send a postcard ((to))

    e-hagaki（絵はがき） a picture postcard

    ôfuku-hagaki（往復はがき） a reply card, a double postal card

hagane 〈はがね：鋼〉 steel.

hagayui 〈はがゆい：歯がゆい〉 feel impatient ((at)).

hage- 〈はげ-〉

    hage-atama（はげ頭） a bald head

    hage-yama（はげ山） a bare hill

hageitô 〈はげいとう〉 an amaranth.

hagemasu 〈はげます：励ます〉 encourage, cheer up, inspire.

hagemi 〈はげみ：励み〉 encouragement.

 hagemi-ni-naru 〈励みになる〉 be encouraging.

 hagemu 〈励む〉 work hard, make an effort.

    gakka-ni hagemu（学課に励む） work hard at one's lessons

hageru 〈はげる〉 become bald, become bare.

 hageta 〈はげた〉 bald, bare.

hageru 〈はげる〉 come off, fall off; fade, discolor.

    Penki ga tokorodokoro hagete-iru.（ペンキが所々はげている.） The paint comes off in places.

 iro-no-hageta 〈色のはげた〉 faded, discolored.

hageshii 〈はげしい：激しい〉 violent, strong, fierce, severe, heavy.

    hageshii kishô no hito（激しい気性の人） a man of violent temper

    hageshii kaze（激しい風） a strong wind

    hageshii itami（激しい痛み） a severe pain

    hageshii kôtsû(-ryô)（激しい交通(量)） heavy traffic

 hageshiku 〈激しく〉 violently, severely, heavily.

    Ame ga hageshiku futteiru.（雨が激しく降っている.） It's raining heavily.

hage-taka 〈はげたか〉 a vulture.

hagi 〈はぎ〉 a bush clover.

ha-gire 〈はぎれ：歯切れ〉

 ha-gire-ga-ii（歯切れがいい） have a crisp and clear way of speaking.

    ha-gire-ga-warui（歯切れが悪い） have a dull way of speaking, be inarticulate

ha-gishiri 〈はぎしり：歯ぎしり〉

　ha-gishiri-suru 〈歯ぎしりする〉 grate one's teeth, gnash one's teeth.

hagi-toru 〈はぎとる：はぎ取る〉 strip off, divest ((a person)) of.

hago-ita 〈はごいた：羽子板〉 a battledore.

ha-gotae 〈はごたえ：歯ごたえ〉

　ha-gotae-ga-aru 〈歯ごたえがある〉 be hard to chew, be tough, be crisp.

　　ha-gotae-ga-nai 〈歯ごたえがない〉 be too soft and require little chewing

hagu 〈はぐ〉 strip off; skin, peel; deprive ((a person)) of.

ha-guki 〈はぐき：歯茎〉 the gum(s).

hagurakasu 〈はぐらかす〉 dodge〔a question〕, shuffle.

hagureru 〈はぐれる：歯茎〉 lose sight ((of)), stray ((from)).

ha-guruma 〈はぐるま：歯車〉 a cogwheel, a gear wheel.

haha 〈はは：母〉 a mother.

　haha-no-yô-na or *haha-rashii* 〈母のような，母らしい〉 motherly, maternal.

ha-hâ 〈ははあ〉 well, indeed, I see.

hâhâ 〈はあはあ〉

　　hâhâ-iu 〈はあはあいう〉 gasp, pant.

　　hâhâ-ii-nagara 〈はあはあいいながら〉 puffing and blowing

　　　hâhâ-ii-nagara hashitte-kuru 〈はあはあいいながら走って来る〉 come running out of breath

hahen 〈はへん：破片〉 a broken piece, a fragment, a splinter.

　　garasu no hahen 〈ガラスの破片〉 pieces of broken glass

hai 〈はい：杯〉 a cup, a glass.

hai 〈はい〉 yes, certainly, all right, sure, O.K.; no; yes, sir; Here it is. / Here you are.

　　"Mikan-wa-suki-desu-ka?" "Hai, suki-desu." （"みかんは好きですか." "はい，好きです."） "Do you like oranges?" "Yes, I do."

　　"Ringo-wa-suki-dewa-ari-masen-ka?" "Hai, suki-dewa-ari-masen." （"りんごは好きではありませんか." "はい，好きではありません."） "Don't you like apples?" "No, I don't."

　　Hai, shôchi-shimashita. （はい，承知しました.） Yes, certainly.

hai 〈はい〉 an embryo.

hai 〈はい：灰〉 ash(es).

　　yakete-hai-ni-naru 〈焼けて灰になる〉 be reduced to ashes

hai 〈はい：肺〉 the lungs.

　　hai-katsuryô 〈肺活量〉 lung capacity

　　hai-kishu 〈肺気しゅ〉 emphysema of the lungs

hai-shinjun（肺浸潤） infiltration of the lungs

hai-gan（肺がん） lung cancer

haian〈はいあん：廃案〉

Sono gian wa haian-ni-natta.（その議案は廃案になった.） The bill has become null and void.

haiben〈はいべん：排便〉

haiben-suru〈排便する〉evacuate the bowels.

haibi〈はいび：配備〉*see.* haichi.

haiboku〈はいぼく：敗北〉(a) defeat.

kettei-teki-na haiboku o kissuru（決定的な敗北を喫する） suffer a decisive defeat

haiboku-suru〈敗北する〉be defeated, be beaten.

haibun〈はいぶん：配分〉distribution, allotment.

haibun-suru〈配分する〉distribute ((among *or* to)), allot ((to)).

haibutsu〈はいぶつ：廃物〉waste material, refuse.

haibutsu o riyō-suru（廃物を利用する） utilize waste material

haichi〈はいち：配置〉arrangement, stationing, posting.

haichi-tenkan（配置転換） a reshuffle

haichi-suru〈配置する〉arrange, station, post.

haiden〈はいでん：拝殿〉the front shrine, a sanctuary.

haiden〈はいでん：配電〉supply of electric power, power distribution.

haiden-ban（配電盤） a switchboard

haiden-suru〈配電する〉supply electricity.

haiei〈はいえい：背泳〉the backstroke.

haiei-o-suru（背泳をする） swim on one's back

haieki〈はいえき：廃液〉factory waste, drainage.

haien〈はいえん：肺炎〉pneumonia.

hai-fai〈ハイファイ〉

hai-fai-no〈ハイファイの〉hi-fi, high-fidelity.

haifu〈はいふ：配布〉distribution, division.

haifu-suru〈配布する〉distribute ((among *or* to)), divide ((among)).

haifun〈ハイフン〉a hyphen.

haifun-de-tsunagu〈ハイフンでつなぐ〉hyphen, hyphenate.

haiga〈はいが：はい芽〉an embryo bud, a germ.

haiga-mai（はい芽米） rice with germs

haigeki〈はいげき：排撃〉

haigeki-suru〈排撃する〉reject, denounce, condemn.

haigo〈はいご：背後〉the back, the rear.

    teki-no-haigo-o-tsuku〈敵の背後を突く〉 attack the enemy in the rear

haigo-no or *haigo-ni*〈背後の，背後に〉behind, at the rear ((of)), at the back ((of)).

haigo〈はいご：廃語〉an obsolete word.

haigō〈はいごう：配合〉combination, harmony, match.

    iro no haigō（色の配合） the combination of colors

haigō-suru〈配合する〉combine, match, tone.

haigū-sha〈はいぐうしゃ：配偶者〉a spouse, a consort.

haigyō〈はいぎょう：廃業〉

haigyō-suru〈廃業する〉give up one's business, shut up one's shop, give up one's practice, retire from the stage, retire from the ring.

haihin〈はいひん：廃品〉waste materials.

    haihin-kaishū（廃品回収） collection of disused articles

hai-hīru〈ハイヒール〉high-heeled shoes.

haiin〈はいいん：敗因〉the cause of defeat.

hai-iro(-no)〈はいいろ(の)：灰色(の)〉gray, grey.

haijo〈はいじょ：排除〉exclusion, removal, elimination.

haijo-suru〈排除する〉exclude, remove, eliminate, put out of the way.

haika〈はいか：配下〉a follower, one's man; a following.

    hito-no-haika-de hataraku（人の配下で働く） work under a person

haikai〈はいかい〉

haikai-suru〈はいかいする〉loiter about, hover about, hang about, prowl about.

haikan〈はいかん：配管〉pipe arrangement, piping, plumbing.

haikan〈はいかん：廃刊〉discontinuance〔of publication〕.

haikan-ni-naru〈廃刊になる〉go out of existence, cease to appear.

haikan-suru〈廃刊する〉discontinue issuing, cease to publish.

haikan〈はいかん：拝観〉a visit.

    haikan-ryō（拝観料） an admission fee

haikan-suru〈拝観する〉have the honor of seeing, visit.

haikei〈はいけい：拝啓〉Dear Sir, Dear Sirs, Gentlemen.

haikei〈はいけい：背景〉a background, scenery, a setting.

    〜*-o-haikei-ni(-shite)*〈〜を背景に(して)〉against... .

hai-kekkaku〈はいけっかく：肺結核〉tuberculosis, consumption.

    hai-kekkaku-ni-kakaru（肺結核にかかる） suffer from consumption

haiken〈はいけん：拝見〉

haiken-suru〈拝見する〉have a look ((at)), see; receive.

    Myaku-o-haiken-shi-mashô.（脈を拝見しましょう.） Let me feel your

pulse.

haiketsu-shô〈はいけつしょう：敗血症〉blood poisoning.

haiki〈はいき：排気〉exhaust.

  haiki-gasu（排気ガス）exhaust gas

haiki〈はいき：廃棄〉abolition, abandonment, abrogation, repeal, reverse.

  haiki-suru〈廃棄する〉abolish, abandon, abrogate, repeal.

haiki-butsu〈はいきぶつ：廃棄物〉waste (matter).

  kôjô-haiki-butsu（工場廃棄物）factory waste

haikingu〈ハイキング〉a hike, (a) hiking.

  haikingu-ni-iku（ハイキングに行く）go on a hike, go hiking

haikô〈はいこう：廃校〉

  haikô-ni-suru〈廃校にする〉close a school.

  haikô-ni-naru〈廃校になる〉be closed.

haikô〈はいこう：廃坑〉an abandoned mine.

  haikô-ni-naru〈廃坑になる〉be abandoned, be disused.

haiku〈はいく：俳句〉a Japanese seventeen-syllabled poem, a *haiku*.

haikyo〈はいきょ：廃きょ〉the ruins.

  haikyo-ni-naru（廃きょになる）fall into ruins

haikyû〈はいきゅう：配給〉distribution, supply, rationing.

  haikyû-sei(do)（配給制(度)）a distribution system, a rationing system

  haikyû-suru〈配給する〉distribute, supply, ration.

haimon-rimpa-sen-en〈はいもんリンパせんえん：肺門リンパせん炎〉tuberculous adenitis of the hilum of the ((left *or* right)) lung.

hainin(-zai)〈はいにん（ざい）：背任（罪）〉breach of trust, misappropriation.

  hainin-zai-ni-towareru（背任罪に問われる）be charged with breach of trust

hainyô〈はいにょう：排尿〉

  hainyô-suru〈排尿する〉urinate, pass urine.

hairetsu〈はいれつ：配列〉arrangement.

  hairetsu-suru〈配列する〉arrange, put in order.

hairu〈はいる：入る〉enter, come in, get in; join, go ((into)); break ((into)); hold, contain; have, get.

  genkan-kara ie ni hairu（玄関から家に入る）enter a house at the front door

  O-hairi-nasai.（お入りなさい．）Come in.

kurabu ni hairu（クラブに入る）join a club

jitsugyô-kai-ni-hairu（実業界に入る）go into business

Kare-no ie ni dorobô-ga-haitta.（彼の家に泥棒が入った.）His house was broken into.

Kono bin niwa ichi-rittoru-han hairu.（この瓶には一リットル半入る.）This bottle holds one liter and a half.

Kono hiroma niwa hyaku-nin hairu.（この広間には百人入る.）This hall seats one hundred guests.

shû-ni samman-en hairu（週に三万円入る）have a weekly income of thirty thousand yen

hairyo〈はいりょ：配慮〉consideration, care, concern, trouble.

yuki-todoita hiryo（行き届いた配慮）thoughtful consideration

haiseki〈はいせき：排斥〉exclusion, expulsion, rejection.

haiseki-suru（排斥する）exclude, expel, reject, boycott.

haisen〈はいせん：敗戦〉(a) defeat.

haisen-koku（敗戦国）a defeated nation

haisen-tôshu（敗戦投手）a losing pitcher

haisen〈はいせん：配線〉wiring.

haisen-suru〈配線する〉wire.

haisen〈はいせん：配船〉

haisen-suru〈配船する〉assign a ship ((on)), allocate a ship ((to)).

haisetsu〈はいせつ：排せつ〉excretion, discharge.

haisetsu-butsu（排せつ物）excrement, excretion

haisetsu-suru〈排せつする〉excrete, discharge.

ha-isha〈はいしゃ：歯医者〉a dentist.

ha-isha ni mite-morau（歯医者に診てもらう）consult a dentist

haisha〈はいしゃ：敗者〉the defeated (person), a loser.

haisha-fukkatsu-sen〈敗者復活戦〉a repêchage

haisha〈はいしゃ：配車〉

haisha-suru〈配車する〉allocate cars.

haishi〈はいし：廃止〉abolition, abrogation.

haishi-suru〈廃止する〉abolish, abrogate.

haishin〈はいしん：背信〉betrayal, infidelity.

haishin-kôi（背信行為）(a) breach of faith

haishoku〈はいしょく：配色〉a color scheme, coloring.

Haishoku-ga-ii.（配色がいい.）The colors match well.

haishoku〈はいしょく：敗色〉signs of defeat.

Kare-no haishoku ga nôkô-da.（彼の敗色が濃厚だ.）His defeat

seems certain.

haishutsu 〈はいしゅつ：排出〉 discharge, exhaust.
　　haishutsu-kô（排出口） an issue, an outlet
　haishutsu-suru〈排出する〉 dischage, exhaust, issue.

haishutsu 〈はいしゅつ：輩出〉
　haishutsu-suru〈輩出する〉 produce a great many... .

haiso 〈はいそ：敗訴〉 a lost case.
　haiso-suru〈敗訴する〉 lose one's lawsuit, go against〔the plaintiff〕.

haisô 〈はいそう：敗走〉
　haisô-suru〈敗走する〉 be routed, be put to rout.

haisui 〈はいすい：廃水〉 *see.* haieki.

haisui 〈はいすい：配水〉 supply of water.
　　haisui-kan（配水管） a water pipe
　haisui-suru〈配水する〉 supply water.

haisui 〈はいすい：排水〉
　　haisui-kan（排水管） a drainpipe
　　haisui-kôji（排水工事） drainage works
　haisui-suru〈排水する〉 drain, dike, pump out; displace.

haisui-no-jin 〈はいすいのじん：背水の陣〉
　haisui-no-jin-o-shiku〈背水の陣を敷く〉 burn one's bridges (behind one).

haisui-ryô 〈はいすいりょう：排水量〉 displacement.

haisuru 〈はいする：排する〉
　bannan-o-haishite〈万難を排して〉 in defiance of all difficulties.

haisuru 〈はいする：廃する〉 discontinue, give up, abolish, abandon, do
　away ((with)).
　　kyorei-o-haisuru（虚礼を廃する） do away with formalities

haita 〈はいた：排他〉 exclusion.
　　haita-shugi（排他主義） exclusionism
　haita-teki(-na)〈排他的(な)〉 exclusive.

haitai 〈はいたい：敗退〉
　haitai-suru〈敗退する〉 lose a battle, be beaten, lose a game.

haitatsu 〈はいたつ：配達〉 delivery.
　　haitatsu-nin（配達人） a deliveryman, a carrier
　　haitatsu-ryô（配達料） the delivery charge, carriage
　haitatsu-suru〈配達する〉 deliver.
　　machigatte-haitatsu-sareru（間違って配達される） be delivered at the
　　wrong address

haitîn 〈ハイティーン〉 one's late teens.

　　　　haitîn-no shônen〈ハイティーンの少年〉a boy in his late teens

haitô(-kin)〈はいとう（きん）：配当（金）〉a dividend.

　　haitô-suru〈配当する〉pay a dividend.

haiyâ〈ハイヤー〉a hired car.

　　haiyâ-o-tanomu〈ハイヤーを頼む〉hire a car.

haiyaku〈はいやく：配役〉the cast〔of a play〕.

haiyû〈はいゆう：俳優〉an actor, an actress.

　　　　haiyû-ni-naru〈俳優になる〉become an actor, become an actress, go
　　　　　on the stage

haizan〈はいざん：敗残〉

　　　　haizan-sha〈敗残者〉a failure, an underdog

　　haizan-no〈敗残の〉defeated.

hai-zara〈はいざら：灰皿〉an ashtray.

haizen〈はいぜん：配ぜん〉

　　haizen-suru〈配ぜんする〉set the table〔for dinner〕.

haizô〈はいぞう：肺臓〉*see.* hai.

haizoku〈はいぞく：配属〉

　　haizoku-suru〈配属する〉assign ((a person)) to.

haji〈はじ：恥〉shame, disgrace.

　　　　haji o shinobu〈恥を忍ぶ〉bear shame

　　　　Haji-o-shire!〈恥を知れ.〉For shame! / What a disgrace!

　　　　haji-shirazu〈恥知らず〉a shameless person

　　haji-o-kaku〈恥をかく〉be put to shame, disgrace oneself.

　　haji-o-kakaseru〈恥をかかせる〉put ((a person)) to shame.

　　haji-o-shira-nai〈恥を知らない〉shameless.

hajiku〈はじく〉

　　　　mizu o hajiku〈水をはじく〉repel water

　　　　soroban o hajiku〈そろ盤をはじく〉operate an abacus

hajimari〈はじまり：始まり〉the beginning, the start.

　　hajimaru〈始まる〉begin, commence, start, be opened; break out.

　　　　Gakkô wa hachi-ji-ni hajimaru.〈学校は八時に始まる.〉School begins
　　　　　at eight.

　　　　Kai wa komban roku-ji-ni hajimaru.〈会は今晩六時に始まる.〉The
　　　　　meeting will be opened at six this evening.

　　　　Sensô ga hajimatta.〈戦争が始まった.〉A war broke out.

hajime〈はじめ：始(初)め〉the beginning, the start, the opening, (the)
　　first.

　　hajime-kara〈初めから〉from the beginning, from scratch.

hajime-kara-owari-made〈始めから終わりまで〉 from beginning to end, from start to finish

hajime-no〈初めの〉 first, early.

hajime-ni〈初めに〉 at the beginning, first, in the beginning.

kongetsu no hajime-ni〈今月の初めに〉 at the beginning of this month

hachigatsu-no-hajime-ni〈八月の初めに〉 early in August

hajimete〈初めて〉 for the first time, first, not...until.

Watashi-wa roku-sai-no-toki hajimete panda o mita.〈私は六歳の時初めてパンダを見た。〉 I saw a panda for the first time when I was six.

Watashi-wa Hokkaidô wa hajimete-da.〈私は北海道は初めてだ。〉 This is my first visit to Hokkaido.

Kesa-ni-natte-hajimete sono jijitsu o shitta.〈今朝になって初めてその事実を知った。〉 It was not until this morning that I learned the truth.

hajime-wa〈初めは〉 at first.

Hajime-mashite.〈初めまして。〉 How do you do? / I'm very glad to see you.

-hajime〈-はじめ：-初め〉 including, and.

Katô-shi-o-hajime-go-nin〈加藤氏を初め五人〉 five persons, including Mr. Kato, Mr. Kato and four others

hajimeru〈はじめる：始める〉 begin, start, set about.

Ame ga furi-hajimeta.〈雨が降り始めた。〉 It has begun to rain.

shôbai o hajimeru〈商売を始める〉 start in business

shigoto o hajimeru〈仕事を始める〉 set about one's work

hajiru〈はじる：恥じる〉 be ashamed ((of)).

hajô〈はじょう：波状〉

hajô-suto〈波状スト〉 a strike in waves, a piston strike

hajô-no〈波状の〉 wavelike, undulating.

haka〈はか：墓〉 a grave, a tomb.

haka o tateru〈墓を建てる〉 raise a tomb

haka-mairi-o-suru〈墓参りをする〉 visit a grave

haka-ishi〈墓石〉 a gravestone, a tombstone

haka-ba〈はかば：墓場〉 *see.* bochi.

hakabakashiku-nai〈はかばかしくない〉

Kare-no shôbai wa amari hakabakashiku-nai.〈彼の商売は余りはかばかしくない。〉 His business is not doing very well.

Kanojo-no byōjō wa hakabakashiku-nai.（彼女の病状ははかばかしくな
い。） Her progress toward recovery is not satisfactory.

hakadoru 〈はかどる〉 progress, make good progress.
  shigoto-ga-hakadoru（仕事がはかどる） get along with one's work
  hakadora-nai〈はかどらない〉 make little progress.

hakai〈はかい：破壊〉 destruction.
  hakai-ryoku（破壊力） destructive power
  hakai-shugi（破壊主義） destructionism
  hakai-suru〈破壊する〉 destroy.
  hakai-teki(-na)〈破壊的(な)〉 destructive.

hakaku〈はかく：破格〉 an exception.
  hakaku-no〈破格の〉 exceptional, unprecedented.
    hakaku-no shōkyū（破格の昇級） an exceptional promotion
    hakaku-no-taigū-o-ukeru（破格の待遇を受ける） be treated excep-
    tionally well

hakanai〈はかない〉 short-lived, passing, transient, vain, empty; sad,
miserable.
  hakanai jinsei（はかない人生） transient life
  hakanai yume（はかない夢） an empty dream
  hakanai-saigo-o-togeru（はかない最期を遂げる） meet with an untimely death

hakanamu〈はかなむ〉 despair (of)), lose all hopes, become pessimistic.
  yo-o-hakanande jisatsu-suru（世をはかなんで自殺する） kill oneself in
  despair

hakarai〈はからい：計らい〉 arrangement, management, good offices,
discretion, judgment.
  〜-no-hakarai-de〈〜の計らいで〉 through the good offices of... , at one's
  (own) discretion.

hakarau〈はからう：計らう〉 arrange, dispose ((of)), manage, see ((to)).
  ii-yō-ni hakarau（いいように計らう） arrange ((a thing)) as one thinks
  best

hakari〈はかり〉 a balance, a steelyard, scales, a dial scale, a weighing
machine.
  hakari-ni-kakeru（はかりに掛ける） weigh ((a thing)) in the balance

hakarigoto〈はかりごと〉 see. keiryaku.

hakari-uri〈はかりうり：量り売り〉
  hakari-uri-suru〈量り売りする〉 sell by measure.

hakaru〈はかる：測(量,計)る〉 measure, take measure ((of)), weigh, take.

shinchô o hakaru〈身長を測る〉 measure one's height

taijû o hakaru〈体重を量る〉 weigh oneself, take one's weight

taion o hakaru〈体温を計る〉 take one's temperature

hakaru〈はかる：謀る，図る〉plan, devise, plot.

jisatsu o hakaru〈自殺を図る〉 attempt suicide

hakase〈はかせ：博士〉a doctor.

Yamada-hakase〈山田博士〉 Dr. Yamada

hake〈はけ〉a brush.

hake-o-kakeru〈はけをかける〉brush.

hake〈はけ〉drainage; sale.

hake-ga-ii〈はけがいい〉flow well; sell well.

hake-guchi〈はけぐち：はけ口〉an outlet; a market ((for)).

haken〈はけん：派遣〉dispatch, despatch.

haken-suru〈派遣する〉dispatch, despatch, send.

shisetsu o haken-suru〈使節を派遣する〉 send an envoy ((to))

haken〈はけん：覇権〉supremacy, mastery, hegemony, leadership.

haken o arasou〈覇権を争う〉 struggle for supremacy, fight for championship

haken o nigiru〈覇権を握る〉 hold supremacy, have the hegemony ((of))

hakeru〈はける〉

mizu-ga-yoku-hakeru〈水がよくはける〉 drain well

shôhin-ga-yoku-hakeru〈商品がよくはける〉 sell well

haki〈はき：破棄〉abrogation, reversal.

jôyaku no haki〈条約の破棄〉 the abrogation of a treaty

haki-suru〈破棄する〉abrogate, reverse.

hanketsu o haki-suru〈判決を破棄する〉 reverse a judgment

haki〈はき：覇気〉ambition, vigor.

haki-ga-aru〈覇気がある〉be ambitious, be full of pep.

haki-ga-nai〈覇気がない〉 lack spirit

haki-chigaeru〈はきちがえる：履き違える〉wear another's shoes; mistake ((one thing)) for ((another)).

hakihaki(-to)〈はきはき（と）〉briskly, promptly, smartly.

hakihaki henji-o-suru〈はきはき返事をする〉 answer promptly

haki-ke〈はきけ：吐き気〉nausea, a sickly feeling.

haki-ke-ga-suru〈吐き気がする〉feel sick (at the stomach), feel like vomiting, feel nausea.

haki-mono〈はきもの：履き物〉footgear, footwear.

hakka 〈はっか〉 peppermint.

hakka 〈はっか：発火〉 ignition, combustion.

shizen-hakka（自然発火） spontaneous combustion

hakka-suru 〈発火する〉 ignite, catch fire.

hakka-shi-yasui 〈発火しやすい〉 easy to catch fire.

hakkai-shiki 〈はっかいしき：発会式〉 an opening ceremony, an inaugural meeting.

hakkaku 〈はっかく：発覚〉 detection, disclosure, exposure.

hakkaku-o-osorete（発覚を恐れて） for fear of detection ((of))

hakkaku-suru 〈発覚する〉 be detected, be revealed, be disclosed, be found out, come to light.

hakkaku-kei 〈はっかくけい：八角形〉 an octagon.

hakkan 〈はっかん：発刊〉 publication, issue.

hakkan-suru 〈発刊する〉 publish, issue, start〔a magazine〕.

hakkan 〈はっかん：発汗〉 sweating, perspiration.

hakkan-suru 〈発汗する〉 perspire, sweat.

hakke 〈はっけ：八卦〉

Ataru-mo-hakke ataranu-mo-hakke.（当たるも八卦当たらぬも八卦.）
Fortune-telling is a hit-or-miss business.

hakken 〈はっけん：発見〉 discovery.

hakken-sha（発見者） a discoverer

hakken-suru 〈発見する〉 discover.

hakketsu-byô 〈はっけつびょう：白血病〉 leukemia.

hakki 〈はっき：発揮〉

hakki-suru 〈発揮する〉 display, exhibit, show.

jitsuryoku o hakki-suru（実力を発揮する） display one's ability

hakkin 〈はっきん：白金〉 platinum.

hakkiri 〈はっきり〉 clearly, distinctly, explicitly.

hakkiri hanasu（はっきり話す） speak distinctly

hakkiri-shita 〈はっきりした〉 clear, distinct, explicit.

hakkiri-shita koe-de（はっきりした声で） in a clear voice

hakkô 〈はっこう：発光〉 luminescence.

hakkô-toryô（発光塗料） a luminous paint

hakkô 〈はっこう：発酵〉 fermentation.

hakkô-kin（発酵菌） a ferment bacillus

hakkô-so（発酵素） ferment, yeast

hakkô-suru or *hakkô-saseru* 〈発酵する，発酵させる〉 ferment.

hakkô 〈はっこう：発行〉 publication, issue.

    hakkô-sho〔発行所〕a publishing office

    hakkô-suru〈発行する〉publish, issue, bring out.

hakkō〈はっこう：発効〉

    hakkô-suru〈発効する〉come into effect, become effective.

hakkō〈はっこう：薄幸〉

    hakkô-no〈薄幸の〉unfortunate, ill-fated.

hakkotsu〈はっこつ：白骨〉a bleached bone, a skeleton.

hakkutsu〈はっくつ：発掘〉excavation.

    hakkutsu-suru〈発掘する〉dig out, dig up, excavate.

hakkyō〈はっきょう：発狂〉madness, craziness, insanity.

    hakkyô-suru〈発狂する〉go mad, become crazy, become insane.

    hakkyô-shita〈発狂した〉mad, crazy, insane.

hako〈はこ：箱〉a box, a case.

    nashi hito-hako〔なし一箱〕a box of pears

    hako-iri-no or *hako-zume-no*〈箱入りの，箱詰めの〉boxed, cased.

hakobi-dasu〈はこびだす：運び出す〉carry ((a thing)) out〔of a room〕.

hakobi-komu〈はこびこむ：運び込む〉carry ((a thing)) into〔a room〕.

hakobi-saru〈はこびさる：運び去る〉carry ((a thing)) away.

hakobu〈はこぶ：運ぶ〉carry, take, bring; go on (well).

    tsutsumi o nikai-e hakobu（包みを二階へ運ぶ）take packages up-stairs

    Watashi-tachi-no shigoto wa umaku hakonda.（私たちの仕事はうまく運んだ。）Our work has gone well.

haku〈はく〉foil, leaf, gilt.

    arumi-haku（アルミはく）aluminum foil

haku〈はく：掃く〉sweep.

    yuka o haku（床を掃く）sweep the floor

haku〈はく：吐く〉spit, vomit.

    chi o haku（血を吐く）vomit blood

haku〈はく：履く〉put on, get on.

    kutsu o haku（靴を履く）put on one's shoes

    kutsu-shita o haku（靴下を履く）pull on one's stockings

    haite-iru〈履いている〉wear, have on.

    Kanojo-wa itsu-mo akai kutsu o haite-iru.（彼女はいつも赤い靴を履いている。）She has always red shoes on.

-haku〈-はく：-泊〉stay.

    ni-sampaku-suru（二，三泊する）make two or three nights' stay

    ippaku-ryokô-o-suru（一泊旅行をする）make an overnight trip

hakua〈はくあ：白亜〉chalk.

　hakua-shitsu-no〈白亜質の〉chalky.

hakuai〈はくあい：博愛〉philanthropy, charity, benevolence.

　hakuai-shugi（博愛主義）　philanthropism

hakubo〈はくぼ：薄暮〉(evening) twilight.

　hakubo-gêmu（薄暮ゲーム）　a twi-nighter

hakuboku〈はくぼく：白墨〉chalk.

　hakuboku-de kaku（白墨で書く）　write with chalk

hakubutsu-kan〈はくぶつかん：博物館〉a museum.

　Daiei-hakubutsu-kan（大英博物館）　the British Museum

hakuchi〈はくち：白痴〉idiocy; an idiot.

　hakuchi-no(-yō-na)〈白痴の(ような)〉idiotic.

hakuchô〈はくちょう：白鳥〉a swan.

hakuchû〈はくちゅう：白昼〉broad daylight.

　hakuchû-ni（白昼に）　in broad daylight

hakuchû〈はくちゅう：伯仲〉

　hakuchû-suru〈伯仲する〉match (each other), be equal ((to)), be even ((with)).

hakudatsu〈はくだつ：はく奪〉deprivation.

　kômin-ken-hakudatsu（公民権はく奪）　deprivation of civil rights

　hakudatsu-suru〈はく奪する〉deprive ((a person)) of, strip ((a person)) of.

hakudô〈はくどう：白銅〉nickel.

　hakudô-ka（白銅貨）　a nickel

hakugai〈はくがい：迫害〉persecution, oppression.

　hakugai-suru〈迫害する〉persecute, oppress.

　hakugai-o-kômuru〈迫害を被る〉be persecuted.

hakugaku〈はくがく：博学〉erudition, wide knowledge.

　hakugaku-no〈博学の〉erudite, learned.

hakugeki-hô〈はくげきほう：迫撃砲〉a trench mortar.

hakuhatsu〈はくはつ：白髪〉white hair, gray hair.

　hakuhatsu-no〈白髪の〉white-haired.

hakuhyô〈はくひょう：薄氷〉thin ice, a thin coat of ice.

　hakuhyô-o-fumu-omoi-ga-suru（薄氷を踏む思いがする）　feel as if skating on thin ice, feel that one is constantly exposed to danger

hakuhyô〈はくひょう：白票〉a blank vote.

　hakuhyô o tôjiru（白票を投じる）　cast a blank vote

hakui〈はくい：白衣〉a white robe.

hakujaku〈はくじゃく：薄弱〉

hakujaku-na〈薄弱な〉feeble, weak, infirm.

  ishi-hakujaku-na（意志薄弱な）weak-willed

hakujin〈はくじん：白人〉a white man.

hakujô〈はくじょう：白状〉confession.

 hakujô-suru〈白状する〉confess.

hakujô〈はくじょう：薄情〉

 hakujô-na〈薄情な〉coldhearted, heartless, cruel.

hakumai〈はくまい：白米〉polished rice.

haku-naishô〈はくないしょう：白内障〉cataract.

hakunetsu〈はくねつ：白熱〉white heat, incandescence; the climax.

  hakunetsu-tô（白熱灯）an incandescent electric lamp

 hakunetsu-suru〈白熱する〉be incandescent, glow white; grow excited.

 hakunetsu-shita or *hakunetsu-teki(-na)*〈白熱した，白熱的(な)〉white-hot, most exciting.

hakurai〈はくらい：舶来〉

  hakurai-hin（舶来品）an imported article, a foreign-made article

 hakurai-no〈舶来の〉imported, foreign-made.

hakuran-kai〈はくらんかい：博覧会〉an exposition, a fair, an exhibition.

  bankoku-hakuran-kai（万国博覧会）a world fair

hakuri〈はくり：薄利〉small profits.

  hakuri-tabai（薄利多売）quick sales at small profits

hakuryoku〈はくりょく：迫力〉power, force, strength.

 hakuryoku-ga-aru〈迫力がある〉be powerful, be impressive, be of great appeal ((to)).

  hakuryoku-ga-nai（迫力がない）lack power, have little appeal ((to))

hakusai〈はくさい：白菜〉a Chinese cabbage.

hakusei〈はくせい：はく製〉stuffing; a stuffed specimen.

  dôbutsu-no-hakusei（動物のはく製）a stuffed animal

 hakusei-ni-suru〈はく製にする〉stuff.

 hakusei-no〈はく製の〉stuffed.

hakusha〈はくしゃ：拍車〉a spur.

 hakusha-o-kakeru〈拍車を掛ける〉spur.

hakusha〈はくしゃ：薄謝〉a small token of one's gratitude.

  hakusha o sashi-ageru（薄謝を差し上げる）offer a reward ((to))

hakushi〈はくし：博士〉*see.* hakase.

hakushi〈はくし：白紙〉a blank sheet of paper.

  hakushi-inin-jô（白紙委任状）a blank letter of attorney

  hakushi-no-tôan-o-dasu（白紙の答案を出す）hand in a blank paper

hakushiki〈はくしき：博識〉wide knowledge, erudition.
　hakushiki-na〈博識な〉erudite, learned, well-informed.
hakusho〈はくしょ：白書〉a white paper.
　keizai-hakusho（経済白書）an economic white paper
hakushoku(-no)〈はくしょく(の)：白色(の)〉white.
　hakushoku-jinshu（白色人種）the white race
hakushon!〈はくしょん.〉ah-choo! / atchoo!
hakushu〈はくしゅ：拍手〉hand clapping.
　wareru-yô-na-hakushu（割れるような拍手）a storm of hand clapping
　hakushu-suru〈拍手する〉clap one's hands.
hakushu-kassai〈はくしゅかっさい：拍手喝采〉cheers, applause.
　hakushu-kassai-suru〈拍手喝采する〉applaud, cheer.
hakuyô〈はくよう：舶用〉
　hakuyô-enjin（舶用エンジン）a marine engine
　hakuyô-no〈舶用の〉marine, for shipping.
hakyoku〈はきょく：破局〉collapse, catastrophe.
　hakyoku-ni-chokumen-suru（破局に直面する）be in the face of ruin
hakyû〈はきゅう：波及〉
　hakyû-suru〈波及する〉extend ((to)), spread ((to)), affect, influence.
hama(be)〈はま(べ)：浜(辺)〉the sands; the beach, the shore.
　hama(be)-zutai-ni（浜(辺)づたいに）along the beach
hamaguri〈はまぐり〉a clam.
ha-maki〈はまき：葉巻〉a cigar.
　ha-maki o suu（葉巻を吸う）smoke a cigar
hamaru〈はまる〉fit in, fit into; fall ((into)).
　Fusuma ga hamara-nai.（ふすまがはまらない.）The sliding door will not fit in.
　mizo-ni-hamaru（溝にはまる）fall into a ditch
hamba〈はんば：飯場〉a bunkhouse.
hambai〈はんばい：販売〉(a) sale, selling.
　hambai-kakaku（販売価格）the selling price
　hambai-in（販売員）a salesman, a saleswoman
　hambai-suru〈販売する〉sell, deal ((in)), handle.
hambashin〈はんばしん：半馬身〉a half length.
hambetsu〈はんべつ：判別〉distinction, discrimination.
　hambetsu-suru〈判別する〉distinguish ((between A and B)), tell ((A)) from ((B)).
hambun〈はんぶん：半分〉(a) half.

hambun-ni herasu（半分に減らす）reduce ((a thing)) to half

hambun-ni kiru（半分に切る）cut ((a thing)) in half

hambun-ni suru（半分にする）divide ((a thing)) into halves

kane-o-hambun-tsukau（金を半分使う）spend half of the money

hambun deki-agatte-iru（半分出来上がっている）be half done

hambun-zutsu-wakeru（半分ずつ分ける）go halves

asobi-hambun-ni（遊び半分に）half in play

jôdan-hambun-ni（冗談半分に）half in jest

hame 〈はめ：羽目〉

hame-o-hazushite-sawagu（羽目をはずして騒ぐ）go on a spree, indulge in merrymaking

kurushii-hame-ni-ochiiru（苦しい羽目に陥る）be in a sad plight, be put in a fix

hame-ita（羽目板）a wainscot, wainscotting

hame-komi 〈はめこみ：はめ込み〉inlaying, insertion.

hame-komu 〈はめ込む〉inlay, insert ((in)), inset.

hame-komi-no 〈はめ込みの〉inlaid, built-in.

hameru 〈はめる〉put in, put on, fix.

te-bukuro o hameru（手袋をはめる）put on one's gloves

to-o-hameru（戸をはめる）fit in a door

hamete-iru 〈はめている〉wear, have on.

yubi-wa o hamete-iru（指輪をはめている）have a ring on one of one's fingers

hametsu 〈はめつ：破滅〉ruin, destruction.

hametsu-suru 〈破滅する〉be ruined, go to ruin.

hami-dasu or **hami-deru** 〈はみだす、はみでる：はみ出す、はみ出る〉jet out, swell out, be forced out, be crowded out〔of a room〕.

hammâ 〈ハンマー〉a hammer.

hammâ-nage（ハンマー投げ）hammer throw

hammei 〈はんめい：判明〉

hammei-suru 〈判明する〉become clear, be ascertained, be known, prove to be... , be identified ((as)).

hammen 〈はんめん：半面〉half the face, a profile; one side, the other side.

hammen 〈はんめん：反面〉the other side.

sono-hammen(-ni-oite)（その反面（において））on the other side

hammo 〈はんも：繁茂〉

hammo-suru 〈繁茂する〉grow thick.

hammo-shite-iru〈繁茂している〉be thickly wooded.

hammo-shita〈繁茂した〉thick, luxuriant, rank.

hammoku〈はんもく：反目〉antagonism, enmity, hostility, feud.

hammoku-suru〈反目する〉be in antagonism ((with)), be hostile ((to each other)).

hamon〈はもん：波紋〉a ripple.

hamon-o-egaku〈波紋を描く〉ripple.

hamon-o-nage-kakeru（波紋を投げ掛ける）bring about a sensation [in the political world]

hamon〈はもん：破門〉excommunication, expulsion.

hamon-suru〈破門する〉excommunicate, expel.

hâmonika〈ハーモニカ〉a harmonica, a mouth organ.

hâmonika o fuku（ハーモニカを吹く）play ((a song)) on a harmonica

ha-mono〈はもの：刃物〉an edged tool; cutlery.

hampa〈はんぱ：半端〉a fragment, an odd thing; an odd sum; the remnant.

hampa-na〈半端な〉fragmentary, odd, fractional.

hampa-na shigoto（半端な仕事）odd jobs

hampa-na kingaku（半端な金額）fractional sum

hampatsu〈はんぱつ：反発〉repulsion, rebounding, resistance.

hampatsu o kanjiru（反発を感じる）feel a repulsion ((toward))

hampatsu-suru〈反発する〉repel, repulse, rebound, resist.

hampatsu-ryoku〈はんぱつりょく：反発力〉repulsive power.

hampatsu-ryoku-no-aru〈反発力のある〉resilient, elastic.

hampatsu-ryoku-no-nai（反発力のない）inert

hampirei〈はんぴれい：反比例〉an inverse proportion.

hampirei-suru〈反比例する〉be in inverse proportion ((to)), be inversely proportional ((to)).

hampu〈はんぷ：頒布〉distribution, circulation.

hampu-suru〈頒布する〉distribute, circulate.

muryô-de hampu-suru（無料で頒布する）distribute free

hampuku〈はんぷく：反復〉repetition, reiteration.

hampuku-renshû-suru-koto（反復練習すること）repeated practice

hampuku-suru〈反復する〉repeat, reiterate, do over again.

hampuku-shite〈反復して〉repeatedly, again and again.

hamu〈ハム〉ham; a (radio) ham.

hamu-eggu（ハムエッグ）ham and eggs

ha-mukau〈はむかう：歯（刃）向かう〉offer resistance ((to)), defy, rise ((against)), turn ((against)).

han 〈はん：判〉a seal, a stamp.

han-o-osu 〈判を押す〉seal.

han 〈はん：範〉an example, a model, a pattern.

han o shimesu（範を示す）　set an example ((to))

han-o-Yôroppa-no-seido-ni-toru（範をヨーロッパの制度に採る）　be modeled upon the European system

han 〈はん：班〉a squad, a group.

han 〈はん：版〉an edition.

shimpan（新版）a new edition

kaitei-ban（改訂版）a revised edition

han 〈はん：半〉half.

han-jikan（半時間）half an hour

ichi-jikan-han（一時間半）　an hour and a half

ku-ji-han（九時半）　half past nine, nine-thirty

han-ne-de（半値で）　at half the value

hannichi（半日）　half a day

han- 〈はん-：反-〉anti-.

han-teikoku-shugi（反帝国主義）anti-imperialism

han- 〈はん-〉Pan-.

han-Taihei-yô-kaigi（はん太平洋会議）the Pan-Pacific Conference

hana 〈はな：花〉a flower, a blossom.

Hana ga saku.（花が咲く.）Flowers bloom.

Hana ga saite-iru.（花が咲いている.）The flowers are out.

Hana ga sukkari chitta.（花がすっかり散った.）The flowers are all gone.

hana o tsukuru（花を作る）grow flowers

hana o tsumu（花を摘む）pick flowers

hana o ikeru（花を生ける）arrange flowers

Wakai-uchi-ga-hana.（若いうちが花.）Youth is a treasure.

hana 〈はな：鼻〉a nose, a trunk, a muzzle, a snout.

hana ga tsumaru（鼻がつまる）one's nose is stopped up

hana o kamu（鼻をかむ）blow one's nose

hana o tsumamu（鼻をつまむ）pinch one's nose

hana-no-ana（鼻の穴）the nostrils

hana-o-susuru 〈鼻をすする〉snivel.

hana-o-tarasu 〈鼻を垂らす〉drivel.

hana-ga-takai 〈鼻が高い〉be proud.

hana-ni-tsuku〈鼻につく〉be offensive to the nose, stink.

hanabanashii〈はなばなしい：華々しい〉splendid, brilliant, glorious.

hanabanashiku〈華々しく〉splendidly, brilliantly, gloriously.

hana-batake〈はなばたけ：花畑〉a flower garden.

    o-hana-batake（お花畑）an Alpine flower zone

hana-bi〈はなび：花火〉fireworks.

    hanabi o ageru（花火を揚げる）let off fireworks

    hana-bi-taikai（花火大会）a fireworks display

hanabira〈はなびら：花びら〉a petal.

hana-fuda〈はなふだ：花札〉Japanese playing cards.

hana-gata〈はながた：花形〉a star, a lion.

    bundan-no-hana-gata（文壇の花形）a literary star, a star writer

hana-ge〈はなげ：鼻毛〉the hairs of the nostrils.

hana-ge-o-nuku〈鼻毛を抜く〉outwit.

hana-goe〈はなごえ：鼻声〉a nasal voice, a twang.

hana-goe-de-hanasu〈鼻声で話す〉talk through the nose.

hana-gumori〈はなぐもり：花曇り〉a hazy sky in springtime.

hanahada〈はなはだ：甚だ〉*see.* hijô-ni.

hanahadashii〈はなはだしい：甚だしい〉extreme, excessive, intense.

    hanahadashii gokai（甚だしい誤解）a serious misunderstanding

    〜-towa-fu-chûi-mo-hanahadashii.（〜とは不注意も甚だしい。）It's too careless of you ((to do))... .

hana-iki〈はないき：鼻息〉

    hana-iki-ga-arai（鼻息が荒い）be very high-spirited, be very high-and-mighty, be unapproachable

    hana-iki-o-ukagau（鼻息をうかがう）curry favor ((with))

hana-ji〈はなぢ：鼻血〉nosebleed.

hana-ji-ga-deru〈鼻血が出る〉bleed at the nose.

hana-kaze〈はなかぜ：鼻風邪〉

hana-kaze-o-hiite-iru〈鼻風邪をひいている〉have a cold in the head.

hana-kotoba〈はなことば：花言葉〉flower language.

hana-kuso〈はなくそ：鼻くそ〉nose dirt, nose wax.

    hana-kuso-o-hojikuru（鼻くそをほじくる）pick one's nose

ha-nami〈はみ：歯並み〉*see.* ha-narabi.

hana-mi〈はなみ：花見〉blossom viewing.

    hana-mi-ni-iku（花見に行く）go to see the blossoms ((at))

hana-michi〈はなみち：花道〉a flower way, a stage passage.

    intai-no-hana-michi-o-shiku（引退の花道を敷く）pave the path of

one's retreat with flowers

hana-mizu 〈はなみず：鼻水〉

hana-mizu-o-tarasu 〈鼻水を垂らす〉 *see.* hana-o-tarasu.

hana-mochi 〈はなもち：鼻持ち〉

hana-mochi-no-nara-nai   otoko（鼻持ちのならない男） a detestable fellow, a mean skunk

hana-moyō 〈はなもよう：花模様〉 a flower pattern.

hana-moyô-no(-tsuita) 〈花模様の（付いた）〉 flowered.

hanamuke 〈はなむけ〉 *see.* sembetsu.

hana-muko 〈はなむこ：花婿〉 a bridegroom.

hanappashi 〈はなっぱし：鼻っぱし〉

hanappashi-no-tsuyoi 〈鼻っぱしの強い〉 strong-minded.

ha-narabi 〈はならび：歯並び〉 a row of teeth.

ha-narabi-ga-warui（歯並びが悪い） have an irregular set of teeth

hanare 〈はなれ：離れ〉 a detached room.

hanarebanare 〈はなればなれ：離れ離れ〉

hanarebanare-ni 〈離れ離れに〉 separately, independently.

hanarebanare-ni-naru 〈離れ離れになる〉 get separated, become scattered.

Ikka wa tôtô hanarebanare-ni-natta.（一家はとうとう離れ離れになった。） The family became scattered at last.

hanare-jima 〈はなれじま：離れ島〉 an isolated island.

hanareru 〈はなれる：離れる〉 separate, part ((from)), part ((with)), leave.

ie-o-hanareru（家を離れる） leave home

hanareta（離れた） separated, detached, isolated; distant, far.

hanarete（離れて） separately ((from)), isolated; at a distance, away from, off.

sukoshi-hanarete（少し離れて） a little way off

hanare-waza 〈はなれわざ：離れ業〉 a feat.

hanare-waza o enjiru（離れ業を演じる） perform a feat

hanaseru 〈はなせる：話せる〉

hanaseru-hito（話せる人） a sensible person, a person of humor

Ano-otoko-wa hanase-nai.（あの男は話せない。） He has no sense (of humor).

hanashi 〈はなし：話〉 a talk, (a) conversation, a chat; a lecture, a speech; a story, a tale; a rumor, an account.

hanashi-aite（話し相手） a person to talk to

hanashi-jôzu（話し上手） a good talker

hanashi-beta（話し下手） a poor talker

hanashi-buri *or* hanashi-kata（話しぶり，話し方）one's manner of speaking

Hanashi-chû.（話し中.）Line's busy. / Number's engaged.

hanashi no tane（話の種）a topic of conversation

hanashi-no-tsuide-desu-ga（話のついでですが）by the way

koko-dake-no-hanashi-desu-ga（ここだけの話ですが）between ourselves

hanashi-o-suru〈話をする〉talk, have a talk ((with)), chat, speak.

hanashi-ai〈はなしあい：話し合い〉consultation, negotiations, an agreement, an understanding.

hanashi-ai-ga-tsuku（話し合いが付く）come to an understanding

hanashi-ai-de〈話し合いで〉by common consent.

hanashi-ai-no-kekka〈話し合いの結果〉as the result of agreement.

hanashi-au〈はなしあう：話し合う〉talk ((with)), discuss ((a matter)) with ((a person)), consult with ((a person)) about.

tettei-teki-ni hanashi-au（徹底的に話し合う）talk ((a matter)) out ((with))

hanashi-gai〈はなしがい：放し飼い〉

hanashi-gai-ni-suru〈放し飼いにする〉pasture, leave ((a dog)) at large.

hanashi-goe〈はなしごえ：話し声〉a voice, voices talking.

hanashi-hambun〈はなしはんぶん：話半分〉

hanashi-hambun-ni-kiku〈話半分に聞く〉take a story at half its face value.

hanashi-kakeru〈はなしかける：話し掛ける〉speak to ((a person)).

hanashi-komu〈はなしこむ：話し込む〉have a long talk ((with)), talk ((with a person)) for hours.

hanashi-kotoba〈はなしことば：話し言葉〉spoken language.

hanashi-zuki〈はなしずき：話し好き〉

hanashi-zuki-na〈話し好きな〉talkative, chatty.

hanasu〈はなす：話す〉talk, speak, tell.

Nani o hanashite-iru-no?（何を話しているの？）What are you talking about?

Eigo-de hanasu（英語で話す）speak in English

Kimi-ni hanashi-tai-koto-ga-aru.（君に話したいことがある.）I have something to tell you.

hanasu〈はなす：放す〉let go, let loose, set free.

inu o hanasu（犬を放す）let a dog loose

hanasu〈はなす：離す〉separate, part, divide; keep away.

Sekiyu-sutôbu o akambô-kara hanashite-oke.（石油ストーブを赤ん坊から離しておけ。） Keep the oil heater away from the baby.

Kare-kara-me-o-hanasu-na.（彼から目を離すな。） Keep an eye on him.

Watashi-wa ima-shigoto-chû-de-te-ga-hanase-nai.（私は今仕事中で手が離せない。） I am engaged.

hana-suji 〈はなすじ：鼻筋〉 the ridge of the nose.

hana-suji-no-tootta 〈鼻筋の通った〉 with a shapely nose.

hana-taba 〈はなたば：花束〉 a bouquet, a bunch of flowers.

hanatsu 〈はなつ：放つ〉

hi-o-hanatsu（火を放つ） set fire ((to)), set ((a house)) on fire

isai o hanatsu（異彩を放つ） cut a brilliant figure

hana-uta 〈はなうた：鼻歌〉 humming.

hana-uta-o-utau 〈鼻歌を歌う〉 hum a song.

hana-wa 〈はなわ：花輪〉 a wreath, a garland, a lei.

hana-ya 〈はなや：花屋〉 a florist; a flower shop, a florist's.

hanayaka 〈はなやか：華やか〉

hanayaka-na 〈華やかな〉 gay, bright, brilliant, splendid, florid, flowery.

hana-yome 〈はなよめ：花嫁〉 a bride.

hana-zakari 〈はなざかり：花盛り〉

hana-zakari-de-aru 〈花盛りである〉 be at their best, be in full bloom.

hana-zono 〈はなぞの：花園〉 a flower garden.

han-byônin 〈はんびょうにん：半病人〉 a sickly person.

han-byônin-ni-naru 〈半病人になる〉 become almost ill.

hanchû 〈はんちゅう：範ちゅう〉 a category.

〜-no-hanchû-ni-zokusuru（〜の範ちゅうに属する） belong to the category of...

handa(-zuke-ni-suru) 〈はんだ（づけにする）：はんだ（付けにする）〉 solder.

handa-zuke-no 〈はんだ付けの〉 soldered.

han-dakuon 〈はんだくおん：半濁音〉 a *p*-sound.

handan 〈はんだん：判断〉 judgment.

handan o kudasu（判断を下す） pass judgment ((on))

handan-o-ayamaru（判断を誤る） make an error in judgment

watashi-jishin-no handan-dewa（私自身の判断では） in my own judgment

handan-suru 〈判断する〉 judge.

gaiken-de handan-suru（外見で判断する） judge from appearances

handi(kyappu) 〈ハンディ（キャップ）〉 a handicap.

handi-o-tsukeru〈ハンディを付ける〉handicap ((a person)).

hando〈ハンド〉a hand touch.

handô〈はんどう：反動〉reaction.

handô-suru〈反動する〉react.

handô-teki(-na)〈反動的(な)〉reactionary.

hando-baggu〈ハンドバッグ〉a handbag, a purse.

handoku〈はんどく：判読〉decipherment, making out, reading.

handoku-suru〈判読する〉decipher, make out, read.

handoru〈ハンドル〉a handle, a handlebar, a (steering) wheel.

handoru-o-nigiru（ハンドルを握る）sit at the wheel, take the wheel

handoru-o-hidari-ni-kiru〈ハンドルを左に切る〉wheel left.

han-dôtai〈はんどうたい：半導体〉a semiconductor.

hane〈はね：羽〉a feather, a plume, plumage; a wing.

hane-buton（羽布団）a feather quilt, a down coverlet

hane〈はね：羽根〉a shuttlecock.

hane-tsuki（羽根つき）battledore and shuttlecock

hane-o-tsuku（羽根をつく）play battledore and shuttlecock

hane-agaru〈はねあがる：跳ね上がる〉jump up; rise suddenly.

hane-ari〈はねあり：羽あり〉a winged ant.

hane-chirasu〈はねちらす：跳ね散らす〉splash, dabble, spatter.

han·ei〈はんえい：繁栄〉prosperity.

han·ei-suru〈繁栄する〉prosper, thrive, flourish.

han·ei〈はんえい：反映〉reflection.

han·ei-suru〈反映する〉reflect, be reflected.

han-eikyû-teki(-na)〈はんえいきゅうてき(な)：半永久的(な)〉semi-permanent.

hane-kaeru〈はねかえる：跳ね返る〉rebound, spring up.

hane-kaesu〈はねかえす：はね返す〉*see.* hane-tsukeru.

hane-kakeru〈はねかける：跳ね掛ける〉splash.

doro-mizu-o　hane-kakerareru（泥水を跳ね掛けられる）be splashed with muddy water

hane-mawaru〈はねまわる：跳ね回る〉jump about, skip about.

hane-mawatte-asobu（跳ね回って遊ぶ）romp

han·en〈はんえん：半円〉a half circle, a semicircle.

han·en o egaku（半円を描く）make a half circle, describe a semicircle

hane-okiru〈はねおきる：跳ね起きる〉jump up, jump out of bed.

haneru〈はねる：跳ねる〉leap, jump, spring; recoil, rebound; splash; be over, close.

    Shibai wa jû-ichi-ji-ni haneta. (芝居は十一時にはねた.) The curtain was dropped at 11p.m.

haneru 〈はねる〉 knock down.

    torakku-ni hanerareru (トラックにはねられる) be knocked down by a truck

hane-tobasu 〈はねとばす：はね飛ばす〉 send ((a person *or* a thing)) flying; spatter, splash.

hane-tsukeru 〈はねつける〉 repel, repulse, reject, refuse.

    yôkyû o hane-tsukeru (要求をはねつける) repel a request

hanga 〈はんが：版画〉 a (woodcut) print.

hangaku 〈はんがく：半額〉 half the price.

    hangaku-de (半額で) at half the price

Hangarî 〈ハンガリー〉 Hungary.

    Hangarî-jin (ハンガリー人) a Hungarian

    Hangarî-go (ハンガリー語) Hungarian

    Hangarî(-jin)-no (ハンガリー(人)の) Hungarian

hangeki 〈はんげき：反撃〉 a counterattack, a counteroffensive.

hangeki-suru 〈反撃する〉 counterattack, make a counterattack, strike back.

hangen 〈はんげん：半減〉 a reduction by half.

hangen-suru 〈半減する〉 reduce by half.

    omoshiro-mi-ga-hangen-suru (面白みが半減する) take off half of the amusement

hangetsu 〈はんげつ：半月〉 a half moon.

hango 〈はんご：反語〉 a rhetorical question.

hangô 〈はんごう：飯ごう〉 a canteen.

han-goroshi 〈はんごろし：半殺し〉

han-goroshi-ni-suru 〈半殺しにする〉 half-kill, beat ((a person)) nearly to death.

han-goroshi-ni-sareru 〈半殺しにされる〉 be half-killed, be nearly killed.

hangyaku 〈はんぎゃく：反逆〉 treason, treachery, (a) rebellion, (a) revolt.

    hangyaku o kuwadateru (反逆を企てる) plot treason ((against))

hangyaku-teki(-na) 〈反逆的(な)〉 treasonous, rebellious.

hanhan 〈はんはん：半々〉

hanhan-ni 〈半々に〉 half-and-half, in half.

    hanhan-ni-wakeru (半々に分ける) halve, divide into halves

han·i 〈はんい：範囲〉a scope, a sphere, (the) limits.

    katsudô-han·i（活動範囲）the sphere of activity

    seiryoku-han·i（勢力範囲）one's sphere of influence

han·i-nai-ni〈範囲内に〉within the limits ((of)).

    han·i-gai-ni（範囲外に）beyond the limits ((of))

han·i-go 〈はんいご：反意語〉an antonym.

hanikamu 〈はにかむ〉be bashful, be shy.

hanikande〈はにかんで〉bashfully, shyly.

haniwa 〈はにわ：はに輪〉a clay figure.

hanji 〈はんじ：判事〉a judge.

    shuseki-hanji（首席判事）a presiding judge

hanjô 〈はんじょう：繁盛〉prosperity.

hanjô-suru〈繁盛する〉prosper, be prosperous, flourish.

hanjuku 〈はんじゅく：半熟〉

hanjuku-no〈半熟の〉half-boiled.

hankachi 〈ハンカチ〉a handkerchief.

hanka-gai 〈はんかがい：繁華街〉busy quarters, an amusement quarter.

hankai 〈はんかい：半壊〉

hankai-suru〈半壊する〉be partially destroyed.

hankan 〈はんかん：反感〉(an) antipathy, ill feeling.

    hankan o idaku（反感を抱く）have an antipathy ((against *or* to)), have ill feeling ((toward))

    hankan o kau（反感を買う）provoke ((another's)) antipathy

hankan-hammin 〈はんかんはんみん：半官半民〉

hankan-hammin-no〈半官半民の〉semi-governmental.

hankei 〈はんけい：半径〉a radius.

    hankei-ni-jussenchi-no en（半径二十センチの円）a circle with a radius of twenty centimeters

    kôdô-hankei（行動半径）a radius of action

hanken 〈はんけん：版権〉copyright.

    hanken-shoyû-sha（版権所有者）a copyright holder

hanken-o-shingai-suru〈版権を侵害する〉infringe the copyright ((of)), pirate.

hanketsu 〈はんけつ：判決〉judgment, a decision.

    hanketsu o ii-watasu（判決を言い渡す）deliver judgment ((on))

    hanketsu o kudasu（判決を下す）give a decision ((upon))

hanketsu-suru〈判決する〉decide ((on)), pass judgment ((on)).

hanki 〈はんき：半期〉a half year.

kami-hanki（上半期）the first half of the year

shimo-hanki（下半期）the latter half of the year

hanki-goto-ni〈半期ごとに〉half-yearly, semiannually.

hanki〈はんき：半旗〉

hanki-o-kakageru〈半旗を掲げる〉hang a flag at half-mast.

hanki〈はんき：反旗〉

hanki-o-hirugaesu〈反旗を翻す〉rise in revolt ((against)).

hankō〈はんこう：犯行〉a crime, an offense.

hankô o jikyô-suru（犯行を自供する）confess one's crime

hankô o hinin-suru（犯行を否認する）deny the offense

hankô-gemba（犯行現場）the scene of an offense

hankō〈はんこう：反抗〉resistance, defiance, rebellion.

hankô-ki（反抗期）one's rebellious age

hankô-suru〈反抗する〉resist, oppose.

hankô-teki(-na)〈反抗的(な)〉defiant, rebellious, hostile.

hankô-teki-na taido o toru（反抗的な態度を取る）take a defiant attitude ((toward))

hankō〈はんこう：反攻〉a counteroffensive.

hankô-suru〈反攻する〉counterattack.

hankyō〈はんきょう：反響〉an echo, reverberation, repercussions, influence, reflection, a response.

hankyô-suru〈反響する〉echo, resound, reverberate.

hankyô-ga-aru or *hankyô-o-okosu*〈反響がある，反響を起こす〉be echoed, have an echo ((in)), elicit a public response.

han-kyōran〈はんきょうらん：半狂乱〉

han-kyôran-to-natte〈半狂乱となって〉half mad, frantically.

hankyū〈はんきゅう：半球〉a hemisphere.

kita-hankyû（北半球）the northern hemisphere

minami-hankyû（南半球）the southern hemisphere

hannen〈はんねん：半年〉*see.* han-toshi.

hannin〈はんにん：犯人〉a criminal, a perpetrator.

hannō〈はんのう：反応〉(a) reaction, an effect.

insei-hannô（陰性反応）a negative reaction

hannô-suru〈反応する〉react ((on *or* to)), respond ((to)).

hannyū〈はんにゅう：搬入〉

hannyû-suru〈搬入する〉carry in, bring in.

han·on〈はんおん：半音〉a semitone.

han·on-ageru〈半音上げる〉sharp.

han·on-sageru〈半音下げる〉 flat

hanran〈はんらん：反乱〉a rebellion, a revolt, an uprising.

  hanran-o-okosu〈反乱を起こす〉rebel ((against)), revolt ((against)), rise ((against)).

hanran〈はんらん：はん濫〉inundation, a flood.

  hanran-suru〈はん濫する〉overflow, flow over, flood, inundate.

hanrei〈はんれい：判例〉a (judicial) precedent.

  hanrei-shû〈判例集〉 law reports

hanro〈はんろ：販路〉a market〔for goods〕, an outlet.

  hanro o kaitaku-suru〈販路を開拓する〉 open (up) a new market ((for))

  hanro o kakuchō-suru〈販路を拡張する〉 extend the market ((for))

hanron〈はんろん：反論〉a counterargument.

  hanron-suru〈反論する〉counterargue.

hanryo〈はんりょ：伴りょ〉a companion.

  isshō-no hanryo〈一生の伴りょ〉 a companion for life

han-sayō〈はんさよう：反作用〉(a) reaction.

  sayô to han-sayô〈作用と反作用〉 action and reaction

  han-sayō-o-oyobosu〈反作用を及ぼす〉react ((upon)).

hansei〈はんせい：半生〉half one's life.

hansei〈はんせい：反省〉introspection, reconsideration.

  hansei-o-unagasu〈反省を促す〉 ask ((a person)) to reconsider

  hansei-suru〈反省する〉introspect, reconsider.

han-seihin〈はんせいひん：半製品〉semimanufactured goods, half-finished goods.

han-seiki〈はんせいき：半世紀〉half a century.

hansen〈はんせん：帆船〉a sailing vessel, a sailboat.

hansen〈はんせん：反戦〉

  hansen-shisô〈反戦思想〉 an antiwar idea

  hansen-shugi-sha〈反戦主義者〉 a pacifist

  hansen-undô〈反戦運動〉 an antiwar movement

hansha〈はんしゃ：反射〉reflection.

  hansha-shinkei〈反射神経〉 reflexes

  hansha-suru〈反射する〉reflect.

han-shakai-teki(-na)〈はんしゃかいてき(な)：反社会的(な)〉antisocial.

  han-shakai-teki kôi〈反社会的行為〉 an antisocial action

hanshi〈はんし：半紙〉common Japanese writing paper.

hanshi-hanshô〈はんしはんしょう：半死半生〉

hanshi-hanshô-no 〈半死半生の〉 more dead than alive, all but dead.

hanshin 〈はんしん：半身〉 half the body; one side of the body.
　　jô-hanshin 〈上半身〉 the upper half of one's body
　　hanshin-zô 〈半身像〉 a half-length statue, a bust

hanshin-hangi 〈はんしんはんぎ：半信半疑〉
　hanshin-hangi-no or *hanshin-hangi-de* 〈半信半疑の，半信半疑で〉 half in doubt.

hanshô 〈はんしょう：半鐘〉 a fire bell, a fire alarm.

hanshô 〈はんしょう：反証〉 counterevidence.
　　hanshô o ageru 〈反証を挙げる〉 produce counterevidence

hanshô 〈はんしょう：半焼〉
　hanshô-suru 〈半焼する〉 be partially destroyed by fire.

hanshoku 〈はんしょく：繁殖〉 breeding, propagation.
　　hanshoku-ki 〈繁殖期〉 a breeding season
　hanshoku-suru 〈繁殖する〉 breed, propagate itself.
　hanshoku-ryoku-no-aru 〈繁殖力のある〉 prolific.

hanshû 〈はんしゅう：半周〉
　hanshû-suru 〈半周する〉 go halfway round.

hanshutsu 〈はんしゅつ：搬出〉
　hanshutsu-suru 〈搬出する〉 carry out.

hanso 〈はんそ：反訴〉 a counterclaim.
　　hanso o okosu 〈反訴を起こす〉 bring a counterclaim ((for))

hansô 〈はんそう：帆走〉
　hansô-suru 〈帆走する〉 sail.

han-sode 〈はんそで：半そで〉 a half-sleeve.
　　han-sode-no shatsu 〈半そでのシャツ〉 an undershirt with half sleeves

hansoku 〈はんそく：反則〉 a foul, foul play.
　hansoku-o-suru 〈反則をする〉 play against the rule, play foul.

hansû 〈はんすう：半数〉 half the number.

hansû 〈はんすう：反すう〉 rumination.
　　hansû-dôbutsu 〈反すう動物〉 a ruminant
　hansû-suru 〈反すうする〉 ruminate.

han-suru 〈はんする：反する〉 be contrary ((to)), be against; violate.
　　kisoku ni hansuru 〈規則に反する〉 violate a rule
　～-ni-hanshite 〈～に反して〉 contrary to... , against... .
　　kitai-ni-hanshite 〈期待に反して〉 contrary to one's expectations
　kore-ni-hanshite 〈これに反して〉 on the contrary, on the other hand.

hansuto 〈ハンスト〉 a hunger strike.

hantai〈はんたい：反対〉opposition, objection; the opposite, the contrary.

 hantai-tô（反対党）an Opposition Party

 hantai-undô（反対運動）an opposition movement

 hantai-jimmon（反対尋問）(a) cross-examination

 hantai-seiryoku（反対勢力）a counterinfluence

 hantai-tôhyô（反対投票）a negative vote

hantai-suru〈反対する〉oppose, be opposed ((to)), object ((to)).

hantai-o-ukeru〈反対を受ける〉meet with opposition, be opposed ((by)).

hantai-no〈反対の〉opposite, contrary.

 hantai-no hôkô-ni（反対の方向に）in the opposite direction

hantai-ni〈反対に〉on the contrary, the other way.

〜-ni-hantai-shite〈〜に反対して〉in opposition to... , against... .

 shokumin-chi-shugi-ni-hantai-shite（植民地主義に反対して）in opposition to colonialism

han-taisei〈はんたいせい：反体制〉

 han-taisei undô（反体制運動）an anti-establishment movement

hantei〈はんてい：判定〉(a) judgment, (a) decision.

 hantei-de-katsu *or* hantei-gachi-suru（判定で勝つ，判定勝ちする）win a decision ((over))

hantei-suru〈判定する〉judge, decide.

hantei-o-ayamaru〈判定を誤る〉misjudge.

han-teishin〈はんていしん：半艇身〉a half-length〔of a boat〕.

hanten〈はんてん：はん点〉a spot, a speck, a speckle.

hanten-no-aru〈はん点のある〉spotted, specked, speckled.

hantô〈はんとう：半島〉a peninsula.

 Atsumi-hantô（渥美半島）the Atsumi Peninsula

hantô-no〈半島の〉peninsular.

han-tômei〈はんとうめい：半透明〉

han-tômei-no〈半透明の〉semitransparent, translucent.

han-toshi〈はんとし：半年〉half a year, a half year.

han-tsuki〈はんつき：半月〉half a month, a half month.

hanzai〈はんざい：犯罪〉a crime, an offense; guilt.

 hanzai o okasu（犯罪を犯す）commit a crime

 hanzai-kôi（犯罪行為）a criminal act

 hanzai-sha（犯罪者）a criminal, an offender

 kanzen-hanzai（完全犯罪）a perfect crime

hanzai(-jô)-no〈犯罪(上)の〉criminal.

han-zubon 〈はんズボン：半ズボン〉 shorts, breeches.

happa 〈はっぱ：発破〉
    happa-o-kakeru 〈発破を掛ける〉 set dynamite; spur ((a person)) to ((do)).

happô 〈はっぽう：八方〉
    happô-bijin (八方美人) everybody's friend
    Happô-fusagari-da. (八方ふさがりだ。) Everything goes against me.
    happô-te-o-tsukusu (八方手を尽くす) try all possible means

happô 〈はっぽう：発泡〉
    happô-suchirôru (発泡スチロール) styro-foam

happô 〈はっぽう：発砲〉
    happô-suru 〈発砲する〉 fire ((upon)), fire off a gun.

happu 〈はっぷ：発布〉 promulgation.
    happu-suru 〈発布する〉 promulgate.

happun 〈はっぷん：発奮〉
    happun-suru 〈発奮する〉 be stimulated ((by)), be inspired ((by)).

happyô 〈はっぴょう：発表〉 (an) announcement, publication.
    happyô-suru 〈発表する〉 announce, make public, publish.
    shiken no kekka o happyô-suru (試験の結果を発表する) announce the results of the examination

hâpu 〈ハープ〉 a harp.
    hâpu o hiku (ハープを弾く) play the harp
    hâpu-sôsha (ハープ奏者) a harpist

hara 〈はら：腹〉 the belly, the bowels, the stomach; anger.
    hara-ga-haru (腹が張る) feel heavy in the stomach, have gas in the stomach
    hara-ga-itamu (腹が痛む) have a stomachache
    hara-ga-heru (腹が減る) get hungry
    hara-ga-dete-kuru (腹が出てくる) develop a potbelly
    hara-ga-tatsu (腹が立つ) get angry
    hara-ni-sue-kaneru (腹にすえかねる) cannot stomach

hara-bai 〈はらばい：腹ばい〉
    hara-bai-ni-naru 〈腹ばいになる〉 lie on one's belly.

hara-chigai 〈はらちがい：腹違い〉
    hara-chigai-no 〈腹違いの〉 of a different mother, half-blood.
    hara-chigai-no kyôdai (腹違いの兄弟) a half brother, a stepbrother

hara-dachi 〈はらだち：腹立ち〉
    hara-dachi-magire-ni 〈腹立ち紛れに〉 in a fit of anger.

haradatashii 〈はらだたしい：腹立たしい〉 provoking, exasperating.

hara-gonashi 〈はらごなし：腹ごなし〉
  hara-gonashi-ni 〈腹ごなしに〉 to help digestion.
hara-guai 〈はらぐあい：腹具合〉
    Hara-guai-ga-warui.（腹具合が悪い.） My bowels are out of order. /
    I have a stomach trouble.
hara-guroi 〈はらぐろい：腹黒い〉 malicious, crafty, scheming.
harahara 〈はらはら〉
  harahara-suru 〈はらはらする〉 feel nervous, feel uneasy, be afraid ((of)),
    be kept in suspense.
  harahara-suru-yô-na 〈はらはらするような〉 thrilling, exciting.
    harahara-suru-yô-na shôbu（はらはらするような勝負）a thrilling
      contest
  harahara-shi-nagara 〈はらはらしながら〉in great fear, with excited
    curiosity.
harai 〈はらい：払い〉(a) payment, an account, a bill.
    harai-ga-ii（払いがいい）be punctual in paying bills
    harai-ga-warui（払いが悪い）be behind in paying bills
    harai o sumasu（払いを済ます）pay a bill, settle an account
    genkin-barai（現金払い）cash payment
harai 〈はらい〉 exorcism, purification.
  o-harai-o-suru 〈おはらいをする〉 get oneself purified.
harai-komi 〈はらいこみ：払い込み〉 payment.
    harai-komi-shihon（払い込み資本）paid-up capital
    zengaku-harai-komi（全額払い込み）payment in full
  harai-komu 〈払い込む〉 pay in, pay up.
harai-modoshi 〈はらいもどし：払いもどし〉(a) refund, (a) repayment.
  harai-modosu 〈払いもどす〉 pay back, refund, repay.
harai-otosu 〈はらいおとす：払い落とす〉 shake down, brush ((dust)) off.
hara-ippai 〈はらいっぱい：腹いっぱい〉 heartily.
    hara-ippai taberu（腹いっぱい食べる）eat heartily
harai-sage 〈はらいさげ：払い下げ〉(a) sale 〔of government property〕,
    disposal.
    harai-sage-hin（払い下げ品）articles sold by the government
  harai-sageru 〈払い下げる〉 sell, dispose ((of)).
hara-ise 〈はらいせ：腹いせ〉
  hara-ise-ni 〈腹いせに〉 by way of revenge, in spite.
harai-sugi 〈はらいすぎ：払い過ぎ〉 overpayment.
  harai-sugiru 〈払い過ぎる〉 overpay, pay in excess.

hara-maki 〈はらまき：腹巻き〉a stomach band.

haramu 〈はらむ〉become pregnant, conceive.

haran 〈はらん：波乱〉

  haran-ni-tonda 〈波乱に富んだ〉eventful, checkered.

    haran-ni-tonda isshō 〈波乱に富んだ一生〉 a checkered career

harasu 〈はらす：晴らす〉clear away, dispel.

    urami o harasu 〈恨みを晴らす〉 pay off old scores

    utagai o harasu 〈疑いを晴らす〉 dispel doubts

harasu 〈はらす〉cause to swell, tumefy.

    naite-me-o-akaku-harasu 〈泣いて目を赤くはらす〉have one's eyes
      swollen red with crying

harau 〈はらう：払う〉pay; brush off, sweep (off).

    daikin o harau 〈代金を払う〉 pay for 〔a book〕

    keii o harau 〈敬意を払う〉 pay one's respect ((to))

    ôbâ-no-hokori-o-harau 〈オーバーのほこりを払う〉 brush an overcoat

harawata 〈はらわた〉the intestines, the guts.

hare 〈はれ：晴れ〉fine weather.

    hare-ma 〈晴れ間〉 an interval of clear weather, a lull in the rain

  hare-no-butai-de 〈晴れの舞台で〉on a grand occasion.

hare 〈はれ〉(a) swelling.

    Hare ga hiku. 〈はれが引く.〉 The swelling goes down.

hare-agaru 〈はれあがる：晴れ上がる〉clear up.

hare-agaru 〈はれあがる：晴れ上がる〉swell up.

harebare 〈はればれ：晴れ晴れ〉

  harebare-suru 〈晴れ晴れする〉feel cheerful, feel refreshed.

  harebare-shita 〈晴れ晴れした〉clear, bright, cheerful, lighthearted,
  refreshing.

    harebare-shita kao-iro 〈晴れ晴れした顔色〉 a bright look

hare-bottai 〈はれぼったい〉somewhat swollen.

    hare-bottai me 〈はれぼったい目〉 swollen eyes

hare-gi 〈はれぎ：晴れ着〉one's best (clothes).

    hare-gi-o-kite 〈晴れ着を着て〉 in one's best clothes

hare-mono 〈はれもの：はれ物〉a swelling.

  hare-mono-ni-demo-sawaru-yô-ni 〈はれ物にでも触るように〉most cautiously, with utmost care, gingerly.

harenchi 〈はれんち：破廉恥〉

  harenchi-na 〈破廉恥な〉shameless, disgraceful.

hareru 〈はれる：晴れる〉clear (up), clear away; be dispelled; be refreshed.

hareru 〈はれる〉 swell, become swollen.
>> ashi-ga-harete-iru（足がはれている） have a swollen foot
>*hareta*〈はれた〉 swollen.

harete 〈はれて：晴れて〉 openly, publicly.

haretsu 〈はれつ：破裂〉 (a) bursting, (an) explosion.
>> suidô-kan no haretsu（水道管の破裂） the bursting of water pipe
>*haretsu-suru*〈破裂する〉 burst, explode.

hare-wataru 〈はれわたる：晴れ渡る〉 clear up.
>*hare-watatta*〈晴れ渡った〉 cloudless, clear.
>> hare-watatta sora（晴れ渡った空） a clear sky

hareyaka 〈はれやか：晴れやか〉
>*hareyaka-na*〈晴れやかな〉 clear, bright, cheerful; gay.
>> hareyaka-na kao（晴れやかな顔） a bright face

hari 〈はり：針〉 a needle, a pin, a hook, a sting, a thorn, a stitch, a hand.
>> hari ni ito-o-toosu（針に糸を通す） thread a needle
>> hari ni esa-o-tsukeru（針にえさを付ける） bait a hook
>> kizu-o go-hari nuu（傷を五針縫う） put five stitches in the wound

hari 〈はり〉 a needle; acupuncture.
>*hari-o-shite-morau*〈はりをしてもらう〉 be punctured with needles.

hari 〈はり〉 a beam, a girder.

hari 〈はり：張り〉 tension, tensity; will power, spirit, pride.

hari-ageru 〈はりあげる：張り上げる〉
>> koe o hari-ageru（声を張り上げる） raise one's voice

hari-ai 〈はりあい：張り合い〉 an inducement.
>*hari-ai-no-nai*〈張り合いのない〉 discouraging, disappointing.

hari-au 〈はりあう：張り合う〉 rival, compete ((with)).
>> o-tagai-ni hari-au（お互いに張り合う） compete against each other

hari-awaseru 〈はりあわせる：張り合わせる〉 paste ((things)) together.

hari-dashi-mado 〈はりだしまど：張り出し窓〉 a bay window.

hari-dasu 〈はりだす：張り出す〉 put up, post up, placard.

hari-gami 〈はりがみ：はり紙〉 a placard, a bill, a poster.
>> hari-gami-o-suru（はり紙をする） put up a poster, stick a bill ((on))
>> Hari-gami-kinshi.（はり紙禁止。） Post no bills.

harigane 〈はりがね：針金〉 (a) wire.
>*harigane-no-yô-na*〈針金のような〉 wiry.

hari-kaeru 〈はりかえる：張り替える〉 repaper, re-cover, reupholster, renew.

hari-kiru 〈はりきる：張り切る〉 be full of vigor, be in high spirits.

　　harikitte hataraku（張り切って働く）　work with zeal

hari-ko 〈はりこ：張り子〉

　　hari-ko-no-tora（張り子のとら）　a papier-mâché tiger, a paper tiger

hari-komi 〈はりこみ：張り込み〉(a) watch, (a) lookout, ambush.

　hari-komu〈張り込む〉keep watch ((against, for *or* on)), be on the lookout ((for)), lie in ambush ((for)).

hari-megurasu 〈はりめぐらす：張りめぐらす〉stretch ((wires)) around.

hari-nezumi 〈はりねずみ〉a hedgehog.

hari-sakeru 〈はりさける：張り裂ける〉burst, break, split.

　　mune-mo-hari-saken-bakari-ni-naku（胸も張り裂けんばかりに泣く）
　　　sob one's heart out

hari-sashi 〈はりさし：針刺し〉a pincushion.

hari-shigoto 〈はりしごと：針仕事〉needlework.

　　hari-shigoto o suru（針仕事をする）　do needlework

hari-taosu 〈はりたおす：張り倒す〉knock ((a person)) down.

haritsuke 〈はりつけ〉crucifixion.

　haritsuke-ni-suru〈はりつけにする〉crucify ((a person)).

hari-tsukeru 〈はりつける：はり付ける〉stick ((on)), paste ((on)).

hari-tsumeru 〈はりつめる：張り詰める〉

　　ki-o-hari-tsumeru（気を張り詰める）　strain one's mind

　　koori-ga-hari-tsumeru（氷が張り詰める）　be frozen all over

harô 〈はろう：波浪〉waves, a billow.

　　harô-chûi-hô（波浪注意報）　a high sea warning

haru 〈はる：春〉spring.

　　haru-kaze（春風）　a spring breeze

　　haru-same（春雨）　spring rain

　haru-no-yô-na〈春のような〉springlike.

　haru-saki-ni〈春先に〉in early spring.

haru 〈はる：張る〉stretch, spread; be frozen; fill.

　　rôpu o haru（ロープを張る）　stretch a rope

　　netto o haru（ネットを張る）　put up a net

　　tento o haru（テントを張る）　pitch a tent

　　tarai ni mizu-o haru（たらいに水を張る）　fill a tub with water

　　ki-ga-haru（気が張る）　feel strained

　　mie-o-haru（見えを張る）　make a display

haru 〈はる〉put, stick, paste, apply.

tegami-ni kitte o haru（手紙に切手をはる） put a stamp on a letter

kokuban-ni keiji o haru（黒板に掲示をはる） stick a notice on the blackboard

kôyaku o haru（こう薬をはる） apply a plaster ((to))

harubaru 〈はるばる〉all the way.

harubaru Hokkaidô-kara yatte-kuru（はるばる北海道からやって来る）come all the way from Hokkaido

haruka(-ni) 〈はるか(に)〉far away, in the distance; far, much.

haruka-kaijô-ni（はるか海上に） far out on the sea

haruka-ni Fuji o nozomu（はるかに富士を望む） see Mt. Fuji a long way off

Kono jisho-no-hô ga haruka-ni ii.（この辞書の方がはるかにいい．）This dictionary is far better.

hasami 〈はさみ〉scissors, shears, clippers; a punch.

hasami-de mono o kiru（はさみで物を切る） cut a thing with scissors

hasami-o-ireru 〈はさみを入れる〉trim, punch.

hasami 〈はさみ〉claws, nippers.

hasami-de hasamu（はさみで挟む） nip with its claws

hasami-uchi 〈はさみうち：挟み撃ち〉

hasami-uchi-ni-suru 〈挟み撃ちにする〉attack ((the enemy)) from both sides.

hasamu 〈はさむ：挟む〉put between, pinch; insert, put in.

hon-no-aida-ni empitsu o hasamu（本の間に鉛筆を挟む） put a pencil between the leaves of a book

yubi o doa-ni hasamu（指をドアに挟む） pinch one's finger(s) in the door

kotoba-o-hasamu（言葉を挟む） put in a word

hasan 〈はさん：破産〉bankruptcy.

hasan-senkoku-o-ukeru（破産宣告を受ける） be declared bankrupt

hasan-suru 〈破産する〉go bankrupt.

haseru 〈はせる〉

meisei-o-haseru（名声をはせる） win fame

hasha 〈はしゃ：覇者〉a supreme ruler; a champion.

hashagu 〈はしゃぐ〉frolic, romp about, make merry.

hashaide-iru 〈はしゃいでいる〉be in jolly spirits.

hashi 〈はし〉chopsticks.

hashi-ichi-zen（はし一ぜん） a pair of chopsticks

hashi 〈はし：橋〉a bridge.

hashi o kakeru（橋を架ける）build a bridge〔over a river〕

hashi o wataru（橋を渡る）cross a bridge

hashi〈はし：端〉an end, the edge.

hashi-kara-hashi-made（端から端まで）from end to end

têburu no hashi（テーブルの端）the edge of a table

hashigaki〈はしがき〉a foreword, a preface, an introduction.

hashigo〈はしご〉a ladder.

kabe-ni hashigo o kakeru（壁にはしごを掛ける）set (up) a ladder against the wall

hashigo o noboru（はしごを登る）go up a ladder

hashigo o oriru（はしごを降りる）climb down a ladder

hashigo-dan（はしご段）a step, a stair, a staircase, a stairway, stairs

nawa-bashigo（縄ばしご）a rope ladder

hinan-bashigo（避難ばしご）a fire escape

hashigo-zake（はしご酒）barhopping, pub-crawling

hashika〈はしか〉the measles.

hashika ni kakaru（はしかにかかる）catch (the) measles

hashike〈はしけ〉a lighter, a barge.

hashira〈はしら：柱〉a pillar, a column, a post, a pole.

hashira o tateru（柱を立てる）set up a pillar

hashira-dokei（柱時計）a wall clock

hashiraseru or **hashirasu**〈はしらせる，はしらす：走らせる，走らす〉run; sail, drive.

kuruma o hashiraseru（車を走らせる）drive a car

hashiri-gaki〈はしりがき：走り書き〉

hashiri-gaki-suru〈走り書きする〉scribble, write hurriedly.

hashiri-haba-tobi〈はしりはばとび：走り幅跳び〉a running broad jump.

hashiri-taka-tobi〈はしりたかとび：走り高跳び〉a running high jump.

hashiru〈はしる：走る〉run.

hashiri-mawaru（走り回る）run about

hashiri-saru（走り去る）run away

hashiri-suguru（走り過ぎる）run past

hashitte-kaeru（走って帰る）run back

hashita〈はした〉a fraction, an odd sum; a fragment, a scrap.

hashita o kiri-suteru（はしたを切り捨てる）omit fractions

hashita-gane（はした金）a small sum of money

hashita-nai〈はしたない〉low, mean, base, vulgar, immodest.

    hashita-nai mono-no-ii-kata o suru（はしたないもののいい方をする）
    use vulgar language
    hashita-nai-furumai-o-suru（はしたない振る舞いをする）behave
    shamefully

hashi-watashi〈はしわたし：橋渡し〉mediation, good offices.
 hashi-watashi-o-suru〈橋渡しをする〉mediate ((between)), intermediate
 ((between)), act as go-between.

hashôfû〈はしょうふう：破傷風〉tetanus, lockjaw.

hashutsu-jo〈はしゅつじょ：派出所〉a police box.

hason〈はそん：破損〉damage, injury, breakdown.
    hason-kasho（破損箇所）a damaged part
 hason-suru〈破損する〉be damaged, be broken (down), be destroyed, be
 impaired.
 hason-shita〈破損した〉damaged, injured, broken.
 hason-shi-yasui〈破損しやすい〉easy to break, fragile.

hassan〈はっさん：発散〉exhalation, diffusion, radiation, evaporation.
 hassan-suru〈発散する〉give forth, emit, exhale ((from)), emanate
 ((from)), radiate, evaporate.
    miryoku o hassan-suru（魅力を発散する）display one's charms
    ikari o hassan-saseru（怒りを発散させる）blow off steam

hassei〈はっせい：発生〉occurrence, (an) outbreak.
    korera no hassei（コレラの発生）an outbreak of cholera
 hassei-suru〈発生する〉occur, break out, happen.

hassei〈はっせい：発声〉
    hassei-hô（発声法）vocalization
    hassei-renshû（発声練習）vocal exercises

hassha〈はっしゃ：発車〉departure.
 hassha-suru〈発車する〉start ((from)), leave, depart ((from)).

hassha〈はっしゃ：発射〉
 hassha-suru〈発射する〉fire, shoot; launch.

hasshin〈はっしん：発しん〉(an) eruption, a rash.

hasshin〈はっしん：発信〉dispatch.
    hasshin-chi（発信地）the place of dispatch
    hasshin-nin（発信人）an addresser, the sender
 hasshin-suru〈発信する〉dispatch, send.

hasshô-chi〈はっしょうち：発祥地〉the cradle, the birthplace.

hassô〈はっそう：発想〉conception.

hassô〈はっそう：発送〉

hassô-gakari〈発送係〉a forwarding clerk

hassô-suru〈発送する〉send out, forward, dispatch, ship, mail out, post.

hassuru〈はっする：発する〉emanate, radiate, shed; issue, utter; originate ((in)), start ((from)), rise ((from)).

hasu〈はす〉a lotus.

hasu-no hana（はすの花）a lotus flower

hasû〈はすう：端数〉*see.* hashita.

hasû o kiri-suteru（端数を切り捨てる）*see.* hashita o kiri-suteru.

hata〈はた：旗〉a flag.

hata o ageru（旗を揚げる）hoist a flag

hata o furu（旗を振る）wave a flag

hata o orosu（旗を下ろす）take down a flag

hata〈はた：機〉a loom.

hata-o-oru〈機を織る〉weave.

hata〈はた：端〉

hata-kara-miru-to（端から見ると）to bystanders, to outsiders

Hata-de-miru-hodo muzukashiku-wa-nai.（端で見るほど難しくはない。）It's not so difficult as it may seem to others.

hatachi〈はたち：二十，二十歳〉twenty years of age, one's twentieth year.

hata-iro〈はたいろ：旗色〉the tide of war, the outlook, the situation.

Aite-no-hô ga hata-iro-ga-ii.（相手の方が旗色がいい。）The chances are in their favor.

hata-iro-o-miru（旗色を見る）sit on the fence

hatake〈はたけ：畑〉a cultivated field, a farm; one's specialty.

hatake o tagayasu（畑を耕す）plow a field

hatake-shigoto（畑仕事）farm work

Shôbai wa watashi-no hatake-dewa-nai.（商売は私の畑ではない。）Business is not in my line.

hataki〈はたき〉a duster.

hataki-o-kakeru or *hataku*〈はたきをかける，はたく〉dust.

hata-meiwaku〈はためいわく：端迷惑〉

hata-meiwaku-ni-naru〈端迷惑になる〉be a nuisance to others.

hatameku〈はためく〉flutter〔in the wind〕.

hatan〈はたん：破たん〉failure, a rupture.

hatan-suru〈破たんする〉fail, come to a rupture.

Sono keikaku wa kanzen-ni hatan-shita.（その計画は完全に破たんした。）The plan has failed completely.

hatarakasu 〈はたらかす：働かす〉 set ((a person)) to work, make ((a person)) work, work, use, exercise.
　atama o hatarakasu (頭を働かす) use one's head
hataraki 〈はたらき：働き〉 work, (a) function, (an) activity.
　kanzô no hataraki (肝臓の働き) the function of the liver
　hataraki-bachi (働きばち) a worker bee
　hataraki-guchi (働き口) a position, a situation
　　hataraki-guchi o mitsukeru (働き口を見つける) find employment
　hataraki-mono (働き者) a hard worker
　hataraki-zakari-de-aru (働き盛りである) be in the prime of life
　hataraki-sugiru (働きすぎる) overwork oneself
hataraki-kakeru 〈はたらきかける：働き掛ける〉 work ((on)), make approaches ((to)), appeal ((to)).
hataraku 〈はたらく：働く〉 work, serve ((at)), operate, operate ((on)).
　yoku hataraku (よく働く) work hard
　Kanojo-wa wêtoresu-to-shite hataraite-iru. (彼女はウェートレスとして働いている。) She serves as a waitress.
hatashite 〈はたして：果して〉 just as one thought, as expected, sure enough; really; ever.
hatasu 〈はたす：果たす〉 carry out, accomplish, achieve, attain, complete, finish, fulfill.
　nimmu o hatasu (任務を果たす) fulfill one's duty
hata-zao 〈はたざお：旗ざお〉 a flagpole, a flagstaff.
hatchaku 〈はっちゃく：発着〉 departure and arrival.
　hatchaku-jikan-hyô (発着時間表) a timetable, a schedule
hatchū 〈はっちゅう：発注〉
　hatchū-suru 〈発注する〉 order.
hate 〈はて：果て〉 the end, the extreme, the limit(s), (the) bound(s).
　sekai no hate (世界の果て) the end of the earth
hate! or **hate-na!** 〈はて．はてな．〉 Dear me! / Good gracious! / well / let me see.
-hateru 〈-はてる：-果てる〉
　tsukare-hateru (疲れ果てる) be tired out, be exhausted
hateshi- 〈はてし-：果てし-〉
　hateshi-ga-nai 〈果てしがない〉 be endless, be boundless, be eternal.
　hateshi-nai 〈果てしない〉 endless, boundless, eternal.
　　hateshi-nai oo-unabara (果てしない大海原) the boundless ocean
　hateshi-naku 〈果てしなく〉 endlessly, eternally.

hato〈はと〉a pigeon, a dove.

　hato-ha-no〈はと派の〉dovish.

hatoba〈はとば：波止場〉*see.* futô（ふ頭）.

hato-me〈はとめ：はと目〉an eyelet.

hato-mune〈はとむね：はと胸〉a pigeon breast.

　hato-mune-no〈はと胸の〉pigeon-breasted.

hatoron-shi〈ハトロンし：ハトロン紙〉brown paper, kraft paper.

-hatsu〈-はつ：-発〉departure, sending; a round, a shot, a shell.

　roku-ji-go-fun-hatsu-no-ressha（六時五分発の列車）the train leaving
　　at 6:05, the 6:05 train

　Nagoya-hatsu-kyûkô（名古屋発急行）an express from Nagoya

　Ôsaka-hatsu-Nikkô-ki（大阪発日航機）a JAL plane leaving Ôsaka

　Rondon-hatsu-tokuden（ロンドン発特電）a dispatch datelined
　　London

　nana-hatsu utsu（七発撃つ）fire seven shots

hatsuan〈はつあん：発案〉a suggestion, a proposal, an idea.

　hatsuan-sha（発案者）a proposer, an originator

　hatsuan-suru〈発案する〉suggest, make a suggestion, propose, devise.

hatsubai〈はつばい：発売〉sale.

　hatsubai-kinshi（発売禁止）prohibition of sale

　hatsubai-suru〈発売する〉sell, put ((a thing)) on sale.

　hatsubai-sareru〈発売される〉be put on sale.

hatsu-butai〈はつぶたい：初舞台〉one's first appearance on the stage,
　one's debut.

hatsubyô〈はつびょう：発病〉

　hatsubyô-suru〈発病する〉be taken ill, become sick.

hatsuden〈はつでん：発電〉the generation of electricity.

　hatsuden-ki（発電機）a dynamo, a generator

　hatsuden-sho（発電所）a power station

　hatsuden-suru〈発電する〉generate electricity.

hatsuden〈はつでん：発電〉dispatch of a telegram.

　ni-gatsu-itsuka　Pari-hatsuden-ni-yoreba（二月五日パリ発電によれば）
　　according to a Paris telegram dated February 5

hatsudô〈はつどう：発動〉

　hatsudô-suru〈発動する〉exercise, invoke.

　kyôken o hatsudô-suru（強権を発動する）take strong measures

hatsudô-ki〈はつどうき：発動機〉a motor, an engine.

hatsuen-tô〈はつえんとう：発煙筒〉a smoke candle.

hatsuga 〈はつが：発芽〉 germination, sprouting.

   hatsuga-suru 〈発芽する〉 germinate, sprout, bud.

hatsugan 〈はつがん：発がん〉

   hatsugan-sei-no 〈発がん性の〉 carcinogenic, cancer-developing.

hatsugen 〈はつげん：発言〉 (an) utterance, speaking; a proposal.

   hatsugen o tori-kesu （発言を取り消す） retract one's words

   hatsugen-suru 〈発言する〉 utter, speak; propose.

hatsugen-ken or **hatsugen-ryoku** 〈はつげんけん，はつげんりょく：発言権，発言力〉 a voice.

   hatsugen-ken-ga-nai （発言権がない） have no voice

hatsugi 〈はつぎ：発議〉 a proposal, a suggestion.

   Takagi-shi-no hatsugi-de （高木氏の発議で） at Mr. Takagi's proposal

hatsuhi(-no-de) 〈はつひ(ので)：初日(の出)〉 the sunrise on New Year's Day.

hatsuiku 〈はついく：発育〉 growth, development.

   hatsuiku-zakari-no kodomo （発育盛りの子供） a growing child

   hatsuiku-suru 〈発育する〉 grow, develop.

hatsuka 〈はつか：二十日〉 twenty days; the twentieth.

hatsuka-nezumi 〈はつかねずみ〉 a mouse.

hatsu-kôen or **hatsu-kôgyô** 〈はつこうえん：はつこうぎょう：初公演，初興行〉 the first public presentation of a play.

hatsu-koi 〈はつこい：初恋〉 one's first love.

   hatsu-koi no hito （初恋の人） the partner of one's first love

hatsu-kôkai 〈はつこうかい：初公開〉 the first public exhibition.

hatsu-kôkai 〈はつこうかい：初航海〉 a maiden voyage; one's first voyage.

hatsumei 〈はつめい：発明〉 invention.

   hatsumei-ka （発明家） an inventor

   hatsumei-suru 〈発明する〉 invent.

hatsu-mimi 〈はつみみ：初耳〉

   Soitsu-wa hatsu-mimi-da. （そいつは初耳だ．） I've heard it for the first time.

hatsu-mono 〈はつもの：初物〉 the first product of the season.

   hatsu-mono-no 〈初物の〉 early.

   hatsu-mono-no ichigo （初物のいちご） early strawberries

hatsunetsu 〈はつねつ：発熱〉 (an attack of) fever.

   hatsunetsu-suru 〈発熱する〉 be attacked with fever, become feverish.

hatsuon 〈はつおん：発音〉 pronunciation.

　　　hatsuon-ga-ii（発音がいい）　have a good pronunciation
　　　hatsuon-ga-warui（発音が悪い）　have a bad pronunciation
　　　hatsuon-kigô（発音記号）　a phonetic sign
　hatsuon-suru〈発音する〉pronounce.
hatsurei〈はつれい：発令〉(an) official announcement.
　hatsurei-suru〈発令する〉announce ((a person's appointment)) officially.
hatsu-shimo〈はつしも：初霜〉the first frost of the year.
hatsu-yuki〈はつゆき：初雪〉the first snow of the year.
hatsu-yume〈はつゆめ：初夢〉the first dream of the New Year.
hattari〈はったり〉(a) bluff, (a) claptrap.
　hattari-o-kakeru〈はったりをかける〉bluff, play to the crowd.
hattatsu〈はったつ：発達〉development, growth, progress, advance.
　　　mezamashii hattatsu（めざましい発達）　remarkable progress
　hattatsu-suru〈発達する〉develop, grow, make progress, advance.
hatten〈はってん：発展〉expansion, development.
　　　hatten-tojô-koku（発展途上国）　a developing country
　hatten-suru〈発展する〉expand, develop.
hatto〈はっと〉
　hatto-suru〈はっとする〉be startled, be surprised, be taken aback.
　hatto-shite〈はっとして〉with a start.
　　　hatto-shite ware-ni-kaeru（はっとして我に返る）　come to oneself with
　　　a start
hau〈はう〉crawl, creep.
　hatte-aruku〈はって歩く〉crawl about, go on all fours.
Hawai〈ハワイ〉Hawaii.
　　　Hawai-jin（ハワイ人）　a Hawaiian
　　　Hawai(-jin)-no（ハワイ（人）の）　Hawaiian
hayaba-mai〈はやばまい：早場米〉an early crop of rice.
haya-bike〈はやびけ：早引け〉
　haya-bike-suru〈早引けする〉leave the class before school is over, leave
　office before the closing time.
haya-de〈はやで：早出〉early attendance.
　　　Asu-wa haya-de-da.（明日は早出だ。）　I must go to the office earlier
　　　tomorrow.
haya-gaten〈はやがてん：早合点〉
　haya-gaten-suru〈早合点する〉jump to a conclusion, be hasty in forming
　a conclusion.
haya-gawari〈はやがわり：早変わり〉

haya-gawari-suru 〈早変わりする〉 transform oneself quickly ((into)), turn quickly ((into)).

hayai 〈はやい：早(速)い〉 early; fast, quick, rapid.

   hayai yûshoku（早い夕食）an early dinner

   hayai ressha（速い列車）a fast train

   keisan-ga-hayai（計算が速い）be quick at figures

   hayai nagare（速い流れ）a rapid stream

   Hayai-mono-gachi.（早い者勝ち。）First come, first served.

hayaku 〈早(速)く〉 early, soon, fast, quick(ly).

   asa-hayaku（朝早く）early in the morning

   dekiru-dake-hayaku（できるだけ早く）as soon as possible

   totemo hayaku hanasu（とても速く話す）speak so fast

haya-jimai 〈はやじまい：早じまい〉

haya-jimai-ni-suru 〈早じまいにする〉 close up ((the store)) early, knock off ((work)) early.

haya-jini 〈はやじに：早死に〉 an early death.

haya-jini-suru 〈早死にする〉 die young.

hayakereba 〈はやければ：早ければ〉 at the earliest chance, if nothing goes awry.

haya-kuchi 〈はやくち：早口〉

haya-kuchi-ni-hanasu 〈早口に話す〉 speak fast.

hayamaru 〈はやまる：早まる〉 be hasty, be rash.

hayamatta 〈早まった〉 hasty, rash, indiscreet.

   hayamatta-koto-o-suru（早まったことをする）commit a rash act, act rashly

hayamatte 〈早まって〉 in one's hurry, rashly, without due consideration.

hayame-ni 〈はやめに：早目に〉 (a little) earlier, in good time.

   sukoshi-hayame-ni　chûshoku　o　toru（少し早めに昼食を取る）have lunch a little earlier

hayameru 〈はやめる：早(速)める〉 quicken, hasten, accelerate.

   ashi o hayameru（足を速める）quicken one's steps

   shi o hayameru（死を早める）hasten one's death

   sokudo o hayameru（速度を速める）accelerate the speed

hayamimi 〈はやみみ：早耳〉

hayamimi-no 〈早耳の〉 quick-eared.

haya-ne-haya-oki 〈はやねはやおき：早寝早起き〉 early to bed and early to rise.

haya-ne-haya-oki-suru 〈早寝早起きする〉 go to bed early and get up early, keep early hours.

haya-nomi-komi 〈はやのみこみ：早のみ込み〉 *see.* haya-gaten.

haya-oki 〈はやおき：早起き〉 early rising; an early riser.

haya-oki-suru 〈早起きする〉 rise early, get up early.

hayari 〈はやり〉 (the) fashion, (the) vogue, popularity; prevalence.

hayari-no 〈はやりの〉 fashionable, popular; epidemic.

hayaru 〈はやる〉 be in fashion, come into fashion; prosper, have a large custom, have a large practice; be prevalent.

Mini-sukâto ga hayatte-iru. （ミニスカートがはやっている.） Mini-skirts are in fashion.

hayaru mise （はやる店） a prospering store

yoku-hayaru byôin （よくはやる病院） a hospital with a large practice

Ryûkan ga hayatte-iru. （流感がはやっている.） Influenza is prevalent.

hayaru 〈はやる〉 be rash, be hasty, be impatient.

hayaru-kokoro-o-osaeru （はやる心を抑える） control oneself, restrain oneself

hayasa 〈はやさ：速さ〉 quickness, swiftness, speed.

hayashi 〈はやし：林〉 a wood, a grove.

matsu-bayashi （松林） a pine grove

hayashi 〈はやし〉 a musical accompaniment.

hayashi-kata （はやし方） a musical accompanist, a band

hayashi-raisu 〈ハヤシライス〉 rice with hashed meat.

hayasu 〈はやす：生やす〉 grow, cultivate.

hige o hayasu （ひげを生やす） grow a beard

hayasu 〈はやす〉 accompany, play music; cheer.

haya-temawashi 〈はやてまわし：早手回し〉

haya-temawashi-o-suru 〈早手回しをする〉 make early preparations, anticipate.

haya-waza 〈はやわざ：早業〉 quick work, a (clever) feat.

denkô-sekka-no haya-waza （電光石火の早業） a lightning trick

haya-zaki 〈はやざき：早咲き〉

haya-zaki-no 〈早咲きの〉 early.

haya-zaki-no chûrippu （早咲きのチューリップ） early tulips

hazakai-ki 〈はざかいき：端境期〉 an off(-crop) season.

haze 〈はぜ〉 a goby.

hazeru 〈はぜる〉 burst open, pop open; split.

-hazu 〈-はず〉 be due ((to do)), be to, be expected, must, ought to, should.

Ressha wa go-ji-ni tôchaku-suru-hazu-desu.（列車は五時に到着するはずです。） The train is due at 5 o'clock.

Kare-wa kyô watashi-ni-ai-ni-kuru-hazu-desu.（彼は今日私に会いに来るはずです。） He is expected to come and see me today.

Kimi-wa sono-koto o shitte-iru-hazu-da.（君はそのことを知っているはずだ。） You ought to know that.

Kanojo-wa ima-goro-wa Tôkyô ni tsuite-iru-hazu-da.（彼女は今ごろは東京に着いているはずだ。） She should have reached Tokyo by this time.

-hazu-ga-nai〈-はずがない〉 cannot.

Kare-ga sonna koto o iu-hazu-ga-nai.（彼がそんなことを言うはずがない。） He cannot say such a thing.

hazu-beki〈はずべき：恥ずべき〉 shameful, disgraceful, dishonorable.

hazu-beki kôi（恥ずべき行為） disgraceful conduct

hazukashi-gari-ya〈はずかしがりや：恥ずかしがりや〉 a shy person.

hazukashi-garu〈はずかしがる：恥ずかしがる〉 be shy, be bashful.

hazukashi-gatte〈恥ずかしがって〉 shyly, bashfully.

hazukashii〈はずかしい：恥ずかしい〉 be ashamed ((of)); shameful.

hazukashiku-nai〈はずかしくない：恥ずかしくない〉 worthy ((of)), decent.

hazukashi-sô-ni〈恥ずかしそうに〉 bashfully, coyly.

hazukashikute or *hazukashi-sa-de*〈恥ずかしくて，恥ずかしさで〉 in shame, with shame.

hazukashime〈はずかしめ：辱め〉 (a) shame, an insult, (a) disgrace.

hazukashime-o-ukeru〈辱めを受ける〉 be put to shame, be insulted.

hazukashimeru〈辱める〉 put ((a person)) to shame, insult.

hazumi〈はずみ：弾み〉 momentum, an impulse; the moment, (a) chance.

toki no hazumi-de（時のはずみで） on the spur of the moment

chotto-shita hazumi-de（ちょっとしたはずみで） by a mere chance

dô-shita-hazumi-ka（どうしたはずみか） by some chance

hazumu〈はずむ：弾む〉 spring, bound, bounce; be lively.

yoku hazumu（よく弾む） bound well

Hanashi ga hazunda.（話が弾んだ。） The conversation became lively.

hazure〈はずれ：外れ〉 the end, the verge, the outskirts; a miss, a disappointment, a blank, a poor harvest.

machi no hazure-ni（町の外れに） on the outskirts of a town

hazure o hiku（外れを引く） draw a blank

hazure-no-nai〈外れのない〉unerring, infallible, unfailing.

hazureru〈はずれる：外れる〉come off, miss, go wrong.

    mato o hazureru（的を外れる）miss the mark

    Kare-no okusoku wa yoku hazureru.（彼の憶測はよく外れる。）His guess does often go wrong.

hazurete-iru〈外れている〉be off.

    Dai-ichi-botan ga hazurete-iru.（第一ボタンが外れている。）Your top button is off.

    yôten o hazurete-iru（要点を外れている）be beside the point

hazusu〈はずす：外す〉take off, unfasten, slip away.

    megane o hazusu（眼鏡を外す）take off one's glasses

    botan-o-hazusu（ボタンを外す）unbutton

    seki o hazusu（席を外す）leave one's seat

he〈へ〉

    he-o-suru（へをする）break wind, fart

    he-tomo-omowa-nai（へとも思わない）make nothing ((of))

hê!〈へえ。〉Dear me! / Indeed! / What? / Well?

hebari-tsuku〈へばりつく〉*see.* shigami-tsuku.

hebaru〈へばる〉be much exhausted ((from *or* with)), be done up.

hebereke〈へべれけ〉

hebereke-ni-you〈へべれけに酔う〉be dead drunk.

hebi〈へび：蛇〉a snake, a serpent.

hebî-kyû〈ヘビーきゅう：ヘビー級〉the heavyweight.

hebî-kyû-no〈ヘビー級の〉heavyweight.

hebo〈へぼ〉

    hebo-shôgi（へぼ将棋）a poor Japanese game of *shôgi*

Hebon-shiki〈ヘボンしき：ヘボン式〉the Hepburn system.

    Hebon-shiki-rôma-ji（ヘボン式ローマ字）the Hepburn system Romanization

Heburai〈ヘブライ〉Hebrew.

    Heburai-jin（ヘブライ人）a Hebrew

    Heburai-go（ヘブライ語）Hebrew

    Heburai-no（ヘブライの）Hebraic, Hebrew

hechima〈へちま〉a sponge cucumber.

hedatari〈へだたり：隔たり〉(a) distance, an interval; (a) difference, a disparity.

    nenrei no hedatari（年齢の隔たり）a disparity of age

hedatete〈へだてて：隔てて〉at a distance, at intervals ((of)), beyond, across.

Kanojo-no ie wa michi-o-hedatete-sugu-soko-da. 〈彼女の家は道を隔て
てすぐそこだ.〉 Her house stands just across the street.

heddo-raito 〈ヘッドライト〉 a headlight.

heddo-raito o tsukeru 〈ヘッドライトを付ける〉 turn on the headlight

hedo 〈へど〉

hedo-o-haku 〈へどを吐く〉 spew.

hedoro 〈ヘドロ〉 sludge.

hei 〈へい：兵〉 *see.* heishi.

hei 〈へい：塀〉 a wall, a fence.

heibon 〈へいぼん：平凡〉

heibon-na 〈平凡な〉 common, ordinary, commonplace.

heibon-na ningen 〈平凡な人間〉 an ordinary person

heichara or **hetchara** 〈へいちゃら, へっちゃら〉

heichara-da or *hetchara-da* 〈へいちゃらだ, へっちゃらだ〉 do not care a
damn.

heichi 〈へいち：平地〉 a flat, level (ground).

heidan 〈へいだん：兵団〉 an army corps.

heiei 〈へいえい：兵営〉 barracks.

heieki 〈へいえき：兵役〉 military service.

heieki ni fukusuru 〈兵役に服する〉 do military service

heifuku 〈へいふく：平服〉 plain clothes.

heigai 〈へいがい：弊害〉 an evil, a harmful influence, an ill effect.

heigai o oyobosu 〈弊害を及ぼす〉 exert an evil influence ((on))

heigen 〈へいげん：平原〉 a plain, a prairie.

heigō 〈へいごう：併合〉 (an) annexation, (an) amalgamation.

heigō-sareru 〈併合される〉 be annexed ((to)), be amalgamated ((into)).

heihatsu 〈へいはつ：併発〉 concurrence, complication.

heihatsu-suru 〈併発する〉 break out at the same time, be complicated
((by)).

Yobyô-ga-heihatsu-shita. 〈余病が併発した.〉 A complication has set
in.

heihei 〈へいへい〉

heihei-suru 〈へいへいする〉 *see.* pekopeko-suru.

heihei-bonbon 〈へいへいぼんぼん：平々凡々〉

heihei-bonbon-na 〈平々凡々な〉 *see.* heibon-na.

heihō 〈へいほう：平方〉 a square.

go-mêtoru-heihô 〈五メートル平方〉 five meters square

　　　go-heihô-mêtoru（五平方メートル）　five square meters

　　　heihô-kon（平方根）　a square root

heihô〈へいほう：兵法〉tactics, strategy.

heii〈へいい：平易〉

　heii-na〈平易な〉plain, simple, easy.

　　　heii-na buntai-de（平易な文体で）in a simple style

　heii-ni〈平易に〉plainly, simply, easily.

heiin〈へいいん：兵員〉strength of troops; army(*or* navy) personnel.

heiji〈へいじ：平時〉time of peace; ordinary times.

　heiji-wa〈平時は〉in peacetime; ordinarily, usually.

heijitsu〈へいじつ：平日〉a weekday; ordinary days.

　　　heijitsu-wa（平日は）on weekdays; on ordinary days

　　　heijitsu-doori（平日どおり）as usual

heijô(-wa)〈へいじょう（は）：平常（は）〉usually, normally.

　　　heijô ni fukusuru（平常に復する）return to normal

　heijô-no〈平常の〉usual, normal.

　heijô-doori〈平常どおり〉as usual.

heika〈へいか：陛下〉His Majesty, Her Majesty; Your Majesty.

heika〈へいか：平価〉par, parity.

　　　heika-kiri-sage（平価切り下げ）devaluation

　　　　heika-kiri-sage-o-suru（平価切り下げをする）devaluate, devalue

heikai〈へいかい：閉会〉the closing.

　　　heikai-no ji o noberu（閉会の辞を述べる）give a closing address

　　　heikai-shiki（閉会式）a closing ceremony

　heikai-suru〈閉会する〉close, be closed.

heikan〈へいかん：閉館〉

　　　Honjitsu heikan.（本日閉館.）Closed for today.

　heikan-suru〈閉館する〉close〔its doors〕, be closed.

heiki〈へいき：兵器〉arms, a weapon.

heiki〈へいき：平気〉

　heiki-na〈平気な〉calm, cool; unconcerned, indifferent.

　heiki-de〈平気で〉calmly, coolly; unconcernedly, with indifference.

　　　heiki-de-aru（平気である）don't mind, don't care

　　　heiki-de-iru（平気でいる）remain calm, be indifferent ((to))

heikin〈へいきん：平均〉an average, balance.

　　　heikin-nenrei（平均年齢）the average age

　　　heikin-ten（平均点）the average mark

　　　heikin-dai（平均台）a balance beam

heikin-ijô-de〈平均以上で〉above the average
heikin-ika-de〈平均以下で〉below the average
heikin-suru〈平均する〉average.
heikin-no or *heikin-teki-na*〈平均の，平均的な〉average, mean.
heikin-shite〈平均して〉on the average.
heikô〈へいこう：平衡〉equilibrium, balance.
heikô o tamotsu〈平衡を保つ〉keep one's balance
heikô o ushinau〈平衡を失う〉lose one's balance
heikô-kankaku〈平衡感覚〉the sense of equilibrium
heikô〈へいこう：平行〉parallel.
heikô-bô〈平行棒〉parallel bars
heikô-sen〈平行線〉parallel lines
heikô-shi-hen-kei〈平行四辺形〉a parallelogram
heikô-suru〈平行する〉run parallel ((to *or* with)).
heikô-no〈平行の〉parallel.
～-to-heikô-shite〈～と平行して〉in parallel with... .
heikô〈へいこう：閉口〉
heikô-suru〈閉口する〉be nonplused, be embarrassed, be annoyed ((at *or* with)), be defeated.
Kono samusa-ni-wa-heikô-da.（この寒さには閉口だ.）I can't stand this cold weather.
heikô-saseru〈閉口させる〉nonplus, strike ((a person)) dumb, silence.
heikô〈へいこう：閉校〉the closing down of a school.
heikô-suru〈閉校する〉close a school.
heimen〈へいめん：平面〉a plane, a level.
heimen-zu〈平面図〉a plan
heimen-no〈平面の〉plane, level, flat.
heinen〈へいねん：平年〉the normal year, the common year.
heinen-saku〈平年作〉an average crop
heinetsu〈へいねつ：平熱〉the normal temperature.
heion〈へいおん：平穏〉
heion-na〈平穏な〉calm, quiet, tranquil.
heion-buji-na〈平穏無事な〉peaceful, pacific, uneventful.
heion-buji-ni〈平穏無事に〉in peace and quiet.
heiretsu〈へいれつ：並列〉
denchi o heiretsu-ni tsunagu（電池を並列につなぐ）connect cells in parallel
heiryoku〈へいりょく：兵力〉military force; the strength of an army.

heisa 〈へいさ：閉鎖〉 closing, closure, shutdown.
    kôjô-heisa（工場閉鎖） a lockout
    heisa-suru〈閉鎖する〉 close, shut, lock out.

heisatsu 〈へいさつ：併殺〉 a double play.

heisei 〈へいせい：平静〉 calm, serenity, tranquility.
    kokoro-no-heisei o tamotsu（心の平静を保つ） keep one's presence of mind
    kokoro-no-heisei o ushinau（心の平静を失う） lose one's composure
    heisei-na〈平静な〉 calm, serene, tranquil, peaceful.

heishi 〈へいし：兵士〉 a soldier, a private; soldiers.

heishin-teitô 〈へいしんていとう：平身低頭〉
    heishin-teitô-shite ayamaru（平身低頭して謝る） beg ((another's)) pardon on one's knees

heiso 〈へいそ：平素〉 *see.* fudan.

heisoku 〈へいそく：閉そく〉 (a) blockade, stoppage, occlusion.
    chô-heisoku（腸閉そく） intestinal obstruction

heitai 〈へいたい：兵隊〉 a soldier.

heitan 〈へいたん：平担〉
    heitan-na〈平担な〉 even, flat, level.

heitan 〈へいたん：兵たん〉 supply trains.
    heitan-kichi（兵たん基地） a supply base

heitei 〈へいてい：閉廷〉
    heitei-suru〈閉廷する〉 adjourn the court.

heitei 〈へいてい：平定〉 suppression, subjugation.
    heitei-suru〈平定する〉 suppress, subjugate.

heiten 〈へいてん：閉店〉
    heiten-suru〈閉店する〉 close (a) shop.

heiwa 〈へいわ：平和〉 peace.
    heiwa o iji-suru（平和を維持する） maintain peace
    heiwa-undô（平和運動） a peace campaign
    heiwa-na〈平和な〉 peaceful.
    heiwa-ni〈平和に〉 peacefully, in peace.
    heiwa-ni-kurasu（平和に暮らす） live in peace

heiya 〈へいや：平野〉 a plain, plains.
    Kantô-heiya（関東平野） the Kanto plain

heiyô 〈へいよう：併用〉
    heiyô-suru〈併用する〉 use together ((with)), take (together) ((with)).

heizen 〈へいぜん：平然〉

heizen-taru 〈平然たる〉 calm, cool, composed.
    heizen-taru taido (平然たる態度) a calm attitude
heizen-to 〈平然と〉 calmly, coolly, with composure.
    heizen-to-shite-iru (平然としている) remain cool, never turn a hair

hekichi 〈へきち：へき地〉 an out-of-the-way place.

hekiga 〈へきが：壁画〉 a wall painting, a fresco, a mural.

hekomu 〈へこむ〉 become dented, become hollow, sink, cave in, yield ((to)).

hekotareru 〈へこたれる〉 lose heart, be discouraged, be disheartened; be tired out; give in, fail.

hema 〈へま〉 a blunder, a bungle, a mess.
hema-o-yaru 〈へまをやる〉 make a blunder, bungle, make a mess of it.
hema-na 〈へまな〉 awkward, bungling.

hembō 〈へんぼう：変ぼう〉 (a) transfiguration, (a) transformation.
hembô-suru 〈変ぼうする〉 undergo a change, transfigure.

hemmei 〈へんめい：変名〉 an assumed name.
    ∼-to-iu-hemmei-de (∼という変名で) under the (assumed) name of ...

hempei 〈へんぺい：へん平〉 flatness.
    hempei-soku (へん平足) a flatfoot
hempei-na 〈へん平な〉 flat.

hempi 〈へんぴ：辺ぴ〉
hempi-na 〈辺ぴな〉 remote, out-of-the-way.
    hempi-na basho (辺ぴな場所) an out-of-the-way place

hempin 〈へんぴん：返品〉 returned goods, articles sent back.
hempin-suru 〈返品する〉 return 〔goods〕.

hen 〈へん：篇〉 a chapter.
    dai-ippen (第一篇) the first chapter

hen 〈へん：編〉
    Yamada-hakase-hen-no kyôka-sho (山田博士編の教科書) a textbook compiled by Dr. Yamada

hen 〈へん：偏〉 a left-handed radical 〔of a Chinese character〕.

hen 〈へん：変〉
hen-na 〈変な〉 strange, queer.
    hen-na-koto-o-iu-yô-desu-ga (変なことを言うようですが) strange as it may sound
hen-ni 〈変に〉 strangely, singularly.
    hen-ni-omou (変に思う) feel ((it)) strange

hen 〈へん：辺〉 a part, neighborhood; a side.

    kono-hen-ni（この辺に）in this neighborhood

      doko-ka-kono-hen-ni（どこかこの辺に）somewhere about here

    san-kakkei no ippen（三角形の一辺）a side of a triangle

hen atsu 〈へんあつ：変圧〉 transformation.

    hen·atsu-ki（変圧器）a transformer

henchô 〈へんちょう：変調〉 irregularity, abnormality, anomaly.

    henchô-o-kitasu〈変調を来す〉become irregular, become abnormal, change for the worse.

henchô 〈へんちょう：偏重〉

    henchô-suru〈偏重する〉give too much importance ((to)).

henden 〈へんでん：返電〉 a reply telegram.

    henden-suru〈返電する〉wire back, reply by cable.

henden-sho 〈へんでんしょ：変電所〉 a (transformer) substation.

hendô 〈へんどう：変動〉 (a) change, fluctuation(s).

    bukka-no hendô（物価の変動）fluctuations in prices

    hendô-kawase-sôba（変動為替相場）the floating exchange rate

    hendô-suru〈変動する〉change, undergo a change, fluctuate, vary.

    hendô-no-hageshii〈変動の激しい〉fluctuating.

    hendô-no-nai（変動のない）unchanged.

henji 〈へんじ：返事〉 an answer, a reply.

    henji o uke-toru（返事を受け取る）receive an answer

    Go-henji-o-matteimasu.（御返事を待っています。）I am waiting for your answer.

    Ori-kaeshi go-henji-kudasai.（折り返し御返事下さい。）Please answer my letter by return (of) mail.

    henji-ni-komaru（返事に困る）be at a loss for an answer

    tegami-no-henji-o-dasu〈手紙の返事を出す〉answer a letter, reply to a letter.

    tegami-de henji-o-suru〈手紙で返事をする〉reply by letter.

henjin 〈へんじん：変人〉 an eccentric person, an oddity, a bigot.

henjô 〈へんじょう：返上〉

    henjô-suru〈返上する〉return, send back.

    kyûka o henjô-suru（休暇を返上する）give up one's vacation

henka 〈へんか：変化〉 (a) change, (a) variation.

    henka-suru〈変化する〉change, vary.

    henka-shi-yasui〈変化しやすい〉changeable, variable.

    henka-ni-tonda or *henka-no-aru*〈変化に富んだ，変化のある〉varied.

henka-ni-toboshii　*or*　henka-no-nai〈変化に乏しい，変化のない〉monotonous

henkaku〈へんかく：変革〉a change, a reform, a revolution.

henkan〈へんかん：返還〉return, restoration, retrocession.
　henkan-suru〈返還する〉return, restore, retrocede.

henkei〈へんけい：変形〉transformation, a modification, a variety.
　henkei-suru〈変形する〉change, transform, change ((into)), turn ((into)), be transformed ((into)).

henken〈へんけん：偏見〉(a) prejudice.
　henken-o-idaku〈偏見を抱く〉be prejudiced ((against)).
　henken-no-nai〈偏見のない〉without prejudice, impartial.

henkin〈へんきん：返金〉repayment, refundment.
　henkin-suru〈返金する〉pay back, repay, refund, reimburse.

henkô〈へんこう：変更〉(an) alteration, (a) change.
　　henkô o kuwaeru〈変更を加える〉make alterations ((in)), make a change ((in))
　henkô-suru〈変更する〉alter, change.
　ichibu-henkô-suru〈一部変更する〉modify.

henkô〈へんこう：偏向〉
　　sayoku-henkô〈左翼偏向〉leftwing leanings

henkutsu〈へんくつ：偏屈〉eccentricity; a bigot.
　henkutsu-na〈偏屈な〉bigoted.

henkyaku〈へんきゃく：返却〉return, repayment.
　henkyaku-suru〈返却する〉return, repay.

henkyô〈へんきょう：辺境〉a frontier, a border district.

henkyô〈へんきょう：偏狭〉
　henkyô-na〈偏狭な〉narrow-minded.

henkyoku〈へんきょく：編曲〉(an) arrangement.
　henkyoku-suru〈編曲する〉arrange.
　　kangen-gaku-ni-henkyoku-suru〈管弦楽に編曲する〉orchestrate

henkyû〈へんきゅう：返球〉
　henkyû-suru〈返球する〉return the ball ((to)).

hennyû〈へんにゅう：編入〉admission; incorporation.
　　hennyû-shiken〈編入試験〉an examination for entrance into a certain class
　hennyû-suru〈編入する〉admit ((into)), incorporate ((into)).

henrei〈へんれい：返礼〉a return present, a return call.
　henrei-suru〈返礼する〉make ((a person)) a present in return, return a

call.

~-no-henrei-ni〈～の返礼に〉in return for... .

hensa〈へんさ：偏差〉(a) deflection, (a) deviation, (a) variation.

　hyôjun-hensa（標準偏差）the standard deviation

hensai〈へんさい：返済〉repayment.

hensai-suru〈返済する〉pay back, return, repay.

hensai-o-semaru〈返済を迫る〉urge ((a person)) to pay back, press ((a person)) for repayment ((of)).

hensai-kigen-ga-kuru〈返済期限が来る〉be due.

　hensai-kigen-ga-sugite-iru（返済期限が過ぎている）be overdue

hensan〈へんさん：編さん〉compilation, editing.

　hensan-sha（編さん者）a compiler, an editor

hensan-suru〈編さんする〉compile, edit.

hensei〈へんせい：編成〉organization, formation, composition.

hensei-suru〈編成する〉organize, form, compose, draw up, make up.

　ressha o hensei-suru（列車を編成する）compose a train

　terebi-bangumi o hensei-suru（テレビ番組を編成する）draw up a TV program

　yosan o hensei-suru（予算を編成する）make up a budget

hensen〈へんせん：変遷〉changes, (a) transition, vicissitudes.

　jidai no hensen（時代の変遷）the change of times

hensen-suru〈変遷する〉change, shift.

hensha〈へんしゃ：編者〉an editor, a compiler.

henshi〈へんし：変死〉an unnatural death.

henshi-suru〈変死する〉die an unnatural death, be accidentally killed.

henshin〈へんしん：返信〉an answer, a reply.

　henshin-yô-hagaki（返信用はがき）a reply card

　henshin-ryô（返信料）return postage

henshin〈へんしん：変心〉a change of mind.

henshin-suru〈変心する〉change one's mind, play ((a person)) false.

henshin〈へんしん：変身〉metamorphosis.

henshin-suru〈変身する〉be metamorphosed ((into)).

henshitsu〈へんしつ：変質〉

　henshitsu-sha（変質者）a degenerate, a pervert

henshitsu-suru〈変質する〉change in quality, degenerate, deteriorate.

henshoku〈へんしょく：変色〉change of color.

henshoku-suru〈変色する〉change color, become discolored, fade.

henshoku〈へんしょく：偏食〉

henshoku-suru 〈偏食する〉 have an unbalanced diet.

henshu 〈へんしゅ：変種〉 a variety, a sport, a monster.

henshû 〈へんしゅう：編集〉 editing, compilation.

     henshû-bu（編集部） the editorial staff

     henshû-chô（編集長） the chief editor

     henshû-in（編集員） a staff member

     henshû-sha（編集者） an editor

henshû-suru 〈編集する〉 edit, compile.

hensô 〈へんそう：変装〉 (a) disguise.

hensô-suru 〈変装する〉 disguise oneself ((as)), be disguised ((as)).

hensô-shite 〈変装して〉 in disguise.

hensô 〈へんそう：返送〉

hensô-suru 〈返送する〉 return, send back.

hensoku 〈へんそく：変則〉 (an) irregularity, (an) anomaly.

hensoku-na 〈変則な〉 irregular, anomalous.

hen-suru 〈へんする：偏する〉 be partial, be biased, be one-sided.

hen-shita 〈偏した〉 partial, biased, prejudiced.

hentai 〈へんたい：変態〉 (an) abnormality.

     hentai-seiyoku（変態性欲） abnormal sexuality

hentai-teki(-na) 〈変態的(な)〉 abnormal.

hentai 〈へんたい：編隊〉 a formation.

     hentai-de tobu *or* hentai-hikô-o-suru（編隊で飛ぶ, 編隊飛行をする）
     fly in formation

hentô 〈へんとう：返答〉 *see.* henji.

hentô-sen 〈へんとうせん：へん桃せん〉 the tonsils.

     hentô-sen-en（へん桃せん炎） tonsillitis

     hentô-sen-hidai（へん桃せん肥大） swollen tonsils

henzô 〈へんぞう：変造〉 forgery.

     henzô-kahei（変造貨幣） a forged coin

henzô-suru 〈変造する〉 forge, falsify.

hen-zutsû 〈へんずつう：偏頭痛〉

hen-zutsû-ga-suru 〈偏頭痛がする〉 have a migraine.

hera 〈へら〉 a (tracing) spatula.

herasu 〈へらす：減らす〉 reduce, decrease, lessen, cut.

heru 〈減る〉 decrease, lessen, run low; wear out.

     taijû ga heru（体重が減る） lose weight

     Gasorin ga hette-kita.（ガソリンが減ってきた.） Gas is running low.

heri 〈へり〉 *see.* fuchi.

he-rikutsu〈へりくつ：へ理屈〉a pointless argument, quibbles.

　he-rikutsu-o-naraberu〈へ理屈を並べる〉argue for argument's sake, chop logic, quibble.

heru〈へる：経る〉pass, elapse, go by, pass(*or* go) through.

　Nyû-Yôku-o-hete（ニューヨークを経て）via New York

herunia〈ヘルニア〉(a) hernia, (a) rupture.

heso〈へそ〉the navel.

heso-kuri〈へそくり〉secret savings.

　heso-kuri-o-suru〈へそくりをする〉save up secretly〔for one's dress〕.

heta〈へた〉the calyx, the stem.

heta〈へた：下手〉

　〜-ga-heta-da〈〜が下手だ〉be poor at... .

　Kare-wa e-ga-heta-da.（彼は絵が下手だ.）He is poor at drawing.

　heta-na〈下手な〉poor.

hetabaru〈へたばる〉fall flat; become exhausted, be worn out, break down.

hetoheto〈へとへと〉

　hetoheto-ni-tsukareru（へとへとに疲れる）be dead tired, be tired out, be done up.

hetsurau〈へつらう〉flatter.

hetto〈ヘット〉beef fat.

heya〈へや：部屋〉a room, a chamber.

　roku-jō-no heya（六畳の部屋）a six-mat room

hi〈ひ：日〉a day, a date; the sun.

　hi ga tatsu-ni-tsurete（日がたつにつれて）as days go by

　hi-ni-hi-ni（日に日に）day by day

　hi o kimeru（日を決める）fix a date

　aru-hi（ある日）one day

　Hi ga noboru.（日が昇る.）The sun rises.

　Hi ga shizumu.（日が沈む.）The sun sets.

　Hi ga teru.（日が照る.）The sun shines.

　Hi ga kureru.（日が暮れる.）It gets dark.

　hi-de kawakasu（日で乾かす）dry ((a thing)) in the sun

　hi-ni ateru（日に当てる）expose ((a thing)) to the sun

hi〈ひ：火〉fire, a fire.

　hi o okosu（火を起こす）make a fire, build a fire

　hi-ni-ataru（火に当たる）warm oneself at the fire

　hi o kesu（火を消す）put out the fire

hi-o-tsukeru（火を付ける）set fire ((to)), set on fire
    tabako ni hi-o-tsukeru（たばこに火を付ける）light a cigarette
hi-ga-tsuku（火が付く）catch fire, take fire
Hi-no-yôjin.（火の用心。）Look out for fire.

hi〈ひ：灯〉a light.
    hi o tsukeru（灯を付ける）turn on the light
    hi o kesu（灯を消す）turn off the light
hi-ga-kieta-yô-ni-naru〈灯が消えたようになる〉become still as death, become deserted.

hi〈ひ：妃〉a princess, a consort.

hi〈ひ：碑〉a tombstone, a monument.

hi〈ひ：比〉(a) ratio; (a) comparison, a match.
    Ê-to-Bî no hi（AとBの比）the ratio of A to B
    Watashi-wa kanojo-no-hi-dewa-nai.（私は彼女の比ではない。）I am no match for her.

hi〈ひ：非〉a mistake, an error, a fault.
    hi o abaku（非を暴く）discover one's faults
    hi o satoru（非を悟る）see one's error
hi-no-uchi-dokoro-ga-nai〈非の打ちどころがない〉be faultless, be impeccable.

hi-〈ひ-：非-〉non-, un-, anti-, in-.
    hi-sentô-in（非戦闘員）a noncombatant
    hi-kagaku-teki(-na)（非科学的(な)）unscientific
    hi-geijutsu-teki(-na)（非芸術的(な)）inartistic

hi-agaru〈ひあがる：干上がる〉dry up, run dry.

hiai〈ひあい：悲哀〉(a) sorrow, (a) grief, sadness.
    jinsei no hiai（人生の悲哀）the sorrows of life
    gemmetsu-no-hiai-o-kanjiru（幻滅の悲哀を感じる）have a sad disillusionment
hiai-ni-michita〈悲哀に満ちた〉sorrowful, full of sorrow.

hi-atari〈ひあたり：日当たり〉
hi-atari-no-ii〈日当たりのいい〉sunny.
    hi-atari-no-warui（日当たりの悪い）unsunny, sunless, shadowy

hibachi〈ひばち：火鉢〉a brazier.
    hibachi-ni-ataru（火鉢に当たる）warm oneself at a brazier

hibai-hin〈ひばいひん：非売品〉an article not for sale, 'Not for sale.'

hibaku〈ひばく：被爆〉
hibaku-suru〈被爆する〉suffer from bombing.

hiban 〈ひばん：非番〉 off duty.
  hiban-no hi〈非番の日〉 a day off, an off day
hi-bana 〈ひばな：火花〉 a spark.
  hi-bana-o-chirasu〈火花を散らす〉 spark, give out sparks.
hibari 〈ひばり〉 a skylark, a lark.
hi-bashi 〈ひばし：火ばし〉 (a pair of) tongs.
hi-bashira 〈ひばしら：火柱〉 a pillar of flames.
hibi 〈ひび：日々〉 every day, day, day after day.
  hibi-no〈日々の〉 everyday, daily.
    hibi-no seikatsu（日々の生活） one's daily life
hibi 〈ひび〉 a crack.
  hibi-ga-hairu〈ひびが入る〉 crack, be cracked.
  hibi-no-haitta〈ひびの入った〉 cracked.
hibi 〈ひび〉 chaps.
  hibi-ga-kireru〈ひびが切れる〉 be chapped, chap.
  hibi-no-kireta〈ひびの切れた〉 chapped.
hibiki 〈ひびき：響き〉 a sound; an echo, an effect ((on)).
  hibiku〈響く〉 sound; be echoed, affect.
hibon 〈ひぼん：非凡〉
  hibon-na〈非凡な〉 extraordinary, uncommon, rare, unique, unusual, remarkable.
    hibon-na hito（非凡な人） a remarkable person
hi-boshi 〈ひぼし：日干し〉
  hi-boshi-ni-suru〈日干しにする〉 dry in the sun.
  hi-boshi-no〈日干しの〉 sun-dried.
hi-boshi 〈ひぼし：干ぼし〉
  hi-boshi-ni-naru〈干ぼしになる〉 be starved to death.
hibu 〈ひぶ：日歩〉 daily interest per 100 yen.
hi-bukure 〈ひぶくれ：火ぶくれ〉 a blister.
  hi-bukure-ga-dekiru〈火ぶくれができる〉 blister.
    yakedo-de hi-bukure-ni-naru（やけどで火ぶくれになる） get one's skin blistered from a burn
hi-busô 〈ひぶそう：非武装〉 demilitarization.
    hi-busô-chitai（非武装地帯） a demilitarized zone
  hi-busô-no〈非武装の〉 demilitarized, unarmed.
hi-buta 〈ひぶた：火ぶた〉
  hi-buta-o-kiru〈火ぶたを切る〉 open fire, fire the first gun.
    senkyo-sen-no-hi-buta-o-kiru（選挙戦の火ぶたを切る） start an e-

lection campaign

hida〈ひだ〉a pleat, a tuck.

   hida-o-toru〈ひだを取る〉pleat.

hidachi〈ひだち：肥立ち〉convalescence, recovery.

     sango-no-hidachi-ga-ii（産後の肥立ちがいい）be doing well after one's childbirth

hidai〈ひだい：肥大〉hypertrophy.

     shinzô-hidai（心臓肥大）hypertrophy of the heart

   hidai-shô-no〈肥大性の〉hypertrophic.

   hidai-shita〈肥大した〉swollen, enlarged, hypertrophied.

hidari〈ひだり：左〉(the) left.

     hidari-e mawaru（左へ回る）turn to the left

     hidari-te（左手）the left hand

   hidari-no〈左の〉left.

hidari-gawa〈ひだりがわ：左側〉the left side.

     Hidari-gawa-tsûkô.（左側通行.）Keep to the left.

   hidari-gawa-no〈左側の〉left(-hand).

   hidari-gawa-ni〈左側に〉on the left side.

hidari-kiki〈ひだりきき：左利き〉

   hidari-kiki-no〈左利きの〉left-handed.

hidari-mawari〈ひだりまわり：左回り〉

   hidari-mawari-no or *hidari-mawari-ni*〈左回りの，左回りに〉counterclockwise.

hidari-uchiwa〈ひだりうちわ：左うちわ〉

   hidari-uchiwa-de kurasu〈左うちわで暮らす〉live in great comfort.

hi-daruma〈ひだるま：火だるま〉

   hi-daruma-ni-naru〈火だるまになる〉be covered with flames.

hiden〈ひでん：秘伝〉a secret, the mysteries.

     hiden-o-tsutaeru（秘伝を伝える）initiate ((a person)) into the secrets ((of))

hi-denka〈ひでんか：妃殿下〉Her Imperial Highness.

hideri〈ひでり：日照り〉dry weather, a drought.

     hideri-tsuzuki（日照り続き）a spell of dry weather

hidô〈ひどう：非道〉

   hidô-na〈非道な〉inhuman, cruel, atrocious, infernal.

hidoi〈ひどい〉heavy, severe, bitter, serious, terrible, cruel, bad.

     hidoi ame（ひどい雨）a heavy rain

     hidoi samusa（ひどい寒さ）severe cold

　　　hidoi atsusa（ひどい暑さ）　terrible heat
　　　hidoi-me-ni-au（ひどい目に遭う）　have bitter experiences
　　　hidoi shiuchi（ひどい仕打ち）　cruel treatment
　　　hidoi kaze（ひどい風邪）　a bad cold
　hidoku〈ひどく〉heavily, severely, bitterly, seriously, terribly, cruelly, badly.
　　　hidoku shikarareru（ひどくしかられる）　be severely scolded
　　　hidoku shukketsu-suru（ひどく出血する）　bleed badly
　　　hidoku kane-ni-komatte-iru（ひどく金に困っている）　be badly in want of money
hi-dori〈ひどり：日取り〉the date.
　　　hi-dori o kimeru（日取りを決める）　fix the date
hiebie〈ひえびえ：冷え冷え〉
　hiebie-shita or *hiebie-suru*〈冷え冷えした，冷え冷えする〉chilly, cold.
hi-eisei-teki(-na)〈ひえいせいてき(な)：非衛生的(な)〉insanitary, unwholesome.
hie-komu〈ひえこむ：冷え込む〉get cold severely.
hieru〈ひえる：冷える〉get cold; feel chilly.
　　　Hie-nai-uchi-ni　meshi-agare.（冷えないうちに召し上がれ.）　Take it before it gets cold.
　　　Kesa wa totemo hiemasu-ne?（今朝はとても冷えますね.）　It's awfully chilly this morning, isn't it?
hie-shō〈ひえしょう：冷え性〉
　hie-shō-de-aru〈冷え性である〉have a cold constitution.
hifu〈ひふ：皮膚〉the skin.
　　　hifu-ga-arete-iru（皮膚が荒れている）　have a rough skin
　　　hifu-ga-yowai（皮膚が弱い）　have a delicate skin
　　　hifu-byō（皮膚病）　a skin disease
　　　hifu-ka（皮膚科）　dermatology
hifuku〈ひふく：被服〉clothing.
　　　hifuku-hi（被服費）　clothing expense
hifun〈ひふん：悲憤〉indignation, resentment.
　　　hifun no namida o nagasu（悲憤の涙を流す）　shed tears of indignation
　hifun-kōgai-suru〈悲憤こう慨する〉be indignant ((at or over)), deplore.
hi-gaeri〈ひがえり：日帰り〉
　　　hi-gaeri-ryokō（日帰り旅行）　a day's trip
　hi-gaeri-suru〈日帰りする〉go and return on the same day.

higai〈ひがい：被害〉damage, (an) injury, harm.

    higai-o-ataeru〈被害を与える〉do damage ((to))

    higai-o-kômuru〈被害を被る〉suffer damage ((from)), be damaged ((by))

    higai-o-manukareru〈被害を免れる〉come out undamaged

    higai-chi〈被害地〉the damaged district

    higai-sha〈被害者〉a sufferer, the injured, a victim

    higai-ga-karui〈被害が軽い〉suffer slightly ((from)).

    higai-ga-ookii〈被害が大きい〉suffer heavily ((from))

higami〈ひがみ〉a bias, (a) prejudice, (a) warp, (a) jaundice.

    higami-konjô〈ひがみ根性〉a jaundiced mind

    higamu〈ひがむ〉become jaundiced ((against)), be biased ((against)).

    higanda〈ひがんだ〉biased, prejudiced, jaundiced.

higan〈ひがん：彼岸〉the equinoctial week.

    higan-no-chûnichi〈彼岸の中日〉the spring equinox, the autumn equinox

hi-gasa〈ひがさ：日傘〉a parasol.

hi-gashi〈ひがし：干菓子〉dry confectionery.

higashi〈ひがし：東〉the east.

    higashi-kaze〈東風〉an east wind

    higashi-no〈東の〉east, eastern.

    higashi-e or *higashi-ni*〈東へ，東に〉east, eastward.

    ~-no-higashi-ni〈～の東に〉in the east of... , on the east of... , to the east of... .

hige〈ひげ：卑下〉

    hige-suru〈卑下する〉humble oneslf.

    hige-shite〈卑下して〉humbly, with humility.

hige〈ひげ〉a mustache, a beard, whiskers.

    hige o hayashite-iru〈ひげを生やしている〉wear a mustache

    hige-o-soru〈ひげをそる〉shave, get shaved.

higeki〈ひげき：悲劇〉(a) tragedy.

    higeki-teki(-na)〈悲劇的(な)〉tragic(al).

hi-genjitsu-teki(-na)〈ひげんじつてき(な)：非現実的(な)〉unreal.

    hi-genjitsu-teki-na keikaku〈非現実的な計画〉an impracticable plan

higo〈ひご：ひ護〉protection, patronage.

    higo-suru〈ひ護する〉protect, shelter, shield.

    ~-no-higo-no-moto-ni〈～のひ護の下に〉under the protection(*or* patronage) of... .

hi-gôhô 〈ひごうほう：非合法〉
hi-gôhô-ka-suru 〈非合法化する〉illegalize, outlaw.
hi-gôhô-na 〈非合法な〉illegal, unlawful.

higoro 〈ひごろ：日ごろ〉usually, always.
　　higoro-no okonai （日ごろの行い）one's everyday conduct
higoro-kara 〈日ごろから〉for a long time.

hi-gure 〈ひぐれ：日暮れ〉nightfall, twilight, evening.
hi-gure-mae-ni 〈日暮れ前に〉before dark.

hihan 〈ひはん：批判〉(a) criticism.
　　jiko-hihan （自己批判）(a) self-criticism
hihan-suru 〈批判する〉criticize.
hihan-o-ukeru 〈批判を受ける〉be criticized ((by)), face criticism.
hinan-teki(-na) 〈批判的(な)〉critical.

hihei 〈ひへい：疲弊〉impoverishment, exhaustion, ruin.
hihei-suru 〈疲弊する〉become impoverished, be exhausted.

hihô 〈ひほう：悲報〉sad news, the news of ((a person's)) death.

hihô 〈ひほう：秘法〉a secret method, a secret recipe.

hihyô 〈ひひょう：批評〉(a) critique, (a) criticism, a review.
　　hihyô-ka （批評家）a critic, a reviewer
hihyô-suru 〈批評する〉criticize, review.

hiideru 〈ひいでる：秀でる〉surpass, excel.
hiideta 〈秀でた〉distinguished, prominent.
　　hiideta sainô （秀でた才能）unusual ability

hiiki 〈ひいき〉(a) favor, patronage; partiality.
hiiki-ni-suru or *hiiki-suru* 〈ひいきにする，ひいきする〉favor, patronize; be partial ((to)).
hiiki-me-ni miru 〈ひいき目に見る〉see ((a thing)) in a favorable light.
hiiki-no 〈ひいきの〉favorite.

hiiragi 〈ひいらぎ〉a holly (tree).

hiji 〈ひじ〉an elbow.
　　hiji o tsuku （ひじをつく）rest one's elbows ((upon))

hi-jindô-teki(-na) 〈ひじんどうてき(な)：非人道的(な)〉inhumane.

hijô 〈ひじょう：非常〉an emergency.
　　hijô-jitai （非常事態）a state of emergency
　　hijô-shudan （非常手段）an emergency measure
　　Hijô-guchi. （非常口.）Emergency Exit. / Fire Exit.
　　hijô-no-sai-niwa （非常の際には）in case of emergency

hijô 〈ひじょう：非情〉

hijō-no〈非情の〉inanimate; coldhearted.

hi-jôkin〈ひじょうきん：非常勤〉(a) part-time service.
hi-jôkin-kôshi（非常勤講師）a part-time teacher
hi-jôkin-no〈非常勤の〉part-time.

hijô-ni〈ひじょうに：非常に〉very, much, greatly, highly, extremely.
hijô-ni omoshiroi hon（非常に面白い本）a very interesting book
Watashi-wa sore ga hijô-ni suki-desu.（私はそれが非常に好きです。）I like it very much.
hijô-ni omonjiru（非常に重んじる）esteem highly

hijô-sen〈ひじょうせん：非常線〉a (police) cordon, a fire line.
hijô-sen o haru（非常線を張る）form a cordon
hijô-sen o toppa-suru（非常線を突破する）break through a cordon

hi-jôshiki〈ひじょうしき：非常識〉lack of common sense.
hi-jôshiki-mo-hanahadashii〈非常識も甚だしい〉be quite ridiculous.
hi-jôshiki-na〈非常識な〉thoughtless, absurd, ridiculous.

hijū〈ひじゅう：比重〉specific gravity; relative importance.
〜-yori-mo-ookina-hijū-o-shimeru〈〜よりも大きな比重を占める〉have a greater importance than ((in)), be given much weight ((in)).

hijun〈ひじゅん：批准〉ratification.
hijun-suru〈批准する〉ratify.

hijutsu〈ひじゅつ：秘術〉a secret art, the mysteries.
hijutsu-o-tsukushite-tataku（秘術を尽くして戦う）fight to the best of one's skill

hika-〈ひか-：皮下-〉
hika-chûsha（皮下注射）hypodermic injection
hika-shibô（皮下脂肪）subcutaneous fat
hika-no〈皮下の〉hypodermic, subcutaneous.

hikae〈ひかえ：控え〉a note, a memo, a copy.
hikae o toru（控えを取る）take a copy ((of))

hikae-me〈ひかめ：控え目〉
hikae-me-no〈控え目の〉moderate, conservative.
hikae-me-no mitsumori（控え目の見積もり）a conservative estimate
hikae-me-ni〈控え目に〉moderately, conservatively.
hikae-me-ni-suru（控え目にする）be moderate ((in))

hikaeru〈ひかえる：控える〉be moderate ((in)), refrain ((from)); take notes ((of)), write down; have.
tabe-mono-o-hikaeru（食べ物を控える）be moderate in eating
tabako-o-hikaeru（たばこを控える）refrain from smoking

nyūshi-o-mokuzen-ni-hikaete〈入試を目前に控えて〉with the entrance examination just before one

hikae-shitsu〈ひかえしつ：控え室〉an anteroom, an antechamber, a waiting room.

hikage〈ひかげ：日陰〉the shade.

hikage-de yasumu（日陰で休む）take a rest in the shade

hikage-no〈日陰の〉shady, in the shade.

hikaku〈ひかく：皮革〉hides, leather.

hikaku-seihin（皮革製品）a leather article

gōsei-hikaku（合成皮革）synthetic leather

hikaku〈ひかく：比較〉comparison.

hikaku-ni-nara-nai（比較にならない）cannot compare ((with))

hikaku-suru〈比較する〉compare ((A with B)).

hikaku-teki(-ni)〈比較的(に)〉comparatively.

〜-to-hikaku-suru-to〈〜と比較すると〉compared with... , in comparison with... .

hikan〈ひかん：悲観〉pessimism, disappointment.

hikan-suru〈悲観する〉be pessimistic ((about *or* of)), be disappointed.

hikan-teki(-na)〈悲観的(な)〉pessimistic.

hikan-teki-ni〈悲観的に〉pessimistically.

hi-karabiru〈ひからびる：干からびる〉dry up, be dried up.

hi-karabita〈干からびた〉dried-up, withered, wizened.

hikarasu〈ひからす：光らす〉make ((a thing)) shine, luster, polish.

hikareru〈ひかれる〉be fascinated, be charmed ((by *or* with)).

hikari〈ひかり：光〉(a) light, rays.

hoshi-no-hikari（星の光）starlight

taiyō-no hikari（太陽の光）the rays of the sun

hikaru〈ひかる：光る〉shine, flash, twinkle, glitter, sparkle.

Inazuma ga hikatta.（稲妻が光った.）The lightning flashed.

hikasareru〈ひかされる：引かされる〉

oya-ko-no-jō-ni-hikasareru〈親子の情に引かされる〉be drawn by the ties of parent and child.

hike〈ひけ：引け〉a defeat, a weak point.

hike-o-toru〈引けを取る〉be beaten ((by)), be defeated ((by)), be inferior ((to)).

hike-o-tora-nai（引けを取らない）be second to none, be behind nobody, prove oneself equal to anyone

hike-doki〈ひけどき：引け時〉the closing hour.

hike-me 〈ひけめ：引け目〉 a weak point, a drawback.

  hike-me-o-kanjiru〈引け目を感じる〉 feel small, feel cheap, feel inferior ((to)).

hikeru 〈ひける：引ける〉

    Kaisha wa go-ji-ni hikeru.（会社は五時に引ける。） The office closes at five.

    Ikura-ka hikemasu-ka?（いくらか引けますか？） Can you make any reduction?

    ki-ga-hikeru（気が引ける） feel ill at ease, become self-conscious

hiketsu 〈ひけつ：秘けつ〉 a secret ((of)), a key ((to)).

    seikô no hiketsu（成功の秘けつ） the secret of success

hiketsu 〈ひけつ：否決〉 rejection.

  hiketsu-suru〈否決する〉 reject, vote against.

hiki 〈ひき：悲喜〉

    hiki-komogomo-de-aru（悲喜こもごもである） have a mingled feeling of joy and sorrow

hiki 〈ひき：引き〉 patronage, (a) favor, backing, support, help, influence, a pull.

  ii-hiki-ga-aru〈いい引きがある〉 have a good backing, be well-connected ((with)), have a strong pull ((with)).

  〜-no-hiki-de〈〜の引きで〉 through the influence of... .

hiki-age 〈ひきあげ：引き上(揚)げ〉 drawing up; (a) withdrawal; salvage; a raise.

    chingin no hiki-age（賃金の引き上げ） a raise in wages

  hiki-ageru〈引き上(揚)げる〉 draw up; withdraw ((from)); salvage; raise.

    guntai o hiki-ageru（軍隊を引き揚げる） withdraw the armies

    chimbotsu-sen o hiki-ageru（沈没船を引き上げる） salvage a sunken ship

hiki-ai 〈ひきあい：引き合い〉 reference; an inquiry.

    takusan hiki-ai-ga-aru（たくさん引き合いがある） have many inquiries

  hiki-ai-ni-dasu〈引き合いに出す〉 refer ((to)), cite as an example.

hiki-au 〈ひきあう：引き合う〉 pay (off), be profitable.

    hiki-au shôbai（引き合う商売） a paying business

hiki-awase 〈ひきあわせ：引き合わせ〉 (an) introduction, (a) presentation; (a) comparison, (a) check.

  hiki-awaseru〈引き合わせる〉 introduce, present; compare, check.

    gembo-to hiki-awaseru（原簿と引き合わせる） check ((it)) with the ledger

hiki-chigiru〈ひきちぎる：引きちぎる〉tear off, wrench off.

hiki-dashi〈ひきだし：引き出し〉a drawer.
　　hiki-dashi o akeru（引き出しを開ける）open a drawer

hiki-dasu〈ひきだす：引き出す〉pull out, draw out.
　　ginkô-kara kane o hiki-dasu（銀行から金を引き出す）draw some of
　　　one's money from the bank

hikide-mono〈ひきでもの：引き出物〉a present, a gift.

hiki-do〈ひきど：引き戸〉a sliding door.

hiki-gaeru〈ひきがえる〉a toad.

hiki-gane〈ひきがね：引き金〉a trigger.
　hiki-gane-o-hiku〈引き金を引く〉pull the trigger, trigger.

hiki-gatari〈ひきがたり：弾き語り〉
　hiki-gatari-o-suru〈弾き語りをする〉accompany oneself ((on)).

hiki-geki〈ひきげき：悲喜劇〉a tragicomedy.

hiki-hanasu〈ひきはなす：引き離す〉draw ((persons *or* things)) apart;
　run ahead ((of)), outdistance, outrun.

hiki-harau〈ひきはらう：引き払う〉
　　Tôkyô-o-hiki-harau（東京を引き払う）remove from Tokyo
　　ie-o-hiki-harau（家を引き払う）clear out of a house

hiki-ireru〈ひきいれる：引き入れる〉take ((a person)) into, drag into; win
　((a person)) over ((to)), entice ((a person)) into.

hikiiru〈ひきいる：率いる〉lead, command, be in command ((of)).

hiki-kae〈ひきかえ：引き換え〉exchange.
　　hiki-kae-ken（引換券）an exchange ticket
　　daikin-hiki-kae-barai（代金引換払い）cash on delivery
　hiki-kaeru〈引き換える〉exchange.
　hiki-kae-ni〈引き換えに〉in exchange ((for)).

hiki-kaesu〈ひきかえす：引き返す〉turn back, return.
　　tochû-de hiki-kaesu（途中で引き返す）turn back halfway

hiki-komoru〈ひきこもる：引きこもる〉stay indoors.
　　byôki-de-hiki-komoru（病気で引きこもる）be confined to one's bed,
　　　be laid up

hiki-komu〈ひきこむ：引き込む〉*see.* hiki-ireru.

hiki-korosu〈ひきころす：ひき殺す〉kill ((a person)) by running over.

hikin〈ひきん：卑近〉
　hikin-na〈卑近な〉familiar, common, plain, simple.
　　hikin-na rei o ageru（卑近な例を挙げる）give a familiar example

hiki-nige〈ひきにげ：ひき逃げ〉

　　hiki-nige-jiken〈ひき逃げ事件〉a hit-and-run case

　　hiki-nige-suru〈ひき逃げする〉hit and run.

hiki-niku〈ひきにく：引き肉〉minced meat.

hiki-nobashi〈ひきのばし：引き伸(延)ばし〉enlargement; prolongation.

　　hiki-nobashi-shashin〈引き伸ばし写真〉an enlarged photograph

　　hiki-nobashi-saku〈引き延ばし策〉a delay move, a filibustering

　　hiki-nobasu〈引き伸(延)ばす〉enlarge; prolong, extend, stretch out.

hiki-nuki〈ひきぬき：引き抜き〉pulling out; picking out.

　　hiki-nuku〈引き抜く〉extract, pull out, uproot; pick out, hire away.

hi-kinzoku〈ひきんぞく：非金属〉a nonmetal.

hiki-okosu〈ひきおこす：引き起こす〉cause, bring about.

　　mendô o hiki-okosu〈面倒を引き起こす〉get into trouble

hiki-sagaru〈ひきさがる：引き下がる〉retire, withdraw ((from)), leave; bow oneself off, beg off.

hiki-sage〈ひきさげ：引き下げ〉reduction, lowering, a cut.

　　bukka no hiki-sage〈物価の引き下げ〉the reduction of prices

　　chingin-no hiki-sage〈賃金の引き下げ〉a wage cut

　　hiki-sageru〈引き下げる〉reduce, lower, cut down.

hiki-saku〈ひきさく：引き裂く〉tear up, tear in pieces.

　　tegami o hiki-saku〈手紙を引き裂く〉tear a letter in pieces

hiki-shimaru〈ひきしまる：引き締まる〉tighten, be tightened, be braced up.

　　hiki-shimatta〈引き締まった〉tightened, tight, firm.

　　hiki-shimatta kao〈引き締まった顔〉firm features

　　hiki-shimatta karada〈引き締まった体〉a firm-fleshed body

hiki-shime〈ひきしめ：引き締め〉tightening.

　　kin･yû-hiki-shime-seisaku〈金融引き締め政策〉a tight money policy

　　hiki-shimeru〈引き締める〉tighten, stiffen, brace.

　　ki o hiki-shimeru〈気を引き締める〉brace oneself up

hikishio〈ひきしお：引き潮〉an ebb tide.

hiki-taosu〈ひきたおす：引き倒す〉pull down.

hiki-tate〈ひきたて：引き立て〉(a) favor, patronage, support, backing (up), recommendation.

　　〜-no-hiki-tate-de〈〜の引き立てで〉under the patronage of... .

　　hiki-tateru〈引き立てる〉favor, patronize, support, back (up); rouse; set off, enhance.

　　ki-o-hiki-tateru〈気を引き立てる〉cheer up

hiki-tate-yaku〈ひきたてやく：引き立て役〉a setoff, a foil.

hiki-tatsu 〈ひきたつ：引き立つ〉look better, improve.

hiki-te 〈ひきて：引き手〉a handle, a knob, a catch.

hiki-tomeru 〈ひきとめる：引き止める〉detain.
　nagaku-hiki-tomeru（長く引き止める）keep ((a person)) long

hiki-tori-nin 〈ひきとりにん：引き取り人〉a claimant.
　Itai-no-hiki-tori-nin-ga-nakatta.（遺体の引き取り人がなかった.）No
　one claimed the body.

hiki-toru 〈ひきとる：引き取る〉take over, take (back).
　Watashi-ga sono ko o hiki-tori-mashô.（私がその子を引き取りましょ
　う.）I'll take over the child.
　iki-o-hiki-toru（息を引き取る）breathe one's last, die

hiki-tsugi 〈ひきつぎ：引き継ぎ〉taking over, handing over.
　hiki-tsugu 〈引き継ぐ〉take over.
　jimu o hiki-tsugu（事務を引き継ぐ）take over ((another's)) duties

hiki-tsuke 〈ひきつけ：引き付け〉(a) convulsion.

hiki-tsukeru 〈ひきつける：引き付ける〉draw, attract, charm, fascinate,
magnetize.
　hito-o-hiki-tsukeru-chikara（人を引き付ける力）attraction, charm,
　magnetism

hiki-tsuru 〈ひきつる：引きつる〉have a cramp, be cramped, twitch.
　ashi-ga-hiki-tsuru（足が引きつる）have a cramp in the leg

hiki-tsuzuite 〈ひきつづいて：引き続いて〉*see.* hiki-tsuzuki.

hiki-tsuzuki 〈ひきつづき：引き続き〉
　Hiki-tsuzuki Y-shi-no-kôen-ga-aru-yotei.（引き続きY氏の講演がある予
　定.）Then Mr.Y will give a lecture.
　hiki-tsuzuki go-aiko-o-kou（引き続き御愛顧を請う）solicit a contin-
　uance of ((a person's)) favor

hiki-tsuzuku 〈ひきつづく：引き続く〉continue, keep, last, follow one
after another.
　hiki-tsuzuku ame（引き続く雨）a continuous rain

hiki-uke 〈ひきうけ：引き受け〉undertaking; acceptance.
　hiki-uke-nin（引き受け人）a guarantor, an acceptor
　hiki-ukeru 〈引き受ける〉undertake, take over; accept; guarantee, vouch
　((for)).
　muzukashii shigoto o hiki-ukeru（難しい仕事を引き受ける）under-
　take a difficult task
　tegata o hiki-ukeru（手形を引き受ける）accept a bill
　mimoto-o-hiki-ukeru（身元を引き受ける）vouch for a person

hiki-wake 〈ひきわけ：引き分け〉a drawn game, a draw, a tie.
hiki-wake-ni-naru or *hiki-wake-ni-owaru* 〈引き分けになる，引き分けに終わる〉end in a tie, draw ((with)).

hiki-watashi 〈ひきわたし：引き渡し〉delivery, transfer, handing over.
hiki-watasu 〈引き渡す〉deliver, transfer, hand over.

hiki-yoseru 〈ひきよせる：引き寄せる〉draw ((a thing)) near.

hiki-zan 〈ひきざん：引き算〉subtraction.
hiki-zan-suru 〈引き算する〉subtract.

hiki-zuru 〈ひきずる：引きずる〉drag.
ashi-o-hikizutte-aruku〈足を引きずって歩く〉drag oneself along
hiki-zuri-komu〈引きずり込む〉drag in
hiki-zuri-mawasu〈引きずり回す〉drag about

hikkakaru 〈ひっかかる：引っ掛かる〉catch, be caught ((by or in)); get entangled ((with)); be tricked, be cheated.
kugi-ni-hikkakaru〈くぎに引っ掛かる〉catch on a nail
warui onna-ni hikkakaru〈悪い女に引っ掛かる〉be entangled with a bad woman
hikkakeru 〈引っ掛ける〉have ((one's coat)) caught; entrap, cheat.

hikkaki-mawasu 〈ひっかきまわす：引っかき回す〉ransack, rummage; carry matters with a high hand.

hikkaku 〈ひっかく：引っかく〉scratch, claw.
kao-o-hikkakareru〈顔を引っかかれる〉be scratched on the face

hikkei 〈ひっけい：必携〉
hikkei-no 〈必携の〉indispensable ((to)).

hikki 〈ひっき：筆記〉
hikki-shiken〈筆記試験〉a written examination
hikki-suru 〈筆記する〉write down, take notes ((of)).

hikkiri-nashi-ni 〈ひっきりなしに：引っ切り無しに〉incessantly, continually, without a break, without interruption.
hikkiri-nashi-ni denwa-ga-kakaru〈ひっきりなしに電話が掛かる〉have telephone calls without a break

hikkomeru 〈ひっこめる：引っ込める〉pull in, move back; withdraw, drop, disclaim.
yôkyû o hikkomeru〈要求を引っ込める〉drop the demand

hikkomi(-) 〈ひっこみ(-)：引っ込み(-)〉
hikkomi-sen〈引っ込み線〉a railway siding, a service wire, a lead-in wire
hikkomi-ga-tsuka-nai 〈引っ込みが付かない〉go too far to retreat.

hikkomi-gachi-no 〈引っ込みがちの〉 retiring, stay-at-home.

hikkomi-jian-no 〈引っ込み思案の〉 conservative, retiring, shy, backward.

hikkomu 〈ひっこむ：引っ込む〉 draw back, retire; stand back.

  inaka-e hikkomu 〈田舎へ引っ込む〉 retire into the country

  ie-ni-hikkonde-iru 〈家に引っ込んでいる〉 keep indoors

  Sono biru wa oo-doori-kara-hikkonda-tokoro-ni-aru. 〈そのビルは大通りから引っ込んだ所にある.〉 The building stands back from the main street.

hikkoshi 〈ひっこし：引っ越し〉

  hikkoshi-nimotsu 〈引っ越し荷物〉 one's property to be moved

hikkosu 〈引っ越す〉 move ((in *or* to)), remove ((in *or* to)).

hikkuri-kaeru 〈ひっくりかえる：引っくり返る〉 be upset, capsize, tumble down; fall on one's back.

  Watashi-tachi-no bôto ga hikkuri-kaetta. 〈私たちのボートが引っくり返った.〉 Our boat capsized.

hikkuri-kaesu 〈引っくり返す〉 upset, capsize, tumble down; turn upside down, turn inside out.

hikkurumeru 〈ひっくるめる：引っくるめる〉

hikkurumete 〈引っくるめて〉 (al)together, in all.

  -~-o-hikkurumete 〈～を引っくるめて〉 including...

hikô 〈ひこう：非行〉 an evil deed.

  hikô-shônen 〈非行少年〉 a juvenile delinquent

hikô 〈ひこう：飛行〉 a flight, flying.

  yakan-hikô 〈夜間飛行〉 a night flight

hikô-suru 〈飛行する〉 fly, make a flight.

hikô-gumo 〈ひこうぐも：飛行雲〉 a vapor trail.

hikô-jô 〈ひこうじょう：飛行場〉 an airfield, an airdrome, an airport.

hi-kôkai 〈ひこうかい：非公開〉

hi-kôkai-de okonawareru 〈非公開で行われる〉 be held behind closed doors

hi-kôkai-no 〈非公開の〉 exclusive, secret, not open to the public, closed-door.

hikô-ki 〈ひこうき：飛行機〉 an airplane.

  hikô-ki ni noru 〈飛行機に乗る〉 take an airplane

  hikô-ki-ni-you 〈飛行機に酔う〉 get airsick

hikoku 〈ひこく：被告〉 a defendant, the accused.

  hikoku-seki 〈被告席〉 the dock

hi-kôshiki 〈ひこうしき：非公式〉

hi-kôshiki-no〈非公式の〉informal, unofficial.

hi-kôshiki-ni〈非公式に〉informally, unofficially.

hikô-tei〈ひこうてい：飛行艇〉a flying boat.

hiku〈ひく：引く〉draw, pull; attract; lay on, install; catch; consult, look up; subtract, reduce; draw.

> kâten o hiku（カーテンを引く）draw a curtain

> kuruma o hiku（車を引く）pull a cart

> chûi o hiku（注意を引く）attract ((a person's)) attention

> gasu o hiku（ガスを引く）lay on gas

> kaze o hiku（風邪をひく）catch cold

> jisho-o-hiku（辞書を引く）consult a dictionary, look up a word in a dictionary

> hachi-kara san o hiku（八から三を引く）subtract 3 from 8

> nedan o hiku（値段を引く）reduce the price

> kuji o hiku（くじを引く）draw lots

> abura-o-hiku（油を引く）oil

hiku〈ひく：引く〉retreat; retire, resign, leave; abate, ebb, sink.

> Netsu ga hiku.（熱が引く.）The fever abates.

> Shio ga hiiteiru.（潮が引いている.）The tide is ebbing.

> Mizu ga hiiteiru.（水が引いている.）The water is going down.

hiku〈ひく：弾く〉play.

> piano o hiku（ピアノを弾く）play the piano

hiku〈ひく〉run over, knock ((a person)) down.

hikareru〈ひかれる〉be run over, be knocked down.

hiku〈ひく〉saw; grind.

> maruta-o-hiite-ita-ni-suru（丸太をひいて板にする）saw a log into boards

> ko-mugi-o-hiite-kona-ni-suru（小麦をひいて粉にする）grind wheat into flour

hikui〈ひくい：低い〉low, short; low.

> hikui yama（低い山）a low hill

> se-no-hikui hito（背の低い人）a short person

> hikui koe-de（低い声で）in a low voice

hikuku〈低く〉low.

> hikuku-naru（低くなる）become low

> hikuku-suru（低くする）make low, lower

hiku-te〈ひくて：引く手〉

hiku-te-amata-de-aru〈引く手あまたである〉be much sought after, have a number of suitors.

hikutsu 〈ひくつ：卑屈〉
　hikutsu-na 〈卑屈な〉 mean-spirited, servile, sneaking, unmanly.
　　hikutsu-na taido 〈卑屈な態度〉 a sneaking attitude

hikyô 〈ひきょう：卑きょう〉 cowardice.
　　hikyô-mono 〈卑きょう者〉 a coward
　hikyô-na 〈卑きょうな〉 cowardly, unmanly, mean, unfair.

hikyô 〈ひきょう：秘境〉 mysterious regions.

hi-kyôryoku 〈ひきょうりょく：非協力〉
　hi-kyôryoku-teki(-na) 〈非協力的(な)〉 uncooperative.

hima 〈ひま：暇〉 time, leisure, spare time, time to spare.
　　hima o tsubusu 〈暇をつぶす〉 kill time
　　hima-doru 〈暇取る〉 take time, be delayed
　　hima-na-toki-ni 〈暇なときに〉 at one's leisure
　　hima-ga-aru 〈暇がある〉 have time to spare, be free
　　hima-ga-nai 〈暇がない〉 have no time to spare, be engaged
　　Kyô-gogo o-hima-desu-ka? 〈今日午後お暇ですか。〉 Will you be free
　　　this afternoon?

himan 〈ひまん：肥満〉
　　himan-ji 〈肥満児〉 an obese child
　himan-suru 〈肥満する〉 grow corpulent.
　himan-shita 〈肥満した〉 obese, corpulent.

himashi-ni 〈ひましに：日増しに〉 day by day.

himashi-yu 〈ひましゆ：ひまし油〉 castor oil.

hima-tsubushi 〈ひまつぶし：暇つぶし〉
　　hima-tsubushi-o-suru 〈暇つぶしをする〉 *see.* hima o tsubusu
　　hima-tsubushi-ni 〈暇つぶしに〉 to kill time

himawari 〈ひまわり〉 a sunflower.

hime 〈ひめ：姫〉 a princess.

himei 〈ひめい：碑銘〉 an epitaph.

himei 〈ひめい：悲鳴〉 a shriek, a scream.
　himei-o-ageru 〈悲鳴を上げる〉 scream, shriek.

himen 〈ひめん：罷免〉 dismissal, discharge.
　himen-suru 〈罷免する〉 dismiss, discharge.
　himen-ni-naru 〈罷免になる〉 be dismissed, be discharged.

himeru 〈ひめる：秘める〉
　　mune-ni himeru 〈胸に秘める〉 keep ((something)) all to oneself
　himerareta 〈秘められた〉 hidden, secret.

hi-minshu-teki(-na) 〈ひみんしゅてき(な)：非民主的(な)〉 undemocratic.

himitsu 〈ひみつ：秘密〉 a secret.

    himitsu o mamoru （秘密を守る） keep a secret

    himitsu o morasu （秘密を漏らす） let out a secret

    himitsu o abaku （秘密を暴く） reveal a secret

    himitsu-kessha （秘密結社） a secret society

    himitsu-shorui （秘密書類） a secret document

    kōzen-no himitsu （公然の秘密） an open secret

    himitsu-no 〈秘密の〉 secret.

    himitsu-ni 〈秘密に〉 secretly, in secret.

    himitsu ni suru （秘密にする） keep ((a matter)) secret

himmoku 〈ひんもく：品目〉 a list of articles; an item.

    eigyō-himmoku （営業品目） business items

himo 〈ひも〉 a string, a cord, a band, a strap.

    himo o musubu （ひもを結ぶ） tie the strings

    himo o toku （ひもを解く） untie the strings

    himo ga tokeru （ひもが解ける） strings come untied

himojii 〈ひもじい〉 hungry.

    himojii-omoi-o-suru （ひもじい思いをする） feel hungry

hi-mono 〈ひもの：干物〉 dried fish.

    hi-mono-ni-suru 〈干物にする〉 dry fish.

hi-moto 〈ひもと：火元〉 the origin of a fire.

himo-tsuki 〈ひもつき：ひも付き〉

    himo-tsuki-no 〈ひも付きの〉 with strings attached.

himpan 〈ひんぱん：頻繁〉

    himpan-na 〈頻繁な〉 frequent.

    kōtsū-no-himpan-na toori （交通の頻繁な通り） a busy street

    himpan-ni 〈頻繁に〉 frequently, very often.

    Chikagoro-wa kōtsū-jiko ga himpan-ni okoru. （近ごろは交通事故が頻繁に起こる。） Traffic accidents frequently happen lately.

himpatsu 〈ひんぱつ：頻発〉 frequent occurrence, frequency.

    himpatsu-suru 〈頻発する〉 occur frequently.

himpin-to 〈ひんぴんと：頻々と〉 frequently, very often.

himpu 〈ひんぷ：貧富〉 wealth and poverty, (the) rich and (the) poor.

    himpu-no-sa （貧富の差） the gulf between rich and poor

himpyō 〈ひんぴょう：品評〉 (a) criticism, (a) comment.

    himpyō-kai （品評会） a competitive show, a contest, a fair

    himpyō-suru 〈品評する〉 criticize, comment ((on)).

hin 〈ひん：品〉elegance, (a) grace, dignity, refinement.

  hin-no-aru 〈品のある〉elegant, graceful, dignified, refined.

    hin-no-nai〈品のない〉 unrefined, coarse

hina 〈ひな〉a chicken, a chick, a young bird.

hina- 〈ひな-〉

    hina-matsuri〈ひな祭り〉 the Doll's Festival

    hina-ningyô〈ひな人形〉 a doll

hinabita 〈ひなびた〉rustic, countrified.

hi-naga 〈ひなが：日長〉a long day.

    haru-no-hi-naga-ni〈春の日長に〉 in springtime when the days are long

hina-gata 〈ひながた：ひな形〉a model, a pattern, a specimen; a form.

hina-geshi 〈ひなげし〉a red poppy.

hina-giku 〈ひなぎく：ひな菊〉a daisy.

hinan 〈ひなん：非難〉blame, criticism.

    hinan no mato〈非難の的〉 the target of criticism

  hinan-suru〈非難する〉blame, censure.

  hinan-no-yochi-ga-nai〈非難の余地がない〉be beyond reproach

  hinan-su-beki〈非難すべき〉blamable.

hinan 〈ひなん：避難〉refuge, shelter,

    hinan-suru〈避難する〉 take refuge ((in)), find shelter ((in))

hinata 〈ひなた：日なた〉a sunny place.

  hinata-de〈日なたで〉in the sun.

    hinata-de hosu〈日なたで干す〉 dry in the sun

hinata-bokko 〈ひなたぼっこ：日なたぼっこ〉

  hinata-bokko-suru〈日なたぼっこする〉bask in the sun.

hindo 〈ひんど：頻度〉frequency.

    shiyô-hindo〈使用頻度〉 frequency in use

hinekureru 〈ひねくれる〉become crooked, become perverse, be warped.

  hinekureta〈ひねくれた〉crooked, perverse, distorted.

    hinekureta seishitsu〈ひねくれた性質〉 a crooked disposition

    hinekureta kangae〈ひねくれた考え〉 a distorted view

hineri- 〈ひねり-〉

    hineri-dasu〈ひねり出す〉 squeeze out, devise, work out

    hineri-mawasu〈ひねり回す〉 play ((with)), tinker ((with))

    hineri-tubusu〈ひねりつぶす〉 crush ((a thing)) with one's fingers

hineru 〈ひねる〉twist, incline.

　　sen-o-hinette-gasu-o-dasu（栓をひねってガスを出す）turn on the gas

hineta〈ひねた〉precocious.

hin・i〈ひんい：品位〉dignity.
　　hin・i o tamotsu（品位を保つ）keep one's dignity
　hin・i-no-aru〈品位のある〉dignified.

hiniku〈ひにく：皮肉〉(a) cynicism, (a) sarcasm, (an) irony.
　　ummei no hiniku（運命の皮肉）the irony of fate
　　hiniku-ya（皮肉屋）a cynic, an ironist
　hiniku-o-iu〈皮肉を言う〉make cynical remarks, speak ironically.
　hiniku-na〈皮肉な〉cynical, sarcastic, ironical.
　hiniku-ni-mo〈皮肉にも〉ironically.

hinin〈ひにん：否認〉denial, disavowal.
　hinin-suru〈否認する〉deny, disavow.

hinin〈ひにん：避妊〉contraception, birth control.
　　hinin-yaku（避妊薬）a contraceptive (pill)
　hinin-suru〈避妊する〉prevent conception, practice birth control.

hinjaku〈ひんじゃく：貧弱〉
　　naiyô-ga-hinjaku-da（内容が貧弱だ）be poor in content
　hinjaku-na〈貧弱な〉poor, scanty, meager.

hinketsu〈ひんけつ：貧血〉anemia.
　hinketsu-shô-no〈貧血症の〉anemic.

hinkô〈ひんこう：品行〉conduct, behavior, demeanor.
　　hinkô-hôsei-na hito（品行方正な人）a man of good conduct

hinkon〈ひんこん：貧困〉poverty, lack.
　　seiji-no hinkon（政治の貧困）political poverty

hinku〈ひんく：貧苦〉hardships of poverty.

hinkyû〈ひんきゅう：貧窮〉*see.* hinkon *or* hinku.

hi-nobe〈ひのべ：日延べ〉postponement, adjournment, deferment, extension of the term.
　hi-nobe-suru〈日延べする〉postpone, put off, defer, extend.

hi-no-de〈ひので：日の出〉sunrise.

hi-no-iri〈ひのいり：日の入り〉sunset.

hi-no-ke〈ひのけ：火の気〉heat of fire.
　hi-no-ke-no-nai〈火の気のない〉unheated.

hinoki〈ひのき〉a Japanese cypress.

hinoki-butai〈ひのきぶたい：ひのき舞台〉
　　hinoki-butai-o-fumu（ひのき舞台を踏む）perform on a first-class stage, stand in the limelight

hi-no-ko 〈ひのこ：火の粉〉 sparks (of fire).

Hi-no-ko ga mai-agari-dashita.〔火の粉が舞い上がり出した.〕 Sparks began to shoot up in the air.

hi-no-kuruma 〈ひのくるま：火の車〉

Kaisha wa zutto hi-no-kuruma-da.〔会社はずっと火の車だ.〕 The company has been hard up for money.

hi-no-maru 〈ひのまる：日の丸〉 the rising-sun flag.

hi-no-me 〈ひのめ：日の目〉

hi-no-me-o-miru 〈日の目を見る〉 see the light of day, be realized.

hi-no-me-o-mi-nai（日の目を見ない） be shelved, be tabled

hi-no-te 〈ひので：火の手〉 the flames, the fire.

hi-no-te-ga-agaru 〈火の手が上がる〉 burst into flame, flame up.

hinsei 〈ひんせい：品性〉(a) character.

hinsei-no-geretsu-na hito（品性の下劣な人） a person of mean character

hinshi 〈ひんし：ひん死〉

hinshi-no 〈ひん死の〉 dying.

hinshi-no jôtai（ひん死の状態） a dying condition

hinshi-no-jûshô-o-ou（ひん死の重傷を負う） be fatally injured

hinshi 〈ひんし：品詞〉a part of speech.

hinshitsu 〈ひんしつ：品質〉 quality.

hinshitsu-no-ii（品質のいい） of good quality

hinshitsu-no-otoru（品質の劣る） of inferior quality

hinshu 〈ひんしゅ：品種〉a kind, a sort, a breed.

hinshu no kairyô（品種の改良） improvement of breed(*or* plants)

hinsô 〈ひんそう：貧相〉

hinsô-na 〈貧相な〉 poor-looking.

hinsuru 〈ひんする〉

hametsu-ni-hinsuru（破滅にひんする） be on the brink of ruin

shi-ni-hinshite-iru（死にひんしている） be on the verge of death

hinto 〈ヒント〉a hint.

hinto o ataeru（ヒントを与える） give a hint

hinyô-ki 〈ひにょうき：泌尿器〉the urinary organs.

hinyô-ki-ka（泌尿器科） urology

hi-ooi 〈ひおおい：日覆い〉a sunshade, a sunscreen, a blind.

hippaku 〈ひっぱく：ひっ迫〉 pressure, stringency, tightness.

hippaku-suru 〈ひっ迫する〉be tight, be stringent, be pressed ((for)).

Kin·yû ga hippaku-shite-iru.〔金融がひっ迫している.〕 The money

market is tight.

hippari-dako 〈ひっぱりだこ：引っ張りだこ〉
 hippari-dako-ni-naru 〈引っぱりだこになる〉 be eagerly sought after 〔by others〕, be in great demand.

hipparu 〈ひっぱる：引っ張る〉 pull, draw.
 mimi-o-hipparu（耳を引っ張る） pull ((a person)) by the ear

hippô 〈ひっぽう：筆法〉a style of penmanship.

hira-ayamari 〈ひらあやまり：平謝り〉
 hira-ayamari-ni-ayamaru 〈平謝りに謝る〉 make a humble apology.

hirai-shin 〈ひらいしん：避雷針〉a lightning rod.

hirakeru 〈ひらける：開ける〉 develop, be opened to traffic; become sensible.
 Kono machi wa dandan hirakete-kita.（この町はだんだん開けてきた.）
  This town has developed gradually.
 hiraketa hito（開けた人） a sensible person

hiraki 〈ひらき：開き〉a (hinged) door; (a) difference, (a) disparity.
 ryôsha-no nenrei no hiraki（両者の年齢の開き） the disparity in age between the two

hiraki-naoru 〈ひらきなおる：開き直る〉 assume a defiant attitude, turn ((upon))

hiraku 〈ひらく：開く〉 open, uncover, unbind; hold, give; bloom.
 Ginkô wa ku-ji-ni hiraku.（銀行は九時に開く.） The bank opens at 9.
 mise o hiraku（店を開く） open a store
 kai o hiraku（会を開く） hold a meeting

hirame 〈ひらめ〉a flatfish, a flounder.

hirameki 〈ひらめき〉a flash.
 inazuma no hirameki（稲妻のひらめき） a flash of lightning
 tensai no hirameki（天才のひらめき） a flash of genius
 hirameku 〈ひらめく〉flash.

hira-oyogi 〈ひらおよぎ：平泳ぎ〉the breaststroke.

hiratai 〈ひらたい：平たい〉flat, even, level.

hira-te 〈ひらて：平手〉
 hira-te-de-utsu 〈平手で打つ〉slap, give ((a person)) a slap.

hira-ya 〈ひらや：平屋〉a one-story house.

hire 〈ひれ〉a fin.

hirei 〈ひれい：比例〉(a) proportion, (a) ratio.
 hirei-suru 〈比例する〉be proportionate ((to)), be in proportion ((to)).
 〜*-ni-hirei-shite* 〈〜に比例して〉in proportion to... .

hire-niku〈ヒレにく：ヒレ肉〉a fillet, (a) tenderloin, (an) undercut.

hiretsu〈ひれつ：卑劣〉

hiretsu-na〈卑劣な〉mean, base, iow.

 hiretsu-na shudan（卑劣な手段）a mean trick

hiretsu-na-koto-o-suru〈卑劣なことをする〉play ((a person)) foul.

hirihiri〈ひりひり〉

hirihiri-suru〈ひりひりする〉smart; taste hot.

hirihiri-saseru〈ひりひりさせる〉bite.

hiritsu〈ひりつ：比率〉(a) ratio, (a) percentage.

 go-san-ni-no hiritsu（五、三、二の比率）the five-three-two ratio

hirô〈ひろう：披露〉(an) announcement, (an) introduction.

 kekkon-hirô-en（結婚披露宴）a wedding reception, an after-wedding celebration

hirô-suru〈披露する〉announce, introduce.

hirô〈ひろう：疲労〉fatigue, exhaustion.

 hirô-ga-toreru（疲労が取れる）get over one's fatigue

hirô-suru〈疲労する〉be tired, become fatigued.

hiro-ba〈ひろば：広場〉an open space, a square, a plaza.

 eki-mae-hiro-ba（駅前広場）a station square

hirobiro-to〈ひろびろと：広々と〉

hirobiro-to-shita〈広々とした〉open, extensive, wide, spacious.

 hirobiro-to-shita nohara（広々とした野原）an open field

 hirobiro-to-shita heya（広々とした部屋）a spacious room

hirogari〈ひろがり：広がり〉an extent, an expanse.

 hateshi-nai hirogari（果てしない広がり）a boundless expanse

hirogaru〈ひろがる：広がる〉spread, get abroad, expand, extend.

 Sono uwasa wa patto hirogatta.（そのうわさはぱっと広がった.）The rumor spread rapidly.

hirogeru〈広げる〉spread, expand, extend, enlarge, widen

 chizu o hirogeru（地図を広げる）spread a map

 te-o-hirogeru（手を広げる）expand one's business

 mise o hirogeru（店を広げる）enlarge a shop

 michi o hirogeru（道を広げる）widen a road

hiroi〈ひろい：広い〉wide, broad, extensive, spacious.

 hiroi chishiki（広い知識）wide knowledge

 hiroi kokoro（広い心）a broad mind

 hiroi robî（広いロビー）a spacious lobby

 kôsai-no-han·i-ga-hiroi（交際の範囲が広い）have a large circle of

acquaintances

hiroku 〈広く〉 widely, extensively.

    hiroku-shirarete-iru 〈広く知られている〉 be widely known

hiroku-suru 〈広くする〉 widen, broaden, enlarge.

hiroku-naru 〈広くなる〉 be widened, be broadened, be enlarged.

hiroi-mono 〈ひろいもの：拾い物〉 a thing found 〔on the road〕.

hiroi-mono-o-suru 〈拾い物をする〉 find something ((on)), make a rare find.

hiroi-nushi 〈ひろいぬし：拾い主〉 the finder 〔of lost property〕.

hiroi-yomi 〈ひろいよみ：拾い読み〉

hiroi-yomi-suru 〈拾い読みする〉 skip ((over)), skim (through), browse in the pages, read here and there.

hiro-ma 〈ひろま：広間〉 a hall, a saloon.

hiromaru 〈ひろまる：広まる〉 spread, get abroad; become popular.

    Uwasa wa sugu hiromaru. 〈うわさはすぐ広まる。〉 Rumors spread fast.

hiromeru 〈広める〉 spread, diffuse, propagate; extend, widen, broaden.

    atarashii shûkyô o hiromeru 〈新しい宗教を広める〉 propagate a new religion

hi-ronri-teki(-na) 〈ひろんりてき(な)；非論理的(な)〉 illogical.

hirosa 〈ひろさ：広さ〉 (an) extent, (an) area.

    hirosa hyaku-heihô-mêtoru 〈広さ百平方メートル〉 one hundred square meters in area

hirou 〈ひろう：拾う〉 pick up, find, gather.

    ko-ishi o hirou 〈小石を拾う〉 pick up a pebble

    michi-de saifu o hirou 〈道で財布を拾う〉 find a purse on the street

    kai-gara o hirou 〈貝殻を拾う〉 gather shells

hiru 〈ひる〉 a leech.

hiru 〈ひる：昼〉 the daytime, day, noon.

    hiru-wa 〈昼は〉 in the daytime

    hiru-hinaka-ni 〈昼日中に〉 in broad daylight

    hiru-mae-ni 〈昼前に〉 before noon

    hiru-sugi-ni 〈昼過ぎに〉 early in the afternoon

hirugaeru 〈ひるがえる：翻る〉 wave, flutter.

    kaze-ni hirugaeru 〈風に翻る〉 flutter in the wind

hirugaesu 〈ひるがえす：翻す〉 change; wave; fly.

    zengen o hirugaesu 〈前言を翻す〉 eat one's words

    Nihon-no kokki o hirugaesu 〈日本の国旗を翻す〉 fly the Japanese flag

mi-o-hirugaeshite nigeru〈身を翻して逃げる〉swing round and run away

hirugao〈ひるがお：昼顔〉a bindweed.

hiru-gohan〈ひるごはん：昼御飯〉*see.* hiru-meshi.

hirui〈ひるい：比類〉
hirui-no-nai〈比類のない〉matchless, unequaled, unrivaled, unparalleled.

hiru-ma〈ひるま：昼間〉day, the daytime.

hiru-meshi〈ひるめし：昼飯〉lunch.

hirumu〈ひるむ〉flinch ((from)), shrink ((from)), be daunted ((by)).
hirumazu-ni〈ひるまずに〉without flinching, nothing daunted.

hiru-ne〈ひるね：昼寝〉a nap.
hiru-ne-suru〈昼寝する〉take a nap.

hiru-yasumi〈ひるやすみ：昼休み〉a lunch break, a noon recess.

hiryô〈ひりょう：肥料〉manure, (a) fertilizer.
kagaku-hiryô（化学肥料）chemical fertilizer
hiryô-o-yaru〈肥料をやる〉manure, fertilize.

hisai〈ひさい：被災〉*see.* risai.

hisan〈ひさん：悲惨〉misery, wretchedness.
hisan-na〈悲惨な〉miserable, wretched.
hisan-na seikatsu（悲惨な生活）a wretched life

hisan〈ひさん：飛散〉
hisan-suru〈飛散する〉scatter, fly.

hisashi〈ひさし〉eaves, a pent roof; a visor, a peak.
hisashi-no-tsuita bôshi（ひさしの付いた帽子）a peaked cap

hisashi-buri〈ひさしぶり：久し振り〉
hisashi-buri-no or hisashi-buri-ni〈久し振りの，久し振りに〉after a long time.
hisashi-buri-no-ame（久し振りの雨）rain after a long spell of fine weather
hisashi-buri-ni ie-ni-kaeru（久し振りに家に帰る）return home after a long absence
hisashi-buri-ni au（久し振りに会う）meet after a long separation
hisashi-buri-ni tegami o morau（久し振りに手紙をもらう）receive a letter ((from a person)) after a long silence

hisashii〈ひさしい：久しい〉long.
hisashiku〈久しく〉long, for a long time.

hi-seisan-teki(-na)〈ひせいさんてき(な)：非生産的(な)〉unproductive, unfruitful.

hi-senkyo-ken〈ひせんきょけん：被選挙権〉eligibility for election.
hisha〈ひしゃ：飛車〉a castle, a rook.
hi-shakô-teki(-na)〈ひしゃこうてき(な)：非社交的(な)〉unsociable.
hishaku〈ひしゃく〉a ladle, a dipper.
　hishaku-de-mizu-o-kumu〈ひしゃくで水をくむ〉ladle water.
hisha-tai〈ひしゃたい：被写体〉a subject.
hishi-gata〈ひしがた：ひし形〉a rhomb, a rhombus.
　hishi-gata-no〈ひし形の〉rhombic, diamond-shaped.
hishihishi-to〈ひしひしと〉
　hishihishi-to-mune-ni-kotaeru〈ひしひしと胸にこたえる〉come　home　to
　　one's heart.
hishimeku〈ひしめく〉jostle, throng ((to)); clamor.
hishi-to〈ひしと〉
　hishi-to　daki-shimeru〈ひしと抱きしめる〉press　((a　person　*or*　a　thing))
　　tightly to one's bosom.
hisho〈ひしょ：秘書〉a secretary.
hisho〈ひしょ：避暑〉summering.
　　　hisho-chi〈避暑地〉a summer resort.
　hisho-ni-iku〈避暑に行く〉go to a summer resort.
　　　Izu-e hisho-ni-iku〈伊豆へ避暑に行く〉go to Izu for the summer
hiso〈ひそ：ひ素〉arsenic.
　　　hiso-chûdoku〈ひ素中毒〉arsenical poisoning
hisô〈ひそう：皮相〉
　hisô-na〈皮相な〉superficial, shallow.
　　　hisô-na mikata〈皮相な見方〉a superficial view ((of))
hisô〈ひそう：悲壮〉
　hisô-na〈悲壮な〉pathetic, tragic.
　　　hisô-na saigo o togeru〈悲壮な最期を遂げる〉meet a tragic death
　　　hisô-na kakugo-de〈悲壮な覚悟で〉with a grim resolution
hisohiso〈ひそひそ〉
　　　hisohiso-banashi〈ひそひそ話〉a whispering talk
　hisohiso-banashi-o-suru or *hisohiso-to hanashi-o-suru*〈ひそひそ話をする,
　　ひそひそと話をする〉talk in whispers.
hisoka-ni〈ひそかに〉secretly, in secret.
　　　kokoro-hisoka-ni〈心ひそかに〉in one's heart
hisomeru〈ひそめる：潜める〉
　　　mi o hisomeru〈身を潜める〉conceal oneself ((behind, in *or* under))
　　　koe o hisomeru〈声を潜める〉lower one's voice

koe-o-hisomete（声を潜めて）in a low voice

hisomu〈潜む〉lie concealed, conceal oneself ((in)).

hisomeru〈ひそめる〉knit, frown.

mayu-o-hisomete〈まゆをひそめて〉with knitted brows, with a frown.

hissan〈ひっさん：筆算〉doing sums on a piece of paper.

hisseki〈ひっせき：筆跡〉handwriting.

hisseki-kantei（筆跡鑑定）handwriting analysis

hissha〈ひっしゃ：筆者〉the writer, the author.

hisshi〈ひっし：必至〉

hisshi-de-aru〈必至である〉be inevitable, be unavoidable.

hisshi〈ひっし：筆紙〉

hisshi-ni-tsukushi-gatai〈筆紙に尽くしがたい〉be beyond description.

hisshi〈ひっし：必死〉

hisshi-no〈必死の〉desperate, frantic.

hisshi-no doryoku o suru（必死の努力をする）make desperate efforts

hisshi-ni-natte〈必死になって〉desperately, frantically.

hisshō〈ひっしょう：必勝〉

hisshō-o-kisu（必勝を期す）be certain of victory

hisshō-o-kishite tatakau（必勝を期して戦う）fight with a firm conviction of ultimate victory

hisshū-kamoku〈ひっしゅうかもく：必修科目〉*see*. hissu-kamoku.

hissori〈ひっそり〉

hissori-shita〈ひっそりした〉quiet, still, silent, hushed, deserted.

Machi-wa-hissori-shite-ita.（街はひっそりしていた.）All was hushed in the streets.

hissori-to〈ひっそりと〉quietly, still, silently.

hissu-〈ひっす−：必須−〉

hissu-jōken（必須条件）an essential condition

hissu-kamoku（必須科目）a required subject

hissu-no〈必須の〉indispensable, essential, necessary, requisite.

hisui〈ひすい〉green jadeite.

hisutamin〈ヒスタミン〉histamine.

kô-hisutamin-zai（抗ヒスタミン剤）an antihistamine

hisuterī〈ヒステリー〉hysteria, hysterics.

hisuterî-o-okosu（ヒステリーを起こす）fall into hysterics

hisuterî(-shô)-no〈ヒステリー(性)の〉hysteric(al).

hitahita(-to)〈ひたひた(と)〉

Saza-nami ga hitahita-to kishi-ni uchi-yoseru.（さざ波がひたひたと岸

に打ち寄せる。) Little waves lap against the shore.

hitai 〈ひたい：額〉 the forehead, the brow.

hita-muki 〈ひたむき〉
  hita-muki-na 〈ひたむきな〉 earnest, single-minded.
  hita-muki-ni 〈ひたむきに〉 earnestly, single-mindedly, devotedly.

hitan 〈ひたん：悲嘆〉 grief, sorrow, lamentation.
  hitan-ni-kureru 〈悲嘆に暮れる〉 be grieved ((at)), be heartbroken ((at)).
  hitan-no-amari 〈悲嘆の余り〉 out of grief.

hitasu 〈ひたす：浸す〉 soak ((in)), dip ((in)).

hitasura 〈ひたすら〉 earnestly, from the bottom of one's heart; solely.
  chichi-no kaifuku-no-hayai-koto-o-hitasura-inoru 〈父の回復の早いこと
  をひたすら祈る〉 earnestly pray for my father's speedy recovery

hitchū 〈ひっちゅう：必中〉
  ippatsu-hitchū-o-nerau 〈一発必中をねらう〉 try to hit the target with the
  first shot.

hitei 〈ひてい：否定〉 (a) denial, negation.
  hitei-suru 〈否定する〉 deny.
  hitei-teki(-na) 〈否定的(な)〉 negative.

hito 〈ひと：人〉 man, mankind; a man, a person, one, people; others;
  character.
    shinsetsu-na hito 〈親切な人〉 a kind man
    Katô-san-to-iu-hito 〈加藤さんという人〉 a Mr. Kato
    Hito-wa-mina byôdô-de-aru. 〈人は皆平等である。〉 All men are equal.
    hito-no-warukuchi-o-iu 〈人の悪口を言う〉 speak ill of others
    Kare-wa uso o iu-yô-na-hito-dewa-nai. 〈彼はうそを言うような人ではな
    い。〉 He is not a man to tell a lie.
    hito-o-miru-me-ga-aru 〈人を見る目がある〉 be able to judge people's
    character
  hito-no-ii 〈人のいい〉 good-natured.
    hito-no-warui 〈人の悪い〉 ill-natured

hito-ame 〈ひとあめ：一雨〉
    Hito-ame-hoshii. 〈一雨ほしい。〉 Rain is much needed.

hito-ashi 〈ひとあし：一足〉 a step.
    Gakkô-made hon-no hito-ashi-desu. 〈学校まではんの一足です。〉 It is
    only a step to the school.

hito-atari 〈ひとあたり：人当たり〉
  hito-atari-ga-ii 〈人当たりがいい〉 be affable.

hito-awa 〈ひとあわ：一泡〉

hito-awa-fukaseru〈一泡吹かせる〉confound, take ((a person)) unawares.

hito-ban〈ひとばん：一晩〉a night, one evening.

yûbe-hito-ban-jû（ゆうべ一晩中）all last night

hito-barai〈ひとばらい：人払い〉

O-hito-barai-o-o-negai-shimasu.（お人払いをお願いします。）I should like to speak to you in private.

hitobito〈ひとびと：人々〉men, people.

oozei-no hitobito（大勢の人々）large crowds of people

hito-chigai〈ひとちがい：人違い〉

hito-chigai-o-suru〈人違いをする〉take one person for another.

hito-dakari〈ひとだかり：人だかり〉a crowd〔of people〕.

hito-dakari-ga-suru〈人だかりがする〉a crowd gathers, be crowded with people.

hito-danomi〈ひとだのみ：人頼み〉dependence on others.

hito-danomi-suru〈人頼みする〉ask others to help.

hito-dasuke〈ひとだすけ：人助け〉

hito-dasuke-ni-naru〈人助けになる〉be of some help to others.

hito-dasuke-o-suru〈人助けをする〉help other people in trouble, do ((a person)) a good turn.

hito-de〈ひとで：人手〉a hand; help, assistance.

hito-de-ga-tari-nai（人手が足りない）be short of hands

hito-de-ni-wataru（人手に渡る）pass into other hands

hito-de-o-kari-nai-de（人手を借りないで）without assistance

hito-de〈ひとで：人出〉a crowd (of people).

hito-de-ga-ooi〈人出が多い〉be crowded (with people).

hitode〈ひとで〉a starfish.

hito-doori〈ひとどおり：人通り〉traffic.

Koko-wa hito-doori-ga-ooi.（ここは人通りが多い．）There is a heavy traffic here.

hitoe〈ひとえ〉an unlined *kimono*.

hito-e-mabuta〈ひとえまぶた：一重まぶた〉a single-edged eyelid.

hito-fuki〈ひとふき：一吹き〉a blow; a blast, a puff.

hito-gara〈ひとがら：人柄〉(a) personality.

hito-gara-no-ii〈人柄のいい〉good-natured.

hito-giki〈ひとぎき：人聞き〉

hito-giki-no-ii〈人聞きのいい〉respectable, decent.

hito-giki-no-warui（人聞きの悪い）disreputable, indecent

hito-goe〈ひとごえ：人声〉a (sound of) voice.

hito-gokochi 〈ひとごこち：人心地〉
  hito-gokochi-ga-tsuku 〈人心地がつく〉come to oneself; feel oneself.

hito-gomi 〈ひとごみ：人込み〉a crowd.
    hito-gomi-o-kaki-wakete-susumu（人込みをかき分けて進む）push one's way through a crowd

hito-goroshi 〈ひとごろし：人殺し〉murder; a murderer.
    hito-goroshi o suru（人殺しをする）commit murder

hito-goto 〈ひとごと：人事〉other people's concern.

hito-ichi-bai 〈ひといちばい：人一倍〉
  hito-ichi-bai hataraku（人一倍働く）work harder than others.

hito-iki 〈ひといき：一息〉
    hito-iki-tsuku（一息つく）take breath, take a rest
    Mô hito-iki-da.（もう一息だ。）Make one more effort.

hito-jichi 〈ひとじち：人質〉a hostage.
    hito-jichi-ni-suru（人質にする）take ((a person)) in hostage

hito-kado 〈ひとかど：一かど〉
    hito-kado-no-jimbutsu-ni-naru（一かどの人物になる）make something of oneself
    hito-kado-no-jimbutsu-da-to-omou（一かどの人物だと思う）think oneself somebody

hito-kage 〈ひとかげ：人影〉the shadow of a person, a (human) figure.

hitokata-naranu 〈ひとかたならぬ：一方ならぬ〉
    Oba-niwa hitokata-naranu-o-sewa-ni-natta.（叔(伯)母には一方ならぬお世話になった。）I owe a great deal to my aunt.

hito-ke 〈ひとけ：人気〉
  hito-ke-ga-nai〈人気がない〉be deserted.
  hito-ke-no-nai〈人気のない〉deserted, empty.
    hito-ke-no-nai michi（人気のない道）an empty road

hito-kire 〈ひときれ：一切れ〉a piece, a slice.
    niku-hito-kire（肉一切れ）a slice of meat

hito-kiwa 〈ひときわ：一際〉
  hito-kiwa-medatsu〈一際目立つ〉be conspicuous, stand out conspicuously.

hito-koto 〈ひとこと：一言〉a (single) word.
    hito-koto-mo-iwa-nai-de（一言も言わないで）without saying a word

hito-kuchi 〈ひとくち：一口〉a mouthful, a bite, a draft; a word.
    hito-kuchi-ni taberu（一口に食べる）eat ((something)) at a mouthful
    hito-kuchi-ni nomu（一口に飲む）drink at a draft

　　hito-kuchi-ni-ieba〈一口に言えば〉in a word, in short

hito-kuse〈ひとくせ：一癖〉

　　hito-kuse-ari-sô-na otoko（一癖ありそうな男）a man with a sly look

hito-mae〈ひとまえ：人前〉

　　hito-mae-ni-deru-koto-o-kirau（人前に出ることを嫌う）shun company

　　hito-mae-o-tsukurou（人前を繕う）save appearances

　hito-mae-de〈人前で〉before others, in public, in company.

　hito-mae-o-habakarazu-ni〈人前をはばからずに〉despite of the presence of others, openly.

hito-makase〈ひとまかせ：人任せ〉

　hito-makase-ni-suru〈人任せにする〉leave ((a matter)) to others.

hito-mane〈ひとまね：人まね〉mimicry.

　　hito-mane-ga-umai（人まねがうまい）have a turn for mimicry

　hito-mane-o-suru〈人まねをする〉mimic.

hito-matome〈ひとまとめ：一まとめ〉a bunch, a bundle.

　hito-matome-ni-suru〈一まとめにする〉collect, put together.

　hito-matome-ni-shite〈一まとめにして〉in a bunch, in a bundle.

hito-mawari〈ひとまわり：一回り〉a turn, a round; a size.

　　hito-mawari-ookii（一回り大きい）be a size larger ((than))

　hito-mawari-suru〈一回りする〉take a turn, go one's rounds.

hito-mazu〈ひとまず：一まず〉for a while, for the time being, for the present.

hito-me〈ひとめ：一目〉a look, a glance.

　　hito-me-miru（一目見る）have a look ((at))

　　hito-me-de（一目で）at a glance

hito-me〈ひとめ：人目〉(public) notice, attention.

　　hito-me o hiku（人目を引く）attract attention

　　hito-me o sakeru（人目を避ける）avoid public notice

　　hito-me-o-shinonde（人目を忍んで）in secret, secretly

　　hito-me-ni-tsuku basho（人目に付く場所）a conspicuous place

hitomi〈ひとみ〉the pupil〔of the eye〕.

hito-mishiri〈ひとみしり：人見知り〉

　hito-mishiri-suru〈人見知りする〉be shy of strangers.

hito-mukashi〈ひとむかし：一昔〉an age, a generation, a decade.

　　Jû-nen hito-mukashi.（十年一昔。）Ten years makes an epoch.

　hito-mukashi-mae〈一昔前〉a decade age, an age ago.

hito-nami〈ひとなみ：人並み〉

　hito-nami-no〈人並みの〉common, ordinary, average.

hito-nami-no seikatsu（人並みの生活）　an ordinary standard of living

hito-nami-ijô-no〈人並み以上の〉above the average, more than average.

hito-nami-hazureta〈人並み外れた〉uncommon, extraordinary.

hito-nami-ni〈人並みに〉like others.

hito-nami-ni-kurasu（人並みに暮らす）　make a decent living

hito-natsuk(k)oi〈ひとなつ(っ)こい：人懐(っ)こい〉affable, amiable, friendly.

hito-nemuri〈ひとねむり：一眠り〉

hito-nemuri-suru〈一眠りする〉have a nap.

hitori〈ひとり：一人〉one person.

hitori-hitori *or* hitori-zutsu（一人一人，一人ずつ）one by one, one after another

hitori-nokorazu（一人残らず）every one (of them), all (together), to the last man

hitori-mo〜nai〈一人も〜ない〉no one, nobody.

Hitori-mo sono-koto-o shitte-iru-mono-wa-i²nai.（一人もそのことを知っている者はいない。）Nobody knows it.

hitori-aruki〈ひとりあるき：独り歩き〉

Onna-no-yoru-no-hitori-aruki-wa　abunai.（女の夜の独り歩きは危ない。）It is not safe for a woman to go out alone at night.

hitori-aruki-suru〈独り歩きする〉go alone.

hitori-atari〈ひとりあたり：一人当たり〉a head.

hitori-botchi〈ひとりぼっち：独りぼっち〉

hitori-botchi-ni-naru〈独りぼっちになる〉be left alone.

hitori-botchi-no〈独りぼっちの〉lonely, solitary.

hitori-butai〈ひとりぶたい：独り舞台〉

hitori-butai-de-aru〈独り舞台である〉stand unrivaled.

hitori-butai-no〈独り舞台の〉without a rival.

hitori-dachi〈ひとりだち：独り立ち〉

hitori-dachi-suru〈独り立ちする〉*see.* dokuritsu-suru.

hitori-de〈ひとりで：一人で，独りで〉alone, by oneself, for oneself.

hitori-de kurasu（独りで暮らす）*see.* hitori-gurashi-o-suru

Hitori-de sore-o yari-nasai.（独りでそれをやりなさい。）Do it yourself.

hitori-de-ni〈ひとりでに：独りでに〉of itself.

Genkan-no-to ga hitori-de-ni aita.（玄関の戸が独りでに開いた。）The front door opened of itself.

hitori-gaten〈ひとりがてん：独り合点〉

hitori-gaten-suru〈独り合点する〉take ((it)) for granted ((that)), jump to a conclusion.

hitori-goto〈ひとりごと：独り言〉

hitori-goto-o-iu〈独り言を言う〉talk to oneself.

hitori-gurashi〈ひとりぐらし：独り暮らし〉a single life.

hitori-gurashi-o-suru〈独り暮らしをする〉live by oneself, live alone.

hitorikko〈ひとりっこ：一人っ子〉an only child.

hitori-mono〈ひとりもの：独り者〉*see.* dokushin.

hitori-yogari〈ひとりよがり：独り善がり〉

hitori-yogari-no〈独り善がりの〉self-satisfied, self-complacent.

hitori-zumō〈ひとりずもう：独り相撲〉

hitori-zumō-o-toru〈独り相撲を取る〉beat the air.

hito-sashi-yubi〈ひとさしゆび：人差し指〉a forefinger, an index finger.

hito-sawagase〈ひとさわがせ：人騒がせ〉

hito-sawagase-o-suru〈人騒がせをする〉raise a false alarm, cause a scare, cry wolf.

hito-sawagase-na〈人騒がせな〉sensational.

　hito-sawagase-na-otoko（人騒がせな男）a scaremonger

hitoshii〈ひとしい：等しい〉be equal ((to)), be equivalent ((to)).

hitoshii〈等しい〉equal.

hitoshiku〈等しく〉equally.

　hitoshiku wakeru（等しく分ける）divide equally

hitoshiku-suru〈等しくする〉equalize.

hito-shirenu〈ひとしれぬ：人知れぬ〉unknown to other people, unseen, inward.

hito-shirezu〈人知れず〉secretly, unseen, inwardly.

hito-soroi〈ひとそろい：一そろい〉a set, a suit.

　gorufu-kurabu-hito-soroi（ゴルフクラブ一そろい）a set of golf clubs

hito-suji〈ひとすじ：一筋〉

hito-suji-ni〈一筋に〉earnestly, single-heartedly.

　geidō-hito-suji-ni-ikiru（芸道一筋に生きる）devote oneself all one's life to his art alone

hito-suji-nawa〈ひとすじなわ：一筋縄〉

hito-suji-nawa-de-ikanu〈一筋縄でいかぬ〉be very hard to deal with.

hito-tamari〈ひとたまり：一たまり〉

hito-tamari-mo-naku〈一たまりもなく〉very easily; helplessly.

　hito-tamari-mo-naku makeru（一たまりもなく負ける）be very easily defeated

hito-toki〈ひととき：一時〉a time.

　　　tanoshii hito-toki o sugosu（楽しい一時を過ごす）　have a good time

hito-to-nari〈ひととなり〉one's disposition, one's personality.

hito-toori〈ひととおり：一通り〉in a general way, briefly, thoroughly.

　　　hito-toori-me-o-toosu（一通り目を通す）　run (one's eyes) through

　　　hito-toori-no-koto o hanasu（一通りのことを話す）　give ((a person))
　　　　an outline of the matter

hitotsu〈ひとつ：一つ〉one, each, the same; just.

　　　hitotsu-zutsu（一つずつ）　one by one

　　　hitotsu-ya-futatsu-no　ayamari（一つや二つの誤り）　one　mistake　or
　　　　two

　　　mô-hitotsu（もう一つ）　one more

　　　hitotsu-hyaku-en（一つ百円）　100 yen each

　　　Mono-oto-hitotsu　shi-nakatta.（物音一つしなかった.）　Not　a　sound
　　　　was heard.

　　　hitotsu-heya-ni kurasu（一つ部屋に暮らす）　live in the same room

　　　Hitotsu yatte-goran.（一つやってごらん.）　Just try it.

hito-tsubu〈ひとつぶ：一粒〉a grain, a drop.

hito-tsukami〈ひとつかみ：一つかみ〉a handful.

　　　hito-tsukami-no kome（一つかみの米）　a handful of rice

hito-tsuki〈ひとつき：一月〉a month.

hito-tsumami〈ひとつまみ：一つまみ〉a pinch.

hito-yaku〈ひとやく：一役〉

　　hito-yaku katte-iru〈一役買っている〉bear a part ((in)).

hito-yama〈ひとやま：一山〉a pile, a lot.

　　　ringo-hito-yama（りんご一山）　a pile of apples

　　　hito-yama hyaku-en（一山百円）　100 yen a lot

hito-yasumi〈ひとやすみ：一休み〉a rest.

　　hito-yasumi-suru〈一休みする〉take a rest, take breath.

hito-zukai〈ひとづかい：人使い〉

　　hito-zukai-ga-arai〈人使いが荒い〉work　one's　men　hard,　be　a　hard
　　master.

hito-zuki〈ひとずき：人好き〉

　　hito-zuki-no-suru〈人好きのする〉attractive, affable, amiable.

hito-zuki-ai〈ひとづきあい：人付き合い〉

　　　hito-zuki-ai-no-ii hito（人付き合いのいい人）　a sociable person

　　　hito-zuki-ai-no-warui hito（人付き合いの悪い人）　an unsociable person

hito-zuma〈ひとづま：人妻〉a married woman.

hito-zure〈ひとずれ：人擦れ〉

hito-zure-no-shita〈人擦れのした〉sophisticated.

　　hito-zure-no-shi-nai（人擦れのしない）　unsophisticated, naïve

hito-zute〈ひとづて：人づて〉

hito-zute-ni-kiku〈人づてに聞く〉know ((something)) from hearsay, learn ((something)) at second hand.

hitsû〈ひつう：悲痛〉

hitsû-na〈悲痛な〉grievous, sorrowful, bitter, touching.

hitsudan〈ひつだん：筆談〉

hitsudan-suru〈筆談する〉carry on a talk by writing on paper what one wants to say.

hitsudoku-sho〈ひつどくしょ：必読書〉a must book.

hitsugi〈ひつぎ：柩〉a coffin.

hitsuji〈ひつじ：羊〉a sheep.

　　hitsuji-no-ke（羊の毛）　wool

　　hitsuji-no-niku（羊の肉）　mutton

　　ko-hitsuji（子羊）　a lamb

　　hitsuji-kai（羊飼い）　a shepherd

hitsuju-hin〈ひつじゅひん：必需品〉necessaries, necessities, a requisite.

　　seikatsu-hitsuju-hin（生活必需品）　the necessities of life

hi-tsuke-yaku〈ひつけやく：火付け役〉a troublemaker, an instigator.

hitsuyô〈ひつよう：必要〉necessity, need.

　　hitsuyô-ni-semararete（必要に迫られて）　out of necessity

　　hitsuyô-no baai-niwa（必要の場合には）　in case of necessity

hitsuyô-de-aru〈必要である〉need, be in need ((of)), be necessary.

　　Watashi-wa ima kane-ga-hitsuyô-da.（私は今金が必要だ。）I am in need of money now.

hitsuyô-ga-nai〈必要がない〉need not ((do)), don't have to ((do)).

　　Isogu-hitsuyô-wa nai.（急ぐ必要はない。）You need not be in a hurry.

hitsuyô-na〈必要な〉necessary, needful.

hitsuzen〈ひつぜん：必然〉

　　hitsuzen-sei（必然性）　inevitability

hitsuzen-teki-(na)〈必然的(な)〉inevitable, necessary, natural.

hitsuzen-teki-ni〈必然的に〉inevitably, necessarily, naturally.

hittakuri〈ひったくり：引ったくり〉bag-snatching; a bag-snatcher.

hittakuru〈引ったくる〉snatch ((from *or* off)), take by force.

hitteki〈ひってき：匹敵〉

hitteki-suru〈匹敵する〉be a match ((for)), be equal ((to)), rival, rank ((with)), correspond ((to)).

hitteki-suru-mono-ga-nai 〈匹敵するものがない〉 have no equal ((in)), be unrivaled ((in)).

hitto 〈ヒット〉 a hit.

    hitto o utsu （ヒットを打つ） make a hit

    dai-hitto-suru （大ヒットする） be a big hit

hittô 〈ひっとう：筆答〉

    hittô-shiken （筆答試験） a written examination

hittô 〈ひっとう：筆頭〉

hittô-de-aru 〈筆頭である〉 be at the head ((of)).

hittsuku 〈ひっつく：引っ付く〉 *see.* kuttsuku.

hiya 〈ひや：冷や〉

    hiya-zake （冷や酒） unwarmed (*or* cold) *sake*

sake o hiya-de-nomu 〈酒を冷やで飲む〉 drink *sake* cold.

hiya-ase 〈ひやあせ：冷や汗〉

hiya-ase-o-kaku 〈冷や汗をかく〉 break into a cold sweat.

hiyahiya 〈ひやひや：冷や冷や〉

hiyahiya-suru 〈冷や冷やする〉 be very much afraid, be in great fear.

hiyakashi 〈ひやかし：冷やかし〉 banter, chaff; mere inspection.

    hiyakashi-hambun-ni （冷やかし半分に） partly for fun

hiyakasu 〈冷やかす〉 banter, chaff, jeer ((at)); have a look ((at things)).

hi-yake 〈ひやけ：日焼け〉 sunburn, suntan.

hi-yake-suru 〈日焼けする〉 get sunburnt, get a tan.

hi-yake-shita 〈日焼けした〉 sunburnt, suntanned.

hiyaku 〈ひやく：飛躍〉

    ronri no hiyaku （論理の飛躍） a jump of logic

    hiyaku-teki-ni nobiru （飛躍的に伸びる） increase by leaps and bounds

hiyari 〈ひやり：冷やり〉

hiyari-to-suru 〈冷やりとする〉 be chilled, feel a chill; have a thrill of horror, be frightened.

hiyashinsu 〈ヒヤシンス〉 a hyacinth.

hiyasu 〈ひやす：冷やす〉 cool, ice.

    atama o hiyasu （頭を冷やす） cool one's head

hiyashita 〈冷やした〉 cooled, iced.

hiyayaka 〈ひややか：冷ややか〉

hiyayaka-na 〈冷ややかな〉 cold, icy, frigid, coldhearted.

    hiyayaka-na taido （冷ややかな態度） a cold attitude

hiyayaka-ni〈冷ややかに〉coldly, icily, frigidly, coldheartedly.

hiyô〈ひよう：費用〉expense(s), (a) cost.

　　hiyô o kiri-tsumeru（費用を切り詰める）　cut down expenses

　　hiyô-ga-kakaru〈費用が掛かる〉be expensive, cost.

　　hiyô-no-kakaru〈費用の掛かる〉expensive, costly.

　　　hiyô-no-kakara-nai（費用の掛からない）　inexpensive.

hi-yoke〈ひよけ：日よけ〉a sunshade, an awning, a blind.

　　hi-yoke o orosu（日よけを下ろす）　lower an awning, put down a blind

hiyoko〈ひよこ〉a chicken, a chick.

hiyoku〈ひよく：肥よく〉

　hiyoku-na〈肥よくな〉fertile, rich.

hiyori〈ひより：日和〉weather, fine weather.

　　Ii-hiyori-desu-ne.（いい日和ですね.）　It's really fine today.

hiyori-mi〈ひよりみ：日和見〉

　hiyori-mi-suru〈日和見する〉wait and see, sit on the fence, see how the wind blows.

hi-yowai〈ひよわい：ひ弱い〉weak, delicate, infirm.

hiyu〈ひゆ：比ゆ〉a figure of speech, a metaphor.

　hiyu-teki(-na)〈比ゆ的(な)〉figurative, metaphorical.

hiza〈ひざ〉a knee, a lap.

　　hiza-o-tsuku（ひざをつく）　fall on one's knees

　　akambô o hiza-no-ue-ni noseru（赤ん坊をひざの上に載せる）　hold a baby on one's lap

　　hiza o kumu（ひざを組む）　cross one's legs, sit cross-legged

　　hiza-o-kuzusu（ひざを崩す）　sit at ease

　　hiza-gashira（ひざ頭）　the kneecap

hizamazuku〈ひざまずく〉kneel (down), fall on one's knees.

　hizamazuite〈ひざまずいて〉on one's knees.

hi-zashi〈ひざし：日ざし〉the sunlight, the sunbeam.

　　Hi-zashi-ga-kitsui.（日ざしがきつい.）　The sunbeams glare.

hizô〈ひぞう：ひ臓〉the spleen.

hizô〈ひぞう：秘蔵〉

　　hizôkko（秘蔵っ子）　one's beloved child

　　hizô-suru〈秘蔵する〉treasure, keep ((a thing)) under lock and key.

　　hizô-no〈秘蔵の〉treasured, favorite.

hi-zuke〈ひづけ：日付〉a date, dating.

　　hi-zuke-henkô-sen（日付変更線）　the date line

hi-zuke-o-kaku〈日付を書く〉date.

hi-zuke-no-nai〈日付のない〉undated.

hizume〈ひづめ〉a hoof.

hizumi〈ひずみ〉(a) strain, (a) distortion, a warp.

    keizai-seichô no hizumi（経済成長のひずみ）the strain of the economic growth

  hizumi-ga-aru or *hizumu*〈ひずみがある，ひずむ〉be strained, be distorted, be crooked, warp.

ho〈ほ：帆〉a sail.

    ho o ageru（帆を揚げる）hoist a sail

    ho o orosu（帆を下ろす）lower a sail

ho〈ほ：穂〉an ear.

    ho-ga-deru（穂が出る）come into ears

ho〈ほ：歩〉a step.

    ni-ho mae-e-deru（二歩前へ出る）take two steps forward

    ippo-ippo（一歩一歩）step by step

hô〈ほう：砲〉a gun, a cannon.

hô〈ほう：方〉a way, a direction, a side; one.

    kochira-no hô o miru（こちらの方を見る）look this way

    umi-no-hô-e iku（海の方へ行く）go in the direction of the sea, go toward the sea

    migi-no hô- ni（右の方に）on the right side

    ano hô（あの方）that (one)

hô〈ほう：法〉a law.

    hô o mamoru（法を守る）observe the law

    hô o okasu（法を犯す）break the law

hô〈ほう〉oh, well, why.

-hô〈-ほう：-法〉a method.

    kyôju-hô（教授法）a method of teaching

hoan〈ほあん：保安〉the preservation(*or* maintenance) of public security.

    hoan-yôin（保安要員）the maintenance personnel

    kaijô-hoan-chô（海上保安庁）Japan's Maritime Safety Agency

hôan〈ほうあん：法案〉a bill.

    hôan o teishutsu-suru（法案を提出する）introduce a bill

    hôan o kaketsu-suru（法案を可決する）pass a bill

    hôan o hiketsu-suru（法案を否決する）reject a bill

hôben〈ほうべん：方便〉an expedient, a shift, a means, an instrument.

    Uso-mo-hôben.（うそも方便.）The end justifies the means.

hôbi〈ほうび：褒美〉a reward, a prize.

　hôbi-o-ageru〈褒美を上げる〉reward ((a person)).

　hôbi-o-morau〈褒美をもらう〉be rewarded, win a prize.

hobo〈ほぼ：保母〉a nurse, a kindergarten teacher.

hobo〈ほぼ〉almost, nearly, about, for the most part.

hôbô〈ほうぼう：方々〉every direction, various places, everywhere.

　　hôbô-aruki-mawaru（方々歩き回る）　tramp from place to place, gad
　　　about

　　hôbô-sagasu（方々捜す）　look for ((a person)) everywhere

　hôbô-kara〈方々から〉from several quarters.

　hôbô-ni〈方々に〉in several places, everywhere, here and there.

hôboku〈ほうぼく：放牧〉

　hôboku-suru〈放牧する〉graze〔cattle〕, put ((cattle)) to grass, put
　((cattle)) to pasture, pasture.

hôbun〈ほうぶん：邦文〉the Japanese language, Japanese.

　　hôbun-taipu-raitâ（邦文タイプライター）　a Japanese typewriter

hôbun〈ほうぶん：法文〉the letter of the law.

　hôbun-ka-suru〈法文化する〉enact into a law, codify.

hôbutsu-sen〈ほうぶつせん：放物線〉a parabola.

hôchi〈ほうち：放置〉

　hôchi-suru〈放置する〉leave ((a thing)) alone, leave ((a matter)) as it is.

hôchi-kokka〈ほうちこっか：法治国家〉a constitutional state.

hochô〈ほちょう：歩調〉(a) step, (a) pace.

　　hochô o awaseru（歩調を合わせる）　keep in step ((with))

hôchô〈ほうちょう：包丁〉a kitchen knife.

hochô-ki〈ほちょうき：補聴器〉a hearing aid, an acousticon.

hôdai〈ほうだい：砲台〉a (gun) battery.

-hôdai〈-ほうだい：-放題〉

　　ii-tai-hôdai-no-koto-o-iu（言いたい放題のことを言う）　say as one likes

　　tabe-tai-hôdai-taberu（食べたい放題食べる）　eat one's fill

　　shi-tai-hôdai-ni（したい放題に）　as one pleases

hôdan〈ほうだん：砲弾〉a cannonball, a shell.

hôden〈ほうでん：放電〉discharge of electricity.

　hôden-suru〈放電する〉discharge electricity.

hodo〈ほど：程〉a limit; one's position.

　　Jôdan-nimo-hodo-ga-aru.（冗談にも程がある。）　You carry your joke
　　　too far.

　　mi-no-hodo-o-shira-nai（身の程を知らない）　do not know one's place

-hodo 〈-ほど〉 like... , not so...as, Nothing... , Nobody... ; the more...the more; How long... ?, How far... ?, How much... ?; around, about, some.

Waga-ya-hodo-ii-tokoro-wa-nai.（我が家ほどいい所はない．） There is no place like home.

Sono shigoto wa kimi-ga kangaete-iru-hodo taihen-dewa-nai.（その仕事は君が考えているほど大変ではない．） The work is not so difficult as you think.

Kenkô-hodo taisetsu-na-mono-wa-nai.（健康ほど大切なものはない．） Nothing is more important than health.

Kare-hodo-umaku-oyogeru-mono-wa-i-nai.（彼ほどうまく泳げる者はいない．） Nobody can swim so well as he.

Hayakereba-hayai-hodo-ii.（早ければ早いほどいい．） The sooner, the better.

Koko-kara Nagoya-made dore-hodo-kakari-masu-ka?（ここから名古屋までどれほどかかりますか．） How long does it take from here to Nagoya?

hito-tsuki-hodo（一月ほど） about a month

jû-mairu-hodo（十マイルほど） some ten miles

hodô 〈ほどう：歩道〉 a sidewalk, a pavement.

ôdan-hodô（横断歩道） a pedestrian crossing, a crosswalk

hodô-kyô（歩道橋） a pedestrian bridge, an overbridge

hodô 〈ほどう：舗道〉 see. hosô-dôro.

hodô 〈ほどう：補導〉 guidance, direction, protection and guidance.

hodô o ukeru（補導を受ける） receive guidance ((from))

shokugyô-hodô（職業補導） vocational guidance

gakusei no hodô（学生の補導） protection and guidance of students

hodô-suru 〈補導する〉 guide, direct, lead.

hôdô 〈ほうどう：報道〉 news, a report, information.

hôdô-jin（報道陣） a news front, a reportorial camp

hôdô-suru 〈報道する〉 report.

hodokeru 〈ほどける〉 get loose, get untied.

kutsu-no-himo-ga-hodokeru（靴のひもがほどける） get unlaced

hodoku 〈ほどく〉 untie, undo, unpack.

musubi-me o hodoku（結び目をほどく） undo a knot

ami-mono-o-hodoku（編み物をほどく） unknit

hodokosu 〈ほどこす：施す〉 do, perform, conduct, try, take.

onkei o hodokosu（恩恵を施す） do ((a person)) a favor

kyôiku o hodokosu（教育を施す）conduct education, give education

arayuru shudan o hodokosu（あらゆる手段を施す）take every possible means

Mô-saku-no-hodokoshi-yô-ga-nai.（もう策の施しようがない.）It is past remedy.

hoeru〈ほえる〉bark, howl, roar.

inu-ni hoerareru（犬にほえられる）be barked at by a dog

hôfu〈ほうふ：抱負〉ambition, aspiration.

hôfu o motsu（抱負を持つ）have an ambition

hôfu o noberu（抱負を述べる）express one's hopes

hôfu〈ほうふ：豊富〉(an) abundance, (a) plenty, (a) wealth, richness.

hôfu-de-aru〈豊富である〉abound ((in or with)), be rich ((in)).

tennen-shigen-ga-hôfu-de-aru（天然資源が豊富である）be rich in natural resources

hôfu-na〈豊富な〉abundant, plentiful, rich.

hôfu-na chishiki（豊富な知識）a great stock of knowledge

hôfu-ni〈豊富に〉abundantly, plentifully, richly.

hôfu-ni-suru〈豊富にする〉enrich.

goi o hôfu-ni-suru（語いを豊富にする）enrich one's vocabulary

hôfuku〈ほうふく：報復〉retaliation, (a) reprisal.

hôfuku-suru〈報復する〉retaliate, make a reprisal ((on)).

hôfuku-to-shite〈報復として〉in retaliation ((for)).

hôga〈ほうが：邦画〉a Japanese film.

hôgai〈ほうがい：法外〉

hôgai-na〈法外な〉exorbitant, unreasonable, extravagant, absurd.

hôgai-na nedan（法外な値段）an exorbitant price

hôgai-na yôkyû（法外な要求）an unreasonable demand

hôgaku〈ほうがく：方角〉a direction, a way, one's bearings.

hôgaku-ga-wakara-naku-naru（方角が分からなくなる）lose one's bearings

hôgaku〈ほうがく：邦楽〉traditional Japanese music.

hôgaku〈ほうがく：法学〉law.

hôgaku-bu（法学部）the law department

hôgaku-hakase（法学博士）a doctor of laws; Doctor of Laws (LL. D.)

hôgan-nage〈ほうがんなげ：砲丸投げ〉shot-put.

hôgan-nage-no-senshu（砲丸投げの選手）a shot-putter

hôgan-nage-o-suru〈砲丸投げをする〉put the shot.

hôgan-shi 〈ほうがんし：方眼紙〉plotting paper; graph paper, section paper.

hogaraka 〈ほがらか：朗らか〉

hogaraka-na 〈朗らかな〉cheerful, bright.

hogaraka-na hito（朗らかな人）a cheerful person

hogaraka-ni 〈朗らかに〉cheerfully, merrily.

-hô-ga-yoi 〈〜ほうがよい：〜方がよい〉had better.

Ima-sugu itta-hô-ga-yoi.（今すぐ行った方がよい.）You had better go right now.

hogei 〈ほげい：捕鯨〉whaling, whale fishing.

hogei-sen（捕鯨船）a whaler, a whaling vessel

hôgeki 〈ほうげき：砲撃〉bombardment, shelling.

hôgeki-suru 〈砲撃する〉bombard, shell.

hôgen 〈ほうげん：方言〉a dialect.

hôgen 〈ほうげん：放言〉unreserved speech, an irresponsible remark.

hôgen-suru 〈放言する〉speak unreservedly, talk big, talk through one's hat.

hogo 〈ほご：補語〉a complement.

hogo 〈ほご〉wastepaper.

hogo-kago（ほごかご）a wastebasket

hogo-ni-suru 〈ほごにする〉throw ((a thing)) into the wastebasket, scrap, annul.

yakusoku-o-hogo-ni-suru（約束をほごにする）break one's word, go back on one's pledge

hogo 〈ほご：保護〉protection, care, patronage, preservation.

keisatsu no hogo（警察の保護）police protection

hogo-sha（保護者）a protector, a guardian

hogo-bôeki（保護貿易）protective trade

hogo-chô（保護鳥）a protected bird

hogo-shoku（保護色）a protective color

hogo-suru 〈保護する〉protect, look ((after)).

hogo-o-ukeru 〈保護を受ける〉be protected ((by)).

hohei 〈ほへい：歩兵〉infantry; an infantryman, a foot soldier.

hôhei 〈ほうへい：砲兵〉artillery; an artilleryman.

hôhô 〈ほうほう：方法〉a method, a way, a measure.

sairyô-no hôhô（最良の方法）the best way

iroiro-na hôhô-de（いろいろな方法で）by various methods

sore-o tsukuru-hôhô（それを作る方法）how to make it

　　hôhô-ron〈方法論〉methodology
　　　hôhô-ron-teki(-na)〈方法論的(な)〉methodological
hoho-emi〈ほほえみ：ほほ笑み〉a smile.
　　hoho-emi-o-ukabete〈ほほえみを浮かべて〉with a smile
　hoho-emu〈ほほ笑む〉smile.
　hoho-emashii〈ほほ笑ましい〉pleasant, smile-provoking.
hoi〈ほい：補遺〉a supplement, an addendum.
hôi〈ほうい：方位〉*see.* hôgaku.
hôi〈ほうい：包囲〉(a) siege, besiegement.
　　teki-no-hôi-o-toppa-suru〈敵の包囲を突破する〉break through the
　　　besieging enemy forces
　　hôi o toku〈包囲を解く〉raise the siege ((of))
　hôi-suru〈包囲する〉surround, besiege, throw a cordon round.
hô-igaku〈ほういがく：法医学〉legal medicine, medical jurisprudence.
　hô-igaku(-jô)-no〈法医学(上)の〉medicolegal.
hoiku〈ほいく：保育〉
　　hoiku-en〈保育園〉a day nursery, a nursery school
　hoiku-suru〈保育する〉nurse, bring up, foster.
hoji〈ほじ：保持〉
　　kiroku-hoji-sha〈記録保持者〉a record holder
　hoji-suru〈保持する〉hold, keep.
hôji〈ほうじ：法事〉
　hôji-o-suru〈法事をする〉hold a Buddhist service for the dead.
hôji-cha〈ほうじちゃ：ほうじ茶〉roasted tea.
hojikuru〈ほじくる〉pick.
　　hana o hojikuru〈鼻をほじくる〉pick one's nose
　　mimi o hojikuru〈耳をほじくる〉clean one's ears
hôjin〈ほうじん：邦人〉a Japanese; the Japanese.
hôjin〈ほうじん：法人〉a juridical person, a corporation.
　　hôjin-zei〈法人税〉the corporation tax
　hôjin-soshiki-ni-suru〈法人組織にする〉incorporate.
hojo〈ほじょ：補助〉assistance, help, support, aid.
　　hojo-isu〈補助いす〉a let-down seat, a jump seat
　　hojo-kin〈補助金〉a subsidy
　hojo-suru〈補助する〉assist, help, support, aid, subsidize.
　hojo-o-ukeru〈補助を受ける〉be assisted, be helped, be subsidized.
hojû〈ほじゅう：補充〉supplement, replenishment, recruiting.
　hojû-suru〈補充する〉supplement, replenish, recruit, fill up.

ketsuin o hojû-suru（欠員を補充する） fill (up) a vacancy

hoka〈ほか：外〉

hoka-no〈ほかの〉 other, another, different, else.

hoka-no hito-tachi（ほかの人たち） other people

hoka-no-hi-ni（ほかの日に） some other day

hoka-no mise-dewa（ほかの店では） at other stores

Hoka-no-mono o misete-kudasai.（ほかのものを見せてください.） Please show me another.

dare-ka hoka-no-hito（だれかほかの人） somebody else

nani-ka hoka-no-koto（何かほかのこと） something else

hoka(-ni)〈外(に)〉 except, but, beyond, besides.

Kimi-no-hoka-ni sonna koto o suru-hito-wa-dare-mo-i-nai.（君の外にそんなことをする人はだれもいない.） No one but you will do such a thing.

kono-hoka-ni（この外に） besides this

hoka-ni suru-koto-ga-nai（外にすることがない） have nothing else to do

Hoka-ni shitsumon-wa-ari-masen-ka?（外に質問はありませんか.） Do you have any other questions to ask me?

Yamada-shi-hoka-go-mei（山田氏外五名） Mr. Yamada and five others

hoka-de or *hoka-ni*〈外で，外に〉 somewhere else, elsewhere.

hoka-kara〈外から〉 from outside.

hôka〈ほうか：邦貨〉 Japanese currency, yen.

hôka〈ほうか：法科〉 *see.* hôgaku-bu.

hôka〈ほうか：砲火〉 gunfire.

hôka o majieru（砲火を交える） exchange fire

hôka〈ほうか：放火〉 incendiarism.

hôka-ma（放火魔） an incendiary maniac, a firebug

hôka-suru〈放火する〉 set fire ((to)), set ((a house)) on fire.

hôka-go〈ほうかご：放課後〉 after school.

hôkai〈ほうかい：崩壊〉 (a) collapse, a breakdown, a breakup.

hôkai-suru〈崩壊する〉 collapse.

hokaku〈ほかく：捕獲〉 capture, seizure.

hokaku-daka（捕獲高） a catch〔of fish〕

hokaku-suru〈捕獲する〉 catch, capture, seize.

hokan〈ほかん：保管〉 custody, charge, safekeeping.

hokan-ryô（保管料） charges for custody

hokan-suru〈保管する〉keep ((a thing)) in custody, take charge ((of)).

hokan-shite-morau〈保管してもらう〉ask ((a person)) to keep ((a thing)) for one.

hôkatsu〈ほうかつ：包括〉

hôkatsu-suru〈包括する〉include, contain, comprehend, embrace, cover.

hôkatsu-teki(-na)〈包括的(な)〉inclusive, comprehensive, general.

hôkatsu-teki-ni〈包括的に〉inclusively, comprehensively, generally.

hoken〈ほけん：保健〉health, sanitation; health education.

    sekai-hoken-kikô〈世界保健機構〉 World Health Organization(WHO)

    hoken-jo〈保健所〉a health center

    hoken-taiiku〈保健体育〉 health and physical education

hoken〈ほけん：保険〉insurance.

    hoken-dairi-ten〈保険代理店〉 an insurance agency

    hoken-keiyaku-sha〈保険契約者〉 a policy holder

    hoken-ryô〈保険料〉 an insurance premium

    hoken-shôken〈保険証券〉 an insurance policy

    hoken-kin〈保険金〉 insurance money

      hoken-kin-uketori-nin〈保険金受取人〉 the beneficiary

hoken-o-kakeru〈保険を掛ける〉insure ((oneself)), take out insurance ((on)), buy insurance ((against)).

hôken〈ほうけん：封建〉

    hôken-seido *or* hôken-shugi〈封建制度，封建主義〉 feudalism

hôken-teki(-na)〈封建的(な)〉feudalistic.

hoketsu〈ほけつ：補欠〉filling a vacancy; a substitute.

    hoketsu-senshu〈補欠選手〉 a substitute player, a reserve, a bench warmer

    hoketsu-senkyo〈補欠選挙〉 a by-election

hoketsu-no〈補欠の〉supplementary.

hôki〈ほうき〉a broom.

    hôki-de haku〈ほうきで掃く〉 sweep with a broom

hôki〈ほうき：法規〉laws and regulations.

hôki-ni-terashite〈法規に照らして〉according to the law.

hôki〈ほうき：放棄〉giving up, abandonment, renunciation, renouncement.

hôki-suru〈放棄する〉give up, abandon, renounce.

    kenri o hôki-suru〈権利を放棄する〉 relinquish one's rights

hôki〈ほうき：ほう起〉

hôki-suru〈ほう起する〉rise in revolt.

hokin-sha〈ほきんしゃ：保菌者〉a germ carrier.

hokkai, Hokkai〈ほっかい：北海〉a northern sea, the North Sea.

hokki-nin〈ほっきにん：発起人〉an originator, a promoter, a proposer.

hokku〈ホック〉a hook.

  hokku-o-kakeru〈ホックを掛ける〉hook.

    hokku-o-hazusu（ホックを外す）unhook

Hokkyoku〈ほっきょく：北極〉the North Pole.

    Hokkyoku-chihō（北極地方）the arctic regions

    Hokkyoku-ken（北極圏）the Arctic Circle

    Hokkyoku-kai（北極海）the Arctic Ocean

    Hokkyoku-guma（北極熊）a polar bear

    Hokkyoku-sei（北極星）the polestar, the North Star

  Hokkyoku-no〈北極の〉arctic, polar.

hokô〈ほこう：歩行〉walking.

    hokô-sha（歩行者）a walker, a pedestrian

hôko〈ほうこ：宝庫〉a treasure house, a treasury.

hôkô〈ほうこう：方向〉a direction, a course.

    hôkô-o-ayamaru（方向を誤る）go in the wrong direction

    hôkô-onchi-de-aru（方向音痴である）have no sense of direction

hôkô〈ほうこう：放校〉expulsion from school.

  hôkô-ni-naru〈放校になる〉be expelled from school.

hôkoku〈ほうこく：報告〉a report.

    hôkoku-sho（報告書）a (written) report

  hôkoku-suru〈報告する〉report, make a report ((of *or* on)).

hokori〈ほこり〉dust.

    Hokori ga tatsu.（ほこりが立つ.）Dust rises.

    Hokori ga tamaru.（ほこりがたまる.）Dust collects.

    hokori o tateru（ほこりを立てる）raise dust

    hokori o kaburu（ほこりをかぶる）be covered with dust

  hokori-o-harau〈ほこりを払う〉.

  hokori-darake-no *or* *hokorippoi*〈ほこりだらけの，ほこりっぽい〉dusty.

hokori〈ほこり：誇り〉pride.

  hokoru〈誇る〉be pride ((of)), take pride ((in)), pride oneself ((upon)).

hokorobaseru〈ほころばせる〉

    Kanojo-wa kao-o-hokorobaseta.（彼女は顔をほころばせた.）Her face broadened in a smile.

hokorobi〈ほころび〉an open seam, a rent, a rip.

    hokorobi o tsukurou（ほころびを繕う）sew up a rent

hokorobiru 〈ほころびる〉 open, be rent, rip; begin to bloom.

hoko-saki 〈ほこさき：矛先〉 a spearhead.
    hoko-saki o mukeru (矛先を向ける) direct one's spearhead ((on))

Hokubei 〈ほくべい：北米〉 North America.
    Hokubei-no (北米の) North American.

hokubu 〈ほくぶ：北部〉 the northern part, the north.
    hokubu-no (北部の) northern.

hoku-hoku-sei 〈ほくほくせい：北北西〉 north-northwest(NNW).

hoku-hoku-tô 〈ほくほくとう：北北東〉 north-northeast(NNE).

hokui 〈ほくい：北緯〉 the north latitude.

hokujô 〈ほくじょう：北上〉
    hokujô-suru (北上する) go up north.

Hoku-Ô 〈ほくおう：北欧〉 North(ern) Europe.

hokuro 〈ほくろ〉 a mole.

hoku-sei 〈ほくせい：北西〉 northwest.
    hoku-sei-no (北西の) northwestern.

hokuso-emu 〈ほくそえむ：ほくそ笑む〉 chuckle over ((at)).

hokutan 〈ほくたん：北端〉
    hokutan-ni (北端に) in the northern extremity(*or* end) ((of)).

hoku-tô 〈ほくとう：北東〉 northeast.
    hoku-tô-no (北東の) northeastern.

hokuto-shichisei 〈ほくとしちせい：北斗七星〉 the Big Dipper, the Great Bear.

hokuyô 〈ほくよう：北洋〉 the northern seas.

hokyô 〈ほきょう：補強〉 reinforcement.
    hokyô-suru (補強する) reinforce, strengthen.

hokyû 〈ほきゅう：補給〉 supply, replenishment.
    hokyû-ro (補給路) a supply route
    hokyû-suru (補給する) supply, replenish.

hôkyû 〈ほうきゅう：俸給〉 see. kyûryô.

hôman 〈ほうまん：放漫〉
    hôman-na (放漫な) lax, loose, slack, reckless.
    hôman-na keiei (放漫な経営) reckless management

hôman 〈ほうまん：豊満〉
    hôman-na 〈豊満な〉 plump, voluptuous, well-developed.

hômatsu 〈ほうまつ：泡まつ〉 a bubble.
    hômatsu-gaisha (泡まつ会社) a bubble company
    hômatsu-kôho (泡まつ候補) a fringy candidate

homba 〈ほんば：本場〉 the home, the best place.

    ringo-no homba〈りんごの本場〉 the best place for apples

hombasho 〈ほんばしょ：本場所〉 a seasonal *sumo* tournament.

hombu 〈ほんぶ：本部〉 the headquarters, the administrative building.

hombun 〈ほんぶん：本文〉 the text〔of a book〕, the body〔of a letter〕.

hombun 〈ほんぶん：本分〉 one's duty.

    hombun o tsukusu〈本分を尽くす〉 do one's duty

homburi 〈ほんぶり：本降り〉 a downpour.

    Ame-ga-homburi-ni-natte-kita.〈雨が本降りになってきた。〉 It began
    to rain in real earnest.

hômen 〈ほうめん：方面〉 a district, a direction, a quarter.

    Shikoku-hômen〈四国方面〉 the Shikoku districts

    Asakusa-hômen-de(-e *or* -ni)〈浅草方面で(へ，に)〉 in the direction of
    Asakusa, somewhere in Asakusa

    kaku-hômen-kara〈各方面から〉 from several directions

hômen 〈ほうめん：放免〉 release, discharge, acquittal.

  hômen-suru〈放免する〉 release, discharge, acquit.

    Kare-wa muzai-hômen-ni-natta.〈彼は無罪放免になった。〉 He was
    acquitted of the charge.

homeru 〈ほめる：褒める〉 praise, speak highly ((of)), admire.

  homeru-beki〈褒めるべき〉 praiseworthy, admirable.

hommatsu 〈ほんまつ：本末〉

  hommatsu-tentô-suru〈本末転倒する〉 put the cart before the horse, be
  preposterous.

hommei 〈ほんめい：本命〉 the favorite, a prospective winner.

hommô 〈ほんもう：本望〉 one's long-cherished desire, satisfaction.

    Kore-de-hommô-da.〈これで本望だ。〉 I'm quite satisfied with this.

hommono 〈ほんもの：本物〉

  hommono-no〈本物の〉 real, genuine.

    hommono-no daiya〈本物のダイヤ〉 a genuine diamond

hommyô 〈ほんみょう：本名〉 one's real name.

hômon 〈ほうもん：訪問〉 a visit, a call.

    hômon-gi〈訪問着〉 a visiting dress

    hômon-kyaku〈訪問客〉 a visitor, a caller

    katei-hômon〈家庭訪問〉 a house call

  hômon-suru〈訪問する〉 visit, call ((on)), call ((at)).

hômotsu-den 〈ほうもつでん：宝物殿〉 a treasure house.

hompô 〈ほんぽう：本俸〉 the regular pay, the basic salary.

hompô 〈ほんぽう：奔放〉
hompô-na 〈奔放な〉 wild, free, unrestrained.

hômu 〈ホーム〉 one's home; the home base; a platform.

hômu 〈ほうむ：法務〉
  hômu-shô (法務省) the Ministry of Justice
  hômu-daijin (法務大臣) the Minister of Justice

hômu-ran 〈ホームラン〉 a home run, a homer.
  hômu-ran-o-utsu 〈ホームランを打つ〉 hit a home run, homer.

hômuru 〈ほうむる：葬る〉 bury; kill, hush up.
  shakai-kara-hômurareru (社会から葬られる) go into oblivion, be ostracized

hômu-shikku 〈ホームシック〉 homesickness, nostalgia.
  hômu-shikku-ni-kakaru 〈ホームシックにかかる〉 get homesick.

hon 〈ほん：本〉 a book, a volume, a work.
  hon o yomu (本を読む) read a book
  hon-bako (本箱) a bookcase
  hon-dana (本棚) a bookshelf
  hon-ya (本屋) a bookstore, a bookshop; a bookseller

hon- 〈ほん-：本-〉 this, the same, present; main, head; real, regular, plenary.
  hon-ken (本件) this affair
  hon-doori (本通り) a main street
  hon-kaiin (本会員) a regular member
  hon-kaigi (本会議) a plenary session

hon-chôshi 〈ほんちょうし：本調子〉 one's regular form.
  Dômo hon-chôshi-ja-nai. (どうも本調子じゃない。) Somehow I am not myself.

hondai 〈ほんだい：本題〉 the main subject; the subject in question.

honden 〈ほんでん：本殿〉 the main shrine.

hondo 〈ほんど：本土〉 the mainland.
  Nihon-hondo (日本本土) Japan proper

hondô 〈ほんどう：本堂〉 the main temple, the main sanctuary of a temple.

hone 〈ほね：骨〉 a bone; pains, trouble, effort(s).
  hone o oru (骨を折る) break a bone; take pains, take trouble, make efforts
  hone o tsuide-morau (骨を接いでもらう) have a broken bone set
  hone-o-nodo-ni-tateru (骨をのどに立てる) have a bone stuck in the

throat
　　hone-ni-shimiru-hodo-samui〈骨に染みるほど寒い〉 be frozen to the bone

hone-o-toru〈骨を取る〉bone.
　　sakana-no-hone-o-toru（魚の骨を取る）bone a fish
hone-no-oreru〈骨の折れる〉hard, toilsome, painful, difficult, arduous.
hone-o-otte〈骨を折って〉with (much) effort, with difficulty.
　　hone-o-orazu-ni〈骨を折らずに〉 without effort, easily

hone-gumi〈ほねぐみ：骨組み〉the frame, a skeleton, build.
　　hone-gumi-no-gatchiri-shita otoko（骨組みのがっちりした男）a man of stout build

hone-mi〈ほねみ：骨身〉
hone-mi-ni-shimiru〈骨身に染みる〉be piercingly cold; come home ((to)), strike ((a person)) home.

hônen〈ほうねん：豊年〉a fruitful year, a good harvest.
　　Kotoshi wa hônen-darô.（今年は豊年だろう。）We shall have a rich harvest this year.
　　hônen-iwai（豊年祝い）a harvest festival
　　hônen-odori（豊年踊り）a harvest dance

hone-no-aru or **honeppoi**〈骨のある，骨っぽい〉bony; spirited, mettlesome.

hone-nuki〈ほねぬき：骨抜き〉
hone-nuki-ni-suru〈骨抜きにする〉mutilate.
hone-nuki-ni-naru〈骨抜きになる〉be mutilated.
hone-nuki-ni-natta or *hone-nuki-no*〈骨抜きになった，骨抜きの〉mutilated.

hone-ori〈ほねおり：骨折り〉pains, trouble, effort(s).
　　Hone-ori-zon-no-kutabire-môke.（骨折り損のくたびれもうけ。）I had all my trouble for nothing.

hone-oshimi〈ほねおしみ：骨惜しみ〉
hone-oshimi-suru〈骨惜しみする〉spare oneself.
　　hone-oshimi-shi-nai（骨惜しみしない） spare no pains
　　　　hone-oshimi-shi-nai-de hataraku（骨惜しみしないで働く）work without sparing oneself

hônetsu〈ほうねつ：放熱〉radiation.
hônetsu-suru〈放熱する〉radiate heat.

hone-tsugi〈ほねつぎ：骨接ぎ〉bonesetting; a bonesetter.

hone-yasume〈ほねやすめ：骨休め〉
hone-yasume-suru〈骨休めする〉take a rest, rest oneself.

hon-gimari 〈ほんぎまり：本決まり〉
　hon-gimari-ni-naru 〈本決まりになる〉 be definitely(*or* formally) decided.

hongoku 〈ほんごく：本国〉 one's own country, one's fatherland.
　hongoku-seifu （本国政府） the home government

hongoshi 〈ほんごし：本腰〉
　hongoshi-o-ireru 〈本腰を入れる〉 set about ((a task)) in real earnest.

hongyō 〈ほんぎょう：本業〉 *see.* honshoku.

hon・i 〈ほんい：本位〉 a standard.
　kin-hon・i （金本位） the gold standard
　jiko-hon・i-nohito （自己本位の人） an egoistic person

hōnin 〈ほうにん：放任〉 noninterference.
　hōnin-shugi （放任主義） a let-alone policy
　hōnin-suru 〈放任する〉 let ((a person)) alone, leave ((a matter)) to take its own course.

honjitsu 〈ほんじつ：本日〉 today, this day.
　Honjitsu-kyūgyô. （本日休業.） Closed for Today.

honka 〈ほんか：本科〉 a regular course.

honkaku-teki(-na) 〈ほんかくてき(な)：本格的(な)〉 real, regular, full-scale.
　honkaku-teki-na natsu （本格的な夏） a real summer

honkan 〈ほんかん：本館〉 the main building.

honke 〈ほんけ：本家〉 the head family.
　honke-hommoto （本家本元） the original home, the originator

hon-kenchiku 〈ほんけんちく：本建築〉 a permanent building.

honki 〈ほんき：本気〉 seriousness, earnestness.
　honki-no 〈本気の〉 serious, earnest.
　honki-de 〈本気で〉 seriously, in earnest.
　honki-de-iu （本気で言う） speak in earnest, mean ((it))
　honki-ni 〈本気に〉 in earnest.
　honki-ni-natte hataraku （本気になって働く） work in earnest

honkoku-ban 〈ほんこくばん：翻刻版〉 a reprint.

honkyo 〈ほんきょ：本拠〉 the base, the headquarters, one's stronghold.

honne 〈ほんね：本音〉
　honne-o-haku 〈本音を吐く〉 disclose one's real intention, give oneself away.

honnen 〈ほんねん：本年〉 this year.

honnin 〈ほんにん：本人〉 the person himself; the person in question.
　honnin-jishin-de 〈本人自身で〉 in person.

hon-no〈ほんの〉mere, just, only.

    hon-no sukoshi〈ほんの少し〉just a little

    hon-no kodomo〈ほんの子供〉only a child

honnô〈ほんのう：本能〉instinct.

  honnô-teki(-na)〈本能的(な)〉instinctive.

  honnô-teki-ni〈本能的に〉instinctively.

honnori(-to)〈ほんのり(と)〉faintly, slightly.

honobono〈ほのぼの〉

    Yo-ga-honobono-to-ake-hajimeta.〈夜がほのぼのと明け始めた.〉The day began to dawn.

    Sore-o-kiite honobono-to-shita-kimochi-ni-natta.〈それを聞いてほのぼのとした気持ちになった.〉The story warmed my heart.

honomekasu〈ほのめかす〉hint ((at *or* that)), drop a hint ((to)), suggest, allude ((to)).

honoo〈ほのお：炎〉a flame, a blaze.

  honoo-ni-tsutsumareru〈炎に包まれる〉be in flames, blaze up.

honrai〈ほんらい：本来〉originally, essentially, in itself; properly speaking.

    honrai-ii-mono（本来いい物）a thing good in itself

honrô〈ほんろう：翻ろう〉

  honrô-suru〈翻ろうする〉toss about; trifle ((with)), make fun ((of)).

honron〈ほんろん：本論〉the main issue; this subject.

    honron-ni hairu（本論に入る）proceed to the main issue

honrui〈ほんるい：本塁〉the home base.

    honrui-da（本塁打）a home run, a homer

honryô〈ほんりょう：本領〉

  honryô-o-hakki-suru〈本領を発揮する〉show oneself at one's best, show one's real ability.

honryû〈ほんりゅう：本流〉the main course, a main current.

honseki〈ほんせき：本籍〉one's domicile.

honsen〈ほんせん：本線〉the main line, the trunk (line).

    Tôkai-dô-honsen（東海道本線）the Tokaido Main Line

honsen〈ほんせん：本船〉the mother ship; this ship.

    honsen-watashi（本船渡し）free on board (F.O.B.; f.o.b.)

honsha〈ほんしゃ：本社〉the head office; this office, our firm.

honshi〈ほんし：本紙〉this paper, these columns; the main section.

honshiki〈ほんしき：本式〉

  honshiki-no〈本式の〉regular, formal.

honshiki-no shokuji （本式の食事） a regular dinner

honshiki-ni 〈本式に〉 regularly, formally, in style.

honshiki-ni Eigo o narau （本式に英語を習う） study English in a systematic way

honshin 〈ほんしん：本心〉 one's real intention.

honshin-wa 〈本心は〉 at heart.

honshin-kara 〈本心から〉 from one's heart.

honshitsu 〈ほんしつ：本質〉 essence, substance.

honshitsu-teki-na 〈本質的な〉 essential, substantial.

honshitsu-teki-ni 〈本質的に〉 essentially, in itself, substantially.

honsho 〈ほんしょ：本署〉 the chief police station; this station.

honshô 〈ほんしょう：本性〉

honshô-o-arawasu 〈本性を現わす〉 reveal one's real character, unmask oneself.

honshoku 〈ほんしょく：本職〉 one's principal occupation, one's regular work; an expert, a professional.

bengo-shi-ga-honshoku-de-aru （弁護士が本職である） be a lawyer by profession

Honshû 〈ほんしゅう：本州〉 Japan proper, the Main Island.

honsô 〈ほんそう：奔走〉

honsô-suru 〈奔走する〉 busy oneself ((about)), take an active part ((in)).

hon-suji 〈ほんすじ：本筋〉 the main line.

hon-suji-kara hazureru （本筋から外れる） wander from the main subject

hon-suji-ni modosu （本筋に戻す） resume the thread of one's discourse

hontai 〈ほんたい：本体〉 *see.* jittai （実体）.

hon-tate 〈ほんたて：本立て〉 a bookstand, a bookrack, ((a pair of)) bookends.

honten 〈ほんてん：本店〉 the head office, the main store.

hontô 〈ほんとう：本当〉 truth, reality, a fact.

Sore-wa hontô-kashira? （それは本当かしら.） Can it be true?

hontô-no 〈本当の〉 true, real, right, proper.

hontô-no hanashi （本当の話） a true story

hontô-no koto （本当の事） a real fact

hontô-rashii 〈本当らしい〉 likely, plausible.

ikanimo hontô-rashii （いかにも本当らしい） most likely

hontô-rashii uso o iu （本当らしいうそを言う） tell a plausible lie

hontô-o-ieba〈本当を言えば〉to tell the truth.

hontô-ni〈本当に〉really, truly, in fact, in earnest.

 Hontô-ni utsukushii.（本当に美しい.）It's really beautiful.

 Hontô-ni arigatô.（本当にありがとう.）Thank you very much indeed.

hontô-ni-naru〈本当になる〉come true.

 Kanojo-no kotoba ga hontô-ni-natta.（彼女の言葉が本当になった.）Her words came true.

hontô-ni suru〈本当にする〉believe, take ((it)) seriously.

 Dare-ga omae-no-iu-koto o hontô-ni-suru-mono-ka.（だれがお前の言うことを本当にするものか.）Who would believe you?

hon·yaku〈ほんやく：翻訳〉translation.

 hon·yaku-de yomu（翻訳で読む）read ((some work)) in translation

 hon·yaku-sha（翻訳者）a translator

hon·yaku-suru〈翻訳する〉translate ((into)), put ((into)).

 seisho o Nihon-go-ni hon·yaku-suru（聖書を日本語に翻訳する）translate the Bible into Japanese

honyū-〈ほにゅう-：ほ乳-〉

 honyū-bin（ほ乳瓶）a nursing bottle

 honyū-dôbutsu（ほ乳動物）a mammal

 honyū-rui（ほ乳類）Mammalia

honzan〈ほんざん：本山〉the head temple.

honzon〈ほんぞん：本尊〉the principal image, an idol.

hoo〈ほお〉a cheek.

 hoo-bone（ほお骨）a cheekbone

hoo-o-akarameru〈ほおを赤らめる〉blush.

hôô〈ほうおう：法王〉the Pope.

hoo-beni〈ほおべに：ほお紅〉rouge.

hoo-beni-o-tsukeru〈ほお紅を付ける〉rouge one's cheeks, put on rouge.

hoo-hige〈ほおひげ〉whiskers.

hoo-kaburi or **hoo-kamuri**〈ほおかぶり，ほおかむり〉

hoo-kaburi-suru or *hoo-kamuri-suru*〈ほおかぶりする，ほおかむりする〉cover one's cheeks with a towel; affect ignorance.

hoon〈ほおん：保温〉keeping warm.

hoo-zue〈ほおづえ〉

hoo-zue-o-tsuku〈ほおづえをつく〉rest one's chin on one's hands.

hoo-zuri〈ほおずり〉

hoo-zuri-suru〈ほおずりする〉press one's cheek against another's.

hoppô 〈ほっぽう：北方〉the north.

　hoppô-ni〈北方に〉to the north ((of))

　hoppô-no〈北方の〉north, northern.

Hoppyô-yô〈ほっぴようよう：北氷洋〉the Arctic Ocean.

hora〈ほら〉a brag, a big talk.

　hora-fuki〈ほら吹き〉a braggart, a boaster

　hora-o-fuku〈ほらを吹く〉brag, talk big, boast.

hora!〈ほら〉Look! / There! / Lo!

　Hora-goran!〈ほらごらん.〉Look there!

horaana〈ほらあな：洞穴〉a cave, a cavern.

hora-gai〈ほらがい：ほら貝〉a trumpet shell, a conch.

horebore〈ほれぼれ〉

　horebore-suru〈ほれぼれする〉be charmed, be enchanted.

　horebore-suru-yô-na〈ほれぼれするような〉charming, attractive, fascinating, enchanting.

hôrei〈ほうれい：法令〉laws and ordinances.

　hôrei-ni-yori〈法令により〉by law.

hôren-sô〈ほうれんそう：ほうれん草〉spinach.

horeru〈ほれる〉fall in love ((with)); be attracted ((by a person's personality)).

　hore-au〈ほれ合う〉be in love with each other

hôretsu〈ほうれつ：放列〉a battery.

　kamera no hôretsu o shiku（カメラの放列を敷く）arrange a battery of cameras

hori〈ほり：堀〉a moat, a canal.

hori〈ほり：彫り〉engraving.

　hori-no-fukai kao（彫りの深い顔）a clearcut face

hôri-ageru〈ほうりあげる：ほうり上げる〉throw up.

hori-ateru〈ほりあてる：掘り当てる〉strike.

　yuden o hori-ateru（油田を掘り当てる）strike oil

horidashi-mono〈ほりだしもの：掘り出し物〉a find; a bargain.

hori-dasu〈ほりだす：掘り出す〉dig out.

　chichû-kara hori-dasu（地中から掘り出す）dig ((something)) out of the ground

hôri-dasu〈ほうりだす：放り出す〉throw ((a thing)) out; expel.

　gakkô-o-hôri-dasareru（学校を放り出される）be expelled from school

hôri-gaku〈ほうりがく：法理学〉jurisprudence.

hori-kaesu〈ほりかえす：掘り返す〉dig up.

hôri-komu〈ほうりこむ〉throw in(to).

hori-okosu〈ほりおこす：掘り起こす〉*see.* hori-kaesu.

hori-sageru〈ほりさげる：掘り下げる〉dig down.

     mondai-o-hori-sagete-kangaeru（問題を掘り下げて考える）delve into the problem, probe into the matter

hôritsu〈ほうりつ：法律〉a law, (the) law.

     hôritsu o benkyô-suru（法律を勉強する）read the law

     hôritsu-jimu-sho（法律事務所）a law office

     hôritsu-ka（法律家）a lawyer, a jurist

     hôritsu-jô-no〈法律上の〉legal.

     hôritsu-jô〈法律上〉legally.

hori-wari〈ほりわり：掘り割り〉a canal.

horo〈ほろ〉a hood, a top.

     horo o kakeru（ほろを掛ける）pull up the hood

hôrô〈ほうろう：放浪〉wandering.

     hôrô-heki（放浪癖）vagrant habits

     hôrô-suru〈放浪する〉wander about.

hôrô(-shitsu)〈ほうろう（しつ）：ほうろう（質）〉enamel.

     hôrô-biki-no〈ほうろう引きの〉enameled.

horobiru〈ほろびる：滅びる〉be ruined, perish, cease to exist, die out.

     horobosu〈滅ぼす〉ruin, destroy, overthrow, annihilate.

     mi o horobosu（身を滅ぼす）ruin oneself

     horobosareru〈滅ぼされる〉be overthrown.

horori-to〈ほろりと〉

     horori-to-suru〈ほろりとする〉be moved to tears.

horo-yoi〈ほろよい：ほろ酔い〉

     horo-yoi-no〈ほろ酔いの〉slightly intoxicated, mellow, happy.

horu〈ほる：掘る〉dig.

horu〈ほる：彫る〉carve, engrave, chisel.

hôru〈ほうる〉throw, pitch, toss.

horumarin〈ホルマリン〉formalin.

horumon〈ホルモン〉(a) hormone.

     dansei-horumon（男性ホルモン）a male hormone

     josei-horumon（女性ホルモン）a female hormone

horun〈ホルン〉a horn.

     horun o fuku（ホルンを吹く）play a horn

horyo〈ほりょ：捕虜〉a prisoner, a captive.

     horyo-ni-naru（捕虜になる）be taken prisoner(s)

horyo-shûyô-jo〔捕虜収容所〕 a prisoners' camp

horyû〈ほりゅう：保留〉reservation.

horyû-suru〈保留する〉reserve.

hôryû〈ほうりゅう：放流〉

hôryû-suru〈放流する〉discharge, stock.

kawa ni sakana-o-hôryû-suru〔川に魚を放流する〕 stock a river with fish

hosa〈ほさ：補佐〉aid, assistance; an assistant, an adviser, a counselor.

kachô-hosa〔課長補佐〕 an assistant section head

hosa-suru〈補佐する〉aid, assist, help, advise, counsel.

hôsaku〈ほうさく：豊作〉an abundant harvest, a bumper crop.

hôsaku〈ほうさく：方策〉a plan, a policy, a means, a scheme.

banzen-no hôsaku〔万全の方策〕 a prudential policy

hôsan〈ほうさん：ほう酸〉boric acid.

hosei〈ほせい：補正〉

hosei-yosan〔補正予算〕 a revised budget

hosei-suru〈補正する〉revise, rectify, correct.

hôsei〈ほうせい：砲声〉the sound of firing, the roaring of a gun.

hôsei〈ほうせい：法制〉laws, legislation.

hôseki〈ほうせき：宝石〉a jewel, a gem.

hôseki-rui〔宝石類〕 jewelry

hôseki-shô〔宝石商〕 a jeweler

hosen〈ほせん：保線〉

hosen-kôji〔保線工事〕 track maintenance work

hôsenka〈ほうせんか：ほう仙花〉a balsam.

hôsha〈ほうしゃ：放射〉emission, radiation, emanation.

hôsha-suru〈放射する〉emit, radiate, emanate.

hôsha-jô〈ほうしゃじょう：放射状〉

hôsha-jô dôro〔放射状道路〕 radial roads

hôsha-jô-no〈放射状の〉radiate, radiated, radial.

hôsha-jô-ni〈放射状に〉radiately, radially.

hoshaku〈ほしゃく：保釈〉bail(ment).

hoshaku-shussho-chû-de-aru〔保釈出所中である〕 be out on bail

hoshaku-kin〔保釈金〕 bail (money)

hoshaku-kin o tsumu〔保釈金を積む〕 furnish bail ((for))

hoshaku-suru〈保釈する〉bail.

hôsha-nô〈ほうしゃのう：放射能〉radioactivity.

hôsha-nô-bai〔放射能灰〕 radioactive ashes

hôsha-nô-no or *hôsha-sei-no* 〈放射能の，放射性の〉radioactive.

hôsha-sen 〈ほうしゃせん：放射線〉radioactive rays.

hoshi 〈ほし：星〉a star; a point.
　　hoshi-akari（星明かり）　starlight
　　hoshi-zora（星空）　a starry sky
　　hoshi-jirushi（星印）　an asterisk
　　hoshi-uranai（星占い）　astrology
　　hoshi o kasegu（星を稼ぐ）　score a point

hôshi 〈ほうし：胞子〉a spore.

hôshi 〈ほうし：奉仕〉(a) service.
　　shakai-hôshi（社会奉仕）　public service
　　hôshi-hin（奉仕品）　a bargain
　　hôshi-suru〈奉仕する〉serve, render service(s) ((to)).

hoshi-budô 〈ほしぶどう：干しぶどう〉raisins, currants.

hoshigaru 〈ほしがる：欲しがる〉want, desire, wish ((for)), long ((for)), covet.

hoshii 〈ほしい：欲しい〉want, desire, wish ((for)), care ((for)), would like.
　　hoshii-mono（欲しい物）　a thing desired

hoshiimama 〈ほしいまま〉
　　hoshiimama-ni-suru〈ほしいままにする〉do as one pleases, have one's own way, give (a) loose ((to)), command, wield.
　　　　sôzô-o-hoshiimama-ni-suru（想像をほしいままにする）　give free play to one's imagination
　　　　kensei o hoshiimama-ni-suru（権勢をほしいままにする）　wield power

hôshiki 〈ほうしき：方式〉a formula, a form.

hoshin 〈ほしん：保身〉self-protection.
　　hoshin-jutsu（保身術）　the art of defending one's own interest

hôshin 〈ほうしん：方針〉a course, a policy, a plan.
　　hôshin o tateru（方針を立てる）　make a plan
　　hôshin-o-ayamaru（方針を誤る）　take a wrong policy
　　eigyô-hôshin（営業方針）　a business policy

hôshin 〈ほうしん：放心〉
　　hôshin-suru〈放心する〉be absentminded, be abstracted.
　　hôshin-jôtai-de〈放心状態で〉with an air of abstraction.

hoshô 〈ほしょう：保障〉guarantee, security.
　　shûdan-hoshô（集団保障）　collective security
　　hoshô-suru〈保障する〉guarantee, secure, ensure.

hoshô 〈ほしょう：保証〉 guarantee, security, assurance.
  hoshô-kin（保証金） guaranty money, security
  hoshô-nin（保証人） a guarantor, a surety.
  hoshô-suru 〈保証する〉 guarantee, warrant, assure.
  hoshô-tsuki-no 〈保証付きの〉 guaranteed, warranted, certified.
    san-nen-kan hoshô-tsuki-no denki-reizô-ko（三年間保証付きの電気冷蔵庫） an electric refrigerator guaranteed for three years

hoshô 〈ほしょう：補償〉 (a) compensation, (an) indemnity.
  hoshô-kin（補償金） compensation (money), an indemnity
  hoshô-suru 〈補償する〉 compensate ((for)), make up ((for)), indemnify.

hoshô 〈ほしょう：歩しょう〉 a sentry, a sentinel; a picket.
  hoshô o oku（歩しょうを置く） post a sentry
  hoshô-ni-tatsu（歩しょうに立つ） stand sentinel

hôshô 〈ほうしょう：報奨〉 a bonus.

hôshô 〈ほうしょう：報償〉 compensation, remuneration.
  hôshô-kin（報償金） compensation money

hôshô 〈ほうしょう：褒賞〉 a prize, a reward.

hoshu 〈ほしゅ：捕手〉 a catcher.

hoshu 〈ほしゅ：保守〉 conservatism.
  hoshu-jin·ei（保守陣営） a conservative camp
  hoshu-tô（保守党） the conservative party
  hoshu-teki(-na) 〈保守的(な)〉 conservative.

hoshû 〈ほしゅう：補習〉 a supplementary lesson.
  hoshû o ukeru（補習を受ける） take supplementary lessons

hoshû 〈ほしゅう：補修〉 repair, mending.
  hoshû-kôji（補修工事） repair work(s)
  hoshû-suru 〈補修する〉 repair, mend.

hôshû 〈ほうしゅう：報酬〉 remuneration, a reward, pay, a fee.
  hôshû-nashi-de（報酬なしで） without remuneration
  ～-no-hôshû-to-shite（～の報酬として） in reward for...
  hôshû-o-dasu 〈報酬を出す〉 remunerate, reward, pay.

hôshutsu 〈ほうしゅつ：放出〉
  hôshutsu-suru 〈放出する〉 release.

hosô 〈ほそう：舗装〉 pavement.
  hosô-dôro（舗装道路） a pavement, a paved road
  hosô-suru 〈舗装する〉 pave.

hôsô 〈ほうそう〉 *see.* tennentô.

hôsô 〈ほうそう：法曹〉

hôsô-kai（法曹界）　legal circles

hôsô〈ほうそう：放送〉broadcasting, a broadcast.

hôsô-o-kiku（放送を聞く）　listen to the radio broadcast

hôsô-kyoku（放送局）　a broadcasting station

hôsô-bangumi（放送番組）　a radio program, a TV program

chûkei-hôsô（中継放送）　relay broadcasting

minkan-hôsô（民間放送）　a commercial broadcast

nama-hôsô（生放送）　a live broadcast

terebi-hôsô（テレビ放送）　a television broadcast, a telecast

zenkoku-hôsô（全国放送）　a national network broadcast

hôsô-suru〈放送する〉broadcast; telecast, televise.

hôsô-chû-no〈放送中の〉on the air.

hôsô〈ほうそう：包装〉packing.

hôsô-shi（包装紙）　packing paper, wrapping paper

hôsô-suru〈包装する〉pack, wrap (up).

hoso-biki〈ほそびき：細引き〉a cord, a small-gauge rope, a hempen cord.

hosoboso〈ほそぼそ：細々〉

hosoboso-to-kurasu（細々と暮らす）　make a poor living

hosoboso-to-shôbai-o-tsuzukeru（細々と商売を続ける）　carry on a scanty business

hoso-gaki〈ほそがき：細書き〉

hoso-gaki-no〈細書きの〉fine-pointed, slender-writing.

hosoi〈ほそい：細い〉thin, fine, slender, narrow.

hosoi koe（細い声）　a thin voice

hosoi ito（細い糸）　a fine thread

hosoi kubi（細い首）　a slender neck

hosoi michi（細い道）　a narrow lane

hosoku-naru〈細くなる〉become thin, become slender, taper off.

hosoku-suru〈細くする〉make thin, make slender, narrow.

hosoku〈ほそく：補足〉supplement, (a) complement.

hosoku-suru〈補足する〉supplement, complement.

hôsoku〈ほそく：法則〉a law, a rule.

hoso-me〈ほそめ：細目〉

hoso-me-ni-kiru〈細めに切る〉cut ((something)) fine.

hosomeru〈ほそめる：細める〉narrow.

me-o-hosomete〈目を細めて〉with one's eyes half-closed.

hoso-mi〈ほそみ：細身〉

hoso-mi-no〈細身の〉thin, slender, narrow.

hoso-michi〈ほそみち：細道〉a narrow lane.

hoso-nagai〈ほそながい：細長い〉long and slender, long and narrow.

hossa〈ほっさ：発作〉a fit, a spasm, an attack.

　　hossa-ga-okiru（発作が起きる）have a fit

hossa-teki(-na)〈発作的(な)〉fitful, spasmodic, temporary.

hossa-teki-ni〈発作的に〉fitfully, spasmodically, by fits (and starts).

hossoku〈ほっそく：発足〉starting, inauguration.

hossoku-suru〈発足する〉start, make a start, be inaugurated.

hossori〈ほっそり〉

hossori-shita〈ほっそりした〉slim, slender, slight, thin.

　　karada-tsuki-ga-hossori-shite-iru（体つきがほっそりしている）have a slender figure

hossuru〈ほっする：欲する〉desire, wish, want, would.

hosu〈ほす：干す〉dry, air.

　　hinata-de hosu（日なたで干す）dry in the sun

hôsu〈ホース〉a hose.

shôka-yô-hôsu〈消火用ホース〉a fire hose

hôsui〈ほうすい：放水〉discharge, drainage.

　　hôsui-ro（放水路）a drainage canal

hôsui-suru〈放水する〉drain water off.

hôtai〈ほうたい：包帯〉a bandage.

hôtai-o-suru〈包帯をする〉bandage, apply a bandage ((to)), dress.

　　hôtai-o-toru（包帯を取る）unbandage, remove the bandage

hotaru〈ほたる〉a firefly.

hotate-gai〈ほたてがい：帆立貝〉a scallop.

hotchikisu〈ホッチキス〉a stapler.

hotchikisu-de-tomeru〈ホッチキスで留める〉staple together.

hôtei〈ほうてい：法廷〉a (law) court.

　　hôtei-de-arasou（法廷で争う）go to law ((with))

　　hôtei-tôsô（法廷闘争）courtroom struggle

hôtei〈ほうてい：法定〉

　　hôtei-dairi-nin（法定代理人）a legal representative

　　hôtei-kinri（法定金利）the legal rate of interest

hôtei-no〈法定の〉legal.

hôtei-shiki〈ほうていしき：方程式〉an equation.

hô-teki(-na)〈ほうてき(な)：法的(な)〉legal.

　　hô-teki kenri（法的権利）a legal right

hô-teki konkyo〈法的根拠〉 a legal basis

hôten〈ほうてん：法典〉a code of laws; a canon.

hoteru〈ほてる：火照る〉feel hot, burn, flush.

hôtô〈ほうとう：宝刀〉a treasured sword.

denka-no-hôtô-o-nuku〈伝家の宝刀を抜く〉play one's trump card.

hôtô〈ほうとう：放とう〉dissipation, prodigality, debauchery.

hôtô-mono〈放とう者〉 a fast liver, a debauchee

hôtô-musuko〈放とう息子〉 a prodigal son

hôtô-suru〈放とうする〉dissipate one's fortune, live fast, sow one's wild oats.

hôtô-no〈放とうの〉dissipated, prodigal.

hotobashiru〈ほとばしる〉gush out, spurt out, spout, pour.

hotobori〈ほとぼり〉

hotobori-ga-sameru-made〈ほとぼりが冷めるまで〉till the affair blows over, till the excitement cools down.

hotohoto〈ほとほと〉quite, completely, entirely, utterly.

hotohoto heikô-suru〈ほとほと閉口する〉 be quite at a loss

hotoke〈ほとけ：仏〉the Buddha; the dead, the deceased.

hotoke-no-yô-na-hito〈仏のような人〉 a saint of a man

hotondo〈ほとんど〉almost, nearly, about; little, few, almost not; hardly, scarcely.

hotondo zembu〈ほとんど全部〉 almost all

Hotondo deki-agatte-iru.〈ほとんど出来上がっている。〉 It is nearly finished.

Seikô no mikomi-wa hotondo-nai.〈成功の見込みはほとんどない。〉 There is little hope of success.

Heya-niwa hotondo-hito-ga-nokotte-i-nakatta.〈部屋にはほとんど人が残っていなかった。〉 Few people were left in the room.

Kare-wa hotondo-kane-o-motte-i-nai.〈彼はほとんど金を持っていない。〉 He has almost no money.

Sore-wa hotondo-fu-kanô-da.〈それはほとんど不可能だ。〉 It's hardly possible.

hotori〈ほとり〉

hotori-ni〈ほとりに〉in the neighborhood ((of)), near, (close) by.

hototogisu〈ほととぎす〉a (little) cuckoo.

hottan〈ほったん：発端〉the origin.

koto no hottan〈事の発端〉 the origin of an affair

somosomo-no-hottan〈そもそもの発端〉 the (very) beginning

hottarakasu 〈ほったらかす〉 see. hôtte-oku.

hottate-goya 〈ほったてごや：掘っ立て小屋〉 a hovel, a hut, a shack.

hôtte-oku 〈ほうっておく：放っておく〉 neglect, lay aside, leave alone.

    shigoto o hôtte-oku（仕事を放っておく） leave one's work undone

    moshi-hôtte-okaretara（もし放っておかれたら） if left alone

hotto 〈ほっと〉

hotto-suru 〈ほっとする〉 feel relieved, breathe freely again.

    Sore-o-kiite hotto-shita.（それを聞いてほっとした。） I felt relieved to hear that.

hotto-shite 〈ほっとして〉 with relief.

hotto-kêki 〈ホットケーキ〉 a hot cake, a griddle cake, a pancake.

hottsuki-aruku 〈ほっつきあるく：ほっつき歩く〉 traipse about, gad about.

hôwa(-jôtai) 〈ほうわ（じょうたい）：飽和（状態）〉 saturation.

    hôwa-ten（飽和点） the saturation point

hôwa-jôtai-ni-aru 〈飽和状態にある〉 be saturated, be in saturation.

hoyahoya 〈ほやほや〉 steaming, hot; fresh.

    yaki-tate-no-hoyahoya（焼きたてのほやほや） steaming hot from the oven(*or* the fire)

    daigaku-de-no-hoyahoya（大学出のほやほや） a young man fresh from college

hoyô 〈ほよう：保養〉 recuperation, recreation.

    hoyô-ni iku（保養に行く） go ((to a place)) for one's health

    hoyô-chi（保養地） a health resort

hoyô-suru 〈保養する〉 recuperate oneself, recreate oneself.

hôyô 〈ほうよう：法要〉 a Buddhist service.

    hôyô o itonamu（法要を営む） hold a Buddhist service for the dead

hôyô 〈ほうよう：抱擁〉 an embrace, a hug.

hôyô-suru 〈抱擁する〉 embrace, hug.

hôyô-ryoku 〈ほうようりょく：包容力〉

hôyô-ryoku-no-aru 〈包容力のある〉 broad-minded.

hoyû 〈ほゆう：保有〉 possession.

    hoyû-mai（保有米） rice holdings

hoyū-suru 〈保有する〉 possess, hold, keep, retain.

hozei-sôko 〈ほぜいそうこ：保税倉庫〉 a bonded warehouse.

hozen 〈ほぜん：保全〉 preservation, integrity, maintenance.

    kankyô-hozen（環境保全） the preservation of the environment

    ryôdo-hozen（領土保全） territorial integrity

hozen-suru 〈保全する〉 preserve the integrity ((of)), keep ((one's country)) intact.

hozon 〈ほぞん：保存〉 preservation, conservation.

hozon-suru 〈保存する〉 preserve, keep, conserve.

hyakka-jiten 〈ひゃっかじてん：百科事典〉 an encyclop(a)edia.

hyakka-ten 〈ひゃっかてん：百貨店〉 a department store.

hyaku 〈ひゃく：百〉 a hundred.

  ni-hyaku 〈二百〉 two hundred

  hyaku-bai 〈百倍〉 one hundred times

  hyaku-bun-no-ichi 〈百分の一〉 one hundredth, one percent

  dai-hyaku 〈第百〉 the hundredth

  nambyaku-to-iu-hitobito 〈何百という人々〉 hundreds of people

hyakubun 〈ひゃくぶん：百聞〉

  Hyakubun-wa-ikken-ni-shikazu. 〈百聞は一見にしかず.〉 Seeing is believing.

hyaku-bun-ritsu 〈ひゃくぶんりつ：百分率〉 (a) percentage.

hyakugai 〈ひゃくがい：百害〉

  Hyakugai-atte ichiri-nashi. 〈百害あって一利なし.〉 Far from being beneficial, it does harm to you.

hyaku-hachi-jû-do 〈ひゃくはちじゅうど：百八十度〉 one hundred and eighty degrees.

  hyaku-hachi-jû-do-no-tenkan-o-suru 〈百八十度の転換をする〉 make a complete about-face, make a *volte-face*, make a radical change ((in)).

hyaku-man 〈ひゃくまん：百万〉 a million.

  hyaku-man-chôja 〈百万長者〉 a millionaire, a millionairess

hyaku-nen 〈ひゃくねん：百年〉 a hundred years, a century.

  hyaku-nen-no kei 〈百年の計〉 a farsighted policy

  hyaku-nen-sai 〈百年祭〉 a centenary

  Kô-nattara-hyaku-nen-me-da. 〈こうなったら百年目だ.〉 All is up with me.

hyakunichi-zeki 〈ひゃくにちぜき：百日ぜき〉 whooping cough.

hyaku-pâsento 〈ひゃくパーセント：百パーセント〉 one hundred percent.

  kôka-hyaku-pâsento-de-aru 〈効果百パーセントである〉 be 100 percent efficacious

hyaku-ten 〈ひゃくてん：百点〉 one hundred points, full marks.

hyaku-tô-ban 〈ひゃくとうばん：110番〉 110.

  hyaku-tô-ban ni denwa-suru 〈110番に電話する〉 dial 110

hyakuyaku 〈ひゃくやく：百薬〉

Sake wa hyakuyaku-no-chô.〔酒は百薬の長。〕 *Sake* is the best of all medicines.

hyappatsu-hyakuchû〈ひゃっぱつひゃくちゅう：百発百中〉

hyappatsu-hyakuchû-de-aru〈百発百中である〉never miss the target.

hyô〈ひょう〉a leopard, a panther.

hyô〈ひょう〉hail, a hailstone.

Hyô-ga-furu.〈ひょうが降る。〉It hails.

hyô〈ひょう：票〉a vote.

hyô〈ひょう：表〉a table, a schedule, a list.

jikoku-hyô（時刻表）a time table

teika-hyô（定価表）a price list

hyô-ni-suru〈表にする〉make into a table, make a list ((of)).

hyôban〈ひょうばん：評判〉fame, (a) reputation, popularity, a rumor; notoriety.

hyôban-ga-ii〈評判がいい〉be well spoken of, have a good reputation.

hyôban-ga-warui（評判が悪い）be ill spoken of, have a bad reputation

〜-to-iu-hyôban-da.〈〜という評判だ。〉It is rumored that... .

hyôban-no(-takai)〈評判の（高い）〉famous, popular; notorious.

hyôchaku〈ひょうちゃく：漂着〉

hyôchaku-suru〈漂着する〉be washed ashore, drift ashore.

hyôdai〈ひょうだい：表題〉a title, a heading, a caption.

hyôdai o tsukeru（表題を付ける）give a title ((to))

hyôga〈ひょうが：氷河〉a glacier.

hyôgen〈ひょうげん：表現〉(an) expression, (a) manifestation.

hyôgen-ryoku（表現力）one's power of expression

hyôgen-suru〈表現する〉express, manifest.

hyôgi〈ひょうぎ：評議〉conference, consultation, discussion.

hyôgi-in（評議員）a councilor; a trustee, a board of trustees

hyôgi-kai（評議会）a council, a conference

hyôgi-chû-de-aru（評議中である）be under discussion

hyôgi-suru〈評議する〉confer, counsel together.

hyôgo〈ひょうご：標語〉a slogan, a motto.

hyôgu-shi〈ひょうぐし：表具師〉a paper hanger, a mounter.

hyôhaku〈ひょうはく：漂白〉bleaching.

hyôhaku-zai（漂白剤）a bleaching agent

hyôhaku-suru〈漂白する〉bleach.

hyôhi〈ひょうひ：表皮〉the cuticle, the bark.

hyôhon 〈ひょうほん：標本〉a specimen.

    dōbutsu-no hyôhon 〈動物の標本〉 a zoological specimen

hyoi-to 〈ひょいと〉suddenly, accidentally, lightly.

    hyoi-to mizo o tobi-koeru 〈ひょいと溝を跳び越える〉 leap lightly across a ditch

    hyoi-to arawareru 〈ひょいと現れる〉 bob up

    hyoi-to atama-ni-ukabu 〈ひょいと頭に浮かぶ〉 flash across ((a person's)) mind

    ni-kai-no mado-kara hyoi-to atama o dasu 〈二階の窓からひょいと頭を出す〉 pop one's head out of the upstairs window

hyôji 〈ひょうじ：表示〉(an) indication.

    hyôji-ki 〈表示器〉 an indicator

    hyôji-suru 〈表示する〉indicate.

    ishi o hyôji-suru 〈意思を表示する〉 indicate one's intention

hyôjô 〈ひょうじょう：表情〉a look, (an) expression.

    hyôjô-ni-tonda or *hyôjô-no-aru* 〈表情に富んだ，表情のある〉expressive.

hyôjun 〈ひょうじゅん：標準〉a standard, a level.

    hyôjun-ni tassuru 〈標準に達する〉 come up to (the) standard

    hyôjun-go 〈標準語〉 the standard language

    hyôjun-ji 〈標準時〉 (the) standard time

    hyôjun-ka-suru or *hyôjun-ni-awaseru* 〈標準化する，標準に合わせる〉standardize.

    hyôjun-no or *hyôjun-teki(-na)* 〈標準の，標準的(な)〉standard, average.

    hyôjun-ika-no 〈標準以下の〉below standard.

hyôka 〈ひょうか：評価〉appraisal, valuation, estimation, evaluation, assessment.

    kadai-hyôka 〈過大評価〉 overestimation

    kashō-hyôka 〈過小評価〉 underestimation

    hyôka-suru 〈評価する〉appraise, value, estimate, evaluate, assess.

hyôkai 〈ひょうかい：氷解〉

    hyôkai-suru 〈氷解する〉melt away, be cleared, be dispelled.

hyôketsu 〈ひょうけつ：氷結〉

    hyôketsu-suru 〈氷結する〉freeze, be frozen, be icebound.

hyôketsu 〈ひょうけつ：票決〉a vote, a decision by vote.

    hyôketsu-suru 〈票決する〉vote ((on)), take a vote ((on)).

hyôki 〈ひょうき：表記〉

    hyôki-no 〈表記の〉mentioned on the face.

    hyôki-no tokoro 〈表記の所〉 the address mentioned on the outside

hyōkin 〈ひょうきん〉

    hyôkin-mono〈ひょうきん者〉a facetious person

   hyôkin-na〈ひょうきんな〉funny, jocular, facetious, droll.

hyokkori〈ひょっこり〉suddenly, unexpectedly, by chance.

    hyokkori-arawareru（ひょっこり現れる）appear unexpectedly, bob up

hyōkō〈ひょうこう：標高〉*see.* kaibatsu.

hyōmei〈ひょうめい：表明〉

   hyômei-suru〈表明する〉state, express, show, indicate, manifest.

    shai o hyômei-suru（謝意を表明する）express one's appreciation

    hantai-o-hyômei-suru（反対を表明する）express oneself against, declare against

hyōmen〈ひょうめん：表面〉the surface, the outside, (an) appearance.

    hyômen-chôryoku（表面張力）surface tension

   hyômen-no〈表面の〉surface, external, outside, seeming.

   hyômen-wa〈表面は〉on the surface.

   hyômen-ka-suru〈表面化する〉come to the front.

hyōnō〈ひょうのう：氷のう〉an ice bag.

    hyônô-tsuri（氷のうつり）an ice-bag suspender

hyōri〈ひょうり：表裏〉inside and outside, two sides.

   hyôri-no-aru〈表裏のある〉double-faced, double-dealing, treacherous.

    hyôri-no-aru-hito（表裏のある人）a double-dealer

hyorohyoro(-to)〈ひょろひょろ(と)〉staggeringly, totteringly.

    hyorohyoro aruku（ひょろひょろ歩く）walk staggeringly

    hyorohyoro-tachi-agaru（ひょろひょろ立ち上がる）stagger to one's feet

hyōron〈ひょうろん：評論〉a review, a comment.

    hyôron-ka（評論家）a reviewer, a commentator

   hyôron-suru〈評論する〉review, comment ((on)).

hyoro-nagai〈ひょろながい：ひょろ長い〉long and narrow, spindly, lanky, gangling.

    hyoro-nagai otoko（ひょろ長い男）a lanky man

hyoro-tsuku〈ひょろつく〉stagger, totter.

hyōryū〈ひょうりゅう：漂流〉drifting.

    hyôryû-butsu（漂流物）driftage

   hyôryû-suru〈漂流する〉drift (about).

hyōsatsu〈ひょうさつ：表札〉a nameplate, a doorplate.

    hyôsatu o kakeru（表札を掛ける）put up a nameplate

hyôshi 〈ひょうし：表紙〉a cover.

hyôshi 〈ひょうし：拍子〉time, (a) rhythm; (a) chance.

    hyôshi o toru（拍子をとる）beat time, keep time

    ni-byôshi（二拍子）simple duple time

    yon-bun-no-ni-byôshi（四分の二拍子）two-four time

    nani-ka-no-hyôshi-de（何かの拍子で）by some chance

hyôshi-gi 〈ひょうしぎ：拍子木〉wooden clappers.

hyôshiki 〈ひょうしき：標識〉a mark(ing), a sign.

    hyôshiki-tô（標識灯）a beacon light

hyôshi-nuke 〈ひょうしぬけ：拍子抜け〉

    hyôshi-nuke-suru〈拍子抜けする〉be damped, be disappointed, lose momentum.

hyôshitsu 〈ひょうしつ：氷室〉an icehouse.

hyôshô 〈ひょうしょう：表彰〉official commendation.

    hyôshô-jô（表彰状）a testimonial, a citation

    hyôshô-shiki（表彰式）a commendation, a ceremony of awarding an honor

    hyôshô-shuru〈表彰する〉commend officially.

hyôshô 〈ひょうしょう：表象〉*see*. shôchô（象徴）.

hyôso 〈ひょうそ〉whitlow, felon.

hyôsô 〈ひょうそう：表装〉mounting.

    hyôsô-suru〈表装する〉mount〔a picture on silken cloth〕.

hyôsuru 〈ひょうする：表する〉pay, express, show, offer.

    keii o hyôsuru（敬意を表する）pay one's respects ((to))

    ikan-no-i o hyôsuru（遺憾の意を表する）express one's regret ((to))

    shukui o hyôsuru（祝意を表する）offer one's congratulations

    chôi o hyôsuru（弔意を表する）offer one's condolences

hyôtan 〈ひょうたん〉a (bottle) gourd.

hyôtei 〈ひょうてい：評定〉rating, evaluation.

    kimmu-hyôtei（勤務評定）efficiency rating

    hyôtei-suru〈評定する〉rate, evaluate.

hyôteki 〈ひょうてき：標的〉a target, a mark.

hyôten 〈ひょうてん：氷点〉the freezing point.

    hyôten-ka-jû-do（氷点下十度）ten degrees below the freezing point, ten degrees below zero

hyôten 〈ひょうてん：評点〉examination marks, a grade.

hyotto 〈ひょっと〉by chance, by accident.

    hyotto-shite, hyotto-shitara or *hyotto-suru-to*〈ひょっとして，ひょっとした

ら，ひょっとすると〉 possibly, maybe, by some chance.

Hyotto-shite kare-no jûsho o go-zonji-ari-masen-ka? 〈ひょっとして彼の住所を御存知ありませんか.〉 Do you happen to know his address?

Hyotto-shitara jimu-sho-ni orareru-ka-to-omotte-ukagaimashita. 〈ひょっとしたら事務所におられるかと思って伺いました.〉 I came on the chance of finding you at your office.

hyôzan 〈ひょうざん：氷山〉 an iceberg.

hyôzan no ikkaku 〈氷山の一角〉 the tip of an iceberg

hyûhyû 〈ひゅうひゅう〉 whistling, with a whistle.

Kaze ga hyûhyû-fuku. 〈風がひゅうひゅう吹く.〉 The wind is blowing with a whistle.

hyûzu 〈ヒューズ〉 a fuse.

Hyûzu ga tonda. 〈ヒューズが飛んだ.〉 A fuse has blown out.

hyûzu-o-tsuke-kaeru 〈ヒューズを付け替える〉 replace a fuse, put in a new fuse

I

i 〈い：胃〉 the stomach.

i-ga-jôbu-da 〈胃が丈夫だ〉 have a strong stomach

i-ga-yowai 〈胃が弱い〉 have a weak stomach

i-ga-motareru 〈胃がもたれる〉 lie heavy on the stomach

i-ga-itamu 〈胃が痛む〉 have a stomachache

i-o-kowasu 〈胃をこわす〉 disorder the stomach

iheki 〈胃壁〉 the wall of the stomach

ien 〈胃炎〉 inflammation of the stomach

i-kataru 〈胃カタル〉 the catarrh of the stomach

i-keiren 〈胃けいれん〉 convulsion of the stomach

i-kaiyô 〈胃かいよう〉 an ulcer of the stomach

i-gan〈胃がん〉 cancer of the stomach

i-kamera〈胃カメラ〉 a gastrocamera

i-kakuchô〈胃拡張〉 gastric dilatation

i-kasui〈胃下垂〉 gastroptosis, gastric ptosis

i〈い：意〉(a) mind, heart, (a) will, an intention, a wish, a desire.

i-ni-kaisuru〈意に介する〉 mind, take ((a matter)) to one's heart

i-o-kesshi-kanete-iru〈意を決しかねている〉 be in two minds, be wavering

i-no-mama-ni-suru〈意のままにする〉 do as one pleases, have one's will

i〈い：威〉

tora-no-i-o-karu-kitsune〈とらの威を借るきつね〉 the ass in the lion's skin

i〈い：井〉a well.

I-no-naka-no　kawazu　taikai-o-shirazu.〈井の中のかわず大海を知らず。〉 A frog in the well knows nothing of the great ocean.

-i〈-い：-位〉a place, a rank.

dai-ichi-i〈第一位〉 the first place

dai-ni-i o shimeru〈第二位を占める〉 take the second place

dai-san-i-ni ochiru〈第三位に落ちる〉 drop to the third place

ian〈いあん：慰安〉(a) consolation, (a) comfort, (a) recreation.

ian-kai〈慰安会〉 an entertainment

iatsu〈いあつ：威圧〉

iatsu-suru〈威圧する〉 coerce, overawe.

i-awaseru〈いあわせる：居合わせる〉happen to be (present).

ibara〈いばら〉a bramble, a thorn.

ibara-no michi〈いばらの道〉 a thorny path

ibaru〈いばる：威張る〉be haughty.

ibaru hito〈いばる人〉 a haughty person

ibiki〈いびき〉a snore.

ibiki-o-kaku〈いびきをかく〉snore.

ibiru〈いびる〉*see.* ijimeru.

ibitsu〈いびつ〉

ibitsu-ni-naru〈いびつになる〉become distorted, get warped.

ibitsu-no〈いびつの〉distorted, warped.

ibo〈いぼ〉a wart.

ibo〈いぼ：異母〉

ibo-kyôdai *or* ibo-shimai〈異母兄弟, 異母姉妹〉 a half brother; a half sister

ibo-ji 〈いぼじ〉 blind piles.

ibukuro 〈いぶくろ：胃袋〉 a stomach, a craw.

i-bunshi 〈いぶんし：異分子〉 a foreign element, an outsider.

ibushi-gin 〈いぶしぎん：いぶし銀〉 oxidized silver.

ibusu 〈いぶす〉 smoke, fumigate, oxidize.

ibutsu 〈いぶつ：遺物〉 a relic, remains.

ibyô 〈いびょう：胃病〉 a stomach trouble.

ichatsuku 〈いちゃつく〉 flirt.

ichi 〈いち：市〉 a market, a fair.

ichi 〈いち：位置〉 a situation, a position, a site.

ichi 〈いち：一〉 one.

    ichi-ka-bachi-ka-yatte-miru （一か八かやってみる） take one's chance, run a risk

    ichi-kara-jû-made （一から十まで） in everything

      Kare-wa sono-koto-ni-tsuite ichi-kara-jû-made shitte-iru. （彼はその事について一から十まで知っている.） He knows everything about it.

    ichi-mo-ni-mo-naku （一も二もなく） readily, without hesitation, flatly

      ichi-mo-ni-mo-naku shôdaku-suru （一も二もなく承諾する） consent readily

      ichi-mo-ni-mo-naku kotowaru （一も二もなく断る） refuse flatly

    dai-ichi （第一） the first

ichiba 〈いちば：市場〉 a market.

    uo-ichiba （魚市場） a fish market

ichi-ban 〈いちばん：1番, 一番〉 the first, No. 1.

    ichi-ban ni naru （一番になる） get the first place

    ichi-ban ressha （一番列車） the first train

ichiban 〈いちばん：一番〉 most, best.

    ichiban kirei-na hana （一番きれいな花） the most beautiful flower

    ichiban ii shina （一番いい品） the best quality

ichibu or **ichi-bu** 〈いちぶ：一部〉 a part, a portion; a copy.

    ichi-shô-bubun （一小部分） a small part

    ichibu-no hito-tachi （一部の人たち） some people

    hon ichi-bu （本一部） a copy of book

ichi-bubun 〈いちぶぶん：一部分〉 *see.* ichibu.

ichibu-ichirin 〈いちぶいちりん：一分一厘〉 *see.* sumbun.

ichibu-shijû 〈いちぶしじゅう：一部始終〉 the whole story, full particulars, everything ((about)), from beginning to end.

ichi-dai 〈いちだい：一代〉 one generation, one's lifetime, one's whole life.

ichi-dai-de kyogaku-no tomi o kizuki-ageru（一代で巨額の富を築き上げる） make a big fortune in one generation

ichi-dai-ki（一代記） a biography

ichi-daiji 〈いちだいじ：一大事〉 a serious matter, a great matter.

ichi-dan or **ichidan** 〈いちだん：一段〉 a step, a rung; a degree.

ichidan-to 〈一段と〉 more, further.

ichidan-to shimpo-suru（一段と進歩する） make further progress

ichi-dan 〈いちだん：一団〉 a body, a group, a party.

ichi-dan-to-natte（一団となって） in a group

ichi-danraku 〈いちだんらく：一段落〉

ichi-danraku-tsukeru 〈一段落つける〉 settle ((a matter)) temporarily.

ichi-do or **ichido** 〈いちど：一度〉 once, one time.

ichi-nen-ni ichi-do（一年に一度） once a year

ichi-ni-do（一，二度） once or twice

ichi-do-dake（一度だけ） only once, for once

ichi-do-narazu（一度ならず） more than once

mô ichi-do（もう一度） once more

ichido-ni（一度に） at a time

ichi-do-mo〜-nai（一度も〜ない） never, not once

ichidô 〈いちどう：一同〉 all, everyone.

wareware-ichidô（我々一同） all of us

ichidô 〈いちどう：一堂〉

ichidô-ni kaisuru 〈一堂に会する〉 meet together in a hall.

ichidoku 〈いちどく：一読〉

ichidoku-suru-kachi-ga-aru 〈一読する価値がある〉 be worth reading.

ichigai-ni 〈いちがいに：一概に〉 unconditionally, wholly.

ichigai-ni kenasu（一概にけなす） condemn ((some group)) as a whole

ichigai-ni ronjiru（一概に論じる） make a sweeping statement

ichigan 〈いちがん：一眼〉 one eye.

ichigan-refu（一眼レフ） a single-lens reflex camera

ichigan 〈いちがん：一丸〉

ichigan-to-natte 〈一丸となって〉 united, in a body.

ichigatsu 〈いちがつ：一月〉 January.

ichigei 〈いちげい：一芸〉 an art.

　　　ichigei-ni-hiideru（一芸に秀でる）　be a master of an art

ichigeki〈いちげき：一撃〉a blow.

　　　ichigeki o kuwaeru（一撃を加える）　strike ((a person)) a blow

　 ichigeki-no-moto-ni（一撃の下に）at a blow.

ichigen-ka〈いちげんか：一元化〉

　 ichigen-ka-suru〈一元化する〉unify, centralize.

ichigo〈いちご：一語〉a strawberry.

ichigon〈いちごん：一言〉a word.

　　　ichigon-no-aisatsu-mo-naku（一言のあいさつもなく）　without saying a
　　　single word of greeting, without permission

ichihatsu〈いちはつ〉iris.

ichi-hayaku〈いちはやく：いち早く〉quickly, promptly, at once, without
　a moment's delay.

ichi-i〈いちい：一位〉the first place, the first rank.

ichiichi〈いちいち〉one by one, everything, in detail, fully.

　　　shorui-ni-ichiichi-me-o-toosu（書類にいちいち目を通す）　read all the
　　　documents one by one

　　　ichiichi kuchi-o-dasu（いちいち口を出す）　meddle in everything

ichiin〈いちいん：一員〉a member.

ichiin〈いちいん：一因〉a cause.

ichiji〈いちじ：一事〉one thing.

　　　Ichiji-ga-banji.（一事が万事.）　One who will steal a pin will steal an
　　　ox.

ichiji〈いちじ：一字〉a letter, a character.

　　　ichiji-ikku-tagaezu-ni（一字一句たがえずに）to the letter

ichi-ji or **ichiji**〈いちじ：1時，一時〉one o'clock; at one time, once, for
　a time.

　 ichiji-no（一時の）temporary, momentary, passing

　　　ichiji-no kanjô（一時の感情）an impulse

ichiji〈いちじ：一次〉

　　　ichiji-hôtei-shiki（一次方程式）an equation of the first degree

　　　ichiji-shiken（一次試験）a primary examination

　 ichiji-no（一次の）first, primary.

ichiji-azukari-sho〈いちじあずかりしょ：一時預かり所〉a cloakroom, a
　checkroom.

ichijiku〈いちじく〉a fig, a fig tree.

ichijirushii〈いちじるしい：著しい〉remarkable, conspicuous, striking,
　considerable.

ichijirushii shimpo〈著しい進歩〉remarkable progress

ichijirushiku〈著しく〉remarkably, considerably.

ichijun〈いちじゅん：一巡〉

ichijun-suru〈一巡する〉make a round ((of)), take a round, walk round.

ichi-mai〈いちまい：一枚〉a sheet, a piece.

kami ichi-mai（紙一枚）a sheet of paper

Kare-no-hô-ga kimi-yori yakusha-ga-ichi-mai-ue-da.（彼の方が君より役者が一枚上だ。）He is a cut above you.

ichimai-iwa〈いちまいいわ：一枚岩〉a monolith.

ichimatsu〈いちまつ：一抹〉

ichimatsu-no-fuan-o-kanjiru〈一抹の不安を感じる〉feel slightly uneasy.

ichimatsu-moyô〈いちまつもよう：市松模様〉checks, checkers.

ichimatsu-moyô-no〈市松模様の〉checked, checkered.

ichi-men or **ichimen**〈いちめん：一面〉the first page, one side; the whole surface.

ichimen-ni（一面に）all over

sora-ichimen-ni（空一面に）all over the sky

ichi-menshiki〈いちめんしき：一面識〉

ichi-menshiki-mo-nai-hito（一面識もない人）a perfect stranger

ichimi〈いちみ：一味〉fellow-conspirators, a party, a gang.

imbô-no-ichimi-ni-kuwawaru（陰謀の一味に加わる）take part in the conspiracy

ichimô-dajin〈いちもうだじん：一網打尽〉

ichimô-dajin-ni-kenkyo-suru〈一網打尽に検挙する〉make a wholesale arrest ((of)).

ichimoku〈いちもく：一目〉

ichimoku-oku〈一目おく〉acknowledge one's own inferiority to another.

ichimoku-ryôzen〈いちもくりょうぜん：一目りょう然〉

ichimoku-ryôzen-de-aru〈一目りょう然である〉be obvious, be as clear as day.

ichimokusan〈いちもくさん：一目散〉

ichimokusan-ni〈一目散に〉at the top of one's speed.

ichimokusan-ni nigeru（一目散に逃げる）run head over heels

ichi-mon〈いちもん：一文〉

ichi-mon-nashi-ni-naru（一文無しになる）become penniless

ichi-mon-no-kachi-mo-nai（一文の価値もない）be not worth a straw

ichimotsu〈いちもつ：一物〉

mune-ni ichimotsu-aru〈胸に一物ある〉have an ax to grind.

ichimyaku 〈いちみゃく：一脈〉
　ichimyaku-ai-tsûjiru 〈一脈相通じる〉have something in common ((with)).

ichi-nan 〈いちなん：一難〉
　Ichi-nan-satte mata-ichi-nan. (一難去ってまた一難.) Out of the frying pan into the fire.

ichi-nen 〈いちねん：一年〉one year.
　ichi-nen-han (一年半) one year and a half
　ichi-nen-jû (一年中) all the year round, throughout the year
　ichi-nen-sei (一年生) a first-year student

ichi-nichi 〈いちにち：一日〉one day.
　ichi-nichi-ichi-nichi (一日一日) day by day
　ichi-nichi-jû (一日中) all day (long)
　ichi-nichi-oki-ni (一日おきに) every other day

ichinin 〈いちにん：一任〉
　ichinin-suru 〈一任する〉leave ((a matter)) entirely to ((a person)).

ichinin-mae 〈いちにんまえ：一人前〉one portion; an adult.
　ichinin-mae no sushi (一人前のすし) one portion of *sushi*
　ichinin-mae-ni-naru (一人前になる) become an adult

ichiô 〈いちおう：一応〉once, in outline, for the time being, first.
　ima-ichiô (今一応) once more, again
　ichiô-me-o-toosu (一応目を通す) glance through
　Ichiô honnin-no ikô-o-sagutte-minakereba-nara-nai. (一応本人の意向を探ってみなければならない.) We must first sound him on his opinion.
　Kore-de ichiô ii-darô. (これで一応いいだろう.) This will do for the time being.

ichiran 〈いちらん：一覧〉a look, a sight; a summary.
　ichiran-barai tegata (一覧払手形) a sight bill
　ichiran-go san-jû-nichi-barai (一覧後三十日払い) payable at 30 days after sight
　ichiran-suru 〈一覧する〉take a look ((at)), look through.

ichiran-sei-sôsei-ji 〈いちらんせいそうせいじ：一卵性双生児〉identical twins.

ichi-rei 〈いちれい：一例〉an example.
　ichi-rei-to-shite (一例として) as an example

ichiren 〈いちれん：一連〉a series ((of)).
　ichiren-bangô (一連番号) serial numbers
　ichiren-no 〈一連の〉a series of.

ichiri 〈いちり：一理〉 some truth, some reason.

Kimi-no-iu-koto-ni-mo ichiri-aru.（君の言うことにも一理ある.） There is some truth in what you say.

ichi-rin-zashi 〈いちりんざし：一輪挿し〉a bud vase.

ichiritsu 〈いちりつ：一律〉

ichiritsu-ni 〈一律に〉uniformly, indiscriminately.

ichiro 〈いちろ：一路〉

ichiro-Honoruru-ni-mukau 〈一路ホノルルに向かう〉go straight for Honolulu.

ichirui 〈いちるい：一塁〉first base.

ichirui-shu（一塁手）a first baseman

ichiryô-jitsu 〈いちりょうじつ：一両日〉a day or two.

ichiryô-jitsu-chû-ni（一両日中に）in a day or two

ichiryû 〈いちりゅう：一流〉

ichiryû-no 〈一流の〉first-class, topflight, one of the best, leading, foremost, top-notch.

ichi-wari 〈いちわり：一割〉ten percent.

ichi-ya 〈いちや：一夜〉one night.

ichi-ya o akasu（一夜を明かす）pass a night ((at *or* in)), sit up all night

ichi-ya-zuke-no-benkyô（一夜漬けの勉強）cramming

ichiyaku 〈いちやく：一躍〉at a bound.

ichiyaku-yûmei-ni-naru 〈一躍有名になる〉leap suddenly into fame.

ichiyô-ni 〈いちように：一様に〉equally, alike, in the same way.

ichiza 〈いちざ：一座〉the company; a company, a troupe.

ichizon-de 〈いちぞんで：一存で〉at one's own will, on one's own responsibility.

ichizu-ni 〈いちずに：一ずに〉intently, simply, blindly.

ichizu-ni omoi-komu 〈いちずに思い込む〉be possessed with the idea ((that)), be convinced unshakably ((that)).

i-chô 〈いちょう：胃腸〉the stomach and intestines.

i-chô-ga-tsuyoi（胃腸が強い）have a strong digestion

i-chô-ga-yowai（胃腸が弱い）have a poor digestion

ichô 〈いちょう〉a ginkgo tree, a maidenhair tree.

ichû 〈いちゅう：意中〉one's mind, one's thoughts.

ichû-no hito（意中の人）a man(*or* a girl) of one's heart

idai 〈いだい：偉大〉

idai-na 〈偉大な〉great, mighty, grand, powerful.

idaku 〈いだく：抱く〉 hold, entertain.
    aku-kanjô o idaku 〈悪感情を抱く〉 have ill feeling ((against))
    utagai o idaku 〈疑いを抱く〉 entertain a doubt
    fuan-o-idaku 〈不安を抱く〉 feel uneasy
iden 〈いでん：遺伝〉 heredity.
    iden-shi 〈遺伝子〉 a gene.
  iden-suru 〈遺伝する〉 be inherited.
  iden-no, iden-sei(-no) or *iden-teki(-na)* 〈遺伝の，遺伝性(の)，遺伝的(な)〉 hereditary.
ideorogî 〈イデオロギー〉 ideology.
  ideorogî-teki(-na) 〈イデオロギー的(な)〉 ideological.
ido 〈いど：井戸〉 a well.
    ido o horu 〈井戸を掘る〉 dig a well
    ido-kara mizu o kumu 〈井戸から水をくむ〉 draw water from a well
    ido-mizu 〈井戸水〉 well water
    ido-bata 〈井戸端〉 the well side
        ido-bata-kaigi 〈井戸端会議〉 housewives' gossip
ido 〈いど：緯度〉 latitude.
idô 〈いどう：異動〉 (a) change.
    jinji-idô 〈人事異動〉 personnel changes
idô 〈いどう：移動〉 (a) movement, (a) transfer.
  idô-suru 〈移動する〉 move, transfer.
idokoro 〈いどころ：居所〉 one's address, one's residence, one's whereabouts.
    idokoro o tsuki-tomeru 〈居所を突き止める〉 follow up ((a person's)) residence.
idomu 〈いどむ：挑む〉 challenge, defy.
ie 〈いえ：家〉 a home, a house.
    ie-ni-iru 〈家にいる〉 stay at home
    ie-ni-i-nai 〈家にいない〉 stay away from home
    ie-ni-kaeru 〈家に帰る〉 go home
    ie o tateru 〈家を建てる〉 build a house
    ie o kasu 〈家を貸す〉 rent a house
iede 〈いえで：家出〉
    iede-musume 〈家出娘〉 a runaway girl
  iede-suru 〈家出する〉 leave one's house, run away from home.
iegara 〈いえがら：家柄〉 lineage, birth.
    iegara-ga-ii 〈家柄がいい〉 be of good birth, come of a good family

iemoto 〈いえもと：家元〉 the head master.

ie-yashiki 〈いえやしき：家屋敷〉 one's house and lot.

ifuku 〈いふく：衣服〉 clothes, garments, dress, clothing.

igai 〈いがい：遺がい〉 one's dead body, the corpse, one's remains.

igai 〈いがい：意外〉

igai-na 〈意外な〉 unexpected, surprising, accidental.

igai-ni(-mo) 〈意外に（も）〉 unexpectedly, contrary to one's expectation, to one's surprise.

igai-ni-omou 〈意外に思う〉 be surprised ((at)), be disappointed ((at)).

-igai 〈-いがい：-以外〉

-igai-ni or *-igai-wa* 〈-以外に，-以外は〉 except, but; besides, in addition ((to)).

igaku 〈いがく：医学〉 medical science, medicine.

    igaku-bu 〈医学部〉 the medical department

    igaku-hakase 〈医学博士〉 a doctor of medicine; Doctor of Medicine (M.D., D.M.)

igaku-jō-no, igaku-no or *igaku-teki(-na)* 〈医学上の，医学の，医学的（な）〉 medical.

igami-au 〈いがみあう：いがみ合う〉 snarl at each other, quarrel ((with)), be at outs ((with)).

    igami-atte-kurasu 〈いがみ合って暮らす〉 lead a cat-and-dog life

igan-menkan or **igan-menshoku** 〈いがんめんかん，いがんめんしょく：依願免官，依願免職〉

igan-menkan-to-naru or *igan-menshoku-to-naru* 〈依願免官となる，依願免職となる〉 be relieved of one's post at one's own request.

igarappoi 〈いがらっぽい〉

    Koko-ni-san-nichi nodo-ga-igarappoi. (ここ二，三日のどがいがらっぽい．) I've had a bur in the throat these few days.

igata 〈いがた：鋳型〉 a mold, a cast.

igen 〈いげん：威厳〉 dignity, majesty.

    igen o tamotsu 〈威厳を保つ〉 keep one's dignity

igen-no-aru 〈威厳のある〉 dignified, majestic.

    igen-no-nai 〈威厳のない〉 undignified

igi 〈いぎ：異議〉 an objection.

igi-o-tonaeru 〈異議を唱える〉 object ((to)).

igi-naku 〈異議なく〉 without objection, unanimously.

igi 〈いぎ：意義〉 (a) meaning, (a) sense, significance.

igi-no-aru 〈意義のある〉 significant.

igi-no-nai〈意義のない〉 meaningless

igi〈いぎ：威儀〉 dignity, majesty.

igi-o-tadashite〈威儀を正して〉in a dignified manner, in state, solemnly.

Igirisu〈イギリス〉*see.* Eikoku.

igo〈いご：囲碁〉the game of *go*.

igo〈いご：以後〉after this, from now on, in (the) future.

sore-igo〈それ以後〉 after that, since then

igyō〈いぎょう：偉業〉a great work.

igyō〈いぎょう：遺業〉

chichi-no igyô o tsugu〈父の遺業を継ぐ〉take over one's father's unfinished work.

ihai〈いはい：位はい〉a (Buddhist) memorial tablet.

ihan〈いはん：違反〉violation.

ihan-kôi〈違反行為〉 an offense

ihan-sha〈違反者〉 a violator, an offender

ihan-suru〈違反する〉violate.

ihatsu〈いはつ：遺髪〉the hair of the deceased.

ihen〈いへん：異変〉an accident, something unusual, an emergency.

ihin〈いひん：遺品〉an article left by the departed.

ihô〈いほう：違法〉unlawfulness, illegality.

ihô-kôi〈違法行為〉 an illegal act

ihô-no〈違法の〉unlawful, illegal.

-ihoku〈ーいほく：ー以北〉north (of).

-ihoku-no, -ihoku-ni or -ihoku-wa〈ー以北の，ー以北に，ー以北は〉north of.

ihyô〈いひょう：意表〉

ihyô-o-tsuku〈意表を突く〉take ((a person)) by surprise, do something unexpected.

ii〈いい〉 good, nice, fine, pretty, handsome, mild, sweet; lucky, auspicious; well, all right; right, splendid.

ii ko〈いい子〉 a good child

kenkô-ni-ii〈健康にいい〉 be good for the health

ii tenki〈いい天気〉 a fine day

ii keshiki〈いい景色〉 a fine view

ii otoko〈いい男〉 a handsome man, a nice fellow

ii kikô〈いい気候〉 a mild weather

ii koe〈いい声〉 a sweet voice

Soitsu-wa ii-ne.〈そいつはいいね。〉 That's fine.

ii hi o erabu〈いい日を選ぶ〉 choose a lucky day

Kyô wa kibun-ga-totemo-ii.（今日は気分がとてもいい．） I feel quite well today.

Sore-wa ii kangae-da.（それはいい考えだ．） That's a splendid idea.

Sore-de-ii.（それでいい．） That'll do.

Sugu itta-hô-ga-ii.（すぐ行った方がいい．） You had better go right now.

Watashi-wa ringo-yori-mikan-no-hô-ga-ii.（私はりんごよりみかんの方がいい．） I prefer oranges to apples.

Koko-de tabako-o-sutte-mo-ii-desu-ka?（ここでたばこを吸ってもいいですか．） May I smoke here?

Komban ko-naku-temo-ii.（今晩来なくてもいい．） You don't have to come tonight.

Motto kane-ga-areba-ii-noni.（もっと金があればいいのに．） I wish I had more money.

Dochira-demo-ii.（どちらでもいい．） I don't care which.

Yôi-wa-ii-ka?（用意はいいか．） Are you ready?

iiai〈いいあい：言い合い〉 a quarrel, a dispute, a wrangle.

iiai-o-suru〈言い合いをする〉 quarrel ((with)), have a quarrel ((with)), dispute, wrangle.

ii-arawasu〈いいあらわす：言い表わす〉 express, describe.

umaku ii arawasu（うまく言い表わす） put ((it)) well

ii-arawashi-kata（言い表わし方） expression

ii-ateru〈いいあてる：言い当てる〉 guess right.

ii-awaseru〈いいあわせる：言い合わせる〉 make previous arrangements.

ii-awaseta-yô-ni〈言い合わせたように〉 as if by common consent.

iibun〈いいぶん：言い分〉 one's say, one's claim.

ii-dasu〈いいだす：言い出す〉 speak, begin to speak; suggest, propose.

iie〈いいえ〉 no; yes.

ii-fukumeru〈いいふくめる：言い含める〉 tell ((a person)) carefully, give ((a person)) full instructions beforehand.

ii-furasu〈いいふらす：言い触らす〉 set ((a rumor)) afloat, spread 〔a rumor〕.

iigakari〈いいがかり：言い掛かり〉 a false charge.

iigakari-o-tsukeru〈言い掛かりを付ける〉 accuse ((a person)) falsely, make a false charge ((against)).

iigusa〈いいぐさ：言い草〉 one's words, one's remarks.

Kare-no iigusa ga ki-ni-ira-nai.（彼の言い草が気に入らない．） I don't like his words.

ii-haru 〈いいはる：言い張る〉 insist ((on *or* that)).

ii-hiraki 〈いいひらき：言い開き〉 vindication, justification, an excuse.

　ii-hiraki-o-suru 〈言い開きをする〉 excuse oneself.

ii-kaeru 〈いいかえる：言い換える〉 say in other words, put ((it)) (in) another way.

　ii-kaeru-to 〈言い換えると〉 in other words.

ii-kaesu 〈いいかえす：言い返す〉 talk back, retort.

ii-kagen 〈いいかげん：いい加減〉

　ii-kagen-na 〈いい加減な〉 moderate, right; random, vague.

　　　chôdo ii-kagen-na atsusa （ちょうどいい加減な暑さ） just warm enough

　　　ii-kagen-na henji （いい加減な返事） a random answer, a vague answer

　ii-kagen-ni 〈いい加減に〉 moderately, properly; at random, halfway.

ii-kata 〈いいかた：言い方〉 a way of speaking, a way of expressing, how to speak.

ii-ki 〈いいき：いい気〉

　ii-ki-ni-naru 〈いい気になる〉 be self-conceited, be puffed up ((with)).

　ii-ki-na 〈いい気な〉 easygoing.

　　　Nan-to ii-ki-na-mono-da! （何といい気なものだ。） How easygoing!

ii-kikaseru 〈いいきかせる：言い聞かせる〉 tell, admonish, reason ((with)).

ii-kimi 〈いいきみ：いい気味〉

　　　Ii-kimi-da! （いい気味だ。） It serves you right!

ii-kiru 〈いいきる：言い切る〉 say definitely, state positively, declare, affirm, assert.

ii-komeru 〈いいこめる：言い込める〉

　ii-komerareru 〈言い込められる〉 be argued into silence, be talked down.

ii-mawashi 〈いいまわし：言い回し〉 a mode of expression.

ii-morasu 〈いいもらす：言い漏らす〉 leave ((something)) untold.

iin 〈いいん：委員〉 a member of a committee.

　　　iin-kai （委員会） a committee

　　　iin-chô （委員長） the chairman

　　　shikkô-iin （執行委員） an executive committee

iin 〈いいん：医院〉 a doctor's office.

ii-naosu 〈いいなおす：言い直す〉 correct oneself, restate.

ii-narawashi 〈いいならわし：言い習わし〉 a common saying, an idiom.

iinari 〈いいなり：言いなり〉

　hito-no iinari-ni-naru 〈人の言いなりになる〉 be at a person's beck and call, be under a person's thumb.

　　hito-no-iinari-ni-naru-hito〈人の言いなりになる人〉 a yes-man

iinazuke〈いいなずけ：言い名〉one's betrothed; one's fiance, one's fiancée.

ii-ne〈いいね：言い値〉the price asked.

ii-nikui〈いいにくい：言いにくい〉hard to say, delicate to discuss.

ii-nogare〈いいのがれ：言い逃れ〉an evasion, an elusion.

　ii-nogareru〈言い逃れる〉explain away, dodge, quibble, shuffle.

ii-nokosu〈いいのこす：言い残す〉leave a message with ((a person)).

ii-shiburu〈いいしぶる：言い渋る〉hesitate to say.

ii-sokonai〈いいそこない：言い損ない〉a slip of the tongue.

　ii-sokonau〈言い損なう〉make a slip of the tongue; fail to tell.

ii-sugi〈いいすぎ：言い過ぎ〉saying too much.

　　〜to-itte-mo ii-sugi-dewa-nai.（〜と言っても言い過ぎではない。）It is not too much to say that... .

　ii-sugiru〈言い過ぎる〉say too much.

ii-tasu〈いいたす：言い足す〉make an additional remark.

ii-tsuke〈いいつけ：言い付け〉an order, a bidding.

　　ii-tsuke o mamoru（言い付けを守る）obey ((a person's)) order

　　ii-tsuke-doori-ni-suru（言い付けどおりにする）do as one is bidden

　ii-tsukeru〈言い付ける〉tell, order, bid; tell on ((a person)).

　　yôji o ii-tsukeru（用事を言い付ける）give orders ((to))

ii-tsukurou〈いいつくろう：言い繕う〉gloss over.

ii-tsukusu〈いいつくす：言い尽くす〉tell all, express oneself fully.

　kotoba-de-ii-tsukuse-nai〈言葉で言い尽くせない〉beyond description.

ii-tsutae〈いいつたえ：言い伝え〉a tradition, a legend.

　ii-tsutaeru〈言い伝える〉hand down by tradition.

iiwake〈いいわけ：言い訳〉an apology, an excuse.

　　kurushii iiwake（苦しい言い訳）a poor excuse

　iiwake-suru〈言い訳する〉make an apology, make an excuse ((for)).

　iiwake-no-tata-nai〈言い訳の立たない〉inexcusable, unjustifiable.

　iiwake-ni〈言い訳に〉by way of excuse.

ii-wasureru〈いいわすれる：言い忘れる〉forget to say.

ii-watasu〈いいわたす：言い渡す〉sentence, announce, tell.

　　hanketsu-o-ii-watasu（判決を言い渡す）give judgment, pronounce a sentence ((on))

ii-yoru〈いいよる：言い寄る〉court, woo, make advances ((to)), make passes ((at)).

iji〈いじ：遺児〉a child of the deceased.

kôtsû-iji（交通遺児） a traffic orphan

iji〈いじ：維持〉maintenance.

iji-hi（維持費） maintenance expenses

iji-suru〈維持する〉maintain, keep up.

iji〈いじ：意地〉temper, nature, disposition, obstinacy, will.

iji-o-haru（意地を張る） be obstinate

iji-o-toosu（意地を通す） have one's own way

iji-no-warui（意地の悪い） ill-tempered, ill-natured

ijippari-no（意地っ張りの） stubborn

iji-kitanai（意地汚い） greedy

iji-ni-natte（意地になって） obstinately, perversely

ijikeru〈いじける〉cower, become perverse.

ijimeru〈いじめる〉bully, treat ((a person)) harshly, be hard ((on)), tease.

yowai-mono o ijimeru（弱い者をいじめる） bully the weaker

ijin〈いじん：偉人〉a great man.

ijirashii〈いじらしい〉lovely, sweet; pitiful, touching.

ijiru〈いじる〉finger, play ((with)).

ijô〈いじょう：以上〉more than, over, beyond; the above-mentioned.

go-jikan-ijô（五時間以上） for more than five hours

nana-sai-ijô-no kodomo（七歳以上の子供） children seven and over

shûnyû-ijô-no-seikatsu-o-suru（収入以上の生活をする） live beyond one's income

~-*ijô-wa*〈～以上は〉since, now that, so long as, once.

ikite-iru-ijô-wa（生きている以上は） so long as one lives

ijô〈いじょう：異状〉something wrong, an accident, change, disorder, (an) indisposition.

ijô-ga-aru〈異状がある〉something is wrong, be abnormal, be out of order, be indisposed.

ijô-ga-nai（異状がない） be normal, be in good order, be all right

ijô-no-aru〈異状のある〉abnormal, wrong, faulty, affected.

ijô-na〈いじょうな：異常な〉unusual, extraordinary, abnormal, uncommon, remarkable.

ijô-kishô（異常気象） abnormal weather

ijô-na shimpo（異常な進歩） remarkable progress

ijû〈いじゅう：移住〉migration, emigration, immigration, removal.

ijû-sha（移住者） an emigrant, an immigrant, a settler

ijû-susu〈移住する〉migrate, emigrate, immigrate, remove, move.

ijutsu〈いじゅつ：医術〉the medical art.

ijutsu-no〈医術の〉medical.

ika〈いか：以下〉less than, under, below; the following, the rest.

hyaku-ika（百以下）100 and less

nana-sai-ika-no kodomo（七歳以下の子供）children 7 and under

futsû-ika（普通以下）below the average

go-man-en-ika-no　bakkin（五万円以下の罰金）a fine not exceeding 50,000 yen

ika-dôyô（以下同様）and so forth on

Ika-shôryaku.（以下省略.）The rest is omitted.

ika〈いか：医科〉the medical department.

ika-daigaku（医科大学）a medical college

ika〈いか〉a cattlefish, a squid.

ikada〈いかだ〉a raft.

ikaga〈いかが〉how.

Go-kiġen-ikaga-desu-ka?（御機嫌いかがですか.）How are you?

Ikaga　o-sugoshi-desu-ka?（いかがお過ごしですか.）How are you getting on?

Mô-ippai　kôhî　o　ikaga-desu-ka?（もう一杯コーヒーをいかがですか.）Won't you have another cup of coffee?

Nagasaki-ryokô　wa　ikaga-deshita-ka?（長崎旅行はいかがでしたか.）How did you enjoy your trip to Nagasaki?

Basu-ni-nottewa-ikaga-desu-ka?（バスに乗ってはいかがですか.）How about taking a bus?

ikagawashii〈いかがわしい〉doubtful, questionable, dubious, suspicious, shady, indecent.

ikagawashii jimbutsu（いかがわしい人物）a doubtful character

ikagawashii basho（いかがわしい場所）a dubious place

ikagawashii shôbai（いかがわしい商売）a shady business

ikagawashii uta（いかがわしい歌）an indecent song

ikaku〈いかく：威嚇〉threat, menace, intimidation.

ikaku-shageki-o-suru（威嚇射撃をする）fire warning

ikaku-suru〈威嚇する〉threaten, menace, intimidate.

ikaku-teki(-na)〈威嚇的(な)〉threatening.

ikan〈いかん〉

Ikan-tomo-shi-gatai.（いかんともし難い.）It can't be helped.

Sore-wa jijô-ikan-ni-yoru.（それは事情いかんによる.）It depends.

ikan-ni-kakawarazu（いかんにかかわらず）regardless ((of))

ikan〈いかん：偉観〉

ikan o teisuru〈偉観を呈する〉present a grand sight.

ikan〈いかん：移管〉
ikan-suru〈移管する〉transfer the control ((of)).

ikan〈いかん：遺憾〉regret.
　ikan-no-i o hyômei-suru（遺憾の意を表明する）　express one's regret
ikan-ni-omou〈遺憾に思う〉regret.
ikan-na〈遺憾な〉regrettable, deplorable, lamentable; unsatisfactory.
　ikan na koto（遺憾な事）　a matter for regret
ikan-nagara〈遺憾ながら〉to one's regret, though with much regret.
ikan-naku〈遺憾なく〉perfectly, thoroughly, to the fullest extent, most satisfactorily.

ikanaru〈いかなる〉*see.* donna.

ika-ni〈いかに〉*see.* donna-ni.
　ika-ni-su-beki-ka（いかにすべきか）　how to do

ikanimo〈いかにも〉indeed, certainly, just, very, extremely.
　Ikanimo-sono-toori.（いかにもそのとおり。）　Yes, indeed. / Just so.
　Ikanimo　kare-no-ii-sô-na-koto-da.（いかにも彼の言いそうなことだ。）
　　It's just like him to say so.
　ikanimo koto no shinsô o shitte-iru-ka-no-yô-ni hanasu（いかにも事の
　　真相を知っているかのように話す）　speak as if one knew the rights
　　of a matter

ikaraseru〈いからせる：怒らせる〉
kata-o-ikarasete-aruku〈肩を怒らせて歩く〉swagger along.

ikari〈いかり〉an anchor.
　ikari o ageru（いかりを上げる）　weigh anchor
　ikari o orosu（いかりを下ろす）　cast anchor
　ikari-o-oroshite-iru（いかりを下ろしている）　be at anchor

ikari〈いかり：怒り〉anger, rage.

ikari-gata〈いかりがた：怒り肩〉square shoulders.
ikari-gata-no〈怒り肩の〉square-shouldered.

ikaru〈いかる：怒る〉*see.* okoru.

ikasama〈いかさま〉(a) fraud, a swindle.
　ikasama-shi（いかさま師）　a swindler, a faker

ikasu〈いかす：生かす〉revive, keep ((an animal)) alive, make the most ((of)).
　sakana o ikashite-oku（魚を生かしておく）　keep a fish alive
　jikan-o-dekiru-dake-ikasu（時間をできるだけいかす）　make the most
　　of ((a person's)) time

kane-o-ikashite-tsukau（金をいかして使う） make the best use of ((a person's)) money

ikasu〈いかす〉be groovy.

ike〈いけ：池〉a pond.

ikebana〈いけばな：生け花〉flower arrangement.

ikedori〈いけどり：生け捕り〉capturing alive.

ikedori-ni-suru or *ikedoru*〈生け捕りにする，生け捕る〉capture ((an animal)) alive.

ikegaki〈いけがき：生け垣〉a hedge.

iken〈いけん：意見〉an opinion, an idea, a view; advice.

iken no shôtotsu（意見の衝突） a conflict of opinions

iken o noberu（意見を述べる） express one's opinion

iken-ga-au（意見が合う） be of the same opinion, agree with ((a person)) about

iken-ga-awa-nai（意見が合わない） differ in opinion, disagree with each other

iken o kiku（意見を聞く） ask ((a person's)) advice

iken ni shitagau（意見に従う） take ((a person's)) advice

iken-suru〈意見する〉give advice ((to)), admonish, reprove.

iken〈いけん：違憲〉

iken-de-aru〈違憲である〉be unconstitutional, be against the constitution.

ikenai〈いけない〉don't, must not, ought not to, shall not; bad, wrong; hopeless, won't do, be all over ((with)).

Soko-e itte-wa-ikenai.（そこへ行ってはいけない.） Don't go there.

Uso o tsuite-wa-ikenai.（うそをついてはいけない.） You mustn't tell a lie.

Sorya ikemasen-ne.（そりゃいけませんね.） That's too bad.

Kare-ga ikenai.（彼がいけない.） He is to blame.

Aka-empitsu-dewa ikenai.（赤鉛筆ではいけない.） The red pencil won't do.

～-to-ikenai-kara〈～といけないから〉for fear ((that)), in case.

ame-ga-furu-to-ikenai-kara（雨が降るといけないから） in case it rains

ikenie〈いけにえ：生けにえ〉a sacrifice, a victim.

ikenie o sasageru（生けにえをささげる） offer a sacrifice ((to))

ikeru〈いける：生ける〉arrange〔flowers〕.

ikeru〈いける：行ける〉

Koko-kara machi-e-wa kuruma-de ichi-jikan-de-ikeru.（ここから町へ

は車で一時間で行ける。）You can get to the town from here in an hour by car.

Kono uisukī wa ikeru. (このウイスキーはいける。) This whisky is not bad.

Bîru-nara sukoshi-wa ikeru. (ビールなら少しはいける。) I can drink some beer.

ikesu 〈いけす：生けす〉a fish preserve, a live well.

ike-suka-nai 〈いけすかない：いけ好かない〉disgusting, disagreeable, nasty.

iki 〈いき：息〉a breath, breathing.

    iki-ga-kusai (息が臭い) have a foul breath

    iki-ga-arai (息が荒い) breathe hard

    iki-ga-kireru (息が切れる) get out of breath, lose one's breath

    iki-ga-kurushii *or* iki-gurushii (息が苦しい，息苦しい) breathe with difficulty

    iki o korosu (息を殺す) hold one's breath

    mada iki-ga-aru (まだ息がある) show signs of life

    iki-o-hiki-toru (息を引き取る) breathe one's last, die, expire

    iki-o-fuki-kaesu (息を吹き返す) fetch one's breath, come to life

    hito-iki-ireru (一息入れる) take a short rest

    hotto-hito-iki-tsuku (ほっと一息つく) be somewhat relieved

iki-o-suru 〈息をする〉breathe.

iki-no-tsuzuku-kagiri 〈息の続く限り〉to one's last gasp.

iki-mo-tsukazu-ni 〈息もつかずに〉without taking breath, at a stretch.

iki-o-kirashite 〈息を切らして〉out of breath.

iki 〈いき：意気〉spirit(s), heart, morale.

    iki-ga-agatte-iru (意気が揚っている) be in high spirits

    iki-shôchin-shite-iru (意気消沈している) be in low spirits

    iki-tôgô-shite-iru (意気投合している) be in congenial spirits

iki 〈いき：域〉limits, confines, a stage.

    shirôto no iki-o-dasshi-nai (素人の域を脱しない) be no better than the confines of amateurism

iki 〈いき：遺棄〉abandonment, desertion.

    iki-shitai (遺棄死体) an abandoned corpse

iki-suru 〈遺棄する〉abandon, desert, leave behind.

iki 〈いき：生き〉

iki-no-ii 〈生きのいい〉fresh, lively.

    iki-no-warui (生きの悪い) stale

iki 〈いき〉

  iki-na 〈いきな〉 stylish, smart, chic.

    iki-na-kakkô-o-shite-iru 〈いきな格好をしている〉 be smartly dressed

iki 〈いき：行き〉 going.

    iki-wa-basu-ni-suru 〈行きはバスにする〉 go by bus

    iki-mo-kaeri-mo aruku 〈行きも帰りも歩く〉 walk there and back

-iki 〈-いき：-行き〉 *see.* -yuki.

ikiatari-battari 〈いきあたりばったり：行き当たりばったり〉

  ikiatari-battari-no 〈行き当たりばったりの〉 happy-go-lucky, casual, haphazard.

  ikiatari-battari-ni 〈行き当たりばったりに〉 at haphazard.

    ikiatari-battari-ni yaru 〈行き当たりばったりにやる〉 do in a haphazard way

iki-ataru 〈いきあたる：行き当たる〉 come ((across)), light ((on)), run ((into)).

iki-chigai 〈いきちがい：行き違い〉 *see.* yuki-chigai.

iki-daore 〈いきだおれ：行き倒れ〉 a person dying on the street.

  iki-daore-ni-naru 〈行き倒れになる〉 fall ill(*or* dying) on the street.

iki-dokoro 〈いきどころ：行き所〉

  iki-dokoro-ga-nai 〈行き所がない〉 do not have any place to go.

iki-domari 〈いきどまり：行き止まり〉 *see.* yuki-domari.

ikidooru 〈いきどおる：憤る〉 resent, be indignant ((at)).

iki-gai 〈いきがい：生きがい〉

  iki-gai-no-aru seikatsu 〈生きがいのある生活〉 a life worth living

iki-gakari 〈いきがかり：行き掛かり〉

    kore-made-no-iki-gakari-o-issai-suteru 〈これまでの行き掛かりを一切捨てる〉 forget all that has happened, let bygones be bygones

  iki-gakari-jô 〈行き掛かり上〉 by force of circumstances.

iki-gake 〈いきがけ：行き掛け〉

  iki-gake-ni 〈行き掛けに〉 on one's way ((to)).

iki-gire 〈いきぎれ：息切れ〉 shortness of breath.

  iki-gire-ga-suru 〈息切れがする〉 be short of breath.

iki-gomi 〈いきごみ：意気込み〉 ardor, enthusiasm, eagerness.

    Hajime-no iki-gomi wa doko-e-yara. 〈初めの意気込みはどこへやら.〉 He has lost much of his initial enthusiasm.

  iki-gomu 〈意気込む〉 be enthusiastic ((about *or* for)), be bent ((on)), be eager ((to do)), be determined ((to do)).

iki-gurushii 〈いきぐるしい：息苦しい〉 suffocating, stifling, stuffy.

ikiiki 〈いきいき：生き生き〉
　ikiiki-shita 〈生き生きした〉 lively, vivid, fresh.
　ikiiki-to 〈生き生きと〉 lively, vividly.
iki-jibiki 〈いきじびき：生き字引〉 a walking dictionary.
iki-kaeru 〈いきかえる：生き返る〉 revive, come to life.
iki-kata 〈いきかた：生き方〉 how to live, a way of life.
ikikata 〈いきかた：行き方〉 how to go; one's way of doing things.
iki-kau 〈いきかう：行き交う〉 *see.* yuki-kau.
iki-ki 〈いきき：行き来〉 *see.* yuki-ki.
ikimaku 〈いきまく：息巻く〉 fume, rage, threaten.
iki-mono 〈いきもの：生き物〉 a living thing, a creature.
ikinari 〈いきなり〉 suddenly, abruptly, without notice.
iki-nobiru 〈いきのびる：生き延びる〉 survive, outlive.
iki-nokoru 〈いきのこる：生き残る〉 survive.
　iki-nokotta 〈生き残った〉 surviving.
ikinuki 〈いきぬき：息抜き〉 a rest, a breathing space, recreation.
　ikinuki-o-suru 〈息抜きをする〉 take a pause, take a short rest.
iki-nuku 〈いきぬく：生き抜く〉 live through.
ikioi 〈いきおい：勢い〉 power, force, energy, vigor, spirit, authority, influence, a trend; necessarily, inevitably, naturally.
　　ikioi-ni-jôzuru 〈勢いに乗ずる〉 take advantage of the circumstances
　ikioi-no-aru 〈勢いのある〉 powerful, energetic, forcible, spirited, influential.
　　ikioi-no-nai 〈勢いのない〉 spiritless, lifeless
　ikioi-yoku 〈勢いよく〉 with great force, vigorously.
　môretsu-na-ikioi-de 〈猛烈な勢いで〉 like forty, with great impetus.
ikioizuku 〈いきおいづく：勢い付く〉 cheer up, be encouraged.
ikiru 〈いきる：生きる〉 live.
　　kome-o-kutte-ikiru 〈米を食って生きる〉 live on rice
　　ikiru-ka-shinu-ka no mondai 〈生きるか死ぬかの問題〉 a matter of life or death
　ikite-iru or *ikiteiru* 〈生きている〉 be alive, be living.
　　ikite-iru-uchi-ni 〈生きているうちに〉 while one is alive
　　ikite-iru-kagiri 〈生きている限り〉 as long as one lives
　ikita 〈生きた〉 live.
　　ikita-kokochi-ga-shi-nai 〈生きた心地がしない〉 feel more dead than alive
iki-saki 〈いきさき：行き先〉 *see.* yuki-saki.

ikisatsu 〈いきさつ〉 the circumstances, particulars, the causes.

iki-sugi 〈いきすぎ：行き過ぎ〉 the excesses ((of)).
iki-sugi-de-aru or *iki-sugiru* 〈行き過ぎである，行き過ぎる〉 go too far.

iki-todoku 〈いきとどく：行き届く〉 *see.* yuki-todoku.

iki-tsuke 〈いきつけ：行きつけ〉
iki-tsuke-no 〈行きつけの〉 favorite, accustomed.
　　iki-tsuke-no ryôri-ya 〈行きつけの料理屋〉 one's favorite restaurant

iki-ume 〈いきうめ：生き埋め〉
iki-ume-ni-naru 〈生き埋めになる〉 be buried alive.

iki-utsushi 〈いきうつし：生き写し〉 close resemblance, a living image.
iki-utsushi-da 〈生き写しだ〉 be true to the life.

iki-wakare 〈いきわかれ：生き別れ〉 a lifelong parting.
iki-wakareru 〈生き別れる〉 part from ((a person)) never to see again.

iki-wataru 〈いきわたる：行き渡る〉 *see.* yuki-wataru.

ikizukai 〈いきづかい：息遣い〉 breathing.
ikizukai-ga-kurushii 〈息遣いが苦しい〉 breathe with difficulty.

iki-zumari 〈いきづまり：行き詰まり〉 *see.* yuki-zumari.

iki-zumaru 〈いきづまる：息詰まる〉 be choked, be stifled.
iki-zumaru-yô-na 〈息詰まるような〉 choking, breath-taking, oppressive, thrilling.

iki-zuri 〈いきずり：行きずり〉 *see.* yuki-zuri.

ikka 〈いっか：一家〉 a family; one's family.
　　ikka o sasaeru 〈一家を支える〉 support a family
　　ikka-shinjû 〈一家心中〉 a whole family suicide

ikkai 〈いっかい：一回〉 once, one time; a round, a game.
　　shû-ikkai 〈週一回〉 once a week
　　mô-ikkai 〈もう一回〉 once more
　　ikkai-sen 〈一回戦〉 the first round

ikkai 〈いっかい：一階〉 the first floor, the ground floor.

ikkai 〈いっかい：一介〉
ikkai-no 〈一介の〉 mere, only, nothing but.

ikkaku-senkin 〈いっかくせんきん：一獲千金〉 making a fortune at one stroke.

ikkan 〈いっかん：一貫〉
　　ikkan-sei 〈一貫性〉 consistency, coherence
ikkan-shita 〈一貫した〉 consistent, coherent.
　　ikkan-shita seisaku 〈一貫した政策〉 a consistent policy

ikkatsu 〈いっかつ：一括〉 a bundle, a lump.

ikkatsu-kônyû〈一括購入〉 a blanket purchase

ikkatsu-suru〈一括する〉lump together, summarize.

ikkatsu-shite〈一括して〉in a lump, en bloc, in bulk, in one lot.

ikken〈いっけん：一軒〉

ikken-goto-ni〈一軒ごとに〉from door to door, from house to house.

ikken〈いっけん：一件〉an affair, a matter, a case.

ikken-shorui（一件書類）all the documents relating to the case

ikken〈いっけん：一見〉a look, a sight, a glance.

ikken-suru〈一見する〉have a look ((at)).

ikken-shite〈一見して〉at a glance, at first sight.

ikki〈いっき：一気〉

ikki-ni〈一気に〉at a breath, at a stretch.

ikki-ni nomi-hosu（一気に飲み干す）empty ((the bottle)) at a draft

ikki-ni yomu（一気に読む）read ((a book)) at a sitting

ikki-ichiyû〈いっきいちゆう：一喜一憂〉

ikki-ichiyû-suru〈一喜一憂する〉be now glad, now sad.

ikko〈いっこ：一個〉one, a piece.

ikko go-hyaku-en（一個五百円）500 yen a piece, 500 yen each

ikko〈いっこ：一戸〉

ikko-o-kamaeru（一戸を構える）keep a house of one's own

ikko-atari（一戸当たり）per household

ikkô〈いっこう：一行〉a party, a company.

ikkô ni kuwawaru（一行に加わる）join a party

ikkô-no-hito-bito（一行の人々）the members of the party

ikkô〈いっこう：一考〉consideration, a thought.

ikko-no yochi-ga-aru（一考の余地がある）leave room for consideration

ikkojin〈いっこじん：一個人〉an individual, a private person.

ikkojin-to-shite（一個人として）as an individual, as a private person

ikkoku〈いっこく：一刻〉a minute, a moment.

ikkoku-o-arasou mondai（一刻を争う問題）a burning question

ikkoku-mo-hayaku〈一刻も早く〉without a moment's delay, as soon as possible, at once.

ikkoku〈いっこく：一国〉one country.

ikkoku-ichi-jô-no-aruji（一国一城のあるじ）the head of a family, a man who has a home of his own

ikkô-ni〈いっこうに：一向に〉

Ikkô-ni zonji-masen.（一向に存じません．）I don't know at all.

Ikkô-ni kamai-masen.（一向に構いません。）　I don't care a damn.

ikkyo〈いっきょ：一挙〉

　　ikkyo-ichidô（一挙一動）　one's every action, everything one does

　　ikkyo-ryôtoku-da（一挙両得だ）　kill two birds with one stone, serve two ends

　ikkyo-ni〈一挙に〉at a stroke, by one effort, with a rush, by one charge.

ikkyû〈いっきゅう：一級〉

　　ikkyû-hin（一級品）　an article of the highest quality

　ikkyû-no〈一級の〉first-class, of the highest quality.

ikô〈いこう：以降〉on and after.

　　itsuka-ikô（五日以降）　on and after the 5th

ikô〈いこう：意向〉an intention.

　　ikô o tadasu（意向を正す）　ask ((a person's)) intention

　　ikô o tashikameru（意向を確かめる）　ascertain ((a person's)) intentions

ikô〈いこう：威光〉power, influence, authority.

　　chichi-oya-no-ikô-de（父親の威光で）　through the influence of one's father

ikoji〈いこじ：依こ地〉*see.*　ekoji.

ikoku〈いこく：異国〉a foreign country.

　　ikoku-jôcho（異国情緒）　an exotic mood

　ikoku-fû-no〈異国風の〉foreign, exotic.

ikotsu〈いこつ：遺骨〉one's remains, one's ashes.

iku〈いく：行く〉go, come, lead ((to)).

　　aruite-iku（歩いて行く）　go on foot

　　jitensha-de iku（自転車で行く）　go by bicycle

　　kyôkai-e iku（教会へ行く）　go to church

　　Ashita iki-masu.（あした行きます。）　I'll come to see you tomorrow.

　　Kono michi-o-iku-to Hongô-ni deru.（この道を行くと本郷に出る。）　This street leads to Hongo.

　　soko-e itta-koto-ga-aru（そこへ行ったことがある）　have been there

　　soko-e itta-koto-ga-nai（そこへ行ったことがない）　have not been there

　　Tôkyô-e-itte-kimashita.（東京へ行ってきました。）　I have been to Tokyo.

　　Iki-mashô.（行きましょう。）　Let's go.

　　umaku iku（うまくいく）　go well, be successful

iku-〈いく-：幾-〉*see.*　nan-.

ikubun 〈いくぶん：幾分〉 *see.* ikura-ka.

ikudo 〈いくど：幾度〉 *see.* nando.

iku-dôon 〈いくどうおん：異口同音〉

  iku-dôon-ni 〈異口同音に〉 with one voice, with one consent, in chorus.

ikuei 〈いくえい：育英〉

  ikuei-shikin （育英資金） scholarship

  ikuei-seido （育英制度） a scholarship system

ikuji 〈いくじ：育児〉 childcare, upbringing of a child.

ikuji 〈いくじ：意気地〉

  ikuji-ga-nai 〈意気地がない〉 have no spirit.

  ikuji-no-nai 〈意気地のない〉 spiritless, timid, cowardly.

ikura 〈いくら：幾ら〉 how many, how much, what.

  ichi-kiro-ikura-de uru （一キロ幾らで売る） sell by the kilogram

  ikura o-kane-o-dashite-mo *or* ikura o-kane-o-moratte-mo （幾らお金を
    出しても，幾らお金をもらっても） at any price

  ikura〜-mo 〈幾ら〜も〉 however.

  ikura-hataraite-mo （幾ら働いても） however hard one may work

  ikura-demo 〈幾らでも〉 as many(*or* much) as one likes.

    Ikura-demo motte-iki-nasai. （幾らでも持って行きなさい。） Take as
    many as you like.

  ikura-mo〜nai 〈幾らも〜ない〉 not many, not much.

    Mô o-kane wa ikura-mo-nokotte-i-nai. （もうお金は幾らも残っていな
    い。） We have not much money left now.

ikura-ka 〈いくらか：幾らか〉 some, something, somewhat, a little.

ikusei 〈いくせい：育成〉

  ikusei-suru 〈育成する〉 bring up, foster.

ikutsu 〈いくつ：幾つ〉 how many, how old.

  ikutsu-ka-no （幾つかの） some, several

  ikutsu-mo-no （幾つもの） many

  ikutsu-demo （幾つでも） any number ((of))

ikyô 〈いきょう：異教〉 heathenism, paganism, heresy.

  ikyô-to （異教徒） a heathen, a pagan, a heretic

ikyoku 〈いきょく：医局〉 a medical office.

ima 〈いま：居間〉 a living room, a sitting room.

ima 〈いま：今〉 now, at present, just now, at once, immediately,
another.

  ima-demo （今でも） even now

  ima-dewa （今では） now, in these days, lately

ima-doki（今時）　(in) these days

ima-goro（今ごろ）　at this time

　　asu-no ima-goro（明日の今ごろ）　at this time tomorrow

　　ima-goro-wa-mô（今ごろはもう）　by this time

ima-hitori（今一人）　another person, the other person

ima-ichi-do（今一度）　once more

ima-kara（今から）　from now (on)

ima-made（今まで）　until now

　　ima-made-no-tokoro（今までのところ）　so far

ima-motte（今もって）　yet, still

ima-ni（今に）　soon, before long, sooner or later

ima-nimo～(-shi)-sô-da（今にも～(し)そうだ）　be ready ((to do))

　　Fune　wa　ima-nimo-shizumi-sô-da.（船は今にも沈みそうだ.）　The
　　vessel is ready to sink.

ima-no（今の）　present, of the present day

　　ima-no-tokoro（今のところ）　for the present, for the moment

ima-sara（今更）　now, at this time

　　Ima-sara　tori-kesu-wake-niwa-ika-nai.（今更取り消すわけにもいかな
　　い.）　It is now too late to cancel it.

ima-shibaraku（今しばらく）　a little longer

ima-shigata（今し方）　just now, a moment ago

ima-sugu（今すぐ）　at once

imada〈いまだ〉　yet, as yet.

imada-ni〈いまだに〉　still, even now.

imaimashii〈いまいましい：忌ま忌ましい〉　vexatious, annoying, hateful,
provoking, disgusting, cursed.

　　Kuso, imaimashii!（くそ, 忌ま忌ましい.）　Confound it! / Damn you!

imaimashigaru〈忌ま忌ましがる〉　be vexed ((at *or* by)).

imaimashisô-ni〈忌ま忌ましそうに〉　with vexation, disgustingly.

imashime〈いましめ：戒め〉　(an) admonition, a lesson, instructions, (a)
warning.

　　Kare-no rei wa watashi-ni yoi imashime-to-natta.（彼の例は私によい戒
　　めとなった.）　His example was a good lesson to me.

imashimeru〈戒める〉　admonish, remonstrate ((against)), warn.

imawashii〈いまわしい：忌まわしい〉　abominable, detestable, disgusting.

imbô〈いんぼう：陰謀〉　a plot, an intrigue, a conspiracy.

imbô-o-kuwadateru〈陰謀を企てる〉　plot, intrigue ((against *or* with)).

imbun〈いんぶん：韻文〉　verse, poetry.

imêji 〈イメージ〉 an image.

  imêji-appu-suru 〈イメージアップする〉 improve an image ((of)).

imi 〈いみ：意味〉 (a) meaning, (a) sense, significance, a point.

  imi-suru 〈意味する〉 mean, signify.

  imi-ga-wakara-nai 〈意味が分からない〉 cannot understand.

  imi-no-aru 〈意味のある〉 meaningful, significant.

    imi-no-nai 〈意味のない〉 meaningless, senseless, pointless

  imi-shinchô-na 〈意味深長な〉 full of meaning, profound.

  imi-ari-ge-ni 〈意味ありげに〉 meaningly, significantly.

  aru-imi-dewa 〈ある意味では〉 in a sense.

imin 〈いみん：移民〉 emigration, immigration; an emigrant, an immigrant.

immetsu 〈いんめつ：いん滅〉 destruction.

  immetsu-suru 〈いん滅する〉 destroy, suppress.

    shôko o immetsu-suru（証拠をいん滅する） destroy evidence

imo 〈いも：芋〉 a potato, a sweet potato, a taro.

imomushi 〈いもむし：芋虫〉 a green caterpillar.

imon 〈いもん：慰問〉 consolation, sympathy.

  imon-suru 〈慰問する〉 console, visit.

i-mono 〈いもの：鋳物〉 a casting, a molding, cast metal.

    i-mono-kôjô（鋳物工場） a foundry

imori 〈いもり〉 a newt.

imôto 〈いもうと：妹〉 a younger sister, a little sister.

imu-shitsu 〈いむしつ：医務室〉 a medical treatment room.

inabikari 〈いなびかり：稲光〉 (a flash of) lightning.

i-nagara-ni-shite 〈いながらにして：居ながらにして〉 as one sits, at one's home, without traveling.

inago 〈いなご〉 a locust.

inaho 〈いなほ：稲穂〉 an ear of rice.

-inai 〈-いない：-以内〉

  -inai-no or *-inai-ni* 〈-以内の、-以内に〉 within, less than, not more than.

    ni-shû-kan-inai-ni（二週間以内に） within two weeks

inaka 〈いなか：田舎〉 the country, the provinces, one's home, one's native place.

  inaka-no 〈田舎の〉 rural, rustic, country.

    inaka-no seikatsu（田舎の生活） rural life

  inaka-fû-no 〈田舎風の〉 country-like.

-inan 〈-いなん：-以南〉 south (of).

-inan-no, -inan-ni or *-inan-wa* 〈-以南の，-以南に，-以南は〉 south of.

inanaku 〈いななく〉 neigh, whinny, bray.

i-naoru 〈いなおる：居直る〉 change one's attitude, assume a threatening attitude.

inasaku 〈いなさく：稲作〉 a rice crop.

inase 〈いなせ〉

inase-na 〈いなせな〉 dapper, swanky, rakish.

(-ya)-inaya 〈（や）いなや：（や）否や〉 as soon as, no sooner...than, hardly... when, scarcely...when, the moment.

     Kare-wa watashi-o-miru-ya-inaya, nige-dashita. 〈彼は私を見るや否や，逃げ出した。〉 The moment he saw me, he ran away.

inazuma 〈いなずま：稲妻〉 *see.* inabikari.

inchiki 〈いんちき〉

inchiki-na 〈いんちきな〉 fake, bogus, phony.

inchô 〈いんちょう：院長〉 the director 〔of a hospital〕, the president 〔of an institute〕, the principal, the rector.

in-denki 〈いんでんき：陰電気〉 negative electricity.

in-denshi 〈いんでんし：陰電子〉 a negatron.

Indo 〈インド〉 India.

     Indo-jin（インド人） an Indian

     Indo-go（インド語） Hindustani

     Indo-yô（インド洋） the Indian Ocean

     Indo(-jin)-no（インド(人)の） Indian

Indoneshia 〈インドネシア〉 Indonesia.

     Indoneshia-jin（インドネシア人） an Indonesian

     Indoneshia(-jin)-no（インドネシア(人)の） Indonesian

ine 〈いね：稲〉 a rice plant.

     ine o karu（稲を刈る） cut(*or* reap) rice

in·ei 〈いんえい：陰影〉 shadow, shading.

in·ei-o-tsukeru 〈陰影を付ける〉 shade.

i-nemuri 〈いねむり：居眠り〉 a doze, a nap.

     i-nemuri-unten-o-suru（居眠り運転をする） drive ((a car)) asleep

i-nemuri-suru 〈居眠りする〉 doze, fall into a doze.

infure 〈インフレ〉 inflation.

     akusei-infure（悪性インフレ） spiral inflation

     infure-taisaku（インフレ対策） an anti-inflation measure

infuruenza 〈インフルエンザ〉 influenza, flu.

inga 〈いんが：因果〉 cause and effect.

inga-kankei（因果関係） causal relation

inga-ôhô（因果応報） nemesis

inga〈いんが：陰画〉a negative.

ingai-katsudō〈いんがいかつどう：院外活動〉lobbying.

ingai-katsudô-o-suru〈院外活動をする〉lobby.

inga-shi〈いんがし：印画紙〉photographic paper.

ingo〈いんご：隠語〉secret language, a cant.

ingō〈いんごう：因業〉

ingô-na〈因業な〉hardhearted, stonyhearted, merciless.

inin〈いにん：委任〉trust, charge, delegation, authorization.

inin-jô（委任状） a letter of attorney

inin-suru〈委任する〉entrust ((a person)) with, delegate ((power or authority)) to ((a person)).

inka〈いんか：引火〉ignition.

inka-suru〈引火する〉catch fire, ignite.

inkan〈いんかん：印鑑〉one's seal.

inkan-shômei（印鑑証明） a certificate of one's seal impression

inken〈いんけん：陰険〉

inken-na〈陰険な〉insidious, sinister, treacherous.

inki〈インキ〉ink.

inki〈いんき：陰気〉

inki-na〈陰気な〉gloomy, dismal.

inko〈いんこ〉a parakeet, a macaw.

inkō〈いんこう〉the throat.

inkô-kataru（いんこうカタル） catarrh of the throat

inkyo〈いんきょ：隠居〉retirement from active life; a person retired from active life.

inkyoku〈いんきょく：陰極〉the cathode, the negative pole.

innai-katsudō〈いんないかつどう：院内活動〉activities in the Diet.

innen〈いんねん：因縁〉fate, connection, origin; a pretext.

innen-da-to-akirameru（因縁だとあきらめる） resign oneself to one's fate

innen-o-tsukeru（因縁をつける） invent a pretext for quarreling ((on))

in-niku〈いんにく：印肉〉an inkpad, a stamp pad.

inochi〈いのち：命〉life.

hito-no inochi o tasukeru（人の命を助ける） save another's life

inochi-o-tori-tomeru（命を取り留める） escape death

inochi o ushinau（命を失う） lose one's life

inochi-tori-ni-naru（命取りになる）prove fatal

inochi-no-aru-kagiri-wa（命のある限りは）as long as one lives

inochi-no-tsuna（命の綱）the staff of life, a life line

inochi-karagara-nigeru（命からがら逃げる）have a narrow escape

inochi-gake-de（命懸けで）at the risk of one's life

ino-ichiban〈いのいちばん：いの一番〉

ino-ichiban-ni〈いの一番に〉first of all.

inokoru〈いのこる：居残る〉remain behind, work overtime.

inori〈いのり：祈り〉a prayer.

inori o sasageru（祈りをささげる）offer a prayer

inoru〈祈る〉pray ((to)), say grace, wish.

Kami-ni inoru（神に祈る）pray to God

Go-kôun-o-inorimasu.（御幸運を祈ります。）I wish you good luck.

inoshishi〈いのしし〉a wild boar.

inreki〈いんれき：陰暦〉the lunar calendar.

inreki-kugatsu（陰暦九月）September according to the lunar calendar

inritsu〈いんりつ：韻律〉a rhythm, a meter.

inryô〈いんりょう：飲料〉a drink.

inryô-sui（飲料水）drinking water

seiryô-inryô（清涼飲料）soft drinks

inryoku〈いんりょく：引力〉attraction, gravitation.

insan〈いんさん：陰惨〉

insan-na〈陰惨な〉dismal, weird, gloomy.

insatsu〈いんさつ：印刷〉printing.

insatsu-jo（印刷所）a printing office, a print shop

insatsu-ki（印刷機）a printing machine

insatsu-butsu（印刷物）printed matter

insatsu-suru〈印刷する〉print.

insatsu-chû-de-aru〈印刷中である〉be in the press.

insei〈いんせい：陰性〉

insei-no〈陰性の〉negative, dormant, gloomy.

inseki〈いんせき：いん石〉a meteorite.

inseki〈いんせき：姻せき〉a relative by marriage.

inseki-kankei-o-musubu〈姻せき関係を結ぶ〉get related by marriage ((to)).

inseki〈いんせき：引責〉

inseki-suru〈引責する〉assume the responsibility ((for)).

inseki-jishoku-suru〈引責辞職する〉assume the responsibility (for an incident) and resign

inshi〈いんし：印紙〉a stamp.
shūnyū-inshi（収入印紙）a revenue stamp

inshi〈いんし：因子〉a factor.

inshō〈いんしょう：印象〉an impression.
ii inshō o ataeru（いい印象を与える）give ((a person)) a favorable impression
warui inshō o ataeru（悪い印象を与える）give ((a person)) an unfavorable impression
dai-ichi inshō（第一印象）the first impression
inshō-teki(-na)〈印象的(な)〉impressive.

inshoku〈いんしょく：飲食〉eating and drinking.
inshoku-butsu（飲食物）food and drink
inshoku-ten（飲食店）an eating house, a restaurant
inshoku-suru〈飲食する〉eat and drink.

inshu〈いんしゅ：飲酒〉drinking.

inshū〈いんしゅう：因習〉a long-established custom, convention.
inshū-ni-torawareru（因習に捕らわれる）be a slave to convention
inshū-o-daha-suru（因習を打破する）do away with conventionalities
inshū-no or *inshū-teki(-na)*〈因習の，因習的(な)〉conventional.

insotsu〈いんそつ：引率〉
insotsu-sha（引率者）a leader
insotsu-suru〈引率する〉lead.

insū〈いんすう：因数〉a factor.
insū-ni bunkai-suru（因数に分解する）resolve into factors
insū-bunkai（因数分解）factorization

insutanto〈インスタント〉instant.
insutanto-shokuhin（インスタント食品）precooked food

intabyū〈インタビュー〉an interview.
intabyū ni ōjiru（インタビューに応じる）accord an interview
intabyū-suru〈インタビューする〉interview.

intai〈いんたい：引退〉retirement.
intai-suru〈引退する〉retire ((from)).

interi〈インテリ〉an intellectual, the intelligentsia.

intoku〈いんとく：隠匿〉concealment.
intoku-suru〈隠匿する〉conceal, hide.

inu〈いぬ：犬〉a dog.

inu o kau〔犬を飼う〕 keep a dog
inu-goya〔犬小屋〕 a kennel, a doghouse
inu-neko-byôin〔犬猫病院〕 a pets' hospital
inu-kaki-de-oyogu〔犬かきで泳ぐ〕 dog-paddle

inujini〈いぬじに：犬死に〉
inujini-suru〔犬死にする〕 die to no purpose.

in・yô〈いんよう：引用〉 quotation.
in・yô-bun〔引用文〕 a quotation
in・yô-fu〔引用符〕 quotation marks
in・yô-suru〔引用する〕 quote ((from)).

inyû〈いにゅう：移入〉
inyû-suru〔移入する〕 import, introduce, bring in.

inzei〈いんぜい：印税〉 a royalty.

inzen〈いんぜん：隠然〉
inzen-ţaru seiryoku〔隠然たる勢力〕 a great, though covert, influence

inzû〈いんずう：員数〉 the (total) number.
inzû o tashikameru〔員数を確かめる〕 ascertain the number

iô〈いおう：硫黄〉 sulfur, sulphur.

ippa〈いっぱ：一派〉 a party, a faction; a school; a sect, a denomination.

ippai〈いっぱい：一杯〉 a cup, a glass, a glassful; a drink.
bîru-ippai〔ビール一杯〕 a glass of beer
supûn-ippai-no-satô〔スプーン一杯の砂糖〕 a spoonful of sugar
ippai-nomu〔一杯飲む〕 have a drink

ippai〈いっぱい：一杯〉 full ((of)), crowded ((with)).
me-ni-ippai-namida-o-tamete〔目にいっぱい涙をためて〕 with one's eyes full of tears
hara-ippai taberu〔腹いっぱい食べる〕 eat one's fill
chikara-ippai-yaru *or* sei-ippai-yaru〔力いっぱいやる，精いっぱいやる〕 do one's best
ippai-kuwaseru〔いっぱい食わせる〕 play a trick ((on))
ippai-kuu〔いっぱい食う〕 be taken in
〜-de-ippai-de-aru〈〜でいっぱいである〉 be full of... , be crowded with... .
ippai-ni-suru〔いっぱいにする〕 fill (up).

ippaku〈いっぱく：一泊〉
ippaku-suru〔一泊する〕 spend a night ((at *or* in)), put up ((at a hotel)) for a night.

ippan〈いっぱん：一般〉

　　　ippan-taishû〈一般大衆〉 general public
　ippan-ka-suru〈一般化する〉 generalize.
　ippan-no〈一般の〉 general.
　ippan-ni〈一般に〉 generally, in general, as a rule, on the whole.
ippashi〈いっぱし：一端〉
　ippashi-no〈いっぱしの〉 like others, pretty good.
　　　ippashi-no yakusha〈いっぱしの役者〉 a pretty good actor
ippatsu〈いっぱつ：一発〉 a shot, a round.
　　　ippatsu-utsu〈一発撃つ〉 fire a shot
ippen〈いっぺん：一変〉
　ippen-suru〈一変する〉 change completely, undergo a complete change,
　　be transformed.
　　　taido o ippen-suru〈態度を一変する〉 change one's attitude
ippen〈いっぺん：一遍〉
　ippen-ni〈一遍に〉 at a time, at a sitting, in one lot.
ippentô〈いっぺんとう：一辺倒〉
　Amerika-ippentô-de-aru〈アメリカ一辺倒である〉 be an out-and-out pro-
　　American.
ippiki-ookami〈いっぴきおおかみ：一匹おおかみ〉 a lone wolf, a loner.
ippin〈いっぴん：一品〉 an article, a dish.
　　　ippin-ryôri〈一品料理〉 dishes à la carte
　tenka-ippin-no〈天下一品の〉 unique, superb.
ippin〈いっぴん：逸品〉 an excellent article, a rarity, a gem, a master-
　　piece.
ippo〈いっぽ：一歩〉 a step.
　　　ippo-zenshin-suru〈一歩前進する〉 take a step forward
　　　ippo-mo-yuzura-nai〈一歩も譲らない〉 do not budge a step
　　　ippo-ippo〈一歩一歩〉 step by step
　　　ippo-goto-ni〈一歩ごとに〉 at every step
ippô〈いっぽう：一方〉 one side, one hand, the other side(*or* hand).
　　　ippô-ni katayoru〈一方に偏る〉 lean to one side
　　　ippô-tsûkô〈一方通行〉 one-way traffic
　ippô-teki(-na)〈一方的（な）〉 one-sided.
　ippô-dewa~, mata ippô-dewa~〈一方では～，また一方では～〉 on the one
　　hand... , on the other hand... .
ippon〈いっぽん：一本〉 one, a piece, a bottle.
　　　bôrupen-ippon〈ボールペン一本〉 a ball-point pen
　　　chôku-ippon〈チョーク一本〉 a piece of chalk

bîru-ippon（ビール一本） a bottle of beer

ippon-gi〈いっぽんぎ：一本気〉

ippon-gi-no〈一本気の〉 single-minded.

ippû〈いっぷう：一風〉

ippû-kawatta〈一風変わった〉 eccentric, strange, queer, peculiar, out of the ordinary.

ippuku〈いっぷく：一服〉 a dose; a smoke; a rest.

kusuri-o-ippuku nomu（薬を一服飲む） take a dose of medicine

ippuku-suu（一服吸う） have a smoke

ippuku-suru〈一服する〉 take a rest.

iradatsu〈いらだつ：いら立つ〉 *see.* iraira-suru.

irai〈いらい：以来〉

sore-irai〈それ以来〉 since then.

irai〈いらい：依頼〉 a request; trust, reliance.

irai ni ôjiru（依頼に応じる） grant ((a person's)) request

go-irai-ni-yori（御依頼により） at your request

irai-jô（依頼状） a letter of request

irai-nin（依頼人） a client

irai-suru〈依頼する〉 request, ask, rely ((upon)).

iraira〈いらいら〉

iraira-suru〈いらいらする〉 be irritated, be nervous, fret, be in a fret, be impatient.

iraira-shite〈いらいらして〉 nervously, in a fret, impatiently.

Iraku〈イラク〉 Iraq.

Iraku-jin（イラク人） an Iraqi

Iraku-no（イラクの） Iraqi

Iran〈イラン〉 Iran.

Iran-jin（イラン人） an Iranian

Iran-no（イランの） Iranian

Irasshai!〈いらっしゃい。〉 Come in! / Welcome!

irasuto〈イラスト〉 an illustration.

ire-ba〈いれば：入れ歯〉 a false tooth.

ire-ba-o-suru（入れ歯をする） have a false tooth put in

ire-ba o hameru（入れ歯をはめる） put in one's false tooth

ire-ba o hazusu（入れ歯を外す） take out one's false tooth

ire-chigai〈いれちがい：入れ違い〉

ire-chigai-ni-naru〈入れ違いになる〉 pass each other.

irei〈いれい：異例〉

irei-no〈異例の〉exceptional, unprecedented.

irei-no shôshin (異例の昇進)　an unprecedented promotion

irei-sai〈いれいさい：慰霊祭〉a memorial service for the dead.

irejie〈いれぢえ：入れ知恵〉a suggestion, a hint.

irejie-suru〈入れ知恵する〉put an idea into ((a person's)) head.

ire-kaeru〈いれかえる：入れ替える〉change ((A for B)), replace ((A with B)), put in afresh.

cha-o-ire-kaeru (茶を入れ替える)　make fresh tea

kokoro o ire-kaeru (心を入れ替える)　mend one's ways

ire-mono〈いれもの：入れ物〉a receptacle, a container, a vessel.

ireru〈いれる：入れる〉put in; send, enter; accept; let in, show in; make; include.

kôhî-ni satô o ireru (コーヒーに砂糖を入れる)　put sugar into coffee

kodomo o gakkô-ni ireru (子供を学校に入れる)　send a child to school

hito-no môshi-de o ireru (人の申し出を入れる)　accept a person's offer

Kanojo-o irete-age-nasai. (彼女を入れてあげなさい.)　Let her in.

o-cha o ireru (お茶を入れる)　make tea

watashi-o-irete zembu-de hachi-nin (私を入れて全部で八人)　eight in all, including me

te-ni-ireru〈手に入れる〉get, obtain.

irezumi〈いれずみ：入れ墨〉tattooing; a tattoo.

irezumi-o-suru〈入れ墨をする〉tattoo.

iri〈いり：入り〉

iri-ga-ii (入りがいい)　have a large attendance

iri-ga-warui (入りが悪い)　have a small attendance

tsuyu no iri (梅雨の入り)　setting-in of the rainy season

iribitari〈いりびたり：入り浸り〉

iribitari-de-aru〈入り浸りである〉be a constant visitor ((at)), frequent.

irie〈いりえ：入り江〉an inlet, a cove.

iriguchi〈いりぐち：入り口〉an entrance, a way in.

iriguchi-de (入り口で)　at the entrance

irikawari-tachikawari〈いりかわりたちかわり：入り替わり立ち替わり〉one after another.

iri-kunda〈いりくんだ：入り組んだ〉complicated, intricate, involved, entangled.

iri-kunda setsumei (入り組んだ説明)　an involved explanation

iri-majiru 〈いりまじる：入り交じる〉 mix ((with)), be mixed up.

iri-midareru 〈いりみだれる：入り乱れる〉 be jumbled.

    iri-midarete tatakau (入り乱れて戦う) fight in a melee

iro 〈いろ：色〉 a color, a tint, a shade; complexion.

    iro-ga-usui (色が薄い) be of a light color

    iro-ga-koi (色が濃い) be of a deep color

    iro-empitsu (色鉛筆) a colored pencil

    iro-jiro-no (色白の) fair-complexioned

iro-o-tsukeru 〈色を付ける〉 color.

iro-o-ushinau 〈色を失う〉 lose color, turn pale.

iro-o-konomu 〈色を好む〉 be amorous.

irô 〈いろう：慰労〉

    irô-kin (慰労金) a gratuity

iro-suru 〈慰労する〉 acknowledge ((a person's)) services.

iroai 〈いろあい：色合い〉 a shade of color, a tint.

irodoru 〈いろどる：彩る〉 color, paint, dye.

i-ro-ha 〈いろは〉 the Japanese alphabet, the ABC ((of)).

iroiro 〈いろいろ：色々〉

    Iroiro-arigatô. (いろいろありがとう。) Thank you for everything.

iroiro-na 〈いろいろな〉 various, of different kinds, all kinds of, many, a lot of.

    iroiro-na ten-ni-oite (いろいろな点において) in various respects

iroiro-ni 〈いろいろに〉 variously, in many ways, in every way.

iroke 〈いろけ：色気〉 tender passion ((toward)); an inclination, an interest.

iroke-zuku 〈色気づく〉 begin to think of love

sukoshi-iroke-ga-aru 〈少し色気がある〉 have half a mind ((to do)), have an eye ((to)).

iroke-no-aru 〈色気のある〉 seductive, coquettish.

    iroke-no-nai (色気のない) fancy-free, innocent

iro-me 〈いろめ：色目〉

iro-me-o-tsukau 〈色目を使う〉 cast a coquettish glance ((at)).

iro-megane 〈いろめがね：色眼鏡〉 colored spectacles.

iro-megane-de-miru 〈色眼鏡で見る〉 look at ((a thing)) through colored spectacles.

iron 〈いろん：異論〉 a different opinion; an objection.

iron-o-tonaeru 〈異論を唱える〉 object ((to)), raise an objection ((against *or* to)).

iron-naku 〈異論なく〉 unanimously.

iroppoi〈いろっぽい：色っぽい〉coquettish, amorous, erotic, sexy.

iro-yoi〈いろよい：色よい〉

    iro-yoi henji（色よい返事）a favorable answer

iro-zuku〈いろづく：色づく〉become tinged, turn red.

iru〈いる：射る〉shoot.

    ya o iru（矢を射る）shoot an arrow

iru〈いる〉parch, roast.

iru〈いる：居る〉be, there is(*or* are), remain, stay, occupy, live, be in, be present.

    ie-ni-iru（家にいる）stay at home

    heya-ni-iru（部屋にいる）occupy a room

    oba-no-tokoro-ni-iru（伯母(叔母)のところにいる）live with one's aunt

    Katô-kun wa imasu-ka?（加藤君はいますか.）Is Mr. Kato in?

    hito-no-iru-tokoro-de（人のいるところで）in the presence of a person

    hito-no-i-nai-tokoro-de（人のいないところで）behind a person's back

iru〈いる：要る〉want, need, require.

    sukoshi kane-ga-iru（少し金が要る）want some money

    nani-mo-ira-nai（何も要らない）need nothing

    daibu hitode-ga-iru（だいぶ人手が要る）require a number of hands

iru〈いる〉be ...ing, be at, keep, remain, be engaged ((in)).

    hataraite-iru（働いている）be working, be at work

    zutto-tatte-iru（ずっと立っている）keep standing

    dokushin-de-iru（独身でいる）remain single

    shôbai-o-shite-iru（商売をしている）be engaged in business

irui〈いるい：衣類〉clothing, clothes, garments.

iruka〈いるか〉a dolphin.

i-rusu〈いるす：居留守〉

    i-rusu-o-tsukau〈居留守を使う〉pretend to be out, be not at home ((to)).

iryô〈いりょう：医療〉medical treatment.

    iryô-hi（医療費）medical expenses

    iryô-kikai（医療器械）medical instruments

    iryô-kikan（医療機関）a medical institution

iryô〈いりょう：衣料〉clothing, clothes.

    iryô-hi（衣料費）clothing expenses

iryoku〈いりょく：威力〉power, might, influence.

    iryoku o furuu（威力を振るう）exercise one's power ((over))

    iryoku-o-hakki-suru（威力を発揮する）prove powerful

    iryoku-no-aru〈威力のある〉powerful, mighty.

iryû 〈いりゅう：慰留〉
 iryû-suru 〈慰留する〉 dissuade ((a person)) from ((doing)).
isagiyoku 〈いさぎよく：潔く〉 manfully, with a good grace.
isai 〈いさい：委細〉 details, particulars, the whole circumstances.
   isai o hanasu (委細を話す) tell ((a person)) all the details
   Isai-wa-mendan-no-ue. (委細は面談の上.) Particulars to be arranged
      personally.
isai 〈いさい：異彩〉
 isai-o-hanatsu 〈異彩を放つ〉 be conspicuous, cut a brilliant figure.
isamashii 〈いさましい：勇ましい〉 brave, courageous, valiant.
 isamashiku 〈勇ましく〉 bravely, courageously.
isameru 〈いさめる〉 remonstrate with ((a person)) on, dissuade.
isan 〈いさん：遺産〉 a legacy, a bequest.
   isan o nokosu (遺産を残す) leave a bequest
   isan-arasoi (遺産争い) a quarrel over an inheritance
   isan-sôzoku (遺産相続) succession to property
   isan-sôzoku-nin (遺産相続人) an inheritor, an heir
isan 〈いさん：違算〉 miscalculation.
 isan-suru 〈違算する〉 miscalculate.
isan 〈いさん：胃酸〉 acid in the stomach.
   isan-kata-shô (胃酸過多症) acid dyspepsia
isasaka 〈いささか〉 a bit, a little, slightly, somewhat, rather.
   Isasaka-odoroita. (いささか驚いた.) I was a little surprised.
   isasaka kentô-chigai-da (いささか見当違いだ) be somewhat beside
      the mark
ise-ebi 〈いせえび〉 a lobster.
isei 〈いせい：異性〉 the other(*or* opposite) sex.
isei 〈いせい：威勢〉
 isei-no-ii 〈威勢のいい〉 (high-)spirited.
 isei-yoku 〈威勢よく〉 in high spirits.
-isei 〈-いせい：-以西〉 west of((of)).
 -isei-no, -isei-ni or *-isei-wa* 〈-以西の，-以西に，-以西は〉 west of.
isei-sha 〈いせいしゃ：為政者〉 a statesman, an administrator, a ruler.
iseki 〈いせき：遺跡〉 remains, ruins, relics.
isetsu 〈いせつ：異説〉 a different opinion, conflicting views.
   isetsu o tonaeru (異説を唱える) have a different opinion ((on))
isha 〈いしゃ：医者〉 a doctor, a physician, a surgeon.
   isha o yobu (医者を呼ぶ) send for a doctor

　　　isha-ni-mite-morau〈医者に診てもらう〉consult a doctor
　　　isha-ni-kakatte-iru〈医者にかかっている〉be under medical treatment
isha-ryô〈いしゃりょう：慰謝料〉consolation money.
　　　isha-ryô o seikyû-suru〈慰謝料を請求する〉demand compensation
　　　((for))
ishi〈いし：医師〉*see.* isha.
　　　ishi-kai〈医師会〉a medical association
ishi〈いし：意志〉will.
　　　ishi-no-tsuyoi hito〈意志の強い人〉a person of strong will
　　　ishi-no-yowai hito〈意志の弱い人〉a person of weak will
　ishi-ni-hanshite〈意志に反して〉against one's will.
ishi〈いし：意思〉an intention.
　　　ishi-hyôji-suru〈意思表示する〉indicate one's intention
　ishi-no-sotsû-o-kaite-iru〈意思の疎通を欠いている〉there is a lack of
　　understanding ((between *or* among)), do not understand each other(*or*
　　one another).
ishi〈いし：遺志〉one's last will.
　　　chichi-no ishi-o-tsuide〈父の遺志を継いで〉in pursuance of one's
　　　father's last will
ishi〈いし：石〉a stone, a pebble.
　　　ishi-dan〈石段〉stone steps
　　　ishi-dôrô〈石灯ろう〉a stone lantern
　　　ishi-gaki〈石垣〉a stone wall
　　　ishi-ya〈石屋〉a stone mason, a stone dealer
　ishi-no-ooi〈石の多い〉stony, full of stones.
ishiki〈いしき：意識〉consciousness, one's senses.
　　　ishiki no nagare〈意識の流れ〉the stream of consciousness
　　　ishiki o ushinau〈意識を失う〉lose consciousness
　　　ishiki o kaifuku-suru〈意識を回復する〉recover consciousness
　ishiki-suru〈意識する〉be conscious ((of)).
　ishiki-teki-ni〈意識的に〉consciously.
ishin〈いしん：維新〉
　　　Meiji-ishin〈明治維新〉the Meiji Restoration
ishin〈いしん：威信〉prestige, dignity, authority.
　　　ishin ni kakawaru〈威信にかかわる〉affect one's dignity
　　　ishin o kizutsukeru〈威信を傷つける〉injure the prestige ((of))
　　　ishin o kaifuku-suru〈威信を回復する〉recover one's lost prestige
ishin-denshin〈いしんでんしん：以心伝心〉telepathy.

ishitsu〈いしつ：異質〉

　ishitsu-no〈異質の〉of a different nature, heterogeneous.

ishitsu-butsu〈いしつぶつ：遺失物〉lost articles.

　　ishitsu-butsu tori-atsukai-jo（遺失物取扱所）　the lost and the found

ishiwata〈いしわた：石綿〉asbestos.

isho〈いしょ：遺書〉a note left behind〔by a dead person〕, a will.

ishô〈いしょう：衣装〉clothes, dress, costume.

ishô〈いしょう：意匠〉a design, an idea.

　　ishô-tôroku（意匠登録）　registration of design

i-shoku〈いしょく：衣食〉food and clothing.

ishoku〈いしょく：移植〉transplantation.

　ishoku-suru〈移植する〉transplant.

ishoku〈いしょく：異色〉

　　ishoku-saku（異色作）　a rare work

　ishoku-no〈異色の〉unique, rare, novel.

ishû〈いしゅう：異臭〉an offensive smell, a nasty smell, a foul smell.

　ishû-o-hanatsu〈異臭を放つ〉give out a foul smell, stink.

ishu-gaeshi〈いしゅがえし：意趣返し〉a revenge.

　ishu-gaeshi-o-suru〈意趣返しをする〉revenge oneself ((on)).

ishuku〈いしゅく：い縮〉

　ishuku-suru〈い縮する〉shrink ((from)), flinch, quail, cower.

isô〈いそう：移送〉transference, removal.

　isô-suru〈移送する〉transfer, remove.

iso(be)〈いそ（べ）：いそ（辺）〉a beach, a (sea) shore.

isogashii〈いそがしい：忙しい〉busy, ((be)) engaged.

　　shigoto-de-isogashii（仕事で忙しい）　be busy with one's work

　isogashiku or *isogashi-sô-ni*〈忙しく，忙しそうに〉busily.

isogi〈いそぎ：急ぎ〉haste, hurry.

　isogi-no〈急ぎの〉hasty, hurried, pressing, urgent.

　　isogi-no chûmon（急ぎの注文）　an urgent order

　oo-isogi-de〈大急ぎで〉in a great hurry.

isoginchaku〈いそぎんちゃく〉a sea anemone.

isogu〈いそぐ：急ぐ〉hurry (up), make haste, hasten.

　　Isoge.（急げ.）　Hurry up.

　　Isogu-na.（急ぐな.）　Don't be in a hurry.

　isogaseru〈急がせる〉hasten, hurry up (on).

　　shigoto o isogaseru（仕事を急がせる）　hasten the work

　isoide〈急いで〉in a hurry, in haste.

　　　isoide-dekakeru〈急いで出掛ける〉　hurry out(*or* off)

isoiso(-to)〈いそいそ(と)〉cheerfully, lightheartedly.

isôrô〈いそうろう：居候〉a hanger-on, a parasite.

　isôrô-suru〈居候する〉live on another.

issai〈いっさい：一切〉

　issai-no〈一切の〉all, whole, entire, every.

　　　issai-no hiyô（一切の費用）all the expenses

　issai〜nai〈一切〜ない〉never, not at all.

issaku-jitsu〈いっさくじつ：一昨日〉the day before yesterday.

issaku-nen〈いっさくねん：一昨年〉the year before last.

issan-ka-tanso〈いっさんかたんそ：一酸化炭素〉carbon monoxide.

issatsu〈いっさつ：一札〉

　issatsu-ireru〈一札入れる〉give a written statement ((to)), write an I.O.U.

issei〈いっせい：一世〉the time, the age.

　　　issei-o-fûbi-suru（一世を風びする）sweep the whole country

　　　Erizabesu-issei（エリザベス一世）Elizabeth I

issei〈いっせい：一斉〉

　　　issei-kenkyo（一斉検挙）a wholesale arrest

　issei-ni〈一斉に〉all together, with one voice, in chorus.

isseki-nichô〈いっせきにちょう：一石二鳥〉killing two birds with one stone.

issen〈いっせん：一線〉a line.

　　　issen o hiku（一線を引く）draw a line ((between))

issetsu〈いっせつ：一説〉

　Issetsu-ni-yoreba〜.〈一説によれば〜。〉Some people say that... .

isshiki〈いっしき：一式〉a complete set ((of)), a suit ((of)).

isshin〈いっしん：一心〉

　　　isshin-dôtai（一心同体）one flesh

　　　isshin-furan-ni（一心不乱に）absorbedly

　　　　isshin-furan-ni-benkyô-suru（一心不乱に勉強する）be absorbed in one's studies〉

isshin〈いっしん：一審〉the first trial.

isshin〈いっしん：一新〉renewal, renovation.

　isshin-suru〈一新する〉renew, renovate, change completely, freshen.

isshin-ittai〈いっしんいったい：一進一退〉

　　　isshin-ittai-no shiai（一進一退の試合）a seesaw game

isshin-jô〈いっしんじょう：一身上〉

isshin-jô-no 〈一身上の〉 personal.

　isshin-jô-no tsugô-de (一身上の都合で)　for personal reasons

issho 〈いっしょ：一緒〉

issho-ni 〈一緒に〉 together, with, together with; at the same time; in a (*or* the) lump.

　issho-ni iku (一緒に行く)　go with ((a person))

　issho-ni kurasu (一緒に暮らす)　live together

　ni-ka-getsu-bun-no kyûryô o issho-ni uketoru (二か月分の給料を一緒に受け取る)　receive two months' pay in a lump

issho-ni-naru 〈一緒になる〉 be married ((to)).

issho-ni-suru 〈一緒にする〉 confound ((A with B)), mix up.

isshô 〈いっしょう：一生〉 (all) one's life, a lifetime; to the end of one's life.

isshô-no 〈一生の〉 lifelong.

　isshô-no nozomi (一生の望み)　one's lifelong desire

　isshô-no shigoto (一生の仕事)　one's lifework

isshô-kemmei(-ni) 〈いっしょうけんめい(に)：一生懸命(に)〉 hard, with all one's might.

　isshô-kemmei hataraku (一生懸命働く)　work hard

　isshô-kemmei yaru (一生懸命やる)　do one's best, try as hard as one can

isshoku-sokuhatsu 〈いっしょくそくはつ：一触即発〉 a touch-and-go situation.

isshu 〈いっしゅ：一種〉 a kind, a sort, a variety.

　kiku-no-isshu (菊の一種)　a kind of chrysanthemum

isshu-no 〈一種の〉 a kind of, of a kind.

isshu-dokutoku-na 〈一種独特な〉 peculiar.

isshu-iyô-na 〈一種異様な〉 strange.

isshû 〈いっしゅう：一周〉

　sekai-isshû-ryokô (世界一周旅行)　a round-the-world trip

isshû-suru 〈一周する〉 make a round ((of)), go round, sail round.

isshû 〈いっしゅう：一蹴〉

isshû-suru 〈一蹴する〉 refuse flatly; beat easily.

isshû(-kan) 〈いっしゅう(かん)：一週(間)〉 (during) a week.

　isshû(-kan)-de (一週(間)で)　in a week

　isshû(-kan)-inai-ni (一週(間)以内に)　within a week

isshû-ki 〈いっしゅうき：一周忌〉 the first anniversary of ((a person's)) death.

isshun〈いっしゅん：一瞬〉a moment, an instant.
　　isshun-ni-shite（一瞬にして）in a moment
isso〈いっそ〉
　　Haji-o-kaku-yori　isso-no-koto　shinde-shimai-tai.（恥をかくよりいっそ
　　のこと死んでしまいたい。）I would rather die than dishonor.
issô〈いっそう：一掃〉
　　issô-suru〈一掃する〉sweep away, wipe out, clean out.
issô〈いっそう：一層〉more, still more, all the more.
　　issô-doryoku-suru（一層努力する）make greater efforts, work
　　　harder
issoku〈いっそく：一足〉a pair.
　　kutsu-issoku（靴一足）a pair of shoes
　　issoku-tobi-ni〈一足飛びに〉at a bound, with one bound.
issui〈いっすい：一睡〉
　　issui-mo-shi-nai〈一睡もしない〉cannot sleep a wink.
issun〈いっすん：一寸〉
　　kurakute　issun-saki-mo-mie-nai〈暗くて一寸先も見えない〉be so dark that
　　one cannot see an inch ahead.
issuru〈いっする：逸する〉lose, miss, let go.
　　kikai o issuru（機会を逸する）lose a chance
　　jôki-o-issuru（常軌を逸する）be eccentric
isu〈いす〉a chair.
　　isu-ni-koshi-kakeru（いすに腰掛ける）sit on a chair
Isuraeru〈イスラエル〉Israel.
　　Isuraeru-jin（イスラエル人）an Israeli
　　Isuraeru(-jin)-no（イスラエル(人)の）Israeli
i-suwaru〈いすわる：居座る〉remain〔in power〕, stay ((on)).
ita〈いた：板〉a board, a plank, a plate, a sheet.
　　ita-garasu（板ガラス）plate glass
　　ita-choko（板チョコ）a chocolate bar
　　ita-gami（板紙）pasteboard
　　ita-o-haru〈板を張る〉board, plank.
　　itabasami-ni-naru〈板挟みになる〉be in a dilemma.
　　ita-ni-tsuku〈板につく〉be quite at home ((in)).
　　ita-ni-tsuka-nai（板につかない）be still green ((at))
itachi〈いたち〉a weasel.
　　itachi-gokko（いたちごっこ）a rat race
itadaki〈いただき：頂〉the top, the summit, the peak.

itadaku〈いただく：頂く〉be crowned ((with)), be given, take, have.

  yuki-o-itadaita yama（雪を頂いた山）a snow-crowned mountain

  arigataku-itadaku（有り難く頂く）accept with thanks

  Kono hon o kashite-itadake-masen-ka?（この本を貸していただけませんか。）Do you mind lending me this book?

itade〈いたで：痛手〉a heavy blow.

  itade o kômuru（痛手を被る）get a heavy blow

itai〈いたい：痛い〉painful, sore.

  〜-ga-itai or **〜-ga-itamu**〈〜が痛い，〜が痛む〉have a pain, hurt.

  ashi-ga-itai（足が痛い）have sore feet

  atama-ga-itai（頭が痛い）have a headache

  ha-ga-itai（歯が痛い）have a toothache

  hara-ga-itai（腹が痛い）have a stomachache

  me-ga-itai（目が痛い）have sore eyes

  nodo-ga-itai（のどが痛い）have a sore throat

  senaka-ga-itai（背中が痛い）feel a pain in one's back

  ude-ga-itai（腕が痛い）have a pain in one's arm

  Oo-itai.（おお痛い。）Ouch!

  itai-me-ni-au〈痛い目に遭う〉get hurt, get into trouble, have a bitter experience.

  itagaru〈痛がる〉complain of a pain, be in pain.

  itasa〈痛さ〉pain.

itai〈いたい：遺体〉the remains, a corpse, the (dead) body.

itaike〈いたいけ：いたい気〉

  itaike-na〈いたいけな〉young and helpless, tender.

itaitashii〈いたいたしい：痛々しい〉pitiful, pitiable, painful, pathetic.

  itaitashii-hodo〈痛々しいほど〉miserably, painfully, pathetically.

itaku〈いたく：委託〉trust, charge, consignment.

  itaku-hin（委託品）a trust, a consignment

  itaku-hambai（委託販売）commission sale, consignment sale

  itaku-suru〈委託する〉entrust ((a person)) with.

itamae〈いたまえ：板前〉a cook.

itamashii〈いたましい：痛ましい〉pitiful, heartbreaking, miserable.

itameru〈いためる：痛める〉hurt, injure, spoil; pain, worry, afflict.

  kokoro-o-itameru（心を痛める）be worried ((about))

itameru〈いためる〉fry.

  abura-de itameru（油でいためる）fry in oil

itame-tsukeru〈いためつける：痛めつける〉deal ((a person)) a severe

blow.

itami 〈いたみ：痛(傷)み〉a pain, an ache, a sore; damage, injury.

 itami o kanjiru（痛みを感じる） feel a pain

 itami o shizumeru（痛みを鎮める） relieve the pain

 itami-dome（痛み止め） a pain-killer

 itami-yasui 〈痛みやすい〉fragile, delicate, perishable.

itamu 〈いたむ：痛(傷)む〉feel a pain, ache; be hurt, be damaged.

itamu 〈いたむ：悼む〉lament, grieve ((for *or* over)), mourn ((over)).

 tomo no shi o itamu（友の死を悼む） lament the death of one's friend

 itamu-beki 〈悼むべき〉lamentable.

itan 〈いたん：異端〉heresy.

 itan-sha（異端者） a heretic

ita-no-ma 〈いたのま：板の間〉a wooden floor, a room with a wooden floor.

itareri-tsukuseri 〈いたれりつくせり：至れり尽くせり〉

 itareri-tsukuseri-no 〈至れり尽くせりの〉perfect, thorough.

 itareri-tsukuseri-no motenashi（至れり尽くせりのもてなし） the most hospitable welcome

itari 〈いたり：至り〉

 Kôei-no-itari-desu.（光栄の至りです。） It is my greatest honor.

Itaria 〈イタリア〉Italy.

 Itaria-jin（イタリア人） an Italian

 Itaria-go（イタリア語） Italian

 Itaria(-jin)-no（イタリア(人)の） Italian

itarikku 〈イタリック〉italics.

 itarikku-ni-suru 〈イタリックにする〉italicize.

itaru-tokoro 〈いたるところ：至る所〉everywhere, wherever one goes, all over.

itashi-kayushi 〈いたしかゆし：痛しかゆし〉

 itashi-kayushi-de-aru 〈痛しかゆしである〉be in a fix.

itasu 〈いたす：致す〉

 Kore-wa mina watashi-no futoku-no-itasu-tokoro-desu.（これは皆私の不徳の致すところです。） This is all due to my lack of insight.

 Dô-itashi-mashite.（どう致しまして。） You are welcome. / Not at all.

i-tatamare-nai 〈いたたまれない：居たたまれない〉

 atsukute i-tatamare-nai（暑くて居たたまれない） be too hot to stay in

 hazukashikute i-tatamare-nai（恥ずかしくて居たたまれない） be too

　　　　ashamed to remain there any longer

itawaru 〈いたわる〉 care ((for)), be kind ((to)), console.

　　　　rôjin-o itawaru (老人をいたわる)　be kind to the old

itazura 〈いたずら〉 mischief, a practical joke, a trick.

　　　　itazurakko (いたずらっ子)　a mischievous boy

　　　　itazura-zakari-no ko (いたずら盛りの子)　a child at his(*or* her) most
　　　　mischievous age

　　itazura-suru 〈いたずらする〉 do mischief, play a trick ((on)).

　　itazura-na 〈いたずらな〉 mischievous.

　　itazura-hambun-ni 〈いたずら半分に〉 half in fun, out of mischief.

itazura-ni 〈いたずらに〉 in vain, aimlessly, idly.

　　　　itazura-ni hi-o-kurasu (いたずらに日を暮らす)　live idly

itchaku 〈いっちゃく：一着〉 the first; a suit.

　　　　itchaku-ni-naru (一着になる)　come in first

　　　　fuyu-fuku itchaku (冬服一着)　a winter suit

itchi 〈いっち：一致〉 agreement, harmony, union, unity, cooperation.

　　　　itchi-ten (一致点)　a point of agreement

　　itch-suru 〈一致する〉 agree ((with)), unite.

　　　　itchi-shi-nai　*or*　itchi-o-kaku (一致しない，一致を欠く)　disagree
　　　　((with)), lack unity

　　itchi-no 〈一致の〉 unanimous, united.

　　　　itchi-no-kôdô-o-toru (一致の行動をとる)　act in union

　　itchi-danketsu-shite or *itchi-kyôryoku-shite* 〈一致団結して，一致協力し
　　　　て〉 in union.

itchô-isseki 〈いっちょういっせき：一朝一夕〉

　　itchô-isseki-ni 〈一朝一夕に〉 in one day, in a short period of time.

itchô-ittan 〈いっちょういったん：一長一短〉 merits and demerits.

itchokusen 〈いっちょくせん：一直線〉 a straight line.

　　itchokusen-ni 〈一直線に〉 in a straight line, as the crow flies.

itchûya 〈いっちゅうや：一昼夜〉 a whole day and night.

iten 〈いてん：移転〉 a removal.

　　　　iten-saki (移転先)　one's new address

　　iten-suru 〈移転する〉 move, remove.

ito 〈いと：糸〉 yarn, thread, string, a line.

　　　　ito ga kireru (糸が切れる)　a string breaks

　　　　ito o nuku (糸を抜く)　take out the stitches

　　　　kage-de ito o hiku (陰で糸を引く)　pull the strings

　　　　ito-maki (糸巻き)　a spool

ito-kiri-ba〈糸切り歯〉an eyetooth, a canine (tooth)

ito-o-toosu〈糸を通す〉thread.

ito〈いと：意図〉an intention, an aim, purpose.

ito-suru〈意図する〉intend, aim ((at)).

-itô〈-いとう：-以東〉east (of).

-itô-no, -itô-ni or *-itô-wa*〈-以東の，-以東に，-以東は〉east of.

itoguchi〈いとぐち：糸口〉a beginning, a clue.

itoguchi o tsukamu〈糸口をつかむ〉find a clue

itoko〈いとこ〉a cousin.

mata-itoko（またいとこ）a second cousin

itoma〈いとま〉leave-taking.

Mô o-itoma-itashimasu.（もうおいとまいたします．）Now I must be going.

itome〈いとめ：糸目〉

kane-ni-itome-o-tsukezu-ni〈金に糸目をつけずに〉regardless of expense.

itonamu〈いとなむ：営む〉hold; run, carry on.

gyogyô o itonamu（漁業を営む）carry on fishery

itoshii〈いとしい〉dear, darling, beloved.

itoshiku-omou〈いとしく思う〉think tenderly ((of)).

itsu〈いつ〉when, at what time.

itsudatsu〈いつだつ：逸脱〉deviation.

itsudatsu-suru〈逸脱する〉deviate ((from)).

itsu-demo〈いつでも〉at any time, always, all the time; whenever.

doyô-nara-itsu-demo（土曜ならいつでも）any Saturday

Kare-wa itsu-demo isogashii.（彼はいつでも忙しい．）He is always busy.

itsu-demo-suki-na-toki-ni（いつでも好きなときに）whenever one likes

itsu-ka〈いつか〉some time, some day; once, the other day.

itsu-ka sono-uchi-ni（いつかそのうちに）one of these days

itsu-kara〈いつから〉from what time, how long.

Itsu-kara koko-ni ita-no-da?（いつからここにいたのだ．）How long have you been here?

itsu-made〈いつまで〉how long, till when.

itsu-made-mo〈いつまでも〉as long as one likes, for ever.

itsu-made-ni〈いつまでに〉by what time(*or* day), how soon.

itsu-mo〈いつも〉always, usually.

itsumo-yori-hayaku（いつもより早く）earlier than usual

itsumo-yori-osoku（いつもより遅く）later than usual

itsu-mo-no 〈いつもの〉 usual, ordinary.
itumo-no-yô-ni 〈いつものように〉 as usual.
itsu-ni-naku 〈いつになく〉 unusually.
itsu-no-ma-ni-ka 〈いつのまにか：いつの間にか〉 before one knows, un-
noticed, without one's knowledge.
itsutsu 〈いつつ：五つ〉 *see.* go.
itsuwa 〈いつわ：逸話〉 an anecdote.
itsuwari 〈いつわり：偽り〉 a lie, a falsehood, a deceit.
itsuwari-no 〈偽りの〉 false, untrue, deceitful.
    itsuwari-no-nai 〈偽りのない〉 honest, true, sincere
itsuwaru 〈偽る〉 tell a lie, feign, pretend, cheat.
    byôki-to-itsuwaru 〈病気と偽る〉 pretend to be ill
ittai 〈いったい：一帯〉 a zone, a tract.
    sono-hen-ittai 〈その辺一帯〉 the whole neighborhood
ittai 〈いったい：一体〉 one body; on earth, in the world.
    Ittai nani-o ii-tai-no-da? 〈一体何を言いたいのだ.〉 What on earth do
        you want to say?
ittai-to-natte 〈一体となって〉 in a body.
ittan 〈いったん：一端〉 one end; a part, a general idea.
    Sore-de sono-ittan-ga-ukagawareru. 〈それでその一端がうかがわれる.〉
        That gives you some idea of the matter.
ittan 〈いったん：一たん〉 once.
itte-hambai 〈いってはんばい：一手販売〉 an exclusive sale.
ittei 〈いってい：一定〉
ittei-no 〈一定の〉 fixed, settled, definite, regular, prescribed, standard.
    ittei-no shûnyû 〈一定の収入〉 a regular income
    ittei-no shoshiki 〈一定の書式〉 a prescribed form
    ittei-no kikan-nai-ni 〈一定の期間内に〉 within a given period
itteki 〈いってき：一滴〉 a drop.
    itteki-zutsu 〈一滴ずつ〉 drop by drop
ittembari 〈いってんばり：一点張り〉 persistence.
    shiranu-zonzenu-no-ittembari-de-aru 〈知らぬ存ぜぬの一点張りである〉
        persist in denial
itten 〈いってん：一点〉 a point, a speck, a dot.
    Sora-niwa itten-no-kumo-mo-nai. 〈空には一点の雲もない.〉 There is
        not a speck of cloud in the sky.
    itten-no-yamashii-tokoro-mo-nai 〈一点のやましいところもない〉 have
        a clear conscience

ittetsu 〈いってつ：一徹〉

　ittetsu-na 〈一徹な〉 obstinate, stubborn, headstrong.

ittô 〈いっとう：一等〉 the first class.

　　ittô-senkyaku （一等船客） a first-class passenger

ittô-chi 〈いっとうち：一頭地〉

　ittô-chi-o-nuku 〈一頭地を抜く〉 cut a conspicuous figure ((among)).

ittoku-isshitsu 〈いっとくいっしつ：一得一失〉 a merit and a demerit.

ittô-shô 〈いっとうしょう：一等賞〉 the first prize.

　　ittô-shô o toru （一等賞を取る） win (the) first prize

iu 〈いう：言う〉 say, speak, talk, tell, express, call.

　　uso o iu （うそを言う） tell a lie

　　rei o iu （礼を言う） express one's gratitude

　　ii-tai-koto o iu （言いたいことを言う） have one's say

　　hito-o-yoku-iu （人を良く言う） speak well of a person

　　hito-o-waruku-iu （人を悪く言う） speak ill of a person

　　iu-koto-ga-wakaru （言うことが分かる） understand, follow

　　iu-koto-o-kiku （言うことを聞く） listen to ((a person)), obey

　　iu-koto-o-kika-nai （言うことを聞かない） disobey

　　iwareta-yô-ni-suru （言われたようにする） do as one was told

　　iwa-nai-de-oku （言わないでおく） leave ((a thing)) unsaid

　　amari-mono-o-iwa-nai hito （余り物を言わない人） a person of few
　　　　words

　　～-wa-iu-made-mo-nai. （～は言うまでもない．） It is a matter of
　　　　course that... .

　　iu-made-mo-naku （言うまでもなく） needless to say, of course

　　hitokuchi-de-ieba （一口で言えば） in a word

　　ii-niku-sô-ni （言いにくそうに） hesitatingly

　　nani-mo-iwa-nai-de （何も言わないで） without saying anything

　　Nagata-to-iu-hito （長田という人） a person called Nagata

　　～-to-iu-koto-da. （～ということだ．） It is said that... .

　　～-to-ittemo-ii. （～と言ってもいい．） It may safely be said that... .

　　～-to-ieba （～と言えば） talking of...

iwa 〈いわ：岩〉 a rock, a crag.

　iwa-no-ooi 〈岩の多い〉 rocky, craggy.

iwa 〈いわ：違和〉

　　iwa-kan （違和感） a feeling of physical disorder

iwaba 〈いわば：言わば〉 so to speak, as it were, in a word.

iwai 〈いわい：祝い〉 congratulation, celebration.

iwai-goto〈祝い事〉 a celebration
iwai-mono〈祝い物〉 a congratulatory gift
iwai-no-kotoba〈祝いの言葉〉 congratulations
~-no-iwai-ni〈～の祝いに〉 in celebration of... .

iwana〈いわな〉 a char(r).

iwashi〈いわし〉 a sardine.

iwau〈いわう：祝う〉 congratulate, celebrate.
kekkon o iwau〈結婚を祝う〉 congratulate a person on his marriage

iwayuru〈いわゆる〉 what is called, what we call.

iya〈いや〉 no; yes.

iya〈いや：嫌〉
iya-garu〈嫌がる〉 dislike, hate, be unwilling ((to do)).
iya-ni-naru or *iyaki-ga-sasu*〈嫌になる，嫌気がさす〉 become disgusted ((with)), become tired ((of)).
iya-na〈嫌な〉 disagreeable, unpleasant, offensive, unwelcome, hateful.
iya-na tenki〈嫌な天気〉 disagreeable weather
iya-na aji〈嫌な味〉 an unpleasant taste
iya-na nioi〈嫌なにおい〉 a bad smell
iya-na kyaku〈嫌な客〉 an unwelcome guest
iya-na yatsu〈嫌なやつ〉 a disagreeable fellow
iya-na shigoto〈嫌な仕事〉 an irksome business
iya-na-kao-o-suru〈嫌な顔をする〉 look displeased
iyaiya(-nagara)〈嫌々(ながら)〉 reluctantly, unwillingly, against one's will.

iyagarase〈いやがらせ：嫌がらせ〉
iyagarase-o-iu〈嫌がらせを言う〉 say a disagreeable thing.

iyaku〈いやく：医薬〉 medicine, medical treatment.
iyaku-hin〈医薬品〉 medicines, medical supplies
iyaku-bungyō〈医薬分業〉 separation of dispensary from medical practice

iyaku〈いやく：意訳〉 free translation.
iyaku-suru〈意訳する〉 translate freely.

iyaku〈いやく：違約〉 a breach of promise.
iyaku-kin〈違約金〉 a penalty, an indemnity
iyaku-suru〈違約する〉 break a promise.

iyami〈いやみ：嫌味〉
iyami-o-iu〈いやみを言う〉 say a disagreeable thing, make sarcastic remarks

iyami-no-aru（いやみのある）　disagreeable, sarcastic, affected

iyami-no-nai（いやみのない）　agreeable, pleasant, unaffected, refined

iyarashii〈いやらしい：嫌らしい〉disagreeable, vulgar, indecent, lascivious.

iyashii〈いやしい：卑しい〉humble, low, mean, base; greedy.

iyasu〈いやす〉heal, cure, quench.

iyô〈いよう：異様〉

iyô-na〈異様な〉strange, queer, singular, grotesque.

iyô-ni〈異様に〉strangely, queerly, singularly, grotesquely.

iyô-ni-kikoeru（異様に聞こえる）　sound strange

iyoiyo〈いよいよ〉more and more, all the more, increasingly; at last.

　　Kaze　wa　iyoiyo-hageshiku-natte-kita.（風はいよいよ激しくなってきた。）It brew harder and harder.

　　iyoiyo-to-iu-toki-ni（いよいよというときに）　at the last moment

iyoku〈いよく：意欲〉volition, will, (a) desire.

iyoku-teki(-na)〈意欲的(な)〉eager ((to)), keen ((on)).

iyoku-teki-ni〈意欲的に〉with a (strong) will.

iza〈いざ〉

　　iza-to-iu-toki-ni（いざというときに）　in case of emergency

　　iza-to-nareba（いざとなれば）　at the last moment, if compelled

　　hito-wa-iza-shirazu,　watashi-wa（人はいざ知らず、私は）so far as I am concerned

izakaya〈いざかや：居酒屋〉a saloon, a public house, a pub.

izakoza〈いざこざ〉*see.* gotagota.

izen(-to-shite)〈いぜん(として)：依然(として)〉still, yet, as...as ever, as it was before, as it used to be.

izen(-wa)〈いぜん(は)：以前(は)〉formerly, before.

izoku〈いぞく：遺族〉a bereaved family.

izon〈いぞん：異存〉an objection.

　　izon-wa-nai（異存はない）　have no objection ((to))

izon〈いぞん：依存〉dependence, reliance.

　　sôgo-izon（相互依存）　interdependence

izon-suru〈依存する〉depend ((on)), be dependent ((on)).

izumi〈いずみ：泉〉a spring, a fountain.

izure〈いずれ〉one of these days, some other time, another time, some day, in time; anyway, in any case, at any rate, after all; which, whichever, either, all, any.

　　Izure-mata ukagaimasu.（いずれまた伺います。）I'll come to see you

some day again.

Izure-ni-shitemo yoku-nai.（いずれにしてもよくない.） Anyway it's not good.

izure-no baai-demo（いずれの場合でも） in either case, in all cases

J

ja〈じゃ：蛇〉

    Ja-no-michi-wa-hebi.（蛇の道は蛇.） One devil knows another.

jâ〈ジャー〉a vacuum bottle.

jâ〈じゃあ〉well, then, in that case, if that is the case.

jaaku〈じゃあく：邪悪〉

  jaaku-na〈邪悪な〉wicked, vicious.

jabujabu〈じゃぶじゃぶ〉

  mizu-no-naka-o-jabujabu-aruku〈水の中をじゃぶじゃぶ歩く〉splash one's way in the water.

  jabujabu-to〈じゃぶじゃぶと〉with splash.

jadô〈じゃどう：邪道〉

  jadô-ni-ochiiru〈邪道に陥る〉go astray.

jagaimo〈じゃがいも：じゃが芋〉a potato.

jaguchi〈じゃぐち：蛇口〉a faucet, a tap, a cock.

    jaguchi-o-hinette-akeru（蛇口をひねって開ける） turn on a tap

jaken〈じゃけん：邪険〉

  jaken-ni-suru〈邪険にする〉be hard ((on)).

  jaken-na〈邪険な〉cruel, hard, hardhearted, harsh, unkind.

jaketsu〈ジャケツ〉a jacket, a sweater.

jakki〈ジャッキ〉a jack.

  jakki-de-kuruma-o-ageru〈ジャッキで車を上げる〉jack up a car.

jakku〈ジャック〉the knave, the jack.

jakô〈じゃこう：じゃ香〉musk.

-jaku〈-じゃく：-弱〉a little less than.

jakuden〈じゃくでん：弱電〉
 jakuden-kiki（弱電機器）a light electric appliance

jakuhai〈じゃくはい：若(弱)輩〉
 jakuhai-dewa-arimasu-ga〈若輩ではありますが〉young and inexperienced as I am.

jakuniku-kyôshoku〈じゃくにくきょうしょく：弱肉強食〉The weaker become the victim of the stronger.

jakusha〈じゃくしゃ：弱者〉the weak.

jakushi〈じゃくし：弱視〉weak eyesight.

jakushin〈じゃくしん：弱震〉a slight earthquake.

jakushô〈じゃくしょう：弱小〉puniness.

jakutai〈じゃくたい：弱体〉
 jakutai-naikaku（弱体内閣）an effete Cabinet
 jakutai-ka-suru〈弱体化する〉weaken.
 jakutai-na〈弱体な〉weak.

jakuten〈じゃくてん：弱点〉a weakness, a weak point.

jama〈じゃま：邪魔〉an obstacle, interruption, disturbance, trouble.
 jama-suru〈邪魔する〉interrupt, disturb, trouble.
  hito-no-suimin-no-jama-o-suru（人の睡眠の邪魔をする）disturb a person in his sleep
  O-jama-shimashita.（お邪魔しました.）I'm afraid I have stayed too long.
  jama-mono（邪魔者）a nuisance, a bore
  hito o jama-mono-atsukai-ni-suru（人を邪魔者扱いにする）treat a person as a nuisance

jambo〈ジャンボ〉a jumbo.
 jambo-jetto-ki（ジャンボジェット機）a jumbo jetplane

jampâ〈ジャンパー〉a jumper, a jacket.

jampu〈ジャンプ〉a jump.
 jampu-suru〈ジャンプする〉jump.

janken〈じゃんけん〉
 Janken-de-kime-yô.（じゃんけんで決めよう.）Let's toss up for it.

jareru〈じゃれる〉play ((with)), be playful, fawn ((on)).

jari〈じゃり：砂利〉gravel.
 jari o shiku（砂利を敷く）spread gravel
 jari-michi（砂利道）a gravel road

jasui〈じゃすい：邪推〉

jasui-suru〈邪推する〉suspect ((a person)) (without reason).

jesuchâ〈ジェスチャー〉a gesture, charades.

jetto-ki〈ジェット機：ジェット機〉a jetplane.

jetto-kôsutâ〈ジェットコースター〉a roller coaster.

ji〈じ：字〉a letter, a character; handwriting.
　　ji-ga-umai（字がうまい）write a good hand
　　ji-ga-heta-da（字が下手だ）write a poor hand
　　kanji（漢字）a Chinese character

ji〈じ〉piles, h(a)emorrhoids.
　　Ji-ga-warui.（じが悪い.）I have piles.

-ji〈-じ：-時〉o'clock, time, an hour.
　　Nan-ji-desu-ka?（何時ですか.）What time is it?
　　San-ji-desu.（三時です.）It is three (o'clock).

jiai〈じあい：自愛〉
　　Go-jiai-o-inorimasu.（御自愛を祈ります.）Please take good care of yourself.

jiai〈じあい：慈愛〉affection, love.
　　jiai-bukai or *jiai-ni-michita*〈慈愛深い，慈愛に満ちた〉affectionate, loving.

jiba〈じば：磁場〉a magnetic field.

jiban〈じばん：地盤〉the ground, the foundation; footing, constituency.
　　jiban-chinka（地盤沈下）subsidence of ground
　　jiban o katameru（地盤を固める）solidify the foundation, solidify one's footing, strengthen one's constituency

jibara〈じばら：自腹〉
　　jibara-o-kiru〈自腹を切る〉pay the expenses out of one's own pocket.

jiben〈じべん：自弁〉
　　jiben-de〈自弁で〉at one's own expense.

ji-bi-inkô-ka-byôin〈じびいんこうかびょういん：耳鼻いんこう科病院〉a nose, ear, and throat hospital.

jibiki〈じびき：字引〉*see.* jisho（辞書）.

jibin〈じびん：次便〉
　　jibin-de〈次便で〉by next mail.

jibo〈じぼ：慈母〉an affectionate mother.

jibô-jiki〈じぼうじき：自暴自棄〉
　　jibô-jiki-ni-naru〈自暴自棄になる〉give oneself up to despair.
　　jibô-jiki-ni-natte〈自暴自棄になって〉in despair.

jibun〈じぶん：自分〉self, oneself.
　　jibun-no〈自分の〉one's own, private, personal.

jibun-no-ie〈自分の家〉 a house of one's own

jibun-de〈自分で〉 by oneself, for oneself, in person.

jibun-de shi-nasai.〈自分でしなさい.〉 Do it yourself.

-jibun〈-じぶん：-時分〉 *see.* -goro *or* -koro.

jibun-katte〈じぶんかって：自分勝手〉

jibun-katte-ni-yaru〈自分勝手にやる〉 have ((everything)) one's own way.

jibun-katte-na〈自分勝手な〉 selfish, egoistic, at one's own judgment.

jibutsu〈じぶつ：事物〉 things, affairs.

Nihon-no jibutsu（日本の事物） things Japanese

jibyô〈じびょう：持病〉 a chronic disease, an old complaint.

jichi〈じち：自治〉 self-government, autonomy.

jichi-tai（自治体） a self-governing body, a municipal corporation

jichi-shô（自治省） the Ministry of Autonomy

jichi-daijin（自治大臣） the Minister of Autonomy

jichi-no〈自治の〉 self-governing, autonomous.

jichin-sai〈じちんさい：地鎮祭〉 a ground-breaking ceremony.

jichô〈じちょう：自重〉

jichô-suru〈自重する〉 be prudent, take good care of oneself.

jidai〈じだい：時代〉 an era, an age, the times, days.

Taishô-jidai（大正時代） the Taishô era

kono genshi-ryoku-no-jidai-ni（この原子力の時代に） in this atomic age

jidai-ni-okure-o-tora-nai-yô-ni-suru（時代に遅れを取らないようにする） keep pace with the times

jidai-okure-no（時代遅れの） behind the times, out-of-date, old-fashioned

watashi-no gakusei-jidai-ni（私の学生時代に） in my school days

jidai-geki（時代劇） a historical play

jidai-sakugo（時代錯誤） anachronism

jidai〈じだい：地代〉 land rent.

jidai〈じだい：次代〉 the next generation.

jidai-no〈次代の〉 coming, rising.

jidan〈じだん：示談〉 an out-of-court settlement.

jidan-kin（示談金） money paid by way of compromise, a composition

jidan-ni-suru〈示談にする〉 settle ((a matter)) out of court.

ji-danda〈じだんだ：地団駄〉

ji-danda-funde-kuyashigaru〈地団駄踏んで悔しがる〉 stamp one's foot

with vexation.

ji-daraku〈じだらく：自堕落〉

  ji-daraku-na〈自堕落な〉slovenly, slatternly, loose.

    ji-daraku-na seikatsu o okuru（自堕落な生活を送る）lead a loose life

jiden〈じでん：自伝〉see. jijo-den.

jidô〈じどう：児童〉a juvenile.

    jidô-bungaku（児童文学）juvenile literature

  jidô-no or *jidô-muke-no*〈児童の，児童向けの〉juvenile.

jidô〈じどう：自動〉

    jidô-doa（自動ドア）an automatic door

    jidô-hambai-ki（自動販売機）a vending machine, a slot machine

  jidô-teki(-na)〈自動的(な)〉automatic.

  jidô-teki-ni〈自動的に〉automatically.

jidôsha〈じどうしゃ：自動車〉a car, an automobile, a motorcar.

    jidôsha-de iku（自動車で行く）go by car

    jidôsha-ni noru（自動車に乗る）ride in a car

    jidôsha o unten-suru（自動車を運転する）drive a car

    jidôsha-jiko（自動車事故）an auto accident

jiei〈じえい：自衛〉self-defense.

    jiei-ken（自衛権）the right of self-defense

jiei〈じえい：自営〉

    jiei-jigyô（自営事業）an independent enterprise

jifu(-shin)〈じふ(しん)：自負(心)〉self-conceit, pride.

    jifu-shin o kizutsukeru（自負心を傷つける）hurt one's pride

  ~-to-jifu-suru〈～と自負する〉pride oneself on... , flatter oneself that
    ... .

  jifu-shin-no-tsuyoi〈自負心の強い〉self-conceited.

jifuteria〈ジフテリア〉diphtheria.

jiga〈じが：自我〉self, ego.

  jiga-no-tsuyoi〈自我の強い〉egoistic, egotistic.

jiga-jisan〈じがじさん：自画自賛〉

  jiga-jisan-suru〈自画自賛する〉sing one's own praises, blow one's own
    trumpet.

jigane〈じがね：地金〉ground metal; one's true character.

  jigane-o-dasu〈地金を出す〉reveal one's true character, betray oneself.

jigatame〈じがため：地固め〉

  jigatame-suru〈地固めする〉solidify ground.

jiga-zô〈じがぞう：自画像〉a self-portrait.

jiga-zô-o-kaku〈自画像をかく〉 paint one's own portrait

jigen〈じげん：時限〉

jigen-bakudan（時限爆弾） a time bomb

san-jigen-me-ni（三時限目に） at the third period

jigen〈じげん：次元〉a dimension.

jigen-ga-chigau（次元が違う） belong to a different level

yo-jigen-no（四次元の） four-dimensional

jigo〈じご：事後〉

jigo-hôkoku（事後報告） an ex post facto report

jigo-no〈事後の〉after the fact.

jigô〈じごう：次号〉the next number.

ika-jigô（以下次号） to be continued〔in our next issue〕

jigô-kanketsu（次号完結） to be concluded

jigoe〈じごえ：地声〉one's natural voice.

jigô-jitoku〈じごうじとく：自業自得〉

Jigô-jitoku-da.（自業自得だ.） As one sows, so one reaps.

jigoku〈じごく：地獄〉hell.

jigoku-ni ochiru（地獄に落ちる） go to hell

jigoku-mimi（地獄耳） sharp ears

shiken-jigoku（試験地獄） the examination evil

jigoku-no-yô-na〈地獄のような〉hellish, infernal.

jiguzagu〈ジグザグ〉zigzag.

jiguzagu-ni（ジグザグに） in zigzags

jigyô〈じぎょう：事業〉(a) business, an enterprise, an undertaking.

jigyô-keikaku（事業計画） a business program

shin-jigyô（新事業） a new enterprise

jigyô o shukushô-suru（事業を縮小する） reduce business

jihaku〈じはく：自白〉confession.

jihaku o kyôyô-suru（自白を強要する） force a confession ((from))

jihaku-suru〈自白する〉confess, make (a) confession.

jihatsu-teki(-na)〈じはつてき(な)：自発的(な)〉spontaneous, voluntary.

jihatsu-teki-ni〈自発的に〉spontaneously, voluntarily.

jihei-shô〈じへいしょう：自閉症〉autism.

jihen〈じへん：事変〉an accident, an incident, an emergency.

jihi〈じひ：慈悲〉mercy, charity.

jihi o tareru（慈悲を垂れる） have mercy ((on))

jihi o hodokosu（慈悲を施す） do ((a person)) an act of charity

jihi-bukai〈慈悲深い〉merciful.

jihi〈じひ：自費〉

  jihi-de〈自費で〉at one's own expense.

jihibiki〈じひびき：地響き〉

  jihibiki-o-tatete taoreru〈地響きを立てて倒れる〉fall with a thud.

jihitsu〈じひつ：自筆〉one's own handwriting, an autograph.

  jihitsu-no〈自筆の〉autograph, holograph.

jihō〈じほう：時報〉a time signal.

jihyô〈じひょう：辞表〉a resignation.

      jihyô o teishutsu-suru〈辞表を提出する〉 tender one's resignatio ((to))

      jihyô o tekkai-suru〈辞表を撤回する〉 withdraw one's resignation

jii〈じい：辞意〉

      jii o morasu〈辞意を漏らす〉 intimate one's intention to resign

      jii-ga-katai〈辞意が固い〉 be firmly resolved to resign

      jii-o-hirugaesaseru〈辞意を翻させる〉 dissuade ((a person)) from resigning

jiin〈じいん：寺院〉a temple.

ji-ishiki〈じいしき：自意識〉self-consciousness.

  ji-ishiki-ga-tsuyoi〈自意識が強い〉be very self-conscious.

jiji〈じじ：時事〉current events.

      jiji-mondai〈時事問題〉 current topics

      jiji-kaisetsu〈時事解説〉 comments on current topics, news com mentary

jiji-kokkoku〈じじこっこく：時々刻々〉every moment, from hour to hour.

      jiji-kokkoku henka-suru〈時々刻々変化する〉 change every hour(o from hour to hour)

jijitsu〈じじつ：時日〉time, days.

      jijitsu ga tatsu-ni-tsurete〈時日がたつにつれて〉 as time passes

      kanari-no jijitsu o yôsuru〈かなりの時日を要する〉 take considerable time

jijitsu〈じじつ：事実〉a fact, the truth.

  jijitsu-jô-no〈事実上の〉actual, real.

  jijitsu-mukon-no〈事実無根の〉unfounded, groundless.

  jijitsu-jô〈事実上〉in fact, as a matter of fact.

jijo〈じじょ：次女〉one's second daughter.

jijô〈じじょう：事情〉circumstances, reasons, case.

      donna jijô-ga-atte-mo〈どんな事情があっても〉 in any circumstances

jijô-no-yurusu-kagiri（事情の許す限り） as far as circumstances permit

kô-iu-jijô-dakara（こういう事情だから） under these circumstances

yamu-o-e-nai-jijô-de（やむを得ない事情で） for some unavoidable reasons

katei-no-jijô-de（家庭の事情で） for one's family reasons

Amerika-no jijô-ni-akarui（アメリカの事情に明るい） be well versed in American affairs

jijô 〈じじょう：自乗〉a square.

　jijô-suru 〈自乗する〉square.

jijo-den 〈じじょでん：自叙伝〉an autobiography.

jijû 〈じじゅう：侍従〉a chamberlain.

jijû-chô 〈侍従長〉 the Grand Chamberlain

jika 〈じか：時価〉the current price.

jika 〈じか〉

　jika-ni 〈じかに〉directly, personally, in person.

jika-ni　kôshô-suru 〈じかに交渉する〉 negotiate ((with the other party)) in person

jika- 〈じか−：自家−〉

jika-chûdoku（自家中毒） autointoxication

jika-hatsuden-sôchi-ga-aru（自家発電装置がある） have its own power plant

jikaku 〈じかく：自覚〉(self-)consciousness.

jikaku-shôjô（自覚症状） subjective symptoms

　jikaku-suru 〈自覚する〉be conscious ((of)), realize.

jikan 〈じかん：次官〉a vice-minister, an assistant secretary.

jikan 〈じかん：時間〉time, an hour.

yo-jikan-han（四時間半） four hours and a half

jikan-ga-jûbun-aru（時間が十分ある） have plenty of time

jikan-ga-nai（時間がない） do not have enough time

jikan ga tatsu（時間がたつ） time passes

jikan-ni-ma-ni-au（時間に間に合う） be in time ((for))

jikan-ni-okureru（時間に遅れる） be late ((for)), be behind time ((for))

jikan o tsubusu（時間をつぶす） kill time

jikan o kasegu（時間を稼ぐ） gain time

jikan-tai（時間帯） a time zone

kimmu-jikan（勤務時間） office hours

jikan-gai-teate（時間外手当） an overtime allowance

jikan-doori-ni 〈時間どおりに〉 punctually, on time.

jikatsu 〈じかつ：自活〉

   jikatsu-suru 〈自活する〉 support oneself, earn one's own living.

jika-yō 〈じかよう：自家用〉

   jika-yō-no 〈自家用の〉 for private use.

jiken 〈じけん：事件〉 an event, an affair, a matter, a case.

   satsujin-jiken 〈殺人事件〉 a murder case

jiketsu 〈じけつ：自決〉 self-determination; suicide.

   jiketsu-suru 〈自決する〉 determine by oneself; commit suicide.

jiki 〈じき：時期(季)〉 time, season.

   mainen kono jiki-ni (毎年この時期に) at this time every year

   jiki-hazure-no (時季外れの) out of season

jiki 〈じき：時機〉 an opportunity, a chance, time, an occasion.

   jiki-ga-kuru-no-o-matsu (時機が来るのを待つ) wait for a favorable time to come

   jiki-o-ukagau (時機を伺う) watch for a chance

   jiki-o-eta 〈時機を得た〉 timely.

   jiki-o-shisshita (時機を失した) untimely

jiki 〈じき：磁気〉 magnetism.

jiki 〈じき：磁器〉 porcelain, china.

jiki 〈じき：次期〉 the next term.

   jiki-no 〈次期の〉 next.

   jiki-no kokkai (次期の国会) the next session of the Diet

jikihitsu 〈じきひつ：直筆〉 *see*. jihitsu.

jiki(-ni) 〈じき(に)：直(に)〉 immediately, soon, in a short time, before long; easily.

   Kanojo-wa jiki-ni kaette-kimasu. (彼女は直に帰って来ます。) She will soon be back.

   jiki-ni okoru (直に怒る) get angry easily

jikka 〈じっか：実家〉 one's parents' home.

jikkan 〈じっかん：実感〉

   jikkan-ga-deru (実感が出る) be true to nature

   jikkan-ga-waku (実感がわく) realize fully

jikkei 〈じっけい：実兄〉 one's true elder brother.

jikkei 〈じっけい：実刑〉 a prison sentence.

jikken 〈じっけん：実験〉 an experiment, a test.

   kagaku-no jikken (化学の実験) a chemical experiment

   kaku-jikken (核実験) nuclear tests

jikken-shitsu（実験室）a laboratory

jikken-suru〈実験する〉experiment, make an experiment.

jikken-teki(-na)〈実験的(な)〉experimental.

jikken-teki-ni（実験的に）experimentally.

jikken〈じっけん：実権〉real power.

jikken o nigiru（実権を握る）hold (real) power ((over))

jikkō〈じっこう：実行〉practice, execution.

jikkō-iin-kai（実行委員会）an execution committee

jikkō-suru〈実行する〉put into practice, carry out.

keikaku o jikkō-suru（計画を実行する）carry out a plan

jikkō〈じっこう：実効〉

jikkō-no-aru〈実効のある〉effective, efficacious.

jikkō-no nai（実効のない）ineffective, inefficacious

jikkuri(-to)〈じっくり(と)〉thoroughly, deliberately, without haste.

jikkyō〈じっきょう：実況〉the actual scene.

jikkyō-hōsō-o-suru〈実況放送をする〉broadcast on the spot.

jiko〈じこ：事故〉an accident, a trouble.

jiko o okosu（事故を起こす）cause an accident

jiko-ni-au（事故に遭う）have an accident

kōtsū-jiko-de shinu（交通事故で死ぬ）be killed in a traffic accident

jiko〈じこ：自己〉one's self, self.

jiko-chūshin-shugi（自己中心主義）self-centeredness

jiko-manzoku（自己満足）self-satisfaction

jiko-senden（自己宣伝）self-advertisement

jiko-shōkai-o-suru（自己紹介をする）introduce oneself

jiko-no〈自己の〉one's own, personal, private.

jikō〈じこう：事項〉a matter, a fact; an item, an article.

kanren-jikō（関連事項）relevant matters

jikō〈じこう：時候〉the season, weather.

jikō-no aisatsu（時候のあいさつ）the season's greetings

fujun-na jikō（不順な時候）unseasonable weather

jikō〈じこう：時効〉prescription.

jikō-ni-naru〈時効になる〉be extinguished by prescription, prescribe.

jiko-hon·i〈じこほんい：自己本位〉egoism.

jiko-hon·i-no〈自己本位の〉egotistic.

jikoku〈じこく：時刻〉time.

jikoku-hyō（時刻表）a timetable

jikoku-go〈じこくご：自国語〉one's own language.

jiku 〈じく：軸〉an axis, an axle; a stem.
  matchi-no-jiku（マッチの軸） matchwood, a matchstick
  jiku-uke（軸受け） a bearing
jikyô 〈じきょう：自供〉a (voluntary) confession.
  jikyô-suru〈自供する〉confess.
jikyoku 〈じきょく：時局〉the situation.
  jûdai-jikyoku（重大時局） a critical juncture
jikyû 〈じきゅう：持久〉
  jikyû-ryoku（持久力） staying power, stamina
  jikyû-sen（持久戦） a protracted war
jikyû-jisoku 〈じきゅうじそく：自給自足〉self-sufficiency.
  jikyû-jisoku-suru〈自給自足する〉be self-sufficient.
jiman 〈じまん：自慢〉boast, pride.
  jiman-suru〈自慢する〉be proud ((of)), boast ((of)).
jimbô 〈じんぼう：人望〉popularity.
  jimbô-no-aru〈人望のある〉popular.
  jimbô-no-nai（人望のない） unpopular
jimbun 〈じんぶん：人文〉humanity; civilization, culture.
  jimbun-chiri（人文地理） human geography
  jimbun-kagaku（人文科学） cultural sciences
jimbutsu 〈じんぶつ：人物〉a person, a character.
  jimbutsu-ga（人物画） a figure painting, a portrait
  jimbutsu-hyô（人物評） a personal sketch
  jimbutsu-shiken（人物試験） a character test
  kô-jimbutsu（好人物） a good-natured person
jimei 〈じめい：自明〉
  jimei-no〈自明の〉self-evident.
  jimei-no ri（自明の理） a self-evident truth
jimejime 〈じめじめ〉
  jimejime-shita〈じめじめした〉damp, wet.
jimen 〈じめん：地面〉the ground.
jimetsu 〈じめつ：自滅〉self-destruction, suicide.
  jimetsu-suru〈自滅する〉destroy oneself, cut one's own throat.
  jimetsu-teki(-na)〈自滅的(な)〉self-destructive.
jimi 〈じみ：地味〉
  jimi-na〈地味な〉plain, simple, modest, sober.
  jimi-na seikatsu（地味な生活） a plain living
  jimi-na iro（地味な色） a quiet color

jimichi 〈じみち：地道〉
　jimichi-na 〈地道な〉 straight, honest, sober, steady.
　jimichi-ni 〈地道に〉 straight, honestly, soberly, steadily.
　　jimichi-ni kurasu 〈地道に暮らす〉 live straight, live honestly, make
　　　an honest living

jimma-shin 〈じんましん〉 hives, nettle rash.

jimmei 〈じんめい：人命〉 (human) life.
　　jimmei-kyûjo 〈人命救助〉 lifesaving

jimmei-bo 〈じんめいぼ：人名簿〉 a list of names, a directory.

jimmin 〈じんみん：人民〉 the people.

jimmon 〈じんもん：尋問〉 questioning, an inquiry, examination.
　　hantai-jimmon 〈反対尋問〉 a cross-examination
　jimmon-suru 〈尋問する〉 question, examine.
　jimmon-o-ukeru 〈尋問を受ける〉 be questioned, be examined.

jimoto 〈じもと：地元〉
　　jimoto-min 〈地元民〉 local people
　jimoto-no 〈地元の〉 local.

jimpin 〈じんぴん：人品〉 personal appearance.
　　jimpin-iyashi-karanu　hito 〈人品卑しからぬ人〉 a respectable-looking
　　　person

jimu 〈じむ：事務〉 business, office work.
　　jimu-o-toru 〈事務を執る〉 attend to one's business
　　jimu-in 〈事務員〉 a clerk, an office worker
　　jimu-shitsu 〈事務室〉 an office (room)
　　jimu-sho 〈事務所〉 an office
　jimu-teki(-na) 〈事務的(な)〉 businesslike, practical.
　jimu-teki-ni 〈事務的に〉 in a businesslike way.

-jin 〈−じん：−陣〉
　　kyôju-jin 〈教授陣〉 a teaching staff

jin·ai 〈じんあい：仁愛〉 philanthropy, benevolence.

jinan 〈じなん：次男〉 one's second son.

ji-narashi 〈じならし：地ならし〉 ground leveling.
　ji-narashi-o-suru 〈地ならしをする〉 level the ground.

ji-nari 〈じなり：地鳴り〉
　ji-nari-ga-suru 〈地鳴りがする〉 hear the ground rumble.

jinchi 〈じんち：陣地〉 a position.
　　jinchi o shishu-suru 〈陣地を死守する〉 defend a position to the last

jinchi 〈じんち：人知〉 human knowledge.

jinchi-no-oyoba-nai〈人知の及ばない〉beyond human knowledge

jinchiku〈じんちく：人畜〉
  jinchiku-ni-mugai-de-aru〈人畜に無害である〉do no harm to men and beasts.

jindai〈じんだい：甚大〉
  jindai-na〈甚大な〉very great, serious, heavy.
    jindai-na higai〈甚大な被害〉serious damage

jindô〈じんどう：人道〉humanity; a sidewalk.
    jindô-ni-motoru〈人道にもとる〉be contrary to humanity
    jindô-shugi〈人道主義〉humanism
    jindô-shugi-sha〈人道主義者〉a humanist
  jindô-teki(-na)〈人道的(な)〉humane.

jin-doru〈じんどる：陣取る〉take up one's position, take one's station.

jin-ei〈じんえい：陣営〉a camp.
    wahei-jin-ei〈和平陣営〉the peace camp

jingi〈じんぎ：仁義〉humanity, duty; a moral code.
    jingi-ni-hazureru〈仁義に外れる〉be against the moral code

jingo〈じんご：人後〉
  jingo-ni-ochi-nai〈人後に落ちない〉be second to none ((in)).

jin-i〈じんい：人為〉
  jin-i-teki(-na)〈人為的(な)〉artificial.
  jin-i-teki-ni〈人為的に〉artificially.

jin-in〈じんいん：人員〉the number of persons, the personnel.
    jin-in-seiri〈人員整理〉a personnel cut

jinin〈じにん：辞任〉*see.* jishoku.

jinin〈じにん：自任〉
  jinin-suru〈自任する〉regard oneself ((that *or* to be)), look upon oneself ((as)), consider oneself ((as)).

jinin〈じにん：自認〉
  jinin-suru〈自認する〉acknowledge, admit.

jinja〈じんじゃ：神社〉a (*Shinto*) shrine.

jinji〈じんじ：人事〉
    jinji-o-tsukusu〈人事を尽くす〉do one's best
    jinji-idô〈人事異動〉personnel changes
    jinji-ken〈人事権〉the right of personnel management

jinji-fusei〈じんじふせい：人事不省〉
  jinji-fusei-ni-naru〈人事不省になる〉become unconscious, faint away.
  jinji-fusei-no〈人事不省の〉unconscious.

jinjô〈じんじょう：尋常〉

　jinjô-no〈尋常の〉ordinary, common, usual.

　　jinjô-no shudan（尋常の手段）ordinary measures

　jinjô-de-nai〈尋常でない〉extraordinary, uncommon, out of the common.

jinka〈じんか：人家〉a human habitation, a house, a dwelling.

　　jinka-ga-misshû-shite-iru（人家が密集している）be crowded with houses

jinkai-senjutsu〈じんかいせんじゅつ：人海戦術〉human wave tactics.

jinkaku〈じんかく：人格〉character.

　　nijû-jinkaku（二重人格）double personality

　　jinkaku-sha（人格者）a man of character

jinken〈じんけん：人権〉human rights.

　　jinken-shingai（人権侵害）an infringement on people's rights

　　kihon-teki jinken（基本的人権）the fundamental human rights

jinken-hi〈じんけんひ：人件費〉personnel expenses.

jinkô〈じんこう：人口〉population.

　　jinkô-ga-ooi（人口が多い）have a large population

　　jinkô-ga sukunai（人口が少ない）have a small population

　　jinkô-mondai（人口問題）the population problem

　　jinkô-chôsa o okonau（人口調査を行う）take a census

jinkô〈じんこう：人工〉

　　jinkô-kokyû（人工呼吸）artificial breathing

　jinkô-no or *jinkô-teki(-na)*〈人工の，人工的(な)〉artificial, unnatural.

jinrui〈じんるい：人類〉mankind, the human race.

　　jinrui-ai（人類愛）love for mankind

　　jinrui-gaku（人類学）anthropology

　jinrui-no〈人類の〉human.

jinryoku〈じんりょく：人力〉human power.

　　jinryoku-no-oyoba-nai（人力の及ばない）be beyond human power

jinryoku〈じんりょく：尽力〉effort(s), good offices, services.

　　Yamada-san no jinryoku-de（山田さんの尽力で）through the good offices of Mr. Yamada

　jinryoku-suru〈尽力する〉endeavor, make efforts, render services.

jinsai〈じんさい：人災〉a man-caused calamity.

jinsei〈じんせい：人生〉human life, life.

　　jinsei-kan（人生観）one's view of life

　　jinsei-tetsugaku（人生哲学）a philosophy of life

jinseki〈じんせき：人跡〉

jinseki-mare-na 〈人跡まれな〉 unfrequented, trackless, virgin.

jinsen 〈じんせん：人選〉
   jinsen-suru 〈人選する〉 select a suitable person ((for)).

jinshin 〈じんしん：人心〉 people's minds, the public feeling.
    jinshin-no dôyô (人心の動揺)   public unrest

jinshin 〈じんしん：人身〉
    jinshin-baibai (人身売買)   flesh traffic
    jinshin-kôgeki (人身攻撃)   a personal attack

jinshu 〈じんしゅ：人種〉 a (human) race.
    jinshu-sabetsu (人種差別)   racial discrimination
   jinshu-ni-yoru, jinshu-no or *jinshu-teki(-na)* 〈人種による，人種の，人種的（な）〉 racial.

jinsoku 〈じんそく：迅速〉
   jinsoku-na 〈迅速な〉 quick, rapid, swift, prompt.
   jinsoku-ni 〈迅速に〉 quickly, rapidly, swiftly, promptly.

jintai 〈じんたい：人体〉 the human body.

jin-teki 〈じんてき：人的〉
    jin-teki shigen (人的資源)   human resources

jintô 〈じんとう：陣頭〉
   jintô-ni-tatsu 〈陣頭に立つ〉 take the lead ((in)), lead the van ((of)).

jintoku 〈じんとく：人徳〉 natural virtue.

jintsû 〈じんつう：陣痛〉 labor (pains).

jin·u·en 〈じんうえん：じん炎〉 pyelitis.

jinushi 〈じぬし：地主〉 a landlord, a landowner.

jin·yô 〈じんよう：陣容〉 battle formation, a lineup, a staff.
   jin·yô-o-totonoeru 〈陣容を整える〉 array troops for battle.

jinzai 〈じんざい：人材〉 (a man of) talent.
    jinzai-o-motomeru (人材を求める)   look out for talent

jinzô 〈じんぞう：じん臓〉 the kidney.

jinzô 〈じんぞう：人造〉
   jinzô-no 〈人造の〉 artificial, man-made, imitation, synthetic.

jîpan 〈ジーパン〉 jeans.

jippi 〈じっぴ：実費〉 actual expense(s), the cost price.
    jippi-de uru (実費で売る)   sell ((an article)) at cost

jippu 〈じっぷ：実父〉 one's true father.

jirai 〈じらい：地雷〉 a (land) mine.

jirasu 〈じらす〉 irritate, fret, tantalize, tease.

jirei 〈じれい：辞令〉 a written appointment, a commission.

jiremma 〈ジレンマ〉a dilemma.

jirettai 〈じれったい〉irritating, impatient.

　jirettaku-naru 〈じれったくなる〉get impatient.

　jirettasô-ni 〈じれったそうに〉irritatedly, impatiently.

jiri-hin 〈じりひん：じり貧〉a gradual decline, dwindling.

　jiri-hin-ni-naru 〈じり貧になる〉dwindle away into nothing.

jirijiri 〈じりじり〉

　　jirijiri-oshi-yoseru（じりじり押し寄せる）edge up ((to))

　　jirijiri-to-yake-tsuku-yô-na　taiyô（じりじりと焼け付くような太陽）the
　　　scorching sun

jiriki 〈じりき：自力〉

　jiriki-de 〈自力で〉by one's own efforts, by oneself.

jiritsu 〈じりつ：自立〉

　jiritsu-suru 〈自立する〉become independent, set up for oneself, support
　　oneself.

jiritsu-shinkei 〈じりつしんけい：自律神経〉the automatic nerve.

jirojiro 〈じろじろ〉

　jirojiro-miru 〈じろじろ見る〉stare ((at)).

jirori-to 〈じろりと〉

　jirori-to-miru 〈じろりと見る〉cast a piercing glance ((at)).

jiryoku 〈じりょく：磁力〉magnetism, magnetic force.

　　jiryoku-kei（磁力計）a magnetometer

jisa 〈じさ：時差〉difference in time.

　　jisa-shukkin（時差出勤）staggered office hours

jisaku 〈じさく：自作〉

　　jisaku-jien-suru（自作自演する）act in a play of one's own writing,
　　　play a piece of music of one's own composition

　jisaku-no 〈自作の〉of one's own making.

jisaku-nô 〈じさくのう：自作農〉a landed farmer.

jisan 〈じさん：持参〉

　　jisan-kin（持参金）a dowry

　　jisan-nin（持参人）a bearer

　jisan-suru 〈持参する〉bring ((a thing)) (with one), take ((a thing)) (with
　　one).

jisatsu 〈じさつ：自殺〉suicide.

　　jisatu o hakaru（自殺を図る）attempt suicide

　　jisatsu-misui（自殺未遂）an attempted suicide

　jisatsu-suru 〈自殺する〉kill oneself, commit suicide.

gasu-jisatsu-suru（ガス自殺する） kill oneself by inhaling gas

jisei 〈じせい：時勢〉the times.

jisei-ni-junnô-suru（時勢に順応する） go with the stream

jisei-ni-okurete-iru（時勢に遅れている） be behind the times

jisei-ni-sakarau（時勢に逆らう） go against the times

jisei 〈じせい：時制〉a tense.

jisei(-shin) 〈じせい（しん）：自制（心）〉self-control.

jisei-shin o ushinau（自制心を失う） lose self-control

jisei-suru 〈自制する〉control oneself.

jiseki 〈じせき：自責〉self-reproach.

jiseki-no-nen-ni-karareru（自責の念に駆られる） have a guilty conscience

jiseki-ten（自責点） an earned run

jiseki 〈じせき：次席〉

jiseki-kenji（次席検事） an associate public prosecutor

jisetsu 〈じせつ：時節〉the season, the times, an occasion, an opportunity.

sakura-no jisetsu（桜の時節） the cherry blossom season

Jisetsu ga tôrai-shita.（時節が到来した。） My time has come.

jisetsu 〈じせつ：自説〉one's own opinion.

jisetsu-o-mage-nai（自説を曲げない） stick to one's opinion

jishaku 〈じしゃく：磁石〉a magnet.

jishin 〈じしん：自身〉oneself, itself.

jishin-no 〈自身の〉own.

jishin-de 〈自身で〉by oneself.

jishin 〈じしん：地震〉an earthquake.

dai-jishin（大地震） a big(*or* severe) earthquake

yowai jishin（弱い地震） a slight earthquake

jishin-kei（地震計） a seismometer

jishin 〈じしん：自信〉self-confidence.

jishin-ga-aru *or* jishin-o-motsu（自信がある，自信を持つ） have confidence ((in))

jishin-ga-nai（自信がない） be without self-confidence

jishin-no-aru 〈自信のある〉self-confident.

jisho 〈じしょ：辞書〉a dictionary.

jisho-o-hiku（辞書を引く） refer to a dictionary, look up ((a word)) in a dictionary

jisho 〈じしょ：地所〉land, a lot, an estate.

jishô〈じしょう：自称〉
jishô-sakka（自称作家） a would-be author
jishô-suru〈自称する〉profess oneself ((to be)), call oneself.
jishô-no〈自称の〉self-styled, would-be.

jishoku〈じしょく：辞職〉resignation.
jishoku-suru〈辞職する〉resign, give up one's office.

jishu〈じしゅ：自首〉
jishu-suru〈自首する〉surrender oneself to the police.

jishu(-sei)〈じしゅ(せい)：自主(性)〉independence.
jishu-sei-ni kakeru（自主性に欠ける） lack in independence
jishu-dokuritsu（自主独立） sovereign independence
jishu-teki(-na)〈自主的(な)〉independent.
jishu-teki-ni〈自主的に〉independently, voluntarily.

jishû〈じしゅう：自習〉self-study.
jishû-jikan（自習時間） study hours
jishû-suru〈自習する〉study for oneself.

jishuku〈じしゅく：自粛〉self-discipline.
jishuku-suru〈自粛する〉practice self-control.

jisoku〈じそく：時速〉the speed an hour.
jisoku hyakkiro-de（時速百キロで） at a speed of 100 kilometers an hour

jison-shin〈じそんしん：自尊心〉self-respect, pride.
jison-shin o kizutsukeru（自尊心を傷つける） hurt ((a person's)) pride
jison-shin-no-tsuyoi〈自尊心の強い〉self-respecting.

jissai〈じっさい：実際〉a fact, the truth, actuality.
jissai-no〈実際の〉real, true, actual, practical.
jissai-ni〈実際に〉really, truly, in fact, actually, practically, as a matter of fact.

jisseikatsu〈じっせいかつ：実生活〉actual life, practical life.

jisseki〈じっせき：実績〉actual results, achievements.
jisseki-o-ageru（実績を上げる） give satisfactory results, bear good fruit
eigyô-jisseki（営業実績） business showings

jissen〈じっせん：実践〉practice.
jissen-suru〈実践する〉practice, put in practice.
jissen-teki(-na)〈実践的(な)〉practical.
jissen-teki-ni〈実践的に〉practically.

jisshakai〈じっしゃかい：実社会〉the actual world.

jisshakai-ni-deru〈実社会に出る〉 go into the world

jisshi〈じっし：実施〉enforcement.

  jisshi-suru〈実施する〉enforce, carry into effect.

  jisshi-sarete-iru〈実施されている〉be in force.

jisshin-pô〈じっしんぽう：十進法〉the decimal system.

jisshitsu〈じっしつ：実質〉substance, essence, quality.

  jisshitsu-chingin〈実質賃金〉 real wages

  jisshitsu-jô-no〈実質上の〉substantial, virtual.

  jisshitsu-jô(-wa)〈実質上(は)〉in substance, virtually.

  jisshitsu-teki(-na)〈実質的(な)〉substantial, material.

  jisshitsu-teki-ni〈実質的に〉substantially, materially.

jisshô〈じっしょう：実証〉an actual proof, corroboration.

  jisshô-suru〈実証する〉prove, demonstrate, substantiate.

jisshû〈じっしゅう：実習〉practice, practical exercise.

  jisshû-sei〈実習生〉 a student apprentice

  jisshû-suru〈実習する〉practice, have practical training.

jisshû(nyû)〈じっしゅう(にゅう)：実収(入)〉a net income, the actual profit; actual yield.

jissoku〈じっそく：実測〉(actual) survey.

  jissoku-suru〈実測する〉survey.

jissû〈じっすう：実数〉the real number, a real number.

ji-suberi〈じすべり：地すべり〉a landslip, a landslide.

jisui〈じすい：自炊〉

  jisui-suru〈自炊する〉cook for oneself.

jisutempâ〈ジステンパー〉distemper.

ji-ta〈じた：自他〉

  ji-ta-tomo-ni-mitomeru〈自他共に認める〉be commonly acknowledged, be generally admitted.

jitabata〈じたばた〉

  jitabata-suru〈じたばたする〉(kick and) struggle.

    Jitabata-suru-na!〈じたばたするな.〉 Don't make a scene!

jitai〈じたい：事態〉the situation.

  yôi-naranu jitai〈容易ならぬ事態〉 a serious situation

jitai〈じたい：辞退〉

  jitai-suru〈辞退する〉decline, refuse to accept.

    yûshoku no shôtai o jitai-suru〈夕食の招待を辞退する〉 refuse to accept the dinner invitation

jitai〈じたい：自体〉itself, in itself.

jitai〈じたい：字体〉the form of a character, type.

jitaku〈じたく：自宅〉one's own house.

    jitaku-ni-iru（自宅にいる）be at home

    jitaku-ryôyô-chû-de-aru（自宅療養中である）be under treatment at home

jitchi〈じっち：実地〉practice.

    jitchi-chôsa（実地調査）an on-the-spot survey

 jitchi-no〈実地の〉practical.

 jitchi-ni〈実地に〉practically, in practice.

jitchoku〈じっちょく：実直〉honesty, integrity, sincerity.

 jitchoku-na〈実直な〉honest, sincere, conscientious.

jiten〈じてん：次点〉the second largest number〔of votes〕; the runner-up.

jiten〈じてん：辞典〉*see.* jisho（辞書）.

jiten〈じてん：事典〉a cyclopedia.

jiten〈じてん：自転〉rotation.

 jiten-suru〈自転する〉rotate on its own axis.

jitensha〈じてんしゃ：自転車〉a bicycle.

    jitensha ni noru（自転車に乗る）ride a bicycle.

    jitensha-de　tsûkin-suru（自転車で通勤する）go to one's office by bicycle

jitojito〈じとじと〉

 jitojito-suru〈じとじとする〉be damp, be wet.

jitsu〈じつ：実〉the truth, the reality, the actuality.

 jitsu-no〈実の〉true, real, actual.

 jitsu-ni〈実に〉truly, really; very, very much, indeed.

 jitsu-no-tokoro, jitsu-wa or *jitsu-o-iuto*〈実のところ，実は，実を言うと〉in fact, in truth, to tell the truth, the fact is that... .

jitsubutsu〈じつぶつ：実物〉the real thing.

 jitsubutsu-dai-no〈実物大の〉full-size(d), life-size(d).

jitsudan〈じつだん：実弾〉a live cartridge, a loaded shell.

    jitsudan-shageki（実弾射撃）target practice with loaded shells

jitsudô〈じつどう：実働〉

    jitsudô-jikan（実働時間）actual working hours

jitsueki〈じつえき：実益〉

 shumi-to-jitsueki-o-kanete-iru〈趣味と実益を兼ねている〉be not only interesting but profitable.

jitsuen〈じつえん：実演〉a demonstration, a performance on the stage.

　　jitsuen-suru〈実演する〉give a demonstration, perform on the stage.

jitsugen〈じつげん：実現〉realization.

　　jitsugen-suru〈実現する〉realize, come true.

　　jitsugen-fu-kanô-na〈実現不可能な〉unrealizable, infeasible.

jitsugyô〈じつぎょう：実業〉business.

　　　　jitsugyô-ni-tsuku（実業に就く）enter business, go into business

　　　　jitsugyô-kai（実業界）the business world

　　　　jitsugyô-ka（実業家）a businessman

jitsuin〈じついん：実印〉one's registered seal.

jitsujô〈じつじょう：実情(状)〉the actual circumstances, the true state of affairs.

jitsumu〈じつむ：実務〉business, business practice.

jitsurei〈じつれい：実例〉an example.

　　　　jitsurei o ageru（実例を挙げる）give an example

jitsuri〈じつり：実利〉utility.

　　　　jitsuri-shugi（実利主義）utilitarianism

jitsuryoku〈じつりょく：実力〉real ability.

　　　　jitsuryoku-sha（実力者）an influential person

　　jitsuryoku-no-aru〈実力のある〉able, capable, talented.

jitsuwa〈じつわ：実話〉a true story.

jitsuyô〈じつよう：実用〉practical use, utility.

　　　　jitsuyô-hin（実用品）a useful article, daily necessaries

　　jitsuyô-teki(-na)〈実用的(な)〉practical.

　　　　jitsuyô-teki-ni-wa　amari　yaku-ni-tata-nai（実用的には余り役に立たない）be of little practical use

jitsuzai〈じつざい：実在〉existence, reality.

　　jitsuzai-suru〈実在する〉exist, be.

　　jitsuzai-no〈実在の〉real, existent.

　　　　jitsuzai-shi-nai（実在しない）unreal, nonexistent

jitsuzon〈じつぞん：実存〉existence.

　　　　jitsuzon-shugi（実存主義）existentialism

ji-tsuzuki〈じつづき：地続き〉

　　ji-tsuzuki-no〈地続きの〉adjoining, adjacent, contiguous.

jittai〈じったい：実体〉substance.

jittai〈じったい：実態〉the actual condition.

jitto〈じっと〉still, quiet; patiently.

　　　　jitto-shite-iru（じっとしている）keep still

　　　　jitto gaman-suru（じっと我慢する）bear patiently

jitto mi-tsumeru（じっと見詰める） gaze ((at)), look hard ((at))

jiu〈じう：慈雨〉a beneficial rain.

jiwajiwa〈じわじわ〉
jiwajiwa-semeru（じわじわ攻める） make a slow but steady attack
jiwajiwa-niru（じわじわ煮る） boil steadily

ji-ware〈じわれ：地割れ〉a fissure in the ground.

jiyô〈じよう：滋養〉nourishment, nutrition.
jiyô-butsu（滋養物） nutritious food, nourishment
jiyô-bun-no-ooi〈滋養分の多い〉nutritious, nourishing.
jiyô-bun-no-sukunai（滋養分の少ない） lean

jiyū〈じゆう：自由〉freedom, liberty.
jiyû-hambai（自由販売） free sale
jiyû-ishi（自由意志） free will
jiyû-kôdô（自由行動） free action
jiyû-shugi（自由主義） liberalism
jiyû-shugi-sha（自由主義者） a liberalist
jiyû-gata（自由形） free style
jiyû-na〈自由な〉free, liberal.
jiyû-ni〈自由に〉freely, at will, as one likes.
jiyû-ni-naru（自由になる） become free, be set free
jiyû-ni-suru（自由にする） do as one pleases, set ((a person)) free

jiyū-jizai〈じゆうじざい：自由自在〉
jiyû-jizai-ni〈自由自在に〉freely, with perfect freedom, at will.

jiyū-ka〈じゆうか：自由化〉liberalization.
jiyû-ka-suru〈自由化する〉liberalize.

jizake〈じざけ：地酒〉(*sake* of) local brew.

jizen〈じぜん：慈善〉charity.
jizen-ongaku-kai（慈善音楽会） a charity concert
jizen-jigyô（慈善事業） charitable work
jizen-ka（慈善家） a charitable person
jizen-no〈慈善の〉charitable.

jizen〈じぜん：事前〉
jizen-kyôgi（事前協議） a prior consultation
senkyo-no-jizen-undô（選挙の事前運動） preelection campaigning
jizen-ni〈事前に〉beforehand, in advance.

jizoku〈じぞく：持続〉
jizoku-suru〈持続する〉support, sustain, keep up, continue.

jô〈じょう：条〉an article.

dai-ichi-jô（第一条） Article 1

jô 〈じょう：畳〉a mat.
hachi-jô-no heya（八畳の部屋） an eight-mat room

jô 〈じょう：嬢〉a girl, a daughter, Miss.
kawaii o-jô-san（かわいいお嬢さん） a lovely little girl
Nakano-san-no o-jô-san（中野さんのお嬢さん） Mr. Nakano's daughter
Tanaka-jô（田中嬢） Miss Tanaka

jô 〈じょう：錠〉a lock, a padlock.
jô-o-kakeru〈錠を掛ける〉lock.
jô-o-akeru（錠を開ける） unlock
jô-ga-kakete-aru〈錠が掛けてある〉be locked.

jô 〈じょう：情〉feeling, sentiment, emotion, affection, love.
oya-ko-no-jô（親子の情） the affection between parent and child
jô-ga-nai〈情がない〉be unfeeling, be heartless.
jô-ni-moroi〈情にもろい〉be emotional.
jô-no-fukai〈情の深い〉kindhearted, warmhearted, affectionate.
jô-no-usui（情の薄い） coldhearted

-jô 〈-じょう：-乗〉
ni o san-jô-suru〈2を3乗する〉raise two to the third power.

jôai 〈じょうあい：情愛〉*see.* aijô *or* jô（情）.

jôba 〈じょうば：乗馬〉horse riding.
jôba-kurabu（乗馬クラブ） a riding club

jôbi 〈じょうび：常備〉
jôbi-gun（常備軍） a standing army
jôbi-yaku（常備薬） a household medicine

jôbu 〈じょうぶ：上部〉the upper part, the top.
jôbu-kôzô（上部構造） a superstructure

jôbu 〈じょうぶ：丈夫〉
jôbu-de-aru〈丈夫である〉be in good health.
jôbu-ni-naru〈丈夫になる〉become healthy.
jôbu-na〈丈夫な〉strong, healthy, robust; solid, firm, durable
jôbu-na kire（丈夫な切れ） durable cloth

jobun 〈じょぶん：序文〉a preface, a foreword.

jôbun 〈じょうぶん：条文〉the text, the provisions.

jôbutsu 〈じょうぶつ：成仏〉
jôbutsu-suru〈成仏する〉depart from life peacefully.

jochô 〈じょちょう：助長〉promotion.

jochô-suru〈助長する〉promote, further, conduce ((to)).

jôcho〈じょうちょ：情緒〉sentiment, emotion.

jôcho-no-aru〈情緒のある〉sentimental, emotional.

jôdan〈じょうだん：冗談〉a joke, fun.

　　Jôdan-ja-nai-yo!〈冗談じゃないよ.〉 It's no joke!

jôdan-o-iu〈冗談を言う〉joke.

　　Jôdan-o-iu-nowa-yame-nasai.〈冗談を言うのはやめなさい.〉 Stop your joking. / No kidding.

jôdan-hambun-ni〈冗談半分に〉half in joke

jôdan-ni〈冗談に〉in joke

jôdan-wa-sate-oki〈冗談はさておき〉joking aside

jôdan〈じょうだん：上段〉the upper berth.

jô-deki〈じょうでき：上出来〉

jô-deki-de-aru〈上出来である〉be well done, be a great success.

　　Jô-deki-da!〈上出来だ.〉 Well done!

jô-deki-no〈上出来の〉well-done, very good.

jo-dôshi〈じょどうし：助動詞〉an auxiliary verb.

jôei〈じょうえい：上映〉screening.

　　jôei-chû-no-eiga〈上映中の映画〉 the picture now showing

　　jôei-jikan〈上映時間〉 the running time

jôei-suru〈上映する〉show, screen, put on the screen.

jôen〈じょうえん：上演〉performance.

　　jôen-chû〈上演中〉 be on now ((at))

jôen-suru〈上演する〉put on the stage.

jogai〈じょがい：除外〉exception, exclusion.

jogai-suru〈除外する〉except, exclude, leave ((a thing *or* a person)) out.

jôgai〈じょうがい：場外〉

　　jôgai-hômu-ran〈場外ホームラン〉 an out-of-the-park homer

jôgai-de or *jôgai-ni*〈場外で，場外に〉outside the hall.

jogaku-sei〈じょがくせい：女学生〉*see.* joshi-gakusei.

jô-ge〈じょうげ：上下〉up and down, top and bottom.

　　jô-ge-sen(-tomo)〈上下線(とも)〉 both up and down lines

jô-ge-suru〈上下する〉rise and fall.

jô-ge-ni〈上下に〉up and down.

jogen〈じょげん：助言〉advice.

　　jogen o motomeru〈助言を求める〉 ask advice 〔of another person〕

　　jogen-sha〈助言者〉 an adviser

jogen-suru〈助言する〉advise, give ((a person)) advice.

jôgi 〈じょうぎ：定規〉a ruler, a square.

    kumo-gata-jôgi（雲形定規） a curved rule

    san-kaku-jôgi（三角定規） a set square

jôgo 〈じょうご〉a funnel.

    jôgo-gata-no 〈じょうご形の〉funnel-shaped.

jôgo 〈じょうご：上戸〉a drinker.

    naki-jôgo（泣き上戸） a maudlin drinker

    warai-jôgo（笑い上戸） a merry drinker

jô-hanshin 〈じょうはんしん：上半身〉the upper half of the body, the bust.

jôhatsu 〈じょうはつ：蒸発〉evaporation; disappearance.

    jôhatsu-suru 〈蒸発する〉evaporate; disappear.

jôheki 〈じょうへき：城壁〉a castle wall.

    jôheki-o-megurasu 〈城壁を巡らす〉wall ((a town)) in.

jôhin 〈じょうひん：上品〉

    jôhin-na 〈上品な〉elegant, refined, graceful.

    jôhin-na shumi-no hito（上品な趣味の人） a man of refined taste

    jôhin-ni 〈上品に〉elegantly, gracefully.

jôho 〈じょうほ：譲歩〉concession, compromise.

    jôho-suru 〈譲歩する〉concede, make a concession, compromise, give way ((to)).

jôhô 〈じょうほう：情報〉information, intelligence, news.

    jôhô o teikyô-suru（情報を提供する） give information ((on))

    jôhô o uru（情報を得る） get information ((about *or* on))

    jôhô-mô（情報網） an intelligence network

    jôhô-shori（情報処理） data processing

joi 〈じょい：女医〉a female doctor.

jôi 〈じょうい：上位〉a higher rank.

    jôi-ni-aru 〈上位にある〉be above, be placed above, rank high(er) ((than)).

jôin 〈じょういん：上院〉the Upper House; the Senate, the House of Lords.

    jôin-giin（上院議員） a member of the Upper House, a senator

jôji 〈じょうじ：情事〉a love affair.

jôjiru 〈じょうじる：乗じる〉multiply; take advantage ((of)).

    hito-no muchi-ni-jôjiru（人の無知に乗じる） take advantage of a person's ignorance

    ～-ni-jôjite 〈～に乗じて〉taking advantage of... , under cover of... .

    yain-ni-jôjite（夜陰に乗じて） under cover of darkness

joji-shi〈じょじし：叙事詩〉an epic.
joji-shi-teki(-na)〈叙事詩的(な)〉epic.

jôjitsu〈じょうじつ：情実〉favoritism, personal considerations.
jôjitsu-ni sayû-sareru（情実に左右される）be influenced by private considerations

jojo〈じょじょ：徐々〉
jojo-ni〈徐々に〉slowly, gradually, by degrees, little by little, step by step.

jôjô〈じょうじょう：情状〉
jôjô-o-shakuryô-suru（情状を酌量する）take the circumstances into consideration
Jôjô-shakuryô-no-yochi-ga-nai.（情状酌量の余地がない.）There are no extenuating circumstances.

jôjô〈じょうじょう：上場〉
jôjô-kabu（上場株）listed stocks
jôjô-suru〈上場する〉list [stocks].

jôjô〈じょうじょう：上々〉the best.
Kondishon-wa-jôjô-da.（コンディションは上々だ.）I'm in the best of condition.

jojô-shi〈じょじょうし：叙情詩〉a lyric.
jojô-shi-teki(-na)〈叙情詩的(な)〉lyric.
jojô-shi-teki-ni〈叙情詩的に〉lyrically.

jôju〈じょうじゅ：成就〉achievement, accomplishment, realization, success.
jôju-suru〈成就する〉achieve, accomplish, realize, succeed ((in)).

jôjun〈じょうじゅん：上旬〉the first ten days of a month.
nigatsu-jôjun-ni（二月上旬に）early in February

jojutsu〈じょじゅつ：叙述〉description.
jojutsu-suru〈叙述する〉describe.

jôjutsu〈じょうじゅつ：上述〉see. jôki (上記).

jôka〈じょうか：浄化〉purification, purgation, a cleanup.
jôka-sô（浄化槽）a water-purifier tank; a septic tank
jôka-suru〈浄化する〉purify; purge, clean up.

jôka-machi〈じょうかまち：城下町〉a castle town.

jô-kampan〈じょうかんぱん：上甲板〉the upper deck.

jôkan〈じょうかん：上官〉a higher officer, a senior officer.

jôkei〈じょうけい：情景〉a scene, a sight.

jôken〈じょうけん：条件〉a condition.

jôken-tsuki-no〈条件付きの〉conditional.
  mu-jôken-no〈無条件の〉unconditional
jôken-tsuki-de〈条件付きで〉conditionally.
  mu-jôken-de〈無条件で〉unconditionally
  ~-to-iu-jôken-de〈～という条件で〉on condition that... .
jôki〈じょうき：上記〉
  jôki-no〈上記の〉above-mentioned.
  jôki-no-yô-ni〈上記のように〉as mentioned above.
jôki〈じょうき：常軌〉
  jôki-o-issuru〈常軌を逸する〉be abnormal, be eccentric.
  jôki-o-isshita〈常軌を逸した〉abnormal, eccentric.
jôki〈じょうき：蒸気〉steam, vapor.
  jôki-kikan〈蒸気機関〉 a steam engine
jôki〈じょうき：上気〉
  jôki-suru〈上気する〉be flushed.
  jôki-shita〈上気した〉flushed.
jô-kigen〈じょうきげん：上機嫌〉good humor.
  jô-kigen-no〈上機嫌の〉good-humored.
  jô-kigen-de〈上機嫌で〉in good humor.
jôkin〈じょうきん：常勤〉
  jôkin-no〈常勤の〉full-time.
  jôkin-de〈常勤で〉full time, on a regular basis.
jokki〈ジョッキ〉a mug.
  jokki-ippai-no-bîru（ジョッキ一杯のビール） a mug of beer
jokô〈じょこう：徐行〉
  jokô-suru〈徐行する〉go slow, slow down.
jôkô〈じょうこう：条項〉articles, clauses, terms, an item.
jôkô〈じょうこう：乗降〉
  jôkô-kyaku〈乗降客〉 passengers getting on and off
jôkoku〈じょうこく：上告〉a final appeal.
  jôkoku o kikyaku-suru（上告を棄却する） reject a final appeal
  jôkoku-suru〈上告する〉appeal to a higher court.
jôkû〈じょうくう：上空〉the sky, the upper air.
  nana-sen-mêtoru no jôkû-de（七千メートルの上空で） at a height of 7,000 meters
jokun〈じょくん：叙勲〉
  jokun-o-ukeru〈叙勲を受ける〉be decorated.
jôkyaku〈じょうきゃく：乗客〉a passenger.

jokyo 〈じょきょ：除去〉removal, elimination.
　jokyo-suru 〈除去する〉remove, eliminate.
jôkyô 〈じょうきょう：状(情)況〉circumstances, conditions, a situation.
　　mokka-no-jôkyô-dewa（目下の状況では）under the present circumstances
　　jôkyô-handan（状況判断）circumstantial judgment
jôkyô 〈じょうきょう：上京〉
　　jôkyô-chû-de-aru（上京中である）be in Tokyo now
　jôkyô-suru 〈上京する〉go up to Tokyo.
jo-kyôju 〈じょきょうじゅ：助教授〉an assistant professor.
jokyoku 〈じょきょく：序曲〉an overture.
jôkyû 〈じょうきゅう：上級〉
　　jôkyû-sei（上級生）a senior student
　jôkyû-no 〈上級の〉higher(-grade), superior, senior.
jômae 〈じょうまえ：錠前〉a lock.
　　jômae-ya（錠前屋）a locksmith
jomaku-shiki 〈じょまくしき：除幕式〉a ceremony of unveiling.
jôman 〈じょうまん：冗漫〉
　jôman-na 〈冗漫な〉diffuse, verbose, wordy.
　　jôman-na buntai（冗談な文体）a diffuse style
　　jôman-na enzetsu（冗漫な演説）a long and tiresome speech
jomei 〈じょめい：助命〉
　　jomei-o-kou（助命を請う）ask for ((a person's)) life
　jomei-suru 〈助命する〉spare ((a person's)) life.
jomei 〈じょめい：除名〉
　jomei-suru 〈除名する〉strike a person's name off, expel.
jômu-in 〈じょうむいん：乗務員〉a crewman, a trainman, a carman; a crew.
jômu-torishimari-yaku 〈じょうむとりしまりやく：常務取締役〉an executive director.
jômyaku 〈じょうみゃく：静脈〉a vein.
　　dai-jômyaku（大静脈）the main vein
　　jômyaku-chûsha（静脈注射）a venous injection
jônai 〈じょうない：場内〉
　jônai-de 〈場内で〉in the hall.
jônetsu 〈じょうねつ：情熱〉passion.
　jônetsu-teki-na 〈情熱的な〉passionate.
jônin 〈じょうにん：常任〉

jônin-iin（常任委員）a member of the permanent committee

jônin-no〈常任の〉standing, permanent.

joô〈じょおう：女王〉a queen.

joô-bachi（女王ばち）a queen bee

jôrei〈じょうれい：条例〉regulations, an ordinance.

shi-jôrei（市条例）a municipal ordinance

jôren〈じょうれん：常連〉regular visitors, frequenters.

jôri〈じょうり：条理〉reason.

jôri-ni-kanau（条理にかなう）stand to reason

jôriku〈じょうりく：上陸〉landing.

jôriku-suru〈上陸する〉land ((at *or* in)), go ashore ((at)).

joro *or* **jôro**〈じょろ，じょうろ：如露，如雨露〉a watering can.

joron〈じょろん：序論〉an introduction.

joryoku〈じょりょく：助力〉help, assistance.

joryoku-sha（助力者）a helper, an assistant.

joryoku-suru〈助力する〉help, assist.

jôryoku-ju〈じょうりょくじゅ：常緑樹〉an evergreen tree, evergreens.

joryû〈じょりゅう：女流〉the fair sex.

joryû-sakka（女流作家）a woman writer

jôryû〈じょうりゅう：蒸留〉distillation.

jôryû-sui（蒸留水）distilled water

jôryû-suru〈蒸留する〉distil.

jôryû〈じょうりゅう：上流〉the upper stream.

jôryû-no, jôryû-de, jôryû-e or *jôryû-ni*〈上流の，上流で，上流へ，上流に〉
upstream.

jôryû-e kogi-noboru（上流へこぎ上る）row upstream

jôryû-shakai〈じょうりゅうしゃかい：上流社会〉the upper classes.

jôryû-shakai no fujin-tachi（上流社会の婦人たち）the women of the
upper classes

josai〈じょさい：如才〉

josai-no-nai〈如才のない〉smart, tactful.

josampu〈じょさんぷ：助産婦〉a midwife.

josei〈じょせい：女性〉a woman, the fair sex.

josei-teki(-na)〈女性的(な)〉womanly, womanish.

josei-rashii〈女性らしい〉feminine.

josei〈じょせい：女声〉a female voice.

josei-gasshô（女声合唱）a female chorus

josei〈じょせい：助成〉

josei-kin（助成金） a subsidy, a bounty.

josei-suru〈助成する〉assist, aid, foster, promote.

jôsei〈じょうせい：情（状）勢〉the state of things, the situation, conditions.

    sekai-jôsei〈世界情勢〉the world situation

jo-seito〈じょせいと：女生徒〉a schoolgirl, a girl student.

joseki〈じょせき：除籍〉

joseki-suru〈除籍する〉strike ((a person's name)) off the register, expel.

jôseki〈じょうせき：定石〉established tactics.

jôseki-doori-ni〈定石どおりに〉(play) by the book.

jôsen〈じょうせん：乗船〉

    jôsen-ken（乗船券） a passage ticket

jôsen-suru〈乗船する〉go on board 〔a ship〕.

josetsu〈じょせつ：除雪〉

    josetsu-sha（除雪車） a snowplow

josetsu-suru〈除雪する〉remove the snow 〔from the street〕.

jôsha〈じょうしゃ：乗車〉

    jôsha-ken（乗車券） a ticket

jôsha-suru〈乗車する〉take a train, get in a car, get on a car.

joshi〈じょし：女子〉a woman, a female, a girl.

    joshi-kôtô-gakkô（女子高等学校） a girls' senior high school

    joshi-daigaku（女子大学） a women's college

    joshi-gakusei（女子学生） a female student

    joshi-ryô（女子寮） a women's dormitory

    joshi-ten·in（女子店員） a saleswoman, a salesgirl

joshi〈じょし：女史〉Madame, Mrs., Miss.

joshi-taipu-no〈女史タイプの〉highbrow-looking.

joshi〈じょし：助詞〉a postpositional word.

jôshi〈じょうし：上司〉one's superior.

jôshi〈じょうし：城し〉the ruins of a castle.

jôshi〈じょうし：情死〉a lovers' suicide.

jôshiki〈じょうしき：常識〉common sense, good sense.

    jôshiki-ga-aru（常識がある） have common sense

    jôshiki-ga-nai（常識がない） have no common sense

    Sonna-koto wa jôshiki-da.（そんなことは常識だ.） Everybody knows it.

jôshiki-teki-na〈常識的な〉sensible, practical.

jôshiki-teki-ni〈常識的に〉sensibly, in a practical manner

jôshô〈じょうしょう：上昇〉

jôshô-kiryû〈上昇気流〉 an ascending current, an updraft

jôshô-suru〈上昇する〉 rise, go up.

jôshoku〈じょうしょく：常食〉staple food.

    kome-o-jôshoku-to-suru（米を常食とする） live on rice

joshu〈じょしゅ：助手〉a helper; an assistant.

jôshû〈じょうしゅう：常習〉

    tobaku-jôshû-sha（とばく常習者） a confirmed gambler

    jôshû-han（常習犯） a habitual crime, recidivism; a habitual criminal

jô-shubi〈じょうしゅび：上首尾〉(a great) success.

    Sore-wa jô-shubi-datta.（それは上首尾だった.） It was a great success.

jô-shubi-no〈上首尾の〉successful.

josô〈じょそう：助走〉an approach run.

josô〈じょそう：除草〉

    josô-zai（除草剤） a weed killer, a herbicide.

josô〈じょそう：女装〉

josô-suru〈女装する〉disguise oneself as a woman.

josô-no〈女装の〉in a woman's dress.

jôsô〈じょうそう：上層〉the upper classes, the upper stratum, the upper story.

jôsô〈じょうそう：情操〉(a) sentiment.

    jôsô-kyôiku（情操教育） culture of esthetic sentiments

josû〈じょすう：序数〉an ordinal (number).

josû〈じょすう：除数〉a divisor.

jôsui〈じょうすい：上水〉water supply; service water.

    jôsui-dô（上水道） waterworks

jôsui-jô〈じょうすいじょう：浄水場〉a filtration plant.

jotai〈じょたい：除隊〉

jotai-suru〈除隊する〉be discharged from military service.

jôtai〈じょうたい：状態〉a state, a condition.

    seishin-jôtai（精神状態） a mental state

jôtai〈じょうたい：常態〉a normal state, normal(cy).

    jôtai-ni fukusuru（常態に復する） be restored to normal(cy)

jôtai〈じょうたい：上体〉the upper part of the body.

jôtatsu〈じょうたつ：上達〉progress, improvement, proficiency.

    jôtatsu-ga-hayai（上達が早い） make rapid progress ((in))

jôtatsu-suru〈上達する〉make progress ((in)), improve ((in)), become proficient ((in)).

jô-tenki〈じょうてんき：上天気〉fair weather.

jôto〈じょうと：譲渡〉

  jôto-suru〈譲渡する〉transfer, hand over.

    zaisan o jôto-suru（財産を譲渡する）transfer property ((to))

  jôto-dekiru〈譲渡できる〉transferable, negotiable.

    jôto-deki-nai（譲渡できない）untransferable, nonnegotiable

jôtô〈じょうとう：常とう〉

    jôtô-shudan（常とう手段）one's old trick, familiar ways

jôtô〈じょうとう：上等〉

  jôtô-no〈上等の〉fine, very good, first-class, superior.

jô-tokui〈じょうとくい：常得意〉a regular customer, a patron.

joya〈じょや：除夜〉New Year's Eve, the watch night.

    joya-no kane（除夜の鐘）the watch-night bell

joyaku〈じょやく：助役〉

    eki-no-joyaku（駅の助役）an assistant stationmaster

    shi-no-joyaku（市の助役）a deputy mayor

jôyaku〈じょうやく：条約〉a treaty.

    jôyaku ni chôin-suru（条約に調印する）sign a treaty

    jôyaku o teiketsu-suru（条約を締結する）conclude a treaty

    jôyaku o haki-suru（条約を破棄する）annul a treaty

    heiwa-jôyaku（平和条約）a peace treaty

jôyo〈じょうよ：剰余〉

    jôyo-kin（剰余金）a surplus (fund)

jôyô〈じょうよう：常用〉common use.

    jôyô-go（常用語）words in common use

    mayaku-jôyô-sha（麻薬常用者）a drug addict

  jôyô-suru〈常用する〉use commonly, make habitual use ((of)).

jôyoku〈じょうよく：情欲〉sexual desire, sensual pleasures.

jôyô-sha〈じょうようしゃ：乗用車〉a passenger car.

joyû〈じょゆう：女優〉an actress.

jôzai〈じょうざい：錠剤〉a tablet.

jôzô〈じょうぞう：醸造〉brewing.

    jôzô-sho（醸造所）a brewery, a distillery

  jôzô-suru〈醸造する〉brew, distil.

jôzu〈じょうず：上手〉

  jôzu-de-aru〈上手である〉be skillful ((at *or* in)), be good ((at)).

    Eigo-ga-jôzu-de-aru（英語が上手である）be good at English

  jôzu-na〈上手な〉good, skillful.

jôzu-ni 〈上手に〉 well, skillfully.

    jôzu-ni-naru（上手になる）become skillful ((at)), become proficient ((in)), improve oneself ((in)).

jû 〈じゅう：十〉 ten.

    jutchû-hakku（十中八九）in nine cases out of ten, ten to one

    dai-jû（第十）the tenth

jû 〈じゅう：銃〉 a gun, a rifle.

    jû o ninau（銃を担う）shoulder a gun

    hito-ni jû o mukeru（人に銃を向ける）level a gun at a person

-jû 〈-じゅう：-中〉 through, throughout, in the course of; all over.

    ichi-nichi-jû（一日中）all day long

    hito-ban-jû（一晩中）all through the night

    raishû-jû-ni（来週中に）in the course of next week

    ni-san-nichi-jû-ni（二, 三日中に）in a few days

    ichi-nen-jû（一年中）all the year round

    sekai-jû（世界中）all over the world

    Ôsaka-jû（大阪中）all over Osaka, everywhere in Osaka

jûatsu 〈じゅうあつ：重圧〉 (heavy) pressure.

    jûatsu o kuwaeru（重圧を加える）put pressure ((on))

jûbako 〈じゅうばこ：重箱〉 a nest of lacquered boxes.

jûbun 〈じゅうぶん：十分〉

    kane-wa-jûbun-aru（金は十分ある）have enough money

    Jûbun-itadakimashita.（十分頂きました.）I have had enough.

jûbun-na 〈十分な〉 enough, sufficient, full.

jûbun-ni 〈十分に〉 enough, sufficiently, fully.

jûbun 〈じゅうぶん：重文〉 a compound sentence.

jûbyô 〈じゅうびょう：重病〉 a serious sickness.

    jûbyô-kanja（重病患者）a serious case

jûbyô-de-aru 〈重病である〉 be seriously sick.

jûchin 〈じゅうちん：重鎮〉 a leading figure, a prominent person.

juchû 〈じゅうちゅう：受注〉

juchû-suru 〈受注する〉 accept an order.

jû-dai 〈じゅうだい：十代〉 one's teens.

    Kare-ra-wa jû-dai-desu.（彼らは十代です.）They are in their teens.

    jû-dai-no-hito（十代の人）a teen-ager; a teen-age boy, a teen-age girl.

jûdai 〈じゅうだい：重大〉

jûdai-na 〈重大な〉 important, of great importance, serious, grave.

　　　ichiban-jûdai-na mondai〈一番重大な問題〉 the most important problem
　　　jûdai-na jiken〈重大な事件〉 a serious affair

judaku〈じゅだく：受諾〉 acceptance.
　judaku-suru〈受諾する〉 accept.

jûdan〈じゅうだん：銃弾〉 a bullet, a shot.

jûdan〈じゅうだん：縦断〉
　jûdan-suru〈縦断する〉 run through.

jûden〈じゅうでん：充電〉
　jûden-suru〈充電する〉 charge, be charged.
　　　batterî ni jûden-suru（バッテリーに充電する） charge a storage battery

judô〈じゅどう：受動〉
　　　judô-tai（受動態） the passive voice
　judô-teki(-na) or *judô-sei-no*〈受動的(な)，受動性の〉 passive.

jûdô〈じゅうどう：柔道〉 judo, jujutsu.

jueki〈じゅえき：樹液〉 sap.

jûgatsu〈じゅうがつ：十月〉 October.

jû-go〈じゅうご：十五〉 fifteen.
　　　dai-jû-go（第十五） the fifteenth

jûgo-ya〈じゅうごや：十五夜〉 a full moon night.
　　　jûgo-ya-no-tsuki（十五夜の月） a full moon, the harvest moon

jûgun〈じゅうぐん：従軍〉
　　　jûgun-kisha（従軍記者） a war correspondent
　jûgun-suru〈従軍する〉 serve in a war.

jugyô〈じゅぎょう：授業〉 teaching, a lesson, a class.
　　　Kyô wa jugyô-ga-nai.（今日は授業がない.） We have no school today.
　　　Kyô wa jugyô-ga-roku-jikan-aru.（今日は授業が六時間ある.） We have six lessons today.
　　　jugyô-jikan（授業時間） school hours
　　　jugyô-ryô（授業料） a school fee, tuition fee
　jugyô-suru〈授業する〉 teach, give lessons.
　jugyô-chû-ni〈授業中に〉 during the lesson.

jûgyô-in〈じゅうぎょういん：従業員〉 an employee, a worker.

jû-hachi〈じゅうはち：十八〉 eighteen.
　　　jû-hachi-kin（十八金） 18-carat gold
　　　dai-jû-hachi（第十八） the eighteenth

jūhan 〈じゅうはん：重版〉
nan-kai-mo-jūhan-ni-naru (何回も重版になる) go into many editions
jūhan-suru 〈重版する〉 print another edition.

jūhan(-sha) 〈じゅうはん(しゃ)：従犯(者)〉 an accessory 〔to a crime〕.

juhi 〈じゅひ：樹皮〉 the bark.

juhyō 〈じゅひょう：樹氷〉 trees covered with ice.

jūi 〈じゅうい：獣医〉 a veterinarian, a vet.

jū-ichi 〈じゅういち：十一〉 eleven.
dai-jū-ichi (第十一) the eleventh

jūichigatsu 〈じゅういちがつ：十一月〉 November.

jūji 〈じゅうじ：従事〉
jūji-suru 〈従事する〉 engage ((in)).
jūji-shite-iru 〈従事している〉 be engaged ((in)).

jūji(-ka) 〈じゅうじ(か)：十字(架)〉 a cross.
jūji-ro (十字路) a crossroads
jūji-o-kiru 〈十字を切る〉 cross oneself.
jūji(-gata)-no 〈十字(形)の〉 cross-shaped, crossed.

jūjitsu 〈じゅうじつ：充実〉
jūjitsu-shita 〈充実した〉 full, complete, substantial.
jūjitsu-shita seikatsu o okuru (充実した生活を送る) live a full life

jūjun 〈じゅうじゅん：従順〉 obedience.
jūjun-na 〈従順な〉 obedient.
jūjun-ni 〈従順に〉 obediently.

jūkan 〈じゅうかん：縦貫〉 *see.* jūdan (縦断).

jūkei 〈じゅうけい：重刑〉
jūkei-ni-shosuru 〈重刑に処する〉 inflict a heavy penalty ((upon)), punish ((a person)) heavily.

jukei-sha 〈じゅけいしゃ：受刑者〉 a convicted person, a convict.

jūkei-shō 〈じゅうけいしょう：重軽傷〉 a serious or slight injury.
jūkei-shō-o-ou 〈重軽傷を負う〉 be seriously or slightly injured.

juken 〈じゅけん：受験〉
juken-sei (受験生) a candidate for an examination, an examinee
juken-kamoku (受験科目) subjects of examination
juken-bangō (受験番号) an examinee's (seat) number
juken-suru 〈受験する〉 take an examination.

jūken 〈じゅうけん：銃剣〉 a bayonet.

jūketsu 〈じゅうけつ：充血〉
jūketsu-suru 〈充血する〉 be congested, be bloodshot.

jūketsu-shita〈充血した〉congested, bloodshot.

　jūketsu-shita me（充血した目）bloodshot eyes

jukkō〈じゅっこう：熟考〉deliberation, (due) consideration.

　jukkō-suru〈熟考する〉think over, deliberate, consider ((a matter)) carefully.

jūkō〈じゅうこう：銃口〉the muzzle〔of a gun〕.

　jūkō-o-tsuki-tsukete〈銃口を突き付けて〉at the point of a gun.

jū-kōgyō〈じゅうこうぎょう：重工業〉heavy industries.

juku〈じゅく：塾〉a private school.

jū-ku〈じゅうく：十九〉nineteen.

　dai-jū-ku（第十九）the nineteenth

jukuchi〈じゅくち：熟知〉

　jukuchi-suru〈熟知する〉know well, be well informed ((of)), be familiar ((with)), be well acquainted ((with)).

jukudoku〈じゅくどく：熟読〉careful reading.

　jukudoku-suru〈熟読する〉read thoroughly.

jukugo〈じゅくご：熟語〉an idiom, a phrase.

jukuren〈じゅくれん：熟練〉

　jukuren-kō（熟練工）a skilled worker

　jukuren-suru〈熟練する〉become skillful ((at *or* in)).

　jukuren-shita〈熟練した〉skilled, expert.

jukuryo〈じゅくりょ：熟慮〉*see.* jukkō.

jukushita〈じゅくした：熟した〉ripe, mature.

jukusui〈じゅくすい：熟睡〉a sound sleep.

　jukusui-suru〈熟睡する〉sleep well, sleep soundly.

　jukusui-shite-iru〈熟睡している〉be fast asleep.

jūkyo〈じゅうきょ：住居〉a dwelling, a residence.

jūkyū〈じゅうきゅう：需給〉demand and supply.

jū-man〈じゅうまん：十万〉a hundred thousand.

　nan-jū-man（何十万）hundreds of thousands

jūman〈じゅうまん：充満〉

　jūman-suru〈充満する〉be full ((of)), be filled ((with)).

　doku-gasu-ga-jūman-suru（毒ガスが充満する）be filled with poisonous gas

jumban〈じゅんばん：順番〉order, turn.

　jumban-o-matsu（順番を待つ）wait for one's turn

jumbi〈じゅんび：準備〉preparation(s), arrangement, provision.

　Yūshoku-no-jumbi-ga-dekimashita.（夕食の準備ができました．）Dinner

　　　is ready.

jumbi-o-suru〈準備をする〉prepare ((for)), make preparations ((for)), get ready ((for)).

　　　chôshoku-no-jumbi-o-suru（朝食の準備をする）prepare breakfast

　　　ryokô-no-jumbi-o-suru（旅行の準備をする）get ready for a trip

jumboku〈じゅんぼく：純朴〉

jumboku-na〈純朴な〉unsophisticated, simplehearted.

jûmin〈じゅうみん：住民〉inhabitants, dwellers, residents.

　　　jûmin-tôroku（住民登録）resident registration

jumoku〈じゅもく：樹木〉trees.

jumoku-no-shigetta〈樹木の茂った〉wooded, woody.

jumon〈じゅもん：じゅ文〉a spell, an incantation.

jû-monji〈じゅうもんじ：十文字〉a cross.

jû-monji-no〈十文字の〉cross-shaped.

jū-monji-ni〈十文字に〉crosswise.

jumpô〈じゅんぽう：遵(順)法〉

　　　jumpô-seishin（遵法精神）a law-abiding spirit

jumpû〈じゅんぷう：順風〉a favorable wind.

　　　jumpû-ni-ho-o-agete-hashiru（順風に帆を揚げて走る）sail before the wind

jumyô〈じゅみょう：寿命〉the span of life, life.

　　　jumyô-ga-nobiru（寿命が延びる）prolong one's life

　　　jumyô o chijimeru（寿命を縮める）shorten one's life

jumyô-ga-nagai〈寿命が長い〉be long-lived.

　　　jumyô-ga-mijikai（寿命が短い〉be short-lived

jun〈じゅん：純〉

　　　junkin（純金）pure gold

　　　jummen（純綿）pure cotton

　　　jummô（純毛）pure(*or* all) wool

　　　jun-eki（純益）net profit

　　　jun-do（純度）purity

　　　jumpaku（純白）snow white

jun-na〈純な〉pure, innocent.

　　　jun-na kokoro（純な心）a pure heart

jun〈じゅん：順〉order, turn (an another expression 'jumban').

　　　jun-ni（順に）in order, in turn, by turns, one by one, one after another

　　　　　ê-bî-shî-jun-ni（ＡＢＣ順に〉in alphabetical order

nenrei-jun-ni（年齢順に）in order of age

jun-o-otte（順を追って）in due order

junan〈じゅなん：受難〉sufferings, severe trial.

Kirisuto no junan（キリストの受難）the sufferings of Christ

jūnan〈じゅうなん：柔軟〉

jūnan-sei（柔軟性）softness, pliability, suppleness, flexibility, elasticity

jūnan-taisō（柔軟体操）calisthenics

jūnan-na〈柔軟な〉soft, pliable, supple, flexible, elastic.

junchō〈じゅんちょう：順調〉

junchō-na〈順調な〉favorable, smooth, normal.

junchō-ni〈順調に〉favorably, smoothly, normally.

Shigoto wa junchō-ni hakondeiru.（仕事は順調に運んでいる.）The work is going on favorably.

junchō-ni-ikeba〈順調にいけば〉in the natural course of events.

jun·en〈じゅんえん：順延〉

Uten-jun·en.（雨天順延.）In case of rain, it will be put off till the next fine day.

jū-nen〈じゅうねん：十年〉ten years, a decade.

jū-nen-ichi-nichi-no-gotoku（十年一日のごとく）for years without a break

jungyō〈じゅんぎょう：巡業〉a tour of the country, a provincial tour.

jungyō-suru〈巡業する〉make a provincial tour.

jungyō-chū-de-aru〈巡業中である〉be on the road, be on tour.

jun·i〈じゅんい：順位〉order, ranking.

jun·i o kettei-suru（順位を決定する）decide ranking

jū-ni〈じゅうに：十二〉twelve.

dai-jū-ni（第十二）the twelfth

jūnibun-ni〈じゅうにぶんに：十二分に〉*see.* jūbun-ni.

jūnigatsu〈じゅうにがつ：十二月〉December.

jū-nin〈じゅうにん：十人〉

Jū-nin-to-iro.（十人十色.）So many men, so many minds.

Jū-nin-nami-no〈十人並の〉average, ordinary.

jūnin〈じゅうにん：住人〉an inhabitant, a dweller.

jūnishi-chō〈じゅうにしちょう：十二指腸〉the duodenum.

jūnishi-chō-kaiyō（十二指腸かいよう）a duodenal ulcer

junjiru〈じゅんじる：殉じる〉sacrifice oneself ((for)).

junjiru〈じゅんじる：準じる〉apply correspondingly, be proportionate ((to)), correspond ((to)).

～-ni-junjite〈〜に準じて〉in accordance with... , according to... , in proportion to... .

junjo〈じゅんじょ：順序〉order.
　junjo-yoku（順序よく）in good order
　junjo-datte（順序立って）in due order, systematically

junjō〈じゅんじょう：純情〉
　junjō-na〈純情な〉naïve, pure in heart.

junjun〈じゅんじゅん：順々〉
　junjun-ni〈順々に〉*see.* jun-ni.

junjun〈じゅんじゅん〉
　junjun-to〈じゅんじゅんと〉earnestly.
　junjun-to toku（じゅんじゅんと説く）talk ((a person)) earnestly

junkai〈じゅんかい：巡回〉a round; a patrol.
　junkai-tosho-kan（巡回図書館）a traveling library
　junkai-suru〈巡回する〉go round; patrol.

junkan〈じゅんかん：循環〉circulation, cycle.
　ketsueki no junkan（血液の循環）circulation of blood
　junkan-ki（循環器）a circulatory organ
　aku-junkan（悪循環）a vicious cycle
　junkan-suru〈循環する〉circulate.

junkatsu-yu〈じゅんかつゆ：潤滑油〉lubricating oil.

junketsu〈じゅんけつ：純潔〉purity, chastity.
　junketsu-na〈純潔な〉pure, chaste.

junketsu-shu〈じゅんけつしゅ：純血種〉
　junketsu-shu-no〈純血種の〉thoroughbred.

junkyo〈じゅんきょ：準拠〉
　junkyo-suru〈準拠する〉be based ((upon)), conform ((to)).
　～-ni-junkyo-shite〈〜に準拠して〉in conformity to... , in accordance with... .

junkyō-sha〈じゅんきょうしゃ：殉教者〉a martyr.

junkyû〈じゅんきゅう：準急〉a local express, a semi-express.

junnō〈じゅんのう：順応〉adaptation, adjustment.
　junnō-sei（順応性）adaptability
　junnō-suru〈順応する〉adapt oneself ((to)), adjust oneself ((to)).
　jisei-ni-junnō-suru（時勢に順応する）go with the tide
　junnō-sei-no-aru〈順応性のある〉adaptable.

junrei〈じゅんれい：巡礼〉a pilgrimage; a pilgrim.

junrei-suru 〈巡礼する〉make a pilgrimage.

junretsu 〈じゅんれつ：順列〉(a) permutation.

   junretsu-kumi-awase（順列組み合わせ）permutations and combinations

junro 〈じゅんろ：順路〉the (fixed) route.

junsa 〈じゅんさ：巡査〉a policeman.

   junsa-hashutsu-jo（巡査派出所）a police box

junshi(-suru) 〈じゅんし（する）：巡視（する）〉patrol.

junshin 〈じゅんしん：純真〉

junshin-na 〈純真な〉naïve, pure, innocent.

junshoku 〈じゅんしょく：殉職〉death on duty.

   junshoku-sha（殉職者）a victim to one's post of duty

junshoku-suru 〈殉職する〉die at one's post of duty.

junsui 〈じゅんすい：純粋〉

junsui-na 〈純粋な〉pure, genuine, unmixed.

juntō 〈じゅんとう：順当〉

juntō-ni-ikeba 〈順当にいけば〉if everything goes well, if nothing intervenes.

junyū 〈じゅにゅう：授乳〉

junyū-suru 〈授乳する〉nurse, suckle.

junzen-taru 〈じゅんぜんたる：純然たる〉pure, absolute, downright, out-and-out, thorough.

   junzen-taru wairo（純然たる賄ろ）a bribe pure and simple

jûô 〈じゅうおう：縦横〉

jûô-ni 〈縦横に〉in all directions, to all points.

   jûô-ni-hashiru-tetsudô-mô（縦横に走る鉄道網）a network of railways

   jûô-ni-kôsa-suru-dôro（縦横に交差する道路）a crisscross of streets

jû-oku 〈じゅうおく：十億〉a billion, a thousand million(s).

jûrai 〈じゅうらい：従来〉up to now, so far, formerly, in the past.

jûrai-no 〈従来の〉old, usual, former, conventional.

   jûrai-no-toori（従来のとおり）as usual, as before

jurei 〈じゅれい：樹齢〉the age of a tree.

juri 〈じゅり：受理〉acceptance.

juri-suru 〈受理する〉accept, receive.

jûrin 〈じゅうりん〉

jûrin-suru 〈じゅうりんする〉trample ((on)), infringe ((on)), overrun.

juritsu 〈じゅりつ：樹立〉

juritsu-suru 〈樹立する〉establish, set up, found.

shin-kiroku o juritsu-suru〈新記録を樹立する〉 establish a new record

jū-rôdô〈じゅうろうどう：重労働〉 heavy labor.

jū-roku〈じゅうろく：十六〉 sixteen.
　　dai-jū-roku（第十六） the sixteenth

juryô〈じゅりょう：受領〉 receipt, acceptance.
　　juryô-sho（受領書） a receipt
　juryô-suru〈受領する〉 receive, accept.

jûryô〈じゅうりょう：重量〉 weight.
　　jûryô-age（重量挙げ） weight lifting

jûryoku〈じゅうりょく：重力〉 gravity.
　　mu-jûryoku-jôtai（無重力状態） a state of weightlessness

jū-san〈じゅうさん：十三〉 thirteen.
　　dai-jū-san（第十三） the thirteenth

jûsatsu〈じゅうさつ：銃殺〉
　jûsatsu-suru〈銃殺する〉 shoot ((a person)) dead.

jusei〈じゅせい：受(授)精〉 fertilization, pollination.
　　jinkô-jusei（人工授精） artificial insemination
　jusei-suru〈受精する〉 be fertilized, be pollinated.
　jusei-suru〈授精する〉 fertilize, pollinate.

jûsei〈じゅうせい：銃声〉 the report of a gun.

jûseki〈じゅうせき：重責〉
　jûseki-o-ou〈重責を負う〉 assume a heavy responsibility.

jushi〈じゅし：樹脂〉 resin.

jū-shi〈じゅうし：十四〉 fourteen.
　　dai-jū-shi（第十四） the fourteenth

jûshi〈じゅうし：重視〉
　jûshi-suru〈重視する〉 attach importance ((to)).

jū-shichi〈じゅうしち：十七〉 seventeen.
　　dai-jū-shichi（第十七） the seventeenth

jūshimatsu〈じゅうしまつ〉 a lovebird.

jushin〈じゅしん：受信〉
　　jushin-ki（受信機） a receiver
　jushin-suru〈受信する〉 receive a message.

jûshin〈じゅうしん：重心〉 the center of gravity.

jûshin〈じゅうしん：銃身〉 the barrel [of a gun].

jushô〈じゅしょう：受賞〉 receiving a prize.
　　jushô-sha（受賞者） a prize winner

　jushô-suru〈受賞する〉receive a prize, win a prize.

jushô〈じゅしょう：授賞〉
　　jushô-shiki（授賞式）　an awarding ceremony
　jushô-suru〈授賞する〉award a prize.

jûsho〈じゅうしょ：住所〉one's address, one's dwelling (place).
　　jûsho-ga-futei-da（住所が不定だ）　have no fixed abode
　　jûsho-fumei（住所不明）　address unknown
　　jûsho-roku（住所録）　an address book

jûshô〈じゅうしょう：重傷〉a serious wound, a severe injury.
　　jûshô-sha（重傷者）　a seriously wounded person
　jûshô-o-ou〈重傷を負う〉be seriously wounded.

jûshô〈じゅうしょう：重症〉a serious illness.
　　jûshô-kanja（重症患者）　a serious case

jûshoku〈じゅうしょく：住職〉the chief priest〔of a temple〕.

jûsô〈じゅうそう：重曹〉bicarbonate of soda.

jûsu〈ジュース〉juice; deuce.
　　jûsu-ni-naru（ジュースになる）　go to deuce

jûsui〈じゅうすい：重水〉heavy water.

jutai〈じゅたい：受胎〉conception.
　jutai-suru〈受胎する〉conceive〔a child〕.

jûtai〈じゅうたい：重態〉a serious condition, a critical condition.
　　jûtai-ni-ochiiru（重態に陥る）　fall into a critical condition
　　jûtai-de-aru（重態である）　be in a critical condition, be seriously sick

jûtai〈じゅうたい：渋滞〉delay, stagnation, congestion.
　　kôtsû-jûtai（交通渋滞）　traffic congestion

jûtaku〈じゅうたく：住宅〉a (dwelling) house.
　　jûtaku-chi（住宅地）　a residential quarter
　　jûtaku-mondai（住宅問題）　the housing problem
　　jûtaku-nan（住宅難）　housing shortage

jûtan〈じゅうたん〉a carpet, a rug.
　　jûtan o shiku（じゅうたんを敷く）　spread a carpet

jûten〈じゅうてん：重点〉priority.
　　jûten o oku（重点を置く）　give priority ((to))
　　jûten-shugi（重点主義）　a priority system

jûten〈じゅうてん：充てん〉filling up.
　jûten-suru〈充てんする〉fill up, plug.

jûtô〈じゅうとう：充当〉appropriation.
　jûtô-suru〈充当する〉appropriate.

jutsu 〈じゅつ：術〉an art, a means, a trick, magic.

    jutsu o tsukau（術を使う）practice magic

jutsugo 〈じゅつご：術語〉a technical term.

jutsugo 〈じゅつご：述語〉the predicate.

juwa-ki 〈じゅわき：受話器〉a receiver.

    juwa-ki o toru（受話器を取る）take the receiver

    juwa-ki o kakeru（受話器を掛ける）put back the receiver

jûyaku 〈じゅうやく：重役〉a director, the board of directors.

juyo 〈じゅよ：授与〉conferment, awarding.

  juyo-suru〈授与する〉confer, give, award, present.

juyô 〈じゅよう：需要〉demand.

    juyô to kyôkyû（需要と供給）demand and supply

    juyô o mitasu（需要を満たす）meet the demand

    hijô-ni-juyô-ga-aru（非常に需要がある）be in great demand

jûyô(-sei) 〈じゅうよう（せい）：重要(性)〉importance.

    jûyô-shi-suru（重要視する）*see.* jûshi-suru

  jûyô-na〈重要な〉important, of importance.

    jûyô-de-nai（重要でない）unimportant, of no importance

jûyu 〈じゅうゆ：重油〉heavy oil, crude oil.

jûzai 〈じゅうざい：重罪〉(a) felony, a serious crime.

    jûzai o okasu（重罪を犯す）commit a serious crime

jûzei 〈じゅうぜい：重税〉a heavy tax.

    jûzei o kasuru（重税を課する）impose heavy taxes ((on))

juzô 〈じゅぞう：受像〉

    juzô-ki（受像機）a television receiver

  juzô-suru〈受像する〉receive the television image.

jûzoku 〈じゅうぞく：従属〉subordination, dependency.

    jûzoku-setsuzoku-shi（従属接続詞）a subordinate conjunction

  jûzoku-suru〈従属する〉be subordinate ((to)).

  jûzoku-saseru〈従属させる〉subordinate.

  jûzoku-teki(-na)〈従属的(な)〉subordinate, subsidiary, auxiliary.

juzu 〈じゅず：数珠〉a rosary.

    juzu-dama（数珠玉）a bead

  juzu-tsunagi-ni-naru〈数珠つなぎになる〉be linked together, be tied in a row.

K

ka〈か：蚊〉a mosquito.
    ka-ni kuwareru〈蚊に食われる〉be bitten by a mosquito
    ka-tori-senkō〈蚊取り線香〉a mosquito repellent
ka〈か：課〉a lesson; a section, a department.
    dai-ikka〈第一課〉the First Lesson, Lesson I
    dai-ikka〈第一課〉the First Section, Section I
ka〈か：科〉a course; a department; a family.
    shōgyō-ka〈商業科〉the commercial course
    neko-ka〈猫科〉the cat family
-ka?〈-か？〉
    Sore-wa hontō-desu-ka?〈それは本当ですか.〉Is it true?
-ka(-dō-ka)〈～か(どうか)〉if, whether.
    zaitaku-ka-dō-ka-tazuneru〈在宅かどうか尋ねる〉ask if one is at home
  ～-ka～-ka〈～か～か〉or, either...or.
    kore-ka are-ka〈これかあれか〉this or that
kaba〈かば〉a hippopotamus.
kabâ〈カバー〉a cover, a jacket.
  kabâ-o-kakeru〈カバーを掛ける〉lay a cover, cover, jacket.
kaban〈かばん〉a bag.
kabau〈かばう〉protect, cover, defend.
kaba-yaki〈かばやき：かば焼き〉a spitchcock.
kabe〈かべ：壁〉a wall.
    kabe-ni e o kakeru〈壁に絵を掛ける〉hang a picture on the wall
    kabe o nuru〈壁を塗る〉plaster a wall
    kabe-gami〈壁紙〉wallpaper
    kabe-shimbun〈壁新聞〉a wall newspaper
kaben〈かべん：花弁〉a petal.

kabi 〈かび〉 mold, mould.
   kabi-ga-haeru or *kabiru* 〈かびが生える，かびる〉 become moldy.
   kabi-no-haeta or *kabi-kusai* 〈かびの生えた，かび臭い〉 moldy, musty.

kabin 〈かびん：花瓶〉 a vase.

kabin 〈かびん：過敏〉 oversensitiveness.
   kabin-shô〔過敏症〕 hypersensitiveness
   kabin-na 〈過敏な〉 oversensitive.

kabocha 〈かぼちゃ〉 a pumpkin.

kâbon 〈カーボン〉 carbon.
   kâbon-shi〔カーボン紙〕 carbon paper

kabu 〈かぶ：下部〉 the lower part.
   kabu-soshiki〔下部組織〕 a substructure

kabu 〈かぶ〉 a turnip.

kabu 〈かぶ：株〉 a stump; stocks, shares.
   kabu-ka〔株価〕 a stock price
   kabu-ken〔株券〕 a stock certificate, a share

kâbu 〈カーブ〉 a curve.
   kyû-kâbu〔急カーブ〕 a sharp curve
   kâbu o nageru〔カーブを投げる〕 throw a curve

kabu-nushi 〈かぶぬし：株主〉 a stockholder, a shareholder.
   kabu-nushi-sôkai〔株主総会〕 a general meeting of stockholders

kabure 〈かぶれ〉 a rash, a skin eruption.
   kabureru 〈かぶれる〉 have a rash, have a skin eruption; be imbued ((with)).

kaburitsuki 〈かぶりつき〉 the front row.

kaburi-tsuku 〈かぶりつく〉 bite ((at *or* into)).

kaburu 〈かぶる〉 put on, wear.
   bôshi o kaburu〔帽子をかぶる〕 put on a hat

kabuseru 〈かぶせる〉 cover ((with)), put ((a thing)) on.

kabushiki 〈かぶしき：株式〉 stocks, shares.
   kabushiki-gaisha〔株式会社〕 a joint-stock company, a corporation

kabuto 〈かぶと〉 a helmet.

kabuto-mushi 〈かぶとむし〉 a beetle.

kachi 〈かち：価値〉 worth, value, merit.
   ningen-no kachi〔人間の価値〕 a man's worth
   o-kane no kachi〔お金の価値〕 the value of money
   hon no kachi〔本の価値〕 the merit of a book
   kachi-kan〔価値観〕 a sense of values

〜-no-kachi-ga-aru 〈〜の価値がある〉 be worth ...ing.

kachi-no-aru 〈価値のある〉 worthy, valuable, of value.

     kachi-no-nai 〈価値のない〉 worthless, valueless, of no value

kachi 〈かち：勝ち〉 a win, a victory.

     Kimi-no-kachi-da-yo. (君の勝ちだよ.) The game is yours.

kachi-au 〈かちあう：かち合う〉 conflict ((with)), collide ((with)).

kachi-hokoru 〈かちほこる：勝ち誇る〉 be triumphant ((over)).

kachi-hokotte 〈勝ち誇って〉 triumphantly, in triumph.

kachikachi 〈かちかち〉

     kachikachi-ni-naru 〈かちかちになる〉 be dried and hardened, be frozen stiff

     kachikachi-ni-natte suwatte-iru 〈かちかちになって座っている〉 sit with an air of stiffness

kachiki 〈かちき：勝気〉 an unyielding spirit.

kachiki-na 〈勝気な〉 unyielding, strong-minded.

     kachiki-na josei 〈勝気な女性〉 a strong-minded woman

kachi-kosu 〈かちこす：勝ち越す〉 have ((two)) wins against ((a person)), be ahead ((of)).

kachiku 〈かちく：家畜〉 domestic animals, cattle.

kachi-make 〈かちまけ：勝ち負け〉 see. shô-hai.

kachi-me 〈かちめ：勝ち目〉 chances, odds.

     Wareware-ni-wa kachi-me-ga-nai. (我々には勝ち目がない.) The odds are against us. / The game is hopeless.

kachi-me-no-nai 〈勝ち目のない〉 hopeless, losing, lost.

     kachi-me-no-nai sensô 〈勝ち目のない戦争〉 a hopeless war

kachi-nuku 〈かちぬく：勝ち抜く〉 fight successfully through, win through.

kachi-toru 〈かちとる：勝ち取る〉 gain, obtain, win.

kadai 〈かだい：課題〉 a subject, a theme; homework, exercises.

kadai 〈かだい：過大〉

kadai-na 〈過大な〉 excessive, unreasonable, exaggerated, too much.

     kadai-na-yôkyû 〈過大な要求〉 an excessive demand

kadai-ni 〈過大に〉 excessively, unreasonably, exaggeratedly, too much.

     kadai-ni hyôka-suru 〈過大に評価する〉 overestimate

kadan 〈かだん：花壇〉 a flower bed.

kado 〈かど：角〉 a corner.

     kado no mise 〈角の店〉 a shop at the corner

     kado o magaru 〈角を曲がる〉 turn a corner

kado-o-magatte-sugu-no-biru〈角を曲がってすぐのビル〉 the building just around the corner

kado〈かど〉a charge, suspicion, ground, a point.

~-no-kado-de〈〜のかどで〉 on a charge of... , on the ground that...

kado〈かど：過度〉excess.

kado-no〈過度の〉too much, excessive.

kado-ni〈過度に〉too much, excessively.

kadō〈かどう：華道〉the art of flower arrangement, floral art.

kâdo〈カード〉a card.

kô-kâdo〈好カード〉 a drawing card

kado-matsu〈かどまつ：門松〉the (New Year's) decoration pines.

kae-dama〈かえだま：替え玉〉a substitute, a dummy.

kae-dama o tsukau〈替え玉を使う〉 employ a substitute, use a dummy

kaede〈かえで〉a maple tree.

kaen-bin〈かえんびん：火炎瓶〉a gasoline bomb.

kaeri〈かえり：帰り〉return, coming back(*or* home).

kaeri-ga-osoi〈帰りが遅い〉 be late (in) coming back

kaeri-o-isogu〈帰りを急ぐ〉 hurry back

kaeri-ni〈帰りに〉on one's way home(*or* back).

kaeri-zaki〈かえりざき：返り咲き〉a comeback.

kaeri-zaku〈返り咲く〉make one's comeback ((on)).

kaeru〈かえる：帰(返)る〉return, come(*or* go) back, be back, say good-by.

gaikoku-kara kaeru〈外国から帰る〉 return from abroad

ie-ni-kaeru〈家に帰る〉 come home

O-kaeri!〈お帰り.〉 Welcome home!

Mô kaera-nakereba-narimasen.〈もう帰らなければなりません.〉 I must say good-by now.

ware-ni-kaeru〈我に返る〉 return to oneself

kaeru〈かえる〉be hatched, hatch.

kaesu〈かえす〉hatch.

kaeru〈かえる〉a frog.

Kaeru-no-ko wa kaeru.〈かえるの子はかえる.〉 Like breeds like.

kaeru〈かえる：変(替, 換, 代)える〉change, alter, convert, exchange.

kao-iro o kaeru〈顔色を変える〉 change color

shôbai o kaeru〈商売を替える〉 change one's occupation

shinro o kaeru〈針路を変える〉 alter the course

genkin-ni kaeru（現金に換える） convert ((a thing)) into cashes

Amerika-doru-shihei o en-ni kaeru（アメリカドル紙幣を円に替える）
exchange American dollar bills for yen in Japanese currency

kaeshi〈かえし：返し〉a gift sent in return.

～-no-o-kaeshi-ni〈～のお返しに〉in return for... .

kaesu〈かえす：返す〉return, give(or hand) back, put back, pay back, send back.

hon o kaesu（本を返す） return a book

kane o kaesu（金を返す） pay the money back

kowareta tsubo o kaesu（壊れたつぼを返す） send a broken vase back

kaette〈かえって〉on the contrary, rather, all the more.

kafû〈かふう：家風〉a family tradition.

kafû-ni-awa-nai（家風に合わない） do not harmonize with one's family tradition

kafuku-bu〈かふくぶ：下腹部〉the abdomen.

kafun〈かふん：花粉〉pollen.

kafusu〈カフス〉cuffs.

kafusu-botan（カフスボタン） cuff links, cuff buttons.

kagai〈かがい：課外〉

kagai-katsudô（課外活動） extracurricular activities

kagai-no〈課外の〉extracurricular.

kagai-sha〈かがいしゃ：加害者〉an assailant, a murderer.

kagaku〈かがく：科学〉science.

shizen-kagaku（自然科学） natural science

kagaku-sha（科学者） a scientist

kagaku-no or kagaku-teki(-na)〈科学の，科学的(な)〉scientific.

kagaku-teki-ni〈科学的に〉scientifically.

kagaku〈かがく：化学〉chemistry.

kagaku-kôgyô（化学工業） chemical industry

kagaku-yakuhin（化学薬品） chemicals

ôyô-kagaku（応用化学） applied chemistry

kagaku-no〈化学の〉chemical.

kagameru〈かがめる〉stoop, bend.

koshi-o-kagamete-aruku（腰をかがめて歩く） stoop in walking

kagamu〈かがむ〉stoop down, bend forward(or over), crouch.

kagande-hon-o-hiroi-ageru（かがんで本を拾い上げる） stoop down to pick up a book

kagami〈かがみ：鏡〉a mirror, a looking glass.

  kagami-ni utsuru〈鏡に映る〉 be reflected in a mirror

  kagami-no-yō-ni-nameraka-na〈鏡のように滑らかな〉 as smooth as glass

kagari-bi〈かがりび：かがり火〉a bonfire, a campfire.

kagaru〈かがる〉whip, cross-stitch, hemstitch, darn.

  botan-ana o kagaru（ボタン穴をかがる） work button holes

kagayakasu〈かがやかす：輝かす〉light up, brighten.

  me-o-kagayakashite〈目を輝かして〉with bright eyes.

kagayaki〈かがやき：輝き〉brilliancy, radiance, brightness.

  kagayakashii〈輝かしい〉brilliant, radiant, bright.

kagayaku〈かがやく：輝く〉shine, glitter, twinkle, sparkle, light up, brighten.

  yorokobi-ni kagayaku（喜びに輝く） sparkle with joy

  kagayaku〈輝く〉twinkling, sparkling, bright.

    kagayaku hoshi（輝く星） twinkling stars

    kagayaku yōkō（輝く陽光） bright sunshine

kage〈かげ：影(陰)〉a shadow, a reflection, shade.

  kage-bōshi（影法師） a shadow, a silhouette

  ko-kaga-de（木陰で） in the shade of a tree

  kage-o-otosu〈影を落とす〉cast a shadow ((on)).

  kage-no-ooi〈陰の多い〉shadowy.

  kage-no-usui〈影の薄い〉unimpressive.

  kage-de〈陰で〉behind ((a person's)) back, in secret, behind the scenes.

kage-boshi〈かげぼし：陰干し〉

  kage-boshi-ni-suru〈陰干しにする〉dry in the shade.

kage-guchi〈かげぐち：陰口〉backbiting.

  kage-guchi-o-kiku〈陰口をきく〉speak ill of ((others)) in ((their)) absence.

kage-hinata〈かげひなた：影日なた〉

  kage-hinata-no-aru〈影日なたのある〉double-hearted, double-dealing.

    kage-hinata-no-nai（影日なたのない） honest, conscientious

kageki〈かげき：歌劇〉an opera.

  kageki-dan（歌劇団） an opera company

kageki〈かげき：過激〉

  kageki-ha（過激派） the extremists

  kageki-na〈過激な〉extreme, excessive, radical.

    kageki-na undō（過激な運動） excessive exercise

kagen〈かげん：加減〉allowance; a degree, an extent; seasoning;

adjustment, fixing; one's condition; addition and subtraction.

　　Yu-kagen wa ikaga-desu-ka? (湯加減はいかがですか.) How is the bath?

　　Kono shichû wa ii aji-kagen-da. (このシチューはいい味加減だ.) This stew is well seasoned.

　　Kyô-wa o-kagen wa ikaga-desu-ka? (今日はお加減はいかがですか.) How do you feel today?

　　kagen-jôjo (加減乗除) addition, subtraction, multiplication, and division

kagen-suru 〈加減する〉 allow ((for)), make allowance ((for)); season; moderate, adjust.

ii-kagen-ni 〈いい加減に〉 in a perfunctory manner.

kagerô 〈かげろう〉 a dayfly.

kagerô 〈かげろう〉 heat waves.

kageru 〈かげる：陰る〉 get dark; be clouded, be obscured [by the clouds].

kagi 〈かぎ〉 a key.

　　doa no kagi (ドアのかぎ) a key to a door

　　seikô no kagi (成功のかぎ) the key to success

　　kagi-ana (かぎ穴) a keyhole

　　kagikko (かぎっ子) a door-key child

kagi-o-kakeru 〈かぎを掛ける〉 lock.

　　kagi-o-akeru (かぎを開ける) unlock

kagi 〈かぎ〉 a hook.

kagi-gata-no 〈かぎ形の〉 hooked, hook-shaped.

kagiri 〈かぎり：限り〉 a limit, an end, bounds.

kagiri-no-nai 〈限りのない〉 limitless, endless.

kagiri-naku 〈限りなく〉 without limit, endlessly.

-kagiri 〈-かぎり：-限り〉 as long as, as far as, as...as.

　　ikite-iru-kagiri (生きている限り) as long as one lives

　　shitte-iru-kagiri (知っている限り) as far as one knows

　　dekiru-kagiri-hayaku (できる限り早く) as soon as possible

　　kondo-kagiri (今度限り) for this once, (for) this time only

　　kon・ya-ni-kagitte (今夜に限って) just for tonight

kagiru 〈かぎる：限る〉 limit, restrict.

kagirareru 〈限られる〉 be limited.

〜-to-wa-kagira-nai 〈〜とは限らない〉 be(or do) not always(or necessarily) ... , not all(or every)...be.

kagi-tsukeru〈かぎつける：かぎ付ける〉smell out.

kago〈かご〉a basket, a cage.
　　kai-mono-kago（買い物かご）a shopping basket
　　kago-no tori（かごの鳥）a bird in a cage

kagō〈かごう：化合〉chemical combination.
　　kagō-butsu（化合物）a (chemical) compound
　kagô-suru〈化合する〉combine ((with)).

kagu〈かぐ：家具〉furniture.
　　kagu-ten（家具店）a furniture store(*or* shop)
　kagu-tsuki-no〈家具付きの〉furnished.

kagu〈かぐ〉smell, sniff.
　　kagi-mawaru（かぎ回る）sniff about, nose about

kagyô〈かぎょう：家業〉one's trade, one's business, one's occupation.
　　kagyô-ni-sei-o-dasu（家業に精を出す）attend closely to one's business

kahan〈かはん：河畔〉the banks of a river, the riverside.
　　kahan-no-yado（河畔の宿）a riverside inn

ka-hanshin〈かはんしん：下半身〉the lower half of the body.

ka-han-sū〈かはんすう：過半数〉the greater part ((of)), the majority, more than half.
　　ka-han-sū o uru（過半数を得る）hold a majority
　　ka-han-sū o waru（過半数を割る）lack a majority

kahei〈かへい：貨幣〉money, currency, a coin.

ka-hi〈かひ：可否〉right or wrong, propriety, aye and no.
　　tôhyô-de teian-no-ka-hi o kimeru（投票で提案の可否を決める）decide one's proposal by vote

kahitsu〈かひつ：加筆〉
　kahitsu-suru〈加筆する〉correct, touch up, revise.

kahō〈かほう：家宝〉an heirloom, a family treasure.

kahō〈かほう：果報〉luck, (good) fortune.
　　Kahô wa nete-mate.（果報は寝て待て．）Everything comes to those who wait.
　　kahô-mono（果報者）a lucky fellow

ka-hogo〈かほご：過保護〉
　ka-hogo-na〈過保護な〉over-protective; over-protected.
　　ka-hogo-na haha-oya（過保護な母親）an overly protective mother
　　ka-hogo-na musume（過保護な娘）an over-protected daughter

kai〈かい：会〉a meeting, a party, a meet; a club, a society.

kai o hiraku（会を開く）open a meeting

kai ni shusseki-suru（会に出席する）attend a meeting

kai〈かい：櫂〉an oar, a paddle, a scull.

kai de kogu〈かいでこぐ〉oar, paddle.

kai〈かい：貝〉a shellfish.

kai〈かい：下位〉a low(er) rank.

kai-dasha（下位打者）low-ranking batters

kai-ni-ochiru〈下位に落ちる〉sink in the scale.

kai〈かい：階〉a story, a floor.

ikkai（一階）the first floor, the ground floor

ni-kai-date-no-ie（二階建ての家）a two-story house

kai〈かい：回〉a time, a round, an inning.

ikkai（一回）once

ni-kai（二回）two times, twice

san-kai（三回）three times

nen yon-kai（年四回）four times a year

jukkai-sen（十回戦）a ten-rounder

san-kai no ura（三回の裏）the second half of the third inning

kai〈かい〉

kai-ga-aru〈かいがある〉be rewarded, be worth while.

Kare-wa doryoku-no-kai-ga-atta.（彼は努力のかいがあった.）His efforts have been rewarded.

yomi-gai-ga-aru（読みがいがある）be worth while reading

kai-ga-nai〈かいがない〉be of no use, be in vain.

doryoku-no-kai-naku（努力のかいなく）in spite of one's efforts

-kai〈-かい：-界〉a world, a circle, a kingdom.

bungaku-kai（文学界）the literary world

jitsugyô-kai（実業界）business circles

dôbutsu-kai（動物界）the animal kingdom

kai-age〈かいあげ：買い上げ〉purchase, buying.

seifu-no kai-age-kakaku（政府の買い上げ価格）the government's purchasing price

kai-ageru〈買い上げる〉purchase, buy.

kaiaku〈かいあく：改悪〉

kaiaku-suru〈改悪する〉change ((a thing)) for the worse.

kai-bashira〈かいばしら：貝柱〉an adductor〔of a shellfish〕.

kaibatsu〈かいばつ：海抜〉above the sea.

kaibatsu sen-mêtoru（海抜千メートル）1,000 meters above the sea

kaibô〈かいぼう：解剖〉dissection.

    kaibô-gaku〈解剖学〉anatomy

    kaibô-suru〈解剖する〉dissect.

kai-bunsho〈かいぶんしょ：怪文書〉a mysterious document, a reprehensive document.

kaibutsu〈かいぶつ：怪物〉a monster.

kaichiku〈かいちく：改築〉rebuilding, reconstruction.

    kaichiku-chû-de-aru（改築中である）be under reconstruction

    kaichiku-suru〈改築する〉rebuild, reconstruct.

kai-chô〈かいちょう：会長〉the president, the chairman.

kaichô〈かいちょう：快調〉

    kaichô-de-aru〈快調である〉be in the best condition, be going on smoothly.

kaichû〈かいちゅう：回虫〉a roundworm.

    kaichû ga waku（回虫がわく）get roundworms

kaichû〈かいちゅう：海中〉

    kaichû-ni〈海中に〉in the sea.

kaichû-dentô〈かいちゅうでんとう：懐中電灯〉a flashlight, an electric torch.

kaidai〈かいだい：改題〉

    kaidai-suru〈改題する〉change the title ((of)).

kaidaku〈かいだく：快諾〉

    kaidaku-suru〈快諾する〉consent willingly, give a ready consent.

kai-dame〈かいだめ：買いだめ〉hoarding.

    kai-dame-suru〈買いだめする〉hoard.

kaidan〈かいだん：階段〉(a flight of) stairs, steps, a staircase.

    kaidan-o-agaru（階段を上がる）go up the stairs, go upstairs

    kaidan-o-oriru（階段を降りる）go down the stairs, go downstairs

kaidan〈かいだん：会談〉a conversation, a talk, a conference.

    shunô-kaidan（首脳会談）a summit conference

    kaidan-suru〈会談する〉talk together, have a talk ((with)), have a conference ((with)).

kaidan〈かいだん：怪談〉a ghost story.

kai-dasu〈かいだす：かい出す〉bail (out).

kaidô〈かいどう：街道〉a highway.

    hon-kaidô（本街道）the main road

kaidoku〈かいどく：解読〉

    kaidoku-suru〈解読する〉decipher, decode.

kaien〈かいえん：開演〉
  kaien-suru〈開演する〉raise the curtain, open performance.
kaifû〈かいふう：開封〉
  kaifû-suru〈開封する〉open〔an envelope〕, unseal.
kaifuku〈かいふく：回復〉recovery, restoration.
    tenkô no kaifuku（天候の回復）improvement of the weather
  kaifuku-ni-mukau〈回復に向かう〉be getting better.
  kaifuku-suru〈回復する〉recover, restore.
    genki o kaifuku-suru（元気を回復する）recover one's spirits
    kenkô o kaifuku-suru（健康を回復する）recover one's health
    kanzen-ni kaifuku-suru（完全に回復する）be completely recovered〔from illness〕
  kaifuku-ryoku-no-aru〈回復力のある〉recuperative.
kaifuku-shujutsu〈かいふくしゅじゅつ：開腹手術〉an abdominal operation, laparotomy.
kaiga〈かいが：絵画〉pictures, paintings, drawings.
kaigai〈かいがい：海外〉
    kaigai-hôsô（海外放送）overseas broadcasting
    kaigai-jijô（海外事情）foreign affairs
    kaigai-ryokô（海外旅行）a foreign travel
  kaigai-no〈海外の〉foreign, oversea(s).
  kaigai-de, kaigai-e or *kaigai-ni*〈海外で、海外へ、海外に〉abroad, oversea(s).
  kaigai-kara〈海外から〉from abroad.
kaigan〈かいがん：海岸〉the seashore, the seaside, the coast, the beach.
    kaigan-sen（海岸線）the shoreline, the coastline
  kaigan-de, kaigan-ni or *kaigan-o*〈海岸で、海岸に、海岸を〉on the shore, at the seaside, on the beach.
  kaigan-ni-sotte or *kaigan-zoi-ni*〈海岸に沿って、海岸沿いに〉along the seashore, along the coast.
kai-gara〈かいがら：貝殻〉a shell.
    kai-gara o hirou（貝殻を拾う）gather shells
    kai-gara-zaiku（貝殻細工）shellwork
kaigen-rei〈かいげんれい：戒厳令〉(the) martial law.
    kaigen-rei o shiku（戒厳令を敷く）impose martial law ((on))
    kaigen-rei o toku（戒厳令を解く）withdraw martial law
kaigi〈かいぎ：会議〉a conference, a meeting.
    kaigi o hiraku（会議を開く）hold a conference

　　　kaigi-shitsu〈会議室〉 a conference room
　　kaigi-suru〈会議する〉confer, meet.
　　kaigi-chû-de-aru〈会議中である〉be in conference.
kaigi(-shin)〈かいぎ(しん)：懐疑(心)〉doubt, skepticism.
　　kaigi-teki(-na)〈懐疑的(な)〉skeptic(al).
kaigô〈かいごう：会合〉a meeting, a gathering, an assembly.
　　kaigô-suru〈会合する〉meet, gather, assemble.
kaigun〈かいぐん：海軍〉the navy.
　　kaigun-no〈海軍の〉naval.
kaigyô〈かいぎょう：開業〉opening of (a) business.
　　　kaigyô-i〈開業医〉 a medical practitioner
　　kaigyô-suru〈開業する〉start (a) business, start practice.
kaigyô〈かいぎょう：改行〉
　　kaigyô-suru〈改行する〉start a new paragraph.
kaihan〈かいはん：改版〉revision; a revised edition.
　　kaihan-suru〈改版する〉revise; issue a revised edition.
kaihatsu〈かいはつ：開発〉development, exploitation.
　　　kaihatsu-tojô-koku〈開発途上国〉 a developing country
　　kaihatsu-suru〈開発する〉develop, exploit.
kaihei〈かいへい：海兵〉a marine.
　　　kaihei-tai〈海兵隊〉 the Marine Corps
kaihei-ki〈かいへいき：開閉器〉a switch.
　　　jidô-kaihei-ki〈自動開閉器〉 an automatic switch
kai-hi〈かいひ：会費〉a (membership) fee.
kaihi〈かいひ：回避〉evasion, avoidance.
　　kaihi-suru〈回避する〉evade, avoid.
kaihô〈かいほう：介抱〉nursing.
　　kaihô-suru〈介抱する〉nurse, look ((after)), care ((for)), attend ((on)).
　　　byônin o kaihô-suru〈病人を介抱する〉 nurse a sick person
kaihô〈かいほう：快方〉
　　kaihô-ni-mukau〈快方に向かう〉get better, become convalescent.
kaihô〈かいほう：会報〉a bulletin, the transactions.
kaihô〈かいほう：解放〉release, emancipation.
　　kaihô-suru〈解放する〉release, emancipate, set ((a person)) free.
kaihô〈かいほう：開放〉opening.
　　　Kaihô-genkin.〈開放厳禁.〉 Don't leave the door open.
　　kaihô-suru〈開放する〉open, leave open.
　　kaihô-teki-na〈開放的な〉openhearted, frank, candid.

kaihyô〈かいひょう：開票〉

kaihyô-suru〈開票する〉open the ballot boxes.

kaihyô〈かいひょう：解氷〉thawing (of ice).

kaihyô-suru〈解氷する〉thaw.

kaiin〈かいいん：会員〉a member, membership.

kaiin-meibo〈会員名簿〉 a list of members

kaiin-sei〈会員制〉 the membership system

kaiin-ni-naru〈会員になる〉become a member, join a society.

kaiin〈かいいん：海員〉a seaman, a crew.

kai-inu〈かいいぬ：飼い犬〉a house dog, a pet dog.

kai-ire〈かいいれ：買い入れ〉purchase, buying.

kai-ireru〈買い入れる〉purchase, buy, lay in.

kaiji〈かいじ：海事〉maritime affairs.

kaijin〈かいじん：灰じん〉ashes.

kaijin-ni-kisuru〈灰じんに帰する〉 be reduced to ashes

kaijo〈かいじょ：解除〉cancellation, release.

kaijo-suru〈解除する〉cancel, release.

keiyaku o kaijo-suru〈契約を解除する〉 cancel a contract

kaijô〈かいじょう：会場〉the place of meeting.

kaijô〈かいじょう：階上〉

kaijô-de or *kaijô-ni*〈階上で，階上に〉upstairs.

kaijô〈かいじょう：海上〉

kaijô-hoken〈海上保険〉 marine insurance

kaijô-de or *kaijô-ni*〈海上で，海上に〉on the sea, at sea.

kaijô〈かいじょう：開場〉

kaijô-suru〈開場する〉open, open the doors.

kaijû〈かいじゅう：怪獣〉a monster.

kaijû〈かいじゅう：懐柔〉conciliation.

kaijû-saku〈懐柔策〉 a conciliatory measure

kaijû-suru〈懐柔する〉consiliate.

kaika〈かいか：階下〉

kaika-de or *kaika-ni*〈階下で，階下に〉downstairs.

kai-kaburu〈かいかぶる：買いかぶる〉overestimate, think too highly(or much) ((of)).

kaikai〈かいかい：開会〉

kaikai-no kotoba〈開会の言葉〉 an opening address

kaikai-shiki〈開会式〉 an opening ceremony

kaikai-suru〈開会する〉open a meeting.

kaikai-chû-de-aru〈開会中である〉be open, be in session.

kaikaku〈かいかく：改革〉(a) reform, reformation.
    kaikaku o okonau（改革を行う）carry out a reform
kaikaku-suru〈改革する〉reform.

kaikan〈かいかん：会館〉a hall, an assembly hall, a club-house.

kaikan〈かいかん：開館〉the opening.
kaikan-suru〈開館する〉open〔a hall〕.

kaikan〈かいかん：快感〉a pleasant sensation.
kaikan-o-oboeru〈快感を覚える〉feel pleasure.

kaikatsu〈かいかつ：快活〉
kaikatsu-na〈快活な〉cheerful, merry.
kaikatsu-ni〈快活に〉cheerfully, lightheartedly.

kaikei〈かいけい：会計〉accounts, finance.
    kaikei-bo（会計簿）an account book
    kaikei-gakari（会計係）an accountant, a cashier
    kaikei-hôkoku（会計報告）a financial report
    kaikei-kensa（会計検査）auditing
    kaikei-nendo（会計年度）a fiscal year

kaiken〈かいけん：会見〉an interview.
    kaiken-o-môshi-komu（会見を申し込む）ask for an interview ((with))
    kisha-kaiken（記者会見）a press interview
kaiken-suru〈会見する〉interview, have an interview ((with)), meet.

kaiketsu〈かいけつ：解決〉solution, settlement.
kaiketsu-suru〈解決する〉solve, settle.
kaiketsu-ga-tsuku〈解決が付く〉be solved, be settled, come to a settlement.

kaiketsu-byô〈かいけつびょう：壊血病〉scurvy.

kaiki〈かいき：会期〉a session, a period, a term.
    kaiki o enchô-suru（会期を延長する）extend the session

kaikin〈かいきん：解禁〉removal of an embargo, the opening.
kaikin-suru〈解禁する〉remove an embargo ((on)).

kaikin〈かいきん：皆勤〉
kaikin-suru〈皆勤する〉attend regularly.

kai-kiru〈かいきる：買い切る〉reserve, book; buy up.

kaiki-sen〈かいきせん：回帰線〉the tropics.
    kita-kaiki-sen（北回帰線）the tropic of Cancer
    minami-kaiki-sen（南回帰線）the tropic of Capricorn

kaiki-shoku〈かいきしょく：皆既食〉a total eclipse.

kaiko 〈かいこ：蚕〉a silkworm.

kaiko o kau〈蚕を飼う〉 raise silkworms

kaiko 〈かいこ：解雇〉discharge, dismissal, layoff.

kaiko-suru〈解雇する〉discharge, dismiss, turn off, fire.

kaiko 〈かいこ：回顧〉recollection, retrospection.

kaiko-roku〈回顧録〉 reminiscences, memoirs

kaiko-suru〈回顧する〉recollect, look back ((at, over *or* upon)), recall.

kaikō 〈かいこう：開校〉the opening of a school.

kaikô-kinen-bi〈開校記念日〉 an anniversary of the founding of a school

kaikô-suru〈開校する〉open a school.

kaikō 〈かいこう：海溝〉a deep, a trench.

Nihon-kaikô〈日本海溝〉 the Japan Deep

kaikoku 〈かいこく：戒告〉a warning.

kai-komu 〈かいこむ：買い込む〉purchase, lay in.

kaikon 〈かいこん：開墾〉reclamation.

kaikon-suru〈開墾する〉reclaim.

are-chi o kaikon-suru〈荒れ地を開墾する〉 reclaim waste land

kaikyo 〈かいきょ：快挙〉a brilliant deed.

kaikyō 〈かいきょう：回教〉Mohammedanism, Islamism.

kaikyô-to〈回教徒〉 a Mohammedan, an Islamite

kaikyô-no〈回教の〉Moslem, Islamitic.

kaikyō 〈かいきょう：海峡〉a strait, a channel.

Tsushima-kaikyô〈対馬海峡〉 the Straits of Tsushima

Igirisu-kaikyô〈イギリス海峡〉 the Channel

kaikyū 〈かいきゅう：階級〉(a) class.

kaikyû-ishiki〈階級意識〉 class consciousness

chûryû-kaikyû〈中流階級〉 the middle class(es)

kaimaku 〈かいまく：開幕〉

kaimaku-jiai〈開幕試合〉 a season opener

Gogo-yo-ji-kaimaku.〈午後四時開幕。〉 The curtain rises at 4p.m.

kaimei 〈かいめい：解明〉elucidation, explication.

kaimei-suru〈解明する〉make clear, elucidate, throw light ((upon)), explicate.

kaimei 〈かいめい：改名〉

kaimei-suru〈改名する〉change one's name.

kaimen 〈かいめん：海綿〉a sponge.

kaimen-jô-no or *kaimen-no-yô-na*〈海綿状の，海綿のような〉spongy.

kaimen 〈かいめん：海面〉 the surface of the sea, the sea level.

kaimetsu 〈かいめつ：壊滅〉 destruction.
kaimetsu-suru 〈壊滅する〉 be destroyed.
kaimetsu-saseru 〈壊滅させる〉 destroy.
kaimetsu-teki(-na) 〈壊滅的（な）〉 crushing, deadly.
   kaimetsu-teki dageki 〈壊滅的な打撃〉 a crushing blow

kai-modoshi 〈かいもどし：買い戻し〉 repurchase.
kai-modosu 〈買い戻す〉 buy back, repurchase, redeem.

kaimoku 〈かいもく：皆目〉 quite, altogether, utterly; ((not)) at all.

kai-mono 〈かいもの：買い物〉 shopping.
   kai-mono-ni-iku 〈買い物に行く〉 go shopping
   kai-mono-o-suru 〈買い物をする〉 do one's shopping
   kai-mono-ni-dete-iru 〈買い物に出ている〉 be out shopping

kaimyô 〈かいみょう：戒名〉 a posthumous·Buddhist name.

kain 〈かいん：下院〉 the Lower House, the House of Representatives, the House of Commons.

kainan 〈かいなん：海難〉 a disaster at sea.
   kainan-kyûjo 〈海難救助〉 sea rescue

kai-narasu 〈かいならす：飼いならす〉 domesticate, tame.
kai-narasareta 〈飼いならされた〉 tame, domesticated.

kai-ne 〈かいね：買い値〉 the purchase price.

kai-neko 〈かいねこ：飼い猫〉 a house cat, a pet cat.

kainin 〈かいにん：解任〉
kainin-suru 〈解任する〉 dismiss, release ((a person)) from office.

kai-nushi 〈かいぬし：飼い主〉 a pet owner.

kai-nushi 〈かいぬし：買い主〉 a buyer, a purchaser.

kainyû 〈かいにゅう：介入〉 intervention.
kainyû-suru 〈介入する〉 intervene.

kaiô-sei 〈かいおうせい：海王星〉 Neptune.

kairai 〈かいらい〉 a puppet.
   kairai-seifu 〈かいらい政府〉 a puppet government

kairaku 〈かいらく：快楽〉 pleasure.
   kairaku-ni-fukeru 〈快楽にふける〉 be given to pleasure

kairan 〈かいらん：回覧〉 circulation.
   kairan-ban 〈回覧板〉 a circular notice
kairan-suru 〈回覧する〉 circulate, read and pass on.

kairi 〈かいり：海里〉 a nautical mile.

kairitsu 〈かいりつ：戒律〉 Buddhist precepts, commandments.

kairo〈かいろ：懐炉〉a body warmer.

kairo〈かいろ：海路〉a sea route.

kairo〈かいろ：回路〉a circuit.

kairô〈かいろう：回廊〉a corridor, a gallery.

kai-rui〈かいるい：貝類〉shellfish.

kairyô〈かいりょう：改良〉(an) improvement, (a) reform, betterment.

    kairyô-no-yochi-ga-aru（改良の余地がある）have some room for
    further improvement

  kairyô-suru〈改良する〉improve, reform, make ((a thing)) better.

  kairyô-shita〈改良した〉improved, reformed.

kairyû〈かいりゅう：海流〉an ocean current.

kaisai〈かいさい：開催〉

  kaisai-suru〈開催する〉hold〔a meeting〕.

kaisan〈かいさん：解散〉breakup; dissolution.

  kaisan-suru〈解散する〉break up; be dissolved.

kaisan-butsu〈かいさんぶつ：海産物〉marine products.

kaisatsu〈かいさつ：改札〉the examination of tickets.

    kaisatsu-gakari（改札係）a ticket examiner

    kaisatsu-guchi（改札口）a wicket

  kaisatsu-suru〈改札する〉examine(punch *or* collect) tickets.

kaisei〈かいせい：改正〉(a) revision, (an) amendment, (an) alteration, (a)
  change.

  kaisei-suru〈改正する〉revise, amend, alter, change.

kaisei〈かいせい：快晴〉fair weather.

kaiseki〈かいせき：解析〉analysis.

    kaiseki-kika-gaku（解析幾何学）analytical geometry

kaisen〈かいせん：海戦〉a naval battle.

kaisen〈かいせん：回線〉a circuit.

    denwa-kaisen（電話回線）a telecommunication line

kaisen〈かいせん〉the itch, scabies.

kaisen〈かいせん：開戦〉the outbreak of war.

  kaisen-suru〈開戦する〉open war ((against)), make war ((on)).

kaisen〈かいせん：改選〉reelection.

  kaisen-suru〈改選する〉reelect.

kaisetsu〈かいせつ：解説〉(an) explanation, a comment, a commentary.

    nyûsu-kaisetsu（ニュース解説）a news commentary

    kaisetsu-sha（解説者）a commentator

  kaisetsu-suru〈解説する〉explain, comment ((on)).

kaisetsu 〈かいせつ：開設〉establishment, opening, installation.
kaisetsu-suru 〈開設する〉establish, open, install.
kaisha 〈かいしゃ：会社〉a company, a corporation, a firm.
    kaisha o setsuritsu-suru〈会社を設立する〉 establish a company
    kaisha-ni tsutomeru〈会社に勤める〉 serve in a company
    kaisha-in〈会社員〉 a company employee, an office worker
kaishaku 〈かいしゃく：解釈〉(an) interpretation, (an) explanation.
kaishaku-suru 〈解釈する〉interpret, explain.
    zen·i·ni kaishaku-suru〈善意に解釈する〉 interpret favorably
kaishi 〈かいし：開始〉beginning, start, opening.
kaishi-suru 〈開始する〉begin, start, open.
kaishi 〈かいし：怪死〉a mysterious death.
kai-shime 〈かいしめ：買い占め〉a corner.
kai-shimeru 〈買い占める〉buy up, corner.
kaishin 〈かいしん：改心〉reform, amendment.
kaishin-suru 〈改心する〉reform oneself, mend one's ways.
kaishin 〈かいしん：会心〉
kaishin-no-saku 〈会心の作〉a work after one's heart.
kaishin 〈かいしん：回診〉
kaishin-suru 〈回診する〉make a round of visits to one's patients.
kaisho 〈かいしょ：かい書〉the square style of Chinese character writing.
kaishō 〈かいしょう：かい性〉
kaishō-no-nai 〈かい性のない〉good-for-nothing, shiftless.
kaishō 〈かいしょう：解消〉(a) dissolution, (a) cancellation.
kaishō-suru 〈解消する〉dissolve, be dissolved, cancel, be canceled.
    kekkon o kaishō-suru〈結婚を解消する〉 dissolve one's marriage
kaishō 〈かいしょう：改称〉
kaishō-suru 〈改称する〉change the name(*or* title)((to)).
kaishō 〈かいしょう：快勝〉a sweeping victory.
kaishō-suru 〈快勝する〉win a sweeping victory.
kaishoku 〈かいしょく：会食〉
kaishoku-suru 〈会食する〉dine with, dine together.
kaishû 〈かいしゅう：回収〉withdrawal, collection.
kaishû-suru 〈回収する〉withdraw, draw back, collect.
    uri-kake-kin o kaishû-suru〈売り掛け金を回収する〉 collect bills
kaishû 〈かいしゅう：改宗〉conversion.
kaishû-suru 〈改宗する〉be converted ((to)).
kaishû 〈かいしゅう：改修〉repair, improvement.

　　　kasen-kaishû〈河川改修〉 river improvement

　kaishû-suru〈改修する〉repair, improve.

kaishun〈かいしゅん：改しゅん〉repentance, penitence.

　kaishun-suru〈改しゅんする〉repent ((of)), be penitent ((of)).

kaisô〈かいそう：海そう〉 seaweeds.

kaisô〈かいそう：回想〉*see.*　kaiko（回顧）.

kaisô〈かいそう：会葬〉

　kaisô-suru〈会葬する〉attend a funeral.

kaisô〈かいそう：回送〉

　　　kaisô-sha（回送車）　an out-of-service car

　kaisô-suru〈回送する〉forward, send on.

kaisô〈かいそう：改装〉

　kaisô-suru〈改装する〉remodel, refit, do over.

　　　mise o kaisô-suru（店を改装する）　refit a store

kaisô〈かいそう：かい走〉

　kaisô-suru〈かい走する〉be routed, be put to rout.

kaisoku〈かいそく：快速〉a high speed.

　　　kaisoku-densha（快速電車）　a rapid service train.

kaisoku〈かいそく：会則〉the regulations of an association.

kaison〈かいそん：海損〉an average.

　　　kyôdô-kaison（共同海損）　a general average

kaisû〈かいすう：回数〉the number of times.

　　　kaisû-ken（回数券）　a commutation(*or* coupon) ticket

kaisui〈かいすい：海水〉seawater, saltwater.

　　　kaisui-gi（海水着）　a bathing suit

kaisui-yoku〈かいすいよく：海水浴〉sea bathing.

　　　kaisui-yoku-ni-iku（海水浴に行く）　go sea bathing

　　　kaisui-yoku-jô（海水浴場）　a bathing place, a seaside resort

kaitai〈かいたい：解体〉

　kaitai-suru〈解体する〉disjoint, take to pieces, break up, pull down; disorganize.

kaitaku〈かいたく：開拓〉reclamation; development, exploitation.

　　　kaitaku-sha（開拓者）　a pioneer, a colonist, a settler

　kaitaku-suru〈開拓する〉reclaim, develop, exploit.

　　　atarashii shijô o kaitaku-suru（新しい市場を開拓する）　open a new market ((for))

kai-tate〈かいたて：買いたて〉

　kai-tate-no〈買いたての〉newly-bought.

kai-te〈かいて：買い手〉a buyer, a consumer.
  kai-te-ga-tsuku（買い手が付く）find a ready buyer
  kai-te-ga-nai（買い手がない）have no demand
  kai-te-shijô（買い手市場）a buyers' market
kaitei〈かいてい：海底〉the bottom of the sea.
  kaitei-ni shizumu（海底に沈む）sink to the bottom of the sea
  kaitei-tonneru（海底トンネル）an undersea tunnel
  kaitei-yuden（海底油田）a submarine oil field
kaitei〈かいてい：改訂〉revision.
  kaitei-zôho-ban（改訂増補版）a revised and enlarged edition
  kaitei-suru〈改訂する〉revise.
kaitei〈かいてい：開廷〉
  kaitei-suru〈開廷する〉open a court, sit.
kaiteki〈かいてき：快適〉
  kaiteki-na〈快適な〉comfortable, pleasant, agreeable.
  kaiteki-na heya（快適な部屋）a comfortable room
kaiten〈かいてん：回転〉revolution, rotation.
  kaiten-doa（回転ドア）a revolving door
  kaiten-isu（回転いす）a swivel chair
  kaiten-mado（回転窓）a pivoted window
  kaiten-mokuba（回転木馬）a merry-go-round
  kaiten-suru〈回転する〉revolve, rotate, turn round, run.
kaiten〈かいてん：開店〉
  kaiten-suru〈開店する〉open a store(*or* shop).
kaitô〈かいとう：解答〉an answer, a solution.
  kaitô-suru〈解答する〉answer, solve.
  tadashii-kaitô-o-suru（正しい解答をする）answer correctly
kaitô〈かいとう：回答〉a reply, an answer.
  kaitô-suru〈回答する〉reply ((to)), give a reply ((to)), answer, give an answer ((to)).
kaitô〈かいとう：解凍〉thawing.
kaitsū〈かいつう：開通〉
  kaitsû-shiki（開通式）an opening ceremony〔of a railway〕
  kaitsû-suru〈開通する〉be opened to traffic, be reopened for service.
kai-tsuke〈かいつけ：買い付け〉
  kai-tsuke-no mise（買い付けの店）one's favorite store
kai-tsumamu〈かいつまむ：かい摘まむ〉
  kai-tsumande-ieba〈かいつまんで言えば〉in short, in a word, to make a

long story short, to be short.

kaiun 〈かいうん：海運〉 shipping, marine transportation.

    kaiun-kai（海運界） the shipping world

kaiun 〈かいうん：開運〉

    kaiun no o-mamori（開運のお守り） a charm for luck

kaiwa 〈かいわ：会話〉 (a) conversation.

    Doitsu-go-kaiwa-ga-umai（ドイツ語会話がうまい） be good at German conversation

    Furansu-go-kaiwa-o-narau（フランス語会話を習う） take lessons in French conversation

kaiwai 〈かいわい：界わい〉 *see.* fukin（付近）.

kaiyaku 〈かいやく：解約〉

    kaiyaku-suru〈解約する〉cancel a contract.

kaiyô 〈かいよう：海洋〉 the sea(s), the ocean.

kaiyô 〈かいよう：潰瘍〉 an ulcer.

    kaiyô-ga-aru（かいようがある） have an ulcer

kaiyû-gyo 〈かいゆうぎょ：回遊魚〉a migratory fish.

kaizai 〈かいざい：介在〉

    kaizai-suru〈介在する〉lie between, exist among.

kaizen 〈かいぜん：改善〉improvement, betterment.

    kaizen-suru〈改善する〉improve, make ((a thing)) better.

    seikatsu o kaizen-suru（生活を改善する） improve one's living

kaizô 〈かいぞう：改造〉reconstruction, rebuilding, reorganization.

    kaizô-suru〈改造する〉reconstruct, rebuild, reorganize.

    naikaku o kaizô-suru（内閣を改造する） reshuffle the Cabinet

kaizoku 〈かいぞく：海賊〉a pirate.

    kaizoku-ban（海賊版） a pirate edition

    kaizoku-sen（海賊船） a pirate ship

kaizu 〈かいず：海図〉a (marine) chart.

kai-zuka 〈かいづか：貝塚〉a shell mound.

kaji 〈かじ：火事〉a fire.

    Kaji-da!（火事だ.） Fire!

    Kaji ga okita.（火事が起きた.） A fire broke out.

    kaji-ni-naru（火事になる） take fire

    kaji-ni-au（火事に遭う） suffer from a fire

    kaji-de yakeru（火事で焼ける） be destroyed in a fire

    kaji o kesu（火事を消す） put out a fire

    kajiba（火事場） the scene of a fire

kaji 〈かじ〉 a rudder, a helm, a wheel.
　kaji-o-toru 〈かじを取る〉 steer.
kaji 〈かじ：家事〉 household affairs.
　kaji-o-yaru 〈家事をやる〉 keep house.
kajikamu 〈かじかむ〉 be benumbed 〔with cold〕.
kajin 〈かじん：歌人〉 a poet, a poetess.
kajiri-tsuku 〈かじりつく：かじり付く〉 bite ((at)); hold on ((to)), stick ((to)).
kajiru 〈かじる〉 bite (at), gnaw, nibble (at).
　oya-no-sune-o-kajiru（親のすねをかじる） hang on one's parents
kajitsu 〈かじつ：果実〉 *see.* kudamono.
kajitsu 〈かじつ：過日〉 the other day, some days ago.
kajiya 〈かじや：かじ屋〉 a smith, a blacksmith.
kajô 〈かじょう：箇条〉 an article, a clause, an item, a point.
　go-kajô-kara-naru（五箇条から成る） consist of 5 articles
　kajô-gaki-ni-suru 〈箇条書きにする〉 itemize.
kajô 〈かじょう：過剰〉 an excess, a surplus.
　kajô-jinkô（過剰人口） surplus population
　seisan-kajô（生産過剰） overproduction
　kajô-no 〈過剰の〉 surplus, excessive, too much.
kaju 〈かじゅ：果樹〉 a fruit tree.
　kaju-en（果樹園） an orchard
kajû 〈かじゅう：果汁〉 fruit juice.
kajû 〈かじゅう：過重〉 overweight.
　kajû-rôdô（過重労働） overwork
kakae 〈かかえ：抱え〉
　hito-kakae-no-takigi（一抱えの薪） an armful of firewood
kakaeru 〈かかえる：抱える〉 hold ((a thing)) in one's arms, hold ((a thing)) under one's arm.
kakageru 〈かかげる：掲げる〉 hoist, hang out, put up.
kakaku 〈かかく：価格〉 price, cost.
　shôhi-sha kakaku（消費者価格） the consumers' price
kakari 〈かかり：係〉 charge, duty.
　kakari-no hito（係りの人） a person in charge
　〜-no-kakari-de-aru（〜の係りである） be in charge of...
kakari-ai 〈かかりあい：掛かり合い〉
　kakari-ai-ni-naru or *kakari-au* 〈掛かり合いになる，掛かり合う〉 be implicated ((in)), be concerned ((with)); have dealings ((with)), have

something to do ((with)).

kakari-tsuke〈かかりつけ：掛かり付け〉

kakari-tsuke-no isha〈掛かり付けの医者〉 one's family doctor

kakaru〈かかる：掛かる〉hang ((on *or* from)).

kabe-ni-kakatte-iru-e〈壁に掛かっている絵〉 a picture hanging on the wall

kakaru〈かかる：掛かる〉begin, start, set about; take, need, require; cost; consult.

shigoto-ni-kakaru〈仕事に掛かる〉 set to work

nagai jikan-ga-kakaru〈長い時間が掛かる〉 take a long time

hiyô-ga-daibu-kakaru〈費用がだいぶ掛かる〉 cost ((one)) much money

isha-ni-kakaru〈医者に掛かる〉 consult a doctor

kakaru〈かかる〉suffer from, get, catch.

byôki-ni-kakaru〈病気にかかる〉 fall ill

hashika ni kakaru〈はしかにかかる〉 catch the measles

kakaru〈かかる：掛かる〉fall ((into)), be caught.

wana-ni-kakaru〈わなに掛かる〉 be caught in a trap

-kakaru〈－かかる〉be ready ((to do)), be about ((to do)), be going ((to do)), set about ((to do)), be on the edge of ((doing)).

Taiyô ga de-kakatte-iru.〈太陽が出かかっている。〉 The sun is about to rise.

Kodomo-ga-futari obore-kakatte-iru.〈子供が二人おぼれかかっている。〉 There are two children drowning.

kakashi〈かかし〉a scarecrow.

kakasu〈かかす：欠かす〉miss, fail〔to attend〕.

ichi-nichi-mo-kakasazu-ni〈一日も欠かさずに〉 without missing a day

kakato〈かかと〉the heel.

kakawarazu〈かかわらず〉

〜*(-ni-)kakawarazu* or 〜*(-nimo-)kakawarazu*〈(〜に)かかわらず，(〜にも)かかわらず〉in spite of… , with all… , regardless of… , whether…or … .

arashi-nimo-kakawarazu〈あらしにもかかわらず〉 in spite of the storm

tenkô-ni-kakawarazu〈天候にかかわらず〉 regardless of the weather

konomu-to-konomazaru-ni-kakawarazu〈好むと好まざるにかかわらず〉 whether one likes it or not

sei-u-ni-kakawarazu〈晴雨にかかわらず〉 rain or shine

sore-nimo-kakawarazu〈それにもかかわらず〉nevertheless.

kakawari〈かかわり：係わり〉*see.* kankei.

kakawaru〈係わる〉*see.* kankei-ga-aru.

kake〈かけ〉a bet, betting, gambling.

kake ni katsu（かけに勝つ）win a bet

kake-o-suru〈かけをする〉make a bet ((on)), bet ((on)).

-kake〈-かけ：-掛け〉

bōshi-kake（帽子掛け）a hatrack

sui-kake-no tabako（吸いかけのたばこ）a half-smoked cigarette

tate-kake-no biru（建てかけのビル）a building in course of construction

shi-kaketa shigoto（しかけた仕事）an unfinished work

kake-agaru〈かけあがる：駆け上がる〉run up.

ni-kai-e kake-agaru（二階へ駆け上がる）run upstairs

kake-ashi〈かけあし：駆け足〉a run; a gallop.

kake-ashi-de（駆け足で）at a run

kake-buton〈かけぶとん：掛け布団〉a coverlet, a quilt.

kake-dashi〈かけだし：駆け出し〉

kake-dashi-no〈駆け出しの〉cub, sucking, newly-fledged.

kake-dashi-no shimbun-kisha（駆け出しの新聞記者）a cub reporter

kake-dasu〈かけだす：駆け出す〉run out, bolt.

kake-gae〈かけがえ：掛け替え〉a substitute.

kake-gae-no-nai〈掛け替えのない〉irreplaceable, irrecoverable.

kake-gae-no-nai inochi（掛け替えのない命）one's irrecoverable life

kake-gae-no-nai kodomo（掛け替えのない子供）one's dearest child

kake-goe〈かけごえ：掛け声〉a shout, a call, a cheer, a yell.

kake-goe-o-kakeru〈掛け声を掛ける〉shout time, shout encouragement.

kake-goto〈かけごと：かけ事〉*see.* kake.

kake-hanareru〈かけはなれる：かけ離れる〉be wide apart ((from)), be far ((from)), be quite different ((from)).

kake-hashi〈かけはし：掛(懸)け橋〉a suspension bridge, a bridge over a gorge.

kake-hiki〈かけひき：駆け引き〉bargaining, negotiation, tactics, stratagem.

kake-hiki-ga-umai（駆け引きがうまい）be a good hand at bargaining

kake-hiki-suru〈駆け引きする〉bargain with ((a person)) over, use tactics.

kakei〈かけい：家計〉household economy.

kakei-ga-yutaka-de-aru（家計が豊かである）be well off

kakei-ga-kurushii（家計が苦しい）be badly off

kakei-bo〔家計簿〕 a domestic account book

kakei〈かけい：家系〉a family line, lineage.

kakei-zu〔家系図〕 a family tree

kake-jiku〈かけじく：掛け軸〉a hanging scroll.

kake-kin〈かけきん：掛け金〉an instalment, a premium.

kakekko〈かけっこ：駆けっこ〉a race, a footrace.

kakekko o suru（駆けっこをする） run a race

kake-komu〈かけこむ：駆け込む〉run ((in *or* into)), seek shelter ((at *or* in)).

kake-mawaru or **kake-meguru**〈かけまわる，かけめぐる：駆け回る，駆け巡る〉run about(*or* around), busy oneself ((about)), be on the run.

kake-mochi〈かけもち：掛け持ち〉

kake-mochi-suru〈掛け持ちする〉have business in two or more places.

kake-mono〈かけもの：掛け物〉*see*. kake-jiku.

kake-ne〈かけね：掛け値〉an overcharge, a fancy price, two prices.

kake-ne-o-iu〔掛け値を言う〕 overcharge, ask two prices.

kake-ne-o-iwa-nai（掛け値を言わない） do not overcharge, ask only one price

kakera〈かけら〉a fragment, a broken piece.

kakeru〈かける：駆ける〉run, gallop.

kakeru〈かける：掛ける〉hang, suspend, put up, lay, cover ((a thing)) with; sit, sit down; sprinkle ((on *or* over)); put on, have; call, ring up; multiply; start, turn on, switch on; spend.

kabe-ni e o kakeru（壁に絵を掛ける） hang a picture on the wall

kamban o kakeru（看板を掛ける） put up a signboard

kata-ni te o kakeru（肩に手を掛ける） lay a person's hand on ((another's)) shoulder

têburu-ni kurosu o kakeru（テーブルにクロスを掛ける） cover a table with a cloth

Dôzo o-kake-kudasai.（どうぞお掛けください.） Please sit down.

hana-ni mizu o kakeru（花に水を掛ける） sprinkle water on the flowers

megane o kakeru（眼鏡を掛ける） have spectacles on

go ni san o kakeru（五に三を掛ける） multiply five by three

enjin o kakeru（エンジンをかける） start an engine

rajio o kakeru（ラジオをかける） switch on the radio

ie-o-tateru-no-ni zuibun kane o kakeru（家を建てるのに随分金を掛ける） spend a lot of money to get a house built

kakeru 〈かける：懸ける〉bet, wager, stake; risk.
   ari-gane o kakeru（有り金をかける）stake all the money one has
   inochi o kakeru（命を懸ける）risk one's life
kakeru 〈かける：欠ける〉break (off), be broken (off); lack, be wanting ((in)), be short ((of)); wane.
   jôshiki-ni-kakeru（常識に欠ける）be lacking in common sense.
-kakete 〈-かけて〉(extending) over, from...to... ; by.
   aki-kara-fuyu-ni-kakete（秋から冬にかけて）from autumn to winter
   kami-ni-kakete（神にかけて）by God
kaketsu 〈かけつ：可決〉
  kaketsu-suru〈可決する〉pass, carry, vote.
   gian o kaketsu-suru（議案を可決する）pass a bill
kake-tsukeru 〈かけつける：駆け付ける〉run ((to)), hasten ((to)), hurry ((to)).
   gemba-e kake-tsukeru（現場へ駆け付ける）hasten to the scene
kake-uri 〈かけうり：掛け売り〉sale on credit.
   Kake-uri o-kotowari.（掛け売りお断り。）For cash only.
  kake-uri-suru〈掛け売りする〉sell on credit.
kake-zan 〈かけざん：掛け算〉multiplication.
  kake-zan-o-suru〈掛け算をする〉multiply.
kaki 〈かき〉an oyster.
kaki 〈かき：火器〉firearms.
kaki 〈かき：火気〉fire.
   Kaki-genkin.（火気厳禁。）No fire. / Flammables.
kaki 〈かき：下記〉
  kaki-no〈下記の〉the following, undermentioned.
  kaki-no-toori〈下記のとおり〉as follows.
kaki 〈かき：夏期〉summer, summertime.
   kaki-kôshû-kai（夏期講習会）a summer school
kaki 〈かき〉a Japanese persimmon.
   kaki-no-ki（かきの木）a persimmon tree
kaki-ageru 〈かきあげる：書き上げる〉finish writing.
kaki-ageru 〈かきあげる：掻き上げる〉comb up, run one's hand through 〔one's hair〕.
kaki-aratameru 〈かきあらためる：書き改める〉see. kaki-naosu.
kaki-arawasu 〈かきあらわす：書き表す〉state in writing, write, describe.
kaki-atsumeru 〈かきあつめる：かき集める〉gather up, rake up.

ochiba o kaki-atsumeru〈落ち葉をかき集める〉 rake up fallen leaves

kaki-chigai〈かきちがい：書き違い〉a mistake in writing.
　kaki-chigai-o-suru or *kaki-chigaeru*〈書き違いをする，書き違える〉make a mistake in writing.
　　atena-o-kaki-chigaeru〈あて名を書き違える〉 address ((a letter)) wrongly

kaki-dashi〈かきだし：書き出し〉the opening sentence.

kakiire-doki〈かきいれどき：書き入れ時〉the best season ((for)), the busiest season ((for)), the highest season ((for)).

kaki-ireru〈かきいれる：書き入れる〉write in, fill in.
　yôshi ni kaki-ireru〈用紙に書き入れる〉 fill in a form, fill out a blank.

kaki-kae〈かきかえ：書き換え〉rewriting, renewal, transfer.
　kaki-kaeru〈書き換える〉rewrite, renew, transfer.
　　ie-yashiki o musuko-no meigi-ni kaki-kaeru〈家屋敷を息子の名義に書き換える〉 transfer one's house and its lot to one's son

kaki-kata〈かきかた：書き方〉penmanship; how to write, a style of writing.

kaki-kesu〈かきけす：かき消す〉
　Wareware-no hanashi wa sôon-de-kaki-kesareta.〈我々の話は騒音でかき消された.〉 Our talks were drowned in the noise.

kaki-kizu〈かききず：かき傷〉a scratch.

kaki-komi〈かきこみ：書き込み〉an entry, notes.
　rangai-no kaki-komi〈欄外の書き込み〉 marginal notes
　kaki-komu〈書き込む〉write in, fill out, fill up.

kaki-kuwaeru〈かきくわえる：書き加える〉add, insert.

kaki-mawasu〈かきまわす：かき回す〉stir (up), churn; ransack.

kaki-mazeru〈かきまぜる：かき混ぜる〉mix up.

kaki-midasu〈かきみだす：かき乱す〉disturb, confuse.

kaki-mono〈かきもの：書き物〉writing.
　kaki-mono-o-suru〈書き物をする〉write.

kaki-mushiru〈かきむしる〉tear, rend.
　kami o kaki-mushiru〈髪をかきむしる〉 tear one's hair

kaki-naguru〈かきなぐる：書きなぐる〉write off, dash off.

kaki-naoshi〈かきなおし：書き直し〉a rewrite.
　kaki-naoshi-o-suru or *kaki-naosu*〈書き直しをする，書き直す〉rewrite, write over again.

kaki-ne〈かきね：垣根〉a fence, a hedge.
　kaki-ne-goshi-ni〈垣根越しに〉 over a fence

kaki-nokosu〈かきのこす：書き残す〉leave a note behind.

kaki-oki〈かきおき：書き置き〉a note left behind.

　kaki-oki-o-suru〈書き置きをする〉*see.*　kaki-nokosu.

kaki-oroshi〈かきおろし：書き下ろし〉

　　kaki-oroshi-no shōsetsu（書き下ろしの小説）a newly written story

kaki-otosu〈かきおとす：書き落とす〉leave out, miss.

kaki-owaru〈かきおわる：書き終わる〉finish writing.

kaki-sokonai〈かきそこない：書き損ない〉a mistake in writing.

　kaki-sokonau〈書き損なう〉write amiss.

kaki-tasu〈かきたす：書き足す〉*see.*　kaki-kuwaeru.

kaki-tateru〈かきたてる：書き立てる〉write up, play up, air, write down.

　　shimbun-de kaki-tateru（新聞で書き立てる）play up in the newspapers

kaki-tateru〈かきたてる：かき立てる〉stir (up), rake (up), poke up.

　　kōki-shin o kaki-tateru（好奇心をかき立てる）stir up curiosity

kakitome〈かきとめ：書留〉registered mail.

　　kakitome-kozutsumi（書留小包）a registered parcel

　kakitome-ni-suru〈書留にする〉have ((a letter)) registered.

　kakitome-no〈書留の〉registered.

kaki-tomeru〈かきとめる：書き留める〉write down, make a note of ((something)).

kaki-tori〈かきとり：書き取り〉dictation.

　　kaki-tori-o-suru（書き取りをする）have dictation

kaki-toru〈かきとる：書き取る〉take(*or* write) down.

kaki-wakeru〈かきわける：かき分ける〉push aside.

　　hito-gomi-no-naka-o-kaki-wakete-iku（人込みの中をかき分けて行く）push one's way through the crowd

kaki-yoseru〈かきよせる：かき寄せる〉*see.*　kaki-atsumeru.

kaki-zome〈かきぞめ：書き初め〉the New Year's writing.

kakke〈かっけ〉beriberi.

kakketsu〈かっけつ：かっ血〉

　kakketsu-suru〈かっ血する〉cough out blood.

kakki〈かっき：活気〉vigor, spirit, liveliness, animation.

　　kakki-ni-michite-iru（活気に満ちている）be full of spirit

　kakki-no-aru〈活気のある〉vigorous, lively, animated.

　　kakki-no-nai（活気のない）spiritless, lifeless, dull

kakkiri(-ni)〈かっきり（に）〉just, exactly, sharp, punctually.

　　sanji kakkiri-ni〈三時かっきりに〉 just at 3

kakki-teki(-na)〈かっきてき(な)：画期的(な)〉 epoch-making.

kakko〈かっこ：各個〉

　kakko-gekiha-suru〈各個撃破する〉 defeat one by one.

kakko〈かっこ：括弧〉a parenthesis, a bracket, a brace.

　　kakko-ni-ireru（括弧に入れる） put in parentheses(*or* brackets)

kakko〈かっこ：確固〉

　kakko-taru〈確固たる〉firm, determined, unshakable.

　　kakko-taru shinnen（確固たる信念） a firm belief

kakkō〈かっこう〉a cuckoo.

kakkō〈かっこう：格好〉a shape, a form, appearance, presence, dress.

　kakkō-no-ii〈格好のいい〉well-formed, well-cut.

　　kakkō-no-warui（格好の悪い） ill-formed, ill-cut

kakkō〈かっこう：滑降〉a descent.

　　kakkō-kyōgi（滑降競技） a downhill race

kakko-ii〈かっこいい〉smart, groovy.

kakkoku〈かっこく：各国〉every country, each nation.

kakkomu〈かっこむ：かっ込む〉shovel ((food)) into one's mouth.

kakkyō〈かっきょう：活況〉activity, briskness.

　kakkyō-o-teisuru〈活況を呈する〉show activity, become active.

kako〈かこ：過去〉the past.

　　kako-jū-nen-kan（過去十年間） for the past ten years

　kako-no〈過去の〉past.

　kako-ni-oite〈過去において〉in the past.

kakō〈かこう：河口〉the mouth of a river, an estuary.

kakō〈かこう：火口〉a (volcanic) crater.

kakō〈かこう：下降〉a fall, a descent, a drop.

　　kakō-sen（下降線） a downward curve

　kakō-suru〈下降する〉go down, fall, descend, drop.

kakō〈かこう：加工〉processing.

　　kakō-shokuhin（加工食品） processed food

　kakō-suru〈加工する〉process.

　kakō-no〈加工の〉processed.

kakō-gan〈かこうがん：花こう岩〉granite.

kakoi〈かこい：囲い〉an enclosure, a fence.

　kakoi-o-suru or *kakou*〈囲いをする，囲う〉enclose, fence round.

kakoku〈かこく：か酷〉

　kakoku-na〈か酷な〉severe, harsh, hard, cruel, merciless.

kakoku-na toɪi-atsukai（か酷な取り扱い） cruel treatment

kakomu〈かこむ：囲む〉enclose, surround, lay siege ((to)).

têburu-o-kakonde suwaru（テーブルを囲んで座る） be seated around the table

kakon〈かこん：禍根〉the root of evil.

kakon o tatsu（禍根を断つ） eliminate the root of evil

shôrai-ni kakon-o-nokosu（将来に禍根を残す） be the cause of trouble in the future

kakou〈かこう：囲う〉enclose, fence; preserve, store.

kaku〈かく：核〉a nucleus, a core, a kernel.

kaku-heiki（核兵器） a nuclear weapon

kaku-kazoku（核家族） a nuclear family

kaku-no〈核の〉nuclear.

kaku〈かく：画〉a stroke.

san-kaku no ji（三画の字） a character of three strokes

kaku〈かく：角〉an angle; a square; a bishop.

kaku〈かく：書く〉write, put down, describe.

kaku〈かく〉draw, paint.

chizu o kaku（地図をかく） draw a map

abura-e-o-kaku（油絵をかく） paint in oil

kaku〈かく〉scratch.

atama o kaku（頭をかく） scratch one's head

kaku〈かく：欠く〉lack, be wanting(*or* lacking) ((in)), be short ((of)).

kaku-koto-no-deki-nai〈欠くことのできない〉indispensable ((to)).

kaku-koto-no-deki-nai-mono（欠くことのできない物） a requisite, necessaries, necessities

kaku〈かく：格〉(a) standing, a rank, a class, a grade.

kaku-ga-agaru（格が上がる） rise in rank

kaku-ga-sagaru（格が下がる） fall in rank

kaku-ga-chigau（格が違う） belong to a different class ((from))

kaku-〈かく-：各〉every, each.

kaku-ji（各自） each, each one.

kaku-jin（各人） each person, every one, everybody.

kaku-〈かく-：隔-〉every other(*or* second).

kaku-jitsu（隔日） every other day

kaku-shû（隔週） every other week

kaku-getsu（隔月） every other month

kaku-nen（隔年） every other year

kakû〈かくう：架空〉
　kakû-no〈架空の〉imaginary, fictitious.
　　kakû-no jimbutsu〈架空の人物〉a fictitious character
kaku-batta〈かくばった：角張った〉square, angular.
kakubetsu〈かくべつ：格別〉
　　Kyô-no-atsusa-wa-kakubetsu-da.（今日の暑さは格別だ。）This is an
　　　exceptionally hot day.
　kakubetsu-no〈格別の〉particular, special; remarkable.
kaku-bin〈かくびん：角瓶〉a square bottle.
kakuchi〈かくち：各地〉every place, various places.
kakuchô〈かくちょう：拡張〉extension, expansion, enlargement.
　kakuchô-suru〈拡張する〉extend, expand, enlarge.
　　jigyô o kakuchô-suru（事業を拡張する）expand one's business
　　dôro o kakuchô-suru（道路を拡張する）widen a street
kakudai〈かくだい：拡大〉magnification.
　kakudai-suru〈拡大する〉magnify, spread, enlarge.
kakudan〈かくだん：格段〉
　　kakudan-no sa（格段の差）a great difference ((between))
kakudo〈かくど：角度〉an angle.
　　kyû-jû-do-no-kakudo-de（九十度の角度で）at an angle of 90°
　　iroiro-na kakudo-kara（いろいろな角度から）from various angles
kaku-eki〈かくえき：各駅〉each station.
　　kaku-eki-ni teisha-suru（各駅に停車する）stop at every station
　　kaku-eki-teisha-no ressha（各駅停車の列車）a local train
kakugen〈かくげん：格言〉a proverb, a maxim.
kakugi〈かくぎ：閣議〉a Cabinet council.
kakugo〈かくご：覚悟〉
　kakugo-suru〈覚悟する〉be prepared ((for)), make up one's mind.
　kakugo-shite-iru〈覚悟している〉be resolved, be resigned.
kakuhan〈かくはん〉
　　kakuhan-ki（かくはん器）an agitator, a stirrer, a churn, an egg
　　　beater
　kakuhan-suru〈かくはんする〉agitate, stir (up), churn, beat.
kakuho〈かくほ：確保〉
　kakuho-suru〈確保する〉secure, insure, guarantee, maintain.
　　yusô-ryoku o kakuho-suru（輸送力を確保する）secure transport-
　　　ation facilities
kaku-hômen〈かくほうめん：各方面〉

kaku-hômen-ni〈各方面に〉 in every direction, in all quarters

kaku-hômen-kara〈各方面から〉 from all quarters

kakuitsu〈かくいつ：画一〉

kakuitsu-ka-suru〈画一化する〉 standardize, unify.

kakuitsu-teki(-na)〈画一的(な)〉 standardized, uniform.

kakuitsu-teki-ni〈画一的に〉 uniformly.

kakuji〈かくじ：各自〉*see.* kaku-〈各-〉.

kakujitsu〈かくじつ：確実〉 certainty, reliability, soundness.

kakujitsu-na〈確実な〉 certain, sure, reliable, sound.

kakujitsu-ni〈確実に〉 certainly, surely, steadily.

kakujû〈かくじゅう：拡充〉 (an) expansion, (an) amplification.

kakujû-suru〈拡充する〉 expand, amplify.

kakukai〈かくかい：各階〉 each floor.

kakukai-ni-tomaru〈各階に止まる〉 stop at every floor

kakukai〈かくかい：各界〉 every field of life, various circles.

kakukai-no meishi〈各界の名士〉 notables from various circles

kakumaku〈かくまく：角膜〉 the cornea.

kakumau〈かくまう〉 shelter, harbor, give refuge ((to)).

kakumei〈かくめい：革命〉 a revolution.

kakumei o okosu〈革命を起こす〉 start a revolution

kakumei-teki(-na) or *kakumei-no*〈革命的(な), 革命の〉 revolutionary.

kakunin〈かくにん：確認〉 confirmation, affirmation, certification.

kakunin-suru〈確認する〉 confirm, affirm, certify.

kakunô〈かくのう：格納〉

kakunô-ko〈格納庫〉 a hangar

kakunô-suru〈格納する〉 house.

kakuran〈かくらん：かく乱〉 disturbance.

kakuran-suru〈かく乱する〉 disturb, throw into confusion.

heiwa o kakuran-suru〈平和をかく乱する〉 disturb peace

kakure-ga〈かくれが：隠れ家〉 a hiding place, a den, a hideout, an agitating point.

kakurembô〈かくれんぼう：隠れん坊〉 hide-and-seek.

kakurembô o suru〈隠れんぼうをする〉 play hide-and-seek

kakureru〈かくれる：隠れる〉 hide oneself, conceal oneself.

kakureta〈隠れた〉 concealed, unknown.

kakureta tensai〈隠れた天才〉 an unknown genius

kakurete〈隠れて〉 out of sight, in secret, secretly, under cover.

kakurete au〈隠れて会う〉 meet in secret

shûkyô-no-bimei-ni-kakurete〈宗教の美名に隠れて〉under cover of religion

kakuri〈かくり：隔離〉isolation, insulation.

kakuri-byôtô〈隔離病棟〉an isolation ward

kakuri-suru〈隔離する〉isolate, insulate.

kakuritsu〈かくりつ：確率〉probability.

seikô no kakuritsu〈成功の確率〉the probability of success

kakuritsu〈かくりつ：確立〉establishment, settlement.

kakuritsu-suru〈確立する〉establish, settle.

heiwa o kakuritsu-suru〈平和を確立する〉establish peace

kakuron〈かくろん：各論〉a discussion of a particular branch ((of)).

kakuron-ni-hairu〈各論に入る〉go into details of a subject.

kakuryō〈かくりょう：閣僚〉a Cabinet member, a Cabinet minister.

kakusa〈かくさ：格差〉a gap, difference, a differential.

chingin-no kakusa〈賃金の格差〉a pay differential

kaku-sage〈かくさげ：格下げ〉

kaku-sage-suru〈格下げする〉downgrade, reduce ((a person)) to a lower rank.

kakusaku〈かくさく：画策〉

kakusaku-suru〈画策する〉plan, project, scheme, map out a plan, maneuver.

kakusei〈かくせい：隔世〉

Tôji-o-omou-to, kakusei-no-kan-ga-aru.（当時を思うと，隔世の感があ る.）When I think of those days, I feel as if I were living in quite a different age.

kakusei-iden〈隔世遺伝〉atavism

kakusei-zai〈かくせいざい：覚せい剤〉a stimulant, a pep pill.

kakushaku〈かくしゃく〉

kakushaku-to-shita〈かくしゃくとした〉hale and hearty.

kakushi-〈かくし-：隠し-〉

kakushi-gei〈隠し芸〉a parlor trick, a stunt

kakushi-kamera〈隠しカメラ〉a concealed camera

kakushi-date〈かくしだて：隠し立て〉

kakushi-date-o-suru〈隠し立てをする〉keep ((a matter)) secret.

kakushi-date-o-shi-nai〈隠し立てをしない〉have no secret from ((a person))

kakushi-date-no-nai〈隠し立てのない〉open, openhearted.

kakushiki〈かくしき：格式〉status, social standing; a formality, a rule.

kakushiki-baru〈格式ばる〉stick to formalities.

kakushiki-batta〈格式ばった〉ceremonious, stiff-mannered.

kakushiki-no-aru〈格式のある〉prestigious.

kakushin〈かくしん：核心〉the core, the kernel, the point.

kakushin ni fureru（核心に触れる）touch the core, come to the point

kakushin〈かくしん：確信〉conviction, firm belief, confidence.

kakushin-suru〈確信する〉believe firmly, be convinced(*or* assured) ((of *or* that)).

kakushin〈かくしん：革新〉(a) reform.

kakushin-seitô（革新政党）a reformist political party

kakushin-suru〈革新する〉reform, make a reform ((in)).

kakushin-teki(-na)〈革新的(な)〉reformist.

kakusho〈かくしょ：各所〉

kakusho-ni〈各所に〉in every place, in various places.

shi-nai-kakusho-ni（市内各所に）in various places of the city

kakushô〈かくしょう：確証〉(a) positive proof.

kakushô o nigiru（確証を握る）secure positive proof ((of))

kakushu〈かくしゅ：各種〉

kakushu-no〈各種の〉various, of every kind, all sorts of.

kakusu〈かくす：隠す〉hide, conceal, cover, veil, screen, put ((a thing)) out of sight, keep ((a matter)) secret.

sugata o kakusu（姿を隠す）hide oneself

toshi o kakusu（年を隠す）conceal one's age

jijitsu o kakusu（事実を隠す）cover up a fact

kakusazu-ni〈隠さずに〉without concealing, frankly, openly.

kakusuru〈かくする：画する〉draw.

issen o kakusuru（一線を画する）draw a line

kakutei〈かくてい：確定〉decision, settlement, confirmation.

kakutei-shinkoku（確定申告）the final income tax return

kakutei-suru〈確定する〉decide ((upon)), be decided, settle, be settled, fix, be fixed, confirm.

kakutei-shita〈確定した〉decided, settled, fixed, certain, final.

kakutei-teki-ni〈確定的に〉definitely, conclusively.

kakuteru〈カクテル〉a cocktail.

kakuteru-pâtî（カクテルパーティー）a cocktail party

kakutô〈かくとう：格闘〉a hand-to-hand fight.

kakutô-suru〈格闘する〉fight hand to hand ((with)).

kakutô〈かくとう：確答〉a definite answer.
　　kakutô o sakeru（確答を避ける）evade (any) definite answer
　kakutô-suru〈確答する〉give a definite answer.
kakutoku〈かくとく：獲得〉acquisition.
　kakutoku-suru〈獲得する〉get, win, acquire, secure.
kakuyaku〈かくやく：確約〉
　kakuyaku-suru〈確約する〉give a definite promise, give one's word
　　((to)).
kakuyasu〈かくやす：格安〉
　　kakuyasu-hin（格安品）a bargain, a good purchase
　kakuyasu-na〈格安な〉cheap, low-priced.
　kakuyasu-ni〈格安に〉cheap, at a bargain.
kakuzai〈かくざい：角材〉square lumber.
kaku-zatô〈かくざとう：角砂糖〉lump sugar, cube sugar.
kakuzetsu〈かくぜつ：隔絶〉
　kakuzetsu-suru〈隔絶する〉be separated ((from)).
　　gekai-to-kakuzetsu-suru（外界と隔絶する）be separated from the
　　　outer world
ka-kyaku-sen〈かきゃくせん：貨客船〉a cargo-passenger boat.
kakyô〈かきょう：架橋〉bridge-building, bridging.
kakyô〈かきょう：華きょう〉overseas Chinese merchants.
kakyoku〈かきょく：歌曲〉a (classical) song.
kakyû〈かきゅう：火急〉urgency, emergency.
　kakyû-no〈火急の〉urgent, pressing.
　kakyû no baai-ni-wa〈火急の場合には〉in case of emergency.
kakyû〈かきゅう：下級〉
　　kakyû-sei（下級生）a lower-class boy(or girl)
　kakyû-no〈下級の〉lower, junior.
kama〈かま〉a sickle, a scythe.
kama〈かま〉an iron pot, a kettle, a teakettle.
kama〈かま：窯〉a stove, an oven, a furnace.
kamaboko〈かまぼこ〉boiled fish-paste.
kamae〈かまえ：構え〉structure, construction, a style, an appearance.
　　kamae-ga-rippa-da（構えが立派だ）have a grand appearance
kamaeru〈かまえる：構える〉keep, set up; be ready ((for)).
　　ikko-o-kamaeru（一戸を構える）set up one's own home
　　nonki-ni kamaeru（のんきに構える）take it(or things) easy
kamakiri〈かまきり〉a mantis.

kama-kubi〈かまくび：かま首〉a gooseneck.

  kama-kubi o motageru〈かま首をもたげる〉raise ((its)) head.

kamasu〈かます〉a saury-pike.

kamau〈かまう：構う〉mind, care, trouble oneself ((about)), bother ((about *or* with)), take notice ((of)); meddle ((in *or* with)); tease.

    Kare-ga dô-iô-ga-kamawa-nai.（彼がどう言おうが構わない。）I don't mind whatever he may say.

    Watashi-niwa o-kamai-naku.（私にはお構いなく.）Please don't bother about me.

    Watashi-ni kamawa-nai-de-kure!（私に構わないでくれ.）Leave me alone!

kamban〈かんばん：看板〉a signboard, a sign.

  kamban o dasu（看板を出す）set up a sign

kambashii〈かんばしい：芳しい〉sweet, fragrant.

  kambashii nioi（芳しいにおい）(a) fragrant smell

  kambashiku-nai〈芳しくない〉poor, bad, unsatisfactory, shameful.

  kambashiku-nai hyôban（芳しくない評判）a bad reputation

kambatsu〈かんばつ〉a drought, a spell of dry weather.

kamben〈かんべん：勘弁〉

  kamben-suru〈勘弁する〉pardon, forgive.

kamben〈かんべん：簡便〉

  kamben-na〈簡便な〉simple, easy, convenient, handy.

kambi〈かんび：完備〉perfection, completeness.

  kambi-shita〈完備した〉perfect, complete, full-equipped.

  setsubi-no-kambi-shita hoteru（設備の完備したホテル）a hotel with complete facilities

kambô〈かんぼう：感冒〉a cold.

  ryûkô-sei-kambô（流行性感冒）influenza

kambô〈かんぼう：官房〉the secretariat(e).

  naikaku-kambô-chôkan（内閣官房長官）the Chief Secretary of the Cabinet

kambô〈かんぼう：監房〉a cell, a ward.

Kambojia〈カンボジア〉Cambodia.

  Kambojia-jin（カンボジア人）a Cambodian

  Kambojia(-jin)-no（カンボジア（人）の）Cambodian

kamboku〈かんぼく：かん木〉a shrub, a bush.

kambotsu〈かんぼつ：陥没〉sinking, (a) subsidence, a cave-in.

  kambotsu-suru〈陥没する〉sink, subside, cave in.

kambu 〈かんぶ：幹部〉the staff, the executives, the leaders.

kambu 〈かんぶ：患部〉the affected part.

kambun 〈かんぶん：漢文〉Chinese composition, Chinese classics.

kambutsu 〈かんぶつ：乾物〉groceries.

 kambutsu-ya〈乾物屋〉a grocer; a grocery store.

kambyô 〈かんびょう：看病〉nursing.

 kambyô-suru〈看病する〉nurse.

kame 〈かめ〉a jar, a jug.

kame 〈かめ〉a tortoise, a turtle.

 kame-no kô（かめの甲）(a) tortoise(*or* turtle) shell.

kamei 〈かめい：家名〉the family name; the family honor.

kamei 〈かめい：加盟〉joining, participation, affiliation.

 kamei-koku（加盟国）a member nation〔of the United States〕

 kamei-suru〈加盟する〉join, participate ((in)), take part ((in)), be affiliated ((with)).

kamei 〈かめい：仮名〉an assumed name, an alias.

 〜-to-iu-kamei-de（〜という仮名で）by the alias of...

kamen 〈かめん：仮面〉a mask.

 kamen o kaburu（仮面をかぶる）wear a mask

 kamen-o-hagu（仮面をはぐ）unmask, throw off the mask

kamereon 〈カメレオン〉a chameleon.

kami 〈かみ：神〉a god, God.

 kami-o-shinjiru（神を信じる）believe in God

kami 〈かみ：加味〉

 kami-suru〈加味する〉add ((to)), include, contain.

kami 〈かみ：紙〉paper.

 kami ichi-mai（紙一枚）a sheet of paper

 kami-ni kaku（紙に書く）write on paper

 kami-ni tsutsumu（紙に包む）wrap in paper

 kami-kire（紙切れ）a slip of paper

 kami-byôshi-no-hon（紙表紙の本）a paper-backed book

 kami-shibai（紙芝居）a picture-card show

kami 〈かみ：髪〉hair.

 kami o arau（髪を洗う）wash one's hair

 kami o katte-morau（髪を刈ってもらう）have one's hair cut

 kami o mijikaku-kari-agete-morau（髪を短く刈り上げてもらう）have one's hair cut short

 kami o mijikaku-shite-iru（髪を短くしている）wear one's hair short

kami o nagaku-shite-iru（髪を長くしている）wear one's hair long

kami o chijirasete-iru（髪を縮らせている）wear one's hair in curls

kami o wakeru（髪を分ける）part one's hair

kami-au〈かみあう：かみ合う〉gear ((into *or* with)), engage ((with)), mesh ((with)).

kami-awaseru〈かみ合わせる〉clench.

ha o kami-awaseru（歯をかみ合わせる）clench one's teeth

kami-dana〈かみだな：神棚〉a household altar.

kami-gakari〈かみがかり：神懸かり〉

kami-gakari-no〈神懸かりの〉inspirational, fanatic(al).

kami-hitoe〈かみひとえ：紙一重〉

kami-hitoe-no sa（紙一重の差）only a very slight difference

kami-kiru〈かみきる：かみ切る〉bite off, cut off with the teeth.

kami-kudaku〈かみくだく：かみ砕く〉

kami-kudaite-setsumei-suru〈かみ砕いて説明する〉explain in plain language.

kami-kuzu〈かみくず：紙くず〉wastepaper.

kami-kuzu-kago（紙くずかご）a wastebasket, a wastepaper basket

kaminari〈かみなり：雷〉thunder, lightning.

kaminari no oto（雷の音）a roar of thunder

kami-no-ke〈かみのけ：髪の毛〉*see.* kami.

kami-shimeru〈かみしめる：かみ締める〉chew; meditate ((on)), digest.

imi o kami-shimeru（意味をかみ締める）digest the meaning

kamisori〈かみそり〉a razor.

kamisori-no ha（かみそりの刃）a razor blade

denki-kamisori（電気かみそり）an electric razor

kami-te〈かみて：上手〉the upper part; the left stage, the right of the stage.

kamitsu〈かみつ：過密〉

kamitsu-toshi（過密都市）an overpopulated city

kami-tsuku〈かみつく：かみ付く〉bite ((at)), snap ((at)).

kami-waza〈かみわざ：神業〉the work of God, a miracle; a superhuman feat.

kami-yasuri〈かみやすり：紙やすり〉sandpaper.

kami-za〈かみざ：上座〉

kami-za-ni suwaru〈上座に座る〉sit at the head of the table.

kami-zaiku〈かみざいく：紙細工〉paperwork.

kami-zutsumi〈かみづつみ：紙包み〉a paper parcel.

kamman 〈かんまん：干満〉 ebb and flow, tide.
    kamman no sa（干満の差） the range of tide
kamman 〈かんまん：緩慢〉
  kamman-na〈緩慢な〉 slow, sluggish, slack, dull, inactive.
    kamman-na shijô（緩慢な市場） a dull market
kammatsu 〈かんまつ：巻末〉the end of a book.
kammei 〈かんめい：感銘〉*see.* kandô（感動）.
kammei 〈かんめい：簡明〉
  kammei-na〈簡明な〉 terse, concise, short and clear, simple and plain.
  kammei-ni〈簡明に〉 tersely, concisely, simply and plainly.
kammi 〈かんみ：甘味〉
    kammi-ryô（甘味料） sweetening materials
kammon 〈かんもん：関門〉a barrier, a gateway ((to)).
    kammon o tsûka-suru（関門を通過する） get over a barrier
kammon 〈かんもん：喚問〉a summons.
  kammon-suru〈喚問する〉summon.
kamo 〈かも〉a (wild) duck, a pigeon, a gull, an easy mark, a sucker.
    kamo-ni-suru（かもにする） make a sucker ((out of))
    ii-kamo-ni-naru（いいかもになる）fall an easy victim〔to one's trick〕
kamoku 〈かもく：科目〉a subject, a course, a curriculum.
    sentaku-kamoku（選択科目） an optional subject
kamome 〈かもめ〉a (sea) gull.
kamoshika 〈かもしか〉an antelope.
-kamo-shirenai 〈〜かもしれない：〜かも知れない〉may, perhaps, maybe, possibly.
    Sô-kamo-shirenai.（そうかも知れない.） It may be so.
kamotsu 〈かもつ：貨物〉freight, goods, cargo.
    kamotsu-jidôsha（貨物自動車） a truck, a lorry
    kamotsu-ressha（貨物列車） a freight train, a goods train
    kamotsu-sen（貨物船） a freighter, a cargo boat
kampa 〈かんぱ：寒波〉a cold wave.
kampa 〈カンパ〉a campaign.
    shikin-kampa（資金カンパ） a fund-raising campaign
kampai 〈かんぱい：乾杯〉a toast.
  kampai-suru〈乾杯する〉drink the toast ((of)).
    kenkô-o-iwatte-kampai-suru（健康を祝って乾杯する） drink to ((a person's)) health
kampai 〈かんぱい：完敗〉a complete defeat.

kampai-suru〈完敗する〉be beaten all hollow.

kampan〈かんぱん：甲板〉a deck.

　　jô-kampan（上甲板）the upper deck

kampeki〈かんぺき：完璧〉perfection, completeness.

　　kampeki-o-kisuru（完璧を期する）aim at perfection

kampeki-na〈完璧な〉perfect, flawless, thorough.

kampen-suji〈かんぺんすじ：官辺筋〉

　kampen-suji-dewa〈官辺筋では〉in government circles.

kampô〈かんぽう：漢方〉Chinese medicine.

　　kampô-yaku（漢方薬）a herb medicine

kampô〈かんぽう：官報〉an official gazette.

kampu〈かんぷ：還付〉return.

　　kampu-zei（還付税）the refund tax

kampu-suru〈還付する〉return.

kampu〈かんぷ：完膚〉

　kampu-naki-made-ni〈完膚なきまでに〉thoroughly, completely, un-
　　sparingly.

kampû〈かんぷう：完封〉

　kampû-suru〈完封する〉shut out.

kampyô〈かんぴょう：干ぴょう〉dried gourd shavings.

kamu〈かむ〉bite, chew.

　　Tabe-mono o yoku kami-nasai.（食べ物をよくかみなさい。）Chew
　　　your food well.

　　inu-ni kamareru（犬にかまれる）be bitten by a dog

kamu〈かむ〉

　　hana o kamu（鼻をかむ）blow one's nose

kan〈かん：缶〉a can, a tin.

　　sekiyu-kan（石油かん）an oil can

kan〈かん：管〉a pipe, a tube.

　　gomu-kan（ゴム管）a rubber tube

kan〈かん：巻〉a volume, a book, a reel.

　　dai-san-kan（第三巻）the third volume, book 3.

kan〈かん：寒〉

　　kan-no-iri（寒の入り）the beginning of midwinter

kan〈かん：棺〉a coffin.

kan〈かん：勘〉perception.

　　kan-ga-ii（勘がいい）have a quick perception

　　kan-ga-warui（勘が悪い）have a slow perception

kan 〈かん〉

kan-ni-sawaru 〈かんに障る〉 cut ((a person)) to the quick, get on ((a person's)) nerves.

kan 〈かん〉

kan-o-suru 〈かんをする〉 warm up 〔*sake*〕.

-kan 〈-かん：-間〉 for, during, in; between, from...to... , among.

go-nen-kan（五年間） for five years

kako-jû-nen-kan-ni（過去十年間に） during the past ten years

Tôkyô-Hakata-kan（東京博多間） between Tokyo and Hakata, from Tokyo to Hakata

kana 〈かな：仮名〉 the Japanese alphabet, *kana*.

kana-zukai（仮名遣い） the use of *kana*

kata-kana（片仮名） the square form of *kana*

hira-gana（平仮名） the cursive *kana* letters

kana-ami 〈かなあみ：金網〉 wire netting, a wire gauze.

kana-ami-o haru（金網を張る） cover ((a thing)) with wire netting

kana-bô 〈かなぼう：金棒〉 an iron rod.

Kanada 〈カナダ〉 Canada.

Kanada-jin（カナダ人） a Canadian

Kanada(-jin)-no（カナダ(人)の） Canadian

kanaeru 〈かなえる〉 grant, answer.

negai o kanaeru（願いをかなえる） grant ((a person's)) request

kana-gu 〈かなぐ：金具〉 metal fittings.

kana-gu o uchi-tsukeru（金具を打ち付ける） nail metal fittings ((on))

kanai-kôgyô 〈かないこうぎょう：家内工業〉 a cottage industry.

kanakiri-goe 〈かなきりごえ：金切り声〉 a shrill voice.

kaname-ishi 〈かなめいし：かなめ石〉 a keystone.

kana-mono 〈かなもの：金物〉 hardware, ironware, a metal utensil.

kana-mono-ya（金物屋） a hardware dealer; a hardware store

kanarazu 〈かならず：必ず〉 certainly, surely, without fail, by all means.

kanarazu ～(-suru) 〈必ず～(する)〉 be sure ((to do)), never fail ((to do)).

kanarazu-shimo～-de-nai 〈必ずしも～でない〉 not always... , not necessarily... .

kanari 〈かなり〉 pretty, fairly.

kanari yoku *or* kanari jôzu-ni（かなり良く，かなり上手に） pretty well, fairly well

kanari-no 〈かなりの〉 fair, considerable.

kanari-no kingaku（かなりの金額） a considerable sum of money

kanaria〈カナリア〉a canary (bird).

kanashii〈かなしい：悲しい〉sad, sorrowful.

kanashii kao-tsuki〈悲しい顔つき〉a sad look

kanashii kao-tsuki-o-suru〈悲しい顔つきをする〉look sorrowful

kanashii-omoi-ga-suru〈悲しい思いがする〉feel sad

kanashii-koto-ni〈悲しいことに〉sad to say, It is a pity that... .

kanashiku-naru〈悲しくなる〉feel sad.

kanashi-sō-ni〈悲しそうに〉sadly, sorrowfully.

kanashimi〈かなしみ：悲しみ〉sadness, sorrow, grief.

kanashimi-no-amari〈悲しみの余り〉in one's sorrow

Kanashimi-de mune-ga-ippai-da.〈悲しみで胸がいっぱいだ。〉Sorrow fills my heart.

kanashimu〈かなしむ：悲しむ〉be sad ((at)), feel sorrow ((for)), grieve ((at *or* over)), mourn.

kanashimu-beki〈悲しむべき〉regrettable, pitiable, deplorable.

〜-wa-kanashimu-beki-koto-da〈〜は悲しむべきことだ。〉It is regrettable that... , It is a pity that... .

kanashimaseru〈悲しませる〉make ((a person)) sad, cause sorrow ((to)).

kanashinde〈悲しんで〉in sorrow, sorrowfully.

kanau〈かなう〉match, be a match ((for)), be equal ((to)).

〜-ni-kanawa-nai〈〜にかなわない〉be no match for... .

kanau〈かなう〉answer, serve, meet, accord ((with)); be fulfilled, be realized.

mokuteki ni kanau〈目的にかなう〉serve one's purpose

nozomi ni kanau〈望みにかなう〉meet one's wishes

dôri-ni-kanau〈道理にかなう〉accord with reason

nozomi ga kanaerareru〈望みがかなえられる〉have one's wishes realized

kanazuchi〈かなづち：金づち〉a hammer.

kan-chigai〈かんちがい：勘違い〉misunderstanding.

kan-chigai-suru〈勘違いする〉misunderstand, mistake, guess wrong.

kanchô〈かんちょう：官庁〉a government office.

kanchô〈かんちょう：管長〉the superintendent priest.

kanchô〈かんちょう：館長〉a curator, a chief librarian.

kanchô〈かんちょう：艦長〉the captain〔of a warship〕.

kanchô〈かんちょう：干潮〉ebb tide, low tide.

kanchô〈かんちょう：かん腸〉(an) enema.

kanchô-suru〈かん腸する〉give an enema ((to)).

kanchû 〈かんちゅう：寒中〉
    kanchû-suiei（寒中水泳）midwinter swimming

kandai 〈かんだい：寛大〉largeheartedness, generosity, leniency.
  kandai-na〈寛大な〉large-minded, generous, lenient.
  kandai-ni〈寛大に〉large-mindedly, generously, leniently.
    kandai-ni tori-atsukau（寛大に取り扱う）deal leniently ((with))

kan-dakai 〈かんだかい：甲高い〉shrill.
    kan-dakai koe（甲高い声）a shrill voice

kandan 〈かんだん：間断〉
  kandan-naku〈間断なく〉incessantly, ceaselessly, unceasingly, continuously.

kandan-kei 〈かんだんけい：寒暖計〉a thermometer.

kanden 〈かんでん：感電〉
  kanden-suru〈感電する〉be struck by electricity.

kan-denchi 〈かんでんち：乾電池〉a dry cell, a dry battery.

kando 〈かんど：感度〉sensitivity, reception.
  hijô-ni kando-ga-ii〈非常に感度がいい〉be highly sensitive.

kandô 〈かんどう：感動〉impression.
  kandô-o-ataeru〈感動を与える〉impress, move, touch.
  kandô-suru〈感動する〉be impressed ((by *or* with)), be moved ((by)), be touched ((by)).
    fukaku kandô-suru（深く感動する）be deeply impressed

kandô 〈かんどう：勘当〉
  kandô-suru〈勘当する〉disown, disinherit.

kane 〈かね：鐘〉a bell, a gong.
    kane o narasu（鐘を鳴らす）ring a bell
    kane o tsuku（鐘をつく）strike a bell
    kane no oto（鐘の音）a sound of a bell

kane 〈かね：金〉money; a metal.
    kane-ga-aru（金がある）have much money, be rich
    kane-ga-nai（金がない）have no money, be poor
    kane-ga-kakaru（金が掛かる）cost much money, be expensive
    kane-ni-komatte-iru（金に困っている）be short of money
    kane o môkeru（金をもうける）make money
    kane o tameru（金をためる）save money
    kane-o-muda-ni-tsukau（金を無駄に使う）waste money
  kane-o-harau〈金を払う〉pay.

kane-banare 〈かねばなれ：金離れ〉

kane-banare-ga-ii 〈金離れがいい〉 be generous with one's money.

kanegane 〈かねがね〉
O-namae wa kanegane-uketamawatte-orimashita.（お名前はかねがね承っておりました.） I have heard about you.

kane-jaku 〈かねじゃく：金尺〉a metal measure, a carpenter's square.

kane-kashi 〈かねかし：金貸し〉money-lending business; a moneylender.

kane-mawari 〈かねまわり：金回り〉financial conditions.
kane-mawari-ga-ii（金回りがいい） be in funds

kane-me 〈かねめ：金目〉
kane-me-no-mono〈金目の物〉a valuable article, valuables.

kane-mochi 〈かねもち：金持ち〉a rich person, a wealthy person.
kane-mochi-no〈金持ちの〉rich, wealthy.

kane-môke 〈かねもうけ：金もうけ〉moneymaking.
kane-môke-ga-umai（金もうけがうまい） be clever at making money
kane-môke-o-suru〈金もうけをする〉make money.

kanen 〈かねん：可燃〉
kanen-butsu（可燃物） a combustible, an inflammable
kanen-sei-no〈可燃性の〉combustible, inflammable.

kan·en 〈かんえん：肝炎〉hepatitis.

kaneru 〈かねる：兼ねる〉combine ((one thing with another)), possess both ((A and B)), serve both ((as)).
shokudô to ima-to-o-kaneta heya（食堂と居間とを兼ねた部屋） a room serving both as a dining room and a living room

-kaneru 〈-かねる〉cannot, be unable ((to do)), be not in a position ((to do)).
henji o shi-kaneru（返事をしかねる） cannot give ((a person's)) answer
shôdaku-shi-kaneru（承諾しかねる） be unable to consent
Ano-otoko-wa donna-koto-demo-shi-kane-nai.（あの男はどんなことでもしかねない.） He will stop at nothing.

kanete 〈かねて〉previously, beforehand.
kanete-no〈かねての〉previous, prearranged.
kanete-no uchiawase-doori（かねての打ち合わせどおり） according to the previous arrangement
kanete-kara〈かねてから〉for some time past.

kanetsu 〈かねつ：加熱〉heating.
kanetsu-suru〈加熱する〉heat (up).

kanetsu 〈かねつ：過熱〉overheating.

kanetsu-keizai〈過熱経済〉an overheated economy

kanetsu-suru〈過熱する〉overheat.

kane-zukai〈かねづかい：金遣い〉

kane-zukai-ga-arai（金遣いが荒い）spend money like water, be extravagant

kane-zumari〈かねづまり：金詰まり〉financial pressure, tight money.

Doko-mo kane-zumari-da.（どこも金詰まりだ。）Money is tight everywhere.

kanezuru〈かねづる：金づる〉

ii kanezuru o mitsukeru（いい金づるをみつける）find a good financial supporter

kanfuru〈カンフル〉camphor.

kanfuru-chûsha（カンフル注射）(a) camphor injection

kangae〈かんがえ：考え〉an idea, an opinion, thought, an intention, a view; prudence, discretion.

ii kangae（いい考え）a good idea

watashi-no kangae-dewa（私の考えでは）in my opinion

kangae o noberu（考えを述べる）express one's opinion

kangae-ni-fukeru（考えにふける）be lost in thought

kangae o jikkô-ni-utsusu（考えを実行に移す）carry out one's intention

kangae-ga-tari-nai（考えが足りない）lack prudence

Sore-wa kangae-ga-ama-sugiru.（それは考えが甘すぎる。）That's too optimistic.

kangae-kata（考え方）one's way of thinking, one's point of view

kangae-no-nai〈考えのない〉thoughtless, imprudent, indiscreet.

kangae-nashi-ni〈考えなしに〉thoughtlessly.

kangae-chigai〈かんがえちがい：考え違い〉misunderstanding, a mistaken idea.

kangae-chigai-o-suru〈考え違いをする〉misunderstand, mistake.

kangae-dasu〈かんがえだす：考え出す〉devise, think up; begin to think.

kangae-goto〈かんがえごと：考え事〉

kangae-goto-o-suru〈考え事をする〉think about something.

kangae-komu〈かんがえこむ：考え込む〉be lost in thought, be deep in thought, brood ((on *or* over)).

kangae-mono〈かんがえもの：考え物〉

Soryâ kangae-mono-da.（そりゃあ考え物だ。）That is open to question.

kangae-naosu〈かんがえなおす：考え直す〉reconsider, think over again.

kangae-nuku〈かんがえぬく：考え抜く〉think ((a matter)) through, rack one's brains ((for *or* over)).

kangae-nuita-sue〈考え抜いた末〉after thinking and thinking.

kangaeru〈かんがえる：考える〉think ((about, of *or* that)), intend ((to do)), expect, hope, fear, consider, regard.

Nani-o kangaete-iru-no?（何を考えているの.）What are you thinking of?

Hokkaidô-e ikô-to-kangaete-iru（北海道へ行こうと考えている）intend to go to Hokkaido

kangaete-iru-yori muzukashii（考えているより難しい）more difficult than I expect

Mô-ichi-do kangaete-minasai.（もう一度考えてみなさい.）Consider it once more.

kangae-tsuku〈かんがえつく：考え付く〉*see.* omoi-tsuku.

kangae-yô〈かんがえよう：考え様〉

Mono wa kangae-yô-da.（物は考え様だ.）It depends upon your way of thinking.

kangai〈かんがい〉irrigation.

kangai-suru〈かんがいする〉irrigate.

kangai〈かんがい：感慨〉deep emotion.

kangai-muryô-de-aru（感慨無量である）be full of deep emotion

kan-gakki〈かんがっき：管楽器〉a wind instrument.

kangarû〈カンガルー〉a kangaroo.

kangei〈かんげい：歓迎〉(a) reception.

kangei-kai o hiraku（歓迎会を開く）hold a reception (in honor of)

kangei-suru〈歓迎する〉welcome.

kokoro-kara kangei-suru（心から歓迎する）give a hearty welcome

kokoro-kara kangei-sareru（心から歓迎される）be heartily welcomed

kangeki〈かんげき：感激〉

kangeki-suru〈感激する〉be deeply moved ((by)).

kangeki-shite-namida-ga-deru（感激して涙が出る）be moved to tears

kangeki〈かんげき：観劇〉theatergoing.

kangeki-kai（観劇会）a theater-party

kangen〈かんげん：換言〉

kangen-sureba〈換言すれば〉in other words.

kangen〈かんげん：還元〉reduction.

kangen-suru〈還元する〉reduce, deoxidize.

kangen-gaku(-dan) 〈かんげんがく（だん）：管弦楽(団)〉an orchestra.

kango 〈かんご：看護〉nursing.
kango-fu〈看護婦〉a nurse
kango-suru〈看護する〉nurse.

kangoku 〈かんごく：監獄〉a prison, a jail, a gaol.

kani 〈かに〉a crab.

kan·i 〈かんい：簡易〉simplicity.
kan·i-hoken〈簡易保険〉postal life insurance
kan·i-na〈簡易な〉simple, simplified.

kan-i-ka 〈かんいか：簡易化〉simplification.
kan-i-ka-suru〈簡易化する〉simplify.

kan-ippatsu 〈かんいっぱつ：間一髪〉
kan-ippatsu(-no-tokoro)-de〈間一髪(のところ)で〉by a hairbreadth.

kanja 〈かんじゃ：患者〉a patient, a case.

kanji 〈かんじ：幹事〉a manager, a secretary.
kanji-chô〈幹事長〉a chief secretary, a secretary-general

kanji 〈かんじ：漢字〉a Chinese character.

kanji 〈かんじ：感じ〉feeling, sense, touch, an impression.
kanji-ga-suru〈感じがする〉feel.
zara-zara-shita-kanji-ga-suru〈ざらざらした感じがする〉feel rough
kanji-o-ataeru〈感じを与える〉impress.
ii-kanji-o-ataeru〈いい感じを与える〉impress ((a person)) favorably
kanji-yasui〈感じやすい〉sensitive ((to)).
kanji-no-ii〈感じのいい〉agreeable.
kanji-no-warui〈感じの悪い〉disagreeable

kanjin 〈かんじん：肝心〉
kanjin-na〈肝心な〉main, essential, important, vital.
kanjin-na ten〈肝心な点〉a basic point, a vital point
kanjin-na toki-ni〈肝心な時に〉at a critical moment

kanjiru 〈かんじる：感じる〉feel.
fuben o kanjiru〈不便を感じる〉feel inconvenienced
itami o kanjiru〈痛みを感じる〉feel a pain
kûfuku o kanjiru〈空腹を感じる〉feel hungry

kanjô 〈かんじょう：勘定〉counting, accounts, a bill.
Kanjô-ga-au.〈勘定が合う。〉The account balances out.
kanjô o harau〈勘定を払う〉pay a bill
kanjô-suru〈勘定する〉count.

kanjô 〈かんじょう：感情〉feeling(s), emotion, sentiment, passion.

kanjô-ni-hashiru〔感情に走る〕 be carried away by one's feelings

kanjô-o-kao-ni-arawasu〔感情を顔に表す〕 display one's feelings

kanjô o osaeru〔感情を抑える〕 control one's feelings

hito-no kanjô o gaisuru〔人の感情を害する〕 hurt another's feelings

kanjô-teki(-na)〔感情的(な)〕emotional.

kanjô-teki-ni〔感情的に〕emotionally.

kanjô-o-komete〔感情を込めて〕with feeling.

kanjô〈かんじょう：環状〉

kanjô-dôro〔環状道路〕 a loop road

kanjô-sen〔環状線〕 a loop (line)

kanjô-no〔環状の〕ring-shaped, loop.

kanju-sei〈かんじゅせい：感受性〉sensibility.

kanju-sei-no-surudoi〔感受性の鋭い〕sensitive ((to)), recipient, impressionable.

kanka(-suru)〈かんか(する)：感化(する)〉influence.

kanka-o-ukeru〔感化を受ける〕be influenced ((by)).

kankaku〈かんかく：間隔〉a space, an interval.

aru-teido kankaku o oku〔ある程度間隔をおく〕 leave some space ((between))

ittei-no kankaku-o-oite〔一定の間隔をおいて〕 at regular intervals

kankaku〈かんかく：感覚〉sense.

kankaku-ga-surudoi〔感覚が鋭い〕 have keen senses

kankaku-ga-nibui〔感覚が鈍い〕 have dull senses

kankaku o ushinau〔感覚を失う〕 become senseless

shikisai-kankaku〔色彩感覚〕 the color sense

kankaku-no-nai〔感覚のない〕insensible, senseless.

kankan〈かんかん〉

Hi ga kankan tetteiru.〔日がかんかん照っている.〕 The sun is shining hot.

kankan-ni-natte-okoru〔かんかんになって怒る〕 be in a fume, get mad with anger

kankatsu〈かんかつ：管轄〉jurisdiction, control.

〜-no-kankatsu-ka-ni-aru〔〜の管轄下にある〕 be under the jurisdiction of...

kankatsu-kanchô〔管轄官庁〕 the competent authorities

kankatsu-suru〔管轄する〕have jurisdiction ((over)), control.

kankei〈かんけい：関係〉relation, relationship, connection, concern.

missetsu-na kankei〔密接な関係〕 a close relation

ningen kankei〈人間関係〉 human relationship

〜-to-mu-kankei-da〈〜と無関係だ〉 have nothing to do with... , have no relation to... , have no connection with... , have no bearing on ...

kankei-tôkyoku〈関係当局〉 the authorities concerned

kankei-shi〈関係詞〉 a relative.

kankei-suru or *kankei-ga-aru*〈関係する，関係がある〉 be related ((to)), be connected ((with)), have to do ((with)).

〜*-ni*(or 〜*-to)-kankei-naku*〈〜に(〜と)関係なく〉 regardless of... ,.irrespective of... , independently of... .

kanketsu〈かんけつ：完結〉 completion, conclusion, end.

Jigô-kanketsu.〈次号完結．〉 To be concluded.

kanketsu-suru〈完結する〉 complete, conclude, finish; be completed, be concluded, be finished.

kanketsu〈かんけつ：簡潔〉

kanketsu-na〈簡潔な〉 concise, brief.

kanketsu-ni〈簡潔に〉 concisely, briefly.

kanketsu-sen〈かんけつせん：間欠泉〉a geyser.

kanki〈かんき．喚起〉

kanki-suru〈喚起する〉 awaken, rouse, arouse, excite.

seron o kanki-suru〈世論を喚起する〉 rouse public opinion

kanki〈かんき：換気〉ventilation.

kanki-sen〈換気扇〉 a ventilating fan

kanki-ga-ii〈換気がいい〉be well ventilated

kanki-ga-warui〈換気が悪い〉 be ill ventilated

kanki-suru〈換気する〉ventilate.

kankin〈かんきん：監禁〉imprisonment, confinement.

kankin-suru〈監禁する〉imprison, confine.

kankin〈かんきん：換金〉

kankin-suru〈換金する〉realize, convert into money, cash.

kan-kiri〈かんきり：缶切り〉a can opener, a tin opener.

kankitsu-rui〈かんきつるい：かんきつ類〉citrus fruits, oranges.

kan-kô〈かんこう：官公〉

kan-kô-chô〈官公庁〉 government and municipal offices

kan-kô-ri〈官公吏〉 government and municipal officials

kankô〈かんこう：刊行〉publication.

kankô-butsu〈刊行物〉 a publication

kankô-suru〈刊行する〉publish, issue.

kankô 〈かんこう：観光〉 sightseeing.
　　kankô-ni-iku（観光に行く） go sightseeing
　　kankô-chi（観光地） a tourist resort
　　kankô-kyaku（観光客） a sightseer, a tourist
　　kankô-ryokô（観光旅行） a sightseeing tour
　kankô-suru〈観光する〉 see(*or* do) the sights.
kankô 〈かんこう：感光〉 exposure, sensitization.
　　kankô-do（感光度） sensitivity
　　kankô-shi（感光紙） sensitive paper
　kankô-saseru〈感光させる〉 expose 〔to light〕.
kankô 〈かんこう：慣行〉 *see.* kanshû（慣習）.
kankô 〈かんこう：敢行〉
　kankô-suru〈敢行する〉 dare ((to do)), venture ((to do)); carry out.
kanko-dori 〈かんこどり：かんこ鳥〉
　　Sono kanraku-gai wa kanko-dori-ga-naite-iru.（その歓楽街はかんこ鳥
　　が鳴いている。） The amusement center is deserted.
kan-kôhen 〈かんこうへん：肝硬変〉 cirrhosis of the liver.
kankoku 〈かんこく：勧告〉 advice, counsel, recommendation.
　kankoku-suru〈勧告する〉 advise, counsel, recommend.
kankon-sôsai 〈かんこんそうさい：冠婚葬祭〉 ceremonial occasions.
kankyaku 〈かんきゃく：観客〉 an(*or* the) audience, a spectator.
　　tasû-no kankyaku（多数の観客） a large audience
　　shôsû-no kankyaku（少数の観客） a small audience
kankyô 〈かんきょう：環境〉 environment, surroundings.
　　kankyô-no-ii（環境のいい） in good surroundings.
　　kankyô-no-warui（環境の悪い） in bad surroundings.
　　katei-kankyô（家庭環境） home environment
kanna 〈かんな〉 a plane.
　　kanna-kuzu（かんなくず） shavings
　kanna-o-kakeru〈かんなをかける〉 plane.
kannen 〈かんねん：観念〉 an idea, a sense; resignation.
　　gimu-kannen（義務観念） a sense of duty
　　jikan-kannen-ga-nai（時間観念がない） have no sense of time
　kannen-suru〈観念する〉 be resigned ((to)), resolve.
knnen-ron 〈かんねんろん：観念論〉 idealism.
　kannen-ron-teki(-na)〈観念論的(な)〉 ideological, ideal.
kannin 〈かんにん：堪忍〉 patience, forgiveness.
　kannin-suru〈堪忍する〉 forgive.

kannin-bukuro-no-o-ga-kireru〈堪忍袋の緒が切れる〉can no longer put up ((with)).

kanningu〈カンニング〉cheating.

kanningu-o-suru〈カンニングをする〉cheat〔in an examination〕.

kannô〈かんのう：官能〉

kannô-teki(-na)〈官能的(な)〉sensual.

kannô〈かんのう：完納〉

kannô-suru〈完納する〉pay the whole amount ((of)); finish up the delivery ((of)).

kannô〈かんのう：感応〉induction.

kannô-koiru（感応コイル）an induction coil

kannô-suru〈感応する〉induce.

kannon-biraki〈かんのんびらき：観音開き〉

kannon-biraki-no-to（観音開きの戸）a pair of folding doors that opens together on hinges.

kannuki〈かんぬき：閂〉a bolt, a bar.

kannuki-o-kakeru〈かんぬきを掛ける〉bar〔the gate〕.

kannushi〈かんぬし：神主〉a *Shinto* priest.

kanô〈かのう：化のう〉suppuration, maturation.

kanô-kin（化のう菌）suppurative germs

kanô-suru〈化のうする〉suppurate, mature.

kanô-sei-no〈化のう性の〉suppurative, purulent, maturating.

kanô(-sei)〈かのう(せい)：可能(性)〉possibility.

kanô-na or *kanô-sei-no-aru*〈可能な，可能性のある〉possible.

kanô-na-kagiri（可能な限り）as far as possible

fu-kanô-na or *kanô-sei-no-nai*〈不可能な，可能性のない〉impossible.

kano-jo〈かのじょ：彼女〉she.

kano-jo-wa *or* kano-jo-ga（彼女は，彼女が）she

kano-jo-no, kano-jo-ni *or* kano-jo-o（彼女の，彼女に，彼女を）her

kano-jo-no-mono〈彼女のもの〉hers

kano-jo-jishin（彼女自身）herself

kan·oke〈かんおけ：棺おけ〉a coffin.

kanraku〈かんらく：歓楽〉pleasure(s), gaieties.

kanraku-gai（歓楽街）an amusement center, gay quarters.

kanraku(-suru)〈かんらく(する)：陥落(する)〉fall, surrender.

kanran〈かんらん：観覧〉inspection.

kanran-ryô（観覧料）an admission fee

kanran-seki（観覧席）a seat, a stand, bleachers

kanran-suru〈観覧する〉see, visit.

kanrei〈かんれい：慣例〉custom.

    kanrei ni shitagau（慣例に従う）　follow the custom

    kanrei o yaburu（慣例を破る）　break the custom

kanrei-no〈慣例の〉customary, usual.

kanrei-ni-yori〈慣例により〉in accordance with the custom.

kanrei〈かんれい：寒冷〉

    kanrei-chi（寒冷地）　a cold district

    kanrei-zensen（寒冷前線）　a cold front

kanrei-na〈寒冷な〉cold, chilly.

kanreki〈かんれき：還暦〉

kanreki o iwau〈還暦を祝う〉celebrate one's 60th birthday.

kanren〈かんれん：関連〉relation, connection.

    kanren-jikô（関連事項）　related matters

    kanren-sangyô（関連産業）　allied industries

    kanren-sei（関連性）　relevance, relevancy

～-ni-kanren-shite〈～に関連して〉in relation to... , in connection with... .

kanri〈かんり：管理〉administration, management, control, charge.

    kanri-nin（管理人）　an administrator, a manager, an executor, a caretaker

kanri-suru〈管理する〉administer, manage, control, take charge ((of)), care ((for)).

    kôjô o kanri-suru（工場を管理する）　manage a factory

    hito-no zaisan o kanri-suru（人の財産を管理する）take charge of another's property

kanryaku〈かんりゃく：簡略〉

kanryaku-ni-suru〈簡略にする〉make simple, simplify.

    sotsugyô-shiki o dekiru-dake kanryaku-ni-suru（卒業式をできるだけ簡略にする）　make the graduation ceremony as simple as possible

kanryaku-na〈簡略な〉simple, brief, informal.

kanryô〈かんりょう：官僚〉a bureaucrat.

    kanryô-shugi（官僚主義）　bureaucratism

kanryô-teki(-na)〈官僚的(な)〉bureaucratic.

kanryô〈かんりょう：完了〉completion, conclusion.

kanryô-suru〈完了する〉complete, conclude, finish; be completed, be concluded, be finished.

kanryû〈かんりゅう：寒流〉a cold current.

kansa〈かんさ：監査〉inspection, audit.

　　kansa-yaku（監査役）an inspector, an auditor
　kansa-suru〈監査する〉inspect, audit.
kansan〈かんさん：換算〉conversion, change.
　　kansan-hyô（換算表）a conversion table
　　kansan-ritsu（換算率）the exchange rate
　kansan-suru〈換算する〉convert, change ((into)).
kansan〈かんさん：閑散〉
　　kansan-ki（閑散期）an off season, a slack season
　kansan-na〈閑散な〉leisurely, dull, inactive, slack.
kansatsu〈かんさつ：観察〉observation.
　　kansatsu-ga-surudoi（観察が鋭い）be sharp in observation
　　kansatsu-ryoku（観察力）one's power of observation
　kansatsu-suru〈観察する〉observe.
kansatsu〈かんさつ：鑑札〉a license.
　　kansatsu o ukeru（鑑札を受ける）take (out) a license
　　inu-no kansatsu（犬の鑑札）a dog's tag, a dog license
kansatsu〈かんさつ：監察〉inspection.
　　kansatsu-kan（監察官）an inspector, a supervisor
kansei〈かんせい：閑静〉quiet, tranquility.
　kansei-na〈閑静な〉quiet, tranquil.
kansei〈かんせい：慣性〉inertia.
kansei〈かんせい：乾性〉
　kansei-no〈乾性の〉dry, drying.
kansei〈かんせい：完成〉completion, accomplishment.
　　kansei-hin（完成品）finished goods
　kansei-suru〈完成する〉complete, accomplish, finish; be completed, be accomplished, be finished.
kansei〈かんせい：歓声〉a shout of joy, a cheer, a hurrah.
　kansei-o-ageru〈歓声を上げる〉shout for joy.
kansei-hagaki〈かんせいはがき：官製はがき〉an official postcard, a postal card.
kansei-tô〈かんせいとう：管制塔〉a control tower.
kansen〈かんせん：幹線〉a trunk line, a main line.
　　kansen-dôro（幹線道路）a trunk road, an arterial road
kansen〈かんせん：汗腺〉a sweat gland.
kansen〈かんせん：感染〉infection, contagion.
　kansen-suru〈感染する〉be infected ((with)).
　kansen-sei(-no)〈感染性(の)〉infectious, contagious.

kansen〈かんせん：観戦〉
 kansen-suru（観戦する）watch a game
kansetsu〈かんせつ：関節〉a joint.
 kansetsu-en（関節炎）inflammation of a joint
kansetsu〈かんせつ：間接〉
kansetsu-no〈間接の〉indirect.
kansetsu-ni〈間接に〉indirectly.
kansha〈かんしゃ：官舎〉an official residence.
kansha〈かんしゃ：感謝〉thanks, gratitude.
 kansha no shirushi-made-ni（感謝の印までに）as a token of one's
  gratitude
 kansha-jô（感謝状）a letter of thanks
kansha-suru〈感謝する〉thank, be thankful ((for)), be grateful ((for)).
kanshaku〈かんしゃく〉passion, temper.
 kanshaku o okosu（かんしゃくを起こす）lose one's temper, fall into
  a passion
 kanshaku-mochi（かんしゃく持ち）a hot-tempered person
 kanshaku-mochi-no（かんしゃく持ちの）hot-tempered
kanshi〈かんし：漢詩〉Chinese poetry, a Chinese poem.
kanshi〈かんし：冠詞〉an article.
kanshi(-suru)〈かんし（する）：監視（する）〉watch.
kanshiki〈かんしき：鑑識〉judgment, identification.
 kanshiki-gan（鑑識眼）a critical eye ((for))
 kanshiki-ka（鑑識家）a judge, a connoisseur, an appraiser
 kanshiki-ka（鑑識課）the Identification Section
kanshiki-suru〈鑑識する〉judge, be a judge ((of)).
kanshin〈かんしん：関心〉concern, interest.
kanshin-ga-aru〈関心がある〉be concerned ((with)), be interested ((in)).
 kanshin-ga-nai（関心がない）be indifferent ((to))
  hotondo kanshin-ga-nai（ほとんど関心がない）be little concerned
  ((with)), be little interested ((in))
kanshin〈かんしん：感心〉admiration, wonder.
kanshin-suru〈感心する〉admire, be deeply impressed ((by *or* with)).
kanshin-na〈感心な〉admirable, praiseworthy.
kanshin-shite〈感心して〉with admiration, admiringly.
kanshin〈かんしん：寒心〉
 ～-wa-kanshin-ni-tae-nai.〈～は寒心に堪えない。〉It is a matter for regret
 that... .

kanshin〈かんしん：歓心〉favor.

kanshin o kau〈歓心を買う〉win ((a person's)) favor

(-ni)-kanshite〈～(に)かんして：～(に)関して〉see. (-ni)-tsuite.

kansho〈かんしょ：寒暑〉heat and cold, temperature.

Koko-wa kansho-no-sa-ga-hageshii.（ここは寒暑の差が激しい。）The heat and cold are both extreme here.

kanshô〈かんしょう：環礁〉an atoll.

kanshô〈かんしょう：鑑賞〉appreciation.

kanshô-suru〈鑑賞する〉appreciate.

kanshô〈かんしょう：干渉〉(an) interference, (an) intervention.

kanshô-suru〈干渉する〉interfere ((in or with)), intervene ((in)).

kanshô〈かんしょう：完勝〉

kanshô-suru〈完勝する〉win a complete victory ((over)).

kanshô〈かんしょう：感傷〉

kanshô-teki(-na)〈感傷的(な)〉sentimental.

kanshô-chitai〈かんしょうちたい：緩衝地帯〉a buffer zone, a neutral zone.

kanshoku〈かんしょく：閑職〉a sinecure, a leisurely post.

kanshoku〈かんしょく：官職〉a government post.

kanshoku-ni-tsuite-iru（官職に就いている）be in the government service

kanshoku〈かんしょく：感触〉the touch, a feel.

kanshoku-ga-yawarakai（感触が柔らかい）be soft to the touch, feel soft

kanshoku〈かんしょく：間食〉

kanshoku-suru〈間食する〉eat between meals.

kanshu〈かんしゅ：看守〉a prison guard, a jailer, a gaoler.

kanshū〈かんしゅう：慣習〉custom, (a) usual practice.

kanshū〈かんしゅう：観衆〉spectators, an audience.

kanshū〈かんしゅう：監修〉(editorial) supervision.

kanshū-sha（監修者）a supervisor, the chief editor

kanshū-suru〈監修する〉supervise.

kanso〈かんそ：簡素〉simplicity.

kanso-ka（簡素化）simplification

kanso-ka-suru（簡素化する）simplify

kanso-na〈簡素な〉simple, plain.

kansô〈かんそう：乾燥〉drying.

ijô-kansô-chûi-hô（異常乾燥注意報）a dry weather alert

    kansô-zai〈乾燥剤〉a desiccant

kansô-suru〈乾燥する〉dry, become dry.

kansô-shita〈乾燥した〉dry, dried, parched.

kansô〈かんそう：感想〉thoughts, impression(s).

    kansô o noberu（感想を述べる）give one's impressions ((of))

    kansô-bun（感想文）a description of one's impressions

kansô〈かんそう：歓送〉

    kansô-kai（歓送会）a farewell party

kansoku〈かんそく：観測〉observation, a survey.

    kansoku-jo（観測所）an observatory

kansoku-suru〈観測する〉observe, survey.

kansô-kyoku〈かんそうきょく：間奏曲〉an interlude, an intermezzo.

kansû〈かんすう：関数〉a function.

kansui〈かんすい：完遂〉completion, successful execution.

kansui-suru〈完遂する〉complete, carry out.

kansuru〈かんする：関する〉be concerned ((with)), be connected ((with)).

    watashi-ni-kansuru-kagiri（私に関する限り）so far as I am concerned

~-*ni-kansuru* or ~-*ni-kanshite*〈～に関する、～に関して〉on, about, concerning, regarding, in connection with... .

    tori-ni-kansuru hon（鳥に関する本）a book on birds

kono-ten-ni-kanshite〈この点に関して〉in this respect.

kantai〈かんたい：寒帯〉the frigid zones.

kantai〈かんたい：艦隊〉a fleet, a squadron.

kantai〈かんたい：歓待〉a warm reception, hospitality.

kantai-suru〈歓待する〉give a warm reception, treat hospitably.

kantan〈かんたん：感嘆〉admiration ((for *or* of)), wonder, marvel.

    kantan-shi（感嘆詞）an exclamation, an interjection

kantan-suru〈感嘆する〉admire, wonder ((at)), marvel ((at)).

kantan-su-beki〈感嘆すべき〉admirable, wonderful, marvelous.

kantan〈かんたん：簡単〉simplicity, brevity.

kantan-na〈簡単な〉simple, brief, light, easy.

    kantan-na koto（簡単な事）a simple matter

    kantan-na tegami（簡単な手紙）a brief letter

    kantan-na shokuji（簡単な食事）a light meal

    kantan-na mondai（簡単な問題）an easy problem

kantan-meiryô-na〈簡単明りょうな〉simple and clear.

kantan-ni〈簡単に〉simply, briefly, in brief, easily, without difficulty.
　　kantan-ni-ieba（簡単に言えば）in short, in brief
kantan-ni-suru〈簡単にする〉make short, simplify.

kantei〈かんてい：官邸〉an official residence〔of the Prime Minister〕.

kantei〈かんてい：鑑定〉judgment, an expert opinion, legal advice, appraisal, estimation.
　　kantei-ka（鑑定家）a judge, a connoisseur, an appraiser
kantei-suru〈鑑定する〉judge, give an expert opinion ((on)), appraise, estimate.
kantei-shite-morau〈鑑定してもらう〉have ((a thing)) judged (by), have ((a thing)) appraised (by).

kanten〈かんてん：寒天〉agar-agar.

kanten〈かんてん：観点〉a point of view, a viewpoint.
　　rekishi-teki kanten-kara-suru-to（歴史的観点からすると）from the historical point of view

kantetsu〈かんてつ：貫徹〉
kantetsu-suru〈貫徹する〉carry out, carry through, accomplish, realize, attain.

kantô〈かんとう：敢闘〉
　　kantô-seishin（敢闘精神）a fighting spirit
　　kantô-shô（敢闘賞）a fighting spirit award
kantô-suru〈敢闘する〉put up a manly fight ((with)), fight gamely.

kantô〈かんとう：完投〉
kantô-suru〈完投する〉pitch the full innings.

kantoku〈かんとく：監督〉supervision, control, direction; a supervisor, an overseer, a director, a manager.
　　jo-kantoku（助監督）an assistant director
kantoku-suru〈監督する〉supervise, control, oversee, direct, look ((after)).
　　seito-o-kantoku-suru（生徒を監督する）look after one's students
～*-no-kantoku-no-moto-ni*〈～の監督の下に〉under the supervision of... , under the direction of... .

kantô-shi〈かんとうし：間投詞〉an interjection.

kantsû〈かんつう：貫通〉
kantsû-suru〈貫通する〉pass through, penetrate; shoot through; tunnel through; run through.

kantsû〈かんつう：かん通〉
kantsû-suru〈かん通する〉commit adultery ((with)).

kanwa〈かんわ：緩和〉relief, mitigation, relaxation.

kanwa-suru〈緩和する〉ease, lighten, mitigate, relieve, relax.

    seigen o kanwa-suru〈制限を緩和する〉 ease restrictions ((on))

Kan-Wa〈かんわ：漢和〉

    Kan-Wa-jiten〈漢和辞典〉 a dictionary of classical Chinese or Chinese classics explained in Japanese

kan·yaku〈かんやく：完訳〉a complete translation.

kan·yo〈かんよ：関与〉

kan·yo-suru〈関与する〉participate ((in)), take part ((in)).

    seiji-ni-kan·yo-suru〈政治に関与する〉 participate in politics

kan·yō〈かんよう：慣用〉common use, usage.

    kan·yō-go-ku〈慣用語句〉 an idiomatic expression, an idiom

kan·yō-no〈慣用の〉common, usual, idiomatic.

kan·yō〈かんよう：肝要〉

kan·yō-na〈肝要な〉very important, vital ((to)), indispensable, essential.

kan·yō〈かんよう：寛容〉leniency, generosity.

kan·yō-na〈寛容な〉lenient, generous.

kan·yu〈かんゆ：肝油〉cod-liver oil.

kanyū〈かにゅう：加入〉joining, entry, subscription.

    kanyū-sha〈加入者〉 a member, a subscriber

kanyū-suru〈加入する〉join, enter, become a member ((of)), subscribe ((for)).

    kurabu ni kanyū-suru〈クラブに加入する〉 join a club

kan·yū〈かんゆう：勧誘〉invitation, persuasion, inducement, canvassing.

kan·yū-suru〈勧誘する〉invite, persuade, induce, canvass ((for)).

kan·yū-chi〈かんゆうち：官有地〉a demesne of the State.

kanzai〈かんざい：管財〉

    kanzai-nin〈管財人〉 an administrator, a receiver

kanzei〈かんぜい：関税〉customs.

kanzei-no-kakaru〈関税の掛かる〉dutiable, liable to duty.

    kanzei-no-kakara-nai〈関税の掛からない〉 undutiable, duty-free

kanzen〈かんぜん：完全〉perfection, completeness.

kanzen-na〈完全な〉perfect, complete.

    kanzen-na shippai〈完全な失敗〉 a complete failure

kanzen-ni〈完全に〉perfectly, completely.

    kanzen-ni-naru〈完全になる〉 become perfect

    kanzen-ni-suru〈完全にする〉 perfect, make perfect

kanzen〈かんぜん：敢然〉

　kanzen-to〈敢然と〉bravely, boldly, fearlessly.

kanzō〈かんぞう：肝臓〉the liver.

kan-zuku〈かんづく：感付く〉suspect, scent, sense, get wind ((of)).

　kan-zukareru〈感付かれる〉be suspected ((by)).

kanzume〈かんづめ：缶詰〉canned food, tinned food.

　　maguro-no kanzume（まぐろの缶詰）canned tuna

　kanzume-ni-suru〈缶詰にする〉can, tin.

kao〈かお：顔〉a face, a look, an expression, an air, one's honor.

　　utsukushii kao（美しい顔）a beautiful face

　　kao o arau（顔を洗う）wash one's face

　　kao-o-makka-ni-suru（顔を真っ赤にする）blush

　　kao o miru（顔を見る）look ((a person)) in the face

　　kao o mi-awasu（顔を見合わす）look at each other

　　kao o shitte-iru（顔を知っている）know ((a person)) by sight

　　fu-kigen-na kao(-tsuki) *or* muzukashii kao(-tsuki)（不機嫌な顔（つき），
　　　難しい顔（つき））a sullen face

　　odoroita kao(-tsuki)（驚いた顔（つき））a look of surprise

　　okotta kao(-tsuki)（怒った顔（つき））an angry look

　　suzushii kao o suru（涼しい顔をする）assume a nonchalant air

　　kao-ga-hiroi（顔が広い）be widely known

　　kao-ga-tatsu（顔が立つ）save one's face

　　kao-ni-kakawaru（顔に係わる）affect one's honor

kao-awase〈かおあわせ：顔合わせ〉

　kao-awase-o-suru〈顔合わせをする〉meet each other, be pitted against
　each other, appear in the same play.

kao-bure〈かおぶれ：顔触れ〉the personnel, the cast.

　　shin-naikaku no kao-bure（新内閣の顔触れ）the personnel of the
　　new Cabinet

　　haiyû no kao-bure（俳優の顔触れ）the cast of a play

kao-dachi〈かおだち：顔立ち〉features, looks, a face.

　　kao-dachi-ga-ii（顔立ちがいい）have good features

kao-iro〈かおいろ：顔色〉complexion, color.

　　kao-iro o kaeru（顔色を変える）change color

　　kao-iro-ga-ii（顔色がいい）look well

　　kao-iro-ga-warui（顔色が悪い）look pale

　　kao-iro-o-ukagau（顔色をうかがう）study the pleasure ((of a person))

kaoku〈かおく：家屋〉a house, a building.

kaoku-shûsen-nin〈家屋周旋人〉 a house agent

kao-make〈かおまけ：顔負け〉

kao-make-suru〈顔負けする〉be put into the shade, be put to the blush.

kao-mise〈かおみせ：顔見せ〉one's debut, one's first appearance on the stage.

kao-muke〈かおむけ：顔向け〉

Seken-ni　kao-muke-ga-deki-nai.（世間に顔向けができない。） I　dare not show myself in public.

kaori〈かおり：香り〉smell, scent, odor, fragrance.

ii kaori-ga-suru（いい香りがする） smell sweet

kaori-no-ii〈香りのいい〉fragrant.

kao-tsuki〈かおつき：顔つき〉a countenance, a look, an expression.

sabishi-sô-na kao-tsuki（寂しそうな顔つき） a forlorn look

kao-yaku〈かおやく：顔役〉a man of influence, a boss.

kappa〈かっぱ〉a water imp; a good swimmer.

kapparai〈かっぱらい：かっ払い〉pilfering; a pilferer, a sneak thief.

kapparau〈かっ払う〉pilfer, sneak.

kappatsu〈かっぱつ：活発〉liveliness, activity.

kappatsu-na〈活発な〉lively, active.

kappatsu-na giron（活発な議論） lively discussion

kappatsu-ni〈活発に〉livelily, briskly, actively.

kappu〈カップ〉a cup.

yûshô-kappu（優勝カップ） a trophy, a champion cup

kappuku〈かっぷく：かっ幅〉

kappuku-no-ii hito（かっ幅のいい人） a man of stout build.

kapuseru〈カプセル〉a capsule.

kara〈から：殻〉a husk, a hull, a shell.

tamago-no-kara（卵の殻） an eggshell

kara〈から：空〉

kara-ni-naru〈空になる〉become empty.

kara-ni-suru〈空にする〉empty, make ((a bottle)) empty.

kara-no〈空の〉empty, vacant.

-kara〈-から〉from, out of, through, at, in, since, after, of, as, because, since, by.

Tôkyô-kara Ôsaka-made（東京から大阪まで） from Tokyo to Osaka

san-ji-kara go-ji-made（三時から五時まで） from three to five o'clock

asa-kara ban-made（朝から晩まで） from morning till night

haha-kara-no tegami（母からの手紙） a letter from mother

fu-chûi-kara (不注意から) from one's carelessness, because of one's carelessness

kuruma-kara-oriru (車から降りる) get out of a car

kôki-shin-kara (好奇心から) out of curiosity

mado-kara miru (窓から見る) look through the window

katte-guchi-kara-hairu (勝手口から入る) come in at a kitchen door

higashi-kara noboru (東から昇る) rise in the east

sore-kara-zutto (それからずっと) ever since then

kuraku-natte-kara (暗くなってから) after dark

ki-kara-dekiru (木からできる) be made of wood

budô-kara dekiru (ぶどうからできる) be made from grapes

Osoi-kara, 〜 (遅いから〜) As it is late, ...

Anata-ga sô iu-kara, 〜 (あなたがそう言うから〜) Since you say so, ...

gaiken-kara hito o handan-suru (外見から人を判断する) judge a person by a person's appearance

karâ 〈カラー〉 a collar.

karâ 〈カラー〉 color.

karâ-terebi (カラーテレビ) a color television set

kara-buri 〈からぶり：空振り〉

kara-buri-suru 〈空振りする〉 swing wide, fan the air.

karada 〈からだ：体〉 the body, build, constitution, health.

karada-jû (体中) the whole body, all over

gatchiri-shita-karada-no hito (がっちりした体の人) a man of strong build

karada-no-tsuyoi-hito (体の強い人) a man of strong constitution

karada-no-yowai-hito (体の弱い人) a man of weak constitution

karada-ni ii (体にいい) be good for the health

karada-ni warui (体に悪い) be bad for the health

karada-no-chôshi-ga-ii (体の調子がいい) be in good health

karada-no-chôshi-ga-warui (体の調子が悪い) be in poor health

karada o kowasu (体をこわす) injure one's health

karada-ni-ki-o-tsukeru (体に気を付ける) take care of oneself, be careful of one's health

karada-o-yasumeru 〈体を休める〉 have a rest.

karada-tsuki 〈からだつき：体つき〉 one's figure, one's shape.

karada-tsuki-no-ganjô-na 〈体つきの頑丈な〉 strongly-built.

kara-genki 〈からげんき：空元気〉 a show of courage, Dutch courage.

karai 〈からい：辛い〉 hot, salty, severe.

    karai karê（辛いカレー） hot curried rice

    aji-ga-karai（味が辛い） taste salty

    karai-ten-o-tsukeru（辛い点を付ける） be severe in marking

kara-ibari(-suru) 〈からいばり（する）：空威張り（する）〉 bluster, bluff.

kâ-rajio 〈カーラジオ〉 a dashboard radio.

karakara 〈からから〉

    nodo-ga-karakara-da（のどがからからだ） be parched with thirst.

karakau 〈からかう〉 make fun ((of)), tease.

    karakatte（からかって） for fun.

    karakai-hambun-ni（からかい半分に） half for fun.

kara-kuchi 〈からくち：辛口〉

    kara-kuchi-de-aru（辛口である） have a salty tooth

    kara-kuchi-no sake（辛口の酒） dry *sake*

kara-kuji 〈からくじ：空くじ〉 a blank.

    kara-kuji o hiku（空くじを引く） draw a blank in a lottery

karakuri 〈からくり〉 mechanism, works; a trick.

kara-kusa-moyô 〈からくさもよう：唐草模様〉 an arabesque design.

kara-mawari 〈からまわり：空回り〉

    kara-mawari-suru〈空回りする〉 slip, run idle, idle; turn out ineffective.

karami-au 〈からみあう：絡み合う〉 get tangled together.

    Sono ken wa iroiro-na jijô-to-karami-atte-iru.（その件はいろいろな事情
    と絡み合っている.） The matter is entangled with various
    circumstances.

karami-tsuku 〈からみつく：絡み付く〉 twine itself round, entwine.

    No-bara ga kaki-ne-ni-karami-tsuite-iru.（野ばらが垣根に絡み付いてい
    る.） Wild rose bushes entwine the hedge.

karamu 〈からむ：絡む〉 pick a quarrel ((with)).

kara-ni 〈からに：空荷〉

    kara-ni-de〈空荷で〉 unloades, in ballast.

karappo 〈からっぽ：空っぽ〉

    Kono hon wa naiyô-ga-karappo-da.（この本は内容が空っぽだ.） This
    book has no substance.

karari-to 〈からりと〉

    karari-to-hareta sora（からりと晴れた空） a clear sky

karashi 〈からし：辛子〉 mustard.

karasu 〈からす〉 a crow, a raven.

karasu 〈からす〉

koe o karasu（声をからす）talk oneself hoarse

koe-o-karashite（声をからして）in a hoarse voice.

koe-ga-kareru〈声がかれる〉get hoarse.

karasu〈からす：枯らす〉kill, blight, blast, wither, season.

kareru〈枯れる〉die, be blasted, wither, be seasoned.

kareta〈枯れた〉dead, withered, dry.

karasu〈からす〉dry up, exhaust; drain.

kareru〈かれる〉dry up, run dry, be exhausted.

Ido ga kareta.（井戸がかれた。）The well has dried up.

karate〈からて：空手〉a self-defense art, *karate*.

kara-tegata〈からてがた：空手形〉a fictitious bill; an empty promise.

kara-tō〈からとう：辛党〉a drinker.

kara-tsuyu〈からつゆ：空梅雨〉a dry rainy season.

karatto〈からっと〉see. karari-to.

kare〈かれ：彼〉he.

kare-wa *or* kare-ga（彼は，彼が）he

kare-no（彼の）his

kare-ni *or* kare-o（彼に，彼を）him

kare-no-mono（彼のもの）his

kare-jishin（彼自身）himself

kare-〈かれ-：枯れ-〉

kare-eda（枯れ枝）a dead branch

kare-ha（枯れ葉）a dead leaf

kare-ki（枯れ木）a dead tree

kare-kusa（枯れ草）dry grass

karê〈カレー〉curry.

karê-ko（カレー粉）curry powder

karê-raisu（カレーライス）curry and rice, curried rice

karei〈かれい〉a flatfish, a turbot.

karei〈かれい：華麗〉splendor, magnificence.

karei-na〈華麗な〉splendid, magnificent.

karekore〈かれこれ〉about, some, almost, nearly.

Mô karekore san-ji-da.（もうかれこれ三時だ。）It is nearly three o'clock.

karekore-suru-uchi-ni〈かれこれするうちに〉meantime, meanwhile.

karekore-iu〈かれこれ言う〉talk ((about)), say things ((about)), criticize, grumble ((about)), complain ((about *or* of)).

karen〈かれん：可れん〉

karen-na〈可れんな〉pitiful, poor; pretty, lovely.
karendâ〈カレンダー〉a calendar.
kare-ra〈かれら：彼ら〉they.
    kare-ra-wa *or* kare-ra-ga（彼らは，彼らが） they
    kare-ra-no（彼らの） their
    kare-ra-ni *or* kare-ra-o（彼らに，彼らを） them
    kare-ra-no-mono（彼らのもの） theirs
    kare-ra-jishin（彼ら自身） themselves
kari〈かり〉a wild goose.
kari〈かり：狩り〉hunting, a hunt.
    kari-ni-iku（狩りに行く） go hunting
    kari-o-suru〈狩りをする〉hunt, shoot.
kari〈かり：借り〉a debt, a loan, a bill.
    kari o kaesu（借りを返す） pay a debt
    kari-ga-aru〈借りがある〉be in debt ((to)), owe ((a person)) money.
kari〈かり：仮〉
    kari-barai-kin（仮払金） a temporary payment
    kari-chôin（仮調印） an initial signature
    kari-eigyô-sho（仮営業所） a temporary office
    kari-menkyo-shô（仮免許証） a temporary license
    kari-ryôshû-sho（仮領収書） an interim receipt
    kari-shobun（仮処分） provisional disposition
    kari-teiryû-jo（仮停留所） a temporary bus stop
    kari-shakuhô *or* kari-shussho（仮釈放，仮出所） release on parole
    kari-no〈仮の〉temporary, provisional.
    kari-ni〈仮に〉temporarily.
    kari-nimo〈仮にも〉even for a time.
    kari-ni~-to-sureba〈仮に〜とすれば〉suppose... , supposing (that)... .
    kari-ni~-to-shite-mo〈仮に〜としても〉even if.
kari-atsumeru〈かりあつめる：駆り集める〉muster, gather together, round up.
kari-chin〈かりちん：借り賃〉(a) rent, hire.
kari-dasu〈かりだす：狩(駆)り出す〉hunt out, start; urge.
kariesu〈カリエス〉caries.
    sekitsui-kariesu（せきついカリエス） spinal caries
kari-gi〈かりぎ：借り着〉borrowed clothing.
    kari-gi-suru（借り着する） wear borrowed clothes
kari-ire〈かりいれ：刈り入れ〉a harvest, harvesting.

kari-ireru〈刈り入れる〉harvest, reap, gather in.

kari-ire-kin〈かりいれきん：借入金〉a loan (of money).

kari-kata〈かりかた：借方〉the debit, the debtor.

kari-kata-ni kinyū-suru（借方に記入する） enter ((a sum)) on the debtor side

kari-kiru〈かりきる：借り切る〉engage wholly.

ryokan-ikken-o-kari-kiru（旅館一軒を借り切る） engage a whole hotel

kari-komi〈かりこみ：狩り込み〉a round-up.

kari-komi-o-yaru〈狩り込みをやる〉round up〔street girls〕.

kari-komu〈かりこむ：刈り込む〉trim, clip, prune, hack.

kari-koshi〈かりこし：借り越し〉an overdraft.

kari-koshi-ni-natte-iru〈借り越しになっている〉remain outstanding.

kari-mono〈かりもの：借りもの〉a borrowed thing.

kari-nui〈かりぬい：仮縫い〉fitting.

kariru〈かりる：借りる〉borrow, owe, rent, hire, use.

hon o kariru（本を借りる） borrow a book

Kanojo-ni ichi-man-en karite-iru.（彼女に一万円借りている.） I owe her ten thousand yen.

ie o kariru（家を借りる） rent a house

Denwa o o-kari-dekimasu-ka?（電話をお借りできますか.） May I use your telephone?

kari-taosu〈かりたおす：借り倒す〉*see.* fumi-taosu.

kari-tateru〈かりたてる：駆り立てる〉drive, spur ((on)).

kari-te〈かりて：借り手〉a borrower, a debtor, a tenant, a renter, a lessee.

kari-toru〈かりとる：刈り取る〉reap, harvest, mow.

kariumu〈カリウム〉potassium.

karō〈かろう：過労〉overwork.

karō-kara byōki-ni-naru（過労から病気になる） fall ill from overwork

karôjite〈かろうじて：辛うじて〉*see.* yatto.

karonjiru〈かろんじる：軽んじる〉make light ((of)), slight, neglect.

jibun-no jôshi o karonjiru（自分の上司を軽んじる） slight one's superiors

karorî〈カロリー〉a calorie, a calory.

karorî-no-ooi tabe-mono（カロリーの多い食べ物） food of high calorie content

karu〈かる：刈る〉cut, mow, reap, harvest, shear.

kami o katte-morau（髪を刈ってもらう） have a haircut

shibafu o karu〔芝生を刈る〕 mow the lawn
ine o karu〔稲を刈る〕 reap rice
hitsuji-no-ke o karu〔羊の毛を刈る〕 shear a sheep

kâru〈カール〉a curl.
kami o kâru-shite-morau〔髪をカールしてもらう〕 have one's hair in curl

karugaru(-to)〈かるがる(と)：軽々(と)〉easily, without any effort.
karugaru-to hakobu〔軽々と運ぶ〕 carry easily

karugarushii〈かるがるしい：軽々しい〉light, thoughtless, rash, imprudent.
karugarushiku〈軽々しく〉lightly, rashly, hastily, imprudently.
karugarushiku handan-suru〔軽々しく判断する〕 judge hastily

karuhazumi〈かるはずみ：軽はずみ〉
karuhazumi-na〈軽はずみな〉rash, hasty, imprudent, indiscreet, thoughtless, reckless.
karuhazumi-na okonai〔軽はずみな行い〕 a rash act

karui〈かるい：軽い〉light, slight.
karui nimotsu〔軽い荷物〕 a light load
karui shokuji〔軽い食事〕 a light meal
karui kaze〔軽い風邪〕 a slight cold
kuchi-no-karui-hito〔口の軽い人〕 a gossipmonger

karu-ishi〈かるいし：軽石〉(a) pumice.
karu-ishi-de-kosuru〈軽石でこする〉pumice.

karuku〈かるく：軽く〉lightly, easily.
karuku shokuji-o-suru〔軽く食事をする〕 take a light meal
karuku katsu〔軽く勝つ〕 win easily
karuku-suru〈軽くする〉lighten, relieve.
kei o karuku-suru〔刑を軽くする〕 reduce a sentence

karushiumu〈カルシウム〉calcium.

karuta〈カルタ〉cards, a game of cards.
karuta-o-toru〔カルタを取る〕 play cards

karute〈カルテ〉a patient's chart.

karuteru〈カルテル〉a cartel.

karyoku〈かりょく：火力〉heat, heating power.
karyoku-hatsuden〔火力発電〕 steam-power generation

karyû〈かりゅう：下流〉the lower reaches of a stream.
karyû-no, karyû-de, karyû-e or *karyû-ni*〈下流の，下流で，下流へ，下流に〉downstream.

kasa 〈かさ：傘〉an umbrella, a parasol, a sunshade.

    kasa o sasu〈傘を差す〉put up an umbrella

    kasa o tatamu〈傘を畳む〉fold an umbrella

    kasa-no-yôi-o-suru〈傘の用意をする〉take an umbrella with one

    kasa-o-kariru〈傘を借りる〉use another's umbrella

    kasa-o-sashite〈傘を差して〉with an umbrella up.

kasa〈かさ〉a bamboo hat, a sedge hat; a shade, a hood; a cap.

kasa〈かさ〉bulk.

    kasa-no-aru or *kasa-batta*〈かさのある，かさ張った〉bulky.

kasa-buta〈かさぶた〉a scab.

kasai〈かさい：火災〉a fire.

    kasai-hôchi-ki〈火災報知器〉a fire alarm

    kasai-hoken〈火災保険〉fire insurance

kasakasa〈かさかさ〉

    hada-ga-kasakasa-shite-iru〈肌がかさかさしている〉be dry of skin.

kasaku〈かさく：佳作〉a fine work, a good piece of work.

kasamu〈かさむ〉increase, run up.

    Hiyô ga kasamu.〈費用がかさむ.〉The expenses run up.

kasan〈かさん：加算〉addition.

    kasan-zei〈加算税〉an additional tax

    kasan-suru〈加算する〉add, include.

kasanaru〈かさなる：重なる〉be piled up; fall on.

    fukô-ga-kasanaru〈不幸が重なる〉have a series of misfortunes

    Nichiyô-to-saijitsu-ga-kasanaru.〈日曜と祭日が重なる.〉Sunday falls on the national holiday.

    kasanatte〈重なって〉in piles.

kasaneru〈かさねる：重ねる〉pile up, heap up; repeat.

    tsukue-no-ue-ni hon o tsumi-kasaneru〈机の上に本を積み重ねる〉pile up books on the desk

    tsumi o kasaneru〈罪を重ねる〉repeat an offense

    kasanete〈重ねて〉in piles, repeatedly.

kasan-ka〈かさんか：過酸化〉

    kasan-ka-suiso〈過酸化水素〉peroxide of hydrogen

kasegi〈かせぎ：稼ぎ〉work, labor; income, earnings.

    kasegi-ni-deru〈稼ぎに出る〉go for work

    kasegi-ga-sukunai〈稼ぎが少ない〉have a poor income, have small earnings

    kasegu〈稼ぐ〉work, earn.

seikatsu-hi o kasegu（生活費を稼ぐ） work for one's living, earn one's bread

toki o kasegu（時を稼ぐ） gain time

kasei〈かせい：火勢〉the force of the fire.

Kasei ga otoroeta.（火勢が衰えた.） The fire has gone down.

kasei〈かせい：家政〉housekeeping.

kasei-ka（家政科） a course in domestic science

kasei〈かせい：火星〉Mars.

kasei〈かせい：加勢〉help, aid, assistance, support, reinforcements.

kasei-suru〈加勢する〉help, aid, assist, support, take sides ((with)).

kasei-sôda〈かせいソーダ：か性ソーダ〉caustic soda.

kaseki〈かせき：化石〉a fossil.

kasen〈かせん：河川〉rivers.

kasen-kaishû-kôji（河川改修工事） river improvement work

kasen〈かせん：架線〉an aerial line, wiring.

kasen-kôji（架線工事） wiring work

kasen〈かせん：化繊〉synthetic fiber.

kasen〈かせん：下線〉an underline.

kasen-o-hiku〈下線を引く〉underline.

kasen-o-hiita bubun（下線を引いた部分） an underlined part

kasetsu〈かせつ：仮説〉a hypothesis.

kasetsu-o-tateru〈仮説を立てる〉hypothesize.

kasetsu〈かせつ：架設〉construction, building, installation.

kasetsu-suru〈架設する〉construct, build, install.

denwa o kasetsu-suru（電話を架設する） install a telephone

kasha〈かしゃ：貨車〉a freight car, a goods waggon; a freight train.

kashi〈かし〉an oak, oak.

kashi-no-mi（かしの実） an acorn

kashi〈かし：歌詞〉the text, words, the libretto.

kashi〈かし：菓子〉confectionery, cake, candy, sweets.

kashi-ya（菓子屋） a confectioner; a confectionery, a candy store, a sweet shop

kashi〈かし：華氏〉Fahrenheit.

kashi-nana-jû-ni do（華氏七十二度） 72 degrees Fahrenheit

kashi〈かし：河岸〉a riverside, a riverbank; a fish market; a place, a scene.

kashi-o-kaeru（河岸を変える） try another place

kashi〈かし：貸し〉a loan, a bill, hire, lease.

Kare-ni-go-sen-en-kashi-ga-aru.〈彼に五千円貸しがある.〉 He owes me 5,000 yen.

kashi-daore-ni-naru〈貸し倒れになる〉 become uncollectable

kashi-biru〈かしビル：貸ビル〉a building for rent.

kashi-dashi〈かしだし：貸し出し〉a loan, lending, an advance.

kashi-dasu〈貸し出す〉loan out, make a loan ((to)).

kashigeru〈かしげる〉incline, lean, tilt.

kubi o kashigeru（首をかしげる） incline one's head on one side

kashi-hon〈かしほん：貸本〉a book to loan out.

kashi-hon-ya（貸本屋） a rental library

kashi-ishô〈かしいしょう：貸し衣装〉clothes for rent.

kashi-ishô-ya（貸し衣装屋） a costumier, a costumer

kashi-jimu-sho〈かしじむしょ：貸事務所〉an office for rent.

kashi-jôtai〈かしじょうたい：仮死状態〉a state of suspended animation.

ka-shikan〈かしかん：下士官〉a noncommissioned officer, a petty officer.

kashi-kari〈かしかり：貸し借り〉lending and borrowing.

Kore-de-kashi-kari-ga-nai.（これで貸し借りがない.） This makes us even.

kashi-kata〈かしかた：貸方〉the credit side, the creditor.

kashi-kata-ni kinyû-suru（貸方に記入する） enter ((a sum)) on the credit side

kashi-kin〈かしきん：貸し金〉a loan, an advance.

kashi-kinko〈かしきんこ：貸し金庫〉a safe-deposit box.

kashikiri〈かしきり：貸し切り〉

kashikiri-basu（貸し切りバス） a chartered bus

kashikiri-no〈貸し切りの〉reserved, chartered.

kashikoi〈かしこい：賢い〉wise, clever, bright, sagacious.

kashiko-sô-da（賢そうだ） seem bright

kashikomaru〈かしこまる〉

Kashikomarimashita.（かしこまりました.） Certainly, sir. / All right, sir.

kashi-koshi〈かしこし：貸し越し〉an overdraft.

kashi-koshi-ni-natte-iru〈貸し越しになっている〉remain unpaid.

kashi-ma〈かしま：貸間〉a room for rent, a room to let.

Kashi-ma-ari.（貸間あり.） Rooms for rent. / Rooms to let.

kashimiya〈カシミヤ〉cashmere.

kashin〈かしん：過信〉

kashin-suru〈過信する〉put too much trust ((in)).

kashi-nushi〈かしぬし：貸主〉a lender, a renter, a creditor, a lessor.

kashira〈かしら：頭〉the head; a leader, a captain, a chief, a boss.

 Kashira-hidari!〈頭左.〉 Eyes left!

 hito-no-kashira-ni-tatsu（人の頭に立つ）stand at the head of others, lead others

-ka-shira〈－かしら〉I wonder (if, whether, who, what, how, when, where *or* why).

kashira-moji〈かしらもじ：頭文字〉an initial, a capital letter.

kashi-te〈かして：貸し手〉a lender, a creditor, a landlord, a lessor.

kashitsu〈かしつ：過失〉a fault, a mistake, an error.

 kashitsu o okasu（過失を犯す）make a mistake, commit an error

 kashitsu-chishi(-zai)（過失致死(罪)）(an) accidental homicide

kashi-tsuke〈かしつけ：貸し付け〉loaning.

kashi-tsukeru〈貸し付ける〉loan, lend.

kashi-ya〈かしや：貸家〉a house for rent, a house to let.

kasho〈かしょ：箇所〉a place, a spot, a point; a part, a portion, a passage.

 onaji kasho-ni（同じ箇所に）in the same place

kashô〈かしょう：過小〉

kashô-hyôka-suru〈過小評価する〉underestimate, underrate.

kashu〈かしゅ：歌手〉a singer.

kashû〈かしゅう：歌集〉a collection of poems, an anthology.

kaso〈かそ：過疎〉

 kaso-chitai（過疎地帯）underpopulated areas

kasô〈かそう：下層〉a lower layer.

 kasô-un（下層雲）the lower layer of clouds

kasô〈かそう：仮装〉disguise.

 kasô-gyôretsu（仮装行列）a fancy-dress parade

kasô-suru〈仮装する〉disguise oneself ((as)).

kasô-shite〈仮装して〉in disguise.

kasô〈かそう：火葬〉cremation.

 kasô-ba（火葬場）a crematory

kasô-ni-suru〈火葬にする〉cremate.

kasô〈かそう：仮想〉imagination, (a) supposition.

 kasô-tekikoku（仮想敵国）a hypothetical enemy

kasoku(-do)〈かそく(ど)：加速(度)〉acceleration.

kasoku-do-teki-ni〈加速度的に〉at an increasing tempo.

kassai 〈かっさい：喝さい〉 cheers, applause.
 kassai o abiru（喝さいを浴びる）win applause
kassai-suru〈喝さいする〉cheer, give cheers, applaud.
kassei 〈かっせい：活性〉activity.
 kassei-tan（活性炭）activated charcoal
kassen 〈かっせん：合戦〉a battle, a fight.
 uta-gassen（歌合戦）a singing contest
kassha 〈かっしゃ：滑車〉a pulley.
kasshoku(-no) 〈かっしょく（の）：褐色（の）〉brown.
kassō 〈かっそう：滑走〉gliding.
 kassô-ro（滑走路）a runway
kassô-suru〈滑走する〉glide.
kassui 〈かっすい：渇水〉(a) shortage of water.
 kassui-ki（渇水期）the dry season
kasu 〈かす〉dregs, lees; refuse; scum.
kasu 〈かす：貸す〉lend, loan, lease, let, rent.
 chikara o kasu（力を貸す）lend one's aid ((to))
 kane o kasu（金を貸す）lend money
 ie o kasu（家を貸す）rent a house
kasuka 〈かすか〉
kasuka-na〈かすかな〉faint, dim, indistinct.
kasuka-ni〈かすかに〉faintly, dimly, indistinctly.
kasumeru 〈かすめる〉rob, plunder; skim, skirt.
 Kamome-ga-ichi-wa suimen-o-kasumete-tobi-satta.（かもめが一羽水面
 をかすめて飛び去った。）A sea gull skimmed over the water.
 Taifû ga Kii-hantô no nantan-o-kasumete-toori-sugita.（台風が紀伊半
 島の南端をかすめて通り過ぎた。）The typhoon skirted the southern
 end of the Kii Peninsula.
kasumi 〈かすみ〉(a) haze, (a) mist.
kasumi-ga-kakaru〈かすみがかかる〉be hazy, be misty.
kasumu〈かすむ〉be hazy; be dim, be blurred.
 me-ga-kasumu（目がかすむ）have dim eyes
kasureru 〈かすれる〉become hoarse; be scratchy; become blurred.
kasuri-kizu 〈かすりきず：かすり傷〉a scratch.
 honno kasuri-kizu（ほんのかすり傷）a mere scratch
kasuru 〈かする〉graze, rub.
kasuru 〈かする：課する〉impose, assign.
 bakkin o kasuru（罰金を課する）impose a fine ((on))

kasuru 〈かする：化する〉 change ((into *or* to)), turn ((into *or* to)), transform ((into *or* to)), make ((into)), influence; be turned, be transformed.

kasutera 〈カステラ〉 sponge cake.

kasu-zuke 〈かすづけ：かす漬け〉 vegetables pickled in *sake* lees.

kata 〈かた：肩〉 the shoulder.
    kata o sukumeru （肩をすくめる） shrug one's shoulders
    kata o tataku （肩をたたく） pat ((a person)) on the shoulder
    kata-no-ni-ga-oriru （肩の荷が降りる） feel a load off one's shoulders
    kata-o-motsu （肩を持つ） side ((with)), take sides ((with))
    kata-o-naraberu （肩を並べる） rank with ((another)), match, equal
    kata-ni-katsugu 〈肩に担ぐ〉 shoulder, carry on one's shoulder.
    〜-o-kata-ni-shite 〈〜を肩にして〉 with...on one's shoulder.
    kata-o-narabete 〈肩を並べて〉 shoulder to shoulder, side by side.

kata 〈かた：過多〉 excess, superabundance.
    isan-kata （胃酸過多） excess acid in the stomach

kata 〈かた：形(型)〉 (a) shape, a style, a type, a model, a pattern, a size.
    kata-ga-kuzureru （形がくずれる） get out of shape
    sen-kyû-hyaku-hachi-jû-san-nen-gata （1983年型） 1983 model
    kami-de kata o toru （紙で型をとる） make a pattern out of paper
    tokuyô-gata （徳用型） the economy size
    oo-gata-no （大型の） large-sized
    kata-ni-hamatta 〈型にはまった〉 conventional, stereotyped.

kata 〈かた：潟〉 a beach, a lagoon.

kata 〈かた：片〉
    kata-o-tsukeru 〈片を付ける〉 settle ((a matter)).
    kata-ga-tsuku 〈片が付く〉 be settled.

-kata 〈-かた：-方〉 a manner, a way; care of; a side.
    aruki-kata （歩き方） one's manner of walking
    hanashi-kata （話し方） one's way of talking
    kaki-kata （書き方） how to write
    Suzuki-sama-kata Nomoto-sama （鈴木様方野本様） Mr. Nomoto care of Mr. Suzuki
    haha-kata-no （母方の） on the maternal side

kata-ashi 〈かたあし：片足〉 one leg.
    kata-ashi-de tatsu （片足で立つ） stand on one leg

katabô 〈かたぼう：片棒〉
    katabô-o-katsugu 〈片棒を担ぐ〉 take part ((in)), take a hand ((in)).

kata-bôeki 〈かたぼうえき：片貿易〉one-way trade, unbalanced trade.

kata-butsu 〈かたぶつ：堅物〉a square.

katachi 〈かたち：形〉(a) form, (a) shape.

katachi-zukuru 〈形作る〉form, shape.

katachi-no-ii 〈形のいい〉well-shaped, shapely.

katachi-no-warui 〈形の悪い〉ill-shaped, unshapely

katachi-bakari-no 〈形ばかりの〉formal, token, for mere form's sake.

kata-doru 〈かたどる〉model ((after *or* on)), pattern ((after *or* on)), copy ((from)), reproduce.

kata-gaki 〈かたがき：肩書き〉a title, a handle 〔to one's name〕.

kata-gaki-no-aru hito 〈肩書きのある人〉 a man of title

kata-gami 〈かたがみ：型紙〉a paper pattern 〔for a dress〕.

katagata 〈かたがた〉partly...and partly, at the same time.

shôyô-katagata-Hokkaidô-kembutsu-ni-kuru 〈商用かたがた北海道見物に来る〉 come up to Hokkaido partly on business and partly for sightseeing

kata-gawa 〈かたがわ：片側〉one side.

Kata-gawa-tsûkô. 〈片側通行。〉 One-way Traffic.

kata-gawari 〈かたがわり：肩代わり〉

kata-gawari-suru 〈肩代わりする〉take over, subrogate.

kata-gi 〈かたぎ：堅気〉

kata-gi-ni-naru 〈堅気になる〉 begin to live a decent life

kata-gi-de-kurasu 〈堅気で暮らす〉 make an honest life

kata-goshi 〈かたごし：肩越し〉

kata-goshi-ni 〈肩越しに〉 over one's shoulder

kata-guruma 〈かたぐるま：肩車〉

kata-guruma-ni-noseru 〈肩車に乗せる〉have ((a child)) on one's shoulders.

kata-haba 〈かたはば：肩幅〉

kata-haba-ga-hiroi 〈肩幅が広い〉 have broad shoulders

kata-haba-ga-semai 〈肩幅が狭い〉 have narrow shoulders

kata-hiza 〈かたひざ：片ひざ〉one knee.

kata-hiza o tateru 〈片ひざを立てる〉 raise one knee

kata-hô 〈かたほう：片方〉one side, the other one; one of a pair, the fellow ((to)), the mate ((to)).

katai 〈かたい：硬(固，堅)い〉hard, tough, stiff, firm, strict, strong.

katai ishi 〈硬い石〉 a hard stone

katai niku 〈硬い肉〉 tough meat

katai kesshin〈固い決心〉 a firm resolution

katai hito〈堅い人〉 a man of strict morals

kataku〈硬(固,堅)く〉 hard, tightly, fast, firmly, strongly, positively, strictly.

kataku shibaru〈堅く縛る〉 bind tightly

kataku te o nigiru〈堅く手を握る〉 hold ((a person's)) hand firmly

kataku kotowaru〈固く断る〉 refuse positively

kataku kinzuru〈固く禁ずる〉 prohibit strictly

kataku-naru〈固くなる〉become hard.

kata-iji〈かたいじ：片意地〉

kata-iji-na〈片意地な〉stubborn, obstinate, headstrong, perverse.

kata-inaka〈かたいなか：片田舎〉the back country.

kataki〈かたき：敵〉an enemy, a foe; a rival.

kataki-uchi〈敵討ち〉 a vendetta, revenge, vengeance

kataki-yaku〈敵役〉 the villain's part

kata-koto〈かたこと：片言〉baby talk.

kata-koto o iu〈片言を言う〉 talk baby talk

kataku〈かたく：家宅〉a house.

kataku-sôsa〈家宅捜査〉 a house search

kataku-sôsa-o-suru〈家宅捜査をする〉 search a house

kataku-shinnyû-zai〈家宅侵入罪〉 housebreaking, trespass

katakuna〈かたくな〉*see.* ganko.

kata-kuri-ko〈かたくりこ：片くり粉〉dogtooth violet starch.

kata-kurushii〈かたくるしい：堅苦しい〉stiff, formal, strict.

kata-kurushii-koto-wa-nuki-ni-suru〈堅苦しいことは抜きにする〉 do without formalities

kata-kurushiku〈堅苦しく〉stiffly, formally.

katamari〈かたまり：塊(固まり)〉a mass, a lump; a group.

koori no katamari〈氷の塊〉 a lump of ice

yoku no katamari〈欲の固まり〉 a lump of avarice

katamaru〈かたまる：固まる〉harden, become hard; congeal, lump; gather.

Chi ga katamaru.〈血が固まる.〉 Blood clots.

katamatte〈固まって〉in groups.

katameru〈かためる：固める〉harden, make hard; strengthen.

danketsu o katameru〈団結を固める〉 strengthen the bond of union

mi-o-katameru〈身を固める〉 marry and settle down

kata-mi〈かたみ：肩身〉

kata-mi-ga-hiroi〈肩身が広い〉 feel proud

kata-mi-ga-semai〈肩身が狭い〉 feel small

kata-mi〈かたみ：形見〉a keepsake, a memento, a remembrance.

haha no kata-mi-to-shite〈母の形見として〉as a remembrance and keepsake of my deceased mother

kata-michi〈かたみち：片道〉one way.

kata-michi jôsha-ken〈片道乗車券〉a one-way ticket, a single ticket

katamukeru〈かたむける：傾ける〉incline, lean, slant; devote ((one-self)) to.

ongaku-ni-mimi-o-katamukeru〈音楽に耳を傾ける〉listen to music

katamuku〈かたむく：傾く〉incline ((to)), lean ((to or toward)), slope; decline, sink.

shindai-ga-katamuku〈身代が傾く〉sink in fortune.

Taiyô ga nishi-ni katamuiteiru.〈太陽が西に傾いている.〉The sun is sinking in the west.

katamuita〈傾いた〉slant, inclined.

katan〈かたん：荷担〉participation, conspiracy.

katan-suru〈荷担する〉participate ((in)), conspire ((with)).

katana〈かたな：刀〉a sword.

katana o nuku〈刀を抜く〉 draw a sword

kata-narashi〈かたならし：肩ならし〉

kata-narashi-o-suru〈肩ならしをする〉warm up, limber up.

katan-ito〈カタンいと：カタン糸〉cotton thread.

kata-omoi〈かたおもい：片思い〉one-sided love.

kata-oya〈かたおや：片親〉one parent.

kata-oya-no-nai〈片親のない〉fatherless, motherless.

katappashi〈かたっぱし：片っ端〉

katappashi-kara〈片っ端から〉one by one, one after another, one and all.

katari-akasu〈かたりあかす：語り明かす〉talk away the night.

katari-au〈かたりあう：語り合う〉talk together, talk ((with)).

kataru〈かたる：語る〉talk, tell, relate, narrate.

mukashi o kataru〈昔を語る〉 talk about old times

kataru〈かたる〉swindle, defraud, cheat; assume.

na o kataru〈名をかたる〉 assume ((a person's)) name

katasa〈かたさ：硬(固, 堅)さ〉hardness, solidity, stiffness, toughness, consistency, tightness, steadiness.

kata-sukashi〈かたすかし：肩透かし〉

kata-sukashi-o-kuwaseru〈肩透かしを食わせる〉dodge〔a blow〕.

kata-sumi〈かたすみ：片隅〉a corner, a nook.
kata-te〈かたて：片手〉one hand.
kata-tema〈かたてま：片手間〉
　kata-tema-ni〈片手間に〉in one's spare time, in leisure hours, as a side job.
katate-ochi〈かたておち：片手落ち〉
　katate-ochi-no〈片手落ちの〉one-sided, unfair, partial, prejudiced.
　　katate-ochi-no sabaki（片手落ちの裁き）one-sided judgment
kata-toki〈かたとき：片時〉
　kata-toki-mo〈片時も〉even for a moment.
katatsumuri〈かたつむり：片手間〉a snail.
kata-ude〈かたうで：片腕〉one arm; one's right hand.
　　kata-ude-to-shite hataraku（片腕として働く）work as ((another's)) right-hand man
kata-ware〈かたわれ：片割れ〉one of the party, an accomplice.
kata-yaburi〈かたやぶり：型破り〉
　kata-yaburi-no〈型破りの〉unconventional, unusual, extraordinary.
　　kata-yaburi-no aisatsu（型破りのあいさつ）an unconventional address
katayoru〈かたよる：偏る〉
　katayotta〈偏った〉biased, partial, unfair, prejudiced.
　　katayotta kangae（偏った考え）a partial view
　katayora-nai〈偏らない〉unbiased, impartial, fair, unprejudiced, balanced.
　　katayora-nai shokuji（偏らない食事）a balanced diet
kata-zukeru〈かたづける：片付ける〉put...in order, clear away, put away, settle, finish.
　　heya o kata-zukeru（部屋を片付ける）put a room in order
　　têburu-o-kata-zukeru（テーブルを片付ける）clear the table
　　omocha o hako-no-naka-ni kata-zukeru（おもちゃを箱の中に片付ける）put the toys away in a box
　　gotagota o kata-zukeru（ごたごたを片付ける）settle a trouble
　　shukudai o kata-zukeru（宿題を片付ける）finish one's homework
　katazuku〈片付く〉be put in order, be cleared off, be settled, be finished.
kate〈かて：糧〉food, bread.
　　kokoro-no kate（心の糧）one's mental food
katei〈かてい：家庭〉(a) home, a family, a household.

    katei-ka〔家庭科〕 the homemaking course

    katei-kyôiku〔家庭教育〕 home education

    katei-ryôri〔家庭料理〕 home cooking

    katei-saiban-sho〔家庭裁判所〕 a family court

    katei-seikatsu〔家庭生活〕 home life

    katei-kyôshi〔家庭教師〕 a tutor, a governess

    katei-no-shitsuke〔家庭のしつけ〕 home discipline

    katei-teki(-na)〔家庭的(な)〕 homely, domestic.

    katei-yô(-no)〔家庭用(の)〕 for home use.

katei〔かてい：過程〕(a) process, a course.

    seizô-katei〔製造過程〕 a process of production

    ～-no-katei-o-tadoru〔～の過程をたどる〕 go through the process of...

katei〔かてい：課程〕a course, a curriculum.

    kôtô-gakkô-no-katei　o　oeru〔高等学校の課程を終える〕 finish the senior high school course

katei〔かてい：仮定〕supposition.

    katei-suru〔仮定する〕suppose, assume.

    ～-to-katei-shite〔～と仮定して〕supposing that... .

kâten〔カーテン〕a curtain.

    kâten o akeru〔カーテンを開ける〕 undraw a curtain

    kâten o shimeru〔カーテンを閉める〕 draw a curtain to

katô〔かとう：下等〕

    katô-dôbutsu〔下等動物〕 the lower animals

    katô-na〔下等な〕low, inferior, mean.

katô〔かとう：過当〕

    katô-kyôsô〔過当競争〕 an excessive competition

kato-ki〔かとき：過渡期〕a transition(al) period.

katoku〔かとく：家督〕an inheritance.

    katoku-o-sôzoku-suru〔家督を相続する〕 inherit a house and estate

Katorikku〔カトリック〕Catholicism, the Catholic Church.

    Katorikku-kyôkai〔カトリック教会〕 a Catholic Church

    Katorikku-kyô-to〔カトリック教徒〕 a Catholic

    Katorikku-no〔カトリックの〕Catholic.

katsu〔かつ：勝つ〕win, beat, defeat.

    kyôgi ni katsu〔競技に勝つ〕 win a game

    teki ni katsu〔敵に勝つ〕 beat the enemy

    jibun ni katsu〔自分に勝つ〕 conquer oneself

katsu〔かつ：且つ〕besides, moreover, further, at the same time, in addition ((to)), both...and.

katsuai〈かつあい：割愛〉

katsuai-suru〈割愛する〉spare, give up, omit.

katsubô〈かつぼう：渇望〉a longing ((for)), a yearning ((for)), an eager desire ((for)).

katsubô-suru〈渇望する〉long ((for)), yearn ((for)), desire eagerly, be anxious ((for)).

katsudô〈かつどう：活動〉activity, action; energy.

katsudô-ka（活動家）an activist, a hustler

katsudô-suru〈活動する〉be active.

katsudô-teki(-na)〈活動的(な)〉active, energetic.

katsugu〈かつぐ：担ぐ〉carry ((a thing)) on the shoulder, shoulder.

omoi nimotsu o katsugu（重い荷物を担ぐ）carry a heavy load on the shoulder

katsuji〈かつじ：活字〉a printing type, type.

katsuji o kumu（活字を組む）set type

katsuji-no-ayamari（活字の誤り）a misprint

katsuji-tai-de-kaku〈活字体で書く〉print, write in block letters.

katsukatsu〈かつかつ〉

ichi-man-en-katsukatsu（一万円かつかつ）not more than ten thousand yen

katsuo〈かつお〉a bonito.

katsuo-bushi（かつお節）dried bonito

katsura〈かつら〉a wig.

katsura o tsukete-iru（かつらを着けている）wear a wig

katsuretsu〈カツレツ〉a fried cutlet.

katruro〈かつろ：活路〉

katsuro-o-hiraku（活路を開く）find a way out, cut one's way

katsuryoku〈かつりょく：活力〉vital power, vitality, energy.

katsute〈かつて〉once, before, formerly, (at) one time, ever; never.

watashi-ga katsute sunde-ita ie（私がかつて住んでいた家）the house I once lived

katsute-no〈かつての〉former, one-time, ex-.

katsuyaku〈かつやく：活躍〉activity, action.

katsuyaku-suru〈活躍する〉be active ((in)), play an active part ((in)).

jitsugyô-kai-de katsuyaku-suru（実業界で活躍する）play an active part in the business world

katsuyô〈かつよう：活用〉practical use; conjugation, inflection, declension.

katsuyô-suru 〈活用する〉 put ((something)) to practical use; conjugate, inflect, decline.

katte 〈かって：勝手〉 a kitchen; condition, circumstances; one's own convenience; selfishness, one's own way.

    katte-dôgu （勝手道具） kitchenware, kitchen utensils

    katte-guchi （勝手口） a kitchen door

katte-ga-wakara-nai 〈勝手が分からない〉 do not know one's way ((about)), be unfamiliar ((with)), be a stranger ((to)).

katte-na 〈勝手な〉 selfish.

    katte-na kaishaku （勝手な解釈） one's own interpretation

    katte-na-mane-o-suru （勝手なまねをする） have one's own way

katte-ni 〈勝手に〉 as one pleases, freely, without permission.

    Katte-ni-shite-yoroshii. （勝手にしてよろしい。） Do as you please.

    Katte-ni-shiro! （勝手にしろ。） Go to the devil!

katto 〈カット〉 a cut.

katto-suru 〈カットする〉 cut.

katto 〈かっと〉

    katto-naru （かっとなる） fall into a passion, flare up.

    katto-natte （かっとなって） in a fit of passion

kau 〈かう：買う〉 buy, purchase, get, take; incur, invite.

    yasuku-kau （安く買う） buy cheap, make a good bargain

    takaku-kau （高く買う） buy dear, make a bad bargain

    urami o kau （恨みを買う） incur ((a person's)) enmity

    kanshin o kau （歓心を買う） win ((a person's)) favor

    kenka o kau （けんかを買う） take up a challenge

kau 〈かう：飼う〉 keep, raise, rear, feed.

    hitsuji o kau （羊を飼う） keep a sheep

    kaiko o kau （蚕を飼う） rear silkworms

    kachiku o kau （家畜を飼う） feed cattle

kawa 〈かわ：川(河)〉 a river, a stream, a brook, a rivulet.

    kawa-ni-sotte （川に沿って） along a river

    kawa-mukai-ni （川向かいに） across the river, on the other side of the river

    kawa o noboru （川を上る） go up a river

    kawa o kudaru （川を下る） go down a river

    kawa o wataru （川を渡る） cross a river

    Mogami-gawa （最上川） the Mogami River, the River Mogami

kawa 〈かわ：皮（革）〉 the skin, (a) hide, leather, (a) fur, (a) bark, (a) rind, peel, film.

    kawa-goto-taberu（皮ごと食べる）eat ((an apple)) skin and all

    kawa o namesu（革をなめす）tan hide

   kawa-o-muku〈皮をむく〉skin, peel, pare, shell.

kawa 〈かわ：側〉 *see.* gawa.

kawa-doko 〈かわどこ：川床〉a riverbed.

kawa-gishi 〈かわぎし：川岸〉the banks of a river.

kawa-haba 〈かわはば：川幅〉the width of a river.

kawa-himo 〈かわひも：革ひも〉a strap, a thong, a leash.

kawaigaru 〈かわいがる〉love, pet.

kawai-ge 〈かわいげ〉

   kawai-ge-ga-nai〈かわいげがない〉do not have charm of a child.

kawaii 〈かわいい〉charming, lovely, dear, sweet, pretty, cute.

kawaisô 〈かわいそう〉

   kawaisô-na〈かわいそうな〉poor, pitiful, sad, miserable, touching.

    kawaisô-na hanashi（かわいそうな話）a sad story

   kawaisô-ni〈かわいそうに〉pitiably, sadly.

    Kawaisô-ni!（かわいそうに.）What a pity! / Poor thing!

   〜-o-kawaisô-ni-omou〈〜をかわいそうに思う〉feel pity for... .

kawaita 〈かわいた：乾いた〉dry, parched.

    kawaita taoru（乾いたタオル）a dry towel

kawaita 〈かわいた：渇いた〉thirsty.

    Nodo-ga-kawaita.（のどが渇いた.）I'm thirsty.

kawa-kami 〈かわかみ：川上〉*see.* jôryû（上流）.

kawakasu 〈かわかす：乾かす〉dry.

    nureta kimono o hinata-de kawakasu（ぬれた着物を日なたで乾かす）dry one's wet clothes in the sun

kawaki 〈かわき：乾き〉drying, dryness.

    kawaki-ga-hayai（乾きが早い）dry fast

   kawaku〈乾く〉dry, get dry, be parched up.

kawaki 〈かわき：渇き〉thirst.

    kawaki o iyasu（渇きをいやす）quench one's thirst

   kawaku〈渇く〉be thirsty.

kawa-kiri 〈かわきり：皮切り〉

   〜-o-kawa-kiri-ni〈〜を皮切りに〉with... as the start.

kawa-mukô 〈かわむこう：川向こう〉

    kawa-mukô-no（川向こうの）on the other side of the river

　　　kawa-mukô-ni（川向こうに）　across the river

kawara〈かわら〉a tile.

　　　kawara-de yane-o-fuku（かわらで屋根をふく）　roof ((a house)) with tiles

kawara〈かわら：河原〉a river beach.

kawari〈かわり：変わり〉a change, (a) difference.

　kawari-ga-nai〈変わりがない〉remain unchanged, nothing is the matter ((with)), be all right.

　kawari-yasui〈変わりやすい〉changeable, unsettled; fickle.

　kawari-naku〈変わりなく〉constantly, peacefully, well, all right.

　　　kawari-naku kurasu（変わりなく暮らす）　get on well

kawari〈かわり：代わり〉a substitute, a replacement, return.

　　　o-kawari（お代わり）　another helping

　kawari-o-suru or *kawari-o-tsutomeru*（代わりをする，代わりを務める）take another's place, act for another, do duty for a person.

　kawari-no〈代わりの〉substitute, another.

　〜-no-kawari-ni〈〜の代わりに〉instead of... , in place of... , in return for ... .

　〜-no-kawari-ni-naru〈〜の代わりになる〉serve as... , do for...

kawari-bae〈かわりばえ：代わり映え〉

　　　Kawari-bae-ga-shi-nai.（代わり映えがしない.）　It's none the better for the change.

kawari-dane〈かわりだね：変わり種〉an exception, a rare case, a peculiar figure.

kawari-hateru〈かわりはてる：変わり果てる〉be completely changed.

　　　kawari-hateta-sugata-ni-naru（変わり果てた姿になる）　become dead and cold

kawari-me〈かわりめ：変わり目〉a change, a turn, a turning point.

　　　jikô no kawari-me（時候の変わり目）　a change of the seasons

kawari-mono〈かわりもの：変わり者〉an odd fellow, an eccentric, a character, a caution.

　　　Kare-wa kawari-mono-da.（彼は変わり者だ.）　He is quite a character.

kawaru〈かわる：変わる〉change, turn.

　　　ki ga kawaru（気が変わる）　change one's mind

　　　shikisai-ga-kawaru（色彩が変わる）　change in color

　　　jûsho-ga-kawaru（住所が変わる）　have one's address changed

　　　Kare-wa maru-de-hito-ga-kawatta.（彼はまるで人が変わった.）　He is

quite another man.

kawara-nai 〈変わらない〉 be unchanged, be the same.

kawaru 〈かわる：代わる〉 take the place ((of)).

　～*-ni-kawatte* 〈〜に代わって〉 for... , in place of... , instead of... , on behalf of... , in succession to... .

kawaru-gawaru 〈かわるがわる：代わる代わる〉 by turns, in turn, alternately.

　　kuruma o kawaru-gawaru unten-suru （車を代わる代わる運転する） drive a car by turns

kawase 〈かわせ：為替〉 a money order, exchange.

　　kawase-de okuru （為替で送る）　send by money order

　　kawase-tegata （為替手形）　a bill of exchange, a draft

　　gaikoku-kawase （外国為替）　foreign exchange

　　kawase-sôba （為替相場）　the exchange rate

　　ko-gawase （小為替）　a postal note, a postal order

kawa-shimo 〈かわしも：川下〉 *see.* karyû.

kawasu 〈かわす：交わす〉 exchange.

　　aisatsu o kawasu （あいさつを交わす）　exchange greetings

kawasu 〈かわす〉 dodge, avoid.

　　mi o hidari-ni kawasu （身を左にかわす）　dodge oneself to the left

kawatta 〈かわった：変わった〉 unusual, strange.

　　kawatta koto （変わった事）　something unusual

kawa-uso 〈かわうそ〉 an otter.

kawa-zakana 〈かわざかな：川魚〉 a fresh-water fish.

kawa-zan·yô 〈かわざんよう：皮算用〉

　　Toranu-tanuki-no-kawa-zan·yô. （捕らぬたぬきの皮算用.）　Don't count the chickens before they are hatched.

kawa-zoi 〈かわぞい：川(河)沿い〉

　kawa-zoi-no 〈川(河)沿いの〉 riverside, along a river.

　kawa-zoi-ni 〈川(河)沿いに〉 along a river.

kawa-zoko 〈かわぞこ：川底〉 the bottom of a river.

kaya 〈かや：蚊帳〉 a mosquito net.

kaya-buki 〈かやぶき〉

　　kaya-buki-no yane （かやぶきの屋根）　a thatched roof

kayaku 〈かやく：火薬〉 gunpowder, powder.

　　kayaku-ko （火薬庫）　a (powder) magazine

kayô-bi 〈かようび：火曜日〉 Tuesday.

kayoi 〈かよい：通い〉

kayoi-no-meido 〈通いのメイド〉 a maid who lives out

kayô-kyoku 〈かようきょく：歌謡曲〉 a popular song.

kayou 〈かよう：通う〉 go, attend, run.

gakkô-ni kayou（学校に通う） go to school

Takarazuka-Ôsaka-kan-o-kayou-basu（宝塚大阪間を通うバス） a bus which runs between Takarazuka and Osaka

kayowaseru 〈通わせる〉 let go, send.

kodomo o gakkô-e kayowaseru（子供を学校へ通わせる） send a child to school

ka-yowai 〈かよわい：か弱い〉 weak, delicate, tender, frail.

kayu 〈かゆ〉 (rice) gruel.

kayu o susuru（かゆをすする） eat gruel

kayui 〈かゆい〉 itchy; feel itchy, itch.

Senaka ga kayui.（背中がかゆい.） My back itches.

kaza-guruma 〈かざぐるま：風車〉 a windmill, a pinwheel.

kazai(-dôgu) 〈かざい（どうぐ）：家財（道具）〉 household effects.

kaza-kami 〈かざかみ：風上〉 the windward.

kaza-kami-no 〈風上の〉 windward.

kaza-kami-ni-mukatte 〈風上に向かって〉 up the wind.

kaza-muki 〈かざむき：風向き〉 the direction of the wind.

Kaza-muki ga kawatta.（風向きが変わった.） The wind has shifted.

kazan 〈かんざん：火山〉 a volcano.

kakkazan（活火山） an active volcano

kyû-kazan（休火山） a dormant volcano

shi-kazan（死火山） an extinct volcano

kazan-bai（火山灰） volcanic ashes

kazan-katsudô（火山活動） volcanic activity

kazan-tai（火山帯） a volcanic zone

kazan-no 〈火山の〉 volcanic.

kazari 〈かざり：飾り〉 an ornament, a decoration, trimmings.

kazari-botan（飾りボタン） an ornamental button, a fancy button

kazari-mono（飾り物） an ornament, a decoration

kazari-tsuke（飾り付け） decoration, arrangement

kazari-no(-tsuita) 〈飾りの（付いた）〉 ornamental, decorative.

kazari(-ke)-no-nai 〈飾り（気）のない〉 unadorned, unaffected, simple, plain, natural.

kazaru 〈かざる：飾る〉 ornament, decorate, adorn.

kazari-tateru（飾り立てる） decorate richly

kaza-shimo〈かざしも：風下〉the leeward.
　kaza-shimo-no〈風下の〉leeward.
　kaza-shimo-ni〈風下に〉on the leeward ((of)).
　kaza-shimo-ni-atatte〈風下に当たって〉to leeward.
kaze〈かぜ：風〉a wind, a draft, a breeze.
　　　Kaze ga deru.（風が出る。）The wind rises.
　　　Kaze ga fuku.（風が吹く．）The wind blows. / It blows.
　　　Kaze ga yanda.（風がやんだ．）The wind has dropped.
　　　kasuka-na kaze（かすかな風）a slight wind
　　　tsuyoi kaze（強い風）a strong wind
　　　mi-o-kiru-yō-na kaze（身を切るような風）a piercing wind
　　　kaze-ni-mukatte（風に向かって）against the wind
　kaze-no-aru or *kaze-no-tsuyoi*〈風のある，風の強い〉windy.
　　　kaze-no-tsuyoi-hi-ni（風の強い日に）on a windy day
kaze〈かぜ：風邪〉a cold.
　　　kaze-o-hiku（風邪をひく）catch cold
　　　kaze-gimi-da（風邪気味だ）have a slight cold
　　　hidoi-kaze-o-hiku（ひどい風邪をひく）have a bad cold
　　　kaze-o-hiite-nete-iru（風邪をひいて寝ている）be in bed with a cold
　　　kaze-ga-nakanaka-nuke-nai（風邪がなかなか抜けない）cannot　shake
　　　　off one's cold
　　　hana-kaze（鼻風邪）a cold in the head
　　　kaze-goe（風邪声）a hoarce voice from a cold
kaze-atari〈かぜあたり：風当たり〉
　　　kaze-atari-ga-tsuyoi（風当たりが強い）blow　hard　((against)),　be
　　　　wind-swept;　receive severe treatment from the world.
kazei〈かぜい：課税〉taxation, imposition of taxes.
　kazei-no-taishō-to-naru〈課税の対象となる〉be　liable　to　taxation,　be
　　dutiable.
　kazei-suru〈課税する〉tax, impose a tax ((on)).
kaze-tooshi〈かぜとおし：風通し〉ventilation.
　　　kaze-tooshi-ga-ii（風通しがいい）be well ventilated
　　　kaze-tooshi-ga-warui（風通しが悪い）be ill ventilated
kazoe-ageru〈かぞえあげる：数え上げる〉count up.
　　　hitotsu-hitotsu kazoe-ageru（一つ一つ数え上げる）count　up　one　by
　　　　one
kazoeru〈かぞえる：数える〉count, reckon, calculate.
　kazoe-chigaeru〈数え違える〉count wrong, miscalculate.

kazoe-naosu 〈数え直す〉 count again, recount.
kazoerareru 〈数えられる〉 countable.
     kazoerare-nai (数えられない) uncountable
kazoe-kire-nai 〈数え切れない〉 countless, innumerable, numberless.

kazoku 〈かぞく：家族〉 a family.
     kazoku no ichi-in (家族の一員) a member of one's family
     kazoku-ga-ooi (家族が多い) have a large family
     kazoku-ga-sukunai (家族が少ない) have a small family
     san-nin-kazoku (三人家族) a family of three
     kazoku-kaigi (家族会議) a family conference
     kazoku-muki-no-hoteru (家族向きのホテル) a family hotel
     kazoku-zure-no-ryokô (家族連れの旅行) a family trip

kazu 〈かず：数〉 a number.
kazu-ga-ooi 〈数が多い〉 be many, be large in number.
     kazu-ga-sukunai (数が少ない) be few, be small in number
kazu-o-kazoeru 〈数を数える〉 count.
kazu-ooku-no 〈数多くの〉 a large number of.
kazu-kagiri-nai 〈数限りない〉 innumerable, numberless.

kazu-no-ko 〈かずのこ：数の子〉 herring roe.

ke 〈け：毛〉 hair, feather, fur, wool.
     Ke ga nukeru. (毛が抜ける.) Hair falls out.
     ke-ga-usuku-naru (毛が薄くなる) be losing one's hair
     koi-kami-no-ke (濃い髪の毛) thick hair
     usui-kami-no-ke (薄い髪の毛) thin hair
     katai-kami-no-ke (かたい髪の毛) coarse hair
     yawarakai-kami-no-ke (柔らかい髪の毛) soft hair
ke-bukai 〈毛深い〉 hairy.
ke-no-nai 〈毛のない〉 hairless.
ke-no 〈毛の〉 woolen.

ke 〈け：気〉 a sign, an indication, a symptom, touch, a trace.
     kakke-no-ke-ga-aru (かっけの気がある) have symptoms of beriberi
     mattaku hi-no-ke-ga-nai (全く火の気がない) be quite unheated

-ke 〈-け：-家〉
     Tokugawa-ke (徳川家) the Tokugawa family, the Tokugawas

ke-ana 〈けあな：毛穴〉 pores (of the skin).

kebakebashii 〈けばけばしい〉 showy, gaudy.
kebakebashiku 〈けばけばしく〉 showily, gaudily.

kebyô 〈けびょう：仮病〉 pretended sickness.

kebyô-o-tsukau〈仮病を使う〉pretend to be sick.

kechi〈けち〉stinginess.

kechimbô（けちん坊）a miser, a niggard, a closefisted fellow

kechikechi-suru〈けちけちする〉be stingy.

kechi-na〈けちな〉stingy, miserly, sparing, mean.

kechi-na ryôken（けちな料けん）a mean spirit

kechi〈けち〉ill luck.

kechi-ga-tsuku（けちが付く）have an ill omen

kechi-o-tsukeru（けちを付ける）find fault ((with))

ke-chirasu〈けちらす：け散らす〉kick about, put ((the enemy)) to rout.

ke-dakai〈けだかい：気高い〉noble.

ke-dakai hito-gara（気高い人柄）noble character

kedamono〈けだもの〉a beast, a brute.

ke-darui〈けだるい〉listless, languid.

kega〈けが〉an injury, a hurt, a wound.

chotto-shita kega（ちょっとしたけが）a slight injury

oo-kega（大けが）a serious injury

kega-nin（けが人）an injured person, a wounded person; the injured, the wounded

kega-o-suru〈けがをする〉get hurt, be injured, be wounded.

kegarawashii〈けがらわしい：汚らわしい〉dirty, filthy; disgusting, loathsome, obscene.

kegare〈けがれ：汚れ〉uncleanness, impurity, defilement, a stain.

kegare-no-nai〈汚れのない〉clean, pure, undefiled, stainless.

kegareru〈けがれる：汚れる〉be stained, be soiled, be polluted, be defiled.

kegasu〈汚す〉stain, soil, pollute, defile, foul, disgrace.

na o kegasu（名を汚す）soil one's reputation

ke-gawa〈けがわ：毛皮〉a fur.

ke-gawa-seihin（毛皮製品）furs

kegen〈けげん〉

kegen-na〈けげんな〉dubious, suspicious.

kegen-na kao（けげんな顔）a dubious look

kegen-sô-ni〈けげんそうに〉dubiously, suspiciously.

ke-girai〈けぎらい：毛嫌い〉

ke-girai-suru〈毛嫌いする〉have a prejudice ((against)).

kehai〈けはい：気配〉a sign, an indication.

kei〈けい：刑〉a punishment, a penalty, a sentence.

   kei-ni shosuru〔刑に処する〕 condemn ((a person)) to a penalty
   kei o ii-watasu〔刑を言い渡す〕 give a sentence ((on))
   kei ni fukusuru〔刑に服する〕 serve a sentence
   kei o shikkô-suru〔刑を執行する〕 execute (a) sentence
   kei o genjiru〔刑を減じる〕 reduce a sentence

kei〈けい：計〉
   kei go-sen-en-ni-naru〔計五千円になる〕 be 5,000 yen in total

kei〈けい〉 a (ruled) line.
   kei o hiku〔けいを引く〕 rule a line
   keishi〔けい紙〕 ruled paper

-kei〈-けい：-系〉 a system; lineage.
   taiyô-kei〔太陽系〕 the solar system

keiai〈けいあい：敬愛〉
  keiai-suru〈敬愛する〉 love and respect.
   keiai-suru Katô-kun〔敬愛する加藤君〕 My dear Mr. Kato

keiba〈けいば：競馬〉a horse race.
   keiba-jô〔競馬場〕 a race track, a racecourse

keibatsu〈けいばつ：刑罰〉a punishment, a penalty.
  keibatsu-o-kuwaeru〈刑罰を加える〉 punish, inflict a penalty ((on)).

keiben〈けいべん：軽便〉
   keiben-tetsudô〔軽便鉄道〕 a light railway

keibetsu〈けいべつ：軽べつ〉 contempt, scorn.
  keibetsu-suru〈軽べつする〉 despise, scorn, look down ((upon)).
  keibetsu-su-beki〈軽べつすべき〉 contemptible.
  keibetsu-teki(-na)〈軽べつ的(な)〉 contemptuous, scornful, disdainful.

keibi〈けいび：警備〉 guard, defense.
   keibi-in〔警備員〕 a guard
  keibi-suru〈警備する〉 guard, defend.

keibi〈けいび：軽微〉
   keibi-na〔軽微な〕 slight, little, trifling, minor.

keibu〈けいぶ：警部〉a police inspector.
   keibu-ho〔警部補〕 an assistant inspector

keibu〈けいぶ：けい部〉the neck, the cervix.

keichô〈けいちょう：傾聴〉
   keichô-ni-atai-suru〔傾聴に値する〕 be worth listening ((to))
  keichô-suru〈傾聴する〉 listen ((to)).

keidai〈けいだい：境内〉 the precincts, the close.

keido〈けいど：経度〉 longitude.

kei-dômyaku〈けいどうみゃく：けい動脈〉the carotid artery.

keiei〈けいえい：経営〉management, operation.
 kojin-keiei〈個人経営〉private management
 keiei-sha〈経営者〉a manager
 keiei-nan-ni-ochiiru〈経営難に陥る〉be in financial difficulties
 keiei-suru〈経営する〉manage, run, keep.

keien〈けいえん：敬遠〉
 keien-suru〈敬遠する〉keep ((a person)) at a distance, give ((a batter)) a walk intentionally.

keifuku〈けいふく：敬服〉
 keifuku-suru〈敬服する〉admire, respect, think highly ((of)).
 keifuku-su-beki〈敬服すべき〉admirable, worthy of admiration.

keiga〈けいが：慶賀〉
 keiga-suru〈慶賀する〉congratulate ((a person)) on, offer one's congratulations to ((a person)) on.

keigan〈けいがん：けい眼〉a keen insight, perspicacity.
 keigan-na〈けい眼な〉perspicacious, penetrating.

keigen〈けいげん：軽減〉
 keigen-suru〈軽減する〉reduce, lighten, relieve, abate.

keigo(-suru)〈けいご(する)：警護(する)〉guard, escort.
 keigo-no-moto-ni〈警護の下に〉under guard

keigo〈けいご：敬語〉polite expressions.

keigu〈けいぐ：敬具〉Yours faithfully, Yours truly, Yours sincerely, Yours respectfully.

keihaku〈けいはく：軽薄〉
 keihaku-na〈軽薄な〉frivolous, flippant, fickle, insincere.

kei-hanzai〈けいはんざい：軽犯罪〉a minor offense.

keihatsu〈けいはつ：啓発〉enlightenment, development.
 keihatsu-suru〈啓発する〉enlighten, develop, edify.
 keihatsu-sareru〈啓発される〉be enlightened, learn ((from)).

keihi〈けいひ：経費〉expense(s), cost(s).
 keihi o setsugen-suru〈経費を節減する〉cut down the expenses
 eigyô-keihi〈営業経費〉business expenses
 nichijô-keihi〈日常経費〉daily expenses
 bakudai-na keihi-o-kakete〈ばく大な経費を掛けて〉at a great cost
 keihi-ga-kasamu〈経費がかさむ〉be expensive, cost much.

keihin〈けいひん：景品〉a premium, a gift, a giveaway.

keihô〈けいほう：刑法〉criminal law.

keihô〈けいほう：警報〉a warning, an alarm.
　　keihô-sôchi（警報装置）an alarm device
keii〈けいい：敬意〉respect, regard, esteem.
　　keii o hyôsuru（敬意を表する）pay one's respects ((to))
　　~-*ni-keii-o-hyôshite*〈～に敬意を表して〉in honor of... .
keii〈けいい：経緯〉details, particulars, circumstances.
keiji〈けいじ：刑事〉a criminal case; a detective.
　　keiji-soshô（刑事訴訟）a criminal action
keiji〈けいじ：慶事〉a happy event.
keiji〈けいじ：啓示〉revelation.
　　kami no keiji（神の啓示）a revelation of God
keiji〈けいじ：掲示〉a notice, a notification, a bulletin.
　　keiji-ban（掲示板）a notice board, a bulletin board
　keiji-suru〈掲示する〉put up a notice, notify.
keiji-jô-gaku〈けいじじょうがく：形而上学〉metaphysics.
keijô〈けいじょう：形状〉form, shape.
keijô〈けいじょう：計上〉
　keijô-suru〈計上する〉add up, sum up, appropriate.
　　yosan-ni keijô-suru（予算に計上する）appropriate in the budget
keijô-hi〈けいじょうひ：経常費〉working expenses, operating costs.
kei-jômyaku〈けいじょうみゃく：けい静脈〉the jugular vein.
keika〈けいか：経過〉progress, course; passage.
　　keika-ga-ryôkô-de-aru（経過が良好である）be doing well
　keika-suru〈経過する〉pass, go by.
　　toki-ga-keika-suru-ni-tsurete（時が経過するにつれて）in course of
　　　time
keikai〈けいかい：警戒〉(a) precaution, (a) caution, watch, guard.
　　genjû-na keikai（厳重な警戒）stringent precautions
　keikai-suru〈警戒する〉be cautious ((of)), look out, watch ((for)), guard
　　((against)).
　keikai-o-okotara-nai〈警戒を怠らない〉keep one's weather eye open
keikai〈けいかい：軽快〉
　keikai-na〈軽快な〉light, nimble, airy.
　keikai-ni〈軽快に〉lightly, nimbly, airily.
keikai-sen or **keikai-mô**〈けいかいせん，けいかいもう：警戒線，警戒網〉
　　a police cordon.
　　keikai-sen o haru（警戒線を張る）throw a police cordon
　　keikai-sen o toppa-suru（警戒線を突破する）slip through a police

    cordon

keikaku〈けいかく：計画〉a plan, a scheme, a project, a program.

    keikaku o tateru（計画を立てる）make a plan

    keikaku o jikkô-suru（計画を実行する）carry out one's plan

    keikaku o tassei-suru（計画を達成する）fulfil a plan

    kijô-no keikaku（机上の計画）a desk plan

    san-nen keikaku（三年計画）a three-year program

    toshi-keikaku（都市計画）town planning

  keikaku-suru〈計画する〉plan, make a plan, scheme, project.

  keikaku-chû-de-aru〈計画中である〉be planning, be afoot.

  keikaku-teki(-na)〈計画的(な)〉planned, systematic, intentional.

  keikaku-teki-ni〈計画的に〉systematically, intentionally.

  keikaku-doori-ni〈計画どおりに〉according to plan.

keikan〈けいかん：警官〉a policeman, the police.

    fujin-keikan（婦人警官）a policewoman

    keikan-tai（警官隊）a police force

keikan〈けいかん：景観〉a spectacular sight.

keiken〈けいけん：経験〉(an) experience.

    keiken o tsumu（経験を積む）accumulate experience

    keiken-ni-tomu（経験に富む）have rich experience

    keiken-ni-toboshii（経験に乏しい）lack experience

    tanoshii keiken（楽しい経験）a pleasant experience

    nigai keiken（苦い経験）a bitter experience

  keiken-suru〈経験する〉experience.

  keiken-no-aru〈経験のある〉experienced.

    keiken-no-nai（経験のない）inexperienced

keiken〈けいけん：敬けん〉

  keiken-na〈敬けんな〉pious, devout.

keiki〈けいき：計器〉a meter, a gauge.

    keiki-hikô（計器飛行）instrument flying

keiki〈けいき：刑期〉a prison term.

    keiki o oeru（刑期を終える）complete one's sentence

keiki〈けいき：契機〉an opportunity, a chance, a turning-point.

    kore-o-keiki-to shite（これを契機として）taking this opportunity

keiki〈けいき：景気〉the times, business, the market.

    Keiki ga ii.（景気がいい。）Times are good.

    Keiki ga warui.（景気が悪い。）Times are hard.

    Keiki wa dô-desu-ka?（景気はどうですか。）How is your business?

    keiki-hendô〈景気変動〉 business fluctuations

    keiki-kôtai〈景気後退〉 business recession

    kô-keiki〈好景気〉 good times, prosperity

    niwaka-keiki〈にわか景気〉 a boom

kei-kinzoku〈けいきんぞく：軽金属〉 light metals.

keiko〈けいこ：けい古〉 practice, learning, lessons, a rehearsal.

  keiko-suru〈けい古する〉 practice, learn, take lessons ((in)).

    baiorin-no-keiko-o-suru（バイオリンのけい古をする） practice on the
violin, take lessons in violin

keikô〈けいこう：傾向〉a tendency ((to *or* toward)), a trend, an inclination ((for, of *or* to)), a disposition.

  keikô-ga-aru〈傾向がある〉 have a tendency ((to do)), tend ((to do)), be
apt ((to do)).

keikô〈けいこう：蛍光〉

    keikô-tô〈蛍光灯〉 a fluorescent lamp

    keikô-toryô〈蛍光塗料〉 a fluorescent paint

keikô〈けいこう：経口〉

    keikô-hinin-yaku（経口避妊薬） an oral contraceptive pill

kei-kôgyô〈けいこうぎょう：軽工業〉 light industries.

keikoku〈けいこく：警告〉(a) warning, (a) caution, (an) admonition.

  keikoku-suru〈警告する〉 warn ((a person)) of, give warning ((to)),
caution ((a person)) against *or* of, admonish.

keikoku〈けいこく：渓谷〉a ravine, a valley, a gorge, a canyon.

keiku〈けいく：警句〉

  keiku-o-haku〈警句を吐く〉 make a witty remark.

keima〈けいま：けい馬〉a knight.

keimô〈けいもう：啓もう〉 enlightenment.

  keimô-suru〈啓もうする〉 enlighten.

  keimô-teki(-na)〈啓もう的(な)〉 enlightening.

keimu-sho〈けいむしょ：刑務所〉a prison, a jail, a gaol.

keimyô〈けいみょう：軽妙〉

  keimyô-na〈軽妙な〉 light, witty, lambent.

kei-ongaku〈けいおんがく：軽音楽〉 light music.

keiran〈けいらん：鶏卵〉an egg, a hen's egg.

keirei〈けいれい：敬礼〉a salute, a bow.

  keirei-suru〈敬礼する〉 salute, bow ((to)).

keireki〈けいれき：経歴〉one's career, one's personal history.

keiren〈けいれん〉 convulsions, (a) cramp.

keiren-o-okosu〈けいれんを起こす〉 fall into a fit of convulsions, develop a cramp

keiren-suru〈けいれんする〉 be convulsed, be cramped.

keiretsu-gaisha〈けいれつがいしゃ：系列会社〉 an affiliated firm.

keiri〈けいり：経理〉 accounting, accountant's business.

keiri-bu（経理部）　the accountants' department

keirin〈けいりん：競輪〉 a bicycle race.

keiri-shi〈けいりし：計理士〉 a public accountant, a chartered accountant.

keiro〈けいろ：経路〉 a course, a route, a stage, a process.

kansen-keiro（感染経路）　the route of infection

ke-iro〈けいろ：毛色〉

ke-iro-no-kawatta〈毛色の変わった〉 queer, strange, out of the ordinary.

keirô〈けいろう：敬老〉 respect for the aged.

keirô-no hi（敬老の日）　Respect-for-the-Aged Day

keiryaku〈けいりゃく：計略〉 a plot, a plan.

keiryaku-ni-kakaru（計略に掛かる）　fall a prey to ((another's)) plot

keiryaku o megurasu（計略をめぐらす）　work out a plan

keiryô-ki〈けいりょうき：計量器〉 a meter, a gauge, a scale.

keiryô-senshu〈けいりょうせんしゅ：軽量選手〉 lightweights.

keiryû〈けいりゅう：渓流〉 a mountain stream.

keiryû〈けいりゅう：けい留〉

keiryû-bui（けい留ブイ）　a mooring buoy

keiryû-suru〈けい留する〉 moor ((at *or* to)).

keisai〈けいさい：掲載〉

keisai-suru〈掲載する〉 publish, insert, carry.

kôkoku o keisai-suru（広告を掲載する）　insert an advertisement

keisai-sareru〈掲載される〉 appear, be reported.

keisan〈けいさん：計算〉 calculation, reckoning, counting, accounts.

keisan-ga-hayai（計算が早い）　be quick at accounts

keisan-ga-osoi（計算が遅い）　be slow at accounts

keisan-ni ireru（計算に入れる）　take ((a thing)) into account

keisan-ki（計算器）　a calculating machine

keisan-jaku（計算尺）　a slide rule

keisan-sho（計算書）　a statement of accounts

keisan-suru〈計算する〉 calculate, reckon, count, cast accounts.

keisan-ga-au〈計算が合う〉 add up.

keisan-o-machigaeru〈計算を間違える〉 miscalculate, make an error in calculation, miscount.

keisan〈けいさん：けい酸〉silicic acid.

keisatsu〈けいさつ：警察〉the police.

    keisatsu-sho（警察署）a police station

    keisatsu-kan（警察官）*see.* keikan

    keisatsu-ken（警察犬）a police dog

    keisatsu-techô（警察手帳）a policeman's identification

keisei〈けいせい：形勢〉the situation, the state of affairs, the tide.

    keisei-o-miru（形勢を見る）watch the situation, stand on the fence

    keisei-ippen（形勢一変）the turn of the tide

keisei〈けいせい：形成〉formation, making.

    ningen-keisei（人間形成）character formation

  keisei-suru〈形成する〉form, make up.

keiseki〈けいせき：形跡〉traces, marks, indications, evidence(s).

    keiseki o shimesu（形跡を示す）show evidence(s) (of)

    keiseki o kuramasu（形跡をくらます）cover up one's traces

keisen〈けいせん：けい船〉

  keisen-suru〈けい船する〉moor ((at *or* to)), lay up.

  keisen-sareru〈けい船される〉be moored ((at *or* to)), lie up.

keisha〈けいしゃ：傾斜〉(an) inclination, a slope.

  keisha-suru〈傾斜する〉incline, slant, slope.

  keisha-shita〈傾斜した〉inclined, slant, sloping.

keishi〈けいし：軽視〉

  keishi-suru〈軽視する〉make light ((of)), treat lightly, give little attention ((to)).

keishi-chô〈けいしちょう：警視庁〉the Metropolitan Police Office.

keishiki〈けいしき：形式〉(a) form, (a) formality.

    keishiki-ni-torawareru（形式に捕らわれる）stick to forms

  keishiki-teki(-na)〈形式的(な)〉formal.

  keishiki-teki-ni〈形式的に〉formally.

keishô〈けいしょう：軽症〉a slight illness, a mild case.

    keishô-kanja（軽症患者）a mild case

keishô〈けいしょう：軽傷〉a slight injury, a slight wound.

  keishô-o-ou〈軽傷を負う〉be slightly injured, be slightly wounded.

keishô〈けいしょう：敬称〉a title of honor, a term of respect.

keishô〈けいしょう：景勝〉

    keishô-no-chi（景勝地）a place of scenic beauty

keishô〈けいしょう：警鐘〉an alarm bell.

    Kore-wa wareware-subete-e-no-keishô-to-naru-darô.（これは我々すべ

てへの警鐘となるだろう。） This will be a warning to us all.

keishô 〈けいしょう：継承〉 succession, inheritance.

keishô-sha（継承者） a successor, an heir

keishô-suru〈継承する〉 succeed ((to)), inherit, take over.

keishoku〈けいしょく：軽食〉 a light meal.

keiso〈けいそ：けい素〉 silicon.

keisô〈けいそう：係争〉(a) dispute, a lawsuit.

keisô-chû-de-aru〈係争中である〉 be pending in court.

keisô〈けいそう：軽装〉 light dress.

keisô-suru〈軽装する〉 be lightly dressed, be casually dressed.

keisotsu〈けいそつ：軽率〉 rashness, hastiness, carelessness.

keisotsu-na〈軽率な〉 rash, hasty, careless.

keisotsu-na-koto-o-suru（軽率なことをする） act hastily

keisotsu-ni〈軽率に〉 rashly, hastily, carelessly.

keisû〈けいすう：係数〉a coefficient.

keitai〈けいたい：携帯〉

keitai-rajio（携帯ラジオ） a portable radio

keitai-hin（携帯品）one's personal effects, hand baggage, hand luggage

keitai-hin-azukari-sho（携帯品預かり所） a cloakroom, a checkroom

keitai-suru（携帯する）carry, take ((a thing)) with one, have ((a thing)) with one.

keitai-yô-no〈携帯用の〉portable, handy.

keitai〈けいたい：形態〉(a) form, (a) shape.

keitai-gaku *or* keitai-ron（形態学, 形態論） morphology

keiteki〈けいてき：警笛〉an alarm whistle, a horn.

keiteki o narasu（警笛を鳴らす） give an alarm whistle, sound a horn

keito〈けいと：毛糸〉woolen yarn.

keito-no〈毛糸の〉woolen.

keito-no kutsu-shita（毛糸の靴下） woolen socks

keitô〈けいとう：鶏頭〉a cockscomb.

keitô〈けいとう：系統〉a system; lineage, descent.

shinkei-keitô（神経系統） the nervous system

keitô-dateru〈系統立てる〉systematize, organize.

keitô-o-hiku〈系統を引く〉be descended ((from)).

keitô-teki(-na)〈系統的(な)〉systematic.

keitô-teki-ni〈系統的に〉systematically.

keiyaku〈けいやく：契約〉a contract, an agreement, a compact.
  keiyaku o musubu〈契約を結ぶ〉make a contract ((with))
  keiyaku o rikô-suru〈契約を履行する〉carry out a contract
  keiyaku o yaburu〈契約を破る〉break a contract
  keiyaku-ihan〈契約違反〉(a) breach of contract
  keiyaku-sha〈契約者〉a contractor
  keiyaku-sho〈契約書〉a contract, an agreement
  keiyaku-suru〈契約する〉contract.
keiyô〈けいよう：掲揚〉
  keiyô-suru〈掲揚する〉hoist, fly, raise, put up.
  kokki o keiyô-suru〈国旗を掲揚する〉hoist a national flag
keiyô-shi〈けいようし：形容詞〉an adjective.
keiyu〈けいゆ：経由〉
  keiyu-suru〈経由する〉go by way of.
  〜-keiyu-de〈〜経由で〉by way of... .
keiyu〈けいゆ：軽油〉gas oil, light oil.
keizai〈けいざい：経済〉economy, finance.
  keizai-jôtai〈経済状態〉economic conditions
  keizai-kiki〈経済危機〉an economic crisis
  keizai-ryoku〈経済力〉economic strength, financial power
  kokka-keizai〈国家経済〉state economy
  keizai-gaku〈経済学〉economics, political economy
  keizai-jô(-no)〈経済上(の)〉economic, finacial.
  keizai-teki(-na)〈経済的(な)〉economical, economic, financial.
  keizai-jô〈経済上〉economically, financially.
  keizai-teki-ni〈経済的に〉economically.
keizoku〈けいぞく：継続〉continuation, continuance.
  keizoku-kikan〈継続期間〉a period of duration
  keizoku-suru〈継続する〉continue, go on.
  keizoku-teki(-na)〈継続的(な)〉continual, continuous.
  keizoku-teki-ni〈継続的に〉continually, continuously.
keizu〈けいず：系図〉genealogy, lineage, a family tree.
kejime〈けじめ〉
  kejime-o-tsukeru〈けじめを付ける〉draw the line between...and... .
kêki〈ケーキ〉a cake.
kekka〈けっか：結果〉a result, a consequence, an effect, fruit, the end.
  shiken no kekka〈試験の結果〉the results of an examination
  gen·in to kekka〈原因と結果〉cause and effect

kekka-ga~-to-naru〈結果が～となる〉result in... .

~-no-kekka〈～の結果〉as a result of... .

hitsuzen-teki-kekka〈必然的結果〉as a necessary consequence.

kekkai〈けっかい：決壊〉

kekkai-suru〈決壊する〉collapse, be broken.

　　Teibô ga kekkai-shita.（堤防が決壊した.）The bank has collapsed.

kekkaku〈けっかく：結核〉tuberculosis.

　　kekkaku-kanja（結核患者）a tuberculous patient

　　kekkaku-kin（結核菌）a tubercle bacillus

kekkan〈けっかん：血管〉a blood vessel.

kekkan〈けっかん：欠陥〉a defect, a fault, deficiency.

　　kekkan-sha（欠陥車）a defective car

kekkan-no-aru〈欠陥のある〉defective, faulty, deficient.

　　kekkan-no-nai（欠陥のない）faultless, perfect

kekki〈けっき：血気〉

kekki-ni-hayaru〈血気にはやる〉be carried away by youthful ardor.

kekki〈けっき：決起〉

kekki-suru〈決起する〉rise to action.

kekkin〈けっきん：欠勤〉absence, nonattendance.

　　chôki-kekkin（長期欠勤）a long(-term) absence

　　mudan-kekkin（無断欠勤）absence without notice

kekkin-suru〈欠勤する〉be absent from one's office.

kekkô〈けっこう：結構〉very well, well enough, pretty well.

kekkô-na〈結構な〉good, fine, nice, excellent, splendid.

　　kekkô-na o-tenki（結構なお天気）fine weather

　　kekkô-na okuri-mono（結構な贈り物）a nice present

　　Sore-de-kekkô-desu.（それで結構です.）That'll do.

　　Iya, mô-kekkô-desu.（いや，もう結構です.）No, thank you.

kekkô〈けっこう：欠航〉

　　Jibin wa kekkô-to-narimasu.（次便は欠航となります.）The next
　　　　sailing(*or* flight) will be cancelled.

kekkô〈けっこう：血行〉blood circulation.

　　kekkô o yoku-suru（血行をよくする）facilitate blood circulation

kekkô〈けっこう：決行〉

kekkô-suru〈決行する〉carry out (resolutely), venture oneself.

kekkon〈けっこん：血こん〉a bloodstain.

kekkon-no-tsuita〈血こんの付いた〉bloodstained.

kekkon〈けっこん：結婚〉(a) marriage.

kekkon-shiki〈結婚式〉a wedding ceremony
    kekkon-shiki o ageru（結婚式を挙げる）celebrate a wedding
kekkon-seikatsu〈結婚生活〉a married life
kekkon-suru〈結婚する〉marry, be married ((to)).

kekkyoku〈けっきょく：結局〉after all, in the end, in the long run.

kekkyû〈けっきゅう：血球〉a blood corpuscle.
hakkekkyû（白血球）a white corpuscle
sekkekkyû（赤血球）a red corpuscle

kemban〈けんばん：けん盤〉a keyboard.
kemban-gakki（けん盤楽器）a keyed instrument

kemben〈けんべん：検便〉a stool test.
kemben-suru〈検便する〉examine ((a person's)) stool.

kembi-kyô〈けんびきょう：顕微鏡〉a microscope.
kembi-kyô-de shiraberu（顕微鏡で調べる）examine ((a thing)) with a microscope

kembô-shô〈けんぼうしょう：健忘症〉forgetfulness.

kembun〈けんぶん：検分〉
kembun-suru〈検分する〉inspect, examine, look over.
shita-kembun-suru（下検分する）conduct a preliminary inspection

kembun〈けんぶん：見聞〉information, knowledge.
kembun-o-hiromeru（見聞を広める）add to one's knowledge, see more of life.

kembutsu〈けんぶつ：見物〉sightseeing, a visit.
kembutsu-ni-iku（見物に行く）go sightseeing
kembutsu-kyaku（見物客）a sightseer, a visitor
kembutsu-nin（見物人）a spectator, an onlooker
kembutsu-seki（見物席）a seat, a box, a stand
kembutsu-suru〈見物する〉do the sights ((of)), visit, see, look on.

kemmaku〈けんまく：剣幕〉
osoroshii-kemmaku-de〈恐ろしい剣幕で〉with a threatening attitude.

kemmei〈けんめい：賢明〉wisdom, intelligence, sagacity.
kemmei-na〈賢明な〉wise, intelligent, sagacious.

kemmo-hororo〈けんもほろろ：剣もほろろ〉
kemmo-hororo-no〈剣もほろろの〉curt, blunt, brusque.
kemmo-hororo-no aisatsu（剣もほろろのあいさつ）a curt answer

kemmon〈けんもん：検問〉a checkup.
kemmon-jo（検問所）a checkpoint
kemmon-suru〈検問する〉check up.

kemmu〈けんむ：兼務〉*see.* kennin.

kemono〈けもの：獣〉*see.* kedamono.

kempei〈けんぺい：憲兵〉a military policeman, an MP; a shore patrolman, an SP.

kempô〈けんぽう：憲法〉the constitution.

kemui〈けむい：煙い〉smoky.

kemuri〈けむり：煙〉smoke.

    kemuri o ageru（煙を上げる）send up smoke

    kemuri-ga-tachi-komete-iru（煙が立ち込めている）be full of smoke

    kemuri-ni-makarete-shinu（煙に巻かれて死ぬ）be suffocated to death by smoke

    kemuri-ni-makareru（煙に巻かれる）be bewildered, be mystified

    kemuru（煙る）smoke, be smoky; be hazy.

kemushi〈けむし：毛虫〉a hairy caterpillar.

kemutai〈けむたい：煙たい〉be smoky; feel awkward.

ken〈けん：県〉a prefecture.

    Hyôgo-ken（兵庫県）Hyogo Prefecture

    kenchô（県庁）a prefectural office

    ken-chiji（県知事）a prefectural governor

    ken(-ritsu)-no〈県（立）の〉prefectural.

ken〈けん：剣〉a sword.

ken〈けん：件〉a matter, an affair, a case, a subject.

    Rei-no ken wa dô-narimashita-ka?（例の件はどうなりましたか.）What has become of the matter?

ken〈けん〉a tendon.

ken〈けん：券〉a ticket, a coupon, a bond.

ken〈けん：圏〉a sphere, a circle, a range, a radius.

ken〈けん〉a key.

ken〈けん：険〉

  ken-no-aru（険のある）sharp, stern, stinging.

    ken-no-aru kao（険のある顔）a sharp look

-ken〈-けん：-軒〉a house, a door.

    go-ken-no-ie（五軒の家）five houses

    ikken-oite-tonari（一軒おいて隣）next door but one

    kado-o-mawatte ni-ken-me（角を回って二軒目）the second house around the corner

-ken〈-けん：-兼〉and, at the same time.

    shokudô-ken-ima（食堂兼居間）a combined dining and living room

ken·aku 〈けんあく：険悪〉
 ken·aku-na 〈険悪な〉 threatening, stormy; serious, critical, grave.
   ken·aku-na kumo-yuki 〈険悪な雲行き〉 threatening clouds
   ken·aku-na kûki 〈険悪な空気〉 a critical atmosphere
ke-nami 〈けなみ：毛並み〉 the lie of hair.
 ke-nami-ga-ii 〈毛並みがいい〉 have a good coat of hair, have a fine coat
   of fur; come of good stock.
ken·an 〈けんあん：懸案〉 a pending problem.
   naga-nen-no ken·an 〈長年の懸案〉 a long-pending question
kenasu 〈けなす〉 speak ill ((of)), cry down, disparage.
kenchi 〈けんち：見地〉 a point of view, a viewpoint.
   rekishi-teki-kenchi-kara 〈歴史的見地から〉 from a historical point of
   view
kenchiku 〈けんちく：建築〉 construction, building, architecture.
   kenchiku-butsu 〈建築物〉 a building, a structure
   kenchiku-hi 〈建築費〉 the cost of construction
   kenchiku-ka 〈建築家〉 an architect
   kenchiku-gyô-sha 〈建築業者〉 a builder, a constructor
   kenchiku-yôshiki 〈建築様式〉 a style of building
   kenchiku-zairyô 〈建築材料〉 building materials
 kenchiku-suru 〈建築する〉 construct, build.
 kenchiku-chû-de-aru 〈建築中である〉 be under construction.
 kenchiku-jô-no 〈建築上の〉 architectural.
kencho 〈けんちょ：顕著〉
 kencho-na 〈顕著な〉 conspicuous, remarkable, marked, striking.
kendô 〈けんどう：剣道〉 Japanese fencing, swordsmanship, *kendô*.
ken·eki 〈けんえき：検疫〉 quarantine.
   ken·eki-sho 〈検疫所〉 a quarantine station
 ken·eki-suru 〈検疫する〉 quarantine, inspect.
ken·eki 〈けんえき：権益〉 rights and interests.
kenen 〈けねん：懸念〉 *see.* shimpai.
ken·en 〈けんえん：犬猿〉
 ken·en-no-naka-de-aru 〈犬猿の仲である〉 lead a cat-and-dog life, be on
   extremely bad terms ((with)).
ken·etsu 〈けんえつ：検閲〉 censorship, inspection.
   genjû-na ken·etsu 〈厳重な検閲〉 rigid censorship
 ken·etsu-suru 〈検閲する〉 censor, inspect.
kengai 〈けんがい：圏外〉

kengai-ni 〈圏外に〉 outside the range(*or* radius) ((of)).

 tôsen-kengai-ni-aru（当選圏外にある）be outside the running

kengai 〈けんがい：懸がい〉

kengai(-zukuri)-no 〈懸がい（造り）の〉 hanging, cascade.

 kengai-zukuri-no kiku（懸がい造りの菊）a cascade chrysanthemum

kengaku 〈けんがく：見学〉

kengaku-suru 〈見学する〉 visit...for study, make an observation study.

 kôjô o kengaku-suru（工場を見学する）visit a factory for study

kengan 〈けんがん：検眼〉 an eye examination.

kengan-suru 〈検眼する〉 examine ((a person's)) eyes.

kengen 〈けんげん：権限〉 authority.

kengen-ga-aru 〈権限がある〉 have authority ((for *or* to do)).

kengen-o-ataeru 〈権限を与える〉 authorize, invest ((a person)) with authority.

kengen-gai-no 〈権限外の〉 unauthorized, unwarranted.

kengi 〈けんぎ：嫌疑〉 suspicion.

kengi-o-kakeru 〈嫌疑を掛ける〉 suspect ((a person)).

kengi-o-ukeru 〈嫌疑を受ける〉 be suspected ((of)).

〜*-no-kengi-de* 〈〜の嫌疑で〉 on the suspicion of... .

kengyô 〈けんぎょう：兼業〉 a side job, a job on the side.

ken·i 〈けんい：権威〉 (an) authority.

 jishin-gaku no ken·i（地震学の権威）an authority of seismology

 ken·i-suji（権威筋）an authoritative source.

ken·i-no-aru 〈権威のある〉 authoritative.

ken·in-ryoku 〈けんいんりょく：けん引力〉 tractive force, pulling capacity.

kenji 〈けんじ：検事〉 a public prosecutor.

kenji 〈けんじ：堅持〉

kenji-suru 〈堅持する〉 hold fast ((to)), stick ((to)).

kenjitsu 〈けんじつ：堅実〉

kenjitsu-na 〈堅実な〉 steady, sound, reliable.

kenjitsu-ni 〈堅実に〉 steadily, soundly, reliably.

kenjô 〈けんじょう：謙譲〉 modesty, humility.

 kenjô no bitoku（謙譲の美徳）the virtue of modesty

kenjû 〈けんじゅう：けん銃〉 a pistol.

kenka 〈けんか〉 a quarrel, a jangle, a dispute, a fight.

 kenka o uru（けんかを売る）pick up a quarrel ((with))

    Kenka-ryô-seibai.（けんか両成敗.） In a quarrel both sides are to blame.

    fûfu-genka（夫婦げんか） a marital quarrel

    sake-no-ue-no kenka（酒の上のけんか） a drunken brawl

kenka-suru〈けんかする〉quarrel ((with)), wrangle, fight.

kenka-zuki-na〈けんか好きな〉quarrelsome.

kenka-goshi-de〈けんか腰で〉in a defiant attitude.

kenkai〈けんかい：見解〉an opinion, a view.

    kenkai no sôi（見解の相違） a difference of view

    kenkai-o-onajiku-suru（見解を同じくする） have the same opinion

    kenkai-o-koto-ni-suru（見解を異にする） have a different opinion, differ in opinion

kenkai〈けんかい：県会〉a prefectural assembly.

    kenkai-giin（県会議員） a member of a prefectural assembly

kenken-gôgô〈けんけんごうごう〉

kenken-gôgô-taru〈けんけんごうごうたる〉noisy, clamorous, uproarious.

kenketsu〈けんけつ：献血〉blood donation.

    kanketsu-sha（献血者） a (blood) donor

kenketsu-suru〈献血する〉donate one's blood.

kenkin〈けんきん：献金〉a gift of money, a contribution, a donation.

    seiji-kenkin（政治献金） a political donation

kenkin-suru〈献金する〉contribute money ((to)), donate money ((to)).

kenkô〈けんこう：健康〉health.

    kenkô-de-aru（健康である） be healthy, be in good health

    kenkô-ga-sugure-nai（健康が優れない） be unhealthy, be in poor health

    kenkô-ni-ii（健康にいい） be good for health

    kenkô ni tekisuru（健康に適する） suit one's health

    kenkô-ni-warui（健康に悪い） be bad for health

    kenkô o gaisuru（健康を害する） injure one's health

    kenkô o kaifuku-suru（健康を回復する） recover one's health

    kenkô o tamotsu（健康を保つ） keep one's health

    kenkô o zôshin-suru（健康を増進する） promote one's health

    kenkô-hoken（健康保険） health insurance

    kenkô-shindan（健康診断） a medical examination, a physical checkup

kenkô-na〈健康な〉healthy.

kenkô-sô-na〈健康そうな〉healthy-looking.

kenkô-kotsu 〈けんこうこつ：肩甲骨〉a shoulder blade, a scapula.

kenkyo 〈けんきょ：検挙〉an arrest, a roundup.
　kenkyo-suru 〈検挙する〉arrest, round up.

kenkyo 〈けんきょ：謙虚〉
　kenkyo-na 〈謙虚な〉humble, modest.
　kenkyo-ni 〈謙虚に〉in a humble way, modestly.

kenkyû 〈けんきゅう：研究〉study, research, investigation.
　　kenkyû-jo〈研究所〉 a research institute
　　kenkyû-shitsu〈研究室〉 a study room
　kenkyû-suru〈研究する〉study, make a study ((of)), research ((into)),
　　make researches ((in)), investigate.

kennai 〈けんない：圏内〉
　kennai-ni 〈圏内に〉within the range(*or* sphere) ((of)).
　　taifû-kennai-ni〈台風圏内に〉 within the range of the typhoon

kennin 〈けんにん：兼任〉
　kennin-suru〈兼任する〉hold also the post ((of)).

kennyô 〈けんにょう：検尿〉examination of the urine, a urine test.
　kennyô-suru〈検尿する〉examine ((a person's)) urine.

ken·o 〈けんお：嫌悪〉hatred, dislike, disgust, abhorrence, detestation.
　ken·o-suru〈嫌悪する〉hate, dislike, abhor, detest.
　ken·o-su-beki〈嫌悪すべき〉hateful, disgusting, detestable, abominable.

ken·on-ki 〈けんおんき：検温器〉*see.* taion-kei.

kenri 〈けんり：権利〉a right, a claim.
　　kenri o shuchô-suru（権利を主張する） claim a right ((to))
　　kenri o shutoku-suru（権利を取得する） acquire a right
　　kenri o kôshi-suru（権利を行使する） exercise one's rights
　　kenri o ran·yô-suru（権利を濫用する） abuse one's rights
　　kenri o ushinau（権利を失う） lose a right
　　kenri o hôki-suru（権利を放棄する） give up one's rights
　　kenri o shingai-suru（権利を侵害する） infringe on ((another's)) right
　　kenri-kin（権利金） a premium, key money

kenrô 〈けんろう：堅ろう〉
　kenrô-na〈堅ろうな〉solid, stout, substantial, durable.
　　kenrô-na kaoku（堅ろうな家屋） a substantial house

kenryoku 〈けんりょく：権力〉power, authority, influence.
　　kenryoku o furuu（権力を振るう） exercise one's authority ((over))
　　kenryoku-tôsô（権力闘争） a power struggle
　kenryoku-no-aru〈権力のある〉powerful, influential.

kenryoku-no-nai〈権力のない〉 powerless, uninfluential

kensa〈けんさ：検査〉(an) inspection, (an) examination, a checkup, (an) audit.

kensa-suru〈検査する〉 inspect, examine, check (upon), audit.

kensa-o-ukeru〈検査を受ける〉 be inspected, be examined.

kensatsu〈けんさつ：検察〉

kensatsu-kan（検察官） a public prosecutor

kensatsu-gawa（検察側） the prosecution

kensatsu〈けんさつ：検札〉 ticket check.

kensatsu-suru〈検札する〉 examine a ticket, check up a ticket.

kensei〈けんせい：県政〉 the prefectural administration.

kensei〈けんせい：けん制〉 a check, restraint; a feint.

kensei-kyû（けん制球） a feint ball

kensei-suru〈けん制する〉 check, restrain.

kenseki〈けんせき：けん責〉 a reprimand, (a) rebuke, (a) reproof.

kenseki-shobun-o-ukeru〈けん責処分を受ける〉 receive an official reprimand ((for)), be reprimanded ((for)), be reproved ((for)).

kensetsu〈けんせつ：建設〉 construction, building, foundation.

kensetsu-shô（建設省） the Ministry of Construction

kensetsu-daijin（建設大臣） the Minister of Construction

kensetsu-suru〈建設する〉 construct, build, found.

kensetsu-chû-de-aru〈建設中である〉 be under construction.

kensetsu-teki(-na)〈建設的(な)〉 constructive.

kenshi〈けんし：絹糸〉 silk thread.

kenshi〈けんし：犬歯〉 a dogtooth, a canine (tooth).

kenshi〈けんし：検死〉 a coroner's inquest, a postmortem examination, an autopsy.

kenshi-kan（検死官） a coroner

kenshi-suru〈検死する〉 examine (a corpse).

kenshiki〈けんしき：見識〉 views, an opinion, discernment; pride, self-respect, dignity.

ichi-kenshiki-ga-aru（一見識がある） have an opinion of one's own

kenshiki-ga-takai〈見識が高い〉 be self-conceited, be proud.

kenshin〈けんしん：献身〉

kenshin-teki(-na)〈献身的(な)〉 devoted, self-sacrificing.

kenshin-teki-ni〈献身的に〉 devotedly.

kenshin-teki-ni-tsukusu（献身的に尽くす） devote oneself ((to))

kenshin〈けんしん：検診〉 a medical examination, a physical checkup.

    shûdan-kenshin〈集団検診〉a collective medical examination

kenshin〈けんしん：検針〉the inspection of a meter.

    kenshin-suru〈検針する〉read a meter.

kenshô〈けんしょう：懸賞〉a prize contest; a prize.

    kenshô o tsukeru〈懸賞を付ける〉 offer a prize ((for))

    kenshô ni ataru〈懸賞に当たる〉 win a prize

    kenshô-kin〈懸賞金〉 a reward

kenshô〈けんしょう：憲章〉a charter, a constitution.

    jidô-kenshô〈児童憲章〉 the Children's Charter

kenshô〈けんしょう：肩章〉a shoulder strap, an epaulet(te).

kenshô〈けんしょう：検証〉(a) verification, identification, (an) inspection.

kenshô-en〈けんしょうえん：けんしょう炎〉inflammation of a tendon ⌐and its sheath.

kenshû〈けんしゅう：研修〉study and training.

    kenshû-sei〈研修生〉 a trainee

    kenshû-suru〈研修する〉study.

kenshutsu〈けんしゅつ：検出〉

    kenshutsu-suru〈検出する〉detect, find.

    hôsha-nô o kenshutsu-suru〈放射能を検出する〉 detect radioactivity

kenson〈けんそん：謙そん〉modesty, humility.

    kenson-suru〈謙そんする〉be modest, be humble.

    kenson-na〈謙そんな〉modest, humble.

kensû〈けんすう：件数〉the number of cases.

    kôtsû-jiko no kensû〈交通事故の件数〉the number of traffic accidents

kensui〈けんすい：懸垂〉chinning exercises.

    kensui-suru〈懸垂する〉do chinning exercises

kentai-ki〈けんたいき：けん怠期〉a period of lassitude.

kentan-ka〈けんたんか：健たん家〉a heavy eater.

kentei〈けんてい：検定〉official approval, (an) examination.

    kentei-shiken〈検定試験〉 a certificate examination

kentô〈けんとう：見当〉aim, an estimate, a guess.

    kentô-o-tsukeru〈見当を付ける〉aim ((at)), estimate, guess.

    kentô-ga-tsuku〈見当が付く〉suppose, guess.

    daitai-kentô-ga-tsuku〈大体見当が付く〉 have a rough idea ((of))

    kentô-ga-hazureru or *kentô-chigai-suru*〈見当が外れる，見当違いする〉 miss one's aim, make a wrong guess, guess wrong.

    kentô-chigai-no〈見当違いの〉misdirected, misplaced, out of place, wrong.

kentô〈けんとう：けん闘〉boxing.

kentô-suru〈けん闘する〉box ((with)).

kentô〈けんとう：健闘〉strenuous efforts, a good fight.

kentô-suru（健闘する）make strenuous efforts, fight a good fight

kentô〈けんとう：検討〉(an) examination, (an) investigation.

kentô-suru〈検討する〉examine, investigate.

kentô-chû-de-aru〈検討中である〉be under investigation

ke-nuki〈けぬき：毛抜き〉(a pair of) tweezers, nippers.

ken・yaku〈けんやく：倹約〉economy, thrift, frugality.

ken・yaku-suru〈倹約する〉economize, be thrifty, be frugal, save.

ken・yaku-shite kane o tameru（倹約して金をためる）save money by frugality

ken・yô〈けんよう：兼用〉

ken・yô-suru〈兼用する〉use ((a thing)) both as...and... .

kenzai〈けんざい：健在〉

kenzai-de-aru〈健在である〉be well, be going strong, be on the active list.

Ryôshin wa mada kenzai-da.（両親はまだ健在だ.）My parents are still well.

kenzan〈けんざん：検算〉

kenzan-suru〈検算する〉verify the accounts, prove.

kenzen〈けんぜん：健全〉

kenzen-zaisei（健全財政）sound finance

kenzen-na〈健全な〉healthy, sound, wholesome.

kenzô〈けんぞう：建造〉building, construction.

kenzô-butsu（建造物）a building, a structure

rekishi-teki kenzô-butsu（歴史的建造物）a historic structure

kenzô-suru〈建造する〉build, construct.

kenzô-chû-de-aru〈建造中である〉be under construction, be on the stocks.

ke-ori〈けおり：毛織〉

ke-ori-mono（毛織物）woolen goods

ke-ori-no〈毛織の〉woolen.

ke-otosu〈けおとす：け落とす〉kick ((a person)) down.

hito-o-ke-otoshite　shôshin-o-hakaru（人を蹴落として昇進を図る）try to win promotion at the sacrifice of others

keppaku〈けっぱく：潔白〉purity, innocence, integrity.

keppaku-na〈潔白な〉pure, innocent, upright.

keppaku-na hito〈潔白な人〉 a man of integrity

keppeki〈けっぺき：潔癖〉

keppeki-na〈潔癖な〉cleanly, squeamish, overnice.

keppyō〈けっぴょう：結氷〉

keppyō-ki〈結氷期〉 the freezing season

keppyō-suru〈結氷する〉freeze, be frozen over, be ice-locked.

kerai〈けらい：家来〉a retainer, a follower, a vassal.

(-)keredo(-mo)〈(-)けれど(も)〉but, however, though, nevertheless, in spite of.

keri〈けり〉

keri-o-tsukeru〈けりを付ける〉settle, clinch, bring ((a matter)) to an end.

keri-ga-tsuku〈けりが付く〉be settled, come to a close.

keroido〈ケロイド〉keloid.

keroido(-jō)-no〈ケロイド(状)の〉keloidal.

kerori-to or **kerotto**〈けろりと，けろっと〉as if nothing had happened; entirely.

keru〈ける〉kick, give ((a person)) a kick; reject.

kesa〈けさ：今朝〉this morning.

kesa-hayaku〈今朝早く〉 early this morning

kesa-kara〈今朝から〉 since this morning

kesa〈けさ〉a surplice.

keshi〈けし〉a poppy.

keshi-tsubu〈けし粒〉 a poppy seed

keshi-tsubu-hodo-no〈けし粒ほどの〉as small as a pin's head.

keshi-gomu〈けしゴム：消しゴム〉an eraser, an India rubber.

keshi-in〈けしいん：消印〉a postmark.

keshikakeru〈けしかける〉set ((a dog)) on ((a person)); instigate, incite.

keshikaran〈けしからん〉rude, impertinent, scandalous, shameful, unpardonable, outrageous.

keshikaran-furumai-o-suru〈けしからん振る舞いをする〉 behave impertinently ((toward))

keshiki〈けしき：景色〉scenery, a scene, a landscape, a view.

ii keshiki〈いい景色〉 fine scenery

keshi-tobu〈けしとぶ：消し飛ぶ〉fly away, scatter away, be scattered away.

keshi-tomeru〈けしとめる：消し止める〉get ((a fire)) under control, put out.

keshô〈けしょう：化粧〉(a) makeup, (a) toilet, dressing.
    keshô-hin（化粧品）cosmetics, toilet articles
    keshô-sui（化粧水）wash, toilet lotion
    atsu-geshô（厚化粧）heavy makeup
    keshô-renga（化粧れんが）ornamental tiles
    keshô-suru〈化粧する〉make up (one's face), make one's toilet.

kessai〈けっさい：決済〉settlement.
    kessai-suru〈決済する〉make up accounts, settle accounts.

kessai〈けっさい：決裁〉sanction, approval.
    kessai-o-aogu〈決裁を仰ぐ〉submit ((a matter)) for ((a person's)) approval.

kessaku〈けっさく：傑作〉a masterpiece; a blunder.
    dai-kessaku o yaru（大傑作をやる）make an absurd blunder

kessan〈けっさん：決算〉settlement of accounts.
    kessan-hôkoku（決算報告）a statement of accounts
    kessan-ki（決算期）a settlement term
    kessan-suru〈決算する〉settle accounts.

kessei〈けっせい：血清〉(a) serum.

kessei〈けっせい：結成〉
    kessei-suru〈結成する〉form, organize.

kesseki〈けっせき：結石〉a calculus, a stone.
    jinzô-kesseki（じん臓結石）a kidney stone

kesseki〈けっせき：欠席〉absence.
    kesseki-todoke（欠席届）a report of absence
    kesseki-sha（欠席者）an absentee
    byôki-kesseki（病気欠席）absence on account of illness
    kesseki-saiban（欠席裁判）judgment by default
    kesseki-suru〈欠席する〉be absent ((from)), absent oneself ((from)).

kessen〈けっせん：決戦〉a decisive battle, a showdown; a deciding match, a runoff.
    kessen-suru〈決戦する〉wage a decisive battle ((with)), run off.

kessen〈けっせん：決選〉a final election.
    kessen-tôhyô（決選投票）a runoff (ballot)

kessen〈けっせん：血栓〉thrombosis.

kessha〈けっしゃ：結社〉an association, a society, a fraternity.
    himitsu-kessha（秘密結社）a secret society, a junto

kesshi〈けっし：決死〉
    kesshi-no〈決死の〉desperate, death-defying.

kesshi-no-kakugo-de〈決死の覚悟で〉in the face of death

kesshin〈けっしん：決心〉determination, resolution.

kesshin o hirugaesu〈決心を翻す〉give up one's resolution, change one's mind

kesshin-suru〈決心する〉determine, be determined, resolve, be resolved, make up one's mind.

kesshin-ga-tsuka-nai-de-iru〈決心が付かないでいる〉be in two minds ((about *or* whether)).

kesshin〈けっしん：結審〉the conclusion of a trial.

kesshite〈けっして：決して〉

kesshite～nai〈決して～ない〉never, by no means, not at all, on no account.

Kesshite-suru-na!〈決してするな。〉Never do it!

Kare-wa kesshite-namake-mono-dewa-nai.〈彼は決して怠け者ではない。〉He is by no means an idle fellow.

kesshô〈けっしょう：血しょう〉blood plasma.

kesshô〈けっしょう：決勝〉the decision of a contest.

kesshô-sen〈決勝戦〉the final game, the finals

jun-kesshô(-sen)〈準決勝(戦)〉the semifinals

kesshô-ten〈決勝点〉the goal, the home

kesshô〈けっしょう：結晶〉crystallization, a crystal; fruit.

doryoku no kesshô〈努力の結晶〉the fruit of one's efforts

kesshô-suru〈結晶する〉crystallize.

kesshoku〈けっしょく：血色〉(a) complexion, color.

kesshoku-ga-ii〈血色がいい〉have a healthy complexion, look well

kesshoku-ga-warui〈血色が悪い〉have a pale complexion, look pale

kesshû〈けっしゅう：結集〉

kesshû-suru〈結集する〉concentrate, mass.

heiryoku o kesshû-suru〈兵力を結集する〉mass troops

wareware-no sôryoku o kesshû-suru〈我々の総力を結集する〉devote all of our efforts

kesshutsu〈けっしゅつ：傑出〉

kesshutsu-shita〈傑出した〉outstanding, prominent, distinguished.

kessô〈けっそう：血相〉

kessô-o-kaeru〈血相を変える〉change color, be black in the face, turn pale.

kessô-o-kaete〈血相を変えて〉black in the face, with a pale face.

kessoku〈けっそく：結束〉union, combination, unity.

kessoku o kataku-suru〈結束を固くする〉 solidity the bond of union

kessoku-ga-katai〈結束が固い〉 be tightly united

kessoku-suru〈結束する〉 band together, combine, unite, be united.

kessoku-shite-teki-ni-ataru〈結束して敵に当たる〉 band together against the enemy

kesson〈けっそん：欠損〉 a deficit, deficiency, a loss.

kesson o shôjiru〈欠損を生じる〉 suffer a deficit, suffer a loss

kessuru〈けっする：決する〉 determine, decide ((on *or* to do)), settle, come to a decision, be decided, be settled; decide ((on)), judge.

kesu〈けす：消す〉 put out, switch off, turn off, blow out; wipe out, rub out.

kaji o kesu〈火事を消す〉 put out a fire

terebi o kesu〈テレビを消す〉 turn off television

kokuban-no-ji o kesu〈黒板の字を消す〉 rub out the letters on the blackboard

keta〈けた〉 a figure, a place; a beam, a girder.

keta o machigaeru〈けたを間違える〉 misplace a figure

yo-keta no sûji〈四けたの数字〉 a number of four figures

keta-ga-chigau〈けたが違う〉 be widely different ((from)), stand no comparison ((with)).

keta-hazure〈けたはずれ：けた外れ〉

keta-hazure-no〈けた外れの〉 extraordinary.

ketatamashii〈けたたましい〉 noisy, loud, clamorous, piercing, shrill, alarming.

ketatamashii onna-no sakebi-goe〈けたたましい女の叫び声〉 a piercing cry of a woman

ketatamashiku〈けたたましく〉 noisily, loudly, alarmingly.

ketatamashiku nari-hibiku〈けたたましく鳴り響く〉 ring alarmingly

ke-tateru〈けたてる：け立てる〉

nami-o-ke-tatete-susumu〈波をけ立てて進む〉 cleave one's way through the waves.

ketchaku〈けっちゃく：決着〉 *see.* keri.

ketchin〈けっちん：血沈〉 precipitation of blood.

ketchin o hakaru〈血沈を計る〉 measure the precipitation of ((a person's)) blood

ke-tobasu〈けとばす：け飛ばす〉 kick away(*or* off).

ketsu〈けつ：決〉 decision, a vote.

ketsu-o-toru〈決を採る〉 put ((a matter)) to a vote, take a vote ((on))

ketsuatsu 〈けつあつ：血圧〉 blood pressure.

> ketsuatsu o hakaru（血圧を計る） measure ((a person's)) blood pressure

> ketsuatsu ga agaru（血圧が上がる） blood pressure rises

> ketsuatsu ga sagaru（血圧が下がる） blood pressure lowers

> ketsuatsu-ga-takai（血圧が高い） have a high blood pressure

> ketsuatsu ga hikui（血圧が低い） have a low blood pressure

ketsuben 〈けつべん：血便〉 bloody excrement.

ketsubô 〈けつぼう：欠乏〉 (a) want, (a) lack, (a) shortage, scarcity.

ketsubô-suru 〈欠乏する〉 want, lack, run short ((of)).

ketsudan 〈けつだん：決断〉 decision, determination, resolution.

> ketsudan-ga-hayai（決断が早い） be quick in decision

> ketsudan-ga-nibui（決断が鈍い） be slow in decision

ketsudan-suru 〈決断する〉 decide, determine, resolve.

ketsudan-ryoku-ga-aru 〈決断力がある〉 be resolute.

> ketsudan-ryoku-ga-toboshii（決断力が乏しい） be irresolute

ketsueki 〈けつえき：血液〉 blood.

> ketsueki no junkan（血液の循環） the circulation of the blood

> ketsueki-gata（血液型） a blood type

> ketsueki-kensa（血液検査） a blood test

ketsuen 〈けつえん：血縁〉 *see.* ketsuzoku.

ketsugi 〈けつぎ：決議〉 a resolution, a decision.

> ketsugi-an（決議案） a (draft) resolution

ketsugi-suru 〈決議する〉 resolve, decide.

ketsugô 〈けつごう：結合〉 (a) combination, (a) union.

ketsugô-suru 〈結合する〉 combine, unite, join together.

ketsui 〈けつい：決意〉 resolution, determination.

> ketsui-o-arata-ni-suru（決意を新たにする） make a fresh determination

> jûdai-na ketsui o suru（重大な決意をする） take a decisive step

ketsuin 〈けついん：欠員〉 a vacancy, a vacant position.

> ketsuin o shôjiru（欠員を生じる） cause a vacancy

> ketsuin o oginau（欠員を補う） fill up a vacancy

ketsujitsu 〈けつじつ：結実〉 fruition.

ketsujitsu-suru 〈結実する〉 bear fruit, attain success.

ketsumaku-en 〈けつまくえん：結膜炎〉 conjunctivitis.

ketsumatsu 〈けつまつ：結末〉 an end, a conclusion, settlement, a result.

ketsumatsu-ga-tsuku 〈結末が付く〉 come to a conclusion, be settled.

ketsumatsu-ga-tsuka-nai〈結末が付かない〉 come to no conclusion, be still pending

ketsumatsu-o-tsukeru〈結末を付ける〉 bring ((a matter)) to a conclusion, settle

ketsurei〈けつれい：欠礼〉

ketsurei-suru〈欠礼する〉 omit to pay one's compliments.

ketsuretsu〈けつれつ：決裂〉a rupture.

kôshô no ketsuretsu〈交渉の決裂〉 the rupture of the negotiations

ketsuretsu-suru〈決裂する〉come to a rupture.

ketsuron〈けつろん：結論〉a conclusion.

ketsuron-ni tassuru〈結論に達する〉 come to a conclusion

sôkyû-na-ketsuron-o-dasu〈早急な結論を出す〉 jump to a conclusion

ketsuron-suru〈結論する〉conclude.

ketsuron-to-shite〈結論として〉in conclusion, to conclude.

ketsuzei〈けつぜい：血税〉the taxes paid by the sweat of one's brow.

ketsuzen〈けつぜん：決然〉

ketsuzen-taru〈決然たる〉resolute, decisive, determined, firm.

ketsuzen-to-shite〈決然として〉resolutely, decisively, in a decided manner, firmly.

ketsuzoku〈けつぞく：血族〉a blood relative.

ketsuzoku-kankei〈血族関係〉 blood relationship

ketsuzoku-kekkon〈血族結婚〉 a consanguineous marriage, an inter-marriage

kettai〈けったい：結滞〉a pause in the pulse.

kettai-suru〈結滞する〉intermit.

kettaku〈けったく：結託〉conspiracy.

kettaku-suru〈結託する〉conspire ((with)).

〜-to-kettaku-shite〈〜と結託して〉in conspiracy with... .

kettan〈けったん：血たん〉bloody phlegm.

kettei〈けってい：決定〉(a) decision, (a) determination, (a) settlement.

kettei-ken〈決定権〉 decisive power

kettei-da〈決定打〉 a game-winning hit, a clincher

kettei-suru〈決定する〉decide ((on)), determine, settle, fix ((upon)), be decided, be determined, be settled, be fixed.

kettei-teki(-na)〈決定的（な）〉decisive, definite, final.

kettei-teki yôso〈決定的要素〉 a determinant

kettei-teki-ni〈決定的に〉decisively, definitely, finally.

ketten〈けってん：欠点〉a fault, a defect, a weak point; a failure mark.

ketten-no-nai〈欠点のない〉faultless, perfect.

kettô〈けっとう：血統〉

    kettô-sho-tsuki-no〈血統書付きの〉pedigreed.

    kettô-sho-tsuki-no inu（血統書付きの犬）　a pedigreed dog

kettô〈けっとう：決闘〉a duel.

    kettô-suru〈決闘する〉duel ((with)).

kewashii〈けわしい：険しい〉steep, precipitous, sheer.

    kewashii yama-michi（険しい山道）　a steep mountain road

ke-yaburu〈けやぶる：け破る〉break open ((a door)) by kicking.

keyaki〈けやき〉a zelkova tree.

kezuru〈けずる：削る〉shave, plane, sharpen; cut down.

    empitsu o kezuru（鉛筆を削る）　sharpen a pencil

    hiyô o kezuru（費用を削る）　cut down the expenses

ki〈き：気〉spirit, (a) heart, (a) mind, a disposition, mood, will, intention, attention.

    ki-ga-aru（気がある）　have a mind ((to do)), be disposed ((to do))

    ki-ga-nai（気がない）　have no mind ((to do))

    ki-ga-au（気が合う）　be congenial ((to or with))

    ki-ga-chigau（気が違う）　become mad

    ki-ga-hikeru（気が引ける）　feel small, feel mean

    ki-ga-kawaru（気が変わる）　change one's mind

    ki-ga-kiku（気が利く）　be smart

    ki-ga-kika-nai（気が利かない）　be dull-witted

    ki-ga-momeru（気がもめる）　feel uneasy ((about or over))

    ki-ga-omoi（気が重い）　be heavyhearted

    ki-ga-raku-ni-naru（気が楽になる）　feel relieved

    ki-ga-sumu（気が済む）　be satisfied, feel relieved

    〜(shi-)tai-ki-ga-suru（(し)たい気がする）　feel like ((doing))

    ki-ga-susuma-nai（気が進まない）　be unwilling ((to do))

    ki-ga-tatsu（気が立つ）　be excited

    ki-ga-togameru（気がとがめる）　feel compunction

    ki-ga-tooku-naru（気が遠くなる）　faint, swoon, lose one's consciousness

    ki-ga-tsuku（気が付く）　become aware ((of or that)), see, find; come to oneself, recover consciousness

    ki-ga-wakai（気が若い）　be young in spirit

    ki-ni-iru（気に入る）　like, be pleased ((with)), please

    ki-ni-kakaru *or* ki-ni-naru（気に掛かる，気になる）　worry, be anxious

((about)), feel uneasy ((about))

ki-ni-suru〈気にする〉 worry ((about)), care ((about)), mind

ki-ni-shi-nai〈気にしない〉 do not mind

ki-no-arai〈気の荒い〉 violent-tempered

ki-no-ookii〈気の大きい〉 large-hearted

ki-no-chiisai〈気の小さい〉 timid

ki-no-kawari-yasui〈気の変わりやすい〉 capricious, fickle

ki-no-mijikai〈気の短い〉 short-tempered

ki-no-nai〈気のない〉 indifferent, unenthusiastic

ki-no-nuketa〈気の抜けた〉 insipid, vapid, flat, stale

ki-no-tsuyoi〈気の強い〉 bold, strong-minded

ki-no-yowai〈気の弱い〉 weakhearted

ki-o-mawasu〈気を回す〉 suspect, be jealous

ki-o-momaseru〈気をもませる〉 worry, keep ((a person)) in suspense

ki-o-ochitsukeru〈気を落ち着ける〉 calm oneself

ki-o-otosu〈気を落とす〉 be disheartened

ki-o-torareru〈気を取られる〉 be preoccupied ((by)), be absorbed ((in))

ki-o-tori-naosu〈気を取り直す〉 take heart (again)

ki-o-tsukau〈気を遣う〉 care ((about)), worry ((oneself)) ((about)), bother one's brain ((about))

ki-o-tsukeru〈気を付ける〉 take care ((of)), pay attention ((to)), mind, look out

ki-o-tsukete〈気を付けて〉 carefully

ki-o-ushinau〈気を失う〉 *see.* ki-ga-tooku-naru

ki-o-waruku-suru〈気を悪くする〉 be displeased, displease

ki-o-yurumeru〈気を緩める〉 relax one's mind

ki-o-yurusu〈気を許す〉 be off one's guard

ki〈き：木〉 a tree, wood.

ki-no〈木の〉 wooden.

ki-no-shigetta〈木の茂った〉 wooded.

ki〈き：機〉 an opportunity, a chance, an occasion.

ki-ga-jukusuru-no-o-matsu〈機が熟するのを待つ〉 wait for a more favorable opportunity

ki〈き：忌〉 (a period of) mourning, an anniversary of ((a person's)) death.

nana-kai-ki〈七回忌〉 the sixth anniversary of ((a person's)) death.

ki〈き：生〉

ki-no〈生の〉 pure, undiluted, unmixed, raw, straight.

    uisukī o ki-de nomu（ウイスキーを生で飲む）　drink whisky straight

ki〈き：奇〉

    ki-o-konomu（奇を好む）　be eccentric

    ki-o-terau（奇をてらう）　make a display of one's originality

ki-ai〈きあい：気合い〉a yell, a shout, a cry.

    ki-ai-o-ireru〈気合いを入れる〉spirit.

    ki-ai-no-haitta〈気合いの入った〉spirited.

    ki-ai-o-irete〈気合いを入れて〉with spirit.

kiatsu〈きあつ：気圧〉atmospheric pressure.

    kô-kiatsu（高気圧）　high atmospheric pressure

    tei-kiatsu（低気圧）　low atmospheric pressure

kiba〈きば〉a tusk, a fang.

    kiba-o-muku〈きばをむく〉snarl, show one's fangs.

kibaku〈きばく：起爆〉

    kibaku-sôchi（起爆装置）　a triggering device

kiban〈きばん：基盤〉a base, a basis, a foundation.

ki-barashi〈きばらし：気晴らし〉(a) diversion, (a) recreation.

    ki-barashi-ni eiga-ni-iku（気晴らしに映画に行く）　go to a movie for diversion

    ki-barashi-o-suru〈気晴らしをする〉divert oneself, recreate oneself, refresh oneself.

kibatsu〈きばつ：奇抜〉

    kibatsu-na〈奇抜な〉strange; novel, original, unconventional.

    kibatsu-na shukô（奇抜な趣向）　novel idea

kiben〈きべん：詭弁〉(a) sophism, (a) sophistry, a quibble.

    kiben-ka（詭弁家）　a sophist

    kiben-o-rôsuru〈詭弁をろうする〉sophisticate, quibble.

    kiben-teki(-na)〈詭弁的(な)〉sophistic(al), quibbling.

kibikibi〈きびきび〉

    kibikibi-shita〈きびきびした〉brisk, dapper, quick, lively, spirited.

    kibikibi-shita seinen（きびきびした青年）　a dapper young man

kibin〈きびん：機敏〉smartness, shrewdness, quickness.

    kibin-na〈機敏な〉smart, shrewd, quick.

    kibin-ni〈機敏に〉smartly, quickly.

kibishii〈きびしい〉severe, strict, rigid, hard, harsh, intense.

    kibishii tori-shimari（厳しい取り締まり）　strict control

    kibishii seikatsu（厳しい生活）　a hard life

    kibishii samusa（厳しい寒さ）　intense(*or* severe) cold

kibishiku 〈厳しく〉 severely, strictly, rigidly, intensely, closely.

kibishi-sa 〈きびしさ：厳しさ〉 severity, strictness, harshness, intensity.

    genjitsu no kibishi-sa （現実の厳しさ） the harshness of reality

kibo 〈きぼ：規模〉 a scale.

    dai-kibo-ni （大規模に） on a large scale

    shô-kibo-ni （小規模に） on a small scale

kibô 〈きぼう：希望〉 (a) hope, (a) wish.

    kibô-ni-michite-iru *or* kibô-ni-moete-iru （希望に満ちている，希望に燃えている） be full of hope, be hopeful

    kibô ni ôjiru （希望に応じる） meet ((a person's)) wishes

    kibô o tassuru （希望を達する） realize one's wishes

    kibô o ushinau （希望を失う） lose one's hope

    kibô-sha （希望者） one who wishes ((to do))

kibô-suru 〈希望する〉 hope, wish.

    heiwa o kibô-suru （平和を希望する） hope for peace

kibô-teki(-na) 〈希望的（な）〉 wishful.

    kibô-teki kansoku （希望的観測） wishful thinking

kibô-no-nai 〈希望のない〉 hopeless.

kibô-doori-ni, kibô-suru-yô-ni or *kibô-suru-toori-ni* 〈希望どおりに，希望するように，希望するとおりに〉 as one wishes.

    kibô-ni-hanshite （希望に反して） againat one's wishes

ki-bori 〈きぼり：木彫り〉 wood carving.

    ki-bori-no ningyô （木彫りの人形） a wooden doll, a doll carved in wood

ki-bukureru 〈きぶくれる：着膨れる〉 look fat in thick clothing.

kibun 〈きぶん：気分〉 (a) feeling, (a) humor, a mood; an atmosphere.

kibun-ga-ii 〈気分がいい〉 feel well, feel all right.

    kibun-ga-warui *or* kibun-ga-sugure-nai （気分が悪い，気分が優れない） feel unwell, feel ill

kibun-tenkan-ni 〈気分転換に〉 for a change, to get a change, for recreation.

kichaku 〈きちゃく：帰着〉 coming back; conclusion.

    giron no kichaku-ten （議論の帰着点） the logical conclusion of an argument

kichaku-suru 〈帰着する〉 come back; result ((in)), boil down ((to)).

kichi 〈きち：機知〉 wit, quick wits.

kichi-ni-tonda 〈機知に富んだ〉 witty.

kichi 〈きち：基地〉 a base.

　　　chûkei-kichi〈中継基地〉a relay base

kichi〈きち：吉〉good luck, good omen.

　kichi-no〈吉の〉lucky, good, fortunate, auspicious.

ki-chigai〈きちがい：気違い〉madness, insanity, a mania; a madman, a maniac, a fan.

　　　shibai-ki-chigai〈芝居気違い〉a theater maniac

　　　yakyû-ki-chigai〈野球気違い〉a baseball fan

　ki-chigai-ni-naru〈気違いになる〉go mad.

　ki-chigai-no〈気違いの〉mad, crazy.

　ki-chigai-jimita〈気違いじみた〉crazy, mad, frantic.

　ki-chigai-no-yô-ni-natte〈気違いのようになって〉like mad, frantically.

kichijitsu〈きちじつ：吉日〉a lucky day, an auspicious day.

kichin〈きちん〉

　kichin-to〈きちんと〉accurately, exactly, regularly, neatly, tidily, in good order.

　　　kichin-to nikki o tsukeru〈きちんと日記を付ける〉keep one's diary regularly

　　　jibun-no heya o kichin-to-shite-oku〈自分の部屋をきちんとしておく〉keep one's room in good order

　kichin-to-shita〈きちんとした〉neat, tidy, in good order.

　kichin-to-suru〈きちんとする〉put ((a desk)) in order.

kichirei〈きちれい：吉例〉

　kichirei-ni-yori〈吉例により〉according to annual custom.

kichô〈きちょう：機長〉a plane captain.

kichô〈きちょう：貴重〉

　　　kichô-hin〈貴重品〉valuables

　kichô-na〈貴重な〉precious, valuable.

　　　kichô-na jikan〈貴重な時間〉precious time

kichô〈きちょう：記帳〉

　kichô-suru〈記帳する〉make an entry, book, register.

kichô-men〈きちょうめん：き帳面〉

　kichô-men-na〈き帳面な〉precise, exact, regular, punctual.

　kichô-men-ni〈き帳面に〉precisely, exactly, regularly, punctually.

kichû〈きちゅう：忌中〉(in) mourning.

kidan〈きだん：奇談〉a strange but true story.

ki-date〈きだて：気立て〉(a) disposition, (a) nature, (a) temper.

　ki-date-no-ii〈気立てのいい〉good-natured.

　　　ki-date-no-warui〈気立ての悪い〉ill-natured

ki-date-no-yasashii〈気立ての優しい〉tenderhearted.

kidô〈きどう：軌道〉an orbit; a (railway) line, a track.

jinkô-eisei-o-uchi-agete　kidô-ni-noseru（人工衛星を打ち上げて軌道に乗せる）launch an artificial satellite into orbit

kidô〈きどう：機動〉

kidô-ryoku（機動力）mobile power

kidô-sei（機動性）mobility

kidô-tai（機動隊）a riot squad

kido-airaku〈きどあいらく：喜怒哀楽〉emotion, feelings.

kido-airaku　o　kao-ni-arawasu（喜怒哀楽を顔に表す）betray one's feelings

ki-dôraku〈きどうらく：着道楽〉(a) love of finery.

ki-dori〈きどり：気取り〉affectation, frills.

ki-dori-ya（気取り屋）an affected person

ki-doru〈気取る〉be affected.

ki-dotta〈気取った〉affected, conceited.

ki-dora-nai（気取らない）unaffected

ki-dotte〈気取って〉affectedly, in an affected manner, conceitedly.

ki-dotte aruku（気取って歩く）walk in an affected manner

kidô-ryoku〈きどうりょく：起動力〉motive power.

kie〈きえ：帰依〉

kie-suru〈帰依する〉become a believer ((in)), be converted ((to)).

kiei〈きえい：気鋭〉

kiei-no〈気鋭の〉spirited, energetic.

shinshin-kiei-no（新進気鋭の）up-and-coming

kien〈きえん：機縁〉(a) chance, (an) opportunity.

kore-o-kien-to-shite（これを機縁として）taking this opportunity

kien〈きえん：奇縁〉a strange chance.

kieru〈きえる：消える〉go out, be put out; melt away; vanish, disappear; wear away.

kifu〈きふ：寄附〉(a) contribution, (a) donation.

kifu-o-tanomu（寄附を頼む）ask for a contribution

kifu-kin（寄附金）a contribution, a donation

kifu-kin o tsunoru（寄附金を募る）collect contributions

kifû〈きふう：気風〉character, disposition, temper, morale, spirit, characteristics.

kifuku〈きふく：起伏〉ups and downs, undulations.

kifuku-suru〈起伏する〉rise and fall, undulate, wave.

kifuku-no-aru〈起伏のある〉undulating, rolling.

ki-furushita〈きふるした：着古した〉worn-out.

kiga〈きが：飢餓〉hunger, starvation.

ki-gae〈きがえ：着替え〉spare clothes, a change of clothes.

ki-gaeru〈着替える〉change (one's clothes).

kigai〈きがい：気慨〉mettle, backbone, spirit.

kigai-no-aru〈気慨のある〉mettlesome, backboned, spirited.

kigai-no-aru hito〈気慨のある人〉 a man of mettle

kigai〈きがい：危害〉an injury, harm.

kigai o kuwaeru（危害を加える） do ((a person)) an injury

ki-gakari〈きがかり：気掛かり〉*see.* shimpai.

kigaku〈きがく：器楽〉instrumental music.

ki-gamae〈きがまえ：気構え〉expectation, anticipation; readiness, preparedness.

ki-gamae-ga-dekite-iru〈気構えができている〉be ready ((for *or* to do)).

kigan〈きがん：祈願〉(a) prayer, (a) supplication.

kigan-suru〈祈願する〉pray ((to)), supplicate.

ki-gane〈きがね：気兼ね〉

ki-gane-suru〈気兼ねする〉feel constraint, have scruples ((about)).

ki-gane-nashi-ni〈気兼ねなしに〉without reserve.

kigaru〈きがる：気軽〉

kigaru-na〈気軽な〉lighthearted.

kigaru-ni〈気軽に〉lightheartedly.

ki-gata〈きがた：木型〉a wooden model, a shoemaker's last.

kigeki〈きげき：喜劇〉a comedy.

kigeki-haiyû（喜劇俳優） a comic actor.

kigen〈きげん：起源(原)〉the origin, the beginning, the rise.

kigen-o-tazuneru（起源(原)をたずねる） trace ((a thing)) to its origin

kigen〈きげん：期限〉a term, a time limit.

shiharai-kigen（支払期限） the term for payment

kigen-ga-kireru〈期限が切れる〉pass a fixed term, be overdue.

kigen〈きげん：紀元〉an era, an epoch.

kigen〈きげん：機嫌〉(a) humor, a temper, a mood.

kigen-ga-ii（機嫌がいい） be in good humor

kigen-ga-warui（機嫌が悪い） be in ill humor, be out of humor

kigen o naosu（機嫌を直す） recover one's temper

kigen-o-toru〈機嫌をとる〉humor, please, flatter.

kigen-yoku〈機嫌よく〉cheerfully, in a good humor.

　　kigen-yoku hito o mukaeru（機嫌よく人を迎える）　receive a person
　　　with warm hands

kigô〈きごう：記号〉a mark, a sign, a symbol.
　　sûgaku-no kigô（数学の記号）　a mathematical symbol

ki-gokoro〈きごころ：気心〉a disposition, a temper.
　ki-gokoro-no-shireta〈気心の知れた〉old and tried, intimate, familiar,
　　reliable.
　　ki-gokoro-no-shire-nai（気心の知れない）unfamiliar, strange, un-
　　　reliable

kigu〈きぐ：器具〉a tool, a utensil, an implement, an instrument.

kigû〈きぐう：奇遇〉a fortuitous meeting.

ki-gurai〈きぐらい：気位〉
　ki-gurai-ga-takai〈気位が高い〉be proud, be haughty, hold one's head
　　high.

ki-gurô〈きぐろう：気苦労〉worry, care, anxiety.
　ki-gurô-ga-tae-nai〈気苦労が絶えない〉be always worrying ((about)), have
　　constant cares.

kigyô〈きぎょう：企業〉an enterprise, an undertaking.
　　dai-kigyô（大企業）　a large enterprise
　　chû-shô-kigyô（中小企業）　a minor enterprise
　　kigyô-ka（企業家）　an enterpriser

kihaku〈きはく：気迫〉spirit, soul.
　　kihaku-ga-aru（気迫がある）　be full of spirit
　　kihaku-ni-kakete-iru（気迫に欠けている）　be lacking in spirit

kihaku〈きはく：希薄〉
　kihaku-na〈希薄な〉thin, weak, dilute(d), rare, sparse.
　　jinkô-kihaku-na（人口希薄な）　sparsely populated

kihatsu〈きはつ：揮発〉
　　kihatsu-yu（揮発油）　volatile oil
　kihatsu-suru〈揮発する〉volatilize.
　kihatsu-sei(-no) or *kihatsu-shi-yasui*〈揮発性(の), 揮発しやすい〉volatile.

kihei〈きへい：騎兵〉a cavalry soldier, cavalry.

kiheki〈きへき：奇癖〉a queer habit.

kihin〈きひん：気品〉dignity, nobility, grace, refinement.
　kihin-no-aru〈気品のある〉dignified, noble, graceful, refined.

kihin〈きひん：貴賓〉a guest of honor.
　　kihin-seki（貴賓席）　seats reserved for distinguished guests
　　kihin-shitsu（貴賓室）　a room reserved for special guests

kihô 〈きほう：気泡〉a (an air) bubble.

kihô 〈きほう：既報〉
　kihô-no-toori〈既報のとおり〉as reported before.

kihon 〈きほん：基本〉a foundation, a basis, a standard.
　kihon-teki(-na)〈基本的(な)〉fundamental, basic, standard.

kii 〈きい：奇異〉
　kii-na〈奇異な〉strange, queer, singular, odd.
　　kii-na-kanji-ga-suru〈奇異な感じがする〉feel strange

kiin 〈きいん：起因〉
　kiin-suru〈起因する〉originate ((in)), arise ((from)), be due ((to)), be caused ((by)).

ki-ippon 〈きいっぽん：生一本〉
　　Nada-no ki-ippon〈灘の生一本〉pure(*or* genuine) Nada *sake*
　ki-ippon-no〈生一本の〉pure, unmixed, undiluted, straight, genuine.
　ki-ippon-na〈生一本な〉straightforward, single-minded.

ki-iro 〈きいろ：黄色〉yellow.
　ki-iro-no or *kiiro-i*〈黄色の，黄色い〉yellow.
　ki-iro-gakatta〈黄色がかった〉yellowish.

ki-ito 〈きいと：生糸〉raw silk.

kiji 〈きじ：記事〉news, a news item, an article.
　　kiji-sashi-tome〈記事差し止め〉a press ban

kiji 〈きじ：生地〉cloth, suit materials, dress materials; one's true color.
　　waishatsu-kiji〈ワイシャツ生地〉shirting
　kiji-no-mama-no〈生地のままの〉plain, undisguised.

kiji 〈きじ〉a pheasant.

kijitsu 〈きじつ：期日〉a (fixed) date, an appointed day, a term.
　　kijitsu o kimeru〈期日を決める〉fix the date ((for *or* on))
　　kijitsu o mamoru〈期日を守る〉keep one's date
　kijitsu-made-ni〈期日までに〉by the appointed day

kijô 〈きじょう：机上〉
　kijô-no〈机上の〉academic, theoretical.
　　kijô-no keikaku〈机上の計画〉a desk plan

kijô 〈きじょう：気丈〉
　kijô-na〈気丈な〉stouthearted, undaunted.

kijû-ki 〈きじゅうき：起重機〉a crane.

kijun 〈きじゅん：基準〉a standard.
　kijun-ni-awaseru〈基準に合わせる〉standardize.
　kijun-no〈基準の〉standard, basic.

kijū-sôsha〈きじゅうそうしゃ：機銃掃射〉machine-gunning.
  kijū-sôsha-suru〈機銃掃射する〉machine-gun.
kijutsu〈きじゅつ：奇術〉magic, jugglery.
    kijutsu-shi〈奇術師〉a magician, a juggler.
kijutsu〈きじゅつ：記述〉(a) description, an account.
  kijutsu-suru〈記述する〉describe, give an account ((of)).
  kijutsu-teki(-na)〈記述的(な)〉descriptive.
kika〈きか：奇禍〉an accident, a mishap.
    kika-ni-au〈奇禍に遭う〉meet with an accident
kika〈きか：気化〉
  kika-suru〈気化する〉evaporate, vaporize, gasify.
kika〈きか：帰化〉naturalization.
  kika-suru〈帰化する〉be naturalized ((as *or* in)).
kika(-gaku)〈きか(がく)：幾何(学)〉geometry.
    kika-kyûsû-teki-ni〈幾何級数的に〉in geometric progression
kikai〈きかい：器械〉an instrument, an apparatus, an appliance.
    iryô-kikai〈医療器械〉medical instruments
kikai〈きかい：機械〉a machine, machinery.
    kikai o kumi-tateru〈機械を組み立てる〉assemble a machine
    kikai o ugokasu〈機械を動かす〉operate a machine
    kikai o bunkai-suru〈機械を分解する〉take a machine to pieces
    kikai-kôgaku〈機械工学〉mechanical engineering
    kikai-ka〈機械化〉mechanization
      kikai-ka-suru〈機械化する〉mechanize
  kikai-teki(-na)〈機械的(な)〉mechanical.
  kikai-teki-ni〈機械的に〉mechanically.
kikai〈きかい：機会〉an opportunity, a chance, an occasion.
    kikai ni jôzuru〈機会に乗ずる〉take advantage of an opportunity
    kikai o toraeru〈機会を捕らえる〉seize an opportunity
    kikai o nogasu〈機会を逃す〉miss an opportunity
    kikai-ga-areba〈機会があれば〉when occasion comes
    kikai-ga-ari-shidai〈機会があり次第〉at the earliest opportunity
    mata-no-kikai-ni〈又の機会に〉on another occasion, some other day
kikai〈きかい：奇怪〉
  kikai-na〈奇怪な〉strange, mysterious, weird.
kikai-taisô〈きかいたいそう：器械体操〉gymnastics with apparatus.
    kikai-taisô-o-yaru〈器械体操をやる〉perform gymnastics on the bar
kikaku〈きかく：規格〉a standard.

    kikaku-hin〈規格品〉standardized articles

kikaku-ka-suru〈規格化する〉standardize.

kikaku-gai-no〈規格外の〉nonstandard.

kikaku〈きかく：企画〉a plan, planning.

kikaku-suru〈企画する〉plan, make a plan.

kikan〈きかん：機関〉an engine; an organ; a means, facilities; an institution, a system.

    kikan-shitsu（機関室）an engine room

    kikan-shi（機関士）an engineer

    kikan-chô（機関長）the chief engineer

    kikan-shi（機関誌(紙)）an organ

    genron-kikan（言論機関）organs of public opinion

    kôtsû-kikan（交通機関）a means of communication, transportation facilities

    kin・yû-kikan（金融機関）a financial institution

    kikan-sha（機関車）a locomotive, an engine

    kikan-jû（機関銃）a machine gun

kikan〈きかん：器官〉an organ.

    shôka-kikan（消化器官）the digestive organs.

kikan〈きかん：期間〉a term, a period.

kikan〈きかん：気管〉the windpipe.

    kikan-shi（気管支）the bronchus

      kikan-shi-en（気管支炎）bronchitis

kikan〈きかん：奇観〉a wonderful sight.

    kikan o teisuru（奇観を呈する）present a wonderful sight

kikan〈きかん：季刊〉

    kikan-shi（季刊誌）a quarterly (magazine)

kikan-no〈季刊の〉quarterly.

kikan〈きかん：既刊〉

kikan-no〈既刊の〉already published.

kikan〈きかん：帰還〉a return, repatriation.

    kikan-hei（帰還兵）a repatriated soldier

kikaseru〈きかせる：聞かせる〉tell, read ((to)), play ((for)), sing ((for)).

    uta o kikaseru（歌を聞かせる）sing a song ((for)).

kikaseru〈きかせる：利(効)かせる〉use, exercise; season.

    ki o kikaseru（気を利かせる）use one's brains

    koshô o kikaseru（こしょうを効かせる）season ((food)) with pepper

ki-kazaru〈きかざる：着飾る〉dress up, be dressed up.

kikei 〈きけい：奇形〉(a) malformation.

kiken 〈きけん：危険〉(a) danger, (a) hazard, (a) peril, (a) risk.

    kiken o okasu（危険を冒す）run a risk

    kiken-ni-ochiiru（危険に陥る）get into danger

    kiken-o-manukareru（危険を免れる）get out of danger

    kiken-chitai（危険地帯）a danger zone

    kiken-shingō（危険信号）a danger signal

    kiken-jōtai（危険状態）a dangerous condition

kiken-de-aru or *kiken-ni-hinshite-iru*〈危険である，危険にひんしている〉be dangerous, be in danger.

kiken-shi-suru〈危険視する〉regard ((a person *or* a thing)) as dangerous.

kiken-na〈危険な〉dangerous, hazardous, perilous, risky.

kiken-o-okashite〈危険を冒して〉in (the) face of danger.

kiken 〈きけん：棄権〉

kiken-suru〈棄権する〉abstain from voting, abandon one's right; withdraw one's entry, drop out (of a race).

kiketsu 〈きけつ：既決〉

    kiketsu-jikō（既決事項）a matter settled

    kiketsu-shū（既決囚）a convicted person

kiketsu-no〈既決の〉decided, settled, convicted.

kiketsu 〈きけつ：帰結〉a conclusion, an end, a result, a consequence.

    tōzen-no kiketsu-to-shite（当然の帰結として）as a natural result

kiki 〈きき：危機〉a crisis, a critical moment.

    kiki o dassuru（危機を脱する）get through a crisis

    kiki-ippatsu-to-iu-toki-ni（危機一髪という時に）at the critical moment

    zaisei-kiki（財政危機）a financial crisis

kīkî 〈きいきい〉

    kīkî-goe（きいきい声）a squeaky voice

kīkî-iu〈きいきいいう〉creak, squeak, scroop.

kiki-akiru 〈ききあきる：聞き飽きる〉be tired of hearing.

kiki-chigaeru 〈ききちがえる：聞き違える〉hear ((a thing *or* a person)) wrong, mishear.

kiki-chigai〈聞き違い〉mishearing.

kiki-dasu 〈ききだす：聞き出す〉hear, find out, extract.

kiki-gurushii 〈ききぐるしい：聞き苦しい〉disagreeable to hear, offensive to the ear.

kiki-ireru 〈ききいれる：聞き入れる〉comply ((with)), grant, accept, take.

hito-no chūkoku o kiki-ireru〈人の忠告を聞き入れる〉take a person's advice

kiki-iru〈ききいる：聞き入る〉listen attentively ((to)).

kiki-jōzu〈ききじょうず：聞き上手〉a good listener.

kiki-kaesu〈ききかえす：聞き返す〉ask back, throw back a question.

kiki-kajiri〈ききかじり：聞きかじり〉a smattering.

kiki-kajiri-no〈聞きかじりの〉superficial, imperfect.

kiki-komi〈ききこみ：聞き込み〉information, a wrinkle.

kiki-komu〈聞き込む〉have information, hear ((something about)), reach one's ears.

kiki-me〈ききめ：効き目〉(an) effect.

kiki-me-ga-hayai〈効き目が早い〉be fast-acting.

kiki-me-no-aru〈効き目のある〉effective.

kiki-me-no-nai〈効き目のない〉ineffective

kiki-mimi〈ききみみ：聞き耳〉

kiki-mimi-o-tateru〈聞き耳を立てる〉prick up one's ears.

kiki-morasu〈ききもらす：聞き漏らす〉fail to catch 〔a word〕, miss.

kikin〈ききん：基金〉a fund, a foundation.

kikin o tsunoru〈基金を募る〉raise a fund

kikin〈ききん：飢きん〉a famine.

dai-kikin〈大飢きん〉a severe famine

kiki-nagasu〈ききながす：聞き流す〉give no heed ((to)), take no notice ((of)), pay no attention ((to)).

kiki-naosu〈ききなおす：聞き直す〉ask again.

kiki-nareru〈ききなれる：聞き慣れる〉get used to hearing.

kiki-nareta〈聞き慣れた〉familiar.

kiki-nareta koe〈聞き慣れた声〉a familiar voice

kiki-nare-nai〈聞き慣れない〉strange.

kiki-nikui〈ききにくい：聞きにくい〉difficult to hear.

ki-kinzoku〈ききんぞく：貴金属〉the precious metals.

kiki-oboe〈ききおぼえ：聞き覚え〉

kiki-oboe-no-aru〈聞き覚えのある〉*see.* kiki-nareta.

kiki-oboe-no-nai〈聞き覚えのない〉*see.* kiki-nare-nai

kiki-sokonau〈ききそこなう：聞き損なう〉*see.* kiki-chigaeru *or* kiki-morasu.

kiki-tadasu〈ききただす：聞きただす〉ascertain, make sure ((of)); inquire.

kiki-te〈ききて：聞き手〉a hearer, a listener, an audience.

kiki-toru 〈ききとる：聞(聴)き取る〉catch ((a person's words)), follow ((a person)).

　　kiki-tore-nai（聞(聴)き取れない）　be inaudible, cannot catch

kiki-ude 〈ききうで：利き腕〉the more skillful arm.

kiki-wake 〈ききわけ：聞き分け〉

　kiki-wakeru〈聞き分ける〉listen to reason, be reasonable, understand.

　kiki-wake-no-ii〈聞き分けのいい〉reasonable.

　　kiki-wake-no-nai（聞き分けのない）　unreasonable

kiki-zute 〈ききずて：聞き捨て〉

　kiki-zute-ni-suru〈聞き捨てにする〉ignore, overlook.

　kiki-zute-deki-nai〈聞き捨てできない〉cannot overlook, cannot pass over.

　kiki-zute-nara-nai〈聞き捨てならない〉unpardonable, inexcusable.

kikkake 〈きっかけ〉a chance, an opportunity, a start, a beginning, a clue, a cue.

　　kikkake o tsukamu（きっかけをつかむ）　seize an opportunity

kikkari(-ni) 〈きっかり(に)〉just, sharp, exactly.

　　ni-ji-kikkari-ni（二時きっかりに）　just at two

kikkyō 〈きっきょう：吉凶〉good or ill luck.

　kikkyō-o-uranau〈吉凶を占う〉tell ((a person's)) fortune.

kikō 〈きこう：気候〉climate, weather, a season.

　　odayaka-na kikō（穏やかな気候）　a mild climate

　　fujun-na kikō（不順な気候）　unseasonable weather

　　kikō no kawari-me-ni（気候の変わり目に）　at the change of season

kikō 〈きこう：機構〉a mechanism, machinery, a system, structure, organization.

　　seiji-kikō（政治機構）　government machinery

kikō 〈きこう：寄港〉

　　kikō-chi（寄港地）　a port of call

　kikō-suru〈寄港する〉call ((at)), make a call ((at)).

kikō 〈きこう：寄稿〉*see.* tôkō（投稿）.

kikō 〈きこう：起工〉

　kikō-suru〈起工する〉begin work; lay (down) the keel, lay the cornerstone.

kikō-bun 〈きこうぶん：紀行文〉an account of a trip.

kikoe 〈きこえ：聞こえ〉reputation, fame, renown.

　kikoe-ga-ii〈聞こえがいい〉sound well, be reputable.

　　kikoe-ga-warui（聞いえが悪い）　sound bad, be disreputable

kikoeru 〈きこえる：聞こえる〉hear, be heard.

　　　yobeba kikoe.ru-tokoro-ni〈呼べば聞こえる所に〉 within hearing ((of))
　kikoe-nai〈聞こえない〉cannot hear, cannot be heard.

kikoku〈きこく：帰国〉
　kikoku-suru〈帰国する〉return to one's country, go home.

kikon〈きこん：既婚〉
　kikon-no〈既婚の〉married.

ki-konashi〈きこなし：着こなし〉
　ki-konashi-ga-umai〈着こなしがうまい〉wear one's clothes stylishly.

kikori〈きこり〉a woodcutter.

kikotsu〈きこつ：気骨〉*see.* kigai（気概）.

kiku〈きく：菊〉a chrysanthemum.

kiku〈きく：利(効)く〉be effective, have effect ((on)), be good ((for)),
　work ((on)).
　　　Kono kusuri wa kaze-ni-yoku-kiku.（この薬は風邪によく効く.） This
　　　medicine has effect on colds.
　　　Burēki ga kika-nai.（ブレーキが効かない.） The brakes don't work.

kiku〈きく：聞(聴)く〉hear, hear ((of)), listen ((to)), ask, follow, take,
　obey.
　　　rajio-o-kiku（ラジオを聴く） listen to the radio
　　　michi o kiku（道を聞く） ask the way
　　　oya-no-iu-koto o kiku（親の言うことを聞く） obey one's parents
　iu-koto-o-kika-nai〈言うことを聞かない〉disobedient, naughty.
　kiku-tokoro-ni-yoreba〈聞くところによれば〉from what I hear.

kikyaku〈ききゃく：棄却〉
　kikyaku-suru〈棄却する〉turn down, reject, dismiss.

kikyō〈ききょう〉a Chinese bellflower.

kikyō〈ききょう：帰郷〉homecoming.
　kikyō-suru〈帰郷する〉go home, return to one's home country.

kikyû〈ききゅう：危急〉an emergency.
　　　kikyû-no-baai-ni(-wa)（危急の場合に(は)） in case of emergency

kikyû〈ききゅう：気球〉a balloon.
　　　kikyû o ageru（気球を揚げる） fly a balloon
　　　kansoku-kikyû（観測気球） an observation balloon

ki-mae〈きまえ：気前〉generosity, liberality.
　ki-mae-no-ii〈気前のいい〉generous, liberal.
　ki-mae-yoku〈気前よく〉generously, liberally.

ki-magure〈きまぐれ：気まぐれ〉a caprice, a whim.
　ki-magure-na〈気まぐれな〉capricious, whimsical.

ki-magure-na tenki〈気まぐれな天気〉 changeable weather

ki-majime〈きまじめ：生まじめ〉
 ki-majime-na〈生まじめな〉 sincere, serious, sober.

ki-mama〈きまま：気まま〉
 ki-mama-na〈気ままな〉 willful, self-willed, wayward.
 ki-mama-ni〈気ままに〉 as one pleases, at will, arbitrarily.

kimari〈きまり：決まり〉 settlement, conclusion; a rule; a custom, a habit.
 kimari-monku〈決まり文句〉 a conventional expression
 kimari-o-tsukeru〈決まりを付ける〉 settle, fix, bring ((a matter)) to an end.
 kimari-ga-tsuku〈決まりが付く〉 be settled, be brought to an end.
 kimari-no, kimatta or *kimari-kitta*〈決まりの，決まった，決まり切った〉 regular, fixed, usual.
 kimatta shigoto〈決まった仕事〉 regular work
 kimatte〈決まって〉 always, regularly, without fail.
 kimatte~(-suru)〈決まって〜(する)〉 make it a rule ((to do)).

kimari-warui〈きまりわるい：決まり悪い〉 awkward.
 kimari-ga-warui〈決まりが悪い〉 feel awkward
 kimari-waru-sō-ni〈決まり悪そうに〉 awkwardly, bashfully.

kimaru〈きまる：決まる〉 be decided, be settled, be fixed, be agreed upon.
 kimara-nai〈決まらない〉 be undecided, be unsettled, be not fixed
 〜-ni-yotte-kimaru〈〜によって決まる〉 depend on... , be determined by ... .
 〜-(suru)-koto-ni-kimatte-iru〈〜(する)ことに決まっている〉 be certain(*or* sure) ((to do)).

kimatsu〈きまつ：期末〉 the end of a term, a term end.
 kimatsu-teate〈期末手当〉 a term-end allowance
 kimatsu-tesuto〈期末テスト〉 a terminal examination

ki-mazui〈きまずい：気まずい〉 disagreeable, unpleasant, embarrassed, awkward.
 ki-mazui-omoi-o-suru〈気まずい思いをする〉 feel disagreeable(*or* unpleasant), feel embarrassed(*or* awkward).

kimba〈きんば：金歯〉 a gold tooth.

kimben〈きんべん：勤勉〉 diligence, industry.
 kimben-ka〈勤勉家〉 a hard worker
 kimben-na〈勤勉な〉 diligent, industrious.

kimben-ni〈勤勉に〉diligently, industriously.

kimbuchi〈きんぶち：金縁〉

　　kimbuchi-no megane（金縁の眼鏡）　gold-rimmed spectacles

kimbyôbu〈きんびょうぶ：金びょうぶ〉a gold-leafed folding screen.

kime〈きめ：木目〉grain, texture.

　kime-no-arai〈きめの粗い〉rough, coarse.

　　kime-no-komakai（きめの細かい）　fine-grained, of fine texture

kime-dama〈きめだま：決め球〉a winning shot.

kimei〈きめい：記名〉

　　kimei-shiki（記名式）　payable to order

　　kimei-tôhyô（記名投票）　an open vote

　kimei-suru〈記名する〉sign one's name.

　　kimei-natsuin-suru（記名なつ印する）　sign and seal

kime-komu〈きめこむ：決め込む〉take ((it)) for granted; assume, pretend, affect.

kimeru〈きめる：決める〉fix, decide, appoint.

　　nedan o kimeru（値段を決める）　fix a price

　　jikan to basho o kimeru（時間と場所を決める）　decide a time and place

　　kimeta-jikan-ni（決めた時間に）　at the appointed time

　～*(-suru)-koto-ni-kimete-iru*〈～（する）ことに決めている〉make it a rule ((to do))... .

kime-te〈きめて：決め手〉a conclusive factor, conclusive evidence, a winning trick.

ki-mi〈きみ：黄身〉the yolk, the yellow.

kimi〈きみ：君〉you; old chap.

　　kimi-wa *or* kimi-ga（君は，君が）　you

　　kimi-no（君の）　your

　　kimi-ni *or* kimi-o（君に，君を）　you

　　kimi-no-mono（君のもの）　yours

　　kimi-jishin（君自身）　yourself

kimi〈きみ：気味〉(a) feeling, (a) sensation.

　　Ii-kimi-da!（いい気味だ.）　Serve(s) you right!

　kimi-no-warui〈気味の悪い〉uncanny, weird, spooky.

ki-mijika〈きみじか：気短〉

　ki-mijika-na〈気短な〉quick-tempered, impatient.

kimi-tachi〈きみたち：君たち〉you.

　　kimi-tachi-wa *or* kimi-tachi-ga（君たちは，君たちが）　you

kimi-tachi-no〔君たちの〕 your

kimi-tachi-ni or kimi-tachi-o〔君たちに，君たちを〕 you

kimi-tachi-no-mono〔君たちのもの〕 yours

kimi-tachi-jishin〔君たち自身〕 yourselves

kimitsu〈きみつ：機密〉a secret.

kimitsu o morasu〔機密を漏らす〕 let out a secret

kimitsu-bunsho〔機密文書〕 confidential documents

kimitsu-no〈機密の〉secret, confidential.

kimitsu〈きみつ：気密〉

kimitsu-kôzô〔気密構造〕 an airtight structure

kimitsu-no〈気密の〉airtight.

kimmekki〈きんめっき：金めっき〉gilding.

kimmekki-suru〈金めっきする〉gild.

kimmekki-shita〈金めっきした〉gilt.

kimmitsu〈きんみつ：緊密〉

kimmitsu-na〈緊密な〉close, tight.

kimmitsu-na renraku-o-tamotsu〔緊密な連絡を保つ〕 keep in close contact ((with))

kimmitsu-ni〈緊密に〉closely, tightly.

kimmotsu〈きんもつ：禁物〉a prohibited thing, a tabooed thing, an anathema, an injurious thing.

kimmu〈きんむ：勤務〉service, duty.

kimmu-jikan-chû-de-aru〔勤務時間中である〕 be on duty

kimmu-jikan-gai-de-aru〔勤務時間外である〕 be off duty

kimmu-suru〈勤務する〉serve, do duty, work.

kimo〈きも：肝〉the liver.

kimochi〈きもち：気持ち〉a feeling, a mood.

kimochi-ga-ii〈気持ちがいい〉be comfortable, be pleasant, be agreeable, feel well.

kimochi-ga-warui〔気持ちが悪い〕 be uncomfortable, be unpleasant, be disagreeable, feel unwell

kimochi-ga-waruku-naru〈気持ちが悪くなる〉feel sick.

kimochi-yoku〈気持ちよく〉cheerfully, pleasantly, agreeably, willingly.

kimon〈きもん：鬼門〉the northeastern and unlucky quarter.

kimono〈きもの：着物〉a *kimono*, clothes, clothing.

kimono o kiru〔着物を着る〕 put on one's clothes

kimono o nugu〔着物を脱ぐ〕 take off one's clothes

rippa-na kimono-o-kite-iru〔立派な着物を着ている〕 be well dressed

kimpaku 〈きんぱく：金ぱく〉 gold foil, (a) gold leaf.

kimpaku 〈きんぱく：緊迫〉 tension, strain.
kimpaku-suru 〈緊迫する〉 become tense, grow strained.
kimpaku-shita 〈緊迫した〉 tense.
　　kimpaku-shita jôsei 〈緊迫した情勢〉 a tense situation

kimpatsu 〈きんぱつ：金髪〉 golden hair.
kimpatsu-no 〈金髪の〉 blond, blonde.

kimpika 〈きんぴか：金ぴか〉
kimpika-no 〈金ぴかの〉 glittering, gilded.

kimpun 〈きんぷん：金粉〉 gold dust.

ki-muzukashii 〈きむずかしい：気難しい〉 hard to please, particular ((about)), fastidious ((about)), testy.
　　Kare-wa ki-muzukashii. 〈彼は気難しい.〉 He is hard to please.

kimyô 〈きみょう：奇妙〉
kimyô-na 〈奇妙な〉 strange, queer, curious, odd.
　　kimyô-na-koto-ni 〈奇妙なことに〉 strange to say
kimyô-ni 〈奇妙に〉 strangely, curiously, oddly.

kin(-no) 〈きん(の)：金(の)〉 gold.
kin-iro-no 〈金色の〉 gold, golden.

kin 〈きん：菌〉 a fungus; a germ, a bacterium, a bacillus.

ki-naga 〈きなが：気長〉
ki-naga-na 〈気長な〉 slowgoing, leisurely, patient.
ki-naga-ni 〈気長に〉 patiently, without haste.

kina-ko 〈きなこ：黄な粉〉 soybean flour.

kina-kusai 〈きなくさい：きな臭い〉 smell smoke.

kinan 〈きなん：危難〉 (a) danger, (a) peril, (a) distress.

kinchaku 〈きんちゃく：近着〉 recent arrival.
kinchaku-no 〈近着の〉 recently received, just arrived.

kin-chisan 〈きんちさん：禁治産〉 incompetency.
　　kin-chisan-sha 〈禁治産者〉 a person adjudged incompetent
　　　　jun-kin-chisan-sha 〈準禁治産者〉 a quasi-incompetent person

kinchô 〈きんちょう：緊張〉 strain, tension.
　　kinchô ga takamaru 〈緊張が高まる〉 tensions are heightened
　　kinchô o hogusu 〈緊張をほぐす〉 relax the tension
kinchô-suru 〈緊張する〉 be strained, become tense.
kinchô-saseru 〈緊張させる〉 strain, tense, key up.
kinchô-shita 〈緊張した〉 strained, tense.

kindai 〈きんだい：近代〉 recent times, modern ages.

　　　kindai-kagaku〈近代科学〉 modern science

　　　kindai-ka〈近代化〉 modernization

　　　kindai-ka-suru〈近代化する〉 modernize

　kindai-no or *kindai-teki(-na)*〈近代の，近代的(な)〉 modern.

kindan-shôjô〈きんだんしょうじょう：禁断症状〉withdrawal symptoms.

kine〈きね〉a pestle, a pounder.

kinen〈きねん：記念〉commemoration, memory.

　　　kinen-bi〈記念日〉 a commemoration day, an anniversary

　　　kinen-sai〈記念祭〉 a commemoration, an anniversary

　　　kinen-hi〈記念碑〉 a monument

　　　kinen-hin〈記念品〉 a souvenir

　kinen-suru〈記念する〉commemorate.

　kinen-no〈記念の〉commemorative, memorial.

　kinen-ni〈記念に〉in memory ((of)), in remembrance ((of)), as a token
　　((of)).

kin·en〈きんえん：禁煙〉

　　　Kin·en.（禁煙.） No Smoking. / Smoking Prohibited.

　kin·en-suru〈禁煙する〉give up smoking, refrain from smoking.

kingaku〈きんがく：金額〉an amount (of money), a sum (of money).

　kingaku-ni-shite〈金額にして〉in value.

kingan〈きんがん：近眼〉*see.* kinshi〈近視〉.

Kinga-shinnen〈きんがしんねん：謹賀新年〉(A) Happy New Year.

kingen〈きんげん：金言〉a wise saying.

kingyo〈きんぎょ：金魚〉a goldfish.

ki-ni-iri〈きにいり：気に入り〉*see.* o-ki-ni-iri.

kinin〈きにん：帰任〉

　kinin-suru〈帰任する〉return to one's post.

kin·itsu〈きんいつ：均一〉uniformity, equality.

　　　kin·itsu-ryôkin-seido〈均一料金制度〉 the uniform rate system

　kin·itsu-no〈均一の〉uniform, equal.

kinji-chi〈きんじち：近似値〉an approximate value.

kinjiru〈きんじる：禁じる〉forbid, prohibit, ban, bar, lay an embargo
　　((on)); suppress, restrain, cannot help.

　　　shitsubô-o-kinji-e-nai〈失望を禁じ得ない〉 cannot help being disap-
　　　pointed

kin-jisan〈きんじさん：禁治産〉*see.* kin-chisan.

kinji-tô〈きんじとう：金字塔〉a pyramid, a monumental work.

　　　kinji-tô o uchi-tateru〈金字塔を打ち建てる〉 accomplish a monumental work

kinjitsu 〈きんじつ：近日〉

kinjitsu-chû-ni 〈近日中に〉 in a few days, one of these days, before long, shortly.

kinjo 〈きんじょ：近所〉 the neighborhood.

kinjo-no 〈近所の〉 neighboring.

    kinjo-no-hito 〈近所の人〉 a neighbor

kinjo-ni 〈近所に〉 in the neighborhood, near by.

kinjo-zukiai 〈きんじょづきあい：近所付き合い〉

kinjo-zukiai suru 〈近所付き合いする〉 neighbor ((with)).

kinjo-zukiai-no-ii 〈近所付き合いのいい〉 neighborly.

    kinjo-zukiai-no-warui 〈近所付き合いの悪い〉 unneighborly

kinjû 〈きんじゅう：きん獣〉 birds and beasts, animals.

kinka 〈きんか：金貨〉 a gold coin.

kinkai 〈きんかい：近海〉

    kinkai-gyogyô 〈近海漁業〉 inshore fishery

    kinkai-kôro 〈近海航路〉 a coasting line

kinkai 〈きんかい：金塊〉 a gold bar, a nugget.

kinkan 〈きんかん〉 a kumquat.

kinkan 〈きんかん：金冠〉 a gold crown.

ha-ni kinkan-o-kabuseru 〈歯に金冠をかぶせる〉 crown a tooth in gold.

kinkan 〈きんかん：金環〉 a gold ring, a corona.

kinkan 〈きんかん：近刊〉 a recent publication.

kinkan-no 〈近刊の〉 recently published; forthcoming.

kinken-seiji 〈きんけんせいじ：金権政治〉 plutocracy.

kinko 〈きんこ：金庫〉 a safe.

    kashi-kinko 〈貸し金庫〉 a safe-deposit box

kinko 〈きんこ：禁固〉 imprisonment.

    kinko-rokkagetsu-no-kei-ni-shoserareru 〈禁固六ケ月の刑に処せられる〉 be sentenced to six months' imprisonment

kinkô 〈きんこう：近郊〉 the suburbs ((of)), the outskirts ((of)).

kinkô-no 〈近郊の〉 suburban, neighboring.

kinkô 〈きんこう：均衡〉 balance, (an) equilibrium.

    kinkô o tamotsu 〈均衡を保つ〉 keep the balance

    kinkô o ushinau 〈均衡を失う〉 lose (the) balance

kinkô 〈きんこう：金鉱〉 (a) gold ore, a gold mine.

kinkon-shiki 〈きんこんしき：金婚式〉 a golden wedding.

kinkotsu 〈きんこつ：筋骨〉

kinkotsu-takumashii〈筋骨たくましい〉muscular, sinewy, brawny.

kinku〈きんく：禁句〉a tabooed word.

kinkyô〈きんきょう：近況〉the recent state, how one is getting on.

kin-kyori〈きんきょり：近距離〉a short distance.

kinkyû〈きんきゅう：緊急〉

    kinkyû-jitai (緊急事態) a state of emergency, an emergency

    kinkyû-no〈緊急の〉urgent, pressing.

kinnen〈きんねん：近年〉in recent years.

kinniku〈きんにく：筋肉〉muscles.

    kinniku-rôdô (筋肉労働) muscular labor

    kinniku-no〈筋肉の〉muscular.

kinô〈きのう：機能〉(a) function, (a) faculty.

    kinô o hakki-suru (機能を発輝する) fulfill one's function

    shinkei no kinô (神経の機能) the functions of the nerves

    kinô-shôgai-o-okosu (機能障害を起こす) be functionally disordered

    kinô-teki(-na)〈機能的(な)〉functional.

    kinô-teki-ni〈機能的に〉functionally.

kinô〈きのう：昨日〉yesterday.

    kinô-no asa (昨日の朝) yesterday morning

    kinô-no ban (昨日の晩) last night

    kinô-no shimbun (昨日の新聞) yesterday's paper

kinô〈きのう：帰納〉induction.

    kinô-hô (帰納法) the inductive method

    kinô-suru〈帰納する〉induce.

    kinô-teki(-na)〈帰納的(な)〉inductive.

    kinô-teki-ni〈帰納的に〉inductively.

ki-no-doku〈きのどく：気の毒〉

    Sore-wa o-ki-no-doku-desu.（それはお気の毒です。）I'm sorry to hear that. / I sympathize with you.

    ki-no-doku-ni-omou〈気の毒に思う〉be sorry ((for or that)), regret, pity.

    ki-no-doku-na〈気の毒な〉poor, pitiable.

    ki-no-doku-nimo〈気の毒にも〉sorry to say.

kinoko〈きのこ〉a mushroom.

    kinoko-gari (きのこ狩り) mushroom gathering

ki-nomi-ki-no-mama-de〈きのみきのままで：着の身着のままで〉with only the clothes one wears.

kinori〈きのり：気乗り〉

    kinori-ga-shi-nai〈気乗りがしない〉be disinclined ((to do)), do not feel like ((doing)).

kinrai〈きんらい：近来〉lately, recently.
　kinrai-no〈近来の〉late, recent.
kinri〈きんり：金利〉(the rate of) interest.
　　kinri o hiki-sageru（金利を引き下げる）lower the rate of interest
kinrô〈きんろう：勤労〉labor.
　　kinrô-shotoku（勤労所得）an earned income.
kinryô〈きんりょう：禁猟〉prohibition of shooting.
　　kinryô-ki（禁猟期）the closed season
　　kinryô-ku（禁猟区）a game preserve
kinryô〈きんりょう：禁漁〉prohibition of fishing.
　　kinryô-ku（禁漁区）a marine preserve
kinryoku〈きんりょく：筋力〉muscular strength.
kinsa〈きんさ：きん差〉
　kinsa-de katsu〈きん差で勝つ〉win by a narrow margin.
kinsaku〈きんさく：金策〉
　　kinsaku-ni-isogashii（金策に忙しい）be busy raising funds
　kinsaku-suru〈金策する〉raise funds.
kinsei〈きんせい：近世〉modern times.
　　kinsei-shi（近世史）modern history
　kinsei-no〈近世の〉modern.
kinsei〈きんせい：金星〉Venus.
kinsei〈きんせい：禁制〉
　　kinsei-hin（禁制品）contraband goods
kinsei〈きんせい：均整〉balance, symmetry.
　kinsei-no-toreta〈均整のとれた〉well-balanced, well-proportioned, symmetrical.
kinsen〈きんせん：金銭〉money, cash.
　　kinsen-tôroku-ki（金銭登録器）a cash register
　kinsen(-jô)-no〈金銭(上)の〉money, pecuniary, monetary.
kinshi〈きんし：金糸〉gold thread.
kinshi〈きんし：近視〉shortsightedness, nearsightedness.
　kinshi-no or *kinshi-gan-teki(-na)*〈近視の，近視眼的(な)〉shortsighted, nearsighted.
kinshi〈きんし：禁止〉(a) prohibition, a ban.
　　kinshi o toku（禁止を解く）remove the prohibition, lift the ban
　kinshi-suru〈禁止する〉forbid, prohibit, ban.
kinshin〈きんしん：近親〉a close relative.

kinshin〈きんしん：謹慎〉home confinement.
　kinshin-o-meijirareru〈謹慎を命じられる〉be confined to one's house.
kinshu〈きんしゅ：筋しゅ〉a myoma.
kinshu〈きんしゅ：禁酒〉temperance, teetotalism.
　kinshu-suru〈禁酒する〉abstain from drinking, give up drinking.
kinshuku-zaisei〈きんしゅくざいせい：緊縮財政〉a reduced budget.
Kintô〈きんとう：近東〉the Near East.
kintô〈きんとう：均等〉equality.
　kintô-wari（均等割）per capita rate
　kintô-no〈均等の〉equal, even.
　kintô-ni〈均等に〉equally, evenly.
　　kintô-ni-suru（均等にする）equalize, make equal
kinu〈きぬ：絹〉silk.
　kinu-ito（絹糸）silk thread
　kinu-orimono（絹織物）silk goods, silk(s)
　kinu-no〈絹の〉silk.
　kinu-no-yô-na〈絹のような〉silky, silken.
kin·yô-bi〈きんようび：金曜日〉Friday.
kin·yoku〈きんよく：禁欲〉abstinence.
　kin·yoku-shugi（禁欲主義）asceticism, stoicism
　kin·yoku-seikatsu o okuru（禁欲生活を送る）lead an ascetic life
kin·yu〈きんゆ：禁輸〉an embargo on the export(*or* import) ((of)).
　kin·yu-hin（禁輸品）articles under an embargo
kinyû〈きにゅう：記入〉entry.
　kinyû-more（記入漏れ）an omission
　kinyû-suru〈記入する〉enter, write, fill in.
kin·yû〈きんゆう：金融〉circulation of money, finance.
　kin·yû o hiki-shimeru（金融を引き締める）tighten the money market
　kin·yû-kikan（金融機関）a banking organ, a financial institution
kinzoku〈きんぞく：金属〉(a) metal.
　kinzoku-seihin（金属製品）metal goods
　kinzoku-no〈金属の〉metallic.
kinzoku〈きんぞく：勤続〉continuous service.
　kinzoku-nengen（勤続年限）the length of one's service
　kinzoku-suru〈勤続する〉serve long.
　　aru kaisha-ni ju-nen-kan kinzoku-suru（ある会社に十年間勤続する）serve in a firm for ten years

kinzoku-sei〈きんぞくせい：金属性〉metallicity.
　kinzoku-sei-no〈金属性の〉metallic.
　　kinzoku-sei-no oto（金属性の音）a metallic sound
kiô〈きおう：既往〉the past.
　　kiô-ni-sakanoboru（既往にさかのぼる）date back ((to)), be retrospective ((to))
　　kiô-shô（既往症）a disease which one has had before
kioi-tatsu〈きおいたつ：気負い立つ〉get excited.
kioku〈きおく：記憶〉memory, remembrance.
　　kioku-ryoku（記憶力）one's (powers of) memory
　　　kioku-ryoku-ga-ii（記憶力がいい）have a good memory
　　　kioku-ryoku-ga-warui（記憶力が悪い）have a poor memory
　　watashi no kioku ga tadashi-kereba（私の記憶が正しければ）if I remember right
　　kioku-sôshitsu-shô（記憶喪失症）amnesia
　kioku-suru（記憶する）remember, keep in mind, learn by heart.
　kioku-su-beki〈記憶すべき〉memorable.
ki-okure〈きおくれ：気後れ〉
　ki-okure-ga-suru〈気後れがする〉become diffident.
kion〈きおん：気温〉temperature.
　　Kion ga agaru.（気温が上がる.）The temperature rises.
　　Kion ga sagaru.（気温が下がる.）The temperature falls.
　　saikô-kion（最高気温）the maximum temperature
ki-o-tsuke〈きをつけ：気を付け〉
　　Ki-o-tsuke!（気を付け.）Attention!
　ki-o-tsuke-no-shisei-o-toru〈気を付けの姿勢をとる〉stand at attention.
kippari(-to)〈きっぱり(と)〉clearly, distinctly, plainly, candidly, frankly, positively, flatly, definitely.
　　kippari-to kotowaru（きっぱりと断る）decline flatly
　kippari-shita〈きっぱりした〉clear, distinct, candid, frank, positive, flat, definite.
　　kippari-shita henji（きっぱりした返事）a definite reply
kippô〈きっぽう：吉報〉good news.
　　kippô o motarasu（吉報をもたらす）bring good news
kippu〈きっぷ：切符〉a ticket.
　　kippu o kiru（切符を切る）punch a ticket
　　kippu-uri-ba（切符売場）a ticket office, a booking office
　　kippu-jidô-hambai-ki（切符自動販売機）a ticket vending machine

hangaku-kippu（半額切符） a half ticket

kirabiyaka〈きらびやか〉
kirabiyaka-ni-ki-kazatte〈きらびやかに着飾って〉in gala dress.

kirai〈機雷〉a mine.

kirai〈きらい：嫌い〉a dislike ((for, of *or* to)), a hatred ((for *or* toward)), aversion ((for *or* to)).
kirai-na-mono（嫌いな物） what one does not like
kirai-de-aru, kirai-da or *kirau*〈嫌いである，嫌いだ，嫌う〉dislike, don't like, have a dislike ((to)), hate.
kirai-ni-naru〈嫌いになる〉come to dislike, lose interest ((in)), get tired ((of)).

kirakira〈きらきら〉glitteringly.
kirakira-suru, or kirakira-kagayaku〈きらきらする，きらきら輝く〉glitter, twinkle; bright, brilliant, twinkling.

kiraku〈きらく：気楽〉ease, comfort.
kiraku-na〈気楽な〉easy, comfortable, easygoing.
kiraku-ni〈気楽に〉easily, in comfort.
kiraku-ni kurasu（気楽に暮らす） live in comfort

kirameki〈きらめき〉a glitter, sparkling, twinkling, glimmering.
kirameku〈きらめく〉see. kirakira-kagayaku.

kirasu〈きらす：切らす〉be short ((of)), be out of stock.

kire〈きれ：切れ〉cloth; a bit, a piece, a slice.
momen-no kire（木綿の切れ） (a) cotton cloth
niku hito-kire（肉一切れ） a piece of meat
pan futa-kire（パン二切れ） two slices of bread

kire-aji〈きれあじ：切れ味〉
kire-aji-no-ii〈切れ味のいい〉sharp.
kire-aji-no-warui（切れ味の悪い） dull, blunt

kire-gire〈きれぎれ：切れ切れ〉
kire-gire-ni〈切れ切れに〉in pieces.
fûtô o kire-gire ni saku（封筒を切れ切れに裂く） tear an envelope in pieces

kire-hashi〈きれはし：切れ端〉a piece, a scrap.

kirei〈きれい：き麗〉
kirei-na〈きれいな〉beautiful, pretty, clean, tidy, neat, fair.
kirei-na onna-no-hito（きれいな女の人） a beautiful woman
kirei-na hana（きれいな花） a pretty flower
kirei-na mizu（きれいな水） clean water

    kirei-na kao-tsuki〈きれいな顔つき〉 a fair countenance

kirei-zuki-na〈きれい好きな〉 cleanly, tidy, neat.

kirei-ni〈きれいに〉 beautifully, clean, neatly, all, completely.

    kirei-ni fuku（きれいにふく） wipe clean

    kirei-ni wasureru（きれいに忘れる） quite forget

kirei-ni-suru〈きれいにする〉 clean, cleanse, put in order, make neat, tidy (up).

    jibun-no heya o kirei-ni-shite-oku（自分の部屋をきれいにしておく）
       keep one's room tidy

kire-ma〈きれま：切れ間〉 an interval, a break, a rift.

    kumo-no kire-ma（雲の切れ間） a break in the clouds

kire-me〈きれめ：切れ目〉 a rift, a break; a pause.

-kirenai〈-きれない：-切れない〉 be more than one can, be too much for.

    tabe-kirenai（食べ切れない） be more than one can eat

    ikura-homete-mo-home-kirenai（幾ら褒めても褒め切れない） cannot
       praise ((a person)) too much

kireru〈きれる：切れる〉 cut, be sharp; break; be worn out; be cut off; run out; be up.

    Kono naifu wa yoku kireru.（このナイフはよく切れる.） This knife is
       sharp.

    Ito ga kireta.（糸が切れた.） The string broke.

    Damu ga kireta.（ダムが切れた.） The dam was broken down.

    Gasorin ga kire-kakatte-iru.（ガソリンが切れかかっている.） The gas
      is running short.

    Mamonaku jikan ga kireru.（間もなく時間が切れる.） Time will be
      up soon.

kire-nai〈切れない〉 (be) dull, (be) blunt.

kiretsu〈きれつ：き裂〉 a crack, a crevice.

kiretsu-o-shōjiru〈き裂を生じる〉 crack.

kiri〈きり：霧〉 (a) mist, (a) fog; spray.

    fukai kiri（深い霧） a dense fog

    Kiri ga hareta.（霧が晴れた.） The fog has lifted.

kiri-o-fuku〈霧を吹く〉 spray (water).

kiri-no-kakatta〈霧のかかった〉 misty.

kiri-no-fukai〈霧の深い〉 foggy.

kiri〈きり〉 a paulownia.

kiri〈きり〉 a gimlet, a drill.

    kiri-de ana o akeru（きりで穴を開ける） bore a hole with a gimlet

kiri〈きり：切り〉an end, limits, bounds; a period.

  kiri-ga-nai〈切りがない〉be endless, be boundless, there is no end.

  kiri-no-ii-tokoro-de-yameru〈切りのいいところでやめる〉stop one's work
    where it is convenient.

kiri-ageru〈きりあげる：切り上げる〉close, stop, wind up, cut short.

    shigoto o kiri-ageru〈仕事を切り上げる〉 cut one's work short

kiri-bana〈きりばな：切り花〉cut flowers.

kiri-dasu〈きりだす：切り出す〉cut down; quarry; begin to talk, break
    the ice, start.

kiri-fuda〈きりふだ：切り札〉a trump (card).

    kiri-fuda o dasu〈切り札を出す〉 play a trump

kirigirisu〈きりぎりす〉a grasshopper.

kiri-hanasu〈きりはなす：切り離す〉cut off, detach ((from)), sever
    ((from)), separate.

kiri-hiraku〈きりひらく：切り開く〉cut (open), clear.

    are-chi o kiri-hiraku〈荒れ地を切り開く〉 clear waste land

kiri-kabu〈きりかぶ：切り株〉a stump, a stubble.

kiri-kae〈きりかえ：切り替え〉a change(over), a switchover, (a) renewal.

    kiri-kae-suitchi〈切り替えスイッチ〉 a changeover switch

  kiri-kaeru〈切り替える〉change, convert, renew, switch.

    atama-o-kiri-kaeru〈頭を切り替える〉 change one's way of thinking

kirikiri〈きりきり〉

    atama-ga-kirikiri-itamu〈頭がきりきり痛む〉 have a splitting head-
    ache

    Ichi-nichi-jū kirikiri-mai-saserareta.〈一日中きりきり舞いさせられた。〉
       Business kept me hustling all day.

kiri-kizamu〈きりきざむ：切り刻む〉mince, chop (up), cut into pieces.

kiri-kizu〈きりきず：切り傷〉a cut, an incised wound.

kiri-kuchi〈きりくち：切り口〉a cut end, an opening.

kiri-kuzusu〈きりくずす：切り崩す〉cut through; break, split.

    yama o kiri-kuzusu〈山を切り崩す〉 cut through a mountain

    kumiai o kiri-kuzusu〈組合を切り崩す〉 split a labor union

kiri-mawasu〈きりまわす：切り回す〉manage, control, run.

    ie o kiri-mawasu〈家を切り回す〉 manage household affairs

kiri-momi〈きりもみ：切り揉み〉a spin.

    kiri-momi-shi-nagara〈きりもみしながら〉 in a spin

kiri-mori〈きりもり：切り盛り〉

  kiri-mori-suru〈切り盛りする〉*see.* kiri-mawasu.

kirin 〈きりん〉 a giraffe.

kiri-nukeru 〈きりぬける：切り抜ける〉 cut one's way through, get over, tide over.

    nankan o kiri-nukeru (難関を切り抜ける) tide over a difficulty

kiri-nuki 〈きりぬき：切り抜き〉 cutting, clipping, a scrap.

    kiri-nuku 〈切り抜く〉 cut (out) ((from)).

kiri-otosu 〈きりおとす：切り落とす〉 cut down, cut off, prune.

kiri-sage 〈きりさげ：切り下げ〉 (a) reduction, devaluation.

    kiri-sageru 〈切り下げる〉 reduce, devaluate.

kiri-same 〈きりさめ：霧雨〉 a drizzle.

kiri-suteru 〈きりすてる：切り捨てる〉 cut off, cast away, omit.

    jû-en-miman-no-hasû o kiri-suteru (十円未満の端数を切り捨てる) omit the fractional sum smaller than ten yen

Kirisuto 〈キリスト〉 (Jesus) Christ.

    Kirisuto-kyô (キリスト教) Christianity

    Kirisuto-kyô-to (キリスト教徒) a Christian

    Kirisuto(-kyô)-no (キリスト(教)の) Christian

kiri-taosu 〈きりたおす：切り倒す〉 cut down, fell.

kiri-tori 〈きりとり：切り取り〉

    kiri-tori-sen (切り取り線) a dotted line, a perforated line

    kiri-toru 〈切り取る〉 cut off, cut away.

kiritsu 〈きりつ：規律〉 order, discipline.

    kiritsu o mamoru (規律を守る) observe discipline

    kiritsu-tadashii 〈規律正しい〉 orderly, disciplined.

    kiritsu-no-nai (規律のない) disorderly, undisciplined

    kiritsu-tadashiku 〈規律正しく〉 in good order.

Kiritsu! 〈きりつ．：起立．〉 Stand up!

kiri-tsukeru 〈きりつける：切り付ける〉 cut at ((a person)) with.

kiri-tsumeru 〈きりつめる：切り詰める〉 cut down, economize.

    keihi o kiri-tsumeru (経費を切り詰める) cut down expenses

kiritto 〈きりっと〉

    kiritto-shita mehanadachi (きりっとした目鼻立ち) clean-cut features

kiri-uri 〈きりうり：切り売り〉

    kiri-uri-suru 〈切り売りする〉 sell ((things)) by the piece, peddle out.

kiro 〈キロ〉 a kilo.

    kiro-guramu (キログラム) a kilogram

    kiro-mêtoru (キロメートル) a kilometer

    kiro-rittoru (キロリットル) a kiloliter

kiro-watto〈キロワット〉a kilowatt

kiro〈きろ：岐路〉a crossroad(s).

jinsei no kiro-ni-tatsu（人生の岐路に立つ） stand at the crossroads of one's life

kiroku〈きろく：記録〉a record, a document.

kiroku o tsukuru（記録を作る） make a record

kiroku o yaburu（記録を破る） break the record

kiroku o kôshin-suru（記録を更新する） better a record

kiroku-gakari（記録係） a recorder, a scorer

kiroku-hoji-sha（記録保持者） a record holder

sekai-shin-kiroku（世界新記録） a new world record

kiroku-eiga（記録映画） a documentary film

kiroku-suru〈記録する〉record, register, write down.

kiroku-shite-oku〈記録しておく〉keep on record.

kiroku-teki(-na)〈記録的(な)〉record, record-breaking.

kiru〈きる：切る〉cut, chop, hash, carve, saw, clip, slice, cut down, punch, switch off, turn off, ring off, hang up, break with ((a person)), swish ((water)) off.

kiru〈きる：着る〉put on.

kite-iru〈着ている〉wear, have on, be dressed in.

kite-miru〈着てみる〉try on.

-kiru〈-きる：-切る〉finish, be through.

shôsetsu o yomi-kiru（小説を読み切る） finish reading a novel

kane o tsukai-kiru（金を使い切る） spend all the money

tsukare-kitte-iru（疲れ切っている） be tired out

kiryô〈きりょう：器量〉personal appearance, looks.

kiryô-no-ii〈器量のいい〉pretty, good-looking.

kiryô-no-yoku-nai（器量のよくない） plainlooking, homely

kiryoku〈きりょく：気力〉energy, spirit, vitality.

kiryoku-no-aru〈気力のある〉energetic, vigorous.

kiryoku-no-nai（気力のない） spiritless

kiryû〈きりゅう：気流〉an air current.

ran-kiryû（乱気流） (air) turbulence

kisai〈きさい：鬼才〉a genius, a prodigy.

kisai〈きさい：記載〉mention; entry.

kisai-suru〈記載する〉mention, carry, print; enter.

kisai〈きさい：起債〉

kisai-suru〈起債する〉float a loan, issue bonds.

kisaku 〈きさく：気さく〉

  kisaku-na 〈気さくな〉 good-humored, frank, openhearted.

kisan 〈きさん：起算〉

  kisan-suru 〈起算する〉 count from, measure from.

kisei 〈きせい：気勢〉 spirit, vigor.

  kisei-o-ageru 〈気勢を上げる〉 arouse one's enthusiasm.

    kisei-o-sogu （気勢をそぐ） dampen one's enthusiasm

    kisei-ga-agara-nai （気勢が上がらない） be in low spirits

kisei 〈きせい：寄生〉 parasitism.

    kisei-chû （寄生虫） a parasite

  kisei-suru 〈寄生する〉 be parasitic ((on)).

kisei 〈きせい：奇声〉 a queer voice.

    kisei o hassuru （奇声を発する） utter a queer voice

kisei 〈きせい：帰省〉

  kisei-suru 〈帰省する〉 go(come *or* return) home, return to one's native place.

kisei 〈きせい：規制〉 regulation, control.

  kisei-suru 〈規制する〉 regulate, control.

kisei 〈きせい：既成〉

    kisei-jijitsu （既成事実） an established fact

  kisei-no 〈既成の〉 established, existing.

kisei 〈きせい：既製〉

    kisei-fuku （既製服） a ready-made suit

  kisei-no 〈既製の〉 ready-made.

kiseki 〈きせき：奇跡〉 a miracle, a wonder.

  kiseki-teki(-na) 〈奇跡的(な)〉 miraculous.

  kiseki-teki-ni 〈奇跡的に〉 miraculously.

kiseki 〈きせき：軌跡〉 a locus.

kisen 〈きせん：汽船〉 a steamship, a steamer, a liner.

kisen 〈きせん：機先〉

  kisen-o-seisuru 〈機先を制する〉 get the start ((of)), beat ((a person)) to the punch, forestall.

kiseru 〈キセル〉 a Japanese pipe.

  kiseru-o-yaru 〈キセルをやる〉 steal a ride on a train without ticket for the middle part of the way.

kiseru 〈きせる：着せる〉 dress, put on, clothe; charge ((a person)) with 〔a guilt〕.

kisetsu 〈きせつ：季節〉 a season.

kisetsu-hazure-no〔季節外れの〕 out of season

kisetsu-fû〔季節風〕 a seasonal wind

kisha〈きしゃ：汽車〉a train, a car, a carriage.

kisha-chin〔汽車賃〕a railroad fare

kisha-ryokô〔汽車旅行〕 a railway journey

kisha-de〔汽車で〕by train.

kisha〈きしゃ：記者〉a journalist, a pressman, a newsman.

kishi〈きし：岸〉the bank, the shore, the beach, the border.

kishi-ni-uchi-age-rareru〔岸に打ち上げられる〕be washed ashore.

kishimu or **kishiru**〈きしむ、きしる〉creak, squeak, grate, jar.

kishitsu〈きしつ：気質〉a disposition, (a) nature, (a) temper, (a) temperament.

kishô〈きしょう：気象〉weather (conditions).

kishô-tsûhô〔気象通報〕a weather report

kishô-dai〔気象台〕a meteorological observatory

kishô-kansoku〔気象観測〕(a) meteorological observation

kishô〈きしょう：気性〉*see.* kishitsu.

hageshii kishô〔激しい気性〕a sharp temper

kishô〈きしょう：起床〉

kishô-jikan〔起床時間〕 the hour of rising

kishô-suru〔起床する〕get up, rise.

kishô-kachi〈きしょうかち：希少価値〉scarcity value.

kishu〈きしゅ：機首〉the nose.

kishu-o-ageru〔機首を上げる〕nose up.

kishu-o-sageru〔機首を下げる〕 nose down

kishu〈きしゅ：旗手〉a standard-bearer.

kishu〈きしゅ：騎手〉a rider, a horseman, a jockey.

kishu〈きしゅ：気しゅ〉emphysema.

hai-kishu〔肺気しゅ〕emphysema of the lung

kishû〈きしゅう：奇襲〉a sudden attack, a surprise attack.

kishû-suru〔奇襲する〕make a surprise attack ((on)).

kishuku〈きしゅく：寄宿〉lodging, board, board and lodging.

kishuku-sei〔寄宿生〕 a boarding student, a boarder

kishuku-sha〔寄宿舎〕a dormitory

kishuku-suru〔寄宿する〕lodge ((at)), board ((with)).

kiso〈きそ：基礎〉the foundation, the basis, the base.

kiso o katameru〔基礎を固める〕 consolidate the foundation ((of))

kiso-kara benkyô-suru〔基礎から勉強する〕 learn from the beginning

kiso-gakka〔基礎学科〕 the fundamental studies

kiso-kôji〔基礎工事〕 foundation work

kiso-chishiki〔基礎知識〕 a grounding ((in))

kiso-teki(-na)〔基礎的(な)〕fundamental, basic, elementary.

kiso〈きそ：起訴〉prosecution, indictment, legal proceedings.

kiso-jô〔起訴状〕 an indictment

kiso-suru〈起訴する〉prosecute, indict, bring an action ((against)), go to law ((with)), sue.　　　　　　　　　　　　　　　　　　「murder

satsujin-zai-de kiso-sareru〔殺人罪で起訴される〕 be indicted for

kisô〈きそう：起草〉drafting.

kisô-suru〈起草する〉draft〔a bill〕.

kisoku〈きそく：規則〉a rule, regulations.

kisoku o mamoru（規則を守る） observe the rules

kisoku o yaburu（規則を破る） break the rules

kisoku-ihan〔規則違反〕 violation of regulations

kisoku-ihan-de-aru〔規則違反である〕 be against the rules

kisoku-sho〔規則書〕 a prospectus

kisoku-teki(-na) or *kisoku-tadashii*〈規則的(な)，規則正しい〉regular.

kisoku-teki(-ni) or *kisoku-tadashiku*〈規則的(に)，規則正しく〉regularly.

kisoku-doori-ni〈規則どおりに〉according to the rules.

kison〈きそん：き損〉damage, injury.

meiyo-kison〔名誉き損〕 a libel, a slander, defamation (of character)

kison-suru〈き損する〉damage, injure.

kison〈きそん：既存〉

kison-no〈既存の〉existing.

kisou〈きそう：競う〉compete with ((another)) for ((something)).

kisotte〈競って〉competitively.

kissa-ten〈きっさてん：喫茶店〉a tearoom, a coffee shop.

kissui〈きっすい：生粋〉

kissui-no〈生粋の〉trueborn, genuine.

kissui〈きっすい：喫水〉draft, draught.

kissui-no-asai fune（喫水の浅い船） a ship with a light draft

kisu〈キス〉a kiss.

kisu-suru〈キスする〉kiss.

kisū〈きすう：奇数〉an odd number.

kisū〈きすう：基数〉a cardinal number.

kisuru〈きする：帰する〉come ((to)), result ((in)), be reduced ((to)); attribute ((to)).

　　　shippai-ni-kisuru（失敗に帰する）　result in failure

　　　seikō o kôun-ni-kisuru（成功を幸運に帰する）　attribute one's success
　　　　to luck

kisuru-tokoro〈帰するところ〉after all, in the end, in the last analysis.

kisuru〈きする：期する〉expect, hope ((for)), look forward ((to)), rely
　((on)), be sure ((of)), be ready, resolve, promise.

　　　rainen-o-kishite（来年を期して）looking forward to the coming year

ki-sezu-shite〈期せずして〉unexpectedly, accidentally, by chance.

ki-sezu-shite～(-suru)〈期せずして～(する)〉happen ((to do)).

kita〈きた：北〉the north.

　　　kita-kaze（北風）a north wind

kita-no〈北の〉north, northern.

kita-e or *kita-ni*〈北へ，北に〉north, northward.

～-no-kita-ni〈～の北に〉in the north of... , on the north of... , to the
　north of... .

kitaeru〈きたえる：鍛える〉train.

　　　karada o kitaeru（体を鍛える）train oneself

kitai〈きたい：期待〉expectation.

　　　kitai ni sou（期待に添う）meet one's expectation

kitai-suru〈期待する〉expect.

kitai-hazure-no〈期待外れの〉disappointing.

kitai-ni-hanshite〈期待に反して〉against one's expectation

kitai〈きたい：機体〉a body, an airframe.

kitai〈きたい：気体〉gas.

kitai-no〈気体の〉gaseous.

kitaku（きたく：帰宅）

kitaku-suru〈帰宅する〉go(come, *or* return) home.

kitanai〈きたない：汚い〉dirty, filthy, unclean; mean, base.

　　　kitanai te（汚い手）dirty hands

　　　kokoro-no-kitanai hito（心の汚い人）a person of base mind

kitanaku-naru〈汚くなる〉get dirty, become filthy.

kitaru-〈きたる-：来る-〉next, coming.

　　　kitaru-nichiyô-bi-ni（来る日曜日に）next Sunday, on Sunday next

kitchin〈キッチン〉a kitchen.

kitchiri〈きっちり〉punctually, precisely.

　　　kitchiri atte-iru（きっちり合っている）be right to the minute

kitei〈きてい：規定〉stipulations, prescriptions, provisions, rules,
　regulations.

kitei-suru〈規定する〉stipulate, prescribe, provide.

kitei-no〈規定の〉stipulated, prescribed, regular, regulation.

   kitei-doori〈規定どおり〉according to the rules.

kitei〈きてい：既定〉

kitei-no〈既定の〉established, fixed, prearranged.

   kitei-no hôshin（既定の方針）a prearranged plan

kiteki〈きてき：汽笛〉a (steam) whistle.

kiteki-o-narasu〈汽笛を鳴らす〉blow a whistle, whistle.

kiten〈きてん：機転〉quick wit, tact.

kiten-o-kikasu〈機転を利かす〉use one's brains, take the hint.

kiten-ga-kiku〈機転が利く〉be quick-witted.

   kiten-ga-kika-nai（機転が利かない）be dull-witted

kiten〈きてん：起点〉the starting point.

〜-o-kiten-to-suru〈〜を起点とする〉start from... .

kito〈きと：帰途〉

kito-ni〈帰途に〉on one's way home.

   kito-ni-tsuku（帰途に就く）start on one's way home, leave for home

kitô〈きとう：気筒〉a cylinder.

kitô〈きとう：祈とう〉a prayer, grace.

kitô-suru〈祈とうする〉pray, say grace.

kitoku〈きとく：危篤〉

kitoku-de-aru〈危篤である〉be dangerously ill, be in a critical condition.

kitoku-ni-ochiiru〈危篤に陥る〉fall into a dangerous condition.

kitoku〈きとく：奇特〉

kitoku-na〈奇特な〉praiseworthy, laudable, commendable.

   kitoku-na okonai（奇特な行い）a praiseworthy conduct

kitoku-ken〈きとくけん：既得権〉vested rights.

kitsuen〈きつえん：喫煙〉smoking.

   kitsuen-shitsu（喫煙室）a smoking room

kitsui〈きつい〉strong, severe, fierce, hard, tight.

   kitsui kaze（きつい風）a strong wind

   kitsui me（きつい目）fierce eyes

   kitsui shigoto（きつい仕事）hard work

   kitsui kotoba（きつい言葉）a harsh word

   kitsui nittei（きつい日程）tight schedule

   kitsui kutsu（きつい靴）tight shoes

kitsuku〈きつく〉severely, tightly.

   kitsuku shikaru（きつくしかる）scold severely

ki-tsuke 〈きつけ：着付け〉 dressing.

　ki-tsuke-o-shite-yaru 〈着付けをしてやる〉 dress, help ((a young girl)) dress (herself).

ki-tsuke 〈きつけ：気付け〉

　　ki-tsuke-gusuri 〈気付け薬〉 a restorative, a stimulant

kitsumon 〈きつもん：詰問〉 cross-examination, intense questioning.

　kitsumon-suru 〈詰問する〉 cross-examine, examine closely, demand an explanation.

kitsune 〈きつね〉 a fox.

　kitsune-iro(-no) 〈きつね色(の)〉 light brown.

ki-tsutsuki 〈きつつき〉 a woodpecker.

kitte 〈きって：切手〉 a (postage) stamp.

　　kitte o haru 〈切手をはる〉 put a stamp ((on))

　　roku-jū-en-gitte 〈六十円切手〉 a sixty-yen stamp

　　kitte-shūshū 〈切手収集〉 stamp collecting

　　　kitte-shūshū-ka 〈切手収集家〉 a stamp collector

-kitte-no 〈～きっての：～切っての〉 the most...in the whole place(*or* of all).

　　sha-nai-kitte-no-shuwan-ka 〈社内きっての手腕家〉 the ablest man in the whole firm

kitto 〈きっと〉 surely, certainly, without fail.

　kitto~(-suru) 〈きっと～(する)〉 be sure ((to do)).

kiun 〈きうん：機運〉 an opportunity, a chance, the time.

　　Kiun ga jukushita. 〈機運が熟した.〉 The time is ripe ((for)).

ki-utsuri 〈きうつり：気移り〉

　ki-utsuri-ga-suru 〈気移りがする〉 be capricious, be puzzled.

kiwa-datsu 〈きわだつ：際立つ〉 be conspicuous, be prominent.

　kiwa-datta 〈際立った〉 conspicuous, prominent, remarkable, distinct.

　　kiwa-datta sainō 〈際立った才能〉 conspicuous ability

　kiwadatte 〈際立って〉 conspicuously, prominently, remarkably, distinctly.

kiwadoi 〈きわどい：際どい〉 dangerous, critical, risky, close, narrow, delicate, risqué.

　　kiwadoi gêmu 〈際どいゲーム〉 a close game

　　kiwadoi hantei 〈際どい判定〉 a delicate judgment

　　kiwadoi-tokoro-de 〈際どいところで〉 at the critical moment

kiwamaru 〈きわまる：極(窮)まる〉

　　kiwamaru-tokoro-o-shira-nai 〈極まるところを知らない〉 know no bounds

kiken-kiwamaru〈危険窮まる〉 be extremely dangerous

kiwameru〈きわめる：極める〉investigate thoroughly, master, attain, reach; go to extremes.

bôgyaku-o-kiwameru〈暴虐を極める〉 be extremely tyrannical

kiwamete〈きわめて：極めて〉very, exceedingly, extremely.

kiwamete jûyô-na〈極めて重要な〉 very important

kiwami〈きわみ：極み〉the extremity, the height.

ikan-no-kiwami-de-aru〈遺憾の極みである〉 be most regrettable

kiwa-mono-shuppan〈きわものしゅっぱん：際物出版〉a fugitive publication.

kiyaku〈きやく：規約〉an agreement, a contract, a covenant, rules.

ki-yasume〈きやすめ：気休め〉

ki-yasume-ni〈気休めに〉to relieve one's conscience, to ease one's mind.

kiyo〈きよ：寄与〉*see.* kôken〈貢献〉.

kiyô〈きよう：器用〉

kiyô-na〈器用な〉skillful ((in)), dexterous ((at *or* in)).

kiyô-ni〈器用に〉skillfully, dexterously.

kiyô〈きよう：紀要〉a memoir, a bulletin.

kiyô〈きよう：起用〉appointment, employment.

kiyô-suru〈起用する〉appoint, employ the service ((of)).

kiyoi or **kiyoraka-na**〈きよい、きよらかな：清い、清らかな〉clear, clean, pure, innocent.

kiyoi kokoro（清い心） a pure heart

kiyomeru〈きよめる：清める〉purify, cleanse, make clean.

kiza〈きざ〉

kiza-na〈きざな〉affected, foppish, flashy, snobbish, snooty.

kizami(-me)〈きざみ（め）：刻み（目）〉a notch, a nick.

kizami(-me)-o-tsukeru〈刻み（目）を付ける〉notch, nick.

kizamu〈きざむ：刻む〉cut, chop (up), mince; carve; tick.

niku o kizamu（肉を刻む） chop meat

toki o kizamu（時を刻む） tick away the time

kizen〈きぜん：毅然〉

kizen-to-shita〈毅然とした〉resolute, firm, dauntless.

kizen-to-shita taido（毅然とした態度） a resolute attitude

kizen-to-shite〈毅然として〉resolutely, firmly, dauntlessly.

kizetsu〈きぜつ：気絶〉fainting, a swoon.

kizetsu-suru〈気絶する〉faint, swoon, lose consciousness.

kizewashii〈きぜわしい：気ぜわしい〉restless, bustling.

kizô 〈きぞう：寄贈〉 presentation, donation.

    kizô-hin 〈寄贈品〉 a gift, a present

  kizô-suru 〈寄贈する〉 present, donate.

kizoku 〈きぞく：貴族〉 a noble, a nobleman, a peer, a peeress.

  kizoku-teki(-na) 〈貴族的(な)〉 aristocratic.

kizoku 〈きぞく：帰属〉 reversion.

  kizoku-suru 〈帰属する〉 revert ((to)), belong ((to)).

kizu 〈きず：傷〉 an injury, a wound, a hurt, a cut, a bruise, a scratch.

    karui kizu 〈軽い傷〉 a slight wound

    omoi kizu 〈重い傷〉 a serious wound

    kizu-guchi o nuu 〈傷口を縫う〉 stitch a wound

    kizu-ato 〈傷跡〉 a scar

  kizu-o-ou 〈傷を負う〉 get injured, get wounded.

  kizu-tsukeru 〈傷付ける〉 injure, wound, hurt.

  kizu-tsuku 〈傷付く〉 get hurt, be injured.

kizu 〈きず〉 a crack, a flaw, a bruise, imperfectness; a fault, a defect, a blemish, a stain, a weakness.

  kizu-tsukeru 〈きず付ける〉 spoil, hurt, blemish.

    puraido o kizu-tsukeru 〈プライドをきず付ける〉 hurt ((a person's)) pride

  kizu-no-aru 〈きずのある〉 cracked, flawed, bruised.

    kizu-no-nai 〈きずのない〉 flawless, perfect

  kizu-no-tsuita 〈きずの付いた〉 blemished, stained.

ki-zukai 〈きづかい：気遣い〉 anxiety, uneasiness, fear, worry, concern.

  ki-zukau 〈気遣う〉 feel anxious ((about *or* for)), fear, worry ((about)), be concerned ((about *or* for)).

  ki-zukatte 〈気遣って〉 for fear ((of)).

  kizukawashi-ge-ni 〈気遣わしげに〉 anxiously, with anxious looks.

ki-zukare 〈きづかれ：気疲れ〉 worry, mental fatigue.

  ki-zukare-suru 〈気疲れする〉 be mentally fatigued.

-ki-zuke 〈-きづけ：-気付〉 care of... , c/o... .

kizuku 〈きづく：築く〉 build, construct.

    teibô o kizuku 〈堤防を築く〉 construct an embankment

ki-zuku 〈きづく：気付く〉 *see.* ki-ga-tsuku.

kizu-mono 〈きずもの：きず物〉 a flawed article; a ruined girl.

  kizu-mono-ni-suru 〈きず物にする〉 damage, crack; ruin, deflower.

kizuna 〈きずな〉 bonds, ties, fetters.

    inshû no kizuna 〈因習のきずな〉 the fetters of convention

ki-zuyoi 〈きづよい：気強い〉 *see.* kokoro-zuyoi.

ko 〈こ：子〉 a child, a boy, a son, a girl, a daughter; the young.

ko 〈こ：弧〉 an arc.
　　ko o egaku〈弧を描く〉 describe an arc

ko 〈こ：個〉 a piece.
　　mikan-san-ko〈みかん三個〉 three oranges
　　sekken-go-ko〈石けん五個〉 five pieces of soap

ko- 〈こ-：故-〉 the late... .

kô 〈こう：功〉 merits, services, credit, honor.
　　toshi no kô〈年の功〉 the merit of age
　　kô-ni-yori〈功により〉 for one's services
　　kô-nari-na-togeru〈功成り名遂げる〉 win fame and name

kô 〈こう：効〉 efficacy, an effect.
　kô-o-sôsuru〈効を奏する〉 take effect, be effective, bear fruit, succeed, work (well).

kô 〈こう：項〉 a clause, a paragraph, an item; a term.

kô 〈こう：甲〉 a (tortoise) shell; the back, the instep; A.

kô 〈こう：香〉 (an) incense.
　　kô o taku〈香をたく〉 burn incense

kô 〈こう：幸〉
　kô-ka-fukô-ka〈幸か不幸か〉 lnckily or unluckily.

kô 〈こう：港〉 a port, a harbor.
　　Tôkyô-kô〈東京港〉 Tokyo Harbor

kô 〈こう〉 so, like this, thus, (in) this way.
　　kô-itte〈こう言って〉 so saying
　　Kô-shi-nasai.〈こうしなさい。〉 Do it (in) this way.

kôan 〈こうあん：公安〉 public peace.
　　kôan-jôrei〈公安条例〉 a public security regulation

kôan 〈こうあん：考案〉 a plan, design, a device.
　　kôan-sha〈考案者〉 a deviser, an originator
　kôan-suru〈考案する〉 plan, design, devise.

kôatsu 〈こうあつ：高圧〉 high pressure; high-handedness.
　　kôatsu-sen〈高圧線〉 a high-voltage cable
　kôatsu-teki(-na)〈高圧的(な)〉 high-handed.
　　kôatsu-teki-na taido〈高圧的な態度〉 a high-handed manner
　kôatsu-teki-ni〈高圧的に〉 high-handedly.

kôba 〈こうば：工場〉 *see.* kôjô.

kobai 〈こばい：故買〉 receiving, fencing.

kobai-suru 〈故買する〉 fence, receive stolen goods.

kôbai 〈こうばい：購買〉 purchase.

    kôbai-ryoku (購買力) purchasing power

    kôbai-suru 〈購買する〉 purchase, make a purchase.

kôbai 〈こうばい：こう配〉 a slope, an incline, a grade, a gradient.

    kyû-na kôbai (急なこう配) a steep slope

    yurui kôbai (緩いこう配) a gentle slope

    nobori-kôbai (上りこう配) an up grade

    kudari-kôbai (下りこう配) a down grade

kôbai 〈こうばい：紅梅〉 a Japanese plum trees with red blossoms.

kô-baisû 〈こうばいすう：公倍数〉 a common multiple.

    saishô-kô-baisû (最小公倍数) the least common multiple

kobamu 〈こばむ：拒む〉 refuse, reject, decline; resist, oppose.

koban 〈こばん：小判〉 a *koban*, an old and oval Japanese gold coin.

   koban-gata-no 〈小判形の〉 oval, oval-shaped.

kôban 〈こうばん：交番〉 *see.* hashutsu-jo.

ko-banashi 〈こばなし：小話〉 a storiette, a short comic story, a joke.

kobaruto 〈コバルト〉 cobalt.

    kobaruto-ryôhô (コバルト療法) a cobalt treatment

kôbashii 〈こうばしい：香ばしい〉 aromatic, fragrant.

ko-bashiri 〈こばしり：小走り〉

   ko-bashiri-ni-hashiru 〈小走りに走る〉 go at a trot.

kôben 〈こうべん：抗弁〉 a plea, a protest, (a) refutation.

   kôben-suru 〈抗弁する〉 make a plea, plead, protest, refute.

kobetsu 〈こべつ：個別〉

   kobetsu(-teki)-ni 〈個別(的)に〉 individually, separately.

kobetsu 〈戸別〉

    kobetsu-hômon (戸別訪問) a house-to-house visit

   kobetsu-ni 〈戸別に〉 from house to house.

kobi 〈こび〉 flattery, coquetry.

   kobi-o-uru 〈こびを売る〉 flatter for money, sell one's favors, coquet.

kôbi 〈こうび：後尾〉 the rear.

   kôbi-no 〈後尾の〉 rear, back.

kôbi 〈こうび：交尾〉 copulation.

    kôbi-ki (交尾期) the pairing season

   kôbi-suru 〈交尾する〉 copulate.

kôbin 〈こうびん：後便〉

   kôbin-de 〈後便で〉 by next mail, in one's next letter.

kobiri-tsuku〈こびりつく：こびり付く〉stick ((to)), adhere ((to)).

kobiru〈こびる〉see.　kobi-o-uru.

kôbo〈こうぼ：酵母〉yeast.
　　　kôbo-kin（酵母菌）　yeast fungus

kôbo〈こうぼ：公募〉
　kôbo-suru〈公募する〉collect publicly, offer for public subscription, raise by public subscription.

kôbô〈こうぼう：興亡〉rise and fall, existence, destinies.

ko-bone〈こぼね：小骨〉small bones.

ko-bonnô〈こぼんのう：子煩悩〉a fond father, a fond mother.

koboreru〈こぼれる〉fall, drop, spill, be spilt, overflow.

kobosu〈こぼす〉spill, drop, shed;　complain ((about *or* of)),　grumble ((about, at *or* over)).
　　　miruku o kobosu（ミルクをこぼす）　spill milk
　　　namida o kobosu（涙をこぼす）　shed tears
　　　bukka-no-takai-no-o-kobosu（物価の高いのをこぼす）　complain of high prices

kobu〈こぶ〉a wen, a swelling, a lump; a hump; a knot.

kobu〈こぶ：昆布〉*see.* kombu.

kobu〈こぶ：鼓舞〉
　kobu-suru〈鼓舞する〉encourage, stimulate, stir up.
　　　shiki o kobu-suru（士気を鼓舞する）　stir up the morale

kôbu〈こうぶ：後部〉the back part, the hind part, the rear; the stern.
　　　kôbu-zaseki〈後部座席〉　a back seat
　kôbu-no〈後部の〉back, hind, rear.
　kôbu-ni〈後部に〉at the rear.

ko-bun〈こぶん：子分〉a follower, a henchman; a following.

kobun〈こぶん：古文〉ancient writings, classics.

kôbun〈こうぶん：構文〉sentence structure.

kô-bunsho〈こうぶんしょ：公文書〉an official document.

ko-buri〈こぶり：小降り〉
　　　Ame ga ko-buri-ni-natta.（雨が小降りになった.）　The rain is lessening.

kobushi〈こぶし〉a fist.
　　　kobushi o nigiru（こぶしを握る）　make a fist

ko-butori〈こぶとり：小太り〉
　ko-butori-no〈小太りの〉fattish.

kobutsu〈こぶつ：古物〉an antique.

　　　kobutsu-shô〈古物商〉a curio dealer, an antique shop
kôbutsu〈こうぶつ：鉱物〉a mineral, the mineral.
　kôbutsu(-shitsu)-no〈鉱物(質)の〉mineral.
kôbutsu〈こうぶつ：好物〉one's favorite dish.
kôcha〈こうちゃ：紅茶〉black tea.
kôchaku-jôtai〈こうちゃくじょうたい：こう着状態〉
　kôchaku-jôtai-ni aru〈こう着状態にある〉be at a stalemate.
kôchi〈コーチ〉coaching; a coacher.
　kôchi-suru〈コーチする〉coach.
kôchi〈こうち：高地〉highland.
kôchi〈こうち：耕地〉arable soil, a cultivated area.
kochikochi〈こちこち〉
　kochikochi-no〈こちこちの〉hard-boiled, hard-shell.
　　　kochikochi-no　hoshu-shugi-sha〈こちこちの保守主義者〉a confirmed
　　　　conservative
kôchin〈こうちん：工賃〉a wage, wages, pay.
kochira〈こちら〉this way, this place, here; this.
　　　Kochira-e dôzo.（こちらへどうぞ.）Please come this way.
　　　Kochira　Yoshida-san-desu.（こちら吉田さんです.）This　is　Mr.
　　　　Yoshida.
　　　Kochira Yoshida-desu.（こちら吉田です.）This is Yoshida speaking.
kôchi-sho〈こうちしょ：拘置所〉a detention house.
kochô〈こちょう：誇張〉(an) exaggeration.
　kochô-suru〈誇張する〉exaggerate.
　kochô-shite〈誇張して〉exaggeratingly.
kôchô〈こうちょう：校長〉a principal, a schoolmaster, a schoolmistress.
kôchô〈こうちょう：好調〉
　kôchô-de-aru〈好調である〉be in good condition.
　kôchô-ni〈好調に〉favorably, smoothly, satisfactorily.
　　　kôchô-ni hakobu（好調に運ぶ）go off smoothly
kôchô〈こうちょう：高潮〉the high tide; the climax.
　　　(sai-)kôchô ni tassuru（(最)高潮に達する）reach the climax
kôchô〈こうちょう：紅潮〉
　kôchô-suru〈紅潮する〉flush, blush.
kôchô-kai〈こうちょうかい：公聴会〉a public hearing.
　　　kôchô-kai o hiraku（公聴会を開く）hold a public hearing ((on))
kôchoku〈こうちょく：硬直〉stiffness, rigidity.
　　　shigo-kôchoku（死後硬直）rigor mortis

kôchoku-suru 〈硬直する〉 stiffen, become rigid.

kodachi 〈こだち：木立〉 a grove, a cluster of trees.

kodai 〈こだい：古代〉 ancient times.
    kodai-shi 〈古代史〉 ancient history
    kodai-no 〈古代の〉 ancient.

kodai 〈こだい：誇大〉
    kodai-kôkoku 〈誇大広告〉 a sensational advertisement
    kodai-môsô-kyô 〈誇大妄想狂〉 megalomania; a megalomaniac

kôdai 〈広大〉
    kôdai-na 〈広大な〉 vast.

ko-dakai 〈こだかい：小高い〉 slightly elevated.
    ko-dakai-oka 〈小高い丘〉 a low hill, a hillock

kodama 〈こだま：木霊〉 an echo.
    kodama-suru 〈木霊する〉 echo.

kôdan 〈こうだん：講談〉 storytelling, a story.
    kôdan-shi 〈講談師〉 a storyteller

kôdan 〈こうだん：公団〉 a public corporation.
    kôdan-jûtaku 〈公団住宅〉 public housing, a housing corporation apartment

kô-danshi 〈こうだんし：好男子〉 a handsome man, a fine-looking man, a nice fellow.

ko-dashi 〈こだし：小出し〉
    ko-dashi-ni-suru 〈小出しにする〉 take out in small quantities.

kodawaru 〈こだわる〉 obstruct; stick ((to)), be particular ((about)).
    myô-ni-kodawaru 〈妙にこだわる〉 be prejudiced ((against))
    kodawara-nai 〈こだわらない〉 make no bones ((about or of))

kôdei 〈こうでい：拘泥〉
    kôdei-suru 〈拘泥する〉 *see.* kodawaru.

kôden 〈こうでん：香典〉 an obituary present.

kôden 〈こうでん：公電〉 an official telegram.

kodô 〈こどう：鼓動〉 beating, throbbing.
    kodô-suru 〈鼓動する〉 beat, throb.

kôdo 〈こうど：硬度〉 solidity, hardness.

kôdo 〈こうど：光度〉 luminosity.

kôdo 〈こうど：高度〉 (an) altitude, (a) height; a high degree.
    kôdo-kei 〈高度計〉 an altimeter
    kôdo-no 〈高度の〉 strong, powerful, high-degree, high-grade, advanced.

kôdô 〈こうどう：講堂〉 a lecture hall, an auditorium, an assembly hall.

kôdô〈こうどう：行動〉action, conduct, behavior.

  jiyû-kôdô（自由行動）free action

  tandoku-kôdô（単独行動）separate action

  tôitsu-kôdô（統一行動）united action

 kôdô-suru〈行動する〉act, conduct oneself, behave (oneself).

kôdô〈こうどう：公道〉a public way.

kôdô〈こうどう：坑道〉a level, a gallery, a shaft, a pit.

ko-dôgu〈こどうぐ：小道具〉(stage) properties.

kodoku〈こどく：孤独〉solitude, loneliness.

 kodoku-na〈孤独な〉solitary, lonely.

  kodoku-na seikatsu（孤独な生活）a lonely life

kôdoku〈こうどく：購読〉subscription.

  kôdoku-ryô（購読料）a subscription

  kôdoku-sha（購読者）a subscriber, a reader.

 kôdoku-suru（購読する）subscribe ((for *or* to)), take, take in.

kôdoku〈こうどく：講読〉reading, translation.

 kôdoku-suru〈講読する〉read.

kodomo〈こども：子供〉a child.

 kodomo-no〈こどもの〉child's, juvenile.

  kodomo-no-toki ni（子供の時に）when one was a child, as a child

  kodomo-no tsukai（子供の使い）a fool's errand

 kodomoppoi（子供っぽい）childish.

 kodomo-rashii〈子供らしい〉childlike.

koe〈こえ：声〉a voice.

  koe-ga-ii（声がいい）have a sweet voice

  koe-o-dashite yomu（声を出して読む）read aloud

  koe-o-karashite（声をからして）in a hoarse voice

  koe-o-soroete（声をそろえて）with one voice, in chorus

  chiisana koe-de（小さな声で）in a low voice

  ookina koe-de（大きな声で）in a loud voice

ko-eda〈こえだ：小枝〉a twig.

koe-gawari〈こえがわり：声変わり〉

 koe-gawari-suru〈声変わりする〉a boy's voice cracks

kôei〈こうえい：光栄〉honor, glory.

 kôei-aru〈光栄ある〉honorable, glorious.

kôei〈こうえい：後衛〉the back player; a back, a fullback.

kôei〈こうえい：公営〉

  kôei-jûtaku（公営住宅）public housing

　　kôei-no〈公営の〉public, municipal.

kôeki〈こうえき：公益〉the public good.

　　kôeki-hôjin（公益法人）a public-service corporation

　　kôeki-jigyô（公益事業）public utilities

kôen〈こうえん：公園〉a park.

　　kokuritsu-kôen（国立公園）a national park

　　kokutei-kôen（国定公園）a seminational park

kôen〈こうえん：後援〉support, backing, patronage.

　　kôen-sha（後援者）a supporter, a patron

　　〜kôen-kai（〜後援会）a society for the support of...

　　kôen-suru〈後援する〉support, back up.

　　〜*-no-kôen-no-moto-ni*〈〜の後援の下に〉with the support of... , under
　　　the auspices of... .

kôen〈こうえん：講演〉a lecture, an address.

　　kôen-kai（講演会）a lecture meeting

　　kôen-sha（講演者）a lecturer, a speaker

　　kôen-suru〈講演する〉lecture ((on)), give a lecture ((on)).

kôen〈こうえん：公演〉a public performance.

　　kôen-suru〈公演する〉perform publicly.

kôen〈こうえん：好演〉good acting, an excellent performance.

koeru〈こえる：肥える〉grow fat; grow fertile.

　　koeta〈肥えた〉fat; rich, fertile.

koeru〈こえる：越(超)える〉cross, go over, get across, get over; be over,
　　be more than, exceed.

　　hei o nori-koeru（塀を乗り越える）get over a fence

　　roku-jussai-o-koete-iru（六十歳を越えている）be more than sixty

　　jisoku hachi-jukkiro-o-koeru sokudo（時速80キロを超える速度）a
　　　speed exceeding 80 kilometers per hour

kôetsu〈こうえつ：校閲〉

　　kôetsu-suru〈校閲する〉look over, revise.

kofû〈こふう：古風〉

　　kofû-na〈古風な〉old-fashioned, antiquated.

kôfu〈こうふ：公布〉promulgation.

　　kôfu-suru〈公布する〉promulgate.

kôfu〈こうふ：交付〉delivery, grant.

　　kôfu-kin（交付金）a grant

　　kôfu-suru〈交付する〉deliver, grant, issue.

　　　ryoken-o-kôfu-suru（旅券を交付する）issue ((a person)) with a

passport

kôfû 〈こうふう：校風〉 the school spirit, the school tradition.

kôfuku 〈こうふく：幸福〉 happiness, welfare.

　kôfuku-na 〈幸福な〉 happy.

　kôfuku-ni 〈幸福に〉 happily.

　　kôfuku-ni-kurasu （幸福に暮らす） live happily, live a happy life

kôfuku 〈こうふく：降伏〉 (a) surrender.

　　mu-jôken-kôfuku （無条件降伏） an unconditional surrender

　kôfuku-suru 〈降伏する〉 surrender.

kofun 〈こふん：古墳〉 an ancient tomb, an old mound.

kôfun 〈こうふん：興奮〉 excitement.

　　kôfun-zai （興奮剤） a stimulant

　kôfun-suru 〈興奮する〉 be excited.

　kôfun-shi-yasui 〈興奮しやすい〉 excitable, (be) easily excited.

　kôfun-shite 〈興奮して〉 in excitement.

kogai 〈こがい：戸外〉 the open air.

　kogai-de 〈戸外で〉 in the open air, out of doors.

ko-gai 〈こが：子飼い〉

　ko-gai-no 〈子飼いの〉 brought up from young.

kôgai 〈こうがい：郊外〉 the suburbs, the outskirts.

　kôgai-no 〈郊外の〉 suburban.

　kôgai-ni 〈郊外に〉 in the suburbs (of)).

kôgai 〈こうがい：校外〉

　kôgai-no, kôgai-de or *kôgai-ni* 〈校外の，校外で，校外に〉 outside the
　school, out of school.

kôgai 〈こうがい：公害〉 a public nuisance, pollution.

　　sôon-kôgai （騒音公害） noise pollution

kôgai 〈こうがい：口外〉

　kôgai-suru 〈口外する〉 disclose, tell, betray, reveal, let out.

　　kôgai-shi-nai （口外しない） keep ((a matter)) to oneself

ko-gaisha 〈こがいしゃ：子会社〉 a subsidiary company.

kôgaku 〈こうがく：高額〉 a large sum (of money).

　　kôgaku-shotoku-sha （高額所得者） a large income earner

kôgaku 〈こうがく：工学〉 engineering.

　　denki-kôgaku （電気工学） electric engineering

kôgaku 〈こうがく：光学〉 optics.

　　kôgaku-kikai （光学器械） optical instruments

kôgaku 〈こうがく：後学〉

kôgaku-no-tame 〈後学のため〉 for one's information.

kôgaku-shin 〈こうがくしん：向学心〉 love of learning, a desire to learn.

ko-gane 〈こがね：小金〉 a small sum of money.

　　ko-gane-o-tameru（小金をためる） make a small fortune

kogane-mushi 〈こがねむし：黄金虫〉 a gold beetle.

ko-gara 〈こがら：小柄〉 small stature.

　　ko-gara-no（小柄の） of small stature

kogarashi 〈こがらし：木枯らし〉 a cold wintry wind.

kogasu 〈こがす：焦がす〉 burn, scorch, singe, char.

ko-gata 〈こがた：小型〉

　　ko-gata-jidô-sha（小型自動車） a compact, a minicar

ko-gata-no〈小型の〉 small-sized, small, midget, miniature.

ko-gatana 〈こがたな：小刀〉 a knife.

koge-cha(-iro) 〈こげちゃ(いろ)：焦げ茶(色)〉 dark brown (color).

kôgei 〈こうげい：工芸〉 industrial arts.

　　bijutsu-kôgei（美術工芸） arts and crafts

kôgei-no〈工芸の〉 industrial, manufacturing, technical.

kôgeki 〈こうげき：攻撃〉 an attack ((on)).

kôgeki-suru〈攻撃する〉 attack.

koge-kusai 〈こげくさい：焦げ臭い〉 smell something burning.

kôgen 〈こうげん：光源〉 a source of light.

kôgen 〈こうげん：高原〉 a plateau, a tableland.

kôgen 〈こうげん：公言〉

kôgen-suru〈公言する〉 declare (openly), profess.

kôgen 〈こうげん：高言〉 big talk, a brag, a boast.

kôgen-o-haku〈高言を吐く〉 talk big, brag (of), boast ((of *or* that)).

kogeru 〈こげる：焦げる〉 burn, be burned.

　　makkuro-ni-kogeru（真っ黒に焦げる） be charred.

kogetsuki 〈こげつき：焦げ付き〉 an irrecoverable loan, a bad debt.

koge-tsuku〈焦げ付く〉 become irrecoverable; scorch and stick ((to)).

kôgi 〈こうぎ：講義〉 a lecture.

　　kôgi ni deru（講義に出る） attend a lecture

kôgi-suru〈講義する〉 lecture ((on)), give a lecture ((on)).

kôgi 〈こうぎ：抗議〉 a protest, an objection.

　　kôgi o môshi-komu（抗議を申し込む） enter a protest with ((a person)) against

　　kôgi-shûkai（抗議集会） a protest meeting

kôgi-suru〈抗議する〉 protest ((against)), make a protest ((against)), object ((to)).

kōgi〈こうぎ：広義〉a broad sense.

  kōgi-ni（広義に）in a broad sense

ko-girei〈こぎれい：小ぎ麗〉

 ko-girei-ni-suru〈小ぎれいにする〉spruce up.

    mi o ko-girei-ni-suru（身をこぎれいにする）spruce oneself up, be neatly dressed

 ko-girei-na〈小ぎれいな〉neat, trim, tidy.

kogi-tsukeru〈こぎつける：こぎ着ける〉row up ((to)); manage ((to do)).

    yatto kaiten-ni-kogi-tsukeru（やっと開店にこぎ着ける）manage to open a store

ko-gitte〈こぎって：小切手〉a check, a cheque.

    ko-gitte-de harau（小切手で払う）pay by check

    ko-gitte o kiru（小切手を切る）issue a check

    ko-gitte o genkin-ni-kaeru（小切手を現金に換える）cash a check

    yoko-sen-ko-gitte（横線小切手）a crossed check

kōgo〈こうご：口語〉spoken language.

    kōgo-tai（口語体）a colloquial style

 kōgo-no〈口語の〉spoken, colloquial.

kōgo〈こうご：交互〉

 kōgo-no〈交互の〉mutual, alternate.

 kōgo-ni〈交互に〉mutually, alternately.

kōgō〈こうごう：皇后〉an empress.

    kōgō-heika（皇后陛下）Her Majesty the Empress

ko-goe〈こごえ：小声〉a low voice.

kogoeru〈こごえる：凍える〉be benumbed with cold, be frozen.

    kogoe-shinu（凍え死ぬ）be frozen to death

kōgōshii〈こうごうしい：神々しい〉divine, heavenly, holy, awe-inspiring, solemn.

ko-goto〈こごと：小言〉(a) scolding.

 ko-goto-o-iu〈小言を言う〉scold.

kogu〈こぐ〉row.

    bôto o kogu（ボートをこぐ）row a boat

kōgu〈こうぐ：工具〉a tool, an implement.

ko-guchi〈こぐち：小口〉a small lot, a small sum.

 ko-guchi-no〈小口の〉small, petty.

kōgun〈こうぐん：行軍〉a march, marching.

 kōgun-suru〈行軍する〉march.

kogun-funtô 〈こぐんふんとう：孤軍奮闘〉one's unaided effort.
　kogun-funtô-suru 〈孤軍奮闘する〉fight alone, fight unsupported.
kôgyô 〈こうぎょう：工業〉(an) industry.
　　kôgyô-chitai（工業地帯）an industrial area
　　kôgyô-koku（工業国）an industrial country
　　kôgyô-toshi（工業都市）an industrial city
　kôgyô-no or *kôgyô-yô-no* 〈工業の，工業用の〉industrial.
kôgyô 〈こうぎょう：鉱業〉mining, the mining industry.
kôgyô 〈こうぎょう：興行〉show business; (a) performance, a show, a run.
　　kôgyô-ken（興行権）the right of performance
　kôgyô-suru（興行する）give a performance, show, run.
ko-haba 〈こはば：小幅〉single breadth.
　　ko-haba-mono（小幅物）narrow cloth, narrow goods
kôhai 〈こうはい：後輩〉one's junior.
　　ichi-nen-kôhai（一年後輩）one's junior by a year
kôhai 〈こうはい：交配〉mating, crossbreeding, cross-fertilization.
　kôhai-suru 〈交配する〉mate, cross.
kôhai 〈こうはい：荒廃〉desolation, devastation, dilapidation.
　kôhai-suru 〈荒廃する〉be desolated, be devastated, dilapidate.
　kôhai-shita 〈荒廃した〉desolate, devastated, dilapidated.
kohaku 〈こはく〉amber.
　kohaku-iro(-no) 〈こはく色(の)〉amber.
kôhaku 〈こうはく：紅白〉red and white.
　　kôhaku-jiai（紅白試合）a contest between two groups
kohan 〈こはん：湖畔〉a lakeside.
　　kohan-no yado（湖畔の宿）a lakeside hotel
kôhan 〈こうはん：公判〉a public trial.
　　kôhan-ni fusu（公判に付す）bring ((a case)) to trial
kôhan 〈こうはん：後半〉the latter half.
kôhan 〈こうはん：広範〉
　kôhan-na 〈広範な〉extensive, widespread, wide-ranging, far-reaching.
kô-han·i 〈こうはんい：広範囲〉a wide range.
　　kô-han·i ni wataru（広範囲に渡る）cover a wide range
koharu-biyori 〈こはるびより：小春日和〉Indian summer.
kohaze 〈こはぜ〉a clasp.
kôhei 〈こうへい：公平〉impartiality, fairness, justice.
　kôhei-na 〈公平な〉impartial, fair, just.

kôhei-mushi-na〈公平無私な〉 fair and disinterested

kôhei-ni〈公平に〉 impartially, fairly, justly.

　hito o kôhei-ni tori-atsukau〈人を公平に取り扱う〉 treat a person fairly

kôhei〈こうへい：工兵〉 an engineer, a sapper.

kôhen〈こうへん：後編〉 the latter part ((of)), a sequel ((to)), the second volume.

kôhi〈こうひ：工費〉 the cost of construction.

　sô-kôhi〈総工費〉 the total cost〔of construction〕

kôhi〈こうひ：公費〉 public expenditure.

　kôhi-de〈公費で〉 at public expense

kôhî〈コーヒー〉 coffee.

　kôhî o ireru〈コーヒーを入れる〉 make coffee

kô-hisutamin-zai〈こうヒスタミンざい：抗ヒスタミン剤〉 an antihistamine.

ko-hitsuji〈こひつじ：子羊〉 a lamb.

kôho〈こうほ：候補〉 candidacy, candidature.

　kôho-chi〈候補地〉 one of the most suitable places ((for))

　kôho-sha〈候補者〉 a candidate, an applicant

kôho-ni-tatsu〈候補に立つ〉 be a candidate ((for)).

　kôho o jitai-suru〈候補を辞退する〉 withdraw a person's candidacy

kôhô〈こうほう：公報〉 an official report, an official bulletin, an official gazette.

kôhô-ni-noru〈公報に載る〉 be gazetted.

kôhô〈こうほう：広報〉 public relations.

kôhô〈こうほう：公法〉 public law.

kôhô〈こうほう：後方〉 *see*. ushiro.

kôhyô〈こうひょう：公表〉 (an) official announcement, publication.

kôhyô-suru〈公表する〉 announce (publicly), publish.

kôhyô〈こうひょう：好評〉 favorable criticism.

　kôhyô o hakusuru〈好評を博する〉 win popularity

　gakusei-tachi-ni kôhyô-de-aru〈学生たちに好評である〉 be popular with students, be well received by students

koi〈こい：恋〉 love.

　koi-bito〈恋人〉 a lover; a love, a sweetheart

　koi-gataki〈恋敵〉 a rival in love

koi-suru〈恋する〉 love, fall in love ((with)).

koi〈こい〉 a carp.

koi 〈こい：故意〉

koi-no 〈故意の〉 intentional, deliberate.

koi-ni 〈故意に〉 intentionally, deliberately, on purpose, knowingly.

koi 〈こい：濃い〉 dark, deep, thick, strong, heavy.

    koi cha(-iro) 〈濃い茶(色)〉 a dark brown

    koi sûpu 〈濃いスープ〉 thick soup

    koi (o)-cha 〈濃い(お)茶〉 strong tea

koku 〈濃く〉 deep, thick, strong.

    o-shiroi o koku nuru 〈おしろいを濃く塗る〉 powder(*or* paint) ((one's face)) thick

kôi 〈こうい：好意〉 goodwill, kindness.

kôi-o-motsu 〈好意を持つ〉 be favorably disposed ((toward)).

kôi-aru 〈好意ある〉 kind, well-meaning.

kôi-teki(-na) 〈好意的(な)〉 friendly, amicable.

kôi-teki-ni or *kôi-kara* 〈好意的に，好意から〉 out of goodwill, through kindness, with good intentions.

kôi 〈こうい：行為〉 an act, an action, a deed, behavior, conduct.

    seitô-na kôi 〈正当な行為〉 a justifiable act

kôi 〈こうい：校医〉 a school doctor.

kôi 〈こうい：高位〉 a high rank.

    kôi-kôkan-no hito 〈高位高官の人〉 a person of (high) rank and office

ko-iki 〈こいき：小いき〉

ko-iki-na 〈小いきな〉 stylish, smart, chic.

kôin 〈こういん：工員〉 a (factory) worker.

kôin 〈こういん：行員〉 a bank clerk.

kôin 〈こういん：拘引〉 (an) arrest, custody.

    kôin-jô 〈拘引状〉 a warrant of arrest

kôin-suru 〈拘引する〉 arrest, take ((a person)) into custody.

ko-inu 〈こいぬ：小(子)犬〉 a little dog, a puppy.

ko-ishi 〈こいし：小石〉 a pebble.

koishii 〈こいしい：恋しい〉 dear, beloved, affectionate.

koishi-garu 〈恋しがる〉 long ((for)), be sick ((for)), yearn ((after)), miss.

kô-shitsu 〈こういしつ：更衣室〉 a dressing room, a locker room.

kôi-shô 〈こういしょう：後遺症〉 an aftereffect, a sequela.

koitsu 〈こいつ〉 this man, this fellow, this guy.

    Koitsu-me! 〈こいつめ。〉 You scoundrel! / Damn you!

kô-ittsui 〈こういっつい：好一対〉 a good pair.

kô-ittsui-de-aru 〈好一対である〉 be a good match ((for)).

kô-iu 〈こういう〉 *see.* konna.

koji 〈こじ：孤児〉 an orphan.
koji-ni-naru (孤児になる) be left an orphan

koji 〈こじ：故事〉 a historical allusion.
koji-raireki (故事来歴) the origin and history

koji 〈こじ：固持〉
koji-suru 〈固持する〉 persist ((in)).

koji 〈こじ：固辞〉
koji-suru 〈固辞する〉 decline positively.

koji 〈こじ：誇示〉 display, show.
koji-suru 〈誇示する〉 display, flaunt.

kôji 〈こうじ：工事〉 construction.
kôji-chû (工事中) Under Construction

kôji 〈こうじ：公示〉 a public notice.
kôji-suru 〈公示する〉 make known to the public.

kôji 〈こうじ〉 malted rice, malt.

koji-akeru 〈こじあける：こじ開ける〉 prize open, pry open, break open.

ko-jika 〈こじか：子じか〉 a fawn.

kojiki 〈こじき：こ食〉 a beggar.

ko-jima 〈こじま：小島〉 a small island, an islet.

kô-jimbutsu 〈こうじんぶつ：好人物〉 a good-natured person, a good fellow.

ko-jimmari 〈こじんまり〉
ko-jimmari-shita 〈こじんまりした〉 snug, cozy.
ko-jimmari-shita ima (こじんまりした居間) a snug little living room

kojin 〈こじん：個人〉 an individual.
kojin-shugi (個人主義) individualism
kojin-no or *kojin-teki(-na)* 〈個人の，個人的(な)〉 individual, personal, private.
kojin-teki-ni 〈個人的に〉 individually, personally, privately.

kojin 〈こじん：故人〉 the deceased.

kojirasu 〈こじらす〉 make...worse, aggravate, complicate.
mondai o kojirasu (問題をこじらす) complicate the matter
kojireru 〈こじれる〉 get entangled, become complicated.
Kanojo wa kaze-ga-kojirete haien-ni-natta. (彼女は風邪がこじれて肺炎になった。) Her cold grew into pneumonia.

kôjiru 〈こうじる：講じる〉 take, devise, adopt.
tekitô-na shudan o kôjiru (適当な手段を講じる) take a proper step

kôjitsu〈こうじつ：口実〉an excuse, a pretext.
　　kôjitsu o tsukuru（口実を作る）　make an excuse
　　〜-o-kôjitsu-to-shite（〜を口実として）　on the pretext of...
kojitsuke〈こじつけ〉distortion, a forced meaning.
　　kojitsukeru〈こじつける〉strain, force the meaning.
　　kojitsuke-no〈こじつけの〉strained, forced, farfetched.
ko-jiwa〈こじわ：小じわ〉fine wrinkles, crow's-feet.
kôjo〈こうじょ：控除〉subtraction, deduction.
　　kôjo-gaku（控除額）　a deduction, an amount deducted
　　kiso-kôjo（基礎控除）　the basic deduction
　　kôjo-suru〈控除する〉subtract, deduct ((from)).
kôjô〈こうじょう：工場〉a factory, a plant, a work(s), a mill.
　　kôjô-chitai（工場地帯）　a factory district
　　kôjô-chô（工場長）　a factory manager
　　suto-ni-yoru-kôjô-heisa（ストによる工場閉鎖）　a lockout
kôjô〈こうじょう：口上〉a prologue, an epilogue.
　　kôjô o noberu（口上を述べる）　deliver a prologue(or an epilogue)
kôjô〈こうじょう：向上〉rise, improvement, progress.
　　kôjô-shin（向上心）　aspiration
　　kôjô-suru〈向上する〉rise, improve, progress.
　　kôjô-saseru〈向上させる〉raise, improve, make better.
kôjô-sen〈こうじょうせん：甲状せん〉the thyroid gland.
ko-jûto〈こじゅうと：小じゅうと〉one's husband's brother.
ko-jûtome〈こじゅうとめ：小じゅうとめ〉one's husband's sister.
kôjutsu〈こうじゅつ：後述〉
　　kôjutsu-suru〈後述する〉mention later.
kôka〈こうか：効果〉(an) effect.
　　geki-teki kôka（劇的効果）　a dramatic effect
　　onkyô-kôka-gakari（音響効果係り）　a sound-effects man
　　kôka-ga-aru〈効果がある〉take effect, have an effect ((on)), be effective.
　　kôka-no-aru or　*kôka-teki(-na)*〈効果のある，効果的(な)〉effective, effectual.
　　kôka-no-nai（効果のない）　ineffectual
kôka〈こうか：工科〉the department of engineering.
　　kôka-daigaku（工科大学）　an engineering college
kôka〈こうか：校歌〉a school song, a college song.
kôka〈こうか：高価〉
　　kôka-na〈高価な〉expensive, costly, dear.

kôka 〈こうか：硬貨〉 hard money, a coin; coinage.

kôka 〈こうか：硬化〉 stiffening, hardening.
  kôka-suru or *kôka-saseru* 〈硬化する，硬化させる〉 stiffen, harden.
    taido o kôka-saseru 〈態度を硬化させる〉 stiffen one's attitude

kôka 〈こうか：高架〉
  kôka-sen 〈高架線〉 an elevated railroad, an overhead railway
  kôka-no 〈高架の〉 elevated, overhead.

kôka 〈こうか：降下〉 (a) descent, a fall, dropping, (a) landing.
  kôka-suru 〈降下する〉 descend, fall, drop, land.

kô-kagaku 〈こうかがく：光化学〉 photochemistry.
  kô-kagaku-sumoggu 〈光化学スモッグ〉 photochemical smog

ko-kage 〈こかげ：木陰〉 the shade of a tree.

kôkai 〈こうかい：航海〉 a voyage, navigation.
  hatsu-kôkai 〈初航海〉 a maiden voyage
  kôkai-nisshi 〈航海日誌〉 a (ship's) log, a logbook
  kôkai-suru 〈航海する〉 sail, make a voyage ((to)).

kôkai 〈こうかい：公海〉 the open sea, the high seas, international waters.

kôkai 〈こうかい：後悔〉 (a) regret, (a) repentance.
  kôkai-suru 〈後悔する〉 regret, repent (of), be sorry ((for)).

kôkai 〈こうかい：更改〉 *see.* kôshin.

kôkai 〈こうかい：公開〉
  kôkai-suru 〈公開する〉 open to the public.
  kôkai-shi-nai 〈公開しない〉 be closed to the public
  kôkai-no 〈公開の〉 open, public.
  kôkai-no-seki-de 〈公開の席で〉 in public

kôkai-dô 〈こうかいどう：公会堂〉 a public hall, a town hall.

kokain 〈コカイン〉 cocain(e).

kôkaku 〈こうかく：広角〉
  kôkaku-renzu 〈広角レンズ〉 a wide-angle lens

kôkaku-rui 〈こうかくるい：甲殻類〉 Crustacea.

kôkan 〈こうかん：交換〉 (an) exchange.
  kôkan-jôken 〈交換条件〉 a bargaining point
  kôkan-shu 〈交換手〉 a telephone operator
  kôkan-dai 〈交換台〉 a switchboard
  kôkan-renzu 〈交換レンズ〉 an interchangeable lens
  kôkan-suru 〈交換する〉 exchange.
  〜*-to-kôkan-ni* 〈〜と交換に〉 in exchange for... .

kôkan〈こうかん：高官〉a high official, a high officer.

kôkan〈こうかん：好感〉(a) good feeling, (a) goodwill, a favorable impression.

    kôkan o ataeru〈好感を与える〉make a favorable impression ((on))

    kôkan o idaku〈好感を抱く〉have a friendly feeling ((toward))

kôkan〈こうかん：交歓〉an exchange of goodwill.

    kôkan-jiai〈交歓試合〉a friendly game

    kôkan-suru〈交歓する〉exchange courtesies ((with)), fraternize ((with)).

kôkan〈こうかん：公館〉

    zaigai-kôkan〈在外公館〉embassies and legations abroad

kôkan-shinkei〈こうかんしんけい：交感神経〉the sympathetic nerve.

kokatsu〈こかつ：枯渇〉drying up; exhaustion, drain.

    kokatsu-suru〈枯渇する〉be dried up; be exhausted, be drained.

kôkatsu〈こうかつ〉

    kôkatsu-na〈こうかつな〉cunning, sly, artful.

koke〈こけ〉moss.

    koke-mushita〈こけむした〉moss-grown, mossy.

kokei〈こけい：固形〉

    kokei-nenryô〈固形燃料〉solid fuel

    kokei-sûpu〈固形スープ〉a soup square

    kokei-no〈固形の〉solid.

kôkei〈こうけい：光景〉a spectacle, a scene, a sight.

kôkei〈こうけい：口径〉a caliber.

kôkei〈こうけい：後継〉succession.

    kôkei-naikaku〈後継内閣〉the succeeding Cabinet

    kôkei-sha〈後継者〉a successor, an heir

kô-keiki〈こうけいき：好景気〉prosperity, good times, a boom.

    kô-keiki-no〈好景気の〉prosperous, lively, booming.

kô-kekka〈こうけっか：好結果〉a satisfactory result.

    kô-kekka o umu〈好結果を生む〉bring about good results

kokekokkô〈こけこっこう〉

    kokekokkô-to-naku〈こけこっこうと鳴く〉cry cock-a-doodle-doo.

kôken〈こうけん：後見〉guardianship; a prompter.

    kôken-nin〈後見人〉a guardian

        kôken-nin-to-naru〈後見人となる〉act as a guardian

kôken〈こうけん：貢献〉a contribution.

    kôken-suru〈貢献する〉contribute ((to)), make a contribution ((to)).

kokera-otoshi〈こけらおとし：こけら落とし〉the opening of a new

theater.

kokeru〈こける〉be sunken, be hollow.
  hoo-no-koketa〈ほおのこけた〉with hollow cheeks.

kôketsu〈こうけつ：高潔〉
  kôketsu-na〈高潔な〉noble, noble-minded, high-minded.
    kôketsu-na hito〈高潔な人〉a person of noble character

koki〈こき：古希〉
  koki-no-iwai〈古希の祝い〉the celebration of one's 70th birthday

kôki〈こうき：高貴〉
  kôki-na〈高貴な〉high, noble.

kôki〈こうき：綱紀〉official discipline.
  kôki-binran〈綱紀びん乱〉the slack discipline of the office
  kôki-shukusei〈綱紀粛正〉enforcement of official discipline

kôki〈こうき：好機〉a good chance, a good opportunity.
  kôki o toraeru〈好機を捕らえる〉seize an opportunity
  kôki o issuru〈好機を逸する〉miss a (good) chance

kôki〈こうき：校旗〉a school banner.

kôki〈こうき：後期〉the latter period, the latter half year.

kôki〈こうき：後記〉a postscript.

kôki〈こうき：広軌〉a broad gauge.
  kôki-tetsudô〈広軌鉄道〉a broad-gauge railroad

kô-kiatsu〈こうきあつ：高気圧〉*see.* kiatsu.

ko-kimi〈こきみ：小気味〉
  ko-kimi-yoi〈小気味よい〉smart, delightful, pleasant.
  ko-kimi-yoku〈小気味よく〉smartly, delightfully, pleasantly.
    ko-kimi-yoku-omou〈小気味よく思う〉find ((it)) gratifying, gloat ((over))

kôkin〈こうきん：公金〉public funds.
  kôkin o ôryô-suru〈公金を横領する〉embezzle public funds

kôkin〈こうきん：拘禁〉confinement, detention.
  kôkin-suru〈拘禁する〉confine, detain.
  kôkin-sareru〈拘禁される〉be confined, be detained.

koki-orosu〈こきおろす：こき下ろす〉denounce, disparage, run down, write down.

kôki-shin〈こうきしん：好奇心〉curiosity.
  kôki-shin-no-tsuyoi〈好奇心の強い〉curious, full of curiosity.
  kôki-shin-kara〈好奇心から〉out of curiosity.

koki-tsukau〈こきつかう：こき使う〉work ((a person)) hard, sweat.

ko-kizami 〈こきざみ：小刻み〉
  ko-kizami-ni〈小刻みに〉little by little, piecemeal.
    ko-kizami-ni aruku（小刻みに歩く）walk with short steps
kokka 〈こっか：国家〉a nation, a state, a country.
    kokka-shugi（国家主義）nationalism
  kokka-no or *kokka-teki(-na)*〈国家の，国家的(な)〉national.
kokka 〈こっか：国歌〉the national anthem.
kokka 〈こっか：国花〉a national flower.
kokkai 〈こっかい：国会〉the Diet, Congress, Parliament.
    kokkai-giin（国会議員）a member of the Diet
    kokkai-giji-dô（国会議事堂）the Diet Building
    kokkai-tosho-kan（国会図書館）the Diet Library
kokkaku 〈こっかく：骨格〉a framework; build, physique.
kokkan 〈こっかん：酷寒〉severe cold.
kokkei 〈こっけい〉
  kokkei-na〈こっけいな〉humorous, comical, funny, ridiculous, facetious.
kokki 〈こっき：国旗〉the national flag.
kokki(-shin) 〈こっき(しん)：克己(心)〉self-control, self-restraint, stoicism.
kokko 〈こっこ：国庫〉the National Treasury.
    kokko-shishutsu-kin（国庫支出金）national treasury disbursements
kokkô 〈こっこう：国交〉diplomatic relations.
    kokkô o danzetsu-suru（国交を断絶する）break off diplomatic relations ((with))
    kokkô o seijô-ka-suru（国交を正常化する）normalize diplomatic relations
kokkoku(-to) 〈こっこく(と)：刻々(と)〉every moment, moment by moment, momentarily.
    kokkoku henka-suru（刻々変化する）change momentarily
kokku 〈コック〉a cook; a cock, a tap, a faucet.
kokkyô 〈こっきょう：国境〉the frontier, the border.
    kokkyô o koeru（国境を越える）cross the border
    kokkyô-sen（国境線）a border line
kokkyô 〈こっきょう：国教〉a state religion.
koko 〈ここ：個々〉
  koko-no〈個々の〉individual, respective.
  koko-ni〈個々に〉individually, one by one.
koko 〈ここ〉

koko, koko-de, koko-e or **koko-ni**〈ここ，ここで，ここへ，ここに〉here, (in *or* to) this place.

　　koko-kara（ここから）　from here
　　koko-kashiko（ここかしこ）　here and there
　　koko-made（ここまで）　up to here, thus far
　　koko-ra（ここら）　around here
　　koko-shibaraku（ここしばらく）　for the time being

kôko〈こうこ：公庫〉the municipal treasury.

　　kin·yû-kôko（金融公庫）　a finance corporation

kôkô〈こうこう：孝行〉filial piety.

　kôkô-suru〈孝行する〉be a good son(or a daughter).

kôkô〈こうこう：航行〉navigation, sailing.

　kôkô-chû〈航行中〉at sea, under way.

　　kôkô-chû-no-sempaku（航行中の船舶）　vessels now under way

　kôkô-suru〈航行する〉navigate, sail.

kôkô〈こうこう：高校〉an abbreviation of 'kôtô-gakkô'.

kôkô〈こうこう〉

　kôkô-taru〈こうこうたる〉brilliant, bright.

　kôkô-to〈こうこうと〉brilliantly, brightly.

　　akari-ga-kôkô-to　kagayaite-iru（明かりがこうこうと輝いている）　be brilliantly lighted with electricity

kôkô〈こうこう〉so and so, such and such.

　　kôkô-iu hito（こうこういう人）　such and such a person
　　kôkô-iu-wake-de（こうこういう訳で）　such being the case

kokochi〈ここち：心地〉

　　i-gokochi-ga-ii（居心地がいい）　be comfortable, feel at home
　　　i-gokochi-ga-warui（居心地が悪い）　be uncomfortable
　　ki-gokochi-ga-ii（着心地がいい）　be comfortable to wear
　　ne-gokochi-ga-ii（寝心地がいい）　be comfortable to sleep (in)
　　nori-gokochi-ga-ii（乗り心地がいい）　be comfortable to ride in
　　sumi-gokochi-ga-ii（住み心地がいい）　be comfortable to live in
　　suwari-gokochi-ga-ii（座り心地がいい）　be comfortable to sit in(or on)

kôko-gaku〈こうこがく：考古学〉archaeology.

kokoku〈ここく：故国〉one's native country.

kôkoku〈こうこく：広告〉an advertisement, an ad.

　　shimbun-kôkoku（新聞広告）　a newspaper advertisement

　kôkoku-suru〈広告する〉advertise.

kôkoku 〈こうこく：抗告〉 a complaint, an appeal ((from)).

kôkoku-suru 〈抗告する〉 complain ((against)), appeal ((from)).

kokoro 〈こころ：心〉 mind, heart, thought, will.

kokoro-ni tomeru (心に留める) bear in mind

kokoro-ga-ugoku 〈心が動く〉 be inclined ((to do)), be moved.

kokoro-o-nayamasu 〈心を悩ます〉 worry ((about)), be anxious ((about)).

kokoro-o-ire-kaeru 〈心を入れ替える〉 reform oneself.

kokoro-bakari-no 〈心ばかりの〉 trifling, slight, small.

kokoro-aru 〈心ある〉 thoughtful.

kokoro-nai （心ない） thoughtless, heartless, inhumane

kokoro-kara-no 〈心からの〉 hearty, sincere.

kokoro-kara 〈心から〉 from the bottom of one's heart.

kokoro-no-naka-de 〈心の中で〉 in one's heart.

kokoro-narazu-mo 〈心ならずも〉 against one's will.

kokoro-atari 〈こころあたり：心当り〉

kokoro-atari-no basho （心当たりの場所） a likely place

kokoro-atari-ga-aru 〈心当たりがある〉 know of, have in mind.

kokoro-atari-ga-nai （心当たりがない） have no idea ((of))

kokoro-bosoi 〈心ぼそい：心細い〉 helpless, lonely.

kokoro-bosoi-omoi-ga-suru （心細い思いがする） feel helpless, feel lonely

kokoro-gake 〈こころがけ：心掛け〉

kokoro-gakeru 〈心掛ける〉 aim ((at)), try, bear in mind.

kokoro-gake-no-ii 〈心掛けのいい〉 right-minded.

kokoro-gake-no-warui （心掛けの悪い） wrongheaded

kokoro-gamae 〈こころがまえ：心構え〉 the attitude of mind, preparation.

kokoro-gamae-o-suru 〈心構えをする〉 be prepared ((for)), get ready ((for)).

kokoro-gawari 〈こころがわり：心変わり〉 a change of mind.

kokoro-gawari-suru 〈心変わりする〉 change one's mind, be fickle.

kokoro-gurushii 〈こころぐるしい：心苦しい〉 painful, regrettable.

kokoro-gurushiku-omou 〈心苦しく思う〉 be sorry, feel bad ((about)), be painful, weigh on ((a person's)) mind.

kokoro-jôbu 〈こころじょうぶ：心丈夫〉

kokoro-jôbu-de-aru 〈心丈夫である〉 feel reassured.

kokoro-machi 〈こころまち：心待ち〉

kokoro-machi-ni-matsu 〈心待ちに待つ〉 eagerly look forward ((to)).

kokoromi 〈こころみ：試み〉a trial, an attempt.

kokoromi-ni 〈試みに〉for trial.

kokoromiru 〈試みる〉try, make an attempt ((at)).

kokoro-mochi 〈こころもち：心持ち〉somewhat, a little, a bit, slightly.

kokoro-mochi mijikaku-suru（心持ち短くする）make ((a thing)) a little shorter

kokoro-nikui 〈こころにくい：心憎い〉excellent, admirable, perfect, striking.

kokoro-nikui-bakari-no udemae（心憎いばかりの腕前）a unique skill

kokoro-nokori 〈こころのこり：心残り〉regret.

kokoro-nokori-ga-suru 〈心残りがする〉regret, feel reluctant [to leave].

kokoro-nokori-ga-nai（心残りがない）have nothing to regret

kokoro-yasui 〈こころやすい：心安い〉intimate, familiar.

kokoro-yasuku-shite-iru 〈心安くしている〉be on intimate terms ((with)).

kokoroyoi 〈こころよい：快い〉pleasant, comfortable, agreeable, refreshing.

kokoroyoku 〈快く〉pleasantly, comfortably, agreeably; gladly, willingly, with pleasure.

kokoroyoku tetsudau（快く手伝う）help one willingly

kokorozashi 〈こころざし：志〉(a) will, (an) intention, an aim, (an) ambition, kindness.

hito-no kokorozashi-o-mu-ni-suru（人の志を無にする）let a person's kindness be of no avail

kokorozasu 〈志す〉intend, aim ((at)).

kokoro-zukai 〈こころづかい：心遣い〉consideration, thoughtfulness, concern, care.

shinsetsu-na kokoro-zukai（親切な心遣い）kind consideration

kokoro-zuke 〈こころづけ：心付け〉a tip, gratuity, a consideration.

kokoro-zukushi 〈こころづくし：心尽くし〉(a) kindness, attentions, consideration, care, solicitude, assiduities.

kokoro-zuyoi 〈こころづよい：心強い〉reassuring, encouraging.

kokoro-zuyoku-omou 〈心強く思う〉feel reassured, feel encouraged.

kôkô-ya 〈こうこうや：好々や〉a good-natured old man.

koku 〈こく〉body.

koku-no-aru sake（こくのある酒）*sake* with good body

koku 〈こく：酷〉

koku-na 〈酷な〉severe, harsh, cruel.

kôkû 〈こうくう：航空〉aviation, flying.

kôkû-ro〈航空路〉 an air route

kôkû-shashin〈航空写真〉 an aerial photograph

kôkû-bin-de〈航空便で〉 by air mail

kôkû〈こうくう：高空〉

kôkû-hikô〈高空飛行〉 high-altitude flight

kokuban〈こくばん：黒板〉a blackboard.

kokuban-fuki〈黒板ふき〉 a wiper, an eraser

kokubetsu〈こくべつ：告別〉leave-taking, farewell.

kokubetsu-shiki〈告別式〉 a farewell service

ko-kubi〈こくび：小首〉

ko-kubi-o-kashigeru〈小首をかしげる〉incline one's head slightly on one side.

kokubô〈こくぼう：国防〉national defense.

kokubô-hi〈国防費〉 national defense expenditure

kokubun〈こくぶん：国文〉the Japanese language.

koku-bungaku〈こくぶんがく：国文学〉Japanese literature.

koku-byaku〈こくびゃく：黒白〉black and white; right and wrong.

koku-byaku-o-arasou〈黒白を争う〉 contend as to which is right

kokuchi〈こくち：告知〉a notice, an announcement.

kokuchi-ban〈告知板〉 a notice board

kokuchi-suru〈告知する〉give notice ((to)), announce.

kokudo〈こくど：国土〉a country, a territory.

kokudo-bôei〈国土防衛〉 national defense

kokudo-kaihatsu〈国土開発〉 land development

kokudo-keikaku〈国土計画〉 national land planning

kokudô〈こくどう：国道〉a national road.

kokuei〈こくえい：国営〉

kokuei-ni-suru〈国営にする〉nationalize.

kokuei-no〈国営の〉government-managed, state-run.

kokuen〈こくえん：黒煙〉black smoke.

kokufuku〈こくふく：克服〉conquest.

kokufuku-suru〈克服する〉conquer, overcome, get over.

kokugai〈こくがい：国外〉

kokugai-de or *kokugai-ni*〈国外で，国外に〉abroad.

kokugai-ni-tsuihô-suru〈国外に追放する〉 expatriate

kokugi〈こくぎ：国技〉a national sport.

kokugo〈こくご：国語〉a language; one's mother tongue; the Japanese language.

　　ni-ka-kokugo〈二か国語〉 two languages

kokuhaku〈こくはく：告白〉(a) confession.
　　kokuhaku-suru〈告白する〉confess, make a confession ((of)).

kokuhatsu〈こくはつ：告発〉prosecution, accusation.
　　kokuhatsu-suru〈告発する〉prosecute, indict, accuse.

kokuhi〈こくひ：国費〉national expenditure.
　　kokuhi-de〈国費で〉 at the expense of the state

kokuhin〈こくひん：国賓〉a national guest.
　　kokuhin-taigū〈国賓待遇〉 a person treated as a national guest

kokuhō〈こくほう：国法〉the national law, the laws of the country.

kokuhō〈こくほう：国宝〉a national treasure.

kokuhyō〈こくひょう：酷評〉severe criticism.
　　kokuhyō-suru〈酷評する〉criticize severely.

kokuin〈こくいん：刻印〉a (carved) stamp.

kokuji〈こくじ：告示〉a notice, a notification.
　　kokuji-ban〈告示板〉 a bulletin board
　　kokuji-suru〈告示する〉give notice ((of)), notify.

kokuji〈こくじ：酷似〉a close resemblance.
　　kokuji-suru〈酷似する〉resemble closely, bear a close resemblance ((to)), be strikingly similar ((to)).

kokujin〈こくじん：黒人〉colored people.

kokujō〈こくじょう：国情〉the state of affairs in a country.

kokujoku〈こくじょく：国辱〉a national disgrace.

kokumei〈こくめい：克明〉
　　kokumei-ni〈克明に〉scrupulously, faithfully.
　　kokumei-ni-kisai-suru〈克明に記載する〉 make a minute description

kokumin〈こくみん：国民〉a nation, a people.
　　kokumin-kanjō〈国民感情〉 a national sentiment
　　kokumin-sei〈国民性〉 the national character, nationality
　　kokumin-no〈国民の〉national.

kokumotsu〈こくもつ：穀物〉cereals; grain, corn.

kokumu〈こくむ：国務〉the affairs of state, state affairs.
　　kokumu-daijin〈国務大臣〉 a minister of state, a minister without portfolio
　　kokumu-chōkan〈国務長官〉 the Secretary of State

kokunai〈こくない：国内〉
　　kokunai-hōsō〈国内放送〉 domestic broadcasting
　　kokunai-jijō〈国内事情〉 domestic affairs

kokunai-mondai〈国内問題〉 domestic problems

kokunai-sangyô〈国内産業〉 domestic industries

kokunai-no〈国内の〉home, domestic, internal.

kokunai-de or *kokunai-ni*〈国内で，国内に〉in the country.

kokuô〈こくおう：国王〉a king, a monarch.

kokuren〈こくれん：国連〉the United Nations (an abbreviation of 'kokusai-rengô').

kokuren-kenshô〈国連憲章〉 the United Nations Charter

kokuren-kanyû-koku〈国連加入国〉 a member of the United Nations

kokuren-riji-koku〈国連理事国〉 a member of the Council of the United Nations

kokuren-sôkai〈国連総会〉 the United Nations General Assembly

kokuren-taishi〈国連大使〉 the ambassador to the United Nations

kokuritsu〈こくりつ：国立〉

kokuritsu-byôin〈国立病院〉 a national hospital

kokuritsu-daigaku〈国立大学〉 a national university

kokuritsu-gekijô〈国立劇場〉 a national theater

kokuritsu-no〈国立の〉national.

kokuron〈こくろん：国論〉public opinion.

kokurui〈こくるい：穀類〉*see.* kokumotsu.

kokuryoku〈こくりょく：国力〉national power, national resources.

kokusai〈こくさい：国債〉a national debt, a national bond.

kokusai o hakkô-suru〈国債を発行する〉 issue a national bond

kokusai〈こくさい：国際〉

kokusai-hô〈国際法〉 public international law

kokusai-jôsei〈国際情勢〉 an international situation

kokusai-kankei〈国際関係〉 international relations

kokusai-mondai〈国際問題〉 an international problem

kokusai-kaigi〈国際会議〉 an international conference

kokusai-kôryû〈国際交流〉 international exchange

kokusai-mihon-ichi〈国際見本市〉 an international trade fair

kokusai-rengô〈国際連合〉 *see.* kokuren

kokusai-no, kokusai-kan-no or *kokusai-teki(-na)*〈国際の，国際間の，国際的(な)〉international.

kokusaku〈こくさく：国策〉a national policy.

kokusan〈こくさん：国産〉

kokusan-hin〈国産品〉 home products, domestic products

kokusan-no〈国産の〉homemade.

kokusei 〈こくせい：国政〉the national administration, the government of a country.

kokusei-chôsa 〈こくせいちょうさ：国勢調査〉a census.
kokusei-chôsa o okonau（国勢調査を行う） take a national census

kokuseki 〈こくせき：国籍〉nationality, citizenship.
kokuseki-fumei no hikô-ki（国籍不明の飛行機） a plane of unknown nationality

kokushi 〈こくし：酷使〉
kokushi-suru 〈酷使する〉work ((a person)) hard, overdrive, overwork, overtax.

kokusho 〈こくしょ：酷暑〉intense heat.

kokuso 〈こくそ：告訴〉a complaint, an accusation.
kokuso-suru 〈告訴する〉make a complaint ((against)), bring a suit ((against)), accuse ((a person)) of.

kokusô 〈こくそう：国葬〉a state funeral.
kokusô ni suru（国葬にする） hold a state funeral ((for))

kokusô-chitai 〈こくそうちたい：穀倉地帯〉a granary.

kôkusu 〈コークス〉coke.

kokusui-shugi 〈こくすいしゅぎ：国粋主義〉(ultra)nationalism.

kokutai 〈こくたい：国体〉the National Athletic Meet (an abbreviation of 'kokumin-taiiku-taikai').

kokutan 〈こくたん：黒たん〉an ebony.

kokuten 〈こくてん：黒点〉a black spot.
taiyô-no-kokuten（太陽の黒点） a sunspot

kokuun 〈こくうん：国運〉the destiny of a nation.
kokuun o kakeru（国運を懸ける） stake the destiny of a nation

kokuyû 〈こくゆう：国有〉
kokuyû-rin（国有林） a state forest.
kokuyû-tetsudô（国有鉄道） a state railway
kokuyû-ni-suru or *kokuyû-ka-suru* 〈国有にする，国有化する〉nationalize.
kokuyû-no 〈国有の〉state-owned, state.

kokuzei 〈こくぜい：国税〉a national tax.

kokyô 〈こきょう：故郷〉one's home, one's native place.

kôkyo 〈こうきょ：皇居〉the Imperial Palace.

kôkyô 〈こうきょう：公共〉
kôkyô-butsu（公共物） public property
kôkyô-dantai（公共団体） a public body
kôkyô-jigyô（公共事業） a public enterprise

    kôkyô-kigyô-tai〈公共企業体〉a public corporation
    kôkyô-kikan〈公共機関〉a public institution
    kôkyô-ryôkin〈公共料金〉public utility charges
    kôkyô-shin〈公共心〉public spirit
  kôkyô-no〈公共の〉public, common.

kôkyô〈こうきょう：好況〉*see.* kô-keiki.

kôkyô〈こうきょう：交響〉
    kôkyô-kyoku〈交響曲〉a symphony
    kôkyô-gaku-dan〈交響楽団〉a symphony orchestra

kokyû〈こきゅう：呼吸〉a breath, respiration.
    kokyû-konnan〈呼吸困難〉difficult breathing, laboring breath
    kokyû-ki〈呼吸器〉the respiratory organs
  kokyû-suru〈呼吸する〉breathe.

kôkyû〈こうきゅう：硬球〉a hard ball.

kôkyû〈こうきゅう：高級〉
    kôkyû-hin〈高級品〉high-grade articles
  kôkyû-na〈高級な〉high-class, high-grade.

kôkyû〈こうきゅう：高給〉a high salary.
  kôkyû-o-moratte-iru〈高給をもらっている〉be highly paid, draw a high salary.

kôkyû〈こうきゅう：好球〉a nice ball.
    kôkyû o mi-nogasu〈好球を見逃す〉miss a nice ball

kôkyû(-sei)〈こうきゅう（せい）：恒久(性)〉permanency.
    kôkyû-kikan〈恒久機関〉permanent machinery
  kôkyû-no〈恒久の〉permanent, eternal, perpetual, everlasting.

kôkyû(-bi)〈こうきゅう（び）：公休(日)〉a regular holiday, a day off.

koma〈こま〉a top.
    koma o mawasu〈こまを回す〉spin a top

koma〈こま〉a chessman, a piece.
    koma o naraberu〈こまを並べる〉set out pieces

koma-gire〈こまぎれ：細切れ〉chopped meat, mincemeat.
  koma-gire-ni-suru〈細切れにする〉chop, hash, mince.

komagoma〈こまごま：細々〉
  komagoma-shita〈細々した〉small, petty, sundry.
  komagoma-to〈細々と〉minutely, in detail.

kômai〈こうまい：高まい〉
  kômai-na〈高まいな〉high, lofty, noble.
    kômai-na risô〈高まいな理想〉a lofty ideal

komakai〈こまかい：細かい〉small, fine, minute, close, delicate, elaborate; stingy, closefisted, miserly.

 komakai kane（細かい金）small change

 komakai ame（細かい雨）a fine rain

 komakai ten（細かい点）minute details

 komakai chûi（細かい注意）close attention

 shinkei-ga komakai（神経が細かい）be sensitive

 kane-ni-komakai（金に細かい）be strict in money

komakaku〈細かく〉to pieces, minutely, in detail, closely.

 komakaku kiru（細かく切る）cut into small pieces

 komakaku shiraberu（細かく調べる）examine closely

komaku〈こまく：鼓膜〉the tympanic membrane.

ko-mame〈こまめ：小まめ〉

ko-mame-na〈こまめな〉brisk, active, diligent.

ko-mame-ni〈こまめに〉briskly, actively, diligently.

 ko-mame-ni-hataraku（こまめに働く）be as brisk as a bee

koma-mono〈こまもの：小間物〉fancy goods, notions, haberdashery.

 koma-mono-ya（小間物屋）a fancy goods dealer, a haberdasher, a fancy store, a fancy shop

kôman〈こうまん：高慢〉

kôman-na〈高慢な〉proud, haughty, uppish.

komari-kiru〈こまりきる：困り切る〉be sorely perplexed, be greatly embarrassed, be at a loss, be up a tree.

komari-mono〈こまりもの：困り者〉a good-for-nothing (fellow), a nuisance, a trouble.

komaru〈こまる：困る〉be troubled ((by *or* with)), be in trouble, suffer ((from)), be perplexed ((about, at *or* with)), be at a loss.

 kane-ni komaru（金に困る）be in trouble over money

 ashi-ga-itakute-komatte-iru（足が痛くて困っている）suffer from sore foot

 Kare-wa dô-shitara-ii-ka komatte-iru.（彼はどうしたらいいか困っている。）He is at a loss what to do.

 henji-ni-komaru（返事に困る）do not know what answer to make

komaraseru〈困らせる〉annoy, embarrass.

komatta〈困った〉troubled, bad, annoyed, embarrassed.

 komatta koto（困ったこと）a bad business

Komatta-koto-ni~.〈困ったことに~。〉The trouble is (that)... .

komashakure-ta〈こましゃくれた〉precocious, pert, cocky.

ko-mata〈こまた：小また〉
ko-mata-ni-aruku〈小またに歩く〉walk with short strides.

ko-mawari〈こまわり：小回り〉
ko-mawari-ga-kiku〈小回りが利く〉be capable of small sharp turns.

komayaka〈こまやか：細やか〉
komayaka-na〈細やかな〉warm, tender, close.
　komayaka-na aijô（細やかな愛情）　warm affection

komban〈こんばん：今晩〉this evening, tonight.
　Komban-wa!（今晩は。）Good evening!

kombi〈コンビ〉combination.
　mei-kombi（名コンビ）a happy combination
　〜-to-kombi-de〈〜とコンビで〉in combination with...

kômbîfu〈コーンビーフ〉corn beef, corned beef.

kombinâto〈コンビナート〉an industrial complex.
　sekiyu-kagaku-kombinâto（石油化学コンビナート）a petrochemical
　　complex

kombô〈こんぼう：こん棒〉a club.

kombô〈こんぼう：混紡〉mixed spinning.
kombô-no〈混紡の〉mixed.

kombu〈こんぶ：昆布〉a (sea) tangle.

kombun〈こんぶん：混文〉a compound-complex sentence.

kome〈こめ：米〉rice.
　kome o tsukuru（米を作る）raise rice
　kome-o-jôshoku-ni-suru（米を常食にする）live on rice
　kome-tsubu（米粒）a grain of rice

kômei-seidai〈こうめいせいだい：公明正大〉
kômei-seidai-na〈公明正大な〉fair, just, open, just and fair.
kômei-seidai-ni〈公明正大に〉fairly, justly, openly.

komekami〈こめかみ〉the temple.

komeru〈こめる：込める〉load, charge; concentrate ((on)).
　jû-ni dangan-o komeru（銃に弾丸を込める）load a gun with a shot
chikara-o-komete〈力を込めて〉with all one's strength, emphatically.
kokoro-o-komete〈心を込めて〉with all one's heart.

komi〈こみ：込み〉
zei-komi-de〈税込みで〉inclusive of taxes, taxes included.

komi-ageru〈こみあげる：込み上げる〉be filled ((with)).
　ikari-ga-komi-ageru（怒りが込み上げる）have a fit of anger

komi-au〈こみあう：込み合う〉be crowded, be jammed.

ko-michi 〈こみち：小道〉a (narrow) path, a lane.

komi-itta 〈こみいった：込み入った〉complicated.
  komi-itta mondai (込み入った問題) a complicated problem

kômin-kan 〈こうみんかん：公民館〉a public hall, a community center.

komma 〈コンマ〉comma.

kommei 〈こんめい：混迷〉bewildering confusion.
  kommei-shita seikyoku (混迷した政局) a confused political situation

kommori 〈こんもり〉
  kommori-shigetta 〈こんもり茂った〉thick, dense, luxuriant.
  kommori-to 〈こんもりと〉thickly, densely, luxuriantly.

kommyônichi 〈こんみょうにち：今明日〉
  kommyônichi-jû-ni 〈今明日中に〉in a day or two, sometime today or tomorrow.

ko-mochi 〈こもち：子持ち〉
  ko-mochi-no sakana (子持ちの魚) a seed fish
  ko-mochi-de-aru 〈子持ちである〉have a family, be a mother(*or* father).

ko-moji 〈こもじ：小文字〉a small letter.

kômoku 〈こうもく：項目〉a head, an item, a clause, a provision.

komon 〈こもん：顧問〉an adviser, a counselor.
  komon-bengo-shi (顧問弁護士) a legal adviser, a corporation lawyer

kômon 〈こうもん：校門〉a school gate.

kômon 〈こうもん：こう門〉the anus.
  kômon-no 〈こう門の〉anal.

ko-monjo 〈こもんじょ：古文書〉paleography, antique documents.

ko-mono 〈こもの：小者〉a person of no importance.

ko-mori 〈こもり：子守〉nursing; a nursemaid, a baby-sitter.
  ko-mori-uta (子守歌) a lullaby
  ko-mori-suru 〈子守する〉look after a baby, baby-sit.

kômori 〈こうもり〉a bat.

komoru 〈こもる〉be confined ((in)); be filled ((with)).
  kaze-de ie-ni-komotte-iru (風邪で家にこもっている) be confined to one's home with cold
  kemuri-ga-ippai-ni-komotte-iru (煙がいっぱいにこもっている) be filled with smoke

kompa 〈コンパ〉a social, a party.

kompasu 〈コンパス〉(a pair of) compasses; a mariner's compass; legs.
  kompasu-ga-nagai (コンパスが長い) have long legs

kompô 〈こんぽう：こん包〉packing.

kompô-suru〈こん包する〉pack up.

kompon〈こんぽん：根本〉the foundation, the basis, the root.

　　kompon-mondai（根本問題）a fundamental problem

　kompon-teki(-na)〈根本的(な)〉fundamental, basic.

　kompon-teki-ni〈根本的に〉fundamentally, basically.

kompyûtâ〈コンピューター〉a computer.

　　kompyûtâ-ni puroguramu o ireru（コンピューターにプログラムを入れる）feed a program into a computer

　　kompyûtâ-de keisan-suru（コンピューターで計算する）run up figures on a computer

komu〈こむ：込む〉be crowded, be jammed.

　　konda basu（込んだバス）a crowded bus

kômu〈こうむ：公務〉official business, public duties.

　　kômu-in（公務員）a public official

　　kômu-shikkô-bôgai（公務執行妨害）interference with a government official in the performance of his duties

ko-mugi〈こむぎ：小麦〉wheat, corn.

　　ko-mugi-ko（小麦粉）(wheat) flour

komura-gaeri〈こむらがえり：こむら返り〉a cramp in the calf.

　　komura-gaeri-o-okosu（こむら返りを起こす）be seized with a cramp in the calf

kômuru〈こうむる：被る〉suffer.

　　songai o kômuru（損害を被る）suffer a loss

kômu-ten〈こうむてん：工務店〉a building contractor's office.

kômyaku〈こうみゃく：鉱脈〉a vein, a lode.

kômyô〈こうみょう：光明〉light, hope, a bright future.

　　zento-ni-kômyô-ga aru（前途に光明がある）have a bright future

kômyô〈こうみょう：巧妙〉

　kômyô-na〈巧妙な〉skillful, dexterous.

　kômyô-ni〈巧妙に〉skillfully, dexterously.

kômyô〈こうみょう：功名〉a great exploit, a glorious deed, distinction, fame.

　　kega-no-kômyô（けがの功名）a chance hit, a fluke

　　kômyô-shin（功名心）ambition, aspiration

　　　kômyô-shin-ni karareru（功名心に駆られる）be driven by ambition

komyunike〈コミュニケ〉a communiqué.

　　kyôdô-komyunike（共同コミュニケ）a joint communiqué

kon〈こん：根〉a root, a radical; perseverance, patience.

　　heihô-kon（平方根）　a square root
　　kon-kurabe（根比べ）　a patience game
kon(-no)〈こん（の）：紺（の）〉dark blue.
kona〈こな：粉〉flour, powder.
　　kona-gusuri（粉薬）　powdered medicine
　　kona-miruku（粉ミルク）　powdered milk
　　kona-sekken（粉石けん）　soap powder
　　kona-yuki（粉雪）　powdery snow
　kona-ni-suru〈粉にする〉powder.
　　hiite kona-ni-suru（ひいて粉にする）　grind...into flour
kona-gona〈こなごな：粉々〉
　kona-gona-ni(-natte)〈粉々に(なって)〉in pieces.
　　kona-gona-ni kudaku（粉々に砕く）　break...to pieces
kônai〈こうない：構内〉the premises, the precincts; the college grounds,
　　the campus; the yard.
kônai〈こうない：港内〉
　kônai-de or *kônai-ni*〈港内で，港内に〉in the port.
kônai〈こうない：校内〉
　kônai-de or *kônai-ni*〈校内で，校内に〉in the school.
kônai-en〈こうないえん：口内炎〉stomatitis.
kônan〈こうなん：後難〉future trouble, the consequences.
　　kônan-o-osorete（後難を恐れて）　for fear of future troubles
konashi〈こなし〉
　mi-no-konashi-ga-ii〈身のこなしがいい〉carry oneself well.
konasu〈こなす〉digest; sell; perform; handle.
　　kazu-de-konasu（数でこなす）　make a profit by quantity sales
　　yaku o umaku konasu（役をうまくこなす）　perform one's part well
　　nan-mondai o konasu（難問題をこなす）　handle a difficulty
konchû〈こんちゅう：昆虫〉an insect.
　　konchû-saishû（昆虫採集）　insect collecting
kondan〈こんだん：懇談〉
　　kondan-kai（懇談会）　a round-table conference, a social gathering
　kondan-suru〈懇談する〉have a familiar talk ((with)), chat ((with)).
kondate〈こんだて：献立〉a menu.
kondo〈こんど：今度〉now, this time; next time.
　kondo-no〈今度の〉new; next, coming, last.
　　kondo-no kin·yô-bi（今度の金曜日）　next Friday
　　kondo-no shiken（今度の試験）　the coming (*or* last) examination

kondo-dake-wa〈今度だけは〉for this once.

kondo-kara-wa〈今度からは〉from now on.

kondo-koso-wa〈今度こそは〉this time, now.

kondô〈こんどう：混同〉confusion.

kondô-suru〈混同する〉confuse ((one thing with another)).

kone〈コネ〉a connection, a pull.

　　kone-ga-aru〈コネがある〉have a pull ((on *or* with))

ko-neko〈こねこ：小〈子〉猫〉a kitten, a kitty.

kônen〈こうねん：光年〉a light-year.

kônen〈こうねん：後年〉in future years, in one's later years.

kônen-ki〈こうねんき：更年期〉the menopause.

　　kônen-ki-shôgai〈更年期障害〉a menopausal disorder

koneru〈こねる〉knead, work, mix up.

kônetsu〈こうねつ：高熱〉(an) intense heat; a high fever.

　　kônetsu-ni-okasareru〈高熱に冒される〉catch a high fever

kônetsu-hi〈こうねつひ：光熱費〉expenses for light and fuel.

kongan〈こんがん：懇願〉(an) entreaty.

　　kongan-suru〈懇願する〉entreat ((a person to do)).

kongaragaru〈こんがらがる〉get confused, get complicated.

kongari(-to)〈こんがり(と)〉

　kongari-to-yakeru〈こんがりと焼ける〉be done to a beautiful brown.

kongen〈こんげん：根元〉the root, the origin, the source.

　　sho-aku no kongen〈諸悪の根元〉the root of all evils

kongetsu〈こんげつ：今月〉this month.

　　kongetsu-jôjun-ni〈今月上旬に〉at the beginning of this month

　　kongetsu-jū-ni〈今月中に〉in the course of this month

kongo〈こんご：今後〉after this, from now on, hereafter, in future.

　　kongo-san-nen-kan-wa〈今後三年間は〉for the coming three years

　　Kongo ki-o-tsuke-nasai.〈今後気をつけなさい。〉Be careful in future.

kongo-no〈今後の〉future.

kongô(-butsu)〈こんごう(ぶつ)：混合(物)〉a mixture, a blend.

　　kongô-daburusu〈混合ダブルス〉a mixed doubles

kongô-suru〈混合する〉mix, mingle, blend.

kongô-shita〈混合した〉mixed.

kon·i〈こんい：懇意〉

　kon·i-ni-shite-iru〈懇意にしている〉be friends ((with)), be on intimate terms ((with)).

　kon·i-na〈懇意な〉intimate, familiar, friendly.

ko-nimotsu〈こにもつ：小荷物〉a parcel, a package.
    ko-nimotsu-tori-atsukai-jo（小荷物取扱所）a parcels office
kon·in〈こんいん：婚姻〉marriage, matrimony.
    kon·in-todoke（婚姻届）registration of one's marriage
        kon·in-todoke-o-dasu（婚姻届を出す）register one's marriage
kônin〈こうにん：公認〉official recognition.
    kônin-kôho(-sha)（公認候補〔者〕）a recognized candidate
    kônin-sekai-kiroku（公認世界記録）an international official record
  kônin-suru〈公認する〉recognize officially, approve publicly.
  kônin-no〈公認の〉recognized, official, authorized.
kônin〈こうにん：後任〉a successor ((to)).
  kônin-ni-naru〈後任になる〉succeed, take over.
  kônin-no〈後任の〉incoming.
konji〈こんじ：根治〉
  konji-suru〈根治する〉cure completely.
konjô〈こんじょう：根性〉(a) nature; spirit, guts.
    konjô-ga-aru（根性がある）have guts
  konjô-no-warui〈根性の悪い〉ill-natured.
konkai〈こんかい：今回〉this time, lately.
  konkai-no〈今回の〉of this time, late.
konketsu〈こんけつ：混血〉mixed blood.
    konketsu-ji（混血児）a half-blood
  konketsu-no〈混血の〉half-blooded, of mixed blood.
konki〈こんき：婚期〉the marriageable age.
    konki o issuru（婚期を逸する）lose a chance of marriage
konki〈こんき：今期〉this term.
konki〈こんき：根気〉perseverance, patience.
  konki-no-ii〈根気のいい〉persevering, patient.
  konki-yoku〈根気よく〉perseveringly, patiently.
konkon〈こんこん：懇々〉
  konkon-to〈懇々と〉earnestly, repeatedly, seriously.
    konkon-to satosu（懇々と諭す）admonish earnestly
konkon〈こんこん〉
  konkon-to〈こんこんと〉unconsciously.
    konkon-to-nemutte-iru（こんこんと眠っている）be in a state of coma
konkon〈こんこん〉
  konkon-to-waki-deru〈こんこんとわき出る〉gush out, well up.
konku(-ketsubô)〈こんく（けつぼう）：困苦（欠乏）〉hardships, privations.

konku-ketsubô ni taeru〈困苦欠乏に耐える〉 endure hardships

konkurîto〈コンクリート〉concrete.

konkûru〈コンクール〉a contest.

shashin-konkûru〈写真コンクール〉 a photo contest

konkyo〈こんきょ：根拠〉a basis, a base, a ground.

konkyo-chi〈根拠地〉 a base

konkyo-no-aru〈根拠のある〉well-grounded.

konkyo-no-nai〈根拠のない〉 groundless

konna〈こんな〉such, like this.

konna-fû-ni〈こんなふうに〉 in this way, like this

konna hi-ni〈こんな日に〉 on such a day

konna koto〈こんなこと〉 such a thing

konna toki-ni〈こんな時に〉 at such a time

konna-wake-de〈こんな訳で〉 such being the case

konnan〈こんなん：困難〉(a) difficulty, (a) trouble, hardship(s).

konnan-ni-ochiiru〈困難に陥る〉 get into trouble

konnan ni taeru〈困難に耐える〉 bear hardship

konnan ni uchi-katsu〈困難に打ち勝つ〉 overcome difficulties

konnan-na〈困難な〉difficult, hard, troublesome.

konnan-na shigoto〈困難な仕事〉 a hard job

konna-ni〈こんなに〉so, so many, so much, like this.

konnichi〈こんにち：今日〉today, this day, these days, the present day.

konnichi no Nippon〈今日の日本〉 Japan today

Konnichi-wa!〈今日は.〉 Good day!/ Good morning!/ Good afternoon!

konnyaku〈こんにゃく〉a paste made from (the starch of) the devil's-tongue.

konnyû〈こんにゅう：混入〉

konnyû-suru〈混入する〉mix, mingle, blend, adulterate.

kono〈この〉this, these, next, last.

kono inu〈この犬〉 this dog

kono natsu〈この夏〉 this summer

kono ni-san-nichi〈この二，三日〉 these few days

kono jûni-gatsu〈この十二月〉 next(*or* last) December

kônô〈こうのう：効能〉effect, efficacy, good, use.

kônô-gaki〈効能書〉 a statement of virtues

kônô-no-aru〈効能のある〉effective, good ((for)), useful.

kônô-no-nai〈効能のない〉 ineffective, no good ((for)), useless

kono-aida 〈このあいだ：この間〉 the other day, a few days ago, lately, recently.

  tsui kono-aida（ついこの間） only the other day

    tsui kono-aida-made（ついこの間まで） till quite recently

kono-bun 〈このぶん：この分〉

  kono-bun-dewa（この分では） at this rate, as things are, from the present state of things

  kono-bun-de-ikeba（この分でいけば） if things go on like this

kono-goro 〈このごろ〉 (in) these days, recently, lately.

  kono-goro-no 〈このごろの〉 present, recent.

ko-no-ha 〈このは：木の葉〉 leaves, foliage.

kono-hen(-ni) 〈このへん(に)：この辺(に)〉 about here, near here, around here, in this neighborhood.

kono-hoka 〈このほか〉 besides, except this.

kono-kata 〈このかた：この方〉 since; this gentleman, this lady.

  jû-nen-kono-kata（十年この方） these ten years

kono-kurai 〈このくらい〉 about so much(*or* many).

  Kyô wa kono-kurai-ni-shite-okô.（今日はこのくらいにしておこう。） So much for today.

kono-mae 〈このまえ：この前〉 last, last time.

  kono-mae-no 〈この前の〉 last, former.

  kono-mae-no doyô-bi（この前の土曜日） last Saturday

  kono-mae-no chiji（この前の知事） the former governor

kono-mama-ni 〈このままに〉 as it is.

  kono-mama-ni-shite-oku（このままにしておく） leave ((a thing)) as it is

konomashii 〈このましい：好ましい〉 desirable.

  konomashiku-nai（好ましくない） undesirable

konomi 〈このみ：好み〉 taste, liking.

  konomi ni au（好みに合う） suit one's taste

  konomu 〈好む〉 like, be fond of.

  kononde 〈好んで〉 by choice, willingly.

  kononde〜(-suru)（好んで〜(する)） be willing ((to do))

  o-konomi-nara 〈お好みなら〉 if you like (it).

ko-no-mi 〈このみ：木の実〉 a fruit, a nut, a berry.

kono-sai 〈このさい：この際〉 on this occasion.

kono-saki 〈このさき：この先〉 hereafter, in future, after this; beyond this, farther (on).

kono-toori〈このとおり〉like this, in this way.

kônotori〈こうのとり〉a stork.

kono-tsugi〈このつぎ：この次〉next.

kono-tsugi-no〈この次の〉next.
> kono-tsugi-no doyô-ni（この次の土曜に）on Saturday next

kono-tsugi-ni〈この次に〉next (time), another time.
> kono-tsugi-ni suru（この次にする）leave ((it)) until another time

kono-ue〈このうえ：この上〉more, further, any longer; besides, more-over.
> kono-ue gaman-deki-nai（この上我慢できない）cannot bear ((it)) any longer

kono-ue(-mo)-nai〈この上（も）ない〉first-rate, the best, the finest, the greatest, unsurpassed.
> kono-ue-mo-nai meiyo（この上もない名誉）the greatest honor

kono-yo〈このよ：この世〉this world, the present life.
> kono-yo-no jigoku（この世の地獄）a hell on earth

kono-yô〈このよう〉

kono-yô-na〈このような〉see. konna.

kono-yô-ni〈このように〉see. konna-ni.

konran〈こんらん：混乱〉confusion, disorder.

konran-suru〈混乱する〉be confused, be disordered.

konran-ni-jôjite〈混乱に乗じて〉in the confusion ((of)).

konrei〈こんれい：婚礼〉a wedding.

konro〈こんろ：こん炉〉a portable cooking stove.

konsâto〈コンサート〉a concert.
> konsâto o hiraku（コンサートを開く）give a concert

konsei〈こんせい：混声〉a mixed voice.
> konsei-gasshô（混声合唱）a mixed chorus

konseki〈こんせき：こん跡〉traces, marks, vestiges.
> konseki o todome-nai（こん跡をとどめない）leave no traces

konsen〈こんせん：混戦〉a confused fight, a melee.

konsen〈こんせん：混線〉

konsen-suru〈混線する〉get entangled, be crossed.

konsento〈コンセント〉an outlet, a plug receptacle, a plug socket.

konsento-ni-sashi-komu〈コンセントに差し込む〉plug in.

konsetsu-teinei〈こんせつていねい：懇切丁寧〉

konsetsu-teinei-na〈懇切丁寧な〉kind, cordial, obliging, exhaustive.

konsetsu-teinei-ni〈懇切丁寧に〉kindly, cordially, obligingly, exhaustively.

konshin〈こんしん：混信〉interference, jamming.

konshin〈こんしん：こん身〉

konshin-no-chikara-o-komete〈こん身の力を込めて〉with all one's might, with might and main.

konshin-kai〈こんしんかい：懇親会〉a social gathering, a social, a get-together.

konsyû〈こんしゅう：今週〉this week.

　　konshû-ippai（今週いっぱい）through this week

　　konshû-jû（今週中）during this week

　　　konshû-jû-ni（今週中に）within this week

　　konshû-no-doyô（今週の土曜）Saturday this week

konsui〈こんすい：こん睡〉a coma, a trance.

konsui-jôtai-ni-ochiiru〈こん睡状態に陥る〉fall into a comatose state.

konsui-jôtai-no〈こん睡状態の〉comatose.

kontan〈こんたん：魂胆〉an intention, a secret design, a plot.

kontei〈こんてい：根底〉

kontei-kara〈根底から〉fundamentally, thoroughly, from the bottom up.

　　kontei-kara kutsugaesu（根底から覆す）overthrow from its bottom

　　kontei-made yurugasu（根底まで揺るがす）shake...to its foundation

kontenâ〈コンテナー〉a container.

　　kontenâ-sen（コンテナ船）a containership

kontesuto〈コンテスト〉a contest.

　　bijin-kontesuto（美人コンテスト）a beauty contest

kontô〈こんとう：こん倒〉

kontô-suru〈こん倒する〉swoon, fall into a swoon, faint (away), fall unconscious.

konton〈こんとん：混とん〉chaos.

konton-to-shita〈混とんとした〉chaotic.

　　konton-to-shita jôtai-ni-aru（混とんとした状態にある）be in a chaotic state

kontorasuto〈コントラスト〉a contrast.

　　Kontorasuto ga tsuyoi.（コントラストが強い。）The contrast is striking.

kontorasuto-no-nai〈コントラストのない〉flat.

kontserun〈コンツェルン〉a combine.

konwa-kai〈こんわかい：懇話会〉a social gathering, a conversazione.

konwaku〈こんわく：困惑〉*see.* tôwaku.

kon·ya〈こんや：今夜〉 see. komban.

kon·yaku〈こんやく：婚約〉 an engagement.
　　kon·yaku-sha（婚約者） one's betrothed, one's fiancé, one's fiancée
　kon·yaku-suru〈婚約する〉 engage oneself ((to)), be engaged ((to)).

kônyû〈こうにゅう：購入〉
　kônyû-suru〈購入する〉 buy, purchase, make a purchase.

konzatsu〈こんざつ：混雑〉 confusion, a bustle.
　konzatsu-suru〈混雑する〉 be confused, be crowded, be bustling.

konzetsu〈こんぜつ：根絶〉 extermination, eradication.
　konzetsu-suru〈根絶する〉 exterminate, eradicate, root out, uproot.

koô〈こおう：呼応〉
　koô-suru〈呼応する〉 act in concert ((with)), act in unison ((with)).
　～-to-koô-shite〈～と呼応して〉 in concert with... , in response to... .

ko-odori〈こおどり：小躍り〉
　ko-odori-shite-yorokobu〈小躍りして喜ぶ〉 dance for joy.

kôon〈こうおん：高温〉 a high temperature.
　　kôon-tashitsu（高温多湿） high temperature and humidity

koori〈こおり：氷〉 ice.
　　koori no katamari（氷の塊） a block of ice
　　koori-makura（氷まくら） an ice pillow
　koori-de-hiyasu〈氷で冷やす〉 cool with ice, ice.
　koori-no-hatta〈氷の張った〉 frozen.
　koori-no-yô-na or *koori-no-yô-ni-tsumetai*〈氷のような，氷のように冷たい〉 icy.

koori-tsuku〈こおりつく：凍り付く〉 freeze ((to)), be frozen hard ((to)).

koori-zatô〈こおりざとう：氷砂糖〉 crystal sugar.

koorogi〈こおろぎ〉 a cricket.

kooru〈こおる：凍る〉 freeze, be frozen over.
　　kooru-yô-ni-samui（凍るように寒い） be freezing cold
　koorasu〈凍らす〉 freeze.

kopî〈コピー〉 a copy.
　kopî-suru〈コピーする〉 copy, take a copy ((of)), duplicate.

koppa〈こっぱ：木っ端〉 a chip, a splinter.
　koppa-mijin-ni kudakeru〈木っ端みじんに砕ける〉 be smashed to pieces.

koppidoku〈こっぴどく〉 harshly, severely, scathingly, smartly.
　　koppidoku-shikaru（こっぴどくしかる） scold scathingly, give ((a person)) a good scolding

koppu〈コップ〉 a glass.

kora 〈こら〉 hi, hey, I say, (look) here.

kôra 〈こうら：甲羅〉 a shell, a carapace.

  kôra-o-hosu〈甲羅を干す〉 bask in the sun.

koraeru 〈こらえる〉 endure, bear, stand.

kôraku 〈こうらく：行楽〉

    kôraku-chi（行楽地） a holiday resort

    kôraku-kyaku（行楽客） a weekender, a holidaymaker

Kôran 〈コーラン〉 the Koran.

korashime 〈こらしめ：懲らしめ〉 (a) chastisement, (a) punishment.

  korashimeru or *korasu*〈懲らしめる，懲らす〉 chastise, punish.

korasu 〈こらす：凝らす〉

    iki o korasu（息をこらす） bate one's breath

    kufû o korasu（工夫を凝らす） exercise one's ingenuity

kore 〈これ〉 this, these; here, look here, listen, I·say.

    kore-dake *or* kore-kurai（これだけ，これくらい） so much, so many

    kore-de（これで） with this

    kore-hodo（これ程） as this, so, such

    kore-ijô（これ以上） *see.* kono-ue

    kore-kara（これから） from now on, hereafter

      kore-kara-no（これからの） future

    kore-kore-no（これこれの） such and such

    kore-made（これまで） so far, till now, up to this time

    kore-made-doori（これまでどおり） as before, as ever

    are-ya kore-ya（あれやこれや） this and that

kôrei 〈こうれい：恒例〉 the custom, the usual practice.

  kôrei-no〈恒例の〉 customary, usual.

  kôrei-ni-yori〈恒例により〉 according to the custom, as usual.

kôrei 〈こうれい：好例〉 a good example.

kôrei 〈こうれい：高齢〉 a great age.

    kôrei-sha（高齢者） the aged, a very old person

korera 〈コレラ〉 cholera.

    korera-kin（コレラ菌） a cholera germ

    shinsei-korera（真性コレラ） a genuine case of cholera

    giji-korera（疑似コレラ） a suspected case of cholera

kôretsu 〈こうれつ：後列〉 the rear rank, the back row.

kori 〈こり：凝り〉 stiffness.

    kata-no kori（肩の凝り） stiffness in the shoulders

kôri 〈こうり：高利〉 a high rate of interest.

kôri 〈こうり：功利〉 utility.

　　kôri-shugi（功利主義）　utilitarianism

　　kôri-teki(-na)（功利的(な)）utilitarian.

kori-katamaru 〈こりかたまる：凝り固まる〉curdle, clot; be fanatical, be bigoted; be given up ((to)), be absorbed ((in)).

ko-rikô 〈こりこう：小利口〉

　　ko-rikô-na〈小利口な〉knowing, smart(ish).

ko-rikutsu 〈こりくつ：小理屈〉 see. he-rikutsu.

koriru 〈こりる：懲りる〉grow wiser by experience.

　　Are-niwa-korita.（あれには懲りた.）It has been a lesson to me.

kori-shô 〈こりしょう：凝り性〉

　　kori-shô-no〈凝り性の〉single-minded, fastidious.

koritsu 〈こりつ：孤立〉isolation.

　　koritsu-shugi（孤立主義）isolationism

　　koritsu-suru〈孤立する〉be isolated, stand alone.

　　koritsu-shita〈孤立した〉isolated, solitary.

kôritsu 〈こうりつ：効率〉efficiency.

kôritsu 〈こうりつ：公立〉

　　kôritsu-no〈公立の〉public, prefectural, municipal.

　　kôritsu-no tosho-kan（公立の図書館）a public library

-koro 〈-ころ〉when, time.

　　wakai-koro（若いころ）when young

　　watashi-ga　achira-ni　tsuku-koro-ni-wa（私があちらに着くころには）by the time when I get there

　　sono-koro（そのころ）in those days, then, at that time

kôro 〈こうろ：航路〉a route, a course, a shipping lane, a line.

　　kôro-hyôshiki（航路標識）a nautical mark, a beacon

kôro 〈こうろ：香炉〉an incense burner.

kôrô 〈こうろう：功労〉services, merits.

　　kôrô-ni-yori（功労により）in recognition of one's services

　　kôrô-sha（功労者）a person who has done good services

　　kôrô-ga-aru〈功労がある〉do much ((for)).

　　kôrô-no-aru〈功労のある〉of merit.

korobu 〈ころぶ：転ぶ〉fall (down), tumble (down), fall to the ground.

korogaru 〈ころがる：転がる〉roll, tumble, fall.

　　korogasu〈転がす〉roll.

koroge-ochiru 〈ころげおちる：転げ落ちる〉tumble down, fall down.

korogeru 〈ころげる：転げる〉see. korogaru.

korokke 〈コロッケ〉a croquette.

korokoro 〈ころころ〉
　korokoro-korogaru 〈ころころ転がる〉roll over and over.

koromo 〈ころも：衣〉coating.

koromo-gae 〈ころもがえ：衣替え〉change of dress.
　koromo-gae-suru 〈衣替えする〉change one's dress.

kôron 〈こうろん：口論〉a dispute, a quarrel.
　kôron-suru 〈口論する〉dispute ((with)), quarrel ((with)).

korori 〈ころり〉
　korori-to 〈ころりと〉easily; suddenly.
　　korori-to mairu 〈ころりと参る〉yield without any resistance
　　korori-to shinu 〈ころりと死ぬ〉die suddenly

koroshi 〈ころし：殺し〉killing, a murder.
　　koroshi-monku 〈殺し文句〉a killing expression
　　koroshi-ya 〈殺し屋〉a hired killer, a professional gunman
　korosu 〈殺す〉kill, murder; hold back; catch out.
　　iki o korosu 〈息を殺す〉hold one's breath

koru 〈こる：凝る〉be absorbed ((in)), be crazy ((about)); grow stiff.
　　go-ni koru 〈碁に凝る〉be crazy about *go*
　　kata-ga-koru 〈肩が凝る〉have a stiff shoulder

kôrudo-gêmu 〈コールドゲーム〉a called game.
　　Kôrudo-gêmu-ni-naru.（コールドゲームになる．）The game is called.

koruku 〈コルク〉(a) cork.
　　koruku-nuki（コルク抜き）a corkscrew
　koruku-no-sen-o-nuku 〈コルクの栓を抜く〉uncork.

kôrutâ(ru) 〈コールター（ル）〉coal-tar.
　kôrutâ(ru)-o-nuru 〈コールター（ル）を塗る〉tar.

kôru-ten 〈コールテン〉corduroy.

kôryaku 〈こうりゃく：攻略〉
　kôryaku-suru 〈攻略する〉carry, capture, reduce.

kôryo 〈こうりょ：考慮〉consideration.
　　kôryo-no-yochi-ga-nai（考慮の余地がない）leave no room for consideration
　kôryo-suru 〈考慮する〉consider.
　jûbun kôryo-shite 〈十分考慮して〉after careful consideration.
　kôryo-chû 〈考慮中〉under consideration.

kôryô 〈こうりょう：香料〉spices, perfume.

kôryô 〈こうりょう：綱領〉general principles; a party platform, a party program.

kôryô 〈こうりょう：校了〉 final proofreading, O.K.

　kôryô-ni-suru 〈校了にする〉 finish proofreading.

kôryoku 〈こうりょく：効力〉 effect.

　　kôryoku o shôjiru（効力を生じる） come into effect, take effect

　　kôryoku o ushinau（効力を失う） lose effect, go out of force

　kôryoku-no-aru 〈効力のある〉 effective.

　　kôryoku-no-nai（効力のない） ineffective

kôryū 〈こうりゅう：拘留〉 detention.

　kôryū-suru 〈拘留する〉 detain.

kôryū 〈こうりゅう：交流〉 interchange.

　　bunka-no kôryū（文化の交流） cultural exchange

kôryū 〈こうりゅう：交流〉 an alternating current (AC).

kôryū 〈こうりゅう：興隆〉 rise, prosperity.

　kôryū-suru 〈興隆する〉 rise, prosper, flourish.

kosa 〈こさ：濃さ〉 depth, thickness, strength, density.

　　iro no kosa（色の濃さ） the depth of a color

kôsa 〈こうさ：考査〉 a test, an examination.

　kôsa-suru 〈考査する〉 test, examine.

kôsa 〈こうさ：交差〉 cross, crossing.

　　kôsa-ten（交差点） a crossing

　kôsa-suru 〈交差する〉 cross, intersect.

kôsai 〈こうさい：交際〉 association, company, intercourse.

　　kôsai-ga-hiroi（交際が広い） have a wide circle of acquaintance

　　kôsai-hi（交際費） social expenses

　kôsai-suru 〈交際する〉 associate socially ((with)), keep company ((with)).

　kôsai-o-tatsu 〈交際を絶つ〉 break off friendship ((with)), be through ((with)).

　kôsai-zuki-no 〈交際好きの〉 sociable.

kôsai 〈こうさい：公債〉 a public loan, a public loan bond.

kôsaku 〈こうさく：耕作〉 cultivation, farming.

　kôsaku-ni-tekisuru 〈耕作に適する〉 be tillable.

　kôsaku-suru 〈耕作する〉 cultivate, farm, till.

kôsaku 〈こうさく：工作〉 construction, engineering work; handicraft; maneuvering, activities.

　　kôsaku-kikai（工作機械） a machine tool

　　seiji-kôsaku（政治工作） political maneuvering

　　chika-kôsaku（地下工作） underground activities

kôsaku-suru〈工作する〉construct, build, make; maneuver, scheme.

kôsaku〈こうさく：交錯〉mixture, complication.

kôsaku-suru〈交錯する〉cross each other, be complicated.

ko-same〈こさめ：小雨〉a light rain, a drizzle.

    Ko-same ga futteiru.（小雨が降っている。） It is drizzling.

kôsan〈こうさん：降参〉surrender.

kôsan-suru〈降参する〉surrender ((to)), be beaten.

kôsan〈こうさん：公算〉probability.

    〜-no-kôsan-ga-ookii（〜の公算が大きい） there is a strong probability that...

kôsatsu〈こうさつ：考察〉consideration, (a) study.

kôsatsu-suru〈考察する〉consider, study.

kôsatsu〈こうさつ：絞殺〉strangulation.

kôsatsu-suru〈絞殺する〉strangle, strangulate, hang.

kosei〈こせい：個性〉individuality, personality.

    kosei-no-tsuyoi hito（個性の強い人） a person of forceful personality

    kosei-teki-na hito（個性的な人） a person with personality

kôsei〈こうせい：後世〉after ages, future generations.

    kôsei-ni-oite（後世において） in later ages

kôsei〈こうせい：恒星〉a fixed star.

kôsei〈こうせい：構成〉making, composition, construction.

    kôsei-yôso（構成要素） a component, a constituent

kôsei-suru〈構成する〉make, compose, construct.

kôsei〈こうせい：公正〉justice, fairness, impartiality.

kôsei-na〈公正な〉just, fair, impartial.

kôsei〈こうせい：厚生〉public welfare.

    kôsei-shô（厚生省） the Ministry of Public Welfare

    kôsei-daijin（厚生大臣） the Minister of Public Welfare

kôsei〈こうせい：校正〉proofreading.

    kôsei-zuri（校正刷り） a proof sheet

kôsei-suru〈校正する〉read the proofs.

kôrei〈こうせい：更正〉

kôsei-suru〈更正する〉be born again, start one's life anew.

kôsei〈こうせい：攻勢〉the offensive.

    kôsei-ni tenjiru（攻勢に転じる） turn to the offensive

    heiwa-kôsei（平和攻勢） a peace offensive

kôsei-no〈攻勢の〉offensive.

kôsei-busshitsu〈こうせいぶっしつ：抗生物質〉an antibiotic.

kô-seinô〈こうせいのう：高性能〉high effectiveness.
kô-seinô-no〈高性能の〉highly efficient.
kô-seiseki〈こうせいせき：好成績〉
kô-seiseki o ageru〈好成績を上げる〉attain good results.
koseki〈こせき：古跡〉a historic spot.
koseki〈こせき：戸籍〉a census register.
koseki-tôhon（戸籍謄本）a copy of one's family register
kôseki〈こうせき：鉱石〉an ore.
kôseki-umpan-sen（鉱石運搬船）an ore carrier
kôseki〈こうせき：功績〉services, merits.
ooi-ni-kôseki-o-tateru（大いに功績を立てる）render remarkable services ((to))
kôseki〈こうせき：航跡〉a wake, a furrow.
kosekose〈こせこせ〉
kosekose-suru〈こせこせする〉make a fuss about trifles.
kosekose-shita〈こせこせした〉fussy, narrow-minded.
kôsen〈こうせん：口銭〉(a) commission, brokerage.
kôsen o toru（口銭を取る）take a commission
kôsen〈こうせん：鉱泉〉a mineral spring, mineral water.
kôsen〈こうせん：光線〉light, a beam, a ray.
kôsen〈こうせん：公選〉public election.
kôsen-suru〈公選する〉elect by popular vote.
kôsen〈こうせん：交戦〉hostilities, a battle, an engagement.
kôsen-koku（交戦国）a belligerent
hi-kôsen-koku（非交戦国）a nonbelligerent
kôsen-suru〈交戦する〉fight ((against *or* with)), be at war ((with)).
kôsen〈こうせん：抗戦〉resistance.
kôsen-suru〈抗戦する〉make resistance ((against *or* to)), resist.
ko-senjô〈こせんじょう：古戦場〉an ancient battlefield.
kôsen-teki(-na)〈こうせんてき(な)：好戦的(な)〉warlike, bellicose.
kôsetsu〈こうせつ：降雪〉(a) snowfall.
kôsetsu〈こうせつ：公設〉
kôsetsu-ichiba（公設市場）a public market
kôsetsu-no〈公設の〉public, prefectural, municipal.
kôsha〈こうしゃ：校舎〉a schoolhouse, a school building.
kôsha〈こうしゃ：公社〉a public corporation.
Nihon-kôtsû-kôsha（日本交通公社）the Japan Travel Bureau
kôsha〈こうしゃ：後者〉the latter.

kôsha-no 〈後者の〉 latter.

kôsha 〈こうしゃ：降車〉
    kôsha-guchi 〈降車口〉 the exit, the way out

kôsha-kikan-jû 〈こうしゃきかんじゅう：高射機関銃〉 an A.A.-machine gun.

koshaku 〈こしゃく：小しゃく〉
    koshaku-na 〈小しゃくな〉 saucy, pert, impudent, cheeky.

kôshaku 〈こうしゃく：講釈〉 *see.* kôdan.

koshi 〈こし：腰〉 the waist, the hip.
    koshi-no-magatta rôjin 〈腰の曲がった老人〉 an old man bent with age
    koshi-o-kakeru 〈腰を掛ける〉 sit down, take a seat.
    koshi-o-nukasu 〈腰を抜かす〉 be paralyzed with terror.
    koshi-no-hikui 〈腰の低い〉 modest, very polite, unassuming.

kô-shi 〈こうし：公私〉 public and private matters.
    kô-shi o kondô-suru 〈公私を混同する〉 mix up public and private matters
    kô-shi-tomo 〈公私とも〉 both in public and private.

kôshi 〈こうし：公使〉 a minister.

kôshi 〈こうし：講師〉 a lecturer, an instructor.
    hi-jôkin-kôshi 〈非常勤講師〉 a part-time lecturer

kôshi 〈こうし：行使〉
    kôshi-suru 〈行使する〉 use, appeal ((to)), exercise.

kôshi 〈こうし：格子〉 a lattice, a grille.
    kôshi-zukuri-no 〈格子造りの〉 latticed, grilled.

koshi-bone 〈こしぼね：腰骨〉 the hipbone, the hucklebone.

koshi-kake 〈こしかけ：腰掛け〉 a seat, a chair, a stool, a bench.
    koshi-kake-shigoto 〈腰掛け仕事〉 a makeshift (*or* stopgap) job

kôshiki 〈こうしき：公式〉 a formula; formality.
    kôshiki-seimei 〈公式声明〉 an official statement
    kôshiki-no 〈公式の〉 formal, official.
    kôshiki-ni 〈公式に〉 formally, officially.

kôshiki 〈こうしき：硬式〉
    kôshiki-tenisu 〈硬式テニス〉 (regulation-ball) tennis
    kôshiki-yakyû 〈硬式野球〉 hard-ball baseball

koshi-kudake 〈こしくだけ：腰砕け〉
    koshi-kudake-ni-naru 〈腰砕けになる〉 weaken in one's attitude.

kôshin 〈こうしん：交信〉
    kôshin-suru 〈交信する〉 exchange (radio) messages ((with)).

kôshin〈こうしん：更新〉renewal, renovation.

　kôshin-suru〈更新する〉renew, renovate.

　　kiroku-o-kôshin-suru（記録を更新する）make a new record

kôshin〈こうしん：行進〉a march, a parade.

　　kôshin-kyoku（行進曲）a march

　kôshin-suru〈行進する〉march, parade.

kôshin〈こうしん：後進〉a junior, a younger person.

　　kôshin-no-tame-ni michi o hiraku（後進のために道を開く）open the way for the promotion of one's juniors

kôshin-jo〈こうしんじょ：興信所〉an inquiry agency, a commercial inquiry agency.

koshi-nuke〈こしぬけ：腰抜け〉a milksop.

　koshi-nuke-no〈腰抜けの〉spineless, yellow.

koshiraeru〈こしらえる〉make, prepare, raise, earn.

　　doresu o koshiraeru（ドレスをこしらえる）make a dress

　　zaisan o koshiraeru（財産をこしらえる）make a fortune

　　yûshoku o koshiraeteiru（夕食をこしらえている）be preparing dinner

kôshisei〈こうせい：高姿勢〉an aggressive attitude, a high posture.

　　kô-shisei o toru（高姿勢を取る）assume an aggressive attitude

koshi-tantan〈こしたんたん：こ視たんたん〉

　koshi-tantan-to-shite〈こ視たんたんとして〉vigilantly.

koshitsu〈こしつ：個室〉a private room, a room of one's own, a single room.

koshitsu〈こしつ：固執〉*see.* koshu.

kôshitsu〈こうしつ：皇室〉the Imperial Household.

kôshitsu〈こうしつ：硬質〉

　kôshitsu-no〈硬質の〉hard.

kosho〈こしょ：古書〉an old book, a rare book.

koshô〈こしょう〉pepper.

koshô〈こしょう：故障〉trouble, an accident, a hitch, an obstacle.

　　enjin-no koshô（エンジンの故障）engin trouble

　koshô-suru〈故障する〉get out of order, go wrong.

　koshô-shite-iru〈故障している〉be out of order.

　koshô-naku〈故障なく〉without a hitch.

kôshô〈こうしょう：交渉〉negotiation(s).

　kôshô-suru〈交渉する〉negotiate with ((a person)) about.

kôshô〈こうしょう：公称〉

　　kôshô-bariki（公称馬力）　nominal horsepower

　kôshô-no〈公称の〉nominal, official, authorized.

kôshô〈こうしょう：高尚〉

　kôshô-na〈高尚な〉high, lofty, noble, elegant.

kôshoku〈こうしょく：公職〉(a) public office.

　　kôshoku ni tsuku（公職に就く）　take up a public office

kôshoku〈こうしょく：交織〉a combined weave.

　　men-mô-kôshoku（綿毛交織）　wool-cotton fabric

kôshoku〈こうしょく：好色〉

　　kôshoku-bungaku（好色文学）　pornographic literature

　　kôshoku-ka（好色家）　a lecher

　kôshoku-no〈好色の〉amorous, lustful, lewd.

kôshô-nin〈こうしょうにん：公証人〉a notary public.

　　kôshô-nin-yakuba（公証人役場）　a notary's office

koshu〈こしゅ：固守〉

　koshu-suru〈固守する〉adhere ((to)), persist ((in)), insist ((on)).

kô-shu〈こうしゅ：攻守〉offense and defense.

　　kô-shu-tokoro-o-kaeru（攻守所を変える）　turn the tables

kôshu〈こうしゅ：絞首〉

　　kôshu-kei-ni　shoserareru（絞首刑に処せられる）　be　sentenced　to
　　　　death by hanging

　　kôshu-dai-ni noboru（絞首台に登る）　go to the gallows

kôshû〈こうしゅう：公衆〉the (general) public.

　　kôshû-benjo（公衆便所）　a public lavatory

　　kôshû-denwa（公衆電話）　a public telephone

　　kôshû-dôtoku（公衆道徳）　public morality

　　kôshû-eisei（公衆衛生）　public hygiene

　kôshû-no〈公衆の〉public, common.

kôshû〈こうしゅう：講習〉a short course, a class.

　　kaki-kôshû-kai（夏期講習会）　a summer course

kôshû〈こうしゅう：口臭〉(a) foul breath.

　　kôshû-ga-aru（口臭がある）　have (a) foul breath

kô-shûha〈こうしゅうは：高周波〉high frequency.

-koso〈-こそ〉the very, just, indeed.

　　kanojo-wa　toshi-koso-wakai　ga（彼女は年こそ若いが）　young　as　she
　　　　is

　　Kore-koso　watashi-ga　sagashiteita-mono-da.（これこそ私が捜していた
　　　　物だ。）　This is the very thing that I have been searching for.

Watashi-koso o-wabi-shi-nakereba-nari-masen.〔私こそおわびしなければ
ばなりません.〕 It is I, not you, that have to apologize.

kôso 〈こうそ：酵素〉ferment, enzym(e).

kôso 〈こうそ：控訴〉an appeal.
  kôso-suru 〈控訴する〉appeal ((to)) [a higher court].

kôsô 〈こうそう：構想〉(a) conception, an idea, a plan, a plot.
  kôsô o neru（構想を練る）work over one's plan

kôsô 〈こうそう：高層〉
  kôsô-kenchiku（高層建築）a multistory building
  kôsô-kiryû（高層気流）an upper air current

kôsô 〈こうそう：抗争〉a contention, (a) struggle.
  naibu-kôsô（内部抗争）an internal struggle

kôsô 〈こうそう：後送〉
  kôsô-suru 〈後送する〉send back.
  kôsô-sareru 〈後送される〉be sent back, be invalided home.

kôsô 〈こうそう：広壮〉
  kôsô-na 〈広壮な〉stately, magnificent.
  kôsô-na teitaku（広壮な邸宅）a magnificent residence

kosobai or **kosobayui** 〈こそばい，こそばゆい〉(be) ticklish.

koso-doro 〈こそどろ：こそ泥〉a sneak thief.
  koso-doro-o-hataraku 〈こそ泥を働く〉pilfer, sneak.

koso-koso 〈こそこそ〉*see.* kossori.
  koso-koso hanasu（こそこそ話す）talk in whispers

kosoku 〈こそく：こ息〉
  kosoku-na 〈こそくな〉temporizing, makeshift.
  kosoku-na shudan（こそくな手段）a makeshift

kôsoku 〈こうそく：校則〉school regulations.

kôsoku 〈こうそく：拘束〉(a) restriction, (a) restraint.
  kôsoku-ryoku（拘束力）binding force
  kôsoku-suru 〈拘束する〉restrict, restrain, bind.
  kôsoku-sare-nai 〈拘束されない〉free, unrestrained.

kôsoku 〈こうそく：高速〉a high-speed.
  kôsoku-dôro（高速道路）an expressway, a freeway, a motorway
  kôsoku-de（高速で）at high speed

kossetsu 〈こっせつ：骨折〉(a) fracture of a bone.
  tanjun-kossetsu（単純骨折）a simple fracture
  fukuzatsu-kossetsu（複雑骨折）a compound fracture
  kossetsu-suru 〈骨折する〉fracture.

kosshi〈こっし：骨子〉the main point(s), the substance, the essentials, the gist.

kossori〈こっそり〉secretly, stealthily.
kossori-hairu〈こっそり入る〉steal in.
kossori-deru（こっそり出る）slip off.

kosu〈こす：越(超)す〉pass, spend, exceed, be more than, be over, move.
toshi o kosu（年を越す）pass the old year
go-sen-nin-o-kosu shigan-sha（五千人を越す志願者）the applicants which exceeded five thousand in number
shinkyo-e-kosu（新居へ越す）move into a newly-built house
Sore-ni-koshita-koto-wa-nai.（それに越したことはない.）Nothing can be better than that.

kosu〈こす〉filter, strain, percolate.

kosû〈こすう：戸数〉the number of houses.

kosû〈こすう：個数〉the number (of articles).

kôsu〈コース〉a course, a lane.
dai-ichi-kôsu（第一コース）Lane No. 1
kôsu o toru（コースをとる）take a course

kosui〈こすい：湖水〉a lake.

kosui〈こすい〉cunning, sly, tricky, underhand.

kôsui〈こうすい：香水〉a perfume, a scent.
kôsui o tsukeru（香水を付ける）use perfume

kôsui〈こうすい：硬水〉hard water.

kosuru〈こする〉rub, scrub, scrape.

kosuto〈コスト〉cost.
seisan-kosuto（生産コスト）the cost of production
kosuto-daka（コスト高）an increase in cost

kotae〈こたえ：答え〉an answer, a reply.
kotaeru〈答える〉answer.
shitsumon ni kotaeru（質問に答える）answer a question

kotaeru〈こたえる〉
karada-ni-kotaeru〈体にこたえる〉tell on oneself.

kotai〈こたい：固体〉a solid (body).
kotai-nenryô（固体燃料）solid fuel
kotai-no〈固体の〉solid.

kôtai〈こうたい：交代(替)〉change, a shift.
kôtai-suru〈交代する〉take one's turn, take another's place, change.

kôtai-de 〈交代で〉by turns, in shifts.
  hachi-jikan-kôtai-de〈八時間交代で〉in eight-hour shifts

kôtai 〈こうたい：後退〉(a) retreat.
  keiki-kôtai〈景気後退〉(a) recession
  kôtai-suru〈後退する〉retreat, go back.

kô-taishi 〈こうたいし：皇太子〉the Crown Prince.
  kô-taishi-hi（皇太子妃）the Crown Princess

kôtaku 〈こうたく：光沢〉luster, a gloss, a polish.
  kôtaku-o-dasu〈光沢を出す〉polish, burnish, shine.
  kôtaku-no-aru〈光沢のある〉lustrous, glossy, polished.
  kôtaku-no-nai（光沢のない）lusterless

kôtan 〈こうたん：降誕〉birth, nativity.
  Kirisuto-kôtan-sai（キリスト降誕祭）Christmas

kotatsu 〈こたつ〉a fireplace with a coverlet, a portable foot warmer.

kotchi 〈こっち〉
  Mô-kotchi-no-mono-da.（もうこっちのものだ.）The game is ours.

kote 〈こて〉an iron, a curling iron, a trowel.

kote 〈こて：小手〉fencing gloves.

kotei 〈こてい：固定〉fixation.
  kotei-kannen（固定観念）a fixed idea
  kotei-suru〈固定する〉fix, be fixed, settle.

kô-tei 〈こうてい：高低〉undulations, rise and fall, pitch.
  kô-tei-no-aru〈高低のある〉undulating, uneven.
  kô-tei-no-nai（高低のない）even, level

kôtei 〈こうてい：皇帝〉an emperor.

kôtei 〈こうてい：工程〉a process of manufacture.

kôtei 〈こうてい：校庭〉a schoolyard.

kôtei 〈こうてい：行程〉(a) distance, a journey, a march.
  ichi-nichi-no kôtei（一日の行程）a day's journey

kôtei 〈こうてい：肯定〉affirmation.
  kôtei-suru〈肯定する〉affirm.
  kôtei-teki(-na)〈肯定的(な)〉affrmative.

kôtei 〈こうてい：公定〉
  kôtei-buai（公定歩合）the official rate
  kôtei-no〈公定の〉official, legal, fixed.

kôteki 〈こうてき：好適〉
  kôteki-na〈好適な〉suitable, good, fitted, ideal.

kôteki(-na) 〈こうてき(な)：公的(な)〉public, official.

kôteki-seikatsu〈公的生活〉 public life

kô-tekishu〈こうてきしゅ：好敵手〉a good rival, a worthy opponent.

koteki-tai〈こてきたい：鼓笛隊〉a drum and fife band.

koten〈こてん：古典〉classics.

koten-no or *koten-teki(-na)*〈古典の，古典的(な)〉classic, classical.

koten〈こてん：個展〉a private exhibition.

kôten〈こうてん：荒天〉stormy weather.

kôten〈こうてん：好転〉

kôten-suru〈好転する〉turn for the better, improve.

kô-tenki〈こうてんき：好天気〉fine weather.

kotenkoten〈こてんこてん〉

kotenkoten-ni yattsukeru（こてんこてんにやっつける） beat ((a person)) to a pulp

kotenkoten-ni makeru（こてんこてんに負ける） be beaten hollow

kôten-teki(-na)〈こうてんてき(な)：後天的(な)〉acquired.

kôten-teki-ni〈後天的に〉*a posteriori.*

kote-shirabe〈こてしらべ：小手調べ〉

hon-no kote-shirabe-ni（ほんの小手調べに）for a mere tryout.

kôtetsu〈こうてつ：鋼鉄〉steel.

kôtetsu-sei-no〈鋼鉄性の〉of steel.

kôtetsu〈こうてつ：更迭〉a change, a switch, a reshuffle.

kôtetsu-suru〈更迭する〉change, switch.

koto〈こと：琴〉a *koto*, a harp.

koto o hiku〈琴を弾く〉 play the *koto*

koto〈こと：事〉a thing, a matter, a fact, a question; circumstances, a case; an incident, an event, an occurrence; a business, a task, a duty.

suru-koto-ga-takusan-aru（する事がたくさんある） have many things to do

jûdai-na koto（重大な事）a serious matter

meihaku-na koto（明白な事）an obvious fact

donna-koto-ga-attemo（どんな事があっても） under any circumstances

koto-ni-yoru-to（事によると） as the case may be

koto-naku（事なく） without incident, uneventfully

koto-aru-goto-ni（事あるごとに） whenever occasion arises

O-mae-no-shitta-koto-ka.（お前の知った事か。） None of your business.

-koto〈-こと〉

    kitte o atsumeru-koto（切手を集めること） collecting stamps

    kanojo-no-iu-koto（彼女の言うこと） what she says

    shigoto o suru-koto（仕事をすること） to do business

    Gaikoku-go o kanzen-ni masutâ-suru-koto-wa muzukashii.（外国語を
完全にマスターすることは難しい.）It is difficult to master any
language completely.

kotô〈ことう：孤島〉an isolated island.

kôtô〈こうとう：高等〉

    kôtô-dôbutsu（高等動物） a higher animal

    kôtô-gakkô（高等学校） a senior high school

    kôtô-kyôiku（高等教育） (a) higher education

kôtô-no〈高等の〉high, higher, advanced, high-grade.

kôtô〈こうとう：口頭〉

    kôtô-shimon（口頭試問） an oral examination

kôtô-no〈口頭の〉oral.

kôtô-de〈口頭で〉orally.

kôtô〈こうとう：こう頭〉the larynx.

    kôtô-gan（こう頭がん） cancer of the larynx

kôtô〈こうとう：高騰〉a sudden rise, a jump.

kôtô-suru〈高騰する〉make a sudden rise, jump.

kôtô〈こうとう：好投〉nice pitching.

kôtô-suru〈好投する〉pitch well.

kotoba〈ことば：言葉〉language, speech, a word.

    kotoba-zukai-ni-ki-o-tsukeru（言葉遣いに気を付ける） be careful in
one's speech

    kotoba-de-ii-arawasu（言葉で言い表す） express...in words, put
((one's feelings)) into words

    kotoba-de-ii-arawase-nai（言葉で言い表せない） be beyond descrip-
tion

    kotoba-o-kaete-ieba（言葉を換えて言えば） in other words

    kotoba-takumi-ni（言葉巧みに） with honeyed words

    kotoba-sukunaku（言葉少なく） in a few words

kôtô-bu〈こうとうぶ：後頭部〉the back part of the head, the occipital
region.

-koto-ga-aru〈-ことがある〉have been to.

    -koto-ga-nai（-ことがない） have never been to

koto-gara〈ことがら：事柄〉a matter, an affair.

kotogotoku〈ことごとく〉*see.* subete.

kotogoto-ni 〈ことごとに：事ごとに〉in everything.

    kotogoto-ni shippai-suru（事ごとに失敗する）fail in everything

    kotogoto-ni hantai-suru（事ごとに反対する）oppose in every way

koto-kaku 〈ことかく：事欠く〉lack, want.

    shikin-ni-koto-kaku（資金に事欠く）lack for funds

    shikin-ni-koto-kaka-nai（資金に事欠かない）be free from want of funds

koto-nakare 〈ことなかれ：事なかれ〉

    koto-nakare-shugi（事なかれ主義）a peace-at-any-price principle, the principle of 'safety first', prudentialism

kotonaru 〈ことなる：異なる〉differ ((from)), be different ((from)), vary.

 kotonatta 〈異なった〉different, various.

koto-ni 〈ことに：殊に〉especially, particularly, exceptionally, above all.

koto-ni-suru 〈ことにする：異にする〉see. kotonaru.

koto-no-hoka 〈ことのほか：殊の外〉exceedingly, extremely, unusually, exceptionally, unexpectedly.

ko-tori 〈ことり：小鳥〉a little bird.

    ko-tori o kau（小鳥を飼う）keep a little bird

    ko-tori-ya（小鳥屋）a bird dealer, a bird shop

kotosara(-ni) 〈ことさら(に)：殊更(に)〉especially, particularly; intentionally, on purpose.

kotoshi 〈ことし：今年〉this year.

    kotoshi-no natsu（今年の夏）this summer

kotowari 〈ことわり：断り〉declining, (a) refusal; an excuse, an apology; a notice; permission, leave.

    kotowari-jô（断り状）a letter of apology

 kotowari mo-naku 〈断りもなく〉without notice, without leave.

kotowaru 〈ことわる：断る〉decline, refuse; excuse oneself ((from)), apologize ((to)); give ((a person)) notice, warn, ask leave.

    shôtai o kotowaru（招待を断る）decline an invitation

    môshi-de o kotowaru（申し出を断る）refuse one's offer

    mae-motte kotowaru（前もって断る）give ((a person)) previous notice

kotowaza 〈ことわざ〉a proverb.

    kotowaza-ni-mo-aru-yô-ni（ことわざにもあるように）as the proverb says

koto-zuke 〈ことづけ：言付け〉a message.

 kotozukeru 〈言付ける〉send a message.

kotsu〈こつ〉a knack, secret, know-how.

    kotsu o shitte-iru（こつを知っている）know the ropes

kôtsū〈こうつう：交通〉traffic, communication, transportation.

    kôtsû no ben（交通の便）facilities of communication

        kôtsû-no-ben-o-hakaru（交通の便を図る）facilitate transportation

    kôtsû-seiri-o-suru（交通整理をする）control traffic

    kôtsû-ihan（交通違反）violation of traffic regulations

    kôtsû-jiko（交通事故）a traffic accident

    kôtsû-junsa（交通巡査）a traffic policeman

    kôtsû-kikan（交通機関）a means of transportation

    kôtsû-kisoku（交通規則）traffic regulations

    kôtsû-shingô（交通信号）a traffic signal

    kôtsû-hi（交通費）carfare

    Kôtsû-ryô ga ooi.（交通量が多い.）Traffic is heavy.

kotsuban〈こつばん：骨盤〉the pelvis.

ko-tsubu〈こつぶ：小粒〉a small grain.

    ko-tsubu-no〈小粒の〉fine.

kô-tsugô〈こうつごう：好都合〉

    kô-tsugô-na〈好都合な〉favorable, convenient, fortunate, satisfactory.

    kô-tsugô-ni〈好都合に〉well, favorably, conveniently, satisfactorily, smoothly, successfully.

kotsukotsu〈こつこつ〉untiringly; a tap, a rap.

    kotsukotsu benkyô-suru（こつこつ勉強する）study untiringly

    kotsukotsu-to-o-tataku（こつこつ戸をたたく）tap at the door

kotsu-maku〈こつまく：骨膜〉the periosteum.

    kotsu-maku-en（骨膜炎）periostitis

kotsun〈こつん〉

    kotsun-to〈こつんと〉with a bump.

    atama o kotsun-to-butsukeru（頭をこつんとぶつける）bump one's head ((against))

    atama-o-kotsun-to-tataku（頭をこつんとたたく）rap ((a person)) on the head

kotsu-niku〈こつにく：骨肉〉

    kotsu-niku-no arasoi（骨肉の争い）domestic feud

kotsuzui〈こつずい：骨髄〉the marrow.

    urami-kotsuzui-ni-tessuru（恨み骨髄に徹する）bear ((a person)) a deep grudge

    kotsuzui-en（骨髄炎）osteomyelitis

kotta 〈こった：凝った〉elaborate, fancy.
    kotta kazari-tsuke（凝った飾り付け）elaborate decorations
kotteri(-to) 〈こってり（と）〉thickly, heavily.
  kotteri-shita 〈こってりした〉thick, heavy, rich.
    kotteri-shita aji（こってりした味）rich taste
kottô(-hin) 〈こっとう（ひん）：骨とう（品）〉a curio, an antique.
    kottô-shûshû-ka（骨とう収集家）a virtuoso
    kottô-ya（骨とう屋）a curio dealer, a curio shop
kou 〈こう：請う〉ask, request, beg.
    enjo-o-kou（援助を請う）ask for ((a person's)) assistance
    shusseki o kou（出席を請う）request ((a person)) to attend
kôu 〈こうう：降雨〉a rainfall.
    (kô-)u-ki（（降)雨季）the rainy season
    kôu-ryô（降雨量）the amount of rainfall, precipitation.
ko-uma 〈こうま：小馬〉a pony.
kôun 〈こううん：幸運〉good fortune, (good) luck.
    Kôun o inorimasu.（幸運を祈ります。）I wish you good luck.
  kôun-na 〈幸運な〉fortunate, lucky.
  kôun-ni-mo 〈幸運にも〉fortunately, luckily.
kôun-ki 〈こううんき：耕うん機〉a cultivator.
ko-uri 〈こうり：小売り〉retail sale.
    kouri-shô（小売商）a retail dealer, a retailer; a retail store
  ko-uri-suru 〈小売りする〉retail.
ko-ushi 〈こうし：子牛〉a calf.
ko-uta 〈こうた：小唄(歌)〉a kouta song, a little song, a ditty.
kôwa 〈こうわ：講和〉peace, reconciliation.
    kôwa-kaigi（講和会議）a peace conference
    kôwa-jôyaku（講和条約）a peace treaty
    tandoku-kôwa（単独講和）a separate peace
  kôwa-suru 〈講和する〉make peace ((with)).
kowabaru 〈こわばる：こわ張る〉become stiff, stiffen.
  kowabatta 〈こわばった〉stiff, hard.
    kowabatta kao-tsuki-de（こわばった顔つきで）with a stiffened look
kowagaru 〈こわがる：怖がる〉fear, be afraid ((of)).
    Nani-mo kowagaru-koto-wa-nai.（何も怖がることはない。）You have
      nothing to fear.
  kowagarasu 〈怖がらす〉frighten, scare.
kowagowa 〈こわごわ：怖々〉timidly, with fear.

kowai 〈こわい：怖い〉 fearful, dreadful, terrible, horrible; be afraid ((of)).
 kowai hanashi（怖い話）a dreadful story
 kowai-me-ni-au（怖い目に遭う）have a dreadful experience
 hebi-ga-kowai（蛇が怖い）be afraid of snakes
kowaku-naru〈怖くなる〉get frightened ((at)).
 〜*-ga-kowakute*〈〜が怖くて〉for fear of... .

kowai 〈こわい〉 tough, hard, stiff.
 kowai kami-no-ke（こわい髪の毛）wiry hair

kowa-iro 〈こわいろ：声色〉
kowa-iro-o-tsukau〈声色を使う〉imitate the voice of ((someone)), take off another's voice.

kôwan 〈こうわん：港湾〉 harbors.
 kôwan-shisetsu（こうわんしせつ：港湾施設）harbor facilities

koware-mono 〈こわれもの：壊れ物〉a fragile article.
 Koware-mono, chûi.（壊れ物, 注意.）Fragile—Handle with Care.

kowareru 〈こわれる：壊れる〉break, be broken, be damaged, get out of order.
koware-yasui〈壊れやすい〉easy to break, fragile, brittle.
kowareta〈壊れた〉broken.

kowasu 〈こわす：壊す〉break, destroy, smash; pull down; injure.
 kona-gona-ni kowasu（粉々に壊す）smash to bits
 ie o kowasu（家を壊す）pull down a house
 karada o kowasu（体をこわす）injure one's health

koya 〈こや：小屋〉a hut, a cottage.
 yama-goya（山小屋）a mountain cottage

kôya 〈こうや：荒野〉a wilderness, a wasteland, a desert land.

ko-yagi 〈こやぎ：子やぎ〉a kid.

ko-yaku 〈こやく：子役〉a child's part; a child actor, a child actress.

kôyaku 〈こうやく：公約〉a public pledge.
 kôyaku o hatasu（公約を果たす）carry out one's campaign pledges
kôyaku-suru〈公約する〉pledge oneself publicly.

kôyaku 〈こうやく：こう薬〉a plaster, a salve, (an) ointment.

kô-yakusû 〈こうやくすう：公約数〉a common measure.
 saidai-kô-yakusû（最大公約数）the greatest common measure

ko-yama 〈こやま：小山〉a hill, a hillock, a mound.

ko-yami 〈こやみ：小やみ〉a lull, a break.
ko-yami-ni-naru〈小やみになる〉abate.

koyasu 〈こやす：肥やす〉manure, fertilize, enrich.

koyô〈こよう：雇用〉engagement, employment, hire.

  koyô-keiyaku（雇用契約） a contract of employment

  kanzen-koyô〈完全雇用〉full employment

  koyô-suru〈雇用する〉engage, employ, hire.

kôyô〈こうよう：効用〉use, utility, (an) effect.

  kôyô-no-aru〈効用のある〉useful, of use, effective.

  kôyô-no-nai〈効用のない〉 of no use

kôyô〈こうよう：公用〉official business.

  kôyô-de〈公用で〉 on official business

kôyô〈こうよう：紅葉〉red leaves.

  kôyô-suru〈紅葉する〉turn red.

kôyô-ju〈こうようじゅ：広葉樹〉a broadleaf tree.

koyomi〈こよみ：暦〉a calendar, an almanac.

  koyomi-no-ue-dewa〈暦の上では〉according to the calendar.

koyori〈こより〉a paper string.

  koyori-o-yoru〈こよりをよる〉twist paper into a string.

koyû〈こゆう：固有〉

  koyû-meishi（固有名詞） a proper noun

  koyû-no〈固有の〉peculiar ((to)), proper ((to)).

  Nihon-koyû-no shûkan（日本固有の習慣） customs peculiar to Japan

kôyû〈こうゆう：校友〉a schoolfellow, a schoolmate, an alumnus, an alumna.

  kôyû-kai〈校友会〉 an alumni association

kôyû〈こうゆう：公有〉

  kôyû-chi〈公有地〉 public land

  kôyû-no〈公有の〉public, public(ly)-owned.

ko-yubi〈こゆび：小指〉a little finger, a little toe.

kôyû-kankei〈こうゆうかんけい：交友関係〉one's company, one's associates.

  kôyû-kankei o shiraberu（交友関係を調べる） check up one's associates

ko-yuki〈こゆき：小雪〉a light snow.

kôza〈こうざ：講座〉a course.

  rajio-Eigo-kôza（ラジオ英語講座） a radio English course

kôza〈こうざ：口座〉an account.

  kôza o hiraku（口座を開く） open an account ((with))

kôza〈こうざ：高座〉the stage.

  kôza-ni noboru（高座に上る） go on the stage

kôzai〈こうざい：功罪〉merits and demerits.

kôzai〈こうざい：鋼材〉steel (materials).

ko-zaiku〈こざいく：小細工〉

ko-zaiku-o-yaru〈小細工をやる〉resort to petty tricks.

ko-zakana〈こざかな：小魚〉small fish.

ko-zakashii〈こざかしい：小ざかしい〉smartish, shrewd.

kôzan〈こうざん：高山〉a high mountain.

　　kôzan-byô〈高山病〉mountain sickness

　　kôzan-shokubutsu〈高山植物〉an alpine plant

kôzan〈こうざん：鉱山〉a mine.

ko-zappari〈こざっぱり：小ざっぱり〉

ko-zappari-shita〈小ざっぱりした〉neat and clean, tidy.

　　ko-zappari-shita-fukusô-o-shite-iru（小ざっぱりした服装をしている）
　　be neatly dressed

kôzen〈こうぜん：公然〉

kôzen-no〈公然の〉open, public, official.

　　kozen-no himitsu（公然の秘密）an open secret

kôzen-to〈公然と〉openly, in public, officially.

ko-zeni〈こぜに：小銭〉small money, change.

ko-zeriai〈こぜりあい：小競り合い〉a skirmish, a brush; a petty quarrel.

kôzô〈こうぞう：構造〉structure, (a) construction, organization.

kôzô-jô〈構造上〉structurally.

kôzoku〈こうぞく：皇族〉royalty, a member of the Imperial family.

kôzoku〈こうぞく：航続〉

　　kôzoku-kyori〈航続距離〉a cruising(*or* flying) range

　　kôzoku-ryoku〈航続力〉a cruising(*or* flying) capacity

kôzoku〈こうぞく：後続〉

kôzoku-no〈後続の〉following, succeeding.

kozotte〈こぞって〉all, one and all, in a body, as a unit, with one accord, unanimously.

　　kozotte hantai-suru（こぞって反対する）oppose as a unit

kôzu〈こうず：構図〉composition.

kôzu-ga-ii〈構図がいい〉be well composed(designed *or* planned).

kozue〈こずえ〉a treetop.

kôzui〈こうずい：洪水〉a flood, an inundation.

　　dai-kôzui（大洪水）a disastrous flood

kôzui-ni-au〈洪水に遭う〉suffer from a flood, be flooded, be inundated.

kôzu-ka〈こうずか：好事家〉a dilettante.

ko-zukai 〈こづかい：小遣い〉 pocket money.

ko-zuku 〈こづく：小突く〉 poke, thrust, push.

   kozuki-mawasu〈小突き回す〉 shake ((a person)) by, push ((a person)) around.

ko-zutsumi 〈こづつみ：小包〉 a parcel, a package.

   kozutsumi(-bin)-de（小包(便)で）by parcel post

ku 〈く：九〉 nine.

   dai-ku（第九） the ninth

ku 〈く：句〉 a phrase.

ku 〈く：区〉 a ward, a district, a division, a section.

   ku-yakusho（区役所） a ward office

   yûbin-ku（郵便区） a postal district

ku 〈く：苦〉 (a) pain, anxiety, worry; difficulty.

  ku-ni-suru〈苦にする〉 worry (oneself) ((about)).

  ku-mo-naku〈苦もなく〉 without difficulty, with ease.

kûbaku 〈くうばく：空爆〉 an air blow, an air raid.

kubaru 〈くばる：配る〉 distribute, deliver, deal.

   bira o kubaru（ビラを配る） distribute handbills

kuberu 〈くべる〉 put ((fuel)) on the fire, put ((paper)) into the fire, burn.

kubetsu 〈くべつ：区別〉 distinction, difference.

  kubetsu-suru〈区別する〉 distinguish ((between A and B)).

kubi 〈くび：首〉 a neck, a head.

   kubi-o-tate-ni-furu（首を縦に振る） nod assent

   kubi-o-yoko-ni-furu（首を横に振る） shake one's head

   kubi-o-kukuru *or* kubi-o-tsuru（首をくくる，首をつる） hang oneself

   kubi-ni-suru（首にする） dismiss, fire

   kudi-ni-naru（首になる） be dismissed, be fired

kubi-jikken 〈くびじっけん：首実検〉 identification.

  kubi-jikken-o-suru〈首実検をする〉 identify (a suspect).

kubippiki 〈くびっぴき：首っ引き〉

  jisho-to-kubippiki-de〈辞書と首っ引きで〉 frequently referring to a dictionary.

kubire 〈くびれ〉 a constricted part, a compression.

   hyôtan no kubire（ひょうたんのくびれ） the narrow part of a gourd

  kubireru〈くびれる〉 be constricted, be compressed.

kubi-suji 〈くびすじ：首筋〉 the scruff of the neck.

kubittake 〈くびったけ：首っ丈〉

   kubittake-de-aru（首ったけである） be deeply in love ((with))

kubittake-ni-naru（首ったけになる）　fall headlong in love ((with))

kubi-wa〈首輪〉a collar.

inu-ni kubi-wa o tsukeru（犬に首輪を付ける）　put a collar on a dog

kubomi〈くぼみ〉a hollow.

kubomu〈くぼむ〉become hollow.

kubonda〈くぼんだ〉hollow, sunken.

me-no-kubonda hito（目のくぼんだ人）　a hollow-eyed person

kubu〈くぶ：九分〉nine parts.

kubu-doori（九分どおり）　almost, nearly

kubu-kurin（九分九厘）　ten to one, in all probability

kubun〈くぶん：区分〉division, classification.

kubun-suru〈区分する〉divide ((into)), classify.

kûbun〈くうぶん：空文〉a dead letter, a scrap of paper.

kuchi〈くち：口〉a mouth, tongue, speech; work, a job, a post, a position.

kuchi-ga-karui（口が軽い）　be talkative

kuchi-ga-omoi（口が重い）　be slow of speech

kuchi-ga-umai（口がうまい）　be fair-spoken

kuchi-ga-warui（口が悪い）　have a sharp tongue

kuchi-ga-kusai（口が臭い）　have (a) bad breath

kuchi-ga-koete-iru（口が肥えている）　be fastidious about one's food

kuchi-ni-au（口に合う）　suit one's taste

kuchi-ni-dasu *or* kuchi-o-dasu（口に出す，口を出す）　put into words

kuchi-ni-dasa-nai（口に出さない）　do not say

kuchi-ni-suru（口にする）　speak ((of)), talk ((of)); take, have

kuchi o akeru（口を開ける）　open one's mouth

kuchi-o-kiku（口をきく）　speak ((to *or* with)), talk ((to *or* with))

kuchi-kara kuchi-e tsutawaru（口から口へ伝わる）　pass from mouth to mouth

ookina-kuchi-o-kiku（大きな口をきく）　talk big

kuchi-o-sagasu（口を探す）　look for a job

kuchi-o-soroete（口をそろえて）　in chorus

kuchi-ippai（口いっぱい）　a mouthful

hito-kuchi-ni（一口に）　at a gulp

kuchi-atari〈くちあたり：口当たり〉

kuchi-atari-ga-ii〈口当たりがいい〉be pleasant to the taste, taste good.

kuchi-atari-ga-warui（口当たりが悪い）　be unpleasant to the taste, taste bad

kuchibashi〈くちばし〉a bill, a beak.

kuchi-bashiru〈くちばしる：口走る〉
 wake-no-wakara-nai koto o kuchi-bashiru〈訳の分からないことを口走る〉
  utter a lot of incoherent things.

kuchi-beni〈くちべに：口紅〉rouge, a lipstick.
   kuchi-beni o tsukeru（口紅を付ける） put on lipstick

kuchi-beta〈くちべた：口下手〉a poor talker.

kuchi-bi〈くちび：口火〉
 kuchi-bi-o-kiru〈口火を切る〉trigger, touch off.

kuchibiru〈くちびる：唇〉a lip.
   uwa-kuchibiru（上唇） the upper lip
   shita-kuchibiru（下唇） the lower lip

kuchi-bue〈くちぶえ：口笛〉a whistle.
 kuchi-bue-o-fuku〈口笛を吹く〉whistle.

kuchi-buri〈くちぶり：口振り〉
 kimi-no-kuchi-buri-dewa〈君の口振りでは〉by the way you talk... .

kuchi-dashi〈くちだし：口出し〉
 yokei-na-kuchi-dashi-o-suru〈余計な口出しをする〉poke one's nose
  ((into)).

kuchi-dome〈くちどめ：口止め〉
   kuchi-dome-ryô（口止め料） hush money
 kuchi-dome-suru〈口止めする〉muzzle.

kuchi-e〈くちえ：口絵〉a frontispiece.

kuchi-genka〈くちげんか：口げんか〉a (wordy) brawl.

kuchi-gitanai〈くちぎたない：口汚い〉foulmouthed, abusive.
 kuchi-gitanaku〈口汚く〉abusively.
   kuchi-gitanaku-nonoshiru（口汚くののしる） abuse ((a person))

kuchi-gomoru〈くちごもる：口ごもる〉mumble, falter.

kuchi-gotae〈くちごたえ：口答え〉a retort.
 kuchi-gotae-suru〈口答えする〉answer back, talk back, retort.

kuchiguchi〈くちぐち：口々〉
 kuchiguchi-ni〈口々に〉severally, unanimously.

kuchi-guruma〈くちぐるま：口車〉
 kuchi-guruma-ni-noru〈口車に乗る〉be taken in by ((a person's))
  honeyed words.

kuchi-guse〈くちぐせ：口癖〉one's favorite phrase.
 kuchi-guse-no-yô-ni-iu〈口癖のように言う〉always say, be never tired of
  saying.

kuchi-hige 〈くちひげ：口ひげ〉a moustache.

kuchi-himo 〈くちひも：口ひも〉a drawstring.

kuchi-kazu 〈くちかず：口数〉
　kuchi-kazu-no-ooi 〈口数の多い〉talkative.
　　kuchi-kazu-no-sukunai (口数の少ない)　silent

kuchi-kiki 〈くちきき：口利き〉
　～-*no-kuchi-kiki-de* 〈～の口利きで〉through the good offices of... .

kuchiku 〈くちく：駆逐〉
　　kuchiku-kan (駆逐艦)　a destroyer
　kuchiku-suru 〈駆逐する〉expel, drive away.

kuchi-mane 〈くちまね：口まね〉
　kuchi-mane-o-suru 〈口まねをする〉mimic another's way of speaking.

kuchi-moto 〈くちもと：口元〉the mouth, shape of the mouth.
　　kuchi-moto-ga-kawaii (口元がかわいい)　have a lovely mouth
　　kuchi-moto-ni-bishô-o-ukabete (口元に微笑を浮かべて)　with a smile
　　　playing about one's lips

kuchi-naoshi 〈くちなおし：口直し〉
　kuchi-naoshi-ni 〈口直しに〉to take the bad taste out of one's mouth.

kuchiru 〈くちる：朽ちる〉rot, decay, molder.
　kuchita 〈朽ちた〉rotten, decayed.
　kuchi-kaketa 〈朽ちかけた〉crumbling, moldering.

kuchi-saga-nai 〈くちさがない：口さがない〉gossipy, scandal-loving.

kuchi-saki 〈くちさき：口先〉
　kuchi-saki-dake-no 〈口先だけの〉specious.
　　kuchi-saki-dake-no-oseji (口先だけのお世辞)　lip service
　kuchi-saki-no-umai 〈口先のうまい〉honey-tongued.

kuchi-yakamashi 〈くちやかましい：口やかましい〉nagging, censorious,
　particular.
　　kuchi-yakamashii oku-san (口やかましい奥さん)　one's nagging wife

kuchi-yakusoku 〈くちやくそく：口約束〉a verbal promise.
　kuchi-yakusoku-suru 〈口約束する〉promise by word of mouth.

kuchi-zoe 〈くちぞえ：口添え〉recommendation, good offices.
　kuchi-zoe-suru 〈口添えする〉recommend, put in a good word ((on behalf
　of)).

kuchi-zusamu 〈くちずさむ：口ずさむ〉hum.

kuchi-zutae 〈くちづたえ：口伝え〉an oral tradition.
　　kuchi-zutae-ni (口伝えに)　by oral tradition

kuchô 〈くちょう：口調〉a tone, a turn of expression.

hageshii kuchô-de〈激しい口調で〉in a sharp tone.

kûchû〈くうちゅう：空中〉the air, the sky.

　　kûchû-bunkai-suru〈空中分解する〉fall apart in midair.

　　kûchû-no〈空中の〉in the air, aerial.

　　kûchû-de or *kûchû-ni*〈空中で，空中に〉in the air, in the sky.

kuda〈くだ：管〉a pipe, a tube.

kudakeru〈くだける：砕ける〉break, be broken, be crushed, be smashed.

　　konamijin-ni kudakeru〈粉みじんに砕ける〉be crushed to pieces

　　kudaku〈砕く〉break (into pieces), crush, smash, shatter.

kudaketa〈くだけた：砕けた〉easy, plain, simple, familiar, friendly.

　　kudaketa taido-de〈砕けた態度で〉in an easy manner

　　kudaketa setsumei〈砕けた説明〉a plain explanation

kudamono〈くだもの：果物〉(a) fruit.

　　kudamono-ya〈果物屋〉a fruiterer, a fruit store

kudaranai〈くだらない〉*see.* tsumaranai.

kudari〈くだり：下り〉a descent, going down.

　　kudari-zaka〈下り坂〉a downward slope, a descent

　　kudari-ressha〈下り列車〉a down train

kudaru〈くだる：下る〉go down, descend; be less than.

　　kawa o kudaru〈川を下る〉go down a river

　　Fushô-sha-wa-sambyaku-nin-o-kudara-nai.〈負傷者は三百人を下らない。〉No less than 300 were injured.

-kudasai〈-ください：-下さい〉please; Will you...?, Would you...?

　　Kono mado o akete-kudasai.〈この窓を開けてください。〉Please open this window.

　　Kono mado o akete-kudasai-masen-ka?〈この窓を開けてくださいませんか。〉Will you please open this window?

kudasu〈くだす：下す〉

　　hanketsu o kudasu〈判決を下す〉pass judgment ((on))

　　ketsuron o kudasu〈結論を下す〉draw a conclusion

　　meirei o kudasu〈命令を下す〉give a command, issue orders

　　hara-o-kudasu〈腹を下す〉have loose bowels

kûdetâ〈クーデター〉a coup d'état.

kûdô〈くうどう：空洞〉a cave, a cavern, a cavity; a vomica.

kudoi〈くどい〉tedious, wordy, lengthy, finical, long-winded, importunate.

　　kudoi setsumei〈くどい説明〉a long-winded explanation

kudoku〈くどく〉tediously, repeatedly, importunately.

kudoku-iu or *kudokudo-to-iu*〈くどく言う，くどくどと言う〉talk tediously, dwell ((on)), harp on the same string.

kudoku〈くどく：功徳〉charity, a pious act, an act of merit.

kudoku o hodokosu（功徳を施す）do an act of charity

kudoku-no-tame〈功徳のため〉for charity's sake.

kudoku〈くどく：口説く〉persuade; make love ((to)), make a pass ((at)).

kudoki-otosu〈口説き落とす〉talk ((a person)) around, win ((a person)) to consent; woo and win a woman.

kue-nai〈くえない：食えない〉not good to eat, inedible; be unable to get along; shrewd, crafty, sly.

kue-nai yatsu（食えないやつ）a crafty fellow

kufû〈くふう：工夫〉a device, a plan, a means.

kufû-suru〈工夫する〉devise, plan, think out.

kûfuku〈くうふく：空腹〉hunger.

kûfuku-o-kanjiru〈空腹を感じる〉feel hungry.

kûfuku-na〈空腹な〉hungry.

kugatsu〈くがつ：九月〉September.

kuge〈くげ：公家〉a court noble.

kugen〈くげん：苦言〉

kugen-o-teisuru〈苦言を呈する〉give ((a person)) bitter but candid advice.

kugi〈くぎ〉a nail.

kugi o utsu（くぎを打つ）drive a nail

kugi o nuku（くぎを抜く）pull out a nail

kugi-nuki（くぎ抜き）a nail puller

kugiri〈くぎり：区切り〉punctuation; a pause, an end.

kugiri-o-tsukeru〈区切りを付ける〉punctuate; put an end ((to)).

shigoto ni kugiri-o tsukeru（仕事に区切りを付ける）put an end to one's work.

kugiru〈くぎる：区切る〉punctuate; cut off, mark off.

kugi-zuke〈くぎづけ：くぎ付け〉

kugi-zuke-ni-suru（くぎ付けにする）nail up, fasten with nails

sono ba-ni kugi-zuke-ni-naru（その場にくぎ付けになる）stand transfixed to the spot

kûgun〈くうぐん：空軍〉an air force.

kûgun-kichi（空軍基地）an air base

kuguri-do〈くぐりど：くぐり戸〉a side door(*or* gate).

kuguru 〈くぐる〉 pass through, go through.
  tonneru o kuguru（トンネルをくぐる） pass through a tunnel

kuhai 〈くはい：苦杯〉
 kuhai-o-kissuru〈苦杯を喫する〉drink a bitter cup, suffer a defeat.

kûhaku 〈くうはく：空白〉blank space, a vacuum.
  seiji-no kûhaku（政治の空白） a political vacuum

kûhi 〈くうひ：空費〉
 kûhi-suru〈空費する〉waste, idle away.

kûhô 〈くうほう：空砲〉
 kûhô o utsu〈空砲を撃つ〉fire a blank shot.

kui 〈くい〉a stake, a post.
  kui o utsu（くいを打つ） drive (in) a stake

kui 〈くい：悔い〉regret, repentance.
  kui o nokosu（悔いを残す） leave some repentance behind

kûi 〈くうい：空位〉a vacant post.

kui-arasu 〈くいあらす：食い荒らす〉eat up and spoil.

kui-aratameru 〈くいあらためる：悔い改める〉repent ((of)), reform one-self.

kui-chigai 〈くいちがい：食い違い〉(a) discrepancy, (a) difference.
  iken no kui-chigai（意見の食い違い） a difference of opinion
 kui-chigau〈食い違う〉differ ((from *or* with)), go wrong.

kui-chigiru 〈くいちぎる：食いちぎる〉bite off, tear off with one's teeth.

kui-chirasu 〈くいちらす：食い散らす〉*see.* kui-arasu.

kui-dôraku 〈くいどうらく：食い道楽〉epicurism; an epicure.

kui-hagureru 〈くいはぐれる：食いはぐれる〉miss a meal.

kui-iji 〈くいいじ：食い意地〉
 kui-iji-no-hatta〈食い意地の張った〉greedy, gluttonous.

kui-iru 〈くいいる：食い入る〉
 kui-iru-yô-ni-mi-tsumeru〈食い入るように見詰める〉stare into〔another's face〕.

kui-ke 〈くいけ：食い気〉appetite.
  kui-ke-zakari-no wakamono-tachi（食い気盛りの若者たち） young men with a hearty appetite

kuiki 〈くいき：区域〉the limits, a zone, an area, a district.
  〜-no-kuiki-nai-de（〜の区域内で） within the limits of...
  kiken-kuiki（危険区域） a danger zone

kui-komu 〈くいこむ：食い込む〉cut ((into)), encroach ((upon)), make an inroad ((into *or* on)).

kata-ni-kui-komu（肩に食い込む）cut into the flesh of one's shoulders

hantai-ha-no senkyo-ku-jiban-ni-kui-komu（反対派の選挙区地盤に食い込む）encroach upon one's antagonist's constituency

hiru-yasumi-ni-kui-komu（昼休みに食い込む）make inroads upon the lunch break

kui-mono〈くいもの：食い物〉food, provisions; a victim, a prey.

kui-mono-ni-suru〈食い物にする〉live on, prey on.

kui-nige〈くいにげ：食い逃げ〉

kui-nige-suru〈食い逃げする〉bilk.

kuiru〈くいる：悔いる〉*see.* kôkai-suru.

kui-sagaru〈くいさがる：食い下がる〉

shitsumon-shite-kui-sagaru〈質問して食い下がる〉repeat questions harassingly.

kui-shibaru〈くいしばる：食いしばる〉

ha o kui-shibaru〈歯を食いしばる〉clench〔one's teeth〕.

kui-shimbô〈くいしんぼう：食いしんぼう〉a glutton.

kui-shimbô-na〈食いしんぼうな〉greedy, gluttonous.

kui-sugi〈くいすぎ：食い過ぎ〉*see.* tabe-sugi.

kui-tari-nai〈くいたりない：食い足りない〉have not eaten enough; be unsatisfied, be unsatisfactory.

kui-tomeru〈くいとめる：食い止める〉check, hold in check, prevent, stop.

ruishô o kui-tomeru（類焼を食い止める）check the spread of a fire

bukka no jôshô o kui-tomeru（物価の上昇を食い止める）stop the rise of prices

kui-tsubusu〈くいつぶす：食いつぶす〉eat ((oneself)) out of house and home.

kui-tsuku〈くいつく：食い付く〉bite ((at)), snap (at).

kui-tsuite-hanare-nai〈食い付いて離れない〉stick like a leech.

kui-tsukusu〈くいつくす：食い尽くす〉eat up, run through, consume.

kui-tsumeru〈くいつめる：食い詰める〉become unable to earn one's livelihood, be down and out.

kuizu〈クイズ〉a quiz.

kuizu-bangumi（クイズ番組）a quiz program

kujaku〈くじゃく〉a peacock, a peahen.

kuji〈くじ〉a lot, a lottery.

kuji o hiku（くじを引く）draw lots

kuji ni ataru（くじに当たる） draw a prize

kuji-biki（くじ引き） drawing lots

kujikeru〈くじける〉be discouraged, lose courage.

kujiku〈くじく〉sprain; crush, break.

kurubushi o kujiku（くるぶしをくじく） sprain one's ankle

tsuyoki o kujiki yowaki-o-tasukeru（強きをくじき弱きを助ける）
crush the stronger and side with the weaker

kujira〈くじら：鯨〉a whale.

kujo〈くじょ：駆除〉

kujo-suru〈駆除する〉get rid ((of)), exterminate.

kujô〈くじょう：苦情〉a complaint.

kujô-o-iu〈苦情を言う〉make a complaint, complain ((of)).

kukai〈くかい：句会〉a haiku gathering.

kukaku〈くかく：区画〉(a) division, a section, a block, a lot〔of land〕.

kukaku-seiri（区画整理） readjustment of (town) lots

kukaku-suru〈区画する〉divide, partition, draw a line ((between)), mark off.

kukan〈くかん：区間〉the section.

kûkan〈くうかん：空間〉space, the infinite.

kukei〈くけい：く形〉a rectangle.

kukeru〈くける〉blindstitch.

kuki〈くき：茎〉a stalk, a stem.

kûki〈くうき：空気〉air; atmosphere.

shinsen-na-kûki（新鮮な空気） fresh air

yogoreta kûki（汚れた空気） foul air

kinchô-shita kûki（緊張した空気） a tense atmosphere

kûki-jû（空気銃） an air gun

kûki-o-suu〈空気を吸う〉breathe.

kûki-o-ire-kaeru〈空気を入れ替える〉air out.

kûki-no-nuketa〈空気の抜けた〉flat.

kukkiri(-to)〈くっきり(と)〉clearly, distinctly.

kukkyô〈くっきょう：屈強〉

kukkyô-na〈屈強な〉strong, sturdy, muscular, powerfully-built.

kukkyoku〈くっきょく：屈曲〉

kukkyoku-suru〈屈曲する〉be crooked, bend, wind, be indented.

kukkyoku-shita〈屈曲した〉crooked, winding, indented, zigzagging.

kûkô〈くうこう：空港〉an airport.

kuku〈くく：九々〉the multiplication table.

kukuru〈くくる〉bind, bundle, tie up, fasten.

kukyō〈くきょう：苦境〉adverse circumstances, difficulties, straits, a fix.

    kukyô-ni-tatsu（苦境に立つ）be in difficulties, find oneself in a fix

kūkyo〈くうきょ：空虚〉

    kûkyo-na〈空虚な〉empty, vacant, hollow, gassy.

    kôkyo-na seikatsu（空虚な生活）a hollow life

kuma〈くま〉a bear.

kuma〈くま〉

    kuma-naku〈くまなく〉all over, everywhere, thoroughly.

    kuma-naku-sagasu（くまなく捜す）comb ((a place)) for ((something))

kuma-bachi〈くまばち〉a hornet.

kuma-de〈くまで：くま手〉a rake.

    kuma-de-de-kaku〈くま手でかく〉rake.

kumen〈くめん：工面〉

    kumen-suru〈工面する〉manage, contrive, make (a) shift, make a raise.

kumi〈くみ：組〉a class; a party, a group, a team; a set, a pair, a pack.

    Ei-kaiwa-no-kumi（英会話の組）an English conversation class

    go-nin-zutsu kumi-ni-natte（五人ずつ組になって）in groups of five

    cha-ki hito-kumi（茶器一組）a tea set

    karuta hito-kumi（カルタ一組）a pack of cards

kumi-ageru〈くみあげる：くみ上げる〉draw up, scoop up, pump up.

kumiai〈くみあい：組合〉an association, a partnership, a union.

    rôdô-kumiai（労働組合）a labor union, a trade union

kumi-awase〈くみあわせ：組み合わせ〉(a) combination, (an) assortment, matching.

    kumi-awaseru〈組み合わせる〉combine, assort, match ((A against B)).

kumi-dasu〈くみだす：くみ出す〉dip out, ladle out, pump out.

kumi-fuseru〈くみふせる：組み伏せる〉hold ((a person)) down.

kumi-himo〈くみひも：組みひも〉a braid, a plaited cord.

kumi-kae〈くみかえ：組み替え〉rearrangement.

    kumi-kaeru〈組み替える〉rearrange.

kumi-kawasu〈くみかわす：酌み交わす〉drink ((sake)) together ((with)).

kumi-kyoku〈くみきょく：組曲〉a suite.

kumi-suru〈くみする〉take part ((in)), participate ((in)), join, side ((with)).

    dochira-ni-mo-kumi-shi-nai〈どちらにも組しない〉maintain neutrality.

kumi-tate〈くみたて：組み立て〉construction, assembly.

kumi-tate-kôjô〈組み立て工場〉 an assembly factory

kumi-tateru〈組み立てる〉construct, put together, assemble.

jidô-sha o kumi-tateru〈自動車を組み立てる〉 assemble an automobile

kumi-toru〈くみとる：くみ取る〉

hito-no-kimochi-o-kumi-toru〈人の気持ちをくみ取る〉enter into a person's feelings, guess a person's idea.

kumo〈くも〉a spider.

Kumo ga su-o-haru.（くもが巣を張る。）A spider spins its web.

kumo-no-su（くもの巣） a spider web, a cobweb

kumo〈くも：雲〉a cloud, the clouds.

Kumo ga kireta.（雲が切れた。）The clouds broke.

kumo-ma-kara arawareru（雲間から現れる）appear from between the clouds

kumo-no-kakatta〈雲のかかった〉clouded.

kumon〈くもん：苦もん〉agony, anguish.

kumon-suru〈苦もんする〉be in agony, agonize ((over)).

kumorasu〈くもらす：曇らす〉cloud; make dim; frown.

Kare-wa kao-o-kumoraseta.（彼は顔を曇らせた。）He frowned.

kumori〈くもり：曇り〉cloudy weather.

komori nochi hare（曇り後晴れ） cloudy, fine later

kumori-zora（曇り空） a cloudy sky

kumoru〈くもる：曇る〉become cloudy, cloud; become dim.

kumotta〈曇った〉cloudy, overcast.

kumo-yuki〈くもゆき：雲行き〉the sky, the weather; the situation, the turn of affairs.

Kumo-yuki ga ayashii.（雲行きが怪しい。）The weather is threatening.

kumu〈くむ：組む〉braid, plait; fold, cross; unite ((with)).

ashi o kumu（足を組む） cross one's legs

ude o kumu（腕を組む） fold one's arms

ude-o-kunde（腕を組んで） arm in arm

kunde shigoto-o-suru（組んで仕事をする） unite with ((another)) in business

kumu〈くむ〉draw, ladle, dip up, pump.

ido-no-mizu-o-kumu（井戸の水をくむ） draw water from a well

pompu-de-mizu-o-kumu（ポンプで水をくむ） pump water

kun〈くん：訓〉the Japanese reading of Chinese characters.

-kun〈-くん：-君〉Mr., Master.

kunai-chô〈くないちょう：宮内庁〉the Imperial Household Agency.

kunan〈くなん：苦難〉distress(es), suffering(s), affliction(s), hardship(s).
　　kunan ni taeru〈苦難に耐える〉stand any kind of hardships

kuneru〈くねる〉
　　karada o kunerasu〈体をくねらす〉twist oneself
　　magari-kunetta michi〈曲りくねった道〉a winding road

kuni〈くに：国〉a country, one's native place.
　　sekai no kuni-guni〈世界の国々〉the countries of the world

kuni-gara〈くにがら：国柄〉national character.

kuniku-no-saku〈くにくのさく：苦肉の策〉a desperate measure taken inevitably.

kunji〈くんじ：訓示〉
　　kunji-suru〈訓示する〉give an address of instructions.

kunkai〈くんかい：訓戒〉
　　kunkai-suru〈訓戒する〉exhort, admonish, caution.

kunkun〈くんくん〉
　　kunkun-hana-o-narasu〈くんくん鼻を鳴らす〉whine.

kunô〈くのう：苦悩〉suffering(s), distress, affliction, anguish.
　　kunô-suru〈苦悩する〉suffer, be anguished, anguish.

kunrei〈くんれい：訓令〉instructions, an order.
　　kunrei o hassuru〈訓令を発する〉*give instructions

kunren〈くんれん：訓練〉training, (a) drill, (a) discipline.
　　kunren-suru〈訓練する〉train, drill, discipline.
　　yoku kunren-sarete-iru〈よく訓練されている〉be well trained, be highly disciplined

kunrin〈くんりん：君臨〉
　　kunrin-suru〈君臨する〉reign ((over)), rule ((over)), dominate.

kunsei〈くんせい：くん製〉smoking.
　　kunsei-no〈くん製の〉smoked.
　　kunsei-no sake〈くん製のさけ〉smoked salmon

kunshi〈くんし：君子〉
　　Kunshi ayauki-ni-chikayorazu.（君子危うきに近寄らず.）A wise man does not court danger.

kunshô〈くんしょう：勲章〉a decoration, an order.

kunshu〈くんしゅ：君主〉a monarch, a sovereign.

kunugi〈くぬぎ〉a kind of oak.

kunwa〈くんわ：訓話〉a moral discourse.

kuppuku〈くっぷく：屈服〉submission, surrender.

kuppuku-suru 〈屈服する〉 submit ((to)), surrender ((to)), yield ((to)), knuckle under ((to)).

kura 〈くら：倉, 蔵〉 a warehouse, a storehouse.

kura 〈くら〉 a saddle.

kûrâ 〈クーラー〉 a cooler, an air conditioner.

kuraberu 〈くらべる：比べる〉 compare.

    ～*-to-kurabe-mono-ni-nara-nai* 〈～と比べ物にならない〉 cannot compare with... , cannot be compared with... .

    kurabe-mono-ni-nara-nai-hodo 〈比べ物にならないほど〉 beyond compare, without comparison.

    ～*-ni-kurabereba* or ～*-to-kurabereba* 〈～に比べれば, ～と比べれば〉 in comparison with... , (as) compared with... .

kurabu 〈クラブ〉 a club; clubs.

    tenisu-kurabu （テニスクラブ） a tennis club

    kurabu-katsudô （クラブ活動） club activities

    kurabu no êsu （クラブのエース） the ace of clubs

kuragari 〈くらがり：暗がり〉 a dark place, the dark.

    kuragari-de 〈暗がりで〉 in a poor light.

kurage 〈くらげ〉 a jellyfish.

kurai 〈くらい：位〉 grade, rank.

    kurai-ga-agaru （位が上がる） rise in rank

    kurai-suru 〈位する〉 rank, be ranked; be situated, lie.

    dai-ichi-i-ni-kurai-suru （第一位に位する） rank first

kurai 〈くらい：暗い〉 dark, gloomy.

    kurai heya （暗い部屋） a dark room

    kurai-uchi-ni （暗いうちに） before daybreak

    kurai-kimochi-ni-naru （暗い気持ちになる） feel gloomy

    kuraku-naru 〈暗くなる〉 get dark.

    kuraku-natte-kara （暗くなってから） after dark

    kuraku-nara-nai-uchi-ni （暗くならないうちに） before dark

    kuraku-suru 〈暗くする〉 darken.

-kurai 〈-くらい〉 about, around, some, or so, as...as, so...as; rather(*or* sooner) than, at all.

    ni-kiro-kurai （二キロくらい） about two kilometers

    san-jikan-kurai （三時間くらい） some three hours

    san-jussai-kurai （三十歳くらい） thirty years or so

    kare-to-onaji-kurai-se-ga-takai （彼と同じくらい背が高い） be as tall as he kare-to-onaji-kurai-jôzu-ni Eigo ga hanase-nai（彼と同じくらい上手に英語が話せない）cannot speak English as well as he

kono-kurai（このくらい）this much

sono kurai（そのくらい）that much

Haji-o-kaku-kurai-nara shinda-hô-ga-mashi-da.（恥をかくくらいなら死んだ方がましだ。）I would rather die than be disgraced.

kuraimakkusu〈クライマックス〉a climax.

kuraimakkusu-ni-tassuru（クライマックスに達する）come to the climax

ku-raku〈くらく：苦楽〉joys and sorrows.

ku-raku-o-tomo-ni-suru（苦楽を共にする）share one's joys and sorrows ((with))

kurakura〈くらくら〉

kurakura-suru〈くらくらする〉feel dizzy, swim.

kuramasu〈くらます〉conceal, hide.

sugata-o-kuramasu（姿をくらます）disappear, conceal oneself

kuramu〈くらむ〉grow dizzy, be dazzled, be blinded.

me-mo-kuramu-bakari-no takasa（目もくらむばかりの高さ）a dizzy height

kane-ni me-ga-kuramu（金に目がくらむ）be blinded by money

kûran〈くうらん：空欄〉a blank (space).

kuranku〈クランク〉a crank.

kuranku-in-suru〈クランクインする〉start filming.

kurarinetto〈クラリネット〉clarinet.

kurarinetto-sôsha（クラリネット奏者）a clarinetist

kurashi〈くらし：暮らし〉(a) living, (a) livelihood, life.

shisso-na kurashi（質素な暮らし）plain living

zeitaku-na kurashi（ぜい沢な暮らし）a luxurious life

anraku-na-kurashi-o-suru（安楽な暮らしをする）live in comfort

sono-hi-gurashi-o-suru（その日暮らしをする）live from hand to mouth

Ikaga-o-kurashi-desu-ka?（いかがお暮らしですか。）How are you getting on?

kurashi-muki-ga-ii〈暮らし向きがいい〉be well off.

kurashi-muki-ga-warui（暮らし向きが悪い）be badly off

kurashiki-ryô〈くらしきりょう：倉敷料〉storage (charges), warehouse charges.

kurashikku〈クラシック〉a classic, classics.

kurashikku-ongaku（クラシック音楽）　classical music

kurasu〈クラス〉a class.

kurasu-kai（クラス会）　a class meeting

kurasu〈くらす：暮らす〉live, get on.

shiawase-ni kurasu（幸せに暮らす）　live happily

kuratchi〈クラッチ〉a clutch, a crutch.

kuratchi-o-ireru（クラッチを入れる）　throw in the clutch

kura-yami〈くらやみ：暗やみ〉the dark, darkness.

kura-yami-de（暗やみで）　in the dark, in darkness

kure〈くれ：暮れ〉nightfall, sunset; the end of the year.

kuregure-mo〈くれぐれも〉earnestly.

Kuregure-mo　o-karada-o-daiji-ni.（くれぐれもお休お大事に.）　Please take good care of yourself.

O-kâ-san-ni　kuregure-mo-yoroshiku.（お母さんにくれぐれもよろしく.）　Please give my best regards to your mother.

kûrei〈くうれい：空冷〉

kûrei-shiki-enjin（空冷式エンジン）　an air-cooled engine

kureosôto〈クレオソート〉creosote.

kureru〈くれる：暮れる〉get dark; end, come to an end.

hi-ga-kure-nai-uchi-ni（日が暮れないうちに）　before dark

hi-ga-kurete-kara（日が暮れてから）　after dark

Kotoshi mo kureta.（今年も暮れた.）　This year has come to an end.

hitan-ni-kureru（悲嘆に暮れる）　be overwhelmed with sorrow

kureru〈くれる〉give.

〜-o-kure-to-iu〈〜をくれと言う〉ask ((a person)) for... .

-kureru〈-くれる〉((do)) ((something)) for ((a person)), be kind enough ((to do)).

〜-(shite-)kure-to-iu（〜して）くれと言う）　ask ((another to do))...

kureyon〈クレヨン〉(a) crayon.

kureyon-de e o kaku（クレヨンで絵をかく）　draw a picture in crayon

kurezôru〈クレゾール〉cresol.

kuri〈くり〉a chestnut, a chestnut tree.

kuri-hiroi-ni-iku（くり拾いに行く）　go gathering chestnuts

kuri-ageru〈くりあげる：繰り上げる〉advance, move up.

kijitsu o kuri-ageru（期日を繰り上げる）　advance the date

kuri-awaseru〈くりあわせる：繰り合わせる〉make time, arrange matters, manage ((to do)).

kuri-dasu〈くりだす：繰り出す〉send out.

arate o kuri-dasu（新手を繰り出す） send out fresh troops

kuri-ire〈くりいれ：繰り入れ〉a transfer.

   kuri-ire-kin（繰入金） money transferred ((to))

kuri-ireru〈繰り入れる〉transfer ((to)), put in.

kuri-kaeshi〈くりかえし：繰り返し〉repetition.

kuri-kaesu〈繰り返す〉repeat, do ((something)) over again.

kuri-kaeshite or *kuri-kaeshi-kuri-kaeshi*〈繰り返して，繰り返し繰り返し〉 repeatedly, over and over (again).

kuri-koshi〈くりこし：繰り越し〉a transfer, a carry-over, bringing over.

kuri-kosu〈繰り越す〉transfer ((to *or* from)), carry forward ((to)), bring forward ((from)).

kurikuri〈くりくり〉

   kurikuri-shita me（くりくりした目） big, round eyes

kurîmu〈クリーム〉cream.

   nama-kurîmu（生クリーム） fresh cream

   keshô-yô-kurîmu（化粧用クリーム） cosmetic cream

kurîmu-jô-no〈クリーム状の〉creamy.

kurîmu-iro-no〈クリーム色の〉cream-colored.

kurîningu〈クリーニング〉cleaning.

   Kôto o kurîningu-shite-morau（コートをクリーニングしてもらう） have one's coat cleaned

   kurîningu-ya（クリーニング屋） a cleaner, a laundry

kuri-noberu〈くりのべる：繰り延べる〉postpone, put off.

kuri-nuku〈くりぬく：くり抜く〉hollow out.

kurippu〈クリップ〉a clip.

kurippu-de-tomeru〈クリップで留める〉clip, fasten with a clip.

Kurisumasu〈クリスマス〉Christmas.

   Kurisumasu-o-medetô.（クリスマスおめでとう.） Merry Christmas to you.

kuro(-no)〈くろ(の)：黒(の)〉black.

kurô〈くろう：苦労〉trouble(s), care(s), worry, anxiety.

   Go-kurô-sama-deshita.（御苦労さまでした.） Thank you very much for your trouble.

   kurô-ga-ooi（苦労が多い） be full of cares

   kurô-no-nai（苦労のない） free from care

   kurôshô-de-aru（苦労性である） be a natural worrier

kurô-suru〈苦労する〉have trouble, have a hard time of it, take pains, be worried ((about)), be anxious ((about)).

kûro〈くうろ：空路〉an air route.

　kûro kikoku-suru（空路帰国する） return home by air

kurôbâ〈クローバー〉a clover.

　yotsu-ba-no kurôbâ（四つ葉のクローバー） a four-leaf clover

kuro-bikari〈くろびかり：黒光り〉

　kuro-bikari-suru〈黒光りする〉shine black, have a black luster.

kuro-bîru〈くろビール：黒ビール〉black beer, porter.

kuro-boshi〈くろぼし：黒星〉a defeat mark, (a) failure.

　kuro-boshi tsuzuki-da（黒星続きだ） make a series of failures

kuroguro-to〈くろぐろと：黒々と〉in deep black.

kuroi〈くろい：黒い〉black, dark.

　iro-ga-kuroi（色が黒い） have a dark complexion

　kuroku〈黒く〉black(ly).

　kuroku-naru（黒くなる） become black; be tanned, be sunburnt

　kuroku-suru（黒くする） black, blacken

kuro-ji〈くろじ：黒字〉a black-ink balance.

　kuro-ji-de-aru（黒字である） be in (the) black

kuro-ko〈くろこ：黒子〉a prompter.

kuro-koge〈くろこげ：黒焦げ〉

　kuro-koge-ni-naru〈黒焦げになる〉be charred, be burnt black.

　kuro-koge-no〈黒焦げの〉charred.

　kuro-koge-no shitai（黒焦げの死体） a charred body

kuro-maku〈くろまく：黒幕〉a wirepuller.

　kuro-maku-ni-naru〈黒幕になる〉pull the wires, work behind the scenes.

kuro-mame〈くろまめ：黒豆〉a black soybean.

kuro-mi〈くろみ：黒み〉

　kuro-mi-gakatta〈黒みがかった〉blackish, darkish.

kurômu〈クローム〉chromium, chrome.

　kurômu-mekki-no〈クロームめっきの〉chromium-plated.

kûron〈くうろん：空論〉an empty theory.

　kijô-no-kûron（机上の空論） a paper plan

kuro-pan〈くろパン：黒パン〉brown bread.

kurorohorumu〈クロロホルム〉chloroform.

kurôru〈クロール〉the crawl (stroke).

Kuro-shio〈くろしお：黒潮〉the Black Current, the Japan Current.

kurôto〈くろうと：玄人〉an expert, a professional.

kuro-waku〈くろわく：黒枠〉

　kuro-waku-no〈黒枠の〉black-framed.

　　　kuro-waku-no hagaki〈黒枠のはがき〉 a mourning card

kuro-yama〈くろやま：黒山〉
　　　kuro-yama-no-yō-na-hito-dakari〈黒山のような人だかり〉 a large crowd of people

kuro-zatō〈くろざとう：黒砂糖〉unrefined sugar.

kurôzu-appu〈クローズアップ〉a close-up.
　　kurôzu-appu-sareru〈クローズアップされる〉be highlighted.

kuru〈くる：来る〉come, be here, be close, be near.
　　　Kanojo-wa go-ji-made-niwa kuru-deshô.（彼女は五時までには来るでしょう。）She will be here by 5.

-kuru〈-くる〉come to, get, begin, become.
　　　suki-ni-natte-kuru〈好きになってくる〉 come to like
　　　Atatakaku-natte-kita.（暖かくなってきた。）It is getting warm.
　　　Ame ga futte-kita.（雨が降ってきた。）It has begun to rain.
　　　omoshiroku-natte-kuru〈面白くなってくる〉 become interesting
　　　〜-e-itte-kita〈〜へ行ってきた〉 have been to...

kurubushi〈くるぶし〉*see.* ashi-kubi.

kuru-byô〈くるびょう：くる病〉rickets, rachitis.

kurui〈くるい：狂い〉madness; warp, disorder, confusion.
　　　kurui-jini〈狂い死に〉 death from madness
　　　kurui-zaki〈狂い咲き〉 unseasonable flowering

kurukuru〈くるくる〉
　　kurukuru-mawaru〈くるくる回る〉turn round and round.

kuruma〈くるま：車〉a car, a cart, a wagon; a wheel.
　　　kuruma-de iku〈車で行く〉 go by car
　　　kuruma-isu〈車いす〉 a wheelchair

kuruma-ebi〈くるまえび：車えび〉a prawn.

kurumaru〈くるまる〉be wrapped up ((in)).
　　kurumu〈くるむ〉wrap ((a thing)) up.

kurumi〈くるみ〉a walnut.
　　　kurumi-wari〈くるみ割り〉 nutcrackers

kururi-to〈くるりと〉
　　kururi-to muki-o-kaeru〈くるりと向きを変える〉turn round.

kurushii〈くるしい：苦しい〉painful, hard, awkward, needy.
　　　Mune ga kurushii.（胸が苦しい。）I have a pain in my chest.
　　　kurushii-me-ni-au〈苦しい目に遭う〉 have a hard time
　　　kurushii tachiba〈苦しい立場〉 an awkward position
　　　kakei-ga-kurushii〈家計が苦しい〉 be in needy circumstances

kurushi-magire 〈くるしまぎれ：苦し紛れ〉
kurushi-magire-ni（苦し紛れに） driven by pain, in desperation, as a last resort.

kurushimi 〈くるしみ：苦しみ〉 (a) pain, agony, sufferings, (a) hardship.
kurushimi o yawarageru（苦しみを和らげる） ease one's sufferings
shi-no kurushimi（死の苦しみ） death agony

kurushimu 〈くるしむ：苦しむ〉 feel pain, suffer ((from)), be worried ((by)).
jûzei ni kurushimu（重税に苦しむ） suffer from heavy taxation
kurushimeru〈苦しめる〉 give ((a person)) pain, trouble, worry.

kuruu 〈くるう：狂う〉 go mad; get out of order, go wrong, be upset.
Kare-wa ki-ga-kurutte-iru.（彼は気が狂っている。） He is mad.
Kimi-no tokei wa kurutte-iru.（君の時計は狂っている。） Your watch is out of order.

kuryo 〈くりょ：苦慮〉
kuryo-suru〈苦慮する〉 worry oneself ((about *or* over)), have much trouble ((in)).

kusa 〈くさ：草〉 grass, a weed, a herb.
niwa-no-kusa o toru（庭の草を取る） weed a garden
kusa-o-taberu〈草を食べる〉 graze.

kusa-bana 〈くさばな：草花〉 a flowering plant, a flower.

kusabi 〈くさび〉 a wedge.
kusabi-o-utsu（くさびを打つ） drive in a wedge

kusai 〈くさい：臭い〉 ill-smelling; smell bad, smell of.
Kono niku wa kusai.（この肉は臭い。） This meat smells bad.
Kono sûpu wa tamanegi-kusai.（このスープはたまねぎ臭い。） This soup smells of onion.

kusa-iro(-no) 〈くさいろ(の)：草色(の)〉 green.

kusa-kari 〈くさかり：草刈り〉 mowing.
kusa-kari-ki（草刈り機） a mower
kusa-kari-o-suru〈草刈りをする〉 mow.

kusa-ki 〈くさき：草木〉 trees and plants, vegetation.

kusakusa 〈くさくさ〉
kusakusa-suru〈くさくさする〉 be in the mopes.

kusa-mi 〈くさみ：臭み〉 a bad smell.
kusa-mi-ga-aru〈臭みがある〉 be ill-smelling.
kusa-mi-ga-nai（臭みがない） be free from smell

kusamura 〈くさむら〉 a bush.

kusa-mushiri〈くさむしり：草むしり〉weeding.

  kusa-mushiri-o-suru〈草むしりをする〉weed.

kusarasu〈くさらす：腐らす〉spoil, rot, corrode, addle.

  ki-o-kusarasu（気を腐らす）mope

kusare-en〈くされえん：腐れ縁〉an inseparable relation, a fatal connection.

kusari〈くさり：鎖〉a chain.

  kusari-de-tsunagu〈鎖でつなぐ〉chain up.

kusaru〈くさる：腐る〉rot, go bad; be depressed.

  kusatta（腐った）rotten, bad.

  kusari-yasui〈腐りやすい〉easy to go bad.

kusasu〈くさす〉*see.* kenasu.

kusa-wake〈くさわけ：草分け〉a pioneer, an early settler.

kusa-yakyū〈くさやきゅう：草野球〉sandlot baseball.

kuse〈くせ：癖〉a habit, a peculiarity.

    kuse-ga-tsuku（癖が付く）fall into a habit ((of))

    ～-no-kuse-ga-aru（～の癖がある）have the habit of...

    kuse o naosu（癖を直す）get rid of a habit

    kotoba-no-kuse（言葉の癖）one's peculiarity in speech

kūseki〈くうせき：空席〉a vacant seat, room, a vacant post.

kuse-mono〈くせもの：くせ者〉an old fox.

kusen〈くせん：苦戦〉a desperate battle, a tough game.

  kusen-suru〈苦戦する〉fight against heavy odds, have a tough game.

-kuse-ni〈-くせに〉though, in spite of, and yet, when.

    kane-mochi-no-kuse-ni（金持ちのくせに）though one is rich

kushakusha〈くしゃくしゃ〉

  kushakusha-suru〈くしゃくしゃする〉*see.* kusakusa-suru.

  kushakusha-no〈くしゃくしゃの〉crumpled, wrinkled, tangled.

    kushakusha-no hankachi（くしゃくしゃのハンカチ）a crumpled handkerchief

kushami〈くしゃみ〉sneezing, a sneeze.

  kushami-o-suru or *kushami-ga-deru*〈くしゃみをする，くしゃみが出る〉sneeze.

kushi〈くし〉a comb.

  kushi-de-kami-o-toku〈くしで髪を解く〉comb one's hair.

kushi〈くし〉a spit, a skewer.

    sakana o kushi-ni-sashite-yaku（魚をくしに刺して焼く）broil a fish on a skewer

kushin〈くしん：苦心〉pains.

  kushin-dan〈苦心談〉an account of one's hard experiences

kushin-suru〈苦心する〉take pains.

kushin-no〈苦心の〉laborious.

kushin-shite〈苦心して〉with great pains, by hard work.

kushô〈くしょう：苦笑〉a wry smile.

kushô-suru〈苦笑する〉smile a wry smile.

kûsho〈くうしょ：空所〉(a) space, a blank (space).

  kûsho o umeru（空所を埋める） fill a blank

kûshû〈くうしゅう：空襲〉an air raid.

  kûshû-keihô（空襲警報） an air-raid alarm

kûshû-suru〈空襲する〉make an air raid ((on)).

kuso〈くそ〉

  Kuso!（くそ．） Damn it! / Hang it!

  kuso-dokyô-no-aru（くそ度胸のある） foolhardy, daredevil

  kuso-majime-na（くそまじめな） too serious, humorless

kûsô〈くうそう：空想〉a fancy, a daydream.

  tanoshii kûsô-ni-fukeru（楽しい空想にふける） indulge in pleasant
  fancies

  kûsô-ka（空想家） a dreamer, a daydreamer

kûsô-suru〈空想する〉fancy, dream, imagine.

kûsô-teki(-na)〈空想的(な)〉fanciful, imaginary.

kussetsu〈くっせつ：屈折〉refraction.

kussetsu-suru〈屈折する〉refract, be refracted.

kusshi〈くっし：屈指〉

kusshi-no〈屈指の〉one of the best, leading, foremost.

kusshin〈くっしん：屈伸〉bending and stretching.

  kusshin-undô o suru（屈伸運動をする） do bending and stretching
  exercises

kussuru〈くっする：屈する〉*see*. kuppuku-suru.

kussezu-ni〈屈せずに〉undauntedly.

kusu〈くす〉a camphor tree.

kusuburu〈くすぶる〉smoke, smolder; stay indoors.

  inaka-ni kusuburu（田舎にくすぶる） lie buried in the country

kusuguru〈くすぐる〉tickle.

kusuguttai〈くすぐったい〉ticklish.

kusukusu〈くすくす〉

kusukusu-warau〈くすくす笑う〉titter, chuckle, giggle.

kusunda〈くすんだ〉somber, dull, sober.

    kusunda-iro〈くすんだ色〉a subdued color

kusuri〈くすり：薬〉(a) medicine, a drug.

    kusuri o chôgô-suru（薬を調合する） compound (a) medicine

    kusuri o nomu（薬を飲む） take medicine

    kusuri-ippuku（薬一服） a dose of medicine

    nomi-gusuri（飲み薬） an internal medicine

    kusuri-ya（薬屋） a drugist, a chemist, a drugstore, a chemist's

    kusuri-yubi（薬指） the third finger, the ring finger

kutabaru〈くたばる〉die, kick the bucket, kick off.

    Kutabatte-shimae!（くたばってしまえ.） Go to hell!

kutabire〈くたびれ〉fatigue.

    kutabireru〈くたびれる〉be fatigued, be tired.

kutakuta〈くたくた〉

    kutakuta-ni-tsukareru〈くたくたに疲れる〉be exhausted, be fagged out, be worn to a frazzle.

kutô〈くとう：句読〉punctuation.

    kutô-ten（句読点） punctuation marks

kutô〈くとう：苦闘〉*see.* kusen.

kutsu〈くつ：靴〉shoes, boots.

    kutsu-issoku（靴一足） a pair of shoes

    kutsu o haku（靴を履く） put on one's shoes

    kutsu o nugu（靴を脱ぐ） take off one's shoes

    kutsu o migaku（靴を磨く） polish shoes

    kutsu-bera（靴べら） a shoehorn

    kutsu-himo（靴ひも） shoelaces, shoestrings

    kutsu-migaki（靴磨き） a bootblack, a shoeblack

    kutsu-ya（靴屋） a shoemaker, a shoemaker's, a shoe store

    kutsu-zumi（靴墨） shoe polish

    kutsu-zure（靴擦れ） a shoe sore

    Kono kutsu wa kitsu-suguru.（この靴はきつすぎる.） These shoes are too tight for me.

kutsû〈くつう：苦痛〉(a) pain, a pang, agony.

    kutsû o kanjiru（苦痛を感じる） feel a pain

    kutsû o yawarageru（苦痛を和らげる） soothe the pain

kutsugaeru〈くつがえる：覆る〉be upset, be overturned, capsize.

    kutsugaesu〈覆す〉upset, overturn, capsize; overthrow, overrule, reverse.

teisetsu o kutsugaesu〈定説を覆す〉overthrow the established
theory

hyôketsu o kutsugaesu〈評決を覆す〉reverse a verdict

kutsujoku〈くつじょく：屈辱〉(a) humiliation, (a) disgrace.

kutsujoku-kan〈屈辱感〉a sense of humiliation

amanjite-kutsujoku-o-ukeru〈甘んじて屈辱を受ける〉eat humble pie.

kutsujoku-teki(-na)〈屈辱的(な)〉humiliating, disgraceful.

kutsurogu〈くつろぐ〉make oneself at home, be at ease.

Dôzo o-kutsurogi-kudasai.（どうぞおくつろぎください。）Please make
yourself at home.

kutsuroide〈くつろいで〉without reserve, at ease.

kutsu-shita〈くつした：靴下〉socks, stockings.

kutsu-shita-issoku〈靴下一足〉a pair of socks

kutsuwa〈くつわ〉a bit.

kutsuwa-o-hameru〈くつわをはめる〉bit〔a horse〕.

kuttaku〈くったく：屈託〉

kuttaku-no-nai〈屈託のない〉free from care, carefree, easygoing, happy-
go-lucky.

kuttaku-no-nai-kao-o-suru（屈託のない顔をする）look carefree

kutte-kakaru〈くってかかる：食って掛かる〉turn ((upon)), bite ((at)).

kuttsukeru〈くっつける：くっ付ける〉join, attach, stick, paste, glue.

kuttsuku〈くっ付く〉stick ((to)), cling ((to)).

kuu〈くう：食う〉*see.* taberu.

kane o kuu〈金を食う〉eat up money

ka-ni kuwareru〈蚊に食われる〉be bitten by a mosquito

jiban o kuwareru（地盤を食われる）be encroached upon ((a
person's)) constituency

Sono-te-wa-kuwanu.（その手は食わぬ.）I know that trick of yours.

hito-o-kutta kao-tsuki（人を食った顔つき）a provoking look

kuu-ka-kuwareru-ka-no tatakai（食うか食われるかの戦い）a life-and-
death struggle

kuwa〈くわ〉a hoe.

kuwa〈くわ：桑〉a mulberry (tree).

kuwadate〈くわだて：企て〉a plan, a project, an attempt, a plot.

kuwadateru〈企てる〉plan, project, attempt.

kuwaeru〈くわえる：加える〉add.

San ni go o-kuwaeruto hachi.（三に五を加えると八.）Three and four
makes eight.

kuwaeru 〈くわえる〉 take in one's mouth.

　　paipu-o-kuwaete（パイプをくわえて） pipe in one's mouth

kuwai 〈くわい〉 an arrowhead.

kuwa-ire-shiki 〈くわいれしき：くわ入れ式〉a ground-breaking ceremony.

kuwase-mono 〈くわせもの：食わせ物(者)〉a fake, a sham, a phony; an impostor, a humbug, a fraud.

kuwaseru 〈くわせる：食わせる〉feed; support, maintain, keep, provide ((for)).

kuwashii 〈くわしい：詳しい〉full, detailed, minute, further; know well, be familar ((with)), be versed ((in)).

　　kuwashii setsumei（詳しい説明） a detailed explanation

　　Nihon-no jijô-ni kuwashii（日本の事情に詳しい） be familiar with Japanese affairs

　　kuwashii-koto（詳しいこと） details, particulars

　kuwashiku〈詳しく〉fully, in detail, minutely.

kuwawaru 〈くわわる：加わる〉join, take part ((in)).

　　ikkô ni kuwawaru（一行に加わる） join the party

kuwazu-girai 〈くわずぎらい：食わず嫌い〉

　kuwazu-girai-de-aru〈食わず嫌いである〉be prejudiced ((against some food)).

kuyami 〈くやみ：悔やみ〉condolence; repentance, regret.

　　kuyami-jô（悔やみ状） a letter of condolence

　kuyami-o-noberu〈悔やみを述べる〉condole ((with)), express one's condolences ((to)).

　kuyamu〈悔やむ〉lament, mourn ((for or over)); regret, be sorry ((for)).

　　hito-no shi o kuyamu（人の死を悔やむ） lament a person's death

kuyashii 〈くやしい：悔しい〉vexing, regrettable.

　kuyashigaru〈悔しがる〉be vexed ((at)).

　kuyashi-sa〈悔しさ〉vexation, chagrin, regret.

　　kuyashi-sa-no-amari（悔しさの余り） in one's vexation

kuyashi-namida 〈くやしなみだ：悔し涙〉tears of vexation.

kuyô 〈くよう：供養〉a memorial service ((for)).

　kuyô-suru〈供養する〉hold a memorial service ((for)).

kuyokuyo 〈くよくよ〉

　kuyokuyo-suru〈くよくよする〉worry (oneself) ((about or over)), grieve (or brood) ((over)).

　　Kuyokuyo-suru-na!（くよくよするな.） Don't worry!

kûyu〈くうゆ：空輸〉air transport.

kûyu-suru〈空輸する〉transport by air.

kûzen〈くうぜん：空前〉

kûzen-no〈空前の〉unprecedented, unexampled, record-breaking.

kûzen-no kiroku（空前の記録）an all-time record

kuzu〈くず〉waste, rubbish, trash.

kuzu-kago（くずかご）a wastebasket, a trash basket

kuzureru〈くずれる：崩れる〉crumble, fall to pieces, break, give way; get out of shape.

kuzusu〈くずす：崩す〉destroy, demolish; change, simplify.

sen-en-satsu o hyaku-en-kôka-ni kuzusu（千円札を百円硬貨にくずす） change a 1,000 yen note into 100 yen coins

ji-o-kuzushite-kaku（字を崩して書く）write a character in a simplified form

kyâ〈きゃっ〉

kyatto-sakebu〈きゃっと叫ぶ〉shriek, scream.

kyabetsu〈キャベツ〉a cabbage.

kyabine〈キャビネ〉a cabinet.

kyabine-ban（キャビネ版）a cabinet size

kyakka〈きゃっか：却下〉(a) rejection, (a) dismissal.

kyakka-suru〈却下する〉reject, dismiss.

kyakkan〈きゃっかん：客観〉

kyakkan-sei（客観性）objectivity

kyakkan-teki(-na)〈客観的(な)〉objective.

kyakkan-teki-ni〈客観的に〉objectively.

kyakkan-teki-ni mite（客観的にみて）objectively speaking

kyakkô〈きゃっこう：脚光〉footlights, floats.

kyakkô-o-abiru〈脚光を浴びる〉be staged, be spotlighted.

kyaku〈きゃく：客〉a caller, a visitor, a guest, a customer, a passenger.

manekarezaru kyaku（招かれざる客）an unwelcome guest

kyaku-ashi〈きゃくあし：客足〉

kyaku-ashi-ga-tooi〈客足が遠い〉attract few customers.

kyaku-atsukai〈きゃくあつかい：客扱い〉

kyaku-atsukai-ga-umai〈客扱いがうまい〉give good service.

kyaku-atsukai-ga-warui（客扱いが悪い）give poor service

kyakuchû〈きゃくちゅう：脚注〉footnotes.

kyaku-dane〈きゃくだね：客種〉

kyaku-dane-ga-ii〈客種がいい〉have customers from the upper classes.

kyaku-hiki 〈きゃくひき：客引き〉touting; a tout, a barker.

kyakuhon 〈きゃくほん：脚本〉a play, a drama, a scenario.
 kyakuhon-ka（脚本家）a playwright, a dramatist, a scenario writer

kyakuin 〈きゃくいん：客員〉
 kyakuin-kyôju（客員教授）a guest professor

kyakuma 〈きゃくま：客間〉a drawing room, a parlor, a guest room.

kyakuseki 〈きゃくせき：客席〉seats (in a theater).

kyakusen 〈きゃくせん：客船〉a passenger boat.

kyakusen-bi 〈きゃくせんび：脚線美〉the beauty of leg lines.
 kyakusen-bi-no〈脚線美の〉with shapely legs.

kyakusha 〈きゃくしゃ：客車〉a passenger car, a passenger coach; a passenger train.

kyakushitu 〈きゃくしつ：客室〉a guest room, a cabin.

kyaku-shôbai 〈きゃくしょうばい：客商売〉the entertainment business.

kyakushoku 〈きゃくしょく：脚色〉dramatization.
 kyakushoku-suru〈脚色する〉dramatize.

kyaku-yose 〈きゃくよせ：客寄せ〉
 kyaku-yose-ni〈客寄せに〉to attract customers.

kyâkyâ 〈きゃあきゃあ〉
 kyâkyâ-warau〈きゃあきゃあ笑う〉scream.
  onaka-o-kakaete-kyâkyâ-warau（おなかを抱えてきゃあきゃあ笑う）
   scream with laughter

kyampu 〈キャンプ〉a camp, camping.
 kyampu-ni-iku（キャンプに行く）go camping

kyankyan 〈きゃんきゃん〉
 kyankyan-naku〈きゃんきゃん鳴く〉yip, yelp.

kyappu 〈キャップ〉a cap, a point protector.

kyarako 〈キャラコ〉calico, muslin.

kyasha 〈きゃしゃ〉
 kyasha-na〈きゃしゃな〉delicate, slender.

kyatatsu 〈きゃたつ：脚立〉a stepladder.

kyatchi-bôru 〈キャッチボール〉
 kyatchi-bôru-o-suru〈キャッチボールをする〉play catch.

kyo 〈きょ：虚〉
 kyo-o-tsuku〈虚を突く〉catch ((a person)) off his guard.

kyo 〈きょ：居〉
 kyo o sadameru〈居を定める〉take up one's abode ((at or in)).

kyô 〈きょう：今日〉today, this day.

kyō-no gogo（今日の午後）this afternoon

kyō-no shimbun（今日の新聞）today's paper

kyō-kara-zutto（今日からずっと）from this day on

kyō-jū-ni（今日中に）in the course of today, before the day is out

raishū-no-kyō *or* senshū-no-kyō（来週の今日，先週の今日）this day week

kyō〈きょう：凶〉ill luck, misfortune.

kyō-no〈凶の〉unlucky, bad, ill-omened.

kyō〈きょう：経〉a sutra.

kyō o yomu（経を読む）recite a sutra

kyō〈きょう：興〉interest, fun.

kyō o sogu〈興をそぐ〉spoil the fun.

-kyō〈-きょう：-強〉a little more than.

kyōaku〈きょうあく：凶悪〉

kyōaku-na〈凶悪な〉atrocious, heinous, fiendish.

kyōaku-na hanzai（凶悪な犯罪）a heinous crime

kyōbai〈きょうばい：競売〉auction.

kyōbai-ni-fusuru or *kyōbai-suru*〈競売に付する，競売する〉sell at auction.

kyōbai-sareru〈競売される〉be auctioned off.

kyōben〈きょうべん：教べん〉

kyōben-o-toru〈教べんを執る〉teach at a school.

kyōbō〈きょうぼう：凶暴〉

kyōbō-na〈凶暴な〉atrocious, ferocious, brutal, outrageous.

kyōbō〈きょうぼう：共謀〉(a) conspiracy, collusion.

kyōbō-sha（共謀者）a conspirator, an accomplice

kyōbō-suru〈共謀する〉conspire ((with)), collude ((with)).

∼-to-kyōbō-shite〈〜と共謀して〉in conspiracy with... , in collusion with ... .

kyōbu〈きょうぶ：胸部〉the breast, the chest.

kyōbu-shikkan（胸部疾患）a chest disease

kyōchi〈きょうち：境地〉a state, a stage.

∼-no kyōchi ni tassuru（〜の境地に達する）attain the stage of...

kyōchiku-tō〈きょうちくとう：きょう竹桃〉an oleander.

kyōcho〈きょうちょ：共著〉collaboration, joint authorship; a joint work.

kyōcho-sha（共著者）a collaborator, a joint author

∼-to-kyōcho-de〈〜と共著で〉in collaboration with... , under joint authorship with... .

kyōchô〈きょうちょう：協調〉cooperation, conciliation.

kyôchô-suru〈協調する〉cooperate.

kyôchô-teki(-na)〈協調的(な)〉cooperative, conciliatory.

kyôchô〈きょうちょう：強調〉emphasis, stress.

  kyôchô-suru〈強調する〉emphasize, lay emphasis ((on *or* upon)), stress, point up.

kyôchû〈きょうちゅう：胸中〉

  kyôchû-o-sassuru〈胸中を察する〉enter into ((a person's)) feelings.

kyôda〈きょうだ：強打〉a heavy blow.

  kyôda-sha〈強打者〉a heavy hitter, a slugger

  kyôda-suru〈強打する〉deal a heavy blow, hit hard; slug, swat.

kyodai〈きょだい：巨大〉

  kyodai-na〈巨大な〉huge, gigantic.

kyôdai〈きょうだい：兄弟〉a brother, a sister.

  kyôdai-genka〈兄弟げんか〉a quarrel between brothers(*or* sisters)

  giri-no-kyôdai〈義理の兄弟〉a brother-in-law, a sister-in-law

kyôdai〈きょうだい：鏡台〉a dresser, a dressing table.

kyôdai〈きょうだい：強大〉

  kyôdai-na〈強大な〉mighty, powerful, strong.

kyôdan〈きょうだん：教壇〉the platform.

  kyôdan-ni-tatsu〈教壇に立つ〉stand on the platform, teach a class.

kyôdan〈きょうだん：教団〉an order, a religious brotherhood.

kyodatsu-jôtai〈きょだつじょうたい：虚脱状態〉a state of lethargy, absentmindedness.

  kyodatsu-jôtai-ni-aru〈虚脱状態にある〉be in a state of lethargy, be utterly absentminded.

kyodô〈きょどう：挙動〉behavior, demeanor.

  kyodô-fushin-no-kado-de〈挙動不審のかどで〉on account of one's suspicious behavior

kyôdo〈きょうど：郷土〉one's native place.

  kyôdo-shoku〈郷土色〉local color

    kyôdo-shoku-yutaka-na〈郷土色豊かな〉rich in local color

kyôdo〈きょうど：強度〉

  kyôdo-no〈強度の〉strong, powerful, intense.

    kyôdo-no-kingan-de-aru〈強度の近眼である〉be very nearsighted

kyôdô〈きょうどう：協同〉cooperation, partnership.

  kyôdô-kumiai〈協同組合〉a cooperative society, a co-op

kyôdô〈きょうどう：共同〉community.

  kyôdô-bokin〈共同募金〉the community chest

kyôdô-bochi〈共同墓地〉a public cemetery

kyôdô-bôei〈共同防衛〉a joint defense

kyôdô-seikatsu〈共同生活〉community life

kyôdô-seimei〈共同声明〉a joint statement

kyôdô-no〈共同の〉common, public, joint, united.

kyôdô-no teki〈共同の敵〉a common enemy

kyôei〈きょうえい：競泳〉a swimming race.

kyoei-shin〈きょえいしん：虚栄心〉vanity.

kyoei-shin-no-tsuyoi〈虚栄心の強い〉vain.

kyôen〈きょうえん：きょう宴〉a banquet, a feast, a dinner.

kyôen〈きょうえん：共演〉

kyôen-suru〈共演する〉do a play with, coact, costar.

kyôfu〈きょうふ：恐怖〉fear, (a) terror, horror, (a) dread.

kyôfu-ni-osowareru〈恐怖に襲われる〉be seized with fear

kyôfû〈きょうふう：強風〉a strong wind.

kyô-fû-chûi-hô〈強風注意報〉a strong-wind warning

kyôfu-shô〈きょうふしょう：恐怖症〉a phobia, morbid fear.

kyogaku〈きょがく：巨額〉an enormous sum, a large amount.

kyogaku-no〈巨額の〉enormous, huge.

kyôgaku〈きょうがく：共学〉coeducation, mixed education.

kyôgen〈きょうげん：狂言〉a *Noh* farce; a trick, a sham, a fake; a play.

kyôgen-jisatsu〈狂言自殺〉a sham suicide

atari-kyôgen〈当たり狂言〉a successful play

kyogi〈きょぎ：虚偽〉falsehood.

kyogi-no〈虚偽の〉false, sham, untrue.

kyogi-no môshi-tate o suru〈虚偽の申し立てをする〉make a false statement, give false evidence

kyôgi〈きょうぎ：競技〉a game, a sport, a match, a contest; an event.

kyôgi-ni-sanka-suru〈競技に参加する〉take part in a game

kyôgi ni katsu〈競技に勝つ〉win a game

kyôgi ni makeru〈競技に負ける〉lose a game

kyôgi-shumoku〈競技種目〉a sporting event

kyôgi〈きょうぎ：協議〉conference.

kyôgi-suru〈協議する〉confer ((with)), consult ((with)), talk with ((a person)) over.

kyôgi〈きょうぎ：教義〉a doctrine, a dogma, a creed.

kyôgi〈きょうぎ：狭義〉a narrow sense.

kyôgi-no〈狭義の〉in a narrow sense.

kyôgû 〈きょうぐう：境遇〉circumstances, one's lot.
　　mijime-na kyôgû〈惨めな境遇〉wretched circumstances
kyôha 〈きょうは：教派〉a (religious) denomination, a sect.
kyôhaku 〈きょうはく：脅迫〉a threat, a menace.
　　kyôhaku-jô〈脅迫状〉a threatening letter
　kyôhaku-suru〈脅迫する〉threaten, menace.
　kyôhaku-teki(-na)〈脅迫的(な)〉threatening, menacing.
　kyôhaku-sarete〈脅迫されて〉under threat(*or* duress(e)).
kyôhan-sha 〈きょうはんしゃ：共犯者〉an accomplice.
kyohi 〈きょひ：拒否〉(a) denial, refusal, a veto.
　　kyohi-ken〈拒否権〉the veto right, a veto
　　　kyohi-ken o kôshi-suru〈拒否権を行使する〉place a veto ((on))
　kyohi-suru〈拒否する〉deny, refuse, veto.
kyohi 〈きょひ：巨費〉a huge sum of money.
　kyohi-o-tôjite〈巨費を投じて〉at a great cost.
kyôho 〈きょうほ：競歩〉heel-and-toe walking.
kyôi 〈きょうい：驚異〉(a) wonder, a miracle.
　　kyôi-no-me-o-mi-haru〈驚異の目を見張る〉stare in wonder
　kyôi-teki(-na)〈驚異的(な)〉wonderful, marvelous.
kyôi 〈きょうい：脅威〉a menace, a threat.
　kyôi-to-naru or *kyôi-o-ataeru*〈脅威となる，脅威を与える〉menace,
　　threaten.
kyôi 〈きょうい：胸囲〉the girth of the chest.
　　kyôi-ga-hiroi〈胸囲が広い〉have a broad chest
　　kyôi-ga-semai〈胸囲が狭い〉have a narrow chest
　　kyôi o hakaru〈胸囲を計る〉measure ((a person's)) chest
kyôiku 〈きょういく：教育〉(an) education.
　　kyôiku-iin〈教育委員〉a member of a board of education
　　gakkô-kyôiku〈学校教育〉school education
　　gimu-kyôiku〈義務教育〉*see.* gimu.
　　katei-kyôiku〈家庭教育〉*see.* katei〈家庭〉.
　kyôiku-o-ukeru〈教育を受ける〉get an education, be educated.
　kyôiku-suru〈教育する〉educate.
　kyôiku-no-aru〈教育のある〉educated.
　kyôiku-teki-na or *kyôiku-jô-no*〈教育的な，教育上の〉educational.
kyôin 〈きょういん：教員〉a teacher.
　　kyôin-shitsu〈教員室〉a teachers' room
kyojaku 〈きょじゃく：虚弱〉

kyojaku-na〈虚弱な〉weak, weakly.
　　kyojaku-na taishitsu（虚弱な体質）a weak constitution
kyôji〈きょうじ：凶事〉an unfortunate incident, a calamity, an evil.
kyôji〈きょうじ：教示〉instruction, teaching.
　kyôji-suru〈教示する〉instruct, teach.
kyojin〈きょじん：巨人〉a giant.
kyôjin〈きょうじん：狂人〉*see.* ki-chigai.
kyôjin〈きょうじん：強じん〉
　kyôjin-na〈強じんな〉strong, tough, iron, tenacious.
　　kyôjin-na ishi（強じんな意志）a strong will
kyojū〈きょじゅう：居住〉
　　kyojū-sha（居住者）a dweller, a resident, an inhabitant
　　kyojū-ken（居住権）the right of residence
　kyojū-suru〈居住する〉live, dwell, reside.
kyôju〈きょうじゅ：教授〉teaching, instruction; a professor.
　　kyôju-hô（教授法）a method of teaching
　　Nomoto-kyôju（野本教授）Professor Nomoto
　　sei-kyôju（正教授）a full professor
　　kyôju-kai（教授会）a faculty meeting
　kyôju-suru〈教授する〉teach, instruct.
kyôju〈きょうじゅ：享受〉
　kyôju-suru〈享受する〉enjoy, have, be given.
kyôjutsu〈きょうじゅつ：供述〉testimony, deposition.
　　kyôjutsu-sha（供述者）a testifier, a deponent
　　kyôjutsu-sho（供述書）a written statement
　kyôjutsu-suru〈供述する〉testify, depose.
kyoka〈きょか：許可〉permission, approval, license, admission.
　　kyoka-o-ete（許可を得て）by permission ((of))
　　kyoka-nashi-ni（許可なしに）without permission
　kyoka-suru〈許可する〉permit, approve, give a license, admit.
kyôka〈きょうか：教科〉a subject.
kyôka〈きょうか：狂歌〉a comic *tanka.*
kyôka〈きょうか：強化〉
　kyôka-suru〈強化する〉strengthen.
kyôka〈きょうか：教化〉
　kyôka-suru〈教化する〉enlighten, educate, civilize.
kyôkai〈きょうかい：境界〉a boundary, a border.
　　kyôkai o kimeru（境界を決める）fix the boundary

kyôkai-sen〈境界線〉a boundary line, a border line

kyôkai〈きょうかい：教会〉a church.

  kyôkai-e iku〈教会へ行く〉 go to church

kyôkai〈きょうかい：協会〉an association, society.

kyôkaku〈きょうかく：きょう客〉a chivalrous person.

kyôkan〈きょうかん：凶漢〉a villain, a ruffian, an assailant, an assassin.

kyôkan〈きょうかん：共感〉sympathy, a response.

  kyôkan o eru〈共感を得る〉 win the sympathy ((of))

  kyôkan o yobu〈共感を呼ぶ〉 rouse ((a person's)) sympathy

  kyôkan-suru or *kyôkan-o-oboeru*〈共感する，共感を覚える〉sympathize ((with)), feel sympathy ((with)).

kyôka-sho〈きょうかしょ：教科書〉a (school) textbook.

kyôkatsu〈きょうかつ：恐喝〉a threat, a menace.

  kyôkatsu-suru〈恐喝する〉threaten, menace.

kyôken〈きょうけん：狂犬〉a mad dog.

  kyôken-byô〈狂犬病〉 rabies, hydrophobia

kyôken〈きょうけん：強権〉

  kyôken o hatsudô-suru〈強権を発動する〉invoke legal authority ((against)).

kyôken〈きょうけん：強健〉

  kyôken-na〈強健な〉robust, stout, strong.

  kyôken-na hito〈強健な人〉 a person of robust health

kyôki〈きょうき：凶器〉a lethal weapon.

kyôki〈きょうき：狭軌〉a narrow gauge.

  kyôki-tetsudô〈狭軌鉄道〉 a narrow-gauge railroad

kyôki〈きょうき：きょう気〉a chivalrous spirit.

  kyôki-no-aru〈きょう気のある〉chivalrous, gallant.

kyokkai〈きょっかい：曲解〉a strained interpretation.

kyokkei〈きょっけい：極刑〉capital punishment.

  kyokkei-ni-shosuru〈極刑に処する〉 condemn ((a person)) to capital punishment

kyokô〈きょこう：挙行〉

  kyokô-suru〈挙行する〉hold, give, perform.

  kyokô-sareru〈挙行される〉be held, take place.

kyokô〈きょこう：虚構〉(a) fabrication, (a) fiction, a figment, a fake.

  kyokô-no〈虚構の〉fabricated, fictitious, false, groundless.

kyôko〈きょうこ：強固〉

  kyôko-ni-suru〈強固にする〉solidify, strengthen.

kyôko-na〈強固な〉firm, stable, solid, strong.
　　kyôko-na ishi〈強固な意志〉 a strong will
kyôkô〈きょうこう：凶行〉(an act of) violence, murder.
　　kyôkô-ni-oyobu〈凶行に及ぶ〉 commit a heinous crime
kyôkô〈きょうこう：恐慌〉a panic.
　kyôkô-o-kitasu〈恐慌を来す〉cause a panic, be panic-stricken.
kyôkô〈きょうこう：強硬〉
　kyôkô-na〈強硬な〉strong, firm, stout, resolute.
　　kyôkô-na taido o toru〈強硬な態度を取る〉 take a firm attitude
　kyôkô-ni〈強硬に〉strongly, firmly, stoutly, resolutely.
　　kyôkô-ni-hantai-suru〈強硬に反対する〉 offer a strong opposition
　　((to))
kyôkô〈きょうこう：強行〉
　　kyôkô-saiketsu-suru〈強行採決する〉 force a vote
　kyôkô-suru〈強行する〉force, enforce.
kyô-kôgun〈きょうこうぐん：強行軍〉
　kyô-kôgun o suru〈強行軍をする〉make a forced march.
kyôkoku〈きょうこく：峡谷〉*see.* keikoku〈渓谷〉.
kyoku〈きょく：局〉a bureau, a department; the central, the exchange; a post office; a broadcasting station.
kyoku〈きょく：極〉a pole; the extremity, the height, the bottom.
　hirô-no-kyoku-ni-tassuru〈疲労の極に達する〉 be dead tired.
kyoku〈きょく：曲〉music, a piece of music, a tune.
kyokubu-masui〈きょくぶますい：局部麻酔〉local anesthesia.
kyokuchi〈きょくち：極地〉the pole, the polar regions.
kyokuchi〈きょくち：局地〉
　kyokuchi-teki(-na)〈局地的(な)〉local.
kyokuchō〈きょくちょう：局長〉the chief of a bureau, a postmaster.
kyokudai〈きょくだい：極大〉the maximum.
　　kyokudai-chi〈極大値〉 the maximum value
kyokudo〈きょくど：極度〉
　kyokudo-no〈極度の〉extreme, utmost.
　kyokudo-ni〈極度に〉extremely, to the utmost.
　　kyokudo-ni kinchô-suru〈極度に緊張する〉 be strained to the limit
kyoku-dome〈きょくどめ：局留〉general delivery, poste restante; To be called for.
kyokugei〈きょくげい：曲芸〉an acrobatic feat.
　　kyokugei-hikô〈曲芸飛行〉 a flying stunt

kyokugen〈きょくげん：極限〉the utmost limits, the extremity.
　　kyokugen ni tassuru（極限に達する）reach the limit ((of))

kyokugen〈きょくげん：極言〉
　　kyokugen-suru〈極言する〉go so far as to say ((that)).

kyokugen〈きょくげん：局限〉
　　kyokugen-suru〈局限する〉localize, set limits ((to)).

kyokumen〈きょくめん：局面〉an aspect, a situation.
　　kyokumen-ga-ippen-suru〈局面が一変する〉take a new turn.

kyokumoku〈きょくもく：曲目〉a program, one's repertoire, a number.

kyōkun〈きょうくん：教訓〉a lesson, instruction.
　　kyōkun o ataeru（教訓を与える）give a lesson ((to))
　　kyōkun o manabu（教訓を学ぶ）learn a lesson ((from))

kyokuron〈きょくろん：極論〉
　　kyokuron-suru〈極論する〉*see.* kyokugen-suru.

kyokuryoku〈きょくりょく：極力〉to the utmost, with all one's might, as...as possible.
　　kyokuryoku-tsutomeru〈極力努める〉do one's best, make every effort.

kyokusa〈きょくさ：極左〉the extreme left.

kyokusen〈きょくせん：曲線〉a curve, a curved line.
　　kyokusen-bi（曲線美）the beauty of one's curves

kyokushō〈きょくしょう：極小〉the minimum.
　　kyokushō-chi（極小値）the minimum value

kyokutan〈きょくたん：極端〉an extreme, extremity.
　　kyokutan-na〈極端な〉extreme, excessive.
　　kyokutan-ni〈極端に〉extremely, excessively, too far.
　　kyokutan-ni hashiru（極端に走る）go too far, run to an extreme

Kyokutō〈きょくとう：極東〉the Far East.
　　kyokutō-no〈極東の〉Far Eastern.

kyokuu〈きょくう：極右〉the extreme right.

kyokyo-jitsujitsu〈きょきょじつじつ：虚々実々〉
　　kyokyo-jitsujitsu no kake-hiki（虚々実々の駆け引き）a case of diamond cut diamond

kyōkyū〈きょうきゅう：供給〉supply, service.
　　kyōkyū-suru〈供給する〉supply ((with)).
　　kyōkyū-o-ukeru〈供給を受ける〉be supplied ((with)).

kyōmei〈きょうめい：共鳴〉*see.* kyōkan（共感）.

kyōmi〈きょうみ：興味〉interest.
　　kyōmi-o-motsu〈興味を持つ〉take interest ((in)), be interested ((in)).

kyômi-no-aru 〈興味のある〉 interesting.

 kyômi-no-nai〈興味のない〉 uninteresting, of no interest

kyomu 〈きょむ：虚無〉

kyomu-teki(-na) 〈虚無的(な)〉 nihilistic.

kyômu 〈きょうむ：教務〉 school affairs.

 kyômu-ka〈教務課〉 the instruction department

kyonen 〈きょねん：去年〉 last year.

kyônen 〈きょうねん：享年〉

 kyônen-hachi-jussai〈享年八十歳〉 died at eighty

kyôô 〈きょうおう：供応〉 an entertainment, a treat, a feast.

kyôô-suru〈供応する〉 entertain, treat ((a person)) to a dinner, wine and dine ((a person)).

kyôraku 〈きょうらく：享楽〉 enjoyment.

kyôraku-suru〈享楽する〉 enjoy.

kyôraku-teki(-na)〈享楽的(な)〉 pleasure-seeking.

kyorei 〈きょれい：虚礼〉 empty forms, useless formalities.

 kyorei-o-haishi-suru〈虚礼を廃止する〉 dispense with empty forms

kyôretsu 〈きょうれつ：強烈〉

kyôretsu-na〈強烈な〉 intense, strong.

 kyôretsu-na panchi〈強烈なパンチ〉 a vicious punch

kyori 〈きょり：距離〉 (a) distance.

 en-kyori〈遠距離〉 a long distance

 kin-kyori〈近距離〉 a short distance

kyori-ga-aru〈距離がある〉 be distant, be far.

kyôri 〈きょうり：郷里〉 one's native place, one's home.

 kyôri-e-kaeru〈郷里へ帰る〉 return home

kyorokyoro 〈きょろきょろ〉

kyorokyoro-suru〈きょろきょろする〉 look around restlessly.

kyôryô 〈きょうりょう：狭量〉

kyôryô-na〈狭量な〉 narrow-minded.

kyôryoku 〈きょうりょく：協力〉 cooperation.

 kyôryoku-sha〈協力者〉 a cooperator

kyôryoku-suru〈協力する〉 cooperate ((with)), work together, unite one's efforts ((with)).

kyôryoku-teki-de-aru〈協力的である〉 be cooperative.

～-to-kyôryoku-shite〈～と協力して〉 in cooperation with... .

kyôryoku 〈きょうりょく：強力〉

kyôryoku-na〈強力な〉 strong, powerful, mighty.

kyôsa 〈きょうさ：教唆〉abetment, instigation.
　kyôsa-suru〈教唆する〉abet, instigate.
kyôsai〈きょうさい：共催〉
　～*-no-kyôsai-de*〈～の共催で〉under the joint auspices of... .
kyôsai-ka〈きょうさいか：恐妻家〉a hen-pecked husband.
kyôsai-kumiai〈きょうさいくみあい：共済組合〉a mutual aid association.
kyôsaku〈きょうさく：凶作〉a bad crop.
kyôsan〈きょうさん：協賛〉approval, support.
　　kyôsan o eru（協賛を得る）obtain the approval ((of))
　kyôsan-suru（協賛する）approve, support.
kyôsan〈きょうさん：共産〉
　　kyôsan-shugi（共産主義）communism
　　　kyôsan-shugi-sha（共産主義者）a communist
　　kyôsan-tô（共産党）the Communist Party
　　　kyôsan-tô-in（共産党員）a communist
kyosei〈きょせい：虚勢〉
　kyosei-o-haru〈虚勢を張る〉bluff, make a bluff.
kyosei〈きょせい：去勢〉
　kyosei-suru〈去勢する〉castrate, emasculate.
kyôsei〈きょうせい：強勢〉emphasis, (a) stress.
　kyôsei-o-oku〈強勢を置く〉put emphasis ((on)), emphasize, accent.
kyôsei〈きょうせい：強制〉compulsion.
　　kyôsei-rôdô（強制労働）compulsory labor
　　kyôsei-shikkô（強制執行）compulsory execution
　kyôsei-suru〈強制する〉compel, force.
　kyôsei-teki(-na)〈強制的(な)〉compulsory, forced.
　kyôsei-teki-ni〈強制的に〉compulsorily, by force.
　kyôsei-sarete〈強制されて〉under compulsion.
kyôsei〈きょうせい：矯正〉
　kyôsei-suru〈矯正する〉rectify, redress, reform, correct, cure.
　　domori-o-kyôsei-suru（どもりを矯正する）cure ((a person)) of stammering
kyôsha〈きょうしゃ：強者〉the strong.
kyôsha〈きょうしゃ：香車〉a spear.
kyôshi〈きょうし：教師〉*see.* kyôyu.
kyoshiki〈きょしき：挙式〉a ceremony, a celebration.
　　kyoshiki-no hi-dori（挙式の日取り）the wedding date
kyôshin〈きょうしん：強震〉a severe earthquake.

kyôshin 〈きょうしん：狂信〉
  kyôshin-teki(-na) 〈狂信的(な)〉fanatic(al).
kyôshin-shô 〈きょうしんしょう：狭心症〉stricture of the heart, heart attack.
kyôshin-zai 〈きょうしんざい：強心剤〉a cardiac, a cordial.
kyoshi-teki(-na) 〈きょしてき(な)：巨視的(な)〉macroscopic.
kyôshitsu 〈きょうしつ：教室〉a classroom, a schoolroom.
kyoshô 〈きょしょう：巨匠〉a master, a maestro.
kyôsho 〈きょうしょ：教書〉a message.
    Amerika-daitôryô-no nentô-kyôsho (アメリカ大統領の年頭教書) the President's annual State of the Union message to Congress
kyôshoku 〈きょうしょく：教職〉the teaching profession.
    kyôshoku-katei (教職課程) a teaching course
    kyôshoku-ni-aru 〈教職にある〉be a teacher, teach school.
kyô-shokuin 〈きょうしょくいん：教職員〉the teaching staff.
kyoshu 〈きょしゅ：挙手〉a show of hands.
    kyoshu-saiketsu-o-suru (挙手採決をする) decide ((on something)) by a show of hands
kyoshû 〈きょしゅう：去就〉
  kyoshû-ni-mayou 〈去就に迷う〉do not know which course to take.
kyôshû 〈きょうしゅう：郷愁〉homesickness, nostalgia ((for)).
    kyôshû-o-kanjiru (郷愁を感じる) feel homesick, feel nostalgia ((for))
kyôshû 〈きょうしゅう：強襲〉an assault.
  kyôshû-suru 〈強襲する〉assault.
kyôshû-jo 〈きょうしゅうじょ：教習所〉a training school, a drivers' school.
kyôshuku 〈きょうしゅく：恐縮〉
  kyôshuku-suru 〈恐縮する〉be much obliged ((to)), be thankful to ((a person)) for; be sorry ((for)), be ashamed.
kyôso 〈きょうそ：教祖〉the founder of a religion.
kyôsô 〈きょうそう：競走〉a race.
  kyôsô-suru 〈競走する〉run a race ((with)).
kyôsô 〈きょうそう：競争〉(a) competition, a contest, rivalry.
    kyôsô-aite (競争相手) a competitor, a rival
    kyôsô-ishiki (競争意識) a competitive sense
    kyôsô-ryoku (競争力) competitive power
    kyôsô-shin (競争心) a competitive spirit
  kyôsô-suru 〈競争する〉compete ((with)), rival.

kyôsô-kyoku 〈きょうそうきょく：協奏曲〉a concerto.

kyôsô-kyoku 〈きょうそうきょく：狂想曲〉a rhapsody.

kyôson 〈きょうそん：共存〉coexistence.

  kyôson-suru 〈共存する〉coexist.

kyôsô-zai 〈きょうそうざい：強壮剤〉a tonic.

kyôsuru 〈きょうする：供する〉offer, present, submit, supply.

  etsuran ni kyôsuru (閲覧に供する) submit ((a document)) to ((a person)) for inspection

kyotai 〈きょたい：巨体〉a big body, a gigantic figure.

kyôtai 〈きょうたい：狂態〉

  kyôtai-o-enjiru 〈狂態を演じる〉behave scandalously, get wild in drink.

kyôtaku 〈きょうたく：供託〉deposition, deposit.

  kyôtaku-kin (供託金) a deposit

  kyôtaku-suru 〈供託する〉deposit ((in *or* with)).

kyôtan 〈きょうたん：驚嘆〉admiration, wonder.

  kyôtan-suru 〈驚嘆する〉admire, wonder ((at)).

  kyôtan-su-beki 〈驚嘆すべき〉admirable, wonderful.

kyôtei 〈きょうてい：協定〉an agreement.

  kyôtei-kakaku (協定価格) a price agreed upon

  shinshi-kyôtei (紳士協定) a gentlemen's agreement

  kyôtei-suru 〈協定する〉agree ((upon)), make an agreement ((with)), arrange ((with)).

kyôtei 〈きょうてい：競艇〉a speedboat race.

kyôteki 〈きょうてき：強敵〉a formidable enemy, a powerful rival.

kyô-teki 〈きょうてき：狂的〉

  kyô-teki-na 〈狂的な〉insane, crazy, fanatic(al), wild.

kyoten 〈きょてん：拠点〉a lodgment, a foothold, a position; a base.

kyôten 〈きょうてん：経典〉scripture, sutras.

kyotô 〈きょとう：巨頭〉a leader, a magnate, a bigwig.

  kyotô-kaidan (巨頭会談) a summit conference

kyôtô 〈きょうとう：教頭〉an assistant principal.

kyôtô 〈きょうとう：共闘〉a joint struggle.

  kyôtô-suru 〈共闘する〉struggle jointly ((against *or* for)).

kyôtô-ho 〈きょうとうほ：橋頭堡〉a bridgehead, a beachhead.

  kyôtô-ho o tsukuru (橋頭ほを造る) establish a bridgehead

kyoton-to 〈きょとんと〉

  kyoton-to-shita-kao-o-suru (きょとんとした顔をする) look stupefied

  kyoton-to-shite (きょとんとして) blankly, dazedly

kyôtsû〈きょうつう：共通〉

 kyôtû-no〈共通の〉common.

  kyôtsû-no rigai（共通の利害）common interests.

kyôtsû-ten〈きょうつうてん：共通点〉

 kyôtsû-ten-ga-aru〈共通点がある〉have something in common ((with)).

kyôwa〈きょうわ：共和〉

  kyôwa-koku（共和国）a republic

  kyôwa-sei（共和政）a republican form of government

  kyôwa-seiji（共和政治）republican government

kyôwa-on〈きょうわおん：協和音〉a concord, a consonance.

kyôyaku〈きょうやく：協約〉an agreement, a convention.

  rôdô-kyôyaku（労働協約）a labor agreement

kyoyô〈きょよう：許容〉

  kyoyô-gendo（許容限度）a tolerance limit

  saidai-kyoyô-ryô（最大許容量）the allowable maximum

 kyoyô-suru〈許容する〉permit, allow, admit, tolerate.

kyôyô〈きょうよう：教養〉culture, education.

  ippan-kyôyô（一般教養）a liberal education

  kyôyô-gakubu（教養学部）the department of liberal arts

 kyôyô-no-aru〈教養のある〉cultured, educated.

  kyôyô-no-nai（教養のない）uncultured, uneducated

kyôyô〈きょうよう：強要〉

 kyôyô-suru〈強要する〉exact, compel, force, coerce.

  kifu o kyôyô-suru（寄附を強要する）exact a subscription

kyôyu〈きょうゆ：教諭〉a teacher, an instructor.

kyôyû〈きょうゆう：共有〉joint ownership, community.

  kyôyû-zaisan（共有財産）common property

 kyôyû-suru〈共有する〉hold in common, own jointly.

kyôzai〈きょうざい：教材〉teaching materials.

kyô-zame〈きょうざめ：興冷め〉

 kyô-zame-de-aru〈興冷めである〉see. kyô o sogu.

kyozetsu〈きょぜつ：拒絶〉(a) refusal, (a) rejection.

  kyozetsu-hannô（拒絶反応）a rejection reaction

 kyozetsu-suru〈拒絶する〉refuse, reject.

kyôzô〈きょうぞう：胸像〉a bust.

kyôzon〈きょうぞん：共存〉see. kyôson.

kyû〈きゅう：球〉a globe, a sphere, a ball, a bulb.

kyû〈きゅう：九〉see. ku（九）.

kyû 〈きゅう〉 moxa cautery.

  kyû-o-sueru 〈きゅうを据える〉 cauterize with moxa; chastise.

kyû 〈きゅう：級〉 a class, a grade, a rate.

  watashi-yori ikkyû-ue-da（私より一級上だ） be a grade above me

  dai-ikkyû-no〈第一級の〉 first-rate

kyû or kyû- 〈きゅう，きゅう-：旧，旧-〉

  kyû-ni fukusuru〈旧に復する〉 be restored to the former state

  kyûaku〈旧悪〉 one's past misdeed, one's old crime

  kyû-shichô〈旧市長〉 an ex-mayor

  kyû-shôgatsu〈旧正月〉 the New Year according to the old calendar

  kyû-no〈旧の〉 old, former, ex-.

kyû 〈きゅう：急〉

  kyû-na〈急な〉 urgent, pressing; sudden; steep, sharp, rapid.

  kyû-na-yô-de *or* kyûyô-de（急な用で，急用で） on urgent business

  tenkô no kyû-na henka *or* tenkô no kyûhen（天候の急な変化，天候の急変） a sudden change of the weather

  kyû-na saka（急な坂） a steep slope

  kyû-na kâbu（急なカーブ） a sharp curve

  kyû-na nagare *or* kyûryû（急な流れ，急流） a rapid stream, rapids

  kyû-o-yôsuru〈急を要する〉 urgent, pressing, requiring immediate attention.

  kyû-ni〈急に〉 immediately, suddenly, without notice, sharply.

  kyû-ni tomaru（急に止まる） stop short

  kyû-ni magaru（急に曲がる） turn sharply

kyûai 〈きゅうあい：求愛〉 courting, courtship.

  kyûai-suru〈求愛する〉 court, woo.

Kyûba 〈キューバ〉 Cuba.

  kyôba-jin（キューバ人） a Cuban

  kyûba(-jin)-no（キューバ(人)の） Cuban

kyû-ba 〈きゅうば：急場〉 an emergency, a crisis.

  kyûba o shinogu（急場をしのぐ） tide over a crisis

kyûban 〈きゅうばん：吸盤〉a sucker.

kyûbyô 〈きゅうびょう：急病〉 a sudden illness.

  kyûbyô-nin（急病人） an urgent case

  kyôbyô-ni-kakaru〈急病にかかる〉 be suddenly taken ill.

kyûchi 〈きゅうち：窮地〉 a difficult situation, a fix, a scrape, a dilemma.

  kyûchi-ni-ochiiru（窮地に陥る） get into a scrape

kyûchû 〈きゅうちゅう：宮中〉 the Imperial Court.

kyûchû-de〈宮中で〉at Court.

kyûdai-ten〈きゅうだいてん：及第点〉a pass mark.

kyûdan〈きゅうだん：球団〉a professional baseball team.

kyûdan〈きゅうだん：糾弾〉impeachment.

kyûdan-suru〈糾弾する〉impeach.

kyûden〈きゅうでん：宮殿〉a palace.

kyûen〈きゅうえん：救援〉relief, rescue.

　　kyûen-ni omomuku（救援に赴く）　go to the rescue ((of))

　　kyûen-busshi（救援物資）　relief goods

　　kyûen-tai（救援隊）　a rescue party

kyûen〈きゅうえん：休演〉

kyûen-suru〈休演する〉suspend the performance, absent oneself from the stage.

kyûfu〈きゅうふ：給付〉presentation, delivery, (a) benefit.

　　kyûfu-kin（給付金）　a benefit

　　hantai-kyûfu（反対給付）　a counter-presentation

kyûfu-suru〈給付する〉make a presentation ((of)), deliver, pay.

kyûgaku〈きゅうがく：休学〉temporary absence from school.

kyûgaku-suru〈休学する〉absent oneself from school temporarily.

kyûgeki〈きゅうげき：急激〉

kyûgeki-na〈急激な〉sudden, abrupt, rapid, drastic.

　　kyûgeki-na henka（急激な変化）　a sudden change

kyûgeki-ni〈急激に〉suddenly, abruptly, rapidly, drastically.

kyûgi〈きゅうぎ：球技〉a ball game.

kyûgo〈きゅうご：救護〉relief, aid.

　　kyûgo-han（救護班）　a relief squad

kyûgyô〈きゅうぎょう：休業〉closure.

　　Honjitsu kyûgyô.（本日休業．）　Closed today.

kyûgyô-suru〈休業する〉be closed.

kyûhaku〈きゅうはく：急迫〉

kyûhaku-suru〈急迫する〉become tense, grow acute.

kyûhaku-shita〈急迫した〉pressing, urgent, imminent.

kyûhaku〈きゅうはく：窮迫〉

kyûhaku-shite-iru〈窮迫している〉be in distress.

　　zaisei-teki-ni-kyûhaku-shite-iru（財政的に窮迫している）　be in financial difficulty

kyûhen〈きゅうへん：急変〉a sudden turn.

　　kyûhen-suru（急変する）　take a sudden turn〔for the worse〕

kyûhô〈きゅうほう：急報〉an urgent report.
　kyûhô-suru〈急報する〉report promptly, give the alarm, send an emergency call.
kyûin-ryoku〈きゅういんりょく：吸引力〉sucking force.
kyûjin〈きゅうじん：求人〉the offer of situation.
　　kyûjin-kôkoku〈求人広告〉a want ad., a situation-vacant advertisement
kyûjitsu〈きゅうじつ：休日〉a holiday, a day off.
kyûjo〈きゅうじょ：救助〉rescue, relief, aid.
　kyûjo-suru〈救助する〉rescue, aid, help.
kyûjô〈きゅうじょう：宮城〉the Imperial Palace.
kyûjô〈きゅうじょう：球場〉a baseball ground, a base park.
kyûjô〈きゅうじょう：窮状〉a sad plight, distress, straitened circumstances.
kyûjô〈きゅうじょう：休場〉closure (of a theater); absence.
　kyûjô-suru〈休場する〉be closed; absent oneself (from the stage), be absent (from the ring).
kyûjô〈きゅうじょう：球状〉
　kyûjô-no〈球状の〉spherical, globular.
kyû-jû〈きゅうじゅう：九十〉ninety.
　dai-kyû-jû-(no)〈第九十(の)〉ninetieth.
kyûjutsu〈きゅうじゅつ：弓術〉archery, bowmanship.
kyûka〈きゅうか：旧家〉an old family.
kyûka〈きゅうか：休暇〉a vacation, holidays.
　　ni-shû-kan-no-kyûka o toru（二週間の休暇を取る）take two weeks' vacation
　　kaki-kyûka（夏期休暇）the summer vacation
　kyûka-de or *kyûka-o-totte*〈休暇で，休暇を取って〉on vacation.
kyûkai〈きゅうかい：休会〉adjournment, recess.
　kyûkai-suru〈休会する〉adjourn, take a recess, recess.
kyûkaku〈きゅうかく：きゅう覚〉the sense of smell.
　kyûkaku-no-surudoi〈きゅう覚の鋭い〉sharp-nosed.
kyû-kakudo〈きゅうかくど：急角度〉a sharp angle.
　　kyû-kakudo-ni-magaru（急角度に曲がる）make a sharp turn
kyûkan〈きゅうかん：旧館〉the old building.
kyûkan〈きゅうかん：急患〉an emergency case.
kyûkan〈きゅうかん：休館〉closure (of a museum).
kyûkan〈きゅうかん：休刊〉

kyûkan-suru〈休刊する〉stop issuing.

kyûkan-chô〈きゅうかんちょう：九官鳥〉a hill myna.

kyûkei〈きゅうけい：休憩〉(a) rest, a break.

　　kyûkei-jikan（休憩時間）a rest period, a recess, an intermission, an interval.

kyûkei-suru〈休憩する〉rest, take a rest.

kyûkei〈きゅうけい：求刑〉

kyûkei-suru〈求刑する〉demand a penalty ((for)).

kyûkei〈きゅうけい：球形〉a globular shape.

kyûkei-no〈球形の〉spherical, globe-shaped.

kyûketsu-ki〈きゅうけつき：吸血鬼〉a vampire, a bloodsucker.

kyûkô〈きゅうこう：急行〉an express.

　　Tôkyô-yuki hachi-ji-hatsu kyûkô（東京行き八時発急行）the 8:00 express for Tokyo

　　kyûkô-ken（急行券）an express ticket

　　kyûkô-ryôkin（急行料金）an express charge

　　tokubetsu-kyûkô（特別急行）*see.* tokkyû

kyûkô-suru〈急行する〉hurry ((to)).

kyûkô-saseru〈急行させる〉send ((a person)) posthaste ((to)).

kyûkô-de〈急行で〉by express.

kyûkô〈きゅうこう：旧交〉old friendship.

　　kyûkô o atatameru（旧交を温める）renew one's old friendship ((with))

kyûkô〈きゅうこう：休校〉closure of a school.

kyûkô-suru〈休校する〉close, be closed.

kyûkô〈きゅうこう：休講〉

　　Yamaguchi-kyôju honjitsu kyûkô.（山口教授本日休講.）No class— Prof. Yamaguchi.

kyû-kôbai〈きゅうこうばい：急こう配〉a steep slope.

kyû-kôbai-no〈急こう配の〉steep.

kyû-kôka〈きゅうこうか：急降下〉a nose dive.

kyô-kôka-suru〈急降下する〉(nose-)dive.

kyûkon〈きゅうこん：球根〉a bulb.

kyûkon〈きゅうこん：求婚〉a proposal of marriage.

kyûkon-suru〈求婚する〉propose ((to)), court.

kyûkutsu〈きゅうくつ：窮屈〉

kyûkutsu-na〈窮屈な〉narrow, tight; formal, rigid, uncomfortable.

　　kyûkutsu-na heya（窮屈な部屋）a narrow room

kyûkutsu-na uwagi〈窮屈な上着〉 a tight coat

kyûkutsu-na kisoku〈窮屈な規則〉 rigid regulations

kyûkyô〈きゅうきょう：旧教〉Catholicism, the Catholic Church.

kyûkyô-to〈旧教徒〉 a Catholic.

kyûkyû〈きゅうきゅう：救急〉first aid.

kyûkyû-bako〈救急箱〉 a first-aid box

kyûkyû-yaku〈救急薬〉 first-aid medicine

kyûkyû-byôin〈救急病院〉 an emergency hospital

kyûkyû-sha〈救急車〉 an ambulance

kyûkyû〈きゅうきゅう〉

～-ni-kyûkyû-to-shite-iru〈～にきゅうきゅうとしている〉think only of... , be bent on... .

kyûmei〈きゅうめい：救命〉lifesaving.

kyûmei-gu〈救命具〉 a life preserver

kyûmei〈きゅうめい：糾明〉

kyûmei-suru〈糾明する〉examine ((a matter)) closely.

kyûmei〈きゅうめい：究明〉

kyûmei-suru〈究明する〉study, investigate, inquire ((into)).

gen·in-o-kyûmei-suru〈原因を究明する〉 inquire into the cause ((of))

kyûmu〈きゅうむ：急務〉urgent business.

～-ga-kyûmu-de-aru.〈～が急務である。〉It is urgently needed that... .

kyûnan-sagyô〈きゅうなんさぎょう：救難作業〉rescue work, salvage work.

kyûnyû〈きゅうにゅう：吸入〉inhalation.

sanso-kyûnyû-ki〈酸素吸入器〉 an oxygen inhaler

kyûnyû-suru〈吸入する〉inhale, imbibe, breathe in.

kyûrai〈きゅうらい：旧来〉

kyûrai-no〈旧来の〉old, traditional, conventional.

kyûrai-no akushû〈旧来の悪習〉 old abuses

kyûraku〈きゅうらく：急落〉a sharp drop, a slump.

kyûraku-suru〈急落する〉drop sharply.

Sôba ga kyûraku-shita.（相場が急落した.） The quotations have declined sharply.

kyûreki〈きゅうれき：旧暦〉the lunar calendar.

kyûri〈きゅうり〉a cucumber.

kyûryô〈きゅうりょう：給料〉pay, a salary, wages.

kyûryô-bi〈給料日〉 a payday

kyûryô〈きゅうりょう：丘陵〉a hill, a hillock.

kyûryô-chitai〔丘陵地帯〕 hilly districts

kyûsai〈きゅうさい：救済〉relief, help, aid.

kyûsai-jigyô〔救済事業〕 relief work

kyûsai-suru〈救済する〉relieve, give relief ((to)), help.

kyûsai〈きゅうさい：休載〉

kyûsai-suru〈休載する〉do not carry, do not appear (in a newspaper).

kyûsei〈きゅうせい：旧姓〉one's former name, one's maiden name.

    Yoshida Kazuo, kyûsei-Yamaguchi〔吉田和夫旧姓山口〕 Kazuo
    Yoshida, formerly Yamaguchi

    Yoshiyama Yoshiko, kyûsei-Taniguchi〔良山義子，旧姓谷口〕 Mrs.
    Yoshiko Yoshiyama, née Taniguchi

kyûsei〈きゅうせい：旧制〉the old system.

kyûsei-no〈旧制の〉under the old system.

kyûsei〈きゅうせい：急性〉

kyûsei-haien〔急性肺炎〕 acute pneumonia

kyûsei-no〈急性の〉acute.

kyûsei-shu〈きゅうせいしゅ：救世主〉the Savior.

kyûseki〈きゅうせき：旧跡〉a historic spot, a historic site, ruins.

kyûsempô〈きゅうせんぽう：急先ぽう〉a champion, a forerunner, a
leader.

kyû-sempô-ni-tatsu〈急先ぽうに立つ〉lead the van ((of)).

kyûsen〈きゅうせん：休戦〉an armistice, a truce; a cease-fire.

kyûsen-kyôtei〔休戦協定〕 a cease-fire agreement

kyûsen-suru〔休戦する〕 conclude an armistice ((with)), make a
truce ((with))

kyûsha〈きゅうしゃ：きゅう舎〉a stable.

kyû-shamen〈きゅうしゃめん：急斜面〉*see.* kyû-kôbai.

kyûshi〈きゅうし：九死〉

kyûshi-ni-isshô-o-eru〔九死に一生を得る〕 have a narrow escape from
death

kyûshi〈きゅうし：きゅう歯〉a molar.

kyûshi〈きゅうし：休止〉a pause, cessation, suspension, stoppage,
discontinuance, a letup.

unten-kyûshi〔運転休止〕 suspension of the service

kyûshi-suru〈休止する〉pause, cease, suspend, stop, discontinue.

kyûshi〈きゅうし：急死〉a sudden death.

kyûshi-suru〈急死する〉die suddenly.

kyûshiki〈きゅうしき：旧式〉

kyûshiki-no〈旧式の〉old-fashioned, outmoded.

kyûshin〈きゅうしん：球審〉the plate umpire.

kyûshin〈きゅうしん：急進〉

kyûshin-teki(-na)〈急進的(な)〉radical.

kyûshin〈きゅうしん：休診〉

    Honjitsu-kyûshin.（本日休診.） No consultation today.

kyûshin-suru〈休診する〉see no patients.

kyûshin-ryoku〈きゅうしんりょく：求心力〉centripetal force.

kyûsho〈きゅうしょ：急所〉the vital point, a vital part, a sore spot, the raw.

    kyûsho-o-tsuku（急所を突く）hit ((a person)) on a sore spot, touch ((a person)) on the raw

    kyûsho o hazureru（急所を外れる） miss the vital parts

    kyûsho-o-tsuita shitsumon（急所を突いた質問）a question to the point

kyûshoku〈きゅうしょく：給食〉(provision of) meals.

kyûshoku-suru〈給食する〉provide meals ((for)).

kyûshoku〈きゅうしょく：求職〉

    kyûshoku-sha（求職者） a job hunter

kyûshoku-suru〈求職する〉seek employment.

kyûshoku〈きゅうしょく：休職〉suspension from duty, a layoff.

kyûshoku-chû-de-aru〈休職中である〉be under suspension.

kyûshû〈きゅうしゅう：旧習〉an old custom.

    kyûshû-ni-shigami-tsuku（旧習にしがみ付く） cling to old customs

kyûshû〈きゅうしゅう：吸収〉absorption.

    kyûshû-zai（吸収剤） an absorbent

kyûshû-suru〈吸収する〉absorb.

kyûshû〈きゅうしゅう：急襲〉

kyûshû-suru〈急襲する〉make a sudden attack ((on)).

kyûsô〈きゅうそう：急送〉

kyûsô-suru〈急送する〉send ((a thing)) by express, rush.

kyûsoku〈きゅうそく：休息〉(a) rest.

kyûsoku-suru〈休息する〉rest, take a rest.

kyûsoku〈きゅうそく：急速〉

kyûsoku-na〈急速な〉rapid, swift, quick.

    kyûsoku-na shimpo o suru（急速な進歩をする） make rapid progress

kyûsoku-ni〈急速に〉repidly, swiftly, quickly.

kyûsu〈きゅうす：急す〉a (small) teapot.

kyûsû〈きゅうすう：級数〉a series.

kyûsui〈きゅうすい：給水〉water supply.
    kyûsui-sha（給水車）a water wagon
    kyûsui-tô（給水塔）a water tower
  kyûsui-suru〈給水する〉supply ((a town)) with water.

kyû-suru〈きゅうする：窮する〉
    hentô-ni-kyû-suru（返答に窮する）be at a loss for an answer
    Kyû-sureba-tsûzu.（窮すれば通ず。）There is always a way out.

kyûtai〈きゅうたい：旧態〉the old state of things.
    kyûtai-o-todome-nai（旧態をとどめない）be changed beyond recognition

kyûtei〈きゅうてい：宮廷〉the Court.

kyûtei〈きゅうてい：休廷〉
  kyûtei-suru〈休廷する〉hold no court.

kyû-teisha〈きゅうていしゃ：急停車〉
  kyû-teisha-suru〈急停車する〉stop suddenly.

kyûteki〈きゅうてき：きゅう敵〉a sworn enemy.

kyû-tempo〈きゅうテンポ：急テンポ〉
  kyû-tempo-de〈急テンポで〉in quick tempo, rapidly.

kyûten〈きゅうてん：急転〉
  kyûten-suru〈急転する〉change suddenly, take a sudden turn.
  kyûten-chokka（急転直下）all of a sudden, precipitately.

kyûtô〈きゅうとう：急騰〉a sudden rise, a jump.
    bukka-no kyûtô（物価の急騰）a sudden jump in prices
  kyûtô-suru〈急騰する〉jump.

kyûyo〈きゅうよ：給与〉(an) allowance, supplies, pay.
    kyûyo-shotoku（給与所得）earned income
    kyûyo-suijun（給与水準）a wage level
    kyûyo-taikei（給与体系）a pay system

kyûyo〈きゅうよ：窮余〉
    kyûyo-no-issaku（窮余の一策）the last resort

kyûyô〈きゅうよう：休養〉(a) rest.
  kyûyô-suru〈休養する〉rest, take a rest.

kyûyô〈きゅうよう：急用〉urgent business.
    kyûyô-de（急用で）on urgent business

kyûyu〈きゅうゆ：給油〉
  kyûyu-suru〈給油する〉refuel, fill.

kyûyû〈きゅうゆう：旧友〉an old friend.

kyûyû〈きゅうゆう：級友〉a classmate.
kyûzô〈きゅうぞう：急造〉
 kyûzô-suru〈急造する〉build in haste.
kyûzô〈きゅうぞう：急増〉a sudden increase.
 kyûzô-suru〈急増する〉increase suddenly.

M

ma〈ま：魔〉a demon, a devil, an evil spirit.
  ma-yoke（魔よけ） a charm against evil
  ma-no-fumikiri（魔の踏切） a fatal(*or* dangerous) railroad crossing
 ma-ga-sasu〈魔が差す〉be possessed by an evil spirit.
ma〈ま：真〉
 jôdan o ma-ni ukeru〈冗談を真に受ける〉take a joke seriously.
ma〈ま：間〉a room, a chamber; time; an interval.
  yo-ma-no ie（四間の家） a house with four rooms
  Watashi-wa isogashikute neru-ma-mo-nai-kurai-da.（私は忙しくて寝る
   間もないくらいだ。） I'm so busy that I have hardly time to sleep.
  sukoshi-ma-o-oite（少し間をおいて） after a short interval
ma-〈まー：真-〉just, right, due; pure.
  mapputatsu-ni（真っ二つに） right in two
  ma-minami(-ni)（真南(に)） due south
mâ〈まあ〉just; well, say, I think, I should say; Oh!/ Dear me!/ Oh, my!/
 Indeed!
  Mâ-sô-itta-tokoro-desu.（まあそういったところです。） Yes, (it's) something like that.
  Mâ-odoroita!（まあ、驚いた。） What a surprise!
ma-atarashii〈まあたらしい：真新しい〉brand-new, spick-and-span(-new).
mabara〈まばら〉
 mabara-na〈まばらな〉sparse, thin, scattered, straggling.

　　mabara-na jinka〈まばらな人家〉 straggling houses
mabara-ni〈まばらに〉sparsely, thinly, scatteredly, stragglingly.
　　mabara-ni-naru（まばらになる） become sparse, thin (out)
mabataki〈まばたき〉a wink, a blink.
mabataki-mo-sezu(-ni)〈まばたきもせず(に)〉without a wink, unblinkingly.
mabataku〈まばたく〉wink, blink.
mabiki〈まびき：間引き〉
　　mabiki-unten（間引き運転） a thinned-out operation
mabiku〈間引く〉thin out, cut out.
maboroshi〈まぼろし：幻〉a phantom, a vision, a dream, an illusion.
maboroshi-no(-yô-na)〈幻の(ような)〉phantom, visionary, dreamlike, illusive.
mabushii〈まぶしい〉dazzling, glaring, blinding.
mabushiku-kagayaku〈まぶしく輝く〉dazzle, glare.
mabuta〈まぶた〉an eyelid.
machi〈まち：町(街)〉a town, a city; a street.
machi-agumu〈まちあぐむ：待ちあぐむ〉grow tired of waiting ((for)).
machiai-shitsu〈まちあいしつ：待合室〉a waiting room.
machi-awaseru〈まちあわせる：待ち合わせる〉meet, wait ((for)).
machi-bôke〈まちぼうけ：待ちぼうけ〉
　　machi-bôke-o-kuwaseru（待ちぼうけを食わせる） keep ((a person)) waiting in vain, stand up ((a person))
　　machi-bôke-o-kuu（待ちぼうけを食う） wait for ((a person)) in vain
machibuse〈まちぶせ：待ち伏せ〉
machibuse-suru or *machi-buseru*〈待ち伏せする，待ち伏せる〉lie in wait ((for)), ambush, waylay.
machibuse-o-kuu〈待ち伏せを食う〉be waylaid ((by)).
machi-dooshii〈まちどおしい：待ち遠しい〉be long (in) coming, be impatient for ((something)).
　　Tsugi-no saijitsu ga machi-dooshii.（次の祭日が待ち遠しい.） The coming national holiday seems long in coming.
　　O-machi-doo-sama.（お待ち遠さま.） I am very sorry to have kept you waiting.
machigaeru〈まちがえる：間違える〉mistake, make a mistake, commit an error, take ((A)) for ((B)).
　　michi-o-machigaeru（道を間違える） take the wrong way
machigai〈まちがい：間違い〉a mistake, an error, a fault, a slip, a

failure, a blunder; an accident, a mishap.

machigai-nai 〈間違いない〉 correct, sure, certain, reliable.

machigai-naku 〈間違いなく〉 correctly, surely, without fail.

machigai-de 〈間違いで〉 by accident.

machigatta 〈まちがった：間違った〉 wrong, mistaken, incorrect.

machigatta-koto-o-suru 〈間違ったことをする〉 do wrong

machigatte 〈間違って〉 by mistake, by accident.

Kimi-ga-machigatte-iru.〈君が間違っている。〉 You are mistaken. / You are wrong.

machigau 〈まちがう：間違う〉 *see.* machigaeru.

machi-hazure 〈まちはずれ：町外れ〉

machi-hazure-ni 〈町外れに〉 on the outskirts of a town.

machi-kado 〈まちかど：街角〉 a street corner.

machi-kaneru 〈まちかねる：待ち兼ねる〉 wait impatiently ((for)), look forward ((to)).

machi-kogareru 〈まちこがれる：待ち焦がれる〉 wait anxiously ((for)).

machi-kutabireru 〈まちくたびれる：待ちくたびれる〉 *see.* machi-agumu.

machi-nami 〈まちなみ：町並み〉 the row of houses on a street.

machi-ukeru 〈まちうける：待ち受ける〉 wait for, expect.

mada 〈まだ〉 yet, as yet, still, more, only.

"Yomi-oemashita-ka?" "Ie, mada-desu." （"読み終えましたか."　"いえ，まだです."） "Have you finished reading it?" "No, not yet."

Mada-ame-ga-futteiru.（まだ雨が降っている。） It is still raining.

Mada go-kiro-aru.（まだ五キロある。） We still have more five kilometers to go.

Mada yo-ji-da.（まだ四時だ。） It is only four o'clock.

madamada 〈まだまだ〉 still, still more.

Madamada hataraka-nakucha.（まだまだ働かなくちゃ。） You must work still harder.

madamu 〈マダム〉 Mrs., Madam, the proprietress.

madara 〈まだら〉 spots, speckles, patches.

madara-no 〈まだらの〉 spotted, speckled, varicolored.

madara-ni 〈まだらに〉 in spots, in patches.

madarukkoi 〈まだるっこい：間だるっこい〉 slow, tedious, dull, slow-moving, sluggish.

-made 〈-まで〉 till, until, to; to, as far as; to, so far as, even.

asa-kara ban-made（朝から晩まで） from morning till night

yoru-osoku-made（夜遅くまで） till late at night

hachi-jussai-made-ikiru（八十歳まで生きる） live to be eighty

Doko-made-ikimasu-ka?（どこまで行きますか.） How far are you going?

Hokkaidô-made ikimasu.（北海道まで行きます.） I'm going to(or as far as) Hokkaido.

Mizu wa mune-made-atta.（水は胸まであった.） The water came up to my chest.

saigo-made（最後まで） to the last

Kare-made watashi-o mikubitte-iru.（彼まで私を見くびっている.） Even he despises me.

-made-ni 〈−までに〉 by, by the time.

tsugi-no getsuyô-made-ni（次の月曜までに） by next Monday

mado 〈まど：窓〉a window.

mado o akeru（窓を開ける） open a window, roll down the window

mado o shimeru（窓を閉める） shut a window

mado-kara-soto-o-miru（窓から外を見る） look out of the window

mado-garasu（窓ガラス） window glass, a windowpane

mado-giwa 〈まどぎわ：窓際〉

mado-giwa-no seki（窓際の席） a window seat

mado-giwa-de or *mado-giwa-ni*〈窓際で, 窓際に〉at(or by) the window.

mado-guchi 〈まどぐち：窓口〉a window, a clerk at the window.

ma-dori 〈まどり：間取り〉the plan of a house, room arrangement.

ma-dori-no-ii ie（間取りのいい家） a well-planned house

madoromu 〈まどろむ〉doze (off), fall into a doze.

mae 〈まえ：前〉

mae-no〈前の〉front, fore; previous, last, former.

mae-no seki（前の席） the front seat

mae-no doyô-ni（前の土曜に） last Saturday, on Saturday last

sono mae-no ban-ni（その前の晩に） on the previous night

kanojo-no mae-no ie（彼女の前の家） her former residence

mae-e, mae-ni or *mae-o*〈前へ, 前に, 前を〉in front ((of)), before; ago, before, previously, formerly; forward, ahead, before.

ie-no-mae-ni（家の前に） in front of a house

san-nen-mae-ni（三年前に） three years ago(or before)

yo-ji-jûgo-fun-mae-ni（四時十五分前に） at a quarter of(or to) four

ippo mae-ni-deru（一歩前に出る） take a step forward

hito-no ie-no-mae-o-tooru（人の家の前を通る） pass a person's house

mae-motte〈前もって〉beforehand, in advance, previously.

hito-no-mae-de 〈人の前で〉 *see.* hito-mae-de.

-mae 〈－まえ：－前〉

    bifu-katsu-o-ni-nin-mae taberu 〈ビフカツを二人前食べる〉 eat two portions of fried beef cutlet

    san-nin-mae-hataraku 〈三人前働く〉 do the work of three men

mae-ashi 〈まえあし：前足〉 a forefoot, a foreleg, a paw.

mae-ba 〈まえば：前歯〉 a foretooth, a front tooth.

mae-barai 〈まえばらい：前払い〉 advance payment, payment in advance.

    unchin-mae-barai(-de) 〈運賃前払い(で)〉 freight prepaid

 mae-barai-suru 〈前払いする〉 pay in advance, advance.

mae-bure 〈まえぶれ：前触れ〉 previous notice.

 mae-bure-mo-naku 〈前触れもなく〉 without notice, without warning.

mae-gaki 〈まえがき：前書き〉 a preface, a foreword, an introduction.

mae-gari 〈まえがり：前借り〉

 mae-gari-suru 〈前借りする〉 borrow in advance.

mae-gashi 〈まえがし：前貸し〉

 mae-gashi-suru 〈前貸しする〉 pay in advance.

mae-iwai 〈まえいわい：前祝い〉 celebration in advance.

 mae-iwai-suru 〈前祝いする〉 celebrate beforehand.

mae-kagami 〈まえかがみ：前かがみ〉

 mae-kagami-ni-natte aruku 〈前かがみになって歩く〉 walk with a slouch.

mae-kin 〈まえきん：前金〉 *see.* mae-barai.

 mae-kin-de-harau 〈前金で払う〉 *see.* mae-barai-suru.

mae-muki 〈まえむき：前向き〉

 mae-muki-no 〈前向きの〉 positive, constructive.

    mae-muki-no shisei-de 〈前向きの姿勢で〉 in a positive attitude

 mae-muki-ni 〈前向きに〉 positively, constructively.

mae-oki 〈まえおき：前置き〉 an introductory remark, a preliminary.

 mae-oki-suru 〈前置きする〉 make introductory remarks.

 ～-to-mae-oki-shite 〈～と前置きして〉 with the preliminary that... .

 mae-oki-nashi-ni 〈前置きなしに〉 without preliminaries.

mae-uri 〈まえうり：前売り〉 advance sale.

    mae-uri-ken 〈前売券〉 a ticket sold in advance

 mae-uri-suru 〈前売りする〉 sell in advance.

ma-fuyu 〈まふゆ：真冬〉 midwinter.

magai(-mono) 〈まがい(もの)：まがい(物)〉 an imitation, a sham.

 magai(-mono)-no 〈まがい(物)の〉 imitation, sham.

ma-gao 〈まがお：真顔〉

ma-gao-de 〈真顔で〉with a serious look.

ma-gari 〈まがり：間借り〉
ma-gari-nin (間借り人) a lodger, a roomer
ma-gari-suru 〈間借りする〉rent a room.

magari-kado 〈まがりかど：曲がり角〉a street corner, a road bend, a turning.
magari-kado-ni-kita　Nihon-keizai (曲がり角に来た日本経済) Japanese economy at a turning point

magari-kuneru 〈まがりくねる：曲がりくねる〉turn and twist, meander.
magari-kunetta 〈曲がりくねった〉winding, tortuous, crooked, meandering.

magarinari 〈まがりなり：曲がりなり〉
magarinari-ni-mo 〈曲がりなりにも〉anyhow, somehow or other, though not satisfactorily.

magaru 〈まがる：曲がる〉turn; bend, be bent, be crooked; be awry.
hidari-e magaru (左へ曲がる) turn to the left
Kono-saki-de michi wa kyū-ni-magatte-iru. (この先で道は急に曲がっている。) The road bends sharply ahead.
toshi-o-totte　koshi-ga-magatte-iru (年を取って腰が曲がっている) be bent with age
Kimi-no　nekutai　wa　magatte-iru. (君のネクタイは曲がっている。) Your tie is awry.

magatta 〈まがった：曲がった〉bent, curved, winding; crooked, perverse, wicked.
magatta kugi (曲がったくぎ) a curved nail
magatta koto (曲がった事) a crooked deed

mageru 〈まげる：曲げる〉bend, curve, crook; pervert, distort, twist.
hiza o mageru (ひざを曲げる) bend one's knees
harigane o mageru (針金を曲げる) curve a wire
hō o mageru (法を曲げる) pervert the law
imi-o-magete-kaishaku-suru (意味を曲げて解釈する) twist the meaning
shugi-o-mageru (主義を曲げる) depart from one's principle

magirasu 〈まぎらす：紛らす〉
sake-de　usa-o-magirasu 〈酒で憂さを紛らす〉drown one's sorrows in drink.

magirawashii 〈まぎらわしい：紛らわしい〉misleading, confusing, ambiguous, equivocal, indistinct.

magire-komu 〈まぎれこむ：紛れ込む〉be lost ((among *or* in)).

    hito-gomi-no-naka-ni　magire-komu（人込みの中に紛れ込む）disappear into the crowds

magire-mo-nai 〈まぎれもない：紛れもない〉unmistakable, obvious, evident, certain.

    magire-mo-nai jijitsu（紛れもない事実）a plain fact

magire-mo-naku 〈紛れもなく〉unmistakably, evidently, beyond doubt, certainly, surely.

-magire-ni 〈-まぎれに：-紛れに〉

    dosakusa-magire-ni-umai-shiru-o-suu（どさくさまぎれにうまい汁を吸う）fish in troubled waters

    hara-dachi-magire-ni（腹立ちまぎれに）in a fit of anger

    kurushi-magire-ni（苦しまぎれに）in one's agony, as the last resort

    ureshi-magire-ni（うれしまぎれに）in the excess of one's joy

magireru 〈まぎれる：紛れる〉be diverted, be beguiled.

    ki-ga-magireru（気が紛れる）be diverted from care, forget one's cares for a time

magiwa-ni 〈まぎわに：間際に〉just before, on the point ((of)).

    shinu-magiwa-ni（死ぬ間際に）just before one's death

    hassha-magiwa-ni（発車間際に）when the train was about to start

magiwa-ni-natte 〈間際になって〉at the last moment, at the eleventh hour.

mago 〈まご：孫〉a grandchild; a grandson, a granddaughter.

magokoro 〈まごころ：真心〉sincerity, faith.

magokoro-kometa 〈真心込めた〉sincere, faithful.

magokoro-komete 〈真心込めて〉sincerely, with one's whole heart, faithfully, devotedly.

magomago-suru 〈まごまごする〉hang around; be flurried, be confused, be bewildered, be at a loss.

    Magomago-shite-iru-toki-dewa-nai.（まごまごしている時ではない.）We have no time to lose.

    Kanojo-ni-shitsumon-sarete　magomago-shite-shimatta.（彼女に質問されてまごまごしてしまった.）I was confused at her question.

magomago-shite 〈まごまごして〉in a flurry.

magomago-sezu-ni 〈まごまごせずに〉without hesitation.

mago-tsuku 〈まごつく〉*see.* magomago-suru.

maguchi 〈まぐち：間口〉a frontage, width.

    maguchi-ga-semai（間口が狭い）have a narrow frontage

magure-atari 〈まぐれあたり：まぐれ当たり〉a chance hit, a fluke.
    magure-atari-de katsu（まぐれ当たりで勝つ）win by a fluke

maguro 〈まぐろ〉a tuna.

magusa 〈まぐさ〉fodder, hay.
  uma-ni-magusa-o-yaru〈馬にまぐさをやる〉fodder a horse, give fodder to a horse.

mahha 〈マッハ〉a Mach (number).
    mahha-ni-de tobu（マッハ 2 で飛ぶ）fly at Mach two

mahi 〈まひ：麻ひ〉paralysis, palsy, numbness.
  mahi-suru（麻ひする）be paralyzed, be palsied, go numb, be benumbed.

ma-higashi(-ni) 〈まひがし(に)：真東(に)〉due east.

ma-hiru 〈まひる：真昼〉broad daylight, midday.
  ma-hiru-ni（真昼に〉in broad daylight, at midday, at noon.

mahô 〈まほう：魔法〉magic, witchcraft, the black art.
    mahô o tsukau（魔法を使う）use magic
    mahô-tsukai（魔法使い）a magician, a wizard, a witch
    mahô-bin（魔法瓶）a thermos (bottle), a vacuum bottle
  mahô-o-kakeru〈魔法をかける〉cast a spell ((on)), bind ((a person)) by a spell.
  mahô-no(-yô-na)（魔法の(ような)〉magic(al).

Mahometto 〈マホメット〉Mohammed, Mahomet.
    Mahometto-kyō（マホメット教）Mohammedanism
      Mahometto-kyō-to（マホメット教徒）a Mohammedan, a Moslem

mai 〈まい：舞〉dancing, a dance.
  mai-o-mau〈舞を舞う〉dance, perform a dance.

-mai 〈-まい：-枚〉a sheet, a leaf, a piece, a page.
    kami-go-mai（紙五枚）five sheets of paper
    hyaku-en-kitte roku-mai（百円切手六枚）six 100-yen stamps

mai-agaru 〈まいあがる：舞い上がる〉fly high, soar, be blown up.

mai-asa 〈まいあさ：毎朝〉every morning.

mai-ban 〈まいばん：毎晩〉every evening, every night.

maibotsu 〈まいぼつ：埋没〉
  maibotsu-suru〈埋没する〉be buried (in the ground).

maido 〈まいど：毎度〉(very) often, frequently; always; every time.
    Maido go-tesû-o-o-kakeshite-ai-sumi-masen.（毎度御手数をお掛けして相すみません。）I'm sorry to trouble you so often.

mai-getsu 〈まいげつ：毎月〉*see.* mai-tsuki

mai-go 〈まいご：迷子〉a stray child.

mai-go-ni-naru〈迷子になる〉be missing, be lost, lose one's way.

mai-hômu-shugi〈マイホームしゅぎ：マイホーム主義〉a family-oriented way of life.

mai-kâ〈マイカー〉one's own car.

　mai-kâ-zoku（マイカー族）owner drivers

mai-kai〈まいかい：毎回〉each time.

maiko〈まいこ：舞子〉a dancing girl, a dancer.

mai-komu〈まいこむ：舞い込む〉visit, drop in.

　hen-na tegami-ga-mai-komu（変な手紙が舞い込む）have a strange letter

maiku(rohon)〈マイク（ロホン）〉a microphone, a mike.

　kakushi-maiku（隠しマイク）a concealed mike

maiku-ni-mukatte〈マイクに向かって〉at a mike.

maiku-o-tsûjite〈マイクを通じて〉through a mike.

maikyo〈まいきょ：枚挙〉

maikyo-ni-itoma-ga-nai〈枚挙にいとまがない〉be too numerous to mention.

mainasu〈マイナス〉minus.

　Hachi-mainasu-san wa go.（八マイナス三は五.）Eight minus three leaves five.

　mainasu-go-do（マイナス五度）minus five degrees

mai-nen〈まいねん：毎年〉every year, annually.

mainen-no〈毎年の〉annual.

mai-nichi〈まいにち：毎日〉every day, daily.

mai-nichi-no〈毎日の〉everyday, daily.

mairu〈まいる：参る〉

　Asu-gogo soko-e mairimasu.（明日午後そこへ参ります.）I'm going there tomorrow afternoon.

　Maitta!（参った.）You've got me there. / I'm done for.

　Kono atsusa-ni-wa-maitta.（この暑さには参った.）I can't stand this heat.

　shinkei ga mairu（神経が参る）one's nerves break down

maishoku〈まいしょく：毎食〉every meal.

mai-shû〈まいしゅう：毎週〉every week, weekly.

mai-shû-no〈毎週の〉weekly.

maisô〈まいそう：埋葬〉burial.

maisô-suru〈埋葬する〉bury.

maisô-sareru〈埋葬される〉be buried.

mai-toshi 〈まいとし：毎年〉 *see.* mai-nen.

mai-tsuki 〈まいつき：毎月〉 every month.

mai-tsuki-no 〈毎月の〉 monthly

maizō 〈まいぞう：埋蔵〉

maizō-ryō（埋蔵量） reserves, an estimated amount ((of))

maizō-suru（埋蔵する）bury in the ground.

maizō-sarete-iru 〈埋蔵されている〉be buried underground.

mâjan 〈マージャン〉mahjong.

majika 〈まぢか：間近〉

majikai 〈間近い〉 very near.

kansei-ga-majikai（完成が間近い） be nearing completion

majika-ni 〈間近に〉near by, close at hand.

majikku-inki 〈マジックインキ〉 marking ink.

majimaji 〈まじまじ〉

majimaji-to miru 〈まじまじと見る〉stare hard ((at)).

majime 〈まじめ〉

majime-na 〈まじめな〉 serious, sober, earnest, grave.

majime-na-kao-o-suru（まじめな顔をする） look serious

majime-kusatte 〈まじめくさって〉with a serious look.

majime-ni 〈まじめに〉seriously, soberly, earnestly.

majime-ni-naru（まじめになる） become serious, turn over a new leaf

majinai 〈まじない〉a charm, a spell, an incantation.

majinai-o-suru 〈まじないをする〉charm, use a charm, cast a spell ((upon)).

majiri 〈まじり：混じり〉

Ame-majiri-no-yuki-ga-futteiru.（雨混じりの雪が降っている．） It is sleeting.

majiri-ke 〈まじりけ：混じり気〉mixture, impurity.

majiri-ke-no-nai 〈混じり気のない〉pure, unadulterated, genuine.

majiru 〈まじる：交(混)じる〉mix ((with)), mingle ((with)), join, be mixed, be mingled, be blended.

Abura to mizu wa majira-nai.（油と水は混じらない．） Oil and water will not mix.

majiwari 〈まじわり：交わり〉acquaintance, association, intercourse, company, friendship.

majiwaru 〈まじわる：交わる〉associate ((with)), keep company ((with)), hold intercourse ((with)); cross, intersect.

shitashiku-majiwaru（親しく交わる）be on intimate terms ((with)), be good friends ((with))

majiwara-nai（交わらない）keep away ((from)), avoid

Ni-hon-no dōro ga chokkaku-ni majiwatte-iru.（二本の道路が直角に交わっている．）The two roads intersect each other at right angles.

majo〈まじょ：魔女〉a witch.

majutsu-shi〈まじゅつし：魔術師〉a magician, a juggler.

makanai〈まかない：賄い〉board, meals, fare.

makanai-zuki-geshuku（賄い付き下宿）board and lodging

makanau〈まかなう：賄う〉board, provide ((a person)) with meals; pay, cover, finance.

ryohi o makanau（旅費を賄う）pay the traveling expenses

makari-machigau〈まかりまちがう：まかり間違う〉

makari-machigaeba（まかり間違えば）if the worst happens, if things go wrong

makari-machigattemo（まかり間違っても）even in the worst case, at the worst

makaseru〈まかせる：任せる〉leave ((a matter)) to ((a person)), trust ((a person)) with.

Watashi-ni makasete-kure.（私に任せてくれ．）Leave it to me.

ashi-ni-makasete aruku（足に任せて歩く）walk as one's legs lead one

un-o-ten-ni-makaseru（運を天に任せる）trust to chance, leave everything to chance, resign oneself to one's fate

makasu〈まかす：負かす〉beat, defeat.

giron-de hito o makasu（議論で人を負かす）beat a person in argument

make〈まけ：負け〉(a) defeat, a loss, a lost game.

Kono-gêmu-wa-kimi-no-make-da.（このゲームは君の負けだ．）You've lost this game.

make-inu〈まけいぬ：負け犬〉an underdog.

makeji-damashii〈まけじだましい：負けじ魂〉an unyielding spirit.

make-kosu〈まけこす：負け越す〉lose more games than ((one's opponent)), lose the majority of one's matches.

make-oshimi〈まけおしみ：負け惜しみ〉(a case of) sour grapes.

make-oshimi-no-tsuyoi-hito〈負け惜しみの強い人〉a poor loser

make-oshimi-o-iu〈負け惜しみを言う〉refuse to own one's defeat.

makeru〈まける：負ける〉be defeated, be beaten, lose; give way ((to)), bow ((to)), yield ((to)); be inferior ((to)), fall behind, be second ((to)); reduce, lower, make ((it)) cheaper; be poisoned.

　　shiai ni makeru〔試合に負ける〕 lose a game

　　kanjô-ni makeru〔感情に負ける〕 give way to one's feelings

　　ummei-ni makeru〔運命に負ける〕 bow to fate

　　yûwaku-ni makeru〔誘惑に負ける〕 yield to temptation

　　Kare-wa Eigo-dewa dare-ni-mo-make-nai.〔彼は英語ではだれにも負けない。〕 He is second to none in English.

　　Sukoshi-makerare-masen-ka?〔少し負けられませんか.〕 Can you make any reduction?

　　urushi-ni-makeru〔うるしに負ける〕 be poisoned with lacquer

makezu-girai〔まけずぎらい：負けず嫌い〕

　makezu-girai-no〔負けず嫌いの〕 unyielding, competitive.

makezu-otorazu〔まけずおとらず：負けず劣らず〕 equally, neck and neck.

maki〔まき〕 firewood, wood.

-maki〔−まき：−巻き〕 a roll; winding.

　　kami-hito-maki〔紙一巻〕 a roll of paper

　　yôka-maki-no tokei〔八日巻きの時計〕 an eight-day clock

maki-ageru〔まきあげる：巻き上げる〕 wind up, roll up; take away, fleece ((a person)) of, swindle ((a person)) out of.

makiba〔まきば：牧場〕 a pasture, a meadow, a ranch.

maki-chirasu〔まきちらす：まき散らす〕 scatter about, strew, sprinkle; squander.

maki-e〔まきえ：まき絵〕 gold lacquer, silver lacquer.

maki-ge〔まきげ：巻き毛〕 a curl, a ringlet.

maki-jaku〔まきじゃく：巻き尺〕 a tape measure.

　maki-jaku-de-hakaru〔巻き尺で測る〕 tape-measure.

maki-jita〔まきじた：巻き舌〕

　maki-jita-de-hanasu〔巻き舌で話す〕 trill one's r's.

maki-kaeshi〔まきかえし：巻き返し〕

　　maki-kaeshi-seisaku〔巻き返し政策〕 a rollback policy

　maki-kaesu〔巻き返す〕 roll back.

maki-komu〔まきこむ：巻き込む〕 roll in, wrap in; engulf; involve in, entangle in.

　　nami-ni maki-komareru〔波に巻き込まれる〕 be engulfed in the waves

　　jiken-ni maki-komareru〔事件に巻き込まれる〕 be involved in a

certain affair

sensô-ni　maki-komareru（戦争に巻き込まれる）be dragged into a war

kikai-ni　maki-komareru（機械に巻き込まれる）be caught in a machine

maki-modosu 〈まきもどす：巻き戻す〉roll back.

maki-mono 〈まきもの：巻き物〉a *makimono*, a roll, a scroll.

makishi 〈マキシ〉a maxi dress, a maxi.

ma-kita(-ni) 〈まきた(に)：真北(に)〉due north.

makitori-gami 〈まきとりがみ：巻き取り紙〉a roll of newsprint.

maki-tsukeru 〈まきつける：巻き付ける〉twist ((something)) around.

maki-tsuku 〈巻き付く〉coil around, twine around; wind itself around.

makizoe 〈まきぞえ：巻き添え〉

makizoe-o-kuu 〈巻き添えを食う〉get involved ((in)), get entangled ((in)), get mixed up ((in)).

makka 〈まっか：真っ赤〉

makka-ni-naru 〈真っ赤になる〉turn red, flush deeply, blush scarlet, blush violently, flame red.

makka-ni-natte-okoru（真っ赤になって怒る）be red with anger

makka-na 〈真っ赤な〉deep-red, crimson; downright.

makka-na uso（真っ赤なうそ）a downright lie

makki 〈まっき：末期〉the last stage, the last years, the close.

makki-teki-shôjô-o-teishite-iru（末期的症状を呈している）be heading for a collapse

makkura 〈まっくら：真っ暗〉

makkura-na 〈真っ暗な〉pitch-dark.

makkuro 〈まっくろ：真っ黒〉

hi-ni-yakete-makkuro-ni-naru 〈日に焼けて真っ黒になる〉be tanned deeply by the sun.

makkuro-na 〈真っ黒な〉deep-black, coal-black.

makoto 〈まこと：誠〉sincerity, a true heart, faithfulness; the truth, the reality, the fact.

makoto-no-aru 〈誠のある〉sincere, true, faithful.

makoto-no-aru hito（誠のある人）a sincere person

makoto-no 〈誠の〉true, real, genuine, actual.

makoto-ni 〈誠に〉sincerely, truly, really, indeed, very, much.

Makoto-ni　arigatô-gozaimasu.（誠にありがとうございます.）Thank you very much.

makoto-shiyaka 〈まことしやか〉
makoto-shiyaka-na 〈まことしやかな〉plausible.
makoto-shiyaka-ni 〈まことしやかに〉plausibly, as if it were true.

maku 〈まく：幕〉a curtain; an act.
　　Maku ga aku.（幕が開く.）　The curtain rises.
　　maku-ai（幕間）　an intermission, an interval
　　maku-gire（幕切れ）　the fall of the curtain

maku 〈まく：膜〉a membrane, a film.

maku 〈まく〉sow.
　　hatake ni ko-mugi-o-maku（畑に小麦をまく）sow the field with
　　　　wheat

maku 〈まく〉scatter; sprinkle, water; give ((a person)) the slip.
　　mizu o maku（水をまく）　sprinkle water
　　keiji o maku（刑事をまく）　give a detective the slip

maku 〈まく：巻く〉roll, wind, coil, bind, tie up.

mâku 〈マーク〉a mark.
　　mâku-suru or *mâku-o-tsukeru*〈マークする，マークを付ける〉mark, put a
　　　　mark ((on)).
　　mâku-sarete-iru jimbutsu（マークされている人物）a marked person

makura 〈まくら〉a pillow.
　　makura o suru（まくらをする）　use a pillow
　　makura-o-narabete〈まくらを並べて〉side by side.
　　makura-moto-no, makura-moto-de or *makura-moto-ni*〈まくらもとの，ま
　　　　くらもとで，まくらもとに〉at one's bedside.

makura-gi 〈まくらぎ：まくら木〉a (railroad) tie, a crosstie, a sleeper.

makura-kotoba 〈まくらことば〉a set epithet.

makureru 〈まくれる〉be turned up.
　　makuru〈まくる〉turn up, roll up.
　　ude o makuru（腕をまくる）　roll up one's sleeves

maku-shita-rikishi 〈まくしたりきし：幕下力士〉a junior-grade *sumo*
wrestler.

makushi-tateru 〈まくしたてる：まくし立てる〉shoot off at the mouth,
rattle away(*or* on).

maku-uchi-rikishi 〈まくうちりきし：幕内力士〉a senior-grade *sumo*
wrestler.

mama 〈まま〉
　　sono-mama-ni-shite-oku（そのままにしておく）　leave ((a thing)) as it
　　　　is

omotta-mama-o-iu（思ったままを言う） speak just as one feels

hito-no-iu-mama-ni-naru（人の言うままになる） be at a person's beck and call

omou-mama-ni（思うままに） as one pleases

meizerareru-mama-ni（命ぜられるままに） as one is told

mâmâ〈まあまあ〉come, come / now, now / there, there / moderately.

  "O-shigoto-wa-dô-desu-ka?" "Mâmâ-desu."（"お仕事はどうですか。" "まあまあです。"） "How is your business?" "So-so."

mama-goto〈ままごと：まま事〉

 mama-goto-o-suru〈まま事をする〉play house, play at keeping house.

mama-haha〈ままはは：まま母〉a stepmother.

mama-ko〈ままこ：まま子〉a stepchild; a stepson, a stepdaughter.

mamben-naku〈まんべんなく：万遍なく〉equally, evenly, uniformly, thoroughly.

  mamben-naku kubaru（万遍なく配る） distribute evenly

mambiki〈まんびき：万引き〉shoplifting; a shoplifter.

 mambiki-suru〈万引きする〉shoplift.

mame〈まめ：豆〉a bean, a pea, a soybean; a blister, a corn.

mame〈まめ〉

 mame-na〈まめな〉diligent, hardworking, active.

 mame-ni〈まめに〉diligently, assiduously.

  mame-ni hataraku（まめに働く） work as busy as a beaver

mame-〈まめ-：豆-〉miniature, midget.

  mame-denkyû（豆電球） a miniature bulb

mame-deppô〈まめでっぽう：豆鉄砲〉a popgun.

mametsu〈まめつ：摩滅〉wear (and tear), defacement.

 mametsu-suru〈摩滅する〉be worn out, be defaced.

ma-mizu〈まみず：真水〉fresh water.

mamman〈まんまん：満々〉

 mamman-taru〈満々たる〉full of.

  mamman-taru jishin-de（満々たる自信で） in full self-confidence

 mamman-to〈満々と〉full to the brim.

  mamman-to mizu-o-tataete-iru（満々と水をたたえている） be filled with water to the brim

mamma-to〈まんまと〉

 mamma-to ippai-kuwasareru〈まんまと一杯食わされる〉be nicely taken in.

mammen〈まんめん：満面〉the whole face.

mammen-ni-emi-o-ukabete〈満面に笑みを浮かべて〉with one's face beaming (with smiles).

mammosu〈マンモス〉a mammoth.
　mammosu-kigyō（マンモス企業）a mammoth enterprise

ma-mo-naku〈まもなく：間もなく〉soon, presently, shortly, before long.
　sono-go-ma-mo-naku（その後間もなく）soon after

ma-mono〈まもの：魔物〉a demon, a devil.

mamori〈まもり：守り〉(a) defense, protection, a safeguard.
　mamori o katameru（守りを固める）strengthen the defense
mamoru〈守る〉defend, protect, guard; obey, observe; keep, fulfill.
　mi o mamoru（身を守る）defend oneself ((against)), protect oneself ((against))
　kōtsū-hōki o mamoru（交通法規を守る）observe traffic regulations
　yakusoku o mamoru（約束を守る）keep one's word

mampuku〈まんぷく：満腹〉a full stomach.
　Mampuku-da.（満腹だ.）I've had enough.

ma-mukai〈まむかい：真向かい〉
ma-mukai-ni〈真向かいに〉right opposite, just in front ((of)).

mamushi〈まむし〉a viper.

man〈まん：万〉ten thousand.
　ni-man（二万）twenty thousand
　man-bun-no-ichi（万分の一）a ten-thousandth
　nan-man-to-iu（何万という）tens of thousands of

man-〈まん−：満−〉full.
　man-ni-jussai-de-aru（満二十歳である）be a full twenty years old

manabu〈まなぶ：学ぶ〉study, learn.

manaita〈まないた〉a chopping board.
　manaita-no-koi-no-yō-na-mono-da（まないたのこいのような ものだ）be entirely left to one's fate

ma-natsu〈まなつ：真夏〉midsummer.
　ma-natsu-ni（真夏に）in midsummer

manazashi〈まなざし〉a look.

manchō〈まんちょう：満潮〉high water, a high tide.
manchō-ji-ni〈満潮時に〉at high tide.

mandan〈まんだん：漫談〉random talk, a comic chat.

mane〈まね〉imitation, mimicry.
mane-o-suru or *maneru*〈まねをする，まねる〉imitate, mimic, pretend.

maneki〈まねき：招き〉an invitation.

maneki-ni-yori（招きにより）by ((a person's)) invitation

maneku（招く）invite, ask; incur, court, cause, bring about.

kiken o maneku（危険を招く）court danger

man·en〈まんえん：まん延〉

man·en-suru（まん延する）spread, prevail, be prevalent, sweep ((over)).

man·etsu〈まんえつ：満悦〉

go-man·etsu-de-aru（御満悦である）look very much satisfied ((with)).

manga〈まんが：漫画〉a comic strip, a caricature, a cartoon.

manga-eiga（漫画映画）a cartoon film, an animated cartoon

manga-ka（漫画家）a cartoon artist, a cartoonist

mangan〈マンガン〉manganese.

mangetsu〈まんげつ：満月〉a full moon.

mania〈マニア〉a mania ((for)), a craze ((for)); a maniac, a fan.

ma-ni-au〈まにあう：間に合う〉be in time ((for)), make; will do, be enough, be of use; can do without.

go-ji-no-ressha ni ma-ni-au（五時の列車に間に合う）make the 5 o'clock train

Ichi-man-en-areba ma-ni-au.（一万円あれば間に合う.）A ten thousand yen will do.

Kimi-ga-inakute-mo jūbun ma-ni-au.（君がいなくても十分間に合う.）We can do very well without you.

ma-ni-awase〈まにあわせ：間に合わせ〉

ma-ni-awase-no（間に合わせの）makeshift, temporary.

ma-ni-awase-ni（間に合わせに）for a shift, as a makeshift ((for)), to temporize.

ma-ni-awaseru（間に合わせる）make shift ((with)), make do ((with)), make ((a thing)) do, temporize.

man·ichi〈まんいち：万一〉

man·ichi-ni-sonaeru（万一に備える）provide against an emergency

man·ichi no baai-ni-wa（万一の場合には）in case of emergency, in time of need

man·ichi-no-koto-ga-atte-mo（万一の事があっても）at the worst

man·ichi-shippai-shitara（万一失敗したら）if I should fail

man·ichi sonna koto ga okottara（万一そんな事が起こったら）if such a thing should happen

manikyua〈マニキュア〉(a) manicure.

manikyua-o-shite-morau（マニキュアをしてもらう）have a manicure

-manimani〈-まにまに〉

nami-no-manimani-tadayou 〈波のまにまに漂う〉 drift at the mercy of the waves.

man·in 〈まんいん：満員〉

Man·in.（満員.） House Full. / Sold out.

man·in-densha（満員電車） a crowded car

man·in-de-aru 〈満員である〉 be full, be crowded, draw a full house.

chô-man·in-de-aru（超満員である） be filled to ((its)) fullest capacity

man·in-no 〈満員の〉 full, crowded, capacity.

man·in-no kankyaku（満員の観客） capacity audience

ma-ningen 〈まにんげん：真人間〉

ma-ningen-ni-naru 〈真人間になる〉 see. majime-ni-naru.

Manira 〈マニラ〉 Manila.

Manira-asa（マニラ麻） Manila hemp

ma-nishi(-ni) 〈まにし(に)：真西(に)〉 due west.

manjiri 〈まんじり〉

manjiri-tomo-shi-nai 〈まんじりともしない〉 pass a sleepless night.

manjô 〈まんじょう：満場〉 the whole house, the whole audience.

manjô-no-kassai-o-abiru（満場の喝さいを浴びる） bring down the house

manjô-itchi-de 〈満場一致で〉 unanimously, by common consent.

manjū 〈まんじゅう〉 a bean-jam bun.

mankai 〈まんかい：満開〉 full bloom.

mankai-de-aru 〈満開である〉 be in full bloom, be at ((their)) best.

mankai-no 〈満開の〉 full-blown.

manki 〈まんき：満期〉 expiration, maturity.

manki-bi（満期日） the expiration date, the date of maturity

manki-ni-naru 〈満期になる〉 expire, mature, fall due; serve out one's time.

mankitsu 〈まんきつ：満喫〉

mankitsu-suru 〈満喫する〉 enjoy to the full.

mannaka 〈まんなか：真ん中〉 the middle, the center, the heart.

mannaka-no 〈真ん中の〉 middle, central.

mannaka-ni 〈真ん中に〉 in the middle ((of)), in the heart ((of)), halfway, midway.

mannen- 〈まんねん-：万年-〉

mannen-kôho（万年候補） a permanent unsuccessful candidate

mannen-yuki（万年雪） permanent snow, an icecap

mannen-hitsu 〈まんねんひつ：万年筆〉 a fountain pen.

mannen-hitsu-ni-inku-o-ireru〈万年筆にインクを入れる〉 fill a pen

manneri or **mannerizumu**〈マンネリ, マンネリズム〉a mannerism.
manneri-ni-ochiiru〈マンネリに陥る〉become stereotyped.

ma-no-atari(-ni)〈まのあたり(に): 目の当たり(に)〉before one's eyes,
with one's own eyes, actually.

ma-no-atari-ni miru（目の当たりに見る）see ((some scene)) with one's
own eyes

ma-nobi〈まのび: 間延び〉
ma-nobi-no-shita〈間延びのした〉tedious, stupid-looking.

manriki〈まんりき: 万力〉a vise, a vice.

manrui〈まんるい: 満塁〉loaded bases.
Manrui-de-aru.（満塁である.）The bases are full.
Ni-shi-manrui-de-aru.（二死満塁である.）The bases are loaded with
two out.
manrui-hômâ o utsu（満塁ホーマーを打つ）hit a grand slam homer

manryô〈まんりょう: 満了〉expiration, termination.
manryô-ni-naru〈満了になる〉expire, terminate, come to an end.

mansai〈まんさい: 満載〉
mansai-suru〈満載する〉be loaded to capacity ((with)), be fully loaded
((with)), carry a full load ((of)).
jôkyaku-o-mansai-suru（乗客を満載する）be crowded with passengers

mansei〈まんせい: 慢性〉
mansei-no〈慢性の〉chronic.

manshin〈まんしん: 満身〉
manshin-sôi-de-aru（満身創いである）be covered all over with
wounds
manshin-no-chikara-o-komete（満身の力を込めて）with all one's
might

manshin〈まんしん: 慢心〉
manshin-suru〈慢心する〉be puffed up, have a swollen head.
manshin-shi-kitte-iru〈慢心し切っている〉be eaten up with pride.

man-tan〈まんタン: 満タン〉
man-tan-ni-suru〈満タンにする〉fill up the tank.

manten〈まんてん: 満点〉full marks.
manten o toru（満点を取る）get full marks

manukareru〈まぬかれる: 免れる〉escape, avoid, evade, be exempt(ed)
((from)), be immune ((from)).

kega-o-manukareru〈けがを免れる〉 get off unhurt

sekinin o manukareru〈責任を免れる〉 shift off one's responsibility

zeikin-o-manukareru〈税金を免れる〉 be exempt from taxation

manuke〈まぬけ：間抜け〉stupidity; a stupid fellow, a blockhead, an ass, a fool.

manuke-na〈間抜けな〉stupid, inane, foolish, silly.

manzai〈まんざい：漫才〉a cross-talk comedy.

manzai-shi〈漫才師〉 a cross-talk comedian

manzara〈まんざら：満更〉

Manzara-waruku-nai.〈満更悪くない.〉 It is not too bad.

manzen〈まんぜん：漫然〉

manzen-to〈漫然と〉at random, aimlessly, indifferently.

manzen-to-jinsei-o-okuru〈漫然と人生を送る〉 drift through life

manzoku〈まんぞく：満足〉satisfaction, gratification, contentment.

manzoku-suru〈満足する〉be satisfied ((with)), be contented ((with)).

manzoku-na〈満足な〉satisfactory, perfect, sufficient, enough, proper.

Manzoku-na   sara wa ichi-mai-mo-nai.〈満足な皿は一枚もない.〉 There is not a plate which remains unbroken.

manzoku-ni〈満足に〉satisfactorily, perfectly, sufficiently, enough, properly.

manzoku-sô-ni〈満足そうに〉contentedly.

maō〈まおう：魔王〉Satan, the Devil.

mappadaka〈まっぱだか：真っ裸〉

mappadaka-ni-naru〈真っ裸になる〉strip oneself bare.

mappadaka-de〈真っ裸で〉with nothing on.

mappira〈まっぴら：真っ平〉

Sake wa mô-mappira-da.〈酒はもう真っ平だ.〉 No *sake* for me.

mappiruma〈まっぴるま：真っ昼間〉

mappiruma-ni〈真っ昼間に〉in broad daylight.

mappitsu〈まっぴつ：末筆〉

Mappitsu-nagara go-kazoku-ni-yoroshiku.〈末筆ながら御家族によろしく.〉 With best wishes for your family.

mararia〈マラリア〉malaria.

mararia(-sei)-no or *mararia-ni-okasareta*〈マラリア(性)の, マラリアに冒された〉malarial, malarian, malarious.

marason〈マラソン〉a marathon (race).

marason-senshu〈マラソン選手〉 a marathon runner

mare〈まれ〉

mare-na〈まれな〉rare, uncommon, unusual, scarce, few.

　　mare-na deki-goto〈まれな出来事〉 a rare occurrence

mare-ni〈まれに〉rarely, seldom.

mari〈まり〉a ball.

　　mari o tsuku〈まりをつく〉 bounce a ball

Maria〈マリア〉Maria.

　　Seibo-Maria〈聖母マリア〉 the Blessed Virgin (Mary)

marifana〈マリファナ〉marijuana.

maronie〈マロニエ〉a horse chestnut.

maru〈まる：丸〉a circle; full, whole.

　　maru-itsuka〈丸五日〉 five full days

　　maru-ichi-nen〈丸一年〉 for a whole year

maru-de-kakomu〈丸で囲む〉circle, enclose ((a figure)) with a circle.

maru-anki〈まるあんき：丸暗記〉

maru-anki-suru〈丸暗記する〉learn by rote.

maru-arai〈まるあらい：丸洗い〉

maru-arai-suru〈丸洗いする〉wash ((a *kimono*)) whole.

maru-batsu〈まるばつ〉

　　maru-batsu-shiki tesuto〈まるばつ(○×)式テスト〉 a multiple choice
　　　test

marudashi〈まるだし：丸出し〉

inaka-ben-marudashi-de hanasu〈田舎弁丸出しで話す〉speak with a broad
　provincial accent.

maru-de〈まるで〉quite, completely, perfectly, utterly, entirely, all; as
　if, just like, as it were.

　　Watashi-wa maru-de oboete-i-nai.〈私はまるで覚えていない。〉 I don't
　　　remember it at all.

　　Kanojo-wa maru-de-ki-chigai-no-yô-da.〈彼女はまるで気違いのよう
　　　だ。〉 She looks as if she were mad.

maru-gao〈まるがお：丸顔〉a round face.

maru-gao-no〈丸顔の〉round-faced.

maru-gari〈まるがり：丸刈り〉close clipping.

maru-gari-ni-suru〈丸刈りにする〉have one's hair cut close, have a close
　crop.

maru-gari-no〈丸刈りの〉close-cropped.

maru-goto〈まるごと：丸ごと〉wholly, entirely.

　　ringo-o-maru-goto-kajiru〈りんごを丸ごとかじる〉 eat an apple skin
　　　and all

　　　sakana-o-maru-goto-taberu（魚を丸ごと食べる）　eat a fish bone and all

maru-hadaka〈まるはだか：丸裸〉
　　　Ano yama wa maru-hadaka-da.（あの山は丸裸だ.）　The mountain is bare of trees.

marui〈まるい：丸(円)い〉round, circular, globular, spherical.

maru-ki-bashi〈まるきばし：丸木橋〉a log bridge.

maruku〈まるく：丸(円)く〉round, in a circle; peacefully, amicably, smoothly.
　　　maruku-suru（丸(円)くする）　round, make round
　　　　　kado-o-kezutte-maruku-suru（角を削って丸くする）　round off the corners
　　　maruku-kiru（円く切る）　cut ((a thing)) round
　　　maruku-natte-neru（丸くなって寝る）　curl oneself up
　　　me-o-maruku-shite（目を丸くして）　with one's eyes wide open
　　　maruku-osameru（丸く治める）　settle ((a matter)) amicably
　　　maruku-osamaru（丸く治まる）　be amicably settled
　　　Kare-mo-ningen-ga-maruku-natta.（彼も人間が丸くなった.）　The corners of his character have been rounded off.

maru-kubi〈まるくび：丸首〉
　　　maru-kubi-no sêtâ（丸首のセーター）　a turtleneck sweater
　　　maru-kubi-no-shatsu（丸首のシャツ）　a T-shirt

Marukusu〈マルクス〉
　　　Marukusu-shugi（マルクス主義）　Marxism
　　　Marukusu-Rênin-shugi（マルクスレーニン主義）　Marxism-Leninism

marumaru〈まるまる：丸々〉completely, entirely, wholly, totally.
　　　Marumaru-son-ni-wa-nara-nai.（丸々損にはならない.）　That won't prove a complete loss.

marumaru-to〈まるまると：丸々と〉
　　marumaru-to-koeta〈丸々と肥えた〉plump, rotund.

marume-komu〈まるめこむ：丸め込む〉cajole, wheedle, win ((a person)) over.
　　marume-konde〜(-saseru)〈丸め込んで〜(させる)〉wheedle ((a person)) into ((doing)).

marumeru〈まるめる：丸める〉round, make round, round off, curl up.

marumi〈まるみ：丸(円)み〉
　　　marumi-o-tsukeru（丸(円)みを付ける）　round, make round
　　　marumi-no-aru（丸(円)みのある）　roundish

maru-mie 〈まるみえ：丸見え〉
maru-mie-de-aru 〈丸見えである〉be fully exposed to view ((from)).

maru-môke 〈まるもうけ：丸もうけ〉
maru-môke-suru 〈丸もうけする〉make a clear profit.

maru-nomi 〈まるのみ：丸のみ〉
maru-nomi-ni-suru 〈丸のみにする〉swallow up, swallow ((a thing)) whole.

maru-pocha 〈まるぽちゃ：丸ぽちゃ〉
maru-pocha-no 〈丸ぽちゃの〉plump, chubby.

maruta 〈まるた：丸太〉a log.
　　maruta-goya 〈丸太小屋〉 a log cabin

maru-tenjô 〈まるてんじょう：丸天井〉a vault, a dome.

maru-tsubure 〈まるつぶれ：丸つぶれ〉
　　Watashi-no mentsu wa maru-tsubure-da. （私のメンツは丸つぶれだ.）
　　　　My face is utterly lost.

maru-yake 〈まるやけ：丸焼け〉
maru-yake-ni-naru 〈丸焼けになる〉be completely burnt, be totally destroyed by fire.

maru-yaki 〈まるやき：丸焼き〉a barbecue.
maru-yaki-ni-suru 〈丸焼きにする〉barbecue, roast ((a hog)) whole.

maru-yane 〈まるやね：丸屋根〉a dome, a cupola.

maru-zon 〈まるぞん：丸損〉
maru-zon-o-suru 〈丸損をする〉suffer a total loss.

maryoku 〈まりょく：魔力〉magical power, (a) charm.

masaka 〈まさか〉
　　Masaka! （まさか.） You don't say so. / Well, I never! / Impossible!
　　　　/ Indeed?
　　Masaka-sonna-koto-wa-nai-darô. （まさかそんなことはないだろう.） It
　　　　is not at all likely.

masaka-no-toki 〈まさかのとき〉an emergency.
masaka-no-toki-ni 〈まさかのときに〉in case of emergency, in case of
　　need.
　　masaka-no-toki-ni-sonaeru （まさかのときに備える） prepare for the
　　　　worst

masakari 〈まさかり〉a broadax(e).

masa-me 〈まさめ：まさ目〉the straight grain.

masa-ni 〈まさに：正に〉just, exactly, surely, certainly, no doubt, duly.
　　Masa-ni sono-toori. （正にそのとおり.） That's right. / You are right.
　　　　/ You said it.

masa-ni〈まさに〉
 masa-ni〜-(-shiyô)-to-suru〈まさに〜(しよう)とする〉be going ((to do)), be about ((to do)), be ready ((to do)).

masaru〈まさる：勝る〉surpass, excel, exceed, be better ((than)), outdo, be superior ((to)).
  Kenkô wa tomi-ni-masaru.（健康は富に勝る。） Health is above wealth.

masatsu〈まさつ：摩擦〉rubbing, friction, (a) discord.
  masatsu o shôjiru（摩擦を生じる） cause friction
  masatsu o fusegu（摩擦を防ぐ） prevent friction
  masatsu-on（摩擦音） a frictional sound, a fricative (sound)
 masatsu-suru〈摩擦する〉rub ((against *or* with)), chafe.

masa-yume〈まさゆめ：正夢〉
  Are-wa masa-yume-datta.（あれは正夢だった。） The dream came true.

maseru〈ませる〉
 masete-iru〈ませている〉be precocious, be smart for one's age.
 maseta〈ませた〉precocious.

mashi〈まし：増し〉(an) increase, (an) addition, (an) extra.
  kyûryô-juppâsento-mashi（給料十パーセント増し） a 10 percent salary increase

mashi〈まし〉
 mashi-de-aru〈ましである〉be better ((than)), be preferable ((to)).
  Konna mijime-na seikatsu o suru-yori shinda-hô-ga-mashi-da.（こんな惨めな生活をするより死んだ方がましだ。） I would rather die than lead such a wretched life.

ma-shikaku〈ましかく：真四角〉a regular square.
 ma-shikaku-no〈真四角の〉square.

ma-shita〈ました：真下〉
 ma-shita-ni〈真下に〉just under, directly below.

mashite〈まして〉still more, still less.
  Kare-datte-sono-kurai-no-koto-no-dekiru, mashite boku-ni-deki-nai-hazu-ga-nai.（彼だってそのくらいのことはできる、まして僕にできないはずがない。） He can do that much, still more it must be possible for me to do that.

ma-shômen〈ましょうめん：真正面〉
 ma-shômen-ni〈真正面に〉just opposite ((to)), right in front ((of)).

massaichû〈まっさいちゅう：真っ最中〉

massaichû-de-aru 〈真っ最中である〉 be at ((its)) height, be in full swing.

massaichû-ni 〈真っ最中に〉 in the midst ((of)), at the height ((of)).

massâji 〈マッサージ〉 (a) massage.

　　massâji-shi 〈マッサージ師〉 a massager; a masseur, a masseuse

massâji-o-suru 〈マッサージをする〉 massage, give ((a person)) a massage.

massâji-o-shite-morau 〈マッサージをしてもらう〉 have a massage, have oneself massaged.

massakari 〈まっさかり：真っ盛り〉

　　Ume wa ima-ya massakari-de-aru. (梅は今や真っ盛りである。) The plum-blossoms are at their best.

massakasama 〈まっさかさま：真っ逆さま〉

massakasama-ni 〈真っ逆さまに〉 headlong, head foremost, head over heels.

massaki 〈まっさき：真っ先〉

massaki-ni 〈真っ先に〉 first of all; at the head ((of)).

massao 〈まっさお：真っ青〉

massao-ni-naru 〈真っ青になる〉 turn deadly pale, blanch.

massao-na 〈真っ青な〉 deep blue; deadly pale, as white as a sheet.

massatsu 〈まっさつ：抹殺〉

massatsu-suru 〈抹殺する〉 erase, strike out, efface; liquidate.

masseki 〈まっせき：末席〉

masseki-o-kegasu 〈末席を汚す〉 have the honor of being present ((at)), have the honor of being a member ((of)).

masshigura 〈まっしぐら〉

masshigura-ni 〈まっしぐらに〉 at full tilt, at full speed.

　　masshigura-ni-tosshin-suru (まっしぐらに突進する) dash ((against *or* for))

masshiro 〈まっしろ：真っ白〉 pure white.

masshiro-na 〈真っ白な〉 pure-white, snow-white, (as) white as snow.

masshô 〈まっしょう：末しょう〉

　　masshô-shinkei 〈末しょう神経〉 a peripheral nerve.

masshô-teki(-na) 〈末しょう的(な)〉 trifling, trivial, insignificant.

masshôjiki 〈まっしょうじき：真っ正直〉

masshôjiki-na 〈真っ正直な〉 downright honest, straightforward.

masshôjiki-ni 〈真っ正直に〉 very honestly, straightforwardly.

massugu 〈まっすぐ：真っすぐ〉

massugu-na 〈真っすぐな〉 straight, (as) straight as an arrow, direct, upright.

massugu-ni〈真っすぐに〉straight, in a straight line, direct, upright.

    massugu-ni iku（真っすぐに行く） go straight

massugu-ni-suru〈真っすぐにする〉straighten, make straight.

masu〈ます：升〉a box (seat); a measure.

masu〈ます〉a trout.

masu〈ます：増す〉increase, gain, rise, go up.

    ninki-ga-masu（人気が増す） gain in popularity

    taijū-ga san-kiro masu（体重が三キロ増す） gain three kilograms in weight

    Kawa-no-mizu ga mashita.（川の水が増した.） The river has risen.

masui〈ますい：麻酔〉anesthesia.

    kyokubu-masui（局部麻酔） local anesthesia

    zenshin-masui（全身麻酔） general anesthesia

    masui-yaku（麻酔薬） an anesthetic, a narcotic

masui-o-kakeru〈麻酔をかける〉put ((a person)) under anesthesia, anesthetize.

masu-komi〈マスコミ〉mass communications, journalism.

    masu-komi-de sawagareru（マスコミで騒がれる） be given much publicity by journalism

    masu-komi-kikan（マスコミ機関） the mass media

masuku〈マスク〉a mask, a respirator; features, looks.

    masuku o kakeru（マスクを掛ける） wear a mask

    hori-no-fukai masuku（彫りの深いマスク） clear-cut features

masumasu〈ますます〉more and more, still more, still less, increasingly.

    Hi ga masumasu-mijikaku-natte-iku.（日がますます短くなっていく.） The day becomes shorter and shorter.

    masumasu-waruku-naru（ますます悪くなる） go from bad to worse

    masumasu-shinkoku-ni-nari-tsutsu-aru-zaisei-jōtai（ますます深刻になりつつある財政状態） the increasingly desperate financial situation

masu-puro〈マスプロ〉mass production.

    masu-puro-kyōiku（マスプロ教育） education conducted on a mass-production basis

masutâ〈マスター〉a master, a proprietor.

    masutâ-kôsu（マスターコース） a Master's program

masutâ-suru〈マスターする〉master.

mata〈また〉the crotch, the thigh.

    oo-mata-ni aruku（大またに歩く） walk with big strides

mata〈また〉a fork.

mata〈また：又〉again, once more; too, also, as well; and, moreover, further(-more).

> Chikai-uchi-ni mata irasshai.（近いうちにまたいらっしゃい。）Please come again soon.
>
> mata-itsu-ka（またいつか）some other time
>
> Watashi-mo(-mata) motte-iru.（私も（また）持っている。）I have it too.
>
> yama-mata-yama（山また山）range upon range of mountains

mata-gari〈またがり：又借り〉

> *mata-gari-suru*〈又借りする〉borrow ((something)) secondhand, sublease.

matagaru〈またがる〉ride, mount.

mata-gashi〈またがし：又貸し〉

> *mata-gashi-suru*〈又貸しする〉underlet, sublet, sublease.

mata-giki〈またぎき：又聞き〉

> *mata-giki-suru*〈又聞きする〉hear secondhand, learn by hearsay.

matagu〈またぐ〉step over, cross.

> shikii o matagu（敷居をまたぐ）cross the threshold

mata-itoko〈またいとこ〉a second cousin.

matamata or **mata-mo(-ya)**〈またまた，またも（や）：又々，又も（や）〉again, once again.

mata-no-hi〈またのひ：又の日〉another day, some other day.

mata-no-na〈またのな：又の名〉another name.

> *mata-no-na o〜-to-iu*〈又の名を〜と言う〉also called... .

mataseru〈またせる：待たせる〉keep ((a person)) waiting.

matataki〈またたき：瞬き〉a wink, winking, a twinkle, twinkling.

> *matataku*〈瞬く〉wink, twinkle.
>
> *matataku-ma-ni*（瞬く間に）in a twinkling, in the twinkling of an eye, in an instant.

mata-to-nai〈またとない：又とない〉

> mata-to-nai chansu（又とないチャンス）a golden opportunity

mata-wa〈または：又は〉or, either...or.

matcha〈まっちゃ：抹茶〉powdered tea.

matchi〈マッチ〉a match.

> matchi o suru（マッチを擦る）strike a match
>
> matchi-de-hi-o-tsukeru（マッチで火を付ける）light a match
>
> Kono matchi wa tsuka-nai.（このマッチは付かない。）This match won't strike.
>
> matchi-bako（マッチ箱）a matchbox

maten-rô 〈まてんろう：摩天楼〉a skyscraper.

mato 〈まと：的〉a mark, a target, an object, the point.

    mato ni ataru 〈的に当たる〉 hit the mark

    kôgeki no mato 〈攻撃の的〉 the target of criticism

    sembô no mato 〈せん望の的〉 an object of envy

    mato-ga-hazurete-iru 〈的が外れている〉 be off the point

matomari 〈まとまり〉(a) settlement, (a) conclusion, completion; coherence, unity, coordination.

matomari-ga-tsuku 〈まとまりが付く〉 *see*. matomaru.

matomari-o-tsukeru 〈まとまりを付ける〉 *see*. matomeru.

matomari-no-nai 〈まとまりのない〉 loose, rambling, incoherent.

    matomari-no-ii 〈まとまりのいい〉 well-coordinated

matomaru 〈まとまる〉be settled, be concluded, be completed, come to an agreement; be collected; be well arranged; be coherent, be in union.

    Kôshô wa yatto matomatta. 〈交渉はやっとまとまった.〉 The negotiations have been concluded at last.

    Tônai wa yoku-matomatte-iru. 〈党内はよくまとまっている.〉 The party is in perfect union.

matomatta 〈まとまった〉large, round; definite, coherent.

    matomatta chûmon 〈まとまった注文〉 a large order

    matomatta kane 〈まとまった金〉 a round sum of money

    matomatta kangae 〈まとまった考え〉 a definite idea

matomeru 〈まとめる〉settle, conclude, complete, finish; collect, put in order.

    kôshô o matomeru 〈交渉をまとめる〉 conclude negotiations

    mi-no-mawari-hin o matomeru 〈身の回り品をまとめる〉 collect one's personal effects

    ikkan-ni matomerareta rombun 〈一巻にまとめられた論文〉 theses which have been collected together in one volume

    kangae o matomeru 〈考えをまとめる〉 collect one's thoughts

matomete 〈まとめて〉together, in a lump, in one lot.

    matomete kau 〈まとめて買う〉 purchase ((things)) in a lot

matome-yaku 〈まとめやく：まとめ役〉a mediator, an arbitrator.

matomo 〈まとも〉

matomo-na 〈まともな〉 honest, straight.

    matomo-na koto 〈まともな事〉 a straight thing

matomo-ni 〈まともに〉 straight, seriously; right, direct(ly), in one's face.

matomo-ni kurasu（まともに暮らす）　live straight

matomo-ni uke-toru（まともに受け取る）　take ((a matter)) seriously

hito-no-kao-o-matomo-ni-miru（人の顔をまともに見る）　look　((a person)) full in the face

kaze-o-matomo-ni-ukete（風をまともに受けて）　in the teeth of the wind

matsu〈まつ：松〉a pine (tree).

matsu-ba（松葉）　a pine needle

matsu-kasa（松かさ）　a pine cone

matsu-yani（松やに）　(pine) resin

matsu〈まつ：待つ〉wait ((for)), await, expect.

nagai-koto hito-o-matsu（長いこと人を待つ）　wait a long time for a person

Chotto-o-machi-kudasai.（ちょっとお待ちください。）　Wait a moment. / Just a moment. / Hold on a moment, please.

O-matase-shite-sumi-masen.（お待たせしてすみません。）　I'm very sorry to have kept you waiting.

Kare-no-kuru-no-o-ima-ka-ima-ka-to-matteiru.（彼の来るのを今か今かと待っている。）　I am expecting him to come immediately.

tanoshimi-ni-shite-matsu（楽しみにして待つ）　look forward ((to))

matsuba-zue〈まつばづえ：松葉づえ〉(a pair of) crutches.

matsuba-zue-o-tsuite aruku（松葉づえをついて歩く）　walk on crutches

matsuge〈まつげ〉eyelashes.

tsuke-matsuge（付けまつげ）　false eyelashes

matsujitsu〈まつじつ：末日〉the last day.

matsu-kazari〈まつかざり：松飾り〉the New Year's pine decorations.

matsu-no-uchi〈まつのうち：松の内〉the first seven days of the New Year.

matsuri〈まつり：祭り〉a festival, a fete.

o-matsuri-sawagi-o-suru〈お祭り騒ぎをする〉make a fuss about it.

matsuri-ageru〈まつりあげる：祭り上げる〉exalt, set up.

iin-chô-ni matsuri-ageru（委員長に祭り上げる）　set ((a person)) up as the head of the committee

matsuro〈まつろ：末路〉the last days, the end.

matsuru〈まつる：祭る〉deify; enshrine.

matsu-take〈まつたけ：松たけ〉a mushroom.

matsuwari-tsuku〈まつわりつく：まつわり付く〉hang about, dangle

about.

matsuwaru 〈まつわる〉 be related ((to)).

 〜-ni-matsuwaru-densetsu（〜にまつわる伝説） a legend told of...

matta 〈まった：待った〉

 Matta!（待った.） Wait! / Hold on!

 matta-o-suru（待ったをする） retract a move

mattaku 〈まったく：全く〉 quite, entirely, thoroughly, totally, altogether.

 Mattaku-sono-toori.（全くそのとおり.） You are quite right.

 mattaku 〜*nai*〈全く〜ない〉 not at all, not in the least.

 Mattaku-shira-nai.（全く知らない.） I know nothing about it at all.

 Mattaku-dô-shitara-ii-ka-wakara-nai.（全くどうしたらいいか分からない.） I am wholly at a loss what to do.

 mattaku-no〈全くの〉 entire, total, perfect, sheer.

 mattaku-no muda（全くの無駄） sheer waste

mattan 〈まったん：末端〉 the end, the tip.

 shakai no mattan-made（社会の末端まで） to every inch of the society

mattô-suru 〈まっとうする：全うする〉 accomplish, fulfill, perform, complete.

 shimei o mattô-suru（使命を全うする） fulfill one's mission

mau 〈まう：舞う〉 dance, fly, wheel, whirl, flutter around.

 Tobi ga sora-o matteiru.（とびが空を舞っている.） A kite is circling in the air.

ma-ue 〈まうえ：真上〉

 ma-ue-no or *ma-ue-ni*〈真上の，真上に〉 just above, right overhead.

maundo 〈マウンド〉 the mound.

 maundo-ni-tatsu（マウンドに立つ） take the mound

ma-ushiro 〈まうしろ：真後ろ〉

 ma-ushiro-no or *ma-ushiro-ni*〈真後ろの，真後ろに〉 just behind.

maware-migi 〈まわれみぎ：回れ右〉

 Maware-migi!（回れ右.） Right about turn!

 maware-migi-o-suru（回れ右をする）turn to the right-about.

mawari 〈まわり：回(周)り〉 circumference, surroundings; by way of.

 Kono-ki-no-mawari-wa dore-kurai arimasu-ka?（この木の周りはどれくらいありますか.） How big is this tree around?

 mawari-o-mi-mawasu（周りを見回す） look around

 Hokkyoku-mawari-de tobu（北極回りで飛ぶ） fly by the North Pole

route

〜-no-mawari-ni〈〜の周りに〉round, around, about.

　tēburu-no-mawari-ni suwaru（テーブルの周りに座る）sit around the table

mawari-butai〈まわりぶたい：回り舞台〉a revolving stage.

mawari-kudoi〈まわりくどい：回りくどい〉roundabout, devious.

　mawari-kudoi-ii-kata-o-suru（回りくどい言い方をする）beat about the bush

mawari-michi〈まわりみち：回り道〉

　mawari-michi-o-suru〈回り道をする〉go by a roundabout way, make a detour.

mawaru〈まわる：回る〉revolve, rotate, turn round, spin; make a round, go one's rounds, go round ((to)); take effect.

　Koma ga mawatteiru.（こまが回っている。）The top is spinning.

　tokui-saki-o-mawaru（得意先を回る）go the rounds of one's customers

　sōpâ-e mawaru（スーパーへ回る）go round to a supermarket

　Shiberia-o-mawatte Pari-e-iku（シベリアを回ってパリへ行く）go to Paris by way of Siberia

　sake-ga-daibu-mawatte-iru（酒がだいぶ回っている）be well under the influence of *sake*

mawashi-mono〈まわしもの：回し者〉a secret agent, a spy.

mawasu〈まわす：回す〉revolve, turn, spin; send round, pass, forward, transmit; transfer; invest, lend.

　shorui o kakari-ni-mawasu（書類を係りに回す）send round the papers to the man in charge

　kaikei-e mawasareru（会計へ回される）be transferred to the account section

　kane o yûri-na jigyō-ni mawasu（金を有利な事業に回す）invest one's money in some profitable enterprise

ma-wata〈まわた：真綿〉floss (silk).

mayakashi〈まやかし〉*see.* magai(-mono).

mayaku〈まやく：麻薬〉a narcotic, a drug, a dope.

　mayaku-jōyō-sha *or* mayaku-kanja（麻薬常用者, 麻薬患者）a drug addict, a narcotic, a dope fiend

　mayaku-mitsubai-sha（麻薬密売者）a drug peddler, a narcotic trafficker

mayoi〈まよい：迷い〉perplexity, bewilderment, (a) delusion, (an) illusion.

mayoi-ga-sameru〈迷いが覚める〉be undeceived, be brought to one's senses.

ma-yonaka〈まよなか：真夜中〉
ma-yonaka-ni〈真夜中に〉at midnight, at dead of night.

mayou〈まよう：迷う〉lose one's way, get lost, go astray; be perplexed, be bewildered, be at a loss, hesitate, waver; be tempted, be captivated.
　　handan-ni-mayou（判断に迷う）waver in one's judgment
　　onna-no utsukushi-sa-ni mayou（女の美しさに迷う）be captivated by a woman's beauty

mayowasu〈まよわす：迷わす〉perplex, bewilder; lead astray; charm, captivate, tempt, seduce.

mayu〈まゆ〉an eyebrow.
　　futoi mayu（太いまゆ）strong eyebrows
　　koi mayu（濃いまゆ）thick eyebrows
　　mayu o kaku（まゆをかく）pencil one's eyebrows
mayu-o-shikameru〈まゆをしかめる〉knit one's brows, frown.

mayu〈まゆ：繭〉a cocoon.
　　mayu-kara ito o toru（繭から糸を取る）reel silk off cocoons

mazamaza〈まざまざ〉
mazamaza-to〈まざまざと〉clearly, vividly, realistically.
　　mazamaza-to omoi-ukaberu（まざまざと思い浮かべる）recall ((a scene)) vividly

mazaru〈まざる：交(混)ざる〉see. majiru.

mazek(k)aesu〈まぜ(っ)かえす：混ぜ(っ)返す〉interrupt.
　　hito-no hanashi-o-mazekaesu（人の話を混ぜ返す）break in on another's talk

mazeru〈まぜる：交(混)ぜる〉mix, mingle, blend, adulterate.
　　semento-to-jari-o-mazeru（セメントと砂利を混ぜる）mingle cement and gravel
　　sake ni mizu-o-mazeru（酒に水を混ぜる）adulterate *sake* with water

mazohizumu〈マゾヒズム〉masochism.

mazu〈まず〉first of all, to begin with; about, nearly, almost.
　　Mazu-sonna-tokoro-da-ne.（まずそんなところだね。）That's about right.

mazui〈まずい〉unsavory, unpalatable; poor, awkward, clumsy, unskillful, unwise.

　　mazu-sô-da（まずそうだ）do not look tasty

　　mazui Eigo-de kakareta tegami（まずい英語で書かれた手紙）a letter
　　　written in poor English

　　Ima sô-suru-no-wa mazui.（今そうするのはまずい.）It is not wise to
　　　do so now.

mazushii〈まずしい：貧しい〉poor, needy.

　　mazushii-kurashi-o-suru（貧しい暮らしをする）live in poverty

me〈め：目〉an eye; a look, a stare, a glance, eyesight; attention, notice,
watch, observation; a viewpoint, a point of view; discernment,
discrimination, judgment, insight; an experience; care, favor; texture,
grain; a pip, a spot.

　　me-ga-sameru（目が覚める）wake up, become awake

　　me-ga-saeru（目がさえる）become wide awake

　　me-ga-itai（目が痛い）have sore eyes

　　me-ga-kuramu（目がくらむ）be dazzled ((by))

　　　yoku-ni me-ga-kuramu（欲に目がくらむ）be blind with avarice

　　me-ga-mawaru（目が回る）be dizzy

　　　me-ga-mawaru-hodo-isogashii（目が回るほど忙しい）be in a whirl
　　　　of business

　　me-ga-mie-nai（目が見えない）be blind

　　me-no-fu-jiyû-na hito（目の不自由な人）a visually handicapped person

　　me-ni warui（目に悪い）be injurious to the eyes

　　me-no-ue-no-kobu（目の上のこぶ）an eyesore

　　me o tojiru（目を閉じる）close one's eyes

　　me o fuseru（目を伏せる）lower one's eyes

　　me-o-kagayakashite（目を輝かして）with one's eyes aglow

　　me o hosomeru（目を細める）narrow one's eyes

　　me-o-maruku-shite-odoroku（目を丸くして驚く）stare with wonder

　　me-o-mawasu（目を回す）faint, swoon, lose consciousness

　　me-o-suete（目を据えて）with one's eyes set ((on))

　　me-ga-ii（目がいい）have good eyesight

　　me-ga-warui（目が悪い）have bad eyesight

　　me-ni-amaru（目に余る）be unpardonable, be too much for ((one))

　　me-ni-mie-nai（目に見えない）be unseen, be invisible

　　me-no-surudoi（目の鋭い）sharp-sighted

　　me-no-todoku-kagiri（目の届く限り）as far as the eye can reach

　　me o itameru（目を痛める）impair one's eyesight

　　me ni tomaru（目に留まる）attract one's attention

me-o-hikarasu *or* me-o-kubaru（目を光らす，目を配る） keep a sharp watch ((on))

me o hiku（目を引く） draw one's attention

me o sorasu（目をそらす） turn one's gaze ((off))

me-o-toosu（目を通す） look over

me-o-tsuburu（目をつぶる） connive ((at))

gaijin-no-me-kara-miru-to（外人の目から見ると） from a foreigner's point of view

me-ga-koete-iru（目が肥えている） have a critical eye, be a good judge ((of))

me-ni-kurui-wa-nai（目に狂いはない） have an unerring eye

hidoi-me-ni-au（ひどい目に遭う） have a hard time of it

me-o-kakeru（目を掛ける） look ((after)), take care ((of)), be kind ((to)).

me-no-arai（目の粗い） rough, coarse-grained

me〈め：芽〉a sprout, a shoot, a germ, a bud.

me-o-dasu〈芽を出す〉sprout, shoot, bud (out).

-me〈-め：-目〉

kado-kara ni-ken-me-no-tate-mono（角から二軒目の建物） the second building from the corner

Nihon-ni-tsuite yokka-me-ni（日本に着いて四日目に） on the fourth day after one arrived in Japan

mae-kara samban-me-no hito（前から三番目の人） the third person from the front

ooki-me-no〈大きめの〉rather large.

chiisa-me-no（小さめの） rather small

me-atarashii〈めあたらしい：目新しい〉novel, new, original.

me-ate〈めあて：目当て〉an aim, an end, an object.

me-ate-ga-hazureru（目当てが外れる） miss one's aim

〜-o-me-ate-ni(-shite)〈〜を目当てに(して)〉for... , in expectation of... .

me-bae〈めばえ：芽生え〉a sprout, a bud.

me-baeru〈芽生える〉spring up, bud out.

me-bana〈めばな：雌花〉a female flower.

me-bari〈めばり：目張り〉

me-bari-suru〈目張りする〉seal up, weather-strip.

me-beri〈めべり：目減り〉

me-beri-suru〈目減りする〉lose in weight.

meboshi〈めぼし：目星〉an aim.

meboshi-o-tsukeru〈目星を付ける〉aim ((at)), spot.

meboshii 〈めぼしい〉 important, valuable.

me-bunryô 〈めぶんりょう：目分量〉

me-bunryô-de 〈目分量で〉 by eye measure, at a rough estimate.

mecha 〈めちゃ〉

    mechakucha-na-koto-o-iu（めちゃくちゃなことを言う）say unreasonable things, talk nonsense

    mechamecha-ni-suru（めちゃめちゃにする）spoil, louse up, make a mess ((of)), upset, ruin

    mechamecha-ni-naru（めちゃめちゃになる）be spoiled, go to pieces, come unstuck

medaka 〈めだか〉 a killifish.

medama-yaki 〈めだまやき：目玉焼き〉 fried eggs, a sunny side up.

medama-yaki-ni-suru 〈目玉焼きにする〉 fry eggs sunny side up.

medatsu 〈めだつ：目立つ〉 be conspicuous, be striking, stand out.

    Ano shiroi tate-mono wa medatsu.（あの白い建物は目立つ。）That white building stands out.

medataseru 〈目立たせる〉 make conspicuous, highlight.

medatta（目立った）conspicuous, striking, marked, remarkable.

medata-nai（目立たない）inconspicuous, quiet.

    medata-nai iro（目立たない色）a quiet color

medatte（目立って）conspicuously, strikingly, markedly, remarkably.

medata-nai-yô-ni〈目立たないように〉inconspicuously, in a quiet way, unobtrusively.

Mê-dê 〈メーデー〉 May Day.

medetai 〈めでたい〉 happy, joyous, auspicious; half-witted.

    medetai-koto（めでたい事）a happy event, a matter for congratulation

    medetai-yatsu（めでたいやつ）a simpleton

    O-medetô!（おめでとう．）Congratulations!

medo 〈めど〉 a prospect, an outlook.

    medo-ga-tsuka-nai（めどが付かない）be not in smooth water

medorê 〈メドレー〉 a medley.

    yon-hyaku-mêtoru-kojin-medorê（四百メートル個人メドレー）the individual 400-meter medley

me-gakeru 〈めがける：目掛ける〉 aim ((at)).

~-o-megakete 〈～を目掛けて〉 at... , toward... .

me-gami 〈めがみ：女神〉 a goddess.

megane 〈めがね：眼鏡〉 glasses, spectacles.

    megane o kakeru〈眼鏡を掛ける〉 put on one's glasses
    megane o hazusu〈眼鏡を外す〉 take off one's glasses
    megane o fuku〈眼鏡をふく〉 polish one's glasses
    do-no-tsuyoi megane〈度の強い眼鏡〉 powerful spectacles

me-gashira〈めがしら：目頭〉
 me-gashira-ga-atsuku-naru〈目頭が熱くなる〉 be moved to tears.

megumi〈めぐみ：恵み〉(a) blessing, grace, (a) favor, (a) kindness, mercy, benevolence.
    kami no megumi〈神の恵み〉 the grace of God
 megumi-bukai〈恵み深い〉 merciful, benevolent, kind.

megumu〈めぐむ：恵む〉bestow a favor ((on)), have mercy ((on)).
 megumareru〈恵まれる〉be blessed ((with)).
    tennen-shigen-ni-megumareru〈天然資源に恵まれる〉 be blessed with abundant natural resources
 megumareta〈恵まれた〉blessed, favored.
    megumare-nai〈恵まれない〉 unfortunate, underprivileged

megurasu〈めぐらす〉surround ((by *or* with)), enclose ((in *or* with)); think out, contrive, devise.
    hei-o-megurasu〈塀をめぐらす〉 surround ((a person's house)) with walls
    saku o megurasu〈策をめぐらす〉 devise a scheme

meguri〈めぐり：巡り〉circulation; a tour, a round.
    chi-no-meguri-ga-warui〈血のめぐりが悪い〉 have a bad circulation
    chi-no-meguri-no-warui〈血のめぐりの悪い〉 slow-witted
    meisho-meguri-o-suru〈名所巡りをする〉 make the rounds of noted places

meguriai〈めぐりあい：巡り合い〉an unexpected meeting
 meguri-au〈巡り合う〉meet by chance.

meguri-awase〈めぐりあわせ：巡り合わせ〉
 fushigi-na meguri-awase-de〈不思議な巡り合わせで〉by a strange coincidence.

meguru〈めぐる〉
 ～-o-megutte〈～をめぐって〉centering around... , concerning... , in connection with... .

me-gusuri〈めぐすり：目薬〉eyewash, (an) eye lotion.
    me-gusuri o sasu〈目薬を差す〉 apply eye lotion

me-hana〈めはな：目鼻〉
 me-hana-ga-tsuku〈目鼻が付く〉take shape.

me-hana-ga-tsuka-nai〈目鼻が付かない〉 remain unsettled

mehanadachi〈めはなだち：目鼻立ち〉features, looks.

　mehanadachi-ga-totonotte-iru〈目鼻立ちが整っている〉be　well-favored, have regular features.

mei〈めい：命〉

　~*-no-mei-ni-yori*〈～の命により〉by order of... .

mei〈めい：銘〉an inscription, an epitaph; a signature.

mei〈めい〉a niece.

mei-〈めい-：名-〉noted, celebrated, distinguished, great, excellent.

　　mei-pianisuto〈名ピアニスト〉 an excellent pianist

mei-an〈めいあん：明暗〉light and darkness.

　　jinsei no mei-an〈人生の明暗〉the bright side and the dark one of life

meian〈めいあん：名案〉a good idea, a splendid idea.

　　Sore-wa meian-da.〈それは名案だ。〉 That's a capital idea.

meibin〈めいびん：明敏〉

　zunō-ga-meibin-de-aru〈頭脳が明敏である〉have a clear head.

　meibin-na〈明敏な〉intelligent, clever, sagacious.

meibo〈めいぼ：名簿〉a register of names, a roll.

　　kaiin-meibo〈会員名簿〉 a membership list

　　kurasu-meibo〈クラス名簿〉 a class list

meibun〈めいぶん：名文〉a beautiful composition, a beautiful passage.

meibun-ka〈めいぶんか：明文化〉stipulation.

　meibun-ka-suru〈明文化する〉stipulate.

meibutsu〈めいぶつ：名物〉a　noted　product, a　special　product, a speciality.

　　meibutsu-otoko〈名物男〉 a popular figure

meicho〈めいちょ：名著〉a famous book, a masterpiece.

meichū〈めいちゅう：命中〉a hit.

　meichû-suru〈命中する〉hit.

　　mokuhyô ni meichû-suru〈目標に命中する〉 hit the mark

meidai〈めいだい：命題〉a proposition.

meido〈めいど：めい土（途）〉Hades, the other world.

meifuku〈めいふく：めい福〉

　meifuku-o-inoru〈めい福を祈る〉pray　for　the　repose　of　((a　person's)) soul.

meiga〈めいが：名画〉a famous picture, a masterpiece.

meigara〈めいがら：銘柄〉a brand, a description; a name (of a stock).

　　meigara-baibai（銘柄売買）　sales on description

meigen〈めいげん：名言〉a wise saying, a witty remark.
　　Sore-wa meigen-da.（それは名言だ。）　That's well said.

meigen〈めいげん：明言〉
meigen-suru〈明言する〉assert, say definitely.

meigetsu〈めいげつ：明(名)月〉a bright moon, a full moon.
　　chûshû-no-meigetsu（仲秋の名月）　the harvest moon

meigi〈めいぎ：名義〉one's name.
　　meigi-henkô（名義変更）　transfer
　　meigi-o-henkô-suru（名義を変更する）　transfer ((to))
meigi-dake-no or *meigi-jô-no*〈名義だけの，名義上の〉nominal.
meigi-jô(-wa)〈名義上(は)〉nominally.
〜*-no-meigi-de*〈〜の名義で〉under the name of... .

meihaku〈めいはく：明白〉
meihaku-na〈明白な〉clear, plain, evident, obvious, apparent, distinct.
meihaku-ni〈明白に〉clearly, plainly, evidently, obviously, manifestly, distinctly.

mei-i〈めいい：名医〉a noted physician.

meiji〈めいじ：明示〉
meiji-suru〈明示する〉state plainly, specify.

meijin〈めいじん：名人〉a master, a master-hand, an expert.
　　meijin-gei（名人芸）　a virtuoso performance
　　meijin-hada-no-tokoro-ga-aru（名人肌のところがある）　have something of a master artist

meijiru〈めいじる：命じる〉order, tell, bid, direct; appoint.
meijirareta-toori-ni〈命じられたとおりに〉as one is told.

meijiru〈めいじる：銘じる〉
kimo-ni-meijiru〈肝に銘じる〉take ((one's advice)) to heart.

mei-jitsu〈めいじつ：名実〉
mei-jitsu-tomo-ni〈名実共に〉both in name and reality.

meikai〈めいかい：明快〉
meikai-na〈明快な〉clear, clear-cut, lucid.

meikaku〈めいかく：明確〉
meikaku-na〈明確な〉clear, accurate, precise, distinct, definite.
meikaku-ni〈明確に〉clearly, accurately, precisely, distinctly, definitely.

meiki〈めいき：明記〉
meiki-suru〈明記する〉write clearly, specify.

meiki〈めいき：銘記〉

meiki-suru 〈銘記する〉 impress on one's mind, bear ((a fact)) in mind.

meikô 〈めいこう：名工〉 a skillful craftsman.

meikyoku 〈めいきょく：名曲〉 a famous work of music, an excellent piece of music.

meikyû 〈めいきゅう：迷宮〉 a labyrinth, a maze.

meikyû-iri-suru 〈迷宮入りする〉 be still unsolved.

meikyû-iri-no 〈迷宮入りの〉 unsolved.

meimei 〈めいめい：銘々〉 everyone, each; individually, severally, respectively.

meimei-no 〈銘々の〉 each, respective.

meimei 〈めいめい：命名〉

     meimei-shiki 〈命名式〉 a christening ceremony

meimei-suru 〈命名する〉 name, give a name ((to)), christen.

meimoku 〈めいもく：名目〉 a name, a title.

meimoku-jô-no 〈名目上の〉 nominal, ostensible.

〜-to-iu-meimoku-de 〈〜という名目で〉 under the pretext of... .

meimon 〈めいもん：名門〉 a distinguished family.

     meimon-no-de-de-aru 〈名門の出である〉 come of a noble family

meinichi 〈めいにち：命日〉 the anniversary of ((a person's)) death.

meirei 〈めいれい：命令〉 an order, a command, a direction, instructions.

     meirei ni shitagau 〈命令に従う〉 obey ((a person's)) order

     meirei-bun 〈命令文〉 an imperative sentence

meirei-suru 〈命令する〉 order, command, direct, give instructions.

〜-no-meirei-de 〈〜の命令で〉 on(*or* under) orders of... , according to the orders of... .

meiro 〈めいろ：迷路〉 a maze, a labyrinth.

meiro-no(-yô-na) 〈迷路の(ような)〉 labyrinthian, labyrinthic.

meirô 〈めいろう：明朗〉

meirô-na 〈明朗な〉 bright, clear, cheerful.

     meirô-na seiji 〈明朗な政治〉 clean politics

meirô-ka-suru 〈明朗化する〉 make bright, brighten up.

meiru 〈めいる〉 feel gloomy, be depressed, be dispirited.

ki-no-meiru-yô-na 〈気のめいるような〉 gloomy, depressing, melancholy.

meiryô 〈めいりょう：明りょう〉

meiryô-na 〈明りょうな〉 clear, plain, distinct, obvious.

meiryô-ni 〈明りょうに〉 clearly, plainly, distinctly, obviously.

meisai 〈めいさい：明細〉 particulars, details.

     meisai-sho 〈明細書〉 a detailed statement, specifications, a detailed account

meisai-na〈明細な〉particular, detailed, minute.

meisai-ni〈明細に〉in every particular, in detail, minutely, fully.

meisaku〈めいさく：名作〉a fine piece, a fine work, a masterpiece.

meisan〈めいさん：名産〉a noted product, a speciality.

meisei〈めいせい：名声〉fame, renown, (a) reputation.

    meisei-o-hakusuru〈名声を博する〉win fame, win a reputation

    meisei o kizu-tsukeru〈名声を傷つける〉hurt one's reputation

meisei-no-aru〈名声のある〉noted, renowned, celebrated, famous.

    sekai-teki-meisei-no-aru〈世界的名声のある〉of worldwide fame

meiseki〈めいせき：明せき〉

zunô-meiseki-na〈頭脳明せきな〉clear-headed.

me-isha〈めいしゃ：目医者〉an eye doctor, an oculist.

meishi〈めいし：名士〉a noted person, a prominent figure, a personage, a celebrity, a notable.

    chihô-no meishi〈地方の名士〉local celebrities

    chotto-shita meishi〈ちょっとした名士〉a bit of a celebrity

meishi〈めいし：名刺〉a visiting card, a calling card.

    meishi o kôkan-suru〈名刺を交換する〉exchange cards

    meishi-gata〈名刺型〉a carte de visite

meishi〈めいし：名詞〉a noun.

meishin〈めいしん：迷信〉(a) superstition.

    meishin o daha-suru〈迷信を打破する〉do away with a superstition

meishin-teki(-na)〈迷信的(な)〉superstitious.

meisho〈めいしょ：名所〉a noted place, a place of interest, sights (to see).

    meisho o annai-suru〈名所を案内する〉show ((a person)) around places of note

    meisho-kyûseki〈名所旧跡〉places of scenic and historical interest

meishô〈めいしょう：名称〉a name, a title, a designation.

meishô-o-tsukeru〈名称を付ける〉name, designate.

meishu〈めいしゅ：名手〉a master-hand, an expert.

    shageki-no-meishu〈射撃の名手〉an expert shot

meishu〈めいしゅ：盟主〉the leader.

meisô〈めいそう：めい想〉meditation, contemplation.

    meisô-ni-fukeru〈めい想にふける〉be lost in meditation

meisô-suru〈めい想する〉meditate ((on)), contemplate.

meitei〈めいてい〉

meitei-suru〈めいていする〉be intoxicated, be in a drunken condition.

meitei-shita〈めいていした〉intoxicated, drunken.

meiten〈めいてん：名店〉a famous store.

　　meiten-gai（名店街）　a quarter of well-known stores

meitô〈めいとう：名答〉a correct answer, an excellent answer.

　　Go-meitô!（御名答.）　You're quite right.

meiwaku〈めいわく：迷惑〉trouble, annoyance, inconvenience.

meiwaku-o-kakeru〈迷惑を掛ける〉trouble ((a person)), cause ((a person)) trouble, get ((a person)) into trouble, annoy, bother, put ((a person)) to inconvenience.

meiwaku-suru〈迷惑する〉be troubled, get into trouble, be annoyed, be bothered, be inconvenienced.

meiwaku-na〈迷惑な〉troublesome, annoying, bothering, inconvenient.

　　Nan-to meiwaku-na-hanashi-da!（何と迷惑な話だ.）　It is a nuisance! / How annoying it is!

meiyo〈めいよ：名誉〉honor, credit, (a) fame, (a) reputation, (a) distinction, dignity.

　　meiyo-ni-naru（名誉になる）　be a credit ((to)), be to one's honor

　　meiyo ni kakawaru（名誉にかかわる）　affect the honor ((of))

　　meiyo o omonjiru（名誉を重んじる）　prize honor

　　meiyo o kizu-tsukeru（名誉を傷つける）　stain ((a person's)) honor

　　meiyo-kyôju（名誉教授）　an honorary professor

　　meiyo-shimin（名誉市民）　an honorary citizen

　　meiyo-shoku（名誉職）　an honorary post

　　meiyo-yoku（名誉欲）　love of fame, a desire for fame

meiyo-ni-kakete〈名誉にかけて〉as a point of honor, upon one's honor.

　　meiyo-ni-kakete〜(-suru)（名誉にかけて〜(する)）　make it a point of honor ((to do))

meiyû〈めいゆう：名優〉a great actor(or actress), a star.

me-jiri〈めじり：目じり〉the corner of the eye.

　　me-jiri-o-sageru（目じりを下げる）　make eyes ((at))

　　me-jiri-no-shiwa（目じりのしわ）　the lines at the corners of the eyes, crow's-feet

mejiro〈めじろ〉a Japanese white-eye.

me-jirushi〈めじるし：目印〉a mark, a sign, a landmark, a pylon.

me-jirushi-o-suru〈目印をする〉mark, put a mark ((on)).

mêkâ〈メーカー〉a maker, a manufacturer.

　　mêkâ-hin（メーカー品）　articles produced by well-known and big

manufacturers

mekake〈めかけ〉a mistress, a concubine.

mekake o oku（めかけを置く）keep a concubine

me-kakushi〈めかくし：目隠し〉

me-kakushi-o-suru〈目隠しをする〉put a bandage over ((a person's)) eyes.

mekasu〈めかす〉dress oneself up, adorn oneself.

mekata〈めかた：目方〉weight.

mekata-de uru（目方で売る）sell by weight

mekata-o-gomakasu（目方をごまかす）give short weight

mekata-o-hakaru〈目方を量る〉weigh, take one's weight.

mekata-ga-tari-nai〈目方が足りない〉be underweight.

mekiki〈めきき：目利き〉judging; a judge, a connoisseur, a critic.

mekiki-o-suru〈目利きをする〉judge.

mekimeki〈めきめき〉perceptibly, remarkably, fast, rapidly.

Byôki ga mekimeki yoku-natta.（病気がめきめきよくなった．）My health improved perceptibly.

mekimeki-ude-ga-agaru（めきめき腕が上がる）show marked improvement in one's skill

Mekishiko〈メキシコ〉Mexico.

Mekishiko-jin（メキシコ人）a Mexican

Mekishiko(-jin)-no（メキシコ(人)の）Mexican

mekki〈めっき〉gilt, gilding, plating, coating.

mekki-ga-hageru（めっきがはげる）The gilt comes off. / betray oneself, show one's true colors

mekki-suru〈めっきする〉gild, plate.

-mekki-no or *-mekki-shita*〈-めっきの，-めっきした〉-plated.

mekkiri〈めっきり〉considerably, remarkably, noticeably.

mekkiri-atatakaku-naru（めっきり暖かくなる）get quite warm

mekkiri-yaseru（めっきりやせる）lose much flesh

-meku〈-めく〉look (like), become like.

Haru-meite-kata.（春めいてきた．）It has become springlike.

Hiniku-meku-kamo-shirenai-ga～.（皮肉めくかも知れないが～．）It may sound ironical, but... .

me-kubase〈めくばせ：目配せ〉

me-kubase-suru〈目くばせする〉make a sign with one's eye(s), wink ((at)).

mekura-ban〈めくらばん：めくら判〉

mekura-ban-o-osu 〈めくら判を押す〉stamp one's seal ((on documents)) unread.

mekura-meppô 〈めくらめっぽう：めくら滅法〉

mekura-meppô-ni 〈めくらめっぽうに〉recklessly, aimlessly, at random.
  mekura-meppô-ni utsu（めくらめっぽうに撃つ）shoot without aim

mekuru 〈めくる〉turn over, turn up, take off.
  pêji o mekuru（ページをめくる）turn the pages ((of))
  sode o mekuru（そでをめくる）turn up the sleeves
  karendâ o mekuru（カレンダーをめくる）tear off a sheet of the calendar

me-kyabetsu 〈めキャベツ：芽キャベツ〉Brussels sprouts.

mêkyappu 〈メーキャップ〉make-up.

mêkyappu-suru 〈メーキャップする〉make (oneself) up.

mêkyappu-shita 〈メーキャップした〉made-up.

me-magurushii 〈めまぐるしい：目まぐるしい〉dizzy, dazing, bewildering.
  me-magurushii yo-no-naka（目まぐるしい世の中）a fast-moving world

me-magurushiku 〈目まぐるしく〉at a dizzy speed.

me-mai 〈めまい〉giddiness, dizziness.

me-mai-ga-suru 〈めまいがする〉get giddy, feel dizzy.

membâ 〈メンバー〉a member, a lineup.
  membâ o soroeru（メンバーをそろえる）make up a four, make up a nine

memboku 〈めんぼく：面目〉face, honor, (a) reputation; appearance, an aspect.
  memboku o tamotsu（面目を保つ）save one's honor
  memboku ni kakawaru（面目に係わる）affect one's reputation
  memboku o ushinau（面目を失う）lose one's face, disgrace oneself
  memboku-o-isshin-suru（面目を一新する）undergo a complete transformation

memboku-nasa-sô-ni 〈面目なさそうに〉shamefacedly.

memeshii 〈めめしい：女々しい〉effeminate, womanish.

memmitsu 〈めんみつ：綿密〉

memmitsu-na 〈綿密な〉minute, close, detailed, careful, scrupulous.
  memmitsu-na keikaku（綿密な計画）a careful plan

memo 〈メモ〉a memorandum, a memo.
  memo o toru（メモを取る）make a note ((of *or* on)), take notes ((of))

memo-yōshi〈メモ用紙〉memo paper

memo-chô〈メモ帳〉a memo pad

me-mori〈めもり：目盛り〉a scale, graduations.

me-mori-o-tsukeru〈目盛りを付ける〉mark with degrees, graduate.

me-moto〈めもと：目もと〉the eyes.

me-moto-ga-patchiri-shite-iru（目もとがぱっちりしている）have a bright pair of eyes

mempu〈めんぷ：綿布〉cotton (cloth), cotton stuff.

men〈めん：面〉a face; a mask, a face guard; the surface, a side, an aspect, a page.

men-to-mukatte-iu（面と向かって言う）say to one's face

men o kaburu（面をかぶる）wear a mask

shakai no kurai men-o-miru（社会の暗い面を見る）look on the dark side of society

arayuru men-kara（あらゆる面から）in every aspect

shakai-men〈社会面〉the social page

men〈めん：綿〉cotton.

men-seihin〈綿製品〉cotton goods

mendan〈めんだん：面談〉an interview.

Isai-mendan.〈委細面談.〉Apply in person (for particulars).

mendan-suru〈面談する〉have an interview ((with)), talk personally ((with)).

mendô〈めんどう：面倒〉trouble, (a) difficulty, a nuisance, complications; attention, care.

mendô-garu〈面倒がる〉think ((it)) troublesome.

mendô-ni-naru〈面倒になる〉become troublesome, become complicated, become serious.

koto o mendô-ni-suru〈事を面倒にする〉complicate matters.

mendô-o-kakeru〈面倒を掛ける〉trouble ((a person)), give ((a person)) trouble, put ((a person)) to trouble.

mendô-o-miru〈面倒を見る〉take care ((of)), look ((after)).

mendô-na〈面倒な〉troublesome, worrisome, difficult, annoying.

mendô-kusai〈めんどうくさい：面倒臭い〉

mendô-kusaku-naru〈面倒臭くなる〉get tired of ((doing)).

mendôkusa-garu〈面倒臭がる〉*see*. mendô-garu.

men-dori〈めんどり〉a hen.

men·eki(-sei)〈めんえき（せい）：免疫(性)〉immunity.

men·eki-ni-naru〈免疫になる〉become immune ((against, from *or* to)).

menjite 〈めんじて：免じて〉

kimi-ni-menjite〔君に免じて〕 for your sake

toshi-ni-menjite〔年に免じて〕 out of respect for ((a person's)) age

menjo 〈めんじょ：免除〉(an) exemption, remission.

menjo-suru〈免除する〉exempt ((from)), remit.

jugyō-ryō-o-menjo-sareru〔授業料を免除される〕 be given free instruction

zeikin-o-menjo-sareru〔税金を免除される〕 be exempted from taxes

menjô 〈めんじょう：免状〉a diploma, a license.

menjô o morau〔免状をもらう〕 obtain a diploma

menka 〈めんか：綿花〉raw cotton, cotton wool.

menkai 〈めんかい：面会〉a meeting, an interview.

menkai-o-motomeru〔面会を求める〕 ask for an interview ((with)), ask ((a person)) to see

menkai-o-kotowaru〔面会を断る〕 refuse an interview ((with)), decline to see

menkai-bi〔面会日〕 a visiting day

menkai-jikan〔面会時間〕 visiting hours

menkai-nin〔面会人〕 a visitor, a caller

Menkai-shazetsu.〔面会謝絶.〕 No Visitors.

menkai-suru〈面会する〉meet, see, have an interview ((with)).

menkan 〈めんかん：免官〉dismissal from office.

igan-menkan-ni-naru〔依願免官になる〕 be dismissed from office at one's request

men-kurau 〈めんくらう：面食らう〉be confused, be confounded, be flurried, be bewildered, be taken aback.

menkyo 〈めんきょ：免許〉license, permission.

menkyo o toru〔免許を取る〕 obtain a license

menkyo o teishi-sareru〔免許を停止される〕 have one's license suspended

menkyo o tori-kesareru〔免許を取り消される〕 have one's license revoked

menkyo o tori-agerareru〔免許を取り上げられる〕 forfeit one's license

menkyo-shô〔免許証〕 a license, a certificate

kari-menkyo-shô〔仮免許証〕 a temporary license, a learner's license

menô 〈めのう〉agate.

me-no-iro 〈めのいろ：目の色〉

me-no-iro-ga-kawaru or *me-no-iro-o-kaeru*〈目の色が変わる，目の色を変える〉 change color.

me-no-iro-o-kaete〈目の色を変えて〉excitedly, with a frenzied look.

me-no-kataki〈めのかたき：目の敵〉

me-no-kataki-ni-suru〈目の敵にする〉regard ((a person)) with hatred.

me-no-mae〈めのまえ：目の前〉

me-no-mae-de（目の前で）before one's eyes, in one's presence

me-no-mae-ni（目の前に）near at hand, just ahead

menrui〈めんるい：めん類〉noodles, vermicelli.

menseki〈めんせき：面積〉(an) area.

mensetsu〈めんせつ：面接〉an interview.

mensetsu-shiken（面接試験）an oral test, an interview

menshi〈めんし：綿糸〉cotton yarn, cotton thread.

menshiki〈めんしき：面識〉acquaintance.

ichi-menshiki-mo-nai-hito（一面識もない人）a total stranger

menshiki-ga-aru〈面識がある〉be acquainted ((with)).

menshoku〈めんしょく：免職〉discharge, dismissal from office.

menshoku-ni-naru〈免職になる〉be discharged, be dismissed.

menso〈めんそ：免訴〉acquittal.

menso-ni-naru〈免訴になる〉be acquitted, be discharged.

mensuru〈めんする：面する〉face, look out ((on)), border ((on)).

men-tooshi〈めんとおし：面通し〉an identification parade, a lineup.

mentsu〈メンツ〉*see.* memboku.

menuki〈めぬき：目抜き〉

menuki-doori（目抜き通り）a main street

menuki-no〈目抜きの〉principal, main.

men·yō〈めんよう：綿羊〉a sheep.

menyū〈メニュー〉a menu, a bill of fare.

menzei〈めんぜい：免税〉exemption from taxation.

menzei-hin（免税品）articles free from taxes, tax-free commodities

menzei-suru〈免税する〉exempt from taxation.

menzen〈めんぜん：面前〉

menzen-de〈面前で〉*see.* me-no-mae-de.

meramera〈めらめら〉

meramera-moe-agaru〈めらめら燃え上がる〉burst into flames, flare up.

meriken-ko〈メリケンこ：メリケン粉〉flour.

meri-komu〈めりこむ：めり込む〉sink ((into)).

doro-ni-meri-komu（泥にめり込む）stick in the mud

merimeri 〈めりめり〉
　merimeri-iu 〈めりめりいう〉 creak, crack.
　merimeri-to 〈めりめりと〉 with a crack.
meriyasu 〈メリヤス〉 knit goods.
　meriyasu-no shatsu (メリヤスのシャツ)　a knit shirt
mesaki 〈めさき：目先〉
　mesaki-ga-kiku (目先が利く)　have foresight, be farsighted
　mesaki-ga-kika-nai (目先が利かない)　lack foresight, be shortsighted
　mesaki-no-koto-bakari-kangaeru (目先の事ばかり考える)　think　only
　　of the present, take a short view of things
　mesaki-no-kawatta (目先の変わった)　out of the common, novel
　mesaki-ni-chiratsuku (目先にちらつく)　haunt ((a person's)) eyes
meshi 〈めし：飯〉 boiled rice, meal; livelihood.
　meshi o taku 〈飯を炊く〉 boil rice.
　meshi-o-kuu 〈飯を食う〉 take a meal, dine; make one's living.
　meshi-ga-kue-nai (飯が食えない)　cannot make a living
me-shibe 〈めしべ：雌しべ〉 a pistil.
mesomeso 〈めそめそ〉
　mesomeso-naku 〈めそめそ泣く〉 sob, weep.
mesu 〈めす：雌〉 a female.
　mesu-neko (雌猫)　a she-cat
mesu 〈メス〉 a surgical knife, a scalpel.
　mesu-o-ireru 〈メスを入れる〉 probe ((a matter)) to the core.
mêtâ 〈メーター〉 a (gas) meter, a (taxi) meter, a (water) meter.
　mêtâ o shiraberu (メーターを調べる)　read the meter
metan 〈メタン〉 methane.
mêtoru 〈メートル〉 a meter.
　mêtoru-hô (メートル法)　the metric system
metsubô 〈めつぼう：滅亡〉 a fall, a downfall, ruin, destruction.
　metsubô-suru 〈滅亡する〉 fall, be ruined, perish, cease to exist.
me-tsuki 〈めつき：目付き〉 a look.
　me-tsuki-ga-warui (目つきが悪い)　have a sinister look
　yasashii me-tsuki-de (優しい目つきで)　with a tender look
　kowai me-tsuki-de (怖い目つきで)　with a menacing look
metta 〈めった：滅多〉
　metta-na 〈滅多な〉 rash, reckless, thoughtless.
　Metta-na-koto-o-iu-na. (滅多なことを言うな。)　Be　careful　about　what

you say.

metta-ni 〈滅多に〉 rarely, seldom.

    Konna koto wa metta-ni-nai. (こんなことは滅多にない。) Such a thing rarely happens.

metta-uchi-ni-suru 〈滅多打ちにする〉 beat ((a person)) up.

me-ushi 〈めうし：雌牛〉 a cow.

me-utsuri 〈めうつり：目移り〉

me-utsuri-suru 〈目移りする〉 be puzzled which one to choose.

me-yani 〈めやに：目やに〉 eye mucus, gum (in the corner of the eye).

mezamashi(-dokei) 〈めざまし（どけい）：目覚まし（時計）〉 an alarm clock.

    mezamashi o roku-ji-ni awasete-oku (目覚ましを六時に合わせておく) set the alarm for six (o'clock)

mezamashii 〈めざましい：目覚ましい〉 striking, wonderful, remarkable, conspicuous, splendid, brilliant.

    mezamashii hatten o suru (めざましい発展をする) make remarkable progress

mezameru 〈めざめる：目覚める〉 wake up, awake; come to one's senses; awake ((to)).

ma-zashi 〈めざし：目刺し〉 dried sardines.

me-zasu 〈めざす：目指す〉 aim ((at)).

me-zatoi 〈めざとい：目ざとい〉 (be) sharp-eyed, (be) quick-eyed.

me-zawari 〈めざわり：目障り〉 an eyesore, an offense to the eye.

me-zawari-de-aru 〈目障りである〉 be an eyesore, offend the eye.

mezurashigaru 〈めずらしがる：珍しがる〉

mezurashigatte-miru or *mezurashi-ge-ni miru* 〈珍しがって見る，珍しげに見る〉 look ((a thing)) with curiosity.

mezurashii 〈めずらしい：珍しい〉 new, novel, rare, curious, unusual, uncommon, extraordinary.

    mezurashii-mono (珍しい物) a novelty, a rare article

    mezurashii rei (珍しい例) a rare example

    mezurashii deki-goto (珍しい出来事) an extraordinary event

    mezurashii-kyaku-ga-kuru (珍しい客が来る) have a visitor whom one hasn't seen for a long time

mezurashiku(-mo) 〈珍しく（も）〉 unusually, exceptionally.

mi 〈み：身〉 one's body; oneself; one's standing, one's social status; heart, mind; life; flesh, meat.

    mi-ni-tsukeru (身に着（つ）ける) put on, wear; keep ((a thing)) about one; acquire, master

mi-o-motte-nogareru（身をもって逃れる） have a narrow escape

mi-o-kiru-yôna（身を切るような） piercing

Mi-kara-deta-sabi.（身から出たさび.） As they sow, so let them reap.

mi-ni-oboe-ga-aru（身に覚えがある） know ((a thing)) by personal experience

mi-no-furi-kata（身の振り方） a plan for one's future

mi o horobosu（身を滅ぼす） ruin oneself

mi-ni-amaru（身に余る） undeserved

mi-o-katameru（身を固める） settle down in marriage

mi-ni-shimiru（身に染みる） touch ((a person)) to the heart

mi-ni-naru（身になる） be nutritious

mi〈み：実〉(a) fruit, a nut, a berry.

mi o musubu（実を結ぶ） bear fruit

mi-ageru〈みあげる：見上げる〉look up ((at)).

miai〈みあい：見合い〉

miai-kekkon（見合い結婚） an arranged marriage

miai-suru（見合いする）meet each other with a view to marriage

mi-akiru〈みあきる：見飽きる〉get tired of seeing.

mi-ataru〈みあたる：見当たる〉find, be found.

Saifu ga mi-atara-nai.（財布が見当たらない.） My wallet is missing.

mi-awaseru〈みあわせる：見合わせる〉look at each other, exchange glances; put off, postpone.

shuppatsu o mi-awaseru（出発を見合わせる） put off one's departure

mi-ayamaru〈みあやまる：見誤る〉fail to recognize, mistake, take ((a thing)) for ((another)).

mi-bae〈みばえ：見栄え〉

mi-bae-ga-suru〈見栄えがする〉look nice, make a good show.

mi-bae-no-suru〈見栄えのする〉nice-looking, attractive.

mi-bae-no-shi-nai（見栄えのしない） poor-looking, unattractive

mi-biiki〈みびいき：身びいき〉

mi-biiki-suru〈身びいきする〉be partial to one's relatives.

mibōjin〈みぼうじん：未亡人〉a widow.

mibōjin-ni-naru〈未亡人になる〉lose one's husband, be widowed.

mibun〈みぶん：身分〉one's standing, one's social status.

mibun-shômei-sho（身分証明書） an identification card

miburi〈みぶり：身振り〉a gesture, (a) gesticulation.

mi-burui 〈みぶるい：身震い〉a shiver, a shudder, a tremble, a quake.
　mi-burui-ga-suru 〈身震いがする〉shiver ((with)), shudder ((with)), tremble ((for)), quake in one's shoes.
　　Omotta-dake-de-mo　mi-burui-ga-suru.（思っただけでも身震いがする.）The mere thought of it makes me tremble.

michi 〈みち：未知〉
　michi-no 〈未知の〉unknown, strange.
　　michi-no sekai（未知の世界）the unknown world

michi 〈みち：道〉a road, a way, a passage, a path, a lane; a course, a means.
　　michi-ni-mayou（道に迷う）lose one's way
　　michi-o-machigaeru（道を間違える）take the wrong way
　　michi o kiku（道を聞く）ask one's way ((to))
　　michi o oshieru（道を教える）tell ((a person)) the way ((to))
　　michi-annai（道案内）guidance, a guide
　　　michi-annai-o-suru（道案内をする）show ((a person)) the way ((to)), act as a guide
　　michibata（道端）the roadside, the wayside
　　michi-jun（道順）a route, the way, a course
　　michi-shirube（道しるべ）a guidepost, a signpost, a waymark; a guide ((to)), a handbook
　　Hoka-ni-toru-beki-michi-ga-nai.（ほかにとるべき道がない.）This is the only course open to us.

michibiku 〈みちびく：導く〉guide, lead; show in(*or* into).

mi-chigaeru 〈みちがえる：見違える〉take ((a thing *or* a person)) for ((another)).
　　mi-chigaeru-hodo-kawaru（見違えるほど変わる）be changed beyond recognition

michikusa 〈みちくさ：道草〉
　michikusa-o-kuu 〈道草を食う〉loiter on the way, waste one's time on the way.

michinori 〈みちのり：道のり〉(a) distance, (a) journey.
　　jitensha-de　san-juppun-hodo-no　michinori（自転車で三十分ほどの道のり）about half an hour's ride by bicycle

michiru 〈みちる：満ちる〉be full ((of)), be filled ((with)); be full; rise, flow.

michi-shio 〈みちしお：満ち潮〉see. manchô.

michi-sū 〈みちすう：未知数〉an unknown quantity.

michi-tariru 〈みちたりる：満ち足りる〉 be contented ((with)).
  michi-tarita seikatsu-o-suru〈満ち足りた生活をする〉 live a full life

michi-zure 〈みちづれ：道連れ〉 a fellow traveler, a traveling companion.

midara 〈みだら〉
  midara-na 〈みだらな〉 indecent, lewd, obscene, bawdy, wanton.

midare-gami 〈みだれがみ：乱れ髪〉 unkempt hair.

midareru 〈みだれる：乱れる〉 be disordered, fall into disorder, be disturbed, be confused, be disheveled, be loose, be lax.
  Kare-no heya wa midarete-ita.（彼の部屋は乱れていた.） His room was in disorder.
  Fūki ga midarete-iru.（風紀が乱れている.） Public morals are lax.

midari 〈みだり〉
  midari-ni 〈みだりに〉 without permission, without reason, at random, recklessly.

midashi 〈みだし：見出し〉 an index; a title, a headline, a heading.

mi-dashinami 〈みだしなみ：身だしなみ〉
  mi-dashinami-ga-ii 〈身だしなみがいい〉 be careful about one's personal appearance, keep oneself neat.

midasu 〈みだす：乱す〉 put out of order, put into disorder, break, disturb, agitate, corrupt, distract.
  retsu o midasu（列を乱す） break the line
  kokoro o midasu（心を乱す） distract one's mind

mi-dokoro 〈みどころ：見所〉 a good point, a merit, promise; the highlight.
  mi-dokoro-no-aru 〈見所のある〉 with some good points, promising.

midori(-iro) 〈みどり(いろ)：緑(色)〉 green.
  midori-no 〈緑の〉 green, verdant.
  midori-gakatta 〈緑がかった〉 greenish, greeny.

midoru-kyū 〈ミドルきゅう：ミドル級〉 the middleweight.
  midoru-kyū-no 〈ミドル級の〉 middleweight.

mie 〈みえ：見え〉 show, (a) display, vanity.
  mie-o-haru 〈見えを張る〉 show off, make a show.

mie-gakure 〈みえがくれ：見え隠れ〉
  mie-gakure-suru 〈見え隠れする〉 appear and disappear, be now in sight and now out of sight.
  mie-gakure-ni-ato-o-tsukeru 〈見え隠れに跡をつける〉 shadow ((a person)).

mieru 〈みえる：見える〉 see, be seen, be visible, be in sight; look, seem; appear, come.

Tooku-ni Fuji-san ga mieru.（遠くに富士山が見える。） Mt. Fuji can be seen in the distance.

Kare-wa　byôki-no-yô-ni-mie-nai.（彼は病気のように見えない。） He does not look sick.

O-tô-san wa mamonaku mieru-deshô.（お父さんは間もなく見えるでしょう。） Your father will appear before long.

mie-suku〈みえすく：見え透く〉

mie-suita〈見え透いた〉plain, transparent, obvious, hollow.

　mie-suita uso o iu（見え透いたうそを言う） tell a transparent lie

migaki〈みがき：磨き〉polish, burnishing.

　migaki-ko（磨き粉） polishing powder

migaki-o-kakeru〈磨きをかける〉give ((a thing)) a polish, polish, burnish, brush up.

migaki-no-kakatta〈磨きのかかった〉polished.

migaku〈みがく：磨く〉polish, burnish, rub, cleanse, brush, clean; cultivate, improve.

　kutsu o migaku（靴を磨く） polish one's shoes

　ha o migaku（歯を磨く） clean one's teeth

　ude o migaku（腕を磨く） improve one's skill

mi-gamae〈みがまえ：身構え〉an attitude, a posture.

mi-gamaeru〈身構える〉assume a stance, stand in readiness ((for *or* to do)), pull oneself up ((for)), stand on (one's) guard.

mi-gara〈みがら：身柄〉one's person.

　mi-gara o hiki-toru（身柄を引き取る） take over ((a person))

migaru〈みがる：身軽〉

migaru-na〈身軽な〉light, nimble.

　migaru-na-fukusô-o-suru（身軽な服装をする） be lightly dressed

migaru-ni〈身軽に〉lightly, nimbly.

　migaru-ni tabi-o-suru（身軽に旅をする） travel light

mi-gatte〈みがって：身勝手〉selfishness.

　Kimi-wa mi-gatte-da.（君は身勝手だ。） You are selfish.

mi-gawari〈みがわり：身代わり〉a substitute, a sacrifice.

mi-gawari-ni-naru〈身代わりになる〉sacrifice oneself ((for)).

~-no-mi-gawari-ni〈～の身代わりに〉in place of... .

migi〈みぎ：右〉(the) right.

　migi-e mawaru（右へ回る） turn to the right

　migi-te（右手） the right hand

~-no-migi-ni-deru〈～の右に出る〉be superior to... , surpass, excel.

migi-no〈右の〉right.

migi-gawa〈みぎがわ：右側〉the right side.

　migi-gawa-no〈右側の〉right(-hand).

　migi-gawa-ni〈右側に〉on the right side.

migi-kiki〈みぎきき：右利き〉

　migi-kiki-no〈右利きの〉right-handed.

migi-mawari〈みぎまわり：右回り〉

　migi-mawari-no〈右回りの〉right-handed.

　migi-mawari-ni〈右回りに〉clockwise.

migoro〈みごろ：身頃〉the body (of a garment).

migoro〈みごろ：見ごろ〉

　migoro-de-aru〈見ごろである〉be in full bloom, be at ((their)) best.

migoroshi〈みごろし：見殺し〉

　migoroshi-ni-suru〈見殺しにする〉leave ((a person)) to ((his)) fate.

migoto〈みごと：見事〉

　migoto-na〈見事な〉beautiful, fine, splendid, admirable, excellent, skillful.

　migoto-ni〈見事に〉beautifully, finely, splendidly, admirably, excellently, skillfully, completely, fairly.

　　migoto-ni makeru〈見事に負ける〉be fairly beaten

　　migoto-ni-shippai-suru〈見事に失敗する〉end in a complete failure

mi-gurushii〈みぐるしい：見苦しい〉dishonorable, disgraceful, unsightly, unbecoming, ugly, shabby.

　　mi-gurushii-furumai-o-suru〈見苦しい振る舞いをする〉act dishonorably, behave unbecomingly

　　mi-gurushii-fukusô-o-suru〈見苦しい服装をする〉be shabbily dressed

mi-hakarai〈みはからい：見計らい〉

　　mi-hakarai-chûmon〈見計らい注文〉an open order

　mi-hakarau〈見計らう〉use one's discretion.

　koro-ai-o-mihakaratte〈ころ合いを見計らって〉at the proper time.

mi-hanasu〈みはなす：見放す〉abandon, forsake, turn one's back ((on)), give up.

　　Kare-wa　isha-ni　mi-hanasareta.〔彼は医者に見放された．〕He was given up by the doctor.

mi-harai〈みはらい：未払い〉

　　mi-harai-kanjô〈未払い勘定〉an outstanding account

　mi-harai-no〈未払いの〉unpaid, unsettled, outstanding.

mi-harashi〈みはらし：見晴らし〉a view, an outlook.

mi-harashi-ga-ii〈見晴らしがいい〉 have a fine view ((of))

mi-harashi-no-ii〈見晴らしのいい〉 with a view, with a beautiful outlook.

mi-hari〈みはり：見張り〉 watch, lookout, guard.

　　mi-hari-nin（見張り人） a watchman, a guard

mi-hari-o-suru〈見張りをする〉 *see.* mi-haru.

mi-haru〈みはる：見張る〉 watch, keep (a) watch, stand guard, be on the lookout ((for)); open ((one's eyes)) wide.

　　(odoroki-no-)me-o-mi-hatte（(驚きの)目を見張って） with one's eyes wide open (in astonishment)

mihon〈みほん：見本〉 a sample, a specimen, a pattern.

　　mihon-ichi（見本市） a trade fair

mi-idasu〈みいだす：見いだす〉 find (out), discover, detect.

miira〈ミイラ〉 a mummy.

mi-iri〈みいり：実入り〉 (an) income, gains, profit.

mi-iri-ga-ii〈実入りがいい〉 earn a large income, be profitable.

mi-iru〈みいる：見入る〉 gaze ((at)), fix one's eyes ((on)).

mijika〈みじか：身近〉

mijika-ni-kanjiru〈身近に感じる〉 feel familiar(*or* close)((to)).

mijikai〈みじかい：短い〉 short, brief.

　　mijikai inochi（短い命） a short life

mijikaku〈短く〉 short, briefly, close.

　　tsume o mijikaku-kiru（つめを短く切る） cut one's nails close

mijikaku-naru〈短くなる〉 shorten, become short.

mijikaku-suru〈短くする〉 shorten, make short, cut short.

mijime〈みじめ：惨め〉

mijime-na〈惨めな〉 pitiful, miserable, wretched.

　　mijime-na-omoi-o-suru（惨めな思いをする） feel miserable

mijin〈みじん〉

koppa-mijin-ni-kudakeru〈木っ端みじんに砕ける〉 be broken to pieces.

mi-jitaku〈みじたく：身支度〉 dress, equipment, outfit.

mi-jitaku-o-suru〈身支度をする〉 dress oneself, fit oneself up ((for)).

　　isoide mi-jitaku-o-suru（急いで身支度をする） dress in haste

mijuku〈みじゅく：未熟〉

　　mijuku-ji（未熟児） a premature baby

mijuku-na〈未熟な〉 unripe, immature; inexperienced, unskilled.

　　mijuku-na shisô（未熟な思想） an immature thought

mi-kaesu〈みかえす：見返す〉 triumph over (one's old enemy), get one's own back ((on)).

mikage-ishi〈みかげいし：みかげ石〉granite.

mi-kagiru〈みかぎる：見限る〉give up, abandon, desert.

mikai〈みかい：未開〉

　mikai-no〈未開の〉uncivilized, savage, barbarous.

mi-kaihatsu〈みかいはつ：未開発〉

　mi-kaihatsu-no〈未開発の〉undeveloped, unexploited.

mi-kaiketsu〈みかいけつ：未解決〉

　mi-kaiketsu-no〈未解決の〉unsolved, unsettled, pending.

mikake〈みかけ：見掛け〉

　　Hito wa mikake-ni-yora-nai.（人は見掛けによらない。）A man is not
　　　to be judged by his looks.

　　mikake-daoshi-de-aru（見掛け倒しである）be not so good as it looks

mi-kakeru〈みかける：見掛ける〉see, find, notice.

　　yoku-mi-kakeru fûkei（よく見掛ける風景）a familiar sight

mikaku〈みかく：味覚〉the (sense of) taste, the palate.

　　mikaku o manzoku-saseru（味覚を満足させる）please one's palate

　mikaku-o-sosoru-yô-na〈味覚をそそるような〉tempting, appetizing.

mikan〈みかん〉a mandarin orange, a tangerine (orange).

mi-kaneru〈みかねる：見かねる〉cannot remain indifferent ((to)).

mi-kansei〈みかんせい：未完成〉incompletion.

　mi-kansei-no〈未完成の〉incomplete, unfinished.

　　mi-kansei-no sakuhin（未完成の作品）an unfinished work

mi-kata〈みかた：見方〉a way of looking, a (point of) view.

　mi-kata-ga-chigau〈見方が違う〉see ((things)) differently.

mikata〈みかた：味方〉a supporter, a friend, an ally, one's side.

　mikata-o-suru〈味方をする〉be on ((a person's)) side, stand by, back,
　　support.

　　Wareware-wa anata-no mikata-o-shimasu.（我々はあなたの味方をしま
　　　す。）We will be on your side.

mika-zuki〈みかづき：三日月〉a new moon, a crescent.

mi-keiken〈みけいけん：未経験〉

　　mi-keiken-sha（未経験者）an inexperienced person

　mi-keiken-de-aru〈未経験である〉have no experience ((in)).

　mi-keiken-no〈未経験の〉inexperienced, unexperienced, untrained.

miken〈みけん：眉間〉the brow, the middle of the forehead.

　　miken ni shiwa-o-yoseru（眉間にしわを寄せる）knit one's brows

mike-neko〈みけねこ：三毛猫〉a tortoise-shell cat.

miketsu〈みけつ：未決〉

miketsu-shû〈未決囚〉 an unconvicted prisoner

miketsu-no〈未決の〉 undecided, unsettled, pending, unconvicted.

mi-kettei〈みけってい：未決定〉

mi-kettei-no〈未決定の〉 undecided, undetermined.

miki〈みき：幹〉a trunk.

mikiri〈みきり：見切り〉

mikiri-hin（見切り品） sacrifice (goods), a bargain

mikiri-o-tsukeru〈見切りを付ける〉 wash one's hands ((of)), give up, abandon.

mi-kiwameru〈みきわめる：見極める〉 probe ((a matter)) to the core.

mikka-bôzu〈みっかぼうず：三日坊主〉 one who can stick to nothing.

mikkô〈みっこう：密航〉a secret passage.

mikkô-suru〈密航する〉 stow away, smuggle oneself ((into)).

mikkoku〈みっこく：密告〉 secret information.

mikkoku-suru〈密告する〉 inform ((the police)) secretly.

tomodachi-o-mikkoku-suru（友達を密告する） inform against one's friend

mikomareru〈みこまれる：見込まれる〉 win ((a person's)) confidence.

mikomi〈みこみ：見込み〉hope, promise; possibility, likelihood; expectation(s), anticipation.

Kare-ga-kaifuku-suru-mikomi-wa-hotondo-nai.（彼が回復する見込みはほとんどない.） There is little hope of his recovery.

mikomi-ga-hazureru〈見込みが外れる〉 be disappointed of one's expectations, misjudge.

mikomi-chigai-o-suru〈見込み違いをする〉miscalculate, make a wrong estimate.

mikomi-no-aru〈見込みのある〉 hopeful, promising.

mikomi-no-nai（見込みのない） hopeless, unpromising

mi-komu〈みこむ：見込む〉expect, anticipate, rely ((on)); estimate, allow (for)).

rieki o juppâsento-to-mi-komu（利益を十パーセントと見込む） estimate the profit at 10 percent

～-o-mikonde〈～を見込んで〉in expectation(*or* anticipation) of... , counting on... .

mikon〈みこん：未婚〉

mikon-no〈未婚の〉 unmarried, single.

mi-koshi〈みこし：神輿〉 a portable shrine.

mikosu〈みこす：見越す〉anticipate, expect, foresee.

mikubiru〈みくびる：見くびる〉hold ((a person)) cheap, make light ((of)), underestimate, despise.

mi-kudasu〈みくだす：見下す〉look down ((upon)), despise.

mi-kuraberu〈みくらべる：見比べる〉compare ((two things)) with the eye, look one from the other.

mikuron〈ミクロン〉a micron.

mimai〈みまい：見舞い〉an inquiry.

 mimai-ni-iku（見舞いに行く）go to inquire after ((a person's)) condition

 mimai-jô（見舞い状）a letter of inquiry

 mimai-kyaku（見舞い客）a visitor

 mimai-kin（見舞い金）a present of money

 mimau〈見舞う〉inquire after ((a person's)) health, visit.

mi-mamoru〈みまもる：見守る〉watch (intently), gaze ((at)).

miman〈みまん：未満〉under, less than.

 roku-sai-miman-no kodomo（六歳未満の子供）children under 6 years of age

 hyaku-en-miman（百円未満）less than 100 yen

mimawari〈みまわり：見回り〉a patrol; a patrolman, a watchman.

 mi-mawaru〈見回る〉patrol, inspect, go round.

mi-mawasu〈みまわす：見回す〉look around.

mimei〈みめい：未明〉

 mimei-ni〈未明に〉before dawn, before daybreak.

mimi〈みみ：耳〉an ear, hearing.

 mimi-ga-hayai（耳が早い）be quick of hearing

 mimi-ga-tooi（耳が遠い）be hard of hearing

 mimi-ga-itai（耳が痛い）have a pain in the ear, be ashamed to hear ((it))

 mimi-ga-kikoe-nai（耳が聞こえない）be deaf

  mimi-ga-kikoe-nai-hito（耳が聞こえない人）a deaf person

 mimi-ga-warui（耳が悪い）have a bad ear

 mimi-ni-hairu（耳に入る）reach one's ears, come to one's knowledge

 mimi-ni-ireru（耳に入れる）tell, inform

 mimi-o-fusagu（耳をふさぐ）stop one's ears

 mimi o kasu（耳を貸す）lend one's ears ((to))

 mimi-o-kasa-nai（耳を貸さない）be deaf〔to all advice〕

 mimi-o-sumashite-kiku（耳を澄まして聞く）listen with strained ears

mimi-o-soroete-harau〈耳をそろえて払う〉 pay in full

mimi-aka〈耳あか〉 earwax

mimi-dare〈耳垂れ〉 discharge from the ears

mimi-kaki〈耳かき〉 an earpick

mimi-nari〈耳鳴り〉 a singing in the ears

mimi-ooi〈耳覆い〉 earflaps, earmuffs.

mimi-tabu〈耳たぶ〉 an earlobe

mimi-uchi〈みみうち：耳打ち〉

mimi-uchi-suru〈耳打ちする〉whisper in ((a person's)) ear.

mimi-yori〈みみより：耳寄り〉

mimi-yori-na〈耳寄りな〉welcome.

mimi-yori-na hanashi〈耳寄りな話〉 welcome news

mimi-zawari〈みみざわり：耳障り〉

mimi-zawari-ni-naru〈耳障りになる〉be offensive to the ear.

mimi-zawari-na〈耳障りな〉ragged, rough, rude, harsh, strident.

mimizu〈みみず〉an earthworm, an angleworm.

mimizu-bare〈みみずばれ〉 a wale, a welt

mi-mochi〈みもち：身持ち〉

mi-mochi-ga-warui〈身持ちが悪い〉be of loose morals, lead a dissolute life.

mi-mono〈みもの：見物〉a sight, a spectacle.

Mi-mono-datta-yo.（見物だったよ.） It was a sight to see.

mi-moto〈みもと：身元〉one's birth and parentage, one's identity.

mi-moto-o-shiraberu〈身元を調べる〉 inquire into ((a person's)) antecedents, check up ((a person's)) record

mi-moto-hoshō-nin〈身元保証人〉 a surety

mi-moto-fumei-no〈身元不明の〉unidentified.

mi-moto-fumei-no-shitai〈身元不明の死体〉 the body of an unidentified person

mimpō〈みんぽう：民法〉the civil law.

mi-muki〈みむき：見向き〉

mi-muki-mo-shi-nai〈見向きもしない〉do not even look ((at)).

mi-muki-mo-shi-nai-de〈見向きもしないで〉without a look ((at)).

mina〈みな：皆〉all, everyone, everything.

mina-de〈皆で〉in all, all told; all together; in a body.

mi-nage〈みなげ：身投げ〉

mi-nage-suru〈身投げする〉drown oneself, throw oneself into the water.

minagiru〈みなぎる〉be full ((of)), be filled ((with)).

Kaisha-kambu-ni-taisuru fushin-kan ga minagitte-iru.（会社幹部に対する不信感がみなぎっている。） A feeling of distrust toward the executives of the company pervades.

mina-goroshi〈みなごろし：皆殺し〉

　mina-goroshi-ni-suru〈皆殺しにする〉kill to a man, annihilate.

　　ikka-mina-goroshi-ni-suru（一家皆殺しにする） murder the whole family

minami〈みなみ：南〉the south.

　　minami-kaze（南風） a south wind

　　Minami-jūji-sei（南十字星） the Southern Cross

　minami-no〈南の〉south, southern.

　minami-e or *minami-ni*〈南へ，南に〉south, southward.

　〜-no-minami-ni〈〜の南に〉in the south of... , on the south of... , to the south of... .

minamoto〈みなもと：源〉the source, the fountainhead.

　〜-ni-minamoto-o-hassuru〈〜に源を発する〉have its origin in... , rise(or spring) from... .

mi-naosu〈みなおす：見直す〉have a better opinion ((of)).

mi-narai〈みならい：見習い〉

　　mi-narai-kikan（見習い期間） a probationary period

　mi-narau〈見習（倣）う〉follow ((a person's)) example; learn.

mi-nareru〈みなれる：見慣れる〉get used to seeing, be familiar ((to)).

　mi-nareta〈見慣れた〉familiar.

　　mi-nare-nai（見慣れない） unfamiliar, strange

minari〈みなり：身なり〉dress, one's personal appearance.

　minari-ga-kichin-to-shite-iru〈身なりがきちんとしている〉be neat in one's dress, be neatly dressed.

mina-san〈みなさん：皆さん〉hello, folks, ladies and gentlemen; all of you.

minashigo〈みなしご〉*see.* koji.

mi-nasu〈みなす：見なす〉regard ((as)), consider, think of ((as)), look upon ((as)).

minato〈みなと：港〉a port, a harbor.

　　minato-ni-hairu（港に入る） arrive in port

mine〈みね：峰〉a peak, the ridge.

min·ei〈みんえい：民営〉

　min·ei-de-aru〈民営である〉be under private management.

mingei〈みんげい：民芸〉folk art, folkcraft.

　　mingei-hin〈民芸品〉 a folk-art object

min·i〈みんい：民意〉 the will of the people.

　　min·i o han·ei-suru〈民意を反映する〉 reflect the will of the people

minikui〈みにくい：醜い〉 ugly, plain; unseemly, unsightly, ignoble.

　　minikui arasoi〈醜い争い〉 an unpleasant quarrel

minji〈みんじ：民事〉 civil affairs.

　　minji-jiken〈民事事件〉 a civil case

　　minji-soshô〈民事訴訟〉 a civil action

minka〈みんか：民家〉a private house.

minkan〈みんかん：民間〉

　minkan-no〈民間の〉 private, nonofficial, civilian, civil.

minna〈みんな〉see. mina.

minô〈みのう：未納〉

　　minô-kin〈未納金〉 the amount in arrears

　minô-no〈未納の〉 unpaid, in arrears.

mi-nogasu〈みのがす：見逃す〉overlook, pass by, pass over, connive ((at)); miss.

　　hanzai-o-mi-nogasu〈犯罪を見逃す〉 connive at a crime

　　kôkyû o mi-nogasu〈好球を見逃す〉 miss a good ball

mi-no-hodo〈みのほど：身の程〉

　mi-no-hodo o shira-nai〈身の程を知らない〉do not know one's place.

mi-no-ke〈みのけ：身の毛〉

　mi-no-ke-no-yodatsu-yô-na〈身の毛のよだつような〉hair-raising, blood-curdling.

mi-no-mawari〈みのまわり：身の回り〉

　　mi-no-mawari-hin〈身の回り品〉 one's personal effects

mino-mushi〈みのむし：みの虫〉a bagworm, a fagot worm.

minori〈みのり：実り〉a crop, a harvest.

　　minori-no-aki〈実りの秋〉 the harvest season

　minori-no-aru or minori-no-ooi〈実りのある，実りの多い〉fruitful.

　minoru〈実る〉bear fruit, ripen.

minoshiro-kin〈みのしろきん：身の代金〉(a) ransom.

　　sen-man-en-no-minoshiro-kin o yôkyû-sareru〈千万円の身の代金を要求される〉 have a ten-million-yen ransom demanded

mi-no-ue〈みのうえ：身の上〉one's lot, one's personal affairs, welfare; one's life.

　　mi-no-ue-o-sôdan-suru〈身の上を相談する〉 consult ((a person)) about one's personal affairs mi-no-ue-o-anzuru〈身の上を案ずる〉feel concerned about ((a person's)) welfare

    mi-no-ue-banashi〈身の上話〉the story of one's life

    mi-no-ue-sôdan-ran〈身の上相談欄〉a home council column

minsei〈みんせい：民生〉public welfare.

    minsei-iin〈民生委員〉a public welfare commissioner

minshin〈みんしん：民心〉popular feelings, public sentiment.

    minshin o ushinau〈民心を失う〉lose the support of the people

minshu〈みんしゅ：民主〉

    minshu-shugi〈民主主義〉democracy

    minshu-shakai-shugi〈民主社会主義〉democratic socialism

    minshu-shugi-koku〈民主主義国〉a democratic country

minshu-ka〈民主化〉democratization.

    minshu-ka-suru〈民主化する〉democratize

minshu-teki(-na)〈民主的(な)〉democratic.

minshuku〈みんしゅく：民宿〉a tourist home.

mi-nuku〈みぬく：見抜く〉see through, look ((a person)) through, divine.

    imbô o mi-nuku〈陰謀を見抜く〉see through ((a person's)) plot

    jimbutsu-o-sukkari-mi-nuku〈人物をすっかり見抜く〉have ((a person's)) measure to an inch

min‧yô〈みんよう：民謡〉a folk song, a folk ballad.

min‧yû〈みんゆう：民有〉

    min‧yû-chi〈民有地〉private land

minzoku〈みんぞく：民族〉a race.

    minzoku-sei〈民族性〉racial characteristics

    minzoku-shugi〈民族主義〉nationalism

minzoku-no〈民族の〉racial.

minzoku〈みんぞく：民俗〉folkways.

mi-oboe〈みおぼえ：見覚え〉

mi-oboe-ga-aru〈見覚えがある〉remember, recognize, recollect.

mi-oboe-no-aru〈見覚えのある〉familiar.

    mi-oboe-no-nai〈見覚えのない〉unfamiliar, strange

miokuri〈みおくり：見送り〉seeing ((a person)) off.

    miokuri-ni eki-made iku〈見送りに駅まで行く〉go to a station to see ((a person)) off

    miokuri-nin〈見送り人〉senders-off

mi-okuru〈見送る〉see ((a person)) off, give ((a person)) a send-off, follow ((a person)) with one's eyes; leave ((a matter)) over.

mi-orosu 〈みおろす：見下ろす〉 look down ((at *or* on)), overlook.

mi-osame 〈みおさめ：見納め〉

　Sore-ga　kanojo-no-mi-osame-datta.（それが彼女の見納めだった．）
　　That was the last that I saw her.

mi-otori 〈みおとり：見劣り〉

　mi-otori-ga-suru 〈見劣りがする〉 compare poorly ((with)), cannot stand
　comparison ((with)), suffer by comparison ((with)).

mi-otoshi 〈みおとし：見落とし〉 an oversight, an omission.

　mi-otosu 〈見落とす〉 overlook, pass by, fail to notice, make an over-
　sight.

mippei 〈みっぺい：密閉〉

　mippei-suru 〈密閉する〉 shut tight(ly), make airtight.

mippû 〈みっぷう：密封〉

　mippû-suru 〈密封する〉 seal up.

mirai 〈みらい：未来〉(the) future.

　mirai-no 〈未来の〉 future, prospective.

　mirai-ni 〈未来に〉 in (the) future.

miren 〈みれん：未練〉 attachment, affection, regret; cowardice, ir-
　resolution.

　miren-ga-aru 〈未練がある〉 be still attached ((to)), feel ((some)) regret.

　miren-na 〈未練な〉 cowardly.

　miren-gamashii 〈未練がましい〉 irresolute, unmanly.

mirin 〈みりん：味りん〉 a sweet kind of *sake* used for seasoning.

miru 〈みる：見(診)る〉 see, look ((at)), have a look ((at)); observe, look
　((at)), see; read; see, do, visit; look over, examine; judge; look ((after)),
　take care ((of)); try, have a try ((at)).

　　Dare-ga-kita-no-ka-itte-mite-goran.（だれが来たのか行って見てごら
　　ん．）Go and see who it is.

　　yoku-miru（よく見る）have a good look ((at))

　　chûi-shite-miru（注意して見る）watch

　　miru-ni-tae-nai（見るに堪えない）cannot bear to see

　　mite-iru-aida-ni　*or* mirumiru（見ている間に，見る見る）in a moment,
　　　in an instant

　　chotto-mite　*or* chotto-mita-dake-de（ちょっと見て，ちょっと見ただけ
　　　で）at a glance

　　Amerika-jin-no-mita　Nihon（アメリカ人の見た日本）Japan as seen by
　　　an American

　　watashi-kara-miru-to〈私から見ると〉from my point of view

　　〜-o-miru-to〈〜を見ると〉seeing that...

　　dô-mite-mo〈どう見ても〉in every respect, to all appearance(s)

　　daitai-kara-mite〈大体から見て〉on the whole

　　shimbun o miru〈新聞を見る〉read the papers

　　terebi o miru〈テレビを見る〉watch television

　　isha ni mite-morau〈医者に診てもらう〉consult a doctor

　　〜-de-miru-to〈〜で見ると〉judging from...

　　Shibaraku futari-no kodomo-o-mite-kudasai.〈しばらく二人の子供を見てください。〉Please look after my two children for a while.

　　haite-miru, kabutte-miru or kite-miru〈履いてみる、かぶってみる、着てみる〉try on

　　Ima-ni-mite-iro!〈今に見ていろ。〉You shall smart for this!

　　Sore-mita-koto-ka!〈それ見たことか。〉I told you so!

miru-kage〈みるかげ：見る影〉

　miru-kage-mo-nai〈見る影もない〉be a mere shadow of one's former self.

miryoku〈みりょく：魅力〉(a) charm, (a) fascination.

　miryoku-ga-aru〈魅力がある〉have an appeal ((to)).

　miryoku-no-aru or *miryoku-teki(-na)*〈魅力のある、魅力的(な)〉charming, fascinating, attractive.

　　miryoku-no-nai〈魅力のない〉unattractive, unprepossessing

misa〈ミサ〉(a) mass.

　　misa-o-okonau〈ミサを行う〉say mass

mi-sage-hateru〈みさげはてる：見下げ果てる〉

　mi-sage-hateta〈見下げ果てた〉mean, contemptible, despicable, ignominious.

misairu〈ミサイル〉a missile.

　　yûdô-misairu〈誘導ミサイル〉a guided missile

mi-sakai〈みさかい：見境〉discrimination.

　mi-sakai-ga-tsuka-nai〈見境が付かない〉cannot discriminate.

　mi-sakai-mo-naku〈見境もなく〉indiscriminately, imprudently.

misaki〈みさき：岬〉a cape, a promontory.

mise〈みせ：店〉a store, a shop, a stall, an office, a firm.

　　mise-o-hiraku〈店を開く〉open a store; set up in business

　　mise-o-shimeru〈店を閉める〉close up a store; wind up business

　　mise-saki〈店先〉the storefront

mise-birakasu〈みせびらかす：見せびらかす〉show off, make a show

((of)), sport.

mi-seinen〈みせいねん：未成年〉minority.
　　mi-seinen-sha〈未成年者〉a minor
　mi-seinen-de-aru〈未成年である〉be under age.

mise-kake〈みせかけ：見せ掛け〉look, appearance, (a) sham, (a) pretense, a make-believe.
　mise-kakeru〈見せ掛ける〉assume the appearance ((of)), sham, pretend, feign, make a show ((of)), make believe.
　mise-kake-no〈見せ掛けの〉apparent, sham, feigned, pretended, make-believe.

mise-mono〈みせもの：見せ物〉a show, an exhibition.
　　Mise-mono-dewa-nai-zo.（見せ物ではないぞ.）This is not meant for a show.

miseru〈みせる：見せる〉show, let ((a person)) see.
　　E-hagaki o misete-kudasai.（絵はがきを見せてください.）Show me some picture postcards.

miseshime〈みせしめ：見せしめ〉a lesson, a warning, an example.
　miseshime-ni〈見せしめに〉as a warning to others.
　　miseshime-ni-suru（見せしめにする）make an example ((of))

mise-tsukeru〈みせつける：見せ付ける〉*see.* mise-birakasu.

mishimishi〈みしみし〉
　mishimishi-iu〈みしみしいう〉creak.
　mishimishi-to〈みしみしと〉with a creak.

mishin〈ミシン〉a sewing machine.
　　mishin-o-kakeru（ミシンをかける）sew with a machine

mi-shiranu〈みしらぬ：見知らぬ〉strange, unfamiliar.
　　mi-shiranu-hito（見知らぬ人）a stranger

miso〈みそ：味そ〉bean paste, *miso.*
　　miso-shiru（みそ汁）*miso* soup

mi-sokonau〈みそこなう：見損なう〉miss; make a mistake, misjudge.
　　Ano manga o mi-sokonatta.（あの漫画を見損なった.）I missed the cartoon film.
　　Aitsu o mi-sokonatta.（あいつを見損なった.）I'm disappointed in him.

mi-someru〈みそめる：見初める〉fall in love ((with a person)) (at first sight).

mi-soreru〈みそれる：見それる〉
　　O-mi-sore-shite-sumi-masen.（お見それしてすみません.）Pardon me

　　　　for not recognizing you.

missei〈みっせい：密生〉

　missei-suru〈密生する〉grow thick, grow in clusters.

missetsu〈みっせつ：密接〉

　missetsu-na〈密接な〉close, intimate.

　　　missetsu-na-kankei-ga-aru（密接な関係がある）be closely related ((with))

misshi〈みっし：密使〉a secret messenger, a confidential agent.

misshitsu〈みっしつ：密室〉a secret room.

missho〈みっしょ：密書〉a secret letter.

misshû〈みっしゅう：密集〉

　misshû-suru〈密集する〉crowd, swarm, cluster together.

　　　Jinka ga misshû-shite-iru.（人家が密集している.）The houses stand close together.

missô〈みっそう：密葬〉a funeral held only by the family members.

misu〈ミス〉a mistake, an error.

misu〈ミス〉Miss.

misuborashii〈みすぼらしい：見すぼらしい〉shabby, poor-looking, miserable, seedy.

　misuborashii-fukusô-o-shite-iru〈見すぼらしい服装をしている〉be shabbily dressed.

misui〈みすい：未遂〉

　　　satsujin-misui（殺人未遂）attempted murder

　　　misui-zai（未遂罪）an attempted crime

misumisu〈みすみす：見す見す〉

　　　Misumisu chansu o nogashita.（みすみすチャンスを逃した.）I passed up the opportunity before my eyes.

misu-purinto〈ミスプリント〉a misprint, a printer's error.

mi-suteru〈みすてる：見捨てる〉forsake, desert, throw over, give up, abandon.

-mitai〈-みたい〉

　-mitai-na〈-みたいな〉like, a sort of... .

　　　o-mae-mitai-na yatsu（お前みたいなやつ）a fellow like you

mitasu〈みたす：満たす〉fill, pack; supply, cover, satisfy.

　　　juyô o mitasu（需要を満たす）supply the demand

mi-tate〈みたて：見立て〉(a) diagnosis; (a) choice, (a) selection.

　　　mi-tate-ga-umai（見立てがうまい）make a good choice

　　　mi-tate-chigai（見立て違い）a wrong diagnosis

mitateru〈見立てる〉diagnose; choose, select.

mita-tokoro〈みたところ：見たところ〉to all appearance(s), judging from the appearance.

    mita-tokoro-genki-sô-da（見たところ元気そうだ）seem to be healthy

mitchaku〈みっちゃく：密着〉close adhesion.

mitchaku-suru〈密着する〉adhere closely ((to)), stick fast ((to)).

mitchaku-saseru〈密着させる〉stick ((A)) fast to ((B)).

mitchiri〈みっちり〉

    mitchiri-renshû-sureba（みっちり練習すれば）with a severe training

    mitchiri-benkyô-suru（みっちり勉強する）study hard

mitei〈みてい：未定〉

    Kaigi no hi-dori wa mitei-desu.（会議の日取りは未定です.）The date of the conference is not yet fixed.

mitei-no〈未定の〉undecided, unfixed, unsettled.

mite-minu-furi-o-suru〈みてみぬふりをする：見て見ぬ振りをする〉blink ((a fact)), pretend not to see.

mi-todokeru〈みとどける：見届ける〉ascertain, make sure ((of *or* that)), see with one's own eyes.

mitome〈みとめ：認め〉a private seal, a signet.

    mitome o osu（認めを押す）stamp one's private seal ((to))

mitomeru〈みとめる：認める〉see, notice, find; recognize, realize; approve ((of)), admit, accept, acknowledge, grant.

    sakka-to-shite mitomerareru（作家として認められる）be recognized as a writer

    yo-ni-mitomerareru（世に認められる）win public recognition

    jibun-no tsumi o mitomeru（自分の罪を認める）admit one's guilt

    haiboku o mitomeru（敗北を認める）accept defeat

    〜-ga-jijitsu-de-aru-koto-o-mitomeru（〜が事実であることを認める）grant the truth of...

mi-tooshi〈みとおし：見通し〉visibility, a prospect, a forecast, (an) insight ((into)).

    Mi-tooshi ga ii.（見通しがいい.）The visibility is good.

    Mi-tooshi ga warui.（見通しが悪い.）The visibility is poor.

    Mi-tooshi ga akarui.（見通しが明るい.）The prospects seem bright.

    mi-tooshi-ga-tsuku（見通しが付く）can see far into the future

mi-toosu〈みとおす：見通す〉get an unobstructed view ((of)), foresee, see through.

    shôrai o mi-toosu（将来を見通す）foresee the future

mitoreru 〈みとれる：見とれる〉 gaze at ((something)) with rapture, be fascinated(*or* charmed) ((by *or* with)), be lost in admiration ((of)).

mitori-zu 〈みとりず：見取り図〉 a (rough) sketch.
mitori-zu-o-toru 〈見取り図をとる〉 sketch, make a sketch ((of)).

mitsu 〈みつ：蜜〉 honey.
     mitsu-bachi 〈みつばち〉 a (honey)bee
     mitsu-bachi-no-su 〈みつばちの巣〉 a honeycomb, a beehive

mitsu 〈みつ：密〉
mitsu-na 〈密な〉 close, intimate; dense, thick; minute, careful.

mitsubai 〈みつばい：密売〉 an illicit sale.
     mitsubai-hin 〈密売品〉 smuggled goods
     mitsubai-sha 〈密売者〉 a secret trader(*or* dealer)
mitsubai-suru 〈密売する〉 deal secretly, sell in secret.

mitsu-bôeki 〈みつぼうえき：密貿易〉 smuggling.
     mitsu-bôeki-sha 〈密貿易者〉 a smuggler

mitsudan 〈みつだん：密談〉
mitsudan-suru 〈密談する〉 talk secretly ((with)), have a confidential talk ((with)).

mitsudo 〈みつど：密度〉 density.

mitsu-domoe 〈みつどもえ：三つどもえ〉
mitsu-domoe-no 〈三つどもえの〉 triangular, three-cornered.

mitsugi 〈みつぎ：密議〉
mitsugi-suru 〈密議する〉 hold a secret conference.

mitsu-go 〈みつご：三つ子〉
     Mitsu-go-no-tamashii-hyaku-made. (三つ子の魂百まで.) As a child, so the man.

mitsukaru 〈みつかる：見付かる〉 be found, be discovered, be detected, be caught; find.
     Nôto ga mitsukara-nai. (ノートがみつからない.) I can't find my notebook.
mitsukeru 〈みつける：見付ける〉 find, discover, detect.

mi-tsumeru 〈みつめる：見詰める〉 gaze ((at *or* on)), look fixedly ((at)), study.

mitsumori 〈みつもり：見積もり〉 an estimate, (an) estimation.
     mitsumori-kakaku 〈見積もり価格〉 an estimated value
     mitsumori-sho 〈見積書〉 an estimate sheet
mitsumori-o-dasu or *mi-tsumoru* 〈見積もりを出す，見積もる〉 make an estimate ((of)), estimate.

ikura-uchiwa-ni-mi-tsumottemo〈幾ら内輪に見積もっても〉at the lowest
　estimate.

mitsu-nyûgoku〈みつにゅうごく：密入国〉
　　mitsu-nyûgoku-sha〈密入国者〉a smuggler, a stowaway
　mitsu-nyûgoku-suru〈密入国する〉smuggle oneself into.

mitsurin〈みつりん：密林〉a thick forest, a jungle.

mitsuryô〈みつりょう：密猟(漁)〉
　　mitsuryô-sha〈密猟(漁)者〉a poacher
　　mitsuryô-sen〈密漁船〉a poaching boat
　mitsuryô-suru〈密猟(漁)する〉poach ((for)).

mitsuyaku〈みつやく：密約〉a secret promise, a secret agreement.
　　mitsuyaku o musubu〈密約を結ぶ〉conclude a secret treaty(*or* a-
　　greement)

mitsu-yunyû〈みつゆにゅう：密輸入〉
　　mitsu-yunyû-sha〈密輸入者〉a smuggler, a runner
　mitsu-yunyû-suru〈密輸入する〉smuggle, run.

mitsu-yushutsu〈みつゆしゅつ：密輸出〉
　mitsu-yushutsu-suru〈密輸出する〉smuggle ((goods)) abroad.

mitsuzô〈みつぞう：密造〉
　　mitsuzô-shu〈密造酒〉home brew, moonshine
　mitsuzô-suru〈密造する〉manufacture illicitly.

mitsu-zoroi〈みつぞろい：三つぞろい〉a suit of clothes.

mittomo-nai〈みっともない：見っともない〉indecent, unbecoming, dis-
　graceful, shameful, dishonorable, shabby.
　　mittomo-nai-furumai-o-suru〈みっともない振る舞いをする〉behave
　　disgracefully

mittsu〈みっつ：三つ〉*see.* san（三).

mi-uchi〈みうち：身内〉one's relations(*or* relatives).

mi-ugoki〈みうごき：身動き〉
　mi-ugoki-deki-nai〈身動きできない〉cannot move at all.

mi-uri〈みうり：身売り〉
　mi-uri-suru〈身売りする〉sell oneself.

mi-ushinau〈みうしなう：見失う〉lose sight ((of)), miss, lose.

mi-wake〈みわけ：見分け〉distinction, discrimination.
　mi-wake-ga-tsuku〈見分けが付く〉know ((A from B)).
　　mi-wake-ga-tsuka-nai〈見分けが付かない〉cannot tell ((A from B))
　mi-wake-no-tsuka-nai〈見分けの付かない〉indistinguishable.
　mi-wake-mo-tsuka-nai-hodo(-ni)〈見分けも付かないほど(に)〉out of

recognition.

mi-wakeru〈見分ける〉know ((A from B)), distinguish ((A from B)).

miwaku〈みわく：魅惑〉

miwaku-suru〈魅惑する〉fascinate, charm, captivate.

miwaku-teki-na〈魅惑的な〉fascinating, charming, captivating.

mi-watasu〈みわたす：見渡す〉look out ((over)), take an extensive view ((of)).

mi-watasu-kagiri〈見渡す限り〉as far as one can see.

miya〈みや：宮〉a shrine.

mi-yaburu〈みやぶる：見破る〉see through, penetrate.

miyage(-mono)〈みやげ(もの)：土産(物)〉a souvenir.

miyage-mono-ya（土産物屋）a souvenir shop

miyako〈みやこ：都〉a capital, a metropolis.

Sumeba-miyako.（住めば都.）There is no place like home.

miya-zukae〈みやづかえ：宮仕え〉

miya-zukae-suru〈宮仕えする〉be in the government service.

miyō〈みよう：見様〉

miyô-mi-mane-de〈見様見まねで〉following another's example.

mi-yori〈みより：身寄り〉a relative, a person to depend on.

mizen〈みぜん：未然〉

mizen-ni-fusegu〈未然に防ぐ〉obviate, nip ((a plot)) in the bud.

mizo〈みぞ：溝〉a ditch, a gutter, a drain; a groove, a chamfer; a gap.

o-tagai-ni-mizo-ga-dekiru（お互いに溝が出来る）be estranged from each other

mizo-ochi〈みぞおち〉*see.* mizu-ochi.

mizore〈みぞれ〉sleet.

Mizore-ga-furu.（みぞれが降る.）It sleets.

mizou〈みぞう：未曽有〉

mizou-no〈未曽有の〉unprecedented, record-breaking, unparalleled.

mizu〈みず：水〉water.

mizu-o-dasu（水を出す）turn on the water

mizu o kakeru（水を掛ける）sprinkle water, pour water

mizu-o-yaru（水をやる）water

mizu-de yusugu（水でゆすぐ）rinse with water

mizu-ni-nagasu（水に流す）forgive and forget

mizu-no-awa-to-naru（水の泡となる）come to nothing

mizu-abi〈みずあび：水浴び〉

mizu-abi-suru〈水浴びする〉bathe, have a dip.

mizu-age〈みずあげ：水揚げ〉takings, gross earnings.

mizu-bitashi〈みずびたし：水浸し〉

　mizu-bitashi-ni-naru〈水浸しになる〉be flooded, be inundated with water, be under water, be submerged.

mizu-bōsō〈みずぼうそう：水ぼうそう〉the chicken pox.

mizu-bukure〈みずぶくれ：水膨れ〉a (water) blister.

　mizu-bukure-ga-dekiru（水膨れが出来る）raise a blister

mizu-dori〈みずどり：水鳥〉a waterfowl, a water bird.

mizu-gi〈みずぎ：水着〉a swimming suit, a bathing suit.

mizu-giwa〈みずぎわ：水際〉the water's edge, the waterside, the shore.

　mizu-giwa-datta〈水際立った〉splendid.

mizu-gusuri〈みずぐすり：水薬〉a liquid medicine, a liquor.

mizu-hake〈みずはけ：水はけ〉drainage.

　mizu-hake-ga-ii〈水はけがいい〉be well drained, drain well.

　　mizu-hake-ga-warui（水はけが悪い）be ill drained, do not drain well

mizuhiki〈みずひき：水引〉a ceremonial red-(*or* black)and-white paper cord.

mizu-irazu〈みずいらず：水入らず〉

　Kare-wa-kazoku-ichidō-mizu-irazu-de kiraku-ni kurashite-iru.（彼は家族一同水入らずで気楽に暮らしている。）All his family members live by themselves in comfort.

mizu-iro〈みずいろ：水色〉a sky blue, a light blue.

mizukake-ron〈みずかけろん：水掛け論〉an endless and futile dispute.

mizukaki〈みずかき：水かき〉a web.

　mizukaki-de-oyogu〈水かきで泳ぐ〉paddle.

mizukara〈みずから：自ら〉oneself, in person, personally.

　mizukara-susunde〈自ら進んで〉of one's own accord(free will *or* choice).

mizu-kasa〈みずかさ：水かさ〉the (volume of) water.

　Kawa-no-mizu-kasa ga mashita.（川の水かさが増した.）The river has risen.

mizu-ke〈みずけ：水気〉

　mizu-ke-no-aru〈水気のある〉moist, damp, watery, juicy.

　　mizu-ke-no-nai（水気のない）dry

mizu-kemuri〈みずけむり：水煙〉spray.

　　mizu-kemuri o ageru（水煙を上げる）raise spray

mizu-kiri〈みずきり：水切り〉the cutwater.

mizu-kusa〈みずくさ：水草〉a water plant.

mizu-kusai〈みずくさい：水臭い〉reserved, cold, lacking in frankness.

mizu-maki 〈みずまき：水まき〉
  mizu-maki-o-suru 〈水まきをする〉water, sprinkle water.
mizu-makura 〈みずまくら：水まくら〉a water pillow.
mizu-mashi 〈みずまし：水増し〉
  mizu-mashi-suru 〈水増しする〉water down, pad.
mizumizushii 〈みずみずしい〉young and fresh, fresh-looking, unspoiled.
mizu-mono 〈みずもの：水物〉a gamble, an uncertain affair.
mizu-mushi 〈みずむし：水虫〉a water insect; athlete's foot.
mizu-ochi 〈みずおち〉the pit of the stomach, the solar plexus.
mizuppoi 〈みずっぽい：水っぽい〉(wishy-)washy, watery, thin.
mizusaki-annai 〈みずさきあんない：水先案内〉piloting, a pilot.
mizu-sashi 〈みずさし：水差し〉a pitcher, a jug, a ewer.
mizu-shirazu 〈みずしらず：見ず知らず〉
  mizu-shirazu-no 〈見ず知らずの〉strange.
    mizu-shirazu-no-hito 〈見ず知らずの人〉 a stranger
mizu-shōbai 〈みずしょうばい：水商売〉a gay trade, a profession of entertainment.
mizu-sumashi 〈みずすまし〉a water beetle.
mizu-tama 〈みずたま：水玉〉a drop of water, a dewdrop.
    mizu-tama-moyō 〈水玉模様〉 polka dots
mizu-tamari 〈みずたまり：水たまり〉a pool, a puddle.
    mizu-tamari-ga-dekiru 〈水たまりが出来る〉 be pitted with puddles
mizuumi 〈みずうみ：湖〉a lake.
mizu-wari 〈みずわり：水割り〉
  mizu-wari-no 〈水割りの〉watered, diluted with water.
    mizu-wari-no uisukî 〈水割りのウイスキー〉 watered whisky, whisky and water
mo 〈も：喪〉mourning.
    mo-ni-fukusuru 〈喪に服する〉 go into mourning ((for))
    mo-chû-de-aru 〈喪中である〉 be in mourning ((for))
    mo-ga-akeru 〈喪が明ける〉 go out of mourning
    mo-fuku 〈喪服〉 mourning dress, widow's weeds
    mo-shô 〈喪章〉 a mourning badge, a crape
    moshu 〈喪主〉 the chief mourner
mo 〈も：藻〉an alga, seaweed.
-mo 〈-も〉and, both...and, as well as, neither...nor; too, also, (not)... either; either...or, whether...or not; even if, (al)though; as many

(much, far *or* long) as; even, so much as.

Eigo-mo-Furansu-go-mo kakeru（英語もフランス語も書ける） be able to write both English and French

Furansu-go-mo-Doitsu-go-mo hanase-nai（フランス語もドイツ語も話せない） be able to speak neither French nor German

Kanojo-mo tsurete-itte-kureru?（彼女も連れて行ってくれる.） Can you take her, too?

Kare-ga ika-nai-no-nara watashi-mo-ika-nai.（彼が行かないのなら私も行かない.） If he doesn't go, I will not either.

Kimi-wa itte-mo-ii-shi ika-naku-temo-ii.（君は行ってもいいし行かなくてもいい.） You may either go or stay here.

ame-ga-futte-mo（雨が降っても） even if it rains

ichi-man-en-mo（一万円も） as much as ten thousand yen

henji-mo-shi-nai（返事もしない） do not even give an answer

mô〈もう〉now; already, yet, no longer; by now, by this (time); another, the other, more.

Mô aki-desu.（もう秋です.） It is autumn now.

Mô kaigi wa hajimatte-iru.（もう会議は始まっている.） The conference has already begun.

Mô-kore-ijô aruke-nai.（もうこれ以上歩けない.） I cannot walk any farther.

Mô kare-wa tsuite-iru-deshô.（もう彼は着いているでしょう.） He may have reached there by now.

Mô-ippai-kôhî-wa-ikaga-desu?（もう一杯コーヒーはいかがです.） Will you have another cup of coffee?

mô-hitori（もう一人） another person, the other person

mô-ichi-do（もう一度） once more

mô-sukoshi（もう少し） a few more, a little more, a little longer

mô-a〈もうあ：盲あ〉

mô-a-gakkô（盲あ学校） a blind and dumb school

mô-benkyô〈もうべんきょう：猛勉強〉

mô-benkyô-suru〈猛勉強する〉study hard.

mochi〈もち：持ち〉wear, durability; charge.

mochi-ga-ii（持ちがいい） wear well, last long, be durable

mochi-ga-warui（持ちが悪い） wear badly, do not last long, be not durable

hiyô-wa-jibun-mochi-de（費用は自分持ちで） at one's own expense

mochi〈もち〉rice cake.

mochi-o-tsuku（もちをつく）　make rice cake

Mochi-wa-mochi-ya.（もちはもち屋。）　Every man to his trade.

mochi-ageru〈もちあげる：持ち上げる〉raise, lift (up); flatter.

mochi-aji〈もちあじ：持ち味〉a peculiar flavor, a characteristic.

mochi-aji-o-ikasu（持ち味を生かす）　make the most of ((its)) characteristics, turn ((its)) peculiar quality to account

mochi-awase〈もちあわせ：持ち合わせ〉things on hand, money on hand, goods in stock.

Ainiku kane-no-mochi-awase-ga-nai.（あいにく金の持ち合わせがない。）　Unfortunately I don't have any money with me.

mochi-awaseru〈持ち合わせる〉have on hand.

mochi-ba〈もちば：持ち場〉one's post.

mochi-ba o mamoru（持ち場を守る）　hold one's post

mochi-bun〈もちぶん：持ち分〉one's share (of the expenses).

mochi-dashi〈もちだし：持ち出し〉

mochi-dashi-o-kinjiru（持ち出しを禁じる）　forbid ((a person)) to take out (books)

mochi-dasu〈持ち出す〉take out, carry out; propose, bring up, broach.

mondai o tôgi-ni-mochi-dasu（問題を討議に持ち出す）　bring a matter up for discussion

mochifu〈モチーフ〉a motif, a motive.

mochi-fuda〈もちふだ：持ち札〉the cards in one's hand.

mochi-goma〈もちごま：持ちごま〉a captured chessman.

mochi-gome〈もちごめ：もち米〉glutinous rice.

mochi-gusare〈もちぐされ：持ち腐れ〉

Takara-no-mochi-gusare-da.（宝の持ち腐れだ。）　It is of no use in my possession.

mochi-hakobi〈もちはこび：持ち運び〉carrying, conveyance.

mochi-hakobi-no-dekiru〈持ち運びのできる〉portable.

mochi-hakobi-ni-benri-na〈持ち運びに便利な〉handy.

mochiiru〈もちいる：用いる〉use, make use ((of)); adopt, take, apply; employ, engage.

mochiirare-naku-naru〈用いられなくなる〉go out of use.

mochi-kabu〈もちかぶ：持ち株〉one's holdings, one's shares.

mochi-kaeru〈もちかえる：持ち替える〉pass ((a thing)) from one hand to the other.

mochi-kakeru〈もちかける：持ち掛ける〉offer, propose, approach.

keikaku-o-mochi-kakeru（計画を持ち掛ける）　approach ((a person))

with a plan

mochi-kata 〈もちかた：持ち方〉
　ki-no-mochi-kata（気の持ち方） a frame of mind

mochi-kiri 〈もちきり：持ち切り〉
　~-no-hanashi-de-mochi-kiri-da.（～の話で持ち切りだ。）be much on the lips of people (in the town).

mochi-komu 〈もちこむ：持ち込む〉carry in.
　shanai-ni sukī o mochi-komu（車内にスキーを持ち込む） carry skis into a car

mochi-kosu 〈もちこす：持ち越す〉carry over, bring over.

mochi-kotaeru 〈もちこたえる：持ちこたえる〉hold on(or out), last, endure, stand, keep up.

mochi-kuzusu 〈もちくずす：持ち崩す〉
　mi-o-mochi-kuzusu〈身を持ち崩す〉ruin oneself, go wrong.

mochi-mae 〈もちまえ：持ち前〉
　mochi-mae-no〈持ち前の〉natural, peculiar, characteristic.
　　mochi-mae-no akarusa（持ち前の明るさ） one's native brightness

mochi-mono 〈もちもの：持ち物〉one's personal effects, one's belongings; one's property.

mochi-naosu 〈もちなおす：持ち直す〉improve, rally.
　　Tenki wa mochi-naoshita.（天気は持ち直した.） The weather has improved.
　　Byônin wa mochi-naoshita.（病人は持ち直した.） The invalid has rallied.

mochi-nige 〈もちにげ：持ち逃げ〉
　mochi-nige-suru〈持ち逃げする〉run away with.

mochi-nushi 〈もちぬし：持ち主〉the owner, the possessor, the proprietor.
　　mochi-nushi-fumei-no shina-mono（持ち主不明の品物） unidentified articles

mochiron 〈もちろん〉of course, to be sure, naturally, needless to say.

mochi-yoru 〈もちよる：持ち寄る〉gather ((somewhere)) each bringing something.

môchô 〈もうちょう：盲腸〉the c(a)ecum, the blind gut.
　　môchô-en（盲腸炎） appendicitis

môda 〈もうだ：猛打〉a heavy blow, slugging.
　　môda-sha（猛打者） a slugger

modae 〈もだえ〉(an) agony, anguish.

modaeru〈もだえる〉be agonized, be anguished.

moderu〈モデル〉a model.

　　jitsuzai-no moderu-o-moto-ni-shite kaku（実在のモデルを基にして書く）write from a living model

　　moderu-shōsetsu（モデル小説）a *roman à clef*

môdo〈モード〉(a) mode, (a) fashion.

modokashi-garu〈もどかしがる〉be irritated, be impatient.

modokashii〈もどかしい〉irritating, impatient.

modokashi-sô-ni〈もどかしそうに〉impatiently.

môdô-ken〈もうどうけん：盲導犬〉a guide dog.

môdoku〈もうどく：猛毒〉(a) deadly poison.

modoru〈もどる：戻る〉go back, return, turn back, go back ((to)).

　　seki-ni modoru（席に戻る）go back to one's seat

modosu〈もどす：戻す〉return, give back, put back; vomit.

　　hon o hondana-ni-modosu（本を本棚に戻す）return a book to the shelf

　　tokei o san-juppun modosu（時計を三十分戻す）put back a watch (by) 30 minutes

moe-agaru〈もえあがる：燃え上がる〉blaze up, burst into flames.

moeru〈もえる：燃える〉blaze, burn, be in flames.

moeru-yô-na〈燃えるような〉blazing, burning, flaming, glaring.

moe-yasui〈燃えやすい〉be easy to burn, catch fire easily.

moe-sashi〈もえさし：燃えさし〉a brand, embers.

moe-utsuru〈もえうつる：燃え移る〉spread ((to)), catch fire.

môfu〈もうふ：毛布〉a blanket, a rug.

mogaku〈もがく〉struggle, writhe, wriggle; be impatient ((for)).

mogeru〈もげる〉come off, be broken off.

mogi〈もぎ：模擬〉

　　mogi-kunren（模擬訓練）a simulated training

　　mogi-shiken（模擬試験）a sham examination

mogi-no〈模擬の〉sham, mock, mimic.

mogi-toru or **mogu**〈もぎとる，もぐ：もぎ取る〉pick(pluck, tear *or* break) off, wrest(*or* wrench) away ((from)).

mogumogu(-to)〈もぐもぐ(と)〉mumblingly.

　　kuchi-o-mogumogu-sase-nagara-iu（口をもぐもぐさせながら言う）mumble.

mogura〈もぐら〉a mole.

moguri〈もぐり：潜り〉

moguri-no〈潜りの〉unlicensed, unregistered, unqualified, bogus.
　moguri-no isha（潜りの医者）an unlicensed doctor
moguri-de〈潜りで〉without a license.

moguri-komu〈もぐりこむ：潜り込む〉get into.
　beddo-ni-moguri-komu（ベッドに潜り込む）get into bed
　kossori-moguri-komu〈こっそり潜り込む〉slip in(*or* into).

moguru〈もぐる：潜る〉dive ((in, into *or* under)); get in.
　chika-ni-moguru（地下に潜る）go underground

mogusa〈もぐさ〉moxa.

mohan〈もはん：模範〉a model, an example, a pattern.
　mohan o shimesu（模範を示す）set an example ((to))
　mohan-to-naru（模範となる）become an example ((of))
　mohan-to-suru（模範とする）follow the example ((of)), model ((after))
mohan-teki(-na)〈模範的(な)〉model, exemplary.
mohan-to-shite〈模範として〉after the example ((of)).

môhitsu〈もうひつ：毛筆〉a writing(*or* painting) brush

mohô〈もほう：模倣〉imitation.
mohô-suru〈模倣する〉imitate.

môi〈もうい：猛威〉
môi-o-furuu〈猛威を振るう〉rage in all its fury.

mojamoja〈もじゃもじゃ〉
mojamoja-no〈もじゃもじゃの〉scraggly, shaggy, disheveled, unkempt.
　mojamoja-no kami-no-ke（もじゃもじゃの髪の毛）disheveled hair

moji〈もじ：文字〉a letter, a character.
　moji-ban（文字盤）a dial plate
moji-doori(-ni)〈文字どおり(に)〉literally, to the letter.

mojimoji〈もじもじ〉
mojimoji-suru〈もじもじする〉fidget, be restless, hesitate.
mojimoji-shi-nagara〈もじもじしながら〉nervously, hesitatingly.

môjû〈もうじゅう：猛獣〉a fierce animal, a beast of prey.

môjû〈もうじゅう：盲従〉blind obedience.
môjû-suru〈盲従する〉obey blindly.

môka〈もうか：猛火〉raging flames, a conflagration.
　môka-ni tsutsumareru（猛火に包まれる）be enveloped in raging flames

môkan〈もうかん：毛管〉a capillary (tube).
　môkan-genshô（毛管現象）a capillary phenomenon

môkaru〈もうかる〉make a profit, gain, earn, be profitable, pay.

　　　môkaru shôbai（もうかる商売）a profitable business
　　môkara-nai〈もうからない〉be unprofitable, do not pay.
môke〈もうけ〉profits, gains, earnings.
　　　môke o seppan-suru（もうけを折半する）divide the gains into halves
　　　môke-guchi（もうけ口）a profitable job
　　　môke-mono（もうけ物）a good bargain, a windfall
　　môke-no-ooi〈もうけの多い〉profitable, gainful.
　　　môke-no-sukunai（もうけの少ない）unprofitable
　　môkeru〈もうける〉make a profit.
　　　raku-ni-môkeru（楽にもうける）make easy money
mokei〈もけい：模型〉a model, a pattern.
　　　shukushaku-mokei（縮尺模型）a scale model
　　　jitsubutsu-dai-mokei（実物大模型）a mock-up
môken〈もうけん：猛犬〉a fierce dog.
　　　Môken-chûi!（猛犬注意.）Beware of the dog!
môkeru〈もうける：設ける〉prepare, arrange; establish, set up; lay down.
　　　jimu-sho o môkeru（事務所を設ける）establish an office
　　　tokubetsu-no kitei o môkeru（特別の規定を設ける）lay down a special rule
môkin〈もうきん：猛きん〉a bird of prey.
mokka〈もっか：目下〉now, at present.
　　　mokka-no-tokoro（目下のところ）for the present, for the moment, for the time being
　　　mokka-no-jôtai-dewa（目下の状態では）as things stand now, in the present circumstances
mokke-no-saiwai〈もっけのさいわい：もっけの幸い〉a stroke of good luck.
mokkin〈もっきん：木琴〉a xylophone.
mokkô〈もっこう：木工〉woodworking.
Môko〈もうこ：もう古〉Mongolia.
　　　Môko-jin（もう古人）a Mongol, a Mongolian
　　　Môko-go（もう古語）Mongolian
　　　Môko(-jin)-no（もう古(人)の）Mongol, Mongolian
mô-kô(geki)〈もうこう（げき）：猛攻（撃）〉
　　mô-kô(geki) o kuwaeru〈猛攻（撃）を加える〉make a violent attack ((on)).
môkon〈もうこん：毛根〉the root of a hair.
mokuba〈もくば：木馬〉a wooden horse, a rocking horse, a horse.

mokugeki 〈もくげき：目撃〉
    mokugeki-sha（目撃者）an eyewitness
  mokugeki-suru〈目撃する〉witness, see with one's own eyes.

mokugyo 〈もくぎょ：木魚〉a wooden gong.

mokuhan 〈もくはん：木版〉wood engraving, wood-block printing.

mokuhen 〈もくへん：木片〉a block, a chip of wood.

mokuhi-ken 〈もくひけん：黙秘権〉
  mokuhi-ken o kôshi-suru〈黙秘権を行使する〉use the right of silence.

mokuhyô 〈もくひょう：目標〉a mark, a sign, a target, a goal, an aim.
    seisan-mokuhyô（生産目標）one's production goal
    mokuhyô-gaku（目標額）a target figure

mokuji 〈もくじ：目次〉a table of contents.

moku-me 〈もくめ：木目〉the grain of wood.
  moku-me-no-komakai〈木目の細かい〉fine-grained.
    moku-me-no-arai（木目の粗い）coarse-grained

mokumoku 〈もくもく：黙々〉
  mokumoku-to(-shite)〈黙々と（して）〉silently, in silence, without saying anything.

mokunin 〈もくにん：黙認〉
  mokunin-suru〈黙認する〉permit tacitly, connive ((at)).

mokurei 〈もくれい：黙礼〉
  mokurei-suru〈黙礼する〉bow in silence.

mokurei 〈もくれい：目礼〉
  mokurei-suru〈目礼する〉nod ((to)), give ((a person)) a nod.

mokuren 〈もくれん：木れん〉a magnolia.

mokuroku 〈もくろく：目録〉a catalog(ue).
    sô-mokuroku（総目録）a general catalog(ue)

mokuro-mi 〈もくろみ〉a plan, a project, an intention, an object, an aim.
    Mokuro-mi ga hazureta.（もくろみが外れた.）My plan has gone wrong.
    nani-ka mokuro-mi-ga-aru（何かもくろみがある）have some object in view
  mokuromu〈もくろむ〉plan, project, intend.

mokusan 〈もくさん：目算〉expectation(s), (a) calculation.
    mokusan-ga-hazureru（目算が外れる）be disappointed in one's expectations, come short of one's expectations

mokusatsu 〈もくさつ：黙殺〉

mokusatsu-suru〈黙殺する〉take no notice ((of)), ignore.

moku-sei〈もくせい：木製〉

moku-seihin（木製品）wooden ware, woodwork

moku-sei-no〈木製の〉wooden, made of wood.

mokusei〈もくせい：木星〉Jupiter.

mokushi〈もくし：黙視〉

mokushi-suru〈黙視する〉remain a mere spactator.

mokusoku〈もくそく：目測〉eye measurement.

mokusoku-o-ayamatte　furai　o　otosu（目測を誤ってフライを落とす）misjudge a fly ball and let it fall

mokutan〈もくたん：木炭〉charcoal.

mokuteki〈もくてき：目的〉a purpose, an aim, an object, an end, a goal.

mokuteki ni kanau（目的にかなう）answer (one's) purpose

mokuteki o tassuru（目的を達する）attain one's purpose

mokuteki-go（目的語）an object

mokuteki-kaku（目的格）an objective case

mokuteki-chi（目的地）one's destination

mokuteki-no-aru〈目的のある〉purposeful.

mokuteki-no-nai（目的のない）purposeless

mokuteki-nashi-ni〈目的なしに〉without aim, for no purpose.

～-no-mokuteki-de〈～の目的で〉with the object of... , with a view to... , for the purpose of... .

mokutô〈もくとう：黙とう〉

mokutô-suru〈黙とうする〉pray silently.

mokuyô-bi〈もくようび：木曜日〉Thursday.

mokuzai〈もくざい：木材〉wood, timber, lumber.

mokuzen〈もくぜん：目前〉

mokuzen-no〈目前の〉before one's eyes, imminent.

mokuzen-ni〈目前に〉before one's eyes, under one's nose.

mokuzen-ni-semaru（目前に迫る）be close at hand

～-no-mokuzen-de〈～の目前で〉in the face of... , in the presence of... .

mokuzô〈もくぞう：木造〉

mokuzô-kaoku（木造家屋）a wooden house, a house built of wood

mokuzô-no〈木造の〉wooden, built of wood.

mômaku〈もうまく：網膜〉the retina.

momareru〈もまれる〉be jostled, be tossed about.

mombatsu〈もんばつ：門閥〉noble lineage, a distinguished family; lineage.

mombu 〈もんぶ：文部〉
　　mombu-shô（文部省）　the Ministry of Education
　　mombu-daijin（文部大臣）　the Minister of Education

mome-goto 〈もめごと：もめ事〉a quarrel, (a) discord, trouble.
　　katei-no mome-goto（家庭のもめ事）　a family discord

momen 〈もめん：木綿〉cotton, cotton cloth.
　　momen-ito（木綿糸）　cotton thread, cotton yarn

momeru 〈もめる〉get into trouble, have a dispute ((with)).
　　ki-ga-momeru（気がもめる）　be worried ((about)), feel uneasy(or anxious) ((about))

momi 〈もみ〉a fir (tree).

momi 〈もみ〉unhulled rice.
　　momi-gara（もみ殻）　chaff

momi-age 〈もみあげ：もみ上げ〉sideburns.
　　momi-age-o-nagaku-shite-iru（もみ上げを長くしている）　wear long sideburns

momi-de 〈もみで：もみ手〉
　　momi-de-o-suru〈もみ手をする〉rub one's hands (together).

momiji 〈もみじ：紅葉〉a maple; autumnal leaves, red leaves.

momi-kesu 〈もみけす：もみ消す〉rub out, smother, hush up, suppress.
　　tabako-no-hi　o　momi-kesu（たばこの火をもみ消す）　crush out a cigarette
　　jiken o momi-kesu（事件をもみ消す）　hush up an affair

momi-ryôji 〈もみりょうじ：もみ療治〉(a) massage.
　　momi-ryôji-o-ukeru〈もみ療治を受ける〉be massaged.

mommô 〈もんもう：文盲〉illiteracy.
　　mommô-ritsu（文盲率）　the illiteracy rate
　　mommô-no〈文盲の〉unlettered, illiterate.

momo 〈もも〉a thigh.

momo 〈もも：桃〉a peach (tree).
　　momo-no-sekku（桃の節句）　the Doll's Festival
　　momo-iro-no〈桃色の〉rosy, pink.

mômô 〈もうもう〉
　　mômô-taru〈もうもうたる〉dense, turbid.
　　mômô-taru-sajin（もうもうたる砂じん）　clouds of dust
　　mômô-taru-kemuri（もうもうたる煙）　volumes of black smoke
　　mômô-to〈もうもうと〉densely, thickly.

yuge-ga-mômô-to-tachi-komete-iru（湯気がもうもうと立ち込めている）be thick with white steam

mômoku〈もうもく：盲目〉blindness.

 mômoku-no or *mômoku-teki(-na)*〈盲目の，盲目的（な）〉blind.

 mômoku-teki-ni〈盲目的に〉blindly, recklessly.

momu〈もむ〉rub; massage.

mon〈もん：門〉a gate.

monchû（門柱）a gatepost

montô（門灯）a gate lamp

dôdô-taru mon-gamae-no uchi（堂々たる門構えのうち）a house with a stately gate

mon〈もん：紋〉a crest, a coat of arms.

mon-tsuki（紋付）a *kimono* bearing one's family crest

monchaku〈もんちゃく：もん着〉trouble, complications, a dispute, a quarrel.

monchaku o okosu（もん着を起こす）cause trouble

mondai〈もんだい：問題〉a question, a problem, a subject, an issue, a matter, trouble.

mondai-de-aru（問題である）be a question, be doubtful

mondai-ni-naru *or* mondai-ka-suru（問題になる，問題化する）become an issue, be at issue

mondai-ni-nara-nai（問題にならない）do not matter

Sore-wa　taishita-mondai-dewa-nai.（それは大した問題ではない。）That is a small matter.

mondai-gai-de-aru（問題外である）be out of the question

mondai-ni-suru（問題にする）call ((a matter)) in question

mondai-ni-shi-nai（問題にしない）take no notice ((of)), do not care, be out of the question

mondai o teiki-suru（問題を提起する）give a question

mondai o kaiketsu-suru（問題を解決する）settle a question

mondai o toku（問題を解く）solve a problem

mondai o okosu（問題を起こす）cause trouble

shakai-mondai（社会問題）a social problem

gaikô-mondai（外交問題）diplomatic issues

dai-mondai（大問題）a serious problem

 mondai-no〈問題の〉in question, at issue.

mondai-no jimbutsu（問題の人物）the person in question

mondai-no ten（問題の点）the point at issue

mondô 〈もんどう：問答〉 questions and answers, a dialogue.
　mondô-suru 〈問答する〉 exchange questions and answers ((with)).
mondori 〈もんどり〉
　mondori-utte 〈もんどり打って〉 head over heels.
mongai-kan 〈もんがいかん：門外漢〉 an outsider, a layman.
mongen 〈もんげん：門限〉 the closing time, lockup.
　　mongen-made-ni kaeru (門限までに帰る) come back by closing time
monju 〈もんじゅ：文殊〉
　　San-nin-yoreba monju-no-chie. (三人寄れば文殊の知恵.) Two heads
　　are better than one.
monka-sei 〈もんかせい：門下生〉 a pupil under one's tuition.
monku 〈もんく：文句〉 words, a phrase; a complaint, (an) objection.
　　kimari-monku (決まり文句) a stock phrase
　monku-o-iu 〈文句を言う〉 complain ((of)), make a complaint ((about)),
　　grumble ((about)), find fault ((with)).
　monku-nashi-no 〈文句なしの〉 perfect.
　　monku-nashi-no sakuhin (文句なしの作品) a perfect work
　monku-nashi-ni 〈文句なしに〉 without any objection, perfectly, satisfac-
　　torily.
mon-nashi 〈もんなし：文無し〉
　mon-nashi-ni-naru 〈文無しになる〉 become penniless.
　mon-nashi-no 〈文無しの〉 penniless.
mono 〈もの：物〉 a thing, something, an object, an article, (a) substance,
　material; reason.
　　Nani-ka-taberu-mono o kudasai. (何か食べる物を下さい.) Give me
　　something to eat.
　　mono-ni-naru (物になる) materialize; make the grade, be successful
　　mono-ni-nara-nai (物にならない) end in failure, come to nothing
　　mono-ni-suru (物にする) master, become proficient ((in)); make
　　something ((of a person))
　　mono-o-iu (物を言う) tell, count ((for)), be helpful
　　　Kane ga mono-o-iu. (金がものをいう.) Money talks.
　　kane-ni-mono-o-iwasete (金にものをいわせて) by the power of
　　money
　　mono-no-wakatta (物の分かった) sensible
　　mono-no-ie-nai (物の言えない) dumb
　　　mono-no-ie-nai hito (物の言えない人) a dumb person
mono 〈もの：者〉 a person, one, a fellow.

mono-gatari 〈ものがたり：物語〉 a story, a tale, a narrative, an account, a fable.
mono-gataru〈物語る〉 tell, narrate, relate, give an account ((of)).

mono-gokoru 〈ものごころ：物心〉
mono-gokoro-ga-tsuite-kara〈物心が付いてから〉 since one can remember.

mono-goto 〈ものごと：物事〉 a matter, things; everything.

mono-hoshi 〈ものほし：物干し〉
  mono-hoshi-zao （物干しざお） a clothes pole
  mono-hoshi-zuna （物干し綱） a clothesline

mono-mane 〈ものまね：物まね〉 mimicry, miming.
  mono-mane-ga-umai （物まねがうまい） be a good mimic
mono-mane-suru〈物まねする〉 mimic, mime.

monomono-shii 〈ものものしい：物々しい〉 showy, pretentious, stately, pompous, imposing.
  monomono-shii gyôretsu （物々しい行列） a stately procession
monomono-shiku〈物々しく〉 pretentiously, pompously, imposingly.

mono-morai 〈ものもらい：物もらい〉 a sty(e).
  me-ni mono-morai-ga-dekiru （目に物もらいが出来る） have a sty in one's eye

mono-no-aware 〈もののあわれ：物の哀れ〉 pathos.
  mono-no-aware o kanjiru （物の哀れを感じる） feel the pathos of nature

mono-oboe 〈ものおぼえ：物覚え〉
mono-oboe-ga-ii〈物覚えがいい〉 have a good memory; be quick at learning.
  mono-oboe-ga-warui （物覚えが悪い） have a poor memory; be slow at learning

mono-oji 〈ものおじ：物おじ〉
mono-oji-suru〈物おじする〉 be skittish.

mono-oki 〈ものおき：物置き〉 a lumber room, a storeroom, a shed, a barn.

mono-omoi 〈ものおもい：物思い〉
mono-omoi-ni-shizumu〈物思いに沈む〉 be lost in deep thought.

mono-oshimi 〈ものおしみ：物惜しみ〉
mono-oshimi-suru〈物惜しみする〉 be stingy, be a miser.
mono-oshimi-sezu-ni〈物惜しみせずに〉 without stint, generously, freely.

mono-oto 〈ものおと：物音〉 a noise, a sound.

mono-sabishii 〈ものさびしい：物寂しい〉 lonely, lonesome, dreary,

desolate.

mono-sashi〈ものさし：物差し〉a rule, a measure.

　　mono-sashi-de hakaru（ものさしで計る）measure with a rule

mono-shiri〈ものしり：物知り〉a well-informed person, a person of extensive knowledge, a learned person.

mono-sugoi〈ものすごい：物すごい〉terrible, horrible.

　　mono-sugoi bakuhatsu（物すごい爆発）a terrific explosion

　　mono-sugoi hito-de（物すごい人出）a tremendous crowd of people

monosugoku〈物すごく〉terribly, horribly, awfully.

mono-tari-nai〈ものたりない：物足りない〉be unsatisfied, be not quite satisfactory.

　　mono-tari-nai-kimochi-ga-suru（物足りない気持ちがする）feel something unsatisfied

mono-wakare〈ものわかれ：物別れ〉

mono-wakare-ni-owaru〈物別れに終わる〉fail to come to an agreement, be broken off.

mono-wakari〈ものわかり：物分かり〉

mono-wakari-no-ii〈物分かりのいい〉understanding, sensible.

mono-warai〈ものわらい：物笑い〉

mono-warai-no-tane-ni-naru〈物笑いの種になる〉become a laughingstock.

mono-wasure〈ものわすれ：物忘れ〉

mono-wasure-suru〈物忘れする〉be forgetful.

mono-zuki〈ものずき：物好き〉curiosity.

mono-zuki-na〈物好きな〉curious, fanciful, whimsical.

mono-zuki-de or *mono-zuki-ni*〈物好きで，物好きに〉from curiosity, for the fun of it.

monsatsu〈もんさつ：門札〉*see.* hyôsatsu.

monshi〈もんし：門歯〉an incisor.

monshô〈もんしょう：紋章〉a crest, family insignia.

montâju〈モンタージュ〉(a) montage.

　　montâju-shashin（モンタージュ写真）a photomontage

mo-nuke-no-kara〈もぬけのから：もぬけの殻〉

　　Beddo wa mo-nuke-no-kara-datta.（ベッドはもぬけの殻だった.）The bed was found empty.

moppara〈もっぱら：専ら〉chiefly, entirely, wholeheartedly, devotedly, persistently.

　　～*-to-iu-uwasa-ga-moppara-da.*〈～といううわさが専らだ.〉It is persistently rumored that... , Everybody talks of... .

môra〈もうら：網羅〉

　môra-suru（網羅する）cover, comprise, include, contain.

　môra-shita or *môra-teki(-na)*（網羅した，網羅的(な)）comprehensive, exhaustive, all-inclusive.

morai-〈もらい-〉

　　morai-go（もらい子）an adopted child

　　　morai-go-o-suru（もらい子をする）adopt a child

　　morai-mono（もらい物）a present, a gift

　　　morai-mono-o-suru（もらい物をする）receive a present ((from))

　　morai-te（もらい手）a receiver; a suitor

　　　Kono　ko-inu-niwa　morai-te-ga-nai.（この子犬にはもらい手がない.）Nobody asks for this puppy.

morasu〈もらす：漏らす〉let leak; express, let fall, reveal, disclose, betray.

　　　shôben-o-morasu（小便を漏らす）wet one's pants

　　　Kono　koto　o　dare-nimo-morasu-na.（この事をだれにも漏らすな.）Keep this matter to yourself.

morau〈もらう〉get, take, have, receive, accept, be given.

　　　tegami o morau（手紙をもらう）receive a letter

　~-shite-morau（～してもらう）get ((a person)) to do, have ((a person)) do.

　~-shite-morai-tai（～してもらいたい）want ((a person)) to do.

more〈もれ：漏れ〉a leak, leakage, a slip; an omission, an oversight.

　　　more o tomeru（漏れを止める）stop a leak

　　　gasu-more（ガス漏れ）a gas leak

　more-naku（漏れなく）without omission, exhaustively.

moreru〈もれる：漏れる〉leak, escape; leak out; be left out.

　　　shôtai-ni-moreru（招待に漏れる）be left out of the invitation

môretsu〈もうれつ：猛烈〉

　môretsu-na（猛烈な）violent, vehement, heavy, fierce, furious, terrible, awful.

　　　môretsu-na supiôdo-de（猛烈なスピードで）at a terrific speed

　môretsu-ni（猛烈に）violently, vehemently, heavily, fiercely, furiously, intensely, terribly, awfully.

　　　môretsu-ni benkyô-suru（猛烈に勉強する）study intently

mori〈もり：森〉a wood, woods, a forest, woodland.

mori〈もり〉a harpoon.

　mori-o-utsu（もりを打つ）harpoon.

mori〈もり：守〉baby-sitting; a nursemaid, a baby-sitter, a keeper.

    akambô-no-mori-o-suru〈赤ん坊の守をする〉take care of a baby

mori-agari〈もりあがり：盛り上がり〉a climax, an upsurge.

  mori-agaru〈盛り上がる〉swell, rise.

  mori-ageru〈盛り上げる〉heap up.

mori-bana〈もりばな：盛り花〉flowers arranged in a basin.

mori-dakusan〈もりだくさん：盛り沢山〉

  mori-dakusan-na〈盛りだくさんな〉many, plenty of, crowded.

  mori-dakusan-ni〈盛りだくさんに〉plentifully.

mori-kaesu〈もりかえす：盛り返す〉rally, make a rally, recover, regain.

morimori〈もりもり〉

    morimori benkyô-suru（もりもり勉強する）study like anything

    morimori-taberu（もりもり食べる）eat like a wolf

mori-tateru〈もりたてる：もり立てる〉support, back (up), bring up.

mori-tsuchi〈もりつち：盛り土〉a fill.

mori-tsuke〈もりつけ：盛り付け〉dishing (up).

  mori-tsuke-o-suru〈盛り付けをする〉dish (up).

môrô〈もうろう〉

  ishiki-ga-môrô-to-naru〈意識がもうろうとなる〉grow faint, have a dim consciousness.

moroi〈もろい〉fragile, brittle, frail; easy.

    namida-moroi（涙もろい）be easily moved to tears

    jô-ni-moroi（情にもろい）be tenderhearted

môroku〈もうろく〉dotage.

  môroku-suru〈もうろくする〉dote.

  môroku-shite-iru〈もうろくしている〉be in one's dotage.

moro-te〈もろて：もろ手〉

  moro-te-o-agete sansei-suru〈もろ手を挙げて賛成する〉support ((something)) wholeheartedly.

moru〈もる：漏る〉leak, escape.

moru〈もる：盛る〉serve, help; pile up; prescribe.

moruhine〈モルヒネ〉morphine, morphia.

    moruhine-chûdoku（モルヒネ中毒）morphine poisoning, morphinism

    moruhine-chûdoku-kanja（モルヒネ中毒患者）a morphinomaniac

morumotto〈モルモット〉a guinea pig.

morutaru〈モルタル〉mortar.

  morutaru-nuri-no〈モルタル塗りの〉mortared.

môsai-kekkan〈もうさいけっかん：毛細血管〉a capillary (vessel).

môsei〈もうせい：猛省〉serious reflection.

　môsei-o-unagasu〈猛省を促す〉urge ((a person)) to reconsider seriously.

môsen〈もうせん：毛せん〉a carpet, a rug.

mosha〈もしゃ：模写〉a copy, a reproduction, a facsimile.

　mosha-suru〈模写する〉copy, reproduce.

moshi〈もし〉if, in case ((of)), provided ((that)).

　　asu　moshi-ame-ga-futtara（明日もし雨が降ったら）if it rains to-morrow

　moshi~-ga-nakatta-ra〈もし～がなかったら〉if it were not for... .

môshi-awase〈もうしあわせ：申し合わせ〉an agreement, arrangement(s).

　　môshi-awase-jikô（申し合わせ事項）items of agreement

　môshi-awase-ni-yori〈申し合わせにより〉by mutual consent.

môshi-awaseru〈もうしあわせる：申し合わせる〉arrange, (mutually) agree ((upon)), appoint.

　　môshi-awaseta-yô-ni（申し合わせたように）as if prearranged

　　môshi-awaseta-jikoku-ni（申し合わせた時刻に）at the appointed time

môshi-bun〈もうしぶん：申し分〉

　môshi-bun-no-nai〈申し分のない〉perfect, most satisfactory, ideal.

　　Kyô-wa　môshi-bun-no-nai　tenki-desu.（今日は申し分のない天気です。）It is a perfect day today.

môshi-deru〈もうしでる：申し出る〉propose, suggest, offer, apply ((at, for *or* to)), request, claim, report.

　　jimu-sho-made-môshi-deru（事務所まで申し出る）apply to the office

môshi-kaneru〈もうしかねる：申しかねる〉

　Môshi-kanemasu-ga,~〈申しかねますが、～〉Excuse me, but... .

moshika-shitara *or* **moshika-suruto**〈もしかしたら，もしかすると〉possibly, by any chance.

môshi-komi〈もうしこみ：申し込み〉a proposal, an offer, request; application.

　　môshi-komi o kotowaru（申し込みを断る）decline a proposal

　　môshi-komi-kigen（申し込み期限）a time limit for application

　　môshi-komi-kin（申し込み金）application money

　　môshi-komi-nin（申し込み人）an applicant, a subscriber

　　môshi-komi-sho *or* môshi-komi-yôshi（申し込み書，申し込み用紙）an application blank, an application form

　môshi-komi-jun-ni〈申し込み順に〉in order of application.

　môshi-komi-shidai〈申し込み次第〉upon request, on application.

môshi-komu〈もうしこむ：申し込む〉propose, offer, apply ((for)), make an application ((for)); book, reserve.

moshimoshi〈もしもし〉Hello!

môshin〈もうしん：盲信〉

　môshin-suru〈盲信する〉believe blindly.

môshi-okuri〈もうしおくり：申し送り〉transfer.

　môshi-okuru〈申し送る〉transfer, hand over.

môshi-tate〈もうしたて：申し立て〉a statement, (a) declaration, testimony.

　môshi-tateru〈申し立てる〉state, declare, put forward, testify.

　　igi o môshi-tateru（異議を申し立てる）raise an objection ((to))

môshi-wake〈もうしわけ：申し訳〉an apology, an excuse.

　　Makoto-ni môshi-wake-arima-sen.（誠に申し訳ありません。）I don't know what excuse to make.

　hon-no môshi-wake-ni〈ほんの申し訳に〉for mere form's sake.

môsô〈もうそう：妄想〉a wild fancy, a fantasy, a delusion.

　　môsô-ni-fukeru（妄想にふける）be lost in wild fancies

môtâ〈モーター〉a motor, an engine.

　　môtâ o kakeru（モーターをかける）start a motor

　　môtâ o tomeru（モーターを止める）shut off a motor

motageru〈もたげる〉lift, raise.

　　atama-o-motageru（頭をもたげる）raise one's head; gain strength and come to the fore gradually

motamota〈もたもた〉

　motamota-suru〈もたもたする〉be slow, be tardy.

motarasu〈もたらす〉bring (about, forth *or* on), cause, produce, result ((in)).

motareru〈もたれる〉lean ((against)); lie heavy ((on the stomach)).

motase-kakeru〈もたせかける：もたせ掛ける〉set ((something)) against ((another)).

mote-amasu〈もてあます：持て余す〉do not know what to do ((with)), be too much ((for)).

　　Ryôshin mo kare-o-mote-amashite-iru.（両親も彼を持て余している。）Even his parents do not know what to do with him.

　　Jikan-o-mote-amashita.（時間を持て余した。）Time lay heavily on my hands.

mote-asobu〈もてあそぶ〉play ((with)), sport ((with)), fool ((with)).

　　josei-o-mote-asobu（女性をもてあそぶ）sport with a woman

mote-hayasu〈もてはやす：持てはやす〉talk much ((about)), make much

((of)).

môten 〈もうてん：盲点〉a blind spot, a scotoma.

   hô no môten〈法の盲点〉 a blind spot of law

mote-nashi 〈もてなし：持て成し〉treatment, reception, service, welcome, entertainment, hospitality.

   kokoro-kara-no mote-nashi〈心からのもてなし〉 hearty hospitality

mote-nashi-no-ii〈もてなしのいい〉hospitable.

   mote-nashi-no-warui（もてなしの悪い） inhospitable

motenasu 〈もてなす：持て成す〉treat, receive, entertain.

   te-atsuku motenasu（手厚くもてなす） treat ((a person)) hospitably

moteru 〈もてる：持てる〉be made much ((of)), be talked much, be lionized, be popular ((with)).

   wakai josei-ni-moteru〈若い女性にもてる〉 be popular with young ladies

moto 〈もと：元（基, 本）〉the beginning, the origin; the foundation, the basis, the source; material; the capital, the cost; formerly, once, before.

   moto-ga-toreru〈元が取れる〉 be able to recover the cost

   zuibun-moto-ga-kakaru〈随分元が掛かる〉 require a large sum of capital

   hi no moto〈火の元〉 the origin of fire

moto-no〈元の〉original, former.

moto-kara〈元から〉from the beginning.

moto-doori〈元どおり〉as before.

moto-wa〈元は〉originally, formerly.

〜-o-moto-ni-shite 〈〜を基にして〉on the basis of... .

moto 〈もと：下〉under.

〜-no-shidô-no-moto-ni 〈〜の指導の下に〉under the direction of... .

moto 〈もと〉

ryôshin-no-moto-de kurasu〈両親のもとで暮らす〉live with one's parents.

môtô 〈もうとう：毛頭〉

môtô〜nai〈毛頭〜ない〉not in the least, not at all, not a bit.

   Môtô-utagai-ari-masen.（毛頭疑いありません。） There is not the slightest doubt about it.

moto-chô 〈もとちょう：元帳〉a ledger.

moto-de 〈もとで：元手〉capital, fund.

motome 〈もとめ：求め〉a request, an appeal, a demand.

   motome-ni-ôjite〈求めに応じて〉 in compliance with ((a person's))

request

motomeru 〈もとめる：求める〉want, wish ((for)); ask, request, demand, claim, call ((for)); search ((for)), seek (after or for).

    setsumei-o-motomeru（説明を求める）call for an explanation

    chii-o-motomeru（地位を求める）seek after a (good) position

motomoto 〈もともと：元々(本々)〉from the first, originally; by nature.

moto-ne 〈もとね：元値〉the cost (price).

    moto-ne-de-uru（元値で売る）sell at cost

    moto-ne-ga-kireru（元値が切れる）lose on the cost price

moto-no-moku-ami 〈もとのもくあみ：元のもくあみ〉

    Moto-no-moku-ami-da.（元のもくあみだ.）I am no better than before.

motozuku 〈もとづく：基づく〉be based ((on or upon)), be grounded ((in, on or upon)), be founded ((on)); come ((from)), originate ((in)), be due ((to)), be attributed ((to)).

    〜-no-kitei-ni-motozuite（〜の規定に基づいて）under the provisions of...

    shiryô-ni-motozuite（資料に基づいて）on the basis of the data

    〜-ni-motozuite kôdô-suru〈〜に基づいて行動する〉act on... .

motsu 〈もつ〉liver, giblets.

motsu 〈もつ：持つ〉have, own, possess, hold, carry; last (long), wear (well), endure, hold (up), keep, live; pay, bear; bear, harbor, cherish; take charge ((of)), be in charge ((of)).

    sutekki-o-motte-aruku（ステッキを持って歩く）carry a cane

    ni-san-nichi motsu（二，三日持つ）keep well for two or three days, hold up for a few days

    hiyô o motsu（費用を持つ）pay the expenses

    kibô o motsu（希望を持つ）cherish a desire

motsure 〈もつれ〉a tangle, (an) entanglement, a snarl, trouble(s), a complication.

    kanjô-no motsure（感情のもつれ）emotional entanglement

    shita-no-motsure（舌のもつれ）a twist in one's tongue

    motsure-o-toku〈もつれを解く〉disentangle.

motsureru 〈もつれる〉get entangled, be snarled, become complicated.

mottai-buru 〈もったいぶる〉assume an air of importance.

mottai-butta〈もったいぶった〉pompous, sententious.

mottai-butte〈もったいぶって〉with an air (of importance), pompously.

mottai-nai 〈もったいない〉wasteful; be too good ((for)), be more than one deserves.

　Jikan-ga-mottai-nai!（時間がもったいない．）　What a waste of time!

　fudan-gi-niwa-mottai-nai（普段着にはもったいない）　be too good for casual wear

motte-koi〈もってこい：持って来い〉

motte-koi-no〈もってこいの〉ideal, capital, the very, just, right.

　Gaishutsu-niwa-motte-koi-no-hi-da.（外出にはもってこいの日だ．）　It's a perfect day for out-going.

　Sono shigoto wa boku-no otôto-niwa motte-koi-da.（その仕事は僕の弟にはもってこいだ．）　The job is just the thing for my brother.

motte-no-hoka〈もってのほか：もっての外〉

motte-no-hoka-da〈もっての外だ〉be outrageous, be absurd, be unreasonable, be unpardonable, be out of the question.

motto〈もっと〉more, some more, longer, farther.

　motto-takusan（もっとたくさん）　much more, many more

mottô〈モットー〉a motto.

mottomo〈もっとも：最も〉(the) most, exceedingly.

　shi-nakereba-naranai mottomo taisetsu-na koto（しなければならない最も大切な事）　the most important thing to do

　mottomo-nagai kawa（最も長い川）　the longest river

mottomo〈もっとも〉

mottomo-da〈もっともだ〉It is right(reasonable *or* natural) ((to)).

　Kare-ga　okoru-nowa-mottomo-da.（彼が怒るのはもっともだ．）　It is reasonable he should get angry.

　Kimi-no-iu-koto　wa　mottomo-da.（君の言うことはもっともだ．）　You are quite right.

mottomo-na〈もっともな〉right, reasonable, natural.

　mottomo-na-koto-o-iu（もっともなことを言う）　speak sense

mottomo-rashii〈もっともらしい〉plausible, specious.

mottomo-rashii kao-o-shite〈もっともらしい顔をして〉with a serious look.

moya〈もや〉haze, mist.

moyamoya〈もやもや〉

kibun-ga-moyamoya-suru〈気分がもやもやする〉feel gloomy.

moyashi〈もやし〉malt, bean sprouts.

moyasu〈もやす：燃やす〉burn, light, kindle.

moyô〈もよう：模様〉a pattern, a design; a look, an appearance, the state of affairs, circumstances.

　sora-moyô（空模様）　the look of the sky

moyô-o-tsukeru〈模様を付ける〉pattern.

moyô-iri-no〈模様入りの〉patterned.

moyô-gae〈もようがえ：模様替え〉

moyô-gae-suru〈模様替えする〉alter, remodel, do over〔a room〕.

moyooshi〈もよおし：催し〉a meeting, a gathering, a function, an entertainment.

　　moyooshi o suru〈催しをする〉 hold a meeting

　　moyooshi-mono〈催し物〉 entertainments, amusements

moyoosu〈もよおす：催す〉hold, give; feel.

moyori〈もより：最寄り〉

moyori-no〈最寄りの〉the nearest, nearby.

mozaiku〈モザイク〉a mosaic.

môzen〈もうぜん：猛然〉

môzen-to〈猛然と〉fiercely, furiously.

mozô〈もぞう：模造〉imitation.

　　mozô-hin〈模造品〉 an imitation, a counterfeit, a fake

mozô-suru〈模造する〉imitate, copy.

mozu〈もず：鵙〉a shrike.

mu〈む：無〉nothing.

　　mu-ni-naru〈無になる〉 come to nothing

　　mu-ni-suru〈無にする〉 bring to naught

　　　kôi o mu-ni-suru〈好意を無にする〉 bring ((a person's)) favor to naught

mubô〈むぼう：無謀〉

mubô-na〈無謀な〉reckless, rash, wild, thoughtless, imprudent.

　　mubô-na koto o suru〈無謀なことをする〉 do reckless things

mubô-ni-mo〈無謀にも〉recklessly, rashly, thoughtlessly.

mu-bôbi〈むぼうび：無防備〉

　　mu-bôbi-toshi〈無防備都市〉 an open city

mu-bôbi-no〈無防備の〉defenseless, unfortified.

mucha〈むちゃ：無茶〉

mucha-o-iu〈無茶を言う〉talk nonsense.

mucha-na〈無茶な〉absurd, unreasonable.

　　mucha-na yôkyû〈無茶な要求〉 an unreasonable and unacceptable demand

muchakucha〈むちゃくちゃ：無茶苦茶〉

muchakucha-na〈無茶苦茶な〉confused, reckless, mad, absurd, unreasonable.

muchakucha-ni 〈無茶苦茶に〉confusedly, recklessly, like mad.
    muchakucha-ni-naru（無茶苦茶になる）get confused utterly
    muchakucha-ni-suru（無茶苦茶にする）make a mess ((of))

muchi 〈むち〉a whip, a lash, a cane.
    muchi-uchi-shô（むちうち症）whiplash
muchi-de-utsu or *muchi-utsu*〈むちで打つ，むち打つ〉whip, lash, use a
    rod.

muchi 〈むち：無知〉ignorance.
muchi-na 〈無知な〉ignorant.

muchin 〈むちん：無賃〉
muchin-jôsha-suru〈無賃乗車する〉steal a ride (on a train).

mu-chitsujo 〈むちつじょ：無秩序〉disorder, chaos.
mu-chitsujo-na〈無秩序な〉disordered, chaotic, lawless

muchû 〈むちゅう：夢中〉
muchû-ni-naru〈夢中になる〉be beside oneself ((with)), forget oneself,
    lose oneself ((in)), be absorbed ((in)), devote oneself ((to)), be crazy
    ((about)), be lost ((in *or* with)).
    hanashi-ni-muchû-ni-naru（話に夢中になる）be deep in conversation
muchû-de〈夢中で〉like one in a dream, for all one is worth.

muda 〈むだ：無駄〉uselessness, futility; waste, wastefulness.
    muda o habuku（無駄を省く）avoid waste
    muda-zukai-suru（無駄使いする）waste (one's money)
    muda-guchi-o-tataku（無駄口をたたく）talk idly
muda-de-aru〈無駄である〉be useless, be of no use, be of no avail.
    Sonna kôka-na mono o kare-ni yattemo muda-da.（そんな高価な物を
    彼にやっても無駄だ.）It's of no use giving him such a precious
    thing.
muda-na〈無駄な〉useless, fruitless, futile, wasteful.
muda-ni〈無駄に〉uselessly, fruitlessly, futilely, wastefully.
    muda-ni-naru（無駄になる）come to nothing, be in vain, be wasted,
    go to waste
    muda-ni-suru（無駄にする）waste, spoil, throw away

mudan 〈むだん：無断〉
    mudan-kekkin（無断欠勤）absence without leave
mudan-de〈無断で〉without leave, without permission, without notice.

muden 〈むでん：無電〉radio, wireless.
    muden o utsu（無電を打つ）send a radio ((to)), send a message by
    wireless

muden-shitsu〈無電室〉 a wireless room

muden-de〈無電で〉by radio, by wireless.

mûdo〈ムード〉a mood.

rakkan-teki-mûdo（楽観的ムード） optimism

hikan-teki-mûdo（悲観的ムード） pessimism

muen〈むえん：無縁〉

muen-botoke（無縁仏） a person who died leaving no relatives behind to attend his grave

muen-no〈無縁の〉unrelated, indifferent, without relations.

mufû〈むふう：無風〉

mufû-jôtai（無風状態） a calm, a settled state

mufû-no〈無風の〉calm, windless.

mu-fumbetsu〈むふんべつ：無分別〉

mu-fumbetsu-na〈無分別な〉indiscreet, imprudent, thoughtless, inconsiderate.

mugai〈むがい：無害〉

mugai-de-aru〈無害である〉do ((a person)) no harm.

mugai-no〈無害の〉harmless.

mugai〈むがい：無がい〉

mugai-kasha（無がい貨車） an open freight car, a truck

mugai-no〈無がいの〉open.

mugaku〈むがく：無学〉illiterateness, ignorance.

mugaku-no〈無学の〉illiterate, ignorant, uneducated.

muge〈むげ：無下〉

muge-ni kotowaru〈無下に断る〉refuse flatly, give ((a person)) a flat refusal.

mugen〈むげん：無限〉infinitude.

mugen-no〈無限の〉limitless, boundless, endless, infinite, immeasurable, inexhaustible, eternal.

mugen-ni〈無限に〉without limitation, boundlessly, endlessly, infinitely, inexhaustibly, eternally.

mugen-dai〈むげんだい：無限大〉infinity, an infinite quality.

mugen-dai-no〈無限大の〉infinite.

mugi〈むぎ：麦〉wheat, barley, oat.

mugi-cha（麦茶） barley tea

mugi-wara（麦わら） (a) straw

mugi-wara-bô（麦わら帽） a straw hat

mugoi〈むごい〉cruel, atrocious, pitiless, inhuman.

mugon〈むごん：無言〉silence, muteness.
　mugon-no〈無言の〉silent, mute.
　mugon-de〈無言で〉silently, mutely.
mugotarashii〈むごたらしい〉cruel, atrocious, tragic.
mu-hai(tô)〈むはい(とう)：無配(当)〉
　　　mu-hai-gaisha（無配会社）a non-dividend-paying company
mu-handô-hô〈むはんどうほう：無反動砲〉a recoilless cannon.
mu-hihan〈むひはん：無批判〉
　mu-hihan-na〈無批判な〉uncritical.
muhô〈むほう：無法〉
　　　muhô-mono（無法者）an outlaw
　muhô-na〈無法な〉unlawful, outrageous, unreasonable, lawless.
muhon〈むほん：謀反〉a revolt, an insurrection, rebellion, treason.
　muhon-o-okosu〈謀反を起こす〉revolt(rebel, rise *or* plot) ((against)).
mu-hôshû〈むほうしゅう：無報酬〉
　mu-hôshû-de〈無報酬で〉without pay, free of charge, without a fee, for
　　nothing.
muhyô〈むひょう：霧氷〉rime, hoarfrost.
mu-hyôjô〈むひょうじょう：無表情〉
　mu-hyôjô-na〈無表情な〉expressionless, impassive, blank, wooden.
　　　mu-hyôjô-na kao（無表情な顔）a wooden face
mu-imi〈むいみ：無意味〉
　mu-imi-na〈無意味な〉meaningless, senseless, absurd.
mu-ishiki〈むいしき：無意識〉
　mu-ishiki-ni〈無意識に〉unconsciously, involuntarily, automatically,
　　mechanically.
mu-jaki〈むじゃき：無邪気〉
　mu-jaki-na〈無邪気な〉innocent, naïve, simple.
muji〈むじ：無地〉
　muji-no〈無地の〉plain, unfigured, solid.
mu-jihi〈むじひ：無慈悲〉
　mu-jihi-na〈無慈悲な〉merciless, heartless, pitiless, cruel.
mu-jiko〈むじこ：無事故〉
　mu-jiko-de〈無事故で〉without an accident.
mujin〈むじん：無人〉
　mujin-no-kyô-o-iku-yô-ni-susumu〈無人の境を行くように進む〉carry
　　everything before ((one)).
mujina〈むじな〉

Kare-ra-wa　hitotsu-ana-no-mujina-da. (彼らは一つ穴のむじなだ.)
　　They are all of a gang.

mujin-zō 〈むじんぞう：無尽蔵〉
　mujin-zō-no (無尽蔵の) inexhaustible, limitless, unlimited.

mujitsu 〈むじつ：無実〉
　　mujitsu-no-tsumi (無実の罪) a false charge, an unreasonable accusation
　　mujitsu-o-shuchō-suru (無実を主張する) insist upon one's innocence

mujō 〈むじょう：無上〉
　mujō-no (無上の) supreme, the highest, the best.
　　mujō-no kōei (無上の光栄) the highest honor

mujō 〈むじょう：無常〉 mutability, uncertainty.
　　Jinsei-wa-mujō-de-aru. (人生は無常である.) Nothing is certain in this world.

mujō 〈むじょう：無情〉
　mujō-na (無情な) heartless, coldhearted, stonyhearted, cruel, merciless.

mu-jōken 〈むじょうけん：無条件〉
　　mu-jōken-kōfuku (無条件降伏) an unconditional surrender
　mu-jōken-de (無条件で) unconditionally, without any condition.

mujun 〈むじゅん：矛盾〉 (a) contradiction, (an) inconsistency, a conflict.
　　mujun-darake-de-aru (矛盾だらけである) be full of inconsistencies
　mujun-suru 〈矛盾する〉 be contradictory ((to)), be inconsistent ((with)), conflict ((with)).
　mujun-shita-koto-o-iu 〈矛盾したことを言う〉 contradict oneself.

mu-jūryoku 〈むじゅうりょく：無重力〉 weightlessness.
　　mu-jūryoku-jōtai (無重力状態) a state of nongravitation

mukade 〈むかで〉 a centipede.

mukae 〈むかえ：迎え〉
　　mukae-ni-iku (迎えに行く) go to meet ((a person))
　　isha-o-mukae-ni-yaru (医者を迎えにやる) send for a doctor
　mukaeru 〈迎える〉 meet, go (out) to meet, welcome, greet.
　　atatakaku mukaeru (温かく迎える) welcome ((a person)) warmly
　　shinnen o mukaeru (新年を迎える) greet the New Year

mukai(-no) 〈むかい(の)：向かい(の)〉 opposite.
　　mukai-no ie (向かいの家) the house opposite
　　mukai-gawa (向かい側) the opposite side
　　mukai-kaze (向かい風) a head wind
　〜-no-mukai-ni 〈〜の向かいに〉 opposite... .

　　　ginkô-no-mukai-ni〈銀行の向かいに〉 opposite the bank

mukai-au〈むかいあう：向かい合う〉face each other, be opposite ((to)).

　　　kare-to mukai-atte-suwaru〈彼と向かい合って座る〉sit face to face with him

mukamuka〈むかむか〉

　mukamuka-suru〈むかむかする〉feel sick, feel nausea; get angry, be offended ((at or by)).

mu-kankaku〈むかんかく：無感覚〉

　mu-kankaku-ni-naru〈無感覚になる〉be insensible ((to)), be benumbed.

　mu-kankaku-na〈無感覚な〉insensible, numb.

mu-kankei〈むかんけい：無関係〉

　mu-kankei-de-aru〈無関係である〉have no relation ((to or with)), have no connection ((with)), have no bearing ((on)), have nothing to do ((with)).

　mu-kankei-no〈無関係の〉unrelated, unconcerned.

mu-kanshin〈むかんしん：無関心〉indifference, unconcern.

　mu-kanshin-de-aru〈無関心である〉be indifferent ((to)), be unconcerned ((about or with)), have no interest ((in)).

mukappara〈むかっぱら：向かっ腹〉

　mukappara-o-tateru〈向かっ腹を立てる〉burst into a fit of anger.

mukashi〈むかし：昔〉ancient times, old days.

　　　mukashi-banashi（昔話）an old tale

　　　mukashi-katagi（昔かたぎ）the old-time spirit

　　　mukashi-najimi（昔なじみ）an old acquaintance

　　　mukashi-no（昔の）ancient, old, former

　　　mukashi-wa（昔は）in ancient times, in the old days

　　　mukashi-mukashi（昔々）once upon a time; long, long ago

　　　mukashi-kara（昔から）from old times

　　　　mukashi-kara-no（昔からの）long-established, long-time

　　　mukashi-fû-no（昔風の）old-fashioned

　　　mukashi-nagara-no（昔ながらの）as it was before

mukau〈むかう：向かう〉face, front; resist, confront, oppose, turn ((on)); go ((to or toward)), make ((for)), head ((toward)), leave ((for)); tend ((toward)).

　　　tsukue-ni-mukau（机に向かう）sit at one's desk

　　　kaze-ni-mukatte hashiru（風に向かって走る）run against the wind

　　　minami-ni-mukatte susumu（南に向かって進む）head south

　　　kaihô-ni-mukau（快方に向かう）take a favorable turn

~**-ni-mukatte** 〈〜に向かって〉 opposite, at, against, in the face of; for, to, toward.

Kare-wa asu Pari-ni-mukatte Narita o tatsu.（彼は明日パリに向かって成田を立つ.） He leaves Narita for Paris tomorrow.

mukei 〈むけい：無形〉

mukei-bunka-zai（無形文化財） intangible cultural properties

mukei-no〈無形の〉 formless, abstract, immaterial, spiritual, invisible, intangible.

mu-keikaku 〈むけいかく：無計画〉

mu-keikaku-na〈無計画な〉 planless, unplanned, reckless.

mu-keiken 〈むけいけん：無経験〉 *see*. mi-keiken.

mu-keisatsu 〈むけいさつ：無警察〉

mu-keisatsu-jôtai-de-aru〈無警察状態である〉 be in a lawless condition.

mukeru 〈むける：向ける〉 turn, direct, point ((at)).

chûi o mukeru（注意を向ける） turn one's attention ((to))

jû o kare-ni-mukeru（銃を彼に向ける） point a gun at him

mukeru 〈むける〉 peel off, come off.

mu-kesseki 〈むけっせき：無欠席〉 regular attendance.

muketsu-kakumei 〈むけつかくめい：無血革命〉 a bloodless revolution.

muki 〈むき：向き〉 a direction; an exposure, situation; suitability.

kaze no muki（風の向き） the direction of the wind

bannin-muki-de-aru（万人向きである） suit all tastes

~**-muki-no**〈〜向きの〉 for... , suited for... .

yushutsu-muki-no（輸出向きの） for exportation

natsu-muki-no doresu（夏向きのドレス） a dress for summer wear

minami-muki-no heya（南向きの部屋） a room facing south

muki 〈むき：無期〉

muki-chôeki（無期懲役） penal servitude for life

muki-enki（無期延期） indefinite postponement

muki-no〈無期の〉 indefinite, unlimited.

muki 〈むき〉

muki-ni-naru〈むきになる〉 become serious.

muki-ni-natte〈むきになって〉 in earnest, with a vengeance.

muki-ni-natte-okoru（むきになって怒る） fly into a passion

muki 〈むき：無機〉

muki-butsu（無機物） an inorganic substance

muki-kagaku（無機化学） inorganic chemistry

muki-no〈無機の〉 inorganic.

muki-dashi〈むきだし：むき出し〉

muki-dashi-no〈むき出しの〉frank, plain, open, unreserved; bare, naked.

muki-dashi-ni〈むき出しに〉frankly, plainly, openly, unreservedly.

    muki-dashi-ni mono-o-iu（むき出しに物を言う）speak plainly

muki-dashi-ni-suru〈むき出しにする〉bare, make bare, expose.

muki-dasu〈むきだす：むき出す〉bare, show.

    ha o muki-dasu（歯をむき出す）show one's teeth

    ha-o-muki-dashite-warau（歯をむき出して笑う）grin

mu-kidô〈むきどう：無軌道〉

    mu-kidô-buri-o-hakki-suru（無軌道ぶりを発揮する）run all lengths of licentiousness

mu-kidô-na〈無軌道な〉aberrant, licentious.

mu-kigen〈むきげん：無期限〉

    mu-kigen-suto（無期限スト）a strike for an indefinite period

mu-kigen-no〈無期限の〉indefinite.

mu-kigen-ni〈無期限に〉indefinitely, for an indefinite period.

mu-kimei〈むきめい：無記名〉

    mu-kimei-tôhyô（無記名投票）an unsigned vote

    mu-kimei-yokin（無記名預金）an uninscribed deposit

mu-kimei-no〈無記名の〉unsigned, unregistered, uninscribed.

mu-kimei-shiki-no〈無記名式の〉blank, general.

muki-mi〈むきみ：むき身〉shucked shellfish.

mukin〈むきん：無菌〉

mukin-no〈無菌の〉without germs, sterilized, pasteurized, aseptic.

muki-naoru〈むきなおる：向き直る〉turn round ((toward)).

mu-kiryoku〈むきりょく：無気力〉

mu-kiryoku-na〈無気力な〉spiritless, nerveless, languid.

mukizu〈むきず：無傷〉

mukizu-no〈無傷の〉unhurt, uninjured; faultless, free from blemish, flawless, perfect.

muko〈むこ：婿〉a son-in-law, a bridegroom.

mukô〈むこう：向こう〉the other side; the opposite direction; beyond; to come, next.

    kawa no mukô-ni（川の向こうに）on the other side of the river

    mukô-kara（向こうから）from the opposite direction

    haruka-mukô-ni（はるか向こうに）in the distance, far away

    yama-no-mukô-ni（山の向こうに）beyond the hill

    mukô-mikka-kan（向こう三日間）for three days ahead, for the next

　　　three days
mukô-no〈向こうの〉over there, over, beyond.

mukô〈むこう：無効〉invalidity, unavailability, ineffectiveness.
mukô-no〈無効の〉invalid, unavailable, ineffective, futile.
mukô-ni-naru〈無効になる〉become ineffective, become unavailable, lose effect.
mukô-ni-suru〈無効にする〉invalidate, make void.

mukô-mizu〈むこうみず：向こう見ず〉
mukô-mizu-na〈向こう見ずな〉rash, reckless.
mukô-mizu-ni〈向こう見ずに〉rashly, recklessly.

mukôzune〈むこうずね：向こうずね〉a shin.

muku〈むく：向く〉turn ((toward)), point ((to)), tend ((toward)), face, be suited ((for)).
　　　ushiro-o-muku〈後ろを向く〉look back, turn around
　　　kyôshi-ni-muite-iru〈教師に向いている〉be suited for a teacher

muku〈むく〉peel, pare, bark.

mukuchi〈むくち：無口〉reticence.
mukuchi-na〈無口な〉reticent, silent.
　　　mukuchi-na hito〈無口な人〉a person of few words

mukui〈むくい：報い〉(a) compensation, (a) reward, a return; (a) punishment.
~-no-mukui-to-shite or *~-no-mukui-de*〈～の報いとして、～の報いで〉in consequence of... , in return for... .

mukuiru〈むくいる：報いる〉recompense, compensate ((for)), reward, give ((something)) in return ((for)); return, requite, repay.
　　　jûbun-ni mukuirareru〈十分に報いられる〉be amply rewarded
　　　mukuirarezu-ni-owaru〈報いられずに終る〉go unrewarded
　　　zen-ni-taishite aku-de-mukuiru〈善に対して悪で報いる〉return evil for good

mukumi〈むくみ〉dropsy, dropsical swelling.
mukumu〈むくむ〉swell.
　　　Ashi ga mukunde-iru.〈足がむくんでいる.〉My legs are swollen.

mukureru〈むくれる〉become sullen.

mu-kyôiku〈むきょういく：無教育〉
mu-kyôiku-na〈無教育な〉uneducated.

mu-kyôsô〈むきょうそう：無競争〉
mu-kyôsô-de〈無競争で〉without a rival.
　　　mu-kyôsô-de-tôsen-suru〈無競争で当選する〉be elected unopposed

mukyû 〈むきゅう：無休〉

　mukyû-de-aru 〈無休である〉 have no holiday.

　　nenjû-mukyû-de-aru（年中無休である） be open throughout the year

mukyû 〈むきゅう：無給〉

　mukyû-de 〈無給で〉 without pay.

mumei 〈むめい：無名〉

　mumei-no 〈無名の〉 anonymous, unnamed, obscure, unknown.

　　mumei-no sakka（無名の作家） an unknown author

mu-menkyo 〈むめんきょ：無免許〉

　mu-menkyo-no 〈無免許の〉 unlicensed.

　mu-menkyo-de 〈無免許で〉 without a license.

mumi-kansô 〈むみかんそう：無味乾燥〉

　mumi-kansô-na 〈無味乾燥な〉 dry, insipid, uninteresting, dull.

muna-ge 〈むなげ：胸毛〉 chest hair.

muna-gi 〈むなぎ：棟木〉 a ridgepole.

munagura 〈むなぐら：胸倉〉

　munagura-o-toru 〈胸倉をとる〉 seize ((a person)) by the coat lapels.

muna-gurushii 〈むなぐるしい：胸苦しい〉 feel oppressed in one's breast.

muna-moto 〈むなもと：胸元〉 the pit of the stomach, the breast.

muna-sawagi 〈むなさわぎ：胸騒ぎ〉 a presentiment.

　muna-sawagi-ga-suru 〈胸騒ぎがする〉 feel uneasy, have a presentiment.

munashii 〈むなしい〉 empty, vain, fruitless, ineffective, unavailing.

　　Kare-no doryoku mo munashikatta.（彼の努力もむなしかった.） His
　　efforts were in vain.

　munashiku 〈むなしく〉 in vain, idly.

　　munashiku toki o sugosu（むなしく時を過ごす） pass one's time idly

muna-zan·yô 〈むなざんよう：胸算用〉 mental arithmetic.

　muna-zan·yô-o-suru 〈胸算用をする〉 calculate mentally.

mune 〈むね：胸〉 the breast, the chest, the bosom, the lungs, heart,
　one's heart.

　　mune o haru（胸を張る） throw out one's chest

　　yutaka-na-mune-o-shita（豊かな胸をした） full-breasted

　　mune-mo-arawa-na（胸もあらわな） bare-bosomed

　　mune-ga-waruku-naru（胸が悪くなる） feel sick at the stomach, feel
　　nausea

　　Mune-ga-dokidoki-suru.（胸がどきどきする.） My heart throbs.

　　mune-no yamai（胸の病） lung trouble

　　mune-ga-ippai-ni-naru（胸がいっぱいになる） fill one's heart (with

gratitude)

O-mae-no-koto-o-kangaeru-to　mune-ga-itamu.（お前のことを考えると胸が痛む.）I feel sorry for you.

mune-mo-hari-sakeru-bakari-ni　naku（胸も張り裂けるばかりに泣く）sob one's heart out

Kanashimi-ni mune-ga-hari-sakeru-omoi-ga-shita.（悲しみに胸が張り裂ける思いがした.）My heart almost burst with grief.

mune-o-utareru（胸を打たれる）be impressed ((with))

mune-o-nade-orosu（胸をなで下ろす）feel relieved

mune-ga-suku（胸がすく）be satisfied

kibō-ni-mune-o-fukuramasete（希望に胸を膨らませて）with one's heart full of hope

mune-ni-ichimotsu-aru（胸に一物ある）have one's own ax(e) to grind

mune〈むね：棟〉the ridge.

mune-age-shiki（棟上げ式）a ceremony after the completion of the framework

mune-kuso〈むねくそ：胸くそ〉

mune-kuso-ga-warui〈胸くそが悪い〉be disgusted ((at, by *or* with)).

munen〈むねん：無念〉

munen-ni-omou〈無念に思う〉regret, be mortified ((by)), be vexed ((at)).

mune-yake〈むねやけ：胸焼け〉heartburn.

mune-yake-ga-suru（胸焼けがする）have heartburn

muni〈むに：無二〉

muni-no〈無二の〉peerless, matchless, unparalleled.

muni-no shin·yū（無二の親友）one's best friend

mu-ninsho〈むにんしょ：無任所〉

mu-ninsho-daijin（無任所大臣）a Minister without portfolio

munô〈むのう：無能〉

munô-na〈無能な〉incompetent, incapable, inefficient.

mu-nôryoku〈むのうりょく：無能力〉incompetence, incapacity, lack of ability.

mu-nôryoku-sha（無能力者）an incompetent, an incapable, a person without capacity

mu-nôryoku-na〈無能力な〉incompetent, incapable.

munyamunya〈むにゃむにゃ〉

munyamunya-negoto-o-iu〈むにゃむにゃ寝言を言う〉mumble in sleep.

mura〈むら：村〉a village.

mura 〈むら〉

　mura-no-aru 〈むらのある〉 uneven, irregular; patched; capricious.

　　mura-no-nai（むらのない） even, uniform.

muragaru 〈むらがる：群がる〉 crowd, throng, flock together, swarm, herd.

mura-hachibu 〈むらはちぶ：村八分〉 village ostracism.

　mura-hachibu-ni-sareru〈村八分にされる〉 be ostracized.

muramura-to 〈むらむらと〉

　~*(-shiyô)-to-iu-ki-ga-muramura-to-okiru*〈~（しよう）という気がむらむらと起きる〉 feel an irresistible temptation ((to do)).

murasaki(-iro)(-no) 〈むらさき（いろ）（の）：紫（色）（の）〉 purple.

murasu 〈むらす：蒸らす〉 steam.

　mureru〈蒸れる〉 be steamed.

mure 〈むれ：群れ〉 a group, a crowd, a throng, a herd, a drove, a flock, a flight, a school, a swarm.

　mure-o-nashite〈群れを成して〉 in groups(crowds, flocks, flights, shoals *or* swarms).

　　mure-o-nashite-oyogu（群れを成して泳ぐ） school.

muri 〈むり：無理〉 unreasonableness, impossibility, compulsion, excessiveness, overwork.

　　muri-nandai（無理難題） an unreasonable demand.

　　muri-shinjû（無理心中） a forced double suicide.

　muri-na〈無理な〉 unreasonable, impossible, forcible, excessive.

　　muri-na yôkyû（無理な要求） an unacceptable demand.

　muri-ni〈無理に〉 unreasonably, by force, against one's will.

　muri-ni-saseru or *muri-jii-suru*〈無理にさせる，無理強いする〉 force ((a person)) to do.

　muri-o-suru〈無理をする〉 strain(overstrain *or* overwork) oneself.

　　Muri-o-suru-na.（無理をするな。） Take it easy.

　muri-mo-nai〈無理もない〉 be natural.

　　Kare-ga　sô　iu-no-mo-muri-wa-nai.（彼がそう言うのも無理はない。） It is natural that he should say so.

mu-rikai 〈むりかい：無理解〉 lack of understanding.

　mu-rikai-na〈無理解な〉 lacking in understanding, unsympathetic.

muryô 〈むりょう：無料〉 no charge.

　　Nyûjô-muryô.（入場無料。） Admission free.

　muryô-no〈無料の〉 free, gratuitous.

　muryô-de〈無料で〉 free (of charge).

muryoku(-sa) 〈むりょく（さ）：無力（さ）〉 powerlessness, helplessness, incapacity.
    muryoku-kan（無力感） a feeling of helplessness
    muryoku-na〈無力な〉 powerless, helpless, incapable.

mu-sabetsu 〈むさべつ：無差別〉 indiscrimination.
    mu-sabetsu-ni〈無差別に〉 without discrimination.
       dan-jo-mu-sabetsu-ni（男女無差別に） without distinction of sex

musaboru 〈むさぼる〉
    bôri-o-musaboru〈暴利をむさぼる〉 make excessive profits.
    musaboru-yô-ni〈むさぼるように〉 greedily, avidly, eagerly.
       musaboru-yô-ni-hon-o-yomu（むさぼるように本を読む） pore over a book

musaku 〈むさく：無策〉
    musaku-de-aru〈無策である〉 lack policy.
    musaku-no〈無策の〉 shiftless.

musa-kurushii 〈むさくるしい〉 foul, filthy, squalid, sordid, dirty, shabby.
       musa-kurushii-minari-o-shite-iru（むさくるしい身なりをしている） be shabbily dressed

musebu 〈むせぶ〉 be choked ((by *or* with)).
    musebi-naku（むせび泣く） be choked with tears

musei-butsu 〈むせいぶつ：無生物〉 an inanimate object.

mu-seifu 〈むせいふ：無政府〉 anarchy.
    mu-seifu-jôtai（無政府状態） a state of anarchy
    mu-seifu-shugi（無政府主義） anarchism
       mu-seifu-shugi-sha（無政府主義者） an anarchist

mu-seigen 〈むせいげん：無制限〉
    mu-seigen-na〈無制限な〉 limitless, unrestricted.
    mu-seigen-ni〈無制限に〉 freely, without any restriction.

musei-ran 〈むせいらん：無精卵〉 an unimpregnated egg.

mu-sekinin 〈むせきにん：無責任〉 irresponsibility.
    mu-sekinin-na〈無責任な〉 irresponsible.
    mu-sekinin-ni〈無責任に〉 without a due sense of responsibility.

musen 〈むせん：無線〉 radio, wireless.
    musen-tsûshin（無線通信） wireless communications

musen 〈むせん：無銭〉
    musen-inshoku-o-suru（無銭飲食をする） jump a restaurant bill
    musen-ryokô-o-suru（無銭旅行をする） travel without money

museru 〈むせる〉 be choked ((by or with)), choke ((on or over)).

mu-sessô 〈むせっそう：無節操〉 inconstancy.
mu-sessô-na 〈無節操な〉 inconstant, unprincipled.

mushakusha 〈むしゃくしゃ〉
mushakusha-suru 〈むしゃくしゃする〉 be irritated, be out of humor.

mushamusha 〈むしゃむしゃ〉
mushamusha-taberu 〈むしゃむしゃ食べる〉 munch.

musha-ningyô 〈むしゃにんぎょう：武者人形〉 a doll warrior.

mushi 〈むし：無死〉
　　Mushi-manrui-de-aru. （無死満塁である.） The bases are full with no outs.

mushi 〈むし：無視〉
mushi-suru 〈無視する〉 ignore, disregard, shut one's eyes ((to)).
　　mushi-sareta-ki-ga-suru（無視された気がする） feel (oneself) left out in the cold

mushi 〈むし：虫〉 an insect, a cricket, a worm, a caterpillar, a moth, vermin.
　　mushi-ga-kuu （虫が食う） be eaten by worms
　　mushi-ga-tsuku （虫が付く） be infested with vermin
　　mushi-ga-waku （虫がわく） become verminous, get worms
　　mushi-no-kutta or mushi-kui-no （虫の食った，虫食いの） worm-eaten, moth-eaten
　　mushi-no-ii （虫のいい） selfish, self-seeking
　　mushi-no-suka-nai （虫の好かない） disagreeable, disgusting
　　mushi-no-idokoro-ga-warui （虫の居所が悪い） be in a poor humor
　　mushi-no-iki-de-aru （虫の息である） be breathing faintly, be dying
　　mushi-ga-shiraseru （虫が知らせる） forebode, have a presentiment
　　mushi-kago （虫かご） an insect cage
　　mushi-yoke （虫よけ） an insect repellent, a moth ball
　　mushi-kudashi （虫下し） a medicine for expelling worms, a vermifuge
　　mushi-boshi （虫干し） (summer) airing

mushi-atsui 〈むしあつい：蒸し暑い〉 sultry, stuffy, close.

mushi-ba 〈むしば：虫歯〉 a decayed(or bad) tooth.

mushibamu 〈むしばむ〉 spoil, affect, undermine.

mushi-buro 〈むしぶろ：蒸しぶろ〉 a steam bath.
mushi-buro-ni-haitta-yô-na 〈蒸しぶろに入ったような〉 sweltering.

mushi-kaesu 〈むしかえす：蒸し返す〉 revive, bring up again, repeat.

furui hanashi o mushi-kaesu〈古い話を蒸し返す〉rehash old stories

mu-shikaku〈むしかく：無資格〉
mu-shikaku-no〈無資格の〉disqualified, unlicensed.

mu-shiken〈むしけん：無試験〉
mu-shiken-de〈無試験で〉without examination.

mushi-kera〈むしけら：虫けら〉
mushi-kera-dôzen-de-aru〈虫けら同然である〉be beneath one's notice, count for nothing in the world.

mushi-megane〈むしめがね：虫眼鏡〉a magnifying glass.

mushimushi〈むしむし：蒸し蒸し〉
mushimushi-suru〈蒸し蒸しする〉see. mushi-atsui.

mushin〈むしん：無心〉
mushin-ni〈無心に〉innocently.

mu-shinjin〈むしんじん：無信心〉see. fu-shinjin.

mu-shinkei〈むしんけい：無神経〉
mu-shinkei-na〈無神経な〉insensible, callous, dull, thick-skinned.

mushin-ron〈むしんろん：無神論〉atheism.
mushin-ron-sha〈無神論者〉an atheist

mushiro〈むしろ〉a straw mat, straw matting.

mushiro〈むしろ〉rather ((than)), better ((than)), sooner ((than)).
Kare-wa shôsetsu-ka-to-iu-yori-wa-mushiro gakusha-da.〈彼は小説家というよりはむしろ学者だ。〉He is a scholar rather than a novelist.

mushiru〈むしる〉pluck, pull, pick, tear.

mushi-yaki〈むしやき：蒸し焼き〉
mushi-yaki-ni-suru〈蒸し焼きにする〉bake in a covered casserole.

mushizu〈むしず：虫酢〉
Mita-dake-de mushizu-ga-hashiru.〈見ただけでむしずが走る。〉The mere sight (of him) makes me sick.

mushô〈むしょう：無償〉
mushô-de〈無償で〉free of charge, without compensation, for nothing.

mushoku〈むしょく：無色〉
mushoku-no〈無色の〉colorless.
mushoku-tômei-no〈無色透明の〉transparent

mushoku〈むしょく：無職〉inoccupation.
mushoku-no〈無職の〉without occupation, jobless, out of work.

mushô-ni〈むしょうに：無性に〉to excess, very much.
Mushô-ni hara-ga-tatta.〈無性に腹が立った。〉I got excessively angry.

mu-shozoku〈むしょぞく：無所属〉
  mu-shozoku-daigishi〈無所属代議士〉 an independent
mu-shozoku-de-aru〈無所属である〉be not affiliated to any (political) party.
mu-shozoku-no〈無所属の〉independent, neutral.
mushû〈むしゅう：無臭〉
mushû-no〈無臭の〉odorless, scentless.
mu-shumi〈むしゅみ：無趣味〉lack of taste.
mu-shumi-na〈無趣味な〉tasteless.
  mu-shumi-na hito（無趣味な人） a man of no tastes
musu〈むす：蒸す〉steam; be sultry.
musû〈むすう：無数〉
musû-no〈無数の〉innumerable, numberless, countless.
musubi〈むすび：結び〉an end, a conclusion; a riceball.
  musubi-me（結び目） a knot, a tie
musubi-no〈結びの〉final, closing.
  musubi-no ichiban（結びの一番） the final (*sumo*) bout
musubi-awaseru〈むすびあわせる：結び合わせる〉tie together, combine, unite.
musubi-tsukeru〈むすびつける：結び付ける〉tie (up), link together, bind(*or* tie) ((one thing)) to ((another)), connect ((A)) with ((B)).
  futatsu-no koto o musubi-tsukete-kangaeru（二つの事を結び付けて考える） consider two things in connection with each other
musubi-tsuku〈結び付く〉be linked ((with)), be related ((with)), combine ((with)), be consistent ((with)).
musubu〈むすぶ：結ぶ〉tie, knot, fasten, bind; close, conclude; join, link; form, organize; ally.
  ribon de musubu（リボンで結ぶ） tie with a ribbon
  enzetsu o jibun-no suki-na kotoba-de musubu（演説を自分の好きな言葉で結ぶ） conclude one's speech with his favorite words
  Narita-Hawai-kan-o-go-jikan-de-musubu-shin-gata-jetto-ki（成田ハワイ間を五時間で結ぶ新型ジェット機） the newly-typed jet liner that links Narita with Hawaii in five hours
  kôgi o musubu（交ぎを結ぶ） form friendship ((with))
musuko〈むすこ：息子〉a son.
musume〈むすめ：娘〉a daughter, a girl.
musume-rashii〈娘らしい〉girlish.
mu-teikô〈むていこう：無抵抗〉nonresistance.

　　　mu-teikô-shugi〈無抵抗主義〉 a principle of nonresistance

　　mu-teikô-de〈無抵抗で〉without making any resistance.

muteki〈むてき：無敵〉

　　muteki-no〈無敵の〉matchless, unrivaled, invincible.

mu-teppô〈むてっぽう：無鉄砲〉

　　mu-teppô-na〈無鉄砲な〉rash, reckless, thoughtless.

　　　mu-teppô-na-koto-o-suru（無鉄砲なことをする） act thoughtlessly

　　mu-teppô-ni〈無鉄砲に〉rashly, recklessly, thoughtlessly.

mu-todoke〈むとどけ：無届け〉

　　　mu-todoke-demo（無届けデモ） an unauthorized demonstration

　　mu-todoke-de〈無届けで〉without notice.

mu-tokuten〈むとくてん：無得点〉

　　mu-tokuten-ni-owaru〈無得点に終わる〉end scoreless.

　　mu-tokuten-no〈無得点の〉scoreless.

mu-tonjaku〈むとんじゃく：無とん着〉indifference, insouciance.

　　mu-tonjaku-de-aru〈無とん着である〉be indifferent ((to)), be careless ((about *or* of)), be unconcerned ((about)).

mutsû〈むつう：無痛〉painlessness.

　　　mutsû-bumben（無痛分べん） painless delivery

　　mutsû-no〈無痛の〉painless.

mutsumajii〈むつまじい〉harmonious, happy, intimate, friendly.

　　mutsumajiku〈むつまじく〉harmoniously, happily.

　　　mutsumajiku kurasu（むつまじく暮らす） live happily

mutto-suru〈むっとする〉be offended ((at, by, over *or* with)), take offense ((at)); be stuffy.

　　mutto-shite〈むっとして〉in a miff.

muttsu〈むっつ：六つ〉*see.* roku.

muttsuri〈むっつり〉

　　muttsuri-shita〈むっつりした〉sullen, morose.

　　muttsuri-to〈むっつりと〉sullenly.

muyami〈むやみ：無やみ〉

　　muyami-ni〈無やみに〉thoughtlessly, recklessly, blindly, excessively, unreasonably.

　　　muyami-ni kawaigaru（無やみにかわいがる）be fond of ((a child)) blindly

　　　muyami-ni-isogu（むやみに急ぐ） make needless haste

muyô〈むよう：無用〉

　　　Shimpai-go-muyô.（心配御無用. ） There is no need for anxiety.

muyô-no〈無用の〉useless, of no use; needless, unnecessary; without business.

  muyô-no-chôbutsu（無用の長物）a good-for-nothing, a useless thing, a white elephant

  Muyô-no-mono tachi-iri-kinshi.（無用の者立ち入り禁止.）No admittance except on business.

muyoku〈むよく：無欲〉

muyoku-na〈無欲な〉unselfish, free from avarice, disinterested.

muyû-byô〈むゆうびょう：夢遊病〉sleepwalking, somnambulism.

  muyû-byô-sha（夢遊病者）a sleepwalker, a somnumbulist

muzai〈むざい：無罪〉innocence, being not guilty.

  muzai o shuchô-suru（無罪を主張する）assert one's innocence

  muzai-no-hanketsu-o-ukeru（無罪の判決を受ける）be declared not guilty

  muzai-ni-naru（無罪になる）be found not guilty

  muzai-hômen-ni-naru（無罪放免になる）be found innocent and acquitted

muzamuza(-to)〈むざむざ(と)〉easily, without resistance, helplessly.

  muzamuza-to damasareru（むざむざとだまされる）be deceived easily

muzan〈むざん：無残〉

muzan-na〈無残な〉cruel, merciless, pitiless, tragic.

  muzan-na saigo-o-togeru（無残な最後を遂げる）meet with a tragic end

muzan-nimo〈無残にも〉cruelly, mercilessly, without pity.

muzei〈むぜい：無税〉

  muzei-yunyû-hin（無税輸入品）duty-free imports

muzei-no〈無税の〉free, duty-free.

muzei-de〈無税で〉free of duties, duty-free.

mu-zôsa〈むぞうさ：無造作〉

mu-zôsa-ni〈無造作に〉with ease, easily, offhand, simply.

muzukaru〈むずかる〉be fretful, be peevish.

muzukashii〈むずかしい：難しい〉hard, difficult, troublesome; doubtful; sullen, serious; particular.

  muzukashii shigoto（難しい仕事）a hard task

  muzukashii jôsei（難しい情勢）a delicate situation

  muzukashii byôki（難しい病気）a serious case

  muzukashii-kao-o-suru（難しい顔をする）look serious

  sasai-na-koto-ni muzukashii（さ細な事に難しい）be particular about

trifling things

muzumuzu〈むずむず〉

muzumuzu-suru〈むずむずする〉itch, feel itchy, tingle; be impatient ((for)), be irritated.

　　Senaka ga muzumuzu-shita.（背中がむずむずした.）I felt my back itchy.

myaku〈みゃく：脈〉the pulse, pulsation; hope.

　　Myaku ga hayai.〈脈が速い.〉The pulse is quick.

　　Myaku-ga-osoi.〈脈が遅い.〉The pulse is slow.

　　Myaku ga yowai.〈脈が弱い.〉The pulse is weak.

　　myaku o kazoeru〈脈を数える〉count ((a person's)) pulse

　　myaku o toru〈脈を取る〉feel ((a person's)) pulse

　　Mô-myaku-ga-nai.（もう脈がない.）The pulse beats no longer. / It's hopeless.

　　fusei-myaku（不整脈）an irregular pulse

myakuhaku〈みゃくはく：脈はく〉pulsation, the pulse.

　　Myakuhaku-hachi-jû.〈脈はく八十.〉The pulse is at 80.

myakumyaku〈みゃくみゃく：脈々〉

myakumyaku-to-shite〈脈々として〉continuously, incessantly.

myô〈みょう：妙〉

myô-na〈妙な〉strange, queer, odd, curious.

　　myô-na-koto-niwa（妙なことには）strange to say

myô-ni-kikoeru-kamo-shirenai-ga〈妙に聞こえるかも知れないが〉strange as it may sound.

myôban〈みょうばん：明晩〉tomorrow evening(*or* night).

myôban〈みょうばん〉alum.

myôchô〈みょうちょう：明朝〉tomorrow morning.

myôgi〈みょうぎ：妙技〉a wonderful performance, a feat.

myôgi-o-miseru〈妙技を見せる〉perform a wonderful feat.

myôgo-nichi〈みょうごにち：明後日〉the day after tomorrow.

myôji〈みょうじ：名字〉a family name, a surname.

myôjô〈みょうじょう：明星〉Venus.

myômi〈みょうみ：妙味〉a charm, beauty, a nice point.

　　myômi ga nai（妙味がない）lack charm

N

na 〈な：名〉 a name, a title, fame.

     na o tsukeru （名を付ける） give a name

     na-o-yobu （名を呼ぶ） call ((a person)) by name

     na o ageru （名を揚げる） win fame, make a name

  na-zukeru 〈名付ける〉 name, call.

  na-no-aru or *na-no-tootta* 〈名のある，名の通った〉 famous, noted, well-known; notorious.

na 〈な：菜〉 greens, vegetables.

     na o tsukeru （菜を漬ける） pickle greens

-na 〈-な〉

     Wasureru-na. （忘れるな.） Don't forget.

     Kesshite-uso-o-tsuku-na. （決してうそをつくな.） Never tell a lie.

-nâ 〈-なあ〉 I wish; what, how.

     O-kane-ga-areba-ii-nâ! （お金があればいいなあ.） I wish I had money.

     Kyôdai-ga-attara-yokatta-no-ni-nâ! （兄弟があったらよかったのになあ.） I wish I had had a brother.

     Kirei-na keshiki-da-nâ! （きれいな景色だなあ.） What a beautiful sight it is!

na-ate 〈なあて：名あて〉 an address.

     na-ate-nin （名あて人） an addressee

na-bakari 〈なばかり：名ばかり〉

  na-bakari-no 〈名ばかりの〉 nominal, token.

     na-bakari-no shachô （名ばかりの社長） the nominal president of the company

     na-bakari-no kifu （名ばかりの寄附） a poor apology for donation

nabe 〈なべ〉 a pan, a pot.

nabiku 〈なびく〉 wave, flutter, bend, bow.

     Yanagi ga kaze-ni nabiiteiru. （柳が風になびいている.） The willows

are flowing in the wind.

kane-no-chikara-ni nabiku（金の力になびく） bow to money

naburi-goroshi〈なぶりごろし：なぶり殺し〉

naburi-goroshi-ni-suru〈なぶり殺しにする〉torture ((a person)) to death.

naburi-mono〈なぶりもの：なぶり者〉a laughingstock.

naburi-mono-ni-naru（なぶり者になる） become a laughingstock

naburi-mono-ni-suru〈なぶり者にする〉make sport ((of)), poke fun ((at)), mock ((at)).

nada〈なだ〉

Genkai-nada（玄海なだ） the Sea of Genkai

nadakai〈なだかい：名高い〉famous, well-known; notorious.

nadameru〈なだめる〉soothe, calm (down).

naku ko o nadameru（泣く子をなだめる） soothe a crying baby

nadameru-yô-ni〈なだめるように〉pacifyingly.

nadaraka〈なだらか〉

nadaraka-na〈なだらかな〉gentle.

nadaraka-na saka（なだらかな坂） a gentle slope

nadaraka-ni〈なだらかに〉gently, smoothly.

nadare〈なだれ：雪崩〉a snowslide, an avalanche.

nadare-komu〈なだれ込む〉rush into.

nade-gata〈なでがた：なで肩〉sloping shoulders.

nade-orosu〈なでおろす：なで下ろす〉

hotto-mune-o-nade-orosu〈ほっと胸をなで下ろす〉give a sigh of relief.

naderu〈なでる〉stroke, pat.

neko o naderu（猫をなでる） stroke a cat

nadeshiko〈なでしこ〉a (fringed) pink.

nade-tsukeru〈なでつける：なで付ける〉comb(smooth, stroke *or* plaster) down (one's hair).

-nado〈-など〉and so on, and so forth, and the like, etc.

nae〈なえ：苗〉a seedling, a (young) plant.

nae-doko（苗床） a seedbed

nae-gi（苗木） a young tree

na-fuda〈なふだ：名札〉a nameplate, a tag.

nafutarin〈ナフタリン〉naphthalene.

naga-ame〈ながあめ：長雨〉a long spell of rainy weather.

naga-banashi〈ながばなし：長話〉a long talk.

denwa-de naga-banashi-o-suru（電話で長話をする） have a long conversation on the telephone

naga-biku 〈ながびく：長引く〉 be prolonged, drag on; be delayed.
> Haha no byôki wa naga-biita.（母の病気は長引いた.） Mother was long in recovering from her sickness.

naga-gutsu 〈ながぐつ：長靴〉 boots, high boots.

nagai 〈ながい：長居〉
nagai-suru 〈長居する〉 stay long, make a long visit.

nagai 〈ながい：長い〉 long.
> Nagai-mono-niwa-makare-ro.（長い物には巻かれろ.） Don't kick against the pricks.

nagai-aida 〈長い間〉 for a long time.
nagai-aida-niwa 〈長い間には〉 in a long time, in the long run.
nagai-me-de-mireba 〈長い目で見れば〉 from the long-range view.

naga-iki 〈ながいき：長生き〉
naga-iki-suru 〈長生きする〉 live long.

naga-isu 〈ながいす：長いす〉 a sofa, a couch.

nagaku 〈ながく：長く〉 long.
> nagaku-kakaru（長く掛かる） take a long time
> nagaku-naru（長くなる） be lengthened, grow longer; lie down
> nagaku-suru（長くする） lengthen, make longer
> nagaku-temo（長くても） at the longest

nagame 〈ながめ：眺め〉 a view, a scene.
> ii nagame（いい眺め） a fine view

nagameru 〈眺める〉 see, look ((at)), watch, gaze ((at)).
> tsuki-o-nagameru（月を眺める） look at the moon

naga-mochi 〈ながもち：長持ち〉
naga-mochi-suru 〈長持ちする〉 be durable, keep long, last long, stay long, wear well.
> Kono tenki wa naga-mochi-shi-nai-darô.（この天気は長持ちしないだろう.） This fine weather will not stay long.

-nagara 〈-ながら〉 while, as, ...ing, with, over; though, but, yet, in spite of.
> terebi o mi-nagara（テレビを見ながら） while watching television
> aruki-nagara uta o utau（歩きながら歌を歌う） sing a song as one is walking
> hohoemi-nagara hanasu（ほほ笑みながら話す） talk with a smile
> cha-o-nomi-nagara hanasu（茶を飲みながら話す） talk over a cup of tea
> mazushii-nagara（貧しいながら） though one is poor

warui-to-wa-shiri-nagara（悪いとは知りながら）though one knows that it is wrong

zannen-nagara～（残念ながら～）I am sorry, but...

yakusoku-shite-oki-nagara（約束しておきながら）in spite of ((a person's)) promise

nagaraku〈ながらく：長らく〉long, for a long time.

Nagaraku go-busata-itashimashita.（長らくごぶさたいたしました.）Excuse me for my long silence.

Nagaraku o-matase-shite sumi-masen.（長らくお待たせしてすみません.）I'm sorry to have kept you waiting so long.

nagare〈ながれ：流れ〉a flow, a stream, a current.

mizu no nagare（水の流れ）the flow of water

hito no nagare（人の流れ）a stream of people

jidai no nagare（時代の流れ）the current of the times

nagare-ni-sakaratte kogu（流れに逆らってこぐ）row against the stream

nagare-boshi（流れ星）a shooting star

nagare-sagyô（流れ作業）assembly-line operation

nagareru〈ながれる：流れる〉flow, run; be washed away; be given up, be dropped.

Kawa ga machi-naka-o nagareru.（川が町中を流れる.）The river runs through the city.

Ase ga kare-no hoo o nagareta.（汗が彼のほおを流れた.）Sweat ran down his cheeks.

Oomizu-de hashi-ga-mittsu nagareta.（大水で橋が三つ流れた.）Three bridges were washed away by the flood.

Ame-de-shiai-ga-nagareta.（雨で試合が流れた.）The game was rained out.

nagare-tsuku〈ながれつく：流れ着く〉drift ((to)), be washed ashore.

nagasa〈ながさ：長さ〉length.

Kono-kawa-no-nagasa-wa-dore-kurai-desu-ka?（この川の長さはどれくらいですか.）How long is this river? / What is the length of this river?

Sono kawa wa nagasa-jukkiro-desu.（その川は長さ十キロです.）That river is ten kilometers long. / That river is ten kilometers in length.

nagasareru〈ながされる：流される〉be carried away, be washed away.

kaze-de oki-e-nagasareru（風で沖へ流される）be driven out to sea in

the wind

Ie-ga-san-gen kôzui-de nagasareta.（家が三軒洪水で流された.） Three houses were washed away by the flood.

nagashi 〈ながし：流し〉 a sink; cruising.

nagashi-no takushî（流しのタクシー） a cruising taxicab

nagashi-komu 〈ながしこむ：流し込む〉 pour ((into)); wash down.

nagasu 〈ながす：流す〉 dash, flush, shed; wash off.

namida o nagasu（涙を流す） shed tears

aka o nagasu（あかを流す） wash off the dirt

naga-tarashii 〈ながたらしい：長たらしい〉 lengthy, very long, long and boring.

naga-tsuzuki 〈ながつづき：長続き〉

naga-tsuzuki-suru〈長続きする〉 last long, continue.

Kare-wa hitotsu-no koto-ni naga-tsuzuki-shi-nai.（彼は一つの事に長続きしない.） He cannot stick to any one thing.

naga-wazurai 〈ながわずらい：長患い〉 a long illness.

naga-wazurai-o-suru（長患いをする） suffer from a long illness

nage-ageru 〈なげあげる：投げ上げる〉 throw up.

nage-dasu 〈なげだす：投げ出す〉 throw out; give up.

ashi o nage-dasu（足を投げ出す） throw out one's legs

shigoto o nage-dasu（仕事を投げ出す） give up one's job

nageire 〈なげいれ：投げ入れ〉 free-style flower arrangement.

nage-ireru 〈なげいれる：投げ入れる〉 throw ((a thing)) in(*or* into).

nage-kaesu 〈なげかえす：投げ返す〉 throw back.

nageki 〈なげき：嘆き〉 grief, sorrow, lamentation.

nageku〈嘆く〉 grieve, lament.

hito-no shi o nageku（人の死を嘆く） lament a person's death

nagekawashii〈嘆かわしい〉 sad, regrettable, lamentable.

nage-komu 〈なげこむ：投げ込む〉 throw in, dump in.

nageru 〈なげる：投げる〉 throw; give up.

ishi o nageru（石を投げる） throw a stone ((at))

shiken o nageru（試験を投げる） give up an examination

nage-suteru 〈なげすてる：投げ捨てる〉 throw away.

nage-taosu 〈なげたおす：投げ倒す〉 throw down.

nage-tsukeru 〈なげつける：投げ付ける〉 throw ((something)) at ((someone)).

nage-uri 〈なげうり：投げ売り〉 a sacrifice sale, a clearance sale, dumping.

nage-uri-suru〈投げ売りする〉sell at a loss, dump.

nageyari〈なげやり：投げやり〉

nageyari-na〈投げやりな〉halfhearted, slovenly, slipshod.
　nageyari-na taido〔投げやりな態度〕 a halfhearted manner

nagi〈なぎ〉a calm, a lull.

nagu〈なぐ〉become calm, calm down, die away, drop, lull.

naginata〈なぎなた〉a halberd, a halbert.

nagisa〈なぎさ〉a beach, a shore, the waterside.

nagi-taosu〈なぎたおす：なぎ倒す〉mow(*or* cut) down.

nagori〈なごり：名残〉parting; remains, traces, relics, vestiges.
　nagori-o-oshimu or *nagori-oshii*〈名残を惜しむ，名残惜しい〉be reluctant
　　to leave, be sorry to part ((from)).
　nagori o todome-nai〈名残をとどめない〉retain no traces ((of)).
　nagori-oshi-ge-ni or *nagori-oshi-sô-ni*〈名残惜しげに，名残惜しそうに〉
　　reluctantly, wistfully.

nagoyaka〈なごやか：和やか〉
　nagoyaka-na〈和やかな〉mild, quiet, peaceful, friendly, amiable,
　　congenial.
　nagoyaka-ni〈和やかに〉mildly, peacefully, amiably.

naguri-ai-o-suru or **naguri-au**〈なぐりあいをする，なぐりあう：殴り合い
　をする，殴り合う〉fight ((with)), exchange blows ((with)).

naguri-gaki〈なぐりがき：殴り書き〉a scribble, a scrawl.
　naguri-gaki-o-suru〈殴り書きをする〉scribble, scrawl.

naguri-kaesu〈なぐりかえす：殴り返す〉hit ((a person)) back.

naguri-kakaru〈なぐりかかる：殴り掛かる〉hit at ((a person)).

naguri-komi-o-kakeru or **naguri-komu**〈なぐりこみをかける，なぐり
　こむ：殴り込みをかける，殴り込む〉make a raid ((on)), attack, storm.

naguri-korosu〈なぐりころす：殴り殺す〉strike ((a person)) to death.

naguri-taosu〈なぐりたおす：殴り倒す〉knock ((a person)) down.

naguru〈なぐる：殴る〉beat, strike, knock, hit.
　　atama-o-naguru〔頭を殴る〕 strike ((a person)) on the head
　　hidoku naguru〔ひどく殴る〕 hit ((a person)) hard
　nagurareru〈殴られる〉be struck, receive a blow.

nagusame〈なぐさめ：慰め〉(a) comfort, (a) consolation.
　　nagusame-no kotoba〔慰めの言葉〕 comforting words
　nagusameru〈慰める〉comfort, console.

nagusami〈なぐさみ：慰み〉(an) amusement, a pastime, (a) pleasure,
　fun, (a) diversion, (a) recreation.

nagusami-hambun-ni〈慰み半分に〉partly for fun.

nai〈ない：無い〉there is no... , have no... , lack, be free from...; be gone.

> Taberu-mono ga zenzen-nai.（食べる物が全然ない。）There is nothing to eat.
>
> Watashi-wa kyôdai-mo-shimai-mo-nai.（私は兄弟も姉妹もない。）I have neither a brother nor a sister.
>
> suru-koto ga nani-mo-nai（する事が何もない）have nothing to do
>
> ketten-ga-nai（欠点がない）be free from faults
>
> Saifu ga-nai.（財布がない。）My purse is gone.

-nai〈-ない〉be not.

> Kare-wa watashi-no itoko-dewa-nai.（彼は私のいとこではない。）He is not my cousin.
>
> Kanojo-wa amari rikô-dewa-nai.（彼女は余り利口ではない。）She is not very clever.

-nai〈-ない〉do not, neither...nor, will not, cannot, never, not...at all, won't, must not.

> Watashi-wa sonna baka-na koto wa shi-nai.（私はそんなばかな事はしない。）I do not do such a foolish thing.
>
> Watashi-wa kanojo-no chichi-mo-haha-mo-shira-nai.（私は彼女の父も母も知らない。）I know neither her father nor her mother.
>
> Watashi-wa kyô gaishutsu-shi-nai.（私は今日外出しない。）I will not go out today.
>
> Kanojo-wa Eigo ga hanase-nai.（彼女は英語が話せない。）She cannot speak English.
>
> Kare-wa kesshite-uso-wa-tsuka-nai.（彼は決してうそはつかない。）He never tells a lie.
>
> Watashi-wa kare-no oji wa zenzen-shira-nai.（私は彼の叔(伯)父は全然知らない。）I don't know his uncle at all.
>
> Mado ga dô-shite-mo aka-nai.（窓がどうしても開かない。）The window won't open.
>
> Detarame o itte-wa-ike-nai.（出たら目を言ってはいけない。）You mustn't talk nonsense.

naibu〈ないぶ：内部〉the interior, the inside.

naibu-no〈内部の〉interior, internal, inside, inner.

naibu-ni〈内部に〉inside, within.

naibu-kara〈内部から〉from within.

nai-bumpi〈ないぶんぴ：内分泌〉internal secretion.

nai-bumpi-eki〈内分泌液〉 an internal secretion

naibun〈ないぶん：内聞〉

naibun-ni-suru〈内聞にする〉keep ((a matter)) secret.

　　Kono ken wa go-naibun-ni-negaimasu.（この件は御内聞に願います．）
　　　I wish you would keep this matter to yourself.

naichi〈ないち：内地〉 the interior; home, mainland.

naidaku〈ないだく：内諾〉an informal consent.

　　naidaku o eru〈内諾を得る〉 obtain ((a person's)) informal consent

naien〈ないえん：内縁〉(a) common-law marriage.

　　naien-no otto〈内縁の夫〉 a common-law husband

　　naien-no tsuma〈内縁の妻〉 a common-law wife

　　naien-kankei-o-musubu〈内縁関係を結ぶ〉 make a common-law
　　　marriage ((with))

naifu〈ナイフ〉a knife.

　　yoku-kireru naifu〈よく切れるナイフ〉 a sharp knife

naifuku〈ないふく：内服〉

　　naifuku-yaku〈内服薬〉 an internal medicine

naifun〈ないふん：内紛〉an internal discord, an intraparty conflict.

naigai〈ないがい：内外〉the inside and the outside.

naigai-no〈内外の〉internal and external, home and abroad.

　　naigai-no jijô〈内外の事情〉 domestic and foreign affairs

naigai-ni〈内外に〉inside and outside, in and out, within and without, at
　home and abroad.

　　shi-no-naigai-ni〈市の内外に〉 in and around the city

naiji〈ないじ：内耳〉the internal ear.

　　naiji-en〈内耳炎〉 inflammation of the internal ear

naiji〈ないじ：内示〉

naiji-suru〈内示する〉show privately, announce unofficially.

naijo〈ないじょ：内助〉

　　naijo-no-kô〈内助の功〉 one's wife's assistance

naijô〈ないじょう：内情〉the inside affairs, the real state of affairs.

　　naijô-ni-akarui〈内情に明るい〉 be familiar with the inside affairs
　　　((of))

naiju〈ないじゅ：内需〉domestic demand, home consumption.

naika〈ないか：内科〉internal medicine.

　　naika-i〈内科医〉 a physician

naikai〈ないかい：内海〉an inland sea.

　　Seto-naikai〈瀬戸内海〉 the Inland Sea of Seto

naikaku〈ないかく：内閣〉a cabinet, a ministry.
    naikaku o soshiki-suru（内閣を組織する）form a Cabinet
    naikaku no kaizô（内閣の改造）the reconstruction of the Cabinet
    naikaku-sô-jishoku（内閣総辞職）a general resignation of the Cabinet
    Naikaku-sôri-daijin（内閣総理大臣）the Prime Minister, the Premier
naikaku〈ないかく：内角〉an interior angle; the in-corner.
    naikakkyû（内角球）an inside ball
naiki〈ないき：内規〉bylaws, private regulations.
naikin〈ないきん：内勤〉desk duty.
  naikin-suru〈内勤する〉be on room duty.
naikô〈ないこう：内攻〉
  naikô-suru〈内攻する〉strike inward, retrocede.
naikô〈ないこう：内向〉
  naikô-sei-no〈内向性の〉introvert(ed).
naimei〈ないめい：内命〉private orders, secret instructions.
naimen〈ないめん：内面〉the inside, the interior.
naimitsu〈ないみつ：内密〉
  naimitsu-no〈内密の〉private, secret, confidential.
  naimitsu-ni〈内密に〉privately, in secret, confidentially.
    naimitsu-ni-shite-oku（内密にしておく）keep ((a thing)) secret
nainen-kikan〈ないねんきかん：内燃機関〉an internal combustion engine.
nairan〈ないらん：内乱〉a civil war.
nairiku〈ないりく：内陸〉inland.
    nairiku-chihô（内陸地方）inland areas
nairon〈ナイロン〉nylon.
    nairon-no kutsu-shita（ナイロンの靴下）nylon stockings, (a pair of) nylons
naisei〈ないせい：内政〉domestic administration.
    naisei-ni-kanshô-suru（内政に干渉する）interfere in the domestic affairs
naisen〈ないせん：内線〉an extension.
    naisen-bangô（内線番号）an extension number
naishin〈ないしん：内申〉a confidential report.
    naishin-sho（内申書）a school report
naishin〈ないしん：内心〉one's mind, one's real intention.
  naishin(-de-wa)〈内心（では）〉at heart.

naishin〈ないしん：内診〉
 naishin-suru〈内診する〉make an internal examination ((of)).

naisho or **naishō**〈ないしょ，ないしょう：内緒，内証〉secrecy, privacy.
　　naisho-goto *or* naishô-goto〈内緒事，内証事〉a secret, a private matter
 naisho-ni-suru or *naishô-ni-suru*〈内緒にする，内証にする〉keep ((a matter)) secret.
 naisho-no or *naishô-no*〈内緒の，内証の〉secret, private.
 naisho-de or *naishô-de*〈内緒で，内証で〉secretly, privately.
 naisho-no-hanashi-da-ga or *naishô-no-hanashi-da-ga*〈内緒の話だが，内証の話だが〉between you and me.

naishoku〈ないしょく：内職〉a side job.
　　naishoku o suru〈内職をする〉do a side job

nai-shukketsu〈ないしゅっけつ：内出血〉internal bleeding.

naitâ〈ナイター〉a night game.

naitei〈ないてい：内偵〉
 naitei-suru〈内偵する〉make secret inquiries ((into)).

naitei〈ないてい：内定〉informal decision.
 naitei-suru〈内定する〉decide informally, be unofficially arranged.

naitsû〈ないつう：内通〉
 naitsû-suru〈内通する〉hold secret communication ((with)), betray.

naiya〈ないや：内野〉the infield.
　　naiya-shu〈内野手〉an infielder
　　naiya-anda〈内野安打〉an infield hit
　　naiya-seki〈内野席〉an infield stand, an infield bleachers

naiyō〈ないよう：内容〉content(s), substance.
　　naiyô-mihon〈内容見本〉sample pages
 naiyô-ga-hôfu-de-aru〈内容が豊富である〉be rich in contents, be substantial.
　　naiyô-ga-hinjaku-de-aru〈内容が貧弱である〉be poor in contents, lack substance

naiyû-gaikan〈ないゆうがいかん：内憂外患〉troubles both at home and abroad.

naizō〈ないぞう：内臓〉the internal organs.
　　naizô-shikkan〈内臓疾患〉an internal disease

najimi〈なじみ〉familiarity, intimacy; an old acquaintance, a friend.
　　osana-najimi〈幼なじみ〉a childhood friend
 najimi-no〈なじみの〉familiar, intimate, favorite.

najimu 〈なじむ〉 become familiar ((with)), make friends ((with)), take kindly ((to)), grow accustomed ((to)), become acclimated ((to)).

　Kodomo-tachi wa nakanaka-watashi-ni-najima-nai. （子供たちはなかなか私になじまない。） Children don't take easily to me.

naka 〈なか：仲〉 relations, relationship, terms.

　naka-ga-ii（仲がいい） be on good terms ((with)), be good friends ((with))

　naka-ga-warui（仲が悪い） be on bad terms ((with))

　naka-no-ii tomodachi（仲のいい友達） a good friend

　naka-yoku-suru（仲良くする） make friends ((with))

　naka-yoku-yatte-iru（仲良くやっている） get along well ((with))

　atsuatsu-no-naka-de-aru（熱々の仲である） be deeply in love with each other

naka 〈なか：中〉 the inside, content(s).

　naka-kara 〈中から〉 from within.

　　naka-kara kagi-o-kakeru（中からかぎを掛ける） lock ((a door)) on the inside

　~*(-no)-naka-de,* ~*(-no)-naka-e* or ~*(-no)-naka-ni* 〈(～の)中で, (～の)中へ, (～の)中に〉 between, among; in, into.

　　Saburô to Sachiko-no-naka-ni tachi-nasai.（三郎と幸子の中に立ちなさい。） Stand between Saburo and Sachiko.

　　heya-no-naka-de（部屋の中で） in a room

　　hiki-dashi-no-naka-e hon o ireru（引き出しの中へ本を入れる） put some books into a drawer

　　ie-no-naka-ni hairu（家の中に入る） go into a house

　~*(-no)-naka-o* 〈(～の)中を〉 through, in the midst of.

　　mori-no-naka-o tootte-iku（森の中を通って行く） pass through the woods

　　oo-ame-no-naka-o dete-iku（大雨の中を出て行く） go out in the heavy rain

　naka-wa 〈中は〉 inside, within.

　　Naka-wa atatakai-ga, soto-wa totemo samui.（中は暖かいが, 外はとても寒い。） It is warm inside, but very cold outside.

nakaba 〈なかば：半ば〉 half; the middle; partly.

　nakaba-deki-agatte-iru（半ば出来上がっている） be half finished

　kongetsu-nakaba-ni（今月半ばに） in the middle of this month

　Watashi-no chichi wa nakaba-shôyô-nakaba-asobi-de yoku ryokô-shimasu.（私の父は半ば商用半ば遊びでよく旅行します。） My father often travels partly on business and partly for pleasure.

naka-darumi 〈なかだるみ：中だるみ〉
 naka-darumi-no-jôtai-de-aru〈中だるみの状態である〉fall into a slump, slacken off.

naka-gai〈なかがい：仲買〉brokerage; a broker, a commission merchant.

naka-goro〈なかごろ：中ごろ〉about the middle.
 raigetsu-naka-goro（来月中ごろ）about the middle of next month

naka-hodo〈なかほど：中程〉the middle, halfway.
 naka-hodo-ni aru（中程にある）lie halfway between

naka-iri〈なかいり：中入り〉a recess, an intermission, an interval.

naka-ma〈なかま：仲間〉a company, a companion, a fellow, a mate.
 asobi-naka-ma（遊び仲間）a playmate
 gakusei-naka-ma（学生仲間）a fellow student
 naka-ma-ni-hairu〈仲間に入る〉join, take part ((in)).

naka-ma-hazure〈なかまはずれ：仲間外れ〉
 naka-ma-hazure-ni-sareru〈仲間外れにされる〉be left out in the cold.

naka-ma-ware〈なかまわれ：仲間割れ〉a split among friends.
 naka-ma-ware-suru〈仲間割れする〉fall out with each other.

naka-mi〈なかみ：中身〉*see.* naiyô.

nakanaka〈なかなか〉very, quite, rather; (not) easily.
 nakanaka-kashikoi（なかなか賢い）quite clever
 Basu wa nakanaka-ko-nakatta.（バスはなかなか来なかった.）The bus was long (in) coming.

naka-naori〈なかなおり：仲直り〉(a) reconciliation, peacemaking.
 naka-naori-suru〈仲直りする〉become reconciled ((with)).
 naka-naori-saseru〈仲直りさせる〉reconcile.

naka-niwa〈なかにわ：中庭〉a courtyard, a quadrangle, a quad.

-nakase〈-なかせ：-泣かせ〉
 oya-nakase（親泣かせ）the plague to one's parents

naka-tagai〈なかたがい：仲たがい〉estrangement, discord, a quarrel.
 naka-tagai-suru〈仲たがいする〉fall out ((with)).

(-ga)-nakattara〈(-が)なかったら〉without, but for.
 Kare-no enjo-ga-nakattara, shippai-shite-ita-darô.（彼の援助がなかったら、失敗していただろう.）But for his help, I would have failed.

naka-yasumi〈なかやすみ：中休み〉
 naka-yasumi-suru〈中休みする〉*see.* ippuku-suru.

naka-yoshi〈なかよし：仲良し〉an intimate friend.
 naka-yoshi-ni-naru（仲良しになる）make friends ((with))

Watashi-wa kare-to-wa naka-yoshi-da.（私は彼とは仲良しだ.） I am (good) friends with him.

naka-yubi〈なかゆび：中指〉the middle finger.

(-ga)-nakereba〈（が）なければ：（が）無ければ〉without, but for; unless, if ...not.

Mizu-ga-nakereba, dare-mo ikiru-koto-wa-deki-nai-darô.（水がなければ、だれも生きることはできないだろう.）Without water, nobody could live.

isshô-kemmei-hataraka-nakereba（一生懸命働かなければ）unless you work hard, if you don't work hard

naki〈なき：亡き〉

ima-wa-naki-haha（今は亡き母）my dead mother

naki-dasu〈なきだす：泣き出す〉begin to cry, burst into tears.

naki-gao〈なきがお：泣き顔〉a tearful face.

naki-gara〈なきがら：亡きがら〉*see.* itai.

naki-goe〈なきごえ：泣(鳴)き声〉a cry; a song, chirping.

akambô-no naki-goe（赤ん坊の泣き声）a baby's cry

tori no naki-goe（鳥の鳴き声）the singing of birds

naki-goto〈なきごと：泣き言〉

naki-goto-o-iu〈泣き言を言う〉make complaints, complain ((about *or* of)).

naki-harasu〈なきはらす：泣きはらす〉

Kanojo-wa me-o-naki-harashite-ita.（彼女は目を泣きはらしていた.） Her eyes were swollen with tears.

naki-jakuru〈なきじゃくる：泣きじゃくる〉sob, blubber.

naki-jôgo〈なきじょうご：泣き上戸〉a crying drunk.

naki-kuzureru〈なきくずれる：泣き崩れる〉break down crying, burst into tears.

naki-mushi〈なきむし：泣き虫〉a crybaby.

naki-neiri〈なきねいり：泣き寝入り〉

naki-neiri-suru〈泣き寝入りする〉resign oneself to〔fate〕.

naki-otoshi〈なきおとし：泣き落とし〉

naki-otoshi-de shôchi-saseru〈泣き落としで承知させる〉wring consent from ((a person)) by force of tears.

naki-sakebu〈なきさけぶ：泣き叫ぶ〉scream, cry, wail.

naki-tsuku〈なきつく：泣き付く〉implore, entreat.

nakittsura〈なきっつら：泣きっ面〉

Nakittsura-ni-hachi.（泣きっ面にはち.）Misfortunes never come singly.

naki-yamu 〈なきやむ：泣きやむ〉 stop crying.

nakôdo 〈なこうど：仲人〉 a go-between.

    nakôdo-o-suru（仲人をする） act as go-between

naku 〈なく：泣く〉 cry, weep, sob.

    ureshi-naki-ni-naku（うれし泣きに泣く） weep for joy

naku 〈なく：鳴く〉 cry, howl, growl; bark, mew, moo, neigh, bleat, roar, squeal, squeak, crow, cluck, quack, coo, caw, croak.

naku-naru 〈なくなる：無(亡)くなる〉 be lost, be gone; run out ((of)), run short ((of)); die, pass away.

    Gasorin ga naku-natta.（ガソリンが無くなった.） The gas has run out.

    Kare-no o-tô-san ga naku-natta.（彼のお父さんが亡くなった.） His father has passed away.

nakusu 〈なくす：無(亡)くす〉 lose.

    tokei o nakusu（時計を無くす） lose a watch

naku-te 〈なくて：無くて〉 in want ((of)), without.

    kane-ga-naku-te-komatte-iru（金が無くて困っている） be badly in want of money

    naku-te-sumasu（無くて済ます） do without

naku-te-mo-ii 〈無くてもいい〉 can do without.

naku-te-wa-nara-nai 〈無くてはならない〉 be indispensable, cannot do without.

    Sanso wa wareware-ni naku-te-wa-nara-nai-mono-da.（酸素は我々に無くてはならないものだ.） Oxygen is indispensable to us.

nama 〈なま：生〉

    nama-tamago（生卵） a raw egg

    nama-yasai（生野菜） green vegetables

    nama-bîru（生ビール） draught beer

    nama-de-taberu（生で食べる） eat ((fish)) raw

nama-no 〈生の〉 raw, uncooked, fresh.

nama-boshi 〈なまぼし：生干し〉

nama-boshi-no 〈生干しの〉 half-dried.

namae 〈なまえ：名前〉 a name.

    namae-wa-shitte-iru（名前は知っている） know ((a person)) by name

nama-gusai 〈なまぐさい：生臭い〉 smelling of (raw) fish, fishy.

    nama-gusai nioi（生臭いにおい） a fishy smell

nama-hanka 〈なまはんか：生半可〉

nama-hanka-na 〈生半可な〉 shallow, superficial.

nama-hanka-na chishiki〈生半可な知識〉 shallow knowledge

nama-henji〈なまへんじ：生返事〉a vague answer, a reluctant answer.

nama-iki〈なまいき：生意気〉

Nama-iki iu-na!〈生意気言うな。〉 None of your cheek!

nama-iki-ni-mo～(suru)〈生意気にも～(する)〉 have the cheek ((to do))

nama-iki-na〈生意気な〉impudent, cheeky, saucy, conceited.

namake〈なまけ：怠け〉idleness, laziness, indolence.

namake-guse〈怠け癖〉 an indolent habit

namake-mono〈怠け者〉 a lazy fellow, an idler

namakeru〈怠ける〉be idle, be lazy, neglect.

benkyô o namakeru〈勉強を怠ける〉 neglect one's studies

namakete kurasu〈怠けて暮らす〉idle away one's time.

nama-ki〈なまき：生木〉a live tree, unseasoned wood, green wood.

nama-ki-o-saku〈生木を裂く〉force lovers to separate.

nama-kizu〈なまきず：生傷〉a fresh wound, a fresh bruise.

Kare-wa itsu-mo nama-kizu-ga-tae-nai.〈彼はいつも生傷が絶えない。〉 He has always some cuts or bruises on his body.

namako〈なまこ〉a trepang, a sea cucumber.

namakura〈なまくら〉a dull blade.

namakura-na〈なまくらな〉dull, blunt.

namamekashii〈なまめかしい〉charming, coquettish, voluptuous.

namanamashii〈なまなましい：生々しい〉fresh, vivid.

namanamashii kioku〈生々しい記憶〉 a fresh memory

nama-nie〈なまにえ：生煮え〉

nama-nie-no〈生煮えの〉half-boiled, underdone.

nama-nurui〈なまぬるい：生ぬるい〉lukewarm, tepid; too mild.

namari〈なまり：鉛〉lead.

namari-no, namari-no-yō-na, namari-iro-no or *namari-sei-no*〈鉛の，鉛のような，鉛色の，鉛製の〉leaden.

namari〈なまり〉an (a provincial) accent, a dialect.

namaru〈なまる〉speak with an accent, be corrupted.

nama-yake〈なまやけ：生焼け〉

nama-yake-no〈生焼けの〉half-roasted, underdone.

nama-zakana〈なまざかな：生魚〉raw fish, fresh fish.

namazu〈なまず〉a catfish.

nama-zume〈なまづめ：生づめ〉

nama-zume-o-hagasu〈生づめをはがす〉have a nail torn off.

nambâ-purêto〈ナンバープレート〉a license plate, a number plate.

nambaringu〈ナンバリング〉a numbering machine.

Nambei〈なんべい：南米〉South America.
 Nambei-no〈南米の〉South American.

namben〈なんべん：何遍〉*see.* nan-do, nan-kai.
 namben-mo〈何遍も〉*see.* nan-do-mo.

namboku〈なんぼく：南北〉north and south.

nambu〈なんぶ：南部〉the southern part, the South.
 nambu-no〈南部の〉southern.

nambyô〈なんびょう：難病〉an incurable disease.

namekuji〈なめくじ〉a slug.

nameraka〈なめらか：滑らか〉
 nameraka-na〈滑らかな〉smooth.
 nameraka-ni〈滑らかに〉smoothly.
   namaraka-ni-suru〈滑らかにする〉 make ((the surface)) smooth

nameru〈なめる〉lick, taste; despise.
   satô o nameru〈砂糖をなめる〉 taste sugar
   Ore-o sô nameru-na-yo.（おれをそうなめるなよ．） Don't despise me so.

nameshi-gawa〈なめしがわ：なめし革〉tanned skin, leather.
 namesu〈なめす〉tan, dress, taw.

nami〈なみ：波〉a wave, a ripple, a billow, a surge.
   Nami ga takai.（波が高い．） The waves are high. / The sea is rough.
   nami-ni-noru〈波に乗る〉 ride on (the crest of) the waves
   nami-no-ma-ni-ma-ni〈波のまにまに〉 at the mercy of the waves

nami〈なみ：並〉the average.
 nami-no〈並の〉average, common, ordinary.
   nami-no ningen〈並の人間〉 an average person
 nami-hazureta〈並外れた〉out of the common, uncommon, above the average.
 nami-taitei-no-koto-dewa-nai〈並大抵の事ではない〉be no easy task.

namida〈なみだ：涙〉a tear.
   Namida ga kare-no hoo o tsutawatta.（涙が彼のほおを伝わった.）
     Tears ran down his cheeks.
   namida o nagasu〈涙を流す〉 shed tears
   namida o fuku〈涙をふく〉 wipe one's tears away
   namida o osaeru〈涙を抑える〉 keep back one's tears

namida-gumu 〈涙ぐむ〉 one's eyes dim with tears, be moved to tears

namida-moroi 〈涙もろい〉 be easily moved to tears

me-ni namida-o-ukabete 〈目に涙を浮かべて〉 with tears in one's eyes

namida-nagara-ni 〈涙ながらに〉 in tears

nami-ki 〈なみき：並木〉 a row of trees.

nami-ki-michi 〈並木道〉 a tree-lined street, an avenue

naminami-naranu 〈なみなみならぬ：並々ならぬ〉 uncommon, extraordinary, great.

naminami-to 〈なみなみと〉 to the brim, to the full.

sakazuki ni naminami-to sake-o-tsugu 〈杯になみなみと酒をつぐ〉 fill a glass to the brim with *sake*

nami-uchi-giwa 〈なみうちぎわ：波うち際〉 the beach.

nammin 〈なんみん：難民〉 refugees, displaced persons.

nammon(dai) 〈なんもん(だい)：難問(題)〉 a difficult problem, a knotty problem.

nampa 〈なんぱ：難破〉

nampa-sen 〈難破船〉 a wrecked ship

nampa-suru 〈難破する〉 be shipwrecked, be wrecked.

nampô 〈なんぼう：南方〉 the south.

nampô-ni 〈南方に〉 to the south ((of))

nampô-no 〈南方の〉 south, southern.

Nampyô-yô 〈なんぴょうよう：南氷洋〉 the Antarctic Ocean.

nan- 〈なん-：何-〉

nan-byaku-to-iu 〈何百という〉 hundreds ((of))

nan-zen-to-iu 〈何千という〉 thousands ((of))

nana-korobi-ya-oki 〈ななころびやおき：七転び八起き〉

Jinsei wa nana-korobi-ya-oki-da. 〈人生は七転び八起きだ.〉 Life is full of ups and downs.

nana-kusa 〈ななくさ：七草〉 the seven spring herbs; the seven autumn flowers.

naname 〈ななめ：斜め〉

naname-no 〈斜めの〉 slanting, oblique, skew.

naname-ni 〈斜めに〉 aslant, obliquely, askew.

naname-ni-katamuku or *naname-ni-naru* 〈斜めに傾く, 斜めになる〉 slant, incline.

nanatsu-dôgu 〈ななつどうぐ：七つ道具〉 one's paraphernalia.

nan-chakuriku 〈なんちゃくりく：軟着陸〉 soft landing.

nan-chakuriku-suru〈軟着陸する〉soft-land ((on)).

nanchô〈なんちょう：難聴〉hardness of hearing.

nan-da〈なんだ：何だ〉what!, why!

Nan-da! Kimi-ka.（何だ．君か．）What! Is that you?

Ame-kurai-nan-da.（雨くらい何だ．）I don't care two straws about the rainy weather.

Nan-da-to.（何だと．）What? / Say it again.

nan-da-ka〈なんだか：何だか〉somewhat, somehow.

Nan-da-ka ki-ni-naru.（何だか気になる．）Somehow I feel uneasy.

nan-demo〈なんでも：何でも〉any, anything, whatever, everything.

Omoshiroi-hon-nara-nan-demo-ii.（おもしろい本なら何でもいい．）Any book will do, if it is interesting.

nan-demo-suki-na-mono（何でも好きな物）whatever one likes

nan-demo-nai〈なんでもない：何でもない〉nothing, nothing serious.

Jû-man-en-kurai-no-kane wa kare-ni-totte nan-demo-nai.（十万円くらいの金は彼にとって何でもない．）One hundred thousand yen is nothing to him.

"Dô-ka-shita-no-ka?" "Nan-demo-nai."（"どうかしたのか．""何でもない．"）"What's the matter with you?" "Nothing serious."

nan-do〈なんど：何度〉how many degrees, what degrees; how many times, how often(*see*. nan-kai).

Ondo-kei wa nan-do-desu-ka?（温度計は何度ですか．）What degrees does the thermometer read?

Kono shô o nan-do-yomimashita-ka?（この章を何度読みましたか．）How many times have you read this chapter?

nan-do-mo〈なんども：何度も〉many times, often, over and over (again).

Watashi-wa nan-do-mo Nikkô-e itta-koto-ga-aru（私は何度も日光へ行ったことがある．）I have been to Nikko many times.

nan-gatsu〈なんがつ：何月〉what month.

Ima nan-gatsu-desu-ka?（今何月ですか．）What month is it now?

nani〈なに：何〉what?; what!, why!

Kore-wa nani-desu-ka?（これは何ですか．）What is this?

Nani-o sagashiteiru-no-desu-ka?（何を捜しているのですか．）What are you looking for?

Nani! Ki-ni-suru-na.（何．気にするな．）Why! Never mind!

nan•i〈なんい：南緯〉the south latitude.

nani-bun〈なにぶん：何分〉

Nani-bun-tomo-yoroshiku-o-negai-shimasu.（何分ともよろしくお願いします。）I leave it entirely to your kind consideration.

nanige-naku〈なにげなく：何気なく〉unintentionally, unconcernedly, casually, inadvertently.

nani-goto〈なにごと：何事〉what, whatever.

Nani-goto-desu-ka?（何事ですか。）What's the matter?

nani-goto-ga-okite-mo（何事が起きても）whatever may happen

nani-goto-mo-naku（何事もなく）without any accident, peacefully

nani-ka〈なにか：何か〉something, anything.

Nani-ka nomi-mono ga hoshii.（何か飲み物がほしい。）I want something to drink.

Kono-koto-ni-tsuite nani-ka shitte-imasu-ka?（この事について何か知っていますか。）Do you know anything about this?

nani-ka-shira〈何かしら〉see. nan-da-ka.

Nani-kuso!〈なにくそ。：何くそ。〉Damn it!

nani-kuwanu-kao〈なにくわぬかお：何食わぬ顔〉

nani-kuwanu-kao-o-shite〈何食わぬ顔をして〉affecting ignorance, as if nothing had happened.

nani-mo～nai〈なにも～ない：何も～ない〉not...anything, nothing.

Sono-koto-ni-tsuite-wa kanojo-wa nani-mo shira-nai.（その事については彼女は何も知らない。）She knows nothing about it.

nani-shiro〈なにしろ：何しろ〉anyhow, at any rate, at all events, for, as you know.

Nani-shiro fu-keiki-desu-kara.（何しろ不景気ですから。）Times are bad, you know.

nani-wa-sate-oki〈なにはさておき：何はさておき〉above all, first of all, before everything else.

nani-wa-tomo-are〈なにはともあれ：何はともあれ〉in any case, at any rate, at all events.

Nani-wa-tomo-are tabe-mono-ga-hitsuyô-da.（何はともあれ食べ物が必要だ。）At all events we need something to eat.

nani-yori〈なにより：何より〉

O-genki-de nani-yori-desu.（お元気で何よりです。）I am very glad that you are well.

nani-yori-no〈何よりの〉most, best.

nani-yori-no shina（何よりの品）a most beautiful present

nani-yori-mo〈何よりも〉above all, first of all, before everything, more than anything else.

nanjaku 〈なんじゃく：軟弱〉

nanjaku-gaikō（軟弱外交） weak-kneed diplomacy

nanjaku-na〈軟弱な〉weak, feeble, weak-kneed.

nan-ji 〈なんじ：何時〉what time, when.

Nan-ji-desu-ka?（何時ですか.） What time is it?

nan-jikan 〈なんじかん：何時間〉how many hours, how long.

nan-jikan-mo〈何時間も〉for hours.

nanka 〈なんか：南下〉

nanka-suru〈南下する〉go down south.

nanka 〈なんか：軟化〉softening.

nanka-suru or *nanka-saseru*〈軟化する，軟化させる〉soften.

taido o nanka-saseru（態度を軟化させる） soften one's attitude

-nanka 〈-なんか〉

O-mae-nanka-no-deru-maku-dewa-nai.（お前なんかの出る幕ではない.） That's none of your business.

nan-ka-getsu 〈なんかげつ：何か月〉how many months, how long.

nan-ka-getsu-mo〈何か月も〉for (many) months.

nan-kai 〈なんかい：何回〉how many times, how often.

Furansu-e-wa nan-kai ikare-mashita-ka?（フランスへは何回行かれましたか.） How many times have you been to France?

nankai 〈なんかい：難解〉

nankai-na〈難解な〉difficult to understand.

nankan 〈なんかん：難関〉a difficulty, a barrier, an obstacle.

nankan o toppa-suru（難関を突破する） tide over a difficulty

nankin 〈なんきん：軟禁〉

nankin-suru〈軟禁する〉confine ((a person)) informally ((in)).

jitaku-ni nankin-sareru（自宅に軟禁される） be confined in one's own house

nankin-mushi 〈なんきんむし：なんきん虫〉a bedbug.

nankō 〈なんこう：難航〉

nankō-shiteiru〈難航している〉be having a hard going.

nankō 〈なんこう：軟こう〉(an) ointment, salve.

nankō o nuru（軟こうを塗る） apply ointment ((to))

nankotsu 〈なんこつ：軟骨〉cartilage.

nan-kuse 〈なんくせ：難癖〉

nan-kuse-o-tsukeru〈難癖を付ける〉criticize, find fault ((with)).

dare-ka-ni nani-ka-to nan-kuse-o-tsukeru（だれかに何かと難癖を付ける） criticize someone for one thing or another

Nankyoku〈なんきょく：南極〉the South Pole.

　Nankyoku-kai（南極海） the Antarctic Ocean

　Nankyoku-tairiku（南極大陸） the Antarctic Continent

nankyoku〈なんきょく：難局〉a difficult situation, a crisis.

　nankyoku-ni-ataru（難局に当たる） deal with a difficult situation, face a difficulty

nankyû〈なんきゅう：軟球〉a soft ball.

nan-naku〈なんなく：難無く〉without difficulty, easily.

nan-nan-sei〈なんなんせい：南南西〉south-southwest (SSW).

nan-nan-tô〈なんなんとう：南南東〉south-southeast (SSE).

nan-nara〈なんなら：何なら〉if you please, if possible, if necessary, if convenient.

　Nan-nara asu-no-gogo mata kite-mimashô.（何なら明日の午後また来てみましょう.） I'll call on you again tomorrow afternoon, if necessary.

nan-nen〈なんねん：何年〉how many years, how long.

nan-nichi〈なんにち：何日〉what day (of the month); how many days, how long.

　Kyô-wa nan-nichi-desu-ka?（今日は何日ですか.） What day of the month is it today?

　nan-nichi-demo（何日でも） for any number of days

nan-nimo〈なんにも：何にも〉

　nan-nimo-nara-nai（何にもならない） come to nothing, be of no avail.

　Anna-ni-kurô-shita-noni-nan-nimo-nara-nakatta.（あんなに苦労したのに何にもならなかった.） All our efforts were of no avail.

nan-nin〈なんにん：何人〉how many people.

nan-no〈なんの：何の〉

　Nan-no-tame-ni sonna koto o shiteiru-no-da?（何のためにそんな事をしているのだ.） What are you doing such a thing for?

　nan-no-kankei-mo-nai（何の関係もない） have nothing to do ((with))

　nan-no-yaku-ni-mo-tata-nai（何の役にも立たない） be good for nothing

　nan-no-ki-nashi-ni（何の気なしに） unintentionally, quite accidentally

Nan-Ô〈なんおう：南欧〉Southern Europe.

na-noru〈なのる：名乗る〉give one's name ((as)), introduce oneself ((as)).

nan-ra〈なんら：何ら〉

　nan-ra-ka-no（何らかの） some, any.

　nan-ra-ka-no riyû-de（何らかの理由で） for some reason (or other)

nan-sai〈なんさい：何歳〉how old.

Nan-sai-desu-ka?（何歳ですか．）How old are you?

nan-sei〈なんせい：南西〉southwest.

nan-sei-no〈南西の〉southwestern.

nanshiki〈なんしき：軟式〉

nanshiki-tenisu（軟式テニス）soft-ball tennis

nanshiki-yakyû（軟式野球）rubber-ball baseball

nansho〈なんしょ：難所〉a dangerous place.

saidai-no nansho（最大の難所）the most difficult stage ((of))

nanshoku〈なんしょく：難色〉

nanshoku o shimesu〈難色を示す〉show disapproval ((of)).

nansui〈なんすい：軟水〉soft water.

nantai-dôbutsu〈なんたいどうぶつ：軟体動物〉a mollusk.

nantan〈なんたん：南端〉

nantan-ni〈南端に〉in the southern end(*or* extremity) ((of)).

nanten〈なんてん：難点〉a difficult point; a fault, weakness.

nanten〈なんてん：南天〉a nandin(a).

nan-to〈なんと：何と〉what, how.

'Subarashii' o Eigo-de-nan-to-iimasu-ka?（'素晴らしい'を英語で何と言いますか．）What is the English for 'subarashii'?

Kono ki o Furansu-go-de nan-to-iimasu-ka?（この木をフランス語で何と言いますか．）What do you call this tree in French?

Nan-to ii o-tenki-deshô!（何といいお天気でしょう．）What a beautiful day it is!

Kono hana wa nan-to utsukushii-n-darô!（この花は何と美しいんだろう．）How beautiful this flower is!

nan-tô〈なんとう：南東〉southeast.

nan-tô-no〈南東の〉southeastern.

nan-toka〈なんとか：何とか〉somehow, anyhow.

nan-toka yatte-iku（何とかやっていく）get along somehow

nan-toka-shite〈何とかして〉somehow or other, by some means or other.

Nan-toka-shite sore-o te-ni-ire-tai.（何とかしてそれを手に入れたい．）I want to get it by some means or other.

nan-tomo〈なんとも：何とも〉

Isha wa haha-wa-nan-tomo-nai-to-itta.（医者は母は何ともないと言った．）The doctor said that there was nothing the matter with my mother.

Omoshiroku-mo-nan-tomo-nai.（面白くも何ともない．）I don't feel

any interest at all in it.

Nan-tomo o-rei-no-môshi-age-yô-ga-ari-masen.〔何ともお礼の申し上げようがありません.〕 I can never thank you enough.

Nan-tomo môshi-wake-gozai-masen.〔何とも申し訳ございません.〕 I have no word of excuse for it.

Nan-tomo-ie-nai-utsukushisa-da.〔何とも言えない美しさだ.〕 It is indescribably beautiful.

nanto-naku〈なんとなく：何となく〉*see.* nan-da-ka.

Nan·yô〈なんよう：南洋〉the South Seas.

Nan·yô-shotô〔南洋諸島〕 the South Sea Islands

nan-yôbi〈なんようび：何曜日〉what day (of the week).

Kyô-wa nan-yôbi-desu-ka?〔今日は何曜日ですか.〕 What day of the week is it today?

nanzan〈なんざん：難産〉difficult delivery, hard labor.

Shin-naikaku wa nakanaka-no-nanzan-datta.〔新内閣はなかなかの難産だった.〕 The new Cabinet was formed after much difficulty.

nao〈なお〉(still) more, still.

Kono-hô ga nao-ii.〔この方がなおいい.〕 This is still better.

nao-warui-koto-ni-wa〔なお悪いことには〕 to make matters worse, and what is worse

Kare-wa hachi-jû-da-ga, nao kakushaku-to-shite-iru.〔彼は八十だが, なおかくしゃくとしている.〕 He is eighty and still he is hale and hearty.

nao-mata〈なおまた：なお又〉besides, further, in addition to ((it)).

naoru〈なおる：直(治)る〉be mended, be repaired, be fixed; be corrected; get well, get over, be restored, be cured.

Machigai wa mina naotte-iru.〔間違いは皆直っている.〕 The mistakes are all corrected.

kaze-ga-naoru〔風邪が治る〕 get over one's cold

byôki-ga-naoru〔病気が治る〕 be cured of a disease

naoshi〈なおし：直し〉

naoshi-ni-dasu〈直しに出す〉send ((a watch to a watchmaker's)) to be repaired.

naoshi-ga-kiku〈直しが利く〉be repairable.

naoshi-ga-kika-nai〔直しが利かない〕 be unrepairable

naosu〈なおす：直(治)す〉mend, repair, fix; correct; cure, heal; reform; do over again.

kikai o naosu〔機械を直す〕 repair a machine

ayamari o naosu（誤りを直す）　correct an error

byōki o naosu（病気を治す）　cure a disease

warui kuse-o-naosu（悪い癖を直す）　get over a bad habit, cure oneself of a bad habit

tegami o kaki-naosu（手紙を書き直す）　write a letter all over again

naozari〈なおざり〉

naozari-ni-suru〈なおざりにする〉neglect, make light ((of)).

nara〈なら〉a Japanese oak.

-nara(-ba)〈－なら（ば）〉if, in case, supposing, provided, on condition that... .

hitsuyō-nara（必要なら）　if necessary

watashi-ga anata-nara（私があなたなら）　if I were you

naraberu〈ならべる：並べる〉put ((things)) side by side, arrange, display.

narabi〈ならび：並び〉a row, a side.

hito-narabi-no-ki（一並びの木）　a row of trees

kono-narabi-no kado-kara-ni-ken-me-no ie（この並びの角から二軒目の家）　the second house from the corner on this side

narabu〈ならぶ：並ぶ〉stand in a line, line up; equal, rival.

hito-to narande-suwaru（人と並んで座る）　sit side by side with a person

narabu-mono-ga-nai（並ぶ者がない）　have no equal, stand unrivaled

narai〈ならい：習い〉a habit, a custom, the way.

yo no narai（世の習い）　the way of the world

-nara-nai〈－ならない〉must, have to, should, ought to, must not, should not, ought not to.

Ie wa shūzen-shi-nakereba-nara-nai.（家は修繕しなければならない.）The house must be repaired.

Kimi-wa sugu ika-neba-nara-nai.（君はすぐ行かねばならない.）You have to go right now.

Oya-ni-wa shitagawa-nakereba-nara-nai.（親には従わなければならない.）One should obey one's parents.

Kyō gaishutsu-shitewa-nara-nai.（今日外出してはならない.）You must not go out today.

Hito no kage-guchi o itte-wa-nara-nai.（人の陰口を言ってはならない.）You should not speak ill of others in their absence.

narasu〈ならす：慣らす〉accustom.

samusa-ni jibun-no-karada o narasu（寒さに自分の体を慣らす）

accustom oneself to the cold

narasu 〈ならす〉 tame, domesticate, train.

    raion o narasu（ライオンをならす） tame a lion

    inu o narasu（犬をならす） train a dog

narasu 〈ならす〉 level, make even, roll.

    jimen o narasu（地面をならす） level the ground

narasu 〈ならす：鳴らす〉 ring, sound, blow, beat.

    beru o narasu（ベルを鳴らす） ring a bell

    keiteki o narasu（警笛を鳴らす） sound the horn

narau 〈ならう：習う〉 learn, practice, take lessons ((in)).

    Eigo o narau（英語を習う） learn English

    ongaku o narau（音楽を習う） practice music

narau 〈ならう：倣う〉 imitate, follow.

    senrei ni narau（先例に倣う） follow the precedent

～-ni-naratte〈～に倣って〉 in imitation of... , after... , after the example of... , in the manner of... , following the example of... .

narawashi〈ならわし：習わし〉 a custom, a practice.

narazu-mono〈ならずもの：ならず者〉 a rogue, a scoundrel, a rascal.

nare-ai〈なれあい：なれ合い〉 collusion, conspiracy.

    ～-to-nare-ai-de（～となれ合いで） in collusion with...

narekko〈なれっこ〉

narekko-ni-naru〈なれっこになる〉 *see.* nareru（慣れる）→ narete-iru.

narenareshii〈なれなれしい〉 familiar.

    narenareshii-taido-de（なれなれしい態度で） with too much familiarity

narenareshiku〈なれなれしく〉 familiarly, in a friendly manner.

    narenareshiku-suru（なれなれしくする） take liberties with

nareru〈なれる：慣れる〉 be used ((to)), be accustomed ((to)).

    Watashi-wa asa-hayaku-okiru-koto-ni-narete-iru.（私は朝早く起きることに慣れている。） I am accustomed to getting up early.

nareta〈慣れた〉 familiar, practiced, experienced.

    nareta-te-tsuki-de（慣れた手つきで） skillfully

nare-nai〈慣れない〉 unfamiliar, unaccustomed, unexperienced.

nareru〈なれる〉 become tame.

    Kono ko-inu wa watashi-ni yoku narete-iru.（この子犬は私によくなれている。） This puppy is quite tame with me.

nareta〈なれた〉 domesticated, tame.

    nareta neko（なれた猫） a tame cat

nare-nai 〈なれない〉 tameless, wild.

nari 〈なり：鳴り〉

nari-o-hisomeru 〈鳴りを潜める〉 be hushed, be silent, be inactive.

nari-agari(-mono) 〈なりあがり（もの）：成り上がり（者）〉 an upstart.

nari-agari-no 〈成り上がりの〉 upstart.

nari-furi 〈なりふり：なり振り〉 appearance.

nari-furi-kamawazu-ni 〈なり振り構わずに〉 regardless of one's appearance.

nari-hibiku 〈なりひびく：鳴り響く〉 ring (out), resound, echo.

nari-kawaru 〈なりかわる：成り代わる〉

〜-ni-nari-kawatte 〈〜に成り代わって〉 for... , in the place of... , on behalf of... .

nari-kin 〈なりきん：成金〉 a new rich, a *nouveau riche*.

nari-kin-ni-naru 〈成金になる〉 become rich suddenly.

nari-mono 〈なりもの：鳴り物〉

nari-mono-iri-de 〈鳴り物入りで〉 with a flourish of trumpets.

nari-sagaru 〈なりさがる：成り下がる〉 be reduced ((to)), fall low.

nari-sokonau 〈なりそこなう：成り損なう〉 miss becoming 〔a rich person〕.

nari-sumasu 〈なりすます：成り済ます〉 pose as, set up for.

nari-tatsu 〈なりたつ：成り立つ〉 consist ((of)), be made up ((of)), be realized, be concluded.

nari-yuki 〈なりゆき：成り行き〉 the course (of events), the turn (of events)

     koto o shizen-no nari-yuki-ni makasu（事を自然の成り行きに任す） leave a matter to take its own natural course

naru 〈なる：鳴る〉 ring, sound, strike, blow, roll.

     Denwa ga natteiru.（電話が鳴っている.） The telephone is ringing.

     Go-ji ga natta.（五時が鳴った.） The clock struck five.

     Kiteki ga tooku-de natta.（汽笛が遠くで鳴った.） The whistle blew in the distance.

     Kaminari ga naru.（雷が鳴る.） The thunder rolls.

     mimi-ga-naru（耳が鳴る） have a singing in one's ears

naru 〈なる：生る〉 bear, grow.

     Kono mikan-no-ki wa mi ga yoku naru.（このみかんの木は実がよくなる.） This orange tree bears well.

(-ni)-naru 〈（〜に）なる〉 get, grow, become, be, come, set in, come ((to do)), make, turn ((into *or* to)), change ((into)), end ((in)), turn out, come out, begin, consist ((of)), be made up ((of))

   samuku-naru〈寒くなる〉get cold

   dandan-takaku-naru〈だんだん高くなる〉 grow taller and taller

   himashi-ni atatakaku-naru〈日増しに暖かくなる〉become warmer and warmer day by day

   Watashi-wa shôrai isha-ni-nari-tai.〈私は将来医者になりたい.〉I wish to be a doctor in the future.

   Watashi-ga Nihon-ni-kite san-nen-ni-naru.〈私が日本に来て三年になる.〉It is three years since I came to Japan.

   seinen-ni-naru〈青年になる〉come of age

   Fuyu-ni-natta.〈冬になった.〉Winter has come.

   Tsuyu-ni-natta.〈梅雨になった.〉The rainy season has set in.

   suki-ni-naru〈好きになる〉come to like

   Ikura-ni-narimasu-ka?〈幾らになりますか.〉What do you make it?

   San-zen-en-ni-narimasu.〈三千円になります.〉It comes to three thousand yen.

   aoku-naru〈青くなる〉turn pale

   Kemushi ga chô-ni-natta.〈毛虫がちょうになった.〉A caterpillar has changed into the butterfly.

   uso-ni-naru〈うそになる〉turn out false

   Itsu-kara-sake-o-nomu-yô-ni-natta-no-desu-ka?〈いつから酒を飲むようになったのですか.〉When did you start drinking?

narubeku〈なるべく〉as...as possible, as...as one can.

   narubeku-hayaku〈なるべく速(早)く〉as quickly as possible, as soon as possible

naruhodo〈なるほど〉indeed, it is true, I see.

   Naruhodo〜da-ga, shikashi〜.〈なるほど〜だが, しかし〜.〉It is true ～, but... .

nasake〈なさけ：情け〉sympathy, pity, mercy, kindness, affection.

  nasake-bukai〈情け深い〉sympathetic, kindhearted, tenderhearted, merciful, affectionate.

  nasake-shirazu-no〈情け知らずの〉coldhearted, heartless, merciless.

nasake-nai〈なさけない：情けない〉pitiable, pitiful, heartless; shameful.

   nasake-nai koto o suru〈情けない事をする〉do a shameful thing

  nasakenaku-naru〈情けなくなる〉feel miserable.

nashi〈なし〉a pear.

-nashi-de〈-なしで：-無しで〉without.

   〜-nashi-de yatte-iku〈〜なしでやっていく〉do without

nashi-kuzushi〈なしくずし：なし崩し〉
　nashi-kuzushi-de-harau〈なし崩しで払う〉pay by installments.

nashi-togeru〈なしとげる：成し遂げる〉accomplish, achieve, carry out, succeed ((in)).
　　mokuteki o nashi-togeru（目的を成し遂げる）achieve one's purpose

nasu〈なす〉an eggplant, an egg apple.

nasu〈なす：為(成)す〉do; accomplish, achieve.

nasuri-〈なすり-〉
　　nasuri-ai（なすり合い）recrimination
　　tsumi o hito-ni nasuri-tsukeru（罪を人になすり付ける）put the blame on a person

natoriumu〈ナトリウム〉sodium.

natsu〈なつ：夏〉summer.
　　natsu-no-hajime-ni（夏の初めに）early in summer
　　natsu-no-sakari-ni（夏の盛りに）in midsummer
　　natsu-gare（夏枯れ）the summer slackness
　　natsu-yasumi（夏休み）the summer vacation
　　natsu-yase-suru（夏やせする）lose weight in summer

natsuin〈なついん：なつ印〉*see.* ôin.

natsukashii〈なつかしい：懐かしい〉dear, longed-for.
　　natsukashii furusato（懐かしい古里）one's dear old home
　natsukashigaru or *natsukashiku-omou*〈懐かしがる，懐かしく思う〉long ((for)).
　natsukashi-sô-ni〈懐かしそうに〉longingly, fondly.

natsuku〈なつく：懐く〉become attached ((to)); be tamed.
　　Kodomo-tachi wa watashi-ni-natsuite-iru.（子供たちは私に懐いている。）Children are attached to me.

natsume〈なつめ〉a jujube (tree).

natte-i-nai〈なっていない：成っていない〉be no good, be a failure, make no sense.

nattô〈なっとう：納豆〉fermented soybeans.

nattoku〈なっとく：納得〉understanding.
　nattoku-suru〈納得する〉listen to reason, be convinced ((of *or* that)), understand.
　nattoku-saseru〈納得させる〉make ((a person)) listen to reason, convince ((a person)) of.
　nattoku-zuku-de〈納得ずくで〉with mutual understanding.

nawa〈なわ：縄〉a rope, a cord.

nawa-bashigo（縄ばしご）a rope ladder

nawa-noren（縄のれん）a rope curtain

nawa-tobi（縄跳び）rope skipping

　nawa-tobi-o-suru（縄跳びをする）skip rope

nawa-o-kakeru〈縄を掛ける〉rope, bind (with a rope).

nawa-o-toku〈縄を解く〉unbind, set free.

nawa-bari〈なわばり：縄張〉one's sphere of influence.

nawa-bari-o-arasu（縄張を荒らす）trespass on ((a person's)) territory

nawa-bari-arasoi（縄張争い）rivalry for spheres of influence, a jurisdictional dispute

naya〈なや：納屋〉a shed, a barn.

nayami〈なやみ：悩み〉worry, trouble, distress, sufferings, pain.

nayami no tane（悩みの種）the source of trouble

nayami-ga-aru（悩みがある）have worries, be in trouble

nayamasu〈悩ます〉annoy, worry, trouble, afflict.

sôon-ni nayamasareru（騒音に悩まされる）be annoyed by the noises

bukka-daka-ni-nayamasareru（物価高に悩まされる）suffer from high prices

nayamu〈悩む〉be annoyed ((at, by *or* with)), be worried ((about)), be troubled ((with)), suffer ((from)).

na-zashi〈なざし：名指し〉nomination.

na-zashi-de yobu〈名指しで呼ぶ〉call by name.

naze〈なぜ〉why, for what reason.

Watashi-wa naze-ka-shira-nai.（私はなぜか知らない。）I don't know why.

naze-nara(-ba) or *naze-ka-to-ieba*（なぜなら（ば）、なぜかといえば）for, because.

Watashi-wa-ika-nai, naze-nara iki-taku-nai-kara.（私は行かない、なぜなら行きたくないから。）I don't go, because I don't want to.

nazo〈なぞ〉a riddle, a puzzle, a mystery; a hint.

nazo o toku（なぞを解く）solve a riddle, answer a puzzle

nazo o kakeru（なぞをかける）drop a hint

nazoru〈なぞる〉trace, follow.

nazuke-oya〈なづけおや：名付け親〉a godparent.

na-zukeru〈なづける：名付ける〉name, call.

ne〈ね：値〉a price, a cost.

Ne ga agaru.（値が上がる。）The price rises.

Ne ga sagaru.（値が下がる。）The price falls.

ne o ageru（値を上げる）　raise the price

ne o sageru（値を下げる）　reduce the price

ne-o-tsukeru（値を付ける）　price; name a price ((for))

ii ne-de ureru（いい値で売れる）　sell at a good price

ne-no-takai〈値の高い〉expensive.

ne-no-yasui（値の安い）　low-priced, moderate in price, cheap

ne〈ね：根〉a root; nature; the origin, the source.

ne ga tsuku（根が付く）　take root

ne-ga-shôjiki-na（根が正直な）　good at heart

ne-mo-ha-mo-nai uwasa（根も葉もないうわさ）　a groundless rumor

ne〈ね：音〉(a) sound, (a) tone, (a) note, (a) ring.

mushi no ne（虫の音）　the chirping of insects

ne-o-ageru〈音を上げる〉be done up.

ne or **nê**〈ね、ねえ〉I say, say, look here, listen, dear; you know, you see; isn't it? / don't you?

ne-agari〈ねあがり：値上がり〉a rise in price.

ne-agari-keikô（値上がり傾向）　a rising tendency in price

ne-agari-suru〈値上がりする〉rise in price.

ne-age〈ねあげ：値上げ〉a rise in price, a raise in wages.

chingin-no-ne-age-o-yôkyû-suru（賃金の値上げを要求する）　ask for higher wages

ne-age-suru〈値上げする〉raise the price(the fare, the wages *or* the rates).

ne-ase〈ねあせ：寝汗〉night sweat.

ne-ase-o-kaku〈寝汗をかく〉have night sweat, sweat at night.

nebaneba〈ねばねば〉

nebaneba-suru〈ねばねばする〉(be) sticky, (be) clammy, (be) gummy.

nebari〈ねばり：粘り〉stickiness; tenacity, perseverance.

nebari-zuyoi〈粘り強い〉tenacious, persevering.

nebaru〈粘る〉be sticky; persevere, stick ((to)); stay long.

ne-bie〈ねびえ：寝冷え〉

ne-bie-suru〈寝冷えする〉catch cold while sleeping.

ne-biki〈ねびき：値引き〉(a) reduction in price, (a) discount.

ne-biki-suru〈値引きする〉reduce the price, discount.

ne-bô〈ねぼう：寝坊〉late rising; a late riser.

ne-bô-suru〈寝坊する〉get up late, oversleep (oneself).

ne-boke〈ねぼけ：寝ぼけ〉

ne-boke-manako（寝ぼけ眼）　sleepy eyes, a drowsy look

ne-bokeru 〈寝ぼける〉 be half asleep.

ne-bukai 〈ねぶかい：根深い〉 deep-rooted; incurable.

ne-bumi 〈ねぶみ：値踏み〉 appraisal, (a) valuation, estimation.

ne-bumi-suru 〈値踏みする〉 appraise, value, estimate.

nêburu 〈ネーブル〉 a navel orange.

ne-busoku 〈ねぶそく：寝不足〉 want of sleep.

　　ne-busoku-de 〈寝不足で〉　from want of sleep

nechanecha 〈ねちゃねちゃ〉

nechanecha-suru 〈ねちゃねちゃする〉 (be) gummy, (be) greasy, (be) slimy, (be) sticky.

ne-chigaeru 〈ねちがえる：寝違える〉 wrick(*or* strain)〔one's neck *or* arm〕in one's sleep.

nedan 〈ねだん：値段〉 *see.* ne 〈値〉.

nedaru 〈ねだる〉 ask ((a person)) importunately for, tease.

ne-doko 〈ねどこ：寝床〉 a bed.

　　ne-doko-de tabako-o-suu 〈寝床でたばこを吸う〉　smoke in bed

　　ne-doko-ni-hairu 〈寝床に入る〉　go to bed

　　ne-doko-o-hanareru 〈寝床を離れる〉　get out of bed

nega 〈ネガ〉 a negative.

ne-gaeri 〈ねがえり：寝返り〉

ne-gaeri-suru 〈寝返りする〉 toss about(*or* roll over) in bed.

ne-gaeru 〈ねがえる：寝返る〉 betray, go over (to the other party).

negai 〈ねがい：願い〉 a wish, a desire, a request, (a) favor.

　　hi-goro-no negai 〈日ごろの願い〉　one's cherished desire

　　negai o kiki-todokeru 〈願いを聞き届ける〉　grant a request

　　O-negai ga aru-no-desu-ga. 〈お願いがあるのですが.〉　May I ask a favor of you?

ne-gao 〈ねがお：寝顔〉 one's sleeping face.

Negattari-kanattari. 〈ねがったりかなったり.：願ったりかなったり.〉 I can wish for nothing better.

negau 〈ねがう：願う〉 wish, desire, hope, ask ((for)), beg, pray.

　　heiwa-o-negau 〈平和を願う〉　wish for peace

　　Ori-kaeshi go-henji-nagaimasu. 〈折り返し御返事願います.〉　I ask you to answer my letter by return mail.

　　Tanaka-san o o-negai-shimasu. 〈田中さんをお願いします.〉　I want Mr. Tanaka on the phone, please.

negawaku-wa 〈ねがわくは：願わくは〉 I pray, I hope, I wish ((I could)).

negi 〈ねぎ〉 a Welsh onion.

negirau 〈ねぎらう〉

 rô-o-negirau 〈労をねぎらう〉thank ((a person)) for his trouble, reward ((a person)) for his services.

ne-giru 〈ねぎる：値切る〉beat down the price, haggle.

 dekiru-dake-negiru （できるだけ値切る） drive the hardest bargain

ne-goto 〈ねごと：寝言〉

 ne-goto-o-iu 〈寝言を言う〉talk in one's sleep.

ne-gurushii 〈ねぐるしい：寝苦しい〉have a bad sleep.

 ne-gurushii-ichi-ya-o-sugosu 〈寝苦しい一夜を過ごす〉 pass a wakeful night

nehan 〈ねはん〉nirvana.

nehori-hahori 〈ねほりはほり：根掘り葉掘り〉

 nehori-hahori-kiku 〈根掘り葉掘り聞く〉ask ((a person)) about ((a matter)) to the minutest details.

ne-iro 〈ねいろ：音色〉a tone quality.

ne-iru 〈ねいる：寝入る〉drop off to sleep, fall asleep.

 naki-nagara-ne-iru （泣きながら寝入る） sob itself to sleep

neji 〈ねじ〉a screw, a (stop-)cock; a spring.

 neji o shimeru （ねじを締める） drive a screw

 neji o yurumeru （ねじを緩める） loosen a screw

 neji-mawashi （ねじ回し） a screwdriver

 neji-o-maku 〈ねじを巻く〉wind 〔a watch〕.

neji- 〈ねじ-〉

 neji-akeru （ねじ開ける） wrench open

 neji-fuseru （ねじ伏せる） get ((a person)) under

 neji-komu （ねじ込む） thrust ((into)), demand an explanation ((of a person))

 neji-mageru （ねじ曲げる） bend ((a thing)) by twisting

nejireru 〈ねじれる〉be twisted, be distorted; become perverse, get crooked.

 nejireta 〈ねじれた〉twisted, distorted; perverse, crooked, warped.

ne-jiro 〈ねじろ：根城〉a base of operations.

 ~-o-nejiro-to-shite 〈～を根城として〉with...as the base of operations.

nejiru 〈ねじる〉twist, wrench, distort.

nekasu 〈ねかす：寝かす〉put ((a child)) to sleep, lay down; let ((goods)) lie idle.

nekki 〈ねっき：熱気〉(a blast of) hot air, heat, fevered air.

nekko 〈ねっこ：根っ子〉a root, a stump.

　　　　nekko-kara-hiki-nuku〈根っ子から引き抜く〉pull up ((a plant)) by the roots

nekkyō〈ねっきょう：熱狂〉enthusiasm, excitement.

　nekkyō-suru〈熱狂する〉be wildly excited ((at, by *or* over)).

　nekkyō-teki(-na)〈熱狂的(な)〉enthusiastic, wild.

　nekkyō-shite〈熱狂して〉with feverish excitement.

neko〈ねこ：猫〉a cat.

　　　　ko-neko（子猫）a kitten

　　　　neko-mo-shakushi-mo（猫もしゃくしも）all the world and his wife, everybody

　　　　neko-ni-ko-ban（猫に小判）caviare to the general

　　　　neko-no-me-no-yō-ni-kawaru（猫の目のように変わる）make chameleonic changes

　　　　neko-o-kaburu（猫をかぶる）assume an air of innocence, look as if butter would not melt in one's mouth

　　　　neko-baba-o-kimeru（猫ばばを決める）pocket, embezzle

　　　　neko-jita-de-aru（猫舌である）be unable to eat hot food

　　　　neko-nade-goe（猫なで声）an insinuating voice

　　　　neko-irazu（猫入らず）rat poison

ne-komi〈ねこみ：寝込み〉

　ne-komi-o-osou（寝込みを襲う）surprize ((a person)) in sleep.

ne-komu〈ねこむ：寝込む〉be laid up ((with)), be sick in bed.

　　　　kaze-de ne-komu（風邪で寝込む）be laid up with a cold

ne-korobu〈ねころぶ：寝転ぶ〉lie down, throw oneself down.

　　　　shibafu-no-ue-ni ne-korobu（芝生の上に寝転ぶ）throw oneself down on the lawn

ne-kosogi〈ねこそぎ：根こそぎ〉all, completely, entirely.

　ne-kosogi-ni-suru〈根こそぎにする〉root up, uproot.

nekutai〈ネクタイ〉a necktie, a bow.

ne-maki〈ねまき：寝巻き〉nightclothes, a nightgown, a nightdress.

nembutsu〈ねんぶつ：念仏〉a Buddhist prayer.

　　　　Uma-no-mimi-ni-nembutsu.（馬の耳に念仏。）It is like water off a duck's back.

ne-mimi-ni-mizu〈ねみみにみず：寝耳に水〉a great surprise, a bolt from the blue.

nemmaku〈ねんまく：粘膜〉a mucous membrane.

nemmatsu〈ねんまつ：年末〉the end of the year, the year-end.

　　　　nemmatsu-chōsei（年末調整）year-end adjustment

ne-moto 〈ねもと：根元〉 the root, the base.

 ki o ne-moto-kara kiru（木を根元から切る）cut down a tree at the root

nempai 〈ねんぱい：年配〉 age, years.

 go-jū-nempai no hito（五十年配の人）a person of about fifty

nempai-no 〈年配の〉 elderly.

 nempai-no hito（年配の人）an elderly person

nempō 〈ねんぽう：年俸〉 an annual salary.

nempō 〈ねんぼう：年報〉 an annual report.

nempyô 〈ねんぴょう：年表〉 a chronological table.

nêmu-baryû 〈ネームバリュー〉

 nêmu-baryû-no-aru sakka（ネームバリューのある作家）a name novelist

nemui 〈ねむい：眠い〉 be sleepy, feel sleepy.

nemuku-naru 〈眠くなる〉 become sleepy.

nemu-ke 〈ねむけ：眠気〉

 nemu-ke-ga-sasu（眠気がさす）become sleepy

 nemu-ke-zamashi-ni（眠気覚ましに）to keep oneself awake

nemuri 〈ねむり：眠り〉 (a) sleep, (a) slumber.

 asai nemuri（浅い眠り）a light sleep

 fukai nemuri（深い眠り）a deep sleep

 nemuri-ga-asai（眠りが浅い）have a poor sleep

 nemuri-gusuri（眠り薬）a sleeping pill

nemuru 〈ねむる：眠る〉 sleep.

 gussuri nemuru（ぐっすり眠る）sleep soundly

 yoku nemuru（よく眠る）sleep well

 yoku-nemutte-iru（よく眠っている）be fast asleep

nemure-nai 〈眠れない〉 cannot get to sleep, sleep badly, be sleepless.

nemu-sô 〈ねむそう：眠そう〉

nemu-sô-na 〈眠そうな〉 sleepy, drowsy.

nemu-sô-ni 〈眠そうに〉 sleepily, drowsily.

nen 〈ねん：年〉 a year.

 nen-ni-ichi-do（年に一度）once a year

 Shôwa-go-jû-hachi-nen（昭和五十八年）the 58th year of Showa

 nen-jû（年中）all the year round

  nenjû-gyôji（年中行事）annual events

 nen-nen（年々）year by year, every year

 nen-nai-ni（年内に）within the year, before the end of the year

nen 〈ねん：念〉 a sense, a feeling; attention, care, caution.

    kansha no nen (感謝の念) a sense of gratitude

    nen-o-ireru (念を入れる) pay attention ((to)), be careful ((in))

        Nen-niwa-nen-o-ire-nasai. (念には念を入れなさい。) You cannot be too careful.

    nen-o-irete (念を入れて) attentively, carefully, with care

    nen-o-osu (念を押す) tell emphatically, call ((a person's)) special attention ((to)), make sure ((of or that))

    nen-no-tame (念のため) to make sure ((of it)), by way of precaution

nenchaku 〈ねんちゃく：粘着〉 adhesion, viscosity.

    nenchaku-ryoku (粘着力) adhesive power, viscosity

    nenchaku-ryoku-no-aru or *nenchaku-sei-no-aru* 〈粘着力のある，粘着性のある〉 adhesive, viscous, sticky.

nenchô-sha 〈ねんちょうしゃ：年長者〉 a senior, an elder.

nendai 〈ねんだい：年代〉 an age, a period.

    sen-kyû-hyaku-hachi-jû-nendai-ni (1980年代に) in the nineteen-eighties

    nendai-jun-ni 〈年代順に〉 chronologically.

nendo 〈ねんど：粘土〉 clay.

    nendo-zaiku (粘土細工) clay work

    nendo-no 〈粘土の〉 clay.

    nendo-no-yô-na or *nendo-shitsu-no* 〈粘土のような，粘土質の〉 clayey.

nendo 〈ねんど：年度〉 a year, a fiscal year.

    jigyô-nendo (事業年度) a business year

    nendo-gawari-ni (年度替わりに) at the change of the fiscal year

nen·eki 〈ねんえき：粘液〉 mucus.

    nen·eki-shitsu-no 〈粘液質の〉 mucous, phlegmatic.

nenga 〈ねんが：年賀〉 the New Year's greetings.

    nenga-jô (年賀状) a New Year's card

nengaku 〈ねんがく：年額〉 an annual sum.

nengan 〈ねんがん：念願〉 one's heart's desire, one's dearest wish.

    naga-nen-no nengan (長年の念願) one's long-cherished desire

nen-gappi 〈ねんがっぴ：年月日〉 a date.

nengen 〈ねんげん：年限〉 a term, a period.

    Nengen ga kireta. (年限が切れた。) The term has expired.

nengetsu 〈ねんげつ：年月〉 years (and months).

    nagai nengetsu o yôsuru (長い年月を要する) take years

nengô 〈ねんごう：年号〉 the name of an era.

nengoro-ni 〈ねんごろ：懇ろ〉
itai o nengoro-ni hōmuru 〈遺体を懇ろに葬る〉bury ((a person's)) body with due ceremony.

nengu 〈ねんぐ：年貢〉
Aitsu-mo-nengu-no-osame-doki-da. 〈あいつも年貢の納め時だ。〉It's the time for him to reap the harvest of crimes.

nen-iri 〈ねんいり：念入り〉
nen-iri-na 〈念入りな〉careful, scrupulous, elaborate.
nen-iri-ni 〈念入りに〉carefully, scrupulously, elaborately.

nenkan 〈ねんかん：年鑑〉a yearbook, an almanac.

nenkan 〈ねんかん：年間〉
Nenkan-yushutsu-sōgaku wa hyaku-oku-doru-ni-tassuru. 〈年間輸出総額は百億ドルに達する。〉The total export amounts to ten billion dollars a year.
nenkan-keikaku 〈年間計画〉a program for the year
san-nenkan-ni 〈三年間に〉in three years

nenki 〈ねんき：年季〉experience, training.
nenki-no-haitta 〈年季の入った〉experienced, trained, practiced.

nenkin 〈ねんきん：年金〉an annuity, a pension.
nenkin-de kurasu 〈年金で暮らす〉live on a pension
rōrei-nenkin 〈老齢年金〉an old-age pension

nenkō-joretsu 〈ねんこうじょれつ：年功序列〉a seniority system.

nenrai 〈ねんらい：年来〉for years, these years.
nenrai-no kibō 〈年来の希望〉one's long-cherished desire
san-jū-nenrai-no oo-yuki 〈三十年来の大雪〉the heaviest snowfall we have had in 30 years

nenrei 〈ねんれい：年齢〉age.
heikin-nenrei 〈平均年齢〉the average age
nenrei-sō 〈年齢層〉an age bracket

nenri 〈ねんり：年利〉annual interest.
nenri-go-bu-de 〈年利五分で〉at an annual interest of 5 percent

nenrin 〈ねんりん：年輪〉an annual ring.

nenryō 〈ねんりょう：燃料〉fuel.
nenryō-hi 〈燃料費〉fuel expenses

-nensai 〈-ねんさい：-年祭〉an anniversary ((of)).
jū-nensai 〈十年祭〉the tenth anniversary
hyaku-nensai 〈百年祭〉the centennial, the centenary

nensan 〈ねんさん：年産〉a yearly output.

-nensei 〈-ねんせい：-年生〉a year, a grade.

"Kimi-wa nan-nensei-desu-ka?" "(Watashi-wa) Go-nensei-desu."
（「君は何年生ですか。」「(私は)五年生です．」）"What grade are you
in?" "I am in the fifth grade."

nenshi 〈ねんし：年始〉the beginning of the year, New Year's Day.

nenshô 〈ねんしょう：燃焼〉combustion.

nenshô-suru 〈燃焼する〉burn.

nenshô-sha 〈ねんしょうしゃ：年少者〉a youth, young people.

nenshû 〈ねんしゅう：年収〉an annual income.

nenshutsu 〈ねんしゅつ：ねん出〉

nenshutsu-suru 〈ねん出する〉devise, work out, contrive, raise.

nentô 〈ねんとう：念頭〉

nentô-ni-oku 〈念頭に置く〉keep ((something)) in mind, take ((something)) into consideration.

nentô-ni-oka-nai （念頭に置かない）give no heed ((to)), take no
thought ((of)), do not care ((about))

nentô 〈ねんとう：年頭〉

nentô-ni 〈年頭に〉at the beginning of the year.

nenza 〈ねんざ〉a sprain.

nenza-suru 〈ねんざする〉sprain.

ne-oki 〈ねおき：寝起き〉

ne-oki-ga-ii 〈寝起きがいい〉wake in good humor.

ne-oki-ga-warui （寝起きが悪い）be fretful on waking

neon 〈ネオン〉neon.

neon-sain （ネオンサイン）a neon sign

Nepâru 〈ネパール〉Nepal.

Nepâru-jin （ネパール人）a Nepalese

Napâru-go （ネパール語）Nepali

Nepâru(-jin)-no （ネパール(人)の）Nepalese

nerai 〈ねらい〉aim.

nerai o sadameru （ねらいを定める）take aim ((at))

nerai ga hazureru （ねらいが外れる）miss one's aim

nerai-uchi （ねらい撃ち）sharpshooting; place hitting

nerai-uchi-ni-suru （ねらい撃ちにする）snipe ((at))

nerau 〈ねらう〉aim ((at)), watch ((for)).

mato-o-nerau （的をねらう）aim at a target

kikai-o-nerau （機会をねらう）watch for a chance

kâka-o-neratte （効果をねらって）for effect

neru 〈ネル〉 flannel.

neru 〈ねる：練る〉 knead; elaborate.

　kona o neru〈粉を練る〉 knead flour

　keikaku o neru〈計画を練る〉 elaborate a plan

neru 〈ねる：寝る〉 sleep, go to bed, lie down; be laid up, be sick in bed.

　nezu-ni-iru〈寝ずにいる〉 sit up.

ne-sagari 〈ねさがり：値下がり〉 a fall in price.

　ne-sagari-suru〈値下がりする〉 fall in price.

ne-sage 〈ねさげ：値下げ〉 a reduction in price.

　ne-sage-suru〈値下げする〉 reduce the price(the fare *or* the freight).

neshina 〈ねしな：寝しな〉

　neshina-ni〈寝しなに〉 just before going to bed.

ne-shizumaru 〈ねしずまる：寝静まる〉 fall fast asleep.

ne-shōben 〈ねしょうべん：寝小便〉 bed-wetting.

　ne-shōben-o-suru〈寝小便をする〉 wet the bed at night.

ne-sobireru 〈ねそびれる：寝そびれる〉 fail to get to sleep.

nessen 〈ねっせん：熱戦〉 a hot contest, heated competition.

　　Nessen-ga-kuri-hirogerarete-iru.（熱戦が繰り広げられている。） A hot contest is under way.

nesshin 〈ねっしん：熱心〉

　nesshin-na〈熱心な〉 eager, zealous, earnest.

　nesshin-ni〈熱心に〉 eagerly, zealously, earnestly.

nessuru 〈ねっする：熱する〉 heat, become heated; get excited.

　nesshi-yasui〈熱しやすい〉 excitable.

ne-sugosu 〈ねすごす：寝過ごす〉 oversleep (oneself).

neta 〈ねた〉 a news item, material(s); (a) proof, evidence.

neta-kiri 〈ねたきり：寝たきり〉

　neta-kiri-no〈寝たきりの〉 bedridden.

netami 〈ねたみ〉 jealousy, envy.

　netamu〈ねたむ〉 be jealous ((of)), be envious ((of)), envy.

　netamashii or *netami-bukai*〈ねたましい，ねたみ深い〉 jealous, envious.

　netande〈ねたんで〉 out of jealousy.

netchū 〈ねっちゅう：熱中〉 enthusiasm, absorption.

　netchū-suru〈熱中する〉 be enthusiastic ((about, in *or* over)), be absorbed ((in)).

ne-tomari 〈ねとまり：寝泊まり〉

　ne-tomari-suru〈寝泊まりする〉 lodge ((at *or* in)).

　　kawa-bata-no　maruta-goya-ni-ne-tomari-suru（川端の丸太小屋に寝泊ま

りする）lodge in a log cabin on the riverside

netsu〈ねつ：熱〉heat, fever, temperature, enthusiasm.
taiyô-netsu（太陽熱）solar heat
netsu o hakaru（熱を計る）take one's temperature
netsu-ga-aru（熱がある）have (a) fever
netsu-ga-takai（熱が高い）have a high fever
Netsu ga sagatta.（熱が下がった.）My temperature has gone down.
yakyû-netsu（野球熱）baseball fever

netsuai〈ねつあい：熱愛〉
netsuai-suru〈熱愛する〉love ardently.

netsubô〈ねつぼう：熱望〉an eager desire.
netsubô-suru〈熱望する〉desire eagerly, desire earnestly, be anxious
((for *or* to do)).

netsubyô〈ねつびょう：熱病〉a fever.
netsubyô ni kakaru（熱病にかかる）catch a fever

netsuen〈ねつえん：熱演〉an impassioned performance.
netsuen-suru〈熱演する〉perform enthusiastically.

netsui〈ねつい：熱意〉zeal, enthusiasm.
netsui-o-motte〈熱意を持って〉zealously, with much enthusiasm.

netsujô〈ねつじょう：熱情〉passion.
netsujô-teki(-na)〈熱情的(な)〉passionate.

ne-tsuki〈ねつき：寝付き〉
ne-tsuki-ga-ii〈寝付きがいい〉fall asleep easily.
ne-tsuki-ga-warui（寝付きが悪い）be wakeful

ne-tsuku〈ねつく：寝付く〉go to sleep, fall asleep; be ill in bed.

netsuppoi〈ねっぽい：熱っぽい〉feverish; enthusiastic, ardent,
zealous.
netsuppoi-kao-o-shite-iru（熱っぽい顔をしている）look feverish
netsuppoi-chôshi-de hanasu（熱っぽい調子で話す）speak enthusiastically

netsuretsu〈ねつれつ：熱烈〉
netsuretsu-na〈熱烈な〉ardent, passionate, fervent, fervid.
netsuretsu-na-kangei-o-ukeru（熱烈な歓迎を受ける）be ardently
welcomed
netsuretsu-ni〈熱烈に〉ardently, passionately, fervently, fervidly.

netsu-rikigaku〈ねつりきがく：熱力学〉thermodynamics.

netsu-shori〈ねつしょり：熱処理〉heat treatment.
netsu-shori-o-suru〈熱処理をする〉treat with heat.

netsuzô〈ねつぞう：ねつ造〉(a) fabrication, (an) invention.
　netsuzô-suru〈ねつ造する〉fabricate, forge, invent, fake.
nettai〈ねったい：熱帯〉the torrid zone, the tropics.
　　nettai-chihô（熱帯地方）the tropics
　　nettai-gyo（熱帯魚）a tropical fish
　　nettai-shokubutsu（熱帯植物）a tropical plant
　nettai-no or *nettai-sei(-no)*〈熱帯の，熱帯性(の)〉tropical.
　　nettai-sei tei-kiatsu（熱帯性低気圧）a tropical depression
netto〈ネット〉a net.
　　netto o haru（ネットを張る）put up a (tennis) net
　　netto-ura（ネット裏）the grandstand
nettô〈ねっとう：熱湯〉boiling water.
ne-uchi〈ねうち：値打ち〉value, worth, merit.
　ne-uchi-no-aru〈値打ちのある〉valuable, worthy.
　　ne-uchi-no-nai（値打ちのない）valueless, worthless, of no merit
ne-zame〈ねざめ：寝覚め〉
　ne-zame-ga-warui〈寝覚めが悪い〉be conscience-stricken.
ne-zô〈ねぞう：寝相〉
　ne-zô-ga-warui〈寝相が悪い〉toss about in one's sleep.
nezumi〈ねずみ〉a rat, a mouse.
　　nezumi-tori（ねずみ捕り）a rattrap, a mousetrap.
ne-zuyoi〈ねづよい：根強い〉deep-rooted, firmly-rooted.
　　ne-zuyoi henken（根強い偏見）a deep-rooted prejudice
　ne-zuyoku〈根強く〉firmly.
ni〈に：二〉two.
　　dai-ni（第二）the second
ni〈に：荷〉a load, a burden, a cargo, a freight, goods, baggage, luggage.
　ni-o-tsumu〈荷を積む〉load〔a cart〕, pack〔a horse〕.
　　ni-o-orosu　*or*　ni-age-suru（荷を降ろす，荷揚げする）unload, discharge, land
-ni〈-に〉at, in, on; at; at, in; on, to, in; to, for, in; for; by, with; at, with; a, per, for.
　　shichi-ji-han-ni（七時半に）at half past seven
　　raigetsu-matsu-ni（来月末に）at the end of next month
　　ichi-gatsu-ni（一月に）in January
　　sen-kyû-hyaku-hachi-jû-san-nen-ni（1983年に）in 1983
　　ni-gatsu-itsu-ka-ni（二月五日に）on February 5

doyô-bi-no-asa-ni（土曜日の朝に）　on Saturday morning

jû-ni-sai-no-toki-ni（十二歳の時に）　at the age of twelve

Suda-chô-ni-sumu（須田町に住む）　live at Suda-cho

Tôkyô-ni sumu（東京に住む）　live in Tokyo

kokuban-ni（黒板に）　on the blackboard

Kyôto no nishi-ni（京都の西に）　to the west of Kyoto

hako-ni（箱に）　in a box

hidari-ni mawaru（左に回る）　turn to the left

Rondon-ni tatsu（ロンドンに立つ）　leave for London

nishi-ni（西に）　in the west

sampo-ni-iku（散歩に行く）　go for a walk

sensei-ni homerareru（先生に褒められる）　be praised by a teacher

yuki-ni oowareru（雪に覆われる）　be covered with snow

sono shirase-ni odoroku（その知らせに驚く）　be surprised to hear the news

shû-ni ichi-do（週に一度）　once a week

go-hyaku-en-ni jukko（五百円に十個）　10 for 500 yen

ni-ai〈にあい：似合い〉

ni-ai-no〈似合いの〉well-matched.

ni-ai-no fûfu（似合いの夫婦）　a well-matched couple

ni-au〈にあう：似合う〉become, suit, match.

Sono sukâto wa anata-ni yoku ni-au.（そのスカートはあなたによく似合う.）　The skirt becomes you well.

Sono nekutai wa kimi-no aoi waishatsu ni yoku ni-au.（そのネクタイは君の青いワイシャツによく似合う.）　The tie matches your blue shirt well.

ni-atta〈似合った〉becoming, well-matched.

ni-bai〈にばい：二倍〉double, twice.

ni-bai-ni-suru〈二倍にする〉double.

ni-bai-no〈二倍の〉double, twofold.

ni-ban〈にばん：二番〉the second, number two.

ni-ban-me-no〈二番目の〉the second.

nibe〈にべ〉

nibe-mo-naku〈にべもなく〉flatly, bluntly, point-blank.

nibe-mo-naku kotowaru（にべもなく断る）　refuse bluntly

ni-boshi〈にぼし：煮干し〉dried small sardines.

ni-bu〈にぶ：二部〉two parts, the second part; two copies.

ni-bu-gasshô（二部合唱）　chorus in two parts.

nibui 〈にぶい：鈍い〉 dull, slow.
　niburu 〈鈍る〉 become dull.
ni-bun 〈にぶん：二分〉
　　ni-bun-suru 〈二分する〉 divide ((a thing)) in two, halve
　　ni-bun-no-ichi 〈二分の一〉 one half
ni-chaku 〈にちゃく：二着〉 the second place, a runner-up.
　　ni-chaku-ni-naru 〈二着になる〉 come in second
nichi 〈にち：日〉
　　ni-gatsu-jû-go-nichi 〈二月十五日〉 the fifteenth of February
Nichi-Bei 〈にちべい：日米〉 Japan and America.
　　Nichi-Bei-kankei 〈日米関係〉 the relations between Japan and the
　　United States
　Nichi-Bei-no 〈日米の〉 Japanese-American.
nichibotsu 〈にちぼつ：日没〉 sunset, sundown.
　　nichibotsu-ni 〈日没に〉 at sunset
　　nichibotsu-mae-ni 〈日没前に〉 before sunset
Nichi-Doku 〈にちどく：日独〉 Japan and Germany.
　Nichi-Doku-no 〈日独の〉 Japanese-German.
Nichi-Ei 〈にちえい：日英〉 Japan and England.
　Nichi-Ei-no 〈日英の〉 Anglo-Japanese.
Nichi-Futsu 〈にちふつ：日仏〉 Japan and France.
　Nichi-Futsu-no 〈日仏の〉 Franco-Japanese.
Nichi-Gô 〈にちごう：日豪〉 Japan and Australia.
　Nichi-Gô-no 〈日豪の〉 Japanese-Australian.
Nichi-I 〈にちい：日伊〉 Japan and Italy.
　Nichi-I-no 〈日伊の〉 Japanese-ltalian.
nichiji 〈にちじ：日時〉 the time, the date.
nichijô 〈にちじょう：日常〉
　nichijô-no 〈日常の〉 everyday, daily.
　　nichijô-no deki-goto 〈日常の出来事〉 a daily occurrence
nichiya 〈にちや：日夜〉 night and day, day and night.
nichiyô 〈にちよう：日用〉 daily use.
　　nichiyô-hin 〈日用品〉 daily necessaries
　nichiyô-no 〈日用の〉 for everyday use.
nichiyô-bi 〈にちようび：日曜日〉 Sunday.
ni-dashi(-jiru) 〈にだし（じる）：煮出し（汁）〉 (soup) stock, broth.
ni-do 〈にど：二度〉 twice, two times; again.
　　Ni-do-aru-koto-wa　san-do-aru. 〈二度ある事は三度ある.〉 What hap-

　　pens twice will happen thrice.

　　Ni-do-to asoko-e-wa ika-nai.〈二度とあそこへは行かない.〉 I will nev-
　　er go there again.

　　ni-do-to-nai kikai〈二度とない機会〉 the opportunity of a lifetime

ni-do-me-no〈二度目の〉 the second.

ni-do-me-ni〈二度目に〉 for the second time.

nie-kira-nai〈にえきらない：煮え切らない〉indecisive, irresolute, undetermined, vague, dubious, lukewarm, noncommittal.

　　nie-kira-nai henji〈煮え切らない返事〉 a vague reply, a noncommittal
　　reply

nie-kuri-kaeru〈にえくりかえる：煮えくり返る〉

　　Harawata ga nie-kuri-kaetta.〈はらわたが煮えくり返った.〉 My blood
　　boiled with rage.

nieru〈にえる：煮える〉 boil, cook, be boiled, be cooked.

yoku-nieta〈よく煮えた〉 well-cooked, well-done.

nie-yu〈にえゆ：煮え湯〉 boiling water.

nie-yu-o-nomasu〈煮え湯を飲ます〉 play ((a person)) false.

ni-fuda〈にふだ：荷札〉a tag, a label.

ni-fuda-o-tsukeru〈荷札を付ける〉 fasten a tag ((to)), tag.

nigai〈にがい：苦い〉 bitter; hard.

　　nigai kusuri（苦い薬）　bitter medicine

　　nigai kao（苦い顔）　a sour face

　　nigai keiken（苦い経験）　a hard experience

niga-mi〈にがみ：苦み〉a bitter taste, bitterness.

niga-mi-no-aru〈苦みのある〉 of a bitter taste.

niga-mi-bashitta〈にがみばしった：苦み走った〉

　　niga-mi-bashitta kao（苦み走った顔）　a stern and handsome face

niga-mushi〈にがむし：苦虫〉

niga-mushi-o-kami-tsubushita-kao o suru〈苦虫をかみつぶした顔をする〉
make a sour face.

nigan〈にがん：二眼〉

　　nigan-refu（二眼レフ）　a twin-lens reflex camera

niganigashii〈にがにがしい：苦々しい〉unpleasant, disgusting, shameful.

ni-gao(-e)〈にがお(え)：似顔(絵)〉a likeness, a portrait.

nigari〈にがり：苦汁〉 brine, bittern.

nigari-kiru〈にがりきる：苦り切る〉look sour ((at)).

nigari-kitte〈苦り切って〉with a sour face.

nigasu〈にがす：逃がす〉let go, set free; miss, lose.

ko-tori o nigashite-yaru〈小鳥を逃がしてやる〉 set a little bird free

zekkô-no chansu o nigasu〈絶好のチャンスを逃がす〉 miss a rare chance

sakana o nigasu〈魚を逃がす〉 lose a fish

niga-te〈にがて：苦手〉 a weak point; an ugly customer to deal with.

Furansu-go wa watashi-no niga-te-da.〈フランス語は私の苦手だ.〉 French is my weak point.

nigatsu〈にがつ：二月〉 February.

niga-warai〈にがわらい：苦笑い〉 a bitter smile, a forced smile.

niga-warai-suru〈苦笑いする〉 smile bitterly.

nige-ba〈にげば：逃げ場〉

nige-ba-o-ushinau〈逃げ場を失う〉 be cut off from escape, be trapped.

nige-dasu〈にげだす：逃げ出す〉 run away, take to flight.

kossori-nige-dasu〈こっそり逃げ出す〉 sneak away

nige-goshi〈にげごし：逃げ腰〉

nige-goshi-ni-naru〈逃げ腰になる〉 make ready to flee, take an evasive attitude.

nige-komu〈にげこむ：逃げ込む〉 run ((into)), take refuge ((in)), seek shelter ((at *or* in)).

nige-mawaru〈にげまわる：逃げ回る〉 run about trying to escape.

nige-michi〈にげみち：逃げ道〉 a way of escape, a way out, a retreat.

nigen〈にげん：二元〉 duality.

nigen-hôsô〈二元放送〉 a simultaneous broadcast from two stations

nigen-teki(-na)〈二元的(な)〉 dual.

nige-okureru or **nige-sokonau**〈にげおくれる, にげそこなう：逃げ遅れる, 逃げ損なう〉 fail to escape.

nigeru〈にげる：逃げる〉 run away, escape; fly away.

inochi-karagara nigeru〈命からがら逃げる〉 run for one's life

nigiraseru〈にぎらせる：握らせる〉

kane o nigiraseru〈金を握らせる〉 slip money into ((a person's)) hand, bribe.

nigiri-kobushi〈にぎりこぶし：握りこぶし〉 a fist.

nigiri-meshi〈にぎりめし：握り飯〉 a rice ball.

nigiri-shimeru〈にぎりしめる：握り締める〉 hold ((a thing)) tight in one's hand, grasp tightly.

nigiri-tsubusu〈にぎりつぶす：握りつぶす〉 crush ((something)) in the hand; shelve, pigeonhole.

nigiri-zushi〈にぎりずし：握りずし〉 hand-rolled *sushi*.

nigiru 〈にぎる：握る〉 hold, grasp, grip.
    himitsu o nigiru（秘密を握る） hold ((a person's)) secret
    seiken-o-nigiru（政権を握る） come into power
nigiwau 〈にぎわう〉 be crowded, be lively; be prosperous.
nigiyaka 〈にぎやか〉
  nigiyaka-na 〈にぎやかな〉 lively, merry, crowded, busy.
    nigiyaka-na ongaku（にぎやかな音楽） lively music
    nigiyaka-na toori（にぎやかな通り） a busy street
nigori 〈にごり：濁り〉 muddiness, impurity.
    nigori-mizu（濁り水） muddy water
nigoru 〈にごる：濁る〉 become muddy, become impure, become cloudy.
  nigotta 〈濁った〉 muddy, impure, cloudy.
    nigotta kûki（濁った空気） foul air
nigosu 〈にごす：濁す〉 speak ambiguously.
    henji-o-nigosu（返事を濁す） give a vague answer
nigun 〈にぐん：二軍〉 a farm team.
ni-guruma 〈にぐるま：荷車〉 a cart, a wagon.
Nihon 〈にほん：日本〉 Japan.
    Nihon-jin（日本人） a Japanese
    Nihon-go（日本語） Japanese
    Nihon-ga（日本画） a picture in Japanese style
    Nihon-kai（日本海） the Japan Sea
    Nihon(-jin)-no（日本(人)の） Japanese
nihon-date 〈にほんだて：二本立て〉 a double feature.
ni-i 〈にい：二位〉 *see.* ni-chaku.
niji 〈にじ：二次〉
    niji-hôtei-shiki（二次方程式） a quadratic equation
    niji-kai（二次会） a second party
      niji-kai-o-suru（二次会をする） have another spree at another
        place
  niji-no 〈二次の〉 second, secondary.
  niji-teki(-na) 〈二次的(な)〉 secondary.
    niji-teki-na mondai（二次的な問題） a secondary problem
niji 〈にじ〉 a rainbow.
nijimi-deru 〈にじみでる：にじみ出る〉 ooze out.
nijimu 〈にじむ〉 blot, run, blur, be blotted.
    Kono kami wa nijimu.（この紙はにじむ。） This paper blots.
ni-jû 〈にじゅう：二十〉 twenty.

dai-ni-jû 〈第二十〉 the twentieth.

nijû 〈にじゅう：二重〉
    nijû-jinkaku (二重人格) double personality
    nijû-kakaku (二重価格) a double price
    nijû-kokuseki (二重国籍) dual nationality
    nijû-mado (二重窓) a double window
    nijû-seikatsu (二重生活) a double life
    nijû-sô (二重奏) a duet
nijû-no 〈二重の〉 double.
nijû-ni 〈二重に〉 doubly.
    nijû-ni-naru *or* nijû-ni-suru (二重になる，二重にする) double

ni-kai 〈にかい：二回〉 twice, two times.
    nen-ni ni-kai (年に二回) twice a year
dai-ni-kai-no or *ni-kai-me-no* 〈第二回の，二回目の〉 the second.

ni-kai 〈にかい：二階〉 the second floor, the first floor.
    ni-kai-ya (二階家) a two-storied house
    ni-kai-date-basu (二階建てバス) a double-decker
ni-kai-no 〈二階の〉 upstairs.
    ni-kai-no mado (二階の窓) an upstairs window
ni-kai-de, ni-kai-e or *ni-kai-ni* 〈二階で，二階へ，二階に〉 upstairs.
    ni-kai-de neru (二階で寝る) sleep upstairs
    ni-kai-e agaru (二階へ上がる) go upstairs
    ni-kai-ni iru (二階にいる) be upstairs
    ni-kai-kara-oriru (二階から降りる) come downstairs

ni-kata 〈にかた：煮方〉 how to cook.
ni-kata-ga-warui 〈煮方が悪い〉 be not properly cooked.

nikawa 〈にかわ〉 glue.

nikibi 〈にきび〉 a pimple.
nikibi-darake-no kao 〈にきびだらけの顔〉 a pimpled face.

nikka 〈にっか：日課〉 a daily task, daily work; a daily lesson.

nikkan 〈にっかん：日刊〉 daily publication.
    nikkan-shimbun (日刊新聞) a daily
nikkan-no 〈日刊の〉 daily.

nikkan 〈にっかん：肉感〉
nikkan-teki(-na) 〈肉感的(な)〉 sensual.

nikkei 〈にっけい：日系〉
    nikkei-Beijin (日系米人) an American of Japanese descent

nikkeru 〈ニッケル〉 nickel.

nikki 〈にっき：日記〉a diary.

  nikki o tsukeru (日記を付ける)　keep a diary

nikkô 〈にっこう：日光〉sunshine, sunlight, the sun's rays.

nikkori 〈にっこり〉

  nikkori-warau 〈にっこり笑う〉smile sweetly.

nikkô-yoku 〈にっこうよく：日光浴〉a sunbath.

  nikkô-yoku-o-suru 〈日光浴をする〉bathe in the sun.

nikkyû 〈にっきゅう：日給〉daily wages.

  nikkyû-de-hataraku 〈日給で働く〉work by the day.

nikochin 〈ニコチン〉nicotine.

  nikochin-chûdoku（ニコチン中毒）　nicotinism

ni-kogori 〈にこごり：煮こごり〉congealed food.

ni-komu 〈にこむ：煮込む〉boil well; cook together.

nikoniko 〈にこにこ〉

  nikoniko-gao（にこにこ顔）　a smiling face

  nikoniko-suru 〈にこにこする〉smile ((at)).

  nikoniko-shite 〈にこにこして〉smilingly, with a smile, with a smiling face.

nikori 〈にこり〉

  nikori-tomo-shi-nai-de 〈にこりともしないで〉unsmilingly.

nikoyaka 〈にこやか〉

  nikoyaka-na 〈にこやかな〉smiling, radiant, genial-looking.

  nikoyaka-na kao（にこやかな顔）　a radiant face

  nikoyaka-ni 〈にこやかに〉smilingly, radiantly.

niku 〈にく：肉〉meat, flesh.

  niku-kiri-bôchô（肉切り包丁）　a carving knife

  niku-ya（肉屋）　a butcher; a meat shop, a butcher's

niku-banare 〈にくばなれ：肉離れ〉

  niku-banare-o-okosu 〈肉離れを起こす〉tear a muscle.

niku-buto 〈にくぶと：肉太〉

  niku-buto-ni-kaku 〈肉太に書く〉write thick.

  niku-buto-no 〈肉太の〉bold-faced.

nikugan 〈にくがん：肉眼〉the naked eye.

  nikugan-dewa mie-nai（肉眼では見えない）　be invisible to the naked eye

nikui 〈にくい：憎い〉hateful, detestable; spiteful.

-nikui 〈-にくい〉hard, difficult, awkward.

  Nihon-go-de jûbun hyôgen-shi-nikui kotoba（日本語で十分表現しにく

い言葉）a word difficult to express fully in Japanese

nikumare-guchi 〈にくまれぐち：憎まれ口〉abusive language, a brickbat.

    nikumare-guchi-o-kiku（憎まれ口をきく）say spiteful things

nikumarekko 〈にくまれっこ：憎まれっ子〉a bad child.

    Nikumarekko-yo-ni-habakaru.（憎まれっ子世にはばかる。）Ill weeds grow apace.

nikumare-yaku 〈にくまれやく：憎まれ役〉an ungracious part, a thankless role.

nikumu 〈にくむ：憎む〉hate, detest.

  nikumu-beki〈憎むべき〉hateful, detestable.

nikurashii 〈にくらしい：憎らしい〉odious, hateful, provoking.

  nikurashi-ge-ni〈憎らしげに〉spitefully, hatefully, provokingly.

nikuromu-sen 〈ニクロムせん：ニクロム線〉nichrome wire.

nikusei 〈にくせい：肉声〉one's natural voice.

nikushimi 〈にくしみ：憎しみ〉hatred.

    nikushimi-o-komete（憎しみを込めて）with hatred

nikushin 〈にくしん：肉親〉blood relationship; a blood relation.

nikushoku 〈にくしょく：肉食〉meat-eating, a meat diet, flesh food.

    nikushoku-dōbutsu（肉食動物）a carnivorous animal

nikushu 〈にくしゅ：肉しゅ〉a sarcoma.

nikutai 〈にくたい：肉体〉the body.

    nikutai-bi（肉体美）physical beauty

    nikutai-rōdō（肉体労働）physical labor

  nikutai-no〈肉体の〉bodily, physical.

niku-zuke 〈にくづけ：肉付け〉

  niku-zuke-suru〈肉付けする〉give body and substance ((to)), flesh out.

niku-zuki 〈にくづき：肉付き〉

  niku-zuki-no-ii〈肉付きのいい〉well-fleshed, fleshy.

nimai-gai 〈にまいがい：二枚貝〉a bivalve.

nimai-jita 〈にまいじた：二枚舌〉

  nimai-jita-o-tsukau〈二枚舌を使う〉be double-tongued, tell a lie.

nimai-me 〈にまいめ：二枚目〉a lover's part; a beau-part actor.

ni-mame 〈にまめ：煮豆〉boiled beans.

nimmei 〈にんめい：任命〉appointment, nomination.

  nimmei-suru〈任命する〉appoint, nominate.

nimmu 〈にんむ：任務〉a duty, a part, (a) function, a mission.

    nimmu o hatasu（任務を果たす）carry out one's duty

　　　nimmu o okotaru〈任務を怠る〉 neglect one's duties

ni-mono〈にもの：煮物〉 cooking, cooked food.

　　ni-mono-o-suru〈煮物をする〉cook.

nimô-saku〈にもうさく：二毛作〉two crops a year.

nimotsu〈にもつ：荷物〉a load, a burden, baggage, luggage, goods, freight.

　　　nimotsu o hakobu〈荷物を運ぶ〉 carry a load, carry one's baggage

　　nimotsu-o-tsumu〈荷物を積む〉load.

　　　nimotsu-o-orosu〈荷物を降ろす〉 unload

nimpu〈にんぷ：妊婦〉*see.* nin-sampu.

ninchi〈にんち：任地〉one's (new) post.

　　　ninchi-ni-omomuku〈任地に赴く〉leave for one's new post

ninchi〈にんち：認知〉recognition, acknowledgment.

　　ninchi-suru〈認知する〉acknowledge ((a child)) as one's own.

ningen〈にんげん：人間〉a man, a human being; man, mankind.

　　　ningen-kankei〈人間関係〉 human relations

　　　ningen-mi〈人間味〉 a human touch, humanity

　　　　ningen-mi-ga-aru〈人間味がある〉 be humane, be warmhearted

　　　　ningen-mi-ga-nai〈人間味がない〉 be coldhearted

　　　ningen-sei〈人間性〉 human nature, humanity

　　ningen-no〈人間の〉 human.

ningyo〈にんぎょ：人魚〉a mermaid, a merman.

ningyô〈にんぎょう：人形〉a doll, a puppet.

　　　nui-gurumi-ningyô〈縫いぐるみ人形〉 a rag doll

　　　ningyô-geki〈人形劇〉 a puppet show

ni-nin-san-kyaku〈ににんさんきゃく：二人三脚〉a three-legged race.

nin·i-shuttô〈にんいしゅっとう：任意出頭〉voluntary appearance.

　　　nin·i-shuttô o motomeru〈任意出頭を求める〉 ask ((a person)) voluntary appearance ((at))

ninjin〈にんじん〉a carrot.

ninjô〈にんじょう：人情〉human nature, humaneness, kindness.

　　　ninjô-ka〈人情家〉 a person of heart

　　ninjô-no-aru or *ninjô-no-atsui*〈人情のある，人情の厚い〉humane, kind.

　　　ninjô-no-nai *or* ninjô-no-usui〈人情のない，人情の薄い〉 unfeeling, unkind

ninjû〈にんじゅう：忍従〉submission, subservience.

　　　ninjû no seikatsu〈忍従の生活〉 a life of submission

ninka〈にんか：認可〉approval, authorization, permission, license, (official) sanction.

    ninka o ukeru（認可を受ける）get authorization ((from)), obtain a license ((from))

ninka-suru〈認可する〉approve, authorize, permit, give license ((to)), sanction.

ninkan〈にんかん：任官〉(an) appointment, a commission.

ninkan-suru〈任官する〉be appointed ((to)), be commissioned.

ninki〈にんき：任期〉one's term of office, one's tenure.

    ninki-ippai-tsutomeru（任期いっぱい勤める）serve one's full term in office

ninki〈にんき：人気〉popularity.

    ninki-ga-ochiru（人気が落ちる）fall in popularity

    ninki-kashu（人気歌手）a popular singer

    ninki-tôhyô（人気投票）a popularity vote

    ninki-mono（人気者）a popular person, a favorite

    ninki-dori-suru（人気取りする）try for popularity

ninki-ga-aru〈人気がある〉be popular ((among *or* with)).

    ninki-ga-nai（人気がない）be unpopular ((among *or* with))

ninniku〈にんにく〉(a) garlic.

ni-no-ashi〈にのあし：二の足〉

ni-no-ashi-o-fumu〈二の足を踏む〉hesitate ((at *or* to do)), recoil ((from)).

ni-no-ku〈にのく：二の句〉

ni-no-ku-ga-tsuge-nai〈二の句が継げない〉be at a loss what to answer.

ni-no-mai〈にのまい：二の舞〉

ni-no-mai-o-enjiru〈二の舞を演じる〉repeat ((a person's)) failure.

ni-no-tsugi〈にのつぎ：二の次〉

ni-no-tsugi-de-aru〈二の次である〉be of secondary importance.

nin-sampu〈にんさんぷ：妊産婦〉expectant and nursing mothers.

ninshiki〈にんしき：認識〉recognition, understanding.

    ninshiki-busoku（認識不足）lack of understanding

    ninshiki-busoku-de-aru（認識不足である）have little understanding

ninshiki-suru〈認識する〉recognize, understand.

ninshiki-o-arata-ni-suru〈認識を新たにする〉see ((it)) in a new light.

ninshin〈にんしん：妊娠〉pregnancy, conception.

    ninshin-rokkagetsu-de-aru（妊娠六か月である）be in the sixth month of pregnancy

ninshin-suru〈妊娠する〉become pregnant, conceive.

ninshin-shite-iru〈妊娠している〉be pregnant.

ninshō〈にんしょう：人称〉person.
    ichi-nin-shô〈一人称〉the first person

ninshō〈にんしょう：認証〉certification, attestation.
    ninshô-shiki〈認証式〉an attestation ceremony
ninshô-suru〈認証する〉certify, attest.

ninsō〈にんそう：人相〉looks.
ninsô-no-yoku-nai〈人相のよくない〉ill-looking.

nintai〈にんたい：忍耐〉perseverance, patience, endurance.
nintai-ryoku-no-nai〈忍耐力のない〉lacking in perseverance.

nintei〈にんてい：認定〉recognition, acknowledgment, approval, authorization.
    shikaku-nintei-shiken（資格認定試験）a qualification test
nintei-suru〈認定する〉recognize, acknowledge, approve ((of)), authorize.

ni-nushi〈にぬし：荷主〉a shipper, a consignor.

ninzū〈にんずう：人数〉the number of persons.
    ninzû-ga-fueru（人数が増える）increase in number
    ninzû-ga-heru（人数が減る）decrease in number
    ninzû-o-soroeru（人数をそろえる）get the required number of persons
    ninzû-o-kazoeru（人数を数える）count heads

nioi〈におい〉(a) smell, (a) scent, (a) perfume, fragrance, a stink.
    ii nioi（いいにおい）a sweet smell
    warui nioi（悪いにおい）a bad smell, a foul smell
nioi-ga-suru〈においがする〉smell.
    Kono hana wa ii-nioi-ga-suru.（この花はいいにおいがする．）This flower smells sweet.
    〜*-no-nioi-ga-suru*〈〜のにおいがする〉smell of... .
    Kono heya wa sakana-no-nioi-ga-suru.（この部屋は魚のにおいがする．）This room smells of fish.
nioi-o-kagu〈においをかぐ〉smell, take a smell ((at)).
ii-nioi-no-suru〈いいにおいのする〉sweet-smelling, fragrant, balmy.
    warui-nioi-no-suru（悪いにおいのする）foul-smelling.
nioi-no-nai〈においのない〉scentless.

niou〈におう〉smell ((of)); be fragrant, stink.

niowasu〈におわす〉drop a hint ((of)), insinuate.

Nippon〈にっぽん：日本〉*see.* Nihon.

niramekko〈にらめっこ〉

niramekko-suru 〈にらめっこする〉 have an outstaring game.

nirami 〈にらみ〉 a glare; authority ((over)).
nirami-ga-kiku (にらみが利く) have much authority ((over *or* with)), have a great influence ((among *or* with)).

nirami-au 〈にらみあう：にらみ合う〉 glare at each other; be at odds with each other.

nirami-awasu 〈にらみあわす：にらみ合わす〉
~*-to-nirami-awasete* 〈～とにらみ合わせて〉 in the light of... , in consideration of... .

nirami-tsukeru *or* **niramu** 〈にらみつける，にらむ：にらみ付ける〉 glare ((at)), look angrily ((at)).
niramareru 〈にらまれる〉 be watched, fall under ((a person's)) displeasure, be suspected.

niran-sei-sôsei-ji 〈にらんせいそうせいじ：二卵性双生児〉 two-egg twins.

nire 〈にれ〉 an elm.

niru 〈にる：煮る〉 boil, cook, do.
ni-sugiru (煮すぎる) overboil, overcook, overdo

niru 〈にる：似る〉 resemble, take ((after)), be like, look like.
Kare-wa haha ni nite-iru. (彼は母に似ている。) He resembles his mother.

nirui 〈にるい：二塁〉 second base.
nirui-shu (二塁手) a second baseman
nirui-da (二塁打) a two-base hit

niryû 〈にりゅう：二流〉
niryû-no 〈二流の〉 second-rate, middling, petty, minor.

ni-san 〈にさん：二，三〉
ni-san-nichi (二，三日) two or three days
ni-san-no 〈二，三の〉 two or three, a few, some, a couple of.

nisanka 〈にさんか：二酸化〉
nisanka-butsu (二酸化物) a dioxide
nisanka-tanso (二酸化炭素) carbon dioxide

nise 〈にせ：偽〉
nise-mono (偽物) an imitation, a sham, a counterfeit, a fake
nise-satsu (偽札) a forged note
nise-no 〈偽の〉 sham, forged, false.

nisei 〈にせい：二世〉 the second; a *Nisei*.
Erizabesu-nisei (エリザベス二世) Elizabeth the Second

niseru 〈にせる：似せる〉 imitate, model ((a thing)) after; counterfeit, forge.

nishi 〈にし：西〉the west.

　　nishi-kaze〈西風〉a west wind

　　nishi-bi（西日）the afternoon sun

　nishi-no〈西の〉west, western.

　nishi-e or *nishi-ni*〈西へ，西に〉west, westward.

　～-no-nishi-ni〈～の西に〉in the west of... , on the west of... , to the west of... .

nishiki 〈にしき〉Japanese brocade.

　　nishiki-e（にしき絵）a color print

　　nishiki-goi（にしきごい）a colored carp

nishiki-hebi 〈にしき蛇〉an Indian python.

ni-shime 〈にしめ：煮染め〉vegetables boiled hard with soy.

nishin 〈にしん〉a herring.

-ni-shite-wa 〈～にしては〉for... , considering... .

　　Kare-wa　go-jû-ni-shite-wa　wakaku　mieru.（彼は五十にしては若く見え
　　る。）He looks young for 50.

nisoku 〈にそく：二足〉

　nisoku-no-waraji-o-haku〈二足のわらじを覆く〉run　after　two　different
　things at the same time.

nisoku-sammon 〈にそくさんもん：二束三文〉

　nisoku-sammon-de-kau〈二束三文で買う〉buy ((a thing)) for a song.

　nisoku-sammon-de-uru〈二束三文で売る〉go for a song

nissan 〈にっさん：日参〉

　nissan-suru〈日参する〉visit ((a place)) daily.

nissan 〈にっさん：日産〉a daily output.

nissha-byô 〈にっしゃびょう：日射病〉sunstroke.

　　nissha-byô-ni-kakaru（日射病にかかる）suffer from sunstroke

nisshin-geppo 〈にっしんげっぽ：日進月歩〉

　nisshin-geppo-no〈日進月歩の〉ever-progressing.

nisshô-ken 〈にっしょうけん：日照権〉a right to receive sunlight.

nisshoku 〈にっしょく：日食〉a solar eclipse.

Nisso 〈にっソ：日ソ〉Japan and the Soviet Union.

　Nisso-no〈日ソの〉Japanese-Soviet, Soviet-Japanese.

nissû 〈にっすう：日数〉(the number of) days.

　　Nissû　wa　dono-kurai-kakarimasu-ka?（日数はどのくらいかかります
　　か。）How many days will it take?

nisu 〈ニス〉varnish.

nisu-o-nuru〈ニスを塗る〉varnish.

nisu-biki-no〈ニス引きの〉varnished.

nitari-yottari〈にたりよったり：似たり寄ったり〉

nitari-yottari-da〈似たり寄ったりだ〉be much the same, be six of one and half-a-dozen of the other.

ni-tatsu〈にたつ：煮立つ〉boil up, come to the boil.

nitchi-mo-satchi-mo〈にっちもさっちも〉

nitchi-mo-satchi-mo-ika-nai〈にっちもさっちもいかない〉be in a fix, be at a pinch, be stranded.

Nitchû〈にっちゅう：日中〉Japan and the People's Republic of China.

Nitchû-no〈日中の〉Japanese-Chinese.

nitchû〈にっちゅう：日中〉the daytime.

nitchû-wa（日中は）in the daytime, during the day, by day

nitô〈にとう：二等〉the second class.

nitô-shô（二等賞）the second prize

ni-tôbun〈にとうぶん：二等分〉

ni-tôbun-suru〈二等分する〉divide ((a line)) into two equal parts, divide equally.

ni-tôhen-sankakkei〈にとうへんさんかっけい：二等辺三角形〉an i-sosceles triangle.

nitoro-guriserin〈ニトログリセリン〉nitroglycerine.

ni-tsuke〈につけ：煮付け〉

sakana-no-ni-tsuke（魚の煮付け）hard-boiled fish

ni-tsumaru〈につまる：煮詰まる〉be boiled down.

ni-tsumeru〈煮詰める〉boil down.

nittei〈にってい：日程〉a day's schedule.

nittei-hyô（日程表）a schedule

nittô〈にっとう：日当〉*see.* nikkyû.

ni-ugoki〈にうごき：荷動き〉movements of goods.

ni-ugoki-no-hayai shôhin（荷動きの速い商品）fast-moving mer-chandise

ni-uke-nin〈にうけにん：荷受人〉a consignee.

niwa〈にわ：庭〉a garden, a yard.

-niwa〈-には〉on; for, to; in order to.

ame-no-hi-niwa（雨の日には）on a rainy day

Sore-wa watashi-niwa muzukashii.（それは私には難しい。）It is difficult for me.

Seikô-suru-niwa isshô-kemmei hataraka-neba-naranai.（成功するには

一生懸命働かねばならない.) You must work hard in order to succeed.

niwaka〈にわか〉

　niwaka-ni〈にわかに〉suddenly, unexpectedly.

niwaka-ame〈にわかあめ：にわか雨〉a shower.

niwatori〈にわとり：鶏〉a chicken, a hen, a cock.

　　niwatori o kau（鶏を飼う）　keep hens

　　niwatori-goya（鶏小屋）　a hen house

　　niwatori-no-niku（鶏の肉）　chicken

niyaketa〈にやけた〉foppish, namby-pamby.

　　niyaketa-otoko（にやけた男）　a namby-pamby

ni-yaku〈にやく：荷役〉stevedoring.

niyaniya〈にやにや〉

　niyaniya-warau〈にやにや笑う〉grin ((at)), give ((a person)) a broad grin.

ni-zakana〈にざかな：煮魚〉fish boiled with soy (and sugar).

ni-zukuri〈にづくり：荷造り〉packing.

　ni-zukuri-o-suru〈荷造りをする〉pack (up), package.

no〈の：野〉a field, a plain.

　　no-michi（野道）　a field path

　no-no〈野の〉wild.

　　no-no hana（野の花）　a wild flower

-no〈-の〉-'s, of; at, in; in, on, of; for, to; by, of; of, in.

　　watashi-no (anata-no, kare-no *or* kanojo-no) hon（私の(あなたの, 彼の, 彼女の)本）　my(your, his *or* her) book

　　wareware-no (anata-tachi-no *or* kare-ra-no) kuruma（我々の(あなたたちの, 彼らの)車）　our(your *or* their) car

　　watashi-no-mono (anata-no-mono, kare-no-mono *or* kanojo-no-mono)（私のもの(あなたのもの, 彼のもの, 彼女のもの)）　mine(yours, his *or* hers)

　　wareware-no-mono (anata-tachi-no-mono *or* kare-ra-no-mono)（我々のもの(あなたたちのもの, 彼らのもの)）　ours(yours *or* theirs)

　　watashi-no ane-no ie（私の姉の家）　my sister's house

　　kyō-no shimbun（今日の新聞）　today's newspaper

　　hon no hyōshi（本の表紙）　the cover of a book

　　Kanda no gakkō（神田の学校）　a school at Kanda

　　Tôkyô no oba（東京の叔(伯)母）　one's aunt in Tokyo

　　kika no shiken（幾何の試験）　an examination in geometry

　　seibutsu no hon（生物の本）　a book on biology

Eigo no sensei〔英語の先生〕 a teacher of English

ni-man-en no ko-gitte〔二万円の小切手〕 a check for twenty thousand yen

heya no kagi〔部屋のかぎ〕 a key to the room

Gohho no e〔ゴッホの絵〕 a painting by Goch

tetsu no mon〔鉄の門〕 a gate of iron

dairiseki no zō〔大理石の像〕 a statue in marble

nô〈のう：脳〉the brain, brains.

nô-geka〔脳外科〕 brain surgery

nôha〔脳波〕 brain waves

nô-hinketsu〔脳貧血〕 cerebral anemia

nô-ikketsu〔脳いっ血〕 apoplexy

nô-nanka-shō〔脳軟化症〕 softening of the brain

nô-shintō〔脳震とう〕 a brain concussion

nô-shukketsu〔脳出血〕 (a) cerebral hemorrhage

nô-shuyō〔脳しゅよう〕 a brain tumor

nô-sei-mahi〔脳性麻ひ〕 cerebral paralysis

nômaku-en〔脳膜炎〕 meningitis

Nihon-nô-en〔日本脳炎〕 Japanese encephalitis

dai-nô〔大脳〕 the cerebrum

shō-nô〔小脳〕 the cerebellum

nô-no〔脳の〕cerebral.

nô〈のう：能〉talent, ability, capacity; a *No(h)* play.

Nô-aru-taka-wa-tsume-o-kakusu.〔能あるたかはつめを隠す。〕 Still waters run deep.

nô-nashi〔能無し〕 a good-for-nothing

nô-kyōgen〔能狂言〕 a *No(h)* farce

no-banashi〈のばなし：野放し〉

no-banashi-ni-suru〔野放しにする〕leave ((a dog)) loose, let ((a person)) do as he pleases.

nobasu〈のばす：伸(延)ばす〉lengthen, extend, stretch; develop, cultivate; put off, postpone; smooth out.

kigen o nobasu〔期限を延ばす〕 extend the term

karada o nobasu〔体を伸ばす〕 stretch oneself

sainō o nobasu〔才能を伸ばす〕 develop one's abilities

taizai o nobasu〔滞在を延ばす〕 prolong one's stay

nobe-〈のべ-：延べ-〉

nobe-jikan〔延べ時間〕 the total man-hours

　　nobe-jin·in（延べ人員）the total number of persons

nobe-barai〈のべばらい：延べ払い〉deferred payment.

nobe-bô〈のべぼう：延べ棒〉a (metal) bar.

　　kin-no nobe-bô（金の延べ棒）a gold bar

noberu〈のべる：述べる〉state, speak, express, tell.

　　shinjitsu o noberu（真実を述べる）state the truth

　　rei o noberu（礼を述べる）express one's thanks ((to))

　　iken o noberu（意見を述べる）give one's opinion

Nôberu-shô〈ノーベルしょう：ノーベル賞〉a Nobel prize.

　　Nôberu-heiwa-shô（ノーベル平和賞）a Nobel prize for peace

　　Nôberu-shô-jushô-sha（ノーベル賞受賞者）a Nobel prize winner

nobi〈のび：伸び〉

　　nobi-o-suru〈伸びをする〉stretch (oneself).

nobi-agaru〈のびあがる：伸び上がる〉stand on tiptoe.

nobi-chijimi〈のびちぢみ：伸び縮み〉

　　nobi-chijimi-suru〈伸び縮みする〉expand and contract, be elastic.

nobi-nayamu〈のびなやむ：伸び悩む〉do not progress so much as was expected.

nobinobi〈のびのび：伸び伸び〉

　　nobinobi-sodatsu〈伸び伸び育つ〉grow free from all restraint.

nobinobi〈のびのび：延び延び〉

　　nobinobi-ni-naru〈延び延びになる〉be long delayed from day to day.

nobiru〈のびる：伸（延）びる〉lengthen, extend, stretch; grow, increase; make progress, develop; be put off, be postponed.

　　Kono michi wa ken-zakai-made nobite-iru.（この道は県境まで延びている。）This road extends to the prefectural border.

　　se-ga-nobiru（背が伸びる）grow taller

　　Ano seito wa mada-nobiru.（あの生徒はまだ伸びる。）The student has a future before him.

　　Pâtî wa raishû-no getsuyô-ni nobita.（パーティーは来週の月曜に延びた。）The party has been postponed till next Monday.

nobori〈のぼり：上り〉(an) ascent, rise.

　　nobori-kudari（上り下り）the ascent and descent, the ups and downs

　　nobori-ressha（上り列車）an up train

　　nobori-zaka（上り坂）an ascent, an uphill road

noboru〈のぼる：上（登，昇）る〉rise, climb, go up, go ((on)); amount ((to)).

　　Taiyô ga nobotteiru.（太陽が昇っている。）The sun is rising.

Fuji-san ni noboru（富士山に登る）climb Mt. Fuji

kawa o noboru（川を上る）go up a river

butai-ni-noboru（舞台に登る）go on the stage

Shûri-hi wa jû-man-en-ni-noboru.（修理費は十万円に上る.）The cost of repairing amounts to a hundred thousand yen.

nobose〈のぼせ〉

nobose-shô-no〈のぼせ性の〉liable to a rush of blood to the head; easily excitable.

nobose-agaru〈のぼせあがる：のぼせ上がる〉become self-conceited, be puffed up with self importance, be infatuated ((with)).

Chotto-seikô-shita-node kare-wa nobose-agatte-iru.（ちょっと成功したので彼はのぼせ上がっている.）The small success has turned his head.

noboseru〈のぼせる〉have a rush of blood to the head, be dizzy; get excited.

Atsusa-de kare-wa nobosete-iru.（熱さで彼はのぼせている.）The heat has gone to his head.

nochi〈のち：後〉

Hare-nochi-kumori.（晴れ後曇り.）Fine, later cloudy.

nochi-no〈後の〉later, future, coming.

nochi-no yo（後の世）the future life

nochi-ni〈後に〉later (on), afterwards, in future.

～(-no)-nochi-ni〈〈～の〉後に〉after... .

kare-ga-shinda-nochi-ni（彼が死んだ後に）after his death, after he died

nôchi〈のうち：農地〉agricultural land, farmland.

nochi-hodo〈のちほど：後程〉afterward(s), later (on).

-node〈-ので〉because of, owing to, on account of, since, as.

byôki-ni-natta-node（病気になったので）because I got sick

nodo〈のど〉a throat.

nodo-ga-itai（のどが痛い）have a sore throat

nodo-ga-kawaku（のどが渇く）be thirsty

nodo-kara-te-ga-deru-hodo-hoshii（のどから手が出るほど欲しい）covet

Nodo-moto-sugireba atsusa-o-wasureru.（のど元過ぎれば熱さを忘れる.）Once on shore, we pray no more.

nôdo〈のうど：濃度〉density, thickness.

nôdô〈のうどう：能動〉

nôdô-tai（能動態）the active voice

nôdô-teki(-na)〈能動的(な)〉active.

nodoka〈のどか〉

nodoka-na〈のどかな〉tranquil, calm, quiet, peaceful.

　　nodoka-na umi（のどかな海） a calm sea

nôen〈のうえん：農園〉a farm.

　　nôen-de hataraku（農園で働く） work on the farm

nôfu〈のうふ：農夫〉*see.* nômin.

nôfu〈のうふ：納付〉

　　nôfu-sho（納付書） a statement of payment

nôfu-suru〈納付する〉pay.

nôgaku〈のうがく：農学〉agriculture.

　　nôgaku-bu（農学部） the department of agriculture

nogareru〈のがれる：逃れる〉escape, get out ((of)), be rid ((of)); evade.

　　sekinin o nogareru（責任を逃れる） evade one's responsibility

nôgei〈のうげい：農芸〉agricultural technology.

　　nôgei-kagaku（農芸化学） agricultural chemistry

no-giku〈のぎく：野菊〉a wild chrysanthemum.

nôgu〈のうぐ：農具〉a farm implement.

nôgyô〈のうぎょう：農業〉agriculture, farming.

nôgyô-no〈農業の〉agricultural.

nôhan-ki〈のうはんき：農繁期〉the farming season.

no-hara〈のはら：野原〉a field, a plain.

nôhin〈のうひん：納品〉delivery of goods.

　　nôhin-sho（納品書） a statement of delivery

nôhin-suru〈納品する〉deliver goods.

noirôze〈ノイローゼ〉(a) neurosis.

nôjô〈のうじょう：農場〉*see.* nôen.

nojuku〈のじゅく：野宿〉

nojuku-suru〈野宿する〉have the night out.

nôka〈のうか：農家〉a farmhouse; a farmer.

nôkai〈のうかい：納会〉the last meeting of the year, the last session of the month.

nôkan-ki〈のうかんき：農閑期〉the leisure season for farmers.

noke-mono〈のけもの：のけ者〉

noke-mono-ni-suru〈のけ者にする〉leave ((a person)) out, exclude.

　　Dare-datte　noke-mono-ni-sareru-no-wa-iya-da.（だれだってのけ者にされるのは嫌だ。） No one likes to be excluded.

nokeru〈のける〉remove, move aside, put out of the way.

noke-zoru〈のけぞる：のけ反る〉bend oneself back.

noki〈のき：軒〉the eaves.

　noki-nami-ni〈軒並みに〉at every door.

nôki〈のうき：納期〉time for payment, the appointed date of delivery.

nô-kigu〈のうぐ：農機具〉farm machines and implements.

nokku〈ノック〉a knock; a fungo.

　nokku-suru〈ノックする〉knock ((at)); hit fungoes.

nokku-auto〈ノックアウト〉a knockout.

　nokku-auto-suru〈ノックアウトする〉knock out.

nôkô〈のうこう：農耕〉farming, tillage.

nôkô〈のうこう：濃厚〉

　nôkô-na〈濃厚な〉thick, dense, heavy, rich.

　　nôkô-na tabe-mono（濃厚な食べ物）a rich food

　　nôkô-ni-naru〈濃厚になる〉become strong, become conspicuous.

nokogiri〈のこぎり〉a saw.

　nokogiri-de-hiku〈のこぎりでひく〉saw.

nokonoko(-to)〈のこのこ(と)〉shamelessly, unconcernedly.

nokorazu〈のこらず：残らず〉all, entirely, without exception.

　　hitori-nokorazu（一人残らず）every one, to the last man

nokori〈のこり：残り〉the remainder, the remnant, the rest.

　　Nokori wa totte-oki-nasai.（残りは取っておきなさい。）Keep the rest for yourself.

　nokori-no〈残りの〉remaining, remnant, surplus.

　　nokori-no shigoto（残りの仕事）the remaining work

　nokori-sukunaku-naru〈残り少なくなる〉run short, draw to an end.

nokori-mono〈のこりもの：残り物〉leftovers, leavings, remains, remnants, odds and ends.

　　Nokori-mono-niwa fuku ga aru.（残り物には福がある。）There is luck in the last helping.

nokoru〈残る〉remain, be left, stay.

　　Mikan-ga-ikura-ka têburu-ni nokotte-iru.（みかんが幾らかテーブルに残っている。）A few oranges remain on the table.

　　Hyaku-en-shika nokotte-i-nai.（百円しか残っていない。）There is only one hundred yen left.

　　ie-ni nokoru（家に残る）stay at home

nokosu〈のこす：残す〉leave (behind), keep back(*or* in).

　　zaisan o nokosu（財産を残す）leave a fortune behind

　　hôka-go nokosareru（放課後残される）be kept after school

nôkotsu〈のうこつ：納骨〉
  nôkotsu-dô〈納骨堂〉 a charnel
  nôkotsu-suru〈納骨する〉 lay ((a person's)) ashes to rest.

noku〈のく〉 get out of the way, step aside.
  Noke, noke!〈のけ，のけ.〉 Get out of the way!

nomareru〈のまれる：飲まれる〉 be swallowed (up); be overawed ((by)).

nomaseru〈のませる：飲ませる〉 make ((a person)) drink, give ((a person)) a drink, administer a medicine ((to a person)), water.

nombiri〈のんびり〉
  nombiri-shita〈のんびりした〉 calm, peaceful, quiet, carefree.
  nombiri-to〈のんびりと〉 calmly, peacefully, quietly, free from all cares.
    nombiri-to inaka-de kurasu〈のんびりと田舎で暮らす〉 enjoy a quiet life in the country

nomeru〈のめる〉 tumble forward.

nomeru〈のめる：飲める〉 drink.
    nome-nai〈飲めない〉 do not drink

nomi〈のみ〉 a flea.

nomi〈のみ〉 a chisel.
  nomi-de-horu〈のみで彫る〉 chisel.

nomi-gusuri〈のみぐすり：飲み薬〉 a medicine.

nomi-komi〈のみこみ：飲み込み〉
  nomi-komi-no-hayai or *nomi-komi-no-ii*〈飲み込みの早い，飲み込みのいい〉 quick-witted, quick of understanding, quick to learn.

nomi-komu〈のみこむ：飲み込む〉 swallow, gulp down; understand, grasp, take in.

nomi-kui〈のみくい：飲み食い〉 eating and drinking.

nomi-mono〈のみもの：飲み物〉 something to drink, a drink, a beverage.

nômin〈のうみん：農民〉 a farmer, a peasant.

-nomi-narazu〈-のみならず〉 not only...but (also), as well as.
    kare-nomi-narazu-kanojo-mo（彼のみならず彼女も） not only he but (also) she, she as well as he

nomi-sugi〈のみすぎ：飲み過ぎ〉 intemperance.

nomu〈のむ：飲む〉 drink, have, take; accept.
    mizu o nomu（水を飲む） drink water
    o-cha o nomu（お茶を飲む） have tea
    sake-o-nomu（酒を飲む） have a drink
    kusuri o nomu（薬を飲む） take medicine

sûpu o nomu（スープを飲む）eat soup

yôkyû o nomu（要求を飲む）accept a request

nomeru〈飲める〉be good to drink.

Sono mizu wa nomemasu-ka?（その水は飲めますか.）Is that water good to drink?

nômu〈のうむ：濃霧〉a dense fog.

no-nezumi〈のねずみ：野ねずみ〉a field mouse.

-noni〈-のに〉though, in spite of; when, while; for; I wish.

ame-ga-hidoku-futteiru-noni（雨がひどく降っているのに）in spite of the heavy rain

Shiken-ga-chikai-noni kare-wa benkyô-shi-nai.（試験が近いのに彼は勉強しない.）He doesn't study when the examination is in sight.

Kugi-o-nuku-noni kugi-nuki-ga-iru.（くぎを抜くのにくぎ抜きが要る.）I want pincers to pull out a nail.

Kimi-mo-issho-ni-kureba-yokatta-noni.（君も一緒に来ればよかったのに.）You ought to have come with us.

nonki〈のんき〉

nonki-na〈のんきな〉easy, easygoing, carefree, leisurely.

nonki-ni〈のんきに〉at ease, leisurely.

nonoshiru〈ののしる〉call ((a person)) names, abuse.

non-puro〈ノンプロ〉

non-puro-no〈ノンプロの〉nonprofessional, nonpro.

nopperi〈のっぺり〉

nopperi-shita〈のっぺりした〉smooth, expressionless, blank.

noppiki-nara-nai〈のっぴきならない：のっ引きならない〉

noppiki-nara-nai-yôji-de〈のっぴきならない用事で〉on unavoidable business.

nora-〈のら：野良〉

nora-shigoto（野良仕事）farm work

nora-inu（野良犬）a stray dog

nora-neko（野良猫）a stray cat

norakura〈のらくら〉idly, lazily, aimlessly.

norakura-kurasu（のらくら暮らす）lead an idle life

noren〈のれん〉a shop curtain; credit, goodwill.

noren o kegasu（のれんを汚す）affect the credit of a shop

nori〈のり〉paste, starch.

nori-de-haru〈のりではる〉paste, stick with paste.

nori-o-tsukeru〈のりを付ける〉starch.

nori 〈のり〉laver.

  aji-tsuke-nori〈味付けのり〉 toasted and seasoned laver

-nori 〈-のり：乗り〉

  roku-nin-nori-no jidôsha〈六人乗りの自動車〉 a six-passenger car

nori-ageru 〈のりあげる：乗り上げる〉run aground, be stranded.

nori-awaseru 〈のりあわせる：乗り合わせる〉happen to ride in the same car.

nori-dasu 〈のりだす：乗り出す〉lean forward; set about, launch out ((on)), enter ((upon)).

  mado-kara-karada-o-nori-dasu〈窓から体を乗り出す〉 lean out of a window

  seikai-ni-nori-dasu〈政界に乗り出す〉 enter upon a political career

nori-ireru 〈のりいれる：乗り入れる〉extend (a bus service) ((into)).

nori-kae 〈のりかえ：乗り換え〉a change, transfer.

nori-kaeru〈乗り換える〉change, transfer.

  Nagoya-de Takayama-sen-ni nori-kaeru〈名古屋で高山線に乗り換える〉 change at Nagoya to the Takayama Line

nori-kakaru 〈のりかかる：乗り掛かる〉

  Nori-kakatta-fune-da, ima-sara-ato-e-hike-nai.〈乗りかかった船だ，今更後へ引けない。〉 I have gone too far to go back.

nori-ki 〈のりき：乗り気〉

nori-ki-ni-naru〈乗り気になる〉become interested ((in)), show much enthusiasm ((for)), be enthusiastic ((about)).

nori-ki-ni-natte〈乗り気になって〉with much interest, enthusiastically.

nori-kiru 〈のりきる：乗り切る〉weather, ride through, sail across; tide over.

nori-koeru 〈のりこえる：乗り越える〉get over, climb over; tide over.

nori-komu 〈のりこむ：乗り込む〉get into, go on board; march into, arrive ((at or in)), enter.

  kuruma-de nori-komu〈車で乗り込む〉 arrive in a car

nori-konasu 〈のりこなす：乗りこなす〉manage 〔a horse〕.

nori-koshi 〈のりこし：乗り越し〉

  nori-koshi-ryôkin〈乗り越し料金〉 an excess fare

nori-kosu〈乗り越す〉ride past 〔one's destination〕.

norikumi-in 〈のりくみいん：乗組員〉a crew, a member of a crew.

nori-kumu 〈のりくむ：乗り組む〉be on board.

nori-mawasu 〈のりまわす：乗り回す〉drive ((a car)) around.

nori-mono 〈のりもの：乗り物〉a vehicle, a conveyance.

nôrin 〈のうりん：農林〉
 nôrin-shô（農林省）the Ministry of Agriculture and Forestry
 nôrin-daijin（農林大臣）the Minister of Agriculture and Forestry

nori-nige 〈のりにげ：乗り逃げ〉
 nori-nige-suru〈乗り逃げする〉steal a ride, ride away ((with)).

nori-okureru 〈のりおくれる：乗り遅れる〉miss, fail to catch.
 saishû-ressha ni nori-okureru（最終列車に乗り遅れる）fail to catch the last train

nori-ori 〈のりおり：乗り降り〉getting on and off.
 nori-ori-ni-chûi-suru〔乗り降りに注意する〕be careful in getting on and off
 nori-ori-suru〈乗り降りする〉get on and off.

nori-suteru 〈のりすてる：乗り捨てる〉get off, leave〔a car〕; abandon〔a car〕.

nori-te 〈のりて：乗り手〉a rider; a passenger.

norito 〈のりと：祝詞〉a *Shinto* prayer.

nôritsu 〈のうりつ：能率〉efficiency.
 nôritsu o ageru（能率を上げる）increase efficiency
 nôritsu-kyû（能率給）efficiency pay
 nôritsu-teki(-na)〈能率的(な)〉efficient.

nori-tsubusu 〈のりつぶす：乗りつぶす〉drive ((a car)) to scraps.

nori-tsukeru 〈のりつける：乗り付ける〉ride up ((to)); get used to riding.

noroi 〈のろい〉slow, tardy.
 ashi-ga-noroi（足がのろい）be slow of foot
 shigoto-ga-noroi（仕事がのろい）be slow in one's work

noroi 〈のろい〉a curse.
 norou〈のろう〉curse.
 norou-beki or *norowareta*〈のろうべき，のろわれた〉cursed.

noro-ke 〈のろけ：のろ気〉
 noro-ke-o-iu or *norokeru*〈のろけを言う，のろける〉talk about one's love affairs.
 saikun-no-noroke-o-iu（妻君ののろけを言う）speak fondly of one's own wife

noronoro(-to) 〈のろのろ(と)〉slowly, tardily, at a snail's pace.

noroshi 〈のろし〉a signal fire, a beacon.

noru 〈のる：乗(載)る〉ride, ride ((in)), take, go on board; appear; join, participate ((in)); be deceived, be taken in.
 jitensha ni noru（自転車に乗る）ride a bicycle

kuruma-ni-noru（車に乗る） ride in a car
takushî ni noru（タクシーに乗る） take a taxi
kisha ni noru（汽車に乗る） take a train
hikô-ki ni noru（飛行機に乗る） take an airplane
fune ni noru（船に乗る） go on board a ship
shimbun-ni-noru（新聞に載る） be reported in a newspaper
hanashi-ni-noru（話に乗る） show some interest in a matter
Sono-te-niwa-nora-nai-yo.（その手には乗らないよ。） That trick won't
do with me.
〜(-ni)-notte-iku《（〜に）乗って行く》go by... .
basu-ni-notte-iku（バスに乗って行く） go by bus
kuruma-ni-notte-iku（車に乗って行く） go by car

noru-ka-soru-ka〈のるかそるか：伸るか反るか〉
Noru-ka-soru-ka-yatte-miyô.（伸るか反るかやってみよう。） Win or
lose, I will try.

noruma〈ノルマ〉one's assigned task.
noruma o hatasu（ノルマを果たす） fulfill the work assigned to one

Noruwê〈ノルウェー〉Norway.
Noruwê-jin（ノルウェー人） a Norwegian
Noruwê-go（ノルウェー語） Norwegian
Noruwê(-jin)-no（ノルウェー（人）の） Norwegian

nôryô〈のうりょう：納涼〉
nôryô-no-tame-ni〈納涼のために〉to enjoy the evening cool.

nôryoku〈のうりょく：能力〉ability, capacity, faculty, power(s).
nôryoku o hakki-suru（能力を発揮する） exhibit one's ability
nôryoku-kyû（能力給） pay according to ability
chô-nôryoku（超能力） superhuman ability
shiharai-nôryoku（支払い能力） the ability to pay
seisan-nôryoku（生産能力） productive capacity
〜(-suru)-nôryoku-ga-aru〈〜(する)能力がある〉be able ((to do)), be
capable of ((doing)).
nôryoku-no-aru〈能力のある〉able, capable.

nosabaru〈のさばる〉act important, act haughtily, push oneself forward.

nôsaku-butsu〈のうさくぶつ：農作物〉the crops, farm product.

nô-sambutsu〈のうさんぶつ：農産物〉agricultural products.

nôsatsu〈のうさつ：悩殺〉
nôsatsu-sareru〈悩殺される〉be under the spell of ((a person's)) charms.

nôsei 〈のうせい：農政〉 agricultural administration.

noseru 〈のせる：載(乗)せる〉 put; place, load, take in, give ((a person)) a ride; put, publish.

    Sono kabin o têburu-no-ue-ni nose-nasai.（その花瓶をテーブルの上に載せなさい。） Put the vase on the desk.

    ni-guruma ni nimotsu-o noseru（荷車に荷物を載せる） load a cart with goods

    jôkyaku-o-noseru（乗客を乗せる） take in passengers

    Kyôkai-made nosete-itte-ageyô.（教会まで乗せて行ってあげよう。） I'll give you a ride to the church.

    Mainichi-shimbun-ni kôkoku o noseru（毎日新聞に広告を載せる） put an ad in the Mainichi

noshi-agaru 〈のしあがる：のし上がる〉 rise in the world ((to)).

nôshuku 〈のうしゅく：濃縮〉

    nôshuku-uran（濃縮ウラン） uranium concentrate, enriched uranium

    nôshuku-suru〈濃縮する〉 concentrate, enrich.

nôson 〈のうそん：農村〉 a farm village, an agricultural district.

    nôson-no〈農村の〉 rural, agricultural.

nosonoso(-to) 〈のそのそ(と)〉 slowly, lazily.

nô-tan 〈のうたん：濃淡〉 light and shade.

    nô-tan-o-tsukeru〈濃淡を付ける〉 shade〔a drawing〕.

noten 〈のてん：野天〉 the open air.

    noten-burn（野天風ろ） an open-air bath

    noten-no〈野天の〉 open-air, outdoor.

    noten-de〈野天で〉 in the open air, outdoors.

nôto 〈ノート〉 a note, a notebook.

    nôto-o-toru〈ノートを取る〉 note down, take notes ((of)).

nottoru 〈のっとる：乗っ取る〉 supplant, usurp, hijack.

    kaisha o nottoru（会社を乗っ取る） take over a company

no-usagi 〈のうさぎ：野うさぎ〉 a hare, a jackrabbit.

nôyaku 〈のうやく：農薬〉 agricultural chemicals.

no-zarashi 〈のざらし：野ざらし〉

    no-zarashi-ni-suru〈野ざらしにする〉 expose ((a thing)) to the weather.

nôzei 〈のうぜい：納税〉 payment of taxes.

    nôzei-sha（納税者） a taxpayer, a ratepayer

    nôzei-shinkoku-yôshi（納税申告用紙） a tax form

    nôzei-suru〈納税する〉 pay one's taxes.

(-o)-nozoite 〈～(を)のぞいて：～(を)除いて〉 except, but.

nichiyô-bi-o-nozoite　mainichi（日曜日を除いて毎日）every day except Sundays

ni-san-no　machigai-o-nozoite（二，三の間違いを除いて）with the exception of a few mistakes

nozoki-ana〈のぞきあな：のぞき穴〉a peephole, a spyhole.

nozoki-komu〈のぞきこむ：のぞき込む〉look into, peep into.

nozoku〈のぞく〉look〔out of the window〕, look〔in at the window〕, peep〔into a room〕.

nozoku〈のぞく：除く〉take off, put away, remove, exclude, omit.

nozomashii〈のぞましい：望ましい〉desirable, advisable, welcome.

nozomashiku-nai（望ましくない）undesirable, unwelcome

nozomi〈のぞみ：望み〉(a) desire, (a) wish, hope.

nozomi o idaku（望みを抱く）cherish a desire

nozomi ga kanau（望みがかなう）fulfill one's desire

nozomi-no-aru〈望みのある〉hopeful, promising.

nozomi-no-nai（望みのない）hopeless

nozomi-doori〈望みどおり〉as one wishes.

nozomu〈のぞむ：望む〉desire, wish, hope.

nugaseru〈ぬがせる：脱がせる〉strip ((a person)) of.

nugeru〈ぬげる：脱げる〉come off.

Undô-gutsu ga nakanaka-nuge-nai.（運動靴がなかなか脱げない.）My sports shoes will not come off.

nugu〈ぬぐ：脱ぐ〉take off, remove, strip oneself ((of)), pull off.

bôshi o nugu（帽子を脱ぐ）take off one's hat

te-bukuro o nugu（手袋を脱ぐ）pull off one's gloves

kimono-o-nugu（着物を脱ぐ）undress (oneself)

nuguu〈ぬぐう〉wipe.

nui-awaseru〈ぬいあわせる：縫い合わせる〉sew together.

nui-bari〈ぬいばり：縫い針〉a (sewing) needle.

nui-ito〈ぬいいと：縫い糸〉sewing thread.

nui-komu〈ぬいこむ：縫い込む〉sew in.

nui-me〈ぬいめ：縫い目〉a seam.

nui-me ga hokorobiru（縫い目がほころびる）a seam opens

nui-mono〈ぬいもの：縫い物〉sewing, needlework.

nui-mono-o-suru〈縫い物をする〉sew, do needlework.

nui-tori〈ぬいとり：縫い取り〉embroidery.

nui-tori-o-suru〈縫い取りをする〉embroider.

nui-tsukeru〈ぬいつける：縫い付ける〉sew on.

nuka 〈ぬか〉 rice bran.

> **nuka-miso** 〈ぬかみそ〉 salted rice bran paste for pickling

>> **nuka-miso-zuke** 〈ぬかみそ漬け〉 vegetables pickled in rice-bran paste

> **nuka-ni-kugi** 〈ぬかにくぎ〉 plow the sand(s), have no effect ((on))

> **nuka-yorokobi** 〈ぬか喜び〉 a premature joy

nukari 〈ぬかり：抜かり〉 a slip, a blunder, an oversight.

> Oba wa yaru-koto-ni-nukari-ga-nai. (叔(伯)母はやる事に抜かりがない.) My aunt knows what she is about.

> *nukari-naku* 〈抜かりなく〉 cautiously, shrewdly, without an oversight.

nukaru 〈ぬかる〉 be muddy, be slushy.

> *nukaru-mi* 〈ぬかるみ〉 mud, a muddy place.

> *nukaru-mi-no* 〈ぬかるみの〉 muddy.

nukasu 〈ぬかす：抜かす〉 omit, leave out, skip.

> **ni-go nukasu** (二語抜かす) leave out two words

> **san-gyô nukasu** (三行抜かす) skip three lines

nuke-ana 〈ぬけあな：抜け穴〉 a secret passage, an underground way, a loophole.

nuke-deru or **nuke-dasu** 〈ぬけでる, ぬけだす：抜け出る, 抜け出す〉 slip out of.

> **sotto beddo-o nuke-dasu** (そっとベッドを抜け出す) slip out of the bed

nuke-gake 〈ぬけがけ：抜け駆け〉

> *nuke-gake-no-kômyô-o-tateru* 〈抜け駆けの功名を立てる〉 steal a march ((on)).

nuke-gara 〈ぬけがら：抜け殻〉 a cast-off skin.

> **hebi-no-nuke-gara** (蛇の抜け殻) a slough

> **semi-no nuke-gara** (せみの抜け殻) a cicada's shell

nuke-kawaru 〈ぬけかわる：抜け替わる〉 slough, molt.

nuke-me 〈ぬけめ：抜け目〉

> *nuke-me-nai* 〈抜け目ない〉 shrewd, smart, canny, cunning, careful.

> *nuke-me-naku* 〈抜け目なく〉 shrewdly, smartly, cannily, carefully.

nuke-michi 〈ぬけみち：抜け道〉 a byway, a secret path, a loophole.

nukenuke(-to) 〈ぬけぬけ（と）〉 impudently, brazenly, unashamedly.

> *nukenuke-to～(-suru)* 〈ぬけぬけと～（する）〉 make no scruple ((to do)).

nukeru 〈ぬける：抜ける〉 come out, fall out; be missing; be gone, get rid ((of)).

> Kyûshi ga nuketa. (きゅう歯が抜けた.) The molar (tooth) came out.

Jû-roku-pêji nukete-iru.（十六ページ抜けている.） Sixteen pages are missing.

Chikara ga sukkari-nukete-shimatta.（力がすっかり抜けてしまった.）
All my strength was gone.

Warui shûkan wa nuke-nai-mono-da.（悪い習慣は抜けないものだ.） It is hard to get rid of a bad habit.

nuki〈ぬき：抜き〉

chôshoku-nuki-de〈朝食抜きで〉 without taking breakfast

aisatsu-wa-nuki-ni-shite〈あいさつは抜きにして〉 without formalities

jôdan-wa-nuki-ni-shite〈冗談は抜きにして〉 joking apart

nuki-gaki〈ぬきがき：抜き書き〉an extract.

nuki-gaki-suru〈抜き書きする〉make extracts ((from)).

nuki-sashi〈ぬきさし：抜き差し〉

nuki-sashi-nara-nai-hame-ni-ochiiru〈抜き差しならない羽目に陥る〉find oneself in a dilemma.

nuki-uchi〈ぬきうち：抜き打ち〉

nuki-uchi-kensa（抜き打ち検査） a surprise inspection

nuki-uchi-teki-ni〈抜き打ち的に〉without any notice.

nuku〈ぬく：抜く〉draw out, pull out; remove, take out; outstrip, excel; skip over.

ha o nuite-morau（歯を抜いてもらう） have a tooth pulled out

shimi o nuku（染みを抜く） take out a stain

gôru-chikaku-de hitori o nuku（ゴール近くで一人を抜く） outstrip ((a person's)) opponent near the goal

te-o-nuku（手を抜く） skimp the work

nukumori〈ぬくもり〉warmth.

Beddo-ni-mada-kanojo-no-nukumori-ga-nokotte-iru.（ベッドにまだ彼女のぬくもりが残っている.） The bed is still warm from her body.

nukunuku(-to)〈ぬくぬく(と)〉

nukunuku-to-kurashite-iru〈ぬくぬくと暮らしている〉lead an easy life.

numa〈ぬま：沼〉a swamp, a marsh.

numa-chi（沼地） marshland, a bog

nuno〈ぬの：布〉cloth.

nuno-gire（布切れ） a piece of cloth

nurari-kurari〈ぬらりくらり〉

nurari-kurari-to-shita〈ぬらりくらりとした〉evasive, noncommittal.

nurasu〈ぬらす〉wet, moisten, soak.

Ashi o nurasa-nai-yô-ni shi-nasai.（足をぬらさないようにしなさい.）

      Take care not to get your feet wet.

nureru 〈ぬれる〉 get wet, be damp, be moistened, be soaked.

  tsuyu-ni nureru (露にぬれる)　get wet with dew

nureta 〈ぬれた〉 wet, damp, moist.

nure-ginu 〈ぬれぎぬ〉 a false charge.

nure-ginu-o-kiseru 〈ぬれぎぬを着せる〉 make a false charge ((against)).

nure-ginu-o-kiserareru 〈ぬれぎぬを着せられる〉 be falsely accused ((of)).

nure-nezumi 〈ぬれねずみ〉

nure-nezumi-ni-naru 〈ぬれねずみになる〉 be drenched to the skin, get wet through.

nurete 〈ぬれて：ぬれ手〉

nurete-de-awa-o-tsukamu 〈ぬれ手であわをつかむ〉 make easy money.

nuri 〈ぬり：塗り〉 coating, lacquering, varnishing, painting, plastering.

nuri-ga-ii 〈塗りがいい〉 be excellently lacquered.

nuri-e 〈ぬりえ：塗り絵〉 a line drawing for coloring.

nuri-gusuri 〈ぬりぐすり：塗り薬〉 an ointment, an unguent.

nuri-kae 〈ぬりかえ：塗り替え〉 repainting, recoating.

nuri-kae-o-suru or *nuri-kaeru* 〈塗り替えをする，塗り替える〉 repaint, recoat.

nuri-mono 〈ぬりもの：塗り物〉 lacquer ware.

nuri-tate 〈ぬりたて：塗りたて〉

nuri-tate-no 〈塗りたての〉 freshly-painted.

nuri-tsubusu 〈ぬりつぶす：塗りつぶす〉 paint out.

nuru 〈ぬる：塗る〉 paint, varnish, plaster; spread; apply.

  chizu ni iro-o-nuru (地図に色を塗る)　color a map

  pan-ni batâ o nuru (パンにバターを塗る)　spread butter on bread

  kizu-ni nankô o nuru (傷に軟こうを塗る)　apply some ointment to the wound

nurui 〈ぬるい〉 tepid, lukewarm.

  O-furo ga nuruku-nai-desu-ka? (お風ろがぬるくないですか.)　Is the bath warm enough?

nuruma-yu 〈ぬるま湯〉 lukewarm water.

nurunuru 〈ぬるぬる〉

nurunuru-shita 〈ぬるぬるした〉 slippery, slimy, clammy, greasy.

nusumi 〈ぬすみ：盗み〉 theft, stealing, pilfering.

nusumu 〈盗む〉 steal.

    Tokei o nusumareta. (時計を盗まれた.)　I had my watch stolen.

nusumi-giki 〈ぬすみぎき：盗み聞き〉

nusumi-giki-suru〈盗み聞きする〉eavesdrop ((on)), overhear, tap, listen in ((on)).

nutto〈ぬっと〉suddenly, unexpectedly.

nuu〈ぬう：縫う〉sew, stitch.

　　kizu-guchi o nuu（傷口を縫う）　sew up a wound

　　hokorobi o nuu（ほころびを縫う）　stitch up a rip

　　hito-naka-o　nuu-yô-ni-shite-aruku（人中を縫うようにして歩く）　thread one's way through a crowd

nyô〈にょう：尿〉urine.

　　nyô-kensa（尿検査）　urine analysis

　　nyôdô（尿道）　the urethra

　　　　nyôdô-en（尿道炎）　urethritis

　　nyôdoku-shô（尿毒症）　uremia

　　nyô-no〈尿の〉urinary, uric.

nyôbô〈にょうぼう：女房〉a wife, one's better half.

　　nyôbô-yaku-o tsutomeru〈女房役を務める〉assist ((a person)) as his right-handed person.

nyojitsu〈にょじつ：如実〉

　　nyojitsu-ni〈如実に〉truly, realistically, vividly, graphically.

　　　　nyojitsu-ni-mono-gataru（如実に物語る）　give a vivid account ((of)).

nyokinyoki〈にょきにょき〉one after another, here and there, all over.

Nyorai〈にょらい：如来〉Buddha.

nyôso〈にょうそ：尿素〉urea.

nyuansu〈ニュアンス〉a nuance, a shade of difference.

nyûbai〈にゅうばい：入梅〉the beginning of the rainy season.

nyû-chô〈にゅうちょう：入超〉an excess of imports over exports, an unfavorable balance of trade.

nyûden〈にゅうでん：入電〉a telegram received.

　　～-kara-no-nyûden-ni-yoreba〈～からの入電によれば〉according to a telegram from... .

nyûdô-gumo〈にゅうどうぐも：入道雲〉gigantic columns of clouds, a thunderhead.

nyûeki〈にゅうえき：乳液〉milky lotion; latex.

nyûgaku〈にゅうがく：入学〉admission into a school, entrance into a school.

　　nyûgaku-gansho（入学願書）　an application for admission

　　nyûgaku-shigan-sha（入学志願者）　an applicant for admission

　　nyûgaku-shiken（入学試験）　an entrance examination

nyûgaku-shiken o ukeru〈入学試験を受ける〉take an entrance examination

nyûgaku-shiken ni gôkaku-suru〈入学試験に合格する〉pass an entrance examination

nyûgaku-kin〈入学金〉an entrance fee

nyûgaku-shiki〈入学式〉an entrance ceremony

nyûgaku-o-kyoka-sareru〈入学を許可される〉be admitted to a school.

nyûgaku-suru〈入学する〉enter a school.

nyûgan〈にゅうがん：乳がん〉cancer of the breast.

nyûgyû〈にゅうぎゅう：乳牛〉a milch cow.

nyûhaku-shoku(-no)〈にゅうはくしょく(の)：乳白色(の)〉milk white.

nyûin〈にゅういん：入院〉entrance to a hospital.

nyûin-kanja〈入院患者〉an inpatient

nyûin-suru〈入院する〉enter hospital.

nyûin-chû-de-aru〈入院中である〉be in (the) hospital.

nyûjaku〈にゅうじゃく：柔弱〉

nyûjaku-na〈柔弱な〉weak, effeminate, weak-kneed.

nyûji〈にゅうじ：乳児〉a suckling, a baby, an infant.

Nyûjîrando〈ニュージーランド〉New Zealand.

Nyûjîrando-jin（ニュージーランド人）a New Zealander

nyûjô〈にゅうじょう：入場〉admission, entrance.

nyûjô-ken（入場券）an admission ticket

nyûjô-seiri-ken（入場整理券）an admission order card

nyûjô-ryô（入場料）an admission fee

Nyûjô-muryô（入場無料）Admission Free

nyûjô-sha（入場者）a visitor, an attendance

nyûjô-shiki（入場式）an opening ceremony

nyûjô-suru〈入場する〉enter, get in; be admitted ((into)).

nyûka〈にゅうか：入荷〉arrival of goods.

nyûka-suru〈入荷する〉arrive, be received.

nyûkai〈にゅうかい：入会〉admission, entrance.

nyûkai-o-môshi-komu（入会を申し込む）apply for admission

nyûkai-kin（入会金）an entrance fee

nyûkai-sha（入会者）a person admitted to membership

nyûkai-suru〈入会する〉join a society, become a member of a society.

nyûkaku〈にゅうかく：入閣〉

nyûkaku-suru〈入閣する〉become a Cabinet member.

nyûkin〈にゅうきん：入金〉receipt of money, payment, money received.

　　nyûkin-dempyô〈入金伝票〉 a paying-in slip
　nyûkin-suru〈入金する〉receive.
nyûko〈にゅうこ：入庫〉
　nyûko-suru〈入庫する〉stock, be stocked; enter the shed.
nyûkô〈にゅうこう：入港〉arrival in port.
　nyûkô-suru〈入港する〉arrive in a port, enter (a) port, make (a) port.
nyûkoku〈にゅうこく：入国〉entrance into a country, immigration.
　　nyûkoku-o-kyoka-suru〈入国を許可する〉 admit ((a person)) into a
　　　country
　　fuhô-nyûkoku〈不法入国〉 illegal entry
　nyûkoku-suru〈入国する〉enter a country, immigrate into a country.
nyûkyo〈にゅうきょ：入居〉
　　nyûkyo-sha〈入居者〉 a tenant
　nyûkyo-suru〈入居する〉move into〔a flat〕.
nyûmaku〈にゅうまく：入幕〉
　nyûmaku-suru〈入幕する〉rise to the senior grade of *sumo*.
nyûmon〈にゅうもん：入門〉
　　Ei-kaiwa-nyûmon〈英会話入門〉 a first step to English conversation
　　nyûmon-sho〈入門書〉 a guide ((to)), a primer ((of))
　nyûmon-suru〈入門する〉become a pupil ((of)), be initiated ((into)).
nyûnen〈にゅうねん：入念〉
　nyûnen-na〈入念な〉deliberate, elaborate, scrupulous.
　nyûnen-ni〈入念に〉carefully, with great care.
nyûsan〈にゅうさん：乳酸〉lactic acid.
　　nyûsan-inryô〈乳酸飲料〉 a lactic acid beverage
nyûsatsu〈にゅうさつ：入札〉a bid, a tender.
　　nyûsatsu-ni-fusu〈入札に付す〉 sell ((a thing)) by tender
　　nyûsatsu-o-tsunoru〈入札を募る〉 call for bids ((for)), invite tenders
　　　((for))
　　nyûsatsu-sha〈入札者〉 a bidder, a tenderer
　nyûsatsu-suru〈入札する〉bid ((for)), tender ((for)).
nyû-seihin〈にゅうせいひん：乳製品〉dairy products.
nyûseki〈にゅうせき：入籍〉entry in a family register.
　nyûseki-suru〈入籍する〉have one's name entered in the family register.
nyûsen〈にゅうせん：乳せん〉a mammary gland.
　　nyûsen-en〈乳せん炎〉 mastitis
nyûsen〈にゅうせん：入選〉
　　nyûsen-sakuhin〈入選作品〉 a winning (piece of) work

　　　nyûsen-sha〈入選者〉a winner

　nyûsen-suru〈入選する〉be accepted, be selected.

nyûsha〈にゅうしゃ：入社〉

　nyûsha-suru〈入社する〉enter a company.

nyûshi〈にゅうし：乳歯〉a milk tooth, a baby tooth.

nyûshi〈にゅうし：入試〉an abbreviation of 'nyûgaku-shiken'.

nyûshô〈にゅうしょう：入賞〉

　　　nyûshô-sha〈入賞者〉a prize winner

　nyûshô-suru〈入賞する〉win a prize.

　　　ittô-ni-nyûshô-suru（一等に入賞する）win the first prize

nyûshu〈にゅうしゅ：入手〉

　nyûshu-suru〈入手する〉obtain, get, receive, come to hand.

nyûsu〈ニュース〉news.

　　　nyûsu-eiga（ニュース映画）a news film, newsreel

　　　nyûsu-kaisetu（ニュース解説）news commentary

　　　nyûsu-sokuhô（ニュース速報）a news flash

　　　denkô-nyûsu（電光ニュース）an electric news tape

　　　kaigai-nyûsu（海外ニュース）foreign news

nyûtai〈にゅうたい：入隊〉enlistment.

　nyûtai-suru〈入隊する〉join the army.

nyûtô〈にゅうとう：入党〉

　nyûtô-suru〈入党する〉join a political party.

nyûwa〈にゅうわ：柔和〉

　nyûwa-na〈柔和な〉gentle, mild, tender, soft, meek.

　　　hijô-ni-nyûwa-na（非常に柔和な）meek as a lamb

nyûyô〈にゅうよう：入用〉*see.* hitsuyô.

nyûyô-ji〈にゅうようじ：乳幼児〉infants, babies.

nyûyoku〈にゅうよく：入浴〉a bath.

　　　nyûyoku-suru（入浴する）take a bath

　　　nyûyoku-saseru（入浴させる）give ((a baby)) a bath

nyûzai〈にゅうざい：乳剤〉an emulsion.

O

o 〈お：尾〉 *see.* shippo.

ō 〈おう：王〉 a king.

> hyaku-jū no ō〈百獣の王〉 the king of beasts

oashisu 〈オアシス〉 an oasis.

oba 〈おば：叔(伯)母〉 an aunt.

ōbā 〈オーバー〉 an overcoat.

ōbā 〈オーバー〉

> *ōbā-na* 〈オーバーな〉 exaggerated, overdone.
> *ōbā-na-ii-kata-o-suru* 〈オーバーな言い方をする〉 exaggerate.

oba-chan 〈おばちゃん：叔(伯)母ちゃん〉 an auntie(*or* an aunty).

o-bā-chan 〈おばあちゃん〉 a grandma.

ōbāhōru 〈オーバーホール〉 an overhaul.

> *ōbāhōru-suru* 〈オーバーホールする〉 overhaul.

o-bake 〈おばけ：お化け〉 a ghost, a goblin, a monster.

o-bā-san 〈おばあさん〉 a grandmother, an old woman.

Ō-Bei 〈おうべい：欧米〉 Europe and America.

> Ō-Bei-jin〈欧米人〉 Europeans and Americans
> Ō-Bei-shokoku〈欧米諸国〉 countries in Europe and America

obekka *or* **o-benchara** 〈おべっか，おべんちゃら〉 flattery.

> *obekka-o-tsukau* *or* *o-benchara-o-iu* 〈おべっかを使う，おべんちゃらを言う〉 flatter.

obi 〈おび：帯〉 a belt, a sash, an *obi*.

> Obi-ni-mijikashi tasuki-ni-nagashi.〈帯に短したすきに長し。〉 Good for neither one thing nor the other.

ō-bī 〈オービー〉 an O.B., an old boy.

obieru 〈おびえる〉 be frightened ((at)), be scared ((at)).

obiki-dasu 〈おびきだす：おびき出す〉 lure away ((from)).

obiki-yoseru 〈おびきよせる：おびき寄せる〉 decoy ((into)).

obitadashii〈おびただしい〉a great number of, a great deal of, numerous, countless, vast, enormous, abundant.

 obitadashii-hito-de（おびただしい人出）a great crowd of people

 obitadashiku〈おびただしく〉innumerably, abundantly.

obiyakasu〈おびやかす：脅かす〉threaten, menace, be a menace ((to)), intimidate.

 Sore-wa sekai-heiwa-o-obiyakasu-mono-da.（それは世界平和を脅かすものだ。）It is a menace to world peace.

ôbo〈おうぼ：応募〉subscription, application, answer.

 ôbo-sha〈応募者〉a subscriber, an applicant

 ôbo-suru〈応募する〉subscribe ((for *or* to)), apply ((for)).

ôbô〈おうぼう：横暴〉oppression, tyranny, high-handedness.

 ôbô-na〈横暴な〉oppressive, tyrannical, high-handed, unreasonable.

oboe〈おぼえ：覚え〉memory, remembrance.

 oboe-ga-ii（覚えがいい）have a good memory

 oboe-ga-warui（覚えが悪い）have a bad memory

 oboe-ga-aru〈覚えがある〉remember, recall.

 mi-ni-oboe-ga-nai（身に覚えがない）be innocent ((of))

ôboe〈オーボエ〉an oboe.

 ôboe-sôsha（オーボエ奏者）an oboist

oboe-gaki〈おぼえがき：覚え書き〉a memorandum, a memo, a memorial, a note.

 oboe-gaki no kôkan（覚え書きの交換）an exchange of notes

oboeru〈おぼえる：覚える〉remember, know, memorize, learn by heart; feel.

 itami o oboeru（痛みを覚える）feel a pain

 oboete-iru〈覚えている〉remember, keep in mind, know by heart.

oboreru〈おぼれる〉be drowned, drown.

 Oboreru-mono wa wara-o-mo-tsukamu.（おぼれる者はわらをもつかむ。）A drowning man will catch at a straw.

oboro-ge〈おぼろげ：おぼろ気〉

 oboro-ge-na〈おぼろげな〉vague, indistinct, dim.

 oboro-ge-ni〈おぼろげに〉vaguely, faintly, indistinctly, dimly.

 oboro-ge-ni-kioku-shite-iru（おぼろげに記憶している）remember dimly, have a faint recollection ((of))

obutsu〈おぶつ：汚物〉dirt, filth.

ôchaku〈おうちゃく：横着〉

 ôchaku-na〈横着な〉impudent, brazen, rude.

ochi-au 〈おちあう：落ち合う〉 meet, rendezvous, come together.

ochiba 〈おちば：落ち葉〉 fallen leaves.

ochibureru 〈おちぶれる：落ちぶれる〉 be ruined, be reduced to poverty, go under, fall in one's circumstances.

ochibureta 〈落ちぶれた〉 ruined, reduced, down-and-out, broken-down.

ochido 〈おちど：落ち度〉 a fault, an error, blame.

Kore-wa watashi-no ochido-da. (これは私の落ち度だ。) This is my fault.

ochido-no-nai 〈落ち度のない〉 faultless, blameless.

ochiiru 〈おちいる：陥る〉 fall ((into)), run ((into)), lapse ((into)).

kiken-ni-ochiiru （危険に陥る） run into danger

ochi-me 〈おちめ：落ち目〉

ochi-me-ni-naru 〈落ち目になる〉 go down on one's luck.

ochiochi 〈おちおち〉

ochiochi-nemure-nai 〈おちおち眠れない〉 cannot have a quiet sleep.

ochiru 〈おちる：落ちる〉 fall, drop, fail, go down, come off.

ki-kara ochiru （木から落ちる） fall from a tree

beddo-kara ochiru （ベッドから落ちる） fall out of the bed

shiken ni ochiru （試験に落ちる） fail (in) an examination

ninki-ga-ochiru （人気が落ちる） fall in popularity

ochitsuki 〈おちつき：落ち着き〉 calmness, presence of mind.

ochitsuki-no-nai 〈落ち着きのない〉 restless, nervous.

ochitsuku 〈おちつく：落ち着く〉 settle (down); calm(*or* cool) down.

shinkyo-ni-ochitsuku 〈新居に落ち着く〉 settle in one's new house

Ochitsuki-nasai. （落ち着きなさい。） Calm down.

ochitsuita 〈落ち着いた〉 calm, quiet, cool.

ochitsuite 〈落ち着いて〉 calmly.

ôchô 〈おうちょう：王朝〉 a dynasty.

o-chôshi-mono 〈おちょうしもの：お調子者〉 a person easily elated.

o-dabutsu 〈おだぶつ：おだ仏〉

o-dabutsu-ni-naru 〈おだ仏になる〉 die, kick the bucket.

ôdâ-mêdo 〈オーダーメード〉

ôdâ-mêdo-no 〈オーダーメードの〉 made-to-order, tailor-made.

ôdan 〈おうだん：横断〉 crossing.

ôdan-suru 〈横断する〉 cross, go across, traverse.

Taihei-yô o hikô-ki-de-ôdan-suru （太平洋を飛行機で横断する） fly across the Pacific

tairiku-ôdan-no 〈大陸横断の〉 transcontinental.

ôdan 〈おうだん：黄だん〉jaundice.

odate 〈おだて〉
　odate-ni-noru 〈おだてに乗る〉be easily flattered.
　　odate-ni-nora-nai（おだてに乗らない）be above flattery

odateru 〈おだてる〉instigate, flatter.
　　Kare-wa sukoshi odateru-to sugu-ii-ki-ni-naru.（彼は少しおだてるとすぐいい気になる.）A little flattery will fetch him.

odayaka 〈おだやか：穏やか〉
　odayaka-na 〈穏やかな〉calm, quiet, peaceful, mild, gentle.
　　odayaka-na umi（穏やかな海）a calm sea
　　odayaka-na kikō（穏やかな気候）a mild climate
　　odayaka-na kaze（穏やかな風）a gentle wind
　odayaka-ni 〈穏やかに〉calmly, quietly, peacefully, mildly, gently.
　　odayaka-ni hanasu（穏やかに話す）speak quietly

odeko 〈おでこ〉the brow, the forehead.
　odeko-no 〈おでこの〉with a prominent forehead.

oden 〈おでん〉Japanese hotchpotch.

odokasu or **odosu** 〈おどかす，おどす：脅かす，脅す〉threaten, menace, frighten.

odokeru 〈おどける〉joke, jest, be funny.
　odoketa 〈おどけた〉jesting, funny.
　odokete 〈おどけて〉jokingly, jestingly, humorously, in fun.

odoodo 〈おどおど〉
　odoodo-suru 〈おどおどする〉be timid, be nervous, be frightened, have the jitters.
　odoodo-shita 〈おどおどした〉timid, nervous.
　odoodo-shite 〈おどおどして〉timidly, nervously.

odori 〈おどり：踊り〉a dance, dancing.
　　odori-ba（踊り場）a landing

odori-agaru 〈おどりあがる：躍り上がる〉jump up.
　　odori-agatte-yorokobu（躍り上がって喜ぶ）jump for joy

odorokasu 〈おどろかす：驚かす〉surprise, astonish, amaze, shock.

odoroki 〈おどろき：驚き〉surprise, astonishment, amazement, wonder.

odoroku 〈おどろく：驚く〉be surprised, be astonished, be amazed, wonder ((at)).
　〜*-wa-odoroku-ni-tari-nai.*〈〜は驚くに足りない.〉It is no wonder that... .
　odoroku-beki 〈驚くべき〉surprising, astonishing, amazing, startling, wonderful.

odoroite 〈驚いて〉 in surprise, in wonder.

 odoroite-ki-o-ushinau〈驚いて気を失う〉 be frightened out of one's senses

odoroita-koto-ni〈驚いたことに〉 to one's surprise.

odoru〈おどる：踊る〉dance; jump, leap.

 piano-ni-awasete odoru（ピアノに合わせて踊る） dance to the piano

 odori-mawaru（踊り回る） jump about

odoshi〈おどし：脅し〉

 odoshi-monku（脅し文句） threatening words

ôen〈おうえん：応援〉help, assistance, aid, support, cheering, rooting.

 ôen-dan（応援団） a cheering party

  ôen-dan-chô（応援団長） a cheerleader, a head rooter

ôen-suru〈応援する〉help, assist, aid, support, cheer, root ((for)).

o-eragata〈おえらがた：お偉方〉a dignitary, a personage, a panjandrum.

oeru〈おえる：終える〉finish, end, complete, get through ((with)), accomplish, graduate ((from)).

 shigoto o oeru（仕事を終える） finish one's work

 kôkô-no-katei o oeru（高校の課程を終える） complete a senior high school course

o-fuda〈おふだ：お札〉a charm, a talisman, an amulet.

ôfuku〈おうふく：往復〉going and returning.

 ôfuku-tomo takushî ni noru（往復ともタクシーに乗る） take a taxicab both ways

 Tôkyô-made-ôfuku（東京まで往復） Tokyo and back

ôfuku-suru〈往復する〉go and return(*or* come back).

o-fukuro〈おふくろ：お袋〉one's mother, one's mater.

o-furu〈おふる：お古〉a used article.

 ane-no o-furu-no doresu（姉のお古のドレス） a hand-me-down dress from my sister

oga-kuzu〈おがくず〉sawdust.

ogami-taosu〈おがみたおす：拝み倒す〉win over ((a person)) by entreaty.

ogamu〈おがむ：拝む〉worship, pray ((to)).

 te-o-awasete ogamu（手を合わせて拝む） pray with joined hands

ogawa〈おがわ：小川〉a brook, a stream.

ôgi〈おうぎ：扇〉a fan, a folding-fan.

ôgi-gata-no〈扇形の〉fan-shaped.

ôgi-gata-ni〈扇形に〉fanwise.

ôgi-gata-ni-hirogeru（扇形に広げる）fan out

oginau〈おぎなう：補う〉supply, make up (for), fill up.

    sonshitsu o oginau（損失を補う）make up for the loss

    ketsuin o oginau（欠員を補う）fill up a vacancy

ôgon〈おうごん：黄金〉gold.

    ôgon-jidai（黄金時代）the golden age

  ôgon-no〈黄金の〉golden.

ogori〈おごり〉a treat.

    Kore-wa boku-no ogori-da.（これは僕のおごりだ.）This is my treat.

  ogoru〈おごる〉treat ((a person)) to.

ogori〈おごり〉pride, arrogance.

  ogoru〈おごる〉be proud, be arrogant.

    Ogoru-Heike-wa   hisashi-karazu.（おごる平家は久しからず.）Pride goes before a fall.

ogosoka〈おごそか：厳か〉

  ogosoka-na〈厳かな〉grave, solemn.

  ogosoka-ni〈厳かに〉gravely, solemnly.

ogyâ〈おぎゃあ〉

  ogyâogyâ-to-naku〈おぎゃあおぎゃあと泣く〉mewl.

o-hajiki〈おはじき〉marbles.

o-hanabatake〈おはなばたけ：お花畑〉a field of Alpine flowers.

o-harai〈おはらい〉the *Shinto* purification.

Ohayô.〈おはよう.〉Good morning.

ôhei〈おうへい：横柄〉

  ôhei-na〈横柄な〉arrogant, haughty.

    ôhei-na-taido-o-toru（横柄な態度を取る）behave haughtily

ôhi〈おうひ：王妃〉a queen, an empress.

o-hire〈おひれ：尾ひれ〉

  o-hire-o-tsukete-hanasu〈尾ひれを付けて話す〉exaggerate, embellish one's story.

o-hitoyoshi〈おひとよし：お人よし〉a good-natured person; an easy mark.

Ohôtsuku-kai〈オホーツクかい：オホーツク海〉the Sea of Okhotsk.

oi〈おい：老い〉

  oi-mo-wakaki-mo〈老いも若きも〉both young and old.

Oi!〈おい.〉Hello, Hey, Say, I say.

oi〈おい〉a nephew.

ôi〈おうい：王位〉the throne, the crown.

　　　ôi-o-keishô-suru（王位を継承する）　succeed to the throne

oi-chirasu〈おいちらす：追い散らす〉scatter, drive away.

oi-dasu〈おいだす：追い出す〉turn(*or* drive) out, turn ((a person)) out-of-doors, expel ((a person from some position)), put ((a tenant)) out; dismiss.

oie-gei〈おいえげい：お家芸〉one's specialty.

oie-sôdô〈おいえそうどう：お家騒動〉a family trouble.

oihagi〈おいはぎ：追いはぎ〉a highwayman, a footpad, a holdup man.

oi-harau〈おいはらう：追い払う〉drive ((a person)) away, turn(*or* send) away, disperse, shoo.

oi-kaesu〈おいかえす：追い返す〉send away, repel.

oi-kakeru〈おいかける：追い掛ける〉chase, run ((after)), pursue.

oi-kaze〈おいかぜ：追い風〉a fair wind, a tail wind.

oikomi〈おいこみ：追い込み〉the last spurt, the last lap.

　　　saigo-no oikomi o kakeru（最後の追い込みを掛ける）　put on the last spurt

oi-komu〈おいこむ：追い込む〉
　　kyûchi-ni oi-komu〈窮地に追い込む〉drive ((a person)) into a corner.

oi-komu〈おいこむ：老い込む〉grow old.
　　　kyû-ni oi-komu（急に老い込む）　age rapidly

oikoshi〈おいこし：追い越し〉
　　　Oikoshi-kinshi.（追い越し禁止.）　No passing.
　　oi-kosu〈追い越す〉pass, outrun, get ahead ((of)).

oi-mawasu〈おいまわす：追い回す〉chase around, follow around, dangle about.

ôin〈おういん：押印〉sealing.
　　ôin-suru〈押印する〉seal, affix one's seal ((to)).

oioi〈おいおい〉
　　oioi-naku〈おいおい泣く〉cry bitterly.

oiru〈おいる：老いる〉grow old, age.
　　　oite masumasu-sakan-de-aru（老いてますます盛んである）　be hale and hearty

oisen〈おいせん：追い銭〉
　　　nusutto-ni-oisen（盗っとに追い銭）　throw good money after bad

oi-shigeru〈おいしげる：生い茂る〉grow thickly, luxuriate.

oishii〈おいしい〉*see.* umai.
　　　Â, oishii!（ああ，おいしい.）　It tastes good!

oi-sore-to〈おいそれと〉at a moment's notice, readily, easily, offhand.

Oi-sore-to kime-kaneru.（おいそれと決めかねる.）I cannot decide offhand.

oite〈おいて〉at, in, on, as for, as to.

oite〈おいて：追い風〉*see.* oi-kaze.

oi-tsuku〈おいつく：追い付く〉overtake, catch up ((with)).

oi-tsumeru〈おいつめる：追い詰める〉*see.* oi-komu（追い込む）.

oi-uchi〈おいうち：追い打ち〉

oi-uchi-o-kakeru〈追い打ちを掛ける〉attack the routed enemy.

oi-yaru〈おいやる：追いやる〉drive ((a person)) away, order ((a person)) off, relegate.

ojan〈おじゃん〉

ojan-ni-naru〈おじゃんになる〉come to nothing, fall through, end in a failure.

Subete-no keikaku ga ojan-ni-natta.（すべての計画がおじゃんになった.）All the plans fell through.

oji〈おじ：叔(伯)父〉an uncle.

ôji〈おうじ：王子〉a prince.

o-jî-chan〈おじいちゃん〉a grandpa.

o-jigi〈おじぎ：お辞儀〉a bow.

o-jigi-suru〈お辞儀する〉bow ((to)), make a bow ((to)).

ojike〈おじけ：おじ気〉

ojike-zuku〈おじけ付く〉be frightened, be scared, grow timid, become nervous.

ojike-zuite-mono-ga-ie-nai（おじけ付いて物が言えない）be too scared to speak

ôjiru〈おうじる：応じる〉answer, reply ((to)), obey, accept, comply ((with)), meet.

shitsumon ni ôjiru（質問に応じる）answer a question

shôtai ni ôjiru（招待に応じる）accept an invitation

irai ni ôjiru（依頼に応じる）comply with ((a person's)) request

juyô ni ôjiru（需要に応じる）meet the demand

〜-ni-ôjite〈〜に応じて〉in answer to... , according to... .

nôryoku-ni-ôjite（能力に応じて）according to one's ability

o-jî-san〈おじいさん〉a grandfather, an old man.

ôjo〈おうじょ：王女〉a princess.

ôjô〈おうじょう：往生〉

Aitsu-ni-wa ôjô-suru-yo.（あいつには往生するよ.）He is impossible.

ôjô-giwa-ga-warui（往生際が悪い）be a bad loser

o-jô-san〈おじょうさん：お嬢さん〉a young lady, your daughter, miss.

oka〈おか：丘〉a hill, a height.

ôka〈おうか：おう歌〉

　ôka-suru〈おう歌する〉sing the praises ((of)).

　　seishun-o-ôka-suru（青春をおう歌する）　sing the praises of youth

o-kabu〈おかぶ：お株〉

　o-kabu-o-ubawareru〈お株を奪われる〉be outdone by another in one's forte.

o-kadochigai〈おかどちがい：お門違い〉

　　Boku-no-tokoro-e-kuru-no-wa-o-kadochigai-da-yo.（僕の所へ来るのはお門違いだよ.）　You've come to the wrong shop.

O-kaeri-nasai.〈おかえりなさい.：お帰りなさい.〉Welcome home.

o-kaeshi〈おかえし：お返し〉a return〔for a gift received〕.

　o-kaeshi-o-suru〈お返しをする〉give ((a person)) something in return.

o-kage〈おかげ：お陰〉

　o-kage-de〈お陰で〉thanks to, by ((a person's)) help.

　　"O-genki-desu-ka?"　"Hai, okage-sama-de genki-desu."（"お元気ですか." "はい, お陰さまで元気です."）　"How are you?"　"I'm fine, thank you."

ôkaku-maku〈おうかくまく：横隔膜〉the diaphragm.

okame〈おかめ：岡目〉

　　Okame-hachimoku.（岡目八目.）　The outsider sees the best of the game.

okami〈おかみ〉a landlady; a mistress, a proprietress.

okan〈おかん：悪寒〉a chill.

　　okan-ga-suru（悪寒がする）　feel a chill

ôkan〈おうかん：王冠〉a crown.

o-kâ-san〈おかあさん：お母さん〉mother, mamma, mammy.

okashii〈おかしい〉amusing, funny; strange, queer.

　　okashii koto o iu（おかしいことを言う）　say funny things

okasu〈おかす：犯す〉commit, violate, break.

　　tsumi o okasu（罪を犯す）　commit a crime

okasu〈おかす：冒す〉risk, face, run, attack.

　　kiken o okasu（危険を冒す）　face a danger

　　yamai-ni okasareru（病に冒される）　be attacked with a disease

　～-o-okashite〈～を冒して〉in spite of... , in the face of... .

　～-no-kiken-o-okashite〈～の危険を冒して〉at the risk of... .

okasu〈おかす：侵す〉invade, violate.

puraibashī o okasu（プライバシーを侵す） violate ((a person's)) privacy

o-kawari 〈おかわり：お代わり〉another helping.

o-kawari-o-suru（お代わりをする） ask for a second helping

o-kazu 〈おかず〉a (side) dish.

oke 〈おけ〉a tub, a pail, a (wooden) bucket.

ōkesutora 〈オーケストラ〉an orchestra.

oki 〈おき：沖〉the offing, the open sea.

oki-de 〈沖で〉off.

Kishû-oki-de（紀州沖で） off Kishu

oki-ni 〈沖に〉in the offing, offshore, out at sea.

-oki 〈-おき：-置き〉

〜*-oki-ni* 〈〜おきに〉every, at interval of... .

ichi-nichi-oki-ni（一日おきに） every other day

ichi-gyō-oki-ni（一行おきに） on every other line

go-fun-oki-ni（五分おきに） every five minutes, at intervals of five minutes

oki-agaru 〈おきあがる：起き上がる〉get up, rise.

okiba 〈おきば：置場〉a yard, a place ((for)).

zaimoku-okiba（材木置場） a lumberyard, a timberyard

oki-chigaeru 〈おきちがえる：置き違える〉misplace, put in a wrong place.

oki-dokei 〈おきどけい：置き時計〉a table clock.

oki-kaeru 〈おきかえる：置き換える〉rearrange, displace.

oki-miyage 〈おきみやげ：置き土産〉a parting present.

oki-mono 〈おきもの：置物〉an ornament.

o-ki-ni-iri 〈おきにいり：お気に入り〉one's favorite, a pet.

o-ki-ni-iri-no 〈お気に入りの〉favorite, pet, darling.

okippanashi 〈おきっぱなし：置きっ放し〉

okippanashi-ni-suru 〈置きっ放しにする〉leave ((a thing)) about.

okiru 〈おきる：起きる〉get up, rise, wake up.

asa-hayaku-okiru（朝早く起きる） get up early in the morning

Oki-nasai.（起きなさい.） Get up.

okite-iru 〈起きている〉be up.

nezu-ni-okite-iru（寝ずに起きている） sit up

okiru 〈おきる：起きる〉happen, take place, occur, break out; arise ((from)), come ((of)), originate ((from, in *or* with)).

donna-koto-ga-okitemo(donna-koto-ga-okottemo)（どんな事が起きても

（どんな事が起こっても）） whatever may happen

Kenka wa gokai-kara-okita.(Kenka wa gokai-kara-okotta.)（けんかは誤解から起きた.(けんかは誤解から起こった.)） The quarrel has arisen from (a) misunderstanding.

Kare-no byôki wa nomi-sugi-kara-okita-n-da.（彼の病気は飲み過ぎから起きたんだ.） His illness comes of drinking too much.

okishifuru〈オキシフル〉 oxygenated water, peroxide.

okite〈おきて〉a law, a rule, a regulation.

　　okite o yaburu（おきてを破る） break the law

oki-tegami〈おきてがみ：置き手紙〉

　oki-tegami-o-suru〈置き手紙をする〉leave a message at home.

oki-wasureru〈おきわすれる：置き忘れる〉leave ((a thing)) behind, forget, mislay.

　　kasa o oki-wasureru（傘を置き忘れる） leave one's umbrella behind

oki-zari〈おきざり：置き去り〉

　oki-zari-ni-suru〈置き去りにする〉leave ((a person)) in the lurch.

okkû〈おっくう：億くう〉

　okkû-na〈億くうな〉bothersome, annoying, tiresome.

ôkoku〈おうこく：王国〉a kingdom, a monarchy.

okonai〈おこない：行い〉an act, an action, a deed, one's doings; behavior, conduct.

okonau〈おこなう：行う〉do, act; behave; hold, give.

　　akuji o okonau（悪事を行う） do wrong

　　shiki o okonau（式を行う） hold a ceremony

　　shiken o okonau（試験を行う） give an examination

　okonawareru〈行われる〉be carried out, be put in force, be held, go on.

okoraseru〈おこらせる：怒らせる〉make ((a person)) angry, offend.

okori〈おこり：起こり〉the origin, the source, the beginning, the rise, the cause.

okorippoi〈おこりっぽい：怒りっぽい〉peevish, quick-tempered.

okoru〈おこる：起こる〉*see.* okiru (happen,...).

okoru〈おこる：怒る〉get angry ((at *or* with)), lose one's temper ((with)).

　okotta〈怒った〉angry, irate, indignant.

　　okotta-kao-o-suru（怒った顔をする） look angry

　okotte〈怒って〉angrily.

　okotte-iru〈怒っている〉be angry ((at *or* with)).

　　hi-no-yô-ni-okotte-iru（火のように怒っている） be hot with anger

okosu〈おこす：起こす〉wake (up), awake; start; raise (up); rise, cause.

Roku-ji-ni okoshite-kudasai.（六時に起こしてください。）Wake me up at six, please.

oku.

undô o okosu（運動を起こす）start a movement

taoreta tsukue o okosu（倒れた机を起こす）raise a fallen desk

muhon o okosu（謀反を起こす）rise in revolt

mendô o okosu（面倒を起こす）cause a trouble

okotaru〈おこたる：怠る〉neglect.

oku〈おく：億〉a hundred million.

jû-oku（十億）a billion, a thousand million

oku〈おく：奥〉the inner part, the interior, the depths, the heart, the recesses.

yama no oku（山の奥）the heart of a mountain

oku-zashiki（奥座敷）an inner room

oku〈おく：置く〉put, place, lay, set, keep.

hon o tsukue-no-shita-ni oku（本を机の下に置く）put a book under the table

fude o oku（筆を置く）lay down a pen

geshuku-nin o oku（下宿人を置く）keep boarders

Kono sakana wa asu-made oke-nai.（この魚は明日まで置けない。）This fish does not keep overnight.

-oku〈-おく〉leave, keep.

Sono-mama-ni-shite-oki-nasai.（そのままにしておきなさい。）Leave them as they are.

to o aketa-mama-ni-shite-oku（戸を開けたままにしておく）keep a door open

oku-ba〈おくば：奥歯〉a back tooth, a molar.

okubyô〈おくびょう：おく病〉cowardice, timidity.

okubyô-mono（おく病者）a coward

okubyô-kaze-ni-fukareru（おく病風に吹かれる）get nervous, get into a funk

okubyô-na〈おく病な〉cowardly, timid.

oku-chi〈おくち：奥地〉the interior.

okugai〈おくがい：屋外〉

okugai-supôtsu（屋外スポーツ）outdoor sports

okugai-no〈屋外の〉outdoor, open-air.

okugai-de〈屋外で〉outdoors, in the open air.

okujô〈おくじょう：屋上〉the roof.

okujô-teien（屋上庭園）a roof garden

oku-man 〈おくまん：億万〉
  oku-man-chôja（億万長者） a billionaire
okumatta 〈おくまった：奥まった〉inner, secluded.
  okumatta heya（奥まった部屋） an inner room
okunai 〈おくない：屋内〉
  okunai-no〈屋内の〉indoor.
  okunai-de〈屋内で〉indoors, within doors.
o-kuni 〈おくに：お国〉your home town, your native country.
oku-no-te 〈おくのて：奥の手〉
  oku-no-te-o-dasu（奥の手を出す） play one's best card
  oku-no-te-to-shite-motte-iru（奥の手として持っている） have in the
    bottom of the bag
okurasu 〈おくらす：遅らす〉set back.
  tokei o san-juppun okurasu（時計を三十分遅らす） set back a watch
    half an hour
okure 〈おくれ：後れ〉(a) delay, a lag; backwardness.
  bunka-no okure（文化の後れ） a cultural lag
  okure-o-toru〈後れを取る〉get behind, be inferior ((to)), yield ((to)).
  okure-o-tori-modosu〈後れを取り戻す〉make up leeway, catch up (with).
okureru 〈おくれる：遅(後)れる〉be late ((for)), be behind time, be
  delayed, be behind, lose, be slow.
  gakkô-ni-okureru（学校に遅れる） be late for school
  jisei-ni-okureru（時勢に後れる） be behind the times
  hi-ni ni-fun okureru（日に二分後れる） lose two minutes a day
  ni-fun okurete-iru（二分後れている） be two minutes slow
okuri-dasu 〈おくりだす：送り出す〉see ((a person)) out.
  kodomo o gakkô-e okuri-dasu（子供を学校へ送り出す） send a child
    off to school
okuri-jô 〈おくりじょう：送り状〉an invoice.
okuri-kaesu 〈おくりかえす：送り返す〉send back, return.
okuri-mono 〈おくりもの：贈り物〉a present, a gift.
  okuri-mono o suru（贈り物をする） give ((a person)) a present
okuri-nushi 〈おくりぬし：送り主〉a sender, a consignor, a remitter.
okuri-saki 〈おくりさき：送り先〉the destination, the consignee, the
  address.
okuru 〈おくる：送る〉send, dispatch, ship, remit; see off, see ((a
  person)) home; pass, spend.
  jisho o okuru（辞書を送る） send ((a person)) a dictionary

oji-o-okuri-ni eki-made-iku〈叔(伯)父を送りに駅まで行く〉 go to the station to see my uncle off

jidōsha-de-ie-made-okuru〈自動車で家まで送る〉 drive ((a person)) home

yosei o okuru〈余生を送る〉 spend the rest of ((a person's)) life

okuru〈おくる：贈る〉present ((a person)) with, give ((a person a thing)) as a gift.

oku-san〈おくさん：奥さん〉a married lady, your(*or* his) wife, madam, Mrs.

okusoku〈おくそく：憶測〉a guess, a conjecture.

okusoku-suru〈憶測する〉guess, conjecture.

okutâbu〈オクターブ〉an octave.

ichi-okutâbu-ageru（一オクターブ上げる） raise ((one's voice)) an octave higher

ichi-okutâbu-sageru（一オクターブ下げる） drop ((one's voice)) an octave lower

okutan-ka〈オクタンか：オクタン価〉octane number.

okutan-ka-no-takai〈オクタン価の高い〉high-octane.

okute〈おくて：奥手〉late crops.

okute-de-aru〈奥手である〉be slow to mature.

okute-no〈奥手の〉late.

oku-yukashii〈おくゆかしい：奥床しい〉modest, gentlemanlike.

okuyuki〈おくゆき：奥行き〉depth.

okuyuki-no-fukai〈奥行きの深い〉deep.

ôkyû〈おうきゅう：応急〉

ôkyû-shûri（応急修理） temporary repairs

ôkyû-teate o suru（応急手当てをする） give first aid treatment ((to))

ôkyû-no〈応急の〉emergency, temporary, makeshift.

o-make〈おまけ：お負け〉an addition, a premium, an extra.

omake-ni〈おまけに〉in addition ((to)); to make matters worse.

o-mamori〈おまもり：お守り〉an amulet, a charm, a talisman.

o-matsuri-sawagi〈おまつりさわぎ：お祭り騒ぎ〉merrymaking, merriment.

o-mawari〈おまわり：お巡り〉a policeman, a cop.

O-mawari-san.（お巡りさん.） Mister Officer.

ombin〈おんびん：穏便〉

ombin-ni〈穏便に〉peaceably, privately.

ombin-ni koto-o-sumasu（穏便に事を済ます） settle a matter

privately

ombu〈おんぶ〉

　akambô-o-ombu-suru（赤ん坊をおんぶする）　carry a baby pickaback

　tanin-ni-ombu-suru（他人におんぶする）　rely upon another

o-medeta〈おめでた〉a happy event.

O-medetô!〈おめでとう。〉Congratulations!

　Tanjô-bi o-medetô!（誕生日おめでとう。）　A happy birthday to you!

　Kurisumasu o-medetô!（クリスマスおめでとう。）　A Merry Christmas!

　Shinnen o-medetô!（新年おめでとう。）　A Happy New Year!

omei〈おめい：汚名〉dishonor, disgrace.

　omei o sosogu（汚名をそそぐ）　cleanse one's dishonor, wipe off a
　　disgrace

ômen〈おうめん：凹面〉

　ômen-renzu（凹面レンズ）　a concave lens

　ômen-no〈凹面の〉concave.

omeome(-to)〈おめおめ（と）〉shamelessly, ignominiously.

o-miki〈おみき：お神酒〉sacred *sake*, *sake* offered before the altar.

o-mikuji〈おみくじ〉a sacred lot.

　o-mikuji o hiku（おみくじを引く）　draw a sacred lot

omocha〈おもちゃ〉a toy, a plaything.

　omocha-no kisha（おもちゃの汽車）　a toy train

　omocha-ya（おもちゃ屋）　a toy dealer; a toy store

　omocha-ni-suru〈おもちゃにする〉play ((with)).

omo-datta〈おもだった：重立った〉leading, chief, main, principal,
important.

omoi〈おもい：思い〉thought, mind, love, wish, expectation, experience.

　omoi-ni-fukeru（思いにふける）　be lost in one's thought

　omoi-o-yoseru（思いを寄せる）　be in love ((with))

　omoi ga kanau（思いがかなう）　realize one's wishes

　iya-na omoi o suru（嫌な思いをする）　have a bitter experience

omoi〈おもい：重い〉heavy; grave, severe, serious, important.

　omoi kaban（重いかばん）　a heavy bag

　omoi tsumi（重い罪）　a grave crime

　omoi byôki-ni-kakaru（重い病気にかかる）　be seriously ill

omoi-agari〈おもいあがり：思い上がり〉conceit, vanity.

　omoi-agaru〈思い上がる〉be conceited, be puffed up ((with)).

　omoi-agatta〈思い上がった〉conceited, swollen.

omoi-amaru〈おもいあまる：思い余る〉be at a loss〔what to do〕.

omoi-ataru〈おもいあたる：思い当たる〉occur ((to)), recall.

omoi-chigai〈おもいちがい：思い違い〉misunderstanding, (a) misapprehension, a mistake.

omoi-chigai-o-suru〈思い違いをする〉misunderstand, mistake.

omoi-dasu〈おもいだす：思い出す〉remember, recall, recollect.

omoi-de〈おもいで：思い出〉recollections, a memory, a reminiscence.

omoi-de-ni-fukeru〈思い出にふける〉indulge in one's reminiscence

omoigakenai〈おもいがけない：思い掛けない〉unexpected.

omoigakenai hômon-kyaku（思い掛けない訪問客）an unexpected visitor

omoigakenaku〈思い掛けなく〉unexpectedly.

omoikiri〈おもいきり：思い切り〉resolution, decision; vigorously, to one's heart's content, with all one's might, to the utmost.

omoikiri-no-warui（思い切りの悪い）irresolute, lacking decision

omoikiri-yasuku（思い切り安く）at the lowest possible price

omoikiri-yaru（思い切りやる）do one's best, let oneself go

omoi-kiru〈おもいきる：思い切る〉give up, abandon.

omoi-kitta〈おもいきった：思い切った〉drastic, radical.

omoi-kitta shochi o toru（思い切った処置を取る）take a drastic measure

omoi-kitte〈思い切って〉resolutely, boldly, daringly.

omoikitte~(-suru)（思い切って~(する)）venture ((to do)), dare ((to do))

omoi-komu〈おもいこむ：思い込む〉fully believe, set one's heart ((on)).

omoi-mo-yoranu〈おもいもよらぬ：思いも寄らぬ〉unexpected; unthinkable, out of the question.

Konna tokoro-de o-me-ni-kakarô-to-wa-omoi-mo-yori-masen-deshita.（こんな所でお目にかかろうとは思いも寄りませんでした。）You were the last person I expected to see in such a place.

omoi-naosu〈おもいなおす：思い直す〉think better of, change one's mind.

omoi-nayamu〈おもいなやむ：思い悩む〉be worried ((about)), be at a loss〔what to do〕.

omoi-no-hoka〈おもいのほか：思いの外〉unexpectedly, beyond one's expectations.

Shiken wa omoi-no-hoka-muzukashikatta.（試験は思いの外難しかった。）The examination was harder than I had expected.

omoi-nokosu〈おもいのこす：思い残す〉

Omoi-nokosu-koto-wa-nani-mo-nai.（思い残す事は何もない。）I have nothing to look back on with regret.

omoi-okosu〈おもいおこす：思い起こす〉see. omoi-dasu.

omoiomoi-ni〈おもいおもいに：思い思いに〉as one pleases, according to one's own way, each in his own way.

omoi-shiru〈おもいしる：思い知る〉come to know, know to one's cost.

Kondo-koso　omoi-shitta-ni-chigai-nai.（今度こそ思い知ったに違いない。）He must have learned his lesson this time.

Omoi-shirasete-yaru.（思い知らせてやる。）He shall smart for it.

omoi-tatsu〈おもいたつ：思い立つ〉

Omoi-tatta-ga-kichijitsu.（思い立ったが吉日。）There is no time like the present.

omoi-todomaru〈おもいとどまる：思いとどまる〉be dissuaded from ((doing)).

omoi-todomaraseru〈思いとどまらせる〉dissuade ((a person)) from ((doing)).

omoi-tsuki〈おもいつき：思い付き〉an idea, a plan, a suggestion.

ii omoi-tsuki〈いい思い付き〉a good idea

omoi-tsuku〈思い付く〉think ((of)), hit ((upon)), take ((it)) into one's head ((to do *or* that)), come into one's mind.

mei-an-o-ni-san　omoi-tsuku（名案を二、三思い付く）hit upon some good plans

omoi-tsumeru〈おもいつめる：思い詰める〉brood ((on *or* over)).

omoi-yarareru〈おもいやられる：思いやられる〉

Kimi-no　shōrai-ga-omoi-yarareru.（君の将来が思いやられる。）I feel uneasy about your future.

omoi-yari〈おもいやり：思いやり〉sympathy, compassion, consideration.

omoi-yari-no-aru〈思いやりのある〉kind ((to)), sympathetic ((with)), considerate ((of)), thoughtful ((for *or* of)).

omoi-yari-no-nai（思いやりのない）unkind, unsympathetic, inconsiderate, thoughtless

omokage〈おもかげ：面影〉

omokage-ga-ikura-ka-nokotte-iru（面影が幾らか残っている）retain something of one's former self

mukashi-no-omokage-wa-nai（昔の面影はない）be not what one used to be, be but the ruin of what one was

Omo-kaji!〈おもかじ。：面かじ。〉Starboard! / Right!

omoki〈おもき：重き〉

omoki-o-oku 〈重きを置く〉 lay emphasis ((on)), set importance ((on)).

omokurushii 〈おもくるしい：重苦しい〉 oppressive, heavy, gloomy.
    omokurushii chimmoku （重苦しい沈黙） an oppressive silence
    omokurushii sora-moyô （重苦しい空模様） a gloomy sky

omo-na 〈おもな：主な〉 chief, principal, main.
    omo-na sambutsu （主な産物） principal products

omo-ni 〈主に〉 chiefly, principally, mainly; mostly, for the most part.

omo-naga 〈おもなが：面長〉
omo-naga-na 〈面長な〉 long-faced, oval-faced.

omo-ni 〈おもに：重荷〉 a heavy load, a burden.

omonjiru 〈おもんじる：重んじる〉 respect, value, make much ((of)).
    meiyo o omonjiru （名誉を重んじる） value honor
omonji-nai 〈重んじない〉 make little ((of)).

omoomoshii 〈おもおもしい：重々しい〉 grave, solemn, imposing.
    omoomoshii kuchô-de （重々しい口調で） in a grave tone
omoomoshiku 〈重々しく〉 gravely, solemnly, with an important air.

omori 〈おもり〉 a weight, a sink.

omo-sa 〈おもさ：重さ〉 weight.
omo-sa-o-hakaru or *omo-sa-ga~aru* 〈重さを量る，重さが～ある〉 weigh.

omoshi 〈おもし〉 a weight, a heavy stone.

omoshiroi 〈おもしろい：面白い〉 interesting, entertaining, amusing, pleasant, funny, exciting.
    omoshiroi-hon （面白い本） an interesting book
    omoshiroi hanashi （面白い話） an amusing story
    omoshiroi kao （面白い顔） a funny face
    omoshiroi gêmu （面白いゲーム） an exciting game
omoshiroku 〈面白く〉 merrily, pleasantly, amusingly.
    omoshiroku-toki-o-sugosu （面白く時を過ごす） have a pleasant time
omoshiroku-nai 〈面白くない〉 uninteresting, dull, unamusing, unpleasant, unsatisfactory, unwelcome.
    omoshiroku-nai gêmu （面白くないゲーム） a dull game
omoshiro-sô-ni 〈面白そうに〉 with interest, merrily, pleasantly, delightedly.
omoshiro-hambun-ni 〈面白半分に〉 for fun.
omoshiro-garu 〈面白がる〉 enjoy, be amused ((at, by *or* with)).

omoshiro-mi 〈おもしろみ：面白み〉 interest, fun.
    Keiba-no-omoshiro-mi-ga wakara-nai. （競馬の面白みが分からない．） I cannot understand why horse racing is such fun.

omote 〈おもて：表(面)〉 the face, the surface, the right side, the head, the outside; the first half; front.

    omote-o-ue-ni-shite (表を上にして) the right side up

    omote to ura (表と裏) the head and tail

    omote-doori (表通り) the main street

    rokkai no omote (六回の表) the first half of the sixth inning

    fûtô no omote (封筒の表) the front of an envelope

    omote-genkan (表玄関) the front door

    omote-Nihon (表日本) the Pacific side of Japan

 omote-ni 〈表に〉 out of doors, outdoors.

omotedatte 〈おもてだって：表立って〉 openly, in public.

    omotedatte hantai-suru (表立って反対する) oppose openly

omote-muki(-wa) 〈おもてむき(は)：表向き(は)〉 officially, ostensibly.

omote-zata 〈おもてざた：表ざた〉

 omote-zata-ni-naru 〈表ざたになる〉 be made public, be brought before the court.

omou 〈おもう：思う〉 think ((about *or* of)), mind, care, feel, believe, regard, consider, expect, remember, imagine, suppose, wish, want, intend ((to do)), be afraid.

    okashii-to-omou (おかしいと思う) think(*or* feel) ((it)) strange

    yoku-omou (良く思う) think well ((of))

    waruku-omou (悪く思う) think ill ((of))

    nan-tomo-omowa-nai (何とも思わない) do not care a bit ((about))

    kanojo-no hanashi-o-hontô-da-to-omou (彼女の話を本当だと思う) believe her story

    meiyo-na-koto-da-to-omou (名誉なことだと思う) regard ((it)) an honor

    omotta-toori (思ったとおり) as one expected, as one feared

    Kanojo-ni doko-ka-de atta-to-omou. (彼女にどこかで会ったと思う。) I remember seeing her somewhere.

    Kare-ni sonna koto wa deki-nai-to-omou. (彼にそんなことはできないと思う。) I suppose it is impossible for him to do such a thing.

    omou-yô-ni (思うように) as one wishes

    omou-zombun(-ni) (思う存分(に)) to one's heart's content, as much as one likes

    seiji-ka-ni-narô-to-omou (政治家になろうと思う) intend to be a statesman

omowaku 〈おもわく：思惑〉 thought, a view; speculation, expectation, calculation.

omowaku-ga-hazureru〈思惑が外れる〉 fall short of one's calculation

omowaku-gai〈思惑買い〉 speculative buying

omowaku-doori〈思惑どおり〉 just as one wished.

omowareru〈おもわれる：思われる〉

hito-ni yoku-omowareru〈人に良く思われる〉 be well thought of by other people.

omowase-buri〈おもわせぶり：思わせ振り〉

omowase-buri-na〈思わせ振りな〉 tantalizing, suggestive, coquettish.

omowashii〈おもわしい：思わしい〉 satisfactory, desirable, favorable.

omowashiku-nai〈思わしくない〉 unsatisfactory, undesirable, unfavorable.

　　Kare-no byôjô wa omowashiku-nai.（彼の病状は思わしくない。） His sickness has not taken a favorable turn.

omowazu〈おもわず：思わず〉 in spite of oneself, unintentionally, unconsciously.

　　omowazu fuki-dasu（思わず吹き出す） burst out laughing in spite of oneself

omo-yatsure〈おもやつれ：面やつれ〉

omo-yatsure-shita〈面やつれした〉 emaciated, gaunt.

omo-yu〈おもゆ：重湯〉 thin rice gruel.

ompa〈おんぱ：音波〉 a sound wave.

ompu〈おんぷ：音符〉 a (musical) note.

ômu〈おうむ〉 a parrot.

omuretsu〈オムレツ〉 an omelet(te).

o-mutsu〈おむつ〉 a diaper, a (baby's) napkin.

o-mutsu-o-tori-kaeru〈おむつを取り替える〉 change〔a baby〕.

on〈おん：恩〉 a favor, a benefit, an obligation, kindness.

　　on-o-kaesu *or* on-gaeshi-o-suru（恩を返す，恩返しをする） return ((a person's)) kindness

　　on-o-ada-de-kaesu（恩をあだで返す） return evil for good

　　Go-on wa kesshite-wasure-masen.（御恩は決して忘れません。） I'll never forget your kindness.

on-shirazu-no〈恩知らずの〉 ungrateful.

onaji〈おなじ：同じ〉 the same ((as *or* with)), equal ((to)), similar ((to)), like, alike.

　　onaji ookisa（同じ大きさ） the same size ((as))

　　hotondo-onaji-de-aru（ほとんど同じである） be almost the same ((as))

onaji-yô-ni-mieru（同じように見える）look alike

onaji-kurai〈同じくらい〉as...as.

    Kanojo-wa watashi-to-onaji-kurai-no-se-no-takasa-da.（彼女は私と同じくらいの背の高さだ。）She is about as tall as I.

o-naka〈おなか〉the belly, the stomach.

    O-naka-ga-suita.（おなかがすいた。）I am hungry.

    O-naka-ga-ippai-da.（おなかがいっぱいだ。）My stomach is full.

    O-naka-ga-itai.（おなかが痛い。）I have a stomachache.

    Kanojo-wa o-naka-ga-ookii.（彼女はおなかが大きい。）She is pregnant.

onchi〈おんち：音痴〉

onchi-no〈音痴の〉tone-deaf.

onchû〈おんちゅう：御中〉Messrs.

    Takata-shôkai-onchû（高田商会御中）Messrs. Takata & Co.

ondan〈おんだん：温暖〉warmth.

ondan-na〈温暖な〉warm.

ondo〈おんど：温度〉temperature.

    ondo o hakaru（温度を計る）take the temperature

    Ondo ga agaru.（温度が上がる。）The temperature rises.

    Ondo ga sagaru.（温度が下がる。）The temperature falls.

    ondo-henka（温度変化）a temperature change

    shitsu-nai-ondo（室内温度）the indoor temperature

    ondo-kei（温度計）a thermometer

ondo〈おんど：音頭〉

ondo-o-toru〈音頭をとる〉lead the song, lead a cheer.

ondoku〈おんどく：音読〉

ondoku-suru〈音読する〉read aloud.

ondori〈おんどり〉a cock, a rooster.

one〈おね：尾根〉a ridge, a spine.

ônen〈おうねん：往年〉

ônen-no〈往年の〉former, onetime.

ongaku〈おんがく：音楽〉music.

    ongaku-gakkô（音楽学校）a music school

    ongaku-ka（音楽家）a musician

    ongaku-kai（音楽会）a concert

ongaku-no or *ongaku-teki(-na)*〈音楽の，音楽的(な)〉musical.

oni〈おに：鬼〉an ogre, a fiend, a devil, a demon.

    shigoto no oni（仕事の鬼）a demon for work

oni-gawara〈鬼がわら〉a gargoyle, a ridge-end tile

oni-no-yô-na〈鬼のような〉fiendish, inhuman.

oni-gokko-o-suru〈鬼ごっこをする〉play tag.

onjin〈おんじん：恩人〉a benefactor.

onjô〈おんじょう：温情〉a warm heart.

onjô-shugi（温情主義）paternalism

onjô-aru〈温情ある〉warmhearted.

onkai〈おんかい：音階〉the (musical) scale.

onkan〈おんかん：音感〉

onkan-kyôiku（音感教育）acoustic training

onkei〈おんけい：恩恵〉a favor, a benefit.

onkei-ni-yokusuru（恩恵に浴する）share in the benefit

onken〈おんけん：穏健〉

onken-ha（穏健派）the moderates

onken-na〈穏健な〉moderate, temperate, sound.

onkô〈おんこう：温厚〉

onkô-na〈温厚な〉gentle.

onkyô〈おんきょう：音響〉(a) sound

onkyô-kôka（音響効果）sound effects

onkyû〈おんきゅう：恩給〉a pension.

onna〈おんな：女〉a woman.

onna-no-ko（女の子）a girl

onna-gata（女形）a female role (player)

onna-gokoro（女心）a woman's heart

onna-rashii〈女らしい〉womanly, feminine.

ono〈おの〉an ax(e), a hatchet.

onoono〈おのおの：各々〉*see.* meimei（銘々）.

onryô〈おんりょう：音量〉volume〔of the radio music〕.

onryô o ookiku-suru（音量を大きくする）turn up the volume

onsei-gaku〈おんせいがく：音声学〉phonetics.

onsen〈おんせん：温泉〉a hot spring, a spa.

onsetsu〈おんせつ：音節〉a syllable.

onsetsu-ni-kugiru〈音節に区切る〉syllabicate.

onsha〈おんしゃ：恩赦〉an amnesty.

onsha-ni-yokusuru（恩赦に浴する）be granted amnesty

onshi〈おんし：恩師〉one's (respected) teacher.

onshin〈おんしん：音信〉correspondence, (a) communication.

Kare-kara koko-ni-ka-getsu onshin-ga-nai.（彼からここ二か月音信がな

い.）　I have heard nothing from him for two months.

onshitsu〈おんしつ：温室〉a hothouse, a greenhouse.

onshō〈おんしょう：温床〉a hotbed.

　　aku no onshō（悪の温床）　a hotbed of vice

onsoku〈おんそく：音速〉the speed of sound.

　　chō-onsoku（超音速）　supersonic (speed)

onsu〈オンス〉an ounce.

onsui〈おんすい：温水〉

　　onsui-pūru（温水プール）　a heated swimming pool

ontai〈おんたい：温帯〉the temperate zones.

　　ontai-chihō（温帯地方）　the temperate regions

ontai〈おんたい：御大〉the boss, the chief.

ontei〈おんてい：音程〉a musical interval.

　ontei-ga-atte-iru〈音程が合っている〉be in tune.

onten〈おんてん：恩典〉

　onten-ni-yokusuru〈恩典に浴する〉receive special favors.

ontō〈おんとう：穏当〉

　ontō-na〈穏当な〉just and proper, reasonable, moderate.

onwa〈おんわ：温和〉

　onwa-na〈温和な〉mild, gentle, temperate.

　　onwa-na kikō（温和な気候）　a mild climate

oo〈おお〉Oh!, well.

oo-ame〈おおあめ：大雨〉a heavy rain.

　　Oo-ame ga futta.（大雨が降った.）　It rained heavily.

oo-ana〈おおあな：大穴〉a great loss; a big hit.

　　oo-ana-o-akeru（大穴をあける）　suffer a great loss

　　oo-ana-o-ateru（大穴を当てる）　make a big hit

oo-arashi〈おおあらし：大あらし〉a heavy storm.

oo-asa〈おおあさ：大麻〉hemp.

oo-atari〈おおあたり：大当たり〉a big hit, a great success.

　oo-atari-suru〈大当たりする〉win a great success.

oo-bune〈おおぶね：大船〉

　　Oo-bune-ni-notta-tsumori-de-i-nasai.（大船に乗ったつもりでいなさい.）
　　Put yourself at ease.

oo-buroshiki〈おおぶろしき：大風呂敷〉

　oo-buroshiki-o-hirogeru〈大風呂敷を広げる〉talk big, brag.

oo-datemono〈おおだてもの：大立て者〉a leading figure, a great figure,
　a bigwig.

seikai-no oo-datemono〔政界の大立て者〕 a leading figure in politics

zaikai-no oo-datemono〔財界の大立て者〕 a financial magnate

oo-de〈おおで：大手〉

oo-de-o-futte〈大手を振って〉with nothing to fear, in triumph, with impunity.

oo-dōgu〈おおどうぐ：大道具〉(stage) setting, a set scene.

oo-doori〈おおどおり：大通り〉a main street.

oo-gakari〈おおがかり：大掛かり〉

oo-gakari-na〈大掛かりな〉large-scale(d), on a large scale.

oo-gakari-na mitsu-yu〔大掛かりな密輸〕 smuggling on a large scale

oo-gakari-ni〈大掛かりに〉on a large scale.

oo-gara〈おおがら：大柄〉large build; a large pattern.

oo-gara-no〈大柄の〉of large build, of great stature; of large patterns.

oo-gata〈おおがた：大型〉

oo-gata-no〈大型の〉large-sized, large, oversize(d).

oogesa〈おおげさ：大げさ〉

oogesa-na〈大げさな〉exaggerated.

oogesa-ni〈大げさに〉exaggeratedly.

oogesa-ni-iu〔大げさに言う〕 exaggerate

oo-goe〈おおごえ：大声〉a loud voice.

oo-goe-de〈大声で〉in a loud voice, loudly.

oo-gosho〈おおごしょ：大御所〉see. oo-datemono.

oo-goto〈おおごと：大事〉a serious matter.

oo-goto-ni-naru〈大事になる〉become serious.

oo-guchi〈おおぐち：大口〉

oo-guchi-no chūmon〔大口の注文〕 a big order

oo-guchi-o-akete〔大口を開けて〕 agape, with one's mouth wide open

oo-guchi-o-tataku〔大口をたたく〕 talk big, brag

oo-haba〈おおはば：大幅〉full breadth.

oo-haba-mono〔大幅物〕 broadcloth

oo-haba-na〈大幅な〉steep, sharp, large, wholesale.

oo-haba-na ne-sage〔大幅な値下げ〕 a sharp fall in prices

oo-haba-na jin・in-seiri〔大幅な人員整理〕 a wholesale discharge

oo-haba-ni〈大幅に〉sharply, by a large margin.

oo-hiroma〈おおひろま：大広間〉a (grand) hall.

Ooi!〈おおい。〉Hullo!, Hallo!, Hi!, Hoy!

ooi〈おおい：多い〉a lot of, lots of, plenty of, many, much, frequent, rich.

     yuki-ga-ooi（雪が多い） have much snow

     Kotoshi wa jishin-ga-ooi.（今年は地震が多い．） Earthquakes are frequent this year.

     Bitamin-bî-ga-ooi（ビタミンBが多い） be rich in vitamin B

ooi〈おおい：覆い〉a cover, a casing, a shade.

  ooi-o-kakeru or *ooi-o-suru*〈覆いを掛ける，覆いをする〉cover.

     ooi-o-toru（覆いを取る） uncover

  ooi-no-aru〈覆いのある〉covered.

     ooi-no-nai（覆いのない） uncovered

ooi-ni〈おおいに：大いに〉very, much, greatly, largely, exceedingly, a great deal.

     ooi-ni yorokobu（大いに喜ぶ） be much pleased

     ooi-ni odoroku（大いに驚く） be greatly surprised

     ooi-ni yaku-ni-tatsu（大いに役に立つ） help ((a person)) a great deal

ooi-iri〈おおいり：大入り〉a full house, a good audience.

     oo-iri-bukuro（大入り袋） a full-house bonus

     Oo-iri-man·in.（大入り満員．） House Full.

oo-isogi〈おおいそぎ：大急ぎ〉

  oo-isogi-no〈大急ぎの〉hurried, urgent.

     oo-isogi-no chûmon（大急ぎの注文） a rush order

  oo-isogi-de〈大急ぎで〉hurriedly, in a great hurry, in great haste.

     oo-isogi-de kaku（大急ぎで書く） write hurriedly

oo-kaji〈おおかじ：大火事〉a big fire.

ookami〈おおかみ〉a wolf.

ookare-sukunakare〈おおかれすくなかれ：多かれ少なかれ〉more or less.

oo-kata〈おおかた：大方〉probably; almost, for the most part.

oo-kaze〈おおかぜ：大風〉a strong wind.

     Oo-kaze-ga-fuiteiru.（大風が吹いている．） It is blowing very hard.

ookii〈おおきい：大きい〉big, large, great, mighty, gigantic, huge, loud.

     ookii ie（大きい家） a big house

     ookii toshi（大きい都市） a large city

     jimbutsu-ga-ookii（人物が大きい） be a great man

     ookii-koe-de（大きい声で） in a loud voice

     ookii-koto-o-iu（大きいことを言う） talk big

  ookiku〈大きく〉big, large, on a large scale, wide.

     ookiku kuchi o akeru（大きく口を開ける） open one's mouth wide

  ookiku-naru〈大きくなる〉grow larger, grow up, become serious.

ookiku-suru〈大きくする〉make larger, enlarge, extend, bring up.

ookisa〈おおきさ：大きさ〉size, dimensions, magnitude, volume, bulk.

ookisa-ga-chigau（大きさが違う）be different in size

ookisa-no-wari-niwa omoi（大きさの割には重い）be heavy for ((its)) size

〜*-to-hotondo-onaji-ookisa-da*〈〜とほとんど同じ大きさだ〉be about as large as... .

ooku〈おおく：多く〉

ooku-no〈多くの〉a lot of, lots of, plenty of, much, many.

ooku-wa〈多くは〉mostly, largely, for the most part.

Kare-ra-no ooku wa〜da.（彼らの多くは〜だ。）Most of them are... .

ooku-temo〈多くても〉at most.

ookura〈おおくら：大蔵〉

ookura-shô（大蔵省）the Ministry of Finance

ookura-daijin（大蔵大臣）the Minister of Finance

oo-machigai〈おおまちがい：大間違い〉a great mistake, a blunder, a gross error.

Sô omou-no-wa oo-machigai-da.（そう思うのは大間違いだ。）It's a great mistake to think so.

oomaka〈おおまか：大まか〉

oomaka-na〈大まかな〉rough, broad, generous, liberal.

oomaka-ni〈大まかに〉roughly.

oomaka-ni mi-tsumoru（大まかに見積もる）estimate roughly

oomaka-ni ieba（大まかに言えば）roughly speaking

oo-mata〈おおまた：大また〉a long stride.

oo-mata-ni aruku（大またに歩く）walk with long strides

oo-me〈おおめ：大目〉

oo-me-ni-miru〈大目に見る〉overlook.

oo-medama〈おおめだま：大目玉〉a good scolding.

oo-medama-o-kuu〈大目玉を食う〉be scolded severely.

oo-misoka〈おおみそか：大みそか〉New Year's Eve, the last day of the year.

oo-mizu〈おおみず：大水〉a (heavy) flood, an inundation, an overflow.

oo-moji〈おおもじ：大文字〉a capital letter.

oo-mono〈おおもの：大物〉a very important person, a VIP.

oo-mugi〈おおむぎ：大麦〉barley.

oo-nata〈おおなた：大なた〉a big hatchet.

oo-nata-o-furuu〈大なたを振るう〉take a drastic measure, make a drastic curtailment 〔in the personnel *or* the budget〕.

ooppira-ni 〈おおっぴらに〉 openly, in public.

ooraka 〈おおらか〉

ooraka-na 〈おおらかな〉 broad-minded, magnanimous, placid.

oo-sawagi 〈おおさわぎ：大騒ぎ〉

oo-sawagi-o-suru 〈大騒ぎをする〉 raise the roof, make a fuss ((about *or* over)).

oo-shio 〈おおしお：大潮〉 the flood tide.

oo-sôji 〈おおそうじ：大掃除〉 general housecleaning.

oo-sôji-o-suru 〈大掃除をする〉 clean the whole house.

oote 〈おおて：大手〉 big enterprisers, large corporations.

oo-tsubu 〈おおつぶ：大粒〉 a large drop.

oo-tsubu no ame 〈大粒の雨〉 a large drop of rain

oou 〈おおう：覆う〉 cover.

yuki-de oowarete-iru 〈雪で覆われている〉 be covered with snow

oo-uridashi 〈おおうりだし：大売り出し〉 a special sale, a bargain sale.

oo-utsushi 〈おおうつし：大写し〉 a close-up.

oo-utsushi-ni-suru 〈大写しにする〉 bring into a close-up

oo-warai 〈おおわらい：大笑い〉 a great laughter, a hearty laugh.

oo-warai-suru 〈大笑いする〉 burst into laughter, have a hearty laugh.

ooya 〈おおや：大家〉 a landlord.

ooyake 〈おおやけ：公〉

ooyake-no 〈公の〉 public, official, formal.

ooyake-no-basho-de 〈公の場所で〉 in public

ooyake-ni 〈公に〉 publicly, officially, formally.

ooyake-ni-suru 〈公にする〉 make public, publish, bring to light

ooyake-ni-naru 〈公になる〉 be made known, be published, come to light

oo-yasuuri 〈おおやすうり：大安売り〉 a bargain sale.

ooyô 〈おおよう：大様〉

ooyô-na 〈大様な〉 broad-minded, liberal, generous, lordly.

ooyô-ni 〈大様に〉 liberally, generously.

ooyô-ni-sodatsu 〈大様に育つ〉 be brought up in easy circumstances

oo-yorokobi 〈おおよろこび：大喜び〉

oo-yorokobi-de 〈大喜びで〉 with great delight.

oo-yuki 〈おおゆき：大雪〉 a heavy snow, a heavy snowfall.

oo-zake 〈おおざけ：大酒〉

oo-zake-o-nomu 〈大酒を飲む〉 drink heavily.

oozappa 〈おおざっぱ：大ざっぱ〉

oozappa-na 〈大ざっぱな〉 rough.

oozappa-ni 〈大ざっぱに〉 roughly.

     oozappa-ni mi-tsumoru (大ざっぱに見積もる)   estimate roughly

oozei 〈おおぜい：大勢〉

oozei-no 〈大勢の〉 a crowd of, a large number of, many.

     oozei-no hitobito (大勢の人々)   a crowd of people

oozei-de 〈大勢で〉 in great numbers, in crowds.

oozeki 〈おおぜき：大関〉 a *sumo* wrestler of the second highest rank.

oo-zume 〈おおづめ：大詰め〉 the finale, the end, the conclusion.

     oo-zume-o-mukaeru (大詰めを迎える)   be close to the end

oo-zumô 〈おおずもう：大相撲〉 a grand *sumo* tournament; a long-drawn *sumo* match.

opâru 〈オパール〉 opal.

opera 〈オペラ〉 an opera.

ôrai 〈おうらい：往来〉 comings and goings, traffic; a street.

ôrai 〈オーライ〉 all right.

Oranda 〈オランダ〉 Holland, the Netherlands.

     Oranda-jin (オランダ人)   a Dutchman

     Oranda-go (オランダ語)   Dutch

     Oranda(-jin)-no (オランダ(人)の)   Dutch

orenji 〈オレンジ〉 an orange.

orenji-iro-no 〈オレンジ色の〉 orange(-colored).

oreru 〈おれる：折れる〉 break, be broken.

     futatsu-ni oreru (二つに折れる)   be broken in two

ori 〈おり〉 a cage, a pen.

ori 〈おり：折〉 an opportunity, a chance, an occasion.

     ori-ga-areba (折があれば)   when an opportunity occurs

     itsu-ka ori-o-mite (いつか折をみて)   at some convenient time

ori-ni-furete 〈折に触れて〉 at times, occasionally.

ori-yoku 〈折よく〉 fortunately.

〜-ori-ni 〈〜折に〉 when.

     jôkyô-shita-ori-ni (上京した折に)   when I came up to Tokyo

ori(-bako) 〈おり(ばこ)：折り(箱)〉 a chip box [for packing lunch].

oriai 〈おりあい：折り合い〉

     oriai-ga-warui (折り合いが悪い)   do not get on well ((with)), be on bad terms ((with))

     oriai-ga-tsuku (折り合いが付く)   come to terms, arrive at an

understanding

ori-au〈おりあう：折り合う〉agree, come to terms, make concessions.

oribu〈オリーブ〉an olive.

oribu-yu（オリーブ油）olive oil

ori-gami〈おりがみ：折り紙〉folding paper.

ori-gami-de-inu-o-oru（折り紙で犬を折る）fold a piece of colored paper into the figure of a dog

ori-gami-tsuki-no〈折り紙付きの〉certified, guaranteed; notorious.

ori-itte〈おりいって：折り入って〉

Ori-itte-o-negai-shi-tai-koto-ga-arimasu.（折り入ってお願いしたい事があります。）I have a special favor to ask of you.

ori-kaeshi〈おりかえし：折り返し〉the turnups, a turn; by return of post.

ori-kaeshi henji-o-suru（折り返し返事をする）answer by return of post

ori-kaeshi-unten（折り返し運転）shuttle service

ori-kaeshi-unten-o-suru（折り返し運転をする）turn back

ori-kaesu〈折り返す〉turn up, make a turn ((for)).

ori-kasanaru〈おりかさなる：折り重なる〉overlap one another, lie one upon another.

ori-kasanatte-taoreru（折り重なって倒れる）fall one upon another

ori-komu〈おりこむ：織り込む〉weave ((into)).

kare-no kangae o gen·an·ni-ori-komu（彼の考えを原案に織り込む）incorporate his idea into the plan

ori-komu〈おりこむ：折り込む〉tuck in; insert.

ori-mageru〈おりまげる：折り曲げる〉fold, turn up.

ori-me〈おりめ：折り目〉a fold, a crease.

kichin-to ori-me-no-tsuita〈きちんと折り目の付いた〉well-creased, neatly-pressed.

ori-me-tadashii〈おりめただしい：折り目正しい〉well-mannered.

ori-me-tadashiku〈折り目正しく〉courteously.

orimono〈おりもの：織物〉cloth, textile.

Orimpikku〈オリンピック〉the Olympic Games, the Olympiad.

oriru〈おりる：降(下)りる〉come(go *or* get) down, get off.

ni-kai-kara oriru（二階から降りる）come downstairs

yûshoku-ni orite-kuru（夕食に降りて来る）come down to dinner

densha o oriru（電車を降りる）get off a train

ori-tatami〈おりたたみ：折り畳み〉

　　　ori-tatami-isu〈折り畳みいす〉 a folding chair
　ori-tatami-shiki-no〈折り畳み式の〉 folding.
　ori-tatamu〈折り畳む〉 fold up.
ori-zume〈おりづめ：折り詰め〉 food packed in a chip box.
ori-zuru〈おりづる：折りづる〉 a folded paper-crane.
oroka〈おろか：愚か〉
　　　oroka-mono（愚か者） a fool
　oroka-na〈愚かな〉 foolish.
　oroka-nimo〈愚かにも〉 foolishly enough.
orooro〈おろおろ〉
　orooro-suru〈おろおろする〉 be flustered, snivel.
oroshi〈おろし：卸〉 wholesale trade.
　　　oroshi-de-kau（卸で買う） buy wholesale
　　　oroshi-uri-shô（卸売商） a wholesale dealer, a wholesaler
　orosu〈卸す〉 wholesale.
oroshi-gane〈おろしがね：卸し金〉 a grater.
orosoka〈おろそか〉
　orosoka-ni-suru〈おろそかにする〉 neglect, slight.
　　　benkyô o　orosoka-ni-suru（勉強をおろそかにする） neglect one's
　　　studies
orosu〈おろす：降(下)ろす〉 take down, unload, drop, set ((a passenger))
　down, draw down.
　　　tana-kara jisho o orosu（棚から辞書を降ろす） take down a dictionary
　　　from the shelf
　　　wagon-kara-nimotsu-o-orosu（ワゴンから荷物を降ろす） unload a
　　　wagon
　　　Tsugi-no　eki-de　oroshite-kudasai.（次の駅で降ろしてください。） Drop
　　　me at the next station.
　　　buraindo o orosu（ブラインドを下ろす） draw down a blind
oru〈おる：織る〉 weave.
oru〈おる：折る〉 break, snap; fold, bend.
　　　migi-ude-o-oru（右腕を折る） have one's right arm broken
　　　futatsu-ni oru（二つに折る） fold in two
ôru〈オール〉 an oar.
ôrudo-misu〈オールドミス〉 an old maid.
orugan〈オルガン〉 an organ.
　　　orugan o hiku（オルガンを弾く） play the organ
orugôru〈オルゴール〉 a music box.

orugu 〈オルグ〉 an organizer.

ôryô 〈おうりょう：横領〉 (a) usurpation.
　　ôryô-zai（横領罪） embezzlement
　　ôryô-suru（横領する）usurp.

osae 〈おさえ：押さえ〉
　osae-ga-kika-nai〈押さえが利かない〉 be unable to control〔one's men〕.

osaeru 〈おさえる：押さえる，抑える〉 check, restrain, control, stop, hold (down).
　　uma o osaeru（馬を押さえる） check a horse
　　bukka-no jôshô o osaeru（物価の上昇を抑える） check the rise in prices
　　ikari o osaeru（怒りを抑える） restrain one's anger
　　kanjô o osaeru（感情を抑える） control one's passion
　　migi-te de kuchi-o-osaeru（右手で口を押さえる） hold the right hand over one's mouth

o-sagari 〈おさがり：お下がり〉(clothes) handed down〔from one's brother *or* sister〕.

o-saki 〈おさき：お先〉
　　Dôzo o-saki-ni.（どうぞお先に.） Please go first.
　　O-saki-ni shitsurei.（お先に失礼.） Excuse me for going first.

osamaru 〈おさまる：治まる〉 be governed well; calm down, quiet down, be suppressed; be settled, come to an end, be over.

osameru 〈おさめる：治める〉 govern, rule(*or* reign) ((over)); suppress, subdue.
　　kuni o osameru（国を治める） govern a country
　　nairan o osameru（内乱を治める） subdue a rebellion

osameru 〈おさめる：収（納）める〉 obtain, realize; pay; put back.
　　kô-kekka o osameru（好結果を収める） obtain good results
　　zeikin o osameru（税金を納める） pay a tax
　　moto-no-basho-ni-osameru（元の場所に納める） put ((a thing)) back in its place

o-san 〈おさん：お産〉 childbirth, delivery, confinement.
　　o-san-ga-karui（お産が軽い） have an easy delivery
　　o-san-o-suru〈お産をする〉have a baby, give birth to a baby.

osanai 〈おさない：幼い〉
　osanai-toki-ni〈幼い時に〉 when a child, in one's childhood, as a child.

osana-tomodachi 〈おさなともだち：幼友達〉 a childhood friend.

o-sarai 〈おさらい〉 a review.

o-sarai-o-suru〈おさらいをする〉review one's lessons.

o-sato〈おさと：お里〉one's home, one's origin.

o-sato-ga-shireru〈お里が知れる〉betray oneself, betray one's origin.

o-seji〈おせじ：お世辞〉a compliment, (a) flattery.

o-seji-o-iu〈お世辞を言う〉pay ((a person)) a compliment, flatter.

o-seji-ni〈お世辞に〉as a compliment.

o-sekkai〈おせっかい：お節介〉officiousness, meddlesomeness.

o-sekkai-na〈お節介な〉officious, meddlesome.

   o-sekkai-na hito〈お節介な人〉an officious person

osen〈おせん：汚染〉pollution.

   kankyō-osen〈環境汚染〉environmental pollution

osen-suru〈汚染する〉pollute.

ōsen〈おうせん：横線〉

   ōsen-ko-gitte〈横線小切手〉a crossed check

ōsen-o-hiku〈横線を引く〉cross.

ōsen〈おうせん：応戦〉

ōsen-suru〈応戦する〉fight back, return the fire.

ōsetsu〈おうせつ：応接〉reception.

   ōsetsu-shitsu〈応接室〉a drawing room, a reception room, a parlor

ōsetsu-suru〈応接する〉receive.

o-shaberi〈おしゃべり〉chattering; a chatterbox.

o-shaberi-suru〈おしゃべりする〉chat, chatter.

o-shaberi-na〈おしゃべりな〉talkative, chattering.

o-share〈おしゃれ〉dandyism, foppery.

oshi〈おし：押し〉

   Nani-goto-mo-oshi-no-itte.（何事も押しの一手.）Push   generally succeeds in everything.

oshi-ga-kiku〈押しが利く〉have influence ((with)).

oshi-no-tsuyoi〈押しの強い〉pushing, aggressive, audacious.

   oshi-no-yowai〈押しの弱い〉fainthearted

oshiai-heshiai〈おしあいへしあい：押し合いへし合い〉

oshiai-heshiai-suru〈押し合いへし合いする〉hustle   and   jostle,   push   and shove.

oshi-akeru〈おしあける：押し開ける〉push(*or* force) ((a door)) open.

oshi-au〈おしあう：押し合う〉jostle(*or* push) one another.

oshi-ba〈おしば：押し葉〉pressed leaves.

oshi-bana〈おしばな：押し花〉pressed flowers.

o-shibe〈おしべ：雄しべ〉a stamen.

oshi-botan 〈おしボタン：押しボタン〉a push button.

oshi-dashi 〈おしだし：押し出し〉
    oshi-dashi-no-itten-o-ageru〈押し出しの一点をあげる〉force in a run with a bases-loaded walk
  oshi-dasu〈押し出す〉push out, force out, crowd out.

oshie 〈おしえ：教え〉teaching(s), a lesson, a doctrine.
    oshie-go〈教え子〉one's pupil
  oshie-o-ukeru〈教えを受ける〉take lessons ((in)), be taught ((by)).

oshie-komu 〈おしえこむ：教え込む〉inculcate, instil, indoctrinate, have a good training ((in)).

oshieru 〈おしえる：教える〉teach, instruct, show, tell, recommend.

oshige-mo-naku 〈おしげもなく：惜しげもなく〉unsparingly, without regret, freely.

oshi-hakaru 〈おしはかる：推し量る〉*see.* suisoku-suru.

oshii 〈おしい：惜しい〉regrettable, pitiful; precious, dear; too good ((for)), wasteful.
  oshi-sô-ni〈惜しそうに〉grudgingly, reluctantly, unwillingly.

oshiire 〈おしいれ：押し入れ〉a closet.

oshi-iru 〈おしいる：押し入る〉force into, break into.

oshi-kaesu 〈おしかえす：押し返す〉push back, force back.

oshi-kakeru 〈おしかける：押し掛ける〉force oneself ((into *or* on)), crash, throng.

oshi-kiru 〈おしきる：押し切る〉carry through, overcome, face it out.
    hantai o oshi-kiru〈反対を押し切る〉overcome the opposition ((of))
  hantai-o-oshi-kitte〈反対を押し切って〉in spite of ((a person's)) opposition.

oshikomi-gôtô 〈おしこみごうとう：押し込み強盗〉a burglar.

oshi-komu 〈おしこむ：押し込む〉push in, thrust in, jam into.
    kuchi-e oshi-komu〈口へ押し込む〉stuff ((a thing)) in one's mouth

oshi-makuru 〈おしまくる：押しまくる〉push and push.

oshi-mondô 〈おしもんどう：押し問答〉
  oshi-mondô-o-suru〈押し問答をする〉bandy words ((with)).

oshimu 〈おしむ：惜しむ〉spare, grudge, regret, be sorry ((for)).
    jikan o oshimu〈時間を惜しむ〉grudge the time
    doryoku o oshima-nai〈努力を惜しまない〉spare no efforts ((to do))
    wakare-o-oshimu〈別れを惜しむ〉be sorry to part ((from *or* with))
    hiyô-o-oshimazu-ni〈費用を惜しまずに〉regardless of expenses
  oshimu-beki〈惜しむべき〉regrettable.

ôshin〈おうしん：往診〉

　　ôshin-ryô（往診料）a doctor's fee for a visit

　ôshin-suru〈往診する〉visit a patient to examine.

oshi-nagasu〈おしながす：押し流す〉wash away, sweep away.

oshi-nokeru〈おしのける：押しのける〉push away(*or* aside).

oshiroi〈おしろい〉face powder.

　oshiroi-o-nuru〈おしろいを塗る〉powder〔one's face〕.

oshi-susumeru〈おしすすめる：押し進める〉push.

　　keikaku-o-oshi-susumeru（計画を押し進める）　push on with a plan

oshi-taosu〈おしたおす：押し倒す〉push(*or* force)((a person)) down.

oshi-toosu〈おしとおす：押し通す〉persist to the end; push through.

　　shinnen-o-oshi-toosu（信念を押し通す）　persist in one's belief

ôshitsu〈おうしつ：王室〉the royal family.

oshi-tsubusu〈おしつぶす：押しつぶす〉crush, smash, squash.

oshi-tsukeru〈おしつける：押し付ける〉push(*or* press)((against)), press
　down, force.

　　karada-ni pisutoru o oshi-tsukeru（体にピストルを押し付ける）　press
　　　a pistol against ((a person's)) body

　　shigoto o oshi-tsukeru（仕事を押し付ける）　force work on ((a per-
　　　son))

oshi-tsumaru〈おしつまる：押し詰まる〉approach the end of the year.

oshi-uri〈おしうり：押し売り〉an importunate peddler.

　oshi-uri-suru〈押し売りする〉force (a person) to buy.

oshi-wakeru〈おしわける：押し分ける〉push one's way through.

oshi-yoseru〈おしよせる：押し寄せる〉bear down ((on)), surge ((on)).

　　oshi-yoseru gunshû（押し寄せる群集）　surging crowds

oshô〈おしょう：和尚〉a Buddhist priest.

ôshô〈おうしょう：王将〉the king.

o-shôban〈おしょうばん〉

　o-shôban-suru〈おしょうばんする〉partake ((of)).

oshoku〈おしょく：汚職〉(official) corruption, bribery.

　　oshoku-jiken（汚職事件）　a bribery case

ôshoku-jinshu〈おうしょくじんしゅ：黄色人種〉the yellow race.

Ôshû〈おうしゅう：欧州〉Europe.

　　Ôshû-kyôdô-tai（欧州共同体）　the European Community (EC)

ôshû〈おうしゅう：押収〉

　ôshû-suru〈押収する〉seize, confiscate, impound.

ôshû〈おうしゅう：応酬〉a reply, a response, a return, an exchange.

    yaji no ôshû〔野次の応酬〕an exchange of heckling
ôshû-suru〈応酬する〉respond, give a retort.

osoi〈おそい：遅い〉late, behind time, slow.
    kaeri-ga-osoi〔帰りが遅い〕be late (in) coming home
    aruku-no-ga-osoi〔歩くのが遅い〕be a slow walker
osoku〈遅く〉late, slow, slowly.
    osoku okiru〔遅く起きる〕get up late
    yoru-osoku-made〔夜遅くまで〕until late at night
    itsumo-yori-osoku〔いつもより遅く〕later than usual
osoku-tomo〈遅くとも〉at the latest.
osokare-hayakare〈遅かれ早かれ〉sooner or later.

o-sonae〈おそなえ：お供え〉an offering, a rice-cake offering.

osoraku〈おそらく：恐らく〉perhaps, probably, maybe, I'm afraid, I
fear.
    Osoraku kanojo-wa ko-nai-deshô.（恐らく彼女は来ないでしょう。）I'm
    afraid she will not come.

osore〈おそれ：恐れ〉fear, terror, dread, anxiety; danger.
    osore o idaku（恐れを抱く）entertain fears
osore-o-nasu〈恐れをなす〉stand in awe ((of)), be frightened.
〜-no-osore-ga-aru〈〜の恐れがある〉be in danger of... , There is the
possibility that... , It is feared that... .
osore-o-shiranu〈恐れを知らぬ〉fearless, intrepid.

osore-iru〈おそれいる：恐れ入る〉
    Go-shinsetsu-ni-osore-irimasu.（御親切に恐れ入ります。）Thank you
    very much for your kindness.
    Osore-irimasu-ga sono e o misete-itadake-masen-ka?（恐れ入りますが
    その絵を見せていただけませんか。）I am sorry to trouble you, but
    will you show me the picture?
    Kare-ga-kuchi-ga-tatsu-no-niwa-osore-itta.（彼が口が立つのには恐れ入
    った。）I cannot but admire his eloquence.
    Kare-no shitsumon-niwa mina osore-itta.（彼の質問には皆恐れ入っ
    た。）His question floored us.

osore-ononoku〈おそれおののく：恐れおののく〉tremble with fear.

osoreru〈おそれる：恐れる〉fear, be afraid ((of)).
osorete〈恐れて〉with fear.
〜-(shi)-nai-ka-to-osorete〈〜（し）ないかと恐れて〉for fear that... .

o-soroi〈おそろい〉
    o-soroi-no-fuku（おそろいの服）suits of the same cloth

osoroshii 〈おそろしい：恐ろしい〉 fearful, terrible, dreadful, fierce, awful.

    osoroshii jiko〈恐ろしい事故〉 a fearful accident

    osoroshii yume〈恐ろしい夢〉 a terrible dream

    osoroshii hito-de〈恐ろしい人出〉 a tremendous crowd

    osoroshii kao o shita〈恐しい顔をした〉 fierce-looking

  osoroshiku〈恐ろしく〉 terribly, awfully.

    osoroshiku atsui〈恐ろしく暑い〉 be awfully hot

  osoroshisa〈恐ろしさ〉 fear, terror, horror.

    osoroshisa-no-amari〈恐ろしさの余り〉 for fear, with horror

osoruosoru 〈おそるおそる：恐る恐る〉 timidly, humbly.

osou 〈おそう：襲う〉 attack.

    bô-fûu-ni-osowareru〈暴風雨に襲われる〉 be attacked by a storm

osowaru 〈おそわる：教わる〉 be taught, learn.

oso-zaki 〈おそざき：遅咲き〉

  oso-zaki-no〈遅咲きの〉 late.

    oso-zaki-no sakura〈遅咲きの桜〉 late cherry blossoms

osu 〈おす：雄〉 a male, a cock.

  osu-no〈雄の〉 male, he-.

osu 〈おす：押す〉 push, press, stamp.

    doa o karuku osu〈ドアを軽く押す〉 push the door lightly

    beru o osu〈ベルを押す〉 press the bell button

    han o osu〈判を押す〉 stamp a seal

    osu-na-osu-na-no dai-konzatsu-de-aru〈押すな押すなの大混雑である〉 be jammed with people

osu 〈おす：推す〉 judge ((by *or* from)), guess, suppose; recommend.

osui 〈おすい：汚水〉 filthy water, sewage.

    osui-shori-jô〈汚水処理場〉 a sewage disposal plant

o-suso-wake 〈おすそわけ：おすそ分け〉

  o-suso-wake-suru〈おすそ分けする〉 share a gift ((with)).

Ôsutoraria 〈オーストラリア〉 Australia.

    Ôsutoraria-jin〈オーストラリア人〉 an Australian

    Ôsutoraria(-jin)-no〈オーストラリア(人)の〉 Australian

Ôsutoria 〈オーストリア〉 Austria.

    Ôsutoria-jin〈オーストリア人〉 an Austrian

    Ôsutoria(-jin)-no〈オーストリア(人)の〉 Austrian

otafuku-kaze 〈おたふくかぜ：お多福風邪〉 mumps.

o-tagai 〈おたがい：お互い〉 *see.* tagai.

ōtai〈おうたい：応対〉

   ōtai-suru〈応対する〉 receive, wait ((on)) 〔customers〕.

otamajakushi〈おたまじゃくし：お玉じゃくし〉 a tadpole.

otazune-mono〈おたずねもの：お尋ね者〉 a wanted man, a fugitive from justice.

otchokochoi〈おっちょこちょい〉 a careless person.

Ōte!〈おうて。：王手。〉 Check!, Checkmate!

o-temba〈おてんば：お転婆〉 a romp.

   o-temba-na〈おてんばな〉 romping.

oten〈おてん：汚点〉 a blot, a stain.

     meisei-ni oten o nokosu（名声に汚点を残す） leave a stain on one's reputation

ōten〈おうてん：横転〉

   ōten-suru〈横転する〉 turn sideways, make a barrel roll.

o-tenki-ya〈おてんきや：お天気屋〉 a fickle person.

ote-no-mono〈おてのもの：お手の物〉 one's forte, one's strong point, one's speciality.

     Sukêto-nara-ote-no-mono-da.（スケートならお手の物だ。） Skating is in my line.

o-tetsudai〈おてつだい：お手伝い〉 a (home) help, a maid.

ote-yawaraka-ni〈おてやわらかに：お手柔らかに〉

     Ote-yawaraka-ni-negaimasu.（お手柔らかに願います.） Please be easy with us. / Don't be too hard on us.

oto〈おと：音〉 a sound, a noise, a roar.

     oto o tateru（音を立てる） make a sound(*or* a noise)

     nami no oto（波の音） the roar of waves

   oto-o-tatete〈音を立てて〉 with a (great) noise, noisily.

ōto〈おうと：おう吐〉 vomiting.

   ōto-suru〈おう吐する〉 vomit.

ōtō〈おうとう：応答〉 an answer, a reply.

     shitsugi-ōtō（質疑応答） questions and answers

ōtobai〈オートバイ〉 a motorcycle, an autocycle.

o-tō-chan〈おとうちゃん：お父ちゃん〉 dad(dy).

otogi-banashi〈おとぎばなし：おとぎ話〉 a fairy(*or* a nursery) tale.

otoko〈おとこ：男〉 a man.

     otoko-no-ko（男の子） a boy

     ichinin-mae-no-otoko-ni-naru（一人前の男になる） become a man

     otoko-o-ageru（男を上げる） raise one's population

otoko-rashii 〈男らしい〉 manly, manful.

otoko-rashiku 〈男らしく〉 manfully.

　otoko-rashiku-nai 〈男らしくない〉 unmanly

otoko-buri-no-ii 〈男振りのいい〉 good-looking.

otome 〈おとめ：乙女〉 a maiden, a virgin, a girl.

ôtome-ka-suru 〈オートメかする：オートメ化する〉 automate.

ôtomêshon 〈オートメーション〉 automation.

ôtomiru 〈オートミール〉 oatmeal, porridge.

otona 〈おとな：大人〉 a grown-up (person), an adult, a man, a woman.

otona-ni-naru 〈大人になる〉 grow up.

otona-biru 〈大人びる〉 look like a grown-up person, become precocious.

otona-ge-nai 〈大人気ない〉 childish.

otonashii 〈おとなしい：大人しい〉 gentle, mild, well-behaved, good.

otonashi-sô-na 〈大人しそうな〉 mild-looking.

otonashiku 〈大人しく〉 gently, quietly, meekly.

otonashiku-suru 〈大人しくする〉 be good, behave well, keep quiet.

　　Otonashiku-shi-nasai.（大人しくしなさい.） Be a good boy(*or* girl).

otori 〈おとり〉 a decoy, a call bird.

　　otori-ni-tsukau 〈おとりに使う〉 use ((a person)) as a decoy, use ((a bird)) for calling

otoroe 〈おとろえ：衰え〉 weakening, decline.

otoroeru 〈衰える〉 become weak, decline, fall off, fail, dwindle.

　kenkô-ga-otoroeru 〈健康が衰える〉 decline in health

otoru 〈おとる：劣る〉 be inferior ((to)), be worse ((than)), be second ((to)), be not so good ((as)).

dare-nimo-otora-nai 〈だれにも劣らない〉 be second to none.

masaru-tomo-otoranai 〈勝るとも劣らない〉 be not at all inferior ((to)).

ototta 〈劣った〉 inferior.

　ototta hinshitsu 〈劣った品質〉 an inferior quality

o-tô-san 〈おとうさん：お父さん〉 father, papa.

oto-sata 〈おとさた：音さた〉 news, tidings.

　　Kare-kara sono-go oto-sata-ga-nai.（彼からその後音さたがない.） I have not heard from him since then.

otoshi-ana 〈おとしあな：落とし穴〉 a pitfall, a trap.

o-toshidama 〈おとしだま：お年玉〉 a New Year's present(*or* gift), a handsel.

otoshiireru 〈おとしいれる：陥れる〉 entrap, land.

otoshi-mono 〈おとしもの：落とし物〉 a lost article.

otoshi-nushi 〈おとしぬし：落とし主〉 the loser.

otosu 〈おとす：落とす〉 drop, let fall, lose.

    gurasu o otosu（グラスを落とす） drop a glass

    saifu o otosu（財布を落とす） lose one's purse

    shin·yô o otosu（信用を落とす） lose one's credit

otôto 〈おとうと：弟〉 a younger(*or* a little) brother.

    sue-no otôto（末の弟） one's youngest brother

ototoi 〈おととい〉 the day before yesterday.

    ototoi-no-ban（おとといの晩） the night before last

ototoshi 〈おととし〉 the year before last.

ôtotsu 〈おうとつ：凹凸〉

   ôtotsu-no-aru〈凹凸のある〉 uneven, irregular, rugged.

otozure 〈おとずれ：訪れ〉 a visit, a call.

    haru no otozure（春の訪れ） the coming of spring

otozureru 〈おとずれる：訪れる〉 *see*. hômon-suru.

otte 〈おって：追って〉 later on.

otte 〈おって：追っ手〉 a pursuer.

    Otte-ga-kakatta.（追っ手がかかった.） A hue and cry went up.

Otto! 〈おっと.〉 Oh!

    Otto-abunai!（おっと危ない.） Oh, take care!

otto 〈おっと：夫〉 a husband.

ottori 〈おっとり〉

   ottori-shita〈おっとりした〉 gentle, quiet, composed.

ottosei 〈おっとせい〉 a fur seal.

ou 〈おう：追う〉 run ((after)), chase, pursue; drive; follow.

    kachiku o ou（家畜を追う） drive the cattle

    hae o ou（はえを追う） drive flies away

    ryûkô o ou（流行を追う） follow the fashion

    shôsetsu-no-suji o ou（小説の筋を追う） follow the plot

   hi-o-otte〈日を追って〉 day by day.

   toshi-o-otte〈年を追って〉 year after year.

   jun-o-otte〈順を追って〉 in order.

ou 〈おう：負う〉 bear, carry...on one's back; owe, assume; receive.

    omo-ni o ou（重荷を負う） bear a heavy load

    gimu o ou（義務を負う） owe a duty ((to))

    sekinin o ou（責任を負う） assume the responsibility ((for))

    jûshô-o-ou（重傷を負う） get seriously injured

o-ushi 〈おうし：雄牛〉 a bull, an ox.

owari 〈おわり：終わり〉 an end, a close, a conclusion.

    owari-made 〈終わりまで〉 to the end, to the last

        hajime-kara owari-made 〈始めから終わりまで〉 from beginning to end

  owari-no 〈終わりの〉 last, final.

  owari-ni 〈終わりに〉 at the end, finally.

    kongetsu no owari-ni 〈今月の終わりに〉 at the end of this month

  owari-ni-nozonde 〈終わりに臨んで〉 in conclusion.

  owari-ni-chikazuku 〈終わりに近づく〉 draw to a close.

owaru 〈おわる：終わる〉 end, come to an end, close, be over, finish, complete, break up, result ((in)).

    Natsu-yasumi wa owatta.〈夏休みは終わった.〉 The summer vacation is over.

    O-cha-no-kai wa san-ji-ni owatta.〈お茶の会は三時に終わった.〉 The tea party broke up at 3.

    shippai-ni-owaru 〈失敗に終わる〉 result in failure

owaseru 〈おわせる：負わせる〉

    sekinin-o-owaseru 〈責任を負わせる〉 make ((a person)) responsible

    kizu-o-owaseru 〈傷を負わせる〉 inflict injuries ((upon))

Oya! 〈おや.〉 Oh! / Oh dear! / Dear me! / Oh my!

    Oya-mâ! 〈おやまあ.〉 O my! / Dear me!

oya 〈おや：親〉 a parent, parents; the dealer, the banker.

    oya-ko 〈親子〉 parent and child

    oya-kôkô-de-aru 〈親孝行である〉 be faithful to one's parents

    oya-omoi-de-aru 〈親思いである〉 be devoted to one's parents

    oya-fukô-mono 〈親不孝者〉 an undutiful son

    oya-yuzuri-de-aru 〈親譲りである〉 be inherited from one's parents

    oya-gokoro 〈親心〉 parental affection

    oya-baka-ni-naru 〈親ばかになる〉 develop into fond parents

    oya-gaisha 〈親会社〉 a parent company

  oya-no 〈親の〉 parental.

    oya-no ikô 〈親の威光〉 parental authority

oyabun 〈おやぶん：親分〉 a boss, the chief, the head.

  oyabun-hada-no 〈親分肌の〉 magnanimous.

oyaji 〈おやじ：親じ〉 one's father, an old man, one's boss.

oya-kata 〈おやかた：親方〉 a master.

o-yama-no-taishô 〈おやまのたいしょう：お山の大将〉 (the) cock of the walk.

Oya-shio〈おやしお：親潮〉the Kurile current.

oya-shirazu〈おやしらず：親知らず〉a wisdom tooth.
　oya-shirazu ga haeru（親知らずが生える）cut one's wisdom tooth

O-yasumi.〈おやすみ。〉Good night!

o-yatsu〈おやつ：お八つ〉afternoon tea, refreshments.

oya-yubi〈おやゆび：親指〉the thumb, the big toe.

ôyô〈おうよう：応用〉application.
　ôyô-kagaku（応用化学）applied chemistry
　ôyô-mondai（応用問題）an applied question, exercises
　ôyô-suru〈応用する〉apply, put into practice.
　ôyô-dekiru〈応用できる〉applicable.

oyobazu-nagara〈およばずながら：及ばずながら〉
　Oyobazu-nagara o-chikara-ni-nari-mashô.（及ばずながらお力になりましょう。）I will do what I can to help you.

oyobosu〈およぼす：及ぼす〉
　eikyô-o-oyobosu（影響を及ぼす）affect, have an effect ((on))
　gai-o-oyobosu（害を及ぼす）do harm ((to))

oyobu〈およぶ：及ぶ〉reach, come (up) ((to)), extend; match, equal.
　chikara-no-oyobu-kagiri（力の及ぶ限り）to the best of one's ability
　oyoba-nai〈及ばない〉do not reach, be beyond; be inferior ((to)), be no equal ((for)); need not, do not have ((to do)).
　　sôzô-mo-oyoba-nai（想像も及ばない）be beyond imagination
　　chikara-ni-oyoba-nai（力に及ばない）be beyond one's power
　　Kimi-wa iku-ni-wa-oyoba-nai.（君は行くには及ばない。）You do not have to go.
　oyobu-mono-ga-nai〈及ぶ者がない〉have no equal ((in)).

oyogi〈およぎ：泳ぎ〉swimming, a swim.
　oyogi-ni-iku（泳ぎに行く）go swimming
　oyogi-ga-umai（泳ぎがうまい）be a good swimmer
　oyogi-ga-heta-da（泳ぎが下手だ）be a poor swimmer
　oyogu〈泳ぐ〉swim.

oyoso〈およそ〉*see.* yaku-（約-）.
　oyoso-no kentô（およその見当）a rough guess

ôza〈おうざ：王座〉the throne.
　ôza-o-arasou（王座を争う）contend with ((another)) for the premier position

o-zendate〈おぜんだて：おぜん立て〉
　o-zendate-o-suru〈おぜん立てをする〉make arrangements ((for)).

ozon 〈オゾン〉 ozone.
ozuozu(-to) 〈おずおず(と)〉 timidly, hesitatingly.

P

pachapacha 〈ぱちゃぱちゃ〉
  pachapacha-suru or *pachapacha-saseru* 〈ぱちゃぱちゃする，ぱちゃぱちゃ させる〉 splash.
pachin 〈ぱちん〉
  pachin-to 〈ぱちんと〉 with a snap.
    pachin-to-shimeru 〈ぱちんと閉める〉 snap
pachinko 〈パチンコ〉 a pinball game.
    pachinko o suru 〈パチンコをする〉 play a pinball machine
    pachinko-ya 〈パチンコ屋〉 a pinball house
pachipachi 〈ぱちぱち〉
    pachipachi-moeru 〈ぱちぱち燃える〉 crackle
    pachipachi-shashin-o-toru 〈ぱちぱち写真を撮る〉 snap off pictures
      one after another
    pachipachi-te-o-tataku 〈ぱちぱち手をたたく〉 clap one's hands
pai 〈ぱい〉 a tile.
paipu 〈パイプ〉 a pipe, a tube; a pipe, a cigarette holder.
Pakisutan 〈パキスタン〉 Pakistan.
    Pakisutan-jin 〈パキスタン人〉 a Pakistani
    Pakisutan(-jin)-no 〈パキスタン(人)の〉 Pakistani
pakupaku 〈ぱくぱく〉
  pakupaku-taberu 〈ぱくぱく食べる〉 munch, devour, eat with relish.
paku-tsuku 〈ぱくつく〉 bite ((at)), munch.
pâma(nento) 〈パーマ(ネント)〉 a permanent (wave), a perm.
  pâma-o-kakeru 〈パーマをかける〉 have one's hair permed, have a perm.
pan 〈パン〉 bread.

pan o yaku（パンを焼く） bake bread, toast bread

pan-hito-kire（パン一切れ） a slice of bread

pan-ya（パン屋） a baker; a bakery

panchi〈パンチ〉a punch.

ago-ni panchi-o-mimau（あごにパンチを見舞う） punch ((a person)) on the jaw

kippu ni panchi-o-ireru（切符にパンチを入れる） punch a ticket

panfuretto〈パンフレット〉a pamphlet, a leaflet, a brochure.

pan-ko〈パンこ：パン粉〉bread crumb.

panku〈パンク〉a puncture, a blowout.

panku o naosu（パンクを直す） mend a puncture, fix a flat tire

panku-suru〈パンクする〉be punctured, go flat.

panorama〈パノラマ〉a panorama.

panorama-no-yô-na〈パノラマのような〉panoramic.

pantsu〈パンツ〉briefs, shorts, panties, pants.

pan・ya〈パンヤ〉kapok.

parapara〈ぱらぱら〉

Ame-ga-parapara-futte-kita.（雨がぱらぱら降って来た.） The rain has begun to patter.

hon o parapara-mekuru（本をぱらぱらめくる） riffle through a book

parashûto〈パラシュート〉a parachute.

parashûto-de-oriru（パラシュートで降りる） make a parachute descent

paripari〈ぱりぱり〉

paripari-no〈ぱりぱりの〉trueborn, to the backbone, genuine, leading.

paripari-no Edokko（ぱりぱりの江戸っ子） an *Edokko* to the backbone

parupu〈パルプ〉pulp.

parupu-zai（パルプ材） pulpwood

pâsento〈パーセント〉per cent, percent.

go-pâsento（五パーセント） five percent

paseri〈パセリ〉parsley.

pasu〈パス〉a pass, a free ticket.

pasu-suru〈パスする〉pass.

bôru o pasu-suru（ボールをパスする） pass a ball〔to another〕

shiken ni pasu-suru（試験にパスする） pass an examination

patchiri〈ぱっちり〉

me-no-patchiri-shita〈目のぱっちりした〉bright-eyed.

pâtî 〈パーティー〉 a party.
　　pâtî o hiraku 〈パーティーを開く〉 hold a party
patokâ 〈パトカー〉 a patrol car.
patoron 〈パトロン〉 a patron.
patorôru 〈パトロール〉 a patrol.
　patorôru-suru 〈パトロールする〉 go on patrol.
pâto-taimu 〈パートタイム〉
　pâto-taimu-no 〈パートタイムの〉 part-time.
　pâto-taimu-de 〈パートタイムで〉 on a part-time basis.
pattari 〈ぱったり〉
　　pattari-de-au 〈ぱったり出会う〉 come across
　　pattari-onshin-ga-to-daeru 〈ぱったり音信が途絶える〉 hear no more ((from))
patto 〈ぱっと〉
　　patto akaruku-naru 〈ぱっと明るくなる〉 become bright suddenly
　　patto-moe-agaru 〈ぱっと燃え上がる〉 burst into flame(s)
　　Uwasa ga patto hirogaru. 〈うわさがぱっと広がる.〉 A rumor spreads in a flash.
patto-shi-nai 〈ぱっとしない〉 unattractive, dull, unsatisfactory.
pechakucha 〈ぺちゃくちゃ〉
　pechakucha-shaberu 〈ぺちゃくちゃしゃべる〉 chatter, prate, prattle, babble.
pechanko 〈ぺちゃんこ〉
　　Kuruma ga pechanko-ni-natta. 〈車がぺちゃんこになった.〉 My car was badly crushed.
pedaru 〈ペダル〉 a pedal.
　pedaru-o-fumu 〈ペダルを踏む〉 pedal.
pêji 〈ページ〉 a page.
　　pêji o mekuru 〈ページをめくる〉 turn over the pages.
　　go-pêji-ni 〈五ページに〉 on page 5
　　juppêji o akeru 〈十ページを開ける〉 open at page 10
pekopeko 〈ぺこぺこ〉
　　O-naka ga pekopeko-da. 〈おなかがぺこぺこだ.〉 I am very hungry.
　　pekopeko-suru 〈ぺこぺこする〉 bow and scrape, be obsequious ((to))
pen 〈ペン〉 a pen
　　pen-de kaku 〈ペンで書く〉 write with a pen, write with pen and ink
　　pen-jiku 〈ペン軸〉 a penholder
　　pen-saki 〈ペン先〉 a pen point, a nib

　　　pen-shûji〈ペン習字〉 penmanship
penanto〈ペナント〉 a pennant.
　　　penanto-o-arasou〈ペナントを争う〉 compete for the pennant
penchi〈ペンチ〉 cutting pliers, pinchers.
penishirin〈ペニシリン〉 penicillin.
　　　yon-jû-man-tan·i-no　penishirin（四十万単位のペニシリン）　400,000
　　　　units penicillin
penki〈ペンキ〉 paint.
　　　Penki-nuri-tate.（ペンキ塗りたて.）　Wet paint. / Fresh paint.
　　　Penki ga hageta.（ペンキがはげた.）　The paint has come off.
　　　penki-ya（ペンキ屋）　a painter
　　penki-o-nuru〈ペンキを塗る〉 paint.
　　penki-o-nuri-kaeru〈ペンキを塗り替える〉 paint afresh.
pêpâ〈ペーパー〉 sandpaper.
　　　pêpâ-o-kakeru（ペーパーをかける）　polish with sandpaper
perapera〈ぺらぺら〉
　　　Eigo o perapera shaberu（英語をぺらぺらしゃべる）　speak English
　　　　fluently
　　　pêji o perapera-mekuru（ページをぺらぺらめくる）　turn the leaves of
　　　　a book one after another
　　perapera-no〈ぺらぺらの〉 thin.
　　　perapera-no kami（ぺらぺらの紙）　thin paper
perori-to〈ぺろりと〉
　　　perori-to shita-o-dasu（ぺろりと舌を出す）　thrust out one's tongue
　　　　((at))
　　　perori-to tairageru（ぺろりと平らげる）　eat up, put away
Perû〈ペルー〉 Peru.
　　　Perû-jin（ペルー人）　a Peruvian
　　　Perû(-jin)-no（ペルー(人)の）　Peruvian
pêsu〈ペース〉 (a) pace.
　　　jibun-no pêsu-de（自分のペースで）　at one's own pace
pesuto〈ペスト〉 (the) pest, (the) plague.
petan-to〈ぺたんと〉
　　petan-to suwaru〈ぺたんと座る〉 sit down with a flop.
petapeta〈ぺたぺた〉
　　petapeta-haru〈ぺたぺたはる〉 plaster.
peten〈ぺてん〉 trickery, swindle, imposture.
　　　peten-shi（ぺてん師）　a swindler, an impostor

peten-ni-kakeru〈ぺてんに掛ける〉swindle, play a trick ((upon)).

pettari〈ぺったり〉

pettari-kuttsuku〈ぺったりくっ付く〉stick fast ((to)).

piano〈ピアノ〉a piano.

　　piano o hiku（ピアノを弾く）play the piano

pîaru〈ピーアール〉public relations.

　　pîaru-katsudô（ピーアール活動）public relations activities

pîaru-suru〈ピーアールする〉publicize.

pichapicha〈ぴちゃぴちゃ〉

　　doro-mizu-no-naka-o　pichapicha-aruku（泥水の中をぴちゃぴちゃ歩く）
　　　　go splashing in the mud

　　pichapicha-oto-o-tate-nagara-sûpu-o-susuru（ぴちゃぴちゃ音を立てなが
　　　　らスープをすする）slurp soup

pichipichi〈ぴちぴち〉

pichipichi-shita〈ぴちぴちした〉young and lively.

piipii〈ぴいぴい〉

　　piipii-naku（ぴいぴい鳴く）peep, cheep

　　itsu-mo　piipii-shite-iru（いつもぴいぴいしている）be always hard up
　　　　for money

pika-ichi〈ぴかいち：ぴか一〉a No. 1, an A 1, a star, an ace.

pikapika〈ぴかぴか〉

　　pikapika-suru（ぴかぴかする）glitter, sparkle

　　pikapika-hikaru（ぴかぴか光る）twinkle

　　kutsu-o-pikapika-ni-migaku（靴をぴかぴかに磨く）put a good shine
　　　　on one's shoes

pikari-to〈ぴかりと〉

pikari-to-hikaru〈ぴかりと光る〉flash.

pike〈ピケ〉a picket.

pike-o-haru〈ピケを張る〉picket.

pikkeru〈ピッケル〉a pickel, an ice ax(e).

pîku〈ピーク〉a peak.

pîku-ji-ni〈ピーク時に〉at peak hours.

pikunikku〈ピクニック〉a picnic.

　　pikunikku-ni-iku（ピクニックに行く）go on a picnic

pikupiku〈ぴくぴく〉

mimi o pikupiku-ugokasu〈耳をピクピク動かす〉twitch one's ears.

pîman〈ピーマン〉a green pepper, a pim(i)ento.

pimpin〈ぴんぴん〉

pimpin-shite-iru 〈ぴんぴんしている〉be very much alive, be hale and hearty, be fresh.

pimpon 〈ピンポン〉ping-pong, table tennis.

    pimpon o suru (ピンポンをする) play ping-pong

pin 〈ピン〉a pin, a hairpin.

    nekutai-pin (ネクタイピン) a tiepin

    pin-de-tomeru 〈ピンで留める〉pin (up), fasten with a pin.

pin 〈ピン〉

    Pin-kara-kiri-made-aru. 〈ピンからキリまである。〉There are all sorts of ... . / There are various classes of... .

pīnatsu 〈ピーナツ〉a peanut.

pin-boke 〈ピンぼけ〉

    pin-boke-de-aru 〈ピンぼけである〉see. pinto-ga-hazurete-iru.

pinchi 〈ピンチ〉a pinch.

    pinchi-o-maneku (ピンチを招く) find oneself in a pinch

    pinchi o kiri-nukeru (ピンチを切り抜ける) tide over a crisis

pin-hane 〈ピンはね〉a kickback.

    pin-hane-o-suru (ピンはねをする) pocket a kickback ((from))

pinsetto 〈ピンセット〉a pair of tweezers.

pin-to 〈ぴんと〉

    pin-to-tsuna-o-haru (ぴんと綱を張る) stretch a rope tight

    pin-to-kuru (ぴんと来る) come home to one, appeal to one, impress one

pinto 〈ピント〉a focus, the point.

    pinto-ga-atte-iru (ピントが合っている) be in focus, be to the point

    pinto-ga-hazurete-iru (ピントが外れている) be out of focus, be off the point

    pinto-o-awaseru 〈ピントを合わせる〉focus, bring ((an object)) into focus.

piramiddo 〈ピラミッド〉a pyramid.

    piramiddo-gata-no 〈ピラミッド形の〉pyramidal.

piripiri 〈ぴりぴり〉

    piripiri-suru 〈ぴりぴりする〉smart, prick, bite, burn.

piritto 〈ぴりっと〉prickingly, spicily.

pishari-to 〈ぴしゃりと〉

    pishari-to-to-o-shimeru (ぴしゃりと戸を閉める) slam the door

    pishari-to hon o tojiru (ぴしゃりと本を閉じる) shut a book with a snap

    pishari-to-shiri-o-utsu (ぴしゃりとしりを打つ) slap ((a person)) on

the back

pisutoru 〈ピストル〉 a pistol, a revolver, a gun.

    pisutoru-o-tsuki-tsukete *or* pisutoru-o-tsuki-tsukerarete（ピストルを突き付けて，ピストルを突き付けられて）at the point of a pistol

    pisutoru-gôtô（ピストル強盗）an armed burglar

pitari-to 〈ぴたりと〉

    pitari-to ateru（ぴたりと当てる）guess right

    pitari-to tomaru（ぴたりと止まる）stop short

    karada o pitari-to kabe-ni-tsukeru（体をぴたりと壁に付ける）hold one's body close to the wall

pitchâ 〈ピッチャー〉 a pitcher.

    hidari-pitchâ（左ピッチャー）a left-handed pitcher, a southpaw

pitchâ-o-yaru 〈ピッチャーをやる〉 pitch.

pitchi 〈ピッチ〉

    pitchi-o-ageru（ピッチを上げる）quicken one's pace, accelerate

    kyû-pitchi-de（急ピッチで）at high speed

pî-tî-ê 〈ピーティーエー〉 a PTA, a Parent-Teacher Association.

pittari 〈ぴったり〉

pittari-au（ぴったり合う）fit ((a person)) to a T; be perfectly correct.

piyopiyo 〈ぴよぴよ〉

piyopiyo-naku（ぴよぴよ鳴く）peep.

pochapochatto-shita 〈ぽちゃぽちゃっとした〉 *see.* fukkura-shita.

pointo 〈ポイント〉 the point; a point; a switch, points.

    hanashi no pointo（話のポイント）the point of a story

pokan-to 〈ぽかんと〉 vacantly, absentmindedly, stupidly; with a bump.

    pokan-to mi-tsumeru（ぽかんと見詰める）stare at ((a person *or* something)) stupidly

    bô-de inu o pokan-to naguru（棒で犬をぽかんと殴る）whack a dog with a club

pokapoka 〈ぽかぽか〉

    pokapoka-atatakai（ぽかぽか暖かい）feel comfortably warm

    pokapoka-shite-kuru（ぽかぽかしてくる）grow warm

    pokapoka-naguru（ぽかぽか殴る）rain several hard blows ((on))

poketto 〈ポケット〉 a pocket.

    poketto-ni-te-o-irete aruku（ポケットに手を入れて歩く）walk with one's hands in one's pockets

poketto-gata-no 〈ポケット型の〉 pocket-size(d), pocketable.

pokin-to 〈ぽきんと〉 with a snap.

　　　pokin-to oreru（ぽきんと折れる）　break ((a branch)) with a snap
pokkuri〈ぽっくり〉suddenly.
　　　pokkuri shinu（ぽっくり死ぬ）　die suddenly
pompon〈ぽんぽん〉
　　　pompon-te-o-narasu（ぽんぽん手を鳴らす）　clap one's hands
　　　Hana-bi ga pompon-agatta.（花火がぽんぽん揚がった.）　Bang! bang!
　　　　went off the fireworks.
　　　nan-demo pompon-iu（何でもぽんぽん言う）　say anything without
　　　　reserve
pompu〈ポンプ〉a pump.
　　pompu-de-mizu-o-kumi-ageru〈ポンプで水をくみ上げる〉pump up water.
pon〈ぽん〉pop, plop.
　　pon-to〈ぽんと〉
　　　pon-to hyaku-man-en dasu（ぽんと百万円出す）　give one million yen
　　　　on the spot for the asking
　　　pon-to-kata-o-tataku（ぽんと肩をたたく）　tap ((a person)) on the
　　　　shoulder
　　　pon-to nukeru（ぽんと抜ける）　come out (with a) pop
pondo〈ポンド〉a pound.
ponkotsu〈ぽんこつ〉
　　　ponkotsu-guruma（ぽんこつ車）　a jalopy, a junker
Pôrando〈ポーランド〉Poland.
　　　Pôrando-jin（ポーランド人）　a Pole
　　　Pôrando-go（ポーランド語）　Polish
　　　Pôrando(-jin)-no（ポーランド(人)の）　Polish
poriechiren〈ポリエチレン〉polyethylene.
poriesuteru〈ポリエステル〉polyester.
poroporo〈ぽろぽろ〉
　　namida o poroporo kobosu〈涙をぽろぽろこぼす〉shed tears copiously.
poruno〈ポルノ〉pornography.
　　　poruno-eiga（ポルノ映画）　a pornographic movie
Porutogaru〈ポルトガル〉Portugal.
　　　Porutogaru-jin（ポルトガル人）　a Portuguese
　　　Porutogaru-go（ポルトガル語）　Portuguese
　　　Porutogaru(-jin)-no（ポルトガル(人)の）　Portuguese
posutâ〈ポスター〉a poster.
　　　posutâ o haru（ポスターをはる）　put up a poster
posuto〈ポスト〉a mailbox, a pillar-box; a post.

gaikô-kan-no posuto〈外交官のポスト〉a post as diplomat

tegami o posuto-ni-ireru〈手紙をポストに入れる〉mail a letter, post a letter.

potapota〈ぽたぽた〉
potapota-tareru〈ぽたぽた垂れる〉drip, dribble, trickle.

potsupotsu〈ぽつぽつ〉
Potsupotsu ame-ga-furi-dashita.（ぽつぽつ雨が降り出した.）It began to rain in drops.

potsuripotsuri(-to)〈ぽつりぽつり(と)〉
potsuripotsuri-hanasu〈ぽつりぽつり話す〉talk bit by bit, talk with frequent pauses.

potto〈ぽっと〉
potto-kao-o-akarameru〈ぽっと顔を赤らめる〉blush.

pôtto〈ぼうっと〉
pôtto-naru〈ぼうっとなる〉be fascinated, be charmed; swoon, faint.

pôzu〈ポーズ〉a pose.
pôzu-o-toru〈ポーズを取る〉pose, strike a pose.

pui-to〈ぷいと〉
pui-to yoko-o-muku〈ぷいと横を向く〉look away with a sullen look.

pukapuka〈ぷかぷか〉
tabako o pukapuka-fukasu〈たばこをぷかぷか吹かす〉puff a cigarette.

pumpun〈ぷんぷん〉
pumpun-niou（ぷんぷんにおう）smell strongly
pumpun-okoru（ぷんぷん怒る）fume
pumpun-okotte（ぷんぷん怒って）in a fume

pun-to〈ぷんと〉
pun-to-niou〈ぷんとにおう〉smell ((of)), be fragrant, stink ((of)).

purachina(-no)〈プラチナ(の)〉platinum.

puraibashî〈プライバシー〉privacy.
puraibashî no shingai（プライバシーの侵害）an invasion of privacy

purakâdo〈プラカード〉a sign, a placard.
purakâdo o kakageru（プラカードを掲げる）put up a placard

puran〈プラン〉a plan.
puran o tateru（プランを立てる）make a plan

puranetariumu〈プラネタリウム〉a planetarium.

purasu〈プラス〉plus.
Hachi-purasu-ichi wa kyû.（八プラス一は九.）Eight plus one is nine.
Ochitsuku-tokoro purasu-mainasu-zero-da.（落ち着くところプラスマイ

ナスゼロだ。） It would mean no gain for you after all.

purasu-arufa〈プラスアルファ〉 plus something

purasuchikku〈プラスチック〉(a) plastic.

purasuchikku-seihin〈プラスチック製品〉 a plastic

purattohômu〈プラットホーム〉a platform.

nobori purattohômu（上りプラットホーム） an up platform

purê-gaido〈プレーガイド〉a theater ticket agency.

purehabu〈プレハブ〉prefabrication.

purehabu-jûtaku（プレハブ住宅） a prefabricated house, a prefab

puremiamu〈プレミアム〉a premium.

puremiamu-tsuki-de〈プレミアム付きで〉at a premium.

purêyâ〈プレーヤー〉a player; a record player.

purin〈プリン〉pudding.

purinto〈プリント〉a print, a mimeographed copy; print, calico.

puripuri〈ぷりぷり〉

puripuri-okoru〈ぷりぷり怒る〉 see. pumpun-okoru.

purîtsu〈プリーツ〉a pleat.

purîtsu-no(-aru)〈プリーツの（ある）〉 pleated.

puro〈プロ〉a professional, a production.

puro-iri-suru（プロ入りする） turn professional

puro-yakyû（プロ野球） a professional; baseball

purodakushon〈プロダクション〉a production, a movie studio.

purofiru〈プロフィール〉a profile.

puroguramu〈プログラム〉a program.

puroguramu-ni-noseru（プログラムに載せる） put on the program

puropan-gasu〈プロパンガス〉propane gas.

puropera〈プロペラ〉a propeller.

puropera-ki（プロペラ機） a prop(-driven) plane

puropôzu〈プロポーズ〉proposal.

puropôzu-suru〈プロポーズする〉propose ((to)).

puroresu〈プロレス〉professional wrestling.

puroretaria〈プロレタリア〉a proletarian.

puroretaria-kaikyû（プロレタリア階級） the proletariat

pûru〈プール〉a swimming pool; a pool.

pûru-suru〈プールする〉pool (a fund).

purutoniumu〈プルトニウム〉plutonium.

puttsuri〈ぷっつり〉

ito-ga-puttsuri-kireru（糸がぷっつり切れる） snap (off)

Sake-to-wa-puttsuri-en-ga-kireta.（酒とはぷっつり縁が切れた.）I gave up drinking once for all.

pyokon-to 〈ぴょこんと〉
pyokon-to-o-jigi-suru〈ぴょこんとお辞儀する〉bob one's head (in a bow).

pyompyon 〈ぴょんぴょん〉
pyompyon-tobu〈ぴょんぴょん跳ぶ〉hop, skip.
　　pyompyon-tobi-mawaru（ぴょんぴょん跳び回る）hop about, romp about

pyûpyû 〈ぴゅうぴゅう〉
　　Pyûpyû-kaze-ga-fuku.（ぴゅうぴゅう風が吹く.）The wind whistles.

pyutto 〈ぴゅっと〉
pyutto-mizu-o-dasu〈ぴゅっと水を出す〉squirt water.

R

raba 〈らば：ら馬〉a mule.

raberu 〈ラベル〉a labal.
raberu-o-haru〈ラベルをはる〉label.

rachi 〈らち〉
rachi-ga-aka-nai〈らちが明かない〉remain unsettled.

rafu 〈らふ：裸婦〉a woman in the nude.

ragubî 〈ラグビー〉Rugby, rugger.

-rai 〈-らい：-来〉
　　sakunen-rai（昨年来）since last year
　　ni-jû-nen-rai-no oo-yuki（二十年来の大雪）the heaviest snowfall in twenty years

raichô 〈らいちょう：来聴〉

Minasan-no-go-raichô-o-o-machi-shimasu.（皆さんの御来聴をお待ちします。）We are cordially waiting for your attending the lecture.

raigetsu〈らいげつ：来月〉next month.

    raigetsu no kyô（来月の今日）this day next month

raihin〈らいひん：来賓〉a guest, a visitor.

    raihin-seki（来賓席）the seats for invited guests

raihô〈らいほう：来訪〉a visit, a call.

    raihô-sha（来訪者）a visitor, a caller

  raihô-suru〈来訪する〉pay ((a person)) a visit, visit.

raikyaku〈らいきゃく：来客〉a caller, a visitor, company.

    raikyaku-ga-aru（来客がある）have company

raimei〈らいめい：雷鳴〉thunder, the rumbling of thunder.

rain〈ライン〉a line.

    rain o hiku（ラインを引く）draw a line

    rain-dansu（ラインダンス）precision dance

rainâ〈ライナー〉a liner, a line drive.

rainen〈らいねん：来年〉next year.

    rainen no ima-goro（来年の今ごろ）about this time next year

rai-Nichi〈らいにち：来日〉a visit to Japan.

    rai-Nichi-chû-no Y-fusai（来日中のY夫妻）Mr. and Mrs. Y, now on a visit to Japan

  rai-Nichi-suru〈来日する〉visit Japan.

raion〈ライオン〉a lion, a lioness.

raireki〈らいれき：来歴〉a career, one's personal history.

raisan〈らいさん：礼賛〉

  raisan-suru〈礼賛する〉adore, praise, glorify.

raise〈らいせ：来世〉the life after death, the world to come, the hereafter.

raishin-shi〈らいしんし：頼信紙〉a telegram form, a telegram blank.

raishû〈らいしゅう：来週〉next week.

    raishû-no-getsuyô-bi-ni（来週の月曜日に）next Monday, on Monday next

raishun〈らいしゅん：来春〉next spring, the coming spring.

raito〈ライト〉a light; the right field, a right fielder; a right.

    raito-o-tsukezu-ni kuruma o hashirasu（ライトを付けずに車を走らす）drive a car without a light

raito-hebî-kyû〈ライトヘビーきゅう：ライトヘビー級〉a light heavy-weight class.

raito-hebî-kyû-senshu〈ライトヘビー級選手〉a light heavyweight

raito-kyû〈ライトきゅう：ライト級〉the lightweight class.

raito-kyû-no〈ライト級の〉lightweight.

raito-midoru-kyû〈ライトミドルきゅう：ライトミドル級〉a light middleweight class.

raito-midoru-kyû-senshu（ライトミドル級選手）a light middleweight

raito-werutâ-kyû〈ライトウェルターきゅう：ライトウェルター級〉a light welterweight class.

raito-werutâ-kyû-senshu（ライトウェルター級選手）a light welterweight

raiu〈らいう：雷雨〉a thunderstorm, a thundershower.

rajio〈ラジオ〉a radio (set).

rajio o kakeru（ラジオをかける）turn on the radio

rajio o kesu（ラジオを消す）switch off the radio

rajio-o-kiku（ラジオを聴く）listen to the radio

rajio-de ongaku-o-kiku（ラジオで音楽を聴く）listen to the music on the radio

Kono rajio-de gaikoku-hôsô-ga-kikeru.（このラジオで外国放送が聴ける。）We can get the foreign stations on this set.

rajio-taisô（ラジオ体操）radio gymnastics

rajiumu〈ラジウム〉radium.

rajiumu-kôsen（ラジウム鉱泉）a radium spring

raketto〈ラケット〉a racket, a bat.

rakka〈らっか：落下〉

rakka-suru〈落下する〉fall, come down, drop.

rakkan〈らっかん：楽観〉optimism.

rakkan-o-yurusa-nai（楽観を許さない）do not warrant any optimism

rakkan-ron（楽観論）an optimistic view

rakkan-ron-sha（楽観論者）an optimist

rakkan-suru〈楽観する〉be optimistic ((about)).

rakkan-teki(-na)〈楽観的(な)〉optimistic.

rakkasei〈らっかせい：落下生〉a peanut.

rakko〈らっこ〉a sea otter.

rakkyô〈らっきょう〉a shallot.

raku〈らく：楽〉

raku-na〈楽な〉easy, comfortable.

raku-na shigoto（楽な仕事）an easy task

raku-ni〈楽に〉comfortably, in comfort, easily, without difficulty.

　　raku-ni kurasu〈楽に暮らす〉 live in comfort
　　Dôzo o-raku-ni.〈どうぞお楽に.〉 Make yourself at home.
　　raku-ni katsu〈楽に勝つ〉 win easily
raku-ni-naru〈楽になる〉 be mitigated, feel relief.
　　Kono　kusuri-o-nomu-to　raku-ni-naru.（この薬を飲むと楽になる.）
　　　This medicine will bring you relief.

rakuban〈らくばん：落盤〉a cave-in.

rakuchaku〈らくちゃく：落着〉settlement.

rakuchaku-suru〈落着する〉 be settled, come to a settlement.
　　Honken　mo　yatto　rakuchaku-shita.（本件もやっと落着した.）　This
　　matter has been finally settled.

rakuchô〈らくちょう：落丁〉a missing page.
　　rakuchô-bon（落丁本） a book with missing pages

rakuda〈らくだ〉a camel.

rakudai〈らくだい：落第〉failure.
　　Kare-wa　teishu-to-shite　rakudai-da.（彼は亭主として落第だ.）He is a
　　failure as (a) husband.
　　Kono sakuhin wa rakudai-darô.（この作品は落第だろう.）This work
　　will be rejected, I'm afraid.
rakudai-suru〈落第する〉fail an examination, flunk, get ploughed; be
　rejected.

rakuen〈らくえん：楽園〉a paradise.

rakugaki〈らくがき：落書き〉scribbling, scrawling.
rakugaki-suru〈落書きする〉scribble, scrawl.

rakugo〈らくご：落ご〉
　　rakugo-sha（落ご者） a straggler, a failure
rakugo-suru〈落ごする〉drop behind, fall to the rear.

rakugo〈らくご：落語〉a comic story.
　　rakugo-ka（落語家） a person who tells a comic story as a
　　professional

rakuin〈らくいん：らく印〉a brand mark.
rakuin-o-osareru〈らく印を押される〉be branded, be stigmatized.

rakunô〈らくのう：酪農〉dairy farming.
　　rakunô-jô（酪農場） a dairy
　　rakunô-seihin（酪農製品） dairy products

rakurai〈らくらい：落雷〉
rakurai-suru〈落雷する〉be struck by lightning.

rakuraku-to〈らくらくと：楽々と〉with great ease, very easily.

rakusa 〈らくさ：落差〉a head.

rakusatsu 〈らくさつ：落札〉a successful bid.
    rakusatsu-nin（落札人）a successful bidder
    rakusatsu-ne（落札値）the highest bid price
  rakusatsu-suru〈落札する〉make a successful bid, be knocked down ((to)).

rakusei 〈らくせい：落成〉completion.
    rakusei-shiki（落成式）an inauguration ceremony
  rakusei-suru〈落成する〉be completed, be finished.

rakuseki 〈らくせき：落石〉a falling rock.

rakusen 〈らくせん：落選〉defeat; rejection.
  rakusen-suru〈落選する〉be defeated in an election; be rejected, be not accepted.

rakushô 〈らくしょう：楽勝〉an easy victory, a walkover.
  rakushô-suru〈楽勝する〉win an easy victory ((over)), win ((a game)) hands down, walk over.

rakutan 〈らくたん：落胆〉discouragement.
  rakutan-suru〈落胆する〉be discouraged, lose courage.
  rakutan-saseru〈落胆させる〉discourage.

rakuten 〈らくてん：楽天〉optimism.
    rakuten-ka（楽天家）an optimist
    rakuten-shugi（楽天主義）optimism
  rakuten-teki(-na)〈楽天的(な)〉optimistic.

raku-yaki 〈らくやき：楽焼き〉hand-molded earthenware.

rakuyô 〈らくよう：落葉〉fall of leaves; fallen leaves.
    rakuyô-ju（落葉樹）a deciduous tree
  rakuyô-suru〈落葉する〉shed ((its)) leaves, fall.

Rama 〈ラマ〉
    Rama-kyô（ラマ教）Lamaism

rambai 〈らんばい：乱売〉underselling.

rambatsu 〈らんばつ：濫伐〉reckless deforestation.
  rambatsu-suru〈濫伐する〉fell trees indiscriminately.

rambô 〈らんぼう：乱暴〉violence, rudeness, roughness.
    rambô-rôzeki（乱暴ろうぜき）violence and lawlessness
  rambô-suru〈乱暴する〉use violence, be rough, behave rudely.
    Kare-ra-wa watashi-ni rambô-suru.（彼らは私に乱暴する。）They are rude to me.
  rambô-na〈乱暴な〉violent, rude, rough, disorderly.

rambō-na kotoba〈乱暴な言葉〉 violent language

rambō-ni〈乱暴に〉 roughly, carelessly.

rambō-ni atsukau〈乱暴に扱う〉 handle roughly

ramma〈らんま：欄間〉a transom.

rammyaku〈らんみゃく：乱脈〉disorder, confusion.

rammyaku-o-kiwameru〈乱脈を極める〉be in a chaotic state, be in utter disorder.

rammyaku-na〈乱脈な〉disordered, disorderly, confused, chaotic.

rammyaku-na keiri〈乱脈な経理〉disorderly accounting

rampatsu〈らんぱつ：濫(乱)発〉an excessive issue.

rampatsu-suru〈濫(乱)発する〉overissue.

rampi〈らんぴ：濫(乱)費〉waste, extravagance.

rampi-suru〈濫(乱)費する〉waste, be extravagant.

kōkin o rampi-suru〈公金を濫(乱)費する〉 spend public money wastefully

rampitsu〈らんぴつ：乱筆〉scratchy writing.

ran〈らん：欄〉a column, a section.

supōtsu-ran〈スポーツ欄〉 the sports section

ran〈らん〉an orchid.

ranchi〈ランチ〉lunch; a launch.

ranchō〈らんちょう：乱丁〉incorrect pagination.

ranchō-bon〈乱丁本〉 a book with incorrect pagination

randa〈らんだ：乱打〉

randa-suru〈乱打する〉pommel, strike ((a bell)) violently.

randoku〈らんどく：濫(乱)読〉

randoku-suru〈濫(乱)読する〉read at random.

randoseru〈ランドセル〉a satchel, a knapsack.

randoseru o se-ou〈ランドセルを背負う〉 have a satchel on one's back

rangai〈らんがい：欄外〉the margin.

rangai-no chū〈欄外の注〉 marginal notes

ran-hansha〈らんはんしゃ：乱反射〉diffused reflection.

ranjuku〈らんじゅく：乱熟〉overripeness.

ranjuku-ki〈らん熟期〉 the stage of overripeness

ranjuku-shita〈らん熟した〉highly-developed, full-grown.

rankaku〈らんかく：濫(乱)獲〉reckless fishing, indiscriminate hunting.

rankaku-suru〈濫(乱)獲する〉fish recklessly, overhunt.

rankan〈らんかん：欄干〉a rail(ing), a parapet.

ranningu 〈ランニング〉 running.

ranningu-hômâ（ランニングホーマー） an inside-the-park homer

rannyû 〈らんにゅう：乱入〉

runnyû-suru 〈乱入する〉 barge into, force one's way into.

ranritsu 〈らんりつ：乱立〉

Sono senkyo-ku wa kôho-sha-ga-ranritsu-shite-iru.（その選挙区は候補者が乱立している。） Too many candidates are running from the constituency.

ransaku 〈らんさく：濫(乱)作〉 excessive production.

ransaku-suru 〈濫(乱)作する〉 overproduce, overwrite.

ransen 〈らんせん：乱戦〉 a confused fight, a dogfight, a melee.

ransha 〈らんしゃ：乱射〉 random firing.

ransha-suru 〈乱射する〉 fire at random.

ranshi 〈らんし：卵子〉 an ovum.

ranshi 〈らんし：乱視〉 astigmatism.

ranshi-no 〈乱視の〉 astigmatic.

ranshin 〈らんしん：乱心〉 insanity, madness.

ranshin-suru 〈乱心する〉 go mad, lose one's mind.

ransô 〈らんそう：卵巣〉 an ovary.

ransô-horumon（卵巣ホルモン） ovarian hormones

rantô 〈らんとう：乱闘〉 a confused fight, a rough-and-tumble.

ran·yô(-suru) 〈らんよう(する)：濫(乱)用(する)〉 abuse, misuse.

shokken o ran·yô-suru（職権を濫(乱)用する） abuse one's official authority

ranzatsu 〈らんざつ：乱雑〉 disorder, confusion, mess.

ranzatsu-na 〈乱雑な〉 disorderly, confused.

ranzatsu-ni 〈乱雑に〉 in disorder, confusedly, in a disorderly manner.

hon o ranzatsu-ni tsumi-ageru（本を乱雑に積み上げる） pile books up in a disorderly manner

ranzatsu-ni-natte-iru 〈乱雑になっている〉 be in disorder, be in a mess.

Raosu 〈ラオス〉 Laos.

Raosu-jin（ラオス人） a Laotian

Raosu(-jin)-no（ラオス(人)の） Laotian

rappa 〈らっぱ〉 a trumpet, a bugle.

rappa o fuku（らっぱを吹く） blow a bugle

rappa-nomi-suru（らっぱ飲みする） drink from a bottle

rappa-zubon（らっぱズボン） bell-bottom(ed) pants

raretsu 〈られつ：羅列〉

raretsu-suru 〈羅列する〉 enumerate, cite.

rasen 〈らせん：ら旋〉 a spiral, a screw.

rasen-kaidan (ら旋階段) a spiral staircase

rasen-jô(-no) or *rasen-kei(-no)* 〈ら旋状(の)，ら旋形(の)〉 spiral.

-rashii 〈-らしい〉 seem, look, be likely, be worthy ((of)).

Sore-wa hontô-rashii. (それは本当らしい。) It seems to be true.

Kare-wa shôjiki-mono-rashii. (彼は正直者らしい。) He looks honest.

Ame-ni-naru-rashii. (雨になるらしい。) It is likely to rain.

Kare-no kôi wa shinshi-rashii. (彼の行為は紳士らしい。) His conduct is worthy of a gentleman.

Kono-atari-ni kôen-rashii-kôen-wa-nai. (このあたりに公園らしい公園はない。) There is no park around here to speak of.

rashin-ban 〈らしんばん：羅針盤〉 a compass.

rasseru-sha 〈ラッセルしゃ：ラッセル車〉 a (Russel) snowplow.

ratai 〈らたい：裸体〉 a naked body.

ratai-ga (裸体画) a nude

ratai-ga-o-egaku (裸体画を描く) paint ((a woman)) in the nude

han-ratai (半裸体) seminudity

ratai-no 〈裸体の〉 naked, nude.

Raten-go 〈ラテンご：ラテン語〉 Latin.

ratsuwan 〈らつわん：らつ腕〉 shrewdness, sharpness.

ratsuwan o furuu (らつ腕を振るう) display one's unusual shrewdness

ratsuwan-ka (らつ腕家) a shrewd person, a go-getter

ratsuwan-no 〈らつ腕の〉 shrewd, sharp.

rebâ 〈レバー〉 liver; a lever; a gearshift.

rêdâ 〈レーダー〉 (a) radar.

rêdâ-kichi (レーダー基地) a radar base

rêdâ-mô (レーダー網) a radar fence

refu 〈レフ〉 a reflex camera.

refuto 〈レフト〉 the left field, a left fielder; a left.

regyurâ 〈レギュラー〉 a regular member.

rei 〈れい：例〉 an example, an instance, a case, an illustration; a precedent; a custom, a practice.

rei o ageru (例を挙げる) give an example

ii rei o tsukuru (いい例を作る) establish a good precedent

rei-no 〈例の〉 usual.

rei-no basho-de (例の場所で) at the usual place

rei-no-gotoku〈例のごとく〉as usual.

rei-o-ageru-to〈例を挙げると〉for example.

〜*-no-rei-ni-naratte*〈〜の例に倣って〉following the example of... .

rei-ni-naku〈例になく〉unusually.

rei〈れい：零〉zero, naught.

 107(ichi-rei-nana)〈一零七〉one zero seven

rei〈れい：霊〉the soul, the spirit.

rei〈れい：礼〉a bow, a salutation; etiquette, politeness; thanks, gratitude; a reward.

 rei o suru（礼をする）make a bow ((to))

 rei-o-iu（礼を言う）express one's thanks ((to))

 rei-o-shissuru（礼を失する）be impolite

 rei o morau（礼をもらう）receive a reward

reibô〈れいぼう：冷房〉air conditioning, air cooling.

 Reibô-kambi.（冷房完備.）Air-conditioned.

 reibô-sôchi（冷房装置）an air conditioner

  reibô-sôchi-ga-aru（冷房装置がある）be air-conditioned

reibô-suru〈冷房する〉air-condition, air-cool.

reibô-no-kiite-iru or *reibô-o-shita*〈冷房の効いている，冷房をした〉air-cooled.

reibun〈れいぶん：例文〉an example, an illustrative sentence.

reichô〈れいちょう：霊長〉

 Jinrui wa bambutsu no reichô-de-aru.（人類は万物の霊長である.）Man is the lord of all creation.

reidai〈れいだい：例題〉an example, an exercise.

reido〈れいど：零度〉zero (degrees).

 reido-ika-ni-sagaru（零度以下に下がる）fall below zero

reifuku〈れいふく：礼服〉full dress, formal dress, a dress suit.

reigai〈れいがい：冷害〉damage from cold weather.

reigai〈れいがい：例外〉an exception.

 Reigai-no-nai-kisoku-wa-nai.（例外のない規則はない.）There is no rule without exceptions.

reigai-teki(-na)〈例外的(な)〉exceptional.

reigai-naku〈例外なく〉without exception.

〜*-wa-reigai-to-shite*〈〜は例外として〉with the exception of... .

reigen〈れいげん：霊験〉

reigen-arataka-na〈霊験あらたかな〉wonder-working, miraculous in its effect.

reigi〈れいぎ：礼儀〉courtesy, etiquette, civility, politeness, good manners.

reigi-tadashii〈礼儀正しい〉courteous, polite, civil.

reigi-o-shira-nai〈礼儀を知らない〉ill-mannered.

reigi-tadashiku〈礼儀正しく〉courteously, politely.

reigi-jô〈礼儀上〉out of courtesy.

reigū〈れいぐう：冷遇〉

reigū-suru〈冷遇する〉treat ((a person)) coldly.

reihai〈れいはい：礼拝〉worship, church service.

　　reihai-dô（礼拝堂）a chapel

reihai-suru〈礼拝する〉worship.

reihai〈れいはい：零敗〉

reihai-suru〈零敗する〉be shut out, fail to score.

reihai-saseru〈零敗させる〉shut out.

reihô〈れいほう：礼砲〉a salute gun.

　　reihô o hanatsu（礼砲を放つ）fire a salute

reiji〈れいじ：零時〉twelve o'clock, noon.

　　gozen-reiji（午前零時）twelve o'clock midnight

reiji〈れいじ：例示〉illustration, exemplification.

reiji-suru〈例示する〉illustrate, exemplify.

reijô〈れいじょう：礼状〉a letter of thanks.

reijô〈れいじょう：令状〉a warrant, a writ.

　　reijô o hakkô-suru（令状を発行する）issue a warrant

　　reijô o shikkô-suru（令状を執行する）execute a warrant ((for))

　　sôsa-reijô（捜査令状）a search warrant

reika〈れいか：零下〉below zero.

　　reika-jû-do（零下十度）10 degrees below zero

reikai〈れいかい：例会〉a regular meeting.

　　mai-tsuki-no reikai（毎月の例会）a monthly meeting

reikai〈れいかい：例解〉

reikai-suru〈例解する〉explain by examples.

reikan〈れいかん：霊感〉(an) inspiration.

　　reikan-ni-yotte（霊感によって）by inspiration

reiketsu〈れいけつ：冷血〉

　　reiketsu-dôbutsu（冷血動物）a cold-blooded animal

reiketsu-no〈冷血の〉cold-blooded.

reikin〈れいきん：礼金〉a reward, a remuneration, a fee.

reikô〈れいこう：励行〉strict enforcement, rigorous execution.

reikô-suru〈励行する〉enforce strictly, carry out strictly, observe strictly.

reikoku〈れいこく：冷酷〉

reikoku-na〈冷酷な〉cruel, unfeeling, heartless, coldhearted, hard-hearted.

reikon〈れいこん：霊魂〉the soul, the spirit.

reikon-fumetsu（霊魂不滅）the immortality of the soul

reikyaku〈れいきゃく：冷却〉cooling, refrigeration.

reikyaku-kikan（冷却期間）a cooling-off period

reikyaku-sôchi（冷却装置）a cooling device

reikyaku-sui（冷却水）cooling water

reikyaku-suru〈冷却する〉cool down, cool, refrigerate.

reikyû-sha〈れいきゅうしゃ：霊きゅう車〉a hearse.

reinen〈れいねん：例年〉

reinen-no〈例年の〉normal, usual, annual.

reinen-no-toori〈例年のとおり〉as usual.

reinen-ni-naku〈例年になく〉unusually.

reiraku〈れいらく：零落〉

reiraku-suru〈零落する〉be ruined, be in reduced circumstances, be reduced to poverty.

reisai〈れいさい：零細〉

reisai-kigyô（零細企業）a small-scale business

reisai-na〈零細な〉small, trifling, petty.

reisei〈れいせい：冷静〉calmness, coolness, composure.

reisei-o-tamotsu（冷静を保つ）keep cool

reisei o ushinau（冷静を失う）lose one's presence of mind

reisei-na〈冷静な〉calm, cool, composed.

reisei-na handan（冷静な判断）cool judgment

reisei-ni〈冷静に〉calmly, coolly, composedly.

reisei-ni mono-goto-o-kangaeru（冷静に物事を考える）think things over coolly

reisen〈れいせん：冷戦〉a cold war.

reisen〈れいせん：冷泉〉a cold mineral spring.

reishô〈れいしょう：冷笑〉a cold smile, a sneer.

reishô-suru〈冷笑する〉sneer ((at)).

reishô〈れいしょう：例証〉(an) illustration, an example.

reishô-suru〈例証する〉give an illustration.

reisô〈れいそう：礼装〉full dress.

reisô-de〈礼装で〉in full dress

reisui〈れいすい：冷水〉

reisui-masatsu-o-suru〈冷水摩擦をする〉rub oneself with a cold wet towel.

reitan〈れいたん：冷淡〉

reitan-na〈冷淡な〉cool, indifferent, coldhearted.

reitan-na taido〈冷淡な態度〉an indifferent attitude

reitan-na ningen〈冷淡な人間〉a coldhearted person

reitan-ni〈冷淡に〉coolly, indifferently, coldheartedly.

reitan-ni-naru〈冷淡になる〉grow cold

rei-ten〈れいてん：零点〉(a) zero.

shiken-de rei-ten o toru〈試験で零点を取る〉get zero in an examination

reitô〈れいとう：冷凍〉freezing.

reitô-shokuhin〈冷凍食品〉frozen foods

reitô-suru〈冷凍する〉freeze.

reitô-o-modosu〈冷凍を戻す〉unfreeze.

reizen〈れいぜん：霊前〉

reizen-ni-nukazuku〈霊前にぬかづく〉bow before the altar〔praying for the repose of the spirit of the deceased〕

reizen-ni-sasageru〈霊前にささげる〉offer ((a thing)) on the altar

reizô-ko〈れいぞうこ：冷蔵庫〉a refrigerator.

reizoku〈れいぞく：隷属〉subordination.

reizoku-suru〈隷属する〉be subordinate ((to)).

reji〈レジ〉a (cash) register, a cashier.

rekidai〈れきだい：歴代〉

rekidai-no〈歴代の〉successive.

rekidai-no naikaku〈歴代の内閣〉successive cabinets

rekihô〈れきほう：歴訪〉

rekihô-suru〈歴訪する〉make a tour ((of)), make a round of calls.

Ajia-shokoku-o-rekihô-suru〈アジア諸国を歴訪する〉make a tour of various countries in Asia

rekinin〈れきにん：歴任〉

rekinin-suru〈歴任する〉hold various posts successively.

rekisen〈れきせん：歴戦〉

rekisen-no-yûshi〈歴戦の勇士〉a soldier who has experienced many battles in the front

rekishi〈れきし：歴史〉history.

Rekishi wa kuri-kaesu.（歴史は繰り返す.） History repeats itself.

Nihon no rekishi（日本の歴史）the history of Japan

rekishi-ka（歴史家）a historian

rekishi-shôsetsu（歴史小説）a historical novel

rekishi-jô-no〈歴史上の〉historical, historic.

rekishi-jô-no jimbutsu（歴史上の人物）a historical figure

rekishi-teki(-na)〈歴史的(な)〉historical, historic, traditional.

rekishi-teki jijitsu（歴史的事実）a historical fact

rekishi-teki-na gyôji（歴史的な行事）a traditional function

rekishi-izen-no〈歴史以前の〉prehistoric.

rekishi-jô〈歴史上〉from the historical point of view.

rekishi-jô-yûmei-na-tokoro（歴史上有名な所） a place of historic interest

rekishi〈れきし：れき死〉

rekishi-suru〈れき死する〉be run over and killed.

rekizen〈れきぜん：歴然〉

rekizen-taru〈歴然たる〉clear, obvious, evident, unmistakable.

rekizen-taru jijitsu（歴然たる事実）an obvious fact

rekizen-taru shôko（歴然たる証拠） an unmistakable evidence

rekkâ-sha〈レッカーしゃ：レッカー車〉a wrecking car.

rekki-to-shita〈れっきとした〉clear, obvious; respectable, decent.

rekki-to-shita iegara（れっきとした家柄）a respectable family

rekkoku〈れっこく：列国〉the Powers, the nations of the world.

rekkyo〈れっきょ：列挙〉

rekkyo-suru〈列挙する〉enumerate.

rekkyô〈れっきょう：列強〉the great Powers.

rekôdo〈レコード〉a record, a disk; a record.

rekôdo o kakeru（レコードをかける） play a record

rekôdo-ni-fuki-komu（レコードに吹き込む） record ((a piece of music)) on a disk

eru-pî-rekôdo（ＬＰレコード） an LP record, a long-playing record

rekôdo o tsukuru（レコードを作る） set up a new record

rekôdo o yaburu（レコードを破る） break the record

rekôdo-hoji-sha（レコード保持者）a record holder

rembai〈れんばい：廉売〉

rembai-suru〈廉売する〉sell at low prices, sell at a bargain rate.

remmei〈れんめい：連盟〉a league, a union, a federation.

remmei〈れんめい：連名〉a joint signature.

remmei-de〈連名で〉in ((one's)) joint names.

rempai〈れんぱい：連敗〉successive defeats.

rempai-suru〈連敗する〉suffer straight defeats.

rempatsu〈れんぱつ：連発〉

rempatsu-jû〈連発銃〉a repeater

rempatsu-suru〈連発する〉fire shots at ((a person)) in succession.

shitsumon o rempatsu-suru〈質問を連発する〉fire questions ((at))

rempô〈れんぽう：連邦〉a federation, a union.

rempô-seifu〈連邦政府〉the federal government

rempô〈れんぽう：連峰〉a mountain range, a chain of mountains.

ren·ai〈れんあい：恋愛〉love.

ren·ai-kekkon〈恋愛結婚〉a love marriage

ren·ai-kekkon-o-suru〈恋愛結婚をする〉marry for love

ren·ai-shôsetsu〈恋愛小説〉a love story, a romance

ren·ai-shite-iru〈恋愛している〉be in love ((with)).

renchû〈れんちゅう：連中〉a company, a set, a lot, a crowd.

yukai-na renchû〈愉快な連中〉a jolly crowd

renda〈れんだ：連打〉

renda-suru〈連打する〉deliver a succession of blows ((against *or* at)).

renga〈れんが〉(a) brick.

keshô-renga〈化粧れんが〉(a) dressed brick

taika-renga〈耐火れんが〉(a) fireproof brick

renga-zukuri-no tatemono〈れんが造りの建物〉a brick building

renge-sô〈れんげそう：れんげ草〉a Chinese milk vetch.

rengô〈れんごう：連合〉combination, union, concert, league, confederation, coalition, a combine, an alliance.

rengô-suru〈連合する〉combine ((with)), form a union ((with)), be allied ((with)).

rengô-shite〈連合して〉in concert ((with)), in league ((with)), in alliance ((with)).

Rênin〈レーニン〉Lenin.

Rênin-shugi〈レーニン主義〉Leninism

Rênin-shugi-sha〈レーニン主義者〉a Leninist

renjitsu〈れんじつ：連日〉every day, day after day.

renjitsu-ren·ya〈連日連夜〉day(s) and night(s)

renkei〈れんけい：連携〉cooperation.

～-to-renkei-shite〈～と連携して〉in cooperation with... .

renketsu〈れんけつ：連結〉coupling, connection, joining.

　　jû-ryô-renketsu-no ressha（十両連結の列車）a ten-car train

　　renketsu-ki（連結器）a coupler, a connector

　　renketsu-shu（連結手）a coupler hand

renketsu-suru〈連結する〉couple, connect, join, attach.

　　Kono ressha-niwa shokudô-sha ga renketsu-shite-arimasu-ka?（この列車には食堂車が連結してありますか。）Is there any dining car attached to this train?

renkin-jutsu〈れんきんじゅつ：錬金術〉alchemy.

renko〈れんこ：連呼〉

renko-suru〈連呼する〉call ((one's name)) repeatedly.

renkô〈れんこう：連行〉

yôgi-sha o sho-ni renkô-suru〈容疑者を署に連行する〉take a suspect to a police station.

renkon〈れんこん：連根〉a lotus root.

renkyû〈れんきゅう：連休〉consecutive holidays.

　　yokka-no-renkyû-ga-aru（四日の連休がある）have four consecutive holidays

rennyû〈れんにゅう：練乳〉condensed milk.

renraku〈れんらく：連絡〉(a) connection, (a) contact, touch, communication.

　　renraku-o-toru（連絡を取る）get in touch ((with))

　　renraku-o-tamotsu（連絡を保つ）keep in contact ((with))

　　renraku-ga-umaku-iku（連絡がうまくいく）make good connections

　　renraku o ushinau（連絡を失う）lose contact ((with))

　　renraku o tatsu（連絡を絶つ）cut off communications ((with))

　　renraku-saki（連絡先）where to make contact

　　renraku-sho（連絡所）a liaison office

renraku-suru〈連絡する〉contact, let ((a person)) know, connect ((with)), be connected ((with)).

　　Kono ressha wa Shin-Ôsaka-de San·yô-sen-ni-renraku-shite-iru.（この列車は新大阪で山陽線に連絡している。）This train connects with the San·yo Line at Shin-Osaka Station.

renritsu〈れんりつ：連立〉

　　renritsu-naikaku（連立内閣）a coalition cabinet

　　renritsu-hôtei-shiki（連立方程式）simultaneous equations

rensa-hannô〈れんさはんのう：連鎖反応〉(a) chain reaction.

　　rensa-hannô o okosu（連鎖反応を起こす）trigger a chain reaction

rensai〈れんさい：連載〉serial publication, serialization.

rensai-mono〔連載物〕 a serial

rensai-shôsetsu〔連載小説〕 a serial novel

rensai-suru〈連載する〉 publish serially, serialize.

rensa-jô-kyûkin〈れんさじょうきゅうきん：連鎖状球菌〉a streptococcus.

rensen〈れんせん：連戦〉

rensen-renshô-suru〔連戦連勝する〕 win successive victories

rensen-rempai-suru〔連戦連敗する〕 be defeated in every battle

renshô〈れんしょう：連勝〉

renshô-suru〈連勝する〉 *see.* rensen-renshô-suru.

renshû〈れんしゅう：練習〉 practice, (an) exercise, training, a drill, (a) rehearsal.

renshû-jiai〔練習試合〕 a practice game

renshû-mondai〔練習問題〕 an exercise

yoku-renshû-o-tsunde-iru〔よく練習を積んでいる〕 be well trained

renshû-busoku-de-aru〔練習不足である〕 be not sufficiently trained

renshû-suru〈練習する〉 practice, train, drill, rehearse.

piano o renshû-suru〔ピアノを練習する〕 practice the piano

rensô〈れんそう：連想〉 association (of ideas).

rensô-suru〈連想する〉 associate ((A with B)), be reminded ((of)).

rensô-saseru〈連想させる〉 remind ((a person)) of, suggest.

rentai〈れんたい：連帯〉

rentai-ishiki *or* rentai-kannen〔連帯意識, 連帯観念〕 the feeling of togetherness

rentai-hoshô〔連帯保証〕 joint liability on guarantee

rentai-hoshô-nin〔連帯保証人〕 a joint surety

rentai-saimu〔連帯債務〕 joint obligation

rentai〈れんたい：連隊〉a regiment.

rentai-chô〔連隊長〕 the regimental commander

rentai-ki〔連隊旗〕 the regimental colors

renta-kâ〈レンタカー〉a rental car.

rentan〈れんたん：れん炭〉a briquet(te).

rentô〈れんとう：連投〉

rentô-suru〈連投する〉 take the (pitcher's) mound in ((two)) consecutive games.

rentogen〈レントゲン〉X-rays, Röntgen rays.

rentogen-shashin o toru〔レントゲン写真を撮る〕 take an X-ray photograph ((of))

renzoku〈れんぞく：連続〉 continuation, succession.

renzoku-eiga〈連続映画〉a serial film

renzoku-suru〈連続する〉continue.

renzoku-teki(-na)〈連続的(な)〉continuous, successive, consecutive.

renzoku-teki-ni〈連続的に〉continuously, successively, consecutively, without a break.

renzu〈レンズ〉a lens.

ô-renzu（凹レンズ）a concave lens

totsu-renzu（凸レンズ）a convex lens

repâtorî〈レパートリー〉a repertory, a repertoire.

repâtorî-ga-hiroi（レパートリーが広い）have a large repertoire ((of))

repôto〈レポート〉a report, a term paper.

rêru〈レール〉a rail, a (railway) line, a (railroad) track.

kâten-no rêru（カーテンのレール）a curtain rod

ressei〈れっせい：劣勢〉

ressei-no〈劣勢の〉inferior in numbers(or strength).

ressei-iden〈れっせいいでん：劣性遺伝〉recessive heredity.

resseki〈れっせき：列席〉attendance, presence.

resseki-sha（列席者）attendants, attendance

resseki-suru〈列席する〉attend, be present ((at)).

ressha〈れっしゃ：列車〉a train.

ressha-bôgai（列車妨害）railway obstruction

ressha-jiko（列車事故）a train accident

nobori-ressha（上り列車）an up train

kudari-ressha（下り列車）a down train

gogo-ni-ji-juppun-no-ressha-de（午後二時十分の列車で）by the 2:10 p.m. train

resshô〈れっしょう：裂傷〉a laceration.

kao ni resshô-o-ou（顔に裂傷を負う）have one's face lacerated

rêsu〈レース〉a lace; a race.

rêsu-no-kazari-no-tsuita〈レースの飾りの付いた〉lace-trimmed.

resuringu〈レスリング〉wrestling.

resuringu-no-senshu（レスリングの選手）a wrestler

retsu〈れつ：列〉a row, a line, a file, a column, a rank.

retsu o tsukuru（列を作る）form a line

retsu-o-tsukutte-narabu（列を作って並ぶ）stand in line, queue

retsu o midasu（列を乱す）break a line

retsu-ni narabu（二列に並ぶ）stand in two lines

□-ni-natte（三列になって）in three rows(or columns)

retsu-o-nashite〈列を成して〉in a line, in a row.

retteru〈レッテル〉a label.

retteru-o-haru〈レッテルをはる〉label.

rettô〈れっとう：列島〉a chain of islands.

  Ryûkyû-rettô（りゅう球列島） the Ryukyu Islands

rettô〈れっとう：劣等〉inferiority.

  rettô-kan（劣等感）a sense of inferiority

rettô-na〈劣等な〉inferior, base.

rêzâ-kôsen〈レーザーこうせん：レーザー光線〉laser beams.

ri〈り：利〉an advantage, benefit.

  chi no ri（地の利）the advantage of position

  ri-ni-satoi（利にさとい）have a quick eye for gain

ri〈り：理〉reason.

ri-ni-kanau〈理にかなう〉be reasonable.

ribêto〈リベート〉a rebate.

ribêto-o-harau〈リベートを払う〉rebate, give a rebate.

  ribêto o uke-toru（リベートを受け取る）receive a kickback

ribetsu〈りべつ：離別〉

ribetsu-suru〈離別する〉part ((from)), separate ((from)); divorce.

richakuriku〈りちゃくりく：離着陸〉taking off and landing.

richi〈りち：理知〉intellect, intelligence.

richi-teki-na〈理知的な〉intellectual.

rîchi〈リーチ〉reach.

  rîchi-ga-nagai（リーチが長い） have a long reach

richigi〈りちぎ：律義〉

richigi-na〈律義な〉upright, honest, faithful, conscientious.

ricgigi-ni〈律義に〉faithfully.

rîdâ〈リーダー〉a leader; a reader.

ridatsu〈りだつ：離脱〉

ridatsu-suru〈離脱する〉leave, desert, renounce, secede ((from)).

  tô-seki-o-ridatsu-suru（党籍を離脱する） secede from a party

rîdo〈リード〉a lead.

rîdo-suru〈リードする〉lead, take the lead.

  ni-ten-rîdo-suru（二点リードする） lead by two points

rieki〈りえき：利益〉(a) profit, gain(s), benefit, advantage, interests.

  rieki o ageru（利益を上げる）make a profit

  rieki-ni-naru（利益になる）be to one's benefit, be for one's interests

  o-tagai-no rieki-no-tame-ni（お互いの利益のために）for mutual

advantage
rieki-haitô〈利益配当〉distribution of profits, a dividend
jun-rieki〈純利益〉a net profit
rieki-no-aru〈利益のある〉profitable.
rieki-no-nai〈利益のない〉unprofitable
rien〈りえん：離縁〉
rien-suru〈離縁する〉divorce, disown.
ri-fujin〈りふじん：理不尽〉
ri-fujin-na〈理不尽な〉unreasonable, unfair, unjust.
rifuto〈リフト〉a (chair) lift.
rigai〈りがい：利害〉interests.
rigai no shôtotsu〈利害の衝突〉a clash of interests
rigai-tokushitsu〈利害得失〉advantages and disadvantages, merits
and demerits
rigai-kankei-ga-aru〈利害関係がある〉be interested ((in))
rigai-kankei-sha〈利害関係者〉the persons interested
rigai-o-chôetsu-shita〈利害を超越した〉disinterested.
rigaku〈りがく：理学〉(physical) science.
rigaku-bu〈理学部〉the department of science
rîgu〈リーグ〉a league.
rîgu-sen（リーグ戦）the league series
Roku-daigaku-rîgu-sen（六大学リーグ戦）the Big Six University
Baseball League Tournament
rigui〈りぐい：利食い〉profit taking.
rihan〈りはん：離反〉
rihan-suru〈離反する〉be alienated ((from)).
rihâsaru〈リハーサル〉a rehearsal.
rihâsaru-o-suru〈リハーサルをする〉rehearse.
rihatsu〈りはつ：理髪〉a haircut, hairdressing.
rihatsu-shi〈理髪師〉a barber, a hairdresser
rihatsu-ten〈理髪店〉a barber shop, a barber's
riji〈りじ：理事〉a director, a trustee.
riji-kai〈理事会〉the board of directors(*or* trustees)
riji-chô〈理事長〉the chairman of the board of directors(*or* trustees)
rijun〈りじゅん：利潤〉(a) profit.
rijun o ou〈利潤を追う〉pursue a profit
rika〈りか：理科〉science.

rika-gaku〈りかがく：理化学〉physics and chemistry.

rikai〈りかい：理解〉understanding, comprehension.

　　rikai o fukameru（理解を深める）　deepen one's understanding

　　sōgo-no rikai（相互の理解）　mutual understanding

　　rikai-ryoku（理解力）　understanding, the comprehensive faculty

　rikai-ga-aru〈理解がある〉be sympathetic ((about)), understand.

　　rikai-ga-nai（理解がない）　be unsympathetic, lack understanding

　rikai-suru〈理解する〉understand, comprehend, apprehend, grasp.

　rikai-shi-yasui〈理解しやすい〉easy to understand.

　　rikai-shi-nikui（理解しにくい）　difficult to understand

riken〈りけん：利権〉rights and interests, concessions.

　　riken-o-asaru（利権をあさる）　hunt for concessions

　　riken-ya（利権屋）　a concession hunter, a grafter

riki〈りき：利器〉a convenience.

　　bummei-no-riki（文明の利器）　a modern convenience

rikiei〈りきえい：力泳〉

　rikiei-suru〈力泳する〉swim with powerful strokes.

rikigaku〈りきがく：力学〉dynamics.

rikimu〈りきむ：力む〉swagger, bluff.

rikiryō〈りきりょう：力量〉ability, capacity.

　rikiryō-ni-ōjite〈力量に応じて〉according to one's ability.

rikisaku〈りきさく：力作〉one's labored great work.

rikisetsu〈りきせつ：力説〉

　rikisetsu-suru〈力説する〉emphasize, lay stress ((on)), insist ((upon)).

rikishi〈りきし：力士〉a *sumo* wrestler.

rikisō〈りきそう：力走〉

　rikisō-suru〈力走する〉run as fast as one can, make a spurt.

rikisō〈りきそう：力漕〉

　rikisō-suru〈力漕する〉row with all one's might.

rikitō〈りきとう：力投〉

　rikitō-suru〈力投する〉pitch with all one's might.

rikken〈りっけん：立憲〉

　　rikken-seiji（立憲政治）　constitutional government

rikkōho〈りっこうほ：立候補〉candidacy, candidature.

　　rikkōho-sha（立候補者）　a candidate

　rikkōho-suru〈立候補する〉run as a candidate, run ((for)), stand ((for)).

rikkyaku〈りっきゃく：立脚〉

　rikkyaku-suru〈立脚する〉be based ((on)).

rikkyō〈りっきょう：陸橋〉a viaduct.

riko〈りこ：利己〉selfishness, egoism.
    riko-shugi（利己主義） egoism
        riko-shugi-sha（利己主義者） an egoist
    riko-teki-na〈利己的な〉selfish, egoistic.
        riko-teki-de-nai（利己的でない） unselfish

rikō〈りこう：履行〉
    rikō-suru〈履行する〉fulfill, perform, carry out, implement.

rikō〈りこう：利口〉
    rikō-na〈利口な〉clever, bright, wise, intelligent; shrewd, smart.
        rikō-na ko（利口な子） a bright child

rikōgaku-bu〈りこうがくぶ：理工学部〉the department of science and engineering.

rikon〈りこん：離婚〉a divorce.
    rikon-soshō（離婚訴訟） a divorce suit
    kyōgi-rikon（協議離婚） a divorce by consent
    rikon-todoke（離婚届） a report of divorce
    rikon-suru〈離婚する〉divorce.

rikōru〈リコール〉(a) recall.
    rikōru-sei（リコール制） the recall system
    rikōru-suru〈リコールする〉recall.

riku〈りく：陸〉(the) land, (the) shore.

riku-age〈りくあげ：陸揚げ〉
    riku-age-suru〈陸揚げする〉land, discharge, unload.

riku-chi〈りくち：陸地〉(the) land.

rikugun〈りくぐん：陸軍〉the army.
    rikugun-no〈陸軍の〉military, army.

rikujō〈りくじょう：陸上〉
    rikujō-kimmu（陸上勤務） shore duty, ground duty
    rikujō-kyōgi（陸上競技） athletic sports
    rikujō-yusō（陸上輸送） land transportation
    rikujō-de or *rikujō-ni*〈陸上で，陸上に〉on land.

riku-kai-kū〈りくかいくう：陸海空〉
    riku-kai-kū-no-san-gun（陸海空の三軍） the land, sea and air forces

rikuro〈りくろ：陸路〉by land, overland.

rikutsu〈りくつ：理屈〉theory, (an) argument.
    rikutsu-o-iu or *rikutsu-o-koneru*〈理屈を言う，理屈をこねる〉put forward an argument, chop logic.

rikutsuppoi〈理屈っぽい〉argumentative.

rikutsu-no-ue-dewa〈理屈の上では〉in theory.

rikyûru〈リキュール〉liqueur.

ri-mawari〈りまわり：利回り〉yield, interest, return(s).
　　Sono　saiken　wa　nen-roku-bu-san-rin-no-ri-mawari-ni-naru.（その債券 は年六分三厘の利回りになる。）The bond yields 6.3%.
　　ri-mawari-ga-ii（利回りがいい）yield a good return
　　ri-mawari-ga-warui（利回りが悪い）yield a bad return

rimban〈りんばん：輪番〉turn, rotation.
　　rimban-sei（輪番制）a rotation system
　rimban-de or *rimban-sei-de*〈輪番で，輪番制で〉by　turns,　under　a rotation system.

rimbyô〈りんびょう：りん病〉gonorrh(o)ea, the clap.

rimen〈りめん：裏面〉the back, the inside, the background, the other side.
　　rimen-kôsaku（裏面工作）behind-the-scene maneuvering

rimokon〈リモコン〉remote control.
　rimokon-de ugoku〈リモコンで動く〉be remote-controlled.
　rimokon-no〈リモコンの〉remote-controlled.

rimpa(-eki)〈リンパ（えき）：リンパ（液）〉lymph.
　　rimpa-sen（リンパせん）a lymph gland
　　　rimpa-sen-en（リンパせん炎）lymphadenitis

rin〈りん〉phosphorus.

rinchi〈リンチ〉lynching.
　rinchi-o-kuwaeru〈リンチを加える〉lynch.

rinen〈りねん：理念〉an idea, a doctrine.

Ringeru-chûsha〈リンゲルちゅうしゃ：リンゲル注射〉an　injection　of Ringer's solution.

ringetsu〈りんげつ：臨月〉the last month of pregnancy.
　　Kanojo-wa　kongetsu　ga　ringetsu-da.（彼女は今月が臨月だ。）Her time comes this month.

ringo〈りんご〉an apple (tree).

ringyô〈りんぎょう：林業〉forestry.

ri-Nichi〈りにち：離日〉a departure from Japan.
　ri-Nichi-suru〈離日する〉depart from Japan.

rinji〈りんじ：臨時〉
　　rinji-kokkai（臨時国会）a special session of the Diet
　　rinji-kyûgyô（臨時休業）a special holiday

　　　rinji-nyûsu（臨時ニュース）news special
　　　rinji-ressha（臨時列車）a special train
　　　rinji-yatoi（臨時雇い）a temporary employee
　　rinji-no〈臨時の〉special, extra, extraordinary, temporary.
　　rinji-ni〈臨時に〉specially, extraordinarily, temporarily.
rinjin〈りんじん：隣人〉a neighbor.
rinjû〈りんじゅう：臨終〉one's deathbed.
　　　rinjû-no-kotoba（臨終の言葉）one's last words
　　　rinjû-ni-saishite（臨終に際して）on one's deathbed
rinkai-gakkô〈りんかいがっこう：臨海学校〉a seaside school.
rinkaku〈りんかく：輪郭〉an outline.
　　　rinkaku o noberu（輪郭を述べる）give an outline ((of))
　　　rinkaku o tsukamu（輪郭をつかむ）grasp the outline ((of))
　　rinkaku-no-hakkiri-shita〈輪郭のはっきりした〉clear-cut.
rinkan-gakkô〈りんかんがっこう：林間学校〉an open-air school.
rinken〈りんけん：臨検〉an official inspection, a search, a raid, boarding.
　　rinken-suru〈臨検する〉visit and inspect, raid and search.
rinki-ôhen〈りんきおうへん：臨機応変〉
　　rinki-ôhen-ni〈臨機応変に〉according to the requirements of the case.
rinkô〈りんこう：りん光〉phosphorescence.
　　　rinkô-seki（りん光石）a phosphate rock
　　rinkô-sei-no〈りん光性の〉phosphorescent.
rinneru〈リンネル〉linen.
rinoriumu〈リノリウム〉linoleum.
rinri〈りんり：倫理〉ethics, morals.
　　　rinri-gaku（倫理学）ethics
　　rinri-teki(-na)〈倫理的(な)〉ethical, moral.
rinrin〈りんりん〉
　　rinrin-naru〈りんりん鳴る〉ring, jingle, tinkle.
rinsan〈りんさん：りん酸〉phosphoric acid.
　　　rinsan-hiryô（りん酸肥料）phosphatic fertilizer
rinsetsu〈りんせつ：隣接〉
　　rinsetsu-suru〈隣接する〉be adjacent ((to)), adjoin.
　　rinsetsu-shita〈隣接した〉neighboring, adjacent ((to)), adjoining.
rinshô〈りんしょう：臨床〉
　　　rioshô-igaku（臨床医学）clinical medicine
　　　rinshô-jikken（臨床実験）clinical demonstration

rinshô-no〈臨床の〉clinical.
rinshô-teki-ni〈臨床的に〉clinically.

rinten-ki〈りんてんき：輪転機〉a rotary press.

rinyô-zai〈りにょうざい：利尿剤〉a diuretic.

rinyû〈りにゅう：離乳〉
　　rinyû-ki（離乳期）the weaning period
rinyû-suru〈離乳する〉wean.

rippa〈りっぱ：立派〉
rippa-na〈立派な〉fine, nice, excellent, splendid, brilliant, stately, respectable, honorable, noble, admirable, praiseworthy.
　　rippa-na ie（立派な家）a splendid house
　　rippa-na gyôseki（立派な業績）a brilliant achievement
　　rippa-na taido（立派な態度）a stately manner
　　rippa-na hito（立派な人）a respectable person
　　rippa-na jinkaku-sha（立派な人格者）a man of noble character
　　rippa-na okonai（立派な行い）a praiseworthy conduct
　　rippa-na-fukusô-o-shita hito（立派な服装をした人）a well-dressed person
rippa-ni〈立派に〉finely, nicely, excellently, splendidly, brilliantly, respectably, admirably, creditably.
　　rippa-ni yatte-nokeru（立派にやってのける）acquit oneself creditably

rippô〈りっぽう：立法〉legislation, lawmaking.
　　rippô-ken（立法権）legislative power
　　rippô-kikan（立法機関）a legislative organ
rippô-no〈立法の〉legislative.

rippô〈りっぽう：立方〉cube.
　　rippô-kon（立方根）the cube root
　　rippô-tai（立方体）a cube
　　rippô-mêtoru（立法メートル）a cubic meter
rippô(-tai)-no〈立方(体)の〉cubic.

rira〈リラ〉a lilac; a lira.

rirê〈リレー〉a relay (race).

rireki〈りれき：履歴〉one's personal record, one's career.
　　rireki-sho（履歴書）one's personal history, one's curriculum vitae

rirîfu〈リリーフ〉
　　rirîfu-tôshu（リリーフ投手）a relief pitcher, a reliever
rirîfu-suru〈リリーフする〉relieve.

ririku〈りりく：離陸〉a takeoff.

ririku-suru〈離陸する〉take off.

ririshii〈りりしい〉gallant, imposing, manly.

riritsu〈りりつ：利率〉the rate of interest.

riron〈りろん：理論〉(a) theory.

 riron-butsuri-gaku（理論物理学）theoretical physics

 riron-tôsô（理論闘争）a theoretical dispute

 riron-ka（理論家）a theorist

riron-jô-no or *riron-teki(-na)*〈理論上の，理論的(な)〉theoretical.

 riron-teki kenkyû（理論的研究）a theoretical study

riron-jô or *riron-to-shite-wa*〈理論上，理論としては〉theoretically, in theory.

riro-seizen〈りろせいぜん：理路整然〉

riro-seizen-to-shita〈理路整然とした〉consistent, logical.

rîru〈リール〉a reel, a spool.

ri-sage〈りさげ：利下げ〉a reduction in the rate of interest.

ri-sage-suru〈利下げする〉reduce the interest.

risai〈りさい：り災〉

 risai-sha（り災者）a sufferer ((from)), a victim ((of))

risai-suru〈り災する〉suffer ((from)), fall a victim ((to)), be hit ((by)).

risan〈りさん：離散〉

risan-suru〈離散する〉scatter, be scattered, disperse, be dispersed, be broken up.

 Kare-no ikka wa risan-shita.（彼の一家は離散した.）His family was broken up.

risei〈りせい：理性〉reason.

 risei o ushinau（理性を失う）lose one's reason

rishi〈りし：利子〉interest.

 rishi ga tsuku（利子が付く）yield interest

 rishi-o-tsukete kaesu（利子を付けて返す）pay back ((money)) with interest

 takai rishi-de（高い利子で）at high interest

 mu-rishi-de（無利子で）free of interest

rishoku〈りしょく：利殖〉moneymaking.

rishoku-no-sai-ga-aru〈利殖の才がある〉be clever at making money.

rishoku〈りしょく：離職〉

 rishoku-sha（離職者）an unemployed person, the unemployed

rishoku-suru〈離職する〉quit one's job, lose employment.

rishû〈りしゅう：履修〉

rishû-suru〈履修する〉complete, finish.

    daigaku-katei o rishû-suru（大学課程を履修する）finish a college course

risô〈りそう：理想〉an ideal.

    takai risô（高い理想）a lofty ideal

    risô-shugi（理想主義）idealism

    risô-ka *or* risô-shugi-sha（理想家，理想主義者）an idealist

risô-no or risô-teki(-na)〈理想の，理想的（な）〉ideal.

    risô-no josei（理想の女性）an ideal woman

risô-teki-ni〈理想的に〉ideally, perfectly.

risoku〈りそく：利息〉*see.* rishi.

risshi-den〈りっしでん：立志伝〉

    risshi-den-chû-no hito（立志伝中の人）a self-made man

risshin-shusse〈りっしんしゅっせ：立身出世〉success in life.

risshin-shusse-suru〈立身出世する〉rise in the world.

risshô〈りっしょう：立証〉proof.

risshô-suru〈立証する〉prove, establish.

    muzai o risshô-suru（無罪を立証する）establish ((a person's)) innocence

risshû〈りっしゅう：立秋〉the first day of autumn.

risshun〈りっしゅん：立春〉the first day of spring.

rissui〈りっすい：立すい〉

rissui-no-yochi-mo-nai〈立すいの余地もない〉there isn't even standing room.

risu〈りす〉a squirrel.

ritchi-jôken〈りっちじょうけん：立地条件〉

ritchi-jôken-ga-ii〈立地条件がいい〉be located favorably.

ritei〈りてい：里程〉mileage, (a) distance.

    ritei-hyô（里程標）a milestone, a milepost

riten〈りてん：利点〉an advantage.

ritô〈りとう：離党〉

ritô-suru〈離党する〉leave a party.

ritomasu〈リトマス〉litmus.

    ritomasu-shiken-shi（リトマス試験紙）litmus paper

ritsu〈りつ：率〉a rate.

    shibô-ritsu（死亡率）a death rate

ritsuan〈りつあん：立案〉

    ritsuan-sha（立案者）a deviser, a planner, a framer

ritsuan-suru〈立案する〉make a plan, devise, draw up.

ri-tsuki〈りつき：利付き〉

    ri-tsuki-kôsai（利付き公債）an interest-bearing bond

ritsuzen〈りつぜん：りつ然〉

ritsuzen-to-suru〈りつ然とする〉be horror-struck.

rittai〈りったい：立体〉a solid (body).

    rittai-kôsa（立体交差）a two-level crossing, grade separation, a cloverleaf

rittai-no〈立体の〉solid, cubic.

rittai-teki(-na)〈立体的(な)〉three-dimensioned.

rittai-teki-ni〈立体的に〉in three dimensions, from all viewpoints.

rittô〈りっとう：立冬〉the first day of winter.

rittoru〈リットル〉a liter.

riyô〈りよう：利用〉utilization, use.

    riyô-kachi（利用価値）utility value

    riyô-sha（利用者）a user, a visitor, a reader

riyô-suru〈利用する〉use, utilize, make (good) use ((of)), take advantage ((of)), avail oneself ((of)).

    jikan-o-kyokuryoku-riyô-suru（時間を極力利用する）make the best use of one's time

    hito-no muchi-o-riyô-suru（人の無知を利用する）take advantage of another's ignorance

    kikai-o-riyô-suru（機会を利用する）avail oneself of an opportunity

riyoku〈りよく：利欲〉greed, avarice.

    riyoku-ni me-ga-kuramu（利欲に目がくらむ）be blinded by greed

riyû〈りゆう：理由〉(a) reason, cause, ground(s), account; a pretext, an excuse.

    mottomo-rashii riyû（もっともらしい理由）a plausible reason

    nantoka-kantoka-riyû-o-tsukete（何とかかんとか理由を付けて）on some pretext or other

riyû-no-tatsu〈理由の立つ〉excusable, justifiable.

    riyû-no-tata-nai（理由の立たない）inexcusable, unjustifiable

~-no-riyû-de〈～の理由で〉for the reason that... , by reason of... , on account of... , on the ground of(*or* that)... .

    kenkô-jô-no-riyû-de（健康上の理由で）for reasons of health

riyû-naku〈理由なく〉without reason, without provocation.

rizaya〈りざや：利ざや〉a profit margin.

ri-zume〈りづめ：理詰め〉

ri-zume-de 〈理詰めで〉by logical reasoning, by (sheer) force of argument.

rizumu 〈リズム〉(a) rhythm.
     hayai rizumu-de（速いリズムで）in quick rhythm
     rizumu-kan（リズム感）rhythmical sense

rizumu-o-toru 〈リズムをとる〉time.

rizumu-o-tsukete 〈リズムをつけて〉rhythmically.

ro 〈ろ〉a scull, an oar.
     ro o kogu（ろをこぐ）work a scull

ro 〈ろ：炉〉a fireplace, a hearth; a furnace.
     ro-ni-ataru（炉に当たる）warm oneself at the hearth
     ro-bata（炉端）the fireside

rô 〈ろう〉wax.
     rô-ningyô（ろう人形）a wax doll

rô-o-hiku 〈ろうを引く〉wax.

rô 〈ろう〉a prison, a jail, a gaol.
     rô o yaburu（ろうを破る）break prison

rô 〈ろう：労〉trouble, labor, toil, pains, service(s).

roba 〈ろば：ろ馬〉an ass, a donkey.

rôba 〈ろうば：老婆〉an old woman.

rôbai 〈ろうばい〉confusion.

rôbai-suru 〈ろうばいする〉be confused, be thrown into confusion, be upset, lose one's head, be panic-stricken.
     rôbai-shi-nai（ろうばいしない）remain calm

rôbai-shite 〈ろうばいして〉in confusion.

rôba-shin 〈ろうばしん：老婆心〉kindness.
     Watashi-wa rôba-shin-kara kimi-ni kô-iu-no-da.（私は老婆心から君にこう言うのだ。）I tell you this out of kindness.

robî 〈ロビー〉a lobby, a lounge.

robotto 〈ロボット〉a robot; a figurehead.

rôchin 〈ろうちん：労賃〉wages, pay.

rôden 〈ろうでん：漏電〉a short circuit, a leakage of electricity.

rôden-suru 〈漏電する〉short-circuit.

rôdô 〈ろうどう：労働〉labor.
     rôdô-sha（労働者）a laborer, a worker
     rôdô-kumiai（労働組合）a labor union, a trade union
        rôdô-kumiai-in（労働組合員）a union man, a unionist
     rôdô-sensen（労働戦線）a labor front

rôdô-undô（労働運動）a labor movement
rôdô-kôsei（労働攻勢）a labor offensive
rôdô-sôgi（労働争議）a labor trouble
rôdô-jikan（労働時間）working hours
rôdô-kijun-hô（労働基準法）the Labor Standards Law
rôdô-shô（労働省）the Ministry of Labor
rôdô-daijin（労働大臣）the Minister of Labor
rôdô-suru〈労働する〉labor, work.

rôdoku〈ろうどく：朗読〉
rôdoku-suru〈朗読する〉read aloud, recite.

roei〈ろえい：露営〉
roei-suru〈露営する〉camp out, bivouac.

rôei〈ろうえい：漏えい〉leakage.
rôei-suru〈漏えいする〉leak out.

rôgan〈ろうがん：老眼〉presbyopia.
Rôgan-ni-natta.（老眼になった.）My eyes got dim with age.
rôgan-kyô（老眼鏡）spectacles for the aged, farsighted eyeglasses

rôgo〈ろうご：老後〉one's old age.
rôgo-ni-sonaeru（老後に備える）provide for one's old age

rôhi〈ろうひ：浪費〉
rôhi-suru〈浪費する〉waste, dissipate, throw away, squander.
jikan o rôhi-suru（時間を浪費する）waste time

rô-hîru〈ローヒール〉low-heeled shoes.

rôhô〈ろうほう：朗報〉good news.

roji〈ろじ：路地〉an alley, a lane.

rôjin〈ろうじん：老人〉an old man, the aged, the old.
rôjin-byô（老人病）the diseases of the aged
rôjin-hômu（老人ホーム）a home for the aged

roka〈ろか：ろ過〉filtration, percolation.
roka-suru〈ろ過する〉filter, percolate.

rôka〈ろうか：廊下〉a passage(way), a corridor, a hallway.

rôka-genshô〈ろうかげんしょう：老化現象〉the symptoms of senility.

rôkai〈ろうかい：老かい〉
rôkai-na〈老かいな〉crafty, cunning, foxy.

rôkaru〈ローカル〉
rôkaru-hôsô（ローカル放送）a local broadcast
rôkaru-sen（ローカル線）a local line

roke〈ロケ〉a location.

roke-tai（ロケ隊） a location unit

roken〈ろけん：露見(顕)〉

roken-suru〈露見(顕)する〉be found out, be detected, be exposed, be laid bare, come out.

Akuji wa roken-suru.（悪事は露見(顕)する.） Murder will out.

rôketsu-zome〈ろうけつぞめ：ろうけつ染〉bat(t)ik.

roketto〈ロケット〉a rocket; a locket.

roketto-hassha-ki（ロケット発射機） a rocket launcher

tsuki-roketto（月ロケット） a moon rocket

rokkaku(-kei)〈ろっかく(けい)：六角(形)〉a hexagon.

rokkaku-kei-no〈六角(形)の〉hexagonal.

rokkan〈ろっかん：ろっ間〉

rokkan-shinkei-tsû（ろっ間神経痛） intercostal neuralgia

rokkotsu〈ろっこつ：ろっ骨〉a rib, the ribs.

rokku-auto〈ロックアウト〉a lockout.

rokku-auto-suru〈ロックアウトする〉lock out.

rokô〈ろこう：露光〉exposure.

rôkô〈ろうこう：老巧〉

rôkô-na〈老巧な〉experienced, trained, veteran.

rokotsu〈ろこつ：露骨〉

rokotsu-na〈露骨な〉plain, undisguised, frank, broad; indecent, suggestive.

rokotsu-ni〈露骨に〉plainly, frankly, broadly, outspokenly.

rokotsu-ni iu〈露骨に言う〉speak plainly

rokotsu-ni-ieba〈露骨に言えば〉to be plain with you.

roku〈ろく：六〉six.

dai-roku（第六） the sixth

rôku〈ろうく：労苦〉labor, pains, toil, effort(s).

rôku o oshima-nai（労苦を惜しまない） spare no pains

roku-de-nashi〈ろくでなし〉a good-for-nothing.

rokuga〈ろくが：録画〉video recording, telerecording.

rokuga-suru〈録画する〉record, videotape.

rokugatsu〈ろくがつ：六月〉June.

roku-jû〈ろくじゅう：六十〉sixty.

dai-roku-jû（第六十） the sixtieth

rokumaku〈ろくまく：ろく膜〉the pleura.

rokumaku-en（ろく膜炎） pleurisy

roku-na〈ろくな〉

Roku-na-koto-ga-nai.（ろくなことがない.）Everything goes wrong with me.

roku-na-koto-o-iwa-nai（ろくなことを言わない）talk nonsense

roku-ni〈ろくに〉

roku-ni-kangae-mo-sezu（ろくに考えもせず）without due consideration

roku-ni-mi-mo-sezu（ろくに見もせず）without looking at it well

Yûbe-kara roku-ni-tabete-i-nai.（ゆうべからろくに食べていない.）I have scarcely had anything to eat since last night.

rokuon〈ろくおん：録音〉recording.

rokuon-têpu（録音テープ）a magnetic tape, a recording tape

rokuon-gakari（録音係）a record man

rokuon-suru〈録音する〉record.

rokushô〈ろくしょう：緑青〉verdigris, green rust.

rôkyô〈ろうきょう：老境〉(one's) old age.

rôkyô-ni-hairu〈老境に入る〉be advanced in life, grow old.

rôkyû〈ろうきゅう：老朽〉

rôkyû-shisetsu（老朽施設）superannuated equipment

rôkyû-ka-suru〈老朽化する〉become superannuated.

rôkyû-no or *rôkyû-ka-shita*〈老朽の，老朽化した〉superannuated, time-worn, worn-out.

Rôma〈ローマ〉Rome.

Rôma wa ichi-nichi-ni-shite narazu.（ローマは一日にして成らず.）Rome was not built in a day.

Rôma-ji〈ローマじ：ローマ字〉Roman letters, *romaji*.

romanchikku-na〈ロマンチックな〉romantic.

romanesuku〈ロマネスク〉Romanesque.

romanesuku-yôshiki（ロマネスク様式）Romanesque style

roman-ha〈ロマンは：ロマン派〉the romantic school；a romanticist.

roman-ha-no shijin（ロマン派の詩人）a romantic poet

romansu〈ロマンス〉a romance.

romansu-kâ（ロマンスカー）a deluxe carriage

romansu-shîto（ロマンスシート）a love seat

rombun〈ろんぶん：論文〉an essay, a thesis.

sotsugyô-rombun（卒業論文）a graduation thesis

romen〈ろめん：路面〉a road surface.

romen-densha（路面電車）a streetcar, a tramcar

rompô〈ろんぽう：論法〉logic, reasoning.

san-dan-rompô〈三段論法〉 a syllogism

rompyô〈ろんぴょう：論評〉(a) criticism, a comment, a review.

rompyô o sakeru（論評を避ける） eschew comment ((on))

rompyô-suru〈論評する〉criticize, comment ((on)), review.

rômu〈ろうむ：労務〉

rômu-sha（労務者） a worker, a laborer

ron〈ろん：論〉(an) argument.

Ron-yori-shôko.（論より証拠.） The proof of the pudding is in the eating.

ronchô〈ろんちょう：論調〉the tone of argument.

shimbun-ronchô（新聞論調） the press comments

rônen〈ろうねん：老年〉old age.

rongai〈ろんがい：論外〉

rongai-de-aru〈論外である〉be out of the question, go to an extreme.

rongi〈ろんぎ：論議〉(a) discussion, (an) argument, (a) debate.

rongi-suru〈論議する〉discuss, argue ((about)), debate ((about *or* on)).

sakan-ni rongi-sareru（盛んに論議される） be hotly argued

Rongo〈ろんご：論語〉the Analects of Confucius.

Rongo-yomi-no-Rongo-shirazu（論語読みの論語知らず） a learned fool

rônin〈ろうにん：浪人〉a lordless *samurai;* a senior high-school graduate failing to enter a college and waiting for another chance to be enrolled.

ronjiru〈ろんじる：論じる〉discuss, argue ((about *or* on)), dispute ((about *or* on)); deal ((with)).

ronjiru-ni-tari-nai〈論じるに足りない〉do not matter at all, be not worth consideration.

ronkyo〈ろんきょ：論拠〉the basis of an argument.

ronri(-gaku)〈ろんり（がく）：論理（学）〉logic.

ronri-teki(-na)〈論理的（な）〉logical.

hi-ronri-teki(-na)（非論理的（な）） illogical

ronri-teki-ni or *ronri-jô*〈論理的に，論理上〉logically.

ronsen〈ろんせん：論戦〉verbal blows, a controversy.

ronsetsu〈ろんせつ：論説〉an editorial, a leading article.

ronsetsu-iin（論説委員） an editorial writer

ronsetsu-de-tori-atsukau〈論説で取り扱う〉editorialize ((on)).

ronshi〈ろんし：論旨〉the point of an argument.

ronshi-o-akiraka-ni-suru（論旨を明らかにする） make one's point of argument clear

ronsô 〈ろんそう：論争〉 an argument, a dispute, a controversy.
　ronsô-suru 〈論争する〉 argue, dispute, have a controversy ((with)).
　ronsô-no-yochi-no-nai 〈論争の余地のない〉 indisputable, incontrovertible.

ronten 〈ろんてん：論点〉 the point at issue.

rô-nyaku-nan-nyo 〈ろうにゃくなんにょ：老若男女〉
　rô-nyaku-nan-nyo-o-towazu 〈老若男女を問わず〉 without distinction of age or sex.

roppô-zensho 〈ろっぽうぜんしょ：六法全書〉 a compendium of laws, a statute book.

rôrei 〈ろうれい：老齢〉 old age.

rôren 〈ろうれん：老練〉
　rôren-na 〈老練な〉 experienced, veteran, old.

roretsu 〈ろれつ〉
　yotte roretsu-ga-mawara-nai 〈酔ってろれつが回らない〉 drink too much and cannot speak distinctly.

rôru 〈ロール〉
　rôru-kyabetsu （ロールキャベツ） a cabbage roll
　rôru-pan （ロールパン） a roll (of bread)

rôryoku 〈ろうりょく：労力〉 labor, toil, effort.
　rôryoku o habuku （労力を省く） save labor

rôsai-hoken 〈ろうさいほけん：労災保険〉 workmen's accident compensation insurance.

rôsaku 〈ろうさく：労作〉 a laborious work.

rosen 〈ろせん：路線〉 a line, a route.
　shihon-shugi-rosen （資本主義路線） the capitalist line

roshi 〈ろし：ろ紙〉 filter paper.

rô-shi 〈ろうし：労資〉 capital and labor, labor and management.
　rô-shi-kankei （労資関係） labor-management relations
　rô-shi-funsô （労資紛争） a conflict between labor and capital
　rô-shi-kyôchô （労資協調） cooperation between capital and labor

Roshia 〈ロシア〉 Russia.
　Roshia-jin （ロシア人） a Russian
　Roshia-go （ロシア語） Russian
　Roshia(-jin)-no （ロシア(人)の） Russian

roshutsu 〈ろしゅつ：露出〉 exposure.
　roshutsu-jikan （露出時間） time of exposure
　roshutsu-busoku （露出不足） underexposure
　roshutsu-ôbâ （露出オーバー） overexposure

roshutsu-kei〈露出計〉an exposure meter

roshutsu-suru〈露出する〉expose.

rôso〈ろうそ：労組〉*see.* rôdô-kumiai.

rôsoku〈ろうそく〉a candle.

rôsoku o tomosu（ろうそくをともす）light a candle

rôsoku o fuki-kesu（ろうそくを吹き消す）blow out a candle

rôsoku-no-hi（ろうそくの火）candlelight

rôsoku-no-shin（ろうそくのしん）a candlewick

rôsoku-tate（ろうそく立て）a candlestick

rosu〈ロス〉loss.

ni-jikan-no-rosu-o-tori-kaesu（二時間のロスを取り返す）make up for two hours lost

rôsu〈ロース〉sirloin.

rôsui〈ろうすい：老衰〉senile decay.

rôsui-de-shinu（老衰で死ぬ）die of old age

rôsuru〈ろうする：労する〉labor.

rôsezu-shite〈労せずして〉without labor(*or* trouble).

roten〈ろてん：露店〉a street stall, a booth.

roten-shô（露天商）a stall keeper, a pitchman

roten〈ろてん：露天〉

roten-buro（露天風ろ）an open-air bath

roten-bori（露天掘り）open-air mining

roten-de〈露天で〉in the open (air).

rôtêshon〈ローテーション〉rotation.

rôtêshon-kara-hazusareru（ローテーションから外される）be put out of rotation

rôtîn〈ローティーン〉one's early teens.

rotô〈ろとう：路頭〉

rotô-ni-mayou〈路頭に迷う〉be thrown on the streets, be left without any support.

rôzeki〈ろうぜき〉

rôzeki-mono（ろうぜき者）a rioter, a rascal, an outlaw, a trespasser

rôzeki-suru〈ろうぜきする〉run riot, play havoc ((among *or* with)).

rubi〈ルビ〉an agate, a ruby.

rubi-o-furu〈ルビを振る〉print *kana*.

rufu〈るふ：流布〉circulation, spread.

rufu-suru〈流布する〉circulate, spread, get about.

rui〈るい：塁〉a base, a bag.

rui-o-fumu〈塁を踏む〉 tread on the base

rui-ni-deru〈塁に出る〉 go to first

rui〈るい：累〉

tanin-ni rui o oyobosu〈他人に累を及ぼす〉cause trouble to others.

rui〈るい：類〉

Rui-o-motte-atsumaru.（類をもって集まる.） Birds of a feather flock together.

ruibetsu〈るいべつ：類別〉classification.

ruibetsu-suru〈類別する〉classify.

ruida〈るいだ：塁打〉a base hit.

ruida-sū（塁打数） total bases

ruigo〈るいご：類語〉a synonym.

ruiji〈るいじ：類似〉(a) resemblance, (a) similarity, (a) likeness.

ruiji-ten（類似点） a point of similarity

ruiji-hin（類似品） an imitation, a similar article

ruiji-suru〈類似する〉resemble, be similar ((to)), be alike ((in)).

ruijin-en〈るいじんえん：類人猿〉an anthropoid (ape).

ruikei〈るいけい：累計〉the total, the sum total, the aggregate.

ruikei-suru-to~-ni-naru〈累計すると〜になる〉total... , amount to... .

ruirei〈るいれい：類例〉a similar example, a parallel case.

ruirei-no-nai〈類例のない〉unexampled, unparalleled, unprecedented, unique.

ruiseki〈るいせき：累積〉accumulation.

ruiseki-akaji（累積赤字） accumulated deficit

ruiseki-suru〈累積する〉accumulate.

ruiseki-shita〈累積した〉accumulated.

ruisen〈るいせん：涙せん〉a lac(h)rymal gland.

ruishin〈るいしん：塁審〉a base umpire.

ruishin〈るいしん：累進〉successive promotion.

ruishin-suru〈累進する〉be promoted from one position to another.

ruishin-teki-ni〈累進的に〉on a graduated scale.

ruishin-teki-ni kazei-suru（累進的に課税する） impose taxes (upon a person) on a graduated scale

ruisho〈るいしょ：類書〉similar books, books of the same kind.

ruishô〈るいしょう：類焼〉

ruishô-suru〈類焼する〉be burnt down by the spreading fire.

ruisui〈るいすい：類推〉(an) analogy.

ruisui-suru〈類推する〉analogize, infer.

～-kara-ruisui-shite〈～から類推して〉on the analogy of... .

Rûmania〈ルーマニア〉Rumania.

    Rûmania-jin（ルーマニア人）a Rumanian

    Rûmania-go（ルーマニア語）Rumanian

    Rûmania(-jin)-no（ルーマニア(人)の）Rumanian

rûmu-kûrâ〈ルームクーラー〉an air conditioner.

rupo〈ルポ〉a report ((on)), reportage.

ruri(-iro)〈るり(いろ)：るり(色)〉lapis lazuli.

rurô〈るろう：流浪〉vagabondage, wandering.

 rurô-suru〈流浪する〉vagabond, wander about.

rûru〈ルール〉a rule.

    rûru-ni-hansuru（ルールに反する）be against the rules

rusu〈るす：留守〉absence.

 rusu-de-aru〈留守である〉be away from home, be absent from home, be out.

 rusu-chû-ni〈留守中に〉during(*or* in) one's absence.

rusu-ban〈るすばん：留守番〉caretaking; a caretaker.

 rusu-ban-o-suru〈留守番をする〉take care of the house〔in a person's absence〕, look after the house〔in another's absence〕.

rûto〈ルート〉a route, a channel.

    seiki-no rûto-de（正規のルートで）through a legal channel

rutsubo〈るつぼ〉a melting pot.

    kôfun-no-rutsubo-to-kasuru（興奮のるつぼと化する）turn into a state of feverish excitement

rûzu〈ルーズ〉

 rûzu-na〈ルーズな〉loose, slovenly.

    rûzu-na yari-kata-de（ルーズなやり方で）in a slovenly manner

ryakudatsu〈りゃくだつ：略奪〉plunder.

 ryakudatsu-suru〈略奪する〉plunder, pillage, loot, sack.

ryakugo〈りゃくご：略語〉an abbreviation, an abbreviated word.

ryakuji〈りゃくじ：略字〉an abbreviation, an abbreviated form.

ryakureki〈りゃくれき：略歴〉a brief personal record.

ryakushiki〈りゃくしき：略式〉informality.

 ryakushiki-no〈略式の〉informal.

    ryakushiki-no fukusô（略式の服装）informal clothes

ryaku-suru〈りゃくする：略する〉abbreviate, abridge, shorten, omit, leave out, dispense ((with)).

 ryaku-shite〈略して〉for short.

ryaku-sazu-ni 〈略さずに〉 in full.

ryakuzu 〈りゃくず：略図〉a rough sketch, a sketch map, a rough plan.

ryô 〈りょう：猟, 漁〉shooting, hunting, fishing; game.
  ryô-ni-iku（猟(漁)に行く）go shooting(hunting *or* fishing)
  ryô-ga-takusan-aru（猟(漁)がたくさんある）have much game, make a big catch

ryô 〈りょう：寮〉a dormitory.
  ryô-sei（寮生）a boarder
  ryô-bo（寮母）a housemother

ryô 〈りょう：量〉(a) quantity, (an) amount, volume.
  ryô-ga-ooi（量が多い）be large in quantity
  ryô-ga-sukunai（量が少ない）be small in quantity
ryô-o-sugosu 〈量を過ごす〉eat too much, take an overdose.
  sake-no-ryô-o-herasu（酒の量を減らす）reduce drinking

ryô 〈りょう：涼〉the cool.
  ryô-o-motomeru（涼を求める）seek for the cool

ryô 〈りょう〉
ryô-to-suru 〈りょうとする〉understand, appreciate.

ryôba 〈りょうば：両刃〉
ryôba-no 〈両刃の〉double-edged.

ryôbun 〈りょうぶん：領分〉a territory, a province.
  Sore-wa watashi-no ryôbun-dewa-nai.（それは私の領分ではない。）It is not in my territory.

ryodan 〈りょだん：旅団〉a brigade.
  konsei-ryodan（混成旅団）a mixed brigade
  ryodan-chô（旅団長）a brigade commander

ryôdo 〈りょうど：領土〉(a) territory, (a) dominion, (a) possession.
  ryôdo o okasu（領土を侵す）invade a territory
  ryôdo-teki yashin o motsu（領土的野心を持つ）have territorial ambitions

ryôen 〈りょうえん：良縁〉a good match.
  ryôen o uru（良縁を得る）make a good match

ryôga 〈りょうが〉
ryôga-suru 〈りょうがする〉surpass, excel, exceed, stand above.
  giryô-de hito o ryôga-suru（技量で人をりょうがする）surpass a person in skill

ryôgae 〈りょうがえ：両替〉money exchanging.
  ryôgae-shô（両替商）a money exchanger; an exchange house

　　ryôgae-suru〈両替する〉exchange, change.

ryôgan〈りょうがん：両眼〉both eyes.

ryôgawa〈りょうがわ：両側〉both sides.
　　michi no ryôgawa-ni（道の両側に）on both sides of the street

ryôhashi〈りょうはし：両端〉both ends.

ryohi〈りょひ：旅費〉traveling expenses.

ryôhô〈りょうほう：療法〉a treatment, a remedy, a cure.
　　kagaku-teki ryôhô（化学的療法）a chemical remedy

ryôhô(-tomo)〈りょうほう（とも）：両方（とも）〉both, neither.
　　Ryôhô-tomo hoshii.（両方とも欲しい。）I want both of them.
　　Ryôhô-tomo hoshiku-nai.（両方とも欲しくない。）I want neither.
　　ryôhô-no〈両方の〉both.

ryôiki〈りょういき：領域〉a territory, a domain, a sphere.
　　kagaku no ryôiki（科学の領域）the sphere of science

ryôji〈りょうじ：領事〉a consul.
　　ryôji-kan（領事館）a consulate

ryôjoku〈りょうじょく：りょう辱〉
　　ryôjoku-suru〈りょう辱する〉rape, violate, outrage.

ryôjû〈りょうじゅう：猟銃〉a hunting gun, a shotgun.

ryôkai〈りょうかい：領海〉territorial waters.
　　Nihon　no　ryôkai-nai-de（日本の領海内で）within the territorial
　　　　waters of Japan

ryôkai〈りょうかい：了解〉understanding, comprehension, consent.
　　ryôkai-ga-tsuku（了解が付く）come to an understanding ((with))
　　ryôkai o uru（了解を得る）obtain ((a person's)) consent
　　ryôkai-suru〈了解する〉understand, comprehend, see, grasp.
　　ryôkai-shi-gatai〈了解し難い〉difficult to understand, incomprehensible.

ryokaku〈りょかく：旅客〉a passenger, a traveler.
　　ryokakki（旅客機）a passenger plane

ryokan〈りょかん：旅館〉an inn, a hotel.
　　ryokan-ni tomaru（旅館に泊まる）put up at an inn

ryôke〈りょうけ：良家〉a good family.
　　ryôke-no-de-de-aru（良家の出である）come of a good family

ryoken〈りょけん：旅券〉a passport.
　　ryoken-o-shinsei-suru（旅券を申請する）apply for a passport

ryôken〈りょうけん：料けん〉an idea, a thought, a design, an intention,
　　a motive, a decision.
　　warui-ryôken　o　okosu（悪い料けんを起こす）conceive an evil

    intention

    Ittai-dô-iu-ryôken-da? (一体どういう料けんだ.) What on earth is your intention?

    Kare-wa ryôken-ga-semai. (彼は料けんが狭い.) He is narrow-minded.

    Sore-wa o-mae-no-ryôken-shidai-da. (それはお前の料けん次第だ.) That is up to you.

    O-mae-no-ryôken-chigai-da. (お前の料けん違いだ.) You are mistaken.

ryôken 〈りょうけん：猟犬〉a hunting dog, a hound, a hunter.

ryôki 〈りょうき：猟期〉a shooting(*or* hunting) season, an open season.

ryôkin 〈りょうきん：料金〉a charge, a rate, a fee, a fare, a toll.

    go-hyaku-en no ryôkin-de (五百円の料金で) at a charge of 500 yen

    ryôkin-chôshû-jo (料金徴収所) a tollgate

  ryôkin-o-toru 〈料金を取る〉charge, make a charge.

    san-byaku-en-no-ryôkin-o-toru (三百円の料金を取る) make a charge of 300 yen

  ryôkin-o-torazu-ni 〈料金を取らずに〉free of charge.

ryokka 〈りょっか：緑化〉

    ryokka-undô (緑化運動) a tree-planting campaign

  ryokka-suru 〈緑化する〉plant trees.

ryokô 〈りょこう：旅行〉a travel, a journey, a tour, a voyage, a trip, traveling.

    ryokô-ni-dekakeru (旅行に出掛ける) go on a tour

    ryokô-kara kaeru (旅行から帰る) return from one's jouney ((to))

    ryokô-annai (旅行案内) a traveler's handbook

    ryokô-nittei (旅行日程) an itinerary

    ryokô-sha (旅行者) a traveler, a tourist

  ryokô-suru 〈旅行する〉travel, make a tour.

    Amerika-jû-o-kumanaku-ryokô-suru (アメリカ中をくまなく旅行する) travel throughout America

  ryokô-chû 〈旅行中〉during one's journey, while on a tour.

ryôkû 〈りょうくう：領空〉territorial air.

    ryôkû-shimpan (領空侵犯) violation of territorial airspace

ryokucha 〈りょくちゃ：緑茶〉green tea.

ryokuchi 〈りょくち：緑地〉a green tract of land.

    ryokuchi-ka (緑地化) afforestation

    ryokuchi-tai (緑地帯) a green belt

ryoku-naishō 〈りょくないしょう：緑内障〉glaucoma.

ryō-kyokutan 〈りょうきょくたん：両極端〉both extremes.
    Kare-ra-no iken wa ryô-kyokutan-da. (彼らの意見は両極端だ。) Their opinions are poles apart.

ryōme 〈りょうめ：量目〉weight.
    ryôme-ga-tari-nai (量目が足りない) be short of weight
    ryôme-o-gomakasu (量目をごまかす) give short weight

ryōmen 〈りょうめん：両面〉both sides.

ryōri 〈りょうり：料理〉cooking, cookery, cuisine, a dish.
    Kanojo-wa ryôri-ga-umai. (彼女は料理がうまい。) She is a good cook.
    ryôri-nin (料理人) a cook
    ryôri-ya (料理屋) a restaurant
  ryôri-suru 〈料理する〉cook, dress.

ryōritsu 〈りょうりつ：両立〉
  ryôritsu-suru 〈両立する〉be compatible ((with)), be consistent ((with)), coexist ((with)).
    ryôritsu-shi-nai (両立しない) be incompatible ((with)), be inconsistent ((with)), do not go ((with))

ryōsai-kembo 〈りょうさいけんぼ：良妻賢母〉a good wife and worthy mother.

ryōsan 〈りょうさん：量産〉mass production.
  ryôsan-suru 〈量産する〉mass-produce.

ryōsei 〈りょうせい：両性〉both sexes.
    ryôsei no gôi (両性の合意) the mutual consent of both sexes

ryōsei 〈りょうせい：両せい〉
    ryôsei-dôbutsu (両せい動物) an amphibious animal
    ryôsei-rui (両せい類) the Amphibia

ryōsen 〈りょうせん：りょう線〉the ridge of a mountain.

ryōshi 〈りょうし：猟(漁)師〉a hunter, a huntsman, a fisherman.

ryōshiki 〈りょうしき：良識〉good sense.
    ryôshiki o hatarakasu (良識を働かす) use good sense
    ryôshiki ni kakete-iru (良識に欠けている) lack good sense

ryōshin 〈りょうしん：両親〉one's parents.

ryōshin 〈りょうしん：良心〉conscience.
    ryôshin-ni-haji-nai (良心に恥じない) have a clear conscience
    ryôshin-ga-togameru (良心がとがめる) feel a prick of conscience
  ryôshin-teki(-na) 〈良心的(な)〉conscientious.

hi-ryôshin-teki(-na)〈非良心的(な)〉 unconscientious

ryôshin-teki-ni〈良心的に〉conscientiously.

ryôshô〈りょうしょう：了承〉acknowledgment.

ryôshô-suru〈了承する〉acknowledge, understand.

ryôshû〈りょうしゅう：領収〉receipt.

ryôshû-shô〈領収証〉a receipt

ryôshû-suru〈領収する〉receive.

Kin-jû-man-en-nari masa-ni-ryôshû-itashimashita.（金十万円なり正に領収いたしました。）Received the sum of ¥100,000.

ryôte〈りょうて：両手〉both hands.

ryôte o hirogeru（両手を広げる）extend one's hands

ryôte-ni-hana（両手に花）sit between two beautiful women

ryôte-de〈両手で〉with both hands.

ryotei〈りょてい：旅程〉an itinerary; the distance to be covered.

ryôtei〈りょうてい：料亭〉a Japanese restaurant.

ryô-tembin〈りょうてんびん：両天びん〉

ryô-tembin-o-kakeru〈両天びんを掛ける〉aim at two objects at a time, sit on the fence.

ryôyaku〈りょうやく：良薬〉a good medicine.

Ryôyaku-kuchi-ni-nigashi.（良薬口に苦し.）A good medicine tastes bitter.

ryôyô〈りょうよう：療養〉(a) medical treatment.

ryôyô-jo（療養所）a sanatorium, a nursing home

ryôyô-suru〈療養する〉recruit oneself, receive medical treatment.

ryôyû〈りょうゆう：両雄〉two great men.

Ryôyû-narabi-tatazu.（両雄並び立たず.）A great man cannot brook a rival.

ryôyû〈りょうゆう：領有〉possession.

ryôyû-suru〈領有する〉possess, be in possession ((of)).

ryû〈りゅう：竜〉a dragon.

-ryû〈-りゅう：-流〉

Nihon-ryû-no-mono-no-kangae-kata（日本流の物の考え方）a Japanese way of thinking

Amerika-ryû-ni（アメリカ流に）in American style

Sôgetsu-ryû（早月流）the Sogetsu school

ryûboku〈りゅうぼく：流木〉driftwood.

ryûchi〈りゅうち：留置〉detention.

ryûchi-jô（留置場）a detention ward

ryûchi-suru〈留置する〉detain, lock up, hold.

ryûchô〈りゅうちょう：流ちょう〉fluency.

　ryûchô-na〈流ちょうな〉fluent.

　ryûchô-ni〈流ちょうに〉fluently.

ryûdan〈りゅうだん：りゅう弾〉a howitzer shell.

　　ryûdan-hô（りゅう弾砲）　a howitzer

ryûdô〈りゅうどう：流動〉a flow, floating.

　　ryûdô-shisan（流動資産）　floating assets

　　ryûdô-shoku（流動食）liquid food, a liquid diet

　　ryûdô-sei（流動性）　liquidity, fluidity

　ryûdô-suru〈流動する〉flow, float, be liquid.

ryûgaku〈りゅうがく：留学〉studying abroad.

　　ryûgaku-sei（留学生）　a student studying abroad

　ryûgaku-suru〈留学する〉study abroad, go abroad for study.

　ryûgaku-chû〈留学中〉during one's stay ((in...to study...)).

ryûgen〈りゅうげん：流言〉

　ryûgen o tobasu〈流言を飛ばす〉circulate a false rumor.

ryûgi〈りゅうぎ：流儀〉a school, a fashion, a style, a way, a manner.

　　jibun-no ryûgi-de（自分の流儀で）　in one's own way

　〜-no-ryûgi-de〈〜の流儀で〉after the fashion of... , in the style of... .

ryûha〈りゅうは：流派〉a school.

ryûho〈りゅうほ：留保〉reservation.

　ryûho-suru〈留保する〉reserve.

　　kenri o ryûho-suru（権利を留保する）　reserve the right ((to do))

ryûhyô〈りゅうひょう：流氷〉floating ice, an ice floe.

ryûi〈りゅうい：留意〉

　ryûi-suru〈留意する〉give consideration ((to)), pay attention ((to)).

ryûiki〈りゅういき：流域〉a basin, a valley.

　　Yôsu-kô-ryûiki（揚子江流域）　the Yangtze valley

ryûin〈りゅういん：りゅう飲〉

　ryûin-ga-sagaru〈りゅう飲が下がる〉feel great satisfaction ((at *or* over)).

　ryûin-o-sageru〈りゅう飲を下げる〉satisfy oneself ((by)).

ryûka-butsu〈りゅうかぶつ：硫化物〉a sulfide.

ryûkai〈りゅうかい：流会〉

　ryûkai-ni-naru〈流会になる〉be adjourned, be called off.

ryûkan〈りゅうかん：流感〉influenza, (the) flu(e).

　　ryûkan-ni-kakaru（流感にかかる）　get the flu

ryûketsu〈りゅうけつ：流血〉

　　ryûketsu-no-sanji〈流血の惨事〉a bloodshedding affair

　　ryûketsu-o-mizu-ni〈流血を見ずに〉without bloodshed.

ryûki〈りゅうき：隆起〉upheaval.

　ryûki-suru〈隆起する〉upheave.

ryukku(-sakku)〈リュック(サック)〉a rucksack, a knapsack.

ryûkô〈りゅうこう：流行〉(a) fashion, (the) vogue, popularity, a craze, a
　fad, a rage.

　　Ryûkô wa kuri-kaesu.〈流行は繰り返す。〉 Fashion repeats itself.

　　saishin-no ryûkô〈最新の流行〉the latest fashion

　　ryûkô-shite-kuru〈流行してくる〉come into fashion

　　ryûkô-shinaku-naru〈流行しなくなる〉go out of fashion

　　ryûkô o ou〈流行を追う〉follow the fashion

　　ryûkô-ni-okureru〈流行に後れる〉be behind the fashion

　　ryûkô-ka〈流行歌〉a popular song

　ryûkô-shite-iru or *ryûkô-suru*〈流行している，流行する〉be in fashion, be
　　in vogue, be popular.

　ryûkô-okure-no〈流行後れの〉old-fashioned, outmoded, out of fashion.

ryûkotsu〈りゅうこつ：竜骨〉the keel.

Ryûkyû〈りゅうきゅう：りゅう球〉Ryukyu.

　Ryûkyû-no〈りゅう球の〉Ryukyuan.

ryûmachi〈リューマチ〉rheumatism.

　　ryûmachi-ga-okoru（リューマチが起こる）have an attack of rheu-
　　matism

　　ryûmachi-ni-nayamu（リューマチに悩む）suffer from rheumatism

　　mansei-ryûmachi（慢性リューマチ）chronic rheumatism

　　ryûmachi-kanja（リューマチ患者）a rheumatic

ryûnen〈りゅうねん：留年〉

　ryûnen-suru〈留年する〉stay for another year in the same class.

ryûnin〈りゅうにん：留任〉

　ryûnin-suru〈留任する〉stay in office.

ryûryû〈りゅうりゅう：隆々〉

　kinkotsu-ryûryû-taru〈筋骨隆々たる〉muscular.

ryûryû〈りゅうりゅう：粒々〉

　ryûryû-shinku-suru〈粒々辛苦する〉toil and moil ((at)).

ryûsan〈りゅうさん：硫酸〉sulfuric acid.

ryûsei〈りゅうせい：流星〉a shooting star, a meteor.

ryûsei〈りゅうせい：隆盛〉prosperity.

　ryûsei-o-kiwameru〈隆盛を極める〉be in full prosperity.

ryûsen-kei〈りゅうせんけい：流線形〉a streamline shape.

　ryûsen-kei-no〈流線形の〉streamline(d).

ryûshi〈りゅうし：粒子〉a particle.

ryûshitsu〈りゅうしつ：流失〉

　ryûshitsu-suru〈流失する〉be washed away.

ryûshutsu〈りゅうしゅつ：流出〉(an) outflow.

　　　kin no ryûshutsu（金の流出）the outflow of gold

　　　zunô-no ryûshutsu（頭脳の流出）the brain drain

　ryûshutsu-suru〈流出する〉flow out, run out.

ryûtô-dabi〈りゅうとうだび：竜頭蛇尾〉an anticlimax.

　　　ryûtô-dabi-ni-owaru（竜頭蛇尾に終わる）end in an anticlimax

ryûtsû〈りゅうつう：流通〉circulation, currency, negotiation, distribution; ventilation.

　　　ryûtsû-kahei（流通貨幣）circulating money

　　　ryûtsû-kakumei（流通革命）a distribution revolution

　　　ryûtsû-shôken（流通証券）a negotiable document

　　　kûki-no-ryûtsû-ga-ii（空気の流通がいい）be well ventilated

　ryûtsû-suru〈流通する〉circulate, float; ventilate.

ryûyô〈りゅうよう：流用〉(a) diversion.

　ryûyô-suru〈流用する〉divert.

　　　kôkin o ryûyô-suru（公金を流用する）misappropriate public funds

ryûzan〈りゅうざん：流産〉(an) abortion.

　ryûzan-suru〈流産する〉have a miscarriage, miscarry, fall through.

ryûzu〈りゅうず：竜頭〉a crown, a stem.

　　　ryûzu o hiki-dasu（竜頭を引き出す）pull out the crown

S

sa〈さ：差〉(a) difference.

　sa-ga-aru〈差がある〉there is a difference ((between)), it differs.

　　　sa-ga-nai〈差がない〉it makes no difference

sâ〈さあ〉come now, now, here, well, let me see.
　　　Sâ koi!〈さあ来い.〉Come on!

saba〈さば〉a mackerel.
　saba-o-yomu〈さばを読む〉cheat ((a person)) in counting.

sabaketa〈さばけた〉
　　　sabaketa hito〈さばけた人〉a man of the world

sabaki〈さばき：裁き〉judgment, decision.
　sabaki-o-ukeru〈裁きを受ける〉be judged, be tried.

sabaku〈さばく：砂漠〉a desert.

sabaku〈さばく：裁く〉judge, decide.

sabaku〈さばく〉sell; deal ((with)), handle.
　　　goro-o sabaku〈ゴロをさばく〉field a grounder

sabasaba〈さばさば〉
　sabasaba-suru〈さばさばする〉feel refreshed, feel relieved.

sabetsu〈さべつ：差別〉(a) distinction, (a) discrimination.
　　　sabetsu-taigû-suru〈差別待遇する〉treat ((a person)) with dis-
　　　　　crimination
　sabetsu-suru〈差別する〉differentiate.
　sabetsu-teki(-na)〈差別的(な)〉discriminative, prejudiced.
　sabetsu-naku〈差別なく〉without discrimination.

sabi〈さび〉rust.
　sabi ga tsuku or *sabiru*〈さびが付く，さびる〉rust, get rusty.
　　　sabi-o-otosu *or* sabi-o-toru〈さびを落とす，さびを取る〉remove the
　　　　　rust
　sabi-tsuita or *sabita*〈さび付いた，さびた〉rusty, rusted.
　sabi-dome-no〈さび止めの〉rustproof.

sabireru〈さびれる：寂れる〉become desolate.
　sabireta〈寂れた〉desolate.
　　　sabireta mura〈寂れた村〉a desolate village

sabishii〈さびしい：寂しい〉lonely, lonesome; feel lonely, miss.
　　　sabishii tokoro〈寂しい所〉a lonely place
　　　Kimi-ga-inakute-sabishii.〈君がいなくて寂しい.〉I miss you.

sabishi-sa〈さびしさ：寂しさ〉loneliness.

sâbisu〈サービス〉service.
　　　sâbisu-gyô〈サービス業〉a service industry
　　　sâbisu-ryô〈サービス料〉a service charge
　sâbisu-suru〈サービスする〉give one's service, attend ((on)).

sabô 〈さぼう：砂防〉 sand erosion control, sandbank fixing.
  sabô-kôji (砂防工事) sand guard work, anti-sand erosion work
  sabô-rin (砂防林) an erosion control forest
saboru 〈さぼる〉 loaf ((on)), play truant ((from)), cut.
  shigoto o saboru (仕事をさぼる) loaf on the job
saboten 〈サボテン〉 a cactus.
sâbu 〈サーブ〉 a service, a serve.
  sâbu o ukeru (サーブを受ける) receive the service
  sâbu-suru 〈サーブする〉 serve [a ball].
sachi 〈さち：幸〉
  Sachi-are-kashi-to-inorimasu. (幸あれかしと祈ります.) I wish you good luck.
sadamaru 〈さだまる：定まる〉 be fixed, be settled.
  sadamara-nai tenkô (定まらない天候) unsettled weather
sadameru 〈さだめる：定める〉 decide, fix; establish.
sadameshi 〈さだめし：定めし〉 surely.
  Go-ryôshin wa sadameshi-o-yorokobi-no-koto-de-shô. (御両親は定めしお喜びのことでしょう.) Your parents must be very glad (of it).
sae 〈さえ〉
  atama-no-sae (頭のさえ) keen intelligence
  ude-no sae o miseru (腕のさえを見せる) show one's skill ((in))
-sae 〈さえ〉 even, (if) only.
  kodomo-de-sae (子供でさえ) even a child
  jikan-sae-areba (時間さえあれば) if only one had time, whenever one has time to spare
  koko-ni suwatte-i-sae-sureba-ii (ここに座っていさえすればいい) have only to sit down here
saegiru 〈さえぎる：遮る〉 interrupt, obstruct, block, intercept.
  michi o saegiru (道を遮る) block the way
  kôsen o saegiru (光線を遮る) intercept the light
saeru 〈さえる〉 be clear, be serene.
  me-ga-saeru (目がさえる) be wakeful
  Tsuki ga saete-iru. (月がさえている.) The moon shines brightly.
  kibun-ga-sae-nai (気分がさえない) be in the blues
  saeta 〈さえた〉 clear, bright.
  saeta ne-iro (さえた音色) a clear tone
  saeta iro (さえた色) a bright color
  saeta yo-zora (さえた夜空) a keenly cold night sky

saezuri 〈さえずり〉 a chirp, a twitter.
saezuru 〈さえずる〉 sing, chirp, twitter.

sâfin 〈サーフィン〉 surfing, surf-riding.

sagaku 〈さがく：差額〉 the difference, the balance.
　　bôeki no sagaku（貿易の差額） the balance of trade

sagaru 〈さがる：下がる〉 hang (down); fall, drop, go down; step back.
　　Ondo ga sagatta.（温度が下がった。） The temperature has gone down.
　　ippo sagaru（一歩下がる） take a step backward

sagashi-mono 〈さがしもの：捜し物〉
sagashi-mono-o-suru〈捜し物をする〉look for something.

sagasu 〈さがす：捜(探)す〉look ((for)), search ((for)), seek ((for)).
　　shigoto-guchi o sagasu（仕事口を探す） hunt for a job
sagashi-dasu〈捜(探)し出す〉look up, find out, discover.
　　jisho-de go o sagashi-dasu（辞書で語を探し出す） look up a word in a dictionary
sagashi-mawaru〈捜(探)し回る〉look about for ((a thing)).

sagen 〈さげん：左げん〉 the port.

sageru 〈さげる：下げる〉 hang, drop, wear, lower.
　　kunshô o sageru（勲章を下げる） wear a decoration
　　atama o sageru（頭を下げる） lower one's head
　　nedan o sageru（値段を下げる） lower the price

sagi 〈さぎ〉 a heron.

sagi 〈さぎ：詐欺〉 (a) fraud, a swindle.
　　sagi-shi（詐欺師） a swindler
sagi-o-hataraku〈詐欺を働く〉swindle, shark.

saguri 〈さぐり：探り〉
saguri-o-ireru〈探りを入れる〉feel out, sound.

saguri-dasu 〈さぐりだす：探り出す〉 spy out, smell out.

saguru 〈さぐる：探る〉 search, look ((for)), grope ((after *or* for)), feel ((after *or* for)).

sagyô 〈さぎょう：作業〉 work.
　　sagyô-fuku（作業服） working clothes, overalls
　　sagyô-jikan（作業時間） working hours
　　sagyô-chû(-ni)（作業中(に)） while at work

saha 〈さは：左派〉 the left wing, the left faction, the leftists.
saha-no〈左派の〉left-wing, leftist.

sahan-ji 〈さはんじ：茶飯事〉a matter of no importance.

　　　nichijô-sahan-ji〈日常茶飯事〉 an everyday occurrence

sahô〈さほう：作法〉 manners, etiquette.

　　　sahô-o-shira-nai〈作法を知らない〉 have no manners

sahodo~(-de-nai)〈さほど～（でない）〉((not)) so, ((not)) much, ((not)) very, ((not)) particularly.

sai〈さい〉 a rhinoceros.

sai〈さい：差異〉 (a) difference.

sai〈さい：才〉 *see.* sainô.

sai〈さい〉 a die.

　　　sai o furu〈さいを振る〉 cast dice

　　　Sai wa nagerareta!〈さいは投げられた．〉 The die is cast!

　　　sai-no-me-ni-kiru〈さいの目に切る〉 cut into dice

sai〈さい：際〉 the time, when.

　　　kono-sai〈この際〉 at this time, at this juncture

　　　hitsuyô-no-sai-ni-wa〈必要の際には〉 in case of need

sai-〈さい-：再-〉 re-.

sai-〈さい-：最-〉 the most, the extreme.

-sai〈-さい：-歳〉 age, years.

　　　Nan-sai-desu-ka?〈何歳ですか．〉 How old are you?

　　　Jussai-desu.〈十歳です．〉 I am ten years old.

　　　jû-ni-sai-no shôjo〈十二歳の少女〉 a twelve-year-old girl

　　　go-sai-no-toki-ni〈五歳の時に〉 at the age of five

saiai〈さいあい：最愛〉

　saiai-no〈最愛の〉 dearest, beloved.

saiaku(-no)〈さいあく（の）：最悪（の）〉 the worst.

　　　saiaku-no baai-niwa〈最悪の場合には〉 in the worst case

saibai〈さいばい：栽培〉 cultivation, raising, growing.

　saibai-suru〈栽培する〉 cultivate, raise, grow.

saiban〈さいばん：裁判〉 a trial, judgment.

　　　saiban ni katsu〈裁判に勝つ〉 win a suit

　　　saiban ni makeru〈裁判に負ける〉 lose a suit

　　　saiban-kan〈裁判官〉 a judge

　　　saiban-chô〈裁判長〉 the chief judge

　　　saiban-sho〈裁判所〉 a court of law, a law court

　saiban-o-okonau〈裁判を行う〉 try, judge.

　saiban-o-ukeru〈裁判を受ける〉 be tried.

　saiban-zata-ni-suru〈裁判ざたにする〉 take ((a case)) into court.

　　　saiban-zata-ni-narazu-ni　kaiketsu-suru　〈裁判ざたにならずに解決する〉

　　　be settled out of court

sai-bashiru 〈さいばしる：才走る〉be cleverish.

saibetsu 〈さいべつ：細別〉subdivision.

　saibetsu-suru 〈細別する〉subdivide.

saibô 〈さいぼう：細胞〉a cell.

　　saibô-bunretsu（細胞分裂）　cell division

saibu 〈さいぶ：細部〉details.

　　saibu-ni-watatte-chôsa-suru（細部にわたって調査する）　go into details

saibun-ka 〈さいぶんか：細分化〉diversification.

　saibun-ka-suru 〈細分化する〉diversify.

saichi 〈さいち：才知〉wit, intelligence.

　saichi-no-aru 〈才知のある〉witty, intelligent.

sai-chôsa 〈さいちょうさ：再調査〉reexamination, reinvestigation.

　sai-chôsa-suru 〈再調査する〉reexamine, reinvestigate.

saichû 〈さいちゅう：最中〉

　saichû-ni 〈最中に〉in the middle ((of)), in the course ((of)).

sai-chûmon 〈さいちゅうもん：再注文〉a repeat order.

saidâ 〈サイダー〉a soda pop.

saidai 〈さいだい：細大〉

　saidai-morasazu hôkoku-suru 〈細大漏らさず報告する〉explain　((an　affair))
　　to the minute detail.

saidai(-no) 〈さいだい（の）：最大（の）〉the　largest,　the　biggest,　the
　　greatest.

saidai-gen(do) 〈さいだいげん（ど）：最大限（度）〉the maximun.

　saidai-gen-no 〈最大限の〉maximum.

saidan 〈さいだん：祭壇〉an altar.

saidan 〈さいだん：裁断〉cutting.

　　saidan-shi（裁断師）　a cutter

　saidan-suru 〈裁断する〉cut.

saien 〈さいえん：再演〉a repeat performance.

　saien-suru 〈再演する〉stage ((a play)) again.

saien 〈さいえん：菜園〉a vegetable garden.

saifu 〈さいふ：財布〉a purse, a pocketbook, a wallet.

　　saifu-no-himo　o　shimeru（財布のひもを締める）　tighten　the　purse
　　strings

saigai 〈さいがい：災害〉(a) disaster, a calamity.

　　saigai-o-ukeru（災害を受ける）　suffer from a disaster

　　saigai-chi（災害地）　a stricken district

saigen 〈さいげん：際限〉 limits, an end.
　　saigen-ga-nai〈際限がない〉 there is no end
　saigen-no-nai〈際限のない〉 limitless, endless.
　saigen-naku〈際限なく〉 endlessly, boundlessly.
saigen 〈さいげん：再現〉 reappearance, (a) reproduction ((of)).
saigetsu 〈さいげつ：歳月〉 time, years.
　　saigetsu-ga-tatsu-ni-tsurete〈歳月がたつにつれて〉 as time passes on
　　Saigetsu hito-o-matazu.〈歳月人を待たず。〉 Time and tide wait for
　　no man.
saigi(-shin) 〈さいぎ（しん）：さい疑（心）〉 suspicion, jealousy.
　saigi-shin-ga-tsuyoi〈さい疑心が強い〉 be of a suspicious nature.
sai-gimmi 〈さいぎんみ：再吟味〉 (a) reexamination.
　sai-gimmi-suru〈再吟味する〉 reexamine, review.
saigo 〈さいご：最後〉 the last, the end.
　saigo-no〈最後の〉 last, final.
　saigo-ni〈最後に〉 lastly, in conclusion, in the end.
　saigo-made〈最後まで〉 to the last, to the end.
saigo 〈さいご：最期〉 one's last moment, one's death, one's end.
　　hisan-na saigo-o-togeru〈悲惨な最期を遂げる〉 meet a tragic end
sai-gumbi 〈さいぐんび：再軍備〉 rearmament.
　sai-gumbi-suru〈再軍備する〉 rearm ((itself)).
saihai 〈さいはい：さい配〉
　saihai-o-furu〈さい配を振る〉 direct, have the command ((of)), lead, take
　the management ((of)).
sai-hakkô 〈さいはっこう：再発行〉
　sai-hakkô-suru〈再発行する〉 reissue.
saihan 〈さいはん：再版〉 a second edition.
saihan-kakaku 〈さいはんかかく：再販価格〉 resale price.
saihatsu 〈さいはつ：再発〉 relapse, return, recurrence.
　saihatsu-suru〈再発する〉 relapse, have a second attack ((of)), return,
　recur.
sai-hensei 〈さいへんせい：再編成〉 reorganization.
　sai-hensei-suru〈再編成する〉 reorganize.
saihô 〈さいほう：裁縫〉 sewing, needlework, tailoring.
　saihô-suru〈裁縫する〉 sew, do needlework.
sai-hôsô 〈さいほうそう：再放送〉
　sai-hôsô-suru〈再放送する〉 rebroadcast.
sai-hyôka 〈さいひょうか：再評価〉 revaluation, reassessment.

sai-hyôka-suru〈再評価する〉revaluate, reassess.

saihyô-sen〈さいひょうせん：砕氷船〉an icebreaker.

saijitsu〈さいじつ：祭日〉a national holiday, a festival day.

saijô〈さいじょう：斎場〉a funeral hall.

saijô(-no)〈さいじょう(の)：最上(の)〉the best.

sai-jôei〈さいじょうえい：再上映〉a rerun.

sai-jôei-suru〈再上映する〉rerun.

sai-kai〈さいかい：最下位〉the lowest rank, the cellar.

　　sai-kai-ni tenraku-suru（最下位に転落する）tumble down into the cellar

saikai〈さいかい：再開〉

saikai-suru〈再開する〉reopen, resume.

saikai〈さいかい：再会〉

saikai-suru〈再会する〉meet ((a person)) again.

sai-kakunin〈さいかくにん：再確認〉reaffirmation, reconfirmation.

sai-kakunin-suru〈再確認する〉reaffirm, reconfirm.

saike-chô〈サイケちょう：サイケ調〉

saike-chô-no〈サイケ調の〉psychedelic.

saikei-koku〈さいけいこく：最恵国〉a most favored nation.

sai-keirei〈さいけいれい：最敬礼〉

sai-keirei-suru〈最敬礼する〉make a deep bow ((to)).

saiken〈さいけん：債券〉a (loan) bond, a debenture.

　　saiken o hakkô-suru（債券を発行する） issue bonds

saiken〈さいけん：債権〉credit, a claim.

　　Watashi-wa kare-ni saiken-ga-aru.（私は彼に債権がある。）I have a claim against him.

　　saiken-sha（債権者）a creditor

saiken〈さいけん：再建〉reconstruction, rebuilding.

saiken-suru〈再建する〉reconstruct, rebuild.

sai-kentô〈さいけんとう：再検討〉reexamination.

sai-kentô-suru〈再検討する〉reexamine.

saiketsu〈さいけつ：裁決〉(a) decision, (a) judgment.

　　saiketsu-o-aogu（裁決を仰ぐ）ask for ((the president's)) decision

saiketsu-suru〈裁決する〉decide, give one's decision ((on)).

saiketsu〈さいけつ：採決〉a vote.

saiketsu-suru〈採決する〉vote ((on)), take a vote ((on)).

saiki〈さいき：才気〉

saiki-kampatsu-na〈才気かん発な〉brilliant, very clever, of great

resources.

saiki 〈さいき：再起〉a comeback, recovery, restoration.

  saiki-suru 〈再起する〉come back, recover, be restored.

  saiki-funô-de-aru 〈再起不能である〉be beyond hope of recovery.

saikin 〈さいきん：細菌〉a bacillus, a bacterium, a germ.

saikin 〈さいきん：最近〉recently, lately.

    saikin-made（最近まで）up to recently

        tsui saikin-made（つい最近まで）till quite recently

  saikin-no 〈最近の〉the latest.

saikō 〈さいこう：採光〉lighting.

  saikô-no-ii 〈採光のいい〉well-lighted.

saikō 〈さいこう：再考〉reconsideration.

  saikô-suru 〈再考する〉reconsider, think over again.

saikō 〈さいこう：再興〉revival, restoration.,

  saikô-suru 〈再興する〉revive, restore.

saikō 〈さいこう：採鉱〉mining.

  saikô-suru 〈採鉱する〉mine.

saikō(-no) 〈さいこう（の）：最高（の）〉the highest, the supreme.

    saikô-saiban-sho（最高裁判所）the Supreme Court

    saikô-ten（最高点）the highest marks, the largest poll

    sekai-no saikô-hô（世界の最高峰）the highest mountain in the world

sai-kōchō 〈さいこうちょう：最高潮〉the climax, the peak.

    sai-kôchô ni tassuru（最高潮に達する）reach the climax

sai-kōfu 〈さいこうふ：再交付〉

  sai-kôfu-suru 〈再交付する〉reissue.

saikon 〈さいこん：再婚〉a second marriage, remarriage.

  saikon-suru 〈再婚する〉marry again.

saikoro 〈さいころ〉a die.

    saikoro o furu（さいころを振る）*see.* sai o furu

saiku 〈さいく：細工〉work, a handiwork.

  saiku-suru 〈細工する〉work ((in *or* on)).

saikuringu 〈サイクリング〉cycling.

    saikuringu-ni-iku（サイクリングに行く）go cycling

saikutsu 〈さいくつ：採掘〉mining.

  saikutsu-suru 〈採掘する〉mine, work.

sai-kyōiku 〈さいきょういく：再教育〉reeducation.

  sai-kyôiku-suru 〈再教育する〉reeducate.

saimatsu 〈さいまつ：歳末〉the end of the year, the year-end.

saimatsu-oo-uridashi〈歳末大売り出し〉a special year-end sale

saimin-jutsu〈さいみんじゅつ：催眠術〉hypnotism, mesmerism.
saimin-jutsu-o-kakeru〈催眠術をかける〉hypnotize, mesmerize.

saimoku〈さいもく：細目〉details, items.

saimu〈さいむ：債務〉a debt, an obligation, liabilities.
saimu-ga-aru〈債務がある〉be in ((a person's)) debt
saimu o seisan-suru〈債務を清算する〉clear up one's debts
saimu-fu-rikô〈債務不履行〉default of obligations

sain〈サイン〉a sign, a signal, a signature, an autograph.
sain-chô〈サイン帳〉an autograph book
sain-suru〈サインする〉sign one's name ((on *or* to)).
sain-o-okuru〈サインを送る〉signal, motion.

sainan〈さいなん：災難〉(a) misfortune, (a) disaster, an accident.
sainan ni au〈災難に遭う〉meet a misfortune
sainan o manukareru〈災難を免れる〉escape a disaster
furyo-no sainan〈不慮の災難〉an unforeseen accident

sainen〈さいねん：再燃〉recrudescence.
sainen-suru〈再燃する〉come to the fore again.

sai-ninshiki〈さいにんしき：再認識〉
sai-ninshiki-suru〈再認識する〉have a new understanding ((of)).

sainô〈さいのう：才能〉talent, ability, capability.
sainô o hakki-suru〈才能を発揮する〉show one's ability
umare-nagara-no sainô o nobasu〈生まれながらの才能を伸ばす〉
develop one's natural ability
sainô-no-aru〈才能のある〉talented, able, capable.
sainô-no-nai〈才能のない〉talentless, incapable.

sainyû〈さいにゅう：歳入〉(annual) revenue.

sairai〈さいらい：再来〉a second advent.
Kirisuto no sairai〈キリストの再来〉the Second Advent of Christ
sairai-suru〈再来する〉come again.

sairen〈サイレン〉a siren.
sairen o narasu〈サイレンを鳴らす〉blow a siren

sairui〈さいるい：催涙〉
sairui-dan〈催涙弾〉a tear(-gas) bomb
sairui-gasu〈催涙ガス〉tear gas

sairyô〈さいりょう：裁量〉discretion.
jibun-jishin-no sairyô-de〈自分自身の裁量で〉at one's own discretion
〜-no-sairyô-ni makasu〈〜の裁量に任す〉leave ((a matter)) to ((a

person's)) discretion

sairyô 〈さいりょう：最良〉

sairyô-no 〈最良の〉 the best.

　sairyô-no hôhô (最良の方法)　the best way

saisaki 〈さいさき：さい先〉 an omen.

　Koitsu-wa saisaki-ga ii. (こいつはさい先がいい.) This is a good start.

saisan 〈さいさん：採算〉 profit.

　dokuritsu-saisan-sei (独立採算制)　a self-supporting system

saisan-ga-toreru 〈採算がとれる〉 be profitable, pay.

　saisan-ga-tore-nai (採算がとれない)　be unprofitable, do not pay

saisan 〈さいさん：再三〉 again and again.

　saisan-saishi (再三再四)　over and over again

saisei 〈さいせい：再生〉 reclamation, regeneration, reproduction.

　saisei-gomu (再生ゴム)　reclaimed rubber

saisei-suru 〈再生する〉 reclaim, regenerate, reproduce.

　rokuon-têpu o saisei-suru (録音テープを再生する) play back the recorded tape

saisei-ki 〈さいせいき：最盛期〉 the height of prosperity, the golden age; the (peak) season.

　Mikan wa ima saisei-ki-da. (みかんは今最盛期だ.) Oranges are now in season.

saiseki 〈さいせき：採石〉 quarrying.

　saiseki-jô (採石場)　a quarry

saisen 〈さいせん：さい銭〉 a money offering.

　saisen o ageru (さい銭をあげる)　make a money offering ((to))

　saisen-bako (さい銭箱)　an offertory chest

saisen 〈さいせん：再選〉 reelection.

saisen-sareru 〈再選される〉 be reelected, win reelection.

sai-senkyo 〈さいせんきょ：再選挙〉

sai-senkyo-suru 〈再選挙する〉 hold a reelection, hold a recall election.

sai-shi 〈さいし：妻子〉 one's wife and child(ren), one's family.

　sai-shi o yashinau (妻子を養う)　support one's family

sai-shiken 〈さいしけん：再試験〉 (a) reexamination.

　sai-shiken o ukeru (再試験を受ける)　take a reexamination

sai-shiken-suru 〈再試験する〉 reexamine, examine again.

saishiki 〈さいしき：彩色〉

saishiki-suru 〈彩色する〉 color, paint.

saishin 〈さいしん：再審〉(a) renewal of procedure, a retrial, a new trial, (a) review.

saishin o meizuru（再審を命ずる） order a new trial

saishin-suru〈再審する〉retry, reexamine, review.

saishin 〈さいしん：細心〉

saishin-no〈細心の〉prudent.

saishin-no chûi o harau（細心の注意を払う） pay close attention ((to))

saishin 〈さいしん：最新〉

saishin-no〈最新の〉the newest, the latest, up-to-date.

sai-shinri 〈さいしんり：再審理〉*see.* saishin（再審）.

saisho 〈さいしょ：最初〉the first, the beginning.

saisho-no〈最初の〉the first, initial.

saisho-ni〈最初に〉first, at the beginning.

saisho-wa〈最初は〉at first, at the start.

saisho-kara〈最初から〉from the beginning.

saishô(-no) 〈さいしょう（の）：最小（の）〉the smallest, the least.

saishô-gen(do) 〈さいしょうげん（ど）：最小限（度）〉the minimum.

saishô-gen-ni-suru〈最小限にする〉minimize.

saishô-gen-no〈最小限の〉minimum.

saishoku 〈さいしょく：菜食〉a vegetable diet.

saishoku-shugi（菜食主義） vegetarianism

saishû 〈さいしゅう：採集〉collection, collecting, gathering.

shokubutsu-saishû（植物採集） plant collecting

saishû-suru〈採集する〉collect, gather.

saishû(-no) 〈さいしゅう（の）：最終（の）〉the last, the final.

saishû-kai（最終回） the last inning, the last round

saishû-ressha（最終列車） the last train

sai-shuppatsu 〈さいしゅっぱつ：再出発〉

sai-shuppatsu-suru〈再出発する〉make a fresh start.

saishutsu 〈さいしゅつ：歳出〉(annual) expenditure.

saisoku 〈さいそく：催促〉

saisoku-suru〈催促する〉press ((a person)) for, urge ((a person to do)).

sai-soshiki 〈さいそしき：再組織〉reorganization.

sai-soshiki-suru〈再組織する〉reorganize.

saitai-sha 〈さいたいしゃ：妻帯者〉a married man.

saitaku 〈さいたく：採択〉

saitaku-suru〈採択する〉adopt.

saitan 〈さいたん：採炭〉coal mining.

saitan-suru 〈採炭する〉 mine coal.

saitan 〈さいたん：最短〉
saitan-kyori （最短距離） the shortest distance
saitan-no 〈最短の〉 the shortest.

saitei 〈さいてい：裁定〉 (a) decision, a ruling, arbitration.
saitei ni shitagau （裁定に従う） obey the decision
saitei-an （裁定案） an arbitration proposal
saitei-suru 〈裁定する〉 decide.

saitei 〈さいてい：最低〉
saitei-chingin （最低賃金） the minimum wages
saitei-no 〈最低の〉 the lowest.

saiteki 〈さいてき：最適〉
saiteki-na 〈最適な〉 optimum, the most suitable, the fittest.

saiten 〈さいてん：祭典〉 a festival.

saiten 〈さいてん：採点〉 marking, scoring.
saiten-ga-amai （採点が甘い） be liberal in marking
saiten-ga-karai （採点が辛い） be severe in marking
saiten-suru 〈採点する〉 mark.

saiwai 〈さいわい：幸い〉 happiness, (good) luck, good fortune.
saiwai-ni 〈幸いに〉 happily, luckily, fortunately.

saiyô 〈さいよう：採用〉 adoption, appointment, employment.
saiyô-tsûchi （採用通知） a notification of appointment
saiyô-suru 〈採用する〉 adopt, engage, employ.

sai-yunyû 〈さいゆにゅう：再輸入〉
sai-yunyû-suru 〈再輸入する〉 reimport.

sai-yushutsu 〈さいゆしゅつ：再輸出〉
sai-yushutsu-suru 〈再輸出する〉 reexport.

saizen(-no) 〈さいぜん（の）：最善（の）〉 the best.
saizen o tsukusu （最善を尽くす） do one's best

sai-zenretsu 〈さいぜんれつ：最前列〉 the front row, the first row.

saizu 〈サイズ〉 size.
saizu ga au （サイズが合う） be one's size
saizu-ga-awa-nai （サイズが合わない） be out of one's size
saizu o hakaru （サイズを計る） take the size ((of))

saji 〈さじ〉 a spoon.
oo-saji （大さじ） a tablespoon
ko-saji （小さじ） a teaspoon
ko-saji-ippai-no-satô （小さじ一杯の砂糖） a heaping teaspoonful of

    sugar

sâji 〈サージ〉 serge.

    kon-sâji〈紺サージ〉 blue serge

sajiki 〈さじき：桟敷〉a box, a gallery, the grand tier, the dress circle; a stand.

sajin 〈さじん：砂じん〉a cloud of sand, a dust storm.

saka(-michi) 〈さか（みち）：坂（道）〉a slope.

    saka o noboru（坂を上る） go up a slope

    saka o kudaru（坂を下る） go down a slope

    nobori-zaka（上り坂） an upward slope

    kudari-zaka（下り坂） a downward slope

    yuruyaka-na saka（緩やかな坂） a gentle slope

saka-ba 〈さかば：酒場〉a bar, a saloon, a pub.

saka-dachi 〈さかだち：逆立ち〉a handstand, a headstand.

 saka-dachi-suru〈逆立ちする〉 stand on one's head, do a handstand.

saka-dai 〈さかだい：酒代〉drink money.

saka-daru 〈さかだる：酒だる〉a *sake* cask.

saka-dateru 〈さかだてる：逆立てる〉set on end, bristle up, erect.

 saka-datsu〈逆立つ〉 stand on end, bristle up.

sakaeru 〈さかえる：栄える〉prosper, flourish, thrive.

saka-gura 〈さかぐら：酒蔵〉a *sake* cellar.

sakai 〈さかい：境〉a border, a boundary.

saka-maku 〈さかまく：逆巻く〉surge, roll, rage.

    saka-maku dotō（逆巻く怒とう） rolling waves

saka-mori 〈さかもり：酒盛り〉a drinking bout, a carousal.

    saka-mori-o-suru（酒盛りをする） have a drinking bout

sakan 〈さかん：左官〉a plasterer.

sakan 〈さかん：盛ん〉

 sakan-na〈盛んな〉prosperous, flourishing; vigorous, active, lively; hearty.

 sakan-ni〈盛んに〉vigorously, actively, briskly; heartily.

    hi-ga-sakan-ni-moeteiru（火が盛んに燃えている） be burning briskly

 sakan-ni-naru〈盛んになる〉prosper, flourish, become active.

sakana 〈さかな：魚〉a fish.

    sakana-ya（魚屋） a fish dealer, a fishmonger; a fish shop

sakana 〈さかな〉a relish (taken with *sake*).

saka-nade 〈さかなで：逆なで〉

 saka-nade-suru〈逆なでする〉rub ((a person)) the wrong way.

saka-neji 〈さかねじ：逆ねじ〉
 saka-neji-o-kuwasu〈逆ねじを食わす〉retort ((against *or* on)).
saka-noboru〈さかのぼる〉go up; go back.
    kawa o saka-noboru（川をさかのぼる）go up a stream
    kako-ni saka-noboru（過去にさかのぼる）go back to the past
sakarau〈さからう：逆らう〉oppose, disobey.
    oya ni sakarau（親に逆らう）disobey one's parents
 ～*-ni-sakaratte*〈～に逆らって〉against..., contrary to... .
    kaze-ni-sakaratte（風に逆らって）in the teeth of the wind
sakari〈さかり：盛り〉the height, full bloom, prime.
    natsu no sakari-ni（夏の盛りに）in the height of summer
    hana-ga-mi-zakari-de-aru（花が見盛りである）be in full bloom
    hataraki-zakari-de-aru（働き盛りである）be in one's prime
    sakari o sugite-iru（盛りを過ぎている）be past one's prime
sakari-ba〈さかりば：盛り場〉amusement quarters.
sakasa(ma)〈さかさ（ま）：逆さ（ま）〉
 sakasama-ni〈逆さまに〉upside down.
    sakasama-ni-suru（逆さまにする）turn ((a thing)) upside down
saka-ya〈さかや：酒屋〉a *sake* dealer, a *sake* shop.
saka-yume〈さかゆめ：逆夢〉a dream which is just contrary to the
    truth.
sakazori〈さかぞり：逆ぞり〉
 sakazori-suru〈逆ぞりする〉shave against the grain.
sakazuki〈さかずき：杯〉a *sake*-cup.
    sakazuki ni sake-o-tsugu（杯に酒をつぐ）fill a cup
sake〈さけ〉a salmon.
sake〈さけ：酒〉liquor, *sake*, wine.
    sake-ga-tsuyoi（酒が強い）be a heavy drinker
    sake-ga-yowai（酒が弱い）be a light drinker
    sake-ni-you（酒に酔う）get drunk
    sake-o-yameru（酒をやめる）give up drinking
    sake-nomi（酒飲み）a drinker
    sake-guse-ga-warui（酒癖が悪い）be a vicious drunk
    sake-kusai（酒臭い）have liquor on one's breath
 sake-o-nomu〈酒を飲む〉drink.
 sake-no-ue-de〈酒の上で〉under the influence of wine.
sakebi〈さけび：叫び〉a shout, a cry, a shriek.
    tasukete-kure-to-iu-sakebi-goe（助けてくれという叫び声）a cry for

help

sakebu 〈叫ぶ〉 shout, cry, shriek.

oo-goe-de-sakebu（大声で叫ぶ） cry out

sakei 〈さけい：左傾〉

sakei-suru 〈左傾する〉 turn to the left.

sakei-shita 〈左傾した〉 left-leaning, leftist.

sake-kasu 〈さけかす：酒かす〉 *sake* lees.

sake-me 〈さけめ：裂け目〉 a tear, a crack, a fissure.

sakeru 〈さける：裂ける〉 tear, be torn.

sake-yasui（裂けやすい） tear easily

sakeru 〈さける：避ける〉 avoid, keep away ((from)).

sakerare-nai 〈避けられない〉 unavoidable, inevitable.

saki 〈さき：左記〉 the undermentioned, the following.

saki-no-toori 〈左記のとおり〉 as undermentioned, as follows.

saki 〈さき：先〉 a tip, an end, a point; ahead, beyond, off; the future; the first; beforehand; earlier than, before; previously; a destination.

yubi no saki（指の先） the tip of a finger, a fingertip

empitsu no saki（鉛筆の先） the point of a pencil

saki-ni-tatte-aruku（先に立って歩く） walk ahead ((of a person))

sugu-saki-ni（すぐ先に） right ahead

Kare-wa kyôkai-no-san-gen-saki-ni sunde-iru.（彼は教会の三軒先に住んでいる.） He lives three doors beyond the church.

Sono tatemono wa ni-kiro-saki-desu.（その建物はニキロ先です.） The building is two kilometers off.

Kono shigoto wa saki-ga-shirete-iru.（この仕事は先が知れている.） This work has no future.

kore-kara-saki（これから先） from now on, in (the) future

Rieki ga nani-yori-saki-da.（利益が何より先だ.） Gain is the first requisite.

Watashi-no-hô-ga kare-yori-saki-ni soko-e tsuita.（私の方が彼より先にそこへ着いた.） I got there earlier than he.

saki-ni kane-o-harau（先に金を払う） pay in advance

saki-ni nobeta-yô-ni（先に述べたように） as previously stated

saki-e tsuite-kara（先へ着いてから） when I get there

saki-barai 〈さきばらい：先払い〉

saki-barai-suru 〈先払いする〉 pay in advance.

unchin-saki-barai-de 〈運賃先払いで〉 carriage forward, freight forward, freight to collect.

saki-bashiru 〈さきばしる：先走る〉 be too hasty in ((doing)).

saki-boso 〈さきぼそ：先細〉

saki-boso-no 〈先細の〉 tapering.

saki-bosori 〈さきぼそり：先細り〉

saki-bosori-suru 〈先細りする〉 taper off, peter out.

saki-bure 〈さきぶれ：先触れ〉 a previous notice.

saki-buto 〈さきぶと：先太〉

saki-buto-no 〈先太の〉 claviform, club-shaped.

sakidatsu 〈さきだつ：先立つ〉

Sakidatsu-mono wa kane. 〈先立つものは金.〉 Money is the first consideration.

oya-ni-sakidatsu 〈親に先立つ〉 die before one's parents

shuppatsu-ni-sakidachi 〈出発に先立ち〉 prior to one's departure

saki-dori 〈さきどり：先取り〉

saki-dori-suru 〈先取りする〉 receive in advance; anticipate.

saki-gake 〈さきがけ：先駆け〉 a herald, the lead.

haru no saki-gake 〈春の先駆け〉 a harbinger of spring

saki-gake-o-suru 〈先駆けをする〉 herald, be the first ((to do)), take the lead ((in)).

ryûkô-no-saki-gake-o-suru 〈流行の先駆けをする〉 lead the fashion

saki-goro 〈さきごろ：先ごろ〉 the other day, some time ago.

saki-hodo 〈さきほど：先ほど〉 a little while ago, some time ago.

saki-hodo kara 〈先ほどから〉 for some time

saki-mawari 〈さきまわり：先回り〉

saki-mawari-suru 〈先回りする〉 forestall; beat ((a person)) to it.

saki-midareru 〈さきみだれる：咲き乱れる〉 bloom all over, bloom in profusion.

saki-mono 〈さきもの：先物〉 futures.

saki-mono-gai 〈先物買い〉 forward buying, speculation

sakin 〈さきん：砂金〉 gold dust, alluvial gold.

sakin-o-toru 〈砂金を採る〉 wash for gold, pan gold.

sakinzuru 〈さきんずる：先んずる〉 go ahead ((of)), forestall, get the start ((of)).

jidai-ni-sakinzuru 〈時代に先んずる〉 be ahead of the times

Sakinzureba hito-o-seisu. 〈先んずれば人を制す.〉 First come, first served.

saki-ototoi 〈さきおととい〉 three days ago.

saki-ototoshi 〈さきおととし〉 three years ago.

sakisohon〈サキソホン〉a saxophone.
    sakisohon-sôsha（サキソホン奏者）a saxophonist
sakka〈さっか：作家〉a writer, an author, a novelist.
sakkâ〈サッカー〉soccer, association football.
sakkaku〈さっかく：錯覚〉an illusion.
 sakkaku-o-okosu〈錯覚を起こす〉have an illusion.
    sakkaku-o-okosaseru（錯覚を起こさせる）produce illusions
sakkarin〈サッカリン〉saccharin.
sakki〈さっき〉*see.* saki-hodo.
sakki〈さっき：殺気〉bloodthirstiness.
 sakki-o-obiru〈殺気を帯びる〉reek of murder.
 sakki-datsu〈殺気立つ〉get excited, look ferocious.
 sakki-datta〈殺気立った〉excited.
sakkin〈さっきん：殺菌〉sterilization.
    sakkin-ryoku（殺菌力）sterilizing power
    sakkin-zai（殺菌剤）a sterilizer
 sakkin-suru〈殺菌する〉sterilize, pasteurize.
sakku〈サック〉a fingerstall, a case.
sakkyoku〈さっきょく：作曲〉musical composition.
    sakkyoku-ka（作曲家）a composer
 sakkyoku-suru〈作曲する〉compose.
sakoku〈さこく：鎖国〉national isolation.
 sakoku-suru〈鎖国する〉close the country to foreigners.
sakotsu〈さこつ：さ骨〉the collarbone.
saku〈さく：策〉a plan, a scheme, a policy, a step, a measure.
    banzen-no saku o kôziru（万全の策を講じる）take a safe plan
    saku-ga-tsukiru（策が尽きる）be at one's wits' end, be at the end of one's resources
    Saku-no-hodokoshi-yô-ga nai.（策の施しようがない.）There is nothing to be done.
saku〈さく〉a fence.
 saku-de-kakomu〈さくで囲む〉fence up.
saku〈さく：作〉a work; a harvest, a crop.
    Matsumoto-saku-no-shôsetsu（松本作の小説）a novel written by Mr. Matsumoto
    heinen-saku（平年作）an average crop
saku〈さく：裂（割）く〉tear; spare.
    zuta-zuta-ni-saku（ずたずたに裂く）tear into shreds

jikan o saku（時間を割く）spare time ((for))

saku〈さく：咲く〉bloom, come out, open.

saite-iru（咲いている）be in bloom, be out, be open

sakuban〈さくばん：昨晩〉last evening, last night.

sakubun〈さくぶん：作文〉a composition.

sakubun o kaku（作文を書く）write a composition

jiyû-sakubun（自由作文）free composition

sakudō〈さくどう：策動〉maneuvers, scheming, machination.

sakudô-suru〈策動する〉maneuver, scheme, machinate.

saku-gara〈さくがら：作柄〉a crop, a harvest.

saku-gara-ga-ii（作柄がいい）have a good crop

saku-gara-ga-warui（作柄が悪い）have a bad crop

sakugen〈さくげん：削減〉reduction, curtailment, a cut.

yosan-no sakugen（予算の削減）a cut in the budget

sakugen-suru〈削減する〉reduce, curtail, cut (down).

jin·in o sakugen-suru（人員を削減する）curtail the staff

sakugo〈さくご：錯誤〉a mistake, an error.

shikô-sakugo（試行錯誤）trial and error

sakuhin〈さくひん：作品〉a work.

bungei-sakuhin（文芸作品）a literary work

geijutsu-sakuhin（芸術作品）a work of art

sakui〈さくい：作為〉artificiality; commission.

sakui-no or *sakui-teki(-na)*〈作為の，作為的（な）〉intentional, deliberate.

sakuin〈さくいん：索引〉an index.

sakuin-o-tsukeru〈索引を付ける〉index.

sakujitsu〈さくじつ：昨日〉yesterday.

sakujo〈さくじょ：削除〉elimination, cancellation.

sakujio-suru〈削除する〉eliminate, cancel, strike out, cross out, strike off.

ni-go sakujo-suru（二語削除する）eliminate two words

san-gyô sakujo-suru（三行削除する）cross three lines out

sakumotsu〈さくもつ：作物〉a crop, crops.

sakumotsu o tori-ireru（作物を取り入れる）gather a crop

Kotoshi wa sakumotsu-no-deki-ga totemo warui.（今年は作物のできがとても悪い。）We have very bad crops this year.

sakunen〈さくねん：昨年〉last year.

sakura〈さくら：桜〉a cherry tree, cherry blossoms.

sakura-iro(-no)〈桜色（の）〉pink.

sakura 〈さくら〉 a decoy, a shill, a bonnet, a claquer, claque.
  sakura-ni-naru (さくらになる) act as a decoy
sakurambo 〈さくらんぼ：桜んぼ〉 a cherry.
sakuran 〈さくらん：錯乱〉 distraction, derangement.
  seishin-sakuran (精神錯乱) mental derangement
  seishin-ga-sakuran-suru 〈精神が錯乱する〉 be mentally distracted.
sakura-sô 〈さくらそう：桜草〉 a primrose.
sakuryaku 〈さくりゃく：策略〉 a trick, an artifice.
  sakuryaku o mochiiru (策略を用いる) use tricks
  sakuryaku-ni-tomu 〈策略に富む〉 be resourceful.
sakusan 〈さくさん：酢酸〉 acetic acid.
sakusei 〈さくせい：作成〉
  sakusei-suru 〈作成する〉 draw up, write out, make out.
  hôkoku-sho o sakusei-suru (報告書を作成する) make out a report
sakusen 〈さくせん：作戦〉 military operations, tactics.
  sakusen-o-neru (作戦を練る) elaborate a plan of operations
  sakusen-o-ayamaru (作戦を誤る) commit a tactical error
sakusha 〈さくしゃ：作者〉 an author, a writer.
sakushi 〈さくし：策士〉 a tactician, a man of resources, a schemer.
sakushi 〈さくし：作詞〉
  sakushi-ka (作詞家) a songwriter
  sakushi-suru 〈作詞する〉 write the lyric.
sakushu 〈さくしゅ：搾取〉 exploitation, sweating, squeezing.
  chûkan-sakushu (中間搾取) intermediary exploitation
  sakushu-suru 〈搾取する〉 exploit, sweat, squeeze.
sakuya 〈さくや：昨夜〉 last night.
sakuzu 〈さくず：作図〉
  sakuzu-suru 〈作図する〉 draw a figure, construct.
sakyû 〈さきゅう：砂丘〉 a dune, a sandhill.
-sama 〈-さま：-様〉 Mr., Mrs., Miss.
samasu 〈さます：覚ます〉 wake up, awake; make ((a person)) sober.
  asa hayaku me-o-samasu (朝早く目を覚ます) wake up early in the
    morning
  mono-oto-de me-o-samasu (物音で目を覚ます) be waked by a sound
  Yo-naka-ni-nan-do-mo-me-o-samashita. (夜中に何度も目を覚ました.)
    I had a wakeful night.
samasu 〈さます：冷ます〉 cool, let ((a thing)) cool.
  yu o samasu (湯を冷ます) cool hot water

samatageru 〈さまたげる：妨げる〉 disturb, obstruct.

  suimin o samatageru（睡眠を妨げる） disturb one's sleep

  kôtsû o samatageru（交通を妨げる） obstruct the traffic

samayou 〈さまよう〉 wander.

  achi-kochi samayou（あちこちさまよう） wander about

samazama 〈さまざま：様々〉

  Yo-wa-samazama.（世はさまざま.） It takes all sorts of men to make (up) a world.

  Hito-no-kokoro-wa-samazama-da.（人の心はさまざまだ.） So many men, so many minds.

  samazama-na 〈さまざまな〉 various, of all kinds, of all sorts.

samba 〈さんば：産婆〉 a midwife.

sambashi 〈さんばし：桟橋〉 a pier, a wharf.

sambi 〈さんび：賛美〉 praise, glorification, admiration.

  sambi-suru〈賛美する〉 praise, glorify, admire.

sambi-ka 〈さんびか：賛美歌〉 a hymn.

sambô 〈さんぼう：参謀〉 a staff officer, the staff; an adviser, a counselor.

  sambô-chô（参謀長） the chief of staff

sambu 〈さんぶ：三部〉

  sambu-gasshô（三部合唱） a chorus of three parts

  sambu-saku（三部作） a trilogy

sambun 〈さんぶん：散文〉 prose.

sambutsu 〈さんぶつ：産物〉 a product, produce.

same 〈さめ〉 a shark.

sameru 〈さめる：覚める〉 wake up, awake; become sober.

sameru 〈さめる：冷める〉 cool, get cold.

sameru 〈さめる〉 fade, be discolored.

  same-yasui iro 〈さめやすい色〉 a fading color.

  same-nai iro（さめない色） a fast color

samezame-to 〈さめざめと〉 bitterly.

  samezame-to naku（さめざめと泣く） cry bitterly

samidare 〈さみだれ：五月雨〉 early summer rain.

samitto 〈サミット〉 the summit.

  samitto-kaidan（サミット会談） a summit conference

samma 〈さんま〉 a Pacific saury.

sammai-me 〈さんまいめ：三枚目〉 a comic actor.

samman 〈さんまん：散漫〉

samman-na〈散漫な〉loose, vague, distracted, scattered.

sammen〈さんめん：三面〉

　　sammen-kiji（三面記事）　city news

　　sammen-kyô（三面鏡）　a three-sided mirror

sammi〈さんみ：酸み〉acidity, sourness.

sammi-no-aru〈酸みのある〉acid, sour.

sammon〈さんもん：三文〉

　　Haya-oki wa sammon-no-toku.（早起きは三文の得。）　The early bird catches the worm.

　　Sore-wa sammon-no-ne-uchi-mo-nai.（それは三文の値打ちもない。）　It is not worth a penny.

sammon〈さんもん：山門〉the main gate of a Buddhist temple.

sammyaku〈さんみゃく：山脈〉a mountain range.

samo〈さも〉

　　samo-manzoku-sô-ni（さも満足そうに）　with evident satisfaction

　　samo-oishi-sô-ni（さもおいしそうに）　with much gusto

　　Samo-ari-sô-na-koto-da.（さもありそうな事だ。）　That is very likely.

　　samo-nai-to（さもないと）　or else, otherwise

samon〈さもん：査問〉inquiry, inquisition.

　　samon-iin-kai（査問委員会）　an inquiry commission

samon-suru〈査問する〉inquire ((into)), interrogate.

samoshii〈さもしい〉mean, base, low.

　　samoshii konjô（さもしい根性）　a base spirit

sampai〈さんぱい：参拝〉

　　sampai-sha（参拝者）a worship(p)er

sampai-suru〈参拝する〉go and worship ((at)).

sampatsu〈さんぱつ：散髪〉a haircut.

sampatsu-suru〈散髪する〉have one's hair cut.

sampatsu〈さんぱつ：散発〉

sampatsu-suru〈散発する〉scatter (hits).

sampatsu-teki(-na)〈散発的(な)〉sporadic.

sampatsu-teki-ni〈散発的に〉sporadically.

sampi〈さんぴ：賛否〉approval or(*or* and) disapproval.

　　sampi-ryôron（賛否両論）　pros and cons

sampi-o-tou〈賛否を問う〉put ((a matter)) to a vote.

sampo〈さんぽ：散歩〉a walk.

　　sampo-ni-iku（散歩に行く）　go out for a walk

sampo-suru〈散歩する〉take a walk.

sampô 〈さんぼう：山砲〉 a mountain gun, mountain artillery.

sampu 〈さんぷ：産婦〉 a woman in childbed.

sampu 〈さんぷ：散布〉
　sampu-suru 〈散布する〉 scatter, sprinkle, spread, drop.

sampuku 〈さんぷく：山腹〉 a hillside, a mountainside.

samugari 〈さむがり：寒がり〉 a person exceedingly sensitive to cold.
　samugaru 〈寒がる〉 feel the cold.

samui 〈さむい：寒い〉 cold, chilly.
　　samuku-naru 〈寒くなる〉　get cold
　　samukute furueteiru 〈寒くて震えている〉　be shivering with cold
　　samu-sô-na-kao-o-shite-iru 〈寒そうな顔をしている〉　look cold
　samusa 〈寒さ〉 (the) cold, coldness.
　　hidoi samusa 〈ひどい寒さ〉　the severe cold

samu-ke 〈さむけ：寒気〉 a chill, a cold fit, rigor.
　　samu-ke-ga-suru 〈寒気がする〉　have a chill, have a cold fit

samu-zora 〈さむぞら：寒空〉 cold weather.

san 〈さん：桟〉 a frame, a bolt.

san 〈さん：酸〉 an acid.

san 〈さん：産〉 a product.
　　Hokkaidô-san-no kuma 〈北海道産のくま〉　a bear from Hokkaido
　　Kariforunia-san-no　gurêpu-furûtsu 〈カリフォルニア産のグレープフルーツ〉　grapefruit of California growth

san 〈さん：三〉 three.
　　dai-san 〈第三〉　the third
　　san-bai 〈三倍〉　three times
　　san-bun-no-ichi 〈三分の一〉　a third

sanagara 〈さながら〉 *see*. atakamo.

sanagi 〈さなぎ〉 a pupa.

sanatoriumu 〈サナトリウム〉 a sanatorium, a sanitarium.

sanchi 〈さんち：産地〉 a producing district.

sanchi 〈さんち：山地〉 a mountainous district.

sanchô 〈さんちょう：山頂〉 the summit of a mountain.

sanchû 〈さんちゅう：山中〉
　sanchû-no, sanchû-de or *sanchû-ni* 〈山中の，山中で，山中に〉 in the mountains.

sandan 〈さんだん：三段〉
　　sandan-tobi 〈三段跳び〉　hop, step, and jump

sandan 〈さんだん：算段〉

   sandan-suru〈算段する〉contrive, manage.

     nan-toka-shite　kane-o-sandan-suru（何とかして金を算段する）　manage to raise money

san-do〈さんど：三度〉three times.

     san-do-no-shokuji（三度の食事）　daily meals

sandô〈さんどう：参道〉the approach to a shrine.

san-fujin-ka〈さんふじんか：産婦人科〉obstetrics and gynecology.

sangai〈さんがい：三階〉the third floor, the second floor.

sangaku〈さんがく：山岳〉mountains.

     sangaku-chihô（山岳地方）　*see.*　sanchi（山地）

sangatsu〈さんがつ：三月〉March.

sangeki〈さんげき：惨劇〉a tragedy, a tragic event.

Sangi-in〈さんぎいん：参議院〉the House of Councilors.

     Sangi-in-giin（参議院議員）　a member of the House of Councilors

sango〈さんご〉coral.

     sango-shô（さんご礁）　a coral reef

sango〈さんご：産後〉

   sango-no〈産後の〉after childbirth.

sangoku〈さんごく：三国〉

     dai-sangoku（第三国）　the third power

sangyô〈さんぎょう：産業〉industry.

     sangyô-kakumei（産業革命）　the Industrial Revolution

     sangyô-supai（産業スパイ）　a corporate spy

   sangyô-no〈産業の〉industrial.

san・i〈さんい：賛意〉approval.

     san・i o hyôsuru（賛意を表する）　express one's approval

sanji〈さんじ：賛辞〉

   sanji-o-teisuru〈賛辞を呈する〉pay a tribute ((to)), compliment.

sanji〈さんじ：惨事〉a disaster, a tragedy.

sanji〈さんじ：産児〉a newborn.

     sanji-seigen（産児制限）　birth control

sanji〈さんじ：三次〉

     sanji-hôtei-shiki（三次方程式）　a cubic equation

san-jigen〈さんじげん：三次元〉three dimensions.

sanjô〈さんじょう：山上〉*see.*　sanchô.

sanjô〈さんじょう：惨状〉a disastrous scene.

     sanjô o teisuru（惨状を呈する）　present a terrible sight

sanjô〈さんじょう：三乗〉cube.

Ni no sanjô wa hachi.〈二の三乗は八.〉 The cube of two is eight.

sanjô-suru〈三乗する〉cube.

sanjoku〈さんじょく：産じょく〉childbed, confinement.

sanjoku-netsu（産じょく熱）childbed fever

san-jû〈さんじゅう：三十〉thirty.

dai-san-jû（第三十）the thirtieth

sanjû〈さんじゅう：三重〉

sanjû-shô, sanjû-sô（三重唱，三重奏）a trio

sanjû-no〈三重の〉threefold, triple.

sanjutsu〈さんじゅつ：算術〉arithmetic.

sanka〈さんか：傘下〉

sanka-no〈傘下の〉subsidiary, affiliated.

sanka-ni〈傘下に〉under ((a person's)) control.

sanka〈さんか：惨禍〉calamity, disaster, ravages.

sanka〈さんか：産科〉obstetrics; the maternity division.

sanka〈さんか：酸化〉oxidation.

sanka-butsu（酸化物）an oxide

sanka-suru〈酸化する〉oxidize, be oxidized.

sanka-shi-yasui〈酸化しやすい〉easily oxidizable.

sanka〈さんか：参加〉participation.

sanka-koku（参加国）a participating nation

sanka-sha（参加者）a participant, an entrant

sanka-suru〈参加する〉participate ((in)), take part ((in)), join.

kyôgi-ni sanka-suru（競技に参加する）take part in a game

san-kai〈さんかい：山海〉

sankai-no-chimmi（山海の珍味）all sorts of dainties

sankai〈さんかい：散会〉

sankai-suru〈散会する〉break up, adjourn, close.

Kai wa gogo-hachi-ji-ni sankai-shita.（会は午後八時に散会した.）The meeting broke up at eight p.m.

sankai〈さんかい：散開〉

sankai-suru〈散開する〉deploy, spread out.

sankai〈さんかい：参会〉attendance.

sankai-suru〈参会する〉attend〔a meeting〕.

sankaku〈さんかく：三角〉a triangle.

sankaku-jôgi（三角定規）a set square

sankaku-kankei（三角関係）a lovers' triangle

sankaku-kansû（三角関数）trigonometrical function

　　　sankaku-no *or* sankakkei-no（三角の，三角形の）triangular, three-cornered.

sankan〈さんかん：山間〉

　　　sankan-no hekison（山間のへき村）a remote hamlet among the mountains

sankan〈さんかん：参観〉a visit, inspection.

　　　sankan-nin（参観人）a visitor

　sankan-suru〈参観する〉visit, make a visit ((of)), inspect.

　　　jugyô o sankan-suru（授業を参観する）visit a class

sankan-ô〈さんかんおう：三冠王〉a triple crown.

sanke〈さんけ：産気〉

　sanke-zuku〈産気付く〉labor starts, feel labor pains.

sankei〈さんけい：参けい〉

　　　sankei-sha（参けい者）a visitor, a worshipper

　sankei-suru〈参けいする〉visit〔a temple *or* a shrine〕.

sanken〈さんけん：散見〉

　sanken-sareru〈散見される〉be found here and there.

sanken-bunritsu〈さんけんぶんりつ：三権分立〉division of administration, legislation, and judicature.

sankô〈さんこう：参考〉reference, consultation.

　　　sankô-shiryô（参考資料）reference data

　　　sankô-sho（参考書）a reference book

　　　sankô-nin（参考人）a witness

　sankô-suru〈参考する〉refer ((to)), consult.

　sankô-ni-naru〈参考になる〉be of help ((to)), furnish ((a person)) with much information.

　sankô-no-tame〈参考のため〉for reference.

sankyaku〈さんきゃく：三脚〉a tripod.

sankyû〈さんきゅう：産休〉maternity leave.

sanran〈さんらん：産卵〉laying eggs.

　　　sanran-ki（産卵期）a spawning season

　sanran-suru〈産卵する〉lay eggs, spawn.

sanran〈さんらん：散乱〉scattering, dispersion.

　sanran-suru〈散乱する〉be scattered about, be littered ((with)).

sanretsu〈さんれつ：参列〉attendance.

　　　sanretsu-sha（参列者）an attendant

　sanretsu-suru〈参列する〉attend, be present ((at)).

　　　sôgi ni sanretsu-suru（葬儀に参列する）attend a funeral

sanrin 〈さんりん：山林〉a forest on a mountain.

sanrin-sha 〈さんりんしゃ：三輪車〉a tricycle.

sanroku 〈さんろく：山ろく〉the foot of a mountain.

sanrui 〈さんるい：三塁〉third base.

 sanrui-shu (三塁手) a third baseman

 sanrui-da (三塁打) a three-base hit

sanryû 〈さんりゅう：三流〉

 sanryû-no 〈三流の〉third-rate.

sansan 〈さんさん〉

 sansan-to-furi-sosogu-taiyô 〈さんさんと降り注ぐ太陽〉brilliant rays of
the sun

sansan-kudo 〈さんさんくど：三々九度〉

 sansan-kudo-no-sakazuki-o-suru 〈三々九度の杯をする〉exchange nuptial
cups.

sansei 〈さんせい：酸性〉acidity.

 sansei-ni-naru 〈酸性になる〉become acid.

 sansei-ni-suru 〈酸性にする〉acidify.

 sansei(-no) 〈酸性(の)〉acid.

sansei 〈さんせい：賛成〉agreement.

 Kimi-ni sansei-desu. (君に賛成です。) I agree with you.

 sansei-suru 〈賛成する〉agree ((to or with)).

sansei-ken 〈さんせいけん：参政権〉suffrage, franchise, the right to vote.

sansen 〈さんせん：三選〉election for the third term.

 sansen-sareru 〈三選される〉be elected for the third term.

sansen 〈さんせん：参戦〉entry into a war.

 sansen-suru 〈参戦する〉enter the war, participate in the war.

sansha 〈さんしゃ：三者〉

 Sansha-bontai. (三者凡退。) All the three batters were easily put
out.

sanshi 〈さんし：蚕糸〉silk yarn.

sanshin 〈さんしん：三振〉a strikeout.

 sanshin-suru 〈三振する〉be struck out.

 sanshin-saseru 〈三振させる〉strike out.

sanshô 〈さんしょう：山しょう〉(a) Japanese pepper (tree).

sanshô 〈さんしょう：参照〉reference, comparison.

 sanshô-suru 〈参照する〉refer ((to)), compare ((with)).

sanshô 〈さんしょう：三唱〉

 banzai-o-sanshô-suru 〈万歳を三唱する〉give three cheers ((for)).

sanshoku〈さんしょく：三食〉three meals.

sanshoku-sumire〈さんしょくすみれ：三色すみれ〉a pansy.

sanshô-uo〈さんしょううお：山しょう魚〉a salamander.

sanshutsu〈さんしゅつ：産出〉

    sanshutsu-gaku（産出額）production, output

 sanshutsu-suru〈産出する〉produce, yield, turn out.

sanshutsu〈さんしゅつ：算出〉calculation, computation.

 sanshutsu-suru〈算出する〉calculate, compute.

 sanshutsu-suru-to~-ni-naru〈算出すると～になる〉work out at... .

sanso〈さんそ：酸素〉oxygen.

    sanso-kyûnyû（酸素吸入）oxygen inhalation

sansô〈さんそう：山荘〉a mountain villa.

sanson〈さんそん：山村〉a mountain village.

sansû〈さんすう：算数〉arithmetic.

sansui〈さんすい：散水〉

 sansui-suru〈散水する〉sprinkle ((a garden)) with water, water.

sansui-ga〈さんすいが：山水画〉landscape (painting).

sansuru〈さんする：産する〉produce, yield.

santan〈さんたん：賛嘆〉praise, admiration.

 santan-suru〈賛嘆する〉praise, be filled with admiration ((at)).

santan〈さんたん：惨たん〉

 santan-taru〈惨たんたる〉wretched, miserable, terrible, frightful, horrible, pitiful.

    santan-taru jôtai（惨たんたる状態）a wretched plight

santei〈さんてい：算定〉calculation, estimate.

 santei-suru〈算定する〉calculate, estimate.

sanwari-dasha〈三割打者〉a three hundred hitter.

san-ya〈さんや：山野〉fields and mountains.

san・yaku〈さんやく：三役〉the *sumo* wrestlers of the three highest ranks; the three top-ranking officials〔of a political party〕.

san・yo〈さんよ：参与〉participation.

 san・yo-suru〈参与する〉participate ((in)), take part ((in)).

    kokusei-ni-san・yo-suru（国政に参与する）take part in the conduct of state affairs

san・yô-sûji〈さんようすうじ：算用数字〉Arabic figures.

sanzai〈さんざい：散在〉

 sanzai-suru〈散在する〉be scattered, be dotted ((with)).

sanzai〈さんざい：散財〉squandering.

sanzai-suru〈散財する〉squander money ((on)).

sanzan〈さんざん：散々〉

　　sanzan-meiwaku-o-kakeru（散々迷惑を掛ける）give ((a person)) much trouble

　　sanzan-matasu（散々待たす）keep ((a person)) waiting for a long time

　　sanzan-warukuchi-o-iu（散々悪口を言う）call ((a person)) all sorts of names

　　sanzan-na-me-ni-au（散々な目に遭う）have a very hard time of it

sanzen〈さんぜん：参禅〉

sanzen-suru〈参禅する〉practice *Zen* meditation.

sanzen〈さんぜん：燦然〉

sanzen-to-shite kagayaku〈さん然として輝く〉shine brilliantly.

sanzen-sango〈さんぜんさんご：産前産後〉before and after childbirth.

　　sanzen-sango-no kyûka（産前産後の休暇）maternity leave

sanzoku〈さんぞく：山賊〉a bandit, a mountain robber.

sanzu-no-kawa〈さんずのかわ：三ずの川〉the Styx.

sao〈さお〉a pole, a rod.

sappari〈さっぱり〉

sappari-suru〈さっぱりする〉feel refreshed.

sappari-shita〈さっぱりした〉clean, neat; frank, plain.

sappari～(-nai)〈さっぱり～(ない)〉(not) at all.

　　sappari-wakara-nai（さっぱり分からない）cannot get ((it)) at all

sappûkei〈さっぷうけい：殺風景〉

sappûkei-na〈殺風景な〉tasteless, prosaic, dull, dreary.

　　sappûkei-na otoko（殺風景な男）a prosaic man

　　sappûkei-na seikatsu（殺風景な生活）a dull life

　　sappûkei-na nagame（殺風景な眺め）a dreary sight

sara〈さら：皿〉a plate, a dish, a platter, a saucer.

sara-ni-moru〈皿に盛る〉dish up.

sara-ni-mori-wakeru〈皿に盛り分ける〉dish out.

me-o-sara-no-yô-ni-shite〈目を皿のようにして〉with one's eyes wide open.

sarada〈サラダ〉a salad.

　　sarada o tsukuru（サラダを作る）mix a salad

　　sarada-yu（サラダ油）salad oil

　　yasai-sarada（野菜サラダ）a vegetable salad

sa-raigetsu〈さらいげつ：再来月〉the month after next.

sa-rainen 〈さらいねん：再来年〉the year after next.

sa-raishū 〈さらいしゅう：再来週〉the week after next.

sarake-dasu 〈さらけだす：さらけ出す〉disclose, expose, lay bare.

te-no-uchi-o-sarake-dasu (手の内をさらけ出す) lay one's cards on the table

sara-ni 〈さらに：更に〉further, still more.

sara-ni-warui-koto-ni-wa (更に悪いことには) to make matters worse

sara-ni doryoku-suru (更に努力する) make further efforts

sararî 〈サラリー〉a salary.

sarari-man (サラリーマン) a salaried man, a white-collar worker

sarari 〈さらり〉

sarari-to 〈さらりと〉entirely, altogether; lightly.

sake o sarari-to yameru (酒をさらりとやめる) give up drinking entirely

sarari-to uke-nagasu (さらりと受け流す) parry lightly

sarasa 〈さらさ〉printed cotton.

sarasara 〈さらさら〉

sarasara-to oto-o-tatete 〈さらさらと音を立てて〉with a rustle.

sarashi 〈さらし〉bleaching, bleached cotton.

sarashi-ko (さらし粉) bleaching powder

sarasu 〈さらす〉expose; bleach.

hi-ni sarasu (日にさらす) expose to the sun

mempu o sarasu (綿布をさらす) bleach cotton

fûu-ni-sarasareta (風雨にさらされた) weather-beaten

sarau 〈さらう〉clean (out), dredge.

mizo o sarau (溝をさらう) clean out a ditch

sarau 〈さらう〉carry off; sweep away; kidnap.

nami-ni ashi-o-sarawareru (波に足をさらわれる) be swept away one's feet by the waves

kodomo o sarau (子供をさらう) kidnap a child

saridomaido 〈サリドマイド〉

saridomaido-ji (サリドマイド児) a thalidomide baby

sarige-naku 〈さりげなく〉indifferently, nonchalantly, casually.

saron 〈サロン〉a saloon; a sarong.

saru 〈さる：猿〉a monkey, an ape.

saru 〈さる：去る〉leave, go away; pass, be over.

Ôsaka o saru (大阪を去る) leave Osaka

Saru-mono-hibi-ni-utoshi. (去る者日々に疎し.) Out of sight, out of

mind.

Taifû ga satta.〔台風が去った.〕 The typhoon has passed.

Natsu ga satta〔夏が去った.〕 Summer is over.

kono-yo-o-saru〔この世を去る〕 pass away, die

saru〈さる：去る〉 last.

saru-nanuka〔去る七日〕 on the seventh day of this month

sarufa-zai〈サルファざい：サルファ剤〉 sulfas.

sarugutsuwa〈さるぐつわ：猿ぐつわ〉a gag.

sarugutsuwa-o-hameru〈猿ぐつわをはめる〉gag, put a gag in ((a person's)) mouth.

sarugutsuwa-o-hamerareru〈猿ぐつわをはめられる〉 be gagged.

saru-jie〈さるぢえ：猿知恵〉shallow cunning.

saru-mane〈さるまね：猿まね〉indiscriminate imitation.

saru-mane-o-suru〈猿まねをする〉imitate ((another)) blindly.

saru-mono〈さるもの：さる者〉no mean adversary.

Teki mo saru-mono.〔敵もさる者.〕 The enemy is no mean adversary.

sasa〈ささ〉bamboo grass.

sasae〈ささえ：支え〉a prop, a support.

sasaeru〈支える〉support, prop.

ikka o sasaeru〔一家を支える〕 support one's family

sasage-mono〈ささげもの：ささげ物〉an offering.

sasageru〈ささげる〉life up; devote, offer.

isshô o kenkyû-ni sasageru〔一生を研究にささげる〕 devote one's life to the study

sasai〈ささい：さ細〉

sasai-na〈さ細な〉trifling, small, slight, petty.

sasai-na koto〔さ細な事〕 a trifling matter, a trifle

sasaru〈ささる：刺さる〉stick, be stuck.

sasatsu〈ささつ：査察〉(an) inspection, investigation.

kûchû-sasatsu〔空中査察〕 an aerial inspection

sasatsu-suru〈査察する〉inspect, investigate.

sasayaka〈ささやか〉

sasayaka-na〈ささやかな〉small, tiny.

sasayaka-na shihon-de shôbai o hajimeru〔ささやかな資本で商売を始める〕 start a business with a small capital

sasayaki〈ささやき〉a whisper, a murmer.

sasayaku〈ささやく〉whisper, talk in whispers, murmer.

sasen 〈させん：左遷〉relegation, demotion.

sasen-suru 〈左遷する〉relegate, demote.

(-)saseru 〈(-)させる〉make, let, allow, force, have, get.

    kare-ni saseru〈彼にさせる〉make him do, let him do, allow him to do, have him do, get him to do

    kodomo-tachi o suki-na-yô-ni sasete-oku〈子供たちを好きなようにさせておく〉let one's children have their own way

sasetsu〈させつ：左折〉

sasetsu-suru〈左折する〉turn to the left.

sashi-ageru〈さしあげる：差し上げる〉give, present.

    O-tanjô-bi-ni nani-o sashi-age-mashô-ka?（お誕生日に何を差し上げましょうか.）What shall I give you for your birthday?

    Nani-o sashi-age-mashô-ka?（何を差し上げましょうか.）What can I do for you?

sashi-atatte〈さしあたって：差し当たって〉for the present, for the time being, for the moment.

    sashi-atatte nani-mo suru-koto-ga-nai（差し当たって何もする事がない）have nothing to do for the moment

sashidashi-nin〈さしだしにん：差し出し人〉the sender.

sashi-dasu〈さしだす：差し出す〉present; send; hold out.

    migi-te o sashi-dasu（右手を差し出す）hold out one's right hand

sashide-gamashii〈さしでがましい：差し出がましい〉

Sashide-gamashii-yô-desu-ga~.〈差し出がましいようですが~.〉I am afraid this is none of my business, but... .

sashie〈さしえ：挿絵〉an illustration, a cut.

sashie-iri-no〈挿絵入りの〉illustrated.

sashi-gane〈さしがね：差し金〉instigation, suggestion.

~-no-sashi-gane-de〈~の差し金で〉at the instigation of... , on the suggestion of... .

sashi-hikaeru〈さしひかえる：差し控える〉withhold, refrain ((from)), be moderate ((in)).

    iken o sashi-hikaeru（意見を差し控える）reserve one's opinion

    shokuji-o-sashi-hikaeru（食事を差し控える）be moderate in eating

sashi-hiki〈さしひき：差し引き〉a balance, (a) deduction.

    sashi-hiki-zandaka（差し引き残高）the balance

sashi-hiki-suru or *sashi-hiku*〈さしひきする, さしひく：差し引きする, 差し引く〉balance, deduct, take off.

    kyûryô-kara-sashi-hiku（給料から差し引く）take ((a sum)) out of

one's salary

sashi-kakaru 〈さしかかる：差し掛かる〉come ((to)), approach.

tonneru-ni-sashi-kakatta-toki-ni（トンネルに差し掛かった時に）just when I came to the tunnel

sashi-ki 〈さしき：挿し木〉a cutting.

sashi-ki-o-suru〈挿し木をする〉plant a cutting.

sashi-komi 〈さしこみ：差し込み〉insertion; a plug, an outlet; a spasm of pain.

sashi-komi-ga-kuru（差し込みが来る）be seized with a spasm

sashi-komu 〈さしこむ：差し込む〉insert; plug in; shine in; have a griping pain.

kôdo o konsento-ni sashi-komu（コードをコンセントに差し込む）plug a cord into an outlet

Nikkô ga mado-kara sashi-komu.（日光が窓から差し込む。）The sunlight streams in the window.

kyû-ni i-ga-sashi-komu（急に胃が差し込む）have acute pain in the stomach

sashi-korosu 〈さしころす：刺し殺す〉stab ((a person)) to death.

sashimi 〈さしみ：刺身〉slices of raw fish.

maguro-no-sashimi（まぐろの刺身）sliced raw tuna

sashimodosu 〈さしもどす：差し戻す〉refer ((a case)) back〔to the original court〕.

sashi-mono-shi 〈さしものし：指物師〉a carpenter, a joiner.

sashi-mukai 〈さしむかい：差し向かい〉

sashi-mukai-ni suwaru〈差し向かいに座る〉sit face to face ((with)).

sashi-ne 〈さしね：指し値〉the limits.

sashi-noberu 〈さしのべる：差し伸べる〉hold out, stretch out, extend.

sashi-oku 〈さしおく：差し置く〉ignore, neglect.

kantoku-o-sashi-oite ônâ-to-dampan-suru（監督を差し置いてオーナーと談判する）negotiate directly with the owner of a pro-ball team over the manager

nani-o-sashi-oite-mo〈何を差し置いても〉first of all.

sashi-osae 〈さしおさえ：差し押さえ〉attachment, seizure.

sashi-osae-reijô（差し押さえ令状）a warrant of seizure

sashi-osaeru〈差し押さえる〉attach, seize.

sashi-osae-o-kuu〈差し押さえを食う〉have one's property attached.

sashi-sawari 〈さしさわり：差し障り〉offense.

sashi-sawari-ga-aru-to-ikenai-kara〈差し障りがあるといけないから〉for

fear of giving offense ((to)).

sashi-semaru〈さしせまる：差し迫る〉be imminent, be impending.

sashi-sematta〈差し迫った〉pressing, urgent.

  sashi-sematta mondai（差し迫った問題）a pressing question

sashi-shimesu〈さししめす：指し示す〉show, point out.

sashi-tomeru〈さしとめる：差し止める〉prohibit, forbid, place a ban ((on)), suspend.

  sono ken-ni-kansuru kiji no keisai-o-sashi-tomeru（その件に関する記事の掲載を差し止める）place a ban on the publication of the news about the matter

sashi-tsukae〈さしつかえ：差し支え〉a hindrance, objection, inconvenience.

  o-sashi-tsukae-nakereba（お差し支えなければ）if it is not inconvenient for you

  〜-to-ittemo-sashi-tsukae-nai.（〜と言っても差し支えない。）One may safely say that... . / It may safely be said that... .

sashi-tsukaeru〈差し支える〉be interrupted, be engaged, be pressed ((for)), be short ((of)).

sashizu〈さしず：指図〉orders, directions, instructions.

  sashizu o ukeru（指図を受ける）receive instructions ((from))

  sashizu ni shitagau（指図に従う）follow ((a person's)) directions

  sashizu-nin（指図人）an order

  sashizu-nin-barai（指図人払い）payable to order

sashizu-suru〈指図する〉order, direct, instruct.

sashô〈さしょう：査証〉a visa.

sashô-suru〈査証する〉visé, endorse.

sashô〈さしょう：詐称〉

sashô-suru〈詐称する〉assume a false name, represent oneself falsely ((as)).

sashu〈さしゅ：詐取〉

sashu-suru〈詐取する〉swindle, obtain ((money)) by fraud, cheat ((a person)) out of.

sasoi〈さそい：誘い〉(an) invitation; (a) temptation, (an) allurement.

sasoi-ni-noru〈誘いに乗る〉be tempted, fall a victim to ((a person's)) allurement.

sasoi-komu〈さそいこむ：誘い込む〉allure ((a person)) into.

sasori〈さそり〉a scorpion.

sasou〈さそう：誘う〉invite, ask, call ((for)); allure, tempt.

pâtî-ni sasowareru〈パーティに誘われる〉 be invited to a party

kai-mono-ni-sasou〈買物に誘う〉 ask ((a person)) to go shopping

Watashi-ga kimi-o sasou-yo.〈私が君を誘うよ。〉 I'll call for you.

sassa〈さっさ〉

sassa-to〈さっさと〉 quickly, fast, in a hurry.

Sassa-to aruke.〈さっさと歩け。〉 Walk quickly.

sasshi〈さっし：察し〉 conjecture, guess, understanding, consideration, sympathy.

sasshi-ga-ii〈察しがいい〉 be sensible, be understanding, be considerate.

sasshi-ga-warui〈察しが悪い〉 be insensible, be dull of understanding, be inconsiderate

sasshi-ga-tsuku〈察しが付く〉 can guess, can understand.

sasshin〈さっしん：刷新〉 (a) reform, (a) renovation, (an) innovation.

kompon-teki-na sasshin o okonau〈根本的な刷新を行う〉 make a radical reform

sasshin-suru〈刷新する〉 reform, renovate, innovate, clean up.

sasshō〈さっしょう：殺傷〉 bloodshed.

sasshō-suru〈殺傷する〉 kill and wound, shed blood.

sassô〈さっそう〉

sassô-taru〈さっそうたる〉 gallant, dashing, smart.

sassô-taru sugata〈さっそうたる姿〉 a gallant figure

sassô-to〈さっそうと〉 gallantly, dashingly.

sassoku〈さっそく：早速〉 at once, immediately, right away.

sempô-e tsuitara-sassoku〈先方へ着いたら早速〉 as soon as I get there

sassuru〈さっする：察する〉 guess, judge, suppose, imagine, sympathize ((with)).

Kare-no-kanashimi-wa-sassuru-ni-amari-aru.〈彼の悲しみは察するに余りある。〉 His grief is beyond imagination.

O-sasshi-itashimasu.〈お察しいたします。〉 I quite sympathize with you.

sassuru-tokoro〈察するところ〉 I suppose, perhaps.

~*-kara-sassuru-to*〈～から察すると〉 judging from... .

sasu〈さす：刺す〉 stab, prick, stick; bite, sting.

naifu-de hito-no-nodo-o-sasu〈ナイフで人ののどを刺す〉 stab a person in the throat with a knife

yubi o hari-de sasu〈指を針で刺す〉 prick a finger with a needle

ka-ni sasareru〈蚊に刺される〉 be bitten by mosquitoes

hachi-ni sasareru （はちに刺される） get stung by a bee

sasu 〈さす：指(差,挿)す〉 point ((to)); hold up; put ((into)), insert; pour ((into)); drop ((into)); rise; shine ((into)); play.

Jishaku no hari ga kita o sashite-iru.（磁石の針が北を指している.） The needle of a magnet points to the north.

kasa o sasu （傘を差す） hold up an umbrella

kabin-ni hana o sasu （花瓶に花を挿す） put flowers in a vase

me-gusuri-o-sasu（目薬を差す） drop some lotion into one's eyes

Shio ga sasu.（潮が差す.） The tide rises.

Hi ga sashiteiru.（日が差している.） The sun is shining ((into)).

shôgi o sasu （将棋を指す） play Japanese chess

sasuga 〈さすが〉

Kare-wa sasuga-ni erai.（彼はさすがに偉い.） He is indeed a great man.

sasuga-no-yûshi-mo （さすがの勇士も） brave as he was

sasuru 〈さする〉 rub, pat, stroke.

senaka o sasuru （背中をさする） rub one's back

satchû-zai 〈さっちゅうざい：殺虫剤〉 an insecticide, an insect powder.

sate 〈さて〉 well, now.

Sate dô-shiyô.（さてどうしよう.） What shall I do now?

satei 〈さてい：査定〉 assessment.

satei-gaku （査定額） an assessed amount

satei-suru 〈査定する〉 assess, make an assessment ((of)), value.

sate-oki 〈さておき〉

nani-wa-sate-oki （何はさておき） first of all

satetsu 〈さてつ：砂鉄〉 iron sand.

satetsu 〈さてつ：さ鉄〉 a setback, a snag.

satetsu-o-kitasu 〈さ鉄を来す〉 be deadlocked.

sato 〈さと：里〉 a village, the country, one's old home.

sato-ni-kaeru （里に帰る） go home to one's parents

sato-gaeri-suru （里帰りする） make her first call at her old home after her marriage

satô 〈さとう：砂糖〉 sugar.

o-cha ni satô o ireru （お茶に砂糖を入れる） put sugar in one's tea

satô-kibi （砂糖きび） a sugar cane

sato-go 〈さとご：里子〉 a foster child, a child put out to nurse.

sato-imo 〈さといも：里芋〉 a taro.

sato-oya 〈さとおや：里親〉 a foster parent.

satori〈さとり：悟り〉comprehension, understanding; *satori*, spiritual awakening.

satori-o-hiraku〈悟りを開く〉be spiritually awakened.

satoru〈さとる：悟る〉perceive, understand, comprehend, realize.

satorare-nai-yô-ni〈悟られないように〉stealthily.

satosu〈さとす：諭す〉advise, reason ((with)), admonish.

　　fu-kokoroe-o-satosu（不心得を諭す）reason with ((a person)) on his mistake

satoshite-yame-saseru〈諭してやめさせる〉dissuade ((a person)) from ((doing)).

satsu〈さつ：札〉a bill, a note, paper money.

　　ichi-man-en-satsu（一万円札）a ten-thousand-yen note

　　satsu-taba（札束）a roll of notes

-satsu〈-さつ：-冊〉a volume, a copy.

　　kono jisho o ni-satsu（この辞書を二冊）two volumes of this dictionary

satsubatsu〈さつばつ：殺伐〉

satsubatsu-to-shita〈殺伐とした〉bloody, brutal, savage, warlike.

satsuei〈さつえい：撮影〉

　　satsuei-jo（撮影所）a cinema studio

　　satsuei-shitsu（撮影室）a studio

satsuei-suru〈撮影する〉take a picture ((of)), photograph, film.

satsugai〈さつがい：殺害〉killing, murder.

satsugai-suru〈殺害する〉kill, murder, put to death.

satsui〈さつい：殺意〉a murderous intent, malice aforethought.

satsui-o-idaku〈殺意を抱く〉conceive a murderous intent, intend to kill.

satsujin〈さつじん：殺人〉homicide, murder.

　　satsujin-jiken（殺人事件）a murder case

　　satsujin-hannin（殺人犯人）a murderer, a murderess

satsujin-teki〈殺人的〉deadly, terrific.

　　satsujin-teki atsusa（殺人的暑さ）deadly heat

satsuki〈さつき：五月〉an azalea.

satsuma-imo〈さつまいも：さつま芋〉a sweet potato.

satsuriku〈さつりく：殺りく〉massacre, slaughter, butchery.

satto〈さっと〉quickly.

　　satto toori-suguru（さっと通り過ぎる）pass quickly

sattô〈さっとう：殺到〉a rush.

sattô-suru〈殺到する〉rush ((to)), make a rush ((for)).

iri-guchi-ni sattô-suru（入り口に殺到する）　rush to an entrance

chûmon-ga-sattô-suru（注文が殺到する）　have a rush of orders

sawagashii〈さわがしい：騒がしい〉noisy; troubled, turbulent.

sawagashiku（騒がしく）noisily.

sawagashiku-suru（騒がしくする）　make a noise

sawagi〈さわぎ：騒ぎ〉a noise; a disturbance, an agitation, a row, fuss, excitement.

sawagi o okosu（騒ぎを起こす）　make a row, create a commotion, cause excitement

sawagi-tateru〈さわぎたてる：騒ぎ立てる〉make a great fuss.

tsumaranai-koto-de sawagi-tateru（つまらない事で騒ぎ立てる）　make a great fuss about trifles

sawagu〈さわぐ：騒ぐ〉make a noise, be noisy, be agitated, make a fuss.

Sonna-ni sawagu-na!（そんなに騒ぐな.）　Don't be so noisy!

sake-o-nonde-sawagu（酒を飲んで騒ぐ）　have a drinking spree

sawa-kai〈さわかい：茶話会〉a tea party.

sawaru〈さわる：触る〉touch, feel.

kata-ni sawaru（肩に触る）　touch ((a person)) on the shoulder

sawaru〈さわる：障る〉

karada-ni-sawaru（体に障る）affect one's health.

sawayaka〈さわやか〉

sawayaka-ni-naru〈さわやかになる〉feel refreshed.

sawayaka-na〈さわやかな〉fresh, refreshing; fluent.

sawayaka-na tenki（さわやかな天気）　refreshing weather

sawayaka-na asa（さわやかな朝）　a crisp morning

benzetsu-sawayaka-ni〈弁舌さわやかに〉fluently, eloquently.

saya〈さや〉a pod, a shell; a case, a sheath, a cap.

saya-endô〈さやえんどう：さやえん豆〉a field pea.

sayô〈さよう：作用〉(an) action, an effect, a function.

kagaku-sayô（化学作用）　a chemical action

sayô-suru〈作用する〉act ((on)), affect.

sayoku〈さよく：左翼〉the left wing, a leftist; the left field.

sayoku-undô（左翼運動）　a leftist movement

sayoku-shu（左翼手）　a left fielder

sayoku-teki(-na)〈左翼的(な)〉left-wing, leftist.

Sayônara.〈さようなら.〉Good-by(e). / Bye-bye. / So long.

sayû〈さゆう：左右〉right and left.

sayû o miru（左右を見る）look right and left

sayû ni wakareru（左右に分かれる）part right and left

sayû-suru〈左右する〉command, govern, control, affect, influence.

ummei o sayû-suru（運命を左右する）control one's destiny

kanjô-ni sayû-sareru（感情に左右される）be swayed by one's feeling

sazae〈さざえ〉a turbo.

sazae-no-tsubo-yaki（さざえのつぼ焼き）a turbo cooked in its own shell

saza-nami〈さざなみ：さざ波〉ripples.

saza-nami-ga-tatsu or *saza-nami-o-tateru*（さざ波が立つ，さざ波を立てる）ripple, ruffle.

sazanka〈さざんか〉a *sasanqua*.

sazo〈さぞ〉how, surely, no doubt, certainly, I am sure.

Go-ryōshin wa sazo-o-yorokobi-deshô.（御両親はさぞお喜びでしょう.）How glad your parents must be!

sazukeru〈さずける：授ける〉grant, confer, award.

kunshô o sazukeru（勲章を授ける）award ((a person)) a decoration

se〈せ：背〉the back.

se o nobasu（背を伸ばす）straighten one's back

se o mukeru（背を向ける）turn one's back ((on))

isu no se（いすの背）the back of a chair

se-bangô〈せばんごう：背番号〉a uniform number.

se-biro〈せびろ：背広〉a sack coat, a lounge suit.

sebiru〈せびる〉tease.

ko-zukai-o-sebiru（小遣いをせびる）tease ((a person)) for pocket money

se-bone〈せぼね：背骨〉the backbone, the spine.

sechi-garai〈せちがらい：世知辛い〉hard to live.

Sechi-garai-yo-no-naka-da.（世知辛い世の中だ.）It's very hard to live nowadays.

sadai〈せだい：世代〉a generation.

tsugi-no sedai（次の世代）the next generation

sû-sedai-ni-wattate（数世代にわたって）for generations

sagamu〈せがむ〉pester.

kane-o-segamu（金をせがむ）pester ((a person)) for money

sei〈せい：背〉height, stature.

sei o hakaru（背を測る）take ((a person's)) height

sei-ga-takai（背が高い）be tall

    sei-ga-hikui（背が低い）be short

    sei-ga-nobiru（背が伸びる）grow tall(er)

    "Sei ga dono-kurai-arimasu-ka?" "Hyaku-nana-jussenchi-arimasu." （"背がどのくらいありますか。""百七十センチあります。"）"How tall are you?" "I am 170 centimeters tall."

sei〈せい：精〉a spirit; energy, vitality.

    hana no sei（花の精）the spirit of a flower

    sei-o-dashite-hataraku〈精を出して働く〉work hard.

sei〈せい：姓〉a family name, a surname.

sei〈せい：性〉(a) sex.

    sei-kyôiku（性教育）sex education

    sei-seikatsu（性生活）one's sex life

    sei-no or *sei-teki(-na)*〈性の，性的(な)〉sexual.

    sei-teki miryoku（性的魅力）sexual attractiveness

sei〈せい：正〉right.

    sei-no〈正の〉positive, plus.

    sei-no kazu（正の数）a positive number, a plus quantity

sei〈せい：生〉

    sei-o-ukeru（生を受ける）be born, come into this world

    sei o tanoshimu（生を楽しむ）enjoy life

    sei-aru-mono（生あるもの）all living things

sei〈せい〉

    toshi-no-sei-de（年のせいで）owing to one's age

    yôki-no-sei-de（陽気のせいで）due to the weather

    shippai o hito no sei-ni-suru（失敗を人のせいにする）lay the failure at a person's door

sei〈せい：聖〉a sage, a saint.

    sei-naru〈聖なる〉holy, sacred, sainted.

-sei〈-せい：-制〉a system, an organization.

    hachi-jikan-sei（八時間制）an eight-hour day

    yo-nen-sei-daigaku（四年制大学）a four-year college

-sei〈-せい：-製〉make, manufacture.

    gaikoku-sei-no（外国製の）foreign-made, of foreign manufacture

    kokunai-sei-no（国内製の）homemade, of home manufacture

    Nihon-sei-no tokei（日本製の時計）a watch of Japanese make, a watch made in Japan, a Japanese-made watch

seiatsu〈せいあつ：制圧〉

    seiatsu-suru〈制圧する〉bring under one's control, gain mastery ((over)).

seibatsu 〈せいばつ：征伐〉 subjugation, suppression.
　seibatsu-suru 〈征伐する〉 subjugate, conquer, suppress.
seibetsu 〈せいべつ：性別〉 the distinction of sex.
　　seibetsu-ni-kankei-naku 〈性別に関係なく〉 irrespective of sex
seibi 〈せいび：整備〉 maintenance, preparation.
　　chijô-seibi-in 〈地上整備員〉 ground crew
　seibi-suru 〈整備する〉 service, fix.
　　jidôsha o seibi-suru 〈自動車を整備する〉 fix a car
seibo 〈せいぼ：聖母〉 the Holy Mother.
　　seibo Maria 〈聖母マリア〉 the Virgin Mary
seibo 〈せいぼ：生母〉 one's (real) mother.
seibo 〈せいぼ：歳暮〉 the end of the year; a year-end present.
　　seibo-oo-uri-dashi 〈歳暮大売り出し〉 a year-end bargain sale
seibô 〈せいぼう：制帽〉 a regulation cap, a school cap.
seibu 〈せいぶ：西部〉 the western part, the west.
　　seibu-geki 〈西部劇〉 a western(*or* Western) (film)
　seibu-no 〈西部の〉 west, western.
seibun 〈せいぶん：成分〉 an ingredient, a component.
　　shu-seibun 〈主成分〉 the main ingredients ((of))
seibun 〈せいぶん：成文〉
　　seibun-hô 〈成文法〉 a statute law, a written law
　　seibun-ka 〈成文化〉 codification
　　　seibun-ka-suru 〈成文化する〉 codify, put in statutory form
seibutsu 〈せいぶつ：生物〉 a living thing, a creature; life.
seibutsu-ga 〈せいぶつが：静物画〉 a picture of still life.
　　seibutsu-ga-ka 〈静物画家〉 a still-life painter
seibutsu-gaku 〈せいぶつがく：生物学〉 biology.
　　seibutsu-gaku-sha 〈生物学者〉 a biologist
seibyô 〈せいびょう：性病〉 a venereal disease (V.D.).
seichi 〈せいち：聖地〉 a sacred ground, the Holy Land.
seichi 〈せいち：生地〉 one's birthplace.
seichi 〈せいち：精ち〉
　seichi-na 〈精ちな〉 fine, minute, subtle.
seichi 〈せいち：整地〉
　seichi-suru 〈整地する〉 level the ground, prepare the soil.
seichô 〈せいちょう：清聴〉
　　Go-seichô-kansha-itashimasu. 〈ご清聴感謝いたします。〉 I thank you
　　for your kind attention.

seichô 〈せいちょう：成(生)長〉growth.
  seichô-kabu（成長株）a growth stock
  seichô-ki（成長期）a growing period
 seichô-suru〈成(生)長する〉grow.
  seichô-suru-ni-shitagatte（成長するに従って）as one grows older
 seichô-shita〈成(生)長した〉grown-up.
seichû 〈せいちゅう：成虫〉an imago.
seidai 〈せいだい：盛大〉
 seidai-na〈盛大な〉prosperous, splendid, grand.
  seidai-na kangei o ukeru（盛大な歓迎を受ける）receive a very warm
    welcome
 seidai-ni〈盛大に〉splendidly, on a large scale.
sei-daku 〈せいだく：清濁〉
 sei-daku-awase-nomu〈清濁あわせ飲む〉be so broad-minded as to be
  tolerant of all sorts of men
sei-denki 〈せいでんき：静電気〉static electricity.
seido 〈せいど：制度〉a system, an organization.
  kyôiku-seido（教育制度）an educational system
 seido-ka-suru〈制度化する〉institutionalize.
seido 〈せいど：精度〉accuracy, precision.
 seido-ga-takai〈精度が高い〉be very accurate, be highly precise.
seidô 〈せいどう：青銅〉bronze.
seidô 〈せいどう：正道〉the right path.
  seidô-o-fumi-hazusu（正道を踏み外す）stray from the right path
seidoku 〈せいどく：精読〉careful reading.
 seidoku-suru〈精読する〉read carefully.
seiei 〈せいえい：精鋭〉the best ((of)), the pick ((of)).
 seiei-na〈精鋭な〉picked, crack.
seieki 〈せいえき：精液〉semen, sperm.
seien 〈せいえん：製塩〉salt manufacture.
  seien-jo（製塩所）a salt factory
seien 〈せいえん：声援〉cheering.
 seien-suru〈声援する〉cheer.
seifu 〈せいふ：政府〉the government.
  seifu-tôkyoku（政府当局）the Government authorities
  Nihon-seifu（日本政府）the Japanese Government
 seifu-no〈政府の〉government, governmental.
sei-fuku 〈せいふく：正副〉principal and vice, original and duplicate.

　　sei-fuku-nitsû-no-shorui　o　sakusei-suru（正副二通の書類を作成する）
　　　make out the document in duplicate

seifuku〈せいふく：制服〉a uniform.
　　seifuku o kiru（制服を着る）wear a uniform
　　seifuku-o-kite-iru（制服を着ている）be in uniform

seifuku〈せいふく：征服〉conquest.
　　seifuku-sha（征服者）a conqueror
　seifuku-suru〈征服する〉conquer, overcome.

seifun〈せいふん：製粉〉(flour) milling.
　　seifun-jo（製粉所）a mill

seigaku〈せいがく：声楽〉vocal music.
　　seigaku-ka（声楽家）a vocalist

seigan〈せいがん：請願〉a petition ((for)), an application ((for)).
　　seigan-sho（請願書）a (written) petition
　seigan-suru〈請願する〉petition, apply ((for)).

seigan-zai〈せいがんざい：制がん剤〉an anticancer medicine.

seigen〈せいげん：制限〉a limit, (a) limitation, (a) restriction.
　　seigen-sokudo（制限速度）regulation speed
　　seigen-nai-de（制限内で）within the limits
　seigen-suru〈制限する〉limit, restrict.
　　karui shokuji-ni seigen-sareru（軽い食事に制限される）be restricted
　　　to a light diet

seigi〈せいぎ：正義〉justice, right.
　　seigi-no-tame-ni tatakau（正義のために戦う）fight in the cause of
　　　justice
　　seigi-kan（正義感）a sense of justice
　seigi-no〈正義の〉just, righteous.

seigo〈せいご：生後〉after one's birth.
　　seigo-ni-ka-getsu-no akambô（生後二か月の赤ん坊）a two-month-old
　　　baby

sei-go-hyô〈せいごひょう：正誤表〉an errata.

seigyo〈せいぎょ：制御〉control, management.
　　seigyo-kan（制御かん）a control rod
　　seigyo-sôchi（制御装置）a control device
　seigyo-suru〈制御する〉control, manage.
　seigyo-shi-yasui〈制御しやすい〉easy to control.
　　seigyo-shi-nikui（制御しにくい）hard to control
　seigyo-deki-nai〈制御できない〉uncontrollable, unmanageable.

seigyô 〈せいぎょう：正業〉an honest calling.

  seigyô-o-itonamu（正業を営む）make an honest living

seiha 〈せいは：制覇〉conquest, domination; championship.

  sekai-seiha（世界制覇）world conquest

  seiha-suru〈制覇する〉conquer, dominate; gain the championship.

seihaku 〈せいはく：精白〉

  seihaku-suru（精白する）refine〔sugar〕, polish〔rice〕.

seihaku-ji 〈せいはくじ：精薄児〉a mentally-handicapped child.

seihan 〈せいはん：製版〉plate-making.

  seihan-suru〈製版する〉make a plate.

sei-hantai 〈せいはんたい：正反対〉the exact opposite.

  Kimi-no iken wa watashi-no-to-wa-sei-hantai-da.（君の意見は私のとは正反対だ.）Your views are diametrically opposed to mine.

  sei-hantai-ni〈正反対に〉in direct opposition ((to)).

seihen 〈せいへん：政変〉a political change, a change of government.

sei-hi 〈せいひ：成否〉success or failure, the issue.

  sei-hi-wa-betsu-to-shite（成否は別として）regardless of the issue

seihin 〈せいひん：製品〉manufactured goods, a product.

  gaikoku-seihin（外国製品）foreign-made articles

  kokunai-seihin（国内製品）domestic articles

  Nihon-seihin（日本製品）Japanese-made articles

seihin 〈せいひん：清貧〉

  seihin-ni-amanjiru〈清貧に甘んじる〉be contented with honest poverty.

sei-hirei 〈せいひれい：正比例〉direct proportion.

  sei-hirei-suru〈正比例する〉be in direct proportion ((to)).

seihô 〈せいほう：製法〉a method of manufacture, how to make... .

seihô 〈せいほう：西方〉the west.

  seihô-ni（西方に）to the west ((of))

  seihô-no〈西方の〉west, western.

sei-hôkei 〈せいほうけい：正方形〉a (regular) square.

  sei-hôkei-no〈正方形の〉square.

sei-hoku 〈せいほく：西北〉the northwest.

  sei-hoku-sei（西北西）west-northwest (WNW)

seihon 〈せいほん：製本〉bookbinding.

  seihon-ya（製本屋）a bookbinder

  seihon-suru〈製本する〉bind〔a book〕.

seihon 〈せいほん：正本〉the original, an attested copy.

seihyô 〈せいひょう：製氷〉ice making.

　　seihyô-ki〈製氷機〉an ice machine
　　seihyô-kôjô〈製氷工場〉an ice plant
seii〈せいい：誠意〉sincerity.
　　seii o kaku〈誠意を欠く〉lack sincerity
seii-no-aru〈誠意のある〉sincere.
　　seii-no-nai〈誠意のない〉insincere
seii-o-motte〈誠意をもって〉with sincerity, sincerely.
sei-ippai〈せいいっぱい：精一杯〉to the utmost, as hard as one can; the best one can do.
　　sei-ippai yaru〈精一杯やる〉do one's best
　　sei-ippai hataraku〈精一杯働く〉work as hard as one can
　　Ikite-iru-no-ga sei-ippai-da.〈生きているのが精一杯だ。〉It is all I can do to be alive.
sei-ja〈せいじゃ：正邪〉right and wrong.
　　sei-ja-o-wakimaeru〈正邪をわきまえる〉know right from wrong
seijaku〈せいじゃく：静寂〉silence, stillness, quiet.
　　seijaku o yaburu〈静寂を破る〉break the silence
seijaku-na〈静寂な〉still, silent, quiet.
seiji〈せいじ：政治〉politics, government, administration, political affairs.
　　seiji o okonau〈政治を行う〉administer the affairs of state
　　seiji o ronjiru〈政治を論じる〉discuss politics
　　akarui seiji〈明るい政治〉clean politics
　　seiji-katsudô〈政治活動〉political activities
　　seiji-kenkin〈政治献金〉a political donation
　　seiji-mondai〈政治問題〉a political issue
　　seiji-ryoku〈政治力〉political power
　　seiji-undô〈政治運動〉a political movement
　　seiji-ka〈政治家〉a statesman, a politician
　　seiji-gaku〈政治学〉politics, political science
　　chihô-seiji〈地方政治〉local politics
seiji(-jô)-no or *seiji-teki(-na)*〈政治上の，政治的(な)〉political.
seiji-jô or *seiji-teki-ni*〈政治上，政治的に〉politically.
seiji〈せいじ：青磁〉celadon porcelain.
　　seiji-iro〈青磁色〉celadon green
seijin〈せいじん：聖人〉a sage, a saint, a holy man.
seijin〈せいじん：成人〉an adult, a grownup.
　　seijin-no-hi〈成人の日〉Adults' Day, Coming-of-Age Day

    seijin-byô〈成人病〉 adult diseases

seijin-suru〈成人する〉 grow up.

seijitsu〈せいじつ：誠実〉 sincerity, honesty, faithfulness.

seijitsu-na〈誠実な〉 sincere, honest, faithful.

    seijitsu-de-nai〈誠実でない〉 insincere, dishonest

seijitsu-ni〈誠実に〉 sincerely, honestly, faithfully.

seijô〈せいじょう：政情〉 a political situation.

seijô〈せいじょう：正常〉 normalcy, normality.

    seijô-ni fukusuru〈正常に復する〉 return to normalcy

seijô-ka-suru〈正常化する〉 normalize, be normalized.

seijô-na〈正常な〉 normal, regular.

    seijô-de-nai〈正常でない〉 abnormal, irregular

seijô-ki〈せいじょうき：星条旗〉 the Stars and Stripes, the Star-Spangled Banner.

seijuku〈せいじゅく：成熟〉 maturity, ripeness.

    seijuku-ki〈成熟期〉 the period of maturity, the age of puberty

seijuku-suru〈成熟する〉 mature, ripen, be ripe.

seijuku-shita〈成熟した〉 mature, ripe.

seijun〈せいじゅん：清純〉

seijun-na〈清純な〉 pure and innocent.

seika〈せいか：聖火〉 the sacred fire, a sacred torch.

    seika-rirê（聖火リレー） a sacred-fire relay

    seika-dai（聖火台） a flame-holder

    Orimpikku-seika（オリンピック聖火） the Olympic Flame

seika〈せいか：聖歌〉 a sacred song, a hymn.

    seika-tai（聖歌隊） a choir

seika〈せいか：盛夏〉 midsummer.

seika〈せいか：正課〉 the regular curriculum.

seika〈せいか：成果〉 a result, a fruit.

    rippa-na seika o osameru（立派な成果を収める） get good results

    seika-naku owaru（成果なく終わる） end without result

seika〈せいか：製菓〉 confectionery.

    seika-gaisha（製菓会社） a confectionery company

seika〈せいか：生家〉 the house where one was born.

seika(-butsu)〈せいか（ぶつ）：青果（物）〉 vegetables and fruits.

    seika-ichiba（青果市場） a vegetable and fruit (wholesale) market

sei-kagaku〈せいかがく：生化学〉 biochemistry.

seikai〈せいかい：政界〉 the political world, political circles.

seikai ni hairu（政界に入る）　enter the political world

seikai o shirizoku（政界を退く）　retire from political life

seikai〈せいかい：正解〉a correct answer.

seikai-sha（正解者）　one who gives a correct answer

seikai-suru〈正解する〉give a correct answer.

seikai〈せいかい：盛会〉a successful meeting.

Kai wa seikai-de-atta.（会は盛会であった.）　The meeting was a great success.

sei-kaiin〈せいかいいん：正会員〉a regular member.

seikai-ken〈せいかいけん：制海権〉the command of the sea.

seikai-ken o nigiru（制海権を握る）　have the command of the sea

seikaku〈せいかく：性格〉character, personality.

tsuyoi seikaku-o-shite-iru（強い性格をしている）　have a strong personality

yowai seikaku-o-shite-iru（弱い性格をしている）　have a weak personality

seikaku-haiyû（性格俳優）　a character actor(*or* actress)

seikaku-teki(-na)〈性格的(な)〉characteristic.

seikaku〈せいかく：正確〉accuracy, exactness, correctness.

Kimi-no tokei wa seikaku-desu-ka?（君の時計は正確ですか.）　Does your watch keep correct time?

seikaku-na〈正確な〉accurate, exact, correct, precise.

seikaku-ni〈正確に〉accurately, exactly, correctly, punctually, precisely.

seikaku-ni hatsuon-suru（正確に発音する）　pronounce correctly

seikaku-ni ieba（正確に言えば）　exactly speaking

seikan〈せいかん：製缶〉can manufacturing; boiler manufacturing.

seikan〈せいかん：生還〉

seikan-suru〈生還する〉return alive; reach the home plate.

seikan〈せいかん：静観〉

seikan-suru〈静観する〉watch calmly, wait and see.

jitai no shinten o seikan-suru（事態の進展を静観する）　watch (calmly) the development of the situation

seikan〈せいかん：精かん〉

seikan-na〈精かんな〉fearless, intrepid, dauntless.

seikatsu〈せいかつ：生活〉(a) life, livelihood, living.

shiawase-na seikatsu o okuru（幸せな生活を送る）　have a happy life

seikatsu-ni-komaru（生活に困る）　find it difficult to make a living

seikatsu-hi（生活費）　living expenses

       seikatsu-hitsuju-hin〈生活必需品〉 necessities of life
       seikatsu-suijun〈生活水準〉 a standard of living
   seikatsu-suru〈生活する〉 live, exist.
seikei〈せいけい：生計〉 livelihood, living.
       seikei o tateru〈生計を立てる〉 earn a living
seikei〈せいけい：西経〉 the west longitude.
seikei〈せいけい：整形〉
       seikei-geka〈整形外科〉 plastic surgery
       seikei-shujutsu〈整形手術〉 a plastic surgery operation
seiken〈せいけん：政見〉 one's political views.
       seiken o happyô-suru〈政見を発表する〉 state one's political views
       seiken-hôsô〈政見放送〉 a broadcast of various political opinions
         stated by election candidates
seiken〈せいけん：政権〉 political power.
       seiken-o-nigiru〈政権を握る〉 come into power
       seiken-o-ushinau〈政権を失う〉 get out of power
       futatabi-seiken-o-nigiru〈再び政権を握る〉 come back to power
seiketsu〈せいけつ：清潔〉 cleanliness, neatness.
   seiketsu-ni-suru〈清潔にする〉 clean, make clean.
       karada o seiketsu-ni-shite-oku〈体を清潔にしておく〉 keep oneself
         clean
   seiketsu-na〈清潔な〉 clean, neat.
seiki〈せいき：世紀〉 a century.
       ni-jusseiki〈二十世紀〉 the twentieth century
seiki〈せいき：性器〉 sexual organs.
seiki〈せいき：生気〉 animation, life, vitality, vigor.
   seiki-no-aru〈生気のある〉 animated, lively, vital.
       seiki-no-nai〈生気のない〉 lifeless, spiritless, inanimate
seiki〈せいき：正規〉
   seiki-no〈正規の〉 regular, formal, legal.
       seiki-no tetsuzuki o fumu〈正規の手続きを踏む〉 follow the regular
         procedure
seikin〈せいきん：精勤〉 dilligence; regular attendance.
       seikin-sha〈精勤者〉 a regular attendant
   seikin-suru〈精勤する〉 be diligent, be assiduous.
seikô〈せいこう：政綱〉 a political program, a platform.
seikô〈せいこう：製鋼〉 steel manufacture.
       seikô-jo〈製鋼所〉 a steelworks

seikô 〈せいこう：性向〉 inclination, disposition.
seikô 〈せいこう：成功〉 (a) success.
 seikô-no-mikomi-ga-jûbun-aru (成功の見込みが十分ある) have a good chance of success
 Go-seikô-o-inorimasu. (御成功を祈ります。) I wish you success.
 dai-seikô (大成功) a great success
 seikô-sha (成功者) a successful man
 seikô-suru 〈成功する〉 succeed ((in)), be successful ((in)).
 seikô-shita 〈成功した〉 successful.
 seikô-shi-nai (成功しない) unsuccessful
seikô 〈せいこう：性交〉 sexual intercourse.
 seikô-suru 〈性交する〉 have sex ((with)).
seikô 〈せいこう：精巧〉
 seikô-na 〈精巧な〉 elaborate.
 seikô-ni 〈精巧に〉 elaborately.
seikô-hô 〈せいこうほう：正攻法〉 the regular tactics for attack.
seikon 〈せいこん：精根(魂)〉 energy, vitality.
 seikon-o-katamukeru (精根を傾ける) devote all one's energy ((to))
 seikon o tsukai-hatasu (精根を使い果たす) exhaust one's energy
seiku 〈せいく：成句〉 a set phrase, an idiomatic expression.
seikû-ken 〈せいくうけん：制空権〉 the command of the air.
 seikû-ken-o-nigiru (制空権を握る) win the air
seikyo 〈せいきょう：盛況〉 prosperity, a success.
 seikyô-de-aru 〈盛況である〉 be prosperous.
seikyoku 〈せいきょく：政局〉 a political situation.
 seikyoku o antei-saseru (政局を安定させる) stabilize the political situation
 seikyoku o dakai-suru (政局を打開する) break a political deadlock
 seikyoku-no kiki (政局の危機) a political crisis
seikyô-to 〈せいきょうと：清教徒〉 a Puritan.
seikyû 〈せいきゅう：請求〉 a demand, a claim, a request.
 seikyû-ken (請求権) a (right of) claim
 seikyû-sho (請求書) a bill, an account
 seikyû-suru 〈請求する〉 ask ((for)), demand, claim, request.
 seikyû-ni-ôjite 〈請求に応じて〉 in compliance with ((a person's)) request.
seikyû 〈せいきゅう：性急〉
 seikyû-na 〈性急な〉 impatient, hasty, quick-tempered.
seimai 〈せいまい：精米〉 polished rice, cleaned rice.

seimai-jo（精米所）a rice mill

seimei〈せいめい：生命〉life.

seimei-zaisan（生命財産）life and property

seimei-ryoku（生命力）life force

seimei-hoken（生命保険）life insurance

seimei-hoken-gaisha（生命保険会社）a life insurance

seimei-hoken-ni-hairu（生命保険に入る）insure one's life

seimei〈せいめい：姓名〉one's full name.

seimei〈せいめい：声明〉a declaration, a statement, an announcement.

seimei-suru〈声明する〉declare, announce.

seimei-sho〈せいめいしょ：声明書〉a (public) statement.

seimei-sho o dasu（声明書を出す）issue a statement ((on))

seimitsu〈せいみつ：精密〉minuteness, precision, accuracy.

seimitsu-kikai（精密機械）a precision machine

seimitsu-na〈精密な〉minute, close, detailed, precise, accurate.

seimitsu-na chizu（精密な地図）a detailed map

seimitsu-ni〈精密に〉minutely, closely, in detail, precisely, accurately.

seimitsu-ni kensa-suru（精密に検査する）examine closely

seimon〈せいもん：正門〉the front gate.

sei-nan〈せいなん：西南〉the southwest.

sei-nan-sei（西南西）west-southwest (WSW)

seinen〈せいねん：成年〉full age, majority.

seinen-ni-tassuru（成年に達する）come of age, reach full age, attain one's majority

seinen〈せいねん：青年〉a youth, a young man; young people.

seinen-danjo（青年男女）young men and women

seinen-jidai（青年時代）one's younger days

sei-nengappi〈せいねんがっぴ：生年月日〉the date of one's birth.

seinô〈せいのう：性能〉efficiency, power, capacity.

seinô-no-ii〈性能のいい〉efficient.

seinô-no-takai（性能の高い）highly efficient, high-powered

Seiô〈せいおう：西欧〉Western Europe.

Seiô-bummei（西欧文明）Western civilization

seirai〈せいらい：生来〉by nature, by birth.

seirai-no〈生来の〉natural, born, congenital.

seirei〈せいれい：政令〉a government ordinance.

seirei-ihan（政令違反）violation of a government ordinance

seirei〈せいれい：精励〉diligence.

seirei-suru〈精励する〉be diligent, work hard.

seireki〈せいれき：西暦〉the Christian Era, A.D.
    seireki-sen-kyû-hyaku-hachi-jû-nen-ni（西暦1980年に） in 1980 A.D., in A.D. 1980

seiren〈せいれん：精錬〉refining.
    seiren-jo（精錬所） a refinery
    seiren-suru〈精錬する〉refine.

seiren〈せいれん：清廉〉
    seiren-keppaku-na hito（清廉潔白な人） a man of integrity
    seiren-na〈清廉な〉upright.

seiretsu〈せいれつ：整列〉
    Seiretsu!（整列） Fall in!
    seiretsu-suru〈整列する〉stand in a row, form in line, line up.

seiri〈せいり：生理〉physiology.
    seiri-kyûka（生理休暇） a monthly physiological leave
    seiri-teki(-na)〈生理的(な)〉physiological.

seiri〈せいり：整理〉arrangement.
    seiri-dansu（整理だんす） a commode, a chest of drawers
    seiri-suru〈整理する〉arrange, put in order.

seiritsu〈せいりつ：成立〉existence, formation, conclusion.
    seiritsu-suru〈成立する〉come into existence, be formed, be concluded.
    Yosan ga seiritsu-shita.（予算が成立した.） The budget was approved.

seiron〈せいろん：正論〉a sound argument.

seiryaku〈せいりゃく：政略〉a political maneuver, a policy.
    seiryaku-kekkon（政略結婚） a marriage of convenience
    seiryaku-teki(-na)〈政略的(な)〉political.

seiryô〈せいりょう：声量〉the volume of voice.
    seiryô-ga-aru（声量がある） have a powerful voice

seiryô-inryô〈せいりょういんりょう：清涼飲料〉a soft drink.

seiryoku〈せいりょく：勢力〉influence, power, might, strength.
    seiryoku no kinkô（勢力の均衡） the balance of power
    seiryoku-arasoi（勢力争い） a struggle for power
    seiryoku-han·i（勢力範囲） a sphere of influence
    seiryoku-ka（勢力家） a man of influence, an influential man
    seiryoku-no-aru〈勢力のある〉influential, powerful, mighty.
    seiryoku-no-nai（勢力のない） uninfluential, powerless

seiryoku〈せいりょく：精力〉energy, vigor, vitality.

seiryoku-ka（精力家） a man of energy

seiryoku-teki-na or *seiryoku-ôsei-na*〈精力的な，精力おう盛な〉energetic, vigorous.

seiryû〈せいりゅう：整流〉rectification, commutation.

seiryû-ki（整流器） a rectifier

seryû-suru〈整流する〉rectify, commute.

seisai〈せいさい：制裁〉punishment, sanction.

seisai-o-kuwaeru〈制裁を加える〉inflict punishment ((upon)), take sanction ((against)).

seisai〈せいさい：精(生)彩〉

seisai-ga-nai or *seisai-o-kaku*〈精彩がない，精彩を欠く〉be lifeless, lack vividness.

seisaku〈せいさく：政策〉(a) policy.

keizai-seisaku（経済政策） an economic policy

taigai-seisaku（対外政策） a foreign policy

seisaku〈せいさく：製作〉manufacture, production.

seisaku-hi（製作費） production cost

seisaku-sha（製作者） a maker, a manufacturer

seisaku-sho（製作所） a factory, a works, a workshop

seisaku-suru〈製作する〉make, manufacture, produce.

seisaku〈せいさく：制作〉a work, a production.

seisaku-suru〈制作する〉produce, turn out.

seisan〈せいさん：正さん〉a dinner.

seisan〈せいさん：青酸〉hydrocyanic acid.

seisan-kari（青酸カリ） potassium cyanide

seisan〈せいさん：生産〉production.

seisan-butsu（生産物） a product, produce

seisan-chi（生産地） a producing district

seisan-daka（生産高） an output, an outturn

seisan-ryoku（生産力） producing power

seisan-sha（生産者） a producer, a maker

tairyô-seisan（大量生産） mass production

seisan-suru〈生産する〉produce, make.

seisan〈せいさん：成算〉

seisan-ga-nai〈成算がない〉have little hope of success.

seisan〈せいさん：清算〉liquidation.

seisan-gaisha（清算会社） a company in liquidation

seisan-nin（清算人） a liquidator

seisan-suru〈清算する〉liquidate.

seisan〈せいさん：精算〉settlement of accounts, adjustment, exact calculation.

   seisan-sho（精算書）a statement of accounts

   unchin-seisan-jo（運賃精算所）a fare adjustment office

seisan-suru〈精算する〉settle accounts, adjust, calculate accurately.

seisan〈せいさん：せい惨〉

seisan-na〈せい惨な〉ghastly, gruesome, grim.

sei-sankakkei〈せいさんかっけい：正三角形〉a regular triangle.

seisei〈せいせい：清々〉

seisei-suru〈清々する〉feel refreshed; feel relieved.

seisei〈せいせい：精製〉refining.

   seisei-yu（精製油）refined oil

seisei-suru〈精製する〉refine.

seisei-shita〈精製した〉refined.

seisei-dôdô〈せいせいどうどう：正々堂々〉

seisei-dôdô-no or *seisei-dôdô-taru*〈正々堂々の，正々堂々たる〉fair and square.

seisei-dôdô-to〈正々堂々と〉fairly.

   seisei-dôdô-to tatakau（正々堂々と戦う）play fair

seiseki〈せいせき：成績〉a result, a record, merit.

   gakkô-no-seiseki-ga-ii（学校の成績がいい）do well at school

   gakkô-no-seiseki-ga-warui（学校の成績が悪い）do poorly at school

   ii-seiseki o toru（いい成績を取る）make a good record

   warui-seiseki o toru（悪い成績を取る）make a poor record

   seiseki-hyô（成績表）a report card

seisen-shokuhin〈せいせんしょくひん：生鮮食品〉perishable foods.

seishi〈せいし：生死〉life and death, fate.

   seishi-no-sakai-o-samayou（生死の境をさまよう）hover between life and death

   seishi o tomo-ni-suru（生死を共にする）share one's fate ((with))

seishi〈せいし：製紙〉paper manufacture.

   seishi-kôjô（せいしこうじょう：製紙工場）a paper mill

seishi〈せいし：正視〉

seishi-suru〈正視する〉look ((a person)) in the face.

   Kare-o-seishi-suru-ni-shinobi-nakatta.（彼を正視するに忍びなかった.）I could not bear to look at him.

seishi〈せいし：制止〉(a) restraint, a check, control.

seishi-suru〈制止する〉restrain, check, control, stop.
　　gunshû o seishi-suru（群集を制止する）control the crowd
seishi〈せいし：静止〉stillness, rest, a standstill.
　seishi-suru〈静止する〉rest, stand still.
seishiki〈せいしき：正式〉
　seishiki-no〈正式の〉formal, regular.
　seishiki-ni〈正式に〉formally, regularly.
　　seishiki-ni-hômon-suru（正式に訪問する）pay a formal visit ((to))
seishin〈せいしん：精神〉spirit, mind, soul, will.
　　seishin o shûchû-suru（精神を集中する）concentrate one's attention
　　　((on))
　　seishin-ryoku（精神力）spiritual strength
　　seishin-jôtai（精神状態）a state of mind
　　seishin-antei-zai（精神安定剤）a tranquilizer
　　seishin-kantei（精神鑑定）a psychiatric test
　　seishin-byô（精神病）a mental disease
　　seishin-byôin（精神病院）a mental hospital
　　seishin-bunretsu-shô（精神分裂症）schizophrenia
　seishin-no or *seishin-teki(-na)*〈精神の，精神的(な)〉spiritual, mental.
　　seishin-teki dageki（精神的打撃）a mental blow
seishin〈せいしん：清新〉
　seishin-na〈清新な〉fresh, new.
seishin-seii〈せいしんせいい：誠心誠意〉sincerely, faithfully.
　　seishin-seii　koto-o-shori-suru（誠心誠意事を処理する）deal with a
　　matter in all sincerity
seishitsu〈せいしつ：性質〉nature, temper, character.
　　seishitsu-no-ii hito（性質のいい人）a good-natured person
　　seishitsu-no-warui hito（性質の悪い人）an ill-natured person
seisho〈せいしょ：聖書〉the Bible.
　　kyûyaku-seisho（旧約聖書）the Old Testament
　　shin·yaku-seisho（新約聖書）the New Testament
seisho〈せいしょ：清書〉a fair copy.
　seisho-suru〈清書する〉make a fair copy ((of)).
seishô〈せいしょう：斉唱〉a unison.
　　seishô-suru（斉唱する）sing in unison
sei-shoku〈せいしょく：聖職〉(holy) orders.
　　sei-shoku-ni-tsuku（聖職に就く）take (holy) orders
seishoku〈せいしょく：生殖〉reproduction, generation.

seishoku-ryoku-no-aru〈生殖力のある〉reproductive, generative.

sei-shô-nen〈せいしょうねん：青少年〉youth, juveniles.

　sei-shô-nen-hanzai（青少年犯罪）juvenile delinquency

　sei-shô-nen-muki-no〈青少年向きの〉for juniors and teen-agers.

seishu〈せいしゅ：清酒〉(refined) *sake.*

seishuku〈せいしゅく：静粛〉

　seishuku-na〈静粛な〉silent, quiet, still.

　seishuku-ni〈静粛に〉silently, quietly.

　　Seishuku-ni negai-masu.（静粛に願います。）Please be quiet.

　seishuku-ni-suru〈静粛にする〉keep quiet.

seishun〈せいしゅん：青春〉the springtime of life, youth.

　　seishun-jidai（青春時代）one's youth, one's youthful days

　seishun-no〈青春の〉youthful, young.

seiso〈せいそ：清そ〉

　seiso-na〈清そな〉neat and clean, tidy.

seisô〈せいそう：政争〉a political strife.

sesô〈せいそう：清掃〉cleaning.

　　seisô-sha（清掃車）a garbage wagon

　seisô-suru〈清掃する〉clean, scavenge.

seisô〈せいそう：正装〉full dress.

　seisô-suru〈正装する〉dress up, be in full dress.

　seisô-shite〈正装して〉in full dress.

seisô〈せいそう：盛装〉gala dress.

　seisô-suru〈盛装する〉be in gala dress.

　seisô-shite〈盛装して〉in gala dress.

seisô-ken〈せいそうけん：成層圏〉the stratosphere.

seisoku〈せいそく：生息〉

　　seisoku-chi（生息地）a habitat

　seisoku-suru〈生息する〉inhabit, live ((in)).

seisû〈せいすう：正数〉a positive number.

seisû〈せいすう：整数〉an integral number.

seisuru〈せいする：制する〉control, suppress, restrain, check.

　　Sakinzureba hito-o-seisu.（先んずれば人を制す。）Take the initiative, and you will win.

seitai〈せいたい：生態〉a mode of life, ecology.

　　hebi no seitai（蛇の生態）the ecology of a snake

seitai〈せいたい：政体〉a from of government.

　　kyôwa-seitai（共和政体）the republican form of government

seitai 〈せいたい：声帯〉 the vocal chords.
　　seitai-mosha（声帯模写） vocal mimicry
seitan 〈せいたん：生誕〉 birth.
　　seitan-hyaku-nen-sai（生誕百年祭） a centenary of a birth ((of))
seitei 〈せいてい：制定〉 enactment, institution, establishment.
　seitei-suru〈制定する〉 enact, institute, establish.
seiteki 〈せいてき：政敵〉 a political opponent.
seiteki(-na) 〈せいてき（な）：静的（な）〉 static(al).
seiten 〈せいてん：聖典〉 a sacred book.
seiten 〈せいてん：晴天〉 fair weather.
　　seiten-tsuzuki（晴天続き） a long spell of fair weather
seiten 〈せいてん：青天〉 the blue sky.
　　seiten no hekireki（青天のへきれき） a bolt from the blue
seitetsu 〈せいてつ：製鉄〉 iron manufacture.
　　seitetsu-jo（製鉄所） an iron mill
seito 〈せいと：生徒〉 a schoolboy, a schoolgirl, a pupil, a student.
seitô 〈せいとう：正統〉 orthodoxy, legitimacy.
　　seitô-ha（正統派） an orthodox school
　seitô-na〈正統な〉 orthodox, legitimate.
seitô 〈せいとう：政党〉 a political party.
　　seitô-seiji（政党政治） party politics
seitô 〈せいとう：製糖〉 sugar manufacture.
　　seitô-gaisha（製糖会社） a sugar-manufacturing company
seitô 〈せいとう：正当〉
　　seitô-bôei（正当防衛） legal defense
　seitô-ka-suru〈正当化する〉 justify.
　seitô-na〈正当な〉 just, right, proper, fair, lawful, legal.
　　seitô-na shudan（正当な手段） fair means
　seitô-ni〈正当に〉 justly, rightly, properly, fairly, lawfully, legally.
seiton 〈せいとん：整とん〉 order.
　seiton-suru〈整とんする〉 put in order.
　　seiton-shite-oku（整とんしておく） keep ((something)) in good order
　seiton-shita〈整とんした〉 in good order, orderly.
　　seiton-shite-i-nai（整とんしていない） out of order
seitsû 〈せいつう：精通〉
　seitsû-suru〈精通する〉 be well versed ((in)), be well acquainted ((with)),
　　be familiar ((with)).
seiu 〈せいう：晴雨〉

　　seiu-kei〈晴雨計〉　a barometer

seiu-ni-kakawarazu〈晴雨にかかわらず〉rain of shine, whether it may rain or not.

seiyaku〈せいやく：制約〉(a) restriction, (a) limitation.

seiyaku-o-ukeru〈制約を受ける〉be restricted ((by)).

seiyaku〈せいやく：製薬〉medicine manufacture.

　　seiyaku-gaisha（製薬会社）　a pharmaceutical company

seiyaku〈せいやく：誓約〉an oath, a vow, a pledge.

　　seiyaku o mamoru（誓約を守る）　keep one's pledge

　　seiyaku o yaburu（誓約を破る）　break one's vow

　　seiyaku-sho（誓約書）　a written oath

seiyaku-suru〈誓約する〉make an oath, vow, pledge, swear.

seiyô〈せいよう：西洋〉the West, Europe.

　　seiyô-shokoku（西洋諸国）　the Western countries

seiyô-no〈西洋の〉Western, European.

seiyô〈せいよう：静養〉(a) rest, recuperation.

seiyô-suru〈静養する〉take a rest, rest quietly, recuperate oneself.

seiyô-no-tame-ni〈静養のために〉for one's health, for a rest.

seiyoku〈せいよく：性欲〉sexual appetite.

seiyu〈せいゆ：製油〉oil manufacture.

　　seiyu-jo（製油所）　an oil factory

seiyû〈せいゆう：声優〉a radio actor(*or* actress).

seiza〈せいざ：星座〉a constellation.

seiza〈せいざ：正座〉

seiza-suru〈正座する〉sit upright.

seizai〈せいざい：製材〉lumbering, sawing.

　　seizai-sho（製材所）　a lumber mill, a sawmill

seizai-suru〈製材する〉saw (up).

seizei〈せいぜい：精々〉at (the) most, at (the) best; as much(*or* far) as possible.

　　seizei-jussai（せいぜい十歳）　ten years old at the most

　　seizei-too-ka（せいぜい十日）　ten days at the longest

　　Seizei hataraki-nasai.（せいぜい働きなさい．）　Work as hard as you can.

seizen〈せいぜん：生前〉

seizen-no or *seizen-ni*〈生前の，生前に〉during one's lifetime, before one's death, while alive.

seizen〈せいぜん：整然〉

seizen-taru〈整然たる〉orderly, well-ordered, regular, systematic.

seizen-to〈整然と〉in good order, in a regular manner, systematically.

seizô〈せいぞう：製造〉manufacture, production.

    seizô-gyô（製造業）the manufacturing industry

    seizô-gyô-sha, seizô-moto（製造業者，製造元）a manufacturer, a maker, a producer

    seizô-sho（製造所）a factory, a mill, a works.

seizô-suru〈製造する〉manufacture, produce, make.

seizon〈せいぞん：生存〉existence, survival.

    seizon-kyôsô（生存競争）the struggle for existence

    seizon-sha（生存者）a survivor

seizon-suru〈生存する〉exist, live, survive.

sei-zoroi〈せいぞろい：勢ぞろい〉

sei-zoroi-suru〈勢ぞろいする〉muster in full array, line up.

seizu〈せいず：製図〉drafting, drawing.

    seizu-yôshi（製図用紙）drafting(*or* drawing) paper

seizu-suru〈製図する〉draft, draw.

seji〈せじ：世事〉see. seko.

sekai〈せかい：世界〉the world.

    sekai-kakkoku（世界各国）all the countries of the world

    sekai-jôsei（世界情勢）the world situation

sekai-teki(-na)〈世界的(な)〉world, worldwide.

    sekai-teki-na fu-keiki（世界的な不景気）a worldwide depression

sekai-teki-ni-yûmei-na〈世界的に有名な〉of worldwide fame, world-famous.

sekai-de〈世界で〉in the world.

sekai-jû-ni〈世界中に〉all over the world.

sekaseka〈せかせか〉

sekaseka-suru〈せかせかする〉be fidgety, be restless.

sakaseka-shita〈せかせかした〉fidgety, restless.

sekasu〈せかす〉see. isogaseru.

seken〈せけん：世間〉the world.

    seken-o-shitte-iru（世間を知っている）have seen much of the world

    seken-shirazu-de-aru（世間知らずである）know nothing of the world

    Seken-wa-kuchi-ga-urusakarô.（世間は口がうるさかろう.）People will talk.

    Seken-ni-kao-muke-ga-deki-nai.（世間に顔向けができない.）I cannot look the world in the face again.

　　　seken-banashi〈世間話〉a gossip, a chat

seken-banare-shita〈世間離れした〉strange, queer, uncommon, extraordinary.

seken-nami-no〈世間並の〉average, common, ordinary.

　　　seken-nami-no seikatsu o suru（世間並の生活をする）make a decent living

seken-zure-no-shita〈世間擦れのした〉sophisticated.

　　　seken-zure-no-shite-i-nai（世間擦れのしていない）unsophisticated

seken-tei〈せけんてい：世間体〉appearance, decency.

　　　seken-tei-o-tsukurou（世間体を繕う）keep up appearances

　　　seken-tei o kamawa-nai（世間体を構わない）don't care what other people will say ((of a person))

　　　Sore-dewa　seken-tei-ga-warui-darô.（それでは世間体が悪いだろう。）That will be shameful.

seki〈せき：籍〉the census register, one's domicile; membership.

　　　seki-o-ireru（籍を入れる）have ((a person's)) name entered in the register

　　　seki-o-nuku（籍を抜く）have ((a person's)) name removed from the register

　　　Nagoya-ni seki-ga-aru（名古屋に籍がある）be domiciled in Nagoya

　　　seki-o-oku（籍を置く）become a member ((of))

seki〈せき：積〉the product.

seki〈せき：席〉a seat, one's place.

　　　seki ni tsuku（席に着く）take one's seat

　　　seki-o-tatsu（席を立つ）rise from one's seat

　　　seki o hanareru（席を離れる）leave one's seat

　　　seki ni modoru（席に戻る）resume one's seat

　　　seki o toru（席を取る）get a seat, get a table, reserve a seat

　　　seki o yuzuru（席を譲る）offer one's seat ((to))

seki〈せき〉a dam.

　　　seki-o-kitta-yô-ni-shaberi-dasu（せきを切ったようにしゃべり出す）burst out speaking

seki-o-tsukuru〈せきを造る〉construct a dam, dam.

seki〈せき〉a cough, coughing.

　　　seki-dome（せき止め）a cough medicine

seki-o-suru〈せきをする〉cough, have a cough.

　　　hidoi seki o suru（ひどいせきをする）cough violently

　　　karui seki-ga-deru（軽いせきが出る）have a slight cough

seki-barai〈せきばらい：せき払い〉hawking, a cough.
seki-barai-o-suru〈せき払いをする〉clear one's throat, give a cough.
sekibun〈せきぶん：積分〉integral calculus.
sekichū〈せきちゅう：せき柱〉the spinal column, the spine.
sekidô〈せきどう：赤道〉the equator.
sekidô-no〈赤道の〉equatorial.
sekidô-chokka-de or *sekidô-chokka-ni*〈赤道直下で，赤道直下に〉right on the equator.
sekiei〈せきえい：石英〉quartz.
sekigai-sen〈せきがいせん：赤外線〉infrared rays.
sekigai-sen-shashin〈赤外線写真〉an infrared photograph
sekihai〈せきはい：惜敗〉
sekihai-suru〈惜敗する〉be defeated by a narrow margin, lose a close game.
sekihan〈せきはん：赤飯〉rice boiled together with red beans.
sekihi〈せきひ：石碑〉a tombstone, a stone monument.
sekiji〈せきじ：席次〉class standing, the seating order.
sekiji-ga ni-ban-agaru〈席次が二番上がる〉gain in class standing by two places
seki-jūji〈せきじゅうじ：赤十字〉
Seki-jūji-sha〈赤十字社〉the Red Cross (Society)
Seki-jūji-byôin〈赤十字病院〉a Red Cross Hospital
seki-komu〈せきこむ：せき込む〉have a fit of coughing.
sekimen〈せきめん：赤面〉
sekimen-suru〈赤面する〉blush.
hazukashikute sekimen-suru〈恥ずかしくて赤面する〉blush with shame
sekinin〈せきにん：責任〉responsibility.
sekinin-ga-aru〈責任がある〉be responsible ((for))
sekinin o ou〈責任を負う〉bear the responsibility ((for or of))
sekinin o hatasu〈責任を果たす〉fulfil one's responsibility
sekinin o tenka-suru〈責任を転嫁する〉shift the responsibility ((on to))
sekinin-kan-ga-tsuyoi〈責任感が強い〉have a strong sense of responsibility
sekinin-nogare-o-suru〈責任逃れをする〉shirk one's responsibility
sekinin-aru chii〈責任ある地位〉a responsible post
sekinin-sha〈責任者〉a person in charge ((of))

sekiran-un 〈せきらんうん：積乱雲〉a cumulonimbus.

seki-rara 〈せきらら：赤裸々〉
　seki-rara-ni 〈赤裸々に〉plainly, frankly, without reserve.

sekiri 〈せきり：赤痢〉dysentery.
　sekiri-kanja 〈赤痢患者〉a case of dysentery

sekiryô 〈せきりょう：席料〉a cover charge, the charge for a room.

sekiryô 〈せきりょう：責了〉O.K. with corrections.
　sekiryô-ni-suru 〈責了にする〉O.K. ((a proof)) with corrections.

sekisai 〈せきさい：積載〉
　sekisai-suru 〈積載する〉load, carry.

sekisetsu 〈せきせつ：積雪〉(fallen) snow.
　sekisetsu-no-tame-tachi-ôjô-suru 〈積雪のため立ち往生する〉be snowed up, be snowbound.

sekitan 〈せきたん：石炭〉coal.
　sekitan o horu 〈石炭を掘る〉dig out coal
　sekitan o taku 〈石炭をたく〉burn coal
　sekitan-gara 〈石炭殻〉coal cinders

seki-tateru 〈せきたてる：せき立てる〉see. isogaseru.

sekitô 〈せきとう：石塔〉see. sekihi.

seki-tomeru 〈せきとめる：せき止める〉dam up, check, intercept.

sekitsui 〈せきつい：脊椎〉the vertebra.
　sekitsui-dôbutsu 〈せきつい動物〉a vertebrate (animal)

sekiwake 〈せきわけ：関脇〉a second champion *sumo* wrestler.

sekiyu 〈せきゆ：石油〉petroleum, kerosene.
　sekiyu-kiki 〈石油危機〉a petroleum crisis

sekizai 〈せきざい：石材〉building stone.

sekizô 〈せきぞう：石像〉a stone statue.

sekizui 〈せきずい：せき髄〉the spinal cord.
　sekizui-en 〈せき髄炎〉myelitis

sekkachi 〈せっかち〉
　sekkachi-na 〈せっかちな〉hasty, impatient, quick-tempered.

sekkai 〈せっかい：石灰〉lime.
　sekkai-gan 〈石灰岩〉limestone

sekkai 〈せっかい：切開〉incision.
　sekkai-shujutsu 〈切開手術〉a surgical operation
　sekkai-suru 〈切開する〉cut open, incise.

sekkaku 〈せっかく：折角〉with much trouble, kindly.
　sekkaku-tameta o-kane 〈せっかくためたお金〉the money one has

saved with much effort

sekkaku-no〈せっかくの〉kind, precious, long-awaited.
　　sekkaku-no o-maneki（せっかくのお招き）one's kind invitation
　　sekkaku-no kyûjitsu（せっかくの休日）the long-awaited holiday

sekkan〈せっかん：折かん〉
sekkan-suru〈折かんする〉chastise, thrash.

sekkei〈せっけい：設計〉a plan, a design.
　　seikatsu-sekkei（生活設計）life planning
　　sekkei-sha（設計者）a designer
　　sekkei-zu（設計図）a plan
sekkei-suru〈設計する〉plan, design, lay out.

sekken〈せっけん：石けん〉soap.
　　sekken-de-arau（石けんで洗う）wash with soap and water
　　kona-sekken（粉石けん）soap powder
　　sentaku-sekken（洗濯石けん）washing soap
　　yokuyô-sekken（浴用石けん）bath soap

sekken〈せっけん：席けん〉
sekken-suru〈席けんする〉carry everything before one, sweep ((over)), make a conquest ((of)).

sekki〈せっき：石器〉a stone implement.
　　sekki-jidai（石器時代）the Stone Age

sekkin〈せっきん：接近〉approach, access.
sekkin-suru〈接近する〉approach, come near, get close ((to)).

sekkô〈せっこう：石こう〉plaster (of Paris), gypsum.
　　sekkô-zaiku（石こう細工）plaster work
　　sekkô-zô（石こう像）a plaster statue

sekkô〈せっこう：斥候〉a scout.
　　sekkô o dasu（斥候を出す）send out scouts

sekkotsu〈せっこつ：接骨〉bonesetting.
　　sekkotsu-i（接骨医）a bonesetter
sekkotsu-suru〈接骨する〉set a bone.

sekku〈せっく：節句〉a seasonal festival.
　　tango-no-sekku（端午の節句）the Boys' Festival

sekkyô〈せっきょう：説教〉a sermon, preaching; scolding.
sekkyô-suru〈説教する〉preach, preach a sermon; scold.

sekkyoku〈せっきょく：積極〉
sekkyoku-teki(-na)〈積極的(な)〉positive, active.
sekkyoku-teki-ni〈積極的に〉positively, actively.

seko 〈せこ：世故〉 worldly affairs.

  seko-ni-takete-iru 〈世故にたけている〉 be a man of the world.

    seko-ni-utoi 〈世故に疎い〉 be ignorant of the world

seku 〈せく〉 hasten, make haste, hurry.

    Seite-wa koto-o-shi-sonjiru. 〈せいては事を仕損じる．〉 Haste makes waste.

sekuto 〈セクト〉 a sect.

    sekuto-shugi 〈セクト主義〉 sectarianism

semai 〈せまい：狭い〉 narrow, small.

    semai michi 〈狭い道〉 a narrow path

    semai heya 〈狭い部屋〉 a small room

    kôsai-ga-semai 〈交際が狭い〉 have only a small circle of acquaintances

  semaku-naru 〈狭くなる〉 become narrower, narrow.

  semaku-suru 〈狭くする〉 make narrower, narrow.

sema-kurushii 〈せまくるしい：狭苦しい〉 narrow and close.

semaru 〈せまる：迫る〉 press, urge; approach, draw near, be close at hand, be pressing.

    hentô-o-semaru 〈返答を迫る〉 press ((a person)) for an answer

    Jikan ga sematte-iru. 〈時間が迫っている．〉 Time is pressing.

sembai 〈せんばい：専売〉 monopoly.

    sembai-hin 〈専売品〉 monopoly goods

    sembai-tokkyo 〈専売特許〉 a patent

semban 〈せんばん：旋盤〉 a lathe.

    semban-kô 〈旋盤工〉 a latheman, a turner

sembatsu 〈せんばつ：選抜〉 selection, choice, picking out.

    sembatsu-chîmu 〈選抜チーム〉 a selected team

    sembatsu-shiken 〈選抜試験〉 a selective examination

  sembatsu-suru 〈選抜する〉 select, choose, pick out.

sembei 〈せんべい〉 a Japanese rice cracker.

sembetsu 〈せんべつ：せん別〉 a parting gift, a farewell present.

sembi 〈せんび：戦備〉 war preparations.

  sembi-o-totonoeru 〈戦備を整える〉 prepare for war.

sembi 〈せんび：船尾〉 the stern.

sembin 〈せんびん：先便〉 a previous letter.

  sembin-de 〈先便で〉 by the last mail.

sembô 〈せんぼう：せん望〉 envy.

    sembô no mato 〈せん望の的〉 an object of envy

sembô-kyô〈せんぼうきょう：潜望鏡〉a periscope.

sembotsu〈せんぼつ：戦没〉death in battle.

　　sembotsu-sha（戦没者）the war dead

sembyô-shitsu〈せんびょうしつ：せん病質〉

　sembyô-shitsu-na〈せん病質な〉sickly.

seme〈せめ：責め〉responsibility, blame, a charge.

　　seme o ou（責めを負う）take the responsibility ((of))

semento(-o-nuru)〈セメント（をぬる）：セメント（を塗る）〉cement.

semeru〈せめる：攻める〉attack, assault.

semeru〈せめる：責める〉blame, reproach.

　　kashitsu-o semeru（過失を責める）blame ((a person)) for his fault

semete〈せめて〉at least, at most, just.

　　Semete shû-ni ichi-do-gurai kitatte-ii-darô.（せめて週に一度ぐらい来た
　　っていいだろう。）You might come and see me once a week at
　　least.

　　Tsuri ga semete-mono nagusami-desu.（釣りがせめてもの慰みです。）
　　Fishing is my only consolation.

semi〈せみ〉a cicada.

semmai-dooshi〈せんまいどおし：千枚通し〉an eyeleteer.

semman〈せんまん：千万〉ten million.

　　san-zen-man-en（三千万円）thirty million yen

semmei〈せんめい：鮮明〉

　semmei-na〈鮮明な〉clear, distinct, vivid.

　　semmei-na gazô（鮮明な画像）a distinct picture

　semmei-ni〈鮮明に〉clearly, distinctly, vividly.

semmen〈せんめん：洗面〉

　　semmen-ki（洗面器）a washbowl, a basin

　　semmen-jo（洗面所）a washroom, a toilet room, a lavatory

　semmen-suru〈洗面する〉wash one's face.

semmon〈せんもん：専門〉a specialty, a speciality.

　　semmon-ka（専門家）a specialist ((in)), an expert ((on)), a
　　professional ((on))

　　semmon-ten（専門店）a specialty store

　　semmon-go（専門語）a technical term, technics

　　semmon-teki-chishiki（専門的知識）expert knowledge

　～-o-semmon-ni-kenkyû-suru〈～を専門に研究する〉make a special study
　　of... , major in... .

　semmon-ka-suru〈専門化する〉specialize.

semmon-gai-de-aru〈専門外である〉be out of one's line.

semmu〈せんむ：専務〉
　　semmu-tori-shimari-yaku（専務取締役）　a managing director

sempai〈せんぱい：先輩〉one's senior.
　　ni-nen-sempai（二年先輩）　one's senior by two years

sempaku〈せんぱく：船舶〉a vessel, a ship, shipping.

sempaku〈せんぱく：浅薄〉
　sempaku-na〈浅薄な〉shallow, superficial.
　　sempaku-na chishiki（浅薄な知識）　a superficial knowledge

sempatsu〈せんぱつ：先発〉
　　sempatsu-tai（先発隊）　an advance party
　　sempatsu-tôshu（先発投手）　a starting pitcher
　sempatsu-suru〈先発する〉start in advance ((of)).

sempatsu〈せんぱつ：洗髪〉a shampoo.
　sempatsu-suru〈洗髪する〉wash one's hair.

sempi〈せんぴ：戦費〉war expenditure.

sempô〈せんぼう：戦法〉tactics, strategy.

sempô〈せんぼう：先方〉the other party, he, she, they; one's destination.

sempô〈せんぼう：先ぼう〉the van, the vanguard.
　　kyû-sempô（急先ぼう）　the most active leader
　sempô-to-naru〈先ぼうとなる〉lead the van.

sempu〈せんぷ：先夫〉one's former husband.

sempû〈せんぷう：旋風〉a whirlwind, a cyclone.
　sempû-o-maki-okosu〈旋風を巻き起こす〉create a great sensation.

sempû-ki〈せんぷうき：扇風機〉an electric fan.
　　sempû-ki o kakeru（扇風機をかける）　turn on an electric fan
　　sempû-ki o tomeru（扇風機を止める）　turn off an electric fan

sempuku〈せんぷく：船腹〉bottoms, shipping.
　　sempuku no kajô（船腹の過剰）　excess of bottoms

sempuku〈せんぷく：潜伏〉concealment, hiding; incubation.
　　sempuku-kikan（潜伏期間）　the latent period
　sempuku-suru〈潜伏する〉conceal oneself, lie hidden, hide out; be latent.

sen〈せん：千〉a thousand.
　　san-zen（三千）　three thousand
　　nan-zen-to-iu-hitobito（何千という人々）　thousands of people

sen〈せん：栓〉a stopper, a cork, a stopcock, a plug.

bin-no-sen-o-suru（瓶の栓をする） stopper a bottle

bin-no-sen-o-nuku（瓶の栓を抜く） uncork a bottle

suidô-no-sen-o-akeru（水道の栓を開ける） turn on the water

gasu-no-sen-o-shimeru（ガスの栓を閉める） turn off the gas

sen〈せん：線〉a line, a track, a wire.

sen o hiku（線を引く） draw a line

Tôkaidô-sen（東海道線） the Tokaido Line

samban-sen（三番線） the third track, Track Three

denwa-sen（電話線） telephone wires

sen〈せん：選〉selection, choice.

sen-ni-hairu〈選に入る〉be selected, be chosen, be accepted.

sen-ni-moreru *or* sen-gai-to-naru（選に漏れる，選外となる） be left out of selection, be not accepted

sen〈せん〉a gland.

senaka〈せなか：背中〉the back.

senaka o mukeru（背中を向ける） *see.* se o mukeru

senaka o arau（背中を洗う） wash one's back

senaka-awase-ni-suwaru（背中合わせに座る） sit back to back ((with))

sencha〈せんちゃ：せん茶〉green tea.

senchaku〈せんちゃく：先着〉first arrival.

senchaku-jun-ni〈先着順に〉in the order of arrival.

senchi〈せんち：戦地〉the front, a battlefront.

senchi-e iku（戦地へ行く） go to the front

senchi(mentaru)〈センチ（メンタル）〉

senchi(mentaru)-ni-naru〈センチ（メンタル）になる〉become sentimental.

senchi(mentaru)-na〈センチ（メンタル）な〉sentimental.

senchi(-mêtoru)〈センチ（メートル）〉a centimeter.

senchô〈せんちょう：船長〉a captain.

senchû〈せんちゅう：船中〉

senchû-no or *senchû-de*〈船中の，船中で〉in a ship, on board.

sendai〈せんだい：先代〉one's father, one's predecessor.

sendai〈せんだい：船台〉a shipway, stocks.

sendan〈せんだん：船団〉a fleet of vessels.

sendatte〈せんだって：先だって〉*see.* senjitsu.

senden〈せんでん：宣伝〉propaganda, advertisement.

senden-hi（宣伝費） advertising expenses

senden-kôka（宣伝効果） propaganda effect

senden-suru〈宣伝する〉propagandize, advertise.

sendo〈せんど：鮮度〉degree of freshness.
　　sendo-ga-ochiru（鮮度が落ちる）lose ((its)) freshness
sendô〈せんどう：船頭〉a boatman.
sendô〈せんどう：先導〉guidance, leadership.
　　〜-no-sendô-no-moto-ni（〜の先導の下に）under the guidance of...
　sendô-suru〈先導する〉lead, take the lead, guide.
sendô〈せんどう：扇動〉instigation, agitation.
　　sendô-sha（扇動者）an instigator, an agitator
　sendô-suru〈扇動する〉instigate, agitate, stir up.
sen·ei〈せんえい：先鋭〉
　　sen·ei-bunshi（先鋭分子）radicals
　sen·ei-ka-suru〈先鋭化する〉become acute, be radicalized.
　sen·ei-na〈先鋭な〉acute, radical.
sen·etsu〈せんえつ：僭越〉
　sen·etsu-na〈僭越な〉audacious, presumptuous.
　　sen·etsu-na-koto-o-suru（僭越なことをする）exceed one's author-
　　　ity, be presumptuous
　sen·etsu-nagara〈僭越ながら〉with your permission.
senga〈せんが：線画〉(a) line drawing.
sengan〈せんがん：洗眼〉eyewashing.
　sengan-suru〈洗眼する〉wash one's eyes.
sengen〈せんげん：宣言〉a declaration, a proclamation.
　　dokuritsu-sengen（独立宣言）the declaration of independence
　　sengen-sho（宣言書）a declaration, a manifesto, a statement
　sengen-suru〈宣言する〉declare, proclaim.
sengetsu〈せんげつ：先月〉last month.
　　sengetsu-too-ka-ni（先月十日に）on the tenth of last month
sen-giri〈せんぎり：千切り〉
　sen-giri-no〈千切りの〉julienne, shredded.
sengo〈せんご：戦後〉
　sengo-no〈戦後の〉postwar.
sengyo〈せんぎょ：鮮魚〉fresh fish.
sengyô〈せんぎょう：専業〉a special occupation, a specialty.
sen·i〈せんい：繊維〉a fiber.
　　sen·i-seihin（繊維製品）textile goods
sen·i〈せんい：船医〉a ship's doctor.
sen·i〈せんい：戦意〉a fighting spirit.
　　sen·i o ushinau（戦意を失う）lose one's fighting spirit

sen·in 〈せんいん：船員〉a seaman; the crew.

    kôkyû-sen·in〈高級船員〉 a ship's officer

sen·itsu 〈せんいつ：専一〉

    Go-jiai-sen·itsu-ni.〈御自愛専一に.〉Please take good care of yourself.

senji 〈せんじ：戦時〉wartime.

    senji-chû-ni〈戦時中に〉in wartime, during the war.

senji-gusuri 〈せんじぐすり：せんじ薬〉a medical decoction.

senjiru 〈せんじる〉boil, decoct, infuse.

senjitsu 〈せんじつ：先日〉the other day, a few days ago.

senji-tsumeru 〈せんじつめる：せんじ詰める〉boil down.

    senji-tsumeru-to〈せんじ詰めると〉when boiled down, in short, after all, in the end.

        Senji-tsumeru-to-kô-narimasu, sunawachi〜.〈せんじ詰めるとこうなります, すなわち〜.〉 It boils down to this that... .

senjô 〈せんじょう：戦場〉a battlefield.

    senjô-de〈戦場で〉 on the battlefield

senjô 〈せんじょう：洗浄〉washing.

    senjô-yaku〈洗浄薬〉 a wash, a lotion

    senjô-suru〈洗浄する〉wash, rinse.

    i o senjô-suru〈胃を洗浄する〉 wash out one's stomach

senjô 〈せんじょう：せん情〉

    senjô-teki-na〈せん情的な〉inflammatory, sensational, suggestive.

senjû-sha 〈せんじゅうしゃ：専従者〉a full time union officer.

senjutsu 〈せんじゅつ：戦術〉tactics, strategy.

    senjutsu-ka〈戦術家〉 a tactician

    senjutsu-jô-no〈戦術上の〉tactical, strategical.

senka 〈せんか：戦火〉

    Senka ga Yôroppa-ni hirogatta.〈戦火がヨーロッパに広がった.〉 The war has spread to Europe.

senka 〈せんか：戦果〉war results.

senka 〈せんか：戦禍〉war damage.

senka 〈せんか：専科〉a special course.

    senka-sei〈専科生〉 a special-course student

senkai 〈せんかい：旋回〉revolution, turning, circling.

    senkai-hikô〈旋回飛行〉 a circular flight

    senkai-suru〈旋回する〉revolve, turn, circle, rotate.

senkaku-sha 〈せんかくしゃ：先覚者〉a pioneer, a forerunner.

senken〈せんけん：先見〉foresight.
senken-no-mei-no-aru〈先見の明のある〉foresighted, farseeing.
senketsu〈せんけつ：鮮血〉fresh blood.
senketsu-ni somaru〈鮮血に染まる〉be covered with blood
senketsu〈せんけつ：先決〉
senketsu-mondai〈先決問題〉a question to be settled before anything else
senki〈せんき：戦記〉a record of war, a military chronicle.
senki〈せんき：戦機〉the time for fighting.
Senki-jukusu.〈戦機熟す.〉The time has matured for opening a battle.
senkin〈せんきん：千金〉
senkin-no-atai-ga-aru〈千金の値がある〉be priceless.
senkō〈せんこう：線香〉an incense stick.
senkō o ageru〈線香をあげる〉offer incense sticks
senkō〈せんこう：せん光〉a flash.
senkō-o-hanatsu〈せん光を放つ〉flash.
senkō〈せんこう：戦功〉distinguished war services.
senkô-o-tateru〈戦功を立てる〉distinguish oneself in war.
senkō〈せんこう：専攻〉special study.
senkô-kamoku〈専攻科目〉a subject of special study
senkô-suru〈専攻する〉major ((in)), specialize ((in)).
senkō〈せんこう：選考〉choice, selection.
senkô-iin〈選考委員〉a selection committee
senkô-suru〈選考する〉make choice, select.
senkō〈せんこう：潜航〉underwater navigation.
senkô-suru〈潜航する〉navigate under water.
senkō〈せんこう：潜行〉
senkô-suru〈潜行する〉go underground.
senkō〈せんこう：先攻〉
senkô-suru〈先攻する〉go to bat first.
senkō〈せんこう：先行〉
senkô-suru〈先行する〉go ahead ((of)), precede.
jidai-ni-senkô-suru〈時代に先行する〉be ahead of the times
senkō-hanabi〈せんこうはなび：線香花火〉toy fireworks.
senkô-hanabi-teki(-na)〈線香花火的(な)〉short-lived.
senkô-hanabi-shiki-ni-patto-kieru〈線香花火式にぱっと消える〉fizzle out.
senkoku〈せんこく：宣告〉a sentence, adjudication.

shikei-no-senkoku-o-suru〈死刑の宣告をする〉 sentence ((a person)) to death

senkoku-suru〈宣告する〉 sentence, adjudicate.

senku-sha〈せんくしゃ：先駆者〉a pioneer, a forerunner.

senkyaku〈せんきゃく：先客〉

　Senkyaku ga atta-ni-chigai-nai.（先客があったに違いない.） There should have been some visitors before us.

senkyaku〈せんきゃく：船客〉a passenger.

　senkyaku-meibo（船客名簿） a passenger list

senkyaku-banrai〈せんきゃくばんらい：千客万来〉

　Ano mise wa senkyaku-banrai-no-dai-hanjô-da.（あの店は千客万来の大繁盛だ.） That store is doing a flourishing trade.

senkyo〈せんきょ：選挙〉election.

　senkyo-ku（選挙区） an electoral precinct, a constituency

　senkyo-undô（選挙運動） an election campaign

　senkyo-enzetsu（選挙演説） a campaign speech

　senkyo-bi（選挙日） the election day

　senkyo-ken（選挙権） the franchise, the suffrage

　senkyo-nin（選挙人） an elector, a voter

　senkyo-ihan（選挙違反） election irregularities

　sô-senkyo（総選挙） a general election

　hoketsu-senkyo（補欠選挙） a by-election

senkyo-suru〈選挙する〉elect.

senkyo〈せんきょ：占拠〉occupation.

senkyo-suru〈占拠する〉occupy.

　fuhô-senkyo-suru（不法占拠する） occupy ((an office)) illegally

senkyô〈せんきょう：船橋〉a bridge.

senkyô〈せんきょう：戦況〉

　Senkyô wa kambashiku-nakatta.（戦況は芳しくなかった.） The war was not going in our favor.

senkyoku〈せんきょく：戦局〉the tide of war.

　Senkyoku wa wareware-ni-yûri-ni tenkai-shita.（戦局は我々に有利に展開した.） The tide of war turned in our favor.

senkyô-shi〈せんきょうし：宣教師〉a missionary.

senkyû-gan〈せんきゅうがん：選球眼〉

senkyû-gan-ga-aru〈選球眼がある〉have a good batting eye.

sennen〈せんねん：先年〉some years ago, the other year.

sennen〈せんねん：専念〉*see.* senshin（専心）.

sennin 〈せんにん：先任〉

    sennin-sha（先任者）a senior member

    sennin-shôkô（先任将校）a senior officer

sennin 〈せんにん：専任〉

    sennin-kôshi（専任講師）a full-time lecturer

 sennin-no〈専任の〉full-time, in full service.

sennin 〈せんにん：選任〉election, nomination.

 sennin-suru〈選任する〉elect, nominate.

sennô 〈せんのう：洗脳〉brainwashing.

 sennô-suru〈洗脳する〉brainwash.

sen-nuki 〈せんぬき：栓抜き〉a bottle opener, a corkscrew.

sennyû 〈せんにゅう：潜入〉infiltration.

 sennyû-suru〈潜入する〉infiltrate, smuggle oneself ((into)).

sennyû-kan 〈せんにゅうかん：先入観〉a preconceived idea, a pre-conception.

    sennyû-kan-o-suteru（先入観を捨てる）get rid of one's preconceived notion ((against))

 sennyû-kan-to-naru〈先入観となる〉preoccupy, be prepossessed ((with)).

se-nobi 〈せのび：背伸び〉

 se-nobi-suru〈背伸びする〉stretch oneself, stand on tiptoe.

senran 〈せんらん：戦乱〉the disturbances of war.

senrei 〈せんれい：先例〉see. zenrei.

senrei 〈せんれい：洗礼〉baptism, christening.

    senrei-mei（洗礼名）one's Christian name

 senrei-o-hodokosu〈洗礼を施す〉baptize.

 senrei-o-ukeru〈洗礼を受ける〉be baptized.

senren 〈せんれん：洗練〉

 senren-sareta〈洗練された〉polished, refined, elegant.

senretsu 〈せんれつ：戦列〉a line of battle.

    senretsu o hanareru（戦列を離れる）leave the battle line

senri-gan 〈せんりがん：千里眼〉clairvoyance; a clairvoyant(e).

 senri-gan-no〈千里眼の〉clairvoyant.

senri-hin 〈せんりひん：戦利品〉a trophy, booty, spoils〔of war〕.

senritsu 〈せんりつ：旋律〉melody.

 senritsu-teki(-na) or *senritsu-no-utsukushii*〈旋律的(な)，旋律の美しい〉melodious.

senritsu 〈せんりつ：戦りつ〉a shiver, a shudder.

 senritsu-suru〈戦りつする〉shiver, shudder, tremble with fear.

senritsu-su-beki 〈戦りつすべき〉 terrible, horrible.

senro 〈せんろ：線路〉 a (railway) line, a track.

     senro o shiku（線路を敷く） lay a line

senryaku 〈せんりゃく：戦略〉 strategy, a stratagem.

     senryaku-busshi（戦略物資） strategic goods

senryaku-jô-no or *senryaku-teki(-na)* 〈戦略上の，戦略的(な)〉 strategic.

senryaku-jô or *senryaku-teki-ni*〈戦略上，戦略的に〉 from the strategical point of view, strategically.

senryô 〈せんりょう：染料〉 dyes, dyestuffs.

senryô 〈せんりょう：占領〉 occupation.

senryô-suru〈占領する〉 occupy, carry.

senryoku 〈せんりょく：戦力〉 war potentials, fighting power.

     senryoku-no zôkyô（戦力の増強） increase in war potential

sensa-bambetsu 〈せんさばんべつ：千差万別〉

sensa-bambetsu-no〈千差万別の〉 an infinite variety of... .

sensai 〈せんさい：先妻〉 one's former wife.

sensai 〈せんさい：戦災〉 war damage.

     sensai-sha（戦災者） a war sufferer

sensai 〈せいさい：繊細〉

sensai-na〈繊細な〉 delicate, fine, subtle.

sensaku 〈せんさく〉

sensaku-suru〈せんさくする〉 poke and pry.

sensaku-zuki-no〈せんさく好きの〉 inquisitive, prying.

sensei 〈せんせい：先生〉 a teacher, a professor, a doctor.

     Yoshida-sensei（吉田先生） Mr. Yoshida, Mrs. Yoshida, Miss. Yoshida, Prof. Yoshida, Dr. Yoshida

sensei 〈せんせい：宣誓〉 an oath.

sensei-suru〈宣誓する〉 take an oath, swear.

sensei(-shugi) 〈せんせい（しゅぎ）：専政(主義)〉 despotism.

sensei-no or *sensei-teki(-na)*〈専政の，専政的(な)〉 despotic.

senseki 〈せんせき：船籍〉 the nationality of a ship.

     senseki-kô（船籍港） the port of registry

sensen 〈せんせん：戦線〉 the front, the battle line.

     kyôdô-sensen o haru（共同戦線を張る） form a united front

sensen 〈せんせん：宣戦〉 a declaration of war.

sensen-o-fukoku-suru〈宣戦を布告する〉 declare war ((against *or* on)).

sen-sengetsu 〈せんせんげつ：先々月〉 the month before last.

sensen-kyôkyô 〈せんせんきょうきょう：戦々きょうきょう〉

sensen-kyôkyô-to-shite〈戦々きょうきょうとして〉with fear and trembling.

sensen-kyôkyô-to-shite-iru〈戦々きょうきょうとしている〉be in constant fear.

sensêshon〈センセーション〉sensation.

　　sensêshon o maki-okosu（センセーションを巻き起こす）create a sensation

sensêshon-na〈センセーションな〉sensational.

sensha〈せんしゃ：戦車〉a tank.

　　sensha-tai（戦車隊）a tank corps

senshi〈せんし：先史〉prehistory.

senshi〈せんし：戦士〉a soldier, a warrior.

　　mumei-senshi（無名戦士）an unknown soldier(*or* warrior)

senshi〈せんし：戦死〉death in battle.

　　senshi-sha（戦死者）a person killed in action; the war dead

senshi-suru〈戦死する〉fall in battle.

senshin〈せんしん：線審〉a linesman.

senshin〈せんしん：専心〉

senshin-suru〈専心する〉devote oneself ((to)).

senshin-koku〈せんしんこく：先進国〉an advanced nation.

senshitsu〈せんしつ：船室〉a cabin.

　　nitô-senshitsu（二等船室）a second-class cabin

senshô〈せんしょう：戦勝〉a victory, a triumph.

　　senshô-koku（戦勝国）a victorious country

senshô〈せんしょう：戦傷〉a war wound.

　　senshô-sha（戦傷者）a(*or* the) war wounded

senshô〈せんしょう：先勝〉

senshô-suru〈先勝する〉score the first point, win the first game.

senshoku〈せんしょく：染色〉dyeing.

　　senshoku-kôjô（染色工場）a dye works

　　senshoku-tai（染色体）a chromosome

senshoku〈せんしょく：染織〉dyeing and weaving.

senshu〈せんしゅ：船主〉a shipowner.

senshu〈せんしゅ：船首〉the bow.

　　senshu-zô（船首像）a figurehead

senshu〈せんしゅ：選手〉a player.

senshu〈せんしゅ：先取〉

　　senshu-ten（先取点）points(*or* runs) scored first

senshu-ten o ageru *or* senshu-suru〈先取点をあげる，先取する〉score first points(*or* runs)

senshû〈せんしゅう：先週〉last week.

senshû-no-kyô〈先週の今日〉this day week

senshû-no suiyô-bi-ni〈先週の水曜日に〉last Wednesday, on Wednesday last

senshû〈せんしゅう：選集〉selected works, a selection, an anthology.

senshu-ken〈せんしゅけん：選手権〉a championship.

senshu-ken o kakutoku-suru〈選手権を獲得する〉win the championship

senshu-ken o ushinau〈選手権を失う〉lose the championship

sekai-senshu-ken〈世界選手権〉the world championship

senshû-raku〈せんしゅうらく：千秋楽〉the last day of public performance, a close, an end.

senshutsu〈せんしゅつ：選出〉election.

senshutsu-suru〈選出する〉elect.

sensô〈せんそう：戦争〉(a) war, a battle.

Sensô ga okita.〈戦争が起きた。〉A war broke out.

sensô ni katsu〈戦争に勝つ〉win a war

sensô ni makeru〈戦争に負ける〉lose a war

sensô-chû-ni〈戦争中に〉during the war

seosô-suru〈戦争する〉make war ((with)), do battle.

sensô〈せんそう：船窓〉a porthole.

sensu〈センス〉a sense.

sensu-ga-aru〈センスがある〉have good sense

sensu-ga-nai〈センスがない〉have no sense

sensu〈せんす：扇子〉a fan.

sensu-o-tsukau〈扇子を使う〉fan oneself.

sensui〈せんすい：潜水〉diving.

sensui-fu〈潜水夫〉a diver

sensui-fuku〈潜水服〉a diving suit

sensui-byô〈潜水病〉caisson disease

sensuikan〈潜水艦〉a submarine

sensui-suru〈潜水する〉dive.

sentâ〈センター〉center field, a center fielder; a center.

sentai〈せんたい：船体〉the hull, a ship.

sentai〈せんたい：戦隊〉a squadron.

sentaku〈せんたく：洗濯〉wash, washing, laundry, cleaning.

　　sentakki（洗濯機）a washing machine, a washer
　　sentaku-mono（洗濯物）washing
　　sentaku-basami（洗濯ばさみ）a clothespin
　　sentaku-ya（洗濯屋）a laundry
　sentaku-suru〈洗濯する〉wash, clean, launder.

sentaku〈せんたく：選択〉selection, choice, option.
　　sentaku-kamoku〈選択科目〉an elective subject, an optional subject
　sentaku-suru〈選択する〉select, choose, make a choice.

sentan〈せんたん：先端〉a point, a tip; the vanguard.
　ryûkô-no-sentan-o-iku〈流行の先端を行く〉lead the fashion.

sentan〈せんたん：戦端〉hostilities.
　　sentan o hiraku〈戦端を開く〉open hostilities ((with))

sente〈せんて：先手〉forestalling.
　sente-o-toru or *sente-o-utsu*〈先手を取る，先手を打つ〉take the initiative ((from)), forestall.

sentei〈せんてい：選定〉selection.
　　sentei-tosho（選定図書）a selected book
　sentei-suru〈選定する〉select.

sentei〈せんてい：せん定〉pruning.
　　sentei-basami（せん定ばさみ）pruning shears
　sentei-suru〈せん定する〉trim, prune.

senten-teki(-na)〈せんてんてき(な)：先天的(な)〉inborn, native, congenital, inherent, inherited.
　senten-teki-ni〈先天的に〉by nature, congenitally, inherently.

sentetsu〈せんてつ：銑鉄〉pig iron.

sentô〈せんとう：銭湯〉a public bath, a bathhouse.

sentô〈せんとう：せん塔〉a steeple, a spire, a pinnacle.

sentô〈せんとう：先頭〉the head, the top, the lead.
　　sentô-ni-tatte-aruku（先頭に立って歩く）walk at the head ((of))
　sentô-ni-tatsu〈先頭に立つ〉take the lead, lead.

sentô〈せんとう：戦闘〉a battle, a fight, a combat.
　　sentô-in（戦闘員）a combatant
　　hi-sentô-in（非戦闘員）a noncombatant
　　sentô-ki（戦闘機）a fighter (plane)
　sentô-suru〈戦闘する〉fight (a battle).
　sentô-teki(-na)〈戦闘的(な)〉militant, aggressive, combative.

sen·yaku〈せんやく：先約〉a previous engagement.
　　sen·yaku-ga-aru（先約がある）have a previous engagement

sen·yô〈せんよう：専用〉exclusive use.

sen·yô-ki（専用機）a plane for one's personal use

〜-no-sen·yô-de-aru〈〜の専用である〉be for...only, be only for...use.

sen·yô-no〈専用の〉exclusive, private.

sen·yû〈せんゆう：占有〉occupancy, occupation, possession.

sen·yû-ken（占有権）the right of possession

sen·yû-sha（占有者）an occupant, a possessor

sen·yû-suru〈占有する〉occupy, possess, take possession ((of)).

senzai〈せんざい：洗剤〉a cleanser, a detergent.

chûsei-senzai（中性洗剤）a neutral detergent

senzai〈せんざい：潜在〉latency, dormancy.

senzai-kôbai-ryoku（潜在購売力）latent purchasing power

senzai-ryoku（潜在力）potentiality

senzai-ishiki（潜在意識）subconsciousness

senzai-suru〈潜在する〉be latent, be dormant, lurk.

senzai-teki(-na)〈潜在的(な)〉potential, latent, dormant.

senzen〈せんぜん：戦前〉

senzen-no〈戦前の〉prewar.

senzo〈せんぞ：先祖〉an ancestor.

senzo-daidai-no〈先祖代々の〉ancestral.

senzoku〈せんぞく：専属〉

senzoku-suru〈専属する〉belong exclusively ((to)).

senzoku-no〈専属の〉under exclusive contract ((with)).

se-ou〈せおう：背負う〉carry ((something)) on one's back, bear, be burdened ((with)).

seppaku〈せっぱく：切迫〉pressure, urgency.

seppaku-suru〈切迫する〉draw near, press; grow tense.

seppaku-shita〈切迫した〉pressing, urgent.

seppan〈せっぱん：折半〉

seppan-suru〈折半する〉halve, go halves ((on)), go fifty-fifty.

seppa-tsumaru〈せっぱつまる：切羽詰まる〉be driven into a corner.

seppa-tsumatte〈切羽詰まって〉under the pressure of necessity, as a last resort.

seri〈せり：競り〉auction.

seri-de uru（競りで売る）sell by auction

seri-de kau（競りで買う）buy at auction

seri-ageru〈競り上げる〉bid up〔the price〕.

seri-otosu〈競り落とす〉knock ((a thing)) down, make a successful bid.

seri-ai〈せりあい：競り合い〉competition.
　　hageshii seri-ai（激しい競り合い）　a keen competition
　seri-au〈競り合う〉compete with ((a person)) for.
serifu〈せりふ〉words, one's line.
　　serifu o iu（せりふを言う）　speak one's lines
serofan〈セロファン〉cellophane.
　　serofan-shi（セロファン紙）　cellophane paper
seron〈せろん：世論〉public opinion.
　　seron-chôsa（世論調査）　a public opinion census
serotêpu〈セロテープ〉cellophane adhesive tape.
seru〈せる：競る〉bid ((for)), make a bid ((for)).
seruroido〈セルロイド〉celluloid.
sesekomashii〈せせこましい〉narrow, pok(e)y.
seseragi〈せせらぎ〉a little stream; the murmur of a stream.
sesera-warai〈せせらわらい：せせら笑い〉a scornful smile.
　sesera-warau〈せせら笑う〉laugh mockingly ((at)).
seshimeru〈せしめる〉do ((a person)) out of.
　　haha-oya-kara　kane　o　seshimeru（母親から金をせしめる）　do　one's
　　mother out of the money
seshiumu〈セシウム〉cesium.
seshû〈せしゅう：世襲〉heredity.
　　seshû-zaisan（世襲財産）　hereditary estate
　seshû-no〈世襲の〉hereditary.
sesô〈せそう：世相〉social conditions, aspects of life.
　　sesô o han・ei-suru（世相を反映する）　reflect social conditions
sessei〈せっせい：摂生〉
　sessei-suru〈摂生する〉be careful of one's health.
　　sessei-o-okotaru（摂生を怠る）　take little care of one's health
sessi〈せっせい：節制〉moderation, temperance.
　sessei-suru〈節制する〉be moderate ((in)), be temperate ((in)).
sessen〈せっせん：接線〉a tangent (line).
sessen〈せっせん：接戦〉a close contest.
　　sessen-o-enjiru（接戦を演じる）　have a close contest
sesse-to〈せっせと〉diligently, hard.
　　sesse-to hataraku（せっせと働く）　work diligently
sesshi〈せっし：摂氏〉Celsius, centigrade (C.).
　　sesshi hachi-do（摂氏八度）　eight degrees C.
sesshi-yakuwan〈せっしやくわん：切歯やく腕〉

sesshi-yakuwan-suru〈切歯やく腕する〉grind one's teeth (with vexation), feel deeply chagrined ((at)).

sesshô〈せっしょう：殺生〉destruction of life.
sesshô-suru〈殺生する〉destroy life, kill animals.
sesshô-na〈殺生な〉cruel, heartless.
　　Sonna-sesshô-na.（そんな殺生な。）That's too cruel of you.

sesshô〈せっしょう：折衝〉negotiation(s).
　　sesshô-no-umai-hito（折衝のうまい人）a clever negotiator
sesshô-suru〈折衝する〉negotiate with ((a person)) for.

sesshoku〈せっしょく：接触〉contact, touch.
　　Sesshoku ga warui.（接触が悪い。）The contact is bad.
　　sesshoku-o-tamotsu（接触を保つ）keep in contact ((with))
sesshoku-suru〈接触する〉touch, contact, make contact ((with)), come in contact ((with)).

sesshu〈せっしゅ：摂取〉intake, ingestion, adoption.
　　ichi-nichi-no　karorî-sesshu-ryô（一日のカロリー摂取量）caloric intake a day
sesshu-suru〈摂取する〉take, take in, ingest, adopt, assimilate.
　　gaikoku-no　bunka　o　sesshu-suru（外国の文化を摂取する）adopt foreign culture

sesshu〈せっしゅ：接種〉inoculation, vaccination.
sesshu-suru〈接種する〉inoculate, vaccinate.

sesshû〈せっしゅう：接収〉requisition.
sesshû-suru〈接収する〉requisition, take over.
　　sesshû-o-kaijo-suru（接収を解除する）release, derequisition

sessô〈せっそう：節操〉constancy, fidelity, chastity.
　　sessô o mamoru（節操を守る）keep one's principles
　　sessô-no-aru hito（節操のある人）a person of principle
　　sessô-no-nai hito（節操のない人）an unprincipled person

sessui〈せっすい：節水〉water saving.
sessui-suru〈節水する〉economize (in) water.

sessuru〈せっする：接する〉touch ((with)), contact ((with)); adjoin, border ((on)); receive, serve; receive.
　　Kanada wa Amerika-gasshû-koku-ni sesshite-iru.（カナダはアメリカ合衆国に接している。）Canada borders on the United States of America.
　　kyaku ni sessuru（客に接する）serve a guest
　　kyûhô ni sessuru（急報に接する）receive urgent news

se-suji〈せすじ：背筋〉
　　se-suji-ga-itamu（背筋が痛む）have a pain in one's back
　　Se-suji ga samuku-natta.（背筋が寒くなった.）I felt a cold shiver
　　　down my spine.
setai〈せたい：世帯〉a household.
　　setai-nushi（世帯主）the head of a household
se-take〈せたけ：背丈〉*see.* shinchô（身長）.
setchaku-zai〈せっちゃくざい：接着剤〉an adhesive agent.
setchi〈せっち：設置〉establishment, foundation.
　setchi-suru〈設置する〉establish, set up, found, create.
　　iin-kai o setchi-suru（委員会を設置する）set up a committee
setchû(-an)〈せっちゅう（あん）：折衷（案）〉a compromise.
seto〈せと：瀬戸〉a strait, a channel.
seto-giwa〈せとぎわ：瀬戸際〉a critical moment, a crisis.
seto-mono〈せともの：瀬戸物〉porcelain, china, earthenware, pottery.
　　seto-mono-ya（瀬戸物屋）a china store
setsu〈せつ：説〉an opinion, a view; a theory.
　　atarashii-setsu（新しい説）a new theory
setsu〈せつ：節〉time; a paragraph, a clause.
　　sono-setsu（その節）at that time
　　o-hima-no-setsu-wa（お暇の節は）when you are free
　　dai-ni-shô dai-san-setsu（第二章第三節）Chapter 2, Paragraph 3
　　shu-setsu（主節）the principal clause
setsu〈せつ：切〉
　setsu-naru〈切なる〉eager, earnest, fervent, ardent.
　　setsu-naru negai（切なる願い）one's fervent desire
　　setsu-naru omoi（切なる思い）an ardent love
setsubi〈せつび：設備〉equipment, conveniences, accommodations.
　　setsubi no kaizen（設備の改善）improvement of equipment
　　setsubi-tôshi（設備投資）equipment investment
　　bôka-setsubi（防火設備）fire-prevention devices
　　kindai-teki setsubi（近代的設備）modern conveniences
　　hoteru-no setsubi（ホテルの設備）hotel accommodations
　～-no-setsubi-ga-aru〈～の設備がある〉be equipped with... .
　setsubi-no-ii〈設備のいい〉well-equipped.
　　setsubi-no-warui（設備の悪い）poorly-equipped
setsubô〈せつぼう：切望〉an earnest desire, an eager wish.
　setsubô-suru〈切望する〉desire earnestly, wish eagerly.

setsubun〈せつぶん：節分〉the day before the (calendric) beginning of spring.

setsudan〈せつだん：切断〉cutting, amputation.

setsudan-suru〈切断する〉cut off, amputate.

　　migi-ashi-o-setsudan-suru（右足を切断する）have one's right leg amputated

setsuden〈せつでん：節電〉power saving.

setsuden-suru〈節電する〉economize (in) electricity.

setsudo〈せつど：節度〉

setsudo-o-mamoru〈節度を守る〉be moderate, use moderation ((in)).

setsugen〈せつげん：節減〉reduction, curtailment, economy.

setsugen-suru〈節減する〉reduce, curtail, cut down.

　　keihi o setsugen-suru（経費を節減する）cut down expenses

setsugô〈せつごう：接合〉joining, union.

setsugô-suru〈接合する〉join, unite, connect, put together.

setsujitsu〈せつじつ：切実〉

setsujitsu-na〈切実な〉earnest, fervent, keen.

　　setsujitsu-na negai（切実な願い）an earnest desire

　　setsujitsu-na mondai（切実な問題）an urgent problem

setsujitsu-ni〈切実に〉earnestly, keenly.

　　hitsuyô-sei o setsujitsu-ni kanjiru（必要性を切実に感じる）feel keenly the necessity ((of))

setsjo〈せつじょ：切除〉erasion, a resection.

setsujo-suru〈切除する〉cut off, resect.

setsujoku〈せつじょく：雪辱〉vindication of one's honor, revenge.

　　setsujoku-sen（雪辱戦）a return match(*or* game)

setsujoku-suru〈雪辱する〉vindicate one's honor, remove one's disgrace, avenge one's defeat.

setsujô-sha〈せつじょうしゃ：雪上車〉a snowmobile, a snow car.

setsumei〈せつめい：説明〉(an) explanation.

　　setsumei-sho（説明書）an explanation, an explanatory (note)

setsumei-suru〈説明する〉explain, give an explanation ((of)).

setsumei-no-dekiru〈説明のできる〉explainable, explicable.

　　setsumei-no-dekinai（説明のできない）unexplainable, inexplicable

setsuna〈せつな〉a moment.

setsuna-teki(-na)〈せつな的(な)〉momentary.

setsuri〈せつり：摂理〉providence.

　　kami-no setsuri（神の摂理）divine providence

setsuritsu 〈せつりつ：設立〉 establishment, foundation, organization.

    setsuritsu-sha（設立者） the founder, the organizer

  setsuritsu-suru〈設立する〉establish, found, set up, organize.

setsuwa〈せつわ：説話〉a tale, a story, a narrative.

    setsuwa-tai（説話体）a narrative form

      setsuwa-tai-no shôsetsu（説話体の小説） a novel in narrative form

  setsuwa-teki(-na)〈説話的(な)〉narrative.

setsuyaku〈せつやく：節約〉saving, economy.

  setsuyaku-suru〈節約する〉save, economize, cut (down).

  totemo-setsuyaku-shite〈とても節約して〉with strict economy.

setsuyu〈せつゆ：説諭〉admonition, reproof.

    setsuyu-no-ue hômen-suru（説諭の上放免する） release ((a person)) on reprimand

  setsuyu-suru〈説諭する〉admonish, reprove.

setsuzoku〈せつぞく：接続〉connection.

    setsuzoku-shi（接続詞）a conjunction

  setsuzoku-suru〈接続する〉connect.

    Kono basu wa hachi-ji-hatsu-no-kyûkô-ni setsuzoku-shimasu-ka?（こ のバスは八時発の急行に接続しますか。） Does this bus connect with the 8:00 express?

settai〈せったい：接待〉(a) reception, a welcome.

    settai-gakari（接待係） a reception committee

    settai-hi（接待費） reception expenses

  settai-suru〈接待する〉receive, entertain, welcome.

settei〈せってい：設定〉establishment, creation, institution.

  settei-suru〈設定する〉establish, create, institute, set up.

setten〈せってん：接点〉a point of contact.

setto〈セット〉a set.

    kôhî-setto（コーヒーセット） a coffee set

    san-ten-setto（三点セット） a three-piece set

    tenisu-o-san-setto-yaru（テニスを三セットやる） play three sets of tennis

    kami o setto-shite-morau（髪をセットしてもらう） have one's hair set

settô〈せっとう：窃盗〉a thief; (a) theft, pilferage.

    settô-zai（窃盗罪） larceny

  settô-o-hataraku〈窃盗を働く〉commit a theft, steal, pilfer.

settoku〈せっとく：説得〉persuasion.

    settoku-ryoku（説得力） persuasive power

settoku-ryoku-no-aru〈説得力のある〉 persuasive

settoku-suru〈説得する〉 persuade.

settoku-shite yame-saseru（説得してやめさせる） dissuade ((a person)) from ((doing))

sewa〈せわ：世話〉 care, trouble; help, aid, assistance; good offices.

Kanojo-wa oba-no-sewa-o-ukete-iru.（彼女は叔(伯)母の世話を受けている。） She is under the care of her aunt.

O-sewa-ni-narimashita.（お世話になりました。） Thank you for your kind help.

Katô-san-no o-sewa-de（加藤さんのお世話で）through the good offices of Mr. Katô

Yokei-na-o-sewa-da.（余計なお世話だ。）That's none of your business.

sewa-yaki（世話焼き） a meddlesome person, a busybody

sewa-zuki〈世話好き〉 an obliging person

sewa-suru〈世話する〉take care ((of)), look ((after)); help, aid, assist; do ((a person)) a service.

sewa-no-yakeru〈世話の焼ける〉troublesome, annoying.

sewashii〈せわしい〉 busy, restless.

-seyo〈-せよ〉 though, even if.

nani-goto-ni-seyo（何事にせよ） whatever it may be

sezoku〈せぞく：世俗〉vulgar customs, the world.

sezoku-ni-toraware-nai（世俗に捕らわれない） stand aloof from the world

shaba〈しゃば：しゃ婆〉this world; the outside world.

Mô-shaba-ni-yô-wa-nai.（もうしゃ婆に用はない。） I have no more use for this world.

shaba-e-deru（しゃ婆へ出る） leave prison

shaberi-makuru〈しゃべりまくる〉rattle on, shoot off one's mouth.

shaberu〈シャベル〉a shovel.

shaberu-de-sukuu〈シャベルですくう〉shovel.

shaberu〈しゃべる〉talk, chat.

yoku-shaberu-hito（よくしゃべる人） a great talker

shabon〈シャボン〉soap.

shabon-dama（シャボン玉） a soap bubble

shaboten〈シャボテン〉*see.* saboten.

shaburu〈しゃぶる〉suck.

yubi o shaburu（指をしゃぶる） suck one's finger

shachi〈しゃち〉a grampus.

shachihoko〈しゃちほこ〉
　　kin-no shachihoko（金のしゃちほこ）two golden dolphins (on the top of a castle roof)
shachō〈しゃちょう：社長〉the president, the head.
　　fuku-shachō（副社長）a vice-president
shachū〈しゃちゅう：社中〉a troupe, a company.
shadan〈しゃだん：遮断〉interception, isolation.
　　shadan-ki（遮断器(機)）a breaker, a crossing gate
　　shadan-suru〈遮断する〉intercept, cut off, isolate.
　　　gaibu-to-no-kōtsū o subete shadan-suru（外部との交通をすべて遮断する）cut off from all communication with the outside world
shadan-hōjin〈しゃだんほうじん：社団法人〉a corporation, an incorporated body, a corporate juridical person.
shadō〈しゃどう：車道〉a roadway, a driveway.
shafutsu〈しゃふつ：煮沸〉boiling.
　　shafutsu-shōdoku-suru（煮沸消毒する）sterilize by boiling
　　shafutsu-suru〈煮沸する〉boil.
shagamu〈しゃがむ〉sit (down) on one's heels, crouch.
　　shagande〈しゃがんで〉in a crouching posture.
shagare-goe〈しゃがれごえ：しゃがれ声〉a hoarse voice.
　　shagare-goe-de〈しゃがれ声で〉in a hoarse voice, huskily.
shagareru〈しゃがれる〉become hoarse, hoarsen.
shageki〈しゃげき：射撃〉firing, shooting, fire.
　　shageki-suru〈射撃する〉fire ((at or on)), shoot.
shahei〈しゃへい：遮へい〉cover, shelter.
　　shahei-suru〈遮へいする〉cover, shelter, shade.
shahen〈しゃへん：斜辺〉the hypotenuse.
shahi〈しゃひ：社費〉the company's expenses.
　　shahi-de（社費で）at one's company's expense
shahon〈しゃほん：写本〉a manuscript, a hand-written copy.
shai〈しゃい：謝意〉gratitude, thanks; apology.
　　shai o hyōsuru（謝意を表する）express one's gratitude, tender an apology ((for))
shain〈しゃいん：社員〉a member, a clerk, an employee; the staff.
　　sei-shain（正社員）a regular member, a staff member
shajiku〈しゃじく：車軸〉an axle.
shajitsu〈しゃじつ：写実〉
　　shajitsu-shugi（写実主義）realism

shajitsu-teki(-na)〈写実的（な）〉realistic.

shajitsu-teki-ni〈写実的に〉realistically.

Shaka〈しゃか〉Gautama, Buddha.

shakai〈しゃかい：社会〉society, the world.

    shakai-ka（社会科）social studies

    shakai-jōsei（社会情勢）social conditions

    shakai-mondai（社会問題）a social problem

    shakai-seido（社会制度）the social system

    shakai-teki chii（社会的地位）one's social position

    shakai-shugi（社会主義）socialism

    shakai-jin-ni-naru（社会人になる）go out into the world

 shakai-no or *shakai-teki(-na)*〈社会の，社会的（な）〉social.

shakan〈しゃかん：舎監〉a dormitory inspector.

shakan-kyori〈しゃかんきょり：車間距離〉the distance between cars.

 shakan-kyori-o-jūbun-ni-tora-nai〈車間距離を十分にとらない〉drive too close to the front car.

shaken〈しゃけん：車検〉an automobile inspection.

shakkan〈しゃっかん：借款〉a loan.

    shakkan-o-mōshi-komu（借款を申し込む）apply for a loan

shakkin〈しゃっきん：借金〉a debt, a loan.

    shakkin-ga-aru（借金がある）be in debt ((to *or* with))

    shakkin-de-kubi-ga-mawara-nai（借金で首が回らない）be deeply in debt

    shakkin o kaesu（借金を返す）pay back one's debt

 shakkin-suru〈借金する〉borrow money ((from)), run into debt.

shakkuri〈しゃっくり〉a hiccup.

    shakkuri-ga-tomara-nai（しゃっくりが止まらない）cannot get rid of one's hiccups

 shakkuri-o-suru〈しゃっくりをする〉hiccup.

shako〈しゃこ：車庫〉a garage, a car shed, a tram depot.

shako〈しゃこ〉a giant clam; a squilla.

shakō〈しゃこう：社交〉social intercourse.

    shakō-ka（社交家）a sociable person

    shakō-kai（社交界）society circles

    shakō-sei（社交性）sociability

      shakō-sei-ni-toboshii（社交性に乏しい）lack sociability, be unsociable

 shakō-teki(-na)〈社交的（な）〉social, sociable.

shakô〈しゃこう：射幸〉

    shakô-shin〈射幸心〉a speculative spirit

        shakô-shin o sosoru〈射幸心をそそる〉increase popular speculation, stir up the gambling spirit

  shakô-teki(-na)〈射幸的(な)〉speculative.

shaku〈しゃく：酌〉

  shaku-o-suru〈酌をする〉serve ((a person)) with *sake*.

shaku〈しゃく〉

    Kanojo-ni-makeru-no-wa-shaku-da.（彼女に負けるのはしゃくだ.）I just can't stand being beaten by her.

  shaku-ni-sawaru〈しゃくに障る〉sting ((a person)) to the quick.

shakuchi〈しゃくち：借地〉leased land.

    shakuchi-ken〈借地権〉a lease, a leasehold

shakudo〈しゃくど：尺度〉a measure, a scale, a gauge, a standard.

shakuhachi〈しゃくはち：尺八〉a bamboo clarinet with five holes.

shakuhô〈しゃくほう：釈放〉release, discharge, acquittal.

  shakuhô-suru〈釈放する〉release, set free, discharge, acquit.

shakui〈しゃくい：爵位〉a title of nobility.

shakumei〈しゃくめい：釈明〉explanation, an apology, vindication.

  shakumei-suru〈釈明する〉explain, apologize ((for)), vindicate.

shakunetsu〈しゃくねつ：しゃく熱〉incandescence, red heat.

    shakunetsu-no taiyô〈しゃく熱の太陽〉a scorching sun

shakuryô〈しゃくりょう：酌量〉consideration, allowance(s).

    Jôjô-shakuryô-no-yochi-nashi.（情状酌量の余地なし.）Nothing can extenuate his guilt.

  shakuryô-suru〈酌量する〉consider, take into consideration, make allowance(s) ((for)).

  jôjô-o-shakuryô-shite〈情状を酌量して〉in consideration of extenuating circumstances.

shakushi〈しゃくし：しゃく子〉a dipper, a ladle, a scoop.

shakushi-jôgi〈しゃくしじょうぎ：しゃく子定規〉formalism.

    shakushi-jôgi-de-yaru〈しゃくし定規でやる〉go by rule and measure, stick fast to rules

    shakushi-jôgi-na-hito〈しゃくし定規な人〉a formalist, a stickler

shakuya〈しゃくや：借家〉a rented house.

    shakuya-dai〈借家代〉a house rent

    shakuya-nin〈借家人〉a tenant

shakuyaku〈しゃくやく〉a peony.

shakuyô 〈しゃくよう：借用〉borrowing, loan.
　　shakuyô-shôsho（借用証書）a bond of debt, an IOU
　shakuyô-suru〈借用する〉borrow.
shamen〈しゃめん：斜面〉a slope.
shamen〈しゃめん：赦免〉
　shamen-suru〈赦免する〉pardon, remit, let ((a person)) off, discharge, set ((a person)) free.
shamo〈しゃも〉a gamecock, a fighting cock.
shamoji〈しゃもじ〉a large wooden ladle, a rice scoop.
shampen〈シャンペン〉champagne.
　　shampen-o-pon-to-nuku（シャンペンをポンと抜く）pop open a champagne bottle
shampû〈シャンプー〉a shampoo.
　shampû-de-kami-o-arau〈シャンプーで髪を洗う〉shampoo.
Shamu-neko〈シャムねこ：シャム猫〉a Siamese cat.
shanarishanari(-to)〈しゃなりしゃなり（と）〉gracefully, mincingly.
　shanarishanari-to aruku〈しゃなりしゃなりと歩く〉mince gracefully about.
shani-muni〈しゃにむに：遮二無二〉
　shani-muni-tosshin-suru〈遮二無二突進する〉make a rush ((against)), dash recklessly.
shanson〈シャンソン〉a chanson, a song.
shaon〈しゃおん：謝恩〉
　　shaon-kai（謝恩会）a dinner party given ((by the graduates)) in honor of their teachers
　　shaon-uri-dashi（謝恩売り出し）thank-you sales
shâpu-penshiru〈シャープペンシル〉an automatic pencil.
share〈しゃれ〉a joke, a pun.
　　share-ga-umai（しゃれがうまい）be good at jokes
　share-o-iu〈しゃれを言う〉joke, pun, make a joke, make a pun.
sharei〈しゃれい：謝礼〉thanks; a reward, a fee.
sharekôbe〈しゃれこうべ〉a skull.
shareta〈しゃれた〉humorous, smart; stylish, chic.
sharin〈しゃりん：車輪〉a wheel.
sharyô〈しゃりょう：車両〉vehicles, cars; the rolling stock.
shasai〈しゃさい：社債〉a debenture, a bond.
　　chôki-shasai（長期社債）a long-term debenture
　　tanki-shasai（短期社債）a short-term debenture

shasatsu〈しゃさつ：射殺〉

shasatsu-suru〈射殺する〉shoot ((a person)) dead, kill by shooting.

shasei〈しゃせい：写生〉sketching.

    shasei-ni-dekakeru〈写生に出掛ける〉 go sketching

    shasei-chô〈写生帳〉 a sketchbook

shasei-suru〈写生する〉sketch, make a sketch ((of)).

shasen〈しゃせん：車線〉a lane.

    yon-shasen(-dôro)〈四車線(道路)〉 a four-lane road

shasen〈しゃせん：斜線〉an oblique line.

shasetsu〈しゃせつ：社説〉an editorial, a leading article.

shâshâ〈しゃあしゃあ〉

shâshâ-shite-iru〈しゃあしゃあしている〉look quite unperturbed.

shâshâ-shita〈しゃあしゃあした〉shameless, brazenfaced.

shâshâ-to〈しゃあしゃあと〉shamelessly, brazenfacedly.

    Yoku-mo shâshâ-to anna uso-ga-ieru-ne!〈よくもしゃあしゃあとあんな
    うそが言えるね。〉 How shameless you are to tell a lie like that!

shashi〈しゃし：斜視〉a squint.

    shashi-de-aru〈斜視である〉 have a squint

shashin〈しゃしん：写真〉a photograph, a photo, a picture; a photo-
graphy.

    shashin o toru〈写真を撮る〉 take a picture

    shashin o totte-morau〈写真を撮ってもらう〉 have one's photograph
    taken

    shashin-utsuri-ga-ii〈写真写りがいい〉 come out well in a photograph

    shashin-girai-de-aru〈写真嫌いである〉 be camera-shy

    shashin-ki〈写真機〉 a camera

    shashin-hantei〈写真判定〉 a photo decision

    shashin-seihan〈写真製版〉 phototype process

    shashin-shokuji *or* shashoku〈写真植字，写植〉 phototypesetting

shashô〈しゃしょう：車掌〉a conductor, a guard.

shashutsu〈しゃしゅつ：射出〉

shashutsu-suru〈射出する〉emit, project, shoot out, jet, radiate.

shasô〈しゃそう：車窓〉a car(*or* train) window.

    shasô-kara nagameru-fûkei〈車窓から眺める風景〉 the scenery seen
    from a train window

shatai〈しゃたい：車体〉a car body.

shataku〈しゃたく：社宅〉a company's house 〔for its employees〕.

shatei〈しゃてい：射程〉a (shooting) range.

shatei-nai-ni-hairu（射程内に入る）　come within range

shateki-ba〈しゃてきば：射的場〉a shooting gallery.

shatsu〈シャツ〉a shirt, an undershirt.

shattâ〈シャッター〉a shutter.

shattâ o kiru（シャッターを切る）　release the shutter

shattâ o orosu（シャッターを下ろす）　pull down a shutter

shatto-auto〈シャットアウト〉shutting out; a shutout.

shawâ〈シャワー〉a shower.

shawâ o abiru（シャワーを浴びる）　take a shower

shayō〈しゃよう：社用〉

shayô-de〈社用で〉on the business of one's firm.

shayō〈しゃよう：斜陽〉

shayô-sangyô（斜陽産業）　a declining industry

shayô-zoku（斜陽族）　the declining upper-class families

shazai〈しゃざい：謝罪〉(an) apology.

shazai o yôkyû-suru（謝罪を要求する）　demand an apology ((from))

shazai-kôkoku o shimbun-ni dasu（謝罪広告を新聞に出す）　publish an apology in a newspaper

shazai-suru〈謝罪する〉apologize, make an apology.

shazetsu〈しゃぜつ：謝絶〉refusal.

shazetsu-suru〈謝絶する〉refuse, decline.

menkai-o-shazetsu-suru（面会を謝絶する）　decline to see a visitor

shepâdo〈シェパード〉a German shepherd (dog).

shi〈し：市〉a city.

shi(ritsu)-no〈市(立)の〉city, municipal.

shi〈し：死〉death; out.

shi-o-kakugo-suru（死を覚悟する）　prepare oneself for death

shi o manukareru（死を免れる）　escape death

shi o maneku（死を招く）　cause one's death

shi o hayameru（死を早める）　quicken one's death

jiko-shi（事故死）　an accidental death

kyû-shi（急死）　a sudden death

shokku-shi（ショック死）　death from the shock ((of))

shi-no-yô-na seijaku（死のような静寂）　a deathlike silence

ni-shi-manrui（二死満塁）　bases loaded full with two outs

shi〈し：詩〉a poem, poetry, verse.

shi o tsukuru（詩を作る）　write a poem

shi-no or *shi-teki-na*〈詩の，詩的な〉poetic, poetical.

shi 〈し：四〉 four.

    dai-shi（第四） the fourth

shi 〈し：師〉 a teacher, an instructor, (the) Rev.

shi 〈し：史〉 history, the annals.

    kinsei-shi（近世史） modern history

-shi 〈-し：-氏〉 Mr.

    Yamada-shi（山田氏） Mr. Yamada

    Yamada-shi-fusai（山田氏夫妻） Mr. and Mrs. Yamada

-shi 〈-し〉 and, moreover, besides, what with and (what with).

    Samui-shi-onaka-wa-suku-shi mi-o-irete-benkyô-deki-nai.（寒いしおな
      かはすくし身を入れて勉強できない。） What with coldness and
      hunger, I cannot devote myself to my studies.

shī 〈しっ〉 hush!, hist!, sh!, mum!, whist!, shoo!.

shi-agaru 〈しあがる：仕上がる〉 be finished, be completed.

shi-age 〈しあげ：仕上げ〉 finish, completion.

    shi-age-ga-ii（仕上げがいい） have a nice finish

    shi-ageru 〈仕上げる〉 finish, complete.

shiai 〈しあい：試合〉 a game, a match.

    yakyû-no shiai（野球の試合） a baseball game

    shiai o suru 〈試合をする〉 play a match(*or* a game) ((with)).

shian 〈しあん：思案〉 thought, consideration, meditation.

    shian-gao（思案顔） a thoughtful look

    shian-suru 〈思案する〉 think ((about)), meditate ((on)), ponder ((over)).

shian 〈しあん：試案〉 a tentative plan, a draft (plan).

shian 〈シアン〉 cyanogen.

shi-assatte 〈しあさって〉 two days after tomorrow.

shiatsu-ryôhô 〈しあつりょうほう：指圧療法〉 a finger-pressure therapy
    (*or* cure).

shiawase 〈しあわせ：幸せ〉 (good) fortune, happiness.

    shiawase-na 〈幸せな〉 fortunate, happy.

    shiawase-ni-mo 〈幸せにも〉 fortunately, happily.

shiba 〈しば：芝〉 turf, grass.

    shiba-kari-ki（芝刈り機） a lawn mower

shiba-fu 〈しばふ：芝生〉 a lawn, a turf.

    shiba-fu o karu（芝生を刈る） mow the lawn

    Shiba-fu-hairu-bekarazu.（芝生入るべからず。） Keep off the grass.

shibai 〈しばい：芝居〉 a play, a drama.

    shibai-kembutsu（芝居見物） theatergoing, playgoing

shibai-kembutsu-ni-iku（芝居見物に行く） go to the theater

shibai-gakatta or *shibai-jimita*〈芝居がかった，芝居染みた〉theatrical, stagy.

shibai-hin〈しばいひん：試売品〉goods on trial sale.

shibaraku〈しばらく〉for a while, for some time, for a long time.

Shibaraku koko-de o-machi-kudasai.（しばらくここでお待ちください.） Please wait here for a while.

Shibaraku-deshita.（しばらくでした.） It's a long time since I saw you last.

shibaraku-shite(-kara)〈しばらくして（から）〉after a while.

shibaraku-sureba〈しばらくすれば〉in a short time.

shibari-tsukeru〈しばりつける：縛り付ける〉bind ((a person)) to 〔a tree〕.

shibaru〈しばる：縛る〉bind, tie, fasten, restrict, chain.

shikkari shibaru（しっかり縛る） tie fast

jikan-ni-shibarareru（時間に縛られる） be restricted by time

shigoto-ni-shibarareru（仕事に縛られる） be chained to one's business

shibashiba〈しばしば〉*see.* tabitabi.

Shiberia〈シベリア〉Siberia.

Shiberia-no〈シベリアの〉Siberian.

shibetsu〈しべつ：死別〉

shibetsu-suru〈死別する〉be bereaved ((of)).

shibin〈しびん：し瓶〉a chamber pot.

shibire〈しびれ〉numbness, paralysis.

Ashi-ni-shibire-ga-kireta.（足にしびれが切れた.） My feet are asleep.

shibire-o-kirasu（しびれを切らす） lose one's patience, grow impatient

shibireru〈しびれる〉become numb, be benumbed, be paralysed.

shibo〈しぼ：思慕〉longing ((for)), yearning ((for)), deep attachment ((to)).

shibô〈しぼう：死亡〉death.

shibô-sha（死亡者） the dead

shibô-ritsu（死亡率） death rate

shibô-kiji（死亡記事） an obituary (notice)

shibô-suru〈死亡する〉die.

shibô〈しぼう：志望〉a desire, an aspiration, a choice.

shibô-kô（志望校） the school of one's choice

shibô-sha（志望者） an aspirant ((to)), an applicant ((for)), a

candidate ((for))

shibô-suru〈志望する〉desire, wish, aspire ((to)), choose.

shibō〈しぼう：脂肪〉fat.

     shibō-ga-tsuku（脂肪が付く）put on fat

     shibō-o-toru（脂肪を取る）remove surplus fat, exercise fat off

     shibō-kata（脂肪過多）obesity, excess of fat

shibō-no-ooi〈脂肪の多い〉fatty.

shibomu〈しぼむ〉fade (away), wither, droop, wilt, deflate.

shibori〈しぼり：絞り〉an iris (of a camera); tie-dyed fabrics.

     shibori-hachi-de-utsusu（絞り八で写す）take a picture at f. 8

shibori-ageru or **shibori-toru**〈しぼりあげる，しぼりとる：絞り上げる，絞り取る〉squeeze ((a person)) dry, bleed ((a person)) white.

shibori-dashi〈しぼりだし：絞り出し〉

     shibori-dashi-enogu（絞り出し絵の具）tube colors

shibori-ki〈しぼりき：絞り機〉a (clothes) wringer.

shiboru〈しぼる：絞(搾)る〉wring, squeeze; press, milk; scold.

     tenugui o shiboru（手ぬぐいを絞る）wring a towel

     mikan-no-shiru o shiboru（みかんの汁を搾る）press the juice from an orange

     miruku o shiboru（ミルクを搾る）milk a cow

     renzu o shiboru（レンズを絞る）stop (down) the lens

     atama o shiboru（頭を絞る）rack one's brains

     sensei-ni shiborareru（先生に絞られる）be scolded by a teacher

shibu〈しぶ：支部〉a branch, a chapter, a local.

shibu〈しぶ：渋〉astringent juice.

     shibu o nuku（渋を抜く）remove the astringency (from persimmons)

     shibu-gaki（渋がき）an astringent persimmon

shibui〈しぶい：渋い〉astringent; sullen; sober, tasteful.

     shibui budō-shu（渋いぶどう酒）rough wine

     shibui-kao-o-suru（渋い顔をする）look sullen

     shibui iro（渋い色）a sober color

shibuki〈しぶき〉a spray, a splash.

     shibuki o ageru（しぶきを上げる）send up spray

shibuki-o-tobasu〈しぶきを飛ばす〉spray, splash.

shibun〈しぶん：詩文〉prose and poetry.

shiburu〈しぶる：渋る〉

     henji-o-shiburu（返事を渋る）hesitate to answer

kane o dashi-shiburu〈金を出し渋る〉 grudge money

shibushibu(-to)〈しぶしぶ(と)：渋々(と)〉reluctantly, unwillingly.

shibutoi〈しぶとい〉stubborn, obstinate, stiff-necked, audacious, impudent.

Nan-to　aitsu-wa　shibutoi-yatsu-da!（何とあいつはしぶといやつだ.）What nerve he's got!

shibutsu〈しぶつ：私物〉one's (private) property, one's personal effects.

shichi〈しち：七〉seven.

dai-shichi〈第七〉 the seventh

shichi〈しち：質〉a pawn.

shichi-ya〈質屋〉 a pawnbroker; a pawnbroker's shop, a pawnshop

shichi-ni-ireru〈質に入れる〉pawn.

shichi-kara-dasu〈質から出す〉 take out a pawn

Shichi-fukujin〈しちふくじん：七福神〉the Seven Gods of Good Fortune.

shichigatsu〈しちがつ：七月〉July.

shichi-go-san〈しちごさん：七五三〉the gala day for children of three, five and seven years old.

shichi-jû〈しちじゅう：七十〉seventy.

dai-shichi-jû〈第七十〉 the seventieth

shichi-ken〈しちけん：質権〉the right of pledge.

shichi-ken o settei-suru〈質権を設定する〉 establish the right of pledge

shichi-ken-settei-sha〈質権設定者〉 a pledger

shichi-ken-sha〈質権者〉 a pledgee

shichimen-chô〈しちめんちょう：七面鳥〉a turkey.

shichirin〈しちりん：七輪〉a portable clay cooking stove.

shichiten-battô〈しちてんばっとう：七転八倒〉

shichiten-battô-no-kurushimi-o-suru〈七転八倒の苦しみをする〉writhe in agony.

shichô〈しちょう：市長〉a mayor.

shichô〈しちょう：視聴〉

shichô-kaku〈視聴覚〉 the visual and auditory senses

shichô-kaku-kyôiku〈視聴覚教育〉 audiovisual education

shichô-sha〈視聴者〉 a (television) viewer

shichô-ritsu〈視聴率〉 audience rating

shi-chô-son〈しちょうそん：市町村〉cities, towns, and villages; municipalities.

shichû 〈シチュー〉a stew.

  shichû-ni suru 〈シチューにする〉stew.

shichû-ginkô 〈しちゅうぎんこう：市中銀行〉a city bank.

shida 〈しだ〉a fern, fernery.

-shidai 〈-しだい：-次第〉as soon as, on.

    Kyôto-ni-tsuki-shidai（京都に着き次第）as soon as I get to Kyoto

    ko-gitte-o-uketori-shidai（小切手を受け取り次第）on receipt of ((a person's)) check

    tsugô-ga-tsuki-shidai-hayaku（都合がつき次第早く）at one's earliest convenience

  〜-shidai-da 〈〜次第だ〉depend on... .

    Sore-wa kimi-no doryoku-shidai-da.（それは君の努力次第だ．）It depends on your own efforts.

shidai-ni 〈しだいに：次第に〉gradually, by degrees.

shidan 〈しだん：師団〉a division.

    shidan-shirei-bu（師団司令部）the division headquarters

shidare-yanagi 〈しだれやなぎ：枝垂れ柳〉a weeping willow.

shi-dashi 〈しだし：仕出し〉

    shi-dashi-ya（仕出し屋）a caterer; a caterer's shop

  shi-dashi-o-suru 〈仕出しをする〉supply dishes to order.

shi-dekasu 〈しでかす：仕出かす〉

    Ano-otoko wa nani-o-shi-dekasu-ka-wakara-nai.（あの男は何を仕出かすか分からない．）There is no knowing what he will do.

shiden 〈市電〉a streetcar, a tram.

shidô 〈しどう：指導〉guidance, leading.

    shidô-o-ayamaru（指導を誤る）misguide, misdirect

    shidô-sha（指導者）a leader, a guide

    shidô-ryoku（指導力）the capacity as a leader

  shidô-suru 〈指導する〉guide, lead.

  shidô-teki-yakuwari o enjiru 〈指導的役割を演じる〉play the part of the leader.

  〜-no-shidô-no-moto-ni 〈〜の指導の下に〉under the guidance of... .

shidô 〈しどう：私道〉a private road.

shidô 〈しどう：始動〉starting.

  shidô-suru 〈始動する〉start.

shîdo(-suru) 〈シード（する）〉seed.

    shîdo-senshu（シード選手）a seeded player

shidoro-modoro 〈しどろもどろ〉

shidoro-modoro-na〈しどろもどろな〉faltering, confused, incoherent.

shidoro-modoro-na-tôben-o-suru（しどろもどろな答弁をする）answer falteringly

shidoro-modoro-ni〈しどろもどろに〉falteringly, confusedly, incoherently.

shidoro-modoro-ni-naru（しどろもどろになる）falter, be thrown into confusion

shiei〈しえい：市営〉

shiei-jûtaku（市営住宅）a municipal dwelling-house

shiei-basu（市営バス）a city bus

shiei-no〈市営の〉municipal, city-operated.

shiei〈しえい：私営〉

shiei-jigyô（私営事業）a private enterprise

shiei-no〈私営の〉privately operated.

shien〈しえん：支援〉

shien-suru〈支援する〉support, back up.

shifuku〈しふく：私腹〉

shifuku-o-koyasu〈私腹を肥やす〉fill one's own pocket.

shifuku〈しふく：私服〉plain clothes.

shifuku-keiji（私服刑事）a plainclothes man

shigai〈しがい：市外〉the suburbs.

shigai-tûwa（市外通話）a toll call, a trunk call

shigai-no〈市外の〉suburban.

shigai-ni〈市外に〉in the suburbs, on the outskirts of a city.

shigai〈しがい：市街〉the streets, a town.

shigai-densha（市街電車）a streetcar, a tram car

kyû-shigai（旧市街）the old town

shigai〈しがい：死がい〉*see.* shitai（死体）.

shigai-sen〈しがいせん：紫外線〉ultraviolet rays.

shigai-sen-ryôhô（紫外線療法）(an) ultraviolet treatment

shigaku〈しがく：私学〉a private educational institution.

shigaku〈しがく：史学〉historical science.

shigaku-bu（史学部）the history department

shigaku〈しがく：歯学〉dentistry.

shigaku-bu（歯学部）the department of dentistry

shigami-tsuku〈しがみつく：しがみ付く〉cling ((to)), hold on ((to)), hold fast ((to)).

shigan〈しがん：志願〉(an) application, (a) desire.

shigan-sha〔志願者〕an applicant

shigan-suru〔志願する〕apply ((for)), desire, wish.

shigatsu〔しがつ：四月〕April.

shigeki〔しげき：刺激〕(a) stimulus, excitement.

shigeki-o-motomeru（刺激を求める）look for excitement

shigeki-butsu（刺激物）a stimulus, an irritant

shigeki-suru〔刺激する〕give a stimulus ((to)), stimulate, excite.

shigeki-sei-no or *shigeki-teki(-na)*〔刺激性の，刺激的(な)〕stimulative.

shigeki-no-tsuyoi〔刺激の強い〕thrilling, exciting.

shigeki-no-nai〔刺激のない〕monotonous.

shigeki-no-nai seikatsu（刺激のない生活）a dull life

shigemi〔しげみ：茂み〕a thicket, a bush.

shigen〔しげん：資源〕resources.

shigen-ni tomu（資源に富む）be rich in natural resources

shigen o kaihatsu-suru（資源を開発する）develop natural resources

shigen〔しげん：至言〕a wise saying.

Kanojo-ga itta-koto wa makoto-ni shigen-da.（彼女が言ったことは誠に至言だ。）What she said is really a wise saying.

shigeru〔しげる：茂る〕grow thick, become dense.

shigeshige(-to)〔しげしげ(と)：繁々(と)〕

shigeshige-kayou（しげしげ通う）visit frequently, frequent

shigeshige-to miru（しげしげと見る）gaze hard ((at))

shigi〔しぎ〕snipe.

shigin〔しぎん：詩吟〕recitation of a Chinese poem.

shigo〔しご：死後〕after one's death.

Shitai wa shigo-ni-shû-kan-keika-shita-mono-to-omowareru.（死休は死後二週間経過したものと思われる。）The body is supposed to have been dead for two weeks.

shigo〔しご：死語〕a dead language.

shigoku〔しごく：至極〕very, most, quite, exceedingly.

Emono o nigashite-zannen-shigoku.（獲物を逃して残念至極。）I'm most regretful for my missing the game.

shigoku〔しごく〕put ((a person)) through hard training.

shigo-sen〔しごせん：子午線〕the meridian (line).

shigoto〔しごと：仕事〕work, business, a task, a job.

shigoto-ni-iku（仕事に行く）go to work

shigoto-ni-tori-kakaru（仕事に取り掛かる）set to work

shigoto-o-yasumu（仕事を休む）stay away from work

shigoto-o-sagasu〈仕事を探す〉look for work

shigoto-de Furansu-e iku〈仕事でフランスへ行く〉go to France on business

shigoto-no-hayai-hito〈仕事の早い人〉a quick worker

shigoto-shi〈仕事師〉a workman, a man of enterprise

shigoto-chû-de-aru〈仕事中である〉be at work

shigoto-o-suru〈仕事をする〉work.

shigure〈しぐれ：時雨〉a drizzling rain, a late-autumn shower.

shigureru〈時雨れる〉drizzle.

shigyô-shiki〈しぎょうしき：始業式〉the opening ceremony.

shihai〈しはい：支配〉management, control, rule.

shihai-nin〈支配人〉a manager

   sô-shihai-nin〈総支配人〉a general manager

shihai-suru〈支配する〉manage, control, rule.

kankyô-ni shihai-sareru〈環境に支配される〉be influenced by one's circumstances

shihai〈しはい：賜杯〉a trophy given ((by)).

shihan〈しはん：師範〉a teacher, an instructor, a coach.

shihan〈しはん：市販〉

shihan-suru〈市販する〉market, place on the market, sell at a market.

shihan〈しはん：紫はん〉a purple spot.

shihan-byô〈紫はん病〉purpura

shi-hanki〈しはんき：四半期〉a quarter.

honnen-do no dai-ichi-shi-hanki〈本年度の第一四半期〉the first quarter of this year

shiharai〈しはらい：支払い〉payment.

shiharai-jôken〈支払条件〉terms of payment

shiharai-kijitsu〈支払期日〉the date of payment

shiharai-nin〈支払人〉a payer

shiharai-saki〈支払先〉a payee

shiharai-zumi-no〈支払済みの〉paid

shiharau〈支払う〉pay.

shihatsu〈しはつ：始発〉the first train.

shihatsu-eki〈始発駅〉the starting station

shihei〈しへい：紙幣〉paper money, a note, a bill.

sen-en-shihei〈千円紙幣〉a thousand-yen bill

shihen〈しへん：紙片〉a piece of paper.

shihen-kei〈しへんけい：四辺形〉a quadrilateral, a quadrangle.

shihō 〈しほう：四方〉 four sides, all directions.

  shihō-happô-ni〈四方八方に〉 on all sides, in all directions, all around

  shihō-happô-kara〈四方八方から〉 from every direction

  jū-mairu-shihō〈十マイル四方〉 ten miles around

shihō 〈しほう：司法〉 administration of justice.

  shihō-ken〈司法権〉 judicial power

  shihō-gyôsei〈司法行政〉 judicial administration

  shihō-seido〈司法制度〉 the judicial system

  shihō-shiken〈司法試験〉 judicial examination

shihō 〈しほう：至宝〉 the greatest treasure.

  kokka-no-shihō〈国家の至宝〉 a great national asset

shihō 〈しほう：私法〉 private law.

shi-hôdai 〈しほうだい：仕放題〉

  shi-hôdai-o-suru〈仕放題をする〉 have one's own way, do as one pleases.

shihon 〈しほん：資本〉 (a) capital, a fund.

  shihon o tôjiru〈資本を投じる〉 invest capital

  shihon-o-nekaseru〈資本を寝かせる〉 let capital lie idle

  shihon no chikuseki〈資本の蓄積〉 accumulation of capital

  ryûdô-shihon〈流動資本〉 floating capital

  shihon-ka〈資本家〉 a capitalist

  shihon-shugi〈資本主義〉 capitalism

  shihon-shugi-keizai〈資本主義経済〉 capitalistic economy

shihyô 〈しひょう：指標〉 an index.

shiika 〈しいか：詩歌〉 poems, poetry.

shiiku 〈しいく：飼育〉

  shiiku-suru〈飼育する〉 breed, rear, raise, keep.

shiin 〈しいん：子音〉 a consonant.

shiin 〈しいん：死因〉 the cause of ((a person's)) death.

  Kare-no shiin wa izen-to-shite fumei-de-aru.（彼の死因は依然として不明である。） The cause of his death is still unknown.

shiin 〈しいん：試飲〉

  shiin-suru〈試飲する〉 try, sample 〔wine〕.

shi-ire 〈しいれ：仕入れ〉 stocking, laying in stock.

  shi-ire-daka〈仕入高〉 the amount of goods laid in

  shi-ire-kakaku〈仕入価格〉 a cost price

  shi-ire-saki〈仕入先〉 a supplier, a vendor, a wholesaler

  shi-ireru〈仕入れる〉 stock, lay in.

shiiru〈しいる：強いる〉force, compel, press.
　　shiite〜saseru〈強いて〜させる〉force ((a person)) to do

shiitageru〈しいたげる：虐げる〉oppress, tyrannize ((over)), persecute.
　　yowai-mono o shiitageru〈弱い者を虐げる〉oppress the weak
　　shiitagerareta hito-bito〈虐げられた人々〉the oppressed

shii-take〈しいたけ〉a *shiitake* (mushroom).

shiji〈しじ：支持〉support, backing.
　　zen-kokumin no shiji-o-ukeru〈全国民の支持を受ける〉have the support of the whole nation
　　seron no shiji〈世論の支持〉the backing of public opinion
　　shiji-sha〈支持者〉a supporter, a backer
　shiji-suru〈支持する〉support, back (up).

shiji〈しじ：指示〉indication, instructions.
　　shiji ni shitagau〈指示に従う〉follow ((a person's)) instructions
　　shiji-o-matsu〈指示を待つ〉wait for instructions
　shiji-suru〈指示する〉indicate, instruct.

shiji〈しじ：師事〉
　shiji-suru〈師事する〉study under ((a person's)) instruction, look up to ((a person)) as one's teacher.

shijimi〈しじみ〉a corbicula.

shijin〈しじん：詩人〉a poet, a poetess.

shijitsu〈しじつ：史実〉a historical fact.

shijo〈しじょ：子女〉
　　ryôke no shijo〈良家の子女〉young men and women of good families

shijô〈しじょう：市場〉a market.
　　shijô-chôsa〈市場調査〉a market research
　　kaigai-shijô〈海外市場〉a foreign market

shijô〈しじょう：私情〉personal feelings.
　　shijô-ni-torawareru〈私情に捕らわれる〉be influenced by personal feelings
　　shijô o sashi-hasamu yochi-ga-nai〈私情をさしはさむ余地がない〉there is no room to admit personal feelings
　　shijô o suteru〈私情を捨てる〉set aside one's personal feelings

shijô〈しじょう：詩情〉poetic(al) sentiment.
　shijô-yutaka-na〈詩情豊かな〉full of poetical sentiment.

shijô〈しじょう：紙上〉
　shijô-de〈紙上で〉in the newspapers.

shijô 〈しじょう：誌上〉
 shijô-de 〈誌上で〉 in the magazine.

shijô 〈しじょう：試乗〉 a trial ride.

shijô 〈しじょう：至上〉
  shijô-meirei（至上命令） a supreme order
 shijô-no 〈至上の〉 supreme, highest.

shijô 〈しじょう：史上〉
  shijô-saidai-no〜〈史上最大の〜〉 the greatest...in history
  shijô-saikô-no〜〈史上最高の〜〉 the highest...in history.

shi-jû 〈しじゅう：四十〉 forty.
  dai-shi-jû（第四十） the fortieth

shijû 〈しじゅう：始終〉 very often, always, all the time.

shijû-hatte 〈しじゅうはって：四十八手〉 the forty-eight ways of attacking in *sumo* wrestling.

shijû-shô 〈しじゅうしょう：四重唱〉 a (vocal) quartet(te).

shijû-sô 〈しじゅうそう：四重奏〉 a quartet(te).
  gengaku-shijû-sô（弦楽四重奏） a string quartet(te)

shika 〈しか：市価〉 the market price.
  shika-no-san-wari-biki-de（市価の三割引きで） at a discount of 30% below the market price
  shika-no hendô（市価の変動） market fluctuations

shika 〈しか〉 a deer; a stag, a hind.
  shika-no-tsuno（しかの角） an antler

shika 〈しか：史家〉 a historian.

shika 〈しか：歯科〉 dentistry.
  shika-i（歯科医） a dentist
  shika-iin（歯科医院） a dentist's
  shika-gikô-shi（歯科技工師） a dental technician

-shika 〈しか〉 only, but, no more than.
  Hyaku-en-shika mochi-awase-ga-nai.（百円しか持ち合わせがない.） I have only one hundred yen with me.
  Sore-dake-shika shira-nakatta.（それだけしか知らなかった.） I knew no more than that.

shikabane 〈しかばね〉
  ikeru shikabane（生けるしかばね） a living corpse

shi-kaeshi 〈しかえし：仕返し〉
 shikaeshi-suru 〈仕返しする〉 revenge oneself ((on)), retaliate ((on)).

shikai 〈しかい：市会〉 a municipal assembly.

shikai-giin（市会議員）a member of the municipal assembly

shikai〈しかい：司会〉

shikai-sha（司会者）the chairman, the master of ceremonies (M.C.)

shikai-suru〈司会する〉preside ((at)), take the chair ((at)).

shikai〈しかい：視界〉sight, view, visibility.

shikai-ni hairu（視界に入る）come into sight

shikai-kara-kieru（視界から消える）go out of sight

Shikai ga ii.（視界がいい。）The visibility is good.

Shikai ga warui.（視界が悪い。）The visibility is poor.

shikake〈しかけ：仕掛け〉a device, a mechanism.

shikake-hana-bi（仕掛け花火）set fireworks

denki-jikake（電気仕掛け）an electric device

shi-kakeru〈しかける：仕掛ける〉

bakudan o shi-kakeru（爆弾を仕掛ける）plant a bomb

kenka o shi-kakeru（けんかを仕掛ける）pick a quarrel ((with))

wana o shi-kakeru（わなを仕掛ける）set a trap ((for))

shi-kaketa shigoto（仕掛けた仕事）work in hand

shikaku〈しかく：四角〉a square.

ma-shikaku（真四角）a regular square

shikaku-na〈四角な〉square.

shikaku〈しかく：資格〉qualification, capacity.

shikaku-shinsa（資格審査）an examination of the applicants' qualification

kojin-no shikaku-de（個人の資格で）in one's private capacity

kyôin-no shikaku o toru（教員の資格を取る）obtain a teacher's license

shikaku-o-ataeru〈資格を与える〉qualify ((a person)) for.

shikaku-o-ubau（資格を奪う）disqualify ((a person)) from

shikaku-ga-aru〈資格がある〉be qualified ((for *or* to do)).

shikaku-ga-nai（資格がない）have no qualifications ((for *or* to do))

shikaku〈しかく：死角〉the dead angle.

shikaku〈しかく：視覚〉(the sense of) sight, vision, eyesight.

shikaku-baru〈しかくばる：四角張る〉be formal, stand on ceremony.

shikaku-barazu-ni〈四角張らずに〉informally, without ceremony.

shikameru〈しかめる〉

kao-o-shikameru〈顔をしかめる〉make a wry face, frown ((at *or* on)).

kao-o-shikamete〈顔をしかめて〉frowningly.

shikamettsura〈しかめっつら：しかめっ面〉a wry face.

shikamettsura-o-suru 〈しかめっ面をする〉 *see.* (kao-o-)shikameru.

shikamo 〈しかも〉 moreover, and that, and yet, nevertheless.

shikan 〈しかん：士官〉 an officer.

shi-kane-nai 〈しかねない：仕兼ねない〉 be capable of ((doing)), do not hesitate ((to do)).

   hito-goroshi-mo-shi-kane-nai （人殺しもしかねない） be capable of committing murder

shikari-tsukeru 〈しかりつける〉 call down, give ((a person)) a good scolding.

shikaru 〈しかる〉 scold.

shikarareru 〈しかられる〉 be scolded.

shikaru-beki 〈しかるべき〉 proper, due, suitable, right, respectable, decent, reasonable, competent.

   shikaru-beki hito-kara-no shôkai-jô 〈しかるべき人からの紹介状〉 a letter of introduction from a competent person

shikaru-beku 〈しかるべく〉 properly, duly, as one thinks best.

shikashi 〈しかし〉 but, however.

shikata 〈しかた：仕方〉 a way, a method.

   tadashii benkyô-no-shikata （正しい勉強の仕方） the right way of studying

shikata-ga-nai 〈しかたがない：仕方がない〉 cannot help, cannot be helped; it is no use; cannot stand; be anxious ((to do)).

   Shikata-ga-nai! 〈仕方がない.〉 It cannot be helped!
   Naitatte-shikata-ga-nai. （泣いたって仕方がない.） It is no use crying.
   Atsukute-shikata-ga-nai. （暑くて仕方がない.） It is unbearably hot.
   Sukî-ni-itte-mitakute-shikata-ga-nakatta. （スキーに行ってみたくて仕方がなかった.） I wanted very much to go skiing.

shikata-naku or **shikata-nashi-ni** 〈しかたなく，しかたなしに：仕方なく，仕方なしに〉 helplessly, against one's will, reluctantly.

shikatsumerashii 〈しかつめらしい〉 formal, grave, serious, solemn.

shikatsumerashii-kao-o-suru 〈しかつめらしい顔をする〉 look grave.

shikatsu-mondai 〈しかつもんだい：死活問題〉 a matter of life or death, a vital question.

shike 〈しけ〉 stormy weather.

shikeru 〈しける〉 be stormy, get turbulent.

shikei 〈しけい：死刑〉 (a) capital punishment, (a) death penalty.

   shikei-ni-shosuru （死刑に処する） put ((a person)) to death
   shikei o haishi-suru （死刑を廃止する） abolish the death penalty

shikei-shû〔死刑囚〕 a condemned criminal

shiken〔しけん：試験〕an examination, an exam; an experiment, a test.

　shiken o ukeru（試験を受ける） take an examination

　shiken ni gôkaku-suru（試験に合格する） pass an examination

　shiken-ni ochiru（試験に落ちる） fail in an examination

　hikki-shiken（筆記試験） a written examination

　kôtô-shiken（口頭試験） an oral examination

　chûkan-shiken（中間試験） a midterm examination

　gakkimatsu-shiken（学期末試験） a term examination

　tsui-shiken（追試験） another examination

　nyûgaku-shiken（入学試験） an entrance examination

　kokka-shiken（国家試験） a state examination

　shiken-hikô（試験飛行） a test flight

　shiken-kan（試験管） a test tube

　shiken-suru〈試験する〉examine, make an experiment ((in *or* on)), test.

　shiken-teki-ni〈試験的に〉tentatively, on trial.

shiketsu〔しけつ：止血〕stopping of bleeding.

　shiketsu-zai（止血剤） a hemostatic

　shiketsu-suru〈止血する〉stop bleeding.

shiki〔しき：四季〕the four seasons.

　shiki-o-tsûjite（四季を通じて） all the year around, in all seasons

shiki〔しき：死期〕the time of death.

　shiki o hayameru（死期を早める） hasten one's death

shiki〔しき：士気〕morale, fighting spirit.

　Shiki-ga-agaru.（士気が上がる.） One's morale is high.

　Shiki-ga-agara-nai.（士気が上がらない.） One's morale is low.

　shiki ni eikyô-suru（士気に影響する） affect the morale

　shiki o kobu-suru（士気を鼓舞する） raise the morale ((of))

　shiki-sosô-suru〈士気阻喪する〉become demoralized.

shiki〔しき：指揮〕command, direction.

　shiki-kan（指揮官） a commander

　shiki-sha（指揮者） a leader, a conductor

　shiki-suru〈指揮する〉command, lead, direct, conduct.

　～-no-shiki-de〈～の指揮で〉conducted by... .

shiki〔しき：式〕a ceremony; a method, a style; a formula.

　shiki o okonau（式を行う） hold a ceremony

　kanojo-shiki-no-yari-kata（彼女式のやり方） her method of doing things *shiki-de-arawasu*〈式で表す〉formulate.

shikibetsu〈しきべつ：識別〉discrimination, discernment.

shikibetsu-suru〈識別する〉discriminate(*or* distinguish) ((A from B)).

shikibetsu-shi-uru〈識別し得る〉distinguishable.

shikibetsu-deki-nai〈識別できない〉indistinguishable

shiki-buton〈しきぶとん：敷布団〉a mattress, a sleeping mat.

shikichi〈しきち：敷地〉a site, the ground.

shikichō〈しきちょう：色調〉a color tone.

shikifu〈しきふ：敷布〉a (bed) sheet.

shikifu o kaeru（敷布を替える）change a sheet

shikii〈しきい：敷居〉a threshold.

shiki-ishi〈しきいし：敷石〉a pavement, a paving stone.

shiki-ishi-o-shiku〈敷石を敷く〉pave ((a road)) with stone.

shikijaku〈しきじゃく：色弱〉color weakness.

shikiji〈しきじ：式辞〉a ceremonial address.

shikiji o noberu（式辞を述べる）give an address

shikijô〈しきじょう：式場〉a ceremonial hall.

shikiken〈しきけん：識見〉judgment, discernment, vision, insight, intelligence.

shikiken-no-takai-hito（識見の高い人）a man of great insight

shiki-kin〈しききん：敷金〉a deposit.

shiki-kin-o-ireru（敷金を入れる）make a deposit

shikimō〈しきもう：色盲〉color blindness.

seki-ryoku-shikimō（赤緑色盲）red-green blindness

shikimō-de-aru〈色盲である〉be color-blind.

shiki-mono〈しきもの：敷物〉a carpet, a rug, a floorcloth; carpeting.

shikin〈しきん：資金〉funds, a fund, (a) capital.

kaiten-shikin（回転資金）revolving funds

unten-shikin（運転資金）working funds

shikin-guri-ga-kurushii（資金繰りが苦しい）have difficulty in raising funds ((for))

shikin-nan（資金難）financial difficulty

shikin〈しきん：至近〉

shikin-dan（至近弾）a near hit

shikin-kyori（至近距離）the shortest range, point-blank range

shikin-seki〈しきんせき：試金石〉a touchstone, a test case.

shikiri〈しきり：仕切り〉partition, division, a compartment; settlement of accounts; toeing the mark.

shikiri-kabe〈仕切り壁〉 a partition wall

shikiri-sho〈仕切り書〉 an invoice

shikiri-naoshi〈仕切り直し〉 toeing the mark again

shikiru〈仕切る〉 partition, divide, settle accounts; toe the mark.

shikiri-ni〈しきりに〉eagerly, anxiously, very hard, very often.

shikiri-ni iki-tagaru〈しきりに行きたがる〉 be eager(*or* anxious) to go

Ame ga shikiri-ni futteiru.（雨がしきりに降っている。） It is raining very hard.

shikiri-ni watashi-ni tegami-o-yokosu（しきりに私に手紙をよこす） write to me a letter very often

shikisai〈しきさい：色彩〉a color.

shikisai-kankaku（色彩感覚） color sensation

shikisai-kôka（色彩効果） a color effect

seiji-teki shikisai-o-obiru（政治的色彩を帯びる） take on a political coloration

shikisai-ni-tonda〈色彩に富んだ〉colorful.

shikisai-ni-toboshii（色彩に乏しい） colorless

shikisha〈しきしゃ：識者〉men of intelligence, the wise.

shikishi〈しきし：色紙〉a square piece of fancy paper.

shikiso〈しきそ：色素〉coloring matter, a pigment.

shikitari〈しきたり：仕来り〉conventions, old customs.

shikiten〈しきてん：式典〉a ceremony, rites.

shiki-tsumeru〈しきつめる：敷き詰める〉spread ((gravel)) all over〔a road〕.

shikka〈しっか：失火〉an accidental fire.

shikkaku〈しっかく：失格〉disqualification.

shikkaku-sha（失格者） a disqualified person

shikkaku-suru〈失格する〉be disqualified ((for *or* from)).

shikkan〈しっかん：疾患〉a disease, a trouble.

kyôbu-shikkan（胸部疾患） a lung trouble

shikkari(-to)〈しっかり(と)〉firmly, tightly, fast, hard.

shikkari musubu（しっかり結ぶ） tie fast

shikkari tsukamaru（しっかりつかまる） hold on fast ((to))

shikkari-mono（しっかり者） a person of steady character

shikkari-suru〈しっかりする〉become strong, be strong-minded, take courage.

Shikkari-shiro!（しっかりしろ。） Cheer up! / Be yourself!

shikkari-shita〈しっかりした〉strong, firm, reliable.

shikkari-shita otoko（しっかりした男） a reliable man

shikke〈しっけ：湿気〉 *see.* shikki.（湿気）.

shikkei〈しっけい：失敬〉 *see.* shitsurei.

shikki〈しっき：漆器〉 lacquer ware.

shikki〈しっき：湿気〉 moisture, humidity, damp.

shikki-no-ooi〈湿気の多い〉 moist, damp, humid.

shikki-no-nai（湿気のない） dry

shikkô〈しっこう：執行〉 execution, performance, enforcement, service.

shikkô-te-tsuzuki（執行手続き） execution proceedings

shikkô-reijô（執行令状） a writ of execution

shikkô-meirei（執行命令） an order of execution

shikkô-kikan（執行期間） the term for execution

shikkô-kikan（執行機関） an executive organ

shikkô-sha（執行者） an executor

shikkô-ri（執行吏） a bailiff

shikkô-yûyo（執行猶予） a stay of execution, probation

shikkô-bu（執行部） the executives

shikkô-suru〈執行する〉 execute, perform, enforce, carry out, serve.

shikkô〈しっこう：失効〉 invalidation.

shikkô-suru〈失効する〉 become null and void.

shikku〈シック〉

shikku-na〈シックな〉 stylish, tasteful, chic.

shikkui〈しっくい：漆食〉 mortar, plaster, stucco.

shikkui-o-nuru〈漆食を塗る〉 plaster, stucco.

shikkuri〈しっくり〉

shikkuri-ika-nai〈しっくりいかない〉 do not get on well with each other.

shikkyaku〈しっきゃく：失脚〉 a downfall, a fall, loss of position.

shikkyaku-suru〈失脚する〉 fall from grace, lose one's position.

shikô〈しこう：し好〉 (a) taste, (a) liking, one's likes.

shikô-ni-au（し好に合う） suit one's taste, be to one's liking

shikô-hin（し好品） one's favorite food, an article of luxury

shikô〈しこう：思考〉 thinking, thought, consideration.

shikô-ryoku（思考力） thinking faculty

shikô-suru〈思考する〉 think, consider.

shikô〈しこう：施行〉 enforcement, operation.

shikô-suru〈施行する〉 enforce, put in force, carry into effect.

shikô〈しこう：指向〉

shikô-sei antena（指向性アンテナ） a directional antenna

shikō-suru〈指向する〉point ((to)).

shi-komi〈しこみ：仕込み〉training, education, teaching; stocking, laying in.

    shi-komi-ga-ii（仕込みがいい）be well educated

    Igirisu-jikomi-no shinshi（イギリス仕込みの紳士）a gentleman educated in England

shi-komu〈しこむ：仕込む〉train, educate, teach; stock, lay in.

    musume-ni sahō o shi-komu（娘に作法を仕込む）teach good manners to one's daughter

    inu ni gei-o-shi-komu（犬に芸を仕込む）teach a dog to do tricks

shikori〈しこり〉a stiffness, an induration; an ill feeling.

    kata-ni shikori-ga-aru（肩にしこりがある）have got a stiffness in the shoulder

shikō-sakugo〈しこうさくご：試行錯誤〉trial and error.

shikotama〈しこたま〉

shikotama-mōkeru〈しこたまもうける〉earn a lot of money.

shiku〈しく：敷く〉lay, spread, pave.

    goza o shiku（ござを敷く）spread a mat

    futon-o-shiku（布団を敷く）make a bed

shiku-hakku〈しくはっく：四苦八苦〉

shiku-hakku-suru〈四苦八苦する〉be in an agony, writhe, be in great distress.

shikujiru〈しくじる〉fail, blunder, make a mistake, commit an error.

shi-kumi〈しくみ：仕組み〉construction, a setup, a contrivance, a mechanism, a plan, (an) arrangement, a plot.

shi-kumu〈仕組む〉contrive, devise, plan, arrange, plot.

    Kono shibai wa migoto-ni shi-kunde-aru.（この芝居は見事に仕組んである。）This play is skillfully got up.

shikushiku〈しくしく〉

    shikushiku-naku（しくしく泣く）sob, snivel

    o-naka-ga-shikushiku-itamu（おなかがしくしく痛む）have a griping pain in one's bowels

shikutsu〈しくつ：試掘〉prospecting, trial boring.

shikutsu-suru〈試掘する〉prospect, make a trial boring.

shikyō〈しきょう：司教〉a bishop.

shikyō〈しきょう：市況〉market conditions, the movements of the market, the market.

    kappatsu-na shikyō（活発な市況）a brisk market

　　　kansan-na shikyô〈閑散な市況〉 a dull market

shikyoku〈しきょく：支局〉a branch (office).

shikyû〈しきゅう：子宮〉the womb, the uterus.

　　　shikyû-gan〈子宮がん〉 uterine cancer

shikyû〈しきゅう：支給〉

　shikyû-suru〈支給する〉supply ((a person)) with, pay, give.

shikyû(-ni)〈しきゅう(に)：至急(に)〉urgently, at once, as soon as possible.

　shikyû-no〈至急の〉urgent, pressing.

　　　shikyû-no baai-ni-wa〈至急の場合には〉 in an urgent case

shikyû-bin〈しきゅうびん：至急便〉

　shikyû-bin-de〈至急便で〉by express.

shikyû-shiki〈しきゅうしき：始球式〉

　shikyû-shiki-o-okonau〈始球式を行う〉throw the first ball.

shima〈しま：島〉an island.

　　　shima-guni（島国） an island country

　　　　　shima-guni-konjô（島国根性） an insular spirit, insularism

shima〈しま〉stripes.

　shima-no(-aru)〈しまの(ある)〉striped.

　　　shima-no zubon（しまのズボン） striped trousers

shimai〈しまい：姉妹〉sisters.

　　　shimai-toshi（姉妹都市） a sister city

　　　shimai-gaisha（姉妹会社） an affiliated company

　　　shimai-hen（姉妹編） a companion (volume) ((to)), a sequel ((to))

shimai〈しまい：仕舞い〉an end, a close, (a) conclusion; a *Noh* dance in plain clothes.

　shimai-ni(-wa)〈しまいに(は)〉in the end, in the long run.

　shimai-made〈しまいまで〉to the end.

　　　Watashi-no-iu-koto o shimai-made-kike.（私の言うことをしまいまで聞け.） Hear me out.

shimari〈しまり：締まり〉

　shimari-no-aru〈締まりのある〉firm, tight.

　shimari-no-nai〈締まりのない〉loose, lax, slovenly, stupid.

　　　shimari-no-nai kuchi-moto〈締まりのない口もと〉 loosely-closed lips

shimari-ya〈しまりや：締まり屋〉a tightwad, a closefisted person.

shimaru〈しまる：閉まる〉be shut, be closed.

　　　To wa shimatte-iru.（戸は閉まっている.） The door is shut.

shimatsu〈しまつ：始末〉

shimatsu-sho〈始末書〉a written apology

shimatsu-ya〈始末屋〉a frugal person

shimatsu-suru〈始末する〉manage, deal ((with)), dispose ((of)); economize, save.

shimatsu-o-tsukeru〈始末を付ける〉settle, liquidate.

koto-no-shimatsu-o-tsukeru（事の始末を付ける）settle a matter

shimatsu-ni-oenaku-naru〈始末に負えなくなる〉get beyond control, get out of (one's) hand.

shimatsu-ga-warui, shimatsu-ni-komaru or *shimatsu-ni-oe-nai*〈始末が悪い，始末に困る，始末に負えない〉difficult to deal with, unmanageable, intractable, incorrigible.

Shimatta!〈しまった。〉My goodness! / Dash it! / Hang it!

shimau〈しまう：仕舞う〉put away, keep, close.

koppu o shimau（コップをしまう）put away the cups

mise o shimau（店をしまう）close a shop

(-shite-)shimau〈〈～して〉しまう〉finish, get through, put an end ((to)).

Shukudai o shite-shimatta.（宿題をしてしまった。）I have finished my homework.

shima-uma〈しまうま：しま馬〉a zebra.

shimbi〈しんび：審美〉

shimbi-gan（審美眼）an eye for the beautiful, a sense of the esthetic

shimbi-teki(-na)〈審美的(な)〉esthetic(al).

shimbō〈しんぼう：心棒〉an axle, a shaft, a stem.

shimbō〈しんぼう：辛抱〉patience, endurance, perseverance, persistence.

shimbō-suru〈辛抱する〉be patient, endure, persevere, put up ((with)).

shimbō-zuyoi〈辛抱強い〉patient, persevering.

shimbō-zuyoku〈辛抱強く〉patiently, with perseverance.

shimbō〈しんぼう：信望〉confidence, popularity.

shimbō-ga-aru（信望がある）enjoy the confidence ((of))

shimbō o ushinau（信望を失う）lose the confidence ((of))

shimboku〈しんぼく：親ぼく〉friendship.

shimboku o hakaru（親ぼくを図る）cultivate mutual friendship

shimboku-kai（親ぼく会）a social gathering, a get-together (meeting)

shimbun〈しんぶん：新聞〉a newspaper, a paper; the press.

shmbun o toru（新聞を取る）take a newspaper

shimbun o haitatsu-suru（新聞を配達する） deliver newspapers
shimbun-ni-yoru-to（新聞によると） according to the newspapers
Shimbun-ni〜-to-dete-iru.（新聞に〜と出ている。）The paper says that
　　… .
shimbun-de-kôhyô-de-aru（新聞で好評である） have a good press
shimbun-de tatakareru（新聞でたたかれる） be attacked in the press
shimbun-dane（新聞種） a news item
　　shimbun-dane-ni-naru（新聞種になる） reach the newspaper
shimbun-kiji（新聞記事） a newspaper story
shimbun-kisha（新聞記者） a newsman, a newspaperman, a
　　journalist, a pressman
shimbun-sha（新聞社） a newspaper office

shime-dashi〈しめだし：締め出し〉
shime-dashi-o-kuwasu〈締め出しを食わす〉 shut the door ((on)), shut out.
shime-dashi-o-kuu〈締め出しを食う〉 be shut out, be locked out.
shime-dasu〈しめだす：締め出す〉 *see.* shime-dashi-o-kuwasu.
shime-gane〈しめがね：締め金〉a buckle, a clasp.
shimei〈しめい：氏名〉a (full) name.
　　jûsho-shimei（住所氏名） one's name and address
shimei〈しめい：使命〉a mission.
　　shimei o hatasu（使命を果たす） fulfill one's mission
shimei〈しめい：死命〉
shimei-o-seisuru〈死命を制する〉 have a hold ((upon *or* over)).
shimei〈しめい：指名〉nomination.
　　shimei-kaiko（指名解雇） a dismissal of workers by designation
　　shimei-tehai（指名手配） arrangements for the search of an
　　　identified criminal
shimei-suru〈指名する〉nominate, name.
　　gichô-ni-shimei-sareru（議長に指名される） be nominated for
　　　chairman
shimei-jun-ni〈指名順に〉in the order of the persons called.
shime-kili〈しめきり：締め切り〉closing.
　　shime-kiri-ni-ma-ni-au（締め切りに間に合う） make the deadline
　　shime-kiri-bi（締め切り日） the closing day, the deadline
shime-kiru〈締め切る〉close; close up, keep shut.
shime-korosu〈しめころす：絞め殺す〉strangle ((a person)) to death.
shime-kukuri〈しめくくり：締めくくり〉supervision, management,
　control; completion, (a) conclusion, (a) settlement.

shime-kukuri-o-tsukeru〈締めくくりを付ける〉complete, finish, bring to a finish.

shime-kukuru〈しめくくる：締めくくる〉settle, bring to a finish; bind fast, hold together.

shimen〈しめん：紙面〉space.

  shimen o saku（紙面を割く）allow space ((for))

  shimen-ga-kagirarete-iru-node（紙面が限られているので）for want of space

  shimen-ga-yuruseba（紙面が許せば）if space allows

  shimen-no-tsugō-de（紙面の都合で）on account of limited space

shime-nawa〈しめなわ：しめ縄〉a sacred straw festoon.

shimen-soka〈しめんそか：四面そ歌〉

shimen-soka-de-aru〈四面そ歌である〉be surrounded by foes on all sides.

shimeppoi〈しめっぽい：湿っぽい〉damp, moist, wet.

  shimeppoi tenki（湿っぽい天気）damp weather

shimeri〈しめり：湿り〉dampness, moisture.

shimeru〈湿る〉become damp, become moist, become wet.

shimetta〈湿った〉damp, moist, wet.

shimeru〈しめる：占める〉occupy, hold, take (up).

  ichi-i o shimeru（一位を占める）hold the first place

  jūyō-na chii o shimeru（重要な地位を占める）hold an important position

  gaikoku-bōeki no san-wari-o-shimeru（外国貿易の三割を占める）account for 30 percent of all the foreign trade

shimeru〈しめる：閉める〉shut, close.

  mado o shimeru（窓を占める）shut a window

shimeru〈しめる：締める〉tighten, fasten; strangle; sum up, add up; economize.

  zaseki-beruto o shimeru（座席ベルトを締める）fasten one's seat belt

  kanjō o shimeru（勘定を締める）add up accounts

shimeshi〈しめし：示し〉

shimeshi-ga-tsuka-nai〈示しがつかない〉set a bad example ((to)).

shimeshi-awaseru or **shimeshi-awasu**〈しめしあわせる、しめしあわす：示し合わせる、示し合わす〉prearrange, conspire ((with)).

shimeshi-awasete-oita-toori〈示し合わせておいたとおり〉as previously arranged, according to a previous arrangement.

shimesu〈しめす：示す〉show, indicate.

  Ondo-kei wa sesshi-san-jū-do o shimeshite-iru.（温度計は摂氏三十度を

示している.）The thermometer shows 30 degrees C.

jitsuryoku o shimesu〈実力を示す〉show one's ability

Shimeta!〈しめた．：占めた．〉Good! / Capital! / I've got it! / How lucky!

Kô-narya shimeta mono-da.（こうなりゃしめたものだ.）Success is almost mine.

shime-te〈しめて：締めて〉in all, altogether.

Shime-te ikura-ni-narimasu-ka?（締めていくらになりますか.）How much does it come to?

shimetsu〈しめつ：死滅〉extinction, annihilation.

shimetsu-suru〈死滅する〉become extinct, be annihilated, perish, die out.

shime-tsuke〈しめつけ：締め付け〉binding fast, pressure, a squeeze.

keizai-teki-shime-tsuke（経済的締め付け）a tightening of the economic squeeze

shime-tsukeru〈締め付ける〉fasten tight, compress.

shimeyaka〈しめやか〉

shimeyaka-na〈しめやかな〉quiet, soft, dismal.

shimeyaka-na tsuya（しめやかな通夜）a quiet (and sorrowful) wake

shimi〈しみ〉a moth, a bookworm.

shimi-no-kutta〈しみの食った〉moth-eaten.

shimi-yoke-no〈しみよけの〉mothproof.

shimi〈しみ：染み〉a stain, a blot, a spot.

shimi o nuku（染みを抜く）take out a stain

shimi-ga-tsuku〈染みが付く〉become stained.

shimi-no-aru〈染みのある〉stained, blotted, spotted.

shimijimi〈しみじみ〉

musuko-ni shimijimi ii-kikasu〈息子にしみじみ言い聞かす〉talk seriously to one's son.

shimi-komu〈しみこむ：染み込む〉soak into, permeate.

shimin〈しみん：市民〉a citizen.

shimin-ken（市民権）citizenship

shimin-zei（市民税）a municipal tax

shimiru〈しみる：染みる〉soak into, permeate; smart.

Kono me-gusuri wa shimiru.（この目薬は染みる.）This eye lotion smarts.

Oji-no chûkoku ga mi-ni-shimita.（叔(伯)父の忠告が身に染みた.）My uncle's advice sank deeply into my mind.

shimi-tooru〈しみとおる：染み通る〉soak through, pierce through,

penetrate, infiltrate ((into)).

shimizu〈しみず：清水〉spring water.

shimmai〈しんまい：新米〉new rice; a new hand, a freshman, a fresher, a greenhorn.

　　shimmai-kisha〈新米記者〉a cub reporter

　shimmai-no〈新米の〉new, green, cub.

shimmei〈しんめい：神明〉God.

　　shimmei-ni chikau〈神明に誓う〉swear by God

shimmi〈しんみ：親身〉

　shimmi-ni-natte sewa-o-suru〈親身になって世話をする〉look after ((a person)) with parental affection.

shimmiri〈しんみり〉

　　shimmiri-hanashi-o-suru（しんみり話をする）have a heart-to-heart talk ((with))

　　shimmiri-suru（しんみりする）become sad, feel sympathy ((for))

shimmitsu〈しんみつ：親密〉intimacy.

　shimmitsu-na〈親密な〉intimate, friendly.

　　shimmitsu(-na-aidagara)-de-aru（親密〔な間柄〕である）be very good friends ((with)), be on intimate terms ((with)).

shimmotsu〈しんもつ：進物〉a present, a gift.

　　shimmotsu-yôhin〈進物用品〉articles for presents

shimmyô〈しんみょう：神妙〉

　shimmyô-na〈神妙な〉tame, docile, meek, faithful.

　　shimmyô-na kao-o-shite〈神妙な顔をして〉with a serious look

　shimmyô-ni〈神妙に〉tamely, meekly, without resistance, faithfully.

　　shimmyô-ni-shite-iru〈神妙にしている〉be on one's good behavior

shimo〈しも：霜〉frost.

　　shimo-bashira〈霜柱〉frost columns

　　shimo-doke〈霜解け〉thawing, a thaw

　　shimo-tori-sôchi〈霜取り装置〉a defrosting device

　　shimo-yoke-suru〈霜よけする〉shelter ((a tree)) from the frost

　Shimo ga oriru.〈霜が降りる。〉It frosts.

　shimo-no〈霜の〉frosty.

　　shimo-no-orita-asa-ni〈霜の降りた朝に〉on a frosty morning

shimo-bukure〈しもぶくれ：下膨れ〉

　shimo-bukure-no〈下膨れの〉full-cheeked, plumpy.

shimon〈しもん：試問〉a question, an interview, an examination.

shimon〈しもん：諮問〉a question, an inquiry.

shimon-iin-kai〈諮問委員会〉an advisory committee

shimon-kikan〈諮問機関〉an advisory organ

shimon-suru〈諮問する〉inquire, put a question ((to)), consult.

shimon〈しもん：指紋〉a fingerprint.

shimon o nokosu（指紋を残す）leave one's fingerprints ((on))

shimon-o-toru〈指紋を取る〉take a person's fingerprints, fingerprint.

shimo-no-ku〈しものく：下の句〉the second half (of a *tanka*).

shimo-te〈しもて：下手〉the lower part; the right stage, the left of the stage.

shimo-yake〈しもやけ：霜焼け〉a frostbite, chilblains.

shimo-yake-ga-dekiru or *shimo-yake-ni-naru*〈霜焼けができる、霜焼けになる〉be frostbitten.

shimo-za〈しもざ：下座〉

shimo-za-ni-suwaru〈下座に座る〉take a lower seat.

shimpa〈しんぱ：新派〉a new school.

shimpa-haiyû（新派俳優）an actor of the new school

shimpa〈シンパ〉a sympathizer.

shimpai〈しんぱい：心配〉anxiety, uneasiness, (a) fear, worry, care, trouble.

shimpai no tane（心配の種）a cause of anxiety

shimpai-goto（心配事）troubles, worries, cares

umaretsuki-no shimpai-shō（生まれつきの心配性）a natural worrier

shimpai-o-kakeru〈心配を掛ける〉cause anxiety ((to)), give ((a person)) trouble, trouble.

shimpai-suru〈心配する〉be anxious ((about)), worry ((about)), feel uneasy ((about)).

shimpai-sô-na-kao-o-suru〈心配そうな顔をする〉look worried.

shimpai-na〈心配な〉anxious, uneasy.

shimpai-no-nai（心配のない）easy, carefree

shimpai-shite〈心配して〉with anxiety.

shimpai-naku（心配なく）at ease

shimpai-sô-ni〈心配そうに〉anxiously, uneasily.

shimpai-no-amari〈心配の余り〉in the excess of anxiety.

shimpan〈しんぱん：審判〉judgment; umpireship.

shimpan-in（審判員）an umpire, a referee, a judge

shimpan-suru〈審判する〉umpire, referee.

shimpan〈しんぱん：侵犯〉(an) invasion, (a) violation.

ryôkû-shimpan（領空侵犯）a violation of another country's

territorial air space

shimpan-suru〈侵犯する〉invade, violate.

shimpan〈しんぱん：新版〉*see.* shinkan.

shimpei〈しんぺい：新兵〉a recruit, a new conscript.

shimpen〈しんぺん：身辺〉

shimpen-o-keikai-suru〈身辺を警戒する〉watch over ((a person)) and protect ((him)) from danger.

shimpi〈しんぴ：神秘〉mystery.

shimpi-teki(-na)〈神秘的(な)〉mysterious.

shimpin〈しんぴん：新品〉a new article.

shimpin-dôyô-de-aru〈新品同様である〉look as good as new, look brand-new

shimpo〈しんぽ：進歩〉progress, advance.

shimpo-suru〈進歩する〉make progress, progress, advance.

    kyûsoku-ni-shimpo-suru（急速に進歩する）make rapid progress

    hotondo-shimpo-shi-nai（ほとんど進歩しない）make little progress

shimpo-teki(-na)〈進歩的(な)〉progressive, advanced.

shimpo-shita〈進歩した〉advanced.

shimpô〈しんぼう：信奉〉belief, faith.

    shimpô-sha（信奉者）a believer ((in)), a devotee ((of))

shimpô-suru〈信奉する〉believe ((in)), have faith ((in)), follow.

shimpojiumu〈シンポジウム〉a symposium.

shimpu〈しんぷ：新婦〉a bride.

shimpu〈しんぷ：神父〉a father.

shimpuku〈しんぷく：振幅〉amplitude (of vibration).

shimpuku〈しんぷく：心服〉

shimpuku-suru〈心服する〉respect highly, have a high regard ((for)).

    tomodachi-kara-shimpuku-sarete-iru（友達から心服されている）enjoy the esteem of one's friends

shimpyô-sei〈しんぴょうせい：信ぴょう性〉credibility, reliability, authenticity.

    shimpyô-sei ni kakeru（信ぴょう性に欠ける）lack credibility

shi-muke-chi〈しむけち：仕向け地〉the destination.

shi-mukeru〈しむける：仕向ける〉induce ((a person to do)), force ((to do)).

shin〈しん：心〉lead; a wick.

shin〈しん：心〉a heart; the core, the marrow.

    shin-kara（心から）from the bottom of one's heart

　　　Kanojo-wa　shin-wa　ii-hito-desu.（彼女は心はいい人です。）　She is
　　　good at heart.
　　　shin-made kusatte-iru（しんまで腐っている）　be rotten to the core
　　　shin-made kooru（心まで凍る）　be frozen to the marrow

shin〈しん：真〉truth, reality, genuineness.
　shin-no〈真の〉true, real, genuine.
　shin-ni〈真に〉truly, really, genuinely, in a true sense.
　　　shin-ni-semaru（真に迫る）　be true to life

shin-〈しん-：新-〉new.
　　　shin-shichō（新市長）　the new mayor

shin-〈しん-：親-〉pro-.
　　　shin-Nichi-ka（親日家）　a Japanophile
　　shin-Nichi-no or *shin-Nichi-teki(-na)*〈親日の，親日的(な)〉pro-Japanese.

shina〈しな：品〉an article, a thing, goods; quality.
　　　arayuru shurui-no shina（あらゆる種類の品）　all sorts of goods
　　　shina-ga-ii（品がいい）　be of good quality
　　　shina-ga-warui（品が悪い）　be of poor quality

shinabiru〈しなびる〉wither, shrivel.
　shinabita〈しなびた〉withered, shriveled.

shina-busoku〈しなぶそく：品不足〉a shortage of goods.

shinadare-kakaru〈しなだれかかる：しな垂れ掛かる〉lean　coquettishly
　((against)).

shina-gire〈しなぎれ：品切れ〉
　shina-gire-de-aru〈品切れである〉be out of stock, be sold out.
　shina-gire-ni-naru〈品切れになる〉run out of stock.

shinai〈しない：市内〉
　shinai-de or *shinai-ni*〈市内で，市内に〉in the city.

shin·ai〈しんあい：親愛〉
　shin·ai-naru〈親愛なる〉dear, beloved.

shina-kazu〈しなかず：品数〉the number of articles, items of mer-
　chandise.

shina-mono〈しなもの：品物〉*see.* shina.

shinan〈しなん：至難〉
　　　shinan no waza（至難の業）　a most difficult task

shin·an〈しんあん：新案〉a new idea, a new device, a novelty.
　　　shin·an-tokkyo（新案特許）　a new device patent

shinau〈しなう〉bend, be pliant, be flexible, be supple.

shina-usu〈しなうす：品薄〉a scarcity of goods.

shina-usu-de-aru〈品薄である〉be in short supply.

shinayaka〈しなやか〉

  shinayaka-na〈しなやかな〉pliant, supple, flexible.

    shinayaka-na yubi（しなやかな指）flexible fingers

shin-butsu〈しんぶつ：神仏〉gods and Buddah.

    shin-butsu-no kago（神仏の加護）divine protection

shincha〈しんちゃ：新茶〉the first tea of the season.

shinchaku〈しんちゃく：新着〉(a) new arrival.

  shinchaku-no〈新着の〉newly-arrived.

shinchiku〈しんちく：新築〉

  shinchiku-suru〈新築する〉build.

  shinchiku-no〈新築の〉newly-built.

    shinchiku-no ie（新築の家）a newly-built house

shinchin-taisha〈しんちんたいしゃ：新陳代謝〉metabolism, renewal, replacement of the old with the new.

  shinchin-taisha-suru〈新陳代謝する〉be renewed, be replaced.

shinchō〈しんちょう：身長〉height, stature.

    shinchō o hakaru（身長を測る）measure ((a person's)) height

    shinchō-ga-nobiru（身長が伸びる）grow in stature, become taller

shinchō〈しんちょう：新調〉

  shinchō-suru〈新調する〉make (a new suit), have ((a thing)) made.

  shinchō-no〈新調の〉newly-made, new.

shinchō〈しんちょう：慎重〉

  shinchō-na〈慎重な〉prudent, careful, cautious, deliberate.

  shinchō-ni〈慎重に〉prudently, carefully, cautiously, deliberately.

shinchoku〈しんちょく：進ちょく〉(an) advance, progress.

  shinchoku-suru〈進ちょくする〉advance, make (good) progress.

  shinchoku-shite-iru〈進ちょくしている〉be in progress.

shinchū〈しんちゅう：心中〉the heart, one's inmost thoughts.

  shinchū-o-sassuru〈心中を察する〉sympathize ((with)).

  shinchū-o-uchi-akeru〈心中を打ち明ける〉take ((a person)) into one's confidence.

shinchū〈しんちゅう：真ちゅう〉brass.

  shinchū-sei-no or *shinchū-iro-no*〈真ちゅう製の，真ちゅう色の〉brazen.

shinchū〈しんちゅう：進駐〉

    shinchū-gun（進駐軍）the occupation forces

  shinchū-suru〈進駐する〉stay, be stationed ((in)), occupy.

shindai〈しんだい：身代〉a fortune, one's property.

shindai o tsubusu（身代をつぶす）ruin one's fortune

shindai〈しんだい：寝台〉a bed, a berth.

shindai-ken（寝台券）a berth ticket

shindai-sha（寝台車）a sleeping car, a sleeper

shindan〈しんだん：診断〉(a) diagnosis.

shindan-o-ayamaru（診断を誤る）make a wrong diagnosis

sôki-shindan（早期診断）an early diagnosis

shindan-sho（診断書）a medical certificate

shindan-suru〈診断する〉diagnose, make a diagnosis ((of)).

shinden〈しんでん：神殿〉a shrine, a sanctuary.

shinden-zu〈しんでんず：心電図〉an electrocardiogram (ECG).

shindo〈しんど：震度〉the (seismic) intensity, a magnitude.

shindo-go no jishin（震度五の地震）an earthquake of magnitude 5

shindô〈しんど：震動〉a shock, a quake.

shindô-suru〈震動する〉shake, quake.

　　Kono kuruma wa shindô-ga-sukunai.（この車は震動が少ない．）This car drives smoothly.

shindô〈しんどう：振動〉(a) vibration, a swing.

shindô-suru〈振動する〉vibrate, swing.

shin·ei〈しんえい：新鋭〉

shin·ei-butai（新鋭部隊）a fresh troop

shin·ei-no〈新鋭の〉new and powerful.

shin-fuzen〈しんふぜん：心不全〉cardiac insufficiency.

shingai〈しんがい：心外〉

shingai-de-aru〈心外である〉regret, be very sorry, be vexed ((at *or* with)).

shingai-na〈心外な〉regrettable, vexatious.

shingai〈しんがい：侵害〉infringement, encroachment, trespass.

kojin-no kenri-no-shingai（個人の権利の侵害）a trespass on ((a person's)) individual right

shingai-suru〈侵害する〉infringe ((on)), encroach ((on)), trespass ((on)).

shingaku〈しんがく：神学〉theology, divinity.

shingaku〈しんがく：進学〉

shingaku-suru〈進学する〉enter a school of higher grade.

shin-gao〈しんがお：新顔〉a new face, a newcomer, a stranger, a new member.

shin-gara〈しんがら：新柄〉a new pattern.

shingari〈しんがり〉

shingari-o-tsutomeru〈しんがりを務める〉bring up the rear.

shingata〈しんがた：新型〉a new style.

　　shingata-sha〈新型車〉　a new style car

shingeki〈しんげき：進撃〉

　shingeki-suru〈進撃する〉advance ((against *or* on)).

shingen〈しんげん：進言〉advice, counsel, a proposal.

　shingen-suru〈進言する〉advise, counsel, propose.

shingen-chi〈しんげんち：震源地〉the seismic center.

shingetsu〈しんげつ：新月〉a new moon, a crescent.

shingi〈しんぎ：真偽〉truth or falsehood.

　　shingi-no-hodo o shiraberu（真偽の程を調べる）　examine whether it
　　　is true or not

shingi〈しんぎ：信義〉faith, fidelity, loyalty.

　　shingi o mamoru（信義を守る）　keep faith ((with))
　　kokusai-shingi（国際信義）　international faith

shingi〈しんぎ：審議〉consideration, deliberation, careful discussion.

　　shingi-chû-de-aru（審議中である）　be under consideration, be on the
　　　carpet

　shingi-suru〈審議する〉consider, deliberate (on), discuss.

shingo〈しんご：新語〉a new word, a new coinage.

shingô〈しんごう：信号〉a signal.

　　shingô o mushi-suru（信号を無視する）　disregard a signal
　　kôtsû-shingô（交通信号）　a traffic signal
　　tebata-shingô（手旗信号）　flag signaling

　shingô-suru〈信号する〉signal, make a signal.

shingu〈しんぐ：寝具〉bedding, bedclothes.

shingun〈しんぐん：進軍〉(a) march, (an) advance.

　　shingun-chû-de-aru（進軍中である）　be on the march

　shingun-suru〈進軍する〉march, advance.

shinguru〈シングル〉

　　shinguru-hitto（シングルヒット）　a single, a base hit
　　danshi-shingurusu-jun-kesshô-sen（男子シングルス準決勝戦）　a men's
　　　singles semifinal match

shin･i〈しんい：真意〉one's real intention; the true meaning.

shini-basho〈しにばしょ：死に場所〉a place to die in.

shini-gami〈しにがみ：死に神〉Death.

　　shini-gami-ni-tori-tsukarete-iru（死に神に取りつかれている）　be pos-
　　　sessed by Death, be in the grip of Death

shini-gane 〈しにがね：死に金〉

shini-gane-o-tsukau〈死に金を使う〉spend money in vain.

shini-giwa 〈しにぎわ：死に際〉

shini-giwa-ni〈死に際に〉at the point of death, on one's deathbed, in one's last moment.

shini-me 〈しにめ：死に目〉

shini-me-ni-ae-nai〈死に目に会えない〉be unable to be present at ((a person's)) death.

shinimono-gurui 〈しにものぐるい：死に物狂い〉

shinimono-gurui-no〈死に物狂いの〉desperate, frantic.

　　shinimono-gurui-no doryoku o suru（死に物狂いの努力をする）make desperate efforts

shinimono-gurui-de or *shinimono-gurui-ni*〈死に物狂いで，死に物狂いに〉desperately, frantically.

shinin 〈しにん：死人〉a dead person, the dead.

　　Shinin-ni-kuchi-nashi.（死人に口なし。）Dead men tell no tales.

shinise 〈しにせ〉a store of old standing.

shini-wakareru 〈しにわかれる：死に別れる〉be separated from ((a person)) by death.

　　Kanojo-wa otto-ni-shini-wakareta.（彼女は夫に死に別れた。）She was bereaved of her husband.

shini-zokonai 〈しにぞこない：死に損ない〉

　　Kono shini-zokonai-me!（この死に損ないめ！）You bastard!

shinja 〈しんじゃ：信者〉a believer, a devotee.

shinjin 〈しんじん：信心〉faith, belief, piety.

shinjin-bukai〈信心深い〉religious, devout, pious.

shinjin 〈しんじん：新人〉a newcomer, a new star, a rookie.

　　shinjin-ô（新人王）the rookie king

shinjiru 〈しんじる：信じる〉believe, trust, be sure ((of)).

　　hito-no-iu-koto o shinjiru（人の言うことを信じる）believe what one says

　　kami-o-shinjiru（神を信じる）believe in God

shinjitsu 〈しんじつ：真実〉truth, reality, fact; truly, really.

　　shinjitsu o mageru（真実を曲げる）bend the truth

shinjitsu-no〈真実の〉true, real.

shinjô 〈しんじょう：身上〉one's merit, a strong point.

　　Soko-ga kare-no shinjô-da.（そこが彼の身上だ。）That's his sole merit.

shinjô 〈しんじょう：真情〉 one's true feelings.
　　shinjô o toro-suru (真情を吐露する) express one's genuine feelings
shinjô 〈しんじょう：信条〉 a principle, a belief, a creed.
shinju 〈しんじゅ：真珠〉 a pearl.
　　jinzô-shinju (人造真珠) an imitation pearl
　　yôshoku-shinju (養殖真珠) a cultured pearl
　　shinju-gai (真珠貝) a pearl oyster
shinjû 〈しんじゅう：心中〉 a double suicide.
　　ikka-shinjû (一家心中) a (whole) family suicide
　　muri-shinjû (無理心中) a forced double suicide
　　shinjû-misui (心中未遂) an attempted double suicide
　shinjû-suru 〈心中する〉 commit a double suicide, die together.
shinka 〈しんか：真価〉 real value, real worth, true merit.
　　shinka o hakki-suru (真価を発揮する) prove one's worth
　　shinka o mitomeru (真価を認める) recognize the worth ((of))
shinka 〈しんか：進化〉 evolution.
　　shinka-ron (進化論) the theory of evolution
　shinka-suru 〈進化する〉 evolve.
　shinka-no 〈進化の〉 evolutional, evolutionary.
shinkai 〈しんかい：深海〉 a deep sea.
　　shinkai-gyo (深海魚) a deep-sea fish
shinkai-chi 〈しんかいち：新開地〉 a newly-opened land.
shinkan 〈しんかん：神官〉 a *Shinto* priest.
shinkan 〈しんかん：新刊〉 new publication.
　　shinkan-sho (新刊書) a new publication
　　shinkan-shôkai (新刊紹介) a book review
　shinkan-no 〈新刊の〉 newly-published.
shinkan 〈しんかん：新館〉 a new building, an annex.
shinkan 〈しんかん：信管〉 a fuse.
shinkan 〈しんかん：震かん〉
　shinkan-saseru 〈震かんさせる〉 shake.
　　sekai-o-shinkan-saseru jiken (世界を震かんさせる事件) the world-shaking event
shin-kansen 〈しんかんせん：新幹線〉 the new trunk line.
　　Tôkaidô shin-kansen (東海道新幹線) the New Tokaido Line
shinkei 〈しんけい：神経〉 a nerve, sensitivity.
　　shinkei o nuku (神経を抜く) extract a nerve
　　Kare-wa shinkei-ga-maitte-iru. (彼は神経が参っている。) His sen-

sitivity is quite fatigued.

　shinkei-suijaku〈神経衰弱〉a nervous breakdown

　shinkei-tsû〈神経痛〉neuralgia

shinkei-ga-futoi〈神経が太い〉be bold, have a lot of nerve.

shinkei-o-tsukau〈神経を遣う〉strain one's nerves, worry ((about)), be worried ((over)).

　shinkei o tsukai-sugiru〈神経を遣いすぎる〉overstrain one's nerves

shinkei-ga-takabutte-iru〈神経が高ぶっている〉be highly strung.

shinkei-no〈神経の〉nerval.

　shinkei-no-nai〈神経のない〉nerveless

shinkei-no-surudoi, shinkei-shitsu-na or *shinkei-sei(-no)*〈神経の鋭い, 神経質な, 神経性(の)〉nervous.

　shinkei-no-nibui〈神経の鈍い〉insensitive, dull

shinkei-kabin-na〈神経過敏な〉oversensitive.

shinken〈しんけん：真剣〉

shinken-na〈真剣な〉earnest, serious.

　shinken-na kao〈真剣な顔〉a serious face

shinken-ni〈真剣に〉in earnest, seriously.

shinken-sha〈しんけんしゃ：親権者〉a person in parental authority.

shinketsu〈しんけつ：心血〉

shinketsu-o-sosogu〈心血を注ぐ〉put one's heart and soul ((into)), devote all one's energy ((to)).

shinki〈しんき：新規〉

　shinki-makinaoshi-o-suru〈新規まき直しをする〉make a fresh start, start afresh

shinki-no〈新規の〉new, fresh.

shinki-ni〈新規に〉anew, newly, afresh.

shinki-itten〈しんきいってん：心機一転〉

shinki-itten-suru〈心機一転する〉change one's mind, become a new man.

shin-kijiku〈しんきじく：新機軸〉a new device.

　shin-kijiku-o-uchi-dasu〈新機軸を打ち出す〉make an innovation

shinki-kusai〈しんきくさい：辛気くさい〉impatient, boring, fretful, depressing.

shinkin-kan〈しんきんかん：親近感〉a feeling of intimacy.

shinkin-kôsoku〈しんきんこうそく：心筋こうそく〉cardiac infarction.

shinki-ro〈しんきろう：しん気楼〉a mirage.

shin-kiroku〈しんきろく：新記録〉a new record.

shinkô〈しんこう：親交〉friendship, friendly relations.

　　shinkô-ga-aru〈親交がある〉 be on friendly terms ((with))
　　shinkô o musubu〈親交を結ぶ〉 contract a friendship ((with))
shinkô〈しんこう：信仰〉faith, belief.
　shinkô-suru〈信仰する〉have faith ((in)), believe ((in)).
　shinkô-no-atsui〈信仰の厚い〉pious, devout.
　shinkô-shin-no-nai〈信仰心のない〉unbelieving, impious.
shinkô〈しんこう：進行〉progress, (an) advance.
　　shinkô-chû-de-aru〈進行中である〉 be in progress
　shinkô-suru〈進行する〉progress, make progress, advance, go on.
　　chakuchaku-shinkô-suru〈着々進行する〉 make steady progress
shinkô〈しんこう：新興〉
　　shinkô-seiryoku〈新興勢力〉 the new emerging forces
　　shinkô-shûkyô〈新興宗教〉 a newly-risen religion
　shinkô-no〈新興の〉new, rising.
shinkô〈しんこう：振興〉promotion, advancement.
　shinkô-suru〈振興する〉promote, advance, encourage, inspire.
shinkoku〈しんこく：申告〉a report, a return, a declaration.
　　ao-iro-shinkoku〈青色申告〉 a blue-paper report
　　kakutei-shinkoku〈確定申告〉 a final return
　　shûsei-shinkoku〈修正申告〉 a revised return
　　shinkoku-sha〈申告者〉 a reporter
　　shinkoku-sho〈申告書〉 a report, a declaration, a statement
　shinkoku-suru〈申告する〉report, declare, file
shinkoku〈しんこく：深刻〉
　shinkoku-ka-suru〈深刻化する〉become　aggravated,　become　more
　　strained.
　shinkoku-na〈深刻な〉serious, grave, severe.
　　shinkoku-na-kao-o-shite-iru〈深刻な顔をしている〉 look serious
　shinkoku-ni〈深刻に〉seriously.
　　mono-goto　o　shinkoku-ni　kangaeru〈物事を深刻に考える〉 take　a
　　　thing serious
shin-kokyû〈しんこきゅう：深呼吸〉deep breathing.
　shin-kokyû-suru〈深呼吸する〉breathe deeply, draw a deep breath.
shinkon〈しんこん：新婚〉
　　shinkon-fûfu〈新婚夫婦〉 a newly-married couple
　　shinkon-ryokô〈新婚旅行〉 a honeymoon
　　shinkon-seikatsu〈新婚生活〉 newly-married life
　shinkon-no〈新婚の〉newly-married.

shinkô-shoku(-no) 〈しんこうしょく（の）：深紅色（の）〉crimson.

shinkû 〈しんくう：真空〉a vacuum.
    shinkû-kan（真空管）　a vacuum tube
  shinkû-no 〈真空の〉vacuous.

shinkyo 〈しんきょ：新居〉a new house.
    shinkyo-ni utsuru（新居に移る）　move to a new house

shinkyô 〈しんきょう：新教〉Protestantism.
    shinkyô-to（新教徒）　a Protestant

shinkyô 〈しんきょう：信教〉
    shinkyô no jiyû（信教の自由）　freedom of religion

shinkyô 〈しんきょう：心境〉a state of mind.
    genzai-no shinkyô（現在の心境）　one's present state of mind

shinkyô 〈しんきょう：進境〉progress.
    shinkyô-ga-ichijirushii（進境が著しい）　make remarkable progress

shinkyû 〈しんきゅう：進級〉(a) promotion.
    shinkyû-shiken（進級試験）　an examination for promotion
  shinkyû-suru 〈進級する〉be promoted.

shin-kyû 〈しんきゅう：新旧〉
    shin-kyû-kôtai（新旧交替）　the old giving way to the new
  shin-kyû-no 〈新旧の〉old and new.

shin-me 〈しんめ：新芽〉a sprout, a bud, a shoot.
  shin-me-o-dasu 〈新芽を出す〉sprout, bud.

shin-memmoku 〈しんめんもく：真面目〉one's true character.
    shin-memmoku o hakki-suru（真面目を発揮する）　show one's true character

shinnâ 〈シンナー〉thinner.
    shinnâ-asobi（シンナー遊び）　glue-sniffing

shinnen 〈しんねん：新年〉a new year, the New Year.
    shinnen o iwau（新年を祝う）　celebrate the New Year
    Sinnen o-medetô!（新年おめでとう。）　(A) Happy New Year!

shinnen 〈しんねん：信念〉belief, (a) faith, (a) conviction.
    shinnen o motsu（信念を持つ）　hold faith ((in))

shinnin 〈しんにん：新任〉
  shinnin-no 〈新任の〉newly-appointed.
    shinnin-no aisatsu o noberu（新任のあいさつを述べる）　make an inaugural address

shinnin 〈しんにん：信任〉confidence, trust.
    shinnin o ete-iru（信任を得ている）　enjoy the confidence ((of))

shinnin-no-atsui-hito〈信任の厚い人〉 a trusted person

shinnin-tôhyô〈信任投票〉 a vote of confidence

shinnin-jô〈信任状〉 credentials

shinnin-suru〈信任する〉 confide ((in)), trust.

shinnyû〈しんにゅう：侵入〉 (an) invasion, (an) intrusion.

shinnyû-sha〈侵入者〉 an invader, an intruder

shinnyû-suru〈侵入する〉 invade, intrude ((into)).

shinnyû〈しんにゅう：進入〉

shinnyû-suru〈進入する〉 go ((into)), enter.

shinnyû-sei〈しんにゅうせい：新入生〉a new student, a freshman.

shinobi-ashi〈しのびあし：忍び足〉

shinobi-ashi-de〈忍び足で〉 with stealthy steps, stealthily.

shinobi-komu〈しのびこむ：忍び込む〉 steal into.

shinobi-yoru〈しのびよる：忍び寄る〉 steal near, sneak up ((on *or* to)).

shinobu〈しのぶ：忍ぶ〉bear, endure, put up ((with)), persevere; conceal oneself, hide oneself.

fuben-o-shinobu〈不便を忍ぶ〉 put up with the inconveniences

shinobi-nai〈忍びない〉be intolerable ((to)), do not have the heart ((to do)), cannot allow oneself ((to do)).

shinobu〈しのぶ〉 recollect, think ((of)).

arishi-hi-o-shinobu〈在りし日をしのぶ〉 think of the bygone days

shinogi〈しのぎ〉

shinogi-o-kezuru〈しのぎを削る〉have a cutthroat competition ((with)).

-shinogi〈-しのぎ〉

ichiji-shinogi-ni〈一時しのぎに〉 for a shift

taikutsu-shinogi-ni〈退屈しのぎに〉 just to kill time

shinogu〈しのぐ〉stand, endure, bear; tide over, pull through; exceed, surpass, excel.

Kono samusa wa shinoge-nai.（この寒さはしのげない．） I cannot stand this cold.

kyûba o shinogu〈急場をしのぐ〉 pull through a crisis

ue o shinogu〈飢えをしのぐ〉 satisfy one's appetite

Sapporo wa jinkô-de Hakodate o shinoide-iru.（札幌は人口で函館をしのいでいる．） Sapporo exceeds Hakodate in population.

shinrai〈しんらい：信頼〉reliance, trust, confidence.

shinrai-ni-kotaeru〈信頼にこたえる〉 prove worthy of ((a person's)) trust

shinrai o uragiru〈信頼を裏切る〉 betray ((a person's)) trust

　　　shinrai o ushinau〈信頼を失う〉 lose credibility

shinrai-suru〈信頼する〉 rely ((on)), trust.

shinrai-dekiru〈信頼できる〉reliable, trustworthy.

　　　shinrai-deki-nai〈信頼できない〉 unreliable, untrustworthy

shinratsu〈しんらつ：辛らつ〉

shinratsu-na〈辛らつな〉bitter, sharp, biting, cutting, acrid, poignant, severe.

　　　shinratsu-na hiniku〈辛らつな皮肉〉 cutting sarcasm

shinreki〈しんれき：新暦〉the new(*or* solar) calendar.

shinri〈しんり：真理〉truth.

shinri〈しんり：心理〉a mental state, psychology.

　　　ijô-shinri〈異常心理〉 abnormal mentality

shinri-teki(-na)〈心理的(な)〉mental, psychological.

shinri-teki-ni〈心理的に〉mentally, psychologically.

shinri〈しんり：審理〉(a) trial, (an) inquiry, (a) hearing, (an) examination.

　　　shinri-chû-de-aru〈審理中である〉 be under trial

shinri-suru〈審理する〉try, inquire ((into)), hear, examine.

shinri-gaku〈しんりがく：心理学〉psychology.

　　　shinri-gaku-sha〈心理学者〉 a psychologist

shinrin〈しんりん：森林〉a forest, a wood.

shinro〈しんろ：進路〉a course, a way.

　　　shinro o kiri-hiraku〈進路を切り開く〉 cut one's way ((through))

　　　shinro o samatageru〈進路を妨げる〉 block one's way

shinro〈しんろ：針路〉a course.

　　　shinro-o-ayamaru〈針路を誤る〉 take a wrong course

　　　shinro o kaeru〈針路を変える〉 turn one's course ((toward))

shinrô〈しんろう：新郎〉a bridegroom.

　　　shinrô-shimpu〈新郎新婦〉 the bride and bridegroom

shinrô〈しんろう：心労〉anxiety, care, worry.

shinrui〈しんるい：親類〉a relative, a relation.

　　　chikai shinrui〈近い親類〉 a near relative

　　　tooi shinrui〈遠い親類〉 a distant relative

　　　shinrui-zukiai〈親類付き合い〉 intercourse between relatives

　　　shinrui-kankei〈親類関係〉 kinship, relationship

shinrui〈しんるい：進塁〉

shinrui-suru〈進塁する〉advance 〔to second〕.

shinryaku〈しんりゃく：侵略〉(an) invasion, (an) aggression.

　　　shinryaku-sha〈侵略者〉 an invader, an aggressor.

shinryaku-suru〈侵略する〉invade.

shinryaku-tekí(-na)〈侵略的(な)〉aggressive.

shinryō-jo〈しんりょうじょ：診療所〉a clinic.

shinryoku〈しんりょく：新緑〉fresh green.

　　shinryoku no kô〈新緑の候〉the season of fresh green

shinsa〈しんさ：審査〉(an) examination, judgment.

　　shinsa-in〈審査員〉an examiner, a judge

shinsa-suru〈審査する〉examine, judge.

shinsai〈しんさい：震災〉an earthquake disaster.

　　shinsai-ni-au〈震災に遭う〉suffer from an earthquake

shinsaku〈しんさく：新作〉a new work, a new composition.

shinsatsu〈しんさつ：診察〉medical examination.

　　shinsatsu-shitsu〈診察室〉a consulting room

shinsatsu-suru〈診察する〉examine.

shinsatsu-o-ukeru〈診察を受ける〉see a doctor.

shinsei〈しんせい：申請〉application.

　　shinsei-sho〈申請書〉an (a written) application

shinsei-suru〈申請する〉apply ((for)).

shinsei〈しんせい：神聖〉sacredness, sanctity.

shinsei-na〈神聖な〉sacred, holy, divine.

shinsei〈しんせい：真性〉genuineness.

　　shinsei-korera〈真性コレラ〉genuine cholera

shinsei-no〈真性の〉genuine, true.

shin-seihin〈しんせいひん：新製品〉a new product.

shinseki〈しんせき：親せき〉*see.* shinrui〈親類〉.

shinsen(-mi)〈しんせん(み)：新鮮(み)〉freshness.

　　shinsen-mi ni toboshii〈新鮮みに乏しい〉lack freshness

shinsen-ni-suru〈新鮮にする〉make fresh, freshen.

shinsen-na〈新鮮な〉fresh, new.

　　shinsen-na kûki〈新鮮な空気〉fresh air

shinsetsu〈しんせつ：親切〉kindness.

　　chotto-shita shinsetsu〈ちょっとした親切〉a little act of kindness

shinsetsu-ni-suru〈親切にする〉be kind ((to)), show ((a person)) kindness.

shinsetsu-na〈親切な〉kind, kindly, good.

　　shinsetsu-na okonai〈親切な行い〉a kind act

shinsetsu-ni(-mo)〈親切に(も)〉kindly, with kindness.

　　Nan-to go-shinsetsu-ni!〈何と御親切に．〉How kind of you!

shinsetsu-gokashi-ni〈親切ごかしに〉under the show of kindness.

shinsetsu〈しんせつ：新雪〉new-fallen snow.

shinsetsu〈しんせつ：新設〉

　shinsetsu-suru〈新設する〉establish, organize, found.

　shinsetsu-no〈新設の〉newly-established.

shinsetsu〈しんせつ：新説〉a new theory, a new view.

　　shinsetsu o tonaeru（新説を唱える）　advance a new theory

shinshaku〈しんしゃく：しん酌〉consideration, allowance(s).

　shinshaku-suru〈しん酌する〉consider, take ((something)) into consideration, allow ((for)), make allowance(s) ((for)).

shinshi〈しんし：紳士〉a gentleman.

　　shinshi-kyôtei（紳士協定）　a gentleman's agreement

　shinshi-buru〈紳士ぶる〉play the gentleman.

　shinshi-teki(-na) or　*shinshi-rashii*〈紳士的(な)，紳士らしい〉gentlemanly, gentlemanlike.

shinshi〈しんし：真し〉

　shinshi-na〈真しな〉sincere.

　　shinshi-na taido（真しな態度）　a sincere attitude

shinshiki〈しんしき：神式〉

　shinshiki-de-okonau〈神式で行う〉hold ((a ceremony)) according to *Shinto* rites.

shinshiki〈しんしき：新式〉a new type.

　shinshiki-no〈新式の〉new, new-type, modern.

shinshin〈しんしん：心身〉mind and body.

　　shinshin-tomo-ni-sôkai-de-aru（心身共にそう快である）　feel refreshed in mind and body

shinshin〈新進〉

　shinshin-no〈新進の〉rising.

　　shinshin-no sakka（新進の作家）　a rising writer

shinshin-to〈しんしんと：深々と〉

　　Yo ga shinshin-to-fukete-iku.（夜が深々と更けていく.）　The night is getting far advanced.

shinshitsu〈しんしつ：寝室〉a bedroom.

shinsho〈しんしょ：信書〉a letter, correspondence.

shinshô〈しんしょう：心証〉a conviction; an impression.

　　shinshô-o-gaisuru（心証を害する）　give ((a person)) an unfavorable impression, hurt ((a person's)) feeling

shinshô〈しんしょう：辛勝〉

　shinshô-suru〈辛勝する〉win ((a game)) narrowly after a hard struggle, nose out.

shinshoku〈しんしょく：浸食〉erosion, corrosion.
  shinshoku-sayô（浸食作用）erosive action
  shinshoku-suru〈浸食する〉erode, corrode.

shinshoku〈しんしょく：寝食〉food and sleep.
  shinshoku o tomo-ni-suru（寝食を共にする）share board and room ((with))
  shinshoku-o-wasurete〈寝食を忘れて〉without sparing oneself, devotedly.

shinshô-sha〈しんしょうしゃ：身障者〉*see.* shintai-shôgai-sha.

shinshuku〈しんしゅく：伸縮〉expansion and contraction.
  shinshuku-sei（伸縮性）elasticity
  shinshuku-sei-ga-nai（伸縮性がない）lack elasticity
  shinshuku-suru〈伸縮する〉expand and contract, be elastic.
  shinshuku-jizai-no〈伸縮自在の〉elastic, flexible.

shinshun〈しんしゅん：新春〉the New Year.

shinshutsu〈しんしゅつ：進出〉
  shinshutsu-suru〈進出する〉advance ((into)), find one's way ((into)), go ((into)).
  kaigai-shijô-ni-shinshutsu-suru（海外市場に進出する）find a larger market abroad

shinsô〈しんそう：真相〉the truth, the actual state of things.
  shinsô o akiraka-ni-suru（真相を明らかにする）disclose the truth

shinsô〈しんそう：新装〉
  shinsô-natta hyakka-ten（新装なった百貨店）the refurbished department store
  shinsô-o-korasu〈新装を凝らす〉refurbish, redecorate, refurnish, remodel.

shin-soko〈しんそこ：心底〉
  shin-soko-kara〈心底から〉from the bottom of one's heart, sincerely, with all one's heart.

shinsotsu〈しんそつ：新卒〉a fresh graduate.

shinsui〈しんすい：浸水〉flood, inundation.
  shinsui-kaoku（浸水家屋）flooded houses, houses under water
  shinsui-suru〈浸水する〉be flooded, be inundated.

shinsui〈しんすい：進水〉launching.
  shinsui-shiki（進水式）a launching ceremony
  shinsui-suru〈進水する〉be launched.

shinsui〈しんすい：心酔〉
 shinsui-suru〈心酔する〉be fascinated ((with)), be devoted ((to)), idolize.

shintai〈しんたい：身体〉the body.
   shintai-kensa（身体検査）a physical examination
     shintai-kensa o ukeru（身体検査を受ける）undergo a physical examination
   shintai-shôgai-sha（身体障害者）a physically handicapped person
 shintai-no〈身体の〉bodily, physical.

shintai〈しんたい：進退〉
   shintai-kiwamaru（進退窮まる）be driven to the corner, be in a dilemma, find oneself between the devil and the deep sea
   shintai-o-ayamaru（進退を誤る）take a wrong course
   shintai-o-tomo-ni-suru（進退を共にする）act in line ((with))

shintaku〈しんたく：信託〉trust.
   shintaku-ginkô（信託銀行）a trust bank
   kashi-tsuke-shintaku（貸付信託）loan trust
   kinsen-shintaku（金銭信託）money trust
 shintaku-suru〈信託する〉trust ((a person)) with.

shintan〈しんたん：心胆〉
 shintan-o-samukarashimeru〈心胆を寒からしめる〉make one's blood run cold.

shintei〈しんてい：心底〉one's inmost thought(s).
   shintei o mi-nuku（心底を見抜く）see through ((a person's)) real intention
   shintei-o-uchi-akeru（心底を打ち明ける）unbosom oneself ((to))

shintei〈しんてい：進呈〉presentation.
 shintei-suru〈進呈する〉present ((a person)) with.

shin-teki〈しんてき：心的〉mental, psychological.
   shin-teki genshô（心的現象）a mental phenomenon

shinten〈しんてん：進展〉development, progress, evolvement.
   jiken no shinten（事件の進展）the development of the affair
 shinten-suru〈進展する〉develop, progress, evolve.

shinten〈しんてん：親展〉Confidential.
 shinten-no〈親展の〉confidential, personal, private.

shin-to〈しんと〉
   Heya-wa-shin-to-shizumari-kaette-ita.（部屋はしんと静まりかえっていた。）A deep silence fell upon the room.
 shin-to-shita〈しんとした〉silent as the grave, deadly still.

shinto〈しんと：信徒〉a believer, a devotee, a follower.

shintō〈しんとう：浸透〉permeation, infiltration.

shintô-suru〈浸透する〉permeate, infiltrate.

shintō〈しんとう：親等〉the degree of relationship.

    isshintô（一親等）a relation in the first degree

shintsū〈しんつう：心痛〉mental agony, heartache.

shinu〈しぬ：死ぬ〉die, pass away.

    wakakute-shinu（若くて死ぬ）die young

    go-jussai-de-shinu（五十歳で死ぬ）die at the age of forty

    kôtsû-jiko-de-shinu（交通事故で死ぬ）be killed in a traffic accident

shini-kakaru〈死にかかる〉be dying.

shinde-tsumetaku-natte-iru〈死んで冷たくなっている〉be as dead as mutton.

shinda〈死んだ〉dead.

    shinda haha（死んだ母）my dead mother

shindemo〈死んでも〉at the risk of one's life, even after one's death.

shinu-made〈死ぬまで〉to the end; to the last hour of one's life.

shinwa〈しんわ：神話〉a myth, mythology.

shin·ya〈しんや：深夜〉midnight.

    shin·ya-hôsô（深夜放送）midnight broadcasting

shin·ya-ni〈深夜に〉at midnight.

shin·ya-made〈深夜まで〉until midnight.

shin·yō〈しんよう：信用〉confidence, trust, reliance, faith, credit.

    shin·yô o kizutsukeru（信用を傷つける）injure one's credit

    seken-no shin·yô o ushinau（世間の信用を失う）lose public confidence

    shin·yô-chôsa（信用調査）credit research

    shin·yô-jô（信用状）a letter of credit

    shin·yô-jôtai（信用状態）one's credit standing

shin·yô-suru〈信用する〉trust, rely ((on)).

shin·yô-ga-aru〈信用がある〉be trusted ((by)), have the confidence ((of)).

shin·yô-dekiru〈信用できる〉trustworthy, reliable.

shin·yô-deki-nai〈信用できない〉untrustworthy, unreliable.

shin·yō-ju〈しんようじゅ：針葉樹〉a needle-leaf tree.

shin·yū〈しんゆう：親友〉a close friend, one's best friend.

    shin·yû-ni-naru（親友になる）become great friends ((with))

shinzen〈しんぜん：神前〉

    shinzen-ni chikau（神前に誓う）pledge before God

shinzen-kekkon（神前結婚） a wedding in *Shinto* rites

shinzen〈しんぜん：親善〉friendship, goodwill.

shinzen-jiai （親善試合） a friendship game

shinzen-shisetsu（親善使節） a goodwill mission

shin-zen-bi〈しんぜんび：真善美〉the true, the good and the beautiful.

shinzô〈しんぞう：心臓〉the heart.

shinzô-ga-tsuyoi（心臓が強い） have a strong heart; have much nerve, be cheeky

shinzô-ga-yowai（心臓が弱い） have a weak heart; be nerveless

shinzô-ga-warui（心臓が悪い） have heart trouble

shinzô-byô（心臓病） a heart disease

shinzô-bemmaku-shô（心臓弁膜症） valvular disease of the heart

shinzô-geka（心臓外科） heart surgery

shinzô-mahi（心臓麻ひ） heart failure

shinzô-no-katachi-o-shita〈心臓の形をした〉heart-shaped.

shinzoku-kaigi〈しんぞくかいぎ：親族会議〉a family council.

shinzu-beki〈しんずべき：信ずべき〉trustworthy, reliable.

shinzu-beki suji（信ずべき筋） a reliable source

shio〈しお：塩〉salt.

hito-tsumami-no-shio（一つまみの塩） a pinch of salt

shio-ni-tsukeru〈塩に漬ける〉salt, preserve in salt.

shio-karai or *shio-ke-no-aru*〈塩辛い，塩気のある〉salty.

shio〈しお：潮〉the tide, a current.

Shio ga michiru.（潮が満ちる.） The tide flows.

Shio ga hiku.（潮が引く.） The tide ebbs.

shio-doki〈しおどき：潮時〉a chance, an opportunity.

shio-doki-o-matsu（潮時を待つ） wait for a good chance

shio-doki-o-mite～(-suru)（潮時をみて～(する)） seize an opportunity ((to do))

Mono-goto-niwa-subete-shio-doki-to-iu-mono-ga-aru.（物事にはすべて潮時というものがある.） There is a time for everything.

shiohi-gari〈しおひがり：潮干狩り〉shellfish gathering.

shiohi-gari-ni-iku〈潮干狩りに行く〉go gathering shellfish.

shio-kagen〈しおかげん：塩加減〉

shio-kagen-ga-ii〈塩加減がいい〉be well seasoned with salt.

shiokara〈しおから：塩辛〉salted fish guts.

shio-kaze〈しおかぜ：潮風〉a sea breeze.

shi-okuri〈しおくり：仕送り〉(an) allowance, (a) remittance.

tsukizuki-no shi-okuri（月々の仕送り）a monthly allowance

gakuhi-no-shi-okuri-o-suru（学費の仕送りをする）supply ((a person))
with his school expenses

shi-okuri-suru〈仕送りする〉send money ((to)), make a ((person)) an
allowance.

shiomizu *or* **shio-mizu**〈しおみず：潮水，塩水〉seawater; salt water.

shiorashii〈しおらしい〉gentle, sweet, pretty, modest.

shiorashii koto o iu（しおらしいことを言う）say pretty things

shiorashii taido-de（しおらしい態度で）in a modest attitude

shioreru〈しおれる〉wither, droop.

shiori〈しおり〉a bookmark; a guide.

shioshio(-to)〈しおしお（と）〉dejectedly, crestfallen, with a heavy heart.

shio-yaki〈しおやき：塩焼き〉

shio-yaki-ni-suru〈塩焼きにする〉broil ((fish)) with sprinkled salt.

shio-zuke〈しおづけ：塩漬け〉salted food.

shio-zuke-ni-suru〈塩漬けにする〉salt.

shio-zuke-no〈塩漬けの〉salted.

shippai〈しっぱい：失敗〉failure.

shippai-ni owaru（失敗に終わる）end in failure

shippai-suru〈失敗する〉fail ((in)), be unsuccessful ((in)).

shippe(i)-gaeshi〈しっぺ（い）がえし：しっぺ（い）返し〉tit for tat, retaliation.

shippe(i)-gaeshi-o-suru〈しっぺ（い）返しをする〉give ((a person)) tit for
tat, retaliate.

shippitsu〈しっぴつ：執筆〉writing.

shippitsu-o-irai-suru（執筆を依頼する）ask ((a person)) to write

shippitsu-suru〈執筆する〉write〔for a magazine〕.

shippo〈しっぽ〉a tail.

shippo-o-maite-nigeru（しっぽを巻いて逃げる）run away with one's
tail between one's legs

shippo-o-dasu〈しっぽを出す〉show one's true colors.

shippo-o-tsukamaeru〈しっぽを捕まえる〉find ((a person's)) fault.

shippô-yaki〈しっぽうやき：七宝焼〉*cloisonné* ware.

shippu〈しっぷ：湿布〉a compress, a pack.

on-shippu（温湿布）a hot compress

shippu-suru〈湿布する〉put a compress ((on)).

shira〈しら〉

shira-o-kiru〈しらを切る〉pretend not to know, affect ignorance.

shirabakureru 〈しらばくれる〉 *see.* shira-o-kiru.

shirabe 〈しらべ：調べ〉 (an) examination, (an) inspection, (an) inquiry; a note, a melody.

shirabe-mono（調べ物） a matter for inquiry

shirabe-o-ukeru（調べを受ける） be examined ((by)), be subjected to examination, be questioned ((by))

shiraberu 〈調べる〉 examine, look over, inquire ((into)), inspect.

Watashi no sūtsukêsu o shirabete-kudasai.（私のスーツケースを調べてください.） Please examine my suitcase.

shorui o shiraberu（書類を調べる） look over the papers

gen·in o shiraberu（原因を調べる） inquire into the cause

buki-o-motte-inai-ka-to-hito-no-karada-o-shiraberu（武器を持っていないかと人の体を調べる） search a person for a weapon

shirafu 〈しらふ〉

shirafu-no 〈しらふの〉 sober, not drunk.

shirafu-no-toki-ni（しらふのときに） when not drunk

shiraga 〈しらが：白髪〉 white hair, gray hair.

shiraga-o-someru（白髪を染める） have one's white hair dyed black

shiraga-atama-no 〈白髪頭の〉 gray-haired.

shirajirashii 〈しらじらしい：白々しい〉

shirajirashii uso（白々しいうそ） a transparent falsehood

shirakaba 〈しらかば：白かば〉 a white birch.

shirakeru 〈しらける：白ける〉 become chilled, be spoiled.

Kare-no-tame-ni za-ga-shiraketa.（彼のために座が白けた.） He cast a chill over the whole room.

shira-ko 〈しらこ：白子〉 milt, soft roe.

shirami 〈しらみ〉 a louse.

shirami o toru（しらみを取る） hunt a louse

shirami-tsubushi-ni-shiraberu 〈しらみつぶしに調べる〉 make a thorough search ((of)).

shiramu 〈しらむ：白む〉 grow light, turn gray.

Sora ga shirande-kita.（空が白んできた.） The sky was turning gray.

shira-nami 〈しらなみ：白波〉 white-crested waves, breakers.

shiran-kao 〈しらんかお：知らん顔〉

shiran-kao-o-suru 〈知らん顔をする〉 cut ((a person)) (dead), give ((a person)) the go-by.

shirareru 〈しられる：知られる〉 become known, become well known.

shirase 〈しらせ：知らせ〉 news, a notice, a report, information.

~-to-iu-shirase-ga-haitta.（～という知らせが入った.） The news came in that... .

shiraseru〈知らせる〉let know, tell, inform ((a person)) of, report, make known.

    mae-motte shiraseru（前もって知らせる）give ((a person)) notice beforehand

shirasezu-ni-oku〈知らせずにおく〉keep ((a matter)) secret.

shira-taki〈しらたき：白滝〉stringy *konnyaku*.

shira-tama-ko〈しらたまこ：白玉粉〉refined rice flour.

shira-uo〈しらうお：白魚〉a whitebait.

shirazushirazu(-ni)〈しらずしらず(に)：知らず知らず(に)〉without knowing it, unconsciously.

shirei〈しれい：指令〉an order, instructions.

shirei-suru or *shirei-o-dasu*〈指令する，指令を出す〉order, give instructions.

shirei〈しれい：司令〉

    shirei-bu（司令部）the headquarters

       sô-shirei-bu（総司令部）the General Headquarters

    shirei-kan（司令官）a commander

    shirei-chôkan（司令長官）a commander-in-chief

shiren〈しれん：試練〉a trial, a test, an ordeal.

    jinsei no ookuno shiren ni taeru（人生の多くの試練に耐える）stand a lot of trials of life

shireru〈しれる：知れる〉become known.

    seken-ni-shireru（世間に知れる）become generally known

shire-nai〈知れない〉there is not knowing, remain unknown, do not come to light; perhaps, maybe.

    Kanojo-no shiin wa mada shire-nai.（彼女の死因はまだ知れない.） The cause of her death still remains unknown.

    Hontô-kamo-shire-nai.（本当かも知れない.） It may be true.

shireta〈知れた〉plain; trifling.

    Shireta-koto-da.（知れた事だ.） It's a matter of course.

    Kare-no syûnyû wa shireta-mono-da.（彼の収入は知れたものだ.） His income is but a trifle.

shiretsu〈しれつ：し烈〉

shiretsu-na〈し烈な〉keen, sharp, severe.

    shiretsu-na kyôsô（し烈な競争）keen competition

shiri〈しり：私利〉personal profit.

shiri o hakaru（私利を図る） seek one's own interests

shiri〈しり〉the buttocks, the hips, the bottom.

shiri o furu（しりを振る） swing one's hips

shiri-ga-omoi（しりが重い） be lazy, be indolent

shiri-ni-hi-ga-tsuku（しりに火が付く） be pressed by urgent business

nyôbô-no-shiri-ni-shikareru（女房のしりに敷かれる） be dominated by one's wife, be henpecked

shiri-agari〈しりあがり：しり上がり〉

shiri-agari-no chôshi（しり上がりの調子） a rising intonation

shiri-agari-ni-fueru（しり上がりに増える） show a rising tendency

shiri-ai〈しりあい：知り合い〉an acquaintance.

shiri-ai-ga-ooi（知り合いが多い） have a large circle of acquaintances

shiri-ai-ni-naru〈知り合いになる〉become acquainted ((with)).

shiri-gomi〈しりごみ：しり込み〉

shiri-gomi-suru〈しり込みする〉flinch ((from)), shrink ((from)), hesitate.

shirikire-tombo〈しりきれとんぼ：しり切れとんぼ〉

shirikire-tombo-ni-naru〈しり切れとんぼになる〉be left unfinished.

shiri-metsuretsu〈しりめつれつ：支離滅裂〉

shiri-metsuretsu-ni-naru〈支離滅裂になる〉become incoherent, lose consistency, fall into a chaos.

shiri-metsuretsu-na〈支離滅裂な〉incoherent, inconsistent.

shiri-mochi〈しりもち〉

shiri-mochi-o-tsuku（しりもちをつく） fall on one's buttocks.

shiri-nugui〈しりぬぐい〉

shiri-nugui-o-suru〈しりぬぐいをする〉pay for ((another's)) blunder, pay ((a person's)) debt.

shiri-oshi〈しりおし：しり押し〉backing, support; instigation.

shiri-oshi-suru〈しり押しする〉support, back; instigate.

shiri-subomi〈しりすぼみ〉

shiri-subomi-ni-naru〈しりすぼみになる〉taper, narrow toward the end.

shiritsu〈しりつ：市立〉

shiritru-gakkô（市立学校） a municipal school

shiritsu-no〈市立の〉municipal.

shiritru〈しりつ：私立〉

shiritsu-gakkô（私立学校） a private school

shiritsu-no〈私立の〉private.

shirizokeru〈しりぞける：退ける〉drive away; keep away; refuse, reject.

shirizoku〈しりぞく：退く〉retreat, move backward; retire ((from)).

ippo shirizoku（一歩退く）take a step backward

shoku-o-shirizoku（職を退く）retire from one's office

shiro〈しろ：白〉white; innocence.

Aitsu-wa shiro-da.（あいつは白だ。）He is innocent.

shiroku-naru〈白くなる〉become white, turn gray.

shiroi〈白い〉white, fair.

yuki-no-yô-ni shiroi（雪のように白い）white as snow

shiroi-hada（白い肌）a fair complexion

shiro〈しろ：城〉a castle.

-shiro〈-しろ〉

nani-goto-ni-shiro〈何事にしろ〉no matter what it may be.

shiro-ari〈しろあり：白あり〉a white ant, a termite.

shiro-ari-no su（白ありの巣）a termites' nest

shiro-ato〈しろあと：城跡〉the site of a castle, the ruins of a castle.

shiro-bai〈しろバイ：白バイ〉a motorcycle policeman, a police motorcycle.

shirohon〈シロホン〉a xylophone.

shiro-ji〈しろじ：白地〉

shiro-ji-uragaki（白地裏書き）(a) blank endorsement

shirokuji-chû〈しろくじちゅう：四六時中〉around the clock, a whole day; always.

shiro-kuma〈しろくま：白くま〉a polar bear.

shiro-me〈しろめ：白目〉the white of the eye.

shiro-mi〈しろみ：白身〉

tamago no shiro-mi（卵の白身）the white of an egg

shiro-mono〈しろもの：代物〉a thing, stuff; an article; a fellow.

kudaranai shiro-mono（くだらない代物）a wretched stuff

yakkai-na shiro-mono（厄介な代物）an ugly customer

shiro-muku〈しろむく：白むく〉a pure-white dress.

shiro-muku-no-kimono-o-kite-iru（白むくの着物を着ている）be dressed all in white

shiro-nuri〈しろぬり：白塗り〉

shiro-nuri-no〈白塗りの〉white-painted.

shirôto〈しろうと：素人〉an amateur.

shirôto-kangae（素人考え）a layman's idea

shirôto-me（素人目）an untrained eye

shirôto-ryôhô（素人療法）home treatment

shirôto-banare-shite-iru〈素人離れしている〉be as good as professional.

shirôto-kusai〈素人くさい〉amateurish.

shiro-zatô〈しろざとう：白砂糖〉refined sugar.

shiru〈しる：汁〉juice, soup.

shiru o shiboru（汁を搾る）extract juice ((from)), express the juice

amai-shiru-o-suu（甘い汁を吸う）take the lion's share ((of))

shiru-no-ooi〈汁の多い〉juicy, watery.

shiru〈しる：知る〉know, be aware ((of)), be acquainted ((with)), be conscious ((of)); be concerned ((with)); experience; guess.

tashô shitte-iru（多少知っている）know a little something ((about))

mattaku-shira-nai（全く知らない）know nothing ((about))

namae-wa shitte-iru（名前は知っている）know ((a person)) by name

Shiranu-ga-hotoke.〈知らぬが仏.〉Ignorance is bliss.

O-mae-no-shitta-koto-ka.（お前の知ったことか.）It's none of your business.

sensô o shira-nai（戦争を知らない）have had no experience of a war

Ta-wa-oshite-shiru-beshi.（他は推して知るべし.）You can easily imagine the rest.

watashi-ga shitte-iru-kagiri-dewa〈私が知っている限りでは〉so far as I know.

shira-nai-aida-ni〈知らない間に〉before one is aware of it.

shirushi〈しるし：印〉a sign, a mark; a brand; a token.

o-rei no shirushi-to-shite（お礼の印として）in token of one's gratitude

shirushi-o-tsukeru〈印を付ける〉mark.

shirusu〈しるす：記す〉write down, mark, mention, give an account ((of)).

shiryo〈しりょ：思慮〉thought, consideration, prudence.

shiryo-no-aru or *shiryo-bukai*〈思慮のある，思慮深い〉thoughtful, prudent.

shiryo-no-nai（思慮のない）thoughtless, imprudent

shiryô〈しりょう：史料〉historical materials.

shiryô〈しりょう：資料〉materials, data.

shiryô o atsumeru（資料を集める）gather materials ((for))

shiryô〈しりょう：飼料〉feed, fodder, forage.

shiryoku〈しりょく：視力〉eyesight, sight.

shiryoku-ga-yowai（視力が弱い）be weak in sight

Kanojo-wa shiryoku-ga-otoroeteiru.（彼女は視力が衰えている.）Her

　　　eyesight is impairing.
　　　shiryoku o kaifuku-suru〈視力を回復する〉 recover one's sight
　　　shiryoku o kensa-suru〈視力を検査する〉 test ((a person's)) eyesight
　　　shiryoku o ushinau〈視力を失う〉 lose one's eyesight
shiryoku〈しりょく：資力〉means, resources, funds.
　　　shiryoku-no-aru hito〈資力のある人〉 a man of means
　　　shiryoku-no-nai hito〈資力のない人〉 a man of no means
shiryoku〈しりょく：死力〉
　shiryoku-o-tsukushite-tatakau〈死力を尽くして戦う〉fight a desperate
　　fight.
shiryû〈しりゅう：支流〉a tributary, a feeder, a branch.
shisa〈しさ：示唆〉suggestion.
　　　shisa-ni-tomu〈示唆に富む〉 be full of suggestions
　shisa-suru〈示唆する〉suggest, hint (at).
shisai〈しさい：司祭〉a priest.
shisai〈しさい：市債〉a municipal loan, a municipal bond.
shisai〈しさい：し細〉reasons, circumstances; meaning, significance;
　　particulars.
　　　shisai-atte〈し細あって〉 for some reason
　　　shisai-ari-ge-ni〈し細ありげに〉 meaningly, significantly
　　　shisai-ni〈し細に〉 in detail, minutely
shisaku〈しさく：思索〉speculation, meditation.
　　　shisaku-ni-fukeru〈思索にふける〉 be lost in meditation
　shisaku-suru〈思索する〉speculate ((on)), meditate ((on)).
shisaku〈しさく：試作〉trial manufacture.
　　　shisaku-hin〈試作品〉 a trial product
　shisaku-suru〈試作する〉manufacture by way of trial.
shisan〈しさん：資産〉property, a fortune, assets.
　　　shisan-ka〈資産家〉 a man of property
shisan-hyô〈しさんひょう：試算表〉a trial balance.
shisatsu〈しさつ：視察〉(an) inspection, observation.
　　　shisatsu-ryokô〈視察旅行〉 a tour of inspection
　shisatsu-suru〈視察する〉inspect, observe.
shisei〈しせい：姿勢〉a posture, a carriage, an attitude.
　　　shisei-ga-ii〈姿勢がいい〉 have a fine carriage
　　　shisei-ga-warui〈姿勢が悪い〉 have a poor carriage
　　　tei-shisei〈低姿勢〉 a low attitude
shisei〈しせい：市制〉municipal organization.

shisei-o-shiku〈市制を敷く〉municipalize.

shisei〈しせい：市政〉municipal administration.

shisei〈しせい：施政〉administration, government.
　　shisei-hôshin（施政方針）an administrative policy, a party line
　　shisei-enzetsu（施政演説）a speech on one's administrative policies

shisei〈しせい：至誠〉sincerity, devotion.

shisei-hagaki〈しせいはがき：私製はがき〉a private postcard, a postcard.

shisei-ji〈しせいじ：私生児〉a natural child, a love child.

shi-seikatsu〈しせいかつ：私生活〉one's private life.

shiseki〈しせき：史跡〉a historic spot(*or* site).
　　shiseki o hozon-suru（史跡を保存する）preserve historic remains

shiseki〈しせき：歯石〉tartar.

shiseki-o-toru〈歯石を取る〉scale ((a person's)) teeth.

shisen〈しせん：死線〉a life-or-death crisis.
　　shisen o koeru（死線を越える）pass through a life-or-death crisis
　　shisen-o-samayou（死線をさまよう）hover between life and death

shisen〈しせん：支線〉a branch line.

shisen〈しせん：視線〉one's eyes, a glance, one's gaze.
　　Shisen ga atta.（視線が合った。）Their eyes met.
　　shisen o sakeru（視線を避ける）avoid ((a person's)) eye
　　shisen o sorasu（視線をそらす）turn one's eyes ((from))

shisetsu〈しせつ：私設〉

shisetsu-no〈私設の〉private.

shisetsu〈しせつ：使節〉an envoy, a mission.
　　shisetsu-dan（使節団）a mission, a delegation

shisetsu〈しせつ：施設〉an institution, an establishment, facilities.
　　kôkyô-shisetsu（公共施設）a public service, a public institution
　　goraku-shisetsu（娯楽施設）facilities for recreation
　　kyôiku-sihsetsu（教育施設）educational facilities

shisha〈ししゃ：支社〉a branch (office).

shisha〈ししゃ：使者〉a messenger, an emissary.

shisha〈ししゃ：死者〉a dead person, the dead.
　　tasû-no shisha（多数の死者）a heavy loss of lives

shisha〈ししゃ：試写〉a preview.
　　shisha o okonau（試写を行う）give a preview

shisha-gonyû〈ししゃごにゅう：四捨五入〉
　　shôsû-ten-san・i-ika-o-shisha-gonyû-suru（小数点三位以下を四捨五入す

る） round off the fractions to three decimal places.

shishi 〈しし〉 a lion, a lioness.

shishi-funjin-no-ikioi-de 〈しし奮迅の勢いで〉 with irresistible force.

shishin 〈ししん：指針〉 a compass needle, an indicator, a pointer; a guide, a guideline.

shishin 〈ししん：私心〉 selfishness.

shishin-no-nai 〈私心のない〉 unselfish.

shi-shinkei 〈ししんけい：視神経〉 the optic nerve.

shishi-sonson 〈ししそんそん：子々孫々〉 posterity, descendants, offspring.

    shishi-sonson ni tsutaeru 〈子々孫々に伝える〉 hand down ((a thing)) to one's offspring

    shishi-sonson-ni-itaru-made 〈子々孫々に至るまで〉 to one's remotest descendants

shisho 〈ししょ：支署〉 a substation.

shishô 〈ししょう：師匠〉 a master, a mistress, a teacher.

shishô 〈ししょう：支障〉 a hindrance, an obstacle, an impediment.

shishô-o-kitasu 〈支障を来す〉 hinder, impede, interfere ((with)).

shishô-naku 〈支障なく〉 without a hitch.

shisho-bako 〈ししょばこ：私書箱〉 a post-office box(P.O.B.), a call box.

shishoku 〈ししょく：試食〉 sampling.

    shishoku-kai 〈試食会〉 a sampling party

shishoku-suru 〈試食する〉 sample, try, taste.

shishô-sha 〈ししょうしゃ：死傷者〉 casualties, the killed and the injured.

shishu 〈ししゅ：死守〉

shishu-suru 〈死守する〉 defend to the last, defend desperately.

shishû 〈ししゅう：刺しゅう〉 embroidery.

    shishû-ito 〈刺しゅう糸〉 embroidery thread

shishû-suru 〈刺しゅうする〉 embroider.

shishû 〈ししゅう：詩集〉 poetical works ((of)), a collection of poems.

shishun-ki 〈ししゅんき：思春期〉 puberty.

shishun-ki-no 〈思春期の〉 pubescent.

shishutsu 〈ししゅつ：支出〉 expenditure, expenses, (an) outgo.

shishutsu-suru 〈支出する〉 expend, pay.

shiso 〈しそ〉 a beefsteak plant.

shisô 〈しそう：思想〉 thought, an idea.

    shisô-ka 〈思想家〉 a thinker

shîsô 〈シーソー〉 a seesaw, a teeter.

shîsô-o-shite-asobu〈シーソーをして遊ぶ〉play at seesaw

shi-sokonau〈しそこなう：仕損なう〉*see.* shi-sonjiru.

shison〈しそん：子孫〉a descendant, posterity.

shi-sonjiru〈しそんじる：仕損じる〉fail, make a mistake, make a blunder.

shîsô-nôrô〈しそうのうろう：歯槽のう漏〉pyorrhea, Riggs' disease.

shissaku〈しっさく：失策〉an error, a mistake, a blunder.
　　dai-shissaku〈大失策〉a gross error
　shissaku-o-suru〈失策をする〉err, make a mistake, commit a blunder.

shissei〈しっせい：失政〉mal administration, misgovernment, misrule.

shissei〈しっせい：湿性〉
　shissei-no〈湿性の〉wet.

shisshin〈しっしん：湿しん〉eczema, moist tetter.

shisshin〈しっしん：失神〉
　shisshin-suru〈失神する〉swoon, faint, fall unconscious.

shisshoku〈しっしょく：失職〉unemployment.

shisso〈しっそ：質素〉simplicity, frugality.
　shisso-na〈質素な〉simple, modest, plain, frugal.
　　shisso-na seikatsu o suru〈質素な生活をする〉live a simple life

shissô〈しっそう：失そう〉disappearance, missing.
　shissô-suru〈失そうする〉disappear, run away, be missing.

shissô〈しっそう：疾走〉
　shissô-suru〈疾走する〉run at full speed, dash.

shissoku〈しっそく：失速〉a stall.
　shissoku-suru〈失速する〉stall.

shissuru〈しっする：失する〉lose, miss, forget.
　　jiki o shissuru〈時機を失する〉lose a chance
　　rei-o-shissuru〈礼を失する〉be rude

shisû〈しすう：指数〉an index (number).

shita〈した：舌〉a tongue.
　　shita o dasu〈舌を出す〉put out one's tongue ((at))
　　shita-ga-mawara-nai〈舌が回らない〉be unable to speak distinctly
　　areta shita〈荒れた舌〉a furred tongue

shita〈した：下〉the lower part, the bottom, the foot.
　　pêji no shita-kara-san-gyô-me〈ページの下から三行目〉the third line from the bottom of the page
　shita-no〈下の〉under, lower, downstair(s).
　　tansu no shita-no hiki-dashi〈たんすの下の引き出し〉the lower

drawer of a bureau

shita-no heya-ni〈下の部屋に〉 in the downstair room

shita-e, shita-ni or *shita-o*〈下へ，下に，下を〉under, below, down, downstairs.

tsukue-no-shita-ni〈机の下に〉 under a desk

chihei-sen-no-shita-ni〈地平線の下に〉 below the horizen

shita-ni oku〈下に置く〉 lay down

shita-e oriru〈下へ降りる〉 go downstairs

shita-bara〈したばら：下腹〉the abdomen, the underbelly.

shita-bi〈したび：下火〉

shita-bi-ni-naru〈下火になる〉burn down, go out of vogue.

shita-dori〈したどり：下取り〉

shita-dori-suru〈下取りする〉take a trade-in ((on)).

shita-dori-shite-morau〈下取りしてもらう〉trade ((in)).

shita-e〈したえ：下絵〉a rough sketch, a dessein, a design.

shitagaeru〈したがえる：従える〉be attended ((by)).

shita-gaki〈したがき：下書き〉a rough copy, a draft.

shita-gaki-suru〈下書きする〉make a rough copy ((of)), make a draft ((of)).

shitagatte〈したがって：従って〉accordingly, consequently, therefore.

(-ni)-shitagatte〈(-に)したがって：(-に)従って〉according to, as.

kare-no sashizu-ni-shitagatte〈彼の指図に従って〉 according to his instructions

taiyô ga shizumu-ni-shitagatte〈太陽が沈むに従って〉 as the sun sets

kare-no kotoba-ni-shitagatte〈彼の言葉に従って〉 at his suggestion

shitagau〈したがう：従う〉obey; follow, accompany.

meirei ni shitagau〈命令に従う〉 obey ((a person's)) order

shita-geiko〈したげいこ：下げい古〉(a) rehearsal.

shita-geiko-suru〈下げい古する〉rehearse, have a rehearsal ((of)).

shita-gi〈したぎ：下着〉underwear, an undershirt, lingerie.

shita-gokoro〈したごころ：下心〉a secret intention.

shita-gokoro-ga-aru〈下心がある〉 have a secret intention, have an ax to grind

shita-goshirae〈したごしらえ：下ごしらえ〉*see.* shita-jumbi.

shitai〈したい：肢体〉a limb, a member.

shitai-fu-jiyû-ji〈肢体不自由児〉 a physically handicapped child

shitai〈したい：姿態〉a figure, a pose.

shitai〈したい：死体〉a dead body, a corpse.

　　shitai-to-natte-hakken-sareru〈死体となって発見される〉be　found
　　dead
　　shitai-kaibô〈死体解剖〉necrotomy, an autopsy
-shi-tai〈～したい〉want to do, wish to do, should like to do, feel like
doing.
　　shi-tai-hôdai-suru〈したい放題する〉have everything one's own way
shita-ji〈したじ：下地〉groundwork, foundation; the first coat.
shita-jiki〈したじき：下敷き〉a celluloid board.
　shita-jiki-ni-naru〈下敷きになる〉be pressed(*or* held) under... .
shita-jumbi〈したじゅんび：下準備〉prearrangement, preparations.
　shita-jumbi-o-suru〈下準備をする〉prearrange,　arrange　beforehand,
　make preparations ((for)).
shita-kembun〈したけんぶん：下検分〉
　shita-kembun-suru〈下検分する〉examine beforehand.
shitaku〈したく：支度〉preparations.
　　shokuji-no-shitaku-o-suru（食事の支度をする）get the dinner ready
　　tabi-no-shitaku-o-suru（旅の支度をする）equip oneself for a trip
　shitaku-suru〈支度する〉prepare, make preparations, get ready; dress
　oneself.
shita-machi〈したまち：下町〉the downtown.
　shita-machi-de, shita-machi-e or *shita-machi-ni*〈下町で，下町へ，下町に〉
　downtown.
　　shita-machi-ni sumu（下町に住む）live downtown
shita-mawaru〈したまわる：下回る〉be less ((than)), fall below.
shita-mi〈したみ：下見〉a preliminary inspection.
　shita-mi-suru〈下見する〉inspect beforehand.
　shita-mi-mo-sezu-ni〈下見もせずに〉sight unseen.
shita-muki〈したむき：下向き〉
　shita-muki-ni-naru〈下向きになる〉look　down,　show　a　downward
　tendency.
shitan〈したん：紫たん〉a red sandalwood.
shita-namezuri〈したなめずり：舌なめずり〉
　shita-namezuri-suru〈舌なめずりする〉lick one's lips.
shita-nuri〈したぬり：下塗り〉the first coat, undercoating.
　　shita-nuri-o-suru（下塗りをする）give　the　first　coat　((to)), put　the
　　undercoating ((on))
shita-saki〈したさき：舌先〉
　shita-saki-sanzun-de　gomakasu〈舌先三寸でごまかす〉cheat　((a　person))

by a glib tongue.

shitashii 〈したしい：親しい〉 intimate, familiar, close, friendly.

　shitashii yūjin（親しい友人） one's close friend

shitashiku-naru〈親しくなる〉 make friends ((with)), become familiar ((with)).

shitashiku-suru〈親しくする〉 be on friendly terms ((with)), be friends ((with)).

shitashimi 〈したしみ：親しみ〉 intimacy, familiarity, friendship, affection.

shitashimi-no-aru〈親しみのある〉 intimate, familiar.

　shitashimi-no-nai（親しみのない） cold, unfamiliar

shitashimi-yasui〈親しみやすい〉 friendly and approachable.

shitashimu〈親しむ〉 be intimate ((with)), make friends ((with)).

　shizen-ni-shitashimu（自然に親しむ） commune with nature

shita-shirabe 〈したしらべ：下調べ〉 preparation; a preliminary inquiry.

shita-shirabe-o-suru〈下調べをする〉 prepare, inquire beforehand.

shitataka 〈したたか〉 severely, soundly, hard, heavily.

　shitataka kogoto-o-iwareru（したたか小言を言われる） be scolded severely

　shitataka utareru（したたか打たれる） be beaten soundly

　shitataka sake-o-nomu（したたか酒を飲む） drink heavily

shitataka-mono 〈したたかもの：したたか者〉 an old wily fox, a vicious woman.

shitatari 〈したたり：滴り〉 dripping, a drop, a trickle.

shitataru〈滴る〉 drip, drop, trickle.

shita-te 〈したて：下手〉

　shita-te-ni-deru（下手に出る） humble oneself, condescend ((to do))

　shita-te-nage-tōshu（下手投げ投手） an underhand pitcher

shitate 〈したて：仕立て〉 tailoring, sewing, a cut.

shitate-no-ii〈仕立てのいい〉 well-tailored.

　shitate-no-warui（仕立ての悪い） ill-tailored

shitateru 〈したてる：仕立てる〉 make, tailor; bring up.

　ichinin-mae-no-otoko-ni-shitateru（一人前の男に仕立てる） make a man of ((a person))

shita-tsuzumi 〈したつづみ：舌鼓〉

shita-tsuzumi-o-utte-taberu〈舌鼓を打って食べる〉 eat ((a thing)) with gusto.

shitau 〈したう：慕う〉 yearn ((after *or* for)), love ((a person)) dearly.

shita-uchi〈したうち：舌打ち〉
shita-uchi-suru〈舌打ちする〉click one's tongue.

shita-uke〈したうけ：下請け〉a subcontract.
shita-uke-gyôsha（下請け業者）a subcontractor
shita-uke-kôjô（下請け工場）a subcontract factory
shita-uke-ni-dasu〈下請けに出す〉sublet, subcontract.

shita-zawari〈したざわり：舌触り〉
shita-zawari-ga-ii〈舌触りがいい〉be soft and pleasant to the tongue.
shita-zawari-ga-warui（舌触りが悪い）be rough and unpleasant to the tongue

shita-zumi〈したづみ：下積み〉
shita-zumi-ni-natte-iru　nimotsu（下積みになっている荷物）goods in the lower layer
kaisha-de　shita-zumi-de-aru（会社で下積みである）hold an ignominious position in a firm

shitchi〈しっち：湿地〉damp ground, marsh.

shitchi〈しっち：失地〉(a) lost territory.
shitchi o kaifuku-suru（失地を回復する）recover the lost territory

shitei〈してい：私邸〉one's private residence.

shitei〈してい：師弟〉master and pupil, teacher and student.
shitei-kankei（師弟関係）the relation between teacher and student

shitei〈してい：子弟〉sons, children.

shitei〈してい：指定〉appointment.
shitei-no-jikan（指定の時間）the appointed time
shitei-seki（指定席）a reserved seat
shitei-suru〈指定する〉appoint.
kaigô-no　basho　o　shitei-suru（会合の場所を指定する）appoint the place for meeting

shiteki〈してき：指摘〉
shiteki-suru〈指摘する〉point out, indicate.
ayamari o shiteki-suru（誤りを指摘する）point out a mistake

shi-teki(-na)〈してき(な)：私的(な)〉private, personal.
shi-teki-na mondai（私的な問題）a private affair

shi-teki(-na)〈してき(な)：詩的(な)〉poetic(al).
shi-teki-ni〈詩的に〉poetically.

shiten〈してん：支点〉a fulcrum.

shiten〈してん：支店〉a branch office.
shiten-chô（支店長）a branch manager

shiten〈してん：視点〉a viewpoint, a point of view.

shitetsu〈してつ：私鉄〉a railroad under private management.

-shite-wa〈-しては〉for, as.

Hachigatsu-ni-shite-wa suzushii.（八月にしては涼しい.）It's cool for August.

Kare-wa keiei-sha-to-shite-wa shippai-da.（彼は経営者としては失敗だ.）He is a failure as an executive.

shite-yaru〈してやる〉

Shite-yattari.（してやったり.）Success is mine.

shite-yarareru〈してやられる〉be cheated, be taken in, be outsmarted.

mamma-to shite-yarareru（まんまとしてやられる）be nicely taken in

shito〈しと：使徒〉an apostle.

shito〈しと：使途〉

tagaku-no shito-fumei-no kane（多額の使途不明の金）a large expenditure of money unaccounted for

shitô〈しとう：死闘〉a desperate struggle.

shitô〈しとう：至当〉

shitô-na〈至当な〉proper, just, fair, right, reasonable.

shi-togeru〈しとげる：仕遂げる〉see. nashi-togeru.

shi-tomeru〈しとめる：仕留める〉kill, shoot dead, bring down.

shîto-nokku〈シートノック〉fielding practice.

shitoshito〈しとしと〉softly, gently.

Ame ga shitoshito futteiru.（雨がしとしと降っている.）It is raining softly.

shitoyaka〈しとやか〉

shitoyaka-na〈しとやかな〉graceful, gentle.

shitoyaka-ni〈しとやかに〉gracefully, gently.

shitsu〈しつ：質〉quality.

shitsu-ga-ii（質がいい）be of good quality

shitsu-ga-warui（質が悪い）be inferior in quality

shitsu-teki-ni〈質的に〉qualitatively.

shitsu-teki-ni-mo ryô-teki-ni-mo（質的にも量的にも）both in quality and in quantity

shîtsu〈シーツ〉a sheet.

shitsubô〈しつぼう：失望〉disappointment, despair.

shitsubô-suru〈失望する〉be disappointed ((at, in, of *or* with)), despair ((of)).

shitsubô-teki(-na)〈失望的(な)〉disappointing.

shitsubô-shite 〈失望して〉 disappointedly, in despair.

shitsudo 〈しつど：湿度〉 humidity.
　　shitsudo-kei (湿度計) a hygrometer

shitsugai 〈しつがい：室外〉
　shitsugai-no 〈室外の〉 outdoor.
　shitsugai-de or *shitsugai-ni* 〈室外で，室外に〉 outdoors, out of doors.

shitsugen 〈しつげん：失言〉 a slip of the tongue.
　　shitsugen o tori-kesu (失言を取り消す) retract one's words
　shitsugen-suru 〈失言する〉 make a slip of the tongue.

shitsugi 〈しつぎ：質疑〉 a question.
　　shitsugi-ôtô (質疑応答) questions and answers

shitsugyô 〈しつぎょう：失業〉 unemployment.
　　shitsugyô-sha (失業者) a person out of employment
　shitsugyô-suru 〈失業する〉 lose one's work.
　shitsugyô-shite-iru 〈失業している〉 be out of work.

shitsui 〈しつい：失意〉 disappointment, despair, a broken heart.
　　shitsui-no-donzoko-ni-aru (失意のどん底にある) be at the nadir of
　　one's fortune

shitsuke 〈しつけ〉 breeding, training, discipline, teaching manners.
　shitsuke-no-ii 〈しつけのいい〉 well-bred, well-mannered.
　　shitsuke-no-warui (しつけの悪い) ill-bred
　shitsukeru 〈しつける〉 breed, train, discipline, teach manners.

shitsuke-ito 〈しつけいと：仕付け糸〉 tacking thread, basting.

shitsukoi 〈しつこい〉 persistent, obstinate, importunate; heavy.
　　shitsukoi byôki (しつこい病気) an obstinate disease
　　shitsukoi tabemono (しつこい食べ物) heavy food
　shitsukoku 〈しつこく〉 persistently, importunately.
　　shitsukoku sasou (しつこく誘う) invite ((a person)) persistently

shitsumei 〈しつめい：失明〉
　　shitsumei-sha (失明者) a blind person
　shitsumei-suru 〈失明する〉 become blind, lose one's eyesight.

shitsumon 〈しつもん：質問〉 a question.
　　shitsumon o abiseru (質問を浴びせる) rain questions ((on))
　　shitsumon ni kotaeru (質問に答える) answer a question
　　shitsumon-zeme-ni-au (質問攻めに遭う) face a barrage of questions
　shitsumon-suru 〈質問する〉 ask ((a person)) a question, put a question to
　　((a person)).

shitsumu 〈しつむ：執務〉

shitsumu-jikan〈執務時間〉 office hours.

shitsumu-suru〈執務する〉attend to one's business.

shitsunai〈しつない：室内〉

shitsunai-sôshoku〈室内装飾〉 interior decoration

shitsunai-yûgi〈室内遊戯〉 an indoor game

shitsunai-gaku〈室内楽〉 chamber music

shitsunai-no〈室内の〉indoor.

shitsunai-de or *shitsunai-ni*〈室内で，室内に〉indoors, in a room.

shitsunai-ni toji-komoru〈室内に閉じ込もる〉 stay indoors

shitsunen〈しつねん：失念〉

shitsunen-suru〈失念する〉forget, escape one's memory.

shitsurei〈しつれい：失礼〉impoliteness, rudeness, bad manners.

shitsurei-suru〈失礼する〉Excuse me, I'm sorry; say good-by(e).

Chotto shitsurei-shimasu.（ちょっと失礼します。） Excuse me just a moment.

Mô shitsurei-shi-nakereba-narimasen.（もう失礼しなければなりません。） I must be going now.

Shitsurei-desu-ga,～.〈失礼ですが，～.〉Excuse me, but... .

shitsurei-na〈失礼な〉impolite, rude.

shitsurei-na-koto o iu〈失礼なことを言う〉 say rude things

shitsurei-na-koto-o-suru〈失礼なことをする〉 act rudely

shitsuren〈しつれん：失恋〉

shitsuren-suru〈失恋する〉be disappointed in love.

shitsuryô〈しつりょう：質量〉mass; quality and quantity.

shitsuyô〈しつよう：執よう〉

shitsuyô-na〈執ような〉obstinate, stubborn, persistent.

shitsuyô-ni〈執ように〉obstinately, stubbornly, persistently.

shitsuyô-ni kui-sagaru〈執ように食い下がる〉 stubbornly refuse to back down

shittai〈しったい：失態(体)〉

shittai-o-enjiru〈失態を演じる〉commit an indiscretion, make a fool of oneself.

shittakaburi〈しったかぶり：知ったか振り〉

shittakaburi-o-suru〈知ったか振りをする〉pretend as if one knew.

shitto〈しっと〉jealousy, envy.

shitto-suru〈しっとする〉be jealous ((of or over)), envy.

shitto-bukai〈しっと深い〉jealous, envious.

shitto-no-amari〈しっとの余り〉from jealousy, out of envy.

shittô 〈しっとう：執刀〉

Tanaka-hakase-no-shittô-de shujutsu wa okonawareta.（田中博士の執刀で手術は行われた。）The operation was performed by Dr. Tanaka.

     shittô-i（執刀医）an operator

shittô 〈しっとう：失投〉

shittô-suru〈失投する〉throw a ball carelessly.

shittori 〈しっとり〉

shittori-ase-bamu〈しっとり汗ばむ〉get moist with sweat.

shittori-shita 〈しっとりした〉quiet, gentle.

     shittori-shita kimochi（しっとりした気持）a quiet mood

shittsui 〈しっつい：失墜〉fall, loss.

     ishin no shittsui（威信の失墜）loss of prestige

shittsui-suru〈失墜する〉lose, fall.

shiuchi 〈しうち：仕打ち〉treatment, behavior, action, conduct.

     hidoi shiuchi o ukeru（ひどい仕打ちを受ける）receive a bad treatment

shi-unten 〈しうんてん：試運転〉a trial run, a trial cruise, test working.

     shi-unten-o-okonau（試運転を行う）make a trial run

shiwa 〈しわ〉wrinkles.

shiwa-ga-yoru〈しわが寄る〉wrinkle.

shiwa-o-nobasu〈しわを伸ばす〉smooth out wrinkles, iron out wrinkles.

shiwa-no-yotta〈しわの寄った〉wrinkled.

shiwa-darake-no or *shiwa-kucha-no*〈しわだらけの，しわくちゃの〉full of wrinkles.

shiwake 〈しわけ：仕訳(分け)〉assortment, classification; journalizing.

     shiwake-chô（仕訳帳）a journal

shi-wakeru〈仕分ける〉assort, classify, journalize.

shiwasu 〈しわす：師走〉December, the year end.

shiwa-yose 〈しわよせ：しわ寄せ〉

shiwa-yose-suru〈しわ寄せする〉shift ((the loss)) on ((to)).

shiwa-yose-sareru or *shiwa-yose-o-ukeru*〈しわ寄せされる，しわ寄せを受ける〉be shifted ((to)).

shiwaza 〈しわざ：仕業〉one's doing.

     Kore-wa dare-no-shiwaza-da?（これはだれの仕業だ。）Who has done this?

shiya 〈しや：視野〉a field of vision, one's view.

     shiya-ga-hiroi（視野が広い）take a broad view of things

shiya-ga-semai〈視野が狭い〉 take a narrow view of things

shiyaku〈しやく：試薬〉a (chemical) reagent.

shi-yakusho〈しやくしよ：市役所〉a city hall, a municipal office.

shiyō〈しよう：子葉〉a seed leaf.

shiyō〈しよう：止揚〉sublation.

shiyō-suru〈止揚する〉sublate.

shiyō〈しよう：使用〉use, employment.

shiyō-sha〈使用者〉 a user, a consumer; an employer.

shiyō-hō〈使用法〉 how to use, directions (for use)

shiyō-ryō〈使用料〉 the rent, the hire

shiyō-suru〈使用する〉use, make use ((of)), employ.

shiyō〈しよう：私用〉private business; private use.

shiyō-de dekakeru〈私用で出掛ける〉 go out on private business

shiyō〈しよう：試用〉(a) trial.

shiyō-suru〈試用する〉try〔a drug〕.

shiyō〈しよう：仕様〉a way, a means.

Sō suru-yori-hoka-ni-dō-nimo-shiyō-ga-nai.（そうするよりほかにどうにも仕様がない。） There is nothing for it but to do so.

shiyō-no-nai〈仕様のない〉good-for-nothing, unmanageable.

shiyoku〈しよく：私欲〉a selfish desire, self-interest.

shiyoku-ni-me-ga-kuramu（私欲に目がくらむ） be blinded by self-interest

shiyoku-no-nai〈私欲のない〉unselfish, disinterested.

shiyū〈しゆう：雌雄〉male and female; victory or defeat.

shiyū-o-kessuru〈雌雄を決する〉fight it out.

shiyū〈しゆう：私有〉private ownership.

shiyū-zaisan〈私有財産〉 private property

shiyū-no〈私有の〉privately-owned.

shizai〈しざい：私財〉private funds.

shizai-o-tōjite〈私財を投じて〉at one's own expense.

shizai〈しざい：資材〉materials.

shizan〈しざん：死産〉

shizan-no〈死産の〉stillborn.

shizen〈しぜん：自然〉nature.

shizen-bi（自然美） the beauty of nature

shizen-kagaku（自然科学） natural science

shizen-kai（自然界） the natural world

shizen-tōta（自然とうた） natural selection

shizen-no 〈自然の〉natural; spontaneous.
  shizen-no　nari-yuki-ni-makasu（自然の成り行きに任す）leave ((a matter)) to take its own(*or* natural) course
shizen-ni 〈自然に〉naturally, spontaneously.
  shizen-ni naoru（自然に治る）heal of itself
shizô 〈しぞう：死蔵〉
shizô-suru 〈死蔵する〉hoard, keep ((a thing)) idle.
shizuka 〈しずか：静か〉
shizuka-na 〈静かな〉quiet, silent, calm, peaceful, gentle.
  shizuka-na umi（静かな海）a calm sea
  shizuka-na ame（静かな雨）a gentle rain
shizuka-ni 〈静かに〉quietly, silently, calmly, peacefully, gently.
  Shizuka-ni!（静かに.）Be silent!
shizuka-ni-naru 〈静かになる〉become quiet.
shizuka-ni-shite-iru 〈静かにしている〉keep quiet.
shizukesa 〈しずけさ：静けさ〉stillness, silence, quiet(ness), calm.
  arashi-no-mae-no shizukesa（あらしの前の静けさ）the silence before the storm
shizuku 〈しずく：滴〉a drop.
shizuku-ga-tareru 〈滴が垂れる〉drip, trickle.
shizumari-kaeru 〈しずまりかえる：静まりかえる〉become as silent as death.
shizumaru 〈しずまる：静(鎮)まる〉become quiet, go down.
shizumeru 〈静(鎮)める〉calm, quiet.
shizumu 〈しずむ：沈む〉sink, go down.
shizumeru 〈沈める〉sink.
shîzun 〈シーズン〉a season.
  yakyû-no shîzun（野球のシーズン）the baseball season
  shîzun-ofu（シーズンオフ）an off-season
shizushizu(-to) 〈しずしず(と)：静々(と)〉gently and slowly.
sho 〈しょ：書〉penmanship.
sho-ga-umai 〈書がうまい〉write a good hand.
sho 〈しょ：署〉an office, a station.
shô 〈しょう：省〉a ministry, a department.
shô 〈しょう：賞〉a prize, a reward.
  shô o toru（賞を取る）win a prize
shô 〈しょう：性〉nature, temperament, character.
shô-ni-awa-nai 〈性に合わない〉be uncongenial ((to)), be not in one's line.

shō 〈しょう：章〉 a chapter.

　　dai-ni-shō〈第二章〉 Chapter II

shō 〈しょう：商〉 the quotient.

shō 〈しょう：勝〉 a victory, a win.

　　yon-shō-ni-hai〈四勝二敗〉 four victories and two defeats

(-de)-shō 〈〜（で）しょう〉 will, shall; I suppose.

(-ma)-shō 〈〜（ま）しょう〉 let us, let's.

　〜*(-ma)-shō-ka?*〈〜（ま）しょうか〉 Shall I... ?

shōaku 〈しょうあく：掌握〉

　shōaku-suru〈掌握する〉 hold, grasp, command, seize.

　　jinshin-o-shōaku-suru〈人心を掌握する〉 have a hold on people

shōbai 〈しょうばい：商売〉 (a) trade, business, an occupation.

　　shōbai o hajimeru〈商売を始める〉 begin business

　　Kare-wa shōbai-ga-umai.〈彼は商売がうまい。〉 He is a good businessman.

　　shōbai-ga-hanjō-suru〈商売が繁盛する〉 do a flourishing business

　　shōbai o kaeru〈商売を替える〉 change one's occupation

　　shōbai o yameru〈商売をやめる〉 give up one's business

　　shōbai-nin〈商売人〉 a merchant, a tradesman; a professional, an expert

　　shōbai-gataki〈商売敵〉 a trade rival

　shōbai-o-suru〈商売をする〉 do business, deal ((in)).

shobatsu 〈しょばつ：処罰〉 punishment.

　shobatsu-suru〈処罰する〉 punish.

　　genjū-ni shobatsu-suru〈厳重に処罰する〉 punish severely

shōbatsu 〈しょうばつ：賞罰〉 reward and punishment.

　　Shō-batsu-nashi.〈賞罰なし。〉 No reward and no punishment.

shōben 〈しょうべん：小便〉 urine.

　shōben-suru〈小便する〉 urinate, pass water.

shōbō 〈しょうぼう：消防〉 fire fighting.

　　shōbō-shi〈消防士〉 a fireman

　　shōbō-sho〈消防署〉 a fire station

　　shōbō-jidō-sha〈消防自動車〉 a fire engine

shoboshobo 〈しょぼしょぼ〉

　　Ame ga shoboshobo-futteiru.〈雨がしょぼしょぼ降っている。〉 It is drizzling.

　　shoboshobo-shita me〈しょぼしょぼした目〉 blear eyes

shōbu 〈しょうぶ：勝負〉 a match, a game, a contest.

shōbu ni katsu〈勝負に勝つ〉 win a game

shōbu ni makeru〈勝負に負ける〉 lose a game

shōbu-o-tsukeru〈勝負を付ける〉 fight to the finish

Shōbu-atta.〈勝負あった.〉 The game is over.

shōbu-ni-nara-nai〈勝負にならない〉 be no match ((for))

shōbu-goto〈勝負事〉 a game, gambling

shōbu-goto-o-suru〈勝負事をする〉 gamble

shōbu-suru〈勝負する〉play, have a match ((with)), contest.

shōbu〈しょうぶ〉an iris.

shobun〈しょぶん：処分〉disposal; punishment.

shobun-suru〈処分する〉dispose ((of)), deal ((with)); punish.

shōbun〈しょうぶん：性分〉nature.

motte-umareta shōbun（持って生まれた性分） one's nature

shōbun-ni-awa-nai（性分に合わない） go against the grain

shōbyō-hei〈しょうびょうへい：傷病兵〉the sick and wounded (soldiers).

shochi〈しょち：処置〉disposal, a measure, treatment.

hitsuyō-na shochi o toru（必要な処置をとる） take a necessary measure

shochi-o-ayamaru（処置を誤る） take a wrong measure

shochi-ni-komaru（処置に困る） do not know what to do (with))

shochi-suru〈処置する〉dispose ((of)), deal ((with)), treat.

shōchi〈しょうち：承知〉

shōchi-suru〈承知する〉know, be aware ((of)); consent ((to)); permit, allow, forgive.

yoku-shōchi-shite-iru（よく承知している） be well aware of it

Shōchi-shimashita.（承知しました.） Certainly. / All right.

Iwareta-toori-ni-yare, sō-de-naito shōchi-shi-nai-zo.（言われたとおりにやれ, そうでないと承知しないぞ.） Do as you were told, or you'll be sorry for it.

go-shōchi-no-yō-ni〈御承知のように〉as you know.

shōchi〈しょうち：招致〉

shōchi-suru〈招致する〉invite, call.

shochō〈しょちょう：署長〉the head, the chief〔of police〕.

shōchō〈しょうちょう：消長〉rise and fall, prosperity and decay, ebb and flow.

shōchō〈しょうちょう：象徴〉a symbol.

shōchō-suru〈象徴する〉symbolize.

shōchō-teki(-na)〈象徴的(な)〉symbolical.

shochū〈しょちゅう：暑中〉midsummer, high summer.
  shochū-mimai-o-dasu（暑中見舞を出す）write ((a person)) a letter to
    inquire after ((a person's)) health in the hot season
shōchū〈しょうちゅう：掌中〉
  shōchū-ni-osameru〈掌中に治める〉have ((something)) in the hollow of
    one's hand.
shodai〈しょだい：初代〉the founder, the first generation.
shōdaku〈しょうだく：承諾〉consent.
  shōdaku-o-ezu-ni（承諾を得ずに）without ((a person's)) consent
  shōdaku-suru〈承諾する〉consent ((to)).
shodan〈しょだん：初段〉the first grade〔in *judo*〕.
shōdan〈しょうだん：商談〉a business talk, negotiations.
  shōdan-o-tori-kimeru（商談を取り決める）strike a bargain ((with)),
    conclude negotiations ((with))
  shōdan-suru〈商談する〉have a business talk ((with)), negotiate ((with)).
sho-dana〈しょだな：書棚〉a bookshelf.
shodō〈しょどう：書道〉calligraphy, penmanship.
shōdo〈しょうど：焦土〉
  shōdo-to-kasuru〈焦土と化する〉be reduced to ashes.
shōdō〈しょうどう：衝動〉an impulse, an urge.
  shōdō-gai（衝動買い）impulse buying
  shōdō-ni-karareru〈衝動に駆られる〉be urged by impulse.
  shōdō-teki-ni〈衝動的に〉impulsively.
shōdoku〈しょうどく：消毒〉disinfection, sterilization.
  shōdoku-zai（消毒剤）a disinfectant
  shōdoku-ki（消毒器）a sterilizer
  shōdoku-suru〈消毒する〉disinfect, sterilize.
shoen〈しょえん：初演〉the first performance.
shōfuda〈しょうふだ：正札〉a price tag.
  shōfuda-nedan（正札値段）a fixed price
shōfuku〈しょうふく：承服〉
  shōfuku-suru〈承服する〉consent ((to)), accept.
  shōfuku-deki-nai〈承服できない〉unacceptable.
shōga〈しょうが〉ginger.
shōgai〈しょうがい：生涯〉a life, a lifetime; for life.
  shiawase-na shōgai o okuru（幸せな生涯を送る）live a happy life
  shōgai o Doitsu-de sugosu（生涯をドイツで過ごす）live in Germany
    all one's life

shōgai〈しょうがい：渉外〉public relations.
 shōgai-jimu（渉外事務） public relations business
shōgai〈しょうがい：傷害〉(an) injury.
 shōgai-chishi（傷害致死） a bodily injury resulting in death
 shōgai-hoken（傷害保険） accident insurance
shōgai〈しょうがい：障害〉an obstacle; trouble
 shōgai ni de-au（障害に出遭う） meet with an obstacle
 shōgai o nori-koeru（障害を乗り越える） get over an obstacle
 shōgai-butsu（障害物） an obstacle, a hurdle, a bar
  shōgai-butsu-kyōsō（障害物競争） an obstacle race, a hurdle race, a steeplechase
 nō-shōgai（脳障害） brain trouble
shō-gakkō〈しょうがっこう：小学校〉an elementary school, a grade school, a primary school.
sho-ga-kottō〈しょがこっとう：書画骨とう〉objects of art and curios.
shōgaku〈しょうがく：商学〉commercial science.
 shōgaku-bu（商学部） the department of commercial science
 shōgaku-hakase（商学博士） a doctor of commercial science, Doctor of Commercial Science (D.C.S.)
shōgaku〈しょうがく：少額〉a small sum.
 shōgaku-no-kane（少額の金） a small sum of money
shōgaku-kin〈しょうがくきん：奨学金〉a scholarship.
 shōgaku-kin o ukeru（奨学金を受ける） gain a scholarship
 shōgaku-kin-o-moratte-iru gakusei（奨学金をもらっている学生） a student who is on a scholarship
shōgaku-sei〈しょうがくせい：小学生〉a school boy, a school girl; school children.
shogaku-sha〈しょがくしゃ：初学者〉a beginner.
shōgatsu〈しょうがつ：正月〉the New Year, January.
shōgeki〈しょうげき：衝撃〉a shock.
 shōgeki-o-ukeru〈衝撃を受ける〉have a shock, be shocked.
shōgen〈しょうげん：証言〉verbal evidence, witness, testimony.
 mokugeki-sha-no shōgen（目撃者の証言） eyewitness evidence
 shōgen-suru〈証言する〉give evidence, testify, swear ((to)), attest (to).
shogeru〈しょげる〉be dispirited, be cast down, be in the blues, be down in the mouth.
shōgi〈しょうぎ：将棋〉Japanese chess, *shogi*.
 shōgi o sasu（将棋を指す） play *shogi*

shôgi-ban〈将棋板〉a *shogi* board
shôgi-daoshi-ni-naru〈将棋倒しになる〉fall down one upon another.

shôgo〈しょうご：正午〉noon.
　　shôgo-ni〈正午に〉at noon

shôgô〈しょうごう：称号〉a title, a degree.

shôgô〈しょうごう：照合〉verification, collation.
　shôgô-suru〈照合する〉verify, collate ((with)).

shôgun〈しょうぐん：将軍〉a general, a *shogun*.

shôgyô〈しょうぎょう：商業〉commerce, business, trade.
　　shôgyô-dôtoku〈商業道徳〉commercial morality
　　shôgyô-tori-hiki〈商業取引〉a commercial transaction
　　shôgyô-shugi〈商業主義〉commercialism
　shôgyô-no〈商業の〉commercial, business, mercantile.

shoha〈しょは：諸派〉the minor parties.

shô-hai〈しょうはい：勝敗〉victory or defeat, the issue.
　　shôhai o kessuru〈勝敗を決する〉decide the issue〔of a game〕

shôhai〈しょうはい：賞杯〉a trophy, a prize cup.

shôhai〈しょうはい：賞はい〉a medal.

shohan〈しょはん：初版〉the first edition.

shôhei〈しょうへい：招へい〉(an) invitation, a call.
　　shôhei ni ôjiru〈招へいに応じる〉accept a call
　shôhei-suru〈招へいする〉invite.

shôhen〈しょうへん：小片〉a small piece, a bit, a fragment.

shôhi〈しょうひ：消費〉consumption, spending.
　　shôhi-sha〈消費者〉a consumer
　　　shôhi-sha-kakaku〈消費者価格〉a consumer price
　　shôhi-zai〈消費財〉consumption goods
　　shôhi-zei〈消費税〉a consumption tax
　shôhi-suru〈消費する〉consume, spend.

shôhin〈しょうひん：商品〉a commodity, goods, merchandise.
　　shôhin-mihon〈商品見本〉a sample of no value
　　shôhin-ken〈商品券〉a gift certificate, an exchange ticket

shôhin〈しょうひん：賞品〉a prize.
　　shôhin o morau〈賞品をもらう〉get a prize

shôhin〈しょうひん：小品〉a short piece, a sketch.

shoho〈しょほ：初歩〉the elements, the first steps, the ABC ((of)).
　shoho-no〈初歩の〉elementary.
　　shoho-no Eigo〈初歩の英語〉elementary English

shôhô〈しょうほう：商法〉commercial law.

shôhon〈しょうほん：抄本〉an extract, an abstract.

shohô-sen〈しょほうせん：処方せん〉a prescription.
　shohô-sen o kaku〈処方せんを書く〉 make out a prescription

shohyô〈しょひょう：書評〉a book review.

shôhyô〈しょうひょう：商標〉a trademark, a brand.
　tôroku-shôhyô〈登録商標〉 a registered trademark

shôi〈しょうい：少尉〉a second lieutenant, an ensign.

shô-iin-kai〈しょういいんかい：小委員会〉a subcommittee.

shoi-komu〈しょいこむ：しょい込む〉be saddled ((with)).
　bakudai-na　shakkin-o-shoi-komu（ばく大な借金をしょい込む） be
　saddled with a heavy debt

shoin〈しょいん：所員〉a member of the staff, the staff.

shôin〈しょういん：勝因〉the cause of victory.

shoji〈しょじ：所持〉possession.
　shoji-hin（所持品） one's personal effects
　shoji-suru〈所持する〉possess, have.

shôji-gaisha〈しょうじがいしゃ：商事会社〉a commercial firm.

shôjiki〈しょうじき：正直〉honesty, uprightness.
　Shôjiki-wa sairyô-no saku.（正直は最良の策.） Honesty is the best
　policy.
　shôjiki-mono（正直者） an honest person
　shôjiki-na〈正直な〉honest, upright.
　shôjiki-ni〈正直に〉honestly.
　shôjiki-ni-ieba〈正直に言えば〉to tell the truth, to be frank with you,
　frankly speaking.

shôjin-ryôri〈しょうじんりょうり：精進料理〉a vegetable diet.

shôjiru〈しょうじる：生じる〉produce, bear; cause, give rise ((to)), bring
　about; happen, occur, take place.
　ichi-dai-henka o shôjiru（一大変化を生じる） bring about a great
　change

shojo〈しょじょ：処女〉a virgin, a maiden.
　shojo-kôkai（処女航海） a maiden voyage
　shojo-saku（処女作） one's maiden work

shôjo〈しょうじょ：少女〉a little(*or* young) girl.
　shôjo-jidai（少女時代） one's girlhood
　shôjo-rashii〈少女らしい〉girlish.

shôjô〈しょうじょう：症状〉symptoms, the condition of a patient(*or* disease).

    chûdoku-shôjô〈中毒症状〉 toxic symtoms

shôjô〈しょうじょう：賞状〉a certificate of merit.

shôjû〈しょうじゅう：小銃〉a rifle, small arms.

    shôjû-dan（小銃弾）a bullet

shojun〈しょじゅん：初旬〉the first ten days of a month.

    ichigatsu-shojun-ni（一月初旬に）early in January

shôjun〈しょうじゅん：照準〉

shôjun-o-awaseru〈照準を合わせる〉aim (at)), sight.

shôjutsu〈しょうじゅつ：詳述〉a full account.

shôjutsu-suru〈詳述する〉explain in full.

shoka〈しょか：初夏〉early summer.

    shoka-ni（初夏に）early in summer

shôka〈しょうか：商科〉a commercial course.

    shôka-daigaku（商科大学）a commercial college

shôka〈しょうか：消火〉fire extinguishing.

    shôka-ki（消火器）a fire extinguisher

    shôka-sen（消火栓）a hydrant

shôka-ni-tsutomeru〈消火に努める〉fight a fire.

shôka〈しょうか：消化〉digestion.

    shôka-ga-hayai（消化が早い）be quick of digestion

    shôka-ki（消化器）digestive organs

    shôka-furyô（消化不良）indigestion, dyspepsia

shôka-suru〈消化する〉digest.

shôka-shi-yasui〈消化しやすい〉digestible.

    shôka-shi-nikui（消化しにくい）indigestible

shôkai〈しょうかい：商会〉a company, a firm.

    Tanaka-shôkai（田中商会）Tanaka & Co.

shôkai〈しょうかい：紹介〉(an) introduction.

    shôkai-jô（紹介状）a letter of introduction

    jiko-shôkai（自己紹介）(a) self-introduction

shôkai-suru〈紹介する〉introduce.

shôkai〈しょうかい：照会〉(an) inquiry, (a) reference.

    shôkai-jô（照会状）a letter of inquiry

    shôkai-saki（照会先）a reference

shôkai-suru〈照会する〉inquire of ((a person)) about.

shôkai(-suru)〈しょうかい（する）：しょう戒（する）〉patrol.

    shôkai-tei（しょう戒艇）a patrol boat

shōkai〈しょうかい：詳解〉a minute explanation.
　shōkai-suru〈詳解する〉explain minutely.
shōkaku〈しょうかく：昇格〉
　shōkaku-suru〈昇格する〉be promoted to a higher status.
　　daigaku-ni shōkaku-suru（大学に昇格する）be raised to the status of university
shokan〈しょかん：所感〉one's impression(s).
　　shokan o noberu（所感を述べる）give one's impressions ((of))
shokan〈しょかん：書簡〉a letter, a note.
　　shokan-sen（書簡せん）letter paper, a writing pad
shōkan〈しょうかん：将官〉a general, an admiral.
shōkan〈しょうかん：小寒〉the second severest cold in midwinter.
shōkan〈しょうかん：召喚〉a summons, a call.
　　shōkan-jō（召喚状）a (writ of) summons
　shōkan-suru〈召喚する〉summon, call.
shōkan〈しょうかん：召還〉
　shōkan-suru〈召還する〉recall.
　　hongoku-e shōkan-sareru（本国へ召還される）be summoned home
shōkan〈しょうかん：償還〉repayment, redemption.
　　shōkan-kigen（償還期限）the period of redemption
　shōkan-suru〈償還する〉repay, redeem.
shō-kanshū〈しょうかんしゅう：商慣習〉commercial usage.
shokatsu〈しょかつ：所轄〉jurisdiction.
　　shokatsu-kanchō（所轄官庁）the authorities concerned
shokei〈しょけい：処刑〉punishment, execution.
　shokei-suru〈処刑する〉punish, execute.
shōkei〈しょうけい：小計〉a subtotal.
　shōkei-suru〈小計する〉subtotal.
shōkei-moji〈しょうけいもじ：象形文字〉a hieroglyph.
shoken〈しょけん：所見〉one's view, one's opinion.
　　shoken o noberu（所見を述べる）set forth one's view ((on))
shōken〈しょうけん：証券〉a bill, a bond, a security.
　　shōken-gaisha（証券会社）a securities company
　　shōken-ichiba（証券市場）a security market
shoki〈しょき：初期〉the early days, the beginning; the early stage.
　　Shōwa-no-shoki-ni（昭和の初期に）early in the Showa era
　shoki-no〈初期の〉early, initial.
　　Chikamatsu-no shoki-no-saku no hitotsu（近松の初期の作の一つ）one

of Chikamatsu's early works

shoki〈しょき：書記〉a clerk, a secretary.

    shoki-chô（書記長）a chief secretary, a secretary-general

    shoki-kan（書記官）a secretary

shoki〈しょき：所期〉

 shoki-no〈所期の〉expected, desired.

    shoki-no mokuteki o hatasu（所期の目的を果たす）achieve the desired end

shôki〈しょうき：商機〉a business opportunity.

    shôki o issuru（商機を逸する）let slip a business opportunity

shôki〈しょうき：勝機〉

 shôki o tsukamu〈勝機をつかむ〉seize a chance to win.

shôki〈しょうき：正気〉consciousness; sanity.

    shôki o ushinau（正気を失う）lose one's senses

    shôki-ni-naru（正気になる）come to one's senses

    shôki-de-aru（正気である）be in one's senses

    shôki-de-nai（正気でない）be out of one's senses

    Shôki-no-sata-dewa-nai.（正気のさたではない。）It's sheer madness.

 shôki-no〈正気の〉sane, sober.

shôkin〈しょうきん：賞金〉a prize, a purse.

    shôkin o kifu-suru（賞金を寄附する）give a purse

shokkaku〈しょっかく：触角〉an antenna, a feeler, a tentacle.

shokkaku〈しょっかく：触覚〉a sense of touch.

shokken〈しょっけん：食券〉a meal ticket.

shokken〈しょっけん：職権〉official power, one's authority.

    shokken o kôshi-suru（職権を行使する）exercise one's authority

    shokken o ran‧yô-suru（職権を濫(乱)用する）abuse one's authority

shokki〈しょっき：食器〉tableware, a dinner set.

    shokki-dana（食器棚）a cupboard

shokku〈ショック〉a shock.

    shokku o ataeru（ショックを与える）give a shock

    shokku-ryôhô（ショック療法）a shock treatment

    shokku-shi-suru（ショック死する）die of shock

 shokku-o-ukeru〈ショックを受ける〉be shocked, get a shock.

shoko〈しょこ：書庫〉a library, a stack room.

shokô〈しょこう：初校〉the first proof.

shôko〈しょうこ：証拠〉(a) proof, evidence.

    shôko o immetsu-suru（証拠をいん滅する）destroy evidence ((of))

shôko-shirabe〈証拠調べ〉 the taking of evidence

shôko-shorui〈証拠書類〉 documentary evidence

tashika-na shôko〈確かな証拠〉 reliable evidence

shôko-fu-jûbun-de〈証拠不十分で〉 for lack of (good) evidence

shôko-dateru〈証拠立てる〉 prove, attest.

shôkô〈しょうこう：将校〉an officer.

kôkyû-shôkô〈高級将校〉 a high-ranking officer

shô-kô〈しょうこう：商工〉

shô-kô-gyô〈商工業〉 commerce and industry

shô-kô-kaigi-sho〈商工会議所〉 a chamber of commerce and industry

shôkô〈しょうこう：小康〉a lull.

Kare-no-byôjô-wa-shôkô-o-tamotte-iru.（彼の病状は小康を保ってい
る。）There has been a lull(*or* slight improvement) in his
condition.

shôkô〈しょうこう：焼香〉

shôkô-suru〈焼香する〉 burn incense for the repose of the dead.

shôkô-guchi〈しょうこうぐち：昇降口〉an entrance, a hatch(way).

shô-kôi〈しょうこうい：商行為〉a commercial transaction.

shokoku〈しょこく：諸国〉various countries, various provinces.

shôkoku〈しょうこく：小国〉a small country, a minor power.

shokon〈しょこん：初婚〉one's first marriage.

shôkon〈しょうこん：商魂〉a commercial spirit.

shôkon-takumashii〈商魂たくましい〉 be aggressive and shrewd in
business.

shôkô-netsu〈しょうこうねつ：しょう紅熱〉scarlet fever.

shôkori〈しょうこり：性懲り〉

shôkori-mo-naku〈性懲りもなく〉 in spite of one's bitter experiences,
without any repentance

shoku〈しょく：食〉food, a meal, appetite.

shoku-ga-susumu〈食が進む〉 have a good appetite

shoku-ga-susuma-nai〈食が進まない〉 have a poor appetite

hi-ni ni-shoku taberu〈日に二食食べる〉 take two meals a day

tei-karorî-shoku〈低カロリー食〉 a low-caloric diet

shoku〈しょく：職〉work, a job, employment, a place, a position.

shoku o ushinau〈職を失う〉 lose one's employment

shoku o yameru〈職をやめる〉 quit one's job

shoku-o-sagasu〈職を探す〉 seek employment, look for a job

shoku ni aritsuku〈職にありつく〉 get a job

shoku-atari〈しょくあたり：食当たり〉*see.* shoku-chûdoku.

shokuba〈しょくば：職場〉one's place of work, one's post, a workshop.
　　shokuba-o-mamoru（職場を守る）stick to one's post
　　shokuba-o-hôki-suru（職場を放棄する）walk off one's job, walk out
　　shokuba-ni-fukki-suru（職場に復帰する）be back to work
　　shokuba-kekkon-o-suru（職場結婚をする）marry a man(*or* woman)
　　　working in the same place
　　shokuba-taikai（職場大会）a work(shop) rally

shokubai〈しょくばい：触媒〉a catalyzer, a catalyst.

shokubô〈しょくぼう：嘱望〉
　shokubô-suru〈嘱望する〉expect much ((of)).

shokubutsu〈しょくぶつ：植物〉a plant, vegetation.
　　kôzan-shokubutsu（高山植物）an alpine plant
　　shokubutsu-en（植物園）a botanical garden
　　shokubutsu-gaku（植物学）botany
　　shokubutsu-gaku-sha（植物学者）a botanist

shoku-chûdoku〈しょくちゅうどく：食中毒〉food poisoning.

shokudai〈しょくだい：しょく台〉a candlestick.

shokudô〈しょくどう：食堂〉a dining room, a restaurant.
　　shokudô-sha（食堂車）a dining car, a diner

shokudô〈しょくどう：食道〉the gullet, the esophagus.

shokuen〈しょくえん：食塩〉(table) salt.
　　shokuen-sui（食塩水）a solution of salt

shokugo〈しょくご：食後〉after a meal.
　　Ichi-nichi　san-kai　mai-shokugo-ichi-jikan-ni-fukuyô.（一日三回毎食後
　　　一時間に服用。）To be taken three times a day an hour after each
　　　meal.

shokugyô〈しょくぎょう：職業〉an occupation, a profession, a trade.
　　Kare-no　shokugyô　wa　nan-desu-ka?（彼の職業は何ですか。）What is
　　　his occupation?
　　Kare-no　shokugyô　wa　isha-desu.（彼の職業は医者です。）He is a
　　　doctor by profession.
　　shokugyô-byô（職業病）an occupational disease
　　shokugyô-hodô（職業補導）vocational guidance
　　shokugyô-ishiki（職業意識）a sense of vocation
　　shokugyô-betsu-denwa-chô（職業別電話帳）a classified telephone
　　　directory

shokuhi〈しょくひ：食費〉food expenses; board, table expenses.

shokuhin〈しょくひん：食品〉food.

shuyô-shokuhin（主要食品）staple food

shokuhin-eisei（食品衛生）food sanitation

shokuin〈しょくいん：職員〉the staff, the personnel; a member of the staff.

shokuin-kaigi（職員会議）a staff meeting

shokuji〈しょくじ：食事(じ)〉a meal, a dinner, a diet, board.

shokuji-no-yôi-o-suru（食事の用意をする）prepare a meal

shokuji-chû-de-aru（食事中である）be at table

shokuji-ni manekareru（食事に招かれる）be invited to dinner

shokuji-ryôhô（食じ療法〉a diet cure

shokuji-ryôhô-o-suru（食じ療法をする）go on a diet

shokuji-tsuki-de（食事付きで〉with board

shokuji-o-suru〈食事をする〉take a meal, dine.

shokuji-chû-ni〈食事中に〉during a meal.

shokuju〈しょくじゅ：植樹〉planting.

shokuju-sai（植樹祭）Arbor Day

shokuju-suru〈植樹する〉plant trees.

shokumei〈しょくめい：職名〉the name of one's occupation, an official title.

shokumin〈しょくみん：植民〉colonization, settlement.

shokumin-chi（植民地）a colony, a settlement.

shokumin-suru〈植民する〉colonize, settle.

shokumotsu〈しょくもつ：食物〉food.

jiyô-bun-no-aru shokumotsu（滋養分のある食物）nourishing food

shokumu〈しょくむ：職務〉duty, an office.

shokumu-ni chûjitsu-de-aru（職務に忠実である）be faithful to one's duties

shokumu o hatasu（職務を果たす）do one's duties

shokumu o okotaru（職務を怠る）neglect one's duties

shokumu-taiman-no-kado-ni-yori（職務怠慢のかどにより）on the charge of neglect of duties

shokumu-shitsumon（職務質問）a police checkup

shokumu-jô-no〈職務上の〉official.

shokun〈しょくん：諸君〉gentlemen, my friends.

shokuniku〈しょくにく：食肉〉(edible) meat.

shokunin〈しょくにん：職人〉an artisan, a craftsman.

shokunô〈しょくのう：職能〉(a) function.

　　shokunô-daihyô（職能代表）　vocational representation

shoku-pan〈しょくパン：食パン〉(a loaf of) bread.

shokureki〈しょくれき：職歴〉one's occupational career.

shokurin〈しょくりん：植林〉afforestation, a plantation.
　shokurin-suru〈植林する〉afforest, plant trees.

shokuryô〈しょくりょう：食料(糧)〉food, provisions.
　　shokuryô-mondai（食糧問題）　a food problem
　　shokuryô-hin（食料品）　an article of food, provisions
　　　shokuryô-hin-ten（食料品店）　a grocery, a grocer's
　　　shokuryô-hin-shô（食料品商）　a grocer

shoku-seikatsu〈しょくせいかつ：食生活〉
　shoku-seikatsu-o-kaizen-suru〈食生活を改善する〉improve one's diet.

shokuseki〈しょくせき：職責〉responsibilities incident to one's work, one's duty.
　　shokuseki o hatasu（職責を果たす）　do one's duty

shokushi〈しょくし：食指〉
　shokushi-ga-ugoku〈食指が動く〉have a desire ((for)).

shokushô〈しょくしょう：食傷〉
　shokushô-gimi-de-aru or *shokushô-suru*〈食傷気味である，食傷する〉be fed up ((with)), be surfeited ((with)).

shokushô〈しょくしょう：職掌〉
　shokushô-gara〈職掌がら〉as a matter of duty, in view of one's (official) position.

shokutaku〈しょくたく：食卓〉a dining table.
　　shokutaku-ni-tsuku（食卓に着く）　sit down to table, sit at table
　　shokutaku-en（食卓塩）　table salt

shokutaku〈しょくたく：嘱託〉non-regular engagement; a non-regular employee.

shokuyô〈しょくよう：食用〉
　　shokuyô-abura（食用油）　edible oil
　shokuyô-ni-tekisuru〈食用に適する〉be good to eat, be edible.
　shokuyô-no〈食用の〉edible, used for food.

shokuyoku〈しょくよく：食欲〉appetite.
　　shokuyoku-ga-aru（食欲がある）　have a good appetite
　　shokuyoku-ga-amari-nai（食欲が余りない）　have a poor appetite
　　shokuyoku-ga-nai（食欲がない）　have no appetite
　　shokuyoku o sosoru（食欲をそそる）　stimulate one's appetite
　　shokuyoku-ôsei（食欲おう盛）　a hearty appetite

shokuyoku-zôshin〈食欲増進〉 increase of appetite

shokuyoku-fushin〈食欲不振〉 lack of appetite

shokuzen〈しょくぜん：食前〉

shokuzen-ni〈食前に〉before a meal.

shôkyaku〈しょうきゃく：焼却〉destruction by fire.

shôkyaku-ro（焼却炉） an incinerator

shôkyaku-suru〈焼却する〉destroy by fire, burn up.

shôkyaku〈しょうきゃく：償却〉(a) repayment, (a) refundment, redemption.

genka-shôkyaku（減価償却） depreciation

shôkyaku-suru〈償却する〉repay, refund, redeem, pay off.

shôkyo〈しょうきょ：消去〉elimination.

shôkyo-suru〈消去する〉eliminate.

shôkyoku〈しょうきょく：消極〉

shôkyoku-teki(-na)〈消極的(な)〉negative, passive.

shôkyoku-teki seisaku（消極的の政策） a negative policy

shôkyoku-teki-ni〈消極的に〉negatively, passively.

shokyû〈しょきゅう：初級〉the beginners' class.

shôkyû〈しょうきゅう：昇級〉promotion.

shôkyû-ga-hayai（昇級が早い） get speedy promotion

shôkyû-suru〈昇級する〉be promoted ((to)).

shôkyû〈しょうきゅう：昇給〉a rise in salary.

shôkyû-suru〈昇給する〉have one's salary raised.

shombori〈しょんぼり〉

shombori-shite-iru〈しょんぼりしている〉be dejected.

shombori-to〈しょんぼりと〉dejectedly, in dejection.

shomei〈しょめい：書名〉the title of a book.

shomei〈しょめい：署名〉a signature, an autograph.

shomei-undô（署名運動） a signature-collecting campaign

shomei-natsuin-suru（署名なつ印する） sign and seal

shomei-suru〈署名する〉sign〔one's name〕.

shomei-iri-no〈署名入りの〉autographed, signed.

shômei〈しょうめい：証明〉(a) proof, testimony, demonstration, certification.

shômei-sho（証明書） a certificate

shômei-suru〈証明する〉prove, testify ((to)), demonstrate, certify.

mujitsu o shômei-suru（無実を証明する） prove one's innocence

shômei〈しょうめい：照明〉lighting, illumination.

shômei-tô〔照明灯〕 street lighting

shômei-kigu〔照明器具〕 an illuminator

shômei-dan〔照明弾〕 a light bomb

shômei-suru〔照明する〕light up, illuminate.

shomen〔しょめん：書面〕a letter, a document.

shomen-de〔書面で〕by letter, in writing.

shômen〔しょうめん：正面〕the front.

shômen-genkan〔正面玄関〕 the front door

shômen-shôtotsu〔正面衝突〕 a head-on collision, a frontal clash

shômen-zu〔正面図〕 a front view

shômen-no〔正面の〕front, frontal.

shômen-ni〔正面に〕in front ((of)).

shômetsu〔しょうめつ：消滅〕extinction, disappearance, extinguishment, lapse.

shizen-shômetsu〔自然消滅〕 natural extinction

kenri no shômetsu〔権利の消滅〕 lapse of one's rights

shômetsu-suru〔消滅する〕cease to exist, disappear, become void, be extinguished, lapse.

shizen-shômetsu-suru〔自然消滅する〕 go out of existence in process of time

shômi〔しょうみ：正味〕

shômi-jûryô〔正味重量〕 the net weight

shômi go-kiro〔正味五キロ〕 5 kilograms net

shômi-kakaku〔正味価格〕 a net price

shômi-hachi-jikan〔正味八時間〕 eight full hours

shômi-no〔正味の〕net.

shômi〔しょうみ：賞味〕appreciation.

shômi-suru〔賞味する〕relish, appreciate.

shomin〔しょみん：庶民〕the (common) people.

shomin-teki(-na)〔庶民的(な)〕common, popular.

shomô〔しょもう：所望〕

shomô-suru〔所望する〕desire, ask ((for)), wish ((for)).

shômô〔しょうもう：消耗〕consumption, waste.

shômô-hin〔消耗品〕 articles of consumption.

shômô-suru〔消耗する〕consume, waste, use up.

shômô-shita〔消耗した〕exhausted, emaciated.

shômon〔しょうもん：証文〕a bond, a deed.

shômon o kaku〔証文を書く〕 execute a deed

shomotsu〈しょもつ：書物〉*see.* shoseki *or* hon.

shomu〈しょむ：庶務〉general affairs.

shomu-ka（庶務課）the general affairs section

shône〈しょうね：性根〉nature, character.

shône-o-ire-kaeru〈性根を入れ替える〉mend one's ways, turn over a new leaf.

shône-no-kusatta〈性根の腐った〉corrupt, depraved.

shonen〈しょねん：初年〉the first year; the early years.

Shôwa-shonen-ni（昭和初年に）in the early years of Showa

shônen〈しょうねん：少年〉a boy.

shônen-jidai（少年時代）one's boyhood

shônen-muki-no〈少年向きの〉for children, juvenile.

shôni〈しょうに：小児〉a little child, an infant.

shôni-ka（小児科）pediatrics.

shôni-ka-i（小児科医）a children's doctor

shôni-mahi（小児麻ひ）infantile paralysis, polio

shonichi〈しょにち：初日〉the opening day, the première.

shônin〈しょうにん：商人〉a merchant, a tradesman, a shopkeeper, a dealer.

shônin〈しょうにん：証人〉a witness.

shônin o shôkan-suru（証人を召喚する）call a witness

shônin-to-naru（証人となる）bear ((a person)) witness

shônin-dai-ni-tatsu（証人台に立つ）take the witness stand, enter the witness box

shônin〈しょうにん：承認〉approval, consent, admission, recognition.

shônin-o-motomeru（承認を求める）ask for ((a person's)) approval

shônin o eru（承認を得る）obtain ((a person's)) approval

shônin-suru〈承認する〉approve, consent (to), admit, recognize.

dokuritsu o shônin-suru（独立を承認する）recognize the independence ((of))

shonin-kyû〈しょにんきゅう：初任給〉a starting salary.

shônô〈しょうのう：しょう脳〉camphor.

shônyû〈しょうにゅう：鐘乳〉

shônyû-dô（鐘乳洞）a stalactite cave

shônyû-seki（鐘乳石）stalactite

shôon-ki〈しょうおんき：消音器〉a muffler, a sound arrester, a silencer.

shôrai〈しょうらい：将来〉the future; in (the) future, some time.

kagayakashii shôrai（輝かしい将来）a bright future

chikai-shôrai-ni（近い将来に） in the near future

shôrai-sei-no-aru or *shôrai-yūbô-na*〈将来性のある，将来有望な〉 promising.

shôrei〈しょうれい：奨励〉 encouragement, promotion.

shôrei-kin（奨励金） a bounty

shôrei-suru〈奨励する〉 encourage, promote.

shori〈しょり：処理〉 management, disposal, treatment.

shori-suru〈処理する〉 manage, dispose ((of)), treat.

shôri〈しょうり：勝利〉 (a) victory.

shôri o eru（勝利を得る） gain a victory

kettei-teki shôri（決定的勝利） a decisive victory ((over))

shôri-sha（勝利者） a victor

shôri-tôshu（勝利投手） the winning pitcher

shôritsu〈しょうりつ：勝率〉 the percentage of victories (to the total number of games).

shorô〈しょろう：初老〉

shorô-no〈初老の〉 middle-aged, elderly.

shôrô〈しょうろう：鐘楼〉 a bell tower, a belfry.

shôron〈しょうろん：詳論〉 full discussion.

shôron-suru〈詳論する〉 state in detail.

shorui〈しょるい：書類〉 documents, papers.

shôryaku〈しょうりゃく：省略〉 (an) omission, (an) abbreviation, (an) abridgment.

shôryaku-suru〈省略する〉 omit, abbreviate, abridge, shorten.

shôryo〈しょうりょ：焦慮〉

shôryo-suru〈焦慮する〉 be impatient ((to do)), worry (oneself) ((about)).

shôryô〈しょうりょう：少量〉 a small quantity ((of)), a little.

shôryô-no shio（少量の塩） a small quantity of salt

shôsa〈しょうさ：少差〉 a narrow margin.

shôsa-de katsu（少差で勝つ） win by a narrow margin, nose out

shôsa〈しょうさ：少佐〉 a major, a lieutenant (commander).

shosai〈しょさい：書斎〉 a study.

shôsai〈しょうさい：商才〉 business ability.

shôsai-ni-takete-iru（商才にたけている） be shrewd in business

shôsai〈しょうさい：詳細〉 details.

shôsai-na〈詳細な〉 detailed.

shôsai-ni〈詳細に〉 in detail.

shôsai-ni-wataru（詳細にわたる） go into details

shosan〈しょさん：所産〉a product, fruit, a result.

shôsan〈しょうさん：硝酸〉nitric acid.

   shôsan-gin（硝酸銀）nitrate of silver

shôsan〈しょうさん：勝算〉a chance of success, prospects of victory.

   Wareware-ni-shôsan-ga-aru.（我々に勝算がある.）The odds are in our favor.

shôsan〈しょうさん：賞(称)賛〉praise, admiration.

   shôsan no kotoba（賞(称)賛の言葉）a word of praise

   shôsan o hakusuru（賞(称)賛を博する）win the admiration ((of))

   shôsan-suru〈賞(称)賛する〉praise, admire.

   shôsan-su-beki〈賞(称)賛すべき〉praiseworthy, admirable.

shôsei〈しょうせい：招請〉invitation.

   shôsei-koku（招請国）an inviting country, the host nation

   shôsei-suru〈招請する〉invite.

shosei-jutsu〈しょせいじゅつ：処世術〉how to get on in the world.

   shosei-jutsu-ni-takete-iru（処世術にたけている）know well how to get on in the world

shoseki〈しょせき：書籍〉a book.

   shoseki-shô（書籍商）a bookseller; a bookstore, a bookshop

shôseki〈しょうせき：硝石〉saltpeter.

   Chiri-shôseki（チリ硝石）Chile saltpeter

shôsen〈しょうせん：商船〉a merchant ship.

   shôsen-tai（商船隊）a mercantile fleet

shosetsu〈しょせつ：諸説〉various opinions.

   shosetsu-funpun-to-shite-iru（諸説紛々としている.）opinions are divided ((on))

shôsetsu〈しょうせつ：小説〉a story, a novel; fiction.

   shôsetsu o kaku（小説を書く）write a novel

   suiri-shôsetsu（推理小説）a mystery story

   shôsetsu-ka（小説家）a novelist

   shôsetsu-ni-suru or *shôsetsu-ka-suru*〈小説にする, 小説化する〉make a novel ((out of)), fictionize.

shôsetsu〈しょうせつ：詳説〉detailed explanation.

   shôsetsu-suru〈詳説する〉explain in full.

shôsetsu〈しょうせつ：小節〉a bar, a measure.

shôsha〈しょうしゃ：商社〉a trading company, a business firm.

shôsha〈しょうしゃ：勝者〉a winner, a victor.

shôsha〈しょうしゃ：照射〉irradiation.

shôsha-suru〈照射する〉irradiate.

rentogen-o-shôsha-suru（レントゲンを照射する） apply X-rays ((to))

shoshi〈しょし：初志〉one's original intention.

shoshi o tsuranuku（初志を貫く） carry out one's original intention

shôshi〈しょうし：笑止〉

shôshi-semban-de-aru〈笑止千万である〉be extremely ridiculous.

shôshi〈しょうし：焼死〉

shôshi-tai（焼死体） a charred body

shôshi-suru〈焼死する〉be burnt to death.

shoshiki〈しょしき：書式〉a (prescribed) form.

shoshiki-doori-ni〈書式どおりに〉according to the form prescribed, in due form.

shoshin〈しょしん：初心〉one's original resolution.

shoshin-sha（初心者） a beginner

shoshin-no〈初心の〉inexperienced.

shoshin〈しょしん：初診〉the first medical examination.

shoshin-ryô（初診料） the fee charged for the first medical examination

shoshin〈しょしん：所信〉one's belief, one's opinion.

shoshin o noberu（所信を述べる） express one's belief

shôshin〈しょうしん：小心〉timidity, cowardice, prudence, circumspection.

shôshin-mono（小心者） a timid person, a coward

shôshin-na〈小心な〉timid, cowardly, prudent, cautious.

shôshin-yokuyoku-to-shite〈小心翼々として〉cautiously, with circumspection.

shôshin〈しょうしん：昇進〉promotion, rise〔in rank〕.

shôshin-suru〈昇進する〉be promoted ((to)), rise.

shôshin-saseru〈昇進させる〉promote, raise.

shôshin〈しょうしん：傷心〉heartbreak.

shôshin-no〈傷心の〉heart-broken.

shôshin-jisatsu〈しょうしんじさつ：焼身自殺〉self-burning.

shôshin-jisatsu-suru〈焼身自殺する〉burn oneself to death.

shôshin-shômei〈しょうしんしょうめい：正真正銘〉

shôshin-shômei-no〈正真正銘の〉genuine, authentic, regular.

shôshitsu〈しょうしつ：焼失〉

shôshitsu-kaoku（焼失家屋） houses burnt down

shôshitsu-suru〈焼失する〉be burnt down.

shōsho〈しょうしょ：証書〉a bond, a deed, a certificate.

shōshō〈しょうしょう：少将〉a major general, a rear admiral.

shōshō〈しょうしょう：少々〉*see.* sukoshi.

shōshoku〈しょうしょく：少(小)食〉

  shōshoku-ka（少(小)食家）a small eater

  shōshoku-de-aru〈少(小)食である〉do not eat much, have a small appetite.

shoshū〈しょしゅう：初秋〉early fall.

  shoshū-ni（初秋に）early in fall

shōshū〈しょうしゅう：召集〉a call, a summons, a muster, convocation.

  shōshū-suru〈召集する〉call, convene, summon.

  rinji-kokkai o shōshū-suru（臨時国会を召集する）convene an extra session of the Diet

shōso〈しょうそ：勝訴〉

  shōso-to-naru〈勝訴となる〉gain a case.

shōsō〈しょうそう：少壮〉

  shōsō-no〈少壮の〉young.

  shōsō-yūi-no（少壮有為の）young and promising

shōsō〈しょうそう：尚早〉

  Jiki-shōsō-de-aru.（時期尚早である．）The time has not yet come to do it.

  shōsō-no〈尚早の〉premature, too early.

shōsō〈しょうそう：焦燥〉fretfulness, impatience, irritation.

  shōsō-kan-ni-karareru〈焦燥感に駆られる〉be in a fret, be irritated.

  shōsō-kan-ni-karare-nagara〈焦燥感に駆られながら〉with impatience.

shōsoku〈しょうそく：消息〉news; movements.

  shōsoku-suji（消息筋）(well-)informed circles

  shōsoku-tsū（消息通）a well-informed person

  shōsoku-ga-aru〈消息がある〉hear ((from)).

  shōsoku-ga-nai（消息がない）hear nothing ((from))

  shōsoku-o-kiku〈消息を聞く〉hear ((of)).

  shōsoku-ni-tsūjite-iru〈消息に通じている〉be well informed ((of)).

shōsū〈しょうすう：少数〉

  shōsū-iken（少数意見）the opinion of the minority

  shōsū-no〈少数の〉a small number of, a few.

  shōsū-no hitobito（少数の人々）a small number of people

shōsū〈しょうすう：小数〉a decimal.

  shōsū-ten（小数点）a decimal point

shôsui 〈しょうすい〉
　shôsui-suru 〈しょうすいする〉 become emaciated, become haggard.
　shôsui-shita 〈しょうすいした〉 emaciated, gaunt, haggard.
shosuru 〈しょする：処する〉
　　nankyoku-ni-shosuru（難局に処する） deal with a difficulty
　　shikei-ni shoserareru（死刑に処せられる） be sentenced to death
shôsuru 〈しょうする：称する〉 call, name; pretend.
　　Yamamoto-to-shôsuru otoko（山本と称する男） a man named Yamamoto, a man who calls himself Yamamoto
　　byôki-to-shôsuru（病気と称する） pretend to be ill
　~-to-shôshite 〈～と称して〉 on the pretext of... , under the pretense of ... .
shotai 〈所帯〉 a household, a home.
　　shotai-o-motsu（所帯を持つ） make a new home
　　shotai-dôgu（所帯道具） household goods
　　shotai-nushi（所帯主） a householder
　　dai-shotai（大所帯） a large family
　shotai-jimiru 〈所帯染みる〉 be domesticated.
shotai 〈しょたい：書体〉 a style of handwriting, a style of type.
shôtai 〈しょうたい：正体〉 one's true colors; consciousness.
　　shôtai o arawasu（正体を現す） show one's true colors
　　shôtai-o-kakusu（正体を隠す） wear a mask
　　shôtai-naku-you（正体なく酔う） be blind drunk
　shôtai-o-abaku 〈正体を暴く〉 unmask.
shôtai 〈しょうたい：招待〉 (an) invitation.
　　shôtai ni ôjiru（招待に応じる） accept an invitation
　　shôtai o kotowaru（招待を断る） decline an invitation
　　shôtai-jô（招待状） a letter of invitation
　shôtai-suru 〈招待する〉 invite.
　shôtai-sareru 〈招待される〉 be invited ((by)), receive an invitation ((from)).
shôtai 〈しょうたい：小隊〉 a platoon.
　　shôtai-chô（小隊長） a platoon leader
sho-taimen 〈しょたいめん：初対面〉 the first interview ((with)).
shotei 〈しょてい：所定〉
　shotei-no 〈所定の〉 fixed, prescribed.
　　shotei-no jikan（所定の時間） the fixed time
shoten 〈しょてん：書店〉 a bookseller's; a bookstore, a bookshop.

shôten〈しょうてん：商店〉a store, a shop.
　　shôten-gai（商店街）a shopping center
shôten〈しょうてん：焦点〉a focus.
　　shôten-ga-atte-iru（焦点が合っている）be in focus
　　shôten-ga-atte-i-nai（焦点が合っていない）be out of focus
　shôten-o-awaseru〈焦点を合わせる〉focus.
shotô〈しょとう：諸島〉
　　Hawai-shotô（ハワイ諸島）the Hawaiian Islands
shotô〈しょとう：初冬〉early winter.
　　shotô-ni（初冬に）early in winter
shotô〈しょとう：初等〉
　　shotô-ka（初等科）an elementary course
　　shotô-kyôiku（初等教育）primary education
　shotô-no〈初等の〉elementary, primary.
shotô〈しょとう：初頭〉the beginning.
　　ni-jusseiki-shotô-ni（二十世紀初頭に）at the beginning of the 20th
　　century
shôto〈ショート〉a shortstop; a short circuit.
　shôto-suru〈ショートする〉short-circuit, short.
shôtô〈しょうとう：消灯〉
　　shôtô-jikan（消灯時間）lights-out
　shôtô-suru〈消灯する〉put out lights.
shotoku〈しょとく：所得〉income, earnings.
　　shotoku-gaku（所得額）the amount of one's income
　　shotoku-zei（所得税）an income tax
shô-tori-hiki〈しょうとりひき：商取引〉a commercial transaction, commercial dealings.
shôtotsu〈しょうとつ：衝突〉a collision, a clash.
　　sanjû-shôtotsu（三重衝突）a three-way collision
　shôtotsu-suru〈衝突する〉collide ((with)), run ((against *or* into)), clash ((with)).
　　gâdorêru-ni-shôtotsu-suru（ガードレールに衝突する）run into a
　　guardrail
shou〈しょう〉*see.* se-ou.
shô-uchû〈しょううちゅう：小宇宙〉a microcosm(os).
shoya〈しょや：初夜〉the bridal night.
shoyô〈しょよう：所要〉
　　shoyô-jikan（所要時間）the time required

shoyô-no〈所要の〉necessary, required, needed.

shōyo〈しょうよ：賞与〉a reward, a bonus.

nemmatsu-shōyo（年末賞与）a year-end bonus

shôyô〈しょうよう：商用〉business.

shôyô-de（商用で）on business

shoyū〈しゅゆう：所有〉possession, ownership.

shoyū-butsu（所有物）one's possessions

shoyû-ken（所有権）(the right of) ownership

shoyû-sha（所有者）a possessor, an owner

shoyû-kaku（所有格）the possessive case

shoyū-suru〈所有する〉possess, have, own.

shōyu〈しょうゆ：しょう油〉soy, soy sauce.

shozai〈しょざい：所在〉one's whereabouts, the seat.

shozai o kuramasu（所在をくらます）conceal one's whereabouts

Kanojo-no shozai wa wakara-nai.（彼女の所在は分からない。）Her whereabouts is unknown.

sekinin-no-shozai o akiraka-ni-suru（責任の所在を明らかにする）make clear where the resposibility lies

kenchô-shozai-chi（県庁所在地）the seat of prefectural office

shozai-nasa〈しょざいなさ：所在なさ〉tedium, boredom.

shozai-nai〈所在ない〉be bored, have nothing to do.

shôzen〈しょうぜん：しょう然〉

shôzen-to〈しょうぜんと〉see. shombori-to.

shozô〈しょぞう：所蔵〉

Yamada-shi-shozô-no〈山田氏所蔵の〉owned by Mr. Yamada.

shôzô-ga〈しょうぞうが：肖像画〉a portrait.

shôzô-ga o kaite-morau（肖像画をかいてもらう）have one's portrait painted

shozoku〈しょぞく：所属〉

shozoku-suru〈所属する〉belong ((to)), be attached ((to)).

shozoku-no〈所属の〉belonging ((to)), attached ((to)).

shu〈しゅ：主〉the Lord, our Lord; the chief thing.

shu-taru〈主たる〉main, chief, principal, primary.

shu-taru mokuteki（主たる目的）one's main object

shu-to-shite〈主として〉mainly, chiefly, principally, primarily, for the most part.

shu〈しゅ：朱〉cinnabar, vermilion.

Shu-ni-majiwareba-akaku-naru.（朱に交われば赤くなる。）He who

touches pitch shall be defiled therewith.

shu-nuri-no 〈朱塗りの〉 vermilion-lacquered.

shu 〈しゅ：種〉 a kind, a sort, a class, a type; a species.

    kono shu no shina （この種の品） articles of this kind

    "shu no kigen" （"種の起源"） "the Origin of Species"

shû 〈しゅう：州〉 a state, a county; a continent; a province.

shû 〈しゅう：周〉 a circuit, a lap.

    san-shû-me-ni （三周目に） on one's third lap

shû 〈しゅう：週〉 a week.

    shû-ni ichi-do （週に一度） once a week

    maishû （毎週） every week

    raishû （来週） next week

    senshû （先週） last week

shû 〈しゅう〉 a hiss, a swish.

shû-to-iu 〈しゅうという〉 hiss.

shûban 〈しゅうばん：終盤〉 the end game, the last stage 〔of an election campaign〕.

shubi 〈しゅび：守備〉 (a) defense; fielding.

shubi-o-suru 〈守備をする〉 defend, guard.

shubi-ni-tsuku 〈守備に着く〉 take to the field.

shubi 〈しゅび：首尾〉

shubi-yoku 〈首尾よく〉 successfully, with success.

    shubi-yoku　nyûshi-ni-gôkaku-suru （首尾よく入試に合格する） succeed in passing an entrance examination

shûbi 〈しゅうび：愁び〉

shûbi-o-hiraku 〈愁びを開く〉 feel relieved.

shubi-ikkan 〈しゅびいっかん：首尾一貫〉

shubi-ikkan-shita 〈首尾一貫した〉 consistent, coherent.

shubi-ikkan-shite 〈首尾一貫して〉 consistently, coherently.

shûbô 〈しゅうぼう：衆望〉 popularity.

    shûbô-o-ninatte rikkôho-suru （衆望を担って立候補する） run for ((the Diet)) with popular support

shûbô-sha 〈しゅうぼうしゃ：首謀者〉 a ringleader.

shûbun 〈しゅうぶん：醜聞〉 a scandal.

shûbun 〈しゅうぶん：秋分〉 the autumnal equinox.

    shûbun-no-hi （秋分の日） Autumnal Equinox Day

shûchaku 〈しゅうちゃく：執着〉 attachment, persistence.

shûchaku-suru 〈執着する〉 be attached ((to)), adhere ((to)).

shûchaku-eki〈しゅうちゃくえき：終着駅〉a terminal station.

shûchi〈しゅうち：周知〉

　shûchi-no〈周知の〉well-known.

　　shûchi-no jijitsu（周知の事実）a well-known fact

　shûchi-no-gotoku〈周知のごとく〉as is generally known.

shûchi〈しゅうち：衆知〉

　shûchi-o-atsumeru〈衆知を集める〉seek wise counsels of many people.

shûchi-shin〈しゅうちしん：しゅう恥心〉a sense of shame.

　　shûchi-shin-ga-nai（しゅう恥心がない）be lost to shame

shuchô〈しゅちょう：主張〉one's point, one's opinion, (an) assertion, a claim.

　　shuchô o mageru（主張を曲げる）concede a point

　　shuchô-o-mage-nai　or　shuchô-o-toosu（主張を曲げない，主張を通す）
　　　stick to one's opinion

　shuchô-suru〈主張する〉assert, insist.

　　kenri o shuchô-suru（権利を主張する）assert one's right(s) ((to))

shuchô〈しゅちょう：首長〉a head, a chief.

　　shuchô-senkyo（首長選挙）election of the heads of local government

shuchô〈しゅちょう：主潮〉the main current.

shuchû〈しゅちゅう：手中〉

　　shuchû-ni-osameru（手中に収める）capture, secure, take possession ((of))

　　〜-no-shuchû-ni-aru（〜の手中にある）be in the possession of...

shûchû〈しゅうちゅう：集中〉concentration.

　　shûchû-da（集中打）a rally of hits

　　shûchû-gôu（集中豪雨）a torrential rain concentrated on some area

　　shûchû-hôka（集中砲火）concentrated fire

　shûchû-suru〈集中する〉concentrate ((on)).

　　chûi o shûchû-suru（注意を集中する）concentrate one's attention ((on))

shudai〈しゅだい：主題〉the subject, the theme.

　　shudai-ka（主題歌）a theme song

shudan〈しゅだん：手段〉a means, a measure, a way, a step, a shift, a resort.

　　fusei-na shudan（不正な手段）a foul means

　　shudan-o-erabazu-ni（手段を選ばずに）by fair means or foul

　　arayuru shudan o tsukusu（あらゆる手段を尽くす）try every possible means

omoi-kitta shudan o toru（思い切った手段をとる） take a drastic step
saigo-no shudan-to-shite（最後の手段として） in the last resort

shûdan〈しゅうだん：集団〉a group, a mass.
　　shûdan-hassei（集団発生） a mass outbreak
　　shûdan-kenshin（集団検診） a group examination, a group checkup
　　shûdan-kyôgi（集団競技） a mass game
　shûdan-no〈集団の〉collective.
　shûdan-de〈集団で〉in a group.
　shûdan-teki-ni〈集団的に〉collectively, as a group.

shû-den(sha)〈しゅうでん(しゃ)：終電(車)〉the last train.

shudô〈しゅどう：手動〉manual operation.
　　shudô-burêki（手動ブレーキ） a hand brake
　shudô-no〈手動の〉manually operated, hand-operated.

shûdô〈しゅうどう：修道〉
　　shûdô-in（修道院） a monastery, a convent
　　shûdô-jo（修道女） a nun, a sister

shudô-ken〈しゅどうけん：主導権〉leadership, initiative.
　　shudô-ken o nigiru（主導権を握る） take the leadership ((in))
　　shudô-ken-arasoi（主導権争い） a struggle for leadership

shei〈しゅえい：守衛〉a guard, a doorkeeper.

shûeki〈しゅうえき：収益〉earnings, gains, proceeds, profits.

shûeki〈しゅうえき：就役〉
　shûeki-suru〈就役する〉go into commission, be placed ((on)).

shuen〈しゅえん：主演〉
　　shuen-sha（主演者） a leading actor(or actress), a star
　shuen-suru〈主演する〉play the leading part ((in)), star.

shûen〈しゅうえん：終演〉the end of a show.

shufu〈しゅふ：主婦〉a housewife, a mistress.

shufu〈しゅふ：首府〉a capital, a metropolis.

shûfuku〈しゅうふく：修復〉restoration.
　shûfuku-suru〈修復する〉restore ((to)).

shûgaku〈しゅうがく：就学〉
　　shûgaku-nenrei（就学年齢） the school age
　shûgaku-suru〈就学する〉enter school.
　　shûgaku-saseru（就学させる） put ((a child)) to school

shûgaku-ryokô〈しゅうがくりょこう：修学旅行〉a school excursion.
　　shûgaku-ryokô-ni-iku（修学旅行に行く） go on a school excursion

shugan〈しゅがん：主眼〉the principal object, the chief aim, the point.

shugei〈しゅげい：手芸〉handicraft.

    shugei-hin（手芸品）handiwork

shûgeki〈しゅうげき：襲撃〉an attack, an assault.

  shûgeki-suru〈襲撃する〉attack, make an attack ((on)), assault.

shugi〈しゅぎ：主義〉a principle.

    shugi-to-shite（主義として）on principle

shûgi〈しゅうぎ：祝儀〉a tip, a gratuity; a celebration.

    shûgi o yaru（祝儀をやる）give ((a person)) a gratuity

    shûgi-bu-shûgi-no-dochira-no-baai-ni-mo（祝儀不祝儀のどちらの場合に
      も）on both occasions, happy and sad

shûgi〈しゅうぎ：衆議〉

  shûgi-ikketsu-suru〈衆議一決する〉be decided unanimously.

Shûgiin〈しゅうぎいん：衆議院〉the House of Representatives.

    Shûgiin-giin（衆議院議員）a member of the House of Re-
      presentatives

shugo〈しゅご：主語〉the subject.

shugô〈しゅごう：酒豪〉a heavy drinker, a tippler.

shûgô〈しゅうごう：集合〉gathering, meeting.

    shûgô-basho（集合場所）a meeting place

  shûgô-suru〈集合する〉gather, meet.

shugo-shin〈しゅごしん：守護神〉a guardian deity.

shugyô〈しゅぎょう：修行〉ascetic practices.

  shugyô-suru〈修行する〉practice asceticism.

shûgyô〈しゅうぎょう：修業〉study, pursuit of knowledge.

    shûgyô-nengen（修業年限）the course of study, the years required
      for graduation

shûgyô〈しゅうぎょう：終業〉the closs of work, the closs of school.

    shûgyô-jikan（終業時間）the closing hour

    shûgyô-shiki（終業式）the closing ceremony

shûgyô〈しゅうぎょう：就業〉

    shûgyô-chû-de-aru（就業中である）be at work

    shûgyô-jikan（就業時間）the working hours

  shûgyô-suru〈就業する〉begin work, start work.

shûha〈しゅうは：宗派〉a (religious) sect, a denomination.

shûha〈しゅうは：周波〉a cycle.

    shûha-sû（周波数）frequency

shûhai〈しゅうはい：集配〉collection and delivery.

    yûbin-shûhai-nin（郵便集配人）a mailman, a postman

shuhan〈しゅはん：首班〉the head.

    naikaku no shuhan（内閣の首班）the head of a cabinet

shuhan〈しゅはん：主犯〉the principal (offender).

shûhen〈しゅうへん：周辺〉the circumference, the outskirts, the environs.

    Tôkyô-shûhen-ni（東京周辺に）on the outskirts of Tokyo

shuhin〈しゅひん：主賓〉the guest of honor.

    〜-o-shuhin-to-shite〈〜を主賓として〉in honor of... .

shuhitsu〈しゅひつ：主筆〉the editor in chief.

shuhō〈しゅほう：手法〉a technique, a method.

shui〈しゅい：首位〉the first place, the top.

    shui-ni-tatsu（首位に立つ）be at the head (of)

    shui-o-shimeru（首位を占める）hold (the) first place, rank first ((in))

shûi〈しゅうい：周囲〉the circumference, surroundings.

    shûi-o-mi-mawasu（周囲を見回す）look around

    shûi-jû-mairu-no shima（周囲十マイルの島）an island twenty miles around

    shûi-no〈周囲の〉surrounding, neighboring.

    shûi-no yamayama（周囲の山々）the surrounding mountains

    shûi-no hitobito（周囲の人々）those around one

    shûi-ni〈周囲に〉around, round.

shuin〈しゅいん：主因〉the principal cause, the main factor.

shuji〈しゅじ：主事〉a manager, a director, a superintendent.

shûji〈しゅうじ：習字〉penmanship.

    shûji o narau（習字を習う）practice penmanship

    shûji-chô（習字帳）a copybook

shûji〈しゅうじ：修辞〉a figure of speech, rhetoric.

    shûji(-gaku)-jô-no or *shûji(-gaku)-teki(-na)*〈修辞(学)上の，修辞(学)的(な)〉rhetorical.

shuji-i〈しゅじい：主治医〉the physician in charge ((of)), one's doctor.

shujin〈しゅじん：主人〉the head [of a family], one's husband; the host, the hostess; the landlord, the landlady; the employer, the master.

    shujin-yaku o tsutomeru（主人役を務める）play the host(*or* hostess)

shûjin〈しゅうじん：囚人〉a prisoner, a jailbird.

shûjitsu〈しゅうじつ：週日〉a weekday.

shûjitsu〈しゅうじつ：終日〉the whole day, all day (long).

shuju〈しゅじゅ：種々〉

    shuju-no〈種々の〉various, sundry, all sorts of.

shujutsu〈しゅじゅつ：手術〉an operation.

　shujutsu-suru〈手術する〉perform an operation ((on)), operate ((on)).

　shujutsu-o-ukeru〈手術を受ける〉undergo an operation, be operated on.

shûka〈しゅうか：集荷〉collection of cargo.

shûkai〈しゅうかい：集会〉a meeting, a gathering, an assembly.

　　shûkai o hiraku（集会を開く）hold a meeting

　　shûkai-jo（集会所）a meeting place; an assembly hall

shukaku〈しゅかく：主格〉the nominative case.

shukaku〈しゅかく：主客〉

　　Sore-wa shukaku-tentô-da.（それは主客転倒だ。）That is putting the cart before the horse.

　　Shukaku-ga-tentô-shita.（主客が転倒した。）The tables were turned.

shûkaku〈しゅうかく：収穫〉a harvest, a crop.

　　shûkaku-ga-ooi（収穫が多い）have a good harvest

　　shûkaku-ga-sukunai（収穫が少ない）have a poor harvest

　　shûkaku-ki（収穫期）the harvest time

　　shûkaku-daka（収穫高）the yield, the crop

　shûkaku-suru〈収穫する〉harvest, reap.

shukan〈しゅかん：主観〉subjectivity.

　shukan-teki(-na)〈主観的（な）〉subjective.

　shukan-teki-ni〈主観的に〉subjectively.

shukan〈しゅかん：主幹〉the chief editor.

shûkan〈しゅうかん：習慣〉a habit, a custom.

　　shûkan o tsukeru（習慣を付ける）form a habit

　　warui shûkan-o-naosu（悪い習慣を直す）get rid of a bad habit

　　mukashi-kara-no　shûkan-ni-shitagatte（昔からの習慣に従って）according to the traditional custom

　shûkan-de or *shûkan-jô*〈習慣で，習慣上〉from habit.

shûkan〈しゅうかん：週間〉

　　aichô-shûkan（愛鳥週間）Bird Week

shûkan〈しゅうかん：週刊〉weekly publication.

　　shûkan-shi（週刊誌）a weekly

　shûkan-no〈週刊の〉weekly.

shukei〈しゅけい：主計〉a paymaster.

shûkei〈しゅうけい：集計〉totalization, a total.

　shûkei-suru-to〜-ni-naru〈集計すると〜になる〉total to... .

shuken〈しゅけん：主権〉sovereignty.

　　shuken-o-shingai-suru（主権を侵害する）violate the sovereignty ((of))

shûketsu 〈しゅうけつ：終結〉(a) conclusion, a close.
  shûketsu-suru〈終結する〉be concluded, close, come to a close.
shûketsu 〈しゅうけつ：集結〉
  shûketsu-suru〈集結する〉concentrate, be concentrated, collect, gather, assemble.
shuki 〈しゅき：手記〉a note, a memorandum.
shuki 〈しゅき：酒気〉the smell of liquor.
  shuki-o-obite-iru〈酒気を帯びている〉be under the influence of liquor.
shûki 〈しゅうき：臭気〉a bad smell.
    shûki o hanatsu（臭気を放つ）give out a bad smell
    shûki-ga-hana-o-tsuku（臭気が鼻をつく）stink to heaven
shûki 〈しゅうき：周忌〉the anniversary of ((a person's)) death.
shûki 〈しゅうき：周期〉a period, a cycle.
  shûki-teki(-na)〈周期的(な)〉periodical.
  shûki-teki-ni〈周期的に〉periodically.
shûkin 〈しゅうきん：集金〉collection of money.
    shûkin-nin（集金人）a money collector, a bill collector
  shûkin-suru〈集金する〉collect money, collect bills.
shukka 〈しゅっか：出火〉an outbreak of fire.
  shukka-suru〈出火する〉a fire breaks out.
shukka 〈しゅっか：出荷〉shipment, forwarding.
    shukka-annai（出荷案内）an advice of shipment
  shukka-suru〈出荷する〉ship, forward.
shukkan 〈しゅっかん：出棺〉
    Gogo-ni-ji shukkan-no-yotei.（午後二時出棺の予定.）The hearse will leave home at 2 p.m.
shukke 〈しゅっけ：出家〉
  shukke-suru〈出家する〉become a bonze.
shukketsu 〈しゅっけつ：出欠〉
  shukketsu-o-toru〈出欠をとる〉call the roll.
shukketsu 〈しゅっけつ：出血〉bleeding.
    shukketsu o tomeru（出血を止める）stop bleeding
    shukketsu-taryô-no-tame-shibô-suru（出血多量のため死亡する）die from excessive bleeding
    shukketsu-hambai（出血販売）a sacrifice sale
  shukketsu-suru〈出血する〉bleed.
shukkin 〈しゅっきん：出金〉payment.
shukkin 〈しゅっきん：出勤〉attendance.

shukkin-bo〔出勤簿〕 an attendance book

shukkin-jikan〔出勤時間〕 the office-going hour

shukkin-suru〈出勤する〉attend one's office, go to office.

shukkin-shite-iru〈出勤している〉be at office.

shukkô〈しゅっこう：出港〉

shukkô-suru〈出港する〉set sail ((from)), leave port.

shukkô〈しゅっこう：出講〉

shukkô-suru〈出講する〉give lectures ((at)), teach ((at)).

shukkô〈しゅっこう：出向〉

shukkô-o-meijirareru〈出向を命じられる〉be ordered to be transferred ((to)).

shukô〈しゅこう：趣向〉a plan, a contrivance, a device, a design.

shukô-o-korasu〔趣向を凝らす〕 think out an elaborate plan

shukô-o-kaete〈趣向を変えて〉for a change.

shukô〈しゅこう：手工〉manual training.

shûkô〈しゅうこう：就航〉commission, service.

shûkô-suru〈就航する〉go into commission, enter service.

shu-kôgei〈しゅこうげい：手工芸〉handicraft, manual work.

shu-kôgyô〈しゅこうぎょう：手工業〉manual industry, handicraft.

shukuchoku〈しゅくちょく：宿直〉night duty.

shukuchoku-no isha〔宿直の医者〕 a doctor on night duty

shukuchoku-suru〈宿直する〉be on night duty.

shukudai〈しゅくだい：宿題〉homework, a home task, an assignment.

shukudai o suru〔宿題をする〕 do one's homework

shukuden〈しゅくでん：祝電〉a congratulatory telegram.

shukuden o utsu〔祝電を打つ〕 send a congratulatory telegram ((to))

shukuen〈しゅくえん：祝宴〉a feast given in honor ((of)), a banquet held in celebration ((of)).

shukufuku〈しゅくふく：祝福〉(a) blessing.

shukufuku-suru〈祝福する〉bless.

shukufuku-sareta〈祝福された〉blessed.

shukuga〈しゅくが：祝賀〉(a) celebration, congratulations.

shukuga-kai〔祝賀会〕 a celebration (party)

shukuga-kai o hiraku〔祝賀会を開く〕 hold a celebration

shukuga-suru〈祝賀する〉celebrate, congratulate.

shukugan〈しゅくがん：宿願〉

shukugan o tassuru〈宿願を達する〉realize one's long-cherished desire.

shukuhai〈しゅくはい：祝杯〉

shukuhai-o-ageru〈祝杯を挙げる〉toast〔a person's health〕, drink in celebration ((of)).

shukuhaku〈しゅくはく：宿泊〉(a) lodging.
   shukuhaku-jo（宿泊所）one's lodgings
   shukuhaku-ryô（宿泊料）hotel charges
shukuhaku-suru〈宿泊する〉lodge ((at *or* in)), put up ((at)).

shukuhô〈しゅくほう：祝砲〉a salute of guns.
shukuhô-o-hanatsu〈祝砲を放つ〉fire a salute.

shukui〈しゅくい：祝意〉one's best wishes.
   ~*-ni-shukui-o-hyôshite*〈～に祝意を表して〉in celebration of... , in honor of... .

shukuji〈しゅくじ：祝辞〉congratulations.
   shukuji o noberu（祝辞を述べる）offer one's congratulations ((to))

shukujitsu〈しゅくじつ：祝日〉a festival, a red-letter day, a public holiday.

shukumei〈しゅくめい：宿命〉fate, destiny.
   shukumei-ron（宿命論）fatalism
shukumei-teki(-na)〈宿命的(な)〉fatal.

shukun〈しゅくん：殊勲〉distinguished services.
   shukun-da（殊勲打）a winning hit
   saikô-shukun-senshu（最高殊勲選手）the most valuable player

shûkurîmu〈シュークリーム〉a cream puff.

shukusaijitsu〈しゅくさいじつ：祝祭日〉*see.* shukujitsu.

shukusatsu-ban〈しゅくさつばん：縮刷版〉a reduced-size edition.

shukusei〈しゅくせい：粛清〉a purge, a cleanup.
shukusei-suru〈粛清する〉purge, clean up.

shukusha〈しゅくしゃ：宿舎〉a lodging house, quarters.

shukusha〈しゅくしゃ：縮写〉
shukusha-suru〈縮写する〉make a reduced copy ((of)).

shukushaku〈しゅくしゃく：縮尺〉a reduced scale.
   shukushaku-zu（縮尺図）a map on a reduced scale
shukushaku-suru〈縮尺する〉scale down.

shukushô〈しゅくしょう：縮小〉(a) reduction.
shukushô-suru〈縮小する〉reduce, cut down.
   jigyô o shukushô-suru（事業を縮小する）reduce the business

shukushô-kai〈しゅくしょうかい：祝勝会〉a victory celebration.

shukuteki〈しゅくてき：宿敵〉an old enemy.

shukuten〈しゅくてん：祝典〉a celebration, a festival.

shukuten-o-ageru〈祝典を挙げる〉hold a celebration, celebrate.

shukuzu〈しゅくず：縮図〉a reduced drawing, an epitome.

　　jinsei no shukuzu（人生の縮図）an epitome of life

shukyô〈しゅきょう：主教〉a bishop.

　　dai-shukyô（大主教）an archbishop

shûkyô〈しゅうきょう：宗教〉a religion.

shûkyô-jô-no or *shûkyô-teki(-na)*〈宗教上の，宗教的(な)〉religious.

shûkyô-shin-no-aru〈宗教心のある〉religious, pious.

shûkyoku〈しゅうきょく：終局〉an end, a close, a conclusion.

　　shûkyoku-o-tsugeru（終局を告げる）come to an end, be concluded

shûkyoku-no〈終局の〉final, ultimate.

shûkyû〈しゅうきゅう：しゅう球〉football.

shûkyû〈しゅうきゅう：週休〉a weekly holiday.

　　shûkyû-futsuka-sei（週休二日制）a five-day week

shûkyû〈しゅうきゅう：週給〉a weekly pay.

　　shûkyû-samman-en-de-aru（週給三万円である）draw a salary of
　　thirty thousand yen a week

shûmaku〈しゅうまく：終幕〉an end, a close, a curtainfall.

shûmaku-to-naru〈終幕となる〉end, come to an end, close.

shûmatsu〈しゅうまつ：週末〉the weekend.

　　shûmatsu-ryokô-ni dekakeru（週末旅行に出掛ける）go on a weekend
　　trip

shumbun〈しゅんぶん：春分〉the vernal equinox.

　　shumbun-no-hi（春分の日）Vernal Equinox Day

shûmei〈しゅうめい：襲名〉

shûmei-suru〈襲名する〉succeed to ((a person's)) stage name.

shumi〈しゅみ：趣味〉(a) taste, (an) interest, a hobby.

　　shumi-no-ii-hito（趣味のいい人）a person of refined taste

　　shumi-no-warui-hito（趣味の悪い人）a person of bad taste

shumi-ga-aru or *shumi-o-motsu*〈趣味がある，趣味を持つ〉be interested
　　((in)), have a taste ((for)).

shumoku〈しゅもく：種目〉an item, an event.

　　eigyô-shumoku（営業種目）items of business

shûmoku〈しゅうもく：衆目〉all eyes, public attention.

　　shûmoku no mato（衆目の的）the focus of public attention

shûmon〈しゅうもん：宗門〉*see.* shûha（宗派）.

shun〈しゅん〉the season.

shun-no〈しゅんの〉in season.

　　　shun-hazure-no〈しゅん外れの〉out of season

shundan〈しゅんだん：春暖〉
　　　shundan-no-kô〈春暖の候〉the mild spring season

shûnen〈しゅうねん：執念〉
　shûnen-o-moyasu〈執念を燃やす〉devote oneself exclusively ((to)).
　shûnen-bukai〈執念深い〉tenacious, revengeful, spiteful.
　shûnen-bukaku〈執念深く〉tenaciously, revengefully, spitefully.

shûnen〈しゅうねん：周年〉an anniversary.
　　　jusshûnen-kinen-ni〈十周年記念に〉in commemoration of the tenth
　　　anniversary

shungen〈しゅんげん：しゅん厳〉
　shungen-na〈しゅん厳な〉strict, stern, rigid, severe.

shuniku〈しゅにく：朱肉〉a vermilion inkpad.

shunin〈しゅにん：主任〉a head, a chief.
　　　eigyô-bu-shunin〈営業部主任〉the business manager
　　　kaikei-shunin〈会計主任〉a chief treasurer

shûnin〈しゅうにん：就任〉inauguration.
　　　shûnin-shiki〈就任式〉an inaugural ceremony
　shûnin-suru〈就任する〉take office ((as)), take one's post ((with)), be
　inaugurated ((as)).

shunkan〈しゅんかん：瞬間〉a moment, an instant.
　shunkan-no or *shunkan-teki(-na)*〈瞬間の，瞬間的(な)〉momentary, in-
　stantaneous.
　shunkan(-teki)-ni〈瞬間(的)に〉in a moment, in an instant, in-
　stantaneously.

shun-ka-shû-tô〈しゅんかしゅうとう：春夏秋冬〉the four seasons.

shunkô〈しゅんこう：しゅん工〉completion.
　　　shunkô-shiki〈しゅん工式〉a completion ceremony
　shunkô-suru〈しゅん工する〉be completed.

shunô〈しゅのう：首脳〉a head, a leader.
　　　shunô-kaidan〈首脳会談〉a top-level(*or* summit) conference
　　　seifu-shunô〈政府首脳〉the leaders of the government

shunôkeru〈シュノーケル〉a snorkel.

shunsetsu〈しゅんせつ〉dredging.
　　　shunsetsu-sen〈しゅんせつ船〉a dredger
　shunsetsu-suru〈しゅんせつする〉dredge.

shunsoku〈しゅんそく：しゅん速〉
　shunsoku-no〈しゅん速の〉swift-footed.

shûnyû〈しゅうにゅう：収入〉an income, earnings; revenue.
　shûnyû-ga-ooi（収入が多い）　have a large income
　shûnyû-ga-sukunai（収入が少ない）　have a small income
　shûnyû-inshi（収入印紙）　a revenue stamp

shuppan〈しゅっぱん：出版〉publication.
　shuppan-butsu（出版物）　a publication
　shuppan-kai（出版界）　the publishing world
　shuppan-sha（出版社）　a publishing company
　shuppan-sha（出版者）　a publisher
　shuppan-suru〈出版する〉publish.
　　jihi-shuppan-suru（自費出版する）　publish ((a book)) on one's own account

shuppan〈しゅっぱん：出帆〉sailing.
　shuppan-suru〈出帆する〉set sail.

shuppatsu〈しゅっぱつ：出発〉departure, starting.
　shuppatsu-jikoku（出発時刻）　the departure time
　shuppatsu-suru〈出発する〉depart ((from)), start ((from)), leave, set out ((from)).
　　Tôkyô-muke　Ôsaka　o　shuppatsu-suru（東京向け大阪を出発する）leave Osaka for Tokyo

shuppei〈しゅっぺい：出兵〉
　suppei-suru〈出兵する〉send troops ((to)).

shuppi〈しゅっぴ：出費〉expenses, expenditure.
　shuppi o kiri-tsumeru（出費を切り詰める）　cut down expenses
　Shuppi ga kasamu.（出費がかさむ。）　The expenses increase.

shuppin〈しゅっぴん：出品〉
　shuppin-suru〈出品する〉send (a picture) ((to)) (an exhibition).

shupurehikôru〈シュプレヒコール〉
　shupurehikôru-o-suru〈シュプレヒコールをする〉shout in chorus.

shûrai〈しゅうらい：襲来〉an invasion, a raid, an attack.
　shûrai-suru〈襲来する〉invade, raid, attack; visit.

shuran〈しゅらん：酒乱〉drunken frenzy.

shû-ressha〈しゅうれっしゃ：終列車〉the last train.

shûri〈しゅうり：修理〉repair, mending.
　jidôsha-shûri-kôjô（自動車修理工場）　an auto repair shop
　shûri-suru〈修理する〉repair, mend.

shuro〈しゅろ〉a hemp palm.

shûrô〈しゅうろう：就労〉

shûrô-chû-de-aru〈就労中である〉be at work.

shûroku〈しゅうろく：収録〉

shûroku-suru〈収録する〉collect, contain, record.

shurui〈しゅるい：種類〉a kind, a sort, a variety.
    arayuru-shurui-no（あらゆる種類の）all kinds of
    iroiro-na shurui-no（いろいろな種類の）different sorts of
    onaji-shurui-no（同じ種類の）of the same kind

shurui-betsu-ni-suru〈種類別にする〉classify, assort.

shûrurearizumu〈シュールレアリズム〉surrealism.

shuryô〈しゅりょう：狩猟〉hunting, shooting.
    shuryô-ni-iku（狩猟に行く）go hunting, go shooting
    shuryô-ka（狩猟家）a hunter
    shuryô-kinshi-ki（狩猟禁止期）the close season

shuryô〈しゅりょう：首領〉a leader, a chief, a boss, a chieftain.

shuryô〈しゅりょう：酒量〉one's drinking capacity.

shuryô-ga-ooi〈酒量が多い〉drink much, be a heavy drinker.

shûryô〈しゅうりょう：修了〉completion [of a course].

shûryô-suru〈修了する〉complete, finish.

shûryô〈しゅうりょう：終了〉an end, a close, (a) conclusion.

shûryô-suru〈終了する〉end, come to an end, close, be over, be concluded.

shuryoku〈しゅりょく：主力〉the main strength.

shuryoku-o-sosogu〈主力を注ぐ〉concentrate one's efforts ((on)).

shuryû〈しゅりゅう：主流〉the main current.
    shuryû-ha（主流派）the leading faction, the faction in power

shusai〈しゅさい：主催〉sponsorship, auspices.
    shusai-sha（主催者）the sponsor
    shusai-koku（主催国）the host nation

～-no-shusai-de〈～の主催で〉under the auspices of... .

shusai〈しゅさい：主宰〉superintedence, presidency.
    shusai-sha（主宰者）the chairman, the leader

shusai-suru〈主宰する〉superintend, preside ((over)).

shûsai〈しゅうさい：秀才〉a brilliant person.

shûsan〈しゅうさん：集散〉collection and distribution.
    shûsan-chi（集散地）a trading center.

shûsan-suru〈集散する〉gather and distribute.

shusei〈しゅせい：守勢〉the defensive.
    shusei-ni tatsu（守勢に立つ）stand on the defensive

shûsei〈しゅうせい：終生〉all one's life.

 shûsei-no〈終生の〉lifelong.

shûsei〈しゅうせい：習性〉a habit.

shûsei〈しゅうせい：修正〉(an) amendment, (a) revision, (a) correction; a retouch.

  shûsei-an〈修正案〉an amendment

 shûsei-suru〈修正する〉amend, revise, correct; retouch.

shu-seibun〈しゅせいぶん：主成分〉the chief elements, the principal ingredients.

shuseki〈しゅせき：主(首)席〉the top, the head.

  shuseki-zenken〈首席全権〉the chief delegate

 shuseki-de-sotsugyô-suru〈首席で卒業する〉graduate first.

shûseki〈しゅうせき：集積〉accumulation, integration.

  shûseki-kairo〈集積回路〉an integrated circuit

 shûseki-suru〈集積する〉accumulate, integrate.

shûsen〈しゅうせん：終戦〉the end of the war.

shûsen〈しゅうせん：周旋〉good offices, recommendation, agency.

  shûsen-nin *or* shûsen-ya〈周旋人，周旋屋〉an agent, a broker

  shûsen-ryô〈周旋料〉a commission, a brokerage

 shûsen-suru〈周旋する〉exercise one's good offices, recommend, act as an agent.

shusen-do〈しゅせんど：守銭奴〉a miser, a skinflint.

shusen-tôshu〈しゅせんとうしゅ：主戦投手〉an ace pitcher.

shusha〈しゅしゃ：取捨〉adoption or rejection, choice, selection.

 shusha-suru〈取捨する〉adopt or reject, choose, select.

shushi〈しゅし：種子〉a seed, a pip, a pit.

shushi〈しゅし：趣(主)旨〉the meaning, the point, an object.

shûshi〈しゅうし：収支〉income and outgo, revenue and expenditure.

  shûshi-o-awaseru〈収支を合わせる〉make both ends meet

  kokusai-shûshi〈国際収支〉balance of international payments

shûshi〈しゅうし：宗旨〉one's religion, a sect; one's taste.

  shûshi-ga-chigau〈宗旨が違う〉be different in religion

  shûshi-o-kaeru〈宗旨を変える〉change one's religion, be converted to another sect

shûshi〈しゅうし：修士〉Master of Arts (M.A.), Master of Science (M. S.).

  shûshi-katei〈修士課程〉the master's course ((in))

shûshi〈しゅうし：終始〉from beginning to end, throughout, all the time, constantly, always.

shûshi-ikkan-shita〈終始一貫した〉consistent.

shûshi-ikkan-shite〈終始一貫して〉consistently.

shûshi-fu〈しゅうしふ：終止符〉a full stop, a period.

　　shûshi-fu o utsu（終止符を打つ）put an end ((to))

shushin〈しゅしん：主審〉the chief umpire.

shûshin〈しゅうしん：終身〉all one's life.

　　shûshin-kaiin（終身会員）a life member

　　shûshin-kei（終身刑）a life sentence

　　shûshin-koyô（終身雇用）life-time employment

　　shûshin-nenkin（終身年金）a life annuity

shûshin〈しゅうしん：執心〉attachment, infatuation.

shûshin-suru〈執心する〉be attached ((to)), be bent ((on)), be infatuated ((with)).

shushô〈しゅしょう：主将〉the captain.

shushô〈しゅしょう：首相〉the prime minister, the premier.

shushô〈しゅしょう：殊勝〉

shushô-na〈殊勝な〉laudable, admirable, praiseworthy.

shûshô〈しゅうしょう：愁傷〉lamentation, deep sorrow, grief.

　　Go-shûshô-ni-zonjimasu.（御愁傷に存じます。）I heartily sympathize with you in your misfortune.

shushoku〈しゅしょく：主食〉the staple food.

　　kome-o-shushoku-to-suru（米を主食とする）live on rice

shushoku〈しゅしょく：酒色〉

shushoku-ni-oboreru〈酒色におぼれる〉be addicted to sensual pleasures.

shûshoku〈しゅうしょく：就職〉

　　shûshoku-guchi（就職口）a position, a situation

　　　　shûshoku-guchi-o-sagasu（就職口を探す）look for a position

　　shûshoku-nan（就職難）the difficulty of getting a job

　　shûshoku-ritsu（就職率）the rate of employment

　　shûshoku-shiken（就職試験）an examination for employment

　　shûshoku-undô（就職運動）job hunting

shûshoku-suru〈就職する〉find employment, get a position ((in)), get a job.

shûshoku〈しゅうしょく：修飾〉ornamentation, (an) adornment; modification.

shûshoku-suru〈修飾する〉ornament, adorn; modify.

shûshû〈しゅうしゅう：収集〉(a) collection.

kitte-shûshû（切手収集） stamp collecting

shûshû-ka（収集家） a collector

shûshû-suru（収集する） collect.

shûshû〈しゅうしゅう：収拾〉

shûshû-suru（収拾する） deal ((with)), manage, save, control, get under control.

nankyoku-o-shûshû-suru（難局を収拾する） deal with a difficult situation

shûshuku〈しゅうしゅく：収縮〉 contraction, shrinking.

shûshuku-sei（収縮性） contractibility

shûshuku-suru〈収縮する〉 contract, shrink.

shûso〈しゅうそ：臭素〉 bromine.

shussan〈しゅっさん：出産〉 (a) childbirth, (a) birth.

shussan-todoke（出産届） a report of a birth

shussan-ritsu（出産率） a birthrate

shussan-suru〈出産する〉 give birth to a child.

shussatsu〈しゅっさつ：出札〉

shussatsu-gakari（出札係） a ticket clerk, a booking clerk

shussatsu-guchi（出札口） a ticket window

shusse〈しゅっせ：出世〉 success in life.

shusse-suru〈出世する〉 succeed in life.

shusseki〈しゅっせき：出席〉 attendance, presence.

shusseki-o-toru（出席をとる） call the roll

shusseki-bo（出席簿） a roll book

shusseki-ritsu（出席率） the percentage of attendance

shusseki-sha（出席者） a person present; attendance

shusseki-suru〈出席する〉 attend, be present ((at)).

shussha〈しゅっしゃ：出社〉

shussha-suru〈出社する〉 go to office.

shusshi〈しゅっし：出資〉 (an) investment.

shusshi-gaku（出資額） the amount of investment

shusshi-sha（出資者） an investor

shusshi-suru〈出資する〉 invest money ((in)).

shusshin〈しゅっしん：出身〉

shusshin-chi（出身地） one's native place

shusshin-kô（出身校） one's Alma Mater

~*-no-shusshin-de-aru*〈～の出身である〉 come from... , be a graduate of ... .

Kyûshû-no-shusshin-de-aru（九州の出身である）come from Kyushu

Keiô-no-shusshin-de-aru（慶応の出身である）be a graduate of Keio University

shussho〈しゅっしょ：出所〉the origin, the source; release from prison.

shussho-no-tashika-na jôhô（出所の確かな情報）information from a reliable source

shussho-suru〈出所する〉be discharged from prison.

shusshô-chi〈しゅっしょうち：出生地〉one's birthplace.

shussho-shintai〈しゅっしょしんたい：出処進退〉

shussho-shintai-o-ayamaru（出処進退を誤る）take the wrong course of action.

shusu〈しゅす〉satin.

shutai〈しゅたい：主体〉the subject, the nucleus.

shutai-sei（主体性）subjectivity, individuality, independence

shutai-sei o kakuritsu-suru（主体性を確立する）establish one's independence

shutai-teki(-na)〈主体的(な)〉subjective, independent.

shûtai〈しゅうたい：醜態〉shameful conduct, an unseemly sight, a scandalous condition.

shûtai-o-enjiru（醜態を演じる）behave (oneself) in a shameful manner

shutchô〈しゅっちょう：出張〉

shutchô-jo（出張所）a local office

shutchô-suru〈出張する〉take an official trip, make a business trip.

shutchô〈しゅっちょう：出超〉an excess of exports over imports.

shûten〈しゅうてん：終点〉the terminal, the terminus.

shuto〈しゅと：首都〉a capital, a metropolis.

shuto-ken（首都圏）the metropolitan circle

shuto-no〈首都の〉metropolitan.

shutô〈しゅとう：種痘〉(a) vaccination.

shutô-o-suru〈種痘をする〉vaccinate.

shutô-o-ukeru〈種痘を受ける〉be vaccinated.

shûto〈しゅうと〉one's father-in-law.

shûtô〈しゅうとう：周到〉

shûtô-na〈周到な〉scrupulous, careful, close.

shutoku〈しゅとく：取得〉(an) acquisition.

shutoku-zei（取得税）an acquisition tax

shutoku-suru〈取得する〉acquire.

shûtoku〈しゅうとく：拾得〉
  shûtoku-butsu（拾得物）a find, something found
 shûtoku-suru〈拾得する〉pick up, find.
shûtoku〈しゅうとく：習得〉learning, acquirement, mastery.
 shûtoku-suru〈習得する〉learn, acquire, master.
  Doitsu-go o shûtoku-suru（ドイツ語を習得する）master German
shûtome〈しゅうとめ〉one's mother-in-law.
shutsuba〈しゅつば：出馬〉
 shutsuba-suru〈出馬する〉run ((for)) (the Diet).
shutsubotsu〈しゅつぼつ：出没〉
 shutsubotsu-suru〈出没する〉infest, make frequent appearances.
shutsudo〈しゅつど：出土〉
  shutsudo-hin（出土品）an excavated article
 shutsudo-suru〈出土する〉be excavated ((from)).
shutsudô〈しゅつどう：出動〉
  guntai no shutsudô（軍隊の出動）the mobilization of troops
 shutsudô-suru〈出動する〉take the field, be dispatched ((to)).
shutsuen〈しゅつえん：出演〉appearance on the stage.
  shutsuen-sha（出演者）a performer, the cast
  shutsuen-ryô（出演料）an actor's(*or* singer's) fee
 shutsuen-suru〈出演する〉appear on the stage.
  terebi-ni shutsuen-suru（テレビに出演する）appear on television
shutsugan〈しゅつがん：出願〉(an) application.
 shutsugan-suru〈出願する〉apply ((for)), make an application.
shutsugeki〈しゅつげき：出撃〉a sally, a sortie.
 shutsugeki-suru〈出撃する〉sally, make a sortie.
shutsugen〈しゅつげん：出現〉appearance, advent.
 shutsugen-suru〈出現する〉appear, make one's appearance, turn up.
shutsugoku〈しゅつごく：出獄〉
 shutsugoku-suru〈出獄する〉be released from prison.
shutsujô〈しゅつじょう：出場〉
  shutsujô-sha（出場者）a participant, a player, a performer, a contestant; the entry
 shutsujô-suru〈出場する〉take part ((in)), participate ((in)).
shutsurui〈しゅつるい：出塁〉
 shutsurui-suru〈出塁する〉get to (first) base.
shutsuryô〈しゅつりょう：出漁〉
 shutsuryô-suru〈出漁する〉go out fishing.

shutsuryoku〈しゅつりょく：出力〉

shutsuryoku-sen-bariki-no-enjin（出力千馬力のエンジン）　an　engine that develops 1,000 h.p.

shutsuryoku-san-jû-man-kiro-watto-no-hatsuden-sho（出力三十万キロワットの発電所）　a power plant that generates 300,000 kilowatts of electricity

shuttei〈しゅってい：出廷〉

shuttei-suru〈出廷する〉appear in court.

shutten〈しゅってん：出典〉the source.

shutten o akiraka-ni-suru（出典を明らかにする）　indicate the source ((of))

shuttô〈しゅっとう：出頭〉appearance, presence, attendance.

shuttô-meirei（出頭命令）　a summons

nin·i-shuttô（任意出頭）　voluntary appearance

shuttô-suru〈出頭する〉appear, present oneself ((at)), be present ((at)), attend.

hôtei-ni shuttô-suru（法廷に出頭する）　appear in court

keisatsu-ni shuttô-suru（警察に出頭する）　present oneself at a police station

shûu〈しゅうう：しゅう雨〉a shower, a squall.

shuwa〈しゅわ：手話〉talking with the hands(*or* fingers).

shûwai〈しゅうわい：収賄〉acceptance of a bribe, corruption.

shûwai-jiken（収賄事件）　a bribery case

shûwai-sha（収賄者）　a bribee, a grafter

shûwai-suru〈収賄する〉accept a bribe.

shuwan〈しゅわん：手腕〉ability, capability.

shuwan o miseru（手腕を見せる）　show one's ability

gyôsei-teki shuwan（行政的手腕）　administrative ability

shuwan-ka（手腕家）　a man of ability

shuwan-no-aru〈手腕のある〉able, capable, talented.

shûya〈しゅうや：終夜〉all night, all the night through.

shûya-unten（終夜運転）　an all-night service

shuyaku〈しゅやく：主役〉the leading part, a leading actor(*or* actress), a star.

shuyaku-o-tsutomeru（主役を務める）　play the leading part, star.

shûyaku〈しゅうやく：集約〉

shûyaku-nôgyô（集約農業）　intensive agriculture

shûyaku-teki(-na)〈集約的(な)〉intensive.

shuyô〈しゆよう：主要〉
 shuyô-jimbutsu（主要人物）the leading characters
 shuyô-sangyô（主要産業）key industries
 shuyô-na〈主要な〉principal, chief, main, leading, important.
shuyô〈しゆよう：腫瘍〉a tumor.
 akusei-shuyô（悪性しゆよう）a malignant tumor
shûyô〈しゆうよう：収容〉accommodation.
 shûyô-jin·in（収容人員）the number of persons to be admitted
 shûyô-ryoku（収容力）a seating capacity
 shûyô-setsubi（収容設備）accommodations
 shûyô-jo（収容所）an asylum, a concentration camp
 shûyô-suru〈収容する〉accommodate, receive, take in, seat, admit, house.
shûyô〈しゆうよう：修養〉mental culture, cultivation of the mind, mental training.
 seishin-shûyô（精神修養）moral training
 shûyô-suru〈修養する〉cultivate one's mind, improve oneself.
shûyô〈しゆうよう：収用〉expropriation.
 shûyô-suru〈収用する〉expropriate.
 tochi o shûyô-suru（土地を収用する）expropriate land
shûyû〈しゆうゆう：周遊〉an excursion.
 shûyû-suru（周遊する）make an excursion
 shûyû-ken（周遊券）an excursion ticket
shuzai〈しゆざい：取材〉
 shuzai-suru〈取材する〉gather data, cover, be based ((on)).
shuzan〈しゆざん：珠算〉calculation on the abacus.
shuzei〈しゆぜい：酒税〉the liquor tax.
shûzen〈しゆうぜん：修繕〉*see.* shûri.
shuzô〈しゆぞう：酒造〉*sake* brewing.
 shuzô-gyô（酒造業）the brewing industry
 shuzô-ka（酒造家）a brewer
shuzoku〈しゆぞく：種族〉a tribe.
 shuzoku-no〈種族の〉tribal.
so〈そ：祖〉an ancestor, the founder, the originator.
sô〈そう：僧〉a priest, a monk.
sô〈そう：層〉a layer, a stratum, a bed, a class.
 (seki)tansô（(石)炭層）a coal bed
 chishiki-sô（知識層）the intellectual class

sô〈そう〉so.

Sô-desu-ka?（そうですか.）Is that so?

moshi-sô-nara（もしそうなら）if so

moshi-sô-de-nakereba（もしそうでなければ）if not so

"Kare-wa　Nihon-jin-desu." "Watashi-mo　sô-desu."（"彼は日本人です." "私もそうです."）"He is Japanese." "So am I."

Sô-okoru-na.（そう怒るな.）Don't be so angry.

Sô-waruku-mo-nai.（そう悪くもない.）It's not so bad.

sô-〈そう-：総-〉all, whole, gross, general, total.

sô-jinkô（総人口）the total population

sô-shotoku（総所得）a gross income

-sô〈-そう〉seem, look, appear; be ready ((to do)), threaten ((to do)); ought.

Kanojo-wa　ureshi-sô-datta.（彼女はうれしそうだった.）She looked happy.

Ima-nimo-ame-ga-furi-dashi-sô-da.（今にも雨が降り出しそうだ.）It is threatening to rain.

Kimi-nara-wakari-sô-na-mono-da.（君なら分かりそうなものだ.）You ought to know it.

~-da-sô-da.〈～だそうだ.〉It is said that... .

soaku〈そあく：粗悪〉

soaku-hin（粗悪品）goods of inferior quality

soaku-na〈粗悪な〉coarse, crude, inferior.

sôan〈そうあん：草案〉a (rough) draft.

sôan-o-kisô-suru〈草案を起草する〉draft a bill, draw up a draft.

sôan〈そうあん：創案〉an original idea.

sô-atari-sen〈そうあたりせん：総当たり戦〉a round robin.

soba〈そば〉buckwheat (noodles).

soba-ko（そば粉）buckwheat flour

soba〈そば〉a side; neighborhood.

Soba-o-hanare-nai-yô-ni-shi-nasai.（そばを離れないようにしなさい.）Keep close to me.

soba-ni〈そばに〉by, beside, near.

soba-ni suwaru（そばに座る）sit by ((a person's)) side

sugu-soba-ni（すぐそばに）close by

sôba〈そうば：相場〉(a) speculation; the market price, a quotation, the current price; estimation.

sôba-ni-te-o-dasu（相場に手を出す）engage in speculation

　　　sôba-de môkeru（相場でもうける）　make money in speculation
　　　kôtei-sôba（公定相場）　an official quotation
　　　oroshi-uri-sôba（卸し売り相場）　the wholesale price
　　〜-to-sôba-ga-kimatte-iru〈〜と相場が決まっている〉be generally considered ((to be))... .

sobadateru〈そばだてる〉
　　　mimi-o-sobadateru（耳をそばだてる）　prick up one's ears

sobakasu〈そばかす〉a freckle.
　　sobakasu-darake-no〈そばかすだらけの〉freckly.

sôban〈そうばん：早晩〉sooner or later.

sô-bana〈そうばな：総花〉
　　sô-bana-teki(-na)〈総花的（な）〉all-round.
　　sô-bana-teki-ni〈総花的に〉to please everybody.

soba-zue〈そばづえ〉
　　soba-zue-o-kuu〈そばづえを食う〉be involved ((in)), get a by-blow ((in)).

sôbetsu〈そうべつ：送別〉a farewell, a send-off.
　　　sôbetsu-no-kotoba（送別の言葉）　a farewell speech
　　　sôbetsu-kai（送別会）　a farewell party

sôbi〈そうび：装備〉equipment.
　　sôbi-suru〈装備する〉equip.
　　jû-sôbi-no〈重装備の〉heavy-equipped.

sobieru〈そびえる〉rise, tower, soar.

Sobieto〈ソビエト〉
　　　Sobieto-shakai-shugi-kyôwa-koku-rempô（ソビエト社会主義共和国連邦）　the Union of Soviet Socialist Republics (U.S.S.R.)

-sobireru〈-そびれる〉fail ((to do)), miss a chance ((to do)).

sobiyakasu〈そびやかす〉
　　　kata o sobiyakasu（肩をそびやかす）　raise one's shoulders
　　　kata-o-sobiyakashite-aruku（肩をそびやかして歩く）　swagger

sobo〈そぼ：祖母〉a grandmother.

sobô〈そぼう：粗暴〉
　　sobô-na〈粗暴な〉wild, rough, violent.

soboku〈そぼく：素朴〉simplicity, artlessness.
　　soboku-na〈素朴な〉simple, artless.

soburi〈そぶり：素振り〉a manner, behavior, an attitude, an air, a look.
　　soburi-o-suru〈素振りをする〉behave oneself.
　　　yosoyososhii-soburi-o-suru（よそよそしい素振りをする）　behave oneself like a stranger ((toward))

socha 〈そちゃ：粗茶〉tea.

Socha-desu-ga.（粗茶ですが.） Please take a cup of tea.

sochi 〈そち：措置〉a measure, a step.

sochi o toru（措置をとる） take a step

sochi-o-ayamaru（措置を誤る） take a wrong step

sôchi 〈そうち：装置〉equipment, a device, an apparatus.

anzen-sôchi（安全装置） a safety device

rei-dambô-sôchi（冷暖房装置） an air-conditioning apparatus

sôchi-suru〈装置する〉equip ((with)), fit ((with)), install.

sochira 〈そちら〉your place, your family.

Sochira-wa　minasan　o-genki-desu-ka?（そちらは皆さんお元気ですか.）
How are you all getting on?

sôchô 〈そうちょう：総長〉the president〔of a university〕.

sôchô 〈そうちょう：早朝〉

sôchô-ni〈早朝に〉early in the morning.

sôchô 〈そうちょう：荘重〉

sôchô-na〈荘重な〉solemn, grave.

sôchô-ni〈荘重に〉solemnly, gravely.

sôda 〈ソーダ〉soda.

sôda-sui（ソーダ水） soda water, a soda

sodachi 〈そだち：育ち〉breeding; growth.

sodachi-no-ii（育ちのいい） well-bred

sodachi-no-warui（育ちの悪い） ill-bred

sodachi-no-hayai（育ちの早い） of rapid growth

sodachi-zakari-no（育ち盛りの） growing

sôdachi 〈そうだち：総立ち〉

sôdachi-ni-naru〈総立ちになる〉get up on one's feet all at once.

sôdai 〈そうだい：総代〉a representative.

sotsugyô-sei-sôdai（卒業生総代） the representative of the graduates

〜*-no-sôdai-to-shite*〈〜の総代として〉representing... .

sôdai 〈そうだい：壮大〉

sôdai-na〈壮大な〉grand, magnificent, imposing.

sôdai-na keshiki（壮大な景色） a grand spectacle

sôdan 〈そうだん：相談〉(a) consultation, a talk, advice.

sôdan-ni-iku　（相談に行く） go to ((a person)) to ask for his advice
((about))

sôdan-aite（相談相手） an adviser

sôdan-suru〈相談する〉consult, talk ((with)), counsel.

sôdan-o-ukeru〈相談を受ける〉be consulted ((by)).

sôdan-no-ue〈相談の上〉after consultation.

sodate-no-oya〈そだてのおや：育ての親〉one's foster parent.

sodateru〈そだてる：育てる〉bring up, rear, raise, nurse, foster, breed, cultivate.

sodatsu〈そだつ：育つ〉grow (up), be brought up.

sôdatsu-sen〈そうだつせん：争奪戦〉a scramble ((for)).

sode〈そで〉a sleeve.

　　sode o makuru〈そでをまくる〉roll up one's sleeves

　　Nai-sode-wa-furenu.〈ないそでは振れぬ。〉Nothing comes out of the sack but what was in it.

　　sode-guchi〈そで口〉a cuff

sode-nashi-no〈そでなしの〉sleeveless.

sôde〈そうで：総出〉

sôde-de〈総出で〉all together, in a body.

sôden〈そうでん：送電〉transmission of electricity, electric supply.

　　sôden-sen（送電線）a power cable

sôden-suru〈送電する〉transmit electricity, supply power ((to)).

sôdô〈そうどう：騒動〉(a) disturbance, a trouble, a quarrel, a riot.

　　sôdô o okosu（騒動を起こす）cause a disturbance

　　Hito-sôdô okoru.（一騒動起こる。）A riot breaks out.

sô-dôin〈そうどういん：総動員〉general mobilization.

soegi〈そえぎ：そえ木〉a splint.

soen〈そえん：疎遠〉estrangement, one's long silence.

soen-ni-naru〈疎遠になる〉be estranged ((from)).

soeru〈そえる：添える〉attach ((to)), add ((to)), accompany.

　　rireki-sho-ni shashin o soeru（履歴書に写真を添える）attach a photo to a curriculum vitae

sofu〈そふ：祖父〉a grandfather.

sôfu〈そうふ：送付〉

sôfu-suru〈送付する〉send, forward.

sôfû〈そうふう：送風〉ventilation.

　　sôfû-ki（送風機）an air blower, a ventilator

sôfû-suru〈送風する〉send air ((to)), ventilate.

sofuto-kurîmu〈ソフトクリーム〉soft ice cream.

sogai〈そがい：阻害〉an impediment, an obstruction, a hindrance.

sogai-suru〈阻害する〉impede, obstruct, hinder, check, arrest.

sogai〈そがい：疎外〉alienation.

sogai-kan〈疎外感〉a sense of alienation

sogai-suru〈疎外する〉alienate.

sô-gakari〈そうがかり：総掛かり〉

sô-gakari-de〈総掛かりで〉with united efforts, all together.

sôgaku〈そうがく：総額〉the total amount, the sum total.

sôgaku-de〈総額で〉in all, in total.

sôgaku-de 〜-ni-naru〈総額で〜になる〉 amount to... , total...

sogan〈そがん：訴願〉a petition, an appeal.

sogan-suru〈訴願する〉petition, appeal.

sôgan-kyô〈そうがんきょう：双眼鏡〉binoculars.

sogeki〈そげき：狙撃〉

sogeki-hei〈狙撃兵〉 a sniper, a sharpshooter

sogeki-suru〈狙撃する〉snipe (at).

sôgen〈そうげん：草原〉a plain, a grassland.

sôgi〈そうぎ：争議〉a dispute, a trouble.

rôdô-sôgi〈労働争議〉 a labor trouble

sôgi〈そうぎ：葬儀〉a funeral (service).

sôgi o okonau〈葬儀を行う〉 hold a funeral

sôgi ni sanretsu-suru〈葬儀に参列する〉 attend a funeral

sogo〈そご〉(a) discrepancy, (a) contradiction; (a) frustration, (a) miscarriage.

keikaku-ni-sogo-o-kitasu〈計画にそごを来す〉 frustrate one's plan

sôgo〈そうご：相互〉

sôgo-kankei〈相互関係〉 mutual relation

sôgo-no〈相互の〉mutual.

sôgo-ni〈相互に〉mutually, each other, one another.

sôgô〈そうごう：総合〉(a) synthesis.

sôgô-byôin〈総合病院〉 a general hospital

sôgô-kyôgi〈総合競技〉 combined exercises

sôgô-suru〈総合する〉synthesize.

sôgô-teki(-na)〈総合的(な)〉synthetic.

sôgô-teki-ni〈総合的に〉synthetically.

sôgô〈そうごう：相好〉

sôgô-o-kuzushite-yorokobu〈相好をくずして喜ぶ〉be all smiles.

sôgon〈そうごん：荘厳〉solemnity, sublimity.

sôgon-na〈荘厳な〉solemn, sublime.

sôgon-ni〈荘厳に〉solemnly, sublimely.

sogu〈そぐ〉reduce, diminish, take from, spoil, weaken.

kyômi o sogu〈興味をそぐ〉 spoil one's interest

sôgû〈そうぐう：遭遇〉

sôgû-suru〈遭遇する〉encounter, come across, meet ((with)).

sôgyô〈そうぎょう：創業〉the commencement of an enterprise; establishment.

sôgyô-irai〈創業以来〉 since the firm was established

sôgyô-suru〈創業する〉commence, start.

sôgyô〈そうぎょう：操業〉operation, work.

sôgyô o tanshuku-suru〈操業を短縮する〉 reduce operation

sôgyô-suru〈操業する〉operate, run, work.

sôha〈そうは：走破〉

sôha-suru〈走破する〉run the whole distance.

sôhaku〈そうはく：そう白〉

sôhaku-na〈そう白な〉 pale, pallid, white.

sôheki〈そうへき：双璧〉the two greatest authorities.

sôhô〈そうほう：双方〉both parties, both sides.

sôhô-no〈双方の〉both, mutual.

sôhô-no-ii-bun o kiku〈双方の言い分を聞く〉 hear both sides

sôhô-no-tame-ni〈双方のために〉 for mutual interests

sôi〈そうい：創意〉originality.

sôi-ni-tonda〈創意に富んだ〉 original, creative, ingenious.

sôi〈そうい：総意〉the general will.

sôi〈そうい：相違〉(a) difference.

sôi-ten〈相違点〉 a point of difference

sôi-suru〈相違する〉differ ((from)), be different ((from)), vary ((from)), disagree ((with)).

~-ni-sôi-nai〈～に相違ない〉must ((be))... , there is no doubt that... , it is certain that... .

sôi-naku〈相違なく〉without fail, certainly.

an-ni-sôi-shite〈案に相違して〉contrary to one's expectations

sô-ieba〈そういえば：そう言えば〉

Sô-ieba ano-hi-wa-oo-yuki-datta.（そう言えばあの日は大雪だった.） It reminds me that it was snowing heavily on that day.

sôin〈そういん：僧院〉a monastery, a cloister.

sôin〈そういん：総員〉the whole number, all hands.

sôin-hyaku-mei〈総員百名〉 one hundred persons in all

soi-ne〈そいね：添い寝〉

soi-ne-suru〈添い寝する〉lie with (a baby).

sô-iu 〈そういう〉 such, like that.

    sô-iu-baai-ni-wa (そういう場合には) in such a case

    sô-iu-fû-ni (そういうふうに) that way, like that

    sô-iu-koto-nara (そういうことなら) if so, then

    sô-iu-wake-de (そういう訳で) such being the case

sôji 〈そうじ：相似〉 (a) resemblance, (a) similarity.

    sôji-kei (相似形) a similar figure

sôji 〈そうじ：掃除〉 cleaning, sweeping, dusting.

    oo-sôji (大掃除) general housecleaning

    sôji-ki (掃除機) a cleaner

sôji-suru 〈掃除する〉 clean, sweep.

    heya o sôji-suru (部屋を掃除する) clean a room

sô-jishoku 〈そうじしょく：総辞職〉 general resignation.

sô-jishoku-suru 〈総辞職する〉 resign in a body.

sôjô 〈そうじょう：僧正〉 a bishop.

    dai-sôjô (大僧正) an archbishop

sôjû 〈そうじゅう：操縦〉 management, handling, operation, control.

    sôjû-sha (操縦者) an operator, a driver

    sôjû-shi (操縦士) a pilot

sôjû-suru 〈操縦する〉 manage, handle, operate, control, drive, pilot, steer.

sôjuku 〈そうじゅく：早熟〉

sôjuku-na 〈早熟な〉 precocious, premature.

sôkai 〈そうかい：総会〉 a general meeting.

    kabu-nushi-sôkai (株主総会) a general meeting of stockholders

sôkai 〈そうかい：掃海〉 mine sweeping.

    sôkai-tei (掃海艇) a mine sweeper

sôkai-suru 〈掃海する〉 sweep up mines.

sôkai 〈そうかい：壮快〉

sôkai-na 〈壮快な〉 stirring, exciting.

sôkai 〈そうかい：そう快〉

sôkai-na 〈そう快な〉 refreshing, exhilarating.

    sôkai-na-kibun-ni-naru (そう快な気分になる) feel refreshed

sokaku 〈そかく：組閣〉

sokaku-suru 〈組閣する〉 form a cabinet.

sôkan 〈そうかん：総監〉 an inspector general.

    keishi-sôkan (警視総監) the Superintendent-General of the Metropolitan Police

sôkan〈そうかん：壮観〉a grand sight.
  sôkan o teisuru〈壮観を呈する〉 present a grand sight
sôkan〈そうかん：送還〉
 sôkan-suru〈送還する〉send back, repatriate.
sôkan〈そうかん：創刊〉
  sôkan-gô〈創刊号〉 the first issue
 sôkan-suru〈創刊する〉start〔a periodical〕.
sôkan(-kankei)〈そうかん（かんけい）：相関（関係）〉correlation, mutual relation.
 sôkan-teki(-na)〈相関的（な）〉correlative, mutually related.
 sôkan-teki-ni〈相関的に〉correlatively.
sôkatsu〈そうかつ：総括〉generalization, summary.
 sôkatsu-suru〈総括する〉generalize, sum up, summarize.
 sôkatsu-teki(-na)〈総括的（な）〉all-inclusive.
 sôkatsu-shite-ieba〈総括して言えば〉generally speaking, to sum up.
sôke〈そうけ：宗家〉the head family.
sôkei〈そうけい：総計〉the total, the sum total.
 sôkei-suru〈総計する〉total, sum up.
sôkei〈そうけい：早計〉
 sôkei-na〈早計な〉premature, too hasty.
sôken〈そうけん：双肩〉
 sôken-ni-kakaru〈双肩に掛かる〉fall on one's shoulders.
sôken〈そうけん：送検〉
 sôken-suru〈送検する〉commit ((a culprit)) for trial.
  shorui-sôken-suru〈書類送検する〉 send the papers to the prosecutor's office
sôken〈そうけん：壮健〉
 sôken-de-aru〈壮健である〉be healthy, be in good health.
 sôken-na〈壮健な〉healthy.
soketto〈ソケット〉a socket.
  futa-mata-soketto〈二またソケット〉 a two-way socket
sôki〈そうき：早期〉an early stage.
  shôjô o sôki-ni hakken-suru（症状を早期に発見する） detect the symptoms in its early stages
sôki〈そうき：想起〉
 sôki-suru〈想起する〉remember, recollect, call to mind.
sôkin〈そうきん：送金〉(a) remittance.
  sôkin-ko-gitte〈送金小切手〉 a remittance check

sôkin-suru〈送金する〉remit money, send money.

sokke-nai〈そっけない：素っ気無い〉curt, blunt, cold.

    sokke-nai henji（素っ気ない返事）　a curt reply

  sokke-naku（素っ気なく）curtly, bluntly, flatly.

    sokke-naku kotowaru（素っ気なく断る）　refuse bluntly

sokketsu〈そっけつ：即決〉a prompt decision, a summary decision.

  sokketsu-suru〈即決する〉decide on the spot.

sokki〈そっき：速記〉shorthand, stenography.

    sokki-sha（速記者）　a shorthand writer, a stenographer

    sokki-roku（速記録）　a stenographic record

  sokki-suru〈速記する〉take down in shorthand, stenograph.

sokkin〈そっきん：側近〉

    shushô-sokkin（首相側近）　those close to the Prime Minister

sokkin〈そっきん：即金〉cash payment.

    sokkin-de harau（即金で払う）　pay in cash

sokkô〈そっこう：即効〉an immediate effect.

    sokkô-ga-aru（即効がある）　have an immediate effect ((on))

sokkô-jo〈そっこうじょ：測候所〉a meteorological observatory.

sokkoku〈そっこく：即刻〉immediately, without delay, at once, right away.

sokkuri〈そっくり〉the exact image; all, entirely, wholly, completely.

    Kare-wa haha-oya-ni sokkuri-da.（彼は母親にそっくりだ。）He is the exact image of his mother.

    sakana o hone-goto-sokkuri taberu（魚を骨ごとそっくり食べる）eat a fish, bone and all

    Watashi-no heya o sokkuri-sono-mama-ni-shite-oite-kudasai.（私の部屋をそっくりそのままにしておいてください。）Please leave my room just as it is.

sokkyô〈そっきょう：即興〉

    sokkyô-shijin（即興詩人）　an improvisator

  sokkyô-no or *sokkyô-teki-ni*〈即興の、即興的に〉impromptu.

sokkyû〈そっきゅう：速球〉a fast ball.

    sokkyû-tôshu（速球投手）　a speedballer

soko〈そこ：底〉the bottom, the sole.

    kokoro no soko-kara（心の底から）　from the bottom of one's heart

  soko-o-tsuku〈底を突く〉reach the bottom, touch (the) bottom.

  soko-no-shire-nai or *soko-nashi-no*〈底の知れない、底なしの〉bottomless, unfathomable, abysmal.

soko-nashi-no numa（底なしの沼） a bottomless swamp

soko〈そこ〉there, that place.

    soko-koko-ni（そこここに） here and there

    soko-de（そこで） there; then

    soko-no, soko-e *or* soko-ni（そこの，そこへ，そこに） there

    soko-kara（そこから） from there

    soko-made（そこまで） so far

sokō〈そこう：素行〉conduct, behavior.

    sokō-ga-osamara-nai（素行が修まらない） be loose in one's morals

sōko〈そうこ：倉庫〉a warehouse, a storehouse.

sōkō〈そうこう：草稿〉a draft, notes, a manuscript.

    sōkō o tsukuru（草稿を作る） make a draft ((of)), make notes ((for))

sōkō〈そうこう：装甲〉armoring.

    sōkō-ban（装甲板） an armor plate, armor plating

soko-bie〈そこびえ：底冷え〉

    soko-bie-suru〈底冷えする〉be chilled to the bone.

sō-kōgeki〈そうこうげき：総攻撃〉a general attack.

sokohi〈そこひ：底ひ〉cataract, amaurosis.

soko-jikara〈そこぢから：底力〉potential power.

sokoku〈そこく：祖国〉one's fatherland(*or* motherland).

    sokoku-ai（祖国愛） love of one's motherland

sōkō-kyori〈そうこうきょり：走行距離〉mileage〔on a car〕.

sōkon〈そうこん：早婚〉(an) early marriage.

    Kare-wa sōkon-da.（彼は早婚だ.） He married young.

sokonau〈そこなう：損なう〉hurt, injure, spoil.

    kanjō o sokonau（感情を損なう） hurt ((a person's)) feelings

-sokonau〈-そこなう：-損なう〉fail ((to do)), miss.

    zasshi o kai-sokonau（雑誌を買い損なう） fail to buy a magazine

    kisha ni nori-sokonau（汽車に乗り損なう） miss the train

    go-chisō-o-tabe-sokonau（ごちそうを食べ損なう） miss out on a capital dinner

soko-ne〈そこね：底値〉the bottom price.

sokonuke〈そこぬけ：底抜け〉

    sokonuke-no zennin（底抜けの善人） a good man to the core

sokora〈そこら〉about there, around there; or so.

    doko-ka-sokora（どこかそこら） somewhere about there

    sokora-jū（そこら中） all over the place

    go-mairu-ka-sokora（五マイルかそこら） five miles or so

sokosoko-ni〈そこそこに〉hurriedly, in haste.
　　asa-meshi-mo-sokosoko-ni（朝飯もそこそこに）taking a hasty
　　　breakfast
sokotsu〈そこつ：粗こつ〉
　　sokotsu-mono（粗こつ者）a careless fellow
　sokotsu-na〈粗こつな〉careless, thoughtless, hasty.
-soku〈-そく：-足〉a pair.
　　kutsu-shita issoku（靴下一足）a pair of socks
sokubai〈そくばい：即売〉a spot sale.
　sokubai-suru〈即売する〉sell on the spot.
sokubaku〈そくばく：束縛〉(a) restraint, (a) restriction, fetters.
　sokubaku-suru〈束縛する〉restrain, restrict, fetter.
　sokubaku-o-ukeru or *sokubaku-sareru*〈束縛を受ける，束縛される〉be
　　restrained, be restricted.
sokudan〈そくだん：速断〉a hasty conclusion.
　sokudan-suru〈速断する〉make a hasty conclusion, jump to a
　　conclusion.
sokudo〈そくど：速度〉speed.
　　ichi-jikan　yon-jū-mairu-no-sokudo-de（一時間四十マイルの速度で）at
　　　a speed of 40 miles an hour
　　sokudo-seigen（速度制限）a speed limit
　　sokudo-kei（速度計）a speedometer
　sokudo-o-masu〈速度を増す〉increase speed, speed up.
　sokudo-o-yurumeru〈速度を緩める〉reduce speed, slow down.
sokuhô〈そくほう：速報〉a quick announcement, a news flash.
　sokuhô-suru〈速報する〉make a quick report ((on)).
sokui〈そくい：即位〉accession to the throne, enthronement.
　　sokui-shiki（即位式）an enthronement ceremony
　sokui-suru〈即位する〉accede to the throne.
sokuji〈そくじ：即時〉*see.* sokkoku.
　　sokuji-barai（即時払い）spot payment
sokujitsu〈そくじつ：即日〉(on) the same day.
sokumen〈そくめん：側面〉the side, the flank.
　　mono-goto-o-sokumen-kara-miru（物事を側面から見る）take a side
　　　view of a thing
　　sokumen-zu（側面図）a side view
　　sokumen-kôgeki（側面攻撃）a flank attack
sokuô〈そくおう：即応〉

sokuô-suru 〈即応する〉 conform ((to)), adapt oneself ((to)), meet.

~-*ni-sokuô-shite* 〈～に即応して〉 in conformity with... , in response to ... .

     jôsei-ni-sokuô-shite（情勢に即応して）in conformity with the circumstances

sokuryô 〈そくりょう：測量〉a survey; sounding.

     sokuryô-zu（測量図）a survey map

     sokuryô-gishi（測量技師）a surveyor, a surveying engineer

sokuryô-suru 〈測量する〉survey, make a survey ((of)), sound.

sokuryoku 〈そくりょく：速力〉speed.

     keizai-sokuryoku（経済速力）an economic speed

     zen-sokuryoku-de（全速力で）at full speed

sokusei 〈そくせい：速成〉an intensive training, quick mastery.

     Furansu-go-sokusei-ka（フランス語速成科）an intensive course in French

sokusei-saibai 〈そくせいさいばい：促成栽培〉forcing culture.

     sokusei-saibai-no yasai（促成栽培の野菜）forced vegetables

sokusei-suru 〈促成する〉force.

sokuseki 〈そくせき：即席〉

sokuseki-no or *sokuseki-ni* 〈即席の，即席に〉offhand.

sokushi 〈そくし：即死〉

sokushi-suru 〈即死する〉be killed on the spot.

sokushin 〈そくしん：促進〉promotion, hastening, facilitation.

     hambai-sokushin（販売促進）sales promotion

sokushin-suru 〈促進する〉promote, hasten, facilitate.

sokusuru 〈そくする：即する〉conform ((to)), agree ((with)), be adapted ((for *or* to)), be based ((on)).

     jidai no yôkyû-ni-sokushita mono-no-kangae-kata（時代の要求に即した物の考え方）a way of thinking to meet the demands of the times

sokutatsu 〈そくたつ：速達〉special delivery, express delivery.

     sokutatsu-no tegami（速達の手紙）a special delivery letter

sokutei 〈そくてい：測定〉measurement.

sokutei-suru 〈測定する〉measure, gauge, find.

sokutô 〈そくとう：即答〉a ready answer.

sokutô-suru 〈即答する〉give a ready answer.

sôkutsu 〈そうくつ：巣くつ〉a den, a haunt, a hangout.

Sôku-wakuchin 〈ソークワクチン〉the Salk vaccine.

sokuza 〈そくざ：即座〉

sokuza-ni〈即座に〉instantly, promptly, at once.

sô-kuzure〈そうくずれ：総崩れ〉a rout.

　sô-kuzure-ni-naru〈総崩れになる〉be routed.

sôkyo〈そうきょ：壮挙〉a heroic attempt, a grand project.

sôkyoku-sen〈そうきょくせん：双曲線〉a hyperbola.

sokyû〈そきゅう：そ及〉retroactivity.

　sokyû-suru〈そ及する〉retroact ((to)).

　sokyû-teki(-na) or *sokyû-ryoku-no-aru*〈そ及的(な)，そ及力のある〉retroactive.

sôkyû〈そうきゅう：送球〉

　sôkyû-suru〈送球する〉throw a ball ((to)), toss a ball ((to)).

sôkyû〈そうきゅう：早急〉

　sôkyû-ni〈早急に〉with dispatch, as quickly as possible.

somaru〈そまる：染まる〉dye, be dyed; be stained ((with)), be tainted ((with)).

　　chi-ni-somaru〈血に染まる〉be stained with blood

　　aku-ni-somaru〈悪に染まる〉sink in vice

sôma-tô〈そうまとう：走馬灯〉a revolving lantern.

somatsu〈そまつ：粗末〉

　somatsu-na〈粗末な〉coarse, plain, poor, humble; careless, rude, rough.

　　somatsu-na tabemono〈粗末な食べ物〉coarse food

　　somatsu-na tori-atsukai〈粗末な取り扱い〉rough handling

　somatsu-ni〈粗末に〉carelessly, rudely, roughly.

　somatsu-ni-suru〈粗末にする〉neglect, slight, waste.

　　oya o somatsu-ni-suru〈親を粗末にする〉neglect one's parents

　　tabe-mono o somatsu-ni-suru〈食べ物を粗末にする〉waste one's food

some〈そめ：染め〉dyeing, coloring.

　　some-mono〈染め物〉dyeing, dyed goods

　　　some-mono-ya〈染め物屋〉a dyer; a dyehouse

　some-ga-ii〈染めがいい〉be well dyed.

　　some-ga-warui〈染めが悪い〉be badly dyed

　someru〈染める〉dye, color.

　　kami o someru〈髪を染める〉dye one's hair

sômei〈そうめい：そう明〉sagacity, intelligence, wisdom.

　sômei-na〈そう明な〉sagacious, intelligent, wise, bright.

sômen〈そうめん〉vermicelli, fine noodles.

sommin〈そんみん：村民〉a villager.

sômu〈そうむ：総務〉general affairs.

　　　sômu-bu〈総務部〉the general affairs department

sômu-keiyaku〈そうむけいやく：双務契約〉a bilateral contract.

somukeru〈そむける：背ける〉
　　　kao o somukeru（顔を背ける）turn one's face away ((from))
　　　me o somukeru（目を背ける）avert one's eyes ((from))
　　　me-o-somukete（目を背けて）with averted eyes

somuku〈そむく：背く〉disobey.
　　　oya-no-ii-tsuke ni somuku（親の言い付けに背く）disobey one's parents

son〈そん：損〉(a) loss, (a) disadvantage.
　　　son o kakeru（損を掛ける）inflict a loss ((upon))
　son-o-suru〈損をする〉suffer a loss, lose.
　　　son-o-shite uru（損をして売る）sell at a loss
　son-ni-naru〈損になる〉do not pay.
　son-na〈損な〉unprofitable, disadvantageous.
　　　son-na kai-mono（損な買い物）a bad bargain
　　　son-na tachiba（損な立場）a disadvantageous position

sonae〈そなえ：備え〉provision, preparations.
　　　Sonae-areba urei-nashi.（備えあれば憂いなし.）Providing is preventing.
　sonaeru〈備える〉prepare ((for)), provide ((against or for)), furnish.
　　　man·ichi-ni sonaeru（万一に備える）prepare for the worst
　　　shôrai-ni-sonaeru（将来に備える）provide for the future
　sonae-no-aru〈備えのある〉provided.
　　　sonae-no-nai（備えのない）unprovided.

sonae-mono〈そなえもの：供え物〉an offering.
　　　sonae-mono o suru or sonaeru（供え物をする, 供える）make an offering

sonae-tsuke〈そなえつけ：備え付け〉equipment, fitting.
　　　kyôin-shitsu-ni-sonae-tsuke-no tosho（教員室に備え付けの図書）books kept in the teachers' room
　sonae-tsukeru〈備え付ける〉provide, furnish, equip, fit.
　　　heya ni terebi-o-sonae-tsukeru（部屋にテレビを備え付ける）equip a room with a television

sô-name〈そうなめ：総なめ〉
　sô-name-ni-suru〈総なめにする〉win a sweeping victory; make a clean sweep ((of)).

sônan〈そうなん：遭難〉a disaster, a mishap, (a) shipwreck, distress.

sônan-shingô〈遭難信号〉a signal of distress

sônan-sha〈遭難者〉a victim, a sufferer

sônan-suru〈遭難する〉meet with a disaster, be wrecked.

sonawaru〈そなわる：備わる〉

kihin-ga-sonawatte-iru〈気品が備わっている〉be endowed with dignity.

sonchô〈そんちょう：村長〉a village headman.

sonchô(-suru)〈そんちょう（する）：尊重（する）〉respect, esteem.

sonchô-su-beki〈尊重すべき〉respectable, estimable.

sondai〈そんだい：尊大〉arrogance, haughtiness.

sondai-na〈尊大な〉arrogant, haughty.

son-eki〈そんえき：損益〉loss and gain, profit and loss.

son-eki-keisan-sho〈損益計算書〉a statement of profit and loss

sonemi〈そねみ〉see.　netami.

songai〈そんがい：損害〉damage, a loss.

songai o ataeru〈損害を与える〉do damage ((to))

songai o kômuru〈損害を被る〉suffer damage, suffer a loss

dai-songai〈大損害〉a heavy loss

songai-hoken〈損害保険〉insurance against loss

songai-baishô〈そんがいばいしょう：損害賠償〉compensation for damage, reparation for injury.

songai-baishô o seikyû-suru〈損害賠償を請求する〉demand damages

songai-baishô-o-suru〈損害賠償をする〉compensate ((a person)) for damages, pay damages ((to)).

songen〈そんげん：尊厳〉dignity, majesty.

sonjiru〈そんじる：損じる〉injure, damage, hurt.

kigen-o-sonjiru〈機嫌を損じる〉hurt ((a person's)) feelings, offend

sonkei〈そんけい：尊敬〉respect.

sonkei-suru〈尊敬する〉respect, honor, think highly ((of)), look up ((to)).

sonkei-su-beki〈尊敬すべき〉respectable, honorable.

sonna〈そんな〉such, like that.

sonna-toki-niwa〈そんなときには〉in such a case

sonna-ni〈そんなに〉so, like that.

Watashi-wa sonna-ni-takusan o-kane-o-motte-i-masen.〈私はそんなにたくさんお金を持っていません.〉I don't have so much money.

sono〈その〉the, that, its.

sono-ba〈そのば：その場〉

sono-ba-ni-i-awaseta hito〈その場に居合わせた人〉those who happened to be there sono-ba-kagiri-no-koto-o-iu〈その場限りのことを言う〉 say something just to suit the occasion

sono-ba-de〈その場で〉 there and then, on the spot.

sono-go〈そのご：その後〉 after that, (ever) since.

sono-go san-nen-shite〈その後三年して〉 three years after that

Sono-go kanojo-ni atte-i-nai.〈その後彼女に会っていない.〉 I have not seen her since.

sono-hen〈そのへん：その辺〉 about there.

doko-ka-sono-hen〈どこかその辺〉 somewhere about there

sono-hi〈そのひ：その日〉 (on) that day.

sono-hi-no-uchi-ni〈その日のうちに〉 before the day is over

sono-hi-gurashi-o-suru〈その日暮しをする〉 live from day to day

sono-hoka-ni〈そのほかに〉 besides, moreover, further.

sono-koro〈そのころ〉 at that time, then, in those days.

sono-kurai〈そのくらい〉 so many, so much, that much, to that extent.

sono-kurai-no〈そのくらいの〉 such, so trifle.

Sono-kurai-no-koto-ni jikan o rōhi-suru-nowa bakagete-iru.〈そのくらいの事に時間を浪費するのはばかげている.〉 It is foolish to waste time on such a trifling matter.

sono-kuse〈そのくせ〉 and yet, still, for all that, nevertheless.

Ano-otoko wa kane-wa-aru-no-da-ga sono-kuse dare-nimo-shin·yô-sare-nai.〈あの男は金はあるのだが, そのくせだれにも信用されない.〉 He is rich, and yet he is not trusted by anyone.

somo-mama〈そのまま〉

sono-mama-ni-shite-oku〈そのままにしておく〉 leave ((a thing)) as it is.

sono-michi〈そのみち：その道〉 the line, the profession, the field.

sono-michi-no taika〈その道の大家〉 an authority in the line

sono-mono〈そのもの：その物〉 the very thing.

Kare-wa shôjiki-sono-mono-da.〈彼は正直その物だ.〉 He is honesty itself.

sono-suji〈そのすじ：その筋〉 the authorities concerned.

sono-suji no mei-ni-yori〈その筋の命により〉 by order of the authorities

sono-ta〈そのた：その他〉 the others, the rest; and so on.

sono-tame〈そのため〉 so, therefore, for that reason, consequently, for that (purpose).

sono-te〈そのて：その手〉

Sono-te-wa-kuwa-nai-yo!〈その手は食わないよ.〉 None of your tricks!

sono-toki 〈そのとき：その時〉then, at that time.

  chôdo sono-toki（ちょうどその時） just then

sono-toori 〈そのとおり〉just so, just like that, just as you say.

  Sono-toori.（そのとおり。） That's right.

sono-uchi 〈そのうち：その内〉among the rest.

  Kanojo-mo sono-uchi-no-hitori-da.（彼女もその内の一人だ。） She is one of them.

sono-uchi-ni 〈そのうちに〉soon, before long, some day, in the meantime, in time.

  Sono-uchi-ni mata o-ukagai-shimasu.（そのうちに又お伺いします。） I will call on you again before long.

sono-ue 〈そのうえ：その上〉besides, moreover.

  sono-ue komatta-koto-ni-wa 〈その上困ったことには〉to make the matters worse, what is worse.

sonraku 〈そんらく：村落〉a village, a hamlet.

sonshitsu 〈そんしつ：損失〉(a) loss.

sonshô 〈そんしょう：損傷〉damage, (an) injury.

sonshoku 〈そんしょく：そん色〉

  sonshoku-ga-nai 〈そん色がない〉be by no means inferior ((to)), be equal ((to)).

son-toku 〈そんとく：損得〉loss and gain, profit and loss, interests.

  son-toku-zuku-de（損得尽くで） for mere gain

  son-toku-o-hanarete（損得を離れて） apart from selfish interest

sônyû 〈そうにゅう：挿入〉insertion.

  sônyû-suru 〈挿入する〉insert, put in.

sonzai 〈そんざい：存在〉existence, being.

  sonzai-riyû（存在理由） justification for existence

  sonzai-suru 〈存在する〉exist, be in existence.

sonzoku 〈そんぞく：存続〉continuance.

  sonzoku-suru 〈存続する〉continue (to be).

  sonzoku-saseru 〈存続させる〉continue, keep up, retain.

sonzoku 〈そんぞく：尊属〉an ascendant, an ancestor, a lineal descendant.

sôô 〈そうおう：相応〉

  sôô-na 〈相応な〉suitable ((for)), suited ((to)), becoming, befitting, adequate, reasonable, proper, fair.

  mibun-sôô-ni-kurasu（身分相応に暮らす） live within one's means

sôon 〈そうおん：騒音〉(a) noise, (a) din.

soppa〈そっぱ：そっ歯〉a projecting (front) tooth.

soppo〈そっぽ〉

 soppo-o-muku〈そっぽを向く〉turn away, look the other way.

sopurano〈ソプラノ〉soprano.

  sopurano-kashu（ソプラノ歌手） a soprano

sora〈そら：空〉there!, look!, here!

sora〈そら：空〉the sky, the air.

  sora-takaku（空高く） high up in the sky

sora〈そら：空〉memory.

  sora-de oboeru（空で覚える） learn by heart

sora-danomi〈そらだのみ：空頼み〉an empty hope.

 sora-danomi-suru〈空頼みする〉hope vainly ((for)).

sora-iro〈そらいろ：空色〉sky blue, azure.

 sora-iro-no〈空色の〉sky-blue, azure.

soramame〈そらまめ：そら豆〉a horsebean.

sora-mimi〈そらみみ：空耳〉mishearing.

  Dare-ka genkan-no-to-o-nokku-shita-yô-ni-omotta-ga sora-mimi-
   datta.（だれか玄関の戸をノックしたように思ったが空耳だった。） I
   only fancied I heard someone knocking on the front door.

sora-moyô〈そらもよう：空模様〉weather.

  Sora-moyô ga ayashii.（空模様が怪しい。） The weather looks
   threatening.

sôran〈そうらん：騒乱〉

  sôran-zai（騒乱罪） the crime of riot act

sora-namida〈そらなみだ：空涙〉sham tears.

  sora-namida o nagasu（空涙を流す） shed sham tears

sora-ni〈そらに：空似〉an accidental resemblance.

sora-osoroshii〈そらおそろしい：空恐ろしい〉feel a vague fear.

sorasu〈そらす：反らす〉bend, curve.

  karada-o-sorasu（体を反らす） bend oneself backward

sorasu〈そらす〉turn away, divert.

  me o sorasu（目をそらす） turn away one's eyes ((from))

  chûi o sorasu（注意をそらす） divert one's attention ((from))

  hanashi o sorasu（話をそらす） change the subject ((from))

sorazorashii〈そらぞらしい：空々しい〉feigned, empty, hollow, thin,
 transparent.

  sorazorashii o-seji-o-iu（空々しいお世辞を言う） make empty
   compliments

sorazorashii uso o iu (空々しいうそを言う) tell a thin lie

sore 〈それ〉 it, that.

sore-da-kara (それだから) so, so that, therefore

sore-dake (それだけ) that much, so much, as much, the more

sore-de-ite *or* sono-kuse (それでいて，そのくせ) and yet, still, nevertheless

sore-demo *or* sore-ni-shitemo (それでも，それにしても) but, nevertheless, however, still

sore-dewa (それでは) if so, then

soredokoro-ka (それどころか) on the contrary, far from that

sore-hodo (それ程) so much, so far, (not) very

sore-jitai (それ自体) in itself

sore-kara *or* sorekkiri (それから，それっきり) since (then), after that

sore-kara-zutto (それからずっと) ever since

sore-made (それまで) till then

sore-made-ni (それまでに) by that time

sore-mo (それも) and that, at that

Sore-mo-sô-da. (それもそうだ。) That's true.

Sore-mo-sô-daga〜. (それもそうだが〜。) It may be so, but... .

sore-ni (それに) besides, moreover

sore-ni-shitewa〜 (それにしては〜) considering...

sore-tomo (それとも) or

soreto-naku (それとなく) indirectly

sorewa-sôto (それはそうと) by the way

sore 〈それ〉 there! / look (out)!

sôrei 〈そうれい：壮麗〉

sôrei-na 〈壮麗な〉 magnificent, grand, imposing, splendid.

Soren 〈ソれん：ソ連〉 see. Sobieto.

soreru 〈それる〉 turn away, miss, deviate ((from)).

hanashi-ga-waki-michi-e-soreru (話がわき道へそれる) stray from the subject

sôretsu 〈そうれつ：壮烈〉

sôretsu-na 〈壮烈な〉 heroic, brave, glorious.

sôretsu-na saigo-o-togeru (壮烈な最期を遂げる) die a heroic death

sorezore 〈それぞれ〉 each, respectively.

sorezore-no 〈それぞれの〉 each, respective.

sori 〈そり〉 a sleigh, a sledge, a sled.

sori〈そり：反り〉a warp, a curve.

　sori-ga-awa-nai〈反りが合わない〉cannot get along ((with)).

sôri(-daijin)〈そうり（だいじん）：総理（大臣）〉*see.* shushô〈首相〉.

　　sôri-fu〈総理府〉the Prime Minister's Office

sori-kaeru〈そりかえる：反り返る〉warp; throw back one's head.

sôritsu〈そうりつ：創立〉establishment, foundation.

　　sôritsu-sha〈創立者〉the founder

　sôritsu-suru〈創立する〉establish, found.

soroban〈そろばん：そろ盤〉an abacus.

　soroban-ga-au〈そろ盤が合う〉pay.

　soroban-o-hajiku〈そろ盤をはじく〉be given to calculation.

soroeru〈そろえる〉arrange, put in order; make uniform; complete.

　　surippa o kichin-to soroete-oku（スリッパをきちんとそろえておく）put one's slippers neatly side by side

　　ita no hashi o soroeru（板の端をそろえる）true up the edges of the boards

　　Sutainbekku no sakuhin-o-soroeru（スタインベックの作品をそろえる）have a complete set of Steinbeck

soroi〈そろい〉a set, a suit, a suite.

　　hito-soroi-no kagu（一そろいの家具）a suite of furniture

　soroi-no〈そろいの〉uniform.

sôron〈そうろん：総論〉general remarks, an introduction ((to)), an outline ((of)).

sorosoro〈そろそろ〉slowly, gradually; soon.

　　Haha wa sorosoro kaette-kimasu.（母はそろそろ帰って来ます。）Mother will be back soon.

sorotte〈そろって〉in a body, all together.

　　sorotte dekakeru（そろって出掛ける）go all together

　soroi-mo-sorotte〈そろいもそろって〉without a single exception, one and all.

sorou〈そろう〉be complete; be equal, be uniform.

　　sei-ga-sorou（背がそろう）be of the uniform height

soru〈そる：反る〉warp, curve, be curved, bend back(ward).

soru〈そる〉shave.

　　kao-o-soru（顔をそる）shave oneself, get one's face shaved

sôrui〈そうるい：走塁〉base running.

sôryo〈そうりょ：僧りょ〉a (Buddhist) priest.

sôryô〈そうりょう：送料〉carriage, postage.

sô-ryôji〈そうりょうじ：総領事〉a consul general.

sôryoku〈そうりょく：総力〉all one's energy.

    sôryoku-sen（総力戦）a total war

    sôryoku-o-agete〈総力を挙げて〉with all one's energies.

so-ryûshi〈そりゅうし：素粒子〉an elementary particle.

sôsa〈そうさ：捜査〉(criminal) investigation, a search.

    sôsa-mô（捜査網）the police dragnet

    sôsa-suru〈捜査する〉investigate, search ((for)).

sôsa〈そうさ：操作〉(an) operation, (a) manipulation, management.

    shijô-sôsa（市場操作）market manipulation

    sôsa-suru〈操作する〉operate, manipulate, manage.

sôsai〈そうさい：総裁〉a president, a governor.

    fuku-sôsai（副総裁）a vice-president

sôsai〈そうさい：相殺〉a setoff, an offset.

    sôsai-kanjô（相殺勘定）an offset account

    sôsai-suru〈相殺する〉offset each other.

sôsaku〈そうさく：創作〉creation, an original work; to write a story, a story.

    sôsaku-ka（創作家）a story writer

    sôsaku-sha（創作者）an originator

    sôsaku-suru〈創作する〉create, write a story.

sôsaku〈そうさく：捜索〉a search, (a) quest.

    sôsaku-tai（捜索隊）a searching party

    sôsaku-negai-o-dasu（捜索願いを出す）ask the police to search ((for))

    sôsaku-suru〈捜索する〉search ((for)).

sosei〈そせい：粗製〉slipshod manufacture.

    sosei-ranzô（粗製濫造）overproduction of coarse articles

    sosei-ranzô-suru〈粗製濫造する〉overproduce articles of inferior quality.

sosei〈そせい：組成〉

    sosei-bun（組成分）a component, a constituent

    sosei-suru〈組成する〉compose, constitute, make up.

sosei〈そせい：蘇生〉resuscitation, reanimation.

    sosei-suru〈蘇生する〉resuscitate, be resuscitated, be restored to life.

    sosei-saseru〈蘇生させる〉bring ((a person)) back to life, restore ((a person)) to consciousness.

sôsei-ji〈そうせいじ：双生児〉twins, a twin.

soseki〈そせき：礎石〉a foundation stone, a cornerstone.

sosen〈そせん：祖先〉an ancestor, a forefather.

sosen(-denrai)-no〈祖先(伝来)の〉ancestral, hereditary.

sô-senkyo〈そうせんきょ：総選挙〉a general election.

sôsha〈そうしゃ：走者〉a (base) runner.

sôsha〈そうしゃ：壮者〉a man in his prime.

sôsha〈そうしゃ：操車〉marshaling.
　　sôsha-jô〈操車場〉a marshaling yard

soshaku〈そしゃく：租借〉a lease.
　　soshaku-ken〈租借権〉(a) lease, leasehold
　　soshaku-suru〈租借する〉hold ((a territory)) by lease, lease.

soshaku〈そしゃく〉chewing, mastication.
　　soshaku-suru〈そしゃくする〉chew, masticate.

soshi〈そし：阻止〉
　　soshi-suru〈阻止する〉hinder, impede, check, block, stop.

sôshi〈そうし：創始〉origination, creation, foundation.
　　sôshi-sha〈創始者〉an originator, a founder
　　sôshi-suru〈創始する〉originate, create, found.

soshiki〈そしき：組織〉(an) organization, formation, construction, a system.
　　soshiki-ryoku〈組織力〉organizing ability
　　soshiki-suru〈組織する〉organize, form, construct.
　　soshiki-dateru〈組織立てる〉systematize.
　　soshiki-teki(-na) or *soshiki-datta*〈組織的(な), 組織立った〉systematic.
　　soshiki-teki-ni or *soshiki-datte*〈組織的に, 組織立って〉systematically.

sôshiki〈そうしき：葬式〉*see.* sôgi〈葬儀〉.

sôshin〈そうしん：送信〉transmission of a message.
　　sôshin-suru〈送信する〉transmit a message ((to)).

so-shina〈そしな：粗品〉a small gift.
　　So-shina-desu-ga　o-uketori-kudasai.〈粗品ですがお受け取りください。〉I hope you'll accept this.

sôshin-gu〈そうしんぐ：装身具〉personal ornaments, accessories.

soshiru〈そしる〉slander, abuse, speak ill ((of)), censure.

soshite〈そして〉and, (and) then, (and) now.

soshitsu〈そしつ：素質〉a nature, makings, quality, a genius.
　　gogaku-no　soshitsu-ga-aru〈語学の素質がある〉have linguistic genius

sôshitsu〈そうしつ：喪失〉loss.
　　jishin-sôshitsu〈自信喪失〉loss of confidence

soshô〈そしょう：訴訟〉a lawsuit, a suit, an action.

　　soshô o okosu〈訴訟を起こす〉raise a suit
　　soshô-ni-katsu〈訴訟に勝つ〉win a lawsuit
　　soshô ni makeru〈訴訟に負ける〉lose a lawsuit
　　soshô o tori-sageru〈訴訟を取り下げる〉drop a suit

sôsho〈そうしょ：草書〉the cursive style of Chinese character or *kana* writing.

sôsho〈そうしょ：双書〉a series, a library.

sôshô〈そうしょう：宗匠〉a master, a teacher.

sôshô〈そうしょう：総称〉a general term.
　sôshô-suru〈総称する〉name generically.

soshoku〈そしょく：粗食〉plain food.
　soshoku-suru〈粗食する〉eat plain food.

sôshoku〈そうしょく：装飾〉ornament, decoration, adornment.
　　sôshoku-hin〈装飾品〉an ornament, a decoration
　sôshoku-suru〈装飾する〉ornament, decorate, adorn.
　sôshoku-teki(-na)〈装飾的(な)〉ornamental, decorative.
　sôshoku-yô(-no)〈装飾用(の)〉for ornamental purposes.

sôshoku-dôbutsu〈そうしょくどうぶつ：草食動物〉a grass-eating animal.

sôshun〈そうしゅん：早春〉early spring.
　　sôshun-ni〈早春に〉in early spring

sosô〈そそう：粗相〉carelessness, a blunder.
　　Kore-wa-sosô-itashimashita.（これは粗相いたしました.）I was awkward.
　sosô-suru〈粗相する〉make a blunder, have a toilet accident.

sosô〈そそう：阻喪〉
　iki-sosô-suru〈意気阻喪する〉be depressed, be disheartened, be in low spirits, be demoralized.

sôsô〈そうそう：早々〉
　　kitaku-sôsô〈帰宅早々〉as soon as one comes home
　　raigetsu-sôsô〈来月早々〉early next month
　　sôsô-ni-hiki-ageru〈早々に引き揚げる〉hurry off

sosogu〈そそぐ：注ぐ〉pour ((into)), flow ((into)), drain ((into)); give, devote ((to)).
　　Kono kawa wa Ôsaka-wan-ni-sosogu.（この川は大阪湾に注ぐ.）This river flows into Osaka Bay.
　　aijô o sosogu〈愛情を注ぐ〉give one's love ((to))

sosokkashii〈そそっかしい〉see. sokotsu-na.

sōsoku 〈そうそく：総則〉 general rules(*or* provisions).

sosokusa(-to) 〈そそくさ（と）〉 in haste, in a hurry.

sosonokasu 〈そそのかす：唆す〉 tempt, entice, instigate, stir up.

sosoru 〈そそる〉 excite, stimulate, arouse, tempt.
  kôki-shin o sosoru 〈好奇心をそそる〉 excite one's curiosity
  shokuyoku o sosoru 〈食欲をそそる〉 tempt one's appetite

sossen 〈そっせん：率先〉
  sossen-suru 〈率先する〉 take the lead.
  sossen-shite～(-suru) 〈率先して～(する)〉 take the lead in ((doing))

sosū 〈そすう：素数〉 a prime number.

sōsu 〈ソース〉 sauce.
  sōsu o kakeru 〈ソースを掛ける〉 put sauce ((on))

sōsui 〈そうすい：送水〉 water supply.
  sôsui-kan 〈送水管〉 a water pipe
  sōsui-suru 〈送水する〉 supply water ((to)).

sō-sureba 〈そうすれば〉 if so, then; and.
  Hidari-ni mawari-nasai, sô-sureba renga-date-no tatemono ga miemasu. 〈左に回りなさい、そうすればれんが建ての建物が見えます。〉 Turn left, and you'll see a brick building.

sōsuru 〈そうする：奏する〉 play, perform.

sōtai 〈そうたい：早退〉 *see*. haya-bike.

sōtai(-sei) 〈そうたい（せい）：相対（性）〉 relativity.
  sôtai-sei-genri 〈相対性原理〉 the theory of relativity
  sôtai-teki(-na) 〈相対的（な）〉 relative.
  sôtai-teki-ni 〈相対的に〉 relatively.

sōtan 〈そうたん：操短〉
  sôtan-suru 〈操短する〉 *see*. sôgyô o tansyuku-suru.

sotchi 〈そっち〉
  sotchi-noke-ni-suru 〈そっちのけにする〉 lay aside, neglect, pay no attention ((to)).

sotchoku 〈そっちょく：率直〉 frankness, candidness.
  sotchoku-na 〈率直な〉 frank.
  sotchoku-ni 〈率直に〉 frankly.
  sotchoku-ni-ieba 〈率直に言えば〉 frankly speaking, to be frank with you

sotchū 〈そっちゅう：卒中〉 apoplexy.

sōtei 〈そうてい：想定〉 (a) supposition, (an) assumption.
  sôtei-suru 〈想定する〉 suppose, imagine, assume.

sôtei〈そうてい：装丁〉binding.

　　sôtei-no-ii hon（装丁のいい本）　a well-bound book

　sôtei-suru〈装丁する〉bind.

sôten〈そうてん：争点〉the point at issue.

sôten〈そうてん：装てん〉loading, a charge.

　sôten-suru〈装てんする〉load, charge.

sotetsu〈そてつ〉a cycad.

soto〈そと：外〉the outside, the open (air).

　soto-no〈外の〉outer, outside, outward, outdoor.

　soto-de, soto(-de)-wa, soto-e or *soto-ni*〈外で，外(で)は，外へ，外に〉out,
　　without, outside, out of doors, in the open (air).

　　　soto-e deru（外へ出る）　go out (of doors)

　　　soto-de asobu（外で遊ぶ）　play in the open

　～-kara-soto-e〈～から外へ〉out (of)～.

　　　heya-kara-soto-e-deru（部屋から外へ出る）　go out of the room

　soto-kara〈外から〉from the outside.

　　　soto-kara to o akeru（外から戸を開ける）　open the door from the
　　　　outside

sôtô〈そうとう：掃とう〉

　　　sôtô-sen（掃とう戦）　a mopping-up operation

　sôtô-suru〈掃とうする〉sweep, mop up.

sôtô〈そうとう：相当〉

　sôtô-suru〈相当する〉be equal ((to)), be proportional ((to)).

　sôtô-na〈相当な〉suitable, proper, reasonable, decent, respectable, good,
　　considerable.

　　　sôtô-na nedan（相当な値段）　a reasonable price

　　　sôtô-na katei（相当な家庭）　a respectable family

　　　sôtô-na shûnyû（相当な収入）　a good income

　sôtô-ni〈相当に〉decently, respectably, fairly, pretty, considerably.

sotoba or **sotôba**〈そとば，そとうば：そ塔婆〉a *stupa*.

soto-bori〈そとぼり：外堀〉an outer moat.

soto-gawa〈そとがわ：外側〉the outside, the exterior.

　soto-gawa-no〈外側の〉outer, outside, exterior.

　soto-gawa-kara〈外側から〉from without.

soto-mawari〈そとまわり：外回り〉circumference; the outer tracks.

sotsu〈そつ〉

　sotsu-no-nai〈そつのない〉perfect, faultless, prudent, tactful.

sotsû〈そつう：疎通〉understanding, communication.

ishi-no-sotsû-o-kaku（意思の疎通を欠く） there is lack of understanding

sotsugyô〈そつぎょう：卒業〉graduation.

sotsugyô-rombun（卒業論文） a graduation thesis

sotsugyô-shiki（卒業式） a graduation ceremony

sotsugyô-shôsho（卒業証書） a diploma

sotsugyô-sei（卒業生） a graduate

sotsugyô-suru〈卒業する〉graduate ((from)), complete a course.

(-ni)-sotte〈(に)そって：(に)沿って〉along, by, with.

kawa-ni-sotte-aruku（川に沿って歩く） walk along the river

sotto〈そっと〉softly, quietly, gently; stealthily, secretly.

sotto-hairu〈そっと入る〉steal into.

sotto-shite-oku〈そっとしておく〉leave ((a thing)) as it is.

sottô〈そっとう：卒倒〉a faint, a swoon.

sottô-suru〈卒倒する〉faint, swoon, fall senseless.

sou〈そう〉accompany, meet, answer, act up ((to)), satisfy.

kibô ni sou（希望にそう） meet one's wishes

kitai-ni sou（期待にそう） act up to one's expectations

mokuteki ni sou（目的にそう） answer one's purpose

sôutsu-byô〈そううつびょう：そううつ病〉manic-depressive psychosis.

sôwaki〈そうわき：送話器〉a transmitter.

sowasowa〈そわそわ〉

sowasowa-suru〈そわそわする〉be restless, be nervous.

sowasowa-shita〈そわそわした〉restless.

sowasowa-shite〈そわそわして〉restlessly.

soya〈そや：粗野〉

soya-na〈粗野な〉rough, coarse, vulgar.

soyô〈そよう：素養〉knowledge, attainments.

Kare-wa Furansu-go-no-soyô-ga-aru.（彼はフランス語の素養がある.）
He has some knowledge of French.

soyogu〈そよぐ〉rustle, sway, wave.

soyo-kaze〈そよかぜ：そよ風〉a gentle breeze.

soyosoyo(-to)〈そよそよ(と)〉gently, softly.

sozai〈そざい：素材〉a material, a subject matter, a copy.

sôzai〈そうざい：総菜〉daily dishes.

sôzan〈そうざん：早産〉a premature birth.

sôzan-suru〈早産する〉give birth to a baby prematurely, be born prematurely.

sozatsu 〈そざつ：粗雑〉

sozatsu-na 〈粗雑な〉 coarse, rough, crude, loose.

sozei 〈そぜい：租税〉 taxes, taxation.

sôzei 〈そうぜい：総勢〉 the whole persons.

 sôzei-hyaku-mei 〈総勢百名〉 one hundred persons in all

sôzen 〈そうぜん：騒然〉

sôzen-to-shita 〈騒然とした〉 noisy, confused, agitated, uproarious, tumultuous.

sôzen-to 〈騒然と〉 in an uproar, in a tumult.

sôzen-to-naru 〈騒然となる〉 be thrown into an uproar.

 Jônai wa sôzen-to-natta.（場内は騒然となった.） The hall was thrown into an uproar.

sôzô 〈そうぞう：創造〉 creation.

 sôzô-ryoku（創造力） creative power

sôzô-suru 〈創造する〉 create.

sôzô-teki(-na) 〈創造的(な)〉 creative.

sôzô 〈そうぞう：想像〉 imagination.

 sôzô-ryoku（想像力） imagination, imaginative power

  sôzô-ryoku-ni-tomu（想像力に富む） be imaginative

  sôzô-ryoku-ni-toboshii（想像力に乏しい） have little imagination

sôzô-suru 〈想像する〉 imagine, suppose.

sôzô-dekiru 〈想像できる〉 imaginable, thinkable.

 sôzô-deki-nai（想像できない） unimaginable, unthinkable

sôzoku 〈そうぞく：相続〉 succession, inheritance.

 sôzoku-zei（相続税） an inheritance tax, a death duty

 sôzoku-nin（相続人） a successor; an heir, an heiress.

sôzoku-suru 〈相続する〉 succeed ((to)), inherit.

sôzôshii 〈そうぞうしい：騒々しい〉 noisy, clamorous, uproarious.

sôzôshiku 〈騒々しく〉 noisily, clamorously, uproariously.

 sôzôshiku-suru（騒々しくする） make a noise, raise a racket

su 〈す：州〉 a sandbank, a (sand) bar, a shoal.

su 〈す：巣〉 a nest, a web, a comb.

 su o tsukuru（巣を造る） build a nest

 su o haru（巣を張る） spin a web

su 〈す：酢〉 vinegar.

 su-no-mono（酢の物） a vinegared dish

sû 〈すう：数〉 a number, a figure.

sû-ni-oite 〈数において〉 in number, numerically.

sû-〈すう-：数-〉several, a few, some.

    sû-jitsu（数日）　several days

    jû-sû-jitsu（十数日）　more than ten days

    sû-jitsu-mae（数日前）　a few days ago

su-ashi〈すあし：素足〉*see.* hadashi.

subarashii〈すばらしい：素晴らしい〉splendid, wonderful.

    subarashiku〈素晴らしく〉splendidly, wonderfully.

subashikoi〈すばしこい〉nimble, quick, smart.

    subashikoku〈すばしこく〉nimbly, quickly, smartly.

subayai〈すばやい：素早い〉quick, agile.

    subayaku〈素早く〉quickly, agilely.

sube〈すべ〉a means, a way, how to ((do)), what to ((do)).

    nasu-sube-o-shira-nai（なすすべを知らない）　be at a loss what to do

suberasu〈すべらす：滑らす〉let slip.

    kuchi-o-suberasu（口を滑らす）　make a slip of the tongue

    ashi-o-suberasu（足を滑らす）　miss one's footing

suberi-dai〈すべりだい：滑り台〉a slide.

    suberi-dai-de suberu（滑り台で滑る）　slide on a slide

suberi-dashi〈すべりだし：滑り出し〉

    suberi-dashi-ga-ii〈滑り出しがいい〉make a good start ((in)).

suberi-dome〈すべりどめ：滑り止め〉

    suberi-dome-no-shite-aru　taiya（滑り止めのしてあるタイヤ）　a skid-proof tire

suberi-komi〈すべり込み：滑り込み〉sliding.

    suberi-komi-de　yatto-kaisha-ni-ma-ni-au（滑り込みでやっと会社に間に合う）　enter the office barely in time

    suberi-komu〈滑り込む〉slide ((into)).

    honrui-ni-suberi-komu（本塁に滑り込む）　slide into home base

suberu〈すべる：滑る〉slide, skate, glide, slip.

    koori-no-ue-o suberu（氷の上を滑る）　skate on the ice

    subette-korobu（滑って転ぶ）　slip and fall

    suberi-yasui〈滑りやすい〉slippery.

    suberu-yô-ni〈滑るように〉glidingly.

subete〈すべて〉all.

    Subete ga owatta.（すべてが終わった。）　All is over.

    subete-no〈すべての〉all, every, entire, whole.

    subete-no ten-de（すべての点で）　in all points, in every respect

subomeru〈すぼめる〉make ((a thing)) narrower.

  kasa o subomeru〈傘をすぼめる〉 shut an umbrella

  kata o subomeru〈肩をすぼめる〉 shrug one's shoulders

  kuchi o subomeru〈口をすぼめる〉 pucker up one's mouth

sûchi〈すうち：数値〉numerical value.

suchîmu〈スチーム〉steam.

 suchîmu-ga-tootte-iru〈スチームが通っている〉be steam-heated.

sudare〈すだれ〉a reed screen, a bamboo blind.

su-datsu〈すだつ：巣立つ〉leave the nest; graduate ((from)), start in life.

su-de〈すで：素手〉

 su-de-de〈素手で〉empty-handed, with bare hands.

sude-ni〈すでに：既に〉already, yet; previously.

su-doori〈すどおり：素通り〉

 su-doori-suru〈素通りする〉pass through without stopping, pass ((a person's)) door without dropping in.

sue〈すえ：末〉the end, the close; the future.

  shigatsu no sue-goro〈四月の末ごろ〉about the end of April

  Kono-ko-no-sue-wa-dō-naru-koto-yara.（この子の末はどうなることやら.）I wonder what will become of this child.

suekko〈すえっこ：末っ子〉the youngest child.

sue-oki〈すえおき：据え置き〉

 sue-oki-ni-suru〈据え置きにする〉leave ((a matter)) as it is, defer, leave ((a loan)) unredeemed.

 sue-oki-no〈据え置きの〉deferred, unredeemed, unredeemable.

  san-nen-sue-oki-no kôsai〈三年据え置きの公債〉a loan deferred for three years

sueru〈すえる：据える〉

 hara-o-sueru〈腹を据える〉make up one's mind.

sue-tsuke〈すえつけ：据え付け〉installation, fitting.

 sue-tsuke-no〈据え付けの〉fixed, stationary.

sue-tsukeru〈すえつける：据え付ける〉install, set up, fix.

sûgaku〈すうがく：数学〉mathematics, math.

  sûgaku-sha〈数学者〉a mathematician

 sûgaku-no〈数学の〉mathematical.

 sûgaku-jô or *sûgaku-teki-ni*〈数学上，数学的に〉mathematically.

su-gao〈すがお：素顔〉an unpainted face.

sugaru〈すがる〉cling ((to)), hang ((on)), lean ((on)); depend ((on)); appeal ((to)).

  tsue-ni-sugaru〈つえにすがる〉lean on a stick

hito-no-nasake-ni-sugaru (人の情けにすがる) appeal to a person for mercy

sugasugashii 〈すがすがしい〉 refreshing, fresh.

sugasugashii kûki (すがすがしい空気) the fresh air

sugata 〈すがた：姿〉 a figure, a form, a shape.

sugata-ga-ii 〈姿がいい〉 have a good figure.

sugata-o-arawasu 〈姿を現す〉 appear, show oneself.

sugata-o-kuramasu 〈姿をくらます〉 hide oneself.

sugata-mi 〈すがたみ：姿見〉 a full-length mirror.

sugenai 〈すげない〉 cold, blunt, curt, flat.

sugenai henji (すげない返事) a curt answer

sugenaku 〈すげなく〉 coldly, bluntly, curtly, flatly.

sugenaku-kotowaru (すげなく断る) give a flat refusal

sugenaku-suru 〈すげなくする〉 treat ((a person)) coldly, turn the cold shoulder ((to)).

sugi 〈すぎ：杉〉 a Japanese cedar.

-sugi 〈-すぎ：-過ぎ〉 past, after; over, over-.

Ima ni-ji-go-fun-sugi-da. (今二時五分過ぎだ.) It is five minutes past two now.

roku-ji-sugi-made (六時過ぎまで) till after six

Kare-wa go-jû-sugi-da. (彼は五十過ぎだ.) He is over fifty.

tabe-sugi (食べすぎ) overeating

nomi-sugi (飲みすぎ) overdrinking

(-ni)-suginai 〈（に）すぎない〉 only, merely, be nothing but... , be no more than... .

Sore-wa hon-no ichi-rei-ni-suginai. (それはほんの一例にすぎない.) It is only one example.

sugiru 〈すぎる：過ぎる〉 pass.

Mô Nagoya-eki o sugita. (もう名古屋駅を過ぎた.) We have already passed Nagoya Station.

Are-kara san-nen-sugita. (あれから三年過ぎた.) Three years have passed since then.

-sugiru 〈-すぎる：-過ぎる〉 too, to excess.

Kare-wa hataraki-sugiru. (彼は働きすぎる.) He works too hard.

Kono sokkusu wa watashi-ni-wa chiisa-sugiru. (このソックスは私には小さすぎる.) These socks are too small for me.

sugoi 〈すごい〉 dreadful, horrible, terrible, ghastly; wonderful, awful.

sugoi me-tsuki (すごい目つき) a dreadful look

　　　sugoi ude（すごい腕）　wonderful ability
sugoku〈すごく〉extremely, awfully.
　　　sugoku-samui（すごく寒い）　extremely cold
sugo-mi〈すごみ〉
sugo-mi-o-kikaseru　or　*sugomu*〈すごみを利かせる，すごむ〉threaten, intimidate.
sugo-mi-no-aru〈すごみのある〉grim, ghastly.
　　　sugo-mi-no-aru　monku-o-narabe-tateru（すごみのある文句を並べ立てる）make threatening remarks
sugoroku〈すごろく：双六〉backgammon.
sugosu〈すごす：過ごす〉pass, spend, get on.
　　　yasumi o Kyûshû-de sugosu（休みを九州で過ごす）spend one's vacation in Kyushu
　　　Ikaga o-sugoshi-desu-ka?（いかがお過ごしですか.）How are you getting on?
　　　tanoshiku toki-o-sugosu（楽しく時を過ごす）have a good time
　　　do-o-sugosu（度を過ごす）go too far, overdo
sugosugo(-to)〈すごすご（と）〉dejectedly, crestfallenly.
sugu〈すぐ〉at once, right away, immediately, as soon as; soon, before long; easily; right, just.
　　　ima-sugu（今すぐ）right now
　　　Mô-sugu-go-ji-da.（もうすぐ五時だ.）It'll soon be five o'clock.
　　　Kare-no ie wa sugu-wakaru.（彼の家はすぐ分かる.）You can find his house easily.
　　　sugu-me-no-mae-de（すぐ目の前で）right under ((a person's)) nose
sugureru〈すぐれる：優れる〉be better ((than)), be superior ((to)), surpass, be excellent.
sugureta〈優れた〉superior, surpassing, excellent, eminent.
sugure-nai〈優れない〉
　　　kibun-ga-sugure-nai（気分が優れない）feel unwell
　　　kenkô-ga-sugure-nai（健康が優れない）be in poor health
suhada〈すはだ：素肌〉bare skin.
sûhai〈すうはい：崇拝〉worship, admiration, cult.
　　　sûhai-sha（崇拝者）a worshiper, an admirer
sûhai-suru〈崇拝する〉worship, admire.
sui〈すい：酸い〉sour, acid.
　　　Kare-wa　yo-no-naka-no-sui-mo-amai-mo-kami-waketa-hito-da.（彼は世の中の酸いも甘いもかみ分けた人だ.）He has tasted the sweets

and bitters of life.

sui-ageru 〈すいあげる：吸い上げる〉suck up, pump up.

suiatsu 〈すいあつ：水圧〉water pressure.

suibaku 〈すいばく：水爆〉an abbreviation of 'suiso-bakudan'.

suiban 〈すいばん：水盤〉a basin.

suibi 〈すいび：衰微〉a decline, decay.
  suibi-suru 〈衰微する〉decline, decay, fall into decay.

suibô 〈すいぼう：衰亡〉a decline, decay, a downfall, a fall.
  suibô-suru 〈衰亡する〉decline, decay, fall.

suibun 〈すいぶん：水分〉water, juice.
  suibun-no-ooi 〈水分の多い〉watery, juicy.

suichoku 〈すいちょく：垂直〉
    suichoku-sen （垂直線） a vertical line
  suichoku-no 〈垂直の〉vertical, perpendicular.
  suichoku-ni 〈垂直に〉vertically, perpendicularly.

suichû 〈すいちゅう：水中〉
  suichû-no 〈水中の〉underwater.
  suichû-ni 〈水中に〉in the water, under water.
  suichû-kara 〈水中から〉from(*or* out of) the water.

sui-dasu 〈すいだす：吸い出す〉suck(*or* draw) out, aspirate.

suiden 〈すいでん：水田〉a paddy field.

suidô 〈すいどう：水道〉water service, city water; a channel.
    suidô-o-hiku （水道を引く） have water supplied
    suidô o dasu （水道を出す） turn on the tap
    suidô o tomeru （水道を止める） turn off the tap
    suidô-kôji （水道工事） waterworks
    suidô-ryô （水道料） water charges
    Bungo-suidô （豊後水道） the Bungo Channel

suiei 〈すいえい：水泳〉swimming.
    suiei-ga-umai （水泳がうまい） be good at swimming
    suiei-ni-iku （水泳に行く） go swimming
  suiei-suru 〈水泳する〉swim.

suigai 〈すいがい：水害〉damage by a flood, a flood disaster.
    suigai-o-kômuru （水害を被る） suffer from a flood

sui-gara 〈すいがら：吸い殻〉a cigarette end.
    sui-gara o suteru （吸い殻を捨てる） throw away a cigarette end

suigen(-chi) 〈すいげん（ち）：水源（地）〉the source 〔of a river〕.

suigin 〈すいぎん：水銀〉mercury.

suigyū〈すいぎゅう：水牛〉a (water) buffalo.

suihan-ki〈すいはんき：炊飯器〉a rice cooker.

suihei〈すいへい：水兵〉a sailor.

suihei〈すいへい：水平〉

    suihei-sen（水平線）the horizon

 suihei-no〈水平の〉level, horizontal.

 suihei-ni〈水平に〉at a level ((with)), horizontally.

    suihei-ni-suru（水平にする）make level

suihō〈すいほう：水泡〉

 suihō-ni-kisuru〈水泡に帰する〉come to nothing, be in vain, end in a failure.

suihō〈すいほう：水ほう〉a blister, a vesicle, a bulla.

suii〈すいい：水位〉a water level.

suii〈すいい：推移〉(a) transition, (a) change.

 suii-suru〈推移する〉change, undergo a change, shift.

    jidai-ga-suii-suru-ni-tsurete（時代が推移するにつれて）with the change of times

suiiki〈すいいき：水域〉the water area, waters.

suijaku〈すいじゃく：衰弱〉weakening.

    suijaku-ga-hidoku-naru（衰弱がひどくなる）become much weaker

 suijaku-suru〈衰弱する〉weaken, grow weak.

 suijaku-shite-iru〈衰弱している〉be weak.

suiji〈すいじ：炊事〉cooking.

    suiji-dōgu（炊事道具）cooking utensils

    suiji-ba（炊事場）a kitchen

 suiji-suru〈炊事する〉cook.

suijō〈すいじょう：水上〉

    suijō-keisatsu（水上警察）the water police

    suijō-kyōgi（水上競技）water sports

    suijō-resutoran（水上レストラン）a floating restaurant

 suijō-de or *suijō-ni*〈水上で，水上に〉on the water.

suijōki〈すいじょうき：水蒸気〉steam, vapor.

suijun〈すいじゅん：水準〉a level, a standard.

    suijun ni tassuru（水準に達する）reach the level

    suijun-ika-de-aru（水準以下である）be below the level

    seikatsu-suijun（生活水準）the standard of living

    suijun-ki（水準器）a level

suika〈すいか〉a watermelon.

suikei〈すいけい：推計〉(an) estimation.
 suikei-suru〈推計する〉estimate.
suikô〈すいこう：遂行〉accomplishment, performance, execution.
 suikô-suru〈遂行する〉accomplish, perform, execute.
sui-komu〈すいこむ：吸い込む〉breathe in, inhale; suck in, absorb.
suikyô〈すいきょう：酔狂〉
 suikyô-na〈酔狂な〉whimsical, fanciful, eccentric.
suikyū〈すいきゅう：水球〉water polo.
suimen〈すいめん：水面〉the surface of the water.
 suimen-ni ukabu（水面に浮かぶ）float on the surface of the water
suimin〈すいみん：睡眠〉sleep.
 suimin-busoku（睡眠不足）want of sleep
 suimin-jikan（睡眠時間）hours of sleep, sleeping hours
 suimin-yaku *or* suimin-zai（睡眠薬，睡眠剤）a sleeping drug
 suimin-o-toru〈睡眠をとる〉sleep, have a sleep.
suimon〈すいもん：水門〉a floodgate, a sluice gate, a lock gate.
sui-mono〈すいもの：吸い物〉soup.
 sui-mono-wan（吸い物わん）a soup bowl
suimyaku〈すいみゃく：水脈〉a water vein.
suinan〈すいなん：水難〉a disaster by water.
suion〈すいおん：水温〉the temperature of the water.
suirei〈すいれい：水冷〉
 suirei-shiki-no〈水冷式の〉water-cooled.
suiren〈すいれん：睡れん〉a water lily.
suiri〈すいり：推理〉reasoning, (an) inference.
 suiri-ryoku（推理力）reasoning power
 suiri-shôsetsu（推理小説）a detective story, a mystery
 suiri-suru〈推理する〉reason, infer ((from)).
suiri〈すいり：水利〉water supply.
 suiri-ga-ii（水利がいい）have sufficient water supply
sui-riku〈すいりく：水陸〉land and water.
 sui-riku-ryôyô-no〈水陸両用の〉amphibious.
suiro〈すいろ：水路〉a waterway, a water course, a channel.
 suiro-hyôshiki（水路標識）a beacon
 suiro-zu（水路図）a hydrographic map
suiron〈すいろん：推論〉ratiocination, (an) inference.
 suiron-suru〈推論する〉ratiocinate, infer ((from)).
suiryô〈すいりょう；水量〉the quantity of water.

suiryô〈すいりょう：推量〉*see.* suisoku.

suiryoku〈すいりょく：水力〉water power.

    suiryoku-hatsuden-sho（水力発電所）a hydroelectric power station

suiryoku〈すいりょく：推力〉impellent force.

suiryû〈すいりゅう：水流〉a (water) current, a stream.

suisai-ga〈すいさいが：水彩画〉a watercolor.

suisan〈すいさん：水産〉

    suisan-butsu（水産物）marine products

    suisan-gyô（水産業）fisheries

suisan-ka-butsu〈すいさんかぶつ：水酸化物〉a hydroxid(e).

sui-sashi〈すいさし：吸いさし〉a half-smoked cigarette, a cigarette butt.

suisatsu〈すいさつ：推察〉*see.* suisoku.

    Shinchû-no-hodo-go-suisatsu-môshi-agemasu.（心中の程御推察申し上げ
    ます。）I deeply sympathize with you.

suisei〈すいせい：水星〉Mercury.

suisei〈すいせい：すい星〉a comet.

suisei〈すいせい：水せい〉

    suisei-dôbutsu（水せい動物）an aquatic animal

  suisei-no〈水せいの〉aquatic.

suisei-toryô〈すいせいとりょう：水性塗料〉water paint.

suisen〈すいせん：水仙〉a narcissus, a jonquil, a daffodil.

suisen〈すいせん：垂線〉a perpendicular (line).

suisen〈すいせん：推薦〉recommendation.

    suisen-jô（推薦状）a letter of recommendation

    suisen-sha（推薦者）a recommender

  suisen-suru（推薦する）recommend.

  ～-no-suisen-de〈～の推薦で〉through the recommendation of... .

suisen-benjo〈すいせんべんじょ：水洗便所〉a flush toilet.

suisha〈すいしゃ：水車〉a water wheel.

    suisha-goya（水車小屋）a (water) mill

suishi〈すいし：水死〉death by drowning.

suishin〈すいしん：垂心〉an orthocenter.

suishin〈すいしん：水深〉the depth of water.

    suishin o hakaru（水深を測る）sound the depth of water

suishin〈すいしん：推進〉propulsion, drive.

suishitsu〈すいしつ：水質〉the quality of water.

suishô〈すいしょう：水晶〉crystal.

    suishô-tai（水晶体）the crystalline lens

    murasaki-suishō〈紫水晶〉amethyst

suishō〈すいしょう：推奨〉recommendation, commendation.

 suishô-suru〈推奨する〉recommend, commend.

 suishô-su-beki〈推奨すべき〉commendable.

suiso〈すいそ：水素〉hydrogen.

    suiso-bakudan（水素爆弾）a hydrogen bomb, an H-bomb

suisô〈すいそう：水槽〉a (water) tank, a cistern, an aquarium.

suisô〈すいそう：水葬〉

 suisô-ni-suru〈水葬にする〉bury at sea.

suisô〈すいそう：吹奏〉

    suisô-gakki（吹奏楽器）a wind instrument

    suisô-gaku（吹奏楽）wind-instrument music

      suisô-gaku-dan（吹奏楽団）a brass band

 suisô-suru〈吹奏する〉blow, play.

suisoku〈すいそく：推測〉a guess, (a) conjecture, (an) inference.

 suisoku-suru〈推測する〉guess, conjecture, infer ((from)).

Suisu〈スイス〉Switzerland.

    Suisu-jin（スイス人）a Swiss

    Suisu(-jin)-no（スイス(人)の）Swiss

suisui〈すいすい〉lightly.

 suisui-tobu〈すいすい飛ぶ〉flit.

suitchi〈スイッチ〉a switch.

 suitchi-o-ireru〈スイッチを入れる〉switch on.

    suitchi-o-kiru（スイッチを切る）switch off

suitei〈すいてい：推定〉(a) presumption, (an) assumption, (an) inference.

    suitei-kakaku（推定価格）the presumed value

 suitei-suru〈推定する〉presume, assume, infer.

suiteki〈すいてき：水滴〉a drop of water.

suitô〈すいとう：出納〉receipts and disbursements.

    suitô-bo（出納簿）a cashbook, an account book

    suitô-gakari（出納係）a cashier, a teller

suitô〈すいとう：水筒〉a canteen, a flask.

suitori-gami〈すいとりがみ：吸い取り紙〉blotting paper.

sui-toru〈すいとる：吸い取る〉absorb, suck up, soak up.

sui-tsuku〈すいつく：吸い付く〉adhere(*or* stick) ((to)).

    sui-tsuite-hanare-nai（吸い付いて離れない）stick fast ((to))

suiyô-bi〈すいようび：水曜日〉Wednesday.

suiyô-sei〈すいようせい：水溶性〉

suiyô-sei-no〈水溶性の〉water-soluble.

suizô〈すいぞう：すい臓〉the pancreas.

suizokkan〈すいぞっかん：水族館〉an aquarium.

suji〈すじ：筋〉a line, a stripe; a tendon; a string; a plot; reason, logic; quarters, a source; an aptitude.

  monogatari no suji〈物語の筋〉the plot of a story

  tashika-na suji〈確かな筋〉a reliable source

  suji-ga-ii〈筋がいい〉have a natural aptitude ((for))

suji-o-chigaeru〈筋を違える〉sprain.

suji-no-ooi〈筋の多い〉stringy.

suji-no-tootta〈筋の通った〉logical, reasonable, coherent.

  suji-no-toora-nai〈筋の通らない〉illogical, unreasonable, incoherent

sûji〈すうじ：数字〉a figure, a numeral.

  Arabia-sûji〈アラビア数字〉an Arabic numeral

sujiai〈すじあい：筋合い〉reason.

  Kimi-ni-sonna-koto-o-iwareru-sujiai-wa-nai.〈君にそんなことを言われる筋合いはない。〉You have no right to say such a thing (to me).

suji-chigai〈すじちがい：筋違い〉a wrick; unreasonableness.

suji-chigai-no〈筋違いの〉illogical, unreasonable, absurd, wrong.

suji-gaki〈すじがき：筋書き〉a synopsis; a plan, a program, a schedule.

suji-gaki-doori-ni〈筋書きどおりに〉as planned, according to schedule.

suji-gane〈すじがね：筋金〉

suji-gane-iri-no〈筋金入りの〉dyed-in-the-wool.

suji-kai〈すじかい：筋交い〉a diagonal beam, a brace.

sujiko〈すじこ：筋子〉salmon roe.

sûjiku〈すうじく：すう軸〉a pivot, an axis, an axle; a central point, the center.

suji-michi〈すじみち：筋道〉reason, logic.

suji-michi-no-tootta or *suji-michi-no-tatta*〈筋道の通った，筋道の立った〉*see.* suji-no-tootta.

  suji-michi-no-toora-nai *or* suji-michi-no-tata-nai〈筋道の通らない，筋道の立たない〉*see.* suji-no-toora-nai

suji-mukai〈すじむかい：筋向かい〉

suji-mukai-no or *suji-mukai-ni*〈筋向かいの，筋向かいに〉diagonally opposite.

sûjitsu〈すうじつ：数日〉(for) a few days.

sûjitsu-chû-ni〈数日中に〉in a few days.

sujô〈すじょう：素性〉birth, blood, origin; identity.

sūjū-〈すうじゅう‐：数十‐〉
　　sūjū-nin-no-hito（数十人の人）　dozens of people
　　sūjū-nen-kan（数十年間）　for several decades
Sukanjinabia〈スカンジナビア〉Scandinavia.
sukasazu〈すかさず〉without a moment's delay, at once, without hesitation.
sukashi〈すかし：透かし〉a watermark, openwork.
sukasu〈すかす：透かす〉make transparent.
　sukashite-miru〈透かして見る〉look through, peer ((into)), hold ((a thing)) against the light.
sukasu〈すかす〉
　o-naka-o-sukasu〈おなかをすかす〉feel hungry.
sukasu〈すかす〉coax, cajole, wheedle, persuade.
sukâto〈スカート〉a skirt.
　　sukâto o haku（スカートをはく）　put on one's skirt
　　sukâto o nugu（スカートを脱ぐ）　take off one's skirt
sukejûru〈スケジュール〉a schedule.
　　sukejûru o tateru（スケジュールを立てる）　make out a schedule
　sukejûru-doori-ni〈スケジュールどおりに〉as scheduled.
sukeru〈すける：透ける〉be transparent.
　sukete-mieru〈透けて見える〉be seen through.
　　sukete-mieru burausu（透けて見えるブラウス）　a sheer blouse
sukêru〈スケール〉a scale.
　sukêru-no-ookii〈スケールの大きい〉large-scaled.
　　sukêru-no-chiisai（スケールの小さい）　small-scaled
suketchi〈スケッチ〉sketching, a sketch.
　　suketchi-ni-iku（スケッチに行く）　go sketching
　suketchi-suru〈スケッチする〉sketch, make a sketch ((of)).
sukêto〈スケート〉skating, skates.
　　sukêto-ni-iku（スケートに行く）　go skating
　　sukêto-gutsu（スケート靴）　a pair of skates
　　sukêto-jô（スケート場）　a skating rink
suki〈すき〉a spade, a plow.
suki〈すき〉an opening, a gap; a chance, an opportunity; an unguarded point.
　　suki-o-nerau（すきをねらう）　watch for a chance
　　ichibu-no-suki-mo-nai（一分のすきもない）　be thoroughly on the alert
suki〈すき：好き〉liking, fondness.

suki-de-aru〈好きである〉like, be fond ((of)).

suki-na〈好きな〉favorite.

    suki-na supôtsu（好きなスポーツ）one's favorite sport

suki-na-yô-ni-suru〈好きなようにする〉do as one pleases.

sukī〈スキー〉skiing, skis.

    sukī-ni-iku（スキーに行く）go skiing

    sukī-gutsu（スキー靴）ski boots

    sukī-jô（スキー場）a skiing ground

sûki〈すうき：数奇〉

sûki-na-ummei-o-tadoru〈数奇な運命をたどる〉be the sport of fortune.

suki-bara〈すきばら：すき腹〉an empty stomach.

    Suki-bara-ni-mazui-mono-nashi.（すき腹にまずい物なし.）Hunger is the best sauce.

suki-kirai〈すききらい：好き嫌い〉likes and dislikes, taste.

    tabe-mono-ni suki-kirai-ga-aru（食べ物に好き嫌いがある）have likes and dislikes in food

suki-ma〈すきま：透き間〉an opening, a gap.

    suki-ma-kaze（すき間風）a draft

suki-ma-naku〈透き間なく〉closely, compactly.

suki-tooru〈すきとおる：透き通る〉be transparent, be seen through.

suki-tootta〈透き通った〉transparent, clear.

    suki-tootta mizu（透き通った水）clear water

sukkarakan〈すっからかん〉

sukkarakan-ni-naru〈すっからかんになる〉become quite penniless.

sukkari〈すっかり〉quite, all, completely, perfectly, entirely.

    sukkari kuraku-naru（すっかり暗くなる）become quite dark

    sukkari wasureru（すっかり忘れる）forget all

    sukkari kawaru（すっかり変わる）change completely

sukkiri〈すっきり〉

sukkiri-suru〈すっきりする〉feel refreshed.

sukkiri-shita〈すっきりした〉refreshed; neat.

sûkô〈すうこう：崇高〉

sûkô-na〈崇高な〉sublime, lofty, noble, grand.

sukoâ〈スコアー〉a score.

    san-tai-ni-no-sukoâ-de（三対二のスコアーで）by a score of 3 to 2

sukoppu〈スコップ〉a shovel, a scoop.

sukoshi〈すこし：少し〉a few, a little, some; a moment; a little way.

    Sukoshi kane o motte-iru.（少し金を持っている.）I have a little

money with me.

Sukoshi-shika　kane　o　motte-i-nai.（少ししか金を持っていない。）I have little money with me.

mô-sukoshi-ato-de（もう少し後で）a little later

sukoshi-mae（少し前）a little while ago

Sukoshi　o-machi-kudasai.（少しお待ちください。）Just a moment, please.

sukoshi-hanarete（少し離れて）a little way off

sukoshi-mo ～nai〈少しも～ない〉not at all, not in the least.

Kono jisho wa sukoshi-mo yaku-ni-tata-nai.（この辞書は少しも役に立たない。）This dictionary is of no use at all.

sukoshi-zutsu〈少しずつ〉little by little, gradually.

Sukottorando〈スコットランド〉Scotland.

Sukottorando-jin（スコットランド人）the Scotch; a Scotchman, a Scotchwoman

Sukottorando(-jin)-no（スコットランド(人)の）Scotch, Scottish

sukoyaka〈すこやか：健やか〉

sukoyaka-na〈健やかな〉healthy, sound, robust.

suku〈すく：好く〉like, be fond ((of)).

sukareru〈好かれる〉be liked, be loved, be popular ((with)).

Kanojo-wa　dare-ni-demo　sukareru.（彼女はだれにでも好かれる。）She is liked by everybody.

suku〈すく〉comb, card.

suku〈すく〉make〔paper〕.

suku〈すく〉plow, plough.

suku〈すく〉

Kono basu wa suite-iru.（このバスはすいている。）This bus is not crowded.

hara-ga-suku（腹がすく）feel hungry

te-ga-suite-iru（手がすいている）be free, be unoccupied

sukui〈すくい：救い〉help, rescue, aid, salvation.

sukui-o-motomeru（救いを求める）ask for help

sukui-ageru〈すくいあげる：救い上げる〉bring ((a person)) to land.

sukui-ageru〈すくいあげる：すくい上げる〉dip up.

sukui-dasu〈すくいだす：救い出す〉rescue ((a person)) from.

sukui-dasu〈すくいだす：すくい出す〉ladle(*or* bail) out.

sukuizu〈スクイズ〉a squeeze play.

sukuizu o yaru（スクイズをやる）run a squeeze

sukumeru〈すくめる〉duck, shrug.

kubi o sukumeru（首をすくめる）duck one's head

sukumu〈すくむ〉cower.

sukunai〈すくない：少ない〉few, little, scarce, rare, short of.

sukunakarazu〈少なからず〉not a few, not a little.

sukunakarazu-odoroku（少なからず驚く）be not a little surprised

sukunaku-tomo〈少なくとも〉at least.

sukuramu〈スクラム〉a scrummage, a scrum.

sukuramu o kumu（スクラムを組む）form a scrummage

sukurappu〈スクラップ〉(a) scrap.

sukurappu-to-shite uru（スクラップとして売る）sell as scrap

sukurappu-ni-suru〈スクラップにする〉scrap.

sukusuku〈すくすく〉

sukusuku-sodatsu〈すくすく育つ〉grow up rapidly.

sukuu〈すくう：救う〉rescue, save, help, relieve, redeem.

hito-ga-obore-kakatte-iru-no-o-sukuu（人がおぼれかかっているのを救う）save a person from drowning

sukuu〈すくう〉scoop (up), dip (up), ladle out; trip ((a person)) (up).

sukuu〈すくう：巣食う〉build a nest, nest; haunt, have one's den ((at or in)).

sumai〈すまい：住まい〉a dwelling, a house.

Dochira-ni o-sumai-desu-ka?（どちらにお住まいですか.）Where do you live?

sumanai〈すまない：済まない〉

sumanai-to-omou（すまないと思う）feel sorry ((for)), be conscience-stricken

sumanai-koto-o-suru（すまないことをする）do ((a person)) wrong

sumashi-jiru〈すましじる：澄まし汁〉clear soup.

sumasu〈すます：済ます〉finish, settle.

shigoto o sumasu（仕事を済ます）finish one's work

kanjō o sumasu（勘定を済ます）settle one's accounts ((with))

～-nashi-de-sumasu〈～なしで済ます〉do without... .

sumasu〈すます：澄ます〉clear, clarify; look prim, look unconcerned, play the innocent, put on airs; prick up〔one's ears〕.

sumashite〈澄まして〉with a serious face, with an indifferent air, with an affected air.

sumâto〈スマート〉

sumâto-na〈スマートな〉smart, stylish.

sumbun〈すんぶん：寸分〉
 sumbun-tagawa-nai〈寸分たがわない〉be not a bit different ((from)), be just the same ((as)).
 sumbun-tagawazu-ni〈寸分たがわずに〉exactly to an inch.
sumi〈すみ：炭〉charcoal.
 sumi-bi（炭火） charcoal fire
sumi〈すみ：墨〉India(n) ink, an ink stick.
 sumi o suru（墨をする） rub an ink stick
 sumi-e（墨絵） an Indian-ink drawing
sumi〈すみ：隅〉a corner, a nook.
 sumi-ni〈隅に〉in a corner.
　Kare-wa nakanaka sumi-ni-oke-nai.（彼はなかなか隅に置けない．） He is a very smart fellow.
sumi-komi〈すみこみ：住み込み〉living in.
 sumi-komi-no-meido（住み込みのメイド） a maid who lives in
 sumi-komu〈住み込む〉live in.
sumi-masen〈すみません〉I am sorry, Excuse me.
　O-matase-shite-sumi-masen.（お待たせしてすみません．） I am sorry to have kept you waiting.
　Sumi-masen-ga kyōkai-e-iku-michi-o-oshiete-kudasai-masen-ka?（すみませんが教会へ行く道を教えてくださいませんか．） Excuse me, but will you show me the way to the church?
sumi-nareta〈すみなれた：住み慣れた〉
 sumi-nareta ie（住み慣れた家） one's dear old house
 sumi-nareta tochi（住み慣れた土地） a place where one has lived long
sumire〈すみれ〉a violet.
 sumire-iro（すみれ色） a violet color
 san-shoku-sumire（三色すみれ） a pansy
sumi-tsuku〈すみつく：住み着く〉settle ((in)).
sumiyaka〈すみやか：速やか〉
 sumiyaka-na〈速やかな〉rapid, prompt, immediate, quick.
 sumiyaka-ni〈速やかに〉rapidly, promptly, immediately, quickly.
sumizumi〈すみずみ：隅々〉all the corners ((of)).
　heya-no-sumizumi-made-yoku-sôji-o-suru（部屋の隅々までよく掃除をする） sweep all the corners of a room
sumô〈すもう：相撲〉*sumo* (wrestling).
 sumô-o-toru〈相撲を取る〉wrestle ((with)).

sumoggu 〈スモッグ〉 smog.

sumoggu-no-ooi or *sumoggu-no-kakatta* 〈スモッグの多い，スモッグのかかった〉 smoggy.

sumomo 〈すもも〉 a (Japanese) plum.

sumpô 〈すんぽう：寸法〉 measure, dimensions, size.

sumpô-o-toru 〈寸法をとる〉 measure, take ((a person's)) measure(*or* measurements).

sumpô-doori-ni 〈寸法どおりに〉 according to one's measurements.

sumu 〈すむ：住む〉 live, dwell, reside.

　　Ane wa Hokkaidô-ni-sunde-iru. (姉は北海道に住んでいる。) My sister lives in Hokkaido.

　　Watashi-wa ima oba-no-ie-ni-sundeiru. (私は今叔(伯)母の家に住んでいる。) I am living now with my aunt.

sumu 〈すむ：済む〉 end, come to an end, be finished, be done, be over.

　　Chôshoku wa sumimashita-ka? (朝食は済みましたか。) Have you finished your breakfast?

　　Kyô-no shigoto wa yo-ji-ni-wa sumimasu. (今日の仕事は四時には済みます。) My day's work will be done by four.

　　Sunda-koto-wa-shikata-ga-nai. (済んだ事は仕方がない。) What is done is done.

　　buji-ni-sumu (無事に済む) come off(*or* be settled) without a mishap, get away with (it)

sumu 〈すむ：澄む〉 become clear, clarify.

sunda 〈澄んだ〉 clear, lucid, transparent.

　　sunda sora (澄んだ空) a clear sky

suna 〈すな：砂〉 sand.

　　suna-hama *or* suna-ji (砂浜，砂地) the sands

suna-no(-ooi) 〈砂の(多い)〉 sandy.

suna-bokori 〈すなぼこり：砂ぼこり〉 a cloud of dust.

sunao 〈すなお：素直〉

sunao-na 〈素直な〉 gentle, obedient, docile.

sunao-ni 〈素直に〉 gently, obediently.

sunappu-shashin 〈スナップしゃしん：スナップ写真〉 a snapshot, a snap.

　　sunappu-shashin o toru (スナップ写真を撮る) take a snapshot ((of)), snap.

sunawachi 〈すなわち〉 namely, that is.

sundan 〈すんだん：寸断〉

sundan-suru 〈寸断する〉 cut to pieces.

sune 〈すね〉 the shank, the shin.
　oya-no-sune-o-kajiru 〈親のすねをかじる〉 hang on one's parents.

sûnen 〈すうねん：数年〉 several years.
　sûnen-mo-sureba 〈数年もすれば〉 in a few years.
　koko-sûnen-rai 〈ここ数年来〉 in the last few years.

suneru 〈すねる〉 be sulky(*or* peevish), sulk.

sungeki 〈すんげき：寸劇〉 a short play, a skit.

sunka 〈すんか：寸暇〉
　sunka-o-oshinde 〈寸暇を惜しんで〉 utilizing every odd moment.

sunnari(-to) 〈すんなり（と）〉
　　sunnari katsu 〈すんなり勝つ〉 win easily
　　sunnari yôkyû o nomu 〈すんなり要求をのむ〉 accept ((a person's)) request so simply

sunoko 〈すのこ：すの子〉 a drainboard.

sunshi 〈すんし：寸志〉 a little token of one's gratitude.

sunzen 〈すんぜん：寸前〉
　sunzen-ni 〈寸前に〉 immediately before.

supai 〈スパイ〉 a spy.
　　supai-kôi （スパイ行為） spying, espionage
　　nijû-supai （二重スパイ） a double agent
　supai-o-suru 〈スパイをする〉 spy.

supaiku 〈スパイク〉 a spike.
　　supaiku-shûzu （スパイクシューズ） spiked shoes
　supaiku-suru 〈スパイクする〉 spike.

Suparuta 〈スパルタ〉 Sparta.
　Suparuta-shiki-no 〈スパルタ式の〉 Spartan.

supasupa 〈すぱすぱ〉
　tabako-o-supasupa-suu 〈たばこをすぱすぱ吸う〉 puff away at one's cigarette.

Supein 〈スペイン〉 Spain.
　　Supein-jin （スペイン人） a Spaniard
　　Supein-go （スペイン語） Spanish
　　Supein(-jin)-no （スペイン（人）の） Spanish

supekutoru 〈スペクトル〉 a spectrum.
　　supekutoru-bunseki （スペクトル分析） spectrum analysis

supîdo 〈スピード〉 speed.
　　jisoku go-jukkiro no supîdo-de （時速五十キロのスピードで） at the speed of 50 kilometers an hour

supîdo-ihan （スピード違反） speeding

supîdo-o-ageru 〈スピードを上げる〉 speed up, get up speed.

supîdo-o-otosu （スピードを落とす） slow down, reduce speed

supîkâ 〈スピーカー〉 a loudspeaker.

suponji 〈スポンジ〉 sponge.

supôtsu 〈スポーツ〉 sports, a sport.

supôtsu-o-yaru （スポーツをやる） take part in a sport

supôtsu-gi （スポーツ着） sportswear

supôtsu-hôsô （スポーツ放送） sportscasting

supôtsu-kisha （スポーツ記者） a sportswriter

supôtsu-ran （スポーツ欄） a sports section

supôtsu-seishin （スポーツ精神） sportsmanship

supôtsu-yôhin （スポーツ用品） sporting goods

suppai 〈すっぱい：酸っぱい〉 sour.

suppai-aji-ga-suru （酸っぱい味がする） taste sour

suppaku-naru （酸っぱくなる） turn sour

suppa-nuku 〈すっぱぬく：素っ破抜く〉 disclose, expose, give away, debunk.

suppokasu 〈すっぽかす〉 give ((a person)) the slip, stand up, leave ((a task)) undone.

yakusoku-o-suppokasu （約束をすっぽかす） break one's word

suppon 〈すっぽん〉 a snapping turtle.

tsuki-to-suppon-no-chigai-ga-aru （月とすっぽんの違いがある） be as different as light from darkness

suppori 〈すっぽり〉

fûdo-o-suppori-kaburu 〈フードをすっぽりかぶる〉 cover one's head completely with a hood.

sûpu 〈スープ〉 soup.

sûpu o nomu （スープを飲む） eat soup

supûn 〈スプーン〉 a spoon.

supûn-ippai-no-satô （スプーン一杯の砂糖） a spoonful of sugar

-sura 〈-すら〉 *see.* -sae.

Surabu 〈スラブ〉

Surabu-jin （スラブ人） a Slav

Surabu-minzoku （スラブ民族） the Slavs

Surabu-go （スラブ語） Slavic

Surabu-jin-no *or* Surabu-minzoku-no （スラブ人の，スラブ民族の） Slavic

suraido〈スライド〉a slide.

    suraido o eisha-suru（スライドを映写する）project a slide

    suraido-sei（スライド制）a sliding scale system

surampu〈スランプ〉a slump.

    surampu-ni-ochiiru（スランプに陥る）get into a slump

    surampu-o-dassuru（スランプを脱する）come out of a slump

surari-to-shita〈すらりとした〉slender, slim, graceful.

surasura(-to)〈すらすら(と)〉smoothly, easily, fluently.

    Banji surasura-to hakonda.（万事すらすらと運んだ.）Everything went on smoothly.

    muzukashii mondai o surasura-to toku（難しい問題をすらすらと解く）solve a difficult question easily

    Eigo o surasura-to shaberu（英語をすらすらとしゃべる）speak English fluently

sure-chigau〈すれちがう：擦れ違う〉pass each other.

sureru〈すれる：擦れる〉rub, wear; lose one's native simplicity.

suresure(-ni)〈すれすれ(に)：擦れ擦れ(に)〉

    suresure-ni-ma-ni-au（擦れ擦れに間に合う）be barely in time ((for))

    kaimen-suresure-ni-tobu（海面擦れ擦れに飛ぶ）skip the surface of the sea

surêto〈スレート〉a slate.

    surêto-buki-no ie（スレートぶきの家）a slate-roofed house

sûretsu〈すうれつ：数列〉a sequence of numbers.

    tôhi-sûretsu（等比数列）geometrical progression

suri〈すり〉a pickpocket.

    suri-ni saifu-o-surareru（すりに財布をすられる）have one's pocket picked of a purse

sûri〈すうり：数理〉a mathematical principle.

    sûri-tôkei-gaku（数理統計学）mathematical statistics

sûri-teki(-na)〈数理的(な)〉mathematical.

sûri-teki-ni or *sûri-jô*〈数理的に，数理上〉mathematically.

suri-agari〈すりあがり：刷り上がり〉completion of printing.

    suri-agari-ga-ii（刷り上がりがいい）be well printed

suri-agaru〈刷り上がる〉be off the press.

suri-bachi〈すりばち：すり鉢〉an earthenware mortar.

suri-bachi-gata-no〈すり鉢形の〉cone-shaped, conic(al).

suri-garasu〈すりガラス：擦りガラス〉frosted(*or* ground) glass.

suri-herasu〈すりへらす：すり減らす〉wear away, rub off.

shinkei o suri-herasu〔神経をすり減らす〕 exhaust one's nerves

suri-kaeru〈すりかえる：すり替える〉substitute ((one thing for another)) secretly.

suri-kireru〈すりきれる：擦り切れる〉wear out, be worn out.

suri-kireta〈擦り切れた〉worn-out.

suriko-gi〈すりこぎ：すり粉木〉a wooden pestle.

suri-komu〈すりこむ：擦り込む〉rub in.

suri-muku〈すりむく：擦りむく〉graze, abrade, chafe, bark, skin.

surippa〈スリッパ〉slippers, scuffs.

suriru〈スリル〉a thrill.

suriru-ni-tonda〈スリルに富んだ〉thrilling.

suri-tsubusu〈すりつぶす〉grind down, mash.

suri-yoru〈すりよる：すり寄る〉nestle ((to)).

surôgan〈スローガン〉a slogan, a motto.

suru〈する：刷る〉print, put in print.

suru〈する〉pick ((a person's)) pocket ((of)).

suru〈する：擦る〉rub, strike.

matchi o suru（マッチを擦る） strike a match

suru〈する〉lose, forfeit.

ari-gane o nokorazu suru（有り金を残らずする） lose all one's money

suru〈する〉grind, bray.

suru〈する〉do; play; make; cost.

shigoto o suru（仕事をする） do one's work

suru-koto-ga-nai（することがない） have nothing to do

yakyû-o-suru（野球をする） play baseball

hito o shiawase-ni-suru（人を幸せにする） make a person happy

Ikura shimashita-ka?（幾らしましたか.） How much did you pay for it?

surudoi〈するどい：鋭い〉sharp, keen, piercing; biting, cutting, acute.

surudoi ha（鋭い刃） a sharp edge

shûkaku-ga-surudoi（臭覚が鋭い） be keen of scent

surudoi hihan（鋭い批判） a biting criticism

surudoku〈鋭く〉sharply, keenly, acutely.

surudoku-suru *or* surudoku-naru（鋭くする, 鋭くなる） sharpen

surume〈するめ〉dried cuttlefish.

sururi-to〈するりと〉

sururi-to-hazureru〈するりと外れる〉slip out of place.

surusuru(-to)〈するする（と）〉

surusuru-to ki-ni-noboru 〈するすると木に登る〉 climb up a tree with ease.

suruto 〈すると〉 then, and just then, thereupon.

sûryô 〈すうりょう：数量〉 quantity, volume.

susamajii 〈すさまじい〉 terrible, horrible, terrific, dreadful, tremendous, amazing.

     susamajii oto（すさまじい音） a terrific sound

susamu 〈すさむ〉 grow wild.

     susanda-seikatsu o okuru（すさんだ生活を送る） lead a dissolute life

sûsei 〈すうせい：すう勢〉 a tendency, a trend.

sushi 〈すし〉 *sushi*, vinegared rice ball with raw fish and shellfish, etc. on.

sûshi 〈すうし：数詞〉 a numeral.

sushi-zume-no 〈すしづめの：すし詰めの〉 jam-packed.

suso 〈すそ〉 the skirt, the cuffs; the foot.

     Kare-wa zubon no suso o makuri-ageta.（彼はズボンのすそをまくり上げた。） He rolled up the cuffs of his trousers.

suso-no 〈すその：すそ野〉 the foot of a mountain.

susu 〈すす〉 soot.

     susu o harau（すすを払う） sweep away soot

susu-darake-no 〈すすだらけの〉 sooty.

susugu 〈すすぐ〉 wash, rinse.

susukeru 〈すすける〉 become sooty.

susuki 〈すすき〉 Japanese pampas grass.

susume 〈すすめ：勧め〉 recommendation, advice, encouragement.

     hito-no susume-de（人の勧めで） by a person's advice

susumeru 〈勧める〉 recommend, advise, encourage, urge; offer.

     sake o susumeru（酒を勧める） offer ((a person)) a drink

susumu 〈すすむ：進む〉 advance, go forward, progress, make progress; gain, be fast.

     Doitsu-go-ga-susunde-iru（ドイツ語が進んでいる） be advanced in German

     daigaku-e susumu（大学へ進む） go on to college

     Watashi-no tokei wa ni-fun-susunde-iru.（私の時計は二分進んでいる。） My watch is two minutes fast.

     shoku-ga-susumu（食が進む） have a good appetite

     byôjô-ga-kanari-susunde-iru（病状がかなり進んでいる） be pretty far gone in one's illness

susumeru 〈進める〉 advance, put forward; hasten, speed (up).

　　　tokei o juppun susumeru（時計を十分進める）put a clock forward by
　　　　ten minutes
　　　kôji-o-susumeru（工事を進める）go ahead with the works

susuri-naki〈すすりなき：すすり泣き〉sobbing
　susuri-naku〈すすり泣く〉sob.

susuru〈すする〉sip, sup, suck (up).
　　　cha o susuru（茶をすする）sip tea.

sutâ〈スター〉a star.
　　　eiga-sutâ（映画スター）a film star

sutaffu〈スタッフ〉a staff.
　　　sutaffu-no-ichi-in-de-aru（スタッフの一員である）be on the staff ((of))
　sutaffu-o-ire-kaeru〈スタッフを入れ替える〉restaff.

sutairu〈スタイル〉a style, a figure.
　　　saishin-ryûkô-no sutairu（最新流行のスタイル）the latest style
　　　sutairu-ga-ii（スタイルがいい）have a good figure
　　　sutairu-ga-warui（スタイルが悪い）have a poor style

sutajiamu〈スタジアム〉a stadium.

sutajio〈スタジオ〉a studio.

sutakora(-to)〈すたこら(と)〉hurriedly.
　sutakora-nigeru〈すたこら逃げる〉beat a hasty retreat.

sutamina〈スタミナ〉stamina.
　　　sutamina-ga-aru（スタミナがある）have stamina
　　　sutamina-ga-nai（スタミナがない）lack stamina
　　　sutamina o tsukeru（スタミナを付ける）build up stamina

sutampu〈スタンプ〉a stamp, a datemark, a postmark.
　　　kinen-sutampu（記念スタンプ）a commemorative stamp
　sutampu-o-osu〈スタンプを押す〉stamp.

sutando〈スタンド〉a stand, bleachers; a desk lamp, a floor lamp.

sutando-purê〈スタンドプレー〉a grandstand play.
　sutando-purê-o-yaru〈スタンドプレーをやる〉make a grandstand.

sutareru〈すたれる：廃れる〉be out of use, become obsolete, go out of
　fashion, be done away ((with)).
　sutareta（廃れた）disused, out of fashion.

sutasuta〈すたすた〉briskly, quickly, rapidly.

sutâto〈スタート〉a start.
　　　sutâto-gakari（スタート係）a starter
　sutâto-o-kiru〈スタートを切る〉start, make a start.
　sutâto-ga-ii〈スタートがいい〉start well, make a good start.

sute-ba〈すてば：捨て場〉a dumping place, a dump.
gomi-no-sute-ba-ga-nai〈ごみの捨て場がない〉find no place to throw the rubbish into.

sute-bachi〈すてばち：捨て鉢〉
sute-bachi-ni-naru〈捨て鉢になる〉become desperate, abandon oneself to despair.
sute-bachi-ni-natte〈捨て鉢になって〉out of despair.

sute-go〈すてご：捨て子〉a foundling, an abandoned child.
sute-go-o-suru〈捨て子をする〉abandon one's child.

suteki〈すてき：素敵〉
suteki-na〈素敵な〉capital, splendid, marvelous, wonderful.

sutēki〈ステーキ〉a steak, a beefsteak.

sutekki〈ステッキ〉a walking stick, a cane.

sute-mi〈すてみ：捨て身〉
sute-mi-de or *sute-mi-ni-natte*〈捨て身で，捨て身になって〉at the risk of one's life.

sute-ne〈すてね：捨て値〉
sute-ne-de〈捨て値で〉dirt-cheap, for a mere song.
　　sute-ne-de uru（捨て値で売る）　sell for a mere song

sutenresu〈ステンレス〉stainless steel.

suteppu〈ステップ〉a step.
suteppu-o-fumu〈ステップを踏む〉step, dance, execute dance steps.

sutereo〈ステレオ〉a stereo, a stereophonic sound system.
　　sutereo-de-kiku（ステレオで聴く）　listen to ((a record)) on a stereo
sutereo-no〈ステレオの〉stereophonic.

suteru〈すてる：捨てる〉throw away; abandon, give up.
　　shiai o suteru（試合を捨てる）　throw away a game

sutētomento〈ステートメント〉a statement.
　　sutētomento　o　happyô-suru（ステートメントを発表する）　announce one's statement

sute-zerifu〈すてぜりふ：捨てぜりふ〉
sute-zerifu-o-iu〈捨てぜりふを言う〉cry something over one's shoulder.

suto〈スト〉a strike (an abbreviation of 'sutoraiki').
　　suto-ni-totsunyû-suru（ストに突入する）　go on (a) strike
　　suto-chû-de-aru（スト中である）　be on strike
　　suto o chûshi-suru（ストを中止する）　call off a strike
　　zenesuto（ゼネスト）　a general strike
　　bubun-suto（部分スト）　a partial strike

suto-ken〈スト権〉the right to strike

sutôbu〈ストーブ〉a stove, a heater.

    sutôbu-o-taku（ストーブをたく）light a stove, make a fire in the stove

    sekitan-sutôbu（石炭ストーブ）a coal stove

    sekiyu-sutôbu（石油ストーブ）an oil heater

sutokkingu〈ストッキング〉(a pair of) stockings.

sutokku〈ストック〉(a) stock; a ski stick.

    sutokku-ga-aru（ストックがある）be in stock

    sutokku-ga-nai（ストックがない）be out of stock

sutoppu〈ストップ〉a stop.

   sutoppu-suru（ストップする）stop.

sutoraiki〈ストライキ〉*see.* suto.

sutoresu〈ストレス〉stress.

    sutoresu-o-kaishô-suru（ストレスを解消する）be released from stress

sutorêto〈ストレート〉

   sutorêto-de-katsu〈ストレートで勝つ〉win a straight victory ((over)).

    sutorêto-de-makeru（ストレートで負ける）suffer a straight defeat ((from))

sutorippâ〈ストリッパー〉a stripper, a stripteaser.

sutorippu〈ストリップ〉a strip tease, a strip show.

    sutorippu o yaru（ストリップをやる）do a strip

    sutorippu-gekijô（ストリップ劇場）a strip-joint

sutorô〈ストロー〉a sipper.

    sutorô-de nomu（ストローで飲む）suck ((soda water)) through a sipper

sutoronchiumu〈ストロンチウム〉strontium.

sûtsu〈スーツ〉a suit.

sûtsu-kêsu〈スーツケース〉a suitcase.

sutta-monda〈すったもんだ：擦ったもんだ〉

   sutta-monda-no-ageku（擦ったもんだの挙げ句）after much fussing.

sutten-korori(n)〈すってんころり(ん)〉

   sutten-korori-to-korobu〈すってんころりと転ぶ〉fall plump.

sutto〈すっと〉

    sutto-tachi-agaru（すっと立ち上がる）spring to one's feet

    mune-ga-sutto-suru（胸がすっとする）feel refreshed, be gratified ((with))

suu〈すう：吸う〉breathe in, smoke; sip.

suwari〈すわり：座り〉stability.

　suwari-no-ii〈座りのいい〉stable.

　　suwari-no-warui（座りの悪い）　unstable

suwari-komi〈すわりこみ：座り込み〉a sit-in, a sit-down.

　　suwari-komi-senjutsu（座り込み戦術）　sit-in tactics

　suwari-komu〈座り込む〉sit down, plant oneself down.

suwaru〈すわる：座る〉sit (down), take a seat, be seated.

　　isu-ni suwaru（いすに座る）　sit on a chair

　　kichin-to suwaru（きちんと座る）　sit straight

suwaru〈すわる：据わる〉set, be set.

　　me ga suwaru（目が据わる）　one's eyes are set

　　dokyō-ga-suwaru（度胸が据わる）　be emboldened, become bold

Suwêden〈スウェーデン〉Sweden.

　　Suwêden-jin（スウェーデン人）　a Swede

　　Suwêden-go（スウェーデン語）　Swedish

　　Suwêden(-jin)-no（スウェーデン(人)の）　Swedish

su-yaki〈すやき：素焼き〉unglazed pottery.

　su-yaki-no〈素焼きの〉unglazed.

suyasuya(-to)〈すやすや(と)〉

　suyasuya nemuru〈すやすや眠る〉sleep peacefully.

suzu〈すず〉tin.

　　suzu-seihin（すず製品）　tinware

　suzu-sei-no〈すず製の〉(made) of tin.

suzu〈すず：鈴〉a bell.

　　suzu no oto（鈴の音）　the tinkle of a bell

　　suzu o narasu（鈴を鳴らす）　ring a bell

suzuki〈すずき〉a sea bass.

suzume〈すずめ〉a sparrow.

suzumi〈すずみ：涼み〉

　　suzumi-ni-iku（涼みに行く）　go out to enjoy the evening cool

　suzumu〈涼む〉cool oneself, enjoy the evening cool air.

suzunari〈すずなり：鈴なり〉

　suzu-nari-ni-naru〈鈴なりになる〉grow in clusters.

suzuran〈すずらん：鈴らん〉a lily of the valley.

suzuri〈すずり〉an inkstone, an ink slab.

suzushii〈すずしい：涼しい〉cool, refreshing.

　　suzushii tokoro-ni oku（涼しい所に置く）　keep ((a thing)) in a cool place

　　suzushii me〔涼しい目〕 bright eyes
　　suzushii-kao-o-shite-iru〔涼しい顔をしている〕 look unconcerned,
　　　　look indifferent
suzushi-sa〔涼しさ〕coolness.

T

ta〈た：田〉a rice field, a paddy field.
　　ta o tagayasu〔田を耕す〕 till a rice field
　　ta o ueru〔田を植える〕 plant rice
ta〈た：他〉*see.* hoka.
　　Ta wa oshite-shiru-beshi.〔他は推して知るべし.〕 The rest may be
　　　　inferred.
taba〈たば：束〉a bundle, a bunch.
　　hana-taba〔花束〕 a bundle of flowers
　　taba-ni-suru or *tabaneru*〈束にする，束ねる〉bundle, tie up in a bundle.
　　taba-ni-shite〈束にして〉in a bundle, in a bunch.
　　taba-ni-natte〈束になって〉in a bunch.
tabako〈たばこ〉a cigarette, a cigar, tobacco.
　　tabako-ya〔たばこ屋〕 a tobacconist's, a cigar store
　　tabako-o-suu〈たばこを吸う〉smoke.
tabe-akiru〈たべあきる：食べ飽きる〉be tired of eating, have enough
　　((of)).
tabe-kake〈たべかけ：食べかけ〉
　　tabe-kake-no〈食べかけの〉half-eaten.
　　tabe-kake-no-tokoro-e〈食べかけのところへ〉while one is taking a meal.
tabe-kata〈たべかた：食べ方〉how to eat, a way of cooking.
tabe-mono〈たべもの：食べ物〉food, diet.
　　Nani-ka tabe-mono o kudasai.（何か食べ物を下さい.） Give me
　　　　something to eat.

tabe-mono-ga-ii〈食べ物がいい〉be well-fed.

　　tabe-mono-ga-warui〈食べ物が悪い〉be ill-fed

tabe-nokoshi〈たべのこし：食べ残し〉leftover food, leavings〔at the table〕.

tabe-nokoshi-no〈食べ残しの〉leftover.

taberu〈たべる：食べる〉eat, have, take.

　　sukkari-taberu〈すっかり食べる〉eat up

　　ichi-nichi-ni san-do taberu〈一日に三度食べる〉take three meals a day

tabete-miru〈食べてみる〉try ((food)).

tabete-ikite-iru〈食べて生きている〉live on.

taberareru〈食べられる〉eatable, edible, good to eat.

　　Kore-wa taberare-masu-ka?〈これは食べられますか。〉Is this good to eat?

tabe-sugi〈たべすぎ：食べ過ぎ〉overeating.

tabe-sugiru〈食べ過ぎる〉eat too much, overeat (oneself).

tabe-tsukeru〈たべつける：食べつける〉get used to eating.

　　tabe-tsuke-nai mono〈食べつけない物〉unusual diet

tabezu-girai〈たべずぎらい：食べず嫌い〉*see.* kuwazu-girai.

tabi〈たび：足袋〉Japanese socks, *tabi*.

tabi〈たび：旅〉a travel, a journey, a trip.

　　tabi-bito〈旅人〉a traveler, a tourist

tabi〈たび：度〉time.

　　kono-tabi〈この度〉this time

**～*-tabi-ni*〈～度に〉every time, each time, whenever.

　　kuru-tabi-goto-ni〈来る度ごとに〉every time one comes

tabi-kasanaru〈たびかさなる：度重なる〉

　　tabi-kasanaru shippai〈度重なる失敗〉repeated failures

tabitabi〈たびたび：度々〉often, frequently, several times.

tabô〈たぼう：多忙〉pressure of business.

　　tabô-o-kiwameru〈多忙を極める〉be pressed by business

tabô-na〈多忙な〉busy.

　　tabô-na seikatsu o okuru〈多忙な生活を送る〉lead a busy life

tabô-no-tame〈多忙のため〉owing to the pressure of business.

tabû〈タブー〉a taboo, a tabu.

　　tabû-de-aru　*or*　tabû-ni-natte-iru〈タブーである，タブーになっている〉be a taboo, be under taboo

tabun〈たぶん：多分〉perhaps, probably, maybe.

tachi 〈たち〉 nature, character; (a) temper, quality; a kind.

tachi-no-warui 〈たちの悪い〉 ill-natured, bad.

tachi-agaru 〈たちあがる：立ち上がる〉 stand up, rise [to one's feet].

tachiai 〈たちあい：立ち会い〉 presence, attendance; a session.

shōnin-tachiai-no-ue-de（証人立ち会いの上で） in the presence of a witness

tachiai-nin（立会人） an observer, a witness, a teller

tachi-au 〈立ち会う〉 be present ((at)), attend, witness, be (a) witness ((to)).

tachiba 〈たちば：立場〉 a standpoint, a position, a situation.

tachiba-o-kaete-miru（立場を換えて見る） see ((a matter)) from a different standpoint

jibun-no tachiba o akiraka-ni-suru（自分の立場を明らかにする） make one's position clear, explain oneself

muzukashii tachiba-ni-aru（難しい立場にある） be in a difficult situation

tachi-banashi 〈たちばなし：立ち話〉

tachi-banashi-suru 〈立ち話する〉 talk standing, stand talking.

tachi-domaru 〈たちどまる：立ち止まる〉 stop, come to a stop.

tachi-domatte ippuku-suu（立ち止まって一服吸う） stop to smoke

tachi-dooshi 〈たちどおし：立ち通し〉

tachi-dooshi-de-aru or *tachi-doosu* 〈立ち通しである，立ち通す〉 keep standing [all the way to...].

tachi-fusagaru 〈たちふさがる：立ちふさがる〉 stand in ((a person's)) way, confront ((a person)).

iriguchi ni tachi-fusagaru（入り口に立ちふさがる） block the door

tachi-gie 〈たちぎえ：立ち消え〉

tachi-gie-ni-naru 〈立ち消えになる〉 be left off, be dropped, fizzle out.

tachi-giki 〈たちぎき：立ち聞き〉 overhearing, eavesdropping.

tachi-giki-suru 〈立ち聞きする〉 overhear, eavesdrop.

tachi-gui 〈たちぐい：立ち食い〉

tachi-gui-suru 〈立ち食いする〉 eat standing.

tachi-iri 〈たちいり：立ち入り〉

Tachi-iri-kinshi.（立ち入り禁止.） Keep off.

tachi-kiru 〈たちきる：断ち切る〉 cut asunder, cut off, break off, sever.

kankei o tachi-kiru（関係を断ち切る） cut off the relationship

tachi-komeru 〈たちこめる：立ちこめる〉 hang over, envelop, screen.

Kiri ga tani-ma-ni tachi-komete-ita.（霧が谷間に立ちこめていた.）

　　　　Mist hung over the valley.

tachimachi〈たちまち〉in a moment, at once, suddenly.

tachi-mawari〈たちまわり：立ち回り〉a fight, a scuffle; a fighting scene.

　tachi-mawaru〈立ち回る〉move about, act, play one's part.

　　josai-naku tachi-mawaru（如才なく立ち回る）play one's part smartly

tachi-mi〈たちみ：立ち見〉

　　tachi-mi-seki（立ち見席）the gallery, standing room

　tachi-mi-suru〈立ち見する〉see a play from the gallery.

tachi-mukau〈たちむかう：立ち向かう〉face, confront, fight ((against)), stand ((against)).

tachi-naoru〈たちなおる：立ち直る〉recover oneself, rally; improve.

tachi-narabu〈たちならぶ：立ち並ぶ〉stand in a row, line〔a street〕.

tachi-noboru〈たちのぼる：立ち上る〉go up, rise.

tachinoki〈たちのき：立ち退き〉removal, evacuation, dispossession.

　　tachinoki-ryō（立ち退き料）compensation for removal

　tachinoki-o-meijiru〈立ち退きを命じる〉order to leave.

tachi-noku〈たちのく：立ち退く〉move out, leave.

　tachi-nokaseru〈立ち退かせる〉remove, evacuate.

tachi-nomi〈たちのみ：立ち飲み〉

　tachi-nomi-suru〈立ち飲みする〉drink ((beer)) standing.

tachi-ōjō〈たちおうじょう：立ち往生〉

　tachi-ōjō-suru〈立ち往生する〉come to a standstill, be held up; be at one's wits' end.

　　fubuki-no-tame-ni　tachi-ōjō-suru（吹雪のために立ち往生する）come to a standstill in the snowstorm

　　endan-de　tachi-ōjō-suru（演壇で立ち往生する）stand speechless on the platform

tachi-okureru〈たちおくれる：立ち後れる〉make a belated start.

　tachi-okurete-iru〈立ち後れている〉be behind ((in)).

tachi-oyogi〈たちおよぎ：立ち泳ぎ〉

　tachi-oyogi-suru〈立ち泳ぎする〉tread water.

tachi-saru〈たちさる：立ち去る〉leave, depart ((from)), go away.

tachi-shōben〈たちしょうべん：立ち小便〉

　tachi-shōben-suru〈立ち小便する〉urinate by the roadside.

tachi-sukumu〈たちすくむ：立ちすくむ〉stand paralyzed, be unable to move.

tachi-tsuzukeru〈たちつづける：立ち続ける〉keep standing.

tachi-uchi 〈たちうち：太刀打ち〉

　tachi-uchi-suru 〈太刀打ちする〉oppose, compete ((with)).

　　Kare-niwa-tachi-uchi-deki-nai.（彼には太刀打ちできない.）I am　no match for him.

tachiuo 〈たちうお：太刀魚〉a scabbard fish.

tachi-yomi 〈たちよみ：立ち読み〉

　tachi-yomi-suru 〈立ち読みする〉read standing in a bookstore.

tachi-yoru 〈たちよる：立ち寄る〉stop ((at)), drop in.

　　Kochira-e　korareta-toki-ni-wa　dôzo　o-tachi-yori-kudasai.（こちらへ来られたときにはどうぞお立ち寄りください.）Please drop in on us when you come this way.

tachi-yuku 〈たちゆく：立ち行く〉can be kept going, can maintain.

tachi-zume 〈たちづめ：立ち詰め〉*see.* tachi-dooshi.

tada 〈ただ〉only, merely, simply, alone.

　　tada-hitori-de（ただ一人で）all alone, all by oneself

　　tada ichi-do（ただ一度）only once

　tada-no 〈ただの〉common, ordinary.

　　tada-no hito（ただの人）a common(*or* an ordinary) man

　tada-de 〈ただで〉free, for nothing.

　　Tada-de moraeru.（ただでもらえる.）You can have it free.

　　Konna-koto-o-shite　tada-dewa-suma-nai-zo.（こんなことをしてただでは済まないぞ.）You shall smart for this.

tada-bataraki 〈ただばたらき：ただ働き〉free service.

tadachi-ni 〈ただちに：直ちに〉at once, immediately, right now.

tadagoto 〈ただごと：ただ事〉a trifling thing.

　　Tadagoto-dewa-nai.（ただ事ではない.）It's out of the common.

tadai 〈ただい：多大〉

　tadai-no 〈多大の〉great, much, considerable, heavy.

　　tadai-no rieki（多大の利益）a large profit

　　tadai-no songai（多大の損害）a heavy loss

tada-ima 〈ただいま：ただ今〉now, at present, just, just now, in a moment.

　　tada-ima mairimasu.（ただ今参ります.）I am coming now.

　　tada-ima　môshimashita-toori（ただ今申しましたとおり）as I have just said

　　Tada-ima!（ただ今.）Hello, here I am!

　tada-ima-no-tokoro 〈ただ今のところ〉for the present.

tada-naranu 〈ただならぬ〉unusual, uncommon; serious, alarming.

tada-naranu mono-oto〈ただならぬ物音〉 an alarming sound

tada-nori〈ただのり：ただ乗り〉

tada-nori-suru〈ただ乗りする〉steal a ride.

tadare〈ただれ〉a sore, an inflammation, festering.

tadareru〈ただれる〉be sore, be inflamed, fester.

tadareta〈ただれた〉sore, inflamed, festered.

tadashi〈ただし：但し〉but, however, only, provided that... .

tadashi-gaki〈ただしがき：但し書き〉a proviso.

tadashii〈ただしい：正しい〉right, just, upright, honest, proper, correct, legal.

tadashii koto o suru（正しいことをする） do a right thing

tadashii hito（正しい人） a just man, an upright man

tadashii Eigo o hanasu（正しい英語を話す） speak correct English

tadashiku〈正しく〉rightly, justly, honestly, properly, correctly, legally.

tadashiku-nai（正しくない） unjust, dishonest, improper, incorrect, illegal

tadasu〈ただす：正す〉correct.

Ayamari-ga-areba　tadashi-nasai.（誤りがあれば正しなさい.） Correct mistakes, if any.

tadasu〈ただす〉ask ((of)), inquire ((of)), inquire ((into)), ascertain.

mi-moto-o-tadasu〈身元をただす〉 inquire into ((a person's)) antecedents

semmon-ka ni tadasu（専門家にただす） consult an expert

moto-o-tadaseba〈元をただせば〉originally.

tadayou〈ただよう：漂う〉drift (about), float.

tadoku〈たどく：多読〉wide reading, extensive reading.

tadoku-suru〈多読する〉read widely, read extensively.

tadoru〈たどる〉follow, trace.

kioku o tadoru（記憶をたどる） retrace one's memory

tadotadoshii〈たどたどしい〉faltering, tottering, unsteady.

tadotadoshiku〈たどたどしく〉falteringly, totteringly, staggeringly, unsteadily, with difficulty.

taedae〈たえだえ：絶え絶え〉

Kanojo-wa　iki-mo-taedae-datta.（彼女は息も絶え絶えだった.） She was gasping for breath.

taedae-ni〈絶え絶えに〉feebly, gaspingly.

taema〈たえま：絶え間〉an interval, an intermission, a break, a gap.

Kono　toori-wa　kuruma-no-taema-ga-nai.（この通りは車の絶え間がな

い.） There is no intermission of cars in this street.

taema-no-nai 〈絶え間のない〉 continued, unceasing, uninterrupted.

taema-naku 〈絶え間なく〉 continually, unceasingly.

Ototoi-kara taema-naku yuki-ga-futteiru. （おとといから絶え間なく雪が降っている。） It has been snowing since the day before yesterday.

taeru 〈たえる：堪(耐)える〉 endure, bear, put up ((with)), stand.

kanashimi ni taeru （悲しみに耐える） endure one's grief

jûseki ni taeru （重責に堪える） stand the heavy responsibility

kônetsu ni taeru （高熱に耐える） stand intense heat

tae-gatai 〈堪え難い〉 unendurable, unbearable.

tae-gatai atsusa （堪え難い暑さ） unbearable heat

taeru 〈たえる：絶える〉 become extinct; end, come to an end.

iki-ga-taeru （息が絶える） breathe one's last, die.

tae-shinobu 〈たえしのぶ：堪え忍ぶ〉 bear patiently, endure, put up ((with)).

taezu 〈たえず：絶えず〉 constantly, ceaselessly, always, all the time.

Kare-wa taezu tabako-o-sutteiru. （彼は絶えずたばこを吸っている。） He is smoking all the time.

taga 〈たが〉 a hoop.

taga ga yurumu （たがが緩む） the hoops get loose, lose one's strength of character

tagaeru 〈たがえる〉 break; dislocate, sprain.

yakusoku o tagaeru （約束をたがえる） break one's promise

tagai 〈たがい：互い〉

tagai-no 〈互いの〉 mutual.

tagai-ni 〈互いに〉 with each other, with one another, mutually.

tagai-chigai 〈たがいちがい：互い違い〉

tagai-chigai-ni 〈互い違いに〉 alternately.

tagai-chigai-ni-suru （互い違いにする） arrange ((things)) alternately

tagaku 〈たがく：多額〉 a large sum.

tagaku-no 〈多額の〉 a large sum of, considerable, heavy.

tagaku-no sonshitsu （多額の損失） heavy loss

tagane 〈たがね〉 a graver, a burin, a cold chisel.

-tagaru 〈-たがる〉 want ((to do)), wish ((to do)), be eager ((to do)), be anxious ((to do)).

iki-tagaru （行きたがる） want to go

hijô-ni iki-tagaru （非常に行きたがる） be anxious to go

tagau 〈たがう〉

　　　ippun-mo-tagawazu-ni（一分もたがわずに）　punctually to the minute

　　　sumbun-tagawazu-ni（寸分たがわずに）　exactly

tagayasu〈たがやす：耕す〉till, plow, cultivate.

　　　tochi o tagayasu（土地を耕す）　cultivate the soil

tagei〈たげい：多芸〉versatility.

　　tagei-no〈多芸の〉versatile, of varied accomplishments.

tagen〈たげん：多元〉

　　　tagen-hôsô（多元放送）　a broadcast from multiple origination

tagiru〈たぎる〉boil, be on the boil, seethe.

tagon〈たごん：他言〉

　　tagon-suru〈他言する〉tell others, divulge, blab.

　　　tagon-shi-nai（他言しない）　do not tell ((a matter)) to anybody, keep ((a matter)) secret

tagui〈たぐい〉

　　tagui-mare-na〈たぐいまれな〉rare.

taguri-yoseru〈たぐりよせる：手繰り寄せる〉

　　tsuri-ito-o-taguri-yoseru〈釣り糸を手繰り寄せる〉haul in a fishing line.

ta-hata〈たはた：田畑〉fields, a farm.

tahô〈たほう：他方〉another side, the other side.

　　　tahô-de-wa（他方では）　on the other hand(*or* side)

ta-hômen〈たほうめん：多方面〉many quarters, many directions.

　　ta-hômen-no〈多方面の〉various, varied, manifold, many-sided.

　　ta-hômen-ni〈多方面に〉in many directions.

tai〈たい：隊〉a party, a company, a band.

tai〈たい：体〉the body.

　　tai-o-kawasu〈体をかわす〉dodge.

tai〈たい：対〉versus, between, against, to, with; even, equal.

　　　Waseda-tai-Keiô-no　yakyû-jiai（早稲田対慶応の野球試合）　a baseball game between Waseda and Keiô

　　　san-tai-ichi-no-sukoâ-de　katsu（三対一のスコアーで勝つ）　win by a score of 3 to 1

　　　tai-Bei-kankei（対米関係）　relations with America

　　　tai-de shôbu-suru（タイで勝負する）　play a game on equal terms

tai〈タイ〉a tie.

　　　tai-ni-owaru（タイに終わる）　end in a〔4-4〕tie

　　　tai-kiroku（タイ記録）　a tie record

　　tai-ni suru〈タイにする〉tie the score.

Tai〈タイ〉Thailand.

Tai-jin〈タイ人〉a Thai

Tai-go〈タイ語〉Thai

Tai(-jin)-no〈タイ(人)の〉Thai

tai〈たい〉a sea bream.

tai〈たい：他意〉any other intention, a secret purpose, malice, ill will.

Tai-wa ari-masen.〈他意はありません。〉I bear you no malice.

-tai〈-たい〉hope, want ((to do)), wish ((to do)), would like ((to do)), should like ((to do)), feel like.

Issho-ni iki-tai.〈一緒に行きたい。〉I should like to go with you.

taian〈たいあん：対案〉a counterproposal.

taiban〈たいばん：胎盤〉the placenta.

taibatsu〈たいばつ：体罰〉

taibatsu o kuwaeru〈体罰を加える〉inflict corporal punishment ((on)).

taibetsu〈たいべつ：大別〉

taibetsu-suru〈大別する〉classify into large groups, divide roughly.

taibô〈たいぼう：待望〉expectation.

taibô-suru〈待望する〉expect, look forward ((to)).

taibô-no〈待望の〉long-cherished.

taibô-seikatsu〈たいぼうせいかつ：耐乏生活〉a life of austerity.

taibyô〈たいびょう：大病〉a serious illness.

taibyô-ni-kakatte-iru〈大病にかかっている〉be seriously ill.

taichô〈たいちょう：隊長〉a captain, a leader, a commander.

taichô〈たいちょう：体調〉physical condition.

taida〈怠惰〉laziness, idleness, indolence.

taida-na〈怠惰な〉lazy, idle, indolent.

taidan〈たいだん：対談〉a face-to-face talk, a conversation, an interview.

taidan-suru〈対談する〉have a talk ((with)), have an interview ((with)), converse ((with)).

taido〈たいど：態度〉an attitude, behavior, a manner.

kyôkô-na taido〈強硬な態度〉a firm attitude ((toward))

taido-ga-ii〈態度がいい〉have good manners

taido-ga-warui〈態度が悪い〉have bad manners

taidô〈たいどう：胎動〉quickening, fetal movement.

taidô-suru〈胎動する〉quicken.

taidoku〈たいどく：胎毒〉congenital syphilis.

taieki〈たいえき：退役〉retirement〔from service〕.

taieki-shôkô〈退役将校〉a retired officer

taieki-suru〈退役する〉retire from service.

taifû〈たいふう：台風〉a typhoon.

Taifû ga hassei-shita.（台風が発生した.） A typhoon formed.

taifû no me（台風の目） the eye of a typhoon

taifû-kennai-ni-aru（台風圏内にある） be within the typhoon area

taigai〈たいがい：対外〉

taigai-kankei（対外関係） foreign relations

taigai-seisaku（対外政策） a foreign policy

taigai-teki(-na)〈対外的（な）〉foreign, international, overseas, outside.

taigai〈たいがい：大概〉see. taitei.

taigaku〈たいがく：退学〉leaving school, (a) withdrawal.

taigaku-suru〈退学する〉leave school, give up school.

chûto-taigaku-suru（中途退学する） leave school halfway

taigaku-saserareru〈退学させられる〉be dismissed from school

taigan〈たいがん：対岸〉the other side, the opposite bank.

taigan-ni〈対岸に〉on the other side, on the opposite bank, across.

taigen〈たいげん：体現〉embodiment.

taigen-suru〈体現する〉embody.

taigen-sôgo〈たいげんそうご：大言壮語〉big talk, bragging, exaggeration.

taigen-sôgo-suru〈大言壮語する〉talk big, brag.

taigi〈たいぎ：大儀〉

taigi-na〈大儀な〉troublesome, wearisome, tedious, languid.

taigi-sô-ni〈大儀そうに〉wearily, languidly, heavily.

taigo〈たいご：隊ご〉the ranks, a line, formation, a procession.

taigo-o-kunde〈隊ごを組んで〉in line, in formation.

taigû〈たいぐう：待遇〉treatment, service, pay.

taigû-mondai（待遇問題） the question of treatment(or pay)

hoteru-no taigû（ホテルの待遇） hotel service

taigû o kaizen-suru（待遇を改善する） increase the pay

taigû-suru〈待遇する〉treat.

taigû-no-ii〈待遇のいい〉hospitable, well-paid.

taigun〈たいぐん：大群〉a large crowd, a large herd, a large flock, a shoal, a large school.

taigun〈たいぐん：大軍〉a big army, a large force.

taiha〈たいは：大破〉

taiha-suru〈大破する〉be heavily damaged.

taihai〈たいはい：大敗〉a crushing defeat.

taihai-suru〈大敗する〉be beaten hollow.

taihai 〈たいはい：退廃〉 corruption, degeneration, decadence, deterioration.

taihai-suru 〈退廃する〉 be corrupted, be degenerated.

taihai-teki(-na) or *taihai-shita* 〈退廃的(な)，退廃した〉 corrupted, degenerated, decadent.

taihan 〈たいはん：大半〉 *see*. dai-bubun.

taihei 〈たいへい：太(泰)平〉 (perfect) peace, tranquility.

    taihei-mûdo（太(泰)平ムード）the blessings of peace and satisfaction

Taihei-yô 〈たいへいよう：太平洋〉 the Pacific (Ocean).

    Taihei-yô-gan（太平洋岸）the Pacific coast, the West coast

taihen 〈たいへん：対辺〉 the opposite side.

taihen 〈たいへん：大変〉 very, greatly, awfully, very much.

    Taihen arigatô-gozaimashita.（大変ありがとうございました.）Thank you very much.

taihen-na 〈大変な〉 serious, grave, terrible, dreadful, awful.

    taihen-na koto（大変なこと）a serious matter

      taihen-na-koto-ni-naru（大変なことになる）become serious, assume serious proportions

    taihen-na jiken（大変な事件）a terrible accident

taihi(-o-hodokosu) 〈たいひ(をほどこす)：たい肥(を施す)〉 compost.

taihi 〈たいひ：待避〉

taihi-suru 〈待避する〉 take shelter ((in *or* under)).

taihi 〈たいひ：対比〉 contrast, comparison.

taihi-suru 〈対比する〉 contrast, compare.

taiho 〈たいほ：逮捕〉 (an) arrest, (a) capture.

    taiho-jô（逮捕状）a warrant of arrest, an arrest warrant

taiho-suru 〈逮捕する〉 arrest, capture, catch, nab.

taiho 〈たいほ：退歩〉 retrogression, degeneration.

taiho-suru 〈退歩する〉 retrograde, degenerate.

taiho-teki(-na) 〈退歩的(な)〉 retrogressive, backward.

taihô 〈たいほう：大砲〉 a gun, a cannon, ordnance.

taii 〈たいい：大尉〉 a captain, a lieutenant (senior grade).

taii 〈たいい：大意〉 the general idea, an outline.

    taii o kumi-toru（大意をくみ取る）have the general idea ((of))

    taii o noberu（大意を述べる）give an outline ((of))

taii 〈たいい：体位〉 physique.

    taii o kôjô-saseru（体位を向上させる）improve one's physique

taii-no〈体位の〉physical.

taii〈たいい：退位〉(an) abdication.

taii-suru〈退位する〉abdicate.

taii-saseru〈退位させる〉depose.

taiiku〈たいいく：体育〉physical training, physical education, gymnastics, athletics.

　　　taiiku-gaku-bu（体育学部）the department of physical education

　　　taiiku-kan（体育館）a gymnasium, a gym

taiin〈たいいん：退院〉

taiin-suru〈退院する〉leave (the) hospital.

taiin-reki〈たいいんれき：太陰暦〉the lunar calendar.

taiji〈たいじ：胎児〉an embryo, a fetus, an unborn child.

taiji〈たいじ：退治〉

taiji-suru〈退治する〉get rid ((of)), root out, exterminate.

taijin〈たいじん：退陣〉

taijin-suru〈退陣する〉step down, resign, retire.

taijin-kankei〈たいじんかんけい：対人関係〉personal relations.

taijō〈たいじょう：退場〉

taijō-meijiru〈退場を命じる〉order ((a person)) out of.

taijō-suru〈退場する〉leave〔the hall〕, go away ((from)), make one's exit.

taijū〈たいじゅう：体重〉(one's body) weight.

　　　taijū-ga-fueru（体重が増える）gain weight

　　　taijū-ga-heru（体重が減る）lose weight

　　　taijū-o-herasu（体重を減らす）lessen one's weight, reduce

taijū-ga~aru〈体重が～ある〉weigh.

taijū-o-hakaru〈体重を計る〉weigh oneself.

taika〈たいか：大火〉a big fire, a conflagration.

taika〈たいか：大家〉a (great) master, an authority.

　　　ongaku-no-taika（音楽の大家）a great musician

　　　Ei-bungaku-no taika（英文学の大家）an authority on English literature

taika〈たいか：滞貨〉freight congestion.

　　　taika no yama（滞貨の山）a heavy pile of stocks

taika〈たいか：大過〉a serious error, a serious mistake.

　　　taika-naku（大過なく）without making any serious errors

taika〈たいか：退化〉retrogression, degeneration, degradation.

taika-suru〈退化する〉retrograde, degenerate, degrade.

taika-shita〈退化した〉degenerated, degraded.

taika〈たいか：耐火〉

taika-kenchiku（耐火建築）a fire-resistant building

taika-no〈耐火の〉fireproof, fire-resistant.

taikai〈たいかい：大会〉a great meeting, a mass meeting, a general meeting, a convention, a tournament.

shimin-taikai（市民大会）a mass meeting of citizens

tô-taikai（党大会）a party convention

taikaku〈たいかく：対角〉the opposite angle.

taikaku-sen（対角線）a diagonal (line)

taikaku〈たいかく：体格〉(a) physique, constitution, (a) build.

taikaku-ga-ii（体格がいい）have a fine physique

taikaku-ga-warui（体格が悪い）have a poor physique

taikaku-kensa（体格検査）a physical examination

taikan〈たいかん：退官〉

taikan-suru〈退官する〉retire from office.

taikan-shiki〈たいかんしき：たい冠式〉a coronation.

taikan-sôchi〈たいかんそうち：耐寒装置〉winterization.

taikan-sôchi-o-suru〈耐寒装置をする〉winterize.

taike〈たいけ：大家〉a rich family, a distinguished family.

taikei〈たいけい：大系〉an outline〔of history〕.

taikei〈たいけい：体形〉one's form, one's figure.

taikei〈たいけい：体系〉a system, an organization.

taikei-ka-suru or *taikei-zukeru*〈体系化する，体系付ける〉systematize.

taikei-teki(-na)〈体系的(な)〉systematic.

taikei〈たいけい：隊形〉(a) formation, order.

taikei-o-midasazu-ni〈隊形を乱さずに〉in good formation.

taikei〈たいけい：体刑〉penal servitude, a jail sentence; corporal punishment.

taikei-ni-shosuru〈体刑に処する〉sentence ((a person)) to penal servitude, inflict corporal punishment ((on)).

taikei〈たいけい：大計〉a farsighted policy.

taiken〈たいけん：体験〉(personal) experience.

taiken-suru〈体験する〉experience, go through.

taiken〈たいけん：大圏〉a great circle.

taiken-kôsu（大圏コース）the great circle route

taiketsu〈たいけつ：対決〉confrontation, a showdown.

taiketsu-suru〈対決する〉confront, have a showdown ((with)).

taiketsu-saseru〈対決させる〉confront ((a person)) ((with)).

taiki〈たいき：大気〉the atmosphere, the air.
    taiki-ken（大気圏）the atmosphere
        taiki-ken-gai（大気圏外）the outer space
    taiki-osen（大気汚染）air pollution

taiki〈たいき：大器〉a person of great caliber.
    Taiki-bansei.（大器晩成。）Great talents mature late.
taiki-bansei(-gata)-no〈大器晩成(型)の〉late-blooming.

taiki〈たいき：待機〉
taiki-suru〈待機する〉watch and wait, hold oneself in readiness, stand by.
taiki-shite-iru〈待機している〉be on the alert, be on call.

taikin〈たいきん：大金〉a large sum of money, a lot of money.
    taikin o môkeru（大金をもうける）make a lot of money

taiko〈たいこ：太古〉ancient times.
taiko-no-jidai-yori〈太古の時代より〉from time immemorial.

taiko〈たいこ：太鼓〉a drum.
    taiko o tataku（太鼓をたたく）beat a drum

taikō〈たいこう：大綱〉general rules, fundamental principles, an outline.

taiko〈たいこう：対抗〉opposition, rivalry.
    taikō-ba（対抗馬）a rival horse, a rival candidate
    taikō-saku（対抗策）a countermeasure
taikō-suru〈対抗する〉oppose, rival, cope ((with)).
～-ni-taikō-shite〈～に対抗して〉in opposition to... , in rivalry with... , against... .

taikō〈たいこう：対校〉
taikō-no〈対校の〉interschool, intercollegiate.

taiko-ban〈たいこばん：太鼓判〉
taiko-ban-o-osu〈太鼓判を押す〉vouch ((for)).

taikoku〈たいこく：大国〉a large country, a major power.

taikū〈たいくう：滞空〉
    taikû-jikan（滞空時間）duration of flight
    taikû-kiroku（滞空記録）a flight record

taikū〈たいくう：対空〉
    taikû-hôka（対空砲火）antiaircraft fire

taikutsu〈たいくつ：退屈〉tedium, tiresomeness, dullness.
taikutsu-suru〈退屈する〉be bored, be weary ((of)).
taikutsu-saseru〈退屈させる〉bore ((a person)).

taikutsu o magirasu 〈退屈を紛らす〉 beguile the tedium.

taikutsu-na 〈退屈な〉 tedious, boring, tiresome, dull.

taikutsu-shinogi-ni 〈退屈しのぎに〉 to kill time, by way of recreation.

taikyaku 〈たいきゃく：退却〉(a) retreat.

taikyaku-suru 〈退却する〉 retreat ((from *or* to)), make a retreat.

    sô-taikyaku-suru （総退却する） make a general retreat

taikyaku-saseru 〈退却させる〉 retire.

taikyo 〈たいきょ：大挙〉

taikyo-shite 〈大挙して〉 in a body, in great force, in large numbers.

taikyo 〈たいきょ：退去〉(a) departure, leaving, quitting, evacuation.

    taikyo-o-meijiru （退去を命じる） order ((a person)) out of a place

taikyo-suru 〈退去する〉 depart, leave, quit, evacuate.

taikyoku 〈たいきょく：大局〉 the general situation.

    Taikyoku-ni zenzen-eikyô-wa-nai. （大局に全然影響はない.） There is not a change in the general situation.

    taikyoku-o-mi-ayamaru （大局を見誤る） take a wrong view of things

taikyoku-kara-mite 〈大局から見て〉 on the whole.

taikyû-ryoku 〈たいきゅうりょく：耐久力〉 durability, staying power.

taikyû-ryoku-no-aru 〈耐久力のある〉 durable, staying.

    taikyû-ryoku-no-nai （耐久力のない） of poor lasting quality

taima 〈たいま：大麻〉 hemp.

taiman 〈たいまん：怠慢〉 negligence, neglect.

    shokumu-taiman （職務怠慢） neglect of duty

taiman-na 〈怠慢な〉 negligent, neglectful.

taimatsu 〈たいまつ〉 a torch, a torchlight.

    taimatsu o tomosu （たいまつをともす） kindle a torch

taimen 〈たいめん：体面〉 honor, dignity, appearances.

    taimen-ni-kakawaru （体面に係わる） affect one's honor

    taimen o tamotsu （体面を保つ） keep up appearances

taimen-jô 〈体面上〉 for honor's sake, for appearance' sake

taimen 〈たいめん：対面〉 an interview.

    taimen-kôtsû （対面交通） facing traffic

taimen-suru 〈対面する〉 interview, meet, see.

taimingu 〈タイミング〉 timing.

taimingu-ga-ii 〈タイミングがいい〉 be well timed.

    taimingu-ga-warui （タイミングが悪い） be not well timed

taimu 〈タイム〉 time, a time-out.

    taimu o toru （タイムを取る） take a time-out

taimu-rekôdâ〈タイムレコーダー〉 a time clock
taimu-o-hakaru〈タイムを計る〉time.

tainai〈たいない：体内〉the interior of the body.
tainai-no or *tainai-ni*〈体内の，体内に〉in the body.

tainai〈たいない：胎内〉the interior of the womb.
tainai-no or *tainai-de*〈胎内の，胎内で〉in the womb.

tainai〈たいない：対内〉
tainai-seisaku〈対内政策〉 a domestic policy
tainai-teki(-na)〈対内的(な)〉domestic, interior, home, internal.

tainetsu〈たいねつ：耐熱〉
tainetsu-garasu〈耐熱ガラス〉 heat-resisting glass
tainetsu-no〈耐熱の〉heatproof, heat-resisting.

tai-Nichi〈たいにち：対日〉
tai-Nichi-gaikô-kankei〈対日外交関係〉 diplomatic relations with Japan
tai-Nichi-kanjô〈対日感情〉 the feeling toward Japan

tainin〈たいにん：大任〉a great task, an important mission.
tainin o hatasu〈大任を果たす〉 carry through a great task

tainin〈たいにん：退任〉
tainin-suru〈退任する〉resign from one's office.

tainô〈たいのう：滞納〉nonpayment, arrearage, failure to pay.
tainô-kin〈滞納金〉 arrears, arrearage
tainô-sha〈滞納者〉 a defaulter, a delinquent
tainô-shobun〈滞納処分〉 disposition for failure to pay
tainô-suru〈滞納する〉be in arrear(s), be delinquent in payment, fail to pay.

taiô〈たいおう：対応〉correspondence, equivalence.
taiô-suru〈対応する〉correspond ((to)), answer ((to)), be equivalent ((to)), cope ((with)).

taion〈たいおん：体温〉temperature.
taion o hakaru〈体温を計る〉 take one's temperature
Taion ga agaru.〈体温が上がる.〉 My temperature rises.
Taion ga sagaru.〈体温が下がる.〉 My temperature falls.
taion-kei〈体温計〉 a (clinical) thermometer

taipisuto〈タイピスト〉a typist.
hôbun-taipisuto〈邦文タイピスト〉 a typist in Japanese

taipu〈タイプ〉a pattern, a type; a typewriter.
onaji taipu no hito〈同じタイプの人〉 a person of the same type

dendô-taipu〔電動タイプ〕 an electric typewriter

taipu-de-utsu, taipu-o-utsu or *taipu-suru*〈タイプで打つ，タイプを打つ，タイプする〉type, typewrite.

taira〈たいら：平ら〉

taira-ni-suru〈平らにする〉flatten, even, level.

taira-na〈平らな〉flat, even, level.

taira-na michi〔平らな道〕 a level road

tairageru〈たいらげる：平らげる〉eat up; subdue, suppress.

tairiku〈たいりく：大陸〉a continent.

Ajia-tairiku〔アジア大陸〕 the Continent of Asia

tairiku-kan-dandô-dan〔大陸間弾道弾〕 an intercontinental ballistic missile

tairiku-sei(-no) or *tairiku-teki(-na)*〈大陸性(の)，大陸的(な)〉continental.

tairiku-sei kikô〔大陸性気候〕 a continental climate

tairitsu〈たいりつ：対立〉opposition, confrontation.

tairitsu-iken〔対立意見〕 an opposing opinion

tairitsu-suru〈対立する〉be opposed ((to)).

tairo〈たいろ：退路〉the path of retreat.

tairo o shadan-suru〔退路を遮断する〕 cut off ((a person's)) retreat

tairu〈タイル〉a tile.

tairu o haru〔タイルを張る〕 set tiles

tairu-bari-no〈タイル張りの〉tiled.

tairyaku〈たいりゃく：大略〉an outline, a summary.

tairyaku-o-noberu〈大略を述べる〉give an outline ((of)), summarize.

tairyô〈たいりょう：大量〉a large quantity.

tairyô-chûmon〔大量注文〕 a bulk order

tairyô-no〈大量の〉mass.

tairyô-ni〈大量に〉in large quantities.

tairyô〈たいりょう：大漁〉a large catch.

tairyô-de-aru〔大漁である〕 have a large catch of fish

tairyoku〈たいりょく：体力〉physical strength.

tairyoku o yashinau〔体力を養う〕 build up one's physical strength

tairyoku-tesuto〔体力テスト〕 a physical strength test

tairyoku-teki(-na)〈体力的(な)〉physical.

tairyoku-teki-ni〈体力的に〉physically.

tairyû〈たいりゅう：対流〉convection.

tairyû-ken〔対流圏〕 the troposphere

taisa〈たいさ：大差〉a considerable difference.

　　taisa-de katsu〈大差で勝つ〉win by a wide margin

　　taisa-o-tsukeru〈大差を付ける〉gain a great lead ((on))

taisa〈たいさ：大佐〉a colonel, a captain.

taisai〈たいさい：大祭〉a grand festival.

taisaku〈たいさく：大作〉a great work.

taisaku〈たいさく：対策〉a measure, a countermeasure, a counterplan.

　　atarashii taisaku o tateru〈新しい対策を立てる〉work out a new countermeasure

taisan〈たいさん：退散〉

　taisan-suru〈退散する〉disperse.

taisei〈たいせい：体制〉(a) structure, a system, an order, organization, an establishment.

　　seiji-taisei〈政治体制〉a political system

　　kyû-taisei〈旧体制〉an old order

　　han-taisei〈反体制〉anti-establishment

taisei〈たいせい：胎生〉viviparity.

taisei〈たいせい：態勢〉preparation(s), an attitude.

　　taisei o totonoeru〈態勢を整える〉make one's preparations ((to do))

taisei〈たいせい：大勢〉the general trend, the general tendency.

　　taisei ni shitagau〈大勢に従う〉follow the general trend

taisei〈たいせい：たい勢〉

　taisei o bankai-suru〈たい勢をばん回する〉restore the declining fortunes.

taisei〈たいせい：大成〉

　taisei-suru〈大成する〉come to greatness; be crowned with success.

Taisei-yô〈たいせいよう：大西洋〉the Atlantic (Ocean).

taiseki〈たいせき：体積〉volume, capacity.

taiseki〈たいせき：たい積〉accumulation, a pile, a heap.

　taiseki-suru〈たい積する〉accumulate, be piled up, be heaped up.

taiseki〈たいせき：退席〉

　taiseki-suru〈退席する〉leave one's seat, retire, withdraw.

taisen〈たいせん：大戦〉a great war.

　　dai-niji-sekai-taisen〈第二次世界大戦〉World War II

taisen〈たいせん：対戦〉

　taisen-suru〈対戦する〉have a game ((with)), compete ((with)).

taisetsu〈たいせつ：大切〉

　taisetsu-na〈大切な〉important, valuable.

　　taisetsu-na shorui〈大切な書類〉important papers

　　taisetsu-na mono〈大切な物〉valuables

taisetsu-ni〈大切に〉carefully, with care.

   taisetsu-ni-suru（大切にする）make much ((of)), take good care ((of))

taisha〈たいしゃ：大赦〉an amnesty.

   taisha-o-okonau（大赦を行う）grant an amnesty ((to)).

taisha〈たいしゃ：退社〉

   taisha-jikoku（退社時刻）the closing hour

taisha-suru〈退社する〉leave the office; retire from the company.

taishaku〈たいしゃく：貸借〉(a) loan; debit and credit.

   taishaku-kankei-ga-aru（貸借関係がある）have accounts to settle
    ((with))

   taishaku-taishô-hyô（貸借対照表）a·balance sheet

taishi〈たいし：大使〉an ambassador.

   chû-Nichi-taishi（駐日大使）an ambassador to Japan

   taishi-kan（大使館）an embassy

     taishi-kan-in（大使館員）the embassy staff

taishi〈たいし：大志〉an ambition, an aspiration.

taishin〈たいしん：耐震〉

   taishin-kôzô（耐震構造）aseismatic structure

taishin-no〈耐震の〉earthquake-proof.

taishita〈たいした：大した〉many, much, a great deal of, very, great, important.

   taishita kane-mochi（大した金持ち）a very rich man

   taishita gakusha（大した学者）a great scholar

   Ryôsha-no-aida-ni　taishita　chigai-wa-nai.（両者の間に大した違いはない.）There is not much difference between them.

   Taishita-koto-dewa-nai.（大したことではない.）It's of no importance.

   taishita kingaku-ni-naru（大した金額になる）amount to a round sum

taishite〈たいして：大して〉

taishite～nai〈大して～ない〉not very, not much.

   Kyô-wa　taishite-samuku-nai.（今日は大して寒くない.）It's not very cold today.

   Taishite-ame-wa-fura-nai-darô.（大して雨は降らないだろう.）It will not rain much.

(-ni)-taishite〈-(に)たいして：-(に)対して〉to, for, toward; against; per.

   rôjin-ni-taishite　shinsetsu-de-aru（老人に対して親切である）be kind to the old

   teki-ni-taishite（敵に対して）against the enemy

hyaku-ni-taishite san-jû〈百に対して三十〉 30 per 100

taishitsu〈たいしつ：体質〉(physical) constitution.

taishitsu(-no)-kaizen〈体質(の)改善〉the improvement of one's constitution

taishitsu-ga-yowai〈体質が弱い〉be of weak constitution

taishitsu-sei(-no) or *taishitsu-teki(-na)*〈体質性(の)，体質的(な)〉constitutional.

taishitsu-teki kekkan〈体質的欠陥〉a constitutional defect

taishitsu-teki-ni〈体質的に〉constitutionally.

taisho〈たいしょ：対処〉

taisho-suru〈対処する〉cope ((with)), deal ((with)), meet.

taishô〈たいしょう：大将〉a general, an admiral; a head, a boss.

taishô〈たいしょう：対象〉an object.

kenkyû no taishô〈研究の対象〉an object of one's study

taishô〈たいしょう：対称〉symmetry.

taishô-teki(-na)〈対称的(な)〉symmetrical.

taishô-teki-ni〈対称的に〉symmetrically.

taishô〈たいしょう：対照〉contrast, comparison, (a) collation.

~-to ichijirushii taishô-o-nasu〈～と著しい対照をなす〉be in a striking contrast to...

taishô-suru〈対照する〉contrast ((A with B)), compare, collate.

hikaku-taishô-suru〈比較対照する〉compare and contrast

kore-towa-taishô-teki-ni~〈これとは対照的に～〉by contrast, ...

taishô〈たいしょう：大勝〉a great victory, a landslide victory.

taishô-suru〈大勝する〉win a great victory.

taishoku〈たいしょく：退職〉retirement.

taishoku-kin〈退職金〉a retirement allowance, a discharge allowance.

taishoku-suru〈退職する〉retire from office, resign an office.

taishoku〈たいしょく：大食〉gluttony.

taishoku-ka〈大食家〉a great eater

taishoku-suru〈大食する〉eat much, gluttonize.

taishoku-no〈大食の〉gluttonous, greedy.

taishô-ryôhô〈たいしょうりょうほう：対症療法〉allopathy.

taishû〈たいしゅう：大衆〉the masses, the general public.

taishû-teki-na〈大衆的な〉popular.

taishû-muki-no〈大衆向きの〉popular, for everybody, for popular use.

taishû〈たいしゅう：体臭〉body smell.

taisô 〈たいそう：大層〉 *see.* hijô-ni.

taisô 〈たいそう：体操〉 gymnastics, gymnastic exercises.
 taisô o suru（体操をする） have gymnastic exercises
 atama-no taisô（頭の体操） mental gymnastics

taisû 〈たいすう：対数〉 a logarithm.
 taisû-hyô（対数表） a table of logarithms
 taisû-kansû（対数関数） logarithmic function

taisuru 〈たいする：対する〉 face, confront, oppose.

taitei 〈たいてい：大抵〉 generally, mostly, usually, almost.
 Watashi-wa taitei jû-ichi-ji-ni neru.（私は大抵十一時に寝る。） I usually go to bed at eleven.
 taitei ie-ni-iru（大抵家にいる） be almost always at home
 taitei-no 〈大抵の〉 general, most.
 taitei-no hito（大抵の人） most people

taiteki 〈たいてき：大敵〉 a powerful enemy, an archenemy, a great rival.

taitô 〈たいとう：対等〉 equality.
 taitô-de-aru 〈対等である〉 be equal ((with)).
 taitô-no 〈対等の〉 equal.
 taitô-ni 〈対等に〉 on equal terms.

taitô 〈たいとう：台頭〉 rise.
 taitô-suru 〈台頭する〉 come to the fore, gather strength, gain power.

taitoku 〈たいとく：体得〉 experience, mastery.
 taitoku-suru 〈体得する〉 learn from experience, master.

taitoru 〈タイトル〉 a title, a championship.
 taitoru o bôei-suru（タイトルを防衛する） defend the title
 taitoru-hoji-sha（タイトル保持者） a titleholder

taiwa 〈たいわ：対話〉 (a) conversation, a dialogue.
 taiwa-suru 〈対話する〉 talk ((with)), dialogue.
 taiwa-tai-no 〈対話体の〉 written in dialogue.

Taiwan 〈たいわん：台湾〉 Taiwan, Formosa.

taiya 〈タイヤ〉 a tire, a tyre.
 taiya-no ato（タイヤの跡） tire tracks

taiyaku 〈たいやく：大役〉 an important task, an important duty, an important role, an important mission.
 taiyaku-o-oose-tsukaru（大役を仰せ付かる） be charged with an important mission

taiyaku 〈たいやく：対訳〉 a translation printed side by side with the original.

taiyo 〈たいよ：貸与〉 lending, a loan.

　taiyo-suru 〈貸与する〉 lend, loan, grant the use ((of)).

taiyô 〈たいよう：太陽〉 the sun.

　　taiyô-kei（太陽系）　the solar system

　　taiyô-netsu（太陽熱）　solar heat

　　taiyô-reki（太陽暦）　the solar calendar

taiyô 〈たいよう：大洋〉 an ocean.

　taiyô-no 〈大洋の〉 oceanic.

taiyô 〈たいよう：大要〉 a summary, an outline, a general idea, general principles.

　taiyô-o-noberu 〈大要を述べる〉 give an outline ((of)), summarize.

taiyoku 〈たいよく：大欲〉 avarice, greed.

　　Taiyoku-wa-muyoku-ni-nitari.（大欲は無欲に似たり.）　Grasp all, lose all.

taiyô-nensû 〈たいようねんすう：耐用年数〉

　　taiyô-nensû-o-sugita-kôsha（耐用年数を過ぎた校舎）　an old school building no longer safe to use

Taiyô-shû 〈たいようしゅう：大洋州〉 Oceania.

taizai 〈たいざい：滞在〉 a stay.

　　watashi-no Rondon-taizai-chû-ni（私のロンドン滞在中に）　during my stay in London

　　hoteru-ni taizai-chû-de-aru（ホテルに滞在中である）　be staying at a hotel

　taizai-suru 〈滞在する〉 stay ((at *or* in)), remain.

　　oba-no-ie-ni-taizai-suru（叔(伯)母の家に滞在する）　stay with one's aunt

　　nagaku-taizai-suru（長く滞在する）　make a long stay

taizen-jijaku 〈たいぜんじじゃく：泰然自若〉

　taizen-jijaku-to-shite-iru 〈泰然自若としている〉 be perfectly calm and self-possessed.

tajirogu 〈たじろぐ〉 shrink back, flinch.

tajitaji(-to) 〈たじたじ(と)〉

　tajitaji-to-naru 〈たじたじとなる〉 stagger, flinch.

tajitsu 〈たじつ：他日〉 some day, some other time.

tajô 〈たじょう：多情〉

　tajô-na 〈多情な〉 passionate, fickle, amorous.

taka 〈たか〉 a hawk.

　taka-ha-no 〈たか派の〉 hawkish.

taka 〈たか：高〉

taka-o-kukuru 〈高をくくる〉 make light ((of)), think little ((of)).

taka-no-shireta 〈高の知れた〉 trifling, insignificant.

  taka-no-shireta koto (高の知れたこと) a trifling matter

takabisha 〈たかびしゃ：高飛車〉

takabisha-ni-deru 〈高飛車に出る〉 act high-handedly.

takaburu 〈たかぶる：高ぶる〉

  Kanojo-wa shinkei-ga-takabutte-iru. (彼女は神経が高ぶっている。) Her nerves are highly strung.

taka-dai 〈たかだい：高台〉 a height, an eminence.

takadaka 〈たかだか：高々〉 at (the) most, at best, no more than.

takadaka-to 〈たかだかと：高々と〉 high, aloft.

  koe-takadaka-to (声高々と) loudly

  hana-takadaka-to (鼻高々と) very proudly

takai 〈たかい：高い〉 high, tall; dear, expensive; loud.

  takai yama (高い山) a high mountain

  Kare-wa sei-ga-takai. (彼は背が高い。) He is tall.

  Ano hon wa totemo ne-ga-takai. (あの本はとても値が高い。) That book is very expensive.

  takai koe-de (高い声で) in a loud voice

taka-ibiki 〈たかいびき：高いびき〉 a loud snore.

taka-ibiki-o-kaku 〈高いびきをかく〉 snore loudly.

takakkei 〈たかっけい：多角形〉 a polygon.

takakkei-no 〈多角形の〉 polygonal.

takaku 〈たかく：高く〉 high; dear, at a high price.

  sora-takaku (空高く) high up in the sky

  takaku kau (高く買う) buy at a high price

takaku-suru 〈高くする〉 raise, make higher.

takaku-naru 〈高くなる〉 be raised, become higher, become taller, become dear, rise in price.

takaku 〈たかく：多角〉

  takaku-keiei (多角経営) diversified management

takaku-teki(-na) 〈多角的(な)〉 many-sided, multilateral, diversified.

takamaru 〈たかまる：高まる〉 rise, be raised.

  kanjô-ga-takamaru (感情が高まる) get excited

takameru 〈高める〉 raise, heighten, elevate, improve, ennoble.

takami 〈たかみ：高み〉

takami-no-kembutsu-o-suru 〈高みの見物をする〉 remain an unconcerned spectator.

takan 〈たかん：多感〉

  takan-na 〈多感な〉 sensitive, sentimental, emotional.

    takan-na seishun-jidai（多感な青春時代）one's impressionable youth

taka-naru 〈たかなる：高鳴る〉

    Watashi-no mune wa taka-naru.（私の胸は高鳴る。）My heart beats fast.

taka-ne 〈たゝね：高値〉a high price.

    taka-ne o yobu（高値を呼ぶ）fetch a high price

takane 〈たかね：高ね〉

    takane-no-hana（高ねの花）a prize beyond one's reach, an unattainable object

taka-nozomi 〈たかのぞみ：高望み〉

  taka-nozomi-suru 〈高望みする〉be ambitious, set one's hopes too high, have an excessive ambition.

takara 〈たから：宝〉a treasure.

    takara-no-mochi-gusare（宝の持ち腐れ）a miser's gold buried in the ground

takaraka 〈たからか：高らか〉

  takaraka-ni 〈高らかに〉aloud, in a loud voice.

takara-kuji 〈たからくじ：宝くじ〉a public lottery.

    takara-kuji o kau（宝くじを買う）buy a lottery ticket

    takara-kuji-de ittō-ga-ataru（宝くじで一等が当たる）win the first prize in a public lottery

takari 〈たかり〉blackmail, a shakedown; a blackmailer.

takaru 〈たかる〉swarm, flock, collect, gather, crowd; sponge (off).

    Ari ga takaru.（ありがたかる。）Ants swarm.

    Hae ga takaru.（はえがたかる。）Flies collect.

takasa 〈たかさ：高さ〉height, pitch, loudness.

    yama no takasa（山の高さ）the height of a mountain

    hito-no koe no takasa（人の声の高さ）the pitch in one's voice

taka-shio 〈たかしお：高潮〉flood tide, high tide.

taka-tobi 〈たかとび：高跳び〉a high jump.

    tachi-taka-tobi（立ち高跳び）the standing high jump

takatobi 〈たかとび：高飛び〉decampment, bolt.

    takatobi-sunzen-ni（高飛び寸前に）just before one's bolt

  takatobi-suru 〈高飛びする〉decamp, run away, make off, take flight, skip out of town.

taka-tobi-komi 〈たかとびこみ：高飛び込み〉platform diving, a high dive.

taka-warai 〈たかわらい：高笑い〉a loud laugh.

taka-warai-suru 〈高笑いする〉laugh loudly.

take 〈たけ：丈〉length.

    kimono no take（着物の丈） the length of one's *kimono*

take 〈たけ：竹〉a bamboo.

    take-kago（竹かご） a bamboo basket

    take-zaiku（竹細工） bamboo work

    take-zao（竹ざお） a bamboo pole

    take-o-watta-yô-na-seikaku-no otoko（竹を割ったような性格の男） a man of frank disposition

takedakeshii 〈たけだけしい〉fierce, ferocious; audacious, shameless.

takenawa 〈たけなわ〉

takenawa-de-aru 〈たけなわである〉be at ((its)) height, be in full swing.

    Haru-masa-ni-takenawa-de-aru.（春正にたけなわである.） The spring is now in all its glory.

takenoko 〈たけのこ〉a bamboo shoot.

takeri-kuruu 〈たけりくるう：たけり狂う〉rave mad.

take-uma 〈たけうま：竹馬〉stilts.

    take-uma-ni noru（竹馬に乗る） walk on stilts

taki 〈たき：滝〉a waterfall, falls.

    taki-tsubo（滝つぼ） the basin of a waterfall

taki-bi 〈たきび：たき火〉a fire (in the open air), a bonfire.

    taki-bi o suru（たき火をする） build up a fire

takigi 〈たきぎ：薪〉firewood.

    takigi o hirou（薪を拾う） gather firewood

takishīdo 〈タキシード〉a tuxedo, a dinner jacket.

taki-tsuke 〈たきつけ：たき付け〉kindling (wood).

taki-tsukeru 〈たき付ける〉kindle, build (a fire); instigate, incite, stir up, egg ((a person)) on.

takkan 〈たっかん：達観〉

takkan-suru 〈達観する〉take a philosophic view ((of)).

takkyū 〈たっきゅう：卓球〉ping-pong.

    takkyū o suru（卓球をする） play ping-pong

tako 〈たこ〉an octopus.

    tako-tsubo（たこつぼ） an octopus trap; a foxhole

tako 〈たこ〉a kite.

tako o ageru（たこを揚げる）fly a kite

tako-age（たこ揚げ）kite-flying

tako〈たこ〉a callus, a corn.

Ashi-ni tako ga dekiru.（足にたこができる.）A corn forms on my foot.

mimi-ni-tako-ga-dekiru-hodo-kiku（耳にたこができるほど聞く）have heard more than enough ((of))

takô〈たこう：多幸〉

Go-takô-o-inorimasu.（御多幸を祈ります.）I wish you every happiness.

takoku〈たこく：他国〉a foreign country, another province.

takoku-mono（他国者）a stranger

takoku-no〈他国の〉foreign.

ta-kokuseki〈たこくせき：多国籍〉

ta-kokuseki-kigyô（多国籍企業）a multinational enterprise

takô-shiki〈たこうしき：多項式〉a polynomial expression.

taku〈たく：宅〉

Yamada-san-no o-taku（山田さんのお宅）Mr. Yamada's house

O-taku-dewa-minasan-dô-shite-irasshaimasu-ka?（お宅では皆さんどうしていらっしゃいますか.）How is your family?

taku〈たく〉burn, kindle, make a fire.

sekitan o taku（石炭をたく）burn coal

furo o taku（風呂をたく）make a bath

taku〈たく：炊く〉boil, cook.

takuan〈たくあん：沢あん〉pickled radish.

takuchi〈たくち：宅地〉housing land, a house lot.

takuji-sho〈たくじしょ：託児所〉a day nursery.

takujô〈たくじょう：卓上〉

takujô-karendâ（卓上カレンダー）a desk calendar

takumashii〈たくましい〉stout, sturdy.

takumashii sôzô-ryoku（たくましい想像力）vigorous imagination

takumi〈たくみ：巧み〉skill, dexterity.

takumi-na〈巧みな〉skillful, dexterous.

takumi-ni〈巧みに〉skillfully, dexterously.

takurami〈たくらみ〉a design, a trick, a contrivance, a scheme.

takuramu〈たくらむ〉contrive, scheme, plot.

takusan〈たくさん：沢山〉

suru-koto-ga-takusan-aru（する事がたくさんある）have many things

　　　to do, have much to do

　　　Mô kekkô-desu. Takusan-itadakimashita.（もう結構です．たくさん頂きました．）No, thank you. I have had enough.

　takusan-no〈沢山の〉a lot of, lots of, plenty of, many, a great many of, much, a great deal of, enough.

takushî〈タクシー〉a taxi.

　　　takushî o hirou（タクシーを拾う）pick up a taxi

　　　takushî ni noru（タクシーに乗る）take a taxi

　　　nagashi-no takushî（流しのタクシー）a cruising taxi

takushi-ageru〈たくしあげる：たくし上げる〉tuck up.

　　　shatsu-no sode o takushi-ageru（シャツのそでをたくし上げる）roll up the shirt sleeves

takusô〈たくそう：託送〉

　takusô-suru〈託送する〉send ((goods)) by ((a person)).

takusuru〈たくする：託する〉entrust, charge, leave ((a thing)) to ((one's)) care.

takuto〈タクト〉a baton.

　　　takuto o furu（タクトを振る）take the baton

takuwae〈たくわえ：蓄え〉store, stock; savings.

　takuwaeru〈蓄える〉store, lay in a stock; save, lay aside.

tama〈たま：玉（球，弾）〉a ball, a bowl, a bead, a bulb; a precious stone, jewelry; a bullet, a shell.

　　　garasu-dama（ガラス玉）a glass bead

　　　denki-no tama（電気の球）an electric bulb

　　　tama-ni-kizu（玉にきず）a fly in the ointment

　tama-o-komeru〈弾を込める〉load a gun.

tama〈たま〉

　tama-ni〈たまに〉occasionally, at times, now and then; rarely.

　　　Raikyaku-wa-tama-ni-shika-nai.（来客はたまにしかない．）I rarely have visitors.

tamago〈たまご：卵〉an egg.

　　　tamago o umu（卵を産む）lay an egg

　　　tamago o waru（卵を割る）break an egg

　　　tamago-no-kara（卵の殻）an eggshell

　　　umi-tate-no tamago（産みたての卵）a new-laid egg

　　　yude-tamago（ゆで卵）a hard-boiled egg

　　　sutâ-no-tamago（スターの卵）a starlet

　tamago-gata-no〈卵形の〉egg-shaped, oval.

tamamono〈たまもの：賜物〉a present, a gift, a result.
doryoku no tamamono〈努力の賜物〉the result of one's efforts
tamamushi-iro〈たまむしいろ：玉虫色〉
tamamushi-iro-no〈玉虫色の〉iridescent.
tamanegi〈たまねぎ：玉ねぎ〉an onion.
tama-no-koshi〈たまのこし：玉のこし〉
tama-no-koshi-ni-noru〈玉のこしに乗る〉be lucky enough to marry into a family of rank.
tamara-nai〈たまらない〉be unbearable, cannot stand; cannot but, cannot help; be dying ((for *or* to do)).
Atsukute-tamara-nai.〈暑くてたまらない．〉It is unbearably hot.
Okashikute-tamara-nai.〈おかしくてたまらない．〉I cannot but laugh.
Ippai-nomi-takute-tamara-nai.〈一杯飲みたくてたまらない．〉I am dying for a drink of *sake*.
tamari-ba〈たまりば：たまり場〉a haunt, a hangout.
tamaru〈たまる〉collect, gather; save, be saved; pile up.
ana-ni-tamatta mizu〈穴にたまった水〉water collected in the hole
Daibu kane-ga-tamatta.〈だいぶ金がたまった．〉Quite a sum of money has been saved up.
Daibu shigoto-ga-tamatta.〈だいぶ仕事がたまった．〉I have a lot of work left to do.
tamashii〈たましい：魂〉a soul, a spirit.
tamashii-o-ire-kaeru〈魂を入れ替える〉turn over a new leaf
tamashii-o-uchi-konde-yaru〈魂を打ち込んでやる〉do ((a thing)) with all one's heart
tamatama〈たまたま〉accidentally, by chance, unexpectedly.
Tamatama-kanojo-ga-i-awaseta.〈たまたま彼女が居合わせた．〉She happened to be there.
tamatsuki〈たまつき：玉突き〉billiards.
tamatsuki o suru〈玉突きをする〉play billiards
tamatsuki-dai〈玉突き台〉a billiard table
tamawaru〈たまわる：賜わる〉grant, give, bestow, award.
tambo〈たんぼ：田んぼ〉a rice field.
tambô〈たんぼう：探訪〉(private) inquiry.
tambô-kiji〈探訪記事〉a report
shakai-tambô〈社会探訪〉reporting
tambun〈たんぶん：短文〉a short sentence, a short piece.
tambun〈たんぶん：単文〉a simple sentence.

tame 〈ため〉 good, advantage, benefit, profit.
  tame-ni-naru 〈ためになる〉 be beneficial ((to)), be profitable ((to)), be advantageous ((to)), be good ((for)), be instructive ((to)).
    tame-ni-nara-nai 〈ためにならない〉 be of no good, be harmful ((to))

tame-iki 〈ためいき：ため息〉a sigh.
  tame-iki-o-tsuku 〈ため息をつく〉sigh, draw a sigh.
  tame-iki-o-tsuite 〈ため息をついて〉with a sigh.

tame-komu 〈ためこむ：ため込む〉save up, hoard, amass.

tamen 〈ためん：多面〉many sides, many faces.
    tamen-tai（多面体）a polyhedron
  tamenteki(-na) 〈多面的（な）〉many-sided, versatile.

(-no)-tame-ni 〈（～の）ために〉for, for the good of, for the sake of; to, in order to, (so) that...may; because of, on account of, owing to; in consequence of, as a result of.
    seigi-no-tame-ni（正義のために）in the cause of justice
    shakai-no-tame-ni（社会のために）for the good of society
    Ei-bungaku-kenkyû-no-tame-ni Rondon-e-iku（英文学研究のためにロンドンへ行く）go to London to study English literature
    ame-no-tame-ni（雨のために）because of the rain
    byôki-no-tame-ni（病気のために）on account of illness
    kôzui-no-tame-ni（洪水のために）in consequence of the flood

tamerau 〈ためらう〉hesitate.
  tamerawazu-ni 〈ためらわずに〉without hesitation.

tameru 〈ためる〉accumulate, gather, save, store, run up.
    kane o tameru（金をためる）save money
    kanjô o tameru（勘定をためる）run up bills
    me-ni namida-o-tamete（目に涙をためて）with tears in one's eyes

tameshi 〈ためし：試し〉a trial, a try, a test.
  tameshi-ni 〈試しに〉on trial.
    tameshi-ni-yatte-miru（試しにやってみる）try, have a try ((at))

tameshi 〈ためし〉
    Kare-wa yakusoku-o-mamotta-tameshi-ga-nai.（彼は約束を守ったためしがない。）I have never known him to keep his word.

tamesu 〈ためす：試す〉try, test.
    Betsu-no-hôhô-de tameshite-goran.（別の方法で試してごらん。）Try another way.

tammari 〈たんまり〉quite a lot.
    tammari-môkeru（たんまりもうける）gain a tidy profit

tammei 〈たんめい：短命〉 a short life.

　tammei-de-aru 〈短命である〉 die young.

　tammei-na 〈短命な〉 short-lived, ephemeral.

tammono 〈たんもの：反物〉 piece goods, dry goods, drapery, textile fabrics.

ta-mokuteki 〈たもくてき：多目的〉

　ta-mokuteki-no 〈多目的の〉 multipurpose.

tamoto 〈たもと〉 the sleeves.

　tamoto-o-wakatsu 〈たもとを分かつ〉 part ((from *or* with)), break (off) ((with)).

tamotsu 〈たもつ：保つ〉 keep, hold, preserve, maintain.

　　chitsujo o tamotsu〈秩序を保つ〉 keep order

　　taimen o tamotsu〈体面を保つ〉 keep up appearances

tampa 〈たんぱ：短波〉 a shortwave.

　　tampa-hôsô〈短波放送〉 shortwave broadcasting

tampaku 〈たんぱく：淡泊〉

　tampaku-na 〈淡泊な〉 plain, light, simple; candid, frank, openhearted; indifferent ((about *or* to)).

　　tampaku-na tabe-mono〈淡泊な食べ物〉 plain food

　　tampaku-na-seikaku-no hito〈淡泊な性格の人〉 a person of frank disposition

　　kinsen-ni-tampaku-de-aru〈金銭に淡泊である〉 be indifferent about money

tampaku-shitsu 〈たんぱくしつ：たん白質〉 albumin, protein.

　tampaku-shitsu-no 〈たん白質の〉 albuminous, proteinic.

tampei-kyû 〈たんぺいきゅう：短兵急〉

　tampei-kyû-na 〈短兵急な〉 impetuous, precipitate, headlong.

　tampei-kyû-ni 〈短兵急に〉 impetuously, precipitately.

tampen 〈たんぺん：短編〉 a short piece.

　　tampen-shôsetsu〈短編小説〉 a short story

　　tampen-shû〈短編集〉 a collection of short stories

　　tampen-eiga〈短編映画〉 a short film

tampo 〈たんぽ：担保〉 (a) security, a mortgage, a guarantee, a warrant.

　　tampo-bukken〈担保物権〉 real rights granted by way of security

　tampo-ni-ireru 〈担保に入れる〉 mortgage, give as a security ((for)).

　　ie-o-tampo-ni-irete kane o kariru〈家を担保に入れて金を借りる〉 borrow money on the security of one's house

　mu-tampo-de 〈無担保で〉 without security.

tampopo 〈たんぽぽ〉 a dandelion.

tamukeru 〈たむける〉 offer, present.

tamuro 〈たむろ〉

tamuro-suru 〈たむろする〉 gather, group; hang around.

tamushi 〈たむし：田虫〉 a ringworm.

tan 〈たん：反〉 a roll of cloth.

tan 〈たん〉 phlegm.

tan-o-haku 〈たんを吐く〉 cough out phlegm, spit.

tan 〈たん：端〉

〜*-ni-tan-o-hassuru* 〈〜に端を発する〉 originate from... , have its origin in ... , arise from... .

tana 〈たな：棚〉 a shelf, a rack.

　　tana o tsuru （棚をつる）　make a shelf, fix a shelf

　　Tana-kara-bota-mochi. （棚からぼたもち.）　It is a piece of good luck.

　　Jibun-no-koto-o-tana-ni-agete　hito-no-koto-o-iu. （自分のことを棚に上げて人のことを言う.）　The pot calls the kettle black.

tana-age 〈たなあげ：棚上げ〉

tana-age-suru 〈棚上げする〉 shelve, put ((something)) into pigeonhole, table.

tanabata 〈たなばた：七夕〉 the seventh night of the seventh month of the lunar calendar; the Weaver.

　　tanabata-matsuri （七夕祭り）　the Festival of the Star Vega

tana-biku 〈たなびく：棚引く〉 hang over, lie over, trail.

tanan 〈たなん：多難〉

tanan-na 〈多難な〉 full of difficulties.

　　tanan-na toki （多難な時）　an age full of troubles

tana-oroshi 〈たなおろし：棚卸し〉 stocktaking, an inventory.

tana-oroshi-suru 〈棚卸しする〉 take stock, make an inventory of the articles in stock.

tana-zarae 〈たなざらえ：棚ざらえ〉 clearance.

　　tana-zarae-oo-uri-dashi （棚ざらえ大売り出し）　a clearance sale

tanazarashi 〈たなざらし〉

tanazarashi-ni-naru 〈たなざらしになる〉 become shopworn.

tanchi 〈たんち：探知〉 detection.

　　tanchi-ki （探知器）　a detector

tanchi-suru 〈探知する〉 detect.

tan-chô 〈たんちょう：短調〉 a minor (key).

tanchô 〈たんちょう：単調〉 monotony.

tanchô-na〈単調な〉monotonous, dull.

　　tanchô-na seikatsu o okuru〈単調な生活を送る〉lead a monotonous life

tanchô-de-nai〈単調でない〉full of variety.

tanchô-zuru〈たんちょうづる：丹頂づる〉a red crested white crane.

tandoku〈たんどく：単独〉

　　tandoku-kôdô〈単独行動〉independent action

　　tandoku-kaison〈単独海損〉a particular average

tandoku-no〈単独の〉independent, individual, single.

tandoku-de〈単独で〉independently, individually, singly, alone, by oneself.

tane〈たね：種〉a seed, a stone; a cause; a subject, a topic; a trick.

　　momo-no tane〈桃の種〉a peach stone

　　Makanu-tane-wa-haenu.（まかぬ種は生えぬ.）One must sow before one can reap.

　　arasoi no tane〈争いの種〉the seeds of discord

　　shimpai no tane〈心配の種〉a cause of anxiety

　　hanashi no tane〈話の種〉a topic of conversation

　　tejina-no tane〈手品の種〉a juggler's trick

　　tane-maki〈種まき〉sowing

　　tane-ushi〈種牛〉a seed bull

tane-o-maku〈種をまく〉sow seed, sow.

tane-no-ooi〈種の多い〉seedy.

　　tane-no-nai〈種のない〉seedless

tanen〈たねん：多年〉many years.

tanen-no〈多年の〉long, of long standing.

　　tanen-no shûkan〈多年の習慣〉long customs

tanen-ni-watatte〈多年にわたって〉for (many) years, over the years.

tangan〈たんがん：嘆願〉(an) entreaty, (an) appeal, (a) petition.

　　tangan-sho〈嘆願書〉a (written) petition

tangan-suru〈嘆願する〉entreat, implore, appeal ((to)), petition.

tangen〈たんげん：単元〉a unit.

tango〈たんご：端午〉

　　tango-no-sekku〈端午の節句〉the Boys' Festival

tango〈タンゴ〉(a) tango.

　　tango o odoru〈タンゴを踊る〉dance the tango

tango〈たんご：単語〉a word.

　　tango-shû〈単語集〉a wordbook

tangutsu〈たんぐつ：短靴〉shoes.

tani〈たに：谷〉a valley, a ravine.

    tani-zoko〈谷底〉 the bottom of a ravine

tan·i〈たんい：単位〉a unit, a denomination; a credit.

    tan·i o machigaeru〈単位を間違える〉 mistake the unit

    san-juttan·i toru〈三十単位取る〉 take 30 credits

tanin〈たにん：他人〉another person, others, an unrelated person, a stranger.

    aka-no tanin〈赤の他人〉 a complete stranger

tan·itsu〈たんいつ：単一〉singleness, unity, simplicity.

   tan·itsu-ka-suru〈単一化する〉simplify.

tan-jikan〈たんじかん：短時間〉a short time.

    tan-jikan-ni〈短時間に〉 in a short time

tanjô-bi〈たんじょうび：誕生日〉one's birthday.

    tanjô-bi o iwau〈誕生日を祝う〉 celebrate one's birthday

tanjû〈たんじゅう：短銃〉a pistol, a revolver.

tanjû〈たんじゅう：胆汁〉bile, gall.

   tanjû-shitsu-no〈胆汁質の〉of bilious temperament.

tanjun〈たんじゅん：単純〉simplicity.

   tanjun-ka-suru〈単純化する〉simplify.

   tanjun-na〈単純な〉simple.

tanka〈たんか：担架〉a stretcher.

    tanka-de hakobu〈担架で運ぶ〉 carry ((a person)) on a stretcher

tanka〈たんか：単価〉a unit price.

tanka〈たんか：短歌〉a Japanese poem of 31 syllables, a *tanka*.

tanka〈たんか〉

   tanka-o-kiru〈たんかを切る〉swear ((at)), hurl defiance ((at)).

tanka〈たんか：炭化〉carbonization.

    tanka-butsu〈炭化物〉 a carbide

   tanka-suru〈炭化する〉carbonize.

tanken〈たんけん：探検〉exploration, expedition.

    tanken-tai〈探検隊〉 an exploration party

    tanken-ka〈探検家〉 an explorer

   tanken-suru〈探検する〉explore.

tanki〈たんき：短気〉

   tanki-na〈短気な〉quick-tempered, hot-tempered, impatient, irritable.

   tanki-o-okosu〈短気を起こす〉lose (one's) temper, become impatient.

   tanki-o-okoshite〈短気を起こして〉in a fit of ill temper.

tanki 〈たんき：短期〉 a short term.
     tanki-kashi-tsuke（短期貸付け）a short-term loan
     tanki-daigaku（短期大学）a junior college
     tanki-no〈短期の〉short, brief, short-term.

tan-kikan 〈たんきかん：短期間〉a short period of time.

tankô 〈たんこう：炭坑(鉱)〉a coal mine.
     tankô-bakuhatsu（炭鉱爆発）a mine explosion

tankô-bon 〈たんこうぼん：単行本〉a separate volume.
     tankô-bon-to-shite   shuppan-suru（単行本として出版する）publish in book form

tankobu 〈たんこぶ〉a wen.
     me-no-ue-no-tankobu（目の上のたんこぶ）an eyesore

tanku 〈タンク〉a tank, a cistern.
     gasu-tanku（ガスタンク）a gas tank, a gasometer

tan-kyori 〈たんきょり：短距離〉a short distance.
     tan-kyori-kyôsô（短距離競走）a short-distance race, a sprint
     tan-kyori-senshu（短距離選手）a sprinter

tankyû 〈たんきゅう：探究〉research, investigation, study, inquiry.
     tankyû-suru〈探究する〉make researches ((in)), investigate, inquire ((into)).

tankyû 〈たんきゅう：探求〉search, pursuit.
     tankyû-suru〈探求する〉search ((for)), pursue.

tan-naru 〈たんなる：単なる〉mere, simple.
     tan-naru jôdan（単なる冗談）a mere joke

tannen 〈たんねん：丹念〉
     tannen-na〈丹念な〉painstaking, careful, elaborate.
     tannen-ni〈丹念に〉painstakingly, carefully, elaborately.

tan-ni 〈たんに：単に〉only, merely, simply.
     tan-ni~-de-aru-bakari-de-naku~-de-aru〈単に～であるばかりでなく～である〉not only...but also... .

tannin 〈タンニン〉tannin.
     tannin-san（タンニン酸）tannic acid

tannin 〈たんにん：担任〉charge.
     tannin-no kurasu（担任のクラス）a class under one's charge
     tannin-no sensei（担任の先生）a teacher in charge
     tannin-suru〈担任する〉take ((a class)) under one's charge.

tannô 〈たんのう：胆のう〉the gall.
     tannô-en（胆のう炎）inflammation of the gall

tannô〈たんのう：たん能〉
　tannô-de-aru〈たん能である〉be skillful ((at, in *or* of)), be good ((at)), be proficient ((in)).
　　Doitsu-go-ni-tannô-de-aru（ドイツ語にたん能である）be proficient in German
　tannô-suru〈たん能する〉be satisfied ((with)), have enough ((of)).

tanomi〈たのみ：頼み〉a request, a favor; reliance.
　　tanomi-ga-aru（頼みがある）have a favor to ask of ((a person))
　　tanomi-o-kiku（頼みを聴く）do ((a person)) a favor, comply with another's request
　　tanomi-no-tsuna（頼みの綱）one's only hope, one's last prop
　tanomi-ni-suru〈頼みにする〉rely ((on)), depend ((on)).
　tanomi-gai-no-aru〈頼みがいのある〉reliable, dependable, trustworthy.
　　tanomi-gai-no-nai（頼みがいのない）unreliable, undependable, untrustworthy

tanomoshii〈たのもしい：頼もしい〉reliable, trustworthy, promising.
　　sue-tanomoshii seinen（末頼もしい青年）a promising young man

tanomu〈たのむ：頼む〉ask, beg, make a request ((to)); trust, charge; rely ((on)), depend ((on)); engage, hire, call in.
　　enjo-o-tanomu（援助を頼む）ask ((a person)) for help
　　tanomare-mo-shi-nai-noni（頼まれもしないのに）without being asked, unasked
　　tegami-o-tanomu（手紙を頼む）charge ((a person)) with a letter
　　Kare-wa　tanomu-ni-tari-nai.（彼は頼むに足りない.）He cannot be relied on.
　　isha o tanomu（医者を頼む）call in a doctor

tanoshi-ge〈たのしげ：楽しげ〉
　tanoshi-ge-na〈楽しげな〉joyful, cheerful, merry, pleasant, happy, gay.
　tanoshi-ge-ni〈楽しげに〉joyfully, cheerfully, merrily, pleasantly, happily, gaily.

tanoshii〈たのしい：楽しい〉pleasant, happy, delightful.
　　tanoshii omoi-o-suru（楽しい思いをする）have a pleasant time
　　tanoshii omoi-de（楽しい思い出）a happy memory
　　Kinô-wa　tanoshikatta.（昨日は楽しかった.）I enjoyed myself yesterday.
　tanoshiku〈楽しく〉pleasantly, happily, delightfully.
　　tanoshiku kurasu（楽しく暮らす）live happily

tanoshimaseru〈たのしませる：楽しませる〉delight, please, enjoy,

amuse, give pleasure ((to)), feast, entertain.

me o tanoshimaseru（目を楽しませる）feast one's eyes ((on))

tanoshimi 〈たのしみ：楽しみ〉pleasure, delight, happiness, (an) a-musement.

dokusho no tanoshimi（読書の楽しみ）the pleasure of reading

Kare-wa　tozan-o-tanoshimi-ni-shite-iru.（彼は登山を楽しみにしている。）He takes pleasure in going up a mountain.

Raigetsu o-me-ni-kakaru-no-o-tanoshimi-ni-shite-imasu.（来月お目にかかるのを楽しみにしています。）I am looking forward to seeing you next month.

tanoshimu 〈たのしむ：楽しむ〉take pleasure ((in)), enjoy (oneself) ((by *or* over)), amuse oneself ((by *or* with)).

jinsei o tanoshimu（人生を楽しむ）enjoy life

hitori-de tanoshimu（一人で楽しむ）enjoy by oneself

tanrei 〈たんれい：端麗〉

yōshi-tanrei-de-aru（容姿端麗である）have a graceful figure

tanrei-na（端麗な）graceful, elegant, handsome, fair.

tanren 〈たんれん：鍛錬〉training, discipline, drill(ing).

tanren-suru〈鍛錬する〉train, discipline, drill.

shinshin o tanren-suru（心身を鍛錬する）train one's body and mind

tanri 〈たんり：単利〉simple interest.

tan-saibô 〈たんさいぼう：単細胞〉

tan-saibô-no（単細胞の）unicellular.

tan-saibô-teki(-na)〈単細胞的(な)〉with a single-celled mind.

tansaku 〈たんさく：探索〉

tansaku-chû-de-aru（探索中である）be searching〔for the criminal〕

tansaku-suru〈探索する〉search ((for)), make a search ((for)), look ((for)).

tansan 〈たんさん：炭酸〉carbonic acid.

tansan-gasu（炭酸ガス）carbonic acid gas

tansan-sui（炭酸水）soda water

tansei 〈たんせい：丹精〉

tansei-komete〈丹精込めて〉with devotion, with great(*or* utmost) care.

tansei 〈たんせい：嘆声〉a sigh, lamentation; a sigh of admiration.

tansei-o-morasu（嘆声を漏らす）heave a sigh of grief; heave a sigh of admiration ((at))

tanseki 〈たんせき：胆石〉a gallstone.

tansen 〈たんせん：単線〉a single track.

tansen-unten（単線運転）the single-track operation

tansen-no〈単線の〉single-track.

tanshi〈たんし：端子〉a terminal.

tan-shichû〈タンシチュー〉tongue stew.

tanshiki-boki〈たんしきぼき：単式簿記〉bookkeeping by single entry.

tanshin〈たんしん：短針〉the hour hand.

tanshin〈たんしん：単身〉alone, unaccompanied, unattended, singlehanded.

tansho〈たんしょ：短所〉a defect, a fault, a demerit, a weak point.
　　tansho-o-oginau（短所を補う）make up for one's defects

tanshô〈たんしょう：嘆賞(称)〉admiration, praise, applause.
　tanshô-suru〈嘆賞(称)する〉admire, praise, applaud.

tanshoku〈たんしょく：単色〉a single color.

tanshoku〈たんしょく：淡色〉a light color.

tanshô-tô〈たんしょうとう：探照灯〉a searchlight.

tanshuku〈たんしゅく：短縮〉shortening, contraction, reduction.
　　sôgyô-tanshuku（操業短縮）reduction of operation
　tanshuku-suru〈短縮する〉shorten, contract, reduce, cut down.

tanso〈たんそ：炭素〉carbon.

tansoku〈たんそく：嘆息〉a sigh, lamentation.
　tansoku-suru〈嘆息する〉heave a sigh, lament.

tansu〈たんす〉a chest of drawers, a cabinet, a bureau.
　　yôfuku-dansu（洋服だんす）a wardrobe, a dresser

tansû〈たんすう：単数〉the singular number.
　tansû-no〈単数の〉singular.

tansui〈たんすい：淡水〉fresh water.
　　tansui-gyo（淡水魚）a fresh-water fish

tan-suika-butsu〈たんすいかぶつ：炭水化物〉a carbohydrate.

tantan〈たんたん：淡々〉
　tantan-to-shita〈淡々とした〉cool, disinterested, unconcerned, indifferent; plain.

tantei〈たんてい：探偵〉a detective.
　　tantei-shôsetsu（探偵小説）a detective story
　　shiritsu-tantei（私立探偵）a private detective

tanteki〈たんてき：端的〉
　tanteki-na〈端的な〉direct, frank, straightforward, point-blank.
　tanteki-ni〈端的に〉directly, frankly, plainly, straightforwardly, point-blank.
　　tanteki-ni ieba（端的に言えば）frankly speaking

tantô 〈たんとう：短刀〉 a short sword, a dagger.

tantô 〈たんとう：担当〉 charge.

    tantô-sha（担当者）　the person in charge ((of))

    tantô-suru（担当する）take charge ((of)), be in charge ((of)).

tantô-chokunyû 〈たんとうちょくにゅう：単刀直入〉

    tantô-chokunyû-ni-ieba〈単刀直入に言えば〉see.　tanteki-ni ieba.

tan-tsuba 〈たんつば〉 spittle.

    tan-tsuba-o-haku〈たんつばを吐く〉spit.

tan-tsubo 〈たんつぼ〉 a spittoon, a cuspidor.

tanuki 〈たぬき〉 a raccoon dog.

    tanuki-neiri-o-suru〈たぬき寝入りをする〉pretend to be asleep.

taoreru 〈たおれる：倒れる〉fall, come down; break down; be ruined, collapse, fall, fail.

    aomuke-ni taoreru（仰向けに倒れる）　fall on one's back

    kaze-de-taoreru（風で倒れる）　be blown down

    karô-de taoreru（過労で倒れる）　break down from overwork

    Tsui-ni gen-naikaku wa taoreta.（ついに現内閣は倒れた.）　At last the Cabinet has collapsed.

    taore-kakatta〈倒れかかった〉tottering, falling, tumbledown.

taosu 〈たおす：倒す〉blow down, cut down, knock down, push down, throw down, fell; defeat, beat, overthrow, kill.

tappitsu 〈たっぴつ：達筆〉a skillful handwriting.

    tappitsu-na hito（達筆な人）　a skillful penman

tappuri 〈たっぷり〉full, enough, good, plentifully.

    tappuri mikka（たっぷり三日）　full three days

    tappuri go-mairu（たっぷり五マイル）　a good five miles

    Jikan wa tappuri-aru.（時間はたっぷりある.）　We have plenty of time.

    aikyô-tappuri-de-aru（愛きょうたっぷりである）　be overflowing with smiles

tara 〈たら〉a cod.

    tara-ko（たら子）　cod roe

-tara 〈-たら〉if, when.

    ame-ga-futtara（雨が降ったら）　if it rains

tarafuku 〈たらふく：たら腹〉

    tarafuku-taberu〈たらふく食べる〉eat one's fill.

tarai 〈たらい〉a tub, a washbowl.

tarappu 〈タラップ〉a gangway (ladder), a ramp.

　　tarappu o oriru〈タラップを降りる〉step down the ladder

taratara〈たらたら〉

　fuhei-taratara-de-aru〈不平たらたらである〉be full of complaints.

-tarazu〈-たらず：足らず〉less than.

　　ikkagetsu-tarazu（一か月足らず）less than a month

tare〈たれ：垂れ〉sauce, gravy, dripping(s).

tare-komeru〈たれこめる：垂れこめる〉hang (low) ((over)).

　　hikuku-tare-kometa kumo（低く垂れこめた雲）low-hung clouds

tare-maku〈たれまく：垂れ幕〉a hanging screen, a curtain.

tareru〈たれる：垂れる〉hang, droop, dangle; drip, drop.

　　ryô-ashi o darari-to-tareru（両足をだらりと垂れる）dangle one's legs

tare-sagaru〈たれさがる：垂れ下がる〉hang down, dangle.

-tari〈-たり〉now...now... , now...and then... , sometimes...sometimes... .

　　futtari-yandari-suru（降ったりやんだりする）rain off and on

tariki-hongan〈たりきほんがん：他力本願〉reliance on others.

　　Kare-wa nani-goto-mo tariki-hongan-da.（彼は何事も他力本願だ.）He always turns to others for help (in everything).

tariru〈たりる：足りる〉be enough, be sufficient.

　tari-nai〈足りない〉be not enough, be insufficient, lack, be short ((of)); be not worth.

　　majime-sa-ga-tari-nai（まじめさが足りない）lack seriousness

　　hito-de-ga-tari-nai（人手が足りない）be short of hands

　　yomu-ni-tari-nai（読むに足りない）be not worth reading

　　toru-ni-tari-nai（取るに足りない）count for nothing; trifling

taru〈たる〉a cask, a barrel.

　taru-zume-no〈たる詰めの〉casked, barreled.

târu(-o-nuru)〈タール(をぬる)：タール(を塗る)〉tar.

tarumi〈たるみ〉slack(ening), loosening, relaxation.

　tarumi-no-nai〈たるみのない〉tight, tense, strained.

tarumu〈たるむ〉slacken, be loosened; relax.

　　Tsuna ga sukoshi tarunde-iru.（綱が少したるんでいる.）The rope is slackening a little.

taryô〈たりょう：多量〉a large quantity, a great deal.

　taryô-no〈多量の〉a large quantity of, a great deal of, much.

　taryô-ni〈多量に〉in large quantities, much.

tasai〈たさい：多才〉versatile talents.

　tasai-na〈多才な〉versatile.

tasatsu 〈たさつ：他殺〉murder.

Tasatsu no utagai-ga-koi.（他殺の疑いが濃い.）There is a strong suspicion of murder.

tashi 〈たし：足し〉

tashi-ni-suru 〈足しにする〉supplement, help.

shûnyû-no-tashi-ni-suru（収入の足しにする）supplement one's income

tashi-ni-naru 〈足しになる〉help, be of use.

Ichi-man-en-dewa amari-tashi-ni-nara-nakatta.（一万円では余り足しにならなかった.）A ten thousand yen didn't help much.

tashika 〈たしか：確か〉

Sore-wa-tashika-da.（それは確かだ.）I am sure of it. / There is no doubt about it.

tashika-na 〈確かな〉sure, certain, positive, definite; reliable, trustworthy; accurate, correct.

tashika-na jijitsu（確かな事実）a positive fact

tashika-na henji（確かな返事）a definite answer

tashika-na hito（確かな人）a reliable person

tashika-na Furansu-go（確かなフランス語）correct French

tashika-ni 〈確かに〉surely, certainly, to be sure, positively, no doubt, without fail.

Tashika-ni!（確かに.）Certainly. / To be sure.

tashika 〈たしか：確か〉perhaps, if I remember right, if I am correct.

Tashika kongetsu-hajime-no-koto-deshita.（確か今月初めのことでした.）It was at the beginning of this month, if I remember correct.

tashikameru 〈たしかめる：確かめる〉make sure ((of *or* that)), ascertain, see if(*or* whether).

tashinameru 〈たしなめる〉reprove, correct.

manâ-ga-warui-no-o-tashinameru（マナーが悪いのをたしなめる）reprove ((a person)) for his bad manners

tashinami 〈たしなみ〉(a) taste, relish, prudence, modesty, accomplishments.

tashinami-ga-ii（たしなみがいい）have a good taste

tashinami o kaku（たしなみを欠く）lack modesty

bungaku-no tashinami（文学のたしなみ）literary accomplishments

tashinamu 〈たしなむ〉have a taste, like, love.

haiku-o-tashinamu（俳句をたしなむ）have a taste for *haiku*

tashi-zan〈たしざん：足し算〉addition.

　tashi-zan-o-suru〈足し算をする〉add up.

tashô〈たしょう：多少〉a little, some, somewhat; many or few, number, quantity, amount.

　　　tashô Ei-go-ga-hanaseru（多少英語が話せる）be able to speak English a little

　　　Go-chûmon wa tashô-ni-kakawarazu o-uke-itashimasu.（御注文は多少にかかわらずお受けいたします。）All orders, whether large or small, will be gratefully accepted.

ta-shumi〈たしゅみ：多趣味〉

　ta-shumi-na〈多趣味な〉of versatile interests.

tashu-tayô〈たしゅたよう：多種多様〉

　tashu-tayô-na〈多種多様な〉various, diversified.

tasogare〈たそがれ〉dusk; twilight.

　　　tasogare-doki-ni（たそがれ時に）at dusk, in the twilight

tassei〈たっせい：達成〉achievement, attainment.

　tassei-suru〈達成する〉achieve, attain, realize, work out.

tassha〈たっしゃ：達者〉

　　　tassha-de-iru（達者でいる）be in good health

　　　Eigo-ga-tassha-da（英語が達者だ）speak good English

　　　keisan-ga-tassha-da（計算が達者だ）be good at figures

　tassha-na〈達者な〉healthy, well, in good health; good (at), skillful.

　tassha-ni〈達者に〉skillfully, fluently.

tassuru〈たっする：達する〉reach, arrive ((at)); amount ((to)); attain, achieve.

　　　mokuteki-chi-ni-tassuru（目的地に達する）arrive at one's destination

　　　hyaku-man-en-ni-tassuru（百万円に達する）amount to one million yen

　　　mokuteki o tassuru（目的を達する）attain one's object

tasu〈たす：足す〉add.

　　　San-tasu-go wa-hachi.（三足す五は八。）Three and five makes eight.

tasû〈たすう：多数〉a great number, (a) majority.

　　　tasû o shimeru（多数を占める）command a majority

　　　tasû-hyô（多数票）majority vote

　　　tasû-iken（多数意見）a majority opinion

　tasû-no〈多数の〉many, a great many, a large number of.

　　　tasû-no hitobito（多数の人々）a large number of people

tasukaru 〈たすかる：助かる〉 be of help; be saved, be rescued, survive.

    Sô-shite-kudasareba taihen tasukaru-no-desu-ga.（そうしてくだされば大変助かるのですが.） That would be of great help to me.

    un-yoku tasukaru（運よく助かる） be fortunately saved

    yatto-tasukaru（やっと助かる） have a narrow escape

    Kare-no-tasukaru-mikomi-wa-hotondo-nai.（彼の助かる見込みはほとんどない.） There is little hope of his recovery.

    tasukaranai-mono-to-akirameru（助からないものとあきらめる） give up ((a person)) for lost

tasuke 〈たすけ：助け〉 help, aid, assistance; rescue.

    tasuke-o-motomeru（助けを求める） ask ((a person)) for help

    tasuke-ni iku（助けに行く） go to the rescue ((of))

tasuke-au 〈たすけあう：助け合う〉 help each other.

tasuke-bune 〈たすけぶね：助け船〉 a lifeboat, a rescue boat; help.

    tasuke-bune-o-dasu〈助け船を出す〉 come to ((a person's)) rescue.

tasuke-dasu 〈たすけだす：助け出す〉 help ((a person)) out of, rescue ((a person)) from.

tasuke-okosu 〈たすけおこす：助け起こす〉 help ((a person)) to his feet, help ((a person)) up.

tasukeru 〈たすける：助ける〉 help, assist; save, rescue.

    shigoto-o-tasukeru（仕事を助ける） help ((a person)) in his work

    oboreru-kodomo-o-tasukeru（おぼれる子供を助ける） save a child from drowning

    shôka o tasukeru（消化を助ける） promote digestion

tasû-ketsu 〈たすうけつ：多数決〉 decision by majority.

    tasû-ketsu-de kimeru（多数決で決める） decide by majority

tataeru 〈たたえる〉 praise, admire.

    yûki-o-tataeru（勇気をたたえる） praise ((a person)) for his courage

tataeru 〈たたえる〉

    mammen-ni-emi-o-tataeru（満面に笑みをたたえる） be beaming with smiles

tatakai 〈たたかい：戦(闘)い〉 a war; a battle, a fight; a struggle; a contest.

    tatakai ni katsu（戦いに勝つ） win a battle

    rôshi-kan-no tatakai（労資間の闘い） a struggle between capital and labor

    tatakau〈戦(闘)う〉 fight ((against *or* with)).

    heiwa-no-tame-ni tatakau（平和のために戦う） fight for peace

　　konnan-to tatakau〈困難と闘う〉fight against difficulties
　　saigo-made tatakau〈最後まで戦う〉fight to the end
　　yūwaku to tatakau〈誘惑と闘う〉resist a temptation

tatakai-nuku〈たたかいぬく：戦(闘)い抜く〉fight through, fight it out.

tatakawasu〈たたかわす：戦(闘)わす〉
　giron-o-tatakawasu〈議論を闘わす〉have a hot discussion with ((a person)) about.

tataki-ageru〈たたきあげる：たたき上げる〉work one's way up.

tataki-dasu〈たたきだす：たたき出す〉turn ((a person)) out of doors, kick out.

tataki-komu〈たたきこむ：たたき込む〉throw into; hammer ((into)), beat ((something)) into ((a person's head)).

tataki-korosu〈たたきころす：たたき殺す〉beat ((a person)) to death.

tataki-kowasu〈たたきこわす：たたき壊す〉knock ((a thing)) to pieces, break down.

tataki-nomesu〈たたきのめす〉knock ((a person)) down.

tataki-okosu〈たたきおこす：たたき起こす〉knock ((a person)) up, rouse ((a person)) out of bed.

tataki-otosu〈たたきおとす：たたき落とす〉knock ((a thing)) down, knock ((a thing)) out of ((a person's hand)).

tataki-tsukeru〈たたきつける：たたき付ける〉pelt; throw, thrust.
　　Ame ga tataki-tsukeru-yô-ni-futteiru.（雨がたたきつけるように降っている。）Rain is pelting.
　　koppu o yuka-ni-tataki-tsukeru（コップを床にたたきつける）throw a cup against the floor
　　jihyô o tataki-tsukeru（辞表をたたきつける）thrust one's resignation ((at))

tataku〈たたく〉strike, pat, knock, beat; attack, criticize.
　　atama o tataku（頭をたたく）strike ((a person)) on the head
　　kata o tataku（肩をたたく）pat ((a person)) on the shoulder
　　to-o tataku（戸をたたく）knock at the door
　　taiko o tataku（太鼓をたたく）beat a drum
　　ne-o-tataku（値をたたく）beat down
　　shimbun-de tatakareru（新聞でたたかれる）be attacked in the newspaper

tatami〈たたみ：畳〉straw matting.
　　tatami-no-omote-gae-o-suru（畳の表替えをする）re-cover the matting
　　tatami-no-ue-de-shinu（畳の上で死ぬ）die in one's bed, die a natural

death

tatami-komu 〈たたみこむ：畳み込む〉 fold in, turn in.

tatamu 〈たたむ：畳む〉 fold; shut up.

  futon o tatamu（布団を畳む）fold up beddings

  mise o tatamu（店を畳む）shut up one's shop, wind up one's business

tatari 〈たたり〉 a curse, an evil spell.

  Ato-no-tatari-ga-kowai-zo.（後のたたりが怖いぞ.）There will be the devil to pay.

  Yowari-me-ni-tatari-me.（弱り目にたたり目.）Misfortunes never come single.

tataru 〈たたる〉 bring an evil ((upon)), curse, haunt, torment.

  onryô-ni tatarareru（おん霊にたたられる）be haunted by a vengeful spirit

tatasu 〈たたす：立たす〉 make ((a person)) stand, raise, lift ((a person)) to his feet.

tatchi 〈タッチ〉 a touch; kiss.

  Kanojo-wa piano-no-tatchi-ga-katai.（彼女はピアノのタッチが硬い.）She has a hard touch at the piano.

  tatchi-no-sa-de katsu（タッチの差で勝つ）beat ((a person)) by a touch

tatchi-suru 〈タッチする〉 touch; be a party ((to)).

  sôsha ni tatchi-suru（走者にタッチする）touch a runner

  Sonna-koto-ni-tatchi-shite-wa-ikenai.（そんなことにタッチしてはいけない.）You must keep out of that.

tate 〈たて：盾〉 a shield.

〜-o-tate-ni-totte 〈〜を盾に取って〉 on the strength of〔law〕.

tate 〈たて：縦〉 length.

  tate-ni-jussenchi yoko san-jussenchi（縦二十センチ横三十センチ）twenty centimeters long and thirty centimeters wide

tate-no 〈縦の〉 lengthwise, vertical.

  tate-no sen（縦の線）a vertical line

tate-ni 〈縦に〉 lengthwise, vertically.

  tate-ni naraberu（縦に並べる）arrange ((things)) lengthwise

-tate 〈-たて〉 fresh from.

  tori-tate-no sakana（捕りたての魚）fish fresh from the sea

  yaki-tate-no pan（焼きたてのパン）bread hot from the oven

  kai-tate-no bôshi（買いたての帽子）a brand-new hat

tate-ana 〈たてあな：縦穴〉a pit.

tate-fuda 〈たてふだ：立て札〉a bulletin board, a notice board.
　　tate-fuda o tateru〈立て札を立てる〉 set up a bulletin board

tate-gaki 〈たてがき：縦書き〉vertical writing.
　tate-gaki-ni-suru〈縦書きにする〉write vertically.

tategami 〈たてがみ〉a mane.
　tategami-no-aru〈たてがみのある〉maned.

tategu 〈たてぐ：建具〉fittings, fixtures, furnishings.
　tategu-o-ireru〈建具を入れる〉furnish〔a house〕, fit up〔a room〕.

tate-hiza 〈たてひざ：立てひざ〉
　tate-hiza-o-suru〈立てひざをする〉sit with one knee drawn up.

tate-ita 〈たていた：立て板〉
　tate-ita-ni-mizu-o-nagasu-yō-ni〈立て板に水を流すように〉with great fluency.

tate-jima 〈たてじま：縦じま〉vertical stripes, pin stripes.
　tate-jima-no〈縦じまの〉striped.

tate-kae 〈たてかえ：立て替え〉payment for another.
　tate-kaeru〈立て替える〉pay for another.

tate-kaeru 〈たてかえる：建て替える〉rebuild.

tate-kakeru 〈たてかける：立て掛ける〉lean ((something)) against〔a wall〕.

tate-kamban 〈たてかんばん：立て看板〉a standing signboard.

tate-kata 〈たてかた：建て方〉the style of building, structure, the way of building.

tate-komoru 〈たてこもる：立てこもる〉hole up〔in a building〕.

tate-komu 〈たてこむ：立て込む〉be crowded ((with)); be busy ((with)), be pressed〔with business〕.
　　kyaku-ga-tate-konde-iru（客が立て込んでいる）be crowded with customers
　　isogi-no shigoto-ga-tate-konde-iru〔急ぎの仕事が立て込んでいる〕be pressed with rush work

tate-komu 〈たてこむ：建て込む〉be crowded with houses.
　　Kono-hen wa biru-ga-tate-konde-iru.（この辺はビルが建て込んでい
　　る。）The neighborhood is crowded with buildings.

tatemae 〈たてまえ：建て前〉the erection of the framework of a house; a principle, a policy, a rule, a basis.

tate-mashi 〈たてまし：建て増し〉extention of a building.
　tate-mashi-suru〈建て増しする〉extend a building.

hito-heya　tate-mashi-suru（一部屋建て増しする）have one room added to one's house

tatemono〈たてもの：建物〉 a building, a structure, an edifice, architecture.

tate-naosu〈たてなおす：立て直す〉make over, reconstruct, reorganize.

keikaku o tate-naosu（計画を立て直す）make a plan anew

kuni-no　zaisei　o　tate-naosu（国の財政を立て直す）rebuild the national economy

tate-naosu〈たてなおす：建て直す〉rebuild.

ie o tate-naosu（家を建て直す）have one's house rebuilt

tatene〈たてね：建値〉official quotations, market prices.

tateru〈たてる：立てる〉stand, set up, hoist; make, get up; look up ((to)), regard, respect; circulate.

rôsoku o tateru（ろうそくを立てる）stand a candle

hata o tateru（旗を立てる）hoist a flag

keikaku o tateru（計画を立てる）make a plan

oto o tateru（音を立てる）make a noise

yuge o tateru（湯気を立てる）get up steam

sempai-no-kao-o-tateru（先輩の顔を立てる）pay due respect to one's seniors

uwasa o tateru（うわさを立てる）circulate a rumor

tateru〈たてる：建てる〉build, construct, erect, establish, found.

ie o tateru（家を建てる）have one's house built

gakkô o tateru（学校を建てる）found an institution

tate-tsubo〈たてつぼ：建坪〉floor space.

tate-tsuke〈たてつけ：立て付け〉

Kono　to　wa　tate-tsuke-ga-warui.（この戸は立て付けが悪い.）This door doesn't open and shut well.

tate-tsuku〈たてつく：盾突く〉oppose, set oneself ((against)), defy, disobey.

tate-tsuzuke〈たてつづけ：立て続け〉

tate-tsuzuke-ni〈立て続けに〉in succession, running, at a stretch.

tate-tsuzuke-ni　ni-hai-mizu-o-nomu（立て続けに二杯水を飲む）take two glasses of water in quick succession

tate-uri〈たてうり：建て売り〉

tate-uri-no jûtaku（建て売りの住宅）a ready-built house

tate-yakusha〈たてやくしゃ：立て役者〉the leading actor, a leader.

tate-yoko〈たてよこ：縦横〉length and breadth.

tate-yoko-ni〈縦横に〉crosswise, lengthwise and breadthwise.

tatoe〈たとえ：例え〉a fable, a proverb, an example.

tatoe〈たとえ〉even if, even though.

    tatoe-jôdan-demo（たとえ冗談でも）even in joke

    tatoe-donna-ni-atama-ga-yoku-temo（たとえどんなに頭がよくても）however clever one may be

tatoeba〈たとえば：例えば〉for example, such as.

tatoeru〈たとえる：例える〉compare ((to)), liken ((to)).

tatsu〈たつ：立つ〉stand (up), rise; start, leave, depart, set out.

    endan-ni tatsu（演壇に立つ）stand on a platform

    Rondon-e tatsu（ロンドンへ立つ）leave for London

    Tatsu-tori-ato-o-nigosazu.（立つ鳥跡を濁さず。）It is an ill bird that fouls its own nest.

tatsu〈たつ：建つ〉be built, be set up.

    Yamada-shi-no-dôzô-ga-tatta.（山田氏の銅像が建った。）A bronze statue was erected to the memory of Mr. Yamada.

tatsu〈たつ〉pass (by *or* away), go on.

    Are-kara san-nen tatsu.（あれから三年たつ。）Three years have passed since then.

    toki-ga-tatsu-ni-tsurete（時がたつにつれて）as time goes by

tatsu〈たつ：裁つ〉cut.

    futatsu-ni tatsu（二つに裁つ）cut in two

tatsu〈たつ：絶つ〉sever, cut off, break off.

    kôsai o tatsu（交際を絶つ）sever acquaintance with ((a person))

    gaikô-kankei o tatsu（外交関係を絶つ）break off diplomatic relations ((with))

tatsu〈たつ：断つ〉abstain ((from)), give up.

    tabako o tatsu（たばこを断つ）give up smoking

tatsumaki〈たつまき：竜巻〉a waterspout, a windspout, a whirlwind.

tatsu-no-otoshigo〈たつのおとしご：竜の落とし子〉a sea horse.

tatsu-se〈たつせ：立つ瀬〉

    Sore-jâ tatsu-se-ga-nai.（それじゃあ立つ瀬がない。）That will leave me in an awkward position.

tatta〈たった〉only, just.

    tatta ni-jikan（たった二時間）for only two hours

    tatta-hitori-de（たった一人で）all alone, all by oneself

    Chichi wa tatta-ima kaetta-tokoro-desu.（父はたった今帰ったところです。）Father has just come back.

taue〈たうえ：田植え〉rice-planting.

  taue-suru〈田植えする〉plant rice, transplant rice.

tawai-naku〈たわいなく〉

  tawai-naku nemutteiru〈たわいなく眠っている〉be sleeping innocently.

tawamu〈たわむ〉bend, be bent.

  Kaze-ga-tsuyokute eda-ga-tawande-iru.（風が強くて枝がたわんでいる．） The strong wind makes the branches bend.

tawamure〈たわむれ：戯れ〉

  tawamure-ni〈戯れに〉for fun, in joke, out of mere caprice.

  tawamureru〈戯れる〉play, sport, disport oneself, romp; flirt ((with)).

tawara〈たわら：俵〉a straw bag.

  kome-dawara（米俵）a straw rice-bag

tawashi〈たわし〉a pot cleaner, a scrubbing brush.

tawawa〈たわわ〉

  eda-mo-tawawa-ni〈枝もたわわに〉with branches bent low with fruit.

tayasui〈たやすい〉easy, simple.

  tayasuku〈たやすく〉easily, without trouble.

  tayasuku hiki-ukeru（たやすく引き受ける） accept ((something)) so readily

tayô〈たよう：多様〉

  tayô-sei（多様性） diversity

  tayô-ka-suru〈多様化する〉diversify.

tayori〈たより：便り〉a letter, news.

  tayori-ga-aru〈便りがある〉hear ((from))

  tayori-ga-nai（便りがない） have no news ((from))

  tayori-o-suru〈便りをする〉write ((a letter)) to ((a person)).

tayori〈たより：頼り〉reliance, trust, help.

  rôgo-no tayori（老後の頼り） a prop for one's old age

  tayori-nai〈頼りない〉unreliable, undependable, helpless; vague, indefinite.

  tayori-nai henji（頼りない返事） a vague answer

  tayori-ni〈頼りに〉with the help ((of)).

  chizu-o-tayori-ni sagasu（地図を頼りに捜す） look for ((a place)) with the help of a map

  tayori-ni-naru〈頼りになる〉be reliable, be trustworthy.

  tayori-ni-nara-nai（頼りにならない） be unreliable, be untrustworthy

  tayori-ni-suru〈頼りにする〉see. tayoru.

tayoru〈たよる：頼る〉rely ((on)), depend ((on)), fall back ((on)).

Watashi-wa dare-mo tayoru-hito-ga-nai.（私はだれも頼る人がない。） I have no one to rely on.

tayumu〈たゆむ〉

tayumanu〈たゆまぬ〉untiring, unremitting, steady, persistent.

tayumanu doryoku（たゆまぬ努力）an unremitting effort

(umazu-)tayumazu〈（うまず）たゆまず〉unremittingly, steadily.

tayumazu-doryoku-suru（たゆまず努力する）persevere in one's efforts

tazan-no-ishi〈たざんのいし：他山の石〉

Motte-tazan-no-ishi-to-su-beki-de-aru.（もって他山の石とすべきである。）Let this be a good lesson to you.

tazei〈たぜい：多勢〉superiority in number.

tazei-o-tanonde（多勢を頼んで）relying on numbers.

tazuna〈たづな：手綱〉a bridle, reins.

tazuna o hiki-shimeru（手綱を引き締める）tighten the reins

tazuna o yurumeru（手綱を緩める）slacken the reins

tazune-bito〈たずねびと：尋ね人〉a missing person.

tazuneru〈たずねる：訪ねる〉visit, call ((on)), call ((at)), go to see, drop in.

tazuneru〈たずねる：尋ねる〉ask, inquire.

riyû o tazuneru（理由を尋ねる）ask (for) the reason

te〈て：手〉the hand.

te o ageru（手を挙げる）raise one's hand

te o furu（手を振る）wave one's hand

te o nobasu（手を伸ばす）stretch one's hand

te o sashi-dasu（手を差し出す）hold out one's hand

te-o-hanasu（手を放す）loose one's hold ((of *or* on))

te-o-totte annai-suru（手を取って案内する）lead ((a person)) by the hand

te-ni-te-o-totte aruku（手に手を取って歩く）walk hand in hand

te o tsunagu（手をつなぐ）join hands

kaban o te-ni-motte（かばんを手に持って）with a bag in one's hand

te-o-tataite-yorokobu（手をたたいて喜ぶ）clap one's hands with joy

te-ni-ireru〈手に入れる〉get, obtain, take possession ((of)).

te-ni-hairu（手に入る）come to one's hands, come into one's possession

hito-no te-ni-wataru（人の手に渡る）fall into another's hands

te-ga-fusagatte-iru〈手がふさがっている〉be engaged, have one's hands full.

Kyū-na shigoto-de-te-ga-hanase-nai.〔急な仕事で手が離せない.〕 I am held up over an urgent business.

Soko-made-wa te-ga-mawara-nai.〔そこまでは手が回らない.〕 I am unable to do that much.

te-ga-aite-iru〔手が空いている〕 be disengaged, have no work to do now

te-ni-tsuka-nai〔手に付かない〕 be unable to settle to work

te-ga-tari-nai〈手が足りない〉be short of hands, be shorthanded.

te o kasu〔手を貸す〕 lend ((a person)) a helping hand

te-ga-kakaru〈手が掛かる〉take much trouble.

te-ga-habukeru〔手が省ける〕 save trouble

te-no-konda〔手の込んだ〕 elaborate, complicated

te-o-nuku〔手を抜く〕 scamp one's work

te-o-dasu or *te-o-tsukeru*〈手を出す, 手を付ける〉turn one's hand ((to)), attempt, meddle ((in or with)); become intimate ((with)).

te-o-utsu〔手を打つ〕 take a measure; close a bargain ((with))

te-o-hirogeru〔手を広げる〕 extend operations

te-o-hiku or te-o-kiru〔手を引く, 手を切る〕 sever one's connection ((with)), wash one's hands ((of)), break (off) ((with))

te-o-hanareru〔手を離れる〕 be off one's hands

te-o-tsukusu〈手を尽くす〉do all that can be done.

te-o-kaeru〔手を変える〕 try some other means

shi-jū-hatte〔四十八手〕 all the tricks in *sumo* wrestling

te-ni-noru〔手に乗る〕 be taken in

te-ni-amaru or *te-ni-oe-nai*〈手に余る, 手に負えない〉be beyond one's capacity, be unmanageable, be beyond one's control.

te-ga-de-nai〔手が出ない〕 be helpless, be powerless.

te-no-tsuke-yō-ga-nai〔手の付けようがない〕 be at a loss what to do ((with))

te-o-yaku〔手を焼く〕 have a bitter experience ((with))

te-ga-ii〈手がいい〉write a good hand.

kono te-no shina〈この手の品〉goods in this line.

te-aka〈てあか：手あか〉dirt from the hands.

te-aka-de-yogoreru〈手あかで汚れる〉be badly thumbed.

te-ami〈てあみ：手編み〉

te-ami-no〈手編みの〉hand-knit(ted), knit by hand.

tearai〈てあらい：手洗い〉hand-washing.

te-arai or **te-arana** 〈てあらい，てあらな：手荒い，手荒な〉rough, rude, harsh, violent.

  te-araku or *te-arani* 〈手荒く，手荒に〉roughly, rudely, violently.

    te-araku atsukau *or* te-arani atsukau（手荒く扱う，手荒に扱う）handle roughly, treat ((a person)) roughly

te-ashi 〈てあし：手足〉hands and feet, the limbs.

    te-ashi o shibaru（手足を縛る）bind ((a person)) hand and foot

  te-ashi-no-fu-jiyû-na 〈手足の不自由な〉crippled.

te-atari-shidai 〈てあたりしだい：手当たり次第〉

  te-atari-shidai-ni 〈手当たり次第に〉at random.

    te-atari-shidai-ni hon-o-yomu（手当たり次第に本を読む）read at random

teate 〈てあて：手当て〉an allowance; aid, treatment.

    teate o shikyû-suru（手当を支給する）give an allowance

    kazoku-teate（家族手当）a family allowance

    teate o ukeru（手当てを受ける）take treatment

    ôkyû-teate（応急手当て）first aid

  teate-o-suru 〈手当てをする〉treat, dress.

    kanja-no-teate-o-suru（患者の手当てをする）treat a patient

    kizu-no-teate-o-suru（傷の手当てをする）dress an injury

te-atsui 〈てあつい：手厚い〉warm, hearty, cordial, hospitable.

    te-atsui-kango-o-ukeru（手厚い看護を受ける）be nursed kindly

  te-atsuku 〈手厚く〉warmly, heartily, cordially, hospitably.

    te-atsuku motenasu（手厚くもてなす）treat ((a person)) cordially

te-banashi 〈てばなし：手放し〉

  te-banashi-de 〈手放しで〉openly, without reserve.

    Te-banashi-de-rakkan-shite-wa-ikenai.（手放しで楽観してはいけない.）You ought not to be overoptimistic.

te-banasu 〈てばなす：手放す〉dispose ((of)), do away ((with)), part ((with)); sell.

te-bayaku 〈てばやく：手早く〉quickly, smartly.

    shigoto o te-bayaku kata-zukeru（仕事を手早く片付ける）finish one's work quickly

te-biki 〈てびき：手引き〉guidance, lead; a guide, introduction.

  te-biki-suru 〈手引きする〉guide, lead.

tebiroku 〈てびろく：手広く〉extensively, widely, on a large scale.

    tebiroku shôbai-suru（手広く商売する）do business on a large scale

te-bukuro 〈てぶくろ：手袋〉gloves, mittens.

　　te-bukuro o hameru〈手袋をはめる〉 put on one's gloves
　　te-bukuro o hazusu〈手袋を外す〉 take off one's gloves

te-bura〈てぶら：手ぶら〉
　te-bura-de〈手ぶらで〉with empty hands, without taking any present.

têburu〈テーブル〉a table.
　　têburu-supîchi（テーブルスピーチ） an after-dinner speech

te-byôshi〈てびょうし：手拍子〉
　te-byôshi-o-utsu〈手拍子を打つ〉beat time with the hands.

te-chigai〈てちがい：手違い〉a mistake, an accident.
　nani-ka-no te-chigai-de〈何かの手違いで〉by some mistake.

techô〈てちょう：手帳〉a pocket notebook.
　　techô-ni tsukeru（手帳に付ける） write down in one's notebook

tedama〈てだま：手玉〉
　hito o tedama-ni-toru〈人を手玉に取る〉twist a person around one's (little) finger.

te-dashi〈てだし：手出し〉
　te-dashi-o-suru〈手出しをする〉see. te-o-dasu.
　　yokei-na-te-dashi-o-suru（余計な手出しをする） have a finger in the pie, poke one's nose ((into))

te-dasuke〈てだすけ：手助け〉help, assistance.
　te-dasuke-suru〈手助けする〉help, assist.

te-dori〈てどり：手取り〉one's salary after tax (deduction); a net income.

te-fuda〈てふだ：手札〉a card; a hand.
　te-fuda-gata-no〈手札型の〉card-size.

te-gakari〈てがかり：手掛かり〉a clue, a key, a track, a mark.
　　te-gakari o eru（手掛かりを得る） find a clue ((to)), find the trace ((of))
　　te-gakari-ga-nai（手掛かりがない） leave no clue ((to))

te-gakeru〈てがける：手掛ける〉handle, deal ((with)), have experience ((in *or* with)).
　te-gaketa-koto-no-nai〈手掛けたことのない〉unfamiliar, unaccustomed, new, strange.

te-gaki〈てがき：手書き〉handwriting.
　te-gaki-no〈手書きの〉handwritten.

tegami〈てがみ：手紙〉a letter.
　　tegami-de shiraseru（手紙で知らせる） inform ((a person)) of ((something)) by letter
　　tegami o uke-toru（手紙を受け取る） receive a letter

　　　　tegami-no-henji-o-dasu〈手紙の返事を出す〉 answer a letter

　tegami-o-kaku〈手紙を書く〉write a letter, write ((to)).

tegara〈てがら：手柄〉a merit, a feat.

　tegara-o-tateru〈手柄を立てる〉perform a feat, distinguish oneself ((in)).

tegaru〈てがる：手軽〉

　tegaru-na〈手軽な〉easy, simple, light.

　　　　tegaru-na hôhô（手軽な方法）a simple way

　　　　tegaru-na shokuji（手軽な食事）a light meal

　tegaru-ni〈手軽に〉easily, simply, lightly.

tegata〈てがた：手形〉a draft, a bill, a note.

　　　　tegata-de shiharau（手形で支払う）pay by draft

　　　　tegata o furi-dasu（手形を振り出す）draw a bill

　　　　tegata o teiji-suru（手形を呈示する）present a bill

　　　　tegata o hiki-ukeru（手形を引き受ける）accept a bill

　　　　tegata o otosu（手形を落とす）honor a bill

　　　　tegata o kaki-kaeru（手形を書き換える）renew a bill

　　　　tegata o shôkan-suru（手形を償還する）redeem a bill

　　　　kawase-tegata（為替手形）a bill of exchange

　　　　yakusoku-tegata（約束手形）a promissory note

　　　　yûzû-tegata（融通手形）an accommodation bill

　　　　shiharai-tegata（支払手形）a bill payable

　　　　uketori-tegata（受取手形）a bill receivable

　　　　tegata-furi-dashi-nin（手形振出人）a drawer of a bill

　　　　tegata-uketori-nin（手形受取人）a payee of a bill

tegatai〈てがたい：手堅い〉steady, sound, safe, trustworthy, reliable.

　　　　tegatai shôbai（手堅い商売）a safe business

　tegataku〈手堅く〉steadily, prudently, cautiously.

tegire-kin〈てぎれきん：手切れ金〉consolation money for separation.

tegiwa〈てぎわ：手際〉skill, tact, performance.

　tegiwa-no-ii〈手際のいい〉skillful, tactful, clever.

　tegiwa-yoku〈手際よく〉skillfully, tactfully, cleverly.

te-gokoro〈てごころ：手心〉discretion, consideration, allowance.

　te-gokoro-o-kuwaeru〈手心を加える〉use one's discretion, take ((a thing)) into consideration, make allowances ((for)), pull one's punches.

tegoro〈てごろ：手ごろ〉

　tegoro-na〈手ごろな〉handy, suitable, moderate.

　　　　tegoro-na nedan（手ごろな値段）a moderate price

te-gotae〈てごたえ：手ごたえ〉resistance, a response, a reaction, effect.

te-gotae-no-aru 〈手ごたえのある〉resisting, responsive, effectual.

   te-gotae-no-nai（手ごたえのない）passive, irresponsive, ineffectual

te-gowai 〈てごわい：手ごわい〉strong, tough, unyielding, formidable.

teguchi 〈てぐち：手口〉a way of doing, a trick.

   itsumo-no teguchi（いつもの手口）the same old trick

te-gusune 〈てぐすね：手ぐすね〉

te-gusune-hiite-matte-iru 〈手ぐすね引いて待っている〉be eagerly watching ((for)), be on the lookout ((for)).

tehai 〈てはい：手配〉arrangements, preparations, search instruction.

tehai-suru 〈手配する〉make arrangements ((for)), begin a search ((for)).

te-hajime 〈てはじめ：手始め〉

te-hajime-ni 〈手始めに〉in the beginning, to begin with, at the outset.

tehazu 〈てはず：手はず〉a program, a plan, arrangements.

   Tehazu ga kurutta.（手はずが狂った。）The program has gone a-miss.

tehazu-doori-ni 〈手はずどおりに〉as scheduled, according to arrangement.

te-hodoki 〈てほどき：手ほどき〉initiation, introduction, a primer, first steps ((in)), A.B.C. ((to)).

te-hodoki-suru 〈手ほどきする〉initiate ((a person)) into, introduce, give ((a person)) elementary lessons ((in)).

tehon 〈てほん：手本〉a copy; an example, a model.

   tehon-o-mite-kaku（手本を見て書く）write after a copy

   tehon o shimesu（手本を示す）set an example〔to others〕

   tehon-ni-suru（手本にする）take ((someone)) for a model, make ((someone)) an example, take ((a thing)) as a model

tei 〈てい：艇〉a boat.

   teiko（艇庫）a boathouse

tei 〈てい：体〉

tei-yoku 〈体よく〉politely, tactfully.

   tei-yoku kotowaru（体よく断る）refuse politely

teian 〈ていあん：提案〉a proposal, a suggestion.

   teian-sha（提案者）a proposer

teian-suru 〈提案する〉propose, suggest.

teibô 〈ていぼう：堤防〉a bank, an embankment, a dike, a levee.

   teibô o kizuku（堤防を築く）construct a bank

teichaku 〈ていちゃく：定着〉fixing.

   teichaku-eki（定着液）a fixing solution

teichaku-suru〈定着する〉fix, be established.

teichi〈ていち：低地〉low ground, lowlands, bottomland.

tei-chingin〈ていちんぎん：低賃金〉low wages.

teichô〈ていちょう：丁重〉politeness, courtesy, civility.

teichô-na〈丁重な〉polite, courteous, civil.

teichô-ni〈丁重に〉politely, courteously, with courtesy, civilly.

     teichô-ni atsukau（丁重に扱う）treat ((a person)) with courtesy

teichô〈ていちょう：低調〉dullness, weakness.

teichô-na〈低調な〉dull, sluggish.

teiden〈ていでん：停電〉a stoppage in power supply, (a) power failure.

teiden-suru〈停電する〉the electric current is cut off.

teido〈ていど：程度〉(a) degree, extent, (a) grade, (a) standard.

     teido-ga-takai（程度が高い）be of a high grade

     teido-ga-hikui（程度が低い）be of a low standard

     teido-mondai（程度問題）a matter of degree

aru teido-made〈ある程度まで〉to some extent.

teien〈ていえん：庭園〉a garden, a park.

     teien o tsukuru（庭園を造る）lay out a garden

teigaku〈ていがく：定額〉a fixed amount.

teigaku〈ていがく：低額〉a small amount.

teigaku〈ていがく：停学〉suspension from school.

teigaku-o-meijiru or *teigaku-shobun-ni-suru*〈停学を命じる，停学処分にする〉suspend ((a student)) from school.

tei-gakunen〈ていがくねん：低学年〉the lower classes.

teigi〈ていぎ：定義〉a definition.

teigi-suru〈定義する〉define.

teihaku〈ていはく：停泊〉anchorage.

     teihaku-chû-no fune（停泊中の船）a ship at anchor

teihaku-suru〈停泊する〉anchor, cast anchor.

teihen〈ていへん：底辺〉the base.

teihyô〈ていひょう：定評〉an established reputation, a settled opinion.

teihyô-no-aru〈定評のある〉acknowledged, recognized; notorious.

teiin〈ていいん：定員〉the fixed number, the seating capacity, the full strength, the complement.

     teiin ni tassuru（定員に達する）reach the regular number

     teiin o chôka-suru（定員を超過する）exceed the fixed number

     teiin-sen-nin-no gekijô（定員千人の劇場）a theater with a seating capacity of 1,000

teiji〈ていじ：定時〉a fixed time.

teiji-no〈定時の〉regular.

teiji-ni〈定時に〉regularly, at a scheduled time.

    teiji-ni hassha-suru（定時に発車する）leave at the scheduled time

teiji〈ていじ：呈示〉

teiji-suru〈呈示する〉present〔a bill〕.

teiji-sei〈ていじせい：定時制〉

    teiji-sei-kôtô-gakkô（定時制高等学校）a part-time senior high school

teiji-sei-no〈定時制の〉part-time.

teijû〈ていじゅう：定住〉settlement.

teijû-suru〈定住する〉settle down.

teika〈ていか：定価〉a fixed price.

    teika-de uru（定価で売る）sell at a fixed price

    teika-hyô（定価表）a price-list

teika〈ていか：低下〉a fall, a decline, a drop, deterioration.

    kion-no teika（気温の低下）a fall in temperature

    hinshitsu no teika（品質の低下）deterioration in quality

teika-suru〈低下する〉fall, drop, lower, deteriorate.

teikan〈ていかん：定款〉the articles of association.

teikei〈ていけい：てい形〉a trapezoid.

teikei〈ていけい：提携〉cooperation.

    gijutsu-teikei（技術提携）a technical tie-up

teikei-suru〈提携する〉cooperate ((with)).

〜-to-teikei-shite〈〜と提携して〉in cooperation with... .

teiken〈ていけん：定見〉a definite view, a fixed principle.

teiken-no-nai〈定見のない〉without any settled principle.

teiketsu〈ていけつ：締結〉conclusion.

teiketsu-suru〈締結する〉conclude.

    heiwa-jôyaku o teiketsu-suru（平和条約を締結する）conclude a peace treaty ((with))

teiki〈ていき：定期〉

    teiki-bin（定期便）a regular service

    teiki-kashitsuke（定期貸付）a time loan

    teiki-ken（定期券）a commutation ticket, a season ticket

    teiki-kensa（定期検査）a periodical inspection

    teiki-shiken（定期試験）a regular examination

    teiki-yokin（定期預金）a fixed deposit

teiki-no〈定期の〉regular, periodical.

teiki(-teki)-ni 〈定期(的)に〉 regularly, periodically, at regular intervals.

teiki 〈ていき：提起〉

teiki-suru 〈提起する〉 pose, raise.

  mondai o teiki-suru（問題を提起する）　pose a problem

tei-kiatsu 〈ていきあつ：低気圧〉 *see.* kiatsu.

teikô 〈ていこう：抵抗〉 resistance, opposition.

  teikô-o-ukeru（抵抗を受ける）　meet with resistance

  teikô-ryoku（抵抗力）　power of resistance

teikô-suru 〈抵抗する〉 resist, oppose, stand ((against)).

teikô-sezu-ni 〈抵抗せずに〉 without struggle.

teikoku 〈ていこく：定刻〉 the appointed time, the fixed time.

  teikoku-ni（定刻に）　at the appointed time, on schedule, punctually

teikoku 〈ていこく：帝国〉 an empire.

  teikoku-shugi（帝国主義）　imperialism

teikoku-no 〈帝国の〉 imperial.

teikû 〈ていくう：低空〉 a low altitude.

  teikû-hikô（低空飛行）　a low-altitude flight

teikyô 〈ていきょう：提供〉 an offer.

  teikyô o ukeru（提供を受ける）　accept an offer

  teikyô o kotowaru（提供を断る）　decline an offer

teikyô-suru 〈提供する〉 offer, make an offer.

teikyû 〈ていきゅう：庭球〉 *see.* tenisu.

teikyû 〈ていきゅう：低級〉

teikyû-na 〈低級な〉 low, low-grade, vulgar.

  teikyû-na shumi（低級な趣味）　low taste

teikyû-bi 〈ていきゅうび：定休日〉 a regular holiday, a shop holiday.

teimei 〈ていめい：低迷〉

teimei-suru 〈低迷する〉 hang low, hover around.

  Shikyô wa teimei-shite-iru.（市況は低迷している。）　The market is dull.

teimen 〈ていめん：底面〉 the base.

teinei 〈ていねい：丁寧〉 politeness, courteousness; care, thoroughness.

teinei-na 〈丁寧な〉 polite, courteous, careful, thorough.

teinei-ni 〈丁寧に〉 politely, courteously, carefully, with care, thoroughly.

  teinei-ni mono-o-iu（丁寧に物を言う）　speak politely

  teinei-ni atsukau（丁寧に扱う）　handle ((a thing)) with care

teinen 〈ていねん：定年〉 the age limit.

  teinen-de taishoku-suru（定年で退職する）　retire under the age limit

teinen-sei（定年制）the age-limit system

teion〈ていおん：低音〉a low voice; bass, a low-pitched sound.

teion〈ていおん：低温〉a low temperature.

teiô-sekkai〈ていおうせっかい：帝王切開〉a Caesarean operation.

teire〈ていれ：手入れ〉repair(s), mending, trimming; a raid.

teire-suru〈手入れする〉repair, mend, trim, groom; raid.

teire-no-yuki-todoita〈手入れの行き届いた〉well-kept, well-groomed.

teirei〈ていれい：定例〉an established usage, usage.

teirei-ni-yori（定例により）according to usage

teiri〈ていり：定理〉a theorem.

teiri〈ていり：低利〉a low rate of interest.

teiryô〈ていりょう：定量〉a fixed quantity.

teiryô-bunseki（定量分析）quantitative analysis

teiryô-no〈定量の〉quantitative.

teiryû〈ていりゅう：底流〉an undercurrent.

teiryû-o-nashite-iru〈底流をなしている〉underlie.

teiryû-jo〈ていりゅうじょ：停留所〉a stop, a station.

basu-no teiryû-jo（バスの停留所）a bus stop

teisai〈ていさい：体裁〉appearance, show.

teisai-ga-ii（体裁がいい）make a good appearance

teisai-ga-warui（体裁が悪い）make an ill appearance

teisai-o-kamawa-nai（体裁を構わない）be indifferent to one's personal appearance

teisatsu〈ていさつ：偵察〉scouting, reconnaissance.

teisatsu-ni-iku（偵察に行く）go scouting

teisatsu-hikô（偵察飛行）a reconnaissance flight

teisatsu-suru〈偵察する〉scout, reconnoiter.

teisei〈ていせい：訂正〉correction, revision.

teisei-suru〈訂正する〉correct, revise.

ayamari o teisei-suru（誤りを訂正する）correct errors

teisen〈ていせん：停戦〉a cease-fire, an armistice, a truce.

teisen-kyôtei（停戦協定）a cease-fire agreement

teisen-suru〈停戦する〉cease fire, stop fighting.

teisen〈ていせん：停船〉stoppage of a ship.

teisen-o-meijiru（停船を命じる）order a ship to stop

teisen-suru〈停船する〉come to, bring to, heaven to.

nômu-no-tame teisen-suru（濃霧のため停船する）be held up in a thick fog

teisetsu 〈ていせつ：定説〉an established theory, an accepted opinion.

teisetsu 〈ていせつ：貞節〉faithfulness, chastity.

teisetsu-na 〈貞節な〉faithful, chaste, virtuous.

teisha 〈ていしゃ：停車〉stoppage, a stop.

teisha-jikan〔停車時間〕 stoppage time

san-pun-kan-teisha〔三分間停車〕 a three minutes' stop

teisha-suru 〈停車する〉stop.

kakueki-ni teisha-suru〔各駅に停車する〕 stop at every station

teishi 〈ていし：停止〉suspension, stoppage; a stop.

teishi-shingô〔停止信号〕 a stop signal

teishi-suru 〈停止する〉suspend, stop.

eigyô o teishi-suru〔営業を停止する〕 suspend business

teishin 〈ていしん：艇身〉a boat's length.

ichi-teishin-no-sa-de katsu〔一艇身の差で勝つ〕 win ((a race)) by a length

tei-shisei 〈ていせい：低姿勢〉

tei-shisei o toru 〈低姿勢をとる〉take a modest attitude.

teishô 〈ていしょう：提唱〉advocacy, proposal.

teishô-sha〔提唱者〕 an advocate

teishô-suru 〈提唱する〉advocate, propose.

teishoku 〈ていしょく：定食〉a table d'hôte (meal).

teishoku 〈ていしょく：定職〉a regular occupation.

teishoku-ga-nai〔定職がない〕 have no fixed employment

teishoku 〈ていしょく：停職〉suspension from office.

teishoku-o-meijiru or *teishoku-shobun-ni-suru* 〈停職を命じる，停職処分にする〉suspend ((a person)) from office.

teishoku 〈ていしょく：抵触〉conflict, contradiction, collision.

teishoku-suru 〈抵触する〉conflict ((with)), be contradictory ((to)), be contrary ((to)).

hôritsu-ni teishoku-suru〔法律に抵触する〕 be contrary to the law

teishu 〈ていしゅ：亭主〉a husband; a landlord.

teishuku 〈ていしゅく：貞淑〉chastity, (female) virtue.

teishuku-na 〈貞淑な〉chaste, virtuous.

tei-shûnyû 〈ていしゅうにゅう：定収入〉a regular income.

teishutsu 〈ていしゅつ：提出〉presentation.

teishutsu-suru 〈提出する〉present, submit, tender, hand in.

gikai-ni hôan o teishutsu-suru〔議会に法案を提出する〕 present a bill to the Diet shukudai o teishutsu-suru〈宿題を提出する〉 hand in one's home-work

gansho o teishutsu-suru〈願書を提出する〉 file(*or* send in) one's ap-plication

teiso〈ていそ：提訴〉

teiso-suru〈提訴する〉 present a case to the court, take action ((a-gainst)).

teisô〈ていそう：貞操〉 chastity, (feminine) virtue.

teisô-o-mamoru〈貞操を守る〉 remain faithful ((to)).

teisô-no-aru〈貞操のある〉 chaste.

teisô-no-nai（貞操のない） unchaste

teisoku〈ていそく：定則〉 an established rule.

teisû〈ていすう：定数〉 a fixed number, a quorum; a constant.

teisû-ni-mita-nai（定数に満たない） do not come up to a quorum

tei-suru〈ていする：呈する〉 show, display, present.

kakkyô o tei-suru（活況を呈する） show activity

sanjô o tei-suru（惨状を呈する） present a tragic sight

te-itai〈ていたい：手痛い〉 severe, hard, serious, heavy.

te-itai dageki o ukeru（手痛い打撃を受ける） suffer a hard blow

te-itaku〈手痛く〉 severely, hard.

teitai〈ていたい：停滞〉

teitai-suru〈停滞する〉 be stagnant, be sluggish.

Jimu ga hidoku teitai-shite-iru.（事務がひどく停滞している.） Busi-ness is seriously delayed.

teitaku〈ていたく：邸宅〉 a residence, a mansion.

teiten〈ていてん：定点〉 a fixed point.

teitetsu〈ていてつ：てい鉄〉 a horseshoe.

uma ni teitetsu-o-utsu〈馬にてい鉄を打つ〉 shoe a horse.

teitô(-ken)〈ていとう(けん)：抵当(権)〉 mortgage.

teitô-ni-toru（抵当に取る） accept ((a thing)) as security

ichiban-teitô（一番抵当） a first mortgage

teitô-ni-ireru〈抵当に入れる〉 mortgage, give ((a thing)) as security.

teitoku〈ていとく：提督〉 an admiral, a commodore.

teiton〈ていとん：停とん〉 a standstill, a deadlock.

teiton-suru（停とんする） come to a standstill, reach a deadlock

teizoku〈ていぞく：低俗〉

teizoku-na〈低俗な〉 vulgar, lowbrow.

te-jaku〈てじゃく：手酌〉

te-jaku-de-nomu 〈手酌で飲む〉 help oneself to *sake*.

te-jika 〈てぢか：手近〉

te-jika-na 〈手近な〉 close by, near by, familiar.

    te-jika-na rei （手近な例） a familiar example

te-jika-ni 〈手近に〉 close by, near by, near at hand.

tejina 〈てじな：手品〉 jugglery.

    tejina-no-tane o akasu （手品の種を明かす） explain the trick

    tejina-shi （手品師） a juggler, a magician.

tejina-o-tsukau 〈手品を使う〉 juggle.

tejô 〈てじょう：手錠〉 handcuffs.

tejô-o-kakeru 〈手錠を掛ける〉 handcuff.

te-jun 〈てじゅん：手順〉 a process, order, a plan, an arrangement, a program.

te-jun-o-kimeru 〈手順を決める〉 plan (out), arrange ((for)).

te-jun-yoku 〈手順よく〉 smoothly, without a hitch.

te-kagen 〈てかげん：手加減〉 tact, skill.

    te-kagen-ga-iru （手加減が要る） require tact

te-kagi 〈てかぎ：手かぎ〉 a (cargo) hook.

teki 〈てき：敵〉 an enemy; an opponent, a rival, a match.

    teki o tsukuru （敵を作る） make enemies

    teki-mikata （敵味方） friends and foes

      teki-mikata-no-kankei-ni-aru （敵味方の関係にある） be opposed to each other

    shôbai-jô-no teki （商売上の敵） one's business rival

teki-ni-mawasu or *teki-to-suru* 〈敵に回す，敵とする〉 have ((a person)) for an enemy, antagonize.

-teki 〈-てき：-滴〉 a drop.

    ni-san-teki （二，三滴） a few drops

te-kibishii 〈てきびしい：手厳しい〉 severe, harsh, bitter.

    te-kibishii hihyô （手厳しい批評） severe criticism

te-kibishiku 〈手厳しく〉 severely, harshly, bitterly.

teki-chi 〈てきち：敵地〉 the enemy's territory.

tekichû 〈てきちゅう：的中〉

tekichû-suru 〈的中する〉 hit [the mark], hit it (right), come true, guess right.

    Watashi-no yogen ga tekichû-shita. （私の予言が的中した．） My prophecy has come true.

tekidan 〈てきだん：敵弾〉 the enemy's bullets.

tekido 〈てきど：適度〉moderation.

  tekido-no 〈適度の〉moderate, temperate.

    tekido-no undô 〈適度の運動〉 moderate exercise

  tekido-ni 〈適度に〉moderately, temperately.

teki-futeki 〈てきふてき：適不適〉fitness, suitability.

    Hito-ni-yotte-teki-futeki-ga-aru.〈人によって適不適がある.〉 Some people are fit for it, but others are not.

tekigai-shin 〈てきがいしん：敵がい心〉see. tekii.

tekigô 〈てきごう：適合〉conformity, agreement, adaptation.

  tekigô-suru 〈適合する〉be in conformity ((with)), fit, suit, adapt oneself ((to)), be adapted ((for)).

tekigun 〈てきぐん：敵軍〉the enemy troops.

tekihatsu 〈てきはつ：摘発〉exposure, disclosure, prosecution.

  tekihatsu-suru 〈摘発する〉expose, disclose, unmask, prosecute.

    ihan-sha o tekihatsu-suru〈違反者を摘発する〉 prosecute an offender

tekihei 〈てきへい：敵兵〉an enemy soldier, the enemy.

tekihô 〈てきほう：適法〉legality.

  tekihô-no 〈適法の〉legal.

    tekihô-de-nai〈適法でない〉 illegal

tekii 〈てきい：敵意〉hostility, a hostile feeling.

    tekii o idaku〈敵意を抱く〉 entertain a hostile feeling ((against))

  tekii-no-aru 〈敵意のある〉hostile.

tekijin 〈てきじん：敵陣〉the enemy line, the enemy camp.

tekijô 〈てきじょう：敵情〉the enemy's movements.

tekikaku 〈てきかく：的確〉see. tekkaku.

tekikaku 〈てきかく：適格〉see. tekkaku.

tekikoku 〈てきこく：敵国〉see. tekkoku.

tekimen 〈てきめん：てき面〉

  tekimen-ni 〈てき面に〉immediately, swiftly.

    tekimen-ni-kiku〈てき面に効く〉 take immediate effect

tekinin 〈てきにん：適任〉

    tekinin-sha〈適任者〉 a fit person

    Kare-wa kono-shigoto-no-tekinin-sha-da.〈彼はこの仕事の適任者だ.〉 He is just the man for this job.

  tekinin-de-aru 〈適任である〉be fit ((for)), be well qualified ((for)), be competent ((for)).

tekiô 〈てきおう：適応〉adaptation.

    tekiô-sei〈適応性〉 adaptability, flexibility

tekiô-sei-no-aru（適応性のある）adaptable, flexible

tekiô-suru〈適応する〉be adapted ((for *or* to)), adapt oneself ((to)).

tekipaki〈てきぱき〉

tekipaki-shita〈てきぱきした〉prompt, quick, businesslike.

tekipaki(-to)〈てきぱき(と)〉promptly, quickly, in a businesslike way.

tekipaki(-to) shigoto-o-yaru（てきぱき(と)仕事をやる）be prompt in one's work, do one's work in a businesslike way

tekirei〈てきれい：適例〉a good example, an apt instance, a case in point.

tekirei-ki〈てきれいき：適齢期〉marriageable age.

tekiryô〈てきりょう：適量〉a proper quantity.

tekiryô-no sake（適量の酒）*sake* taken in proper quantity

tekisei〈てきせい：適正〉

tekisei-kakaku（適正価格）a reasonable price

tekisei-na〈適正な〉proper, just, right, reasonable.

tekisei-kensa〈てきせいけんさ：適性検査〉an aptitude test.

tekisetsu〈てきせつ：適切〉

tekisetsu-na〈適切な〉fit, apt, appropriate, adequate, proper, happy.

tekisetsu-na shochi（適切な処置）a proper measure

tekisetsu-de-nai〈適切でない〉unfit, inappropriate, inadequate.

tekisetsu-ni〈適切に〉suitably, fitly, appropriately, to the point, happily.

tekisha-seizon〈てきしゃせいぞん：適者生存〉the survival of the fittest.

tekishi〈てきし：敵視〉

tekishi-suru〈敵視する〉look upon ((a person)) as an enemy, show enmity ((toward)).

tekishutsu〈てきしゅつ：摘出〉

tekishutsu-suru〈摘出する〉take out, extract, remove.

tekisuru〈てきする：適する〉suit, fit, be suited ((for *or* to)), be fitted ((to)), be suitable ((for)), be fit ((for)), be good ((for *or* to do)).

shiyô-ni-tekisuru（使用に適する）be fit for use

inryô-ni-tekisuru（飲料に適する）be good to drink

tekishite-iru〈適している〉suited, fit, adapted, qualified.

tekishite-i-nai（適していない）unsuited, unfit, unadapted, unqualified.

tekitai〈てきたい：敵対〉hostility.

tekitai-kôi（敵対行為）hostile actions, hostilities

tekitai-teki(-na)〈敵対的(な)〉hostile.

tekitô〈てきとう：適当〉

tekitô-na 〈適当な〉 fit, suitable, proper.

    tekitô-na toki-ni (適当なときに) at a proper time

tekitô-ni 〈適当に〉 suitably, properly.

tekiyaku 〈てきやく：適役〉 *see.* tekinin.

tekiyaku 〈てきやく：適訳〉 a proper translation.

tekiyō 〈てきよう：摘要〉 a summary, an epitome, a digest, an outline, an abstract.

tekiyô 〈てきよう：適用〉 application.

tekiyô-suru 〈適用する〉 apply.

tekiyô-dekiru 〈適用できる〉 be applicable.

tekizai 〈てきざい：適材〉 the right man.

    tekizai-tekisho (適材適所) the right man in the right place

tekkai 〈てっかい：撤回〉 withdrawal.

tekkai-suru 〈撤回する〉 withdraw.

    zengen o tekkai-suru (前言を撤回する) withdraw one's former statement

tekkaku 〈てっかく：的確〉

tekkaku-na 〈的確な〉 precise, accurate, exact.

    tekkaku-na handan (的確な判断) a precise judgment

tekkaku-ni 〈的確に〉 precisely, accurately, exactly.

tekkaku 〈てっかく：適格〉

    tekkaku-sha (適格者) a qualified person

tekkaku-na 〈適格な〉 qualified, competent.

tekkan 〈てっかん：鉄管〉 an iron tube, an iron pipe.

tekken-seisai 〈てっけんせいさい：鉄けん制裁〉

tekken-seisai o kuwaeru 〈鉄けん制裁を加える〉 administer fist law.

tekki 〈てっき：鉄器〉 ironware, hardware.

    tekki-jidai (鉄器時代) the Iron Age

tekki 〈てっき：敵機〉 an enemy plane.

tekkin 〈てっきん：鉄筋〉

tekkin-konkurīto 〈鉄筋コンクリート〉 ferroconcrete, reinforced concrete.

    tekkin-konkurīto-no tate-mono (鉄筋コンクリートの建物) a ferroconcrete building

tekkiri 〈てっきり〉 surely, beyond all doubt.

tekkiri～-da-to-omou 〈てっきり～だと思う〉 conclude that... .

    Kare-wa tekkiri-nigeta-to-omotta. (彼はてっきり逃げたと思った.) I concluded that he had run away.

tekkō 〈てっこう：鉄鉱〉 iron ore.

tekkô 〈てっこう：鉄鋼〉 steel.

    tekkô-gyô〈鉄鋼業〉 the steel industry

tekkô-jo or **tekkô-jô**〈てっこうじょ，てっこうじょう：鉄工所，鉄工場〉an ironworks.

tekkoku〈てっこく：敵国〉an enemy country.

tekkotsu〈てっこつ：鉄骨〉a steel frame, an iron frame.

    tekkotsu-kôzô〈鉄骨構造〉 steel-frame structure

tekkyo〈てっきょ：撤去〉withdrawal, removal.

  tekkyo-suru〈撤去する〉withdraw, remove.

    shôgai-butsu o tekkyo-suru〈障害物を撤去する〉 remove an obstacle

tekkyô〈てっきょう：鉄橋〉an iron bridge, a railroad bridge.

teko〈てこ〉a lever.

    teko-de mochi-ageru〈てこで持ち上げる〉 raise ((something)) with a lever

  teko-demo-ugoka-nai〈てこでも動かない〉do not budge an inch.

teko-ire〈てこいれ：てこ入れ〉

  teko-ire-suru〈てこ入れする〉prop up, bolster.

tekozuru〈てこずる〉have much trouble ((with)), be utterly puzzled what to do ((with)).

  tekozuraseru〈てこずらせる〉give ((a person)) much trouble, put ((a person)) out.

te-kubi〈てくび：手首〉a wrist.

te-kuse〈てくせ：手癖〉

  te-kuse-ga-warui〈手癖が悪い〉be light-fingered, have light fingers.

tema〈てま：手間〉time; labor, trouble.

    tema-ga-kakaru〈手間が掛かる〉 take time, require much labor

    tema o habuku〈手間を省く〉 save time, save oneself trouble

    tema-chin〈手間賃〉 wages for labor

      tema-chin-o-harau〈手間賃を払う〉 pay for labor

  tema-doru〈手間取る〉be delayed, be kept long ((about)).

têma〈テーマ〉a theme.

    kenkyû-têma〈研究テーマ〉 a subject of study

temae〈てまえ：手前〉this side; out of respect ((for *or* to)), out of consideration ((for)), in the presence ((of)).

    kawa no sugu-temae〈川のすぐ手前〉 just this side of the river

    kodomo no temae〈子供の手前〉 in the presence of one's children

te-makura〈てまくら：手まくら〉

  te-makura-suru〈手まくらする〉rest one's head on one's arm.

te-mane 〈てまね：手まね〉 a gesture, signs.

te-mane-o-suru 〈手まねをする〉 gesture, make gestures.

te-maneki 〈てまねき：手招き〉 beckoning.

te-maneki-suru 〈手招きする〉 beckon ((to)).

temawari-hin 〈てまわりひん：手回り品〉 one's things, one's personal effects; baggage, luggage.

te-mawashi 〈てまわし：手回し〉 preparations, arrangements.

te-mawashi-ga-ii 〈手回しがいい〉 be ready, be fully prepared beforehand.
　　Kanojo-wa itsu-demo te-mawashi-ga-ii. (彼女はいつでも手回しがいい。) She is always ready.

tembai 〈てんばい：転売〉 resale.

tembai-suru 〈転売する〉 resell.

tembatsu 〈てんばつ：天罰〉 Heaven's judgment, the punishment of Heaven.
　　Tembatsu-tekimen. (天罰てき面。) Swift is Heaven's vengeance.

tembiki 〈てんびき：天引き〉 deduction in advance.

tembiki-suru 〈天引きする〉 deduct, reduce, strike off.

tembin 〈てんびん：天びん〉 a balance.
　　tembin-ni-kakeru 〈天びんに掛ける〉 weigh in the balance

tembō 〈てんぼう：展望〉 a view.
　　tembō-ga-kiku 〈展望が利く〉 have a fine view ((of))
　　tembō o samatageru 〈展望を妨げる〉 obstruct the view
　　tembō-dai 〈展望台〉 an observation platform
　　tembō-sha 〈展望車〉 an observation car

tembō-suru 〈展望する〉 view; review, survey.

tembun 〈てんぶん：天分〉 one's natural gifts.
　　tembun-no-aru hito 〈天分のある人〉 a gifted person

tembyō 〈てんびょう：点描〉 a sketch.
　　jimbutsu-tembyō 〈人物点描〉 personal sketches, the personal profile ((of))

temijika 〈てみじか：手短〉

temijika-ni 〈手短に〉 shortly, briefly.
　　temijika-ni-hanaseba 〈手短に話せば〉 to put it briefly, to be brief

te-miyage 〈てみやげ：手土産〉 a caller's present.

temmatsu 〈てんまつ：てん末〉 the circumstances, the course of events, the particulars, the details.
　　koto no temmatsu-o-hanasu 〈事のてん末を話す〉 give ((a person)) a full account of a matter

temmei 〈てんめい：天命〉God's will, Providence; fate, destiny.

  jinji-o-tsukushite temmei-o-matsu（人事を尽くして天命を待つ） do one's best and leave the rest to Providence

  temmei-to-akirameru（天命とあきらめる） resign oneself to fate

temmetsu 〈てんめつ：点滅〉

  temmetsu-suru〈点滅する〉go on and off, turn on and off.

temmon(-gaku) 〈てんもん（がく）：天文（学）〉astronomy.

  temmon-dai（天文台） an astronomical observatory

  temmon-gaku(-jô)-no or temmon-gaku-teki(-na)〈天文学（上）の，天文学的（な）〉astronomical.

-temo 〈-ても〉but, though, (even) if, however, no matter... .

  yuki-ga-futtemo（雪が降っても） even if it snows

  donna-ni kurushiku-temo（どんなに苦しくても） however hard it may be

temochi 〈てもち：手持ち〉stock in hand, holdings.

  temochi-ga-aru（手持ちがある） have goods in stock

  temochi-gaika（手持ち外貨） foreign currency holdings

temochi-busata 〈てもちぶさた：手持ち無さた〉

  temochi-busata-de-aru〈手持ち無さたである〉feel ill at ease, time hangs heavy on one's hands.

te-moto 〈てもと：手もと〉

  te-moto-ga-kuruu（手もとが狂う） miss one's aim

  te-moto-ni〈手もとに〉at hand.

  te-moto-ni oku（手もとに置く） keep ((something)) at hand

  Ima te-moto-ni kane-ga-nai.（今手もとに金がない。） I have no money with me.

tempen-chii 〈てんぺんちい：天変地異〉a natural disaster.

tempi 〈てんび：天火〉an oven.

  tempi-de yaku（天火で焼く） bake in an oven

tempi 〈てんぴ：天日〉

  tempi-de-kawakasu〈天日で乾かす〉dry ((a thing)) in the sun.

tempo 〈てんぽ：店舗〉a store, a shop.

tempo 〈テンポ〉tempo, speed.

  tempo-ga-awa-nai（テンポが合わない） be out of tempo

  tempo-no-hayai〈テンポの速い〉fast-paced.

tempu 〈てんぷ：天賦〉

  tempu-no〈天賦の〉natural, inborn.

  tempu-no sai（天賦の才） a natural gift

tempu 〈てんぷ：添付〉
  tempu-suru 〈添付する〉 attach, append, be accompanied ((by)).
  tempu-no 〈添付の〉 attached, accompanying.
  〜*-o-tempu-shite* 〈〜を添付して〉 with... .

tempuku 〈てんぷく：転覆〉
  tempuku-suru 〈転覆する〉 overthrow, overturn, upset; be overthrown, be overturned, be capsized.

tempura 〈てんぷら：天ぷ羅〉 Japanese fried food, *tempura*.

te-mukai 〈てむかい：手向かい〉 resistance, opposition.
  te-mukai-suru 〈手向かいする〉 resist, oppose, rise ((against)).

ten 〈てん：天〉 the sky, the air, the heavens.
  ten-ni-mukatte tsuba-o-haku 〈天に向かってつばを吐く〉 spit up into the sky
  ten-ni-mo-noboru-kokochi-ga-suru 〈天にも昇る心地がする〉 be in the seventh heaven
  un-o-ten-ni-makasu 〈運を天に任す〉 trust to Heaven

ten 〈てん〉 a sable, an ermine.

ten 〈てん：点〉 a spot, a speck; a dot, a point; a point, a respect; marks; a run, a score, a piece.
  ten-sen 〈点線〉 a dotted line
  sono ten-dewa 〈その点では〉 on that point
  shuppatsu-ten 〈出発点〉 a starting point
  ten o tsukeru 〈点を付ける〉 give marks
  ten-ga-amai 〈点が甘い〉 be generous in marking
  ten-ga-karai 〈点が辛い〉 be severe in marking
  san-ten o ireru 〈三点を入れる〉 score three runs
  irui-jutten 〈衣類十点〉 ten pieces of clothing

tenaga-zaru 〈てながざる：手長猿〉 a long-armed ape, a gibbon.

tenami 〈てなみ：手並み〉
  O-tenami-haiken. 〈お手並み拝見。〉 I'll challenge you to a game to see how skillful you are.

te-narai 〈てならい：手習い〉
  Roku-jû-no-te-narai. 〈六十の手習い。〉 It is never too late to learn.

te-nareru 〈てなれる：手慣れる〉 get used ((to)), get skillful ((in)).
  te-narete-iru 〈手慣れている〉 be quite at home ((in *or* on)).

te-nazukeru 〈てなずける：手懐ける〉 win ((a person's)) heart, influence ((a person)) by money; tame, domesticate.

ten-chi 〈てんち：天地〉 heaven and earth, the universe; top and bottom;

a world, a realm, a land, a sphere.

Ten-chi-muyô.〔天地無用.〕 This side up. / Do not turn over.

bettenchi（別天地）a different world

tenchi〈てんち：転地〉(a) change of air.

tenchi-ryôyô（転地療養）treatment by a change of air

tenchi-suru〈転地する〉go ((to Izu)) for a change of air.

tende〈てんで〉(not) at all, altogether.

Tende sore-wa mondai-ni-nara-nai.（てんでそれは問題にならない.）It is altogether out of the question.

tendon〈てんどん：天どん〉a bowl of rice (topped) with fried fish.

tengan〈てんがん：点眼〉

tengan-suru〈点眼する〉apply eyewash ((to)).

tengoku〈てんごく：天国〉Heaven, Paradise.

tengu〈てんぐ：天ぐ〉a long-nosed goblin; a self-conceited person.

tengu-ni-naru〈てんぐになる〉become conceited ((of)), become vain ((of)).

tengusa〈てんぐさ：天草〉an agar-agar.

tengyô〈てんぎょう：転業〉

tengyô-suru〈転業する〉change one's occupation.

ten·i〈てんい：転移〉

ten·i-suru〈転移する〉spread, metastasize.

te-nimotsu〈てにもつ：手荷物〉baggage, luggage.

te-nimotsu o azukaru（手荷物を預ける）have one's baggage checked

te-nimotsu-tori-atsukai-jo（手荷物取扱所）a baggage office, a luggage office

te-nimotsu-ichiji-azukari-sho（手荷物一時預かり所）a checkroom, a cloakroom

ten·in〈てんいん：店員〉a clerk, a shopman, a shopgirl, a shopwoman, a salesman, a saleswoman.

tenisu〈テニス〉tennis.

tenisu o suru（テニスをする）play tennis

tenji〈てんじ：点字〉braille, raised letters.

tenji-no hon（点字の本）a book in raised letters

tenji〈てんじ：展示〉exhibition, display.

tenji-hin（展示品）an exhibit, exhibition

tenji-kai（展示会）an exhibition, a show

tenji-suru〈展示する〉exhibit, put ((a thing)) on display.

tenjô〈てんじょう：天井〉the ceiling.

tenjô-no-takai〈天井の高い〉high-ceilinged.

tenjô-ura-de〈天井裏で〉in the ceiling.

tenjô〈てんじょう：天上〉the heavens.

tenjô-in〈てんじょういん：添乗員〉a courier, a tour conductor.

tenju〈てんじゅ：天寿〉one's natural span of life.

tenju-o-mattô-suru〈天寿を全うする〉die a natural death.

tenka〈てんか：天下〉the whole country, the realm, the land, the public, the reins of government.

    Tenka-taihei.〈天下泰平.〉Peace reigns over the land.

tenka-o-toru〈天下を取る〉bring the whole land under one's rule, come to power.

tenka-ippin-no〈天下一品の〉unique, peerless, unparalleled.

tenka〈てんか：点火〉ignition.

    tenka-sôchi〈点火装置〉an igniter, a spark plug

tenka-suru〈点火する〉ignite, fire (up), light, kindle.

tenka〈てんか：転嫁〉imputation.

tenka-suru〈転嫁する〉impute, lay, shift.

    sekinin o tenka-suru〈責任を転嫁する〉shift the responsibility ((on))

tenka-butsu〈てんかぶつ：添加物〉an (a food) additive.

tenka-butsu-no-nai〈添加物のない〉additive-free.

tenkai〈てんかい：展開〉unfolding, development, evolution; deployment; expansion.

tenkai-suru〈展開する〉unfold, develop, spread; deploy; expand.

tenkai〈てんかい：転回〉revolution, rotation.

tenkai-suru〈転回する〉revolve, rotate, take a turn.

tenkan〈てんかん〉epilepsy.

tenkan-o-okosu〈てんかんを起こす〉have an epileptic fit.

tenkan〈てんかん：転換〉conversion, a turnabout, diversion, turnover, switchover.

    hyaku-hachi-jû-do-no-tenkan-o-suru〈百八十度の転換をする〉make an about-face

    kibun-tenkan-ni soto-e deru〈気分転換に外へ出る〉go out for a change

    tenkan-ki〈転換期〉a turning point

tenkan-suru〈転換する〉convert, turn, divert, switch.

tenkei〈てんけい：典型〉a type, a model.

tenkei-teki(-na)〈典型的(な)〉typical.

tenken〈てんけん：点検〉inspection, examination.

tenken-suru〈点検する〉inspect, examine, check.

tenki 〈てんき：天気〉 the weather.

Kesa-no tenki-wa-dô-desu-ka? (今朝の天気はどうですか.) How is the weather this morning?

ii tenki (いい天気) fine weather

jô-tenki (上天気) splendid weather

warui tenki (悪い天気) bad weather, rainy weather

iya-na tenki (嫌な天気) wretched weather

kawari-yasui tenki (変わりやすい天気) changeable(*or* unsettled) weather

Tenki-ni-nari-sô-da. (天気になりそうだ.) The weather is likely to clear up.

tenki-ga-yokereba (天気が良ければ) if it is fine

tenki-gaikyô (天気概況) the general weather condition

tenki-yohô (天気予報) a weather forecast

tenki-zu (天気図) a weather map

tenki 〈てんき：転機〉 *see.* tenkan-ki.

tenki 〈てんき：転記〉

tenki-suru 〈転記する〉 post [an item].

tenkin 〈てんきん：転勤〉 transference.

tenkin-suru 〈転勤する〉 be transferred [to another office].

tenko 〈てんこ：点呼〉 (a) roll call.

tenko-suru 〈点呼する〉 call the roll.

tenkô 〈てんこう：天候〉 the weather.

Tenkô ga kuzureru. (天候がくずれる.) The weather breaks.

tenkô-no-kaifuku-o-matsu (天候の回復を待つ) wait for the weather to improve

aku-tenkô-o-tsuite (悪天候を突いて) in spite of inclement weather

tenkô 〈てんこう：転校〉

tenkô-suru 〈転校する〉 change from one school to another, change one's school.

tenkô 〈てんこう：転向〉 a conversion, a turn.

tenkô-suru 〈転向する〉 be converted ((to)), turn ((to)).

tenkyo 〈てんきょ：転居〉 moving, a removal, a change of address.

tenkyo-saki (転居先) one's new address

tenkyo-tsûchi (転居通知) a removal notice

tenkyo-suru 〈転居する〉 move ((to *or* into)), remove ((to *or* into)), change one's address.

ten-mado 〈てんまど：天窓〉 a skylight.

tennen 〈てんねん：天然〉nature.

    tennen-gasu〈天然ガス〉 natural gas

    tennen-kinen-butsu〈天然記念物〉 a natural monument

    tennen-shigen〈天然資源〉 natural resources

tennen-no〈天然の〉natural, unartificial, spontaneous, wild.

    tennen-no ryôkô〈天然の良港〉 a natural good harbor

tennentô〈てんねんとう：天然痘〉(the) smallpox.

    tennentô-ni-kakaru〈天然痘にかかる〉 suffer from smallpox

tennin〈てんにん：転任〉change of post.

tennin-suru〈転任する〉be transferred〔to another post〕.

tennô〈てんのう：天皇〉an emperor.

    Tennô-heika〈天皇陛下〉 His Majesty the Emperor

tennyo〈てんにょ：天女〉a celestial maiden.

tennyû〈てんにゅう：転入〉

tennyû-suru〈転入する〉move into.

te-no-hira〈てのひら：手の平〉the palm.

te-no-hira-ni-nosete〈手の平に載せて〉in the palm of one's hand.

te-no-kô〈てのこう：手の甲〉the back of the hand.

tenôru〈テノール〉tenor.

    tenôru-kashu〈テノール歌手〉 a tenor

te-no-uchi〈てのうち：手の内〉

te-no-uchi-o-miseru〈手の内を見せる〉show one's cards, tip one's hand ((to)).

te-no-ura〈てのうら：手の裏〉

te-no-ura-o-kaesu-yô-ni〈手の裏を返すように〉suddenly, all of a sudden.

    te-no-ura-o-kaesu-yô-ni-kawaru（手の裏を返すように変わる） change one's mind completely all of a sudden

tenraku〈てんらく：転落〉a fall, degradation.

tenraku-suru〈転落する〉fall ((from)), degrade.

tenran-kai〈てんらんかい：展覧会〉an exhibition, a show.

    tenran-kai o hiraku（展覧会を開く） hold an exhibition

    tenran-kai o mi-ni-iku（展覧会を見に行く） visit an exhibition

tensai〈てんさい：天才〉genius, a genius.

tensai-teki(-na)〈天才的(な)〉gifted, talented.

tensai〈てんさい：天災〉a natural calamity.

tensai〈てんさい：てん菜〉a (sugar) beet.

tensai〈てんさい：転載〉reprinting, reproduction.

    Kin-tensai.（禁転載.） All rights reserved.

tensai-suru〈転載する〉reprint, take ((from)).

tensaku〈てんさく：添削〉correction.

tensaku-suru〈添削する〉correct, look over, touch up.

tensei〈てんせい（成）：天性（成）〉nature, temperamental disposition; by nature.

tensei-no〈天性の〉natural, born.

tenseki〈てんせき：転石〉

Tenseki-koke-musazu.（転石こけむさず.）A rolling stone gathers no moss.

tenseki〈てんせき：転籍〉

tenseki-suru〈転籍する〉have one's registered domicile transferred ((to)).

tensha〈てんしゃ：転写〉transcription, copying.

tensha-suru〈転写する〉transcribe, copy ((from)).

tenshi〈てんし：天使〉an angel.

tenshi-no-yô-na〈天使のような〉angelic.

tenshin-ramman〈てんしんらんまん：天真らん漫〉

tenshin-ramman-na〈天真らん漫な〉naïve, innocent.

tenshoku〈てんしょく：天職〉a mission, a vocation, a calling.

tenshoku〈てんしょく：転職〉*see.* tengyô.

tenshu〈てんしゅ：店主〉a storekeeper, a shopkeeper, the proprietor.

tenshukaku〈てんしゅかく：天守閣〉a castle tower, a donjon.

tenshutsu〈てんしゅつ：転出〉

tenshutsu-suru〈転出する〉move out ((to)), be transferred ((to)).

tensô〈てんそう：転送〉transmission, forwarding.

Go-tensô-kudasai.（御転送下さい.）Please forward.

tensô-saki（転送先）a forwarding address

tensô-suru〈転送する〉transmit, forward.

tensoku〈てんそく：天測〉(an) astronomical observation.

tensû〈てんすう：点数〉marks.

tentai〈てんたい：天体〉a heavenly body.

tentai-bôenkyô（天体望遠鏡）an astronomical telescope

tenteki〈てんてき：天敵〉a natural enemy.

tenteki〈てんてき：点滴〉an intravenous drip.

tenteki-o-suru（点滴をする）give an intravenous drip injection

tenteko-mai〈てんてこまい：手手古舞い〉

tenteko-mai-suru〈てんてこまいする〉run about busily, have an extremely busy time.

tenten-to〈てんてんと：転々と〉

　　tenten-to　gakkô-o-kaeru（転々と学校を変える）　change from school
　　　　to school

　　tenten-to　jûsho-o-kaeru（転々と住所を変える）　often change one's
　　　　address

　　tenten-to　shoku-o-kaeru（転々と職を変える）　change one's job
　　　　frequently

　　tenten-to　shoyû-nushi-o-kaeru（転々と所有主を変える）　pass from
　　　　hand to hand

　　Bôru wa sayoku-e tenten-to-shita.（ボールは左翼へ転々とした.）　The
　　　　ball went rolling out into the left field.

tenten-to〈てんてんと：点々と〉here and there, scattered.

tentetsu-ki〈てんてつき：転てつ器〉a (railroad) switch, the points.

tento〈テント〉a tent.

　　tento o haru（テントを張る）　pitch a tent

tentô〈てんとう：店頭〉a shop front.

　tentô-ni-dasu〈店頭に出す〉put ((goods)) on sale.

tentô〈てんとう：点灯〉lighting.

　tentô-suru〈点灯する〉switch on a light.

tentô〈てんとう：転倒〉a (violent) fall, inversion; upset.

　ki-ga-tentô-suru〈気が転倒する〉lose one's presence of mind, be beside
　　oneself.

tentô-mushi〈てんとうむし：てんとう虫〉a ladybird, a ladybug.

tenugui〈てぬぐい：手ぬぐい〉a towel.

　　tenugui-de fuku（手ぬぐいでふく）　wipe with a towel

　　tenugui o shiboru（手ぬぐいを絞る）　wring a towel

te-nui〈てぬい：手縫い〉

　te-nui-no〈手縫いの〉hand-sewn.

te-nukari〈てぬかり：手抜かり〉*see.* te-ochi.

te-nurui〈てぬるい：手ぬるい〉lax, mild, lenient, lukewarm.

ten·ya-mono〈てんやもの：店屋物〉a dish from a caterer.

ten·ya-wan·ya〈てんやわんや〉utter confusion.

　　ten·ya-wan·ya·no·oo·sawagi·ni·naru（てんやわんやの大騒ぎになる）
　　　　be thrown into an utter confusion

ten·yô〈てんよう：転用〉diversion.

　ten·yô-suru〈転用する〉divert〔a thing to some other purpose〕.

tenzai〈てんざい：点在〉

　tenzai-suru〈点在する〉be dotted ((with)).

te-ochi〈ておち：手落ち〉an omission, an oversight, neglect, a careless mistake, a fault.

Sore-wa watashi-no te-ochi-desu.（それは私の手落ちです。） It is my fault.

te-ochi-de or *te-ochi-kara*〈手落ちで，手落ちから〉by(*or* through) an oversight.

te-ochi-naku〈手落ちなく〉without any omission, perfectly, thoroughly.

te-oi〈ており：手負い〉

te-oi-no〈手負いの〉wounded.

te-oke〈ておけ：手桶〉a pail, a wooden bucket.

te-okure〈ておくれ：手後(遅)れ〉

te-okure-da or *te-okure-ni-naru*〈手後(遅)れだ，手後(遅)れになる〉be too late, be past treatment.

te-ono〈ており：手おの〉a hand ax(e), a hatchet.

te-ori〈ており：手織り〉

te-ori-no〈手織りの〉handwoven, homespun.

teppai〈てっぱい：撤廃〉abolition, removal.

teppai-suru〈撤廃する〉abolish, remove, do away ((with)), lift.

tôsei o teppai-suru（統制を撤廃する） lift controls

teppan〈てっぱん：鉄板〉an iron plate, a sheet of iron; a hot plate.

teppei〈てっぺい：撤兵〉

teppei-suru〈撤兵する〉evacuate, withdraw troops ((from)).

teppeki〈てっぺき：鉄壁〉

teppeki-no〈鉄壁の〉impregnable.

teppen〈てっぺん〉the top, the summit, the crown.

atama-no-teppen-kara tsumasaki-made（頭のてっぺんからつま先まで） from top to toe

teppitsu〈てっぴつ：鉄筆〉a stencil pen.

teppô〈てっぽう：鉄砲〉a gun, a rifle.

teppô o utsu（鉄砲を撃つ） fire a gun, shoot a gun

teppô-mizu（鉄砲水） a flash flood

teppun〈てっぷん：鉄粉〉iron filings.

têpu〈テープ〉a tape.

têpu-ni rokuon-suru（テープに録音する） record on a tape

têpu o kiru（テープを切る） breast the tape, cut the tape

têpu o nageru（テープを投げる） throw a paper streamer

jiki-têpu（磁気テープ） (a) magnetic tape

tera〈てら：寺〉a (Buddhist) temple.

terai〈てらい〉(an) affectation, pretension.

terau 〈てらう〉 show off, make a show ((of)), pretend, affect.

tera-sen 〈てらせん：寺銭〉 the rent of a gambling house.

terashi-awasu 〈てらしあわす：照らし合わす〉 check ((with)), tally ((with)).

terasu 〈てらす：照らす〉 shine ((on)), light (up), throw light ((on)), illuminate; refer ((to)), compare ((with)).

　　Taiyô wa chikyû-o terasu.（太陽は地球を照らす.）The sun shines on the earth.

　　rekishi-ni-terashite（歴史に照らして）in the light of history

　　hô-ni-terashite（法に照らして）according to the law

terebi 〈テレビ〉 television, TV.

　　terebi o miru（テレビを見る）watch television

　　yakyû o terebi-de miru（野球をテレビで見る）watch a baseball game on TV

　　terebi-ni deru（テレビに出る）appear on television

　　terebi-no-eizô（テレビの映像）a TV image

　　terebi-hôsô（テレビ放送）a TV broadcast

　　terebi-juzô-ki（テレビ受像機）a television set

　　terebi-shichô-sha（テレビ視聴者）a televiewer, a viewer

terebi-hôsô-o-suru〈テレビ放送をする〉 televise, telecast.

terebin-yu 〈テレビンゆ：テレビン油〉 turpentine oil.

tere-kakushi 〈てれかくし：照れ隠し〉

tere-kakushi-ni〈照れ隠しに〉 to cover one's embarrassment.

tere-kusai or **tere-kusa-sô-na** 〈てれくさい，てれくさそうな：照れ臭い，照れ臭そうな〉 embarrassed, awkward.

teren-tekuda 〈てれんてくだ：手練手管〉 the wiles of the coquette.

tereru 〈てれる：照れる〉 be embarrassed, feel awkward.

teretaipu 〈テレタイプ〉 a teletypewriter.

teretaipu-de-sôshin-suru〈テレタイプで送信する〉 send ((a message)) over the teletype, teletype.

teri-kaeshi 〈てりかえし：照り返し〉 reflection, reflected heat.

teri-tsukeru 〈てりつける：照り付ける〉 shine ((on)), beat ((on)).

teri-yaki 〈てりやき：照り焼き〉 fish boiled with soy.

tero(-kôi) 〈テロ(こうい)：テロ(行為)〉 terrorism.

　　tero-soshiki（テロ組織）a terrorist organization

teru 〈てる：照る〉 shine.

　　tettemo-futtemo（照っても降っても）rain or shine

teruteru-bôzu 〈てるてるぼうず：照る照る坊主〉 a paper charm doll which

Japanese children often make to bring fine weather.

te-ryôri 〈てりょうり：手料理〉a home-cooked dish.

tesage 〈てさげ：手提げ〉a reticule.
　　tesage-kaban（手提げかばん）a briefcase, an attaché case
　　tesage-kinko（手提げ金庫）a portable safe

te-saguri 〈てさぐり：手探り〉groping.
　　te-saguri-de-iku（手探りで行く）grope one's way
　te-saguri-suru〈手探りする〉grope.

te-saki 〈てさき：手先〉a tool, an agent; the fingers.
　　te-saki-to-shite tsukawareru（手先として使われる）be used as an agent ((of))
　te-saki-no-kiyô-na〈手先の器用な〉deft, clever with one's fingers.
　　te-saki-no-bu-kiyô-na（手先の不器用な）clumsy

te-sei 〈てせい：手製〉
　te-sei-no〈手製の〉handmade, of one's own making.

te-shio 〈てしお：手塩〉
　te-shio-ni-kakete sodateru〈手塩に掛けて育てる〉bring up ((a child)) with tender care.

te-shita 〈てした：手下〉a follower, one's men.
　te-shita-to-natte hataraku〈手下となって働く〉work under ((a person)).

te-sô 〈てそう：手相〉the lines of the palm.
　　te-sô-mi（手相見）a palmist
　te-sô-o-miru〈手相を見る〉read ((a person's)) palm, tell ((a person's)) hand.

tessaku 〈てっさく：鉄さく〉an iron railing, an iron fence.

tessen 〈てっせん：鉄線〉iron wire, steel wire.

tesshū 〈てっしゅう：撤収〉withdrawal, removal.
　tesshû-suru〈撤収する〉withdraw, remove.

tessoku 〈てっそく：鉄則〉an iron rule.

tessuru 〈てっする：徹する〉
　　kane-môke-ni-tessuru（金もうけに徹する）devote oneself to money-making
　　yo-o-tessuru（夜を徹する）sit up all night

tesû 〈てすう：手数〉trouble.
　　tesû-ga-kakaru（手数が掛かる）require (much) trouble
　　tesû o habuku（手数を省く）save trouble
　tesû-o-kakeru〈手数を掛ける〉give ((a person)) trouble.
　　O-tesû-o-kakemasu-ga〜.（お手数を掛けますが〜.）I'm sorry to

trouble you, but... .

tesû-no-kakaru〈手数の掛かる〉troublesome.

te-suki-gami〈てすきがみ：手すき紙〉handmade paper.

tesuri〈てすり：手すり〉a handrail, a guardrail, banisters.

tesû-ryô〈てすうりょう：手数料〉a commission, charge, a fee.

tesû-ryô-o-toru〈手数料を取る〉charge.

tesuto〈テスト〉a test.

tesuto o ukeru（テストを受ける）take a test

gakuryoku-tesuto（学力テスト）an achievement test

tesuto-o-suru〈テストをする〉test, give ((a person)) a test.

tetsu〈てつ：鉄〉iron, steel.

Tetsu-wa-atsui-uchi-ni-ute.（鉄は熱いうちに打て.）Strike while the iron is hot.

tetsu-bin（鉄瓶）an iron kettle

tetsu-bô（鉄棒）an iron bar; a horizontal bar

tetsubun（鉄分）iron (content)

tetsu-kuzu（鉄くず）scrap iron

tetsu-no(-yô-na)〈鉄の(ような)〉iron.

tetsu-no-yô-na ishi（鉄のような意志）an iron will

tetsu〈てつ〉a wheel track.

zensha-no-tetsu-o-fumu〈前者のてつを踏む〉follow in another's steps, repeat the mistake of others.

tetsudai〈てつだい：手伝い〉help, assistance; a help, a helper, an assistant, a maid.

tetsudau〈手伝う〉help, assist.

shigoto-o-tetsudau（仕事を手伝う）help ((a person)) to do his work

tetsudô〈てつどう：鉄道〉a railroad, a railway.

tetsudô o fusetsu-suru（鉄道を敷設する）lay a railroad

tetsugaku〈てつがく：哲学〉philosophy.

tetsugaku-sha（哲学者）a philosopher

tetsugaku-teki(-na)〈哲学的(な)〉phlosophical.

tetsugaku-teki-ni〈哲学的に〉philosophically.

tetsujô-mô〈てつじょうもう：鉄条網〉wire entanglements.

tetsujô-mô o haru（鉄条網を張る）stretch wire entanglements

tatsuke(-kin)〈てつけ(きん)：手付け(金)〉a deposit, earnest money.

tetsuke-o-harau（手付けを払う）make a deposit ((on))

te-tsuki〈てつき：手つき〉

bu-kiyô-na-te-tsuki-de（不器用な手つきで）with clumsy hands, awkwardly

tetsuya〈てつや：徹夜〉

　　tetsuya-de-kambyô-suru（徹夜で看病する）sit up all night with an invalid

tetsuya-suru〈徹夜する〉sit up all night.

tetsu-zai〈てつざい：鉄材〉iron material, steel material.

te-tsuzuki〈てつづき：手続き〉procedure, formalities, steps.

　　te-tsuzuki o suru（手続きをする）take proceedings ((for)), go through due formalities, take steps ((in))

　　te-tsuzuki o fumu（手続きを踏む）follow procedure ((of))

　　hôritsu-jô-no te-tsuzuki（法律上の手続き）legal formalities

　　nyûgaku-te-tsuzuki（入学手続き）the entrance procedure

te-tsuzuki-jô-no〈手続き上の〉procedural.

te-tsuzuki-jô〈手続き上〉procedurally.

tettai〈てったい：撤退〉(a) withdrawal, (an) evacuation.

tettai-suru〈撤退する〉withdraw, evacuate, pull ((out of)).

tettei〈てってい：徹底〉thoroughness.

tettei-suru〈徹底する〉be thorough, come home to one's heart.

tettei-shita〈徹底した〉thoroughgoing, downright.

　　tettei-shita nikushoku-ka（徹底した肉食家）a thoroughgoing meat-eater

tettei-teki(-na)〈徹底的(な)〉thorough, exhaustive, complete, out and out.

　　tettei-teki kenkyû（徹底的研究）an exhaustive study

tettei-teki-ni〈徹底的に〉thoroughly, exhaustively, completely, soundly, to the nail.

　　tettei-teki-ni-chôsa-suru（徹底的に調査する）make a thorough investigation ((of))

　　tettei-teki-ni tatakau（徹底的に戦う）fight to the bitter end

tettori-bayai〈てっとりばやい：手っ取り早い〉expeditious.

tettori-bayaku〈手っ取り早く〉expeditiously.

　　tettori-bayaku-ieba（手っ取り早く言えば）in short, to be short, in a word

tettô-tetsubi〈てっとうてつび：徹頭徹尾〉thoroughly, out and out, in every way, from top to bottom, from beginning to end.

tettsui〈てっつい：鉄つい〉

tettsui-o-kudasu〈鉄ついを下す〉give a hard blow ((to)).

teusu〈てうす：手薄〉

bôbi no teusu-na tokoro（防備の手薄なところ）a weak point of defense

te-wake 〈てわけ：手分け〉
te-wake-suru（手分けする）divide (a work) ((among)).
　　te-wake-shite-sagasu（手分けして捜す）search for ((a person)) in several parties

te-watasu 〈てわたす：手渡す〉hand over ((a thing)) into ((a person)).

te-zawari 〈てざわり：手触り〉feel, touch.
te-zawari-ga-ii 〈手触りがいい〉feel smooth.
　　te-zawari-ga-arai（手触りが粗い）feel rough

te-zema 〈てぜま：手狭〉
te-zema-na 〈手狭な〉narrow, too small.

te-zukami 〈てづかみ：手づかみ〉
te-zukami-ni-suru（手づかみにする）seize by hand, take with the fingers.
te-zukami-de（手づかみで）with one's fingers.

te-zukuri-no 〈てづくりの：手作りの〉handmade, homemade, home-grown.

te-zumari 〈てづまり：手詰まり〉a stalemate.
　　te-zumari-ni-naru（手詰まりになる）come to a deadlock

te-zuru 〈てづる：手づる〉*see.* tsute.

tî 〈Ｔ（ティー）〉
　　tîji-tai（Ｔ字体）a T bandage
　　tî-jôgi（Ｔ定規）a T square
　　tî-shatsu（Ｔシャツ）a T shirt

to 〈と：戸〉a door.
　　to o akeru（戸を開ける）open a door
　　to o shimeru（戸を閉める）shut a door
　　　　to o batan-to shimeru（戸をばたんと閉める）shut a door with a bang
　　to-o-tataku（戸をたたく）knock at the door

to 〈と：都〉the Metropolis.
　　Tôkyô-to（東京都）Tokyo Metropolis
　　tomin（都民）a citizen of Tokyo
to(-ei)-no 〈都(営)の〉metropolitan, operated by the metropolis.
　　to-ei-basu（都営バス）a metropolitan bus

-to 〈-と〉and; with, along with, together with; against; when, as, as soon as; if; -ever, no matter...; that.
　　kimi to boku（君と僕）you and I

　　　ane-to-issho-ni（姉と一緒に）　along with my sister
　　　konnan-to tatakau（困難と闘う）　struggle against difficulties
　　　eki-ni tsuku-to（駅に着くと）　when I arrived at the station
　　　asu ame-ga-furu-to（明日雨が降ると）　if it rains tomorrow
　　　kimi-ga doko-e-ikô-to（君がどこへ行こうと）　wherever you may go
　　　Asu wa ame-da-to-omou.（明日は雨だと思う。）　I think (that) it will
　　　　be rainy tomorrow.

tô〈とう：党〉a party, a faction, a clique.
　　　tô no hôshin（党の方針）　the lines of a party
　　　tôin（党員）　a member of a party
　　　tôki or tô-soku（党規，党則）　party rules
　　　tônai-jijô（党内事情）　the intraparty situation
　　　tô-taikai（党大会）　a (party) convention

tô〈とう：塔〉a tower, a pagoda, a steeple.
　　　go-jû-no-tô（五重の塔）　a five-storied pagoda

tô〈とう：糖〉sugar.
　　　nyô-ni tô-ga-deru（尿に糖が出る）　have sugar in one's urine

tô〈とう〉a cane.
　　　tô-zaiku（とう細工）　(a) canework

tô〈とう：当〉
　　　tô-o-ete-iru（当を得ている）　be right, be proper
　　　tô-o-ete-i-nai（当を得ていない）　be wrong, be improper
　　　tô-no-honnin（当の本人）　the person in question

tô〈とう：等〉a class, a degree; and so on.
　　　ittô（一等）　the first class

-tô〈-とう：-頭〉a head.
　　　ushi go-tô（牛五頭）　five head of cattle

tôan〈とうあん：答案〉an examination paper, a paper.
　　　tôan o dasu（答案を出す）　hand in one's paper
　　　tôan o shiraberu（答案を調べる）　look over examination papers

toba〈とば：と場〉a gambling place.

tobaku〈とばく：と博〉gambling.
　　　tobaku-jô（と博場）　see. toba
　　tobaku-o-suru〈と博をする〉gamble.

tôban〈とうばん：当番〉duty, turn.
　　　tôban-de-aru（当番である）　be on duty
　　　sôji-tôban（掃除当番）　one's turn for sweeping

tôban〈とうばん：登板〉

tôban-suru 〈登板する〉take the mound, go to the hill.

tobasu 〈とばす：飛ばす〉fly, make fly; blow off; skip, jump, omit; hurry, hasten; splash, spatter.

 mokei-hikô-ki o tobasu（模型飛行機を飛ばす）fly a model airplane
 kaze-de bôshi o tobasareru（風で帽子を飛ばされる）have one's hat blown off
 go-pêji o tobasu（五ページを飛ばす）skip page five
 eki-e takushî o tobasu（駅へタクシーを飛ばす）hasten to the station in a taxi

tobatchiri 〈とばっちり〉a by-blow.

tobatchiri-o-kuu 〈とばっちりを食う〉get a by-blow, be involved ((in)).

tôbatsu 〈とうばつ：討伐〉subjugation, suppression.

tôbatsu-suru 〈討伐する〉subjugate, suppress.

tôben 〈とうべん：答弁〉a reply, an answer, an explanation, a defense.

 tôben o motomeru（答弁を求める）demand an answer ((of))
 tôben-ni-kurushimu（答弁に苦しむ）be at a loss what explanation to make

tôben-suru 〈答弁する〉reply, answer, defend oneself.

tobi 〈とび〉a kite.

tobi-agaru 〈とびあがる：飛(跳)び上がる〉fly up, jump up.

 bikkuri-shite-tobi-agaru（びっくりして飛び上がる）be startled into a jump

tobi-aruku 〈とびあるく：飛び歩く〉run about, gad about.

tobibako 〈とびばこ：跳び箱〉a vaulting horse.

tobi-chiru 〈とびちる：飛び散る〉fly about, scatter.

tobi-dashi-naifu 〈とびだしナイフ：飛び出しナイフ〉a switchblade knife.

tobi-dasu 〈とびだす：飛び出す〉run out, dash out, jump out.

 toori-e tobi-dasu（通りへ飛び出す）run out into the street

tobi-deru 〈とびでる：飛び出る〉protrude, project.

 me-dama-ga-tobi-deru-hodo-takai nedan（目玉が飛び出るほど高い値段）an exorbitant price

tobi-dôgu 〈とびどうぐ：飛び道具〉a missile, a firearm.

tobi-guchi 〈とびぐち：とび口〉a fire hook, a fireman's hook.

tobi-haneru 〈とびはねる：飛び跳ねる〉hop, jump up and down, romp around.

tobi-hi 〈とびひ：飛び火〉flying sparks, leaping flames.

tobi-hi-suru 〈飛び火する〉flames leap ((to)), spread in unexpected quarters.

tobi-iri 〈とびいり：飛び入り〉participation ((in a contest)) from the outside; an adventitious player.

tobi-iri-suru 〈飛び入りする〉participate ((in a contest)) from the outside.

tobi-ishi 〈とびいし：飛び石〉stepping stones.

tobi-ishi-renkyū 〈飛び石連休〉 off-and-on holidays

tobi-ita 〈とびいた：飛び板〉a springboard.

tobi-ita-tobikomi 〈飛び板飛び込み〉 springboard diving

tobi-kakaru 〈とびかかる：飛び掛かる〉spring ((on)), fly ((at)).

tobikiri 〈とびきり：飛び切り〉exceptionally, beyond comparison.

tobikiri yasui 〈飛び切り安い〉 exceptionally cheap

tobikiri-jōtō-no 〈飛び切り上等の〉 of very best quality

tobikoeru 〈とびこえる：飛び越える〉jump (over).

hei o tobikoeru 〈塀を飛び越える〉 clear a fence

tobikomi 〈とびこみ：飛び込み〉diving.

tobikomi-dai 〈飛び込み台〉 a diving platform

tobikomi-jisatsu 〈飛び込み自殺〉 killing oneself by jumping in front of a train

tobi-komu 〈飛び込む〉jump in, dive into.

kawa-no-naka-ni-tobi-komu 〈川の中に飛び込む〉 dive into the river

tobi-kosu 〈とびこす：飛び越す〉jump over, clear.

mizo o tobi-kosu 〈溝を飛び越す〉 jump over a ditch

bā o tobi-kosu 〈バーを飛び越す〉 clear a bar

tobi-mawaru 〈とびまわる：飛び回る〉fly about, jump about, romp around.

tobi-noku 〈とびのく：飛びのく〉jump back, jump aside.

tobi-noru 〈とびのる：飛び乗る〉jump into.

ressha-ni-tobi-noru 〈列車に飛び乗る〉 jump into a train

tobi-nukete 〈とびぬけて：飛び抜けて〉by far, outstandingly.

tobi-nukete-ii 〈飛び抜けていい〉 by far the best

tobi-nukete-iru 〈飛び抜けている〉 stand out from others

tobi-okiru 〈とびおきる：飛び起きる〉jump out of bed, jump up.

tobi-ori 〈とびおり：飛び降り〉

tobi-ori-jisatsu-o-suru 〈飛び降り自殺をする〉 commit suicide by plunging ((from))

tobi-oriru 〈飛び降りる〉jump down, leap down.

mado-kara tobi-oriru 〈窓から飛び降りる〉 jump down out of a window

tobira 〈とびら：扉〉a door; a title page.

tobi-saru〈とびさる：飛び去る〉fly away.

tobi-shoku〈とびしょく：とび職〉a scaffolding man.

tobi-tatsu〈とびたつ：飛び立つ〉take wing, take off.

tobitobi〈とびとび：飛び飛び〉

  tobitobi-ni〈飛び飛びに〉without order, at random; here and there.

    tobitobi-ni yomu（飛び飛びに読む）read skippingly

tobi-tsuku〈とびつく：飛び付く〉leap ((at)), jump ((at)); snatch at.

    sempô-no môshi-de-ni-tobi-tsuku（先方の申し出に飛び付く）snatch at a person's offer

tobiuo〈とびうお：飛び魚〉a flying fish.

tobi-utsuru〈とびうつる：飛び移る〉

    eda-kara eda-e tobi-utsuru（枝から枝へ飛び移る）fly from branch to branch

tôbô〈とうぼう：逃亡〉(an) escape, (a) flight, desertion.

  tôbô-suru〈逃亡する〉escape ((from)), flee, desert, make one's getaway.

    kokugai-e-tôbô-suru（国外へ逃亡する）flee the country, jump the country

tobokeru〈とぼける〉pretend ignorance, pretend not to know, act blank.

    toboketa-kao-o-suru（とぼけた顔をする）look blank

toboshii〈とぼしい：乏しい〉scanty, meager, scarce; be short ((of)), be poor ((in)), be lacking ((in)).

    toboshii shûnyû（乏しい収入）a scanty income

    miryoku-ni-toboshii（魅力に乏しい）be lacking in charms

    keiken-ni-toboshii（経験に乏しい）have little experience ((in))

  toboshiku-naru〈乏しくなる〉run short, become scarce.

tobotobo〈とぼとぼ〉trudgingly.

  tobotobo-aruku〈とぼとぼ歩く〉trudge along.

tobu〈とぶ：飛(跳)ぶ〉fly; jump, leap.

  tobu-yô-ni〈飛ぶように〉like the wind.

    tobu-yô-ni hashiru（飛ぶように走る）run like the wind

    tobu-yô-ni ureru（飛ぶように売れる）sell like hot cakes

  tonde-kuru〈飛んで来る〉come running.

    tonde-iku（飛んで行く）rush ((to))

tôbu〈とうぶ：頭部〉the head.

tôbu〈とうぶ：東部〉the eastern part, the East.

  tôbu-no〈東部の〉eastern.

to-bukuro〈とぶくろ：戸袋〉a sliding door case.

tôbun 〈とうぶん：糖分〉sugar.

    tôbun o fukumu （糖分を含む） contain sugar

tôbun 〈とうぶん：等分〉

  tôbun-suru 〈等分する〉divide equally, share equally.

tôbun 〈とうぶん：当分〉for the time being, for some time.

    Tôbun-no-aida Tôkyô-ni taizai-suru-tsumori-desu. （当分の間東京に滞在するつもりです。） I intend to stay in Tokyo for some time.

tôbyô 〈とうびょう：闘病〉a struggle against a disease.

    san-nen-kan-no-tôbyô-seikatsu （三年間の闘病生活） three years of struggle against one's disease

tôbyô 〈とうびょう：投びょう〉anchorage.

  tôbyô-suru 〈投びょうする〉anchor, cast anchor.

tôchaku 〈とうちゃく：到着〉arrival.

    tôchaku-jikoku （到着時刻） the time of arrival

  tôchaku-suru 〈到着する〉arrive ((at or in)), get ((to)), reach.

  tôchaku-shidai 〈到着次第〉on one's arrival.

  tôchaku-jun-ni 〈到着順に〉in order of arrival.

tochi 〈とち：土地〉land, a piece of land, a lot, real estate; soil.

    tochi o kau （土地を買う） buy a piece of land

    tochi-tsuki-no ie （土地付きの家） a house with a lot attached

    tochi-bai-bai （土地売買） dealings in real estate

    tochi-daichô （土地台帳） a land ledger

    koeta tochi （肥えた土地） fertile soil

  tochi-no 〈土地の〉local, native.

    tochi-no shûkan （土地の習慣） a local custom

    tochi-no meisan （土地の名産） a well-known local product

tôchi 〈とうち：当地〉this place.

  tôchi-no, tôchi-de or *tôchi-ni* 〈当地の，当地で，当地に〉at this place, here.

tôchi 〈とうち：統治〉rule, reign, government.

    tôchi-sha （統治者） the ruler, the sovereign

  tôchi-suru 〈統治する〉rule over, govern.

  ～-no-tôchi-ka-ni-aru 〈～の統治下にある〉be under the rule of.... .

tochiru 〈とちる〉fumble.

    serifu o tochiru （せりふをとちる） fluff one's lines

tôchô 〈とうちょう：登頂〉

  tôchô-suru 〈登頂する〉reach the summit.

tôchô 〈とうちょう：盗聴〉wiretapping.

tôchô-ki（盗聴器）a concealed microphone, a wall-snooper, a wiretapping device

tôchô-suru〈盗聴する〉tap, listen in.

tôchô〈とうちょう：登庁〉

tôchô-suru〈登庁する〉attend the office.

tôchoku〈とうちょく：当直〉duty, watch.

tôchoku o kôtai-suru（当直を交代する）relieve the watch

tôchoku-in（当直員）a person on duty

tôchoku-suru〈当直する〉be on duty, keep the watch.

tochû-de〈とちゅうで：途中で〉on the way ((from *or* to)), on one's way ((to)), in the middle ((of)), halfway.

gakkô-kara ie-e-kaeru-tochû-de（学校から家へ帰る途中で）on my way home from school

shokuji-no-tochû-de（食事の途中で）in the middle of a meal

tochû-de yameru（途中でやめる）give up halfway

Tochû-made-go-issho-shima-shô.（途中まで御一緒しましょう。）I'll go part of the way with you.

tochû-gesha〈とちゅうげしゃ：途中下車〉a stopover.

tochû-gesha-suru〈途中下車する〉stop over ((at)), break one's journey.

to-daeru〈とだえる：途絶える〉stop, cease.

Hanashi ga to-daeta.（話が途絶えた。）The conversation came to a halt.

Hito-doori-ga-to-daeru.（人通りが途絶える。）The street is deserted.

Tsûshin ga to-daeta.（通信が途絶えた.）The radio communication was interrupted.

tôdai〈とうだい：灯台〉a lighthouse.

to-dana〈とだな：戸棚〉a closet, a locker, a cupboard.

todoke〈とどけ：届け〉a report, a notice, a notification, a written excuse.

byôki-todoke（病気届）a sick report

shibô-todoke（死亡届）a notice of death

todoke-o-dasu〈届けを出す〉report, notify, send in a written excuse.

todokeru〈とどける：届ける〉report; hand over; send, deliver.

keisatsu-e todokeru（警察へ届ける）report to the police

hiroi-mono o keisatsu-e todokeru（拾い物を警察へ届ける）hand over a find to the police

Bîru-o-ichi-dâsu koko-e todokete-kudasai.（ビールを一ダースここへ届けてください。）Please deliver a dozen bottles of beer to this address.

todokoori〈とどこおり：滞り〉arrears, arrearage; a hitch, (a) delay.
kyûryô no todokoori（給料の滞り）arrears of pay
todokoori-naku〈滞りなく〉punctually, promptly, without delay, without a hitch.

todokooru〈とどこおる：滞る〉be left unpaid, be in arrears, be overdue; be delayed, be left undone.
shigoto-ga-todokooru（仕事が滞る）be behind with one's work

todoku〈とどく：届く〉reach, get ((to)).
me-no-todoku-kagiri（目の届く限り）as far as the eye can reach
te-no-todoku-tokoro-ni（手の届く所に）within one's reach
sugu-te-no-todoku-tokoro-ni（すぐ手の届く所に）within easy reach, near at hand
te-no-todoka-nai-tokoro-ni（手の届かない所に）beyond one's reach

todomaru〈とどまる〉stay, remain.

todome〈とどめ〉a finishing stroke.
todome-o-sasu〈とどめを刺す〉give ((a person)) a finishing blow, give ((a person)) a coup de grâce.

todo-no-tsumari〈とどのつまり〉in the end, after all, finally, at last.

tôdori〈とうどり：頭取〉the (bank) president.

todoroki〈とどろき〉a roar, a peal; throbbing, beating.
kaminari no todoroki（雷のとどろき）a peal of thunder
todoroku〈とどろく〉roar, peal; throb.
mune-o-todorokasete〈胸をとどろかせて〉with a beating heart.

toe-hatae〈とえはたえ：十重二十重〉
toe-hatae-ni〈十重二十重に〉thick and fast.
shiro o toe-hatae-ni tori-kakomu（城を十重二十重に取り囲む）surround a castle thick and fast

tôei〈とうえい：投影〉a cast shadow, projection.
tôei-gahô（投影画法）the method of projections

tôfu〈とうふ：豆腐〉bean curd, *tofu*.
tôfu-ya（豆腐屋）a *tofu* maker

toga〈とが〉fault, blame; a crime.

tôgai〈とうがい：等外〉an also-ran.
tôgai-ni-ochiru〈等外に落ちる〉fall under the regular grades.

tôgai〈とうがい：当該〉
tôgai-kanchô（当該官庁）the authorities concerned

togame〈とがめ〉blame, (a) censure, (a) rebuke.

ryôshin no togame（良心のとがめ）the pangs of conscience

togameru〈とがめる〉blame, censure, reproach, reprove, take ((a person)) to task.

kashitsu-o-togameru（過失をとがめる）blame ((a person)) for his fault

Ki-ga-togameru.（気がとがめる.）My conscience pricks me.

tôgan〈とうがん：冬がん〉a wax gourd.

tô-garashi〈とうがらし：唐辛子〉red pepper.

togarasu〈とがらす〉sharpen; get nervous.

empitsu o togarasu（鉛筆をとがらす）sharpen a pencil

kuchi-o-togarasu（口をとがらす）pout

togatta〈とがった〉sharp, pointed.

saki-no-togatta（先のとがった）sharp-pointed

toge〈とげ〉a thorn, a prickle, a splinter, a spine.

toge-o-tateru（とげを立てる）run a thorn ((into))

toge o nuku（とげを抜く）pull out a thorn

toge-no-aru〈とげのある〉thorny, prickly, spiny; barbed, harsh, stinging.

toge-no-aru kotoba（とげのある言葉）harsh language

toge-no-nai〈とげのない〉thornless.

tôge〈とうげ：峠〉a (mountain) pass; the crisis.

tôge o kosu（峠を越す）cross a pass; pass the crisis, turn the corner, be over the hump.

Suzuka-tôge（鈴鹿峠）Suzuka Pass

tôgei〈とうげい：陶芸〉ceramic art, ceramics.

tôgei-ka（陶芸家）a ceramist

togeru〈とげる：遂げる〉accomplish, attain, achieve, realize, carry out.

mokuteki o togeru（目的を遂げる）accomplish one's purpose

omoi o togeru（思いを遂げる）realize one's desire

togerare-nai〈遂げられない〉unattainable, unrealizable.

togetogeshii〈とげとげしい〉sharp, harsh, stinging.

tôgi〈とうぎ：討議〉(a) discussion, (a) debate.

tôgi-ni-noboru（討議に上る）come up for discussion

tôgi-chû-de-aru（討議中である）be under discussion

tôgi o uchi-kiru（討議を打ち切る）close a discussion

tôgi-suru〈討議する〉discuss, debate ((about *or* on)).

tôgi-sezu-ni〈討議せずに〉without debate.

tôgi〈とうぎ：党議〉a party council, a party decision.

tôgi-jô〈とうぎじょう：闘技場〉an arena.

---

togireru 〈とぎれる：途切れる〉 break, pause, be interrupted.

    Hanashi ga kyû-ni togireta. (話が急に途切れた.) There was a sudden pause in the conversation.

togiretogire 〈とぎれとぎれ：途切れ途切れ〉

  togiretogire-no 〈途切れ途切れの〉 broken, disconnected, intermittent.

  togiretogire-ni 〈途切れ途切れに〉 brokenly, disconnectedly, intermittently, off and on, at intervals.

togi-sumasu 〈とぎすます：研ぎ澄ます〉 sharpen well.

  togi-sumashita 〈研ぎ澄ました〉 well-whetted, sharply-honed.

togi-ya 〈とぎや：研ぎ屋〉a grinder, sharpener, a furbisher.

tôgō 〈とうごう：等号〉an equal mark.

tôgō 〈とうごう：統合〉integration, unification, combination, synthesis.

  tôgô-suru 〈統合する〉integrate, unify, combine, put together.

tôgoku 〈とうごく：投獄〉imprisonment.

  tôgoku-suru 〈投獄する〉put ((a person)) in prison.

togu 〈とぐ：研ぐ〉whet, grind, sharpen, hone.

to-guchi 〈とぐち：戸口〉the door, the doorway.

    to-guchi-ni tatsu （戸口に立つ） stand at the door

    to-guchi-no-kaidan （戸口の階段） a doorstep

toguro 〈とぐろ〉a coil.

  toguro-o-maku 〈とぐろを巻く〉coil itself.

tôgyo 〈とうぎょ：闘魚〉a fighting fish.

tôgyo 〈とうぎょ：統御〉rule, control, management.

  tôgyo-suru 〈統御する〉rule, govern, control, manage, administrate.

tôgyû 〈とうぎゅう：闘牛〉a bullfight.

    tôgyû-jô （闘牛場） a bullring

    tôgyû-shi （闘牛士） a bullfighter

tôha 〈とうは：党派〉a party, a faction, a clique.

    tôha o kumu （党派を組む） form a party

    tôha-ni-wakareru （党派に分かれる） split into factions

tôha 〈とうは：踏破〉

  tôha-suru 〈踏破する〉travel through on foot, traverse.

tôheki 〈とうへき：盗癖〉a thieving propensity, kleptomania.

  tôheki-ga-aru 〈盗癖がある〉have a thievish habit, be kleptomaniac, be sticky-fingered.

tôhemboku 〈とうへんぼく：唐変木〉a blockhead.

tô-hi 〈とうひ：当否〉right or wrong, justice, propriety.

tôhi 〈とうひ：党費〉party expenses.

tôhi〈とうひ：逃避〉escape, flight, evasion.
    genjitsu-kara-no tôhi（現実からの逃避）escape from reality
    tôhi-suru〈逃避する〉escape, flee.
tôhin〈とうひん：盗品〉stolen articles.
toho〈とほ：徒歩〉walking.
    toho-ryokô（徒歩旅行）a walking tour, a hike
    toho-de〈徒歩で〉on foot.
tôhô〈とうほう：当方〉we, our part.
    tôhô-de-wa（当方では）on our side, on our part
tôhô〈とうほう：東方〉the east.
    tôhô-ni（東方に）to the east ((of))
    tôhô-no〈東方の〉east, eastern.
tôhoku〈とうほく：東北〉the northeast.
    tôhoku-tô（東北東）east-northeast (ENE)
    Tôhoku-chihô（東北地方）the northeastern district in Japan
    tôhoku-no〈東北の〉northeastern.
tohô-mo-nai〈とほうもない：途方もない〉extraordinary, wild, fabulous, exorbitant, absurd.
    tohô-mo-nai koto-o-iu（途方もないことを言う）talk about absurd things
    tohô-mo-naku〈途方もなく〉fabulously, exorbitantly, absurdly, ridiculously.
    tohô-mo-naku takai（途方もなく高い）exorbitantly high
tôhon〈とうほん：謄本〉a certified copy, a transcript, a duplicate.
tohô-ni-kureru〈とほうにくれる：途方に暮れる〉be puzzled, be at a loss.
    Dô-shitara-ii-no-ka tohô-ni-kurete-iru.（どうしたらいいのか途方に暮れている.）I am puzzled what to do.
tôhon-seisô〈とうほんせいそう：東奔西走〉
    tôhon-seisô-suru〈東奔西走する〉busy oneself ((about)), be always on the move.
tôhyô〈とうひょう：投票〉vote, poll, ballot.
    tôhyô-de kimeru（投票で決める）decide by vote
    tôhyô-sha（投票者）a voter
    tôhyô-sû（投票数）voting figures
    tôhyô-bi（投票日）a polling day
    tôhyô-jo（投票所）a polling place, the polls
    tôhyô-bako（投票箱）a ballot box
    tôhyô-yôshi（投票用紙）a ballot (paper), a voting slip

    tôhyô-ritsu〈投票率〉a turnout

    mukô-tôhyô〈無効投票〉an invalid vote

 tôhyô-suru〈投票する〉vote ((against *or* for)), cast a vote ((for)), poll, ballot ((for)).

toi〈とい〉a water pipe, a gutter.

toi〈とい：問い〉a question.

    toi ni kotaeru（問いに答える）answer a question

toi-awase〈といあわせ：問い合わせ〉(an) inquiry.

 toi-awaseru〈問い合わせる〉inquire of ((a person)) about.

tôi-jô〈とういじょう：糖衣錠〉a sugar-coated tablet.

toi-kaesu〈といかえす：問い返す〉ask again, ask back.

toi-kakeru〈といかける：問い掛ける〉put a question ((to)), ask ((a person)) a question.

toire〈トイレ〉a toilet (room).

to-ishi〈といし：と石〉a whetstone, a grindstone, a hone.

    to-ishi-de togu（と石で研ぐ）sharpen ((a knife)) on a whetstone

toi-tadasu〈といただす：問いただす〉question, cross-examine.

tôitsu〈とういつ：統一〉unity, unification, standardization, concentration, rule.

    tôitsu o kaku（統一を欠く）lack unity

    tôitsu-sensen（統一戦線）a united front

    seishin-tôitsu（精神統一）mental concentration

 tôitsu-suru〈統一する〉unify, standardize, rule.

toi-tsumeru〈といつめる：問い詰める〉question closely, press ((a person)) for an answer.

toji〈とじ〉binding, stitching; sewing.

tôji〈とうじ：当時〉at that time, in those days, then.

 tôji-no〈当時の〉at that time, of those days, then.

tôji〈とうじ：答辞〉a reply, an address in reply.

    tôji o yomu（答辞を読む）read the reply

tôji〈とうじ：冬至〉the winter solstice.

tô-ji-ki〈とうじき：陶磁器〉ceramic ware, china and porcelain, pottery.

toji-komeru〈とじこめる：閉じ込める〉shut up, confine, imprison.

    yuki-ni-toji-komerareru（雪に閉じ込められる）be snowed up

 toji-komoru〈閉じ込もる〉shut oneself up, be confined ((in)).

    isshitsu-ni toji-komoru（一室に閉じ込もる）be confined in a room

toji-komi〈とじこみ：とじ込み〉a file.

 toji-komu〈とじ込む〉keep on file.

to-jimari〈とじまり：戸締まり〉
to-jimari-o-suru〈戸締まりをする〉lock the doors, lock up.

tojiru〈とじる：閉じる〉shut, close.
me o tojiru（目を閉じる）shut one's eyes
kai o tojiru（会を閉じる）close a meeting

tojiru〈とじる〉file, bind; sew.
shorui-o-tojite-oku（書類をとじておく）keep papers in a file

tôjiru〈とうじる：投じる〉
ippyô o tôjiru（一票を投じる）cast a vote.
jigyô-ni-mi-o-tôjiru（事業に身を投じる）embark in an enterprise
shizai-o-tôjite（私財を投じて）at one's own expense

tôji-sha〈とうじしゃ：当事者〉the person concerned, the party concerned.

tôjitsu〈とうじつ：当日〉the day, the appointed day.
tôjitsu-kagiri-yûkô-no kippu（当日限り有効の切符）a day ticket

tôjô〈とうじょう：搭乗〉
tôjô-in（搭乗員）a crewman, a crew
tôjô-sha（搭乗者）a passenger
tôjô-suru〈搭乗する〉board.

tôjô〈とうじょう：登場〉entrance on the stage, appearance.
tôjô-jimbutsu（登場人物）characters, the cast
tôjô-suru〈登場する〉appear on the stage, make an appearance, come into the picture.

-toka〈-とか〉
Yamada-toka-iu-hito（山田とかいう人）a certain Mr. Yamada
inu-toka neko-toka sono-ta iroiro-na dôbutsu（犬とか猫とかその他いろいろな動物）dogs, cats and various other animals
shihon o tôka-suru（資本を投下する）invest capital

tôka〈とうか：糖化〉
tôka-suru〈糖化する〉saccharify.

tôka〈とうか：等価〉equivalence.
tôka-no〈等価の〉equivalent.

tôka〈とうか：灯火〉
Tôka-shitashimu-beki-kô-to-narimashita.（灯火親しむべき候となりました.）The good season for reading has come.

tôka〈とうか：投下〉
tôka-suru〈投下する〉drop, throw down.

tokage〈とかげ〉a lizard.

tokai〈とかい：都会〉a city, a town.

　　tokai-seikatsu（都会生活）　city life, urban living

　tokai-sodachi-no〈都会育ちの〉city-bred.

tôkai〈とうかい：倒壊〉collapse, destruction.

　　tôkai-kaoku（倒壊家屋）　houses collapsed

　tôkai-suru〈倒壊する〉fall down, collapse, be destroyed.

tokaku〈とかく：と角〉

　tokaku～(-shi)-gachi-de-aru〈とかく～（し）がちである〉be apt ((to do)).

　　Watashi-wa　tokaku-kaze-o-hiki-gachi-da.（私はとかく風邪をひきがち
　　だ.）I am apt to catch cold.

　tokaku-no〈とかくの〉various.

　　Kanojo-niwa-tokaku-no-uwasa-ga-aru.（彼女にはとかくのうわさがあ
　　る.）There are unsavory rumors about her.

tôkaku〈とうかく：頭角〉

　tôkaku-o-arawasu〈頭角を現す〉distinguish oneself, make a conspicuous
　figure.

tôkaku〈とうかく：倒閣〉overthrowing the Cabinet.

　　tôkaku-undô（倒閣運動）　a movement to overthrow the Cabinet

tôkan〈とうかん：投かん〉

　tôkan-suru〈投かんする〉post, mail.

tô-kara〈とうから〉for a long time, long since.

tokasu〈とかす：溶かす〉melt, dissolve.

　　tetsu o tokasu（鉄を溶かす）　melt iron

　　satô o mizu-ni tokasu（砂糖を水に溶かす）　dissolve sugar in water

tôkatsu〈とうかつ：統轄〉control, supervision.

　tôkatsu-suru〈統轄する〉control, exercise general control ((over)),
　supervise.

tokei〈とけい：時計〉a watch, a clock.

　　tokei o maku（時計を巻く）　wind a clock(*or* a watch)

　　tokei-o-miru（時計を見る）　look at one's watch

　　tokei o susumeru（時計を進める）　put on a watch

　　tokei o okurasu（時計を遅らす）　put back a watch

　　tokei o jihô-ni awaseru（時計を時報に合わせる）　set the watch by the
　　time signal

　　Kono tokei wa susumu.（この時計は進む.）This watch gains.

　　Ano tokei wa okureru.（あの時計は後れる.）That watch loses.

　　Kare-no　tokei　wa　go-fun　susunde-iru.（彼の時計は五分進んでいる.）
　　His watch is five minutes fast.

Kanojo-no tokei wa sampun okurete-iru.（彼女の時計は三分後れている。） Her watch is three minutes slow.

Anata-no tokei wa atte-imasu-ka?（あなたの時計は合っていますか。） Is your watch correct?

Tokei ga ni-ji o utsu.（時計が二時を打つ。） The clock strikes two.

tokei-dai（時計台） a clock tower

tôkei〈とうけい：統計〉statistics.

tôkei o toru（統計を取る） take the statistics ((of))

tôkei-gaku（統計学） (the science of) statistics

tôkei-hyô（統計表） a statistical table

tôkei-no or *tôkei-teki(-na)*〈統計の，統計的(な)〉statistical.

tôkei-jô(-wa)〈統計上(は)〉statistically, in the statistics.

tôkei〈とうけい：東経〉the east longitude.

tôkei〈とうけい：闘鶏〉a cockfight.

toke-komu〈とけこむ：解け込む〉

kankyô-ni-toke-komu（環境に解け込む） adapt oneself to the environment

tôken〈とうけん：刀剣〉a sword.

tôken〈とうけん：闘犬〉a dogfight; a fighting dog.

tokeru〈とける：解ける〉get loose, be solved, be appeased.

Kutsu-no-himo ga toketa.（靴のひもが解けた。） My shoestring got loose.

Mondai ga toketa.（問題が解けた。） The problem was solved.

Haha-no ikari ga yatto toketa.（母の怒りがやっと解けた。） At last my mother's anger has been appeased.

tokeru〈とける：溶ける〉melt, thaw, dissolve.

Yuki ga sukkari-toketa.（雪がすっかり溶けた。） The snow has melted away.

Satô wa mizu-ni tokeru.（砂糖は水に溶ける。） Sugar dissolves in water.

toke-yasui〈溶けやすい〉soluble, fusible.

toke-nikui（溶けにくい） insoluble, infusible

toketsu〈とけつ：吐血〉vomiting of blood, hematemesis.

toketsu-suru〈吐血する〉vomit blood.

tôketsu〈とうけつ：凍結〉freezing.

shisan-tôketsu（資産凍結） freezing of assets

tôketsu-suru〈凍結する〉freeze.

tôketsu-o-toku〈凍結を解く〉unfreeze.

toki 〈とき：時〉 time, the time, a time, an opportunity.

    Toki wa kane-nari. 〈時は金なり。〉 Time is money.

    toki-ga-tatsu-ni-tsurete 〈時がたつにつれて〉 as time goes by

toki-no 〈時の〉 then, of the time.

    toki-no hito 〈時の人〉 the person of the moment

toki-o-eta 〈時を得た〉 timely, opportune, seasonable.

toki-naranu 〈時ならぬ〉 untimely, inopportune, unseasonable; sudden, unexpected.

toki-o-tagaezu-ni 〈時をたがえずに〉 punctually.

toki-o-utsusazu 〈時を移さず〉 without delay, without losing a moment, immediately.

chôdo-ii-toki-ni 〈ちょうどいい時に〉 just in time

toki-o-mite 〈時を見て〉 at a favorable opportunity.

toki-to-shite-wa 〈時としては〉 occasionally.

toki-to-baai-ni-yotte-wa 〈時と場合によっては〉 according to circumstances.

-toki 〈-とき：-時〉 when, at the time (of), if, in case (of).

    kodomo-no-toki-ni 〈子供の時に〉 when I was a child, in my childhood

    uten-no-toki-wa 〈雨天のときは〉 if it rains

tôki 〈とうき：冬季〉 the winter season.

    tôki-Orimpikku 〈冬季オリンピック〉 the Winter Olympic Games

tôki 〈とうき：冬期〉 the winter, the wintertime.

tôki 〈とうき：陶器〉 earthenware, china(ware), pottery.

tôki(-sei)-no 〈陶器(製)の〉 china, ceramic.

tôki 〈とうき：騰貴〉 a rise, an advance.

    bukka-tôki 〈物価騰貴〉 a rise in prices

tôki-suru 〈騰貴する〉 rise, advance, go up.

tôki 〈とうき：投機〉 (a) speculation.

    tôki-ni-te-o-dashite-shippai-suru 〈投機に手を出して失敗する〉 speculate unfortunately

tôki-o-yaru 〈投機をやる〉 speculate ((in)).

tôki-teki(-na) 〈投機的(な)〉 speculative.

tôki 〈とうき：登記〉 registration.

    tôki-bo 〈登記簿〉 a register

    tôki-sho 〈登記所〉 a registry (office)

    Tôki-zumi. 〈登記済み。〉 Registered.

tôki-suru 〈登記する〉 register, have ((a thing)) registered.

tokidoki〈ときどき：時々〉sometimes, at times, now and then, occasionally, frequently.

toki-fuseru〈ときふせる：説き伏せる〉*see.* settoku-suru.

tokimeki〈ときめき〉a throb.

tokimeku〈ときめく〉beat fast.

Yorokobi-ni mune ga tokimeku.（喜びに胸がときめく.）My heart throbs with joy.

tokimeku〈ときめく：時めく〉enjoy great prosperity.

toki-niwa〈ときには：時には〉at times, once in a while.

toki-ori〈ときおり：時折〉*see.* tokidoki.

toki-tama〈ときたま：時たま〉*see.* tama-ni.

toki-tsukeru〈ときつける：説き付ける〉*see.* settoku-suru.

tokka〈とっか：特価〉a special price.

tokka-de uru（特価で売る）sell at a special price

tokka-hambai（特価販売）a bargain sale

tokka-hin（特価品）an article offered at a special price

tokkan〈とっかん：突貫〉a charge, a rush.

tokkan-kôji（突貫工事）rush work

tokkan-kôji-de-ie-o-tateru（突貫工事で家を建てる）run up a house

tokkei-kanzei〈とっけいかんぜい：特恵関税〉preferential duties.

tokken〈とっけん：特権〉a privilege.

tokken o ataeru（特権を与える）grant ((a person)) a privilege

tokken o kôshi-suru（特権を行使する）exercise a privilege

tokken-kaikyû（特権階級）the privileged classes

shôsû-tokken-kaikyû（少数特権階級）the privileged few

tokki〈とっき：突起〉a projection, a process, an appendix.

chûyô-tokki（虫様突起）the vermiform appendix

chûyô-tokki-en（虫様突起炎）appendicitis

tokki〈とっき：特記〉special mention.

tokki-suru〈特記する〉mention specially.

tokkô〈とっこう：特効〉(a) special efficacy.

tokkô-yaku（特効薬）a specific (medicine)

〜-ni-tokkô-ga-aru（〜に特効がある）be specially good for... .

tokkumi-ai〈とっくみあい：取っ組み合い〉a grapple.

tokkumi-ai-o-suru〈取っ組み合いをする〉grapple ((with)).

tokku-ni〈とっくに〉long ago, quite a while ago.

Ryôshin wa tokku-ni nakunatta.（両親はとっくに亡くなった.）My parents died long ago.

Ressha wa tokku-ni dete-shimatta.（列車はとっくに出てしまった.）
The train was gone quite a while ago.

San-ji-wa-tokku-ni-sugite-ita.（三時はとっくに過ぎていた.）　It was
well past three o'clock.

tokkuri〈とっくり：徳利〉a (*sake*) bottle.

　tokkuri-kubi-no〈とっくり首の〉turtleneck.

tokkyo〈とっきょ：特許〉a patent.

　tokkyo-ken（特許権）　a patent right

　tokkyo-hin（特許品）　a patented article

　tokkyo-o-toru〈特許を取る〉get a patent ((for *or* on)), patent.

tokkyû〈とっきゅう：特急〉a limited express, a special express.

tokkyû-shu〈とっきゅうしゅ：特級酒〉the superior quality *sake*.

toko〈とこ：床〉a bed.

　toko-ni-tsuku（床に就く）　go to bed

　toko-ni-tsuite-iru（床に就いている）　be sick in bed

　toko-o-hanareru（床を離れる）　get up, leave one's sickbed

　toko o ageru（床を上げる）　put away the bedding

tokô〈とこう：渡航〉a passage, a voyage.

　tokô-te-tsuzuki-o-suru（渡航手続きをする）　arrange passage

　tokô-sha（渡航者）　a passenger, a foreign traveler

　tokô-suru〈渡航する〉make a passage ((to)), go over ((to)).

tôkô〈とうこう：陶工〉a potter, a pottery worker, a ceramist.

tôkô〈とうこう：投降〉surrender.

　tôkô-sha（投降者）　a surrenderer

　tôkô-suru〈投降する〉surrender, give up one's arms.

tôkô〈とうこう：投稿〉a contribution.

　tôkô-sha（投稿者）　a contributor

　tôkô-suru〈投稿する〉contribute, write ((for)).

tôkô〈とうこう：登校〉

　tôkô-suru〈登校する〉go to school, attend school.

toko-age〈とこあげ：床上げ〉recovery from illness.

　toko-age-no-iwai-o-suru（床上げの祝いをする）　celebrate one's re-
　covery from illness

　toko-age-o-suru〈床上げをする〉leave one's sickbed, recover from one's
　illness.

toko-bashira〈とこばしら：床柱〉an alcove post.

toko-ita〈とこいた：床板〉an alcove slab.

toko-natsu〈とこなつ：常夏〉everlasting summer.

toko-natsu no kuni（常夏の国）a land of everlasting summer

toko-no-ma〈とこのま：床の間〉an alcove, a *tokonoma*.

tokoro〈ところ：所〉a place, a district, a locality, a scene, space, room; one's address; a point, a feature; moment, time; extent; a case.

Koko-wa watashi-ga umareta-tokoro-desu.（ここは私が生まれた所です。）This is the place where I was born.

Tokoro-kawareba shina-kawaru.（所変われば品変わる。）So many countries, so many customs.

kinō jiko-no-atta-tokoro（昨日事故のあった所）the scene where the accident occurred yesterday

Suwaru-tokoro-ga-nai.（座る所がない。）There is no room to sit.

Takagi-kun-no tokoro o shitte-imasu-ka?（高木君の所を知っていますか。）Do you know Mr. Takagi's address?

Kare-wa ii tokoro-ga-aru.（彼はいいところがある。）He has a good point.

Kanojo-niwa doko-ka-sabishi-sō-na-tokoro-ga-aru.（彼女にはどこか寂しそうなところがある。）There is something lonely in her.

Kare-niwa-shōjiki-na-tokoro-ga-hitotsu-mo-nai.（彼には正直なところが一つもない。）There is not an honest bone in his whole body.

Chōdo-ii-tokoro-e kita.（ちょうどいいところへ来た。）You've come at a good time.

warui-tokoro-e-kuru（悪いところへ来る）come at an ill-chosen time

watashi-no-shitte-iru-tokoro-dewa（私の知っているところでは）so far as I know

ima-made-no-tokoro-dewa（今までのところでは）so far

mokka-no-tokoro（目下のところ）at present, for the present

-tokoro〈-ところ〉be going to, be about to.

Ima-gakkō-e iku-tokoro-desu.（今学校へ行くところです。）I am going to school now.

Chichi wa Tōkyō-kara kaetta-tokoro-desu.（父は東京から帰ったところです。）Father has just returned from Tokyo.

Kanojo-wa oboreru-tokoro-datta.（彼女はおぼれるところだった。）She was nearly drowned.

tokoro-de〈ところで〉well, now, by the way; even if, no matter ((what, who...)).

Tokoro-de kanojo-wa dō-shite-ru?（ところで彼女はどうしてる。）By the way, how is she getting along?

Ima-sugu dekaketa-tokoro-de kisha-ni-ma-ni-awa-nai-darō.（今すぐ出

掛けたところで汽車に間に合わないだろう.）Even if you start right now, you will not be in time for the train.

dare-ga yatta-tokoro-de（だれがやったところで）whoever tries it

tokoro-dokoro〈ところどころ〉here and there, at places.

tokoro-ga〈ところが〉but, however, nevertheless, on the contrary, while.

tokoroten〈ところてん〉gelidium jelly.

tokoroten-shiki-ni〈ところてん式に〉in turn, one after another, successively, mechanically.

tôkô-sen〈とうこうせん：等高線〉a contour line.

tokoton〈とことん〉

tokoton-made〈とことんまで〉to the finish, to the bitter end.

tokoton-made tatakau（とことんまで戦う）fight it out

tokoton-made yaru（とことんまでやる）go the whole way, do it thoroughly

tokoya〈とこや：床屋〉a barber; a barbershop, a barber's.

toko-zure〈とこずれ：床擦れ〉a bedsore.

toku〈とく：解く〉undo, untie, unbind; solve, answer.

tsutsumi o toku（包みを解く）undo a package

musubi-me o toku（結び目を解く）untie a knot

daisû-no mondai o toku（代数の問題を解く）work out a problem in algebra

gokai o toku（誤解を解く）remove a misunderstanding

toku〈とく：説く〉explain, elucidate, interpret; preach, teach, expound; persuade; advocate.

toku〈とく：溶く〉dissolve.

toku〈とく：得〉(a) profit, (a) gain, (an) advantage, benefit.

toku-ni-naru or *toku-o-suru*〈得になる，得をする〉profit, gain, be of advantage ((to)), benefit, be economical, pay.

toku-na〈得な〉profitable, advantageous, beneficial, economical.

toku〈とく：徳〉(a) virtue.

toku-no-takai-hito（徳の高い人）a man of virtue

toku-no-aru〈徳のある〉virtuous, respectable.

tokubai〈とくばい：特売〉a bargain sale.

tokubai-suru〈特売する〉sell at a special price.

tokubetsu〈とくべつ：特別〉

tokubetsu-kyûkô-ressha（特別急行列車）*see.* tokkyû

tokubetsu-seki（特別席）a reserved seat

tokubetsu-na 〈特別な〉 special, particular.

tokubetsu-na riyû 〈特別な理由〉 a particular reason

tokubetsu-ni 〈特別に〉 specially, particularly.

tokuchô 〈とくちょう：特徴〉 a feature, a characteristic, individualities

tokuchô-no-aru 〈特徴のある〉 characteristic, distinctive.

tokuchô-no-nai 〈特徴のない〉 featureless, characterless

tokuchô 〈とくちょう：特長〉 a strong point, a merit, a forte.

toku-dai 〈とくだい：特大〉

toku-dai-no 〈特大の〉 outsized, extra-large, king-sized.

toku-dane 〈とくだね：特種〉 a scoop.

toku-dane-de-kyôsô-shi-o-nuku 〈特種で競争紙を抜く〉 scoop the rival papers.

tokugaku 〈とくがく：篤学〉

tokugaku-no-shi 〈篤学の士〉 a devoted scholar

tokugi 〈とくぎ：特技〉 one's special ability.

tokugi 〈とくぎ：徳義〉 morality.

tokugi-shin 〈徳義心〉 moral sense

tokugi-o-omonjiru 〈徳義を重んじる〉 have a high sense of honor.

tokugi-jô-no 〈徳義上の〉 moral.

tokuha 〈とくは：特派〉 dispatch.

tokuha-in 〈特派員〉 a special correspondent

tokuha-suru 〈特派する〉 dispatch specially, detail.

tokuhitsu 〈とくひつ：等筆〉

tokuhitsu-su-beki 〈特筆すべき〉 worthy of special mention, remarkable, striking, big.

tokuhô 〈とくほう：特報〉 a news flash.

tokuhô-suru 〈特報する〉 flash.

tokuhyô 〈とくひょう：得票〉 the number of votes obtained, one's poll.

tokui 〈とくい：得意〉 one's strong point; pride.

Kare-wa Furansu-go ga tokui-da.（彼はフランス語が得意だ.） He is good at French.

tokui-garu or *tokui-ni-shite-iru* 〈得意がる，得意にしている〉 be proud ((of)).

tokui-no 〈得意の〉 elated, triumphant; favorite.

tokui-no zetchô-ni-aru 〈得意の絶頂にある〉 be at the height of one's glory

tokui-ni-natte or *tokui-mammen-de* 〈得意になって，得意満面で〉 proudly, triumphantly.

tokui〈とくい：得意〉a customer.
 tokui ga dekiru（得意ができる） gain a new customer
 tokui o ushinau（得意を失う） lose a customer
 jô-tokui（上得意） good customers
 tokui-saki（得意先） a client
tokui〈とくい：特異〉
 tokui-sei（特異性） singularity
 tokui-taishitsu（特異体質） an idiosyncrasy, an allergy
tokujitsu〈とくじつ：篤実〉
 tokujitsu-na〈篤実な〉sincere, faithful.
tokuju〈とくじゅ：特需〉special procurements.
 tokuju-keiki（特需景気） a special procurement boom
tokumei〈とくめい：匿名〉anonymity.
 tokumei-no〈匿名の〉anonymous.
 tokumei-de〈匿名で〉anonymously.
tokumei〈とくめい：特命〉
 tokumei-zenken-taishi（特命全権大使） an ambassador extraordinary
  and plenipotentiary
 tokumei-o-obite〈特命を帯びて〉on a special mission.
toku-ni〈とくに：特に〉specially, especially, particularly.
tokurei〈とくれい：特例〉a special case, an exception.
tokusaku〈とくさく：得策〉a good policy, the best plan.
 〜-ga-tokusaku-de-aru〈〜が得策である〉be advisable (wiser *or* better)((to
  do *or* that...)).
tokusan〈とくさん：特産〉a special product, a speciality.
tokusei〈とくせい：特性〉a special quality, a specific character, a
 property, an individuality.
tokusei〈とくせい：特製〉special make.
 tokusei-no〈特製の〉specially made, of special make.
tokusei〈とくせい：徳性〉virtue.
tokusen〈とくせん：特選〉(a) special selection.
 tokusen-ni-naru〈特選になる〉be specially selected.
 tokusen-no〈特選の〉specially selected ((by)).
tokusetsu〈とくせつ：特設〉
 tokusetsu-denwa（特設電話） a specially installed telephone
 tokusetsu-suru〈特設する〉set up specially.
tokusha〈とくしゃ：特赦〉(an) amnesty.
 tokusha-o-okonau（特赦を行う） grant an amnesty ((to))

tokusha-de shussho-suru〈特赦で出所する〉 be released from prison under an amnesty

tokushi〈とくし：特使〉a special envoy.

tokushi-ka〈とくしか：篤志家〉a charitable person, a philanthropist.

tokushin〈とくしん：得心〉consent, conviction, satisfaction.

tokushin-no-iku-yô-ni-setsumei-suru（得心のいくように説明する） give ((a person)) a convincing explanation, explain ((a matter)) to ((a person's)) satisfaction.

tokushin-suru〈得心する〉be convinced ((of)), be satisfied ((of)).

tokushin-saseru〈得心させる〉make ((a person)) consent, persuade ((a person to do)), convince ((a person)), satisfy ((a person)).

tokushitsu〈とくしつ：特質〉*see.* tokusei（特性）.

tokushitsu〈とくしつ：得失〉advantages and disadvantages, merits and demerits, profits and losses.

tokushitsu-o-kangaeru（得失を考える） weigh the relative advantages

tokushoku〈とくしょく：特色〉*see.* tokuchô（特徴）.

tokushoku o hakki-suru（特色を発揮する） display one's characteristic feature(s)

tokushoku-zukeru（特色付ける） characterize, distinguish

tokushu〈とくしゅ：特殊〉

tokushu-kô（特殊鋼） special steel

tokushu-na〈特殊な〉special, particular, characteristic.

tokushu-na jijô（特殊な事情） special circumstances

tokushu-na sainô（特殊な才能） a special ability

tokushû〈とくしゅう：特集〉a special edition.

tokushû-gô（特集号） a special issue

tokushû-kiji（特集記事） features, feature articles

tokusoku〈とくそく：督促〉urge, pressing, demand, dunning.

tokusoku-jô（督促状） a letter of reminder, a dunning note

tokusoku-suru〈督促する〉urge, press, dun.

toku-suru〈とくする：得する〉profit, gain, benefit.

tokutei〈とくてい：特定〉

tokutei-no〈特定の〉specific, specified, special, exceptional.

tokuten〈とくてん：特典〉a privilege, a special favor.

〜-no-tokuten-ga-aru（〜の特典がある） enjoy the privilege of...

tokuten〈とくてん：得点〉marks; a score, a run.

tairyô-tokuten（大量得点） a large score

tokuten-suru〈得点する〉score.

tokutô〈とくとう：特等〉a special grade.
tokutô-seki（特等席）a special seat, a box.

tokutoku-to(-shite)〈とくとくと（して）：得々と（して）〉proudly, in triumph, with elation
tokutoku-to-shite kataru（得々として語る）speak triumphantly

tokuyaku〈とくやく：特約〉
tokuyaku-ten（特約店）a special agent
tokuyaku-suru〈特約する〉make a special contract ((with)).

tokuyô〈とくよう：徳用〉
tokuyô-hin（徳用品）an economical article
tokuyô-no〈徳用の〉economical.

tokuyû〈とくゆう：特有〉
tokuyû-no〈特有の〉peculiar ((to)), its own.
Nihon-tokuyû-no hana（日本特有の花）the flower peculiar to Japan
tokuyû-no utsukushisa（特有の美しさ）a beauty of its own

tôkyoku(-sha)〈とうきょく（しゃ）：当局（者）〉the authorities; a person in authority.
gakkô-tôkyoku（学校当局）the school authorities.

tô-kyori〈とうきょり：等距離〉equal distances, equidistance.
tô-kyori-no〈等距離の〉equidistant ((from)).

tôkyû〈とうきゅう：等級〉a class, a grade, a rank, a degree.
tôkyû-o-tsukeru〈等級を付ける〉classify, grade.

tôkyû〈とうきゅう：投球〉throwing a ball, pitching.
tôkyû-suru〈投球する〉make a throw ((to)), pitch.

to-madoi〈とまどい：戸惑い〉puzzlement, bewilderment.
to-madoi-suru or *to-madou*〈戸惑いする，戸惑う〉be puzzled, be bewildered, be at a loss.

tomari〈とまり：止まり〉stoppage, a stop; an end, a termination.

tomari〈とまり：泊まり〉stopping, a stay; night duty.
hito-ban-domari-de Tôkyô-e iku（一晩泊まりで東京へ行く）go to Tokyo for the night
Wareware-wa kon･ya tomari-da.（我々は今夜泊まりだ。）We are on duty tonight.
tomari-gake-de-iku〈泊まりがけで行く〉go on an overnight visit ((to)).

tomari-gi〈とまりぎ：止まり木〉a perch.

tomaru〈とまる：止まる〉stop, go off, leave; perch.
kaku-eki-ni tomaru（各駅に止まる）stop at every station

kyû-ni tomaru（急に止まる）stop dead

Shukketsu-ga-tomatta.（出血が止まった.）It has stopped bleeding.

Reibô ga kyû-ni tomatta.（冷房が急に止まった.）The air conditioning went off suddenly.

Ha-no-itami ga tomarimashita-ka?（歯の痛みが止まりましたか.）Has the toothache left you?

tomaru〈とまる：泊まる〉stop ((at, in *or* with)), stay ((at, in *or* with)), put up ((at)).

hito-ban tomaru（一晩泊まる）stay overnight

hoteru-ni tomaru（ホテルに泊まる）put up at a hotel

tomato〈トマト〉a tomato.

tombo〈とんぼ〉a dragonfly.

tombo-gaeri〈とんぼがえり：とんぼ返り〉a somersault, a somerset.

tombo-gaeri-o-suru（とんぼ返りをする）turn a somersault

tome-bari〈とめばり：留め針〉a pin.

tome-bari-de-tomeru〈留め針で留める〉pin.

tome-do〈とめど：止めど〉

tome-do-no-nai〈止めどのない〉ceaseless, incessant.

tome-do-naku〈止めどなく〉endlessly, ceaselessly, incessantly.

tome-do-naku shaberu（止めどなくしゃべる）go on talking incessantly

tome-gane〈とめがね：留め金〉a clasp, a hook, a fastening.

tome-gane-de-shimeru〈留め金で締める〉clasp.

tome-gane-o-hazusu（留め金を外す）unclasp

tômei〈とうめい：透明〉transparency.

tômei-na〈透明な〉transparent.

tômen〈とうめん：当面〉

tômen-suru〈当面する〉confront, face.

tômen-no〈当面の〉urgent, pressing, immediate, present.

tômen-no mondai（当面の問題）an urgent question, the problem one is facing, the question at issue

tomeru〈とめる：止める〉stop, turn off, switch off; check, arrest; forbid.

takushî o tomeru（タクシーを止める）stop a taxicab

iki o tomeru（息を止める）hold one's breath

gasu o tomeru（ガスを止める）turn off the gas

terebi o tomeru（テレビを止める）switch off the television set

seichô o tomeru（成長を止める）arrest the growth ((of))

sake-o-tomerarete-iru（酒を止められている）be forbidden to drink

tomeru 〈とめる：留める〉 fasten, fix.

kugi-de tomeru（くぎで留める） fasten ((a thing)) with a nail

tomeru 〈とめる：泊める〉 lodge, put ((a person)) up.

hito o hito-ban tomeru（人を一晩泊める） put a person up for the night

tomi 〈とみ：富〉 riches, wealth.

tomu 〈富む〉 be rich, grow rich.

tennen-shigen-ni-tomu（天然資源に富む） be rich in natural resources

tonda 〈富んだ〉 rich, wealthy.

tomi-kuji 〈とみくじ：富くじ〉 a lottery, a lottery ticket.

tomi-kuji-o-hiku（富くじを引く） take a chance in a lottery

tomi-kuji-ni-ataru（富くじに当たる） win a prize in a lottery

tômin 〈とうみん：冬眠〉 hibernation, winter sleep.

tômin-dôbutsu（冬眠動物） a hibernating animal

tômin-suru 〈冬眠する〉 hibernate.

tomma 〈とんま：とん馬〉 an ass, a donkey, an idiot, a stupid fellow.

tomma-na 〈とんまな〉 stupid, silly, foolish.

tomo 〈とも：友〉 a friend, a companion.

shôgai-no tomo（生涯の友） one's lifelong friend

shomotsu o tomo-to-suru（書物を友とする） have books for companions

tomo 〈とも：供〉 an attendant, a companion, a retinue.

tomo-o-tsurezu-ni-iku（供を連れずに行く） go unattended, go alone

Ei-shi-no-o-tomo-ni-kuwawatte（A氏のお供に加わって） in the retinue of Mr. A

Tochû-made-o-tomo-shi-mashô.（途中までお供しましょう。） I will go part of the way with you.

-tomo 〈－とも〉 of course, indeed, certainly, to be sure; even if, -ever; both, neither.

Sô-desu-tomo!（そうですとも。） Yes, indeed.

dare-ga hantai-shiyô-tomo（だれが反対しようとも） whoever objects

nani-goto-ga okorô-tomo（何事が起ころうとも） whatever may happen

itsu ikô-tomo（いつ行こうとも） whenever you may go

doko-e ikô-tomo（どこへ行こうとも） wherever you may go

donna-ni hatarakô-tomo（どんなに働こうとも） however hard you may work

watashi-tachi-fûfu-tomo（私たち夫婦とも） both my husband and I

Ryôhô-tomo watashi-o shira-nai.（両方とも私を知らない.） Neither of them knows me.

tomodachi〈ともだち：友達〉a friend, a companion.

shitashii tomodachi（親しい友達）a close friend

Warui tomodachi wa sake-nasai.（悪い友達は避けなさい.） Avoid a bad companion.

tomodachi-ni-naru（友達になる） make friends ((with))

tomodachi-zukiai-o-suru（友達付き合いをする） associate with ((a person)) as a friend

tomodachi-gai-ga-nai（友達がいがない） be not true to one's friend

shôbai-tomodachi（商売友達） a business friend

tomo-daore〈ともだおれ：共倒れ〉

tomo-daore-ni-naru〈共倒れになる〉fall together, be ruined together, share the same fate.

tomo-gui〈ともぐい：共食い〉an internecine struggle.

tomo-gui-suru〈共食いする〉prey on each other.

tomo-kaku〈ともかく：とも角〉at any rate, anyhow, anyway; setting aside, aside from, not to mention.

jôdan-wa-tomo-kaku（冗談はともかく） joking aside

tomo-kasegi〈ともかせぎ：共稼ぎ〉

tomo-kasegi-suru〈共稼ぎする〉work in double harness.

tomonau〈ともなう：伴う〉accompany, be accompanied ((by *or* with)), attend, be attended ((by *or* with)), go with.

tashô-no kiken-ga-tomonau（多少の危険が伴う） be attended with some danger, involve some risks

sekinin-ga-tomonau（責任が伴う） carry (with it) responsibilities

tomo-ni〈ともに：共に〉together, with, as.

tomo-ni kurasu（共に暮らす） live together

toshi-to-tomo-ni（年とともに） with the years

toshi-o-toru-to-tomo-ni（年を取るとともに） as one grows older

tomo-ni-suru〈共にする〉share ((with)), partake ((of)).

seikatsu-o-tomo-ni-suru（生活を共にする） live together

ku-raku o tomo-ni-suru（苦楽を共にする） share joys and sorrows ((with))

ummei o tomo-ni-suru（運命を共にする） share one's fate ((with))

tô-morokoshi〈とうもろこし〉Indian corn, maize, corn.

tomoru〈ともる〉burn, be lighted ((by)).

Heya-niwa rampu ga tomotteiru.（部屋にはランプがともっている.） A

lamp is burning in the room.

tomosu〈ともす〉burn, light (up), turn on.

tomoshi-bi〈ともしび：ともし火〉a light, a lamplight.

tomo-sureba〈ともすれば〉

tomo-sureba～(-shi)-gachi-de-aru〈ともすれば～(し)がちである〉be apt ((to do)).

tomo-zuna〈ともづな：とも綱〉a hawser, a mooring line.

tomo-zuna-o-toku〈とも綱を解く〉unmoor.

tompuku〈とんぷく：とん服〉a dose of medicine.

tompuku o nomu (とん服を飲む) take a dose of medicine

tomurai〈とむらい：弔い〉a funeral.

tomurai o dasu (弔いを出す) hold a funeral ((for))

tomurai-gassen (弔い合戦) an avenging battle

tomurau〈とむらう：弔う〉hold a mass ((for)), mourn ((for)), condole ((with)).

tômyô〈とうみょう：灯明〉a taper offered before a god.

ton〈トン〉a ton.

jutton-zumi-torakku (十トン積みトラック) a ten-ton truck

ton-sū〈トン数〉tonnage.

haisui-ton-sū (排水トン数) displacement tonnage

jûryô-ton-sû (重量トン数) deadweight tonnage

sô-ton-sû (総トン数) gross tonnage

tonaeru〈となえる：唱える〉recite, chant; advocate, advance.

nembutsu o tonaeru (念仏を唱える) chant a prayer〔to Amitabha〕

igi o tonaeru (異義を唱える) take objection ((to))

tonakai〈となかい〉reindeer.

tônamento〈トーナメント〉a tournament.

tônamento-de-yûshô-suru (トーナメントで優勝する) win a tournament

tônan〈とうなん：東南〉the southeast.

tônan-Ajia (東南アジア) Southeast Asia

tônan-tô (東南東) east-southeast (ESE)

tônan〈とうなん：盗難〉

tônan-jiken (盗難事件) a case of theft

tônan-hin (盗難品) a stolen article

tônan-hoken (盗難保険) burglary insurance

tônan-todoke-o-dasu (盗難届を出す) report a theft to the police

tônan-ni-au〈盗難に遭う〉be robbed, be stolen, be burglarized.

tonari〈となり：隣〉a next-door house.

    ikken-oite-tonari（一軒おいて隣）next house but one

    tonari-kinjo（隣近所）the neighborhood

  tonari-no〈隣の〉next, neighboring.

    tonari-no heya（隣の部屋）the next room

    tonari-no-hito（隣の人）one's neighbor

  tonari-atte-suwaru〈隣り合って座る〉sit side by side.

    tonari-atte-sumu *or* tonari-awase-ni-sumu（隣り合って住む，隣り合わせに住む）live next door to each other

tonchaku〈とんちゃく：とん着〉*see.* tonjaku.

tonchi〈とんち〉wit.

  tonchi-no-aru〈とんちのある〉witty, quick-witted.

    tonchi-no-kika-nai（とんちの利かない）dull-witted

tonchinkan〈とんちんかん：とん珍漢〉

  tonchinkan-na〈とんちんかんな〉inconsistent, incoherent, irrelevant, absurd.

    tonchinkan-na koto o iu（とんちんかんな事を言う）say inconsistent things

tonda〈とんだ〉

  tonda-me-ni-au〈とんだ目に遭う〉have a hard time of it, have a terrible experience.

tonde-mo-nai〈とんでもない〉absurd, preposterous, outrageous, unexpected.

    Tonde-mo-nai!（とんでもない.）Absurd! / Far from it! / Nothing doing!

    tonde-mo-nai nedan（とんでもない値段）an exhorbitant price

    tonde-mo-nai yôkyû（とんでもない要求）a preposterous demand

    tonde-mo-nai machigai（とんでもない間違い）a gross mistake

    tonde-mo-nai uso-tsuki（とんでもないうそつき）a hell of a good liar

tô-ni〈とうに〉long ago, a long time ago, already.

tonikaku〈とにかく：とに角〉anyhow, anyway, at any rate.

tônin〈とうにん：当人〉the person in question, the man himself.

tonjaku〈とんじゃく：とん着〉

  tonjaku-shi-nai〈とん着しない〉do not care, be indifferent ((to)), be unconcerned ((about)), pay no attention ((to)).

  tonjaku-sezu-ni〈とん着せずに〉regardless ((of)), without regard ((to)).

ton-katsu〈とんカツ：豚カツ〉a pork cutlet.

tonkyô〈とんきょう：とん狂〉

tonkyô-na〈とん狂な〉wild, crazy, hysterical.
　　tonkyô-na-koe-o-dasu（とん狂な声を出す）give a wild cry, screech, scream.
tonneru〈トンネル〉a tunnel.
　　tonneru o nukeru（トンネルを抜ける）go through a tunnel
to-no-ko〈とのこ：との粉〉polishing powder.
tonosama-gaeru〈とのさまがえる：殿様がえる〉a bullfrog.
tonshi〈とんし：とん死〉a sudden death.
　tonshi-suru〈とん死する〉die suddenly.
ton-to〈とんと〉entirely, quite; ((not)) at all, ((not)) in the least.
　　ton-to-go-busata-suru（とんとごぶさたする）have been silent so long
　　ton-to wakara-nai（とんと分からない）cannot understand at all
tonton〈とんとん〉a knock, a rap, a tap; even, equal, quits.
　tonton-to-o-tataku〈とんとん戸をたたく〉tap at the door.
　tonton-de-aru〈とんとんである〉break even.
　　tonton-ni-suru（とんとんにする）make even
tonton-byôshi〈とんとんびょうし：とんとん拍子〉
　tonton-byôshi-ni〈とんとん拍子に〉swimmingly, without a hitch, rapidly.
ton·ya〈とんや：問屋〉a wholesale dealer; a wholesale store.
　　ton·ya-gai（問屋街）a wholesale district
　　Sô-wa-ton·ya-ga-orosa-nai.（そうは問屋が卸さない.）You are expecting too much.
tônyô-byô〈とうにょうびょう：糖尿病〉diabetes.
　tônyô-byô-de-aru〈糖尿病である〉be diabetic.
tônyû〈とうにゅう：投入〉
　tônyû-suru〈投入する〉throw into; invest.
tonza〈とんざ〉a check, a setback.
　tonza-suru〈とんざする〉be checked, receive a setback, be frustrated.
Tô-Ô〈とうおう：東欧〉Eastern Europe.
too-asa〈とおあさ：遠浅〉
　too-asa-ni-natte-iru〈遠浅になっている〉be shallow for a good distance from the shore.
too-boe〈とおぼえ：遠ぼえ〉
　too-boe-suru〈遠ぼえする〉howl.
toode〈とおで：遠出〉
　toode-suru〈遠出する〉go for an outing, make a trip.
tooen〈とおえん：遠縁〉a distant relation.
　～*-no-tooen-ni-ataru*〈～の遠縁に当たる〉be distantly related to... .

tooi 〈とおい：遠い〉 far, distant, remote.
　　tooi shinseki （遠い親せき） a distant relative
　　tooi-tokoro-ni （遠い所に） far away, a long way off
tooka 〈とおか：十日〉 ten days; the tenth.
tookarazu 〈とおからず：遠からず〉 soon, shortly, before long, in the near future.
tooku 〈とおく：遠く〉 a long distance, a distant place; far away, a long way off, in the distance.
　　tooku-e iku （遠くへ行く） go far
　　tooku-kara （遠くから） from far away
　　　tooku-kara kuru （遠くから来る） come from a great distance
　　tooku-ni-mieru kyôkai （遠くに見える教会） a church in the distance
　　tooku-ni sumu （遠くに住む） live far away
　　tooku-oyoba-nai （遠く及ばない） be far behind
too-mawari 〈とおまわり：遠回り〉 a roundabout way, a detour.
　too-mawari-suru 〈遠回りする〉 go by a roundabout way, go a long way about.
too-mawashi 〈とおまわし：遠回し〉
　too-mawashi-ni 〈遠回しに〉 indirectly, in a roundabout way, euphemistically.
　　too-mawashi-ni-iu （遠回しに言う） hint ((at)), suggest, say indirectly, say in a roundabout way
too-me 〈とおめ：遠目〉
　too-me-ga-kiku 〈遠目が利く〉 can see a long distance, have long sight.
　too-me-niwa 〈遠目には〉 from a distance.
too-nari 〈とおなり：遠鳴り〉 distant peals, a distant roar.
too-noku 〈とおのく：遠のく〉 keep away ((from)).
　　ashi-ga-too-noku （足が遠のく） come less frequently 〔than before〕
too-nori 〈とおのり：遠乗り〉 a long-distance drive.
　too-nori-suru 〈遠乗りする〉 make a long drive.
tôon-sen 〈とうおんせん：等温線〉 an isothermal line.
toori 〈とおり：通り〉 a road, a street, a passage.
　　oo-doori （大通り） a main street
-toori(-ni) 〈-とおり(に)〉 as, according to, in accordance with.
　　goran-no-toori （御覧のとおり） as you see
　　itsumo-no-toori （いつものとおり） as usual
　　iwareta-toori-ni （言われたとおりに） as I was told
　　Mattaku sono-toori. （全くそのとおり．） You are quite right.

toori-ame〈とおりあめ：通り雨〉a passing rain, a (sudden) shower.

toori-gakari〈とおりがかり：通り掛かり〉

toori-gakari-no〈通り掛かりの〉passing, chance.

toori-gakari-no hito（通り掛かりの人）a passer-by

toori-gakari-no-setsu-wa（通り掛かりの節は）whenever you happen to come this way

toori-gakari-ni〈通り掛かりに〉as one passes, on the way.

toori-ippen〈とおりいっぺん：通り一遍〉

toori-ippen-no〈通り一遍の〉casual, perfunctory, formal, conventional.

toori-ippen-no aisatsu（通り一遍のあいさつ）perfunctory greetings

toori-kakaru〈とおりかかる：通り掛かる〉happen to pass (by).

toori-kakatta〈通り掛かった〉passing.

toori-kosu〈とおりこす：通り越す〉

Atsui-no-o-toori-koshite-udaru-yô-da.（暑いのを通り越してうだるようだ。）It is rather boiling than hot.

toori-ma〈とおりま：通り魔〉a phantom killer.

toori-michi〈とおりみち：通り道〉a passage, a path, a way.

toori-michi o fusagu（通り道をふさぐ）block up the passage

toori-nukeru〈とおりぬける：通り抜ける〉pass through.

toori-sôba〈とおりそうば：通り相場〉the current price.

toori-sugari〈とおりすがり：通りすがり〉

toori-sugari-no〈通りすがりの〉passing

toori-sugari-ni〈通りすがりに〉when passing by.

toori-sugiru〈とおりすぎる：通り過ぎる〉go past, pass (by).

tooru〈とおる：通る〉go ((along, past *or* through)), pass ((along, by *or* through)), pass ((as *or* for)); do, go down.

ie-no-mae-o-tooru（家の前を通る）pass a house

migi-gawa-o-tooru（右側を通る）keep to the right

Dôzo o-toori-kudasai.（どうぞお通りください。）Please step in.

shiken ni tooru（試験に通る）pass an examination

sekai-no ikkyû-hin-de-tooru（世界の一級品で通る）pass as A-1 quality in the world

Sonna iiwake wa toora-nai.（そんな言い訳は通らない。）Such an excuse won't do.

tooru〈とおる〉penetrate, pierce.

Kare-no koe wa yoku-tooru.（彼の声はよくとおる。）His voice carries very well.

toosen-bô〈とおせんぼう：通せん坊〉

toosen-bô-o-suru〈通せんぼうをする〉bar ((a person's)) way.

tooshi〈とおし：通し〉

　　tooshi-bangô（通し番号）serial numbers

toosu〈とおす：通す〉let ((a person)) pass, let in, show in, let ((a thing)) through, run ((a thing)) through; remain, keep, carry through; carry, pass.

　　Kare-o ni-kai-e tooshi-nasai.（彼を二階へ通しなさい.）Show him upstairs.

　　hari-ni-ito-o-toosu（針に糸を通す）run a thread through a needle

　　isshô dokushin-de-toosu（一生独身で通す）remain a bachelor(*or* an old maid) through life

　　waga-mama-o-toosu（我がままを通す）have one's own way

　　zatto me-o-toosu（ざっと目を通す）look through briefly

　　hôan o toosu（法案を通す）carry a bill

toozakaru〈とおざかる：遠ざかる〉go away ((from)), keep away ((from)).

　　akuyû-kara toozakaru（悪友から遠ざかる）keep away from bad company

toozakeru〈遠ざける〉keep away ((from)), keep ((a person)) at a distance; avoid, shun.

topikku〈トピック〉a topic, a subject.

toppa〈とっぱ：突破〉

toppa-suru〈突破する〉overcome, get over, pass; exceed; break through.

toppa-kô〈とっぱこう：突破口〉

toppa-kô o hiraku〈突破口を開く〉achieve a breakthrough ((in)).

toppan〈とっぱん：凸版〉

　　toppan-insatsu（凸版印刷）relief printing

toppatsu〈とっぱつ：突発〉

　　toppatsu-jiken（突発事件）an unforeseen occurrence

toppatsu-suru〈突発する〉burst out, break out, occur suddenly.

toppatsu-teki(-na)〈突発的(な)〉sudden, unexpected.

toppatsu-teki-ni〈突発的に〉suddenly, unexpectedly.

toppi〈とっぴ：突飛〉

toppi-na〈突飛な〉wild, extravagant, eccentric.

　　toppi-na kangae（突飛な考え）a wild idea

toppu〈トップ〉top.

　　toppu-kiji（トップ記事）a front-page story

toppu-o-kiru〈トップを切る〉be at the top ((of)), take the lead ((in)).

toppu-kurasu-no〈トップクラスの〉leading, top-flight.

toppû 〈とっぷう：突風〉a (sudden) gust of wind.

toppuri 〈とっぷり〉completely, entirely.

    Hi wa toppuri kurete-ita. (日はとっぷり暮れていた.) Night had completely fallen.

toppyôshi-mo-nai 〈とっぴょうしもない：突拍子もない〉see. tonde-mo-nai or toppi-na.

tora 〈とら〉a tiger.

    tora-no-ko (とらの子) a tiger cub; one's treasure, one's precious savings

    tora-no-maki (とらの巻) a key, a crib; secrets

toraeru 〈とらえる：捕らえる〉catch, seize, arrest.

    hito no sode o toraeru (人のそでを捕らえる) catch a person by the sleeve

    kikai o toraeru (機会を捕らえる) seize an opportunity

    zoku o toraeru (賊を捕らえる) arrest a thief

torahômu 〈トラホーム〉trachoma.

torai 〈とらい：渡来〉

    torai-suru 〈渡来する〉come across the sea, visit; be introduced ((into)), be brought over ((from)).

tôrai 〈とうらい：到来〉arrival.

    tôrai-suru 〈到来する〉arrive, come, present itself.

    Kikai ga tôrai-shita. (機会が到来した.) An opportunity has presented itself.

torakku 〈トラック〉a truck, a lorry; a track.

    torakku-kyôgi (トラック競技) track events

tô-raku 〈とうらく：当落〉success(*or* defeat) in an election, the result of an election.

tô-raku 〈とうらく：騰落〉rise and fall.

torampetto 〈トランペット〉a trumpet.

    torampetto o fuku (トランペットを吹く) blow a trumpet

torampu 〈トランプ〉a deck of cards, a playing card.

    torampu o kubaru (トランプを配る) deal cards

    torampu o suru (トランプをする) play cards

    torampu-de uranau (トランプで占う) tell one's fortune from cards

toranku 〈トランク〉a trunk; the trunk, the boot.

toransu 〈トランス〉a transformer.

torasuto 〈トラスト〉a trust.

    torasuto-kinshi-hô (トラスト禁止法) an antitrust law

torawareru〈とらわれる：捕らわれる〉be captured; be swayed ((by)), be seized ((with)).

    kanjô-ni-torawareru（感情にとらわれる）be swayed by sentiment

    mesaki-no-koto-ni-toraware-sugiru（目先の事にとらわれすぎる）be too much swayed by the needs of the moment

    kyôfu-ni-torawareru（恐怖にとらわれる）be seized with panic

tore-daka〈とれだか：取れ高〉a catch, a take, a yield.

torêdo〈トレード〉trading of players.

    torêdo-manê（トレードマネー）transfer fee

torêdo-suru〈トレードする〉trade.

tôrei〈とうれい：答礼〉a return salute.

tôrei-suru〈答礼する〉return a salute(*or* a call).

torepan〈トレパン〉sweat pants.

toreru〈とれる：取(採,捕,撮)れる〉come off; leave; be made, be got, be obtained; be caught; take.

    Botan-ga-hitotsu toreta.（ボタンが一つ取れた.）A button has come off.

    Ha-no-itami ga toreta.（歯の痛みが取れた.）The toothache has left me.

    Budô-kara budô-shu ga toreru.（ぶどうからぶどう酒が採れる.）Wine is made from grapes.

    Kono ike-dewa koi ga toreru.（この池ではこいが捕れる.）Carp is caught in this pond.

    Kono shashin wa totemo yoku torete-iru.（この写真はとても良く撮れている.）This photo is taken very well.

tori〈とり：鳥〉a bird.

    tori o kau（鳥を飼う）keep a bird

    tori-kago（鳥かご）a (bird)cage

tôri〈とうり：党利〉party interests.

toriae-zu〈とりあえず：取りあえず〉for the time being, for the present; first of all.

toriae-zu〜(-suru)〈とりあえず〜(する)〉hasten ((to do)).

tori-ageru〈とりあげる：取り上げる〉take up; take away, deprive; adopt, accept, listen ((to)).

    juwa-ki o tori-ageru（受話器を取り上げる）take up a receiver

    menjô-o-tori-agerareru（免状を取り上げられる）be deprived of one's license

    shikaku-o-tori-agerareru（資格を取り上げられる）be disqualified

    mondai o tori-ageru（問題を取り上げる）take up a problem

tori-ai〈とりあい：取り合い〉a scramble.

  tori-ai-o-suru〈取り合いをする〉scramble ((for)).

tori-atsukai〈とりあつかい：取り扱い〉treatment, handling, dealing.

    teichō-na-tori-atsukai-o-ukeru（丁重な取り扱いを受ける）be treated cordially

    Tori-atsukai-chūi.（取り扱い注意.）Handle with care.

    tori-atsukai-jikan（取扱時間）service hours

    tori-atsukai-ten（取扱店）a dealer

  tori-atsukau〈取り扱う〉treat, handle, deal ((with)).

    inu o zankoku-ni tori-atsukau（犬を残酷に取り扱う）treat a dog cruelly

    rambō-ni tori-atsukau（乱暴に取り扱う）handle roughly

    aru mondai-o-tori-atsukau（ある問題を取り扱う）deal with a problem

tori-au〈とりあう：取り合う〉scramble ((for)); take notice ((of)), have to do ((with)).

    bōru-o-tori-au（ボールを取り合う）scramble for a ball

    kujō-o-tori-awa-nai（苦情を取り合わない）take no notice of ((a person's)) complaints

    Anna yatsu-ni-tori-awa-nai-hō-ga-ii.（あんなやつに取り合わない方がいい.）You had better have nothing to do with such a fellow.

    te-o-tori-atte-naku（手を取り合って泣く）take each other's hands and weep

tori-awase〈とりあわせ：取り合わせ〉an assortment, arrangement, (a) combination.

    myō-na tori-awase（妙な取り合わせ）a strange combination

  tori-awaseru〈取り合わせる〉assort, arrange, combine, group, mix.

tori-bun〈とりぶん：取り分〉one's share, a portion.

tori-chigaeru〈とりちがえる：取り違える〉misunderstand, mistake.

    imi o tori-chigaeru（意味を取り違える）mistake the meaning

tori-chirasu〈とりちらす：取り散らす〉scatter about, put in disorder.

tori-dasu〈とりだす：取り出す〉take out.

toride〈とりで〉a fort, a fortress, a stronghold.

toridori〈とりどり〉

  toridori-no〈とりどりの〉various, diverse.

    iro-toridori-no（色とりどりの）of various colors, various kinds of

  toridori-ni〈とりどりに〉variously, diversely.

torie〈とりえ：取り柄〉worth, (a) merit, one's strong point.

torie-no-nai 〈取り柄のない〉worthless.

tori-goya 〈とりごや：鳥小屋〉an aviary, a henhouse.

tori-hada 〈とりはだ：鳥肌〉gooseflesh.

tori-hada-ga-tatsu 〈鳥肌が立つ〉have gooseflesh.

　　zenshin-ni tori-hada-ga-tatsu 〈全身に鳥肌が立つ〉be gooseflesh all over

tori-hakarai 〈とりはからい：取り計らい〉management, arrangement, discretion, disposal.

　　tokubetsu-no tori-hakarai 〈特別の取り計らい〉 special management

tori-hakarau 〈取り計らう〉manage, arrange, dispose ((of)), deal ((with)).

　　tekitô-ni tori-hakarau 〈適当に取り計らう〉 arrange ((a matter)) as one thinks best

tori-harau 〈とりはらう：取り払う〉remove, take away, get ((a thing)) out of the way, demolish, take down.

tori-hazushi 〈とりはずし：取り外し〉removal, dismantlement, demounting.

tori-hazushi-no-dekiru 〈取り外しのできる〉movable, removable, demountable.

　　tori-hazushi-no-deki-nai 〈取り外しのできない〉 unmovable, fixed

tori-hazusu 〈取り外す〉remove, take away, take down, detach, dismantle.

tori-hiki 〈とりひき：取り引き〉transactions, dealings.

　　tori-hiki-kankei-ga-aru 〈取り引き関係がある〉 have business relations ((with))

　　tori-hiki-daka 〈取引高〉 the volume of business, a turnover

　　tori-hiki-ginkô 〈取引銀行〉 one's bank

　　tori-hiki-saki 〈取引先〉 a customer, a client, a business connection, a correspondent

　　genkin-tori-hiki 〈現金取引〉 cash transactions

　　shin·yô-tori-hiki 〈信用取引〉 credit transactions

　　tori-hiki-jo 〈取引所〉 an exchange, a stock exchange

tori-hiki-suru 〈取り引きする〉transact business ((with)), have dealings ((with)).

torii 〈とりい：鳥居〉a *Shinto* shrine gate, a *torii*.

tori-ire 〈とりいれ：取り入れ〉harvest.

　　tori-ire-doki 〈取り入れ時〉 harvest time

tori-ireru 〈取り入れる〉harvest, gather (in); take in; accept; introduce.

tori-iru 〈とりいる：取り入る〉ingratiate oneself ((with)), curry favor ((with)).

　uwa-yaku-ni-tori-iru（上役に取り入る）curry favor with one's superiors

　onna-ni-tori-iru（女に取り入る）win a girl's heart

tori-isogi〈とりいそぎ：取り急ぎ〉in haste.

　Tori-isogi-go-tsûchi-môshi-agemasu.（取り急ぎ御通知申し上げます。）I hasten to inform you that... .

tori-kae〈とりかえ：取り替え〉(an) exchange, (a) change, (a) renewal, replacing.

tori-kaeru（取り替える）exchange, change, renew, replace.

　aru mono o hoka-no mono-to tori-kaeru（ある物をほかの物と取り替える）exchange one thing for another

　têburu-kurosu o atarashii-no-to tori-kaeru（テーブルクロスを新しいのと取り替える）renew a tablecloth

tori-kaeshi〈とりかえし：取り返し〉

tori-kaeshi-no-tsuka-nai（取り返しのつかない）irrevocable, irretrievable, irreparable.

　tori-kaeshi-no-tsuka-nai sonshitsu（取り返しのつかない損失）an irrecoverable loss

　Sunde-shimatta-koto wa tori-kaeshi-ga-tsuka-nai.（済んでしまった事は取り返しがつかない。）What is done cannot be undone.

tori-kaesu〈とりかえす：取り返す〉take back, regain, recover, make up ((for)).

　son o tori-kaesu（損を取り返す）regain a loss

　okure-o-tori-kaesu（遅れを取り返す）make up for lost time

Tori-kaji!〈とりかじ．：取りかじ．〉Port! / Left!

tori-kakaru〈とりかかる：取り掛かる〉begin, set about, start.

　shigoto-ni-tori-kakaru（仕事に取り掛かる）get to work, set about one's work

tori-kakomu〈とりかこむ：取り囲む〉surround, crowd round, enclose.

　yaji-uma-ni tori-kakomareru（やじうまに取り囲まれる）be surrounded by a rabble

　ie o ishi-gaki-de tori-kakomu（家を石垣で取り囲む）enclose a house with stone walls

tori-kawasu〈とりかわす：取り交わす〉exchange, interchange.

　keiyaku-sho o tori-kawasu（契約書を取り交わす）exchange (written) contracts with each other

tori-keshi〈とりけし：取り消し〉cancellation, revocation, withdrawal.

chûmon no tori-keshi（注文の取り消し）cancellation of an order

tori-keshi-no-deki-nai〈取り消しのできない〉irrevocable.

tori-kesu〈取り消す〉cancel, take back.

yoyaku o tori-kesu（予約を取り消す）cancel a reservation

zengen o tori-kesu（前言を取り消す）take back what one said

tori-kime〈とりきめ：取り決め〉an arrangement, an agreement, (a) settlement.

tori-kimeru〈取り決める〉arrange, settle.

torikku〈トリック〉a trick.

torikku-o-mochiiru（トリックを用いる）resort to a trick

torikku-ni-kakaru〈トリックに掛かる〉be tricked, be taken in.

toriko〈とりこ〉a captive, a prisoner.

toriko-ni-naru〈とりこになる〉be captured, be enslaved, be captivated.

tori-koboshi〈とりこぼし：取りこぼし〉an unexpected defeat through one's carelessness.

tori-komi〈とりこみ：取り込み〉confusion, a misfortune, a trouble.

Kare-no ie-dewa nani-ka-tori-komi ga dekita-ni-chigai-nai.（彼の家では何か取り込みができたに違いない。）Something unfortunate must have happened at his house.

tori-komu〈取り込む〉be in confusion, be busy, be engaged.

tori-komi-sagi〈とりこみさぎ：取り込み詐欺〉a confidence game.

torikoshi-gurô〈とりこしぐろう：取り越し苦労〉needless worries about the future, unnecessary anxiety.

torikoshi-gurô-o-suru〈取り越し苦労をする〉borrow trouble, meet trouble halfway.

Torikoshi-gurô-o-suru-na.（取り越し苦労をするな。）Don't cross the bridge till you come to it.

tori-kowasu〈とりこわす：取り壊す〉pull down, demolish, break up.

tori-kumi〈とりくみ：取組〉a match, a bout.

kô-tori-kumi（好取組）a good match

tori-kumu〈取り組む〉wrestle ((with)), tackle.

nan-mondai to tori-kumu（難問題と取り組む）tackle a difficult problem

tori-magireru〈とりまぎれる：取り紛れる〉be occupied ((with)), be engrossed ((in)).

yôji-ni-tori-magirete〈用事に取り紛れて〉under pressure of business.

tori-maki〈とりまき：取り巻き〉hangers-on.

tori-maku〈取り巻く〉surround, hem ((in)).

tori-matomeru 〈とりまとめる：取りまとめる〉 arrange in order, adjust.

tori-mazeru 〈とりまぜる：取り混ぜる〉 put together, mix, assort.

tori-mazete 〈取り混ぜて〉 all together, in all.

tori-midasu 〈とりみだす：取り乱す〉 put in disorder, disturb; be confused, be upset, lose one's composure, lose self-control, be disheveled.

tori-midashita 〈取り乱した〉 disordered, untidy, confused, distracted.

tori-midashite 〈取り乱して〉 out of order, confusedly, distractedly.

tori-midashita-yôsu-mo-naku 〈取り乱した様子もなく〉 calmly, composedly.

tori-mochi 〈とりもち：鳥もち〉 birdlime.

tori-modosu 〈とりもどす：取り戻す〉 recover, take back.

    kenkô o tori-modosu 〈健康を取り戻す〉 recover one's health

tori-motsu 〈とりもつ：取り持つ〉 go between, act as a go-between.

tori-naosu 〈とりなおす：取り直す〉 take heart, pull oneself together; wrestle again.

tori-nashi 〈とりなし：執り成し〉 mediation, intercession, good offices.

    yûjin-no tori-nashi-de 〈友人の執り成しで〉 through one's friend's good offices

tori-nasu 〈執り成す〉 mediate, intercede ((with)), say a good word ((for)).

tori-nigasu 〈とりにがす：取り逃がす〉 fail to catch, miss.

tori-ni-iku 〈とりにいく：取りに行く〉 go for ((a thing)).

tori-niku 〈とりにく：鳥肉〉 chicken.

tori-ni-kuru 〈とりにくる：取りに来る〉 come for ((a thing)).

tori-ni-yaru 〈とりにやる：取りにやる〉 send ((a person)) for.

tori-nokeru 〈とりのける：取りのける〉 remove, take away, clear out of the way.

tori-nokosu 〈とりのこす：取り残す〉 leave behind.

tori-nokosareru 〈取り残される〉 be left behind.

tori-nozoku 〈とりのぞく：取り除く〉 remove, take away, get rid ((of)).

tori-osaeru 〈とりおさえる：取り押さえる〉 arrest, seize, capture.

tori-sageru 〈とりさげる：取り下げる〉 withdraw, abandon.

    soshô o tori-sageru 〈訴訟を取り下げる〉 call off a suit

tori-saru 〈とりさる：取り去る〉 remove, take away.

tori-shikiru 〈とりしきる：取り仕切る〉 manage ((a job)) all by oneself.

tori-shimari 〈とりしまり：取り締まり〉 control, management, regulation, superintendence.

    tori-shimari-ga-yuki-todoite-iru 〈取り締まりが行き届いている〉 be well controlled *tori-shimaru* 〈取り締まる〉manage, control, keep in order, superintend.

　genjû-ni-tori-shimaru〈厳重に取り締まる〉control strictly, maintain strict discipline ((over))

tori-shimari-yaku〈とりしまりやく：取締役〉a director.

tori-shirabe〈とりしらべ：取り調べ〉(an) investigation, (an) examination, (an) inquiry.

　tori-shirabe-chû-de-aru〈取り調べ中である〉be under investigation

tori-shiraberu〈取り調べる〉investigate, examine, inquire ((into)).

tori-sokonau〈とりそこなう：取り損なう〉fail to get, miss.

tori-soroeru〈とりそろえる：取りそろえる〉put together, assort.

　takusan-tori-soroete-aru〈たくさん取りそろえてある〉have a large assortment ((of))

tori-sugaru〈とりすがる：取りすがる〉cling ((to)).

tori-tate〈とりたて：取り立て〉collection, levying; appointment, promotion.

　tori-tate-tegata〈取立手形〉a collection bill

tori-tateru〈取り立てる〉collect, exact, levy; appoint, promote.

tori-tate〈とりたて：取(採,捕)り立て〉

tori-tate-no〈取(採,捕)り立ての〉fresh.

　tori-tate-no sakana〈捕り立ての魚〉fish fresh from the sea

　tori-tate-no budô〈取り立てのぶどう〉freshly picked grapes

toritate-te〈とりたてて：取り立てて〉in particular, particularly.

　Toritate-te-iu-beki-koto-wa-nani-hitotsu-nai.〈取り立てて言うべきことは何一つない。〉There is nothing worth mentioning.

toritome-no-nai〈とりとめのない：取り留めのない〉rambling, incoherent, vague, absurd, wild.

　toritome-no-nai koto o iu〈取り留めのないことを言う〉say incoherent things

tori-tomeru〈とりとめる：取り留める〉

　ichimei-o-tori-tomeru〈一命を取り留める〉escape death

tori-tsugi〈とりつぎ：取り次ぎ〉agency; intermediation.

　tori-tsugi-o-tanomu〈取り次ぎを頼む〉ask to see ((a person)), ask ((a person)) to send in one's name

　tori-tsugi-ten〈取次店〉an agency

tori-tsugu〈取り次ぐ〉act as an agent; answer the door, convey.

toritsuke〈とりつけ：取り付け〉installation, furnishing.

　denwa no toritsuke〈電話の取り付け〉the installation of a telephone

toritsukeru〈取り付ける〉set up, furnish.

toritsuku 〈とりつく：取り付く〉hold fast ((to)), cling ((to)); possess, take possession ((of)), haunt.

    akuma-ni toritsukareru（悪魔に取り付かれる）be possessed by a devil

   toritsuku-shima-ga-nai〈取り付く島がない〉feel utterly hopeless.

tori-tsukurou 〈とりつくろう：取り繕う〉patch (up); smooth over, temporize.

toriuchi 〈とりうち：鳥打ち〉fowling.

    toriuchi-ni-iku（鳥打ちに行く）go fowling

    toriuchi-bô（鳥打ち帽）a sports cap

toriwake 〈とりわけ〉especially, above all, first of all, particularly.

tori-yame 〈とりやめ：取りやめ〉cancellation.

   tori-yameru〈取りやめる〉cancel, call off.

tori-yoseru 〈とりよせる：取り寄せる〉order ((from)), get ((someone)) to send.

    jisho o Maruzen-kara tori-yoseru（辞書を丸善から取り寄せる）order a dictionary from Maruzen

tori-zata 〈とりざた：取りざた〉a rumor, town talk, gossip.

   iroiro-tori-zata-sareru〈いろいろ取りざたされる〉be talked about, various rumors are afloat.

toro 〈とろ〉fatty meat of tuna.

tôrô 〈とうろう：灯ろう〉a garden lantern, a hanging lantern, a dedicatory lantern.

toro-bi 〈とろび：とろ火〉a slow fire.

   toro-bi-de-niru〈とろ火で煮る〉cook over a slow fire, simmer.

torokeru 〈とろける〉melt away; be charmed ((with)).

torokko 〈トロッコ〉a truck, a trolley.

tôroku 〈とうろく：登録〉registration, entry.

    tôroku-shôhyô（登録商標）a registered trademark

   tôroku-suru〈登録する〉register, enter.

   tôroku-zumi-no〈登録済みの〉registered.

toron 〈とろん〉

   toron-to-shita〈とろんとした〉sleepy, drowsy, heavy.

    toron-to-shita me（とろんとした目）drowsy eyes

tôron 〈とうろん：討論〉a discussion, a debate.

    tôron o uchi-kiru（討論を打ち切る）close a discussion

    tôron-kai（討論会）a forum, a discussion, a debate

      kôkai-tôron-kai（公開討論会）an open forum

tôron-suru 〈討論する〉 discuss, debate.

torori 〈とろり〉

torori-to-shita 〈とろりとした〉 thick〔liquid〕.

tororo 〈とろろ〉 grated yam.

    tororo-imo (とろろ芋) a yam

    tororo-kombu (とろろ昆布) tangle flakes

torôru 〈トロール〉 a trawl.

    torôru-gyogyô (トロール漁業) trawling

    torôru-sen (トロール船) a trawlboat, a trawler

torotoro 〈とろとろ〉

    torotoro-niru (とろとろ煮る) *see.* toro-bi-de-niru

    torotoro-suru (とろとろする) doze off, take a nap

Torotsukî 〈トロツキー〉

    Torotsukî-shugi (トロツキー主義) Trotskyism

toru 〈とる：取る〉 take, pass, hand; take, get, win; take, prefer, choose; take, have; charge, ask; take, book, reserve; take (in); take off, remove; rob....of; take.

    jisho o te-ni-toru (辞書を手に取る) take a dictionary in one's hand

    Koshô o totte-kudasai. (こしょうを取ってください.) Pass me the pepper, please.

    Sono bôru-pen o totte-kudasai. (そのボールペンを取ってください.) Please hand me the ball-point pen.

    gakui o toru (学位を取る) take a degree

    manten o toru (満点を取る) get full marks

    ittô-shô o toru (一等賞を取る) win the first prize

    suki-na-mono o toru (好きな物を取る) take the one one likes

    ichi-nichi-ni san-shoku toru (一日に三食取る) take three meals a day

    chûshoku o toru (昼食を取る) have lunch

    rishi o toru (利子を取る) charge interest

    seki o totte-oku (席を取っておく) book a seat

    Asahi-shimbun-o-toru (朝日新聞を取る) take in the Asahi

    bôshi o toru (帽子を取る) take off one's hat

    hito-kara kane-o-toru (人から金を取る) rob a person of his money

    hito-no-iu-koto o waruku-toru (人の言うことを悪く取る) take a person's words amiss

toru 〈とる：執る〉 take, manage.

    rô o toru (労を執る) take trouble

jimu o toru（事務を執る）do business

toru〈とる：採る〉take, engage, adopt, extract.

shudan o toru（手段をとる）take a measure

sotsugyô-sei-o-go-nin toru（卒業生を五人採る）engage five graduates

goma-kara abura o toru（ゴマから油を採る）extract oil from sesame

toru〈とる：捕る〉take, catch, seize.

kawa-de sakana o toru（川で魚を捕る）catch fish in a river

toru〈とる：撮る〉take.

shashin o toru（写真を撮る）take a picture

tôrui〈とうるい：盗塁〉a steal.

tôrui-suru〈盗塁する〉steal a base.

Toruko〈トルコ〉Turkey.

Toruko-jin（トルコ人）a Turk

Toruko-go（トルコ語）Turkish

Toruko(-jin)-no（トルコ(人)の）Turkish

toru-ni-tara-nai〈とるにたらない：取るに足らない〉insignificant, trifling, trivial, of no account.

tôryaku〈とうりゃく：党略〉a party policy.

toryô〈とりょう：塗料〉paints.

tôryô〈とうりょう：棟りょう〉a master carpenter.

tôryû〈とうりゅう：とう留〉stay, sojourn.

tôryû-kyaku（とう留客）a guest, a house guest

tôryû-suru〈とう留する〉stay, sojourn.

naga-tôryû-suru（長とう留する）make a long stay

tôsai〈とうさい：搭載〉

tôsai-suru〈搭載する〉load, embark, carry.

tosaka〈とさか〉a comb, a crest, a cockscomb.

tôsaku〈とうさく：盗作〉plagiarism.

tôsaku-suru〈盗作する〉plagiarize.

tôsaku〈とうさく：倒錯〉perversion.

sei-teki tôsaku-sha（性的倒錯者）a sexual pervert

tôsan〈とうさん：倒産〉insolvency, bankruptcy.

tôsan-suru〈倒産する〉go into bankruptcy.

tosatsu〈とさつ：と殺〉slaughter, butchery.

tosatsu-jô（と殺場）a slaughterhouse, a butchery

tosatsu-suru〈と殺する〉slaughter, butcher.

tôsei〈とうせい：統制〉control, regulation.

tôsei-keizai（統制経済）controlled economy

tôsei-suru〈統制する〉control, regulate.

tôsei-no-toreta〈統制のとれた〉well-organized, systematic.

   tôsei-no-torete-i-nai（統制のとれていない）unorganized, unsystematic

tôseki〈とうせき：党籍〉the party register.

   tôseki o hanareru（党籍を離れる）leave the party

   tôseki-o-hakudatsu-sareru（党籍をはく奪される）be expelled from the party

tôseki〈とうせき：投石〉

tôseki-suru〈投石する〉throw a stone ((at)).

tôsen〈とうせん：当選〉election, winning.

   tôsen-sha（当選者）an elected person, a successful candidate, a prize winner

tôsen-suru〈当選する〉be elected, win the prize.

   shi-chô-ni-tôsen-suru（市長に当選する）be elected mayor

   ittô-ni-tôsen-suru（一等に当選する）win the first prize

tôsen〈とうせん：当せん〉

   tôsen-bangô（当せん番号）a lucky number

   tôsen-sha（当せん者）a drawer of the lucky number

tôsha〈とうしゃ：投射〉projection, incidence.

   tôsha-kaku（投射角）an angle of incidence

tôsha〈とうしゃ：謄写〉copy, transcription.

tôsha-suru〈謄写する〉copy, transcribe.

tôsha-ban〈とうしゃばん：謄写版〉a mimeograph.

   tôsha-ban-zuri（謄写版刷り）a mimeographed sheet

tôsha-ban-de-insatsu-suru〈謄写版で印刷する〉mimeograph.

tôsha-ban-zuri-no〈謄写版刷りの〉mimeographed.

toshi〈とし：年〉a year, age.

   toshi no hajime-ni（年の初めに）at the beginning of the year

   toshi no kure-ni（年の暮れに）at the end of the year

   toshi-ga-tatsu-ni-tsurete（年がたつにつれて）as years pass by, in the course of years

   jû-hachi-no-toshi-ni（十八の年に）at the age of eighteen, when one was eighteen

   O-toshi-wa-ikutsu-desu-ka?（お年は幾つですか。）How old are you?

   Toshi-to-tomo-ni shiryoku-ga-otoroete-kita.（年とともに視力が衰えてきた。）With age my eyesight is beginning to fail.

   O-toshi-no-wari-ni-wa wakaku-miemasu-ne.（お年の割には若く見えますね。）You look young for your age.

toshi-no-jun-ni〈年の順に〉according to age

toshi-ni-ni-awazu mono-shiri-da〈年に似合わず物知りだ〉be knowledgeable beyond one's age

Toshi-wa-arasoe-nai. / Toshi-niwa-kate-nai.〈年は争えない.：年には勝てない.〉Age will tell.

Toshi-ni-fusoku-wa-nai.〈年に不足はない.〉He is old enough for it.

toshi-o-toru〈年を取る〉grow old(er).

toshi-o-totta〈年を取った〉old, aged.

toshi〈とし：都市〉a city, a town.

chihô-toshi（地方都市）a rural town.

toshi-no〈都市の〉municipal, urban.

tôshi〈とうし：闘志〉a fighting spirit.

tôshi-mamman-de-aru（闘志満々である）be full of fight

tôshi〈とうし：闘士〉a fighter.

tôshi〈とうし：投資〉investment.

tôshi-shintaku（投資信託）investment trust

setsubi-tôshi（設備投資）investment in plant and equipment

tôshi-suru〈投資する〉invest (in).

tôshi〈とうし：凍死〉

tôshi-suru〈凍死する〉be frozen to death.

tôshi〈とうし：透視〉

tôshi-suru〈透視する〉look at ((a person's stomach)) through a fluoroscope.

toshi-gai〈としがい：年がい〉

toshi-gai-mo-nai〈年がいもない〉be thoughtless for one's age, be beneath one's years.

Nan-to-toshi-gai-mo-nai.（何と年がいもない.）Be your age. / You must know better at your age.

toshi-go〈としご：年子〉brothers(*or* sisters) born in two successive years.

toshi-goro〈としごろ：年ごろ〉age, a marriageable age.

onaji toshi-goro no shôjo-tachi（同じ年ごろの少女たち）girls about the same age

toshi-goro-no musume（年ごろの娘）a marriageable daughter

toshi-goto-ni〈としごとに：年ごとに〉every year, year by year.

toshi-kakkô〈としかっこう：年格好〉age.

kimi-kurai-no-toshi-kakkô-no otoko（君くらいの年格好の男）a man about your age

tôshiki〈とうしき：等式〉an equality.

toshi-koshi〈としこし：年越し〉

toshi-koshi-soba〈年越しそば〉New Year's Eve's buckwheat vermicelli

toshi-ma〈としま：年増〉a middle-aged woman.

toshi-mawari〈としまわり：年回り〉

toshi-mawari-ga-ii〈年回りがいい〉be in one's lucky year.

toshin〈としん：都心〉the heart of the city of Tokyo.

tôshin〈とうしん：刀身〉the blade of a sword.

tôshin〈とうしん：等親〉the degrees of kinship.

ni-tôshin〈二等親〉a relation in the second degree

tôshin〈とうしん：等身〉life size.

tôshin(-dai)-no〈等身(大)の〉life-size.

tôshin〈とうしん：投身〉

tôshin-jisatsu-suru〈投身自殺する〉commit suicide by drowning.

tôshin〈とうしん：答申〉

tôshin-suru〈答申する〉submit a report.

toshi-nami〈としなみ：年波〉one's increasing age.

yoru-toshi-nami-ni〈寄る年波に〉under the weight of years.

yoru-toshi-nami-ni　koshi-ga-magatte-iru〈寄る年波に腰が曲っている〉be bent with age

toshi-shita〈としした：年下〉

futatsu-toshi-shita-de-aru〈二つ年下である〉be ((a person's)) junior by two years

toshi-shita-no〈年下の〉younger, junior.

-to-shite〈-として〉as, by way of.

tomodachi-to-shite〈友達として〉as a friend

jôdan-wa-betsu-to-shite〈冗談は別として〉joking apart

-to-shite-mo〈-としても〉even if, though, granting that... .

-to-shite-wa〈-としては〉as for, for.

watashi-to-shite-wa〈私としては〉as for me

Kare-wa　gaijin-to-shite-wa　Nihon-go o jôzu-ni hanasu.〈彼は外人としては日本語を上手に話す。〉He speaks Japanese well for a foreigner.

toshi-tsuki〈としつき：年月〉time, years.

nagai　toshi-tsuki-o-hete〈長い年月を経て〉after a lapse of many years

toshi-ue〈としうえ：年上〉

toshi-ue-no〈年上の〉older, senior.
　toshi-ue-no-hito〈年上の人〉one's senior

toshiyori〈としより：年寄り〉an old person; the old.
　toshiyori-o-daiji-ni-suru〈年寄りを大事にする〉make much of the old
　toshiyori-jimite-iru〈年寄りじみている〉be old before one's time

toshi-yoru〈年寄る〉grow old.

tosho〈としょ：図書〉books.
　tosho-mokuroku〈図書目録〉a catalog of books
　shinkan-tosho〈新刊図書〉new books
　tosho-kan〈図書館〉a library

tôsho〈とうしょ：島しょ〉islands.

tôsho〈とうしょ：投書〉a contribution; an anonymous letter.
　tôsho-bako〈投書箱〉a complaints box, a suggestion box
　tôsho-suru〈投書する〉contribute, write (a letter) ((to)).

tôshô〈とうしょう：凍傷〉frostbite, a chilblain.
　tôshô-ni-kakaru〈凍傷にかかる〉be frostbitten, get chilblains.

toshu〈としゅ：徒手〉
　toshu-taisô〈徒手体操〉free gymnastics

tôshu〈とうしゅ：党首〉the leader of a (political) party.

tôshu〈とうしゅ：投手〉a pitcher.
　tôshu-o-yaru〈投手をやる〉pitch.

tôshû〈とうしゅう：踏襲〉
　tôshû-suru〈踏襲する〉follow in ((a person's)) footsteps, follow.

toso〈とそ〉spiced *sake.*

tosô〈とそう：塗装〉coating, painting.
　tosô-suru〈塗装する〉coat with paint.

tôsô〈とうそう：逃走〉flight, an escape.
　tôsô-chû-de-aru〈逃走中である〉be on the run
　tôsô-suru〈逃走する〉flee, run away, escape.

tôsô〈とうそう：闘争〉a fight, a struggle, a strike.
　chin·age-tôsô〈賃上げ闘争〉a struggle for higher wages
　tôsô-shikin〈闘争資金〉struggle fund
　tôsô-suru〈闘争する〉fight, struggle.

tôsotsu〈とうそつ：統率〉command, leadership.
　tôsotsu-suru〈統率する〉command, lead, direct.

tossa〈とっさ〉
　tossa-no〈とっさの〉momentary, instantaneous.
　tossa-no-kyû-o-sukuu〈とっさの急を救う〉rescue ((a person)) from

an imminent danger

tossa-ni 〈とっさに〉 promptly, off hand, on the spur of the moment.

tosshin 〈とっしん：突進〉 a rush, a dash, a charge.

tosshin-suru 〈突進する〉 rush, dash, make a dash, charge ((at)).

tosshutsu 〈とっしゅつ：突出〉 projection.

tosshutsu-suru 〈突出する〉 project, jut out.

tosshutsu-shita 〈突出した〉 projecting.

tôsui 〈とうすい：統帥〉 the supreme command.

tôsui-ken 〈統帥権〉 the prerogative of supreme command

tôsui 〈とうすい：陶酔〉 intoxication; fascination.

jiko-tôsui 〈自己陶酔〉 narcissism

tôsui-suru 〈陶酔する〉 be intoxicated; be fascinated ((by)).

tôta 〈とうた〉 selection; dismissal.

shizen-tôta 〈自然とうた〉 natural selection

tôta-suru 〈とうたする〉 select, weed out; dismiss.

totan 〈トタン〉 zinc.

totan-ita 〈トタン板〉 a zinced iron sheet

totan 〈とたん：途端〉

totan-ni 〈途端に〉 just as... .

sono-totan-ni 〈その途端に〉 just then, just at that time

tôtatsu 〈とうたつ：到達〉 arrival, attainment.

tôtatsu-suru 〈到達する〉 arrive ((at *or* in)), attain.

mokuteki ni tôtatsu-suru 〈目的に到達する〉 attain one's object

totchimeru 〈とっちめる：取っちめる〉 take ((a person)) to task.

tôtei 〈とうてい：到底〉 *see.* totemo∼-nai.

totemo 〈とても〉 very.

Watashi-wa totemo isogashii. 〈私はとても忙しい.〉 I am very busy.

totemo∼nai 〈とても∼ない〉 not possibly, not at all, by no means, hardly.

Watashi niwa totemo sore wa deki-nai. 〈私にはとてもそれはできない.〉 I cannot possibly do it.

totetsu-mo-nai 〈とてつもない：途てつもない〉 *see.* tohô-mo-nai.

totô 〈ととう：徒党〉 conspirators, a faction, a clique.

totô-o-kumu 〈徒党を組む〉 band together, conspire, clique.

tôtô 〈とうとう：到頭〉 at last, at length, finally, after all.

Tôtô yuki-ni-natta. 〈とうとう雪になった.〉 It began to snow at last.

Tôtô kanojo-wa ko-nakatta. 〈とうとう彼女は来なかった.〉 She didn't come after all.

-tô-tô 〈-とうとう：-等々〉 etc., and so on.

tôtobu 〈とうとぶ：貴(尊)ぶ〉 respect, honor, look up ((to)); think much ((of)), value.

tôtoi 〈とうとい：貴(尊)い〉 respectable, honorable; precious, valuable; noble, sacred.

totonou 〈ととのう：整(調)う〉 be prepared, be ready; be in (good) order; be settled, be arranged.

totonoeru 〈整(調)える〉 prepare ((for)), get ready; put ((things)) in order; arrange, settle; get, purchase.

   totonotta 〈整(調)った〉 well-ordered, well-regulated, neat.

     totonotta kao-dachi〈整った顔立ち〉 a well-featured face

totsuben 〈とつべん：とつ弁〉 slowness of speech.

   totsuben-de-aru 〈とつ弁である〉 be slow of speech.

totsugeki 〈とつげき：突撃〉 a charge, a rush.

   totsugeki-suru 〈突撃する〉 charge (at *or* on), rush ((at)).

totsugu 〈とつぐ：嫁ぐ〉 marry, be married ((to)).

totsumen 〈とつめん：凸面〉

     totsumen-renzu〈凸面レンズ〉 a convex lens

   totsumen-no 〈凸面の〉 convex.

totsunyû 〈とつにゅう：突入〉

   totsunyû-suru 〈突入する〉 rush ((into)), break ((into)).

     masshigura-ni totsunyû-suru〈まっしぐらに突入する〉 rush headlong ((into))

totsuzen 〈とつぜん：突然〉 suddenly, all of a sudden, unexpectedly.

   totsuzen-no 〈突然の〉 sudden, unexpected.

tottan 〈とったん：突端〉 the tip, the point.

     misaki no tottan〈岬の突端〉 the horn of a cape

totte 〈とって：取っ手〉 a handle, a knob, a grip, a pull, an ear.

     totte o mawasu〈取っ手を回す〉 turn the doorknob

(-ni)-totte 〈((に)とって〉 to, for, with.

     watashi-ni-totte〈私にとって〉 to me

tôtei 〈とうてい：突堤〉 a pier, a quay, a breakwater.

totte-kawaru 〈とってかわる：取って代わる〉 take the place ((of)), replace.

totte-kuru 〈とってくる：取って来る〉 fetch, go and get.

totte-oki-no 〈とっておきの：取っておきの〉 reserved; best, choicest.

     totte-oki-no uisukî〈取っておきのウイスキー〉 the whisky reserved for very special occasion

Kanojo-wa totte-oki-no-kimono-o-kite-dekaketa.〔彼女は取っておきの着物を着て出掛けた.〕 She went out in her best.

totte-oku 〈とっておく：取っておく〉 keep, reserve, save, set aside.

seki o totte-oku〔席を取っておく〕 keep a seat, reserve a seat

totte-tsuketa-yô-na 〈とってつけたような：取って付けたような〉 unnatural, studied, artificial, forced.

totte-tsuketa-yô-na warai〔取って付けたような笑い〕 a forced smile

totto-to 〈とっとと〉 hurriedly, at a brisk pace, at once.

Totto-to dete-ike!〔とっとと出て行け.〕 Go out right now!

tottsuki 〈とっつき：取っ付き〉 the beginning.

tottsuki-no-ii or tottsuki-yasui〔取っ付きのいい，取っ付きやすい〕 easy of access.

tottsuki-no-warui *or* tottsuki-nikui〔取っ付きの悪い，取っ付きにくい〕 difficult of access

tou 〈とう：問う〉 ask, put a question ((to)), inquire; care; charge, accuse.

satsujin-zai-ni towareru〔殺人罪に問われる〕 be charged with murder

~-o-towazu 〈～を問わず〉 irrespective of... .

dan-jo-o-towazu〔男女を問わず〕 irrespective of sex

sei-u-o-towazu〔晴雨を問わず〕 rain or shine

-towa 〈～とは〉 as, for; so much; how should... , I am sorry that... .

Kare-wa-dai-gakusha-towa-ie-nai.〔彼は大学者とは言えない.〕 We cannot call him a great scholar.

sanjuppun-towa-kakara-nai〔三十分とはかからない〕 do not take so much as half an hour

Kanojo-ga-shin-henshû-chô-towa!〔彼女が新編集長とは.〕 Just think of her being our new general editor!

towa-ie 〈とはいえ：とは言え〉 but, however, still, nevertheless, though, and yet.

towa-iu-mono-no 〈とはいうものの：とは言うものの〉 *see.* towa-ie.

tôwaku 〈とうわく：当惑〉 perplexity, puzzlement, embarrassment, bewilderment.

tôwaku-suru 〈当惑する〉 be perplexed, be puzzled, be embarrassed, be bewildered, be at a loss.

tôwaku-shita-yôsu-de 〈当惑した様子で〉 with an air of perplexity.

tôwaku-shite 〈当惑して〉 in perplexity, in bewilderment.

tôya 〈とうや：陶冶〉 training, cultivation.

tôya-suru 〈陶冶する〉 train, cultivate, build up.

jinkaku o tôya-suru〔人格を陶冶する〕 cultivate one's character

to-ya-kaku〈とやかく：とや角〉
  to-ya-kaku-iu（とやかく言う）criticize, meddle ((in)), raise objections
  to-ya-kaku-shimpai-suru（とやかく心配する）be worried over one thing or another

tōyaku〈とうやく：投薬〉medication, (medical) prescription.
  tōyaku-suru〈投薬する〉administer medicine ((to)).

Tōyō〈とうよう：東洋〉the East, the Orient.
  Tōyō-jin（東洋人）an Oriental
  Tōyō-no〈東洋の〉Eastern, Oriental.

tōyō〈とうよう：当用〉present use.
  tōyō-kanji（当用漢字）Chinese characters for everyday use

tōyō〈とうよう：盗用〉appropriation.
  tōyō-suru〈盗用する〉appropriate.
    tasha no dezain o tōyō-suru（他社のデザインを盗用する）appropriate the registered designs of other companies

tōyō〈とうよう：登用〉appointment, assignment, promotion.
  tōyō-suru〈登用する〉appoint, promote.
    jinzai o tōyō-suru（人材を登用する）engage able men

tōyu〈とうゆ：灯油〉kerosene, lamp oil, paraffin oil.

tōza〈とうざ：当座〉
  tōza-yokin（当座預金）a current account
  tōza-no〈当座の〉present, current, temporary.
    tōza-no-ma-ni-au（当座の間に合う）be enough for the present
  tōza-shinogi-ni〈当座しのぎに〉as a temporary expedient.
  tōza-wa〈当座は〉for the present.

tōzai〈とうざい：東西〉east and west.
  tōzai-go-kiro（東西五キロ）five kilometers from east to west
  tōzai-namboku（東西南北）north, south, east and west
    tōzai-namboku-kara（東西南北から）from every direction, from all quarters

tozan〈とざん：登山〉mountain climbing, mountaineering.
  Fuji-tozan-o-suru（富士登山をする）climb Mt. Fuji
  tozan-ka（登山家）a mountaineer, an alpinist
  tozan-suru〈登山する〉climb a mountain, go up a mountain.

tozasu〈とざす：閉ざす〉shut, close, lock.
  kuchi-o-tozashite-katara-nai（口を閉ざして語らない）keep one's mouth shut
  koori-ni-tozasareta minato（氷に閉ざされた港）an icebound harbor

tôzen〈とうぜん：当然〉justly, naturally, as a matter of course.

~-wa-tôzen-da.〈～は当然だ。〉It is natural that... .

Kare-ga seikô-suru-no-wa-tôzen-da.〈彼が成功するのは当然だ。〉It is natural that he should succeed.

tôzen-no〈当然の〉just, proper, righteous, natural, deserved.

tôzen-no kekka〈当然の結果〉a natural result

tôzen-no-koto〈当然の事〉a matter of course

tôzen-no-mukui〈当然の報い〉deserts

tozetsu〈とぜつ：途絶〉stoppage, interruption, cessation, suspension.

tozetsu-suru〈途絶する〉be stopped, be cut off, be blocked, be interrupted, be tied up, cease.

Kôtsû ga tozetsu-suru.〈交通が途絶する。〉Traffic is blocked.

tôzoku〈とうぞく：盗賊〉a thief, a robber, a burglar.

tsû〈つう：通〉an authority ((on)), an expert ((at *or* in)), a connoisseur.

tsû-de-aru〈通である〉be an authority ((on)), be well versed ((in)), be well-informed ((in *or* on)), be a connoisseur ((in *or* of)).

-tsû〈-つう：-通〉

shorui-ni-tsû〈書類二通〉two copies of a document

shorui o san-tsû tsukuru〈書類を三通作る〉make out a document in triplicate

tsuba〈つば〉spit, spittle.

tsuba-o-haku〈つばを吐く〉spit.

tsuba〈つば〉a sword guard; a brim.

tsubaki〈つばき〉a camellia.

tsubame〈つばめ〉a swallow.

tsubasa〈つばさ：翼〉the wings.

tsubasa o hirogeru〈翼を広げる〉spread the wings

tsube-kobe〈つべこべ〉

Tsube-kobe-iu-na!〈つべこべ言うな。〉Hold your tongue! / Shut up!

tsuberukurin〈ツベルクリン〉tuberculin.

tsuberukurin-hannô-kensa〈ツベルクリン反応検査〉a tuberculin test

tsubo〈つぼ〉a jar, a pot; the very right spot for applying moxa; what one aims at.

omou-tsubo-ni-hamaru〈思うつぼにはまる〉turn out just as one wished, play into the hands ((of)).

tsubomi〈つぼみ〉a bud.

tsubomi o motsu〈つぼみを持つ〉have buds

fukuranda tsubomi〈膨らんだつぼみ〉a swollen bud

tsubu 〈つぶ：粒〉 a grain, a drop.

    hito-tsubu-no-kome（一粒の米） a grain of rice

    oo-tsubu-no-ame（大粒の雨） a large drop of rain

    tsubu-no-sorotta〈粒のそろった〉even-grained, even-sized.

tsūbun 〈つうぶん：通分〉

    tsūbun-suru〈通分する〉reduce ((fractions)) to a common denominator.

tsubura 〈つぶら〉

    tsubura-na〈つぶらな〉round, beady.

    tsubura-na hitomi（つぶらなひとみ） beady eyes

tsubureru 〈つぶれる〉be smashed, be crushed, be broken, be destroyed; go bankrupt, fail.

    Jishin-de takusan-no ie ga tsubureta.（地震でたくさんの家がつぶれた.） Many houses were destroyed by the earthquake.

    Ano kaisha wa tsubureta.（あの会社はつぶれた.） The company failed.

    koe-ga-tsubureru（声がつぶれる） lose one's voice

    tsubure-yasui〈つぶれやすい〉fragile, brittle.

tsuburu 〈つぶる〉close, shut.

tsubusa-ni 〈つぶさに〉in detail, minutely, fully.

    tsubusa-ni-kataru（つぶさに語る） give a minute account ((of))

tsubushi 〈つぶし〉

    tsubushi-ne（つぶし値） junk value

    tsubushi-ga-kiku〈つぶしが利く〉be serviceable in any other work.

tsubusu 〈つぶす〉crush, smash; dissipate; kill, waste.

    shindai o tsubusu（身代をつぶす） dissipate one's fortune

    jikan o tsubusu（時間をつぶす） kill time

    muda-ni jikan o tsubusu（無駄に時間をつぶす） waste time

tsubuyaki 〈つぶやき〉a mutter, a murmur.

    tsubuyaku〈つぶやく〉mutter, murmur ((against *or* at)), grumble ((about, at *or* over)).

tsubu-yori 〈つぶより：粒より〉

    tsubu-yori-no〈粒よりの〉picked, choice, the best.

tsubu-zoroi 〈つぶぞろい：粒ぞろい〉

    tsubu-zoroi-no〈粒ぞろいの〉uniformly good.

tsuchi 〈つち：土〉earth, soil, the ground.

    koeta tsuchi（肥えた土） rich soil

    ne ni tsuchi-o-kabuseru（根に土をかぶせる） cover the root with earth

tsuchi-o-horu〈土を掘る〉dig in the ground.

tsuchi〈つち〉a hammer, a mallet.

  tsuchi-de-utsu〈つちで打つ〉hammer.

tsûchi〈つうち：通知〉(a) notice, information, an advice.

    tsûchi-jô〈通知状〉a notice, a letter of advice

  tsûchi-suru〈通知する〉inform ((a person)) ((that *or* of)), let ((a person)) know ((that *or* of)), give ((a person)) a notice ((that *or* of)).

  tsûchi-o-ukeru〈通知を受ける〉be informed ((that *or* of)), have notice ((that *or* of)).

tsuchi-bokori〈つちぼこり：土ぼこり〉dust.

tsuchi-fumazu〈つちふまず：土踏まず〉the arch of the foot.

tsuchi-iro〈つちいろ：土色〉earthlike color.

  kao-ga-tsuchi-iro-ni-naru〈顔が土色になる〉turn ghastly pale.

  tsuchi-iro-no〈土色の〉earthlike.

tsuchi-kemuri〈つちけむり：土煙〉a cloud of dust.

tsuchi-tsukazu〈つちつかず：土付かず〉

  tsuchi-tsukazu-de-aru〈土付かずである〉have a clean record.

tsûchô〈つうちょう：通帳〉a passbook, a bankbook.

tsûchô〈つうちょう：通ちょう〉a note, a notification.

    saigo-tsûchô（最後通ちょう）an ultimatum

tsûda〈つうだ：痛打〉

  tsûda-suru〈痛打する〉give a telling blow.

tsudo〈つど：都度〉each time, whenever, as often as.

    jôkyô-no-tsudo（上京の都度）each time one comes up to Tokyo

tsudoi〈つどい：集い〉a gathering, a meeting, a get-together.

tsûdoku〈つうどく：通読〉

  tsûdoku-suru〈通読する〉read through.

tsue〈つえ〉a stick, a cane.

    tsue-o-tsuite aruku（つえをついて歩く）walk with a stick

  tsue-tomo-hashira-tomo-tayori-ni-suru〈つえとも柱とも頼りにする〉rely upon ((a person)) as the sole support.

tsûfû〈つうふう：通風〉ventilation.

  tsûfû-no-ii〈通風のいい〉well-ventilated.

    tsûfû-no-warui（通風の悪い）ill-ventilated

tsûfû〈つうふう：痛風〉gout.

  tsûfû-ni-kakatta or *tsûfû-no*〈痛風にかかった，痛風の〉gouty.

tsugai〈つがい〉a pair, a brace.

tsûgaku〈つうがく：通学〉attending school.

tsûgaku-suru 〈通学する〉 go to school, attend school.

tsuge 〈つげ〉 a box tree.

    tsuge-no kushi（つげのくし）a boxwood comb

tsuge-guchi 〈つげぐち：告げ口〉 taletelling.

tsuge-guchi-suru 〈告げ口する〉 tell ((on)).

tsûgeki 〈つうげき：痛撃〉 a severe blow.

    tsûgeki o ataeru（痛撃を与える）make a severe attack ((on))

tsugeru 〈つげる：告げる〉 tell, let ((a person)) know, inform.

    namae o tsugeru（名前を告げる）give one's name

tsugi 〈つぎ：次〉

tsugi-no 〈次の〉 next, following.

    tsugi-no nichiyô-bi-ni（次の日曜日に）on Sunday next, next Sunday

    tsugi-no bun（次の文）the following sentence

tsugi-ni 〈次に〉 next.

    kono-tsugi-ni（この次に）next time

tsugi-kara-tsugi-e or *tsugi-tsugi-ni* 〈次から次へ，次々に〉 one after another.

tsugi 〈つぎ：継ぎ〉 a patch.

tsugi-o-ateru 〈継ぎを当てる〉 patch (up).

tsugi-no-atatta 〈継ぎの当たった〉 patched.

tsugi-awaseru 〈つぎあわせる：継ぎ合わせる〉 join together.

tsugi-hagi 〈つぎはぎ：継ぎはぎ〉 patching.

    tsugi-hagi-zaiku（継ぎはぎ細工）patchwork

tsugi-ki 〈つぎき：接ぎ木〉 grafting; a grafted tree.

tsugi-ki-suru 〈接ぎ木する〉 graft ((in, into *or* on)).

tsugi-komu 〈つぎこむ：つぎ込む〉 pour in; put ((money)) into, invest in.

tsugi-me 〈つぎめ：継ぎ目〉 a joint, a seam.

tsugi-me-no-nai 〈継ぎ目のない〉 jointless, seamless.

tsugi-tasu 〈つぎたす：継ぎ足す〉 add ((to)), piece out.

tsugô 〈つごう：都合〉 circumstances, a reason, convenience.

    tsugô-ni-yori（都合により）owing to circumstances, for certain reasons

    tsugô-no-ii-toki-ni（都合のいいときに）at one's convenience

    go-tsugô-ga-yoroshikattara（御都合がよろしかったら）if it suits you

    go-tsugô-tsuki-shidai（御都合つき次第）at your earliest convenience

tsugô-no-ii 〈都合のいい〉 favorable, convenient, opportune.

    tsugô-no-warui（都合の悪い）unfavorable, inconvenient, inopportune

tsugô-yoku〈都合よく〉favorably, conveniently, fortunately.

   tsugô-waruku（都合悪く）unfavorably, inconveniently, unfortunately

tsugô-suru〈都合する〉arrange, manage, raise.

   jikan o tsugô-suru（時間を都合する）arrange the hours

   ichi-man-en tsugô-suru（一万円都合する）raise ten thousand yen

tsugu〈つぐ〉pour, fill.

   cha o tsugu（茶をつぐ）pour tea

   wain-o-tsugu（ワインをつぐ）fill a glass with wine

tsugu〈つぐ：接ぐ〉join ((one thing to another)), put together; set.

   hone to tsugu（骨を接ぐ）set a broken bone

tsugu〈つぐ：継ぐ〉succeed, inherit.

   chichi-no zaisan o tsugu（父の財産を継ぐ）inherit one's father's fortune

   yo-o-hi-ni-tsuide（夜を日に継いで）day and night

tsugu〈つぐ：次ぐ〉rank next ((to)), come next ((to)).

   Tôkyô-ni-tsugu dai-tokai（東京に次ぐ大都会）the largest city next to Tokyo

tsugumi〈つぐみ〉a (dusky) thrush.

tsugumu〈つぐむ〉shut, close.

kuchi-o-tsugumu（口をつぐむ）hold one's tongue, clam up.

tsugunai〈つぐない：償い〉compensation, indemnity.

   〜-no-tsugunai-to-shite（〜の償いとして）in compensation for...

tsugunai-o-suru or *tsugunau*〈償いをする, 償う〉make up ((for)), compensate (for), indemnify, atone ((for)).

   tsumi-o-tsugunau（罪を償う）atone for one's crime

tsûhei〈つうへい：通弊〉a common evil.

tsûhô〈つうほう：通報〉a report, a bulletin, information.

tsûhô-suru〈通報する〉report, inform.

tsui〈つい〉only, just, but; by mistake, in spite of oneself.

   tsui-ima-shigata（つい今しがた）only a moment ago, just now, right now

   tsui mi-otoshite-shimau（つい見落としてしまう）just overlook

   tsui waratte-shimau（つい笑ってしまう）laugh in spite of oneself

   tsui dôi-shite-shimau（つい同意してしまう）comply〔with what one says〕without due consideration

tsui〈つい：対〉a pair, a couple, a set.

tsui-no〈対の〉twin.

tsuibamu 〈ついばむ〉 pick up, peck (at).

tsuichô 〈ついちょう：追徴〉 additional collection.

    tsuichô-zei（追徴税） a tax collected in addition

  tsuichô-suru〈追徴する〉 collect in addition, forfeit.

tsuide 〈ついで：次いで〉 after that, subsequently.

  tsuide-okoru〈次いで起こる〉 follow, ensue.

tsuide 〈ついで〉 an occasion, an opportunity.

    o-tsuide-no-setsu-wa（おついでの節は） at your convenience, when
      you have an opportunity

    Tsuide-nagara-môshi-agemasu-ga～.〔ついでながら申し上げますが
      ～.〕 I take this occasion to say... .

    tsuide-no-ari-shidai（ついでのあり次第） at the first opportunity

  tsuide-ni〈ついでに〉 by the way, at the same time, on one's way ((to)).

tsuîdo 〈ツイード〉 tweed.

tsuigeki 〈ついげき：追撃〉 pursuit, chase, give chase ((to)).

  tsuigeki-suru〈追撃する〉 pursue, chase.

tsuihô 〈ついほう：追放〉 banishment, exile, purge.

  tsuihô-suru〈追放する〉 banish, exile, purge, remove.

    kokugai-ni-tsuihô-suru（国外に追放する） banish ((a person)) from
      the country

    kôshoku-kara tsuihô-suru（公職から追放する） remove ((a person))
      from public office

  tsuihô-o-kaijo-suru〈追放を解除する〉 depurge.

tsuijû 〈ついじゅう：追従〉 following, imitation.

    tsuijû-sha（追従者） a follower

  tsuijû-suru〈追従する〉 follow, imitate.

tsuika 〈ついか：追加〉 an addition, a supplement.

    tsuika-chûmon（追加注文） an additional order

  tsuika-suru〈追加する〉 add ((something)) to, supplement.

  tsuika-no〈追加の〉 additional, supplementary.

tsuiki 〈ついき：追記〉 a postscript.

  tsuiki-suru〈追記する〉 add a postscript ((to)).

tsuiku 〈ついく：対句〉 an antithesis, a couplet.

    tsuiku o nasu（対句をなす） make an antithesis

tsuikyû 〈ついきゅう：追求〉 pursuit, chase, search.

  tsuikyû-suru〈追求する〉 pursue, chase, seek ((after)).

  ～-o-tsuikyû-shite〈～を追求して〉 in pursuit of... .

tsuikyû 〈ついきゅう：追究〉 investigation, close inquiry, cross-examination.

tsuikyû-suru〈追究する〉investigate ((a matter)) thoroughly, inquire into ((a matter)) closely, cross-examine.

tsûin〈つういん：通院〉
tsûin-suru〈通院する〉go to hospital regularly.

tsui-ni〈ついに〉at last, at length, finally, in the end, after all.

tsuinin〈ついにん：追認〉ratification, confirmation.
tsuinin-suru〈追認する〉ratify, confirm.

tsuioku〈ついおく：追憶〉*see.* tsuisô.

tsuiraku〈ついらく：墜落〉a fall, a crash.
tsuiraku-suru〈墜落する〉fall, crash.

tsuiseki〈ついせき：追跡〉pursuit, chase, tracking.
    tsuiseki-chôsa〈追跡調査〉a follow-up survey
tsuiseki-suru〈追跡する〉pursue, chase, track.

tsuishi〈ついし：追試〉a supplementary examination, a makeup examination.
    tsuishi o ukeru〈追試を受ける〉take a supplementary examination

tsuishi〈ついし：墜死〉death from a fall.
tsuishi-suru〈墜死する〉fall to death.

tsuishin〈ついしん：追伸〉a postscript.

tsuishô〈ついしょう：追従〉flattery.
    tsuishô-warai〈追従笑い〉a flattering smile
tsuishô-suru〈追従する〉flatter, say flattering things ((to)).

tsuiso〈ついそ：追訴〉
tsuiso-suru〈追訴する〉bring a supplementary suit ((against)).

tsuisô〈ついそう：追想〉recollection, retrospect(ion), reminiscence.
    tsuisô-roku〈追想録〉reminiscences, memoirs
tsuisô-suru〈追想する〉recollect, retrospect, reminisce.

tsuitachi〈ついたち：一日〉the first day of a month.

tsuitate〈ついたて：つい立て〉a (single-leaf) screen.

(-ni)-tsuite〈(〜に)ついて〉of, about, on, over, as to, as for, regarding, with regard ((to)), in respect ((of)), concerning; a, per; under.
    kono ten-ni-tsuite〈この点について〉on this point
    ichi-dâsu-ni-tsuite〈一ダースについて〉per dozen

(〜ni)-tsuite-wa〈(〜に)ついては〉as for... , as to... .

tsuite-iku〈ついていく：付いて行く〉follow ((a person)), keep up ((with)).

tsuite-kuru〈ついてくる：付いて来る〉follow ((a person)).

tsuite-mawaru〈ついてまわる：付いて回る〉pursue, trail, dog.

tsuitô〈ついとう：追悼〉mourning.

    tsuitô-no ji（追悼の辞）a memorial address

    tsuitô-kai（追悼会）memorial services

    tsuitô-suru〈追悼する〉mourn ((for *or* over)).

tsuitotsu〈ついとつ：追突〉a rear-end collision.

    tsuitotsu-suru〈追突する〉dash ((against something)) from behind.

tsuiyasu〈ついやす：費やす〉spend, take, consume, waste.

    ooku-no kane o tsuiyasu（多くの金を費やす）spend a lot of money

    Wareware-wa kenkyû-no-kansei-ni san-nen-o-tsuiyashita.（我々は研究の完成に三年を費やした。）It took us three years to complete our study.

tsuizen〈ついぜん：追善〉a memorial service for the dead.

    tsuizen-kôgyô（追善興行）a memorial performance ((for))

tsui-zo～-nai〈ついぞ～ない〉never, not... at all.

tsuizui〈ついずい：追随〉

    ta-no-tsuizui-o-yurusa-nai〈他の追随を許さない〉be peerless, be without a peer, be unrivaled, be second to none ((in)).

tsuji〈つじ〉a crossroads, a crossing, a street, a street corner.

tsûji〈つうじ：通じ〉passage, an action of the bowels.

    tsûji-ga-aru（通じがある）have an action of the bowels

    tsûji-ga-nai（通じがない）have no passage

tsûjiru〈つうじる：通じる〉run, lead ((to)); be well versed ((in)), be proficient ((in)), be familiar ((with)); be understood; get connected ((with)); be in touch ((with)).

    Furansu-go-ni-tsûjite-iru（フランス語に通じている）be proficient in French

    imi-o-tsûjiru（意味を通じる）make oneself understood

    Kanojo-ni denwa-o-shita-ga-tsûji-nakatta.（彼女に電話をしたが通じなかった。）I could not get through to her by telephone.

    Kono densen-niwa denryû-ga-tsûjite-i-nai.（この電線には電流が通じていない。）This wire is not charged with electricity.

    kimyaku-o-tsûjiru（気脈を通じる）have a secret understanding ((with))

tsûji-te〈つうじて：通じて〉through, throughout, all over.

    terebi ya shimbun-o-tsûji-te（テレビや新聞を通じて）through the television and newspapers

    isshô-o-tsûji-te（一生を通じて）throughout one's life

    zenkoku-o-tsûji-te（全国を通じて）all over the country

ichi-nen-o-tsûji-te〈一年を通じて〉 all the year round

tsuji-tsuma〈つじつま〉
tsuji-tsuma-ga-au〈つじつまが合う〉 be consistent.
    tsuji-tsuma-ga-awa-nai〈つじつまが合わない〉 be inconsistent
tsuji-tsuma-o-awaseru〈つじつまを合わせる〉 make ((one's story)) consistent.
tsuji-tsuma-no-awa-nai-koto-o-iu〈つじつまの合わないことを言う〉 talk inconsistently.

tsûjô〈つうじょう：通常〉 usually, generally, commonly.
    tsûjô-kokkai〈通常国会〉 an ordinary session of the Diet
tsûjô-no〈通常の〉 ordinary, common, usual.

tsuka〈つか〉 the hilt.

tsuka〈つか：塚〉 a mound.
    ichiri-zuka〈一里塚〉 a milestone

tsûka〈つうか：通貨〉 currency, current money.
    tsûka-bôchô〈通貨膨張〉 inflation
    tsûka-no-kiri-sage〈通貨の切り下げ〉 devaluation

tsûka〈つうか：通過〉 passage, passing, transit, carriage.
    tsûka-eki〈通過駅〉 a nonstop station
tsûka-suru〈通過する〉 pass, go through, be carried.
    tonneru o tsûka-suru〈トンネルを通過する〉 go through a tunnel
    gian o tsûka-saseru〈議案を通過させる〉 carry a bill

tsukaeru〈つかえる：仕える〉 serve, wait ((on)).
    kami ni tsukaeru〈神に仕える〉 serve God

tsukaeru〈つかえる〉 be choked, be blocked, be obstructed.
    mune-ni-tsukaeru〈胸につかえる〉 lie heavy on the stomach
    Kuruma-ga-tsukaete-iru.〈車がつかえている。〉 Traffic is held up.
    Shigoto-ga-tsukaete-iru.〈仕事がつかえている。〉 I'm very busy.

tsukaeru〈つかえる：使える〉 be usable, be useful, be serviceable, be fit for use.
    tsukaeru otoko〈使える男〉 a useful man
    tsukae-nai otoko〈使えない男〉 a man who is good for nothing

tsukai〈つかい：使い〉 an errand, a messenger, the bearer.
    tsukai-ni iku〈使いに行く〉 go on an errand
    tsukai-ni yaru〈使いにやる〉 send ((a person)) on an errand

tsûkai〈つうかい：痛快〉
tsûkai-na〈痛快な〉 awfully delightful, thrilling; incisive.

tsukai-furusu〈つかいふるす：使い古す〉 wear out by use.

tsukai-furushita〈使い古した〉worn-out, well-worn.

tsukai-hatasu〈つかいはたす：使い果たす〉spend all, use up, go through, exhaust, drain.

  kane o tsukai-hatasu（金を使い果たす）use up all the money

  zaisan o tsukai-hatasu（財産を使い果たす）go through one's fortune

tsukai-kake〈つかいかけ：使いかけ〉

tsukai-kake-no〈使いかけの〉partially used.

tsukai-kata〈つかいかた：使い方〉how to use.

tsukai-komi〈つかいこみ：使い込み〉defalcation, embezzlement.

tsukai-komu〈使い込む〉defalcate, embezzle, appropriate ((money)) for one's own use; break in, use ((a thing)) for a long time.

tsukai-konasu〈つかいこなす：使いこなす〉manage, handle, master.

tsukai-michi〈つかいみち：使い道〉(a) use.

  tsukai-michi-ga-aru（使い道がある）be of use

  tsukai-michi-ga-hiroi（使い道が広い）be of wide use

  tsukai-michi-ga-nai（使い道がない）be of no use

tsukai-mono〈つかいもの：使い物〉

tsukai-mono-ni-nara-nai〈使い物にならない〉see. tsukai-michi-ga-nai.

tsukai-mono〈つかいもの：使い物〉a present, a gift.

tsukai-narasu〈つかいならす：使い慣らす〉accustom oneself to using, break in.

tsukai-nareru〈使い慣れる〉be accustomed to using.

tsukai-nokosu〈つかいのこす：使い残す〉leave ((something)) unused, leave ((money)) unspent.

tsukai-sugiru〈つかいすぎる：使い過ぎる〉use too much, use in excess, spend too much, overwork.

tsukai-sute〈つかいすて：使い捨て〉

tsukai-sute-no〈使い捨ての〉throwaway, disposable.

  tsukai-sute-no jidai（使い捨ての時代）the 'throwaway age'

tsukai-te〈つかいて：使い手〉a user; an employer.

tsukai-wake〈つかいわけ：使い分け〉proper use.

tsukai-wakeru〈使い分ける〉use properly.

tsukamae-dokoro〈つかまえどころ〉see. tsukami-dokoro.

tsukamaeru〈つかまえる〉catch, seize, take hold ((of)), grasp, grab.

  ude o tsukamaeru（腕をつかまえる）seize ((a person)) by the arm

tsukamaru〈つかまる〉hold (on) ((to)).

  Tsuri-kawa-ni-tsukamatte-i-nasai.（つり革につかまっていなさい.）
    Hold on to a strap.

tsukamaeru 〈つかまえる：捕まえる〉 catch, arrest.

tsukamaru 〈捕まる〉 be caught, be arrested.

    Dorobô ga tsukamatta. （泥棒が捕まった。） A thief was caught.

tsukamaseru 〈つかませる〉 bribe, grease ((a person's)) palm, slip; pass off.

tsukami 〈つかみ〉 a handful; a grip, a hold.

    kome-hito-tsukami （米一つかみ） a handful of rice

tsukami-ai 〈つかみあい：つかみ合い〉 grappling, a scuffle, a tussle.

tsukami-ai-o-suru 〈つかみ合いをする〉 grapple with each other.

tsukami-ai-ni-naru 〈つかみ合いになる〉 come to grips ((with)).

    kôron-no-sue tsukami-ai-ni-naru （口論の末つかみ合いになる） proceed from words to grips

tsukami-dasu 〈つかみだす：つかみ出す〉 take ((something)) out by handfuls; throw ((a person)) out of doors.

tsukami-dokoro 〈つかみどころ〉 a hold, a grip, a point.

tsukami-dokoro-no-nai 〈つかみどころのない〉 slippery, elusive, intangible, vague.

    tsukami-dokoro-no-nai henji （つかみどころのない返事） an elusive answer

tsukami-dori 〈つかみどり：つかみ取り〉

    nure-te-de-awa-no-tsukami-dori （ぬれ手であわのつかみ取り） make easy money

tsukami-kakaru 〈つかみかかる〉 be down ((on)).

tsukamu 〈つかむ〉 seize, catch, grasp, grip.

    shikkari tsukamu （しっかりつかむ） grasp tightly

    yôten o tsukamu （要点をつかむ） grasp the point

    shinsô-o-tsukamu （真相をつかむ） get at the truth

tsûkan 〈つうかん：通関〉

    tsûkan-te-tsuzuki （通関手続） customs formalities

tsûkan-suru 〈通関する〉 clear the customs.

tsûkan 〈つうかん：痛感〉

tsûkan-suru 〈痛感する〉 feel keenly, fully realize.

tsuka-no-ma 〈つかのま：つかの間〉

tsuka-no-ma-no 〈つかの間の〉 brief, momentary, transient.

    tsuka-no-ma-no yorokobi （つかの間の喜び） a transient joy

tsuka-no-ma-mo 〈つかの間も〉 even for a moment.

tsuka-no-ma-ni 〈つかの間に〉 in a moment.

tsukare 〈つかれ：疲れ〉 fatigue.

tsukare-ga-toreru〈疲れがとれる〉recover from one's fatigue

tsukareru〈疲れる〉be tired, get tired.

hetoheto-ni tsukareru, tsukare-hateru *or* tsukare-kiru〈へとへとに疲れる，疲れ果てる，疲れ切る〉be tired out, be dead tired, be exhausted

tsukareru〈つかれる〉be possessed ((by *or* with)), be obsessed ((by *or* with)).

tsukareta-yô-ni〈つかれたように〉as if possessed.

tsukaru〈つかる〉soak ((in)), be soaked ((in)), be flooded ((with)).

Watashi-no ie wa yuka-shita-made mizu-ni-tsukatta.（私の家は床下まで水につかった。）My house was flooded below the floor.

tsukaru〈つかる：漬かる〉be well-seasoned.

tsukatsuka-to〈つかつかと〉straight, directly, without hesitation.

tsukatsuka-to ayumi-yoru（つかつかと歩み寄る）walk directly ((up to))

tsukau〈つかう：使う〉use, make use ((of)), spend; employ, handle; do, practice.

atama o tsukau（頭を使う）use one's brains

dokusho-ni ooku-no jikan o tsukau（読書に多くの時間を使う）spend much time in reading

ooku-no hito o tsukau（多くの人を使う）employ many persons

hito o tsukau-no-ga-umai（人を使うのがうまい）be clever in handling people

ningyô o tsukau（人形を使う）manipulate a puppet

tsuke〈つけ：付け〉a bill, a check; credit.

tsuke o harau（付けを払う）pay a bill

tsuke-de kau（付けで買う）buy on credit

tsuke-agaru〈つけあがる：付け上がる〉be puffed up, grow impudent, take advantage ((of)).

yasashiku-shite-yareba-tsuke-agaru（優しくしてやれば付け上がる）take advantage of ((a person's)) kindness

tsuke-awase〈つけあわせ：付け合わせ〉vegetables added to a meat or a fish, a garnish.

tsuke-awaseru〈付け合わせる〉add ((some vegetables)) as a relish ((to)).

tsuke-bito〈つけびと：付け人〉an attendant, an assistant.

tsuke-hige〈つけひげ：付けひげ〉a false mustache.

tsuke-kaeru〈つけかえる：付け替える〉change, renew, replace.

denkyû o tsuke-kaeru（電球を付け替える）change an electric bulb

tsuke-komu〈つけこむ：付け込む〉take advantage ((of)), presume ((on)), practice ((on)).

    hito-no yowami-ni-tsuke-komu（人の弱みに付け込む）practice on a person's weakness

tsuke-kuwaeru〈つけくわえる：付け加える〉add ((to)).

tsuke-matsuge〈つけまつげ：付けまつげ〉false eyelashes.

tsuke-mawasu〈つけまわす：付け回す〉follow, dangle ((about)).

tsuke-me〈つけめ：付け目〉an object, an aim.

    Soko-ga kare-ra-no-tsuke-me-da.（そこが彼らの付け目だ.）That's what they are trying to take advantage of.

tsukemono〈つけもの：漬け物〉pickles, pickled vegetables.

tsuke-ne〈つけね：付け根〉a joint, the base, the root.

    kubi no tsuke-ne（首の付け根）the base of the neck

tsuke-ne〈つけね：付け値〉a price offered, an offer, a bid.

tsuke-nerau〈つけねらう：付けねらう〉follow after, shadow, dog.

    hito-no inochi o tsuke-nerau（人の命を付けねらう）seek a person's life

tsuke-otoshi〈つけおとし：付け落とし〉an omission〔in a bill〕.

  tsuke-otoshi-o-yaru or *tsuke-otosu*〈付け落としをやる，付け落とす〉fail to enter.

tsukeru〈つける：付ける〉put; enter, put down, keep; fix, attach; apply; light, kindle; turn on; provide; add.

    ne o yasuku tsukeru（値を安く付ける）put the price cheap

    chôbo-ni tsukeru（帳簿に付ける）enter in a book

    nikki o tsukeru（日記を付ける）keep a diary

    doa-ni beru o tsukeru（ドアにベルを付ける）fix a bell to the door

    kiri-kizu-ni nankô o tsukeru（切り傷に軟こうを付ける）apply some ointment to the cut

    pan-ni batâ o tsukeru（パンにバターを付ける）spread butter on bread

    tabako ni hi-o-tsukeru（たばこに火を付ける）light a cigarette

    terebi o tsukeru（テレビを付ける）turn on television

    denki o tsukeru（電気を付ける）switch on the electric light

    hikoku-nin ni bengo-shi-o-tsukeru（被告人に弁護士を付ける）provide the defendant with a lawyer

    kanji-ni kana o tsukeru（漢字に仮名を付ける）add the *kana* to a Chinese character

tsukeru〈つける：着ける〉put on; bring, drive up.

iya-ringu o tsukeru（イヤリングを着ける） put on earrings

fune o sambashi-ni-tsukeru（船を桟橋に着ける） bring a ship alongside the quay

tsukeru 〈つける：漬ける〉soak ((in)); pickle〔vegetables〕.

-tsukeru 〈-つける〉get used to... , be in a habit of... .

tabe-tsukete-iru（食べつけている） be used to eat

tsuketari 〈つけたり：付け足り〉an accessory, an addition.

tsuketari-no 〈付け足りの〉accessory, additional.

tsuke-tashi 〈つけたし：付け足し〉an addition, a supplement.

tsuke-tasu 〈付け足す〉add ((to)), supplement.

tsuke-todoke 〈つけとどけ：付け届け〉an occasional present; a bribe.

bon-kure-no-tsuke-todoke o suru（盆暮れの付け届けをする） make ((a person)) summer and year-end presents

tsukeyaki 〈つけやき：付け焼き〉

tsukeyaki-ni-suru 〈付け焼きにする〉broil with soy.

tsukeyaki-no 〈付け焼きの〉broiled with soy.

tsuke-yakiba 〈つけやきば：付け焼き刃〉

tsuke-yakiba-no 〈付け焼き刃の〉makeshift, borrowed, superficial.

tsuki 〈つき：月〉the moon; a month.

tsuki-no-hikari（月の光） moonlight

tsuki-no-de（月の出） the rise of the moon, moonrise

tsuki-no-iri（月の入り） moonset, moondown

tsuki-ni ichi-do（月に一度） once a month

tsuki 〈つき：突き〉a thrust, a stab, a punto, a stroke.

hito-tsuki-ni 〈一突きに〉with a thrust, at a stroke.

tsuki 〈つき：付き〉luck.

Tsuki ga kawatta.（つきが変わった.） Our luck changed.

-tsuki 〈-つき：-付き〉attached ((to)).

kagu-tsuki-no kashi-ya（家具付きの貸家） a furnished house to let

(-ni)-tsuki 〈(〜に)つき〉per, for; on account of, owing to, because of.

ichi-doru-ni-tsuki go-ko（一ドルにつき五個） five for a dollar

jukko-ni-tsuki sambyaku-en（十個につき三百円） 300 yen for 10

byôki-ni-tsuki（病気につき） on account of illness

tsuki-age 〈つきあげ：突き上げ〉pressure from below, goading.

tsuki-ageru 〈突き上げる〉put pressure ((upon)), goad.

〜-no-tsuki-age-de 〈〜の突き上げで〉under pressure from... , goaded by ... .

tsuki-ai 〈つきあい：付き合い〉association, intercourse, acquaintance, society, company.

　tsuki-ai-ga-hiroi〈付き合いが広い〉have a large circle of acquaintances

　tsuki-ai-ga-semai〈付き合いが狭い〉have few acquaintances

tsuki-ai-no-ii〈付き合いのいい〉sociable.

　tsuki-ai-no-ii-hito〈付き合いのいい人〉a sociable person, a good mixer

　tsuki-ai-no-warui-hito〈付き合いの悪い人〉an unsociable person, a bad mixer

o-tsuki-ai-de or *o-tsuki-ai-ni*〈お付き合いで，お付き合いに〉for company.

tsuki-au〈付き合う〉keep company ((with)), associate ((with)).

　hito-to taitō-ni tsuki-au〈人と対等に付き合う〉associate with a person on equal terms

tsuki-akari〈つきあかり：月明かり〉the moonlight.

　tsuki-akari-de〈月明かりで〉by moonlight

tsuki-atari〈つきあたり：突き当たり〉the end.

　rōka no tsuki-atari-ni〈廊下の突き当たりに〉at the end of the passage

tsuki-ataru〈突き当たる〉come to the end ((of)); run against, run into.

　roji-ni-tsuki-atatte migi-ni-mawaru〈路地に突き当たって右に回る〉turn to the right at the end of the lane

tsuki-awaseru〈つきあわせる：突き合わせる〉place ((a person)) opposite; compare ((with)), collate ((with)), check ((against *or* with)).

　hiza-o-tsuki-awaseru〈ひざを突き合わせる〉sit knee to knee ((with))

　kao-o-tsuki-awaseru〈顔を突き合わせる〉come face to face ((with))

　utsushi o gembun-to-tsuki-awaseru〈写しを原文と突き合わせる〉check the copies up with the original

tsuki-dasu〈つきだす：突き出す〉thrust out, push out.

　mado-kara kao o tsuki-dasu〈窓から顔を突き出す〉stick one's head out of the window

　hannin o keisatsu-ni tsuki-dasu〈犯人を警察に突き出す〉hand over a criminal to the police

tsuki-deru〈つきでる：突き出る〉stand out, jut (out), project.

　umi-ni tsuki-deru〈海に突き出る〉jut out into the sea

tsuki-deta〈突き出た〉projecting, protruding.

tsuki-gime〈つきぎめ：月決め〉

tsuki-gime-no〈月決めの〉monthly.

tsuki-hajime〈つきはじめ：月初め〉

tsuki-hajime-ni 〈月初めに〉 at the beginning of the month, early in the month.

tsuki-hanasu 〈つきはなす：突き放す〉 forsake, desert.

tsuki-hi 〈つきひ：月日〉 time.
　　tsuki-hi ga tatsu-ni-tsurete 〈月日がたつにつれて〉 as time goes on

tsuki-kaesu 〈つきかえす：突き返す〉 reject to accept.

tsuki-kizu 〈つききず：突き傷〉 a stab.

tsukikkiri 〈つきっきり：付きっ切り〉 constant attendance.
　　tsukikkiri-de-kambyô-suru 〈付きっ切りで看病する〉 wait on a patient all the time

tsuki-korosu 〈つきころす：突き殺す〉 stab ((a person)) to death.

tsuki-matou 〈つきまとう：付きまとう〉 persistently follow ((a person)) around, tag along ((after)).

tsuki-mi 〈つきみ：月見〉
tsuki-mi-suru 〈月見する〉 enjoy the moonlight.

tsukimi-sô 〈つきみそう：月見草〉 an evening primrose.

tsuki-mono 〈つきもの：付き物〉 an accompaniment, an indispensable part.
　　~-ni-tsuki-mono-de-aru 〈～に付き物である〉 be always accompanied with ... , be an indispensable accompaniment to... .

tsûkin 〈つうきん：通勤〉 attending office, commutation.
　　tsûkin-densha （通勤電車） a commuter train
　　tsûkin-sha （通勤者） a commuter
　　tsûkin-teate （通勤手当） a commuting allowance
　　tsûkin-teiki(-ken) （通勤定期(券)） a commutation ticket, a season ticket
tsûkin-suru 〈通勤する〉 go to (the) office, commute.

tsuki-nami 〈つきなみ：月並み〉
tsuki-nami-no 〈月並みの〉 conventional, commonplace, hackneyed.

tsuki-nokeru 〈つきのける：突きのける〉 thrust ((a person)) aside.

tsuki-okure 〈つきおくれ：月後(遅)れ〉
　　tsuki-okure-no-zasshi （月遅れの雑誌） a back number of a magazine

tsuki-otosu 〈つきおとす：突き落とす〉 thrust down.
　　kisha-kara hito o tsuki-otosu （汽車から人を突き落とす） push a person off a train

tsukiru 〈つきる：尽きる〉 be exhausted, be used up, run out, come to an end.
　　Shokuryô-ga-tsukita. （食糧が尽きた.） We have run out of pro-

visions.

tsuki-nai 〈尽きない〉 inexhaustible, endless.

tsuki-sasaru 〈つきささる：突き刺さる〉 stick, pierce.

tsuki-sasu 〈突き刺す〉 thrust, pierce, stab.

tsuki-soi 〈つきそい：付き添い〉 attendance.

    tsuki-soi-nin（付き添い人） an attendant, a chaperon

tsuki-sou 〈付き添う〉 accompany, attend ((on)).

    ryôshin-ni-tsuki-sowarete   shuttô-suru（両親に付き添われて出頭する）
        present oneself accompanied by one's parents

tsuki-taosu 〈つきたおす：突き倒す〉 knock down.

tsuki-tarazu 〈つきたらず：月足らず〉 premature birth.

    tsuki-tarazu-no ko（月足らずの子） a premature baby

tsuki-tarazu-de-umareru 〈月足らずで生まれる〉 be born prematurely.

tsuki-tobasu 〈つきとばす：突き飛ばす〉 thrust ((a person)) away, send ((a
person)) flying.

tsuki-tomeru 〈つきとめる：突き止める〉 ascertain, locate, trail, trace,
find out.

    shippai no gen·in o tsuki-tomeru（失敗の原因を突き止める） ascertain
        the cause of the failure

    uwasa-no-de-dokoro-o-tsuki-tomeru（うわさの出所を突き止める）
        trace a rumor to its source

tsuki-tooru 〈つきとおる：突き通る〉 pierce, penetrate.

tsuki-toosu 〈突き通す〉 *see.* tsuki-sasu.

tsuki-tsukeru 〈つきつける：突き付ける〉 thrust ((a thing)) before ((a
person)), place under ((a person's)) nose.

    jihyô o tsuki-tsukeru（辞表を突き付ける） thrust one's resignation
        ((at))

    pisutoru o tsuki-tsukeru（ピストルを突き付ける） point a pistol ((at))

tsuki-tsumeru 〈つきつめる：突き詰める〉

tsukitsumete mono-goto o kangaeru 〈突き詰めて物事を考える〉 take a
matter too seriously.

tsuki-wari 〈つきわり：月割り〉

tsuki-wari-de 〈月割りで〉 on a monthly basis, by monthly installments.

tsuki-yaburu 〈つきやぶる：突き破る〉 crash through.

tsuki-yama 〈つきやま：築山〉 an artificial small hill.

tsuki-yo 〈つきよ：月夜〉 a moonlight night.

tsuki-yubi 〈つきゆび：突き指〉

tsuki-yubi-o-suru 〈突き指をする〉 sprain one's finger.

tsukizuki〈つきづき：月々〉every month.

tsukizuki-no〈月々の〉monthly.

tsukkai(-bô)〈つっかい（ぼう）：突っかい（棒）〉a prop, a support.

tsukkai(-bô)-o-suru〈突っかい（棒）をする〉prop (up), support.

tsukkakaru〈つっかかる：突っ掛かる〉turn ((on)), pick a quarrel ((with)).

tsukkakeru〈つっかける：突っ掛ける〉slip on.

 sandaru o tsukkakeru（サンダルを突っかける）slip on sandals

tsukkendon〈つっけんどん：突っけんどん〉

tsukkendon-na〈つっけんどんな〉sharp, harsh, blunt, gruff.

tsukkendon-ni〈つっけんどんに〉sharply, harshly, bluntly, impolitely.

tsukkiru〈つっきる：突っ切る〉cross, go across.

tsukkomu〈つっこむ：突っ込む〉thrust ((in or into)), plunge ((into)).

 poketto-ni te o tsukkomu（ポケットに手を突っ込む）thrust one's hand into one's pocket

 tsukkonda-shitsumon-o-suru（突っ込んだ質問をする）make a searching inquiry

 tsukkonde-iroiro-tazuneru（突っ込んでいろいろ尋ねる）question ((a person)) closely

tsûkô〈つうこう：通行〉passing, passage, traffic.

 tsûkô o samatageru（通行を妨げる）obstruct the traffic, bar the way

 Tsûkô-dome.（通行止め.）Closed to traffic.

 Kochira tsûkô-kinshi.（こちら通行禁止.）No passage this way.

 Migi-gawa-tsûkô.（右側通行.）Keep to the right.

 tsûkô-nin（通行人）a passerby

tsûkô-suru〈通行する〉pass (through), go through(or along).

tsûkoku〈つうこく：通告〉notice, notification, announcement.

 ippô-teki tsûkoku（一方的通告）one-sided notice

tsûkoku-suru〈通告する〉give notice ((of)), notify.

tsûkon〈つうこん：痛恨〉deep regret.

 tsûkon-ji（痛恨事）a matter for great regret

〜-wa-tsûkon-no-itari-de-aru.〈〜は痛恨の至りである。〉It is to be greatly regretted that... .

tsuku〈つく：突く〉thrust, stab, gore, prick; push, poke, butt; strike; attack, assail; be pungent; brave.

 nodo-o-tsukareru（のどを突かれる）be stabbed in the throat

 hari-de yubi-saki o tsuku（針で指先を突く）prick one's finger with a needle mari o tsuku（まりをつく）　bounce a ball

　　kane o tsuku（鐘をつく）　strike a bell

　　teki-no-haigo-o-tsuku（敵の背後を突く）　attack the enemy in the rear

　　itai tokoro-o tsuku（痛いところを突く）　touch ((a person)) on a sore
　　　place

　　hana o tsuku（鼻を突く）　assail one's nostrils

　　fûu-o-tsuite（風雨を突いて）　in spite of the wind and rain

　　soko o tsuku（底を突く）　touch bottom

tsuku〈つく：付く〉stick ((to)), be stained ((with)); grow, bear; study
　((under)); attend ((on)), wait ((on)); belong ((to)), be attached ((to));
　take; catch, be lighted; side ((with)); be in luck.

　　shikkari tsuku（しっかり付く）　stick fast ((to))

　　inku-ga-tsuite-iru（インクが付いている）　be stained with ink

　　rishi-ga-tsuku（利子が付く）　bear interest

　　sensei-ni-tsuku（先生に付く）　learn under a teacher

　　kango-fu-ga-tsuite-iru（看護婦が付いている）　be attended by a nurse

　　garêji-no-tsuita ie（ガレージの付いた家）　a house with a garage

　　ne-ga-tsuku（根が付く）　take root

　　niku-ga-tsuku（肉が付く）　take on flesh

　　hi-ga-tsuku（火が付く）　catch fire

　　Kare-wa　itsu-mo　haha-oya-ni-tsuku.（彼はいつも母親に付く.）　He
　　　always takes a side with his mother.

　　Saikin　tsuite-i-nai.（最近ついていない.）　I have been out of luck
　　　recently.

tsuku〈つく：着(就)く〉reach, arrive ((at *or* in)), get ((to)); start, set out;
　take; engage ((in)).

　　Tôkyô-ni-tsuku（東京に着く）　arrive in Tokyo

　　kiro-ni-tsuku（帰路につく）　start for home

　　seki-ni-tsuku（席に着く）　take a seat

　　shokutaku-ni-tsuku（食卓に着く）　sit at table

　　toko-ni-tsuku（床に就く）　go to bed

　　shoku-ni-tsuku（職に就く）　engage in an occupation

tsuku〈つく〉cost.

　　takaku-tsuku（高くつく）　prove to be expensive

tsuku〈つく〉pound, hull.

tsukuda-ni〈つくだに：つくだ煮〉food boiled in soy.

tsukue〈つくえ：机〉a desk.

　　tsukue-ni-mukatte-iru（机に向かっている）　be sitting at one's desk

tsukuri 〈つくり：作(造)り〉make, structure, construction, workmanship; growing.

　　Kare-no ie wa tsukuri-ga-shikkari-shite-iru.（彼の家は造りがしっかりしている.）His house is of solid structure.

　　kiku-zukuri（菊作り）the growing of chrysanthemums

tsukuri-ageru 〈つくりあげる：作(造)り上げる〉make up, build up, complete, finish.

tsukuri-banashi 〈つくりばなし：作り話〉a made-up story, a fiction.

　tsukuri-banashi-o-suru〈作り話をする〉make up a story.

tsukuri-dasu 〈つくりだす：作り出す〉manufacture, turn out, produce, create, devise.

tsukuri-goe 〈つくりごえ：作り声〉a feigned voice.

　tsukuri-goe-de〈作り声で〉disguising one's voise, in a feigned voice.

tsukuri-goto 〈つくりごと：作り事〉a fabrication, a fiction.

tsukuri-kaeru 〈つくりかえる：作(造)り替える〉make over, remodel, rebuild, reconstruct, convert, transform, adapt.

　　shokudô o tsukuri-kaeru（食堂を造り替える）remodel a dining-room

　　shôsetsu o geki-ni-tsukuri-kaeru（小説を劇に作り替える）dramatize a novel

tsukuri-kata 〈つくりかた：作り方〉the way of making, how to make.

tsukuri-naosu 〈つくりなおす：作り直す〉remake, make ((a thing)) over.

tsukuri-tsuke 〈つくりつけ：造り付け〉

　tsukuri-tsuke-no〈造り付けの〉built-in, fixed.

tsukuri-warai 〈つくりわらい：作り笑い〉a feigned laugh.

　tsukuri-warai-o-suru〈作り笑いをする〉force a laugh, affect a smile.

tsukuri-zakaya 〈つくりざかや：造り酒屋〉a *sake* brewer, a *sake* brewery.

tsukuroi 〈つくろい：繕い〉patching up, darning.

tsukurou 〈つくろう：繕う〉patch up, darn; adjust, keep up, save.

　　kutsu-shita o tsukurou（靴下を繕う）darn socks

　　minari o tsukurou（身なりを繕う）tidy oneself

　　teisai o tsukurou（体裁を繕う）keep up appearances

tsukuru 〈つくる：作(造)る〉make; brew, distil; write, compose; build, construct; coin, mint; form; raise, grow; organize, found; fix; foster, cultivate; make up.

　　ki-de tsukue o tsukuru（木で机を作る）make a desk of wood

　　sake o tsukuru（酒を造る）brew *sake*

　　hon o tsukuru（本を作る）write a book

    su o tsukuru〈巣を造る〉build a nest

    hashi o tsukuru〈橋を造る〉construct a bridge

    kahei o tsukuru〈貨幣を造る〉mint coins

    retsu o tsukuru〈列を作る〉form a line

    ko-mugi o tsukuru〈小麦を作る〉grow wheat

    kurabu o tsukuru〈クラブを作る〉organize a club

    bentô o tsukuru〈弁当を作る〉fix a lunch

    ii kôkei-sha o tsukuru〈いい後継者を作る〉train a good successor

    kao o tsukuru〈顔を作る〉make up one's face

    tsukutta-hanashi〈作った話〉an invented story

tsukushi〈つくし〉a horsetail.

tsukusu〈つくす：尽くす〉make efforts, do; exhaust, use up.

    saizen o tsukusu〈最善を尽くす〉do one's best

    shakai-no-tame-ni tsukusu〈社会のために尽くす〉do much for the society

    ronji-tsukusu〈論じ尽くす〉discuss ((a subject)) fully

    tabe-tsukusu〈食べ尽くす〉eat up

tsukuzuku〈つくづく〉entirely, utterly, quite, keenly, severely.

    Yo-no-naka-ga-tsukuzuku-iya-ni-natta.（世の中がつくづく嫌になった.）I've got quite sick and tired of life.

tsuma〈つま：妻〉a wife.

tsuma〈つま〉garnishings, a relish.

tsumabiku〈つまびく：つま弾く〉play ((the guitar)) with one's fingers.

tsumabiraka〈つまびらか〉

  tsumabiraka-ni-suru〈つまびらかにする〉ascertain, make ((a matter)) clear.

  tsumabiraka-de-nai〈つまびらかでない〉be little known.

tsuma-hajiki〈つまはじき〉

  tsuma-hajiki-suru〈つまはじきする〉disdain, shun.

tsumami〈つまみ〉a knob, a handle; a pinch; a relish.

    hito-tsumami-no-shio〈一つまみの塩〉a pinch of salt

tsumami-dasu〈つまみだす：つまみ出す〉pick out, throw out, drag out.

tsumami-gui〈つまみぐい：つまみ食い〉

  tsumami-gui-suru〈つまみ食いする〉eat by stealth when nobody is about; embezzle.

tsumamu〈つまむ〉pick, pinch, hold ((a thing)) between one's fingers.

    hana o tsumamu〈鼻をつまむ〉hold one's nose

    Dôzo o-kashi o o-tsumami-kudasai.（どうぞお菓子をおつまみくださ

い.）Please help yourself to the cake.

tsumaranai 〈つまらない〉trifling, trivial, insignificant, of little importance, worthless, useless, stupid, uninteresting, dull.

    tsumaranai koto（つまらない事）a trifle, a matter of no importance

    tsumaranai hon（つまらない本）a stupid book

    Nanda, tsumaranai!（何だ，つまらない．）Nonsense!

tsumaranaku 〈つまらなく〉cheerlessly, in vain.

    jinsei o tsumaranaku-kanjiru（人生をつまらなく感じる）find life a bore

tsumaranasa-sô-ni 〈つまらなさそうに〉with a cheerless look, with a bored look.

tsumari 〈つまり〉after all, in a word, briefly, that is (to say).

tsumaru 〈つまる：詰まる〉be stopped, be choked; be full, be stuffed, be jammed; be pressed ((for)), be hard up, be at a loss.

    Entotsu ga susu-de tsumatte-iru.（煙突がすすで詰まっている．）The chimney is choked up with soot.

    Hana ga zutto tsumatteiru.（鼻がずっと詰まっている．）My nose has been stuffed up.

    Oo-doori wa kuruma-de tsumatte-iru.（大通りは車で詰まっている．）The main street is jammed with traffic.

    kane-ni-tsumatte-iru（金に詰まっている）be pressed for money

    hentô-ni-tsumaru（返答に詰まる）be at a loss for an answer

tsuma-saki 〈つまさき：つま先〉the tip of a toe, tiptoe(s)

    tsuma-saki-de aruku（つま先で歩く）walk on tiptoe(s)

tsumasareru 〈つまされる〉

mi-ni-tsumasareru 〈身につまされる〉be deeply touched ((by)).

tsuma-yôji 〈つまようじ〉a toothpick.

tsumazuki 〈つまずき〉stumbling; a failure.

tsumazuku 〈つまずく〉stumble ((against *or* over)).

    ishi-ni-tsumazuite-korobu（石につまずいて転ぶ）stumble over a stone

tsume 〈つめ：詰め〉checkmating.

tsume 〈つめ〉a nail, a claw, a hoof.

    tsume o kiru（つめを切る）cut one's nails

    tsume-o-nobasu（つめを伸ばす）have one's nails long

    tsume o kamu（つめをかむ）bite one's nail

    tsume no aka（つめのあか）the dirt in the nail

        tsume-no-aka-hodo-mo-nai（つめのあかほどもない）do not have an

atom ((of))

tsume-kiri〈つめ切り〉a nail clipper

tsume-awase〈つめあわせ：詰め合わせ〉an assortment.

tsume-awaseru〈詰め合わせる〉assort, pack together.

tsume-awase-no〈詰め合わせの〉assorted.

tsume-bara〈つめばら：詰め腹〉

tsume-bara-o-kiraseru〈詰め腹を切らせる〉force ((a person)) to resign his post.

tsume-eri〈つめえり：詰め襟〉a stand-up collar.

tsume-eri-no seifuku（詰め襟の制服）a uniform with a stand-up collar

tsume-kaeru〈つめかえる：詰め替える〉repack, refill.

tsume-kakeru〈つめかける：詰め掛ける〉crowd ((into)), throng ((to)), besiege.

tsume-komi〈つめこみ：詰め込み〉cramming.

tsume-komi-shugi（詰め込み主義）the cramming system

tsume-komu〈つめこむ：詰め込む〉stuff, load, cram, pack, crowd.

ana ni kami-o tsume-komu（穴に紙を詰め込む）stuff a hole with paper

atama-ni tsume-komu（頭に詰め込む）cram knowledge into one's head

kaban-ni hon o tsume-komu（かばんに本を詰め込む）pack books in a bag

jōkyaku o basu-ni tsume-komu（乗客をバスに詰め込む）crowd people into a bus

tsume-mono〈つめもの：詰め物〉stuffing, filling, plugging, packing, padding.

tsume-mono-o-suru〈詰め物をする〉stuff, fill, plug, pad.

tsumeru〈つめる：詰める〉cram, stuff, fill, pack; sit up, sit close; take in, shorten; keep up; hold; be stationed ((at)); checkmate.

kaban-ni irui o tsumeru（かばんに衣類を詰める）pack one's clothes in a bag

bin ni mizu-o-tsumeru（瓶に水を詰める）fill a bottle with water

Mō-sukoshi o-tsume-kudasai.（もう少しお詰めください。）Sit up a little closer, please.

sukāto-no-take o tsumeru（スカートの丈を詰める）take in a skirt

tsumete-shigoto-o-suru（詰めて仕事をする）work hard continuously

iki o tsumeru（息を詰める）hold a breath

tsume-sho 〈つめしょ：詰め所〉a station, a guardroom.

tsume-shōgi 〈つめしょうぎ：詰め将棋〉a chess problem.

tsumetai 〈つめたい：冷たい〉cold, chilly.

    tsumetai taido o toru〈冷たい態度を取る〉assume an indifferent attitude ((toward))

 kokoro-no-tsumetai〈心の冷たい〉coldhearted.

 tsumetaku-naru〈冷たくなる〉become cold; die.

tsume-yoru 〈つめよる：詰め寄る〉draw near, draw close ((to)).

tsumi 〈つみ：罪〉a crime, a sin, guilt, (a) punishment.

    tsumi o okasu〈罪を犯す〉commit a crime

    tsumi o kakusu〈罪を隠す〉conceal one's guilt

    tsumi o mitomeru〈罪を認める〉admit one's guilt

    tsumi-o-manukareru〈罪を免れる〉escape punishment, get off scot-free

 tsumi-ni-otoshiireru〈罪に陥れる〉incriminate, frame ((a person)).

 tsumi-no-aru〈罪のある〉guilty, sinful.

    tsumi-no-nai〈罪のない〉not guilty, innocent

tsumi-ageru 〈つみあげる：積み上げる〉pile up, pile one on another.

tsumi-bukai 〈つみぶかい：罪深い〉sinful, guilty.

tsumi-dashi 〈つみだし：積み出し〉shipment.

    tsumi-dashi-kô〈積み出し港〉a port of shipment

 tsumi-dasu〈積み出す〉ship off, send off.

tsumi-horoboshi 〈つみほろぼし：罪滅ぼし〉atonement of sins.

 tsumi-horoboshi-o-suru〈罪滅ぼしをする〉atone ((for)).

 tsumi-horoboshi-ni〈罪滅ぼしに〉for one's atonement.

tsumi-kae 〈つみかえ：積み替え〉transshipment.

 tsumi-kaeru〈積み替える〉transship.

tsumi-kasanaru 〈つみかさなる：積み重なる〉be piled up, accumulate.

tsumi-kasane 〈つみかさね：積み重ね〉a heap, a pile, a stack, accumulation.

    doryoku-no-tsumi-kasane〈努力の積み重ね〉one's continuous efforts

 tsumi-kasaneru〈積み重ねる〉heap up, pile up, stack, accumulate.

tsumi-ki 〈つみき：積み木〉building blocks, bricks.

tsumi-komi 〈つみこみ：積み込み〉loading, shipping.

 tsumi-komu〈積み込む〉load, ship, take on〔a cargo〕.

tsumi-naosu 〈つみなおす：積み直す〉load over again, pile over again.

tsumi-ni 〈つみに：積み荷〉a load, a freight, a cargo.

 tsumi-ni-o-orosu〈積み荷を降ろす〉unload, discharge cargo.

tsumi-nokoshi 〈つみのこし：積み残し〉a shut-out cargo.

  tsumi-nokosu 〈積み残す〉shut out from shipment.

tsumi-oroshi 〈つみおろし：積み卸し〉

  tsumi-oroshi-suru 〈積み卸しする〉load and unload.

tsumi-tate 〈つみたて：積み立て〉laying by, reserving.

    tsumi-tate-kin（積立金）a reserve fund

  tsumi-tateru 〈積み立てる〉lay aside, save, reserve.

tsumi-tori 〈つみとり：積み取り〉loading.

  tsumi-toru 〈積み取る〉load, take on.

tsumi-toru 〈つみとる：摘み取る〉nip off, pick off.

tsumi-tsukuri 〈つみつくり：罪作り〉

  tsumi-tsukuri-na 〈罪作りな〉sinful, cruel, heartless.

tsumori 〈つもり：積もり〉an intention, an idea, a thought, a purpose.

    watashi-no tsumori-dewa（私の積もりでは）in my thought

  ~*(-suru)-tsumori-de-aru* 〈～(する)つもりである〉intend ((to do)), will ((do)), think of ((doing)), be going ((to do)).

  ~*-no-tsumori-de* 〈～のつもりで〉with the intention of... , for the purpose of... .

tsumoru 〈つもる：積もる〉accumulate, be piled up, lie ((on)).

    Yuki ga jussenchi tsumotte-iru.（雪が十センチ積もっている.）Snow lies ten centimeters deep.

    tsumoru-hanashi-ga-aru（積もる話がある）have much to talk about

    tsumoru urami（積もる恨み）a deep-rooted hatred ((toward))

tsumu 〈つむ：詰む〉become close; be checkmated.

  me-no-tsunda 〈目の詰んだ〉close, fine.

    gisshiri-ji-no-tsunda（ぎっしり字の詰んだ）closely printed

tsumu 〈つむ：積む〉pile, load; amass, accumulate.

    kenchiku-shizai-o-tsunda torakku（建築資材を積んだトラック）a truck laden with building materials

    kyoman-no-tomi o tsumu（巨万の富を積む）amass a big fortune

    keiken o tsumu（経験を積む）accumulate experience

tsumu 〈つむ：摘む〉pick, pluck, gather.

    cha o tsumu（茶を摘む）pick tea leaves

    hana o tsumu（花を摘む）gather flowers

tsumugi 〈つむぎ〉pongee.

tsumugu 〈つむぐ：紡ぐ〉spin.

    men-kara ito o tsumugu（綿から糸を紡ぐ）spin yarn out of cotton

tsumuji 〈つむじ〉the whirl of hair on the head.

tsumuji-magari（つむじ曲がり） a perverse fellow, a crank

tsumuji-magari-no（つむじ曲がりの） perverse, crossgrained, eccentric

tsumuji-o-mageru〈つむじを曲げる〉become perverse, get cross.

tsumuji-kaze〈つむじかぜ：つむじ風〉a whirlwind.

tsuna〈つな：綱〉a rope, a cord.

tsuna o haru（綱を張る） stretch a rope

inochi no tsuna（命の綱） the staff of life

tanomi-no-tsuna（頼みの綱） the last hope

tsunagari〈つながり〉connection, relation.

tsunagari-ga-aru or *tsunagaru*〈つながりがある，つながる〉be related ((to *or* with)), be connected ((with)), be jointed together.

chi-ga-tsunagatte-iru（血がつながっている） be related by blood ((with))

tsunagi〈つなぎ〉a connection, a link, an entr'acte.

jikan-tsunagi-ni（時間つなぎに） to fill up the time

tsunagi-me（つなぎ目） a joint, a join

tsunagi-awaseru〈つなぎあわせる：つなぎ合わせる〉connect, join together, tie together.

tsunagu〈つなぐ〉tie, fasten; moor; connect, link, join.

uma o ki-ni tsunagu（馬を木につなぐ） tie a horse to a tree

fune o tsunagu（船をつなぐ） moor a ship

Rondon-ni-tsunaide-kudasai.（ロンドンにつないでください．） Please connect me with London.

te o tsunagu（手をつなぐ） join hands

tsuna-hiki〈つなひき：綱引き〉a tug of war.

tsuna-hiki o suru（綱引きをする） have a tug of war

tsunami〈つなみ：津波〉a tidal wave, a *tsunami*.

tsuna-watari〈つなわたり：綱渡り〉tightrope dancing; a tightrope walker.

tsuna-watari o suru〈綱渡りをする〉walk on a tightrope.

abunai-tsuna-watari-o-suru（危ない綱渡りをする） take a great risk

tsune〈つね：常〉

〜(-suru)-no-ga-tsune-de-aru〈〜(する)のが常である〉make it a rule ((to do)).

〜(-suru)-no-ga-tsune-de-atta〈〜(する)のが常であった〉used ((to do)).

tsune-ni〈常に〉always, ordinarily, usually, habitually.

tsune-ni〜*-to-wa-kagira-nai*〈常に〜とは限らない〉not...always.

tsûnen 〈つうねん：通念〉a common idea, a generally accepted idea.

tsûnen 〈つうねん：通年〉the whole year.

tsuneru 〈つねる〉pinch, give a pinch.

     kitsuku-tsuneru （きつくつねる） give ((a person)) a sharp pinch ((on))

     Waga-mi-o-tsunette-hito-no-itasa-o-shire. （我が身をつねって人の痛さを
     知れ.） He who lives in a glasshouse should not throw stones at
     his neighbors.

tsunezune 〈つねづね：常々〉always, usually.

tsuno 〈つの：角〉a horn, an antler.

     tsuno-bue （角笛） a horn, a bugle

     tsuno-no-aru 〈角のある〉horned.

tsuno-kakushi 〈つのかくし：角隠し〉the bride's hood ﹇at a wedding﹈.

tsunoru 〈つのる：募る〉raise, collect, float, invite.

     shikin o tsunoru （資金を募る） raise funds

     shigan-sha o tsunoru （志願者を募る） invite applicants

tsun-to 〈つんと〉primly; pungently.

     tsun-to-sumasu （つんと澄ます） assume a prime attitude, look prim

     tsun-to-hana-o-tsuku （つんと鼻を突く） assail one's nostrils

tsuntsun 〈つんつん〉

     tsuntsun-suru 〈つんつんする〉be prim, be cross.

tsunzaku 〈つんざく〉break, rend, split, burst, pierce.

     hada-o-tsunzaku-yô-na （肌をつんざくような） cutting, piercing

     mimi-o-tsunzaku-yô-na （耳をつんざくような） ear-splitting, ear-
     piercing

tsû-pîsu 〈ツーピース〉a two-piece suit.

tsuppaneru 〈つっぱねる：突っぱねる〉reject, turn down.

tsuppari 〈つっぱり：突っ張り〉a prop, a support.

     tsupparu 〈突っ張る〉prop up; insist ((on)).

tsuppashiru 〈つっぱしる：突っ走る〉dash forward.

tsura 〈つら：面〉a face, a mug, a pan.

tsura-ate 〈つらあて：面当て〉an allusive hint, spiteful words.

     tsura-ate-suru 〈面当てする〉make an allusive remark, speak a spiteful
     thing.

     tsura-ate-gamashii 〈面当てがましい〉spiteful, malicious.

     tsura-ate-ni 〈面当てに〉out of spite, in allusion ((to)).

tsura-damashii 〈つらだましい：面魂〉a countenance, an expression ﹇of
a face﹈.

tsura-gamae 〈つらがまえ：面構え〉a look.

dômô-na tsura-gamae〈どう猛な面構え〉 a ferocious look

tsurai〈つらい〉 hard, painful, bitter.

　　tsurai-omoi-o-suru（つらい思いをする） have a hard time, have a
　　　bitter experience
　　tsurai-tachiba-ni-aru（つらい立場にある） be in a delicate position

tsuraku〈つらく〉 hardly, painfully, bitterly, cruelly, harshly.

　　tsuraku-ataru（つらく当たる） treat ((a person)) harshly, give ((a
　　　person)) a raw deal

tsuranaru〈つらなる：連なる〉 range, stretch in a row.

　　namboku-ni-tsuranaru（南北に連なる） stretch north and south

tsuraneru〈つらねる：連ねる〉 join, link, put ((things)) in a row, range.

　　na o tsuraneru（名を連ねる） enter one's name (in)
　　kuruma-o-tsuranete（車を連ねて） in a long string of (motor)cars

tsura-no-kawa〈つらのかわ：面の皮〉

tsura-no-kawa-o-hagu〈面の皮をはぐ〉 debunk ((a person)).

tsura-no-kawa-no-atsui〈面の皮の厚い〉 brazenfaced, impudent,
shameless.

tsuranuku〈つらぬく：貫く〉 penetrate, pierce, go through, run through;
carry out, attain.

　　Kawa wa machi-o-tsuranuite-nagarete-iru.（川は町を貫いて流れてい
　　　る.） The river runs through the city.
　　mokuteki o tsuranuku（目的を貫く） attain one's object

tsurara〈つらら〉 an icicle.

tsurasa〈つらさ〉 pain, painfulness, bitterness, sorrow.

　　wakare no tsurasa（別れのつらさ） the sorrow of parting

tsura-yogoshi〈つらよごし：面汚し〉 a disgrace ((to)), a shame ((on)), a
discredit ((to)).

　　tsura-yogoshi-ni-naru（面汚しになる） be a disgrace ((to)).

tsura-yogoshi-na〈面汚しな〉 disgraceful, shameful.

tsure〈つれ：連れ〉 a companion, company.

　　tabi-no tsure（旅の連れ） a traveling companion
　　san-nin-zure-de（三人連れで） with three companions

tsure-dasu〈つれだす：連れ出す〉 take ((a person)) out; abduct.

tsûrei〈つうれい：通例〉 usually, commonly, generally, as a rule.

tsûrei-no〈通例の〉 usual, common, ordinary, general, customary.

tsure-ko〈つれこ：連れ子〉 a child by one's previous marriage.

tsure-komi〈つれこみ：連れ込み〉

　　tsure-komi-yado（連れ込み宿） a hotel catering to lovers

tsure-komu〈連れ込む〉take into.

tsurenai〈つれない〉cold, heartless, hard.

　tsurenaku〈つれなく〉coldly, heartlessly, harshly, cruelly.

　　tsurenaku-suru（つれなくする）be hard ((on))

tsure-ni-iku〈つれにいく：連れに行く〉go for ((a person)), call for ((a person)).

tsureru〈つれる：連れる〉take ((with)), be accompanied ((by)).

tsure-saru〈つれさる：連れ去る〉take ((a person)) away.

tsure-sou〈つれそう：連れ添う〉

　　Tsure-sotte-go-nen-ni-naru.（連れ添って五年になる.）We have been married for five years.

(-ni)-tsurete〈～（に）つれて〉as, with.

　　hi-ga-tatsu-ni-tsurete（日がたつにつれて）as days go by

　　toki-ga-tatsu-ni-tsurete（時がたつにつれて）with the passage of time

　　toshi-o-toru-ni-tsurete（年を取るにつれて）as one grows older

tsurete-iku〈つれていく：連れて行く〉take ((a person)) with ((one)).

tsurete-kaeru〈つれてかえる：連れて帰る〉take ((a person)) home.

tsurete-kuru〈つれてくる：連れて来る〉bring ((a person)) with ((one)).

tsûretsu〈つうれつ：痛烈〉

　tsûretsu-na〈痛烈な〉severe, bitter, sharp, cutting, incisive.

　tsûretsu-ni〈痛烈に〉severely, bitterly, cuttingly.

　　tsûretsu-ni hihan-suru（痛烈に批判する）criticize severely

tsuri〈つり：釣り〉fishing.

　　tsuri-ni-iku（釣りに行く）go fishing

　　tsuri-ba（釣り場）a fishing place

　　tsuri-bari（釣り針）a fishing hook

　　tsuri-bori（釣り堀）a fishing pond

　　tsuri-bune（釣り舟）a fishing boat

　　tsuri-dôgu（釣り道具）fishing tackle

　　tsuri-ito（釣り糸）a fishing line

　　tsuri-nakama（釣り仲間）a fishing companion

　　tsuri-zao（釣りざお）a fishing rod

　tsuri-o-suru〈釣りをする〉fish, angle.

tsuri(-sen)〈つり（せん）：釣り（銭）〉change.

　　tsuri o morau（釣りをもらう）get the change

　　Hai, o-tsuri-desu.（はい，お釣りです.）Here's your change.

tsuri-agaru〈つりあがる：釣り上がる〉be hung up, be lifted.

　me-jiri-no-tsuri-agatta〈目じりの釣り上がった〉slant-eyed.

tsuri-ageru 〈つりあげる：釣り上げる〉 land, fish up; turn up; boost (up).

    ookina sakana o tsuri-ageru（大きな魚を釣り上げる） land a big fish

    me o tsuri-ageru（目を釣り上げる） turn up one's eyes

    shika-o-tsuri-ageru（市価を釣り上げる） raise the price by manipulation

tsuri-ai 〈つりあい：釣り合い〉 balance, equilibrium, proportion, harmony.

tsuri-ai-o-toru：〈釣り合いを取る〉 balance (oneself), bring ((things)) into proportion, keep in harmony ((with)), harmonize.

tsuri-ai-no-toreta〈釣り合いの取れた〉 balanced, well-balanced, well-proportioned.

    tsuri-ai-no-tore-nai（釣り合いの取れない） unbalanced, ill-balanced, ill-proportioned

tsuri-au〈釣り合う〉 balance, be in proportion ((to)), be in harmony ((with)), match.

    tsuri-awa-nai（釣り合わない） be unbalanced, be out of proportion

tsuri-bashi 〈つりばし：つり橋〉 a suspension bridge.

tsuri-dana 〈つりだな：つり棚〉 a hanging shelf.

tsuri-gane 〈つりがね：釣り鐘〉 a hanging bell, a temple bell.

    tsuri-gane-dô（釣り鐘堂） a belfry, a bell tower

    tsuri-gane-sô（釣り鐘草） a dotted bellflower

tsuri-kawa 〈つりかわ：つり革〉 a strap.

    tsuri-kawa-ni bura-sagaru（つり革にぶら下がる） hold on to a strap

tsuri-komareru 〈つりこまれる：釣り込まれる〉 be attracted ((by)), be allured ((by)), be enticed ((by)).

    hanashi-ni-tsuri-komareru（話に釣り込まれる） be attracted by a story

tsuri-sagaru 〈つりさがる：つり下がる〉 hang ((from)), be hung (down), be suspended, dangle.

tsuri-sageru〈つり下げる〉 hang, suspend, dangle.

tsuri-te 〈つりて：釣り手〉 an angler.

tsuri-tenjô 〈つりてんじょう：つり天井〉 a suspended ceiling.

tsuri-wa 〈つりわ〉 the rings.

tsûro 〈つうろ：通路〉 a passage, a way, an aisle.

tsuru 〈つる：弦〉 a bowstring, a string; a chord.

tsuru 〈つる〉 a vine, a tendril, a runner.

tsuru 〈つる〉 a crane.

tsuru 〈つる：釣る〉 fish, angle, catch.

    kawa-de sakana-o-tsuru（川で魚を釣る） fish in a stream

Kyô-wa yoku-tsureta.（今日はよく釣れた.） I have had a good catch today.

tsuru〈つる〉hang, suspend, swing.

kaya o tsuru（蚊帳をつる）hang a mosquito net

tsuru〈つる〉have a cramp, be cramped.

hidari-ashi-ga-tsuru（左足がつる）have a cramp in the left leg

tsurube-uchi〈つるべうち：つるべ打ち〉

tsurube-uchi-ni-utsu〈つるべ打ちに打つ〉fire many shots in rapid succession.

tsuru-hashi〈つるはし〉a pickax(e), a pick.

tsuru-kusa〈つるくさ：つる草〉a vine, a creeper, a climber.

tsururi-to〈つるりと〉

tsururi-to-suberu〈つるりと滑る〉slip (down).

tsurushi-age〈つるしあげ：つるし上げ〉

tsurushi-age-ni-suru or *tsurushi-ageru*〈つるし上げにする，つるし上げる〉gang up and persecute ((a person)) with questions.

tsurushi-age-ni-sareru or *tsurushi-agerareru*〈つるし上げにされる，つるし上げられる〉be subjected to a kangaroo court.

tsurushi-gaki〈つるしがき〉a dried persimmon.

tsurusu〈つるす〉*see.* tsuri-sageru, tsuru.

tsurutsuru〈つるつる〉

tsurutsuru-suberu（つるつる滑る）be slippery

tsurutsuru-ni-hagete-iru（つるつるにはげている）be as bald as an egg

tsurutsuru-shita〈つるつるした〉smooth, slippery.

tsûsan〈つうさん：通産〉

tsûsan-shô（通産省）the Ministry of International Trade and Industry

tsûsan-daijin（通産大臣）the Minister of International Trade and Industry

tsûsan〈つうさん：通算〉summing up, the sum total.

tsûsan-suru〈通算する〉sum up, totalize, include.

tsûsan-suru-to〜-ni-naru（通算すると〜になる）total up to... .

tsûsei〈つうせい：通性〉a common quality.

tsûsetsu〈つうせつ：通説〉a common opinion.

tsûsetsu〈つうせつ：痛切〉

tsûsetsu-na〈痛切な〉keen, severe, acute.

tsûsetsu-ni〈痛切に〉keenly, severely, acutely.

tsûsetsu-ni kanjiru（痛切に感じる） keenly feel

tsûshin 〈つうしん：通信〉correspondence, communication, a dispatch, news.

    tsûshin-kyôiku（通信教育） a correspondence course of education

    tsûshin-eisei（通信衛星） a communications satellite

    tsûshin-kikan（通信機関） a means of communication

    tsûshin-hambai（通信販売） mail order, mail-order sale

    tsûshin-bo（通信簿） a report card

  tsûshin-suru〈通信する〉correspond ((with)), communicate ((with)).

tsûshô〈つうしょう：通商〉commerce, trade.

tsûshô〈つうしょう：通称〉a popular name, (an) alias.

    Yamaguchi Saburô tsûshô-San-chan（山口三郎通称三ちゃん）
    Yamaguchi Saburo alias San-chan

tsuta〈つた〉an ivy.

tsutae-kiku〈つたえきく：伝え聞く〉hear from others.

tsutaeru〈つたえる：伝える〉report, tell; teach, initiate; hand down; transmit; introduce.

    jôhô o tsutaeru（情報を伝える） give information

    O-tô-san-ni-yoroshiku-o-tsutae-kudasai.（お父さんによろしくお伝えください。） Please remember me to your father.

    waza no hiketsu o tsutaeru（技の秘けつを伝える） initiate ((a person)) into the mysteries of an art

    kôsei-ni tsutaeru（後世に伝える） hand down to posterity

    netsu o tsutaeru（熱を伝える） transmit heat

    bukkyô o Nihon-ni tsutaeru（仏教を日本に伝える） introduce Buddhism into Japan

  tsutawaru〈伝わる〉be reported, be told, pass; be handed down; be transmitted; be introduced.

    kuchikara kuchi-e-to tsutawaru（口から口へと伝わる） pass from mouth to mouth

tsûtatsu〈つうたつ：通達〉(a) notification, a notice.

  tsûtatsu-suru〈通達する〉notify.

tsutau〈つたう：伝う〉go along.

    hashigo-o-tsutatte oriru（はしごを伝って降りる） go down by means of a ladder

tsute〈つて〉an intermediary, an introducer, a connection, influence, a pull.

    kaisha-ni tsute-ga-aru（会社につてがある） have a connection in a

firm, have someone in a company who will use his influence for ((a person))

tsutomaru 〈つとまる：勤まる〉 be fit for(*or* be equal to)〔a task〕.
　　Watashi-ni-wa-kono-shigoto-wa-tsutomara-nai.（私にはこの仕事は勤まらない.）I am unfit for this task.

tsutome 〈つとめ：務め〉a duty.
　　tsutome o hatasu（務めを果たす）fulfill one's duties
　　tsutome o okotaru（務めを怠る）neglect one's duties
　tsutomeru（務める）serve, act.
　　gichō-o-tsutomeru（議長を務める）serve as chairman

tsutome 〈つとめ：勤め〉duties, service, business.
　　tsutome-buri（勤めぶり）one's assiduity, one's service
　　tsutome-nin（勤め人）a salaried man, an office worker
　tsutomeru〈勤める〉work ((in *or* for)), serve ((in)), be employed ((in)).

tsutome-guchi 〈つとめぐち：勤め口〉a situation, a position.
　　tsutome-guchi-o-sagasu（勤め口を探す）look for a situation

tsutomeru 〈つとめる：努める〉make efforts, endeavor, try hard.
　　kôjô-ni tsutomeru（向上に努める）endeavor for the promotion ((of))
　tsutomete〈努めて〉as much as one can, to the best of one's ability, diligently.
　　tsutomete～(-suru)（努めて～(する)）make efforts ((to do))

tsutome-saki 〈つとめさき：勤め先〉one's place of employment.
　　tsutome-saki o kaeru（勤め先を変える）change one's job

tsû-ton-karâ 〈ツートンカラー〉
　tsû-ton-karâ-no〈ツートンカラーの〉two-toned.

tsutsu 〈つつ：筒〉a pipe, a tube.

-tsutsu 〈-つつ〉*see.* -nagara.

tsutsuga-naku 〈つつがなく〉safely, without accident, in good health.

tsutsuji 〈つつじ〉an azalea.

tsutsuku 〈つつく〉poke (at), pick (at); peck; nudge; incite, instigate.
　　hi-o-tsutsuku（火をつつく）poke at the fire
　　esa-o-tsutsuku（えさをつつく）peck at the food
　　hiji-de-tsutsuku（ひじでつつく）nudge ((a person)) with one's elbow

tsutsumashii 〈つつましい〉modest, humble, frugal, respectful.
　tsutsumashiku〈つつましく〉modestly, humbly, frugally, respectfully.
　　tsutsumashiku kurasu（つつましく暮らす）live frugally

tsutsumi 〈つつみ：堤〉a bank, an embankment.

tsutsumi 〈つつみ：包み〉a bundle, a package, a parcel.

kami-zutsumi〔紙包み〕a paper package

tsutsumi-gami〈つつみがみ：包み紙〉wrapping paper.

tsutsumi-kakushi〈つつみかくし：包み隠し〉concealment.

tsutsumi-kakushi-no-nai〈包み隠しのない〉honest, straightforward.

tsutsumi-kakusu〈包み隠す〉conceal, keep ((a matter)) secret ((from)).

tsutsumi-kakusazu-ni〈包み隠さずに〉without concealment, openly, frankly.

tsutsumi-kakusazu-ni-iu〔包み隠さずに言う〕tell the plain truth

tsutsumu〈つつむ：包む〉wrap; cover, envelop ((in)), veil ((in)).

kami-ni tsutsumu〔紙に包む〕wrap up in paper

honoo-ni tsutsumareru〔炎に包まれる〕be enveloped in flames

shimpi-ni-tsutsumareru〔神秘に包まれる〕be veiled in mystery

tsutsu-nuke〈つつぬけ：筒抜け〉

tsutsu-nuke-de-aru〈筒抜けである〉leak out (entirely).

tsutsu-nuke-ni〈筒抜けに〉directly, just as told.

tsutsu-nuke-ni-kikoeru〔筒抜けに聞こえる〕come directly to one's ears

tsutsu-saki〈つつさき：筒先〉the muzzle, the nozzle, the snout.

tsutsushimi〈つつしみ：慎み〉discretion, prudence, modesty.

tsutsushimi-bukai〈慎み深い〉discreet, prudent, modest.

tsutsushimi-no-nai〈慎みのない〉indiscreet, imprudent, immodest.

tsutsushimu〈慎む〉be discreet, be careful; refrain ((from)).

genkō-o-tsutsushimu〔言行を慎む〕be discreet in word and deed

sake-o-tsutsushimu〔酒を慎む〕refrain from drinking

tsutsushinde〈つつしんで：謹んで〉respectfully, humbly.

Tsutsushinde-o-wabi-môshi-agemasu.〔謹んでおわび申し上げます。〕I humbly ask your pardon.

tsutsu-sode〈つつそで：筒そで〉a tight sleeve, a tight-sleeved *kimono*.

tsuttatsu〈つったつ：突っ立つ〉stand up (straight), stand.

tsûun〈つううん：通運〉transportation.

tsûun-gaisha〔通運会社〕a transport company, an express company

tsûwa〈つうわ：通話〉a (telephone) call.

ittsûwa〔一通話〕one call

shinai-tsûwa〔市内通話〕a local call

tsûwa-ryō〔通話料〕the charge for a telephone call

tsuwari〈つわり〉morning sickness.

tsuya〈つや：通夜〉a vigil, a wake.

tsuya-o-suru〔通夜をする〕keep vigil, hold a wake.

tsuya 〈つや〉 gloss, luster.
  tsuya-o-dasu 〈つやを出す〉 gloss, bring out the luster, polish up.
    tsuya-o-kesu 〈つやを消す〉 take off the gloss, frost, mat
  tsuya-no-aru 〈つやのある〉 glossy, lustrous, polished, shiny.
    tsuya-no-aru kami 〈つやのある髪〉 glossy hair
  tsuya-no-nai 〈つやのない〉 dim, dull, lusterless.
tsuya-buki 〈つやぶき〉
  tsuya-buki-suru 〈つやぶきする〉 rub and polish.
tsuya-dashi 〈つやだし：つや出し〉 glazing, calendering, burnishing, polishing.
tsuya-keshi 〈つやけし：つや消し〉 grinding, frosting, matting.
  tsuya-keshi-no 〈つや消しの〉 ground, frosted, mat.
tsûyaku 〈つうやく：通訳〉 interpretation; an interpreter.
  tsûyaku-suru 〈通訳する〉 interpret.
tsuyatsuya-shita 〈つやつやした〉 bright, sleek, slick.
  tsuyatsuya-shita kao 〈つやつやした顔〉 a bright complexion
tsûyô 〈つうよう：通用〉
  tsûyô-kikan 〈通用期間〉 the term for which a thing is available
  tsûyô-mon 〈通用門〉 a side gate, a service entrance
  tsûyô-suru 〈通用する〉 pass ((for)), be current, be good ((for)).
tsuyo-bi 〈つよび：強火〉
  tsuyo-bi-ni-kakeru 〈強火にかける〉 set over a blazing fire.
tsuyogari 〈つよがり：強がり〉
  tsuyogari-o-iu 〈強がりを言う〉 bluff.
tsuyo-goshi 〈つよごし：強腰〉 a firm attitude.
  tsuyo-goshi-ni-deru 〈強腰に出る〉 assume a firm attitude
tsuyoi 〈つよい：強い〉 strong, powerful, stout, sound, healthy.
  karada-ga-tsuyoi 〈体が強い〉 have a strong constitution, be strongly built
  tsuyoku 〈強く〉 strongly, hard.
    Ame ga tsuyoku futteiru. 〈雨が強く降っている.〉 It's raining hard.
  tsuyoku-naru 〈強くなる〉 become(*or* grow) strong.
  tsuyoku-suru 〈強くする〉 make strong, strengthen.
tsuyo-ki 〈つよき：強気〉 a bull, a bullish feeling.
  tsuyo-ki-no 〈強気の〉 strong, bullish, aggressive.
tsuyomeru 〈つよめる：強める〉 strengthen, intensify, increase, emphasize, tone up.
  goki-o-tsuyomete iu 〈語気を強めて言う〉 say with emphasis

tsuyo-mi 〈つよみ：強み〉one's strong point, one's strength, one's forte, an advantage.

tsuyo-sa 〈つよさ：強さ〉strength, powerfulness.

tsuyu 〈つゆ〉soup, broth.

tsuyu 〈つゆ：露〉dew, a dewdrop.
> Tsuyu ga oriru.（露が降りる.）The dew falls.
> tsuyu-ni nureru（露にぬれる）be wet with dew

tsuyu 〈つゆ：梅雨〉the rainy season.
> Tsuyu-ni-haitta.（梅雨に入った.）The rainy season has set in.
> Tsuyu ga aketa.（梅雨が明けた.）The rainy season is over.

tsûyû-sei 〈つうゆうせい：通有性〉a common trait.

tsûzoku 〈つうぞく：通俗〉popularity.
> tsûzoku-shôsetsu（通俗小説）a popular novel
> *tsûzoku-no* or *tsûzoku-teki(-na)*〈通俗の，通俗的（な）〉popular, common.
> *tsûzoku-teki-ni*〈通俗的に〉popularly, in a popular style.
> tsûzoku-teki-ni kakarete-iru（通俗的に書かれている）be written in a popular style

tsuzukeru 〈つづける：続ける〉continue, keep up, go on ((with)), keep on ((with)).
> hanashi-o-tsuzukeru（話を続ける）go on talking
> kaki-tsuzukeru（書き続ける）keep on writing
> *tsuzukete* or *tsuzuke-zama-ni*〈続けて，続けざまに〉continuously, without a break, in succession, one after another, running.
> go-do-tsuzukete（五度続けて）five times in succession
> san-jikan-tsuzukete（三時間続けて）three hours running

-tsuzuki 〈-つづき：-続き〉a row, continuance, succession, a series ((of)).
> Zen-gô-kara-no-tsuzuki（前号からの続き）Continued from the last number
> fukô-tsuzuki（不幸続き）a series of misfortunes
> samusa-tsuzuki（寒さ続き）a long spell of cold weather

tsuzuku 〈つづく：続く〉continue, keep on, last, run, follow.
> Ji-gô-ni-tsuzuku.（次号に続く.）To be countinued.
> Tatakai wa ichi-nichi-jû-tsuzuita.（戦いは一日中続いた.）The battle went on all day.
> Ame ga furi-tsuzuita.（雨が降り続いた.）We had a spell of rainy days.
> Kono shibai wa rokkagetsu tsuzuku.（この芝居は六か月続く.）The play will run for six months.

Kare-ga watashi-ni tsuzuita. 〈彼が私に続いた.〉 He followed me.

tsuzuite 〈続いて〉 continuously, in succession, one after another.

tsuzumi 〈つづみ：鼓〉a hand drum, a *tsuzumi.*

tsuzure-ori 〈つづれおり：つづれ織り〉hand-woven brocade.

tsuzuri 〈つづり〉spelling.

tsuzuri-o-machigaeru 〈つづりを間違える〉misspell.

tsuzuri-awasu 〈つづりあわす：つづり合わす〉bind together, file.

tsuzuri-kata 〈つづりかた：つづり方〉(a) composition; how to spell.

tsuzuru 〈つづる〉spell; bind.

tsuzutte-oku 〈つづっておく〉place ((documents)) on file

U

u 〈う〉a cormorant.

ukai 〈う飼い〉 cormorant fishing

uba 〈うば：乳母〉a nurse.

uba-guruma 〈うばぐるま：乳母車〉a baby carriage, a perambulator.

ubai-au 〈うばいあう：奪い合う〉scramble ((for)), struggle ((for)).

ubai-kaesu 〈うばいかえす：奪い返す〉take back, reoccupy, recapture.

ubau 〈うばう：奪う〉take, rob(*or* deprive) ((a person)) of.

inochi o ubau 〈命を奪う〉 take ((a person's)) life

ubawareru 〈奪われる〉be robbed of.

ubu 〈うぶ〉

ubu-na 〈うぶな〉simplehearted, innocent, naïve.

ubuge 〈うぶげ：産毛〉downy hair.

ubugi 〈うぶぎ：産着〉swaddling clothes.

ubugoe 〈うぶごえ：産声〉the first cry of a newborn baby.

ubuyu 〈うぶゆ：産湯〉a newborn baby's first bath.

ubuyu-o-tsukawaseru 〈産湯を使わせる〉bathe a newborn baby.

uchi 〈うち：内〉the inside.

    uchi-ni hairu〈内に入る〉 come inside

uchi〈うち〉a house, one's home(*or* house).

    uchi-e-kaeru〈うちへ帰る〉 go(come *or* return) home

uchi-ni〈うちに〉within, inside, indoors, in, at home.

    uchi-ni-iru〈うちにいる〉 stay at home, keep indoors

    uchi-ni-i-nai〈うちにいない〉 be away from home

uchi, uchi-de or **uchi-kara**〈うち, うちで, うちから：内, 内で, 内から〉between, among, of, out of.

    ryôsha-no-uchi-de〈両者のうちで〉 between the two

    wareware-san-nin-no-uchi-de〈我々三人のうちで〉 among us three, of us three

    jû-nin-no-uchi-kyû-nin-made〈十人のうち九人まで〉 nine out of ten persons

uchi-ni〈内に〉in, within, during; while, before.

    ni-san-nichi-no-uchi-ni〈二，三日のうちに〉 in(*or* within) a few days

    fuyu-yasumi-no-uchi-ni〈冬休みのうちに〉 during the winter vacation

    wakai-uchi-ni〈若いうちに〉 while one is young

    kuraku-nara-nai-uchi-ni〈暗くならないうちに〉 before it gets dark

uchiage〈うちあげ：打ち上げ〉setting off, a launching; the close〔of a run of performances〕.

uchi-ageru〈うちあげる：打ち上げる〉shoot up, launch, fly; wash up on the shore; close, finish.

    jinkô-eisei o uchi-ageru〈人工衛星を打ち上げる〉 launch an artificial satellite

    kishi-ni uchi-agerareru〈岸に打ち上げられる〉 be cast up on the shore

    kôgyô o uchi-ageru〈興行を打ち上げる〉 close the performance

uchiai〈うちあい：打(撃)ち合い〉an exchange of blows, an exchange of shots.

uchi-akeru〈うちあける：打ち明ける〉tell, confess, confide ((in)).

    kokoro o uchi-akeru〈心を打ち明ける〉 speak one's mind

    nanimo-kamo uchi-akeru〈何もかも打ち明ける〉 tell everything ((to))

uchiawase〈うちあわせ：打ち合わせ〉a previous arrangement.

    uchiawase-kai〈打ち合わせ会〉 a preliminary meeting, a consultation

    uchiawase-o-suru〈打ち合わせをする〉make arrangements, arrange.

uchi-barai〈うちばらい：内払い〉partial payment.

uchi-benkei〈うちべんけい：内弁慶〉a lion at home and a mouse abroad.

uchi-bori〈うちぼり：内堀〉an inner moat.

uchidashi〈うちだし：打ち出し〉the closing〔of the show〕, the close〔of the *sumo* wrestling match series for the day〕.

uchi-dasu〈うちだす：打ち出す〉hammer out, work out, strike out, set forth.

> atarashii seisaku o uchi-dasu（新しい政策を打ち出す）hammer out a new policy

uchide-no-kozuchi〈うちでのこづち：打ち出の小づち〉a mallet of luck, an Aladdin's lamp.

uchi-gawa〈うちがわ：内側〉the inside.

uchi-gawa-no〈内側の〉inside, inner.

uchi-gawa-ni〈内側に〉inside, within.

uchi-gawa-kara〈内側から〉from within.

uchi-iwai〈うちいわい：内祝い〉a family celebration.

uchi-jû〈うちじゅう：うち中〉all the family, all over the house.

uchi-kaesu〈うちかえす：打ち返す〉strike back, return a blow ((to)).

> bôru o uchi-kaesu（ボールを打ち返す）return the ball

uchi-katsu〈うちかつ：打ち勝つ〉conquer, overcome, get over.

> konnan ni uchi-katsu（困難に打ち勝つ）overcome a difficulty

uchikeshi〈うちけし：打ち消し〉(a) denial, negation.

uchi-kesu〈打ち消す〉deny.

uchiki〈うちき：内気〉a bashful disposition, shyness.

uchiki-na〈内気な〉bashful, shy.

uchikin〈うちきん：内金〉money paid on account, earnest money.

uchi-kiru〈うちきる：打ち切る〉bring ((a matter)) to an end, call off.

uchi-komu〈うちこむ：打ち込む〉drive in, shoot into; devote oneself ((to)).

> kugi o kabe-ni-uchi-komu（くぎを壁に打ち込む）drive a nail into a wall
>
> tamashii-o-uchi-konde（魂を打ち込んで）with one's heart and soul

uchi-korosu〈うちころす：撃ち殺す〉shoot ((a person)) dead.

uchimaku〈うちまく：内幕〉the inside (facts), the low-down.

> uchimaku-o-shitte-iru（内幕を知っている）have the low-down ((on))

uchi-mata〈うちまた：内また〉

uchi-mata-no〈内またの〉pigeon-toed.

> uchi-mata-ni aruku（内またに歩く）walk pigeon-toed

uchi-mawari〈うちまわり：内周り〉the inner tracks.

uchi-mi〈うちみ：打み身〉a bruise.

uchi-nomesu〈うちのめす：打ちのめす〉knock ((a person)) down.

uchinori 〈うちのり：内のり〉 inside measure.

  uchinori-de 〈内のりで〉 in the clear.

uchi-nuku 〈うちぬく：打(撃)ち抜く〉 punch, penetrate; shoot through.

uchi-otosu 〈うちおとす：打(撃)ち落とす〉 strike down; shoot down.

uchi-poketto 〈うちポケット：内ポケット〉 an inside pocket.

uchi-sokonau 〈うちそこなう：打(撃)ち損なう〉 miss [the mark], fail to hit.

uchi-tokeru 〈うちとける：打ち解ける〉 open one's heart, be frank ((with)).

  uchi-toketa 〈打ち解けた〉 unreserved, familiar.

    uchi-tokete hanasu (打ち解けて話す) talk in a familiar way

uchi-tsukeru 〈うちつける：打ち付ける〉 strike, knock, beat; nail ((on *or* to)).

    atama o hashira-ni uchi-tsukeru (頭を柱に打ち付ける) knock one's head against a post

uchi-tsuzuku 〈うちつづく：打ち続く〉 a series of, a long spell of.

    uchi-tsuzuku fukô (打ち続く不幸) a series of misfortunes

uchiumi 〈うちうみ：内海〉 an inland sea.

uchiwa 〈うちわ〉 a (round) fan.

  uchiwa-de-aogu or *uchiwa-o-tsukau* 〈うちわであおぐ，うちわを使う〉 fan (oneself).

uchiwa 〈うちわ：内輪〉

    uchiwa-genka-o-suru (内輪げんかをする) have a family quarrel, quarrel among themselves

  uchiwa-no 〈内輪の〉 private, inside.

    uchiwa-no hanashi (内輪の話) a private affair

  uchiwa-ni 〈内輪に〉 moderately, conservatively.

    uchiwa-ni mi-tsumoru (内輪に見積もる) estimate conservatively

uchiwake 〈うちわけ：内訳〉 items, details.

    uchiwake o suru (内訳をする) state the items ((of))

uchi-yaburu 〈うちやぶる：打ち破る〉 break down; defeat.

uchi-yoseru 〈うちよせる：打ち寄せる〉 beat upon [the shore], roll on.

uchôten 〈うちょうてん：有頂天〉 ecstasy, rapture.

    uchôten-ni-naru (有頂天になる) go into ecstasies ((over)), fall into raptures

uchû 〈うちゅう：宇宙〉 the universe, space.

    uchû-chûkei (宇宙中継) the space relay

    uchû-heiki (宇宙兵器) a space weapon

uchû-hikô（宇宙飛行） a space flight
　　uchû-hikô-shi（宇宙飛行士） a spaceman
uchû-keikaku（宇宙計画） a space program
uchû-roketto（宇宙ロケット） a space rocket
uchû-sen（宇宙船） a spaceship
uchû-tsûshin（宇宙通信） space communication
uchū-no〈宇宙の〉 universal, cosmic.

udaru〈うだる〉
udaru-yō-na〈うだるような〉 sweltering, boiling.
　udaru-yō-na atsusa（うだるような暑さ） the sweltering heat

udatsu〈うだつ〉
udatsu-ga-agara-nai〈うだつが上がらない〉 cannot get on in the world.

ude〈うで：腕〉an arm; ability, capacity, talent, skill; force.
ude-o-oru（腕を折る） have one's arm broken
ude-gumi-suru（腕組みする） fold one's arms
ude-gumi-shite *or* ude-o-kunde（腕組みして，腕を組んで） with folded arms, arm in arm ((with))
ude o furuu（腕を振るう） exercise one's skill
ude o migaku（腕を磨く） improve one's skill
ude-ga-ochiru（腕が落ちる） fall off in one's skill ((in))
ude-shidai-de（腕次第で） according to one's ability
ude-zumō（腕相撲） arm wrestling
ude-tate-fuse（腕立て伏せ） a push-up
ude-no-aru〈腕のある〉 able, capable, skilled.
　ude-no-nai（腕のない） incapable, incompetent
ude-zuku-de〈腕尽くで〉 by force, by a strong-arm method.

udemae〈うでまえ：腕前〉 ability, capacity, skill.

uderu〈うでる〉 *see.* yuderu.

udo〈うど〉 an *udo.*
udo-no-taiboku（うどの大木） a big useless fellow

udon〈うどん〉 noodles.
udon-ko（うどん粉） (wheat) flour

ue〈うえ：飢え〉 hunger, starvation.
ue o shinogu（飢えをしのぐ） keep off hunger
ue-jini（飢え死に） (death by) starvation
　ue-jini-suru（飢え死にする） die of hunger, be starved to death
ueru〈飢える〉 be hungry, starve.
　aijō-ni-ueru（愛情に飢える） be hungry for affection

ueta〈飢えた〉hungry.

ue〈うえ：上〉upside, the top.

    ue-kara shita-made（上から下まで）from top to bottom

    ue-kara-no meirei（上からの命令）an order from above

    Eigo-o-hanasu-to-iu ten-dewa kimi-no-hô ga boku-yori-ue-da.（英語を話すという点では君の方が僕より上だ.）You are superior to me in speaking English.

ue-no〈上の〉up, upward, upper, higher, above, superior, older, uppermost.

    nana-sai-kara-ue-no shôjo（七歳から上の少女）girls of seven and upward

    ue-no bubun（上の部分）the upper part

    ue-no chii（上の地位）a higher position

    ue-no ko（上の子）the elder child

    ichiban-ue-no hiki-dashi（一番上の引き出し）the top drawer

∼*-no-ue-no* or *-no-ue-ni*〈～の上の、～の上に〉above, over, on, on the top of.

    tsukue-no-ue-ni（机の上に）on the desk

    oka-no-ue-ni（丘の上に）on the top of the hill

∼*-no-ue*〈～の上〉after, on.

    jûbun-kôryo-no-ue（十分考慮の上）after careful consideration

∼*(-)ue-ni*〈（～）上に〉up; besides, in addition ((to)), as well as, moreover.

    ni-kai-ue-ni sumu（二階上に住む）live two floors up

    Kare-wa atama-ga-ii-ue-ni kenkô-da.（彼は頭がいい上に健康だ.）Besides having a clear head, he is blessed with good health.

uehâsu〈ウエハース〉*see*. wehâsu.

uekae〈うえかえ：植え替え〉transplantation.

ue-kaeru〈植え替える〉transplant, replant.

ueki〈うえき：植木〉a garden plant.

    ueki-bachi（植木鉢）a flowerpot

    ueki-ya（植木屋）a gardener

uekomi〈うえこみ：植え込み〉a plantation, a shrubbery.

ueru〈うえる：植える〉plant, grow.

    niwa-ni ki o ueru（庭に木を植える）plant trees in a garden

uerutâ-kyû〈ウエルターきゅう：ウエルター級〉*see*. werutâ-kyû.

uesuto〈ウエスト〉*see*. wesuto.

uetsuke〈うえつけ：植え付け〉planting.

ue-tsukeru〈植え付ける〉plant, implant.

ugai 〈うがい〉
    ugai-gusuri〈うがい薬〉 a gargle
  ugai-suru〈うがいする〉 gargle.
ugatsu〈うがつ〉 dig, drill, pierce.
  ugatta-koto-o-iu〈うがったことを言う〉 make a penetrating remark.
ugen〈うげん：右げん〉 the starboard.
ugo〈うご：雨後〉
  ugo-no-takenoko-no-yô-ni arawareru〈雨後のたけのこのように現れる〉
    appear like so many mushrooms after rain.
ugokasu〈うごかす：動かす〉 move, work, operate; impress, stir, affect,
  influence.
    kikai o ugokasu（機械を動かす） work a machine
    hito-no-kokoro-o-ugokasu hanashi〈人の心を動かす話〉 a moving
    story
  ugokasare-yasui〈動かされやすい〉 be easily affected.
  ugokashi-e-nai〈動かし得ない〉 undeniable, unshakable, positive.
    ugokashi-e-nai jijitsu（動かし得ない事実） an undeniable fact
ugoki〈うごき：動き〉 a movement, motion, activity, action, a trend.
    koma no ugoki（こまの動き） the action of a chessman
    yo-no-naka no ugoki（世の中の動き） the trend of the world
  ugoki-ga-tore-nai〈動きがとれない〉 cannot move, be in a fix.
ugoki-mawaru〈うごきまわる：動き回る〉 move about.
ugoku〈うごく：動く〉 move, go, operate, run, work; be influenced,
  waver, be moved, be touched.
    denki-de ugoku（電気で動く） go by electricity
    kane-de-sugu-ugoku（金ですぐ動く） can be easily bribed
  ugoka-naku-naru〈動かなくなる〉 stop working, run down, come to a
    standstill, break down.
ugomeku〈うごめく：動めく〉 wriggle, squirm.
uguisu〈うぐいす〉 a (Japanese) bush warbler.
uha〈うは：右派〉 the right wing, the right-wing faction, the rightists.
  uha-no〈右派の〉 right-wing, rightist.
Uinna〈ウインナ〉 Vienna.
    Uinna-sôsêji（ウインナソーセージ） a Vienna sausage
uitto〈ウイット〉 wit.
  uitto-no-aru〈ウイットのある〉 witty.
uiuishii〈ういういしい：初々しい〉 fresh and naïve.
uizan〈ういざん：初産〉 one's first childbirth.

ujauja 〈うじゃうじゃ〉 *see.* uyouyo.

uji 〈うじ〉 a maggot, a worm.

ujigami 〈うじがみ：氏神〉 a tutelary deity 〔of a village〕.

ujiko 〈うじこ：氏子〉 people under the protection of a tutelary god.

ukabareru 〈うかばれる：浮かばれる〉 rest in peace; get on in the world.

　　Kore-dewa kare-no rei mo ukabare-mai.（これでは彼の霊も浮かばれまい。） This could not set his soul in peace.

　　Kare-wa-mô-isshô-ukabare-nai.（彼はもう一生浮かばれない。） It's all up with him now.

ukaberu 〈うかべる：浮かべる〉 float.

　　ike-ni bôto o ukaberu（池にボートを浮かべる） float a boat in the pond

　　me-ni-namida-o-ukabete（目に涙を浮かべて） with tears in one's eyes

　　bishô-o-ukabete（微笑を浮かべて） with a smile

ukabi-agaru 〈うかびあがる：浮かび上がる〉 break the surface, rise to the surface, surface.

ukabu 〈うかぶ：浮かぶ〉 float; occur.

　　〜-ga-futo-kokoro-ni-ukanda.（〜がふと心に浮かんだ。） It occurred to me that... .

ukagai 〈うかがい：伺い〉 a visit, a call; an inquiry.

　　go-kigen-ukagai-o-suru（御機嫌伺いをする） pay one's respects ((to))

　　ukagai-o-tateru（伺いを立てる） ask for one's instructions

ukagau〈伺う〉 call ((on)), call ((at)); visit; ask.

　　Kon・ya ukagai-masu.（今夜伺います。） I will call on you tonight.

　　Chotto-ukagaimasu-ga,〜（ちょっと伺いますが、〜） Excuse me, but ...

ukagau 〈うかがう〉 watch ((for)), spy ((on)).

　　ki o ukagau（機をうかがう） wait for an opportunity

　　keisei-o-ukagau（形勢をうかがう） see how the wind blows

ukai 〈うかい：う回〉 a detour, a roundabout way.

　　ukai-suru（う回する） make a detour, take a roundabout way

ukanu 〈うかぬ：浮かぬ〉

ukanu-kao-o-suru〈浮かぬ顔をする〉 pull a long face.

ukareru 〈うかれる：浮かれる〉 make merry.

ukare-aruku〈浮かれ歩く〉 walk lightheartedly.

ukare-sawagu〈浮かれ騒ぐ〉 frolic.

ukaru 〈うかる：受かる〉 pass 〔an examination〕.

ukasareru 〈うかされる：浮かされる〉

netsu-ni-ukasareru 〈熱に浮かされる〉 be delirious with a fever.

ukatsu 〈うかつ〉

    Dômo-ukatsu-deshita. (どうもうかつでした.) It was very careless of me.

  ukatsu-na 〈うかつな〉 careless, thoughtless, stupid.

  ukatsu-ni 〈うかつに〉 carelessly, thoughtlessly, stupidly.

ukauka 〈うかうか〉

    Ukauka-suru-na. (うかうかするな.) Look about you! / Be alert!

uke 〈うけ：受け〉

  uke-ga-ii 〈受けがいい〉 be popular ((with)), be in favor ((with)), stand well ((with)).

    uke-ga-warui 〈受けが悪い〉 be unpopular ((with)), be out of favor ((with))

uke-au 〈うけあう：請け合う〉 undertake; assure, guarantee.

    hinshitsu o uke-au 〈品質を請け合う〉 guarantee the quality

uke-dachi 〈うけだち：受け太刀〉

  uke-dachi-ni-naru 〈受け太刀になる〉 be on the defensive.

uke-dasu 〈うけだす：請け出す〉 take ((a thing)) out of pawn.

ukei 〈うけい：右傾〉

  ukei-suru 〈右傾する〉 turn to the right.

ukeire 〈うけいれ：受け入れ〉 reception, acceptance.

    ukeire-taisei-ga-dekite-i-nai (受け入れ態勢ができていない) be not prepared to receive

uke-ireru 〈うけいれる：受け入れる〉 accept, assent, grant, listen ((to)), comply ((with)).

    yôkyû o uke-ireru (要求を受け入れる) comply with ((a peson's)) request

uke-kotae 〈うけこたえ：受け答え〉 an answer, a reply.

  uke-kotae-suru 〈受け答えする〉 answer, give an answer ((to)).

uke-mi 〈うけみ：受け身〉

  uke-mi-ni-naru 〈受け身になる〉 be on the defensive, be in a passive position.

uke-mi 〈うけみ：受け身〉 the passive.

    uke-mi-no dôshi (受け身の動詞) a passive verb

ukemochi 〈うけもち：受け持ち〉 charge.

    ukemochi-no sensei (受け持ちの先生) the teacher in charge

    ukemochi-jikan (受け持ち時間) one's class hours

  uke-motsu 〈受け持つ〉 have charge ((of)), be in charge ((of)).

uke-nagasu〈うけながす：受け流す〉parry.

ukeoi〈うけおい：請負〉a contract.
>ukeoi-nin（請負人）a contractor
>ukeoi-de（請負で）by contract

ukeou〈請け負う〉contract.

ukeowaseru〈請け負わせる〉give ((a person)) a contract ((for)).

ukeru〈うける：受ける〉receive, get, obtain; catch; undergo, take; suffer; be well received.
>atatakai kangei o ukeru（温かい歓迎を受ける）receive a warm welcome
>ittô-shô o ukeru（一等賞を受ける）get the first prize
>menkyo o ukeru（免許を受ける）obtain a license
>bôru o ukeru（ボールを受ける）catch a ball
>shiken o ukeru（試験を受ける）take an examination
>ma-ni-ukeru（真に受ける）take ((it)) seriously, believe ((it))
>songai o ukeru（損害を受ける）suffer a loss
>kengi-o-ukeru（嫌疑を受ける）be suspected ((of))
>wakai josei-ni ukeru（若い女性に受ける）be popular with young women

uketamawaru〈うけたまわる：承る〉hear, be told, understand; receive.

uke-tomeru〈うけとめる：受け止める〉catch.

uketori〈うけとり：受取〉a receipt.
>uketori o kaku（受取を書く）make a receipt
>uketori-nin（受取人）a recipient, a remittee, a beneficiary, a consignee
>uketori-shidai（受け取り次第）upon receipt

uketoru〈受け取る〉receive, get, accept.

uke-tsugu〈うけつぐ：受け継ぐ〉succeed ((to)), take over, inherit.
>chichi-no shôbai o uke-tsugu（父の商売を受け継ぐ）succeed to one's father's business

uketsuke〈うけつけ：受付〉acceptance; an inquiry office.
>uketsuke-gakari（受付係）a receptionist

uketsukeru〈受け付ける〉receive, accept.
>uketsuke-nai（受け付けない）reject, refuse; lend no ear ((to))

ukeuri〈うけうり：受け売り〉

ukeuri-suru〈受け売りする〉retail; tell at second hand.

ukeuri-no〈受け売りの〉secondhand.
>ukeuri-no chishiki（受け売りの知識）secondhand knowledge

uke-watashi〈うけわたし：受け渡し〉delivery, payment.
　　uke-watashi-bi（受け渡し日）a delivery day
　　uke-watashi-jôken（受け渡し条件）　terms of delivery
　uke-watashi-suru〈受け渡しする〉deliver, hand over.

uke-zara〈うけざら：受け皿〉a saucer.

uki〈うき：雨季〉the rainy season.
　　Uki-ni-haitta.（雨季に入った.）The rainy season has set in.

uki〈うき：浮き〉a float, a buoy.

uki-agaru〈うきあがる：浮き上がる〉come to the surface, surface; be not based ((on)).

ukiashi-datsu〈うきあしだつ：浮き足立つ〉be wavering, be ready to run away.

uki-bori〈うきぼり：浮き彫り〉relief.
　uki-bori-ni-suru〈浮き彫りにする〉carve in relief, emboss.

uki-bukuro〈うきぶくろ：浮き袋〉an air bladder; a float, a life belt, a swim ring.

uki-dokku〈うきドック：浮きドック〉a floating dock.

uki-gashi〈浮き貸し〉an illegal loan.

uki-gumo〈うきぐも：浮き雲〉a floating cloud.

uki-me〈うきめ：憂き目〉
　uki-me-o-miru〈憂き目を見る〉come to grief, have a bitter experience.

uki-shizumi〈うきしずみ：浮き沈み〉*see.* fuchin.

ukiuki〈うきうき：浮き浮き〉
　ukiuki-shita〈浮き浮きした〉buoyant, cheerful, lighthearted.
　ukiuki-to〈浮き浮きと〉buoyantly, cheerfully, lightheartedly.

ukiyo〈うきよ：浮き世〉the world, life.
　　ukiyo no narai *or* ukiyo no tsune（浮き世の習い, 浮き世の常）the way of the world
　ukiyo-banare-no-shita〈浮き世離れのした〉other-worldly, unworldly.

ukiyo-e〈うきよえ：浮世絵〉an *ukiyoe* color-print.

ukkari(-shite)〈うっかり（して）〉carelessly, absentmindedly, by mistake, in spite of oneself.
　ukkari-shite-iru〈うっかりしている〉be absentminded.
　ukkari-shaberu〈うっかりしゃべる〉slip out, blurt out.

ukketsu〈うっけつ：うっ血〉congestion〔of blood〕.
　ukketsu-suru〈うっ血する〉be congested with blood.

uku〈うく：浮く〉float; be saved.
　　ichi-man-en-uku（一万円浮く）can save ten thousand yen

uma〈うま：馬〉a horse, a pony, a colt.
　　uma ni noru（馬に乗る）ride a horse
　　uma-de iku（馬で行く）go on horseback
　　uma o hashiraseru（馬を走らせる）gallop one's horse
　　uma-kara oriru（馬から降りる）get off a horse
　　uma-kara ochiru（馬から落ちる）fall from a horse
　　uma-ga-au（馬が合う）get on well ((with))
　　uma-nori-ni-naru（馬乗りになる）sit astride ((a person))

umai〈うまい〉delicious, sweet, tasty, nice; skillful, good, happy.
　　umai-mono（うまい物）a delicacy
　　umai kangae（うまい考え）a good(or happy) idea
　　umai koto o iu（うまいことを言う）say nice things
　　ji-ga-umai（字がうまい）write a good hand
　　ryôri-ga-umai（料理がうまい）be good at cooking
　　yakyû-ga-umai（野球がうまい）play baseball well
　　Sore-dewa-hanashi-ga-uma-sugiru.（それでは話がうますぎる.）It's
　　　too good to be true.
　　umai-shiru-o-suu（うまい汁を吸う）take the lion's share, get all the
　　　profit ((out of))

umaku〈うまく〉skillfully, well.
　　umaku-iku（うまくいく）go well, be successful
　　umaku-ika-nai（うまくいかない）go wrong, be unsuccessful
　　umaku-yaru（うまくやる）manage ((a thing)) successfully

umami〈うまみ〉deliciousness, taste; a charm.
umami-no-aru〈うまみのある〉profitable.
　　umami-no-aru shôbai（うまみのある商売）a profitable trade

ûman-ribu〈ウーマンリブ〉women's liberation.

umare〈うまれ：生まれ〉birth, lineage.
　　umare-kokyô（生まれ故郷）one's birthplace
　　umare-no-ii（生まれのいい）wellborn
　　umare-tsuki（生まれつき）one's nature; by nature
　　　umare-tsuki-no（生まれつきの）natural
　　umare-tate-no（生まれたての）newly-born

umareru〈生まれる〉be born.
　　umarete-hajimete（生まれて初めて）for the first time in one's life
　　umarete-kono-kata（生まれてこの方）ever since one's birth
　　umare-kawaru（生まれ変わる）be born again, start one's life afresh

umaru〈うまる：埋まる〉be buried; be filled up.

dosha-de-umatta-senro〈土砂で埋まった線路〉 a railroad line buried with earth and sand

kembutsu-nin-de umaru〈見物人で埋まる〉 be filled up with spectators

umeru〈埋める〉bury, fill up; make up ((for)).

kūhaku o umeru〈空白を埋める〉 fill a blank

akaji o umeru〈赤字を埋める〉 make up the deficit

umaya〈うまや〉a stable.

umazu-tayumazu〈うまずたゆまず〉tirelessly, with untiring zeal.

ume〈うめ：梅〉a plum, a plum tree.

ume-boshi〈梅干し〉 a pickled plum

umeawase〈うめあわせ：埋め合わせ〉amends, (a) compensation.

umeawase-o-suru〈埋め合わせをする〉make up ((for)).

umeki(-goe)〈うめき(ごえ)：うめき(声)〉a groan, a moan.

umeku〈うめく〉groan, moan.

umetate〈うめたて：埋め立て〉reclamation.

umetate-chi〈埋め立て地〉 a reclaimed land

ume-tateru〈埋め立てる〉reclaim, fill in, fill up.

umi〈うみ：海〉the sea, the ocean.

naida umi〈ないだ海〉 a calm sea

atari-ichimen hi no umi〈辺り一面火の海〉 a sea of flames all around

umi〈うみ〉pus.

umi o dasu〈うみを出す〉 press out the pus

umu〈うむ〉form pus.

umi〈うみ：産(生)み〉

umi-no-kurushimi〈産みの苦しみ〉 labor pains

umi-no-oya〈生みの親〉 one's real parent

umi-be〈うみべ：海辺〉the beach, the seaside.

umi-dasu〈うみだす：産(生)み出す〉give birth ((to)), bring forth, produce, invent.

umi-game〈うみがめ：海がめ〉a turtle.

umi-hebi〈うみへび：海蛇〉a sea snake.

umi-otosu〈うみおとす：産み落とす〉give birth ((to)), drop.

umisen-yamasen〈うみせんやません：海千山千〉

umisen-yamasen-no-shitataka-mono〈海千山千のしたたか者〉 a sly old dog

umi-tate〈うみたて：産み立て〉

umi-tate-no〈産みたての〉fresh, new-laid.

umi-tate-no tamago（産みたての卵） a new-laid egg

ummei〈うんめい：運命〉(a) destiny, fate, (a) lot, fortune.

　　ummei-ni-amanjiru（運命に甘んじる） submit to fate

　　ummei-o-tomo-ni-suru（運命を共にする） cast one's lot ((with))

　　ummei no itazura（運命のいたずら） a caprice of fate

　　ummei-ron-sha（運命論者） a fatalist

　～-no-ummei-ni-aru or *ummei-zukerareru*〈～の運命にある，運命づけられる〉be destined(*or* doomed) ((to do)).

ummo〈うんも：雲母〉 mica.

umô〈うもう：羽毛〉feathers, plumes; feathering, plumage; down.

umoreru〈うもれる：埋もれる〉*see.* uzumoreru.

umpan〈うんぱん：運搬〉*see.* unsô.

umu〈うむ：有無〉

　　umu-ai-tsûjiru（有無相通じる） supply each other's needs

　umu-o-iwasezu-ni〈有無を言わせずに〉whether one will or not, by force.

umu〈うむ：産(生)む〉lay, bear, give birth ((to)); produce, give rise ((to)).

　　tamago o umu（卵を産む） lay an egg

　　onna-no-ko-o-umu（女の子を産む） give birth to a girl

　　iro-iro-na uwasa o umu（いろいろなうわさを生む） give rise to a variety of rumors

un〈うん：運〉(a) destiny, fate, (a) lot, fortune, luck, chance.

　　un o ten-ni makasu（運を天に任す） leave one's fate to Heaven

　　un o tamesu（運を試す） try one's fortune

　　Un ga muite-kita.（運が向いてきた.） Fortune is smiling upon me.

　　Un-ni-megumareru.（運に恵まれる.） Luck favors me.

　　un no tsuki（運の尽き） the end of one's luck

　un-ga-ii〈運がいい〉be lucky.

　　un-ga-warui（運が悪い） be unfortunate, be unlucky

　un-yoku〈運よく〉fortunately, luckily.

　　un-yoku～(-suru)（運よく～(する)） have the fortune ((to do))

　un-waruku〈運悪く〉unfortunately, unluckily.

　　un-waruku～(-suru)（運悪く～(する)） have the misfortune ((to do))

　un-ga-yokereba〈運がよければ〉with luck.

un〈うん〉yes, all right.

　　un-to-iu（うんと言う） say yes

　　un-tomo-sun-tomo-iwa-nai（うんともすんとも言わない） do not say even a word, remain silent

unadareru〈うなだれる〉droop one's head.

unagasu〈うながす：促す〉urge, press, demand, prompt, quicken.
　　chûi o unagasu（注意を促す）call ((a person's)) attention ((to))

unagi〈うなぎ〉an eel.

unari〈うなり〉a groan, a roar, a beat, humming.
　　unari-goe（うなり声）a groan, a moan
　　unari-goe-o-ageru（うなり声を上げる）groan

unaru〈うなる〉groan, moan, roar, growl, trumpet, hum, howl.
　　unaru-hodo-kane-o-motte-iru（うなるほど金を持っている）be　rolling
　　in riches

unasareru〈うなされる〉have a nightmare.

unazuku〈うなずく〉nod ((at *or* to)), nod assent ((to)).

unchin〈うんちん：運賃〉a fare, freight (rates).
　　unchin-saki-barai（運賃先払い）freight to collect
　　unchin-hyô（運賃表）a tariff, a freight list

undei〈うんでい：雲泥〉
undei-no-sa-ga-aru〈雲泥の差がある〉there　is　a　world　of　difference
　　((between *or* among)).

undô〈うんどう：運動〉exercise(s), sports, games, motion, movement;
　a campaign.
　　tekido-no undô（適度の運動）moderate exercise
　　undô-busoku（運動不足）lack of exercise
　　undô-fuku（運動服）sportswear
　　undô-gutsu（運動靴）sports shoes
　　undô-gu-ten（運動具店）a sporting-goods store
　　undô-jô（運動場）a playground
　　undô-ka（運動家）an athlete
　　undô-kai（運動会）an athletic meeting
　　undô-kyôgi（運動競技）athletic sports
　　undô-shinkei（運動神経）a motor nerve
　　　　undô-shinkei-ga-hattatsu-shite-iru（運動神経が発達している）have
　　　　quick control of one's muscles
　　okunai-undô（屋内運動）indoor games
　　seiji-undô（政治運動）a political movement
　　senkyo-undô（選挙運動）an election campaign
　　shûshoku-undô-o-suru（就職運動をする）make　efforts　to　obtain　a
　　　　position
　　undô-in（運動員）a canvasser, an electioneer

undô-shikin〈運動資金〉 campaign funds

undô-suru〈運動する〉 take exercise, move, campaign, make efforts.

une〈うね：畝〉a ridge〔in the field〕, a furrow.

un·ei〈うんえい：運営〉operation, management, conduct.

un·ei-suru〈運営する〉operate, manage, conduct.

uneri〈うねり〉undulation, winding, a swell.

uneru〈うねる〉undulate, wind, swell.

uneune〈うねうね〉

uneune-to-shita〈うねうねとした〉meandering, winding, zigzag.

unga〈うんが：運河〉a canal.

unga o hiraku（運河を開く） dig a canal

uni〈うに〉a sea urchin; seasoned sea urchin eggs.

unkô〈うんこう：運行〉movement, revolution.

tentai no unkô（天体の運行） the movement of heavenly bodies

unkô〈うんこう：運航〉operation, service.

unkô-suru〈運航する〉operate, run.

unkyû〈うんきゅう：運休〉suspension of the (railway) service.

unkyû-suru〈運休する〉the (train) service is suspended.

un-nun〈うんぬん〉so and so, such and such, and so on.

u-nomi〈うのみ〉

u-nomi-ni-suru〈うのみにする〉swallow ((a thing)) without chewing, swallow.

unsei〈うんせい：運勢〉one's star, fortune, luck.

unsei-ga-ii（運勢がいい） be born under a lucky star

unsei-ga-warui（運勢が悪い） be born under an unlucky star

unsô〈うんそう：運送〉conveyance, transportation, traffic, freight.

unsô-gyô（運送業） forwarding business

unsô-gaisha（運送会社） a transport company

unsô-ryô（運送料） forwarding charges, freight

unsô-suru〈運送する〉convey, transport, carry, forward.

unten〈うんてん：運転〉operation, driving, working; employment.

unten-menkyo（運転免許） a driver's license

unten-shikin（運転資金） working capital

unten-shu（運転手） a motorman, an engineer, a driver, a chauffeur, a cabman, an operator

unten-keitô（運転系統） a route

unten-suru〈運転する〉operate, drive; employ.

unto〈うんと〉hard, severely, heavily, by far, a great deal ((of)), a lot ((of)).

 unto hataraku（うんと働く）work hard
 unto sake-o-nomu（うんと酒を飲む）drink heavily
 unto-kane-o-tsukau（うんと金を使う）spend a lot of money
 unto-shikaru（うんとしかる）give ((a person)) a good scolding

unubore〈うぬぼれ〉self-conceit, vanity, self-importance.
unuboreru〈うぬぼれる〉be conceited, be vain, think highly of oneself.
unubore-no-tsuyoi〈うぬぼれの強い〉self-conceited, vain, self-important.

un・yô〈うんよう：運用〉application, practical use, employment; investment.
un・yô-suru〈運用する〉apply, use, employ; invest.

un・yu〈うんゆ：運輸〉transportation, conveyance, traffic.
 un・yu-kikan（運輸機関）means of conveyance
 un・yu-shô（運輸省）the Ministry of Transport
 un・yu-daijin（運輸大臣）the Minister of Transport

unzan〈うんざん：運算〉operation, calculation.
 unzan-ga-umai（運算がうまい）be good at calculation
unzan-suru〈運算する〉operate, calculate.

unzari〈うんざり〉
unzari-suru〈うんざりする〉be disgusted ((with)), be sick ((of)), become tired ((of)).
 unzari-suru shigoto（うんざりする仕事）a boring work

uo〈うお：魚〉a fish.
 uo-ichiba（魚市場）a fish market

uo-gokoro〈うおごころ：魚心〉
 Uo-gokoro-areba-mizu-gokoro.（魚心あれば水心.）Roll my log and I'll roll yours.

uômingu-appu〈ウオーミングアップ〉*see*. wômingu-appu.

uo-no-me〈うおのめ：魚の目〉a corn.

uô-saô〈うおうさおう：右往左往〉
uô-saô-suru〈右往左往する〉go this way and that, go pell-mell.

uppun〈うっぷん：うっ憤〉resentment, pent-up fury.
 uppun o harasu（うっ憤を晴らす）vent one's pent-up fury ((on))

ura〈うら：裏〉the reverse side, the other side, the inside, the reverse, the opposite, the back, the rear; the lining; the second half.
 rekôdo no ura（レコードの裏）the reverse side of a record
 ura-e mawaru（裏へ回る）go round to the back door
 nana-kai no ura（七回の裏）the second half of the seventh inning

ashi-no-ura〈足の裏〉 the sole

kotoba no ura（言葉の裏） the hidden implications of one's words

ura-o-kaku〈裏をかく〉counterplot.

ura-tsuki-no〈裏付きの〉with a lining.

urabureru〈うらぶれる〉become shabby.

urabureta-sugata-de〈うらぶれた姿で〉in a shabby appearance.

ura-doori〈うらどおり：裏通り〉a back street, a side street.

ura-gaeshi〈うらがえし：裏返し〉

ura-gaeshi-ni〈裏返しに〉inside out.

kutsu-shita o ura-gaeshi-ni-haku（靴下を裏返しに履く） put on one's socks inside out

ura-gaeshi-ni-suru or *ura-gaesu*〈裏返しにする，裏返す〉turn inside out, turn over.

uragaki〈うらがき：裏書き〉endorsement, a visa.

uragaki-nin（裏書人） an endorser

uragaki-suru〈裏書きする〉endorse, visa, prove.

uragiri〈うらぎり：裏切り〉(a) betrayal.

uragiri-mono（裏切り者） a betrayer, a turncoat, an informer, a strikebreaker.

uragiru〈裏切る〉betray, play ((a person)) false.

shinrai o uragiru（信頼を裏切る） betray one's trust

kitai-o-uragiru（期待を裏切る） be contrary to one's expectations

ura-goe〈うらごえ：裏声〉a falsetto.

ura-goe-de utau（裏声で歌う） sing in falsetto

uragoshi〈うらごし：裏ごし〉a strainer.

uragoshi-suru〈裏ごしする〉strain.

ura-guchi〈うらぐち：裏口〉the back door.

ura-guchi-kara dete-iku（裏口から出て行く） go out at the back door

ura-guchi-eigyô（裏口営業） illegal business

ura-hara〈うらはら：裏腹〉the contrary.

Kare-wa iu-koto-to-suru-koto-ga-ura-hara-da.（彼は言うこととすることが裏腹だ.） He acts contrary to what he says.

ura-ji〈うらじ：裏地〉lining (cloth).

urakata〈うらかた：裏方〉a stagehand.

urame〈うらめ：裏目〉the reverse side.

urame-ni-deru〈裏目に出る〉backfire.

urameshii〈うらめしい：恨めしい〉feel bitter ((against)), be reproachful.

urameshi-sô-na〈恨めしそうな〉reproachful, spiteful, rueful.

     urameshi-sô-na kao〈恨めしそうな顔〉a reproachful look
urameshi-sô-ni〈恨めしそうに〉with a reproachful look, reproachfully.

urami〈うらみ：恨み〉a grudge, an ill feeling, hatred.
     urami o idaku〈恨みを抱く〉have a grudge ((against)), bear ((a person)) an ill will
     urami o kau〈恨みを買う〉incur grudge
     urami-o-harasu〈恨みを晴らす〉revenge oneself ((on))
     urami-gamashii koto o iu〈恨みがましいことを言う〉say reproachful things ((against))
     uramu〈恨む〉bear a grudge ((against)), blame.

ura-michi〈うらみち：裏道〉a back street, a byway.

ura-mon〈うらもん：裏門〉a back gate.

uran〈ウラン〉uranium.
     tennen-uran〈天然ウラン〉natural uranium

uranai〈うらない：占い〉fortune-telling.
     uranai-shi〈占い師〉a fortune-teller
     uranau〈占う〉tell ((a person's)) fortune.

ura-Nihon〈うらにほん：裏日本〉the coast of the Japan Sea.

uraniumu〈ウラニウム〉*see.* uran.

ura-niwa〈うらにわ：裏庭〉a back garden, a backyard.

ura-omote〈うらおもて：裏表〉both sides.
     kami no ura-omote〈紙の裏表〉both sides of the paper
     shôbai no ura-omote〈商売の裏表〉the in and outside of the trade
     ura-omote-no-aru〈裏表のある〉double-dealing.
     ura-omote-no-aru-hito〈裏表のある人〉a double-dealer, a double-faced person

uraraka〈うららか〉
     uraraka-na〈うららかな〉bright, beautiful, fine, glorious.
     uraraka-na haru-no-hi〈うららかな春の日〉a bright spring day
     uraraka-na tenki〈うららかな天気〉beautiful weather

ura-te〈うらて：裏手〉the back.
     ura-te-no or *ura-te-ni*〈裏手の，裏手に〉at the rear ((of)), at the back ((of)).

ura-uchi〈うらうち：裏打ち〉lining, backing.
     ura-uchi-suru〈裏打ちする〉line, back.

urayamashii〈うらやましい〉enviable.
     urayamashiku-omou or *urayamu*〈うらやましく思う，うらやむ〉be envious ((of)), envy.

urayamashi-sô-na〈うらやましそうな〉envious.

urayamashi-sô-ni〈うらやましそうに〉enviously.

ura-zuke〈うらづけ：裏付け〉backing, support, corroboration, substantiation.

ura-zukeru〈裏付ける〉back up, support, substantiate.
　　shuchô o ura-zukeru（主張を裏付ける）substantiate a statement

urei〈うれい：憂い〉grief, trouble, anxiety.
　　urei-ni-shizumu（憂いに沈む）be sunk in grief

urei-naku〈憂いなく〉without anxiety.

urekko〈うれっこ：売れっ子〉a popular person, a person of great popularity.

ure-kuchi〈うれくち：売れ口〉*see.* ure-yuki.

ure-nokori〈うれのこり：売れ残り〉unsold goods, remainders; an old maid.

ure-nokoru〈売れ残る〉remain unsold; remain on the shelf.

ureru〈うれる：売れる〉sell, be sold; be well known.
　　yoku ureru（よく売れる）sell well
　　yoku-ureru-shina（良く売れる品）a good seller
　　amari-ure-nai（余り売れない）have a poor sale

ureshi-garu〈うれしがる〉be glad, be pleased, be delighted, be happy.

ureshi-garaseru〈うれしがらせる〉gladden, please, delight, make ((a person)) happy.

ureshii〈うれしい〉(be) glad, (be) pleased, (be) happy.
　　ureshii shirase（うれしい知らせ）happy news

ureshii-koto-ni(-wa)〈うれしいことに(は)〉to one's joy.

ureshikute〈うれしくて〉for joy.

ureshi-sô-ni〈うれしそうに〉joyfully, with joy.

ureshisa-no-amari〈うれしさの余り〉in one's joy.

ureshi-naki-ni-naku or *ureshi-namida-o-nagasu*〈うれし泣きに泣く，うれし涙を流す〉shed tears of joy.

ure-yuki〈うれゆき：売れ行き〉a market, sale(s), demand.
　　ure-yuki-ga-ii（売れ行きがいい）sell well, be in good demand
　　ure-yuki-ga-warui（売れ行きが悪い）be in poor demand

uri〈うり〉a melon.

uri-futatsu-de-aru〈うり二つである〉be as like as two peas, resemble closely.

uri〈うり：売り〉sale, selling.
　　uri-ni-dasu（売りに出す）put ((an article)) to sale

uri-kai〈売り買い〉 selling and buying

uri-age or **uri-age-daka**〈うりあげ, うりあげだか：売り上げ, 売上高〉(the) proceeds.

sō-uri-age-daka〈総売上高〉 the gross proceeds

heikin-uri-age-daka〈平均売上高〉 average sale

uri-age-dempyō〈売上伝票〉 a sales slip

uri-ba〈うりば：売り場〉a counter.

uri-dashi〈うりだし：売り出し〉a bargain sale, a special sale, a clearance sale.

uri-dashi-chū-no bumpitsu-ka（売り出し中の文筆家） a rising literary man

uri-dasu〈売り出す〉offer for sale; become popular, win fame.

Kanojo-wa kono-kyoku-de uri-dashita.（彼女はこの曲で売り出した．） She gained her reputation by this song.

uri-gui〈うりぐい：売り食い〉

uri-gui-suru〈売り食いする〉live by selling one's property.

uri-harau〈うりはらう：売り払う〉sell off, sell out, dispose ((of)).

uri-ie〈うりいえ：売り家〉a house for sale.

uri-isogu〈うりいそぐ：売り急ぐ〉sell in haste.

uri-kake-kin〈うりかけきん：売り掛け金〉credit, accounts.

uri-kata〈うりかた：売り方〉salesmanship; a seller, the selling side.

uri-kireru〈うりきれる：売り切れる〉be sold out.

uri-komi〈うりこみ：売り込み〉sale.

uri-komu〈売り込む〉sell, find a new market and sell.

uri-kotoba〈うりことば：売り言葉〉

uri-kotoba-ni kai-kotoba（売り言葉に買い言葉） give tit for tat

uri-mono〈うりもの：売り物〉an article for sale, For Sale.

uri-mono-ni-naru（売り物になる） be fit for sale

uri-mono-ni-naranai（売り物にならない） be unsalable

uri-mono-ni-dasu（売り物に出す） place ((a thing)) on sale

uri-mono-ni-suru〈売り物にする〉capitalize ((on)).

bibō-o-uri-mono-ni-suru（美ぼうを売り物にする） capitalize on one's beauty

uri-ne〈うりね：売値〉the sale price.

uri-oshimi〈うりおしみ：売り惜しみ〉

uri-oshimi-suru〈売り惜しみする〉be unwilling to sell, restrict the sale ((of)).

uri-sabaku〈うりさばく：売りさばく〉sell, dispose ((of)), work off.

uri-te〈うりて：売り手〉a seller.

    uri-te-ichiba（売手市場）a sellers' market

uri-tobasu〈うりとばす：売り飛ばす〉sell off, dispose ((of)).

uri-tsukeru〈うりつける：売り付ける〉impose ((an article)) on ((a person)).

uri-tsukusu〈うりつくす：売り尽くす〉sell out.

uri-watasu〈うりわたす：売り渡す〉sell ((a thing)) (over) to ((a person)).

uri-ya〈うりや：売家〉 *see.* uri-ie.

urizane-gao〈うりざねがお：うりざね顔〉an oval face.

uroko〈うろこ〉a scale.

  uroko-o-otosu〈うろこを落とす〉scale〔a fish〕.

uro-oboe〈うろおぼえ：うろ覚え〉a faint memory ((for)).

urotaeru〈うろたえる〉be confused, be upset.

    urotae-nai（うろたえない）keep calm

  urotaete（うろたえて）in confusion.

urotsuku〈うろつく〉loiter, hang about(*or* around), wander ((about)).

urouro-suru〈うろうろする〉 *see.* urotsuku.

uru〈うる：得る〉*see.* eru.

  uru-tokoro-ga totemo ooi〈得るところがとても多い〉gain much ((by *or* from)), learn a great deal ((from)).

    uru-tokoro-ga sukoshi-mo-nai（得るところが少しもない）gain nothing ((by *or* from)), learn nothing ((from))

  〜-*shi-uru*〈〜し得る〉can ((do)), be able ((to do)), may ((do)).

uru〈うる：売る〉sell; betray.

    teika-de uru（定価で売る）sell at fixed prices

    takaku uru（高く売る）sell dear

    yasuku uru（安く売る）sell cheap

    môkete-uru（もうけて売る）sell at a profit

    son-shite-uru（損して売る）sell at a loss

    tomo o uru（友を売る）betray one's friend

    na-o-uru（名を売る）become famous ((as *or* for)), win fame

    kenka o uru（けんかを売る）pick a quarrel ((with))

ûru〈ウール〉wool.

    ûru-ji（ウール地）woolens

  ûru-no〈ウールの〉woolen.

urumu〈うるむ：潤む〉be wet.

    namida-de urumu（涙で潤む）be wet with tears

    urunda me（潤んだ目）dim eyes

uruoi 〈うるおい：潤い〉 moisture, damp; charm.

uruoi-no-aru 〈潤いのある〉 charming, tasteful.

uruoi-no-nai 〈潤いのない〉 dry, prosaic.

    uruoi-no-nai seikatsu o suru 〈潤いのない生活をする〉 lead a prosaic life

uruosu 〈うるおす：潤す〉 wet, moisten, dip, irrigate; profit.

    kuchi o uruosu 〈口を潤す〉 moisten one's lips

uruou 〈潤う〉 be moistened; share the profit.

urusai 〈うるさい〉 annoying, bothering, troublesome, pesky, pertinacious, importunate, noisy.

    Urusai! 〈うるさい.〉 Don't bother me!

    urusai yatsu 〈うるさいやつ〉 an annoying fellow

    Hae wa urusai. 〈はえはうるさい.〉 Flies are a nuisance.

    Seken-no-kuchi wa urusai. 〈世間の口はうるさい.〉 People will talk.

urusaku 〈うるさく〉 annoyingly, persistently, importunately.

    urusaku-shitsumon-suru 〈うるさく質問する〉 trouble ((a person)) with questions

urusa-sô-ni 〈うるさそうに〉 with an annoyed look.

urusagaru 〈うるさがる〉 feel annoyed ((at *or* by)).

urushi 〈うるし：漆〉 (Japanese) lacquer.

urushi-o-nuru 〈漆を塗る〉 lacquer.

urushi-nuri-no 〈漆塗りの〉 lacquered.

uruu-doshi 〈うるうどし：うるう年〉 a leap year.

uruwashii 〈うるわしい：麗しい〉 beautiful, sweet, graceful.

uryô 〈うりょう：雨量〉 the amount of precipitation.

    uryô-kei 〈雨量計〉 a rain gauge

usa 〈うさ：憂さ〉 gloom, sorrow.

    usa o harasu 〈憂さを晴らす〉 dispel one's gloom, drown one's sorrow 〔in wine〕

usa-barashi-ni 〈憂さ晴らしに〉 for diversion, for a change.

usagi 〈うさぎ〉 a rabbit, a hare.

usan-kusai 〈うさんくさい：うさん臭い〉 suspicious-looking.

usan-kusa-sô-ni 〈うさん臭そうに〉 suspiciously.

useru 〈うせる〉 disappear, vanish; be missing, be lost.

    Kie-usero! 〈消えうせろ.〉 Get out of my sight!

usetsu 〈うせつ：右折〉

    Usetsu-kinshi. 〈右折禁止.〉 No right turn.

usetsu-suru 〈右折する〉 turn to the right.

ushi 〈うし：牛〉a cow, a bull, an ox; cattle.

    ushi-goya〈牛小屋〉 a cowshed

ushinau 〈うしなう：失う〉lose, miss.

    kibô o ushinau〈希望を失う〉 lose one's hope

    ryôshin-o-ushinau〈両親を失う〉 lose one's parents, become an orphan

    shiryoku-o-ushinau〈視力を失う〉 lose one's sight, be deprived of one's sight

    iro-o-ushinau〈色を失う〉 lose color, turn pale

ushiro 〈うしろ：後ろ〉the back, the rear.

ushiro-no 〈後ろの〉back, rear.

    ushiro-no zaseki〈後ろの座席〉 the back seat

ushiro-ni or *ushiro-o* 〈後ろに，後ろを〉at the back ((of)), behind, backward.

    doa-no-ushiro-ni〈ドアの後ろに〉 behind the door

ushiro-kara 〈後ろから〉from behind.

    ushiro-kara-tsuite-iku〈後ろから付いて行く〉 go behind, follow

ushiro-date 〈うしろだて：後ろ盾〉backing, support; a supporter, a patron.

ushiro-date-ni-naru 〈後ろ盾になる〉back up, support.

ushiro-gami 〈うしろがみ：後ろ髪〉

ushiro-gami-o-hikareru-omoi-ga-suru 〈後ろ髪を引かれる思いがする〉feel as if one's heart were left behind.

ushiro-gurai 〈うしろぐらい：後ろ暗い〉underhand, shady.

    nani-ka-ushiro-gurai-koto-o-yatte-iru〈何か後ろ暗いことをやっている〉 be engaged in something underhand

ushiro-mae 〈うしろまえ：後ろ前〉

ushiro-mae-ni 〈後ろ前に〉with the front side back.

ushirometai 〈うしろめたい：後ろめたい〉have a guilty conscience.

ushiro-muki 〈うしろむき：後ろ向き〉

ushiro-muki-ni-naru 〈後ろ向きになる〉turn one's back ((upon)).

ushiro-sugata 〈うしろすがた：後ろ姿〉one's rear view.

ushiro-yubi 〈うしろゆび：後ろ指〉

    Ushiro-yubi-o-sasare-nai-yô-ni-shi-nasai.〈後ろ指を差されないようにしなさい。〉 Keep yourself above suspicion.

uso 〈うそ〉a lie, (a) falsehood.

    mottomo-rashii uso〈もっともらしいうそ〉 a plausible lie

    tsumi-no-nai uso〈罪のないうそ〉 a white lie

uso-happyaku-o-naraberu〈うそ八百を並べる〉 tell a pack of lies

uso-hakken-ki〈うそ発見器〉 a lie detector

uso-tsuki〈うそつき〉 a liar

uso-o-tsuku〈うそをつく〉 lie, tell a lie.

usseki〈うっせき：うっ積〉

usseki-suru〈うっ積する〉 be pent up.

usseki-shita〈うっ積した〉 pent-up.

ussō〈うっそう〉

ussō-taru〈うっそうたる〉 thick, dense, luxuriant.

ussō-to〈うっそうと〉 thickly, densely, luxuriantly.

ussura(-to)〈うっすら（と）〉 faintly, slightly, lightly.

Yane-ni-ussura-to-yuki-ga-tsumotte-iru.〈屋根にうっすらと雪が積もっている。〉 The roof is slightly white with snow.

usu〈うす〉 a mortar, a hand mill.

usu-〈うす-：薄-〉

usu-cha-iro〈薄茶色〉 light brown

usu-midori〈薄緑〉 light green

usu-murasaki〈薄紫〉 light purple

usu-akari〈うすあかり：薄明かり〉 dim light, twilight.

usu-bi〈うすび：薄日〉 thin sunlight.

Usu-bi ga sashiteiru.〈薄日がさしている。〉 The sun is shedding soft beams of light.

usu-geshō〈うすげしょう：薄化粧〉(a) light makeup.

usu-geshō-suru〈薄化粧する〉 do a little makeup.

usu-geshō-shita〈薄化粧した〉 lightly-powdered.

usu-gi〈うすぎ：薄着〉a light dress, thin clothing.

usu-gi-suru〈薄着する〉 be thinly dressed.

usu-gitanai〈うすぎたない：薄汚い〉 filthy, dirty, untidy, grubby, slovenly.

usu-goori〈うすごおり：薄氷〉 thin ice.

usu-goori-ga-haru〈薄氷が張る〉 be covered with thin ice

usu-gumori〈うすぐもり：薄曇り〉

Usu-gumori-da.〈薄曇りだ。〉 It's a little cloudy.

usu-gurai〈うすぐらい：薄暗い〉 dim, gloomy.

usu-gurai-tokoro-de〈薄暗い所で〉 in the gloom

usu-guraku-naru〈薄暗くなる〉 get dark.

usui〈うすい：薄い〉 thin, weak, light, faint.

usui kami〈薄い紙〉 thin paper

　　　usui cha〈薄い茶〉 weak tea

　　　iro-ga-usui〈色が薄い〉 be light in color

　usuku〈薄く〉 thinly, weakly, lightly, faintly.

　　　usuku-kiru〈薄く切る〉 cut ((meat)) thin, slice

usu-kawa〈うすかわ：薄皮〉a thin skin, a film, a thin layer, a thin membrane.

usu-kimi(-no)-warui〈うすきみ(の)わるい：薄気味(の)悪い〉weird, uncanny, eerie.

usu-me〈うすめ：薄目〉

　usu-me-o-akete miru〈薄目を開けて見る〉look ((at something)) with half-closed eyes.

usu-me〈うすめ：薄め〉comparative thinness.

　usu-me-no〈薄めの〉rather light.

usumeru〈うすめる：薄める〉water down.

usu-mono〈うすもの：薄物〉light stuff, thin silk, a flimsy dress.

usu-moya〈うすもや：薄もや〉a thin mist.

usuppera〈うすっぺら：薄っぺら〉

　usuppera-na or *usupperai*〈薄っぺらな，薄っぺらい〉thin, sleazy; shallow, superficial, frivolous.

usuragu〈うすらぐ：薄らぐ〉

　　　Itami ga usuragu.（痛みが薄らぐ．）The pain mitigates.

　　　Kyômi ga usuragu.（興味が薄らぐ．）one's interest flags

usura-samui〈うすらさむい：薄ら寒い〉chilly.

usuusu〈うすうす：薄々〉

　usuusu-kanzuite-iru〈薄々感付いている〉get an inkling ((of)).

usu-warai〈うすわらい：薄笑い〉a faint smile, a half-smile.

uta〈うた：歌〉a song, a poem.

　　　uta o utau〈歌を歌う〉 sing a song

　　　uta o tsukuru〈歌を作る〉 write(*or* compose) a song(*or* a poem)

utagai〈うたがい：疑い〉(a) doubt, a question, (a) suspicion.

　　　utagai o idaku〈疑いを抱く〉 have a doubt ((about, as *or* to)), have a suspicion ((that)).

　　　utagai o maneku〈疑いを招く〉 incur suspicion

　　　utagai o harasu〈疑いを晴らす〉 clear up ((a person's)) doubts, dispel suspicion

　　　utagai-no-me-de miru〈疑いの目で見る〉 regard ((something)) with suspicion

　utagai-bukai〈疑い深い〉doubting, distrustful, suspicious.

utagai-mo-naku〈疑いもなく〉without doubt.

utagau〈うたがう：疑う〉doubt, suspect.

　　utagau-yochi-ga-nai（疑う余地がない）there is no room for doubt ((that))

　　Jibun-no mimi o utagatta.（自分の耳を疑った.）I could hardly believe my ears.

sukoshi-mo-utagawazu-ni〈少しも疑わずに〉without the least suspicion.

utagawashii〈うたがわしい：疑わしい〉doubtful, questionable, uncertain, unreliable, suspicious.

　　utagawashii ten（疑わしい点）a doubtful point

utagawashi-sô-ni〈疑わしそうに〉doubtfully, incredulously, suspiciously.

uta-goe〈うたごえ：歌声〉a singing voice.

utai〈うたい：謡〉an *utai*, chanting (of) a *No(h)* text.

utai-monku〈うたいもんく：謳い文句〉a catchword, a catchphrase.

uta-kai-hajime〈うたかいはじめ：歌会始め〉the New Year Poetry Party held at the Imperial Court.

utata-ne〈うたたね：うたた寝〉a nap, a doze.

utata-ne-suru〈うたた寝する〉take a nap, nap, fall into a doze, doze.

utau〈うたう：歌う〉sing.

utau〈うたう〉declare, express; extol.

utchari〈うっちゃり：打っちゃり〉

utchari-o-kuwasu〈うっちゃりを食わす〉betray ((a person)) at the last moment.

uten〈うてん：雨天〉rainy weather, a rainy day.

　　uten-tsuzuki（雨天続き）continued rainy weather

　　uten-taisô-jô（雨天体操場）a gymnasium

uten-no-baai-wa〈雨天の場合は〉if it rains.

uten-no-tame〈雨天のため〉owing to the rain.

utoi〈うとい：疎い〉

seji-ni-utoi〈世事に疎い〉know little of the world.

utonjiru〈うとんじる：疎んじる〉

yo-ni utonjirareru〈世に疎んじられる〉be neglected by the world.

utouto(-to)〈うとうと（と）〉drowsily.

utouto-suru〈うとうとする〉doze (off).

utsu〈うつ：打〔撃〕つ〉strike, hit, beat, knock; fire, shoot; move, impress.

　　atama-o-utsu（頭を打つ）strike ((a person)) on the head

　　sokkyû o utsu（速球を打つ）hit a fast ball

　　　　taiko o utsu（太鼓を打つ）　beat a drum
　　　　go-ji o utsu（五時を打つ）　strike five
　　　　Ute!（撃て．）　Fire!
　　　　kokoro-o-utsu（心を打つ）　impress ((a person))
　　　　　　kokoro-o-utareru（心を打たれる）　be touched ((by))
　　　　soba o utsu（そばを打つ）　make buckwheat vermicelli
　　　　ami o utsu（網を打つ）　cast a net
　　　　hito-shibai-utsu（一芝居打つ）　play a trick ((on))
　　　　dempô o utsu（電報を打つ）　send a wire
　　　　chûsha o utsu（注射を打つ）　give ((a person)) an injection

utsubo〈うつぼ〉a moray.

utsubuse〈うつぶせ：うつ伏せ〉
　utsubuse-ni-naru〈うつ伏せになる〉lie on one's face.

utsukushii〈うつくしい：美しい〉beautiful, pretty, lovely, fine, good-looking, noble.
　　　　sugata-no-utsukushii（姿の美しい）　shapely
　　　　kokoro-no-utsukushii（心の美しい）　noble-minded
　utsukushiku〈美しく〉beautifully, prettily, sweetly.
　　　　utsukushiku ki-kazaru（美しく着飾る）　dress oneself colorfully
　utsukushisa〈美しさ〉beauty.

utsumuki〈うつむき〉
　utumuki-ni〈うつむきに〉on one's face.
　utsumuku〈うつむく〉look down, hang one's head.
　　　　utsumuite-aruku（うつむいて歩く）　walk keeping one's head slightly down

utsuri〈うつり：写(映)り〉a reflection.
　　　　Kanojo-wa shashin-utsuri-ga-ii.（彼女は写真写りがいい．）She is photogenic.

utsuri-gi〈うつりぎ：移り気〉
　utsuri-gi-na〈移り気な〉capricious, fickle, whimsical.

utsuri-kawari〈うつりかわり：移り変わり〉(a) change, (a) transition.
　　　　yo no utsuri-kawari（世の移り変わり）　the changes of the times

utsuro〈うつろ〉
　utsuro-na〈うつろな〉hollow, vacant, blank.
　　　　utsuro-na koe（うつろな声）　a hollow voice
　　　　utsuro-na me（うつろな目）　vacant eyes

utsuru〈うつる：映(写)る〉be reflected, be taken; match, become.
　　　　kosui-ni-utsutte-iru Fuji-san（湖水に映っている富士山）　Mt. Fuji

which is reflected in the lake

Kono iro wa anata-ni yoku utsuru. （この色はあなたによく映る.） This color matches you well.

utsuru 〈うつる：移る〉 move ((to)), remove ((to)); catch, be infected; pass ((into *or* to)), turn ((to)); spread ((to)).

Tôkyô-ni-utsuru （東京に移る） move to Tokyo

kanojo no kaze ga utsuru （彼女の風邪が移る） catch cold from her

hanashi ga utsuru （話が移る） the conversation turns ((on))

Hi ga tonari-no ie-ni-utsutta. （火が隣の家に移った.） The flames spread to the next house.

utsuri-yasui 〈移りやすい〉 changeable, infectious, contagious.

utsushi 〈うつし：写し〉 a copy, a duplicate.

utsushi-o-toru 〈写しを取る〉 make a copy ((of)), copy.

utsusu 〈うつす：写（映）す〉 copy, take a picture ((of)), project.

nôto o utsusu （ノートを写す） copy one's notebook

shashin o utsushite-morau （写真を写してもらう） have one's picture taken

sukurîn-ni eiga o utsusu （スクリーンに映画を映す） project a motion picture on a screen

utsusu 〈うつす：移す〉 move ((to)), remove ((to)), transfer ((to)); give, infect; empty.

jimu-sho o Tôkyô-ni utsusu （事務所を東京に移す） move one's office to Tokyo

Kanojo-wa watashi-ni kaze o utsushita. （彼女は私に風邪を移した.） She gave me her cold.

mizu o baketsu-kara joro-ni utsusu （水をバケツから如露に移す） empty the water out of a bucket into a watering pot

keikaku o jikkô-ni-utsusu （計画を実行に移す） put a plan into practice

utsuwa 〈うつわ：器〉 a vessel, a receptacle; capacity, ability.

utsuwa-no-ookii hito （器の大きい人） a man of great capacity

utsuwa-no-chiisai hito （器の小さい人） a man of small capacity

Watashi-wa sono-utsuwa-dewa-nai. （私はその器ではない.） I am not equal to it.

uttae 〈うったえ：訴え〉 a (law) suit, an action, a complaint, a charge, an accusation.

uttaeru 〈訴える〉 sue, go to law, appeal ((to)), complain ((of *or* to)), resort ((to)).

　　　seron-ni uttaeru〈世論に訴える〉 appeal to the public opinion
　　　keisatsu-ni uttaeru〈警察に訴える〉 complain to the police office
　　　zutsû o uttaeru〈頭痛を訴える〉 complain of a headache
　　　wanryoku-ni uttaeru〈腕力に訴える〉 resort to violence
　uttaerareru〈訴えられる〉be accused ((of)).

utte-deru〈うってでる：打って出る〉
　seikai-ni-utte-deru〈政界に打って出る〉enter upon a political career.

utte-kawaru〈うってかわる：打って変わる〉change completely.
　utte-kawatta〈打って変わった〉completely changed.
　～-to-wa-utte-kawatte〈～とは打って変わって〉so far from... .

uttetsuke〈うってつけ：打って付け〉
　uttetsuke-no〈打って付けの〉most suitable.
　　　uttetsuke-no shigoto（打って付けの仕事） the work best suited for a
　　　person
　　　Kare-wa sono yaku-ni-wa uttetsuke-no hito da.（彼はその役には打って
　　　付けの人だ。）He is just the man for the position.

uttori〈うっとり〉
　uttori-suru〈うっとりする〉be enraptured, be enchanted.
　uttori-shita〈うっとりした〉enraptured, rapt.
　uttori-to〈うっとりと〉with rapture, with rapt attention.

uttôshii〈うっとうしい〉depressing, dull.
　　　uttôshii tenki（うっとうしい天気） depressing weather

uwa-baki〈うわばき：上履き〉slippers.

uwa-be〈うわべ：上辺〉the surface, appearance.
　　　uwa-be o kazaru（上辺を飾る） keep up appearances
　uwa-be-no〈上辺の〉surface, seeming.
　uwa-be-dake-de〈上辺だけで〉by mere appearances.
　uwa-be-dake-wa〈上辺だけは〉on the surface, to all appearances.

uwa-gaki〈うわがき：上書き〉an address.
　uwa-gaki-o-kaku〈上書きを書く〉address〔a letter〕.

uwagi〈うわぎ：上着〉a coat, a jacket.
　　　uwagi o kiru（上着を着る） put on a coat
　　　uwagi o nugu（上着を脱ぐ） take off a coat

uwagoto〈うわごと：うわ言〉
　uwagoto-o-iu〈うわ言を言う〉talk in delirium.

uwa-gusuri(-o-kakeru)〈うわぐすり（をかける）：うわぐすり（を掛ける）〉
　glaze, enamel.

uwa-gutsu〈うわぐつ：上靴〉slippers, house shoes.

uwaki 〈うわき：浮気〉
    uwaki-mono（浮気者） a flirt
  uwaki-suru〈浮気する〉 be unfaithful to one's husband(*or* wife).
  uwaki-na〈浮気な〉 fickle, inconstant.
uwamae 〈うわまえ：上前〉 a percentage, a commission.
    uwamae o haneru（上前をはねる） take off a percentage ((from)), pocket a kickback
uwa-mawaru 〈うわまわる：上回る〉 exceed, be more ((than)).
uwa-me 〈うわめ：上目〉
  uwa-me-o-tsukau〈上目を使う〉 cast an upward glance, look at ((a person)) from under one's eyeblows.
uwa-muki 〈うわむき：上向き〉 an upward tendency, an upturn, an uptrend.
  uwa-muki-ni-naru〈上向きになる〉 have a rising tendency, look up, go upward.
uwa-no-sora 〈うわのそら：上の空〉
  uwa-no-sora-de〈上の空で〉 halfheartedly, absentmindedly, inattentively.
      hito-no hanashi-o-uwa-no-sora-de-kiku（人の話を上の空で聞く） be inattentive to a person's talk
uwa-nuri 〈うわぬり：上塗り〉
  uwa-nuri-o-suru〈上塗りをする〉 give the final coating 〔of paint〕.
      haji-no-uwa-nuri-o-suru（恥の上塗りをする） add shame to a shame
uwappari 〈うわっぱり：上っ張り〉 overalls, a wrapper, a smock.
uwasa 〈うわさ〉 a rumor, gossip.
      uwasa-ga-tatsu（うわさが立つ） the rumor is abroad that...
      uwasa o tateru *or* uwasa o hiromeru（うわさを立てる，うわさを広める） spread a rumor
      uwasa o hitei-suru（うわさを否定する） deny the rumor
      uwasa o momi-kesu（うわさをもみ消す） stifle the rumor
      ne-mo-ha-mo-nai uwasa（根も葉もないうわさ） a groundless rumor
      Uwasa-o-sureba-kage.（うわさをすれば影。） Talk of the devil, and he is sure to appear.
      Hito-no-uwasa-mo-shichi-jû-go-nichi.（人のうわさも七十五日。） A wonder lasts but nine days.
  uwasa-o-suru〈うわさをする〉 rumor, gossip about.
  uwasa-ni-naru or uwasa-ni-noboru〈うわさになる，うわさに上る〉 be gossiped about.
  uwasa-o-kiku〈うわさを聞く〉 hear of.

Sono-go kare-no-uwasa-wa-kiki-masen.（その後彼のうわさは聞きません。） He has not been heard of since.

～-to-iu-uwasa-da.〈～といううわさだ。〉 It is said that... .

uwa-shiki〈うわしき：上敷き〉a carpet, a sheet, a mat.

uwa-suberi〈うわすべり：上滑り〉

uwa-suberi-na〈上滑りな〉shallow, superficial.

uwatchôshi〈うわっちょうし：上っ調子〉

uwatchôshi-na〈上っ調子な〉flippant, frivolous.

uwate〈うわて：上手〉

uwate-de-aru〈上手である〉be superior ((to)), be better ((than)), be more skillful ((than)).

uwatsuita〈うわついた：浮ついた〉frivolous, flighty.

uwa-ya〈うわや：上屋〉a shed.

uwa-yaku〈うわやく：上役〉one's superior.

uwa-zei〈うわぜい：上背〉stature, height.

uwa-zumi〈うわづみ：上積み〉the upper load.

uwa-zumi-suru〈上積みする〉load ((something)) on top ((of)).

uwa-zuru〈うわずる：上擦る〉sound hollow, ring false.

uwazutta〈上擦った〉excited, hollow-sounding.

uyamau〈うやまう：敬う〉respect, show respect ((for)).

kami o uyamau（神を敬う） worship God

uyamau-beki〈敬うべき〉respectable, venerable.

uyamuya〈うやむや〉

uyamuya-ni-owaru（うやむやに終わる） end in smoke

uyamuya-ni-shite-oku（うやむやにしておく） leave ((a matter)) undecided

uyauyashii〈うやうやしい：恭しい〉respectful, reverent.

uyauyashiku〈恭しく〉respectfully, reverently.

uyauyashiku-ichirei-suru（恭しく一礼する） make a respectful bow

uyoku〈うよく：右翼〉the right wing, a rightist; the right field.

uyoku-shu（右翼手） a right fielder

uyoku-teki(-na)〈右翼的(な)〉right-wing.

uyo-kyokusetsu〈うよきょくせつ：う余曲折〉

ikuta-no uyo-kyokusetsu-o-hete（幾多のう余曲折を経て）after many turns and twists.

uyouyo〈うようよ〉in swarms.

uyouyo-shite-iru〈うようよしている〉swarm ((with)), teem ((with)), be crowded ((with)), be lousy ((with)).

uyouyo-to 〈うようよと〉 in swarms.

uzu(-maki) 〈うず(まき)：渦(巻き)〉 a whirlpool, an eddy, a maelstrom.

uzu-o-maku or *uzu-maku* 〈渦を巻く，渦巻く〉 whirl, eddy, swirl, curl.

uzuku 〈うずく〉 ache, smart, tingle, throb with pain, fester.

uzukumaru 〈うずくまる〉 crouch, squat down.

uzumoreru 〈うずもれる〉 be buried; live in obscurity.

　　yuki-ni uzumoreru〈雪にうずもれる〉 be buried under snow

　　inaka-ni uzumoreru〈田舎にうずもれる〉 bury oneself in the country

uzura 〈うずら〉 a quail.

uzu-shio 〈うずしお：渦潮〉 an eddying current, whirling waves.

uzu-takaku 〈うずたかく〉

uzu-takaku-tsumu〈うずたかく積む〉 pile up high, be piled high ((with)).

uzuuzu 〈うずうず〉

uzuuzu-suru〈うずうずする〉 have an itch ((to do)), be impatient ((to do)) be burning with a desire ((to do)).

W

wa 〈わ：和〉 the sum, the total; peace, harmony, unity.

　　ni-to-ni-no wa wa yon.（二と二の和は四.） The sum of two and tw is four.

　　wa-o-musubu（和を結ぶ） make peace ((with))

wa 〈わ：輪〉 a circle, a ring, a link, a wheel, a hoop, a loop.

　　wa o kaku（輪をかく） describe a circle

　　wa o tsukuru（輪を作る） form a circle

　　wa-ni-natte odoru（輪になって踊る） dance in a circle

wa 〈わ〉 a bundle.

　　maki-go-wa（まき五わ） five bundles of firewood

wâ 〈わあ〉 Hurrah! / Hurray! / Oh! / Wow!

wabi 〈わび〉 an apology, an excuse.

　　　o-wabi no tegami（おわびの手紙）　a letter of apology

wabiru〈わびる〉apologize.

　　　go-busata-o-wabiru（ごぶさたをわびる）　apologize to ((a person)) for one's long silence

wabishii〈わびしい〉lonely, miserable, wretched.

　　　wabishii seikatsu（わびしい生活）　a lonely life

wabishiku〈わびしく〉solitarily, miserably.

waboku〈わぼく：和睦〉peace, reconciliation.

　　waboku-suru〈和睦する〉make peace ((with)), be reconciled ((with)).

wabun〈わぶん：和文〉Japanese.

　　　wabun-eiyaku（和文英訳）　translation from Japanese into English, Japanese-English translation

wadai〈わだい：話題〉a topic.

　　　wadai-ga-hôfu-de-aru（話題が豊富である）　have an ample store of topics

　　　wadai-ni-noboru（話題に上る）　become the topic of one's conversation

　　　wadai o kaeru（話題を変える）　change the subject

wadakamari〈わだかまり〉troubles, ill feeling, grudge, reserve.

　　　wadakamari o suteru（わだかまりを捨てる）　put ill feeling aside, throw off reserve

　　wadakamari-ga-aru〈わだかまりがある〉be troubled in mind, bear ill feeling ((against)).

wa-ei〈わえい：和英〉Japanese-English.

　　　wa-ei-jiten（和英辞典）　a Japanese-English dictionary

wafû〈わふう：和風〉Japanese style.

　　　wafû-ryôri（和風料理）　Japanese dishes

wafuku〈わふく：和服〉Japanese clothes, a *kimono*.

　　　wafuku-ni-ki-gaeru（和服に着替える）　change into a *kimono*

waga〈わが：我が〉my, our, one's own.

　　　waga-ya（我が家）　my home

　　　waga kuni（我が国）　our country

　　　waga michi o iku（我が道を行く）　go one's own way

waga-mama〈わがまま：我がまま〉selfishness, willfulness, caprice.

　　waga-mama-na〈我がままな〉selfish, willful, capricious.

　　　waga-mama-na kodomo（我がままな子供）　a spoilt child, a willful child

　　waga-mama-ni〈我がままに〉selfishly, willfully, waywardly.

kodomo o waga-mama-ni-sodateru〔子供を我がままに育てる〕 pamper one's child

waga-mi〈わがみ：我が身〉oneself.

Waga-mi-o-tsunette hito-no-itasa-o-shire.〔我が身をつねって人の痛さを知れ。〕 Judge (of) others' feelings by your own.

waga-mono-gao〈わがものがお：我が物顔〉

waga-mono-gao-ni〈我が物顔に〉as if it were one's own.

wagi〈わぎ：和議〉negotiations for peace; composition.

wagi no shinsei〔和議の申請〕 application for composition

wa-giri〈わぎり：輪切り〉

wa-giri-ni-suru〈輪切りにする〉cut in round slices.

wagō〈わごう：和合〉harmony, concord, unity.

wagô-suru〈和合する〉harmonize ((with)), be in accord ((with)).

wagô-shite〈和合して〉in (perfect) harmony.

wa-gomu〈わゴム：輪ゴム〉a rubber band.

wahei〈わへい：和平〉peace.

wahei-kôshô〔和平交渉〕 peace negotiations

wahō〈わほう：話法〉narration, speech.

waidan〈わいだん：わい談〉a filthy(*or* an indecent) talk, smut.

waidan-o-suru〈わい談をする〉have an indecent talk.

waikyoku〈わいきょく：わい曲〉distortion.

waikyoku-suru〈わい曲する〉distort.

wairo〈わいろ：賄ろ〉bribery, a bribe.

wairo o tsukau〔賄ろを使う〕 offer a bribe

wairo o toru〔賄ろを取る〕 accept a bribe

wairo-no-kiku〈賄ろの効く〉bribable, corruptible.

wairo-no-kika-nai〔賄ろの効かない〕 unbribable, incorruptible

waisetsu〈わいせつ〉obscenity, indecency.

waisetsu-kôi〔わいせつ行為〕 an indecent act

waisetsu-na〈わいせつな〉obscene, indecent.

waishatsu〈ワイシャツ〉a shirt.

waishatsu-ji〔ワイシャツ地〕 shirting

waiwai(-to)〈わいわい(と)〉noisily, clamorously, boisterously.

waiwai-sawagu〈わいわい騒ぐ〉make much noise, be noisy.

wajutsu〈わじゅつ：話術〉the art of conversation.

waka〈わか：和歌〉a 31-syllable Japanese poem, *tanka* poetry.

wakaba〈わかば：若葉〉young leaves, fresh verdure.

waka-fûfu〈わかふうふ：若夫婦〉a young couple.

waka-gaeri 〈わかがえり：若返り〉 restoration of youth, rejuvenation.
    waka-gaeri no hiketsu〈若返りの秘けつ〉 the secret of rejuvenation
waka-gaeru〈若返る〉 grow younger.
waka-gaetta-ki-ga-suru〈若返った気がする〉 feel oneself young again.
waka-ge〈わかげ：若気〉youthful spirit.
waka-ge-no-itari-de-aru〈若気の至りである〉be too young and thoughtless.
waka-gi〈わかぎ：若木〉a young tree, a sapling.
waka-hage〈わかはげ：若はげ〉premature baldness.
wakai〈わかい：若い〉young; low.
    wakai hito〈若い人〉 a young person
    Kanojo-wa watashi-yori-mittsu-wakai.（彼女は私より三つ若い.） She is three years younger than I.
    ki-ga-wakai（気が若い） be young in spirit
    wakai bangô（若い番号） a low number
wakai-toki-ni〈若い時に〉when young.
wakai-uchi-ni〈若いうちに〉while young.
wakaku〈若く〉
    toshi-no-wari-ni wakaku-mieru（年の割に若く見える） look young for one's age
wakai〈わかい：和解〉reconciliation, amicable settlement, composition.
wakai-suru〈和解する〉make peace ((with)), be reconciled ((with)), come to terms ((with)), make a composition ((with)).
wakajini〈わかじに：若死に〉early death.
waka-jini-suru〈若死にする〉die young.
waka-kusa〈わかくさ：若草〉young grass.
waka-me〈わかめ：若め〉*wakame* seaweed.
waka-me〈わかめ：若芽〉young buds, fresh shoots, sprouts.
waka-mono〈わかもの：若者〉the young.
wakarazu-ya〈わからずや：分からず屋〉an obstinate person.
wakare〈わかれ：別れ〉parting, separation, farewell.
    wakare no tsurasa（別れのつらさ） the wrench of parting
    wakare-o-oshimu（別れを惜しむ） be loath to part ((from))
    kanashii wakare（悲しい別れ） a sad separation
    wakare-no-akushu-o-suru（別れの握手をする） shake ((a person's)) hand and say goodbye
wakare-banashi〈わかればなし：別れ話〉
Wakare-banashi-ga-mochi-agatte-iru.〈別れ話が持ち上がっている.〉They

are thinking of getting divorced.

wakare-me 〈わかれめ：別れ目〉a parting of the ways; a turning point.

wakare-michi 〈わかれ道：別れ道〉a branch road, a forked road, a crossroads.

wakareru 〈わかれる：分か(別)れる〉branch off ((from)), diverge, be divided; part ((from or with)), separate, be separated, divorce.

    Koko-de michi wa futatsu-ni wakareru.（ここで道は二つに分かれる.）
      Here the road breaks into two.

    iken-ga-wakareru（意見が分かれる）be divided in opinion

    tomodachi-to eki-mae-de wakareru（友達と駅前で別れる）part from
      a friend in front of the station

    tsuma to wakareru（妻と別れる）divorce one's wife

wakarewakare 〈わかれわかれ：別れ別れ〉

    wakarewakare-ni kurasu（別れ別れに暮らす）live separately

    wakarewakare-ni-naru（別れ別れになる）become separated (each
      other)

wakari 〈わかり：分かり〉understanding, comprehension.

    wakari-ga-hayai（分かりが早い）be quick of understanding

    wakari-ga-osoi（分かりが遅い）be slow of understanding

wakari-kitta 〈わかりきった：分かり切った〉plain, obvious, evident, self-evident.

    wakari-kitta koto（分かり切った事）a plain fact

wakari-yasui 〈わかりやすい：分かりやすい〉easy to understand.

wakari-yasuku 〈分かりやすく〉simply, plainly.

    wakari-yasuku-ieba（分かりやすく言えば）to speak in plain language

wakari-nikui 〈分かりにくい〉hard to understand.

wakaru 〈わかる：分かる〉understand, get, see; be sensible, have sense; appreciate; know, can tell, learn, prove ((to be)); recognize; find; be announced.

    Watashi-no-itte-iru-koto-ga-wakarimasu-ka?（私の言っていることが分
      かりますか.）Can you understand me?

    Wakarimashita.（分かりました.）I see. / I get you.

    Kanojo-wa mono-ga-wakaru.（彼女は物が分かる.）She has good
      sense.

    Kanojo-wa jōdan-ga-wakara-nai.（彼女は冗談が分からない.）She has
      no sense of humor.

    ongaku-ga-wakaru（音楽が分かる）have an ear for music

    Watashi-wa e-ga-wakara-nai.（私は絵が分からない.）I am no judge

of pictures.

Dô-shitara-ii-ka-wakara-nai.（どうしたらいいか分からない.） I am at a loss what to do.

Hitome-mireba wakaru.（一目見れば分かる.） I can tell it on sight.

Uwasa wa jijitsu-mukon-de-aru-koto-ga-wakatta.（うわさは事実無根であることが分かった.） The rumor turned out to be groundless.

Kore-kara-saki　nani-ga-okiru-ka-wakara-nai.（これから先何が起きるか分からない.） There is no telling what may happen from now on.

Watashi-ga-sugu-wakarimashita-ka?（私がすぐ分かりましたか.） Did you recognize me at once?

Sono-ie-wa-sugu-wakarimasu-yo.（その家はすぐ分かりますよ.） You will find the house easily.

Shiken no seiseki wa wakarimashita-ka?（試験の成績は分かりましたか.） Were the results of the examination announced?

waka-sa〈わかさ：若さ〉youth, youthfulness.

waka-sa o tamotsu（若さを保つ） remain one's youthfulness

waka-shiraga〈わかしらが：若白髪〉

Kanojo-wa waka-shiraga-da.（彼女は若白髪だ.） She has gray hair, while she is still young.

wakasu〈わかす：沸かす〉boil, heat.

furo o wakasu（風呂を沸かす） heat the bath

cha-o-wakasu（茶を沸かす） make tea

waka-te〈わかて：若手〉a young person, a young(er) member.

wakawakashii〈わかわかしい：若々しい〉youthful, young, fresh.

wakawakashii-kao-o-shita〈若々しい顔をした〉fresh-faced.

waka-zô〈わかぞう：若造〉a stripling.

waka-zukuri〈わかづくり：若作り〉

waka-zukuri-o-suru〈若作りをする〉make oneself up to look young, wear a young dress.

wake〈わけ：訳〉(a) meaning; (a) reason, (a) cause, ground(s); circumstances, the case.

wake-o-tazuneru（訳を尋ねる） inquire into the reason

wake o hanasu（訳を話す） tell the reason ((why))

Sore-niwa wake-ga-aru.（それには訳がある.） There is a reason for it.

Kô-iu-wake-nano-desu.（こういう訳なのです.） This is how it is.

wake-no-wakatta hito（訳の分かった人） a sensible person

wake-no-wakara-nai-koto-o-iu（訳の分からないことを言う） talk

nonsense

Kibishiku ko-goto-o-iwa-nai-wake-ni-ika-nai.〈厳しく小言を言わないわけにいかない。〉 I cannot help speaking severely to him.

kô-iu-wake-de〈こういう訳で〉for this reason.

wake-ga-atte〈訳があって〉for certain reasons.

aru-wake-ga-atte（ある訳があって）for a certain reason

wake-mo-naku〈訳もなく〉without reason.

kô-iu-wake-da-kara〈こういう訳だから〉such being the case.

sô-iu-wake-nara〈そういう訳なら〉if that is the case, if so.

wake-au〈わけあう：分け合う〉share ((something)) with ((a person)).

wake-hedate〈わけへだて：分け隔て〉

wake-hedate-suru〈分け隔てする〉discriminate ((against, between *or* in favor of)).

wake-hedate-naku〈分け隔てなく〉without discrimination, impartially.

wake-mae〈わけまえ：分け前〉a share, a portion.

wake-mae-ni-azukaru（分け前にあずかる）take one's share ((in)), have a share ((in))

wake-mae o toru（分け前を取る）take one's share

wake-mae o yôkyû-suru（分け前を要求する）claim a share ((in)), claim one's portion ((of))

wake-me〈わけめ：分け目〉

tenka-wake-me-no tatakai（天下分け目の戦い）a life-and-death battle

wake-nai〈わけない：訳ない〉easy, simple.

Sô-suru-no-wa-wake-nai.（そうするのは訳ない.）It is quite easy to do it.

wake-naku〈訳なく〉easily, with ease, without difficulty.

wakeru〈わける：分ける〉divide, part, separate, distribute ((among)), divide ((among)), share, classify.

kami o mannaka-de wakeru（髪を真ん中で分ける）part one's hair in the middle

kenka o wakeru（けんかを分ける）separate the fighting persons

rieki o wakeru（利益を分ける）share the profits among themselves

waki〈わき〉the side, the other way, another place.

waki o miru（わきを見る）look the other way

hanashi-o-waki-e-sorasu（話をわきへそらす）turn the subject in another direction

waki-ni〈わきに〉by, by the side ((of)), beside, aside.

waki-ni oku（わきに置く）lay aside

waki-ni yoru〈わきに寄る〉step aside

waki-aiai〈わきあいあい：和気あいあい〉

waki-aiai-taru〈和気あいあいたる〉harmonious, happy, peaceful.

waki-aiai-taru katei（和気あいあいたる家庭）a happy home

waki-aiai-to-shite〈和気あいあいとして〉harmoniously, peacefully.

waki-bara〈わきばら：わき腹〉one's side.

waki-bara-ga-itamu（わき腹が痛む）have a pain in one's side

waki-deru〈わきでる：わき出る〉gush out.

waki-ga〈わきが〉the (offensive) smell of the armpit, body odor.

waki-ga-ga-hidoi（わきがひどい）have a strong body odor

waki-ga-dome（わきが止め）an underarm deodorant

waki-ge〈わきげ：わき毛〉underarm hair.

waki-kaeru〈わきかえる：沸き返る〉boil up; seethe, be in an uproar, be in a ferment.

wakimae〈わきまえ〉discretion.

wakimae-no-aru〈わきまえのある〉discreet, sensible, well-mannered.

wakimae-no-nai（わきまえのない）indiscreet, thoughtless, ill-mannered

zengo-no-wakimae-mo-naku〈前後のわきまえもなく〉thoughtlessly, without thinking of the consequence.

wakimaeru〈わきまえる〉know, discern.

waki-me〈わきめ：わき目〉

waki-me-mo-furazu-shigoto-o-suru〈わき目も振らず仕事をする〉devote oneself closely to one's work.

waki-mi〈わきみ：わき見〉

waki-mi-suru〈わき見する〉look away.

waki-michi〈わきみち：わき道〉a byroad, a side road; a digression.

hanashi-ga-waki-michi-e-soreru（話がわき道へそれる）wander from the subject

waki-mizu〈わきみず：わき水〉spring water.

waki-no-shita〈わきのした：わきの下〉the armpit.

waki-no-shita-ni ase-o-kaku（わきの下に汗をかく）sweat under one's arms

waki-no-shita-o kusuguru（わきの下をくすぐる）tickle ((a person)) under his arm

waki-tatsu〈わきたつ：沸き立つ〉boil up, stir.

waki-yaku〈わきやく：わき役〉a supporting role; a supporting player.

waki-yaku-o-tsutomeru〈わき役を務める〉play a supporting part.

wakkusu(-o-nuru) 〈ワックス(をぬる)：ワックス(を塗る)〉 wax.

waku 〈わく：枠〉 a frame, a tambour, a rim; a limit.
    waku-nai-de (枠内で)   within the limit ((of))

waku 〈わく：沸く〉 boil, grow hot.
    Furo-ga-waita. (風ろがわいた.)   The bath is ready.

waku 〈わく〉 gush out, spring; grow, breed.
    Watashi-no-mune-ni kibō ga waite-kita. (私の胸に希望がわいてきた.)
       Hope sprang in my breast.
    Uji-ga-waita. (うじがわいた.)   Maggots have bred.

wakuchin 〈ワクチン〉 vaccine.
    shōni-mahi-wakuchin (小児麻ひワクチン)   a polio vaccine
    wakuchin-o-chūsha-suru 〈ワクチンを注射する〉 vaccinate.

wakusei 〈わくせい：惑星〉 a planet.

wakuwaku 〈わくわく〉
    wakuwaku-suru 〈わくわくする〉 get nervous, be excited.
    Yorokobi-de mune ga wakuwaku-shita. (喜びで胸がわくわくした.)
       My heart throbbed with joy.
    wakuwaku-shite 〈わくわくして〉 trembling 〔with joy〕.

wameki 〈わめき〉
    wameki-goe (わめき声) a shout, a yell, a scream, a shriek
    wameki-tateru 〈わめき立てる〉 bawl out.

wameku 〈わめく〉 cry, yell, shout, shriek, scream.

wamman 〈ワンマン〉 an autocrat.
    Uchi-no shachō wa wamman-da. (うちの社長はワンマンだ.)   Our
       president runs a one-man business.
    wamman basu (ワンマンバス)   a one-man bus

wampaku 〈わんぱく：腕白〉
    wampaku-kozō (腕白小僧)   a naughty boy, an imp, an urchin
    wampaku-na 〈腕白な〉 naughty, mischievous.

wampīsu 〈ワンピース〉 a one-piece dress.

wan 〈わん：湾〉 a bay, a gulf, an inlet.
    Ōsaka-wan (大阪湾)   Osaka Bay
    Mekishiko-wan (メキシコ湾)   the Gulf of Mexico

wan 〈わん〉 bowwow.
    wan-to-naku 〈わんと鳴く〉 bark.

wan 〈わん〉 a (wooden) bowl.

wana 〈わな〉 a snare, a trap.
    wana-ni-kakaru (わなに掛かる)   fall into a trap

jibun-no-shikaketa-wana-ni-kakaru〈自分の仕掛けたわなに掛かる〉
be hoist with one's own petard

wana-ni-kakeru〈わなに掛ける〉entrap, ensnare.

wa-nage〈わなげ：輪投げ〉quoits.

wa-nage-o-suru〈輪投げをする〉play quoits

wanawana〈わなわな〉

wanawana-furueru〈わなわな震える〉quiver, tremble.

wani〈わに〉a crocodile, an alligator.

wani-gawa-no-hando-baggu〈わに皮のハンドバッグ〉a crocodile(*or* an alligator) handbag

wankyoku〈わんきょく：湾曲〉a curve, a bend.

wankyoku-suru〈湾曲する〉curve, bend.

wanryoku〈わんりょく：腕力〉physical strength, force, violence.

wanryoku-no-tsuyoi〈腕力の強い〉strong-armed.

wanryoku-de〈腕力で〉by force.

wansa-to〈わんさと〉in great numbers.

wansa-to oshi-yoseru〈わんさと押し寄せる〉come in great numbers, come in crowds, flock, throng

wanshō〈わんしょう：腕章〉an armband, a chevron, an arm badge.

wanshō o tsukeru〈腕章を着ける〉wear an armband

wanwan〈わんわん〉(a) bowwow.

wanwan-hoeru〈わんわんほえる〉bark (bowwow).

waon〈わおん：和音〉a chord.

wappen〈ワッペン〉a badge, a sticker.

wara〈わら〉(a) straw.

wara-yane-no ie〈わら屋根の家〉a straw-thatched house

warabi〈わらび〉a bracken.

warai〈わらい：笑い〉a laugh, laughter, a smile, sneer.

warai o osaeru〈笑いを抑える〉suppress a laugh

warai-ga-tomara-nai〈笑いが止まらない〉cannot stop chuckling

warai-banashi〈笑い話〉a funny story

warai-gao〈笑い顔〉a smiling face

warai-goe〈笑い声〉(a peal of) laughter

warai-jôgo〈笑い上戸〉a laughing drunk

warai-mono-ni-naru〈笑い物になる〉be made a laughingstock ((of)), make oneself a laughingstock

Warai-goto-jâ-nai.〈笑い事じゃあない.〉That is no laughing matter, I tell you.

warai-dasu 〈わらいだす：笑い出す〉 begin to laugh, burst into laughter, burst out laughing.

warai-tobasu 〈わらいとばす：笑い飛ばす〉 laugh away.

warau 〈わらう：笑う〉 laugh, smile, chuckle, grin, sneer ((at)).

    dotto-warau（どっと笑う） burst into a roar of laughter

    hara-o-kakaete-warau（腹を抱えて笑う） be couvulsed with laughter ((at))

    namida-no-deru-hodo-warau（涙の出るほど笑う） laugh oneself into tears

    omowazu-warau（思わず笑う） laugh in spite of oneself

    warawazu-ni-irare-nai（笑わずにいられない） cannot help laughing

    hara-no-naka-de-warau（腹の中で笑う） laugh at ((a person)) behind his back

    Warau-kado-niwa-fuku-kitaru.（笑う門には福来たる.） Laugh and be fat.

warawaseru 〈わらわせる：笑わせる〉 make ((a person)) laugh.

    Warawaseru-ne!（笑わせるね.） That's a laugh!

    Warawaseru-na!（笑わせるな.） Don't make me laugh!

ware 〈われ：我〉 oneself, self.

    ware o wasureru（我を忘れる） forget oneself

    ware-ni-kaeru（我に返る） recover one's senses, come to oneself

ware-nagara 〈我ながら〉 I flatter myself that... , though I say it.

    Ware-nagara yoku-yatta.（我ながらよくやった.） I did it well, though I say it.

    Ware-nagara-hazukashii.（我ながら恥ずかしい.） I am ashamed of myself.

ware-gachi-ni 〈われがちに：我勝ちに〉

ware-gachi-ni-seki-o-arasou〈我勝ちに席を争う〉 scramble for seats.

ware-me 〈われめ：割れ目〉 a crack, a chasm, a split, a crevice.

ware-mono 〈われもの：割れ物〉 a fragile article.

    Ware-mono-chûi.（割れ物注意.） Fragile.

wareru 〈われる：割れる〉 break, be broken, split, be split, crack.

    Koori ga wareru.（氷が割れる.） Ice breaks.

    futatsu-ni wareru（二つに割れる） split in two

    atama-ga-wareru-yô-ni-itamu（頭が割れるように痛む） have a splitting headache

    wareru-yô-na-kassai（割れるような喝采） a storm of applause

wareware 〈われわれ：我々〉

wareware-nihon-jin（我々日本人） we Japanese

wareware-wa *or* wareware-ga（我々は，我々が） we

wareware-no（我々の） our

wareware-ni *or* wareware-o（我々に，我々を） us

wareware-no-mono（我々のもの） ours

wareware-jishin（我々自身） ourselves

wari〈わり：割〉percentage, rate, ratio; profit, gain.

san-wari（三割） thirty percent

ichi-nichi go-hyaku-en no wari de（一日五百円の割で） at the rate of 500 yen a day

wari-ni-au〈割に合う〉pay.

wari-ni-awa-nai（割に合わない） do not pay

wari-no-ii〈割のいい〉profitable, paying.

wari-no-warui（割の悪い） unprofitable

wariai〈わりあい：割合〉proportion, rate, ratio, percentage.

san-tai-ni-no-wariai-de（三対二の割合で） by three to two

wariai-ni〈割合に〉*see.* wari-ni.

wari-ate〈わりあて：割り当て〉assignment, allotment, quota.

wari-ate-seido（割り当て制度） a quota system

wari-ateru〈割り当てる〉assign, allot.

waribashi〈わりばし：割りばし〉half-split chopsticks.

waribiki〈わりびき：割引〉(a) discount, (a) reduction.

waribiki-jôsha-ken（割引乗車券） a reduced fare ticket

waribiki-ken（割引券） a discount ticket

dantai-waribiki-ryôkin（団体割引料金） a group rate

waribiki-tegata（割引手形） a discounted bill

waribiki-suru〈割引する〉discount, make a discount, reduce, give a reduction.

Genkin-de-kaeba ikura-ka waribiki-shimasu-ka?（現金で買えば幾らか割引しますか。） Can you make any discount for cash?

Tairyô-ni-katte-kudasaru-nara, waribiki-shimasu.（大量に買ってくださるなら割引します。） We will give you a reduction, if you buy (it) on a quantity.

hito-no-hanashi o waribiki-shite kiku（人の話を割引して聞く） take what one says with a grain of salt

wari-daka〈わりだか：割高〉

wari-daka-ni-naru〈割高になる〉be rather expensive, be comparatively high in price.

wari-dasu〈わりだす：割り出す〉calculate, infer ((from)), deduce ((from)).

wari-in〈わりいん：割り印〉a tally seal.
> wari-in o osu（割り印を押す）affix one's seal simultaneously at the joining of two papers

wari-kan〈わりかん：割り勘〉an equal split.
> Wari-kan-ni-shiyô.（割り勘にしよう.）Let's go Dutch.

wari-kireru〈わりきれる：割り切れる〉be divisible ((by)), can be divided ((by)).
> *wari-kire-nai*〈割り切れない〉be indivisible ((by)), cannot be divided ((by)); be incomprehensible, be still in doubt ((about *or* on)).
> > wari-kire-nai-mono-ga-nokoru（割り切れないものが残る）leave some room for doubt, be not quite satisfied ((with))

wari-kiru〈わりきる：割り切る〉give a definite solution ((for)).
> warikitta taido（割り切った態度）a businesslike attitude

wari-komu〈わりこむ：割り込む〉squeeze oneself in, break in, intrude into.
> man·in-densha-ni-wari-komu（満員電車に割り込む）squeeze oneself into a crowded car
> retsu-ni-wari-komu（列に割り込む）break into a line

wari-mae〈わりまえ：割り前〉a share, one's lot.
> wari-mae o harau（割り前を払う）pay one's share
> wari-mae o morau（割り前をもらう）get one's share

wari-mashi〈わりまし：割り増し〉an extra (pay), a premium, a bonus.
> wari-mashi-ryôkin（割り増し料金）an extra charge
> wari-mashi-kin-tsuki-saiken（割り増し金付き債券）a premium bond

wari-modoshi(-kin)〈わりもどし（きん）：割り戻し（金）〉(a) rebate, (a) drawback, (a) kickback.
> *wari-modoshi-suru* or *wari-modosu*〈割り戻しする，割り戻す〉rebate, allow a drawback, kickback.

wari-ni〈わりに：割に〉comparatively, rather.
> wari-ni toki-yasui（割に解きやすい）be comparatively easy to solve
> wari-ni-amai（割に甘い）be rather sweet than I expected
> 〜*-no-wari-ni*〈〜の割に〉for, considering, in proportion to, in comparison with.
> > toshi-no-wari-ni wakai（年の割に若い）be young for one's age

wari-tsuke〈わりつけ：割り付け〉layout, casting off.
> *wari-tsukeru*〈割り付ける〉lay out, cast off.

wari-yasu 〈わりやす：割安〉
 wari-yasu-ni-naru 〈割安になる〉 be economical, be a good buy.

wari-zan 〈わりざん：割り算〉 division.
 wari-zan-o-suru 〈割り算をする〉 divide.

waru 〈わる：割る〉 divide, cut; split, chop; break, crack, smash; mix ((whisky)) with water, water down, dilute; drop below.
 Roku-o-san-de-waru-to ni-ga-tatsu.（六を三で割ると二が立つ.） Six divided by three gives two.
 maki o waru（まきを割る） chop wood
 mado-garasu o waru（窓ガラスを割る） smash a windowpane
 Ichi-doru ga ni-hyaku-go-jû-en o waru.（一ドルが二百五十円を割る.） The dollar drops below 250 yen.
 kuchi-o-waru（口を割る） confess

waru-agaki 〈わるあがき：悪あがき〉
 waru-agaki-suru 〈悪あがきする〉 make useless struggling.

warubireru 〈わるびれる：悪びれる〉
 warubirezu-ni 〈悪びれずに〉 without flinching, with calm composure, calmly, with a good grace.

waru-dakumi 〈わるだくみ：悪だくみ〉 wiles, an evil design, a scheme, a plot, an intrigue.
 waru-dakumi-o-suru 〈悪だくみをする〉 plot ((against)), intrigue ((against)).

waru-fuzake 〈わるふざけ：悪ふざけ〉
 waru-fuzake-o-suru 〈悪ふざけをする〉 play a practical joke ((on)).

waru-gashikoi 〈わるがしこい：悪賢い〉 cunning, sly, crafty, wily.

waru-gi 〈わるぎ：悪気〉 ill will, harm, an evil intent, malice.
 Waru-gi-ga-atte-shita-no-dewa-nai.（悪気があってしたのではない.） I meant no harm.
 waru-gi-no-nai 〈悪気のない〉 innocent, good-natured, harmless.

warui 〈わるい：悪い〉 bad, evil, ill, wrong, wicked; harmful, injurious; indisposed, unwell; inferior, of inferior make, coarse; rotten, sour; poor, weak, foul; muddy; unlucky.
 warui-nakama-to-tsuki-au（悪い仲間と付き合う） get into bad company
 warui-koto（悪い事） an evil deed, a wrong, a vice, a crime, a sin
 Uso-o-tsuku-no-wa warui.（うそをつくのは悪い.） It is wrong to tell a lie.
 Watashi-ga warui.（私が悪い.） I am to blame.
 me-ni warui（目に悪い） be bad for the eyes

Doko-ka-warui-no-desu-ka? （どこか悪いのですか.） Is anything the matter with you?

kibun-ga-warui （気分が悪い） feel sick

kao-iro-ga-warui （顔色が悪い） look pale

shinzō-ga-warui （心臓が悪い） be troubled with a weak heart

hinshitsu-ga-warui （品質が悪い） be inferior in quality

Gyūnyū wa atsui-to sugu waruku-naru. （牛乳は暑いとすぐ悪くなる.） The milk soon goes sour in hot weather.

kioku(-ryoku)-ga-warui （記憶(力)が悪い） have a poor memory

Tenki ga waruku-natte-kita. （天気が悪くなってきた.） The weather has turned bad.

warui-michi （悪い道） a bad road

warui shirase （悪い知らせ） ill news

hyōban-ga-warui （評判が悪い） have a bad reputation

Kono-kikai-wa-doko-ka-warui. （この機械はどこか悪い.） Something is wrong with this machine.

waru-jie 〈わるぢえ：悪知恵〉 cunning, craft, wiles.

waru-jie-o-tsukeru 〈悪知恵を付ける〉 abet, put ((a person)) up to.

waru-jie-no-aru 〈悪知恵のある〉 cunning, crafty, sly, wily.

waruku 〈わるく：悪く〉 badly, ill.

hito-o-waruku-omou （人を悪く思う） think ill of others

waruku-toru （悪く取る） take ((it)) amiss

waruku-suru-to 〈悪くすると〉 if the worst comes to the worst.

Waruku-suru-to asu mata yuki-da. （悪くすると明日また雪だ.） I fear it may snow tomorrow again.

warukuchi 〈わるくち：悪口〉 abuse, slander.

warukuchi-o-iu 〈悪口を言う〉 say bad things [about others].

waru-mono 〈わるもの：悪者〉 a bad fellow, a rogue, a rascal, a knave.

hito-o-waru-mono-ni-suru （人を悪者にする） lay the blame on a person

jibun-ga-waru-mono-ni-naru （自分が悪者になる） take the blame on oneself

waru-sa 〈わるさ：悪さ〉

waru-sa o suru 〈悪さをする〉 play a trick ((on)).

warutsu 〈ワルツ〉 a waltz.

warutsu-o-odoru 〈ワルツを踊る〉 dance a waltz.

waru-yoi 〈わるよい：悪酔い〉

waru-yoi-suru 〈悪酔いする〉 be sick from drink, give ((a person)) nasty aftereffects.

waru-zure 〈わるずれ：悪擦れ〉

waru-zure-suru 〈悪擦れする〉 become sophisticated.

wasabi 〈わさび〉 a (Japanese) horseradish, a *wasabi*.

wasabi-ga-kiite-iru （わさびが利いている） be highly seasoned with *wasabi*

wasabi-zuke （わさび漬） *wasabi* preserved in *sake* lees

wasai 〈わさい：和裁〉 Japanese dressmaking.

wase 〈わせ〉 an early-ripening rice plant.

wase-no kankitsu （わせのかんきつ） early oranges

wa-sen 〈わせん：和戦〉

wa-sen-ryôyô-no-kamae-o-suru 〈和戦両様の構えをする〉 be prepared both for war and peace.

waserin 〈ワセリン〉 vaseline.

washi 〈わし：和紙〉 Japanese paper.

washi 〈わし〉 an eagle.

washi-bana （わし鼻） a hooked nose

washi-zukami 〈わしづかみ〉

washi-zukami-ni-suru 〈わしづかみにする〉 grab, clutch.

washo 〈わしょ：和書〉a Japanese book.

washoku 〈わしょく：和食〉 Japanese-style food.

wasô 〈わそう：和装〉

wasô-suru 〈和装する〉 be dressed in a *kimono*.

Wasshoi! 〈わっしょい．〉 Heave-ho!

wasure-gachi 〈わすれがち：忘れがち〉

wasure-gachi-de-aru 〈忘れがちである〉 be apt to forget, easily forget.

wasure-gatami 〈わすれがたみ：忘れ形見〉 one's posthumous child.

wasure-momo 〈わすれもの：忘れ物〉a thing left behind.

O-wasure-mono-no-nai-yô-negaimasu．（お忘れ物のないよう願います．） Please take care nothing to be left behind.

wasurena-gusa 〈わすれなぐさ：わすれな草〉 a forget-me-not.

wasureppoi 〈わすれっぽい：忘れっぽい〉 forgetful.

wasureppoi hito （忘れっぽい人） a forgetful person

wasureppoku-naru 〈忘れっぽくなる〉 become forgetful.

wasureru 〈わすれる：忘れる〉 forget, be forgetful ((of)), live down, slip one's mind; leave ((a thing)) behind.

hito-no namae o wasureru （人の名前を忘れる） forget a person's name

Sonna-koto wa wasure-nasai.（そんなことは忘れなさい.）　Forget it.

Wasure-nai-de-okoshite-kudasai.（忘れないで起こしてください.）
Don't forget to wake me.

wasure-nai-uchi-ni（忘れないうちに）　before one forgets

toki-ga-tatsu-ni-shitagatte-kanashimi-o-wasureru（時がたつに従って悲しみを忘れる）　live down one's sorrow

sake-de-usa-o-wasureru（酒で憂さを忘れる）　drown one's sorrow in wine

Tsukue-no-ue-ni jisho o oki-wasurete-kita.（机の上に辞書を置き忘れてきた.）　I left my dictionary on my desk.

wasurerareta-hito（忘れられた人）　a forgotten man

wasurerare-nai omoi-de（忘れられない思い出）　a lasting memory

wata〈わた：綿〉cotton.

wata-gashi（綿菓子）　cotton candy, spun sugar

wata-ire（綿入れ）　wadded clothes

wata(ku)shi〈わた（く）し：私〉

wata(ku)shi-wa *or* wata(ku)shi-ga（私は，私が）　I

wata(ku)shi-no（私の）　my; private, personal

wata(ku)shi-ni *or* wata(ku)shi-o（私に，私を）　me

wata(ku)shi-no-mono（私のもの）　mine

wata(ku)shi-jishin（私自身）　myself

watari〈わたり：渡り〉

watari-ni-fune（渡りに船）　a timely offer

watari-ni-fune-to-môshi-de-o-ukeru（渡りに船と申し出を受ける）　jump at an offer

watari-o-tsukeru（渡りを付ける）　come in contact ((with)), get in touch ((with))

watari-au〈わたりあう：渡り合う〉argue ((with)), bandy words ((with)).

watari-dori〈わたりどり：渡り鳥〉a migratory bird, a bird of passage, a migrant.

watari-rôka〈わたりろうか：渡り廊下〉a connecting corridor, a breezeway.

watari-zome〈わたりぞめ：渡り初め〉the first crossing of a new bridge.

wataru〈わたる：渡る〉go across, go over, cross; pass into another's hands; be introduced, be brought over; get along, walk through the world.

hashi o wataru（橋を渡る）　cross a bridge

Bukkyô wa itsu Nihon-ni-watatte-kimashita-ka?（仏教はいつ日本に渡

ってきましたか.）　When was Buddhism introduced into Japan?

Wataru-seken-ni-oni-wa-nai.（渡る世間に鬼はない.）　There is kindness to be found everywhere.

ishi-bashi-o-tataite-wataru（石橋をたたいて渡る）　be cautious to timidity

wataru〈わたる〉range ((from A to B *or* over)), extend, cover, span, last, spread ((over)).

sû-mairu-ni-wataru（数マイルにわたる）　extend over several miles

kô-han·i ni wataru（広範囲にわたる）　cover a wide field

sû-seiki-ni-watatte（数世紀にわたって）　for centuries

watashi〈わたし：渡し〉a ferry; delivery.

watashi-de kawa o wataru（渡しで河を渡る）　cross a river by ferry

honsen-watashi（本船渡し）　free on board(F.O.B.)

watasu〈わたす：渡す〉ferry; hand (over) ((to)), turn over, deliver; pay; build, lay, stretch.

kawa-o-fune-de-watasu（河を船で渡す）　ferry ((a person)) across a river

tegami o hito-ni watasu（手紙を人に渡す）　hand a letter to a person

Genkin-hiki-kae-ni gempin o o-watashi-shimasu.（現金引き換えに現品をお渡しします.）　We will deliver the article in exchange for cash.

kyûryô o watasu（給料を渡す）　pay wages

mizo-ni ita o watasu（溝に板を渡す）　lay a plank across a ditch

watto〈ワット〉a watt.

hyaku-watto-no denkyû（百ワットの電球）　a 100-watt bulb

watto〈わっと〉

watto-naki-dasu〈わっと泣き出す〉burst out crying, burst into tears.

wâwâ〈わあわあ〉

wâwâ-iu（わあわあ言う）　talk noisily

wâwâ-naku（わあわあ泣く）　cry noisily, blubber

wayaku〈わやく：和訳〉Japanese translation.

eibun-wayaku（英文和訳）　translation from English into Japanese

wayaku-suru〈和訳する〉translate into Japanese.

wayô-setchû〈わようせっちゅう：和洋折衷〉

wayô-setchû-no〈和洋折衷の〉in semi-Western style.

waza〈わざ：業(技)〉work, a deed; art.

Sore-wa yôi-na waza-dewa-nai.（それは容易な業ではない.）　It is no easy task.

waza o migaku（技をみがく）　improve one's arm

waza-to〈わざと〉on purpose, intentionally, deliberately, knowingly.

waza-to yomi-chigaeru（わざと読み違える）intentionally misread a book

waza-to-rashii〈わざとらしい〉unnatural, artificial, forced.

waza-to-rashii emi（わざとらしい笑み）an artificial smile

wazawai〈わざわい：災い〉(an) evil, (a) misfortune, (a) disaster, a calamity, one's ruin.

wazawai o maneku（災を招く）invite a disaster

wazawai-tenjite fuku-to-nasu（災い転じて福となす）turn a misfortune into a blessing

Kuchi-wa-wazawai-no-moto.（口は災いの元.）Out of the mouth comes evil.

wazawaza〈わざわざ〉on purpose, expressly, specially.

Tooi-tokoro-o-wazawaza-oide-kudasatte-arigatô-gozaimasu.（遠い所をわざわざおいでくださってありがとうございます.）It is very kind of you to come all the way to see me.

wazuka〈わずか〉

wazuka go-jû-en（わずか五十円）only fifty yen

wazuka-ni-nen-no-uchi-ni（わずか二年のうちに）in a mere two years

Gakkô-made hon-no-wazuka-desu.（学校までほんのわずかです.）It is only a step to the school.

wazuka-na〈わずかな〉a few, a little, trifling, slight, mere.

wazuka-na kingaku（わずかな金額）a small sum of money

wazuka-na shûnyû（わずかな収入）a small income

wazuka-na sôi（わずかな相違）a slight difference

wazuka-ni〈わずかに〉only, merely, just, barely.

wazurai〈わずらい：患い〉a sickness, an illness.

naga-no wazurai（長の患い）a long illness

wazurau〈患う〉be sick, suffer ((from)).

mune-o-wazuratte-iru（胸を患っている）suffer from lung disease

wazurawashii〈わずらわしい：煩わしい〉troublesome, annoying, complicated, intricate.

wazurawasu〈わずらわす：煩わす〉bother, trouble, give ((a person)) trouble, annoy, worry.

wehâsu〈ウェハース〉a wafer.

werutâ-kyû〈ウェルターきゅう：ウェルター級〉the welterweight class.

werutâ-kyû-no〈ウェルター級の〉welterweight.

wesuto〈ウェスト〉the waist.

wesuto-no-hosoi 〈ウェストの細い〉 small-waisted.
wômingu-appu 〈ウォーミングアップ〉 warming-up.
wômingu-appu-suru 〈ウォーミングアップする〉 warm up.

Y

ya 〈や：矢〉 an arrow.
　　ya o hanatsu〈矢を放つ〉 shoot an arrow ((at))
　　ya-no-yô-ni hayai〈矢のように速い〉 be as swift as an arrow
　　ya-mo-tate-mo-tamara-nai〈矢も盾もたまらない〉 be dying ((for *or* to do))
　　ya-no-saisoku-o suru〈矢の催促をする〉 press ((a person)) hard ((for))
-ya 〈-や〉 and, or; as soon as.
yâ 〈やあ〉 oh / ah / oh my! / my goodness! / dear me!; hullo / hello / hi.
yaban 〈やばん：野蛮〉
yaban-na〈野蛮な〉 savage, barbarous, uncivilized, rude.
yabo 〈やぼ：野暮〉
yabo-na〈野暮な〉 unrefined, rustic, boorish, senseless.
　　yabo-na koto o iu〈野暮なことを言う〉 say senseless things
yabô 〈やぼう：野望〉 (an) ambition.
yabottai 〈やぼったい：野暮ったい〉 unrefined, uncouth.
yabu 〈やぶ〉 a bush, a thicket, a bamboo grove.
yabu-kara-bô-ni〈やぶから棒に〉 suddenly, abruptly.
yabu-hebi 〈やぶへび：やぶ蛇〉
yabu-hebi-ni-naru-to-ikenai-kara〈やぶ蛇になるといけないから〉 lest it should wake up a sleeping dog.
yabu-isha 〈やぶいしゃ：やぶ医者〉 a quack (doctor).
yabu-ka 〈やぶか：やぶ蚊〉 a striped mosquito.
yabure 〈やぶれ：破れ〉 a tear, a rent.
　　fuku-no yabure o tsukurou〈服の破れを繕う〉 mend a rent in one's

clothes

yabure-kabure〈やぶれかぶれ：破れかぶれ〉

yabure-kabure-ni-naru〈破れかぶれになる〉become desperate.

yabure-kabure-de〈破れかぶれで〉desperately.

yabureru〈やぶれる：破れる〉tear, be torn, rend, be rent, rip, become ragged; break, be broken, burst; wear out, be worn out.

yabureta〈破れた〉torn, ripped, ragged, broken, worn-out.

yabureru〈やぶれる：敗れる〉be beaten.

　　shiai ni yabureru〈試合に敗れる〉lose a game

yabureta〈敗れた〉defeated.

yaburu〈やぶる：破る〉tear, rend, rip; break, destroy, disturb; violate; beat, defeat, whip.

　　yakusoku o yaburu〈約束を破る〉break one's promise

　　dentô o yaburu〈伝統を破る〉break away from the convention

yachin〈やちん：家賃〉a (house) rent.

　　yachin ga agaru〈家賃が上がる〉the rent rises

yachô〈やちょう：野鳥〉a wild bird, wild fowl.

yado〈やど：宿〉lodging, a hotel, an inn, lodgings, rooms.

　　yado-chin〈宿賃〉hotel charges, a hotel bill

　　yado-chô〈宿帳〉a hotel register

yado-o-toru〈宿を取る〉put up ((at)), stay ((at *or* with)).

yadokari〈やどかり〉a hermit crab.

yadori-gi〈やどりぎ：宿り木〉a mistletoe, a parasite.

yadosu〈やどす：宿す〉conceive.

yado-ya〈やどや：宿屋〉*see.* ryokan.

yae-ba〈やえば：八重歯〉a double tooth, an oblique tooth.

yae-zakura〈やえざくら：八重桜〉a double-flowered cherry tree, double cherry blossoms.

yagai〈やがい：野外〉the fields, the open air.

　　yagai-ensô-kai〈野外演奏会〉an open-air concert

yagai-de〈野外で〉in the open air, outdoors.

yagate〈やがて〉soon, shortly, before long, in due course, some time.

yagi〈やぎ〉a goat.

　　ko-yagi〈子やぎ〉a kid

　　yagi-gawa〈やぎ皮〉goatskin, kid

yagô〈やごう：屋号〉a store name; a stage title.

yagu〈やぐ：夜具〉bedclothes, a coverlet, a quilt.

yagura〈やぐら〉a turret, a tower; a scaffold, scaffolding.

yagura-daiko〈やぐら太鼓〉the drum-beating announcing the beginning and the end of the *sumo* matches for the day.

yagyû〈やぎゅう：野牛〉a bison, a buffalo.

yahan〈やはん：夜半〉
　yahan-ni〈夜半に〉at midnight, in the middle of the night.

yahari〈やはり〉too, also, as well, ((not)) either; still; after all; none the less, nevertheless.

yahi〈やひ：野卑〉
　yahi-na〈野卑な〉vulgar, base, mean, low, coarse, gross.
　　yahi-na kotoba（野卑な言葉）coarse language

yahō〈やほう：野砲〉a field gun, field artillery.

yai〈やい〉hi, hey, man, bah.

yaiyai〈やいやい〉
　yaiyai-iu〈やいやい言う〉press ((a person)) hard ((for)), clamor ((against *or* for)).

yaji〈やじ：野次〉rooting, jeering, hooting, interruption.
　yaji-o-tobasu or *yajiru*〈野次を飛ばす，野次る〉jeer ((at)), hoot ((at)), disturb, interrupt.
　　yajiri-taosu（野次り倒す）hoot down

yajiri〈やじり：矢じり〉an arrowhead.

ya-jirushi〈やじるし：矢印〉an arrow.
　　Kono ya-jirushi-no-hôkô-ni-o-susumi-kudasai.（この矢印の方向にお進みください。）Please follow this arrow.

yaji-uma〈やじうま：野次馬〉a curious crowd, curiosity seekers.

yajū〈やじゅう：野獣〉a wild animal.
　yajû-no-yô-na〈野獣のような〉brutal, beastly.

yakai〈やかい：夜会〉an evening party, a ball.
　　yakai-fuku（夜会服）(an) evening dress, (a) party dress

yakamashii〈やかましい〉noisy, boisterous, clamorous; findfaulting, strict, hard, severe, rigid, stringent; particular ((about)); much-discussed.
　　Toori ga yakamashii.（通りがやかましい。）The street is noisy.
　　yakamashii oyaji（やかましいおやじ）a strict father
　　Kare wa yakamashii jôshi ni tsukaeta.（彼はやかましい上司に仕えた。）He served a hard superior.
　　yakamashii kisoku（やかましい規則）stringent rules
　　Kare-wa jikan-ni-yakamashii.（彼は時間にやかましい。）He is a stickler for punctuality.

tabe-mono-ni-yakamashii（食べ物にやかましい）be particular about food

yakamashii mondai（やかましい問題）a much-discussed question

yakamashiku〈やかましく〉noisily, boisterously, clamorously; strictly, severely.

yakamashiku-suru（やかましくする）make a noise, raise a racket

yakamashiku-iu（やかましく言う）find fault ((with)), be strict ((with)), be overnice, be particular ((about))

yakan〈やかん：夜間〉

yakan-hikô（夜間飛行）a night flight

yakan-kimmu（夜間勤務）night duty

yakan-bu（夜間部）the evening session of a school

yakan-ni or *yakan-wa*〈夜間に，夜間は〉at night, in the night.

yakan〈やかん〉a kettle, a teakettle.

yakata-bune〈やかたぶね：屋形船〉a houseboat.

yake(-kuso)〈やけ(くそ)〉desperation, despair.

yake(-kuso)-gimi-de-aru（やけ(くそ)気味である）be a little desperate

yake(-kuso)-ni-naru or *yake(-kuso)-o-okosu*〈やけ(くそ)になる，やけ(くそ)を起こす〉become desperate.

yake(-kuso)-ni-natte or *yake(-kuso)-o-okoshite*〈やけ(くそ)になって，やけ(くそ)を起こして〉in desperation, desperately, recklessly.

yake-ni〈やけに〉desperately, awfully, terribly.

yake-ni samui（やけに寒い）be terribly cold

yake-ato〈やけあと：焼け跡〉the ruins of a fire.

yake-dasareru〈やけだされる：焼け出される〉be burnt out (of house and home).

yakedo〈やけど〉a burn, a scald.

yakedo no ato（やけどの跡）the scar of a burn

yakedo-suru〈やけどする〉get burnt, burn oneself, get scalded.

te o yakedo-suru（手をやけどする）burn one's hand

yakei〈やけい：夜景〉a night view.

yakei〈やけい：夜警〉night watch; a night watchman.

yake-ishi〈やけいし：焼け石〉a hot stone.

Sore-wa yake-ishi-ni mizu-da.（それは焼け石に水だ.）It will be like throwing water on thirsty soil.

yaken〈やけん：野犬〉an ownerless dog.

yaken-gari-o-suru（野犬狩りをする）round up ownerless dogs

yake-nohara〈やけのはら：焼け野原〉a wide stretch of burnt-out area.

yake-nokoru〈やけのこる：焼け残る〉be saved from the flames.

yake-ochiru〈やけおちる：焼け落ちる〉be burnt down, be burnt to the ground.

yakeru〈やける：焼ける〉be burnt, be destroyed by fire, be reduced to ashes; be roasted, be broiled, be baked, be toasted; be sunburnt, be sun-tanned; be discolored.

Pan ga yaketa.（パンが焼けた．）The bread has toasted.

hi-ni-yaketa kao（日に焼けた顔）a sunburnt face

ki-iro-ku-yaketa kami（黄色く焼けた紙）paper tarnished yellow

mune-ga-yakeru（胸が焼ける）have heartburn

yake-shinu〈やけしぬ：焼け死ぬ〉be burnt to death.

yake-tsuku〈やけつく：焼け付く〉

yake-tsuku-yô-na atsusa（焼けつくような暑さ）the parching heat of the sun

yake-tsuku-yô-na taiyô（焼けつくような太陽）a scorching sun

yake-zake〈やけざけ：やけ酒〉

yake-zake-o-nomu〈やけ酒を飲む〉drink out of desperation.

yaki〈やき：焼き〉

Kutani-yaki（九谷焼）Kutani ware

yaki-no-ii〈焼きのいい〉well-tempered.

yaki-no-amai（焼きの甘い）not well-tempered

yaki-ami〈やきあみ：焼き網〉a gridiron.

yakiba〈やきば：焼き場〉a crematory.

yaki-buta〈やきぶた：焼き豚〉roast pork.

yaki-dôfu〈やきどうふ：焼き豆腐〉broiled *tofu*.

yakigushi〈やきぐし：焼きぐし〉a skewer, a spit.

yaki-harau〈やきはらう：焼き払う〉burn down, reduce to ashes.

yaki-imo〈やきいも：焼き芋〉baked sweet potatoes.

yaki-in〈やきいん：焼き印〉a brand.

yaki-in-o-osu〈焼き印を押す〉brand.

yaki-kiru〈やききる：焼き切る〉burn off.

yaki-korosu〈やきころす：焼き殺す〉burn to death.

yaki-mashi〈やきまし：焼き増し〉additional printing〔of a photograph〕.

yaki-mashi-suru（焼き増しする）make an extra print

yaki-meshi〈やきめし：焼き飯〉frizzled rice.

yaki-mochi〈やきもち：焼きもち〉jealousy.

yaki-mochi-yaki（焼きもち焼き）a jealous person

yaki-mochi-o-yaku〈焼きもちを焼く〉be jealous ((of)).

yakimoki〈やきもき〉

  yakimoki-suru〈やきもきする〉be nervous ((about)), worry (oneself) ((about)), be impatient ((about)).

    yakimoki-shite-byōki-ni-naru（やきもきして病気になる）worry oneself ill

yakimono〈やきもの：焼き物〉pottery, porcelain, earthenware; a broiled fish.

yakin〈やきん：夜勤〉night duty, a night shift.

    yakin-o-suru（夜勤をする）take night duty

    yakin-teate（夜勤手当）night-work allowance

yakin(-gaku)〈やきんがく：や金(学)〉metallurgy.

yaki-naoshi〈やきなおし：焼き直し〉rebaking; an adaptation ((from)), a rehash ((of)).

  yaki-naosu〈焼き直す〉bake again; adapt ((from)), rehash.

yaki-niku〈やきにく：焼き肉〉roast meat.

yaki-nori〈やきのり：焼きのり〉toasted laver.

yaki-soba〈やきそば：焼きそば〉chow mein.

yaki-sugiru〈やきすぎる：焼き過ぎる〉overdo, overcook; overprint.

yaki-suteru〈やきすてる：焼き捨てる〉burn up, throw into the fire.

yaki-tate〈やきたて：焼きたて〉

  yaki-tate-no〈焼きたての〉hot from the oven, fresh-baked.

yaki-tori〈やきとり：焼き鳥〉grilled chicken.

yakitsuke〈やきつけ：焼き付け〉enameling; printing.

  yaki-tsukeru〈焼き付ける〉enamel; print.

yaki-tsuku〈やきつく：焼き付く〉be branded on one's mind, be burnt into one's memory.

yaki-tsukusu〈やきつくす：焼き尽くす〉burn up, consume by fire.

yakiuchi〈やきうち：焼き討ち〉

  yakiuchi-suru〈焼き討ちする〉attack ((a building)) with fire, set ((a house)) on fire.

yaki-zakana〈やきざかな：焼き魚〉broiled fish.

yakka-daigaku〈やっかだいがく：薬科大学〉a college of pharmacy.

yakkai〈やっかい：厄介〉(a) trouble, annoyance, a burden; dependence, care.

    yakkai-goto（厄介事）a troublesome thing, a trouble, a burden, a difficulty

    yakkai-mono（厄介者(物)）a bother, a nuisance, a handful, a white elephant, a dependent, a hanger-on yakkai-barai-o-suru〈厄介払いをする〉 get rid of a nuisance

yakkai-o-kakeru〈厄介を掛ける〉 trouble, give ((a person)) trouble.

yakkai-ni-naru〈厄介になる〉depend ((on)), be dependent ((on)), stay ((with)), live ((on)), be in trouble ((with)).

yakkai-ni-nara-nai（厄介にならない） be independent ((of)), be self-reliant, stand on one's own legs

yakkai-na〈厄介な〉 troublesome, annoying, burdensome, difficult.

yakkan〈やっかん：約款〉an agreement, a stipulation, a clause.

yakke〈ヤッケ〉a parka.

yakki〈やっき：躍起〉

yakki-ni-naru〈躍起になる〉become excited ((over)), get heated ((over)), become eager, grow desperate.

yakki-ni-natte〈躍起になって〉eagerly, frantically, desperately.

yakki-ni-natte benkai-suru（躍起になって弁解する） excuse oneself with heat

yakko-san〈やっこさん〉the fellow, the chap, the guy.

yakkyō〈やっきょう：薬きょう〉a cartridge (case).

yakkyoku〈やっきょく：薬局〉a pharmacy, a drugstore, a chemist's shop; a pharmacist's office, a (doctor's) medicine room.

yakō〈やこう：夜行〉

yakō-ressha（夜行列車） a night train

yakō-sei-no〈夜行性の〉nocturnal.

yakō-sei-no dōbutsu（夜行性の動物） a nocturnal animal

yakō〈やこう：夜光〉

yakō-dokei（夜光時計） a watch with luminous hands and dial

yakō-toryō（夜光塗料） a luminous paint

yakō-chū（夜光虫） a noctiluca

yaku〈やく：厄〉a calamity, an evil, ill luck.

yakubi（厄日） an unlucky day

yaku-doshi（厄年） an unlucky year(*or* age)

yaku〈やく：役〉an office, a post; duty, a part; a role; use, service, help, assistance.

yaku-ga-tsutomaru（役が勤まる） be fit for the post

Rōjin-tachi-no-sewa-o-suru-no-ga watashi-no yaku-desu.（老人たちの世話をするのが私の役です。） It is my duty to look after the old.

Oferia no yaku o tsutomeru（オフェリアの役を務める） play the role of Ophelia

yaku-ni-tatsu〈役に立つ〉be useful, be serviceable, be helpful, be of use ((for *or* to)), help, serve, do.

　totemo-yaku-ni-tatsu（とても役に立つ）be of great use ((for *or* to))

　O-yaku-ni-tateba　shiawase-desu.（お役に立てば幸せです。）I should
　　be happy to be of any service to you.

yaku-ni-tata-nai〈役に立たない〉be useless, be unserviceable, be of no
　use, be of no service, be of no avail.

　amari-yaku-ni-tatanai（余り役に立たない）go for little

yaku〈やく：訳〉(a) translation, (a) version.

　Kanojo-no-yaku-wa-umai.（彼女の訳はうまい。）Her translation is
　　well done. / She is a good translator.

yaku〈やく：焼く〉burn; roast, broil, bake, toast; make; cremate; print.

　pan o yaku（パンを焼く）bake bread

　sumi o yaku（炭を焼く）make charcoal

　te-o-yaku（手を焼く）burn one's fingers, be unable to control

yaku-〈やく-：約-〉about, some, nearly, or so, almost.

　yaku go-mêtoru（約五メートル）about five meters

　yaku-ni-shûkan（約二週間）two weeks or so

yakuba〈やくば：役場〉an office.

　machi-yakuba（町役場）a town office

yaku-barai〈やくばらい：厄払い〉

yaku-barai-suru〈厄払いする〉exorcize, drive away evils.

yakubun〈やくぶん：訳文〉a translation, a version.

yakubun〈やくぶん：約分〉reduction of a fraction to the lowest term(s).

yakubun-suru〈約分する〉reduce.

yakubutsu〈やくぶつ：薬物〉medicines, drugs, medical substances.

　yakubutsu-chûdoku（薬物中毒）medicinal poisoning

yakubyô-gami〈やくびょうがみ：疫病神〉a pest, a plague.

　yakubyô-gami-ni　tori-tsukareru（疫病神に取り付かれる）be seized by
　　a plague

yakudô〈やくどう：躍動〉

yakudô-suru〈躍動する〉move lively, stir, throb.

yakugaku〈やくがく：薬学〉pharmacy, pharmacology.

　yakugaku-ka（薬学科）the pharmaceutical department

yakugara〈やくがら：役柄〉one's role, the nature of one's part.

yakugo〈やくご：訳語〉words used in translation, an equivalent.

　tekitô-na　Nihon-go-no　yakugo（適当な日本語の訳語）a proper
　　Japanese equivalent

yakuhin〈やくひん：薬品〉a drug, (a) medicine.

kagaku-yakuhin（化学薬品） chemicals

yakuhon〈やくほん：訳本〉a translation.

yakuin〈やくいん：役員〉an officer, an official, the board, the staff; a director, an executive.

    yakuin-kai（役員会） a meeting of officers

    yakuin-shitsu（役員室） an executive office

yakujo〈やくじょ：躍如〉

  yakujo-taru〈躍如たる〉vivid, lifelike, graphic.

    Kare-no-memboku-yakujo-taru-mono-ga-atta.（彼の面目躍如たるものが
    あった.） It was just like him.

yakujō-sho〈やくじょうしょ：約定書〉a (written) contract, an a-greement, a pact.

yakume〈やくめ：役目〉a duty, an office, a business.

    yakume o hatasu（役目を果たす） do one's duties

yakumi〈やくみ：薬味〉spices.

    yakumi-ire（薬味入れ） a cruet, a caster

yakunin〈やくにん：役人〉a government official, a public official.

yakusatsu〈やくさつ：やく殺〉

  yakusatsu-suru〈やく殺する〉strangle ((a person)) to death.

yakuseki-kô-naku〈やくせきこうなく：薬石効無く〉in spite of all the medical treatment.

yakusha〈やくしゃ：訳者〉a translator.

yakusha〈やくしゃ：役者〉a player, an actor, an actress.

    senryô-yakusha（千両役者） a star actor

    yakusha-ga-ichi-mai-ue-de-aru （役者が一枚上である） be a cut above
    ((a person)) [in ability]

yakushin〈やくしん：躍進〉a rush, a dash, rapid progress.

  yakushin-suru〈躍進する〉rush ((at *or* for)), make a dash ((at *or* for)), make rapid progress.

yakusho〈やくしょ：役所〉a government office, a public office.

  yakusho-ni-tsutomeru〈役所に勤める〉serve in an office.

yakusô〈やくそう：薬草〉a medical herb.

yakusoku〈やくそく：約束〉a promise, an engagement, an appointment, a date, an agreement, a bargain.

    yakusoku o tori-kesu（約束を取り消す） call off one's engagement

    San-ji-ni yakusoku-ga-aru.（三時に約束がある.） I have an engage-ment at three.

    yakusoku-no-jikan-ni-okureru（約束の時間に遅れる） lose one's

appointment

yakusoku-suru〈約束する〉promise, make a promise, make an appointment ((with)), agree ((upon)).

yakusoku-doori-ni〈約束どおりに〉according to one's promise, as promised.

yakusoku-no-jikan-ni〈約束の時間に〉at the appointed time.

~-to-iu-yakusoku-de〈～という約束で〉on condition that... .

yakusu〈やくす：訳す〉translate.

Eigo o seikaku-na-Nihon-go-ni yakusu〈英語を正確な日本語に訳す〉translate English into Japanese exactly

Tsugi-no bun o Nihon-go-ni yakushi-nasai.〈次の文を日本語に訳しなさい。〉Put the following into Japanese.

yakusū〈やくすう：約数〉a measure, a divisor.

yakutoku〈やくとく：役得〉a perquisite, an emolument.

yakutoku o uru〈役得を得る〉gain a perquisite

yakuwari〈やくわり：役割〉a part, a role, a cast.

jūdai-na yakuwari o enjiru〈重大な役割を演じる〉play an important part ((in))

yakuyō〈やくよう：薬用〉

yakuyō-arukōru〈薬用アルコール〉medicinal alcohol

yakuyō-sekken〈薬用石けん〉medicated soap

yakuyô-no〈薬用の〉medicinal, medical.

yaku-yoke〈やくよけ：厄よけ〉

yaku-yoke-no-o-mamori〈厄よけのお守り〉a talisman to keep off evils

yaku-yoke-ni-naru〈厄よけになる〉ward off evil fortune, protect ((a person)) from evils

yakuza〈やくざ〉a gangster, a trash, a hooligan.

yakuzai〈やくさい：薬剤〉a medicine, a drug.

yakuzai-shi〈薬剤師〉a pharmacist, a druggist, a chemist

yaku-zuki〈やくづき：役付き〉a responsible person.

kaisha-de yaku-zuki-ni-naru〈会社で役付きになる〉get a responsible post in a firm

yakyoku〈やきょく：夜曲〉a nocturne.

yakyū〈やきゅう：野球〉baseball.

yakyū-o-suru〈野球をする〉play baseball

yama〈やま：山〉a mountain, a peak, a hill; a heap, a pile; (a) speculation, an adventure; the climax, the end.

yama ni noboru〈山に登る〉 climb a mountain

yama o oriru〈山を下りる〉 descend a mountain

yama no chōjō〈山の頂上〉 the summit of a mountain

yama no fumoto-ni〈山のふもとに〉 at the foot of a mountain

yama-no-chūfuku-ni〈山の中腹に〉 on the mountain side

yama-no-ooi chihō〈山の多い地方〉 a mountainous country

yama-no-yô-na oo-nami〈山のような大波〉 mountainous waves

yama-nobori〈山登り〉 mountain climbing

yama-goya〈山小屋〉 a mountain hut

yama-oku-ni〈山奥に〉 in the heart of a mountain

yama-kuzure〈山崩れ〉 a landslide, a landfall

Yama ga atatta.〈山が当たった。〉 The speculation has turned out well.

Yama ga hazureta.〈山が外れた。〉 The speculation has failed.

Koko-ga kono shôsetsu no yama-da.〈ここがこの小説の山だ。〉 This is the climax of this novel.

yama-to-tsumu or *yama-zumi-ni-suru*〈山と積む，山積みにする〉 heap, pile.

yama-o-kakeru〈山を掛ける〉 speculate ((in)), take a chance, gamble.

yamaarashi〈やまあらし：山荒し〉 a porcupine, a hedgehog.

yamabiko〈やまびこ：山びこ〉 an echo.

yama-biraki〈やまびらき：山開き〉 the opening of a mountain to climbers.

yamabuki〈やまぶき〉 a Japanese rose.

yamabuki-iro〈やまぶき色〉 bright yellow

yama-dori〈やまどり：山鳥〉 a copper pheasant.

yamagara〈やまがら〉 a Japanese titmouse.

yamai〈やまい：病〉 a disease, (an) illness.

Yamai-wa-kuchi-kara.〈病は口から。〉 Food is the source of all diseases.

Yamai-wa-ki-kara.〈病は気から。〉 The mind rules the body.

yama-inu〈やまいぬ：山犬〉 a wild dog; a Japanese wolf, a coyote.

yama-kaji〈やまかじ：山火事〉 a forest fire.

yamakan〈やまかん：山勘〉

yamakan-de〈山勘で〉 by guess, at a venture, on speculation.

yama-ke〈やまけ：山気〉 a speculative disposition.

yama-ke-ga-aru〈山気がある〉 have a speculative disposition

yama-ke-o-dasu〈山気を出す〉 be tempted to speculate.

yama-mori 〈やまもり：山盛り〉

oo-saji-ni-yama-mori-ippai-no-satô（大さじに山盛り一杯の砂糖） a full tablespoonful of sugar

yama-mori-ni-suru〈山盛りにする〉heap up.

chawan ni gohan-o-yama-mori-ni-suru（茶わんに御飯を山盛りにする） heap a bowl with rice

yama-neko〈やまねこ：山猫〉a wildcat, a lynx.

yama-neko-sôgi（山猫争議） a wildcat strike

yama-no-imo〈やまのいも：山の芋〉a yam.

yama-no-te〈やまのて：山の手〉the hilly sections, the residential sections, uptown, the Bluff.

yama-shi〈やまし：山師〉a speculator, a mountebank, a swindler; a miner.

yamashii〈やましい〉have a feeling of shame, have a guilty conscience.

yamashii-tokoro-wa-nani-hitotsu-nai（やましいところは何一つない） have nothing to be ashamed of, have a clear conscience

yama-wake〈やまわけ：山分け〉an equal division.

yama-wake-suru〈山分けする〉go halves ((with)), go fifty-fifty ((with)), divide equally ((between, among *or* with)).

yamayama〈やまやま：山々〉

O-ai-shi-tai-no-wa-yamayama-desu-ga〜.（お会いしたいのは山々ですが〜.） I should very much like to go and see you, but... .

yama-zakura〈やまざくら：山桜〉a wild cherry tree, wild cherry blossoms.

yameru〈やめる〉stop, cease, discontinue, break off, lay off, bring ((something)) to an end, put an end ((to)); give up, quit, abandon; abolish, do away ((with)).

hanashi o yameru（話をやめる） stop talking

shigoto o yameru（仕事をやめる） leave off work

tori-hiki o yameru（取り引きをやめる） close an account ((with))

sake o yameru（酒をやめる） give up drinking

tochû-de gakkô o yameru（途中で学校をやめる） quit school halfway

isha o yamete hôritsu-o-yaru（医者をやめて法律をやる） abandon one's medical profession for law

furui kanshû o yameru（古い慣習をやめる） abolish an old usage

yameru〈やめる：辞める〉resign, retire ((from)), leave.

kômu-in-o-yameru（公務員を辞める） retire from government service

kaisha o yameru（会社を辞める） leave a company

yamesaseru〈やめさせる〉stop, cure, put an end ((to)).

 tabako-o-yamesaseru（タバコをやめさせる）make ((a person)) give up smoking

 kenka-o-yamesareru（けんかをやめさせる）put an end to a quarrel, make up a quarrel

yamesaseru〈やめさせる：辞めさせる〉dismiss.

 shoku-o-yamesaseru（職を辞めさせる）dismiss ((a person)) from office

yami〈やみ〉darkness, the dark.

 yami-ni-tsutsumareru（やみに包まれる）be shrouded in darkness

 Issun-saki-wa-yami.（一寸先はやみ.）Who knows what may happen tomorrow?

 yami-kara-yami-ni-hômuru（やみからやみに葬る）hush up

 yami-yo（やみ夜）a pitch-dark night, a moonless night

 yami-busshi（やみ物資）black-market goods

 yami-ne（やみ値）a black-market price

 yami-tori-hiki（やみ取引）black-marketing

  yami-tori-hiki-o-suru（やみ取引をする）black-marketeer

 yami-ni-magirete〈やみに紛れて〉under cover of darkness.

yami-agari〈やみあがり：病み上がり〉

 yami-agari-de mada karada-ga-yowatte-iru〈病み上がりでまだ体が弱っている〉be still weak from one's recent illness.

yamitsuki〈やみつき：病み付き〉

 Kare-wa gorufu-ga-yamitsuki-ni-natte-iru.（彼はゴルフが病み付きになっている.）He is infatuated with playing golf.

yami-uchi〈やみうち：やみ討ち〉a surprise attack.

 yami-uchi-o-kuu〈やみ討ちを食う〉be attacked unawares.

yamome〈やもめ〉a widow.

 otoko-yamome（男やもめ）a widower

yamori〈やもり〉a gecko.

yamu〈やむ：病む〉be taken ill.

 ki-o-yamu（気を病む）worry ((about))

yamu〈やむ〉stop, cease, calm down, drop, lull, end, cease, be over.

 ame-ga-yamu（雨がやむ）stop raining

 Arashi ga yanda.（あらしがやんだ.）The storm has calmed down.

yamu-o-enai〈やむをえない：やむを得ない〉be necessary, be unavoidable, be inevitable.

 yamu-o-enai jijô（やむを得ない事情）unavoidable circumstances

Sore-wa yamu-o-enai.〈それはやむを得ない.〉 It can't be helped.

yamu-o-ezu〈やむを得ず〉 inevitably, from necessity, reluctantly, against one's will.

yamu-o-ezu～(-suru)〈やむを得ず～（する）〉 be compelled ((to do)), be forced ((to do)), be obliged ((to do))

yanagi〈やなぎ：柳〉a willow.

yancha〈やんちゃ〉

yancha-bôzu〈やんちゃ坊主〉 a mischievous boy, an urchin

yancha-na〈やんちゃな〉mischievous, naughty.

yane〈やね：屋根〉a roof.

yane-ura〈屋根裏〉 a garret, an attic

yane-o-fuku〈屋根をふく〉roof.

yani〈やに〉resin, nicotine.

yani-ga-tamaru〈やにがたまる〉 be choked with nicotine

yani-sagaru〈やにさがる：やに下がる〉look complacent.

yaniwa-ni〈やにわに〉suddenly, immediately, instantly.

yanushi〈やぬし：家主〉the owner of a house, a landlord, a landlady.

yanwari(-to)〈やんわり（と）〉softly, gently.

yan·ya-to〈やんやと〉with applause, loudly, enthusiastically.

yan·ya-to kassai-suru〈やんやと喝采する〉 applaud loudly

yanyô-shô〈やにょうしょう：夜尿症〉enuresis, bed-wetting.

yaochô〈やおちょう：八百長〉a put-up job.

yaochô-jiai〈八百長試合〉 a fixed game, a put-up game

yaochô-o-yaru〈八百長をやる〉fix a fight.

ya-omote〈やおもて：矢面〉

ya-omote-ni-tatsu〈矢面に立つ〉bear the brunt ((of)), become the target ((of)).

yao-ya〈やおや：八百屋〉a greengrocer; a vegetable store, a greengrocer's.

yappari〈やっぱり〉*see*. yahari.

-yara〈-やら〉

Naku-yara-wameku-yara kanojo-wa oo-sawagi-o-shita.（泣くやらわめくやら彼女は大騒ぎをした.） She made a scene, crying and screaming.

yuki-yara-kaze-yara-de（雪やら風やらで） what with the snow and (what with) the wind

Takagi-to-yara-iu-hito（高木とやらいう人） a certain Mr. Takagi

dare-yara-san（だれやらさん） Mr. what's-his-name

Kanojo-wa-dô-shite-iru-no-yara.〔彼女はどうしているのやら。〕 How is she getting on, I wonder?

yarareru〈やられる〉be beaten; be struck, be shot; be wounded; be killed, be done for; be stolen; be deceived, be outwitted; have an attack ((of)).

yare〈やれ〉oh, ah.

yareyare〈やれやれ〉

Yareyare, yatto sunda.〔やれやれ，やっと済んだ。〕 Well, well, I've done it at last.

yareyare-to-omou〔やれやれと思う〕 feel relieved, breathe again

yari〈やり〉a spear, a lance, a javelin.

yari-de-tsuku〈やりで突く〉spear, lance.

yari-au〈やりあう：やり合う〉have a quarrel ((with)), argue ((with)).

yari-ba〈やりば：やり場〉

Watashi-wa me-no-yari-ba-ni-komatta.〔私は目のやり場に困った。〕 I did not know which way to look.

yari-dama〈やりだま：やり玉〉a victim, a sacrifice.

yari-dama-ni-ageru〈やり玉に挙げる〉make ((a thing *or* a person)) the object of attack, make a victim ((of)), make an example ((of)).

yari-ika〈やりいか〉a squid.

yari-kaesu〈やりかえす：やり返す〉retort, answer back.

yari-kakeru〈やりかける〉begin to do, make a beginning.

ano-otoko-wa yari-kaketara-saigo〔あの男はやりかけたら最後〕 once he begins to do anything

yari-kaketa or *yari-kake-no*〈やりかけた，やりかけの〉unfinished, half-done.

yari-kaketa shigoto〔やりかけた仕事〕 work in hand

yari-kanenai〈やりかねない〉

Kare-nara donna-koto-de-mo-yari-kanenai.〔彼ならどんな事でもやりかねない。〕 He dares to do anything.

yarikata〈やりかた：やり方〉a way of doing, a method, how to do, a course, a process.

Hito-sorezore-no-yarikata-ga-aru.〔人それぞれのやり方がある。〕 Everybody has his own way of doing.

Sore-wa kimi-no-yarikata-shidai-da.〔それは君のやり方次第だ。〕 It depends on how you do it.

yari-kirenai〈やりきれない：やり切れない〉cannot stand, be unbearable ((to)).

Kono-atsusa-dewa-mattaku-yari-kirenai.（この暑さでは全くやり切れない。） I can't really stand this heat.

yari-komeru 〈やりこめる：やり込める〉 put ((a person)) to silence, talk ((a person)) down.

yari-konasu 〈やりこなす〉 manage 〔a difficult task〕.

yarikuri 〈やりくり：やり繰り〉 makeshift, management.

yarikuri-ga-umai （やり繰りがうまい） be a good manager

yarikuri-suru 〈やり繰りする〉 make (a) shift ((with *or* without)).

sukunai-shūnyū-de   yarikuri-shite-iku （少ない収入でやり繰りしていく） make shift with a small income

jikan-o-yarikuri-suru （時間をやり繰りする） manage time ((to do))

yari-nage 〈やりなげ：やり投げ〉 javelin throw.

yari-nage-no-senshu （やり投げの選手） a javelin thrower

yari-nage-o-suru 〈やり投げをする〉 throw a javelin.

yari-naoshi 〈やりなおし：やり直し〉 redoing.

yari-naosu 〈やり直す〉 do over again, start over again, begin all over again, make a fresh start.

yari-nikui 〈やりにくい〉 difficult to do, delicate.

yari-nuku 〈やりぬく：やり抜く〉 carry ((a thing)) through, accomplish, achieve.

yarippanashi 〈やりっぱなし：やりっ放し〉

yarippanashi-ni-suru 〈やりっ放しにする〉 leave ((a thing)) half-done.

yarippanashi-ni-shite 〈やりっ放しにして〉 without finishing.

yari-sokonai 〈やりそこない：やり損ない〉 a failure, a miss, a blunder, a botch, a slip-up.

yari-sokonau 〈やり損なう〉 fail ((in)), make a blunder, make a botch ((of)).

yari-sugiru 〈やりすぎる：やり過ぎる〉 overdo, go too far; give too much.

yari-sugosu 〈やりすごす：やり過ごす〉 wait till ((a person)) goes past ((one)).

yarite 〈やりて：やり手〉 a person of ability, a shrewd person, a go-getter.

yari-togeru 〈やりとげる：やり遂げる〉 *see*. yari-toosu.

yari-toosu 〈やりとおす：やり通す〉 carry out(*or* through).

yari-tori 〈やりとり：やり取り〉

kotoba-no-yari-tori-o-suru （言葉のやり取りをする） talk back and forth

tegami-no-yari-tori-o-suru （手紙のやり取りをする） exchange letters

((with))

yari-tsukeru〈やりつける：やり付ける〉be used ((to do *or* to doing)).

    yari-tsuketa shigoto（やりつけた仕事）the work one is used to do, the work familiar to one

yari-yasui〈やりやすい〉easy to do.

yarō〈やろう：野郎〉a fellow, a guy, a rogue, a blighter.

    Kono-yarō!（この野郎。）You rascal!

yaru〈やる〉give, let ((a person)) have; do, try, set about, carry on; play; act; hold; run, keep; have, eat, drink.

    sen-en yaru（千円やる）give ((a person)) 1,000 yen

    Nani-o-yatte-irunda?（何をやっているんだ。）What are you doing?

    umaku yaru（うまくやる）do well

    dô-nika-kô-nika-yaru（どうにかこうにかやる）manage to do ((something))

    Yareru-mono-nara-yatte-miro.（やれるものならやってみろ。）I dare you to do it.

    shigoto o yatte-shimau（仕事をやってしまう）get the work finished

    tenisu o yaru（テニスをやる）play tennis

    Hamuretto-o-yaru（ハムレットをやる）play the part of Hamlet

    Koma-gekijô-dewa nani o yatte-imasu-ka?（コマ劇場では何をやっていますか。）What is on now at the Koma Theater?

    o-cha-no-kai o yaru（お茶の会をやる）give a tea party

    sentaku-ya o yaru（洗濯屋をやる）run a laundry

    Ippai-yari-masen-ka?（一杯やりませんか。）Won't you have a drink?

    yaraseru〈やらせる〉make ((a person)) do, compel ((a person)) to do, allow ((a person)) to do.

-yaru〈－やる〉do ((for a person)).

    hito-ni hon o katte-yaru（人に本を買ってやる）buy a book for a person

yâru〈ヤール〉a yard.

yaruse-nai〈やるせない：やる瀬ない〉disconsolate, dreary, wretched.

    yaruse-nai-omoi-o-suru〈やる瀬ない思いをする〉feel disconsolate.

ya-sagashi〈やさがし：家捜し〉a house searching.

    ya-sagashi-suru〈家捜しする〉search a house.

yasai〈やさい：野菜〉vegetables, greens.

    yasai o tsukuru（野菜を作る）grow vegetables

    yasai-batake（野菜畑）a vegetable garden

    yasai-ryôri（野菜料理）a vegetable dish

yasashii 〈やさしい：優しい〉 gentle, tender, mild, affectionate, kind.

    ki-date-no-yasashii 〈気立ての優しい〉 sweet-tempered, kindhearted

    me-tsuki-no-yasashii 〈目付きの優しい〉 gentle-eyed

yasashiku 〈優しく〉 gently, tenderly, affectionately, kindly.

    yasashiku-suru 〈優しくする〉 be affectionate ((to)), be kind ((to))

yasashi-sa 〈優しさ〉 tenderness, kindness.

yasashii 〈やさしい：易しい〉 easy, simple.

yasashiku 〈易しく〉 easily, simply.

yasechi 〈やせち：やせ地〉 barren land.

yase-gaman 〈やせがまん：やせ我慢〉

yase-gaman-o-suru 〈やせ我慢をする〉 endure ((something)) from pride.

yase-hosoru 〈やせほそる：やせ細る〉 lose flesh, become thin.

yasei 〈やせい：野生〉 wildness.

yasei-suru 〈野生する〉 grow wild, live in the wild state.

yasei-ka-suru 〈野生化する〉 become feral.

yasei-no 〈野生の〉 wild.

    yasei-no dôbutsu 〈野生の動物〉 a wild animal

yasei(-mi) 〈やせい（み）：野性（味）〉 wild nature.

yasei-mi-o-obita 〈野性みを帯びた〉 wild.

yase-kokeru 〈やせこける：やせこける〉 become emaciated.

yasen 〈やせん：野戦〉 field operations.

    yasen-byôin 〈野戦病院〉 a field hospital

yasen 〈やせん：野選〉 a fielder's choice.

yase-otoroeru 〈やせおとろえる：やせ衰える〉 grow thin and worn-out.

yaseppochi 〈やせっぽち〉 a skinny person, a bag of bones.

yaseru 〈やせる〉 become lean, get thin, lose flesh, reduce one's weight, reduce flesh; become infertile.

yaseta 〈やせた〉 lean, thin, skinny, weedy; sterile, infertile.

yashi 〈やし〉 a palm (tree).

    yashi-no-mi 〈やしの実〉 a coco(a)nut

yashi 〈やし：野師〉 a mountebank, a quack; a showman.

yashiki 〈やしき：屋敷〉 the premises; a mansion.

yashin 〈やしん：野心〉 an ambition.

    ryôdo-teki yashin 〈領土的野心〉 a territorial ambition

    yashin-ka 〈野心家〉 an ambitious person

    yashin-saku 〈野心作〉 an ambitious work

yashin-o-idaku 〈野心を抱く〉 have an ambition, be ambitious.

yashin-mamman-to-shite-iru 〈野心満々としている〉 be full of ambition, be highly ambitious.

yashin-no-aru or *yashin-teki(-na)*〈野心のある，野心的(な)〉ambitious.

yashinau〈やしなう：養う〉bring up, foster, support; cultivate.

　　san-nin-no kodomo o yashinau（三人の子供を養う）bring up three
　　　children

　　kazoku o yashinau（家族を養う）support one's family

　　yoi shûkan o yashinau（よい習慣を養う）cultivate a good habit

yashiro〈やしろ：社〉a (*Shinto*) shrine.

yashoku〈やしょく：夜食〉a midnight snack.

yashu〈やしゅ：野手〉a fielder.

yashû〈やしゅう：夜襲〉a night attack.

　　yashû o kakeru（夜襲を掛ける）make a night attack ((on))

-yasu〈-やす：-安〉cheap.

　　jû-en-yasu（十円安）down 10 yen

yasu-agari〈やすあがり：安上がり〉

　yasu-agari-de-aru or *yasu-agari-ni-naru*〈安上がりである，安上がりになる〉
　cost little, be economical.

yasu-bushin〈やすぶしん：安普請〉a jerry-built house.

　yasu-bushin-no〈安普請の〉jerry-built.

yasui〈やすい：安い〉cheap, inexpensive, low, moderate, reasonable.

　　nedan-ga-yasui（値段が安い）moderate in price

　　yasui kai-mono（安い買い物）a good bargain

　yasuku〈安く〉cheaply, inexpensively, at a moderate price.

　　yasuku-kau（安く買う）buy cheap(er)

　yasuku-naru〈安くなる〉go down in price, become cheaper, fall, come
　down.

　yasuku-suru〈安くする〉make cheaper, reduce the price.

yasui or **-yasui**〈やすい，-やすい〉easy, be apt ((to do)).

　　O-yasui-goyô-desu.（おやすい御用です。）It's no trouble at all. /
　　　Nothing is easier.

　　kaki-yasui（書きやすい）be easy to write

　　koware-yasui（壊れやすい）be easy to break, be fragile

　　yomi-yasui（読みやすい）be easy to read

　　kaze-o-hiki-yasui（風邪をひきやすい）be liable to take a cold

yasumaru〈やすまる：休まる〉be rested; be set at ease, feel at ease, be
　relieved.

　yasumeru〈休める〉rest, give ((a person)) a rest; set ((a person's mind))
　at ease.

shigoto-no-te-o-yasumeru〈仕事の手を休める〉 rest from one's work

yasumaseru〈やすませる：休ませる〉give ((a person)) a day off, keep ((a child)) out of school.

yasumasete-hoshii〈休ませてほしい〉 wish to have a holiday

yasumi〈やすみ：休み〉(a) rest, a recess, a break; a holiday, a vacation.

san-ji-kara yo-ji-made ichi-jikan-no yasumi〈三時から四時まで一時間の休み〉 an hour's recess from three to four

Asu-wa gakkô wa yasumi-da.〈明日は学校は休みだ。〉 We have no school tomorrow.

yasumi-naku〈休みなく〉 without a break.

Kesa-kara yasumi-naku-yuki-ga-furi-tsuzuiteiru.〈今朝から休みなく雪が降り続いている。〉 It hasn't stopped snowing since this morning.

yasumi-yasumi〈休み休み〉 with frequent stops to rest.

yasu-mono〈やすもの：安物〉a cheap article.

Yasu-mono-gai-no-zeni-ushinai.〈安物買いの銭失い。〉 Penny wise and pound foolish.

yasumu〈やすむ：休む〉rest, take a rest (from), be absent ((from)); sleep, go to bed.

shigoto-o-yasumu〈仕事を休む〉 rest from one's work

yoko-ni-natte-yasumu〈横になって休む〉 lie at rest

ni-shû-kan-yasumu〈二週間休む〉 take two weeks' holiday

gakkô-o-mikka-yasumu〈学校を三日休む〉 be absent from school for three days

Yûbe-wa yoku-yasunda.〈ゆうべはよく休んだ。〉 I slept well last night.

hayaku yasumu〈早く休む〉 go to bed early

yasunde-iru〈休んでいる〉 be at rest.

yasumazu(-ni)〈休まず(に)〉 without rest, without a break.

yasumazu-ni-hataraku〈休まずに働く〉 be kept working

yasu-ne〈やすね：安値〉a low price.

hôgai-na-yasu-ne-de uru〈法外な安値で売る〉 sell at an excessively low price

yasuppoi〈やすっぽい：安っぽい〉cheap-looking, mean; tawdry, flashy.

yasuppoi shina〈安っぽい品〉 a cheap-looking article

yasuppoku〈安っぽく〉 cheaply, meanly.

yasuppoku-mieru〈安っぽく見える〉 look frivolous, look undignified

yasuraka〈やすらか：安らか〉

yasuraka-na〈安らかな〉 peaceful, tranquil, quiet, calm, restful.

　　　yasuraka-na hibi o okuru〈安らかな日々を送る〉 live a peaceful life

yasuraka-ni〈安らかに〉 peacefully, in peace, tranquilly.

　　　yasuraka-ni nemuru〈安らかに眠る〉 sleep peacefully

yasuri〈やすり〉 a file, a rasp.

　　　kami-yasuri〈紙やすり〉 sandpaper

yasuri-o-kakeru〈やすりをかける〉 file, rasp.

yasu-ukeai〈やすうけあい：安請け合い〉

yasu-ukeai-o-suru〈安請け合いをする〉 be too ready to make a promise, undertake ((a task)) lightly.

yasu-uri〈やすうり：安売り〉 a bargain sale.

yasu-uri-suru〈安売りする〉 sell cheap, sell at a bargain.

yasuyasu-to〈やすやすと：安々と〉 easily, with ease, without difficulty, without effort.

　　　yasuyasu-to katsu〈やすやすと勝つ〉 win easily, win hands down

yatai-bone〈やたいぼね：屋台骨〉 the foundation, fortune.

　　　yatai-bone-ga katamuku〈屋台骨が傾く〉 one's fortune declines

yatai(-mise)〈やたい(みせ)：屋台(店)〉 a stall, a stand, a booth.

yatara-ni〈やたらに〉 indiscriminately, at random, recklessly, thoughtlessly, excessively, extremely.

　　　yatara-ni kane o tsukau〈やたらに金を使う〉 spend money freely

　　　yatara-ni hito o homeru〈やたらに人を褒める〉 praise a person excessively

yatô〈やとう：野党〉 the Opposition party, a party out of power.

　　　yatô-tôshu〈野党党首〉 the leader of the Opposition

yatoi-nushi〈やといぬし：雇い主〉 an employer.

yatou〈やとう：雇う〉 engage, employ, take on; hire.

yatowareru〈雇われる〉 be employed, be engaged.

yatsu〈やつ〉 a fellow, a chap, a guy, a blighter, an egg.

　　　ii yatsu〈いいやつ〉 a good egg

yatsu-atari〈やつあたり：八つ当たり〉

yatsu-atari-suru〈八つ当たりする〉 wreak one's anger without reason on everybody.

yatsugibaya-ni〈やつぎばやに：矢継ぎ早に〉 in rapid succession.

　　　yatsugibaya-ni-shitsumon-suru〈矢継ぎ早に質問する〉 shoot question after question ((at))

yatsume-unagi〈やつめうなぎ：八つ目うなぎ〉 a lamprey (eel).

yatsureru〈やつれる〉 get haggard, be worn out.

　　　yatsurete-miru-kage-mo-nai〈やつれて見る影もない〉 be worn to a

shadow

yatsureta 〈やつれた〉 haggard, worn-out, exhausted.

yatsusu 〈やつす〉 disguise oneself ((as)), be disguised ((as)).

    uki-mi-o-yatsusu〈憂き身をやつす〉 be given ((to)), be absorbed ((in))

yatsu-zaki 〈やつざき：八つ裂き〉

    yatsu-zaki-ni-suru〈八つ裂きにする〉 tear ((a person)) limb from limb, tear ((a person)) in pieces.

yatte-iku 〈やっていく：やって行く〉 get along, get on, manage ((to do)).

    shakkin-sezu-ni nan-toka-yatte-iku〈借金せずに何とかやって行く〉 make shift without borrowing money

yatte-kuru 〈やってくる：やって来る〉 come along, make one's appearance, turn up.

yatte-miru 〈やってみる〉 try, have a try ((at)), attempt, try one's hand ((at)).

    mô-ichi-do yatte-miru（もう一度やってみる） have a try once more

    omoi-kitte-yatte-miru（思い切ってやってみる） take one's chance

yatte-nokeru 〈やってのける〉 succeed ((in)), carry out, accomplish.

    rippa-ni yatte-nokeru（立派にやってのける） accomplish ((a thing)) successfully

yatto 〈やっと〉 at last, at length; just, barely, narrowly; with difficulty, with much effort.

    yatto shigoto o oeru（やっと仕事を終える） finish the work at last

    yatto-kisha-ni-ma-ni-au（やっと汽車に間に合う） be just in time for the train

    yatto-nan-o-nogareru（やっと難を逃れる） have a narrow escape

    yatto shiken-ni-gôkaku-suru（やっと試験に合格する） scrape through an examination

    yatto sanchô-ni-tadori-tsuku（やっと山頂にたどり着く） get to the mountaintop with great difficulty

yattoko 〈やっとこ〉 pincers.

yattukeru 〈やっつける〉 defeat, beat, score off; settle; kill, do away ((with)).

yawarageru 〈やわらげる：和らげる〉 soften, moderate; ease, lessen, relieve; appease, pacify.

    koe o yawarageru（声を和らげる） soften one's voice

    kanashimi o yawarageru（悲しみを和らげる） ease ((a person's)) grief

    ikari o yawarageru（怒りを和らげる） appease ((a person's)) anger

yawaragu 〈やわらぐ：和らぐ〉 be softened, moderate, lessen, be

appeased, be mitigated.

    Kaze ga yawaraida.（風が和らいだ。）　The wind has gone down.

    Itami ga yawaraida.（痛みが和らいだ。）　The pain has been eased.

    Kanojo-no ikari ga yawaraida.（彼女の怒りが和らいだ。）　Her anger is mitigated.

yawaraka〈やわらか：柔(軟)らか〉

yawarakai or *yawaraka-na*〈柔(軟)らかい，柔(軟)らかな〉soft, tender, gentle, mild.

    yawarakai hi-zashi〈柔らかい日差し〉 soft sunbeam

    yawarakai niku〈軟らかい肉〉 tender meat

    yawarakai kaze〈柔らかい風〉 gentle breeze

yawarakaku〈柔(軟)らかく〉softly, tenderly, gently, mildly.

    yawarakaku-naru〈柔(軟)らかくなる〉 soften, become tender

    yawarakaku-suru〈柔(軟)らかくする〉 make soft, tenderize

yaya〈やや〉a little, slightly, in some degree, somewhat, pretty, fairly, rather.

    Chichi wa kyô-wa yaya ii-hô-desu.（父は今日はややいい方です。）　Father is a little better today.

yayakoshii〈ややこしい〉complicated, tangled, intricate.

    yayakoshii jiken〈ややこしい事件〉 a tangled affair

yo〈よ：世〉the world, the society, life; the age, the times.

    yo-ni-deru〈世に出る〉 start (in) life, go out into the world

    yo-ni-shirareru〈世に知られる〉 be known to the world

    yo-ni-irerare-nai〈世に入れられない〉 be shut out of society

    yo-ni wasurerareru〈世に忘れられる〉 be forgotten by the world

    yo o suteru〈世を捨てる〉 forsake the world

    yo-o-saru〈世を去る〉 die, pass away

    Meiji no yo〈明治の世〉 the Meiji era

    yo-ni-sakarau〈世に逆らう〉 swim against the current

    yo-ga-yo-nara〈世が世なら〉 in better times, if times were better

yo〈よ：夜〉(a) night, (an) evening.

    Yo ga akeru.（夜が明ける。）　The day breaks.

    Yo ga fuketa.（夜が更けた。）　The night deepened.

    yo o akasu〈夜を明かす〉 spend a night

yô〈よう：用〉business, an engagement, an errand; use, service.

    yô-o-tasu〈用を足す〉 do one's business

    fujin-yô〈婦人用〉 for ladies

yô-ga-aru〈用がある〉have something to do, be busy, be engaged, have business ((with)), want to speak ((to)).

    yô-ga-nai〈用がない〉have nothing to do, be disengaged, do not want; be useless, be of no service

  yô-ga-atte〈用があって〉on business, on an errand.

yô〈よう：陽〉the positive.

    in to yô〈陰と陽〉 the positive and the negative

yô〈よう〉a carbuncle, an anthrax.

yô〈よう：要〉the main point, the aim, the secret.

    yô-o-ete-iru〈要を得ている〉 be to the point

  yô-suru-ni or *yô-wa*〈要するに，要は〉in short, in a word.

yô〈よう：様〉a way, a manner; a sort, a kind; as, like; so that...may; an effect.

    dono-yô-ni〈どのように〉 in what way, how

    Watashi-wa kimi-o uragiru-yô-na-otoko-dewa-nai.（私は君を裏切るような男ではない。）I am not the sort of man to betray you.

    sono-yô-na-shina（そのような品）an article of that kind

    watashi-ga nakushita-no-to-onaji-yô-na mannen-hitsu（私が無くしたのと同じような万年筆） the same fountain pen as I lost

    Suki-na-yô-ni-shi-nasai.（好きなようにしなさい。）Do as you please.

    tenshi-no-yô-na-otome（天使のような乙女）an angel of a girl

    yama-no-yô-na-oo-nami（山のような大波） a mountain of a wave

    Yuki-no-yô-da.（雪のようだ。）It looks like snow.

    Kimi-ga machigatte-iru-yô-da.（君が間違っているようだ。）It seems that you are wrong.

    ari-no-yô-ni hataraku（ありのように働く）work like so many ants

    yuki-no-yô-ni-shiroi（雪のように白い）be as white as snow

    kyûkô-ni-ma-ni-au-yô-ni eki-e isogu（急行に間に合うように駅へ急ぐ） hurry to the station so that one may be in time for the express

    Kanojo-wa sono-yô-na-koto-o tegami-de-itte-kita.（彼女はそのような事を手紙で言ってきた。）She sent me a letter to that effect.

yô〈よう〉hullo, bravo.

    Yô, dekashita!（よう，でかした。）Well done!

yo-akashi〈よあかし：夜明かし〉

  yo-akashi-suru〈夜明かしする〉sit up all night.

yo-ake〈よあけ：夜明け〉dawn, daybreak.

  yo-ake-mae-ni〈夜明け前に〉before dawn.

yo-aruki〈よあるき：夜歩き〉

  yo-aruki-suru〈夜歩きする〉go out at night.

yo-asobi〈よあそび：夜遊び〉

  yo-asobi-suru〈夜遊びする〉go out in the evening for seeking pleasure.

yôbai〈ようばい：溶媒〉a solvent.

yoban〈よばん：夜番〉night watch, a night watchman.

  yoban-o-suru（夜番をする）keep night watch

yobawari〈よばわり：呼ばわり〉

  yobawari-suru〈呼ばわりする〉call.

    hito o dorobô-yobawari-suru（人を泥棒呼ばわりする）brand a person as a thief

yobi〈よび：予備〉a reserve, preparation.

  yobi-chishiki（予備知識）previous knowledge ((of))

  yobi-kôshô（予備交渉）a preliminary talk

  yobi-no〈予備の〉preliminary, reserve, emergency.

  yobi-no megane（予備の眼鏡）an emergency pair of glasses

yôbi〈ようび：曜日〉a day of the week.

    Kyô-wa nan-yô-bi-desu-ka?（今日は何曜日ですか.）What day of the week is it today?

yobi-ageru〈よびあげる：呼び上げる〉call up, call out.

  meibo o yobi-ageru（名簿を呼び上げる）call the roll

yobi-atsumeru〈よびあつめる：呼び集める〉call together.

yobidashi〈よびだし：呼び出し〉a call; a summons; a *sumo* crier.

  keisatsu-no yobidashi ni ô-ji-nai（警察の呼び出しに応じない）ignore the summons from the police

  yobi-dasu〈呼び出す〉call; summon; call ((a person)) to the telephone.

yobi-eki〈よびえき：予備役〉

  yobi-eki-ni-hennyû-sareru〈予備役に編入される〉be registered on the reserve list.

yobi-goe〈よびごえ：呼び声〉a call, a cry; a rumor.

  yobi-goe-ga-takai〈呼び声が高い〉be much talked about ((as)).

yobi-ireru〈よびいれる：呼び入れる〉call ((a person)) into.

yobi-kaesu〈よびかえす：呼び返す〉call back, recall.

yobi-kakeru〈よびかける：呼び掛ける〉call ((to)), speak ((to)), accost; appeal ((to)).

  taishû-ni yobi-kakeru（大衆に呼び掛ける）appeal to the public

yobi-kô〈よびこう：予備校〉a preparatory school, a prep school.

yobi-komu〈よびこむ：呼び込む〉see. yobi-ireru.

yobi-modosu〈よびもどす：呼び戻す〉see. yobi-kaesu.

yobi-mono〈よびもの：呼び物〉a chief attraction, the highlight, a main event.

yobi-na 〈よびな：呼び名〉a given name, an alias.

yobi-ni-iku 〈よびにいく：呼びに行く〉go and fetch.

yobi-ni-kuru 〈よびにくる：呼びに来る〉call for.

yobi-ni-yaru 〈よびにやる：呼びにやる〉send for.

yobi-okosu 〈よびおこす：呼び起こす〉wake up; call ((something)) to mind, be reminded ((of)).

yobi-rin 〈よびりん：呼び鈴〉a bell, a doorbell.
　　yobi-rin o narasu（呼び鈴を鳴らす）ring a bell

yobi-sute 〈よびすて：呼び捨て〉
　yobi-sute-ni-suru 〈呼び捨てにする〉call ((a person)) by name without any honorific title.

yobi-tomeru 〈よびとめる：呼び止める〉call ((a person)) to stop.
　　keikan-ni yobi-tomerareru（警官に呼び止められる）be called to stop by a policeman

yobi-tsukeru 〈よびつける：呼び付ける〉call ((a person)) to one.
　　sensei-ni-yobi-tsukerareru（先生に呼び付けられる）be called before one's teacher

yobi-yoseru 〈よびよせる：呼び寄せる〉call ((a person)) to one, summon; call together.

yobô 〈よぼう：予防〉prevention ((against *or* of)), protection ((against *or* from)), (a) precaution.
　　yobô-chûsha（予防注射）a preventive injection
　　yobô-sesshu（予防接種）(a) protective inoculation ((against))
　　yobô-saku（予防策）preventive measures
　　　yobô-saku o kôjiru（予防策を講じる）take preventive measures
　　yobô-sen-o-haru（予防線を張る）take a precautionary measure ((against)), forestall
　yobô-suru 〈予防する〉prevent, protect ((against *or* from)), take precaution ((against)).

yôbo 〈ようぼ：養母〉a foster mother, an adoptive mother; a mother-in-law.

yôbô 〈ようぼう：要望〉a cry ((for)), a demand ((for)), one's wishes.
　　yôbô ni kotaeru（要望にこたえる）meet the demand ((of))
　yôbô-suru 〈要望する〉cry ((for)), demand.

yôbô 〈ようぼう：容ぼう〉looks, the face.
　yôbô-no-minikui 〈容ぼうの醜い〉plain-looking.

yoboyobo 〈よぼよぼ〉

yoboyobo-aruku〈よぼよぼ歩く〉totter along, walk with tottering steps.

yoboyobo-no〈よぼよぼの〉feeble and tottering.

yobu〈よぶ：呼ぶ〉call, call out ((to)), hail, call after; send for, call in; invite; name.

    tasuke-o-yobu（助けを呼ぶ）call for help

    yobeba-kikoeru-tokoro-ni（呼べば聞こえる所に）within call

    kuruma o yobu（車を呼ぶ）order a taxi

    yūjin-o-sūnin yūshoku-ni yobu（友人を数人夕食に呼ぶ）invite a few friends to dinner

    〜-ni-chinande Kichinosuke-to-yobareru（〜にちなんで吉之助と呼ばれる）be named Kichinosuke after...

yōbu〈ようぶ：腰部〉the waist, the hips.

yobun〈よぶん：余分〉an excess, superfluity, an extra, a surplus.

yobun-no〈余分の〉excessive, superfluous, extra, to spare.

    ichi-doru yobun-no-kane o harau（一ドル余分の金を払う）pay 1 dollar extra, pay 1 dollar too much

    yobun-no jikan（余分の時間）time to spare

yōbun〈ようぶん：養分〉nourishment, nutriment.

yobyō〈よびょう：余病〉a complication.

    yobyō-o-heihatsu-suru（余病を併発する）cause a complication, develop a complication

yochi〈よち：余地〉room, a scope, a blank, space.

    Madamada kenkyû-no-yochi-ga-aru.（まだまだ研究の余地がある．）There is much room for further study.

    gimon-no-yochi-ga-nai（疑問の余地がない）leave no room for doubt

    dakyô-no-yochi-ga-aru（妥協の余地がある）admit of compromise

    Kono-baai kimi-wa benkai-no-yochi-wa-nai.（この場合君は弁解の余地はない．）You have no excuse in this case.

    hitei-no-yochi-ga-nai（否定の余地がない）be beyond denial

yochi〈よち：予知〉foreknowledge.

yochi-suru〈予知する〉foresee, know beforehand, foretell.

    jishin o yochi-suru（地震を予知する）foretell an earthquake

yōchi〈ようち：用地〉a land, a lot, a site ((for)).

yōchi〈ようち：要地〉an important place, a strategic point.

yōchi〈ようち：幼稚〉

yōchi-na〈幼稚な〉childish, crude, primitive.

    yōchi-na kangae（幼稚な考え）a childish idea

yōchi-en〈ようちえん：幼稚園〉a kindergarten.

　　　kodomo o yôchi-en-e yaru〈子供を幼稚園へやる〉send one's child to a kindergarten

　　　yôchi-en-no-hobo〈幼稚園の保母〉a kindergartener

yochiyochi〈よちよち〉

　　　yochiyochi-aruki-no-kodomo〈よちよち歩きの子供〉a toddler

　yochiyochi-aruku〈よちよち歩く〉toddle.

yôchû〈ようちゅう：幼虫〉a larva.

yôdai〈ようだい：容体(態)〉one's condition.

　　　yôdai-ga-omowashiku-nai〈容体が思わしくない〉be in a bad condition

　　　Kare-no yôdai wa kyûgeki-ni-akka-shita.〈彼の容体は急激に悪化した。〉His condition took a sudden change for the worse.

yodan〈よだん：余談〉a digression.

　yodan-desu-ga〈余談ですが〉in this connection I may add that... , incidentally... .

　yodan-wa-sate-oki〈余談はさておき〉to return to the subject.

yodan〈よだん：予断〉(a) prediction.

　yodan-o-yurusa-nai〈予断を許さない〉there is no predicting... , admit of no prediction.

yôdan〈ようだん：用談〉a business talk.

　yôdan-suru〈用談する〉talk with ((a person)) on business.

yô-dansu〈ようだんす：用だんす〉a chest of drawers, a cabinet.

yodare〈よだれ〉slaver, saliva, slobber.

　　　yodare-kake〈よだれ掛け〉a bib, a pinafore

　yodare-o-nagasu〈よだれを流す〉slaver, slobber.

　yodare-no-de-sô-na〈よだれの出そうな〉mouth-watering.

yô-dateru〈ようだてる：用立てる〉lend, accommodate, oblige.

　　　Jû-man-en-yô-datete-kure-masen-ka?〈十万円用立ててくれませんか。〉Could you accommodate me with 100,000 yen?

yodatsu〈よだつ〉

　mi-no-ke-ga-yodatsu〈身の毛がよだつ〉make one's hair stand on end, make one's blood run cold.

　mi-no-ke-ga-yodatsu-yô-na〈身の毛がよだつような〉bloodcurdling.

yô-denki〈ようでんき：陽電気〉positive electricity.

yô-denshi〈ようでんし：陽電子〉a positron.

yôdo〈ヨード〉iodine, iodin.

yodomi〈よどみ〉stagnation, hesitation, (a) sediment, a pool.

　yodomi-naku hanasu〈よどみなく話す〉speak fluently.

yodomu〈よどむ〉stagnate, hesitate, settle, deposit.

yo-dooshi〈よどおし：夜通し〉all night, throughout the night.
>> yo-dooshi kambyō-suru（夜通し看病する）be up with a patient all through the night

yōdō-sakusen〈ようどうさくせん：陽動作戦〉a feint operation, diversionary activities.

yōeki〈ようえき：溶液〉a solution.

yōfu〈ようふ：養父〉a foster father, an adoptive father, a father-in-law.

yōfū〈ようふう：洋風〉
>> yōfū-kenchiku（洋風建築）a house in Western style
> *yōfū-no*〈洋風の〉foreign, European, in Western style.

yo-fukashi〈よふかし：夜更かし〉
>> Yo-fukashi wa karada-ni-warui.（夜更かしは体に悪い.）Sitting up late at night is harmful to health.
> *yo-fukashi-suru*〈夜更かしする〉sit up late at night.

yofuke〈よふけ：夜更け〉
> *yofuke-ni*〈夜更けに〉late at night, in the dead of night.
> *yofuke-made*〈夜更けまで〉far into the night, till late.

yōfuku〈ようふく：洋服〉foreign clothes.
>> yōfuku-dansu（洋服だんす）a wardrobe, a bureau
>> yōfuku-kake（洋服掛け）a coat hanger
>> yōfuku-ya（洋服屋）a tailor; a tailor's

yōga〈ようが：洋画〉(a) Western painting, (an) oil painting; a foreign film.
>> yōga-ka（洋画家）an artist of Western painting

yōga〈ようが：陽画〉a positive.

yōgaku〈ようがく：洋楽〉Western music.

yōgan〈ようがん：溶岩〉lava.

yō-gashi〈ようがし：洋菓子〉Western cakes.
>> yō-gashi-ten（洋菓子店）a confectionery

yōgeki〈ようげき：要撃〉an ambush.
> *yōgeki-suru*〈要撃する〉ambush, lie in wait ((for)).

yogen〈よげん：予言〉(a) prophecy, (a) prediction.
>> Kare-no-yogen-doori-ni-natta.（彼の予言どおりになった.）His prophecy came true.
>> yogen-sha（予言者）a prophet, a prophetess
> *yogen-suru*〈予言する〉foretell, predict, prophesy.

yōgi〈ようぎ：容疑〉suspicion.

    satsujin no-yôgi-de（殺人の容疑で）on suspicion of murder

    yôgi-sha（容疑者）a suspect, a suspected person

yogo〈よご：予後〉prognosis, convalescence.

yôgo〈ようご：用語〉wording, diction, phraseology, a term, terminology, (a) vocabulary.

    semmon-yôgo（専門用語）technical terms

yôgo〈ようご：養護〉protective care, nursing.

    yôgo-gakkyû（養護学級）a weak children's class

yôgo〈ようご：擁護〉protection, defense, assistance, support.

 yôgo-suru〈擁護する〉pretect, defend, support, help.

yogore〈よごれ：汚れ〉a spot, a stain, a blot, a smudge; dirt.

    yogore-mono（汚れ物）soiled things, washing, laundry

 yogore-o-toru〈汚れを取る〉remove stains ((from)), clean.

 yogore-no-nai〈汚れのない〉stainless, spotless, clean.

yogoreru〈よごれる：汚れる〉become dirty, be soiled, be stained, be blotted.

    Shiroi waishatsu wa sugu yogoreru.（白いワイシャツはすぐ汚れる。）A white shirt soils easily.

    Kûki ga yogorete-iru.（空気が汚れている。）The air is polluted.

 yogoreta〈汚れた〉dirty, soiled, stained, unclean.

    ase-de-yogoreta shatsu（汗で汚れたシャツ）a sweat-stained undershirt

yogosu〈よごす：汚す〉make ((a thing)) dirty, soil, stain, pollute.

    fuku o yogosu（服を汚す）soil one's clothes

yôgu〈ようぐ：用具〉a tool, an implement, an instrumemt, an outfit.

    undô-yôgu（運動用具）sporting goods

yôguruto〈ヨーグルト〉yog(h)urt.

yôgyo〈ようぎょ：養魚〉fish breeding.

    yôgyo-jô（養魚場）a fish farm

yôgyô〈ようぎょう：窯業〉(the) ceramic industry, ceramics.

yoha〈よは：余波〉an aftereffect, an aftermath, a trail.

yohaku〈よはく：余白〉a blank, (a) space, a margin.

yôhei〈ようへい：よう兵〉a mercenary (soldier).

yôhin〈ようひん：用品〉

    daidokoro-yôhin（台所用品）kitchen utensils

    katei-yôhin（家庭用品）domestic articles

yôhin〈ようひん：洋品〉haberdashery, men's furnishings.

    yôhin-ten（洋品店）a haberdasher's, a hosier's

yôhi-shi 〈ようひし：羊皮紙〉 parchment.

yohô 〈よほう：予報〉 a forecast, a prediction.
    chôki-yohô（長期予報） a long-range forecast
  yohô-suru（予報する）forecast, predict.

yôhô 〈ようほう：用法〉(a) use, how to use ((a thing)).
    yôhô o shira-nai（用法を知らない） do not know how to use
    yôhô-gaki（用法書き） the directions

yôhô 〈ようほう：養ほう〉 beekeeping, apiculture.
    yôhô-bako（養ほう箱） a wooden beehive
    yôhô-ka（養ほう家） a beekeeper, an apiculturist

yohodo 〈よほど〉
    Haha wa kyô-wa yohodo kibun-ga-ii-rashii.（母は今日はよほど気分がいいらしい.） Mother seems to be much better today.
    Yohodo-chûi-ga-hitsuyô-desu.（よほど注意が必要です.） You cannot be too careful.
    yohodo-no-koto-ga-nai-kagiri（よほどのことがない限り） unless there is some extraordinary reason

yoi 〈よい：良（善）い〉 *see.* ii.

yoi 〈よい：宵〉 the early evening.
    Mada yoi-no-kuchi-da.（まだ宵の口だ.） It is still early in the evening.
    yoi-no-myô-jô（宵の明星） the evening star, Venus

yoi 〈よい：酔い〉 drunkenness, tipsiness, intoxication.
  yoi-ga-mawaru 〈酔いが回る〉 get tipsy, feel the effects of wine.
    yoi-ga-sameru（酔いがさめる） become sober
  yoi-o-samasu 〈酔いをさます〉 make ((a person)) sober, get rid of the effects of wine.

yôi 〈ようい：用意〉 preparation(s), readiness, arrangements, provision.
    Yôi!（用意.） Ready!
    Yûshoku-no-yôi-ga-dekimashita.（夕食の用意ができました.） Dinner is ready.
  yôi-suru or *yôi-o-suru* 〈用意する，用意をする〉 prepare ((for)), get ready ((for)), make arrangements ((for)), provide ((against *or* for)).
    fuyu-no-yôi-o-suru（冬の用意をする） prepare for the winter
    yûshoku-no-yôi-o-suru（夕食の用意をする） get dinner ready
    masaka-no-toki-no-yôi-o-suru（まさかのときの用意をする） provide against an emergency

yôi 〈ようい：容易〉 ease, easiness.

yôi-na〈容易な〉easy, simple.

    yôi-na koto（容易なこと）an easy matter

yôi-naranu〈容易ならぬ〉grave, serious, dangerous.

    yôi-naranu jitai（容易ならぬ事態）a serious situation

yôi-ni〈容易に〉easily, with ease, without difficulty.

    yôi-ni dekiru（容易にできる）be easily done

    Kôshô-wa-yôi-ni-saikai-sare-nakatta.（交渉は容易に再開されなかった.）
        It was long before the negotiations were resumed.

yôi-ni-suru〈容易にする〉make easy, simplify, facilitate.

yoidore〈よいどれ：酔いどれ〉a drunkard.

yôiku〈よういく：養育〉

    yôiku-hi（養育費）the expense of bringing up a child

yôiku-suru〈養育する〉bring up, rear.

yoin〈よいん：余韻〉a lingering tone, reverberations, suggestiveness.

yôin〈よういん：要因〉an essential factor, a main cause.

yôin〈よういん：要員〉needed personnel, workers required.

yoippari〈よいっぱり：宵っ張り〉

    Kare-wa yoippari-no-asa-nebô-da.（彼は宵っ張りの朝寝坊だ.）He
        keeps late hours.

Yoisho!〈よいしょ.〉Yo-ho! / Yo-heave-ho!

yôi-shûtô〈よういしゅうとう：用意周到〉

    yôi-shûtô-na〈用意周到な〉exhaustive, cautious, prudent.

yoi-tsubureru〈よいつぶれる：酔いつぶれる〉be dead drunk.

yoi-zame〈よいざめ：酔いざめ〉

    yoi-zame-no-mizu-o-nomu（酔いざめの水を飲む）cool one's coppers.

yôji〈ようじ：幼児〉a baby, an infant, a little child.

yôji〈ようじ：幼時〉childhood.

    yôji-ni（幼時に）in one's childhood

yôji〈ようじ：用事〉business, an engagement, things to do, an errand.

    sukoshi-yôji-ga-aru（少し用事がある）have some business to do

    amari-yôji-ga-nai（余り用事がない）do not have much to do

    kore-to-itta-yôji-ga-nai（これといった用事がない）have nothing par-
        ticular to do

yôji-de〈用事で〉on business, on an errand.

yôji〈ようじ〉a toothpick.

    yôji o tsukau（ようじを使う）use a toothpick

yôjin〈ようじん：用心〉care, caution, (a) precaution, guard, prudence.

    yôjin-o-okotaru（用心を怠る）neglect to take precautions

Ashi-moto go-yōjin!〔足元御用心.〕 Mind your step!

Kaichū-butsu-go-yōjin!〔懐中物御用心.〕 Beware of pickpockets!

yōjin-bō〈用心棒〉a bodyguard, a muscleman, a bouncer, a chucker(-out)

yōjin-suru〈用心する〉be careful ((of)), take care ((of)), be cautious ((of)), take precautions ((against)), beware ((of)), guard ((against)), look out ((for)).

kaze-o-hika-nai-yō-ni-yôjin-suru〔風邪をひかないように用心する〕 take care not to catch cold

yōjin-shite-iru〈用心している〉be on one's guard, be on the alert.

yōjin-bukai〈用心深い〉careful, thoughtful, scrupulous, cautious, watchful, prudent, circumspect.

yōjin-bukaku〈用心深く〉carefully, scrupulously, cautiously, prudently.

yōjin-bukaku kôdō-suru〈用心深く行動する〉act with care

yōjin〈ようじん：要人〉a very important person, a V.I.P., a prominent person, a leading figure.

yoji-noboru〈よじのぼる：よじ登る〉climb (up), clamber (over *or* up).

yojireru〈よじれる〉*see.* nejireru.

yojiru〈よじる〉*see.* nejiru.

yojō〈よじょう：余剰〉a surplus.

yojō-nō-sambutsu〈余剰農産物〉surplus farm produce

yōjo〈ようじょ：養女〉a foster daughter, an adopted daughter.

yōjō〈ようじょう：養生〉care of health, recuperation.

yōjō-suru〈養生する〉take care of one's health.

yōjō-no-tame〈養生のため〉for one's health, for recuperation.

yōjō〈ようじょう：洋上〉

yôjō-daigaku〈洋上大学〉a floating university

yôjō-de or *yôjō-ni*〈洋上で，洋上に〉on the ocean.

yōjutsu〈ようじゅつ：よう術〉black art, witchcraft.

yoka〈よか：余暇〉leisure, spare time.

yoka-o-riyô-suru〈余暇を利用する〉make use of one's spare time

yō-kagu〈ようかぐ：洋家具〉Western-style furniture.

yōkai〈ようかい：よう怪〉a ghost, an apparition, a phantom, a monster, a goblin.

yōkai〈ようかい：溶解〉melting, solution.

yôkai-ten〈溶解点〉the melting point

yōkai-suru〈溶解する〉melt, dissolve.

yokaku〈よかく：余角〉the complementary angle.

yokan 〈よかん：予感〉a presentiment, a hunch.
    fukitsu-na yokan（不吉な予感）a sinister presentiment
    yokan-ga-suru〈予感がする〉have a hunch ((of *or* that)).

yokan 〈よかん：余寒〉the lingering cold 〔of early spring〕.
    Yokan imada sari-gatashi.（余寒いまだ去り難し.）The cold still lingers.

yôkan 〈ようかん：羊かん〉sweet jelly of beans.

yôkan 〈ようかん：洋館〉a Western-style building.

yokare-ashikare 〈よかれあしかれ：善かれあしかれ〉right or wrong, for better or worse, for good or evil.

-yoke 〈-よけ〉protection, a shelter, a charm.
    mushi-yoke（虫よけ）a protection against moths

yokei 〈よけい：余計〉
    Yokei-na-o-sewa-da!（余計なお世話だ.）It's none of your business!
    Yokei-na-shimpai-o-suru-na.（余計な心配をするな.）You need not worry yourself about it.

yôkei 〈ようけい：養鶏〉poultry farming.
    yôkei-jô（養鶏場）a poultry farm, a chickyard
    yôkei-o-suru〈養鶏をする〉raise poultry.

yoken 〈よけん：予見〉a prevision.
    yoken-suru〈予見する〉foresee.

yôken 〈ようけん：用件〉business.
    Yôken-o-hayaku-ii-nasai.（用件を早く言いなさい.）Come to the point at once.

yôken 〈ようけん：要件〉an essential condition ((of)), a requisite ((for)).

yokeru 〈よける〉avoid, keep away ((from)), get out of the way ((of)), step aside ((from)), take shelter ((from)), dodge.

yoki 〈よき：予期〉expectation(s), (an) anticipation, (a) hope.
    yoki-suru〈予期する〉expect, anticipate, look ((for)).
    yoki-shi-nai〈予期しない〉unexpected, unanticipated, unlooked-for.
    yoki-shita-yô-ni〈予期したように〉as expected, as one expected.
    yoki-ijô-ni〈予期以上に〉beyond (one's) expectation(s).
    yoki-ni-hanshite〈予期に反して〉contrary to expectation.

yôki 〈ようき：容器〉a receptacle, a container, a vessel.

yôki 〈ようき：陽気〉(the) weather; liveliness, cheerfulness, merriment, gaiety.
    yôki-no-kagen-de（陽気の加減で）owing to the weather
    yôki-na〈陽気な〉lively, cheerful, merry, gay.

yôki-ni〈陽気に〉cheerfully, merrily.
　　yôki-ni utau（陽気に歌う）sing merrily
yokin〈よきん：預金〉(a) deposit.
　　yokin o hiki-dasu（預金を引き出す）draw one's money ((from))
　　yokin-tsûchô（預金通帳）a (deposit) passbook
　　yokin-sha（預金者）a depositor
yokin-ga-aru〈預金がある〉have a bank deposit ((of)).
yokin-suru〈預金する〉deposit money in a bank, bank.
yokkyû〈よっきゅう：欲求〉want(s), (a) desire ((for)), a wish ((for)).
　　yokkyû o mitasu（欲求を満たす）satisfy one's wants
　　yokkyû-fuman（欲求不満）frustration
yoko〈よこ：横〉the side, the flank, the width.
　　tate-go-mêtoru yoko-yon-mêtoru（縦五メートル横四メートル）5 by 4
　　meters
yoko-ni〈横に〉across, broadwise, sideways, transversely, horizontally.
　　yoko-ni oku（横に置く）lay ((a thing)) on its side, lay ((a thing)) by
　　one's side
　　yoko-ni sen o hiku（横に線を引く）draw a line horizontally
　　yoko-ni suwaru（横に座る）sit by ((a person))
　　kubi-o-yoko-ni-furu（首を横に振る）say no
　　yoko-ni-naru（横になる）lie down
　　yoko-ni-suru（横にする）lay down
　　tate-kara-mitemo-yoko-kara-mitemo（縦から見ても横から見ても）
　　every inch
　　yoko-kara-kuchi-o-dasu（横から口を出す）poke one's nose ((in)),
　　meddle ((in))
yôkô〈ようこう：要港〉a port of strategic importance.
yôkô〈ようこう：要項〉the essential points, the gist.
yôkô〈ようこう：陽光〉sunshine, sunlight.
yoko-ana〈よこあな：横穴〉a cave, a tunnel, a drift.
yoko-bai〈よこばい：横ばい〉
yoko-bai-suru〈横ばいする〉remain stable, show no fluctuations.
yoko-bara〈よこばら：横腹〉see. waki-bara.
yoko-bue〈よこぶえ：横笛〉a flute.
yoko-chô〈よこちょう：横町〉a bystreet, a side street, a lane, an alley.
　　futatsu-me-no yoko-chô o migi-e magaru（二つめの横町を右へ曲がる）
　　turn the second turning to the right
yoko-daoshi〈よこだおし：横倒し〉

yoko-daoshi-ni-naru〈横倒しになる〉fall down sidelong.

yoko-donari〈よこどなり：横隣〉

　　yoko-donari-no hito（横隣の人）one's next-door neighbor; a person sitting next to one

yoko-dori〈よこどり：横取り〉

　yoko-dori-suru〈横取りする〉seize ((a thing)) by force, snatch away; usurp.

yokô-enshû〈よこうえんしゅう：予行演習〉a rehearsal.

　yokô-enshû-o-suru〈予行演習をする〉rehearse.

yoko-gaki〈よこがき：横書き〉lateral writing.

　yoko-gaki-ni-suru〈横書きにする〉write laterally.

yoko-gao〈よこがお：横顔〉a profile.

　　yoko-gao-ga-utsukushii（横顔が美しい）have a nice profile

yoko-gi〈よこぎ：横木〉a crosspiece, a bar, a (cross) rail, a ledger.

yoko-giru〈よこぎる：横切る〉cross, go across.

yoko-jima〈よこじま：横じま〉horizontal stripes.

　yoko-jima-no〈横じまの〉horizontal-striped.

yokoku〈よこく：予告〉a (previous) notice, a (previous) announcement, (a) warning.

　　yokoku-hen（予告編）a preview

　yokoku-suru〈予告する〉give notice ((to)), announce previously, give ((a person)) warning.

　yokoku-doori-ni〈予告どおりに〉as previously announced.

　yokoku-nashi-ni〈予告なしに〉without notice.

yoko-me〈よこめ：横目〉

　yoko-me-de miru〈横目で見る〉look at ((a person)) sideways.

　　yoko-me-de-jirotto-miru（横目でじろっと見る）give a sharp glance at ((a person)) out of the corner of one's eyes

yoko-michi〈よこみち：横道〉a side road; (a) digression, a wrong way.

　hanashi-ga-yoko-michi-ni-soreru〈話が横道にそれる〉wander from the subject.

yoko-moji〈よこもじ：横文字〉a Western language.

yoko-muki〈よこむき：横向き〉

　yoko-muki-ni〈横向きに〉sideways.

　　yoko-muki-ni neru（横向きに寝る）lie on one's side

yoko-nagashi〈よこながし：横流し〉

　yoko-nagashi-suru〈横流しする〉sell ((goods)) through illegal channels.

yoko-naguri〈よこなぐり：横殴り〉

　　　　yoko-naguri-no ame〈横殴りの雨〉 a slanting rain
yoko-nami〈よこなみ：横波〉a side wave.
　　　　yoko-nami-o-kuu〈横波を食う〉 be hit by side waves
yokoppara〈よっぱら：横っ腹〉*see.* waki-bara.
yô-ko-ro〈ようこうろ：溶鉱炉〉a smelting furnace.
yokoshima〈よこしま〉
　　yokoshima-na〈よこしまな〉 wicked, evil, dishonest, unjust, perverse.
　　　　yokoshima-na kangae〈よこしまな考え〉 an evil thought
yô-koso〈ようこそ〉
　　　　Yô-koso-oide-kudasaimashita.〈ようこそおいでくださいました.〉 I am
　　　　very glad you have come. / I am very glad to see you.
yokosu〈よこす〉
　　　　tegami-o-yokosu〈手紙をよこす〉 write ((a person))
　　　　tegami-de-itte-yokosu〈手紙で言ってよこす〉 write a letter to ((a
　　　　person)) saying that...
yoko-suberi〈よこすべり：横滑り〉a sideslip.
　　yoko-suberi-suru〈横滑りする〉sideslip, skid.
yokotaeru〈よこたえる：横たえる〉lay down.
　　　　karada o yokotaeru〈体を横たえる〉 lay oneself down
　　yokotawaru〈横たわる〉lie down.
yoko-te〈よこて：横手〉
　　yoko-te-ni〈横手に〉at the side ((of)).
yokottsura〈よこつら：横っ面〉
　　yokottsura-o-haru〈横っ面を張る〉box ((a person's)) ear(s), slap ((a
　　person)) on the cheek.
yoko-yari〈よこやり：横やり〉
　　yoko-yari-o-ireru〈横やりを入れる〉interrupt, interfere ((in)), break in.
yoko-zuke〈よこづけ：横付け〉
　　yoko-zuke-ni-suru〈横付けにする〉bring alongside.
　　　　fune o gampeki-ni-yoko-zuke-ni-suru〈船を岸壁に横付けにする〉 lay a
　　　　ship alongside the pier
　　　　kuruma o genkan-ni-yoko-zuke-ni-suru〈車を玄関に横付けにする〉
　　　　bring a car to the front door
yokozuna〈よこづな：横綱〉a grand champion *sumo* wrestler.
yoku〈よく〉well, nicely, right(ly), thoroughly, fully, considerably,
　　skillfully, carefully, exactly, much, a great deal, usually, generally,
　　commonly, often, frequently.
　　　　yoku nemuru〈よく眠る〉 sleep well

yoku-kangaeru〔よく考える〕 think ((a matter)) over

yoku miru〔よく見る〕 look at ((a thing)) carefully

iu-koto-ga-yoku-wakara-nai〔言うことがよく分からない〕 do not understand exactly

yoku hataraku〔よく働く〕 work hard

yoku chikoku-suru〔よく遅刻する〕 be often late

yoku-aru-koto-da-ga〔よくあることだが〕 as too often happens

yoku〜shita-mono-da〔よく〜したものだ〕 used ((to do))

Yoku-mâ-go-buji-de.〔よくまあ御無事で.〕 It is wonder that you were safe.

yoku-naru〔良くなる〕get better, get well, clear up.

Ni-san-nichi-sureba yoku-naru-deshô.〔二，三日すれば良くなるでしょう.〕 I'll be myself again in a few days.

Tenki wa yoku-naru-deshô.〔天気は良くなるでしょう.〕 The weather will clear up.

yoku-suru〔良くする〕improve, be skillful ((in)).

yoku-nai〔良くない〕unwell, poorly.

yoku-ikeba〔良くいけば〕all going well.

yoku-itte-mo〔良くいっても〕if things go well.

yoku-mite-mo〔良く見ても〕at best, at the most.

yoku〔よく：欲〕 avarice, greed; a desire, a wish, a thirst.

yoku-ni-me-ga-kuramu〔欲に目がくらむ〕 be blind with avarice

chishiki-yoku〔知識欲〕 a desire for knowledge

kinsen-yoku〔金銭欲〕 love of money

meiyo-yoku〔名誉欲〕 a desire for fame

yoku-no-fukai〔欲の深い〕avaricious, greedy, selfish.

yoku-no-nai〔欲のない〕 unselfish, disinterested

yoku-o-ieba〔欲を言えば〕if one may be allowed to hope for more.

Yoku-o-ieba-mô-sukoshi-hiroi-niwa-ga-hoshii.〔欲を言えばもう少し広い庭が欲しい.〕 I wish my house had a larger garden to it.

yoku〔よく：翼〕a wing.

yoku-menseki〔翼面積〕 (the) wing area

yoku-〔よく-：翌-〕the next, the following.

yokuchô〔翌朝〕 the next morning

yokujitsu〔翌日〕 the next day

yokunen〔翌年〕 the next year

yokuatsu〔よくあつ：抑圧〕(a) restraint, (an) oppression, (a) suppression, (a) repression.

yokuatsu-suru 〈抑圧する〉 restrain, oppress, suppress, repress.

yoku-bari 〈よくばり：欲張り〉 avarice, an avaricious person.

yoku-baru 〈欲張る〉 be avaricious, be greedy.

yoku-batta 〈欲張った〉 avaricious, greedy.

yoku-batte 〈欲張って〉 avariciously, out of avarice.

yokubô 〈よくぼう：欲望〉 a desire, an appetite, an ambition.

    yokubô o mitasu 〈欲望を満たす〉 gratify one's desires

yokudo 〈よくど：よく土〉 fertile land.

yokujô 〈よくじょう：浴場〉 a bath, a bathroom, a (public) bathhouse.

yokujô 〈よくじょう：欲情〉 *see.* jôyoku.

yoku-me 〈よくめ：欲目〉 a partial view, (a) partiality.

    oya-no yoku-me-de ko o miru 〈親の欲目で子を見る〉 regard one's children with parental partiality

yoku-mo 〈よくも〉

    Yoku-mo watashi-ni-mukatte sonna koto ga ieru-ne. 〈よくも私に向かってそんなことが言えるね.〉 How dare you say such a thing to me?

yokuryû 〈よくりゅう：抑留〉 detention, internment.

    yokuryû-sha 〈抑留者〉 a detainee, an internee

yokuryû-suru 〈抑留する〉 detain, intern, seize.

yokusei 〈よくせい：抑制〉 control, restraint, repression.

yokusei-suru 〈抑制する〉 control, restrain, repress, inhibit.

yokusei-deki-nai 〈抑制できない〉 uncontrollable, unrestrainable.

yokushi 〈よくし：抑止〉 determent.

    yokushi-ryoku 〈抑止力〉 a deterrent power

yokushitsu 〈よくしつ：浴室〉 a bathroom.

yokusô 〈よくそう：浴槽〉 a bathtub.

yokusuru 〈よくする：浴する〉

onkei-ni-yokusuru 〈恩恵に浴する〉 share in the benefit.

yokutoku 〈よくとく：欲得〉

yokutoku-o-hanarete 〈欲得を離れて〉 out of a disinterested motive.

yokutoku-zuku 〈よくとくずく：欲得尽く〉

yokutoku-zuku-no 〈欲得ずくの〉 interested, selfish.

yokutoku-zuku-de 〈欲得ずくで〉 from a selfish motive.

yokuyô 〈よくよう：抑揚〉 intonation, modulation, inflection.

yokuyô-no-aru 〈抑揚のある〉 intoned, modulated.

    yokuyô-no-nai 〈抑揚のない〉 monotonous, unaccentuated

yokuyô 〈よくよう：浴用〉

　　　yokuyô-sekken（浴用石けん）　bath soap
yokuyoku〈よくよく〉
　　　yokuyoku-kane-ni-komatte-iru（よくよく金に困っている）　be badly in
　　　　　need of money
　　　yokuyoku-no jijô（よくよくの事情）　unavoidable circumstances
　　　　　yokuyoku-no-jijô-ga-nakereba（よくよくの事情がなければ）　without
　　　　　　some compelling reasons
yokuyoku-〈よくよく‐：翌々〉
　　　yokuyoku-jitsu（翌々日）　the next day but one
　　　yokuyoku-nen（翌々年）　two years later
yokyô〈よきょう：余興〉an entertainment.
　　yokyô-ni〈余興に〉by way of entertainment.
yôkyoku〈ようきょく：陽極〉the anode, the positive pole.
yôkyû〈ようきゅう：要求〉a demand, a claim, a request, needs.
　　　yôkyû-ni-ôjiru（要求に応じる）　grant ((a person's)) request, yield
　　　　　to ((a person's)) request
　　　jidai no yôkyû（時代の要求）　the requirements of the age
　　　songai-baishô no yôkyû（損害賠償の要求）　a claim for the damages
　　yôkyû-suru〈要求する〉demand, claim, request, call ((on)), ask ((for)).
　　yôkyû-ni-yori〈要求により〉at one's request, on demand.
yôkyû〈ようきゅう：洋弓〉Western-style archery.
yôma〈ようま：洋間〉a Western-style room.
yome〈よめ：夜目〉
　　yome-ni-mo hakkiri mieru〈夜目にもはっきり見える〉be clearly seen even
　　　in the dark.
yome〈よめ：嫁〉a wife, a bride, a daughter-in-law.
　　　yome-ni-iku（嫁に行く）　marry ((a man))
　　　yome-ni-morau（嫁にもらう）　marry ((a woman))
yomei〈よめい：余命〉
　　　Yomei-ikubaku-mo-nai.（余命幾ばくもない.）　His days are num-
　　　　bered. / He has but few days left.
yômei〈ようめい：用命〉
　　　Nan-nari-to-go-yômei-ni-ôjimasu.（何なりと御用命に応じます.）　I am
　　　　at your service.
yome-iri〈よめいり：嫁入り〉wedding, marriage.
　　　yome-iri-jitaku（嫁入り支度）　a trousseau, preparations for marriage
yomeru〈よめる：読める〉be able to read, be legible, make out, can be
　　interpreted; see, understand.

Kare-no ji wa dômo-yome-nai.〈彼の字はどうも読めない.〉 His writing is hardly legible.

iroiro-no imi-ni yomeru〈いろいろの意味に読める〉 can be read in various ways

Sore-de yometa.〈それで読めた.〉 Well, that explains it.

yomi〈よみ：読み〉 reading; judgment, calculation.

yomi-ga-fukai〈読みが深い〉 have a sound judgment.

yomi-ga-asai〈読みが浅い〉 have a poor judgment

yomi-ageru〈よみあげる：読みあげる〉 read out, read aloud; read through, finish reading.

yo-michi〈よみち：夜道〉

yomichi-o-iku〈夜道を行く〉 go by night.

yomi-fukeru〈よみふける：読みふける〉 be absorbed in reading.

yomigaeraseru〈よみがえらせる：〉 revive, revivify; wake; freshen.

kioku o yomigaeraseru〈記憶をよみがえらせる〉 wake one's memories

yomigaeru〈よみがえる〉 revive; be freshened.

yomi-kaesu〈よみかえす：読み返す〉 read over, reread.

yomi-kaki〈よみかき：読み書き〉 reading and writing.

yomi-kata〈よみかた：読み方〉 how to read; pronunciation; a reading lesson.

yomikiri〈よみきり：読み切り〉

yomikiri-shôsetsu〈読み切り小説〉 a complete story

yomi-kiru〈よみきる：読み切る〉 read through, finish reading.

ikki-ni yomi-kiru〈一気に読み切る〉 read through ((a book)) at a stretch

yomi-konasu〈よみこなす：読みこなす〉 read and understand, digest.

yomi-mono〈よみもの：読み物〉 reading (matter).

tsumara-nai yomi-mono〈つまらない読み物〉 cheap reading

yomi-naosu〈よみなおす：読み直す〉 read over again.

yomi-nikui〈よみにくい：読みにくい〉 hard to read, illegible.

yomi-otosu〈よみおとす：読み落とす〉 omit reading, omit...in reading.

yomi-owaru〈よみおわる：読み終わる〉 read through, finish reading, have done with.

yo-mise〈よみせ：夜店〉 a night stall.

yo-mise-o-dasu〈夜店を出す〉 open a night stall

yomi-sute〈よみすて：読み捨て〉

yomi-sute-ni-suru〈読み捨てにする〉 read ((a magazine)) to kill time, throw ((a book)) away after reading ((it)) once.

yomi-toru 〈よみとる：読み取る〉 read 〔another's thought〕.

yomi-yasui 〈よみやすい：読みやすい〉 easy to read, legible.

yômô 〈ようもう：羊毛〉 wool.

  yômô-no 〈羊毛の〉 woolen.

yomogi 〈よもぎ〉 a mugwort.

yômoku 〈ようもく：要目〉 principal items.

yomoya 〈よもや〉 ((not)) possibly, surely ((not)).

  Yomoya-sonna-koto-wa-aru-mai. 〈よもやそんなことはあるまい。〉 That is highly impossible.

  Yomoya watashi-o wasure-wa-su-mai! 〈よもや私を忘れはすまい。〉 Surely you have not forgotten me!

yomoyama 〈よもやま〉

  yomoyama-banashi-o-suru 〈よもやま話をする〉 talk on various topics.

yômô-zai 〈ようもうざい：養毛剤〉 a hair tonic.

yomu 〈よむ：読む〉 read, chant.

  isoide-yomu 〈急いで読む〉 read hurriedly

  koe-o-dashite yomu 〈声を出して読む〉 read aloud

  musabori-yomu 〈むさぼり読む〉 read greedily

  tannen-ni yomu 〈丹念に読む〉 read carefully

  tokorodokoro-tobashite yomu 〈所々飛ばして読む〉 read skipping here and there

  zatto-yomu 〈ざっと読む〉 glance over

  yomu-kachi-ga-aru 〈読む価値がある〉 worth reading

  kyô o yomu 〈経を読む〉 chant a sutra

yomu 〈よむ：詠む〉

  uta-o-yomu 〈歌を詠む〉 compose a *tanka*, write a poem.

yômu 〈ようむ：要務〉 important business.

yômu-in 〈ようむいん：用務員〉 a janitor.

yô-muki 〈ようむき：用向き〉 one's business, an errand.

  yô-muki o tazuneru 〈用向きを尋ねる〉 ask ((a person)) his business

yon 〈よん：四〉 four.

  yon-bun-no-ichi 〈四分の一〉 one-fourth, a quarter

  yon-bun-no-san 〈四分の三〉 three-fourths, three-quarters

yonabe 〈よなべ：夜なべ〉 night work.

  yonabe-o-suru 〈夜なべをする〉 do night work, work nights.

yo-naka 〈よなか：夜中〉

  yo-naka-ni 〈夜中に〉 at midnight, in the middle of the night.

yondokoro-nai 〈よんどころない〉 unavoidable, inevitable.

　yondokoro-nai jijô-de 〈よんどころない事情で〉 under unavoidable circumstances.

yonen 〈よねん：余念〉

　yonen-ga-nai 〈余念がない〉 be absorbed ((in)), be bent ((on)), be devoted ((to)).

　　dokusho-ni-yonen-ga-nai 〈読書に余念がない〉 be absorbed in reading

yônen 〈ようねん：幼年〉 infancy, childhood.

　yônen-jidai-ni 〈幼年時代に〉 in one's childhood.

yonetsu 〈よねつ：余熱〉 remaining heat.

yo-nige 〈よにげ：夜逃げ〉 flight by night.

　yo-nige-suru 〈夜逃げする〉 flee by night.

yôniku 〈ようにく：羊肉〉 mutton, lamb.

yônin 〈ようにん：容認〉

　yônin-suru 〈容認する〉 admit, approve ((of)), tolerate.

yon-jû 〈よんじゅう：四十〉 *see*. shi-jû.

yo-no-naka 〈よのなか：世の中〉 the world, life, the times, an age.

　　Yo-no-naka ga kawatta. (世の中が変わった。) Times have changed.

　　yo-no-naka-ga-iya-ni-naru (世の中が嫌になる) be sick and tired of the world

　　Yo-no-naka-to-wa-sonna-mono-da. (世の中とはそんなものだ。) That is the way of the world.

　　sechigarai yo-no-naka (世知辛い世の中) a hard world

yopparai 〈よっぱらい：酔っ払い〉 a drunken man, a drunk, a drunkard.

　　yopparai-unten (酔っ払い運転) drunken driving

　yopparau 〈酔っ払う〉 get drunk, get intoxicated.

yôran 〈ようらん：揺らん〉 a cradle.

　　yôran-no-chi (揺らんの地) the cradleland, the birthplace

　yôran-ki-ni 〈揺らん期に〉 in the cradle.

yôrei 〈ようれい：用例〉 an example.

yoreru 〈よれる〉 be twisted, be tangled.

yoreyore 〈よれよれ〉

　yoreyore-no 〈よれよれの〉 worn-out, shabby.

yori 〈より〉 a twist.

　　yori-ito (より糸) twisted thread, twine.

　　ude-ni-yori-o-kakeru (腕によりをかける) do one's best

　　ude-ni-yori-o-kakete (腕によりをかけて) to the best of one's ability

　　yori-o-modosu (よりを戻す) get reconciled ((with)), return to the former relations ((with))

-yori〈 -より〉from, on (and after); than, to, above.

raigetsu mikka-yori（来月三日より）on and after the 5th of next month

Kore-wa are-yori-ii.（これはあれよりいい。）This is better than that./ This is superior to that.

-yori〈 -より：-寄り〉

yaya kita-yori-no-tokoro-ni（やや北寄りの所に）a little to the north ((of))

minami-yori-no kaze（南寄りの風）a southerly wind

migi-yori-no seiji-ka（右寄りの政治家）a right-of-center politician

yori-ai〈よりあい：寄り合い〉a meeting, a gathering.

chô-nai-no yori-ai（町内の寄り合い）a town meeting

yori-ai-jotai（寄り合い所帯）a mixed up team, a promiscuous household

yori-atsumaru or **yori-au**〈よりあつまる，よりあう：寄り集まる，寄り合う〉gather, assemble, flock together, draw together.

yori-awaseru〈よりあわせる：より合わせる〉twist together.

yori-dokoro〈よりどころ〉foundation, a ground, authority, a source.

yori-dokoro-no-aru〈よりどころのある〉authenticated, reliable.

yori-dokoro-no-nai（よりどころのない）groundless, uncertain, unreliable

yori-dori〈よりどり：より取り〉choice.

yori-dori-suru〈より取りする〉choose.

yori-gonomi〈よりごのみ：より好み〉see. eri-gonomi.

yori-kakaru〈よりかかる：より掛かる〉lean ((against, on *or* over)); rely ((on)).

kabe-ni-yori-kakaru（壁により掛かる）lean against a wall

yori-michi〈よりみち：寄り道〉

yori-michi-suru〈寄り道する〉stop on the way.

yori-nuki〈よりぬき：より抜き〉see. erinuki.

yori-sou〈よりそう：寄り添う〉draw nearer ((to)), nestle close ((to)), cuddle ((to)).

yôritsu〈ようりつ：擁立〉

yôritsu-suru〈擁立する〉back (up), support.

hito o yôritsu-shite aru chii-ni-tsukeru（人を擁立してある地位に就ける）help a person to a position

yoritsuki〈よりつき：寄り付き〉the opening of a session.

yoritsuki-nedan〈寄り付き値段〉 an opening price

yori-tsuku〈よりつく：寄り付く〉come near, approach.

yori-tsuka-nai〈寄り付かない〉keep away ((from)), shun

yori-wakeru〈よりわける：より分ける〉sort out, assort, classify, pick out, separate.

yôro〈ようろ：要路〉a principal road.

kôtsû no yôro〈交通の要路〉the main artery of traffic

yôrô〈ようろう：養老〉

yôrô-in〈養老院〉an old people's home

yôrô-nenkin〈養老年金〉an old-age pension

yoroi〈よろい〉armor.

yoroi-do〈よろいど：よろい戸〉a louver window, a (folding) shutter.

yorokobashii〈よろこばしい：喜ばしい〉glad, delightful, happy, joyful, joyous, pleasant, gratifying.

yorokobashii tayori〈喜ばしい便り〉 happy news

yorokobasu〈よろこばす：喜ばす〉delight, make ((a person)) happy, please, give pleasure ((to)).

yorokobi〈よろこび：喜び〉joy, delight, rejoicing, pleasure, rapture, congratulation, gratification.

yorokobi-no-amari naku〈喜びの余り泣く〉cry for joy

yorokobi-no-iro-o-ukaberu〈喜びの色を浮かべる〉 show pleasure ((at))

yorokobi o noberu〈喜びを述べる〉 offer one's congratulations ((on))

yorokobu〈よろこぶ：喜ぶ〉be pleased ((at, with *or* to do)), be delighted ((at, with *or* to do)), be rejoiced ((at *or* over)), be glad ((of *or* to do)).

seikô-o-yorokobu〈成功を喜ぶ〉 be pleased with one's success

Kodomo-tachi wa sono kôkei-o-mite yorokonda.〈子供たちはその光景を見て喜んだ.〉 The children were delighted to see the spectacle.

Sono shirase-o-kiite watashi-wa totemo yorokonde-iru.〈その知らせを聞いて私はとても喜んでいる.〉 I am very glad to hear the news.

odori-agatte-yorokobu〈躍り上がって喜ぶ〉 jump for joy

yorokobu-beki〈喜ぶべき〉delightful, pleasant, happy, for congratulation.

yorokobu-beki koto〈喜ぶべき事〉 a matter for congratulation

yorokonde〈喜んで〉with joy, with pleasure, gladly, willingly.

yorokonde mukaeru〈喜んで迎える〉 receive ((a person)) with joy

yorokonde oshieru〈喜んで教える〉 teach ((a person)) with pleasure

yoromeku〈よろめく〉stagger, reel, falter, totter, lurch; have a love affair ((with)).

yoromeki-nagara 〈よろめきながら〉 with faltering steps.

yoron 〈よろん：よ論〉 *see.* seron.

Yôroppa 〈ヨーロッパ〉 Europe.

Yôroppa-tairiku（ヨーロッパ大陸） the European Continent

Yôroppa-jin（ヨーロッパ人） a European

Yôroppa-no（ヨーロッパの） European

yoroshi 〈よろしい〉

Yoroshii-desu-tomo.（よろしいですとも.） Yes, all right.

Dochira-demo-yoroshii.（どちらでもよろしい.） Either will do.

Tabaco-o-suttemo-yoroshii-ka?（たばこを吸ってもよろしいか.） May I smoke?

yoroshiku 〈よろしく〉

Yoroshiku-o-tori-hakarai-kudasai.（よろしくお取り計らいください.） I leave it entirely to your discretion.

Kodomo-o-yoroshiku-o-negai-itashimasu.（子供をよろしくお願いいたします.） I hope you will kindly look after my son.

O-taku-no-minasan-ni yoroshiku-o-tsutae-kudasai.（お宅の皆さんによろしくお伝えください.） Please remember me to your family.

Chichi-kara-mo-yoroshiku-to-no-koto-deshita.（父からもよろしくとのことでした.） Father sends you his best regards.

yoroyoro(-to) 〈よろよろ（と）〉 staggeringly, totteringly, falteringly.

yoroyoro(-to)-aruku（よろよろ（と）歩く） stagger along

yoroyoro(-to)-tachi-agaru（よろよろ（と）立ち上がる） stagger to one's feet

yoru 〈よる：夜〉 night.

yoru-mo-hiru-mo（夜も昼も） night and day, day and night

yoru-osoku-made（夜遅くまで） till late at night

yoru-no-Tôkyô（夜の東京） Tokyo at night

yoru-ni 〈夜に〉 at night, in the night.

yoru-wa 〈夜は〉 by night.

yoru 〈よる〉 twist, twine.

yoru 〈よる：寄る〉 draw near, come near, approach; drop in, call ((at *or* on)), touch ((at)); meet, come together, assemble, swarm.

Motto-hi-no-chikaku-ni-yori-nasai.（もっと火の近くに寄りなさい.） Come nearer to the fire.

Dôzo mata o-yori-kudasai.（どうぞまたお寄りください.） Drop in again, please.

Yoru-to-sawaru-to kare-no-hanashi-da.（寄ると触ると彼の話だ.） Whenever they meet, he is sure to be one of the topics of their conversation.

yotte-takkate-naguru（寄ってたかって殴る）gang up and beat ((a person))

yoru〈よる〉

yori-ni-yotte-sono-hi-ni〈よりによってその日に〉on that day of all days.

(ni)-yoru〈(に)よる〉depend ((on)), be based ((on)), be due ((to)).

Jijô-ikan-ni-yoru.（事情いかんによる。）That depends.

Furansu-no densetsu-ni-yoru（フランスの伝説による）be based on a French legend

fu-chûi-ni-yoru（不注意による）be due to carelessness

~-ni-yori, ~-ni-yotte or **~-ni-yoru-to**〈〜により，〜によって，〜によると〉

go-irai-ni-yori or go-irai-ni-yotte（御依頼により，御依頼によって）in compliance with your request

jijô-ni-yori or jijô-ni-yotte（事情により，事情によって）according to circumstances

hanashi-ai-ni-yori or hanashi-ai-ni-yotte（話し合いにより，話し合いによって）by common consent

shimbun-ni-yoru-to（新聞によると）according to newspapers

kiku-tokoro-ni-yoru-to（聞くところによると）judging from reports

yorube〈よるべ：寄る辺〉

yorube-ga-nai〈寄る辺がない〉have no relative or friend to depend on, have no place to go.

Yorudan〈ヨルダン〉Jordan.

Yorudan-no〈ヨルダンの〉Jordanian.

yoru-hiru〈よるひる：夜昼〉day and night.

yoru-hiru-no-betsu-naku〈夜昼の別なく〉night and day, all the time.

yôryô〈ようりょう：用量〉dosage.

yôryô〈ようりょう：容量〉capacity.

yôryô〈ようりょう：要領〉the point, the gist; a summary; the knack.

yôryô-o-ete-iru（要領を得ている）be to the point

Kanojo-no hanashi wa yôryô-o-e-nakatta.（彼女の話は要領を得なかった。）Her remarks were not to the point.

yôryô-o-eta-koto-o-iu（要領を得たことを言う）speak to the point

yôryô-o-kai-tsumande-hanasu（要領をかいつまんで話す）sum up

yôryô o nomi-komu（要領を飲み込む）get the knack ((of))

yoryoku〈よりょく：余力〉remaining strength, reserve power.

yoryoku o takuwaeru（余力を蓄える）save up one's energy

mada yoryoku-ga-aru（まだ余力がある）still have the energy left

yôryoku〈ようりょく：揚力〉lift.

yôryoku-so〈ようりょくそ：葉緑素〉chlorophyll.

  yôryoku-so(-iri)-no〈葉緑素（入り）の〉chlorophyllous.

yosa〈よさ：良さ〉(a) merit, (a) virtue, (a) good quality, a good point.

kanojo-no　yosa-ga-wakara-nai（彼女のよさが分からない）cannot see her merit

yôsai〈ようさい：洋裁〉dressmaking.

yôsai-gakkô（洋裁学校）a dressmaking school

yôsai〈ようさい：要さい〉a fortress, a stronghold.

yosan〈よさん：予算〉an estimate, a budget.

yosan o tateru（予算を立てる）make an estimate, make a budget

yosan-ni keijô-suru（予算に計上する）include in the budget

yosan o hensei-suru（予算を編成する）compile a budget

yosan o chôka-suru（予算を超過する）exceed the budget

yosan o kiri-tsumeru（予算を切り詰める）cut down a budget

yosan-an（予算案）a budget bill

  yosan-an-o-gikai-ni-teishutsu-suru（予算案を議会に提出する）open the budget

hon-yosan（本予算）the principal budget

zantei-yosan（暫定予算）a provisional budget

hosei-yosan（補正予算）a revised budget

  yosan-nai-de〈予算内で〉within one's budget.

yôsan〈ようさん：養蚕〉sericulture, silk culture.

yôsan-gyô（養蚕業）the sericultural industry

yose〈よせ：寄席〉a vaudeville theater, a variety hall.

yose-atsume〈よせあつめ：寄せ集め〉a mixture, a medley, odds and ends.

yose-atsume-no-chîmu（寄せ集めのチーム）a scratch team

  yose-atsumeru〈寄せ集める〉put together, gather, collect, scratch together.

yose-gaki〈よせがき：寄せ書き〉a collection of autographs.

yose-gi〈よせぎ：寄せ木〉parquetry.

yose-gi-zaiku（寄せ木細工）wooden mosaic, parquetry

yosei〈よせい：余生〉the rest of one's life.

yosei o anraku-ni okuru（余生を安楽に送る）live in comfort for the rest of one's days

yosei〈よせい：余勢〉surplus energy.

yosei-o-katte〈余勢を駆って〉driving on without a stop, following up the victory.

yôsei〈ようせい：よう精〉a fairy, an elf.

yôsei〈ようせい：養成〉training, education, cultivation.
    yôsei-kikan（養成期間）a training period
  yôsei-suru〈養成する〉train, educate, bring up, cultivate.

yôsei〈ようせい：要請〉a demand, a request.
    jidai no yôsei（時代の要請）the needs of the times
  yôsei-suru〈要請する〉demand, request, ask.

yôsei〈ようせい：陽性〉
  yôsei-no〈陽性の〉positive.

yôseki〈ようせき：容積〉capacity, cubic volume, bulk; solid content.

yosen〈よせん：予選〉a preliminary match, a trial heat; a provisional election.
    hyaku-mêtoru-yosen（百メートル予選）the 100 meter preliminary
  yosen-o-tsûka-suru〈予選を通過する〉qualify ((for)).
    yosen-de-ochiru（予選で落ちる）be disqualified ((from)), be e-liminated ((from))

yôsen〈ようせん：用せん〉stationery, letter paper, a writing pad.

yôsen〈ようせん：よう船〉chartering, a chartered ship.
    yôsen-keiyaku（よう船契約）charter

yoseru〈よせる：寄せる〉draw ((a thing)) near; put ((a thing)) aside; gather, collect; call ((people)) together; add, sum up.
    tsukue o mado-no-chikaku-ni-yoseru（机を窓の近くに寄せる）draw up one's desk close to a window
    Mata sono-uchi-ni yosete-itadakimasu.（またそのうちに寄せていただきます。）I'll drop in again some time later.
    〜-ni-omoi-o-yoseru（〜に思いを寄せる）be in love ((with))

yôsetru〈ようせつ：溶接〉welding.
    yôsetsu-bô（溶接棒）a welding rod
    denki-yôsetsu（電気溶接）electric welding
  yôsetsu-suru〈溶接する〉weld ((to *or* together)).

yose-tsukeru〈よせつける：寄せ付ける〉allow ((a person)) to come near.
  yose-tsuke-mai〈寄せつけない〉keep away ((from)), keep ((the enemy)) off.

yose-zan〈よせざん：寄せ算〉addition.
  yose-zan-o-suru〈寄せ算をする〉add up.

yôsha〈ようしゃ：容赦〉pardon, forgiveness, mercy.

yôsha-suru〈容赦する〉pardon, forgive, show leniency ((to)), overlook.

   yôsha-shi-nai〈容赦しない〉show no mercy ((to)), make no allowance ((for))

yôsha-no-nai〈容赦のない〉merciless.

yôsha-naku〈容赦なく〉mercilessly, without mercy.

   yôsha-naku shobatsu-suru（容赦なく処罰する）punish ((a violator)) without mercy

yoshi〈よし：由〉

 ~*-no-yoshi*〈～の由〉I hear that... , I understand that... , they say that ... , it is said that... .

Yoshi!〈よし.〉All right! / Well! / Good!

yôshi〈ようし：用紙〉a (blank) form, paper.

   tôan-yôshi（答案用紙）an examination paper

yôshi〈ようし：要旨〉the point, the substance, the purport, a summary.

yôshi〈ようし：容姿〉figure, one's appearance.

yôshi〈ようし：陽子〉a proton.

yôshi〈ようし：養子〉an adopted child, a son-in-law.

   yôshi-engumi（養子縁組）adoption

 yôshi-ni-suru〈養子にする〉adopt.

 yôshi-ni-iku〈養子に行く〉be adopted ((into)).

yoshi-ashi〈よしあし：善しあし〉good or evil, right and wrong, merits and demerits.

   koto-no-yoshi-ashi-wa-betsu-ni-shite（事のよしあしは別にして）for good or evil

   tenki-no-yoshi-ashi-ni-kakawarazu（天気のよしあしにかかわらず）regardless of weather

   ~*-mo-yoshi-ashi-da*（～もよしあしだ）have both advantages and disadvantages

yôshiki〈ようしき：洋式〉Western style.

yôshiki〈ようしき：様式〉a mode, (a) style.

   seikatsu-yôshiki（生活様式）a mode of living

yoshimi〈よしみ〉friendship, intimacy.

   shin·yû-no-yoshimi-de（親友のよしみで）out of friendship

   mukashi-no-yoshimi-de（昔のよしみで）for old acquaintance' sake

yoshin〈よしん：余震〉an aftershock, an after tremor.

yoshin〈よしん：予審〉a preliminary examination, a pretrial hearing.

yôsho〈ようしょ：要所〉an important position, a strategic point, an important point.

*yôsho*yôsho-ni〈要所要所に〉at every strategic point.

yôsho〈ようしょ：洋書〉a Western book.

yôshô〈ようしょう：要衝〉a point of strategic importance.

yô-shokki〈ようしょっき：洋食器〉dinnerware, a set of dinnerware.

yôshoku〈ようしょく：要職〉an important post.

    yôshoku-ni-tsuku〈要職に就く〉be appointed to an important post

yôshoku〈ようしょく：洋食〉Western dishes.

yôshoku〈ようしょく：養殖〉raising, culture, breeding.

    kaki-no-yôshoku-jô（かきの養殖場）an oyster bed

yôshoku-suru〈養殖する〉raise, cultivate, breed.

yoshû〈よしゅう：予習〉preparation (of lessons).

yoshû-suru〈予習する〉prepare lessons.

yoso〈よそ〉another place.

yoso-de〈よそで〉at another place, elsewhere.

    yoso-de kau（よそで買う）buy elsewhere

    doko-ka yoso-de（どこかよそで）somewhere else

yosô〈よそう：予想〉expectation, anticipation, a forecast, a prospect, imagination, supposition, an estimate.

    kome-no-shûkaku-yosô（米の収穫予想）a prospect for the rice crop

yosô-suru〈予想する〉expect, anticipate, forecast, foresee, presume, imagine, suppose, estimate.

yosô-doori-no or *yosô-doori-ni*〈予想どおりの，予想どおりに〉as expected.

    yosô-doori-ni-naru（予想どおりになる）come up to one's expectations

yosô-gai-no〈予想外の〉unexpected, unforeseen.

yosô-gai-ni〈予想外に〉unexpectedly, beyond expectation(s), against one's expectations.

yosô-ni-hanshite〈予想に反して〉contrary to one's expectations.

yôso〈ようそ：要素〉an element, a factor, a requisite.

    kôsei-yôso（構成要素）a component

yôso〈ようそ：よう素〉iodine.

yôsô〈ようそう：洋装〉

yôsô-suru〈洋装する〉be dressed in Western style.

yôsô〈ようそう：様相〉an aspect, a phase.

    tada-naranu yôsô o teisuru（ただならぬ様相を呈する）assume a serious aspect

yoso-goto〈よそごと：よそ事〉a matter of no concern.

yoso-goto-no-yô-ni〈よそ事のように〉as if it were none of one's concern.

yosoku 〈よそく：予測〉an estimate, a forecast, prediction.

  yosoku-suru 〈予測する〉estimate, forecast, predict.

    yosoku-deki-nai (予測できない)　cannot be foreseen

yoso-me 〈よそめ：よそ目〉

  yoso-me-ni-mo 〈よそ目にも〉even to a casual observer.

yoso-mi 〈よそみ：よそ見〉

  yoso-mi-suru 〈よそ見する〉look aside, take one's eyes ((off)).

    yoso-mi-shi-nagara aruku (よそ見しながら歩く)　walk along looking around one

yosooi 〈よそおい：装い〉dress, array, attire; toilet, make-up.

    natsu-no-yosooi (夏の装い)　the summer attire

    yosooi-mo-arata-na butikku (装いも新たなブティック)　a newly furnished boutique

yosoou 〈よそおう：装う〉dress oneself ((in)), ornament oneself ((with)), make up; pretend, affect, feign, assume.

    byôki-o-yosoou (病気を装う)　pretend to be ill

  〜-o-yosootte 〈〜を装って〉under pretense of... .

    heisei-o-yosootte (平静を装って)　with feigned calm

yosou 〈よそう〉serve, dish up, help oneself ((to)).

yosoyososhii 〈よそよそしい〉distant, cold, frigid, unconcerned, indifferent, standoffish.

    yosoyososhii-taido-o-toru (よそよそしい態度を取る)　give ((a person)) the cold shoulder

  yosoyososhiku 〈よそよそしく〉distantly, coldly, in a frigid manner.

    yosoyososhiku-suru (よそよそしくする)　be cold ((to)), treat ((a person)) coldly

yoso-yuki 〈よそゆき：よそ行き〉

  yoso-yuki-no 〈よそ行きの〉formal, company.

    yoso-yuki-no kotoba (よそ行きの言葉)　unnaturally formal language

    yoso-yuki-no kimono (よそ行きの着物)　one's best clothes

yosu 〈よす〉stop, give up, cut off.

    Mô-yose-yo! (もうよせよ。)　Cut it out!

yôsu 〈ようす：様子〉the state of affairs; (an) appearance, a look, (a) manner; a sign.

    yôsu-o-shitte-iru (様子を知っている)　be familiar ((with))

    yôsu-ga-wakara-nai (様子が分からない)　be ignorant ((of))

      Watashi-wa koko-no-yôsu-ga-mattaku-wakara-nai. (私はここの様子が全く分からない。)　I am quite a stranger here.

bikkuri-shita-yôsu-de（びっくりした様子で）with a look of surprise

Kanojo-ga-ki-ga-tsuita-yôsu-wa-nakatta.（彼女が気が付いた様子はなかった。）There was no sign of her awareness.

yôsui〈ようすい：用水〉service water, water for irrigation, rainwater.

yôsui-ro（用水路）an irrigation channel

yôsuru〈ようする：要する〉require, need, take, want, demand.

saishin-no chûi o yôsuru（細心の注意を要する）require close attention

yôsuru-ni〈ようするに：要するに〉in a word, in short, to sum up, after all.

yosute-bito〈よすてびと：世捨て人〉a hermit, an anchoress.

yôtashi〈ようたし：用足し〉

yôtashi-ni-iku〈用足しに行く〉go on an errand, go out on business.

yotayota〈よたよた〉

yotayota(-to) or yotayota-shita-ashidori-de〈よたよた（と），よたよたした足取りで〉unsteadily, totteringly.

yotayota-aruku〈よたよた歩く〉totter, stagger.

yotei〈よてい：予定〉a program, a plan, a schedule, previous arrangement; an estimate.

yotei o tateru（予定を立てる）make a plan

yotei o henkô-suru（予定を変更する）change the program

yotei-ga-kuruu（予定が狂う）have the schedule broken

yotei-ga-tsumatte-iru（予定が詰まっている）have a tight schedule

shuppatsu-yotei-bi（出発予定日）the expected date of departure

yotei-gaku（予定額）the estimated amount

yotei-suru〈予定する〉plan, schedule, intend, expect, arrange beforehand.

yotei-de-aru〈予定である〉be scheduled, be expected, intend ((to do)), be due ((to do)).

Pâtî wa nichiyô(-bi)-no-yotei-de-aru.（パーティーは日曜（日）の予定である。）The party is scheduled for Sunday.

Ressha wa gogo-san-ji-chaku-no-yotei-de-aru.（列車は午後三時着の予定である。）The train is due at 3p.m.

yotei-no〈予定の〉scheduled, intended, expected, prearranged, appointed, estimated.

yotei-no-jikoku-ni（予定の時刻に）at the appointed time

yôtei-doori〈予定どおり〉as previously arranged, according to plan.

yotei-yori-hayaku〈予定より早く〉earlier than expected, before time.

yotei-yori-osoku〈予定より遅く〉later than expected, behind time.

    yotei-yori futsuka-okurete〈予定より二日遅れて〉two days later than expected, two days behind time

yôten〈ようてん：要点〉the main point, the substance.

    yôten o tsukamu〈要点をつかむ〉catch the point

yôten〈ようてん：陽転〉

    yôten-suru〈陽転する〉change to positive.

yotô〈よとう：与党〉the Government party, the party in power.

    yotô-giin（与党議員）a member of the Government party

yôto〈ようと：用途〉(a) use, service.

    yôto-ga-hiroi〈用途が広い〉have various uses, be used for various purposes.

yotoku〈よとく：余得〉an extra profit, a perquisite.

yôton〈ようとん：養豚〉hog raising, pig keeping.

    yôton-gyô-sha（養豚業者）a hog raiser, a pig breeder

yôtsû〈ようつう：腰痛〉lumbago.

yotsu-ashi〈よつあし：四つ足〉

    yotsu-ashi-no〈四つ足の〉four-footed.

yo-tsugi〈よつぎ：世継ぎ〉a successor; an heir, an heiress.

yotsu-giri〈よつぎり：四つ切り〉a quarter.

yôtsui〈ようつい：腰つい〉the lumbar vertebra.

yotsu-kado〈よつかど：四つ角〉a crossroads; a street crossing, a street corner.

    yotsu-kado o hidari-e magaru（四つ角を左へ曲がる）turn the corner to the left

yotsun-bai〈よつんばい：四つんばい〉

    yotsun-bai-ni-naru〈四つんばいになる〉get on all fours.

    yotsun-bai-ni-natte〈四つんばいになって〉on hands and knees.

yotsu-ori〈よつおり：四つ折り〉a quarto.

yo-tsuyu〈よつゆ：夜露〉the night dew.

you〈よう：酔う〉get drunk; feel sick; be intoxicated.

    uisukī-ni you（ウイスキーに酔う）get drunk on whisky

    fune-ni-you（船に酔う）be seasick

    seikô-ni you（成功に酔う）be intoxicated with success

yowa-bi〈よわび：弱火〉a low flame.

yowa-goshi〈よわごし：弱腰〉

    yowa-goshi-no〈弱腰の〉timid, weak-kneed, faint-hearted.

yowai〈よわい：弱い〉weak, feeble, faint, frail, delicate, light, mild, poor.

　karada-ga-yowai〈体が弱い〉 have a delicate constitution, be poor in health

　fune-ni-yowai〈船に弱い〉 be a bad sailor

　sake ni yowai〈酒に弱い〉 be a poor drinker

　sûgaku-ni-yowai〈数学に弱い〉 be poor at mathematics

yowaku〈弱く〉 weakly, feebly, faintly.

　yowaku-naru〈弱くなる〉 become weak, weaken

　yowaku-suru〈弱くする〉 make weak, weaken

yowai-mono〈よわいもの：弱い者〉a weak person, the weak.

　yowai-mono-ni mikata-suru〈弱い者に味方する〉 stand by the weak

　yowai-mono-ijime-o-suru〈弱い者いじめをする〉 bully the weak

yowa-ki〈よわき：弱気〉faintheartedness; a bear.

yowa-ki-ni-naru〈弱気になる〉be discouraged.

yowa-ki-na〈弱気な〉fainthearted, weak.

yowamaru〈よわまる：弱まる〉become weak, grow fainter, abate.

yowameru〈弱める〉make weak(er), enfeeble, tone down.

yowami〈よわみ：弱み〉a weakness, a weak point.

　yowami o miseru〈弱みを見せる〉 betray one's weak point

yowa-mushi〈よわむし：弱虫〉a weakling, a jellyfish, a coward, a crybaby, a milksop.

yowa-ne〈よわね：弱音〉

yowa-ne-o-haku〈弱音を吐く〉sing small, make complaints.

yowaraseru〈よわらせる：弱らせる〉weaken, enfeeble, emaciate; annoy, embarrass.

yowari-hateru〈よわりはてる：弱り果てる〉be utterly exhausted, be tired out; be much annoyed ((at)), be at one's wit's end.

yowaru〈よわる：弱る〉weaken, grow weak, languish, be run down; be depressed, be perplexed, be annoyed.

　Kono-atsusa-ni-wa-yowaru.（この暑さには弱る。）The heat knocks me down.

　karada-ga-yowatte-iru〈体が弱っている〉 be out of health

yowasa〈よわさ：弱さ〉weakness, frailty, feebleness.

yowaseru〈よわせる：酔わせる〉make ((a person)) drunk; enrapture, charm, intoxicate.

yo-watari〈よわたり：世渡り〉

　yo-watari no michi〈世渡りの道〉 the art of living

yo-watari-ga-umai〈世渡りがうまい〉know how to make a living.

yowayowashii 〈よわよわしい：弱々しい〉weakly, feeble, delicate-looking.

　　yowayowashii koe（弱々しい声）a feeble voice

yoyaku 〈よやく：予約〉preengagement, subscription, reservation.

　　yoyaku o uketsukeru（予約を受け付ける）take reservations

　　yoyaku o tori-kesu（予約を取り消す）cancel a reservation

　　ha-isha-no-yoyaku（歯医者の予約）a dental appointment

　　yoyaku-kin（予約金）a deposit, a subscription price

　　yoyaku-seki（予約席）a reserved seat, Reserved.

　yoyaku-suru〈予約する〉subscribe ((for *or* to)), book ((a seat)) previously, have ((a room)) reserved, make a reservation, engage.

　yoyaku-zumi-no〈予約済みの〉reserved, engaged.

　　Zaseki-wa-subete　yoyaku-zumi-desu.（座席はすべて予約済みです。）

　　　All seats are reserved. / We are all booked up.

yôyaku 〈ようやく：要約〉summation; a summary, an epitome.

　yôyaku-suru〈要約する〉summarize, epitomize, sum up.

　yôyaku-sureba〈要約すれば〉to sum up, in short, in a word.

yôyaku 〈ようやく〉*see.* yatto.

yôyô 〈ようよう：洋々〉

　yôyô-taru〈洋々たる〉boundless, vast.

　　yôyô-taru taiyô（洋々たる大洋）the boundless ocean

　　yôyô-taru zento（洋々たる前途）a bright future

yoyû 〈よゆう：余裕〉room, time (to spare), sufficient time, a margin.

　~-(suru)-yoyû-ga-aru〈~(する)余裕がある〉can afford ((to do)).

yoyû-shakushaku 〈よゆうしゃくしゃく：余裕しゃくしゃく〉

　yoyû-shakushaku-to-shite-iru（余裕しゃくしゃくとしている）have a great reserve of energy, have enough and to spare, be calm and composed.

　yoyû-shakushaku-to-shite〈余裕しゃくしゃくとして〉in a free and easy manner.

yozai 〈よざい：余罪〉other crimes.

yôzai 〈ようざい：用材〉material; timber, lumber.

　　kenchiku-yôzai（建築用材）building materials

yôzai 〈ようざい：溶剤〉a solvent.

yo-zora 〈よぞら：夜空〉a night sky.

yo-zuri 〈よずり：夜釣り〉night fishing.

　yo-zuri-ni-iku〈夜釣りに行く〉go fishing at night.

yu 〈ゆ：湯〉hot water; a bath, a spa.

　　yu-o-wakasu（湯を沸かす）boil water, get the bath ready

yu-ni-hairu（湯に入る）have a bath

yu-o-tsukawaseru（湯を使わせる）give ((a child)) a bath

yu-kagen-o-miru（湯加減をみる）see how hot the bath is

Yu-kagen-wa-ikaga-desu-ka?（湯加減はいかがですか.）How do you find the bath?

yû〈ゆう：優〉A, Excellent.

yû o morau（優をもらう）get an A

yu-agari〈ゆあがり：湯上がり〉

yu-agari-ni-ippai-yaru〈湯上がりに一杯やる〉have a drink of *sake* just after a bath.

yûai〈ゆうあい：友愛〉friendship, fellowship.

yu-aka〈ゆあか：湯あか〉fur, scale.

yu-aka-o-toru〈湯あかを取る〉remove scale〔from a boiler〕, scale.

yuatsu〈ゆあつ：油圧〉oil pressure.

yû-bae〈ゆうばえ：夕映え〉the evening glow.

yûbe〈ゆうべ：昨夜〉last night, yesterday evening.

yûbe〈ゆうべ：夕べ〉an evening.

aki-no yûbe（秋の夕べ）an autumn evening

ongaku-no yûbe（音楽の夕べ）a musical evening

yûben〈ゆうべん：雄弁〉eloquence, fluency.

Chimmoku-wa-kin　yûben-wa-gin.（沈黙は金雄弁は銀.）Silence is golden, speech is silver.

yûben-ka（雄弁家）an eloquent speaker

yûben-o-furuu〈雄弁を振るう〉speak eloquently ((on)).

yûben-na〈雄弁な〉eloquent, fluent.

yûben-ni〈雄弁に〉eloquently, fluently.

〜-o-yûben-ni-mono-gataru（〜を雄弁に物語る）be eloquent of...

yubi〈ゆび：指〉a finger, a toe.

yubi o mageru（指を曲げる）bend one's fingers

yubi o narasu（指を鳴らす）snap one's fingers

yubi o sasu（指を差す）point the finger ((at))

yubi-o-kuwaeru（指をくわえる）put a finger in one's mouth

yubi-o-kuwaete-mite-iru（指をくわえて見ている）remain a mere onlooker, look enviously ((at))

Seikô-sha　wa　go-hon-no-yubi-de-kazoeru-hodo-shika-i-nakatta.（成功者は五本の指で数えるほどしかいなかった.）The successful men could be counted on the fingers of one hand.

yûbi〈ゆうび：優美〉grace, elegance, refinement.

yûbi-na〈優美な〉graceful, elegant, refined.

yubi-kiri〈ゆびきり：指切り〉

yubi-kiri-suru〈指切りする〉hook and cross one's little finger with another's.

yûbin〈ゆうびん：郵便〉mail, post.

yûbin ga okureru（郵便が遅れる）the mail is delayed

yûbin o atsumeru（郵便を集める）collect the mail

yûbin o haitatsu-suru（郵便を配達する）deliver the mail

yûbin-bangô（郵便番号）zip code

yûbin-gawase（郵便為替）a postal money order

yûbin-kyoku（郵便局）a post office

yûbin-ryôkin（郵便料金）postage, postal charges

yûbin-uke（郵便受け）a mailbox, a letter box

yûbin o dasu（郵便を出す）mail, post.

yûbin-de〈郵便で〉by mail, by post.

yûbin-de dasu（郵便で出す）send by mail

yubi-ori〈ゆびおり：指折り〉

yubi-ori-kazoeru〈指折り数える〉count on one's fingers.

yubi-ori-kazoete-matsu（指折り数えて待つ）look forward ((to)), wait eagerly ((for))

yubi-ori-no〈指折りの〉leading, principal, prominent.

yubi-saki〈ゆびさき：指先〉the tip of a finger.

yubi-wa〈ゆびわ：指輪〉a ring.

yûbô〈ゆうぼう：有望〉

yûbô-na〈有望な〉promising, hopeful, bright.

yûboku〈ゆうぼく：遊牧〉nomadism.

yûboku-min（遊牧民）nomads, a wandering tribe

yûboku-seikatsu（遊牧生活）a nomadic life

yubune〈ゆぶね：湯船〉a bathtub.

yuchaku〈ゆちゃく：癒着〉adhesion, conglutination.

yuchaku-suru〈癒着する〉adhere ((to)), heal up.

yûchi〈ゆうち：誘致〉lure, attraction, enticement.

yûchi-suru〈誘致する〉lure, attract, entice.

kôjô o yûchi-suru（工場を誘致する）invite a factory〔to a place〕

yûchô〈ゆうちょう：悠長〉

yûchô-ni-kamaeru（悠長に構える）take things easy

yûchô-na〈悠長な〉leisurely, slow.

yûdachi〈ゆうだち：夕立〉a (sudden) shower, an evening shower.

    yûdachi-ni-au〈夕立に遭う〉 be caught in a shower

yûdai〈ゆうだい：雄大〉grandeur, magnificence.

  yûdai-na〈雄大な〉grand, magnificent.

    yûdai-na nagame（雄大な眺め）a grand sight, a magnificent view

yudan〈ゆだん：油断〉inattention, carelessness, imprudence, incautiousness, unpreparedness.

    Yudan-taiteki.（油断大敵.）There is many a slip 'twixt the cup and the lip.

  yudan-suru〈油断する〉be inattentive, be careless, be unprepared.

    yudan-shi-nai（油断しない）be on one's guard, be on the alert

  yudan-saseru〈油断させる〉throw ((a person)) off his guard.

  yudan-no-nara-nai〈油断のならない〉snaky, cunning, subtle.

  yudan-naku〈油断なく〉with jealousy.

  yudan-shite-iru-uchi-ni〈油断しているうちに〉whike one is off one's guard.

yûdan〈ゆうだん：勇断〉a resolute decision.

yudaneru〈ゆだねる〉entrust ((a person)) with, entrust ((a matter)) to ((a person)).

yûdan-sha〈ゆうだんしゃ：有段者〉a grade holder.

Yudaya〈ユダヤ〉Judea.

    Yudaya-jin（ユダヤ人）a Jew

    Yudaya-kyô（ユダヤ教）Judaism

    Yudaya(-jin)-no（ユダヤ（人）の）Jewish

yuden〈ゆでん：油田〉an oil field.

yuderu〈ゆでる〉boil.

yude-tamago〈ゆでたまご：ゆで卵〉a boiled egg.

yûdô〈ゆうどう：誘導〉induction, inducement, guidance.

    yûdô-dan（誘導弾）a guided missile

    yûdô-sôchi（誘導装置）a guidance system, guidance controls

    yûdô-jimmon（誘導尋問）a leading question

      yûdô-jimmon-o-suru（誘導尋問をする）ask ((a person)) a leading question

  yûdô-suru〈誘導する〉induce, guide, lead.

yûdoku〈ゆうどく：有毒〉

    yûdoku-gas（有毒ガス）poisonous gas

  yûdoku-na〈有毒な〉poisonous, venomous, noxious.

yue〈ゆえ：故〉a reason, a cause; circumstances.

  yue-atte〈故あって〉for a certain reason, under the inevitable

circumstances.

   yue-naku-shite〈故なくして〉 without reason

yûei-jutsu〈ゆうえいじゅつ：遊泳術〉 how to get along in the world.

   yûei-jutsu-ga-umai〈遊泳術がうまい〉 be wise in the ways of life.

yûeki〈ゆうえき：有益〉

   yûeki-na〈有益な〉 beneficial, instructive, wholesome, useful, profitable.

       omoshirokute-yûeki-na（面白くて有益な） instructive as well as interesting

   yûeki-ni〈有益に〉 usefully, to advantage.

       kane-o-dekiru-dake-yûeki-ni-tsukau（金をできるだけ有益に使う） make the most of one's money

yûenchi〈ゆうえんち：遊園地〉 a recreation ground, an amusement park.

yûetsu〈ゆうえつ：優越〉 superiority, predominance.

       yûetsu-kan（優越感） a sense of superiority, superiority complex

   yûetsu-shita〈優越した〉 superior, predominant.

yûfuku〈ゆうふく：裕福〉

   yûfuku-na〈裕福な〉 rich, wealthy, affluent, well-to-do, well-off, prosperous.

yûga〈ゆうが：優雅〉 elegance, grace, daintiness.

   yûga-na〈優雅な〉 elegant, graceful, dainty.

yûgai〈ゆうがい：有害〉

   yûgai-na〈有害な〉 bad, harmful, injurious, noxious, pernicious.

yûgai〈ゆうがい：有がい〉

       yûgai-kasha（有がい貨車） a boxcar, a covered waggon

   yûgai-no〈有がいの〉 covered.

yu-gaku〈ゆがく：湯がく〉 scald, parboil.

yugameru〈ゆがめる〉 pervert, distort, warp, twist; bend, curve.

       jijitsu o yugameru（事実をゆがめる） pervert the fact

       kao o yugameru（顔をゆがめる） distort one's face, make a wry face

yugami〈ゆがみ〉 (a) distortion, a warp, (a) bend.

   yugamu〈ゆがむ〉 be perverted, be distorted, be warped, be bent.

   yuganda〈ゆがんだ〉 perverted, distorted, warped, crooked, slanted, bent.

yûgao〈ゆうがお：夕顔〉 a bottle gourd.

yûgata〈ゆうがた：夕方〉 evening.

       asu-no-yûgata-made-ni（明日の夕方までに） by tomorrow evening

       yûgata-ni（夕方に） in the evening

yûga-tô〈ゆうがとう：誘が灯〉 a light trap.

yuge 〈ゆげ：湯気〉 steam, vapor.

  yuge-ga-tatsu or *yuge-o-tateru* 〈湯気が立つ，湯気を立てる〉 steam.

  yuge-no-tatte-iru 〈湯気の立っている〉 steaming.

yûgeki-shu 〈ゆうげきしゅ：遊撃手〉 a shortstop.

yûgen-gaisha 〈ゆうげんがいしゃ：有限会社〉 a limited responsibility company, a corporation.

yûgi 〈ゆうぎ：遊戯〉 play, sports, a pastime, a game.

yû-giri 〈ゆうぎり：夕霧〉 an evening mist.

yûgô 〈ゆうごう：融合〉 fusion, unity, harmony.

  kaku-yûgô 〈核融合〉 nuclear fusion

  yûgô-suru 〈融合する〉 fuse into one, unite into one, be in harmony ((with)).

Yûgosurabia 〈ユーゴスラビア〉 Yugoslavia.

  Yûgosurabia-jin 〈ユーゴスラビア人〉 a Yugoslavian

  Yûgosurabia(-jin)-no 〈ユーゴスラビア（人）の〉 Yugoslavic

yûgû 〈ゆうぐう：優遇〉 favorable treatment.

  yûgû-suru 〈優遇する〉 treat ((a person)) well, pay a good salary ((to)).

yûgun 〈ゆうぐん：友軍〉 friendly forces, an allied army.

yûgure 〈ゆうぐれ：夕暮れ〉 see. yûgata.

yûhan 〈ゆうはん：夕飯〉 see. yûshoku.

yûhatsu 〈ゆうはつ：誘発〉

  yûhatsu-suru 〈誘発する〉 induce, cause, lead up ((to)), give rise ((to)).

yûhei 〈ゆうへい：幽閉〉 confinement.

  yûhei-suru 〈幽閉する〉 confine, shut up.

  yûhei-sareru 〈幽閉される〉 be confined.

yû-hi 〈ゆうひ：夕日〉 the evening sun, the setting sun.

yûho-dô 〈ゆうほどう：遊歩道〉 a promenade.

yûi 〈ゆうい：優位〉 predominance, a dominant position.

  yûi-ni-tatsu 〈優位に立つ〉 stand at advantage ((over)), have an advantage ((over))

  yûi-o-shimeru 〈優位を占める〉 gain an advantage ((over))

yûi 〈ゆうい：有為〉

  yûi-na 〈有為な〉 promising, able, capable.

yuibi- 〈ゆいび-：唯美-〉

  yuibi-shugi 〈唯美主義〉 (a)estheticism

  yuibi-teki(-na) 〈唯美的（な）〉 (a)esthetic.

yuibutsu- 〈ゆいぶつ-：唯物-〉

  yuibutsu-ron 〈唯物論〉 materialism

yuibutsu-shikan〈唯物史観〉historical materialism

yuibutsu-ron-teki(-na)〈唯物論的(な)〉materialistic.

yuibutsu-ron-teki benshô-hô〈唯物論的弁証法〉materialistic dialectic

yû-igi〈ゆういぎ：有意義〉

yû-igi-na〈有意義な〉significant, useful.

yû-igi-na-seikatsu-o-okuru〈有意義な生活を送る〉lead a significant life, live to some purpose

yuigon〈ゆいごん：遺言〉one's will, one's last wish, a verbal will.

yuigon-jô〈遺言状〉a (written) will, a testament

yuigon-jô-o-nokosazu-ni-shinu〈遺言状を残さずに死ぬ〉die intestate

yuigon-suru〈遺言する〉leave a will.

yuigon-de or *yuigon-ni-yotte*〈遺言で，遺言によって〉by will, under a will, at one's wish.

yuigon-de zaisan-o chônan-ni yuzuru〈遺言で財産を長男に譲る〉leave one's property to his eldest son by will

yuiitsu〈ゆいいつ：唯一〉

yuiitsu-no〈唯一の〉only, sole, one.

yuiitsu-muni-no〈唯一無二の〉the one and only, unique

yûin〈ゆういん：誘因〉an occasion, cause.

yûin-to-naru〈誘因となる〉occasion, be the occasion ((of)), cause, lead up ((to)), bring ((about)).

yuinô〈ゆいのう：結納〉a betrothal present.

yuishin-〈ゆいしん-：唯心-〉

yuishin-ron〈唯心論〉spiritualism, mentalism, idealism.

yuishin-ron-teki(-na)〈唯心論的(な)〉spiritualistic, mentalisitic, idealistic.

yuisho〈ゆいしょ：由緒〉lineage, a history.

yuisho-aru or *yuisho-tadashii*〈由緒ある，由緒正しい〉of good lineage, of noble birth, historic.

yûji〈ゆうじ：有事〉emergency.

yûji-no-sai-niwa〈有事の際には〉in time of emergency.

yûjin〈ゆうじん：友人〉a friend, a companion.

yûjin-daihyô-to-shite〈友人代表として〉on behalf of friends

yûjô〈ゆうじょう：友情〉friendly feelings, friendship.

yûjô-ga-aru or *yûjô-ni-atsui*〈友情がある，友情に厚い〉be kind to one's friend(s).

yûjû-fudan〈ゆうじゅうふだん：優柔不断〉irresolution.

yûjû-fudan-na〈優柔不断な〉irresolute.

yuka〈ゆか：床〉a floor.

yuka-ita〈床板〉floorboards

yuka-undô〈床運動〉floor exercises

yuka-o-haru〈床を張る〉board the floor, floor.

yukai〈ゆかい：愉快〉pleasure, delight.

Komban-wa-jitsu-ni-yukai-deshita.（今晩は実に愉快でした．）Thanks for a very pleasant evening.

yukai-na〈愉快な〉pleasant, delightful, joyful, cheerful, happy.

yukai-ni〈愉快に〉pleasantly, delightfully, cheerfully, happily.

yukai-ni-toki-o-sugosu（愉快に時を過ごす）have a good time

yûkai〈ゆうかい：誘拐〉kidnaping, abduction.

yûkai-han（誘拐犯）a kidnaper, an abductor

yûkai-suru〈誘拐する〉kidnap, abduct.

yûkai〈ゆうかい：融解〉fusion, melting, dissolution.

yûkai-suru〈融解する〉fuse, melt, dissolve.

yûkan〈ゆうかん：夕刊〉an evening paper, an evening edition.

yûkan〈ゆうかん：勇敢〉bravery.

yûkan-na〈勇敢な〉brave, courageous.

yûkan-ni〈勇敢に〉bravely, courageously.

yukari〈ゆかり〉affinity, connection.

en-mo-yukari-mo-nai（縁もゆかりもない）do not have any connection whatever ((with)).

yûkari〈ユーカリ〉an eucalyptus.

yuka-shita〈ゆかした：床下〉

yuka-shita-made shinsui-suru（床下まで浸水する）be flooded below the floor level

yuka-shita-no or *yukashita-ni*〈床下の，床下に〉under the floor.

yûka-shôken〈ゆうかしょうけん：有価証券〉a negotiable instrument(*or* paper), securities.

yukata〈ゆかた：浴衣〉a light cotton *kimono* worn in summer.

yuka-ue〈ゆかうえ：床上〉

yuka-ue-made shinsui-suru（床上まで浸水する）be flooded above the floor level

yuka-ue-no or *yuka-ue-ni*〈床上の，床上に〉on the floor.

yûkei〈ゆうけい：有形〉materiality.

yûkei-mukei-no〈有形無形の〉material and moral.

yûken-sha〈ゆうけんしゃ：有権者〉a voter, an elector.

yuketsu〈ゆけつ：輸血〉a blood transfusion.

yuketsu-suru〈輸血する〉give a blood transfusion ((to)).

yuki 〈ゆき：雪〉 snow, a snowfall.

  yuki ga tsumoru （雪が積もる） snow lies

  yuki ga tokeru （雪が解ける） snow melts

  yuki-geshô （雪化粧） a coat of snow

  yuki-guni （雪国） a snow district

  yuki-kaki （雪かき） snow shoveling, a snow shovel, a snow shoveler

  yuki-otoko （雪男） a snowman, a *yeti*

  yuki-yoke （雪よけ） a shelter, a snowshed, a snowbreak

  yuki-yake-shita （雪焼けした） snow-tanned

yuki-ga-furu 〈雪が降る〉 snow.

  yuki-ga-hidoku-furu （雪がひどく降る） snow heavily

-yuki 〈-ゆき：-行き〉 (bound) for.

  Tôkyô-yuki-no kyûkô （東京行きの急行） an express for Tokyo

yûki 〈ゆうき：勇気〉 courage.

  yûki o dasu （勇気を出す） muster up one's courage

  yûki o ushinau （勇気を失う） lose courage

yûki-zukeru 〈勇気付ける〉 encourage, hearten up.

  yûki-zukerareru *or* yûki-zuku （勇気付けられる，勇気付く） be encouraged ((at *or* by))

yûki-o-kujiku or *yûki-o-sogu* 〈勇気をくじく，勇気をそぐ〉 discourage.

  yûki-o-kujikareru *or* yûki-o-sogareru （勇気をくじかれる，勇気をそがれる） be discouraged

yûki-no-aru 〈勇気のある〉 courageous.

  yûki-no-nai （勇気のない） timid, cowardly, fainthearted

yûki 〈ゆうき：有機〉

  yûki-butsu （有機物） organic matter

  yûki-kagaku （有機化学） organic chemistry

  yûki(-soshiki)-tai （有機(組織)体） an organism

yûki-no or *yûki-teki(-na)* 〈有機の，有機的(な)〉 organic.

yukiatari-battari 〈ゆきあたりばったり：行き当たりばったり〉 *see*. ikiatari-battari.

yuki-ataru 〈ゆきあたる：行き当たる〉 *see*. iki-ataru.

yuki-chigai 〈ゆきちがい：行き違い〉

yuki-chigai-ni-naru 〈行き違いになる〉 cross each other (on the way).

yuki-daore 〈ゆきだおれ：行き倒れ〉 *see*. iki-daore.

yuki-daruma 〈ゆきだるま：雪だるま〉 a snowman.

  yuki-daruma o tsukuru （雪だるまを作る） make a snowman

yuki-daruma-shiki-ni-ookiku-naru 〈雪だるま式に大きくなる〉 snowball.

yuki-doke 〈ゆきどけ：雪解け〉a thaw.
　yuki-doke-no 〈雪解けの〉snow-thawing.
　　yuki-doke-no kisetsu〈雪解けの季節〉the snow-thawing season
　　yuki-doke-no michi〈雪解けの道〉a slushy road
yuki-dokoro 〈ゆきどころ：行き所〉*see.* iki-dokoro.
yuki-domari 〈ゆきどまり：行き止まり〉
　yuki-domari-ni-naru〈行き止まりになる〉come to a dead end.
yuki-gakari 〈ゆきがかり：行き掛かり〉*see.* iki-gakari.
yuki-gake 〈ゆきがけ：行き掛け〉*see.* iki-gake.
yukikata 〈ゆきかた：行き方〉*see.* ikikata.
yuki-kau 〈ゆきかう：行き交う〉come and go, go back and forth.
yuki-ki 〈ゆきき：行き来〉going and coming, traffic.
　　Kono-toori-wa　hito-no-yuki-ki-ga-ooi.（この通りは人の行き来が多い.）
　　　There is a lot of traffic in this street.
yuki-saki 〈ゆきさき：行き先〉one's destination, the place where one has gone(*or* is going).
yuki-sugi 〈ゆきすぎ：行き過ぎ〉*see.* iki-sugi.
yuki-todoku 〈ゆきとどく：行き届く〉be prudent, be careful, be attentive, be perfect, be complete.
　　Ano hito wa yuki-todoita-hito-desu.（あの人は行き届いた人です.）He is a man of scrupulous care.
　　eisei-setsubi-ga-yuki-todoite-iru（衛生設備が行き届いている）have complete sanitary arrangements
　　sōji-ga-yuki-todoite-iru（掃除が行き届いている）be quite clean and tidy
yuki-tsuke 〈ゆきつけ：行きつけ〉*see.* iki-tsuke.
yuki-wataru 〈ゆきわたる：行き渡る〉spread, extend, prevail; go round.
　　Mina-ni-yuki-wataru-dake-sake-ga-nai.（皆に行き渡るだけ酒がない.）There is not enough *sake* to go round.
yuki-zumari 〈ゆきづまり：行き詰まり〉a deadlock, an impasse, a stalemate.
　　yuki-zumari o dakai-suru（行き詰まりを打開する）break the deadlock
　yuki-zumaru〈行き詰まる〉come to a deadlock, be at a standstill.
yuki-zuri 〈ゆきずり：行きずり〉
　yuki-zuri-no〈行きずりの〉passing, casual.
　　yuki-zuri-no hito（行きずりの人）a casual passerby
yukkuri 〈ゆっくり〉slowly, without hurry, gently, leisurely, at one's

leisure.

　yukkuri hanasu（ゆっくり話す）　speak slowly

　yukkuri tachi-agaru（ゆっくり立ち上がる）　get up unhurriedly

　yukkuri-nemuru（ゆっくり眠る）　have a good sleep

　yukkuri-furo-ni-hairu（ゆっくり風ろに入る）　take a long bath

　yukkuri-kangaeru（ゆっくり考える）　ponder ((over))

　Yukkuri-shite-iki-nasai.（ゆっくりしていきなさい.）　Stay as long as you like.

　Dôzo go-yukkuri.（どうぞごゆっくり.）　Please make yourself at home.

yûkô〈ゆうこう：友好〉

　yûkô-kankei（友好関係）　friendly relations ((between *or* with)), (a) friendship

　yûkô-koku（友好国）　a friendly nation

　yûkô-teki(-na)〈友好的(な)〉friendly, amicable.

　yûkô-teki-na fun·iki（友好的な雰囲気）　an amicable and cordial atmosphere

yûkô〈ゆうこう：有効〉

　yûkô-kikan（有効期間）　the term of validity

　yûkô-kyori（有効距離）　the effective range

　yûkô-sûji（有効数字）　a significant figure

　yûkô-tôhyô（有効投票）　a valid ballot

　yûkô-na〈有効な〉valid, good, available, effective.

　yûkô-na keiyaku（有効な契約）　a valid contract

　mikka-kan yûkô-na kippu（三日間有効な切符）　a ticket good for three days

　yûkô-ni〈有効に〉validly, effectively.

　yûkô-ni-naru（有効になる）　come into effect, become effective, take effect

　yûkô-ni-tsukau（有効に使う）　use effectively, make good use ((of))

yûkon〈ゆうこん：雄こん〉

　yûkon-na〈雄こんな〉grand, sublime, vigorous, bold.

　yûkon-na fude-zukai（雄こんな筆使い）　a bold stroke of pen

yuku〈ゆく：行く〉

　yuku-toshi（行く年）　the old year

yuku〈ゆく：逝く〉die, pass away.

yukue〈ゆくえ：行方〉the place where one has gone, one's whereabouts.

　yukue-o-kuramasu（行方をくらます）　conceal oneself, disappear

　　　yukue-o-sagasu〔行方を捜す〕 search ((for))
　　　yukue-o-tsuki-tomeru〔行方を突き止める〕 locate
yukue-fumei〈ゆくえふめい：行方不明〉
　　　yukue-fumei-sha〔行方不明者〕 a missing person, the missing
　　yukue-fumei-ni-naru〔行方不明になる〕 be lost, be missing.
　　yukue-fumei-no〈行方不明の〉 missing.
yuku-saki〈ゆくさき：行く先〉
　　yuku-saki-zaki-de〔行く先々で〕 everywhere one goes.
yuku-sue〈ゆくすえ：行く末〉 one's future.
　　　yuku-sue-o-anjiru〔行く末を案じる〕 be anxious about one's future
yuku-te〈ゆくて：行く手〉 one's way.
　　　yuku-te o saegiru〔行く手を遮る〕 bar one's way
yukuyuku-wa〈ゆくゆくは：行く行くは〉 in future, some day.
yûkyô〈ゆうきょう：遊興〉 merrymaking, (a) spree, (worldly) pleasures.
　　　yûkyô-hi〔遊興費〕 the expense for pleasures
　　yûkyô-suru〔遊興する〕 make merry, be on the spree.
yûkyû〈ゆうきゅう：有給〉
　　　yûkyû-kyûka〔有給休暇〕 a paid holiday
　　yûkyû-no〈有給の〉 paid, salaried.
yûkyû〈ゆうきゅう：遊休〉
　　　yûkyû-shisetsu〔遊休施設〕 idle facilities
　　yûkyû-no〈遊休の〉 idle, unemployed, unused.
yume〈ゆめ：夢〉 a dream, a vision, an illusion.
　　　fukitsu-na yume〔不吉な夢〕 an evil dream
　　　kowai yume〔怖い夢〕 a terrible dream
　　　yume-no-sekai〔夢の世界〕 a dreamland
　　yume-o-miru〈夢を見る〉 dream.
　　　～-no-yume-o-miru〈～の夢を見る〉 dream of...
　　yume-o-samasu〈夢をさます〉 awake ((a person)) from sleep, bring ((a person)) to his senses, disillusion.
　　yume-ga-sameru or *yume-kara-sameru*〈夢がさめる，夢からさめる〉 a-wake from sleep, come to one's senses.
　　yume-ka-to-omou〈夢かと思う〉 feel as if in a dream, can hardly believe one's ears.
　　yume-ni-mo-omowa-nai〈夢にも思わない〉 never dream ((of)).
　　yume-no-yô-na〈夢のような〉 dreamy, dreamlike, visionary.
　　yume-utsutsu-ni〈夢うつつに〉 half awake and half asleep.
yume-gokochi〈ゆめごこち：夢心地〉 a dreamy state of mind.

yume-gokochi-de 〈夢心地で〉as if in a dream.

yume-gokochi-de-aru（夢心地である）feel as if one were in a dream

yûmei 〈ゆうめい：有名〉

yûmei-jin（有名人）a celebrity, a notable

yûmei-kô（有名校）a big-name school

yûmei-ni-naru 〈有名になる〉become famous, win a reputation.

ichiyaku-yûmei-ni-naru（一躍有名になる）leap to fame

yûmei-na 〈有名な〉famous, famed, notable, noted, well-known, celebrated; notorious.

yûmei-na gakusha（有名な学者）a famous scholar

yûmei-na sagi-shi（有名な詐欺師）a notorious swindler

sekai-teki-ni-yûmei-na（世界的に有名な）world-famous, of worldwide reputation

yûmei 〈ゆうめい：勇名〉

yûmei-o-todorokasu 〈勇名をとどろかす〉be famous for one's brave act.

yûmei-mujitsu 〈ゆうめいむじつ：有名無実〉

yûmei-mujitsu-no 〈有名無実の〉nominal, little more than a name, in name only.

yûmei-mujitsu-no iin-chô（有名無実の委員長）the nominal chairman of a committee

yume-mi 〈ゆめみ：夢見〉

yume-mi-ga-ii 〈夢見がいい〉have a good dream.

yume-monogatari 〈ゆめものがたり：夢物語〉a fantastic story.

yumi 〈ゆみ：弓〉a bow, archery.

yumi o iru（弓を射る）shoot an arrow

yumi-ya（弓矢）bow and arrow

yumi-nari 〈ゆみなり：弓なり〉

yumi-nari-no 〈弓なりの〉arched, bowed, curved.

yu-mizu 〈ゆみず：湯水〉

yu-mizu-no-yô-ni kane o tsukau 〈湯水のように金を使う〉spend money like water.

yûmô 〈ゆうもう：勇猛〉

yûmô-kakan-na 〈勇猛果敢な〉of dauntless courage.

yûmoa 〈ユーモア〉humor.

yûmoa-o-kaisuru（ユーモアを解する）have a sense of humor

yûmoa-ga-aru 〈ユーモアがある〉be humorous.

yûmoa-ga-nai（ユーモアがない）be humorless

yu-moto 〈ゆもと：湯元〉the source of a hot spring.

Yunesuko〈ユネスコ〉UNESCO.

yû-ni〈ゆうに：優に〉full(y), well, easily.

 yû-ni go-mêtoru（優に五メートル）a full five meters

 yû-ni-hyaku-man-en-o-koeru（優に百万円を超える）be well over a million yen

 yû-ni hyaku-nin syûyô-dekiru（優に百人収容できる）be able to hold 100 people easily

Yunibâshiâdo〈ユニバーシアード〉the Universiade.

yunifômu〈ユニフォーム〉a uniform.

 yunifômu o kiru（ユニフォームを着る）put on a uniform

yûnô〈ゆうのう：有能〉

yûnô-na〈有能な〉able, capable, competent.

 yûnô-na-hito（有能な人）a man of ability, an able man

yu-nomi〈ゆのみ：湯飲み〉a teacup, a cup.

yu-noshi〈ゆのし：湯のし〉

yu-noshi-o-kakeru（湯のしをかける）steam and iron.

yunyô-kan〈ゆにょうかん：輸尿管〉the ureter.

yunyû〈ゆにゅう：輸入〉import(ation), introduction.

 yunyû-gyô-sha（輸入業者）an importer

 yunyû-hin（輸入品）imports〔from abroad〕

 yunyú-zei（輸入税）an import duty

 yunyû-chôka（輸入超過）an excess of imports, an unfavorable balance of trade

yunyû-suru〈輸入する〉import, introduce.

yuragu〈ゆらぐ：揺らぐ〉sway, swing, flicker, shake.

yurai〈ゆらい：由来〉the origin, the history, the source.

 yurai-o-tazuneru（由来を尋ねる）trace ((a thing)) to its source, inquire into the origin ((of))

yûran〈ゆうらん：遊覧〉an excursion, a pleasure trip, sightseeing.

 yûran-sen（遊覧船）an excursion boat

yûran-suru〈遊覧する〉go sightseeing ((to)), do the sights ((of)).

yure〈ゆれ：揺れ〉shaking, a shake, a sway, (a) vibration, a shock, a tremor, pitching and rolling, tossing, a jolt, a flicker.

yûrei〈ゆうれい：幽霊〉a ghost, an apparition, a specter, a phantom.

 Ano-basho-niwa-yûrei-ga-deru.（あの場所には幽霊が出る。）The place is haunted (by a ghost).

 yûrei-gaisha（幽霊会社）a bogus company

yûrei-no-yô-na〈幽霊のような〉ghostly, ghostlike.

yureru 〈ゆれる：揺れる〉 shake, sway, vibrate, tremble, pitch and roll, toss, joggle, flicker.

Kono fune wa hidoku yureru. (この船はひどく揺れる.) This vessel pitches and rolls badly.

yū-retsu 〈ゆうれつ：優劣〉 superiority or inferiority.

yū-retsu-o-arasou (優劣を争う) vie for superiority ((with)), struggle for mastery

hotondo-yū-retsu-ga-tsuke-gatai (ほとんど優劣が付け難い) there is little to choose ((between or among))

yuri 〈ゆり〉 a lily.

yuri-ne (ゆり根) a lily bulb

yūri 〈ゆうり：有利〉

yūri-na 〈有利な〉 profitable, paying, advantageous, favorable, stronger, better.

yūri-na jōken (有利な条件) favorable conditions

yūri-na-ichi-o-shimeru (有利な位置を占める) be in a better position ((than)), have an advantage ((over)), have an edge ((on))

yūri-to-naru or *yūri-ni-tenkai-suru* 〈有利となる, 有利に展開する〉 turn to one's advantage

yūri-de-aru 〈有利である〉 favor, be in one's favor, be of advantage ((to)).

yūri 〈ゆうり：有理〉

yūri-sū (有理数) a rational number

yūri 〈ゆうり：遊離〉 isolation, separation.

yūri-suru 〈遊離する〉 isolate, separate.

genjitsu-kara-yūri-suru (現実から遊離する) be far from realities

yuri-kaeshi 〈ゆりかえし：揺り返し〉 an aftershock.

yuri-kago 〈ゆりかご：揺りかご〉 a cradle.

yuri-okosu 〈ゆりおこす：揺り起こす〉 shake ((a person)) out of his sleep.

yurugase 〈ゆるがせ〉

yurugase-ni-suru 〈ゆるがせにする〉 neglect, make light ((of)).

nichinichi-no shigoto o yurugase-ni-suru (日々の仕事をゆるがせにする) neglect one's daily work

yurugasu 〈ゆるがす：揺るがす〉 shake, shock.

ten-chi o yurugasu (天地を揺るがす) shake heaven and earth

yurugi 〈ゆるぎ：揺るぎ〉

yurugi-nai 〈揺るぎない〉 firm, secure, solid, steady.

yurui 〈ゆるい：緩い〉 loose, lenient, generous, lax, slack, gentle, slow.

yurui musubi-me (緩い結び目) a loose knot

　　　yurui kâbu（緩いカーブ）　a slow curve

　yuruku〈緩く〉loosely, leniently.

　　　yuruku shibaru（緩く縛る）　tie loosely

yurumeru〈ゆるめる：緩める〉loosen, unfasten, relax, ease, mitigate.

　　　beruto o yurumeru（ベルトを緩める）　loosen the belt

　　　keikai o yurumeru（警戒を緩める）　relax one's guard ((against))

　　　ki o yurumeru（気をゆるめる）　relax one's attention

　　　sokuryoku o yurumeru（速力を緩める）　reduce the speed

yurumi〈ゆるみ：緩み〉relaxation, slackness.

　　　ki-no yurumi（気の緩み）　mental slackness

　yurumu〈緩む〉loosen, become loose, abate, relax, slack(en).

　　　Kutsu-no-himo ga yurunda.（靴のひもが緩んだ.）　The shoestring has got loose.

　　　Samu-sa ga yurunde-kita.（寒さがゆるんできた.）　The cold has abated.

　　　kiritsu ga yurumu（規律が緩む）　discipline is slack

yurushi〈ゆるし：許し〉permission, leave, approval, license, exemption, pardon, forgiveness, excuse.

　　　yurushi-o-kou（許しを請う）　ask for ((a person's)) permission, ask ((a person's)) forgiveness

　　　yurushi o ukeru（許しを受ける）　get permission ((to do)), obtain ((a person's)) pardon ((for))

　yurushi-o-ete〈許しを得て〉with ((a person's)) permission.

　　　yurushi-o-e-nai-de（許しを得ないで）　without ((a person's)) leave

yurusu〈許す〉permit, give ((a person)) leave, approve, grant, admit; license; exempt; acknowledge; trust, confide ((in)); forgive, pardon, excuse; release, set ((a person)) free, let ((a person)) off.

　　　jijô-no-yurusu-kagiri（事情の許す限り）　as far as circumstances permit

　　　tenkô-ga-yuruseba（天候が許せば）　weather permitting

　　　negai o yurusu（願いを許す）　grant ((a person's)) request

　　　nyûgaku-o-yurusu（入学を許す）　admit ((a student)) into a school

　　　Kare wa waga-kuni-saidai-no-gakusha-to-shite-ji-ta-tomo-ni-yurusarete-iru.（彼は我が国最大の学者として自他共に許されている.）
　　　He is acknowledged as the greatest scholar of our country.

　　　hito ni ki-o-yurusu（人に気を許す）　trust a person

　　　kashitsu-o-yurusu（過失を許す）　forgive ((a person)) for his fault

　　　yurusarete-kitaku-suru（許されて帰宅する）　be released and return

home

yurushi-gatai 〈許し難い〉 unpardonable, inexcusable.

yuruyaka 〈ゆるやか：緩やか〉

yuruyaka-na 〈緩やかな〉 loose, slack, lenient, lax, generous, gentle, slow, easy.

yuruyaka-ni 〈緩やかに〉 leniently, generously, gently, slowly.

   yuruyaka-ni nagareru 〈緩やかに流れる〉 flow gently

yûryo 〈ゆうりょ：憂慮〉 anxiety, concern, fear(s), apprehension(s), cares.

yûryo-suru 〈憂慮する〉 be anxious ((about)), be concerned ((about)), be troubled ((about)), worry ((about *or* over)), fear, have fears ((for)).

yûryo-su-beki 〈憂慮すべき〉 serious, grave, alarming.

   yûryo-su-beki jitai 〈憂慮すべき事態〉 a grave situation

yûryô 〈ゆうりょう：有料〉

   yûryô-dôro 〈有料道路〉 a toll road

yûryô-no 〈有料の〉 charged, paid.

yûryô 〈ゆうりょう：優良〉 superiority, excellence.

   yûryô-kabu 〈優良株〉 superior stocks

yûryô-na 〈優良な〉 superior, excellent.

yûryoku 〈ゆうりょく：有力〉

   yûryoku-sha 〈有力者〉 an influential person

yûryoku-na 〈有力な〉 strong, powerful, influential, potent, leading, convincing, valid.

   yûryoku-na sansei 〈有力な賛成〉 a powerful argument in favor ((of))

   yûryoku-na shôko 〈有力な証拠〉 a valid proof

   mottomo-yûryoku-na yûshô-kôho 〈最も有力な優勝候補〉 the likeliest winner 〔of the championship〕

yusaburu 〈ゆさぶる：揺さぶる〉 shake; undermine.

yûsan-kaikyû 〈ゆうさんかいきゅう：有産階級〉 the propertied classes.

yûsei 〈ゆうせい：遊星〉 *see.* wakusei.

yûsei 〈ゆうせい：郵政〉 postal services.

   yûsei-shô 〈郵政省〉 the Ministry of Posts and Telecommunications

   yûsei-daijin 〈郵政大臣〉 the Minister of Posts and Telecommunications

yûsei 〈ゆうせい：優勢〉 superiority, ascendancy.

yûsei-de-aru 〈優勢である〉 be superior ((to)), have the edge ((on *or* over)), have the upper hand ((of)), maintain a superior position.

   kazu-ni-oite yûsei-de-aru 〈数において優勢である〉 be numerically superior ((to)) *yûsei-ni-naru* 〈優勢になる〉 gain in strength, gain ground.

yûsei-na 〈優勢な〉 superior, leading, predominant.

yûsei-gaku 〈ゆうせいがく：優生学〉 eugenics.

yûsei-gaku-jô 〈優生学上〉 from a eugenic point of view.

yûsei-on 〈ゆうせいおん：有声音〉 a vocal(*or* voiced) sound.

yusei-toryô 〈ゆせいとりょう：油性塗料〉 oil paint.

yûsen 〈ゆうせん：優先〉 priority, preference.

　　yûsen-jun・i 〈優先順位〉 the order of priority

yûsen-suru 〈優先する〉 be prior ((to)), have preference ((to)), take precedence ((of *or* over)).

yûsen-teki(-na) 〈優先的(な)〉 preferential.

yûsen-teki-ni 〈優先的に〉 preferentially, with priority ((to)).

　　yûsen-teki-ni-tori-atsukau (優先的に取り扱う) give priority ((to))

　　yûsen-teki-ni-tori-atsukawareru (優先的に取り扱われる) be given the highest priority

yûsen-hôsô 〈ゆうせんほうそう：有線放送〉 wire broadcasting.

yûsen-ken 〈ゆうせんけん：優先権〉 the priority, the preference.

　　yûsen-ken o eru (優先権を得る) acquire a priority

yûsha 〈ゆうしゃ：勇者〉 a brave man.

yushi 〈ゆし：油脂〉 oils and fats.

yûshi 〈ゆうし：雄姿〉 a brave figure.

yûshi 〈ゆうし：有志〉 an interested person, a supporter.

　　yûshi-ichidô (有志一同) all (the persons) concerned

yûshi 〈ゆうし：有史〉

　　yûshi-irai-no (有史以来の) in history, on record, since the dawn of history

　　yûshi-(i)zen-no (有史(以)前の) prehistoric, of prehistoric times

yûshi 〈ゆうし：融資〉 financing, a loan.

yûshi-suru 〈融資する〉 finance, loan, furnish funds ((to)).

yûshikai-hikô 〈ゆうしかいひこう：有視界飛行〉 visual flying.

yû-shikaku-sha 〈ゆうしかくしゃ：有資格者〉 a qualified person.

yûshiki-sha 〈ゆうしきしゃ：有識者〉 a well-informed person.

yûshi-tessen 〈ゆうしてっせん：有刺鉄線〉 barbed wire.

　　yûshi-tessen-no saku (有刺鉄線のさく) a barbwire fence

yûshô 〈ゆうしょう：勇将〉 a brave general.

yûshô 〈ゆうしょう：優勝〉 the victory, championship.

　　yûshô-kôho (優勝候補) a favorite for the championship

　　yûshô-sen (優勝戦) a championship tournament, the finals

yûshô-kettei-sen（優勝決定戦） a playoff
yûshô-sha（優勝者） the winner, a champion, a titleholder
yûshô-hai（優勝杯） a championship cup, a trophy cup
yûshô-ki（優勝旗） a championship flag
yûshô-suru（優勝する） win the victory, win the title, come off winner.

yûshô〈ゆうしょう：有償〉
yûshô-de〈有償で〉for payment.

yûshoku〈ゆうしょく：夕食〉supper, dinner, an evening meal.
yûshoku o toru（夕食を取る） take supper
yûshoku-go-ni〈夕食後に〉after supper.

yûshoku〈ゆうしょく：憂色〉a worried look.
yûshoku-ni-tozasareru〈憂色に閉ざされる〉fall into the state of deep anxiety.

yûshoku-jinshu〈ゆうしょくじんしゅ：有色人種〉a colored race.

yûshû〈ゆうしゅう：優秀〉excellence, superiority.
yûshû-na〈優秀な〉excellent, superior, best.
yûshû-na seiseki（優秀な成績） an excellent record

yûshû〈ゆうしゅう：憂愁〉melancholy, gloom.

yûshû-no-bi〈ゆうしゅうのび：有終の美〉
yûshû-no-bi-o-kazaru〈有終の美を飾る〉carry ((a matter)) to perfection, bring ((a matter)) to a successful conculsion.

yushutsu〈ゆしゅつ：輸出〉export(ation).
yushutsu-hin（輸出品） exports
yushutsu-gyô-sha（輸出業者） an exporter
yushutsu-nyû-gyô-sha（輸出入業者） exporters and importers
yushutsu-chôka（輸出超過） an excess of exports, a favorable balance of trade
yushutsu-suru〈輸出する〉export.

yusô〈ゆそう：輸送〉transport(ation), conveyance, transit.
kaijô-yusô（海上輸送） transportation by sea
yusô-ki（輸送機） a transport (plane)
yusô-ryoku（輸送力） transport capacity, carrying power
yusô-suru〈輸送する〉transport, convey.

yûsô〈ゆうそう：郵送〉
yûsô-suru〈郵送する〉mail, post, send by mail, send through the post.

yûsô〈ゆうそう：勇壮〉
yûsô-na〈勇壮な〉brave, heroic, gallant.

yusô-kan〈ゆそうかん：油送管〉an oil pipe, an oil pipeline.

yûsû〈ゆうすう：有数〉
  yûsû-no〈有数の〉prominent, eminent, distinguished, leading, one of the greatest... , one of the foremost... .

yusugu〈ゆすぐ〉wash out, rinse.
  kuchi o yusugu（口をゆすぐ）wash out one's mouth

yusuri〈ゆすり〉extortion, blackmail, shakedown; an extortioner, a blackmailer.
  yusuru〈ゆする〉extort, blackmail.

yusuru〈ゆする：揺する〉shake, rock, swing, roll.

yû-suzumi〈ゆうすずみ：夕涼み〉
  yû-suzumi-suru〈夕涼みする〉enjoy the evening cool.

yûtai〈ゆうたい：優待〉preferential treatment, hospitality, welcome.
  yûtai-ken（優待券）a complimentary ticket
  yûtai-suru〈優待する〉treat ((a person)) with kindness, receive ((a person)) hospitably.

yûtai〈ゆうたい：勇退〉
  yûtai-suru〈勇退する〉resign one's post of one's own accord.

yutaka〈ゆたか：豊か〉
  yutaka-na〈豊かな〉abundant, plentiful, ample, affluent, rich, wealthy, well-off.
    yutaka-na shakai（豊かな社会）the affluent society
  yutaka-ni〈豊かに〉abundantly, plentifully, amply, in affluence, richly.
    yutaka-ni-kurasu（豊かに暮らす）be well off, be well-to-do

yutampo〈ゆたんぽ：湯たんぽ〉a hot-water bottle.

yû-tân〈ユーターン〉a U-turn.
    Yû-tân-kinshi.（ユーターン禁止.）No U-turns.
  yû-tân-suru〈ユーターンする〉take a U-turn.

yûten〈ゆうてん：融点〉the melting point, the fusing point.

yûtô〈ゆうとう：優等〉excellence, honors.
    yûtô-de sotsugyô-suru（優等で卒業する）graduate with honors
    yûtô-sei（優等生）an honor student
  yûtô-de-aru〈優等である〉be excellent ((in)).

yuttari〈ゆったり〉
  yuttari-shita〈ゆったりした〉calm, quiet, composed, loose.
    yuttari-shita kôto（ゆったりしたコート）a loose coat
    yuttari-shita taido（ゆったりした態度）an easy manner
    yuttari-shita-kibun-ni-naru（ゆったりした気分になる）feel at ease
  yuttari-to〈ゆったりと〉composedly, at one's ease.

yuttari-to　isu-ni-koshi-o-kakeru（ゆったりといすに腰を掛ける）　settle oneself comfortably in a chair

yuu〈ゆう：結う〉dress, do up, tie up.

yûutsu〈ゆううつ：憂うつ〉melancholy, gloom, dejection, depression, low spirits.

yûutsu-shô（憂うつ症）　melancholia, hypochondria

yûutsu-ni-naru〈憂うつになる〉feel melancholy.

yûutsu-na〈憂うつな〉melancholic, gloomy, dejected, out of spirits.

yûutsu-na tenki（憂うつな天気）　gloomy weather

yûutsu-na kao（憂うつな顔）　a long face

yûwa〈ゆうわ：融和〉harmony, reconciliation.

yûwa-suru〈融和する〉harmonize ((with)), get reconciled ((with)).

yu-wakashi〈ゆわかし：湯沸かし〉a kettle.

gasu-yu-wakashi-ki（ガス湯沸かし器）　a gas water heater, a gas geyser

yûwaku〈ゆうわく：誘惑〉temptation, allurement, seduction.

yûwaku ni katsu（誘惑に勝つ）　overcome a temptation

yûwaku-ni-makeru（誘惑に負ける）　yield to temptation

yûwaku to tatakau（誘惑と闘う）　resist temptation

yûwaku-suru〈誘惑する〉tempt, allure, seduce.

yû-yake〈ゆうやけ：夕焼け〉an evening glow.

yû-yake-zora（夕焼け空）　the sky aglow with the setting sun

yûyaku〈ゆうやく：勇躍〉

yûyaku-shite〈勇躍して〉in high spirits.

yûyami〈ゆうやみ：夕やみ〉dusk, twilight.

Yûyami ga sematteiru.（夕やみが迫っている.）　The evening dusk is gathering.

yûyami-semaru-koro〈夕やみ迫るころ〉at dusk, at nightfall.

yûyo〈ゆうよ：猶予〉postponement, grace, extension, a reprieve, (a) delay.

Ikkoku-no-yûyo-mo-nai.（一刻の猶予もない.）　There is no time to lose.

nikagetsu-no-yûyo-kikan（二か月の猶予期間）　two months' grace

yûyo-suru〈猶予する〉postpone, put off, give grace, give time, allow delay, reprieve.

kei-no-shikkô-o　ikkagetsu　yûyo-sareru（刑の執行を一か月猶予される）　be reprieved for one month

yûyo-sezu-ni〈猶予せずに〉without delay, promptly.

yûyō 〈ゆうよう：有用〉
  yûyō-na〈有用な〉useful, of use, serviceable, available.

yûyū 〈ゆうゆう：悠々〉
  yûyū-taru〈悠々たる〉calm, quiet, composed, leisurely, slow, eternal.
  yûyū-to〈悠々と〉calmly, quietly, in a leisurely manner, slowly, without difficulty.
      yûyū-to-katsu〈悠々と勝つ〉win an easy victory ((over))
  yûyū-jiteki-no-seikatsu-o-okuru〈悠々自適の生活を送る〉live in easy retirement.

yuyushii 〈ゆゆしい：由々しい〉serious, grave, fatal.

yûzai 〈ゆうざい：有罪〉being guilty.
      yûzai-ni-naru〈有罪になる〉be found guilty
  yûzai-no〈有罪の〉guilty.

yu-zamashi 〈ゆざまし：湯冷まし〉cooled boiled water.

yu-zame 〈ゆざめ：湯冷め〉
  yu-zame-suru〈湯冷めする〉feel a chill after a bath.

yûzei 〈ゆうぜい：郵税〉postage.
      Yûzei-mae-barai.（郵税前払い.）Postage prepaid.

yûzei 〈ゆうぜい：遊説〉canvassing, electioneering, stumping.
  yûzei-suru〈遊説する〉go canvassing, canvass, take the stump, stump, barnstorm.
      Kansai-chihō-o-yûzei-shite-mawaru（関西地方を遊説して回る）barnstorm through the Kansai districts

yûzen 〈ゆうぜん：悠然〉*see.* yûyū.

yûzen(-zome) 〈ゆうぜん（ぞめ）：友禅（染）〉printed silk, the *Yuzen* process.

yuzu 〈ゆず〉a citron.

yûzû 〈ゆうずう：融通〉accommodation, finance; elasticity, adaptability, flexibility.
  yûzû-suru〈融通する〉accommodate, lend ((a person)) money.
  yûzû-no-kiku〈融通の利く〉elastic, adaptable, flexible.
      yûzû-no-kika-nai〈融通の利かない〉unadaptable, lacking adaptability, hidebound

yuzuri-ai 〈ゆずりあい：譲り合い〉mutual concessions, a compromise.
  yuzuri-ai(-no-seishin)-de〈譲り合い（の精神）で〉by compromising.
  yuzuri-au〈譲り合う〉make mutual concessions, compromise.

yuzuri-ukeru 〈ゆずりうける：譲り受ける〉buy, take over, be transferred, inherit.

yuzuri-watasu 〈ゆずりわたす：譲り渡す〉hand over, transfer.

yuzuru 〈ゆずる：譲る〉hand over, turn over, transfer, give, part ((with)), sell; give way ((to)); yield ((to)); be inferior ((to)); leave, defer, postpone.

    shôbai o musuko-ni yuzuru（商売を息子に譲る）hand over the business to his son

    kenri o yuzuru（権利を譲る）transfer the rights ((to))

    seki o yuzuru（席を譲る）give one's seat ((to))

    mise o yasuku yuzuru（店を安く譲る）sell (a person) a shop cheap

    ippo-mo-yuzura-nai（一歩も譲らない）do not yield an inch

    dare-nimo-yuzura-nai（だれにも譲らない）be second to none ((in))

    Sono-ken-wa gojitsu-ni yuzuri-mashô.（その件は後日に譲りましょう．）
      Let's take up the matter some other time.

Z

za 〈ざ：座〉
  za-ni-tsuku〈座に着く〉seat oneself, take one's seat.
    kenryoku-no-za-ni-iru（権力の座にいる）be in power

zabon 〈ザボン〉a shaddock.

zabun 〈ざぶん〉
  zabun-to-mizu-ni-tobi-komu〈ざぶんと水に飛び込む〉splash into the water.

za-buton 〈ざぶとん：座布団〉a cushion in Japanese style.

zabuzabu 〈ざぶざぶ〉
  zabuzabu-to-mizu-o-karada-ni-kakeru〈ざぶざぶと水を体に掛ける〉dash water on oneself.

zachô 〈ざちょう：座長〉the chairman, the chairwoman; the proprietor.

zadan-kai 〈ざだんかい：座談会〉a round-table talk.

zahyô 〈ざひょう：座標〉coordinates.

zahyô-jiku〔座標軸〕 an axis of coordinates

zai〈ざい：財〉a fortune.

zai o nasu（財を成す）make a fortune

zaiaku〈ざいあく：罪悪〉a sin, a crime.

zaiaku-kan（罪悪感）a sense of guilt

zaibatsu〈ざいばつ：財閥〉a financial clique, a *zaibatsu*.

zaichû〈ざいちゅう：在中〉

Insatsu-butsu-zaichû.（印刷物在中．）Printed matter.

zaidan〈ざいだん：財団〉a foundation, a syndicate.

Rokkuferâ-zaidan（ロックフェラー財団）the Rockefeller Foundation

zaigai〈ざいがい：在外〉

zaigai-hôjin（在外邦人）Japanese residents abroad

zaigai-shisan（在外資産）overseas assets

zaigai-no〈在外の〉abroad, overseas.

zaigaku〈ざいがく：在学〉

zaigaku-sei（在学生）a student

zaigaku-shômei-sho（在学証明書）a school(*or* college) certificate

zaigaku-suru〈在学する〉be in school(*or* college).

zaigaku-chû-ni〈在学中に〉while in school(*or* college).

zaigen〈ざいげん：財源〉a source of revenue.

zaigen o motomeru（財源を求める）seek a source of revenue

zaihô〈ざいほう：財宝〉treasure(s), riches.

zaii〈ざいい：在位〉

zaii-chû-ni〈在位中に〉during the reign ((of)).

zaijô〈ざいじょう：罪状〉(the nature of) a crime.

zaijû〈ざいじゅう：在住〉

Kôbe-zaijû-no-Amerika-jin（神戸在住のアメリカ人）an American resident in Kobe

zaijû-suru〈在住する〉reside, live.

zaikai〈ざいかい：財界〉the business world, the financial world.

zaiko〈ざいこ：在庫〉stock.

zaiko o shiraberu（在庫を調べる）check the stock

zaiko-ga-nai（在庫がない）be out of stock

zaiko-hin（在庫品）stock on hand

zaikô〈ざいこう：在校〉 *see.* zaigaku.

zaimei〈ざいめい：罪名〉charge.

～*-no-zaimei-de*〈～の罪名で〉on a charge of... .

zaimoku〈ざいもく：材木〉wood, lumber, timber.

zaimoku-oki-ba〈材木置場〉a lumberyard, a timberyard.

zaimoku-ya〈材木屋〉a lumber dealer, a timber dealer

zaimoku-o-kiri-dasu〈材木を切り出す〉lumber.

zaimu〈ざいむ：財務〉financial affairs.

zaimu-chôkan〈財務長官〉the Secretary of the Treasury

zain〈ざいん：座員〉a member of the troupe, the company.

zainin〈ざいにん：罪人〉a criminal, an offender.

zainin〈ざいにん：在任〉

zainin-suru〈在任する〉hold office.

zainin-chû-ni〈在任中に〉while in office.

zairai〈ざいらい：在来〉

zairai-no〈在来の〉ordinary, common, conventional.

zairai-no yarikata〈在来のやり方〉the traditional method

zairu〈ザイル〉a (climbing) rope.

zairyô〈ざいりょう：材料〉(a) material, stuff, raw material(s); a factor.

kenchiku-zairyô〈建築材料〉building materials

hikan-teki zairyô〈悲観的材料〉a disheartening factor

zairyoku〈ざいりょく：財力〉financial power, means.

zairyû〈ざいりゅう：在留〉

Pari-zairyû-hôjin〈パリ在留邦人〉Japanese residents in Paris

zaisan〈ざいさん：財産〉a fortune, property.

zaisan o tsukuru〈財産を作る〉make a fortune

zaisan o nokosu〈財産を残す〉leave a fortune

zaisan o sashi-osaeru〈財産を差し押さえる〉seize ((a person's)) property

zaisan o tsukai-hatasu〈財産を使い果たす〉run through one's fortune

zaisan-zei〈財産税〉property tax

shiyû-zaisan〈私有財産〉private property

zaisan-me-ate-ni〈財産目当てに〉for money.

zaisei〈ざいせい：財政〉finance.

zaisei-ga-konnan-de-aru〈財政が困難である〉be in financial difficulty

kenzen-zaisei〈健全財政〉sound finance

zaisei-gaku〈財政学〉public finance

zaisei-teki(-na)〈財政的(な)〉financial.

zaisei-teki-ni〈財政的に〉financially.

zaisei〈ざいせい：在世〉

zaisei-chû-ni〈在世中に〉during one's lifetime.

zaiseki〈ざいせき：在籍〉

zaiseki-suru 〈在籍する〉 be on the (school) register.

zaishitsu 〈ざいしつ：材質〉 the quality of the material.

zaishoku 〈ざいしょく：在職〉

zaishoku-chû-ni 〈在職中に〉 *see.* zainin-chû-ni.

zaitaku 〈ざいたく：在宅〉

zaitaku-suru 〈在宅する〉 be at home, be in.

zakka 〈ざっか：雑貨〉 general goods, sundries.

zakki-chô 〈ざっきちょう：雑記帳〉 a notebook.

zakkin 〈ざっきん：雑菌〉 various germs.

zakkoku 〈ざっこく：雑穀〉 (miscellaneous) cereals.

zakku-baran 〈ざっくばらん〉

zakku-baran-na 〈ざっくばらんな〉 outspoken, frank, candid.

zakku-baran-ni 〈ざっくばらんに〉 outspokenly, frankly, candidly.

　　zakku-baran-ni-ieba 〈ざっくばらんに言えば〉 frankly speaking, to be
　　frank with you

zakkyo 〈ざっきょ：雑居〉 mixed living.

zakkyo-suru 〈雑居する〉 live together.

zako 〈ざこ：雑魚〉 small fish, small fry.

zakô 〈ざこう：座高〉 one's sitting height.

zako-ne 〈ざこね：雑魚寝〉

zako-ne-suru 〈雑魚寝する〉 sleep together all in a huddle.

zakotsu 〈ざこつ：座骨〉 the hucklebone, the hipbone.

　　zakotsu-shinkei-tsû 〈座骨神経痛〉 sciatica, hip gout

zakuro 〈ざくろ〉 a pomegranate.

zakuro-ishi 〈ざくろいし：ざくろ石〉 garnet.

zakuzaku 〈ざくざく〉

　　jari-o-zakuzaku-funde-aruku 〈砂利をざくざく踏んで歩く〉 crunch on
　　gravel

　　tamanegi o zakuzaku-kizamu 〈玉ねぎをざくざく刻む〉 chop an onion

zakyô 〈ざきょう：座興〉 amusement (of the company), fun.

　　zakyô-ni-uta-o-utau 〈座興に歌を歌う〉 amuse the company with a
　　song

zama 〈ざま〉

　　Zama-o-miro! 〈ざまを見ろ。〉 Serve you right!

　　Sono-zama-wa-nan-da! 〈そのざまは何だ。〉 Shame on you!

zambu 〈ざんぶ：残部〉 the remainder, the rest.

zambu 〈ざんぶ〉 *see.* zabun.

zammu 〈ざんむ：残務〉 unsettled affairs.

　　zammu-o-seiri-suru〈残務を整理する〉wind up the affairs ((of)), wind
　　　up a company

zampai〈ざんぱい：惨敗〉

　zumpai-suru〈惨敗する〉suffer a crushing defeat, be defeated
　　overwhelmingly, be defeated utterly.

zampan〈ざんぱん：残飯〉the leftover, the leavings〔of a meal〕.

zampin〈ざんぴん：残品〉the remaining stock(s), unsold goods.
　　zampin-seiri〈残品整理〉a clearance sale, stocktaking sale

zandaka〈ざんだか：残高〉the balance, the remainder.
　　kuri-koshi-zandaka〈繰り越し残高〉the balance carried over

zangai〈ざんがい：残がい〉the remains ((of)), ruins, the wreck ((of)).
　zangai-o-sarasu〈残がいをさらす〉be in ruins, be wrecked.

zangaku〈ざんがく：残額〉the remainder〔of the money〕.

zange〈ざんげ〉repentance, (a) confession.
　zange-suru〈ざんげする〉repent (of), confess.

zangô〈ざんごう〉a trench.

zangyaku〈ざんぎゃく：残虐〉brutality, cruelty.
　　zangyaku-kôi〈残虐行為〉a brutality, a cruel act
　zangyaku-na〈残虐な〉brutal, cruel.

zangyô〈ざんぎょう：残業〉overtime work.
　　zangyô-teate〈残業手当〉overtime pay
　zangyô-suru〈残業する〉work overtime.

zankin〈ざんきん：残金〉the balance, the money left (over).

zankoku〈ざんこく：残酷〉(a) cruelty.
　zankoku-na〈残酷な〉cruel.
　　zankoku-na koto o suru〈残酷なことをする〉do a cruel thing
　zankoku-ni〈残酷に〉cruelly.

zannen〈ざんねん：残念〉regret.
　zannen-garu or *zannen-ni-omou*〈残念がる，残念に思う〉regret, be sorry.
　zannen-na〈残念な〉regrettable.
　zannen-nagara〈残念ながら〉I am sorry, but... ; to my regret.
　zannen-sô-ni〈残念そうに〉regretfully.

zannin〈ざんにん：残忍〉*see.* zankoku.
　　zannin-sei〈残忍性〉one's brutal nature

zanrui〈ざんるい：残塁〉
　zanrui-suru〈残塁する〉be left on base.

zanryû〈ざんりゅう：残留〉
　zanryû-suru〈残留する〉remain behind.

zansatsu〈ざんさつ：惨殺〉
 zansatsu-shitai〈惨殺体〉 a mangled corpse
 zansatsu-suru〈惨殺する〉murder cruelly.
zansetsu〈ざんせつ：残雪〉the remaining snow.
zanshi〈ざんし：惨死〉a violent death.
 zanshi-suru〈惨死する〉be killed in a cruel way.
zanshin(-sa)〈ざんしん（さ）：ざん新（さ）〉novelty, originality.
 zanshin-na〈ざん新な〉novel, original.
zansho〈ざんしょ：残暑〉the lingering summer heat.
 Zansho ga kibishii.〈残暑が厳しい。〉The lingering summer heat is
  severe.
zanson〈ざんそん：残存〉
 zanson-suru〈残存する〉survive, still exist, be still alive, remain.
zantei〈ざんてい：暫定〉
 zantei-sochi〈暫定措置〉a temporary step, a tentative measure
 zantei-yosan〈暫定予算〉a provisional budget
 zantei-teki(-na)〈暫定的（な）〉provisional, temporary, tentative.
 zantei-teki-ni〈暫定的に〉provisionally, temporarily, tentatively.
zantō〈ざんとう：残党〉the remnants of a defeated party.
zan・yo〈ざんよ：残余〉
 zan・yo-no〈残余の〉remaining, residuary.
zappi〈ざっぴ：雑費〉sundry expenses.
zarame〈ざらめ：ざら目〉granulated sugar.
zara-ni〈ざらに〉
 zara-ni-aru〈ざらにある〉be very common, be by no means rare, be met
  with everywhere.
  zara-ni-nai（ざらにない）be (very) rare, be rarely to be found
zarazara〈ざらざら〉
 zarazara-suru〈ざらざらする〉feel rough, be sandy.
 zarazara-shita〈ざらざらした〉rough, coarse, sandy.
zaru〈ざる〉a (bamboo) basket.
 zaru-soba〈ざるそば〉buckwheat noodle served on a wicker
  bamboo-plate
zaseki〈ざせき：座席〉a seat.
 zaseki o yoyaku-suru〈座席を予約する〉reserve a seat
 zaseki-shitei-ken〈座席指定券〉a reserved-seat ticket
zasetsu〈ざせつ：ざ折〉failure, collapse.
 zasetsu-kan〈ざ折感〉frustration

zasetsu-suru 〈ざ折する〉 fail, break down, be frustrated, collapse.

zashiki 〈ざしき：座敷〉 a room, a drawing room.

　　zashiki-ni toosu (座敷に通す) show ((a person)) in the room

zashô 〈ざしょう：ざ傷〉 a contusion, a fracture.

　　zashô-suru (ざ傷する) have a fracture

zashô 〈ざしょう：座礁〉

zashô-suru (座礁する) run on a rock, run aground.

zasshi 〈ざっし：雑誌〉 a magazine, a journal.

　　zasshi o toru (雑誌を取る) take (in) a magazine

zasshu 〈ざっしゅ：雑種〉 a mixed breed, a crossbreed.

zasshu-no 〈雑種の〉 crossbred.

　　zasshu-no inu (雑種の犬) a mongrel

zasshûnyû 〈ざっしゅうにゅう：雑収入〉 miscellaneous incomes, sundry receipts.

zassô 〈ざっそう：雑草〉 weeds.

zassô-o-toru 〈雑草を取る〉 weed.

　　niwa-no-zassô-o-toru (庭の雑草を取る) weed a garden

zassô-no-oi-shigetta 〈雑草の生い茂った〉 weedy, overgrown with weeds.

zatsu 〈ざつ：雑〉

zatsu-na 〈雑な〉 rough, rude, coarse, gross.

　　zatsu-na bunshô (雑な文章) a slipshod style

zatsu-ni 〈雑に〉 roughly, coarsely.

　　zatsu-ni dekite-iru (雑にできている) be roughly made

zatsudan 〈ざつだん：雑談〉 a chat, gossip, idle talk.

zatsudan-suru 〈雑談する〉 have a chat, gossip.

zatsueki 〈ざつえき：雑役〉 odd jobs.

zatsuji 〈ざつじ：雑事〉 miscellaneous affairs, routine work, chores.

　　zatsuji-ni owareru (雑事に追われる) be busy with chores

zatsu-kabu 〈ざつかぶ：雑株〉 minor stocks.

zatsumu 〈ざつむ：雑務〉 miscellaneous business, the routine duties.

zatsunen 〈ざつねん：雑念〉 earthly thoughts.

　　zatsunen-o-saru (雑念を去る) dismiss earthly thoughts from one's mind

zatsuon 〈ざつおん：雑音〉 noises, jarring and grating.

　　Rajio-ni-zatsuon-ga-hairu. (ラジオに雑音が入る。) The radio program is hampered by noises.

zatsuyô 〈ざつよう：雑用〉 miscellaneous affairs, chores.

zatsuzen 〈ざつぜん：雑然〉

zatsuzen-to〈雑然と〉in disorder.

zatta〈ざった：雑多〉

shuju-zatta-na〈種々雑多な〉of every sort and kind.

zatto〈ざっと〉about, around; briefly, roughly.

    zatto nijû-nen（ざっと二十年）about twenty years

    zatto setsumei-suru（ざっと説明する）explain briefly

    zatto-me-o-toosu（ざっと目を通す）glance through

    zatto ieba（ざっと言えば）roughly speaking

zattô〈ざっとう：雑踏〉hustle and bustle, a throng.

zattô-suru〈雑踏する〉be crowded ((with)).

zawameki〈ざわめき〉a stir, (a) commotion, noises; bustle and confusion; a hum of voices; a rustle.

zawameku〈ざわめく〉be astir; be noisy; rustle.

zawatsuki〈ざわつき〉a stir, (a) commotion.

zawatsuku〈ざわつく〉see. zawameku.

zawazawa〈ざわざわ〉

zawazawa-suru〈ざわざわする〉see. zawameku.

zayû〈ざゆう：座右〉

    zayû-no-mei（座右の銘）one's motto

zâzâ〈ざあざあ〉

    Ame ga zâzâ futteiru. （雨がざあざあ降っている.）It's raining heavily.

zazen〈ざぜん：座禅〉

zazen-o-kumu〈座禅を組む〉sit in (religious) meditation.

zehi〈ぜひ：是非〉right and wrong, the propriety ((of)); by all means, without fail, at any cost.

    koto no zehi o ronjiru（事の是非を論じる）discuss the rights and wrongs of the matter

    Kono-natsu zehi Hokkaidô-e ikô. （この夏是非北海道へ行こう.）Let us go to Hokkaido this summer by all means.

    Zehi-irasshai. （是非いらっしゃい.）Do come and see me.

zei〈ぜい：税〉a tax, a duty.

    zei o kasuru（税を課する）impose a tax ((on))

    zei o osameru（税を納める）pay a tax

    zei o chôshû-suru（税を徴収する）collect taxes

zei-no-kakaru〈税の掛かる〉dutiable, taxable.

    zei-no-kakara-nai（税の掛からない）tax-free, free of duty

zei-biki-no or *zei-biki-de*〈税引きの，税引きで〉after tax.

zei-komi-no *or* zei-komi-de（税込みの，税込みで） before tax

zeigaku〈ぜいがく：税額〉the amount of a tax, an assessment.

zeihô〈ぜいほう：税法〉the tax law.

zeikan〈ぜいかん：税関〉a custom(s) house, the customs.

zeikan o tooru（税関を通る） get through the customs

zeikan-te-tsuzuki（税関手続き） customs formalities

zeikin〈ぜいきん：税金〉*see.* zei.

zeimu-sho〈ぜいむしょ：税務署〉a taxation office.

zeimu-sho-in（税務署員） a tax collector

zeiniku〈ぜいにく：ぜい肉〉superfluous flesh.

zeiniku-o-toru（ぜい肉を取る） get rid of superfluous flesh

zeiri-shi〈ぜいりし：税理士〉a licensed tax accountant.

zeiritsu〈ぜいりつ：税率〉the tax rate, a tariff.

zeiritsu o hiki-ageru（税率を引き上げる） raise the tax rates

zeisei〈ぜいせい：税制〉a tax system.

zeishû(nyû)〈ぜいしゅう(にゅう)：税収(入)〉tax yields.

zeitaku〈ぜいたく：ぜい沢〉luxury.

zeitaku-ni-kurasu（ぜい沢に暮らす） live in luxury

zeitaku-hin（ぜい沢品） a luxury

zeitaku-suru〈ぜい沢する〉indulge in luxury.

zeitaku-o-iu〈ぜい沢を言う〉ask too much, expect too much.

zeitaku-na〈ぜい沢な〉luxurious.

zeitaku-ni〈ぜい沢に〉luxuriously, in luxury.

zeizei〈ぜいぜい〉

zeizei-iu〈ぜいぜいいう〉wheeze.

zekkei〈ぜっけい：絶景〉a glorious view.

zekken〈ゼッケン〉the (player's) number.

zekkô〈ぜっこう：絶交〉

zekkô-suru〈絶交する〉break off (friendship) ((with)), be through ((with)).

zekkô〈ぜっこう：絶好〉

zekkô-no〈絶好の〉the best, capital, splendid.

zekkô-no kikai（絶好の機会） a capital opportunity

zekkôchô〈ぜっこうちょう：絶好調〉

zekkôchô-de-aru〈絶好調である〉be in the best (possible) condition, be in the pink.

zekkyô〈ぜっきょう：絶叫〉

zekkyô-suru〈絶叫する〉shout at the top of one's voice.

zemba〈ぜんば：前場〉the morning session, the first session.

zembin〈ぜんびん：前便〉

zembin-de〈前便で〉by last mail, in one's last letter.

zembô〈ぜんぼう：全ぼう〉the whole aspect, the entire picture ((of)).

　　zembô-o-akiraka-ni-suru（全ぼうを明らかにする）bring the whole affair to light

zembu〈ぜんぶ：前部〉the front part, the front, the fore.

zembu〈ぜんぶ：全部〉all, the whole.

　　issatsu-no-hon o zembu yomu（一冊の本を全部読む）read a book from cover to cover

　　zembu shiharau（全部支払う）pay in full

zembu-no〈全部の〉all, whole, entire, every.

zembu-de〈全部で〉in all, all told, altogether.

zembun〈ぜんぶん：前文〉the above sentence.

zembun〈ぜんぶん：全文〉the whole sentence, the full text.

　　zembun o in·yô-suru（全文を引用する）quote the whole sentence

zemmai〈ぜんまい〉a spring; a flowering fern.

　　zemmai o maku（ぜんまいを巻く）wind a spring

　　zemmai-jikake（ぜんまい仕掛け）clockwork

　　　zemmai-jikake-ni-natte-iru（ぜんまい仕掛けになっている）move by clockwork

zemmen〈ぜんめん：前面〉the front, the façade.

zemmen-no〈前面の〉front, in front.

～-no-zemmen-ni〈～の前面に〉in front of... , ahead of... .

zemmen〈ぜんめん：全面〉

　　zemmen-kôwa（全面講和）an overall peace (treaty)

zemmen-teki(-na)〈全面的(な)〉all-out, overall, general, full-scale, complete.

　　zemmen-teki-na kyôryoku（全面的な協力）all-out cooperation

zemmen-teki-ni〈全面的に〉fully, to the fullest extent, completely.

　　zemmen-teki-ni-kaitei-suru（全面的に改訂する）make an overall revision ((of))

　　zemmen-teki-ni-shiji-suru（全面的に支持する）give full support ((to))

zemmetsu〈ぜんめつ：全滅〉

zemmetsu-suru〈全滅する〉be completely destroyed, be annihilated.

zemmon〈ぜんもん：前門〉

　　zemmon-no-tora, kômon-no-ookami（前門のとら，後門のおおかみ）find oneself between the devil and the deep sea

zempai〈ぜんぱい：全敗〉

zempai-suru〈全敗する〉lose all games.

zempai〈ぜんぱい：全廃〉(total) abolition.

zempai-suru〈全廃する〉abolish altogether.

zempan〈ぜんぱん：全般〉the whole.

zempan-no or *zempan-teki(-na)*〈全般の，全般的(な)〉whole, general.

zempan-ni(-watatte) or *zempan-teki-ni*〈全般に(わたって)，全般的に〉generally.

zempen〈ぜんぺん：前編〉the first part, the first volume.

zempô〈ぜんぼう：前方〉the front.

zempô-no〈前方の〉front, forward.

zempô-e, zempô-ni or *zempô-o*〈前方へ，前方に，前方を〉in front, ahead, forward.

　　zempô-o miru（前方を見る）look ahead

　　haruka zempô-ni（はるか前方に）far ahead

zempuku〈ぜんぷく：全幅〉

zempuku-no-shinrai-o-oku〈全幅の信頼を置く〉trust ((a person)) absolutely.

zen〈ぜん：善〉the good, goodness.

　　Zen-wa-isoge.（善は急げ。）Never hesitate in doing what is good.

zen〈ぜん：禅〉Zen.

　　zenshû（禅宗）the Zen sect

zen〈ぜん〉a table, a tray; a meal.

　　zen-o-sueru（ぜんを据える）set the table ((for)), set a meal before ((a person))

　　gohan-ichi-zen（御飯一ぜん）a bowl of rice

　　hashi-ichi-zen（はし一ぜん）a pair of chopsticks

zen-〈ぜん-：前-〉former, ex-, previous.

　　zen-jûsho（前住所）one's former address

　　zen-shushô（前首相）the ex-Prime Minister

zen-〈ぜん-：全-〉whole, entire, all, full, complete.

　　watashi-no zen-kazoku（私の全家族）all my family

zen-aku〈ぜんあく：善悪〉good and evil, right and wrong.

　　zen-aku-o-wakimaeru（善悪をわきまえる）know good from evil

zenchi〈ぜんち：全治〉a complete cure.

　　zenchi-tooka-no-kizu（全治十日の傷）an injury which will take ten days to heal completely

zenchi-suru〈全治する〉be completely cured.

zenchi-shi〈ぜんちし：前置詞〉a preposition.

zenchi-zennô〈ぜんちぜんのう：全知全能〉

    zenchi-zennô-no-kami（全知全能の神）Almighty God, the Almighty

zenchô〈ぜんちょう：前兆〉an omen, a sign.

    yoi zenchô（良い前兆）a good omen

    warui zenchô（悪い前兆）an evil omen

zenchô〈ぜんちょう：全長〉the full length.

    zenchô-jû-mêtoru（全長十メートル）a full length of 10 meters

zendai-mimon〈ぜんだいみもん：前代未聞〉

  zendai-mimon-no〈前代未聞の〉unheard-of, unprecedented, unparalleled in history.

zen-date〈ぜんだて：ぜん立て〉

    Zen-date-wa-totonotta.（ぜん立ては整った.）It's all set.

  zen-date-suru〈ぜん立てする〉set the table ((for)), make preparations ((for)).

zendo〈ぜんど：全土〉the whole land.

  zendo-ni(-watatte)〈全土に（わたって）〉all over the land.

zendô〈ぜんどう：善導〉

  zendô-suru〈善導する〉lead ((a person)) in the right direction.

zen·ei〈ぜんえい：前衛〉a forward (player); the van.

    zen·ei-bijutsu（前衛美術）*avant-garde* art

zenesuto〈ゼネスト〉a general strike.

zengaku〈ぜんがく：全額〉the total amount.

    zengaku-o-harau（全額を払う）pay in full

    zengaku o harai-modosu（全額を払い戻す）refund the full amount (back)

zengaku〈ぜんがく：全学〉

    zengaku-shûkai（全学集会）an all-campus meeting

zengaku(-bu)〈ぜんがく（ぶ）：前額(部)〉the forehead.

Zengakuren〈ぜんがくれん：全学連〉the National Federation of Students' Self-Government Associations, the *Zengakuren*.

zengen〈ぜんげん：前言〉one's previous remarks.

    zengen-o-hirugaesu（前言を翻す）go back on one's word

    zengen o tori-kesu（前言を取り消す）take back one's words

zengen〈ぜんげん：漸減〉(a) gradual decrease.

  zengen-suru〈漸減する〉decrease gradually.

zengo〈ぜんご：前後〉front and rear; order, sequence.

    zengo(-sayû)-o-mi-mawasu（前後(左右)を見回す）look around

zengo-no-mi-sakai-mo-naku〈前後の見境もなく〉thoughtlessly, recklessly

zengo-kankei〈前後関係〉the context

zengo-suru〈前後する〉get out of order.
　Hanashi ga zengo-shite-iru.（話が前後している.）The story lacks in sequence.

zengo-no or *zengo-ni*〈前後の, 前後に〉before and behind, back and forth, before and after.

zengo-ni yureru（前後に揺れる）swing back and forth

zengo-ni-teki-o-ukeru（前後に敵を受ける）be attacked in front and rear

yūshoku-no-zengo-ni（夕食の前後に）before and after dinner

-zengo〈-ぜんご：-前後〉about, around, nearly.

san-jussai-zengo no josei（三十歳前後の女性）a woman of about thirty

zengô〈ぜんごう：前号〉the preceding number.
　Zengô-yori-tsuzuku.（前号より続く.）Continued from the last issue.

zengo-fukaku〈ぜんごふかく：前後不覚〉unconsciousness.

zengo-fukaku-ni-naru〈前後不覚になる〉become unconscious.

zengo-saku〈ぜんごさく：善後策〉

zengo-saku-o-kôjiru〈善後策を講じる〉work out remedial measures, resort to an expedient.

zengun〈ぜんぐん：全軍〉the whole army, the whole team.

zen·han〈ぜんはん：前半〉the first half.

zeni〈ぜに：銭〉see. kane（金）.

zen·i〈ぜんい：善意〉a favorable sense, good intentions; good faith.

zen·i-no〈善意の〉well-intentioned; *bona fide*.

zen·i-no daisan-sha（善意の第三者）a third party in good faith

zen·i-ni〈善意に〉in good part, favorably.

zen·i-ni kaishaku-suru（善意に解釈する）take in good part

zen·iki〈ぜんいき：全域〉the whole (district).

Kantô-zen·iki-ni-watatte〈関東全域にわたって〉throughout the Kanto district.

zenin〈ぜにん：是認〉approval, admission.

zenin-suru〈是認する〉approve ((of)), admit.

zen·in〈ぜんいん：全員〉all the members.

zen·in-itchi〈ぜんいんいっち：全員一致〉

zen·in-itchi-no〈全員一致の〉unanimous.

zen·in-itchi-de〈全員一致で〉unanimously.

zenjin-mitô〈ぜんじんみとう：前人未到〉
zenjin-mitô-no〈前人未到の〉unexplored, virgin.

zenjitsu〈ぜんじつ：前日〉the day before, the previous day.

zenjutsu or **zenki**〈ぜんじゅつ，ぜんき：前述，前記〉
zenjutsu-no or *zenki-no*〈前述の，前記の〉above-mentioned.
zenjutsu-no-toori or *zenki-no-gotoku*〈前述のとおり，前記のごとく〉as mentioned above.

zenka〈ぜんか：前科〉a previous offense, a criminal record.
　　zenka-ga-aru（前科がある）have a criminal record
　　zenka-sampan-no otoko（前科三犯の男）a man with three previous convictions
　　zenka-mono（前科者）an ex-convict

zenkai〈ぜんかい：前回〉the last time.
zenkai-no〈前回の〉the last, preceding.

zenkai〈ぜんかい：全快〉complete recovery.
zenkai-suru〈全快する〉recover completely〔from one's illness〕, get quite well again.

zenkai〈ぜんかい：全壊〉complete collapse.
zenkai-suru〈全壊する〉be completely destroyed.

zenkai-itchi〈ぜんかいいっち：全会一致〉
zenkai-itchi-no〈全会一致の〉unanimous.
zenkai-itchi-de〈全会一致で〉unanimously.

zenkei〈ぜんけい：全景〉a general view.

zenkei〈ぜんけい：前景〉the foreground.

zenken〈ぜんけん：全権〉full power.
　　zenken o inin-suru（全権を委任する）invest ((a person)) with full power ((to do))
　　zenken-taishi（全権大使）an ambassador plenipotentiary

zenki〈ぜんき：前期〉the first term, the first half year.
　　zenki-kuri-koshi-kin（前期繰越金）the balance brought forward〔from the preceding term〕

zenkô〈ぜんこう：全校〉the whole school.
　　zenkô-seito（全校生徒）all the students of a school

zenkô〈ぜんこう：前項〉the foregoing paragraph; the antecedent.

zenkô〈ぜんこう：善行〉a good deed, good conduct.
　　zenkô-shô（善行賞）a prize for good conduct

zenkoku〈ぜんこく：全国〉the whole country.

zenkoku-teki(-na) 〈全国的(な)〉 national, nationwide.

zenkoku(-teki)-ni 〈全国(的)に〉 all over the country, throughout the country.

zennan-zennyo 〈ぜんなんぜんにょ：善男善女〉 pious people.

zennen 〈ぜんねん：前年〉 the preceding year.

sono-zennen 〈その前年〉 the year before.

zennichi-sei 〈ぜんにちせい：全日制〉

　　zennichi-sei-kôtô-gakkô 〈全日制高等学校〉 a full-time senior high school

zennichi-sei-no 〈全日制の〉 full-time.

zen-Nihon(-no) 〈ぜんにほん(の)：全日本(の)〉 all-Japan.

zennin 〈ぜんにん：善人〉 a good person.

zennin-sha 〈ぜんにんしゃ：前任者〉 one's predecessor.

zennô 〈ぜんのう：全能〉

zennô-no 〈全能の〉 almighty, all-powerful.

zennô 〈ぜんのう：前納〉

zennô-suru 〈前納する〉 pay in advance.

zen·on 〈ぜんおん：全音〉 a whole-note.

　　zen·on-kai 〈全音階〉 the whole-note scale

zenra 〈ぜんら：全裸〉 total nudity.

zenra-no 〈全裸の〉 stark naked.

zenra-de 〈全裸で〉 in the nude, in the altogether.

zenrei 〈ぜんれい：前例〉 a former example, a precedent.

　　zenrei o tsukuru 〈前例を作る〉 set a precedent

zenrei-no-nai 〈前例のない〉 unprecedented.

zenreki 〈ぜんれき：前歴〉 one's past record, one's personal history, one's background.

zenretsu 〈ぜんれつ：前列〉 the front row.

zenritsu-sen 〈ぜんりつせん：前立せん〉 the prostate (gland).

zenryaku 〈ぜんりゃく：前略〉

Zenryaku-tori-isogi-o-shirase-itashimasu. 〈前略取り急ぎお知らせいたします。〉 I hasten to inform you that... .

zenryô 〈ぜんりょう：善良〉 goodness.

zenryô-na 〈善良な〉 good, virtuous, right, honest.

　　zenryô-na ichi-shimin 〈善良な一市民〉 a good citizen

zenryoku 〈ぜんりょく：全力〉 all one's power, all one's energies.

zenryoku-o-tsukusu 〈全力を尽くす〉 do one's best, do one's utmost, do all one can.

zenryoku-o-tsukushite〈全力を尽くして〉with all one's might, with might and main.

zensai〈ぜんさい：前菜〉an *hors d'oeuvre*.

zensei〈ぜんせい：全盛〉the height of prosperity.

    zensei-o-kiwameru（全盛を極める）be at the height of one's prosperity

    zensei-ki *or* zensei-jidai（全盛期, 全盛時代）the golden age, one's best days

zensei〈ぜんせい：善政〉good government.

zensei-o-shiku〈善政をしく〉govern well.

zen-sekai〈ぜんせかい：全世界〉the whole world, all the world.

zen-sekai-ni(-watatte)〈全世界に(わたって)〉all over the world.

    zen-sekai-ni shirareru（全世界に知られる）be known all over the world

zen-sekinin〈ぜんせきにん：全責任〉full responsibility.

    zen-sekinin o ou（全責任を負う）assume full responsibility ((for))

zensen〈ぜんせん：前線〉the front line; a front.

    baiu-zensen（梅雨前線）a rainy front

zensen〈ぜんせん：全線〉the whole line.

zensen-ni-watatte〈全線にわたって〉all along the line.

zensen〈ぜんせん：善戦〉

zensen-suru〈善戦する〉put up a good fight.

zensha〈ぜんしゃ：前者〉the former.

zenshi〈ぜんし：全市〉the whole city.

zenshi-o-agete-no〈全市を挙げての〉citywide.

zenshi〈ぜんし：全紙〉a whole sheet of paper, the whole space〔of a newspaper〕.

zenshin〈ぜんしん：全身〉the whole body, the full length.

    zenshin-zô（全身像）a full-length figure

zenshin-ni〈全身に〉all over (the body), from top to toe.

    zenshin-ni yakedo-o-ou（全身にやけどを負う）get burnt all over the body

zenshin〈ぜんしん：前身〉one's antecedents, the predecessor.

zenshin〈ぜんしん：前進〉an advance, a forward movement.

    zenshin-kichi（前進基地）an advance base

zenshin-suru〈前進する〉advance, go ahead.

zenshin〈ぜんしん：漸進〉

zenshin-suru〈漸進する〉progress gradually.

zenshin-teki(-na)〈漸進的(な)〉gradual, moderate.

zenshin-teki-ni〈漸進的に〉gradually, step by step.

zensho〈ぜんしょ：善処〉

zensho-suru〈善処する〉do ((something)) as one thinks fit, handle ((a matter)) with discretion.

zenshô〈ぜんしょう：全勝〉

zenshô-suru〈全勝する〉win all the games.

zenshô〈ぜんしょう：全焼〉

zenshô-suru〈全焼する〉be completely destroyed by fire, be burnt down.

zenshô〈ぜんしょう：前しょう〉

    zenshô-sen（前しょう戦）a (preliminary) skirmish

zenshû〈ぜんしゅう：全集〉one's complete works, a complete collection.

zensoku〈ぜんそく：ぜん息〉asthma.

zen-sokuryoku〈ぜんそくりょく：全速力〉full speed.

    zen-sokuryoku-de（全速力で）at full speed

zensô-kyoku〈ぜんそうきょく：前奏曲〉a prelude.

zenson〈ぜんそん：全損〉total loss.

zentai〈ぜんたい：全隊〉the whole troop.

    Zentai-tomare!（全隊止まれ.）Halt!

zentai〈ぜんたい：全体〉the whole.

zentai-no〈全体の〉whole, entire.

zentai-ni〈全体に〉in general, to all.

zentai-ni-watatte〈全体にわたって〉all over.

zentai-kara-miru-to〈全体から見ると〉on the whole.

zentai-to-shite〈全体として〉as a whole.

zentei〈ぜんてい：前提〉a premise, an assumption.

    zentei-jôken（前提条件）a precondition

〜-o-zentei-to-shite〈〜を前提として〉on the assumption that... , supposing, presupposing... .

zento〈ぜんと：前途〉one's future, prospects.

    zento-yûbô-de-aru（前途有望である）have a bright future before one

    zento-tanan-de-aru（前途多難である）have many difficulties ahead of one

    zento-ryôen-de-aru（前途りょう遠である）have a long way to go, be far off

zento-yûbô-na〈前途有望な〉promising.

zentsû〈ぜんつう：全通〉the opening of the whole line.

zentsû-suru〈全通する〉be opened to thorough traffic.

zen・ya〈ぜんや：前夜〉the previous night, the night before, last night.

zen・yaku〈ぜんやく：全訳〉a complete translation ((of)).

　zen・yaku-suru〈全訳する〉translate completely.

zen・yô〈ぜんよう：善用〉

　zen・yô-suru〈善用する〉make good use ((of)).

zenzen〈ぜんぜん：全然〉wholly, utterly, entirely, quite, completely.

　zenzen～nai〈全然～ない〉not...at all.

　　　　Ano hito wa zenzen-shira-nai.（あの人は全然知らない。）I don't know him at all.

　　　　zenzen yaku-ni-tata-nai（全然役に立たない）be utterly useless

zen-zenjitsu〈ぜんぜんじつ：前々日〉two days before.

zenzô〈ぜんぞう：漸増〉(a) gradual increase.

　zenzô-suru〈漸増する〉increase gradually.

zenzu〈ぜんず：全図〉a complete map.

zeppan〈ぜっぱん：絶版〉

　zeppan-ni-naru〈絶版になる〉go out of print.

　zeppan-de-aru〈絶版である〉be out of print.

zeppeki〈ぜっぺき：絶壁〉a precipice, a cliff.

zeppitsu〈ぜっぴつ：絶筆〉one's last writing.

zerachin〈ゼラチン〉gelatin(e).

　zerachin-jô-no〈ゼラチン状の〉gelatinous.

zerî〈ゼリー〉(a) jelly.

　zerî-jô-ni-naru〈ゼリー状になる〉jelly.

zero〈ゼロ〉zero, nought.

　　　　zero-hai（ゼロ敗）a shutout

　　　　zero-hai-suru（ゼロ敗する）be shut out

zesei〈ぜせい：是正〉

　zesei-suru〈是正する〉correct, put right.

zessan〈ぜっさん：絶賛〉great admiration.

　　　　zessan-ni-atai-suru（絶賛に値する）deserve the highest terms of praise

　　　　zessan o hakusuru（絶賛を博する）win great admiration

zessei〈ぜっせい：絶世〉

　zessei-no〈絶世の〉peerless.

　　　　zessei-no bijin（絶世の美人）a woman of peerless beauty

zessen〈ぜっせん：舌戦〉verbal warfare, a heated discussion ((with)).

zesshoku〈ぜっしょく：絶食〉fasting.

　　　　zesshoku-ryôyô（絶食療養）a fast cure

zesshoku-suru 〈絶食する〉 fast, abstain from food.

zessuru 〈ぜっする：絶する〉

gengo-ni-zessuru （言語に絶する） be beyond description, be indescribable

sôzô-ni-zessuru （想像に絶する） be beyond all imagination

zetchô 〈ぜっちょう：絶頂〉 the summit, the top, the peak.

tokui no zetchô （得意の絶頂） the summit of one's prosperity

zetsubô 〈ぜつぼう：絶望〉 despair, hopelessness.

zetsubô-suru 〈絶望する〉 despair ((of *or* to do)).

zetsubô-teki(-na) 〈絶望的(な)〉 desperate, hopeless.

zetsubô-shite 〈絶望して〉 in despair.

zetsubô-no-amari 〈絶望の余り〉 out of despair.

zetsudai 〈ぜつだい：絶大〉

zetsudai-na 〈絶大な〉 the greatest.

Zetsudai-na go-shien-o-onegai-itashimasu. （絶大な御支援をお願いいたします。） Please give us your (most) generous support.

zetsuen 〈ぜつえん：絶縁〉 insulation, disconnection.

zetsuen-tai （絶縁体） an insulator

zetsuen-suru 〈絶縁する〉 insulate; break off relations ((with)).

zetsugan 〈ぜつがん：舌がん〉 cancer of the tongue.

zetsumetsu 〈ぜつめつ：絶滅〉 extermination, extinction.

zetsumetsu-suru 〈絶滅する〉 exterminate, become extinct.

zetsumyô 〈ぜつみょう：絶妙〉

zetsumyô-na 〈絶妙な〉 exquisite, superb.

zetsurin 〈ぜつりん：絶倫〉

zetsurin-no 〈絶倫の〉 unparalleled, unequaled.

seiryoku-zetsurin-no otoko （精力絶倫の男） a man of unequaled energy

zettai 〈ぜったい：絶対〉 absoluteness.

zettai-chi （絶対値） the absolute value

zettai-ryô （絶対量） the absolute quantity

zettai-tasû （絶対多数） an absolute majority

zettai-ni 〈絶対に〉 absolutely, positively.

zettai-ni fu-kanô-de-aru （絶対に不可能である） be absolutely impossible

zettai-ni hantai-suru （絶対に反対する） be positively against

zettai-zetsumei 〈ぜったいぜつめい：絶対絶命〉

zettai-zetsumei-ni-naru 〈絶対絶命になる〉 be driven to the last extremity.

zeze-hihi 〈ぜぜひひ：是々非々〉

  zeze-hihi-no-taido-o-toru〈是々非々の態度を取る〉adopt the principle of being fair and just.

zô 〈ぞう：象〉an elephant.

zô 〈ぞう：像〉an image, a figure, a statue, a picture, a portrait.

  dairiseki-zô（大理石像）a statue in marble

zôchiku 〈ぞうちく：増築〉

  zôchiku-suru〈増築する〉extend a building.

zôchô 〈ぞうちょう：増長〉

  zôchô-suru〈増長する〉become presumptuous, be puffed up, grow more and more selfish.

zôdai 〈ぞうだい：増大〉enlargement, (an) increase.

  zôdai-gô（増大号）an enlarged number

  zôdai-suru〈増大する〉enlarge, increase.

zôen 〈ぞうえん：増援〉reinforcement.

  zôen-butai（増援部隊）reinforcements

  zôen-suru〈増援する〉reinforce.

zôen(-jutsu) 〈ぞうえん（じゅつ）：造園（術）〉landscape gardening.

  zôen-ka（造園家）a landscape gardener

zôfuku 〈ぞうふく：増幅〉amplification.

  zôfuku-ki（増幅器）an amplifier, a booster

  zôfuku-suru〈増幅する〉amplify.

zôgaku 〈ぞうがく：増額〉an increased amount.

  zôgaku-suru〈増額する〉increase, raise.

zôgan 〈ぞうがん：象眼〉

  zôgan-zaiku（象眼細工）inlaid work

  zôgan-suru〈象眼する〉inlay.

zôge 〈ぞうげ：象げ〉ivory.

  zôge no tô（象げの塔）a tower of ivory

  zôge-zaiku（象げ細工）ivory work

zô-gen 〈ぞうげん：増減〉increase or decrease, rise or fall, variation.

  zôgen-suru〈増減する〉increase or decrease, rise or fall, vary.

zôgo 〈ぞうご：造語〉a coined word.

zôhai 〈ぞうはい：増配〉

  zôhai-suru〈増配する〉pay an increased dividend.

zôhatsu 〈ぞうはつ：増発〉

  rinji-ressha-o-zôhatsu-suru（臨時列車を増発する）run an extra train

  kôsai-o-zôhatsu-suru（公債を増発する）issue additional bonds

zôhei〈ぞうへい：増兵〉*see.* zôen.

zôhei-kyoku〈ぞうへいきょく：造幣局〉the Mint Bureau.

zôho〈ぞうほ：増補〉enlargement.
   zôho-ban（増補版）an enlarged edition
   zôho-suru（増補する〉enlarge.

zôin〈ぞういん：増員〉
   zôin-suru〈増員する〉increase the personnel.

zôka〈ぞうか：造花〉an artificial flower.

zôka〈ぞうか：増加〉(an) increase, addition, gain, rise.
   jinkô no zôka（人口の増加）increase in population
   zôka-ritsu（増加率）the rate of increase
   zôka-suru（増加する〉increase, rise, grow.

zôkan(-gô)〈ぞうかん（ごう）：増刊（号）〉an extra number.

zôkei〈ぞうけい：造けい〉
   zôkei-ga-fukai〈造けいが深い〉be at home ((in)), have a profound knowledge ((of)).

zôkei-bijutsu〈ぞうけいびじゅつ：造形美術〉plastic arts.

zôketsu〈ぞうけつ：増結〉
   zôketsu-sha（増結車）a car(*or* cars) added
   zôketsu-suru〈増結する〉add a car(*or* cars) 〔to a train〕.

zôketsu-zai〈ぞうけつざい：増血剤〉a blood-making medicine.

zôki〈ぞうき：臓器〉internal organs; bowels.

zôki-bayashi〈ぞうきばやし：雑木林〉a copse.

zôkin〈ぞうきん：雑きん〉a floorcloth, a mop.
   zôkin-o-kakeru〈雑きんをかける〉swab, mop.

zokka〈ぞっか：俗化〉vulgarization.
   zokka-suru〈俗化する〉vulgarize, be vulgarized.

zokki-bon〈ぞっきぼん：ぞっき本〉remaindered books.

zokkô〈ぞっこう：続行〉continuation.
   zokkô-suru〈続行する〉continue, go on ((with)).

zokkon〈ぞっこん〉
   zokkon-hore-komu〈ぞっこんほれ込む〉be deeply in love ((with)), have a crush ((on)).

zoku〈ぞく：族〉a family; a tribe, a race.
   bîto-zoku（ビート族）the beat generation

zoku〈ぞく：属〉a genus.
   zokumei（属名）a generic name

zoku〈ぞく：賊〉a thief, a robber, a burglar; a rebel.

zoku 〈ぞく：俗〉

　zoku-ni 〈俗に〉commonly, popularly.

　　zoku-ni-iu〈俗に言う〉 to use a common phrase, as is commonly said, as the saying is

zokuaku 〈ぞくあく：俗悪〉vulgarity.

　zokuaku-na 〈俗悪な〉vulgar.

zokuen 〈ぞくえん：続演〉the continuation of a show.

　zokuen-suru 〈続演する〉run consecutively.

zokugo 〈ぞくご：俗語〉colloquial language, slang.

zokuhatsu 〈ぞくはつ：続発〉a succession, a series.

　　jiken no zokuhatsu〈事件の続発〉 a series of events

　zokuhatsu-suru 〈続発する〉occur in succession.

zokuhen 〈ぞくへん：続編〉a sequel ((of)), a continuation ((of)), a second volume.

zokuji 〈ぞくじ：俗事〉worldly affairs, routine work, daily routine.

　　zokuji-ni-owareru〈俗事に追われる〉 be busy with daily routine

zokumyô 〈ぞくみょう：俗名〉a secular name.

zokunen 〈ぞくねん：俗念〉worldly thoughts, earthly desires.

　　zokunen-o-saru〈俗念を去る〉 free oneself from earthly desires

zokuppoi 〈ぞくっぽい：俗っぽい〉common, popular, vulgar.

zokusei 〈ぞくせい：属性〉a generic character.

zokusetsu 〈ぞくせつ：俗説〉a popular saying.

zokushutsu 〈ぞくしゅつ：続出〉

　zokushutsu-suru 〈続出する〉occur one after another.

zokusuru 〈ぞくする：属する〉belong ((to)).

zoku-uke 〈ぞくうけ：俗受け〉

　zoku-uke-suru 〈俗受けする〉appeal to popular taste.

zokuzoku 〈ぞくぞく〉

　zokuzoku-suru 〈ぞくぞくする〉feel chilly, shiver with cold; feel a thrill.

　　ureshikute-zokuzoku-suru〈うれしくてぞくぞくする〉 be thrilled with joy

zokuzoku(-to) 〈ぞくぞく（と）：続々（と）〉one after another, in succession.

zôkyô 〈ぞうきょう：増強〉reinforcement, (an) increase, (a) buildup.

　zôkyô-suru 〈増強する〉reinforce, increase, build up.

　　gunji-ryoku o zôkyô-suru〈軍事力を増強する〉 build up military strength

zombun(-ni) 〈ぞんぶん（に）：存分（に）〉to one's heart's content, as much as one pleases.

　　zombun-ni taberu〈存分に食べる〉 eat to one's heart's content

　　zombun-ni-ude-o-hakki-suru〈存分に腕を発揮する〉 give full play to
　　　　one's ability

zommei〈ぞんめい：存命〉

　zommei-suru〈存命する〉 be alive, be living.

　zommei-chū(-wa)〈存命中(は)〉 while in life, while one lives.

zômotsu〈ぞうもつ：臓物〉 entrails, guts, giblets, pluck.

zongai〈ぞんがい：存外〉 *see.* angai.

zôni〈ぞうに：雑煮〉 rice cakes boild with vegetables in a soup, *zoni.*

zonzai〈ぞんざい〉

　zonzai-na〈ぞんざいな〉 rude, rough, careless, slapdash.

　　zonzai-na kuchi-no-kiki-kata〈ぞんざいな口のきき方〉 a rough way of
　　　　speaking

　zonzai-ni〈ぞんざいに〉 roughly, carelessly.

　　zonzai-ni atsukau〈ぞんざいに扱う〉 handle roughly, treat un-
　　　　courteously

zôo〈ぞうお：憎悪〉 hatred, detestation.

　zôo-suru〈憎悪する〉 hate, detest.

　zôo-su-beki〈憎悪すべき〉 hateful, detestable.

zôri〈ぞうり：草履〉 Japanese sandals, a *zori.*

zôrin〈ぞうりん：造林〉 afforestation.

zorozoro〈ぞろぞろ〉

　zorozoro-dete-kuru〈ぞろぞろ出てくる〉 troop out [of a room].

zôsaku〈ぞうさく：造作〉 the furnishings [of a building].

　zôsaku-tsuki-no〈造作付きの〉 furnished.

　　zôsaku-no-tsuite-i-nai〈造作の付いていない〉 unfurnished

zôsan〈ぞうさん：増産〉 an increase in production, an increased yield.

　zôsan-suru〈増産する〉 increase production.

zôsa-nai〈ぞうさない：造作ない〉 easy, simple.

　　Sonna-koto-wa zôsa-nai-yo.〈そんなことは造作ないよ。〉 That's quite
　　　　easy.

　zôsa-naku〈造作なく〉 easily, without any difficulty.

　　zôsa-naku yatte-nokeru〈造作なくやってのける〉 finish ((the task))
　　　　without any difficulty

zôsatsu〈ぞうさつ：増刷〉

　zôsatsu-suru〈増刷する〉 print additional ((10,000)) copies.

zôsei〈ぞうせい：造成〉 preparation [of land for building a house].

zôsei-suru 〈造成する〉 prepare.

zôsen 〈ぞうせん：造船〉 shipbuilding.
     zôsen-jo（造船所）a shipyard, a dockyard

zôsetsu 〈ぞうせつ：増設〉
     zôsetsu-suru（増設する）establish more... , install more... .

zôshi 〈ぞうし：増資〉
     zôshi-suru（増資する）increase the capital.

zôshin 〈ぞうしん：増進〉 increase, promotion.
     zôshin-suru（増進する）increase, promote.
         nôritsu o zôshin-suru（能率を増進する）increase efficiency
         kenkô o zôshin-suru（健康を増進する）promote health

zôsho 〈ぞうしょ：蔵書〉 a collection of books, one's library.
     zôsho-ka（蔵書家）a book collector

zôshô 〈ぞうしょう：蔵相〉 *see.* ookura-daijin.

zôshoku 〈ぞうしょく：増殖〉 increase, multiplication, proliferation.
     zôshoku-ro（増殖炉）a breeder (reactor)
     zôshoku-suru（増殖する）increase, multiply, proliferate.

zôshû 〈ぞうしゅう：増収〉 an increase of receipts; an increased yield.

zô-shû-wai 〈ぞうしゅうわい：贈収賄〉 corruption.

zôsui 〈ぞうすい：雑炊〉 a porridge of rice and vegetables.

zôsui 〈ぞうすい：増水〉
     zôsui-suru（増水する）rise, swell.

zôtei 〈ぞうてい：贈呈〉 presentation.
     zôtei-hin（贈呈品）a present, a gift
     zôtei-shiki（贈呈式）a ceremony of the presentation ((of))
     zôtei-suru（贈呈する）present, make a present ((of)).

zôtô 〈ぞうとう：贈答〉 an exchange of presents, gift-giving.
     zôtô-hin（贈答品）a present, a gift

zotto 〈ぞっと〉
     zotto-suru（ぞっとする）shudder, shiver, be horrified.
         kangaeta-dake-demo zotto-suru（考えただけでもぞっとする）shudder at the mere thought ((of))
         mita-dake-demo zotto-suru（見ただけでもぞっとする）be horrified at the mere sight ((of))
     zotto-suru-yô-na（ぞっとするような）blood-curdling, hair-raising, gruesome.

zôwai 〈ぞうわい：贈賄〉 bribery, corruption.
     zôwai-jiken（贈賄事件）a bribery case

　　　　zôwai-zai-ni-towareru〈贈賄罪に問われる〉 be charged with bribery
　　zôwai-suru〈贈賄する〉bribe, give ((a person)) a bribe.
zôyo〈ぞうよ：贈与〉donation, presentation.
　　　　zôyo-zei〈贈与税〉 a donation tax
　　zôyo-suru〈贈与する〉give, present, donate.
zôzei〈ぞうぜい：増税〉a tax increase.
　　zôzei-suru〈増税する〉increase taxes.
zu〈ず：図〉a picture, a diagram, a figure, an illustration.
　　　　zu-de-setsumei-suru〈図で説明する〉 illustrate by a diagram
　　zu-ni-ataru〈図に当たる〉work well.
　　zu-ni-noru〈図に乗る〉be puffed up.
zu〈ず：頭〉
　　zu-ga-takai〈頭が高い〉be haughty, hold one's head too high.
zuan〈ずあん：図案〉a design.
　　zuan-o-tsukuru〈図案を作る〉design.
zuba-nukete〈ずばぬけて：ずば抜けて〉by far.
　　　　Kanojo-wa gakkô-jû-de zuba-nukete yoku-dekiru.（彼女は学校中でず
　　　　ば抜けてよくできる.） She is by far the most excellent student in
　　　　the whole school.
zubari〈ずばり〉
　　　　Sono-mono-zubari-desu.（そのものずばりです.） You hit the mark. /
　　　　You said it.
　　　　zubari-to-iu（ずばりと言う） speak frankly, plump
　　　　zubari-to kotaeru（ずばりと答える） answer decidedly
zubon〈ズボン〉trousers, pants.
　　　　zubon-jita（ズボン下） drawers, underpants, pants
zubora〈ずぼら〉
　　zubora-na〈ずぼらな〉slovenly.
　　　　zubora-na-hito（ずぼらな人） a sloven
zuboshi〈ずぼし：図星〉
　　　　Masa-ni-zuboshi-desu.（正に図星です.） You've hit the mark.
zubu〈ずぶ〉
　　zubu-no〈ずぶの〉utter, entire.
　　　　zubu-no shirôto（ずぶの素人） a rank amateur
zubu-nure〈ずぶぬれ〉
　　zubu-nure-ni-naru〈ずぶぬれになる〉get wet through, be drenched to the
　　　　skin.
　　　　ame-de zubu-nure-ni-naru（雨でずぶぬれになる） be wet through

from the rain

zubutoi〈ずぶとい：図太い〉bold, audacious, impudent, brazen-faced, iron.

zudon〈ずどん〉a bang; a thud.

　　zudon-to ochiru（ずどんと落ちる）fall with a thud

zuga〈ずが：図画〉drawing.

zugai-kotsu〈ずがいこつ：頭がい骨〉the skull.

zuhyô〈ずひょう：図表〉a chart, a diagram.

zui〈ずい：髄〉the marrow, the pith.

　hone-no-zui-made〈骨の髄まで〉to the marrow of one's bone, to the core.

zuibun〈ずいぶん：随分〉fairly, pretty, very, quite, extremely.

　　zuibun atsui（随分暑い）awfully hot

　　Zuibun-hidoi-koto-o-iu-no-ne!（随分ひどいことを言うのね.）What a thing to say!

zuihitsu〈ずいひつ：随筆〉an essay.

　　zuihitsu-ka（随筆家）an essayist

zuii〈ずいい：随意〉

　　zuii-kamoku（随意科目）an optional subject

　zuii-no〈随意の〉voluntary, optional, free.

　zuii-ni〈随意に〉voluntarily, freely, at will, as one pleases.

　　Go-zuii-ni.（御随意に.）Do as you please.

zuiichi〈ずいいち：随一〉

　　tôdai-zuiichi-no-chôkoku-ka（当代随一の彫刻家）the greatest sculptor of the day

zuiin〈ずいいん：随員〉an attendant, a member of ((a person's)) suite.

　　zenken-taishi oyobi sono zuiin（全権大使及びその随員）the ambassador plenipotentiary and his suite

zuiji〈ずいじ：随時〉(at) any time, as occasion calls.

zuikô〈ずいこう：随行〉

　zuikô-suru〈随行する〉attend, accompany.

　~-ni-zuikô-shite〈～に随行して〉in the suite of... .

zuisho-ni〈ずいしょに：随所に〉everywhere, here and there, at every turn.

zuisô-roku〈ずいそうろく：随想録〉one's (fugitive) essays.

zujô〈ずじょう：頭上〉

　zujô-ni〈頭上に〉overhead, over the head.

zukai〈ずかい：図解〉an illustration.

zukai-suru 〈図解する〉 illustrate.

zukan 〈ずかん：図鑑〉 a picture book, an illustrated book.

zukazuka(-to) 〈ずかずか(と)〉 directly, straight, without permission, without ceremony, rudely.

 Kare-wa zukazuka-to boku-no heya-ni haitte-kita. (彼はずかずかと僕の部屋に入ってきた。) He came rudely into my room.

-zuke 〈-づけ：-付け〉

 kongetsu-tooka-zuke-no tegami (今月十日付の手紙) a letter dated the 10th of this month

zukei 〈ずけい：図形〉 a figure.

zukezuke 〈ずけずけ〉

 zukezuke-mono-o-iu 〈ずけずけ物を言う〉 do not mince matters.

-zuki 〈-ずき：-好き〉 a lover ((of)), a fan.

 ongaku-zuki (音楽好き) a lover of music

 yakyû-zuki (野球好き) a baseball fan

-zuki 〈-づき：-付き〉 attached ((to)).

 Amerika-taishi-kan-zuki-bukan (アメリカ大使館付き武官) a military attaché to the American Embassy

zukin 〈ずきん：頭きん〉 a hood.

zukizuki or **zukinzukin** 〈ずきずき：ずきんずきん〉

 zukizuki-itamu or *zukinzukin-itamu* 〈ずきずき痛む, ずきんずきん痛む〉 smart with pain, throb with pain, have a throbbing pain.

zukku 〈ズック〉 canvas.

 zukku-no kutsu (ズックの靴) canvas shoes

-zuku-de 〈-ずくで〉

 sôdan-zuku-de (相談ずくで) by mutual agreement

 ude-zuku-de (腕ずくで) by force

-zume 〈-づめ：-詰め〉

 hako-zume-no (箱詰めの) packed in a case

 bin-zume-no (瓶詰めの) bottled

 tachi-zume-de-aru (立ち詰めである) be kept standing

 honsha-zume-ni-naru (本社詰めになる) be called back to the head office

zumen 〈ずめん：図面〉 a drawing, a plan.

 zumen o hiku (図面を引く) draw a plan

-zumi 〈-づみ：-積み〉

 jutton-zumi-torakku (十トン積みトラック) a ten-ton freight truck

zundô 〈ずんどう〉

zundō-de-aru〈ずんどうである〉have no waist.

zunguri〈ずんぐり〉

  zunguri-shita〈ずんぐりした〉thickset, stocky, dumpy, pudgy, chunky.

    zunguri-shita otoko〈ずんぐりした男〉 a stocky man

zunō〈ずのう：頭脳〉a head, brains.

    zunō-rōdō〈頭脳労働〉 brain work

  zunō-meiseki-de-aru〈頭脳明せきである〉be clear-headed.

zu-nukete〈ずぬけて：図抜けて〉*see.* zuba-nukete.

zunzun〈ずんずん〉quickly, rapidly, steadily, on and on.

    Shigoto ga zunzun-hakadotteiru.〈仕事がずんずんはかどっている．〉
        The work is making rapid progress.

    zunzun-iku〈ずんずん行く〉 go on and on

zurakaru〈ずらかる〉run away, escape, make one's gateway.

zurari-to〈ずらりと〉in a row.

  zurari-to-narabu〈ずらりと並ぶ〉be lined ((with)).

zurasu〈ずらす〉shift; stagger.

zure〈ずれ〉a lag, divergence.

    jikan-no zure〈時間のずれ〉 a time lag

    ryōsha-no-aida-no kangae-kata no zure〈両者の間の考え方のずれ〉 a
      difference of outlook between the two

zure〈-づれ：-連れ〉*see.* tsure.

zureru〈ずれる〉get out of position, be beside the point.

zuri-ochiru〈ずりおちる：ずり落ちる〉slip down.

zuru〈ずる〉a trick, a foul play; a shirk, a dodger.

  zuru-o-kime-komu〈ずるを決め込む〉shirk one's duty.

zuruchin〈ズルチン〉dulcin.

zurui〈ずるい〉sly, cunning, unfair, foul, dishonest.

  zurui-koto-o-suru〈ずるいことをする〉play foul, do a dishonest thing,
  cheat ((at *or* in)).

zurukeru〈ずける〉be idle, shirk one's duty.

zuru-yasumi〈ずるやすみ：ずる休み〉truancy.

  zuru-yasumi-suru〈ずる休みする〉play truant ((from)), stay away ((from
  school *or* office)) without a good reason.

zuruzuru〈ずるずる〉

    zuruzuru-hiki-zuru〈ずるずる引きずる〉 drag along, trail

    zuruzuru-suberu〈ずるずる滑る〉 slither

zuruzuru-bettari-ni〈ずるずるべったりに〉

    zuruzuru-bettari-ni-naru〈ずるずるべったりになる〉 be left unsettled

zuruzuru-bettari-ni-shite-oku（ずるずるべったりにしておく）leave ((a matter)) undecided

zusan〈ずさん〉

zusan-na〈ずさんな〉careless, slipshod, slovenly.

zushi〈ずし：子子〉a miniature shrine.

zushiki〈ずしき：図式〉a diagram, a graph.

zushin〈ずしん〉

zushin-to〈ずしんと〉with a thud, heavily.

zūtai〈ずうたい：ずう体〉

zūtai-no-ookii〈ずう体の大きい〉bulky, hulking.

-zutai-ni〈－づたいに〉

senro-zutai-ni aruku（線路づたいに歩く）walk along the tracks

yane-zutai-ni nigeru（屋根づたいに逃げる）flee from roof to roof

zutazuta〈ずたずた〉

zutazuta-ni〈ずたずたに〉to pieces, into shreds.

zutazuta-ni saku（ずたずたに裂く）tear to pieces

Gôsetsu-de San·in-sen-wa-zutazuta-ni-natta.（豪雪で山陰線はずたずたになった.）The heavy snow tore the San·in line into strips.

-zutsu〈－ずつ〉

hitotsu-zutsu（一つずつ）one by one

futari-zutsu（二人ずつ）two by two

sukoshi-zutsu（少しずつ）little by little

zutsû〈ずつう：頭痛〉a headache.

zutsû-ga-suru（頭痛がする）have a headache

wareru-yô-na zutsû（割れるような頭痛）a splitting headache

zutsû-no-tane-de-aru〈頭痛の種である〉be a constant headache ((to)), be a cause of anxiety ((to)).

zutto〈ずっと〉all the way, all the time, (all) through, far, long, much.

zutto tachi-tsuzukeru（ずっと立ち続ける）be kept standing all the way

asa-kara-zutto（朝からずっと）all through the morning

zutto ato-ni-natte（ずっと後になって）long afterward(s)

zutto-mukashi-ni（ずっと昔に）a long time ago

Watashi-wa kare-yori zutto toshi-ga-wakai.（私は彼よりずっと年が若い.）I am much younger than he.

zūzūshii〈ずうずうしい〉bold, impudent, audacious, cheeky, shameless.

zūzūshiku〈ずうずうしく〉boldly, impudently, audaciously, cheekily, shamelessly.

POCKET
ROMANIZED
JAPANESE-ENGLISH
DICTIONARY
(paperback edition)

FIRST PUBLISHED IN DEC. 1984
SEVENTH PUBLISHED IN FEB. 1990

compiled by Hiroshi Takahashi
Kyōko Takahashi

Publishers: Taiseidô Shobô Co., Ltd.

2-4 Kanda Jimbô-chô, Chiyoda-ku,
Tokyô, Japan
4-3 Aotani-chô 4-chôme, Nada-ku,
Kôbe, Japan

(Printed in Japan)

ポケット
ローマ字和英辞典
著　者：高橋　寛　高橋恭子
出版社：株式会社　大盛堂書房
東京都千代田区神田神保町2-4
03(261)5965
神戸市灘区青谷町4丁目4-13
078(861)3436